HISTORY OF HUMANITY

Scientific and Cultural Development

History of Humanity
Scientific and Cultural Development

Volume I	*Prehistory and the Beginnings of Civilization* ISBN 92–3–102810–3 (UNESCO) ISBN 0–415–09305–8 (Routledge)
Volume II	*From the Third Millennium to the Seventh Century* BC ISBN 92–3–102811–1 (UNESCO) ISBN 0–415–09306–6 (Routledge)
Volume III	*From the Seventh Century* BC *to the Seventh Century* AD ISBN 92–3–102812–X (UNESCO) ISBN 0–415–09307–4 (Routledge)
Volume IV	*From the Seventh to the Sixteenth Century* ISBN 92–3–102813–8 (UNESCO) ISBN 0–415–09308–2 (Routledge)
Volume V	*From the Sixteenth to the Eighteenth Century* ISBN 92–3–102814–6 (UNESCO) ISBN 0–415–09309–0 (Routledge)
Volume VI	*The Nineteenth Century* ISBN 92–3–102815–4 (UNESCO) ISBN 0–415–09310–4 (Routledge)
Volume VII	*The Twentieth Century* ISBN 92–3–102816–2 (UNESCO) ISBN 0–415–09311–2 (Routledge)

In memory of Paulo E. de Berrêdo Carneiro, President of the first International Commission for a Scientific and Cultural History of Mankind (1952–1969) and of the present Commission from 1979 to 1982

The publication of this volume of *History of Humanity* has been made possible thanks to the generous support of the World Islamic Call Society

HISTORY OF HUMANITY

Scientific and Cultural Development

Volume IV
From the Seventh to the Sixteenth Century

EDITED BY

M. A. Al-Bakhit

L. Bazin

S. M. Cissoko

CO-EDITED BY

M. S. Asimov Y. Karayannopoulos

A. Gieysztor J. Litvak King

I. Habib P. Schmidt

CONSULTANT

R. Mantran

Routledge Reference

UNESCO

First published in 2000
by the United Nations Educational, Scientific and Cultural Organization
7 Place de Fontenoy, 75352 Paris 07 SP
and
Routledge
11 New Fetter Lane, London EC4P 4EE
29 West 35th Street, New York, NY 10001

Routledge is an imprint of the Taylor & Francis Group

Typeset by Tek-Art, Croydon, Surrey
Printed in Great Britain by TJ International Ltd, Padstow, Cornwall

Printed on acid-free paper

Index compiled by Leigh Priest

Authors are responsible for the choice and the presentation of the facts contained in this book and for the opinions expressed therein, which are not necessarily those of UNESCO and do not commit the Organization.

The designations employed and the presentation of material throughout this publication do not imply the expression of any opinion whatsoever on the part of UNESCO concerning the legal status of any country, territory, city or area or of its authorities, or concerning the delimitation of its frontiers or boundaries.

The International Commission for the History of the Scientific and Cultural Development of Mankind bears intellectual and scientific responsibility for the preparation of this new edition.

Generic names containing the word 'man' should be understood to refer to both sexes of the species.

British Library Cataloguing in Publication Data
A catalogue record for this book is available on request

Library of Congress Cataloging in Publication Data
A catalog record for this book has been applied for

ISBN 92–3–102813–8 (UNESCO)
ISBN 0–415–09308–2 (Routledge)

PREFACE

by the Director-General of UNESCO

'Our civilization is the first to have for its past the past of the world, our history is the first to be world history.'[1] Now that we have reached the year 2000, the phenomenon described over fifty years ago by Jan Huizinga becomes an ever more sensible reality. In a bounded and increasingly interconnected world, we necessarily find ourselves a part of that emerging global civilization that constitutes the matrix of our collective destinies.

The years immediately following the Dutch historian's assertion were indeed to illustrate, and in the most horrific manner, the interdependence of the world community. The planet on which millions of humans wished for nothing more than to live in peace and well-being presented the unnatural spectacle of a world at war. Land, sea and air routes were patrolled day and night by armadas venting fury on all that was most precious and vital to the inhabitants. The dreadful hurt that the populations sustained, physically and morally, dispelled *in perpetuum* a number of illusions and faced humanity with a stark choice – that of being, in the words of Albert Einstein, 'one or none'.

Thenceforth the grave danger attendant on inter-racial, and consequently inter-cultural, ignorance was conspicuous to thinking minds. A flawed consciousness of our common humanity must be incompatible with the survival of a world armed with knowledge of such awesome potential. Clearly the only course of action, the only way forward, lay in building bridges between peoples, in forging a resilient awareness of the unity inherent in human diversity.

Such was the background to UNESCO's decision in 1947 to produce a truly universal work of international co-operation that would provide 'a wider understanding of the scientific and cultural aspects of the history of mankind and of the mutual interdependence of peoples and cultures and of their contributions to the common heritage'.[2] That initiative, which was one of UNESCO's earliest projects, sprang from the Organization's fundamental principles and was widely acclaimed, although not a few saw in it a Sisyphean undertaking at which past attempts had signally failed.

Three years later, in 1950, the first International Commission for a History of the Scientific and Cultural Development of Mankind began the task of fashioning a history that – in the words of René Maheu – would 'present to man the sum total of his memories as a coherent whole'. As the distinguished international team of collaborators took shape and as the first results of its work began to appear in the Commission's review the *Journal of World History*, it became clear that new ground was being broken in pursuit of this ambitious goal. When some fifteen years later the first edition began to appear in six languages, the reception accorded to the work confirmed – some inevitable reservations apart – the success of this 'first attempt to compose a universal history of the human mind from the varying standpoints of memory and thought that characterize the different contemporary cultures'.

The compilers of the first edition of the *History of Mankind* were conscious that all historiography is 'work in progress', that in the continuous flux of history nothing is fixed, neither facts nor interpretations. In 1969, Paulo de Berrêdo Carneiro declared: 'The day will come when what we have written . . . will, in its turn, have to be replaced. I like to think that our successors will attend to this, and that a revised edition of the work we have begun may be published at the dawn of a new millennium.'

That day is now with us. The General Conference of UNESCO decided in 1978 that the work should be revised, and two years later the Second International Commission met to formulate its aims.

Much has changed since the publication of the first edition. In recent years, the historical sciences have been enriched by contributions from many disciplines, giving rise to new methods of investigation and bringing to light new facts, particularly in the realm of 'prehistory'. At the same time, a heightened awareness of cultural identity has intensified the demand for a corresponding decentralization of historical viewpoints and interpretations. UNESCO has both heeded and nurtured this trend by undertaking a series of regional histories, one of which – *General History of Africa*[3] – is on the point of completion, while others are in active preparation. Finally, history itself has moved on, altering in the process the perspectives from which the past is viewed.

For all these reasons and to take account of some valid criticisms of the original version, it was decided that the new

1 HUIZINGA, J. 1936. A Definition of the Concept of History. In: KLIBANSKY, R.; PATON, H. J. (eds), *Philosophy and History*. Oxford. p. 8.

2 UNESCO. 1947. *General Conference; Second Session*. Paris. Resolution 5.7.

3 The complete version of *General History of Africa* has been published in Arabic, English and French, and the abridged version in English and French.

edition of the History of the Scientific and Cultural Development of Humanity, to be called simply the *History of Humanity*, should not be merely a revision but rather a radical recasting of its predecessor. Its goal – to provide an account of the history of humanity in terms of its varied cultural and scientific achievements – remains unchanged, but the view it offers of its subject is – it is hoped – more detailed, more diverse and broader in scope.

Twenty years after the launching of the project, it is my privilege to present this new *History*, which has built upon and extended the pioneering work of those dedicated scholars responsible for the first edition. I should like to express my admiration and deep gratitude to the members of the Second International Commission and to the some 450 distinguished specialists from all geocultural backgrounds who have contributed to this historic undertaking. Readers will, I feel sure, make known their own views in the years to come. In committing this work to their scrutiny, the International Commission – and, through it, UNESCO – is taking the final step in the task entrusted to it by the community of Member States represented at the General Conference. Each of us, I am sure, stands to benefit from this concerted testimony to our common past and act of faith in our shared future.

CONTENTS

Preface v
Director-General of UNESCO
Foreword x
Charles Morazé, former President of the International Commission
General Introduction xvi
Georges-Henri Dumont, President of the International Commission
The International Commission xviii
Series list xix
List of figures xx
List of maps xxi
List of plates xxii
The contributors xxvi
Acknowledgements xxx

A Introduction 1
Introduction 3
Mohammad Adnan Al-Bakhit, Louis Bazin and Sékéné Mody Cissoko

B Thematic section 9
1 Environment and population 11
Victor I. Kozlov
2 The family, domestic groups, and society 23
Robert Fossier
3 The state and the law 41
Editor's note 41
Louis Bazin
3.1 Europe 42
3.1.1 The principles 42
Rafael Gibert y Sánchez de la Vega
3.1.2 The practice 47
Aleksander Gieysztor
3.2 The Islamic world 50
Majid Khadduri
3.3 Nomadic states in Central Asia 55
Louis Bazin
3.4 South and South-East Asia 57
Irfan Habib
3.5 East Asia 60
Guangda Zhang
3.6 Africa 63
Isidore Ndaywel è Nziem
3.7 The Americas 66
William T. Sanders
4 Economic systems and technologies 71
Richard W. Bulliet
5 Communication and transport 84
Richard W. Bulliet
6 Knowledge and sciences 96
Ahmad Yusuf Al-Hasan
7 Religions, ethics and philosophy 120
Maurice Borrmans
8 Art and expression 143
8.1 The Old World 143
Oleg Grabar
8.2 The New World: the evidence from Mesoamerica 164
Alfonso Arellano Hernández

C Regional section 171
I The heirs of the Graeco-Roman world 173
Introduction 175
Yannis Karayannopoulos

9 Byzantium 178
9.1 Historical summary 178
Ljubomir Maksimovic
9.2 State organization, social structure, economy and commerce 183
Yannis Karayannopoulos
9.3 Cultural achievement 186
Panayotis L. Vocotopoulos
10 Carolingian Europe 195
Pierre Riché

II The configuration of European personality 205
Introduction 207
Jacques Le Goff

11 Medieval Western Europe 209
Jacques Le Goff
12 East and South-East Europe 221
12.1 Ethnic and political changes in the Balkan Peninsula 221
Vasilka Tăpkova-Zaimova
12.2 The Christianization of the Slavs and other ethnic groups, particularly those near the Black Sea 225
Vasilka Tăpkova-Zaimova
12.3 Literary and artistic forms of expression 229

12.3.1 Literary forms of expression 229
12.3.2 Artistic forms of expression 232
Vasilka Tăpkova-Zaimova
13 Central and Northern Europe 235
Lucien Musset
14 The expansion of European influence 242
José-Luis Martín Rodríguez
15 The corridor between Europe and Asia 250
15.1 The Kiev Rus' 250
Anatoly P. Novoseltsev
15.2 The Armenians 252
Viada Arutjonova-Fidanjan
15.3 The Georgians and other Caucasians 254
Viada Arutjonova-Fidanjan
15.4 The Crimeans 257
Sergei P. Karpov

III **The Muslim world and its Arabian zone** 259

Introduction 261
Abdul Aziz Duri

16 The rise of Islam 264
16.1 The rise of Islam in Arabia 264
Abdul Aziz Duri
16.2 The sources of Islam 268
Azmi Taha Al-Sayyed
16.3 The formation of the early Islamic polity and society: general characteristics 271
Clifford Edmund Bosworth
17 Expansion of Islam and aspects of diversity in Asia, Africa and Europe 274
17.1 Poles of Expansion from Arabia 274
Saleh Ahmed Al-Ali
17.2 Arab Expansion in the Muslim world 278
Saleh Ahmed Al-Ali
17.3 The Iranian renaissance and the rise of the national language and literature 281
Ehsan Yarshater
17.4 The Turco-Mongol period 286
Françoise Aubin
17.5 The west of Islam 289
17.5.1 Al-Maghrib, Spain and Sicily 289
Younes Shanwan
17.5.2 The Sudan and countries south of the Sahara 292
Djibril Tamsir Niane
18 The Islamic world: social and material life, classes and communities 295
18.1 Society and material culture of the Islamic world 295
Mounira Chapoutot-Remadi and Radhi Daghfous
18.2 Non-Muslims in Islamic society 311
Benjamin Braude, Irfan Habib, Kamal Salibi and Ahmad Tafazzoli, co-ordinated by *Mounira Chapoutot-Remadi* and *Radhi Daghfous*
19 Arabia and the eastern Arab lands (Al-Mashriq) 314
Farouk Omar Fawzi
20 North and North-East Africa 332
20.1 Miṣr (Egypt) 332
Ayman Fu'ad Sayyid
20.2 Al-Maghrib 338
M'hammad Benaboud
21 Muslims in the Iberian Peninsula, the Mediterranean coast and its islands 348
Manuel Sánchez Martínez

IV **The Asian world** 361

Introduction 363
Irfan Habib

22 Iran 365
Seyyed Hossein Nasr
23 Central Asia 378
Muhammad S. Asimov and *Numan N. Negmatov*
24 Turkish expansion towards the west 387
24.1 Islamization of the Turks, Oghuz and Turkmen 387
Clifford Edmund Bosworth
24.2 The Turkmen forays into western Anatolia and the Balkans 393
Robert Mantran
24.3 The Turkmen in western Anatolia and their emirates 397
Halil Inalcik
25 South Asia 398
25.1 India 398
Irfan Habib
25.2 Sri Lanka 411
Kingsley M. de Silva
25.3 Nepal 414
Alexander W. Macdonald
26 South-East Asia and the Asian islands in the Pacific 416
Denys Lombard
27 China 421
Guangda Zhang
28 Japan and Korea 447
28.1 Japan 447
Francine Hérail
28.2 Korea 458
Li Ogg
29 Siberian–Manchurian hunting peoples 461
29.1 Siberian and Manchurian peoples: nomadism 461
Michail V. Vorobyev
29.2 The Turkish and Mongol peoples of the steppes: pastoral nomadism 465
Louis Bazin
30 The Mongol Empire 470
Shagdaryn Bira
31 The Tibetan cultural area 479
Yonten Gyatso and Fernand Meyer

V **The African continent** 483

Introduction 485
Sékéné Mody Cissoko

32 West Africa 489
32.1 The peoples 489
Sékéné Mody Cissoko
32.2 The economy 492
Sékéné Mody Cissoko
32.3 Societies and political structures 496
Sékéné Mody Cissoko
32.4 Religions 499
32.4.1 Traditional African religions 499
Isaac Adeagbo Akinjogbin

32.4.2 Islam and Christianity 502
Sékéné Mody Cissoko
32.5 Arts and sciences 504
Isaac Adeagbo Akinjogbin
33 Nubia and the Nilotic Sudan 507
Yūsuf Faḍl Ḥasan
34 Ethiopia 515
E. J. Van Donzel
35 The East coast and the Indian Ocean islands 524
35.1 Environment and techniques 524
Edward A. Alpers
35.2 Trade and urban development 526
Edward A. Alpers
35.3 Arab–Muslim cultures and local cultures on the east coast of Africa and the Indian Ocean islands 529
Victor Matveyev
35.4 Mixed cultures of Madagascar and the other islands 531
Rafolo Andrianaivoarivony
35.5 International importance of the region 536
Edward A. Alpers
36 Central and Southern Africa 539
Isidore Ndaywel è Nziem

VI Civilizations of the Americas 549

Introduction 551
Christine Niederberger and Louis Bazin

37 North America 555
37.1 North American Arctic cultures 555
Jean Aigner
37.2 North-western North America 560
Roy L. Carlson
37.3 The eastern woodlands of North America 566
James B. Stoltman
37.4 The greater south-west 573
Linda S. Cordell
37.5 North-eastern Mexico 577
Jeremiah F. Epstein
38 Mesoamerica and Central America 580
38.1 Mesoamerica: central and northern areas 580
Paul Gendrop, Jaime Litvak King and Paul Schmidt
38.2 Central America 589
Wolfgang Haberland
39 South America 593
39.1 The Caribbean area and the Orinoco–Amazon region 593
Mario Sanoja and Iraida Vargas Arenas
39.2 The central Andes 602
Luis Millones
39.3 Southern South America 612
Ana María Lorandi and Daniel Schávelzon

VII Oceania and the Pacific 619
Jacqueline de La Fontinelle and Michel Aufray

Chronological table 627

Index 663

NOTE ON TRANSLITERATION

Every effort has been made to achieve consistency in the transliteration of non-western writing systems but this has not proved possible in every case.

FOREWORD

Charles Morazé,
former President of the International Commission

> Among the great tasks assigned to UNESCO by the Constitution is the duty to promote and encourage mutual knowledge and understanding throughout the world. While many of the divergences which divide people date from a distant past, an analysis of their historical antecedents discloses links which draw them nearer to one another, brings to light their contributions to a common patrimony of humanity, reveals the ebb and flow of cultural exchanges and emphasizes their increasing tendency to become integrated into an international community.

This is how Paulo E. de Berrêdo Carneiro, President of the International Commission (1952–69), expressed himself in the opening paragraph of the Preface to the *History of the Scientific and Cultural Development of Mankind* in 1963. Today, it would be difficult to say anything about humanity's 'increasing tendency to become integrated into an international community' unless an attempt is made to assess the outcome of this 'tendency' as reflected in the state of the world since. Today, few events remain local. Information on any minor or major occurrence is communicated to almost everyone immediately and an action undertaken in one part of the world inevitably has its repercussions on the others. Those who experience fully this 'planetarization' sense the 'integration' of all human beings into an international community less as a 'tendency' than as a *fait accompli*. But what about the subordinates who are more or less associated or the vast excluded majority of people? These others put the question in completely different terms. What they seem to ask is: can a 'common patrimony of humanity' be achieved solely through an integration based on scientific and technical developments? What then can we do to ensure an equal access to such means for all when the more fundamental task of reducing existing differences in the very standards of living lags far behind?

The idea of writing a history of the development of humankind was first put forward by Julian Huxley, the Executive Secretary of the Preparatory Commission of UNESCO. In 1946 Huxley wrote that 'the chief task before the humanities today would seem to be to help in constructing a history of the development of the human mind, notably in its highest cultural achievements'. He underscored the major role that historians would play in the realization of what he called a 'gigantic enterprise'. Huxley later outlined a project which was to be submitted to the future UNESCO. In 1950, in accordance with a resolution passed by the General Conference of UNESCO, an International Commission was set up and the publication of a *History of the Scientific and Cultural Development of Mankind* in six volumes was approved. The first volume appeared in 1963.

What was this 'gigantic enterprise', conceived by Huxley worth? Critics received the volumes more often badly than well. They did not question the data included. What they objected to mainly were the criteria of the selection of data and the interpretations offered. Yet a closer look at these criticisms revealed that, skilled as they were at pointing out certain flaws and misconceptions, these commentators hardly ever came up with concrete suggestions that would lead to any improvement of the work in the future. On the whole, however, we were left with the impression that notwithstanding its shortcomings, a very large number of readers found the work commendable, particularly as a first step towards the achievement of an 'essential task'.

No elucidation, rational or otherwise, of the origins or the evolution of human beings can be offered once and for all, as if by divine revelation. Writing a history of the development of humankind necessarily constitutes a work that one has to return to over and over again. Nearly thirty years passed by before UNESCO decided to take up once more a work that could by no means be regarded as finished. Requested by the new Member States, a recasting of the first edition deserved the wholehearted support of all those who helped establish the Organization. The changes which have taken place over these last thirty years rendered necessary and amply justified a revision and revaluation of history, and the members of the International Commission were the first to acknowledge such a need. There were, of course, other and more imperative reasons. Two of these should be pointed out here.

The first concerns the developments in the area of research methodology since the 1960s. Over the last three decades historical knowledge has increased considerably and has turned from factual history to greater interest in anthropological research. Although they still remain far from being fully capable of answering all the questions that we ask today – or for that matter the more serious of those posed thirty years ago – the added insight that present studies offer us deserves to be transmitted to a larger public. The second, and perhaps less obvious reason, springs from the very role that the writing of history can, and is meant to, play in increasing our level of awareness. A writing or, as in the present case, a rewriting of the history of human scientific and cultural evolution signifies not only taking stock of the new data available but also helping one and all in evaluating and assessing the various implications, positive and also negative, of all the changes. Justifying science in the name of all its benefits and advantages amounts to refusing to accept the damaging effects it can have. We have gradually accustomed ourselves to the presence of many latent nuclear volcanoes without compensating for the technological risks. Not enough has been done to counterbalance the excessive monetary investments needed to build up such arsenals with sufficient funds to help confront the problems and miseries afflicting one section of humanity and which is on the way to becoming a danger for the other. Technological development has also begun seriously to endanger animal and plant life on this planet. Factors such as these plead for greater vigilance.

Universal histories and histories of the world abound. So many have already been published and continue to be published that one could question the need to bring out yet another one. No doubt many readers will be surprised at this venture. Each in his own way will of course judge this work better or worse than another of its kind. There is however one major difference. Other works of history enjoy a certain freedom that has in a sense been denied to the present one. They are free to choose themes, periods and regions that suit best the demands of a particular readership and a specific conception of history. Such works can thereby claim a certain cohesion of the elements introduced; a cohesion which also helps establish a certain uniformity of expression and style. The present work is founded on an entirely different principle: a maximum of diversity. This diversity proves to be, on the one hand, so great that it is difficult to stop it from becoming disparate and, on the other, not great enough to allow for a convenient regrouping of elements into types. The fault lies not in the venture itself nor in those who took up the task. It lies mainly in the present state of historical knowledge. The analytic nature of historical research today blocks the way to synthesis, to the kind of approach required in the writing of a history that can be considered truly universal.

This work can serve only as a history of the world and not as a universal history. This, of course, is already a great deal. We should not count on the diffusion of a universalism, which is the subject of reflection by a very small, privileged minority, as long as all cultures are not equally represented and historians from all parts of the world are not endowed with the same means and cannot claim the same status, social and otherwise.

Not claiming to attain the unattainable does not, however, mean renunciation. The roads to universalism are full of bends and curves. But, they all lead to the same destination: one history for one united world. Since this history could not reach the highest common factor, it had to tend towards the lowest common multiple. And in this respect, the present work has not failed in its mission.

In 1950 we opted in three days for a plan that would take thirteen years to complete. With a view to ensuring a unity of style and presentation, we decided that each of the six volumes would be written by a single author. Such ideas had to be abandoned. Some thirty years later, the new Commission decided to take more time over the distribution of the work to be done between seven and not six volumes, each well co-ordinated with the other and allowing free play to as many authors as would be necessary to cover a maximum of domains. The selection of the criteria on which the new history would be based first led to a detailed examination of the comments made by the readers of the first edition. After many debates and discussions, all agreed that it would not do simply to juxtapose a series of regional histories one after the other. Then one of the two possible solutions had to be chosen: dividing history either into themes or into periods and analysing each according to themes and regions. The first option – an idea that had already been put forward before 1948 – would perhaps have helped bring out in a more significant manner the factors which render manifest the common destiny of mankind. But the present state of historical research, which in most cases and owing to an ever-increasing acquisition of skills, proceeds in the form of temporal as well as regional specializations, constituted a real obstacle to the realization of such a scheme. It was therefore decided that each of the seven volumes would be devoted to a single period and would contain a thematic and regional section.

Yielding to the constraints imposed by the state of knowledge and research today does not, however, solve all probable problems. Let us take a look at the issue point by point.

The idea of splitting up into periods a past that the mission of all historians is to revive as an organic whole pleased no one. But, taking everything into consideration, had the objective been to separate one cultural component from another or, for example, the physical from the cultural or the religious from the profane, this surgery would have turned literally into a vivisection. Opting for the lesser evil, the Commission thus decided to work on chronological sections. This, at least, allowed for the preservation of a certain unity within each group.

Already in the 1950s it had become evident that the form of periodization upheld by the European tradition loses its signification when applied to the other parts of the world. Terms such as 'Antiquity', 'the Middle Ages' or 'modern times' do not correspond to much in so far as Asia is concerned, and perhaps even less for what concerns Africa. Admittedly we continue using such words for the sake of convenience. We cannot totally discard them, but we should try at least not to trust them fully.

The importance of each period is measured more in terms of what humankind has contributed to each than in terms of a duration defined by astronomy. The 'Grand Discoveries' of the sixteenth and the seventeenth centuries led to some spectacular changes in the history of the world. A sudden growth of ideas and of commercial capitalism accompanied by or resulting from military conquests gave rise to migrations that brought about the creation of a new map of the world and new conceptions of humanity's destiny. This moment marks a turning point that we have ever since sensed as an acceleration of history. It was, therefore, decided that three volumes of the present work would be devoted to the period succeeding these significant changes and transformations as against only four which would cover the entire preceding period, starting from the origins of humankind and leading up to the sixteenth century. The Commission also decided to devote more and more pages to the more recent years. The fifth volume thus covers three centuries; the sixth, one and a half; and the seventh only about seventy-five years.

A word of caution is, however, necessary. We often make use of a concept of progress that is based on the quantitative and not the qualitative value of what has been achieved. Manufactured goods, consumer items and exchanges, whether they concern concrete objects or ideas, can be more or less quantified. But, as we do not possess any means of measuring happiness or well-being, we cannot infer therefrom that the quantitative and the qualitative values of this progress are the same, particularly in so far as the world in general is concerned. This notion of progress should not, moreover, hinder a proper appraisal of all that was contributed to history by our ancestors, to whom we owe our existence and our way of living.

Great care was taken to avoid putting an undue emphasis on what could be considered as being only the European landmarks of history. The years 1789 and 1914, although highly significant in the history of Europe, served only nominally as points of reference. It was understood that, depending on the case, the ethnocentrism implied by these dates would be reduced as much as necessary through a proper and adequate treatment of the issues preceding or following them. Similarly, to avoid falling into the traps of Western traditionalism, it was considered necessary to cease using the Christianization of the Roman Empire as a mark of the end of the Ancient World and the beginning of the Middle Ages and, therefore, to include the first years of the Hegira in the third volume, which covers the period from 700 BC to AD 700, the middle of which comes before the beginning of the era acknowledged – belatedly – also by the Muslims.

The Commission's choice does not conflict very much with the Chinese system of dating, because around the same epoch the same phenomenon appeared in both the east and west of Eurasia: the awakening of tribes in these Central Steppes who until then had been restricted to a disorderly, Brownian form of movement of particular groups, henceforth united together and set off to conquer the largest empire that the world has ever known. Events such as this draw our attention to the advantages of following a calendar determined not according to the permanent aspects of the planets but according to the variations of climate. Indeed, the Mongols would not have reached such a high degree of power had the climate not favoured the humidification of the pasture lands which nourished their horses. However, it will be a good while before we have available a calendar based on climatic variations. We still lack information on some vital factors: the evaluation of harvests, the extension or the regression of lacustrine and forest areas, phytographical analyses, and so on. Only when we have obtained such necessary data can we think of establishing a new type of periodization that can be verified through metereological calculations extrapolating and applying to the past our present conjectures about the influence of solar explosions on the atmosphere.

The period to be treated in the fourth volume was therefore set by the end of Volume III (the seventh century) and the beginning (the sixteenth century) of Volume V. Volumes I and II have been devoted to the many thousands of years constituting the origins of humanity. The richness of the new data at our disposal made it necessary to treat separately the period spreading from the third millennium to the beginning of the seventh century before our era.

This division into seven volumes, dictated by a combination of factors ranging from the abstract to the practical – amongst the latter being that of ensuring the more or less equal size of the volumes – is more or less in keeping with historical facts. Beyond all specific differences, five principal stages can be recorded in human evolution: the use of material tools accompanied by the emergence of cultures destined to be full of meaning for a long time to come; the moulding of a geo-politics or a geo-culture signalled by the appearance of major works of all kinds, all of which were to be of lasting value; partitive convulsions that forced in advance the distinction of cultural identities through the play of mutual influences; conceptions resulting from a closed human universe whose planetary course lies within a limitless space; the intensification of centres of development under the pressure of a capitalism that has become industrial and an industry that is becoming scientific – phenomena which push to the outskirts the excess of constraints from which the thus privileged zones escape. The seventh volume will thus deal with the issue of these new currents and the tidal waves that they provoke; facets that lead to the birth of a new type of polarization and as a result of which traditional cultures fall into abeyance.

Such bird's-eye views as those offered here are not misleading because they are crude; they seem questionable because they escape our sight when we keep ourselves too close to the ordinary facts. And it is in this that we mainly confront the limitations of our methods of research. No one is unaware of the difficulties that continue to affect all attempts to provide a synthetic view of humankind's common destiny. There is no answer to these difficulties from which the present subdivision of each volume into themes and regions suffers; into themes to bring out what all human beings share in common; into regions to mark the diversities.

In each volume, the thematic parts should have been the easiest to work out. Several problems were, however, encountered. In order to ensure that the cultures that benefit from the spectacular development that we witness today be no longer favoured beyond measure, it was considered necessary to reduce the importance granted to theoretical innovations and their applications and therefore to refrain from using scientific discoveries as chronological pointers. Had this not been the case, the distribution of themes would have been a simple matter. It would have sufficed to begin with a survey of the scientific and technical knowledge acquired over a given period of time and then retrace the causes in their sequential order.

Now, from the moment when it becomes necessary for history to tone down the privileges conferred on some by the process of evolution – and, more particularly, to question a system of values rooted in an overly univocal notion of progress – it also becomes necessary to standardize the distribution of themes by including more 'ordinary' references, for example by starting with a description of the physical and natural conditions in order to arrive at the scientific through the demographic and the cultural. This not only increased the uniformity of the volumes but also offered the major advantage of emphasizing the ways of living. Whatever they are, these must first satisfy the basic physiological needs – a vital minimum dictated by the instincts of survival and rendered partially relative by the differences of climate. Each culture responds to this in its own manner and according as much to its natural environment as to the habits that it inherits. Certain acquired needs are then added to this vital minimum – superfluous needs turned into necessary ones and established in varying degrees according to the social hierarchies and geohistorical differences. Moreover, as human beings are not only biological but also thinking and feeling entities, each material culture is accompanied by a culture that can be called 'spiritual' in the widest sense of the term and that also varies according to the situation already mentioned. Finally, even though the conditions are not identical, material culture and spiritual culture are interrelated.

This enunciation of the common grounds on which all human lives are established stands to reason and would seem evident to any lay person. It could also, however, lead us to think that it is easy to find historians ready to develop each theme. The present state of historical knowledge proves that it is not so and, as always, for the same reason. Insignificant as this problem may be, the solution lies in turning one's back on analytical methods and adopting an approach that would be one of synthesis.

Undoubtedly, current research and investigations help us in our evaluation of material and spiritual cultures, but separately. We are completely ignorant about the interconnections between the two. Where does this notorious deficiency come from? Two main reasons can be put forward.

The first concerns the elaboration of a global history. Indeed, when it comes to local or regional histories, each confined to a particular epoch, the data that we possess help us either to deal with some of the problems or to contribute by offering some information. But when one or the other problem needs to be looked at from a global point of view, then we confront a major difficulty: which elements of the data available should be included in an inventory of an absolutely common heritage? In other words, what advances made at one place or the other, or at one point of time or another, effectively contributed to what can be called 'general progress'? The workshops of historians can boast of few if any historians at all who specialize in the evaluation of 'generalities'! When the need for one arises, then it has to be admitted that the courageous few who have undertaken such a task suffered from the absence of sufficient information and were compelled to work in conditions that rendered their merits highly eminent but curbed considerably their influence.

This first reason leads to the second, the absence of criteria that would make it possible to distinguish effectively the subjective from the objective as much in the work accomplished as in the reputations won. Here we touch upon an issue that is too important to dismiss without fuller attention.

The studies on primitive or savage societies, particularly those conducted over the last fifty years, carried anthropology to a high degree of what must be called the 'intelligence' of cultures. Indeed, in these societies, myth plays a fundamental role. It legitimizes matrimonial and social behaviour as well as customs and ways of living – the way one eats, dresses and organizes one's life inside and outside one's own dwelling. In an even more significant manner, it legitimizes humankind's spiritual behaviour as much in times of war as in peace. This global aspect of myth itself leads us to the heights from which, at one glance, we can view not only the various behaviours as a whole, but also, and as a result, the very logic that sustains them.

Historical evolution disperses myth, without however abolishing the mythological function. It provokes the growth of branches and favours ramifications. What had been thanks to myth, at one and the same time, religion and literature, moral and political, art and technique, breaks up later into more and more subdivided areas of knowledge; differentiations that led namely to the belief that the logic of myth or of the sacred is gainsaid by that of science. 'Science': this word which obstructs more than all others what we term historical intelligence. In the original sense of the word, science means knowledge, with no distinction implied between knowledge and know-how. Today this same word has taken on such a specific meaning that for a vast majority of the most highly informed minds, science denotes truth, as against the falsity of myth. Yet, many eminent scholars acknowledge that this 'truth' contains a part of myth and that it is indeed thanks to this that methods and knowledge advance. It is by working within the mythological that we reduce the part of myths, something of which always survives in the very heart of science.

The barriers that have been most resolutely built against the 'intelligence' of history have their sources in the gradual formation of separate enclaves of investigation. Social, economic, political, literary history and so on: each domain follows its own path and rarely meets the other, or never enough to allow for the establishment of criteria common to all that could constitute the basis for a truly universal history of scientific and cultural developments. The worst form of such separations can be found in the cosmic distance that has been introduced between the history of religion and that of science, and this in spite of some highly remarkable, though rare, attempts to make them move towards each other via the social and the philosophical. No significant results should be expected until the gaps between ordinary language and scientific language are bridged, particularly when the latter makes use of mathematical terms so fully exploited by the initiated few and so little accessible to the secular mass.

This brings us back to the question of the limitations of this edition referred to earlier: limitations concerning the basic logical presuppositions on which a truly universal history of humankind should be founded. It is only on the basis of certain common features that one culture can comprehend something that is part of another culture and that the people of today can understand a little of what lies in the past. But then, given the present state of our knowledge and the manner in which the basic logical presuppositions are handled, our history will remain beyond the reach of the general public, however enlightened, for which it is intended.

None the less, a certain merit – perhaps less significant than hoped for – makes this second edition worthy of our attention. By eliminating the notion that the cultures rendered marginal by 'progress' represent groups of people 'without history', the study of cultures wherein myth is dispersed among all kinds of domains could only gain from the experience of those whose lives are, even today, steeped in a mythology that they all consider fundamental. We have not as yet reached our goal, but the step taken marks a sure improvement in terms of our understanding of history. And, as the readers will themselves find out, it is this aspect of the thematic part of each volume that makes this work truly exceptional.

We now come to the question of the treatment of regions in each volume. To begin with, let us look at a major ambiguity which threatened the very conception of these sections. An example will suffice. To which region does Newton belong? To Cambridge? England? Europe? The West? The world? There is no doubt that the universality of his law of gravitation makes him a part of the common heritage of humanity. Yet, undoubtedly this law discovered by a particular man, at a particular place and point of time, would seem to have miraculously descended from the skies, if we did not take into account the facts of the discovery, the circumstances leading to it and the manner in which the law was adopted by all. Should we have then talked about Newton in one way in the thematic chapter and in another in the regional? Although the difficulties involved in solving such a problem are great, they turn out to be less so when confronted with yet another problem that would have resulted from any attempt to merge the two parts into one: for, in that case, the question would have been, which one? A fusion of all into the regional would, to a great extent, have simplified the task, given that we are dealing with specializations in different fields. But it would have led to the very unpleasant need to emphasize the merits of one culture at the cost of the others. A fusion of all into the thematic? In that case, Newton's law would have been stripped of its socio-cultural characteristics and this would have led to some kind of sanctification of the 'genius'. Needless to say, what has been noted as regards Newton applies to all thinkers, discoverers and to all that humankind has created.

Some readers will perhaps regret the fact that this history, whose dominant note is certainly transcultural, does not succeed better in overcoming certain problems resulting from habits and preconceived notions. We all talk about Asia, Africa and Europe. Originally, these were names given to Greek nymphs and were used to distinguish the three principal, cardinal points of the world perceived by the Mediterranean navigators: the east, the south and the north, respectively. To these seafarers the west was nothing but a vast indecipherable stretch, presumably a part of the legendary Atlantis. As for the continent of America, its name was curiously given to it by a cartographer who, while outlining a map of this continent, used the information supplied to him by Amerigo Vespucci – thus depriving Christopher Columbus of the recognition he deserved. In the case of the nymphs as well as in that of the cartographer, we can no longer distinguish the subjective from the objective. What was in fact a very subjective decision in the first place now appears to be very objective because it is commonly accepted by everyone. We cannot change something that has been so firmly established over the years, but the often very serious problems and disadvantages that result from the ethnocentrism implied by such customs need to be pointed out.

Depending on the epochs, Egypt is at times best understood when considered as African and at others when its civilization is regarded as having acquired much of its significance from a dual Nile–Euphrates identity. Similarly, instead of remaining Mediterranean, southern Europe became continental when the centre of gravity of exchanges and developments shifted to the Atlantic. China constitutes another example. This Middle Kingdom felt the effects of the existence of other continental regions when its Great Wall no longer protected it from the conquerors it tried later to assimilate, or when it yielded, perhaps for too long a period, to the attacks of the seamen and naval forces coming from the other end of the world, that is, from Europe.

Geographical perspectives change from one era to another. But it is difficult to incorporate such changes and align them with the periodization adopted for a work on history. Those responsible for planning the seven volumes had to devise the ways and means of solving such problems. At times they had to have recourse to certain subterfuges so as to prevent the periodization from turning into some kind of a jigsaw puzzle and requiring a frequent arrangement and rearrangement. This entailed, however, the risks of introducing certain anachronisms.

Such risks are in no way negligible. To a modern mind, for example, the commerce or the conquests in ancient times across the deserts of Sinai appear as manifestations of the hostilities existing between Africa and Asia. This distinction between the two continents becomes nonsensical when applied to the period when Egypt did not see itself as African nor Assyria as Asian. Each region thought of itself first as constituting in itself the whole universe or as representing in itself the whole universe as defined by its own gods. We must be aware of the dangers of accepting such ideas, which still survive in the unconscious, affect our conscious minds, and foster notions of rights and privileges detrimental to the development of universalism.

The need to determine the number of pages to be devoted to each 'continent' arose from certain customs that, although anachronistic, generate at times very strong emotions and influence our decisions. It also arose from the fact that the distrust of ethnocentrism expressed itself in terms that were very ethnocentric. Including Cro-Magnon man in an inventory of 'European' sites amounts to attributing to him a label that contradicts all that was felt in times when existence could not be conceived of except in terms very different from those related to our planetary territoriality. Similarly, the concept of Africa was itself foreign to the African empires or kingdoms, each constituting for each a world in itself and, at the same time, a world which belongs to all. The readers will themselves correct such imperfections, which have resulted from a need to adopt a pragmatic approach.

Applying modern notions of geography to any period of the past relieves us of the dizziness felt when we look down into the immense depths of time, yet it is in these depths that cultural but also natural interactions, direct or indirect, multiplied: a swarming mass much too indecipherable to allow for the delineation of linear ancestry. It is, therefore, better to avoid distinguishing overmuch our distant common ancestors. Physical evolution leads perhaps to the formation of races. But as the human species can be known through its customs, faculties and cerebral activities, this privilege common to all reduces practically to nothing the particularisms that some not always disinterested viewpoints defined formerly as racial.

The human species cannot really be differentiated except as ethnic groups and through customs that defy any simplistic typology. A strong capacity for adaption, peculiar to humans, enables them to invent a practically limitless number of solutions to the problems posed by all kinds of environments, and even more so by circumstances that the smallest events modify and great events transform altogether. In this lies the most amazing aspect of history: the infinite variety of answers that each individual or collectivity finds to the questions put to it by destiny. The more history accelerates its pace and becomes more specific, the more our destiny becomes enigmatic. This is because every human being is a human being and no single one resembles another.

The end of the colonialisms that believed or claimed themselves to be the civilizers of this world led to the birth of many new nations and many new Member States of international organizations. 'New' in what sense? The establishment of a 'New World Order' is bound to remain a Utopian idea as long as history has not explained how a local body of historical cultures finally engendered what it has over the centuries referred to as 'civilization'; a word full of contradictions. Intended as universal and respectful to other cultures, this civilization turned out to be materialist and destroyed many cultures as a result of the superiority that it attributed to its own system of laws and rights. Two heavy tasks thus face historians: acknowledging the universalism that lies hidden beneath all particularisms and agreeing among themselves on what should be made generally known in this respect.

An elucidation of the past requires personal as well as collective efforts. This two-fold process should therefore have found spontaneous expression in a work meant to aid the advancement of knowledge. The Commission recommended therefore that, in addition to the thematic and regional parts, a third part be added that would have comprised specific supplements on details that needed developing, problems that needed solving, and finally an exposition of different and opposing opinions on interpretations in dispute. This project met with overwhelming difficulties and some explanation is called for!

This international history, which had been conceived as a result of dialogues and discussions, would evidently have gained considerably from an exposition of the differences in interpretation in their proper dimensions. It would have been more lively and instructive and have given readers more food for thought. Unfortunately, the dispersion of authors to be included and chosen from the whole world demanded means and time that we did not have. The Editors, who already had a heavy task, could not have undertaken this extra work without assistance, in particular from committees specifically chosen and brought together in the light of the subjects to be discussed. Taking into account the costs of travel and accommodation, the already high cost of the operation would have almost doubled. No doubt a day will come when, debates on themes and regions being easier than they are now, it will be possible to expound history as it is revealed by a confrontation of knowledge and viewpoints on particular questions concerning all humanity.

Until the state of knowledge and of historical research in the world has reached this convergent point, we are obliged to give up the idea of showing the divergences that future workshops of historians will have to face. We have, however, provided notes at the end of articles, which have been written so as to ensure maximum diversity and the broadest possible participation. A certain arbitrariness persists, of course. But this will remain unavoidable as long as the excesses that analyses lead to are not minimized through the elaboration of syntheses based on criteria derived from irrefutable logical presuppositions – presuppositions that help establish universal certitudes. Let us not forget, however, that innovations originate only within the gaps of certitude.

One of the merits of this work lies in that it has succeeded in enlisting the collaboration of a very large number of people, representing a large number of regions and cultures. The Commission also encouraged the formation of local working groups responsible for obtaining and organizing the data to be included in the various chapters. This present work marks perhaps only the beginning of such collective efforts. Nevertheless, it permits us to anticipate satisfactory results. Knowing oneself well in order to make oneself better known constitutes a major contribution to mutual understanding. In this respect, historical research resembles an awareness of unconscious phenomena. It brings into the daylight what in the nocturnal depths of individual or collective existences gives them life, so to say, in spite of themselves or against their will.

This publication will no doubt give rise to many critcisms. If these turn out to be harsh, they will justify the project, whose main objective is to arouse us from our dogmatic slumber. Historical events take care of this much more efficiently, but at a much higher price.

GENERAL INTRODUCTION

Georges-Henri Dumont
President of the International Commission

Societies are making greater demands than ever on history, but urgent as they might be, these demands by various groups are not altogether straightforward. Some societies look to historians to define their identity, to buttress the development of their specific characteristics or even to present and analyse the past as confirming a founding myth. Conversely, other societies, influenced both by the *Annales* school of historiography and by the geographical, chronological and thematic enlargement of history, aspire to the building of bridges, the ending of self-isolation and the smoothing out of the lack of continuity that is characteristic of the short term.

In 1946 those attending the meeting of the first Preparatory Commission of UNESCO agreed that it was part of the fundamental mission of the United Nations Educational, Scientific and Cultural Organization to lay the foundations for a collective memory of humanity and of all its parts, spread all over the world and expressing themselves in every civilization. The International Scientific Commission came into being four years later with the apparently gigantic task of drafting a *History of the Scientific and Cultural Development of Mankind*. Publication of the six volumes began in 1963, marking the successful conclusion of an international endeavour without parallel, but not without risks. Success with the general public was immediate and lasting, notwithstanding the reservations expressed by the critics, who often found certain choices disconcerting but were not consitent in the choices and interpretations they proposed as alternatives.

For its time – not the time of its publication but that of its long preparation – the first edition of the *History of the Scientific and Cultural Development of Mankind* must be seen as a daring achievement, having a number of faults inherent in the very nature of historical knowledge but opening up new avenues and encouraging further progress along them.

In 1978, the General Conference of UNESCO decided to embark on a new and completely revised edition of the *History of the Scientific and Cultural Development of Mankind* because it realized that the considerable development of historiography, the improvement of what are called its auxiliary sciences and its growing links with the social sciences had combined with an extraordinary acceleration of day-to-day history. What it did not know, however, was that the pace of this acceleration would continue to increase until it brought profound changes to the face of the world.

It scarcely needs saying that the task laid upon the International Scientific Commission, under the chairmanship of the late Paulo de Berrêdo Carneiro and then of my eminent predecessor, Professor Charles Morazé, was both enormous and difficult.

First of all, international teams had to be formed, as balanced as possible, and co-operation and dialogue organized between the different views of the major collective stages in the lives of people, but without disregarding the cultural identity of human groups.

Next, attention had to be given to changes in chronological scale by attempting a scientific reconstruction of the successive stages of the peopling of our planet, including the spread of animal populations. This was the goal pursued and largely attained by the authors of the present volume.

Lastly, steps had to be taken to ensure that traditional methods of historical research, based on written sources, were used side by side with new critical methods adapted to the use of oral sources and contributions from archaeology, in Africa for the most part.

To quote what Professor Jean Devisse said at a symposium in Nice in 1986 on 'Being a historian today': 'If we accept that the history of other people has something to teach us, there can be no infallible model, no immutable methodological certainty: listening to each other can lead to a genuine universal history.'

Although historians must be guided by a desire for intellectual honesty, they depend on their own views of things, with the result that history is the science most vulnerable to ideologies. The fall of the Berlin Wall a few weeks after I assumed office symbolized the end of a particularly burdensome ideological division. It certainly makes the work of the International Scientific Commission easier whenever it has to come to grips with the past–present dialectic, from which history cannot escape.

In a way, the impact of ideologies will also be lessened by the fact that the Chief Editors of each volume have sought the invaluable co-operation not only of experienced historians but also of renowned specialists in disciplines such as law, art, philosophy, literature, oral traditions, the natural sciences, medicine, anthropology, mathematics and economics. In any event, this interdisciplinarity, which helps dissipate error, is undoubtedly one of the major improvements of this second edition of the *History of Humanity, Scientific and Cultural Development* over the previous edition.

Another problem faced was that of periodization. It was out of the question systematically to adopt the periodization long in use in European history, that is Antiquity, the Middle Ages, modern times, because it is now being extensively called into question and also, above all, because it would have led to a Eurocentric view of world history, a view whose absurdity is now quite obvious. The seven volumes are thus arranged in the following chronological order:

Volume I	Prehistory and the beginnings of civilization
Volume II	From the third millennium to the seventh century BC
Volume III	From the seventh century BC to the seventh century AD
Volume IV	From the seventh to the sixteenth century
Volume V	From the sixteenth to the eighteenth century
Volume VI	The nineteenth century
Volume VII	The twentieth century.

It must be stated at once that this somewhat surgical distribution is in no way absolute or binding. It will in no way prevent the overlapping that there must be at the turn of each century if breaks in continuity and the resulting errors of perspective are to be avoided. Indeed, it has been said that we are already in the twenty-first century!

In his preface, Professor Charles Morazé has clearly described and explained the structure of each of the volumes, with a thematic chapter, a regional chapter and annexes. This structure, too, may be modified so as not to upset the complementarity of the pieces of a mosaic that must retain its significance.

When the International Scientific Commission, the Chief Editors of the volumes and the very large number of contributors have completed their work – and this will be in the near future – they will be able to adopt as their motto the frequently quoted saying of the philosopher Etienne Gilson:

> We do not study history to get rid of it but to save from nothingness all the past which, without history, would vanish into the void. We study history so that what, without it, would not even be the past any more, may be reborn to life in this unique present outside which nothing exists.

This present will be all the more unique because history will have shown itself to be not an instrument for legitimizing exacerbated forms of nationalism, but an instrument, ever more effective because ever more perfectible, for ensuring mutual respect, solidarity and the scientific and cultural interdependence of humanity.

THE INTERNATIONAL COMMISSION

for the New Edition of the History of the Scientific and Cultural Development of Mankind

President: G.-H. Dumont (Belgium)

Members of the International Commission:
I. A. Abu-Lughod (Palestinian Authority)
A. R. Al-Ansary (Saudi Arabia)
J. Bony (Côte d'Ivoire)
E. K. Brathwaite (Barbados)
G. Carrera Damas (Venezuela)
A. H. Dani (Pakistan)
D. Denoon (Australia)
M. Garašanin (Yugoslavia)
T. Haga (Japan)
H. Inalcik (Turkey)
S. Kartodirdjo (Indonesia)
J. Ki-Zerbo (Burkina Faso)
C. Martínez Shaw (Spain)
E. Mendelsohn (United States of America)
E. M'Bokolo (Democratic Republic of the Congo)
K. N'Ketia (Ghana)
T. Obenga (Congo)
B. A. Ogot (Kenya)
Pang Pu (China)
W. Sauerlander (Germany)
B. Schroeder-Gudehus (Ms) (Canada)
R. Thapar (Ms) (India)
I. D. Thiam (Senegal)
K. V. Thomas (United Kingdom)
S. L. Tikhvinsky (Russian Federation)
N. Todorov (Bulgaria)
G. Weinberg (Argentina)
M. Yardeni (Ms) (Israel)
E. Zürcher (The Netherlands)

Bureau of the International Commission:
A. R. Al-Ansary (Saudi Arabia)
E. K. Brathwaite (Barbados)
G. Carrera Damas (Venezuela)
A. H. Dani (Pakistan)
E. Mendelsohn (United States of America)
R. Thapar (Ms) (India)
I. D. Thiam (Senegal)
K. V. Thomas (United Kingdom)
S. L. Tikhvinsky (Russian Federation)
N. Todorov (Bulgaria)

Honorary Members:
S. A. Al-Ali (Iraq)
P. J. Riis (Denmark)
T. Yamamoto (Japan)

Former Presidents:
P. E. B. Carneiro (Brazil) (deceased)
C. Morazé (France)

Secretariat (UNESCO):
J. P. Bouyain, Principal Programme Specialist
B. Appleyard (Ms)
M. Vallès (Ms)

Former Members:
E. Condurachi (Romania) (deceased)
G. Daws (Australia)
C. A. Diop (Senegal) (deceased)
F. Iglesias (Brazil) (deceased)
A. A. Kamel (Egypt) (deceased)
M. Kably (Morocco)
H. Nakamura (Japan)
J. Prawer (Israel) (deceased)
S. Zavala (Mexico)

HISTORY OF HUMANITY SCIENTIFIC AND CULTURAL DEVELOPMENT IN SEVEN VOLUMES

VOLUME I
Prehistory and the Beginnings of Civilization

Editor: S. J. De Laet (Belgium) (deceased)
Co-Editors: A. H. Dani (Pakistan)
J. L. Lorenzo (Mexico) (deceased)
R. B. Nunoo (Ghana)

VOLUME II
From the Third Millennium to the Seventh Century BC

Editors: A. H. Dani (Pakistan)
J.-P. Mohen (France)
Co-Editors: C. A. Diop (Senegal) (deceased)
J. L. Lorenzo (Mexico) (deceased)
V. M. Masson (Russian Federation)
T. Obenga (Congo)
M. B. Sakellariou (Greece)
B. K. Thapar (India) (deceased)
Xia Nai (China) (deceased)
Zhang Changshou (China)

VOLUME III
From the Seventh Century BC *to the Seventh Century* AD

Editors: E. Condurachi (Romania) (deceased)
J. Herrmann (Germany)
E. Zürcher (The Netherlands)
Co-Editors: J. Harmatta (Hungary)
J. Litvak King (Mexico)
R. Lonis (France)
T. Obenga (Congo)
R. Thapar (Ms) (India)
Zhou Yiliang (China)

VOLUME IV
From the Seventh to the Sixteenth Century

Editors: M. A. Al-Bakhit (Jordan)
L. Bazin (France)
S. M. Cissoko (Mali)
A. A. Kamel (Egypt) (deceased)
Co-Editors: M. S. Asimov (Tajikistan) (deceased)
P. Gendrop (Mexico) (deceased)
A. Gieysztor (Poland) (deceased)
I. Habib (India)
Y. Karayannopoulos (Greece)
J. Litvak King/P. Schmidt (Mexico)

VOLUME V
From the Sixteenth to the Eighteenth Century

Editors: P. Burke (United Kingdom)
H. Inalcik (Turkey)
Co-Editors: I. Habib (India)
J. Ki-Zerbo (Burkina Faso)
T. Kusamitsu (Japan)
C. Martínez Shaw (Spain)
E. Tchernjak (Russian Federation)
E. Trabulse (Mexico)

VOLUME VI
The Nineteenth Century

Editors: P. Mathias (United Kingdom)
N. Todorov (Bulgaria)
Co-Editors: S. Al Mujahid (Pakistan)
A. O. Chubarian (Russian Federation)
F. Iglesias (Brazil) (deceased)
Shu-li Ji (China)
I. D. Thiam (Senegal)

VOLUME VII
The Twentieth Century

Editors: E. K. Brathwaite (Barbados)
S. Gopal (India)
E. Mendelsohn (United States of America)
S. L. Tikhvinsky (Russian Federation)
Co-Editors: I. A. Abu-Lughod (Palestinian Authority)
I. D. Thiam (Senegal)
G. Weinberg (Argentina)
Tao Wenzhao (China)

LIST OF FIGURES

1 The *quipu*, a decimal system of counting (pre-Hispanic Peru)
2 Digging stick (pre-Hispanic Peru)
3 Woman weaving at a backstrap loom (pre-Hispanic Peru)
4 Paired dragons, bronze door-knocker (Iran)
5 A royal official, a suspension bridge and human porterage (pre-Hispanic Peru)
6 The three main forms of horse harness: (a) throat-and-girth (western antiquity); (b) breast strap (ancient and early medieval China); (c) padded horse collar (late medieval China and medieval Europe)
7 Transport and communications in early medieval Northern Europe (France)
8 Uighur script as adapted to Mongolian
9 Arabic script as used in North and West Africa
10 Maya vigesimal numeration
11 The development of numerical notation in India
12 Ibn al-Shātir's model of the motion of the Moon
13 Ox-driven set of wheels and cogs to elevate water (Iraq)
14 *Shaoxing Bencao*: Chinese herbal medicine
15 Chinese acupuncture
16 An anatomy lesson in late fifteenth-century Italy
17 Principles of optics: from a thirteenth-century Spanish manuscript
18 Gateway to al-Azhar Mosque, Cairo (Egypt)
19 Saint Sophia, Kiev (Ukraine)
20 The architect Villard de Honnecourt's drawing of the gothic tower and sculptures of the Cathedral of Laon (France)
21 The temple of Borobudur, Java (Indonesia)
22 Muslim and Christian minstrels in thirteenth-century Spain
23 Sacrificial rites in the ball court: post-classical Maya relief from Chichén Itzá, Yucatán (Mexico)
24 Aztec temple and houses, Aztec codex
25 Early Glagolitic and Cyrillic scripts: (a) the Gospel of Assemanius (Bulgaria); (b) a Cyrillic letter written on elm bark, Novgorod (Russia)
26 Courtyard of a *funduq* or *khān*, a hostelry and storehouse for caravans, merchants and their goods, Cairo (Egypt)
27 Islamic architecture in Cordova (Spain): (a) the mosque: double-horseshoe arches of the main prayer hall; (b) the mosque: multi-lobed arches of the caliph's private prayer space; (c) the mosque: the *mihrāb* or prayer-niche indicating the direction of Mecca; (d) the caliph's palace in the Cordovan suburb of Madīnat al-Zahrā': detail of carved blind window in stone
28 Islamic architecture in Seville: the original appearance of the minaret of the Great Mosque (Spain)
29 The astronomical clock-tower of Kaifeng (China)
30 Early Chinese compass: floating metal fish in a bowl of water
31 Schematic view of Tōdaiji (Japan)
32 Granite tortoise near the ruins of the palace at Qarāqorum (Mongolia)
33 Sculpted windows from three rock churches in Lalibela (Ethiopia): (a) Church of Beta Ghiorghis; (b) Church of Beta Mariam; (c) and (d) Church of Beta Mikael
34 *Átlatl* or spear-thrower, Mitztec or Aztec (Mexico)
35 The 'Staff God' or 'Weeping God' of Tiwanaku or Tiahuanaco (Bolivia)
36 Chimu architectural decoration in moulded mud at Chan Chan (Peru)

LIST OF MAPS

1 Climate and vegetation zones of the world, from the seventh to the sixteenth century
2 Long-distance migrations and conquests in Europe between the seventh and the fifteenth centuries
3 The distribution of universities in Europe during the Middle Ages
4 The boundaries of Byzantium: from glory to decline
5 The Carolingian Empire and the Treaty of Verdun (843)
6 Europe *circa* 1000
7 Intellectual centres in Western Europe during the twelfth century
8 Ethnic movements in Central and South-Eastern Europe during the sixth and seventh centuries
9 Major early medieval towns in the Balkans
10 Northern and Central Europe
11 Christopher Columbus' voyages to America
12 The spread of Islam throughout the world, from the seventh to the fifteenth centuries
13 Central Asia: important medieval geographical areas
14 Iraq in the early ʿAbbāsid era
15 Egypt
16 The Maghrib in the Middle Ages
17 Iran and its neighbours
18 The Sāmānid state between 874 and 999
19 Turkish migrations in the tenth and the eleventh centuries
20 Turkish principalities in Anatolia in the twelfth century
21 Ottoman advances in the fourteenth and fifteenth centuries
22 India in the tenth century
23 India in the fourteenth century
24 The Tang Empire in 755
25 The Northern Song Empire in 1111
26 The Southern Song Empire in 1208
27 Zheng He's voyages between 1405 and 1433
28 Relations between China and Japan between the seventh and the ninth centuries
29 The Mongol Empire: conquests and campaigns (thirteenth century)
30 Africa between the seventh and the fifteenth centuries
31 Island and town of Kilwa, East Africa
32 Archaeological sites known and dated in Madagascar and the Comoros from the period 600 to 1500
33 Bantu expansion in central and southern Africa
34 American culture areas
35 Key to tribal territories in the Arctic
36 Language groups, rivers and significant archaeological sites or localities on the north-west coast of North America, from 700 to 1500
37 Eastern woodlands of North America
38 North America's greater south-west
39 North-eastern Mexico culture area
40 The Mesoamerican culture area
41 Central America
42 The circum-Caribbean and Orinoco–Amazon areas from 700 to 1600
43 The Central Andes from 700 to 1600
44 The southern cone of South America from 700 to 1500

LIST OF PLATES

NOTE

The plates, illustrating this volume were juxtaposed in deliberate compositions by M. Barry, the specialist appointed by UNESCO for this work, not only according to regions, but also to bring out meaningful cultural comparisons between the civilizations of this era and to suggest their influences upon one another. Consequently, the order in which the plates happen to be referred to in the course of the text does not necessarily correspond to their numbered sequence in the Plates section.

1 Codex Fejérváry-Mayer (Mexico), showing the nine 'Lords of Nights' who govern the Aztec calendar
2 Chinese farmer with plough and twin yoked bullocks
3 Muslim farmer with plough and twin yoked bullocks
4 Single camel and pair of oxen draw ploughs in Roman North Africa
5 French farmer with wheeled plough and twin yoked oxen
6 English farmer harrowing by means of 'a horse harnessed with an efficient horsecollar', *Luttrell Psalter* (England)
7 'Modern' horsecollar harnessing in Europe
8 Horse-drawn cart going uphill, *Luttrell Psalter* (England)
9 (a) and (b) Transport in former Chinese capital of Bienjing (modern Kaifeng), 'Spring Festival on the River'
10 Western European heraldry
11 Islamic heraldry (Iraq)
12 Central Asian cavalry, Farāmurz chasing the king of Kabul's army
13 Mongol princess in high-wheeled camel-cart crosses a river
14 Japanese mounted Warrior-Aristocrat
15 West African Equestrian figure (Mali)
16 Depiction of mill and water-wheel, Morocco or Islamic Spain
17 Depiction of water-wheel in France
18 Water-wheel moved by oxen (Iraq)
19 Harnessing water-power in China: (a) the *Niuche*; (b) the *Tongache*; (c) the *bache*
20 Viking ship (Norway)
21 Chinese stern-post rudder, 'Spring Festival on the River' (China)
22 Muslim dhow as used in the Gulf and Indian Ocean (Iraq)
23 Venetian sailing craft, 'The Legend of Saint Ursula' (Italy)
24 Portuguese *caravela* as seen through a Spanish Muslim potter's eyes
25 Fully rigged Portuguese *caravela* under full wind aft (Portugal)
26 Building the Great Mosque of Tīmūr in Samarkand (Uzbekistan)
27 Building Castle Khawarnaq, by Bihzād of Herāt for the Persian-language tales (Āzerbaijān)
28 The Cathedral of Reims (France)
29 Depiction of a contemporary rising Gothic cathedral, Tours (France)
30 Citadel of Aleppo (Syria)
31 Krac des Chevaliers, Crusader castle (Syria)
32 The Bāb Zuwayla, the *city ramparts*, Cairo (Egypt)
33 The Great Zimbabwe (Zimbabwe): (a) aerial view; (b) tower and ramparts
34 Ramparts and minarets of the Mosque of Jingereber, Timbuktu (Mali)
35 Gateway of fort of Kilwa Kisiwani, Kilwa Island (Kenya)
36 Ramparts and moat, Provins (France)
37 Genoese fortress at Soldaia, Crimea (Ukraine)
38 Fortress of Sacsahuamán, Cuzco (Peru)
39 Fortified gateway of the 'Porte du Croux', Nevers (France)
40 Northern European view of Venice (Italy)
41 Italian fortified seaside town (Italy)
42 Demon with fire-lance on Buddhist banner (China)
43 Early bronze cannon cast in 1331 (China)
44 The English Earl of Warwick besieges the French fortified port of Caen with guns
45 The Dome of the Rock, Jerusalem
46 Medieval French view of Jerusalem with the Dome of the Rock (France)
47 Judgment of Solomon, Hebrew prayer book, Tours (France)
48 Solomon with the Queen of Sheba, Notre Dame de Corbeil (France)
49 Solomon, Book of Psalms (Ethiopia)
50 Solomon holds his magic seal, Tabrīz (Iran)
51 Solomon, the Queen of Sheba and their minister Asaph borne by submissive genies, probably Tabrīz (Iran)
52 Ganesh and his *shaktī* or projected female counterpart, Khajuraho (India)
53 Ganesh as Lord of Prosperity and patron of merchants (India)
54 Ganesh and other Hindu deities (China)
55 Ganesh in the royal pose enthroned upon the lotus, Polonnaruva (Sri Lanka)
56 Christ as Pantocrator, in the pose of Imperial Protector, with Saint Menas, Eastern Christendom (Egypt)
57 The Crucified Saviour between the Virgin and Saint John. Eastern Christendom, Byzantine icon, Sinai (Egypt)

58 The Entombment, Eastern Christendom, Thessaloniki (Greece)
59 Christ as Pantocrator, Western Christendom, Catalonia (Spain)
60 The Crucified Saviour, Western Christendom, Arezzo (Italy)
61 Christ bearing the wounds of the Cross, Western Christendom, Prague (Czech Republic)
62 'Ecce Homo', Western Christendom (Portugal)
63 The Ascension of the Virgin as seen before the Imperial Basilica of the Holy Apostles in Constantinople (Turkey)
64 Procession of the Holy Cross before the Basilica of Saint Mark, Venice (Italy)
65 The Great Mosque of Cordova (Spain)
66 The private oratory of the caliphs in the Great Mosque of Cordova (Spain)
67 Striped arches in the nave of the Abbey Church of Sainte Madeleine, Vézelay (France)
68 Striped arches in the cloisters of Notre Dame Cathedral, Le Puy en Vélay (France)
69 Multi-lobed arches of the portal of the Chapel of Saint Michel d'Aiguilhe, Le Puy en Vélay (France)
70 Blind pointed arches of the façade of the Mosque of al-Aqmar, Cairo (Egypt)
71 Pointed vaulting in the prayer hall of the Masjid-i Jāmi' ('Friday Mosque'), Isfahān (Iran)
72 Fātimid-style blind pointed arches on the apse of the cathedral, Monreale (Sicily)
73 Fātimid-style pointed arches in the cathedral cloister, Monreale (Sicily)
74 Durham Cathedral (England)
75 Cathedral of Saint Etienne, Bourges (France)
76 Hebrew page from the *Guide to the Perplexed* by Maimonides (Spain)
77 King David depicted as a contemporary French king, Tours (France)
78 Islamic-style windows in the Synagogue of El Tránsito, Toledo (Spain)
79 Mingled Hebrew and Arabic calligraphies in the Synagogue of El Tránsito, Toledo (Spain)
80 Face of Prince Gautama as a *Bodhisattva,* Ajantā (India)
81 Face of the Bodhisattva Avalokiteshvara, Nara (Japan)
82 The Buddha Shākyamuni, Ankor (Cambodia)
83 The Buddha Akshobhya, Tibet
84 The Bodhisattva Avalokiteshvara, Veragala (Sri Lanka)
85 The Bodhisattva Avalokiteshvara, Song Dynasty (China)
86 The Bodhisattva Avalokiteshvara, Koryo Dynasty (Korea)
87 The Bodhisattva Avalokiteshvara seen as the guide of a human soul, Dunhuang (China)
88 The Great Mosque of Tlemcen (Algeria)
89 Oculus in the dome over the Tomb of the Ṣūfī master Shāh Ni'matullāh Walī, Māhān (Iran)
90 Carpet page to a multi-volume Qur'ān, Cairo (Egypt)
91 Tile decoration over the supposed tomb of the Ṣūfī master Shams-i Tabrīzī, Multān (Pakistan)
92 'The Scribe', Palenque, Chiapas (Mexico)
93 Maya characters or glyphs, Palenque, Chiapas (Mexico)
94 Mixtec writing, Puebla-Oaxaca region (Mexico)
95 Portrait of the poet Li Taibo, Southern Song Dynasty (China)
96 Cursive calligraphy, Yuan Dynasty (China)
97 Classically formed calligraphy (Korea)
98 Portrait of the poet Akahito, Kamakura period (Japan)
99 'Grass' calligraphy of verses by famous poets, Kamakura period (Japan)
100 Educated Indian woman writing on a palm-leaf, Khajuraho (India)
101 Astasāhasrikā-Prajnā-Pāramitā (Nepal)
102 Indian Buddhist missionary to China reading a Sanskrit manuscript
103 Giovanni Boccaccio at his writing-desk, with the figure of Fortune, Paris (France)
104 *Marcus:* initial to the Gospel of Saint Mark from the monastery of Lindisfarne, Anglo-Saxon (England)
105 The Chi-Ro Page or twin Greek initials of the name of Christ (Ireland)
106 Cyrillic script on a ceramic plaque, Preslav (Bulgaria)
107 Page of Kūfī calligraphy from the Qur'ān on parchment (Tunisia)
108 Page of Kūfī calligraphy from the Qur'ān on vellum (Iraq)
109 Blessing in Kūfī calligraphy on a slip-painted earthenware dish, Nīshāpūr (Iran)
110 Page of Naskh (standard cursive) calligraphy from the Qur'ān on paper, Cairo (Egypt)
111 Wall decorations in tiling and stucco with bands of thuluth, Fez (Morocco)
112 Arabic script as used for Persian in Nasta'līq ('hanging cursive') calligraphy, Herāt (Afghanistan)
113 Arabic script as used for Turkish in Nasta'līq ('hanging cursive') calligraphy, Herāt (Afghanistan)
114 Arab scribe writing with a reed-pen upon his knee, Baghdād (Iraq)
115 Chinese printing: block-printing on paper, Dunhuang (China)
116 Arabic block-printing, West Asia
117 The 42-line bible in movable type, Mainz (Germany)
118 The poet François Villon, Paris (France)
119 The world as seen by the Franco-Flemish Jean Mansel: the three continents surrounded by the ocean stream
120 The monstrous creatures: illustration to the works of Solinus Polyhistor, Arnstein (Germany)
121 Marco Polo samples the pepper crop on India's Malabar coast, *Book of Marvels*
122 The Ptolemaic world map as published in Ulm (Germany)
123 The medieval Arab world-view
124 The world map of Henricus Martellus, Florence (Italy)
125 Detail of the Kangnido (Korea)
126 An Arabic translation of *De Materia Medica of Dioscorides*
127 The triumph of Saint Thomas Aquinas, Pisa (Italy)
128 Prince Shōtoku and his sons (Japan)
129 Miniature from a treatise on the dislocation of bones by Apollonios of Kition, Byzantine manuscript
130 Page with a depiction of medicinal plants from an Arabic translation of *De Materia Medica of Dioscorides*
131 The devil blows disease upon Job (France)
132 Church dignitary shown wearing spectacles, Cathedral of Meaux (France)
133 Avicenna's 'Medical canon': (a) lecturing; (b) doctor examining urine; (c) apothecary's shop; (d) doctor's house call; (e) bleeding
134 The astronomical observatory in Beijing (China)
135 The constellation of Perseus (Iran)
136 The constellation of Boötes, Central Asia
137 The constellation of Aquarius, *Liber de stellis fixarum*
138 Celestial globe (Iran)

139 The astrolabe (Iran)
140 The astrolabe (Syria)
141 The astrolabe (France)
142 The astrolabe (Egypt)
143 The astrolabe (Spain)
144 Stone of the Sun or Aztec calendar stone (Mexico)
145 Emperor Constantine as founder of Constantinople
146 Saint Demetrius in the pose of imperial protector over the archbishop, Thessaloniki (Greece)
147 The Christ-child as Imperial Pantocrator with the Virgin enthroned, Byzantium
148 Emperor John II Comnenus and Empress Irene, with the Virgin and Child, Aya Sofya, Constantinople, Byzantium
149 Christ crowns the German emperor Otto II and his Byzantine-born consort, the Empress Theophano, Byzantium
150 Emperor Manuel II Palaeologus, manuscript illumination, Byzantium
151 Tsar Ivan Alexander of Bulgaria and his family, Tŭrnovo (Bulgaria)
152 Prince Milutin of Serbia symbolically offers his church of the annunciation at Gracanica (Federal Republic of Yugoslavia)
153 Baptism of the Bulgarians under Boris I (Bulgaria)
154 Head of an archangel, Sofia (Bulgaria)
155 Saint Theodore, ceramic icon from Preslav (Bulgaria)
156 The Transfiguration (Armenia)
157 Baptism of the Rus' (Russia)
158 Saint Boris and Saint Gleb, Moscow school (Russia)
159 The Trinity by Andrei Rublev (Russia)
160 The Saviour by Andrei Rublev (Russia)
161 Equestrian bronze statuette of Charlemagne, Carolingian Empire
162 Frankish mounted warriors, Carolingian Empire
163 Rabanus Maurus, Abbot of Fulda, presents his book to Pope Gregory IV, Carolingian Empire
164 Saint John's mystic vision of the Adoration of the Lamb, Carolingian Empire
165 Dragon-head, carved head-post from the Viking ship burial at Oseberg (Norway)
166 Dragon-head, ornament to a horse's harness-bow from Mammen (Denmark)
167 Viking warrior's head from Sigtuna (Sweden)
168 Head of King Eystein of Norway, Bergen (Norway)
169 The Frankish emperor Charles the Bald and the Abbot of the Monastery of Saint Martin de Tours (France)
170 Rex a Deo Coronatus, German Emperor Henri II (Germany)
171 Archbishop Thomas Becket slain by the knights of King Henry II of England (England)
172 Robert d'Anjou, king of Naples and the sainted Bishop Louis of Toulouse (Italy)
173 Queen Béatrice de Bourbon in the Basilica of Saint Denis (France)
174 The wedding of the Bruges-based Italian merchant Giovanni Arnolfini to Giovanna Cenami by Jan van Eyck, Bruges (Belgium)
175 Saint Bridget of Vadstena, Ostergötland (Sweden)
176 The Virgin of Kreuzlowa (Poland)
177 The Austrian lyric poet and knight Walther von der Vogelweide (Germany)
178 Courtly love: a kneeling knight and his lady, Westphalia (Germany)
179 Musical notation: detail from the missal of Saint-Denis (France)
180 Dante admonishes the city of Florence by Domenico di Michelino, Florence (Italy)
181 Mecca, Mosque of the Ḥaram with the Ka'ba at the centre
182 Bedouin girl with camel herd, Baghdād (Iraq)
183 The setting out of a pilgrim caravan, Baghdād (Iraq)
184 Travellers in an Iraqi village, Baghdād (Iraq)
185 Nomad families with Turco-Mongol-style round felt tents, Baghdād (Iraq)
186 The feast of Tīmūr's enthronement beneath his royal *yurt,* Herāt (Afghanistan)
187 Prince Bayād plays the lute before the Lady Riyād and her handmaidens
188 The handmaiden Shamūl delivers a letter from the Lady Riyād to Prince Bayād
189 Traditional mansion (Yemen)
190 Pre-Islamic coins
191 Early figure-bearing coins of the Umayyad Dynasty
192 Islamic coins with inscriptions only
193 Impact of Islamic coins on Christian Europe
194 European-wide reversion to the gold standard
195 Mausoleum of Shāh Ismā'īl the Sāmānid, Bukhārā (Uzbekistan)
196 Tomb of Ghiyāṣ u'ddin Tughluq, Delhi (India)
197 *Madrasa* 'of the Citadel', Baghdād (Iraq)
198 Court of Lions in the Alhambra, Granada (Spain)
199 *Mihrāb* in the Friday Mosque, Iṣfahān (Iran)
200 Multi-lobed *mihrāb* of the Juma Mosque on Mafia Island (Kenya)
201 Courtyard to the prayer hall, in the Qarawiyyīn Mosque, Fez (Morocco)
202 Minaret of the Great Mosque of Qayrawān (Tunisia)
203 Minaret of the 'Booksellers' (*Kutubiyya*), Marrakech (Morocco)
204 Minarets of the Mosque of al-Azhar, Cairo (Egypt)
205 Minarets flanking the gateway to the Mosque of Jenne (Mali)
206 Minaret of the Mosque of Sāmarrā (Iraq)
207 Twin stonework minarets flanking the gateway to the 'Blue *Madrasa*', Sivas (Turkey)
208 Minaret of Jām (Afghanistan)
209 The Qutb Minār, Delhi (India)
210 Dimna the Jackal and the Lion-King, Baghdād (Iraq)
211 The Lion-King kills Shanzāba the Bull, while the jackals Kalīla and Dimna look on, Herāt (Afghanistan)
212 Figured tiles with animal and other motifs in cross and star patterns from the Kāshān Workshops, Dāmghān (Iran)
213 Griffin, Islamic work, Pisa (Italy)
214 Pre-Islamic Soghdian lords feasting cup in hand in the Sasanian royal pose, Panjikent (Tajikistan)
215 The 'Abbāsid caliph al-Ma'mūn feasting cup in hand in the Sasanian royal pose
216 Muslim conqueror of north-west India, enthroned in the Sasanian royal pose
217 Mamlūk sultan feasting cup in hand in the conventional royal pose, Cairo (Egypt)
218 Sultan Husayn Mīrzā Bayqarā of Herāt humbles himself by night before a holy man, Herāt (Afghanistan)
219 The Iranian hero Siyāwush with his bride Farangish, Gujerāt (India)
220 The Kalpasutra and the Kalakacharya Katha, Gujerāt (India)
221 The chariot-temple of the Jagamohan, Konarak, Orissa (India)

222 Shiva Natarāja, Tāmilnādu (India)
223 Shiva Natarāja, Polonnaruva (Sri Lanka)
224 Vajranrtya, goddess of the exuberant dance, Java (Indonesia)
225 Lingarāja, Temple of Bhuvaneshwar, Orissa (India)
226 Southern façade of the shrine of Po Klaung Garai, Binh-dinh (Viet Nam)
227 General silhouette of the Bayon, Angkor Wat (Cambodia)
228 Borobudur, Java (Indonesia)
229 Ornamental front to a temple of Shiva at Banteay Srei (Cambodia)
230 The future Buddha Maitreya (Cambodia)
231 Durga Mahisasuramardini (Cambodia)
232 Crowned head of Buddha (Thailand)
233 The drawing on the ceiling of the chamber in the tumulus of Koguryo
234 Gal Vihāra, Polonnaruwa (Sri Lanka)
235 A many-armed Shiva seated upon the bull Nandī, Dandān-oilik (China)
236 Many-armed aspect of the Bodhisattva Avalokiteshvara, Kyōtō (Japan)
237 Emperor Taizong of the Tang Dynasty (China)
238 Emperor Taizu of the Song Dynasty (China)
239 Emperor Hongwu, founder of the Ming Dynasty (China)
240 Three lady musicians, Tang Dynasty (China)
241 Dense urban crowds around the bridge, 'Spring Festival on the River' by Zhang Zeduan (China)
242 A Ming Dynasty recreation of the painting 'Spring Festival on the River' (China)
243 Chinggis Khān (Mongolia)
244 Ögödäy Khān (Mongolia)
245 Qubilay Khān (Mongolia)
246 (a) and (b) Khitan bronze funeral mask (Mongolia)
247 Detail from a fresco in the Palace of Ögödäy Khān, Qarāqorum (Mongolia)
248 Mongol horseman and his quarry, Yuan Dynasty (China)
249 Ceramic tiles of Pohai
250 Metallic amulet of the early inhabitants of the steppe
251 'Hostelry in the Mountains', Song Dynasty (China)
252 'Autumn in the River Valley', Song Dynasty (China)
253 'Autumn Landscape' (Japan)
254 'Five-Coloured Parakeet on Blossoming Apricot Tree', Song Dynasty (China)
255 Sheep and goat, Yuan Dynasty (China)
256 The minister Taira-no-Shigemori (Japan)
257 Portrait of the Lady Kodai-no-Kimi, the poet (Japan)
258 Prince Niu-no-Miya and his spouse Princess Uji (Japan)
259 The Mali Empire in the *Catalan Atlas*
260 Couple: terracotta statuettes (Niger)
261 Hairpin made of iron, Sanga (Mali)
262 Horse's bit made of iron, Kumbi Saleh (Mauritania)
263 Cache-sexe, fibre and straw, Sanga (Mali)
264 Predogon statuette (Mali)
265 Portuguese knight seen through West African eyes, kingdom of Benin (Nigeria)
266 Bronze roped pot, Igbo-Ukwu (Nigeria)
267 Bronze bust of a queen mother, Kingdom of Benin (Nigeria)
268 Head of a young oni (king), Ife (Nigeria)
269 Supposed portrait of Orson, spouse of the olowo (king) Renrengeyen of Owo (Nigeria)
270 Decorative knob for a staff of office, Igbo-Ukwu (Nigeria)
271 The Great Mosque of Kilwa (Tanzania)
272 Arches of the Great Mosque of Kilwa (Tanzania)
273 A royal Palace at Dunqula converted into a Mosque
274 Money: cowries, *Cyprea moneta*
275 Tomb from the classical Kisalian period, Sanga site
276 Bishop Marianos of Faras protected by the Virgin and Child (Sudan)
277 Martha the Queen Mother with the Virgin and Child (Sudan)
278 The Nativity (Sudan)
279 Saint Mark (Ethiopia)
280 Rock-cut church of Beta Ghiorghis, Lalibela (Ethiopia)
281 Cañon (Canyon) de Chelly: the *White House*, Arizona (USA)
282 Painted pottery from Mimbres, New Mexico (USA): (a) Bird; (b) Grasshopper; (c) Turkey; (d) Turtle; (e) Mythological or ritual re-enactment scene
283 Deer figurehead, west coast of Florida (USA)
284 Antlered human head, Spiro, Oklahoma (USA)
285 Warrior's head, Spiro, Oklahoma (USA)
286 Warrior, Tennessee (USA)
287 Dancing shaman, Spiro, Oklahoma (USA)
288 Human head effigy jar, Arkansas (USA)
289 Three-pointed stone, Santo Domingo (Dominican Republic)
290 Three-pointed stone, Río Pedras (Puerto Rico)
291 Spatula, Higüey, Santo Domingo (Dominican Republic)
292 Dagger or scepter, anthropomorphic stone carving, Río Pedras (Puerto Rico)
293 'Belt' or 'collar', Río Pedras (Puerto Rico)
294 Deified ancestor made manifest in the figure of the vision-serpent, Yaxchilan, Chiapas (Mexico)
295 Blood-letting ritual, Yaxchilan, Chiapas (Mexico)
296 Ruler and nobles with war captives, Bonampak (Mexico)
297 Head of a ruler, Palenque, Chiapas (Mexico)
298 Pirámide del Adivino, Uxmal, Yucatán (Mexico)
299 Statue-columns, Tula, Hidalgo (Mexico)
300 Drum with a serpent, Mexico City (Mexico)
301 Quetzalcóatl in both human and serpent form, Mexico City (Mexico)
302 Crouching God, Mexico City (Mexico)
303 Turquoise mask, Mexico City (Mexico)
304 Eagle warrior, Mexico City (Mexico)
305 Quetzalcóatl as lord of the winds offers a sacrifice (Mexico)
306 Double-headed serpent, Mexico City (Mexico)
307 Aztec temple-pyramid, Mexico City (Mexico)
308 Golden frog (Panama)
309 The 'Alligator' God, Río de Jesus, Province of Veraguas (Panama)
310 The 'Alligator' God, Coclé (Panama)
311 Funerary mask, Tolima (Colombia)
312 Stylized gold figure, Tolima (Colombia)
313 Cache figure, Tunja (Colombia)
314 Gold mask, Nazca (Peru)
315 Ceremonial knife or 'Tumi', Tolima (Colombia)
316 Chan Chan, Tschudi (Peru)
317 Anthropomorphic jar (Peru)
318 Pottery vessel with a mythological scene (Peru)
319 Golden funerary mask, Lambayeque (Peru)
320 Pisaq terraces (Peru)
321 The Temple of the Sun, Machu Picchu (Peru)
322 Pottery vessel: the Inca's warriors (Peru)
323 Silver alpaca, Lake Titicaca (Peru - Bolivia)

THE CONTRIBUTORS

Aigner, Jean (USA); spec. prehistory and human palaeoecology – East Asia, Arctic, Circumpolar; Professor of Anthropology, University of Alaska; Director, Office of Faculty Development, University of Alaska.

Akinjogbin, Isaac Adeagbo (Nigeria); spec. history of West Africa, Yoruba language and literature; Professor of History, Awolowo University, Ife.

Al-Ali, Saleh Ahmad (Iraq); spec. social and economic history of early Islam; President of Iraq Academy; Professor of Arabic History, College of Arts, University of Baghdād.

Al-Bakhit, Mohammad Adnan (Jordan); spec. Islamic history; President, Al al-Bayt University, Mafraq (Jordan).

Al-Hasan, Ahmad Yusuf (Syria); spec. history of Islamic science and technology; Professor, Institute for the History of Arabic Science, University of Aleppo, Syria; Professor, University of Toronto.

Al-Sayyed, Azmi Taha (Jordan); Professor, Department of Philosophy, Al-al Bayt University, Mafraq.

Alpers, Edward A. (USA); spec. history of East Africa; Professor, Department of History, University of California.

Andrianaivoarivony, Rafolo (Madagascar); spec. archaeology and cultural heritage; Director, Art and Archaeology Centre, Faculty of Arts, University of Antananarivo; member of Malagasy Academy.

Arellano Hernández, Alfonso (Mexico); spec. Maya writing and culture; Mesoamerican civilizations; Assessor, Humanities Coordination; Professor, Humanities Faculty (Pre-Hispanic Art and Literature), Universidad Nacional Autónoma de México.

Arutjonova-Fidanjan, Viada (Russian Federation); spec. Byzantinology and Armenology; leading researcher of the Institute of Russian History of the Russian Academy of Sciences; member of the scientific body of the East-Christian Centre (Moscow).

Asimov, Muhammad S., *deceased* (Tajikistan); spec. philosophy and history of sciences; Professor; former member, Tajik Academy of Sciences, Dushanbe.

Aubin, Françoise (France); spec. history, sociology and religions of Central and East Asia; Emeritus Director of Research, Centre National de la Recherche Scientifique (CNRS) and Centre d'Etudes et de Recherches Internationales (CERI) at the Fondation Nationale des Sciences Politiques.

Aufray, Michel (France); spec. Oriental languages and civilizations; Lecturer, Institut National des Langues et Civilisations Orientales (INALCO); scientific member of INALCO, Paris.

Barry, Michael (USA); spec. medieval Iberian cultures (Islamic, Christian) and in medieval and modern Afghanistan. Latest book, *Colour and Symbolism in Islamic Architecture* (Thames & Hudson), received 1997 Medal for History of Art from the Académie Française.

Bazin, Louis (France); spec. philology and cultural history of the Turkish-speaking and Turco–Mongol world; Emeritus Professor, Université de Paris III-Sorbonne Nouvelle; Director of Studies (Turkish History and Philology), Ecole Pratique des Hautes Etudes, IVe section; member of the Institut de France (Académie des Inscriptions et Belles-Lettres).

Benaboud, M'hammad (Morocco); spec. social history of Al-Andalus and the Maghrib (medieval period); Professor, Universities of Rabat and Tetuan; Coordinator of the Research Group for the History of Morocco and al-Andalus at the University of Tetuan.

Bira, Shagdaryn (Mongolia); spec. history, religion and culture of Mongolia; Professor and senior researcher, Institute of History, Mongolian Academy of Sciences; Secretary-General, International Association for Mongol Studies; academician of the Mongolian Academy of Sciences; honorary member of the International Academy of Indian Culture.

Borrmans, Maurice (France/Italy); spec. Islamic law, Muslim spirituality and Muslim–Christian relations through history (especially in the Arab world); Editor-in-Chief of its yearly journal *Islamochristiana*; member of the International Academy of Religious Sciences (Brussels); Professor, Pontificio Istituto di Studi Arabi e d'Islamistica (Rome).

Bosworth, Clifford Edmund (UK); spec. history and culture of the Islamic Middle East and India; Professor, University of Manchester; member, British Academy.

Braude, Benjamin (USA); spec. Middle Eastern history; Professor, University of Boston College.

Bulliet, Richard W. (USA); spec. medieval Islamic history; Professor, Columbia University, New York.

Carlson, Roy L. (Canada); spec. archaeology and ethnology, North American prehistory, particularly north-west coast and south-west, primitive art; Professor, Department of Archaeology, Simon Fraser University; Director, Museum of Archaeology and Ethnology, Simon Fraser University.

Chapoutot-Remadi, Mounira (Tunisia); spec. medieval Islamic history, Egypt and Syria during Mamlūk period; Professor of medieval history, Department of Medieval History at the Faculty of Humanities and Social Sciences, University of Tunis I.

Cissoko, Sékéné Mody (Mali); spec. history of medieval Timbuktu; has published various works on the history of western Sudan, from the Middle Ages to the colonial conquest; research worker, IFAN-Dakar; Professor at the University of Cheikh Anta Diop, Dakar and then at the University of Libreville. Now in Mali.

Cordell, Linda S. (USA); spec. US south-west archaeology and history; Director, University of Colorado Museum; Professor, Department of Anthropology, University of Colorado at Boulder.

Daghfous, Radhi (Tunisia); spec. medieval Islamic history, Arabic peninsula and Yemen in the Middle Ages; Director of Department of History at the Faculty of Humanities and Social Sciences; Professor of Medieval History, University of Tunis I.

Donzel, E. J. Van (The Netherlands); spec. history of Ethiopia, Islam; Secretary-General and co-editor of the *Encyclopaedia of Islam*; member of the Academia Europea.

Duri, Abdul Aziz (Jordan); spec. Arab history (esp. economic history); Professor of History, Jordan University; member of the Royal Academy for Islamic Civilization Research; honorary member of the Jordan Academy for the Arabic Language.

Epstein, Jeremiah F. (USA); spec. archaeology of Mesoamerica and Early Man in the New World; Professor Emeritus, Department of Anthropology, University of Texas.

Fawzi, Farouk Omar (Iraq); spec. Islamic history and civilization; Chairman, Department of Islamic History, University of Al-al-Bayt, Mafraq (Jordan).

Fossier, Robert (France); spec. medieval history in Western Europe; Emeritus Professor, la Sorbonne (Paris I); Honorary Director of the Department of History.

Fu'ad Sayyid, Ayman (Egypt); spec. Muslim history, co–dicology of Arabic manuscripts and urban history; Professor of History and Muslim civilization, University Hilwan; adviser to the National Library and National Records of Egypt.

Gendrop, Paul, *deceased* (Mexico); Professor of Pre-hispanic Architecture, especially Maya, School of Architecture of the National University of Mexico.

Gibert y Sanchez de la Vega, Rafael (Spain); spec. history of law; former Professor, History of the Spanish Law; Professor, History of Law and the Institutions; Emeritus member of the Portuguese Academy of History (Lisbon).

Gieysztor, Aleksander, *deceased* (Poland); Professor, University of Warsaw.

Grabar, Oleg (USA); spec. history of art and architecture in Islamic lands; Professor Emeritus, School of Historical Studies, Institute for Advanced Study, Princeton; former Aga Khan Professor of Islamic Art, Harvard University.

Gyatso Yonten (France); spec. history of Tibet and Buddhist philosophy; researcher, Centre of Tibetan Studies, Centre National de la Recherche Scientifique (CNRS), Paris.

Haberland, Wolfgang (Germany); spec. archaeology with emphasis on the archaeology of Central America and the Native American art of North America; former Vice-Director of the Hamburg Museum of Anthropology.

Habib, Irfan (India); spec. socio-economic history of medieval India, history of science and technology in India and links with Islamic science; Professor of Medieval History, Aligarh Muslim University.

Ḥasan, Yūsuf Faḍl (Sudan); spec. history of the Middle East, Sudan and Islam in sub-Saharan Africa; Professor and former Director, Institute of African and Asian Studies, Khartoum; Vice-Chancellor, University of Khartoum; editor, *Sudan Notes and Records*.

Hérail, Francine (France); spec. history of Japan (with emphasis on the Nara-Heian period); Director of Studies, Ecole Pratique des Hautes Etudes, Sciences Historiques et Philologiques.

Inalcik, Halil (Turkey); spec. Ottoman history; Professor, Bilkent University; Emeritus Professor; Department of History, University of Chicago; member of the American Academy of Arts and Sciences, Turkish Academy of Sciences; corresponding member of the British Academy.

Karayannopoulos, Yannis (Greece); spec. Byzantine history; corresponding member, Austrian and Bulgarian Academies of Sciences; Emeritus Professor, University of Thessaloniki.

Karpov, Sergei P. (Russian Federation); spec. economic and political history of Byzantium and Black Sea region in the thirteenth to fifteenth centuries; Professor, Moscow State University; Director, Centre of Byzantine and Black Sea Studies, Moscow State University; President, Russian National Association of Medievalists.

Khadduri, Majid (Iraq); spec. Islamic law; member of the Iraqi delegation to the San Francisco Conference which laid down the United Nations; Professor Emeritus, Johns Hopkins University; member of the Academy of the Arabic Language in Cairo; member of the Iraqi Academy; President of the Shayhani Society of International Law.

Kozlov, Victor I. (Russian Federation); spec. ethnodemography and ethnogeography; Professor and chief researcher, Institute of Ethnology and Anthropology, Russian Academy of Sciences.

La Fontinelle, Jacqueline de (France); spec. Oceanic languages; Professor, Institut des Langues et Civilisations Orientales (INALCO), Paris.

Leboutte, René (Belgium); spec. historical demography; socio-economic history of early modern and modern Europe; Professor at the Department of History and Civilization, European University Institute, Florence, Italy.

Le Goff, Jacques (France); spec. historical anthropology of medieval Western Europe; former President of the Ecole des Hautes Etudes en Sciences Sociales; co-director of the review *Annales, Histoire, Sciences Sociales.*

Li, Ogg (Korea); spec. ancient history of Korea; Emeritus Professor, Department of East Asia, University of Paris VII; former Director, Centre d'Etudes Coréennes, Collège de France.

Litvak King, Jaime (Mexico); spec. Mesoamerican archaeology; member of the Institute of Anthropological Research, University of Mexico.

Lombard, Denys, *deceased* (France); spec. history of South-East Asia; Director of Studies, Ecole des Hautes Etudes en Sciences Sociales; Director, Ecole Française d'Extrême Orient.

Lorandi, Ana María (Argentina); spec. pre-Columbian Andean archaeology and ethnohistory; former Director, Institute of Anthropology, University of Buenos Aires; member of many international academic bodies.

MacDonald, Alexander W. (UK); spec. ethnology of Himalaya and Tibet; Honorary Research Director, Centre National de la Recherche Scientifique (CNRS), Paris.

Maksimovic, Ljubomir (Yugoslavia); spec. Byzantinology, especially history of the society and the state institutions; Professor, University of Belgrade; research councillor, Institute for Byzantine Studies, Serbian Academy of Sciences and Arts.

Mantran, Robert (France); spec. Ottoman history; Emeritus Professor, Université de Provence; Honorary President of the International Committee of Pre-Ottoman and Ottoman Studies; member of the Institut de France (Académie des Inscriptions et Belles-Lettres).

Martín Rodríguez, José-Luis (Spain); spec. medieval Spanish history; Professor, National University of Distance Learning, Madrid.

Matveyev, Victor, *deceased* (Russian Federation); spec. history and ethnography of the peoples of North and East Africa, medieval Arabic works on Africa; former Head of the African Department of the Anthropology and Ethnography Museum in the Russian Academy of Sciences.

Meyer, Fernand (France); spec. Tibetology; Professor, Ecole Pratique des Hautes Etudes, Sciences Historiques et Philologiques (Chair of Sciences and Civilization of the Tibetan World), Paris; Director, UPR 299: Milieux, Sociétés et Cultures en Himalaya, Centre National de la Recherche Scientifique (CNRS), Paris.

Millones, Luis (Peru); spec. ethnohistory of central Andes; Professor of Anthropology, University of San Marcos, Lima; member, Chilean Academy of History; senior researcher, Simon Rodriguez Foundation, Buenos Aires.

Musset, Lucien (France); spec. medieval Scandinavian history; Emeritus Professor, University of Caen; member of the Académie des Inscriptions et Belles-Lettres (Paris).

Nasr, Seyyed Hossein (Iran); spec. history of sciences, philosophy and Islamic studies; former Professor and Dean, Tehrān University; founder and first President, Iranian Academy of Philosophy; currently University Professor, the George Washington University; member, Institut International de Philosophie.

Ndaywel è Nziem, Isidore (Democratic Republic of Congo); spec. history of Central Africa; Titulary Professor, Department of History, Faculty of Arts, University of Kinshasa; Associate Director of Studies, African Studies Centre, Ecole des Hautes Etudes en Sciences Sociales, Paris; President, Society of Congolese Historians.

Negmatov, Numan N. (Tajikistan); spec. archaeology; Head, Section of Culture of the Institute of History; member of Academy of Sciences of Tajik Republic, Dushanbe.

Niane, Djibril Tamsir (Guinea); doctor honoraris causa of Tufts University, Massachussetts; spec. in the Mandigo world; former Director of the Fondation L.S. Senghor, Dakar; editor of Volume IV of *General History of Africa*; former Dean of the Faculty of Literature; Conakry. Palmes académiques.

Niederberger, Christine (France); spec. human relations with the palaeo-environment, traditional agrarian techniques and economic systems; socio-political and iconographic aspects of early Mesoamerica and the Olmec civilization at the Centre of Mexican and Central American Studies, Mexico.

Novoseltsev, Anatoly P., *deceased* (Russian Federation); spec. medieval history of Transcaucasia and Central Asia; Professor, Moscow State University; editor-in-chief of the annual *Ancient States on the USSR Territory*; corresponding member of the Russian Academy of Sciences; Director, Institute of Russian History of RAS.

Riché, Pierre (France); spec. early medieval religious and cultural history of Western Europe; Emeritus Professor, l'Université Paris X-Nanterre; residing member, la Société nationale des Antiquaires de France; member of the Medieval History and Philology Department, Comité des travaux historiques et scientifiques.

Salibi, Kamal (Lebanon); Professor of History and Director of the Center for Arab and Middle Eastern Studies of the American University of Beirut; Director of the Royal Institute for Inter-Faith Studies in Amman (Jordan).

Sánchez Martínez, Manuel (Spain); spec. history of Al-Andalus and late medieval Spain; researcher, CSIC (Institución Milá y Fontanals), Barcelona.

Sanders, William T. (USA); spec. anthropology and Mesoamerican prehistory; Professor, Department of Anthropology, Pennsylvania State University.

Sanoja, Mario (Venezuela); spec. Latin American archaeology, history of agriculture in the Old and the New World; Professor, Universidad Central de Venezuela; member, National Academy of History of Venezuela.

Schávelzon, Daniel (Argentina); spec. urban historical archaeology; Director, Center of Urban Archaeology, University of Buenos Aires; trustee, National Commission of Historical Monuments and Sites.

Schmidt, Paul (Mexico); spec. Mesoamerican archaeology; research associate, National University of Mexico.

Shanwan, Younes (Jordan); spec. Andalusian (Arabic–Spanish) literature; Chairman of the Arabic Department at Yarmouk University, Jordan.

Silva, Kingsley M. de (Sri Lanka); spec. Sri Lankan history; formerly Professor, Sri Lankan History, University of Peradeniya, Sri Lanka; Executive Director, International Centre for Ethnic Studies, Kandy.

Stoltman, James B. (USA); spec. prehistory of Eastern North America; Professor, University of Wisconsin–Madison.

Tafazzoli, Ahmad, *deceased* (Iran); Professor of Ancient Iranian Studies at the University of Tehrān; Vice-President of the Persian Academy of Language and Literature; recipient of an honorary degree from the State University of St Petersburg (1996).

Tăpkova-Zaimova, Vasilka (Bulgaria); spec. Balkan and Byzantine history; former Head of the Mediaeval Byzantium and Balkan Peoples Section, Institute of Balkan Studies; Professeur Extraodinaire, Universities of Veliko Tarnovo and Sofia and at the Academy of Fine Arts; member, International Association of South-East European Studies.

Vargas Arenas, Iraida (Venezuela); spec. archaeology of middle Orinoco, north-east Venezuela and the Antilles; Professor of Archaeological Theory at the Universidad Central de Venezuela, Caracas; President, Society of Venezuelan Archaeologists.

Vocotopoulos, Panayotis L. (Greece); spec. Byzantine and post-Byzantine art and architecture; Professor, Department of History and Archaeology, University of Athens.

Vorobyev, Michail V., *deceased* (Russian Federation); spec. cultural history of East Asia in the early and medieval periods; chief scientific worker, Institute of Oriental Studies, Russian Academy of Sciences.

Yarshater, Ehsan (USA); spec. Persian cultural history, Persian literature, Iranian dialectology; Director, Center for Iranian Studies and Professor Emeritus of Iranian Studies, special lecturer status at Columbia University; editor, *Encyclopaedia Iranica*; general editorship of the Tabari Translation Project.

Zhang, Guangda (China); spec. medieval Chinese history and Dunhuang manuscripts; Professor of History, Beijing University; Professor, International Chair at the Collège de France (1993–94); visiting Professor, University of Pennsylvania.

ACKNOWLEDGEMENTS

The UNESCO International Commission for a New Edition of the History of the Scientific and Cultural Development of Humanity elaborated, following a decision of the General Conference in 1978, the concept of this 'new edition'.

The UNESCO International Commission, the authors and the publishers wish to thank all those who have kindly given permission for the reproduction of the plates in this book.

The Chief Editors of this volume wish to pay tribute to the support received from the President of the Commission: Professor Paulo E. de Berrêdo Carneiro, until his death in 1982; from Professors Charles Morazé and Georges-Henri Dumont; and from their Co-Editors the late Professors M. S. Asimov and A. Gieysztor and Professors I. Habib, Y. Karayannopoulos, J. Litvak King and P. Schmidt. They would especially like to thank Professor Habib for his invaluable help and extend their special gratitude to Professor R. Mantran for acting as consultant.

They also wish to pay tribute to the Chief Editor, the late Professor A. A. Kamel and the former Chief Editor, Professor H. Ahrweiler, and finally all the members and following interns (J. Fredette, A. Karakatsoulis, J. La Coste, C. N'doubi, T. Uteseny, M. L. Vanorio) of the UNESCO Secretariat involved in this volume.

They extend their grateful thanks to the UNESCO National Commissions of Côte d'Ivoire, Kuwait, Morocco and Spain as well as to the Al al-Bayt University of Mafraq (Jordan), which have organized conferences and meetings within the framework of the preparation of this volume.

UNESCO also wishes to express its gratitude to the World Islamic Call Society for its generous financial assistance to this project and finally to A. Arellano Hernández and M. E. Barry for their invaluable contributions to the iconography of this book.

A

INTRODUCTION

INTRODUCTION

Mohammad Adnan Al-Bakhit, Louis Bazin and Sékéné Mody Cissoko

The definition of periods is a major problem that constantly arises in the writing of history. In a collective work which must be split up into a series of volumes in order to be manageable, the limits of the period of each volume must be set in terms of dates of events that can be deemed significant enough in affecting the course of history. Whatever choices are made are bound to be, to some extent, arbitrary and subjective. And in a work as comprehensive in its coverage as the *History of the Scientific and Cultural Development of Humanity* – especially for periods when communication between human groups had not yet developed to the point which in the twentieth century makes it tend towards universality – it is impossible to set dates that are equally significant for all the regions and peoples of our planet.

We must at least try to select the dates of events which, although their repercussions for humanity as a whole might not have been immediate or even rapid, at least set in motion developments which over the following centuries, perhaps even down to our own day, gradually gathered momentum and came to affect a considerable number, in some cases a majority, of the Earth's peoples. This is the approach we have adopted with this fourth volume, and it is also that adopted by the authors of the previous volumes.

As Volume III ends with the preaching of the Prophet Muḥammad between 610 and 632 and the achievements of his disciples, who had emigrated with him from Mecca to Medina in 622 (the year of the 'Hegira' or emigration), in short with the time when Islam, the last of the great universal religions, was beginning to spread and to influence the course of world history, it is the beginning of the seventh century, the first century of the Hegira, that is the overall chronological starting point of Volume IV. This was also the time when, at the eastern extremity of the 'Old World' a new dynasty, the Tang (618–907), united and reorganized China, adopted an expansionist policy in Central Asia and for a time took the Celestial Empire to the height of its power, simultaneously establishing cultural contacts with the West with the Iranian world of Sogdiana and Sasanian Persia and, to the East, fostering the spread to Japan of a Chinese form of Buddhism.

The two major expansionist forces of the period, each of which brought in its wake an original culture and ideology, were to meet in the middle of the eighth century in Central Asia, where in 751 the Battle of the Talas between the armies of Islam, led by the Arabs, and of imperial China of the Tang put an end to Chinese expansion westwards. This Arab victory established an outpost of Islam in an eastern region of Central Asia; it marked the ability of Islam to consolidate itself in the Iranian world, then to gradually extend into the Turkish world, where its expansion accelerated rapidly during the tenth century. The westward migration of Islamized Turks, the Seljuks, in the eleventh century ended in the Turkish conquest of Asia Minor and made possible the subsequent creation of the Ottoman Empire, which, controlling Western Asia, Eastern Europe and North Africa, was to become one of the great world powers.

The chronological starting point for this volume therefore corresponds to events of great significance for the history of the 'Old World'.

The date chosen to close the period (at the end of the fifteenth century) is that of an event whose repercussions continue to be felt today: in 1492 the first Atlantic crossing by Christopher Columbus led to the discovery of the 'New World' by the 'Old' and the establishment of direct, continuous communication between the two. It marks the beginning of the European (Spanish, Portuguese, English and French) colonization of America, which continued through the sixteenth and succeeding centuries and will be discussed in Volume V. A tragedy for the indigenous peoples, but bringing immense profit to some of the conquerors, it was to transform the economic and geopolitical situation in Europe, with myriad consequences.

We chose not to end the period covered in Volume IV with 1453, the date of the fall of Constantinople, which the classical, typically Eurocentric tradition sees as the 'end of the Middle Ages' and the beginning of 'Modern History'. This is because this date, which originally evoked the emotional shock that ran through Christian Europe for essentially symbolic reasons when the Turks conquered the capital of the Eastern Empire, heir to one half of the Christianized Roman Empire, did not have the decisive importance for the world as a whole which is attributed to it. Indeed, by 1453 the Byzantine Empire had already been reduced in Europe to the town and immediate environs of Constantinople, and the Ottomans, who had established their capital at Adrianople as early as 1365, already occupied much of Greece and the Balkans. Nor did the year 1453 mark the apogee of the Ottoman Empire, which had not yet occupied the whole of politically fragmented Anatolia.

While inter-communication between the major regions of the world was not yet general during this period, various events did bring about a significant development of communication in the 'Old World'. The rapid expansion of Islam between the seventh and fifteenth centuries to a large part of Asia, the islands of South-East Asia, North and

East Africa, Spain and the Balkans introduced not only its religious concepts but also a highly developed scientific and technical culture to areas stretching from Guangzhou to Granada. In the thirteenth and fourteenth centuries, the extraordinary expansion of Chinggis Khān's Mongol Empire from the Volga to the Pacific Ocean and from the Indus to the Black Sea revived the Silk Road for a time and, after the massacres and destruction were over, made land travel right across Asia possible again. The Venetian Marco Polo's journey to Beijing and Fujian is the most famous demonstration of this. The remarkable religious eclecticism of the Mongols, who allowed Buddhism, Christianity and Islam to be freely practised and preached, meant that different religions could coexist peacefully.

However, these two examples, and there are a few others, should not obscure the violence of the conflicts and the cruelty of the wars which, as in earlier (and later) periods, ranged religions, factions and States against each other from the seventh to the fifteenth centuries. However, in their tragic way these struggles led to a type of communication between victors and vanquished which although it cannot be recommended with any enthusiasm did give rise to various exchanges: thus it was with the Crusades, which, alongside its disasters, brought the Christian West and the Muslim East into contact with the material, intellectual and technical culture of their adversaries, whom they also came to know better.

As the memory of religious and political wars, wars of conquest, massacres, genocide, persecutions, destruction of material and cultural property can revive or maintain antagonism between peoples, we felt that in a book published by UNESCO, one of whose missions is to promote peace and concord between peoples, we should mention them in their proper context and not allow them to obscure the cultural and scientific history of humanity, the purpose of our work. This should not be interpreted as a negation of established facts or as historical revisionism.

All serious historical writing must respect all nations, ethnic groups, religions and cultures. We have therefore been careful to avoid any statement or formulation which might be interpreted as expressing hostility or contempt even though none was intended. We are happy that all our contributors have followed this principle of their own accord.

In a collaborative work on such a scale as ours, differences of opinion between historians are natural, but these are of a scientific nature. We must accept that no historical account is ever definitive. The available documentation cannot be exhaustive. Sources may be ambiguous or contradictory. Even if the facts are well established, they may be open to varying interpretations. The most objective historian is sometimes obliged to venture a hypothesis. Indeed, he or she is perfectly entitled to support the one which he finds most convincing. But another historian has a perfect right to be of a different opinion. If they cannot come to an agreement, neither of them should be censored: both opinions should be expressed, on the individual responsibility of each. This is what has happened in some cases in this volume.

The formation of modern, then contemporary, states gave rise to conflict and opposition, some of which persist. The desire of ruling groups to justify and consolidate the established order and, conversely, hostility to it from opponents, religious communities, linguistic or ethnic minorities, all advancing as arguments historical facts, many of which go back to the period we cover in this volume, have necessarily led to contradictory assessments. The historian who seeks to be impartial must not ignore them, but it is not his job to resolve them. His role is not to make value judgements about historical facts but to try to establish them more accurately, a difficult task in disputed cases and always open to the challenge of new evidence. The task is particularly difficult when social, religious or political history or particular events still resonate or are transformed in the collective memory and sensibility, as often happens.

Historical research on cultural and scientific development is not altogether free of this sort of difficulty, but there is not the same degree of uncertainty and, except in rare cases, there is much less risk of offending the beliefs of any particular group. Research here can be factual and descriptive, less affected by predefined conceptions. It is another matter that its findings, like those of all historical research, may on occasion suit one or other ideological framework; and, as no one is infallible, the historian's conclusions will always be subject to objective criticism.

The various cultures whose special characteristics are essential components of the identity of the various human societies are not closed groupings, however. To varying degrees, there is always some communication between them, peaceful or otherwise, which leads to borrowings and exchanges. These may form chains and networks, which sometimes extend over great distances. Many examples can be cited: in the spiritual domain, the expansion of universal religions; in the intellectual domain, phonetic writing; for food, transfers of cultivated plants; and so on. Technical and scientific inventions have spread throughout the world: thus paper making, developed in China in the second century, reached Sogdiana around the year 300; the Arabs learned the technique in Central Asia in the middle of the eighth century and took it to Baghdād and Damascus, then to North Africa and Muslim Spain around the year 1000; the Italians acquired it in the thirteenth century and it spread throughout Europe, finally replacing parchment. Decimal positional numbering with nine digits plus zero – a decisive invention – appeared in India in the sixth century and was adopted in the ninth by Islamic scholars, who spread it throughout the Muslim world. Its use gradually expanded in Europe from the twelfth to the fifteenth centuries and finally spread throughout the world.

While the diversity of cultural anthropology maintains a great plurality of identities through specific religious, social, ethical and more generally ideological traditions, scientific and technical achievements tend towards universality. They gradually become the common property of humanity, and the history of their development, even if there are competing claims as to their invention, must be viewed from a unitary perspective. Such, at least, is the approach adopted in this book. It in no way rules out giving credit to inventors whose identity is known, or to those who disseminated or perfected their inventions; the aim is to prevent them becoming bones of contention.

Like its neighbours, Volume III and Volume V, Volume IV is divided into two sections, one *thematic*, the other *regional*.

The eight chapters of the Thematic Section, which form the first half of the volume, give an overall view, by principal themes, of the general state worldwide of the cultural and scientific development of humanity between the seventh and the fifteenth centuries:

1 Environment and populations.
2 Family, domestic groupings and society.

3 State and law (oral law, written law, customary law).
4 Economic systems and technologies.
5 Communication and transport.
6 Knowledge and sciences.
7 Religions, ethics and philosophy.
8 Art and expression.

These themes, the number of which could have been increased only at the risk of fragmentation, were defined in such a way as to cover broadly the main areas of human activity, involving cultures, traditions, and intellectual and spiritual developments. They have been written by experts in general and comparative history.

Some historical disciplines, such as political science and the study of war, which are covered in the Regional section, have been left out, and although the space devoted to the Thematic section is considerable, it was not possible to extend the coverage of each theme to all regions of the world. In fact, the present state of historical knowledge would not in any case have permitted it despite rapid, constant progress: there are still grey areas, notably regarding regions where the absence or shortage of written sources or our inability to decipher them makes it very difficult to reconstruct the past. Recourse to archaeology, however valuable, does not shed light on all aspects, and the projection of current data of cultural anthropology back into the past is always a hazardous undertaking.

In order to establish their arguments on a sufficiently sound basis without exceeding the limits imposed on the length of their articles, the authors have had to select, over a wide enough range to give a general outline, elements whose authenticity is well enough established to satisfy the requirements of historical science. A selection was thus made, guided by their own knowledge, for which they make no claims to universality, and it was necessarily restricted. Other choices might have been possible. The bibliographies appended to the chapters are intended to give some idea of the possibilities of a wider exploration.

The Regional section was planned after extensive consultation over several years, in the Editorial Board of the volume, international in composition, which itself consulted numerous specialists from many countries. The historians consulted and the editors agreed unanimously that all the regions of the world should be covered. Having accepted this, two related problems arose: first, the unequal advance of historical studies in different regions could not be ignored; second, whatever the inequalities, there had to be an equitable quantitative distribution among the regions covered in respect of the space to be devoted to them. This was bound to give rise to some discussion.

In addition to these difficulties, there was the problem of delimiting the regions whose geographic definition, linked to the extension of cultural zones rather than physical geography, varied over the nine centuries covered by the volume. It was logical to resolve this problem first. For the sake of clarity, a limited number of major regions had to be identified, which would then be subdivided into secondary cultural zones, as they presented greater or lesser degrees of cultural diversity, however marked the general features.

The major region, which defined itself by its profound cultural originality, straightforward geographical definition and the novelty of its appearance in world history, was the 'New World', whose discovery by the 'Old' brings the volume to a close. This volume covers the period preceding the region's increasingly intensive penetration by external cultures (most importantly European), a question dealt with in Volume V. Pre-Columbian America was therefore identified as one major region, all the more interesting because the study of its rich history has developed considerably in recent decades.

For diametrically opposed reasons, Europe was also selected as a major region: having to a very large extent inherited the Graeco-Roman culture and the institutions of the Roman Empire, it had acquired a degree of homogeneity in this period as a result of the spread of Christianity, which had become its main characteristic. Furthermore, it has for centuries been the most intensively studied region, with an enormous output of historical work. Its history is dealt with in two chronological parts ('The Heirs of the Graeco-Roman World' and 'The Configuration of European Personality') and occupies about 20 per cent of Volume IV.

The major European and pre-Columbian American cultural groupings having been defined without difficulty, the next task was to define those which, in traditional geographic divisions, are referred to as Africa and Asia (the history of Oceania in this period is a special case, since so little is as yet known about it). It should be pointed out that these divisions were conceived by Europeans (they were named after two provinces of the Roman Empire: Africa, broadly corresponding to northern Tunisia, and Asia, the western part of Anatolia) and their usage spread in the modern period, but they cannot be said to constitute cultural zones as such, still less in ancient times: Greek civilization developed as much in Asia Minor as in Greece, and that of the Roman Empire extended all round the Mediterranean basin, in Europe, Asia and Africa (allowing local cultures to subsist it is true), to cite only major examples; and the Urals, regarded as dividing Europe from Asia (they are in fact simply two parts of one vast continent, Eurasia), were never a real barrier.

Between the seventh and the fifteenth centuries, a historical, religious and cultural phenomenon of exceptional scope emerged in the 'Old World' which, from our point of view, profoundly changed the nature and the distribution of the zones of civilization: the spread of Islam. Starting in Arabia, it encompassed North and East Africa, a (small) part of Europe, Western and Central Asia, the interior of China, and a substantial part of India and the islands of South-East Asia. It is true that the various local cultures were maintained under the surface in this vast territorial expanse, but, along with a religion that in essentials preserved its unity (differences of view on minor points were more political than theological), Islamization introduced changes – in social relationships, institutions, ways of life, knowledge and the arts – that formed a coherent system and, in Arabic, gave intellectuals a common means of expression transcending the great diversity of regional languages.

Some of the authors of Volume IV therefore felt it would be appropriate to abandon the traditional definition of regions by continent in this specific and remarkable case, and to consider the Islamic world as a whole as one of the great cultural regions for this period (without, however, disregarding the regional cultures included in it, which continued to flourish). Other historians agreed that this point of view had something to recommend it, but observed that the history and enduring special characteristics of these regional cultures (for example, the Iranian, Turkish and Indian) might be partially obscured by a presentation in which the dominant theme was Arab–Islamic.

A compromise solution was adopted, which although not ideal in every respect met this objection: a large part (slightly over 20 per cent of the volume) entitled 'The Muslim World and its Arabian Zone', covers not only Arab Islam but also non-Arab Islam, on the basis of its expansion (at different dates) to Iran; Turkish, Tajik and Turko-Mongol Central Asia; North Africa, Spain and Sicily; and Sudan and south of the sub-Saharan Africa. In this part of the book, the history of events is reduced to the minimum necessary to understand the chapters (14 per cent of the volume and therefore 70 per cent of the section) devoted to developments of cultural interest, with inter-regional comparisons and a study of the participation of non-Muslims in the civilization of Muslim countries.

A part entitled 'The Asian Worlds' (30 per cent of the volume) has been devoted to the regions of Asia and its islands that were not part of the Muslim cultural zone during this period, including those where Islamic acculturation either came late, was only partial or sporadic, or was strongly dominated by a local national culture. It includes (1) Iran, Central Asia and the Turkish world; (2) India and its neighbours (South Asia), South-East Asia and Indonesia; (3) China (Han area), Japan and Korea; and (4) Siberia, Mongolia (including the Khanates of the Mongol Empire) and Tibet. Care has been taken to arrange the chapters in an order which successively brings together regions with related cultures. Such an arrangement enables the reader to recognize, through informal sub-groupings, varying degrees of cultural community between these four major sectors, at the same time noting the differences within each one of the specific regional cultures. Furthermore, there are cultural links between the first and the second (partial Islamization), the second and third (Buddhism), and between the third and fourth (Buddhism and Chinese acculturation), which give a degree of cohesion to the whole.

As far as Africa is concerned, as the Muslim acculturation of some regions (particularly in North Africa) is dealt with in the part entitled 'The Muslim World and its Arabian Zone', it was decided to devote a separate part to the other regions, entitled 'The African World'. This part, which occupies about 15 per cent of the volume, deals more particularly with the areas for which sufficient evidence is available on the period from the seventh to the fifteenth century, either in written sources or from archaeological data: West Africa, Nubia and the Nilotic Sudan, Ethiopia, the east coast and the islands of the Indian Ocean (including Madagascar), and central and southern Africa.

Finally, for the Pacific islands lying at a great distance from any continental land mass and of whose existence the rest of the world was only just becoming aware in the centuries in question, we have had to limit ourselves to a very few pages setting out the facts so far established, under the title 'Oceania'.

As has been seen, the major regions, once identified, had to be subdivided. Once these subdivisions had been decided on, with their respective lengths, which led to much discussion, the various subheadings required in each subdivision were formulated. The table of contents thus came to almost 130 items. The corresponding chapters or sub-chapters were entrusted to specialists after various proposals. After much consultation, followed by approaches to prospective authors, about eighty writers from some forty nationalities agreed to contribute to Volume IV. The editors sought to form a team with as broad an international coverage as possible that was also representative of developments in historical research in the various parts of the world.

For a work of this sort, which deals with different cultures, it is easy to imagine the difficulty of reaching agreement as to the choice of such a group of writers, at once competent, interested in the undertaking and concerned to keep constantly in view the larger human perspective. The task of the authors themselves was no less difficult: the number of pages assigned to them was necessarily limited, so in their contributions they have had to compress their specialized knowledge of a large historical field relentlessly without any serious omissions. This has been all the more difficult because, historical events being the central focus, they have had to set out the essentials of the scientific and cultural history of humanity and reduce to the bare minimum mention of the events that had caused their appearance.

In any case, the limits imposed on the size of the volume, and therefore on the chapters, forced the authors to be necessarily restrictive in their selection of materials. As all choices are by their nature reductive, not all those made will satisfy the expectations of every reader. Some may complain that one particular culture has been left out, or insufficiently studied, or that another culture they do not care for has been given too much attention. The editors will be the first to agree that legitimate criticism can be levelled against the work and deny any claim to perfection. To the best of their abilities, they have followed the recommendations set out by UNESCO: 'Care should be taken to ensure that the content of UNESCO's publications covers the greatest possible number of countries and cultures.' The directive is not always easy to apply to a period of nine centuries (the seventh to the fifteenth) that ended half a millennium ago, that saw the configuration of peoples and cultural zones change considerably, and for which there is scant information for many regions. At the same time, the temptation to project present cultures, and still more present states, into the past is historically incorrect and should be resisted.

Relationships between cultures and countries changed profoundly during the period studied in Volume IV, which saw a wide variety of intensive cultural exchanges and many migrations. In many regions, there was an intermingling of peoples and cultures which extended those that followed the great invasions of the fifth and sixth centuries in the 'Old World'. It was essentially as a result of these interminglings that medieval and then modern nationalities were formed, encouraging cultural syntheses that often transcended earlier antagonisms.

We are sure that all our readers will be particularly interested in these syntheses and the generalization of certain cultural components that resulted from contacts between the different peoples, whether in peacetime or in war. In addition to those to which the authors explicitly draw attention, readers will discover others and will doubtlessly also be able to identify remnants of some of them in their own cultures. One may well not wish to see the accumulation of these generalized cultural features result in a uniformity of civilization that would make the life of humanity as a whole one of tedious conformity. But such is not the case, even though such a trend is now emerging, because of developments in communications, in the technical field, some sectors of material life such as clothing, or in sport, games and even artistic activities. But there is still great diversity – in spirituality, ways of life and national traditions; and, if properly understood, this diversity could again be, as it has been in the past, a source of enrichment for humanity. But for this to happen, cultural identities must preserve their originality without seeking to impose themselves by force on those with other identities –

who must in turn respect them. This will not happen of itself but through a mutual understanding, which requires the objective, impartial information that it is the historian's duty to provide.

It was in this spirit that UNESCO sponsored this History and the editors and writers of this volume have been careful to follow.

Planning of our volume began once the division into seven volumes with the same basic structure (thematic section, regional section, appendices) had been decided on. In 1985, a meeting of the chief editors of the seven volumes drew up draft outlines for each of the volumes. Some changes were made to the draft outline for Volume IV, in the light of experience, over the next four years. In May 1990, a dummy of the volume, to which only minor changes were made subsequently, was adopted at an editorial meeting in Ávila (Spain) attended by various specialists.

A year later, misfortune struck: in April 1991 Professor Abdulaziz Kamel, the eminent Egyptian historian, chief editor of the volume, who had played such an important part in its planning, died suddenly. His death saddened everyone who had worked with him on the volume and was a severe blow to its progress.

The programme for the important part entitled 'The Muslim World and its Arabian Zone' had to be revised, new writers found for its key chapters (more than a quarter of this part), which Professor Kamel was to write, and the numbers of the editorial team made up. These arrangements were not completed until early 1992.

While the present volume was in preparation, the editorial team was also grieved to learn of the death of three co-editors: Professors Gendrop from Mexico in 1988, Asimov from Tajikistan in 1996 and Gieysztor from Poland in 1999.

Less serious were the problems resulting from the delays or abandonment by some authors (sometimes difficult to replace); this was to be expected, given the large number of contributors. Some had to be asked to reshape parts of their articles, to abridge them, avoid overlaps, or fill in a gap. This sometimes caused understandable chagrin but was eventually accepted with good grace.

As was decided at the outset, the articles were examined by two successive authorities: an Editorial Board for each volume and an *ad hoc* International Commission for the whole work. The Editorial Board for Volume IV consisted of three chief editors, assisted by six co-editors and a consultant, of various nationalities; Europe, Asia, Africa and America were represented on the Board, which held overall responsibility for the publication. The preparation of the work of the International Commission, with forty members representative of very diverse cultures, was entrusted to its eight-member Bureau. Its approval of the chapters was required, after approval by the Editorial Board, for final acceptance. Neither of these two authorities would presume to alter a text, but each could ask the author to make the required improvements. We are happy that this system operated in a spirit of scientific reflection, co-operation and consensus, and that there were no insurmountable problems, even if this meant presenting two divergent viewpoints on occasion.

The results of such an undertaking can be neither exhaustive nor perfect, and we now willingly submit it for criticism, the essential propellant of historical studies. We only hope that, together with information which is global in scope (though necessarily condensed), it will offer a broad public a thoughtful understanding of the world's broad range of cultures and appreciation of the contribution they have made to the common heritage of humanity.

B

THEMATIC SECTION

I

ENVIRONMENT AND POPULATION*

Victor I. Kozlov

GEOGRAPHICAL CONDITIONS

For a period as long as the nine hundred years that elapsed between the seventh and the sixteenth centuries, to understand just how populations, historically, interacted with the environments where they were fated to live requires at least an initial glance at what were then – as now – two of the world's main binding geographical conditions. One of these is orography – the very lie of the land, its mountains and relief – as wrought by the Earth's own inner forces. The other is climate – as it varies according to how the energy of the sun's rays happens to fall upon the different surfaces of the Earth's sphere: as further modified by relief. But the number and density of populations also shifted depending on just when regions, or indeed whole continents, came to be inhabited, not to mention changes in local modes of production and the vagaries of contact between the regions themselves. Thus, before the turn of the sixteenth century, the lands of the so-called New World – the Americas and also Australia and Oceania – enjoyed virtually no contact whatsoever with the Old: they went their own way, developing more slowly perhaps, at any rate differently. Yet humanity first entered and peopled these same regions at quite a later date than even some of the geographically most utterly remote spots of the so-called Old World (see Map 1).

A glance at Eurasia's map discloses huge mountain chains, running east to west, which nearly bisect the continent. These highlands stretch from the Far Eastern summits of the Kunlun, through the Himalayas, Pamirs ('the Roof of the World') and Caucasus, to the westernmost Carpathians, Alps and Pyrenees. This interlocked series of mountain chains tended rather to delay contact between the northern and southern parts of the Eurasian continent, and instead more easily channelled the movements of whole populations into parallel east–west directions. Almost the entire period under review was stamped by the great migrations of nomadic peoples – mainly Turkic and Mongol – from the high-lying regions of the Altai and Mongolia into areas stretching farther west, and only episodically might such peoples move south. To block the incursions of nomads south into their own homeland, the Chinese had raised their Great Wall of stone by the third century BC. Only much farther west were the nomads to find a gap in the mountain ranges of Turkestan, allowing them to turn south – onto the Iranian plateau or down into India. In the remotest west, such nomad raiders were finally able to follow the valley of the Danube up into the very heart of Central Europe. But the other great migrations of the age – Germanic and Slavonic tribes in Europe, and Arabs into Western and Central Asia – did not, however, follow such a distinct geographic orientation.

Africa's mountain ranges and high plateaux show an altogether contrary orientation. Here they rise in the eastern part of the continent but stretch from north to south. Despite adverse climatic conditions (such as those of the tropical forest zone, to which we shall return), such highlands again served to channel the migrations of whole peoples (mainly here the semi-nomadic Bantu-speaking tribes), although this time in a purely southward direction. The east–west movement of the Arabs along the Mediterranean coast was thus something of an exception.

The distribution of major climatic zones, with their different covers of natural vegetation, also very much determined patterns of human habitation and distribution. Eurasia's map further reveals a long, wide belt of steppe and semi-desert stretching from Mongolia to Central Asia. This zone of flat land then branches out into two directions: one extending from Central Asia into the steppes of southern Russia and onwards to the Danube valley; the other, and increasingly arid branch, turning into the dry steppes and semi-deserts of Iran, Āzerbaijān and Western Asia beyond.

Throughout the period under consideration, pastoral tribes turned this entire zone into their homeland. They drove their herds to pasture essentially between the great forest belt to the north and the mountain ranges to the south. Farming here only proved possible in the moister European steppes, or around such permanent sources of water as were to be found in the oases of Central Asia, although such agricultural spots always lay under hovering threat from nomad raids.

To the north of the steppe extends the boreal forest zone. Europe's mainly mixed and broad-leaved forests enjoy fully adequate precipitation. Where stretches of these forests were cut and cleared, their land offered good farming and might support a rather densely settled population. But woodlands lying to the east of the Urals are drier and colder, turning into *taiga*: that is, cold-climate coniferous forest. In the remote past, only small groups of hunters, fisherfolk, and breeders and herders of reindeer, dwelt there.

But to the south of Asia's arid zone, with its semi-deserts and total deserts bisected by mountain ranges, lies a warmer, moister zone, with broad-leaved and subtropical vegetation. Many parts of this zone are highly favourable to cultivation. The great river valleys, with their fertile alluvial soil – easy to bring under the plough – and their wild food grains (rice,

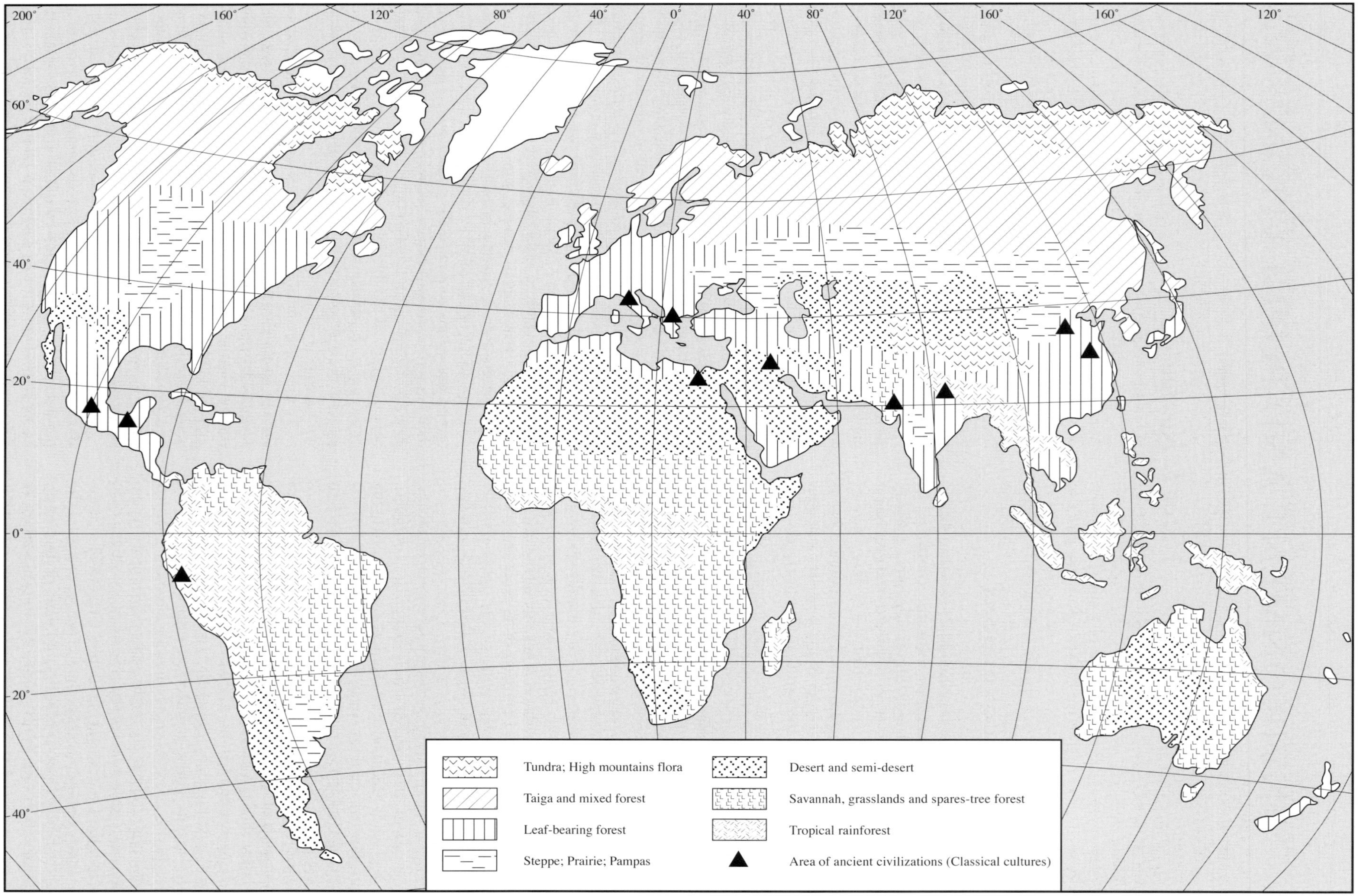

Map 1 Climate and vegetation zones of the world, from the seventh to sixteenth century (Kozlov, V.).

wheat, barley and so on), offered especially encouraging conditions for farming. Such were the rivers Tigris and Euphrates of Mesopotamia; the rivers Indus, Ganges and Brahmaputra in the northern Indian subcontinent; and the rivers Huanghe and Yangtze in China. In just such spots, where opportunities were best for growing crops and irrigating the soil, arose several of the Old World's first great civilizations (4000–1500 BC). Only a small part of Asia lies in the truly tropical zone with monsoon-watered forests, but even here, several areas offered excellent farmland, amongst them Java with its fertile volcanic soil.

In Africa, climatic zones are more sharply marked off from one another than they are in Eurasia. The Equator almost exactly bisects Africa: with the zone of tropical rain forest here occupying the central part of the continent. Both to the north and to the south of this forest belt stretches Africa's own steppe land, the savannah; farther north, the savannah turns into the Sahara, a vast desert with few oases. Africa yielded fewer opportunities for farming than did Eurasia. The continent does boast certain wild cereal plants (such as wheat and rice in East Africa), as well as several wild tuberous food plants (such as yams in West Africa). But Africa also sheltered far fewer animals suitable for domestication: both the goat and the horse, for example, had to be brought in from West Asia. Cattle-breeding in Africa's central regions was rendered impossible by the deadly illness inflicted by the bite of the tsetse fly. Thus in the remote past the bulk of Africa's territory sheltered only small groups of food gatherers and hunters. Belts of good farmland were to be found only along the eastern, northern (Mediterranean) and western rims of the continent. Egypt's great ancient civilization founded on irrigated agriculture could only take root in the lower reaches of the Nile valley.

Geographical conditions in the Americas show some marked differences from those prevailing in the Old World. The belt of mountain chains is narrower here, but runs almost uninterruptedly along the western coast of both continents from northernmost North America to the southernmost tip of South America. Yet the pattern of climatic zones is much the same. Where the Equator cuts through South America; to the north and south stretches the zone of tropical rain forest. Farther south appears the zone of the *pampas,* or savannah, covered mainly by grass. To the north – that is, North America – semi-deserts alternate with prairies rather similar to the south's *pampas.* These yield to broad-leaved forests. Further north again comes a zone of mixed forests, then one of coniferous forests, until finally there remains only a zone of circumpolar tundra.

On the whole, South America's forbidding geographical conditions were hardly more fit for human habitation than were those in Africa. In North America, if anything, they were even worse. Yet human beings, mainly in small groups of hunters and gatherers, did penetrate the Americas 20,000–30,000 years after the first anthropoid ape-descended humans began populating Africa. The Native American descendants of these early groups slowly adapted to local ecological conditions in the course of lengthy migrations from Alaska down to Tierra del Fuego, and from the continent's western seaboard to its eastern one. Some areas of the Western Hemisphere did provide wild plants available for cultivation (maize or Indian corn, potatoes, cotton and so on), but almost no animals for domestication – save, notably, for the llama (and the alpaca) in the highlands of the central Andes. The llama in due course was made to yield its meat and wool, and to bear human beings' loads over mountain trails. Harsh circumstances, however, delayed Native American development, and the number of inhabitants of both Americas in this age remained far below the population of Africa (see Table 1).

Human beings probably reached the Australian continent earlier than they did the Americas, but geographical living conditions here proved the most forbidding of all. Half the territory of this continent is desert or semi-desert. Forest regions are mainly to be found in eastern Australia. Only few animals were there to be hunted; none might be domesticated. Nor were almost any of the indigenous plants fit for cultivation. Before the arrival of Europeans, there were thus in Australia no settled populations, only small migrating Aboriginal groups who subsisted by gathering food (including caterpillars and worms) and by hunting some game (marsupial animals, birds and so forth). Native Australians were not even familiar with the bow, but they did invent such specific weapons as the boomerang.

To round out this geographical and ecological introduction, we should add that the Earth's climate betrayed some fluctuations over this period: rainier centuries thus alternated with drier ones. It has been verified that, at least so far as this period in Eurasia was concerned, heaviest rainfall occurred in the seventh and then in the sixteenth centuries, and the least in the twelfth. Such variations in weather sufficed to make themselves felt upon the vegetation of the different climatic zones, and even to shift their respective borders a little: enough, in any case, to cause ecological change and force whole groups of population to move to other regions.

Always highly sensitive to such changes were the nomads of the steppes and semi-deserts, whose herds remained so crucially dependent upon the quantity, and quality, of natural vegetation: hence the vast migrations of pastoral tribes in this period over considerable distances from their original homes (see Plates 182, 185).

PATTERNS OF HUMAN REPRODUCTION

Historical twists in humanity's fate, we might add, and especially in remoter ages like the period under consideration here, much depended on the size of the population within each given territorial unit or state. Larger populations spurred more intensive cultural and economic exchange, and provided greater reserves of labour or military force, which strengthened the stability of states or ethnic units. Lower demographic numbers, on the other hand, weakened such units.

Unfortunately, we have few reliable statistics to allow us truly to analyse in depth the variations in population in pre-industrial times. We do have ethnographic data, however, compiled by anthropologists, which yield us the size of various tribal formations from the seventeenth into the twentieth centuries, although these more recent figures hardly allow us precisely to assess the exact demography of tribes or migrant groups in the more distant past throughout the world. Then we have archaeological findings: these give us information about ancient technology, the size of rural settlements or cities, the layout of buildings and so on – but not demographic statistics. Still, in some cases we do have access to lists compiled in ancient or medieval states of, say, taxpayers or house owners, or men recruited for military service. Our various demographic calculations therefore take into account a given level of culture and technology; the basic mode of production

Table 1 Medium Estimates of world populations by regions and in countries[1] (in millions)

	AD 1	600	1000	1300	1500
WORLD TOTAL	170–185	195–220	265–290	370–405	440–475
EUROPE (excl. Russia)	30–35	25–30	40–45	75–80	80–85
Italy	7	3.5–4.5	5–7	10	9–10
France	6	4–5	6–7	16–17	15–16
Spain and Portugal	5–6	4	9–10	7–8	7–8
Britain and Ireland	1	1	2–3	4–5	5–6
Germany	2–3	3–4	4–6	8–9	10–11
Russia[2]	5–7	5–6	9–10	12–13	15–16
ASIA (excl. Russia)	115–120	140–150	180–190	230–250	270–290
India	35–40	50–55	70–80	80–90	100–110
China	50–60	50–60	60–70	85–95	110–120
Japan	1	3	4–5	9–10	15–17
Turkey	5–7	5	7	7	6
Syria and Lebanon	3–5	3–4	2–3	2	2
AFRICA	15–20	20–25	30–35	40–45	50–55
Egypt	4–6	3–5	3–5	4–5	4–5
Maghrib	3–4	2–3	4–5	5–6	5–6
West Africa	2–4	4–5	7–8	9–10	12–13
East Africa	2–3	4–5	6–7	8–9	10–11
CENTRAL and SOUTH AMERICA	2–3	4–5	5–10	10–15	20–35
NORTH AMERICA	1	1–2	1–2	2–3	2–3
AUSTRALIA and OCEANIA	1	1	1.5	1.5–2	2

1 Here we used the estimates of all the authors presented in the 'short bibliography' but at the same time suppose that the smaller figures are more trustworthy.
2 Russia is in the borders of the former USSR.

and given subsistence patterns; the size of territory under cultivation; and, most especially, the inferable density of population. (It is known that population density corresponds to a ratio of 2–5 human beings for every 1,000 km^2 in the case of a hunter-gatherer economy; to 7–15 human beings per 10 km^2 where cattle-breeding nomads prevail; to 1–2 human beings per 1 km^2 in regions subject to slash-and-burn cultivation; and finally to 3–10 human beings per 1 km^2 where stable farming exists along with early forms of handicrafts and trade. Nor is this list exhaustive.) All figures given in this text, then, will serve to provide only general bearings.

It is useful to submit at the outset of this chapter that the human population of the planet at the very beginning of the common (AD) era, at any rate according to average estimations, amounted to, say, about 170–185 million. By the beginning of the seventh century AD, this seems to have increased to 195–220 million (see Table 1). But this was a very slow growth in population. By comparison, one might note that the population of the United States increased from 170 million to 190 million between 1957 and 1964 – almost 900 times more swiftly. The reasons for such a low increase in population, and the main features of population distribution between – and within – continents, will be indicated below. At this juncture, we will note only that the three main areas of population concentration in the first six centuries AD were the Mediterranean basin and those European countries lying to the north and west of Italy that had come under Roman rule; northern India; and China. Here lived more than three-quarters of the world's human inhabitants.

Trends in population statistics are determined by two main factors: natality and mortality, or birth rates and death rates. The measured difference between such rates in turn discloses the rate of natural increase, or decrease, in population numbers. The birth rate is itself determined by highly complex factors, which include the physiological, the psychological and the sociological. Such factors influence the average age of marriage, attitudes towards celibacy, the frequency of sexual relations, the respective status of childless and prolific families, resort to contraceptives or abortion, and so on.

It is also important here to mention the role played by prevailing religious norms: these very much influenced birth rates because they oriented a society's priorities, determined the age and general arrangement of marriages, specified family patterns, lay down taboos on sexual relations at given periods, defined attitudes towards childlessness, and the like. The role played in this regard by earlier forms of religion such as animism, fetishism and totemism, or even by such ancient creeds as Zoroastrianism, is not always entirely clear to us, but in the main they probably all encouraged fertility to much the same extent. If we confine our brief survey here to only the four major world religions – Buddhism, Christianity, Hinduism and Islam – we find the two latter, that is Hinduism and Islam, to have exerted a strong and directly positive influence on reproduction, for they both encouraged early marriage and the bearing of many children, especially sons. The influence exerted by Buddhism and Christianity, however, is not so clear-cut, and sometimes even betrays glaring discrepancies. On the one hand, various teachings of these two creeds did not oppose, but rather endorsed, ancient traditions of early marriage. Major doctrines of both creeds ruled out resort to contraceptives and abortion, thus again furthering higher birth rates. On the other hand, these same two religions laid much stress on 'mortification of the flesh', celibacy, monasticism, and the like: thus diminishing the birth rate. For its part, Confucianism, a basically semi-religious system of ethics prevailing mainly in China, again actively promoted natality through its support for the cult of ancestors.

But whether in remoter ages or in the period under review here, differences in birth rate between the populations of various lands or cultures remained, ultimately, rather negligible. Ancient tradition nearly everywhere encouraged prolific birth rates to offset the prevailing steep mortality. Nearly universal custom married off girls almost as soon as they reached puberty.

Indeed, the custom of early marriage was a direct corollary to parallel efforts urging virtually all available nubile women into marital sexual relations – sometimes through polygamy. Female celibacy was rare. Where it existed, this was usually connected with some religious prohibition. Hinduism, for example, especially among its higher castes, ruled out remarriage for widows even when such women might still be very young. Western Europe's endorsement of young women's observance of strict celibacy as members of one of the religious orders was no insignificant tradition either. Still, prolific mothers were everywhere held in high respect; childless families were pitied, and even socially condemned.

As for death rates, we should note that accurate analysis of mortality has the most direct and significant bearing on all studies connected with historical demography. For thousands of years, mortality alone determined what main differences truly existed between various population trends.

Unlike natality, mortality rates do betray the powerful differing effects of varying biological factors, including those pertaining to both ecology and anthropology. Peoples who dwelt in a given natural environment over the course of millennia did adapt biologically. Hence the origin and perpetuation of such racial variations as darker skin, which does serve to protect human beings from the more harmful consequences of solar radiation. The role of certain genetically inherited diseases should also receive at least passing mention here, given in the past the almost universal prevalence of ethnically homogeneous marriages: such diseases might become, as a consequence, very much associated with a particular ethnic group – and indeed become reinforced wherever traditions of cross-cousin marriage prevailed. Moreover, the natural environments of the various geographically localized and ethnically demarcated territories could show very highly marked differences. Ethnic units became closely adapted to a given habitat, then, when impelled to migrate to new regions where other environmental factors came into play (with different climate, relief or solar radiation), their death rates usually rose.

Hence specific diseases and the prevailing level of mortality narrowly reflected given ways of life, including types of economic activity which, indeed, do so much to determine the relation of human beings to their natural and social environment. Those factors for mortality which introduced significant differentiation between various ethnic and cultural groups included the prevailing regime of work, daily routine and diet, as well as the pertinent religious norms or rituals. In many cases, a combination of factors led to ethnically and culturally traceable variations in the death rates of different sex groups or age groups. Hence, for example, a numerical preponderance of males in many Eurasian countries (India, China, Japan and so on) was primarily due to traditional scorn for females[1]: new-born girls received less care and inferior food and clothing. This, and also hard work, early marriage, frequent pregnancies and repeated child bearing, took their toll in terms of higher female mortality and lower viable female birth rates. Also relevant here are the cases where death might be dealt deliberately to certain family members. Among some groups of hunter–gatherers like the aboriginal San tribe of Australia, for example, tradition dictated that all a mother's new-born offspring be killed until her previous offspring was able to walk. A number of hunting groups in harsher northern climes (Eskimos, Athabascans, Chukchas), to avoid winter hunger, caused their elderly to be killed (or to kill themselves). Traditions of head-hunting, ritual sacrifice, even cannibalism, likewise all took their toll in raising death rates.

But the age's three main factors of mortality, hardly 'leashed in like hounds', were starvation, illness and war: the poet's 'famine, sword and fire'. All three, and especially famine, bore the powerful stamp of whatever the given environment. Disease was a most potent factor. Until well into the nineteenth century, human beings were virtually powerless to withstand infections and epidemics, either local or widespread. Plague, typhus, smallpox and cholera (the latter still as late as early nineteenth-century Europe and North America) ruthlessly cut populations down to size.

Famine, however, was a foe against which human beings always found means to struggle, either by inventing new modes of food production or by improving old ones, consonant with whatever their particular environment. Humanity thus progressed from hunting and gathering to slash-and-burn culture and cattle breeding, then on to the regular farming of fields along with irrigated agriculture.

As to war, we should bear in mind that in the period under review, discernible cases of dwindling populations were due not so much to direct battle casualties as to the frequency and duration of armed conflicts, not to mention the cruelty of conquerors towards the conquered and defenceless.

But in all regions lucky enough to be spared, over a lengthy period, by famine (whether this was the result of drought or some other natural calamity), epidemics or drawn-out war, then the size of populations rose – until some new natural or social disaster cut such growth.

WORLD POPULATION *c.* 600 AD

As noted above, the most populated areas of Europe at the beginning of the Christian era were those lying under Roman rule, especially those around the Western Mediterranean basin: Italy, Gaul (roughly modern France) and Iberia (modern Spain and Portugal). The Roman Empire's eastern European provinces at this time were more sparsely inhabited. Greece's demographic decline was partly due to ecological crisis: far too numerous herds of goats had come close to exhausting natural vegetation, while shipbuilders had felled or much reduced once spacious forests. But the population of all European provinces of the Roman Empire dropped in the wake of invasion by various barbarian tribes in what has been termed the *Völkerwanderung*, or great 'migration of peoples'. Marauding war bands lived off the fat of the land, plundering and destroying crops – and so helping to spread disease and epidemics.

A key role in the migrations seems to have been played by those tribal horse nomads known as the Huns, who initially lived in central Mongolia. Early in the fourth century AD, some of these tribes did manage to breach the Great Wall and invade northern China, but the bulk moved west though the steppe zone until they reached Pannonia (roughly modern

Hungary) in the Danube valley and ultimately Gaul, where they terrified native Europeans with their unfamiliar appearance – and ferocity in practice. Pressure from the Huns in turn jolted many Germanic peoples into migration: Goths, Vandals, Franks, Lombards and others. Rome itself, the 'Eternal City', was taken and sacked by the Visigoths or 'West Goths' in AD 410, and again in AD 455 by the Vandals. Rome's population dwindled from about 300,000 in mid-fourth century to less than 50,000, or even 30,000, by the end of the sixth. Most cities of the disintegrating Western Roman Empire in Italy, Gaul, Iberia and other provinces shared this fate. Livestock was slaughtered, irrigated agriculture decayed, farms reverted to bush, forest or swamp, while hunger and attendant disease brought low the survivors of war. When population growth resumed in North-west Europe, population density itself long remained very low, with the bulk of the land now covered by forests or swamps.

In Asia in this age, however, population numbers steadily rose, multiplying both in India and in Indo-China, due to progress in agriculture. But China's population, by contrast, failed to register similar growth, mostly because the country's northern regions, normally the most densely settled, fell repeatedly prey to such nomadic conquerors as the Huns, while the irrigation system of the Huanghe valley consequently suffered much damage. Frequent wars (between Byzantines and Persians) also checked population growth in Western Asia.

In Africa, the most densely populated area of the continent, and indeed in the world in this age, remained Egypt. Along with the rest of North Africa likewise brought under Roman rule, Egypt had been the main granary of the empire. But Egypt suffered severely in the late sixth-century wars between Byzantines and Persians, just as the neighbouring North African provinces when invaded in the fifth century from Iberia by the Vandals (whose migration around the Mediterranean reached this far) – before subsequent recapture in the sixth century by the Byzantines. For hundreds of years after these events, all these countries failed to attain their former population figures again. In sub-Saharan Africa, small, dispersed pockets of settled population practised only slash-and-burn agriculture. In West Africa, to be sure, such societies were becoming increasingly familiar with the earlier forms of iron-based metallurgy. But throughout all regions lying to the south of the Sahara, a hunter–gatherer type of economy prevailed. The population grew in numbers, but slowly.

The density of population in the Americas in AD 600 was even lower than it was in Africa. Only two isolated regions might boast early forms of agriculture along with some forms of state organization: central and south-east Mexico, and the northern Andean area. But none of these cultural areas was at all familiar with iron-based metallurgy or even with the copper-based tools and weapons once known in the Old World; only obsidian and similar materials were used. In other regions of South, Central and North America, small scattered groups of population mainly subsisted by hunting and gathering. Opinions differ as to the total population of the Americas in AD 600, but average estimates put the figure at around 5 to 7 million. Australia and Oceania in this age sheltered for their part only about 1 million inhabitants.

WORLD POPULATION SINCE AD 600

The lengthy historical period that lasted from AD 600 to AD 1500 was varied and complex throughout the world's different regions. Indeed, down to the very close of the fifteenth century, there were essentially two worlds. Only with Columbus' journey in 1492, when the Genoese mariner in Spanish service made his landfall in the Bahamas thinking that he had reached Japan, did the hitherto separate histories of the 'Old World' and the 'New World' become truly linked.

Over the nine centuries under consideration, then, average estimates put the increase in world population at somewhat over double – that is, from 195 million to 440 million. Such demographic inference underscores a decidedly slow overall average growth rate of less than one person per 1,000 in a year. But even such sluggish increase remained erratic, for it varied not only between regions but also from one period to another within the same region. Whole stretches of vast regions even suffered absolute decline in catastrophic periods of war or epidemic.

The world's population mainly owed its increase to development in modes of production. Improvements in farming brought an expansion in land under cultivation, helped by the development and spread of ferrous metallurgy with the manufacture of such tools as iron axes, iron spades, iron-edged hoes and ploughs and so on. Hence, improved handicrafts and the rise of trade played key roles here (see Plates 2–6).

Indeed, in the Old World, a gigantic single network of trade ultimately embraced regions as remote from one another as East Asia and West Africa, North Europe and South and South-East Asia. But conquest, territorial incorporations and recombinations, and widespread trade, were also features of some regions of the New World.

But the main outlines in the pattern of world population distribution actually changed very little over this millennium. There remained, as before, three major concentrations of population on Earth: in China; in India; and around the Mediterranean. Together these three regions accounted for the ovewhelming majority of all humanity, but as the populations of these three areas expanded, their cultural borders became increasingly blurred. It is important, moreover, to note that population densities, in this age, reached maximum figures precisely where the empires or large states came into being: for here is where agricultural technology, urban development and the spread of trade together formed the outstanding features of the prevailing economy.

Such empires or large states, with their stable political institutions and expanding economies, arose mainly in the subtropical zones, or in those zones characterized by warm, rainy or temperate climates. The broad-leaved or mixed forests in such zones came under the axe to make room for farming or to serve the needs of home builders, shipbuilders, metalworkers and the like. The retreat of these forests was a main ecological feature of the age. But zones dominated by cold-weather coniferous forests, or by the treeless circumpolar tundra, remained almost as uninhabited as they had been in the remotest past. Low population density also characterized desert zones and regions covered by tropical rain forest. The pattern of farmland in the dry steppe zones remained rather spotty, for here farmers and pastoralists shared use of such country, with their activities more often than not complementary to one another.

Relatively important changes in population distribution did occur owing to the 'migration of peoples': peasants struck out into new territories, and nomads moved over long distances (see Map 2). Another factor for change was urbanization.

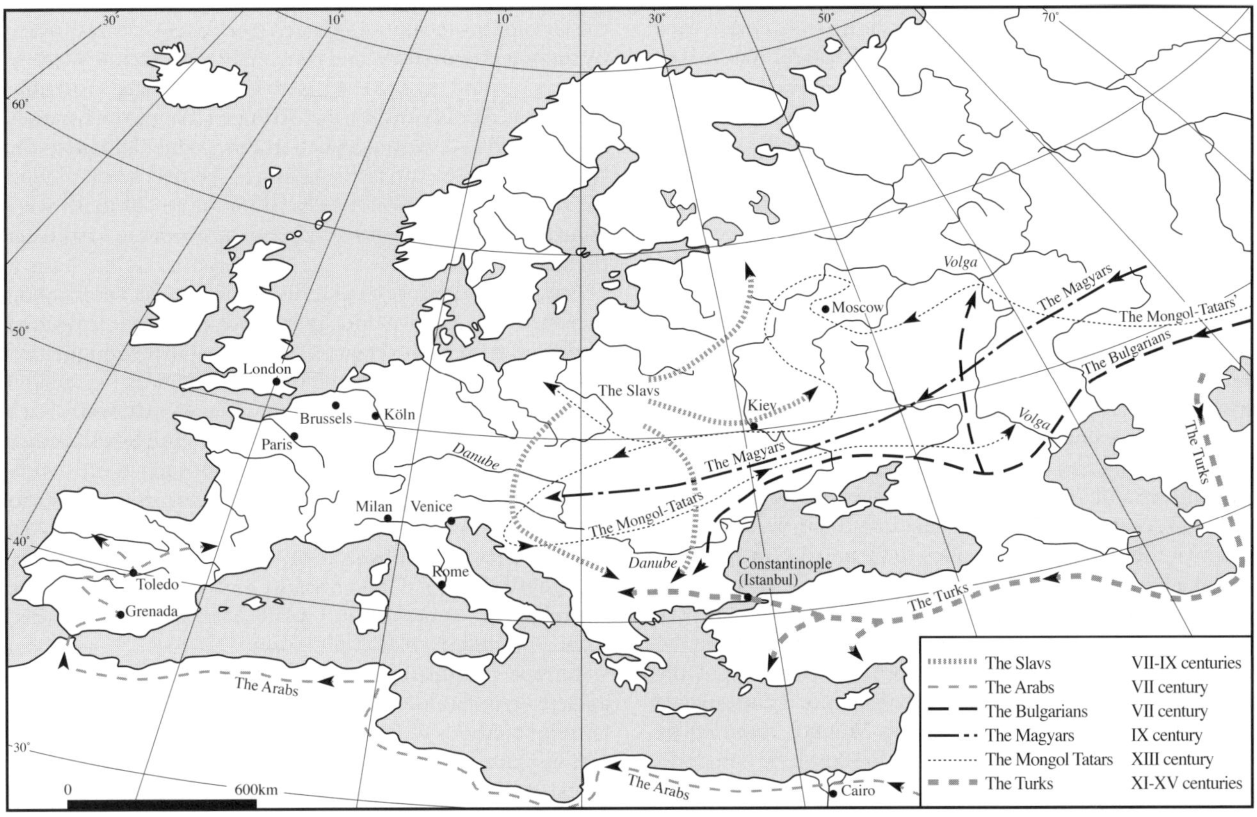

Map 2 Long-distance migrations and conquests in Europe between the seventh and fifteenth centuries (Kozlov, V.).

Europe in the twelfth and thirteenth centuries showed a resumption in urban growth – after the long interruption marked by the flight of urban dwellers to the countryside due to difficulties of defence and lack of supplies. This later medieval urban upsurge was linked to the revival of international trade, with the rise of Venice providing the most remarkable illustration of this trend (see Plates 36, 39, 40, 41).

But nomads in the steppe zones and semi-deserts continued to play an essential and highly characteristic part in Old World history until the very turn of the fifteenth century. For such nomads were far more than mere herders. By tradition, their war bands were as well organized, and equipped, as any military unit. Mounted nomads could hold strategic points, interdict their opponents' movements, and mass in large numbers to storm urban trading centres – as in the oases. But most especially, pastoralists bred livestock with skill. They moved with their herds in search of pasture and water. In turn, however, they depended on the settled peasants to provide them with grain and handicrafts. Hence the relation between pastoralists and farmers, who thus bartered for each other's badly needed products, was usually one of mutual dependence – but one which might also vary according to the respective balance of power between herders and peasants.[2] With their war-mounts – normally horses but also, in the Near East, riding camels – herders enjoyed considerable strategic superiority over settled folk in terms of mobility, surprise tactics and striking power. During many centuries, nomads could launch attacks from very great distances against entire farming areas. The reasons for such nomad aggressiveness are not always altogether clear, but ecological shifts such as drought and shrinking pastures certainly spurred the herders' offensives. In addition, the nomads' tactical capacity to muster large but fast-moving war bands, led by brutally efficient chiefs, obviously served them all too well in battle. But victory in war spawned fresh problems when peace returned. As once said: 'You can win an empire on horseback, but you cannot rule it on horseback.' Pastoral conquerors, therefore, usually adopted wholesale the entire administrative system of those settled peoples whom they overcame. The Mongol nomads who conquered China in the thirteenth century thus borrowed the governing model of the Han Chinese (see Plates 12, 186, 248). The Magyar or Hungarian tribes who penetrated the Danube valley from the southern Urals in the ninth century likewise ended by making Western Christian cultural norms their own.

Many nomad tribes also played a key role in the age's international trade in slaves. Huns and Mongols sold slaves to the Chinese. Turks sold captives taken from the Slavic lands to the various Near Eastern countries. Other nomad slavers dealt in captives from Africa, again for sale in the Arab world, Iran and India.[3]

EUROPE

Europe was harrowed by wars throughout all the centuries surveyed here. From the sixth to the tenth century, such wars mainly followed upon the continual migration of local, mostly very rural, European peoples. Germanic tribes thus drove their way east as far as Gdansk and Silesia, while Slavonic tribes pushed south into the Balkans and eastwards until they reached the Dniepr and the middle Volga.

Other conflicts broke out under pressure from migrations that came from much farther afield.

In the seventh century, the Arab tribes, united by Muḥammad under the green banner of Islam, sallied forth from Arabia to conquer those whom they regarded as 'infidels'. Moving along the North African coast, they mingled with its native Berber tribes, and their mixed offspring so came to be known – to medieval Christian Europeans at least – as 'Moors' (Spanish *Moros*, from the older Latin *Mauri* for inhabitants of this region). By the early eighth century, Arab commanders from Syria, mustering Morocco's Berber tribes, crossed over to the Iberian peninsula, crushed its Visigothic monarchy and conquered nearly all of Spain except its northernmost strip along the Pyrenees. Christian Iberians – Navarrese, Leonese, Castilians, Aragonese and Portuguese – fought for more than seven centuries to push back their Muslim foes.

Other invaders reached Europe more directly from the east. In the ninth century, nomadic Magyar tribes secured a tract of land set almost in the very centre of Europe – Hungary – whence they raided neighbouring countries. Meanwhile, the movement of Turkish tribes from Central towards Western Asia began in the tenth century. But in the thirteenth century, the Mongol and Turkic (or Tatar) tribes to the south of Lake Baikal were welded under Chinggis (Jenghiz) Khān into a single, and formidable, fighting unit. In 1212–13, the Mongols conquered northern China, turned west to annihilate the Central Asian Muslim Turkish state of the *Khwārazm-Shāhs*, then carried raids deep into Transcaucasia and the Azov steppe. In 1237–41, a Mongol army led by Bātū Khān swept through and crushed all the Slavic kingdoms of Eastern Europe, reached the Adriatic, then turned back to settle around the lower Volga, where they created a semi-nomadic state of their own, known as 'the Golden Horde'. The Mongols stormed and burned to the ground, or otherwise destroyed, a large number of urban centres, while killing, enslaving or driving away their inhabitants. Losses from Mongol incursions in several of the Slavic countries of Eastern Europe (especially the Russian principalities) amounted to about one-third of their total populations.

Before the turn of the fifteenth century, the Ottoman Turks, who first entered Asia Minor (Anatolia) from Central Asia, began making their military presence felt in the Balkan peninsula. By the mid-fifteenth century, they had conquered all of it. The native population, where it was mainly Slavic, here too suffered heavy losses. The Kosovo region thus lost its mostly Serbian population (although partly through emigration to northern regions). Constantinople, capital of the Eastern Roman Empire and once the greatest of all medieval cities with a population in the eleventh century of 300,000, shrank drastically: as a result, however, of its sack by Latin Crusaders in 1204 and the visitation of bubonic plague in 1338. The number of its inhabitants had already been reduced many times by the time it fell to the Ottoman Turks in 1453.

Other European states at this time fought one another, or suffered uprisings or civil war. The most protracted conflict came to be called the 'One Hundred Years War' between England and France (1337–1453). The eight Crusades, launched mainly from France and Germany between 1096 and 1270 to rescue the 'Holy Sepulchre' in Palestine, also caused population losses in both Europe and the Near East.

As noted above, medieval peoples were defenceless against epidemics. At the same time, continuous growth in population and increasing demographic concentration in towns and large villages created highly favourable conditions for rapid contagion. The most devastating of all epidemics was bubonic plague, which struck in the mid-fourteenth century. Moving along the trade routes, the plague reached the Crimea from Central Asia by 1339, whence it was carried by trading ships to Italy, and ravaged France, and all Western Europe beyond, in 1347–49, with many renewed visitations thereafter. About one-third of Europe's population, mainly in the south and west, perished in this plague, known as the 'Black Death'. Secondary epidemics claimed many victims as well, with starvation locally felling more: all these were contributing causes to the steep rise in death rates over this period (see Plate 131).

Still, despite such demographic losses, Europe's population managed to increase gradually over the nine-century period dealt with here. On average, it is estimated that its population thus climbed from 25–30 million in AD 600 to 40–45 million in AD 1000, and then to 80–85 million by AD 1500. Such estimates are based on some available medieval census material, as notably gathered in England: such as the census of house owners carried out in 1083–1086 (the *Domesday Book*), or the poll tax census of the adult population taken in 1377. Between the beginning and end of our period, then, the population of Great Britain and Ireland grew from 1 million to 5–6 million, while that of France soared from 4–5 million to 16 million (see Table 1).

Europe's population growth may mainly be explained by a decrease in famines. More land came under the plough as farming methods were bettered. Slash-and-burn cultivation was replaced by the three-field system of agriculture. Metalwork improved, spreading the use of iron tools. Swamps were drained, and many forests were felled – not that the latter occurrence was an entirely favourable ecological development as medieval Europe's woodlands shrank steadily. Meanwhile, the amount of trade rose rapidly between and within states. One advantage enjoyed by Eurasia's 'European peninsula' was its nearness to salt-water routes all along its perimeter, from the Gulf of Finland and the Baltic Sea down to the Eastern Mediterranean. Other water routes were offered by such navigable rivers as the Rhine and Danube for inland trade. When the security of land routes improved as the threat from war bands and robbers receded, regions struck by drought or famine might more readily obtain supplies from less affected areas.

On the whole, then, the predominant trend for medieval Europe was one of decisive population increase, although subject to severe fluctuations both general and regional. Maximum population growth is observable in the more newly settled lands of North-West, Central and Eastern Europe, that is, those lying north of the Alps and Carpathians: including Britain, the Low Countries, Germany and Poland. Woodlands were cleared and swamps drained to make room for cultivated fields. Germany's population thus grew from 3–4 million in AD 600 to more than 15 million in the later fifteenth century. But demographic rise in Southern and Western Europe was less rapid on account of epidemics and war. In the Iberian lands, the population only doubled. But new cities grew apace. By the fifteenth century, Western Europe boasted six cities whose populations were as follows: Paris (274,000), Bruges (125,000), Milan (125,000), Venice (111,000), Genoa (100,000) and Grenada (100,000) – not to mention hundreds of smaller towns. At the same time, the commercial and manufacturing productivity of the urban centres of northern Italy rendered this region the most developed in Europe and the true cradle of the European Renaissance.

We also have some knowledge of demographic change in the European part of Russia even before Peter I instituted a regular census in the early eighteenth century. Thus, in the sixth century AD, we may trace the migration of the ancestors of the eastern Slavonic tribes, who once lived in the region to the north of the Carpathians, into the upper basins of the Dnieper and the Volga. In the ninth century, two states came into being, with Kiev and Novgorod as their urban centres. A trade route connected them, leading from the Baltic to the Black Sea. They were then united into a single kingdom under Kiev, hence the name Kievan Russia, which extended its borders as far as the middle Volga, where Finno-Ugric tribes were living. The steppes of southern Russia were occupied by Turkic-speaking nomadic tribes. By the turn of the eleventh century, European Russia held 4 million people. Their economy was based on slash-and-burn farming, cattle breeding and hunting. Even around Kiev, the density of population amounted to only five persons per 1 km^2 – several times less than the norm in most countries in Western Europe. In northern and eastern European Russia, density was lower still: about one person per 1 km^2.

In the eleventh century, Kievan Russia became divided into several principalities. These were all conquered by the Mongols – or Tatars – in the thirteenth century, and only in the fifteenth century did Russia recover its independence under the authority of the princes of Moscow.

During these two and a half centuries of their ascendancy in Russia, the Tatars, while now the overlords of the settled Slavic peoples whom they had conquered, continued to live as nomads in the steppe zone. They collected tribute from the Slavs but interfered very little with their way of life, and as a result the numbers of the eastern Slavic population began to rise. Losses to the 'Black Death' were not so great among the eastern Slavs as they had been in the rest of Europe, presumably due to lower population density and a colder climate. By AD 1500, the population had grown to 11–12 million. Moscow at the turn of the sixteenth century was a large urban centre boasting more than 50,000 inhabitants, but dense woodland still stretched around the city on every side, while the levels of farming, industry, education and so on, in Muscovite Russia, remained well below standards in Western Europe.

ASIA

In what used to be Soviet Asia, population in Transcaucasia during this period was restricted to about 2 million inhabitants, owing to ceaseless incursions by Central Asian nomads from Transoxania and also Iranian forces. The situation was much the same in Transoxanian Central Asia itself after the thirteenth-century Mongol invasion: ravaged towns, ruined irrigation systems and fields that had reverted to pasture. What economic and cultural improvement occurred in Transoxania was mainly to be noted under the rule of Tīmūr or Tamerlane (r. 1370–1405), who glutted his home region with war plunder seized through his successful conquests elsewhere. But Tīmūr also thus sent many of his male subjects to their deaths, thereby likewise checking Transoxania's level of population at around 2 million inhabitants. The largest city in Tīmūr's Transoxania was his capital, Samarkand, with a population of more than 100,000. But what are now Russia's vast territories in Siberia and Eastern Asia remained very sparsely populated indeed. Even as late as the seventeenth century, estimates put the native population in these regions at only about 240,000, the largest ethnic group of which was made up of the Buriats, a part of the Mongol people, numbering here 35,000 to 40,000.

As noted above, the two chief demographic concentrations in Asia lay in the east and south. In some demographic respects, Chinese patterns of reproduction resembled those of Europe, albeit with fewer regional fluctuations. In ancient China, compact ethnic and political units had gradually taken form, and each of such contending states had already reached huge sizes in comparison with contemporary Western polities. The shaping of the Chinese state was first determined by the agricultural expansion of the Han Chinese into the north-eastern valleys formed by the rivers Ching, Wei and Fen, as well as into the lower valley of the Huanghe. Millet was the main crop in this region until gradually overtaken by wheat after AD 700. China's older political centres were drawn into a closer relation with the rice-growing Yangtze valley, and the two areas became connected by major canals in the seventh century. Migration by ethnic Chinese into the fertile river basins to the south of the Yangtze rapidly increased in the course of the eighth century, spurred by a developing rice-growing technology based on improved tools, better seeds and perfected methods of irrigation. To the south of the now united ethnic Han Chinese dwelt the non-Han or 'barbarian' peoples who spoke Miao, Yao or Tai. As the Chinese moved across the Yangtze into such 'barbarian' territory, they did incorporate or assimilate some of these peoples whose level of culture was not too unlike their own, but also gradually pushed back weaker groups subsisting on hunting or slash-and-burn farming into the more forbidding highlands and other terrain unsuitable for agriculture. Elsewhere, too, migrant farming clans withdrew to protect their societies and way of life from the relentless pressure of the far more economically advanced Chinese. As a result, by the turn of the twelfth and thirteenth centuries, only a remnant population of non-Han minorities survived in the highlands of south-western and western China. What repeatedly interrupted China's demographic growth were popular uprisings (especially those of the ninth and fourteenth centuries), warlike invasions (in the twelfth and thirteenth centuries), floods and famines, and such epidemics as plague and cholera. Thus the population in southern China grew more rapidly than in the north, which remained the main target of Mongol nomad attacks. Nevertheless, China's numbers still managed to rise from an estimated total of 60–70 million in AD 600 to 110–120 million in AD 1500. By the close of the fifteenth century, neighbouring Korea sheltered 4–5 million people, while Japan might boast as many as 15–17 million. Altogether, China, Korea and Japan now held more than one-third of the entire population of the world. Major East Asian cities that should be mentioned here in AD 1500 included Chang'an, Luoyang, Nanjing, Beijing, Yangzhou, Guangzhou (Canton), Quanzhou (Zaytun) and Kyōto (see Table 1).

It is important to bear in mind that the Chinese were far more advanced than contemporary medieval Europeans in many fields of technology and culture. They were familiar with gunpowder by the seventh century and with the art of printing by the eighth, while their use of navigational compasses becomes well noted by the twelfth. For many centuries the Chinese controlled a major portion of the main trade route linking East and West – the so-called 'Silk Route'. At sea, between 1405 and 1433 the Chinese admiral Zheng He's ships rounded South Asia several times and made landings along the coasts of the Red Sea and as far as East Africa. But by the close of the fifteenth century, China's technological edge over Europe was already almost gone (see Plates 21, 42, 43, 115).

Centres of demographic concentration in South Asia appear to have changed very little over our period. Such demographic catastrophes as famine, epidemics and wars wiped out previous gains. All the same, India's population did grow steadily from an estimated 50–55 million in AD 600 to 100–110 million in AD 1500 (see Table 1). Medieval India's demographic lag as compared with China appears to have been caused by its murderous wars in the late fourteenth century: as when Tamerlane ravaged the Sultanate of Delhi.

India's main demographic concentrations lay along the River Ganges and especially in the provinces of Bihar and Bengal. Rice was a major crop, and dams and dykes afforded flood protection in areas receiving more than 80 inches of rain a year. In India, too, the spread of intensive farming pushed hill tribes who subsisted on slash-and-burn cultivation back into inhospitable territory, in this case the tropical forests, as with the Mundas and Oraons of Bihar. Population density in southern India in this age was generally lower than in the north, although thicker along the lowland coasts than in the highlands in the south's interior still blanketed by tropical forest. All the same, south India's population was rising steadily, at a rate much like China's, thus probably more rapidly than in the north, owing to its greater amounts of vacant land still available for farming.

In the vast territories wedged between China and India known as South-East Asia, several countries (including Viet Nam, Thailand and Myanmar) showed similar patterns of development. Their advanced economy was everywhere based on rice farming. The nucleus of irrigated agriculture arose in the lowlands, while highlanders worked farms or resorted to extensive slash-and-burn cultivation in the more mountainous and forbidding interiors. But in the very depth of the area's tropical forests, some tribes perpetuated clan-based social systems and still subsisted on a hunter–gatherer economy alone.

The Western Asian lands over these nine centuries were not, however, able to recover the population levels they had attained in more ancient times. Demographic numbers in Anatolia (modern Turkey) fluctuated between 6 million and 7 million, those in Iran and Arabia alike at around 4–5 million each, and only about 1 million people apparently dwelt in Iraq. The main reasons for such demographic stagnation could be due to the decline of agriculture and to the almost endless wars of conquest waged by the Arabs, Mongols and Turks. In Byzantine and later Seljuk Anatolia, the core area of the future Ottoman Empire, agriculture flourished only along the shores of the Mediterranean and the Black Sea, or along certain routes leading through the mountainous plateau – but the rest of its territory, mainly steppe, was increasingly left to nomads and semi-nomads. The great urban centre of Islam's highly developed civilization was Baghdād, which at its height boasted about 300,000 inhabitants. Other important medieval Islamic West Asian cities included Antioch, Tripoli, Damascus, Tabriz, Herāt and Ghaznī.

AFRICA

North Africa was absorbed into the larger Islamic world after its conquest by the Arabs in the seventh century, but its evolution preserved original traits. North African agriculture was mainly restricted to a Mediterranean strip to the north of the Atlas range, being impeded to the south by dry steppe land and desert. Wheat was grown in littoral areas between Morocco and Tunisia and also in the oases of Libya, but most especially in Egypt's great oasis formed by the River Nile. Egyptian grain had fed Rome in imperial times and continued to supply first Byzantium, then the seat of the Arab caliphate in Damascus and finally – after the Ottoman conquest – Istanbul. But throughout much of North Africa in this period, nomads held a key strategic role. Each of North Africa's towns was mainly a caravan emporium, rising within a ring of cultivated fields and palm groves, and separated from other towns by an intervening stretch of steppe or desert. At the same time, these towns were linked to one another by far-reaching trade routes, although these routes crossed grimly inhospitable territory held by nomads or semi-nomads who had their own interests in mind. For all their apparent isolation, however, the towns enjoyed many ties with their surrounding countryside and its villages, all of whose various ethnic or tribal groups were well represented in distinct urban quarters. The solidarity of Islam, and much intermarriage, further united town and country.

North Africa suffered severe losses in the 'Black Death' but recovered rapidly, for its population then grew at a faster pace than West Asia's. While fifteenth-century Egypt had still failed to reach its ancient population level, the three countries of the Maghrib (Morocco, Algeria, Tunisia) for their part outstripped the number of their ancient inhabitants.

Demographic growth in the savannah and also the moister tropical lands to the south of the Sahara was gaining speed, but population density still remained low. While slash-and-burn farming prevailed in some western and eastern regions, tuber-bearing plants were gaining ground in the west, as was grain in the east. Metallurgy continued to be practised in its ancient centres. Population figures in the so-called 'Sahel' belt, or southern 'shore' of the desert (between Mauritania and Chad), rose from an estimated 1–2 million in AD 600 to 3–4 million in AD 1500; in West Africa (stretching from Senegal to Nigeria) the corresponding figures were from 4–5 million to 12–13 million, and in East Africa (from Sudan and Ethiopia to Tanzania) from 4–5 million to 12–13 million.

The lands of the Sahel and West Africa enjoyed connections with North Africa. Africa's main trade routes led from Cairo along the Mediterranean coast to Fez in Morocco, then turned south and crossed the Sahara by various paths, converging on the towns of Gao and Timbuktu along the bend of the Niger, whence river transport or donkey caravans carried goods deep into the West African heartlands (see Plate 259). Trade across the Sahara with the West African lands was of crucial importance not only to North Africa but also to the Middle East and even to Europe as well. For West Africa's gold mines (in Bambuk and Bure) vitally supplied the Old World's economy with its main source of bullion. Less populated and more isolated was the tropical forest zone, which did, however, export some goods in demand in the Middle East (ivory, coffee, slaves) while importing horses, brass, textiles and food products from North Africa, and also salt from mines in the Sahara. Links between East Africa and the Middle East multiplied when a portion of the local population converted to Islam. The Islamic ports of Zanzibar and Malindi became centres of trade with South Asia. In Malindi, indeed, Vasco da Gama in 1498 secured the Muslim pilot who guided his ships to India (see Plates 22, 200, 271, 272).

Southern Africa remained very sparsely populated. Bantu-speaking tribes, herders and cultivators familiar with the use of iron, entered this area from the north in about the sixth century. In the course of the period dealt with here, they opened up new lands and adapted to their new environment, but they also pushed aside older established populations: these were the Khoisan-speaking peoples (the Khoikhoi and the San), hunter–gatherers who had preceded the Bantu in these regions, and who were now driven into the harsher south-west or even into the Kalahari Desert. In AD 1500, the entire population of southern Africa (including Namibia) amounted to only about 1 million.

THE AMERICAS

The Western Hemisphere's culturally most advanced areas in pre-Columbian times, with the correspondingly largest concentrations of population as well, lay in Central America and in the western highlands of South America. Two such regions in Central America were the lowland area of Maya settlement in the Yucatán Peninsula and the highland area settled by the Toltecs and then the Aztecs on the Mexican plateau. Both these regions relied on the semi-irrigated cultivation of maize. Even before the arrival of Cortés and his Spaniards, Classical Maya civilization had collapsed and many of its settlements lay abandoned. But in central Mexico, a strong Aztec confederation held its own with a population averaging around 5–10 million and even more. Less significant in size were the cultivated areas lying to the north, in territory corresponding to what is now the United States, such as the 'Pueblos', the Mississippi valley and the shores of the Great Lakes.

In South America, in the central Andean region including modern Peru, arose the highly organized Inca state with an economy based on the cultivation of maize in low-lying areas and of potatoes in the highlands. The Incas enjoyed use of a dense network of mountain trails and were also in communication with those tropical forest tribes living around the upper reaches of the Amazon. The Incas herded llamas for meat and wool, and also used them for the transport of goods (see Plate 323). To the north of Peru, potatoes and maize were farmed chiefly by the Chibcha people. The global population of this agricultural area in north-west South America, prior to its conquest by the Spaniards, was probably much the same as the corresponding agricultural area in Central America: 5–10 million.[4] Other American areas, South and North, were only thinly inhabited by hunter–gatherers, whose total number may be estimated at between 2 and 3 million people. One should note here that such demographic estimates of pre-Columbian America have generally varied considerably, ranging from 8–9 million to as many as 90–100 million. Whether these higher figures are accurate or not, all scholars agree that Native Americans suffered a catastrophic decline in population in the first century that followed their initial contact with Europeans. War and conquest were not the only cause for this; a major reason was the spread of such European epidemic diseases as smallpox, measles and malaria, against which the native peoples enjoyed no immunity.

CONCLUSION

The lengthy period extending from AD 600 to AD 1500 was marked by steady, stubborn growth in population, despite steep mortality, and by multiplying contacts between different parts of the planet, despite deep-lying hostility. In the Old World, distant lands were connected by trade routes and exchanged not only goods but also achievements in technology and other forms of knowledge, much to the benefit of Europe's progress. At the end of this period, powerful links were forged between the Old World and the New (except for Australia). In contrast to the haphazard growth of communications within the Old World, bonds across the Atlantic were strengthened at once by massive migration from Spain and Portugal to the lands of Central and South America.

To be sure, the history of these nine centuries was charged with events fraught with contradictions – and cruelty. The routes which furthered trade also spread epidemic diseases or sped aggressive invaders on their way. Improvement in techniques spurred progress in farming – and in weaponry too.

The main ecological trait of this period lay in the planet's shrinking woodlands. Forests were felled to clear farmland, to secure domestic fuel, or to meet the needs of shipbuilding and metallurgy (especially iron works). Forest fires were lit by slash-and-burn farmers, or by hunters to flush out their prey. Portions of Africa's savannahs may be due to such forest fires. Down to the seventeenth century, the forest cover – or what was left of it – constantly retreated before the dense populations of the Mediterranean, northern India and eastern China. Yet this was only a prefiguration of the great ecological crises of our time.

EDITOR'S NOTES

*Irfan Habib and René Leboutte have added certain remarks in order to qualify certain points in this article or to update the bibliography.

1 Females exceeded males amoung foundlings 'by a long way' in medieval Europe (C. Cipolla, 1981, p. 69 and n), and it has been shown that in fifteenth-century Italy there was 'one important social factor which eroded the ranks of little girls more than boys: infanticide and abandonment' (D. Herlihy and Z. C. Klapische, 1987, p. 145). Female infanticide was still more widespread in Japan.

2 The nomad's very important role as long-distance transporters between sedentary zones should also be mentioned. This should dilute somewhat the view of nomads as a purely negative factor in the economic and social environment of the medieval world.

3 An additional fact should be mentioned – that sedentary communities also drew large supplies of slaves from nomadic tribes themselves through raiding expeditions and developing slave-catching agents among the nomads. Thus the large number of Turkish slaves in the Islamic world from the tenth to the thirteenth century. Incidentally, there is the estimate of over 2 million African (Saharan and Guinean coast) slaves transported over the Sahara during 700–1400 (J. D. Tracy, 1990, p. 322).

4 The population of central Mexico in 1518 is now estimated at 25.2 million (with a possible range of 18–30 million) rather than 5–10 million. See S. F. Cook and W. Borah, 1979. pp. 132–68.

BIBLIOGRAPHY

Anthropology and Population Problems. Apr. 1982. Current Anthropology.

BAIROCH, P. 1985. *De Jericho à Mexico: Villes et économie dans l'histoire.* Paris.

BELOCH, J. 1886. *Die Bevolkerung der griechisch-romanischen Welt.* Leipzig.

CARR-SAUNDERS, A. M. 1936. *World Population: Past Growth and Present Trends.* Oxford.

CHAND, T. 1963. *Influence of Islam on Indian Culture,* 2nd edn. Allahabad.

CIPOLLA, C. 1981. *Before the Industrial Revolution,* 2nd edn. London.

COOK, S. F; BORAH, W. 1979. *Essays in Population History: Mexico and California,* Vol. III. Berkeley, Calif.

DAVIS, K. 1951. *The Population of India and Pakistan.* New York.

DENEVAR, W. M. (ed.) 1976. *The Native Population of the Americas in 1492.* Wisconsin.

HERLIHY, D.; KLAPISCHE, Z. C. 1987. *Tuscans and their Families.* New Haven.

HOHENBERG, P.; LEES, L. H. 1992. *La formation de l'Europe urbaine, 1000–1950.* Paris, p. 29.

KOZLOV, V. 1969. *Trends of Numerical Strength of Peoples.* Moscow (in Russian).

LORIMER, F. 1954. *Culture and Human Fertility. A Study of the Relation of Cultural Conditions to Fertility in Non-Industrial and Transitional Societies.* UNESCO. Paris.

MCEVEDY, C.; JONES, R. 1978. *Atlas of World Population History.*

OHLIN, C. 1964. *Historical Outline of World Population Growth.* United Nations, World Population Conference. Belgrade.

PERROT, C. (ed.) 1987. *Démographie historique.* Paris.

POLGAR, S. (ed.) 1975. *Population Ecology and Social Evolution.* The Hague, Paris.

RAYCHAUDHURI, T.; HABIB, I. 1982. *Cambridge Economic History of India c. 1200–1750,* Vol. I., Cambridge.

REINHARD, M.; ARMENGAUD, A. 1961. *Histoire générale de la population mondiale.* Paris.

Review of Historical Demography. 1987. Budapest.

RUSSEL, J. C. 1958. Late ancient and medieval population, *Transactions American Philosophical Society,* New Series, Vol. 48.

TRACY, J. D. (ed.) 1990. *The Rise of Merchant Empires.* Cambridge.

TREWARTHA, G. T. 1969. *A Geography of Population: World Pattern.* New York.

URLANIS, B. Z. 1941. *Growth Population of Europe.* Moscow (in Russian).

USHER, A. P. 1930. The history of population and settlement in Eurasia. In *Geographical Review,* Vol. 20.

2

THE FAMILY, DOMESTIC GROUPS AND SOCIETY

Robert Fossier

The family cell still constitutes today the basic social structure of any human grouping. It may either present a nuclear aspect (that is, the couple and their unwed offspring) or spread to include closer or more distant branches (as with joint families), or further embrace a potentially significant number of clients, domestic servants and friends. Such various forms of groupings are naturally determined by their level or type of economic structure, by the force of psychological or religious constraints, and by the weight of custom or law. In addition, the family is obviously also tantamount to a living organism, one evolving over the course of time and subject to modification from surrounding pressures, or even provoking such pressures in turn. Nevertheless, and under whatever form, the family remains the initial framework for human community. It precedes all other political and economic forms of grouping, corresponds to the very first rung on the scaffold upon which the whole structure of production and consumption rests, and continues to be the place where customs and beliefs are preserved. This is as much as to say that its study must precede – throughout most of human history – that of all other forms of life.

Such preliminary observations are commonplace. But they are very much in order here in so far as the task at hand amounts to nothing less than a scanning of the various forms taken by the family in the course of a thousand years and across the surface of the planet. The sheer number of unequal or even conflicting forms clearly indicates that such a study must restrict itself to pointing out major traits of similarity. By restricting ourselves, as we shall and must, to observations of an anthropological kind, we shall still have enough to say to be able to leave aside the more evolved structures of established societies, limiting ourselves to a few broad features.

APPROACHES TO THE FAMILY

Whether mustered around the couple or spreading its branches wide, the family has always been something *taisible*, a 'hushed matter' as old-fashioned French jurists used to say; that is, it puts a barrier between the enclosed space within which it thrives, and 'other people' who have no business to be privy to its particular problems. There exists no society which fails to exhibit such private traits. Obviously, then, access to intimate knowledge of the family group is an arduous process.

The historian of the family has available to him a considerable stock of written material. Given the weight of religious affairs in the various societies of this period, as we shall have further occasion to see, he finds displayed before him sets of rules assumed to be of supernatural or at least theological origin, under their venerable guises. Humanity was presented with an array of regulations supposed to offer guidance along the way to salvation in matters sexual, matrimonial or ritual, through the teachings of the Bible, then through those of the Christian New Testament or Islamic Qur'ān, followed by their respective glosses, such as the canonical rulings of Christendom or the *ḥadīth* which nourished the Muslim *sharī'a*; and moving further east, through the echoes of the sayings of the Buddha and Manusmriti and the teachings traditionally ascribed to Laozi or (with somewhat more certainty) to Kung Fuzi ('Confucius'), and finally – to cross the ocean – through the prophecies of Native America. Obviously, this considerable mass of normative ordinances, regulating daily life, does point to the different ways in which holy law, perforce, had to come to terms with human laws. But although never devoid of religious inspiration, the *fatwā*'s of Islam, the judicial rulings of Europe, and India's rhymed texts of the *dharmaśāstra*, not to mention the contributions made by Chinese law codes in the age of the Tang and Song dynasties, do compel the historian to take into account the gap between divine will or ideal and human potential. In actual fact, however, regardless of whether the writ invoked was God's or a human judge's, laws mostly amounted to pure theory, pure will, pure ideal. For what was afoot in the huts of humbler folk? The private life of such dwellings we can only hope to penetrate by means of documents bearing on daily practice, or through writings of literary inspiration. The fact is that we can, indeed, make use of written sources here and there, as we shall see further. Nevertheless, such sources are never foolproof, for literary art in these centuries was never spontaneous – it was written to order, adapted itself to the specifications of patrons, or followed prevailing fashions. And regarding documents such as deeds of sale, or marriage contracts, in these, the poor, the weak and the isolated (everywhere the humble were all three of these at once throughout this age) are nowhere to be found, although such people were the overwhelming majority.

The weight of written documents is matched by available stocks of archaeological or artistic material. This is because carved, engraved or painted representations of family groups, in some cases divine family groups, were charged with symbolism and intimate detail. Romanesque, Maya or Buddhist sculpture, as well as miniatures, ceramics and tapestries ranging from the Mediterranean to Japan, depicted couples, kin groups, scenes of piety, and weddings. Here too, a patron's requirements, or given models, might distort. Still, the visual arts speak to us as clearly as written texts, and diggings yield even more telling material. Funerary inscriptions, graveyards or the remains of dwellings offer us unveiled glimpses of family organization, rites of passage or everyday furniture. But Aztec ruins differ from deserted villages in Europe, and Iraqi archaeological sites from diggings in northern China. Yet stones and skeletons mislead us far less than writings.

Than writings? To be sure! But what is to be done when texts are lacking? And worse, when archaeological remains are missing too? Then one must follow the anthropological approach. We know how rich these can be, but how confused their stratification can be as well. By definition, even custom itself must needs be tailored to fit the evolution of human groups. How, then, can one be sure that a given trait remains valid throughout the period we are exploring? And how dare we maintain that a given practice attested on the banks of the Niger can shed light on what was then occurring on the banks of the Seine?

The picture is hardly an encouraging one, especially since we must add a further series of caveats to the reader. For if all the means of access outlined above could be followed through equally and everywhere, then a general fresco, in bold strokes, of the history of the family in the course of a thousand years might be possible. But this is far from being the case. So far as the world of the Pacific is concerned, we are faced with a blanket of silence that can only be pierced through a few oral interviews where several centuries are jumbled together. Pre-Columbian America we can only glimpse through the prism of its Iberian colonizers. Sub-Saharan Africa, at least considerably north of the Equator, does enjoy a rich stock of traditions which have now been appreciably elucidated, but it is still hardly possible for us to go back in time beyond the great West African empires of the fifteenth and sixteenth centuries, and even for these we have no texts. Asia, in turn, presents us with strongly contrasted facets, for though we may proceed only by means of furtive allusions to the north of the Gobi, the Chinese, Korean and Japanese worlds fairly swarm with canonical, normative and literary writings, and also artistic data, although documents concerning everyday practice tend to be lacking. Still, patterns of evolution can be clearly discerned, an encouraging trait which, nevertheless, does complicate our general account. The Indian world, for its part, appears to us more immobile. Islam fails to a great extent to yield us sources on daily life and also presents us with important regional variations, a predictable consequence of a conquest that was rapid and for long remained superficial. We are left with the two branches of Christendom, that of Rome and that of Byzantium. But an unprejudiced reader will quickly perceive that underlying structures here are often more primitive than elsewhere.

Over and beyond inevitable distinctions, the nine or ten centuries we are called upon to survey do display several arresting resemblances. Everywhere, even where evolution was most advanced, identical traits are to be noticed characterizing families' lives. Farming techniques and crafts, and also the means for domination over other human beings such as political and legal structures, were nowhere, at this time, particularly efficient, even in those areas whose progress has been made much of, as in the cases of Eastern Asia or Western Europe. The weight of a still dominant and untamed nature still made itself powerfully felt on all human groups, who could only derive solace and a sense of solidity by resorting to two structures, or, let us say, to two concerns: to stay closely bound together within the group, given the lack of easy contacts with other groups; and to rely upon the religious sphere to provide whatever protection the group was at a loss to furnish on its own. Hence the presence of two powerful factors: a private sphere predominating over the public sphere, and divine beings who exerted crushing pressure on human beings.

Even where a king, an emperor, or one of his vicegerents, claimed to speak on behalf of the commonweal in promulgating a law, he could do so only by assimilating his person to and within the framework of the family. Thus, in China, the example of the emperor's private life was supposed to guide that of his subjects. In Japan, the household or *ie* constituted the natural relay of authority. In Christendom, study of the Roman *res publica* was restricted to clerics: the prince dwelt in his 'hall', governed with his kin, and wove bonds with his subjects through ties of blood. In India, the household was an enclosed space whither no public affairs were suffered to penetrate: the individual was its master. Islam offers perhaps the clearest depiction: the *ḥaram*, where the women held sway, could be entered by no one external to it. Numerous external signs make themselves obvious: the household adopted a defensive attitude towards the outside world, the choice of residence for the spouses was all-important, children remained shut within until they were seven years old; and finally, from India to Italy, there was the veil (*purdah*, *chādor*, *ḥā'iq* and so forth), which every woman, upon leaving the 'private' domain where she held sway, was required to don so as not to become 'public' (see Plate 188).

Most visible, solid and universal was the weight exerted by the religious sphere upon the family's structure and life. The first domain amounted to keen awareness of an order willed by the divine power(s), whose rejection immediately transformed one into an outcast in India, a rebel in China, a heretic in Europe. To the terrestrial representatives of the spiritual power were assigned the task of enforcing this Order. Familiar enough is the success of the Indian Vedic texts, whose import was ultimately adopted by Christendom, concerning the trilogy of functions within the world of humankind. Morality, protection and fertility were so many divine requirements, which the West expressed by describing the service of God as ensured by the *oratores*, the wielding of weapons by the *bellatores*, and the task of production by the *laboratores*.

The Deity's design concerned mastery over all human activities. Its representatives enjoyed control over time, both past and future. Africa's *griots* may have passed for witch doctors in the eyes of Whites, but they, too, were possessed by the Holy Spirit. The shamans of Northern Asia and Oceania were inspired by the spirits which animated the world. Native America's priests, Maya, Aztec, Mochica or Inca, scrutinized the march of time and held sway over life-sustaining labour. Only through the exact observance of rituals and supernatural manifestations could society subsist. It was the Cosmic Order which ruled over the human order, and this belief was shared from India to Mexico. On the fringes of our subject, however, we find some astonishing outcrops such as the idea, imposed both by *Brahmins* and by the Christian Church, that man in his original state was in a state of sin for which he needed to atone. Also, and even squarely set within the field of matters economic, labour was held to have value only if sacralized, as was the case with the trade guilds of Islam and the West, where piety mingled with the wielding of tools.

Between the godhead and humankind, the servants of the former – the *griots*, *Brahmins* or Christian clerics whom we have mentioned – tended to interpose themselves. But this was not an essential issue, for in practical terms there existed no 'clergy' either in the Islamic world or in China, and what clergy did exist in Japan exerted no everyday pressure there. What was essential was a written scripture or, where this did not exist, as in Africa or Oceania, custom. Elsewhere, writings tended to teem, loaded with minute regulations and superimposed glosses. True, we have hardly yet managed to read those of the Maya or Inca peoples, but the Recitation of the Word of God (Qur'ān), along with the *ḥadīth* which followed, laid the foundations for the daily use and wont or *sharī'a* of the faithful of Islam, while the Gospels and, later, the writings of the Fathers, the Papal decretals and the full weight of Canon Law, did the same among Christians. The rights and duties of Indians became progressively fixed, beginning with the Lawbook of Manu (200 BC–AD 200) and extending to the medieval *dharmaśāstra* texts, although the latter were moral rather than legislative codes. The teachings of the Divine Wisdom offered China multiple paths of approach, which all, however, converged upon the notion of a state of universal stability inspired by a divine design. Laozi preached a form of naturalism which we find again among the Japanese devotees of Shintō; Confucius laid down the four principles of order, or *shu*, where obedience and good will were held to express social equilibrium; and Mengzi (Mencius) believed in the power of the Wise Ones. Thus, in contrast to Christianity's ferocious rigorism, Islam was able to embrace a number of different rites on the basis of custom (*sunna*), or better yet, make do with two visions of the Prophetic message, whereby the *Shī'a* Muslims remained faithful to the venerated, 'Medinese' type of family society. Moreover, throughout India and East Asia, the smiling message of the Buddha eased the path of the faithful towards salvation, while India's truly individualistic doctrine, as constituted by Hinduism, multiplied as many ways of approach as there were major deities, with *bhagavata* for the devotees of Vishnu, *paśupata* for those of Shiva, and so forth.

As for the role of the family in all this, it was necessary for us to set it within this period's prevailing religious context, which, in turn, may determine the four levels of study upon which we will now base our argument.

The family and the unknowable

The gods were powerful. What they knew, man did not. Now at this time, everything surrounding man bore the stamp of the incomprehensible; nature oppressed him everywhere and he grasped none of its cogs and wheels; everything which escaped his understanding was 'supernatural', 'miraculous', and accepted as a message from the Other World. Geographical and biological manifestations bore witness to the wrath, or favour, of the Divine. The annual return of life-bestowing vegetation, and better yet, the daily sunrise itself, were benefactions to be celebrated. Even in the kinds of places where scientific accomplishment has been much lauded, where historians have praised major strides in knowledge, such levels were restricted to the learned alone. Other folk always merely believed in the whims of the gods, or at best, in the hazards of the agrarian cycle.

Now, such universally shared resignation touched on problems which are of concern to us here: whence came man, if not from a divine act of creation? What was the meaning of the blood thus coursing through – and then escaping from – his veins? Why should a child inherit the psychological character of his paternal grandfather and the physical traits of his maternal uncle? Were men who died in youth, or who failed to consummate their marriages, somehow 'marked'? No doubt the general scope of knowledge was becoming enlarged. No one can deny the progress then made by Chinese and Aztec astronomy, by Indian and Islamic medicine, and by European technology (see Chapters 4, 5 and 6). But the masses were content to submit. We may restrict ourselves to pointing out that, more often than not, a mother figure was invoked as the intermediary between the masses and Heaven, and we need hardly dwell here upon the figure of the Christian Virgin (see Plate 147). Where a civilization like that of Byzantium made bold to resort to images in order to depict the unknown world whither souls were expected to return – and between the seventh and ninth centuries, the Byzantine Empire indeed tore itself asunder in controversy over the issue of the very propriety of such representations of the Divine and its intermediaries – Islam rejected this sort of approach on principle (see Plate 90). No doubt it was a more confirmed belief in the power of sanctified matter which provided the justification for the statues of gods carved in the Americas or in Central and Eastern Asia (see Plates 236, 301).

Defilement

The world was impure. This was because, as Iranian thinkers taught and Christians came very close to believing as well, it was regarded as a battlefield between the principles of good and evil. Such impurity was also owing to the fact that man himself was fashioned of perishable matter. India, Native America and other civilizations preferred to cremate his body and so purify the earth of him, rather than allow him to rot in the earth as the three great monotheistic cultures of the Mediterranean basin insisted upon. And further, during man's very lifetime, ignoble matter issued forth from his body, to be disposed of in the secrecy of his 'privy'. It was in those civilizations which still remained most subject to nature's power, as in the Americas, Africa and Oceania, that defecation was most regarded as a source of disgust and a sign of blame, whereas such natural calls were considered in a far simpler light wherever greater mastery was wielded over the environment. Public and indeed collective latrines are to be found throughout the area ranging from ancient Rome to medieval India.

From such defilement one had to preserve oneself, and also to be cleansed. In moral terms, this was accomplished through rituals accompanying the delivery of the new-born into the world, through rites of christening and the like around the Mediterranean basin, or those of magical initiation in the Americas and Africa. In more concrete terms as well, minute and repeated care was taken with ablutions, hygiene and gestures of purification, as with India's repeated bathings, Islam's ablutions and resorts to the *ḥammām*, and Japan's frequent changes of clothing along with the destruction of soiled objects. Such obsession was less marked in China (where two baths a month were the rule) and appears to have been seriously in abeyance in a Europe whose population long preserved a deplorable reputation for filth, at least down to the twelfth century, when practicable bathhouses were again opened.

Christendom addressed itself more than other areas to the offence given to God by man's defilement, and identified three fields where this defilement caused ravages. One of these concerned money and its abuse, a subject to which we shall return only incidentally; the second – with which we shall need to deal – had to do with sexuality, whereby man was held to demean his will power; finally came the case of blood issuing forth from the body of a victim, and most especially that which flowed unstaunched from women, thus rendering them the very incarnation of defilement.

Women, between men and the unknown

If there does exist a trait common to all the cultural areas of this age, it centres on the disparaged status of that sex so oddly qualified as the 'weaker'. In precisely the same areas where we shall later attempt to find traces of 'female promotion', as in sub-Saharan Africa, in India or in Europe, we must acknowledge that inequality between the sexes continues to remain the rule. Male grievances drew upon a well-stocked arsenal, in appearance, at least, based on purely moral grounds. Women were cruel, lascivious, fickle, garrulous, jealous, spendthrift and capricious creatures. Now, since it would be just as easy to draw up a parallel – and no less critical – list at masculine expense, it seems quite clear that such grievances hardly constitute the original reason for women's relegation. To a certain but in any case questionable extent, women's relative physical weakness may have contributed to their disqualification in the first budding cultures of hunters and gatherers, although their procreating role and sway over the hearth-fire certainly could have provided them with some compensation here. The original reason for women's eviction should rather be sought elsewhere , and there is no place on Earth where this same reason was not adduced, which is that women destroyed men and devoured their vigour because they seduced them and so caused them to lose their self-control. Woman was *tetzahuitl*: as the Aztec expression put it, she aroused fear. Among the monotheistic civilizations 'of the Book', those which spoke of a Sin and Fall, Woman was responsible for all the miseries of the species. To Hinduism, she was mistress of both life and death. She stood betwixt this world and the next, serving as a go-between and a magician who communicated with the dead or cast spells upon men. In Christendom, she was guilty as if by definition, even for cases of impotence in men.

Her genitalia lay at the source of the distrust which she aroused because they provoked both astonishment and repulsion. In Africa and Oceania it was believed that menstrual blood killed the sperm; elsewhere such blood was thought at the very least to be corrupt, and so to be unrelated to the honourable blood which flowed, say, from a wound. A woman's periods were to be kept hidden. She was isolated from the group and relegated to reserved areas, as in Japan and also in Oceania and the Americas; at the very least she needed to purify herself after her periods, as in India or in Christendom.

Hence women, as victims and devourers at once, were alienated on account of their own sexual activity. Their right to take pride in their own specific form of sexuality was only rarely to be found, in the Islamic world and Japan. Copulation may still have been a woman's weapon, but this too remained a 'hushed' affair. Not only did it behove a woman to hide her genitalia as something mysterious and awesome, but she was also required to cloak her entire person when moving out of doors. Donning the veil was more a matter of protection for her sake and that of others, than a sign of alienation and a mark that she was property.

Obviously the ideal would be to have no contact with the impure sex, or at least it would be necessary to expect that the Divinity which placed woman on man's path, in order to test him, should, at the end of time, be the source of redemption after having been the cause of man's chastisement. Such preoccupations never ceased to absorb the minds of Christendom. Eve had caused humankind to fall, hence the Virgin Mary would save it as the 'new Eve' – whose cult of salvation indeed often savours somewhat of Hinduism. Thus caught in its own contradictions, the Church perforce condemned Eve but necessarily spared Mary. In the meantime, before redemption, women were to be shunned. In India, Manu had already recommended such a course, and farther west, Christian fathers from Saint Jerome to Jacques de Vitry spoke no differently. Virginity was expected to prevail among both men and women, and this 'state' was set by Church thinkers on the level of an 'order' (*ordo virginarum*, *viduarum* or *monachorum*) superior to all others. Likewise prized in Eastern Asia and especially in Japan as a sign of highly moral personal self-control, virginity in Islam acquired an additional dimension: it became a badge of honour. Obviously, everyone was in all places aware that the perpetuation of the species depended upon the sexual act and its attendant defilement, and that God had said: 'Increase and multiply'. The challenge, then, was to curb instinct and establish the fine line of 'chaste behaviour' as a rampart between the extinction of the human species and licentiousness.

Awareness of being

One's relations with such other human beings, which form the basis of all social life, imposed awareness of self and realization of belonging to a group with distinctive traits in regard to all other groups, be it the clan or the narrow family circle. Now, man in this age had no inkling of the origin of his own species or of how the various ethnic entities came to be dispersed. He believed in the primordial couple formed by Adam and Eve in Eden, or in such original human beings as Fuxi or Nügna in the remote Chinese or Korean past, respectively, whence their various issues, but he had little notion of the genes and heredity which went to forge lineages. Islam, as heir to Greek thought, went the furthest in attributing value to physical or moral traits passed on from one generation to another. Elsewhere, Buddhist individualism, Shintō nature worship and Christianity's submission to the designs of God set limits to speculation on heredity or the claims of blood lineage. Wherever the idea did occasionally crop up that an individual might belong to a group enjoying common characteristics, then importance was given not so much to genetics as to the sacred aspect of such a group. Where it had been perceived that an individual might resemble such and such a kinsman, and therefore be entitled to receive an identical surname, still such empirical observations yielded most often to submission to the arbitrary will of the gods. And yet the feeling of prolonging one's lineage in all its power and originality constituted the very basis of the survival of the group. Hence each cultural area, despite very real local differences, revered its ancestors, maintained concern for its shared blood-lines, and remained wary of that fickle element in its midst represented by women.

The place of ancestors

It was through the circumstances of his birth that an individual came to be acknowledged. That is, he was acknowledged as a member of a lineage whose distant roots, invented if need be if proof of these were lacking, furnished a source of prestige for the group as a whole and also a basis for its unity. Whether mythic or real, ancestors belonged to the sphere of the sacred. They could be linked to the gods, as in Japan or among the Maya; be mingled with genii and supernatural 'objects', as in sub-Saharan Africa; be identified with an animal totem such as the wolf, eagle or bear, as in Central and Eastern Europe; or finally, in simple human terms, allow an individual boldly to state his descent from, say, Charlemagne.

In the case of societies where subsistence was difficult, as in the islands of Oceania, in sub-Saharan Africa or in the Americas, the ancestors revered were those regarded as having been the first to clear and plant. It was on their lands, which were thought to have been once shared in common, that life continued to be led. Nomads such as the Bedouin, the Mongols or the Fulani, transferred to the shepherding of the primordial herds the role thus played by the Ancient Ones. Elsewhere, in places where social organization was more advanced, the ancestors served to ensure the judicial unity of the family, as in China; or through the previous lives that they had led, to settle the fate and caste of their descendants, as in India, or their type of economic activity, as in Japan, if they did not simply lay down the foundations for their offspring's duties, goods and honours, as in Christendom.

It was thus befitting to respect the dead and their memory. To render a cult to the ancestors certainly meant attempting to secure their favour but perhaps much further than this, such a cult also helped to prove one's own existence in this world. Rituals might differ, but their underlying principle was universal; feasts, sacrifices and invocations afforded access to the spirit of the particular ancestor who could thereby allow the unknowable to become known. Asia took such cults to an extreme, although not so much in India, where the notion of reincarnation set necessary limits to the idea that ancestors had permanently disappeared from this world, as in China and Japan. In this regard, the Chinese world, for a period of a thousand years or more, witnessed a certain amount of contention between the tradition of respect for elders, whether departed or still alive, and a measure of scepticism imparted by Confucianism and later Buddhism. Korea and Japan, however, made and continue to make of the daily cult of the dead a key pivot of their social lives.

A group of 'elders' tended to weigh upon the lives of the younger. These elders never tired of giving advice; were consulted on marriages and hunts; bore responsibility for adoptions; and loomed as arbiters and witnesses, whose memories were plumbed and who held council together, as in sub-Saharan Africa (the *mansa*), in the Islamic world (the *malā*), in Byzantium, or around the elm tree in the square of European villages. Such elders presided over the initiation of the young (in special reserved places as with the *tsimia* of New Guinea); it was they again who, along with the women, interpreted the signs sent by the Unknown. To ensure the power of the elders, children were turned into their most docile sounding-boards within the family group. This second trait clarified the status – so often disparaged – of childhood by stressing the link between generations as the very justification of the lineage. And finally, within the circle of dwellings, there rose the settlement whither the elders would wend their way at death: the necropolis. This was no mere resting-field where none would presume to disturb the repose of the departed (such as the *atrium* of Christian usage or the *kiwa* of the Antilles). It was also a family temple wherein veneration for preceding generations was perpetuated.

Thus came about 'dynastic awareness' (*Sippenbewusstsein*), with which each powerful individual was invested and which he transmitted in turn as a holy fragment of his power. Thus it was with the princes of Ghana and Mali in Africa, the rulers of the West, and the emperors of China and Japan. And even where ancestral rank was not so exalted, efforts were made to preserve those elements bearing witness to continuity, such as the nails and hair of the dead. Was this not, after all, a sign that death never constitutes an end? Where forgetfulness might occur, then customs of nomenclature served to recall the departed. Thus an individual could bear the name of an ancestor – throughout East Asia, ancestral names became a generic appellation, as in China, where the name of the clan (*xin*) was added to that of the house (*xi*) or otherwise a patronym recalling a common origin, as in Byzantium. Names could also point to ancestors extending back two or three generations, as in Islam. A complete Islamic 'name' included tribe (*nisba*), appended lineage (*nasab*), given name accompanied either by that of the father (introduced by *ibn*) or by that of the son (introduced by *abū*), and a nickname, often honorific (*laqab*). Strangely enough, the West long resisted such usage. Down to the eleventh century, individual christening designated a specific individual only, even if the given name were one traditionally used in his family. The introduction of appellations of ascendance, 'the son of so-and-so', or of transmittable nicknames, spread only after AD 1100 or even 1150.

A common blood-line

It was the notion of a group of people not only belonging to the same blood-line but also extending to cover either the individuals that one loved or by whom one was served which came to embrace the idea of the family in all its fullness. The vocabulary expressing this is unequivocal: African (Swahili) *ujamaa* could signify at once the three notions of kinship, mutual help and community; in Mexico, the *tecalli* likewise could mean a group linked by blood-line, the faithful of a cult and economic partners; Japanese *no ko* included blood kin, political allies and neighbours; the Christian *familia* embraced kin, domestics and those who gave it 'aid and comfort'. The enlarged family cell hence provided the prime framework for social life and also, as has been said, for ancestor cults – and indeed, as we shall see, for economic and political activities as well. Such notions as solidarity and mutual help naturally resulted in the concept of collective responsibility, not only on moral but also on very real practical grounds. In sub-Saharan Africa, the group as a whole was held to suffer the crippling effects of a rival group's witchcraft, and in turn shared as a bloc in retaliatory acts of violence; in East Asia, from the eighth century on, an insult or unaccountable flight from battle could unleash a chain of score settling, verging even on clan warfare with political aims, as in Japan, where bonds of loyalty rivalled those of blood kinship; Islam may in theory have forbidden revenge, especially in the private sphere, but in practice was forced to tolerate bloody rivalries; Western Christendom in turn was hard put to it to stem its family feuds (*faida* and *vendetta* are the well-known Italian terms for these), and in turn public justice often pursued what private custom demanded.

Without going into what are more often than not merely formal subtleties, we may say that, in this period, the kinship patterns which appear most obviously to predominate were the agnatic (or pyramid of kin through male ties only), whose solidity was certainly buttressed by the family ancestor cult; and the patrilinear aspect is the most visible in the transmission of possessions and in the matrimonial structure. Now, since these patterns, in pre-medieval centuries, are found among all Indo-European peoples in the whole of the area of Indian civilization and Christendom, and also throughout the islands of Oceania, in pre-Columbian America, in the Semitic lands and in East Asia, their origins should doubtless be sought in the basic economic structures, that is, among the bands of hunters and warriors, herdsmen and wandering plant gatherers whose values gave predominance to the male members and especially to the male leader of the clan.

These initial patterns, however, became subject to profound alterations during the period under examination here. Whereas the tribes of Oceania and Native America offer us stable patterns in which indications of maternal ascendance remain hidden, in sub-Saharan Africa, by roughly the fourteenth century, we note increasing sedentary settlement bringing about, within the same ethnic groups, clashes between those clans now in possession of landholdings exploited on a common basis, and those clans that were still pastoralists. Among the former, which might include several hundred individuals, differing degrees of wealth – including the possession of slaves – now sometimes tended to disrupt the equality of all clan members in regard to the common ancestor. This is where a matrilineal contribution could introduce precious goods which enhanced the social value of the wife's family. This was also the situation which prevailed in the Islamic world. In principle, a woman with her goods came under the control of her husband and hence of his ancestral lineage. If unmarried, she remained under the control of her brothers. Christendom went even further by blending Roman law, which had gradually come to favour the cognatic principle, with Celtic or Germanic usage, where the share of women and their original lineages was very great indeed. After the twelfth century, progress was such that paternal and maternal lines came to be regarded as virtually equal, as was also the case in Byzantium, where we see – at least among the aristocracy – women revert to using their original patronyms. The situation becomes more complex when we begin to deal with Asia. The agnatic principle hardly evolved in northern India, whereas in the south a matrilineal and even matriarchal pattern came to the fore. The Chinese, Korean and Japanese areas remained loyal to a firmly patrilineal structure, because here the ancestor cult was solidly established and accompanied by thoroughgoing respect for omnipotent fathers. Even so, the maternal portion of the family also came to be worshipped in the family cult.

The 'family' as a whole, that is a collective linked by blood ties, might thus be a group which archaeology – as in Europe for example – has shown could amount to as many as 100 or even 200 individuals down to about the turn of the tenth and eleventh centuries (thus also Japanese *hīwon*: 'those dwelling together'). It is probable that the family's over-structure, that is, the tribe or ethnic group in relation to the clan or lineage (German thus distinguishes *Sippe* and *Geschlecht*), remained all-inclusive only down to the dawning of the period surveyed here. The way of life of humbler folk remains, more often than not, shrouded from us. Nevertheless, striking similarities in kinship patterns do appear wherever we allow ourselves to overlook strictly local differences in terminology. Thus, in Native America, the Mexican *cencaltin* and Peruvian *ayllu* were dwellings grouped around common courtyards in which those linked by blood ties going back as far as four generations lived. In sub-Saharan Africa, the clan council (*mansa* in Mali) wielded control over three generations. Islam maintained an even higher degree of solidarity under the watch of the tribal *malā* (the 'gathering' or 'council'). in Western Christendom, joint families wove the ties of their *proximitas* and *propinquitas* back to the sixth ascending generation, thereby creating a sphere of economic and political power whence the landed aristocracy drew its strength. In Byzantium, within the framework of the village (*chōrion*), the kinship group (*syngeneia*) joined paternal and maternal lines of ascendance and brought them together in order to manage common assets. In India, the *gōtra* corresponded to a clan bound by blood ties covering six generations. In Japan, the *uji* – whose formation between the sixth and ninth centuries AD marks a crucial stage in Japanese social history – linked within a single grouping all the kin of a single ancestor, an assemblage which might absorb all the members of the same village or all those bound to one another within a single framework of allegiance, thus constituting something midway between the ethnically based clan (*daikazoku*) and a kinship system covering only a few generations (*dōzoku*), thus amounting to a number of individuals bound by ties of solidarity and ranging anywhere between 100 and 1,000 people.

While the ancestor cult only concerned those actually sharing a common origin, 'kinship' might be extended to include all those from whom assistance was expected – whether on a voluntary basis or not. 'Artificial kinship' thus included a considerable mass of those whom ties of amity, or dependence, attached to the clan. These could even be slaves, as in Ghana from the seventh century onwards, or among the Aztecs and Incas of the fifteenth century. In Islam, tributaries who had fled their birthplaces or native families could become a dominant tribe's *mawālī* or 'clients', a group which could also number slaves, servants and prisoners. In this as in other known cases, free men could enter into a sort of voluntary personal dependence and be considered as those 'fed' at the expense of a wealthy overlord. Such, for example, were the *oblati* – those 'offered' to the service of a monastery – or even the vassals of Christendom's 'feudal' system. Japan, for its part, had both its 'unconditional' (*noto*) henchmen and its 'participants' (*munchū*) in the clan's worship or labour. A group could thus swell beyond the 1,000 mark. Such dilation, however, caused the entire family structure to go dangerously awry, for it thus evolved from a ritual cell, geared for self-subsistence, into a larger economic, political or military power unit, all in concentric circles radiating from an initial nucleus of blood ties, whether in the Islamic lands, within the Byzantine aristocracy or among the great 'houses' of Western Christendom alike, and as far as China and Japan. At this stage, it is no longer ties of 'kinship' which we find at the centre of the reactions provoked, but only the interests of a few individuals.

Naturally within the vaster family or clan groupings, sub-groupings could appear. The fragmentary character of these sub-groupings could even ultimately cause dissociation from the family cult unit. It is the associations of brothers and brothers-in-law which appear most clearly to us, because these could often derive their existence from the conditions dictated by an inheritance which had to remain undivided: phratries, brotherhoods and *parçonneries* were some of the terms used in the West to describe such partnerships, which often brought closely together several male family members issued from both paternal and maternal lineages. Islam was also familiar with 'such' groupings with its concern to keep watch over 'its' womenfolk. Hence these groupings might take form even before the father's death. Farther east, in China, at least between the seventh and eleventh centuries, associations between brothers and sisters were extant. Later, in the thirteenth and fourteenth centuries, 'brotherhoods' consisting of sisters, so to speak, came into being.

Hence at this stage, we should address the issue of the actual place occupied by couples within such groupings. All the groups, after all, claimed to spring from a primordial couple. But grappling with this problem – if marriage rituals may be left aside for the moment – is all the more difficult because the available material concerning norms was for a long time very discreet about the very 'supporting structure' of all family life. To be sure, the teachings of Buddhism, Shintōism and also Confucianism throughout East Asia, as well as the message of Islam and the Gospels and canonical rulings of Christendom, all stressed the importance of the couple's role, but these were formal texts which might well mask realities. What does argue in favour of the vitality of the conjugal nucleus is the very size of clan groupings. It is possible that in Native America, in Africa and in Oceania, the nature of local economic preoccupations hardly allowed such a structure to develop. Elsewhere, with the reservation that psychological and indeed cultural dependence upon the larger group never ceased to exist, the couple without a doubt was able to continue to strengthen its position throughout the tenth to fourteenth centuries, when the hold of parents, brothers and cousins became somewhat loosened, and productive activities diversified. To the 'house' (*domus*, *ostal*, *haus*) of the West, there corresponded the 'house' (*ghar*) and 'oven' (*chūlhā*) of Northern India and their southern Indian equivalents (*vitu* and *kutumpa*), as well as Japanese *ie*. In all places after the twelfth or thirteenth centuries, archaeology and iconography yield multiple clues of these groupings consisting of one adult male, one or more spouses, and their young, living around their 'hearth' in an isolated dwelling. One might even go so far as to suggest that the lower the social category of this living unit, the better its chances of escaping the control of the larger group.

The world of women

Throughout all these centuries, and in all areas, woman was considered a creature impure and presumed to be frail, a subject of puzzlement for the other half of humanity. On the one hand, it was expected that she should be set apart, or even isolated, on account of the defects believed to stamp her very essence, but on the other, her primordial role, and the natural attraction she exerted, confused churchmen of all cloths. As a result, while she was treated relatively more gently in the cultures of India and Japan than in those of Islam or the Christian West, still the general outlook was unquestionably one of adamant male preponderance.

Since she had to be hidden yet also cared for, the various cultures provided her with reserved areas. In the societies of Native America, of Oceania, and to a lesser degree of sub-Saharan Africa, women were grouped apart (as in the Mexican *citnacalli*). Elsewhere, she was assigned sections of the home which menfolk might penetrate only in exceptional circumstances. There was no real opposition here between the Islamic *ḥaram* and 'hir owne chambir' in the castles of Christendom. East Asia resorted to much the same practices and also to others, such as that of lodging a wife in her father's house, where her husband would then visit her, as in fourteenth-century Japan. But even where she might live together with her spouse, she remained narrowly watched over for a reason which we can only identify as this one: a woman's womb amounted to a form of precious 'family' property, to be sheltered at all costs from the lust of males and from carnal sin. Fathers, husbands, brothers and uncles (with numerous regional variations concerning the latter) were therefore expected to keep close vigil over her out of a sense of honour – or property – especially when she went outdoors. Her veil, as already pointed out, prolonged her privacy in the public sphere.

Though apparently reduced to objects, women, as we shall see, nevertheless had a prominent role to play. But where she proved incapable of correctly discharging her part as mother, educator and guardian of the hearth, then a woman's presence in the family appeared more of a burden than an asset. For instance, were little girls present in too abundant numbers, or unwedded or unweddable daughters, to be spared? The issue of infanticide, whether systematically perpetrated or slyly induced through ill-treatment, corresponds to a practice whose enormity tends to give historians pause. It seems to be averred as a fact, however, among the Incas, in the Japan of the early centuries AD, and even in India. In China, infants were still being exposed in the tenth century. The occurrence has also been affirmed – and hotly denied, though rather shamefacedly and without convincing arguments – regarding Christendom in the earlier Middle Ages.

The positive side to a woman's fate fortunately provided some compensation. Regarded as being by essence unknowable, women, as we have seen, were held to be the natural interpreters of the Other World, and female deities and intercessors were not lacking, beginning with the Christian Virgin. We should note, however, that female access to liturgical functions occurs only in those cultures which, compared with others, still remained most subject to primeval nature. Thus female shamans existed in Oceania and Central Asia, and perhaps also in Mexico; elsewhere, societies were content with women merely devoted to divine service, as in India and South America; these could even include the 'witches' of Christendom. The two domains – but they were fundamental ones – where a woman could play out her role to full potential were obviously those linked to her procreating function and to the sedentary situation of her family group. As a mother, she enjoyed privileged status in all societies, even before expected birth. Her blood price or Anglo-Saxon 'wergild' (German *Wehrgeld*), in the early medieval West, could rise to four times that of a murdered man; in India, she was 'worth a thousand fathers'. The value set on her procreating role was naturally tied to the need to perpetuate the species. It is striking to note here the dissociation made between the initial sex act, lying as it did under a cloud of suspicion, and the resulting conception of children, whose interruption, as we shall see, was regarded as a calamity. Attention has been lavished on the spread of mother veneration among the various civilizations of the thousand-year period surveyed here, especially in the West, where the cult of Mary was resolutely oriented towards maternal protection.

Beyond certain economic demands, it was also no doubt this maternal prestige which assigned the education of children, of both sexes, to their mothers. The watch and care of little males were entrusted to women down to the age of 7 in the West, in Islam, in Africa and in Oceania, and a little later – to the ages of 10 or 12 – in East Asia. Even if this had been the only domain in which women might hold sway, it would still have been enough to restore a fundamental role to them, since character and mind are moulded in the very first years. Thus all males, greater or lesser, of the medieval period were morally shaped by women, and not only taught but also educated, at least in the necessary basics. Yet we should note here a remarkable contrast between those civilizations which took some pains to open the doors of knowledge and even of 'Letters' to their womenfolk, as was the case in Japan and China (thus Ban Zhao's 'Advice to Girls' goes back to the third century AD), and those – such as Islam and Christendom – which opted to maintain women in 'holy ignorance'.

Gradual sedentary settlement, which of course must leave out here the pastoral peoples or those who practised migrant agriculture over long stretches of time, also contributed greatly to the development of women's roles, for as a hunter or woodcutter, husbandman or shepherd, a male could not keep watch over supplies or manage the food stocks, tend the fire or prepare the food. Even the most 'advanced' societies of the age remained narrowly dependent upon their means of subsistence. To be sure, men were the main breadwinners, but it was the women who acted as the managers for what the men brought in. Everything bore witness to the hold exercised by women. To draw the water, to watch over the cistern, to make the pot boil: from Mexico to Japan such functions were allotted to women, as were the tasks of preserving and preparing maize, wheat, barley or rice, and those of feeding and then dispatching the poultry or swine. As 'mistress' of the household, a woman wielded unshared sway over the Western 'hearth' and Japanese *ie*; to her were entrusted the household's keys (whence ancient Germanic *fruwa*) and accounts. With the other women of the village she held her 'parliaments', exchanging news and passing it on around washing trough, mill and well. In the meantime, the menfolk made rowdy in the tavern or at the forge, boasted of things and invented them, then made noisy incursions into their 'private' sphere. But who was truly in charge here?

With the possible single exception of sub-Saharan Africa, women did not enjoy access to the titles and offices of the secular realm. Nevertheless, since history does bear to such a great extent the stamp of Christian princesses, East Asian empresses, and Indian and Muslim confidantes, should such a remark perhaps not be qualified, at any rate for the tenth, eleventh and then fifteenth centuries in Christendom, for the thirteenth century in India, the tenth in Islam, and the fourteenth and fifteenth in East Asia? These are matters of nuance. But were our subject so to require, we might easily attest to those judicial openings which allowed women to act as witnesses in court, bring lawsuits, manage their assets or develop an economic activity.

We should not allow ourselves to be drawn towards an overly optimistic viewpoint. It had to be stressed that, beyond the relegation of women imposed as a matter of principle, there were numerous areas where both sexes had equal status before their bones were laid, without distinction, in the same earth. Certainly, iron-fisted countesses were to be found alongside spinners of yarn and mowers of hay everywhere; there were mothers who were erudite and others who were overbearing, wives who were subtle and others dominating. There were periods of progress and also steps back: synchronism must fail us here because local conditions differed too widely. To take only the twin poles of the Eurasian land mass, the situation of women in Japan was downgraded between the twelfth and fourteenth centuries (the Kamakura Age), while the reverse was true during the same period in the West (see Plates 173, 174, 257, 258).

The need to procreate

The anxiety provoked in our time by uncontrolled growth in the number of human beings to feed is nothing new. There have always been times and places on Earth where the world appeared too 'full', given the technological level of the moment. We know the obvious cause of this occurrence. Human sexuality, like that of all other natural species, is generous and potent to the point of rendering it the basis of all society. Its excesses can only be restrained by humankind's conscious will – or by the furies of nature. This is why manifestations of sexual drive were channelled by societies from early on towards a matrimonial form of organization, judged to constitute the only means of curbing excess. None of the cultural areas surveyed in this period seems to have remained in a prehistoric or protohistoric state of sexual anarchy in which all the males and females of a given territory might be thrown together in common and at random.

The carnal act

The attraction of one sex for the other appears such a normal thing that it seems idle to dwell upon it. Even if such a thing could be proved, a thick veil would prevent us taking full measure of what all this might imply, for the sexual act, performed in public, was always considered a disturbance of order, and so punished everywhere; and if performed in private, it largely escapes our view. Yet documentation is not lacking. There are the rulings of religious authorities, records of family advice, fictionalized anecdotes, poems and drawings.

In the order of Creation, the divine power allowed a most troublesome element to come into play, which is that, for males at least, the sexual act is a source of pleasure, hence a temptation and attraction. The 'Peoples of the Book' might reason that this was a trial to which God wished to subject his creatures, by encouraging them to observe *moderatio*; still, the act remained at once inevitable, agreeable and necessary. While virginity, or even strict chastity, was certainly regarded, as we have seen, as offering humankind a better path, such an approach jeopardized the ancestor cult and ultimately doomed the species. In addition, it disturbed the social order if not shared by all parties. This is why, despite intense anti-matrimonial drives in Iran, Byzantium and the West at the turn of the eleventh century, the legitimate character of *copula carnalis*, as Christians called it, was admitted everywhere. At most, the defenders of moderation in the *pugna carnis*, the 'flesh's struggle' against unrestrained impulse (the sort of sexual delirium which India for its part called *gandharva*), attempted to raise barriers against excess. From the ninth century on, regulations among Christians became minute: indulgence was permitted in view of procreation only, and also only outside the periods of religious holidays, pregnancy and breastfeeding, and even so, only with a *delectatio moderata*, as Thomas Aquinas expressed it. Jews allowed sex only once a week, and Muslims only if the woman so requested. India's regulations could impose abstinence over periods lasting several months. And beyond the confines of the monotheistic civilizations, sex might be forbidden in times of hunting or clearing, or banned from unpropitious areas such as marshes, gardens or cemeteries. Moreover, the very act, even though subject to *discretio* as Church Fathers never tired of demanding from Saint Paul to Saint Albert (Albertus Magnus), remained a defilement because a woman's sexual organs were impure, as said above, and because a man's willpower was demeaned and lost in the process of carnal embrace, hence unsettling the masculine order.

A number of cultures even drew pride in choosing to regard pleasure as something to be shared equally between both partners, and that man's duty lay in seeing to it that he aroused the pleasure of his mate. This was the view in Islam, in India and in Japan. Eroticism might be the natural approach to use towards arousing mutual pleasure. Love treatises were nowhere lacking, describing the attitudes, postures and practices needed to arouse it: from Ovid to the *Liber Gonorrhini* in the West, and from the *Pillow Book of Sei Shōnagon* in eleventh-century Japan to India's *Kāmasūtra* (a technical manual for successful coitus), human beings enjoyed subtle guides. Priests, Brahmins and Buddhist monks thundered in vain. We should, however, observe that a true geography of eroticism still eludes us. Thus stress on nudity in the West yielded in turn to a focus on dress and hair, but reappeared as a stimulant in East Asia and Islam; tipsiness was popular in Peru, and plant-based aphrodisiacs were so in Africa; kissing was banned in New Guinea, but in China bound feet for young girls (which appeared at the latest by the tenth century) were considered a source of eroticism; other examples of fantasies pertaining to each culture might be adduced.

All the cultures yield us evidence of shared love. There are the abundant poetic writings of Arabic, Christendom's romances of the thirteenth and fourteenth centuries, and even the 'Lives' of holy individuals in Byzantium and elsewhere; India reserved a place for 'suttee' (*satī*), whereby a loving and beloved woman accompanied her husband in death, while the recorded adventures of clandestine lovers in Japan if not in China unequivocally bear witness to that cultural fact.

It needs no effort of the imagination to discern that the rigid strictures of the ministers of the Divinity were not spontaneously observed by common folk. We can measure the seriousness of the sanctions that aimed to ensure avoidance of the effects – illegitimate birth, especially – of undesired practices. Such 'sins' were identical everywhere: partaking of a self-aborting potion, smothering a foetus, practice of *coitus interruptus* in the case of a male, a woman's immediate resort to self-cleansing, and indulgence in postures believed to impede conception, not to mention magic invocations before or after the embrace in nearly all places. The attitudes of chastity's guardians varied, and sometimes veered between extremes. Customs considered acceptable in Japan might be punished by death in Mexico; between these poles, Islam condemned with rather more indulgence, and Christianity with more rigour but also with more subtlety. Thus preventive contraception entailed penance, contraception after the act more serious penance still. Infanticide, however, whether at birth or during the last stages of pregnancy, was murder, and an insult to the ancestors; the penalty for those guilty was death.

'Solitary pleasures', obviously, allowed one to avoid all danger; we may infer their universality – by definition as it were – by common sense rather than by extant proof. But laws dealt harshly with such practices, regarding them as wastes of the divine gift. Women stood here more accused than men, no doubt because men were those who wrote the laws. Resort to homosexuality was as a rule placed on the same level, but the ways in which it was dealt with could vary greatly from one place to another. This was probably because social structures might here and there actually encourage it, as for example in the West and in Islam, where the sexes where systematically segregated between the age of 12 and the time of marriage, or wherever there were single-sex organizations, such as among Christian clergy and Christian bodies of monks; bands of warriors, whether Muslim or Western; and Brahmans or other groups resulting from the caste barrier in India. In principle, the penalty for the guilty could again be death. This was so in America and in Islam, but the frequency of occurrences, particularly among women, led authorities to avert their gaze, as was systematically the case in East Asia.

Naturally, what remained to be feared was the uncontrolled violence of masculine impulses. Condemned on all sides, but systematically perpetrated and multiple in form, rape was the sexual plague of this age. Death sanctioned the crime in America and in Islam, and very heavy penalties were imposed in the West because the order of society, of the family, and even of property, were seriously injured both on the spot and in the consequences. And where authorities were forced by necessary circumstances to look the other way, this was because they then chose to regard rape as a sort of virility rite for those men, or at least those young men, taking part. But the dangers inherent in rape were so soon and so obviously recognized as lying beyond what society could bear that official forms of prostitution were set up long before the medieval age. The role expected of women plying this trade, through their contribution to social regularity and to the defence of the family and public order, explains why the Churches tolerated, protected, indeed encouraged the 'services' of prostitutes. It was in temples that India's *devadasī* priestesses and 'hostesses' practised their craft; in Christendom, the houses of those 'gentlewomen that live honestly by the prick of their needles' clustered around churches; street girls in Islam loitered in front of mosques; and Japanese prostitutes welcomed their customers in the 'quarter of blessed flowers', or *yoshiwara*. Native America erected the custom into a rule of life, and in Peru every great house had its own 'service woman' entrusted with the instruction of the household's adolescent males. Statistics were in proportion to the range of the practice. In Dijon in France, at the close of the Middle Ages, 10 per cent of the town's women resorted to prostitution, whether on a regular basis or not. Towards the latter half of the first millennium AD, 500 prostitutes were known in Tanjore in India, 15,000 in Kyōto and 20,000 in Chang'an – not counting transvestites. Sharp geographical differentiation may further be observed. While the *devadasī* of India and the *geisha* ('persons of art') in Japan were lettered, often erudite, and offered cultured conversation in addition to the physical pleasure they bestowed, more often than not prostitutes were country girls.

Marriage

It was union between a man and one or more consorts – if the reverse ever existed among the Celts, in parts of sub-Saharan Africa or in Southern India, this was only a distant memory by the medieval period – that provided the foundations of society in so far as sexual anarchy thereby ceased to exist. Whether durable or not, based on mutual consent or imposed, a matter of simple cohabitation or the result of complicated rites, such union provided the bedrock for relations between the sexes, and hence lies at the very core of our subject. Nevertheless, it is difficult to follow the history of marriage in the course of a thousand years and in so many different places, because wedlock constitutes the most flexible and sharply contrasted link in our survey. Here again, and in fact here more than elsewhere, we shall have to restrict ourselves to generalities.

We should first remind ourselves that although a sexual dimension can hardly be excluded from marriage, it would be a mistake to assign it the leading role. Marriage, whatever its forms, is primarily a contract, and pleasure merely its ornament. At issue are goods to be managed, inheritances to provide for, a lineage to perpetuate. A number of its characteristics narrowly depend upon conflicting circumstances within a given cultural area. Monogamy was most usually the lot of the pauper who could not decently afford to feed several wives, or that of the urban dweller who did not enjoy enough space in which to spread his 'hearth'. Money, age, self-interest and square metres often decided these things far more than the strictures of divines.

The first aspect of this complex whole obviously concerns the number of spouses involved. Monogamous cultures tend to pass harsh judgement on polygamy. They see here a matter of indulgence regarding licentiousness, a form of scorn regarding women, and a refusal of total involvement on the part of one human being towards another. Practitioners of polygamy, for their part, invoke the absolute need for offspring, notably male, in order to perpetuate the species and the religion, and refer as well to the dimension of social and economic prestige, and to the strength represented by the group of women in the household. But while such principles may be clearly enunciated in each culture, realities are something else again since in the one case, the practice of keeping concubines may compensate for monogamy, and in the other, sheer poverty will limit the number of wives. The monogamous group, whether in the name of the primordial couple formed in Eden or elsewhere according to various Asian creation myths, or on account of the sacramental force of the union between the sexes, included the Jews and Christians, East Asia, and India. In this case, the 'hearth', the Japanese *ie*, might include five to seven people, even though this basic unit must be set within a vaster clan. In fact, this situation took a long time to prevail. In the West, especially among the wealthy, polygamy (whether admitted or not) was patently practised until the Conciliar decisions of the eighth and particularly the eleventh centuries. It is known, however, to have survived, under the form of kept concubines, until the fifteenth century, but when the Church placed marriage among the sacraments – albeit at the lowest rank – it bestowed upon wedlock an obvious constraining force. In India, there was opposition between the more lax Buddhists and the more rigorous Brahmins, who went so far as to encourage *satī*, the cremation of a wife upon the pyre of her deceased husband. It is thought that 90 per cent of India's homes were monogamous (see Plates 219, 220). Japan and China were also resolutely monogamous, but here the practice of keeping concubines was also legitimate. In Islam, the Qur'ān authorized four wives, provided one could feed and treat them equally. Less stable societies seem to have been familiar with the principle of outright markets for women, hence of legitimized polygamy. This was true in sub-Saharan Africa undoubtedly, and in Native America most certainly, and notably in Peru, where a minister of the Inca was appointed to allot wives. Oddly enough, the islands of Oceania seem rather to have tended towards monogamous union; satisfactory explanation for this has not been advanced.

There were limitations, however, to these unions. These were mostly raised by the taboo on incest. Even so (as was the case with the Egyptian pharaohs), the Inca wedded his sister and an Aztec could 'know' his daughter, but on the whole, consanguineous copulation was shunned, extending to various degrees. Was this on account of very real fears of physiological effects? Or out of concern not to mingle identical family lines? Or yet again, as a precaution against grouping together too many inheritances? While the Native American world seems to have tolerated contact between close degrees of kin such as with sister or aunt – but under government control, as in Peru – and although union between first cousins seems to have been legitimate in New Guinea, elsewhere degrees of prohibition were set very high. Byzantium by the seventh century had fixed the forbidden limit at the fourth and then at the fifth degree, the West in the ninth century set its own limit at the seventh, ninth-century India took it to the eighth, and Islam and the Far East even extended this to include artificial relations. Naturally, an evolution accompanied the loosening of religious constraints. To a certain extent, the development of the practice of adoption, once so well known to the Graeco-Roman world, served to cover the fault. It was abundantly resorted to in the Christian Near East, and in Islam and India from the seventh century onwards, but it was late in coming to the West (in the thirteenth century). In the latter area, the Church lowered its barrier against incest to the fourth degree when it finally appeared that the material dangers of systematic endogamy were diminishing in intensity (1215).

The term 'endogamy' brings us to the second aspect of the world of marriage. Once the legitimate character of a union was ensured ('banns' were proclaimed so that objections – if any – could be made known), the main question to be resolved became that of whether to bestow one's choice within one's circle of kin (endogamy), or outside it (exogamy). These two options have coexisted in all cultures. To wed one's kin, without incest, was to reinforce the purity of the blood-line, preserve the ancestor cult, avoid the departure of a consort outside the clan, or provide for an easy replacement by an uncle upon the decease of the father, preferably an uncle on the maternal side, because closer in age to the mother. Sub-Saharan Africa, India, Japan and China all clung firmly to this practice, encouraged by an imperious 'house' society. Buddhism also contributed to this tendency, since it refused to countenance inequality between the social levels of the spouses (homogamy). Islam subscribed to all this as well in theory, but the Prophet had not really foreseen the issue, and medieval Muslim practice was more a case of later influences, particularly Iranian. In Christendom, things were even more complex. Both solutions long coexisted in its midst, even in the face of an offensive mounted by the Church in favour of exogamy, which ruled out incest – and so weakened the Church's rival, the warrior aristocracy. This long struggle in fact pitted the Church against the powerful members of society, those who were imbued with awareness of the purity of their blood-lines and were concerned to marry as far as possible above their station (hypergamy), whereas the humble more readily accepted the advice of their priests.

Given these constraints, one may measure just how small was the proportion of 'marriages of love'. This, however, was not the primary goal, which remained procreation, hence fertile sexual union. Deference was due here to the wise ones who made inquiries and decided. These were Africa's 'elders', the Japanese *nakōdō*, and China's *mei jen*, who chose future spouses from those of marriageable age, or else an actual official like the Inca's minister. In India, in Christendom and in Islam, parents entered into often lengthy negotiations, to which the betrothed were not privy at all. They might meet only on their actual wedding day, as in Eastern Asia, or upon the occasion of their exchange of vows (*sponsalia*, *verba de futuro*) among Christians. In Islam, on this same occasion, things were not yet considered binding, however, and a girl could still refuse, something which would have been regarded as an unheard-of aberration anywhere else. Furthermore, there existed betrothals which could concern children still below the age of understanding, an occurrence observable in all these areas. Christendom went furthest towards granting a place to the notion of free will, that is of approval or *consensus*, between the 'betrothed'. Roman law as codified by Justinian, enforced in the sixth century AD in the East and by the tenth century in the West, was predicated upon affection, *dilectio*, which the principle of exogamy as encouraged by the Church was in theory bound to favour. Nevertheless, in Europe as elsewhere, the matrimonial 'model', as a rule, married barely nubile girls to men already 'established', hence ten to fifteen years their seniors. The dependent position of a bride who was too young, the dominant role played by her brothers if her husband were to travel or die, the short span of time of such unions, and the necessity of prostitution to accommodate the many young males waiting to become 'established' or to receive the bride granted them by their fathers (whence the trait so marked in Islam with its *aḥdāth*, its gangs of young unmarried males on the prowl and out for a rape or theft) were the main features of this matrimonial structure.

If marriage amounted to a contract, then it was fitting that it should give occasion to unequivocal public manifestations: the pledge before witnesses, and in Byzantium even before a notary; the form of words or vows exchanged, which made the agreement similar to a commercial pact; the exchange of symbolic and ritual objects, such as a ring signifying the match and worn on the finger (in Christendom), or in a nostril (in India and Africa); carnal consummation, without which the agreement and contract became null and void; and finally, the settlement of the male and his female consort or consorts in a place which would henceforth constitute his 'hearth', even if shared with others. In this regard, numerous variations may be observed. In Christendom, in India, in Islam and in China, settlement took place in the husband's home, but Japan recognized two possibilities, and in sub-Saharan Africa and in Native America, cohabitation – at least temporarily – occurred in the home of the bride's father. The Oceanic world solved the problem in a trenchant manner: each of the partners stayed in their own original homes.

The rites might not suffice, in any case. The agreement had to be made tangible between the contracting parties. Thus the principle of the father's grant of a dowry in order to provide for the bride's upkeep during her married life, while the groom's father in turn gave or promised a dower or bride-price to ensure the spouse's decent widowhood, constituted a universally practised warranty. Jurists in all lands have had no trouble in deciphering this practice as a relic of an age when women were bought and sold. In fact, the twin material elements of the contracts were not always implemented exactly. The bride's contribution could amount to no more than a few items of furniture or such movables on which she retained no monopoly, whereas the husband would provide his father-in-law with provisions and even with a tract of land. This was the situation in America, in Africa and in Japan. In Islam, to the bride-price (*mahr*) put together for the wife was added a gift bestowed at the time of the match; but even where she brought little material wealth with her, a woman in this case remained entitled to it. The situation was almost the reverse in India, where a dowry could even be put together as the result of a collection made in the village, while the groom for his part pledged barely anything at all. China and Christendom provided the most balanced patterns. On the one hand, the bride's family furnished a rich dowry (*maritagium*, *dotalicium*, *exovale*), constituting the bride's property but managed by her spouse under his father-in-law's watchful eye; and on the other hand, the groom set aside part of his assets, often a third, in order to provide if necessary for his wife's ultimate widowhood, with in some cases the addition of an immediate donation (*doarium*, *donatio propter nuptias*, *Morgengab*).

The ending of a match could not fail to be a very serious matter. We can easily discern the main reason for such breaks, which was the lack of consummation in the flesh, or sterility – the latter, by the way, always imputed to the female partner, who at worst might even be suspected of witchcraft. But the wish to repudiate could find other outlets, notably on account of a woman's loss of looks because of age, as in Islam and in the West. Repudiation existed everywhere, in Africa, in China, in India, even in Byzantium on the grounds of verified infertility. While the initiative most often came from the male, in East Asia a woman could take the first steps, or divorce could even result from mutual consent. We may observe here that adultery, although also entailing repudiation, was not invoked as a determining cause. This was because adultery constituted a crime against the family and even against society. Punishment therefore might vary according to the psychological structure of a given society. Among the Incas, the offence was punished with death, but in Mexico, 'compensatory' adultery might wash away the fault. In Eastern Asia, chastisement meant relegation and servile tasks for several years. Islam dictated stoning to death, although as a rule accommodations could be reached. Christendom seems to have favoured stressing the shame and silliness of the offence by resorting to public demonstrations that brought dishonour upon the guilty. Loyalty to one's husband thus appeared as a pillar of the family group. It could lead as far as India's *satī*, or short of this excess, to a prohibition on remarriage, especially for widows – who happened in any event to be more numerous than widowers. While this prohibition remained very much in force in China and India, it finally disappeared in the West and Byzantium by the tenth and eleventh centuries, respectively, probably to encourage the birth rate.

To survive and endure

How to ensure the necessary continuity without which a family group, the human group in fact, could obviously not perpetuate itself and so transmit the physical, material and psychological inheritance of which it is the custodian in its passage through this world?

The place of the child

In a world everywhere confronted with the problem of sheer subsistence, where toil had to be shared in common and solidarity was the rule in order to ensure survival, those individuals incapable of producing could well pass for useless burdens, or at the very least as encumbrances to be put up with for as short a time as possible. That a child represented the obvious promise of the future goes without saying. In expectation of a future womb, or future progenitor, the infant's birth was wished for. It is possible that boys, who actually happen to be physiologically frailer, were given more protection against natural hardships than girls, or even that girls were eliminated outright as in the cases referred to above. In addition, infant mortality struck down rapidly and far more widely than in the most impoverished countries today (the evidence of European cemeteries, in particular, points to a death rate of one in every three – or even of one in every two – children). Living as it were under a suspended death sentence and on borrowed time, superfluous and cumbersome burdens and worthless in economic terms, children endured only on account of what they could become. It has even been argued that the very notion of childhood, as a sentiment, was lacking at this time.

Such a statement ought, however, to be qualified. To begin with, in certain cultures, the coming of a child was held to be a token of Heaven's forgiveness, sent from on high; and even if the child as such had no role to play, he justified the family's existence. It was in India and China that value seems truly to have been set upon the infant in itself, as is the case with us today. The child was considered as 'a good example', or as 'repayment of a debt', and not only as a human cub or worthless runt. Japan showed more reluctance, and Islam more still. In Islam, children, except for elder sons, lay under suspicion, were regarded as irresponsible beings, and were hidden away on principle. Christians for a long time thought along much the same lines, yet there are now convincing archaeological, poetic and iconographic clues which point to interest shown in at least the very first stages of the child's life by the twelfth century in particular. It is true that in these initial stages, a child, as has been pointed out, still remained entirely in the world of the womenfolk, which leads one to think, although this is not necessarily a binding law, that the female sex tended to show more tenderness and attention to these unfinished creatures issued from their wombs.

By the age of 5 (in Africa), 7 (in Europe, Islam and Eastern Asia), and 10 (in India), a child joined the world of men if male, of women if female. Here began the hardest stage in its life, which might last about ten years: somewhat less for girls so soon to be married off, but longer for boys, who would have to wait for their trade, status and spouse. A boy's adolescence might indeed last until the age of 25 (as in Byzantium), corresponding to his period of apprenticeship of life, where the powers of concentration and labour expected of him might go beyond what his mind and body were yet mature enough to cope with. Initiation rites accompanied this 'passage'. In Christendom and in China, mere allusions, often literary, lift only a corner of the veil on the brutal conflicts between rising and established forces; in Japan and in Islam, published texts make special mention of the brutalities perpetrated particularly by young males in villages, or by the gangs of unmarried *aḥdāth* who roamed the streets of 'Arab' towns. India was also familiar with rites of access to puberty, and then to cultural responsibility, but in very peaceful terms as is so often the case in this region. The 'passage' took its harshest forms in America, Africa and the Oceanic zone, with violent abductions of adolescents from their mothers, scourgings, infliction of scars and other marks, almost literally 'faggings', which might be repeated over several years, sometimes accompanied by long periods of isolation or privation conducive to the development of violence, or homosexuality, among members of either sex.

The most widespread, outstanding, and for the adolescent perhaps most painful trait, was the crushingly possessive tutelage exercised by the father over his issue. No doubt the absolute *patria potestas* of ancient Mediterranean law had lost some of its force, but the responsibility of the father still remained unlimited. In Japan, he could still sell, prostitute or even kill his issue where considered useless or guilty, and in India, banish them from the caste with the consensus of the members of the caste – which amounted to fatal isolation. China and Islam seem not to have gone so far, but loyalty and piety regarding one's father were among the pillars of these societies. As usual, India balanced the power of the father, which still remained strong, with that of the mother endowed with certain weight. Curiously enough, it was Christendom which, although it still bore the stamp of Roman law, went furthest in eroding paternal authority.

Transmission of wealth

Judicial data touching on inheritance are among the most ponderous and complicated documents with which a historian may be called upon to deal. This is because the notion of ensuring that the fruit of his toil on Earth should be passed on to his descendants is so deeply rooted in man. Whether his intentions were thereby to give permanence to the worship of his ancestors or whether he was moved by affection or even by interests of the moment, the fact remains that man has multiplied prescriptions, prohibitions and loopholes.

To begin with, a man who wished to bequeath his wealth may have wanted to preserve in their integrity the fruits he had inherited or acquired in the course of his own life. In this case, he had to select a single beneficiary – a simple enough solution, fruitful as far as the solidity of his legacy was concerned, but naturally disastrous for the other heirs to his person. However, he may have shown more concern, out of affection or a sense of justice, in a fair-minded distribution, and so shared out his goods in more or less equal lots, thereby wronging no one but ruining his house. Finally, as a married man threatened with coming death, he may have elected to ponder the fate of his future widow and perhaps also of his daughters. For if ancestor worship were the priority, or, in equal measure, the need to reinforce a legacy, then the bequeather must needs opt for a single heir or, at the least, a preferred heir, so ensuring continuity. But if the group's type of activity required collective efforts, such as hunting, herding or clearing, or if demographic pressures were to make themselves strongly felt as a source of possible disturbance, then an equitable sharing-out might be preferable. But then again, a woman's position might be so solid in a given society that the bequeather could hardly avoid providing for her. In the case of the poor, a single undivided inheritance could prove rather useless, but in the case of the powerful, an undivided legacy could be an asset to be preserved in order to maintain wealth and prestige. If the kin were neither too close nor too finicky, then the bequeather might act as he pleased or on the spur of his last moments. But where the cognatic family system remained very much in force, then the bequeather had to bow to the approval of others who would decide in the interest of the group – and not in that of the dying bequeather. The place of male primogeniture, or if one wishes to put it more simply, of the elder son (although choice might favour the younger son, as among the Mongols, with all the consequent bitterness and disturbances), is the first problem we must deal with. We have gone into the reasons for primogeniture with responsibility for the ancestor cult, the inherited estate and the powers of command going to the eldest. But the transfer of all disposable assets to the eldest son existed nowhere. Even if we do not take into account the share bequeathed to the widow, there always existed hindrances to complete dispossession of the other sons; even wills drawn up under Roman law restricted the implementation of total primogeniture, all the more reason for custom to do so. Even in Japan, where primogeniture was most vigorously observed, to the extent that a still-young elder son would go and live apart with his father, built-in limitations were extant. Thus, there were the cases where a son who ought dutifully to have shown filial piety towards his sire (*kō*) chose instead to give priority to his military or political loyalties (*chū*), and such an attitude would then entail his exclusion from his paternal inheritance. In addition, at least among humbler folk, between a quarter and a third of a legacy was in practice 'reserved' for the other heirs. In India, where the situation was already far less rigid, there existed a willingness to replace, as heir, a deceased elder son by one's son-in-law, and after 1200, the right of primogeniture tended to give way to co-legacies, as in China in much the same period. Islam favoured primogeniture since the preferred heir could buy up the shares of the others, but the practice of division was also very strong there. All in all, Christendom also remained partial to both approaches, depending on the period. As might be expected, it was the aristocracy which opted for primogeniture, but even in this case, the eldest son was only entitled to a preferential share, amounting at most to two-thirds. Probably such limits to the complete transmission of property to one heir owed more to an awareness of the risks involved than to a spirit of justice. One becomes convinced of this when looking at the state of anarchy which loomed over the other possible approach, that of sharing out.

This was where local traditions, whose origins often escape us, became entangled to an extreme. In Western Christendom, for example, Celtic usage made a place for women and recommended sharing out; among the Germanic peoples, males predominated (as in the Salic law) but widows could inherit (Burgundian law); the Lombards apportioned equitably, but the Goths stood for primogeniture; Roman law favoured the eldest son but still endorsed apportioning; the Nordic peoples included uncles and aunts in the inheritance. In the meantime, arrangements regarding widows were no less confused. If such was the disorder prevailing at the western tip of Eurasia, one can hardly hope to make out a clear picture for entire continents. Hence let us restrict ourselves to salient points. To begin with, apportioning could cover only certain assets. In Peru, the Inca and the temples reserved two-thirds of legacies for themselves; in sub-Saharan Africa, common lands were excluded from the possibility of being shared out; in India, paternal and maternal assets were treated differently. In addition, among Christians at least, it was always possible for kinsfolk to interfere in order to approve or oppose, or even to recover goods unfairly allotted (*laudatio parentum*, *retrait lignager*, *ritorn*), or instead to encourage attribution of a vacant patrimonial asset to a *proximus* or *germanus* (this was known as *epibolē* in Byzantium and as *adjectio sterilium* in the West). If one adds that, depending upon his legal status, a man could be despoiled by his own master, often of a good part of his assets, and sometimes of all of them, and that this situation was familiar to Europe, America and India alike, then one can gauge how many sources of conflict might nourish repeated and painful turmoil. We need merely look to Europe and to its practice of sharing out the children resulting from a marriage between a free male partner and a bondswoman, or the relapse of all offspring into bondage wherever custom decreed that 'the worst' was to be followed.

But we do enjoy a clearer view where the third approach is concerned, that regarding inheritance by or for women. In Europe, the custom varied between areas where preferential transmission went through males (*per virgam*), as where a warrior aristocracy set the social tone, and those areas – admittedly on the decline after the early twelfth century – where transmission *per ventrem* was more the rule. A few simple principles can be given here. A girl upon whom a dowry was bestowed, and who was then married off, would be excluded from her father's succession in so far as she had already received an advance, as it were, on her inheritance. This was what happened from the twelfth century in Christendom and India. The reasoning was that where she could preserve the management of her endowment or at least remained its main proprietor, then she could recover whatever was left of it upon her widowhood. A second trend entitled daughters to a share of the inheritance wherever the rule was for the legacy to be apportioned out – but only after yielding primacy to the sons and by drawing upon the mother's assets (*materna maternis*). In this, the daughters' shares were always smaller, amounting to no more than half in Islam.

Obviously, widows were entitled to the most, given their usually still young age as a result of the 'matrimonial model', or because remarriage was forbidden, or on account of the violence of the period, which left them no outlet except poverty or the convent. If we set aside those areas where the custom was to enforce rigid exclusion on women who could no longer bear children and were hence considered useless, as in Oceania and Africa, it was generally admitted that widows were entitled to enjoy their dower (that is, husband's bride-price) and recover whatever remained of their dowry (that is, their father's endowment). This was the minimal solution found in Eastern Asia. Another possibility was that the widow might be entitled, as an additional usufruct, to a portion of what remained of the legacy, amounting to as much as a third in Christendom, but restricted either to the couple's acquired assets or to those which properly pertained to the maternal line; according to this procedure, the widow enjoyed priority over other legatees linked by blood ties or by marriage, particularly sons-in-law.

The most favourable situation existed in India, especially in the south. At the turn of the thirteenth century, a widow was entitled to a normal and occasionally predominant share in her husband's legacy, at least wherever the custom of *satī* did not prevail.

To live together

The different societies of this millennium movingly yearned to reinforce all those ties which might permit them to endure. Some were based if not on mutual affection among men, at least on demonstrations of fellowship in everyday life. Others rather put their trust in the bonds of mutual organization whereby common interests were linked to respect for authority. The ultimate effect was nearly everywhere to structure society into hierarchical orders which alone seemed adequate to hold human groups together and permit them to last.

Fellowship, of course, depends upon cultural impulses whose intensity may vary according to different ethnic groups, their sense of hospitality, inclination for games, or concern for shared meals. We shall therefore be content to throw light on the importance of celebrations, which often took on a powerful religious hue, and brought together men – and far more rarely women – in regular and frequent demonstrations of play (it has been estimated that in the West, more than 100 days in the year were taken up by some sort of festivals, feasts, entertainments or processions). Dances, bonfires, tests of skill, races, animal fights, parades in costume, noise making, existed everywhere, in town and country alike. Naturally, variations were numerous. 'Maypoles' and midsummer bonfires in the West went back to pagan roots; in Native America, play in the ball court preceded bloody sacrifice; drinking bouts in Christendom, archery bouts in China and boat races in Japan could all result in rivalry between families or clans; even apparently peaceful games like chess among the Muslims or cards among the Chinese were often more akin to duels than to playful recreation.

Men 'fraternizing' in the tavern or women socializing around the washing trough present an egalitarian dimension, but this has to be seen against the vertical links binding men inside very powerful structures within which the flesh-and-blood feeling of relationship, artificially created, may run parallel to or even become stronger than the bonds of kinship. There are two cultural areas where this seems to have been most marked. One was Western Christendom, where fellowships of young warriors, at least from the seventh century on, united, within bonds of almost filial loyalty, the 'vassal' (from Celtic *gwass*, 'boy') with his lord ('seigneur' and other variants in the Romance languages, from Latin *senior* or 'elder'). This was the well-known source of the practice of vassalage in the twelfth and thirteenth centuries and beyond. The other was in Eastern Asia, where Japan's military aspect almost presents a curious mirror image of contemporary Christendom, while China's ties were more intellectual and psychological between masters and disciples.

The 'royal model', or the example of an emperor, provided a psychological pole which served to orient society towards a hierarchical summit, making it desirable to attach oneself to the prince's family, or at least to associate one's own family group with the magnificent, religious, and if need be ferocious, authority of the prince. In China, the words for duke and father, count and elder son, carried the same meaning. Concerning Japan, the near-military aspect of the social framework is surprising. Should we attribute it to the conscious will of the various clans jockeying for power since the seventh century? Or to a political system thought up by the *shōguns* of the thirteenth century? Or simply to the compartmented configuration of the terrain, perpetuating traditions of self-defence under difficult conditions, or even to the sense of honour and respect for strength so rooted in the archipelago? Islam also honoured the warrior (whence the word *'aṣabiyya* for a 'fellowship of warriors'), regardless of whether or not such a warrior happened to be fighting for the Faith – but did not ossify such respect into so rigid a mould as Japan's. Nor should we forget that while Western Christendom, so often and so imprudently labelled 'feudal', certainly did grant political importance to its men-at-arms, it nevertheless left large sectors of its society free of military control.

China was altogether exceptional. Here, society was held together not by swordsmen but by scribes. At the outset, the Confucian message lay down knowledge as the rule. Throughout the thousand-year period, the role of 'jurists', of schools and of the *literati,* continued to grow. The Qin Dynasty by the third century BC, the Tang, the Song and the Ming in the eighth, twelfth and fifteenth centuries AD, developed a system of teaching consisting of codes (with several hundred articles), examinations, endless controls, resulting in an omnipotent bureaucracy, graded 'mandarins', civil servants who were masters of everyday life and who were lured by social promotion, respect for the written word and administrative efficiency. In the fifteenth century, there were 80,000 titled officials in the imperial household alone. Naturally, one could hardly compare Western Christendom to the Chinese world, but even here, respect for the law, whether secular or ecclesiastical, written or oral (and in any case earlier oral traditions were being written down by the twelfth and thirteenth centuries), as well as the role granted to 'clerks' at the side of lay princes or in the Church, showed that in this part of the world, too, the social framework could no longer rely on brute force alone to maintain order.

One recourse that might have remained would have been a social administration entrusted to purely religious authorities, but the weight of the various Churches here was unequal, and sometimes indeed non-existent. Thus Islam made no difference between believers, any more than did the Buddhists of the East; India, to be sure, was subject to the powerful pressure of its millions of Brahmins, but these formed a hermetically sealed caste of ultimate concern to itself alone. It was Christendom which most resorted to pious groupings, with its brotherhoods (not without a whiff of paganism about them with their social drinking bouts, or *potaciones*), in which peasants or craftsmen joined together for mutual assistance and devotional exercises. To a certain extent, the monastic establishments, to which the poor, the excluded, younger sons and old maids flocked, in addition to those impelled by more authentic vocations, might be considered in much the same light. In Byzantium, where such religious houses fulfilled multiple functions, they were even referred to as 'family monasteries'.

It will not have escaped attention that the various barriers enclosing individuals, such as horizontal and vertical fellowships and the relative weight of sword or pen, resulted in a powerful hierarchical organization of the world of the living. With the possible exception of those cultures still very much subject to the tyranny of nature, as in the islands of Oceania, profound gulfs isolated individuals from one another. Some, which we shall just mention in passing, concerned the different rights granted to men. Slavery, for example, existed everywhere, an institution fed by prisoners of war, condemned criminals and individuals bought to provide free labour. One may quibble over nuances and argue that the Western form of slavery, which died out towards the tenth century, had been even harsher than the serfdom which followed, that the 5 per cent of slaves in the societies of China and Japan were well treated, and that all things considered the daily fate of bondsmen was no worse than that of others. Still, slavery in the Middle Ages constituted a fact which it is useless to try to hide in the name of Christianity, especially as Christian civilization did not care, as would be seen long after the Middle Ages. Suffice it to say that this shameful institution existed on the fringes of humanity, and it is better not to dwell on these nuances too closely.

Other elements of differentiation may be based on two criteria which were not, for that matter, mutually exclusive. One was the type of activity set aside for a given individual in society, and the other was his economic, political or religious rank. The first would normally place an individual within a group from which he could no longer emerge and where he would no longer be approached by any individual belonging to any other group, since each would be held to enjoy his own role, way of life and law within the harmony of the larger whole. In Japan, for example, one might belong to the group or *sei* of the warriors (*samurai*), craftsmen, peasants, merchants or outcasts (*se min*: those who practised degrading trades such as butchers and tanners) and slaves (*yatsuko*). But it was in India, as is well known, and particularly in the Ganges Plain and in south India, that caste (*jātī*) became the mandatory frame of life. The texts of the *dharmaśāstra* never ceased to affirm as much, and their glosses (*nibandha*) progressively fossilized society. Nearly 3,000 hermetically shut castes existed, opposed to all contact that could mix their blood-lines or manifestations of worship with one another, with each practising its own customs (*āchār*) and having its own usages (*ācharan*), which it was forbidden for others to imitate. Caste spread like a contagion throughout South Asia (India) between the tenth and twelfth centuries, because it was ultimately considered to provide the securest guarantee against disorder, and we see no attempt to overthrow such a system. Indeed, many of these castes were highly regarded, for example those of the warriors (*kshatrya*) often inclined to Buddhism, the Brahmans, the temple servants and even the merchants (*vaishya*). By contrast, the worst fate was to be counted among those practising humiliating and filthy trades. These were 'those below' (*paraiyan*, whence 'pariah'), in the sense of unworthy, untouchable.

Without going to these extremes of disintegration, Christendom and, to a lesser degree, Islam, one might recall, were also tempted by this idea of thus immutably allotting individuals to a given function. The trinitarian pattern, as it happens inherited from India and referred to above, apportioned individuals to those who prayed for others (*oratores*), those who defended them (*bellatores*) and those who fed them (*laboratores*). This view of a balance willed by God blocked any notion of social promotion, since it was a sacrilege towards the Creator to try to escape one's 'order'. The idea of rivalry, however, was introduced within each social order, with struggles between richer and poorer, stronger and weaker, and between those whose blood price or *wergild* was higher than that of others.

Thus there emerged groups which were both united in their family mechanisms and daily needs, and split asunder in their practical values and social relations.

CONCLUSION

At the end of a global survey where, so many nuances – even important ones – have obviously had to be passed over, we may attempt to strike a general balance. We have dealt here neither with Korea nor Tibet, nor southern Africa, the American plains, Northern Asia, Northern Europe, the Jews or the Khmer. Elsewhere, broad coverage has had to ignore definite specific features, and we have spoken of 'sub-Saharan Africa', of 'Oceania', of 'Christendom', and worst of all, of 'Islam'. But this was our only solution to avoid confusion or fragmentation into a welter of detail.

Is it possible, then, to outline a broad conclusion? It is, and on two different planes. In the first place, this thousand-year period was indeed marked by features common to the whole world, although more sharply etched in some places than others. All societies were steeped in a religious atmosphere which coloured everything they did, and this often conferred leading rank on those men who served the divine, the guardians of the rules of family life. In addition, all these societies were firmly organized into hierarchies, 'orders', castes and clans. Their driving element was armed force, that of the state or that of the warriors. Regarding the latter, family practices combined to strengthen their control. If we go even further into the field dealt with here, we shall also find a deterioration in the status of women almost everywhere, albeit with two fundamental qualifications: guarantees of a judicial or even economic character sheltered her, in theory, from want; and within the house, that is, her 'private' sphere, she wielded very real authority, almost unshared, especially over her children. Finally, the pressure of kinship ties, even extended kinship ties, was fundamental, weighing upon marriage, inheritance and the management of assets alike. It was kinship which animated demonstrations of fellowship, the forms of groups and even political activity.

The second area of observation, which might draw upon a very general view of all these components, would lead us to an attempt to classify family types. It would seem possible to identify three groups of these.

The first covers East Asia. Traits observed here seem to form a social pattern of monogamy (on the whole), of sexuality under close surveillance, and of prevailing endogamy. Women were treated with more consideration in Japan than in China, but kinship ties were everywhere all-powerful, even though primogeniture was on the rise. The influence of religion was slight but that of political structures considerable. Demonstrations of fellowship were firm, and so was the social hierarchy. In a word, this was a social and family atmosphere that was very solid, almost rigid, where the law served as guide. All in all, and the comparison might cause surprise, the Andean societies offered rather similar traits, although with more sexual freedom, but also greater control by priests. They were solid societies that were destroyed only by force. What we know of Oceanian customs shows rather comparable family structures again, but here the lack of political structures obviously gives a rather different colouring to the whole.

The second model would be the Indian one, which quickly appears to our eyes as the most flexible, liberal and indeed 'congenial'. Here was no rigidity, either in its matrimonial system, which could juxtapose both monogamy and polygamy, or in the status of woman, wife or offspring. On the one hand, the clergy held no daily sway, and politics was non-existent or nearly so. But on the other, serving as a fundamental guarantee against social breakdown, a strict hierarchy of caste enclosed the whole in a rigid corset. Where East Asia was stable, India offered relative immobility. This is what makes it possible to include neighbouring Islam, which was heir in turn to very various legacies, under the same general type, beyond apparent divergences such as greater strictness regarding women (but only when they went out in 'public'), and greater influence of the religious idea. Still, just as in India, there were few demonstrations of fellowship, and no interference from above. This was a flexible society, taken up with its local customs and remaining nearly immobile. We might be tempted to look for many similar traits in African societies, although these also offered areas of difference, such as a sexuality more tightly reined, more powerful demonstrations of fellowship, and the presence of a priesthood.

This leaves us with the Christian model, where most of the various traits we have just observed are to be found, but pushed as it were to their extremes: an imperious monogamy, a sexuality kept under close surveillance, the difficult position of women, the influence of kinship, powerful fellowships, strict priestly control, interference on the part of the political power, and a firm social hierarchy. To be sure, Byzantium was not Rome; in the East, the state was even more exacting, but women were treated there with more consideration, and kinship ties were less tyrannical, but the society found there was solid, brutal and dynamic. By a strange resemblance, Maya and Aztec Mexico was not without similarities with this pattern, and the sixteenth-century conflict thereby took on all the more the appearance of a fight to the death.

It can well be imagined that no single explanation could entirely account for all three models. Beliefs, different ethnic groups, natural conditions and economic possibilities were all too thoroughly intermingled in them. Their roots must surely be sought very far back in time, and this is a task best left to the anthropologist, not to the historian. At the very least we might say that at the close of the fifteenth century, of the three models outlined here, the East Asian was solid and uniform, preoccupied with its own stability, and closed in upon itself. The second, the Indian, was marked by flexibility and also weakness, which exposed it to faltering under outside blows. The third, the European, is the one which in fact appears as the most vigorous, the most capable of expansion, although certainly not either the most 'humane' or the most balanced, but in the conquest of the world by the Europeans, then just about to begin, perhaps this same structure, in its very dynamism, also perhaps played a contributing role.

EDITOR'S NOTES

The vast scope and extreme complexity of the subject has meant that, given the unavoidable editorial pressure limiting the number of pages of the contributions, the author has had to make difficult choices regarding subject matter and regions, and also to make cuts, which was a far from easy matter, in an original that was fuller and more detailed.

In addition, as the contributors' typescripts were communicated to various specialists, some of them sent us reader's notes, the most detailed of which were from Professor Irfan Habib, a specialist on India and Islam. We are unable to reproduce them in full so we have summarized the substance of his comments below.

1 Professor Habib questions whether the Indian *Vedas*, compiled as they were between 1500 and 800 BC, could have had an influence on Christianity with regard to the 'threefold function' (religious, military and productive), given the disparity between the dates. [Could this not, in a more general fashion, be the persistence of an Indo-European tradition?].

2 The Indian doctrine of *karma* differs from the notion of 'original sin' inasmuch as it holds that a person's position in his present life is determined by his behaviour in his previous life, which could have been virtuous or sinful. His destiny and caste are dependent on this for himself but not his offspring. This individual factor of Hinduism is, however, at variance with the collective caste system. (People are born into a caste but can change caste, after death, in a future life, in accordance with their virtues or failings.)

3 Funeral rites: in India, cremation was compulsory above all for the three upper castes (*varnas*). Burial was permitted for the other castes (and for children). It is only in recent times that cremation became usual in the lower castes, and even amongst the outcastes. The idea that cremation pollutes the ground does not appear in the writings of orthodox Brahmanism. The Parsees, on the other hand, prohibit cremation on the grounds that the corpse pollutes the fire.

4 The status of women: in the canonical writings of orthodox Brahmanism, women are quite badly treated. They are charged with spite and lust and appear as a symbol of impurity. The same is not true of some Tantric sects, not part of mainstream Hinduism, which ascribe certain magical and religious powers to women. The Hindu tradition of *satī* (the voluntary sacrifice of the widow on her husband's funeral pyre) makes it impossible to gain general acceptance for the idea that Indian culture accords women a more favourable status than other cultures. However, the practice of *satī* has never been universal in India, and the remarriage of widows is by tradition customary in India's lower castes and amongst the outcastes, with, notably, a younger brother frequently marrying his elder sibling's widow.

5 With regard to Buddhism, it is to be noted that the teaching it provides, showing how to break free of the cycle of reincarnation and achieve the ultimate liberation of *nirvana,* varies from school to school. In the conservative ones, known as schools of the 'Lesser Vehicle' (Hīnayāna), it is very strict. It is relaxed only in those known as schools of the 'Greater Vehicle' (Mahāyāna), which emerged around the beginning of the Christian age with the acknowledgment of salvation through the mercy of the liberated souls, the *bodhisattvas,* and so secured a wide public following.

6 In Islam, the central body of the doctrine concerned with faith and behaviour is made up of the Qur'ān (the word of God through the voice of the Prophet Muḥammad, not the word of the Prophet) and the *ḥadīth* (a collection of accounts of the Prophet's precepts, and of his actions, which should serve as an example to follow). These together determine Islamic law (the *sharī'a*), a common reference for all Muslims in the strict sense of the word, Sunnis or Shī'ites. The difference between the first (who are in the majority) and the second has its origins in the divisions which arose after the Prophet's death on the question of his succession as supreme leader of the Muslims. With the assassination of his first successor, 'Alī, husband of Fāṭima, the Prophet's daughter and only child, the Shī'ites did not recognize the authority of the caliphs elected from outside the Prophet's lineage, as they held the view that the Prophet's successors had to be his descendants, who were personified only in the sons of 'Alī and Fāṭima. Initially, then, this was simply a conflict between advocates of succession by election (the Sunnis) and advocates of succession by inheritance (the Shī'ites).

7 With regard to Islamic Law on patrimonial inheritance, Professor Habib mentions the fact that sons inherit in equal shares regardless of age, and daughters inherit in equal shares which correspond to half of a son's share. He is not aware of any sources identifying cases of the eldest son purchasing other shares.

8 On the subject of regard for virginity and celibacy in Islam, Professor Habib mentions the fact that the Prophet was married (in fact, he had several wives).

9 Finally, Professor Habib queries the hypothesis in the author's conclusion (which the author does actually qualify to a great extent) about the particular role of the 'Christian model' in the expansion of Europe after 1500.

BIBLIOGRAPHY

ABD EL JALIL, J. M. 1950. *Aspects intérieurs de l'Islam.* Paris.

AHRWEILER, H. 1971. *Etudes sur les structures administratives et sociales de Byzance.* London.

AIYANGAR, S. K. 1941. *Ancient India.* Pune.

ALLEN, M. R. 1967. *Male Cults and Secret Initiation in Melanesia.* Melbourne.

ALTEKAR, A. S. 1973. *The Position of Women in Hindu Civilization.* Hindu University, Varanasi.

AMIRA, K. 1960. *Germanisches Recht,* Vol. I. Berlin.

ANGOLD, M. J. 1984. *The Byzantine Aristocracy from the IXth to the XIIIth Centuries.* Oxford.

ARUGA, K. 1943. [*The Family System and the System of Tenure in Japan*]. Tokyo.

——. 1953. [*The Family in Ancient Japan*]. Tokyo.

ATIYA, A. S. 1968. *A History of Eastern Christianity.* London.

AUGÉ, M. 1975. *Les domaines de la parenté. Filiation, alliance, résidence.* Paris.

BEATTIE, H. J. 1973. *Land and Lineage in China.* London.

BECK, B. E. F. 1972. *Peasant Society in Konku: A Study of Rights and Left Subcastes in South India.* Vancouver.

BENVENISTE, E. 1969. *Le vocabulaire des institutions indo-européennes,* Vol. I. Paris.

BERNAND, C.; GRUZINSKI, S. 1988. *De l'idolâtrie: une archéologie des sciences religieuses.* Paris.

BERQUE, A. 1982. *Vivre l'espace au Japon.* Paris.

BIARDEAU, M. 1981. *L'Hindouisme, anthropologie d'une civilisation.* Paris.

BLUNT, E. A. H. 1931. *The Caste System of Northern India.* London.

BOULEGUE, J. 1987. *Le grand Jolof, XIIIe–XVIe s.* Paris.

BUGGE, J. 1975. *Virginitas: An Essay in the History of a Medieval Ideal.* The Hague.

BUSHNELL, G. H. 1977. *Peru.* London.

CALVERLEY, E. F. 1958. *Islam: An Introduction.* Cairo.

Cambridge Economic History of India. 1983. Cambridge.

Cambridge History of Africa, Vol. III. 1977. Cambridge.

Cambridge History of Islam. 1970. Cambridge.

Cambridge Medieval History, Vol. IV: Byzantium and its Neighbours. 1968. Cambridge.

CAMERON, A. 1981. *Continuity and Change in VIth Century Byzantium.* London.

CHAPELOT, J.; FOSSIER, R. 1980. *Le village et la maison au Moyen Âge.* Paris.

CHARANIS, P. 1973. *Social, Economic and Political Life in the Byzantine Empire.* London.

CHAUNU, P. 1969. *Conquête et exploitation des nouveaux mondes.* Paris.

CHICHEROV, A. I. 1971. *India, Economic Development in the XVIth–XVIIIth Centuries.* Moscow.

CHOWNING, A. 1977. *An Introduction to the Peoples and Cultures of Melanesia.* Menlo Park. California.

CH'U, T. T. 1959. *Law and Society in Traditional China.* Paris.

CISSOKO, S. M. 1975. *Tombouctou et l'empire songhaï.* Dakar.

COE, M. D. 1965. *The Jaguar's Children: Preclassic Central Mexico.* New York.

——. 1966. *The Maya.* London.

COQUERY, G. 1965. *La découverte de l'Afrique.* Paris.

CORNEVIN, E. 1965. *Histoire de l'Afrique.* Paris.

COULSON, N. J. 1978. *A History of Islamic Law.* London.

DAUVILLIER, J. 1933. *Le mariage dans le droit classique de l'Eglise.* Paris.

DAUVILLIER, J.; DECLERCQ, C. 1936. *Le mariage en droit canonique oriental.* Paris.

DIOP, C. A. 1960. *L'Afrique noire précoloniale.* Paris.

DJAIT, H. 1974. *La personnalité et le devenir arabo-islamique.* Paris.

DUBY, G. 1981. *Le chevalier, la femme et le prêtre: le mariage dans la France féodale.* Paris.

DUBY, G.; LE GOFF, J. 1977. *Famille et parenté dans l'Occident médiéval.* Rome (Actes du colloque de Paris, 6–8 Juin 1974).

DUCELLIER, A. 1986. *Byzance et le monde orthodoxe.* Paris.

——. 1994. *Le drame de Byzance; idéal et échec d'une société chrétienne.* Paris.

DUFF, R. 1956. *The Moa-Hunter Period of Maori Culture.* Wellington.

DUMONT, L. 1975. *Dravidiens et Kariera. L'alliance de mariage dans l'Inde du sud et en Australie.* Paris.

——. 1979. *Homo hierarchicus. Le système des castes et ses implications.* Paris.

DUSSOURD, H. 1979. *Au même pot et au même feu. Etudes sur les communautés familiales agricoles du centre de la France.* Moulins.

DUTT, N. K. 1931. *Origin and Growth of Castes in India.* London.

DVORNIK, F. 1970. *Les Slaves. Histoire et civilisation.* Paris.

EBERHARD, W. 1962. *Social Mobility in Traditional China.* Leiden.

EBREY, P. B. 1984. *Family and Property in Sung China.* Princeton.

EMORI, I. 1976. [*The Structure of Japanese Village Society*]. Tokyo.

ESCARRA, J. 1955. *La Chine,* Paris.

EVANS, C.; MEGGERS, B. J. 1966. *Mesoamerica and Ecuador (Handbook of Middle American Indians, IV).* Austin.

FARES, E. B. 1932. *L'honneur chez les Arabes avant l'Islam.* Paris.

Femme au moyen âge (La). 1990 (Colloque international de Maubeuge 6–9 Octobre 1988; éd. par ROUCHE, M.; HENCLIN, J.).

Femme dans les civilisations des Xe–XIIe s. (La). 1977. Poitiers (Actes du colloque tenu de Poitiers, 23–25 Septembre 1976).

FENG, H. Y. 1967. *The Chinese Kinship System.* Cambridge.

FITZGERALD, C. P. 1954. *China: A Short Cultural History.* London.

FLANDRIN, J. L. 1970. *L'Eglise et le contrôle des naissances.* Paris.

——. 1977. *Les amours paysannes.* Paris.

——. 1983. *Un temps pour embrasser. Aux origines de la morale sexuelle occidentale.* Paris.

FOX, R. 1967. *Kinship and Marriage. An Anthropological Perspective.* London.

——. 1972. *Anthropologie de la parenté. Une analyse de la consanguinité et de l'alliance.* Paris.

FREDERIC, L. 1968. *La vie quotidienne au Japon à l'époque des samouraïs.* Paris.

FREEMAN, J. M. 1979. *Untouchable, an Indian Life History.* London.

FUKUO, T. 1972. [*General History of the Japanese Family System*]. Tokyo.

FUKUTAKE, T. 1967. *Japanese Rural Society.* Oxford.

GARDET, L. 1961. *La cité musulmane: vie sociale et politique.* Paris.

——. 1977. *Les hommes de l'Islam.* Paris.

GAUDEMET, J. 1963. *Les communautés familiales.* Paris.

——. 1980. *Société et mariage.* Strasbourg.

GERNET, J. 1959. *La vie quotidienne en Chine à la veille de l'invasion mongole.* Paris.

GODELIER, M. 1982. *La production des grands hommes. Pouvoir et domination masculine chez les Baruya de Nouvelle Guinée.* Paris.

GOODY, J. 1971. *Kinship.* London.

——. 1982. *Parenthood and Social Reproduction. Fostering and Occupational Roles in West Africa.* London.

——. 1985. *L'évolution de la famille et du mariage en Europe.* Paris.

GRANET, M. 1932. *Catégories matrimoniales et relations de proximité dans la Chine ancienne.* Paris.

GRIMAL, P. 1967. *Histoire mondiale de la femme,* Vol. II. Paris.

GROUSSET, R. 1957. *Histoire de la Chine.* Paris.

GRUNEBAUM, G. E. von 1947. *Medieval Islam: A Study in Cultural Orientation.* Chicago.

GRUZINSKI, S. 1985. *Les hommes-Dieu du Mexique.* Paris.

HEERS, J. 1974. *Le clan familial au Moyen Âge.* Paris.

HENIGE, D. P. 1974. *Chronology of Oral Tradition.* Oxford.

HERITIER, F. 1981. *L'exercice de la parenté.* Paris.

Histoire de la famille (éd. Levi-Strauss, Duby), Vol. I, 1986. Paris.

HOGBIN, I. 1973. *Anthropology in Papua New Guinea.* Melbourne.

HOHLFELDER, R. I. 1982. *City, Town and Countryside in the Early Byzantine Era.* New York.

HONJO, E. 1935. *The Social and Economic History of Japan.* Kyōto.

HOWARD, A.; HIGHLAND, G. H. 1967. *Polynesian Culture History.* Honolulu.

INOUE, K. 1965. *A History of Japan*. Tokyo.
JOHNSON, D. J. 1977. *The Medieval Chinese Oligarchy*. Boulder.
JOLLY, J. 1928. *Hindu Law and Custom*. Calcutta.
KAEGI, W. E. 1982. *Army, Society and Religion in Byzantium*. London.
KAPADIA, K. M. 1966. *Marriage and Family in India*. Bombay.
KAWASHIMA, T. 1948. [*The Family Structure of Japanese Society*]. Tokyo.
KAZDAN, A. P. 1960. [*Villages and Towns in Byzantium from the IXth to the Xth centuries*]. Moscow.
KI-ZERBO, J. 1962. *Les civilisations noires*. Paris.
KING, D. P. 1972. *Law and Society in the Visigothic Kingdom*. London.
KURIAN, G. 1974. *The Family in India. A Regional View*. Paris.
LAIOU-THOMADAKIS, A. E. 1977. *Peasant Society in the Late Byzantine Empire*. Princeton.
LE GOFF, J. 1964. *La civilisation de l'Occident médiéval*. Paris.
LEMERLE, P. 1979. *The Agrarian History of Byzantium*. Galway.
Le Moyen âge (éd. Fossier), Vols I et II. 1982. Paris.
LE ROY LADURIE, E. 1975. *Montaillou, village occitan de 1294 à 1324*. Paris.
LEVI-PROVENCAL, E. 1948. *Islam d'Occident*. Paris.
LEVI-STRAUSS, C. 1967. *Les structures élémentaires de la parenté*, Paris; The Hague.
LEYSER, K. 1979. *Rule and Conflict in Early Medieval Society. Ottonian Saxony*. London.
LINANT DE BELLEFONDS, Y. 1965. *Traité de droit musulman*. Paris.
LINGAT, R. 1967. *Les sources du droit dans le système traditionnel de l'Inde*. Paris.
LITAVRIN, G. G. 1977. Vizantičskoe obschestvo i gosudarstvo v 10–11 vv [*Byzantine Society and Government from the Xth to the XIth Centuries*]. Moscow.
LIU WANG, H. C. 1969. *The Traditional Chinese Clan Rules*. New York.
LORCIN, M. T. 1979. *Façons de vivre et de penser: les fabliaux français*. Lyon.
LY, M. 1977. *L'empire du Mali*. Paris.
MACDONALD, C. 1977. *Une société simple: parenté et résidence chez les Palawan (Philippines)*. Paris.
MACDONALD, D. B. 1965. *The Religious Attitude and Life in Islam*. Beirut.
MADAN, T. N. 1965. *Family and Ship. A Study of the Pandits of Rural Kashmir*. Bombay.
MAGLI, I. 1983. *Matriarcat et pouvoir des femmes*. Paris.
MAJUMDAR, R. C. 1952. *Ancient India*. Varanasi.
MALINOWSKI, B. 1987. *The Sexual Life of Savages in North-Western Melanesia*. Boston.
MANDELBAUM, D. G. 1972. *Society in India*. Bombay.
MAQUET, J. 1966. *Les civilisations noires*. Paris.
MASON, J. A. 1966. *The Ancient Civilizations of Peru*. London.
MAZAHERI, A. 1951. *La vie quotidienne des musulmans au Moyen Âge*. Paris.
MEAD, M. 1973. *Moeurs et sexualité en Océanie*. Paris.
MEGGERS, B. J. 1963. *Aboriginal Cultural Development in Latin America*. Washington.
METRAUX, A. 1962. *Les Incas*. Paris.
MEYER, J. J. 1971. *Sexual Life in Ancient India: A Study in the Comparative History of Indian Culture*. Delhi.
MURAKAMI, Y. 1979. [*The Society of the* ie *as a Civilization*]. Tokyo.
MURRAY, A. C. 1983. *Germanic Kinship Structure*. Toronto.
NAKANE, C. 1967. *Kinship and Economic Organization in Rural Japan*. London.
NOONAN, J. T. 1969. *Contraception et mariage*. Paris.
OLIVER, D. L. 1961. *The Pacific Islands*. New York.
OSTROGORSKY, G. 1956. *Quelques problèmes d'histoire de la paysannerie Byzantine*. Brussels.
PATLAGEAN, E. 1977 *Pauvreté économique et pauvreté sociale à Byzance, IVe–VIIe s.* Paris.
——. 1981. *Structure sociale, famille, Chrétienté à Byzance, IVe–XIe s.* London.
PEZU-MASABUAU, J. 1981. *La maison japonaise*. Paris.
POWER, E. 1979. *Les femmes au Moyen Âge*. Paris.
RADCLIFFE-BROWN, A. R. 1950. *African Systems of Kinship and Marriage*. London.
REISCHAUER, E. O. 1953. *Japan, Past and Present*. New York.
RENOU, L. 1950. *La civilisation de l'Inde ancienne*. Paris.
——. 1978. *L'Inde fondamentale*. Paris.
RODINSON, M. 1979. *Les Arabes*. Paris.
ROUCH, J. 1980. *La religion et la magie songhaï*. Paris.
SANSOM, G. B. *Japan: A Short Cultural History*. New York.
SCHACHT, J. 1952. *Esquisse de droit* musulman. Paris.
——. 1964. *An Introduction to Islamic Law*. London.
SONTHEIMER, G. D. 1977. *The Joint Hindu Family. Its Evolution as a Legal Institution*. New Delhi.
SOOTHILL, W. E. 1934. *Les trois religions de la Chine*. Paris.
SOUSTELLE, J. 1955. *La vie quotidienne des Aztèques à la veille de la conquête espagnole*. Paris.
SRINIVAS, M. N. 1978. *The Changing Position of Indian Women*. Delhi.
STONE, L. 1977. *The Family, Sex and Marriage in England, 1500–1800*. London.
TENG, S. Y. 1968. *Family Instructions for the Yen Clan*. Leiden.
TILLON, G. 1966. *Le Harem et les cousins*. Paris.
URVOY, Y. 1949. *Histoire de l'empire du Bornou*. Paris.
USHIOMI, T. 1982. *La communauté rurale au Japon*. Paris.
VAILLANT, G. 1951. *Les Aztèques du Mexique*. Paris.
VAN GENNEP, A. 1909. *Les rites de passage*. Paris; The Hague.
WALTHER, W. 1981. *Femmes en Islam*. Paris.
WEMPLE, S. F. 1981. *Women in Frankish Society: Marriage and the Cloister, 500 to 900*. Philadelphia.
YAWATA, I. 1968. *Prehistoric Culture in Oceania*. Honolulu.
ZIMMERMANN, F. 1972. *La parenté*. Paris.

3

THE STATE AND THE LAW

EDITOR'S NOTE

Louis Bazin

This chapter raises very complex issues, which vary from one region to another. Unfortunately, the very substantial contribution received from the eminent historian Professor Rafael Gibert y Sánchez far exceeded the number of pages allowed for this chapter. In addition, as it was impossible for any specialist to cover all the regions of the world simultaneously on such a broad topic, the author focused attention above all on European phenomena. Considering that other cultural areas existing at that time should also be covered in the chapter on the state and the law, the Editorial Board asked specialists from other regions if they would be willing to submit more concise contributions.

Unfortunately, in order to avoid too excessive an increase in the number of pages originally allocated for this chapter it was also necessary to abridge the contribution of Professor Gibert y Sánchez. The author very kindly consented to this but preferred not to effect the necessary cuts himself. This difficult and perilous task thus falls to the Editorial Board, which is aware that any deletion is likely to be controversial. We should therefore like to assure the reader that omissions from the abridged text are not the responsibility of the eminent scholar, to whom we present our sincere apologies.

3.1
EUROPE

3.1.1
THE PRINCIPLES

Rafael Gibert y Sánchez de la Vega

THE STATE

In AD 600, the Earth was already politically well-mapped out with names, and yet until to AD 1500 new names of states continued to appear. These names were usually derived from the names of peoples or individuals, although not necessarily founders or conquerors, but names sometimes emerged in an arbitrary or casual fashion. Throughout the Middle Ages, from their opening to their closing years, states disappeared due to natural causes, but the most common reason for their destruction was human activities. Then the state, or perhaps the city, might be rebuilt in a more suitable location, or on the original site. The name of the state persisted and sometimes, by way of a resurrection, recovered its corpus. Observation of medieval political reality, or rather state reality, is hindered by the fact that a single state could change its name or, conversely, keep the same name while its territory shrank or grew. The word 'territory' touches upon one of the fundamental elements of any state, since a town standing in complete isolation from its surrounding countryside is inconceivable.

Strictly speaking, the city was a political territory. It was a unique, non-expendable piece of land, chosen either at random or with the aid of omens, selected, measured out and so truly founded, or at least its construction begun. Every city was the work of one or two or more real or mythological founders, whose name it usually took, although circumstances sometimes conspired to give it another name or to keep the name by which the area was known before the city was founded. In AD 600, ancient cities still existed. As in many other periods, and end of every century, the early seventh century saw a so-called 'crisis of urban civilization', that is to say, a return to rural or forest life. The invasion of the city and the country by forest – ruralization in its various forms – was a universal periodic phenomenon. There is no steadfast rule governing the duration of cities. One distinguishing feature of the city in this age was its defensive walls, although the city could continue to grow outside the city walls (see Plates 36, 39, 40, 41).

There were holy cities and cities which were military in nature, commonly because they were originally military camps. Even when the city was born and prospered for other reasons – as a seat of government, or as an industrial or commercial centre – it always had to be defended. This was the role of the castle near the city. Agriculture and cattle farming, two closely related activities, were also closely linked to the city, one of the basic features of which was the market, a specific, specially protected sector which was safe, might even have its own government and was open to foreigners. A principal or eminent city which stood out above all the others served as the capital or chief city of the state with which it became identified. The city-states of the early Middle Ages gradually lost those traits which had characterized them in classical antiquity, notably on account of the barbarian invasions; political power here was exercised only where the reigning monarch resided: but at least down to the tenth century, such a ruler normally shifted his residence from one city to another. Thereafter, however, with more settled government and the development of economic activities – especially in the Mediterranean – as of the turn of the tenth and eleventh centuries, it became possible to distinguish those cities which were outright political capitals from actual trading cities, some of which became completely independent and whose affairs both political and economic were then administered by their own governments (as for example the Italian cities: Venice, Genoa, Florence) (see Plates 40, 41, 64). Similarly, we regard the territorial state as peculiar to the modern age. This is not so. With feudalism, power and law lay squarely in the hands of those who held fortified castles, wielded authority and extended their protection over more or less significant stretches of territory. In the eleventh and twelfth centuries, a new development saw the light, with progressive concentration of power in the hands of a leader imposed by military force or recognized as such through election, choice or necessity. When such a leader was endorsed by the religious authorities, then he became a sovereign, one to whom all subjects owed fealty: this trend resulted in the monarchies of the post-feudal age. The term 'capital city' was bestowed upon the town where such a ruler resided and where governmental, political, military, financial and economic means became concentrated. More often than not, the political capital was also the seat of the territory's highest religious authority; laws and directives issued from such centres were therefore largely marked by religious criteria, and the secular power might on occasion suffer official rebuke – even castigation – by the Church.

POPULATION

A population is not merely a collection of individuals, although for some purposes it is regarded as such by states, including medieval ones. Within the state, we always find the family. A metaphor taken from biology, like others drawn from botany, mechanics or – more aptly – zoology, regards the family as the basic cell of society. The family has always preserved its identity and some of its original vigour within the state. The state itself was regarded as a large family, and the king assumed the characteristics of a father to his people.

The tribe is a group of families which acknowledge a common origin and chief. A given tribe might occupy a territory and also found a city within which they preserved their identity and their own name when a number of tribes shared the same area. Tribes define a particular state structure and transcend government and military service. Genuine political organization brought about the dissolution of the tribal order but, when the link with the state grew weak, the tribal order re-emerged. Tribal order, solidarity and justice existed together.

POWER

The defining feature of a state is its power. By the seventh century, family and tribal chiefs had already emerged, but what was needed was a head of state. Family and tribal reminiscences emerged in state, political power. There is an ultimate, decisive differentiation which makes political power a concrete reality, something autonomous though not independent, frequently in conflict with, but nourished by, the related, affinitive realities of war and morality. Power is something indefinable but evident. Why and how does one rule? The connection with physical force and moral superiority is obvious. Sovereign power is invested in an individual, although it may, in exceptional circumstances and for a short time, be collective in nature. However, it is always personal, taking the form of one or more human beings vested with a higher power, which, in the Middle Ages, was sacred in nature.

> Homage and the oath of fealty instituted mutual duties of non-aggression and assistance between a vassal and his lord, duties which differed little from those expected between kinsmen linked by ties of blood. But the preponderant position held by the fief in feudal-vassal relations contributed to weaken ties of personal feeling, and feudal institutions were ultimately powerless to free aristocratic society from violence and anarchy, despite the efforts of the Church (as with the 'Peace of God'). From the twelfth century onwards, the progress of royal power first made itself felt within the framework of feudal institutions, which then were gradually deflected to impose the person of the ruler.
>
> (G. Duby)

As well as the religious aspect, monarchy carried family connotations. Monarchy entailed government of the state by the family, whether legitimate or not. In the medieval monarchy, power passed from father to son, although it eventually became possible to skip a generation or a degree of kinship when power passed to grandsons, nephews or a more distant relation, whose right was legitimized by virtue of his descent from a former king. Succession sometimes took place in the midst of disturbances and conflicting claims, and literally in wars. Crime, in the form of regicide, even took on a certain institutional nature. Saint Gregory of Tours called this *morbus goticus,* but it is universal. The death of the crown prince helped to channel succession towards another branch of the family. Before 600 AD, and since then too, women had been crowned and seated upon the throne, holding the sceptre and even wielding the sword with singular energy, but this was exceptional. On the other hand, access to the throne through marriage to an heiress was common when there was no male heir in the royal family. Despite the practice of carving up the kingdom among sons, or alternatively among the heads of different factions, in the same way as the rest of the inheritance was divided up, the principle of preserving the inheritance intact or restoring unity remained latent. Succession of the first-born kept the kingdom intact.

RULERS AND THE RULED

The Middle Ages provide cases of stability which coincide with the notion of the state. The people were not a structured society divided into classes which, simply put and depending on one's perspective, could be regarded as upper, middle or lower class. The middle class was the basis of civil normality. When no middle class existed society became polarized, divided into a noble or aristocratic class, which had power under the ruler, and a lower class, which was quashed in the political order. Upper-class status was hereditary and access to it was easy or difficult, depending on marriage, extraordinary merit or royal concession. There were degrees within the nobility. The upper class preferred to remain aloof and not share the benefits of their position, which was accompanied by privileges. Ownership or control of land was the basis and mainstay of the nobility. Possession of land by any class, including the lower classes, meant participation in power. One form of absolute power made ownership of the land the exclusive right of the king and his family. Ownership of the land was thus bound up with political dominion over the territory. Temporary concession of land, subject to payment of rent or a tax, constituted servile status.

A single word might sum up the reciprocal relationship between rulers and the ruled, and that is loyalty. However harsh and oppressive political domination might appear, it was justified by concern for the good of the subjects, who, in return, owed the king homage and service. This relationship was qualified and firmly consolidated by the universal religious practice of the oath of fealty, which, although not exclusive to the Middle Ages, characterizes this period in a conventional way. However, this direct relationship between the sovereign and his subjects was upset when client relationships, involving a bond of loyalty, were established between the subjects themselves. By virtue of such relationships, higher-ranking subjects afforded lower-ranking subjects protection, providing them with land, arms and other possessions. The lower-ranking subject was then obliged to provide his protector with advice, tribute and military service. When relationships of this nature became widespread, they altered the notion of the state and gave rise to a different form of state, the feudal state. Feudalism was a characteristic of the medieval state, but it disappeared completely as a result of the changes which occurred at the outset of the modern age.

THE COURT

As peoples moved around their territories in search of new places to settle, a group of followers accompanied the chief until he had settled in a city. The palace of the previous sovereign or a newly built palace became the visible sign of established power. For military or other reasons, the court became itinerant once again. There were a number of royal residences, some of which were resting places or hunting lodges, hunting being a typically royal pursuit. Even transient domination led to the expansion of the city with the construction of temples, tribunals, theatres and a concentration of facilities for the pursuit of intellectual and artistic life. The courtly seal was set upon these cities. In contrast to these open, expansive courts, other courts existed which were isolated and concerned exclusively with the tasks of government and administration. Hermetic, impenetrable and distant from the people, the latter type of court was where that the king's officials and collaborators were concentrated. The scribe and bearer of the royal seal which authenticated documents (the chancellor) embodied the effective power of government. Depending on the respective personalities of the king and his minister, the latter would remain nothing more than the mere executor of royal decisions or become the effective channel of government.

THE COUNCIL AND THE ASSEMBLY

Sooner or later the general assembly, a basic institution typical of all medieval states, was silenced or abolished by a figure of absolute power who reduced the people to a passive multitude. The existence of such an assembly in turn presupposed that representatives of the various leading social bodies now made up the visible framework of the State and so surrounded the person of the sovereign: such as religious dignitaries, barons, ministers, administrators and judges. Representatives of local communities might also be invited to participate, but for a long time to come, the common people, as such, were nowhere represented. When a people settled in a territory and a central power structure was set up, the role of the assemblies diminished.

THE ADMINISTRATION OF JUSTICE

Justice was twofold in the Middle Ages: the king's justice and justice of the people joined in assembly. The king's secret intervention in the activities of unjust judges and his arbitrary power to correct injustices constituted the penultimate resort available to the oppressed people. Appeal to the king was a right, sometimes interfered with by the alienation of justice, which was equivalent to the dissolution of the state. Appeals against a royal sentence could only be directed to God. Flagrant and repeated injustice led to rebellion, to the deposition and, ultimately, the death of the king. In exceptional cases, some kingdoms enjoyed a tier of justice which mediated between the king and his subjects. An emperor was a judge of kings. Where the king was not also the religious head, appeals could be made to the religious authorities. The Pope might excommunicate emperors and kings on the grounds of their alleged injustice and free subjects from their oath of fealty and obedience.

The purely legalistic aspects of religious law can be distinguished from the spiritual or intimate aspects and those which were arbitrary or social in nature. Religion presupposed a world governed by a Divinity, that God had given certain laws from which the laws of man were derived and that, as the Supreme Judge, His was the final judgement to which humanity might appeal. Humanity's duties towards God could be given a legal framework. The sovereign power had a special relationship with God which ranged from total identification of the sovereign with God, as was the case in a theocratic state, to claiming divine descent and special protection. That all power emanated from God was a universal conviction. The consecration of kings was a religious rite, as was oath taking, which involved God in human relations, certain penal clauses in contracts, and even relationships of trust or credit. To a greater or lesser degree, religion permeated the life of the state and the law. The Church existed alongside the political state, and there might be a double hierarchy of state officials and priests. A code of punishments for specifically religious crimes existed alongside the ordinary legal code, which also contemplated transgressions of a religious nature. Monasteries were centres dedicated to spirituality, science, trade and social service. They also played a role in temporal government, particularly in rural areas. Marriage and parenthood had a religious connotation, and the religious tribunals were charged with solving conflicts in this area. The influence of religious law on secular law constituted a chapter in any legal code.

With the passage of time, more and better laws, absent or scarce at the outset, were promulgated (the terms of quantity and quality are not always compatible) as the need was felt to fix in a precise manner the rules governing social intercourse, which, until that time, had been unwittingly but tacitly observed.

At that point the figure of the jurist emerged. The jurist was a technician who abstracted rules and principles by interpreting pre-existing customs, solving doubtful cases, which, by definition, are all those which come before a judge. The law, which at the outset merely synthesized custom, later became an active element capable of developing or suppressing customs. Once the legal system had been consolidated in a legal code, custom, defined and sustained by the laws, was constrained within that code. Custom was accepted in accordance with or on the fringe of the law. Over time, custom recovered its creative power in a clandestine way, gradually undermining and finally supplanting the legal edifice.

At the height of the period of legislation at the beginning of the Middle Ages, when the *Corpus of Justinian* was being drawn up, custom was recognized in Justinian's Digest. Justinian's jurists (331–63) were of the opinion that when written laws were not applicable, the solution provided by custom should be applied. Not for nothing was ingrained custom observed as law. Since the binding nature of legislation was derived primarily from the will of the people, what was approved by the people but not written down was also binding. Peoples expressed their will by voting or by deeds. In a system as impregnated with authority as the system of canon law, which evolved slowly up till the twelfth century, custom achieved full recognition as a source of Church law and finally even surpassed written legislation, which often gave way before the might of contrary practice. Ultimately, customs or laws became judicial when they were applied or created by a judge: this is what should be investigated everywhere. This task of judges, upon which the vigour of laws and customs rests, is known as jurisprudence. The same term is also used to refer to the doctrine which provides the underlying substance. A distinction was made between territorial and local custom, as well as between the customs of the various social orders, trades and corporations. Custom, which was fixed by survey and codified, continued to evolve despite being written down.

WAR AND PEACE

The matter of the legitimacy of war was questioned in the religious field, where the aspiration to peace was common. There were ongoing, hereditary wars where occasional battles were followed by short interludes of peace, such as a grievance resolved by force of arms.

War in the Middle Ages followed certain formalities, such as the declaration of war, choosing a battleground and fixing a date for the battle. The outcome was accepted. On some famous occasions, the vanquished were slaughtered and the population evicted and sent into exile with the loss of all their possessions. Cities which resisted siege were also sacked and plundered. However, capitulation was also known to occur, in which case both sides received guarantees, particularly covering the life and property of those who had surrendered. The ancient practice of turning the conquered people into slaves was no longer normal practice, but temporary imprisonment with the possibility of a ransom, which was an act of piety, continued to exist.

An alliance is an agreement between two or more states for the pursuit of specific aims. The fundamental point about alliances is that the signatories must abstain from aggressive action among themselves. This term is usually linked to friendship, but friendship and alliance are two different concepts. Friendship gives rise to more effective co-operation. Alliances involve an element of defence against a common enemy and imply a threat, albeit a potential one, to a third party. Medieval belief was to regard as natural an alliance between those who professed the same religion. Alliances between princes of different faiths against another prince of their own faith was regarded as *Impium foedus*.

Treaties could be reinforced by instruments to guarantee their execution and observance. They were accompanied by a religious act, the oath, and divine intervention was invoked against anyone who broke the treaty. The ancient practice of guaranteeing observance of the treaty by taking hostages was still observed at this time.

DIPLOMACY AND INTER-STATE RELATIONS

Historians, influenced by the viewpoint of the sources, have traditionally paid greater attention to inter-governmental relations and, in particular, to relations between the sovereigns of respective states. The personal nature of these relations was apparent when on the death of a sovereign the friendships and alliances made during his reign had to be renewed. Although there was a degree of continuity in hereditary friendships and enmities, every kingdom, and particularly every dynasty, established a new type and style of inter-state relations. The most visible form of such relations was the dispatch of ambassadors to foreign courts.

Diplomacy was a specific activity which enjoyed autonomy within the wider field of politics. A distinction was made between the external policy of each state, inspired by the sovereign or a minister, and the execution of that policy by diplomatic agents. The representative role played by diplomats, as well as the results of their mediation, was reflected in documents. Not for nothing were marriages between reigning families a foremost expression of the harmony and good intentions of different peoples. One consequence of such marriages was the union of states under a single heir. A strong sense of nationhood could prevent this happening in a number of ways. Similarly, marriage conflicts also affected political relations. The practice of giving provinces, regions and cities as a dowry could also change the configuration of a territory and affect the composition of states. Apart from marriage, other instruments of external politics were adoption and the status of godparents. The development of medieval states was inextricably linked to the family history of individual dynasties.

PREMISES OF HUMAN RIGHTS

Two aspects of social law which run counter to natural law were practised in the Middle Ages – slavery and torture. With regard to slavery, we have already mentioned urban and rural freedoms, but in the same environments and at the same time the opposite occurred: settlers who were originally free were subjected to the rules and practices of slavery. To a certain extent, the juridical business of emancipation satisfied the natural right to freedom clearly expressed by many. Turning for a moment to penal law, there is ample evidence that the death penalty, mutilations and other infamous punishments were widely practised. However, it should be observed that over such a long span of time there were periods when the penalties imposed by the public power with its repressive apparatus were suspended, precisely due to the weakness of the organs of power, even their total extinction. At such times, the atavistic practice of private vengeance reappeared. There is evidence to suggest the existence of certain principles which may be regarded as the roots of human rights. In early medieval Spain, where the despotism of the former Roman administration had been combined with 'barbarian' customs, there was formulated the Visigothic so-called *habeas corpus* of the sixth and seventh centuries, by virtue of which no one could be condemned without a public accusation and the presentation of convincing proof at a public trial. That this was meant to ensure the right to a fair trial is made abundantly clear by the fact that this council disposition was left in abeyance (Toledo, 583 AD) because it made the pursuit of traitors to the king difficult. The inviolability of the home has been confirmed in urban environments. The Middle Ages also granted an accused person a period of grace in which to flee and contemplated the possibility of the accused coming to justice voluntarily instead of having to face the consequences of unlimited enmity. Finally, the right to sanctuary in churches and other holy places, even for those pursued for serious crimes, was extremely effective during the Middle Ages but declined in the modern age and is unknown in our own times.

BIBLIOGRAPHY

AMIRA, V. 1907. *Grundriss des germanischen Rechts*. Strasbourg.

BELOW, J. von 1900. *Territorium und Stadt* (2nd edn, 1927).

BRAS, G. LE 1955. *Histoire du Droit et des Institutions de l'Eglise en Occident. Prolégomènes*. Paris.

BRUNNER, H. 1894. *Forschungen zur Geschichte des deutschen und französischen Rechts*. Stuttgart.

BUSSI, E. 1954. *In torno al concetto di diritto commune*. Milan.

CALASSO, 1954. *Medioevo del diritto*. Milan.

CIANI, A; DIURNI, G. (eds) 1991. *Esercitio del potere e prassi della consultazione*. Atti dell'VIII colloquio internazionale romanístico-canonístico (1990).

ERMINI, G. 1952. *Corso di diritto comune*. I. *Genesi ed evoluzione storica. Elementi costitutivi e fonti*. Milan.

FICKER, J. 1891–94. *Untersuchungen zur Erbenfolge der ostgermanischen Rechte*. Innsbruck.

GANSHOF, F. L. 1953. *Le Moyen Âge*. In: RENOUVIN, P. (ed.) *Histoire des relations internationales*. Paris.

GENICOT, L. 1963. *Les lignes du faîte du Moyen Âge*. Tournai.

——. 1980. La loi. In: *Typologie des sources du Moyen Âge Occidental*, fasc. 30. Brepols, Turnhout.

GIBERT, R. 1982. *Elementos formativos del derecho en Europa: germánico, romano, canónico*. Madrid.

HERSCH, J. 1968. *Le droit d'être un homme*. UNESCO.

KANTOROWICK, E. H. 1957. *The King's Two Bodies: A Study in Medieval Politic Theology*. Princeton.

—— 1968. *Les libertés urbaines et rurales du XIe au XIVe siècles*. Collection Histoire, Brussels.

LION, M. 1968. Los derechos humanos en la historia y en la doctrina. In: *Veinte años de evolución de los derechos humanos*. México.

MITTEIS, H. 1940. *Das Staat des hohen Mittelalter*. Böhlaus, Weimar.

OSSORIO, A. 1928. *Derecho y Estado*. Reus, Madrid.

PARADISI, B. 1950. *Storia del diritto internazionale del medioevo*. Jovene, Naples.

PIRENNE, H. 1927. *Les villes du Moyen Âge*. Brussels.

RUIZ DE LA PEÑA, J. I. 1984. *Introducción al estudio de la Edad Media*. Madrid.

SAVIGNY, F. K. von 1834–1851. *Geschichte des römischen Rechts im Mittelalter*, I–VIII (ed. anastática Darmstad, 1951).

SCHRAMM, P. E. 1954–1956. *Herrschaftszeichen und Staatssymbolique. Beiträge zu ihrer Geschichte vom dritten bis zum achtzehnten Jahrhundert, I, II, III*. Stuttgart.

SERRA, A. *Los derechos humanos*. Madrid.

VANDERLINDEN, J. 1967. *Le concept de Code en Europe Occidentale du XIIIe au XXe siècle*. Brussels.

VINOGRADOFF, P. 1929. *Roman Law in Medieval Europe*. Oxford.

3.1.2
THE PRACTICE

Aleksander Gieysztor

At the dawn of the Middle Ages, new realms were established with monarchical institutions on the ruins of the former Western Roman Empire. A few centuries later, similar entities arose out of the tribal societies of Scandinavia, and Central and Eastern Europe. An agrarian way of life predominated everywhere, with land tenure organized into greater or lesser demesnes whose economies stood more or less closed in upon themselves. What luxury trade and crafts existed were to be found in a few pre-urban centres, and catered to the requirements of the tiny elite in power.

In the monarchies of the earlier Middle Ages, and to a certain extent down to the eleventh century and even to the twelfth, notions of power and property remained closely entangled, as indeed were such concepts as public and private law. Monarchy preserved its patrimonial character: a prince stood both at the head of his realm and in actual ownership; thus, when he died, his inheritance was divided amongst all his sons. To such a concept of power, the Carolingian Empire added, however, the notion of anointment (with holy oil): such sacralization of the royal person henceforth bestowed upon the ruler a charismatic character and a dominant position within the institutions of the Church (see Plate 169). Royal and ecclesiastical power henceforth worked closely together on behalf of the *Civitas Dei*, the City of God, and played an active role in moulding ideas on ethics, social relations and spiritual culture. The Church was richly endowed with lands by the secular power, and lords both religious and lay wielded increasing political influence over the reigning prince.

Secular lords enjoyed hereditary title to their demesnes and acquired the prerogative of upholding public order, especially over their own subjects. Such a prerogative formed the basis for the secular lords' various immunities from taxation and judicial interference, confirmed their hold over higher office, and secured them other privileges still.

Public authority at first had been quite powerful for some time, founded as it had been on a personal link between the prince and all his subjects. But then such authority disintegrated into various territorial kingdoms and principalities. Thus arose the feudal link, a contract of vassalage which shaped the relations between a king and his dukes or counts, and in turn between these dukes and counts and lesser lords – thereby bringing about a correlation between personal ties and land tenure. This system, although closely followed in France, was generally observed in only a few other countries, and even there to differing degrees.

However patrimonial the king's power might have been at the outset, through the ruler's sacralization by anointment such royal power finally tended to become hereditary and transmissible to the ruler's eldest son. Even so, royal power remained subject to Divine law in the eyes of a Christian society, and stood limited by the king's need to secure necessary approval from the magnates who sat in council with him. Where conflict might arise between such great lords and their king, legal formulation allowed for the right to resist an unjust prince. Pertaining to the state's organization were the raising of the armed forces (a prince's bodyguard at first, and then the levying of knights); taxation; and the administration of justice. But whether at the central court of the king or at the territorial level of the magnates, the forms of the various government functions remained quite rudimentary – and were moreover often delegated to the landed magnates.

At different periods but as part of a generalized trend (with a few exceptions as in England), the various monarchies bent under the pressure of centrifugal forces represented by the magnates. The West's economic surge made itself felt not only in terms of farming and improvements in the rural way of life but also in the rise of trade, crafts and services increasingly located in cities. The surge also contributed to heightening hierarchical differences of privilege between the various social orders or estates.

Central authority faded away, or became seriously weakened, in the face of the magnates who ruled over *seigneuries* or 'lordships' in France, major territorial principalities in Germany, and autonomous or even altogether independent dukedoms in Poland or Russia. In some of these lands, the monarchy's power survived on a reduced scale; elsewhere, the privileged orders, assembled in councils, took it on themselves to look after public affairs. The apparatus of the state fell apart, allowing the Church entirely to free itself from the sway of secular rulers and so to formulate its own theocratic programme in Rome – albeit at loggerheads with the various lay sovereigns.

Within these broadly synthetic outlines, particular traits stand out, however, with varying degrees of sharpness. At last centripetal trends towards reunification, favoured by the need for defence not only against external threats but also against feudalism's own abuses, began to make themselves felt at the outset of the thirteenth century: especially amongst the knights but also amongst the burghers in the cities. A budding nationalism played a further part in such trends towards unity. Royal reunification was carried out in different ways, but if a monarch handled matters with skill, he might even turn such notions as the fealty owed to him by his vassals, or patrimonial rules of inheritance, to his own advantage: at purely regional levels at first, then increasingly on a national scale. Throughout the thirteenth and fourteenth centuries, in France and also in Central Europe, truly national monarchies came to the fore. In the Holy Roman Empire of the German nation, where claims to universal sway had prevailed in theory even as late as the twelfth century, several great dukedoms emerged as *de facto* sovereign states, one of them being Austria; altogether, the German principalities henceforth formed a disparate and highly complex federation. In Italy, city-states took the form of republics, ruled by oligarchies which increasingly extended their territorial reach and even secured landholdings overseas.

The social basis on which the new monarchies depended was the privileged estates: the clergy, the nobility, the city burghers and, in some cases, the yeomanry or free farmers. The clerical and noble classes, and especially the elites amongst them, were still the most powerful elements, however, and frequently came into conflict with the rising bourgeoisie, whose economic importance in the West was growing ceaselessly.

Thus the power of kings revived, finding support among city burghers, among knights, and also among those great barons who were devoted to the crown. Monarchy henceforth sought its fundamental justification through such symbols as the sacred anointing of the royal person; through such ideas as the realm now to be conceived of as a transpersonal, public and sovereign institution; and through such notions expressed in phrases like the 'king's two bodies' and 'each king is an emperor in his own realm' (*rex imperator in regno suo*). Limits to royal power lay in the privileges granted to various groups, who received these on a basis of collective solidarity and saw to their proper political functioning. Hence the vertical structure, which had characterized the older form of monarchy, was now changed, to a certain degree, into a horizontal structure.

While the higher levels of royal administration developed to the point of showing burgeoning signs of bureaucracy, the assembled councils of the privileged estates clung to a now precarious balance with the monarchy. For the king henceforth had his own court of law, and a renovated territorial administration spread its own network, although considerable local administrative autonomy was yet conceded to provinces, cities, the Church and sometimes even to cultural and confessional minorities. Moreover, royal taxes still largely depended on agreement with the privileged estates before they might be increased: the task of collecting them, however, now fell to competent government departments and staffs.

The fourteenth and fifteenth centuries saw various monarchies – in such European countries as France, England and Spain – finally bring political feudalism to heel, gradually reduce the powers of the privileged orders and effect the territorial unity of the realm, where only a king might legislate, hold sovereign sway, raise permanent taxes, recruit standing armed forces, appoint judges and create public offices. While councils and assemblies still tempered the full force of the ruler's power, nevertheless the trend was now well started in a number of countries that pointed the way to the system of royal absolutism of early modern Europe.

Notions of civil and criminal law, and various judicial procedures, stemmed from an increasingly complex medieval European social culture acquired over the course of time.

The starting point in medieval European legal history coincides with the disappearance of Roman law in the West, although Roman law did continue to exist and to enjoy influence in the East. When Roman institutions collapsed in the West, their place was taken by customary law, which prevailed not only amongst the Germanic peoples who occupied the former territories of the Western Empire but also in the Scandinavian and Slavic lands. In the early Middle Ages, legal norms once shaped over the tribal period, and judicial practice later sanctioned by the authority of the state (although the State legally interfered very little), ensured the overruling predominance of customary law in social life. Customary law had first grown up among scattered human groups, the tribes and ethnic entities outside the Roman Empire. These groups had then carried their legal use and wont with them in their wanderings, so that at the outset, customary law had been perceived as pertaining to a specific group of persons and not to a given territory. As the West became divided into different realms amongst the invading groups, so too did legal usage become particularized, both at a personal and at a territorial level. The oldest texts to deal with customary legal usage thus referred to the 'laws of the barbarians' or *leges barbarorum* – Visigoths, Ostrogoths, Burgundians Lombards or Franks as the case might be – as distinguished from the 'Roman laws' or *leges romanae*, which applied to the Romanized peoples and to the Church.

Civil customary law dealt with personal status, lineage and the family. It addressed the forms of marriage, the family's structure, matters of property and possession direct or indirect, obligations, and rights of succession. In criminal customary law, retaliation for murder might, under the authority of the prince, take the form of imposing compensatory payment of specified amounts of *wergeld* or blood-money, to be paid by the murderer's kin to the kin of the victim: that is, by one family group to another. We know what specific infractions of the public peace or order had to be settled to the advantage of the ruler. The prevailing legal procedure lay in trial by ordeal, which might involve a judicial duel or having to prove one's innocence by undergoing the test of boiling water or a red-hot iron. Here divine authority – pagan at first, and later Christian – was supposed to determine the innocent party.

Important changes intervened in the thirteenth century, when the process of the state's disintegration was halted and finally reversed, and rulers could now make good their claim to legislate. Such royal legislation was buttressed by resort to theoretical argumentation, through the universities' renewal of the study of Roman law and the development of canon law since the twelfth century and well into the thirteenth. The first phase of legislative revival, observable throughout Europe, involved, in each region, the 'setting down to writing of its customs' (*consuetudines in scriptis redactae*). Practising jurists working on their own – although not without royal interference – acquitted themselves of the labour of collecting this material in the form of approved manuals. Then royal legislation took such various forms as the granting of special privileges and statutes in the fourteenth and fifteenth centuries: while autonomous assemblies and governing bodies – as in the cities – passed laws as well. The corporate character of society found expression in the diversity of the customary law binding on nobles and burghers. The clergy were ruled by canon law, and peasants by domanial rights.

In civil legislation, the ascendancy of a resuscitated Roman law, with the glosses of university commentators, became ever more marked: as in the case, for example, of the distinction drawn between *dominium directum* and *dominium utile*, which divided property between its legal owner and its acting usufructuary. Regarding legislation pertaining to persons and to the family, legal capacities were specified according to age and sex, social order and creed; all manner of corporations were accepted as legal personalities; and civil regulations for marriage were drafted according to canon law.

Criminal law addressed the problems of public peace, threatened as this was by private wars, and involved itself with an increasing number of offences which came under the judgment of the ruler – including the 'crime of lese majesty' or *crimen laesae majestatis*, that is, high treason. Stress was now laid on an individual's responsibility and intent, while *wergeld* was limited and profitably transmuted into a taxed fine. The death penalty became more widespread, however, and was often cruelly carried out.

Judicial procedure showed only the beginnings of a distinction between civil and criminal cases. Regardless of whether a civil or a criminal case was involved, it was a plea, brought against an individual, which initiated an oral, public and highly formalized trial. In such a trial, a judge sat in arbitration over the litigation between two contending parties and weighed the respective force of the arguments they submitted. In the high and later Middle Ages, legal procedure was enriched in several fields, with resort of appeal allowed in civil cases to higher jurisdiction in order to obtain reconsideration of a sentence. In Italy, from the thirteenth century, judicial procedures began to be recorded in writing in light of the norms of Roman and canon law, and this way of holding trials increasingly influenced civil procedure in a number of European countries at the dawn of the modern era.

Medieval Europe's institutional and legal legacy prolonged its existence, and continued to show its vitality, down to the very end of Europe's old order.

BIBLIOGRAPHY

CHÉNON, E. 1928. *Histoire générale du droit français public et privé*, Vol. I. Paris.

EBEL, F.; THIEMANN, G. 1989. *Rechtsgeschichte*, Vol. I. Berlin.

HATTENHAUER, H. *Europäische Rechtsgeschichte*. Heidelberg.

IMBERT, J. 1972. *Histoire du droit privé*. Paris.

KANTOROWICZ, E. 1957. *The King's Two Bodies: A Study in Medieval Political Theology*. Princeton.

KOSCHAKER, P. 1993. *Europa und das römische Recht*, 2nd edn. Munich.

LANGUI, A.; LEBIGRE, A. 1979. *Histoire du droit pénal*, Vols I and II. Paris.

LEMARIGRIEN, J. F. 1970. *La France médiévale, institutions et société*. Paris.

MITTEIS, H. 1968. *Deutsches Privatrecht*. Munich.

PLANITZ, H. 1997. *Deutsche Rechtsgeschichte*. Graz.

PLÖHL, W. 1960. *Geschichte der Kirchenrechts*, Vols I and II, 2nd edn. Vienna.

SCZANIECKI, M. 1997. *Powszechna historia panstwa i prawa* [General History of the State and of Law], 9th edn. Warsaw.

SOJKA-ZIELINSKA 1997. *Historia prawa* [History of Law], 6th edn. Warsaw.

3.2
THE ISLAMIC WORLD

Majid Khadduri

Law is a system of social control whose object is the regulation of human conduct in accordance with a certain set of rules. Every mature legal system records human experience and its concern to maintain peace and security in a given society. In that part of the world where Islam prevailed, Islamic law thus recorded its own experience in coming to terms with the issues of maintaining peace and security. But while the law of Islam did assimilate foreign elements into its structure, it nevertheless always preserved its basic character.

THE THEORY OF ISLAMIC LAW

In a society which viewed human beings as essentially weak and therefore incapable of rising above their personal failings, the idea that fallible humans might lay down a set of rules to the satisfaction of all human requirements could hardly be accepted. It was therefore necessary, in the eyes of such a society, that its legal system be perceived as established by some form of superior authority. Since such legislation was seen to proceed from a higher, divine source, embodying God's own will and justice, such legislation formed another category of law. Such legislation might be called holy or sacred law, transmitted through a prophet (Kamali, 1991; Khadduri, 1955). In Islamic legal theory, such law is considered divine and eternal. It preceded society, for it coexisted with God himself; and it is infallible and inviolable because it embodied the very will, power and justice of God.

God's commands as communicated to the Prophet Muḥammad, the 'seal of the Prophets' (Qur'ān 33:40; Calverly, 1936), constituted, in the eyes of the believers, the final and most perfect of all divine legislative revelations. These commands included rules of conduct as well as religious doctrine. Communicated as the very Word of God, compiled in the book known as the Qur'ān or 'Reading', the commands formed a body of legislation which provided the fundamental law of the state, as well as the laws governing the state's foreign relations.

While it is accepted as the source for all legislation, the Qur'ān did not present all its laws with equal clarity and detail. On all matters of law and belief, the Prophet was not held to have spoken out of mere impulse (Q. 53:3); for he had been given divine wisdom, empowering him to apply general principles to particular situations. The Prophet's decisions, transmitted as 'traditions' (*sunna* or *ḥadīth*), provided a fresh source of legal rules, held to be just as binding as the divine revelations (Shāfi'ī, 1961). Neither the Qur'ān nor the *sunna*, however, are considered to provide an actual legal digest. They were sources, from which the jurists (the *'ulamā'*) worked out an elaborate legal structure embodying in detail the entire range of the individual's expected behaviour.

The *sharī'a*, or Holy Law, considered the right path, guides believers through their lifetimes in this world and prepares them for salvation in the next. The *sharī'a* distinguishes between the beautiful (*husn*) to be followed, and the ugly (*qubh*) to be avoided, or, in other terms, between 'right' and 'wrong'. However, the *sharī'a* also grants human beings several choices between the strictly enjoined (*fard*) and the strictly forbidden (*harām*). Between these two extremes, believers enjoy the freedom of fulfilling certain actions deemed 'recommended' (*mandūb*), and of rejecting others deemed 'repellent' (*makrūh*). But neither is the latter utterly forbidden, nor the former absolutely mandatory. Moreover, between these two extremes stands the category of what is *jā'iz* (admissible), to which law is indifferent and where believers enjoy full freedom of action.

The *sharī'a* may be said to possess three fundamental characteristics. The first is its permanent validity regardless of time and place: thus, even where believers might reside in foreign territory, they remain bound by the *sharī'a*. The second is the way this law takes into primary consideration the community's ethical standards and general interests as a whole, while the believer's individual interests find protection only in so far as they conform to the common interests of the society. The third lies in the way the law is expected to be observed with sincerity and good faith.

As a result of their conquests, the Muslims became familiar with the laws and customs of the conquered territories, such as the Byzantine and Sasanian. Some of these laws and customs were adopted in so far as they did not contradict the *sharī'a*. In the same way, legal elements from the Mongol successor states of Chinggis Khān's empire might find a place in the local 'public law' of several Muslim countries. The Ottoman sultans acted likewise in the fifteenth century, with respect to local legal procedures in the Balkan provinces.

THE CONCEPT OF SOCIETY, STATE AND SOVEREIGNTY

Since Islamic law was accepted as eternal, society was necessarily conceived as established according to this law. But, since society is the product of the individual's sociability because by his very nature 'man is a social animal', no individual except God can live alone, because men were created to live together. Muslim thinkers took it for granted that men and women should live together to form societies (al-Fārābī, 1895; Ibn Khaldūn, 1958; Aristotle, 1946). Yet 'men are the enemies of each other', states a Qur'ānic revelation (Q. 20:121); and had it not been for 'God (causing) the restraint of one man (by means) of another, the earth would have been corrupted', as still another revelation puts it (Q. 2:252). Society, in other words, cannot survive except under authority. Thus, just as Islamic doctrine regards society as indispensable for the survival of human beings, so does it consider the existence of a state authority necessary for the survival of society. For while the individual is a social animal by nature, he is not a well-behaved one. Ibn Khaldūn (d. 1406), the philosopher-historian, summed up such a conception of authority thus:

> When mankind has achieved social organization . . . people need someone to exercise a restraining influence and keep them apart, for aggressiveness and injustice are in the animal nature of man. The weapons made for the defence of human beings against the aggressiveness of dumb animals do not suffice against the aggressiveness of man to man, because all of them possess those weapons. Thus, something else is needed for defence against the aggressiveness of human beings toward each other . . . . The person who exercises a restraining influence . . . must dominate them and have power and authority over them, so that no one of them will be able to attack another. This is the meaning of royal authority (*mulk*). It has thus become clear that royal authority is a natural quality of man which is absolutely necessary to mankind.
>
> (Ibn Khaldūn, 1958, pp. 91–92)

To whom, then, does ultimate authority belong? There are several verses in the Qur'ān in which the term *mulk* ('sovereignty' or 'statehood'), and its derivative *mālik* (the 'holder' of such *mulk*), indicate that ultimate authority belongs to God. 'Do you not know that the sovereignty of the Heavens and of the Earth belongs to God?', the Qur'ān thus asks (Q. 2:101). The expressions of God's will have thus been transmitted on Earth through the prophets. Moreover, again according to the Qur'ān, sovereignty can be conceived of as something delegated: 'God gives His sovereignty to whom He pleases' is but one such revelation (Q. 2:248 and 3:25).

When the Prophet Muḥammad passed away, no rule had provided for his immediate succession. But the leading companions of the Prophet met and elected Abū Bakr as his first 'successor' (*khalīfa*: 'caliph'). This election of Abū Bakr then set the precedent for establishing the holder of the office of Caliph as the head of state.

The first Caliph's election was held without any difficulties, because Abū Bakr had received from Muḥammad, before the latter's demise, the mission to lead in prayers; moreover, he was recognized as a competent, wise and influential individual. In turn, Abū Bakr's own choice of a successor in the person of 'Umar was readily ratified by the Companions and the *umma* or 'community' of the believers. Then 'Umar entrusted to a council (*shūrā*) of six members, selected by himself, the task of appointing his own successor, declared to be 'Uthmān. But finally, 'Alī was proclaimed fourth caliph in ambiguous circumstances, after the murder of 'Uthmān. Mu'āwiya, for his part, was not proclaimed caliph as a result of the arbitration at 'Adhruh but became caliph in effect after 'Alī's own assassination in AD 661. Until this time, the principle of a choice in the matter had been reinforced by the notion of *bay'a* or *mubāya'a,* that is, 'approval' on the part of those individuals competent to judge, the jurists or *'ulamā'*, the 'learned ones'.

But then, since Mu'āwiya's time, the institution of the caliphate took on a dynastic form, and the practice of hereditary transmission became a custom, perhaps through Byzantine influence but especially out of necessity: in order to counter possible 'Alid claims, to ensure the transfer of power within Mu'āwiya's family (the Umayyads), to legitimize such power by securing approval, and so to avoid or limit dissent regarding the caliphate. Hereditary transmission has never been recognized as a strictly legal means.

In Shī'ism, the Prophet's mission was prolonged through the Imāmate, whose incumbent enjoyed all the prerogatives of a prophet save revelation; in Shī'ite teaching, the legitimate *imām* is 'Alī, and his descendants are also considered legitimate.

Since ultimate authority and the power to make law remained, in principle, with God, the jurists concluded that earthly authority, or the exercise of sovereignty, remained subordinate to the law. Thus both ruler and people were equally bound by the law, and the ruler's powers were derived from, and defined by, the *sharī'a.*

The Caliph, therefore, though in practice the holder of divine sovereignty, was not considered – in contrast to certain concepts of modern authority – as standing above the law. Both he and the state were deemed as merely instruments, by virtue of which the law was enforced. If the state failed to enforce the law, then in such a case it obviously forfeited its *raison d'être*; while if the Caliph violated the law, according to some jurists then he had no right to remain Caliph; but even in such circumstances, believers remained in theory under full obligation to observe the law. In practice, however, the caliphs did issue orders which, consciously or not, did violate the law.

Owing to the supreme position which the law occupies in the Islamic polity, the state here assumes a character different from that which it holds in other societies, where the law is placed under the state. It has been maintained that such a state should be called a theocracy – a term coined by Josephus – on the assumption that God is the ultimate sovereign of such a state (Māwardī, 1853). However, it is not God but God's law which really governs, for God was never regarded as the direct ruler of his subjects. Only God's representative (Prophet or Caliph), deriving his authority from the divine law, was charged with executive powers. Such a state might thus be called a nomocracy but not a theocracy, for the law was the tangible source of authority.

SCHOOLS OF LAW

Islamic law is not all to be found in the Qur'ān, as the Scripture is often all too brief on matters of detail. Nevertheless, the Qur'ān was still regarded as the basic source of the law. The law's details were worked out by jurists, and these developed elaborate doctrines and schools of law.

The jurists or *ulamā* all agreed that the Qur'ān was the unquestionable basic legal source. But here agreement ended. Four schools of law gradually emerged as to how to develop the law. The first of these schools, the so-called Hanafī School, bore the name of the Iraqi jurist Abū Hanīfa (d. 767); distinguished by its liberal use of analogy (*qiyās*), including resort to opinion (*ra'y*), it grew up in an area where earlier civilizations had flourished and reflected the new conditions outside Arabia. The second school arose in the Hijāz, where Mālik ibn Anas (d. 795) emphasized resort to the traditions of the Prophet; it came to be known as the Hijāzī or Mālikī School. But the corpus of Mālik's legal compilation shows that this school was no less acquainted with resort to 'opinion' than the Iraqi School. (Schacht, 1951; 1964). The third or Shāfi'ī School of Law was created by Shāfi'ī (d. 820), who laid down a systematic method for making use of the legal sources provided by his predecessors. Shāfi'ī was careful, however, in his resort to the traditions of the Prophet, as he insisted that only those traditions that were proved genuine might be binding. Shāfi'ī moreover advocated resort to *ijmā',* (consensus), as a source of law, on the grounds that such consensus would represent the will of the community of Believers on the basis of the Prophet's own traditional saying: 'My people will never agree on an error.' In practice, however, it was taken for granted that only jurists might exercise *ijmā'* or 'consensus' on behalf of the community. As for the fourth school of law, the Hanbalī, founded by Ahmad ibn Hanbal (d. 855), stressed dependence upon the Prophet's *sunna* and objected to the use of analogy, considered as an inadequate source for decisions (Ahmad ibn Hanbal, 1949).

The Shī'ī sect developed its own school, or schools, of law, but there was no restriction – nor is there even now – against a believer shifting his allegiance from one school of law to another. While allegiance to the Hanafī and Shāfi'ī Schools predominated in Iraq, Syria and Egypt, only later, under the Ottomans, was the Hanafī School adopted as official. The Mālikī School progressively lost ground in Arabia itself but spread throughout North Africa and also prevailed in Spain before the latter came under Christian rule. The Shī'ī doctrine ultimately dominated southern Iraq and Iran, and also gained adherents in Central Asia and India.

Neither under the first four Caliphs nor under Umayyad rule did any individual hold the office of head of civil power by the side of the Caliph. High-ranking officials were mainly charged with managing the armed forces, financial matters and the administration of the provinces. Nor was any vizier entrusted with full powers under the early 'Abbāsids either; at a later period, however, and throughout all the Muslim lands, the vizier (known in Spain as the *hājib*) came to enjoy an essential role as a result of the weakening of the Caliph's power, and so ended by assuming full powers himself.

From the tenth and especially the eleventh century, another individual, the *Sulṭān*, acquired pre-eminent rank by the Caliph's side as head of both the military and political powers, and then, in various regions, attained the status of a sovereign henceforth fully independent of any recognition on the part of the Caliph. The *Sulṭān's* role was clearly defined in the *Siyāsat-Nāmeh* by Nizām al-Mulk, and so the office of the sultanate appears among the Seljuks in the second half of the eleventh century, among the Mamlūks of Egypt from 1258, and among the Ottomans by the end of the fourteenth century.

THE ISLAMIC LAW OF NATIONS

The Islamic state, with its universal appeal to humankind, necessarily raised the question as to how its relationship with other states and communities should be conducted. The special branch of Islamic law called the *Siyar,*[1] developed by Muslim jurists to deal with Islam's relationship with non-Muslims, may be called the Islamic law of nations. The basic assumption underlying this law is the principle that only the community of believers is the subject of Islamic law, while all other communities are the object of its system, although these communities are by no means denied certain advantages of the Islamic system. The ultimate objective of Islam was to establish peace and order within the territory brought under the pale of its law, and to expand the area of the validity of that law in order to include the entire world.

But the Islamic state, like other states with universal appeal, could not possibly establish peace and order in the world solely in accordance with its own law. Outside it, there remained other communities with which it had to deal permanently. The world was thus split into two divisions: the territory of Islam (*dār al-Islam*), consisting of the territory over which Islamic law ruled supreme, and the rest of the world, called *dār al-Harb*, or the territory of war, over which other public orders prevailed. The first included the community of believers and others known to have possessed scriptures, who preferred to hold fast to their own laws at the price of paying a poll tax (*jizya*) to Islamic authority. Relations between Islam and other communities were regulated in accordance with special agreements recognizing the canon law of each religious community on all matters relating to personal status.

The world surrounding the *dār al-Islam* is the *dār al-Harb*, the territory of war. The *dār al-Islam* was in theory neither at peace nor necessarily in permanent hostility with the *dār al-Harb*, but in a condition which might be described as a 'state of war', a modern legal terminology. But the *dār al-Harb*, though viewed as in a state of nature, was not treated as a no-man's land without regard to justice.

THE JIHĀD AS A CONCEPT OF JUST WAR

On the assumption that the ultimate objective of Islam was the world, the instrument with which it sought to achieve its objective was the *jihād*. Islam prohibited all kinds of warfare except in the form of *jihād*, but the *jihād,* though often described as a holy war, did not necessarily call for fighting, even though a state of war existed between the *dār al-Islam* and the *dār al-Harb*, as Islam's ultimate objectives might be achieved by peaceful as well as by resort to force. Strictly speaking, the word *jihād* does not mean 'war' in the material sense of the word. Literally, it means 'exertion', 'effort' and 'attempt', denoting that the believer is urged to use his utmost endeavours to fulfil a specific task. Its technical meaning is the exertion of the believer's strength to fulfil a duty prescribed by the law 'in the path of God' (Q. LXI: 10–11), the path of right and justice. Thus the *jihād* may be defined as a religious and legal duty which must be fulfilled by each believer either by the heart and tongue in combating evil and spreading the word of God, or by the hand and sword in the sense of participation in fighting. Only in the latter sense did Islam consider the *jihād* a collective duty which every believer was bound to fulfil, provided he was able to take the field. Such war, called in Western legal tradition 'just war' (*bellum justum*), is the only valid kind of war under the Islamic law of nations.

In early Islam, scholars like Abū Hanifa (d. 768), made no explicit declaration that the *jihād* was a war to be waged against non-Muslims solely on the grounds of disbelief. On the contrary, they stressed that tolerance should be shown to unbelievers and advised the caliph to wage war only when the inhabitants of the *dār al-Harb* came into conflict with Islam. It was Shāfi'ī (d. 820), in his formulation of Islam's relationship with non-Muslims, who advocated the doctrine that the *jihād* had for its intent the waging of war on unbelievers for their disbelief in Islam and not only when they entered into conflict with the Islamic state (Shāfi'ī, 1904–8). The object of the *jihād,* which was not necessarily an offensive war, was thereby transformed into a collective obligation enjoined on the Muslim community to fight unbelievers 'wherever you may find them' (Q. IX: 5), and the distinction between offensive and defensive war became no longer relevant.

But Shāfi'ī's doctrine of the *jihād* was not entirely accepted by all jurists, not even by some of his own followers. When Islamic power began to decline, the state obviously could not assume a preponderant attitude without impairing its internal unity. Thus the duty of the *jihād* was restricted to being binding only when strength of believers was theirs (Q. II: 233). Not only did Islamic states become preoccupied with problems of internal security but also their territorial integrity was exposed to dangers when foreign forces (Crusaders or Mongols) from the *dār al-Harb* challenged their power and threatened their very existence. Ibn Taymiya (d. 1328), a jurist who was gravely concerned with internal disorder, understood the futility of the classical doctrine of the *jihād* when foreign forces were menacing the gates of *dār al-Islam.* He made concessions to reality by reinterpreting the *jihād* to mean waging a defensive war against unbelievers whenever they threatened Islam (Taqi al-Dīn Ahmad bin Taymiya, 1949). No longer construed as a war against the *dār al-Harb* on the grounds of disbelief, the *jihād* became binding on believers only in the defence of Islam, to be declared by Muslim rulers whenever Islam was in danger.

CONDITIONS OF PEACE

Although a state of war was considered the normal condition between Islamic and non-Islamic states, Islamic law permitted the establishment of short-term peaceful relationships with non-Muslims on both the individual and communal levels. On the individual level, it took the form of *amān* (safe conduct). On the official level, it took the form of diplomacy and concluding short-term treaties.

The amān

It is a pledge of security by virtue of which any individual from the *dār al-Harb* was entitled to enter the *dār al-Islam* for a period not exceeding a year. Should a non-Muslim enter the *dār al-Islam* without an *amān*, he would be liable for punishment. The *musta'min* (the person granted an *amān*) had the privilege of bringing his family with him and could visit any place of interest to him, except the holy cities of Mecca and Medina. He could also reside permanently, if he became either a *dhimmi* and paid the poll tax or decided to become a Muslim. While in residence, he had the right to conduct his business and perform any other function provided he observed the laws and traditions of Islam. If he failed to do so and committed a crime, he would be liable for punishment. If he turned out to be a spy, he would be liable to be executed. The *amān* was normally terminated when its period expired. If someone wanted to return, he had to obtain another *amān*. The *amān* served the good purpose of permitting both Muslims and non-Muslims to cross frontiers and travel in each other's countries on the basis of reciprocity. The *amān* may be considered as a factor in promoting peaceful relationships between Muslims and non-Muslims.

Diplomacy

Its adoption by Islam was not necessarily for peaceful purposes, as it was often used as an auxiliary to war. When the *jihād* came to a standstill, it became increasingly important to conduct official relationships between Islamic states and other states. The exercise of the right of legation, however, was not intended to establish permanent representation but primarily to dispatch temporary missions to deliver messages, negotiate treaties and other matters. Foreign emissaries who enter the *dār al-Islam* were supplied with letters of credence and enjoyed diplomatic immunity from the moment they declared themselves to be on an official mission. If the mission, however, proved to be a failure, the emissaries were dismissed with obvious coolness ('Afifi, 1986).

Treaties

The conclusion of a treaty established the condition of peace between Muslims and non-Muslims. Because of the state of war then existing between Islamic states and other states, the duration of the treaty must necessarily be limited. On the strength of the precedent set by the Prophet Muḥammad in a treaty which he had concluded with the people of Mecca for a period of ten years, the rule was set that the duration of peace treaties should not exceed ten years. The treaty-making power after the Prophet Muḥammad's death rested in the hands of the Caliph. His power, however, was often delegated to the commanders in the field or to provincial governors. Once the treaty had been signed, the Muslim authorities were under obligation to observe its terms strictly. As stated in the Qur'ān, Muslims were required 'not to break oaths after making them' (Q. XVI: 19), and, if the non-Muslims did not break them, Muslims were advised to 'fulfil their agreement to the end of their terms' (Q. IX: 4; III: 75–76). Before termination by expiry, the treaty might be declared terminated by mutual consent ('Afifi, 1985; Khadduri, 1955; Fattal, 1958).

CONCLUSION

By the end of the fifteenth century, although a state of war between the *dār al-Islam* and the *dār al-Harb* was still in existence, Islam as a state could no longer continue to expand, but Islam as a religion never stopped spreading in Central and South Asia, as well as in Africa, by cultural and commercial means. Since the fall of the Abbasid dynasty in 1258, the *dār al-Islam* may be said to have formally been divided into three categories of political entities: first, the category of fully independent states; second, the category of entities that were nominally considered under Ottoman or Persian control but were fully independent in domestic affairs; third, the periphery of the *dār al-Islam.*

NOTE

1 The term *Siyar*, plural of *sira*, gained two meanings since the second century of the Islamic era, one used by chronicles in their account to mean life or bibliography, and the other, used by jurists, to mean the conduct of the state in its relationship with other nations (Nāsir Bin Abd-Allah al-Mutarrazi, 1950).

BIBLIOGRAPHY

'AFIFI, M. S. 1985. *Islam and International Treaties.* Cairo. Arabic text.
——. 1986, *Diplomacy in Islam.* Cairo. Arabic text.
AHMAD BIN HANBAL, A. B. 1949. *al-Musnad* (ed. Shakir). Cairo.
ARISTOTLE. *Politics* 1946. (Barker's translation.) Oxford. Book I, p. 6.
CALVERLY E. 1936. *Muhammad, Seal of the Prophets in Moslem World* (Vol. 25), pp. 79–82.
AL-FĀRĀBI. 1895. *Risala Fi Ahl al-Madina al-Fadila* (ed. Dietrici), p. 53.
FATTAL, A. 1958. *Le statut légal des non-musulmans en pays d'Islam.* Beirut.
IBN KHALDŪN. 1958. *al-Muqaddima,* tr. Rosenthal. London. Vol. I, pp. 89–92.
KAMALI, M. H. 1991. *Principles of Islamic Jurisprudence.*Cambridge. Chs. 2–3, 10.
KHADDURI, M. 1955. *War and Peace in the Law of Islam.* Baltimore. pp. 24–25.
MAINE, H. S. 1931. *Ancient Law* (World's Classics). pp. 101, 138–44.
MĀLIK. 1951. *al-Mutta'.* Cairo.
MĀWARDI. 1853. *Kitab al-Ahkan al-Sultāniya* [Book on the Principles of Government] (ed. Enger). Bonn. Ch. 1.
NĀSIR BIN ABD-ALLAH AL-MUTARRAZI. 1950. *al-Mughrib,* Vol. II. Hyderabad. p. 972.
SCHACHT, J. 1950. *Origins of Muhammadan Jurisprudence.* Oxford. pp. 311–314.
——. 1964. *An Introduction to Islamic Law.* Oxford.
SHĀFI'I. *al-Risala Fi Usul al-Fiqh* [Treaties on the Sources of Law], tr. Khadduri, 1961, *Islamic Jurisprudence.* Baltimore. Ch. 8, ch. XVIII.
——. 1904–1908. *Kitab al-Umm.* Vol. IV. Cairo. pp. 84–85.
TAQI AL-DĪN Ahmad bin Taymiya, 1949, Majmu'at *Rasā'il,* (ed. Hamid al-Fiqqi) Cairo. pp. 115–146.

3.3
NOMADIC STATES IN CENTRAL ASIA

Louis Bazin

Around the year AD 600 (and since early antiquity), pastoral nomadism with a tribal structure was the dominant socio-economic regime in the steppes of Central Asia. However, the tribes in the wooded mountainous zones, who roamed over a smaller area than those of the steppe zones, relied more on stock raising than on hunting and were also food gatherers. Hunting provided a valuable complement to the diet of the pastoralists and raids also enabled them to acquire different goods. The agriculture practised by both groups was embryonic.

In such societies, the most highly structured and hierarchical organization was the tribe. Titles corresponded to different steps in the hierarchy and these titles had to be used when people were identified by name. The most important titles, especially on the steppe, were those associated with the military hierarchy of the men that more often than not determined the tribe's power structure.

In Central Asia during the early Middle Ages, the term 'state' as we understand it can be applied quite correctly to areas in the control of sedentary groups, especially Indo-European (Iranians in Sogdiana and in the kingdom of Khotan and 'Tokharians' from the Tarim region), who had their metropolises (such as Samarkand, Bukhārā, Khotan, Kucha, Agni). The concept of a nomadic state with a flexible tribal structure and a capital which moves around with the highest chief's 'palace of tents' requires some clarification, however.

In fact, confederations of tribes were formed on the basis of the defeat in battle of one or more tribes by another, which then imposed both a state structure and a system of laws to perpetuate it. Similarly, it was the use of force that determined the internal structure of the tribe, over and above the hereditary principle. Throughout history, tribes formed, split and reconstituted themselves as a result of coalitions, tribal infighting, changes of allegiance and 'palace revolutions'. These upheavals within tribes and confederations did not mean permanent anarchy. Once one clan had triumphed, its chief or his immediate successor set about restoring the 'state' and the 'laws' using more or less the same principles.

These principles, as far as we can tell from the most reliable historical sources (native and foreign), were fairly homogeneous within the two main ethno-linguistic communities of Central Asia which founded nomadic States that can be called 'empires': the ancient Turks and the Mongols. They, along with their neighbours (mainly Chinese annalists), have left us the most interesting texts on this subject. Our analysis will therefore concentrate on these two key examples.

From the Chinese annals, we learn that in AD 552 the chief of the tribal group called Turk, which had previously lived south of the Altai Mountains, revolted against his suzerain, the Great Khān (*Kagan*) of the *Zhuan-zhuan* (proto-Mongols?), who ruled over what is now Mongolia. He defeated him, forced him to commit suicide and took over his land and title. This conqueror, who became Bumïn Kagan, died shortly after this triumph. His descendants were to control the Mongolian area from the borders of northern China to the basin of the Irtysh until the beginning of the 740s, apart from a half century (630–682) when they were controlled by China. His younger brother Istämi Kagan extended his dominion in the west of Central Asia to the borders of Sasanian Persia, but the Western Turk Khanate that he had created was broken up in 630 without leaving any first-hand accounts of its history. However, the inscriptions on funeral stele erected in Mongolia for the leaders of the Eastern Turk Khanate are very interesting historically and are the oldest datable monuments in the Turkic language. The longest of these inscriptions and the ones that give the most information on state ideology and its legislative application are on the one hand the autobiography of Tonyukuk (d. *c.* 726), military leader and adviser to the Emperor Bilgä Kagan, his son-in-law; and on the other hand the biography of Bilgä Kagan's younger brother Köl Tegin, a heroic warrior who died in 731, and Bilgä Kagan's epitaph written to the people in the first person singular (also used by Tonyukuk), which incorporates some of the material used in the biography and additional autobiographical information as well as proclaiming a doctrine of the state. The biography and the epitaph were both written by Bilgä Kagan himself (d. 734), and all these inscriptions are key sources of information on this period.

All three texts express the same concept of power, not totally dissimilar to that of Imperial China: the state is an institution of divine right, controlled by the Great Sky God, Tengri, of whom the Kagan meaning ('like the sky') is an emanation (*cf.* The Chinese emperors' 'Mandate of Heaven'). If the *Kagan* faithfully performs his celestial mission in the interests of the Turk people (*Türk bodun*) including the commoners (*kara bodun:* 'the dark people'), Tengri will always assist him in government and warfare. But if the *Kagan* makes mistakes, and especially if he disobeys the law (*törü*) of the Turk people (that is to say the customary law handed down by oral tradition, which governs all institutions, public and private, as well as relations between individuals), Tengri will abandon him and he will lose his power (sometimes even his life). In the same way, Tengri will punish or even destroy those who depose their rightful *Kagan*, for instance to submit to the Chinese and become Chinese. The content of this law is not explicit, because it is a law of nature, a sacred law; its provisions are familiar to all the leaders to the extent that they concern them, from the summit of the hierarchy down to the private lives of families and individuals. In action, Tengri is often linked to two important divinities: *Umay*, his divine consort and mother goddess of whom the empress, the *Katun* ('like Umay') is the representative, and *Yer Sub*, the 'Earth and Water' of the Turks, protectress of their living space. Tengri is himself sometimes called Turk Tengrisi ('sky of the Turks').

In the three inscriptions we have described, the term 'Turk' denotes, in the strictest sense, all Bumïn Kagan's Turk tribes and other Turkic-speaking tribes that form an integral part of their confederation and are subject to their *Kagan* and their law. Other tribal groups that were also Turkic-speaking, such as the Oghuz from northern Mongolia and the *Kïrkïz* (early Kirghiz) from the upper reaches of the Yenisei, although they had been subjected to the Turk *Kagan* by force, were not considered Turk because they kept their own internal organization unchanged. They were, however, incorporated into the State (*el*) of the Turks *(Türk eli)* as vassals of its sovereign, to whom they paid tribute.

This ideal state described by Bilgä Kagan, who hoped it would last for ever, never knew long periods of stability. It was undermined by its heterogeneity, by dissension among the tribal chiefs, the Beys (*Bäg*), within the Turk confederation and by rivalry among the princes of the blood (*tegin*). It fell in 744, and the nine *Oguz (Tokuz Oguz)* took power in Mongolia before they themselves were chased out in 840 by the *Kïrkïz*.

Five centuries after the reign of Bilgä Kagan, it would be the turn of the Mongols of Chinggis Khān to form a state and then a vast empire. The oldest text they have left to us, the *Secret History of the Mongols*, completed in 1240 and written by someone in the entourage of Chinggis Khān, outlines concepts of the sovereign, the state and law very reminiscent of the epitaphs of Köl Tegin and Bilgä Kagan. According to the *Secret History,* Täm Üjin, the future Chinggis Khān, was a tenth-generation descendant, by direct male lineage, of the youngest of the three sons that the beautiful widow Alan Qo'a bore to Tenggiri (= Turkish Tengri), who came nightly to visit her in the form of a luminous yellow man. He was thus descended from the Great Sky God, to whom he prayed fervently and who guided his decisions, enabling him, after a miserable childhood, to become Khān of his tribe and then, in 1206 at around the age of 40, to be elected Great Khān (*Kahan* = Turkic *Kagan*) of all the Mongolian and Turkic tribes of Mongolia. Between then and his death in 1227 he subdued all the nomads of the Central Asian steppes and forests and conquered settled areas from northern China to the Caspian Sea. He did all this 'with the strength of the Eternal Sky', a phrase that headed the letters and decrees of his immediate successors, Ögödäy, Güyük and Möngkä, from 1229 to 1259.

Before the enthronement of Chinggis Khān, ties between the Mongolian tribes had been loose and unstable, not of the kind associated with a state. But once he had become Great Khān, he embarked on a vigorous reorganization of Mongolian society, focusing on military structures at the expense of tribal structures and appointing leaders of 10, 100, 1,000 or 10,000 soldiers as he thought fit, without worrying about pre-existing hierarchies. He thus broke the desire for tribal autonomy. During his life, his state did not have a Mongolian name, but before he died he split his empire into different territories (*ulus*) for his sons, and the word '*Ulus*' was used in the end for the states thus formed.

Old Mongolian did not have a word for 'state', but there was one to denote 'custom' (*törä/törü* = Turkic, idem, and law), and another to denote 'law' (*jasah/jasaq*, derived from *jasa*, 'to put in order' = Turkic *yasa*, 'determine'). For the first time in the Turco-Mongolian world, Chinggis Khān ordered the drafting of a code of Mongolian law, as he saw it. The code, of which only extracts survive, incorporated many Mongolian customs, but Chinggis Khān made them tougher (for example, death was the punishment not only for murder but also for serious theft, possession of stolen goods, premeditated lying, adultery, rape, and so on). After he died, in 1227, these laws were less and less strictly enforced.

After the Mongolian Empire dissolved, following its break-up into *Ulus*, the increasing number of settlements and cities progressively lessened the importance of nomadism. Of course there were still nomadic tribes in Mongolia and the steppes of Central Asia, but they no longer formed true states, and their traditional customary laws were affected by conversion to Buddhism and even more (except in Mongolia) to Islam.

BIBLIOGRAPHY

GROUSSET, R. 1941 (and reprints). *L'Empire des steppes*. Paris.

HAENISCH, E. 1948. *Die Geheime Geschichte der Mongolen*. Leipzig. [German translation of the *Secret History* (with commentary).]

LEMERCIER-QUELQUEJAY, C. 1970. *La Paix Mongole*. Paris.

PELLIOT, P. 1949 (printed posthumously). *L'Histoire secrète des Mongols*. Paris. [Transcription of the Mongolian text and French translation of the first six chapters.]

TEKIN, T. 1995. *Les inscriptions de l'Orkhon*. Istanbul. [French version of the book by the same author, *Orhon Yazïtlaï,* 1988. Ankara. Old Turkic text and translation of the three epitaphs mentioned.]

VLADIMIRTSOV, B. Ya. 1934. *Obšcestvennyj stroj Mongolov*. Leningrad. [Interpretation of social structures in terms of feudalism.]

3·4
SOUTH AND SOUTH-EAST ASIA

Irfan Habib

Much of the difficulty of defining the nature of the state as part of a social structure in early medieval India arises out of the blurred perceptions in our sources of its different components, such as the monarchy, the aristocracy, the bureaucracy, and various segments of superior classes claiming some administrative or political authority. It is possible to suppose that a weak monarchy might yet form part of a powerful state if all the latter's various components are considered together. Thus the same 'state' might equally appear as both weak and strong, liberal and harsh, depending on what elements of it we are looking at. This may be illustrated by comparing the Chinese pilgrim Xuan Zhuang's (634–44) depiction of the government in India as 'generous', the 'taxation being light' (Watters, 1904–5, I: p. 176), with the historian Kalhaṇa's (*c.* 1148–9) envisioning (through words attributed to the ideal ruler, Lalitāditya) of a harsh state which should leave the villagers no 'more food supply than required for one year's consumption nor more oxen than wanted for [the tillage of] their fields' (A. Stein, 1900: p. 154).

It is possible that Xuan Zhuang had only the royal establishment and taxes in mind, while Kalhaṇa is thinking of the entire power apparatus in society. There is indeed no evidence that between the seventh and twelfth centuries there occurred any substantial increase in the potency of the king's authority; if anything, considerable evidence has been adduced for a weakening of royal power, through a 'feudalization' of the polity (R. S. Sharma, 1980: pp. 63–90). For south India, B. Stein (1980) has propounded for this period his much-debated thesis of a 'segmentary state', but whether the strength of the state in the larger sense really declined, in tandem with that of the monarchy, is another matter. B. D. Chattopadhyaya (1996, pp. 143–6), points out that the tendency of regional states to replace larger ones during this period did not necessarily arise out of mere fragmentation of earlier empires but rather from local sources of power; and, therefore, presumably these constituted centres of much greater authority than their larger predecessors.

We may suppose, then, that two simultaneous processes were occurring in at least much of northern India and the Deccan (northern parts of the peninsula). On the one hand, there was the growth of hereditary 'feudatories' (*sāmantas, ṭhakkuras;* later, *rāṇakas, rāutas, nāyakas*), and the emergence of 'clan monarchies', creating new units of territorial division, each defined by numbers of villages (12, 42, 84, and so on) (U. N. Ghoshal, 1929: pp. 241, 259–60). On the other, there was a deepening of the control of the superior classes over the population, particularly with the emergence of the class of *rājaputras,* or cavalry troopers, who became the mainstay of north Indian states (I. Habib, 1995: pp. 138–40). As a result, the fiscal pressure on peasants continually increased, with taxes and levies multiplying (Sharma, 1980: pp. 190–92).

The increasing scale of construction of irrigation tanks and canals, such as those by Chandela rulers in central India and Chōlas in the south (tenth–eleventh centuries), shows that these states were capable of harnessing sufficient resources to invest in works yielding fiscal return. Gunawardana (1981) distinguishes between two phases of irrigational activity in Sri Lanka: up to the seventh century, large works were undertaken by kings; subsequently, the works became smaller but more numerous and were built by private owners, with the kings as 'arbiters' standing between the owners and the peasant users of water. Whether these 'owners' were really private, or were in fact local potentates, and so part of the state, is an important question. If the latter was the case, the diffusion of control over hydraulic activity in Sri Lanka need not be seen as a weakening of the state, just as its presence need not also symbolize 'oriental despotism' (*cf.* Wittfogel, 1958).

One area in which the Indian rulers did not usually claim to exercise authority was that of law making. The law largely originated in custom, in the formation of which the ruling class doubtless played a part; and it, then, tended to be codified in the *dharmaśāstra* texts, usually compiled by priestly schools. In the *dharmaśāstra,* the separation of castes (*varna, jāti*) and the superiority of the higher castes played a fundamental role (see Kane, 1930, for the evolution of this body of law). The rulers could defy the law where it mattered to them, as Kalhaṇa so frequently notes in his history of Kashmir; but there is no king from this period who can truly be called a law giver. Rather, the rulers aspired to the titles of protector of the *dharma*, or the preventer of 'the admixture of castes', which occur so frequently in the inscriptions. Priestly influence thus assigned an important function to the state as enforcer of the Brahmanical law, the function being unaffected by the Buddhist or Jain sympathies of individual monarchs and dynasties.

Our evidence for many kingdoms in South-east Asia matches fairly well what we know of their Indian models. Over a large part of South-east Asia, especially Sumatra, Java, parts of Thailand, Cambodia and Annam, during this period, the official language was Sanskrit; the rulers and courts followed Indian political and administrative terminology and patronized religions derived from India, *viz.* Buddhism, Śaivism and Vaishnavism (Majumdar, 1927, 1933, 1937, 1938, 1944). These states, like their Indian counterparts, were essentially agrarian polities with the ability in time to harness sufficient resources to build massive monuments like those at Borobudur in Java (ninth century) and Angkor Wat in Cambodia (twelfth century), the latter dwarfing anything comparable built in India. (The nearest parallel here is offered by the large 'Dravidian' temple complexes of south India.) The South-east Asian states also undertook irrigation works (as at Angkor Tham, Cambodia, *c.* 1200), which deepens the impression of their affinity with peninsular Indian states.

The Ghōrian conquests in northern India around the close of the twelfth century resulted in the creation of a state (the 'Delhi Sultanate', 1206–1526) modelled after the sultanates of the Iranic and Central Asian worlds. There was now no living link with the Caliphate, even though Baghdād was destroyed only in 1258. Individual sultans like Iltutmish (1210–36) or Muḥammad Tughluq (1324–51) might accept diplomas from the caliphs, but these were mere ceremonial gestures to enhance legitimacy: the sultans claimed for themselves absolute sovereignty (*ūlī'l amarī*), untrammelled by any sacred or secular authority. This assertion was backed by a direct claim of the sultan to the total agricultural surplus, a claim enforced in a very large area of the sultanate under 'Alā'u'ddīn Khaljī (1296–1316). From this may well date the tax–rent equation in India, whose political and economic implications were to so greatly intrigue Marx.

This increasing tendency of the sultans to assert absolute power raised important questions, which it is the special merit of the historian Ẕiyā' Baranī (b. 1285) to have addressed. While Baranī wrote a special tract devoted to the problems of government (*Fatāwā-i Jahāndārī*) (*cf.* M. Habib and Afsar Khan, 1957–58), it is in his history of the Delhi Sultanate (1357), that his main ideas, often expressed through words ascribed to historical characters, emerge most clearly and in relation to actual contexts.

Baranī attributes to Balban (1266–86) the claim that the sultan partakes of special divine inspiration; however, the simple Jalālu'ddīn Khaljī (1290–96) is represented as finding, on his becoming sultan, that this was an empty pretence! The truth lay with those nobles present who thereupon muttered among themselves: 'Royalty is nothing but terror, power and the claim to unshared authority' (quoted in I. Habib, 1981: p. 104). No sacred halo or religious sanction thus needed to be cited to justify the sultan's authority. A sultan who freely exercised such authority, like 'Alā'u'ddīn Khaljī or Muḥammad Tughluq, in the early phase of his reign, helped to expand and consolidate the state, and to increase its resources, which would naturally enrich the entire ruling class. Yet the sultan's power always necessarily stood in opposition to the ambitions of individual members of the nobility, who claimed a share in both resources and power, whether as holders of *iqṭā's* (territorial assignments) or as *amīrs* (commanders). Baranī is aghast that powerful sultans could destroy whole segments of the nobility ('men of birth') and recruit officials from outside its ranks. In other words, the power of the monarch and the stability of the ruling class were ever enmeshed in an unresolvable contradiction. If the nobles' aspirations for stability were to prevail, as they did after Fīrūz Tughluq's accession in 1351, then the power to organize conquests or control rebels and suppress local sub-exploiters (*khūṭs*, *chaudhurīs*, and so on), could not but evaporate rapidly (*cf.* I. Habib, 1981: pp. 99–113).

Another important matter that troubled Baranī was the relationship between the sultan and the *sharī'a* (Islamic law). The jurists' codification of Muslim law had been completed long before the establishment of the Delhi Sultanate; and Indian conditions and customs had played no role in its formulation. While no sultan claimed to have the right to alter the *sharī'a*, the sultans' administrative measures contained regulations that would often disregard the *sharī'a*. On the whole, Baranī's attitude in this matter is pragmatic: he weighs the desirability of enforcing the *sharī'a* against the expediency of ignoring it (e.g., in not treating Hindus strictly as *kāfirs*, or in tolerating prostitution). He seems, in fact, to concede that the interests of government had to prevail over the duty of enforcing the law.

The Delhi Sultanate, and the regional states it spawned (besides notable partial imitations, such as the Vijayanagara Empire), had various broad features shared with the earlier Indian states. But the sultanates' major institutions were of a different lineage from their Indian predecessors, the degree and centralization of royal power under them was much greater, and, above all, the rent–tax equation was now far more explicitly acknowledged and enforced. These represented substantive alterations in the character of the state. The rapid acculturation of the sultanate ruling class to Indian conditions, and the quiet overlooking of Islamic law to obtain accommodation with Hindu potentates and subjects, did not really modify the structural characteristics of the sultanates. For their success derived not so much from religious enthusiasm as from their professional army (increasingly drawing upon Hindu elements as well); and, so long as their mounted bowmen prevailed over all opponents, advantageous accommodations with subordinate groups could do the sultanates no harm.

The story of the sultanates in South-East Asia begins as early as the thirteenth century. These arose out of Muslim communities formed by merchants from India (especially Gujarat), the Persian Gulf and the Red Sea. Given the mercantile nature of these communities, the South-East Asian sultanates, such as those of Samudra, Perlak and Aceh in Sumatra, Mataram in Java Island and Malacca (Melaka) in Malaya, had their seats in ports and thence spread into hinterlands. There was almost no Indian and perhaps few Islamic models for such maritime states: these began to conform to the land-based sultanates only when the hinterlands were subdued, a process which was well advanced by the time our period ended (*c.* 1500).

BIBLIOGRAPHY

CHATTOPADHYAYA, B. D. 1996. Change through Continuity: Notes towards an Understanding of the Transition to Early Medieval India. In *Society and Ideology in India: Essays in Honour of Professor R. S. Sharma*, ed. by D. N. JHA. New Delhi.

GHOSHAL, U. N. 1929. *Contributions to the History of the Hindu Revenue System*. Calcutta.

GUNAWARDANA, R. A. L. H. 1981. Total Power or Shared Power? A Study of the Hydraulic State and its Transformation in Sri Lanka from the Third to the Ninth Century A.D. *Indian Historical Review*, Vol. VII, pp. 70–98.

HABIB, I. 1981. Barani's Theory of the History of the Delhi Sultanate. In: *Indian Historical Review*, Vol. VII, pp. 99–115.

——. 1995. *Essays in Indian History: Towards a Marxist Perception*. New Delhi.

HABIB, M.; KHAN, A. S., 1957–58. *Fatāwā-i Jahāndārī* of Ẕiā-u'ddīn Baranī. *Medieval India Quarterly*, Aligarh, Vol. 1957–58, pp. 1–87, 151–252; reprinted as *The Political Theory of the Delhi Sultanate*, Allahabad, n.d.

KANE, P. V. 1930. *History of the Dharmaśāstra*, five vols. Pune.

MAJUMDAR, R. C. 1927. *Champa: History and Culture of an Indian Colonial Kingdom*. Dhaka (reprint, Delhi. 1985).

——. 1933. *Inscriptions of Kambuja*, Calcutta.
——. 1937, 1938. *Swarnadvipa*, two parts. Dhaka; Calcutta.
——. 1944. *Hindu Colonies in the Far East*, Calcutta.
SHARMA, R. S. 1980. *Indian Feudalism, c. A.D. 300–1200*, 2nd edn. Delhi.
STEIN, A. 1900. *Kalhaṇa's Rājataraṅgiṇī* (trans.), two vols. Westminster.
STEIN, B. 1980. *Peasant State and Society in Medieval South India.* Delhi.
WATTERS, T. 1904–5. *On Yuan Chwang's Travels in India (A.D. 629–45)*, ed. by T. W. RHYS DAVIDS. London.
WITTFOGEL, K. A. 1958. *Oriental Despotism, a Comparative Study in Total Power.* New Haven.

3·5
EAST ASIA

Guangda Zhang

CHINA

Sources of authority and underlying principle of law

Since the time when China emerged out of prehistory as a state in about 1766 BC, there has been a dominant belief among the Chinese that sovereigns possessed a mandate of Heaven (*tianmin*) to rule, and the inherited royal or imperial power in family succession could be perpetuated only with Heaven's approval. This idea led every founder of later dynasties to justify his claim to legitimacy by the mere assumption that he was entrusted by Heaven to take good care of the people as Heaven no longer approved of his predecessor. During the Han, a dynasty that lasted four centuries from 202 BC to AD 220, when a highly centralized national administration and legal system were finally established, the ruler further emphasized his claim to be the son of Heaven (*tianzu*) and showed a marked preference for traditional, mainly Confucian, ideals of government. As the emperor was himself above the law, his principal function, propounded in the Confucian ideology of Han times, was to exercise his mandated power in an orderly fashion, act as a moral exemplar, and display virtue and benevolence. During succeeding dynasties, at all times when the laws were systematically integrated into the code or revised, special stress was laid on the principle that the utility of law lay in securing not so much the effective rule of the empire as the maintenance of morals. A wise ruler should govern by example; only the ordinary ruler, one who had failed to educate, would lower moral standards and resort to government by punishment.

Within the context of the Chinese patriarchical kinship system, Chinese imperial statecraft and codified law were also influenced by Confucian ritualist values (see below).

Sui–Tang law

The Sui (581–618) and Tang (618–907) were major dynasties in Chinese history. One of their notable accomplishments lay in applying consistent effort, never seen before or since, to prescribing standards for institutions and administrative procedures by codifying the law and administrative statutes. A number of long-term institution-building trends of the preceding centuries were now incorporated into their political structure, and innovations were grafted onto traditional institutions to reshape the mechanism for governing the vast, reunified empire. From 581 to 737, the Sui and early Tang had all aspects of political and socio-economic institutions and administrative practice codified in terms of uniform norms and rules applicable to the whole empire. Continuous and large-scale efforts culminated in a universal and uniform system of codified law, which was divided into four categories: the criminal law (*lü*), the administrative statutes (*ling*), the regulations (*ge*) and the ordinances (*shi*). In general, this codified system was called *lü-lingge shi* in Chinese and *ritsuryōshi* in Japanese.

The *lü* or codified written law was essentially a code of penal law. It specified categories and degrees of penalty applicable to criminal offences and administrative infractions, varying the punishment according to the social hierarchical status of the offender, while taking into consideration aggravating and mitigating circumstances. An act committed by a slave against his or her master, or by an inferior member of the family against his or her superior, was thus much more harshly punished, but not *vice versa*. Here we can observe the ethical standards of Sui and Tang codified law: it took into account the unequal relationships between father and son, husband and wife, and elder and younger within the kinship system, and the inequality between a master and slave or slavelike sub-commoner, or a ruler and subject prevalent in society relationship, it spelled out appropriate punishment not only in terms of the given crime. The law reflected the fact that the high value set on 'rituals' and 'rites' in Confucianism, as constituting the most important component of law.

The codification of the penal laws began with the revision of existing laws by the founder of the Sui, Wendi, during the years 581–583, and was basically accomplished with the promulgation of one of the most important and influential of all Tang codified laws, called the *Yonghui Code,* in 651, followed by its detailed commentary, called the *Tanglü shuyi*, in 653. The Sui code abolished many severe punishments to demonstrate the emperor's leniency, and simplified its content to 500 articles, about a third of the size of what had been in force under the former dynasty, in order to reduce inconsistencies and redundancies and thus facilitate the conduct of procedure. It supplied a model for the Tang code. The *Tanglü shuyi*, now usually called *The Tang code* in Western literature, remained the most authoritative commentary on Chinese penal law down to the fourteenth century, and survives today in its 737th reissue. *The Penal Code of the Song* (*Song Xingtong*), promulgated in 963, and *The New Code of the Zhih-yuan Era* (*Zhiyuan Xinge*), promulgated under Mongol (Yuan) rule in 1291, were among many echoes of the Tang Code.

The *ling* or administrative Statutes were mainly concerned with the conduct of official business and the regulation of official behavior. They were regularly revised at various intervals (in the years 583, 624, 637, 651, 712 and 737). The *Zhenguanling* (637), for example, consisted of 1,590 articles divided among 30 chapter headings. The first chapter specified the various official posts appropriate to each level of the graded rank system. Aristocrats, dignitaries, and officials were conferred privileges according to or depending on their ranks, honorific titles (*san guan*), military merit titles *(xün)*, and actual official appointments. Chapters 2–5, 11–19, 21, 25 and 26 were concerned with the central and local government offices and institutions, the function of each government bureau and administrative procedures, duties of senior officials and subordinate personnel, the recruitment, discipline, and emolument or salary of the official classes. Chapter 8 ('Households') defined a rigid categorization of population which was classified first into *liang* ('good') and *chien* ('lowborn'), then the 'good' into *chi, nung, kung, shang,* or literati officials, peasants, artisans and merchants, and the 'lowborn' into five groups of servile status. The Household Statute also regulated the census registration, which was carried out regularly every three years. Chapter 9 ('Arable Fields') set forth precise rules for an equal-land allocation system (*chün tian zhi*), and a new economic pattern in land ownership and tenure, during almost three centuries (486–780). Under this system, state-owned agricultural land was subject to periodic reallotment to the individual male for his adult lifetime. The assignment of a certain amount of land imposed duties on adult subjects. Taxes in kind and in labour were collected in turn from each household, in terms of per capita taxation (as formulated in chapter 10, 'Taxation in Kinds and Labour').

As the chief purpose of the codified law and administrative statutes was to provide uniform norms and explicit directives for the conduct of official business at all levels, the system could function properly only as long as its social conditions remained stationary or undisturbed. As economic and social changes led to many deviations from what the integrated codes originally prescribed, specific rules and supplementary regulations had to be promulgated in edicts and decrees. These were later re-promulgated in official legal compendia called *ke* ('Regulations', amending or amplifying to the codified law and Statutes). The *zhenguan ke*, completed in 637, was limited to 700 articles in 18 chapters. They were selected from some 3,000 edicts issued since 618. The *ke* was also systematically revised, and especially compiled in the form of collections of *Edicts subsequent to the Regulations (Kehou chi*, in the years 651, 685, 705, 712, 719, 737, 785, 807, 818, 830, 839 and 851).

Finally, there were the supplementary ordinances, called *shih*, to provide detailed provisions or particular modifications for the implementation of the *lü, ling* and *ke* by different government departments. These were promulgated by the central organ of government under 33 chapter headings.

After the outbreak of the An Lushan rebellion in 755–763, however, many of the rules of statutes fell into disuse.

Private agreements between individuals

As early as the seventh and eighth centuries, private agreements between two parties ('ssu-yueh') evolved outside the formal legal system in order to expedite economic transactions. The stereotyped formula in these contracts ran: 'Officials have government law, and common people follow private contracts'. During the later Tang, the Five Dynasties (907–960), and the Song (960–1279), what with the breakdown of the lüling system and a marked economic growth, Chinese society became more and more market-oriented and diversified. People began to draw up contracts as the only reliable record of changes of ownership. Reliance on written contracts for the purchase and mortgaging of land or other property, for the purchase of commodities, slaves, or a cow or a horse, or for the hiring of wage labourers, for adopting a child, or for the announcing any matrimonial engagement, became a commonplace practice. Business partnerships in commerce and agriculture could be formalized and protected through this increasingly vigorous and effective use of contracts. Contractual practice was also widely followed in daily life under the Mongols (Yuan).

Family instructions and popularized sacred edicts

In imperial times, the primacy of the family was proclaimed in the law codes. A vital instrument for strengthening the family ethic and moral indoctrination from the sixth to the fifteenth centuries lays in the tradition of rendering Confucian values explicit in written colloquial versions. A famous early example is the *Family Instructions for the Yen Clan* (*Yanshi Jiaxun*) of Yen Zhitui, published in the sixth century. A more recent instance is the *Maxims for Family Management* (*Zhijia Geyan*) of Zhu Bailu of the early Qing. Another type was offered by the Sacred Edicts. Ming Taizi (1368–98), the founder of the Ming Dynasty, issued his commandments, six in number, in 1388 and 1399. He also ordered that these maxims be posted on school walls and inscribed on stone tablets: 'Be filial to your parents; be respectful to your elders; live in harmony with your neighbours; instruct your sons and grandsons; be content with your calling; and do not evil' (Rawski, 1985, p. 32). In addition, they were read aloud to villagers six times a month.

JAPAN

Chinese Buddhism was introduced to Japan from Korea in about the mid-sixth century. With Buddhism came its associated fine arts and various Chinese cultural influences, such as Chinese characters. Japan's initial impetus to adopt social and institutional system came from admiration for the prosperous and highly centralized empire of the Sui and Tang. The Japanese began deliberately to organize their state upon the model of the Tang from the seventh century on, although the native tradition, strongly aristocratic, proved powerful also. The period extending from 604, when the Japanese imperial court took the first concrete measures towards establishing bureaucratic institutions, to the year 967, when imperial power became subject to a Regency government, may be considered as the *ritsuryō* period in Japanese history, within which the Nara period (710–94) was the classic age of the flourishing of Chinese civilization in Japan. The government, imitating Chinese practice, instituted a regular programme of legal instruction in the government academy (*Daigakuryō*). The *Yōrō ritsuryō* took effect in 757, its principal model being the Chinese *Yong hui lü* of 651. But Japan had to depart somewhat from Chinese models because of its own particular conditions. The continental militia system, for example, was attempted, but soon abandoned, while the Chinese civil service examination system was never introduced.

SILLA

Silla was a well-organized kingdom in the Korean peninsula, closely modelled on the Tang pattern. The ruling class copied the Tang lüling system, used the Chinese written language, and practised both Confucianism and a sinicized form of Buddhism.

BIBLIOGRAPHY

BALZS, E. 1954. *Le Traité juridique du 'Souei chou'*. Leiden.

CHEN, YIN KO. 1944. Sui T'ang zhi-du yüan-yuan Lue Lun Gao (Brief remarks on the origins of the Sui and T'ang institutions, a preliminary discussion draft), 1st edn Chong ching, latest edn. In: *Chen Yin ko Wen-ji* (Collected Works of Chen Yin ko). Shanghai. 1980.

IKEDO, O. 1993. Tōryō, In: *Chūgoku Hōseishi*, ed. by Shiga Shūzō. Tokyo.

INOUE, M. *et al.* 1976. *Ritsuryō* Tokyo.

JOHNSON, W. 1979. *The Tang Code*, Vol. I, *General Principles*. Princeton.

NIIDA, N. 1933 *Tōryō shūi*. Tokyo. Reprint Tokyo. 1964.

——. 1936–63. *Chūgoku hōseishi kenkyū: hō to kanshu, hō to dōdoku*, four vols, Tokyo. Reprint, Tokyo. 1980.

RASWKI, E. 1985. Economic and social foundations of late imperial culture. In: *Popular Culture in Late Imperial China*. California.

ROTOURS, R. des. 1947–8. *Traité des fonctionnaires et traité de l'armée*. two vols. Leiden.

TWITCHETT, D. 1963. *Financial Administration under the T'ang Dynasty*. Cambridge (2nd rev. edn., 1970).

——. 1979. Sui and T'ang China, 589–906. In: *Cambridge History of China*. Vol. 3, Part I. Cambridge.

YAMAMOTO, T.; IKEDA, O.; OKANO, M. (eds) 1978, 1980. *Tun-huang and Turfan Documents Concerning Social and Economic History*. Vol. 1, *Legal Texts*. Tokyo.

YOSHIDA, K. 1979. Zui Tō Teikoku to Nippon no Risuryō Kokka. In: *Zui Tō Teikoku to Higashi Ajia Sekai*. Tokyo.

3.6
AFRICA

Isidore Ndaywel è Nziem

In sub-Saharan Africa, where many forms of the state were in existence,[1] every people was characterized by a set of institutions and social practices held in common: and admitted by all to be their binding social norms. Along with use of a shared language, such a primary judicial order – which invariably affected the organization of kin and marriage and entailed principles governing both rules of succession and codes for proper social and moral behaviour – offered the surest criterion by which any one group might identify itself. Taken together, such elements made up such a group's 'tradition'. Moreover, whatever each group's particular judicial arrangements might be, the legitimacy of all power remained predicated upon hereditary transmission. Such hereditary transmission, in turn, drew justification from the notion that authority, in its essence, was something extra-human, which might not, in principle, be usurped by those not entitled thereto by fate.

But even though such elements were supposed to provide a guarantee of the permanence of a society, they were not, in themselves, immutable: for they could, after all, prove permeable to evolution. Indeed, outright innovations were on occasion pushed through and made good by outstanding individuals. The most typical case here is provided by the great early nineteenth-century conqueror Chaka, who, contrary to tradition and in a boldly new manner, managed to forge an awesome army, and to carve out a powerful empire, for the Zulu (J. Ki-Zerbo, 1972: 355–56). Although in less spectacular fashion, prohibitions on, say, consuming certain foods, for example, are seen to have evolved over succeeding periods: and to have gone through various stages of adjustment depending on a given economic situation, on migrations, or shifts in the ecological environment. Thus, taboos observed by dwellers of the grasslands could differ from those binding upon inhabitants of the forest.

But even the principle of filiation, once thought to be the most stable element in ethnic tradition, could be susceptible to change. Thus Central Africa's matrilineal belt, stretching from Namibia to the Zambezi and from the Ogoou River to Lake Tanganyika, is probably a vestige of an older archaic matrilineal order which once may have characterized all the peoples dwelling south of the Sahara (Cheikh Anta Diop, 1960; J. Vansina, 1985: 607). In any case, it is recognized that the Luba of Katanga, like the peoples of the forest to the west of Lualaba, were familiar with such a matrilineal order before adopting their current mode of patrilineal filiation (L. de Heusch, 1972; G. P. Murdock, 1959: 287). Evolution in the opposite direction, from a patrilineal to a matrilineal order, while rare, has also been observed, notably among the peoples of the Central Basin (Mumbanza mwa Bawele, 1976) as a result of economic pressures. Indeed, the acknowledgement, to this day, of a system of dual filiation, as among the Lunda (J. Vansina, 1966b), allows us to observe just such a process still in operation: for tradition too, in the past as in days to come, remains subject to the laws of evolution.

The earliest judicial orders already included an array of laws determining the rights and obligations of each. Failure to respect what custom enjoined entailed moral sanctions like the infliction of dishonour, blame, cursing, and banishment to the fringes of the social group.

Over and beyond 'custom', there existed those laws promulgated by political aristocracies, and which thereby stood in close relation to the actual wielding of power. Allegiance to a given court, whether one lying far off or near at hand, would thus have to take the form of a proffered tribute.[2] The rendering of such tribute had to occur on a regular basis, as whenever a successful hunt made it possible to submit the fruits of one's chase. The withholding of one's mandatory tribute, however, in itself signalled political contention and the outbreak of rebellion. Here it was enough to omit the submission of one's tribute to incur royal wrath and risk bringing upon one's head a punitive expedition. But a subject who overcame his lord in battle thereby at once secured his own independence. A situation of just this kind is attested between the kingdoms of the Kongo[3] and Angola. The king of the Kongo thus received tribute from the king of Ndongo (in northern Angola), so entitling the Kongolese ruler to style himself 'Lord of the Ambundu peoples'. The fact that this particular title disappeared in the course of the sixteenth century furnishes proof that the king of Ndongo successfully contended with his political overlord and so finally won his own autonomy (W. Randles, 1968). A relation based upon subordination was thus transformed into one of reciprocity.

The envoys of a central political power, sent on regular missions to the provincial nobilities in order to collect tribute, were actually dispatched for the ultimate purpose of ensuring control over a wide-ranging political area taken as a whole. Political conquest boiled down to imposing acknowledgement of a common superstructure over and above pre-existing political networks. The groups concerned, which had hitherto been autonomous, now found themselves assembled within a new framework, in which they were henceforth expected to function as sub-groups. These now submitted to regular control by agents of the central power through the collection of tribute.

The extension of the state thus ensured the extension of the sway of law. The most typical example of such a process of political integration is offered by Rwanda, where the Hutu lordships were conquered one after the other by the Tutsi clan of the *Nyinginya*, thus bringing about, by the sixteenth century, the feudal kingdom of Rwanda, where farmers and herders dwelt together (B. A. Ogot, 1985).

As for the judiciary power, while dependent upon the political power, it still enjoyed its own distinct manner of functioning. In fact, while the pertinent political authorities oversaw trials, they never did so alone but were always accompanied by the leading local 'headmen': these were custodians of the law, were in charge of education, and, in a rather contradictory manner, were responsible for both the accusation and the defence. Such courts functioned at all levels, from the villages to the highest hierarchies in the realm, according to the gravity of the case being tried and the rank of the parties implicated in the trial. A dispute beween villages could only be settled by the dignitary responsible for the local chieftainship, and one between two opposing dignitaries had to be taken to the king.

The most usual offences, other than those pertaining to common law, concerned disputes over legacies, quarrels regarding inherited landholdings, and cases of 'assassination' through witchcraft. Where sorcery was alleged, trials by ordeal were usually resorted to, in order to determine the identity of whoever was regarded as having 'devoured' the deceased.

There also existed an international code of conduct regulating relations between states. Peaceful coexistence and favoured relations found expression in the forging of ties of political 'kinship', as it were, serving to bind together the various aristocracies in power. 'Family' ties of this sort might imply subordination or reciprocity. In the southern grasslands, that is, south of the equatorial forest zone, the different royal courts which, over time, had undergone the influence of the Lunda culture all claimed to be 'younger siblings' to the *Ant Yav*, the reigning dynasty of this particular people (J. Vansina, 1966b). But the king of the Kongo, in his dealings with the Portuguese monarchy following upon the 'discovery' of the mouth of the Congo River by Diogo Cão in 1483, often referred to his fellow ruler on the throne in Lisbon as his 'brother'. To give practical meaning to such brotherhood, the Kongolese royal family, on receiving baptism, chose to adopt exactly the same Christian names as those borne by the reigning Portuguese sovereigns.[4] The fall of the realm was due mainly to the fact that Dom Afonso (1506–1543), king of the Kongo, totally keen as he was to modernize his domain, took this notion of brotherhood with Portugal's ruler far too seriously, to the point of believing that his own personal intervention could help to end the slave trade – whereas the ultimate grandmaster of the whole trade was none other than the Portuguese monarch himself (L. Jadin and M. Dicorato, 1974: 155–6).

Disputes did not necessarily result in war, because political negotiations could be conducted between states through duly appointed emissaries. Such a role, amongst the Kuba and also amongst the Leele living in what is now the Democratic Republic of the Congo, could be allotted to ranking, and often polyandrous, female personalities (I. Ndaywel è Nziem, 1981: 769–89), who were sent as envoys to the enemy or were entrusted with welcoming the enemy's own delegates (M. Douglas, 1963: 129–130). When war did break out, then it was waged until one of the belligerents acknowledged his submission to the other, or, in the case of an internal revolt, until the central power either managed or failed to overcome a rebellious province, which thus secured its autonomy.

If viewed from the point of view of respect for human rights, the facts of ancient African history admittedly betray considerable weaknesses on this score, linked to what was then a failure to recognize any principle of equality between human beings. Local conceptions, indeed, fully admitted the notion of human inequality. Some individuals held higher social rank than others, in so far as they were considered to enjoy contact with the supernatural world: such as kings and chieftains as opposed to the common folk, masters as opposed to their slaves, men as opposed to women, and elder siblings as opposed to their juniors. It therefore seemed fair enough for a chieftain to be buried with slaves supposed to continue serving him in the other world; for an elder sibling to exert strict control over his juniors whereby every word he uttered, in kindness or wrath, had binding effect upon them; and for the taking of a woman to assume the form of an outright kidnapping, if such a union were regarded as beneficial for the family concerned. Still, such shortcomings did find some compensation through a global perception of life as one which acknowledged a general human preponderance within the natural order of things. No human being could thus ever be confused, in any way, with any animal or thing. Rules enjoining hospitality, and respect for life and motherhood, held their meaning only because they involved, first and foremost, the individual human person.

Taken in all, Africa south of the Sahara could indeed boast its own well-elaborated systems of law, with due injunctions, rules and graded sanctions. The past's judicial order remains to be fully and validly taken into proper account in the perceptions, awareness and current setting of post-colonial, modern Africa.

NOTES

Editor's note: In the Middle Ages, there were state structures in Africa which provide the basis for the history of the continent studied in this chapter, region by region. The author, who is a Central Africa specialist, focuses his study on that sub-Saharan region, where the very foundations of the state and the law in medieval Africa can be seen, that is to say, customs and their evolution towards a structured society and a classic, federalist authority. Outside Central Africa, in the Sudano–Sahelian or Sudano–Ethiopian regions, where forms of statehood are to be found, for instance, in the empires of Ghana (seventh to eleventh century), Mali (thirteenth to fourteenth century), Gao (fifteenth to sixteenth century), the Hausa or Yoruba states, the states of Kānem-Bornu and the Nilotic-Ethiopian world, the state was conducive to the unification of tribes and countries and the development of society on foundations which the author analyses on the basis of the example of Central Africa.

1 There exist attempts to classify and compare the various African political systems: M. Fortes and E. Evans-Pritchard, 1940; J. Vansina 1962, 1966a.

2 At issue here is particularly the case of *noble* tribute – as distinguished from the *common* tribute, mainly consisting of food products derived from hunting and gathering or from farming. Noble tribute required gifts to higher-ranking hierarchies of such symbols of power as the pelts of leopards or panthers, the fangs of beasts of prey, eagle feathers, elephant tusks, and the like.

3 We should distinguish here between the medieval kingdom of the *Kongo* and the two modern republics going by the name of *Congo* (with their respective capitals at Brazzaville and Kinshasa).

4 At the end of the fifteenth century, the crowns of Portugal and the Kongo were worn by Dom João (II) and his queen Dona Eleonor, and by Dom João (Nzinga Nkuwu) and his own queen Dona Eleonor, respectively.

BIBLIOGRAPHY

de HEUSCH, L. 1972. *Le roi ivre ou l'origine de l'Etat.* Gallimard, Paris.

DIOP, C. A. 1960. *L'Afrique noire précoloniale.* Présence Africaine, Paris.

DOUGLAS, M. 1963. *The Lele of Kasai.* Oxford University Press, London.

FORTES, M.; EVANS-PRITCHARD, E. (eds) 1940. *African Political Systems.* IAI, London.

JADIN, L.; DICORATO, M. 1974. *Correspondance de Dom Afonso, roi du Congo (1506–1543).* ARSOM, Brussels.

KI-ZERBO, J. 1972. *Histoire de l'Afrique.* Hatier, Paris.

MUMBANZA MWA BAWELE, 1976. Fondements économiques de l'évolution des sytèmes de filiation dans les sociétés de la Haute-Ngiri et de la Moëka, du XIXè siècle à nos jours. *Communication aux Deuxièmes Journées d'Histoire du Zaïre* (Bukavu, April 1976).

MURDOCK, G. P. 1959. *Africa: its Peoples and their Culture History,* New York.

NDAYWEL È NZIEM, I. 1981. Histoire de l'institution polyandrique dans le Bas-Kasaï (Zaïre). In: *2000 ans d'histoire africaine: Le sol, la parole et l'écrit (Mélanges offerts à Raymond Mauny).* Société Française d'Histoire d'Outre-mer, Paris, pp. 769–89.

OGOT, B. A. 1985. La région des Grands Lacs. In: *Histoire générale de l'Afrique,* IV. UNESCO–NEA, Paris, pp. 543–70.

RANDLES, W. 1968. *L'ancien royaume du Congo, des origines à la fin du XIXè siècle.* Mouton, Paris–The Hague.

VANSINA, J. 1962. A Comparison of African Kingdoms. In: *Africa,* XXXII, 4, pp. 335–42.

——. 1966a. *Kingdoms of the Savanna: a History of the Central African States until European Occupation.* University of Wisconsin Press, Madison.

——. 1966b. *Introduction à l'ethnographie du Congo,* Ed. Universitaires. Kinshasa.

——. 1985. L'Afrique équatoriale et l'Angola, les migrations et l'apparition des premiers Etats. In: *Histoire générale de l'Afrique,* IV, *L'Afrique du XIIè au XVIè siècle.* UNESCO–NEA, Paris, pp. 601–28.

3·7
THE AMERICAS

William T. Sanders

In the New World at the time of European discovery, the social and political organization of the native population varied enormously, from small, egalitarian nomadic hunter–gatherer bands to great empires, with all of the intermediate stages of cultural evolution being represented as well. In only two areas, Mesoamerica and the Central Andes, did native peoples create state-level societies. When the Spaniards arrived in Mexico in 1519, approximately one-third of the cultural area was incorporated into a great tributary empire with its capital at Tenochtitlán, the present site of Mexico City; and virtually all the Central Andean cultural area, including some areas that probably would have been excluded in earlier times, was organized into a single large state with its capital at Cuzco, the largest state created in the New World. The following discussion on the political organization of these two areas focuses on these two states, the Aztec and the Inca Empires.

The period from AD 700–1500 in Mesoamerica is the final period of pre-European cultural development and is also the first period in which we have a combination of relatively detailed recorded history as well as archaeological data, particularly with respect to the final two centuries. For this reason, we have a more detailed picture of political institutions and behaviour than is possible for the earlier period, where most of our reconstructions are based on archaeological remains. One major exception to this latter statement is Classic Maya recorded history on public monuments, but because of the nature of the setting of these documents, the messages are very brief and as yet not entirely understood.

During this period, over much of the area, for most of the time period, states were relatively small. Most of the polities, as in earlier times, had populations of 10,000–20,000. A few were somewhat larger, more often considerably smaller, each ruled by a dynastic family with a hereditary ruler. Also evident was a class of intermediate status, including nobles by birth (i.e., inherited status and landed estates with attached serfs) and a number of nobles of achieved status, based on military service to the state. This class resided in central places, along with the ruling lineage, with average populations of 3,000 to 6,000 people. Professional craftsmen and merchants made up the rest of the population of the town, and these towns were centres of a large number of rural settlements. During this period, however, one of these small states would periodically go through a process of expansion, conquer its neighbours and create a tributary empire, often with populations exceeding 100,000 people. The Aztecs in Central Mexico created the largest state of all and the first pan-Mesoamerican empire, with its capital at Tenochtitlán. The Aztec Empire was the most complex political institution in the entire history of this cultural area in terms of its physical size and internal organization.

The Aztecs, or more properly the Mexica, were a people organized into a small state in 1376 when their first ruler, Acamapichtli, was seated on the throne. Shortly after this, in approximately 1428, the Aztecs embarked on a career of military expansion.

Besides a professional warrior class, and the periodic conscription of the peasantry, the Aztecs established a series of permanent garrisons along the borders of competing states and in strategic locations. Over this period of about ninety years, they created a hegemonic empire in which approximately 500 small local states, distributed over an area of 80,000 square miles, were incorporated into a single polity, with an estimated population of 5–6 million people. The capital city of Tenochtitlán grew steadily in response to this imperial growth to reach a peak population of 150,000–200,000 in 1519, when Cortés arrived.

The original core state, prior to this expansion, probably had a population of 10,000–20,000 people, as with small states over most of Mesoamerica. We will first discuss the organization and structure of that core state and then the administration of the empire. The small states in Central Mexico, like the original Aztec state, had as their head, an individual with the title of *tlatoque* or *tlatoani*. The position was hereditary, within particular lineages, but frequently the succession was not father to son but rather older brother to younger brother, before it moved to the next generation. The power of the *tlatoani* increased dramatically in the case of expanding states, as he established control over small neighbouring states. At a level below the *tlatoani* in Tenochtitlán was an official referred to as the *cihuacoatl*. He was a close relative of the *tlatoani* and acted as a military advisor. Below this level, the city of Tenochtitlán was divided into four major wards with four appointed ward heads, usually men from the warrior class. These were directly responsible to the *Tlatoani*, or his agent the *Cihuacoatl*, and performed primarily administrative roles: the mobilization of manpower for war and the payment of taxes. Below this level, each of the major wards of the city was divided into twelve to fifteen districts, called *calpulli* or *tlaxicalli*. The head of each of these was a hereditary chief, whose position was restricted to a particular lineage of the ward. Writers have debated over the years whether the *calpulli* was some kind of theoretical descent group as well as a spatial division. What we know is that in the rural areas the *calpulli* was the land holding unit and held land in common, which was then apportioned by the head and a council of elders to the individual households that were members of the *calpulli*. It was also a unit of tax collection in which the adult males of the *calpulli* were mobilized by the head to provide either labour or goods for the *tlatoani* of the local state. The *calpulli* was a ceremonial unit, in that each of the *calpullis* had a temple dedicated to its patron god. Finally, it was a unit of military service, in that young men were trained in special schools, called *telpochcalli,* primarily in military skills, and fought in battle as a military unit. In the towns, particularly the larger ones, either the *calpulli* or smaller subdivisions of the *calpulli* were units of occupational specialization.

Separate from this administrative hierarchy was a specialized judiciary with professional judges appointed by the *tlatoani,* either from the hereditary nobility or from the military class. The courts were organized in two levels, one for cases restricted to the noble class and the other for commoners. The noblemen's court also served as an appeal court for commoners. In general, any disputes involving people within a *calpulli* were resolved by the *calpulli* head and his council of elders. Cases went to the official judiciary when the dispute was between members of different *Calpullis*, or disputes between *Calpullis* as corporate groups. The actual proceedings of the court were held in the royal palace, where professional judges listened to the litigants, or their agents, and made the decisions themselves. The proceedings were recorded by professional scribes, who recorded the names of the litigants, the name of the judge, the nature of the case, the date and the results in special books that were kept as a record of court proceedings. There is no reference anywhere in the Spanish accounts that the Aztecs codified laws in books; apparently only the specific judicial cases were recorded.

The Spanish were greatly impressed with the efficiency with which the legal process was carried out in terms of speed and the honesty of the judges, and always compared the Aztec system favorably with the Spanish. In general, punishments for criminal cases were exceedingly harsh, with numerous offences punished by death. For example, if an individual maliciously destroyed the corn field of a farmer, he was executed for this deed. Interestingly, however, a distinction was made between malicious behaviour of this type and stealing corn in times of need. In the latter case, the individual was not punished at all, but the head of the *calpulli* and the council of elders were censured for not assuring that their members had land for their support. A less serious punishment was temporary slavery, in which the accused individual was made a slave of his accuser for a specified period of time.

With respect to military personnel, in the smaller states in Central Mexico virtually all the armies that were mobilized for war against neighbouring states were conscripts from the entire population, i.e. the noble class, the craftsmen and merchants living in the town, and most particularly the peasantry, some residing in the town and some in outlying rural settlements. At the time of the Spanish Conquest, a common pattern in Central Mexico was the capture of enemy warriors for sacrifice to the patron gods of the local states. Individuals who made these captures in battle were given special titles and awards, and a kind of military aristocracy was created, made up of these people. At a certain point in their development as warriors they were given estates and assigned serfs, and became, in essence, a special nobility. They comprised the only standing armies among the small states in Central Mexico. As the Aztec Empire evolved, and as the city grew in size, this warrior class became quite large: a number of Spanish references suggest that the number of people promoted to this status had reached thousands and possibly tens of thousands by 1519.

These people were supported by the state and acted as emergency shock troops to suppress rebellion, and to intervene in major battles to turn the tide of the battle.

Ross Hassig has characterized the Aztec Empire as a 'hegemonic empire'. What he means is that the leaders of these states had very specific and limited objectives, and they invested minimal administrative costs in order to achieve them. The result was a lack of a truly well-developed administrative hierarchy. The major objective of military expansion was to exact goods, particular goods not found in the Valley of Mexico, where the central state was located. In tropical lowland areas, for example, taxes were exacted in cacao, the chocolate bean ; in cotton cloth; feathers from tropical birds; and other exotic goods. In environments similar to the Valley of Mexico, staple goods like maize and other grains were taxed. In most of the 500 conquered states the Aztecs allowed the ruling lineage to continue in office, and to rule their people, with little interference. The local *tlatoani* was responsible for mobilizing the labour and goods to fulfil imperial tax obligations, turn over the goods to the Aztec tax collectors, called *calpixque,* who resided in his town.

The Aztecs grouped the 500 conquered states into thirty-eight provinces, usually selecting one of the local towns as the capital of each province. In residence at these provincial capitals was a governor, whose major purpose was to ensure that the local *calpixque* assigned to the small states in the area collected the taxes and turned them over to him at the provincial capital. The tax was then forwarded to Tenochtitlán, where it was received by a professional class of accountants, who also had the title of *calpixque.* They received the taxes, recorded the amounts and redistributed them from royal store houses. At the head of this hierarchy of accountants was an official called the *huecalpixque.* Some of the tax was in the form of raw goods, for example metal and cotton, and was turned over to royal craftsmen living in the palace, who converted them into finished products. The goods were consumed by the royal lineage and also given as gifts to lower-ranking people who served the state. All of this official class of judges, administrators above the level of the *calpulli* chiefs, governors, and tax collectors and receivers were appointed and the positions held by members of the hereditary nobility or by warrior chiefs.

Prior to the rise of the Aztec Empire during the period AD 900–1200 in Central Mexico, while we do have some recorded history, it was not written contemporaneously with the events, but rather mandated by rulers who lived in the fifteenth century, primarily to legitimize the rights of the ruling family to rule by claiming descent from earlier dynasties. Many of the rulers of the fifteenth–sixteenth centuries in Central Mexico, for example, claimed to be descended from an ancient dynasty of kings who ruled from the city of Tula or Tollán during the period from 900 to approximately AD 1200. The people of Tollán were called Toltecs by the later peoples of Mexico and, according to tradition, were supposedly the creators of urban life and civilization in Central Mexico, and the first great conquest state. As we have seen in Volume III, the first great city and large state in central Mexico actually emerged at Teotihuacán between 100 BC and AD 700. Archaeological evidence has revealed that the city of Tollán had a population of about 60,000 around AD 1100. Its public buildings closely resembled those described by the Spaniards and revealed by archaeology in the Aztec capital in later times, indicating that many of the institutions and political structures found in the Aztec core state were already in existence and probably derived historically from those at Tollán created by the Toltecs. The empire of the Toltecs was approximately equal in size to that of earlier Teotihuacán, but it had a spatial distribution more directed to the north and west of the central plateau. It probably included the state of Mexico, portions of Puebla, all of the modern Mexican states of Hidalgo (where the capital was located), Guanajuato, Querétaro and Aguascalientes and portions of Michoacán and Tamaulipas. In Yucatán, at about the same time, a major polity emerged contemporary with and culturally linked to Tollán, with its centre at the great archaeological site of Chichén Itzá.

Located in the Central Andean cultural area, the Inca Empire was the largest and most thoroughly organized of all of New World polities. At the moment of the Spanish Conquest, in 1532, it covered approximately 1.5 milliion km^2 of space and extended from the present-day Ecuador–Colombia border for a distance of 3,000 km to Central Chile. Its width varied from 200 to 300 km. This peculiar shape, plus the extremely rugged topography due to the mountainous terrain and the extremely arid conditions on the Peruvian coast, posed a formidable administrative problem, which was solved by the Incas in ingenious ways.

As in the Aztec case, the apex of power among the Inca was a hereditary ruler with autocratic powers. A major problem, possibly due to the short period of the existence of the Inca state – i.e. less than 100 years – was that at the death of each ruler a crisis occurred in the succession. On the one hand, selection was limited to one of his sons, but a specific heir was not automatically designated. On the other hand, this may have been a benefit, because out of the competition, at least during the final century of the Inca dynasty, the most vigorous, martial and brilliant leader ended up as the occupant of the office.

In Cuzco resided eleven kin groups or *ayllus,* each one descended from a previous Inca ruler. They formed an upper nobility with a variety of functions for the maintenance and the expansion of the empire. From this class were drawn many of the higher-level administrators, and the able-bodied men from this class served as professional warriors. Ten additional *ayllus,* people who claimed the title Inca, but were of commoner origin, resided at Cuzco and also provided personnel for these two services. During the administration of Pachacutec, a strain, in terms of manpower resources, was already beginning to become evident, but he solved this problem by giving Inca status to a very large population of Quechua speakers who resided in the central highlands. By this ingenious technique, i.e. expanding membership of the Inca ruling group, he provided manpower for both administration and a professional army; this policy also consolidated the loyalty of a much larger, more expanded population.

Below the rank of Inca was a class of nobles who were descendants of the original royal lineages of the conquered states and were referred to as *curacas*. These states ranged in size from a few thousand people up to the Chimu Empire on the north coast, which must have had a population of several hundred thousand people at the time of the Inca conquest. The descendants of these royal lineages were kept as administrators and their positions maintained as hereditary. However, the Inca also required that the *curacas* marry into the Inca royal lineages. If the empire had lasted a few more generations, the process would have created a single ruling aristocracy.

In contrast to the Aztecs, the Incas designed what can be properly referred to as an administrative empire, with a complex hierarchical bureaucracy. One of the distinctive Inca practices was a periodic census of the entire population of the empire by age and sex, a census that was recorded by the use of the famous *quipus* (see Figure 1). This census was recorded by professional record keepers. On the basis of this census, taxes were exacted directly on every able-bodied male, resident in the empire, below the level of the Inca and *curaca* class, in services and goods. This was in sharp contrast to the Aztec system, in which the Aztec simply taxed the local ruler of a state certain quantities of goods, and he was directly responsible for their collection. All the higher-level administrative positions, i.e. the governors of the four great quarters of the empire and the governors of provinces, were filled by Inca nobility. The census apparently functioned to organize the local *curacas* into a hierarchy of officials based upon their supervision of tax payers with respect to units in a decimal system. In areas where the local political polities were small and political organization was highly fragmented, the higher levels in this numerical hierarchy, particularly units of 10,000 tax payers, were also occupied by Incas. With the exception of the 'four lords of the four corners of the empire' and the two lowest levels of the hierarchy, i.e. heads of fifty and ten tax payers, all of these positions were filled by Incas or by local *curacas* and inherited though the male line.

Figure 1 The *quipu:* the domino-like figure to the left suggests the manner in which its decimal system of counting should be understood, pre-Hispanic Peru. Redrawn from the Inca–Spanish chronicler Felipe Guamán Poma de Ayala (sixteenth century), (after Hagen, V. W. von, *Realm of the Incas*, NY 1957, p. 157).

As has been mentioned, the *curacas* were also required to marry women of the Inca royal lineage. A second technique of Inca administration was the creation of a truly extraordinary road system. The Highland Road ran the entire length of the empire, from the border between Ecuador and Colombia to just south of Santiago in Chile. The coastal road ran the entire length of the Peruvian coastal desert. Furthermore, a series of transverse highways connected these two major roads. Along the road, the Inca state constructed *tambos* (rest houses) for personnel moving along the roads, and a postal service based on human runners, that was capable of carrying messages hundreds of kilometres within a few days.

The archaeological manifestations of the empire are so obvious that one Andean researcher pointed out that even if the Inca Empire had occurred well before the Spanish Conquest, we would still have recognized it as an empire, including its extension and the location of its capital, from purely archaeological data. This is because the Inca, aside from the road system, constructed scores of major provincial administrative centres, in pure Inca style, all over the empire, where Incas by blood or by ascription were resettled. These were built by local corvee labour, through the tax structure, and the Inca rulers exacted a much heavier tax on labour for public works than the Aztecs.

The Inca army, like that of the Aztecs, was manned primarily by conscripts, but also like the Aztecs, there was a class of professional warriors. In the Inca case, this consisted of the able-bodied males of the royal lineages and the Inca commoner lineages in residence at Cuzco. These served as a steady source of manpower. Because campaigns, during the eighty years of expansion of the empire, were constant and prolonged, this policy created a professional army. Unlike the Aztecs, who drew their manpower for their conscript armies only from the core area of the Valley of Mexico, the Incas drafted men from all over the empire. In some cases, invading forces were made up almost entirely of these non-Inca, non-Quechua conscripts.

While the Aztecs did move families from the Valley of Mexico to reside in towns at critical points to control the administration of their empire and man garrisons, the Incas carried out this policy on a much more expanded scale. Besides the resettlement of Incas by birth, or by ascription, at the provincial centres built throughout the empire, they also moved local populations from one area to another, particularly from those areas where resistance to Inca conquest was spirited, in order to break up local loyalties and create heterogeneity in all of the local areas of the empire. In some cases, almost the entire population was moved and scattered over the Inca domain. Some of these outsiders were settled in the capital city of Cuzco to provide services for the support of the Inca state. The movement of Quechua speakers from the central highlands to all parts of the empire resulted in homogenization of language. If the process had not been interrupted by the Spanish Conquest, these policies would have created a single homogeneous linguistic and cultural area in the Central Andes. Considering the terrain of the Inca Empire and its vast size, these administrative techniques were remarkably successfully and thorough.

With respect to the judiciary, at Cuzco itself, a special hierarchy of judges was created, similar to that of the Aztecs, to preside over criminal and civil suits. For the rest of the empire, the administrative hierarchy served both administrative and judicial functions.

Prior to the Inca Empire in the Central Andes, the period AD 600–1000 is referred to as the Middle Horizon. The term refers to a major historical process, the widespread dissemination of a highly integrated style and its associated iconography over most of the Central Andes. This style was expressed in painted ceramics, woven textiles, ornaments of precious metals and, in a restricted area, in stone sculpture. As in the case of the Incas, the iconography was a blend of political and religious ideology. Also parallel to the Inca phenomenon is clear and obvious evidence of the existence of large-scale, imperial organization. The periods immediately preceding and succeeding this period are characterized by highly evolved and vigorous regional cultures and styles.

The religious and political ideology is older and more pervasive and, furthermore, expressed on stone monuments and architecture at the great site of Tiahuanaco in the highlands of Bolivia and clearly originated there. The puzzling feature, however, is that the specific style found at Tiahuanaco is limited to the highlands of Bolivia and nearby areas in Chile, Argentina and the tiny coastal valleys of southern Peru. In a much larger area that included the Peruvian highlands and the north and central coastal areas of Peru, a distinctive version of this style was widespread. It is distinguishable from the Tiahuanaco style itself, but clearly derived from it. The origin of this derived Tiahuanaco style had always puzzled archaeologists until the discovery of Wari, a huge urban site near Ayacucho, in the central Peruvian highlands. It appears that some members of the upper class of Tiahuanaco left the city, perhaps as the result of dynastic dissension, took over a portion of the Ayacucho valley, and introduced the elite manifestations of Tiahuanaco culture in terms of organization and associated ideology. From this centre they expanded their power over a period of 100, possibly 200, years to include most of the highlands of Peru and the north and central coast.

Clear evidence of the spread of this power is also found in architecture. A distinctive spatial feature of the capital city of Wari is its organization into large rectangular enclosures, enclosing houses consisting of central courts and rows of rooms arranged, in tandem, along the periphery of these courts. In the highlands, at two major locations, and perhaps a number of others, Pikillacta in the south, and Viracocha Pampa in the north, each marking approximately the southern and northern limits of the diffusion of the style, these architectural features were reproduced. In the coastal areas, for the first time, planned communities were established, with each unit of a city defined by rectangular adobe enclosures. These centres suggest an empire very similar to that of the Incas, a conclusion also reinforced by the presence of roads connecting coastal valleys and connecting them with the highlands. The period AD 600–800, therefore, is a period of the formation of two large Andean Empires, one based at Tiahuanaco, the other at Wari, comparable in many of their characteristics, particular the Wari Empire, to the later Inca polity. Between these two periods of large-scale state formation, the Central Andes were divided into chiefdoms and small kingdoms, with the exception of the north coast, where a number of coastal valleys were conquered and integrated into a single political system with its capital at the great city of Chanchán.

BIBLIOGRAPHY

BRUNDAGE, B. C. 1963. *The Empire of the Inca.* University of Oklahoma Press.

EKHOLM, G. F.; BERNAL, I. (eds) 1971. *The Handbook of Middle American Indians: Archaeology of Northern Mesoamerica,* Part 1. University of Texas Press, Boston, Texas.

GIBSON, C. 1964. *The Aztecs Under Spanish Rule: A History of the Indians of the Valley of Mexico 1519–1810*. Stanford University Press, California.

HASSIG, R. 1985. *Trade, Tribute and Transportation: The 16th Century Political Economy of the Valley of Mexico*. University of Oklahoma Press.

——. 1988. *Aztec Warfare: Imperial Expansion and Political Control.* University of Oklahoma Press.

LANNING, E. P. 1967. *Peru before the Incas*. Prentice-Hall, Englewood Cliffs, New Jersey.

SCHREIBER, K. J. 1989. *Planned Architecture of Middle Horizon Peru: Implications for Social and Political Organization*. University Microfilms, University of Michigan.

4

ECONOMIC SYSTEMS AND TECHNOLOGIES

Richard W. Bulliet

A century ago, the view of human historical development that prevailed in European thought grew from contemplation of so-called 'Western history', an intellectual paradigm embodying the following linkages: Ancient Egypt and Mesopotamia → classical antiquity → Dark Ages → high Middle Ages → Renaissance and Reformation → Enlightenment → modern times. Alternative paradigms conceived by non-Europeans, such as Ibn Khaldūn, were of interest as components of world intellectual history; but the 'Western history' paradigm prevailed as the interpretative model, partly because it contributed so powerfully to explaining and justifying European imperialism and non-European subjugation. The 'Western history' paradigm was taken for granted by professional historical journals, historical societies, university curricula and other institutions deriving from European models in all parts of the world.

A necessary component of this paradigm was the concept of the Middle Ages, the period we are here more appropriately indicating by dates, as an era of economic and technological stasis. Modern times and European world hegemony, it was argued, stemmed from advances in science and industry, often termed 'revolutions', that in turn could not have come about without the secularization and rationalization of thought ineluctably emanating from the Renaissance and Reformation → Enlightenment linkage. However grand the accomplishments of the European Middle Ages may have been in matters spiritual or artistic, qualities like inventiveness, technological imagination, natural curiosity and zeal for change were deemed to have been lacking. This conception was necessary to distinguish the earlier period from the presumed later sequence from enlightened thought to scientific and technological discovery to Industrial Revolution.

As historians ventured to explore the earlier history of non-European parts of the world, potential paradoxes arose. If science and industry depended upon a uniquely European sequence of intellectual stages from the stagnant Dark Ages to modern times, then the absence of a self-developed modern industrial society in other parts of the world must have been the product of an economic and technological stagnation that never received the stimulus of the Enlightenment. Yet it was apparent that this was not invariably the case. A synchronous view of the world showed that Chinese society, Indian society and various Muslim societies were inventive and economically dynamic during Europe's presumed period of stagnation. Moreover, many other societies in Japan, Africa, island and mainland South-east Asia, and South and Central America exhibited more sophisticated technologies and economic organization than Europe in some areas.

As more becomes known about world economic and technological history before the tumultuous changes of the sixteenth century, the more apparent it becomes that stagnation is an entirely inappropriate label, both for Europe and for the rest of the world. The privileged position of European economic and technological development in modeling world history in pre-modern times must accordingly give way to a broader inquiry into the relationships between economic and technological conditions, on the one hand, and intellectual and religious or political and societal formations, on the other.

This chapter will stress diversity, inventiveness and geographical interconnections in an effort to demonstrate the complexity of world economic and technological matters during the period of the European Middle Ages. Inevitably, discussion of many economic patterns and technological developments will be omitted. Constraints of space militate against encyclopedic comprehensiveness and dictate a selection of examples subordinated to the argument outlined above.

POPULATION MOVEMENTS AND TECHNOLOGICAL CHANGE

Historians have attributed much to the displacement of peoples over the face of the Earth. Conquests, folk migrations, forced resettlement, wars of conquest and the implanting of colonies can be shown to have fostered language change, technological diffusion, and alteration of social and political patterns from prehistoric times onward. Some historians and prehistorians have even seen this as the primary mechanism of change in economic systems and technologies, often attributing major changes in technology to invasions or folk migrations that are otherwise poorly attested. This historiographical practice suggests a possible correlation between periods of comparatively extensive population displacement and periods of more rapid economic and technological change. A test of this hypothesis would be to compare the nine-hundred year period 300 BC–AD 600 with the nine-hundred year period AD 600–1500.

The earlier period saw major displacements of people in Europe in the form of Germanic migrations and Hellenistic and Roman imperial growth, with, on occasion, attendant enslavement and displacement of conquered peoples. It also saw the start of Bantu migrations southwards and eastwards from north-west sub-Saharan Africa and a movement of Turkic and Iranian peoples westwards in Central Asia. But overall, this was a period of comparatively limited human displacement. Aside from the likely superiority in agricultural equipment and technique of the Bantu-speaking peoples and the Roman development of a road system and centralized imperial economy, the displacements that did occur were associated with profound economic or technological change only in the waning centuries of the Roman Empire, when Europe suffered severe economic and political regression. The use of horse-mounted warriors, which ultimately became a military factor in many parts of Africa, Asia and Europe, was perhaps the most far-reaching technological development associable with population movement, stemming, as it did, from the example of Central Asian pastoralists encroaching on agricultural lands in the Middle East and Eastern Europe.

By contrast, the period AD 600–1500 saw far more extensive population movements. The Arab conquests of the seventh century not only spread tribespeople from the Arabian peninsula, with their particular beliefs and ways of life, from Afghanistan to Spain, but population movement became commonplace within the geographically enormous caliphate that the Muslim Arabs founded. Zanj slaves from East Africa became common as rural labourers in Iraq. The Jatt (Arabic, Zutt) people from northern India, perhaps already in Iraq before the Arab conquest, were transplanted to Syria and then to the Byzantine frontier, possibly becoming the ancestors of the Gypsies. An Indonesian community in Iraq, the Sayabija, was presumably connected with the general Indonesian migration westwards that resulted in the settling of Madagascar. Slavic military slaves (*saqāliba*) found service in North Africa. And Turkic warriors bought or recruited from Central Asia served wherever the caliphs sent them.

A second population shift of this period saw Turkic and then Mongol tribes move westwards across Central Asia, the former becoming a presence in the Balkans and Iran after AD 950 and in Anatolia after 1071, and the latter conquering the world's largest contiguous territorial empire under the aegis of Chinggis Khān in the thirteenth century. Just as with the Arabs, the Turko-Mongol movement had strong secondary effects. Most notably, invasion and trade disruption led to an economic decline in Iran that prompted many thousands of Iranians, particularly of the educated elite, to migrate to India, Anatolia and the Arab countries.

In Europe, Viking raiders struck Britain and north-west Europe between the ninth and eleventh centuries, establishing a major colony in Normandy. The Norman invasion of Sicily in 1060 and conquest of Britain in 1066 and the presence of vast hoards of Islamic coins in Scandinavia and Poland stemming from Viking trade down the rivers of Russia illustrate the range of their expeditions. In China, a steady advance of Han Chinese from the north into the southern provinces was a hallmark of this period. The Southern Song Dynasty (1127–1279) was the first major Chinese state centred in the south. In Africa, the Bantu migrations and, in the Pacific, the Polynesian advance from island to island add yet further to the picture of an era marked by extraordinary mobility of population. And this without mentioning the European sea ventures that culminated at the very end of the period in the circumnavigation of Africa and the discovery of the Americas.

Was this also a period of technological and economic change commensurate with this unprecedented intermixing of peoples? Arguably it was. Several technologies of truly transformative character spread through population migrations and contacts. Gunpowder, developed in China primarily, but not exclusively, for display purposes, transformed the armies and political systems of the entire world after 1300 (see Plates 42, 43). Paper making and block printing spread from China to Japan and Korea and across Central Asia (see Plates 115, 116). Block printing seemingly developed independently in Western Asia at approximately the same time (Bulliet, 1987). Whether Europeans received the idea from China via Central Asia or from Egypt and Syria may be debated, but European block-printing seems to have provided the spur for the development of movable type printing by Gutenberg in the fifteenth century (see Plate 117). In all of these places, except, curiously, Western Asia, printing had a transformational impact on many aspects of society.

The Chinese compass, developed in connection with geomancy, spread westwards, too, in this period, making possible the remarkable fifteenth-century sailing expeditions of Vasco da Gama, Christopher Columbus, and other Europeans and the equally impressive voyages to Africa of the Chinese admiral Zheng He between 1405 and 1433. On land, major improvements in transport and agricultural output were made after the Europeans became aware of the technical advantages of Chinese-style harnessing. New horse harnesses made for greater efficiency, because land could be ploughed faster, and heavier soils could be worked; and the faster speed of horse-drawn passenger vehicles fostered an interest in comfort that resulted in the invention in Eastern Europe of the coach, a wagon with the passenger compartment suspended by straps or springs (see Plates 7–9).

From a world-historical standpoint, therefore, there seems to be support for the idea that the acceleration of inter-societal contact and population movement during this era did, indeed, foster technological change, just as it fostered artistic change, for example the impact of Chinese painting and pottery styles in Mongol and Tīmūrid Iran; religious change, for example the spread of Islam in India and Indonesia and Buddhism in Japan; and the spread of disease, for example the Eurasian pandemic of bubonic plague, emanating from Central Asia, in the mid-fourteenth century. We will return to this hypothesis at the end of this essay after reviewing the major modalities of economic life prevailing during this period.

HUNTERS, GATHERERS AND FISHERMEN

The turbulent panorama of population movements and accompanying changes in technology and economic affairs provides much of the drama in the social history of the world between 600 and 1500. Nevertheless, it must always be borne in mind that for most people, the forms of economic life and the technologies they deployed for meeting their needs changed little during this period. In North and South America, for example, although agriculture was the dominant mode of food production in parts of the Andes, Mexico and Central America, and eastern North America, many peoples of the forests, plains and deserts lived by harvesting wild plants and hunting wild animals, as they had for several millennia. The same is true for the populations of Australia, New Guinea and other parts of island South-east Asia, for some peoples in the Central African rain forest and southern African deserts, and for some peoples north of the Arctic Circle, although there fishing was also an important means of livelihood. In other parts of the world, too, hunting and gathering persisted as a way of life for small groups of people.

Hunting, fishing and food-gathering societies acquired and transmitted great funds of lore about the fauna and flora in their environments. Today, ethnobotanists study their systems of classifying and identifying plants, and medical researchers interrogate their healers and shamans about natural therapeutic agents. This type of research has proved that despite low population densities and limited manufactures, these peoples were technologically quite sophisticated, understanding technology to include the accumulation and transmission of knowledge needed to exploit and control the environment. Moreover, the lore gathered by hunters and gatherers often persisted well after the groups gained a degree of familiarity with domesticated plants and animals.

Among the Ka'apor people of north-eastern Brazil, for example, adult men spend 20 per cent of their time gardening but 30 per cent hunting, fishing and food gathering (Balée, 1994). Adult women garden 15 per cent of the time and devote 14 per cent to hunting, fishing and gathering. Although pre-literate, they identify 500 or more plant species in their surroundings, only one-seventh of which are domesticated. These plants provide most of their food and materials for clothes, houses and weapons. In addition, they provide personal ornaments, cosmetics, dyes, cleansers, body paints, perfumes, medicines for thirty-seven different conditions, magical amulets, and ritual objects. The Ka'apor also identify various poisonous plants to avoid, and others to use to kill fish.

The botanical lore of the Ka'apor is representative of the vast troves of knowledge, acquired through generations of experimentation with the environment, typical of people who satisfy many, if not all, of their needs by hunting, gathering and fishing. During the period 600–1500, however, little of this knowledge was transmitted outside the immediate group. Agriculturalists typically knew far less about wild plants and animals. Even after 1500, when the plants and animals of the Americas came to be known in Europe and then elsewhere in the Old World, domesticates like corn, potatoes, cacao and tobacco had a far greater impact than wild species.

The most important wild plant to be newly exploited and domesticated during this period came not from the New World but from Somalia and Yemen. The pastoralists and food gatherers of Somalia probably had known for centuries that eating the bean of the coffee plant would keep them awake, but decocting a beverage from the bean (or its husk) became economically significant only in the fourteenth century, starting in Yemen and spreading northward into the Ottoman Empire and then into Europe (Hattox, 1985). Curiously, the mildly energizing effect of chewing the leaves of the *qat* tree, which was as well known in Yemen then as it is today, did not cause its use to spread along with coffee.

PASTORALISTS

Pastoralism is a more specialized economic system particularly adapted to regions that are too rugged or too arid for agriculture. Like hunters and gatherers, pastoralists pay close attention to the natural environment and accumulate great funds of lore regarding the plants that their animals eat and the wild game to be found in their territory. Most also concern themselves with controlling breeding. Typically, most male animals are killed young to increase the proportion of females and thus maximize the reproductive potential of the herd or flock set to graze on sparse pasture. The small number of males kept for breeding limits the extent of the gene pool and is conducive towards the emergence of local breeds. Sometimes special traits are bred for: distinctive horn shapes for cattle, piebald colouring for horses and camels, fat tails for sheep, and many different qualities for dogs. The boundaries between breeds, for example between piebald camels in the southern Sahara and solid-coloured animals in the north, or between fat-tailed sheep in Libya and Tunisia and thin-tailed sheep in Algeria and Morocco, conceal differences that have as yet been little explored by historians.

Yet despite similarities to hunter–gatherers, most pastoral societies have been more or less closely linked to sedentary agricultural societies. Unlike hunters, gatherers and fishermen, whose ways of life were often entirely self-sufficient, most pastoralists made use of some foodstuffs and manufactured goods from settled areas and traded livestock, wool and hides to obtain them.

Even though consuming animal products is a fairly inefficient way to convert vegetation into human sustenance, pastoral societies usually had greater population densities than hunter–gatherer societies living in similar habitats. Pastoral density depended basically on two variables: the type of vegetation, which in turn dictated what animals could be supported, and the competition of agriculturalists for land suitable for growing crops. The Arabian and Somali Deserts had long supported herders of one-humped camels. Since camels could spend a week away from a water source, while sheep and goats had to be watered daily, all but the most arid tracts could be put to use. In Arabia, entire camping groups made up of related families travelled with the herds, while in Somalia men would leave their families for part of the year and take the camels into the inland wastes to graze (see Plates 182–184).

Camel nomadism spread extensively in the Sahara Desert during this period (Bulliet, 1975). Camels had replaced cattle and horses along the southern edge of the desert on a gradual basis from approximately the third century BC onward. A variety of camel-using societies subsequently developed from western Sudan to Mauretania. Camel nomadism did not become important in the northern Sahara, however, until after the third century AD. Just as the southern peoples, for example the Teda of Chad and the Tuareg of Niger and Mali, developed their own distinctive folkways and technologies, notably in camel-saddle design, so the Berbers of the northern Sahara, though linguistically akin to the Tuareg, adopted technologies that derived from Roman and Arab sources. The winter rainfall regime of the north contrasting with the spring rainfall regime in the south tended to keep the herds and peoples apart, since camel breeding was tied physiologically to the rain cycle. Nevertheless, the spread of camel breeding facilitated a growth in trans-Saharan caravan trading that brought northern and sub-Saharan Africa into more consistent contact than they had experienced in many centuries, at least since the desert climate reached its current level of aridity around 2500 BC.

Somalia, Arabia and the Sahara afford a comparison for the notion that population densities deriving from degrees of aridity, best exemplified by the species of animal herded, have a determining impact on the political capacities of different groups of pastoralists. Xavier de Planhol has argued that horse nomads, being more numerous on the ground, are more apt to organize themselves into conquest bands than are widely strewn groups of camel nomads (de Planhol, 1968). Yet while Somali camel pastoralists never chose the path of conquest and empire formation, and Saharan camel herders did so only occasionally, as in the empire created by the Mauretanian *murābiṭūn* or 'Almoravids' in the eleventh century, Arab tribesmen conquered most of Western Asia and North Africa between AD 632 and 711. To be sure, many Arabs came from settled parts of the peninsula, such as Yemen, and others herded sheep and goats on the desert fringes rather than camels, but some of the most frequently mentioned tribal names of the conquest period are those of camel tribes.

The purpose of making this comparison is to caution against the idea that certain types of pastoralism have intrinsic qualities that are conducive towards political activity, or that changes in the pastoral regime *per se*, as might arise, for example, from climatic fluctuations, cause major political events in nomadic zones. The known history of the seventh-century Arab and thirteenth-century Mongol empires, to take the two most important states founded by pastoralists during this period, suggest that many other factors, including conditions in surrounding territories, talents of specific leaders, and incentives for co-operation weigh heavily in triggering momentous historical events.

The horse nomads that provided the economic and military base for the Mongol invasions had been prevalent in Central Asia since the times of the Scythians in the west and the Xiungnu in the east. Historians have tried to interpret their periodic violent eruptions into agricultural lands as responses to climatic change (Huntington, 1907), to periods of Chinese expansion northwards (Lattimore, 1951), or, conversely, to periods of Chinese imperial weakness (Barfield, 1989). However, none of the earlier periods of conquest stands comparison with what Chinggis Khān and his descendants achieved. Not only did they and their Turkic tribal allies bring all of China, Russia and Iran under their sway and attempt an invasion of Japan, but for a century and more they successfully managed relations among the far-flung parts of their empire and maintained their largely peaceful dominance over vast agricultural lands (see Plates 14, 248).

The Arab and Mongol conquests and the development of the Saharan caravan trade overshadow the other varieties of pastoralism of this period because of their impact on inter-regional communication and exchanges of technology and other cultural traits. Nevertheless, pastoralists who seasonally shifted their flocks of sheep, goats or cattle to high summer pastures or low winter pastures were common in mountainous areas of Western Asia (for example, Kurds) and North Africa (for example, Berbers of the Atlas) and, on a smaller scale, in mountainous parts of Europe (see Plate 185). Cattle nomadism was common in the semi-arid Sahel district of sub-Saharan Africa; while reindeer herding supported Lapps in northern Scandinavia and Chukchi in eastern Siberia.

The mobility of pastoral peoples differs greatly depending on climate and terrain. Groups that raise pack animals and migrate over extensive territories may become involved in caravan trading, as happened in Western Asia, North Africa and Central Asia. Even in sedentary regions of India, the Banjara cattle pastoralists transported goods in bulk on large herds of pack oxen (Tracy, 1990). In this fashion, they can become instruments of inter-regional transmission of technology, products and other cultural traits. But pastoralists more often manifest cultural conservatism. Their migratory or semi-migratory existence in generally resource-poor environments militates against the accumulation of goods or major changes in lifestyle that might put their survival at risk. Thus the empires established by the Arabs and the Mongols marked periods of unprecedented inter-regional interaction and exchange, even though the Arab, and Mongol horsemen themselves changed their ways of life but little.

AGRICULTURE

The vast majority of the world's people devoted most of their efforts to growing food plants. The term 'agriculture' usually used for this pursuit often conjures up the image of fields of grain being worked by oxen or horses pulling ploughs. For much of Europe, Western Asia, India and East Asia, this image is reasonably accurate. In these regions, rice, wheat, barley, oats, millet or rye were staple crops. The actual processes of field preparation, sowing, harvesting and processing the grain differed considerably, however. Rice required large amounts of water and was planted densely in carefully ploughed beds to be replanted after 30–50 days. Water buffalo were often used as draft animals in the flooded paddy fields of South and South-east Asia and south and central China (see Plate 19). Irrigation was not only important in many rice-growing areas, where great amounts of water were required, but also in arid zones such as Western Asia, where a large proportion of the available labour was devoted to construction and maintenance of irrigation systems, and superintending the provision of water to the fields, whether by underground channel (*qānāt*) in Iran, by canal from the Tigris or Euphrates in Iraq, or by types of waterwheel in other areas. Europe, by contrast, relied mostly on rainfall (see Plates 16–18). Clearing new land of trees and undergrowth was a major chore, however.

The amount of land that could be cultivated depended on the availability of labour and the efficiency of the technology at hand. Though rice cultivation expanded widely in southern China during this period, the most important technological change in grain farming was probably the introduction, mentioned earlier, of more efficient harnessing into Europe (White, 1962). From classical antiquity, the Europeans had been wedded to the notion that ploughing must be done by a pair of animals, usually yoked oxen. Yoke harnesses for horses were inefficient because the strap around the animal's neck that attached it to the yoke exerted too much pressure on the throat for maximum traction. Evidence for new types of harnessing, the horse collar and the breast strap, date back to the eighth century (see Plates 5–8). Linguistic evidence indicates that some of the technology may have come from China, but the means of transmission is obscure. Similar harnesses had been known in Roman Tunisia and Libya, but they seem not to have spread (see Plates 2–4).

Being faster than oxen, plough horses harnessed by these new devices increased the area that could be cultivated in a given number of man-hours. Their greater strength, in part built up by selective breeding to provide warhorses for heavily mailed knights, facilitated the cultivation of heavy, muddy soils, which had previously been avoided. The use of a mould-board on the plough to turn the soil over instead of just scratching a groove, a practice also known previously in China, was an accompanying technological change. The milling of grain also improved in Europe at the same time. Overshot watermills, in which the gravity of falling water added to the force of the flow, and horizontal-axis windmills became common (Forbes, 1964–1966) (see Plate 17). Yet most other processing operations, such as reaping, threshing and winnowing, continued to rely on human or animal power.

However dominant grain cultivation may have been in these areas in producing staples and establishing a seasonal work cycle, it is only part of the agricultural picture. Non-grain crops were of considerable importance even in grain-producing regions. In East Asia, soybeans provided a vital dietary supplement to rice, and mulberry leaves fed the silkworms that were the basis of China's most important cloth industry. In Western Asia and North Africa, sugar cane and cotton, both originally from India, spread widely in the early centuries of this period, the former becoming a major product in Egypt and the latter in Iran (Watson, 1983). Only towards the end of the period did sugar cane spread to parts of Southern Europe and to European-controlled Mediterranean islands. The same innovative spirit that spurred the popularization of these plants, which had been grown in Western Asia in a very limited way before the Arab conquests, also fostered the spread of citrus trees, aubergines, and other plants native to East Asia. Historians believe that the Silk Road across Central Asia was the primary route of dissemination for these cultivars, but seaborne traders may also have played a role.

Although ploughed fields and rippling expanses of ripening grain are often assumed to epitomize agriculture, sub-Saharan Africa, much of South-east Asia and the Americas resorted to entirely different technologies in growing food plants. Instead of the plough, the hoe or digging stick (see Figure 2) was the instrument used in planting. Instead of broadly scattering grain by throwing it on the ground, the inefficient European practice, seeds or cuttings were carefully planted in individual holes or mounds. Growing corn, developed in Mexico from a wild grass into a sturdy stalk with large ears and planted in parts of North America as well, and similar-looking varieties of sorghum in sub-Saharan Africa involved

Figure 2 Digging stick: men and women, working together in teams, harvest potatoes, pre-Hispanic Peru. Redrawn from Felipe Guamán Poma de Ayala (after Hagen, V. W. von, *Realm of the Incas*, NY 1957, p. 55).

a seasonal cycle of labour analogous to that of the smaller grains. But starchy rhizomes and tubers like potatoes, yams and manioc, staple foods of the Andes, the Caribbean region and island South-east Asia, could be harvested all year round (Sauer, 1972).

Cultivation of these latter plants, which grow from cuttings rather from seeds, is sometimes referred to as vegeculture. Although the territory devoted to plant cultivation in Africa expanded steadily during this period with the spread of people speaking Bantu languages, there was comparatively little technology transfer between agricultural and vegecultural zones. Indeed, the report in Latin texts that the indigenous Berber peoples of North Africa were unfamiliar with agriculture before learning about it from the Romans probably reflects the unfamiliarity of small grain farmers with other types of food growing (Bulliet, 1981). Everywhere, domestic plants and the technologies for growing and processing them were accorded religious and symbolic value.

Arboriculture was yet another form of food growing. Coconuts, breadfruit and bananas were staples in the Pacific and in island South-east Asia. Bananas evidently spread to Africa, possibly during this period, along with migrants from Indonesia. In the hot deserts of North Africa and Western Asia, the date palm was highly valued as a staple. In the Yucatán, the Maya, too, may have relied heavily on tropical fruits (Netting, 1977). In most regions, however, tree products were dietary supplements rather than staple foods.

Just as the variety, worldwide, of techniques of food production is too great to explore here, so the nature of land and resource management varied enormously. The manor of tenth-century Europe with its village of peasant huts huddled around the great house of the lord bespeaks the fragmentation of land holding and inclination towards self-sufficiency characteristic of a region where urban and commercial life were at a low ebb and political power rested on personal bonds of fealty. Yet manors and serfs bound to the soil were also a feature of Song China, a robust and centrally administered empire. By contrast, in Fāṭimid and Mamlūk Egypt, villages were strung along the length of the Nile without focus on a lord's residence, and there was no formal serfdom. Taxes were assessed and collected by agents or officials commanding the usufruct of the land sent from the flourishing new capital of Cairo (Rabie, 1972). In the Andes, the distribution of villages reflected the broader political situation. The great conquests of the Incas in the fifteenth century saw a rearrangement of settlement and food storage patterns along roads to facilitate the movement and supply of the armies (D'Altroy, 1992). This situation reflects the degree of control that the Incan government exercised over its agricultural subjects (see Plate 320).

In general, the organization of agricultural settlement reflected the local circumstances governing the distribution of the harvest. At one extreme, for example in many mountainous and desert areas in Western Asia, farming communities were almost entirely self-sufficient. At the other, for example Song China, elaborate taxation and transportation bureaucracies collected agricultural produce for dispatch by way of the extensive canal system to hungry cities.

Central place theory provides geographical models of spatial distribution appropriate to different patterns of function in different societies (Christaller, 1966). A single farming village, for example, might not provide enough work for a shoemaker, but several villages would. Hence, a small town with a shoemaker and other artisans would theoretically be centred among a group of villages. A group of these small towns, in turn, would be centred around a larger town featuring, perhaps, a weekly market and a church. And the larger towns would be distributed around a city providing yet higher functions, such as tax collection or a law court. Central place theory can be used as a tool for understanding how agricultural settlements are distributed in a society with a more or less well-known hierarchy of functional needs, but it can also be used, as in the example cited above from Peru, to deduce functions from the distribution of settlements, that is, granaries near roads would reflect the need to supply the army even without written descriptions of the logistics of Incan conquest. Spatial distribution adds another dimension to the vast store of knowledge and experience coded in the techniques and patterns of agricultural life.

ARTS, CRAFTS AND MANUFACTURES

All of the world's peoples, regardless of their social organization or means of sustenance, fabricated things. The conventional distinctions between manufactures, crafts and arts are not always helpful in elucidating this enormous range of activity. Cloth making, for example, is usually classed as a manufacture, and historians have devoted great attention to analysing techniques of spinning, weaving, felting, dyeing and so on. Tailoring, sewing and embroidery, on the other hand, have been regarded as crafts, or more simply as types of home industry. One consequence of this difference in classification is that the role of women in the fabrication of goods has largely been neglected. Things made by women in the home, or at the camping sites of pastoralists,

Figure 3 Woman weaving at a backstrap loom, pre-Hispanic Peru. Redrawn from Felipe Guamán Poma de Ayala (after Hagen, V. W. von, *Realm of the Incas*, NY 1957, p. 83).

hunter–gatherers and fishing groups often displayed great artistry, creativity and industry. Embroidery, bead work, feather work and sewing occupied great amounts of female effort in virtually every society in the world (see Figure 3). Moreover, the patterns and motifs found on household goods often influenced the styles of better-studied manufactures. Surviving records rarely permit a correction of this gender bias inherent in studies of arts, crafts and manufactures. Industries outside the home were mostly dominated by men, even when the labour was provided by women and children, as was the case, for example, in much of the weaving industry in Europe and Western Asia and the silk-reeling industry in China, at least until a silk-reeling machine was perfected in the thirteenth century (Elvin, 1973).

Another way of classifying fabricated items is into such categories as everyday, luxury and fine art. These terms derive in part from the comparative scarcity of goods and in part from estimates of the time or skill required to manufacture them. As a consequence, these classifications tend to be relative. In the realm of pottery, for example, Chinese production was abundant and of very high average quality. The large glazed terracotta figurines of horses and camels found in Tang burials, the increasing refinement of colour and glazing technique in Song porcelain, and the rich ornamentation on Ming blue-and-white porcelain, were all known to pottery makers in the Islamic world by way of the Central Asian and Indian Ocean trade routes. But Iranian pottery, the best in the Islamic world during this period, never matched Chinese quality. Imitations of Tang splash-painted and slip-painted wares were popular in Iran in the ninth century, just as imitations of Chinese celadon and porcelain were in the fifteenth. But true porcelain, which results from fusing kaolin and feldspar at very high temperatures, could not be produced, and the delicacy of colour and shape rarely approached the Chinese standard (see Plate 200).

Nevertheless, it is easily possible to distinguish levels of skill in the production of Iranian pottery. In the tenth century, for example, unglazed wares with little or minimal surface decoration were ubiquitous. Glazed wares of a utilitarian character were abundant in cities and probably marketed to the middle social strata, and a few pieces of unusual size and fineness were probably highly valued by the elite. Yet no information has been preserved about the pottery industry, and very few pieces bear the names of potters, who seem, on the whole, to have enjoyed very low status.

Three hundred years later, Iranian pottery had gone through a transformation most strongly marked by the overwhelming popularity of newly developed turquoise glazes (see Plate 212). For the elite, intricately painted *Mīnā'ī* ware, polychrome tilework and ceramic mosaics for architectural ornament show great creativity, and the names of potters are indicated somewhat more frequently. The great tiled tombs and mosques of Tīmūrid Samarkand in the fifteenth century were the culmination of this development (see Plate 26). On the other hand, the abundance and quality of wares destined for the middle class, which had declined greatly during the disorders of the immediately pre-Mongol and Mongol periods, seem to have diminished, particularly by comparison with contemporary Yuan and Ming China.

Extending the comparison further to contrast Iranian pottery with wares made in Muslim Spain and Morocco, the difference in quality is marked indeed. The Western potters were much more limited in their knowledge of chemistry and in the variety of their shapes and designs. The blue of the East never reached the West, where dark green remained the dominant colour in ceramic architectural decoration and in many household wares (see Plate 24).

Yet by comparison with Western Europe, Islamic Spain was a sophisticated centre of ceramic production. Southern European potters used Islamic models to develop glazed wares to add to their earlier repertoire of rather plain earthenware products. Thus a fine piece of pottery executed for elite use in twelfth-century Europe was far inferior to a contemporary product destined for the same class in Iran, or even more so in China.

What holds for pottery holds for most other manufactures as well. Within a given zone of production for goods of a certain type, whether of metal, leather, cloth, precious stone or any other material, comparison allows distinctions to be made between products that exhibit greater or lesser skill, creativity in design, hours of labour, or complexity of manufacturing process. Elite goods are easily distinguished in this way from common goods. Yet techniques of manufacture were so localized and familiarity with products from distant lands (much less with techniques of production) so limited that comparison between zones becomes largely futile.

A European carpenter, for example, customarily used a saw that cut on the forward stroke. No one questioned this traditional way of sawing. But Japanese carpenters customarily used saws that cut on the draw stroke. The difference this made was that a forward-stroke saw had to withstand both the resistance of the wood and the compressive force of the sawyer's hand. Hence, it had to be thick enough and stiff enough to resist bending. The draw-stroke saw, on the other hand, had to overcome the resistance of the wood and the tensile force exerted by the sawyer's hand pulling it. But since iron has greater tensile strength than compressive strength, the Japanese saw could be thinner and make a finer cut, as specimens of Japanese wooden combs with teeth several times denser than those of European combs make clear.

In assessing the history of manufactures, arts and crafts during this period, therefore, the decisions of art historians and museum curators to designate some products 'fine art', others 'minor arts', and others 'popular art' should be used with caution. Gold repoussé masks from Peru, bronze portrait busts from Benin in West Africa, bronze figurines of Hindu deities from the Chōla state in southern India, and bronze incense burners from Seljuk Iran (see Figure 4) are roughly contemporary and represent the highest level of metal craftsmanship in their respective regions (see Plates 222, 267, 319). It would not be difficult, perhaps, to rank specimens comparatively according to aesthetic criteria, refinement of technique or understanding of materials, but it is more important historically to explore the organization of production, the division of labour, and the local traditions and design models that their existence testifies to. Throughout the period under discussion, influence of techniques and styles between geographical areas, such as between Spain and Europe in the field of pottery, was comparatively slow and infrequent.

Figure 4 Paired dragons, bronze door-knocker from Seljuk Iran, twelfth or early thirteenth century. Staatliche Museen, Berlin (after Otto-Dorn, K., *Kunst des Islam*, Baden-Baden 1964, p. 151).

Exceptions to this general statement are associated for the most part with royal or aristocratic patronage, the area most often termed 'fine art'. Rulers with unlimited financial resources frequently sought exotic products from abroad and occasionally imported foreign specialists to teach techniques to local artisans. A notable example of this was the importation of Chinese artworks and artisans during the Mongol and Tīmūrid periods to train Western Asian miniature painters in Chinese styles of design. The clouds, trees and rocks that feature prominently in manuscripts executed in Mongol Tabrīz or Tīmūrid Herāt clearly reflect Chinese origins (see Plates 12, 211). However, the fact that court tastes occasionally spurred dramatic changes in artistic or architectural styles does not contradict the essential localism and slow rate of absorbing lessons or styles from afar of most craft and manufacturing traditions during this period.

INVENTIONS AND THE DIFFUSION OF TECHNOLOGY

Reference has already been made to some of the most noteworthy instances of technological diffusion in this period: the compass, efficient equine harness, paper making, block printing, gunpowder, iron implements in Africa, and so on. These instances say little, however, about the nature of invention and the reasons for diffusion. Historians of technology have long struggled under the burden of European exceptionalism. The model of history presented at the outset of this essay culminates in Europe's creation of the modern industrial world, and that creation is commonly seen as a unique consequence of a much broader intellectual and philosophical evolution, to wit, the emergence of a rationalist, experimental view of the natural world. This exceptionalist schema is reinforced by the abundance of source material pertinent to the study of invention and technological change in Europe after the popularization of printing and the secularization of education from the fifteenth century onwards.

It is apparent, however, that invention was abundant, on a worldwide scale, during the period under consideration despite the general absence of the later European attitude towards reason and experimentation. Although the names of individual inventors and the stories of how they came by their insights are generally unknown, it is evident that technological development thrived in China during the Song and Yuan periods. Every aspect of technology, from mining and irrigation to armaments and shipbuilding, was subject to significant improvement, a detailed exposition of these improvements being available in Joseph Needham's multi-volume *Science and Civilization in China* (Needham, 1954). Likewise, the Islamic world brought forth innovations in chemistry, such as the process of distillation, and in astronomical instrumentation. The latter led to major steps forward in astronomical observation and conceptualization in the fourteenth and fifteenth centuries (Saliba, 1994).

From these instances and countless others in other societies it is apparent that looking at the natural world with curiosity and practicality is quite compatible with both theistic world views, like that of Islam, and non-theistic ones like that of Neo-Confucianism. No heritage of Aristotelian thought or banishment of other-worldly outlooks is necessary for a person to observe a process and think of how to improve it, or consider a need and devise a new way of meeting it. Invention is a universal human attribute.

Technological diffusion, on the other hand, varies considerably over time and space. The changing balance between more innovation-prone segments of a population and more conservative ones interested sociologist Vilfredo Pareto a century ago (Pareto, 1980), and studies of innovation diffusion based on this spectrum of psychological dispositions have been explored further by Everett Rogers and others (Rogers, 1962). These studies broadly conclude that people presented with opportunities for change weigh many factors in making their decisions: What benefit will come from the change? What costs will be incurred? How difficult will it be? Who else is doing it? Will family members and friends accept it? Does it contravene established laws or customs? Will I be considered peculiar or irreverent for doing it?

Economic historians like Robert Heilbroner stress the cost/benefit factor in adopting innovative techniques and see technological change as essentially random prior to the emergence of European capitalist economies in which financial rewards were directly based on competitive performance (Heilbroner, 1994). The technological historian David Landes, on the other hand, adduces ideological factors in attempting to explain why the mechanical clock originated and spread in Europe during this period (Landes, 1983). He suggests that Christian monks had to keep close track of time in order to maintain their prayer schedule, but he overlooks the equal, if not more pressing, exigency of prayer and fasting schedules in Muslim countries.

The factors governing the diffusion of technology in the military area are more clear-cut than elsewhere. New or improved weapons in the hands of one party repeatedly inspired efforts by the other party to copy, acquire or improve them. In this respect, the plethora of independent kingdoms and principalities in Europe afforded more arenas of military contention than in most other parts of the world, and military technology and architecture advanced there rapidly even though the Muslim world learned of the use of gunpowder somewhat earlier.

In non-military situations, the rate of diffusion could vary considerably. Paper making, for example, reportedly reached Samarkand from China in AD 751 but did not get to Nuremberg for another 640 years. Some technologies failed to spread altogether because of social barriers. Block printing, sometimes from moulded tin plates, is attested in Egypt and Iran as early as the ninth century and as late as the fourteenth (Bulliet, 1987). But widespread printing never developed during the intervening centuries. In the later Muslim society of the Ottoman Empire, opposition to printing was led by the religious authorities, who felt it would degrade their holy scripture (and possibly infringe on their scribal monopoly), but the earlier block prints, long forgotten by Ottoman times, were mostly amulets bearing verses from the Qur'ān (see Plate 116). In all likelihood, the failure of printing in the earlier Muslim world was connected to its close association with members of the fraternity of beggars who fobbed off printed amulets on illiterates, who thought they had been written by holy men. In other words, in this instance the barrier to diffusion related to social class rather than economic potential.

Looking at the period as a whole, places where local economic and social circumstances favoured the adoption of new techniques – most notably Song China, but also Islamic cities in the ninth–twelfth centuries and European city-states in the thirteenth–fifteenth centuries – are clearly discernible. But a selective diffusion of technology occurred in other regions as well, often along trade routes or in association with population movements. On balance, the pace of world technological change would appear to be substantially greater than during the preceding millennium, and among non-European peoples unquestionably greater than in the subsequent half millennium.

ORGANIZATION OF PRODUCTION

The organization of agricultural and manufacturing production varied according to the scale of activities, the complexity of operations, the constraints of the environment, and the local political and social structure, although the latter can also be viewed as a manifestation of the organization of production. Since the accumulation of wealth was more often the result of political coercion or religious devotion than of competitive commerce, efficiency of production was not of paramount importance. Nevertheless, slavery as a basis for agricultural production became less common over the period, presumably because of its inefficiency and expense. Agricultural slavery was common, for example, in seventh-century Tang China, but it was largely supplanted under the succeeding Song dynasty by serfdom, or personal bondage to a piece of land and/or to the owner/lord of the land. In the same way, serfdom replaced slavery in much of Europe after the fall of the Roman Empire.

Maintaining the productivity of the land and control of its surplus was the main concern of ruling elites. The Aztecs and Incas maintained their states by military threat and could thereby requisition tribute from subjugated peoples. Most Islamic states asserted taxation rights in return for protecting the local Muslim community from external threat and internal disorder. Taxes were initially assessed and collected by the elaborate revenue bureaucracy of the unified caliphate, but by the tenth century the tendency towards assigning tax-producing lands as usufruct grants (*iqṭā'*) to officials and military officers was well advanced. In Europe, secular lordship derived from service to royal authority, that authority having generally been asserted by force, most often by a Germanic tribe, during the latter days of the Roman Empire. In the resulting system, minor lords owed loyalty upwards through a chain of oaths reaching to a king or count, but they owed nothing to the serfs and free peasants living on their land. Ecclesiastical lords holding lands from the Pope (sometimes with confirmation by secular monarchs) did not allow their care of souls to conflict with their extraction of agricultural surplus. Monastic establishments, particularly the twelfth-century Cistercians, who believed in using lay brethren to work monastic lands, were somewhat more benevolent landlords.

The lot of most of the world's population, therefore, was agricultural toil under coerced or semi-coerced conditions. Production beyond the level of bare sustenance was regularly seized as tax, rent, dues or tribute. Pastoral nomads, even when subject to similar taxes or dues, generally led a freer life because of the difficulty of collecting from them; and hunters, gatherers and fishermen usually lived in self-contained communities that had only limited obligations towards their chiefs. The rewards of agricultural life being so meagre, the cultivator's incentive for change was generally low, and escape to the city, to banditry or to a life of wandering a recurrent temptation, at least for young men.

The burden of organizing production or improving it fell mostly on those who owned or held usufruct of the land and the agents who served them. In less monetized regions, where production was consumed mostly on the manor and only a small amount converted into durable goods or cash, innovation and improvements in efficiency produced only minor results and were seldom undertaken. The same is true of command systems, in which armed tax or tribute collectors from a distant court, capital or chieftain's camp appeared regularly to carry off any surplus. Monetization and the expansion of commercial opportunities, however, opened up possibilities for substantial increases in wealth for landlords who knew how to take advantage of them.

The growth of cities and expansion of inter-regional trade in Iran during the ninth and tenth centuries, for example, touched off a boom in cotton cultivation that vaulted the cotton merchants and cloth makers who bought the crop to the top of the merchant hierarchy. The simultaneous development of sugar cane as the primary export crop of Egypt bespeaks a similar response to the high degree of monetization and safe transportation network established by the caliphate and continued by most of its successor states after the ninth century.

In Song China, an increase in the supply of money and marked improvements in the road and canal networks fostered more and more inter-regional trade, and this, in turn, contributed to a boom in agricultural production and efficiency. New strains of rice, better field preparation, multiple cropping and innovative irrigation techniques all contributed to an agricultural revolution as the zone of rice cultivation was pushed ever further south. Printed treatises on agriculture confirm these developments and demonstrate yet another factor contributing to innovation and growth in production.

In contrast to Western Asia and China, European agriculture changed little during the early centuries of this period, when money was scarce, towns small and transportation difficult. The most significant changes – deep ploughing, improved horse harnesses and extensive clearing of new land – had their impact in the eleventh and twelfth centuries, when cities were beginning to flourish in Italy and Flanders and regional fairs were growing in importance.

With respect to the actual organization of labour in the fields, custom is often difficult to distinguish from deliberate plan. Iranian village lands watered by underground canals, for example, were divided among hereditary work teams called *boneh*, but surviving records provide no indication of when or how this system came into use. The Egyptian practice of redividing village lands among peasant cultivators every year after the Nile flood is of similarly indefinite antiquity.

Turning to the organization of non-agricultural production, the largest and most complex projects were public construction works. In China, and to a lesser extent Iraq, the government recruited and organized masses of labourers to dig canals. In Europe, cathedrals held pride of place as the grandest public enterprises. Many different types of labour were called for in the different stages of cathedral building: designers, quarrymen, stone cutters, scaffold builders, sculptors, glaziers, lead workers, record keepers, paymasters, and so forth. Seeing these massive projects to completion required forceful and persistent organization over long periods of time. The same holds true for the less well-documented construction of large religious edifices elsewhere: the ninth-century Buddhist temple of Borobudur in Java, the eleventh-century Hindu temples at Tanjore in southern India and Khajuraho in northern India, the twelfth-century Vaishnavite (Hindu) temple complex of Angkor Wat in Cambodia, the fourteenth- and fifteenth-century mosque and tomb complexes of Mamlūk Egypt and Mongol and Tīmūrid Iran and Central Asia, and the fourteenth-century pyramidal temples in the Aztec capital of Tenochtitlán. Only slightly less complex was the construction of defensive walls and fortifications. Sacsahuamán, the fifteenth-century Incan fortress outside Cuzco, Peru; Zimbabwe, the eleventh-century walled stone city from which the modern African country takes its name; the Great Wall of China, rebuilt in stone by the Ming rulers after the fourteenth century; and the magnificent castles of the crusading era, for example, the *Krak des Chevaliers* in Syria, Beaufort in Lebanon and the citadel of Cairo, testify to the existence of the capacity to organize grand building projects in almost every part of the world (see Plates 26–41, 221, 229, 307, 320, 321).

Shipyards and armouries were next in scale to massive building projects. In division of labour and volume of production, these were the most important non-agricultural industries, other than textiles, in most large states. Venice, for example, a fledgling city-state in AD 829, when two of its citizens purloined the relics of its patron Saint Mark from Alexandria, pursued a successful policy of commercial imperialism from the twelfth century onwards that enabled it to outstrip its city-state rivals Pisa and Genoa and become a major power in the eastern Mediterranean by 1500. The power of Venice was centred on its Arsenal, a fortified shipbuilding facility that, at its peak, employed 16,000 craftsmen, who could build a fighting galley in a single day. Similarly, much of Song China's iron production, the greatest in the world until the Industrial Revolution, went into armaments. And by the end of the period, cannon founding was a major enterprise in Europe, with handguns and shoulder guns just beginning their rise to eventual battlefield dominance. In both regions, major improvements in the design and construction of sailing ships led to the long-distance voyages of discovery in the fifteenth century and to an increase in the scale of naval combat (see Plates 21–25, 42–44).

In the realm of what would now be called consumer goods, textiles held pride of place as the largest and highest-value industry. But textile production ranged from home weaving for family consumption to large enterprises producing ornamented garments for officials (*ṭirāz*) in the Islamic caliphate or silk damask in Song China. One Chinese entrepreneur had 500 looms for weaving silk in his home (Elvin, 1973). Division of labour in textile production could similarly range from simple home spinning and weaving to complex operations requiring many steps. The production of silver thread in Iran, for example, started with obtaining small cylindrical ingots of silver from a furnace (Wulff, 1966). These were drawn into coarse wire, and then drawn again on a separate machine into fine wire. This wire was run through a roller device that flattened it into a fine ribbon of foil. Then a winding machine wound the foil around a thread and reeled it up. Only then could it be used for weaving or embroidery.

Crafts and trades practised in towns naturally led to feelings of affinity among practitioners. Guilds provided more or less organized expressions of this affinity in different regions. Guilds were economically important in tenth-century Byzantium and twelfth-century Flanders. In Islamic Western Asia, craft affinities, in evidence by the eleventh century, seem not to have developed fully into guilds, that is, into craft bodies that set standards and levels of production, until the fourteenth century. Muslim guild members often belonged to the same Ṣūfī organization – Ṣūfism then being dominated by brotherhoods devoted as much to camaraderie and religious orthopraxy as to mysticism – just as European guilds were often attached to specific Christian saints or sects. In India, occupational divisions were even more religiously and socially marked. Members of one of the many castes (*jātī*) usually engaged in the same craft or activity, and their occupational affinity was reinforced by traditions of endogamy and commensality and accompanying taboos.

THE ROLE OF TOWNS

Consumption of the agricultural surplus and of manufactured goods was concentrated in towns and cities, but the size, organization and function of these centres of population varied greatly. Cities not situated on navigable rivers or canals or near a seaport rarely grew larger than 100,000–200,000. Most were much smaller. The high cost of animal-drawn land transport – due primarily to the cost of feeding the animals, paying the teamsters or camel pullers, and laying out money for tolls or protection – made supplying food to a larger population very difficult, since the larger the population, the larger the radius of agricultural land needed to sustain it and the longer the transport route. On the other hand, ports accessible from the sea like Constantinople and Guangzhou, river cities like Baghdād and Cairo, and canal cities like Beijing and Yangzhou could grow much larger, in some cases to over a million (see Plates 241, 242).

Within a given geographical region, certain functions tended to be provided by the largest city, as the central place theory described above makes clear. Smaller cities and towns ranked downward both in size and in categories of function. A calculation of the percentage of a region's total population resident in its ten largest cities provides a rough comparative index of the degree of urbanization in different parts of the world (Russell, 1972). Although population figures for the period in question are scarce and often of questionable reliability or interpretation, it is apparent that the population of Europe was comparatively rural. In most areas no more than 10 per cent lived in the ten largest cities. Nevertheless, areas with easy access to the sea, such as Tuscany (largest city Florence), the Veneto (Venice) and Flanders (Ghent) were able to double this proportion once seaborne trade began to quicken in the twelfth century (see Plates 40, 41).

In the Islamic cities of Western Asia, North Africa and Spain, the level of urbanization was much higher. Cordova, Cairo, Baghdād, and Nīshāpūr were much larger than the cities of Europe. The proportion of the population living in the top ten cities of north-eastern Iran, the region centered on Nīshāpūr, approached that of the Veneto or Flanders even though there were no navigable waterways or seaports (Bulliet, 1994). Parts of China were even more heavily urbanized under the Southern Song dynasty. The city of Zhenjiang at the juncture of the Grand Canal and the Yangtze river, for example, housed 24 per cent of the people in its county at the beginning of the thirteenth century and 33 per cent by the century's end (Elvin, 1973). Overall, the more heavily settled parts of China seem to have had an urbanization rate of about 20 per cent.

The functions of towns and cities depended in part on their size and the degree of urbanization. The small cities and low urbanization rate of Europe corresponded to the rural locus of much of the landed nobility and of their wealth. Mostly rural monasteries and nunneries echoed this pattern in the ecclesiastical realm. Cities were generally too small, as both producing and consuming centres, to have a dramatic effect on the overall economy until the twelfth century with the rebirth of Mediterranean trade and the burgeoning of textile manufacture in Flanders. Even then, subsequent urban growth outside Italy, southern France and the Low Countries was often affected as much by royal residence and the growing power of monarchs *vis-à-vis* the nobility as by trade and manufacturing.

In Iran, by comparison, the Arab conquests of the seventh century shifted authority from the rural-based petty aristocracy of the Sāsānid Empire to the nodes of Muslim Arab governance in the small cities of the Iranian plateau (Bulliet, 1994). Wealth was drawn from the countryside into these governing nodes by taxation and sale of booty, and the process of conversion drew new Muslims to the nascent cities to share in the Islamic commonweal, escape local persecution or harassment by former co-religionists, and find a community in which a Muslim religious life could be fully realized. The result was an explosion of urban growth that saw some cities grow from under 10,000 in AD 700 to well over 100,000 by 950. This urban growth provided both the market and the financial basis for the growth in trade and manufacturing that became the hallmark of medieval Islamic society. With the exception of Baghdād and Cairo, the presence of a royal court was generally not the main spur to urban wealth and efflorescence.

Once cities anywhere crossed a certain threshold of size, prosperity and commercial activity, whether by virtue of government favour, possession of a holy pilgrimage site or advantageous location on a harbour, at a river crossing or athwart a trade route, their dynamism tended to draw wealth and population from the countryside. Since deaths seem generally to have been more numerous than births in the crowded and insanitary conditions of pre-modern cities, a constant trickle of migration from the countryside was needed simply to maintain size. Rapid urban growth required a major migration. In thirteenth-century Europe, general population growth resulting from technological innovations that improved the efficiency of agriculture provided the basis for such a migration. In Islamic Western Asia, sociological factors associated with conversion spurred migration without an accompanying boom in overall population. In China, improvements in agriculture, a sociological shift of elites from a rural nobility to a city-based scholar class, and general population growth, particularly in the south, all played a role in the greatest surge of urbanization of the period.

These differences from one cultural region to another were reflected in symbolic ways. European literature from the earlier part of the period focused on the exploits of knights and of a nobility that resided in castles surrounded by villages or small towns. Major building projects and art patronage similarly concentrated on rural monasteries and noble residences. By the fourteenth century, however, urban cathedrals, university-based scholarship and writings designed to please the bourgeoisie, such as those of Boccaccio and Chaucer (see Plate 103), reflected the new flourishing of cities. Yet the folk literature of the peasantry continued to feature ominous forests and rural wandering in search of fortune.

By contrast, in comparatively non-urbanized India, the epic *Rāmāyaṇa,* which relates the adventures of Rāma and his wife Sītā during their banishment in the forest, retained unchallenged popularity, just as the decidedly non-urban plays and poems of Kālidāsa, written somewhat before this period, retained their reputation as the most artistic literary works in Sanskrit. The appeal of these works, of course, does not imply an absence of urban life. Sanskrit was primarily the language of a largely urban elite. Rather, it suggests that Indian cities did not develop the allure and cultural self-consciousness found in Europe.

In Islamic Western Asia, the main genre of literature to gain popularity in the wake of the urbanization surge of the ninth–tenth centuries was the *maqāmāt*, a series of linked tales often named after the cities in which they took place (see Plate 184). Patronage of art and architecture, too, was almost entirely urban, except briefly under the Mongols and related dynasties that maintained peripatetic courts. Tīmūr (Tamerlane), one of the world's greatest conquerors, commanded armies composed mostly of pastoral nomads (see Plate 186), but he also sought fame as a city builder. Because of him and his family, Samarkand became a fabled city in the fifteenth century and retains to this day some of the most beautifully ornamented buildings in the world (see Plate 26).

Following Max Weber (Weber, 1992), many historians have expanded the notion of city as symbol to include the phenomenon of judicial autonomy, as established in the twelfth century and afterwards by royal charter or joint oath of the burghers in some European cities. Despite the fact that few cities maintained their autonomy for more than a couple of centuries, these historians have argued that autonomy should be part of the definition of a 'true' city. Through this symbolic definitional route, they have granted the twelfth- and thirteenth-century trading cities of Italy and Flanders a special place not only in the paradigmatic history of Western civilization but also in world history at large. By comparison, the urban agglomerations of Western Asia, India, China and elsewhere have sometimes been stripped of their title as cities and their historical role diminished.

Although no one would deny the importance of royal charters or common oaths in Europe as the means by which certain cities established their own jurisdiction between the competing claims of canon law, feudal law, and royal law, this welter of conflicting legal systems was unique to Europe. In the Islamic world, for example, there was a single religious law to which sultan, merchant and peasant all owed obedience (Bulliet, 1972). Yet this law was not administered by a centralized system of courts. Rulers possessed the authority to name judges in every city; but in practice, most judgeships were granted according to the nomination, or at least with the assent, of the local burghers (merchants, landowners and religious scholars), or even became hereditary in a local family. Since there was no appellate jurisdiction outside the local court, comparable to European appeals to Pope or king, most cities were functionally autonomous even without an oath or charter.

The European and the Islamic situations reflect particular historical conditions that should not be generalized to other parts of the world. In India, for example, villages rather than cities were autonomous, providing they paid their taxes. Cities arose as centres of population, marketing, industrial production, distribution, administration and religious devotion in many parts of the globe. Their growth and functions should be described and evaluated according to the legal, governmental, economic, demographic and cultural conjunctions appropriate to their individual cases rather than to a particular European model.

TRADE

Exchange has been assumed in all of the topics discussed thus far. At the most basic level, barter of goods and services is integral to the working of all non-monetized societies from the Amazon rain forest to the Arctic tundra, to the self-sufficient agricultural villages of Europe, China, Senegal or Malaysia. Barter arrangements can also rise to the level of trade, as is evidenced by long-distance exchanges of goods like obsidian and lapis lazuli dating back to prehistoric times. Trade usually involved a medium of exchange, however, some symbolic token of mutually accepted value. Metallic media of exchange that have no other use are usually termed coins. Non-metallic tokens serving the same function included cacao beans in Central America, cowrie shells in sub-Saharan Africa and South-East Asia, and strings of shell beads or *wampum* in eastern North America. Although some substances used as media of exchange were highly valued because of their alternative uses, as gold and silver were in many places for jewellery, this had nothing to do with their symbolic value in exchange.

In the early part of the period under examination, struck silver, gold or copper coins were the primary medium of exchange in Mediterranean Europe, Byzantium, northern India, and Islamic Western Asia, Central Asia and North Africa. In all these places, it was a joint heritage from the Hellenistic and Roman eras. Over time, coinage revived in outlying parts of the former Roman Europe, such as England and France, but was adopted more slowly in Northern and Eastern Europe. The Islamic coinage zone gradually stretched across India after 1000 and into coastal East Africa. China constituted a separate coinage zone utilizing cast copper coins in all areas and lead and iron coins in some.

The abundance of coins in a given area depended on sources of supply – mines, conversion of metal articles into coin, and import of coins from elsewhere – and their value, either as coins or as bullion, relative to their value in places with which trade was conducted. Regions whose exports were greatly in demand and which imported little tended to accumulate coinage, which could then be reminted or converted into treasure. India, which exported cotton cloth, spices and gems, appears to have had a favourable balance of trade throughout this period. Regions with an appetite for imports that exceeded their export capacity, such as Western Europe, which had little to sell on the international market but woollens, furs and amber but had a strong demand for spices, sugar and cotton cloth, found it difficult to maintain a large supply of high-value currency. The minting of coins was normally the prerogative of rulers, but once minted there were no effective controls on their circulation (see Plates 190–194).

The merchants who traded goods within and between regions realized substantial profits but also ran substantial risks. Shipwreck, banditry, warfare and piracy were ever-present dangers. In addition, the scarcity of information about supply and demand in distant locations could result in a merchant buying when prices were high in one place and being forced to sell on a glutted market elsewhere. Because of the high profit margins on long-distance trade, the presence of merchants in a city or country could add considerably to its wealth. The economic revival of Europe after the eleventh century is positively associated with the increasing role of merchants from southern France and Italy in Mediterranean trade and the diminishing role of the previously dominant Muslim traders. Some regimes, such as that of the Mongols, facilitated the activities of both local and foreign traders as a source of wealth for the state. Others, such as the Mamlūks in Egypt in the fourteenth and fifteenth centuries, discouraged trade by establishing state monopolies on some goods.

Few people had any understanding of why an economy grew or languished. Economic motives prompted wars and raids to seize land or booty, but by themselves these seldom produced prosperity or arrested economic decline. The Vikings, for example, raided the coastal communities of Northern Europe and Britain extensively, but the vast hoards of Iranian coins found in Scandinavia and on islands in the Baltic Sea indicate that peaceful trade was probably a greater source of wealth than booty. Similarly, the opening of regular caravan trade across the Sahara Desert by the eighth century city-states of Tāhert in Algeria and Sijilmāsa in Morocco made these places very wealthy because they were trading salt from the desert for gold dust from the Niger River region. Since African societies south of the Sahara did not use gold coins or objects, they did not initially ascribe high value to gold dust. Eventually, however, Tāhert and Sijilmāsa lost economic prominence and were abandoned. Their fall seems to have been related to changes in trade rather than military conquest.

The organization of local exchange was much more susceptible to regulation than was long-distance trade. Family or sectarian loyalty was a common feature of inter-regional trade, where confidential knowledge of the state of distant markets could mean the difference between profit and loss (Steensgaard, 1974). Jewish and Armenian merchants maintained correspondence and business partnerships over enormous distances. But within a city's market, trade was often overseen by government officials. The *eparch* in Constantinople and the *muḥtasib* in major Islamic cities had wide-ranging authority over prices, weights and measures, and market behaviour. In China, urban market areas were officially demarcated and closely regulated. Foreign merchants might be even more restricted. Arabs and Indians, for example, could trade only in specified seaports, as in the kingdom of Ghana, in the Sahel district of West Africa, Arab merchants from north of the Sahara resided in a separate district of the capital city.

Outside the cities, on the other hand, markets could not be as closely supervised. Weekly or monthly markets and seasonal fairs were important commercial intermediaries between city and countryside. The rotating system of fairs in twelfth- and thirteenth-century Champagne was famous throughout Europe and overseen by special officials, but most rural or periodic markets and fairs in various parts of Africa and Eurasia, including Song China, were less closely supervised. A still more casual mechanism of trade outside the city was that with passing caravans and itinerant pedlars. Caravans are normally thought of as a means of long-distance trade, but many caravan merchants exchanged trade goods for supplies at every stop along the route. Remote towns and villages depended on such occasional visits, and upon pedlars, for contact and trade with the outside world.

CONCLUSION: POPULATION MOVEMENTS AND CHANGE

A portrait of world technological regimes and economic systems over a period of nine centuries within the space here available can at best be a discontinuous series of snapshots. The intention of this chapter has been twofold: first, to sketch the immense variety of technological and economic situations extant in the world between AD 600 and 1500; and second, to show that the historiographical tradition of looking at world history from the vantage point of European history, assumed to be a model, is of little value. Song China was unquestionably the world economic and technological giant of the era. Urbanization and commerce in the Islamic world far outpaced Europe. Inter-regional contacts of great importance for the diffusion of plants and technologies long preceded the European voyages of discovery. And the capacity to innovate technologically and establish those innovations commercially was widespread and generally unrelated to ideological or religious superstructures.

To the degree that the pace of technological change and inter-regional contact can be argued, on balance, to have accelerated during these centuries, it seems more plausible to attribute the change to the greater degree of human movement and migration in comparison with the preceding centuries than to any particular political or ideological cause. Although the conquests of Alexander, the Roman Empire, and the Han Dynasty provided dramatic instances of politically based interregional interaction and exchange between 300 BC and AD 300, the expansive ethnic movements of the Arabs, the Turks, the Mongols, the Han Chinese (into southern China) and the Bantu had greater impact on technological and cultural exchange.

It is noteworthy that Western Europe remained isolated from most of these major population movements. The history of Europe will always be an important part of world history because of the developments that transpired from the sixteenth century onwards, but it will be better understood if historians place it in the context of the world as a whole.

BIBLIOGRAPHY

ADAMS, R. E. W. (ed.). 1977. *The Origins of Maya Civilization*. Albuquerque.

BALEE, W. 1994. *Footprints of the Forest: Ka'apor Ethnobotany – The Historical Ecology of Plant Utilization by an Amazonian People*. New York.

BARFIELD, T. 1989. *The Perilous Frontier: Nomadic Empires and China*. Oxford.

BULLIET, R. W. 1972. *The Patricians of Nishapur*. Cambridge, Mass.: Ch. 3.

——. 1975. *The Camel and the Wheel*, Cambridge, Mass.

——. 1981. Botr et Baranès: Hypothèses sur l'histoire des Berbères. In: *Annales: Economies, Sociétés, Civilisations*, Jan.–Feb. pp. 104–16.

——. 1987. Medieval Arabic *Tarsh*: a forgotten chapter in the history of printing. In: *Journal of the American Oriental Society*, 107/3, pp. 427–38.

——. 1994a. *Islam: The View from the Edge*. New York.

——. 1994b. Medieval Arabic *Tarsh*, *op. cit.* and Determinism and pre-industrial technology. In: SMITH, M. R.; MARX, L. (eds) *op. cit.* pp. 201–15.

CHRISTALLER, W. 1966. *Central Places in Southern Germany*, tr. Carlisle W. Baskin. Englewood Cliffs, New Jersey.

D'ALTROY, T. N. 1992. *Provincial Power in the Inka Empire*. Washington, DC.

DE PLANHOL, X. 1968. *Les fondements géographiques de l'histoire de l'Islam*. Paris.
DUBY, G. 1977. *L'économie rurale et la vie des campagnes dans l'Occident*. Paris.
——. 1988. *La société chevaleresque*. Paris.
DYER, C. 1989. *Standards of Living in the Later Middle Ages: Social Change in England c. 1200–1520*. Cambridge.
EL FASI, M.; HRBEK, I. 1988. *General History of Africa*, Vol. 3, *Africa from the Seventh to the Sixteenth Century*. London.
ELVIN, M. 1973. *The Pattern of the Chinese Past*. Stanford.
FORBES, R. J. 1964–66. *Studies in Ancient Technology*, six vols. Leiden.
GERNET, J. 1978. *La vie quotidienne en Chine à la veille de l'invasion mongole, 1250–1276*. Paris.
GOITEIN, S. D. 1967–83. *A Mediterranean Society: The Jewish Communities of the Arab World as Portrayed in the Documents of the Cairo Geniza*, five vols. Berkeley.
HATTOX, R. S. 1985. *Coffee and Coffeehouses: The Origin of a Social Beverage in the Medieval Near East*. Seattle.
HEILBRONER, R. L. 1994. Do Machines Make History? Technological Determinism Revisited. In: SMITH, M. R.; MARX, L. (eds) *Does Technology Drive History?* Cambridge, Mass.: pp. 53–78.
HUNTINGTON, E. 1907. *The Pulse of Asia*. Boston.
LAIOU-THOMADAKIS, A. E. 1977. *Peasant Society in the Late Byzantine Empire: A Social and Demographic Study*. Princeton.
LANDES, D. 1983. *Revolution in Time: Clocks and the Making of the Modern World*. Cambridge, Mass.
LATTIMORE, O. 1951. *The Inner Asian Frontiers of China*. New York.
MOKHTAR, G. 1981. *General History of Africa*, Vol. 2, *Ancient Civilizations of Africa*. London.
MOKYR, J. 1990. *The Lever of Riches: Technological Creativity and Economic Progress*. New York.
MUMFORD, L. 1961. *The City in History*. Harmondsworth.
NEEDHAM, J.; WANG, L. *et al*. 1954. *Science and Civilization in China*, 6 Vol., Cambridge.
NETTING, R. MC. C. 1977. Maya Subsistence: Mythologies, Analogies, Possibilities. In: ADAMS, R. E. W. (ed.) *The Origins of Maya Civilization*. Albuquerque: pp. 299–333.
PARETO, A. 1980. *Compendium of General Sociology*, Minneapolis.
RABIE, H. M. 1972. *The Financial System of Egypt AH 564–741*/AD *1169–1341*. London.
RICHÉ, P. 1973. *La vie quotidienne dans l'Empire Carolingien*. Paris.
RODINSON, M. 1966. *Islam et Capitalisme*.
ROGERS, E. 1962. *Diffusion of Innovations*. New York.
RUSSELL, J. C. 1972. *Medieval Cities and their Regions*. Bloomington.
SALIBA, G. 1994. *A History of Arabic Astronomy: Planetary Theories during the Golden Age of Islam*. New York.
SAUER, C. 1972. *Seeds, Spades, Hearths, and Herds: The Domestication of Animals and Foodstuffs*. Cambridge, Mass.
SJOBERG, G. 1960. *The Preindustrial City: Past and Present*. New York.
STEENSGAARD, N. 1974. *The Asian Trade Revolution of the Seventeenth Century: The East India Companies and the Decline of the Caravan Trade*. Chicago.
THAPAR, R. 1966. *A History of India*, Vol. 1. Harmondsworth.
TRACY, J. D. (ed.) 1990. *The Rise of Merchant Empires: Long-distance Trade in the Early Modern World, 1350–1750*. Cambridge: pp. 372–379.
WATSON, A. M. 1983. *Agricultural Innovation in the Early Islamic World: The Diffusion of Crops and Farming Techniques*. Cambridge.
WEBER, M. 1962. *The City*, tr. New York.
WIET, G. 1960. *L'évolution des techniques dans le monde musulman medieval*. In: *Cahiers d'histoire mondiale*, Vol. VI–I, UNESCO.
WHITE, L. JR. 1962. *Medieval Technology and Social Change*. Oxford.
WULFF, H. 1966. *The Traditional Crafts of Persia: Their Development, Technology, and Influence on Eastern and Western Civilizations*. Cambridge, Mass.

5

COMMUNICATION AND TRANSPORT

Richard W. Bulliet

The century beginning in AD 600 witnessed two episodes of extraordinary political expansion, that of the Arab Muslim caliphate centred in Western Asia, with successive capitals at Medina in Arabia, Damascus in Syria and Baghdād in Iraq; and that of the Tang Dynasty in China. By 711, Arab armies, with assistance in the most distant reaches from North African Berbers and Persian-speaking Central Asians, carried their conquest to Spain and southern France in the west to Central Asia's Tarim Basin in the east. Their northern frontier, however, stabilized at the Taurus Mountains in Turkey and their southern frontier near the Egyptian–Sudanese border and along the northern oases of the Sahara Desert. These latter frontiers were not significantly penetrated, at least politically, until the twelfth century. At the other end of Asia, the Tang Dynasty took control of large portions of Korea, Manchuria, Mongolia, Tibet and Turkestan; and Tang culture deeply influenced Japan. At one point, these two expansive forces actually collided in a battle between Arabs and Chinese on the Talas River in Kyrgyzstan in AD 751.

The other end of the time period to be covered by this essay is also marked by an epochal event, the arrival of Christopher Columbus in the West Indies. Vasco da Gama's voyage around Africa five years later brought the Europeans into the Indian Ocean, and the return of Magellan's fleet to Spain in 1522 completed the circumglobal linkage of lands that is presumed in all later history.

Both types of expansion, Arab and Chinese primarily by land and European by sea, depended upon, and at the same time altered, world communications and transport. By bringing into contact peoples who had previously known little of one another, they stimulated profoundly influential exchanges of manufactured goods, natural products and ideas. Not only did greatly increased numbers of people engage in long-distance travel, but the aggregate world economy surged forward, in part because of an expanded international flow of goods.

However, the maritime adventures of the Europeans at the end of the period never would have been attempted had it not been for overland travel. The establishment by the Mongols in the thirteenth century of a single empire stretching from China to Eastern Europe repeated, though only for about a century, the continent-spanning achievements of the Muslim Arabs and Tang Chinese. Once again, products, ideas and knowledge of other peoples were exchanged freely over vast areas. But whereas the Europeans had largely been isolated from those earlier episodes of world interconnection, this time people like Marco Polo travelled all the way to China and came back to inform Europeans about the vastness of Asia and the high level of its civilizations.

Meanwhile, on the African continent, the Saharan caravan trade, which brought great quantities of gold from sub-Saharan Africa to Morocco, made the rulers of Spain and Portugal aware of a distant source of wealth that their perennial Muslim enemies had sole access to. Outflanking Islam and finding the source of the African gold thus became an important goal in their launching of the voyages that brought Europe into direct contact with the rest of the world.

However, transport and communication during these centuries, despite their great importance, have seldom been viewed as subjects of special historical interest. After all, the great mass of continental people everywhere lived comparatively parochial lives, dependent for their sustenance upon their fields, flocks or fisheries and seldom venturing far from their villages or accustomed pastures. For them, transport was mostly local, and more often than not pedestrian.

An illustration may be taken from eleventh-century Iran, where the pack camel was the standard means of heavy transport. The landlocked city of Nīshāpūr had approximately 150,000 non-farming inhabitants in AD 1000. The primary mode of heavy transport in the region was by camel, each load weighing approximately 225 kg. If, therefore, each of these people had to be provisioned with 1 kg of staple grain per day, no fewer than 600 laden camels or equivalent pack animals per day had to make their way into the city, be unloaded and their burdens distributed by donkey or human porters to mills, bakeries, stables and homes. In order to account for other necessities of life – such things as grain and straw for animals, other agricultural produce, firewood and sun-dried bricks – this number should be at least doubled, yielding a total of 1,200 laden camels, or their equivalent, entering the city daily. This number is vastly higher than any plausible estimate of long-distance caravan traffic passing through Nīshāpūr on a daily basis.

From this perspective, it is apparent that most transport, everywhere, was local. This must be kept in mind even though much of this chapter will be concerned with long-distance travel and transport. Contacts between parts of the world did, indeed, increase significantly between 600 and 1492; and the lives of millions were affected by the increase. But most of this effect was indirect. Most of the world's people stayed close to home, both physically and mentally.

LAND TRANSPORT

William McNeill has observed that heavy transport in the medieval and pre-modern world may be classified into three broad technological zones, characterized by camels, carts and canals, respectively (McNeil; 1987). Although pack animals were used extensively in all three zones, the Middle East and North Africa were particularly characterized by this form of transport.

By contrast, carts and wagons, and in later time periods roads to facilitate them, developed most extensively in Europe. Carts were also used in India, China, Central Asia and Japan. The hypothesis that all of these wheeled societies received their impetus from a common point of origin of wheeled transport in Europe or the Middle East belongs to an earlier period (Piggott, 1983; Littauer and Crouwel, 1979). In any case, the hypothesized early connections did not persist, and India and China developed their own characteristics.

A general need in wheeled societies that also developed differently in different regions was for bridges. Bridge design varied considerably according to the materials available and the nature of the river to be crossed. The great city of Baghdād on the Tigris River, for example, was served only by pontoon bridges because of the river's unpredictable and often devastating spring flooding. In the Andes, where wheeled transport was unknown, suspension bridges built under the Inca stretched as much as 60 metres across gorges (see Figure 5). China, India, Europe and the Islamic Middle East all had distinctive bridging traditions (see Plates 30, 31, 40, 241, 242).

Canals, in later centuries to have a major impact on Europe, were during this period a distinctive feature of transport in China. They will be discussed below in the section on inland waterways.

Figure 5 A royal official, a suspension bridge and human porterage in pre-Hispanic Peru. Redrawn from Felipe Guamán Poma de Ayala (after Hagen, V. W. von, *Realm of the Incas*, NY 1957, p. 169).

A fourth zone, which McNeill does not mention, should be added to these three. That is the zone of human portage. In the pre-Columbian Americas, none of the domestic animals, except the llamas of the Andes, were suited to carrying loads; and even the llamas were not very strong. Likewise, extensive regions of sub-Saharan Africa were infested by tsetse flies, which preyed lethally on the animals – cattle, camels and to a lesser degree horses – used for transportation along the Sudan belt between the tsetse region and the desert. In both regions, human labour was the only alternative. Unfortunately, for the period under investigation, little detailed information is available on transport by porter, and it will therefore not be specifically discussed.

The Middle East, Central Asia, North Africa and the Sahara Desert

The camel zone came into being through the abandonment of wheeled transport during the centuries immediately prior to the period under consideration. Middle Eastern and North African society are unique historically in turning away from this proverbial triumph of human ingenuity during a period that was otherwise comparatively prosperous and peaceful, namely, that of the late Roman and Sasanid empires. This apparent technological devolution is all the more surprising in view of the likelihood that the Middle East, if not the birthplace of wheeled transport, was at least a region in which major technical improvements are attested during ancient times.

The deterioration of Roman roads was probably more an effect of the abandonment of wheels, since camels prefer softer surfaces, than a cause. The absence of a technical vocabulary for cart and wheel manufacture, in both Arabic and the New Persian that came to be written in Arabic script, reinforced by the extreme rarity of references to wheeled vehicles in Islamic texts, all but proves that the disappearance of the wheel was largely complete prior to the Arab conquests of the seventh century (Bulliet, 1975: Chs 1, 3–4).

It is beyond the chronological limits of this chapter to develop at length the hypothesis that the abandonment of the wheel resulted from the intrinsic economy of exploiting the low cost of desert-bred camels rather than oxen or mules, and from a deliberate, if only fragmentarily attested, determination by Arab camel breeders to sell, rent or personally use their animals in all aspects of heavy and long-distance transport, and to suppress competition by rival carters. This hypothesis must be mentioned, however, because the consequences of the Arabs' gradual assumption of primacy in the transport economy of the Middle East during the pre-Islamic centuries set the stage for the later conquests and for the great efflorescence of trade and travel that followed them. The caliphate established by Muḥammad's followers not only exercised political dominion from Portugal to the Indus River but also, from the very outset, in keeping with the developing Arab penchant for travel, fostered extensive interconnections between its far-flung provinces.

The technology of animal transport in the Islamic world before the twelfth century was comparatively uniform. Pack saddles for camels and donkeys were inexpensive and efficient. Camel saddles in particular preserved the mark of their Arabian origin from Morocco to Afghanistan. Only in Central Asia did the Arabian influence meet a limit (Bulliet, 1975: Ch. 5). One-humped Arabian camels rapidly displaced the indigenous two-humped camels of Iran, possibly before the rise of Islam, but the cold winters of Central Asia constituted an insurmountable barrier. Loads that were carried along the Silk Road from Mesopotamia to the Oxus River by one-humped camels were reloaded in the commercial cities of Transoxania onto two-humped camels for the rest of the journey across the Tarim basin and then south-east through Gansu to northern China. The saddles of the two-humped camels were entirely different from the Arabian saddles and derived from an independent technological tradition.

The disappearance of wheeled vehicles and the rise of camel transport affected economic and social life in a number of ways (Bulliet, 1975: Ch. 8). Roads were typically beaten tracks rather than smoothed or paved surfaces. Certain barriers that elsewhere inhibited wheeled traffic, such as defiles, steep grades, trees and large rocks, could readily be bypassed or negotiated single file. No village was beyond the reach of the pack animal. Rivers, on the other hand, though infrequently encountered in the arid zone, were as troublesome for pack animals as for wagons. Hence it is not surprising that building bridges, as well as caravanserais for overnight stops between towns, was a common sign of strong government (see Plates 13, 184, 241, 242).

One specific industry came into being to service the Central Asian caravan trade and in early modern times disappeared almost without a trace. This was the breeding of hybrid camels born of a cross between one-humped and two-humped parents (Bulliet, 1975: Ch. 5). The hybrid, called a *bukht* in Arabic, was unusually large and strong, stood up reasonably well to cold weather and carried more than the average load. Since the offspring of two *bukhts* was a weakling, fresh breeding had to be done for every generation, just as it did for sterile mules.

Caravan routes typically passed through or skirted deserts. Major trajectories, in addition to the Silk Road across Central Asia and northern Iran were those paralleling the Euphrates and Tigris Rivers in Mesopotamia; the pilgrimage routes in Arabia, east and west from the Euphrates to Mecca, and north and south along the mountains of Hijaz province from Syria to Yemen; the Nile route, with a southern offshoot that struck off across the desert around Aswan to reach the Sudan belt of sub-Saharan Africa; and a route across the high plain of North Africa from Tunisia to Morocco.

Routes across the Sahara present a special problem. Scholars disagree strongly on the subject of Saharan trade. Although some historians, relying on textual evidence, retain the view that camels were not introduced into the Sahara until Roman imperial times, and then from the north, technological evidence suggests that the camel actually spread into the Sahara earlier than that along the desert's southern edge and central highlands and massifs (Bulliet, 1975: Ch. 4). Although the pack saddles found in the Sahara are south Arabian in design, the riding saddles of the Sahara are diverse, remarkably efficient and unparalleled elsewhere. In particular, they are never used by tribes in the northern parts of the Sahara. Although in all likelihood they derive technologically from the north Arabian saddle, these Saharan riding saddles, which are useless for pack work, must have undergone a long period of development in isolation from other saddling traditions and from the need felt elsewhere to build saddles that could be used either for cargo or for riding. This condition is best fulfilled by assuming a non-trade oriented dissemination of camels in the southern Sahara followed by a gradual percolation northward.

Following this hypothesis, it seems likely that significant trans-Saharan trade developed only in Islamic times, notably after the rebellions against the central rule of the caliphate beginning in AD 740. The new trade routes were concentrated first in the west (Morocco, Mauritania, Mali), away from the remaining outpost of the caliphate in Tunisia, but after the suppression of minor North African states by the Fāṭimids in the early tenth century, central routes from the northern bend of the Niger to Tunisia and Tripolitania acquired greater prominence. While all of these routes were probably pioneered by merchants from the north who were in touch with the market for gold dust, slaves, and other sub-Saharan products, the role of the peoples of the southern Sahara, particularly in developing the several step exchange of south Saharan salt for Senegalese and Nigerian gold dust, which, given the fact that the need for salt is not bounded by time, probably antedated the opening of the trans-Saharan routes, remains to be investigated (see Plate 259).

Since all products were carried by pack animal, singling out particular items would unduly skew a portrayal of land transport as a whole. Suffice it to say that long caravan journeys favoured high-value, low-bulk products such as precious metals, spices, fine cloth and *objets d'art*. Yet most caravans traded as they went, purchasing provisions in the towns they passed through. This was less true for the winter caravans across the desolate Tarim basin, or caravans across the sparsely populated Arabian and Saharan Deserts. However, despite the popular image of the desert caravan, most long-distance trade went through populated agricultural lands with comparatively brief stages of desert transit. The role of the long-distance caravan in maintaining regular commercial contact and spreading news between intermediate points on the route, large and small, is important to any understanding of the transport system.

The cost of overland pack transport is assumed to have been quite high, but pertinent data are scarce. In any case, the lack of inland water transport, the barren hinterlands of most seaports, which prevented them serving large regions, and the absence of wheeled vehicles eliminated much potential price competition. While it is apparent that goods from afar commanded much higher prices than they brought at their sources, a good part of the mark-up does not derive from the cost of transport *per se*. Given the slow pace of a camel caravan, normally 20 miles per day, long-distance traders had to wait months, if not years, for delivery of the goods they had invested their capital to procure, or the proceeds earned by their travelling partners. The price they eventually sold them for, therefore, included not just the cost of transport (animals, personnel, provisions, protection money, breakage and pilferage, and so on) but also the opportunity cost represented by shorter-term or less risky investments bypassed by the merchant in hopes of making a larger profit.

Europe

The period under consideration began at the low point of European economic decline accompanying and following the fall of the Roman Empire in the west, and there was little improvement over the next four centuries. Roman cities had contracted into small towns. Money had largely fallen out of use. Agriculture centred more on subsistence, and the delivery of goods to local lords, than upon market trade. Tiny polities, linguistic differentiation, and bondage of the tiller to the soil or to his lord militated against extensive travel. In addition, much of Europe was heavily forested and scored with rivers. Few of the high-quality roads that the

Romans had built for imperial communications and military movement, usually by foot, were still in use (Forbes, 1965: pp. 161–164).

Yet Europe inherited a long tradition of wheeled transport. Although the earliest datable depictions of wheeled vehicles come from the Middle East, archaeological finds of wheels and carts in Northern Europe and the plains of Eastern Europe point to the use of sophisticated and innovative wheeled vehicles, not obviously derived from Middle Eastern models, well back into the prehistoric period (Piggot, 1983). This transport tradition appears to be related more to social status than to trade. Prehistoric rock engravings of schematized carts and yoked animals, always unladen, are found from Scandinavia to the Pamir and Tian Shan mountains of Central Asia, and many vehicles have been found buried in the graves of the elite.

Moreover, Europe inherited from classical antiquity a quasi-religious regard for wheeled vehicles. The chariot race in commemoration of the death of Patroklos in the Iliad is the earliest description of a racing tradition that continues through Roman times, taking on particular importance in the Byzantine East. The fact that the pagan gods of classical antiquity customarily rode in chariots should not be disregarded. Just as in early Rome a chariot, though no longer militarily functional, was the vehicle in which a triumphant general paraded through the streets painted red to look like the statue of Jupiter on the Capitoline Hill, Germanic tradition obliged the Merovingian kings of eighth-century France to use a wagon drawn by oxen whenever they wished to travel. Anything else was beneath their royal dignity (Haupt, 1986: p. 189).

Thus medieval Europe inherited a cultural fixation upon wheeled vehicles but little economic incentive to develop them. Nevertheless, the terms used in medieval Latin texts – *biga*, *carpentum*, *carrus*, *esseda*, *vehiculum* and so on – preserve an archaic Roman vocabulary that indicates little more than that a vehicle had two or four wheels and hence may possibly conceal technological innovations (Haupt, 1986: pp. 194–195).

Carts were almost certainly the most common vehicles, but carts were better for passenger use than for heavy hauling. Balancing a heavy or bulky load – stones for cathedral building, for example – directly over a cart's axle was difficult, but failure to do so could make the burden difficult for the draft team to manage. A four-wheeled wagon was much more sensible for such heavy hauling, but turning a wagon was difficult. Unless its front axle pivoted at the centre, a wagon had to follow an enormous arc in turning. But the front axle could only be pivoted if some way were found to prevent the large wheels from hitting the body of the wagon as they turned. Different solutions had different drawbacks. Raising the body of the wagon entirely above the wheels risked making it top-heavy and unstable. Narrowing the body but keeping the axle as wide as the roads permitted reduced the cargo space. Making the wheels smaller so they fitted under the body put greater strain on the wheels, particularly on rough surfaces (see Plates 7, 8).

Many forms of steerable front axle were eventually adopted in one region or another, but the chronology and locus of innovation are obscure (Haupt, 1986: pp. 191–4). Urban street patterns that lack large turn-around areas would suggest that steerable front axles were in use by, perhaps, the beginning of the thirteenth century; but the first explicit depiction of such an arrangement comes from a fourteenth-century military manual.

Associated with the problem of steering was the question of how the body of the wagon related to the wheeled chassis. Building the body as a separate structure may have facilitated thinking about how to turn the wheels, but it also stimulated ideas about how to make the ride more comfortable (Wackernagel, 1986: pp. 197–205). One idea was the wagon body with arches and a fabric or solid roof to protect the passengers from the elements. Another set wagon developers on the path that eventually led to the invention of the wagon spring.

Whether paved with cobbles, as came to be common with the expansion of cities from the twelfth century on; surfaced with stone, as was the case with some of the surviving Roman roads; or simply levelled surfaces of dirt, sand and rubble, the roads caused great discomfort to riders in springless carts and wagons. As early as 1000, there is evidence of wagons that suspended a riding hammock or chair from iron hooks attached to raised posts at front and rear. This could not have been very practical for just one person, but by the end of the period under consideration the idea had formed of suspending the entire enclosed body from hooks so that it could swing freely above the bouncing wheels. It was from this that the idea of springs later developed.

It might be noted that comparatively little study has been made of the wheeled vehicles of Southern Europe. Although it might be presumed that developments there kept company with those in Northern and Eastern Europe, some evidence indicates a different tradition in the all-important area of harnessing. In 1962, Lynn White Jr published an influential book highlighting, among other technological innovations, the adoption of horse-collar and breast-strap harnessing as a key element in Europe's recovery of economic vitality (White, 1962).[1] The throat-and-girth strap harnesses of classical antiquity presumed that every vehicle had to be drawn by two animals yoked together. Since horses held their heads higher than oxen and had no anchor point on their backs analogous to the protruding thoracic vertebrae of bovine animals, the only way to attach the yoke was to tie it around the horse's neck and chest (see Plates 6, 7, 8). This procedure situated the point of traction mostly on the horse's neck muscles, rather than on its skeleton, and thereby made strangulation rather than strength the limiting factor in determining how much force could be exerted. The new harnesses (see Figure 6), predicated upon shafts or traces

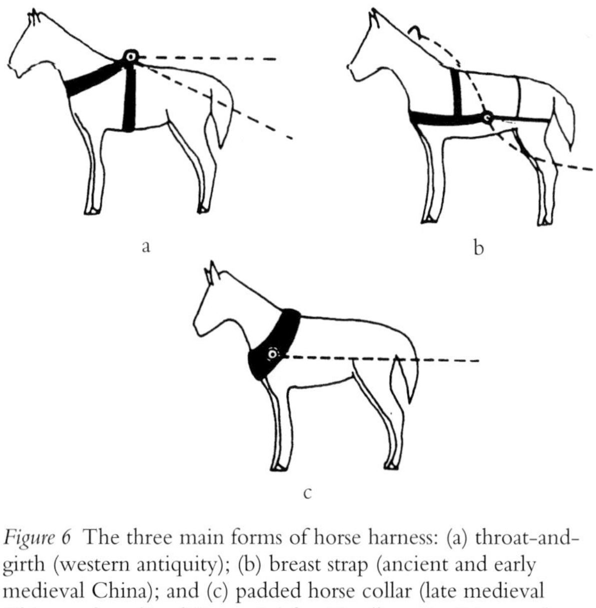

Figure 6 The three main forms of horse harness: (a) throat-and-girth (western antiquity); (b) breast strap (ancient and early medieval China); and (c) padded horse collar (late medieval China and medieval Europe) (after Needham, J., *Science and Civilization in China*, Cambridge 1952).

extending from the vehicle along either side of each horse, shifted the point of traction to the animal's shoulders (horse collar) or breast (breast strap), thus permitting it to use all of its strength for pulling. White argued that these new harnesses, first attested in the eighth century, permitted faster ploughing, ploughing of heavier soils and pulling of heavier loads.

White's thesis raised the question of where the new harnesses came from and exactly when they were developed. He and others argued, partly linguistically, for a Merovingian-period diffusion across Central Asia from China, where efficient single-animal harnessing appeared much earlier (Haudricourt, 1948: p. 61; Needham and Ling, 1965: pp. 243–53, 303–28). However, efficient harnessing of both the breast-strap and horse-collar type is attested as an independent development in Roman Tunisia and Tripolitania. Ploughs drawn by efficiently harnessed single camels (and perhaps horses) and single horses harnessed to carts by horse collars are depicted on North African bas reliefs and lamps of the third and fourth centuries BC, and there is a textual reference to a camel-drawn cart (Bulliet, 1975, pp. 192–202; Deneauve, 1986: p. 152, figs 12–13). Moreover, the same technology survives to the present day in the oases of southern Tunisia and on the Cap Bon peninsula.

The question of whether efficient harnessing may have diffused northwards into Southern Europe in late Roman times arises from linguistic considerations (Bulliet, 1975: pp. 202–08). Spanish, Portuguese, Italian, Maltese and the current Arabic speech of the rather isolated oases of southern Tunisia have key harnessing terms, words for breast strap and whipple-tree, seemingly derived from a common Roman origin. French and Provençal, on the other hand, have distinctly different terms. While it is possible that refugees from the Christian reconquest of Andalusia brought these crucial terms to southern Tunisia, it is difficult to explain in this way why *kirrita* (= Latin *carretta*), for example, is only used in the Arabic of the oases and not in other parts of Tunisia. It is more plausible to assume continuous use in this area, but this would imply a common harnessing zone of late Roman origin linking Tunisia and Tripolitania with the northern Mediterranean littoral. And this, in turn, would imply an earlier knowledge, and different source, of efficient harnessing in Europe, possibly including diffusion to Northern Europe during the Merovingian period.

It is apparent from the foregoing discussion that issues surrounding the adoption and impact of efficient harnessing in Europe between AD 600 and 1492 remain unresolved. But from the point of view of transport *per se*, as opposed to ploughing, it is questionable whether better harnessing would have made much difference during the early centuries of this period, when cities were still small, roads unimproved and volume of trade low. Under these circumstances, it is perhaps understandable that improvements are more evident in passenger than in freight vehicles.

Land routes in Europe during the period under consideration cannot be summarized simply. The network of Roman roads, many still passable, linked major points in some regions, but freight volume was low, one estimate indicating 1,000 tonnes per year towards the end of the period (Forbes, 1965). Pilgrimage routes, however, including several across France to Santiago de Compostela and north-west Spain, and those converging on Rome and Constantinople, were very popular. Overall, the image of a mixed traffic of horse riders, pedestrians with packs or wheelbarrows, and wheeled vehicles, more often than not travelling in groups and stopping at rudimentary inns after a day's travel of 30–50 km, seems appropriate to most regions in Western Europe. Further to the east, such an important route as the long trek from the Baltic Sea to the Islamic lands around the Caspian Sea is well attested archaeologically, but little is known about the traders or modes of conveyance.

CHINA AND INDIA

Just as the abundant evidence of the Roman period obscures European transport developments over the following centuries, so discussions of land transport in China and India tend to focus on earlier periods. Carts were in use in China as early as the fourteenth century BC. Early ideograms, grave finds and depictions show them to be very similar to the contemporary carts of Central Asia, Europe, and the Middle East (von Dewall, 1986: pp. 168–86; Needham and Ling, 1965). Two to four horses are shown harnessed by means of a yoke to a vehicle with spoked wheels. Given this similarity, and the absence of earlier finds or indications of solid or composite wheels, it is generally assumed that the Chinese adopted the cart from Central Asia.

By the beginning of the Han Dynasty in the third century BC, however, a major change had taken place in harnessing technology. The central tongue and yoke attested earlier had been replaced by a pair of shafts extending from the cart along each side of a single horse and rising to an arched juncture across the animal's back. Traction was provided by a breast strap attached to the shafts. Thus the invention of efficient harnessing in China occurred several centuries before the similar developments discussed in the previous section took place in Europe and North Africa.

From that time on, comparatively little technological change took place in Chinese vehicles down to the nineteenth century. Perhaps because of the early development of efficient single-animal harnessing, the Chinese consistently preferred carts to wagons and thus avoided the problems and challenges represented by four-wheeled wagons drawn by multi-animal teams. Since such important developments as springs, pivoting axles, brakes, and complex harnesses stemmed more from wagon use than cart use (as did road improvements to accommodate very heavy loads), it might be concluded that China early on entered a state of equilibrium in wheeled transport that precluded further change. An exception to this generalization lies in the area of wheelbarrows. Although the chronology is insecure, China developed a sophisticated array of wheelbarrow designs (see Plates 9a, 9b). Interestingly, there seem to be no connections between Chinese wheelbarrows and the less developed European wheelbarrows, and wheelbarrow use seems to be unknown elsewhere in the world, including in Central Asia.

The Silk Road from Beijing through Gansu and Xinjang (the Tarim basin) affords a comparison of transport by cart and by pack camel. Carts, sometimes drawn by camels, commonly carried passengers along the parts of the route under Chinese control, and some Central Asian pastoralists transported their *yūrts* (see Plate 185)– felt huts – on wheeled vehicles; but heavy loads were normally carried all the way to Beijing by two-humped pack camel. The importance of this route and its valuable commodities is testified to in the early centuries of the period under discussion (Tang Dynasty – seventh–tenth centuries) by an abundance of glazed and unglazed pottery figurines of laden camels found in graves (Bulliet, 1975: pp. 161–70, pp. 209–13; Häusler, 1986: pp. 139–52). It seems apparent that as in the Middle East and North Africa, pack camels were more efficient than carts for heavy loads, but without easy access to the desert herding areas found in the arid zone, most of China was too distant (and much of it too warm) to make economic use of the Mongolian-bred animals (see Plate 13).

In any case, heavy hauling in the broad Chinese flood plains focused upon canals rather than roads, as will be discussed below. Transport routes concentrated on moving goods to and from these canals, and to and from the busy seaports of China's coastal trade.

In India, wheeled vehicles are attested as early as the third millennium BC in the form of model oxcarts from the Indus valley civilization. During the Vedic period of the second millennium, when the literary evidence of the Vedas tells more about the recently arrived speakers of Indo-European tongues than about the pre-existing population, lighter vehicles make an appearance, particularly in the form of war chariots. All of these vehicles, whether drawn by zebu bullocks or horses, featured paired animals with a yoke harness (Gail, 1986: pp. 153–67). The main change apparent in depictions of Indian bullock carts at the beginning of the period under consideration and at its close is a type of half-spring suspension system, not found in other regions, that continues to be used in modern times. Exactly when this improvement in riding comfort developed is uncertain. Pack oxen were also used for grain transport in pre-modern times.

Efficient harnessing of horses never became necessary, because horses were always scarce in India and monopolized by the military. Chariots were gradually abandoned as cavalry rendered them militarily obsolete. Many later manuscript illustrations of war scenes from the epic *Mahābhārata*, part of which, the *Bhavagad Gītā*, portrays the god Krishna in the guise of a chariot driver, indicate that the artists had no idea of what a chariot actually may have looked like.

Another Indian transport development, datable to the period after 1000, is the introduction of the one-humped camel (Bulliet, 1975: pp. 153–56; 188–90). A twelfth-century frieze from Mandor in the north-west depicts both baggage camels and a camel-drawn cart.[2] Two-humped camels were probably indigenous to Afghanistan and familiar in the north-west as pack, riding and cart animals. But the one-humped camels of the Baluch, who migrated around the turn of the millennium to what is now southern Afghanistan and Pakistan, provided competition for their two-humped cousins. Two-humped camel transport gradually disappeared, and one-humped camels, which are better adapted to heat, became common as pack animals throughout northern India. Camel carts remain today a competitive form of freight hauling in parts of Pakistan and India.

The major routes of western India connected the valley of the Indus with Afghanistan and eventually the Silk Road through the Kabul valley in the north, and with Iran by way of Qandahār in the south (Schwartzberg, 1978: plates III.C.5a, III.D.4, IV.3e.). From the Punjab, or upper Indus valley, a major route went eastwards, skirting the extensive Thar Desert, to connect with the Doab, the combined valley of the Ganges and the Jumna. Routes then roughly paralleled those rivers all the way to the Bay of Bengal. Another route, skirting south of the desert, connected the Indus valley with Gujarat and the western edge of the Deccan peninsula. The escarpment of the Western Ghats behind the coastal plain made east–west transport in the Deccan difficult, however. The main routes to interior Deccan and to ports on the east coast came southwards from the Doab.

Little can be said about the mix of traffic and goods on these routes during this period. Divided, like Europe, into numerous smaller states, and challenged from outside first by Arab Muslim occupiers of the lower Indus valley in the eighth century, and more cataclysmically by Turco-Iranian invaders from Afghanistan after 1000, India went through a complex and turbulent period in its political history. Yet the routes to the Islamic lands to the northwest particularly prospered after the establishment of the Muslim Delhi Sultanate in northern India after 1200.

SEA TRANSPORT

The half century or so of Portuguese and Spanish seafaring that brought Europe into contact with the rest of the world reached a first climax with Christopher Columbus' arrival in the New World in 1492 and Vasco da Gama's landfall in India in 1498. The former date is also the end of the period under consideration because it symbolizes a turning point in world history when Europe ended its millennium of post-Roman isolation and began to interact in significant ways with the rest of the world.

Yet it would be a mistake to look upon these important European voyages as unparalleled feats of long-distance sailing and discovery. Unfortunately, except for the almost contemporary voyages of the Chinese fleets commanded by Zheng He, equally impressive achievements by the mariners of the Indian and Pacific Oceans during the period 600–1492 have left no direct record. Although the later historical consequences of their deeds had less impact on world history as a whole than those of the Europeans, their skill, daring, persistence and technical competence deserve special mention despite the paucity of direct historical evidence.

Through archaeological and linguistic dating techniques, and other scraps of evidence, scholars have determined that the islands of Polynesia began to be settled after AD 500, Tahiti, for example, apparently being reached in the fourteenth century. Similarly, Madagascar was settled by seafaring peoples from Indonesia over a lengthy period ending in approximately the fifteenth century. Although the latter voyages may not have involved crossing such long stretches of open water as those in the Pacific, the Indonesian origins of the Malagasy language testify to the fact that large numbers of colonizers must have traversed a distance comparable with that between Europe and North America.

Although the compass was not yet in use, these Polynesian and Indonesian seafarers, in their small outrigger vessels and sailing rafts, proved to be excellent navigators and fearless adventurers. The sail designs of their vessels, which with catamaran hulls could be as long as European ships of Columbus' era, indicate a long period of innovation and development, apparently focusing on Indonesia as the original home of the spritsails from which they all derive (Bowen, 1953: pp. 81–117, 185–211; Hornell, 1946). This tradition of sail design differs significantly from the lateen sails of the western Indian Ocean, and from Chinese mat sails stiffened by battens.

Thus, it must be assumed that during the period under consideration, the island region from Indonesia to Hawaii had a rich history, now regrettably lost, of risk taking, inventiveness, thirst for new experience, and true discovery (Dodd, 1972). Although this history was eventually overshadowed and terminated by European maritime expansion after 1500, it is desirable to keep it in mind as a caution against facile assumptions about the innate boldness, acumen, or technical and scientific skill of the Europeans who carried out that expansion.

The Indian Ocean

Seafaring in the Indian Ocean was well developed long before AD 600. Sailing craft, known generically as *dhows,* carried on a coastal trade up the East African coast from Madagascar; across southern Arabia and southern Iran, with heavy activity in the Persian Gulf, where trading contact was made with Mesopotamia; and down India's west, or Malabar, coast to Sri Lanka. Coastal trading around the ocean's eastern perimeter – along the east, or Coromandel, coast of India; across the Bay of Bengal; and then down the Malay peninsula to Indonesia – seems to have been conducted more by Indians and Indonesians than by the Arabs and Persians who dominated the western routes; but sailors and traders of many languages and cultures could be found in the cosmopolitan world of Indian Ocean trade. Moreover, seafaring technology was fairly uniform over the entire area.

The spritsails of the Pacific islands are generally characterized by a triangular shape with the sail attached to a boom at the bottom. The lateen sails found throughout the Indian Ocean are similarly of a roughly triangular shape, but they do not have a boom at the bottom. In all likelihood, these sail types evolved from different primitive versions: a sail stretched between two vertical poles in the case of the spritsail, and a square sail hanging from a horizontal yard lashed to a vertical mast in the case of the lateen.

The fact that these types evolved separately indicates that the Indian Ocean world and that of the seas further east did not form part a single maritime system in ancient times. Yet by the seventh century AD, sails of Chinese design on an Indian ship are depicted in the Ajanta caves of western India, and Arab traders were beginning to form a prosperous community in southern China. In short, the earlier separation between maritime regions was already breaking down at the start of the period under consideration.

Since much of the textual evidence concerning Indian Ocean seafaring between 600 and 1492 comes from Muslim sources, it is likely that the role of the Arabs has been somewhat exaggerated. The notion that Islam was somehow a causative factor in stimulating maritime activity also remains to be demonstrated.

The greater likelihood is that sailors from Indonesia, India, Iran and Arabia were all active in a trade that carried both high-value goods, such as spices from the East Indies, and bulk cargoes, such as wood from East Africa. The fact that in AD 711 a portion of an Arab army was transported by ship to invade Sindh, the southern part of the Indus valley, attests to the maritime skill, the shipping capacity and the knowledge of promising coastal targets readily available in the Persian Gulf seventy-five years after the start of the Arab conquests. The presence in Iraq of an ethnic group of Indonesians, called in Arabic the *Sayābija,* at roughly the same period proves a similar fund of skills and knowledge for the other side of the ocean. Knowledge of this sort doubtless improved significantly with the introduction into the region of the magnetic compass from China in the thirteenth century (Needham, 1954: p. 247).

Throughout the period under consideration, therefore, it is reasonable to assume that the littoral regions of the Indian Ocean were in regular contact and affected by a more or less common maritime culture involving sailors and traders from many lands. But this does not mean that the hinterlands of these coasts were equally in contact. Archaeological remains in East Africa do not indicate a broad extension inland of the Swahili culture of the coast (in Arabic, *sāḥil*; plural *sawāḥil* = Swahili). As for Somalia and southern Arabia, as well as the relatively minor extension of seafaring about halfway up the Red Sea, most of the harbours were situated on barren shores. And even where there were settled hinterlands, as in the Ḥadhramaut valley and the highlands of Yemen, and the Green Mountains (*Jabal Akhḍar*) of Oman, deserts and mountains denied these regions easy overland contact with other lands. In other words, the areas in contact with the Indian Ocean maritime system were themselves in poor communication with the rest of the Islamic world.

The same is true of most of the Persian Gulf, bounded by waterless deserts on both the Arabian and the Persian sides, and of Iran's Makran coast and Pakistan's Baluchistan coast. The Shaṭṭ al-'Arab confluence of the Tigris and Euphrates entering the Persian Gulf and the Indus River entering the Arabian Sea provided valuable points of entry into broader agricultural regions, as, to a lesser extent, did a few spots where caravan tracks ended at small harbours. But overall, despite the enormous length of their coastlines, East Africa and Western Asia remained land-oriented even while occasionally enjoying the benefits of goods imported by the vibrant and cosmopolitan trading society they were tangentially in contact with. North-western India shared this disjuncture between sea and land to some extent because of deserts and the precipitous Western Ghats, but further to the south, the Malabar coast had a deeper hinterland.

The coast of the Bay of Bengal, extending down the Malay peninsula to the islands of Indonesia, provided easier access to agricultural hinterlands, in some areas, or else were strongly oriented towards communications by sea. It is hardly surprising, therefore, that aspects of Hindu and Buddhist culture were diffused from India throughout island and mainland South-East Asia while leaving no trace of a similar maritime expansion westwards.

Unfortunately, the paucity of information on the early history of the eastern Indian Ocean precludes a discussion of specific dates and modalities of intercommunication.

The Mediterranean Sea

Since the opening of the Suez Canal in 1869, people have become accustomed to thinking of the Red Sea as a natural link between the Mediterranean Sea and the Indian Ocean. In reality, the Red Sea was a dead end surrounded on its northern reaches by broad deserts so lacking in fresh water that the few seaports could never grow beyond small town size. Moreover, the prevailing northerly winds of the upper Red Sea made sailing very difficult for ships rigged as they were between 600 and 1492.

Looking at Western Asia as a formidable land barrier between the commerce of the eastern Mediterranean and that of the Indian Ocean, the existence of a technological disjuncture between these two maritime zones is hardly surprising. Indian Ocean vessels were normally, but perhaps not exclusively, constructed of planks fastened to each other by palm-fibre ropes tied through holes bored for the purpose. The seams were then caulked with bitumen, readily available in what has now become the oil region of the Persian Gulf (see Plate 22). Mediterranean shipbuilders, by contrast, used nails as fasteners, and at some point during the period under consideration began to construct some vessels by nailing planks to an internal frame that was laid down first.

By the ninth century, however, a new sail design of Indian Ocean, probably Persian Gulf, origin began to appear in the

Mediterranean (Bowen, 1953: pp. 197–198). The square sails of antiquity were replaced by triangular lateen sails, surely a result of the cross-fertilization of cultures inspired by the Muslim unification of Byzantine Egypt and Syria with Sasanian Mesopotamia and Iran.

Yet even with the new sail design, oar power remained a crucial element in Mediterranean seafaring. Galleys were used as both military and cargo vessels until the fourteenth century, when cogs (*kogge*), clumsy, slow, square-sailed ships with capacious hulls that had evolved for trade in the North Atlantic, acquired a predominance in commercial shipping (Parry, 1963: pp. 60–61). A fourteenth-century cargo ship of conventional Mediterranean design and rigged with a lateen sail might require a crew of fifty sailors to transport 250 tonnes of cargo. A cog could do the same job with little more than twenty seamen (see Plate 23).

Slow cargo ships of limited manoeuvrability accentuated the need for fast, flexible war vessels. Thus the galley, with a lateen sail, continued to dominate naval conflicts throughout the period. Indeed, naval warfare and piracy play a stronger role in the history of the Mediterranean than elsewhere, at least until the fifteenth century. Abounding in small islands, convenient harbours and narrow passages, the Mediterranean was ideal for galley warfare. War galleys could put out from a base on shore and overtake passing cargo ships, but they could not remain at sea for long periods of time. They carried too many men, and their military sleekness severely limited storage space for fresh water.

The later naval warfare concept that emphasized defeating an enemy's navy and blockading its ports with ships that could hold station at sea for long periods of time did not apply in the Mediterranean (Guilmartin, 1974). A fleet engagement might yield a victory, but it could not be followed up with a blockade unless the victor also held points on land to base galleys. Consequently, fortified harbours and coastal forts receive much greater attention in Mediterranean history than they do elsewhere. By the same token, the development of gunnery at the end of the period involves coastal guns much more than naval guns. A galley crew stroking at attack speed to ram an enemy closed distance too rapidly to allow for the reloading of guns that had been discharged at long range. Hence cannon shot was reserved for the final moment before contact, and there was no impetus to develop the galley as a gunnery platform, as happened with ships in the North Atlantic (see Plates 25, 44).

Mediterranean shipping at the start of the period was primarily coastal. Mariners seldom sailed long distances out of sight of land, and winter weather precluded sailing altogether. Although the Mediterranean has seemed to some historians and political leaders a natural focus for unity because of its narrowness and the geographical similarities of the surrounding lands, throughout most of this period it still posed a major barrier between the south and north sides, except at its ends, where Spain and Morocco almost touched and the Levant coast enjoyed easy connections with Egypt and Greece, and at its waist, where Sicily and Malta provided a bridge between Italy and Tunisia.

The European commercial resurgence of the twelfth century, led by the Italian city-states of Venice, Pisa and Genoa, redeveloped the potential for trans-Mediterranean contact that had been languishing since the decline of the Roman Empire. Egypt, Tunisia and the Black Sea all became major ports of call for Italian vessels, and Europeans became important consumers of goods made in or transhipped through the Islamic world (Ashtor, 1983). This new age of transportation is marked by the development of *portolans*, nautical charts showing the coastlines of the Mediterranean with great accuracy and marked with compass directions, which allowed captains to travel with confidence over broad stretches of open water. While most surviving *portolans* are by southern European map makers, a few North African charts in Arabic, dating as early as 1330, are still extant (Soucek, 1992: pp. 263–65). The earliest European *portolans* date to the late thirteenth century (Parry, 1963: p. 101). This new development seems not to have percolated through the Islamic world, however, since comparable nautical charts remain unknown in the Indian Ocean until the end of this period (Tibbetts, 1992: pp. 256–262) (see Plates 122–124, 259).

Mediterranean trade was also facilitated at this time by the legal development of business partnerships in both Christian and Islamic societies. The Italian *commenda* partnership is directly comparable to the Muslim *muḍāraba* (Udovitch, 1970). Both made legal provision for one merchant to supply the capital with which another would undertake to travel abroad and buy and sell goods, the profits being split between the two. Since this sort of relationship relied on trust, and the prices of goods in various markets were difficult to learn about, trading networks often developed around other sorts of affinity. Citizens of city-states made partnerships and carried on commercial correspondence with fellow citizens. Jews maintained close trading connections with other Jews on both sides of the Mediterranean and as far away as Indonesia. And somewhat later, Armenians and India's *Banyās* did likewise.

The North Atlantic

Isolated from the Mediterranean maritime domain, and challenged by a wealth of estuaries and fjords, the peoples living along Europe's Atlantic and Baltic coasts developed their naval skills along different lines. The square sail of antiquity retained its dominance but became more efficiently rigged. Oars, on the other hand, gradually became restricted to small boats. The Viking galleys of the eighth and ninth centuries demonstrated that oars and a single square sail could overcome all the challenges of the North Atlantic, a fact best testified to by Leif Ericsson's voyage to North America in the eleventh century (see Figure 7; Plate 20). But the general trajectory of maritime development ran towards constructing wider, high-sided ships propelled by square sails. In the fifteenth century, influenced by sailing practices in the Mediterranean, with which the northern shipmasters had reconnected in the previous century, shipbuilders in all parts of Europe began to experiment with additional sails and masts on high hulls of the North Atlantic type, thus confirming this trajectory (Parry 1963: pp. 62–63) (see Plates 23, 24).

The reasons for the decline of galleys are not hard to find. The Iberian Atlantic coast, the Bay of Biscay and the North Sea were not congenial to the type of galley warfare practised in the narrow seas of the Mediterranean. The Atlantic was rough, islands were comparatively few, and distances to ports on the opposite side were great. Sails were a necessity; high sides protected against heavy seas; and greater width provided more cargo space. A galley carrying 250 tonnes of cargo required a crew of 200 men. A typical North Atlantic sailing ship of the fourteenth century needed little more than twenty (Parry, 1963: pp. 55, 61).

The gains in efficiency represented by the development of wide-hulled sailing vessels increased the profitability of

Figure 7 Transport and communications in early medieval Northern Europe: Viking-type ship, coastal watch-tower and messengers on horseback with early form of saddle and stirrups. Redrawn from the 'Bayeux Tapestry', eleventh century, Bayeux Museum, Normandy, France (after a drawing by Jean Thouvenin, in Parisse M., *La tapisserie de Bayeux*, Paris 1983, p. 21).

shipping high-bulk, low-value commodities. Wool, grain, and wine came to typify North Atlantic commerce in the way that spices and other high-value Eastern goods typified Mediterranean trade, although neither type of cargo was totally excluded in either region.

Although the ship designs of the North Atlantic proved eventually to be an important factor in establishing European dominance of the world's seas, many advances in seafaring came to the area relatively late, including the compass and the pilot-book (*routier* or *rutter* = *portolan*), both borrowed from the Mediterranean. Marine charts and tables indicating traverse lines that showed the compass headings for open-sea sailing were available to Italian and Catalan sailors by the late thirteenth century but were unknown in Northern Europe until the sixteenth.

The historical importance of North Atlantic seafaring accelerates during the decades preceding the voyages of Columbus with which the period under consideration ends. Prince Henry of Portugal (d. 1460) sponsored a series of expeditions along the Atlantic coast of Africa. The overflow of the *reconquista* into Africa, in the form of attacks on Moroccan seaports, provided the Portuguese with an incentive to outflank the Muslims and discover their sources of gold. From 1434, when Gil Eanes first rounded Cape Bojador, just south of the Canary Islands and only 1,000 miles from Lisbon, until 1488, when Bartolomeu Dias returned from sea to inform his monarch that he had rounded the tip of Africa and thus opened the way for direct voyages to India, the Portuguese were consumed with a national venture that gradually changed from outflanking the Moors to discovering a route to India. By comparison, Spain supported the voyages of the Genoese sailor Columbus, who had experience sailing on Portuguese ships to Guinea, in a more speculative enterprise in that they proposed to go well beyond the Atlantic islands that had been reached in the earlier decades. Had Columbus not had the good fortune to encounter a completely unpredicted continental obstacle, of course, he and his men would have died at sea just as his critics predicted.

The China Sea

Chinese seafaring was highly developed during the period under discussion. The junks and sampans of China's rivers and coastal waters bespeak a technological domain quite independent of the Indian Ocean and South-East Asia (Needham and Ronan, 1986: Chs 2, 5, 6).[3] Unlike the keeled ships of Indonesia, called in Malay *jong* (presumably the original of the word 'junk'), junks normally had flat bottoms and compartmented hulls, the latter concept eventually being adopted by European shipbuilders. Their rudders were suspended from large housings cantilevered over the middle of the stern, as opposed to the *jong* design of two lateral rudders. And the quadrilateral Chinese sails had not only a yard at the top and a boom at the bottom, but also a series of horizontal poles, or battens, bracing the strips of cloth or matting making up the sail. With sails rigged from three or more masts, a practice also followed in Indonesia, the Chinese ships surprised the Europeans who first arrived in Eastern waters, and may have contributed to the transition to multiple masts in Europe. For war, the navy deployed 'tower ships' featuring a miniature castle, with catapult, on the deck (as opposed to the fore-and-aft castles developed on Atlantic vessels) and oars, for manoeuvrability, as well as sails (Needham and Ronan, 1986: p. 91, fig. 189).

Though inland waterways seem to have been most important for the development of Chinese shipbuilding at the outset of this period, China came to make good use of its long coastline and good harbours for coastal shipping of grain and trade goods, particularly under the Mongol Yuan dynasty in the late thirteenth century. Chinese vessels also sailed to Japan and various parts of Southeast Asia, as is visually attested by a detailed carving of a junk at Angkor Thom in Cambodia dated to about 1185. Ships constructed in southern China shared characteristics of both the junk and the *jong*, being nailed instead of sewn and having an axial rudder like the vessels of northern China but having a keel like those of Indonesia (Manguin, 1993: pp. 253–80). Yet Chinese shipping seems not to have been plentiful in the Indian Ocean, nor are there indications of Chinese vessels trading in Middle Eastern ports. Instead, a thriving overseas trading community of Arabs grew up at Zaytūn, north of Amoy in southern China, during the Islamic period (see Plate 21).

The most striking episode in Chinese seafaring took place between 1405 and 1433, when the admiral Zheng He, who came to be known proverbially as 'the Three-Jewel Eunuch who went down into the west', led seven great voyages throughout the East and South China Seas and across the Indian Ocean as far as Africa (Needham and Ronan, 1986: pp. 128–32). The Chinese were well aware of the lands of the Indian Ocean from centuries of trade, largely through Arab intermediaries but to some degree by Chinese themselves, and from trips to India by Chinese Buddhist pilgrims. Thus Zheng He's expeditions are not directly comparable with the voyages into the unknown Atlantic by the Europeans later in the century, but they nevertheless demonstrated China's ability to traverse broad seas and, if the emperor so desired, influence foreign lands.

Chinese naval ambition had become apparent with the establishment in the twelfth century of an admiralty by the Song Dynasty, then in the midst of a period of great economic growth and technological development (Needham and Ronan, 1986: pp. 120–126). Eleven squadrons of ships became twenty within a century, and catapults launching gunpowder bombs became a standard shipboard weapon. Some vessels used newly invented paddle-wheels, either stern- or side-mounted, operated by treadmills; and early in the thirteenth century experiments were made with iron plating. With the coming to power of the Yuan Dynasty shortly thereafter, territorial expansion by sea became a political goal. In 1274, 900 ships transported 250,000 soldiers across the Sea of Japan to attack that country, only to be frustrated by bad weather. In 1281, 4,400 ships attempted a second invasion of Japan; again the Japanese were saved, this time by a 'divine wind' or typhoon.

Early in the fifteenth century, under the succeeding Ming Dynasty, Chinese shipyards turned out a flood of new vessels. The largest were 135 m long and almost 55 m wide, with crews of 400–500 men and sails rigged to as many as nine masts (Needham and Ronan, 1986: p. 123). By comparison, a contemporary Mediterranean war galley was about 40 m long and 5 m wide (Parry, 1963: p. 55). The tonnage of the Chinese ships was an order of magnitude greater than that of the Spanish and Portuguese ships that sailed to the Western Hemisphere and around Africa. These were the ships that made up Zheng He's fleet.

Zheng He's first voyage (1405–1407) visited Java, Sumatra, Sri Lanka and the west coast of India. Some squadrons of the fourth expedition (1413–1415) reached Iran, while others sailed throughout the East Indies. In 1417–1419, Chinese squadrons reached Kenya and Somalia and brought back, among other things, giraffes. Finally, in 1431, a last expedition, manned by 27,550 officers and sailors, made contact with twenty separate kingdoms and voyaged even further down the coast of Africa (Needham and Ronan, 1986: pp. 132–8). Two years after the fleet's return in 1433, the second of the two Ming emperors who had sponsored the expeditions died, and the succeeding emperors, following the advice of a new group of officials, turned away from the sea to concentrate on agricultural policy. Further naval efforts were limited to protecting coastal shipping from pirates, and China's opportunity to establish itself as a world sea power passed.

Inasmuch as the expeditions of Zheng He, unlike those sent out later by the rulers of Portugal and Spain, discovered no hitherto unknown lands and brought back no reports, much less concrete evidence, of exploitable sources of gold and silver, the decision to turn away from expensive sea exploration may have been a sensible one. A similar decision had been made by the Norse four centuries earlier when they chose not to exploit their discovery of land on the far side of the North Atlantic.

Comparisons of this sort highlight the fortuitous character of the later European voyages in terms of their captains finding great wealth comparatively early in their collective endeavour.

INLAND WATERWAYS

William McNeill, in the article cited earlier, maintains that the overall Eurasian situation with regard to inland transport in the period under consideration was one in which riverboats were normally more efficient and more heavily relied on than land transport. And in the case of China, where several centuries of canal building reached a first climax in AD 605 with the completion of the Grand Canal connecting the Huanghe with the Yangtze River, riverboats were supplemented by canal boats. Where navigable rivers and canals existed, overland transport tended to radiate out from river ports as a subsidiary transport network for collecting and distributing produce and merchandise (see Plates 241, 242).

The early Chinese canal system generally followed the lay of the land. The engineers of the Yuan Dynasty, however, attempted the difficult task of building locks to raise the Grand Canal over hills to reach Beijing (Elvin, 1973: pp. 104–5). They were only partially successful. Not until 1411, during the Ming Dynasty, was a system of fifteen locks constructed to complete a new waterway that was thirteen Chinese feet deep and thirty-two wide. As a result, the volume of grain reaching Beijing annually by canal increased tenfold.

The conditions of river transport differed greatly from region to region and cannot easily be summarized. Europe was plentifully supplied with rivers, and vessels of many kinds plied the river routes. Small oar-propelled boats made of skins, basketry, wood and even pottery served in different places for transporting small numbers of people and for fishing. In speaking of small craft, it should be noted that the Western Hemisphere was home to a wide variety of designs, often quite innovative, from the skin kayaks of the Inuit to the birch bark canoes of the woodland Native Americans, to the balsa sailing rafts of Peru (Hornell: pp. 148–75).

Some of these vessels were used in coastal communication, and others on inland waterways and lakes. Unfortunately, most information about this transportation domain comes from later periods and can only be inferred for the period before 1492.

Heavier cargos relied on sails as well as on rowing and poling. In some regions, notably on the Tigris and Euphrates, where travel upstream was easier by caravan, rafts were normally used.

Transport on these rivers by means of wooden platforms lashed to inflated animal skins is attested as early as the second millennium BC and remained a principal means of supplying cities from Baghdād northwards throughout the period under discussion (Hornell: pp. 26–30). Their advantage here and elsewhere, such as on rivers descending from the Himalaya, was that the wood could be sold, and the skins deflated and returned upstream by pack animal.

Worldwide, the most developed system of inland water transport was in China. The Grand Canal made it possible to ship rice from southern China down the Yangtze River and then northwards to connect with the Huanghe for distribution in northern China. Marco Polo remarked of the Yangtze River in the late thirteenth century that 'more dear things, and of greater value, go and come by this river, than go by all the rivers of the Christians together, nor by all their seas' and estimated the number of craft on its lower reaches at 15,000 (Needham and Ronan, 1986: p. 115).

Yet the Grand Canal was not truly an all-season system until the fifteenth century. The early Chinese canal system generally followed the lie of the land. The engineers of the Yuan Dynasty, however, attempted the difficult task of building locks to raise the Grand Canal over hills to reach Beijing (Elvin, 1973: pp. 104–5). They were only partially successful. Only under the Ming Dynasty, in 1411, was an intricate system of fifteen locks constructed to complete a new waterway that was 13 Chinese feet deep and 32 wide. As a result, the volume of grain reaching Beijing annually by canal increased tenfold. After that, the transport of grain through coastal waters by junk, which had grown greatly during the Yuan Dynasty, declined precipitously. The size and effectiveness of the sea-going navy rapidly followed the same path. By 1474, the main fleet had gone from 400 warships to 140.

OTHER ASPECTS OF COMMUNICATION

This chapter has concentrated on means of transportation with the tacit implication that wherever people travel, they also communicate. It should be noted, however, that many large states instituted special relay systems for transmitting messages, usually for official purposes only. In the Islamic caliphate, this was called *barīd*, a word that betrays its Roman origin from Latin *veredus*, or post horse. The Mongols called their relay system *yam*. Both of these systems relied on horses. In India, however, runners were used, as they were in Incan Peru, where a message could be transmitted 150 miles in one day with a relay every mile. Communications systems like these, needless to say, also served as intelligence systems informing the rulers of what was afoot in distant parts of their realms.

Another aspect of communication proper to this period is the development of block-printing in China around the ninth century and of printing with movable type in Korea in the thirteenth. Much of what was printed initially answered religious needs. In Central Asia, most surviving specimens are from religious texts, as they are in Egypt, where block-printing seems to have developed independently at about the same time as it appeared in China. By the time of the Song dynasty in China, however, printing was commonly used for books of every sort (see Plates 115, 116).

Communication by letter or book depended, however, on literacy and possession of a common language. In China, universal use of a single system of characters to represent words that were very differently pronounced in various regional dialects greatly facilitated literate communication and helped to bind an enormous country together. In somewhat different ways, Latin in Europe and Arabic in the Islamic world served similar functions. Latin was virtually the only written language commonly represented in written form in Europe at the outset of this period, and it remained the dominant language of educated people down to its end even though vernacular literatures were then becoming very popular. A common command of Latin permitted all educated Europeans to communicate with one another irrespective of their mother tongues (see Plates 117, 118).

The same was true of Arabic for educated Muslims, although it did not develop fully as an instrument for technical prose until the eighth century. Its status as the language of the Qur'ān established it in an immutable form as the first language of instruction for children. This kept the written language from following the spoken versions of Arabic as they diverged more and more over the centuries to a point where they probably would have become separate languages except for the grammatical and lexical benchmark of the Qur'ānic text.

Other languages served literate communication needs in a more limited fashion. Jews normally wrote the vernacular languages of the regions they resided in Hebrew script. This afforded them a number of languages – Judaeo-Arabic, Judaeo-Persian, and so on – for written communication that could not be read to other people, a particular advantage in the area of trade. The Armenian language and script gave Armenian traders the same advantage.

Finally, mention should be made of hybrid trade languages that enabled people from different lands to communicate with one another. Such languages, sometimes called pidgins, are grammatically simpler than the tongues they derive from. The original *Lingua Franca* was the trade language of the Mediterranean during this period. Now extinct, it was based on Italian but incorporated words from Spanish, French, Greek and Arabic. The trade language that developed in East Africa during this period was called Swahili, 'the language of the coastal people'. Its grammar is based on Bantu, but it contains an abundance of Arabic words. Island and mainland South-East Asia also had a trade language based on a simplified form of Malay. In modern times, this has become the official language of Malaysia and Indonesia.

CONCLUSION

Looked at on a worldwide basis, transport and communication between 600 and 1492 is best analysed regionally, as has been done above. China and its neighbouring seas constituted a single system with regard to most technological, economic and military matters. Local land routes serviced river and canal systems with an active, but normally not expansive, seaborne trade. Island South-East Asia and Polynesia, despite the paucity of data about them, also seem to have constituted a maritime system with only a negligible land component. This is mainly determined by technological continuities and evidence of far-reaching migration of people and products during this period. The Indian Ocean littoral was similarly a system, but in many of its parts, for geographical reasons, it was poorly linked to the lands behind the coasts. As a cosmopolitan realm with sailors and passengers of many lands and faiths, it was not really an extension of any of the cultures that bordered it. But it affected them all by affording connections between them. Primarily land systems include India, the Middle East and Central Asia, and the northern and southern littorals of the Sahara Desert. And Europe can be seen either as a single system based on river and coastal transport with a subsidiary network of roads, or as two subsystems focusing on the Mediterranean Sea and the North Atlantic.

The criteria that make for classifying all of these as systems include substantial technological continuity, ready exchange of economic and cultural goods within the system, and absence of internal barriers to communication as substantial as those separating each system from the others, these barriers being sometimes geographical and at other times cultural, religious or political. There was unquestionably a significant degree of communication and exchange of goods between these systems, but this did not make of them a unified or 'world' system. Inter-system links remained slow and difficult, and information reaching one system about another was often treated as a subject of wonder and amazement.

Yet contact between the systems, much of it maintained by people with great technical acumen, repeatedly stimulated improvements in efficiency that ultimately converged in the comparatively uniform transport systems of modern times. Indian Ocean lateen sails entered the Mediterranean. Mediterranean multiple masts, possibly influenced by reports about China, influenced Atlantic shipbuilders. Camel saddle designs travelled from the Middle East to Morocco, India and Central Asia. And efficient vehicle harnesses travelled from China to Europe.

The story of the compass is illustrative of this elusive pattern of technological exchange. In 1088, a century before the earliest European reference to the compass, a Chinese engineer and astronomer wrote:

> Magicians rub the point of a needle with the lodestone; then it is able to point to the south. But it always inclines slightly to the east, and does not point directly to the south. [It may be made to] float on the surface of water, but then it is rather unsteady. It may be balanced on the finger-nail, or on the rim of a cup, where it can be made to turn more easily, but these supports being hard and smooth, it is liable to fall off.
>
> (Needham and Ronan, 1986: pp. 9–10)

Centuries of observations and experiments by Chinese geomancers seem to underlie this description of a compass. But regardless of its other uses, the compass as a maritime instrument is clearly indicated in documents of the period immediately following that of the cited passage. Whether the Chinese compass reached Europe during the following century through the medium of the Indian Ocean has long been debated. Without rehearsing the arguments for and against this hypothesis, suffice it to say that in this, as in so many other aspects of transportation history before 1492, the paucity, ambiguity and discontinuity of data make it difficult to see things whole. Thus the history of transport and communication between 600 and 1492 remains a topic of great importance where new discoveries and analyses may be hoped for in the years to come.

NOTES

1 The person who first raised changes in harnessing as a significant historical question, and whose collection of illustrations is still of value, was Richard Lefebvre des Noëttes, 1924, 1931.
2 *Archaeological Survey of India, Annual Report, 1909–10*, Plate XLIVa, text, p. 98. I am indebted to Professor I. Habib for this valuable reference.
3 This work collects in one manageable volume the dispersed discussions of maritime matters scattered over two volumes of the longer work.

BIBLIOGRAPHY

ABU LUGHOD, J. 1989. *Before European Hegemony: The World System AD 1250–1350*. New York, Oxford.

ASHTOR, E. 1983. *Levant Trade in the Later Middle Ages*. Princeton.

BOWEN, R. LE BARON. JR. 1953. Eastern Sail Affinities. In: *American Neptune*, Vol. 13, pp. 81–117, 185–211. Salem, Mass.

BULLIET, R. W. 1975. *The Camel and the Wheel*. Cambridge, Mass.

DENEAUVE, J. 1986. Note sur quelques lampes africaines du IIIe siècle. *Antiquités Africaines*, Vol. 22. Paris.

DEWALL M. VON, 1986. Der Wagen in der Frühzeit Chinas. In: TREUE, W. (ed.), *Achse, Rad, und Wagen: fünftausend Jahre Kultur- und Technikgeschichte*, Vendenhoeck & Ruprecht, Göttingen, pp. 158–186.

DODD, E. 1972. *Polynesian Seafaring*. New York.

ELVIN, M. 1973. *The Pattern of the Chinese Past*. Stanford, pp. 104–5.

FORBES, R. J. 1965. *Studies in Ancient Technology*, Vol. 2. Leiden.

GAIL, A. J. 1986. Der Wagen in Indien. In: TREUE, W. (ed.) *Achse, Rad, und Wagen: fünftausend Jahre Kultur- und Technikgeschichte*. Göttingen, pp. 153–7.

GUILMARTIN, J. 1974. *Gunpowder and Galleys*. London.

HAUDRICOURT, A. 1948. Contribution à la géographie et à l'ethnologie de la voiture. *La Revue de Géographie humaine et d'Ethnologie*, Vol. 1. Paris.

HAUPT, H. 1986. Der Wagen im Mittelalter. In: TREUE, W. (ed.) *Achse, Rad, und Wagen: fünftausend Jahre Kultur- und Technikgeschichte*. Göttingen, pp. 187–96.

HÄUSLER, A. 1986. Rad und Wagen zwischen Europa und Asien. In: TREUE, W. (ed.) *Achse, Rad, und Wagen: fünftausend Jahre Kultur- und Technikgeschichte*. Göttingen, pp. 139–52.

HORNELL, J. 1946. *Water Transport: Origins and Early Evolution*, Cambridge.

LEFEBVRE DES NOËTTES, R. 1924. *La Force motrice animale à travers les âges*. Paris.

——. 1931. *L'Attelage: le cheval de selle à travers les âges*. Paris.

LITTAUER, M.; CROUWEL, J. 1979. *Wheeled Vehicles and Ridden Animals in the Ancient Near East*. Leiden.

MCNEILL, W. H. 1987. The Eccentricity of Wheels, or Eurasian Transportation in Historical Perspective. In: *American Historical Review*, Vol. 92, pp. 1111–26. Washington.

MANGUIN, P. Y. 1993. Trading Ships of the South China Sea. In: *Journal of the Economic and Social History of the Orient*, 36, pp. 253–280.

NEEDHAM, J. 1954. *Science and Civilisation in China*, Vol. II (I). Cambridge. p. 247.

NEEDHAM, J.; LING, W. 1965. *Science and Civilisation in China*, Vol. 4, parts 2–3. Cambridge.

NEEDHAM, J.; RONAN, C. A. 1986. *The Shorter Science and Civilisation in China*, Vol. 3. Cambridge.

PARRY, J. H. 1963. *The Age of Reconnaissance: Discovery, Exploration and Settlement 1450–1650*. Berkeley.

PIGGOTT, S. 1983. *The Earliest Wheeled Transport: From the Atlantic Coast to the Caspian Sea*. London.

SCHWARTZBERG, J. E. 1978. *A Historical Atlas of South Asia*. Chicago.

SOUCEK, S. 1992. Islamic Charting in the Mediterranean. In: HARTLEY, J. B.; WOODWARD, D. (eds) *The History of Cartography, Vol. 2b, Cartography in the Traditional Islamic and South Asian Societies*, Chicago, pp. 263–292.

TIBBETTS, G. R. 1992. The Role of Charts in Islamic Navigation in the Indian Ocean. In: HARTLEY, J. B.; WOODWARD, D. (eds) *The History of Cartography, Vol. 2b, Cartography in the Traditional Islamic and South Asian Societies*. Chicago, pp. 256–62.

UDOVITCH, A. L. 1970. *Partnership and Profit in Medieval Islam*. Princeton.

WACKERNAGEL, R. H. 1986. Zur Geschichte der Kutsche bis zum Ende des 17. Jahrhunderts. In: TREUE, W. (ed.) *Achse, Rad, und Wagen: fünftausend Jahre Kultur-und Technikgeschichte*. Göttingen, pp. 197–235.

WHITE, L. JR. 1962. *Medieval Technology and Social Change*. Oxford.

6

KNOWLEDGE AND SCIENCES

Ahmad Yusuf Al-Hasan

THE DEVELOPMENT OF KNOWLEDGE

East Asia

China has enjoyed a continuous civilization since ancient times. In 589, it was reunited by the Sui Dynasty (581–618), under which the Grand Canal was completed. The period of the Tang dynasty (618–907) was marked by an advance in education, art and literature. Education was under the influence of Confucianism. There were government and private schools in each district, town and village. In the capital there were colleges for higher studies. The written examination system for the selection of government officials became firmly established. Besides the university, an Imperial Academy was founded. Block-printing was invented; this supplied the textbooks needed for the civil service examinations and satisfied the demand for Buddhist and Daoist prayers and charms. Although it was an age of literature, there was some scientific activity by Buddhists and alchemical works by Daoists. There was an influx of new religions, including Zoroastrianism, Nestorian Christianity and Manichaeism.

The period of the Song dynasty (960–1279) was one of great cultural achievements. The traditional views of Confucianism were re-examined and this resulted in the emergence of Neo-Confucianism. The invention of movable-type printing led to the multiplication of books and stimulated the spread of literacy and culture. Alchemical pursuits by Daoists resulted in a formula for gunpowder. The biological sciences flourished, and compilation literature and encyclopedic works increased.

The Yuan (Mongol) Dynasty (1279–1368) was less fruitful in cultural achievements, but the Mongol Empire extended over a vast area and foreign contacts increased. The court of the Khān was full of Muslims and Europeans. The increase in foreign contacts, especially with Islam, brought new ideas in science and technology, and knowledge of the world outside China increased. Such cultural contacts encouraged the establishing of an astronomical observatory. But due to an overall decrease in opportunities for employment, Chinese scholars increasingly applied their talents to the drama and the novel. They used the vernacular, which was a significant development in Chinese culture (see Plates 95, 96, 115, 134).

The Ming Dynasty (1368–1644) restored native Chinese culture. During the early Ming, the Chinese encyclopedic movement reached its climax, and the *Yongle Dadian* encyclopedia was commissioned in 1403. It ran to more than 11,000 volumes. In the fifteenth century, Chinese admiral Zheng He led major maritime exploration.

Japan began its development by acquiring aspects of Chinese civilization. In the sixth century, the ideographic Chinese script, Confucianism and Buddhism came through Korea. In the seventh century, Prince Shōtoku Taishi, initiated direct relations with the Sui Dynasty (see Plate 128). Envoys were exchanged and Japanese students were sent to China. In 701, a university system was inaugurated and schools were built in the provinces.

In 710, the imperial capital was shifted to Nara, and there was a brilliant flowering of culture. Four times within seventy years, official missions went to the Tang court, accompanied by large numbers of students. The compilation of Japan's two most ancient histories, the *Kojiki and Nihon shoki*, took place. In 794, the capital was shifted to Heian. The Heian period (794–1185) was one of great literary brilliance, and histories were compiled. The earliest writings of the period, however, were almost all in Chinese.

During the tenth century, a truly Japanese culture developed, one of the most important contributing factors being the emergence of indigenous scripts, the *kana* syllabaries. The two scripts, *hiragana* and *katakana,* made it possible to write the national language, and their invention was a seminal event in the history of Japan. A great amount of writing in Japanese was produced. The *hiragana* script enabled some talented women to create works of literature (see Plate 257). The establishment of a military government, or shōgunate, saw the beginning of rule by the *samurai* warrior class and the end of the role of the aristocracy. During the Kamakura period (1192–1333), overseas trade fostered new cultural developments such as the introduction of Zen Buddhism and neo-Confucianism from Song China. Chinese influences left their mark on the formation of *samurai* culture and on everyday life (see Plates 14, 98, 256, 257, 258).

Korea acquired much of Chinese culture, such as Chinese characters, laws, Confucianism and Buddhism. The unified Silla dynasty (668–935) adhered to the Tang culture of China. The language of Silla became the forerunner of the modern Korean language. There was belief in Buddhism as a religion, and in Confucianism for its political and ethical principles (see Plate 86). The Yi dynasty was established in 1392. Hanyang (now Seoul) was made the capital. The Confucian ethical system was adopted officially and replaced Buddhism. Neo-Confucian scholars gained government posts through civil service examinations. The early Yi dynasty flourished culturally. Through the technique of movable-type printing,

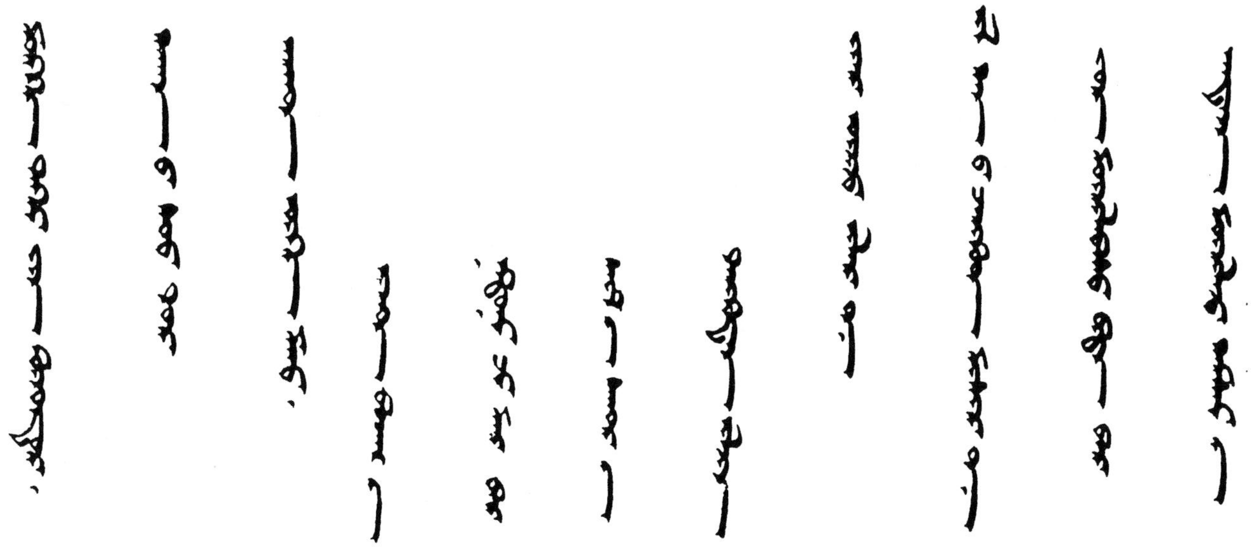

Figure 8 Uighur script as adapted to Mongolian. Letter from the Ilkhān or 'vassal khān' of Persia, Arghūn, to King Philip IV 'the Fair' of France, AD 1288 (from Mostaert, Cleaves, Woodman 1962; p. 105, plate I).

developed in Korea in 1234, many publications in scientific subjects were produced. In 1420, a royal academy was established. In 1443, the Korean phonetic alphabet was completed (see Plates 97, 125).

Chinggis Khān adopted the Uighur script for the Mongolian language in 1204 (see Figure 8). The Tibetan language was reduced to writing in the seventh century, the script here being derived from the Brahmi.

India and South-East Asia

The first centuries of the Christian era represent the classical age of Hindu science, which was a glorious period in its history. The period from Harsha (606–46) until the end of the eighth century was a continuation of the Gupta period. Major achievements continued to be made until about 1200. After that, Indian science followed two paths: one was a continuation of the earlier tradition and the other developed as a result of the Islamic presence.

Primary education was largely confined to upper castes. The teaching language was mostly Sanskrit (see Plate 100). Higher education was pursued at universities and colleges, which were set up first by the Buddhists and later by the Hindus. In north India, there were several cultural centres, the most important being Nalanda, Valabhi and Vikramasīla. The university of Nalanda was established in the Gupta period. Its fame attracted students from abroad. Universities and colleges were numerous in the north and in the south and were part of Buddhist monasteries or Hindu temples. Some Hindu higher schools of learning were conducted by Brahmin scholars in their own homes. Indian mathematics and astronomy flourished and reached their peak of achievement in the classical period. There were distinguished works in medicine, alchemy and agricultural science. Legal texts and commentaries were abundant. Literature continued to be composed in Sanskrit, and there was a revival of interest in prosody, grammar and lexicography.

Sanskrit and later Prakrit were the medium of learning before the rise of vernacular languages. The Sinhalese alphabet is a modification of the Brahmi in which Pali had earlier been written. Prakrit languages stand halfway between Sanskrit and some of the living vernaculars of India (see Plates 101, 102). The literature in Prakrit is chiefly known as the literature of Jainism, one of India's main religions.

In the fourteenth century, 'Bhakti' saints preached in local languages and not in Sanskrit. One of these was Namdev, who preached in Marathi. Religious preachers of other traditions such as the Nath-Yogis in the north and the Lingayats in Karnataka began using local spoken dialects a little earlier. This led to a gradual breaking away from Sanskrit and Prakrit, and the eventual emergence of vernaculars. Bengali, Hindi, Gujarati and Marathi developed as vernacular languages between the seventh and fourteenth centuries. All of these belong to the Indo-Aryan group of languages. Among the Dravidian family of languages, the most important are Telugu, Tamil, Kannada and Malayalam. With the exception of Tamil, literature developed in the three other languages during this period, with influences from Sanskrit (see Plate 220). From the eleventh century, the Persian language became the language of culture and of the court (see Plate 219). Modern Indian languages are full of Persian words.

Indian and Chinese influences penetrated South-East Asia in the early centuries AD. Indian civilization exerted the most profound influence. Chinese influence affected Viet Nam only because this region was annexed to the Chinese empire for many centuries. Indian influence affected what has been called 'farther India' (Myanmar, southern Thailand, Cambodia and southern Viet Nam), west Malaya, eastern Sumatra and northern Java. Indian Sanskrit scholars and monks settled and helped to consolidate these communities into regional, theocratic and socially stratified states, which were at different times either Buddhist or Hindu-Brahman. In Java and Cambodia, where society developed the institution of a god-king, scholars of Sanskrit were part of the king's court, but literary activity in Sanskrit was confined to the elite and never reached the people. In Myanmar, Hinduism was never widely accepted and the more open Pali studies were pursued not at the court but at Buddhist monasteries throughout the kingdom, and were thus more available to the public.

Vernacular literature emerged in the fourteenth and fifteenth centuries. Vietnamese began to be used after independence from China in the fifteenth century, using a modified Chinese script. Malay became a literary language in the thirteenth century after the adoption of Islam, using an Arabic-based script, and learning became available to all. In Myanmar, the first writers were monks and later laymen educated in their monasteries. The Thai kings of Laos and Siam developed their own vernacular literature, but in Cambodia no vernacular literature emerged in this period.

The world of Islam

Islamic science had its first beginnings in South-West Asia and Egypt, an area which had been the heart of the Old World for about 4,000 years before Islam. The period between 622 and 750 was the formative period of Islamic science. By the middle of the ninth century, the majority of the population had been Islamized. Among the populations of the core Islamic lands, Arabic became the vernacular language in Syria, Iraq and Egypt, while in Iran, Arabic became the language only of learning. Similar variations in the degree of linguistic Arabization were repeated in other regions of Islam. The first centres of Islamic learning were Medina and Mecca. After the conquests in the seventh century, new schools of learning were established in the newly built cities of al-Baṣra and al-Kūfa in Iraq. When the seat of the caliphate moved to Damascus with the Umayyads, the new capital also became an important cultural centre. Muslim learning truly began with the commencement of the writing of the Qur'ān in AD 650. The importance which Arabic assumed as the language of the Qur'ān led to the development of Arabic grammar and linguistic studies in the eighth century. Muslim theological sciences and jurisprudence flourished, and various cultural, religious and philosophical movements appeared. The rational sciences were still studied in Greek, Syriac and Pahlavi, but this period witnessed the beginnings of translations from these languages.

With the rise of the 'Abbāsids to power in AD 750, the groundwork had already been prepared for the scientific renaissance which followed, and the second phase of Islamic culture started. Al-Manṣūr (754–775) laid the cornerstone for Baghdād in 762. In a few years, the city had become the cultural centre of the Islamic Empire. Under Al-Manṣūr and the succeeding caliphs, Islamic science and scholarship reached their peaks. Scientific research in Arabic increased in momentum at the beginning of the ninth century. The time was ripe for the translation of the natural sciences into Arabic on a large scale. The translation movement began with Al-Manṣūr and continued for about 150 years.

Islamic learning spread to all towns and cities in eastern and western Islam, and great scholars flourished in all regions. By the middle of the eighth century, a popular system of elementary school education had been adopted, and these schools or *maktabs* were found in almost every town and village. Advanced studies were undertaken in the early centuries under independent teachers, who conducted their lectures in mosques. The system of lecturing in mosques gave rise to the college, or *al-madrasa*, which started to appear in the eleventh century. Enough endowments provided teachers with generous salaries, and board, lodging and clothing for students. Colleges spread to all regions of Islam. Some colleges were in fact universities, such as al-Mustanṣiriyyah in Baghdād (1234) (see Plate 197). Many independent teachers gave lectures in philosophy, astronomy, astrology, geometry, medicine, pharmacy, natural science and alchemy. More often medical subjects were taught in medical schools attached to hospitals, and the exact sciences (mathematics, astronomy and physics) were taught in observatories. Research effort was undertaken in research institutes such as the Bayt al-Ḥikma ('House of Wisdom'), founded by al-Ma'mūn in Baghdād in AD 830. It comprised an astronomical observatory, a translation bureau and a great library. In 1005, Caliph al-Ḥākim founded an institute for research and advanced study in Cairo. During the Sāmānid period in the tenth century, Bukhārā also became a great centre of learning with a famous library. The extensive spread of libraries was made possible by the spread of paper manufacturing, which created the new profession of the *warrāq*, that is, one who dealt with paper and copied manuscripts. Paper spread to all regions of Islam, finally reaching Europe (see Plates 114, 126, 130).

In Iran, after the seventh century, Pahlavi declined until it ceased to be used. A new Persian language was taking shape, but literary activity in this new Persian did not begin until the ninth century. In this period, the great Iranian poet Firdawsī (d. *c.* 1020–1026), completed the national epic of his people, the *Shāh-Nāmeh* (see Plates 12, 219). By the thirteenth century, Persian had become a language containing considerable scientific and historical writings. These included one of the first known geographical works, *Ḥudūd al-'Ālam* ('The Limits of the World'; tenth century), and Ibn Sīna's *Dānishnāmeh-yi 'Alā'ī*. The Uighur script was used for Turkish. After conversion to Islam, however, the Turks of Central Asia, after the Tajiks, adopted the Arabic alphabet (see Plates 112, 113). Turkish literary work appeared in the eleventh century. Aramaic was the vernacular language of Syria until it was replaced by Arabic. Syriac remained the ecclesiastical language of Monophysitism. Hebrew was used as a literary and a liturgical language. Arabic was the language of learning for Jewish scholars who were natives of Islamic regions (see Plates 76–79). Arabic also became the literary language for Berber-speaking peoples, and Arabic script was used to write most Berber languages. Coptic was replaced by Arabic but continued as a liturgical language.

Sub-Saharan Africa

Between the eighth and the fifteenth centuries, Africa south of the Sahara witnessed the rise of several flourishing kingdoms and empires. The African peoples had highly organized networks of long-distance trade, a developed agriculture, and mining and metallurgical activities. The most prominent states in West Africa were the Sudanese empires of Ghana, Mali, the Songhai and the Kanem-Bornu. Some of these were greater in size and population than those which existed at the time in Europe. The eastern coast of the continent, from the Horn to Sofala, had direct trade relations with the Islamic world and the Far East. This led to the founding of coastal trading city-states, among which Kilwa attained prominence. Mingling of Arabs, Persians and Asians with the indigenous Bantu resulted in a new Swahili culture and population. Madagascar, also saw a symbiosis of Eastern and African cultures. Early in the fourth century, the kingdom of Axum, the forerunner of Ethiopia, adopted Monophysite Christianity. In Central Africa, several states were established. The Kongo kingdom in the west and the Mwene Mutapa Empire in the east were prominent. In the southern tip of the continent, there are indications that a civilization flourished in this period.

Sub-Saharan African education was designed to prepare children for responsibility in the home, the village and society.

It provided religious and vocational education and full initiation into society. An Islamic system of education based on writing was adopted in all areas where Islam had spread. Elementary schools based on the study of the Qur'ān developed. By the end of our period, Timbuktu had 180 elementary schools and a famous university. Prosperity made possible the development of a literate class devoted to worship and study. The book trade flourished. The universities of the Sudanese (in medieval Arabic, *Sūdān* referred to the entire sub-Saharan Sahel strip from West to East Africa) taught the humanities, which included Islamic subjects, as well as grammar, rhetoric, logic, astrology, astronomy, history and geography. The Sudanese elite reached the height of Islamic learning. African Islamic literature emerged throughout the Sudan, from the Atlantic coast to the Red Sea. Besides this written material, oral tradition (see historiography below) remained a rich source of knowledge and the sciences in Africa.

Africa is a vast linguistic area comprising at least 1,000 languages. Four main families are recognized: Afro-Asiatic, Niger–Congo, Nilo-Saharan and Khoisan. The Niger–Congo is the largest family, having spread across all of sub-Saharan Africa. Among the important languages are Swahili, Fulani, Igbo, Wolof, Yoruba and Zulu. The Afro-Asiatic family is found in North Africa, the Horn of Africa and South-West Asia. The most important are Galla, Somali and Beja from the Cushitic branch; Hausa from the Chadic; Arabic, Hebrew and Amharic from the Semitic; Berber; and Coptic. Nilo-Saharan languages are spoken in an area extending from Mali in the west to Ethiopia in the east and

Figure 9 Arabic script as used in North and West Africa. Page from an account of the kingdom of Mali, in the *Rihla* ('Journey') by the Moroccan traveller Ibn Baṭṭūṭa, fourteenth century AD (Bibliothèque Nationale, Paris, MS arabe 2291, f°103).

from Egypt in the north to Tanzania in the south. Songhai is one major language in this family. Languages of the Khoisan family are spoken in the extreme south.

Ideographic writing systems similar to Egyptian hieroglyphics were employed. An old Nubian writing system derived from Coptic was used and later Nubian was written in Arabic script. Ge'ez, Amharic, Tigre and Tigrinya are written in the Ethiopic alphabet, itself derived from a south Arabian Sabaean script (see Plate 279). Standard literary Hausa and Swahili during this period were written in Arabic script (see Figure 9).

Europe, Byzantium and early Russia

In the seventh century, the nations of northern and western Europe were still in their formative stages, emerging from the migrations of peoples during this period. Not until the tenth century did the linguistic and ethnic map of Northern Europe stabilize and begin to take its modern shape. In this period, the Church became the heir to the Roman Empire and the patron of education through its creation and support of schools. Most men of learning were priests or monks, and all branches of learning were made subordinate to theology. The works of Isidore (d. 636) and Bede (d. 735) are representative of the scientific literature of the early period. Their only purpose was to preserve the inherited remnants of classical learning. The renaissance of science which took place in Europe in the twelfth century was of more importance to science than was the later revival of classical antiquity in Italy. This renaissance acquainted Europe with the whole corpus of the philosophy, logic, exact sciences, non-mathematical natural sciences and medicine of the Greeks and Muslims. It took no less than two centuries, the fourteenth and fifteenth, to assimilate this knowledge and to start to develop a new science.

The translation movement was accompanied by the rise of higher learning in the West. Western Europe was on the eve of its political, social and economical revival. The increase in population and urbanization encouraged the growth of schools. Cathedral schools emerged, notably at Reims, Chartres and Paris. With the appearance of translated Greek and Arabic works after the twelfth century, large numbers of students were attracted to these schools from all parts of Europe. When students and teachers multiplied in numbers, the universities emerged. Starting with Paris and Bologna in the latter part of the twelfth century and the early part of the thirteenth, universities spread throughout Europe. It was in these universities that the adaptation and assimilation of Greek and Islamic learning was achieved, and where most of the intellectual activity took place. Their importance to the emergence of modern science is even greater. They provided the institutional foundation upon which the achievements of later centuries were built (see Plates 127, 133, 137, 141 and Map 3).

Meanwhile, Constantinople assumed pre-eminence over Christianity in the East, as Rome did in the West. The schism between the Western and Eastern churches began in the eighth century and became final in 1054. Byzantium reached its golden age between the ninth and eleventh centuries; decline followed. It was attacked by the Seljuks from the east and by the Normans, Bulgars and Patzinaks (or Petchenegs) from the west. Commercial supremacy passed to Venice. Constantinople fell to the Crusaders in 1204, was recaptured in 1261 and was finally lost to the Ottomans in 1453.

In Byzantine higher education, rhetoric was more important than original thinking. Philosophical teaching was

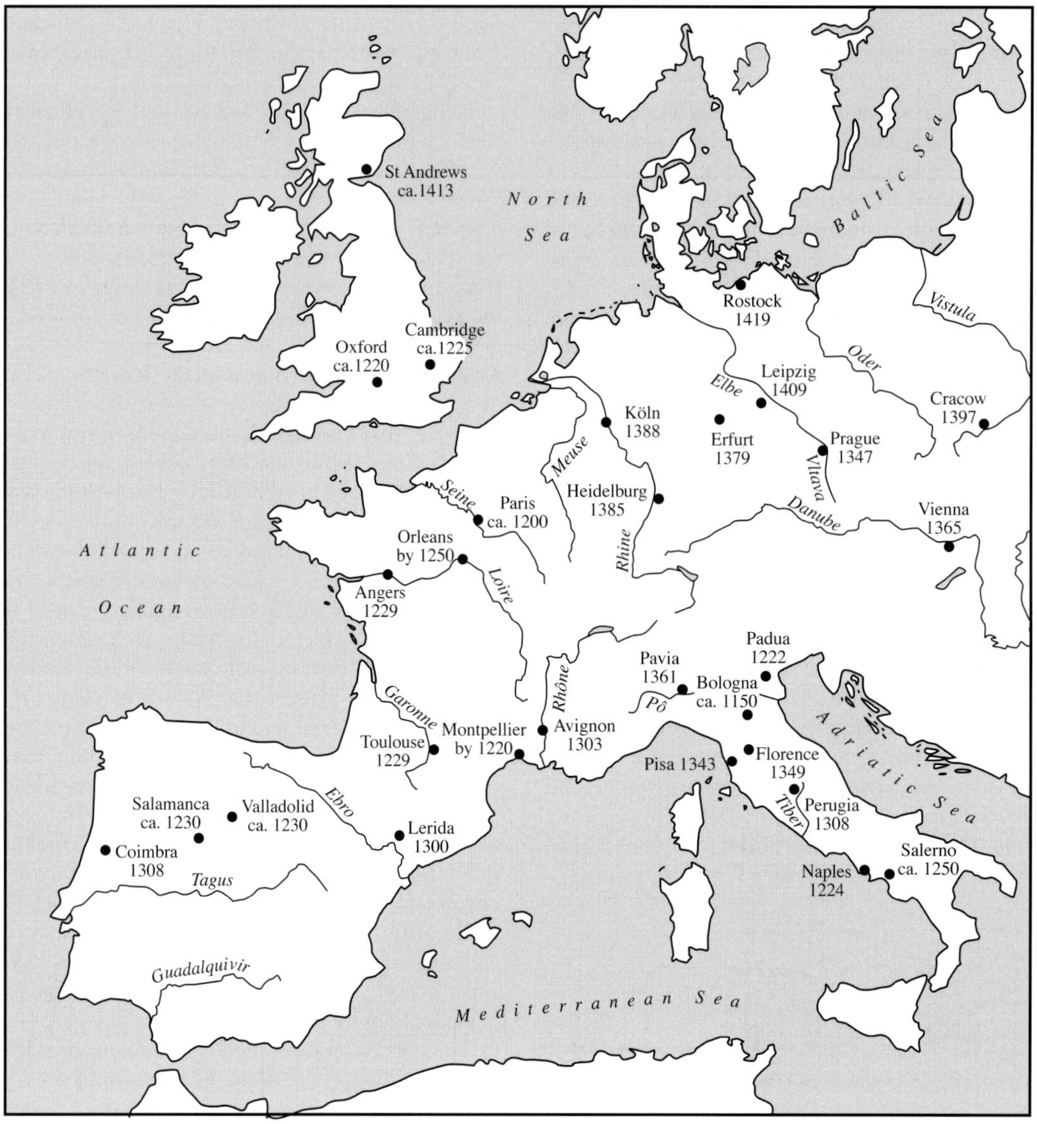

Map 3 The distribution of universities in Europe during the Middle Ages (after Lindberg, D. C., 1992, *The Beginnings of Western Sciences*, Chicago University Press, p. 207).

concerned with explanation rather than with analysis, and originality in the sciences was lacking. But despite these limitations the Byzantines preserved the literature, science and philosophy of classical Greece in recopied manuscripts, some of which were carried to the West (see Plate 127).

The Slavs can be subdivided into east, west and south Slavs. In religion, they are divided into two main groups: those associated with the Eastern Orthodox Church and those associated with the Roman Catholic Church. With few exceptions, the division is further marked by the use of the Cyrillic alphabet by the former and the Latin alphabet by the latter (see Plates 105, 106).

The west Slavs had their cultural and political life integrated into the general European pattern; they experienced, more than other Slavs, all the cultural, philosophical, political and economic changes in the West. Universities were established in Bohemia, Poland and Hungary. On the other hand, the Russians and Balkan Slavs, whose lands were invaded by Mongols and Turks, remained for many centuries without any close contact with the West; they therefore did not share in the renaissance of science which started with the translation of Arabic works. The schism between the two churches was another factor in isolation. A major difference was that the Orthodox Church in each country used the vernacular language in religious services, so Greek did not become the universal language of culture as Latin was in the West.

In 1240, the Tatar Empire, also known as the Golden Horde, imposed its control over Russia until 1451. This had a crippling effect on Russian culture, including the Church, which became more formalistic and ritualistic. By the time Tatar rule came to an end, Russia, now united under Moscow, had entered a new phase in its development. At the end of this period, the various countries of Eastern Europe, after witnessing the rise and fall of their own kingdoms, fell under Ottoman rule for the next four centuries.

Latin remained the language of learning in Western Europe during this period, and the Romance languages developed from spoken Latin. French was the first to develop into a literary language; followed by Italian, Spanish, Portuguese, Provençal and Catalan. For political reasons, Provençal and Catalan declined and gave way to French and Spanish, respectively. The Germanic family (English, German, Dutch and the Scandinavian languages) were fully developed into literary languages in this period. Icelandic developed out of Norwegian. It was itself a learned language and Latin never entirely displaced it for literary works. Yiddish is a West

Germanic language which became identified with the Jewish people of Central Europe around the ninth century. It is a mixture of Germanic and Hebrew elements, with some Slavic. Gaelic or Irish was a literary language in the eighth century with extensive medieval literature. Ireland was wholly Gaelic-speaking in this period (see Plate 104).

Greek was preserved by its literary heritage and by the Byzantine Empire. The Greek language changed considerably throughout the centuries and was marked by internal diglossia between its spoken and written forms. Finally, alongside the classical, a vernacular Greek arose which was used for light literature. Saint Cyril in the ninth century used a southern form of Slavic for his translation of the Septuagint, and 'Old Church Slavonic' remained the vehicle of Russian Orthodoxy. The Cyrillic alphabet is used to write all the East Slavic languages (see Plates 106, 153), while the West Slavs and most Croatians use the Latin alphabet. The outstanding Slavonic language in this period was Bohemian or Czech. The earliest Czech texts go back to the thirteenth century. Russian literature is represented by some religious and travel literature. Botanical glosses which appeared in Polish establish its existence. Among the Finno-Ugric branch of languages, Hungarian was written in a modified Latin alphabet from the thirteenth century. The earliest Georgian inscriptions date from the fifth century. New Georgian developed as a secular literary medium in the twelfth century. It is written in the Mkhedruli alphabet. Saint Mesrop (fifth century) invented a special alphabet for Armenian. By the ninth century, spoken Armenian became distinct from the literary idiom and was utilized in writing, beside the classical, in the twelfth century (see Plate 156).

Pre-Columbian America

The term 'pre-Columbian civilizations', refers to the Native American cultures that evolved prior to the Spanish conquest in the sixteenth century. The outstanding cultural achievements of these civilizations are often compared with those of the ancient Old World.

The Maya possessed one of the greatest civilizations of the Western Hemisphere. They practised agriculture, built large stone buildings and pyramid temples, worked gold and copper, developed a precise calendar and made use of hieroglyphic writing. Decisive breakthroughs in deciphering this script have only occurred recently. The Maya paid great regard to their priesthood: to become a priest, the trainee had to receive rigorous education in school, where he was taught history, writing, divining, medicine and the calendar system (see Plates 92, 93, 294, 295). The Aztecs created a great empire of about 6 million people with remarkable systems of agriculture, irrigation and reclamation. The Aztec calendar was the one common to much of Mesoamerica (see Plate 144). The Mexicans did develop a written language, but it might more correctly be described as picture writing (see Plate 94), and cultural preservation relied heavily upon oral transmission of important events and knowledge.

In the central Andes, the greatest cultural development was that of the Inca empire, which at its height had a population of about 6 million. Inca technology and architecture were highly developed, and their irrigation systems, palaces, temples and fortifications can still be seen. They built a vast network of roads. The Incas did not possess a written or recorded language, so their history and culture were preserved by oral tradition. Their education was divided into two distinct categories: vocational education for the common people; and a highly formalized training for the nobility.

THE EXACT SCIENCES

Mathematics in Pre-Columbian America

Maya mathematics involved two outstanding developments: the positional notation and zero. In the number system, the ratio of increase of successive units was 20 in all positions except the third. Thus 20 units of the lowest order (*kin* or days) make one unit of the next higher order (*uinal* or 20 days); 18 *uinals* make one unit of the third order (*tun* or 360 days); 20 *tuns* make one unit of the fourth order (*katun* or 7,200 days); and so on until the high order of *alautun*. One *alatun* equals 64 million *tuns*. In the Maya codices, the symbols for 1 to 19 were expressed by bars and dots. Each bar stands for five units and each dot for one unit. The zero is represented by a symbol that looks like a half-closed eye. The numbers are arranged vertically, the lowest order being assigned the lowest position (see Figure 10).

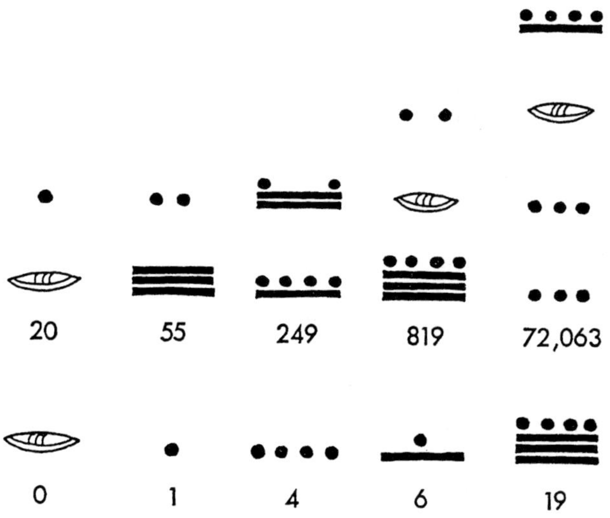

Figure 10 Maya vigesimal numeration (after Coe, M. D., *The Maya*, London 1966, p. 183).

Mathematics in China and Japan

During the Tang dynasty (618–906), Wang Xiaotong (fl. 625), wrote the *Qigu Suanjing*, in which he dealt with cubic and quadratic equations. At the end of the eighth century, the decimal system was simplified, and Han Yan simply wrote the word '*duan*' to separate decimals. In the same century, the zero symbol was mentioned in the work of the Hindu-Chinese astronomer Qutan Xida. During the Song and Yuan dynasties, four great mathematicians appeared. Qin Jiushao wrote *Notes on the Mathematical Treatise in Nine Sections* in 1247. He dealt with indeterminate equations and gave solutions to equations of the tenth degree. Li Ye wrote the *Sea Mirror of Circle Measurement* in 1248. He dealt with the problem of inscribing a circle inside a triangle and wrote the resulting equations with four unknowns. Yang Hui wrote the *Detailed Analysis of Mathematical Rules in Nine Chapters*, in which he gave the sums of various series and solved equations with five unknowns, in 1261. The last great mathematician was Zhu Shijie who wrote the *Introduction to Mathematical Studies* in 1299, and the *Precious Mirror of Four Elements*, which marks the peak of Chinese algebra, in 1303. The first was the main vehicle by which Chinese algebra reached Japan. In the *Precious Mirror*, Zhu used a diagram identical to Pascal's triangle to find the coefficients in the binomial theorem.

Chinese mathematical works reached Japan first through Korea and later directly from China. Prince Shōtoku Taishi (d. 622) is called the father of Japanese arithmetic. A school of arithmetic was founded around AD 670, and nine Chinese works were specified for students of mathematics. This period was one of preparation, contributing nothing new to what China had already developed.

Indian mathematics

Before AD 600, mathematics had already reached a mature stage of development. Two important earlier developments are worthy of mention. The decimal place-value system (base ten) became known to the Indians at the beginning of the sixth century, probably inspired by the Babylonians (see Figure 11). Another achievement was in trigonometry. The earliest sine tables originated in India. Among the mathematicians who appeared after 600, three were most prominent. Brahmagupta (b. 589) developed a lemma for the solution of indeterminate equations of the second degree, and a formula for the sum of arithmetic progressions. The arithmetical operations of Mahāvīra (*c.* 850), are based on decimal place-value notation, some involving zero. He studied the summation of geometric progressions. Bhāskara II (b. 1114), represents the culmination of Indian mathematics. He was the first to state that the division of a number by zero is infinite. He dealt with linear and quadratic equations, both determinate and indeterminate, simple mensuration, arithmetic and geometric progressions, surds, and Pythagorean triads.

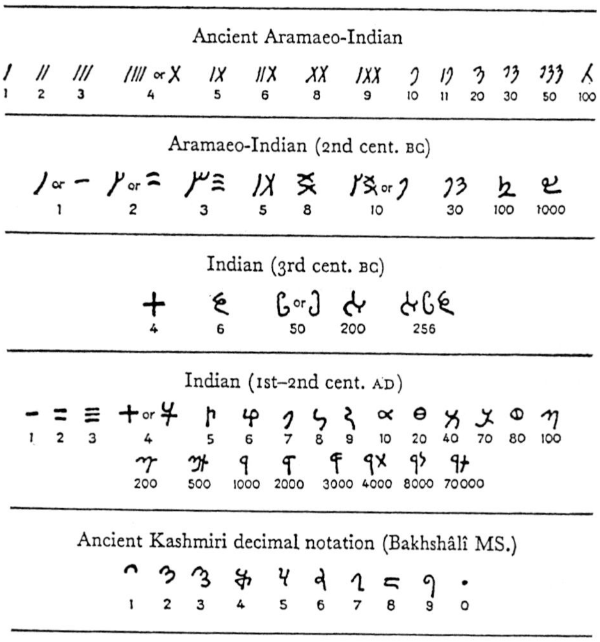

Figure 11 The development of numerical notation in India (after Taton (ed.), 1963, p. 149).

Islamic mathematics

Hindu numerals were introduced into Syria in the seventh century. Hindu arithmetic came with the translation of astronomical works in the eighth century. The first treatise on Arabic–Hindu reckoning was that of Muḥammad ibn Mūsā al-Khwārizmī (d. *c.* 850). A fundamental development was the use of decimal fractions, which were first used by al-Uqlīdisī (fl. 950) and were fully worked out by al-Kāshī (fl. 1420). Iterative procedures enabled mathematicians to produce numerical tables with unprecedented precision. Al-Māhānī (fl. 860) and others studied the theory of ratios and proportions and developed a definition for irrational numbers. In the theory of numbers, Thābit ibn Qurra (d. 901) put forward a most important theorem for amicable numbers.

Islamic algebra began by assimilating Babylonian, Greek and Indian knowledge, but it was al-Khwārizmī who laid the foundations of algebra as an independent discipline. He gave solutions to six types of quadratic equation. Algebra was further developed by several eminent successors, notably 'Umar al-Khayyām (d. 1131), who classified all types of cubics and gave their solutions. 'Pascal's' triangle was discovered by al-Karajī (fl. 1011) and used by al-Khayyām and Naṣīr al-Dīn al-Ṭūsī (d. 1274). Signs instead of words in algebra were employed by al-Qalasādī (*c.* 1486).

Geometry was founded on Greek works, especially Euclid's *Elements*. After the translation of Archimedes, Banū Mūsā (ninth century) wrote *On the Measure of Simple and Spherical Figures*. Another classical problem which received attention was the theory of parallels. In their search for better solutions, mathematicians proved some non-Euclidean theorems. A proof by al-Ṭūsī was translated into Latin.

In trigonometry, Muslims adopted the sine function of the Sanskrit works. In the ninth century, Ḥabash al-Ḥāsib introduced the notion of the 'shadow' or tangent and compiled a table of tangents which was the earliest of its kind. Muslims defined the six trigonometric functions and compiled their tables to a very high degree of precision. In 1260, Naṣīr al-Dīn al-Ṭūsī wrote a book on trigonometry, *Shakl al-qiṭā'*, which marked the emergence of trigonometry as an independent branch of mathematics (see Plate 139).

Mathematics in Europe

Gerbert (d. 1003), was the first to introduce Arabic numerals into Europe, for use with the abacus. In the twelfth century, al-Khwārizmī's treatise on arithmetic was translated into Latin: from the Latin title of this work came the word 'algorithm'. Arabic–Hindu numerals were also introduced by Leonardo of Pisa (Fibonacci) (d. *c.* 1245), who learned arithmetic while residing in Arab countries. In 1202, he wrote the *Book of the Abacus*. Around 1240, John of Holywood wrote the *Algorismus vulgaris* based on the work of al-Khwārizmī, which became the standard university text for several centuries. But the new system met with resistance, and it was not until the sixteenth century that Arabic–Hindu numerals finally replaced the Roman system.

Al-Khwārizmī's treatise on algebra was also translated into Latin (the word 'algebra' comes from the Arabic *al-Jabr*). Fibonacci's book discusses algebra and gives the results of al-Khwārizmī and al-Karajī. These works on algebra did not attract much academic attention, and few mathematicians became familiar with them. Only in the late fifteenth century was algebra adopted at the University of Leipzig. In geometry, the *Elements* of Euclid with some works of Archimedes and Banū Mūsā's treatise were rendered into Latin. But Euclid's *Elements* was not an easy work to comprehend, and time was needed for its assimilation.

Trigonometry was first introduced with the translation of Arabic astronomical works. Robert of Chester, in 1249, was the first to use the word 'sinus', from the Arabic *jaib*. It is not known whether al-Ṭūsī's independent work on trigonometry was known in Europe, but Wallingford (d. 1335) and Regiomontanus (d. 1476) also treated trigonometry as an independent discipline.

Astronomy in Pre-Columbian America

The duration of the solar year was calculated with amazing accuracy, as well as the synodical revolution of Venus. In the Dresden Codex, there are very precise Venusian and lunar tables and a method for predicting solar eclipses. The Maya had a sacred year of 260 days, an official year of 360 days and a solar year of 365+ days.

Chinese astronomy

In 1092, Su Song described a large water-driven astronomical clock with escarpment which turned a celestial globe and an armillary sphere. Zhamaluding (Jamāl al-Dīn) was a Muslim astronomer who devised a new calendar for Qubilai Khān in 1267. He also introduced some Islamic astronomical instruments into China. At the same time, Guo Shoujing (d. 1316) compiled a list of astronomical instruments, including the Arab *torquetum* (see Plate 134).

Indian astronomy

During the fourth–sixth centuries, several astronomical works appeared under the name of *Siddhanta*. These were the result of a long history of contacts with Babylonian and Greek cultures and of original contributions. The *Sūryasiddhānta* was the best and most accurate. It underwent periodic revisions over the centuries and served as a standard astronomical text. Brahmagupta wrote two astronomical treatises. Bhāskara II followed the general lines of the *Sūryasiddhānta,* and his work was a continuation of his predecessors, especially Brahmagupta. He made a further elaboration of epicyclic–eccentric theories of planetary motions.

Islamic astronomy

Islamic astronomy began with the translations of Sanskrit, Pahlavi and Greek works, notably the *Almagest*. Muslim astronomers reached prominence in their knowledge. The greatest astronomer of the ninth century was Al-Battānī, who made observations and compiled a catalogue of stars for AD 880. He determined the various astronomical coefficients with great accuracy, discovered the motion of the solar apsides and wrote an elaborate treatise which remained authoritative until the sixteenth century. Numerous Arabic treatises discussed the planetary theory. Astronomical literature became more sophisticated and culminated in launching criticisms of the *Almagest*. Ibn al-Haytham (Alhazen), al-'Urdī and al-Ṭūsī argued against Ptolemy's astronomy and proposed alternative planetary models. Al-Ṭūsī introduced a new mathematical theorem, now known as the Ṭūsī couple. Al-Shīrāzī proposed a model for the motion of Mercury. In the fourteenth century, Ibn al-Shāṭir produced the first model of the motion of the Moon (see Figure 12). Recent research shows that the Copernican model for the movement of the farther planets uses the techniques of al-'Urdī and al-Ṭūsī, and the model for the Moon is identical to that of Ibn al-Shāṭir. This precise correspondence raised the question of the possible transmission to Europe of Islamic models.

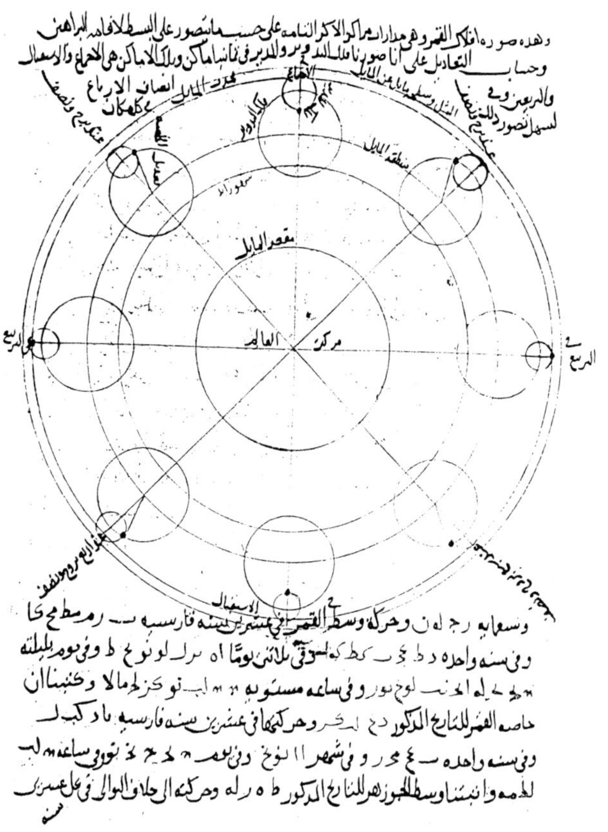

Figure 12 Ibn al-Shātir's model of the motion of the Moon, fourteenth century AD, elaborated upon Ptolemy's theory of planetary motion (after Badeau *et al.*, 1978, p. 127).

Islamic observatories were centres of astronomical research and education, and between the ninth and the fifteenth centuries they were established in numerous cities, notably Baghdād, Damascus, Cairo, Shīrāz, Khwārizm, Marāghah and Samarkand. The Samarkand observatory was established by the enlightened prince Ulūgh Beg (d. 1449). It was completed in 1420 and its work lasted nearly thirty years under his continued patronage. Besides Ulūgh Beg, who was himself a scientist, the observatory included distinguished astronomers and mathematicians such as al-Kāshī. Their work resulted in the *Zīj-i Ulūgh Beg*, a masterpiece of observational astronomy. This was the peak achievement of Islamic observatories, and from here on the Islamic tradition of founding observatories was transmitted to Europe (see Plates 135, 136, 138–40, 142, 143).

Astronomy in Europe

In the tenth century, Gerbert introduced the armillary sphere and the astrolabe through contacts with Arab science in northern Spain. The use of the astrolabe necessitated a set of astronomical tables (see Plate 141), and Adelard of Bath translated the astronomical tables of al-Khwārizmī in 1126. The *zīj* of al-Battānī and the *Toledan Tables* (by al-Zarqalī) were also translated. Besides the astrolabe and the tables, astronomers needed deeper knowledge of astronomical theories. The *Almagest* was translated from Greek and Arabic, but it was too advanced to be used as a textbook. A non-mathematical treatise of al-Farghāni, the *Rudimenta astronomica*, served as an introduction to theoretical astronomy. To serve the needs of the universities, a curriculum developed around manuals written by John of Holywood. To these were added the anonymous *Theorica planetarum*, some treatises by Thābit and the *Alphonsine Tables*. Under Alfonso X (1252–84) in Spain, a collection of treatises on astronomical instruments and tables, the *Libros del saber de astronomía*, was compiled in Castilian and consisted mainly of translations from Arabic. In the fifteenth century, Peuerbach wrote the *Theoricae novae planetarum* (1454). Regiomontanus set up a small private astronomical observatory at Nuremberg, but the real observatories with large and permanently mounted instruments had to await the sixteenth century (see Plates 137, 141).

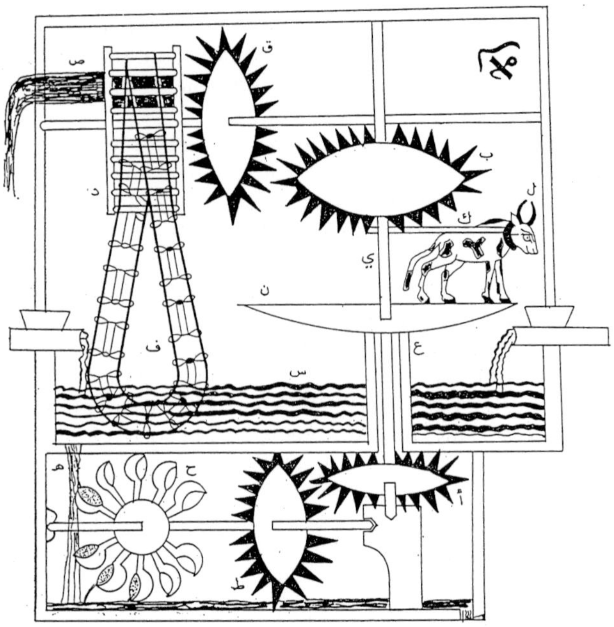

Figure 13 Water-driven set of wheels and cogs to elevate water (showing a dummy ox). Redrawn from the treatise on *Automata* by al-Jazarī, Iraq, AD 1206, preserved in the Topkapi Palace Library, Istanbul (after al-Hassan, A. Y. and Hill, D. R., 1986).

Chinese physics

The Chinese were more disposed towards a concept of waves and did not adopt an atomic philosophy. Their main achievement was the development of the magnetic compass. The earliest clear mention of the magnetic needle was by Shen Gua in 1086 and the earliest mention of its use for navigation occurs after 1100 by Zhu Yu. In optics, we find that the *Hua shu*, written in 940, mentions four kinds of lens. Shen Gua knew about the camera obscura. In acoustics, Zhang Zai explained that the formation of sound is due to the friction between material things in 1060.

Indian physics

This was not studied separately, and each of the several religious schools had their own notions of atom, space and time. Atomism was known from the sixth century BC. The elements of the impetus theory appeared in the seventh century BC, but it became recognizable from the fifth century AD.

Islamic physics

Statics and hydrostatics were studied under 'the science of weights'. The Arabic books on this subject dealt with the theory, construction and use of scientific weighing instruments. Several works were written on the *Qarastūn*, like that of Thābit ibn Qurra. Al-Bīrūnī wrote on the measurement of specific gravities. Al-Khāzinī's book *The Balance of Wisdom* is one of the most remarkable books on mechanics, hydrostatics and physics of the Middle Ages. The results obtained by al-Bīrūnī and al-Khāzinī for specific gravities were among the finest achievements in experimental physics. The laws of hydrostatics were applied extensively in the *Kitāb al-Ḥiyal* by the Banū Mūsa brothers. Al-Bīrūnī applied these laws to explain the working of natural springs and artesian wells. Some original theorems on hydrodynamics were formulated for the movement of bodies in fluids and the effect of shape on the amount of resistance to motion.

Although kinematics was not a separate branch of science, uniform circular motion was defined. Thābit ibn Qurra came close to defining instantaneous velocity. We also find in the works of Ibn Sīnā and Ibn Rushd notions relating to rates of change of place. In dynamics, Ibn Sīnā developed the concept of *mayl* or 'impetus' to explain projectile motion. Another important concept was that of 'momentum', or *quwwat al-harakah* as described by Ibn al-Haytham. Gravity was the subject of extensive studies by numerous scientists, who formulated ideas of great interest. Al-Khāzinī defined gravity as a universal force directed towards the centre of the Earth. The dynamics of Ibn Bājja was known in Europe and was influential.

A special category of works dealt with the science of ingenious devices (*'ilm al-ḥiyal*). The earliest was the book by the Banū Mūsā brothers. Al-Murādī (eleventh century), in Spain, described large water-clocks and automata (see Figure 13) driven by full-sized waterwheels. These compare with the large water-clock of Su Song. The most important treatise on machines in the Middle Ages was al-Jazarī's book (thirteenth century). All these works illustrated ingenious machines that were designed for productive purposes as well as for amusement.

Optics was one subject in which Islamic scientists made major contributions. It was Ibn al-Haytham who made the most profound developments in this science. His *Kitāb al-Manāẓir* is a comprehensive work, which gave a new theory of vision and discussed the propagation, reflection and refraction of light. Among his other important findings, he discussed the magnifying power of lenses. Kamāl al-Dīn al-Fārisī, following in the footsteps of Ibn al-Haytham, was able to give a satisfactory account of both the primary and secondary rainbows.

Physics in Europe

The most influential source for medieval statics was Thābit ibn Qurra's *Liber Karastonis*. The *Elementa Super Demonstrationem Ponderis* of Jordanus Nemorarius (d. 1237) gave some original ideas on statics. This was followed by a larger and better work, the anonymous *De Ratione Ponderis*, which corrected many of the inadequacies of the earlier treatise. Great attention was given to the nature of motion. Among the commentators who dealt with this question were William of Ockham (d. 1347) from Oxford and Jean Buridan (d. *c.* 1358) from Paris. The concept that motion is a quality became common in the second half of the fourteenth century. In kinematics, motion is described without any reference to causation. Gerard of Brussels wrote the *Book of Motion* and thus started the kinematic tradition in the Latin West. The distinction between kinematics and dynamics was further elaborated by a group at Merton College, Oxford, including Bradwardine and others. They developed such technical vocabulary as velocity and instantaneous velocity. Nicholas Oresme in Paris developed a geometric system for the representation of motion.

In dynamics, John Philoponus of Alexandria in the sixth century AD rejected the views of Aristotle on motion. He assumed that the hurled body acquires a self-expending motive force or inclination from the agent producing the initial motion. Ibn Sīnā modified this by saying that the violent inclination was not self-expending; it was a permanent force whose effect became dissipated only as a result of external agents such as air resistance. In the fourteenth century, ideas on impressed force were further elaborated by Jean Buridan and his successors into a mature theory. Buridan called this impressed force 'impetus'. He went a step further by declaring that impetus is dependent on the quantity of matter in the body, and on its velocity.

The work of al-Kindī on optics and the views of Ibn Sīnā about the nature of light became known in Europe. But the work by Ibn al-Haytham, *Optical Thesaurus*, was of the greatest importance and continued to be the major work on this subject. Western European interest in optics began with Robert Grosseteste (d. 1253) and Roger Bacon (d. 1292). Pecham (d. 1292) and Witelo (d. after 1281) wrote treatises on optics following the lead of Ibn al-Haytham (Alhazen), and it was due to their work that Ibn al-Haytham's optical theories became dominant. Theodore of Freiburg (d. *c.* 1310) used Ibn al-Haytham's theories to develop a theory of the rainbow. A Muslim contemporary of Theodore, al-Fārisī, developed a similar theory as we have seen.

THE NATURAL SCIENCES

Chinese natural science

The Chinese kept meteorological records of such things as rainfall and earthquakes, compiled tide tables and made meteorological forecasts. An analysis of the contents of Shen Gua's work (eleventh century) indicates that he devoted considerable space to observations in meteorology, geology and mineralogy. Du Wan, in 1133, discussed fossils and Mu Biao wrote the *Synonymic Dictionary of Minerals and Drugs* in 806. The Chinese herbals (*Bencao*) were a unique tradition which continued throughout the centuries (see Figure 14). Numerous editions appeared and new items continued to be added. Among the numerous editions of this period was the *Zhenglei Bencao*, compiled in 1108 by Tang Shenwei. An important edition, the *Shaoxing Bencao*, was compiled and printed in 1159 in thirty-three books. The most original edition was the *Jiuhuang Bencao*, compiled in 1406 by the Ming prince Zhu Xiao (d. 1425). A botanical dictionary,

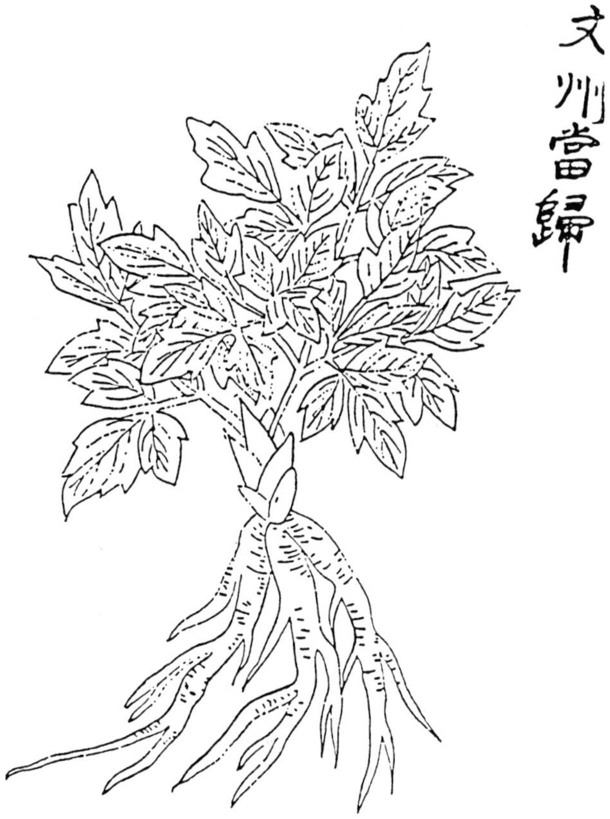

Figure 14 *Shaoxing Bencao*: Chinese herbal medicine. Chinese herbals, or bencao, were based on unique principles. This plant contains an oxytoxic active principle. From the *Shaoxing Bencao*, AD 1159 (after Needham, J., 1970, p. 413).

Quanfang Beizu, was compiled in 1256 by Chen Jingyi. An elaborate treatise on husbandry, *Nongsang jiyao*, was completed in 1273. Wang Zhen wrote a treatise on agriculture, the *Nongshu*, in 1314. Treatises were also written on specific subjects such as tea and bamboo. Animals were listed and described in the *Bencao* books. There were works on specific species such as birds and crickets.

Indian natural science

Plants and animals were subjects of interest to lexicographers, encyclopedists and poets. There were classification systems for animals and plants. Specific texts were devoted to agriculture and horticulture, such as the *Ḳrisi-Parasara*.

Islamic natural science

Following Aristotle, Muslim philosophers discussed meteorological questions and came up with new ideas. Ibn Sīnā studied the changes occurring near the surface of the Earth: the formation of river deposits, the structure of mountains, fossils and the formation of stones, and gave the most complete treatment of geology of the Middle Ages. Al-Bīrūnī also made important observations of geological changes like earthquakes. He remarked that the Indus valley was probably an ancient sea basin. The Ikhwān al-Ṣafā ('Brethnen of Purity') gave a correct interpretation of fossils and of the hydrological cycle. Work on mineralogy resulted in the 'lapidaries', and sometimes dealt with metallurgy and petrology. Among these are Al-Kindī's treatises on precious stones and the metallurgy of steel and the *Kitāb al-Jamāhir* ('Book of Gems') by al-Bīrūnī. Works on alchemy and cosmography also dealt with similar subjects.

Botany was related to medicine and agriculture. Works of a philological nature were written on specific plants (see Plate 130). The most important Arabic work on botany was *Kitāb al-Nabāt* ('Book of Plants') by al-Dīnawarī (ninth century). Medical works devoted a section to herbs, as did encyclopaedic works like those by al-Nuwayrī. Books on agriculture (*'ilm al-filāḥa*) such as *Nabataean Agriculture* by Ibn Waḥshiyya (tenth century), are good sources. From the tenth century, almost all Arabic works on *al-filāḥa* were written in al-Andalus. Ibn Baṣṣāl and Ibn al-'Awwām were among a long succession of agriculturists, and agricultural practices in Yemen were documented in the thirteenth century by two of the Rasūlī kings.

Zoology was related to veterinary medicine, medicine and agriculture. The earliest Arabic works on animals were the philological treatises dealing with individual domestic animals such as horses. Of the early zoological works, the most prominent is *Kitāb al-Ḥayawān* by al-Jāḥiẓ (ninth century), which gave some novel theories. All encyclopaedic and cosmographic works of the thirteenth and fourteenth centuries and some treatises on agriculture devoted sections to animals. In the fourteenth century, Kamāl al-Dīn al-Damīrī wrote *The Great Book on the Life of Animals*, the most complete extant Arabic work on zoology.

Veterinary medicine developed as a separate discipline, one of the earliest works beings written by Ḥunayn ibn Isḥāq. In the same period (ninth century), Ibn Akhī Khizām wrote the first book on the treatment of horses (hippiatrics). The greatest work was *Kāmil al-Ṣīnā'atayn* by Abū Bakr al-Bayṭār (d. 1340). A special branch of veterinary medicine was falconry, dealing with birds of prey. Treatises appeared from the early days of the 'Abbāsids, but the crowning work was *al-Qānūn al-Wāḍiḥ* by Ibn Qushtimur (thirteenth century).

Natural History in Europe

Meteorology became of interest after the twelfth century. The European Jewish scholar Themon (fl. fourteenth century) compiled *Questions on the Four Books of Aristotle's Meteorologica*. Ibn Sīnā's treatise *On the Formation of Stones and Mountains* was made available in Latin. Albertus Magnus (d. 1280), in his *Book of Minerals*, discussed the material, hardness and fissility of stones and gave much first-hand information. Jean Buridan (d. 1358) formulated ideas on geology.

Books known as lapidaries were common; they included material of a fabulous nature, such as the magical virtues of stones. The collection of scholarly works patronized by King Alfonso X (1252–84) included a lapidary which expounded astrological and occult notions.

Two kinds of botanical literature were written: treatises on theoretical botany and books on herbs. The theoretical works were mostly inspired by the pseudo-Aristotle's *On Plants*, on which Albertus Magnus wrote an important commentary. The most important book on herbs was *De Materia Medica* by Dioscorides. Around 1300, Simon of Genoa compiled *Synonyma Medicinae*, a dictionary of about 6,000 articles, drawing on both Late Classical and Arab sources.

In zoology, the writings of Albertus Magnus were the finest yet written in Europe. His *Questions 'On Animals'*, based on Aristotle's *On Animals*, was made available with the addition of the influential commentaries of Ibn Sīnā. Another source of medieval knowledge was the bestiaries, books on animal lore that flourished in the twelfth century and further expanded in size as they were copied. A famous work on falconry was that by Emperor Frederick II (d. 1250), *On the Art of Hunting with Birds*. It was based on Aristotle but also on Arabic sources, as well as on his own direct observations.

Chinese alchemy

Alchemy in China is associated with Daoism. Its basic foundation is the belief in physical immortality and the possibility of attaining it through an elixir. Probably the most famous alchemical treatise is *Danjing Yaojue*, attributed to Sun Simo (d. after 673). One of the main works was a collection of alchemical treatises, known as *Yunji Qigian*, which was compiled by Zhang Junfang in 1022. Another important source is the *Daozang*. The elixirs of immortality or longevity were varied in composition, the main materials being cinnabar, mercury, lead, silver, gold and sulphur. In their search for the elixir of immortality, Daoist alchemists performed many chemical operations and thus made several discoveries, including gunpowder. There is a wealth of chemical information in their treatises.

Indian alchemy

Alchemy made its appearance in the fifth or sixth century AD under twin aspects: pursuit of the elixir of life; and attempts to transmute base metals into gold. In the next seven or eight centuries, Indian alchemy attracted a large following due to its association with Tantrism. It seems likely that the male–female concept in Indian alchemy came from China, where alchemy was based on the *yin* and the *yang*, and where cinnabar was considered the main ingredient of the elixir of immortality. Alchemy, or *rasavidyā*, developed into a methodical knowledge and a number of texts, known as the *rasashāstra*, appeared as of the tenth century AD, embodying a large amount of alchemical knowledge, including materials, processes and alchemical apparatus.

Islamic alchemy

Pre-Islamic Alexandrian alchemy was based on the idea that all substances are composed of four elements – air, fire, water and earth – and on the belief that it is possible to transmute one metal into another. Islamic alchemy began with the Umayyad prince Khālid ibn Yazīd (d. 704), but the greatest alchemist, before the rise of modern chemistry, was Jābir ibn Ḥayyān ('Geber') (d. 813). He stressed the importance of experiment and made notable advances in the theory and practice of chemistry. Jābir adopted the concept of sulphur and mercury in the formation of metals. He was well acquainted with the usual chemical operations. He had his own laboratory and described a great number of experiments, which resulted in the discovery of nitric and other mineral acids. His books are full of technological innovations, such as the production of cast iron and steel. The works attributed to Jābir are very large in number, but only some were written by him, others by his followers. Like many other Arabic works, some of Jābir's writings are extant only in their Latin versions, while others have been lost. In Jābir's time, Arabic versions of such late Greek works as the pseudo-epigraph *Turba Philosophorum* and the pseudo-Apollonius *Secret of Creation*, with the *Tabula Smaragdina* appended to it, were in circulation. The next most important figure in Islamic alchemy was Abū Bakr Muḥammad ibn Zakariyyā al-Rāzī (Rhazes) (d. 925). With Jābir, he was responsible for initiating the transformation of alchemy into chemistry. His most important extant works are *The Book of Secrets, The Book of the Secret of Secrets* and *Liber de Aluminibus et Salibus*, which is available only in Latin. One of al-Rāzī's main contributions is his classification of mineral substances. He also gave a detailed description of chemical laboratory equipment and its main processes and described a large number of experiments in which he produced several mineral acids and chemicals. Al-Rāzī's chemical knowledge was applied by him to medicine, and thus he might be considered the ancestor of iatrochemistry. Ibn Sīnā (d. 1037) was not a chemist, but he did discuss alchemy; he refuted the theory of transmutation. Many other prominent Muslim scientists wrote on alchemy and chemical technology. In the large number of manuscripts which remain to be studied, there is abundant information concerning the properties of substances; the necessary apparatus and processes for the production of mineral and organic acids and alkalis; the distillation of wine; the technology of products like soap, glass, ceramics and dyes; and metallurgy. Extensive Arabic literature also exists on incendiaries, including gunpowder.

Alchemy in Europe

There were some early technical books of recipes on such topics as paints and pigments, but the science of alchemy was not yet known. In the thirteenth century, al-Rāzī's *De Aluminus et salibus* and *Liber Secretum Secretorum*, and Ibn Sīnā's *De Anima in Arte Alchimiae* were most influential. At the end of the thirteenth century, four treatises attributed to Jābir appeared, including *Summa Perfectionis Magesterii*, which became the main chemical textbook of medieval Europe. Despite doubts raised about the authorship of Jābir's Latin works, it is known that they are representative of Arabic alchemy. From the middle of the thirteenth century, alchemy began to appear in writings attributed to such celebrated names as Albertus Magnus and Raymond Lull.

MEDICINE

Chinese and Japanese medicine

Ancient Chinese natural philosophy was based upon the idea of two fundamental forces, the *yang* and the *yin*. Ancient Chinese physicians assumed that all diseases were divided into six classes derived from excess of one or other of six fundamental *qi*. The naturalists classified all natural phenomena into five groups associated with the five elements: water, fire, wood, metal and earth. These were regarded as intimately allied with the organs of the human body. Thus the fire of the heart is red like cinnabar, which can ensure the perpetual regeneration of the human body. State organization of medicine began early in China. Medical examinations were held and the teaching and practice of medicine were regulated. *The Treatise on the Causes and*

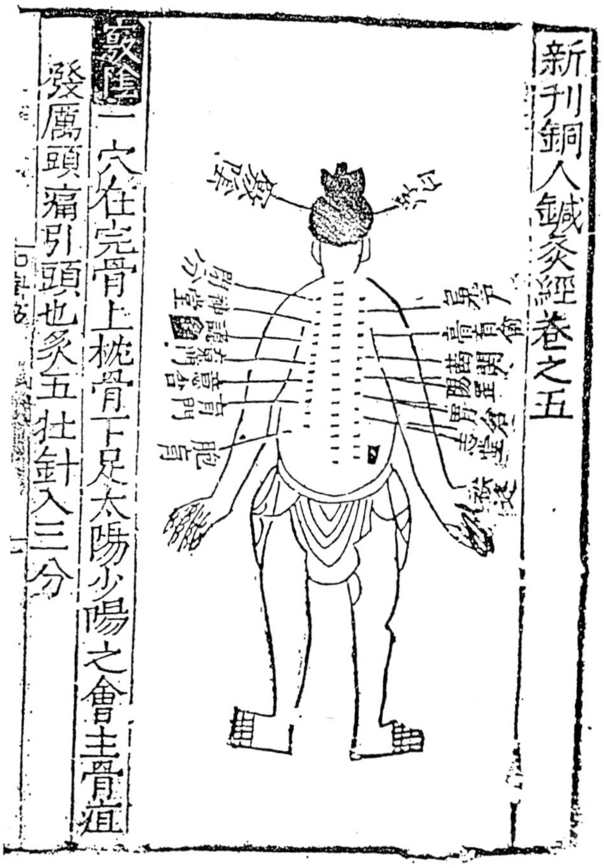

Figure 15 Chinese acupuncture: a page from the *Manual of Acupuncture* by Wang Wei-I, AD 1026 (after Needham, J., 1970, p. 290).

Symptoms of Diseases was written in AD 610 by Chao Yuanfang by imperial order. This is a major work on theoretical medicine, in which clinical knowledge was expanded. It contains descriptions of genito-urinary troubles and smallpox. Another important physician was Sun Simo. His book *Thousand Golden Remedies*, is an immense collection of recipes. He prescribed the use of calomel for venereal diseases. Another comprehensive treatise, *Important Family Practice of a Frontier Official* by Wang Tao, was published in 752. It includes every branch of medicine and therapeutics and a brief treatment of veterinary medicine. During the Song Dynasty, many works were written. Wang Weide (fl. *c.* 1027) wrote a treatise on the art of acupuncture (see Figure 15), and Song Ci (fl. 1247) compiled a treatise on forensic medicine. There were works on pediatrics, the pulse, diseases of women and fevers. Social and personal hygiene and preventive medicine were given special attention, and oral vaccination was applied. Special diets were prescribed for diseases like pellagra.

Korean physicians introduced Chinese medicine into Japan in the sixth century AD. Japanese medical students were sent to China in 608, and some Chinese physicians were occupying high positions in Japan in the eighth century. The earliest Japanese hospital was founded in 758. By the ninth century, Chinese medicine completely superseded the old medical lore of Japan. Waké Hiroyo wrote a treatise on materia medica derived from Chinese works, in the ninth century. In the same century, Fukuyoshi Omura wrote the earliest Japanese treatise on surgery, which was of Chinese derivation.

Indian medicine

Theories of Indian medicine, *ayurveda*, had already been formulated before this period. *Ayurveda* means knowledge of longevity. Its basic theory is that of organ functions and their disequilibrium. The human body, like the universe, is constituted of five elements: water, fire, wind, space and earth. The task of *ayurveda* is to maintain their balance. Vāgbhata (fl. *c.* 625) is considered of equal importance to such physicians as Charaka and Susruta. His *Astangahrdaya* was an authoritative exposition of the Ayurvedic knowledge. The *Rugvinischaya* of Madhavakara (fl. eighth or ninth century), which deals mainly with diagnostic methods, became a standard text. The Indian *materia medica* consisted mainly of vegetable substances, with some minerals, which were introduced at later dates. Surgeons used a variety of instruments to perform such operations as removing bladder stones and cataracts.

Islamic medicine

When Islam spread throughout the Near East, there were schools of medicine in Alexandria and Jundishāpūr. In the ninth century, Ḥunayn ibn Isḥāq and his school of translators rendered Greek works into Arabic. Other works were translated from Pahlavī and Sanskrit. Some translators were accomplished physicians and wrote works of their own. Ḥunayn wrote many treatises, including an *Introduction to Medicine*. The first medical encyclopedia in Arabic was *Paradise of Wisdom* by 'Alī ibn Sahl Rabbān al-Ṭabarī (d. after 861). Al-Rāzī (d. 925) is considered the greatest physician of Islam. Among his important works are *Kitāb al-Hāwī fī al-Tibb* in twenty-three volumes, *Kitāb al-ṭibb al-Manṣūrī* and the *Treatise on Smallpox and Measles*. Another notable physician was 'Alī ibn 'Abbās al-Majūsī (Haly Abbas) (d. *c.* 994). He wrote *The Perfection of the Art of Medicine*. Abū al-Qāsim al-Zahrāwī (Albucasis) (d. *c.* 1009), from Spain, wrote *Kitāb al-Taṣrīf* ('The Book of Concessions'); it included an illustrated treatise on surgery which is considered the greatest achievement in medieval surgery. Another most celebrated figure in Islamic medicine was Ibn Sīnā (Avicenna) (d. 1037). His most important medical work is *al-Qānūn* ('The Canon of Medicine'). Because of its formal perfection and intrinsic value *al-Qānūn* surpassed all other medical works and remained supreme in Europe for six centuries. It dominated the teaching of medicine in Europe until the end of the sixteenth century and continued to be published until the end of the seventeenth (see Plates 133a–e).

Islamic physiology was based on the humoral system, a concept that came with the Greek medical writings. In this system, everything is considered to be made up of a mixture of four 'humours'. In normal health, these humours were regarded as present in a balanced mixture in the body. In the field of anatomy, Galen was the primary source. Some were critical of Galen, such as al-Rāzī, who wrote *The Book of Doubts about Galen*. It was thought that the heart has two ventricles, left and right, separated by a wall which has an opening. Ibn al-Nafīs (d. 1288) rejected this and declared that there is no opening and the wall is compact. He thus discovered the pulmonary circulation.

External factors played a part in the formation of disease, such as the environment, and the patient's age, sex and habits. This gave an explanation for some infectious diseases. In diagnosis, attention was paid to the organ's temperature, to the pulse, to urine and faeces. What we might today term clinical pathology was an essential part of diagnosis at the time. A large number of diseases, such as smallpox, hay fever, meningitis and whooping cough, were diagnosed.

Al-Zahrāwī explained that surgery should be based on a sufficient knowledge of anatomy. The use of an anaesthetic sponge is said to have been described by him and also the use of antiseptics in the treatment of wounds. Works on ophthalmology reached their peak about AD 1000, when 'Alī ibn 'Īsā al-Kaḥḥāl wrote his book, *Tadhkirat al-kaḥḥālīn*. His contemporary 'Ammār al-Mawṣilī was the first to introduce the technique of suction removal of the cataract. In pharmacology there was a distinction between simple drugs and compound drugs. Several treatises on simple drugs were written. All the medical works included sections on drugs. Al-Bīrūnī's *Kitāb al-Saydala*, and the treatise of Abū Manṣūr Muwaffaq, were two important works on pharmacy. In al-Andalus, Ibn Juljul wrote a commentary on Dioscorides. Ibn al-Bayṭār (d. 1248) wrote the largest pharmaceutical encyclopedia. On compound drugs Ṣābūr ibn Sahl (d. 869) wrote the first known formulary. The hospital was known before Islam. The first Islamic hospital was established in the seventh century. Numerous others were established in Baghdād and they spread very quickly to most other cities. Hospitals became major scientific institutions devoted to the treatment of all kinds of diseases, with medical schools attached to them.

Medicine in Western Europe

During the early Middle Ages, some practical medical writings of Galen and Hippocrates were available in Latin. At one time medicine was practiced at the monasteries where the religious tradition of miraculous cures and the cult of saints prevailed. Medical education shifted gradually from the monasteries to the urban schools and by 1200 the practice of medicine was almost secular. At the end of the eleventh century Salerno became a centre of medical education. Constantine the African (d. 1087) came from North Africa and began to translate medical works into Latin from Arabic. After 1150, more medical works were translated. The assimilation of Graeco-Arabic medical literature which began in Salerno helped the emergence of medicine as a learned profession, and medical faculties were established in Paris, Montpellier, Bologna and other universities. Constantine's translations led to the formation of a collection of medical texts, the *Articella*, which became the heart of the curriculum of Latin medicine. This was supplemented by the works of Galen, al-Rāzī, Ibn Sīnā and others. With these, the medical curriculum acquired a strong philosophical orientation. The medieval medical theories were the same as the Graeco-Arabic ones. Medico-botanical lexicons gave the medicinal properties of plants. Many collections of recipes and prescriptions were in common use such as the *Antidotarium Nicolai*, which acquired a special authority by the end of the thirteenth century.

The study of anatomy at Salerno began with the *Pantegni* of Haly Abbas and was accompanied by the anatomical study of pigs. Human dissection began probably in Bologna late in the thirteenth century. Mondino dei Luzzi (d. 1326) of Bologna, wrote a dissection manual, *Anatomia*, which became a guide to human dissection for two centuries. During the fourteenth century, dissection became a standard part of medical instruction (see Figure 16). Despite this, the

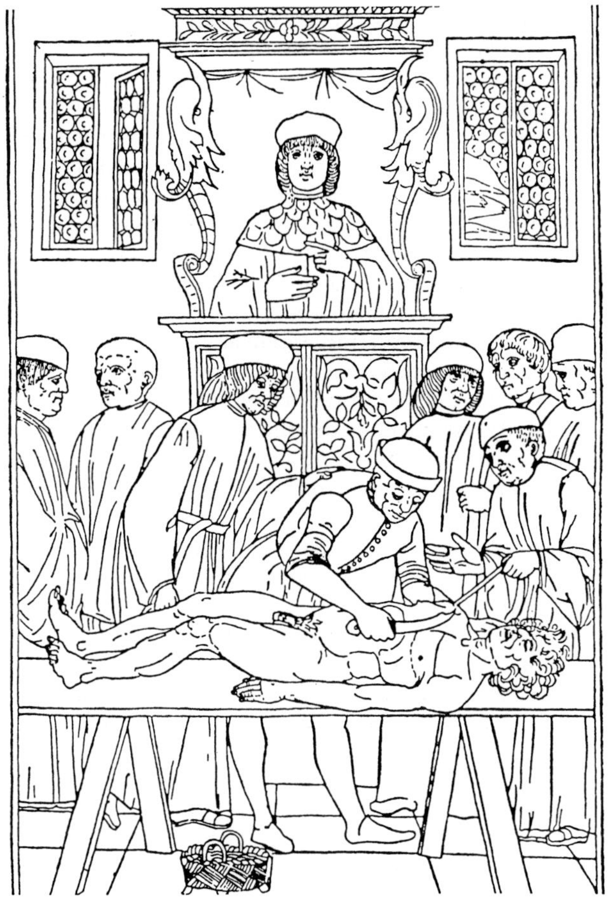

Figure 16 An anatomy lesson in late fifteenth-century Italy. Dissections of the human body became part of medical education in Italy in the fourteenth century. The subject of this late fifteenth-century Italian woodcut is a pioneering dissection performed more than a century earlier under the supervision of the renowned physician Mondino dei Luzzi (d. 1326) (from Goldstein, 1980, p. 149).

anatomical theories of Galen remained prevalent. Surgery first acquired full 'intellectual' status in Italian universities. The *Chirurgia Magna* of Guy de Chauliac (d. *c.* 1370) remained a standard work in Western Europe up to the end of the sixteenth century. Some daring procedures, such as the removal of cataracts and bladder stones, were performed.

HUMAN AND SOCIAL SCIENCES

Geography

Chinese geography

More attention was given to making observations than to the formulation of theory. There were weather records, surveys of resources and products, studies of the nature of the soil, and descriptions of the waterways. Gauges were used to measure rain and snow precipitation, and the compass was used for navigation. The nature of the hydrological cycle was understood, and at the time when Ibn Sīnā was writing his theories about the erosion of mountains, Shen Gua (fl. 1070) entertained similar ideas.

There were a number of Chinese travellers who left records of historical importance. One was Buddhist monk Xuanzang, who travelled to India in the seventh century to study Buddhism. Then there was the Nestorian Christian monk, Bar Sauma, who went on a mission to Europe in the thirteenth century. In the same period, Zhou Daguan visited Cambodia and wrote a detailed account of the customs of the Cambodians. Chinese merchants sailed to Java and Malaya, India and the Persian Gulf. The major work of exploration was carried out by the Chinese admiral Zeng He in the fifteenth century. His voyages covered Java, Sumatra, Malaya, Sri Lanka and the west coast of India. He also reached the Persian Gulf, the Red Sea and the east coast of Africa.

Two examples of maps for China, carved in stone, date from the twelfth century. Under Mongol rule, maps began to span the entire Asian continent. The geographer Zhu Sifen prepared a comprehensive map of China, and his successors added other countries. An extant Korean revision from the fifteenth century gives many European and African places (see Plate 125).

Indian geography

Hindu geographic knowledge can be found in the sacred *Purānas,* where we find material on regional and general geography. These writings also discuss meteorology, climatology and oceanography. The *Siddhanta* treatises on astronomy deal with geographical matters. Brahmanical geographical works are rare, but four titles are reported to have been written between the tenth and thirteenth centuries. It is reported also that the Jainas did substantial work on geography before 1200. It may be said in general that the Indians were aware of the geography of India, and that Hindu literature reflects a fair knowledge of other countries.

Islamic geography

Muslim scientific geography arose at the beginning of the 'Abbāsid period. Pre-Islamic geographical knowledge was the starting point. Al-Khwārizmī's *Kitāb Ṣūrat al-arḍ* of the ninth century came the nearest to Ptolemy's *Geography.* The basis of his system was to divide the inhabited world into seven 'climes', parallel with the Equator. Life to the south and to the north of the climes was assumed to be impossible. The other hemisphere, 'which is below us', was also thought not to be populated. In this system, the prime meridian passes through the Canary Islands, going east as far as the extremity of Korea, where the longitude is 180°. This span comprises half the hemisphere. While meditating on the sphericity of the Earth, geographers conceived the possibility of arriving east by travelling west. And in describing the lands to be encountered if one travels along the Ocean Sea 'which encircles all lands', geographers gave interesting accounts of the hypothetical circumnavigation of Africa from a starting-point in the Atlantic Ocean. On the basis of concrete evidence, al-Bīrūnī concluded that the Indian Ocean and the Atlantic Ocean were connected. He also made the interesting suggestion that towards the South Pole, night ceases to exist. al-Ṭūsī and al-Bīrūnī argued against the classical idea of an uninhabited southern quarter because of the sun's heat. The Balkhī school, and others, did not follow the clime system and adopted instead a division of provinces on a territorial basis. This was a human geography of sorts.

Throughout this period, a rich geographical literature was written, describing all the regions of Islam in detail. Other countries in Asia, Africa and Europe were also frequented and described. The long list of geographers and travellers includes al-Iṣṭakhrī, Ibn Ḥawqal, al-Muqaddasī, al-Mas'ūdī, al-Bīrūnī, Nāṣir-i Khusraw, Ibn Jubayr and Ibn Baṭṭūṭa. Several works described India, China and South-East Asia. Korea was visited and Japan identified. Exploration missions went deep into Central and North Asia. Journeys were made to the Niger and the equatorial regions of West Africa. East Africa was known until a latitude of about 24°S. In the Atlantic, Muslim ships sailed along the western coasts of Europe, including England, Scotland and Ireland and also south of Morocco for a considerable distance. Such Atlantic islands as the Canaries were known. Al-Mas'ūdī and al-Idrīsī give stories about adventurous missions into the Atlantic. Countries of Western Europe were described by several geographers. Travellers gave accounts about Byzantium, the Aral–Caspian region, the empire of the Khazars and the 'Rus' state (Russia).

A world map was prepared by al-Khwārizmī in the ninth century in addition to other maps based on the latitude and longitude of places. Longitudes were determined by calculations. What is known as the *Atlas of Islam* of al-Balkhī consisted of a set of twenty maps representing the various regions. It was accompanied by a map of the world. Al-Idrīsī's work included a set of seventy maps based on the tradition of climes (see Plate 123). They were accompanied by a large map of the world engraved in silver. Ḥamdallah Musṭawfī's works, *Tārīkh-i Guzīdeh* (1329–1330) and *Nuzḥat al-Qulūb* (1339–1340), were accompanied by maps.

Arabic navigational literature, which flourished in the eleventh century, forms a corpus of highly specialized writings. All the extant literature is concerned with the Indian Ocean, the Red Sea and the Persian Gulf. Aḥmad ibn Mājid (fifteenth century), who was one of the greatest navigators of all times, wrote about fifty works on navigation and according to a sixteenth-century Arab chronicler, has been believed to have served as Vasco da Gama's pilot from Malindi to Calicut. Sulaymān al-Mahrī wrote five works early in the sixteenth century. The works of Ibn Mājid and al-Mahrī represent the height of the Arabs' knowledge of nautical geography. They used excellent sea charts, with the lines of the meridian and parallels. They also used many fine instruments, including the compass, and made full use of astronomical knowledge for navigation.

Geography in sub-Saharan Africa

The merchants of the western Sudan had a fair idea of the geography of the Muslim world and perhaps of the rest of the known world. In the fifteenth century, Wangara merchants were usually literate, and had a very clear knowledge of their environment. Owing to royal pilgrimages, many people of the Sudan enjoyed accurate knowledge of the Maghrib, Egypt and Arabia. On the eastern coast of Africa, the Zanj and Swahili were thoroughly familiar with the eastern Arab world, with India, and perhaps with distant China. Geography was taught in the schools of Timbuktu. Africans had carried out navigational activities along the West and East African coasts. The fourteenth-century West African prince *Mansa* Mūsā told the story of a predecessor who sent a mission of 200 vessels into the Atlantic. Some scholars have tried to find in this interesting story evidence of a hypothetical discovery of America by sailors from Mali.

Geography in Western Europe

In the early Middle Ages, most Western Europeans thought of the Earth as a disc or rectangle. There were, however, scholars who accepted the idea of a spherical Earth. In the twelfth century, both the *Almagest* of Ptolemy and Arabic geographical knowledge became available in Latin. In the beginning of the fifteenth century, two important books appeared. One was the Latin translation of Ptolemy's *Geography,* and the other was the *Imago mundi* of Pierre d'Ailly, who disputed Ptolemy's idea of an enclosed Indian Ocean (see Plate 122). He was also among the first in Europe to contend that India might be reached by sailing west. Although the information conveyed in these two works was not new to Latin scholars, their publication at this time stressed the basic notions essential for the great geographical discoveries to come.

Until the eleventh century, European geographic horizons were narrow, and many of those who lived in Europe were familiar only with their immediate surroundings. The Scandinavians were known to live in a world of their own, in lands otherwise considered uninhabitable, but in the ninth century, these same Vikings reached Iceland and established a settlement there. They discovered Greenland a century later, and landed in North America in 1003. In the eleventh century, people started to travel to the Near East in the wake of the Crusades, and Europe was brought into contact with the Mongols. From the thirteenth century on, missionaries and merchants travelled extensively, reaching China and leaving accounts of their journeys. The most prominent among these was Marco Polo (d. 1324). He journeyed from Europe to Asia in 1271–1295, remaining in China for seventeen of those years. His *Il millione*, known as *The Travels of Marco Polo,* became a classic (see Plate 121).

At the beginning of the fifteenth century, the stage was set for the next step in the discovery of the world. There was progress in geographical knowledge. Better ships for Atlantic navigation became available. Navigational instruments, including the compass, were improved and the use of the astrolabe to determine latitude became more common. The Portuguese Prince Henry the Navigator (d. 1460) took the initiative by sending expeditions into the Atlantic along the coasts of Africa in an effort to reach India. In his lifetime, the Gold Coast was explored. In 1487, Bartolomeu Dias rounded the southern tip of Africa, and finally, Vasco da Gama completed the trip and reached Calicut in 1498 (see Plate 124).

Christopher Columbus was influenced by the geographical ideas of the time and believed in the possibility reaching India by sailing west. He sailed from Spain in 1492 and by perservering in his course and due to geographical inevitability, he discovered America.

Later medieval map makers were clearly aware of the Earth's sphericity, but for the most part maps remained small and schematic. The inhabited world was represented by a circular figure surrounded by the ocean. In the midst of the land area was a T-shaped arrangement of continental bodies. The three divisions – Europe, Asia and Africa – were accepted as standard. The centre of the inhabited world, just above the centre of the T, was Jerusalem (see Plate 119). The late fourteenth century witnessed a notable improvement in the art of mapping. *Portolano* charts became standard devices for sea captains. The famous Catalan map of the world, made in 1375, incorporated material from numerous *portolano* charts. It also included parts of the west coast of Africa and East and South-East Asia based on reports by Marco Polo. Geographical knowledge was profoundly increased by the end of the fifteenth century. Charts showing the new discoveries of Columbus, Vasco da Gama and others gradually transformed world maps.

Historiography

Chinese historiography

China had the longest continuous past and the most abundant written history, unequalled by any other country. Chinese scholars showed great interest in the history of China from the earliest times. Confucius stressed the importance of the lessons of history. According to his teachings, the conscientious transmission of authentic records was a main duty. Several centuries after his death, the recording of history and the careful preservation of records became one of the main functions of the Chinese government, both at the central and the local levels. Most of these histories were written by official historians. Although the content of such histories was imposed by what interested the higher officialdom, there appeared men of genuine historical insight and cardinal integrity. One of the greatest of these was Liu Zhiji (661–721), who wrote an epochal work on historical criticism, *Shitong*, published about 710. Believing that he could not exercise his own judgement under government control, he retired in order to write his independent historical critique. The first comprehensive general history of China was the *Zizhi tongjian* of Sima Guang (1019–1086), which covered the period from 402 BC to 959 AD. He worked for nineteen years, assisted by three other scholars, and their sources were chosen from more than 320 historical works.

Japanese historiography

Genealogies and mythological records were kept in Japan, at least from the sixth century. Emperor Temmu (seventh century) ordered the compilation of myths and genealogies that finally resulted in the *Kojiki* and *Nihon shoki*. While the *Kojiki* is richer in genealogy and myth, the *Nihon shoki* adds a great deal to scholarly understanding of both the history and the myth of early Japan. These two works are extremely important because there is no other authority on the history of ancient Japan, and because all the Shintō mythology is contained in them. The *Nihon Shoki* was the first of six national histories which appeared until the tenth century.

Indian historiography

Ancient and medieval India lacked a properly Hindu historiography. The only Hindu historical work in this period is *Rājatarangini* by the twelfth-century Kashmiri poet Kalhana, written in Sanskrit. It seems that this work is much more than a mere annalistic narration. Other works may be regarded as quasi-historical literature, such as the bardic literature of Rajputana, and the ballads, the heroic poems, the chronicles of Rajasthan and of Assam. Although they are unsuitable as political history, they contain valuable data for the social and cultural historian.

Ḍiyā' al-Dīn Barānī, or Barnī (d. after 1357), wrote a history of India in Persian. He was a significant figure in Indo-Muslim thought on government. In his *Fatāwā-i Jahāndāri,* he expounded a politico-religious philosophy of history. In his *Tārīkh-i Firūz-Shāhi* he gives the history of the Sultanate of Delhi and shows what happens in history when the precepts of the *Fatāwā* are disregarded. His history is a continuation of Minhāj Sirāj's history of the early sultans of Delhi and their nobility, the *Ṭabaqāt-i Nāṣiri,* completed in 1260.

Muslim historiography

Chronology begins with the Ḥijra in AD 622. By the time of the establishment of the 'Abbāsid Caliphate in 750 the science of history had already reached maturity. A feature of historiography is the meticulous scrutiny by historians of the sources they used. Down to the time of al-Ṭabarī (d. 923), when historians were still near to the main events surrounding the birth of Islam, they developed a special technique called *isnād*, which comprised a chain of authorities through which information percolated to later periods. When later historians became far removed from the early periods, they were careful to use all the accumulated reliable sources of their predecessors, and to list these sources. The methods for the scrutiny of historical facts were perfected by Ibn Khaldūn, who concluded that historical narratives are to be tested by their inherent possibility or credibility.

The earliest Muslim historians dealt with the life of the Prophet and the missionary campaigns. These were followed by a series of histories of the *futūḥ* or conquests. Prominent among the *futūḥ* historians were al-Wāqidī (d. 823) and al-Balādhurī (d. 892). General histories began to appear in the ninth century. The general history of al-Ṭabarī (d. 923), known in the West as the *Annals*, is the soundest and most reliable work of its kind. Al-Ṭabarī applied the method of *isnād* with rigour and reported only reliable information. The greatest achievements of Muslim historiography was the history of Ibn al-Athīr (d. 1232), known as *The Perfect in History*. Ibn al-Athīr was an impartial historian who compiled his work from all available sources. Another major work was the *Jāmi' al-Tawārīkh* by Rashīd al-Dīn (d. 1318), the Īl-Khānīd minister. This history of the world was issued in both Persian and Arabic. It was compiled after extensive research drawing on Arabic, Persian, Uighur, Mongolian and Chinese sources.

Besides the general histories, there appeared histories of special important events such as the history of Siffīn. Local histories started to appear in the ninth century. Among the great historians of Egypt were al-Maqrīzī (d. 1442) and Ibn Taghrībardī (d. 1469). A long series of Andalusian and Maghribī historians wrote on the local histories of western Islam. An important later historian was the Andalusian *wazīr (vizier)* Lisān al-Dīn Ibn al-Khaṭīb (d. 1347). Histories of some heroes of Islam, such as Ṣalāḥ al-Dīn ('Saladin'), were written. There were histories of important Muslim towns such as Baghdād and Damascus. Books of genealogy were also written, as well as books on the viziers and scribes of Islam. Biographical and autobiographical works formed important historical sources, and probably the most important of these was the *Biographical Dictionary*, by Ibn Khallikān (d. 1282).

The most celebrated historian of the medieval period, and one of the most distinguished of all time, was Ibn Khaldūn (d. 1406). He inaugurated a new school of thought. He was the author of *Muqaddima* ('Introduction to History'), in which he tried to treat history as a science (see Plate 123). He saw that history covered such things as economics and sociology, as well as purely political, military and religious events. He developed a concept of growth and change in history comparable to the growth of an individual organism, and explained how societies rise, develop and decay. Besides, he examined social solidarity and its basis, climatic and occupational influences on group character, laws of social change and political stability and economic and religious influences on behaviour.

Sub-Saharan African historiography

The renaissance of learning which took place in sub-Saharan Africa in the fourteenth and fifteenth centuries resulted in the appearance of a distinctive African historical literature, written in Arabic, in the sixteenth and seventeenth centuries, such as the *Tā'rīkh al-Fattāsh* written by several generations of the Ka'tī family (starting from 1519), and the *Tā'rīkh al-Sūdān* by al-Sa'dī (completed in 1655). In the same period, African historical literature appeared on the east coast of Africa. Many more African historical manuscripts remain to be discovered.

Oral tradition was also an important source for African history. It included myths, songs of praise, epic poetry, folk songs, children's songs, magical incantations, riddles and proverbs. The collection and conservation of oral traditions is now no longer left to foreigners. Some of the best collections have been made by African scholars, and many universities in Africa are engaged in recording and interpreting this material.

European historiography

Throughout most of this period, historiography in Western Europe was a Christian Latin literature, written by men of religion, mainly monks. The figurative language of the Bible revealed patterns of world history. The biblical narratives were usually paratactic in style, without causal or connecting words. This style then became characteristic of earlier medieval historiography. From the ninth century onwards, however, historians augmented their sources by borrowing from Roman rhetoric and literature. By the end of the ninth century, there were a variety of historical writings, including annals, universal chronicles and tribal histories. One feature of medieval historiography is the presence of a copious literature on the lives of saints, characterized by supernatural events. Another feature was the attempt by ecclesiastical writers to link the tribal history of the various 'barbarian' peoples to the Bible, such as histories of the English, Germanic tribes, Franks and Spanish Visigoths.

The period from the tenth to the end of the twelth century included the most productive years for medieval historiography. Gradually, historians' horizons expanded, as Europeans had more contact with each other and with other cultures such as the Islamic. The Crusades inspired some of the best historical narratives of the whole medieval period. By the fourteenth century, history no longer belonged entirely to the Church and was being written in the vernacular languages. A change was coming over the study and writing of history that was to cause historians to concern themselves more with the affairs of this world. In France, the monks of the Royal Abbey of Saint Denis compiled the Great Chronicles of France between the mid-thirteenth century to the late fifteenth. In England, the monks of St Albans kept a national history for more than two centuries from 1214. Similar histories were abundant in Italy, the Low Countries and Germany. Town chronicles, such as the Nuremberg Chronicle and the History of Florence, became common.

The Renaissance brought far-reaching changes to historical methods and writing. Many more of those writing history were laymen rather than churchmen. Francesco Petrarch (d. 1374) composed a history of Rome. Giovanni Villani (d. 1348) was Florence's first important historical writer. His history of his own city, in Italian, is noteworthy for its use of statistics. Lorenzo Valla (d. 1457) is considered the pioneer of modern historical criticism.

In the Byzantine Empire, historians consciously held to the classical tradition of the Greeks. Thus they were more concerned with contemporary worldly events and less governed by the Church. The Byzantines gave the world one of the first and best women historians, Anna Comnena (d. 1148), daughter of Emperor Alexius I. When she was a young girl, she saw the armies of the First Crusade march through Constantinople.

Grammar and lexicography

China

Chinese writing is ideographic as opposed to alphabetic. Symbols of pictorial origin are used to represent ideas expressed in the Chinese language. The most common writing combines a semantic element (called a radical) with a phonetic element. The number of radicals was reduced to 214, at which figure they remain today. Chinese words have only one syllable. The tones constitute an integral part of the monosyllabic morpheme. In many cases, they help to define differences of meaning between syllables that are otherwise identical.[1] In the seventh century, Lu Fayan compiled the earliest phonetic dictionary of the Chinese language, the *Qieyun*, the words being classified under 204 rhymes. In 1067, Sima Guang, in his dictionary *Leipian*, included a key to the *Qieyun*. This elaborate dictionary included over 31,000 words.

Japan

The first encyclopedic Chinese–Japanese dictionary was compiled in the eleventh century. Other dictionaries followed between the twelth and fifteenth centuries.

Tibet

The *Tenjur* includes a Tibetan–Sanskrit dictionary and treatises on grammar, logic, medicine and other topics.

India

Sanskrit was a scholarly language, like Latin in the West. Initial education was in Sanskrit and thus it was the only language common to all Indians. Grammar developed quite early, but the development of lexicography was much slower. Sanskrit dictionaries were compiled between the sixth and the twelth centuries. The spread of Buddhism resulted in the compilation of bilingual dictionaries with Chinese, Tibetan, Korean, Mongolian and Japanese. Pali was the language in which, according to tradition, the Buddha preached. Several grammarians wrote Pali grammars and dictionaries. Sinhalese is derived from Pali, but with a strong admixture of Dravidian words; its grammar is close to that of Pali.

The Islamic world

Arabic grammar originated in Baṣra and Kūfa in Iraq in the seventh century. Sībawayh (eighth century), in his great work *al-Kitāb,* was the first to undertake a complete description of Arabic at the three levels of syntax, morphology and phonology within the framework of a unified grammatical model. The tenth century was a golden age for grammar in Baghdād. Several noted grammarians taught there. During the following centuries, until the fourteenth, a galaxy of grammarians appeared. One of the most brilliant was Ibn Jinnī (tenth century). Outstanding among his works was *Khaṣā'iṣ al-'Arabiyyah*. This was a search for the uniform organizing principles of Arabic at all levels from phonology to syntax, from a semantic and psychological standpoint. Ibn Hishām (fourteenth century) wrote *Kitāb Mughnī al-Labīb fī al-Naḥw*, which became the standard manual for the teaching of Arabic.

Al-Khalīl Ibn Aḥmad (eighth century), who systematized Arabic prosody, was the first lexicographer to compile a general Arabic dictionary. Between the eighth and fifteenth centuries, more than a dozen comprehensive Arabic dictionaries were compiled. In the tenth century, al-Jawharī compiled *al-Siḥāḥ*, which comprised 40,000 entries arranged alphabetically according to the last radical of the word. Two outstanding dictionaries appeared during the thirteenth and fourteenth centuries. One was *Lisān al-'Arab* by Ibn Manẓūr. This vast dictionary with over 80,000 entries was by far the greatest lexicographic monument of the Middle Ages in any language. The second work was *al-Qāmūs al-Muḥīt* by al-Firūzābādī.

A large number of specialized word lists or dictionaries on specific topics were compiled. The most complete example of this kind of dictionary of synonyms is the massive *al-Mukhaṣṣaṣ* of Ibn Sīda (eleventh century). In addition, technical dictionaries of the various sciences, such as *Mafātīḥ al 'Ulūm* by al-Khwārizmī (tenth century), also appeared.

Other languages of the Islamic world

In the eleventh century, the *Dīwān lughat al-Turk*, a vocabulary of eastern Turkish including grammatical remarks was compiled. A Turkish–Arabic glossary and a Persian–Turkish–Mongol one were made public in the thirteenth century. The first systematic Turkish grammar was written in the same period. *Lughat-i furs* by 'Alī ibn Aḥmad Asadī Ṭusī is the oldest surviving Persian dictionary, from the eleventh century. Two other Persian dictionaries were compiled in Iran in the fourteenth century. Still more were compiled in India, or by the Turks. A large number of specialized glossaries were also produced.

The earliest systematic treatise on Syriac grammar was composed in the first half of the seventh century. The most comprehensive Syriac dictionary was compiled by Bar Bahlul in the tenth century. Between the eleventh and thirteenth centuries, a series of works on grammar following Arabic methods appeared.

Sa'ādia, in Iraq (tenth century), composed two works on Hebrew grammar and a Hebrew dictionary. He is considered the founder of Hebrew philology. The study of Hebrew grammar flourished at Cordova. Ibn Janāḥ (tenth century), the greatest Hebrew philologist of the Middle Ages, compiled a Hebrew grammar and a Hebrew dictionary, both works being written in Arabic. In this same period, the first complete Hebrew dictionary of biblical language was composed; similarly, new Hebrew rules of prosody were drawn up, based upon Arabic. The grammar and dictionary of the European Jewish scholar David Qimḥi (d. *c.* 1235), *Mikhlol*, was influential. The greater task of adapting the language for scientific and philosophical purposes was initiated by Judah ibn Tibbon (d. 1190).

There are a few Coptic grammatical and lexicographical writings dating from the eleventh century, also written in Arabic.

Europe and Byzantium

The Latin grammars of Donatus (fourth century) and Priscian (late fifth century), were the two most popular grammatical textbooks of the Middle Ages. Between the tenth and thirteenth centuries, several treatises on grammar appeared based on them. John of Garland (thirteenth century) was one of the first speculative grammarians to lift grammar to a higher philosophical level. In the fourteenth century, work on speculative grammar was quite active. This was highly theoretical and was directed at university education, whereas school grammar continued to be written on the basis of the old grammars of Donatus and Priscian.

Although Latin was the established language of the West, at the beginning of this era lexicography was far from developed. A large number of glossaries were prepared for individual works. Later, glosses from different sources were collected and combined. This was still not a dictionary. The first Latin lexicographic work of importance was that of Papias of Lombardy (eleventh century). Other lexicographic works followed, such as *De Utensilibius* by Ṇeckham. The *Dictionarius* of John of Garland was also a list of words. This title represents the first use of the word 'dictionary'. The most important work of the thirteenth century was the *Catholicon* of John Balbi. This was a combination of grammar, prosody, rhetoric, etymology and a dictionary. More specialized vocabularies began to appear such as that of Simon of Genoa, which included Greek, Arabic and Latin terms.

Other languages of Europe

In England, Aelfric in the ninth century wrote a Latin grammar based on Priscian and Donatus, having in mind the application of that grammar to Old English. But the first true grammar to appear in Europe was a unique Icelandic work called *First Grammatical Treatise*, written in the twelth century by the unknown First Grammarian, who showed a remarkable originality and independence of thought. Troubadour literature fostered a demand for grammatical information and from the thirteenth century several Provençal and Catalan grammatical works were written. *De Vulgari Eloquentia* by Dante (fourteenth century) was the first work on Italian philology. Apart from these works, development of grammar in Western Europe was exceedingly slow. The first French grammar for English students was written in England in the fifteenth century and was based on Latin models. The first Spanish and German grammars appeared in the fifteenth century. The first works on grammar for Italian, French, Middle English and Dutch did not appear before the sixteenth century.

In Eastern Europe, the Greek grammatical work of Moschopoulos appeared in the fourteenth century. The earliest Slavonic grammar was composed in Serbia in the fourteenth century. Further east, Armenian grammatical texts were compiled in the thirteenth century.

The development of lexicography in the vernaculars was very slow. Vocabularies, glosses and word lists only were compiled and continued to appear. Some of these were bilingual. True dictionaries did not appear before the sixteenth century. A Latin–Old English glossary accompanied Aelfric's grammar, which is the earliest Latin–English lexicographic work extant. The earliest Latin–German glossary was also from the ninth century. French lexicography was attempted before the end of the fourteenth century in a French adaptation of the Latin *Catholicon*. An English–Latin dictionary was compiled at the end of the fifteenth century. An Armenian dictionary was composed in this period, and an Armenian–Arabic–Latin glossary also.

TRANSMISSION OF KNOWLEDGE

Diffusion of Chinese culture to Korea and Japan

Chinese civilization penetrated first into Korea and from there reached Japan, until the Japanese made direct contact with China in the seventh century. The *Taika* (Great Reform) era in Japan which followed the establishment of a monarchy in AD 645 saw the beginning of many new institutions, most of which were imitations of those of the Tang Dynasty in China. The *daigakuryo*, or college house, which was established in the capital, and the provincial schools followed at first a curriculum almost identical to that of the Tang Dynasty. Other aspects of Chinese influence on both Korea and Japan have been discussed in preceding sections.

China and India

After the spread of Buddhism into China, many Indian monks visited China, while India in turn became a goal of pilgrimage for Chinese Buddhists. This resulted in a Sino-Indian exchange of culture and scientific knowledge, which intensified in the middle of the fourth century and lasted until the beginning of the eleventh. The official history of the Sui Dynasty, completed in AD 636, contains in its bibliographical catalogue a number of books all beginning with the word Boluomen or Brahmin. Although these works are now lost, their mere listing in an official history is significant. In the seventh century, the Indian *Siddhantas* were taught at Zhangnan, and in the eighth century, there were Indian astronomers in the Tang court. On the other hand, there are examples of the influence of Chinese mathematics on Hindu mathematics. There were also reports of exchanges in alchemy, pharmacopoeia and medicine. At this stage, it is difficult to attempt any balance sheet of the mutual influences between Indian and Chinese.

China, Islam and Western Europe

We can say in general terms that the sciences in China developed independently of both the Islamic and Latin civilizations, but in the Middle Ages, the science and scientific thought of Islam formed very much a single unit with European science. On the other hand, ancient and medieval Chinese science was confined to the boundaries of the ideographic Chinese language and was not translated into either Arabic or Latin. The translation movement from other languages into Arabic took place from the middle of the eighth century until the end of the ninth. During this period the Tang Dynasty was in power and the Arabs had already established good trade relations with China. But although there was an Arab community in Guangzhou, no Chinese scientific works reached the Arabs. This led Ṣā'id al-Andalusī (d. 1070), in his book *The Categories of Nations*, to conclude that Chinese civilization was one of technology only.

During the period of the Mongol Empire in the thirteenth and fourteenth centuries, and due to the incorporation of some Islamic lands into the Mongol Empire, scientific contacts between Islamic and Chinese scholars did take place. At the Marāghah observatory, Naṣīr al-Dīn al-Ṭūsī (d. 1274) had among his team a Chinese astronomer (see Plate 139). It is also probable that this scholar took back home some Islamic mathematical knowledge. Other Muslim astronomers, Jamāl al-Dīn and his mission, were employed by the Mongols at their court in China for several years. Although it is difficult to judge the influence of this mission, it seems likely that they did affect the development of Chinese astronomical instruments and the establishment of a Chinese observatory. Muslim military engineers were in the service of Qubilay Khān and constructed ballistic engines for his armies. In about 1313, Rashīd al-Dīn initiated the preparation of an encyclopedia of Chinese medicine in Persian. During the whole period of Mongol rule, Europe had direct access to China, but this did not result in the translation of any Chinese scientific works into Latin. The story was different concerning the transmission of technological inventions.

India, Islam and Western Europe

India, however, played an important rôle in the transmission and diffusion of scientific ideas between East and West. On one side, India received Babylonian, Egyptian and Greek ideas in science and technology; on the other, its science was transmitted back to Islamic civilization in the earlier centuries of Islam, and thence to the West. With the start of the translation movement into Arabic in the eighth century, the first astronomical book to be translated was one of Brahmagupta's works which came to be known in Arabic as the *Sindhind*. This remained the major source for Islamic astronomy until the translation of the *Almagest*. Many *zījs* (almanacs) were prepared on this basis, the most important of which were those by al-Khwārizmī, revised later by al-Majrīṭī. In arithmetic, we have already discussed how Hindu numerals reached the Arabs and how they were transmitted to Western Europe. A great Muslim scientist, al-Bīrūnī, had the chance to reside in India, learn Sanskrit and study the culture and sciences of India. He is known to have taught there himself both the Greek and Arabic sciences. His *Kitāb al-Hind* (1035) is perhaps the profoundest scrutiny in pre-modern times of one culture by the leading scientist of another.

Indian medical works were translated into Arabic in the eighth century. When Abū al-Ḥasan 'Alī al-Ṭabarī wrote his great medical work *The Paradise of Wisdom* in the ninth century, he devoted part of it to Hindu medicine. This work was not translated into Latin and thus Hindu medical theories did not reach Europe. With the establishment of Muslim Ghaznavid rule in India, and later of the Delhi Sultanate (early thirteenth century), Islamic sciences, incorporating Greek theories in astronomy and medicine, reached India. And although they were studied at first among Muslim circles, they gradually became known to Hindu scholars.

Sub-Saharan Africa, Islam and Asia

This period was a golden age for trans-Saharan trade. As a result, many Berbers and Arabs settled in the cities of the Sudan. The rôle of Islam in the spread of ideas was of paramount importance. Arabic became the language of the literate and of the courts; *Mansa* (prince) Mūsā spoke it correctly. An African literature in Arabic came into being. Scholarly exchanges between the universities of the Sudan and those of the Maghrib lasted from the fourteenth to the sixteenth century; and during the fourteenth century, Cairo also strongly attracted Sudanese scholars. Situated on the pilgrim route, Cairo sheltered a large community of African inhabitants and students. The rulers of the Sudan were surrounded by Arab scholars and counsellors. On returning from his pilgrimage Mansa Mūsā had writers, scholars and architects in his retinue (see Plate 259).

The same can be said about the influence of international trade on the East African coast. A new Swahili civilization was born with strong Islamic and Arabic influences. Ethiopian culture for its part was influenced by Syrian Christian missionaries at an early date, and the Ethiopian language and script were of south Arabian origin. The culture of Madagascar was influenced by settlers from South-East Asia. Chinese trade missions visited the East African coast, and Africans became acquainted with Chinese products.

Translation of Greek, Syriac and Pahlavī works into Arabic

By the middle of the eighth century, with the advent of the 'Abbāsids, the time was ripe for the start of the translation movement from Pahlavī, Syriac, Sanskrit and Greek on a large scale. This movement was launched by al-Manṣūr (r. 754–775) and received special attention from his successors, notably al-Ma'mūn (r. 813–833). Beside the caliphs the translation effort was supported by other influential patrons. Ibn al-Muqaffa' (d. 757) translated from Pahlavī into Arabic works on logic, history and medicine. Members of the al-Nawbakht family translated Pahlavī works of astronomy and astrology. The *Almagest* was translated more than once into Arabic in the ninth century. Al-Ḥajjāj ibn Maṭar made two translations of Euclid's *Elements*, and Isḥāq ibn Ḥunayn made a third, which was corrected later by Thābit ibn Qurra.

The whole medical heritage of the Alexandrian school was translated by Ḥunayn ibn Isḥāq (d. 877) and his school. They rendered the works of Galen, Hippocrates and the herbal work of Dioscorides. In philosophy, they translated almost all the works of Plato and Aristotle. Thābit ibn Qurra (d. 901) was responsible for the translation or revision of some of the most important works of Archimedes, Apollonius, Euclid, Ptolemy, Theodosius and others (see Plates 126, 130). Like Ḥunayn, he headed a school of translators.

Translations from Arabic into Latin

Contacts between Western Europe and Islam existed both on the diplomatic level and in trade. Diplomatic contacts go back to the times of Hārūn al-Rashīd and Charlemagne in the eighth century. In 950, Otto I, in Frankfurt, and 'Abd al-Raḥmān, in Cordova, exchanged ambassadors who were both scholars. Some cultural contacts with Islamic culture took place in northern Spain when students from Western Europe travelled there to study Islamic science. Gerbert made such a pilgrimage in the 960s to study Islamic mathematics. Such contacts created in Western minds an image of Islam as a repository of great intellectual riches. The earliest translations from Arabic were several treatises on mathematics and the astrolabe in the tenth century. In the eleventh century, Constantine the African, whom we mentioned earlier, translated several medical treatises which laid the foundations of medical literature in the West for several centuries. The translation movement gathered momentum in the first half of the twelth century. Spain was most suited as a centre for this activity. It had the advantage of a brilliant Islamic culture and a geographical proximity to Western Europe. In 1085, Toledo fell into Christian hands. In addition to its rich libraries, Toledo also had a large community of Mozarabs and native Jews, who played an essential rôle in the translation from Arabic into Latin. The fall of Toledo provided a golden opportunity for scholars from Western Europe to come to this great city to study Islamic and Arabic culture and science.

One of the pioneers in the translation movement was Adelard of Bath (fl. 1116–1142), from England. He stayed in Syria for several years, during which time he acquired much Arabic learning. Adelard translated the astronomical tables of al-Khwārizmī as revised by al-Majrīṭī, and Euclid's *Elements*. John of Seville (fl. 1133–1142), a Mozarab from Toledo, translated a large number of astrological works. Others from Spain included Mark of Toledo (fl. 1191–1216), who translated several texts of Galen. The list of translators who came to Toledo also included Robert of Chester, from Wales; Hermann the Dalmatian, a Slav; and Plato of Tivoli, from Italy. The greatest translator of the entire movement was Gerard of Cremona (*c.* 1114–1187), who came to Toledo from Italy in search of the *Almagest*. He stayed to learn Arabic. After he had rendered the *Almagest* into Latin, he stayed in Toledo for the next thirty-five or forty years, working with a group of assistants translating the most important Arabic works. The number of his translations exceeded ninety and they included works on astronomy, mathematics, medicine, logic, philosophy and alchemy. The translation movement continued in Spain into the thirteenth century, when we meet such scholars as Alfred of Sarashel, Michael Scot, Marrochini, Arnold of Villanova and Raymond Lull. An important effort of translation from Arabic into Spanish was undertaken by Alfonso X the Wise, as discussed earlier. Outside Toledo and Spain, Stephen of Antioch translated the *Liber regalis* of 'Alī ibn 'Abbās in 1127. A century later, Philip of Tripoli translated the pseudo-Aristotelian *Secret of Secrets*.

Sicily in the twelth century also became a centre for the transmission of Islamic science. Successive kings attracted to their courts men of learning irrespective of their religion or native language. Islamic culture continued to occupy a unique position. This was especially true under Roger II (r. 1101–1154), who was patron to al-Idrīsī. The court of Frederick II (1194–1250) also teemed with learned men of all faiths. The most prominent scholars in Sicily were Michael Scot, Theodore of Antioch and Leonardo of Pisa. These scientists translated treatises on philosophy, zoology, medicine, mathematics, mechanics and cosmography. Frederick founded the University of Naples in 1224 and established there a library with a large collection of Arabic manuscripts. To the universities of Paris and Bologna, he donated copies of the translations of Aristotle and Ibn Rushd which were completed on his orders. Translation activity continued under Manfred and Charles of Anjou. The most impressive translation under Charles was that of the massive *Kitāb al-Ḥāwī* (*Continens*) by al-Rāzī, undertaken by Faraj ben Sālim (see Plate 133).

In the thirteenth century, there were translators working in Italy and France, especially at Montpellier. Although the translation movement had lost its momentum by the end of the thirteenth century, yet translations continued until the sixteenth.

Translations from Greek into Latin

The translation movement of the twelth century gave new life to efforts to translate directly from Greek. There were Greek-speaking communities in Italy, especially in the south, and libraries contained Greek works. Scholars also could obtain Greek works directly from Byzantium. In the twelth century, these efforts resulted in the translation of some of Aristotle's treatises, Ptolemy's *Almagest*, and Euclid's *Elements*, *Optics* and *Catoptrics*. This activity continued into the thirteenth century, most notably through William of Moerbeke, who aimed to provide the Latin West with a complete version of the Aristotelian corpus. He also translated some neo-Platonic works and writings by Archimedes.

In the fifteenth century, the urge to return to Greek sources revived. In 1410, Ptolemy's *Geography* was translated from Greek (see Plate 122). Regiomontanus worked on translating the *Almagest* but left the work unfinished. With the fall of Constantinople in 1453, Byzantine scholars fled to Italy, bringing with them classical Greek works. This further spurred the revival of humanism. But in fact, many Greek scientific texts had already been translated.

THE CONSEQUENCES OF SCIENTIFIC DISCOVERIES

The Origins of Modern Science

Before discussing the consequences of certain scientific discoveries, it is useful to give a general assessment of the legacy of science in this period in history. The pre-modern science of 1492 made significant contributions to modern science, which started to emerge in Europe in the sixteenth and seventeenth centuries. It prepared the ground for later achievements. Although new science started by overthrowing the hitherto dominant systems of Euclid and Aristotle in astronomy and mechanics, science in its new form still preserved the bulk of the material which it inherited from ancient and medieval civilizations. Science in each stage inherits the results of a predecessor civilization or acquires the knowledge of a contemporary one as we have seen. Medieval Western Europe started to build its science by acquiring the Greek and Islamic sciences, mostly through translations of Arabic works. Much of the heritage of the classical and Indian civilizations was incorporated into these translations. It would have taken many hundreds of years more if Europeans had had to discover the same things for themselves, namely to recreate the same scientific knowledge through their own independent inquiry and research. By the same argument, modern science would not have emerged in the sixteenth and seventeenth centuries if Copernicus, Galileo, Kepler and Newton did not have at their disposal the scientific results of their predecessors. Let us take some examples.

We have already mentioned how the Islamic astronomers were working on reforming the Ptolemaic planetary system, and how they succeeded in producing non-Ptolemaic planetary models. These models cropped up again, in Western Europe, in the work of Copernicus. The only basic change in the Copernican planetary system was his readoption of the ancient Greek concept of a heliocentric universe. Copernican astronomy preserved the basic principles of astronomy as they had been practised before.

Concerning the dynamics of motion, we have seen how doubts on Aristotle began with Philiponus and how the concept of impetus was developed by Ibn Sīnā and others, reaching maturity with Buridan. Hindu scientists also discussed the concept of impetus. Historians of science have found a fairly direct connection between Ibn Bājja's (d. 1139) commentaries on Aristotle and Galileo's theory of free fall. They have ascribed to Ibn Bājja (Avempace) an essential rôle that enabled Galileo to generalize Buridan's impetus theory and transform it into general inertial dynamics. Galileo's analysis of the kinematics of falling bodies was, to a very considerable extent, an elaboration and application of kinematic principles developed at Oxford and Paris in the fourteenth century.

Optics is another science which displays a high degree of continuity between pre-modern and early modern science (see Figure 17). Kepler's theory of the retinal image was an important innovation in visual theory, but it was worked out entirely within the medieval conceptual framework, without the need to repudiate any of the fundamental principles. The printed works of Ibn al-Haytham, Witelo and Pecham formed the foundation of Kepler's new theory of the retinal image. Kepler rigorously applied axioms already long established in arriving at his solutions.

Continuity is also evident in the case of mathematics. There is here a continuous evolution throughout the centuries, and whereas there may have been an accelerated pace of progress with the passage of time, we cannot say that a revolution in mathematics took place in any dramatic manner. In this period, arithmetic, algebra and trigonometry were developed into independent disciplines. The sophisticated approaches employed in algebra were the first steps in the creation of new sub-disciplines such as the algebra of polynomials, the numerical solution of equations and indeterminate analysis. This continuity between pre-modern and early modern science is evident in all other disciplines, including the natural sciences, alchemy and medicine.

Having briefly discussed the continuity between the pre-modern and modern science, we shall look into some of the scientific discoveries and their consequences. But the list cannot be exhaustive.

Hindu-Arabic numerals

The importance of the introduction of the Hindu–Arabic numerals cannot be overestimated. They are a milestone in history, arguably similar in importance to the alphabet.

Optics and lenses

The Optical Thesaurus of Ibn al-Haytham (*c.* 1038) discussed lenses and their magnifying powers. Roger Bacon (d. 1294) mentioned their use for aiding the sight of old people. Convex spectacles were probably invented before 1280. By 1300, they were being made in Venice. This gave rise to the trade of lens grinders and spectacle makers (see Plate 132). In 1608, a member of this trade invented the telescope.

Optics and perspective

Ibn al-Haytham formulated an intromission theory which explained the principal facts of visual perception. Optics in Latin became known as *Perspectiva*. In the thirteenth century, Bacon, Pecham and Witelo wrote commentaries on *Perspectiva*. Modern perspective, an offshoot of the science of optics, was born in Florence in the fourteenth century. Its foundation is the concept of the visual cone of rays from an object to the eye. Its first advocate was Lorenzo Ghiberti, the Florentine sculptor. A Latin manuscript of Ibn al-Haytham's work in the Vatican Library is annotated by him. Ghiberti was one of several sculptures, painters and architects, including Leonardo da Vinci, who formed an identifiable school of perspective. Perspective in Renaissance art provided an inspiration for Desargues (d. 1661) in the invention of projective geometry. Increasing interest by mathematicians in perspective continued into later centuries, until it was finally incorporated into geometry and played an important rôle in revolutionizing the subject.

The applied mechanical science of machines, clocks and automata

The Hellenistic mechanical tradition of waterwheels and water clocks continued into Islamic times and gave rise to a

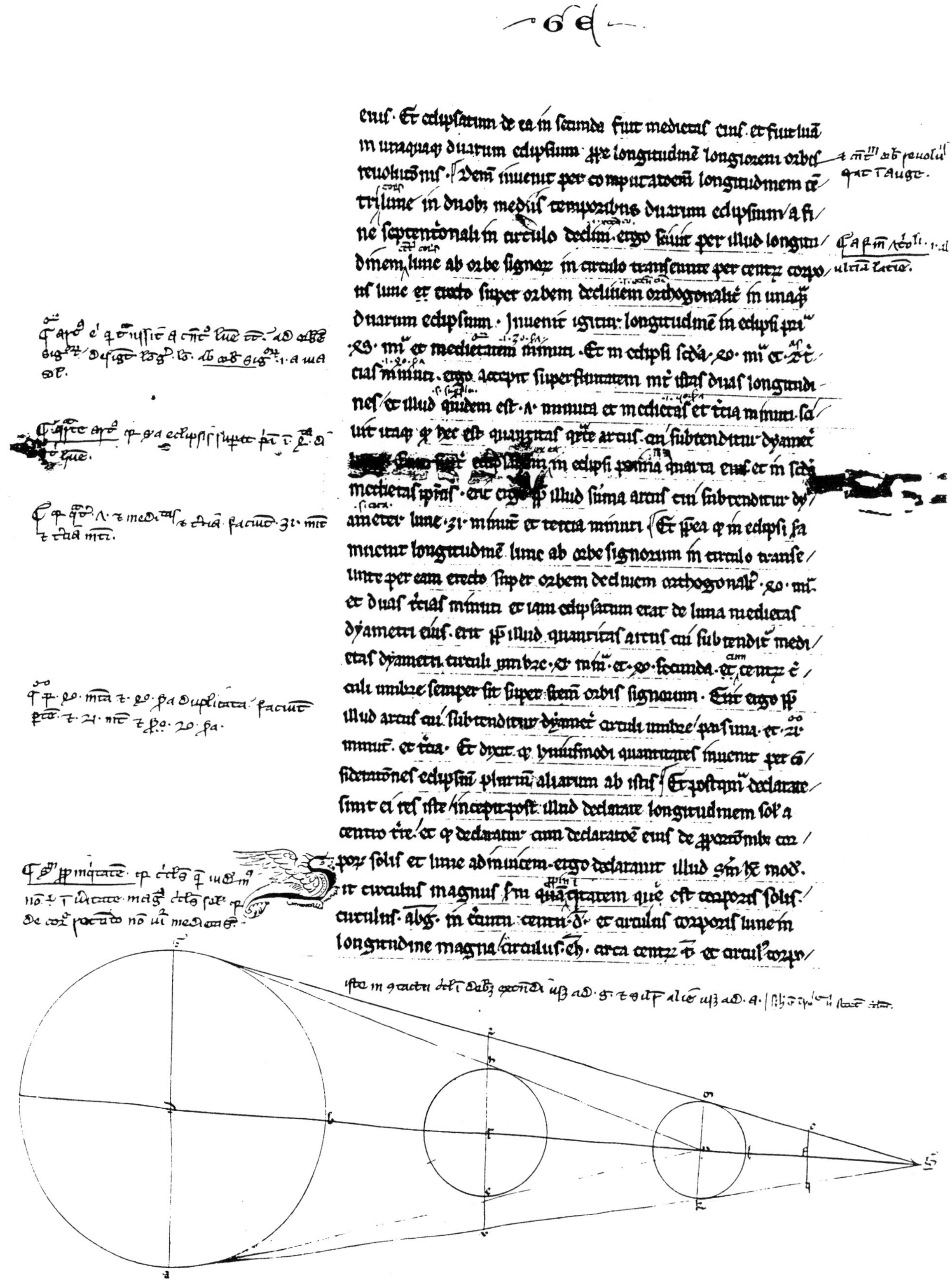

Figure 17 Principles of optics: from a thirteenth-century Spanish manuscript of the twelfth-century Latin translation, completed in Toledo by Gerard of Cremona, of the earlier twelfth-century Arabic Islāh al-Majistī ('Correction to the Almagest of Ptolemy'), by Jābir ibn Aflah of Seville (Biblioteca Nacional de Madrid, manuscrito arabe 10006, f°59 v°).

more developed and elaborate literature on a great variety of designs of water-raising machines, watermills, windmills, siege engines, clocks, automata and other ingenious devices. The mechanical tradition reached the Latin West and culminated in the appearance of the mechanical clock in the fourteenth century. In the sixteenth and seventeenth centuries, a large number of books on machinery appeared in both Arabic and Latin incorporating previous mechanical ideas. In one treatise, for example, (Taqī al-Dīn, 1552), a six-cylinder monoblock piston pump employing a camshaft is described. Such machines were the immediate predecessors of the steam engine and the multi-cylinder engines of modern times.

The influence of geography and astronomy on navigation and the voyages of discovery

The great geographical discoveries of the fifteenth century were made possible through the application of scientific knowledge in improving navigation and in providing the concept of the possibility of reaching India by sailing westwards across the Atlantic Ocean. This was the basic notion which inspired Christopher Columbus to sail west in order to reach India and resulted in the discovery of the New World. In navigating the Atlantic and other oceans, a navigator needed to know his position, and this was made partially possible by the calculation of latitude. North of the Equator, at night, latitude can be calculated by observing the height of the pole star (Polaris) above the horizon. But this star becomes too low in the sky near the Equator and cannot be observed below it. Therefore latitudes were determined by measuring the meridian height of the sun. This necessitated the use of astronomical instruments such as the cross-staff, together with tables of declination. The *Toledan Tables* of al-Zarqālī (Azarquiel), the *Alphonsine Tables*, and fourteenth-century Arabic, Spanish and Portuguese almanacs provided the necessary theoretical data. Calculations were simplified by means of trigonometry. Longitude was determined by the approximate dead-reckoning method. Several other factors were crucial in improving navigation, such as the use of the compass and progress in cartography. The use of the stern-post rudder and the improved construction of ships were important factors. Triangular lateen sails made caravels particularly well suited for beating against the wind (see Plates 21–25).

In addition to the enormous historical effects of the great voyages of discovery, the effects on science were also great. The success of the early voyages created an enormous demand for shipbuilding and navigation. Mathematically trained craftsmen for compass, instrument and map making increased in number. Navigation schools were founded in several countries. The need for astronomical observations and charts gave a direct stimulus to the further development of astronomy, which became less dependent on astrology.

Alchemy and metallurgy

Metals were of major concern to alchemists, and their properties were studied through extensive experimentation. Apart from the alchemical treatises, special works describe the manufacture and heat treatment of steel and swords. Cast iron was produced and its properties were described. Swords made from Damascus steel exhibited desirable qualities. For about a century and a half, attempts were made in Europe to reproduce steel comparable in quality to Damascus steel, involving eminent scientists such as Michael Faraday. This was useful for the development of modern metallurgy. Cast iron increased in importance with the rise in the manufacture of cannon and for the construction of machinery.

Gunpowder and cannon

Gunpowder was an invention of Chinese alchemists, and formulations became abundant in treatises of the thirteenth century. Besides its use in fireworks, it also began to be used in warfare. Its first use for cannons began in the thirteenth century. In the fourteenth century, cannons and hand-guns were used on an increasing scale in both Islamic countries and Europe. The use of gunpowder and cannons had far-reaching consequences in history.

The effects of gunpowder on the development of science

Gunpowder had a profound influence on science. The main ingredient, potassium nitrate or saltpetre, in its impure natural state is not suitable for the manufacture of gunpowder. Pure saltpetre was produced as the result of careful separation and purification of salts, a process which was first described by al-Rammāḥ (d. 1292). The continued demand for pure saltpetre turned attention to the phenomena of solution and crystallization. Further, the explosion of gunpowder could not be explained, since it did not require air like all other fires. After centuries of speculation and experimentation this led to the discovery of oxygen in the eighteenth century, and this marked the end of alchemy and the rise of modern chemistry.

The force of explosion and the expulsion of the ball from the barrel of a cannon gave an indication of the possibility of utilizing such forces, and this was an inspiration in the development of the steam engine. The manufacture of cannons led to the development of boring machines for the barrels. This was of great help in making accurate cylinders for steam engines.

The study of the movement of a cannon ball through the air was very important for predicting its trajectory, and this was a motivating factor in the development of dynamics.

Distillation and mineral acids

Alchemists produced nitric, sulphuric and hydrochloric acids and *aqua regia* by distillation. They were used as powerful solvents and for industrial purposes such as the separation of silver from gold. Methods of production improved in the sixteenth century and later. Acids were of extreme importance in the rise of modern chemistry and chemical industries.

Distillation and alcohol

The production of distilled alcohol was closely related to the development of distillation as a chemical process. Arabic alchemical treatises of the eighth–eleventh centuries referred to the distillation of wine. Jābir noted the inflammable properties of alcohol as early as the eighth century. At Salerno, alcohol was known around 1100. In the fourteenth century, distillers of alcoholic drinks appeared. In this same period, alcohol was used as a component in military fires in Islamic countries. The production of alcohol led to the invention of water-cooled condensers. It became possible to condense other volatiles such as ether. For larger production, the still and condenser supplemented the alembic and retort and made organic chemistry possible. The water-cooled condenser helped James Watt to invent a separate condenser and so to produce the first thermally efficient steam engine.

Chemical drugs and iatrochemistry

The use of chemicals for medical purposes was known in China and India. Islamic physicians, such as al-Rāzī, used chemical remedies. However, popular opinion associates the foundation of iatrochemistry with Paracelsus (d. 1541). In the seventeenth century, confidence in chemical drugs increased when Boyle put the preparation of chemical compounds on a more scientific basis. Pharmaceutical laboratories followed in the eighteenth century.

NOTE

1 This is a very rough approximation. The problem is very complex and would need much space to explain.

BIBLIOGRAPHY

BEAZLEY, C. R. 1949. *The Dawn of Modern Geography*. New York.

BERNAL, J. D. 1969. *Science in History*, Vol. I, *The Emergence of Science*; Vol. II, *The Scientific and Industrial Revolutions*. Middlesex, England.

BOSE, D. M.; SEN, S. N.; SUBBARAYAPPA, B. V. (eds) 1971. *A Concise History of Science in India*. New Delhi.

COLLISON, R. L. 1982. *A History of Foreign Language Dictionaries*. London.

HARTMANN, R. R. K. (ed.) 1986. *The History of Lexicography*. Amsterdam.

AL-HASSAN, A. Y. and HILL, D. R. 1986. *Islamic Technology*. Cambridge University Press and UNESCO.

LINDBERG, D. (ed.) 1978. *Science in the Middle Ages*. Chicago.

NASR, S. H. 1976. *Islamic Science: An Illustrated Study*. London, World of Islam Festival.

NEEDHAM, J. 1954. *Science and Civilization in China*. Cambridge.

ROSENTHAL, F. 1968. *A History of Muslim Historiography*, (2nd rev. edn). Leiden.

SARTON, G. 1927–48. *Introduction to the History of Science*. Baltimore, MD.

TATON, R. (ed.) 1967. *A General History of the Sciences*, Vol. I, *Ancient and Medieval Science*, Vol. II, *The Beginnings of Modern Science*. London.

THOMPSON, J. W.; HOLM, B. J. 1942. *A History of Historical Writing*. New York.

UNESCO *General History of Africa*, 1981–1993, Vol. I, *Methodology and African Prehistory*, KI-ZERBO, J. (ed.); Vol. III, *Africa from the Seventh to Eleventh Century*, EL-FASI, M. (ed.); Vol. IV, *Africa from the Twelfth to Sixteenth Century*, NIANE, D. T. (ed.). UNESCO.

YU-SHAN, Han 1955. *Elements of Chinese Historiography*. California.

7

RELIGIONS, ETHICS AND PHILOSOPHY

Maurice Borrmans

During the nine centuries starting from the beginning of the seventh century, a century which witnessed the birth and spread of Islam in the Middle East, until 1492, the year in which Europe discovered America, all human societies had more or less elaborate forms of religion which are very difficult to classify into rigid categories. Some of them were rooted in the community, land or tribe, constituting the natural or cosmic religions which some people at times group together under the rather vague terms of 'animism', 'shamanism' or 'natural polytheism'. For many centuries, other religions inspired the philosophical and mystical inquiry which has accompanied the rise of brilliant civilizations within rural and urban settings, with some of such religions being characterized by dualism and gnostic quests. Still other religions crystallized into forms of wisdom in which philosophy and spirituality fused into 'world views' which encompassed the entirety of human development, such as Daoism, Shintō and Hinduism, before being renewed or transformed by more personalized forms of religion, such as Jainism and Buddhism. In addition to these religions, concerning which the adjectives 'cosmic' and 'historic', in relation to the latter two, are frequently used, there were the prophetic religions, namely the monotheism of Islam, Judaism and Christianity, which are based on revelation to humankind through privileged intermediaries chosen by a unique God.

The purpose of all these religions – the term 'religion' being used in a broad sense – was to provide answers to the primordial questions which have always troubled the heart of *homo religiosus*: what meaning should one ascribe to human beings, life, good and evil, suffering, happiness, death and the afterlife? Throughout the world, human beings were captivated by the quest for a 'divine essence' which would give 'meaning' to them, and by the quest for a 'sacred essence' which would give them 'dignity'. 'Religions' afforded them the required access to such essences by means of their rites and symbolism, which made it possible to communicate with absolute entities (the supreme being, the gods or God himself), with the spirits (the immaterial world of the suprasensible) and the ancestors (the great continuous human family). This chapter will not be concerned with the concrete history of these 'religions' and their successful or unsuccessful relationships with the economy, culture, aesthetics or politics but will simply describe their ritual manifestations, define the beliefs and dogmas in question, and appreciate the results of their spiritual and mystical inquiry, in more or less close relation to the reigning philosophies.

ANIMISM, SHAMANISM AND POLYTHEISTIC SYSTEMS

Animism, the belief in a supreme essence ('vital force' or 'soul') which is thought to dwell in places and objects, assumes different characteristics depending on the type of local culture and period in history. Throughout the world, the purpose of religions rooted in the land, community or tribe was to afford their followers access to the divine or sacred by means of a symbolism which gave prominence to beings and things in order to ensure the integration of all into the social group and the inclusion of all in the life-giving continuity of the latter. Irrespective of whether such groups were sedentary or nomadic, and of whether such societies were made up of farming, hunting or fishing communities, the objective was to ensure survival through participation in life's mystery and energies by the use of rites and magic which, through their specialized intermediaries, made it possible to participate in the 'supernatural' and give meaning to the essential stages of individual and collective human existence.

Shamanism (a term which applies to the religion of the Tungus people of Siberia) was then the 'form of religion whose philosophical basis was animism', the *shaman* referring to a person able to communicate with the supernatural in order to help the community to cope with the problems of everyday life. A religion in the broad sense of the term, shamanism seems to have existed, during the historical period with which we are concerned, in all areas of the world where the higher 'forms of wisdom' represented by the cosmic, then historic and finally monotheistic religions had not yet appeared or taken root. The examples of numerous historical variants are provided by Europe and Northern Asia, the Pacific, sub-Saharan Africa and America.

Shamanism in Northern Europe and Northern Asia was characterized by 'archaic techniques of ecstasy' which were rooted in 'a complex of beliefs, rituals and traditions based on the figure of the *shaman*' (*táltos* among the Magyars). This 'ecstasy' signified the ascension of the soul of the *shaman* to the deity, whereas 'possession' signified that the *shaman* was visited by spirits who took control of him or her. This represents the twofold ascending and descending movement which was to be found in all natural religions, which, indeed, continue to exist as the substratum of the more elaborate forms of wisdom and religions. The *shaman*, 'he or she who knows', was thought to represent a 'primitive gnosis' and was a necromancer, soothsayer, healer and magician. He or she was a person who was sacred – occasionally or in a professional capacity – and who enabled the group to communicate with the divine or deities and some of its members to be infused with the energies of the *mana*, 'a physical or supernatural power or influence', which were transmitted by the spirits or ancestors which he or she had invoked.

The many different aspects of this shamanism existed among the common people in contemporary China and Japan: communication with the protective deities and spirits of the dead through a 'medium' (*shaman*), male or female, whose trances were interpreted as the cosmic expression of faith. In Tibet, the *Bön* ('truth', 'reality') religion, which was practised before the coming of Buddhism (which was granted royal patronage in the eighth and ninth centuries) and partially assimilated by the latter as a result of constant interaction, had followers (the *Bönpos*) whose objective was to accede to the 'eternal doctrine' thanks to the teaching and practice transmitted by their *shamans* in their holy scriptures, their own *Kanjur* (texts considered to have been submitted by Tönpa Shenrap after he had attained total illumination) and their *Tanjur* (later commentaries and treaties). The shamanism of the Magyars, before they were converted to Christianity after settling down in the Danube plains (tenth and eleventh centuries), was also a set of magic beliefs which encompassed the hierarchical cosmology of many different 'worlds', the reality of the animals and spirits of this 'lower world' whose energies could be secured by the wearing of amulets and the intuitive awareness of a 'supreme being', the master of the universe (*Isten*).

A similar 'animism', providing the questions of *homo religiosus* with answers, was to be found in the numerous Pacific islands (Micronesia, Melanesia and Polynesia), with individual cultural areas exhibiting different nuances. The Micronesians had numerous deities, starting with the high gods of the sky or the individual group's founding heroes, followed by spirits associated with specific places, objects and activities, and, finally, the ancestors. A specialized clergy was in charge of knowledge of myths and tribal genealogies. In Melanesia, little attention seems to have been paid to high gods, while great importance was attached to the 'culture heroes' (*dema*) and 'founders of clans', as well as to the somewhat evil spirits (*masalai*) against which protection was ensured by apotropaic rites (exorcism). Ancestors played a major role in their capacity as transmitters of *mana* (energy) through the agency of the 'masters' of initiation and funeral rites (masks and magic). The Polynesians had a better-structured system with aristocratic families, a more organized clergy and better-structured mythology and theology: a hierarchy among cosmic gods, a sacred world which was awesome and inaccessible (observation of *tapus*, physical and moral restrictions/taboos which were not to be transgressed), and specialists in 'things religious' ('shamanistic figures') who were also the 'masters of praise' (cultic associations or *ka'ioi*). The religion of the Aborigines of Australia was based on the cult (*kunapipi*) of fertility, and deities ('centres or reservoirs of energies', related principally to the seasons) were represented in the visible world by specific creatures and elements. Ritual activities which marked life's essential 'passages' (birth, puberty, marriage, death) formed part of the 'covertly sacred' and the 'overtly sacred', and were closely linked with the cosmogonic myths ('Dream Time') and the liturgical activity designed to ensure the constant renewal of 'life'.

The 'religions of Africa' were relatively heterogeneous in terms of culture and encompassed a great variety of languages. None the less, they all had a unifying vision of existence in which 'vitality' and 'wisdom' were evenly balanced. It was, according to the wording of Marcel Griaule's definition, a 'system of relationships between the visible world of humankind and the invisible world', which was controlled by a Creator and powers which, under different names and as different representative aspects of the unique God, were specialized in all kinds of functions; hence the convergences towards a vital union through the agency of intermediary powers (ancestors, genies, spirits). The 'Other World' was governed by a supreme God, the creator and master of the cosmos of whom one was not to be afraid because of his natural goodness, and who was absent and present at one and the same time. The ancestors played a central and paramount role. They were the tutelary powers who ensured life, fertility and prosperity, and the guardians of family traditions. Ancestor worship, with its rites and beliefs, was complemented by that of the 'secondary gods', local and non-local spirits and genies whose favour had to be won by the performance of specific rites whereby everyone could establish essential relationships with the ancestors and spirits. Such rites concerned the use of the corporeal techniques of dance and rhythm (masks, trances, possessions), basic ritual acts (of a cyclical or occasional nature) in the form of prayers, offerings and sacrifices (with animal substitutes acting as sacrificial intermediaries: totemism) and, above all, the major ceremonial complexes with their sacred symbolism (initiation, funeral and healing rites). In this way, the individual was integrated into the group and human evolution into that of the cosmos in order to ensure a 'survival' which transcended death.

In North America, the Inuit had a very simple religion with neither gods nor priests nor feasts, but an awareness of belonging to a 'cosmic order' in which spirits dwelt in the animal kingdom as well as in the mineral kingdom. This religion, which was profoundly influenced by this form of animism, was headed by the *angakop* (*shaman*), who held moral sway over the group, ensuring observance of the taboos, 'actions constituting a clear violation of the world order'. Among the Native Americans, the greater the level of organization of society and its evolution from hunting to agriculture, the greater was the separation of the profane from the sacred, as was reflected in their beliefs and rites, and the greater was the distinction between the figure of the *shaman* and that of the chief. The profound religiosity of Native Americans was aimed at ensuring respect for and continuation of the harmony of the universe, and consisted of profound attachment to the 'Earth Mother', obeisance to the creative (and sometimes solar) 'great spirit' which gave the heavens their sacred nature, close relationship with certain animals used by the 'mythical figures' who transmitted legends and rites (*tricksters*) and sometimes by the *shamans*, whose prestige was based on their medical and magical art, which guaranteed this universal harmony.

The religions of Central America were much more elaborate and very highly structured. Systems of writing had been developed in the region, with the result that the Maya and Aztecs possessed sacred books. The Toltec–Mayan religion thus had three books, the *Chilam Balam*, the *Ritual of the Bacabs* and the *Popol Vuh*, which gave details of its rituals. Encompassing the ancient Olmec traditions, whose animism raised the feline, the jaguar human-infant and the mother goddess of water and fertility to the rank of 'superior beings', the religion of the Toltecs and their capital Tula (856–1168), of the Maya in the Yucatán peninsula (seventh to fifteenth centuries) and, lastly, of the Aztecs in Mexico (twelfth to fifteenth centuries) merged in a syncretistic way which further complicated pantheons, beliefs and rites (see Plate 144). The Mesoamerican religions all share common traits. The reality of the world they portrayed was precarious and imperilled. It was a world which had undergone four previous destructions by mythical phenomena, and a fifth solar cycle (our own) was destined to be destroyed in a cosmic catastrophe. Hence an elaborate cosmology whose thirteen heavens and nine underworlds had an equivalent number of gods.

Time seems to have been the object of worship, especially among the Maya (*cf.* the steles which they erected at the end of each *katún* of 7,200 days). With remarkable ingenuity, they all established extremely precise calendrical systems which governed activities and festivities as well as the destinies of both individuals and societies. They had a solar calendar of 365 days in which each month of twenty days was under the sign of a specific deity, a ritual calendar of 260 days concerning celebrations and cultic activities, and a divinatory 'Venusian' calendar (based on the revolutions of the planet Venus). The calendrical 'count of days' and 'of destinies' made people believe in a rigorous predestination, starting from birth. Limitless polytheism had developed, initiated by a primordial couple whose 'descendants' multiplied at an identical speed to that of the lush propagation of 'mythological stories'. The Aztecs ended up with a pantheon in which traditional and adopted deities were divided into deities of the land, water, vegetation and the sky (stars), into gods which protected individual groups, into 'corporation' deities for individual trades, and into deities in charge of all types of activity.

The Aztecs inherited four major gods. The two main ones among them, Tezcatlipoca (the god of the smoking mirror) and Quetzalcóatl (the Feathered Serpent-Bird), the former being the god of warriors and the latter being the god of priests, had been at war. Tezcatlipoca had defeated Quetzalcóatl. Quetzalcóatl was the god of the east and the wind as well as the inventor of writing. He disapproved of human sacrifice, and was the supreme civilizing hero. Conversely, Tezcatlipoca was the sorcerer god who came from the north and demanded human sacrifices. He was the god who 'saw everything in his spy-mirror' and, as a result, determined the choice of sovereigns. In fifteenth-century Mexico, twin cults were devoted to Tlaloc, the great rain god who dwelt on the mountain tops and demanded the sacrifice of children because he was the solar deity of sedentary farmers, and Huitzilopochtli (the resuscitated warrior), who had guided the long migration of the Aztecs, indicating the site of Mexico City (1325) to them after an endless series of conquests (see Plates 300, 301, 305, 306, 307).

The gods of this intricate and hierarchical polytheism were both benevolent and dangerous, demanding and jealous, hungry for offerings and thirsting for sacrifices. This led to an abundance of scrupulously organized rituals carried out by the caste of priests who were allocated to as many colleges as there were temples requiring their services. The wonderful architecture and polychrome decorations of such temples bore witness to the consummate art of Aztec civilization. Mesoamerican rites comprised processions, plant offerings, self-scarifications, and animal and even human sacrifice. By the fifteenth century, this latter practice had reached its zenith in the Aztec Empire (victims chosen from the best individuals or from slaves). The victims were put to death by the removal of their hearts, which were offered to the gods because human blood and hearts were to be supplied uninterruptedly 'to our mother and our father, the Earth and the Sun', since this was the only way of guaranteeing the order of the cosmos, the succession of the seasons and the regular reappearance of the Sun. This was the system, comprising polytheistic animism, finely detailed liturgies and a pluralistic syncretism, that the Spanish conquerors were to discover.

In South America, the Incas, whose andean empire reached its zenith during the reign of Pachacuti (1438–1471), had a solar religion which was very closely linked to imperial power. There were different types of rites and beliefs. The popular cult of the *huacas* (objects and places infused with mysterious and supernatural powers because they were associated with the spirits and ancestors) existed side by side with theological speculations concerning the great god Viracocha, the 'creator of the upper world and the lower world, the shaper of the world' and the culture hero who was responsible for the creation of the Sun and the Moon as well as for sharing out land among different peoples. The solar cult of the Inca pantheon concerned both the Sun and its consort, the Moon (*Quilla*), which was also its sister. The priests and 'Chosen Women' (the 'Virgins of the Sun') officiated at religious ceremonies, which were governed by a calendar of twelve months. The practice of divination was prevalent.

The foregoing is an account, for the period between the seventh and fifteenth centuries, of the numerous and varied religions of land, tribe and community which, at times, expanded into the dimensions of an empire. It showed their great diversity and forms, which were favoured or imposed by the requirements of place and time. Myths, symbols and rites worked more or less harmoniously to provide both the individual and the group with a structure, survival and a destiny. *Homo religiosus*, who was filled with anxiety and possessed a keen myth-making mind, used myths, the 'secret preserved at source which leads to the confines of humankind and the gods', the better to reconstruct the known universe and determine the place in it of beings and things (high god, deities, ancestors, relationships, geographical places, plants, animals, objects). As M. Eliade wrote, 'a myth tells a sacred story, narrating an event which occurred during the primeval age'. It is a 'traditional narrative concerning events which took place at the beginning of time and aimed at providing the basis for the ritual activities of present-day people and, in general, at fashioning all the forms of activity and thought through which people gain an understanding of their existence in the world' (P. Ricoeur). The symbol played a central role in this context, establishing intriguing interconnections between mind and matter. It taught about the invisible world, transformed energy, presided over an alliance and channelled prayer. It was thus the symbolic experience of life which universally gave rise to the mythical dimension of the spoken word, which was substantiated by ritual celebrations, and thus gave time its full meaning and significance. This extension beyond earthly horizons by the invocation of spirits, 'communion' with ancestors and desire for eternity was manifest everywhere, although the intermediaries could take the form of as many deities as there were human needs to be satisfied. Magic and witchcraft were readily employed in this context, where the dialectic and conflict between good and evil and between life and death occurred without interruption. Far from being 'pagan', these so-called 'primitive' religions were ethnic, local, family, village, urban and royal religions. They were profoundly human and their devotees were keenly aware that the invisible powers were good or bad, ambivalent or ordinarily beneficent to the community, provided that a whole range of traditional observances whereby the group fashioned its individual identity were maintained.

DUALISTIC CURRENTS AND IRANIAN RELIGIONS

In the seventh century, before the Arab conquest and the gradual conversion of its inhabitants to Islam, the Sasanian Empire (which stretched from Mesopotamia to Turkestan) had Mazdaism as its official religion and the *Avesta* as its sacred book. Mazdaism, the religion of the 'worshippers of Mazda' or Ahura Mazda, an offshoot of the ancient religion of the Achaemenids, was based on a collection of beliefs and rites which were common to the Iranians and Indians, and in which an increasingly strict and well-structured dualism was established with the object of explaining the divine, history and the universe. Zoroaster (or Zarathustra, hence the name Zoroastrianism, which is also attached to Mazdaism) is thought to have been its prophet and priest in Media some time between the seventeenth and sixth centuries BC. He is also the supposed author of the more ancient texts of the *Avesta*, the seventeen hymns (*gāthās*) of the Mazdean liturgy which praised the 'Wise Lord' (Ahura Mazda), the creator and master of the world, and his suite of both divine and human entities. He adopted the old myth of the 'complaint of the ox' who was unjustly sacrificed while forging an alliance between humankind and itself for their mutual benefit. Under the protection of Prince Vishtaspa, Zoroaster explained the history of the world in terms of the struggle between light and darkness, which began with the conflict between the primal twins. So, he prayed to fire, the fire of Ahura Mazda, which was the symbol of justice and an instrument used for ordeals. Zoroaster was subsequently elevated to legendary status, becoming the archetypal priest, warrior and herdsman–farmer. This legendary account is given in Book 7 of the *Dēnkart* ('Acts of Religion'), a Mazdean encyclopedia of nine books written in Pahlavī (tenth century).

Mazdaism expressed belief in the existence of a 'Wise Lord' (Ahura Mazda), the source and mainstay of all the 'good' entities who were both divine and human (collectively called *amesha spentas* ('bounteous immortals') representing the qualities of both god and humankind at the same time: *asha*, fire (justice); *vohu manah*, the ox (the good mind); *khshathra*, the sky (power); *ārmaiti*, the earth (devotion); and *haurvatāt* and *ameretāt*, waters and plants (health and non-death). This hierarchical group existed in symmetrical opposition to the group representing the forces of evil, all of which sprang from a Destructive Spirit (*Ahriman*), the enemy of the Bounteous Spirit. This pantheon included the ancient god Mithra, who had been created by the Wise Lord before becoming his rival or equal who was also to be worshipped. In times past, the Bounteous Spirit had met his twin, the Destructive Spirit, and this led to incessant combat between the forces of good and those of evil, in the vast cosmic context and in each human being. At the close of history, a saviour (*saoshyant*) was supposed to bring about universal renewal (*frasho kareti*). The Bounteous Spirit was merged, from very early on, with the Wise Lord, who thus became locked in almost eternal combat with the Destructive Spirit, both of them having been fathered by Time (*zrvan*). Mazdaism, which was given its precise form and structure by the high priest Kartēr during the reign of Varhrān II and after the Manichaean interlude (third century), was thus a national religion in Ctesiphon in the seventh century, with a priestly hierarchy and the seal of official orthodoxy. The orthodox texts, written in Pahlavī in the ninth century, narrated that the world had been created to serve as a stage for the great combat: the initial immaterial and invisible state of the universe had been succeeded by the world, which was created in six stages (the sky, the water, the earth, the tree, the ox, the man). Ohrmazd and Ahriman were locked in unceasing combat, and the latter (the Destructive Spirit) put to death the first-born ox, whose death was transformed into a 'fertile sacrifice'. The Primal Man (*gaya maretan*) was supposed to be the progenitor of human beings and the source of everything that was useful in the cosmos.

Initiation rites introduced the Zoroastrian to the religious practice of a life in which everything was regulated by a strict liturgy: five daily prayers (standing, facing the Sun), seasonal festivities and ceremonial funerals. The fate of believers in the afterlife depended solely on their moral comportment in this life, and they had to refrain from any impure contact (very precise rules of purification existed) and ensure that their souls were gradually elevated by good thoughts, words and deeds above matter and out of reach of the forces of evil, so that at death they could merge with their individual 'pre-existent souls' (*fravashi*). During the Sasanian period, the cult of fire dominated the official liturgy. Hundreds of temples of fire were constructed and the liturgy of fire was conducted according to a complex ritual and austere prescriptions. Each king had his own fire, the symbol of his power, which was lighted, when he was crowned. Society, which was divided into three social classes (priests, warriors and herdsmen–farmers) waited for the coming of successive saviours, the last of whom was to ensure final victory over evil and darkness. Ahriman would then be thrown into Hell and the wicked would be subjected to their final punishment there before joining the righteous on a regenerated Earth, where Ohrmazd would reign alone. Such were the prophecies found, in about the ninth century, in the main Pahlavī books of a Mazdaism which was then prevalent. Its sacred text, the *Avesta* ('knowledge'), whose twenty-one books are summarized in the *Dēnkart*, has survived only partially in the form of the *Vidēvdāt*. The other amalgamated parts are to be found in the *Yasna* (a kind of missal) and the *Yashts* (prayers for specific occasions). The *Khorda* (little) *Avesta* comprises various prayers and the five daily prayers (*gāh*). Mazdean cosmogony was presented, in the ninth century, in the *Bundahishu* ('Primordial Creation') and, in the tenth century, in this *Dēnkart* ('Acts of Religion'), which is a fully fledged Mazdean encyclopedia. Mazdaism was a dualistic religion established on the basis of ancient Aryan and Iranian religious traditions. In the third century, it was also to become one of the sources of inspiration of Manichaeism.

Manichaeism was founded by Mānī (216–277) in the third century AD in an Elchasaite environment (a gnostic kind of Judaeo-Christian baptism), and was presented as a 'Religion of the Book' which was to take the place of the allegedly 'failed' Zoroaster, Buddha and Jesus. Mānī, who had substituted the Eastern Syriac alphabet for Pahlavī writing, then became the founder of a Church and creator of a veritable treasure of scriptures. An initial canon of seven texts (the Heptateuch) written in Eastern Syriac (*The Living Gospel* or *Major Gospel*, the *Treasure of Life*, the *Book of Secrets* (or of *Mysteries*), the *Pragmateai* or *Treatise on Legends*, the *Book of Giants*, the *Letters of Mānī* and the *Book of Psalms and Prayers*), and two other texts (the *Shābuhrazān*, dedicated to the Sasanian sovereign Shāpūr I, and the *Arzhang Mānī*, a book of iconic images), all revealed that Manichaeism was partially related to Mazdaism while at the same time borrowing extensively from Christianity, of which it seemed to have been a heresy or an alternative Church. It consisted of a dualistic gnosis which preached about the conflict between the two co-eternal and radically opposed principles of Light and Darkness, with Mānī, the Paraclete announced by Jesus, supposedly being the last prophet with a religion to reveal. The New Church 'of Light', namely Manichaeism with its scriptures, clergy and institutions, saw itself as the result of the revelation made by the Paraclete to Mānī in order to complete past religions and incorporate the best aspects of Mazdaism. It taught that at the very beginning, Light and Darkness were separated, thus signifying the irreconcilable opposition of spirit and matter. During the middle period of human existence, that of history, Primal Man had been enticed to follow the 'Archons' of this material world, with the result that human beings were given to the pursuits of the flesh and to sin. It also stated that there had been no lack of gnostic messengers and magnified Jesus, whom it represented as one of three determined figures gathering the sparks of light previously held prisoner in the material realm into his 'Cross of Light'. Thus, akin to the Christian Church, the 'spiritual' Church of Mānī had its doctrine, hierarchy, rites and missions. Its 'gnostic' followers had to adhere to the mysteries, free themselves from fleshly pursuits and matter, pray, fast, give alms, and obey the commandments of justice (truth, chastity, poverty, non-violence, vegetarianism). The Manichaean community, a community of the elect who were 'separated' from the world, possessed its own liturgy, with its holiest ceremony being the *Bēma* (the forgiveness of sins, remembrance of the Passion of Mānī, who died in prison, and the Easter celebration of gnosis).

The similarities between Manichaeism and Mazdaism made it a dangerous rival for the latter. As a result of a great many controversies and persecutions, by the seventh century the practice of Manichaeism had been restricted to the Uighur kingdom (762–840) in Central Asia (see Plate 54). But Manichaeism was fated to reappear in the Christian world in both original and radical forms. The Christian Churches fought against it using non-violent means, then repressed it. It was condemned by the Byzantine emperors and, in the seventh century, was still felt to represent a mortal danger to the Eastern Roman Empire. To be sure, it had its emulators in the form of crypto-Manichaean Christian doctrines, which restricted the Christian world view to a dualistic struggle between good and evil. There was the short-lived case of Messalianism (the way of 'those who pray'), which accepted only the New Testament, rejected the sacraments and magnified prayer and asceticism as the channels by which to liberate penitents from all impure passion (they rejected manual work and adopted the life of mendicants). There was also Paulicianism, which achieved considerable growth in Armenia and Asia Minor before spreading to the Balkans. It was founded by the Armenian Constantine of Mananali, originally a Manichaean who is thought to have revised Mānī's teaching in the light of the New Testament, and the intention of the movement was to reconcile Manichaeism with Christianity. It taught that a malevolent spirit had created the material world and inspired the Old Testament, whereas a good Essence had given rise to the spiritual world and the writings of the New Testament. The ordinary members of the sect adopted this teaching, while its initiates adhered to the spirit of the dualistic tradition, namely that Jesus could in no way have been human, as he could not belong to a material world which was the source of all evil. The Paulicians thus rejected the sacraments, dogmas and structures of the Church, retaining their vocabulary while spurning their content. They advocated a morality of liberation akin to that of Manichaeism but put less emphasis on contemplation and asceticism. They were ready missionaries and formidable 'disputants' who preached a primitive egalitarian anarchy for society. Missionary activities and political deportations brought them, in the mid-eighth century, to the Balkans, where they won converts among both the Bulgarians, who had recently arrived, and the local poor rural folk. Bogomilism grew in their wake.

For over half a millennium, Bogomilism was to represent the 'Balkan variant' of the dualistic religions. It was founded in the mid-tenth century by Bogomil, a Bulgarian priest who was initially active in Macedonia. Bogomil doctrines exhibited serious internal divisions, notwithstanding an attempt to establish a system of doctrine during the eleventh and twelfth centuries (the *Book of Saint John*, also called the *Secret Book*, and the *Sea of Tiberias*). Their dualistic cosmology taught that the 'evil principle' (Satan) was the elder son of God and not his equal, and that Christ was his younger son. As a result, the historic combat between Satan (Satanaël) and his fiends (including the Old Testament and the established Church), and a Jesus who merely effected a 'passage' on Earth ('Docetist' Christology), was merely a series of symbols and allegories of the message contained in the Gospels and the Acts. The Bogomils rejected the cult of the Cross and the sacraments in favour of prayer (the *Pater*) and asceticism, refusing obeisance to princes and bishops, whom they saw as the captives of their own wealth. The faithful were divided into two categories, the 'believers' and the 'perfect'. The latter had to be pure Christians who were free of all passion (*inter alia*, abstinence and non-violence were required of them). And, Satan having created the world and remaining the master of the material sphere, souls had to transmigrate finally to free themselves of the latter through the 'baptism of Christ by the Spirit'. The Bogomils gradually organized themselves into a Church with a hierarchy of 'perfects', and were closely allied to the Cathari of the West. They carried out a doctrinal syncretism and, at the same time, Bogomilism became a patriotic ideology in Bulgaria and more particularly in Bosnia, where it was used by the local nobility in their struggle against the kingdom of Hungary. The Middle Ages ended with some Bogomils being won over to Catholicism by the preaching of the Franciscans, while others embraced the Islam of the Ottoman conquerors.

The Cathari (Cathars) were already present in the West. These 'perfect' Cathari wanted to remedy the deficiencies of Western Christendom and purify it by renouncing the material world, so securing the independence of the 'religious' sphere from the 'political' sphere. The activities of itinerant preachers, who adopted the reformist ideas of Pope Gregory VII, led to the creation of numerous communities from the Rhineland to Spain. They sank their deepest roots in Languedoc–Aquitaine, with the support of local princes, between 1140 and 1170. The Cathari adopted moderate Bogomilism and rejected the Old Testament. They received the support of Nicetas, the head of the Paulician Church of Dragovica (in the Balkans), during their Council of Saint Felix of Caraman (1167) and ended up adopting the radical dualistic views of the Paulicians. They then became the poor and 'perfect' devotees of a rich Church, and a sect with a political orientation ('occitan' ideology). The Dominicans attacked them by word and example, but the main causes of their decline were to be found in the 'Albigensian crusades' and the nascent Inquisition. They had disappeared completely by the fifteenth century.

FORMS OF ETHICAL WISDOM AND RELIGIOUS BELIEFS

Daoism

While these 'dualistic currents' bore the stamp of the ancient religions of Iran, Japan and China established more or less religious forms of wisdom over and above the simplicity of their ancient original shamanism. Daoism took root in China in the second century BC, grew over the centuries, was proclaimed the 'official religion' under the Wei in the North (444), and finally ceased to be the official cult a little before the seventh century. The *Dao* or *Tao* (the 'way'), defined as 'the autonomous Reality which is the source and end of all things', was thought to represent the Ultimate, the Great Unity and the manifestation of the Oneness of living beings. It thus stood for the inner 'Self' of each individual, which transcended the binomial of *yin/yang* (sky/earth, shade/light) but could only be perceived in the alternating nature of these two opposed elements. There were numerous Daoist schools with distinctive definitions of Daoism, and the latter's sects and institutes practised it in widely different ways. The School of 'Perfect Unity' (*Zhengyizong*), or Western School, dated back to Zhang Daoling and was officially approved by the authorities in AD 444. The Northern School (*Beizong*), founded in the tenth century by Wang Zhu, practised an austere asceticism and integrated Daoism with Confucianism and Buddhism. The Southern School (*Nanzong*) was founded by Liu Haichan, and the doctrines of the last two schools were systematized by Lu Dongbin during the Tang Dynasty (618–907). Two other schools were founded under the Yuan (1271–1368): the Schools of the 'Great Unity' (*Taiyizong*) and the 'Authentic Way' (*Zhendaozong*). The teaching of the *Dao* had been greatly systematized by Zhuangzi and Liezi, and, more particularly, by Laozi (the 'Old Master'), who was a contemporary of Confucius. The doctrine of Laozi, a man who lived 'retired from the world', emphasized 'humility and the ineffable'. His work, the *Daodejing* (the 'Classic of the Way and its Power'), contains the teachings of the *Dao*. He himself became the chief exponent of Daoism and was even divinized in AD 666 under the name of Laojun (the 'Old Lord'). Conversely, the *Huainanzi*, another work which was composed by an academy of scholars gathered around Liu An, the vassal king of the Huanan (beginning of the first Han period) is a syncretic encyclopedia. The *Daozang*, the Daoist canon compiled in AD 745, contains 1,464 fascicles which deal with all the sciences and practices of 'longevity'.

The essential feature of Daoism in both its philosophical and religious forms is the search for longevity or immortality through oneness with the immense and peaceful harmony of the universe, whose immanence becomes manifest in anyone who submits to the simple (*su*), the rough (*pu*), the natural (*ziran*), in short, to authentic reality (*dao*). The Daoism of the seventh century can thus be defined as a search for wisdom and longevity based on a well-organized religious structure. Its goal was that of submission to a Supreme Unity (*Taiyi*) which was all-embracing, although accompanied by a Celestial Unity (*Tianyi*) and a Terrestrial Unity (*Diyi*). A now divinized Laozi had his place in it, and, under the Song (960–1279), the 'Three Purities' (*Sanqing*) acted as mediators in the pantheon: the celestial Precious Lord ('who is and who sits'), the spiritual Precious Lord ('who works efficiently') and the divine Precious Lord ('who inspires being'). Daoist schools had different definitions and its sects and institutes, different practices. The 'Sect of the Accumulation of Virtue' (*Jishanpai*) wanted to improve human existence through moral effort; the 'Book Sect' (*Jingdianpai*) pondered over the mysteries of Daoist doctrine. Other sects were the 'Alchemist Sect' or 'Sect of the Tripod' (*Dandingpai*), which systematized pharmaceutical experiments and breathing techniques, the 'Talisman Sect' (*Fulupai*), which worshipped the spirits (*shen*) of Heaven and the ancestors, and the 'Sect of Experimental Divination' (*Zhanyanpai*), which scrutinized signs in Heaven and Earth in order to foretell the future accurately. Asceticism and cultic practices involved activity aimed at self-improvement (embryonic breathing), which was inseparable from piety, and visualization of the gods (*shen*) in order to achieve unity with the *Dao* (the spiritualization of one's entire being). There was a community cult of the 'gods', who were intricately linked to everyday village life, which aimed at ensuring the protection of human beings from all harm. The clergy made ready use of divination, employing a Daoist liturgy in which vestments had great symbolic value.

Confucianism

Within the foregoing context, Confucianism could be defined as an ethic aimed at preserving traditional society and the structure of the state but able, at the same time, to accommodate other religions. It dates back to Confucius (551–479 BC), who, at a time of feudal disorder and internecine strife, advocated a return to a moral dispensation based on the cosmic order (the *Law of Heaven*). Confucianism requires 'a kindly disposition and a taste for respectability, as well as a desire for moral and social advancement' of its followers. It was partially eclipsed by Buddhism but enjoyed renewed vitality under the Tang Dynasty (618–907). Famous poets, most notably Wang Wei (699–759), codified its doctrine in their didactic poetry. An edict of 845 against Buddhism and other foreign religions allowed Confucianism to regain its dominant position in Chinese culture. It subsequently took the form of neo-Confucianist philosophy under the reign of the Song (960–1279): Zhao Yong (1001–1077), Zhou Dunyi (1017–1073), Zhang Zai (1020–1076), and the brothers Cheng Hao (1032–1085) and Cheng Yi (1033–1107), with most emphasis being placed by some on reason, and by others on sentiment. A reformer called Wang Anshi (1021–1086) also had a role to play, and, centuries later, Wang Yangming gave renewed life to its teachings under the Ming Dynasty. Traditional faiths, especially ancestor worship, were still observed alongside Confucianism, but emphasis was now put on *zen* (humanity, kindness). The gradual expansion of family and social piety was expected to enable individuals to gain control over their emotions and to love other people as much as themselves. One then became a 'superior person' (*junzi*), whose superiority resided in one's virtue and culture. The achievement of such personal dignity meant that the individual participated in maintaining the harmony of society, especially if the latter was ruled by a 'sage-king'. Confucian doctrine was condensed into four books, including *The Doctrine of the Mean* (*Zhongyong*), which stated that by their 'nature' individuals helped to maintain the harmony of the cosmos and the metaphysical order which governed all things.

This Chinese humanism was profoundly to influence Japan and Viet Nam. Relinquishing the 'religious' sphere and 'the other world' to Shintō and the Buddha, the purpose of Japanese Confucianism was to regulate human relationships and provide the basis for civic morality in this 'lower world'. Thus, codes, laws, political maxims and educational programmes all served to buttress a rigidly hierarchical society in which the perfect ethic took the layered form of social classes, that of the warrior (*samurai*) rising above those of the farmer, craft worker and merchant, for granted. This can be explained by the fact that the Confucianism which was brought to Japan in the sixth century AD was that of the last Han Dynasty, whose ideology justified and upheld a notion of government centralized around an emperor who received his mandate from Heaven and was therefore under no obligation to be a 'sage-king'. In AD 604, Prince Shōtoku systematized Confucianism in his *Constitution of Seventeen Articles*. Later, in the *Kojiki* (*c*. 680) and *Nihonshoki* (720), virtuous government was defined as that of the emperor, a descendant of the gods. The models of the neo-Confucianism of the Song, which was introduced into Japan at the end of the twelfth century, were also Japanized. Viet Nam, which remained under Chinese influence until 939, likewise witnessed the triumph of a state Confucianism whose ideal was epitomized by the virtue of *nhān* (benevolence) with liturgy centred around the cult of Heaven and the ancestors. Confucius himself was worshipped. Thus, King Ly Thanh Tōn (r. 1054–1072) built the *Shrine of Literature* (*Van Miēu*) in Hanoi in honour of the Great Master.

Shintō

In Japan, Shintō (the 'way of *kami*' or the deities) was based on traditional practices which gave expression to an attitude towards life and a set of beliefs abounding in symbolic models. There existed the Shintō of the imperial household (rites carried out by the emperor in honour of *Amaterasu-ō-mikami*, the goddess of the Sun, and the imperial ancestors), shrine Shintō (a structured set of rites and beliefs) and folk Shintō, with its profound religiosity. Of the first two, 'state Shintō', constituted a governmental institution (proclaimed 'non-religious') which reinforced the Japanese sense of identity. But Shintō, rooted in ancient myths and practices, had to be transformed into a religion, the better to distinguish itself from Confucianism and Buddhism, which were imported from China starting from the sixth century AD. Hence its first literary documents, the *Kojiki* ('Records of Ancient Matters') and the *Nihon Shoki* ('Chronicles of Japan'), were compiled on the orders of the Palace in the eighth century. Shintō was then organized with a mythology, priesthood, rites and shrines. Shintō, a religion of personal faith in the *kami*, fostered community cohesiveness through frequent attendance at its ceremonies, which were held in local shrines, while, at the same time, remaining tolerant of other religions such as Buddhism. The concept of *matsuri* ('celebration of life') is central to Shintō, with the message that life should be lived intensely in the present in harmony with the cosmos and with a comforting web of relationships linking each individual to the thousands of divine beings (*kami*) of Japanese mythology. Thus, through the ages, Shintō came to play the role of a 'national religion'.

Hinduism

In the seventh century, the peoples of India practised a great variety of religions, in which no orthodoxy of any kind can be discerned. Hinduism was a diversified complex of beliefs, attitudes and rites whose central tenet was apparently that of the *dharma* or 'the general restrictive order of things'. This order was unchanging (*sanātanadharma*) and governed all individuals according to their castes (*varnas*), endowing them with a 'guided effort' (*āshrama*) of a moral, spiritual and social nature at each of the four stages of their individual lives. From the seventh to the fifteenth centuries, the adherents of Hinduism, a religion benefiting from the numerous elaborations of the Vedic and Dravidian traditions and also espousing the worship of personal gods who were more accessible to the common people, felt the need to react against the innovative reforms of Buddhism and Jainism. They wrote down their various religious traditions in the form of the *Purānas* or 'ancient stories', which are sacred texts, including the *Bhāgavata Purāna*, of the major religious Shaivite and Vaishnava groups. The *Purānas* concern the creation of the world, its re-creation subsequent to periodic destruction, the genealogy of ancient gods and saints, the succession of the ages and epochs of world history, and royal genealogies. They also include encyclopedias of secular sciences.

Vedism, the ancient form of Hinduism, was polytheistic in practice, if not in theory, with its numerous gods (Indra, Agni, Soma, Mitra and Varuna, Sūrya and so on), although modified and attenuated to enable unification with a 'Lord of creatures', a 'Germ of gold' or 'the One'. The *ātman–brahman* was said to be the starting point of the universe. Each living being has its *ātman*, its Self (distinct from both body and mind). It is a kernel of being, identical in all individuals, and only to be perceived after consistent effort towards internalization. The *brahman* is the supreme *ātman*, the Absolute at the heart of all things and yet transcending all things. Channels to this impersonal and neutral *brahman* are provided by the gods (*Deva*), who are its secondary manifestations. The *brahman* ultimately fuses with the *ātman*, for 'thou art That' (your *ātman* is the *brahman*). To this relative degree of polytheism should be added the vast liturgy of sacrifices, which the caste of Brahmans carried out. Such sacrifices comprised the offering of an elixir of immortality (*soma*) or, simply, milk, rice, flowers or fruits. It was the Brahmans who, through the literary elaboration of the *Upaniṣads*, transformed sacrifice into an internalized practice: 'The sacrifice is personified by the individual.' Society was divided between the castes of the Brahmans, warriors, herders–farmers, merchants, and, below them, the lowly (and often semi-servile) *Sūdras*. Each caste had its own protective gods, and at the time of the *Upaniṣads* the god Brahma, the personification of *brahman*, was even said to have appeared. All individuals, irrespective of caste, strove to free themselves from the 'circular flow' (*samsāra*) of living beings and the unceasing process of births and deaths by ethical and religious 'actions' (*karma*) which might save them, thus freeing the individual from the phenomenal world of plurality. The 'law of *karma*', with its unrelenting retributive punishment of actions, meant that, to escape the unavoidable condition of rebirth in animal, human or divine form, individuals were obliged to secure their liberation through the worship (*bhakti*) of their gods, *yoga* or meditation, and thus become able to gain knowledge of *ātman* at last. The final hurdle was that *ātman* should secure its essential freedom by fusing with Brahman, its original source, after abandoning the phenomenal world of flesh and matter.

The Hinduism of the time made available numerous channels to ensure this liberation of *ātman*. In addition to the ritualism and intellectual mysticism of the Brahmans, and in reaction against the spiritual systems elaborated by Buddhism and Jainism, Hinduism had for centuries provided ordinary people with personalized gods such as Shiva and Vishnu, whose cults became particularly well developed alongside those of Vāsudeva Krishna and Rāma. One of Hinduism's foremost gods, venerated in innumerable temples, celebrated in a great many mythological stories and meditated upon in the heart of philosophical speculations, is Shiva, 'the Auspicious One', a high god who controls all the worlds and intervenes in the organization and development of the universe. Shiva's consort (*shakti*) is the Great Goddess, and he is 'the Great *Yogin*' with astounding powers of concentration and creation, as well as being 'the true *guru*'. This is not a divine manifestation (*avatāra*), however, for Shiva transcends the realm of his creation. He is depicted as the 'King of the dance', a dance cosmic in nature for it creates and destroys worlds. He is also the Supreme Being, releasing the *ātman* of beings who emulate his *yoga* and asceticism to unite themselves to him beyond death. Shivaism flourished from the eighth to the thirteenth century in Kashmir, where its doctrine was systematized by Abhinavagupta (ninth century). Vishnu is named the Supreme Cosmic Person who represents the totality of the universe. He organizes space and is the protector of this world. His consort is the goddess Lakshmī, and his 'divine manifestations' (*avatāra*) are Krishna and Rāma, as well as Brahmā, the creator of the world. His most fervent devotees, *bhaktī* being an essentially Vaishnava phenomenon, endeavoured to reconcile these numerous manifestations, which work to re-establish the cosmic *dharma*, with the immutable nature of Vishnu. Vishnuism is thus a set of beliefs, spiritual practices and also religious groups all centred on Vishnu. The Pañcarātras saw themselves as its authentic representatives, and Rāmānuja gave it final philosophical expression in the eleventh century. The Bhāgavata, or 'followers of the Blissful' Lord Vishnu, had as their sacred texts the *Bhāgavata Purāna* and the *Vishnu Purāna*, which systematized *bhakti* and thus conveyed the divine presence to the worshipper. Krishna, the mythical hero or *avatāra* of Vishnu, is the Master of Wisdom in the *Bhāgavad-Gītā* and the Victorious Warrior in *Bhāgavata Purāna* (a part of the great mythological text *Mahābhārata*). It was in his honour that the poet Jayadeva composed the *Gītā Govinda*, a love poem, in the twelfth century. Finally, Rāma, another *avatāra* of Vishnu, was named the god of mercy and, in the fifteenth century, his followers founded the sect of the Rāmānandis, 'those who put their joy in Rāma'. 'The Romance of Rāma' (*Rāmāyana*) by Vālmīki, which narrates his story, is one of Hinduism's great literary achievements, along with the *Mahābhārata*.

Seventh-century Hinduism, then, espoused these very varied forms all rooted in scholarly or popular religious traditions. In subsequent centuries, but prior to the invasion of the thirteenth century which dealt serious blows to its socio-political underpinnings, Hinduism enjoyed a richly significant period of growth whose main influential development was the composition of the *Purānas*. Worshippers who continued to practise the Vedic cult crystallized their traditions in the *smriti* ('remembered') form, as opposed to the *shruti* ('heard') form of the texts of the Vedas. These concerned cultic activities, private and public morality, family liturgy, and everything which came within the province of *dharma*. Many people persevered in their veneration of the higher gods previously mentioned, *inter alia* Shiva and Vishnu. Devotees of these two gods then composed the *Purānas* ('ancient stories') in which the mythology of the gods and their consorts were interlaced with cosmological and theological speculations. The *Bhāgavata Purāna*, dating back to this period, is a text of 18,000 stanzas arranged in books, Book X being a mythical biography of Krishna. All these different religious systems were systematized by thinkers, philosophers and theologians into increasingly theistic 'disciplines'. The *darśanas*, or methods of approach aimed at reaching a 'vision' of ultimate reality and thereby securing one's final liberation, are but one example of the different schools of asceticism and meditation.

Two of the *darśanas* concern the prescriptions of the Vedas (the *Pūrva-Mīmānsā*, for example, deals with delicate aspects of ritual) and their grand intuitions (the *Vedānta*, an exegesis relating to the nature of the relation between *ātman* and *brahman*). Two others relate to the rules of logic (*Nyāya* or 'method' for direct observation, inference, assimilative comparison and reliable testimony) and the inventory of the categories of reality (*Vaisheshika* or 'physical science' of the nature of things and beings). Still others concern a scale of values and realities (*Sāmkhya* thus establishes dualism between nature, *prakriti*, and the spiritual monads, *purusha*), or asceticism (*yoga*) and devotional practice (*bhaktī*).

The 'paths' of Hinduism are thus manifold, involving the rigid system of social classes (castes). Such aesthetic and liturgical visions found expression in the proliferation of holy images (statues representing the divine presence), the building of sumptuous temples with magnificent architecture and the composing of anthems of great lyrical value. Shivaism and Vishnuism had a pivotal importance and the confraternities to which they gave rise played a decisive role. These included the *Ālvārs*, meaning those 'plunged' by meditation in the love of God, who profoundly influenced the world of the Tamils (sixth to ninth centuries).

Other groups of contemporary Hindus concentrated on the active power of deities whose vital energy (*shaktī*) was personified by their consorts or goddesses. This form of Hinduism, termed Tantrism or Shaktism, emphasized self-realization in order to transcend the human condition through the asceticism or divinations which brought to life in each individual the divine energies (*shaktī*) transmitted by the female deities who were worshipped above all others. Cultic initiation was carried out by a *guru* who guided the novice through the successive stages of perfection, involving rites and sacrifices. The Tantrism of the time seems to have been the extreme form of Hinduism comprising the many contradictory forms which Jainism and Buddhism sought to reform or challenge (see Plates 52, 53, 55, 221–231, 235, 236).

A very important development within Hindu religious thought was initiated by Śankarāchārya (*c.* 800), through his commentaries on the Upaniṣads, in which he offered a pantheistic version of the Vedānta, maintaining the principle of the ultimate non-duality (*advaita*), with Illusion (*māyā*) sustaining the separateness of things imagined through our sensory perceptions. Within some centuries, if not immediately, Śankarāchārya's doctrine became dominant in Hindu religious thought; and he came to be credited in tradition with the rout of Buddhism in India.

COMBINED PHILOSOPHICAL AND RELIGIOUS SYSTEMS

Jainism

A contemporary of the Buddha (sixth to fifth century BC), Mahāvīra, 'the Great Hero' or Jaina, meaning 'conqueror', founded Jainism by example and preaching. The exclusive pursuit of this religion, often seen as a heterodox school (*darśhana*) of Hinduism, is pure asceticism and the primacy of the spiritual domain. The Jaina 'path' has no place for deities and requires a fully internalized sacrifice of its adherents. Jainas are established only in India, where they have always been a minority group which has never been absorbed by Hinduism because of the ascetic austerity of their monks and the interaction between these monks and the creed's lay devotees. Both of these categories have considerably enriched the religious literature of India. The second Jaina Council (*c.* AD 500) led to the systematization, first in Ardhamāgadhi and then in Sanskrit, of a canon including forty-five texts on doctrine, ritual, hagiography and monastic discipline, and representing the teachings of twenty-four masters of asceticism, of whom Mahāvīra is considered to be the last but one. Jainism is widely associated with commerce and urban culture. Its followers include both monks and laity. Jaina monks (*sādhu*) and nuns (*sādhvī*) are expected to lead a wandering life after being initiated by their *guru*, and practise *ahimsā* or the 'desire not to do injury to the life or feelings of living beings' (absolute vegetarianism). Jaina monks fall into two categories: those who dress in white (*shvetambaras*), and those who practise complete nudity, the 'sky-clad' (*digambaras*). Lay adherents observe the same vows albeit on a minor scale, going to temples and places of pilgrimage where they worship the *tīrthankaras*, the twenty-four 'fordmakers' who show the way to liberation. For Jainas, the universe is the one and only reality. It is inhabited by living beings (*jīvas*), devoid of conscious and spiritual in nature, and inanimate beings (*ajīvas*) which are without consciousness and material in nature. The *jīvas* lead an autonomous existence, their essential characteristic being their consciousness (*cetanā*). *Jīvas* have distinct, destructive or non-destructive *karmas*, from which liberation should be secured through 'right vision, right knowledge and right conduct'. To this end, the wandering ascetic vows to abstain from committing the five great vices (harming living and sentient beings, lying, stealing, indulging in sexual acts, and owning material possessions). Fasting, solitude, mortification of the body and the confession of offences ensure control over the mind and discursive reasoning, as a prelude to meditation centred on *ātman*. Jainism has taken the requirement of psychological analysis to its limits, namely through fourteen stages of spiritual qualifications which lead the soul to 'integrate its pure essence' and thereby attain the state of omniscience (perfect conscious knowledge in synergy with the psychological and physical organism) and 'realized' perfection (*siddha*) in which the soul, liberated at last from the body, enjoys bliss. Thus, notwithstanding the austere nature of its system, Jainism extols the primacy of the spiritual, the value of non-violence, the benefits of self-control and desire for the fully realized being.

Buddhism

Buddhism, a historical religion whose founder was a contemporary of Mahāvīra, had spread throughout Asia by the beginning of the seventh century. Evolving in many different ways, it emerged as a universal message expressed by doctrines and schools which profoundly influenced national religions and cultures. Siddhārtha Gautama was born in a Hindu environment in northern India in the middle of the sixth century BC. He became a wandering monk after his personal conversion. Then, after renouncing an overly austere asceticism to devote himself to meditation, he was able to secure release from the 'ceaseless round of births and deaths' (*samsāra*), at last to become the Awakened One (hence the name 'Buddha') and never to be reborn. He described this experience to his companions in his 'sermon of Benares' on the Four Noble Truths, 'the first turning of the Wheel of the Law'. The Buddhist monastic community (*sangha*) thus came to be born. Its 'four sublime states' were as follows: perfect loving kindness (*maitrī*), active compassion (*karma*), the experience of joy in the happiness of other people (*muditā*) and equanimity (*upekkā*), which extended the three preceding virtues to all beings. The four were collectively known as *Brahmā-Vihāra* (Dwelling of Brahmā), for whoever accomplished them became 'Brahmā's equal'. The Buddha Sākyamuni (so-called the ascetic of Sākya after his original clan), who soon became a legendary figure, was seen as one of the numerous beings who became awakened after a great many previous existences. Thus, in response to Hinduism's existential queries, Buddhism provides the central tenet of the non-Self or *anattā* (the illusion of the existence of a Self). It adopted the Vedic concepts of *karma* and *samsāra* but rejected that of *ātman*, the Self at either the individual or universal level (*brahman*). The search for responses to metaphysical questions is futile, and human existence is one of suffering (*dukkha*). It is only through the suppression of the causes of suffering that one can become free to attain *nirvāna*, which is the total extinction of the life cravings (envy, wrath, ignorance, and so on) which hold people captive to an unceasing 'transmigration', akin to the turning of the wheel. The Buddhist path thus leads to a final destination, which is described in negative terms: an absolute reality exists which can neither be known nor expressed in words ('a completely vacuous positive pole'), and the sole resort of human beings is to free themselves of the 'negative pole' of the world of phenomena in which they are submerged and suffer unduly. The nature of one's access to *nirvāna* depends on whether one espouses the teachings and practices of the Lesser Vehicle (Hīnayāna) or those of the Greater Vehicle (Mahāyāna). Mahāyāna Buddhism was thus practised in China, Japan and Viet Nam in the seventh century, while Sri Lanka and South-East Asia remained faithful to the Hīnayāna tradition. The Hīnayāna is highly demanding, being the spiritual 'Lesser Vehicle' on the road to salvation and claiming fidelity to the initial teachings of the Buddha. Four councils had resulted in schisms in the original Buddhist movement.

The Hīnayāna (lesser vehicle) is directed to close adherence to the experience and initial teachings of the Buddha. The Buddhists of this Lesser Vehicle advocated 'strict observance' and kept to the practices of the Theravādins, one of the two groups of the Vibhajyavādins who had condemned the Servāstivādins at the second Council of Patāliputra. They compiled and preserved the Buddhist canon in the Pāli language and also established themselves in Sri Lanka, whence their doctrine spread into Myanmar, Thailand, Laos and Cambodia through the proliferation of schools, monasteries and temples. Hīnayāna, representing 'ancient Buddhism' or School of the South, primarily stressed two fundamental points. The first point relates to its cosmic vision: since the world of phenomena is considered to be real, although non-permanent and insubstantial, and since all suffering stems from its 'established and conditioned' character, *nirvāna* can only be gained by leaving the world. The second point concerns the importance given to wisdom (*prajna*) leading to non-attachment. The genuine Buddhist is thus the monk (*arhat*) who at the end of his present life reaches total extinction (*parinīrvāna*). In the form of the *Theravāda*, this wisdom continued to draw its sustenance from the testimonies of the 'Elders'. It had originally been set down in writing in the Pali canon and commented upon by Buddhaghosa, in the fifth century, in his *Visuddhimagga* (Way to Purity). During this period, the Hīnayāna thus came to represent the essential aspects of the original form of Buddhism, influencing the art, literature and culture of the different countries in which it had become the official wisdom.

Mahāyāna (greater vehicle), which developed later, towards the beginning of the era under discussion, stated that the teachings of the 'Elders' formed only a part of the Buddha's teachings. The Buddha was said to have entrusted chosen followers with his final counsels; these Mahāyānas were considered empowered to transmit, after the Mahasānghikas, so as to lead a greater number of people to freedom by means of the 'Greater Vehicle'. Mahāyāna lays foremost emphasis on the role played by the *bodhisattvas* (Buddhas-to-be) 'for the salvation of all'. In a probably parallel development to *bhaktī* in Hinduism, it replaced asceticism by devotion. The monastic ideal lost its importance, salvation now being possible through devotion to those exceptional beings who had gained access to Enlightenment but remained on Earth, out of great compassion, in order to bring salvation to all. The original vow of the *bodhisattva* in this form of Buddhism in no way dissociates individual salvation from that of the multitude ('I resolve to gain Perfect Enlightenment so that all living beings might be saved'). Hence the significance here of both compassion and the 'Wisdom of Voidness', through which *bodhisattvas* have the appearance of 'beings so transparent that the flow of universal love can pass through them'. Mahāyāna thus gradually came to deify and multiply the Buddha. It distinguished between his historical body (*nirmānakāya*, meaning 'transitory body'), his 'body of bliss' (*sambhogakāya*), transfigured by all the merit acquired in previous lives, and his 'body of the Law' (*dharmakāya*), the absolute essence of the Buddha, a pure spiritual reality which is boundless and coextensive with the universe. The concept even exists of an 'original Buddha' who borders on the Absolute. Mahāyāna goes on to stress that all individuals, be they monks or lay people, should increase their wisdom by reliving the Buddha's experience. Since Absolute Reality is formless and beyond understanding and each Buddhist is a repository of a 'germ of Buddha', one need only cultivate the sense of delving very deeply within oneself, using the meditative practices of Zen Buddhism, for example. With a philosophy based on voidness, Mahāyāna renounces the intellectual approach and sometimes takes on a Tantric form (*Vajrayāna*: a non-dogmatic approach combining compassionate love and transcendental knowledge). This form of Buddhism, which used the 'Greater Vehicle' to put salvation within everyone's reach, was more accessible to the common people and became particularly widespread in Northern Asia.

A chequered fate befell both Buddhist 'vehicles' between the seventh and the fifteenth centuries. The Brahmans in India succeeded in almost entirely eliminating Buddhism from the subcontinent by the twelfth century, although the Hīnayāna Theravāda School did take root in Sri Lanka, whence it spread to Myanmar (eleventh century). In Cambodia, there existed a strange fusion between Mahāyāna and Shivaism. Hīnayāna was introduced into the country by Theravāda monks during the reign of Jayavarman VII (1191–1218) and flourished despite brutal Shivaite persecution at the end of the thirteenth century. Mahāyāna reigned supreme in Thailand until the invasion of Thais (thirteenth century), and the latter then converted to the Hīnayāna of the Theravāda. During this same period, Viet Nam and Indonesia partially accepted Mahāyāna. It was in China, however, that Buddhism spread to an extraordinary extent starting from the first century AD, with the first *sūtras* being translated in Luoyang on the Huanghe River. This Lesser Vehicle Buddhism, seen as a variant of Daoism, was adapted to both the common people and the noble classes, and the Buddha was even worshipped. With the fall of the Han Dynasty (AD 220), Mahāyāna spread throughout China through a second generation of missionaries. The resulting Chinese form of Buddhism was tinged with Daoism, and two schools, the Chan and the Jingtu, informed its philosophy and practice. The Chan made meditation an end in itself because it was considered an immediate experience in which absolute reality was revealed, while the Jingtu ('Pure Land' tradition) emphasized the Indian cult of the Amitābha ('Infinite Light') Buddha, whose intercession was sufficient for rebirth in the 'Paradise of the West' and accession to *nirvāna*. A remarkable feature of the spread of Buddhism in China was the passage to India of a large number of Chinese pilgrims, who went to collect and translate Sanskrit texts of both the Hīnayāna and Mahāyāna traditions. The most outstanding such pilgrim, who has left a detailed record of his travels, was Xuan Zhuang (602–664), followed by Yijing (635–713).

The period between the seventh and ninth centuries, under the Sui (581–618) and Tang Dynasties (618–907), thus marked the golden age of Buddhism in China. Many schools, foundations and monasteries were created, and their wealth and power made them a political force of which the state had to take account. But Buddhism's secular power in China led to its downfall. Confucianist and Daoist leaders lent their support to three periods of persecution in 626, 714 and 842–845. These resulted in the destruction of 40,000 monasteries, the secularization of more than 260,000 monks and nuns, and the confiscation of millions of hectares of fertile land. Although authorized again in 846, Chinese Mahāyāna Buddhism survived only in the shape of a small community which bore witness to a glorious past.

Buddhism also expanded to Japan through Korea in the mid-sixth century. It was well received by the ruling classes of both countries and promptly put to use in the service of the state. During the Nara period (710–784), it comprised six schools which provided Japanese intellectuals with the major currents of Buddhist thought. For the laity, Buddhism represented a magnificent spectacle of temples, statues, rites and ceremonies, with magical connotations. Emperor Shōmu made it the state religion. During the Heian period (794–1185), Dengyō Daishi (767–822) founded the Tendai school from his monastery on Mount Hiei. He defended the universality of salvation (illumination) against his adversaries, maintaining that Buddhahood was present in all sentient beings and that illumination was but the realization of innate Buddhahood. At the same time, Kōbō Daishi (774–835) founded the Shingon School, in which Buddhism took over and transcended the truths of Daoism and Confucianism.

His treatise on the 'Ten Stages of Spiritual Development' formed the basis of a folk religion in Japan, where he came to be honoured as a national hero. A very hierarchical monasticism which enjoyed the support of the state conferred political significance on 'Japanese Buddhism'. Nonetheless, shamanistic figures (itinerant monks) were active among ordinary people. They included Kōya (903–972), who preached the cult of Amida (the Buddha Amitābha means 'Infinite Light'), which afforded protection against the spirits of the dead. Amidism was then an extreme form of bhaktī (devotion) which made asceticism and monastic life completely unnecessary, since the saving power of Amida was guaranteed all the more when it had no ascetic effort with which to contend. Buddhism became fully Japanized during the Kamakura period (1185–1333), with the warrior class now taking over responsibility for its cultural aspects from the court nobles. Thanks to its three new movements, the Pure Land School, Zen and the Nichiren Sect, Tendai doctrine was brought to the common people through the agency of very strong feudal organizations. Only Zen, with its monastic component, saw its spirituality combined with the war-making aspirations of the Shōgunate of Kamakura and would further blossom under the Ikkyu (1394–1481). In this way, the Japanese Buddhism of the period displayed its own individual characteristics: compromises which promoted continuity between gods, humans and Nature; a tendency towards formalism and ritualism; close ties with the state; the association of schools with charismatic individuals; and emphasis on present life and the waiving of monastic rules. All these different aspects made Mahāyāna in this country a distinctively Japanese form of humanism.

Buddhism in Tibet adapted itself to the practices of the Bon religion and to the latter's cult of spirits, which were considered to be deities (see Plate 83). A number of schools were established, including the Red Hats (unreformed Buddhism) and the Yellow Hats (reformed Buddhism). The success of Buddhism was seen in Tibet as the fulfilment of the promise of universal salvation through the compassion and agency of the Bodhisattva. During the reign of King Song-tseu-gampo (seventh century), Buddhism took lasting root with the aid of Indian priests and Tibetan translators. The efforts of the impious King Lang Darma to destroy it in the tenth century were unsuccessful. A second expansion took place with the active support of two *lamas*, Yeshe Woi and Rinchen Sangpo. The teachings of Indian Buddhist universities spread to Tibet, and the following schools were established: the Nyingmapas, 'those who follow the elders' (unreformed Buddhism); the Kagyupas, founded by Marpa (1012–1096), which comprise Tantric lay followers and ascetic as well as solitary *yogins*; the Sa-kya-pas, also founded in the eleventh century; the Karmapas, founded by Dusum Khyenpa (1110–1193) (a system of 'successive reincarnations'); and the Gelukpas, founded by Tson-kha-pa in 1409, who observed celibacy and strict monastic discipline. These schools became the crucibles for the distinctive 'spiritualities' of the *lamas* (the 'superior ones'), the 'true guides who show the way leading to Buddhahood and who are worthy and capable of choosing their reincarnation'. The influence which they wielded in social and political life played a decisive role in the growth of Tibetan Buddhism, which was also influenced by the Tantrism or 'short path' for achieving Enlightenment of Padmasambhava, the 'Lotus Born' (eighth century) and his school, which produced the brilliant scholar Klong-chen (1308–1364). The *Dalai Lamas*, who became the spiritual and temporal rulers of Tibet, first appeared at the close of our period, and transmitted their power through successive reincarnations. The first *lama* was supposedly Gedun Drub, born in 1391 and regarded as a physical manifestation of Chenrezi, one of the *bodhisattvas* of Mahāyāna, the 'Lord of Infinite Compassion' and tutelary deity of Tibet.

In this way, Buddhism, through its numerous manifestations as Hīnayāna, or Mahāyāna managed to maintain a living presence in South-East Asia, Tibet, China and Japan. To be sure, in these lands the Buddha's creed frequently had to compromise with local religious traditions and prevailing social and political conditions: but at this price, it endured and thrived, whereas in India – where Buddhism first arose and developed – it almost completely disappeared (see Plates 80–87, 232–234).

MONOTHEISTIC RELIGIONS

Islam

At the dawn of the seventh century, a new Prophet appeared on the far southern confines of the age's two prevailing religious worlds: the Sasanian Empire of Persia, whose majority observed the Mazdean faith of their rulers while tolerating a Nestorian Christian minority in their midst; and the Byzantine or Eastern Roman Empire, where Christianity held all-powerful sway although one disputed between such contending sects as the Orthodox (known in Syria as the 'Emperor's Party' or Melchites) and the Monophysites (also called the Jacobites). The new prophet was born, to be precise, near the western shore of Arabia, in the oasis city of Mecca, and first won to his faith the people of the neighbouring oasis of Yathrib, which thereby came to be called simply Medina (*Madīna*, the city). The new Prophet's name was Muḥammad ibn 'Abd Allāh ibn 'Abd al-Muṭṭalib. His 'inspiration' or revelations (*waḥy*) came to him, he made known, from God (in Arabic, Allāh). The revelations which he uttered were memorized by his followers, then set down by them in writing, and finally collected in their entirety in a volume known as the Qur'ān, or 'Recitation'. The Prophet's daily 'practice' or *sunna* constituted a supplementary model for his followers' belief and conduct, while his leadership of the new community or *umma* came to serve as a model of earthly government for his 'successors', the *khulafā* (sing. *khalīfa*) or 'caliphs': a title successively adopted by the acting or then figurehead rulers of Medina (632–661), Damascus (661–750), Baghdād (762–1258), Cordova (929–1031), Cairo (969–1171 and 1258–1517), and thereafter Istanbul (after 1453). Following a uniquely personal religious experience, Muḥammad preached to his people, who were mostly polytheistic, first in Mecca, from 610 to 622, then in Yathrib, now Medina, from 622 to 632. His teaching, while bearing close resemblance to certain essential beliefs of Judaism and Christianity, differed from these two 'heavenly religions' in that it set out to reform them on certain points of doctrine and partly to correct them with regard to religious rites and moral obligations. Muḥammad emphasized total surrender (*islām*) to the one and only God (*Allāh*), in the same way that Abraham had submitted fully to the orders of his Lord according to Judaeo-Christian tradition.

When he first began to preach to the people of Mecca, Muḥammad emphasized the demands of social justice protection for the defenceless and the dispossessed. He also stated that on the day of Resurrection, everyone would have to answer for their conduct to their Creator and Lord, who would be both their judge and provider. Accordingly, he preached the existence of a final place of happiness, the Garden (*Janna*), and another place of eternal damnation, the Fire (*Nār*) or Gehenna. When Muḥammad met resistance from his own society, he insisted that prophets (*anbiyā'*, *rusul*) had been sent repeatedly during the course of human history, and that the most significant among these were Noah, Abraham, Moses, Jesus and Muḥammad himself. The message of the God who 'speaks to humans' was always the same: he was All Merciful (*al-Raḥmān*), his providence called for obedience and worship, his justice would come on Judgement Day in the form of final retribution, and his message was laid down in the books of the Torah, the Psalms, the Gospel and the Qur'ān, with the latter being the perfect, Arabic version of original Scripture (*al-Kitāb*), which abrogated all preceding ones. 'Adversaries' were punished and 'the faithful' were made victorious, he declared, because God wished to set down his law (*sharī'a*) for all so that the world might become a 'place of justice and peace'. After sealing an alliance with two Arab tribes which had embraced Islam and also with three Jewish tribes as temporary allies, Muḥammad fled from his native city for Yathrib (Yathrib was renamed Medina, meaning the City of the Prophet) in 622. This was the emigration (*ḥijra*), which marked the beginning of a new era, the Islamic era. Muḥammad would add to his teachings for another ten years. These became increasingly precise and concrete. He entered into controversial discussions with Jews and Christians and waged military campaigns which finally opened the gates of Mecca to him. He thus fashioned the Islamic state, to which he won over all the Arabs living in the peninsula, who either became Muslims (the servants of God and his Messenger) or chose to remain 'protected' Jews and Christians (Najrān).

After his death in 632, Muḥammad was succeeded by four 'rightly guided' (*khulafā' rāshidūn*) caliphs. Abū Bakr (632–634) consolidated the unity of the young State. 'Umar (634–644) undertook the conquest of the Middle East. His victory at al-Yarmūk (636) over the Byzantines yielded Syria–Palestine and Egypt to Islam, while that of al-Qādisīya (637) over the Sasanians brought the Persian Empire into the Islamic fold. Then came 'Uthmān (644–656), under whom the Islamic state further conquered Turkestan in the east and Libya in the west. There was also a final unifying recension of the Qur'ān, which preserved the cohesion of a Muslim community now wielding political power everywhere, while guaranteeing protection for the Christian and Mazdean majorities in conquered countries by the granting of a special and fairly liberal status of tolerance, the *dhimma*. 'Alī (656–661), the fourth caliph, had to withstand serious internal dissensions, which resulted in internecine warfare (*fitna kubrā*) between his followers and those of the cousin of the assassinated 'Uthmān. The conflict ended with the violent death of 'Alī and led to a final division of the Muslim *umma* into the minority Shī'īs, who followed the successors of 'Alī (Ḥasan and Ḥusayn), the dissenting Khārijīs (a small minority which is still active), and the majority Sunnīs, who supported 'Uthmān's cousin Mu'āwiya, governor of Damascus. The latter made his town the new capital from which the dynasty of the Umayyad caliphs (661–750) exercised their sway. They were to extend the Islamic Empire over the north of Spain (Poitiers, 736) and as far as the Indus in India.

After the 'golden age' of the 'Abbāsid caliphs (750–1258), the Ottoman Turks extended the 'Abode of Islam' to the Balkans, until Constantinople, converted to Istanbul in 1453, became the capital of a powerful Islamic state which came to encompass the totality of Islam's lands from Algeria to Iraq, and from the Balkans to Yemen. At the same time, Islam's rulers protected the arts and sciences in an ethnically and religiously cosmopolitan context, while their faith spread further to India and finally reached Sumatra and Java. Islam was also embraced by numerous ethnic groups in sub-Saharan Africa as a result of the commercial activities of Muslims in East Africa and the presence of their missionary brotherhoods in the north and west. In this way, Islam held sway from Senegal to Indonesia and from Turkestan to Sudan.

Islam, which spread so rapidly because of its twin political and military dimensions, was thus presented in the Middle East as the 'perfect monotheistic religion', several centuries after Christianity. It was a combined religious, cultural and political movement which promptly asserted itself in contradistinction to preceding monotheistic religions. Three centuries were required to establish its structure on the basis of the variety of its schools and the multiplicity of its sects. Indeed, Islam had to formulate its 'identity' with respect to Judaism and Christianity wherever the latter religions had systematized the content of their faith, described the nature of their rites and set forth their moral prescriptions. Within a very short space of time, Islam was thus able to 'define' its doctrine, cult and ethic as well as its law and world view in almost immutable terms. Irrespective of whether they are Sunnīs, Shī'īs or Khārijīs, all Muslims respect the same doctrine, practise the same rites and live according to the same moral ideal.

Their doctrine expresses in six articles the twofold declaration of their 'profession of faith' (*shahāda*): 'There is no god but Allāh and Muḥammad is his Messenger'. They all affirm their belief in God, his angels, his books, his prophets, the Resurrection and predestination. The one God is thus at the very heart of the Islamic faith. He is the Creator and Transcendent, for 'nothing is like unto him', and he is also judge and reckoner. It is through the simple act of meditation or the human act of imitation of his ninety-nine 'Most Beautiful Names' that the believer can approach this irreducibly unknowable mystery. The angels are the messengers of this God who also corresponds to a benevolent Providence, which the actions of the great tempter, Satan, in his jealousy of human dignity, give history its dramatic twist. The Qur'ān names twenty-five prophets, many of whom appear in biblical history: Adam, Enoch/Idrīs, Noah, Abraham, Lot, Ishmael, Isaac, Jacob, Joseph, Hūd, Shu'ayb, Sāliḥ, Moses, Aaron, Joshua/Dhū l-Kifl, David, Solomon, Elijah, Elisha, Job, Jonah, Zachariah, John, Jesus and Muḥammad. Four of these had outstanding roles to play: Abraham is a model of the pure monotheism embraced by Muḥammad, Moses was the founder of Judaism through the Torah, which he received from God, Jesus was the founder of Christianity through the Gospel, also given to him by God, and Muḥammad is 'the seal of the Prophets' whose coming had been announced by the others and to whom was entrusted the Qur'ān. Thus, Muslims believe that the latter gives credence to the preceding 'books' of the Torah, Psalms and Gospel while at the same time reforming and abrogating them. Islam is thus defined in terms of the strict monotheism taught by Muḥammad and enshrined in the Qur'ān, which is the ultimate 'book' to which all Muslims refer (see Plates 90, 107, 108, 110). It comprises 114 chapters (*sūras*) and 6,235 verses (*āyāt*) written in a 'clear Arabic' which cannot be imitated (*i'jāz*). For Muslims, it represents a book of meditation and theology as well as a collection of legal and liturgical texts. It provides them with a belief in the resurrection of the body, in a Day of Judgement (on which God will be 'seen'), and in final retribution. The only unpardonable sin, punished by everlasting Fire, is the attribution of partners to God. All other sins of believers are to be either punished (during a short period of time) or forgiven (immediately). The afterlife (*al-ākhira*), in the Garden, will reward the just with all the satisfactions of body and spirit, which are known to God only. With regard to predestination, the Qur'ān abounds in verses which peremptorily declare that 'God guides whomsoever he chooses and misleads whomsoever he chooses', and in others which state the existence of human responsibility ('Whosoever chooses, let him believe, and whosoever does not choose, let him not believe').

Islamic doctrine is accompanied by a sober cult comprising ritual prayer (*ṣalāt*), legal alms-giving (*zakāt*), the fasting (*ṣiyām*) of Ramaḍān and the pilgrimage (*ḥajj*) to Mecca. Pious Muslims are called to prayer five times a day, at fixed times, and pray facing the Shrine (*Ka'ba*) of Mecca after first accomplishing minor (*wuḍū'*) or major (*ghusl*) purification, depending on their degree of impurity. The gestures and phrases used are very simple, take little time and are accomplished alone or communally on Fridays at midday after the preaching of the *imām*. The architecture of the mosques in which Muslims perform this weekly ritual is adapted to such functions (with ablution rooms, courtyard and cloister, prayer room, and apse indicating the direction of Mecca or *miḥrāb*) (see Plates 199–209). The Qur'ān frequently praises those 'who say their prayers and give alms', the latter consisting in giving a tenth of one's income to 'the poor and needy' and other kinds of people (Qur'ān: 9, 60). The daylight fasting of Ramaḍān lasts for a full lunar month (when meals are taken at night) and is a period for reflection and festivities culminating in the 'festival of breaking the fast' (*'īd ṣaghīr*, the 'minor festival'), prior to the 'major festival' (*'īd kabīr*), which, each year, accompany the festivities that take place at the time of pilgrimage. In fact, all Muslims are called upon to accomplish the essential rites of the pilgrimage to Mecca at least once during their lifetime (see Plates 181, 183, 214): doing so, they are thought to experience a sincere 'return to God' (*tawba*). Therefore the pilgrims are truly encouraged to remain faithful to their creed and cult and to live in accordance with the ten commandments which were given to Moses, and of which the Qur'ān reminds them in its moral teachings (most particularly in Chapter 17, verses 22–39). Muslims believe that the Qur'ān is God's will revealed to them concerning the behaviour required of all in the personal and domestic as well as social and political spheres, all these aspects being further specifically dealt with in the *Sharī'a* (Islamic law), itself based on Qur'ānic principles.

Although the Sunnīs, Shī'īs and Khārijīs share a single doctrine, cult and code of ethics, there are differences between them in certain areas which have drifted further apart during the course of the history of Islam. Thus, in addition to the two 'feasts' already mentioned, a feast of the 'birth of the Prophet' (*mawlid nabawī*) was quickly imposed under the influence of the Fāṭimids, while the Shī'īs have always observed the feast of '*Ashūrā*' (the tenth day of the month *muḥarram*) to commemorate the redemptive sufferings of Ḥusayn, the son of 'Alī and grandson of Muḥammad, who was put to death in Karbalā' (680) because he refused to recognize the authority of the Umayyad caliph. The Shī'īs believed that 'Alī inherited Muḥammad's prophetic charisma, and that this charisma was passed on to his direct descendants. Their movement was strongest in Iraq and Iran but was also subdivided into numerous socio-political 'branches' based on particular theological beliefs. Many, notably the 'Twelvers' (*Ithnay 'Asharīya*) of Iraq and Iran, held the belief that this charisma lasted until the twelfth *imām*, Muḥammad al-Mahdī, who disappeared in 940 (the 'major occultation') and who would return at the end of time as the 'sign of the Hour'. The Zaydis of Yemen were followers of the fourth *imām*, 'Alī Zayn al-'Ābidīn (680–714: duration of his imāmate), through his son Zayd. The Ismā'īlīs (who inspired the Qarmaṭian movement from 874 to 1078 and the activities of the notorious 'Old Man of the Mountain' of Alamūt from 1090 to 1256) declared allegiance to Ismā'īl, the son of the sixth *imām*, Ja'far al-Ṣādiq (733–765: duration of his imāmate). The Druze of the Middle East followed the teachings of the Fāṭimid caliph al-Ḥākim (996–1021) and his disciple, Hamzah. Many other dissenting groups seceded for political or religious reasons, thus confirming that Muḥammad was correct when, according to a famous *ḥadīth*, he is supposed to have predicted: 'My community will divide into 73 sects of which only one will be saved.'

It is within the framework of this multi-ethnic religious society, with its innumerable schools and sects, that classical Islam established its exegesis and theology and systematized its sciences and forms of spirituality. Its sacred book, the Qur'ān, was explained and interpreted (*tafsīr* and *ta'wīl*) by such major commentators as the *imām* Ja'far (699–765), Ibn Qutayba (828–889), al-Ṭabarī (839–923), al-Murtaḍā (965–1044), al-Ṭabarsī (d. 1153), al-Zamakhsharī (1075–1144), Fakhr al-dīn al-Rāzī (1148–1209), al-Qurṭubī (d. 1272), al-Bayḍāwī (d. 1286), al-Khāzin (1279–1340), al-Qāshānī (d. 1329), the two al-Jalālayn (1388–1459 and 1445–1505). The words and deeds of Muḥammad, as collected by his 'Companions', were compiled into a corpus of traditions, which constitute the '*sunna* of the Prophet' (a fundamental 'source' after the Qur'ān), and whose collectors were Mālik ibn Anas (d. 795), al-Bukhārī (d. 870), Muslim (d. 865), Ibn Ḥanbal (d. 855), Ibn Mājā (d. 886), Abū Dāwūd (d. 888), al-Tirmidhī (d. 892) and al-Nasā'ī (d. 917). It was on the basis of these main two sources that Islamic Sunnī law became divided into four 'schools of law' (*madhāhib*), whereas the Shī'īs used *imām* Ja'far as their authority. Using distinctive sets of legal techniques (personal opinion, analogical reasoning, consensus, preferential judgement), the Ḥanafī school derived from Abū Ḥanīfa (d. 767), the Mālikī school from Mālik ibn Anas, the Shāfi'ī school from al-Shāfi'i (d. 820) and Ḥan balī school from Aḥmad ibn Ḥanbal (d. 855) produced rules to govern cultic activities, family and contract law, as well as the organization of society and the state. This relatively varied application of the 'texts' to the socio-economic realities of the different cultural areas of the vast Islamic world guaranteed for the faith an intellectual and spiritual pluralism which enabled it to welcome into its ken the philosophy of the Greeks and the wisdom of India. Christian monasteries in the Middle East provided Islam's rulers with translations of Greek philosophical works from Syriac into Arabic, while the poets, prose writers and grammarians of the new Arabic literature converted the ancient language of the Arabs into a linguistic tool which could express all aspects of knowledge.

This period witnessed the growing influence on Muslim thinkers and philosophers of ancient Greek thought in Arabic translations, not only as exemplified by Aristotle but also by such later neo-Platonic works as the so-called *Theology of Aristotle* (a confusing medieval misnomer for writings actually by Plotinus) and the so-called *Book of Causes* (by Proclus). Part of this Hellenistic heritage was absorbed into theology and mysticism, while another developed independently within the context of 'Islamic philosophy'. In the Middle East, al-Kindī (801–866), al-Fārābī (873–950) and Ibn Sīnā (Avicenna) (980–1037) were brilliantly successful in taking up and expounding the principal works of Aristotle and Plato. At the same time, the 'Brethren of Purity' (tenth century), who were Ismā'īlīs, promoted neo-Pythagoreanism and popularized philosophical studies, while Yaḥyā ibn 'Adī (d. 974), al-Tawḥīdī (d. 1023) and Miskawayh (d. 1030) laid emphasis on a 'discipline of manners' in the name of ethics. Later, in Spain, philosophy was once again taken up and given prominence by Ibn Bājja (d. 1138), Ibn Ṭufayl (d. 1185) and Ibn Rushd (Averroës) (1126–1198), with the object of ascribing equal value to reason and revelation, that is, philosophy and theology. It is well known that numerous works of Greek thought, especially those of Aristotle and Plato, were thus relayed during the Middle Ages to the Latin West by the translations and commentaries of Arab philosophers.

Muslim theology as it flourished in Baghdād from the eighth to the tenth century also had to meet the requirements of philosophical reasoning. Its first schools had emphasized free will (*qadarīya*) or insisted on the constraining power of God (*jabarīya*), while others postponed any moral judgement (*murji'a*) on 'Muslim sinners'. In Baṣra and Baghdād, the Mu'tazila endeavoured to integrate the best aspects of Greek philosophy into their theological thought as a way of providing the best possible proof that Islam was 'the religion of reason'. Al-'Allāf (d. 849), al-Naẓẓām (d. 846), al-Jubbā'ī (d. 916) and his son, Abū Hāshim (d. 933), and the qāḍī 'Abd al-Jabbār (d. 1025) used the analogy of being and formulated their philosophy in terms of five basic principles. The oneness of God implies that his attributes are identical to his essence; and as nothing is comparable to him, the Qur'ān was 'created'. Divine justice implies that humans are responsible and are therefore the 'creators' of their actions; as a result, good and evil are 'in the nature of things' and do not come under arbitrary divine intervention. The 'promises and threats of God' are genuine; and people will therefore be judged according to their faith and action. Muslim sinners are not excluded from the *umma*, where they are in an 'intermediate situation'. The *umma* has a duty 'to order good and forbid evil'. The Mu'tazila imposed their doctrine by resort to an outright inquisition (*miḥna*) under the caliph al-Ma'mūn (r. 813–833). The followers of al-Ash'arī, their adversaries, did likewise during the reign of al-Mutawakkil (847–861), and this led to the final triumph of the 'fundamentalist' theology espoused by the Ash'arī, Māturīdī and Ḥanbalī schools, which was closer to the 'original texts' and less amenable to the solicitations of philosophy.

For al-Ash'arī (873–935) and his disciples, al-Bāqillānī (d. 1013), al-Juwaynī (d. 1085) and al-Ghazālī (d. 1111), the arguments of tradition and, therefore, of revelation took precedence over those of reason. They therefore thought that the Qur'ān was 'un-created' and that its anthropomorphic aspects should be acknowledged 'without knowing how' (*bi-lā-kayfa*). Human actions are 'created' by God and merely acquired (*kasb*) by human beings, with good and evil stemming exclusively from divine decision (hence the importance of Islamic law, which expresses divine will). Lastly, faith alone can be sufficient to secure salvation, and God may even 'be seen' in the afterlife. For al-Māturīdī (d. 944) and like-minded philosophers in Turkestan, al-Samarqandī (d. 1002) and al-Nasafī (d. 1142), a compromise was possible between faith and reason because 'effective causality' existed in human beings and the Mu'tazila were partly right. Taking the opposite view, Ibn Ḥanbal (780–855), whose thinking was echoed by Ibn Baṭṭa (d. 997), Ibn Ḥazm (994–1063), Ibn 'Aqīl (d. 1119) and Ibn Taymīya (1263–1328), emphasized the importance of the 'original texts' and interpreted them literally, advocating the strict application of Islamic law (*sharī'a*) down to its finest details so that the 'will of God' could be fully obeyed. He rejected any comparison between God and his creatures (*tashbīh*), giving all the more prominence to his absolute transcendence (*tanzīh*), but acknowledged all the anthropomorphic aspects of the Qur'ān notwithstanding. Such, then, were the tendencies of Islamic theology, to which its various schools gave expression from the eighth to the fifteenth century.

At the same time, a whole movement concerned with asceticism and mysticism (*taṣawwuf*) developed which rejected philosophical speculations and political conflicts, testifying instead to a spiritual life in which the believer 'imitates the behaviour of God' (*al-takhalluq bi-akhlāq Allāh*) and endeavours to promote peace in the *umma*. And, for more than three centuries, there were such witnesses to the 'unity of testimony (*waḥdat al-shuhūd*) in the persons of, for instance, Ḥasan al-Baṣrī (642–728), 'the mystic in the community'; Rābi'a al-'Adawīya (713–801), 'the poetess of disinterested love'; al-Muḥāsibī (781–857), 'the master of self-examination'; al-Junayd (d. 910), 'the prudent spiritual director'; Bisṭāmī (d. 874), 'the herald of absolute oneness'; and al-Ḥallāj (858–922), the witness to 'the relationship of love based on painful passion'. Then came al-Ghazālī, who was able to reconcile Ṣūfism, which was either suspected or condemned by political and religious authorities, with orthodox Sunnī doctrine thanks to his own *Summa Theologica*, which he called the *Revival of the Religious Sciences* (1095–1098). Subsequently, other mystics who were more open to Platonic and Indian philosophies proclaimed a 'unity of existence' (*waḥdat al-wujūd*). These included Ibn 'Arabī in Damascus (1165–1240), Ibn al-Fāriḍ in Cairo (1181–1235), al-Suhrawardī in Aleppo (1151–1191), who advocated 'illuminative wisdom', and Jalāl al-Dīn Rūmī in Konya (1207–1273), the master of 'mystical poetry'. Their personal experiences were entrusted to circles of disciples, who were to develop into 'religious brotherhoods' (*ṭuruq*) which, from the twelfth century, grew in both towns and the countryside to provide the faithful with the support of prayer and charity associations in which the mediation of saints, and techniques of meditation, could satisfy the desires of an 'Islam of the heart'. The thirteenth century thus successively witnessed the establishment of the Qādirīya, the Shādhilīya, the Rifā'īya, the Mawlāwīya, the Badawīya and the Qalandarīya; the fourteenth century, that of the Bektāshīya, the Khalwatīya and the Naqshabandīya; and the fifteenth century, that of the Jazūlīya and the Ni'matallāhīya. By the end of the fifteenth century, both rural and town dwellers had thus been provided with a whole network of religious brotherhoods which provided them with sound religious education and genuine community welfare assistance, before assuming more political roles in the centuries which followed.

Such, then, are the characteristics which the Islamic world, stretching from Senegal to Indonesia and from the Balkans to Yemen, exhibited at the end of the fifteenth century through the great variety of its socio-political institutions, its theological and legal schools, and its spiritual currents and religious brotherhoods. In the intellectual sphere, the eighth to the tenth century had been decisive in Baghdād, but it was only after the decline and fall of the 'Abbāsid caliphate that jurists such as al-Māwardī (991–1031) and Ibn Taymīya (1263–1328) systematized its 'political order' as the 'golden age' of Islamic civilization.

Judaism

Jewish communities became more widely dispersed than ever after Bar-Kokhba's revolt against Rome (AD 135) and the edict of the Emperor Hadrian expelling them from Judaea, but they continued their efforts to comprehend and explain the 'oral Bible'. In about 200–220, Rabbi Yehūdah ha-Nasi, head of the academy of Sepphoris, compiled the *Mishna* by putting together the different *Mishnayot* (collections of oral laws) and thus established a normative *Halakha* (Jewish law), sometimes making an eclectic choice between several opinions. His code became the '*Mishna par excellence*' and comprised six orders (*sedarim*): seeds (*zeraïm*), festivals (*mo'ed*), women (*nashim*), damages (*neziqin*), sacred things (*qodashim*) and purifications (*toharot*), further subdivided into a set of sixty-three tractates. From the sixth to the tenth century, the Hebrew text of the 'written Bible' was codified by the Masoretes in order to ensure correct transmission as well as authentic reading, thanks to the provision of vowel signs. The 'western system' of the school of Tiberias was ultimately victorious over that of the 'eastern Babylonian school', thanks to the work accomplished by Rabbi Aaron ben Moshe ben Asher (ninth to tenth century).

The *Mishna*, written in Hebrew and codifying the normative aspects of the oral Torah, was subsequently to have its contents clarified and adapted to prevailing circumstances. Work on the Talmud then consisted of reproducing the *Mishna* and its commentaries (*Gemara*), written in Aramaic. Completed in about AD 400, through the efforts of five generations of *amoraim* ('interpreters') of Israel, the Talmud of Caesarea, Tiberias and Sepphoris (the 'Jerusalem Talmud'), with a concise style and logical reasoning, dealt with only thirty-nine of the *Mishna*'s tractates and was neither influential nor commented upon because the Byzantine Empire put an end to the 'Jewish institutions' of Palestine in AD 425. It was the 'Babylonian Talmud' which was to influence all Jewish communities and became the object of innumerable commentaries. The Babylonian diaspora had already developed its academies, first that of Sura, which was founded in AD 219 and which continued in Mata Mehasya, and then that of Pumbedita, which was founded in AD 260, after the destruction of the Academy of Nahardea (259), and was subsequently replaced by the Academy of Mahoza, which became the place of residence of the Exilarch (338). It was the work of eight generations of Babylonian *amoraim* which resulted in the Babylonian Talmud, the only Talmud with normative value. The *geonim* ('excellent masters'), who came after the Babylonian academies, gave an increasing number of *responsa* to questions raised, thus making their contribution to the Talmud itself, which dated back to Rab (Abba Arekha), Samuel and Rabina. One third of the Babylonian Talmud, which records the discussions of the masters, comprises the *Halakha* (legal commentaries), and two-thirds, the *Haggada* (narratives and information); it deals with thirty-six tractates of the *Mishna*. This Talmud was reproduced in the form of a *Compendium* by Rabbi Hananel of Kairouan (Qayrawān) (eleventh century) and the *Halakhot* by Rabbi Isaac Alfasi (1013–1103) in North Africa. Then came Moses ben Maimon (Maimonides) (1135–1204), who established an almost definitive codification of Jewish religious law in his *Mishne Torah*.

Jewish philosophy was already well developed, its seminal work being an initial treatise written in Arabic by Sa'adya Gaon (812–942), head of the Academy of Sura, entitled *Emunot we-Deot* ('Beliefs and Opinions'). A whole corpus of philosophical Jewish literature flourished in contemporary Spain, its most renowned writers being Solomon ibn Gabirol (1020–1050); Bahya ibn Pakuda (end of the eleventh century), with his *Duties of the Hearts*, Moses ibn Ezra (1060–1139); Yehudah ha-Levi (1080–1145), with his defence of Judaism ('*Kuzari*'); Abraham ibn Ezra (1092–1167), with his commentary on the Bible; and, lastly, Maimonides, with his *Guide for the Perplexed* (*Moreh Nevukhim*). His codification of Jewish law (*Mishne Torah*) was preceded by *The Book of Knowledge* (*Sefer ha-Mada'*) and followed by a work entitled *The Book of Precepts* (*Sefer ha-Mitswot*). Furthermore, he had summarized the Jewish faith in his *Thirteen Articles of Faith*. Maimonides' work would long serve as a reference, and other scholars followed in his wake (see Plate 76). Thus, Rabbi Moses ben Jacob of Coucy (mid-thirteenth century) compiled all the teachings of the masters of Spain and Germany, and Rabbi Asher ben Yehiel (1250–1327) codified Jewish law anew with the assistance of his son Jacob. At the end of the fifteenth century, Rabbi Joseph Karo (1488–1575) re-established the 'Circle of Safed' in Galilee and established a definitive normative compendium with the title of 'The Well-Laid Table' (*Shūlhan 'arukh*).

All these works, which aimed at commenting on the *Mishna* and Talmud, enriched the liturgy of the synagogue, wherein the communities of the diaspora rediscovered their identity and reasserted their faith. Indeed, Rab 'Amram ben Sheshna (end of the ninth century) in Sura had already compiled all the liturgical texts of the period. Whether they observed the Sefardi rites of Spain and North Africa or the Ashkenazi rites of Central and Eastern Europe, Jewish communities were subjected to the vicissitudes of history, which at times afforded them complete freedom of expression and growth (as in Umayyad Spain and the Early Middle Ages in Europe) and, at other times, forced them to go underground or into exile (Spain under the Almohads (1130–1269) and during the reconquest was hostile to them). The resulting need to adapt led Rabbi Gershom ben Yehudah to abolish polygamy for German Jews (in about 1000) and Rabbi Solomon ben Isaac (*Rashi*) (1040–1105) of Troyes to comment once again on the Babylonian Talmud, before many additional commentaries were added by the Tosefta scholars in Central Europe. The Rhineland pogroms (1096) and the expulsions ordered by the kings of England (1290), France (1306) and Spain (1492) forced a great number of Jewish communities to seek refuge in Islamic countries (mostly in the Ottoman Empire) or in Eastern Europe.

Mystical tendencies nevertheless emerged in some of these communities, promoted by the aforementioned Ibn Pakuda and Maimonides, together with a host of 'masters' who developed their teaching in Spain, Germany and Provence. In the twelfth century, Rabbi Yehūdah the Pious of Ratisbon wrote *The Book of the Pious* (*Sefer Hassidim*), and at the end of the thirteenth century, the 'Bible of the Kabbalists', *The Book of Splendour* (*Sefer ha-zohar*), was said to have been 'discovered' by Rabbi Moses bar Shemtov of León and attributed by him to Rabbi Simeon ben Yohai (second century). The term '*Kabbala*' ('tradition') means the 'mystical tradition of Judaism'. It is an esoteric wisdom based on the cosmogony of creation and the theosophy of the 'Divine Chariot' of Ezekiel (*merkava*). The roots of the Kabbala are thus to be found in an apocalyptic Jewish substratum, but it was enriched by numerous Gnostic and neo-Platonic contributions. On the theoretical side, the Kabbala meditated on the divine principle at work in the world through the ten *Sefirot* (or spiritual forces synonymous with the beautiful names of God). On the practical side, the Kabbala involved magical and Pythagorean aspects. The 'Circle of Safed', with Rabbi Joseph Karo and, later, Rabbi Isaac Luria, was foremost in its emphasis on asceticism and mysticism. Such, then, were the ethical, religious and mystical characteristics of Jewish communities at the end of the fifteenth century, as witnessed in the very great diversity of their socio-cultural situations in both the Muslim and Christian worlds (see Plates 48, 77).

Christianity

At the outset of the fateful seventh century, an apparently triumphant Christendom, whose main preoccupations on Earth still seemed to be how to deal with social and political transformations among the ruins of the Roman Empire in the West, or under the sway of the yet resilient Roman Empire in the East, actually stood poised before the coming onrush of the greatest historical challenge it would ever come to know in this age: the rise and rapid expansion of an Islamic Empire. Early Christianity arose within the very heart of Palestinian Judaism. It first grew up among the scattered Jewish communities of the Diaspora. It had been nourished upon the monotheism of Israel, then had affirmed its own fulfillment of Israel's messianic promise through Jesus Christ. Jesus, the new creed taught, had died on the cross, but had risen from the dead at Easter. The Word of God had been made flesh, and thereby offered salvation and 'communion' to all those 'worthy of God'. Christianity, then, expressed a monotheism wherein God made himself manifest to humanity through the visible person of Jesus, at once 'true God, and true man'. God had thus bestowed his gift of 'grace' on humans (see Plates 56–61). Christianity went on to formulate its doctrine, to give structure to its liturgy, to clarify its ethic teachings and organize its earthly communities among very diverse social and cultural settings. After the persecutions of the first three centuries of its era, which had at once stimulated and tested, tempered and strengthened, the spirit of Christians, it had become the religion of the majority of the peoples of the empire and even the 'official religion' of the state. Its 'oecumenical councils' had established its doctrine and organized its earthly structure. Those of Nicaea (325) and Constantinople (381) had defined the essential content of the Christian faith: faith in one God, the Father of all and Creator of the universe; faith in his Word, Jesus Christ who was consubstantial with him and who became flesh through the Virgin Mary so as to impart 'Divinity' to the human condition and bring salvation to all humans through his crucifixion, death and resurrection; faith in the Holy Spirit 'which comes from the Father and from (or through) the Son', and ensures sanctification of the faithful through the sacraments (baptism, confirmation, communion in the Lord's Supper, penance, holy orders, matrimony, extreme unction); and faith in the Church, which brings them together in this way in a 'communion of saints' waiting for the resurrection of the dead, the second coming of Jesus and a final 'face-to-face' vision of God. Previous councils had been held precisely in order to determine this doctrine and cult, and the resulting philosophy of the Gospels. In Ephesus (431), the oneness of the person (*hypostasis*) of the Word Incarnate, Jesus Christ, was stressed, thus enabling a 'communication of idioms' whereby Christians might call Mary 'the mother of God' (*Theotokos*). In Chalcedon (451), the distinction between the two natures in Jesus Christ was reasserted ('one in two natures united without being confused or merged') against those who attributed only 'one nature' to him after hypostatic union. In Constantinople (553), the doctrine of the preceding councils was reaffirmed by condemnation of the 'three chapters' or theses which adopted positions judged to be heterodox. Explaining the mystery of the Incarnation of the Word in Jesus Christ in the various contemporary languages and cultures of Greek, Syriac, Coptic and Latin (and later Arabic), was no easy task.

Inevitably, the organization and communion of the churches suffered as a result. The church held sway on earth through five historical patriarchates (Jerusalem, Antioch, Alexandria, Rome and Constantinople), with Rome enjoying honorary primacy (because of the martyrdom of Peter) and Constantinople *de facto* primacy (because of the residence of the Emperor), but had become divided after the councils. Schisms and heresies led to separations, which were caused or justified by linguistic preferences and political choices. Thus, after Ephesus, the Churches of Mesopotamia, which had remained faithful to the Christology of Nestorius sought refuge within the Sasanid Empire and flourished there under the name of the Nestorian Church, with a patriarch in Ctesiphon. After Chalcedon, the churches of Syria and Egypt, which were hostile to any form of primacy by Byzantium, asserted their fidelity to Monophysite Christology ('the Word of God Incarnate has only one nature'). In Syria, they were organized by Jacob Baradai within the Syriac context and became the Jacobite Church, while in Egypt, the Coptic Church proclaimed that it had inherited the Christology of the see of Alexandria. The Armenian Church, which was under a Sasanian protectorate, also rejected the decisions of Chalcedon, establishing its own identity at the Katholikosal Synod of Dvin (552). None the less, everywhere from the Balkans to Palestine and from Carthage to Damascus, a great many peoples remained faithful to the orthodoxy of the councils and the faith professed by the emperor. They constituted what became known in Syria as the *Melchite Churches* (*malik* in Syria means 'King') and benefited from the rich theological storehouse of writings of the Fathers of the Greek Church. The individual characteristics of the independent churches were soon reinforced in practice by the expansion of the Islamic Empire, which forced them to keep to themselves for fear of losing their flock. Conversely, those churches linked to Constantinople ran into difficulties because of the increasingly strained relations between Constantinople and Rome, two political entities whose paths began to diverge.

The Nestorian Church, also called the 'Eastern Church', underwent initial reform under the patriarchate of Mar Aba I (540–551) and boasted renowned 'theological schools' at Nisibis and Edessa, to which was added the school of Seleucia-Ctesiphon (which became *Madā'in* after the Arab conquest), a fully fledged theological, biblical and liturgical academy whose fame lasted until the eleventh century. Here resided the 'Patriarch-Catholicus of the East'. Although suffering from continual schisms and vacancies of its patriarchal see, the Nestorian Church none the less managed to spin a whole network of education in the Syriac language. For instance, most of the teaching staff of the University of Gondeshapur in Sasanian Mesopotamia, along with its medical staff, were Nestorian Christians. The five provinces of the interior were also administrative divisions of the Sasanian Empire. Monasticism flourished everywhere as a result of the great reform by Abraham of Kashkar (491–586), the 'father of monks', who had organized coenobitic life. The Nestonian Church's external provinces were those of Fārs (on both sides of the Persian Gulf, with its bishopric at Rew-Ardashir) and Khorāsān (with its twin bishoprics of Merv and Nīshāpūr), to which were added, during the course of the seventh century, those of the country of the Medes (Hulwān, then Hamadan), of Bactria (northern Afghanistan) and Soghdiana, or the country of the Turks (Samarkand), under the patriarchate of Ichoyahb II (628–644). Churches were even established in China.

Under the 'Abbāsid caliphate (750–1258), the Nestorian Church benefited from the cultural and political unification of the Islamic Empire and spread back to Syria, where it competed with the Jacobite Church. To be sure, the Muslim caliph, with his Christian doctors, played a very influential role in the election of the Nestorian patriarchs, and indeed it was the caliph who confirmed the mandate of a given patriarch. The Nestorian Church reached its zenith in the intellectual and missionary spheres during the patriarchate of Timothy I (780–823), who transferred his see to Baghdād. He organized two councils (790 and 805) and wrote the *Eastern Synodicon* and the *Rules Governing Ecclesiastical Judgements and Successions* (805), which gave 'protected' Christians (*dhimmīs*) a code covering their entire personal status in like manner to the *sharī'a* for Muslims. Timothy I was a learned theologian who is also known for his *Dialogues* with the caliph al-Mahdī and his successor. This period witnessed the appearance in Baghdād of a whole range of Christian and Islamic apologetic literature, and the rise to fame of such Nestorian scholars as Ḥunayn ibn Isḥāq (d. 873) and Elias of Nisibis (975–1046) on the Christian side, next to learned men like al-Hāshimī and al-Ṭabarī on the Muslim side. In Asia, between the ninth and the twelfth centuries, some Turkish tribes, the Uighur, Tangut, Keraït and Öngüt, became Christians, and Nestorian Christianity also took root in southern India (Malabar). The stele of Si-ngan-fu, which was erected in China in AD 781, narrates the story of the coming of Christianity under the Tang Dynasty, telling how Timothy I appointed a metropolitan who resided in their empire. The Daoist backlash of AD 843–845 put an end to this missionary effort.

Later, when Chinggis Khān and his successors were at the height of their powers, there was a revival of the Nestorian Church under the Mongol Īl-Khānate of Persia (1256–1353). The patriarchs Denha I (1265–1281) and Yahballaha III (1283–1318) took full advantage of this situation, especially the latter, who was a monk of Öngüt origin and who belonged to the same culture as the Īl-Khān of Persia. Under the protective wing of the 'Mongol peace', the Eastern Church undertook its greatest expansion in the Middle East and Asia, with thirty provinces and 250 bishoprics. Rabban Sauma, the 'master' of the patriarch, was sent as an ambassador to Rome (1286–1288) with a view to securing a holy alliance between the Pope and Īl-Khān Arghūn, but strife, setbacks and persecutions put an end to his patriarchate (Arbela was destroyed in 1310). In 1318, the Nestorian Church held its last synod. It was no doubt too closely associated with the Mongol authorities and went down with the latter in both the Middle East (after the victory of the Muslim Mamlūks at 'Ayn Jālūt, 1260) and East Asia, where the Ming Dynasty expelled the Mongols from China in 1369.

The Coptic Church in Egypt gradually came to be subjected to the vicissitudes of an Arab–Islamic power which alternately tolerated or persecuted it, depending on the dynasty in power or other historical circumstances. It remained faithful to its beliefs stemming from the 'age of the martyrs', which had begun with the persecutions by Diocletian (AD 284) and to the Monophysite doctrine established after Chalcedon and reinforced by its own individual evolution. It thus upheld the testimonies of the great theologians of Alexandria and the 'Desert Fathers', attaching great importance to monasticism (anchoritism and coenobitism). Although still titled 'Patriarch of Alexandria', Christodulus (1044–1075) decided to reside in Babylon–Fusṭāṭ, near the new town of Cairo founded by the Fāṭimids. As in the case of the Eastern Church in Baghdād, the Coptic Church promptly adopted Arab culture. It boasted a large number of reforming patriarchs who sought to restore discipline, renew its liturgy and enrich its theology. They included Christodulus and Cyril I (1078–1092) in the eleventh century, Macarius II (1103–1129) and Gabriel Ibn Ṭāriq (1132–1145) in the twelfth century, and Cyril III ibn Laqlaq (1235–1243) in the thirteenth century, with his *Ordinances*. There were also many ecclesiastical historians, such as Ibn al-Muqaffa' (d. 987), Michael, Bishop of Tanis, and Ibn Bana, with his *History of the Forty-eight Monasteries and Churches of Egypt* (1188). The Coptic Church enjoyed particular renown in the thirteenth century through the writings of the Ibn al-'Assāl brothers: Abū Isḥāq was a theologian and spiritualist, Abū l-Faraj was an exegetist and al-Ṣafī a talented disputant who rigorously countered all the arguments of Muslim polemists against Christianity. A crowning achievement came in the fourteenth century with the Church encyclopaedia compiled by Abū l-Barakāt Ibn Kabar and entitled the *Lamp of Darkness*. Such were the contributions of the Coptic Church to the maintenance of the traditions of the Church of Alexandria.

The Byzantine Church, whose destiny was closely linked to that of the Roman Empire of the East, reached its zenith during the reign of Justinian (527–565) (see Plate 145). Fired by 'theologizing zeal' and 'Christian moderation', Justinian had tried to bring the Monophysite Churches (Coptic and Jacobite) closer to Orthodox doctrine at the second Council of Constantinople (553), all the more so as the empire still united the Middle East, Africa and Italy with the Greek world. The empire was governed by the theocratic power of the *Basileus*, master of all means and ends, who christianized the legacy of ancient Hellenistic culture and subjugated a docile Church, which readily became the 'vehicle of the state'. However, the long war between the Byzantines and Sasanians (572–628), which restored the relics of the 'Holy Cross' to Jerusalem (630) by means of the warlike powers of Heraclius (r. 610–641), severely weakened the empire. Shortly thereafter, an expanding Islam seized all the Byzantine provinces in the Middle East and Africa (Jerusalem, 638; Damascus, 635; Egypt, 643; Carthage, 698), before unsuccessfully laying siege to Constantinople itself (717–718). By the end of the seventh century, the Byzantine Empire stretched only from Asia Minor to Ravenna in Italy. From the seventh to the ninth century, the Church in the empire, under the *de facto* twin authority of the patriarch and the emperor, was rocked by crises in which dogma, piety and politics all played a part. Emperor Heraclius still wanted to win over the Monophysite Churches and, inspired by the patriarch Sergius, in 634 made official the theory of 'monoenergism', which maintained that Christ had two natures, but that they were based on only one 'energy'. This doctrine was received with little enthusiasm and became, in 638, the 'monothelitism', made compulsory by Emperor Constans II (641–668), who did not hesitate to deport Martin I, pope of Rome, to the Crimea (where he died in 656) because he had opposed it. Was there not but 'one will' in the Word Incarnate? Under Constantine IV Pogonate, the sixth oecumenical Council of Constantinople (680–681) complemented Chalcedon with the affirmation that in Christ there was 'human free will', which was distinct from the divine will but entirely consonant with it.

The iconoclastic quarrel which followed came as a natural consequence of such Christological disputes. Emperor Leo III the Isaurian (717–741) prohibited religious images (*icons*) and ordered their destruction, against the advice of Rome (730), in an attempted retort to the Islamic challenge (whose cult rejected human representation) and to reform popular piety (the excesses of which led to icon worship). His son, Constantine V Copronymus (741–775), went further, with the worship of images being compared to idolatry and the image of Christ himself being prohibited at the Synod of Hieria (753), where the bishops none the less confirmed the cult of the Holy Virgin and the intercession of saints. The seventh oecumenical Council of Nicaea–Constantinople (787) put an end to iconoclasm, restored the cult of icons (*iconodulia*) and undertook the reform of the Byzantine Church. But the iconoclasts again gained the upper hand with Emperors Constantine VI, Leo the Armenian (813–820) and Theophilus (829–842), in their struggle against interference from monks and their congregations. The death of Theophilus cleared the way for the triumph of an orthodoxy for which 'the homage paid to the icon represented the honour given to its prototype'. A fully fledged Christology implied this, since 'if art could not represent Christ, that would mean that the Word was not Incarnate' (Theodore Studites). At the end of the iconoclastic disputes, in which the Byzantine Church had opposed imperial decisions, this church once again became independent and took renewed interest in theological developments, as witnessed in its schools and monasteries, which had renowned figures like John Grammatikos and Theodore of Stoudion, who thus continued the tradition of Maximus the Confessor (580–662) and John of Damascus (675–749).

This period also marked the beginning of conflicts with Rome as the Byzantine provinces of Italy were gradually reintegrated into the Latin system, while Constantinople's missionary effort aimed at the Slavs, as demonstrated by the evangelical and cultural activities of the brothers Cyril (827–869) and Methodius (825–885) (inventors of the Slavic liturgy and Cyrillic alphabet), remained one of the bones of contention between Byzantium and Rome. The Byzantine Church intended to reserve the conversion of the Slavs for itself and did precisely that, converting the Bulgarians and their Khān Boris (865–870) (see Plate 153), then the Russians with the baptism of Vladimir I (Kiev, 988). But the Slavs of Central Europe were christianized as a result of missionary activity directed by the Popes of Rome (as with the conversion of the Polish king Mieszko in 967). Byzantine misunderstandings with Rome continued to grow, and in the ninth century came the 'Photius affair' and the schism of 867. The deposition of the Byzantine patriarch Ignatius (858) had enabled the election of a 'learned civil servant' Photius, and Pope Nicholas I (858–867) had recognized him while reasserting the primacy of Rome and other usages, which resulted in the Photian Schism. Photius criticized the Latin West's proclamation that the Holy Spirit proceeded from both the Father and the Son (*Filioque*) instead of 'through the Son' (*per Filium*). Pope Hadrian II then condemned Photius. Happily, the fourth Council of Constantinople (879–880) brought about reconciliation between Rome and Byzantium, although silence was maintained over certain points in the Credo.

As for the situation of the contemporary Byzantine Church, the *Epanagoge* of Basil I defined the origin and extent of patriarchal powers (assisted by a 'permanent Synod') in relation to those of the Emperor. Despite its acceptance of an often restrictive political controls, the Church enjoyed genuine spiritual independence, despite the growing importance of a court clergy and the many problems created by the Church's and the monasteries' wealth (with nepotism, simony and other moral weaknesses in its wake). The Byzantine Church had its fair share of reformers, and its 'spiritual current' served as a seedbed for an elevated culture both sacred and lay, with the 'modest piety' of Anna Comnena, and the writings of Christophorus of Mytilene, Simeon of Euchaïta, Michael Choniates and Cyril the Phileote. In this way, the Church ensured the cultural continuity of Byzantium, organizing its 'Patriarchal Academy' through the three Teachings or *didascalia* (the Psalms, Paul the Apostle, the Gospels) in the mid-twelfth century. Then the compromise between Rome and Byzantium failed. The Popes, with Charlemagne, rejected Byzantine control over Italy and intended to exercise their primacy *urbi et orbi*. Hence the mutual excommunications of 1054, when the papal legate rejected the claims of the patriarch Michael Cerularius (1043–1058), and the latter, with his synod, anathematized Pope Leo IX. This was a case of mutual misunderstanding in which 'Rome failed completely to understand a Byzantine theocracy which seemed unable to distinguish between the objectives of the throne and those of the Church, while Byzantium remained completely ignorant of the spiritual revival of the West and interpreted it solely in terms of political hegemony' (Alain Ducellier). Henceforth, the Byzantine Church was determined to go its own way with a policy of mistrust towards Jews, peace with Muslims and understanging towards Slavs. At the same time, there was renewed growth in monasticism with the rising influence of Mount Athos (as renovated by Athanasius in 960), the practice of *Hesychasm* (silent prayer to Jesus) and the teaching of Symeon the New Theologian (917–1022) in the capital.

Latin enthusiasm for the Crusades (1095) met with incomprehension on the part of Byzantium because of the now wide differences between Greek and Latin Christians in cultural traditions, theological creations, and the spiritual beliefs and practices of monastic life. And, although it was initially endorsed by the Roman pope and the Byzantine Emperor, the Fourth Crusade was perverted by the Venetians who stormed and conquered Constantinople, turning it into the capital of a new 'Latin Empire', whilst the remnants of the Byzantine ruling class clung precariously to Nicaea (1204–1261) until Michael VIII Palaeologus regained possession of his 'city'. But the Byzantine 'Empire' was now restricted to the shores of the Aegean Sea, and the Byzantine Church adopted the alternately pro-Ottoman and pro-Roman policies of its emperors. Slowly but surely, the Ottomans took over from the Seljuks in Asia Minor, and from the Byzantines themselves in the Balkans, during the reigns of their sultans Murad I (1362–1389), Bāyezīd I (1389–1402), Mehmed I (1413–1421) and Murād II (1421–1451). Increasingly, the Byzantines loomed as the champions of Orthodox Christianity against both Turks and Latins. Patriarchs like Athanasius, Kallistos, Nil Kerameus, and talented ecclesiastics like Joseph Bryennios, Gregory Palamas and Isidore Glabas catechized the Orthodox Christian faithful through liturgy, preaching and hagiography, all the more so as they saw the presence of the Genoese and Venetians everywhere as a challenge to their identity. Meanwhile, a reconciliation and 'union' between Rome and Byzantium formed part of deliberate imperial policy. Pope Gregory X and Michael VIII Palaeologus, the Basileus, subscribed to the same 'Roman faith' at the Council of Lyons (1274), but the emperor was not followed in this at all by the Byzantine clergy and the people, and the Byzantine patriarchate thus suffered many schisms and vacancies. Under the pressure of events, the emperor and such Byzantine supporters as he could find for 'union' were reconciled with Pope Eugenius IV and the 'Latins' at the Council of Ferrara–Florence (1438–1439), after first trying to resolve their theological differences (the *Filioque*, papal primacy, purgatory, the use of unleavened wafers and eucharistic epiclesis), as well as minor complaints and misdirected attacks. In Constantinople, however, opposition to 'union', which was headed by Mark of Ephesus and Scholarios, who triumphed over those who endorsed the 'union' (Bessarion and Isidore of Kiev). Constantinople fell at last in 1453 to Mehmed II, who made it his capital, Istanbul, and promptly showed favour to those Byzantines who had 'preferred the turban to the papal mitre'. This lack of understanding between the Byzantine Church and Latin Christendom was to last for many centuries further.

In Rome, the popes took over from increasingly ineffective political authorities as successive waves of 'barbarians' washed over the former provinces of the Western Roman Empire. Indeed, Saint Leo I, pope from 440 to 461, persuasively negotiated Attila's withdrawal and so prevented the Huns from storming the 'city' – thereby deservedly winning the title of *defensor civitatis*, 'defender of the city', for his successors. Gregory I (r. 590–604), famed both as a preacher and as a learned commentator of scripture in his own right, ushered in a new era of reform for the Western Church. He intended that the Roman see both retain its honorary primacy among all bishoprics and assume sole responsibility for dealing with the Eastern Churches in oecumenical ('universal') communion. Through Pope Gregory's zeal, new life was breathed into the drive to convert Northern Europe, a process lasting from the turn of the seventh into the ninth century. Gregory himself designated his missionary Augustine ('Saint Austin of Canterbury') to the Anglo-Saxon lands: where Augustine and his successors laid the foundations of an early English Church, whose leading theological luminary became the Venerable Bede (*Baeda Venerabilis*, 673–735). Meanwhile, the Celtic and Breton Churches were strengthened too, while missionaries belonging to the austere monastic orders established off the coast of Scotland and in Ireland (Iona and Bangor) returned to spread the Gospel on the continent itself in their 'pilgrimage for God'. Ireland's own Saint Columba thus founded the abbeys of Luxeuil in France and Bobbio in Italy (590 and 615). These in turn became seeding grounds for new missionaries and bishop–monks, who preached the Word throughout seventh-century northern Gaul and Flanders (with Saint Amandus) and then in eighth-century Germany and what is now The Netherlands: with Saints Fridolinus and Pirminus (d. 753) in Germany's western reaches, Saints Rupert (d. 715) and Emmeranus in Bavaria, Saint Killian in Thuringia, Saint Willibrord (d. 739) in Friesland, and Saint Boniface (672–754) throughout all the Germanic lands. In Italy, Saint Willibald restored the Benedictine monastery of Monte Cassino in 729 and revived its influence throughout the peninsula. Monks everywhere observed the same basic rule: with praises offered to God ('divine offices'), manual labour (clearing, draining and developing the land), intellectual work (teaching, combined with the copying of manuscripts), and missionary activity (including catechizing, or the teaching of the faith's basic tenets.)

The popes mediated beween the West's various contending rulers in this age (Franks, Lombards and others), and took stands – though from a distance – in the different theological disputes which shook the Eastern Church (the monothelitic and iconoclastic controversies). Meanwhile, the Frankish Merovingian dynasty was on the wane, with the political rise of the Merovingian kings' own all-powerful stewards or 'mayors of the palace': such as Charles 'the Hammer', who himself commanded the Frankish troops which stopped an incursion of Spanish Muslim forces at Poitiers in 732. Charles' own son, Pepin 'the Short', was crowned King of the Franks (r. 751–768). Pepin wrested the lands of the former exarchate of Ravenna from the Lombards in Italy and bestowed these lands upon the pope. His son and successor Charlemagne (r. 768–814) confirmed this donation, and in turn was crowned 'Emperor of the West' by the pope in Rome on Christmas Day 800 (see Plate 161). Charlemagne defended and laid down the guiding organizational lines of this 'Roman Empire of the West', thus resuscitated at long last, which he ruled from his capital at Aachen (Aix-la-Chapelle). The reform of Church and state under Charlemagne went hand in hand in all spheres. Charlemagne's own Palace School, and various schools sponsored by urban bishops (at Lyons, Metz and Orléans) or by the monasteries, nurtured an intellectual revival whose leading lights included such ecclesiastical scholars as Paul the Deacon, Alcuin, Dungal the Recluse and Theodulf of Orléans. The cultural impetus of this 'Carolingian Renaissance' endured, even though the empire itself was dismembered by 843. The Church for its part took advantage of the Carolingian Age's respite to put its own house in order, settling such theological misunderstandings as that arising from the Spanish heresy of 'Adoptionism' (whereby God was held to have 'adopted' as his son the 'man' Jesus' through baptism), while further clarifying its own position on various theological issues in relation to the Byzantines. Meanwhile, the Roman Church's missionary drive to preach the Gospel to the remaining pagan peoples of Northern and Central Europe proceeded apace. First the Saxons in the ninth, then the Danes and Western Slavs in the tenth century were converted. Abbeys were again reformed through the efforts of such figures as Benedict of Aniana. Political divisions resulting from the break-up of the Carolingian Empire could no longer impede the rapid growth of intellectual culture in the German lands or the territories of Lotharingia (the core of future 'Lorraine'). Doctrinal disputes pitting council against council ,which flared up over the Eucharist or the issue of predestination, were fortunatly mostly resolved by the ninth century, while the study of canon law revived. Popes were still frequently called upon to deal with the practical everyday business of the age's political life: such pontiffs as Nicholas I (r. 858–867), Hadrian II (r. 867–872) and John VIII (872–882) took a leading hand in determining the succession of Western Europe's various secular rulers; they appointed bishops; they even again 'defended the city' when Muslim warriors, operating by sea from Sicily, sacked Rome itself in 846.

But finally, the social rivalries which were politically shaking the empire to pieces brought their dissolving force to bear upon the Church as well. For two centuries (888–1057), indeed, the Church actually fell 'into the hands of the laity'. Rome was now rent by the contending factions of its local lay nobility, led by such men as the early tenth-century *patricius* or virtual dictator Theophylactus at the head of his clan, or later by the counts of Tusculum, who struggled for political power not only over the city but over the very persons of the popes. When Germany's kings attempted to revive – and rule – what had been Charlemagne's Western Empire, with Otto I's crowning in Rome on 9 February 962, these northern monarchs too strove to impose their sway over the popes against the Roman nobles. Popes and rival anti-popes were thus enthroned in Rome through elections rigged alternately by fiercely opposed German emperors and Roman nobles, until the resulting welter of family feuds, bloody street clashes, armed German interventions and popular Roman revolts dragged the papacy's prestige into the mire. But two popes did manage to stand out in such an age: Sylvester II (999) and Saint Leo IX (1049–1054). Both attempted to halt the drift and enforce reforms. The number of dioceses was increased, but a Church torn between contending clergy, nobles and common people had itself become feudalized. Bishops were turning into feudal lords with fiefs of their own, and a career in the Church was coming to be sought with an eye to increasing one's earthly wealth rather than under the urge of one's spiritual vocation. Even so, while certain monasteries might so grow in wealth, secular feudal lords retained control over all abbeys on their lands. Clearly, then, only 'exemption' – that is, the securing of the monasteries' independence from all local secular control – might encourage a true monastic revival. This now came. In 910, the abbey of Cluny led the way to reform, thereafter spinning its own network of reformed Cluniac monastic houses throughout Europe. Meanwhile, Latin Christendom resumed its expansion: to the Slavic Wends, to Moravia, to Poland and to all of Scandinavia. Local churches, at the same time, took up anew the struggle to promote 'moral' rule over lay society, as well as an intellectual and even artistic revival, with such leading clerical figures as Odon of Cluny, Liutprand of Cremona and Gerbert of Aurillac. Thus came about the flowering of Romanesque art, which dates from this period: with magnificent frescoes decorating stark, stately architecture and bearing witness thereby to a remarkable surge in creative piety.

The 'Gregorian Reform', so called after the crucial late eleventh-century reign of Pope Gregory VII, heralded the rise of the truly Christian Middle Ages, as such, as a phase in European civilization. For the papacy now entirely freed itself of the supremacy – or 'caesaro-papism' – of the German emperors over the Church. In a Lateran Council, Nicholas II (r. 1059–1061) ruled that papal elections should henceforth be decided by the cardinal bishops alone (Nicholas could rely on new allies, the troops of Normans in Rome, to cast off imperial German influence). The Church ruled out any further investiture of bishops by secular rulers anywhere, condemned 'simony' (the purchasing of ecclesiastical office) and outlawed 'nicholaism' (the possibility for priests to marry or take a concubine). Alexander II (1061–1073) and especially Gregory VII (1073–1085) further championed such reforms, as through the *Dictatus Papae* of 1075. To be sure, a key factor in the Church's new freedom was the Norman alliance: Norman knights in these years were present in southern Italy, where they were militarily wresting Sicily from the Muslims for Christendom, just as they had recently conquered England under their duke William in 1066. But the essential matter was the 'power of Peter', now superseding that of all earthly sovereigns and guaranteeing justice and peace through papal legates. The German Emperor Henry IV had to abase himself before Gregory VII at Canossa in 1077 to lift the pope's sentence of excommunication upon his person. Still, the 'quarrel between pope and emperor' flared up afresh when the emperor again presumed to invest all bishops in his realm, militarily intervened once more in Italy to depose Gregory, put him to flight and set up an anti-pope, Clement III (1084–1100). But nothing the Emperor might do could any longer stop the gradual triumph of 'Gregorian ideas' (see Plates 169–172). Urban II (r. 1088–1099) put all his energy into applying them, with the support not only of such courageous bishops as Hugh of Lyons and outstanding theologians like Saint Anselm of Canterbury, but also of the whole Benedictine Order of Cluny. In 1095, councils held at Piacenza and Clermont further endorsed the reforms. But Urban could also call on another kind of supporter: the knights. He urged the Spanish kingdoms of Aragon, Castile and León to press on with the *Reconquista* – Toledo was permanently taken from the Muslims in 1085, and Valencia and Lisbon were temporarily captured in 1092 and 1093 – and especially mustered the knights of France into the great venture of the Crusades: in response to appeals for help from the Byzantine Emperor Alexis I Comnenus. An anti-Gregorian reaction set in under the pontificate of Pascal II (1099–1118), while the quarrel on bishops' investitures between pope and lay rulers continued to rage until the Concordat of Worms in 1122 confirmed the pope's sole right to invest bishops – while recognizing the emperor's right to veto appointments. 'Gregorian' bishops and doctors of canon law at length united the entire Western Church and made the reform permanent at the ninth oecumenical Lateran Council of 1123. Cluny's abbeys had been so many nourishing grounds for the 'reforming' bishops, but now came the creation of the orders of the Carthusians (with Saint Bruno) in 1084 and of Cîteaux in 1098 (where Saint Bernard would make his reputation), the increase in the number of canons regular (according to the Rule of Saint Augustine), and the founding in 1120 (by Saint Norbert) of the *Premonstratensians* or White Canons. All these orders encouraged local churches to reform the clergy, to edify the faithful, to rehabilitate Christian marriage and to labour for peace but also to buttress the rising organization of knighthood: for the Crusades were stirring a new spirit whereby 'the spiritual power and the secular arm' worked together to 'free the Holy Land'.

Notwithstanding all the blood they shed, the nine Crusading expeditions, which lasted for two centuries, by confronting Christians and Muslims, also forced them to meet – and moreover brought the Latin and Eastern Churches into closer contact. Trade, technology, architecture and the sciences all derived benefit from the Latin West's new receptivity to the ancient Greek heritage as bequeathed through Arab intermediaries. This age witnessed Western Europe's remarkable economic, cultural and religious breakthrough – with the spread of 'communal charters' – although everywhere the 'quarrel between pope and emperor' took local forms of conflict between the papacy and the rising states: especially with the promulgation in 1140 of the monk Gratian's *Decretum* to justify the monarchical stand taken by the popes. Smoother relations might exist, however, as between the Church and the sainted King Louis IX of France (r. 1242–1270). Crusading hardly impeded the development of famous universities in Bologna (1119) and Padua (1221), followed by Paris's Sorbonne (1257). But finally conflict between a lay ruler, France's Philip the Fair, and a pope, Boniface VIII (1294–1303), brought matters to a head: the pope asserted his suzerainty over all Christian princes with the *Unam Sanctam* Bull of 1302, but the storming of Boniface's castle at Anagni by Philip's knights in 1303 resulted in the pontiff's death from shock shortly thereafter. The Church, however, withstood the shock: Innocent III had thoroughly reorganized the life of Western Christendom through the fourth Lateran Council of 1215; the second Council of Lyons had permanently laid down binding rules for electing popes (through conclaves) in 1274. Meanwhile, Honorius III (r. 1216–1227) had recognized a host of new mendicant orders, the Friars Preachers founded by Saint Dominic (1170–1221) and the Friars Minor by Saint Francis of Assisi (1181–1226). By bearing witness to the Christian life through their own lives of poverty, begging and itinerant preaching, together with the Third Order, which brought together lay people, they breathed new life into the preaching of the Gospel in medieval society and furthered 'Gregorian reform' in the midst of still rampant simony and the ever-present dangers of renascent heresy.

The seven popes who dwelt in Avignon between 1305 and 1377, after Clement V quitted Rome, did endeavour to organize properly the papal court or 'Curia Romana': involving authoritarian rule, centralized administration and high taxation. Spiritually minded devotees, however, criticized the 'Avignon popes' for their narrow dependence upon the French king and still narrower association with rich ecclesiastical benefices. Saint Catherine of Siena convinced Gregory XI to return to Rome in 1377, but after his death and the election of Urban VI (r. 1378–1389), a new (anti-)pope raised his rival claim in Avignon, Clement VII (r. 1378–1394). This resulted in the 'Great Schism of the West'. Two further rival popes, Gregory XII in Rome and Benedict XIII in Avignon, were declared deposed by the Council of Pisa in 1409 on grounds of incompetent inactivity. To compensate for their shortcomings, the council elected another pope, Alexander V, himself succeeded by John XXIII (r. 1410–1419) – but both these successive prelates continued to be opposed by Benedict XIII in Avignon and also in Rome by Gregory XII (who still regarded himself as the only legitimate successor to Urban VI). The Council of Constance finally deposed all three contending popes – John, Benedict and Gregory – and agreed on Martin V (1419–1431), whose successor, Eugenius IV (1431–1447), then had to face the 'absolutist' pretensions of the Council of Basel, which declared 'the council is superior to the pope'. The Basel Council dispersed in confusion after again electing an anti-pope, Felix V, who abdicated, however, in 1449. Meanwhile, Eugenius ordered the next council, over which he presided, to assemble in Ferrara (1437–1439), then Florence (1439–1442) and Rome (1443), where it testified to 'the union of the Churches' between Rome and Constantinople. Nicholas V (1447–1455) finally succeeded in calming matters, bringing the contending parties together and stabilized the papacy's 'Roman presence' once more. Indeed, Nicholas became the first Renaissance pope. But the consequences of the 'Great Schism' were nothing if not profound. Divisions everywhere lurked beneath the surface (participants in the councils voted by 'nations'), and nationalist resentment found expression, in France for example, by the 'Gallicanism' defended by the Sorbonne and the country's 'most Christian' kings; elsewhere, such resentment broke out, and far more radically, with the Hussite rising in Bohemia; later still would come the outright Protestant breaks with Rome in Luther's Germany, Calvin's Geneva and Henry VIII's England.

All the same, Western Christendom's theological and spiritual development proceeded apace between the thirteenth and fifteenth centuries, marked as it was with the flowering of the mendicant orders and the revival of monasticism at the hands of such groups as the Cistercians and Carthusians. Theology found expression in a large variety of *summae* and *sententiae* (the example here was set by Peter Lombard, 1110–1160). The thirteenth century's store of knowledge vastly expanded with the West's adoption of the teaching of the Greek philosophers (in the form of translations into Latin from their Arabic versions). The movement to study such philosophy grew in Paris and Oxford, with the Church playing its part to ensure proper Christian discrimination in dealing with ancient pagan texts. The great doctrinal syntheses belong to this period, roughly the middle and second half of the thirteenth century; Saint Bonaventure (1221–1274) defended the organic unity of Christian wisdom; Saint Albert 'the Great' (1193–1280) wished to 'reconsider' pagan thought from a 'Latin Christian perspective'; and Saint Thomas Aquinas (1225–1274), in his *Summa Theologica*, grounded the Christian understanding of faith on a sound philosophy of Being (see Plate 127). Condemnation of many theses of the new learning by the Bishop of Paris in 1277 failed to check its growth in various schools. In the fourteenth century, Duns Scotus stressed reliance on the *via antiqua* or reliance on evangelical practice, while Master Eckhart and his disciples dwelt on the 'deification', through mystic union, of the Christian; Petrarch stressed a humanism based on the teachings of Saint Augustine, and William of Ockham strove, with his *via moderna*, to define a 'nominalism' – whereby abstractions were to be regarded as mere 'names' – not unconnected with pragmatism.

Cultured elites and common folk alike found spiritual nourishment in all these trends. Although Crusades, schism, conflict and the activities of the Inquisition, founded in 1229 to serve as the Church's judicial weapon in fighting heresy in co-operation with secular authorities, all cast their shadow on the life of Western Christendom, its outlook was brightened by those who preached to the masses, reformed the clergy and exercised influence through the abbeys. Liturgy, devotion and the creation of brotherhoods, and sisterhoods, ensured access to the Faith's truths and the grace of sacraments to all. Christians believed in acquired merit and put their trust in salvation through solidarity with the communion of saints. Even before fully exploring the possibility of contacts in Spain between Christian devotees and Muslim Ṣūfīs, scholars have spoken in terms of a 'mystic invasion' in this age, especially in Italy and northern Europe. Lay folk were afforded access to spiritual experience, as mirrored in such works as the *Imitation of Christ* attributed to Thomas à Kempis (1380–1471), through the third orders and the Béguine convents, and also through the various schools of mystical thought, including those of Master Eckhart and the Dominicans Johann Tauler and Heinrich Suso in the Rhineland, of Jan van Ruysbroeck in Flanders, of Julian of Norwich in England, and of Catherine of Siena, a Dominican tertiary, in Italy. The West's devotion to suffering humanity as exemplified in the figure of Christ (*Ecce homo*) or that of Mary as 'Mother of Sorrows' (*Mater dolorosa*) appeared to complement Byzantium's preferred contemplation of the Word Incarnate in glorious majesty. Much here was due to the steadfast and manifold activities of the 'spirituals', who, in all religious congregations, supported a return to 'strict observance' of those models set by their orders' founders. The medieval Church, 'ever in need of reform', yet strove to be 'one, holy and Catholic'. United in such faith, priestly hierarchy and lay believers alike upheld the Church's vertical (or heavenly) dimension and its horizontal (or earthly) one. The art of frescoes, rood screens and altar panels, in churches where Romanesque yielded in glory only to Gothic, everywhere bore witness to this fervour. For every city where a bishop held sway gave full expression to aesthetic yearning through brotherhoods engaged in building heaven-soaring cathedrals, lit with translucid stained glass windows whose symbolism faithfully mirrored the spirituality of their age (see Plates 28, 29, 74, 75).

CULTURAL AND RELIGIOUS INTERACTIONS

These religious worlds maintained constant contact with one another and, as we have seen, their troubled history was marked by both destructive conflicts and constructive encounters. We might thus usefully give an account of the cultural interaction which took place in the different spheres of thought and action. Translation schools enabled the Islamic *madrasas* and Western universities to familiarize themselves with the civilization of 'others'. The 'House of Wisdom' (*Bayt al-Ḥikma*) in Baghdād, which reached its zenith under the caliph al-Ma'mūn (813–833) with an elite group of Muslim and Christian thinkers and the famous translators known as the Banū l-Munajjim, enabled the Arab and Islamic world of the 'Abbāssid period (eighth to ninth century) to assimilate the thought and sciences of the Greeks. This was how Plato, Aristotle, Ptolemy and Galen were taken to the Arabs and gave the Arab–Islamic sciences (philosophy, theology, astronomy, medicine, and so on) a decisive impetus. Later in reconquered Toledo (1085), translators like Robert of Ketton, Hermann of Dalmatia and Pierre of Poitiers transmitted this heritage to the Latin world (indeed, they translated the Qur'ān into Latin), while Constantine the African (1051–1087) translated the works of Hippocrates, Galen and Rāzī for the School of Medicine of Salerno. A little later, Raymond Marti's Dominicans opened a *studium* in Tunis (1250–1259), and Raymond Lull's Franciscans an institute for the study of Islam and Arabic in Miramar, in the Balearic Islands (1274–1287). In addition, the Council of Vienna (1311) decided to found departments of Arabic at the universities of Rome, Bologna, Salamanca, Paris and Oxford.

Such centres of medieval culture were enriched by the stories of travellers (and pilgrims during the Crusades) and the treatises of geographers. Marco Polo (1254–1324) travelled to Mongolia and as far as Beijing (Khānbāliq), where he was employed by the Great Khān Qubilay. On his return to Venice, he wrote his *Book of the Marvels of the World* (1298) (see Plate 121).

The Arab–Islamic world also produced a whole corpus of literature concerning the discovery of the world, beginning with the anonymous *Narrative on China and India* (*Akhbār al-Sīn wa-l-Hind*) (851), to al-'Umarī (1300–1384) and Ibn Baṭṭūṭa (1304–1377) and the stories of their travels. Compendia for the use of government secretaries by Ibn Khurdādhbeh (d. 885), Ibn Rusteh (d. 903) and Qudāma (d. 932), and geographical works for the elite, including those of Ibn al-Faqīh (d. 903), were followed by the stories told by such renowned travellers as Ibn Faḍlān (early tenth century) and Buzurg Ibn Shahriyār (end of the tenth century). Also successful were the 'Books of Routes and Kingdoms' (*Masālik wa-mamālik*) by al-Ya'qūbī (d. 897), al-Balkhī (d. 934), al-Iṣṭakhrī (d. 951), Ibn Ḥawqal (d. 977), al-Muqaddasī (d. 988), al-Bakrī (d. 1091) and al-Idrīsī (1099–1153). Popular too were al-Mas'ūdī (d. 956) and his *Meadows of Gold* (*Murūj al-dhahab*), al-Bīrunī (973–1046) and his *Description of India* (*Ta'rīkh al-Hind*), Yāqūt (d. 1229) and his *Dictionary of Countries* (*Mu'jam al-buldān*), al-Qazwīnī (d. 1283) and his *Marvels of Beings* (*'Ajā'ib al-makhlūqāt*) and Abu l-Fidā' (d. 1331) and his *Localization of Countries* (*Taqwīm al-buldān*). Such books on the history and geography of the other regions of the world were not based on anything like the scientific rigour of the present day, but it did encompass their beliefs, rites and customs. Thus, the description and classification of religions led to the discovery among Muslims of a specific literary genre, books on *'Communities and Sects'* (*Kitāb al-milal wa-l-niḥal*), in which the Andalusian Ibn Ḥazm (994–1064) and the Iranian al-Shahrastānī (1076–1153) were to excel, no doubt drawing their inspiration from what Ibn al-Nadīm (936–995) wrote on the subject in Book IX of his *Fihrist al-'ulūm* (*The Encyclopaedia of Sciences*). One positive aspect of the Crusades was that they compelled Christians and Muslims to recognize their differences and hence to engage in explanations and arguments. They had to put such dialogues and controversies into a philosophical context in which they often used the Graeco-Hellenistic heritage as a 'common language'.

Religious interaction took place in this essentially Mediterranean context in which ancient and secular philosophy posed the same challenges to the monotheistic religions of the Middle East. Countless meetings and debates between Christians and Muslims also occurred there in the Middle East. From the seventh to the tenth century, Melchite Christians like Saint John of Damascus (675–753), with his *De Haeresibus* (which deals with Islam in its conclusion), and Theodore Abū Qurra (740–825), with his *Treatise on the Existence of the Creator and True Religion*; and Nestorians like Timothy I (728–823) with his *Dialogue with the Caliph al-Mahdī*, and 'Ammār al-Baṣrī (800–850), with his *Questions and Answers*, called Islam into question and praised Christianity. Conversely, Muslims like 'Ali al-Ṭabarī (d. 855) and al-Jāḥiẓ (776–869) wrote their *Refutation of the Christians*, while the *Correspondence between al-Hāshimī* [a Muslim] *and al-Kindī* [a Christian] was published in about 820. The Byzantines also contributed to this genre with Nicetas of Byzantium (842–912), Georges Harmotolos (ninth century) and Nicholas the Mystic, patriarch of Constantinople from 901 to 925, with his *Letter to the Emir of Crete* and his *Correspondence between 'Umar* [II, caliph of Damascus] *and Leo* [III, emperor of Byzantium] in about 900.

Christians' and Muslims' knowledge of one another during the eleventh and twelfth centuries readily made references to each other's texts. For instance, on the Muslim side, there were Ibn Ḥazm (994–1064) and his *Book of Discernment between Communities and Sects* (*Kitāb al-fiṣal fī l-milal wa-l-niḥal*), al-Juwaynī (1028–1085) and his *Exposition on the Changes to be Found in the Torah and Gospels* (*Shifā'al-ghalīl fī bayān mā waqa'a fī l-Tawrāt wa-l-Injīl min al-tabdīl*), and al-Ghazālī (1059–1111) and his *Noble Refutation of the Divinity of Jesus based on the Gospels* (*al-Radd al-jamīl li-ilāhiyyat 'Īsā bi-sarīḥ al-Injīl*). On the Christian side, the Nestorian Elias of Nisibis (975–1046) narrated what happened during his numerous 'Sessions' (*Majālis*), in the Middle East, with the emir of

Mosul. And, in the West, the writings of Peter the Venerable (1094–1156) of Cluny (for a while a leading figure of the 'School of Toledo'), a letter from Pope Gregory VII to the Ḥammādid emir of Bijāya (Algeria) in 1076, and the *Letter from a Monk in France to al-Bājī* (1078), all bore witness to a genuine openness of mind, in sharp contrast to the refutation by al-Khazrajī (1125–1187) entitled *Maqāmi' al-ṣulbān*.

Happily, renewed efforts were made during the thirteenth and fourteenth centuries, especially by the Christians, to understand the other side and maintain discussions with them using their language, texts, and philosophical and theological reflection. In the West, Raymond Marti (1230–1284) wrote his *Pugio Fidei adversus Mauros et Judaeos*, Saint Thomas Aquinas (1225–1274) his *Summa contra Gentiles*, William of Tripoli (1220–1291) his *Tractatus de Statu Saracenorum* (after his numerous voyages to the Middle East) and Ricoldo di Montecroce (1243–1320), his treatise *Contra legem Saracenorum* (after long acquaintance with Middle Eastern Muslims). These writers were all Dominicans. The Franciscans provided the example of the peaceful visit of Saint Francis of Assisi (1219) to the king of Egypt, al-Malik al-Kāmil, from the camp of Crusaders: Raymond Lull (1235–1315), the Franciscan tertiary, followed Francis' example with his writings and travels to North Africa. Two religious orders were established during the same period. They were the Trinitarians (founded by John of Matha, 1160–1213, and Felix of Valois) and the Mercedarians (Our Lady of Mercy, founded by Raymond of Peñafort and Peter Nolasco) for the 'redemption of captives' taken by the Saracens. The polemical spirit was still in existence, however, as was demonstrated by the refutation of *The Text of Toledo* (1236) in Spain by al-Qurṭubī and the reactions of Ibn Taymīya (1263–1328) in the Middle East to the writings of the Melchite Paul of Antioch (d. 1180), even though the latter had entitled his treatise *Letter to my Muslim Friends*. But times were about to change and, in the Byzantine world, a 'new spirit' witnessed in the works of Gregory Palamas (1296–1360) and the Emperor Manuel II Palaeologus (1348–1425). It must also be said that in both Spain and the Byzantine Empire, there had been no lack of contacts between the 'spirituals' on both sides. Indeed, had not Islamic Ṣūfism itself been partly influenced by Middle Eastern Christian monasticism between the seventh and the tenth centuries? (Hence, perhaps, Ṣūfism's insistence on the 'unity of testimony', *waḥdat al-shuhūd*, in mystical experience.) And, in the same way, had not Christian 'revivals' in Spain in turn borrowed vocabulary and methods from Andalusian Ṣūfism (Ibn 'Abbād of Ronda, d. 1389) and the North African brotherhoods (witness the exchanges between Ibn Sab'īn and Raymond Lull)?

Cultural exchanges between the Arab–Muslim world and the Latin and Byzantine worlds became too numerous not to lead to renewed inquiry in the spheres of thought, the sciences and the arts. The sack of Baghdād by the Mongols (1258) and the end of the Crusades (1291) seem to have forced Islam to retire somewhat within itself, although the Ottomans and the Tunisian thinker Ibn Khaldūn (1332–1406) remained very much open to the outside world (see Plate 123). Indeed, singular developments arose out of the meeting of the two cultures in Western Europe. Masterpieces of Plato, Aristotle and Plotinus and, more particularly, Aristotelian physics, ethics and metaphysics were made available, in Latin translations, with the commentaries of al-Kindī, al-Fārābī, Avicenna and Averroës, who were Muslims, and Avicebron and Maimonides, who were Jews. The 'doctrinal bloc' of unitary 'Augustinism' was superseded by a 'neo-Platonic Augustinism' under the influence of Avicenna, and then by an Averroist 'Aristotelianism' (with notions such as a world without end, the determinism of nature, the transcendence of God, the negation of providence and monopsychism). With his *Opus Majus*, Roger Bacon, in England (1214–1294) heralded the experimental method and modern mathematics. Siger of Brabant (1235–1281) was greatly influenced by the rationalism of Averroës. Saint Albert the Great and Saint Thomas Aquinas were able to fashion all these philosophical contributions into a novel theological synthesis of a profoundly Christian nature (see Plate 127). Literature itself acquired new expressions with the lyric poetry of the troubadours and the affirmation of 'courtly love'. Indeed, Dante himself (1265–1321) was influenced by certain masterpieces of Arab–Islamic literature in his creation of *The Divine Comedy* (see Plate 180).

In the mid-fifteenth century, Nicholas of Cusa (1401–1464) finally assumed the role of a harbinger of the coming Renaissance. This German humanist and Roman cardinal participated in the Council of Basel (1431) and went to Byzantium as papal legate. He was also active at the Council of Ferrara–Florence, promoting 'union' in his *De Concordantia Catholica*. When informed of the realities of Islam and the 'unknowns' of the other religions, he thought, in his *De Pace Fidei* (*The Peace of Faith*), about the possibility of 'making opposites coincide'. He reasoned that the divine harmony of a God who was Three in One and of whom Jesus Christ was the Word Incarnate signified tolerance between religions, which, indeed, bring about 'the coincidence of opposites' in the world of creatures: the material and the spiritual, body and soul, God and human beings, the one and many, unity and diversity, with the result that religions all inherit a certain wisdom. With its goal of a 'reasonable accord between religions', his Utopian view saw in the order of the cosmos a humanism based on divine wisdom, and paths which might lead to peace between peoples. His *De Pace Fidei* was to serve as a model for Christian humanists in the sixteenth century.

BIBLIOGRAPHY

Dictionnaire des Religions. 1993. POUPARD, P. (ed.), Paris.
Encyclopaedia Britannica. 1966. Chicago.
Encyclopaedia Cattolica. 1949–1954. Vatican City.
Encyclopaedia of Islam. 1960 (new edn). Leiden.
Encyclopaedia Judaica. 1971. Jerusalem.
Encyclopaedia of Buddhism. 1961. Colombo.
Enciclopaedia delle Religioni. 1970–1976. Florence.
Encyclopaedia of Religion. 1987. New York.
Encyclopaedia Universalis. 1970–1973. Paris.
Histoires des Religions. 1970–1976. PUECH, H. Ch. (ed.), Paris.
Homo Religiosus. 1978–1993. Louvain-la-Neuve.
New Catholic Encyclopaedia. 1967. New York.

8

ART AND EXPRESSION

8.1
THE OLD WORLD

Oleg Grabar

All men and women, at all times and in all places, have expressed their feelings, emotions, beliefs, associations, ambitions and modes of behaviour in an immense variety of spoken, written, sung, performed, instrumental, plastic, decorative or representational ways. Some of their statements or messages were meant only for a few close relatives; others were destined for all of humankind. Some were in highly restricted codes whose understanding was accessible only to a few and can only be approximated in our own times; others were meant from the very beginning to have a wide contemporary currency and the hope of a meaning across the ages. Much has been lost for ever; what remains and what can be reconstructed by contemporary scholarship are but statistically unclear fragments of what had existed.

And then there is an issue which applies particularly to religious expression as it predominated during the centuries under consideration. It is that the perception of the expression varies now, as it did in the past, according to the category of the observer or receiver of that expression. Thus, what is an intensely holy statement to the reader of or listener to the Gospels, the Qur'ān or Persian mystical poetry becomes a literary masterpiece of thought, structure or imagery to the non-believer. Christian icons or Hindu mantras can be objects of faith and piety as well as works or art; they can be found in a temple or in a museum and they will be understood quite differently in each case. Such documents are, at the same time, individual and unique sources for concrete moments and places in history and examples for the consideration of poetic, musical or visual experience in general. Both approaches – one directed towards the cultural specificity of a time and place, the other emphasizing universal values and judgements – will be found in the pages which follow.

A balance survey of eight centuries of artistic expression in the whole world is impossible to achieve. This is not the place to indulge in debates about the ethical propriety of extending to specific cultural achievements judgements issued from other cultures. Nor is there any value or purpose in making comparative rosters of accomplisments and to distribute rewards for artistic successes. Instead, four themes affecting artistic creativity have been identified. Each one is discussed as it affects or involves all the arts: architecture, plastic and decorative arts, writing, music, oral and written literature, performing arts. The choice of examples cannot be complete, but it is hoped that guidelines are provided to understand an immense artistic endeavour everywhere. One point, however, needs elaboration. The Islamic world is prominent in this chapter for the reason that its appearance in the seventh century is the crucial event of this period. By its location in the centre of the Afro-Eurasian mass, it affected all other cultures, at times superficially, at other times radically. The arts of Pre-Columbian America are only mentioned in some sections of this sub-chapter because its history developed independently of Eurasia and Africa. It is only at the formal and structural levels that it can be fitted into a general statement of the arts and expressions of a time before the 'great discoveries' (see sub-Chapter 8.2 and Part VI).

Of the four themes around which this chapter is organized, the first two are more peculiar to these centuries than to other periods of world history. They are the movements of people, especially of artists and artisans, and the contrasts (or lack thereof) between the faiths and religious systems which dominate these times. The other two are universal and permanent issues of artistic behaviour, although their specific ways may be original for the period between AD 600 and 1492. One is the nature of patronage, the sponsorship and consumption of the arts. The second one is the apparent opposition with varying degrees of intensity between piety and pleasure, intent and consumption, collective or individual purposes, a contrast which always affects the making of works of art and the social or personal behaviour they evoke.

THE ARTS AND MOVEMENTS OF PEOPLE

From the frontiers of China to the Iberian peninsula and to North Africa, the phenomenon of the great migrations of, at that time, mostly Indo-European but already often enough Turkic and even Mongol peoples was still going on in the early seventh century and affecting areas as diverse as the Pannonian plains of Hungary, southern Russia and Ukraine, the republics of Central Asia, Afghanistan, and Mongolia.

The settled cultures of China, northern India, Iran and the Mediterranean provided much of the vocabulary of motifs found on the objects in metal or the textiles made for or used by nomadic warrior families, who carried these motifs to lands in which they had been unknown. At the same time, an original interpretation of animal forms and a fascination with geometric ornamentation often transfigured people, beasts or plants into exuberant patterns. Graves excavated at the frontiers of China and in the Caucasus or the silver treasure of Nagysentmiklos now in the Vienna Museum are just a few of the many examples of objects apparently of practical use – cups, ewers, plates, clothes, shrouds – whose date, attribution and specific iconographic significance are often a matter of speculation, but whose forms contain fascinating mixes of traditional languages from the Mediterranean, Iran or China with styles from nomadic lands.

Thus, at the very outset of the period under consideration, the visual arts of most of the Eurasian world were affected by the movements of thousands of people in its northern half. Contacts were made between forms which had been only local, and syntheses were made for reasons which can no longer be imagined or reconstructed. Nor do we really know how the patrons and users of the seventh century, in settled lands or in nomadic areas, reacted to these works of art, as the iconographic and expressive meanings of the remaining silver and bronze vessels are still debated. In the last decade of the fifteenth century, the first steps of the dramatic expansion of Western Europe and the growth of new empires created a very different type of relationship between cultures, as domination by European art and misunderstanding or rejection of other arts become the norm, some notable exceptions notwithstanding.

The arts of the intermediate centuries were also affected by numerous movements of people: some slow and almost invisible, others dramatic and highly effective; some ideologically spurred, others purely economic; some involving small numbers of people, others characterized by huge migrations; some with important but temporary effects, others with permanent results. Three examples with particularly striking involvement in the arts are the so-called Silk Road, the three missionary faiths of Buddhism, Christianity and Islam, and the Mongols and Turks. Some of these movements – for instance, the Silk Road and Buddhism or Islam and the Turkish expansion – overlap with each other and some – the spread of Islam and of Christianity, the Mongol invasions – are more dramatic and more important than others. Yet each one illuminates something of the artistic expressions of that time.

The Silk Road

Not much is known about the economics of the Silk Road, which served to move the precious textiles made in China to Mediterranean and Indian markets and which continued even after the Chinese monopoly on the manufacture of silk had been broken in the late sixth century, because the taste for specifically Chinese silks never disappeared. Furthermore, this cross-continents road, as it crossed some of the most forbidding areas of the world, contributed to the movement of other goods, of ideas and of people, even after the Tibetan incursions of the ninth century and its partial revival under Mongol rule.

One artistic consequence was the growth and maintenance at high levels of wealth and artistic creativity of urban centres in Soghd (roughly corresponding to the contemporary republics Uzbekistan and Tajikistan), on the northern and southern edges of the Tarim basin (in modern Xinjiang (Sinkiang) in China), and on the western edges of China proper (from Dun-Huang to Xian). Painting and sculpture in wood and stucco dominated the creativity of these areas, largely because of Buddhism, which became its most visible system of faith, but involving other religions as well such as Christianity, Manichaeism, various forms of Zoroastrianism, shamanism and pagan cults. A visual syncretism with a considerable originality of its own characterizes the art of places like Panjikent, Afrasiyab, Kyzyl or Turfan. It involves themes and ideas from China, India and Iran, and it is probably the availability of these forms which explains the appearance in the Altai region of a strange commemorative sculpture associated with Uighur and other Turkic rulers (see Plates 54, 87, 214, 235).

The Silk Road did not involve large numbers of people, and the objects it carried were relatively few and more or less restricted, in their use, to the upper classes. But these objects became a source of inspiration for the representation of people and for the manufacture of other objects. They expanded the visual vocabulary of artists and consumers who had no connection with the challenging landscape of the road itself. In this sense, the Silk Road is paradigmatic of the importance of relatively small movements of people and goods which can have an effect on the arts because of the prestige attached to what was carried. It also illustrates at least one relatively novel phenomenon of the arts of these centuries. It is the acknowledgement of others than oneself as worthy of honour and representation. Many Soghdian or inner Asian paintings show distinct ethnic groups involved together in religious or other common activities.

Three missionary faiths: Buddhism, Christianity, Islam

These are the three predominant religions of these centuries. All three are missionary religions with universal messages, all three expanded enormously, and all three had major effects on the artistic expression of their followers. This section seeks only to define the effects of their expansion on the development of the arts; more formal questions will be dealt with later.

In the instance of Christianity, the pagans of Northern and Eastern Europe were converted and, as a result, Latin or Cyrillic alphabets became the means by which languages, hitherto (with small exceptions) only spoken, were written down. Furthermore, while some areas were Christianized by slow osmosis affecting a pagan population (Brittany, for instance), in many places colonists and conquerors transformed the land available in their own image. Sometimes the farming, military and urban colonists adopted and developed local languages, at other times they imposed their own or else allowed for the coexistence of two or more literary cultures. One culture was Latin, Greek, or Slavonic: concentrated in the hands of a literate clergy, these usually extra-national languages remained for centuries the languages of learning and of authority. The other one was the vernacular spoken by its inhabitants, and most vernaculars eventually emerged as vehicles for written artistic expression.

The duality of language expression that was derived from movements of people affected literature and thought in all lands except East Asia. In the visual arts, the nature of the investment needed for architecture and the doctrines and practices of the Church, Western or Eastern, led to the development of two major visual expressions of liturgical space and of Christian doctrines, one 'Latin' wherever the Roman Church went, the other 'Greek' wherever the Eastern Church prevailed. Exceptions exist no doubt, but, on a general level, a clear distinction can be established between the longitudinal vision of high naves, multiple apses and fancy sculpted façades of Western Christianity and the dome-centred, inner directed sanctuaries of the Eastern churches, colourfully decorated with paintings and mosaics. When the two meet, as in some twelfth-century buildings in Vladimir in Russia or in Palermo in Sicily, the contrasts are effective but not always harmonious (see Plates 28, 29, 63, 64, 72–75).

Something very similar occurred with Islam. Most early believers were Arabs, and they converted and conquered regions occupied by linguistic cultures other than Arabic. Large numbers of Arab Muslims also settled in areas like southern Spain, Central Asia and, later, the east coast of Africa, which were far removed from the Arabian heartland. The intensity of the conversion process varied from area to area and from time to time, but everywhere Arabic became the language of religion and of learning. Little by little, other languages adapted the Arabic script to their own phonetic systems. For Persian, the first remaining fragments in the new script which are dated come from the tenth century, while the earliest known and dated Turkish text in an Arabic script is a dictionary of the eleventh century. The close relationship between Islam and the Arabic script is clear from an example like that of the fourteenth-century inscriptions from Kilwa in Tanzania, where the script is clear but not the language. In fact, many examples exist, from China to the Christian West, of Arabic letters used apparently as pleasurable ornament, without a written meaning. Thus, even though the local ways of many different cultures remained beyond conversion (as in the cases of Iran and of Africa) and independently from domination by the Muslim ruling classes (as in the Indian subcontinent), the consistent presence of the Arabic alphabet gave a comparable formal patina to regions that often did not share the same language. These changes, in so many different places, were made possible by movements of people and, sometimes, of goods, resulting directly from the existence of the new faith.

Formal matters like letters were not the only result of the Muslim expansion. In the late seventh and especially in the eighth centuries, North Africa became arabicized for ever, Andalusia and Central Asia for more limited periods of time. A related phenomenon was the expansion of Iranian literary culture into India and beyond, which was a direct result of the spread of Islam with an Iranian flavour. On a smaller scale, the oral traditions of Kurds, Berbers, Ethiopians, Malaysians and Indonesians were affected by the arrival of Muslim traders, missionaries or soldiers. And, since most of the new arrivals were men, who married local women, the emerging culture was often the means by which households were held together. A remarkable role was played by women in the maintenance and even in the creation of culture in areas of physical and religious expansion.

Beyond formal features like the Arabic script, literary ones like the spread of Arabic, Persian or Turkish narratives and poetic genres, or cultural ones such as the fostering of locally meaningful amalgams between a new faith and old traditions, the spread of Islam through the movements of Muslims had a significant impact on a number of functions and forms of architecture (see Figure 18). Muslims built mosques wherever they went, and a map could be drawn of the spread of a classical early Islamic hypostyle mosque with its ample spaces on hundreds of columns (Cordova, Kairouan, Cairo, Samarra, Konya, Herāt, Delhi); of an Iranian type based on a courtyard with one to four large vaulted halls (eyvans), developed in the twelfth century (Ardistan, Iṣfahān, Bukhārā, Samarkand); of small nine-bay mosques (Toledo, Cairo, Balkh); and of a dome-centred mosque just appearing in the emerging Ottoman Empire (Bursa, Edirne, the Fatih mosque in Istanbul). It is difficult to know whether the spread of these various types derived from choices made by large numbers of people recalling memories of some common past elsewhere (as may well have been the case with the early art of Andalusia or the later one of northern India), or by some ideological reasoning on the part of rulers and other patrons of architecture. What is certain, however, is that the spread of Islam is most immediately visible through architectural forms like minarets and domes grown in very circumscribed local circumstances but acquiring pan-Islamic meanings (see Plates 195–209).

Buddhism, the third of the missionary universal systems of faith, also spread from its land of birth, northern India, to many other places, mostly, during the period with which we are concerned, to Sri Lanka, Korea and Japan, eventually disappearing from India itself but having already established itself in China before AD 600. This expansion was not the work of large migrations of people but of small groups of missionaries and of pilgrims travelling back to the sites of Gautama's activities, like the Chinese pilgrims, Xuan Zhuang for example, who left wonderful accounts of their travels. As a result, this expansion did not have the linguistic results of Muslim and Christian expansions. But it did affect the imagery of the arts, as will be discussed at greater length later on, with a powerful narrative of a holy life, with tangible visions of an eschatology, and with an emotional relationship to holy representations. Literature, the visual world and the manufacture of objects were more affected than was architecture, although commemorative monuments like stupas did travel from India to China for a short period of time. But, perhaps most importantly, the Buddhist presence provided all of Asia, except for its Semitic western edges, with a vision of beauty, a dream of physical perfection, so that, even when Buddhism had nearly disappeared from Iran and Afghanistan, Persian poetry still described visual perfection as 'Buddha-like'.

Turks and Mongols

As early as the ninth century, Turkish soldiers formed the backbone of the 'Abbasid army in Iraq and often rose to important administrative positions throughout the Muslim world. The Arab *littérateur* al-Jaḥiẓ wrote elegant essays in praise of the Turks. A century later, Turkish dynasties in Central Asia led the first raids of Muslims into the plains of northern India. An expansion began which eventually brought Ottoman armies to Vienna, Turkic rulers to most of southern Russia and the Ukrainian plains, and Turkic or Mongol leaders to South and South-East Asia. These ethnic and military movements revolutionized the linguistic map of Eastern Europe as well as of Western and Central Asia and introduced into many lands of ancient cultures a new set of habits and memories from remote lands and distant pasts. The Turkic expansion acquired an additional impulse

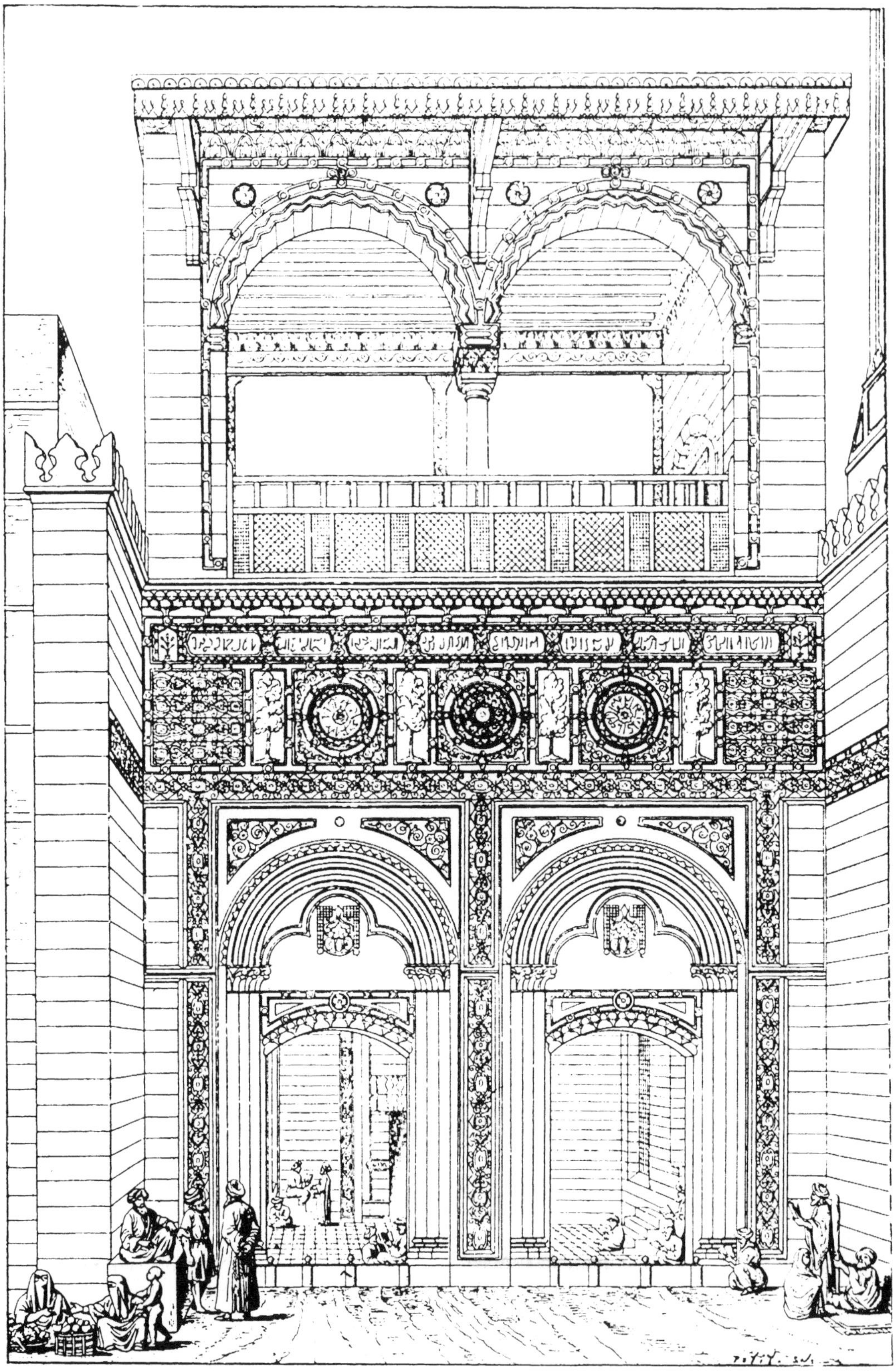

Figure 18 Gateway to al-Azhar Mosque, Cairo (Egypt), founded in the tenth century AD, continually restored and added to from the thirteenth to the fifteenth (after Le Bon, G., *La civilisation des Arabes*, Paris 1883, p. 158).

by becoming tied to the surge of the Mongols in the thirteenth and fourteenth centuries, as only Japan, the Mediterranean and Western Europe, within Eurasia, escaped the appearance of the followers of Chinggis Khān or those of Tīmūr (Tamerlame).

These momentous events and changes in population and in the ethnic composition of different lands left many traces in the arts, but at different levels of importance and of effectiveness. At the most practical and most immediate level, the Mongol states made possible artistic exchanges. Tīmūr and his successors in Iran and Central Asia compelled artisans and architects from Shīrāz in south-west Iran to build, plan and decorate the cities, especially Samarkand and its hinterland, which he and the military aristocracy around him developed and adorned in Khurāsān and Transoxania. The Tīmūrid 'renaissance' in all the arts, painting as well as architecture, can, in part at least, be attributed to this more or less forced migration of artists and artisans. Earlier in the fourteenth century, Persian artisans were sent to China and, at the academy created in Tabrīz (in northwestern Iran) by the vizier Rashīd al-Dīn, Chinese painters helped to train Persian artists in new directions by introducing formulas of composition (grouping of personages into clusters of two or three, landscape arranged on oblique rather than parallel lines, crooked trunks of trees, and so on) and techniques (paint used like ink, economy of colour) which, as a later text put it, 'opened the face of painting' in Iran. And in a similar fashion, even though the exact story is still unclear through lack of neat archaeological data, the growth and eventual spread of 'blue and white' pottery in China and in Iran and its transformation into the most ubiquitous fancy ceramic found in the trading ports of West Africa as well as in most of Europe are the results of the contacts in technical competencies and in artistic taste made possible by the Mongol invasion.

Among the most unexpected effects of these invasions was the appearance in Qarāqorum, the Mongol capital, of the French jeweller Guillaume Boucher. He had been taken prisoner in Hungary and brought to Mongolia as a rare technician specializing in metalwork. In the Mongolian capital, he constructed marvels of gold and silver, including a tree with snakes intertwined in its branches which served as conduits for alcoholic beverages. On top of the tree, an angel with a trumpet would send blasts to the kitchen whenever refills were needed. It has also been suggested, although not universally accepted, that Italian architects were involved in the construction of the spectacular dome over the mausoleum of Oljāytū at Sultāniyeh in northern Iran, as its construction is technically comparable to the equally innovative technique of the Duomo in Florence.

A second level of importance for Turco-Mongol movements of people lies in the contact with old cultures based on written traditions, which led to the writing down of traditions that had remained oral until then. A new Mongol literature came to light which is known best for its historical and religious books, but also for an epic poetry whose texts have been preserved in seventeenth-century histories like those of Sanang-setchen. The old Soghdian alphabet was used to transcribe Uighur literature, and Islamic religious texts appear in Chaghatai, most interestingly the mystical stories of the Prophet's Night Journey. Tatar poems are recorded in Arabic script, but the most significant changes are in Anatolia and Thrace, where first a Turkish popular literature, then a religious Islamic one, and finally a courtly one around the princes, all developed because of the massive immigration of Turks and Turkmens.

The Turkic languages were not alone in blossoming as a result of these migrations and conquests. The culture of the Turkish and Mongol elites was often Persian, because their Islamization took place, most of the time, within regions dominated by Iranian culture. It is this Iranian culture which was transmitted to Turkish courts in Anatolia and in India and, as a result, a literature in Persian and an art of expression, especially miniature painting, with Persian conventions became the norm in the Ottoman world as well as in the Indian sub-continent and in some, but not all, of its South- East Asian extensions (see Plates 113, 219).

There is, finally, a third level to the importance of the Turkic and Mongol migrations and invasions: the mythical level. In Europe, these invasions cut the Eastern Christian world from the Western one and thus contributed to the originality of later, mostly religious, traditions in Lithuania, Ukraine, Russia, Romania, Bulgaria, Serbia and Greece. They also postponed Eastern Europe's direct involvement in the momentous intellectual and artistic changes of the fourteenth and especially fifteenth centuries in Italy, which were about to revolutionize representation and thought. Everywhere, the Mongol world became a myth and the stories of travelers like Marco Polo were enlarged into fancy legends. In China, the tragic stories of Lady Wenji and of Lady Wang Zhaojun involved their journeys in the lands of the Uighurs or of the Mongols, and these journeys were lovingly described in literature as forms of exile into uncultured lands, while painters used the stories to represent, on the one hand, the sophisticated taste of the Chinese and, on the other, the 'different' alienness of Central Asia rulers (see Plate 13). In a more immediate fashion, Japanese scrolls depicted the deities of the seas and of the winds protecting Japan by defeating the Mongol invaders. And the Turco-Mongol world represented itself as a myth in a stunning series of images now in Istanbul and presumably executed in Central Asia. Attributed much later to a mysterious 'Black Pen' (*Siyāh Qalam*), they depict men, women, children and animals in tortured and often monstrously satirical shapes suggesting something of the unreality of the imaginary rather than the precision of concrete memories. The initial artistic language of these representations derives mostly from the representational art of China, occasionally from that of Iran. From China, these images, wherever they were made, did not borrow the sophisticated near-contemporary styles of Song painting but those of the older and somewhat cruder Buddhist paintings from the sanctuaries and commemorative monuments of the ancient Silk Road. The three themes outlined in this section – a commercial venture, the missionary faiths, a migration of conquerors – are not the only aspects of the phenomena of migration or of movements of people which would have affected the artistic expression of these centuries. There were other recurring or unique events which compelled significant movements of people. Such are the Crusades in the twelfth and thirteenth centuries, the spread of Manichaean beliefs in Iran and Central Asia as well as in the Balkans and the Alps, pilgrimages of many faiths and, most particularly, the centripetal obligation for Muslims to go to Mecca once in their lifetimes, Brahmanical and Buddhist expansion into South-East Asia, and many others. The effect of all these movements is a curious paradox. On the one hand, the possibilities for the knowledge of different beliefs and ways of life than one's own increased dramatically and one can point to dozens of artistic and linguistic ways or to ways of living – things as varied as blue and white ceramics, travel literature, clothes, and furniture – which demonstrate awareness of other peoples and of other cultures and appreciation of the qualities of these 'others'. Yet, at the same time, these contacts, migrations and changes often contributed to the development of local languages, of differentiated arts, of individual tastes and cultures. They fostered a sense of separateness and of uniqueness. National or at least ethnic literature appeared during these centuries, and epic traditions often condemned others as enemies, as the perennially dangerous 'Tūrān' facing 'Īrān' in the Persian *Shāh-Nāmeh* composed at the court of a Turkish prince around the year 1000. The paradox is well illustrated by an Arab traveller from Morocco, Ibn Baṭṭūṭa, who visited most of then known Africa and Asia.

As a Muslim, he could find people like him almost everywhere, but he was also very keenly aware that many Muslims, not to speak of non-Muslims, were very different from him.

THE EXPRESSIONS OF BELIEFS

It is common to refer to these centuries as the Age of Faith. This traditional expression is, in many ways, valid. Religion dominated the definitions that men made of themselves and of others, and much of the creative energies of the time were devoted to building, beautifying and otherwise expressing the sacred. But it is also a misleading expression, for it implies that later centuries had developed alternative concerns at the expense of religious ones and that non-religious purposes were absent from the arts between 600 and 1500. In fact, it is only in Western Europe in the sixteenth century and elsewhere in the nineteenth and twentieth centuries that alternative values, avowedly secular ones or national ones, truly competed with pious ones, and, at the same time, purposes remote from holy ones did affect the arts before 1500. Let us say simply that religious values and religious terms were the most common ways for self-definition and for the identification of the groups with which one associated or which one rejected. Towards the end of the period, linguistic identification began to take over as the primary manner of recognizing oneself and others.

This chapter concentrates on three aspects of religions as they affected the arts: the making of restricted or holy spaces, the ways of representing the holy or the divine, and the processes of symbolization of the faith. In each case, examples are selected without any attempt at being exhaustive and especially without any significant concern for chronology and development.

Holy and restricted spaces

All religions have spaces restricted in meaning or in purpose to those who belong to the community of the faithful. Membership in a community was generally automatic and came through birth or marriage, although conversions, willed or forced, took place as well. The acknowledgement of membership usually took place through a ceremony, at home or in specific spaces devoted to the expression of newly sworn allegiance. Such are the baptisms of Christianity, which took place originally in distinct buildings known as baptisteries and eventually incorporated into churches. And public spaces in African villages were transformed into restricted ones by decoration or by the positioning of participants when young men or women were accepted into the community as adults.

Holy places were often built spaces, but they need not be, as one of the more intriguing feature of a sacred space is that, in nearly all cultures, certain types of liturgical behaviour like processions or the forming of a circle transform any space into a holy one, at least for the duration of the ceremony. At times, mountains and valleys in India, Africa or Central Asia become sacred when contemplated or visited by those who believe in their holiness and remain forbidding or isolated natural phenomena for all others. Often these places, invisible to those who do not belong to a community, are connected with memories of an ancient past or with the dead, ancestors buried there and whose graves are lost, as with the Mongol or Turkic rulers of inner Asia, a pattern carried for a while by the Mongols to Iran and to Central Russia. At times, as in China, ancestors were buried in their house and remain for ever the guardians of the living.

In short, religious spaces are much more than categories of building. They can be natural or living areas, but it is the act of building which occasionally transformed these spaces into systems of formal arrangements associated with individual religions and even into works of art. The following three categories of commemorative, congregational and social spaces for religious purposes are examples of a rich and complex typology of religious architecture.

Commemorative spaces

What is meant by this term is, first of all, a single monument or complex, like the Holy Sepulchre in Jerusalem (commemorating the death and burial of Christ, first built in the early part of the fourth century and very much restored over the centuries), the tomb of al-Shāfi'i in Cairo (to the mausoleum founder of one of the four major schools of Islamic law within Sunni Islam, begun in the twelfth century and often redone), or the complex of Imām Rezā in Meshed (begun on a major scale in the fourteenth century on the site of burial of a direct descendant of 'Alī, holy to Shī'ites but continuously redone). In these and thousands of typologically comparable buildings, an individual or an event with an acknowledged relationship to the faith through lineage, martyrdom, prophecy, theophany or witnessing is being recalled by the construction of space. While the monuments expressing the behaviour of men, for instance death for the faith or the glorification of a good life, tend to repeat others and to follow formal patterns which cut across cultures and religions (for instance through the presence of a fancy cupola), monuments commemorating theophanies tend to be unique.

The most remarkable among them is the Ka'ba in Mecca, a pre-Islamic sanctuary of Arabian paganism understood through the actions of and revelations to the Prophet Muḥammad as the 'House of God' built by Abraham, the first agent of the divine revelation which ended with the Prophet Muḥammad. It became the *qibla* or direction of prayer for all Muslims, the focus of the yearly pilgrimage and a pole of attraction to the mystic. From the point of view of this chapter, two features of the Ka'ba are remarkable. One is that it was, in spite of its structural simplicity (an approximate cube of relatively small dimensions, roughly 15 by 12 by 10.5 metres), never copied before some twentieth-century anomalies. The other one is that its holiness extended beyond itself, eventually to include the whole city of Mecca and the area around it. Over the first two centuries of Islam, a visual expression of that holiness was created through the razing of the houses which surrounded the sanctuary and the construction of what is visible today after many enlargements and extensions: a vast open space surrounded by porticoes, and a small number of additional spots sanctified by holy events, like the Zemzem well, which God made available to Hagar in order to feed her infant son Ishmael (see Plate 181).

Equally extraordinary and unique is the case of the Dome of the Rock in Jerusalem, completed in 691–2 by order of the Umayyad caliph 'Abd al-Malik. It is located on the holy area of the ancient Jewish Temple, flattened by the Roman army in the second century AD. Its initial purpose was probably to proclaim the Islamic revelation in the city of Christ, but quite rapidly it and the large area around it (now called the Ḥaram al-Sharīf – the Holy Sanctuary) became a space devoted to the commemoration of the Night Journey of the Prophet, an event which acquired over the centuries profound mystical connotations, and to the expectation of the life to come, as Jerusalem was destined to be the place of the resurrection. The architectural forms of the Dome of the Rock, a cupola on a high drum surrounded by a two-aisled octagon, and its beautiful mosaic decoration, are all in the language of the current art of the Mediterranean, but the combination of artistic terms found in this building was then and has remained unique (see Plates 45, 46).

Such utterly unique religious commemorative monuments are relatively rare. Elsewhere within the Muslim world, tombs of holy men and women abound in many shapes and sizes, but nearly always with highly visible cupolas. Christianity had one monument unique in its holiness, the rotunda around the tomb of Christ in Jerusalem, but even it became a model often meant to be imitated in complex medieval interpretations of its circular forms (see Plate 46). Commemorative implications suffuse the crypts and transepts of many Western churches and the enclosing domes of the Eastern ones. The idea of a *martyrium*-type of building devoted to the memory of individuals and events which testify to the presence of God pervades most forms of Christian church architecture. Similarly, the Muslims developed the idea of the *mashhad*, an Arabic word which has exactly the same meaning as *martyrium*, 'place of witnessing'.

Buddhism and Hinduism did not emphasize to the same extent the individual specificity of the holy place and did not commemorate individuals or holy events in the same manner as Islam and Christianity. Yet stupas, the often huge mounds frequently covered with representations and surrounded by railings and gates, were commemorating the Buddha's presence, as, for instance, in the twelfth-century complex of Polonnaruva in Sri Lanka. In a place like Vārānasi, commemorative sanctuaries were built for the edification of pilgrims. And, in the apparently very alien world of Toltec and Aztec Mexico, commemoration and liturgy ordered the huge spaces of temples.

Commemoration was also an important factor in the manufacture of objects, often sacred souvenirs from holy places, and of representations of the holy (see below). For, in a deeper sense, the true expression of commemoration took place in the practices of the faithful, formal liturgies as in Hinduism and Christianity, or in special events like the Muslim *ḥajj*, as well as in private devotions in all faiths with purposes and expressions as wide as human nature.

Congregational spaces

Assembly for collective or individual prayer, liturgy, sacrifices or any combination of these pious activities was a major source of inspiration for what are essentially congregational buildings.

The simplest, at least in its original shape, was the mosque, the *masjid al-jāmi'*, *masjid-i jum'eh* or simply *masjid* and *jāmi'* (in modern Turkish *cami*), of Islam. The roots from which these words derive have a clear meaning: 'to gather' (*jama'a*) and 'to prostrate one's self [before God]' (*sajada*). Initially, the faithful gathered in the house of the Prophet in Medina, whose court lined with shaded areas to the north and south became the space identified with the presence of the fledgling community. A deeper colonnade indicated the *qibla*, or

Figure 19 Saint Sophia, Kiev (Ukraine), reconstruction of original eleventh-century state (drawing after Brunow, in Schung-Ville, C.; du Ry, C. J., *L'art de Byzance et de l'Islam*, Brussels 1979, p. 11).

direction of prayer toward Mecca; a small pulpit with three steps served for the Prophet to speak and to receive the allegiance of his followers; the call to prayer was made from the roof. Out of these humble beginnings came the classical hypostyle mosque with its enormous covered space on multiple columns or piers, with its courtyard often provided with the façade of an axial nave higher than the surrounding ones, with a fancily decorated niche in the back wall (the *mihrāb*) indicating the presence of the Prophet and indirectly the direction of prayer, with a frequently elaborate chair or pulpit (the *minbar*), much later with one or more tall minarets serving many functions, only one of which was to call to prayer.

In many cities – from Cordova in Spain (examples from the ninth and tenth centuries) to Konya in Turkey (thirteenth century) and, with modifications, to Samarkand in Uzbekistan (early fifteenth century) – where fairly early hypostyle buildings have survived until today or can be reconstructed with a fair degree of certainty, the simple requirements of the faith were transformed into major works of art through fancy decoration (especially around the *mihrāb* area), through elaborate gates, through the quality of the construction techniques, and through artistic modular compositions based on geometry (see Plates 199–209). These transformations were probably the results of two factors other than the liturgical (requirement for collective prayer) and social (for many centuries, the mosque served as the school and a hostel for the community, and some of these functions are still present in contemporary practice) functions of the mosque: the need to show an Islamic presence in non-Muslim lands or to non-Muslims; and the patronage of caliphal or princely authority (see Plates 65, 66). The aesthetic expression of the mosque was often the consequence of its power.

Comparable arguments and conclusions can be developed around Christianity and the medieval church in Europe. It too was affected by the authority of rulers: Carolingian emperors in Aachen; Russian princes in Kiev, Moscow or Vladimir; Serbian and Bulgarian Kings in Sopocani and Boiana, respectively; the kings of France in Saint Denis or the Sainte Chapelle in Paris, all sponsored churches for the celebration of the liturgy but at times combined this congregational purpose with a commemorative one and with the glorification of individual princes and dynasties. The most powerful patron of churches was, however, the Church itself, a complex organization with its own hierarchies of priests and monks and with very varying relationships to the faithful.

The basic plans of churches – longitudinal basilical hall with several naves in Western Europe, dome-centred or cross-in-square in Eastern Europe – had been established by the sixth century and, aside from the formation and elaboration of local styles described elsewhere in this volume, the history of medieval Christian architecture consisted of the structural transformations affecting these two types of buildings and in the decoration applied to them. Two aspects of these modulations can be highlighted.

One is size, as both in breadth and in height, medieval churches changed immensely over the centuries, even though the liturgical necessities of a central altar visible from everywhere and of masses that had to be heard restricted the congregational space of churches, especially by comparison with mosques. There are the small Mozarabic churches of north central Spanish villages in the ninth and tenth centuries, and few medieval churches in the Balkans or in Scandinavia were ever very large. But, already in the eleventh century, the church of Saint Sernin in Toulouse was meant to accommodate thousands of pilgrims, and the huge Hagia Sophia in Kiev (see Figure 19), inspired by the great sixth-century masterpiece in Constantinople, dominated the space around it as well as making room for thousands of worshippers. In these examples, space was limited by the technology of building established in the late Roman Empire and in some of its outlying areas, like Armenia. For centuries, details rather than basic structures were modified. With the technological revolution of the Gothic age – pointed arches, ribs, flying buttresses – striking extensions to the height of churches were made possible and led to the dominating cathedrals of Northern Europe, whose naves and spires towered over the emerging cities of the thirteenth century (see Plates 28, 29, 75). Dozens of examples (Amiens, Beauvais, Laon, Cologne) are over 100 m in height, a size which has no relationship to the practical needs of the liturgy and only serves as a sort of cosmic cover and filter of light (see Figure 20). There is no single explanation for the technological change which took place some time in the twelfth century, but its spread, if not its invention, is certainly connected with the growth

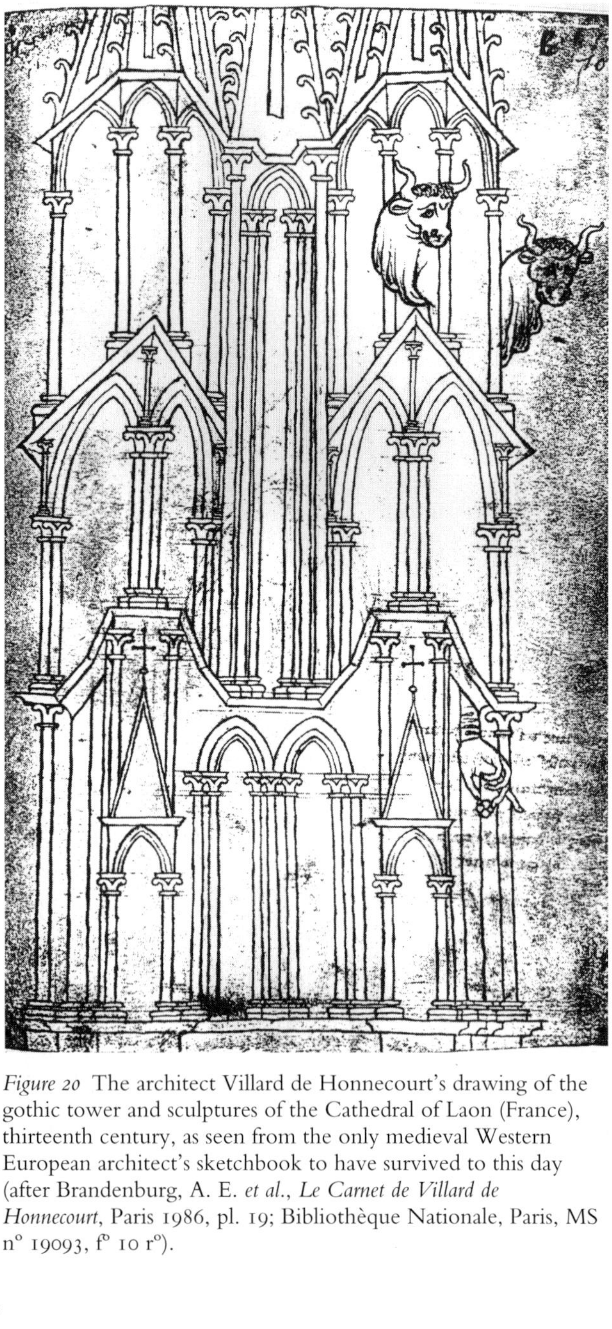

Figure 20 The architect Villard de Honnecourt's drawing of the gothic tower and sculptures of the Cathedral of Laon (France), thirteenth century, as seen from the only medieval Western European architect's sketchbook to have survived to this day (after Brandenburg, A. E. *et al.*, *Le Carnet de Villard de Honnecourt*, Paris 1986, pl. 19; Bibliothèque Nationale, Paris, MS n° 19093, f° 10 r°).

of cities and of a new type of urban pride and wealth. At more or less the same time, the Muslim fascination with the height and ornamentation of minarets (numerous examples in Iran and Cairo) began to grow from the same kind of urban milieu (see Plates 202–209).

The second characteristic of Christian congregational building is its decoration. Paintings and mosaics remained predominant in the East, but in the West, from the eleventh century onwards a renewal occurred in the art of sculpture, as portals and then many other parts of churches acquired a complex religious imagery. Somewhat later, stained glass in windows filtered the light of churches, diffusing on the natural stones of construction the light of divine revelation. Much more than mosques with their subdued decoration limited for the most part to writing and to floral or geometric ornament, churches are provided with a surface, with a skin, which transmits other messages than those of an architecture of technical virtuosity and spatial inventiveness, wrapping the faithful in the celebration of the faith and proclaiming to the outside world the presence of the faith and the wealth or power of its patrons (see Plates 48, 145, 146, 148, 152).

The great Hindu and Jain temples of India, Cambodia and Indonesia share many characteristics with Muslim and Christian congregational buildings (see Figure 21). They occupy large spaces for enormous crowds of worshippers, they are carefully oriented and composed according to very ancient principles of sacred geometry in order to be attuned to the permanent forces of nature, and they usually comprise a central focus in the shape of an elaborate pyramidal structure which is both the home of the holy and the proclamation of that holiness to the surrounding world. Some of the temples, like the celebrated Cambodian ones at Angkor (eighth–thirteenth centuries), were royal foundations and reflect the power and ideological ambitions of monarchies. Most of the surfaces of these temples were covered with sculptures, as they were in the much earlier Buddhist temples of India and Afghanistan (see Plates 221, 225–229). In the early caves of Ajanta and in the Buddhist sanctuaries of

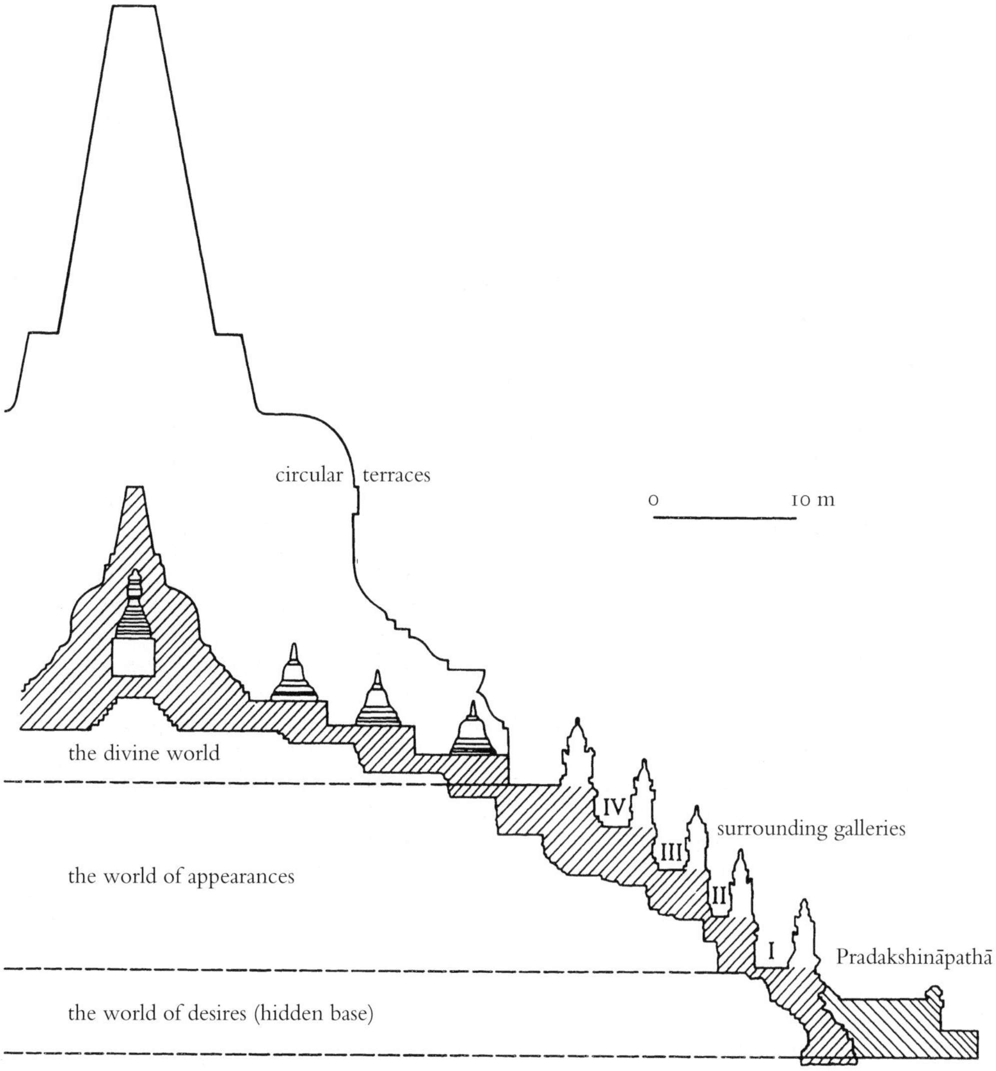

Figure 21 The temple of Borobudur, Java (Indonesia), eighth–ninth century AD original idealized projection, present outline and cosmic symbolism (after Nou, J. L.; Frédéric, L., *Borobudur*, Paris 1994, p. 25).

inner Asia, however, paintings often replaced sculptures (see Plate 80).

Congregational spaces were not always highly structured, specifically built, architectural compositions. In the areas of today's Mongolia, Sinkiang and Kazakhstan, as well as in Central and West Africa, in the oases and deserts of Semitic Arabia before the appearance of Islam, in the high valleys and plateaux of the Atlas, natural spaces like a secluded valley or open spaces within the built environment of villages and other settlements were, at certain times, transformed into collective congregational spaces. They may then acquire temporary props like tents, platforms, flags, and other implements and symbols, which are not well preserved but which constitute an alternative architecture to the permanent one of brick, wood or stone. It is likely that, in the past, as today, this alternative architecture often coexisted with formally built mosques, temples and churches. Such is the case of the *muṣallā*, a well-defined but barely built space outside Muslim cities used for major feasts only. Such is also the case with the transformation of urban spaces in Iran and northern India during the performance of the so-called 'passion plays' of Shīʿism re-enacting the martyrdom of Ḥusayn. The latter, with their buildings of models of architecture, with their portable stages, and with their processions in streets decorated with textiles, are best known after 1500, but some prototypes must have existed in the period under consideration. In the Christian West, too, liturgical plays and processions transfigured, at specific times, the streets and squares of cities. By definition, such temporary arrangements of space do not leave architectural remains, but they often shape the taste of artisans and of the public.

Service spaces

An original development of medieval Islamic culture was to provide a monumental character to service institutions involved in healing the sick, forming religious and legal elites, gathering together men (and, in a few cases, women) belonging to the same sects or claiming the same religious allegiances, and housing veterans of holy wars. The most celebrated of these establishments was the *madrasa* (school for legal and religious thought), which, from the twelfth century onwards, appeared in every city from Morocco to northern India, with many dozens remaining in a city like Cairo. *Khānāqahs* or *khanegāhs* (monastery-like communal establishments), *ribāṭs* or *rabāṭs* (initially residences for warriors, later for members of religious groups), and hospitals also abound and are often difficult to distinguish from the ubiquitous *madrasa*. Nearly all these service buildings consist of variations on a single theme: a fancy portal serving as a sort of proclamation or advertisement to the outside, the domed tomb of the founder and patron, an open court surrounded by rooms for collective functions like praying, tending to the sick or learning, and occasionally living quarters. Many of them, especially the earlier ones in Syria, were relatively modest in size and in presence, even though sponsored by ruling princes and dedicated to the profound ideological purposes of restoring orthodox Islam and protecting it from sectarian dissensions. But in examples like those of the *madrasa* of Sultan Ḥasan in Cairo (mid-fourteenth century), of Gawhar Shād in Meshed (first half of the fifteenth century) or of Khargird (mid-fifteenth century) in eastern Iran, we encounter enormous and monumental establishments on many floors, with elaborate decorative programmes, and with aesthetic ambitions and expectations which surpass their religious purposes. At the other end of a scale of visual presumption lies a place like Bisṭām in northern Iran, where, over several centuries, an aggregate of practical functions ranging from collective mosques to rooms for solitary meditation and gateways built by rulers came to create a small 'city of God'. The Muslim phenomenon of an architecture of high quality for differentiated services commanded and supported by the faith is unique in the scope of the functions involved. But comparable building activities existed elsewhere as well. There are Buddhist monasteries and there are Christian ones. In the West, the most beautiful monastic foundations are the cloisters from Romanesque times, as at Silos in Spain, Moissac in France and, in a different context, Monreale in Sicily. Harmoniously composed spaces with a brilliant array of carved stone capitals and other forms of sculpted decoration served as focal points for the practical and meditative lives of monks and nuns as well as of their guests. Hospitals, chapels, houses and schools appear in cities after the thirteenth century. In Eastern Europe, monastic establishments often became walled and turreted, small or large 'cities of God' with churches, chapels, hostels, libraries, living or guest quarters, even jails, all fitted in or around an open space.

The cultural importance of these service monuments of religious inspiration extends much beyond their architectural significance. They were centres for the copying of books and other means for the transmission of religious and secular lore. Monasteries and *madrasas* formed networks from city to city and area to area through which everything from new ideas to changes in taste for styles of writing could be explored and transformed. Within Christianity and Buddhism, they were also important centres for the invention, performance and growth of music as well as for the preservation of musical information, mostly through manuscripts. Islam was more ambivalent about the pious values of music, but a religious thinker like al-Ghazālī did write on the psychological legitimacy of music, because of its soothing effects on the soul of practitioners and listeners alike.

While it is possible to generalize the functions of an architecture of the faith, the many spaces created for the piety of believers in several different religious systems, it is almost impossible to propose formal generalizations. There is no common style between the architectures of so many different regions and of four or five major religious groups. Styles and technologies of building are for the most part independent of specific religions. And yet, as one looks at the thousands of buildings involved in the remarks of the preceding pages, two partly contradictory concerns seem to dominate all religious architecture during these centuries, and probably at other times as well. One is the concern of proclamation, whereby the religious monument forces itself on the living or natural landscape. Towers, domes, fancy portals, narrow pyramids, flying buttresses and many other devices are used to proclaim the presence of the faith, indeed of the divine, among men. These proclamations are, for the most part, directed to the faithful of the proclaiming monument, as they reassure and exhort by their very presence. But they are also proclamations to those who are not members of the faith: they seek to convert or to dominate, as with the Dome of the Rock in Jerusalem, the Quṭb Minār in Delhi or the Fātiḥ mosque in Constantinople, built shortly after the conquest of the city in 1453 on the site of the Byzantine Church of the Holy Apostles, where all Christian emperors had been buried. These were indeed centuries during which the discourse, visual or oral, of the faith stopped being restricted to believers alone, as diverse communities lived next to each other, and each one wanted to proclaim its truth.

The second concern is that of restriction, as the ceremonies, prayers, liturgies, offerings and sacrifices were meant to take place without alien visitors, even with occasional exceptions made to impress foreigners or barbarians. Most religious architecture required the creation of boundaries, of limits between public functions common and accessible to all men and women and those restricted to the faithful. Walls and barriers are found everywhere, but in gates and portals the two functions of proclamation and of exclusion merge into each other.

Representations of the sacred

Whether fully expressed through learned discussions or operating instinctively, without philosophical or theological explorations, the question of the legitimacy of representing the holy permeates all the major religions of Europe, Asia and Africa. This is particularly true for revealed religions like Christianity and Islam, with their belief in a transcendental and invisible God active in the world now as he had been in the past. His reality is absolute and incomprehensible and, therefore unique and impossible to copy or imitate. The most thorough discussion of these issues of representing the divine occurred during what is known as the crisis of iconoclasm, which shook the Eastern Christian world of Byzantium between the end of the seventh century and 843, when an official doctrine about the nature of images was elaborated and accepted by the main authorities of the Church. The theological, philosophical and historical arguments debated during this century and a half led, ultimately and almost unwittingly, to questions about the very possibility of representing whatever is known but not seen and about the true nature of that which is seen.

The Byzantine phenomenon is called 'iconoclasm' because the social and political consequences of this particular movement were often the physical destruction of images. Such destructions were rare under Muslim rule until much later, but, almost from the very beginning of its existence, the public art of Muslims omits representations of people, animals and anything that can be construed as alive. As a reaction to the prevailing artistic ways of Christianity, paganism, Hinduism and Buddhism, and in answer to very precise questions on the part of the faithful, Islam developed its own doctrine, which is appropriately called 'aniconism' since it does not lead so much to the destruction of representations as to their avoidance altogether. Western Christianity never really abandoned representations, but arguments about their value (or lack thereof) lingered throughout the Middle Ages and explain the Protestant iconoclasm of the sixteenth century. Buddhism was usually quite tolerant of all varieties of behaviour, but, in the ninth century, a relatively short-lived prohibition against representations was proclaimed in China, and some destruction of images took place.

The reasons for this concern for the legitimacy of representing the living world are both general and specific. The specific ones apply primarily to Christianity and to Islam. Both religions were strongly influenced by the ancient and very forceful Jewish proscription against the representation of all living things. But they were also influenced by Platonic and especially Neo-Platonic thought, which had developed elaborate constructs dealing with the relationship between a subject, its representation, and its theoretical and ideal model, or else its true (as opposed to apparent) existence. At the same time, they were under the almost daily impact of a technology of representation issued from classical antiquity which could provide the illusion of almost anything otherwise seen. And finally, all these religions were missionary religions and knew that, in worlds of predominant illiteracy, representations and other visually perceived signs could be used for teaching and conversion. Images could be lessons for the illiterate as well as ways of glorifying the divine and the holy by surrounding it with beauty and with visions of everything from holy history to the afterlife. All religious systems except Islam accepted the notion that images could be used for the purposes of enlightening the faithful or the catechumens and for honouring God, Christ, the Virgin, the Prophets, the Buddha, and all sorts of saints.

But all religions also had to face the possibility, almost the likelihood, of idolatry, that is to say of the transformation of representations into whatever it is that they were supposed to represent. Hence, in Buddhism as in Christianity, all justifications for images argued that the image itself is but a material object which may have acquired some holiness from the personage or story depicted on it, but it is only an intermediary to that personage or to that story. In reality, this last step was not always taken by all believers, and images became operating agents in the lives of men and women. They cured the sick, they saved cities from their enemies, they protected the good from the bad, and occasionally they were even worshipped. To prevent the dangers inherent in the worship of inanimate objects, Islam or, more precisely, the Arab leaders of early Muslim communities, quite instinctively and without initially making a doctrine of it (the Qur'ān does not contain any formal statement opposing images), simply learned to avoid images because of their potential as idols. It is only later, probably not before the middle of the eighth century, that more thoughtful reasoning was provided to justify these early rejections.

For the visual arts at large, however, these debates are important in identifying a key ambition of all the arts inspired by a faith: to define and then to reproduce the intelligible or emotional reality of the sacred. It could be done in narrative fashion, as churches or Hindu temples; illuminated books or portable objects in all faiths outside Islam (with notable exceptions after 1300) depicted sacred histories: the stories of the Old and New Testaments, the life of the Buddha, the adventures of Shiva, the activities of thousands of saints and divinities. It could be done in summary form, as events and stories are picked up and then simplified into expressions required by liturgical obligations or habits (books of prayers and missals in Christianity, mantras in Hinduism); transformed into icons with personally or collectively accepted holiness (best-known examples are Russian or Greek, but there are equivalents from India); or functional ones like liturgical implements or souvenirs from holy places (phials from Jerusalem, chalices and patens for the celebration of mass, boxes for relics, implements bought and carried as souvenirs from temples and holy sites, prayer beads). If not strictly speaking narrative, these images can be descriptive, as sacred events or personages are depicted on the walls of temples and churches. They can be evocative, as God the Father appears, in Byzantine mosaics, as Pantocrator (all-powerful) in the shape of Christ and surrounded by angels and archangels or, in Western European portals, as a paternal ruler or a judge (see Plate 59). In a similar way, tall, smiling and motionless

Buddhas welcome everyone to reach perfection (see Plates 82, 83).

Through these images of the divine and of events, accomplished or not, involving or pertaining to the divine and to the faithful, all major religious systems except Islam raised the fundamental question whether that which is real and intelligible rather than visible can be expressed so as to be seen by the eyes. It is a question to which there never will be a satisfactory answer, and some of the Byzantine theologians realized that the technical concreteness of a work of art almost by definition restricted its ability to 'represent' the intelligible in the ways in which nature or man could be depicted. The Christian doctrine of the incarnation, which proclaimed that the divine had been made flesh, helped to make its representation possible, if not necessary. But some of the theologians and certainly the faithful and practising artists derived two further attitudes about the arts of representation. One was that a style of representation could be made to evoke rather than depict physical reality. Something holy could be shown without being technically represented, because another order than the one derived from visual observation was used for the representation. Stylistic conventions and canons, as much as the subject matter, became vehicles for expressing the sacred. Thus, two-dimensional bodies, repetitive facial types, simplified gestures and arbitrary relationships to the surrounding landscape became, in Christian or Buddhist art, the ways in which the sacred was shown. In Hinduism, on the other hand, it would have been an exaggeration of natural features which provided that impression of impossible plausibility which would have identified sacred images. In Western European art, from the thirteenth century onward, these canons competed with another vision of the divine, one which sees actual nature and physical beauty as living proofs of God's greatness. Within a very different set of conventions and with an entirely different type of piety, a relatable inspiration from a beautiful nature emerges in Chinese and Japanese paintings inspired by Daoism. And, finally, it can be argued that, in Persian miniatures from the early fifteenth century on or in many classical Chinese and Japanese paintings, there ruled a religious pantheism which enlarged everything created as an aspect of the divine or, at any rate, a simple all-encompassing humanism (see Plates 211, 212, 251–255).

Another side to this ambition of making the sacred visible was the growth of what its opponents and critics called idolatry. With very few exceptions in the case of relics of Christ, of the Buddha or of saints, and of a small number of images said to have been made 'without the intervention [of human] hands', few believed that natural items (a bone or a tooth) or things made by men (a cloth) were actually divine. But even medieval Muslim accounts are full of stories about objects, often carrying writing in unknown languages, which could heal and bring other forms of happiness and success. Works of art could operate like magical formulas and thus compete with or reflect divine power.

The real issue raised by the artists and theologians of the Middle Ages is, therefore, that of the power of art, a power for enjoyment or for behaviour and action, a power for pious or immoral thoughts and ways, but always an attraction away from the true and pure expression of the faith. Like the Buddhist Chinese rulers of the ninth century who condemned Buddhist image making, Saint Bernard of Clairvaux in twelfth-century Burgundy argued, in a celebrated sermon to his fellow monks, that the contemplation of beautiful things is an invitation to sin or, at best, a great waste of resources that could be better spent otherwise.

Saint Bernard's arguments would have been accepted by traditional Muslim learned men, as they too, at least most of them, saw the dangers of whatever takes the faithful away from the straight path of the revelation. The issue becomes a controversial one when it is applied to what was unquestionably one of the most original artistic contributions of medieval Islam, the beautification of writing loosely known as calligraphy. The reason for the controversy is the apparent contradiction between two sets of argument. One belongs to our own times and has asserted that calligraphy was the way in which Muslims expressed the emotions and expectations which, in other cultures and religions, were made apparent through images. On the other hand, there are no commonly known medieval or traditional statements which, even remotely, allude to a relationship between the faith and the very well-documented evolution of different kinds of script. What is documented is that the administrators of the huge Muslim empire sought to standardize the writing used in communications between the far-flung provinces of the empire and, as a result, developed a *khaṭṭ al-mansūb*, a 'proportioned script' regulated through various ratios between segments of letters and, initially at least, based on the diamond-shaped dot made by applying a pen on a writing surface. From the tenth century, when proportioned writing was first established, until the twentieth, a series of variants to the initial script were developed, mostly, during the period with which we are dealing, in Baghdād, Tabrīz, and Herāt, the major capital cities of political entities. Such is the sober and severe *muḥaqqaq* script so prized by the copyists of the Qur'ān or the soft and fluid *nasṭa'līq* of so many manuscripts of Persian literature.

It is possible to argue that, even though state concerns were behind the development of calligraphy for writing in the Arabic script, the continuous elaboration of writing and its acknowledgement as the premier aesthetic effort of the Muslim world in written sources derived from or were inspired by the central function of writing in the Islamic revelation. On this score, the debate is still open and we should perhaps accept that the contemporary judgement which associates beautiful writing with an expression of the faith is valid as an emotional and aesthetic judgment, even if it does not agree with historical evidence (see Plates 107–114).

Whatever answers one gives to this question, the transformations of Arabic script were prized outside the Muslim world. Hundreds of Western objects, even portals of churches and in the fifteenth century Italian religious paintings, many Byzantine buildings and certain types of Chinese ceramics, copied Arabic letters and words without being aware of their religious or other meanings. Only in East African examples (as in the mosque of Kilwa in Tanzania and on some of the tombstones found there) do we find instances of the Arabic script which cannot be read in full but which was certainly meant to be holy.

It is also difficult to propose a religious source for the calligraphic arts of China and Japan. There, secular aesthetic values and the veneration of past monuments seem to have been the main factors in sponsoring an art of beautiful writing. And yet, there again, as with later Persian writing (and certainly with writing in Arabic characters after 1500 in the Ottoman Empire or in the Indian subcontinent), it is possible to propose mystical or at least esoteric meanings for the transformations of characters, as sophisticated Daoism may often explain how some of these changes were appreciated and perhaps why they were made (see Plates 95–99).

Two further aspects of the representation of the sacred need mention. One is literature. There are literary genres, like sermons and liturgical prayers, which centred on the practice of the faith and in which rhetorical devices of all sorts were used to enhance precepts or interpretations. Photius in Byzantium (ninth century) and Saint Bernard in the West (twelfth century) composed many sermons of literary merit, while the poetry of Sophronius, patriarch of Jerusalem in the seventh century, of John of Damascus (eighth century: the exact attribution of some of these poems is in doubt) and from the Latin liturgy of the dead (such as the *Dies Irae*) are still used and admired today. Within the Muslim world, less importance was given to rhetorical and decorative devices in the prose dealing with religious matters, and the sermon did not become the literary exercise it was in Christianity. Yet some passages in al-Ghazālī's discussions of beauty and al-Maqdisī's demonstrations of the existence of God are set in dramatic tones which are effective as works of literature. Formulaic though they may be, many introductions to religious books are at times effective compositions of balanced prose. And a literature of prayer, collective or personal, certainly existed in Arabic and was extended to all the linguistic groups of Muslims.

Religious images, pious purposes and powers of persuasion through words are central to mystical writing in prose, as with Ibn al-ʿArabī or Ibn Ḥazm, and especially in poetry, where Muslim writers used the most arcane treasures of the Arabic and Persian languages and all sorts of literary devices in order to proclaim their visions of the divine through alliterations, unexpected associations of images and correspondences between the senses which transform some of these works into masterpieces of world poetry. Jalāl al-Dīn Rūmi in the Islamic thirteenth century and Meister Eckhart in the thirteenth–fourteenth century in the Christian world were authors of poems profoundly imbued with their faith, aesthetically striking, expressing at times a pantheism which led them, and others like them, to be rejected by the official religious establishments of their time. And in India it is primarily the epic tradition which has preserved through literature the religious lore which had been codified in the *purānas* of old. But, like all epic traditions, the Indian one was affected by worldly tastes and expectations, on which more will be said below.

And then there is music with its occasional accessory, dance. Its role was enormous in the Christian liturgy, and Western monasteries were instrumental in developing both plainsong and, from the twelfth century on, polyphony. It is also in monasteries that the earliest recordings of music took place and that a system of notation was developed, since the recording of words and of sound was needed for the proper performance of the liturgy (see Plate 179). The *bhaktī* stream of medieval Hinduism gave prominence to music in prayer and ceremonies, and rhythmic chant and movement is present in Buddhist or Daoist modes of behaviour. Although ways to chant the Scripture and to proclaim the call to prayer were to develop in the Islamic world, the major known developments came out of the Ottoman Empire after 1500. Official Islam was as fearful of the aesthetic pleasures of music as it was of painting. The major earlier exception is that of Ṣūfism, which practised both dancing and music. The spectacular whirling dances of holy men like the *mevlevis* in Anatolia and elsewhere were expressions of piety, but they hardly represent a typical feature of Islam.

In East Asia religious music, mostly instrumental, accompanied public and private ceremonies: the *yüeh-hsüan* was a musical ensemble which performed in a garden in front of a place where ritual ceremonies were held (see Plate 240). But public liturgies and collective pious behaviour were not developed in ways which justified anything comparable to what is known in Christendom. In the Indian subcontinent, on the other hand, devotional poetry was sung, as with the twelfth-century *Gītā Govinda* dealing with Krishna's love with Rādhā. Furthermore, Hindu fascination with logical systems and order led to musical treatises as early as in the eighth and ninth centuries (*Brhad-desi*, a manual of musical logic) and continuing into the thirteenth century with the more elaborate *sangitu-ratnakan*. Dance, with its rhythmic and repetitious recomposition of bodily shapes arbitrarily chosen to represent emotional or other states, was also used in most of South Asia (see Plate 224), in many of the shamanistic cults of Central Asia, and probably in Africa to express religious feelings or to relate sacred narratives. But dance and music, even more than literature or the visual arts, are associated with secular functions and purposes, and the distinction between the realm of the sacred and that of the court or of the city is not always easy to make.

Symbols of faith

The identification of symbols is always difficult to make, and it is easy simply to antedate recent characteristics, as is often done with the assumption that the crescent has been a Muslim symbol from the beginning or that the color green has always been associated with the family of the Prophet. There are in fact relatively few symbols like the cross, which, in its many shapes, acquired fairly early a consistent meaning for Christians themselves and about Christians for others. During the centuries under consideration, only Christianity and Islam, the two religions with missionary programmes and with numerous and consistent relations with other religions, developed symbolic forms identifying them to themselves and to others. There is, for instance, the minaret, which first appeared to show the existence of Muslims in primarily non-Islamic settings and whose connotative and symbolic significance was always ahead of its practical one of calling the faithful to pray. The Quṭb Minār in Delhi, the Jām minaret in a hidden valley of Afghanistan (see Plates 208, 209) and the Kalāyān minaret of Bukhārā in Uzbekistan are striking twelfth and early thirteenth-century examples of architectural and engineering art with an extensive decoration of writing and of geometry, whose function was much more than the call to prayer and which were not addressed to Muslims alone. The spires of churches, and especially of Gothic cathedrals (see Plate 28; Figure 20), or the bell towers adjoining Russian churches, had symbolic much more than practical purposes. And symbolic meanings can be attributed to a host of details in Christian, pagan, Islamic, Buddhist and Hindu arts: the wheel of the Buddha, the mandala of India, images of divinities, the halo of Christianity, the simple proclamation of God's power or of his name in many Iranian mosques, occasionally the name of the Prophet, of ʿAlī and of the first caliphs, the colours of the clothes worn by shamans in Central Asia, and so on. To enter certain chapels or oratories belonging to any religion was often to enter into what the French poet Baudelaire called a 'forest of symbols'. We must assume that, at the time of their original creation and use, these symbolic systems were known more or less instinctively by those who participated in the practice of the various religions involved.

But symbols were meant primarily for the internal consumption and use of separate religious communities. It is only within the inner mechanisms of these communities that they can be recognized in the original fullness of their meanings, and religious systems which had strong ecclesiastical traditions could preserve symbols longer and more effectively than the traditions, like Islam, with a weak one. A secondary or alternative function or use of symbols is that they provide even those who do not fully understand them access to their forms and thereby to the religions they represent. All symbols can be provided with aesthetic merits independent of their significance, and a cross or a mandala are, and probably always have been, items for the adornment of the body as well as carriers of holiness. But the point is particularly striking when one contemplates the powerful sculpture of Aztec and earlier temples, in which little–understood meanings strike by the sheer force of their transformation of matter at the hands of anonymous artists.

PATRONAGE

Artistic expressions require an investment. At times, the investment is purely financial and the object of the investment is its own reward, as funds are made available for the construction of a building, the acquisition of books or of objects, or for the performance of a piece of music. At other times, the investment is social and human, as in the support of creative or performing groups or individuals without prejudice to what they accomplish. There is also a preserving investment focused on the maintenance and safekeeping of things made or built. And, finally, there is a more complicated investment of memory without concomitant funds, which deals with the need to keep and transmit the knowledge and understanding of a culture's artistic expression. More is known about the first two types of investment than about the last two, but all of them can be touched upon through four types of often interlocking patronage.

Ecclesiastical

Large and organized religious establishments, like the Christian Church all over Europe and in parts of Western Asia, Buddhist monasteries in China, Tibet, Japan and Sri Lanka, Hindu and Jain temples in India and South-East Asia, were replete with priests, monks and all sorts of lay functionaries, all organized in carefully delineated hierarchies and usually provided with signs (clothes or symbolic objects) identifying their functions. These individuals, for the most part but not exclusively men, distributed often very extensive funds invested by the mass of the faithful or, more frequently, by rich individuals, and they sponsored everything from architecture to religious souvenirs. Such groups with fully ascertained responsibilities for artistic expression did not exist in the Muslim world, at least not formally, although, by the fourteenth century, it is possible to assume a restricted patronage by Ṣūfī orders and perhaps, in a few areas, by Shī'ite religious leaders.

It is difficult to generalize on the character of the ecclesiastical patronage across Europe and Asia, but two features seem to dominate in their effects. One is safekeeping, as sanctuaries, temples, monasteries and churches preserve objects and settings because of their sacred value and because the maintenance of tradition and the rejection of change are essential pillars of any religious establishment. A particularly striking example is the Shosoin in Nara in Japan, a temple built in 752, regularly taken apart for repairs and reconstructed in exactly the same shape and technique since then. It contains a sealed treasure of objects from the whole world which can only be seen once a year and to which nothing has been added since then. Christian churches and monasteries also kept treasures. Usually, their holdings are a peculiar mix of very remarkable masterpieces and of redundant and repetitive liturgical implements. History has not always been kind to these Christian treasures of Europe and only a few – Burgos in Spain, Sens in France, Aachen in Germany – contain a range of quality which must have been much more common. And within Muslim culture it is only at the very beginning of the tenth century that the Ka'ba in Mecca lost, after looting by a radical religious group, its function of being the repository of expensive and unusual treasures issued from the conquest. But the idea was not lost, as, from the fourteenth century onward, the religious and dynastic shrine at Ardebil in northern Iran kept in its treasury a unique collection of manuscripts, Chinese ceramics and rugs.

The second feature of ecclesiastical patronage is the sponsorship of architecture and of other arts. Sometimes this sponsorship reflected genuine practical needs within religious communities, but quite often it responded to the demands of wealth, as every religious establishment developed ways of soliciting and utilizing funds from the rich and at times the pious. Islam in particular created the institution of the *waqf*, a complicated system for the transfer of private fortunes for public and pious purposes. In most instances, this patronage was extremely conservative. New pagodas and new churches resemble old ones, and traditional techniques, styles and topics are usually preserved in the copying of manuscripts and the making of pious and decorative objects.

Rulers and Courts

One architectural function, the palace, is exclusively associated with rulers and authority. Nearly everywhere, palaces have represented an ideal of beauty and luxury often sung about by poets (see Plates 5, 187–189). In the Iranian epic of the *Shāh-Nāmeh* or in the lyrical poetry of a Niẓāmī, in Russian folk tales like the story of the city of Kitej, or in *The Thousand and One Nights*, the beautiful palace appears at several levels of interpretation. It is an expensive place full of gold and precious stones and of wonderful objects which cannot be found in daily life; it exemplifies power through the accumulation of wealth and of marvels. It is a secluded area carefully separated from the rest of the world through walls, beautiful gardens, strange waterworks and gates; and access to it is difficult and fraught with dangers as well as possible blissful rewards, for the palace is psychologically remote. And, finally, at a symbolic level, the real or imaginary forms of the palace are also the ways in which the divine is imagined, most particularly the visionary divine of the mystic or of eschatology. Royal or imperial gardens are like divine Paradise and the Jerusalem to come in Jewish and Christian traditions. The Paradises of Islam or the places in the clouds or hidden in mountain valleys depicted in Chinese novels inspired by Buddhist pilgrims (many versions of the *Xi-you ji* or *Journey to the West*) all evoke magnificent royal palaces.

Luxurious, remote, marvellous and a foretaste of eternity though they may be, palaces have not survived as well as monuments of religious architecture. Many were destroyed by competing rulers and dynasties erasing the traces of their predecessors, or else they fell into disuse as tastes changed or patrons died. Poets were aware of the short life of palaces and frequently used royal constructions as metaphors for the inevitability of death, the transitory quality of life and the vanity of human efforts.

As a result, we are not well informed on the actual looks and layouts of palaces. The ones in Constantinople (beginning in the fourth century, but primarily from the sixth onwards), Baghdād (mid-eighth century), Cairo under the Fāṭimids (late tenth and eleventh centuries), Tabrīz (first half of the fourteenth century), Samarkand (end of the fourteenth century and beginning of the fifteenth), or Beijing (primarily thirteenth and fourteenth centuries) were all imperial palaces with tremendous impacts on their contemporaries and on foreign visitors, but only a few ruins remain in Istanbul, Cairo, Samarkand and in Vijayanagara in south India (late thirteenth century and onwards). For the most part, we have to depend on descriptions and recollections which are often difficult to interpret, even when they can be related to fairly extensive remains, excavated or still buried, at places like Madīna al-Zahrā (near Cordova, the site of a major royal foundation in the tenth century), Sāmarrā (the huge temporary 'Abbāsid capital built in the ninth century north of Baghdād in Iraq)(see Plate 206) or Qarāqorum (in Mongolia, where extensive remains of the palaces of the Great Khāns were excavated in part) (see Figure 32).

We are better informed about a second tier of palace architecture, the residences of local rather than universal power. Such are the fortified citadels, with dozens of particularly well-preserved examples: the Tower of London; and the old Louvre in Paris; the citadels of Cairo, Herāt, or Aleppo; and the Kremlin in Moscow and in several other capitals of pre-Mongol Russian principalities. Most of these citadels were military establishments for feudal rulers of relatively small kingdoms and they are properly related to the dozens of fortified chateaux for landed aristocrats best known in Western and Central Europe but also present in Western Asia (Krak des Chevaliers and Bosra in Syria, Ajlun and Jerash in Jordan), in North Africa (Qal'a of the Benī Ḥammād and Ashir in Algeria), and in Central Asia (Soghdian countryside and Tajikistan) (see Plates 30–32, 36–41). Their impressive external looks did not always lead into equally impressive interiors, as dark meeting or store rooms, jails, stables, armories and simple oratories predominated for a setting of life that must have been remarkable for its boredom. However, feudal architecture exhibits a high level of technical competency in the construction of walls and especially of vaults in stone, brick and concrete, so as to avoid the vulnerability of wood to fires. And it can be noted that a similar high quality of technical craft occurs in the royal cities of Peru, like Cuzco and Macchu Picchu (see Plates 320, 321).

To the spectacular drabness of most castles and citadels there is one striking exception, the Alhambra in Grenada, whose main features date from the fourteenth century (see Plate 198). There, inside a perfectly typical fortified enclosure of walls and towers and next to a large but common citadel, a delicate ensemble of secluded halls around courtyards with static or running water was planned in the lower part of a hill with highly formal gardens climbing up the side of the mountain. A learned poetry was composed for the Alhambra and then written on the walls of the palace like a sort of guide to the user and to the visitor. It transformed the sensuous splendour of the floral and geometric decoration into an iconographic and ideological statement proclaiming the cosmic meaning of the decoration. Other such brilliant interiors can be imagined from the archaeological remains of a few eighth-century Muslim villas in Syria, Jordan and Palestine, and by the description of the palace built in the tenth century by Armenian King Gagik at Akhtamar in eastern Turkey.

Rulers and their courts exercised their patronage in two additional ways. One was the organization and sponsorship of individual artists or whole ateliers of painters, calligraphers and artisans. The phenomenon is most clearly observable in the Mongol courts, as early as the fourteenth century in Tabrīz, and the courts, like the early Ottomans or the Turkic dynasties of northern India, which were under the cultural influence of the Mongols. The institution of what was eventually called a *kitābkhāneh* (literally 'house for books') or of a *naqqāshkhāneh* (literally 'place of manufacture and decoration') was a mixture of a library-museum and a real atelier-school in which things were made for the court, especially to be distributed as gifts by the ruler. It is probable that the origins of these institutions are to be found in some sort of symbiosis between ancient Roman and Byzantine imperial practices and those of Tang China, but the important point is that they fostered the transfer of styles, of technical competencies, and of objects. It is because of these ateliers that albums could be assembled like the celebrated Istanbul and Berlin ones of the late fifteenth century, in which Chinese, Iranian, Central Asian and Western images and ideas are all found together. And it is possible, thanks to a signed drawing from a Persian album now in Berlin but originally in Istanbul, to reconstruct how an ancient Roman cup in precious stone with mythological figures was given as a gift from a Mamlūk ruler from Egypt to a Mongol one in Persia and how a descendant of the Mongol ruler gave the cup to an Italian, as it ended up as the Tazza Farnese, owned by a Medici and now in the Naples museum.

The other point about the patronage of princes lies in the complex realm of image making. Through their sponsorship of official representations on coins and medals, on the sculpture of cathedrals, on scrolls, and in book illustrations, the courts of Europe and Asia created a set of standard representations of rulers. Few, if any, were portraits in the sense of approximations of reality. Most emphasized signs and symbols of power: crowns, sceptres, orbs, clothes of specific colours like the purple of Byzantine emperors, poses when seated or standing, presence of numerous attendants, and so forth. An iconography of the ruling figure, which had culture-specific forms but universal values,was thus created. In some cases, as, for instance, with the early 'Abbāsid and Fāṭimid caliphates in the Muslim world, the court controlled the manufacture of some of the materials, most particularly textiles, used in princely ceremonies and distributed this material as gifts. In this manner, there was a great deal of sharing of forms in the many different arts of ruling courts. There was also a hierarchy from truly imperial courts – Byzantium, Baghdād, Beijing – to dozens of lesser centres copying, more or less faithfully and more or less effectively, the themes and ideas of imperial capitals. Some of these originally lesser centres in the Balkans, in Iran, in India, in Western and Central Europe, and in central or northern Russia, grew into major creative centres of their own by the end of the fifteenth century (see Plates 145–152, 214–217).

The literary and musical experiences accompanying the visual world of rulers are limited to a panegyric poetry which is only interesting for the convolutions of its images describing princes and emperors. More original are the various ceremonies which controlled and organized the life of the ruler and which served to enhance the importance and prestige of his position. Books of ceremonies have been preserved for Byzantium, the 'Abbāsid Empire and Chinese emperors. In the formality and rigour of dress and gesture involved in most of these activities there was a theatrical quality comparable to religious rituals. The performance side of courtly life was to remain for centuries in the memories of men and to affect the representational arts of all countries. And it is in large part through the sculptures on the walls of temples and palaces that the ceremonies as well as the theatre of Aztec and Inca life could be reconstructed.

Urban patronage

The growth of commercial and manufacturing cities in all areas of Europe, Asia, North Africa and East Africa is one of the major novelties of the centuries under consideration. For the expression of the arts, the patronage associated with these cities exemplifies a curious paradox, already mentioned several times. On the one hand, these cities were forums where people and things from many different origins met, and we know how richly diversified were the art and culture of Soghdian cities on the Silk Road in the seventh and eighth centuries, how Guangzhou and Xian in China, Baṣra in Iraq, Cairo and Alexandria in Egypt, Novgorod in Russia, and Amalfi, Genoa and Venice in Italy were places of knowledge of exotic things and people. Although remarkable for his achievements and for having survived to write them down, Marco Polo was not alone in his century and had many followers in subsequent centuries. Yet the dominant feature of the expression of medieval cities during this millennium was the appearance of local particularisms in written and oral literature, in the visual arts, in music, and in the representational arts. And, in a striking contrast to the arts of rulers, which were easily exchanged between princes, urban expressions tended to remain within their own settings and eventually led to what would become national arts.

A few examples may suffice. From Japan with Lady Murasaki's astonishing *Tale of Genji* (twelfth century) to al-Ḥarīrī's *Maqāmāt* (eleventh century) and the *Tale of Baybars* (fourteenth and later centuries) in the Arab world, and to Chrétien de Troyes and the *roman courtois* in twelfth-century France, an art of story-telling appears everywhere. The heroes and protagonists were taken from courtly and aristocratic circles, from popular sources, or even from a variety of imaginary worlds like those of anthropomorphic animals. But in nearly all cases the language of the expression was highly local, fully aware of vernacular terms, even if difficult as with the pyrotechnics of Ḥarīrī's Arabic. Through a language accessible to geographically restricted groups emerged picaresque heroes like Abū Zayd of Sarūj, noble ones with human weaknesses like the keepers of the Grail, sensitive ones like Japanese ladies, and fantastic ones like Aladdin. The urban milieu provided a public for the buying of books and for listening to stories being read aloud, even for attending theatrical performances. In both China and Western Europe, plays were performed in public places. Some dealt with religious stories, but social issues came out as well in the puppet shows known from Egypt and Anatolia (see Plates 11, 18, 178, 182–184, 258).

Although comparative linguists have been able to identify any number of consistent types of story from one area to another, direct translations were relatively rare during these centuries at this particular level of literary lore. But exceptions do exist, such as the Indian 'Mirror of Princes' around animals known as the *Pancatañtra* translated into Persian and Arabic as *The Book of Kalīlah and Dimna* and spread all over Western and Eastern Europe (see Plates 210, 211).

The visual arts were also significantly affected by the patronage of cities. The phenomenon was a universal one and, for instance, the Hanseatic cities around the Baltic Sea, Novgorod in northern Russia, the cities of the valley of the Meuse, and early medieval Flemish cities sponsored all sorts of artistic endeavours, mostly around churches and other pious establishments. But the most spectacular development of an urban patronage occurred in the cities of the Muslim world. There, beginning in the ninth century in Iraq and then spreading everywhere, the techniques of industrial arts like ceramics, metalwork, glass and textiles grew in variety and quality to meet a wide range of different functions and different tastes. Writing, vegetal or geometric ornament, but, most unexpectedly, an enormous variety of representations of everything from simple animals to astrology and to scenes from epic or lyrical narratives appear on hundreds of objects made primarily for the urban elites. With the Mongol invasions and the social and political changes which followed, the creativity and originality of Muslim cities as patrons of the arts declined considerably, but the baton was taken by China in textiles and especially by Italy and then Northern Europe, where eventually all Western Asian techniques were rediscovered and ameliorated. By 1500, it was often Venice and Lucca that were making 'oriental' brasses and silks and sending them all over Western Asia.

Folk patronage

It is not easy to separate a folk patronage from an urban one, at times even from a courtly one, as many themes, ideas, techniques and modes of behaviour which had originated at popular levels were incorporated into the patronage of the bourgeoisie or of princes, at times even of the ecclesiastical order. This is particularly true of music and of the performing arts. For instance, the percussion and string variations of individual tribes and villages were learned and codified by urban specialists and then performed in cities or at courts. Thus, the innovations of Arabic music in the eighth century are attributed, in later learned treatises on the arts, to Ibn Muja and Ibn Muhrīz, who are alleged to have travelled and collected materials all over Arabia. And it is the very urban Ikhwān al-Ṣafā, 'Brethren of Purity,' followed by al-Kindī and Ibn Sīnā, who developed the philosophical theory of this popular music. In Song China, Korea and Japan, a similar process of codification of popular music took place in the eleventh and twelfth centuries. In India and possibly in Aztec Mexico, the same process affected dance and drama, as a complex theory was developed for the manipulation of the body's movements and their transformation into learned canons. Yet, only too often, we can only guess at the popular roots of the arts, since it is their more learned versions that have been best preserved.

An interesting case in point is that of rugs or carpets. Very few have remained from the centuries with which we deal and, with a few Anatolian, Egyptian and Chinese exceptions, they are mostly fragments. Much is known about them from texts and a little about depictions in paintings from all urban, princely and ecclesiastical centres of patronage. The techniques and the functions of rugs always remained part and parcel of all nomadic cultures and most village cultures. Yet rugs were also made at and for princely courts and in fact it is reasonable to assume that all levels of society used them nearly everywhere except in tropical lands, where mats served comparable purposes. But the visual identification of the hundreds of terms involving types of rugs is almost impossible to make.

Several conclusions about the patronage of these centuries emerge. There existed throughout two relatively 'high' forms of sponsorship of the arts: religion and political power, which maintained fairly common and often interchangeable patterns and procedures, regardless of location. And then there were highly local folk and urban ways, which tended to differ from each other, but which were constantly codified into learned philosophical theories and transformed into either science or rhetoric. Whereas their ways were different, their systematization was curiously consistent across the two continents and almost always led to binary divisions into mutually exclusive types. Thus in Japan, there was a 'music of the left' (*togaku*) containing Chinese- and Indian-derived pieces and a 'music of the right' (*komafuku*) involving Korean and Manchurian ones. Courtly and popular ways competed in Western Europe, and Russian folk tales and popular games formed a different genre from epic stories like the *Tale of Igor*. It is this variety in patronage which created the wealth of the arts of that time and it also began the movement towards individualized and discrete expression which would eventually lead to literatures in different languages and to different styles in art and music.

PIETY AND PLEASURE

Most of the argument of this chapter has dealt so far with the practical and ideological functions and purposes of artistic expressions and with the varieties of sponsorship in the making and the use of the arts. The examples cited outlined the ways in which human creativity reflected social, political and religious needs and also, by extension, shaped behaviour by compelling or restricting access to spaces, images, words or sounds. Relatively little has been said about the forms of artistic expression. The reason is in part that forms are more consistently circumscribed than patronage and religious or political practices. They depend on the materials available locally, on the preservation of restricted traditions, and on the habits of guilds and other associations of artisans and poets. And the economics of artistic expression also militated against the rapid spread of new ideas, new songs, new images and new techniques. Examples of technological or formal transfers exist no doubt. In the early Middle Ages, they are particularly characteristic of the Muslim world which, in the late eighth and the ninth centuries, succeeded in revolutionizing the art of ceramics by discovering local Iraqi, Egyptian and Iranian ways of imitating Chinese models. From obscure origins in ninth- or tenth-century Iraq, the *muqarnas*, the so-called 'stalactite' technique of covering architectural space with carefully composed geometric combinations, spread to Morocco and India as early as the eleventh century and was used in Byzantium and Christian Sicily (see Plates 197, 198, 201, 207, 209).

We do not know how these transfers across seas and deserts were made, but one better-documented example shows that they were relatively rare, since this particular one acquired almost mythical proportions. It is the case of Ziryāb, a poet-singer from Iraq who came to Cordova in Spain in the ninth century and who is alleged to have changed everything in al-Andalus, from the art of singing to table manners and new haircuts. The point of the stories about Ziryāb is simply that, within the rationale of the times, a series of major changes in expression could only be explained through the arbitrary intervention of one individual.

In the later Middle Ages, such examples of technical and formal diffusion are more characteristic and better known for European art, as with the architectural technology associated with Gothic art, but the powerful impact of Chinese forms, especially in painting and poetry, on Korea, Japan and even more remote Iran, is equally striking.

One of the most powerful instruments in making these transfers possible was the spread of paper from China, first to Muslim Asia after the middle of the eighth century and eventually to the Christian world. Its relative cheapness and ease of manufacture made it available in many more places and to many more people than parchment, papyrus, tree bark, clay tablets and other older surfaces for writing or recording information and directions. Drawings and models were easily transmitted, and literature or ideas could be written down and copied for large-scale sale or distribution. Thus, in China, where printing on paper had first developed, a collection of Chinese classics in 130 volumes was begun in 932 under the sponsorship of a minister, Feng Dao. Printing is known for Uyghur texts in the thirteenth century, but it did not spread farther west (see Plate 115).

In short, the means for the transmission of forms on a large scale existed but were limited before the fifteenth century. Movements of people – like the free or forced movements of artisans mentioned earlier; the movements of monks and priests in Christianity and Buddhism; large pilgrimages like the yearly *ḥajj* of the Muslims or the seasonal Hindu pilgrimages in India – were responsible for much of the knowledge of foreign forms and ideas that existed. In spite of these limitations, it is possible to propose three formal attributes of artistic expression between 600 and 1500 which are present nearly everywhere, although not necessarily connected to each other, genetically or otherwise. These attributes are what I have called 'piety', which is understood here as an attitude towards the holy that affects ideas and interpretations as well as behaviour; 'pleasure', the sensuous relationship of affection and desire which is at the root of most artistic needs and expressions; and 'the self', a feature which did not have the importance it would acquire in subsequent centuries, but which deals with the private and exclusive, rather than public and collective, enjoyment of the arts. In all instances, however, it is important to reiterate that these are not exclusive attributes and that the arts of the time, sometimes even the very works to be mentioned here, are also significant at all sorts of other levels and in many other ways.

Piety

The contemplation of a Buddhist painting or sculpture from Dunhuang in China, a Japanese temple or Sri Lanka brings out a number of consistent characteristics: almost total frontality; schematic bodies under regulated folds; faces without the expression of emotions but with consistently frozen smiles; a limited number of gestures with a right hand which often appears to be (and often is) out of scale with the rest of the body; and a small number of signs for which one can assume, even without knowing it, a specific meaning to those who belong to the faith. A nearly similar statement could be made about many Byzantine paintings and mosaics after the ninth century, about Greek or Russian icons, about the frontispieces of Irish, Carolingian and Ottonian manuscripts, and about some of the larger sculptures on the portals of Romanesque churches. On another level, the complex imagery of Jalāl al-Dīn Rūmī, the great thirteenth-century Persian mystical poet living in Anatolia, reflects a system of correspondences between the divine world, nature and human emotions or behaviour. A comparable wealth is found among Western Christian mystic writers and, in a different way, in the writings and sayings of Saint Francis of Assisi. In a phenomenon like that of hesychasm, a spiritual attitude which spread in the fourteenth century from Byzantium to the whole of Eastern Christendom, there are images and practices which are comparable to those of Muslim mysticism and even of Chinese Daoism.

These examples suggest that certain formal qualities of composed simplification and abstraction, of obvious symbolic associations, of richly colourful visions, of diffuse pantheism, became associated with expressions of faith and piety. These same qualities occur in some of the striking West African sculptures from Benin and elsewhere in Africa, which appear towards the end of our period. In the visual arts, the formal result of these attributes is usually called 'iconic', for two reasons. One is that it does occur quite frequently and in all lands on objects for private devotion, like the icons of the Eastern Christian Church. The other is that it is a transformation of representations in a way that allows them to evoke other ideas and personages than themselves and to act on beholders or users as intermediaries towards the divine. They are in truth searches for the expression of the inexpressible and, as such, one of the most extraordinary human endeavours in the history of artistic expression. It can be argued that even the Muslim world, normally less susceptible to such sensuous developments, provided writing with an iconic quality, as when the words 'Allāh', 'God', 'Muḥammad', or 'Alī' grandiosely cover the walls of religious buildings or when a veil covers the faces of prophets because the sight of their beauty would overwhelm those who could see them. Iconic power ultimately transcends the forms and the meanings to which it is applied.

Such is not the case with a second type of expression of piety, the narrative. The need to tell stories pertaining to the holy – the life of Christ or of the Buddha, lives of saints and of holy men and women, accounts of the behaviour of divinities or of humans in their own quests for the divine – is a truly universal phenomenon and even the severe rigidity of orthodox Islam did not escape a hagiography of the Prophet and endless accounts of the lives of earlier prophets or of later holy men. These narratives become artistic expressions when translated into one of many forms. They can be dances enacting the lives and loves of Hindu divinities. They can be dramas, as in Christian Passion plays or in the Shī'ite performances of the tragic death of Ḥusayn. They can be in prose or in poetry, and, most particularly, in painted or sculpted images. The technical styles of these various examples vary, but there are certain common features in the compositional structure of narration through sequential frames like those of comic strips. And, even for a grandiose masterpiece like Dante's *Divine Comedy*, it has been suggested that the progression of the Prophet Muḥammad's ascension into Heaven served as a model (see Plate 180).

Finally, throughout our millennium, the holy and piety were made visible through portable objects, souvenirs from holy places like Mecca, Benares or Jerusalem, prayer rugs for travellers, or little altars or icons for voyagers to be reminded of their religious duties and to accomplish them properly. The use of some of these objects verged on the magic, as, like many phrases or adages derived from liturgical practice, they served to ward off evil and dangers and to beckon favours. The styles, techniques and quality of these objects and of the spoken or written formulas that fulfilled some of the same functions varied enormously. Yet they do represent a practice shared by believers in many different religions. A very special case among these objects are the ones used in formal liturgies, that is to say in predetermined, usually imposed, and relatively inflexible collective behaviour. All sanctuaries, even in Sunnī Islam, used some of the most talented individuals among their worshippers to buy or to make liturgical objects, many of which today adorn the museums of the world.

Pleasure

Pious arts – visual, spoken, sung, spoken or performed – would not have affected so many people if they did not possess the essential qualities of attracting and of pleasing. Some artistic expressions were meant primarily, at times exclusively, to add something special to whatever one was or did, to please by transforming the setting of life, in some ways everyday life and daily behaviour, in other ways special occasions only like private feasts and public festivals.

Continuing antique practices, rulers were providers of public pleasure through ceremonies at the time of their accession to power, at weddings and other family events, on the arrival of foreign ambassadors, or on regional occasions like the cresting of the Nile in Egypt. Accounts of such occasions exist for nearly every major centre of power and culture and they are interesting because they were often written by foreigners like Clavijo, the Spanish envoy from the Portuguese king to Tīmūr in Samarkand (around 1400), or Liudprand of Cremona after his visit to Constantinople in the tenth century. These two were certainly eye witnesses to whatever they relate. Others reused formulas from a special literary genre, the evocation in the guise of a depiction of remote lands. Whether in truth or in legend, spectacles were created which included displays of imperial or royal treasures; covering walls and gates with all sorts of textiles; building fancy tents; dressing soldiers in fancy uniforms; presentation of exotic and wild animals like leopards and giraffes; enormous quantities of food and scents; singing and dancing, at times acrobatic; and other sporting events and occasional performances by clergy or lay attendants. The point was always to show off one's power through one's wealth and through the originality of the performances, but the true vehicle of royal pride was the pleasure given to others. There are few direct visual documents of such displays, but Persian miniatures and, later, the miniatures of the Ottoman and Mughal worlds often depicted the colorful settings of gardens, kiosks and even whole cities decked out in brilliant colours for richly dressed and handsome men and women to drink, eat, play, and listen to music and poetry. Even when miniaturized as illustrations of books, the sensuality of Persian miniatures finds an echo in the magnificence of the *Très*

Riches Heures commissioned by the Duc de Berry in the early fifteenth century and executed by the Limbourg brothers (see Plates 5, 218).

On a less sumptuous level, images reflecting such ceremonies do occur in Byzantine and Western European miniatures from earlier times, in the sculptures of the temples of Angkor in Cambodia, and in objects, like the twelfth-century Mantle of Roger II made in Palermo and kept in Vienna as the coronation robe of the Habsburg emperors, or like the crowns preserved from Hungary or Muscovy. It is often the second-hand luxury of smaller feudal princes which has been preserved rather than that of the emperors or the sultans ruling whole empires.

The arts of pleasure were of even greater import in literature and music. Secular poetry could be a poetry of unrequited love with the troubadours of Western Europe and the lyrical poets of Iran, or of brilliant images, as in Yamoto's poetry of Japan, but everywhere it expressed the whole range of human emotions and feelings by appealing to the auditory or reading pleasure of men. It could be dramatic, even melodramatic, in the eloquent verses of the Persian epic the *Shāh-Nāmeh* or the *Chanson de Roland* in medieval France, exquisitely lyrical with Niẓāmī or Ḥafeẓ, or highly personalized and superbly crafted in Petrarch's sonnets. But in all these instances it served to give pleasure to those who read and especially to those who listened. A secular theatre came into being in China in the fourteenth century, and novels of all sorts proliferated to soothe or enlighten their readers. And it was also in China that appeared the ideal, in part a scholarly convention, of learned literati who have partly separated themselves from the world in order to contemplate and at times to execute themselves paintings and exercises in calligraphy which are exclusively for the pleasure of the eye and the ear. All these examples exhibit a vibrant technical refinement (see Plates 95, 99, 113, 177, 257, 258).

Something similar happened to music, as, in India, China, Iran and Europe, secular singing and playing instruments increasingly dominated musical activities (see Figure 22). Courts sponsored orchestras and an interesting dichotomy emerged between a popular music constantly refreshed in the varieties of folk experience and a learned music which developed and was judged according to sophisticated and often arbitrary canons. Arabic texts distinguish between a 'heavy' (*thaqīl*) and a 'light' (*khafīf*) style of music. A similar distinction existed in China between *ya-sheng* and *cheng-sheng*, 'right' and 'vulgar', ways, and probably elsewhere as well. In Western Europe, a musical treatise by Philippe de Vitry (1291–1361) was called *Ars Nova*, 'New Art', presumably to distinguish it from older traditions. And his near-contemporary Guillaume de Machaut (1300–1361) developed the art of the motet and fixed the new rules of most singing genres (see Plates 179, 187, 240, 258).

Figure 22 Muslim and Christian minstrels in thirteenth-century Spain. Miniature from the Cantigas de Santa María of King Alfonso X 'the Wise' of Castile (after Pidal, R. M., *Poesía arabe y poesía europea*, Madrid 1941, p. 75).

Perhaps the most original and interesting side to the arts of pleasure occurs in the industrial arts, developed primarily under the sponsorship of the cities. Most of the objects involved had in common their prosaic purpose: to cook, to bring light, to drink, to eat, to warm, to write, to dress for public or private occasions. First in China and then in the Muslim world, much later in Europe, the possibility arose of transforming nearly every aspect of life into an art of pleasure by adding colour, images, designs and so on to the implements of daily life. Thus were created the first steps of a style of life, a *genre de vie*, which was no longer restricted to the rich and powerful but which, through the miracle of new technologies, was made available to all. This change in the visually perceived and tangible surroundings of men was undoubtedly related to the literature they knew, the poetry they heard or the music to which they listened; and women as well as men took part in the sponsorship and appreciation of these new surroundings.

A few random examples illustrate the impact and range of the inspiration of pleasure. The merchant citizens of Pisa bought (or looted) an odd Islamic griffin and put it on the top of their cathedral (see Plate 213). Saint Thomas à Becket is buried in a purely Western Asian silk. And, among the sculptures from Benin in West Africa, there are striking representations of European merchants (see Plate 265), while Chinese ceramicists were making blue and white ceramics for foreign markets (see Plate 200). Foreigners were makers of marvels and of wonders. They were represented at times like bizarre monsters or like inventions of folk imagination (see Plate 120), as with Prester John hiding somewhere in Asia or Ethiopia and ready to help Christians against Muslims. But they were also the purveyors of luxury, of beauty, of much that was pleasant and unique in one's life.

Self

Throughout the period with which we deal and especially from the time of the Mongol invasions, the Eurasian and North African continents exhibited the originality of creative minds either marching to different drummers than those around them or cultivating something peculiarly their own. Such were Lady Murasaki in Japan and many of the writers of novels there and in China. Such was 'Omar Khayyām in Persia, a sceptic, who gained fame as a scientist and a poet. Such were the Japanese sculptors who picked the traditional images of Buddhas and altered them into almost portrait-like figures. Such were Dante out of the sheer genius of his writing (see Plate 180); Petrarch, who transformed his private life into public poetry; Chaucer, who depicted the society of his time in a new language; and François Villon, who risked being hanged for his crimes but wrote wonderful lyric verses (see Plate 118). Such were especially the painters and sculptors, from Duccio to Masaccio and the Van Eyck brothers (see Plate 174) or the Pisani to Claus Sluter and Donatello, who created the first of several renaissances by discovering on the one hand the antique heritage and, on the other, the visual specificity of each person and of each thing; or the Song painters Ma Yuan and Chen Xian, who endowed traditional topics with highly personal statements.

On the whole, these were not yet the centuries during which the personalities of individual artists were of greater significance than their technical competencies; artisanal anonymity still predominated. Yet poetry hardly exists without real poets and, as the centuries went by, eccentricities of character and belief were no longer sufficient to compel the recall or the dismissal of artists. Qualities of expression began to be identified with men and women rather than only with their creations or with their sponsors.

Two paradoxes can be proposed as conclusions to this chapter on artistic expression during nine centuries.

The first is the contrast or contrasts between culture-wide or even universal means and techniques of expression on the one hand and, on the other, the importance taken by local, at times parochial and even short-lived, differentiations, competencies and expectations. The latter always existed, but, during the centuries with which we have dealt, the possibility of universal forms and universal means appeared through proselytizing religions no longer ethnically or otherwise restricted, through several empires or imperial ideals without obligatory and fixed functions, and through languages, or at least scripts, which were meant to transcend boundaries. These universal impulses sponsored much of what was new and brilliant in the arts of the times, especially with respect to architecture and to other visual arts, to some degree with music and with certain high literary forms like pious or liturgical poetry, some types of epic and lyrical poetry, and heroic subjects. But it is local potentials and local wills which transformed the universal impulses into expressions accessible and available to all. This contrast would remain a constant in the arts of the world. Its multiple variations over the centuries lie at the very core of any interpretation of works of arts because of the ways in which the Middle Ages extended their presence beyond the areas where they were created.

The second paradox lies in the subjects and the forms of the arts. In one, rather simple-minded, sense, it is the contrast between religious and secular aims, between services or honours rendered to the divine realm or to the ruler on Earth. In practice, no doubt there were similarities between the two and they often influenced each other, but, on the whole, two different audiences were sought, and different behaviour was expected of users of each. In a deeper sense, a contrast existed between visual representations and performances or spoken and sung utterances which sought to please and those which were meant to persuade. The former developed sensory qualities and the latter rhetorical ones. Both sets of qualities sought justifications and models in their own past or in the past of others. In this manner, they regulated not only the diachronic evolution of the arts but also the continuous interpretation and reinterpretation of these arts. Ultimately, towards the end of our period, the complexities of social, political and intellectual growth led to the emergence everywhere of the artist in word, image or design, whose abilities and relationships replaced in large measure the earlier tension between religious and secular aims. That emergence was possible only because of the centuries of ferment within quite a different structure for artistic expressions.

BIBLIOGRAPHY

ADLE, C. (ed.) 1982. *Art et société dans le monde musulman*. Paris.

ALLAN, S. 1991. *The Shape of the Turtle: Myth, Art and Cosmos in Early China*. New York.

ASHENE, E. V. 1978. *Understanding the Traditional Art of Ghana*.

ASTON, W. G. 1971. *History of Japanese Literatuare*. C. E. Tuttle.

AZARPAY, G. 1979. *Soghdian Painting*. Berkeley.

AZHAROV, I.; REMPEL, L. 1971. *Reznoi Shtuk Afrasiaba*. Tashkent.

BADEL, P. 1984. *Introduction à la vie littéraire de Moyen Âge*. Paris.

BECKWITH, J. 1979. *Early Christian and Byzantine Art*. London.

BELENITSKY, A. M.; BENTOVICH, I. B.; BOLSHAKOV, O. G. 1973. *Srednevekoyyi Gorod Srednei Azii*. Leningrad.

BLAIR, S.; BLOOM, J. 1994. *Art and Architecture of Islam: 1200–1600*.

BLIER, S. P. 1987. *The Anatomy of Architecture*. Cambridge.

BRANER, R. 1991. *Dichtung des europaïschen Mittelatler*. Munich.

BROWNE, E. G. 1957. *A Literary History of Persia*, 4 vols. Cambridge. (reprinted several times since.)

BUSSAGLI, M. 1963. *Painting of Central Asia*. Geneva.

BYONG-WON, L. 1974. *An Analytical Study of the Sacred Buddhist Chant of Korea*. (Diss. U. of Washington).

Cambridge History of Arabic Literature, 1983–1990, 3 vols. Cambridge.

CHANDRA, L. (ed.) 1991. *The Art and Culture of South-East Asia*.

COLE, H. M. 1990. *Icons: Ideals and Power in the Art of Africa*. Smithsonian, Washington, DC.

CONANT, K. J. 1979. *Carolingian and Romanesque Architecture*. London.

COSTA, P. M. 1978. *The Pre-Islamic Antiquities at the Yemen National Museum*. Rome.

DODWELL, C. R. 1993. *The Pictorial Arts of the West*. London.

DURLIAT, M. 1985. *L'art roman*. Paris.

ETTINGHAUSEN, R.; GRABAR, O. 1992. *The Art and Architecture of Islam: 650-1250*. Pelican History of Art Series.

ETTINGHAUSEN, R. 1963. *Arab Painting*. Geneva.

FARHAT, H. 1973. *The Traditional Music of Iran*. Tehran.

FOUCHÉCOUR, C. H. DE. 1969. *La description de la nature dans la poésie lyrique persane du XIe siècle*. Paris.

——. 1986. *Moralia*. Paris.

FRANKL, P. 1962. *Gothic Architecture*. London.

GALLY, M.; MARCHELLO-NIZIA, CH. 1985. *Littérature de l'Espagne médiévale*. Paris.

GILES, H. 1985. *The Classical History of Chinese Literature*, 3 vols. Gloucester.

GRABAR, O. 1973. *The Formation of Islamic Art*. New Haven. (French translation, 1987. *La formation de l'art islamique*. Paris.)

——. 1992. *The Mediation of Ornament*. Princeton.

HARLE, J. C. 1986. *The Art and Architecture of the Indian Subcontinent*. London.

HEINRICHS, W. (ed.) 1990. *Orientalisches Mittelalter*. Wiesbaden.

HERBERT, P.; MILNER, A. 1989. *South-East Asian Languages and Literatures: A Select Guide*. Hawaii.

HOBSON, R. L. 1993. *The Master Book of Chinese Art*. Gloucester.

KATO, S. 1989. *A History of the First 1000 Years*. Kodansha.

KOBAYASHI, T. U. 1993. *Portraits from the Floating World*. Kodansha.

KRAUTHEIMER, R. 1988. *Early Christian and Byzantine Architecture*. London.

LANDY, P. 1970. *La musique bouddhique, musique du Japon: les traditions musicales*. Paris.

LAZARD, G. 1962. *Les premiers poètes persans (IX–X siècles)*. Paris; Tehran.

LUCE, G. H. 1969–70. *Old Burma – Early Pagan*. J. J. Augustin.

MASON, P. 1993. *History of Japanese Art*. Abrams.

MEDINA, J. T. 1982. *Introduction to Spanish Literature*. Krieger.

MITCHELL, G. (ed.) 1997. *Architecture of the Islamic World*. London.

NKETIA, J. H. 1963. *African Music in Ghana*. London.

PORTE, J. (ed.) 1968. *Bouddhisme; autres musiques traditionelles en Extreme-Orient: Encyclopedie des musiques sacrées*. Paris.

RAGUSA, O. 1990. *First Readings in Italian Literature*. S. F. Vanni.

RAWSON, P. 1990. *The Art of Southeast Asia: Cambodia, Vietnam, Thailand, Laos, Burma, Java, Bali*. Thames & Hudson, London.

REMPEL, L. I. (ed.) 1983. *Hudozhestvennaia Kultura Srednei Azii*. Tashkent.

RYPKA, J. 1968. *History of Iranian Literature*. Dordrecht.

SADIE, S. (ed.) 1980. *The New Grove Dictionary of Music and Musicians*, 20 vols. REF.ML 100., N.48. London.

SCHIMMEL, A. 1992. *A Two-Colored Brocade, the Imagery of Persian Poetry*. Chapel Hill; London.

SCHMIDT. 1970. *Volksgesang und Volkslied: Proben und Probleme*. Berlin.

SOURDEL-THOMINE, J.; SPULER, B. 1973. *Die Kunst des Islam*. Berlin.

STRACHAN, P. 1990. Pagan: *Art and Architecture*. United Kingdom.

WATSON, W. 1994. *Chinese Art and Architecture*. London.

WRIGHT, O. 1978. *The Modal System of Arab and Persian Music*, AD 1250–1300. London.

ZUMTHOR, P. 1987. *La lettre et la voix*. Paris.

8.2

THE NEW WORLD: THE EVIDENCE FROM MESOAMERICA

Alfonso Arellano Hernández

THE WONDER OF THE WORLD

In the vast area known as Mesoamerica and now occupied by Belize, Guatemala, Honduras and parts of El Salvador and Mexico, many different peoples arose whose intellectual and artistic achievements are among the most outstanding in human history. We have many examples of splendid works of art ranging from large stone sculptures to fragile feather work, and including architecture, ceramics, small sculptures (in basalt, tezontle, silex, onyx, obsidian, pyrite, jade, turquoise, rock crystal, stucco, bone, shell, wood, copper, silver and gold), painting (on walls, vessels and codices) and – as indirect means of reference – literature and music.

These works of art were mainly produced by Huastecs, Maya, Aztecs (Mexicas), Mixtecs, Olmecs, Uacusechas or Purepechas, Teotihuacanos, Toltecs, Totonacs, Xochicalcas and Zapotecs, to mention but a few of the peoples involved. The artistic and historical value of the works left behind by these groups is now universally recognized.

However, although there has been human life in America for at least 50,000 years and there are archaeological remains that reveal the earliest concerns and aesthetic canons of those first inhabitants, scholars generally agree that Mesoamerican art as such began around the seventeenth century BC and continued up to the sixteenth century AD. This long period has been divided into three main sub-periods: the Pre-Classic (Early: 1800–1300 BC; Middle: 1300–500 BC; Late: 500 BC–AD 300), the Classic (Early: AD 300–600; Late: AD 600–900) and Post-Classic (Early: AD 900–1250; Late: AD 1250–1500).

During these thirty-three centuries, scenes of everyday life, views of the world, the gods and myths were given artistic expression in many different and complex forms. In the following pages, I shall indicate *grosso modo* some of the most notable examples.

The water's embrace

One of the places where signs of artistic expression first emerged was the Basin of Mexico. It was during the Early Pre-Classic period that human settlements first appeared, based on advanced stone-working techniques. Such sites include El Arbolillo, Zacatenco and Tlatilco. However, the first works of art were ceramics: in addition to vessels decorated with incisions or slips, there are many examples of 'pretty ladies', small female figures with schematic features and prominent breasts and thighs, which are sometimes painted red.

By the Middle Pre-Classic new sites had appeared, such as Copilco, Tlapacoya and Chalcatzingo, with mounds of beaten earth that would later give rise to dwelling places and temples on pyramids. Sculpture in clay (such as the 'Tlatilco acrobat') and in stone became widespread and reflected Olmec influence, as in Chalcatzingo.

However, it was during the Early Pre-Classic that cities first attained importance with the growth of Azcapotzalco, Teotihuacán, Xico, Ticomán and Cerro de la Estrella as major urban centres. Cuicuilco is noteworthy for its pyramid built on a circular plan incorporating four stepped structures. The pottery has polychrome designs and is often in the form of animals, such as fish and birds, with a combination of schematized and natural features.

Gods, jaguars and men

Notwithstanding the above remarks, it is to the Olmecs that the term 'mother culture' in the history of Mesoamerica is applied. The most important area of their settlements was the coast of the Gulf of Mexico, to the south of Veracruz and west of Tabasco. It was there, from the middle of the Early Pre-Classic onwards, that such important cities as La Venta, Tres Zapotes, San Lorenzo, El Manatí, Cerro de las Mesas and Los Tuxtlas grew up.

La Venta is one of the largest and oldest Olmec sites. The site is laid out on a north–south axis, along which lie courtyards flanked by wide platforms and a number of earthworks of various kinds, the most outstanding example of which is the enormous Mound C, the first pyramid in Mesoamerica.

Works in stone (basalt) include geometrically patterned mosaics laid out at ground level and later buried, representing fantastic faces that may be of deities, and the colossal heads, which are portraits with individualized features, almond-shaped eyes, thick lips and flat noses and adorned with different kinds of head-dress. Mention should also be made of the altars with representations of anthropomorphic beings emerging from the jaws of animals – the 'Monster of the Earth' – and sometimes holding small human figures, which are perhaps children. There are also examples of 'stelae', which are large unpolished stone slabs carved with figures of animals (felines and reptiles) and humans (alone, in various attitudes, or together in complex scenes). Particular mention should be made of 'the wrestler', a muscular figure seated with his legs turned towards the left, his body leaning forward and turned towards the right and his arms bent and raised almost to shoulder level.

There are many objects made of jade and other semi-precious stones carved in the shape of small canoes, axes (smooth or engraved), masks or human figurines with a 'V' cut into the forehead. An example of such work is Offering 4 from La Venta. In addition to vessels of various shapes, the pottery includes figures known as 'baby faces': asexual human figures with oval faces, slant eyes, flat noses and thick lips with the mouth turned down at the corners.

As a result of excavations carried out at El Manatí, we also have evidence of wood carving, the existence of ball games – as revealed by rubber balls – and of human sacrifices. Olmec influence extended to various places in Mesoamerica, including Las Bocas (Puebla), Teopantecuanitlán (Guerrero), Chalcatzingo (Morelos) and Xoc (Chiapas).

The land of the setting sun

Western Mexico (the states of Sinaloa, Querétaro, Guanajuato, Colima, Nayarit, Jalisco, Michoacán and Guerrero) is a case apart from the Pre-Classic period onwards. It is known mainly for its pottery and metalwork, which, although not the only means of expression, revealed extraordinary levels of skill in decoration and the creation of different forms. Most of these works were produced for ritual and funerary purposes and were found in shaft-and-chamber tombs.

From the fifth century BC onwards, vessels were decorated with colours and designs that continued to be used until the end of the Post-Classic period. Red, black, ochre and cream are used by themselves, or sometimes two or more of these colours are combined in complicated geometrical shapes and given a highly polished and almost glazed finish.

During the Pre-Classic period, miniature figurines were produced in Chupícuaro, whereas larger sizes were common in Colima, Nayarit and Jalisco during the Classic period. In Sinaloa, geometrical decoration of red and black on cream was the prevailing style. However, apart from similarities in the shapes of the vessels (stirrup-spout bowls, dishes and 'patojos' (drinking pots)), Colima is known for its animal figures: dogs, armadillos, opossums, parrots, ducks, snakes, lizards, crabs and fish. On the other hand, Jalisco is known for its human figures: large figures in various attitudes, profusely decorated and polychromed (geometrical designs) and small figures grouped in scenes from everyday life: mothers holding their children, people playing amongst themselves or at ball games or accompanied by small dogs, and meetings in buildings or in the open air.

Metalworking achieved an extremely high standard in the Post-Classic period, when the lost-wax process was used to produce various kinds of jewellery and adornments of copper, gold and silver, such as small bells, hatchets and clasps. Finally, in Guerrero, where the particular Mezcala style developed, fine stone pieces were produced, especially schematic figures with straight lines and sharp outlines. This style can be seen to advantage in axes, models, anthropomorphic masks and pectorals and other kinds of jewellery.

As far as architecture during the Post-Classic is concerned, it is worth mentioning the large platforms that support temples or *yácatas*, which are buildings that are rectangular and semicircular in plan.

The domination of the horizontal

One of the largest cities on the high plateau during the Classic period was Teotihuacán. Its situation enabled it to exercise control over the Valley of Mexico and, on archaeological evidence, extend its influence to various regions of Mesoamerica. Teotihuacán is of particular importance on account of its architecture, whose main features are its grid-pattern urban plan laid out along two central axes lying perpendicular to each other (one being the Avenue of the Dead), the use of the *talud* (a low sloping wall) and the *tablero* (a vertical panel surrounded by mouldings so as to form a projecting frame), and the almost complete lack of vertical emphasis in the buildings, which blend in with the surrounding hills and valleys.

These features are particularly visible in the palaces or residential compounds consisting of central patios surrounded by porticoes with pillars, passageways and rooms (Atetelco, the Viking Group, Tetitla and Zacuala).

One of the most important buildings is the Ciudadela (citadel), which consists of a central square surrounded on all sides by a continuous platform surmounted by a number of structures arranged symmetrically around the courtyard. In the midst of the citadel rises the 'Pyramid of Quetzalcóatl', which combines three-dimensional sculpture and painting: the *taludes* and *tableros* are decorated with plumed serpents, the heads of divinities having a mosaic-like appearance, and aquatic elements, and the whole complex was painted in greens, reds, ochres and white.

The Pyramids of the Sun and of the Moon, the main centres of attention along the Avenue of the Dead, present something of an exception on account of both the absence of *talud–tablero* and their size, since they rise to heights of over 60 and 40 metres, respectively.

Another distinctive feature of Teotihuacán is the abundance of colour, since very extensive surfaces are painted, mostly in combinations of reds, greens, blues, ochres, white and black, so as to produce complex geometrical, anthropomorphic or zoomorphic designs. Similar examples of such work are provided by Atetelco, Quetzalpapálotl, Tepantitla, Tetitla, La Ventilla, Yayahuala and Zacuala.

Ceramics of different shapes (pots, bowls, cups, vases) were also highly coloured, ranging from monochrome (black, polished red and the typical 'thin orange' ware) to polychrome, and decorated with scenes often similar in style to wall paintings. Figurines and censers are also often decorated in combinations of colours.

The rigid and schematic geometry of the architecture is also found in the sculpture. This is true of the image thought to be of Chalchiuhtlicue, of three-dimensional sculptures (many in onyx and ceramic) and of the masks made of precious materials. Of particular note is the Stela of La Ventilla, which combines straight and curved lines in both its structure and its decoration so as to form complex interlocking designs.

The lords of the white hill

The mountainous region of Oaxaca was occupied by Zapotecs and Mixtecs, among other peoples, from the Middle Pre-Classic to the end of the Post-Classic. Many cities were built, including Coixtlahuaca, Cuilapan, Dainzú, Etla, Lambytieco, Mitla, Monte Albán, Monte Negro, Teotitlán, Yagul, Yanhuitlán and Zaachila.

One of the main urban centres was Monte Albán, where a number of substantial architectural structures surround a large rectangular space in which various other buildings are placed. They are characterized by the use of 'double scapulary' *tableros*, where double mouldings are set around a frame that is open at the bottom so as to form an inverted U shape. There are also ball courts and a number of residential compounds with porticos and courtyards.

Of particular note are the Temple of the Danzantes (Structure L) and the Observatory (Structure J), which is pentagonal in plan. Both structures are decorated with carved stone slabs: in the former they represent human beings in free, loose postures, perhaps sacrificed prisoners of war, while the second shows the conquests of Monte Albán. There are many stelae with carved scenes accompanied by glyphs indicating dates and historical events, e.g. Stelae 12 and 13 of Monte Albán (end of the Middle Pre-Classic) and the *Stone of Bazán* (middle of the Classic period).

Another interesting aspect of Zapotec art is provided by the many tombs containing paintings of complex scenes symbolizing gods and possible historical figures. Among the most famous are Tomb 105 at Monte Albán and Tomb 1 at Xuchilquitongo. In addition, they contain offerings made to the dead, consisting of both monochrome and polychrome ceramics in the form of utilitarian and effigy urns, together with the so-called 'companions' (almost all with representations of the gods Cocijo and 13 Serpent). Other offerings include jewellery made of jade, rock crystal and bone, an outstanding example of which is the jade mask of the so-called 'Bat God'.

The coast of the smiling faces

In the area lying between the rivers Soto la Marina (Tamaulipas) and Grijalva (Tabasco), a number of different cultures developed, including, in addition to the Olmec, those of the Huastecs and the Totonacs and that associated with Remojadas. It is to the Totonacs that the sites of El Tajín, Yohualichán, Isla de Sacrificios and Tres Picos are attributed. At other sites, such as Quiahuiztlán and Cempoala, there is clear Mexica influence.

As far as the architecture is concerned, a distinctive feature at both El Tajín and Yohualichán is the presence of niches on the *tableros* and of delicate relief carvings on stone slabs, columns, *tableros* (panels) and three-dimensional sculptures with predominant intertwined designs and scroll motives. Examples of such work are to be found in the large ball court at El Tajín, on the 'stone of Tepetlaxco' and in the three kinds of objects – *hachas* ('hatchets'), *yugos* ('yokes') and *palmas* ('palms') – associated with the ball game.

The pottery is notable for the figurines, especially those with 'smiling' faces, which are funerary offerings remarkable for the very fact of representing smiles. There are also the large ceramic figures found at El Zapotal, which are of women – the so-called Cihuatete – with their arms extended and dressed in different ways, and the clay skeletons known as Mictlantecuhtli, the god of death. Both El Tajín and Las Higueras have remains of mural paintings that employ designs very similar to those used in their sculpture.

The Huastecs, whose settlements included Tamuín, Tantoc and Castillo de Teayo, are famous for their jewellery made from shells and gold and the pottery decorated with *chapopote* (black asphalt). However, this culture is mainly identified by its three-dimensional sculptures of naked or semi-naked men and women with their arms crossed across their chests and wearing head-dresses consisting of a conical hat with a sort of fan attached. These figures usually represent some kind of contrast, such as that between life and death, as in the examples of the 'Huastec youth' and a number of female figures.

Jungles and humans

One of the great Mesoamerican cultures was the Maya culture, famed for its scientific achievements and its art. It has been classified on a regional basis – Izapa, Motagua, Petén, Usumacinta, Río Bec, Chenes, Planicies Norteñas, Puuc, Costa Oriental – while cities such as Bonampak, Cerros, Chichén Itzá, Cobá, Copán, Dzibilchaltún, Palenque, Quiriguá, Tikal and Uxmal are only some of the hundreds of examples (see Plates 297, 298).

The architecture is characterized by the use of corbelled vaults and stone causeways or *sacbeob* as well as by the presence of profusely decorated roof combs. Typical features of the architecture of the Yucatán peninsula are also the use of columns (monoliths or consisting of several drums), decoration employing stone mosaics and large masks of deities with prominent noses (Uxmal, Kabah, Chicanná) and towers in the form of pyramids (Río Bec, Xpuhil).

The buildings are mostly palace-like structures, low and wide with one or more superimposed storeys and numerous rooms arranged around courtyards; taller pyramid-like platforms (from 20 to 70 metres high) surmounted by temples, and open-ended ball courts. The buildings are arranged so as to leave open spaces between them and, of course, to allow for the irregularities of the terrain. Most walls were painted, either in monochrome or with geometric designs or scenes, and decorated with sculpture in stucco and stone. For the most part, both divinities and humans are represented (see Plate 296).

Painting was also used to decorate codices and urns. Several codices have been recovered from tombs, although except for three of them, named after the places where they are conserved (Dresden, Madrid and Paris), they have become petrified, with the result that their pages cannot be unfolded. They are illustrated with glyphs, stories of the gods, almanacs and various ritual or mythical scenes.

Another distinctive feature is the presence of altars and stelae accompanying the buildings. These are sculptures representing kings taking part in important acts in their lives: enthronement, the capture of prisoners or the shedding of blood (see Figure 23). Such scenes are also represented on lintels of both stone and wood.

Sculpture and painting also display an undeniable fondness for human and animal forms, both schematized and naturalistic, although mixed with or surrounded by various elements strongly imbued with religious symbolism, as is common in Mesoamerica (see Plates 92, 93, 295, 296, 297).

These characteristics are also to be found in the figurative decoration used on ceramics, particularly the effigy urns. In fact, it is during the Classic period that these features are most clearly apparent, as is shown by the plates, cups, bowls and pots, such as the tetrapod urns of Petén, the Vase of Altar de Sacrificios, the censers of Mayapán and the figurines in the Jaina style.

However, objects of high quality and great beauty were also produced in other materials – shell, stucco, bone, jade, wood, obsidian – either with incisions on the surface or carved in low relief. Examples of some of the various kinds

Figure 23 Sacrificial rites in the ball court. Post-classical Maya relief from Chichén Itzá, Yucatán (Mexico), AD 900–1200 (after Schele, L.; Miller, M. E., *The Blood of Kings*, NY 1986, p. 244).

of superb object produced, representing figures of animals, human beings and deities and decorated with glyphs, are the stucco sculptures of God K from Tikal, the jade mosaic masks of Calakmul, the plaques of Nebaj, the wooden sceptres recovered from the Sacred Cenote of Chichén Itzá and the very many 'eccentrics' in obsidian.

The divine inheritance

With the fall of Teotihuacán, a number of other cities that had escaped the fate of that great metropolis came to the fore. Thus, Cholula, Cacaxtla, Xochicalco and El Tajín, together with various centres in Oaxaca and the Maya area, continued to develop throughout the Post-Classic. Of particular importance were Xochicalco and Cacaxtla.

Xochicalco (in the state of Morelos) is generally known for one single building: the Pyramid of the Plumed Serpents. The *taludes* and *tableros* are carved with reliefs of undulating feathered serpents and water snails, which frame seated figures in rich attire. The distinctive artistic style of the city has long been recognized on account of the ball court marker in the form of a macaw head and a number of carved stelae, although recent excavations have brought to light new works of art that will add to our knowledge of the site.

Similarly, Cacaxtla (in Tlaxcala) is famous for its acropolis, which consists of a number of different structures arranged around courtyards. One of these structures, Portico B, has polychrome murals on its *talud* representing a bloody battle scene in which two groups of enemy warriors with their mouths open as if shouting hack and slash at one another, while blood and entrails are scattered on the ground. Other buildings (Portico A, the Red Temple and the Temple of Venus) also contain paintings representing persons in disguise, animals and glyphs. The artistic style of Cacaxtla mostly reflects Maya and probably Ñuiñe influences, the former being most clearly apparent in the Red Temple and the latter in Portico B.

Dialogues with the heart

In the middle of the seventh century AD, a number of tribes from the north arrived on the Central Plateau. One of these groups, known as the Toltecs, established its main centre at Tula (in the state of Hidalgo)(see Plate 299). They brought with them new artistic styles in architecture and sculpture that were grafted onto the dying Teotihuacán tradition. These included modifications of the *tablero–talud* structure, which they decorated with relief carvings, as well as colonnaded halls or galleries, benches with carved reliefs, serpentine columns, pilasters and walls with friezes of warriors, birds, felines and snakes simulating processions, altars supported by small atlantes, and the *chacmool*, reclining anthropomorphic figures with a receptacle resting on the stomach.

The ceramics are characterized by their colour and design, particularly red on cream and ochre with drawings in wavy lines. A completely separate kind of ceramic is the plumbate pottery (also exported to Guatemala), sometimes encrusted with mother of pearl.

The influence of Tula was so great that it even reached as far as the Yucatán peninsula and merged with the Maya tradition, as is shown by various buildings at Chichén Itzá, such as the Temple of the Warriors, the *tzompantli* or 'skull rack', the Court of the Thousand Columns and the 'Mercado'.

The cloud people

In Oaxaca, the major sites such as Monte Albán gave way to other cities such as Tilantongo, Achiutla and Mitla.

Traditionally assigned to the Mixtec culture, Mitla also has a number of Zapotec features, such as the use of the 'scapulary' moulding on the *tablero* and monolithic columns. Stone mosaics are also used, in combination with some of these features, to create friezes with an endless variety of intricate patterns, mainly '*grecas*'.

The pottery is also distinctive on account of its colours and designs: geometrical and stylized figures of animals and men are brought vividly to life through the use of reds, ochres, browns, blues, greens, black and white. Moreover, there are similarities between ceramic painting and the style employed in such codices as the *Bodley, Borgia* (end of the fifteenth century AD), *Colombino* (twelfth century AD), *Féjérvary-Mayer, Nuttall* and *Selden*. Furthermore, the same pictorial style is to be found on the pottery of Cholula (see Plates 1, 94).

In addition to the carving of bones, rock crystal, amber and turquoise, the Mixtecs were extremely skilful in metalworking, particularly gold work, through the use of the lost-wax process. Some of the most impressive examples come from Tomb 7 at Monte Albán: earrings, bracelets, necklaces, pectorals (particularly the Pectoral of Mictlantecuhtli and the *Chimalli* of Yanhuitlán) and lip rings, together with animal figures, beads and goblets carved in rock crystal.

The final turning

New Chichimeca immigrants settled in the Central Valley of Mexico from the thirteenth century AD onwards. They included the Tenochca or Mexica (Aztecs), who in less than 200 years gained control over an extensive area of Mesoamerica.

Tenochtitlán – the Mexica capital – developed as an urban centre from a small island that was gradually enlarged through the construction of *chinampas* on a grid pattern, so that the city had both earth roads and canals for canoes, as well as causeways connecting it to the mainland. The architecture is characterized, in addition to the residential complexes similar to palaces, by the construction of double pyramidal platforms (with a double staircase flanked by *alfardas* (wide ramps) surmounted by cubes, and with two temples situated on the summit) and circular pyramidal structures dedicated to the wind god (see Figure 24). The sacred precinct was surrounded by a *coatepantli* (wall of serpents), including several *tzompantlis* (see Plate 307).

The sculpture has realistic features but is, at the same time, schematic and rigid. Some extraordinary examples are the head of the 'eagle knight', the *cuauhxicalli* (receptacles for hearts) in the form of felines or birds, obsidian or onyx vessels in the shape of monkeys, and skulls of stone or rock crystal. Examples are also to be found of monumental sculptures: Coatlicue, Xochipilli, the 'stone of the sun', the severed head of Coyolxauhqui, the *xiuhcóatl* or the '*teocalli* of sacred war'.

Figure 24 Aztec temple and houses, with a chieftain marching towards them. Footprints indicate migration or movement (redrawn after Alfredo Beltrán from an Aztec codex, fifteenth century AD, in Hagen, Victor W. von, *The Aztec: Man and Tribe*, NY 1958, p. 46).

Few examples of featherwork have survived until the present day, but there are enough to give us an idea of the delicacy of such articles, such as the so-called 'head-dress of Moctezuma' (now in Vienna) and the shield with the figure of an *ahuizote* (mythical 'water dog').

Finally, several codices have come down to us. These are books containing paintings of the histories of kings, of the gods and their myths, and the tribute lists of the kingdom. They include the Codex *Borbonicus*, the Codex *Boturini* or '*Tira de la Peregrinación*', the *Tonalámatl Aubin, Matrícula de Tributos* (Register of Tribute) and the Codex *Mendoza* (see Plates 300–306).

The arrival of new gods

When the Europeans penetrated into America during the early decades of the sixteenth century, the various peoples of Mesoamerica were at different stages of development. Some had reached the end of their cycle of development, some had begun to decline, while others were destroyed by the newcomers.

Cultural cross-fertilization soon occurred as traditions merged. As a result, architecture and the visual arts in Mexico still preserve some aesthetic features inherited from Mesoamerica and it is from these that they draw their strength, together with the traditions that have come from the Old World. They are voices linking the past with the present, complementing life and death, and are echoes of time past that resound down the centuries and still enthrall us with their harmony.

EDITORS' NOTE

During the final phase of preparation of this volume the Editors decided to devote a sub-chapter to the 'Art and Architeture of pre-Columbian America'. Constraints of time and space compelled author Luis Arellano Hernández to confine the text to Mesoamerica, which is a testimony to the cultural wealth of this sub-region during the period under study. However, at that time America comprised other centres of civilization, particularly in the central Andes, where the Incas founded an equally highly civilized empire. These are dealt with in Part VI of this volume (Introduction and Chapters 37–39) and in the Plates section.

BIBLIOGRAPHY

BENSON, E. (ed.) 1981. *Mesoamerican Sites and World-views*. Dumbarton Oaks. Washington.

BERNAL, I. *et al.* 1974–1976. *México, panorama histórico y cultural*, 10 vols. Instituto Nacional de Antropología e Historia. Mexico City.

CASO, A. *et al.* 1981. *Cuarenta siglos de arte mexicano*, 2 vols. Porrúa-Herrero: I. Mexico City.

COOK DE LEONARD, C. *et al.* (eds) 1959. *Esplendor del México antiguo*, 5 vols. Centro de Investigaciones Antropológicas de México. Mexico City.

COVARRUBIAS, M. 1957. *Indian Art of Mexico and Central America*. Knopf. New York.

DAHLGREN DE JORDÁN, B. 1954. *La Mixteca: su cultura e historia prehispánicas*. Instituto de Investigaciones Antropológicas, UNAM. Mexico City.

FLANNERY, K.; MARCUS, J. 1983. *The Cloud People. Divergent Evolution of the Zapotec and Mixtec Civilizations*. Academic Press. New York.

FONCERRADA DE MOLINA, M. 1993. *Cacaxtla. La iconografía de los olmeca–xicalanca*. Instituto de Investigaciones Estéticas, UNAM. Mexico City.

FONCERRADA DE MOLINA, M.; LOMBARDO DE RUIZ, S. 1979. *Vasijas pintadas mayas en contexto arqueológico (catálogo)*. Instituto de Investigaciones Estéticas, UNAM (Estudios y Fuentes del Arte en México, XXXIX). Mexico City.

FUENTE, B. DE LA, 1965. *La escultura de Palenque*. Instituto de Investigaciones Estéticas. UNAM (Estudios y Fuentes del Arte en México, XX). México City.

——. 1974. *Arte prehispánico funerario. El Occidente de México*. Coordinación de Humanidades, UNAM (Colección de Arte, 27). Mexico City.

——. 1975. *Las cabezas colosales olmecas*. Fondo de Cultura Económica (Testimonios del Fondo). Mexico City.

——. 1978. *Los hombres de piedra. Escultura olmeca*. Instituto de Investigaciones Estéticas, UNAM. Mexico City.

FUENTE, B. DE LA, *et al*. 1982. *Historia del arte mexicano*, 12 vols. Secretaría de Educación Pública-Salvat Mexicana de Ediciones, S.A.: I–III (Pre-Columbian Art). Mexico City.

——. 1995. *La acrópolis de Xochicalco*. Instituto de Cultura de Morelos. Mexico City.

FUENTE, B. DE LA (co-ord.) 1995. *La pintura mural prehispánica en México. Teotihuacán*, 2 vols. Instituto de Investigaciones Estéticas, UNAM. Mexico City.

GENDROP, P. (co-ord.) 1971. *Murales prehispánicos*. Artes de México (Artes de México, 144). Mexico City.

——. 1973. *La escultura clásica maya*. Artes de México (Artes de México, 167). Mexico City.

GUTIÉRREZ SOLANA, N. 1985. *Códices de México. Historia e interpretación de los grandes libros pintados prehispánicos*. Panorama Editorial. Mexico City.

HEYDEN, D. 1983. *Mitología y simbolismo de la flora en el México prehispánico*. Instituto de Investigaciones Antropológicas, UNAM (Serie Antropológica, Etnohistoria, 44). Mexico City.

INSTITUTO NACIONAL DE ANTROPOLOGÕA E HISTORIA. 1993–1996. *Revista de Arqueología Mexicana*, 3 vols. (19 nos.). Consejo Nacional para la Cultura y las Artes–Instituto Nacional de Antropología e Historia. Mexico City.

KELEMEN, P. 1969. *Medieval American Art. Masterpieces of the New World before Columbus*, 3rd edn, 2 vols. Dover Publications. New York.

KUBLER, G. 1962. *The Art and Architecture of Ancient America*. Penguin Books, Harmondsworth.

LOMBARDO DE RUIZ, S. (co-ord.). 1987. *La pintura mural maya en Quintana Roo*. Instituto Nacional de Antropología e Historia–Gobierno del Estado de Quintana Roo (Colección Fuentes). Mexico City.

LÓPEZ AUSTIN, A. 1981. *Tarascos y mexicas*. Secretaría de Educación Pública–Fondo de Cultura Económica (SEP/80, 4). Mexico City.

LÓPEZ AUSTIN, A. *et al*. 1989. *Teotihuacán*. El Equilibrista–Turner Libros, Citicorp–Citybank. México–Madrid.

MANZANILLA, L.; LÓPEZ LUJÁN, L. (co-ord.) 1989. *Atlas histórico de Mesoamérica*. Larousse. Mexico City.

——. 1994. *Historia antigua de México*, 3 vols. Instituto Nacional de Antropología e Historia. Mexico City.

MARQUINA, I. 1951. *Arquitectura prehispánica*, 2 vols. Instituto Nacional de Antropología e Historia. Mexico City.

MILLER, M. E. 1982. *The Murals of Bonampak*. University of Texas Press. Austin.

MORLEY, S. G. 1982. *La civilización maya*, 3rd reprint. Fondo de Cultura Económica (Sección de Obras de Antropología). Mexico City.

NICHOLSON, H. B. (ed.) 1967. *The Origins of Religious Art and Iconography in Preclassic Mesoamerica*. University of California. Los Angeles.

NOGUERA, E. 1965. *La cerámica arqueológica de Mesoamérica*. Instituto de Investigaciones Históricas, UNAM (First Series, 86). Mexico City.

OCHOA, L. (ed.) 1979. *Historia prehispánica de la Huaxteca*. Instituto de Investigaciones Antropológicas, UNAM (Arqueología, Etnohistoria, Serie Antropológica, 26). Mexico City.

O'GORMAN, E. *et al*. 1994. *México en el mundo de las colecciones de arte*, 7 vols. Grupo Azabache: I–II (Mesoamérica). Mexico City.

PIÑA CHAN, R. 1975. *Historia, arqueología y arte prehispánico*, 1st reprint. Fondo de Cultura Económica (Sección de Obras de Antropología). Mexico City.

PROSKOURIAKOFF, T. 1950. *A Study of Classic Maya Sculpture*. Carnegie Institution of Washington (Publication 593). Washington.

RUIZ LHUILLIER, A. 1981. *El pueblo maya*. Salvat Mexicana de Ediciones, S.A.-Fundación Cultural San Jerónimo Lídice. Mexico City.

SÉJOURNÉ, L. 1983. *El pensamiento náhuatl cifrado por los calendarios*, 2nd edn. Siglo XXI (Colección América Nuestra, América Indígena, 35). Mexico City.

SOUSTELLE, J. 1966. *L'Art du Mexique ancien*, Arthaud Paris; Spanish trans., 1969. *El arte del México antiguo*. Editorial Juventud. Barcelona.

——. 1986. *Los olmecas*, 1st reprint. Fondo de Cultura Económica. Mexico City.

THOMPSON, J. E. S. 1966. *The Rise and Fall of Maya Civilization*. University of Oklahoma. Norman.

TOSCANO, S. 1984. *Arte precolombino de México y de la América Central*, 4th edn. Instituto de Investigaciones Estéticas, UNAM. Mexico City.

WAUCHOPE, R. (gen. ed.) 1965. *Handbook of Middle American Indians*, 16 vols. University of Texas Press. Austin.

WEAVER, M. P. 1981. *The Aztecs, Maya and their predecessors. Archaeology of Mesoamerica*, 2nd edn. Academic Press. New York.

WESTHEIM, P. 1957. *Ideas fundamentales del arte prehispánico en México*. Fondo de Cultura Económica. Mexico City.

WHITECOTTON, J. 1985. *Los zapotecos. Príncipes, sacerdotes y campesinos*. Fondo de Cultura Económica. Mexico City.

C

REGIONAL SECTION

I: The Heirs of the Graeco-Roman World

INTRODUCTION

Yannis Karayannopoulos

FROM A MEDITERRANEAN TO A CONTINENTAL EUROPE

The three centuries following the death of Justinian in AD 565 witnessed radical changes in that part of the world which came to be known as Europe. First, it divided once and for all into two main areas, East and West, destined to develop independently. In the West, the centre of gravity shifted northwards, away from the Mediterranean, whereas the Eastern or Byzantine part of Europe, despite its preoccupations with events in the north and east, continued to 'coexist' with the Mediterranean.

In the East, Graeco-Roman tradition and Christianity, with modifications and adaptations here and there to cope with altered circumstances, continued to be the dominant influences on private and public life. In the Western part, however, new forms developed, based on Graeco-Roman tradition and Christianity but also owing much to the influence of the Germanic peoples. These new elements coalesced into new state and social formations and were the source of a way of living and thinking which eventually became what is regarded as essentially European.

Justinian's policy of reconquest was the last significant attempt to restore the Roman Empire in its essentially Mediterranean form. With the occupation of Africa, south-east Spain, the Balearic Islands, Corsica, Sardinia and most of Italy, Mediterranean Europe, centred on the East–West axis, seemed to have been reconstituted. This, however, was just an attractive illusion. In the first place, it included only a very small part of the area formerly occupied by the Romans in Spain, and nothing at all of Gaul and England; similarly, a large part of northern Italy was excluded. Furthermore, the regions outside the reconquered territories were organized into new Germanic states which had no sense of belonging to the Roman Empire. The empire, for them, was just a vague concept devoid of any tangible political content.

Thus the imaginary line running from Illyria to Africa had, since AD 395, been the demarcation line not between two parts of the same state but in reality between the Greek culture of the East and the Germano-Latin culture of the West. Even so, one might have been able to speak of the survival of a Mediterranean axis and a Mediterranean Europe in the fifth and sixth centuries if this axis had not been penetrated by marauding Vandals, whose acts of piracy almost interrupted trade and commerce between the western Mediterranean basin and the other regions for almost 100 years, and if there had been a common language and religious dogma among the Mediterranean peoples.

Justinian's reconquest thus turned out to be an artificial creation which could not last, although it did at least give the impression that an East–West axis still existed and was the one true 'Europe'. Behind the façade, however, the foundations of this 'Europe' were being eaten away. New states were springing up in the West during the seventh century: the Visigoths established limited rule in Spain and Septimania; the Franks formed a state out of Gaul, the area west of the Alps and the Jura; while the Lombards had a state in Italy, side by side with the possessions of the Byzantine exarchate of Ravenna.

To these external factors causing the geographical and political unity of Mediterranean Europe to break up was added a very important event – the expansion of the Arab world. Starting from Arabia in the second year after Muḥammad's death (632), the Arabs, between 637 and 647, occupied Syria, Palestine, Egypt and parts of Persia and North Africa. During the years 673–678 and again in 717–718 they laid siege to Constantinople but were repulsed. Europe was firmly secured from that direction.

The Arabs at almost the same time attempted an invasion of Europe through Spain and advanced as far as Aquitaine but were defeated at Poitiers by Charles Martel in 732. This marked the end of the Arab threat to Europe. But in spite of this favourable outcome, the Arab presence in both the eastern and western Mediterranean undoubtedly shattered the geopolitical unity of the area, since it meant that the two shores of the sea were in separate and hostile hands. Furthermore, having succeeded in repelling the Arabs, the Franks did not venture beyond a line running between Pamplona, Zaragoza and Tortosa. They were bent on expansion to the north-east and south-east and in any case did not pursue any aims of maritime domination in the Mediterranean.

On the other side of Europe, during the last 20 years of the sixth century, the Slavs were moving into the north and north-west of the Balkans. Subsequently, and until the establishment of the Slavic states of the Bulgars, Serbs, Croats and Slovenes, they slowly advanced southwards and entered the Greek peninsula, where they established small, isolated settlements that, over the centuries, became Christian, Hellenized and assimilated into the life of the people of the country.

At the beginning of the seventh century, the Serbs and Croats were settling in the west and north-west Balkans and the Slovenes in what is now Istria, thus forming a barrier that the Emperor Heraclius tried to use against the Avars, although from 626 onwards these no longer represented a threat to Byzantium. After the second third of the seventh century a new enemy appears, the Arabs, who in addition to the aggressive stance of the young Bulgarian state (681) were a cause for concern in Byzantium and drew its attention away from the Western world.

In Italy, Lombard expansion provided a new cause for the separation of the two worlds, this time setting the pope in opposition to the East. In fact, in 751, the Lombards occupied Ravenna and abolished the Byzantine exarchate. As the Byzantines had no forces available to dispatch to Italy, the pope turned to the Franks, who, by the Treaty of Ponthium (754), had promised him their help. When the Lombards again attacked Rome in 756, Pepin the Short crossed the Alps and, having defeated the Lombards, offered the pope the territories governed by the exarchs of Pentapolis and Emilia. Twenty years later, in 774, Charlemagne overthrew the Lombard state and ratified the donation of Pepin, which is how the Papal state came into existence. All these events contributed to the definitive alienation of the pope from Byzantium. In fact, after 781, there is no longer any mention in papal documents of the Byzantine emperor's years of rule.

Also contributing to the political and intellectual estrangement between West and East, to the distancing of the Western world from the Mediterranean, and to its turning towards the north, were the political concerns of the Franks. As a northern people, the Franks were more directly concerned with those regions where they had first settled and less concerned with those areas to the south that they had occupied later. When the Norman invasions at the end of the eighth century began to threaten their northern possessions, the Franks naturally turned their attention to these threatened areas. It should be added that, because of these invasions, the Frankish people were on good terms with their local chiefs who were organizing resistance against the Normans, and this had political and social consequences for the Frankish state.

Given all these developments, it was natural that Byzantium, in the minds of Western 'Europeans', became a distant and almost mythical region. The West and the East, those two halves of the 'unique and indivisible Roman Empire' of days gone by, were in the process of becoming two worlds – strangers to each other. That was not all. Cultural developments, hostility in religious and cultural matters, and clashes between East and West were such that the idea of 'Europe', in the eyes of a Western European, became reduced to the northern and western regions of our continent, which effectively meant the empire of Charlemagne. As the historian Nithard put it, '*Carolus . . . omnem Europem* [sic] *omni bonitate repletam reliquit*'. The eastern regions of Europe formed a different world called the 'East', or at best, the 'Eastern Empire'. This was most in evidence where the way of life was concerned.

The bedrock of European culture in the Mediterranean was Graeco-Roman civilization. But whereas in Byzantium, despite the initial aversion felt by Christianity towards paganism, interest in classical literature continued as before, interest in the West declined and, especially from the sixth century onwards, there was a marked decline in cultural activity, both intellectual and linguistic. This was on a large scale as a result of the destruction of the materials of scholarship. During the continual wars and other calamities of the sixth and seventh centuries, libraries were destroyed and schools were no longer able to function. The only exceptions were Spain under the Visigoths and Ravenna and Rome in Italy.

That the classical tradition survived at all can be attributed to the existence of the monasteries, particularly those in Ireland, which, in those difficult times, offered not only a refuge but also a place where classical texts could be studied and transcribed. From Ireland and, following its conversion to Christianity, from England, elements of classical learning were brought back to Gaul as early as the seventh century (with Saint Columba (530–615)), and in the first half of the eighth century to Germany (with Saint Boniface, 672/3–754).

The fact that this intellectual activity was carried on by the clergy rather than the laity led to changes in its objectives, which instead of being purely cultural now had a religious content. This change of objectives continued the tradition inaugurated by Saint Augustine, namely that the sole object of learning should be human's better understanding of Holy Writ. This development had an impact on the education of the laity, which declined in a surprising way. In continental Europe, all cultural activity became the monopoly of the clergy, and the laity were almost all illiterate (see Chapter 10).

Intellectual and cultural activity at that time was nevertheless not the exclusive preserve of the Church and theologians, because the monarchy, for its own administrative and political purposes, also made use of men who had been trained by the Church. Church and monarchy thus became closely linked institutions which created new opportunities for artistic and intellectual expression. As a result of this collaboration, Rome gradually managed to draw the various local churches under its spiritual wing and thus succeeded in imparting to the Western medieval world one of its characteristics – that of a transnational religious unity alongside multiple political differences.

The activity that we have described led, in the age of Charlemagne, to a flowering of cultural activity, subsequently termed the 'Carolingian renaissance', one essential feature of which was the growth of education. The teaching method was based on that of Isidore of Seville, who had maintained the Roman system, in which the *trivium* (grammar, rhetoric and logic) and *quadrivium* (arithmetic, music, geometry and astronomy) were regarded as the servants of the spiritual queen of all knowledge – theology. This work of education, which created favourable conditions for erecting barriers against ignorance and barbarism, began long before Charlemagne. Monastic schools had been active since the beginning of the eighth century. Their full flowering, however, came later, one famous example being the school of Saint Denis, which began its activities during the final thirty years of that century and where work was done to restore the Latin language to its pure form.

Charlemagne founded a court school, about which we know very little. His main achievement, however, was the court academy, which brought together many learned men from various countries, and whose influence on the development of Western literature was very significant. The academy undertook the work of purging Latin of elements from common Germanic and Romance languages and introduced a particularly elegant form of script (the Carolingian cursive script), used in copying manuscripts and in diplomatic documents.

Elsewhere, in the regions that they conquered, particularly Syria and Egypt, the Arabs discovered important centres of learning whose origins went back to the golden age of classical Greece. They were full of libraries containing large numbers of works by Greek, Hebrew, Persian, Chinese and Indian scholars. Through the Arabs, the Western world, rediscovering Greek science and philosophy, was able to develop its own momentum and make original contributions, above all because it was able to view the fruits of Greek science and philosophy not with the respect of the imitator but with the curiosity of the explorer.

In the East, in Byzantium, the situation was different. Classical scholarship and interest in the ancient world had never vanished. Byzantium cultivated on a broad scale the study of the literature of ancient Greece, even though, to begin with at least, it was more an imitator of the spirit of antiquity.

In literature, science and the arts (Carolingian art), an independent tradition thus began to emerge early in Western Europe. It drew on elements taken from the Germanic peoples, made use of the philosophy and science of ancient Greece, enriched and handed on by the Arabs, and took Christian teaching as its foundation, thus opening up new cultural horizons and leading to intellectual and philosophical concepts very different from those of Byzantium. As a result, the cultural divide between Byzantium and the West, and their linguistic and political differences, created a gulf between them which the hatred caused by their differing dogmas made only deeper.

The Europe based on Mediterranean unity had collapsed. Now, side by side with the Byzantine world was emerging in the West what was to become 'Europe' *par excellence*, with its own political objectives and its own intellectual, artistic, social and scientific life. Thus, slowly at first but with gathering momentum from the eighth century on, the centre of political activity shifted from the Mediterranean to the regions belonging to the Frankish state. Mediterranean Europe was supplanted by continental Europe.

Developments in Europe were not limited to the fields of politics and culture. In society, in the economy and in government there were changes and innovations which made for radical differences in comparable situations in Mediterranean and continental Europe. While in Byzantium the changes kept the old social and administrative structure but transformed it to meet the demands of the day, taking Roman law as the basis, similar changes in the West led to innovations that were certainly influenced by Roman law but were also due to the laws, customs and usages of the Germanic peoples. The consequences of these innovations were to be seen in the changes that occurred in agrarian life and relationships and also, and most importantly, in feudalism. Whereas Western agrarian relationships, despite their differences, do have some points in common with institutions in the East, feudalism was an exclusively Western phenomenon. A great role in the emergence of feudalism was played by the need for a good, well-equipped and hence expensive army, the impossibility of paying for it in cash, given the economy of the period, and the need to administer a state consisting of many different peoples with their customs and traditions, without state servants and without a developed administrative system.

All this meant that a sophisticated Roman style of government could not be applied or used. It was therefore finally rejected and a simpler and more convenient, decentralized feudal system was applied, which was the system that typified the new continental Europe. To reach this point, the Middle Ages made use of late Roman institutions such as the *beneficium*, the Celtic system of *vassi* and the Germanic system of the *Gefolgschaft* to create a new system – feudalism – the characteristic feature of which was the personal relationship between the lord and his vassal, based on mutual loyalty, and a graduated system of property ownership and political power. Despite local variations, feudalism also included the new concept of chivalry, with its attendant code of conduct and social communication.

In Byzantium, on the other hand, feudalism as such never appeared. The power of the Byzantine emperor was absolute and indivisible. Everyone else – the common people, large landowners and senior officials – were directly subordinate to him and had no power other than the conditional authority vested in them by the emperor. Equally, there was no such social group as the knights and no literature specifically inspired by them. These differences, too, helped to transform the old united Mediterranean Europe into a continental Europe, detached and divorced from the Mediterranean world and Byzantium.

The history of Europe from the sixth century AD and even earlier is therefore the history of the separation and estrangement of two halves of the European world – the West and the East. Based upon different cultural foundations, the two parts also went their separate ways in terms of economic and social structures in which the West, in particular, made use of the contribution of foreign peoples. Subsequently, the West developed its own unique approach to its problems. But the East continued to follow the Roman tradition in its system of government. It retained for a long time forms of social organization that were freer and more flexible, but it remained true to the old conservative principles of state intervention in trade and the economy. Only at the end of its existence did it try to introduce new ideas into economics, urban organization and administration, but it was too late. It came under Turkish domination and for four hundred years and more played no part in the life of Europe. During the whole of this critical period – a time of discovery, of invention and of development in science and thought – 'Europe' was represented by its western part alone.

BIBLIOGRAPHY

BOOCKMANN, H. 1985. *Einführung in die Geschichte des Mittelalters.* Munich.

FOLZ, R.; GUILLOU, A.; MUSSET, L.; SOURDEL, D. 1972. *De l'antiquité au monde médiéval.* Paris.

LOPEZ, R. S. 1962. *Naissance de l'Europe.* Paris.

MAIER, F. G. 1968. *Die Verwandlung der Mittelmeerwelt.* Frankfurt.

9

BYZANTIUM

9.1
HISTORICAL SUMMARY

Ljubomir Maksimovic

The early history of Byzantium (fourth to sixth century) is set in the framework of the late Roman period. In the reign of Justinian I (527–565), great efforts were made to reconquer the western territories, while the huge undertaking of the codification of Roman law aimed to lay the foundations of a world imperium. The cost of this grandiose political scheme proved, however, too great a burden for the empire, and there followed a period of stagnation during the second half of the sixth century. In fact, this turned out to be not merely a period of respite, but the advent of a new era.

Meanwhile, along the northern frontiers, pressure from the barbarians represented a much more serious threat than in the past. The Balkan defence system was crumbling and finally collapsed in 602. Slav migrants submerged the peninsula, soon limiting the authority of the empire to the coastal towns. In the east, the age-old enemy, Persia, experienced considerable success at the beginning of the seventh century and seized most of the rich territories in the eastern part of the empire (Syria, Palestine, Egypt). This marked the end of the world of antiquity, whose strength had been drained by the outstanding achievements of the age of Justinian and was totally exhausted under his successors.

The empire of the early seventh century thus faced grave threats, despite the fact that it still controlled the eastern Mediterranean basin. Its territories included most of Italy (the exarchate of Ravenna), the central areas of North Africa and Mediterranean Africa (exarchate of Carthage), the Balkan coastal zones, the Aegean islands, Crete, Cyprus and Asia Minor, the latter subsequently emerging as the true source of Byzantine strength. The empire was cosmopolitan in nature, with the Greek element predominating, both in cultural terms and possibly in terms of numbers. This was the setting in which, despite the trials yet to come, lay the possibilities of rebirth.

BYZANTIUM AND ITS NEIGHBOURS (*c.* 600 TO 1025)

The changes which marked the real beginnings of the Byzantine period took place under Heraclius (610–641) and his successors. It became clear that Constantinople, although its rulers were still proclaimed Roman emperors, was no longer the capital of the whole of Christendom. The emperor officially adopted the ancient Greek title of basileus, while the Greek language completely supplanted Latin in official use, with a corresponding modification of the titles of functionaries. Along with this, the introduction of new structures in provincial administration marked the beginnings of fundamental changes in social and military organization.

The new system of administration took on a military character in response to serious threats from outside. The stationing of troops – the *themes* – on certain territories (in the seventh century, almost exclusively in Asia Minor) ensured the establishment, at low cost, of a powerful indigenous army based on a large number of small landowners. Furthermore, as part of this process, a long-term policy of displacement of populations was instituted, affecting the Balkan Slavs, the Armenians and the tribes of Asia Minor and the Caucasus.

These changes did not take place in particularly propitious conditions. Throughout most of the Balkans, Slav expansion was beginning to take on the character of large-scale settlement. The Avar state of Pannonia, which during the previous century had often seemed like a spearhead for the advancing Slav tribes, organized a last great offensive to bring down the empire. The siege of Constantinople in 626 was the culminating point of this venture and at the same time marked its failure, after which the Avars faded out of the Byzantine political scene for good. The hoped-for assistance from Persia had proved inadequate, for the Sasanian state was already at that time having to face a major Byzantine counter-offensive in the east.

After a series of great victories by the Persian army in the second decade of the seventh century, it was the turn of Heraclius to triumph, carrying war into the heart of the Sasanian Empire between 622 and 628. However, beginning in the fourth decade of the seventh century, the Arab invasion took Byzantium by surprise, creating a dangerous threat. First the countries of the Middle East and North Africa, then Cyprus and the Aegean islands situated on the route to Constantinople fell into Arab hands. The capital itself had difficulty in withstanding two protracted sieges (674–678, 717–718). Although the defeat of the invaders before Constantinople heralded final victory, the Arab conquests had nevertheless wrought lasting changes in the position of the empire. Moreover, the emergence of the Bulgar state – the first foreign state south of the Danube – in the ninth decade of the seventh century added a further complication to the already precarious situation of the empire.

The loss of a large number of prosperous towns led to a deterioration in the previously flourishing trade with the Far East. The religious and political situations also underwent change. The empire had lost three of its great spiritual centres (the patriarchates of Jerusalem, Alexandria and Antioch), while during the seventh century the papacy asserted its claims with increasing insistence. The patriarchate of Constantinople remained the only countervailing spiritual force *vis-à-vis* the imperial power, and its leaders thus became suddenly aware of their importance. The first serious criticisms were made of the domination of secular over religious authority, and the eighth century (officially from 730 onwards) witnessed the outbreak of the iconoclastic controversy, a concentrated expression of the contradictions that had emerged between state and Church. This conflict exacerbated the antagonism between the European and Anatolian provinces and ultimately led to a profound internal crisis which was only temporarily set aside on the occasion of the seventh Ecumenical Council (787).

Externally, the iconoclastic crisis brought about deep changes in the political position of Byzantium and, among other effects, marked the beginning of a process whose consequences were to be felt much later. The dissensions between Constantinople and Rome were thereafter expressed more and more openly, especially following the loss of the Ravenna exarchate (751), a setback which forced the empire to abandon the initiative in Italy to the Frankish rulers. On the other fronts, however, Emperor Constantine V (741–775) won several outstanding victories over the Bulgars and re-established the balance in the struggle between Byzantium and the Arabs.

In the early ninth century, the situation again became more complex. Although the economic difficulties were overcome fairly rapidly thanks to the reforms carried out by Nicephorus I (802-811), the war against the Bulgars ended in an unexpected defeat, made even worse by the death of the emperor on the battlefield. On another level, the empire suffered a second major setback with the coronation of Charlemagne as emperor (800), an act which Byzantium was finally obliged to recognize (812) after having vainly attempted to ignore it. In protest, the Byzantine rulers took to assuming the official title, from that time onwards, of 'Emperor of the Romans', which had previously been only tacitly accepted, thus signalling that the challenge from the West did not affect their position as the hierarchical head of Christendom.

The unstable situation at the beginning of the century encouraged a revival of iconoclasm, although this time the movement was only limited in scope. However, the difficult period was not yet at an end: Byzantium was shaken from within by widespread social and ethnic unrest (821–823), while the Arabs assailed Sicily. It was only after the long iconoclastic crisis was finally laid to rest (842/843) that Byzantium again experienced a strong political and cultural resurgence, whose effects were soon to be felt beyond the frontiers of the empire.

The Byzantine state then endeavoured to build up its own sphere of influence by concentrating its real power on a limited number of countries. This undertaking, which was facilitated by the re-establishment of Byzantine authority over the Balkans outside the Greek ethnic area, combined religious, political and cultural components. It was at this time that Byzantine missionary activity developed, through the joint action of the state and the Church. This activity resulted in the conversion of the Khazars, the Moravians and the Bulgars in the seventh decade of the ninth century and of the Serbs in the eighth decade, while subsequent decades witnessed the spread of writing, directly based on Byzantine models, among the Balkan Slavs.

The cultural and political changes and the consequent effort to propagate those changes beyond the frontiers of the empire found a solid basis in a state structure that had now gained in strength. Autocracy was definitively established as the system of government at the end of the ninth century, while a sweeping codification of law was undertaken during the reigns of Basil I (867–886) and Leo VI (886–912). This strengthening of the state was accompanied by a marked increase in its military power. In the second half of the ninth century, Byzantium was finally able to take the strategic initiative once again in the conflict with the Arabs, capturing the town of Bari in southern Italy in 875.

The rising power of Byzantium also experienced some setbacks, the most serious of which resulted from Bulgaria's aggressive policy during the reign of Simeon (893–927). This state, consolidated on both the ethnic and political levels during the ninth century, was then at the height of its power. After inflicting several crushing defeats on Byzantium (896, 913, 917), Simeon was in a position to challenge its rulers' undivided claim to the imperial crown. Although he was unable to achieve his greatest ambition, that of uniting Bulgaria and Byzantium, he none the less forced the government of Constantinople to recognize him as emperor. The fact that this title held good only on Bulgarian territory did nothing to reduce the impact of the ideological and political concession it implied, but it had no direct effect on the position of the empire, since Constantinople soon came to exert a very strong influence over Simeon's successor.

Although the power of the Byzantine Empire was at that time unequalled in the eastern Mediterranean, the first signs of crisis were starting to appear in the decline of small-scale land ownership. As early as the first decades of the tenth century, the imperial authorities became aware of the danger posed by the disappearance of small landowners to the state's financial and military resources. From the third decade onwards, and several times later in the century, laws were promulgated to try to stem this process and to check the increasing power of the aristocracy, but these measures could only delay for a while a social change that had become inevitable.

The tenth century was nevertheless not one of stagnation; it was, on the contrary, marked by the continuation of the brilliant achievements of the previous century. In the cultural field, the humanist trend reached its height through what is usually termed the 'encyclopaedism' of the intellectual circle that grew up around Constantine VII Porphyrogenitus (913–959). In the political–military sphere, the offensives conducted in the east over a number of years were crowned with remarkable success: Crete, Cyprus, Cilicia and northern Syria, then part of the territories of Armenia, were won back from the Arabs. In the north, the Bulgar state was destroyed (971), while Byzantine missionaries secured the conversion of Kievan Rus (988). Lastly, the restoration on a new basis of the Bulgar state (976–1018) – a further threat – was warded off by Basil II (976–1025), making it possible for the first time since the Slav migrations to establish sustainable frontiers along the Danube. However, soon after Basil's death, the empire suddenly found itself at a long-foreseeable turning point (see Map 4).

BYZANTIUM AND ITS NEIGHBOURS UNTIL THE FALL OF CONSTANTINOPLE TO THE LATINS (1025–1204)

In the first half of the eleventh century the effects of the great social changes of the previous century finally became apparent. This was the beginning of a period of open domination by the aristocracy, or more precisely by the bureaucracy of Constantinople. The jealousy of the civilian aristocracy towards the military aristocracy of the provinces, coming on top of the first serious shortage of financial resources, led to a decline in interest in the army. The result was catastrophic. The uprisings of the Slavs and rebellion within the army seriously undermined Byzantine authority in the Balkans on several occasions (1035, 1040, 1047, 1072), an authority which had moreover been undermined by the Petchenegs. The last attempted offensives in Italy (1043) failed, and it was the Normans and the Seljuk Turks who, in the same tragic year (1071), brought down Byzantine authority in Italy (Bari) and most of Asia Minor, respectively. To cap it all, this catastrophe had been preceded by the final schism between the Churches of Rome and Constantinople in 1054, which for Byzantium meant the loss of its last chance of exerting an influence in Western Europe.

The deep dissatisfaction among the military aristocracy, which had for long been kept out of the affairs of state, led to a further reversal. The new dynasty of the Comneni (1081–1185) inherited a disastrous situation: the state's coffers were empty and it found itself faced with threat from the Normans in the Balkans, the powerful Seljuk sultanate of Rūm (1085) and the disquieting rise in the strength of the Serbian state. The empire reacted by carrying out a first major currency devaluation, while endeavouring to secure the help of outside allies and to strengthen the army.

Although the first of these measures met with some success in temporarily solving the financial difficulties, it opened the way for a steady depreciation of the currency during the following centuries. The support of the new Venetian (and later Genoese) allies was bought at the price of their exemption from all trade taxes (May 1082), which gradually brought national trade to the brink of ruin. One of the few successes scored as a result of this alliance is ascribable to the participants of the First Crusade, who, respecting the agreement concluded with Alexius I (1081–1118), won back for him several towns in Asia Minor from the Seljuks (1096–1097). Lastly, the army was strengthened by the characteristically feudal institution of *pronoia* – the conditional granting, for life, of a source of revenue, usually in the form of an estate with the tenantry tied thereto, in exchange for military duty. In this way, a new army was raised to restore the shaken prestige of the empire.

This recovery made it possible to annihilate the dangerous Petchenegs (in 1091, and finally in 1122), to ward off the Norman threat at the beginning of the twelfth century and during the Second Crusade, and to reduce the danger from the Serbs and Hungarians to the level of brief incursions at times when the main body of the imperial army was occupied elsewhere. Lastly, a series of offensives led to the recovery of vast territories in Syria (1130–1137, 1159) and Italy (1155–1156). The cost of these victories, however, far exceeded the material resources of the empire.

Towards the end of the century, the accumulated weaknesses resulted in a sudden reversal of fortunes. A series of grave defeats inflicted by the Seljuks (1176), the Serbs and the Hungarians (1181–1183) and the Normans (the fall of Thessaloniki in 1185) cancelled out all the previous victories. The Bulgars, throwing off the Byzantine yoke, succeeded in re-establishing their state (1185–1190), while Serbia's independence was recognized in all but name (1190). It was no longer possible to halt the process of decline, which was to lead to final disaster at the time of the Fourth Crusade. Having taken and sacked Constantinople (13 April 1204), the Venetians and the Latins divided up the prostrate empire.

THE GREEK BYZANTINE STATES AND THE LATIN EMPIRE (1204–1261)

The territory of the conquered empire was divided up into several Crusader states, ruled by a Latin emperor enthroned at Constantinople, while the Venetians kept for themselves several enclaves in Constantinople and a whole series of strategic strongpoints on the islands and the mainland. Nevertheless, the Byzantine tradition still managed to survive in three states – Trebizond, Epirus and Nicaea, the last of which was to be the main centre from which the restoration of the empire was organized.

Having held out successfully in the unequal struggle against the Latins and the Seljuks, the Nicaean Empire, ruled by the Lascarids, asserted itself during the second and third decades of the thirteenth century as a power to be reckoned with. Trebizond, on the other hand, on account of its situation on the Black Sea, was to remain a peripheral outpost of the Byzantine world until its fall in 1461, whilst Epirus, on the strength of having recaptured Thessaloniki from the Latins (1224), was also rising to the rank of an empire and attempting to challenge the prestige of Nicaea. Defeated by the Bulgars in 1230, this western Greek state was, however, soon eliminated from the political scene and it was the Empire of Nicaea, strengthened by the entry of its troops into Thessaloniki (1246) which finally emerged as the dominant power, in the eyes of Western Europe too. The Lascarid state then experienced a period of great economic and cultural prosperity. The restoration of Byzantium was only a question of time. When Michael VIII (1258/59–1282), the founder of the Paleologue dynasty, came to power, and despite strong opposition from European and Balkan powers, this aim was finally achieved and Constantinopole was recovered without great effort (25 July 1261).

THE PALAEOLOGI: RECOVERY, DECLINE AND FALL (1282–1453)

The restored Byzantine Empire soon found itself in a highly complex international situation, especially after Charles of Anjou seized the crown of Sicily and Naples (1266) and set his sights on the Byzantine capital. His alliance with the great Balkan states and other European powers, combined with the ultimatum by the Curia, forced Constantinople to accept an ecclesiastical union with Rome (Lyons, 1274). This respite was, however, short-lived, and the danger represented by the Angevin coalition soon re-emerged, still more menacing.

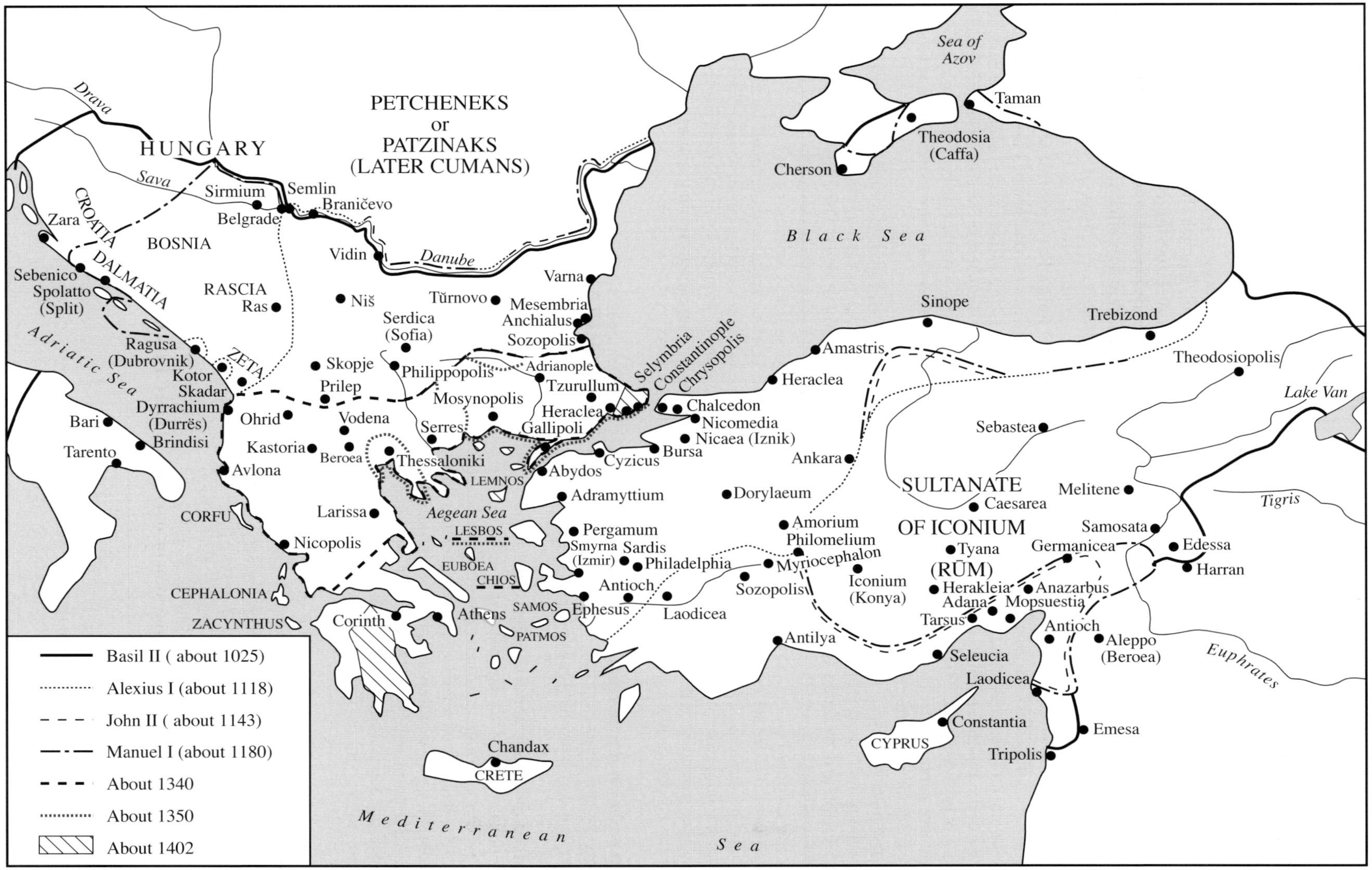

Map 4 The boundaries of Byzantium: from glory to decline (draft Maksimovic, L.).

Finally, Byzantium was saved by the great Sicilian uprising (the Sicilian Vespers, March 1282) which, by putting an end to Angevin domination, at the same time destroyed the Western anti-Byzantine axis.

Byzantium emerged victorious but exhausted from these conflicts, which swallowed up all the financial and military resources inherited from Nicaea. As a result of the steady collapse of finances and the transformation of the pronoia concessions into inherited property, the army on the ground was reduced to a small and second-rate force. The consequences were disastrous, as was shown at the beginning of the fourteenth century by the episode of the Catalan Company of mercenaries who, turning against the empire, plundered most of its European territories.

Towards the end of the thirteenth and the beginning of the fourteenth century, the weakness of the empire became fully apparent. The attacks from Serbia, which took the strategic initiative in Macedonia, now constituted a permanent threat to the northern frontier, while the war between Venice and Genoa (1294–1302) ended in a strengthening of the position of those two Italian republics, to the detriment of Byzantium. To the east, beginning early in the fourteenth century, the Turks gained control of the whole of Asia Minor, with the exception of a few towns or important strongholds.

The deterioration of Byzantium's international position and its chronic internal weakness threw the empire into a series of civil wars that began with a confrontation between rival aristocratic factions (1321–1328) and was succeeded by dynastic conflicts (1341–1347) that at the same time had a social and religious dimension. This period of crisis was also one of constantly increasing pressure from Serbs and Turks. The Serbian state, which occupied a large part of the Balkan territory of the empire, was aiming for the imperial crown (1346), while during the third decade of the century, the Turks captured the last great Byzantine bastions in Asia Minor and very soon began to threaten the European fringes of the empire, thus making even worse the already disastrous effects of civil wars.

The death throes of Byzantium began in the middle of the fourteenth century. Although after the death of the Emperor Dušan (1355) Serbia no longer constituted a threat, the Turks, who had gained a foothold on the mainland of Europe (Gallipoli, 1354), rapidly consolidated their positions in Thrace. Constantinople thus found itself completely encircled, without any real authority over the few territories still belonging to the empire. The only hope then lay in the Christian west, resulting in a series of diplomatic overtures to obtain support from the Catholic powers. However, the reluctance shown by the Western states and the opposition, within the empire itself, to any concessions meant that no positive results could be obtained. The only effort of any consequence to be attempted came to grief at the battle of Nicopolis (1396).

Meanwhile, pressure from the Turks was steadily increasing: the Byzantine emperor became a vassal of the emir and the sultan respectively (1372–1402), Bulgaria disappeared as a state (1393–1396), and a large part of Greece was conquered. The Turkish defeat by Tīmūr at the battle of Ankara (1402) and the ensuing unrest in the Ottoman Empire gave Byzantium a brief period of respite, but the Turks were soon to inflict a further series of bitter blows upon the empire: the siege of Constantinople (1422); the devastation of the Morea, its last relatively rich territory (1423); the obligation again to pay tribute money to the sultan (1424); and the final loss of Thessaloniki (which became Venetian in 1423 and Turkish in 1430). The last vain attempts included the conclusion of the union of the churches at Florence (1439), a further defeat for the Crusaders at Varna (1444) and the proclamation of the Union at Constantinople itself (1452).

In April 1453, Sultan Mehmed II, at the head of an immense army, laid siege to Constantinople, which was defended by only a handful of men. Their heroic resistance was broken on 29 May 1453 by the assault of the Janissaries, during which the last emperor, Constantine XI Dragas, died fighting. The taking of the capital, accompanied by the destruction of treasures of inestimable cultural value, marked the end of the Byzantine Empire, even though a few regions succeeded in holding out, albeit for only a short time, against Turkish domination.

BIBLIOGRAPHY

BECK, H. G. 1978. *Das byzantinische Jahrtausend.* Munich.

BRÉHIER, L. 1970. *Le monde byzantin, I: Vie et mort de Byzance.* Paris.

Cambridge Medieval History. 1966. IV/1: Byzantium and its Neighbours. Cambridge.

ISTORIJA VIZANTII. 1967. *History of Byzantium* I–III. Moscow, pp. 471–519.

OBOLENSKY, D. 1971. *The Byzantine Commonwealth.* London.

OSTROGORSKY, G. 1963. *Geschichte des byzantinischen Staates,* Munich.

VASILIEV, A. A. 1952. *History of the Byzantine Empire.* Madison, Wisconsin.

9.2
STATE ORGANIZATION, SOCIAL STRUCTURE, ECONOMY AND COMMERCE

Yannis Karayannopoulos

The internal history of the Byzantine Empire and its evolution depended on three factors: the old Roman state organization and social structure, the Hellenistic cultural tradition, and Christianity.

The imperial theory of Byzantium was therefore also strongly influenced by these factors. The Byzantine emperor was recognized as the successor of the emperors of Rome and was called *basileus* (emperor) of the Romans. According to the old Roman tradition of the *principatus*, the emperor was selected as the 'best' by the senate, the army and the *demes*, acting as representatives of the Roman people. However, according to the new Christian concepts, at the election of the emperor was manifested the divine will. The emperor was not only the one whom the people had chosen, he was also the one whom God had 'chosen'.

The principle to consider the emperor as the 'best' and 'chosen' of God was not compatible with the practical need for hereditary succession, which could only ensure the normal succession to the throne. To overcome the dissension of the theoretical principle and the practical demand, the Byzantines introduced the institution of co-emperor, the long practice of which created and finally consolidated the dynastic and hereditary succession, although the fiction of a 'real' imperial election and its ceremony remained in effect until the end of the Byzantine Empire.

The administration of the state during the early Byzantine period was based on the reforms of two Roman emperors, Diocletian (245–313) and Constantine (*c.* 285–337); on strict separation between military and civil administration; on the creation of large *praefecturae praetorianae,* which were in turn subdivided into *dioceses* and *provinciae*. However, the continuous attacks of foreign peoples forced the state to abandon little by little the principle of a separation of military and civil authority. These trends were systematized in the years of Justinian, who reorganized the administration of many districts on the basis of the union of the two authorities. After a period of stagnation during the seventh century due to many external distractions, the reorganization was completed in the eighth century through the creation of the civil-military administrative system of themes, as the administrative and military districts into which the empire was divided were now called. But soon the initial *themes* were divided into smaller ones, and thus little by little the thematic institution lost much of its importance. During the later Byzantine period, the *themes* were divided into even smaller districts with only economic authority, and this division ended with the abolition of the thematic institutions, which almost coincided with the time of the conquest of the Byzantine state by the Franks (1204).

After the recapture of Constantinople (1261) whatever remained of the state was administrated by *kephalai* (heads), who resided at towns or fortresses and had authority only over the small areas around their command. At the same time, administrative districts were created with wider powers, mostly of a temporary nature, administered by members of the imperial family. The most important of those administrative entities was the *despotate* of Morea, which lasted even a few years after the fall of Constantinople (1453).

The financial administration of the state during the early Byzantine period was in the hands of three autonomous offices: *the comitiva sacrarum largitionum, the comitiva rerum privatarum and the comitiva sacri patrimonii.* Since the end of the early Byzantine period, the position of the *logothetae*, who were the directors of the offices mentioned above, was strengthened and the financial administration was broken into many special economic departments, the *logothesia*, everyone of which undertook a particular sector of public finances. This new financial organization, although continuously deteriorating, lasted almost until the twelfth century.

After the twelfth century, however, things changed radically. The authority of the *logothesia* fell into the hands of the supervisor of the *vestiarium*, while the financial administration of the provinces was run by the *kephalai* (heads) with the help of special economic employees.

The methods of economic policy remained unchanged and undeveloped, characterized by strong centralization and by continuous state interventions in the sphere of the economic life.

Taxation procedure in the middle and later Byzantine periods comprised three steps: first, the measurement of land by category (arable or pasture land, vineyards, and so on) and by quality (first quality, second, and so on). The result was then converted into *modii*. A *modios* was a unit of land surface varying in size according to the quality of land or cultivation. Afterwards, the state determined the value of the *modios*, again according to the quality of land or cultivation. The product of the number of *modii* of each category of land or cultivation, multiplied by the determined value of the corresponding *modios*, constituted the value of that land or cultivation. This figure served to compute the basic land tax, amounting to 4.16 per cent *ad valorem*. The value of the rest of an estate (for example, kitchen gardens, olive trees, mills) was determined by approximately the same procedure. Animals were taxed at 8.5 per cent of their value.

The *paroikoi* (tenants) were considered part of the total worth of the landowner's estate. Here, each landowner was taxed for each individual *paroikos* family, in proportion to the draught animals which that family possessed.

Taxes in both the middle and later Byzantine state were many and mostly aimed at fiscal purposes, although the social factor was not absent. There were direct taxes (of incomes) but also there were indirect taxes (buying and selling), duties and custom duties.

The monetary taxation was complemented by compulsory services in the early Byzantine Period and later by all kinds of compulsory labour which tax payers had to fulfill.

The results of the estimates of taxable matter were listed in the books of deeds; however, they did not have decisive demonstrative power and were seldom used as documents in disputes about titles.

The army of early Byzantium, organized on the basis of the reforms of Diocletian and Constantine, was divided between defence forces (*limitanei*) and the field army (*comitatenses*).

Both as a general reserve and as forces for deployment and offence, those military units were used around Constantinople (*comitatenses palatini*). The Byzantine army was divided into various *magisteria militum*, the head of which was a *magister militum*.

The Byzantine army during the Early Period was made up of both natives and mercenaries. Since the years of Justinian, the recruiting of natives had been extended, and since the end of the sixth century was imposed on the largest scale.

As noted above, from the seventh century on the *magisteria* were gradually replaced by new military divisions, the *themes*, whose commander or *strategos*, from the mid-eighth century on, exercised both civil and military authority within his *theme*.

The army of the *themes* until the tenth century, as presented to us by the *Tactica* of Emperor Leon VI and other military manuals of the period, was not all that different in organization, generally speaking, from the army of the end of the sixth century, as we know it from the *Strategicon* of Mavrikius. The differences rather lie in military terminology and nomenclature. However, since the eleventh century, the recruiting of natives fell back to second place, and the use of mercenaries gradually became dominant again, mostly because the evolution of the art of war made the existence of well-exercised and experienced professional armies mandatory.

So the majority of the army during the later Byzantine period until the end of the empire was a small mercenary force, consistent in numbers with the poor financial power of the state. The efforts of Manuel Comnenus to reorganize national recruiting on new bases did not yield results.

The navy too, after the middle Byzantine period, was neglected. Practically at the end of this period it was disbanded almost entirely. This situation continued during the later Byzantine period. Since the time of Alexius Comnenus, the state had been forced to ask for assistance from the naval cities of Italy, help bought at too high a price; for the granting of too many commercial privileges undermined the empire's economic strength. Even during the time of the last siege of Constantinople, the fight at sea and on land was only partially fought by Byzantine forces. The state had lost every potential to protect itself and relied solely on foreign help, which was restricted and could not manage to save it from the attacks of its enemies.

The dispensing of justice was the emperor's prerogative. Other judges dispensed justice for reasons of expediency, since the emperor could not judge personally all the cases presented. So there was a hierarchy of judges leading to the emperor who usually judged appeals, with the exception of high treason, which was brought before him immediately. Within the framework of this judiciary system, episcopal courts in the form of *audientia episcopalis* were also developed.

During the later Byzantine period, the institution of 'general judges' of the Romans was created, while in the *castra* and small districts, the duties of judges were performed by the 'heads'.

In the sector of legislation, the early Byzantine period was characterized by a strong effort to codify the laws. The Theodosian Code was published in 438. In its sixteen books were included the laws of all the Byzantine emperors since Constantine. Much more systematic was the codification carried out at the behest of Justinian. In its three separate parts (*Institutes*, *Digest*, *Codex Justinianus*) this codification included all the decisions of the old jurists and all the laws of former emperors still in use. The *novels*, or laws of Justinian which were published after the *Codex*, constituted the fourth part of his legislative work, known to us as the *Corpus Juris Civilis*.

The middle Byzantine period is distinguished by the intense legislative action of its rulers. In the years of the first Isaurian emperor were published the *Ecloga* (726), mainly a collection of customary laws showing the strong influence of Greek law. Unlike the *Ecloga*, the legislation of the Macedonian dynasty – although it had many elements drawn from the legislation of the Isaurians – recalled the model of Justinian's law. Very significant, from a social point of view, were the laws of the Macedonian dynasty, which tried to curb extensive landholdings.

During the later Byzantine period, the state did not show activities equal to those of former periods in the legislative sector. However, such activity could be taken up by private initiative, the main proof being the legal collection put together by Constantine Harmenopoulos, general judge of Thessaloniki in the fourteenth century, known as the *Hexabiblos*.

The social profile of the empire during the early Byzantine period was characterized by the parallel existence of large landowners, free small farmers, free workers attached to leased land or to their professions, and of slaves.

The gap between the *potentiores* (members of the upper class and the great landowners) and the *humiliores* (members of other social strata) was great and was increased by the tendency of the large landholdings to expand at the expense of smaller ones. Justinian, during whose reign the increase of large landed property reached its maximum, managed with wise and strict laws to curb, in some ways, the ambitions of the great landowners and to prepare the way for future developments.

The social measures of Justinian and, in the period of his successors, the attacks of enemies, which reached deep inside the empire, contributed to reducing the power of the great landowners and giving for a while the impression of balance and social security: the small rural communities recovered, excessively large landholdings seemed to come under control, and internal pressures against small landholdings seemed to abate. But after victories against the Arabs there followed a craze for the acquisition of land on the part of the great landowners, who took advantage of the adverse conditions to annex in any way they could the lands of small farmers, soldiers and others, creating serious military and social problems. Military, because with the absorption of their so-called military property, soldiers were left with no income to pay for their needs in arms and equipment; and social, because small free landholdings were destroyed.

The emperors of the Macedonian dynasty tried many times with very strict laws to stop the tendency towards even larger landholdings and to prevent the attendant social misfortune, which threatened the state. But the policy of the Macedonian emperors gave only temporary results. From the eleventh century on, state policy favouring small property holders was abolished, while various kinds of land grant encouraged the consolidation of large property; the *pronoia* system, which originally had been a grant of land taxes otherwise accruing to the state, now evolved from an allotment for a brief period into a lifetime grant and finally into a hereditary concession of the land itself to the grantee.

The continually increasing political instability and weakness, the continually worsening financial situation of the state and the uninterrupted pressures on tax payers determined the profile of Byzantine society during the later Byzantine period. This situation eventually created a dangerous polarization: against a few very rich great landowners stood the great mass of very poor farmers, many of whom became serfs of the landowners since they had no land of their own. Nevertheless, we must say that Byzantine serfdom concerned a particular category of lessors–cultivators, who legally remained perfectly free and who could leave their leased land as soon as they had obtained land of their own. The transitive stage in this trend was made up by the *hypostatikoi* serfs, serfs who were both lessors of land and at the same time owners of land.

The Byzantine economy was a rural one. The lands of Egypt before the Arab conquest, the plains of Asia Minor and of the Balkans, constituted the granaries of the age, but their products were mostly used for local consumption; care was taken only for the provisioning of Constantinople itself by transporting cereals from other provinces. Besides cereals and pulses, wine production, oil, arboriculture, horticulture and apiculture constituted the main rural pursuits of the Byzantines.

Parallel to purely agricultural occupations, cattle-raising was equally developed in Byzantium, especially on the high plains of Asia Minor and the Balkans. Fishing was also very much resorted to, owing to the importance of fish in the Byzantine diet.

Mining was an important sector of the Byzantine economy as well. The state, of course, appropriated the best and most productive mines and marblepits, the mines of alum, and so on, and exploited them using slaves, originally captives of war and convicts as mine workers, the *metallarii*. It granted the less productive mines to citizens for a rent, consistent with the value of their yield, but it also preserved the government's priority in purchasing this yield.

Byzantine economy was actually both rural-oriented and urban-oriented. The urban population, to a limited extent, was also concerned with rural pursuits. Around the towns stretched the lands of town-dwellers who worked these farms and lived by their cultivation, but lived inside the towns, which constituted centres of agricultural trade as well as markets for the products of handicraft. The city, too, was where all services were performed.

Trade, however, was restricted. Whatever was circulated and exchanged was, with a few exceptions, luxuries, small both in bulk and weight, but whose high price offset the expenses and counterbalanced the dangers of their transport. The trade of the age, therefore, was of concern mostly to the wealthy, a small social class, and usually did not have the significance which scholars attribute to it in the economy of this period.

Only international trade was financially important for Byzantium. The merchandise of international trade reached Constantinople or Antioch and Alexandria, from where such goods were transported to the West or made available in Byzantium for the needs of the court, the Church or the wealthy classes.

Since the seventh century, Arab expansion along the Mediterranean coasts had shifted the main axis for trade from east–west to north–south. New commercial roads reached Constantinople from ports on the Black Sea, while Thessaloniki served the Balkan hinterland. Notwithstanding these changes, the east–west trade, while reduced, was not altogether interrupted.

Since the ninth century, foreign merchants had been bringing their products into the large Byzantine towns, and when, by the end of the tenth but mainly from the eleventh century, the Byzantines for political reasons granted to these merchants various privileges and tax exemptions, these same merchants managed gradually to undermine Byzantine commerce and to limit its significance as a main source of income for Byzantium. Later, the advance of the Turks in the Balkans stopped all Byzantine commercial activity.

BIBLIOGRAPHY

AHRWEILER, H. 1979. *Etudes sur les structures administratives et sociales de Byzance*. London.

BRÉHIER, L. 1970. *Les institutions de l'empire byzantin*. Paris.

Cambridge Medieval History 4, II: 1966–67. Government, Church and Civilization. Cambridge.

GROSSE, R. 1920. *Römische Militärgeschichte von Gallienus bis zum Beginn der byzantinischen Themenverfassung*. Berlin.

KARAYANNOPOULOS, Y. 1988. *La théorie politique byzantine*. Thessaloniki (in Greek).

——. 1991. Entwicklungsetappen der agrargesell-schaftlichen Verhältnisse. In: *Byzanz. XXIIIe Congrès International des Etudes Byzantines*, Rapports pléniers, Moscow, pp. 102–51.

KÜHN, H. J. 1991. *Die byzantinische Armee im 10. u. 11. Jh.* Vienna.

LEMERLE, P. 1991. *Histoire de Byzance*, Paris.

RUNCIMAN, S. 1958. *Byzantine Civilization*. New York.

ZACHARIA, K. E. 1892. *v. Lingenthal, Geschichte des griechisch-römischen Rechts*. Berlin.

9.3
CULTURAL ACHIEVEMENT

Panayotis L. Vocotopoulos

CIVILIZATION AND CULTURAL ACHIEVEMENTS

A German historian has called the Byzantine state 'the Holy Roman Empire of the Greek nation'. Byzantine civilization, too, was rooted in these two traditions: the Roman, which can be detected mainly in legislation and, to a lesser degree, in architecture, as it was practised in the eastern provinces of the empire, and the Greek, which became predominant after the loss of Italy and is manifest in literature, science and the arts. All the manifestations of Byzantine culture were at the same time permeated by Christianity, which was ever present in public and private life. Eastern, mainly Arabic, elements are often found in Byzantine decoration, while after the Crusades, different aspects of Byzantine culture were influenced by the Latin West.

Literature

Byzantine literature is a continuation of ancient Greek literature. There was no break with the classical tradition, as there was in the Latin West. A part of it is written in an idiom imitating the Attic dialect of the fifth and fourth centuries BC, while another follows the vernacular and does not differ significantly from modern Greek, as it was spoken in the nineteenth century. Several ancient genres, such as tragedy and comedy, disappeared, owing to the change in outlook of medieval men and to the growing influence of the Church. Lyric poetry produced mainly religious hymns; foremost among hymnographers were Andrew of Crete, John Damascene and Kosmas of Maiouma in the eighth century. The former is credited with the creation of the *kanon*, consisting of nine odes, which replaced the *kontakion*, until then the dominant form of church hymn. The most important epic (twelfth century, but compiled from earlier sources) related the deeds of the legendary defender of the Eastern marches, Digenis Akritas. Romances of the Palaeologan period, such as *Belthandros and Chrysantza*, imitate Western chivalric literature. Many epigrams were composed, especially from the eleventh century onwards (Christopher of Mytilene, eleventh century; Manuel Philes, fourteenth century). Theology always enjoyed a privileged status in Byzantine thought and literature. In the eighth and ninth centuries the debate over icon worship was its main subject. The principal advocates of icon worship were Saint John Damascene and Saint Theodore the Studite. Hagiographical and homiletical literature flourished, especially during the middle Byzantine period. Many florilegia with excerpts dealing with various heresies were compiled in the twelfth century. In the fourteenth century, the Hesychast movement, centring on a specific method of achieving communion with God, provoked heated debates between its advocates, such as Saint Gregory Palamas, and its adversaries, like Demetrios Kydones. The most important Byzantine philosopher was George Gemistos or Plethon (*c.* 1360–1452), a defender of Plato as opposed to Aristotle, who first taught in Constantinople but spent the last forty years of his long life in Mistra in the Peloponnese teaching and writing. Epistolography allows us a glimpse into the private life of the Byzantines, although it stuck too often to stereotyped formulas. Historians such as Laonikos Chalkokondyles (fifteenth century) imitate Thucydides in language and style, while the authors of chronicles wrote histories of humankind in the vernacular, beginning with Adam and ending with their own time. Among historians, one may mention Michael Psellos (eleventh century), Anna Comnene (twelfth century), Niketas Choniates (thirteenth century) and Nikephoros Gregoras (fourteenth century), and among chroniclers Theophanes (ninth century) and John Skylitzes (eleventh century).

Education

Literacy appears to have been more widespread in the Greek East than in the Latin West, at least in the cities. The language and substance of education were Greek; very few people could read or speak Latin. Small children were taught reading and writing from the Bible, especially the psalter. At a later age – ten or twelve – orthography and grammar were taught from Greek classical texts. One has to bear in mind that Greek classical literature and scientific texts were copied again and again and saved from oblivion by Byzantine scholars and scribes (see Plate 129). Educated Byzantines were familiar both with the scriptures and with Greek classical authors and although devout Christians, were often experts in Greek mythology. However, schools in Byzantium were rare, and reading, writing and arithmetic were often taught privately. From the mid-ninth century on, however, a school of higher learning, where rhetoric, philosophy, mathematics and astronomy as well as music, law and medicine were taught, was revived in Constantinople. In the eleventh and twelfth centuries, several higher educational institutions, roughly equivalent to universities, were active in the capital. Teachers included the more famous intellectuals of the time, such as John Mavropous and Michael Psellos, who boasted of his many foreign pupils. These schools ceased to function after the capture of Constantinople by the Latins in 1204. After the city's liberation in 1261, several schools of a university level are mentioned, such as that of Maximos Planoudes (d. *c.* 1305) and some functioned till the Turkish conquest, like the *katholikon mouseion,* where the famous scholars John Argyropoulos and Michael Apostolis taught. Constantinople retained to the end its reputation as a centre of higher education. In the fifteenth century, many of the more famous scholars emigrated to Italy, where they were very much sought after.

Sports

Sports were not as important as in late antiquity. Among those practised after the seventh century were running, wrestling, archery and horse races. The higher classes played *tzykanion* – a ball game of Persian origin on horseback, resembling polo. Tournaments, between both individuals and groups, were introduced at the time of the Crusades.

Science and technology

The Byzantines preserved the scientific treatises of Greek antiquity, and the works of Greek astronomers, mathematicians and scientists were copied and illustrated; they also produced compendia of their writings but did not significantly advance scientific research.

Byzantine geography relied heavily on Strabo; writers, however, endeavoured to reconcile their knowledge with the Bible and with data contained in older sources. The writings of Constantine VII Porphyrogennetos (tenth century) contain information on the Byzantine Empire and neighbouring lands but mix the contemporary situation with that described in ancient treatises. Travel literature developed during the late period (twelfth to fifteenth century). Few Byzantine maps have survived from the period considered here; most date from the thirteenth and fourteenth centuries and illustrate the treatises of Ptolemy (see Plate 122) and Strabo. The Mediterranean was supposed to be the centre of the Earth.

Numbers were represented with twenty-seven letters of the Greek alphabet, including three which were by then out of use. Indian–Arabic numerals were introduced in the thirteenth century, but Greek letters continued also to be used for many centuries.

Apart from sundials, the Byzantines used water clocks to measure time; they do not appear to have manufactured mechanical clocks. Systems of fire beacons allowed messages to be transmitted very quickly.

Although many ancient mines had ceased to function by the sixth century, Byzantium still produced gold, silver, iron and copper. The main source of power was animals. Watermills, known already in late antiquity, became widespread during the middle Byzantine period, while windmills are attested in the fourteenth century. Among technical innovations one may mention the use of the stirrup, which is first documented in the seventh century, and the introduction of the nailed horseshoe in the tenth. The Byzantines used a variety of weapons (different types of spears, bows, swords, maces, axes and slings). Siege machinery was a continuation of devices used in antiquity, such as wooden towers, rams, catapults and crossbows mounted on stands. Tunnels were dug to bring down walls. Although 'Greek fire' (naphtha) was discovered in Byzantium in the sixth century, the Byzantines did not produce firearms, developed in the West in the fourteenth century, and did not have the means during the late period to hire Western gunsmiths.

Byzantine ships were small and fast. They had round hulls, one to three masts and triangular sails. Constantinople was the main shipbuilding centre. As opposed to the outer-shell construction method of late antiquity, the Byzantines first built the frame of a ship.

Byzantine textiles were made of wool, linen and silk; cotton was introduced in the late period. They were woven in state-owned and private establishments, as well as in households. Silk was introduced in the sixth century, and silk factories were established in both the capital and the provinces, for example Thebes and Corinth.

The main writing material was parchment. Paper was introduced by the Arabs in the ninth century, but its use was not widespread before the twelfth century. Oriental paper was supplanted by Italian in the fourteenth century. Byzantine technology, ahead of that of neighbouring states till the tenth century, lagged afterwards behind that of the Western and Islamic powers. In the mid-1440s, Bessarion addressed a letter to Constantine Palaeologus, urging him to send young men to Italy in order to learn engineering, the fabrication of arms and shipbuilding.

Medicine

Byzantine medicine inherited the principles of Graeco-Roman medicine and depended mainly on Hippocrates and Galen. It was, however, enriched by Arab and in later centuries, by Western medicine. Physicians were specialized, practised new theories such as uroscopy and prescribed a variety of drugs for various diseases. The seventh-century physician Paul of Aegina describes in detail dozens of difficult operations. The Byzantines used a wide variety of sophisticated surgical instruments. Military treatises list physicians and men whose task was to rescue casualties among army personnel. Hospitals existed not only in Constantinople but also in the provinces. All major monasteries had a dispensary for the sick. The only well-known hospital from written sources, that of the Pantocrator monastery in the capital, had fifty beds, specialized physicians – including a woman for female patients – and many pharmacists. Treatises of ancient physicians on pharmacology and surgery were copied and illustrated. Alongside scientific medicine, patients sought healing through visits to miraculous shrines or astrology (see Plate 129).

Law

Byzantine law was based on Roman law, as it had been codified and completed under Emperor Justinian in the sixth century. In the second quarter of the eighth century, Leo III issued the Ekloge, which aimed to simplify the complex law system of the sixth century. The so-called Rhodian maritime law, regulating shipping, has been dated between the seventh and ninth centuries. The *Nomos Georgikos* (Farmer's law), which regulated relations within villages and probably dates from the eighth century, was subsequently revised. Many laws were promulgated or codified under Leo VI the Wise (886–912). The *Procheiros Nomos* is a revision of the early legislation of the Macedonian dynasty on private and penal law. The *Basilika* are a collection of laws aiming to simplify Justinian's code. To the tenth century is also dated the Book of the Eparch, which regulated the activities of guilds in Constantinople. The more important law book of the late centuries of Byzantium is the *Hexabiblos* by Constantine Harmenopoulos, a judge in Thessaloniki in the mid-fourteenth century; this was an easy-to-use compilation of secular law which became very popular and was adopted as a law code in Greece until the early twentieth century as well as in several Slavic countries.

Architecture

The regular city planning of antiquity, which survived into the sixth century, gave way to a maze of narrow winding streets with very few open spaces.

As in the preceding period of late antiquity, surviving buildings are almost exclusively churches and fortifications. Very few palaces, houses, baths or monastic buildings are preserved or have been adequately excavated and published.

The main difference in the layout of churches, resulting from changes in the liturgy, consisted of the addition of two bays – the *prothesis* and the *diakonikon* – on either side of the sanctuary. Most churches were now vaulted rather than timber-roofed. It should be noted that, contrary to Latin practice, no particular architectural form was prescribed according to the function of the church building – monastic or parish church, cathedral and so on.

Few churches were erected during the so-called dark period (seventh–mid-ninth century). The most important is perhaps Saint Sophia in Thessaloniki, a large church with a dome resting on massive piers, enveloped on three sides by an ambulatory, which was built in the eighth century. This plan continued to be used until the fourteenth century, mainly in Constantinople and southern Macedonia.

A distinctive feature of Byzantine church architecture after the eighth century is the modest size of churches, compared with their early Christian antecedents. Middle and late Byzantine churches rarely exceed 30 m in length, while some early Christian ones approach or even exceed 100 m. The trend was obviously towards a great number of small churches rather than a few large ones.

The church plan one always associates with middle and late Byzantine architecture is the cross-in-square, which superseded the basilica characteristic of the early Christian period: a dome rose at the intersection of two barrel vaults, which formed a cross and were inserted within a square or rectangle. The corner bays were usually covered with vaults and more rarely with smaller domes.

From the thirteenth century onwards, the lateral arm of the cross was often extended by two lateral apses. This variant, called the athonite plan, was particularly popular in monastic churches until the seventeenth century. In the eleventh century appear two elaborate church types: one with a dome resting on eight supports, exemplified by the main churches of the monasteries of Hosios Loukas in central Greece and of Daphni near Athens; the other consisting of a domed octaconch rising from a square base. Its best example is the church of the Nea Moni on the island of Chios in the Aegean. Other churches had the form of a free-standing domed cross, a vaulted or timber-roofed hall or a three-aisled basilica.

Some churches do not fit any standard plan. During the late Byzantine period, churches in Constantinople, Thrace, Macedonia and Epirus were often surrounded on two or three sides by loggias and chapels.

Façades were austere until the end of the tenth century. They gradually became more colourful and were enlivened with bricks cut into different shapes. In Constantinople, Thrace and Macedonia, they were often articulated with setbacks and pilasters. Sculptural decoration was confined to capitals, cornices and door frames, or was non-existent in the case of more modest buildings. In the more lavish structures, such as the main churches of the monasteries of Hosios Loukas and Nea Moni, the lower part of the walls was covered with a marble revetment and the marble floor was enlivened with geometrical patterns in different colours. The upper part of the interior glittered with mosaics. In most churches, however, the walls and vaults were adorned in the cheaper medium of fresco (see Plates 63, 145, 146, 148).

Very few, if any, large public buildings were constructed in the provinces after the sixth century. Byzantine emperors continued to reside in the Great Palace in Constantinople, which was a complex of buildings within a large precinct like the Kremlin in Moscow, and not a single large building like the palaces of Versailles or Buckingham. In the twelfth century, the Great Palace was abandoned in favour of the smaller palace of Blachernae, which had rather the character of a castle.

The more important houses were built around a courtyard. Construction was generally of poor quality. In the countryside, houses were sometimes built of unbaked red bricks or reeds plastered with mud and had an earthen floor.

The practice of bathing, an important element of late antiquity culture, underwent a radical change after the seventh century. Many baths were abandoned and bathing came to be considered a luxury when not medically prescribed. Monastic regulations prescribed bathing between twice a month and thrice a year; sick monks, however, were allowed frequent baths. Byzantine baths had plans similar to those of the Roman period and comprised vaulted rooms for dressing and cold, warm or hot bathing.

Byzantine fortifications consisted of a wall with projecting towers and fortified gates. Most surrounded towns, but there were also inner citadels and barrier walls, like the Hexamilion, which protected the isthmus yielding access to the Peloponnese. Most important of all were the walls surrounding Constantinople, whose land fortifications comprised a moat, an outer wall and a higher inner wall, from which projected towers. The walls of Thessaloniki are also comparatively well preserved. Byzantine fortifications evolved according to changing needs. In the twelfth century, towers were built for the use of the crossbows, while in the fifteenth century one encounters round ports for firearms.

Monumental painting

Paintings decorating churches or secular buildings were executed in mosaic or, more frequently, in fresco. Few secular paintings have survived, but we know from old descriptions that Byzantine palaces and houses were adorned with hunting or battle scenes. Portraits were quite widespread, not only in mosaic and fresco but also on panels and in miniatures.

Most religious buildings had been decorated till the early eighth century with representations of Christ, the Virgin, saints and scenes either of events of the Old and New Testaments or of an allegorical nature. There was also a trend to decorate churches only with geometric or vegetal motifs. A portion of the clergy and the faithful were opposed to representing Christ, the saints and religious scenes, which reminded them of pagan practices, and this opposition culminated in the iconoclastic crisis, which lasted from the 720s till 843 with a thirty-year interruption. Religious representations were forbidden, destroyed and replaced by non-figural decorations and crosses (see Plates 193 (a) and (b)). After the controversy ended with the victory of the icon worshippers, a system of decorating churches evolved where the cupola was adorned with the figure of Christ surrounded by angels, prophets and apostles, the apse with the Virgin Mary and the more important holy bishops, the vaults with scenes from the life of Christ and Mary, and the lower parts of the walls with various saints.

Some of the works of the century following the restoration of icons, such as the apse mosaics of Saint Sophia in Constantinople, display an impressionistic quality with classic reminiscences, long proportions and an idealistic expression (see Plate 148).

Most wall decorations of the first half of the eleventh century are characterized by motionless stately figures with an ecstatic gaze, thick contours and a system of folds enhancing the various parts of the body, as in Hosios Loukas. New subjects appear in the course of the eleventh century, such as the Last Judgement. A classicizing style with charming lively figures, noble stances and idealized features follows at the end of the eleventh and the early twelfth century; it is best expressed in the mosaics of Daphni near Athens.

An elaborate linear manner with elongated bodies, complicated drapery and a search for dramatic effects evolves in the third quarter of the twelfth century; its masterwork is the fresco decoration of the church of Saint Panteleimon at Nerezi, near Skopje, founded in 1164 by a member of the ruling dynasty and obviously connected with the capital. This tendency is carried to an extreme in the 'dynamic style' of the frescoes of Kurbinovo, near the Lake of Ochrid (1191) and the church of Saint Anarghyri in Kastoria. A reaction was inevitable; during the second and third quarters of the thirteenth century a monumental sculptural style prevailed, whose best works are the frescoes of Mileševa (*c.* 1235) and Sopoćani (1265) in Serbia.

Around 1300, there developed a cubic style, with thick bodies, meaningful gestures and stern faces and fraught moreover with symbolic scenes. Iconography was enriched in the thirteenth and fourteenth centuries with illustrations derived from religious hymns. In the second decade of the fourteenth century, in the decorations of the Holy Apostles in Thessaloniki and of the monastery of Chora in Constantinople, the anonymous artists introduce more figures in each scene, achieve a better sense of plasticity and gradual shading and depict with great ability the emotions of their figures. Elaborate buildings convey a new sense of space.

Two tendencies coexist in metropolitan painting of the second half of the fourteenth and of the early fifteenth century: an expressionistic one, with figures painted summarily with rapid brushstrokes, agitated draperies and awkward stances, as seen in the frescoes of Ivanovo in Bulgaria and Volotovo in Russia; and a more classical style, characterized by rhythmical and symmetrical compositions, restrained gestures and a calm expression, best exemplified by the frescoes of the Peribleptos church in Mistra, which are ascribed to Constantinopolitan masters.

Since the beginning of the fifteenth century, very little artistic activity is attested in Constantinople, practically reduced to an impoverished city-state. It is gradually superseded as a major artistic centre by the island of Crete, where social and economic conditions under Venetian rule were favourable to artistic creation. Crete was to remain the main cultural and artistic centre of Hellenism until its capture by the Turks in 1669.

Panel painting

Icons, that is, religious pictures usually painted on wooden panels, played an important role in both public and private worship in the orthodox world. Very few survive from the sixth to the eleventh century. A few dozen date from the twelfth and thirteenth, many more from the fourteenth and fifteenth centuries, while icons of the sixteenth century are preserved in large quantities.

The style and iconography of icons did not differ significantly from that of monumental or miniature painting. From the twelfth century onwards, the screen shutting off the sanctuary from the rest of the church was gradually covered with icons and was called for that reason an *iconostasis*. The main scenes of the lives of Christ and the Virgin, as well as Christ standing or seated, whom the Virgin, John the Baptist, angels and apostles implored for the salvation of humankind, were depicted on beams or single panels on top of the *iconostasis*, while larger icons of Christ, the Virgin and Saint John were placed at breast level. Other icons were hung on walls or placed on special stands for the faithful to worship. Icons were usually painted in the technique of tempera, but some were made of minute glass or gold tesserae set up on a base of wax (see Plates 56, 57, 147).

Icons, as well as wall paintings or miniatures, were usually anonymous. This is not perhaps due so much to Christian modesty as to the fact that painters were considered in Byzantium as simple artisans, as they also were in medieval Western Europe.

Illuminated manuscripts

Several hundred Byzantine illuminated manuscripts have survived. They were often illustrated by the same artisans who painted frescoes or icons and reflect the same trends in style and, as far as religious subjects are concerned, in iconography. The Gospels were by far the most often illustrated text. Miniatures included portraits of the four evangelists, usually full-page, decorative headings, and scenes illustrating the Gospel text, either full-page or of smaller format, inserted within the text; these scenes may range from four or five to several hundred. Of the other texts of the Bible, the one most often illustrated was the Psalter, with either a few large-format illuminations or scores of small-scale scenes painted in the margins (see Plate 150).

Sculpture

Sculpture in the round practically disappeared in the seventh century, but marble reliefs decorated chancel screens, sarcophagi and numerous buildings, especially churches, which were adorned with carved capitals, portals or cornices. Their decoration included geometric and vegetal motifs and more rarely animals, human figures or motifs derived from Arabic script. Very often the marble used came from ruined older buildings. An increased plasticity is noticeable from the twelfth century onwards.

Very few examples of Byzantine wood carving are preserved, due to the perishable character of this material. They include doors, chancel screens and icons, where the wood was also painted. All date from the last centuries of Byzantium.

Minor arts

Ivory carving, whose tradition had been interrupted in the seventh century, reappeared on an impressive scale in the tenth and eleventh centuries and produced works of very high quality (see Plate 149). Ivory relief plaques with religious representations were used as small-format icons or formed triptychs, while plaques with religious or mythological subjects derived from classical art, and also animal or floral motifs, adorned caskets, most of which were originally jewellery boxes. Contrary to Western practice, ivories did not decorate book covers in Byzantium. From the twelfth century onwards, ivory was replaced by steatite, a usually green-coloured stone that was easier to carve and cheaper, and from which were made not only small icons but also amulets and patens.

Bronze statuary was abandoned in the seventh century, but metals such as gold, silver, bronze and lead were used to produce medallions, jewellery, liturgical vessels and dishes. Embellishments on silver might be in niello, a black-coloured mixture of sulphur with silver, copper or lead. Bronze plaques with niello or engraved decoration were used as revetments of monumental doors, some of which, dating from the eleventh century, are preserved in Italy.

Byzantine jewellery was based on both the Graeco-Roman and the Eastern tradition. It was extensively used by the imperial court and the aristocracy, but ordinary people also wore gilded bronze jewels, imitating gold, while glass paste simulated gems.

Enamels, coloured with metallic oxides and fused with metal, were used to decorate luxury objects such as reliquaries, icons, metal crosses, liturgical vessels and crowns.

The Byzantines produced a wide range of objects from glass, such as cups, bottles, lamps, mosaic cubes and window panels. Exquisite Byzantine glass vessels, some with mythological scenes, are now preserved in the treasury of San Marco in Venice.

The more common raw materials of Byzantine textiles were linen, wool and silk. Ancient costume was gradually abandoned and trousers and sleeves introduced. In the Palaeologan period, costume was much influenced by both Western and Islamic fashions.

Apart from garments, textiles were also used in curtains, which were in wide use in both religious and secular architecture, and for various liturgical cloths. Sumptuous silk textiles, produced in Constantinople, used to be distributed on special occasions or presented to foreign rulers or high officials. They were often decorated with symmetrical vegetal motifs, highly stylized animals or human figures.

Embroideries adorned the costumes of the emperor and high dignitaries, as well as liturgical clothes. They were made with golden and silver threads on silk backing, and were sometimes enhanced with precious stones. Silk threads were used for the faces, which seem sometimes to be painted. The art of embroidery was mainly exercised by men, and reached its peak in the Palaeologan period (see Plate 58).

Medieval pottery did not attain the quality of ancient Greek products. In the seventh century, glazed wares appeared to replace the red-slipped ones of late antiquity. In the ninth–twelfth centuries, geometric, vegetal or figural designs – vivid though stylized animals and sometimes human figures – were painted in various colours on a white fabric. Islamic motifs, especially Kūfic letters, were not uncommon. Among the techniques introduced after the tenth century, partly under Islamic influence, was incised ware. Some of the best workshops have been identified as Constantinopolitan. Apart from pottery for the table or the kitchen, clay was used to produce lamps, censers, bricks and various ornaments, which were often embedded in the façades of buildings from the late tenth century onwards, to great decorative effect.

CIVILIZATION: IRRADIATION, IMPACT AND INTERACTION

The diffusion of Byzantine civilization into other countries and cultures, and the opposite process, are complex phenomena which lasted in some cases for a thousand years and in others for several centuries. Let us consider only mutual relations in the realm of art.

Many of the countries involved had been parts of the Byzantine Empire, former Byzantine subjects lived in them, and they preserved on their soil earlier Byzantine monuments; others had only more indirect contacts with Byzantium. Some countries shared with Byzantium the same Christian faith; others differed in dogma, while the Arabs and Turks belonged to another religion altogether. Several of the peoples with which Byzantium had contacts already enjoyed high cultures of their own, while others were just emerging as states or cultural entities. In some cases, there was mutual interaction; in others, Byzantium influenced the art of other countries without itself being influenced by them. A general consideration is that Byzantine painting enjoyed far more prestige and was far more imitated than its architecture.

In the case of the Latin West, Byzantine influence was much stronger in Italy and the Crusader states than in those countries beyond the Alps. At first, Byzantine art alone exercised its impact on Western art, but in the thirteenth–sixteenth centuries the situation was gradually reversed. Relations with the Islamic world were reciprocal: at times, the Byzantine influence prevailed, as in the eighth or the fourteenth century; at times the Islamic prevailed, as during the middle Byzantine period. The Christian lands of the Caucasus owed much to Byzantine painting but not to Byzantine architecture. Bulgaria does not appear to have developed a distinct style of its own, and its local art is an integral part of Byzantine art. In the case of the other Orthodox countries of Eastern Europe – Serbia, Russia, Romania – Byzantine art and architecture were part of a total religious and cultural package which these countries received as a coherent whole. Byzantine painting exercised a lasting influence, but architecture also depended on Western models or followed its own course.

The Latin West

Byzantium always entertained close relations, friendly or hostile, with the Latin Church and the 'Franks', as all Western Christians were designated in Byzantium. In the West, the

Greek language was not widely known, except in southern Italy. Therefore numerous Greek theological texts and the acts of councils, as well as secular texts such as the 'Alexander Romance', were translated into Latin. Some Greek grammars were written in the West to promote the knowledge of Greek, including one by Roger Bacon. Works of Plato, Aristotle and Proclus were translated in the twelfth and thirteenth centuries. Classical authors, whose texts were carefully preserved in Byzantium, played an essential role in the advent of the Italian Renaissance. Byzantine scholars such as Manuel Chrysoloras and John Argyropoulos had taught Greek in Italy in the fourteenth and fifteenth centuries. The visit of George Gemistos Plethon to Florence in the late 1430s and his defence of Plato in his discussions with Italian scholars probably led to the foundation of the Platonic Academy in that city. Beginning with the early Renaissance, Byzantine manuscripts of ancient authors were avidly collected in the West and copied by Greek scribes who had settled in Italy. Byzantine scholars were also instrumental in the first printed editions of Greek authors.

Greek scientific treatises first came to the attention of Western scholars through Arabic translations. Byzantine medicine influenced Western surgery and pharmacology. The ancient Greek geographers Ptolemy and Strabo were translated into Latin in the fifteenth century. Roman law, as codified by Justinian, enormously influenced Western jurists from the eleventh century onwards. On the other hand, Frankish law in the Latin Crusader principality of Achaia adopted Byzantine usages in dealings with its Greek subjects in the fourteenth century.

The Greek and Latin languages influenced each other. Many Greek words relating to religion, music, medicine, law, navigation, commerce, textiles and cooking were adopted in the West. Byzantine romances of the chivalry of the fourteenth century were adapted from Western originals and betray a mixed vocabulary. There were also mutual influences in customs and everyday life. Tournaments, introduced in the twelfth century from the West, were popular at the Byzantine court. Costume was influenced by Italian styles in the fourteenth and fifteenth centuries.

In the realm of music, the organ was adopted in the Latin West from Byzantine court ceremonial, and Latin musical notation had Greek origins.

Byzantine influence on Western art of the seventh–tenth centuries is more evident in Italy, even in regions outside Byzantine control, as in the case of the frescoes of Santa Maria Antiqua in Rome and Castelseprio near Milan. North of the Alps, indirect contacts with Byzantine art are noticeable in miniature painting, as in the 'Book of Kells' (see Plate 105). The marriage of the German emperor Otto II to the Greek princess Theophano increased Byzantine influence in Germany, as may be seen in an ivory representing the imperial couple blessed by Christ (see Plate 149) or in the miniatures of the Reichenau school. In Italy, Byzantine influence was particularly strong in the eleventh and twelfth centuries in both Venice and Sicily: the later mosaics of San Marco in Venice reflect the style then prevailing in Byzantium. For its part, the architecture of the church of San Marco, begun in about 1063, was modelled on the sixth-century five-domed cruciform Church of the Holy Apostles in Constantinople and not on a contemporary building, because it was designed to house the relics of the apostle Saint Mark, just as its prototype in Byzantium contained those of the apostles Saint Andrew and Saint Luke (see Plate 64). However, several churches in southern Italy, such as those of Rossano and Stilo, follow the current cross-in-square domed plan.

Byzantine art exerted a strong influence on Western painting in the thirteenth century, as may be seen in the frescoes of Aquileia, some Pisan crucifixes or in panels such as the Mellon Madonna in Washington (see Plate 147). In Greece at the same time, Romanesque influence is manifest in the architectural decoration of several churches, and in the sculptures of the Paregoretissa at Arta. Frankish architecture appears to have influenced secular architecture of the thirteenth–fifteenth centuries, for example in the palaces of Trebizond and Mistra. A large group of icons preserved in the monastery of Sinai, where the traditional Byzantine style and iconography are mixed with Western features, have been attributed to Western artists who had settled in the monastery itself or in Palestine during the Crusades. Completely Gothic in style are a few late frescoes decorating Orthodox churches in Greece and Cyprus.

Secular and religious architecture in Latin-occupied regions of Greece, such as Crete and Chios, adopted Western decorative motifs. Church planning was also influenced by the cohabitation of Orthodox Christians and Catholics. Some churches in Chios and the Cyclades have two sanctuaries of different form side by side, with two altars: one for the Orthodox and one for the Catholic rite. Panel and fresco painting of the fifteenth and sixteenth centuries in Crete and Cyprus depended on the late Palaeologan style and iconography but occasionally incorporated Western iconographic and stylistic features. Cretan artists could also paint icons completely Italian in style and iconography. Some Greek painters chose to settle in the West and to follow exclusively the Renaissance style. Foremost among these was Domenikos Theotokopoulos from Candia, where he was already well known in his early twenties but whose career developed mainly in Spain, where he was appropriately called El Greco – 'the Greek'.

Armenia and Georgia

Armenia and Georgia, which were buffer zones between Byzantium on the one hand and Persia, the Arabs and Turkish Muslims on the other, always enjoyed close relations with the Byzantine Empire. Several Byzantine emperors and members of the nobility were themselves of Armenian descent, but thoroughly Byzantinized. Armenian painting often depended on Byzantine models. Relations in the realm of architecture, however, were not as close as has sometimes been suggested. Although church plans which have been linked with Armenia follow early Christian models, building techniques differed, and the reliefs which cover the façades of Armenian churches like a carpet were unknown in Byzantine art (see Plate 156).

The fact that the Georgian Church was Chalcedonian in its dogma encouraged closer contacts with Byzantium. Georgian monks were active in Sinai, Mount Athos and Constantinople. In the realm of art, Byzantine influence was strongest on Georgian painting of the tenth–fourteenth centuries. The programme and style of murals depended heavily on Byzantine models, except for the placement of the image of the cross under the dome and that of Christ in the apse. Illuminated manuscripts and icons reflected current Constantinopolitan tastes, and some manuscripts and icons have bilingual inscriptions.

The Muslim world

In spite of almost continuous warfare, there were tight commercial and cultural relations between Byzantium and the Muslim world. In the early eighth century, Greek mosaicists were invited to adorn mosques in Damascus and Jerusalem, and in the tenth century to work in Cordova. Greek philosophical, medical and scientific works were translated into Arabic (see Plates 126, 130); for example, the compendium of writings of the seventh-century physician Paul of Aegina, who was active in Alexandria, was translated into Arabic and greatly influenced Arabic medicine. Byzantine scholars, such as Leo the Mathematician (ninth century) were invited to the Arab court. Aristotelian philosophy influenced Arabic thought and was thence transmitted to Western Europe *via* Spain and Sicily. Palaces and pavilions built in the ninth century in Constantinople and its suburbs by Theophilos and Basilios I were modelled on buildings of the 'Abbāsid court, which had impressed Byzantine envoys. Byzantine silk textiles were often decorated with motifs inspired by Islamic art. Angular Arab letters derived from the so-called Kūfic alphabet are a common feature in the brick decoration of churches and in the ornamentation of textiles and glass. Ceramics and metalwork were also influenced by Arabic ornamentation. Arabic treatises on geography, the natural sciences and medicine influenced Byzantine geographers, scientists and physicians. Many Arabic words passed into Greek, and *vice versa*.

Sasanian influence, strongly felt during the preceding period, persisted in Byzantine art under the Isaurian and Macedonian dynasties.

Some borrowings from Persian literature are found in the 'Tale of Barlaam and Josaphat' and in the 'Alexander Romance'. Persian astronomical treatises were translated into Greek. The *tzykanion*, a popular polo game played on horseback, was of Persian origin.

Byzantium strongly influenced the art and culture of the Turks and was in turn influenced by them. The court ceremonial of the sultans and the administrative structure of their state betray Byzantine influence. Greek was the language of documents sent to foreign rulers, and many Greek words found their way into Turkish. Ottoman architecture adopted the cloisonné masonry of Byzantium, and mosques from the fifteenth century onwards were domed according to the model of the church of Saint Sophia.

Bulgaria and Serbia

The influence of Byzantium was very strong in Bulgaria, its main enemy in Europe until the tenth century. Proto-Bulgarian inscriptions were written in Greek. Bulgaria was Christianized by Byzantine missionaries who were pupils of the two sainted brothers Constantine – Cyril and Methodius from Thessaloniki, who had first led a mission to Moravia which finally failed due to opposition from the papacy. Cyril and Methodius translated the Old and New Testaments and other texts into Slavonic and invented a special alphabet, the 'glagolitic', rather than imposing the Greek one. Instead of insisting that various rites be held in Greek, as the papal missionaries performed them in Latin, they translated the liturgy into the native languages. 'Glagolitic' was in turn superseded by the Cyrillic alphabet (see Figures 25a and b), which is an adaptation of the Greek as written in the ninth century (see Plate 106). Theological treatises, chronicles and geographical works were translated into Old Slavonic and formed the basis for the development of an indigenous literature. Byzantine culture was preponderant in the tenth century at the court of Symeon of Bulgaria. Byzantine etiquette was introduced, and the palaces and churches erected by Symeon in his capital at Preslav were inspired in plan and decoration by contemporary Constantinopolitan models. In the first Bulgarian capital at Pliska, on the contrary, extant late antique buildings had been reused. During the second Bulgarian empire, a simplified version of Byzantine law was introduced, and both architecture and painting were directly dependent on Byzantine models (see Plates 151, 153–155).

Byzantine influence penetrated the Serbian kingdom of the Nemanids mainly through ecclesiastical relations, the weddings of Byzantine princesses to Serbian royalty, and the annexation of Greek territories. The Serbian court adopted Byzantine ceremonial, costume and titulature. The *Zakonik*, a law code promulgated by Serbian Tsar Stephen Dušan, followed Byzantine models. Greek theological treatises and romances were translated into Serbian, while Greek rhetorical hagiography influenced the biographies of prominent Serbians. Serbian church architecture, which at first relied mainly on Dalmatian models, was strongly influenced by the architecture of Thessaloniki and Epirus in the fourteenth century under Milutin and Dušan in church types, decoration and building techniques. In the fifteenth-century Morava school, most churches belonged to the trefoil 'athonite' plan, with Romanesque sculptural decoration added. Painting closely followed Byzantine models, and some of the best church decorations of the fourteenth century are the work of Greek masters summoned mainly from nearby Thessaloniki (see Plate 152).

Rus'

Relations between Byzantium and Rus' are attested since the ninth century and were intensified in the tenth, especially after the conversion of the Russians to Christianity. The head of the Russian Church, who resided at Kiev, was normally a Greek, as were many of his suffragan bishops. After their conversion, Constantinople became for the Rus' a place of pilgrimage, while they strove to imitate the Byzantines in every respect. Early Rus' literature was strongly influenced by Byzantine models – chronicles, homilies, biographies of saints – but did not try to imitate the more sophisticated genres. Several Russian travellers wrote accounts of their visits to the Greek East, with vivid descriptions of Constantinople.

Greek architects and artists were called upon as early as the late tenth century, but surviving works date mainly from the 1030s. They include the Golden Gate and the Saint Sophia cathedral in Kiev (see Figure 19), and the church of the Transfiguration at Černigov. Masonry was unknown in Russia at that time, so building techniques, architecural decoration and plans prevailing in Constantinople were used. Both Saint Sophia and the church at Černigov are cross-in-square domed structures, with brick and stone masonry, blind arches and engaged brick columns on the exterior, recalling contemporary Constantinopolitan architecture. The Rus' were content with the cross-in-square plan and did not adopt other plans current in Byzantium. From the late eleventh century onwards, the architecture of Rus' elaborated its Byzantine models and developed a distinct style.

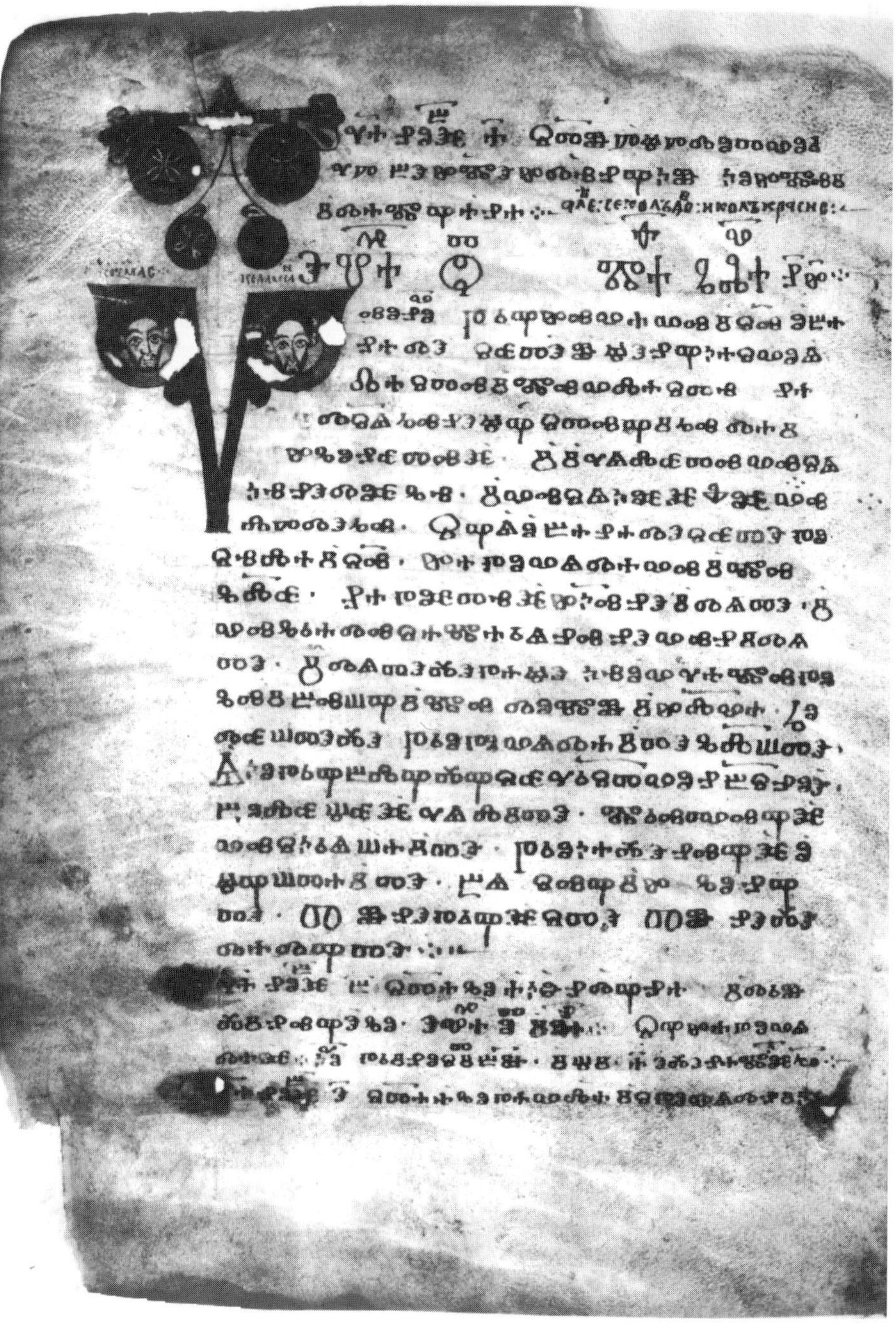

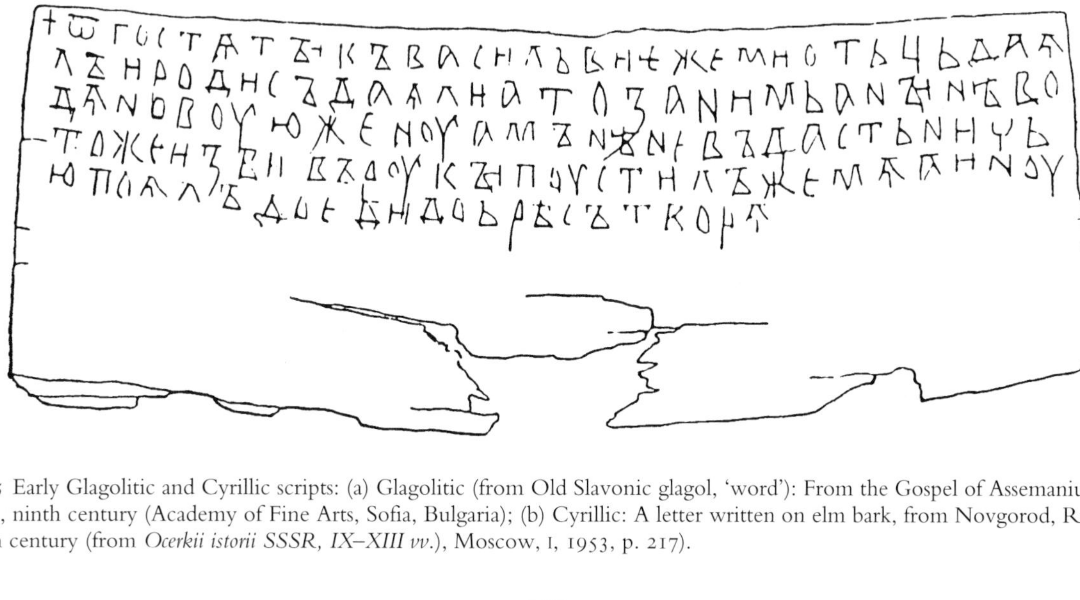

Figure 25 Early Glagolitic and Cyrillic scripts: (a) Glagolitic (from Old Slavonic glagol, 'word'): From the Gospel of Assemanius, Bulgaria, ninth century (Academy of Fine Arts, Sofia, Bulgaria); (b) Cyrillic: A letter written on elm bark, from Novgorod, Russia, eleventh century (from *Ocerkii istorii SSSR, IX–XIII vv.*), Moscow, 1, 1953, p. 217).

The situation is different as far as painting is concerned. Artists adhered more or less closely to Byzantine models until the early fifteenth century, when pupils of Theophanes the Greek, such as Andrei Rublev, abandoned the Byzantine in favour of a distinctively Russian idiom, with delicate flat and linear figures (see Plates 159, 160). The mosaic decoration of Saint Sophia in Kiev, which was the first major undertaking on Rus' soil, is the work of masters sent from Constantinople (see Plate 157). Local Rus' painters, responsible for later decorations, do not depart from the standard iconographic cycles and appear to have been very well informed of the latest developments in Constantinople, whose style they closely follow. The greatest Byzantine painter of the late fourteenth century, Theophanes, left his native Constantinople in search of better commissions in Novgorod and Moscow, where he remained for the rest of his life and strongly influenced the development of Russian painting.

When the Rus' were Christianized, Byzantium provided them not only with clergy but also with icons, manuscripts and liturgical vessels. This export of cult objects continued for many centuries. The famous Virgin of Vladimir was sent from Constantinople to the Rus' in the mid-twelfth century and was widely copied. Local schools of icon painting developed in Rus' which were influenced by Byzantine models but also displayed local characteristics (see Plate 158). Rus' illuminated manuscripts also adhered closely to Byzantine models.

Sculptures of the eleventh century, such as those preserved in Saint Sophia in Kiev, display a distinctively Byzantine style, but later reliefs have a local style and iconography. The sculptural decoration of the façades encountered in the church of Saint Demetrius at Vladimir was unknown in Byzantium. Metalwork, enamels, wood and bone carvings were also influenced by Byzantine art.

Greek icons and embroideries continued to be exported to Rus' in the fifteenth century, but Russian icons, liturgical vessels and vestments were also sent to the Greek East as presents to monasteries and church dignitaries, and were highly appreciated.

Rumania

The principalities of Wallachia and Moldavia were founded in the thirteenth–fourteenth centuries. Earlier architectural remains here are crude versions of Byzantine plans and building techniques. The relations of this region with Byzantium were intensified after its political emancipation from Hungary in the mid-fourteenth century. Court ceremonial was modelled on the Byzantine, and literature was influenced by Byzantine models. The royal church at Curtea de Arges, the most important monument in Wallachia, belongs to the cross-in-square plan, while later churches often belong to the athonite type, where side apses are added. In Moldavia, on the other hand, a local school of architecture developed with a very tall dome resting on the exterior walls, heavy buttresses, and windows and portals of Gothic design.

Fresco decorations in both principalities adhered to Byzantine iconography and style. Later, they were influenced by the frescoes of the Morava school, itself closely connected with late fourteenth-century painting in Thessaloniki. Icons, miniatures, embroideries, ceramics and wood carving equally betray strong Byzantine influence. In Moldavia, frescoes covered the entire exterior surface of churches.

Hungary

A Byzantine mission was active in the tenth century in Hungary, and monasteries of the Greek rite are recorded there in the eleventh and twelfth centuries. Although Latin influence became predominant in the twelfth century, Greek theological treatises were translated. Many Byzantine works of art reached the country in the eleventh and twelfth centuries, among them a crown with enamel portraits donated to King Geza I, which now forms the lower part of the holy crown of Hungary.

BIBLIOGRAPHY

1972. Actes du XXIIe congrès International d'Histoire de l'art, Budapest, 1969. Section II. Le rayonnement des modèles byzantins, Vol. I. Budapest, pp. 111–283.

BAYNES, N.; MOSS, H.; St. L. B. (eds) 1948. *Byzantium*. Oxford.

BECK, H. G. 1959. *Kirche und theologische Literatur im byzantinischen Reich*. Munich (Handbuch der Altertumswissenschaft, XII, 2.1).

——. 1978. *Das byzantinische Jahrtausend*. Munich.

BECKWITH, J. 1970. *Early Christian and Byzantine Art*. Harmondsworth, Penguin Books (Pelican History of Art).

COLLINET, P. 1923. Byzantine Legislation from the Death of Justinian (565) to 1453. In: *Cambridge Medieval History*, Vol. IV. Cambridge, pp. 707–723.

DELVOYE, C. 1967. *L'art byzantin*. Paris.

DEMUS, O. 1970. *Byzantine Art and the West*. New York.

DER NERSESSIAN, S. 1945. *Armenia and the Byzantine Empire*. Cambridge, Mass.

DUMBARTON OAKS PAPERS. 1964. *Papers on the Relations Between Byzantium and the Arabs*, Vol. 18, pp. 1–132.

GUILLOU, A. 1974. *La civilisation byzantine*. Paris.

HAUSSIG, H. W. 1966. *Kulturgeschichte von Byzanz*, 2nd edn. Stuttgart.

HUNGER, H. 1978. *Die hochsprachliche profane Literatur der Byzantiner*. Munich (Handbuch der Altertumswissenschaft, XII, 1.2).

KAHANE, H.; KAHANE, R. 1976. *Abendland und Byzanz: Sprache. Reallexikon der Byzantinistik*, Vol. I. Amsterdam, pp. 347–498.

——. 1982. The Western Impact on Byzantium: The Linguistic Evidence. Dumbarton Oaks Papers, Vol. 36, pp. 127–153.

KRAUTHEIMER, R. 1986. *Early Christian and Byzantine Architecture*, 4th edn. Harmondsworth, Penguin Books (Pelican History of Art).

LAZAREV, V. 1967. *Storia della pittura bizantina*. Torino.

——. 1970. Regard sur l'art de la Russie prémongole. In: *Cahiers de Civilisation Médiévale*, Vol. 13, pp. 195–208; Vol.14, 1971, pp. 221–238; Vol. 16, 1973, pp. 1–15; Vol. 17, 1974, pp. 99–108.

MANGO, C. 1975. *Byzantine Architecture*. New York.

MOURIKI, D. 1981. The Formative Role of Byzantine Art in the Artistic Style of the Cultural Neighbors of Byzantium. Reflections of Constantinopolitan Styles in Georgian Monuments. In: *Jahrbuch der Österreichischen Byzantinistik* Vol. 31/2, pp. 725–757.

OBOLENSKY, D. 1971. *The Byzantine Commonwealth*. London.

SCHÄFER, H. 1973–4. Architekturhistorische Beziehungen zwischen Byzanz und der Kiever Rus im 10. und 11 Jahrhundert. In: *Istanbuler Mitteilungen*, Vol. 23–24, pp. 197–224.

THÉODORIDÈS, J. 1957. La science byzantine. In: *Histoire générale des sciences*, I, pp. 490–502.

10

CAROLINGIAN EUROPE

Pierre Riché

The 'barbarian' invasions of the fifth and sixth centuries broke the Western Roman Empire apart, and several kingdoms were born from its ruins. Some of these – the Vandal, Ostrogoth and Burgundian kingdoms – did not last long, while others – the Visigoth, Lombard and above all Frankish – managed to survive. In the East there remained the old empire, and on one occasion Justinian tried (albeit in vain) to reconquer the West. He was able to hold on only in Italy but did so in spite of the advent of new barbarians, the Lombards.

The 'barbarians' brought with them a new type of civilization, but being few in number they were unable to impose their legislation on the West. They used the Roman legislation for public law, reserving Germanic custom for private law. Roman culture resisted by transforming itself under the influence of Christianity. In practice, the 'barbarians' were gradually converted to Catholicism, and their kings became the leaders of national churches; a new Christian culture was created, especially around the monasteries. Irish, Anglo-Saxon and Merovingian monks favoured study of the Bible, and commentaries upon it employing Latin for the liturgy and the interpretation of sacred texts. The Rule of Saint Benedict, promulgated in Italy during the sixth century, had not yet been disseminated throughout the entire region (see Plates 104, 105).

In short, what characterized the West prior to the Carolingian period was diversity and compartmentalization; no political, moral or religious force was as yet capable of organizing the region. The papacy itself suffered from the repercussions of the invasions; the bishop of Rome succumbed to the domination of the Ostrogoths and then the Byzantines, while the Lombards, who occupied northern and central Italy, wished to unify the peninsula by taking the Byzantine town of Ravenna, and then Rome itself. The future was thus uncertain.

The great merit of the Carolingians was the way in which they grouped the forces of the West and gave Europe its initial outlines. Before then, the word 'Europe' had been only an expression, as used to distinguish the region from 'Asia' or 'Africa'. Yet by the end of the Carolingian period, 'Europe' had developed into what we might call a 'legal entity'. The cultural, political and spiritual activity of the laity and ecclesiastics had fostered conditions in which the first European grouping was able to come into being, and it is the story of that activity that we must now present.

THE INITIAL OUTLINES OF CAROLINGIAN EUROPE

The rise of an aristocratic family

In the seventh-century West, the Visigoths and Franks firmly maintained their position, but at the beginning of the eighth century, Berber and Arab armies from North Africa invaded the Iberian peninsula. The Visigoths were defeated in 711, and their chiefs took refuge in the north-west of the peninsula. The greater part of Spain was subject to Islamic law, a situation that lasted for centuries.

This leaves us with the Frankish kingdom. The Merovingians – masters of that kingdom since the time of Clovis – were unable to maintain the unity of Gaul. After the death in 639 of Dagobert, the dynasty's last great king, the regions to the west, *Neustria*; those to the east, *Austrasia*; and those to the south, *Aquitaine* – which remained faithful to Roman traditions – confronted one another. The Merovingian kings were weak rulers, dominated by their aristocracy and its chief, the 'mayor of the palace'. The aristocrats possessed immense domains, cultivated by free peasants and slaves.

Among these families, special mention is due to the clan from which the Carolingians were descended. It came to notice at the end of the sixth century through the activities of two men: Arnoul, Bishop of Metz, and Pepin (or 'Pippin'), mayor of the Austrasian palace. Arnoul possessed huge domains between the Moselle and the Meuse and in the area surrounding Worms, and at the end of his life he retired to a monastery founded by the disciples of Saint Columban. Pepin, called Pepin of Landen since the thirteenth century, possessed lands in the area of the middle Meuse, the great waterway which became one of the important axes of economic life in Northern Europe. Pepin's daughter married Arnoul's son. At his death, his son Grimoald succeeded him as 'mayor of the palace' and founded monasteries such as those of Stavelot and Malmédy, installing his sister in the monastery of Nivelles. Grimoald's power was such that he sought to oust the Merovingian king of Austrasia and install his son in the latter's place, but this *coup d'état* failed because a large section of the aristocracy remained faithful to the Merovingians. This aristocratic family returned to prominence only with the advent of Pepin II, called Pepin of Herstal. Pepin II succeeded in unifying the household administrations ('mayoralties') of Austrasia and Neustria, in installing his followers in the various counties of the kingdom, and in intervening militarily in Frisia, Alemannia and Bavaria.

The principate of Charles Martel

There was a crisis at the death of Pepin II, but his bastard son Charles or 'Carolus' (who was to give his name to the *Carolingian* lineage) took things in hand. Taking advantage of the decadence of the Church, he gave back the possessions confiscated by Charles and distributed them among his followers, who would soon come to be called 'vassals'. He was thus able to secure considerable power and to acquire the peripheral principalities: Frisia, Thuringia, Hesse and Alemannia; his authority was reinforced by the presence of missionaries, whom he protected: Willibrord in Frisia and Boniface in Germany. Boniface was an Anglo-Saxon. Together with the pope, he laboured to convert pagan Germany and founded monasteries to train future missionaries.

An unexpected event was to provide Charles with the opportunity to penetrate south of the Loire, and so impose his authority in Aquitaine. What happened was that the Muslims of Spain had militarily crossed the Pyrenees, and Eudes, Duke of Aquitaine, appealed to Charles for help. Charles' celebrated victory at Poitiers succeeded in halting the invasion. The appearance of Charles was providential (he would come to be called *Martel* – literally, the 'hammer' – perhaps in recollection of the name given to Judas Maccabeus, warrior hero of the Old Testament). In 739, Pope Gregory even appealed to him for help in the face of ever-increasing danger from the Lombards: Rome was threatened and, since the papacy was in conflict with Byzantium on account of the iconoclastic question, it turned to the West. But Charles needed Lombard support to hold back the Muslims in Provence and refused to intervene.

But Charles Martel did feel strong enough to refrain from replacing the deceased Merovingian king; this forbearance was, in a way, a second, more discreet *coup d'état*. Without adopting the royal title, he conducted himself like a king, even arranging for the division of the realm between his sons Pepin and Carloman. He died on 22 October 741 and was buried in the Abbey of Saint-Denis, thereby foreshadowing its use as France's future royal necropolis.

PEPIN AND CHARLEMAGNE, CREATORS OF THE CAROLINGIAN EMPIRE

Pepin the Short, mayor of the palace

Submission of the principalities

The death of Charles Martel plunged the Frankish kingdom into a fresh crisis, of which the Germanic and Aquitanian princes took advantage by mounting a rebellion. Pepin and his brother Carloman sought and found the means to maintain and consolidate their father's work. They re-established a Merovingian king on the throne, thus satisfying those loyal to the Merovingian dynasty, whose origins lay in a distant past. Thus these rulers would later be called, in French tradition, *'les rois fainéants'* (the idle kings), but continued to reign under the control of the 'mayors of the palace'.

Meanwhile Pepin and Carloman attacked Aquitaine, still stubbornly independent, and forced its duke to swear an oath of fealty. They brought Bavaria under control and made several expeditions into 'Alemanni'. The missionaries, Boniface and Pirmin, gave them full moral support in these operations.

The reform of the Frankish Church

Pepin and Carloman, both pious rulers, wished to reform the Frankish Church, then under the influence of lax, illiterate priests who cared little for their flocks. The people were steeped in superstition. In 742 and 743, Carloman and Pepin, with the full support of Boniface, held councils for reform. These councils enforced on clerics standards of behaviour befitting their office, made the Rule of Saint Benedict mandatory for all monks, re-established the full authority of bishops, and attacked popular superstitions. The two princes dared not, however, reclaim landholdings – for fear of impoverishing, and alienating, too many of their supporters. In any case, not only Boniface but also the popes supported the two princely brothers in their drive to reform. When the devout Carloman retired to an Italian monastery in 747, Pepin, now sole remaining 'mayor of the palace', felt sufficiently powerful to put into effect the plan he had been nurturing for some time – that is, openly to proclaim himself king of the Franks.

The reign of Pepin

Historians tend to deal with Pepin's lifework and that of his son, the future Charlemagne, by misrepresenting the reign of the first Carolingian king as a mere prelude to the splendid rule of the second. Yet it was under Pepin that the great decisions were made, which were to stamp the history of the West over the next century to come: among their key priorities, the Carolingian rulers henceforth set themselves to observe a close alliance with the pope, to receive 'consecration' (through anointment in holy oil by the pope), to enforce full Roman usage in liturgy, to reform the currency, and to bind the main regions of the West in union around a Frankish political core.

Pepin the Short's 'coup d'état'

In order to oust, and replace, the Merovingian king, Pepin first had to secure the necessary support. The monks of the Abbey of Saint-Denis, outside Paris, waged an outright propaganda campaign on behalf of the prince. Pepin and his supporters also decided to involve the Holy See. Pope Zacharias agreed that whoever actually discharged the functions of a king, without holding the title of a king – ought to take the title of king. 'By his apostolic authority', the pope therefore commanded that Pepin be so crowned king. In practical fact, Pepin was elected and raised to the throne by a council of magnates in Soissons. But then – and this was a new development – he had himself 'consecrated' with holy oil by the bishops as well. In so doing, Pepin not only imitated the usage of the Visigothic rulers of Spain: more importantly, he mirrored the hallowed example of Old Testament kings. Pepin made himself the Lord's 'anointed': thereby ensuring his own moral and, indeed, religious power.

Founding of the pontifical state

The popes begged for the new king's aid in their struggle to resist the Lombards: in 751 (the year of Pepin's *coup d'état*), Ravenna, northern Italy's last Byzantine stronghold, had been captured by King Aistolf, and only Rome remained to be taken for Italy to become completely Lombard. Pope Stephen II, to preserve the Holy See's independence, searched

Pepin out in Gaul to enlist his help: the first time that a pope had entered 'barbarian' territory. Pepin could do no other than welcome him and promised to set matters straight in Italy. It is possible that this was the occasion when the pope made available to Pepin that notorious forged document, the 'Donation of Constantine': whereby the first Christian Roman emperor was said to have donated the very city of Rome, and indeed the entire West, to the lordship of the pope – while betaking his own imperial person to his newly founded city of Constantinople (whence to rule, henceforth and for ever, only over the East). During his stay in the French Abbey of Saint-Denis, the pope renewed Pepin's 'consecration' in holy oil, further 'consecrated' his wife and children, and bestowed on them all the title of 'Roman patricians'.

Two expeditions to Italy were necessary for Pepin to force his will on the Lombard king and make him yield part of his territorial conquests to the pope himself. This was the origin of the Papal states, which survived until 1871.

Conquest of Aquitaine

Pepin was determined to end the independence of Aquitaine. From 760 until his death in 768, he campaigned every year, penetrating ever further into the heart of the country, advancing right down to the Garonne and accepting the surrender of the Basques. Aquitaine was subjugated, but devastated; its civilization and culture, which had been preserved since the great invasions, now lay in ruins. The country was to take a long time to recover from the Carolingian trauma.

Continuation of religious reform

Pepin's 'consecration' committed him to expand Christianity throughout his realm. He was supportered in this by the bishop of Metz, Chrodegang, who drafted rules for the canons, drawing inspiration from the Benedictine Rule so that all priests, like monks, should lead a communal life. He helped Pepin to spread the Roman liturgy throughout Gaul in order to unify ritual in all churches. This long-term work was to be continued by Charlemagne.

Pepin's prestige

Pepin's reputation reached far beyond the frontiers of his kingdom, and even beyond Italy: he was the first Frankish ruler to make agreements with Muslim princes and to restore good relations with the Byzantines. The administrative machinery of his court was strengthened, and above all he put an end to monetary anarchy by re-establishing a royal monopoly on coinage. From his reign onwards, until the thirteenth century, his silver issue – the *denarius* – became standard everywhere. Finally, in his offices, clerics now tended to replace lay officials, who were becoming ever less well educated, and this dominance of the bureaucracy by priests was to last in France until the early fourteenth-century reign of Philip the Fair.

When Pepin died, on 24 September 768, at the age of 54, he was buried in the Abbey of Saint-Denis. In his youth, he had been brought up in this abbey; he had undertaken the construction of its new church (for which Pope Stephen II ceremonially laid the cornerstone) and had enjoyed the support of its monks throughout his reign. The Salic Law was drafted at Saint-Denis; its prologue, which praised the Franks as the new chosen people, contained the following sentence: 'Long live Christ, Who loveth the Franks, whose rule He protecteth, whose leaders He filleth even with the light of His grace, over whose army He watcheth, and Who hath granted unto them even the stronghold of His Faith.'

Charlemagne the conqueror

After Pepin's death, his two sons divided the kingdom between them, in accordance with Germanic custom. However, Charlemagne, the elder, was unable to reach an understanding with his brother Carloman. This discord compelled their mother Bertrada to intervene. She secured an alliance not only with the Bavarian king, Tassilo III, but also with Desiderius, king of the Lombards. But after Carloman's death in 771, Charlemagne managed Frankish foreign affairs along very different lines.

The conditions of Charlemagne's conquests

Charlemagne filled the major part of his reign with wars of conquest. According to his biographer Eginhard, he 'dilated' the realm, adding about 1 million square kilometres, corresponding to much of the old Roman West. These conquests were achieved gradually, with no previously established plan, but until the very end, Charlemagne remained faithful to certain principles. On the one hand, he wanted to protect his inherited kingdom against the incursions of pagans, in particular Saxons. On the other hand, as a most Christian king, he sought to contain the Muslims, and also to reconquer part of their territory; his wars thus took on the appearance of expeditions as religious as they were political (see Plates 161, 162). Yet it has to be acknowledged that this man of war, who loved fighting and could never remain inactive, regarded war truly as 'a national institution of the Franks'. It allowed him to accumulate wealth and share it among his churches and followers. So long as the conquests lasted, the king was able to keep his aristocracy in line and be sure of their support. His military success depended upon the might of his army, one perhaps not so large as has been assumed. According to some historians, Charlemagne had only 5,000 fighting men, which explains the difficulties he encountered, especially in Saxony. But other scholars, who take into account the number of *fiscs* (that is, domains), bishoprics and abbeys in the kingdom, believe the king could muster 36,000 horsemen, in addition to foot soldiers and auxiliaries, which would yield a total of 100,000 men. The main element in the Carolingian army was heavy cavalry, a force now becoming increasingly large. Successful military operations depended upon speed of mobilization and the massing of troops at the beginning of each spring. Charlemagne saw to it that roads and highways were properly maintained and the bridges well repaired; he even planned to cut a canal between the Rhine and the Danube; archaeologists have discovered traces of this canal in an area then called the *Fossa Carolina*.

The stages of conquest

Breaking with the Lombard alliance his mother had advocated, Charlemagne decided to respond to a fresh appeal for help by the new pope, Hadrian I, by conquering the Lombard kingdom. The expedition went ahead with no difficulties; King Desiderius surrendered, and Charlemagne became king of the Lombards. He also made a pilgrimage to Rome and confirmed his father's donation of territory to the Holy See twenty years earlier.

The second area of operations was Saxony, where Charlemagne began his campaign of conquest in 772. No prince, whether Roman or Frank, had ever dared to penetrate this land of forests and marshes before, and tackle the Saxon pagans. Charlemagne clearly did not suspect at the outset that he would have to wage a thirty-year war there. He obtained the Saxons' first submission in 777 at his new residence of Paderborn, and hoped to convert the conquered population. At Paderborn, too, he met a Muslim chief, who begged him to intervene against his rivals in northern Spain. Charlemagne therefore crossed Aquitaine and besieged Zaragoza, but the siege failed, and the Frankish rearguard was massacred by the Basques at Roncesvalles. The year 778 was thus a year of difficulties for Charlemagne, since hard upon disaster at Roncesvalles came a Saxon revolt and a threat from Arichis, Duke of Benevento, who sought to increase his duchy at the expense of the pontifical state.

Charlemagne overcame the crisis, proclaimed his son Pepin king of Italy during a second journey to Rome in 781, and at the same time conquered Benevento. He turned back to take Bavaria – until then ruled by his cousin Tassilo – and unleashed a policy of terror in Saxony, forcing Saxons either to surrender and convert, or be killed. This decisive period ended in a new crisis, worse than that of 778. The Muslims crossed the eastern Pyrenees, while both Benevento and the Saxons rose against him; Charlemagne was 46 years of age and once more had to deal with, and finally overcome, such setbacks. In 794, he summoned an assembly at Frankfurt to re-establish order in the Church and decide on economic and monetary matters, while in the same year finally settling his residence at Aachen (Aix-la-Chapelle). From this time on, he prepared for his crowning as emperor.

Charlemagne becomes emperor

Since 476 there had only been a single empire, the Eastern. Charlemagne, master of several Western regions, was encouraged by clerics such as Alcuin to re-establish the empire in the West. Various events favoured him: first the presence of a woman, the Empress Irene, on the throne of Constantinople. To be sure, she had restored the cult of images at the Seventh Council of Nicaea; but she had seized power at the expense of her son. At the Council of Frankfurt, in 794, Charlemagne, too, had condemned iconoclasm though opposed to the cult of images; he too had constructed a palace at Aachen which rivalled the sacred palace at Constantinople; he too styled himself both 'king and priest'; and he too appeared as the leader of a Christian empire. Moreover, the new pope, Leo III, under attack from the Roman aristocracy, needed Charlemagne's help. Therefore, he also favoured the restoration of a Western empire.

The restoration took place on Christmas Day 800. The *Annales Laureshamenses* summed up the situation as follows:

> 'Since in the land of the Greeks there was no longer an Emperor and since they were all under the dominion of a woman, it seemed to Pope Leo and all the fathers who sat in the assembly, and to all the Christian people, that they should give the name of Emperor to Charlemagne, King of the Franks, who occupied Rome – where the Caesars had customarily resided – and also Italy, Gaul and Germany . . . God almighty having consented to place these countries under his authority, it would justly conform to the demand of all the Christian people that he should also bear the imperial title.

Thus the pope crowned Charlemagne emperor, and thereafter, throughout the Middle Ages, rulers would come to Rome to obtain their imperial crowns (see Plate 194a). Yet Charlemagne did not wish to submit to the pontifical authority and be emperor of the Romans; he remained 'King of the Franks and Lombards, governing the Roman Empire'. When in 813 he decided to associate his son Louis with the empire, he himself crowned Louis at Aachen without involving the pope. This marked the opposition of two conceptions of empire, an opposition bearing the seeds of conflict between pope and emperor that would last throughout the history of the medieval West.

Charlemagne consolidated his work to the end of his life in 814, by defending his empire against the attacks of new opponents: Slavs beyond the Elbe and in Bohemia; Danes who ravaged Frisia and against whom he raised a fleet; and, to the south, Muslim raiders in Corsica and Sardinia. Meanwhile, he succeeded in conquering the Avars' stronghold in the Danube plain, and to capture Barcelona, which allowed him to organize the 'Spanish marches': the future Catalonia.

When he died in 814, at almost seventy years of age, Charlemagne could be regarded as 'the father of Europe', whose very diverse regions he had managed to weld under his single authority. But what would be the fate of his 'European empire' under his successors?

THE FATE OF THE EMPIRE FROM 814 TO 877

We can only trace here the main outlines of this story, through the main stages of Carolingian Europe's lifespan (see Map 5).

The attempt to create a unitary empire and its failure

Louis, son of Charlemagne, later nicknamed the 'Pious' or the 'Debonair', was strongly influenced by those clerics who wished to maintain the unity of the empire. Some of them dreamed of the fusion of all its peoples, and the abolition of all 'barbarian' laws. In 817, Louis decided to name his oldest son Lothair co-emperor, with Lothair's brothers having to be content with the title of 'kings'. However, Louis had four sons, the youngest of whom – Charles – was born of a second marriage. According to Germanic tradition, all children were entitled to their share of an inheritance, even a territorial one. This tradition conflicted with the unitary concept favoured by the Church. Thus, after a promising beginning, the reign of Louis the Pious was troubled after 833 by incessant wars between Lothair and his brothers. When Louis died in 840, the unity of the empire was at risk.

The division of Verdun

As the Scandinavian invasion of the West began, the Carolingian princes had to reach an agreement and so decided to share out the empire between them. After several years

Map 5 The Carolingian Empire and the Treaty of Verdun (843), (after Riché, P., 1968, Grandes Invasions et empires, in *Histoire universelle*, Larousse, Paris).

of preparation, the Carolingian Empire was divided at Verdun between Charles 'the Bald', who held all the western part; Louis the German, who held the eastern part; and Lothair, the eldest son, who kept the title of emperor and took the entire central region extending from Aix-la-Chapelle (Aachen) to Rome. Historians have looked for the reasons underlying this new map of the West. The division was based here neither upon language nor upon nationality, nor did it take into account the economic equilibrium of each kingdom. It was made to ensure that each brother had *fiscs*, abbeys and episcopal sees situated in the ancestral lands and held by the great Austrasian families, and that the possessions and benefices their vassals had enjoyed for some years did not fall into another lord's hands.

Obviously, those who divided the empire could not foresee that the frontiers fixed at Verdun, outlining the map of medieval Europe and particularly the frontier separating the kingdom of France from that of Lothair, were destined to last for centuries: this frontier was made up of the River Escaut, which separated the kingdom from the Imperial lands, and the Rivers Saône and Rhône. After Lothair's death, in 855, his own share was further divided into three – and so were drawn the frontiers of the future states of medieval Europe: Lorraine, Provence, Burgundy and Italy.

Break-up of the empire

For a while, the various kings met to combine forces in order to fight against external enemies, above all the Scandinavians. The clerics encouraged these alliances and sought to maintain an appearance of at least moral and religious unity. None the less, the Carolingian princes were concerned essentially with their own interests and those of their vassals.

The papacy, now freed from imperial tutelage, recovered political initiative under the pontificates of Nicholas I (after 867) and John VIII (872–882). John VIII crowned Charles the Bald emperor in 877.

Charles the Bald, the last Carolingian emperor

Charles the Bald, an educated, energetic and ambitious prince, dreamed of restoring his grandfather's empire. He succeeded in containing the Scandinavian invasions by fortifying 'marches' and by building castles. He tidied the monetary system and turned his court into a prestigious cultural centre. Pope John VIII offered him the imperial crown, and on Christmas Day 875 crowned both him and his wife (see Plate 169). Yet history could not be repeated. Charles was threatened by his brother Louis of Bavaria, by new attacks upon the Seine region by the Vikings, and by the indiscipline of his aristocracy. In spite of all this, he responded to John VIII's appeal for military help against Muslim raiders in southern Italy, but he died on 6 October 877 while returning to France to crush a revolt by his nobles.

Seeking a new emperor, Pope John VIII crowned Charles the Fat, son of Louis the German, in 881, but the new emperor failed to defend Italy against Sicilian Muslim corsair raids and was unable to help Paris when the city was besieged by the Vikings in 885–886. The sick emperor was deposed in 888 by the aristocracy, whereupon the nobles in each kingdom elected one of their own number king. This was the end of the Carolingian Empire.

THE INSTITUTIONS OF THE EMPIRE

Even though the Carolingian Empire itself thus lasted for only a few decades, the institutions with which Charlemagne and his successors had endowed it survived long after its demise.

Religious institutions

We should begin with religious institutions, because the 'consecrated' ruler first of all saw to the reform of the Church, and to the proper functioning of its organization on Earth.

Ecclesiastical structures

Pepin and Charlemagne re-established metropolitan provinces, each with a bishop, henceforth known as an archbishop, at its head. '*Charlemagne's Testament*' list these twenty-one provinces. The archbishops exercised full authority over their bishops, and some – for example Hincmar, the powerful archbishop of Reims – declared that they would never relinquish their right to do so. The archbishops of Hamburg, Salzburg and Mainz extended their powers over territories newly won for Christianity: strips of Scandinavia at the time of Louis the Pious, and the Slavic regions. From the middle of the eighth century, councils were regularly convened to discuss moral, religious, doctrinal and even political issues; they enacted canons that contributed to the formation of Church law.

A bishop was assisted in the management of his diocese by his cathedral clergy, who, in principle, led a communal life and observed the rule for canons promulgated by Chrodegang of Metz in the middle of the eighth century. Dioceses that were too large were subdivided into archidiaconates, in turn divided into deaneries. These administrative divisions were to remain in force throughout the entire Middle Ages. In fact, the Carolingians wished to promote instruction and supervision of the faithful, and to give Christianity firm roots among the people by making sure that all children were baptized at birth, that all Christians attended divine service on Sundays, and that all received communion at least three times a year. This respect for external rules was consonant, as it were, with Old Testament legalism.

The Carolingian rulers tended to distrust monks who lived apart and in isolation from the world; they wished to impose the Rule of Saint Benedict everywhere. In 817, Louis the Pious's friend, Benedict of Aniana, presided over a council at Aachen that sought to bring uniformity to monastic legislation and create a common spirit among different monastic foundations. This paved the way for the subsequent development at Cluny in the tenth century.

The Church in submission to the princes

In assisting Church reform and restoring ecclesiastical structures, the rulers counted on the Church's full collaboration with their policies, and upon its submission. Charlemagne, as a new 'David', established a kind of sacred monarchy in which the prince and his representatives took all decisions. The ruler appointed bishops and abbots, and considered that they should divide their time between pastoral duties and service to the prince. The ruler summoned them to his court and entrusted them with administrative and diplomatic missions. The abbots, now the ruler's vassals, might even contribute troops for military expeditions. The rulers also took it upon themselves to supervise the management of the churches' increasing wealth, and ordered inventories of that wealth (see Plate 169). A modern observer might be surprised that the clergy neither protested against such royal control nor sought, in the name of religious vocation, to recover their liberty. Because they participated in power and derived material benefit from this power, and because they confused what pertained to the spiritual and what pertained to the temporal, bishops and abbots could imagine no other system. If some priests in the time of Louis the Pious did declare the primacy of the spiritual, this was in order to usurp political power for their own benefit. Far from liberating the Church, the collapse of the Carolingian Empire, and the ascendancy of the great aristocratic families, curbed it even more firmly under the secular power.

Administrative structures

A Carolingian ruler was no tyrant, and his monarchy was not absolute in the sense that Byzantium's was. He wished to maintain contact with his subjects by holding general assemblies like those held before his own reign. In Charlemagne's time, the great secular and spiritual lords, military chiefs, officials and magnates were summoned before each year's summer campaign to discuss the great issues of the moment. These assemblies resulted in the drawing up of the well-known 'capitularies' – ordinances containing a series of articles or *capitula* – whence their name – to which we owe a great deal of our knowledge of life in the empire.

The general assembly was a kind of extension of the council which helped the ruler to govern, and it resided in the palace. The ruler delegated to his friends various tasks: both 'offices' of the royal household, and more important responsibilities. The 'chamberlain' was responsible for the 'chamber', for here were stored all the riches derived from indirect taxation, annual gifts, tributes, war booty and so on. The head of the bureaux, the 'chancellor', formulated and authenticated royal charters. The Carolingian rulers wished to restore to writing a role it had lost, so documents of all kinds were issued from the court and returned to it, where they were examined by the clerics.

The decisions taken by the ruler in his palace or in the general assembly were transmitted to his local agents – the 'counts'. There were in the empire about 300 counts, who enjoyed extensive powers, as in Merovingian times. Since they sometimes abused these powers, Charlemagne kept watch over them by means of personal envoys, his *missi dominici*, to whom he gave instructions prior to their departure on circuit. In 802, for instance, he wrote:

> Mete out full, equitable justice to churches, widows, orphans and all others, without fraud, corruption or improper delays, and make sure that your subordinates do likewise . . . Above all, let no one hear either you or your subordinates say 'Keep quiet until the *missi* are passed, and we will arrange things afterwards between ourselves.' On the contrary, make it your business to speed up the settlement before our arrival of matters pending. Read and re-read this letter and keep it safe so that it may serve as witness between you and us.

Always concerned to foster personal relations between himself and his subjects, Charlemagne decided to make all free men swear an oath of fealty; he also invited the functionaries serving him to become his 'vassals'. In this way, he was sure of surrounding himself with faithful men able to assist him at all times and to each of whom, in return, he gave a 'benefice', generally in the form of land. The vassal's commitment lasted for life, that is, it was cancelled on the death of either vassal or lord, whereupon his 'benefice' returned to the ruler's possession. So long as the latter wielded considerable authority, the system worked well enough, but when such authority weakened, the vassals tried to keep the lands conceded to them for themselves and their descendants. This is what happened in the second half of the ninth century.

One of the ruler's duties was to ensure that justice and public law prevailed. This function derived not only from his 'consecration' but also from both Roman and Germanic tradition. The ruler had to ensure that the rights of all were respected and that the laws were applied, whether they were 'barbarian' or Roman in origin. The ruler's representative, the count, was obliged to hold three judiciary sessions each year, assisted by legal specialists called *scabini*, from which derived the French word '*échevin*' (alderman). It was during this period that 'major causes' began to be distinguished from 'minor ones'; a count dealt with the former, while leaving the latter to his deputies. In this way, the classical distinction (made throughout the Middle Ages) between 'high' and 'low' justice was established. In cases of conflict, it was possible either to place matters before the royal *missi*, who could quash the count's decisions, or to appeal to the palace tribunal. Under Frankish procedure, the burden of proof lay upon the accused, who had to defend his or her innocence by an oath sworn on relics, or by the judgement of God through an ordeal by boiling water or by a duel. These originally pagan practices were repugnant to some clerics, but they remained in use in the West down to the thirteenth century.

The resources of the empire

The history of the economy in the early Middle Ages in the West has for several years given rise to considerable discussion: some hold that there was recession and stagnation down to the eleventh century, whereas others hold the contrary view that the West experienced an economic renewal after the seventh century. It seems that the Carolingians encouraged recovery through their initiatives and legislation, and in consequence caused an increase in the production of goods and stimulated market transactions.

Charlemagne was a very great landowner, possessing immense domains – some 600 of them – through inheritance and conquest, from the valley of the Loire to the Rhineland, from which he sought to extract the highest returns. He wished good information on the current state of his *villae* and instructed his stewards to compile an inventory of his resources. This was the subject of the famous capitulary *De Villis* (c. 800). The chief steward, helped by the 'mayors', saw to the distribution of agricultural and artisanal work, fixed the dates for sowing, ploughing and harvesting, ensured that the presses were kept in good condition, and looked after the breeding of horses and the upkeep of forests. At this time, forests not only yielded resources of all kinds but also formed a hunting preserve for the ruler.

The great secular and ecclesiastical landowners copied the sovereign and enacted similar regulations for their estates. Under Louis the Pious, the Abbey of Saint-Germain-des-Prés drafted a famous polyptych, which described twenty-five separate domains in the Paris region. Charlemagne's cousin Adalard, Abbot of Corbie, prescribed in detail the work to be carried out by craftsmen and peasants on his lands.

One objective of agricultural regulation was the sale of surplus products, which required the setting up of trading arrangements in local markets. Charlemagne wished to encourage fair dealing in commercial exchange by the 'fair price' concept, a theme often addressed in the Middle Ages. He forbade monopolies and speculation, frequent in times of shortage; in 794, he fixed the maximum price of grain and ordered strict inspection of weights and measures.

From 744 onwards, each episcopal town was obliged to hold a market, the idea being to establish a place where commercial transactions might be supervised by the authorities and so enrich the royal treasury, since the tolls – dues and excises – flowed into the prince's coffers. In 864, Charles the Bald instructed his counts to draw up a list of existing markets showing which had been established under his grandfather and which since his own accession. Market profits were so considerable that bishops and abbots requested that the ruler grant them charters of exemption that would permit them to retain a share of commercial revenues.

A proper commercial policy would not have been feasible without a stable instrument of exchange: coinage. We have seen that Pepin the Short had resumed the striking of coins, and he decided that the silver *denarius* should be struck in several locales under his control. His successors waged war on forgers and had new *denarii* coined regularly. The value of the *denarius* was established at one-twelfth of a *solidus*, the money of account; this duodecimal system was also adopted in England and survived there until 1971. The reforms of the Carolingian rulers thus permitted a 'silver zone' to be set up in Europe, one that lasted until the thirteenth century, when gold coinage reappeared once more.

THE INTELLECTUAL RENAISSANCE

When one thinks of the contribution of the Carolingians, the word 'renaissance' comes immediately to mind. From the eighth century on, a new culture, inspired by Christianity, began to re-emerge in Spain, Italy and the British Isles, from out of the ruins of Roman a culture whose long drawn-out agony had lasted into the seventh century.

The merit of the Carolingians lies in their success in making use of the first signs of cultural revival in the West by restoring schools and by gathering around them artists and men of letters, to whom they gave patronage and encouragement. Contemporaries were highly conscious of the stimulus provided by royal power and spoke of a *renovatio* – a word that can be translated as 'renaissance' – attributing all the merits of this renewal to Charlemagne. However, Charlemagne was not the only one: his father Pepin had begun it before him, and his successors would continue the work.

Educational policy

The emergence of ecclesiastical schools in the West preceded Charlemagne, such schools having existed from the sixth century in the cathedrals, monasteries and even rural parishes, but they had suffered the effects of the crisis that came over the Church at the end of the seventh century and at the beginning of the eighth. Pepin the Short, in applying himself to the reform of the clergy, had laid the groundwork for cultural restoration. Charlemagne went further, wishing to revive the school system altogether; since he was responsible for the clergy, he desired them to acquire enough education to enable them, in turn, to teach the people entrusted to their care. The reform of the liturgy began under Pepin, and the reorganization of the Church could succeed only if the clergy were well enough versed in Latin to be able to read, and meditate upon, the Scriptures. As we have already seen, moreover, the ruler was conscious of the fact that, in order to perfect his administration, it was necessary to fully restore writing to the role it had enjoyed under the Roman Empire.

Charlemagne therefore stipulated, in the *Admonitio Generalis* of 789, that, in every monastery and bishopric, children should be taught the psalms, how to take notes (that is, the stenography of the age), singing, calculation and grammar (that is, Latin). Furthermore, he encouraged the bishops to create rural schools in each village and township, in which children might be taught free of charge. In 813, he even expressed the hope that once home again, these children would in turn teach household members the prayers they had learned at school. Charlemagne was certainly conscious of the difficulties of applying the educational reforms everywhere. The reforms required bishops to ensure that royal orders were reflected at the diocesan level. For a long time it was believed, on the strength of Notker of Saint-Gall's famous anecdote, that Charlemagne had created a school in his own palace. Notker portrayed the ruler as inspecting his school and chiding lazy young aristocrats while lavishing compliments on the pupils of more modest extraction. In fact, those who made up this 'school' were the scribes, notaries, cantors and copyists, busy learning their future professions in the palace's offices and in its chapel.

Louis the Pious and his sons continued Charlemagne's education policy. At the Council of Aachen in 817, Benedict of Aniana expressed the wish that monastic schools might be strictly reserved for young oblates preparing to become monks. For this reason, great abbeys such as that of Saint-Gall had to reopen some day schools where clerics, and even members of the laity, could receive instruction up to a certain level. On the well-known ground plan of Saint-Gall, one can see the outline of a school to the north of the church, with twelve classrooms and a house for the master, while the quarter for novices and brethren was situated to the east of the church. In 822 and 829, Emperor Louis once more addressed the need to set up schools. His son Lothair, as ruler in northern Italy, created nine educational centres where 'pupil teachers', sent from various bishoprics, could undertake further studies.

While it is difficult to assess all the immediate results of such educational legislation, one does note advances in cultural attainment among the clergy, and the production of all kinds of written works, so that the royal efforts had not been in vain. In northern France, Germany and Italy, there were numerous centres of culture; only Aquitaine and Provence had no known schools. The teachers – both clerics and monks – studied, taught, wrote: they also enthusiastically rediscovered the authors of antiquity, its grammarians, rhetoricians, and authors of treatises on astronomy and medicine. They knew that the study of the liberal arts allowed, as Alcuin put it, 'not only the possibility of reaching the peak of Holy Scriptures, but also true wisdom, which is the knowledge of God'. There were increasing numbers of books at their disposal, because, since Charlemagne's time, scribes had undertaken the recopying (in a new writing style) of books until then marred by errors. The new style of penmanship, called the 'Carolingian minuscule' in Charlemagne's honour, was a highly regular script, with spaces now finally separating words. It was gradually adopted throughout the West and has even come down to us, for the first Renaissance printers admired it so much that they adopted it: it became the lower case of modern typefaces.

It would be impossible to overestimate the prodigious labours of the Carolingian scribes, begun during Charlemagne's reign, and whose successors in the use of this script continued without interruption throughout the eleventh century. Thousands of manuscripts – approximately 8,000 have been counted – have come down to us, but these represent only a fraction of the output of the Carolingian *scriptoria*. Thanks to these scribes, the works of the Church Fathers, and of ancient grammarians, rhetoricians, poets and the major Latin prose writers, were made available for conservation in libraries. European culture is greatly indebted to them; without them, knowledge of Latin classical literature would not have been possible (see Plates 163, 164).

The court as the seat of intellectual culture

Restoration of the schools, and measures permitting the acquisition of knowledge and techniques, were indispensable preconditions for an eventual intellectual renaissance, but they were not sufficient in themselves. The rulers had to set the example, turning their courts into meeting places where writers could gather and ordering the production of written works: in short, they had to exercise literary patronage.

Although himself unable to write, Charlemagne took a lively interest in all the disciplines. His biographer, Eginhard, tells us that he received the instruction of an Italian, Peter of Pisa, and afterwards that of Alcuin. He was interested in grammar, rhetoric, astronomy and, above all, theology. Religious, scientific and philosophical questions were discussed in what has been called the 'Palatine Academy'; for example, Charlemagne requested an Anglo-Saxon scholar to discuss the real or imaginary existence of nothingness and shadows. He secured the help of Alcuin and Paulinus, archbishop of Aquileia, in checking the Spanish heresy of 'adoptionism', which held that Jesus was merely the adopted son of God. In reply to the Byzantines' arguments on the cult of images, he appealed to Theodulf, who drafted what are known as the 'Caroline Books'. He opposed Byzantium once more in having the famous *filioque* ('and from the Son') added to the Creed, a clause that was to remain a bone of contention between the Catholic and Orthodox Churches.

The court remained brilliant under Louis the Pious and – especially – Charles the Bald, and strangers were welcomed, whether Spanish, Anglo-Saxon or Irish. The end of political unity in the empire in 843 had few immediate consequences for the Carolingian cultural renaissance.

Many clerics from different regions took stands in the various religious quarrels, especially concerning the dispute over double predestination. The monk Gottschalk declared that, whatever people did, the wicked were predestined for eternal death, just as the good were predestined for eternal life, and this led to a denial of human freedom of choice. Hincmar, archbishop of Reims, condemned this heresy, and called upon the learned Irishman known as John Scotus Erigena (the 'Irishman') to help him to refute it.

Erigena had translated the Greek Fathers and was the first great medieval philosopher. His book *On the Division of Nature* (written *c.* 864) was, as Etienne Gilson puts it, an immense metaphysical epic in which, long before Saint Anselm, the author defined the rights and functions of reason in the face of authority. Erigena's work attracted scholars to the School of Auxerre, such as Heric and later Remigius (Remy), whose importance we are now only beginning to discover.

Another characteristic of the Carolingian renaissance was that some lay aristocrats, modelling themselves upon the rulers, also sought to acquire scholarship. They possessed large numbers of books in their palaces and ordered monks and clerics to produce treatises that would guide them in good conduct and the attainment of salvation. These treatises were called 'mirrors', and they show us what was expected of the perfect aristocrat: energy, justice, loyalty to one's prince, charity to the poor, the practice of penance, recital of divine offices, and reading the Bible. Some of these 'mirrors' were destined for young people called upon to exercise political functions, and they reveal clerics' ideas on the exercise of royal power. Special mention must be made of the 'manual' that a lay aristocrat, Dhuoda, wrote for his 16-year-old son William, a true compendium of theological and moral knowledge.

For lay aristocrats ignorant of Latin, Charlemagne arranged for 'the transcription of the ancient barbarian poems that sang the history and wars of former kings'; the few pieces of evidence at our disposal show that these poems formed the first elements of the *chansons de geste*. Other poets wrote, in the Germanic language, on the life of Christ, Genesis or the Last Judgement. National languages, whether Germanic or Romance – the *Strasbourg Oaths* being the first example – became literary languages.

ARTISTIC RENEWAL

The Carolingian renaissance was also expressed in an astonishing increase in building. A hundred or more royal residences were either erected or transformed; twenty-seven cathedrals were created; hundreds of monasteries had new buildings added to them. The rediscovery of classical treatises on architecture, such as that of Vitruvius, enabled buildings to be constructed in stone, a material still little used in areas north of the Loire. The journeys made by the Carolingians to Italy allowed them to discover the beauty of Roman basilicas, triumphal arches and Palatine chapels. Unfortunately, few examples of Carolingian buildings have been preserved.

The most famous is the Palace at Aachen, which Charlemagne built after 795 to rival that of Constantinople. Certain parts of this palace survive within the *Rathaus* (town hall) of Aachen, and especially the remarkably preserved royal chapel, adorned with marble columns brought from Italy, bronze grilles, and bronze doors. This chapel enjoyed such prestige in the West that it was imitated from the ninth to the eleventh century. When Theodulf, Bishop of Orléans, constructed the oratory for his villa at Germigny, he intended to compete with the emperor, although his square church, still to be seen and admired, drew most of its inspiration from the East and from Visigothic Spain, Theodulf's place of origin.

There is nothing left of the Carolingian cathedrals, because the architects of the Romanesque period replaced them; our knowledge of them derives only from archaeological excavation, which has allowed foundations to be located and ground plans to be drawn. These churches have been shown to have had twin facing apses, a design later reflected in many post-Carolingian buildings. A set of vaulted crypts was built at the extremities of the sanctuaries in order to protect relics and allow the faithful to worship them, such as may still be seen at Saint-Médard Abbey in Soissons, and in the Church of Saint-Germain in Auxerre, whose crypts, consecrated in 859 in the presence of Charles the Bald, were decorated with magnificent frescoes still visible today.

Carolingian churches were richly decorated with marble and stucco facings, capitals, and carved balustrades. While the walls at Auxerre, in the Church of Saint John in Müstair in Graubünden and in Reichenau Abbey were painted with frescoes, the images had a largely aesthetic and pedagogical value and, as affirmed in the 'Caroline Books', were not to be worshipped. In this, the Carolingians were opposed to the Byzantines.

Rulers and great aristocrats had richly ornamented liturgical books in their chapels. The workshops at Tours, Saint-Denis and other monasteries produced bibles, gospels and psalters, which, with their miniatures and their ivory or gold-tooled bindings, bear witness to the mastery of the artists of this age. (see Plate 164).

We may add that the Carolingians, who had introduced plainsong into the churches, encouraged the creation of musical repertoires to embellish the unfolding of the liturgy. At Saint-Riquier, an abbey managed by Charlemagne's son-in-law, the first *tonarium* was composed in about 800; this was a book setting down the pitch of an antiphon. The ninth century was a time of great musical invention – with neumic notations and tropes – and saw the appearance of the first theoretical treatises on harmony and music.

CONCLUSION

Carping minds might say that Carolingian civilization cuts a poor figure in comparison with the magnificence of Byzantium during the Macedonian dynasty, or of Baghdād under the 'Abbāsids. However, thanks to the Carolingian princes, clerics and monks, the West experienced its first flowering. Others would say that Charlemagne's unification of Europe was premature, since his successors were unable to preserve the empire, but we need to recognize that the cultural unity of the West did begin to develop then. The fragmentation of the empire into kingdoms, and the new invasions that ravaged these in the second half of the ninth century, were unable to ruin all the religious and cultural achievements of the Carolingians.

For 'Europe' then became something more than the purely geographical region it had designated at the beginning of the ninth century, as distinct from 'Africa' or 'Asia': it was now a set of territories aware of a common destiny. Charlemagne has been called 'the father of Europe', his grandson Charles the Bald 'the prince of Europe', and Pope John VIII 'the Rector of Europe'. All these expressions, along with many others that might be cited, are not devoid of meaning. Europe was not yet composed of power blocs regarded as national entities; there was as yet no 'Germany', 'France' or 'Italy', but a vast collection of peoples, each with its own character, language and uniqueness. Their antagonisms – which did exist, and which were to endure right down the present day – were however neutralized by the political powers and by the Church. The Carolingian rulers were organizers who, together with the Church, invented a novel idea of the state, founded upon respect for religious law.

This Europe was also one identified with the Latin Church or, as then came more and more to be said, with 'Christendom'. Frisians and Saxons were now converted to Christianity; the Muslims had been compelled to relinquish the north of Spain. The Carolingians maintained good relations with both the Spanish Christian kings of Oviedo and the Anglo-Saxon kings on the other side of the English Channel.

Europe was also an intellectual community, a community of scholars who spoke and wrote in the same language – Latin, whose purity had been restored by the reform of the schools. As one poet has it, 'Charlemagne showed as much ardour in suppressing textual errors as in conquering his enemies on the field of battle'. It has been said that in arresting the evolution of Latin, which was gradually changing into a vernacular (the ancestor of the Romance languages), the Carolingians created a gulf between learned and popular cultures. While there is some truth in this, for the sake of the success of liturgical reform, the renewal of scholarship and the unity of all those governing the empire, it was necessary that Latin recover its precision and universality. Thanks to the Carolingians, for centuries to come, the West would have access to an international linguistic means of communication: and one it was not subsequently to recover.

Knowledge of Latin allowed the literati, with new manuscripts at their disposal, to begin studying those works one calls 'classical'. Whether one considers this is a matter for rejoicing or for disapproval, Western education would now continue to be marked by the rule of grammar, a tradition of virtuosity in rhetoric and a taste for learned poetry. Carolingian writers, encouraged by their princes, left works in verse and prose that, when studied properly, cannot be mistaken for plagiarisms of classical works.

The Carolingian inheritance was as much institutional as cultural. Church structures had been established; the papacy had secured its temporal power from the Carolingians; the pope insisted on 'consecrating' princes as emperors; and hierarchical networks had been woven, with archbishoprics, bishoprics, archidiaconates and deaconries. The Rule of Saint Benedict had been imposed upon every monastery. The system of tithes would disappear only with the French Revolution. As for the 'consecration' of kings, which confirmed the religious character of the sovereign, this custom would survive until the nineteenth century. All European kings would base their kingship upon the foundations of the Carolingian monarchy. The coronation oath derives in direct line from the 'promise' made by the rulers of the ninth century. The concept of a 'royal ministry', one obliging a king to ensure the rule of justice and peace, and to expect help and advice from his bishops, is also of Carolingian origin.

Finally, how can one avoid mentioning that, right down to the very end of the Middle Ages, all Western princes and aristocrats sought, with zeal and ingenuity, to discover ties of kinship between themselves and the Carolingians. For this illustrious family had so many descendants, dispersed across the different regions of Europe, that such claims might even be legitimate. Yet for every genuine affiliation, there were countless false genealogies. The point is that all nobles were proud to count either a Carolingian prince among their ancestor, or at least one of the heroes, peers of Charlemagne, whose exploits were recounted in the *chansons de geste*. Every time we in Europe have sought to achieve unification, whether under Napoleon or in our own time, we have invoked the name of Charlemagne. After all, is the 'Charlemagne Prize' not awarded each year, at Aachen, to the politician who has laboured the hardest for such unification?

BIBLIOGRAPHY

AMANN, E. 1947. L'époque carolingienne. In: FLICHE, A.; MARTIN, V. (eds) *Histoire de l'Eglise*, Vol. VI. Paris.

BLOCH, M. 1939. *La société féodale*. Paris.

BRUANFELS, W. (ed.) 1965–1968. *Karl der Grosse, Lebenswerk und Nachleben*. 5 vols. Dusseldorf.

BUTZER, P. L. and LORZMANN, D. (eds) 1993. *Science in Western and Eastern Civilization in Carolingian Times*. Birkhäuser Verlag, Bale.

BUTZER, P. L., KERNER, M. and OBERSCHELP, W. (eds) 1997. *Charlemagne and his Heritage: 1200 Years of Civilization and Science in Europe*. Brepols.

CONTRENI, J. J. 1992. *Carolingian Learning, Masters and Manuscripts*. Variorum, Great Yarmouth.

FOLZ, R. 1964. *Le couronnement impèrial de Charlemagne*. Paris.

——. 1972. *De l'antiquité au monde médiéval*. Paris. La montée des Carolingiens au pouvoir, pp. 289–310; la formation et l'organisation de l'Empire carolingien, pp. 315–353; les destinées de l'Empire carolingien au IXè siècle, pp. 354–399.

GANSHOF, F. L. 1968. *Frankish Institutions Under Charlemagne*. Providence, Rhode Island.

——. 1971. *The Carolingians and the Frankish Monarchy*. London.

GUADAGNIN, P. (ed.) 1988. *Un village au temps de Charlemagne* (éd. de la réunion des Musées nationaux, Paris).

HALPHEN, L. 1995. *Charlemagne et l'empire carolingien*, 3rd edn. Paris.

HEITZ, C. 1981. *L'architecture religieuse carolingienne*. Paris.

HUBERT, J.; PORCHER, J.; WOLBACH, W. F. 1968. *L'empire carolingien*, 2nd edn. Paris.

LEBECQ, S. 1990. Les origines franques (Vè–IXè siècle). In: *Nouvelle Histoire de la France médiévale*, Vol. 1. Paris.

MCKITTERICK, R. 1989. *The Carolingian and the Written Word*. Cambridge.

Nascita dell'Europa ed Europa Carolingia. 1981. Un' equazione da verificare. *Settimane di studio del centro italiano di studi sull'alto Medioevo*, Vol. XXVII. Spoleto.

PACAUT, M. 1980. L'Europe carolingienne ou le temps des illusions (milieu VIIIè–milieu Xè siècle). In: *Histoire générale de l'Europe*. Vol. I, *L'Europe des origines au début du XVè siècle*. Paris.

PIRENNE, H. 1939. *Mohammed and Charlemagne*. London.

RICHÉ, P. 1986. *La vie quotidienne dans l'Empire carolingien*, 4th edn. Paris (English trans. 1978; Polish trans. 1979; German trans. 1981; Japanese trans. 1993).

——. 1993. Le Christianisme dans l'Occident carolingien (milieu VIIIè–fin IXè siècle). In: A. VAUCHEZ (ed.) *Histoire du Christianisme*, Vol. IV. Paris.

——. (3rd edn) 1999. *Ecoles et enseignement dans le haut Moyen Âge*, Paris (Italian trans., Rome, 1984).

——. 1992. *Les Carolingiens. Une famille qui fit l'Europe* (new edn). Paris.

——. (2nd edn) 1992. *Dhuoda, manuel pour mon fils*. (Introduction and critical edition) 'Sources chrétiennes', Paris.

ROUCHE, M. 1983. Les premiers frémissements de l'Europe. In: FOSSIER, R. (ed.) *Le Moyen Âge*. Vol. I, Paris, pp. 369–397.

SKUBISZEWSKI, P. 1998. *L'Art du Haut Moyen Âge*. Paris.

SULLIVAN, R. E. 1989. The Carolingian Ages. *Speculum*, pp. 267–306.

THEIS, L. 1990. *L'héritage des Charles de la mort de Charlemagne aux environs de l'an mil*. In: *Nouvelle histoire de la France mèdièvale*, Vol. 2. Paris.

TOUBERT, P. 1988. La part des grands domaines dans le décollage économique de l'Occident (VIIIè–Xè siècle). *FLARAN*, 10, pp. 53–86.

ULLMANN, W. 1969. The Carolingian Renaissance and the Idea of Kingship. London. *Law and Politics in the Middle Ages*. Introduction to the sources of medieval political ideas, 1975.

WERNER, K. F. 1984. *Les Origines*. In: FAVIER, J. (ed.) *Histoire de France*, Vol. I. Paris.

WHITE, L. 1962. *Medieval Technologies*. Oxford.

II: The Configuration of European Personality

INTRODUCTION

Jacques Le Goff

Europe came into being in the medieval age, between the sixth and the sixteenth century. What took place here – not without conflict – was a cultural blend between Christianity and several civilizations inherited from the world of antiquity: a mixed legacy bequeathed not only by the Roman Empire but also by the ancient cultures of the Celts, Germans and Slavs.

The Christian religion fashioned a cultural unity – that of Christendom. But Christendom itself became organized into distinct, increasingly varied and increasingly national-minded states. Europe's configuration hence came to be one of both unity and fragmentation, unity and diversity (see Map 6).

But Europe also inherited, in part from its Roman legacy, a yawning cultural chasm. The Roman Empire had not so much united as juxtaposed two distinct worlds: a Latin-speaking West and a Greek-speaking East. Thus arose and developed a dual Europe, one dominated by Roman Catholic Christianity in the West and the other moulded by Greek Orthodox Christianity in the East.

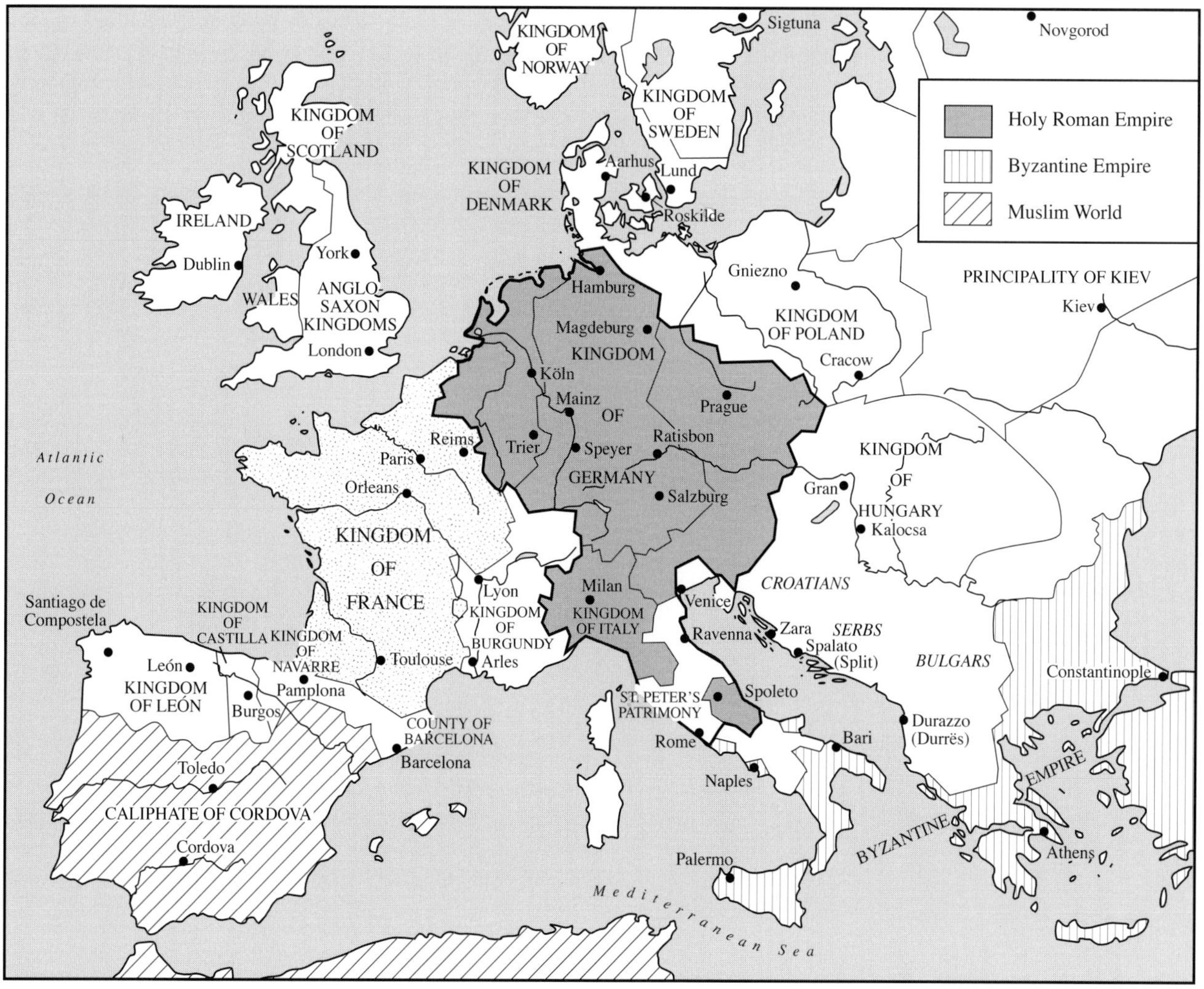

Map 6 Europe *c.* 1000: politically more fragmented, but enriched with the emergence of new Christian states (Le Goff, J., 1964, *Civilisation de l'occident médiéval*, Flammarion-Arthaud).

After a long spell of demographic, economic, political and cultural decline, Western Christian Europe reached stability at the end of the tenth century, then developed under the feudal system, and from the thirteenth century began its lurch towards a pre-capitalist civilization.

Western Europe thus laid in its medieval age the foundations of its future power, one fated, by the turn of the sixteenth century, to dominate the rest of the world. Such power was built upon foundations not only technological, economic, military and political but also intellectual and ideological: foundations, as it were, in the mind. The crucible of this power lay in late Medieval Europe's urban surge. However stubborn the hold of tradition, this urban surge fostered innovation and modernization, based upon the development of science and reason. But hard upon such a surge in Europe's power followed a parallel rise in Europe's spirit of intolerance, repression and persecution within, coupled with a yearn not only to expand but also to conquer, abroad.

Yet medieval Europe also provided the foundations for Europe's unity. What it produced in the realms of science and thought, and what it achieved in art, transcend how it misused all these and came to enrich the culture of the world.

11

MEDIEVAL WESTERN EUROPE

Jacques Le Goff

THE CATHOLIC CHURCH AND THE EARTHLY KINGDOMS

Christianism became the great new religious and ideological movement of the medieval West after its recognition as the official creed of the Roman Empire in the fourth century. But it was a religion which also gradually became divided against itself. In the West, there thus grew up a Latin Church, and in the East a Greek Church, increasingly drifting apart on either side of a long-lasting cultural frontier that hardened over time along political lines: a rift on the ground which reached from Scandinavia all the way to Croatia. Balts, Poles, Czechs, Slovaks, Hungarians and Slovenes thus fell on the Western side of this divide, while on the other side were to be found the Russians and Greeks, amongst many other peoples. The divide was sanctioned and sealed by the Great Eastern Schism of 1054, which permanently removed the Greek Church from the See of Rome and made the separation between Western Christendom, on the one hand, and the Orthodox domains of Byzantium and the eastern Slavic lands, on the other, into something final. The Byzantine world was at first the wealthier of the two domains, and best preserved the legacy of antique culture; but it grew progressively weaker as it fell prey to both economic exploitation by Westerners (especially by Italians) and territorial seizures by Turks – until it collapsed in 1453. The West, for its part, had been a barbarized, divided world; whatever meagre unity it had initially possessed was for a while only poorly symbolized by two figureheads, the pope and the emperor; but then Latin Christendom experienced its extraordinary economic, political and cultural surge which led it to embark on a career of expansion and, increasingly, conquest.

The Roman Empire in the West had not survived invasion and settlement on its soil by the mostly Germanic peoples who, from the third century on, had overwhelmed its military defence lines, known as the *limes*, set up as a barrier against nomad incursions. Nor had the empire been able to outlive the disintegration of its hitherto far-ranging monetary economy and the effects of urban collapse, widening mass poverty, and general crisis in cultural and ethical values which attended the decline of ancient civilization and the spread of Christianity. In its place there arose two new powers.

The first of these was that of the Church, which made its power felt on two levels. On the local level, it was still able to rely on a network of towns, although the towns themselves were shrinking in size, through those urban leaders who combined religious with economic, social and political functions: the bishops. On a more unitary level, the Church sought to occupy the entire space which had been that of the old Western Roman Empire, defunct since the close of the fifth century, and whose legacy the bishop of Rome now sought for himself. As a sort of super-bishop under the title of pope, he claimed supremacy over the Eastern Church, which however increasingly eluded his grasp, and over the Western Church: which he eventually did secure, albeit slowly and painfully. Decisive papal breakthroughs in this direction occurred in the eighth century with support from the Frankish kings and the carving out for the papacy of a territorial base in central Italy: the *Patrimony of Saint Peter*. A major drive for religious reform – known as the Gregorian reform after Pope Gregory VII (1073–1085), who played a leading part – was carried through between the middle of the eleventh and the close of the twelfth century. The intended effect was to remove the Church from its previous subservience to feudal lay power structures and also sharply to separate the clergy from the lay folk by binding celibacy upon the former, and the married state upon the latter – as the normal condition for lay folk.

The second power was represented by the kingdoms. These grew up as a result of the fusion within the borders of the former Roman Empire between the newly installed conquering peoples and the older settled folk, under the authority of the conquering leader, who took the title of king and founded a ruling dynasty. Such were the kingdoms of the Ostrogoths and the Lombards in Italy, of the Visigoths in Aquitania and later in Spain, of the Franks in Gaul, and of the many petty kingdoms of the Anglo-Saxons in Great Britain.

Europe's initial pattern thus emerged, based upon a dual design. The first was boldly communal, starkly marked out in religious and cultural terms: that of Christendom itself. The second design showed greater variety, being made up of a patchwork of different kingdoms founded upon both imported ethnic traditions and more ancient local and multi-cultural traditions (as with the meeting of Germans and Gallo Romans in Gaul, for instance). This second design, as it were, prefigured the Europe of nation-states.

Two major features resulted from this reorganization of the Roman Empire in the West. The first was the rejection of theocratic power. Religious power pertained to the Church and to the pope, political power to kings. This duality of powers was predicated on the Gospel's injunction: 'Render to Caesar the things that are Caesar's' (see Plates 169–172).

The second was the ethnic mingling which came about with the rise of Christendom and the Christian kingdoms: Celts, Germans, Gallo-Romans, British Romans, Italian Romans, Iberian Romans and Jews came to mix with Normans, Slavs, Hungarians and Arabs. Such cultural blendings had already begun in the days of the Roman Empire and foreshadowed a multi-cultural and multi-ethnic Europe open to waves of immigration. Yet already in Visigothic Spain that evil incubus of European civilization: anti-Semitism, began to loom.

Western Christendom strove twice to effect its own political unity in the form of an empire independent of that of the Byzantine Greeks: with Charlemagne, crowned by the pope in Rome in 800, and then with Otto I, likewise crowned by the pope in Rome in 962. Such imperial resurrection spawned an institution more theoretical and symbolic than real, the Holy Roman Empire of the German nation, with Rome fondly idealized as its capital. More often than not, this empire was mostly an empty shell in medieval Europe. Pope and emperor, the two symbolic heads of medieval Christendom, ultimately exhausted their powers in disputes over the supremacy of the spiritual sovereignty over the temporal, or the other way around (see Plates 149, 169, 170).

Meanwhile, since the outset of the eighth century, the great wave of Arab conquest had reached Western Europe. While it washed only thinly and briefly over Provence, and lingered to a further and deeper but still rather limited extent in Sicily, it submerged the greater part of Spain, whence it only receded in the twelfth and especially in the thirteenth century under the counter tide of the wars of the *Reconquista*, waged by the small northern Iberian Christian kingdoms of Castile, León, Navarre, Asturias, Galicia and Aragon. But only in 1492 did a reunified Christian Spain managed to flush Islam from its very last stronghold in the peninsula, the small kingdom of Grenada.

The struggle against the Muslims provided the papacy with an opportunity to unite Western Christians in a common goal: the recapture of the Christian shrines of Palestine, the Holy Land. When the pope preached his Crusade in Clermont in 1095, his purpose was not only to add Palestine to the lands of Christendom but also to deflect Christian aggressiveness from inter-Christian wars and provide an outlet – beyond the confines of the West – for overpopulation and the strains and passions it entailed. Moreover, crusading reflected the collective imaginative stirring of Western Christians fascinated by the mental picture of a Jerusalem for which they yearned as the earthly mirror of the heavenly Jerusalem, and so thought to be situated at the very centre of the Earth's surface. The Crusades failed militarily, however, and Christians ceased to hold any part of Palestine after the fall of Acre in 1291 (see Plates 31, 45, 46).

The Crusades actually weakened the Christian states and their peerages, embittered relations between Latins and Byzantines after the sack of Constantinople by the Crusaders at the beginning of the Fourth Crusade in 1204, sharpened the spirit of holy war (*jihād*) amongst the Muslims themselves, and if anything hampered rather than helped the trade ventures of Christians in the East spearheaded by the Venetians and Genoese – who founded rival commercial empires throughout the eastern Mediterranean and the Aegean as far as Cyprus and the Crimea.

In Sicily and especially in Spain, however, and despite armed confrontation, contact between Muslims and Christians (and Jews) resulted in important cultural borrowings, particularly in the artistic field. Arabic sciences (notably in the fields of medicine and astronomy) left a lasting impact on Western Christendom. Moreover, the Arabs were the bearers of philosophical and scientific traditions bequeathed by the ancient Greeks but which were no longer known to Latin science. All this spurred the development of learning in Western Christendom, which flowered in the scholasticism of the thirteenth century. Arabic poetry also probably played an important role as a model for the early courtly verse of the troubadours in Christian Southern Europe from the close of the eleventh to the middle of the thirteenth century. Cordova, and especially Toledo, which Spanish Christians recaptured as early as 1085, were the great meeting points for the major civilizations of Islam, Judaism and Western Christendom. Palermo too, in the field of science, played a similar although less important part (see Plates 65–69, 70–73, 133, 137, 141).

While Western Christendom thus had to face the external challenge of Islam, it also had to deal with the internal threat posed by the series of heterodox movements, or heresies, which sprang up in its midst from the eleventh century onwards. Care should be taken to distinguish here those heresies primarily directed against the Church and its perceived moral corruption and unjustified monopoly of the sacraments. Such heresies preached a return to what was regarded as having been the primitive poverty, purity and brotherhood of the early Church. In effect, these movements expressed a cry of revolt against the wealth and worldliness which had come over the West since its great economic upsurge at the turn of the eleventh century.

But a still greater threat appeared in the shape of a movement which in fact was not a Christian heresy at all but a completely different religion with its own distinct theology, clergy and ritual practice. This was the movement of the Cathars, adherents of the particular form taken by one of the dualist creeds which had grown up in the Middle East since ancient times, especially Manichaeism in the third century AD. Not until the end of the thirteenth century was the Cathar movement fully overcome.

Through the struggles which it waged against such movements, the Roman Church did at least spare Western Europe from the know-nothingness and oppression which the various fundamentalist religious sects clearly threatened. But in the process it became engaged in general repression, which, beyond the heretics, fell alike on Jews, homosexuals, lepers, beggars and vagabonds. While Europe was buoyed by an expansionist mood and displayed open curiosity about the outside world in the later medieval centuries, such expansion was secured at the price of merciless internal intolerance and exclusion. Europe sought internal scapegoats, and multiplied their number.

MONASTERIES AND MONASTIC CULTURE

A very marked aspect of the great crisis of the third and fourth centuries AD had been the rise of asceticism: the rejection of carnal pleasure in food, clothing and sex. In the East, men had fared forth in quest of salvation to dwell far away from the urban bustle of their fellow humans, in remote spots, either in small groups or entirely alone. This was the 'flight into the desert'. This model of life began to spread in the West at the beginning of the sixth century, and a type of man previously unknown in the West appeared: the monk, the man on his own. The European 'desert' available to such

Western Christian anchorites was the forest, which stretched across vast reaches of their continent. Here the monks built their monasteries for collective living, or their rudimentary lonely hermitages. In successive waves, between the fifth and eighth centuries and then between the tenth and twelfth, Western Europe became filled with monks and hermits (see Plate 163).

One sixth-century Italian monastic institution in particular came to enjoy outstanding success: this was the Rule of Saint Benedict of Nursia, founder of the monastery of Monte Cassino on the southern fringes of Latium. The Benedictine Order, whose monasteries multiplied, owed its success precisely to the very moderation, practicality and sense of balance of its rule, which was moreover actively supported by Charlemagne and Louis the Pious, who further had this rule revised and then imposed it as binding on Western monasticism in general.

Other orders, however, emerged after the tenth century. The powerful Order of Cluny spawned a fresh network of monasteries but remained rather too narrowly linked to the feudal nobility. Anchorite movements sprang up in Italy on a large scale. The Order of Cîteaux, founded in Burgundy in 1098, became famous and influential through its monk Saint Bernard (1091–1153), who was widely celebrated in his own day.

Medieval monasticism oscillated between two poles. One pole was concerned with penitence. Importance was attached to manual labour both as a form of penitence and as a means of attaining economic self-sufficiency so as to allow a monastery to eschew as far as possible all contact with the outside world. This in fact drove the monasteries into becoming active economic agents in the development of the resources of rural and forest zones: and here the Cistercian Order – that of Cîteaux – played a major role. The other pole was liturgical, dwelling upon the *Opus Dei* or Work of God: the service of the Lord, ritual and prayer, and splendid ceremonial that rendered fitting tribute to the creator. Here Cluny stood out.

But monastic organization also contributed a model for the measure and fixing of time. The division of the day into canonical hours for the various services offered a time pattern for the daily use and wont of the world at large. The sound of bells, whose use began to spread in the seventh century, imparted the rhythm of the Church's own daily schedule to the daily life of all Christendom for many hundreds of years to come.

Finally, the monks conferred upon manual labour itself, first undertaken as a penance, something of the very dignity which clung to their own persons and social status. As a result, they went far in rehabilitating the work ethic in the general system of religious and human values.

THE FEUDAL SYSTEM

During the earlier medieval period extending from the fifth to the ninth century, a new historical system arose which linked a mode of production with its own type of society and scale of values: this was the feudal system.

An earlier system, that of the demesne or great estate inherited from the pattern of large estates of late antiquity, evolved into feudalism's own model of 'lordship'. In this model, the demesne yielded its central social place to that of the lordship, which grouped the populations of several castles and villages under the authority of a lord. The lord combined military powers of command (*ban*) with civilian jurisdiction and economic leadership over a peasant population whose personal status gradually evolved from one of outright judicial servitude (*serfs*) to one of semi or even complete freedom. Feudalism, in fact, represented the triumph of regionalization.

But feudalization was complemented and corrected by two other manifestations. The first of these was fresh urban growth between the tenth and fourteenth centuries. The cities were linked to the feudal system but also to an ever wider network of far-reaching trade, and their population was made up of a new social category which stood outside the feudal world's vassal–lord scale of relations. These were the burghers, who evolved their own code of values: one rooted in freedom ('city air makes one free'), autonomy and the search for both profit and new knowledge in the schools.

The second manifestation was the rebirth of central power with the rise of the monarchies and the gradual genesis of the modern state through two models in particular: that of monarchy itself (in England, France, the Iberian peninsula and the case of papal rule), and that provided by the city-states (in Italy and, to a lesser extent, Germany). The power vested in the monarch or city-state opposed its own centralization to the forces of regionalization, spawned bureaucratic institutions and gradually recovered a portion of its sovereign prerogatives touching the army, finance, justice and coinage.

The feudal system was based on two fundamental principles: land and personal links. Personal links within the feudal scale were theoretically the preserve of the upper ranks of society, represented by the nobles. A lower lord, or vassal, swore homage and fealty to a higher lord, who in return pledged to protect his vassal and bestowed upon him a tract of land, or fief.

From the turn of the eleventh century, the outstanding social feature of the feudal order was the class of the *milites*, or knights. The most important knights held their own castles, or castellenies. For the castle was the seat of power and prestige in feudal society – and also a true cultural centre. Along with military expeditions and warlike deeds, the castle was where feudalism's system of values and ways of thought were elaborated and made manifest. In addition to their prowess in battle, nobles strove to win and serve a paramour, and to observe a proper code of manners in the castles of their lords – behaviour which yields us the core of the feudal ideal: courtliness.

A key element in the whole system was the family: that is, the extended family or lineage, around which complex webs of kinship and alliance were spun.

Feudal society cannot be grasped, however, if we neglect the lower class on which this whole interlocked system of lords and vassals ultimately rested for its economic well-being: the peasants, who represented the overwhelming majority of the population. Although this peasant class was by no means uniform, in social practice, all farm labourers tended to be regarded, with contempt, as one indistinct mass of villeins (see Plates 5, 6, 8).

The crucial importance of the Church must never be overlooked in feudal society, of which it was an essential component from the very outset. Numerous and often vast landholdings were so many Church lordships. Bishops, abbey chapters, whole monasteries were lords. The Church moreover underpinned the whole feudal system with religious and ideological justification. God, indeed, was the supreme Lord of all. Original sin had first cast men into thralldom, and the peasants were precisely so many incarnations of human servitude. The Church was perceived as the ally of the temporal lords – and as the keystone to the whole arch of the feudal system.

Medieval Western Christendom's projected and idealized social pattern ultimately stemmed from ancient Indo-European prototypes regarding the three great social functions: first came those who prayed (*oratores*), the clergy who represented the sacred function; then came those who fought (*bellatores*), the warriors, who expressed the function associated with physical force; finally came those who laboured (*laboratores*), the peasants and, later, the craftsmen, incarnations as it were of the productive function. Whatever its limits, this pattern did serve to bestow dignity upon labour, which is one of the characteristics of European identity.

Another ideal was that conveyed by courtly literature, which provided an early form for Europe's idealized notions of courteous behaviour. But the feudal spirit remained essentially a warlike one. Feudal society's chief form of entertainment was the joust, a warrior's game and also – very much like modern sport – a highly lucrative venture.

The nobility, who dominated the feudal structure, bequeathed their notion of 'honour' to Europe's system of values. But they also showed much preoccupation with the prerogatives of 'blood': through the image of 'purity of blood', a notion which reared up in fifteenth-century Spain, this concept came to bedevil Europe in a significant way under the aspect of racism.

REGIONS AND THE NEW STATES OF MEDIEVAL EUROPE

England's rulers, after the Norman Conquest of 1066, annexed Wales in the later thirteenth century but failed to extend their sway over all of Ireland, and still less over Scotland, which remained an independent realm. But the English monarchy did manage to acquire vast domains in western France, from Normandy to the River Loire and as far as Gascony, and even very nearly absorbed the French kingdom altogether – before losing all its French possessions in the wake of the Hundred Years War by the middle of the fifteenth century. For their part, the English nobility, and the English cities, were able to impose limits on their monarchs' powers (Magna Carta in 1215, the Provisions of Oxford in 1258). England thus gave Europe an example of a political power controlled by a constitution and a parliament.

France, once it had settled her contention with England, offered Europe's most far-reaching example of a centralized state. By the close of the Middle Ages, it had almost overcome another major hurdle, the economic, social and political gap which still separated its better-developed northern territories from its southern districts: where the North's political sway had long made almost no headway, where a different language (Provençal) still prevailed, and where a distinct form of civilization steeped in antique traditions and Eastern influences had flowered in an earlier age.

Spain underwent a dual development: the Islamic presence in its midst dwindled and then disappeared, while the number of Christian kingdoms was finally paired down to only two, Castile and Aragon: including the latter's eastern seaboard on the Mediterranean, Catalonia. The joining of these two realms in the late fifteenth century through the wedding of Isabel of Castile and Ferdinand of Aragon further sealed Spanish unity, although both the Basque country and Catalonia preserved a strong linguistic and ethnic identity. Spain's rulers, somewhat like England's, had to reckon with representative assemblies, the *cortes*. In 1492, Ferdinand and Isabel financed Columbus' expedition which reached the West Indies, later to be called 'America' after the Italian navigator Amérigo Vespucci.

Portugal had become detached from Spain by the middle of the thirteenth century and constituted Europe's most important Atlantic seaboard. Turned as it was towards the open ocean and the West African coast, fifteenth- and early sixteenth-century Portugal took a leading role in preparing and carrying out the great maritime discoveries: as Portuguese ships moved down the African shoreline, rounded the Cape of Good Hope, sailed Eastern waters and finally reached India and later Brazil (see Plates 24, 25).

Germany and Italy remained frailer, non-united political entities where the cities came to play a dominant part. Germany's Hanseatic league of powerful trading port cities dominated the shores of the North Sea and the Baltic. At the close of the Middle Ages, however, the Habsburg dynasty began to extend its sway over Central Europe and beyond.

In Italy, true city-states were formed, based on a powerful economy that rested in part on economic positions acquired elsewhere, from Flanders to Cyprus. After the decline of Genoa, Pisa and the south Italian ports, the chief city-states were Milan, Venice and Florence. In the face of the Turkish threat (with the fall of Constantinople in 1453), Italy remained Europe's main gateway to the Mediterranean and the Middle East, and its most important cradle of high urban civilization inherited from the medieval age (see Plate 40).

An original political entity came into being in the very heart of Western Europe: the Swiss Confederation, formed around an initial core of three cantons which united and sealed a treaty of permanent alliance in 1291. The Swiss in fact controlled most of the Alpine passes affording land communication between Southern and Northern Europe (even though from the fourteenth century onwards, ships regularly plied between Italy, England and Flanders).

At about the turn of the eleventh century, two fresh groups of princely states entered the fold of Western or Latin Christendom with the conversion of their rulers and peoples.

The first group corresponded to the Scandinavian states, which took form when the Vikings settled down after injecting a distinct Nordic strain throughout Western Europe – from Normandy and later England down to Sicily – in the tenth and eleventh centuries. The new states were Denmark, Norway and Sweden, next to which should be mentioned Iceland, which added its own strongly original contribution to medieval civilization (see Plate 168).

The second group was that of the western Slavic states along the European divide which separated Latin Catholic from Greek Orthodox Christendom. Poland's relations with the German Empire were more often than not marked by conflict, but the kingdom still saw many German colonists settle on its soil and especially in its cities. Poland enjoyed a brilliant period in the fourteenth and fifteenth centuries which brought union with Lithuania and a trend towards eastern expansion under the Jagellon dynasty (see Plate 176).

Bohemia–Moravia's own golden age under the rule of its Czech Przemyslid kings in the eleventh to thirteenth centuries came to an end when the country became increasingly pulled into a German political orbit. Still, the fifteenth century witnessed a powerful revolutionary movement, at once religious, social and political in scope, that of the Hussites: one of the first strong manifestations of outright nationalism in Europe and a precursor of the Reformation (see Plate 61).

Other Slavic peoples, such as the Slovaks to the east of the Czechs and the Slovenes and Croats to the south, enjoyed only a frail and short-lived period of autonomy around the turn of the eleventh century before falling under Hungarian rule.

Hungary was the last of the new European states to be created, just as its people, of Asian origin, were the latest to enter the world of Latin Christendom, which they joined through the conversion of their king Stephen: who received his crown from Pope Sylvester II on 25 December 1000.

CITIES

The medieval city differed profoundly from its ancient forerunner, for it was not so much a military, political and administrative centre as an economic and cultural one.

Agricultural surpluses fed a growing urban population of immigrant peasants, for an increasing number of men and women found employment in crafts. Building projects, such as the new churches, which sometimes attained great size (cathedrals), made further demands on labour. The spreading network of trade attracted crowds to its markets and fairs, money changers and bankers. The city dominated its surrounding countryside and gave birth to a new society linked to fresh economic activities with their attendant intellectual pursuits: whence the development of judicial teaching, knowledge and practice. The most socially and politically advanced urban trend of the eleventh and twelfth centuries was the communal movement, which made itself sharply felt in northern France and especially in northern and central Italy. The city's administration came into the hands of a group of citizens who formed the town council, regulated economic life and civic affairs, and raised taxes. Power belonged to citizens who were equal at least in theory – although judicial differences in status actually ranged them in a graded hierarchy.

The dominant actor in urban life was the merchant, especially the merchant dealing in large-scale trade which opened foreign and sometimes very distant horizons. A strong small-town patriotism emerged, which nurtured urban imagination. New values appeared, centred on profit, the work ethic, and a sense of beauty, cleanliness and order: for medieval urbanism was founded upon a positive image of the city. Most medieval men and women regarded their city, with its monuments, as a place of beauty and wealth – and one that moreover offered a secure refuge within its walls.

The city also offered its dwellers new forms of social solidarity. These at first were mainly professional. Urban craftsmen organized into more or less highly structured 'trades' (*arti* in Italy, *Zünfte* in Germany, guilds in England). But the lower grade of workers in larger cities were massed into an unskilled labour force subject to haphazard employment and wages on a daily basis only, a proletariat left with no other defence but occasional resort to violence. The first actual strikes broke out in northern France and Flanders in the second half of the thirteenth century. The crisis of the fourteenth century added the blight of unemployment to the deepening wretchedness, squalor, homelessness and dependence on begging, delinquence and prostitution which increasingly clouded the urban atmosphere. Urban riots and outright revolts flared up, as with the great rising of the *ciompi* (poor workers) in Florence in 1378. Rural risings expressed another form of social tension, as with the *jacquerie* in France in 1358, or England's Peasant Revolt of 1381.

Other bonds of solidarity were forged along religious lines. Parish groupings and lay brotherhoods multiplied, placed under the patronage of the Virgin, the Holy Ghost or a variety of saints. Such religious-minded organizations offered brethren the consolation of worship offered in common, support in case of trouble, and, at the time of a member's death, participation in organizing his funeral and holding *post mortem* prayers. With the opening of the thirteenth century, fresh religious orders gathered, no longer now in the 'desert' but in the midst of other people, in the cities. These were the mendicant orders (Dominicans, Franciscans, Augustinian Friars and White Friars). These devoted themselves to preaching the Word in a new urban setting, squarely faced urban problems of labour and money, confessed the city's living, and ministered to its dying.

City-life also imparted a new measure to the flow of time, with a more rational and regularized means of marking hours better adapted to the needs of merchants and to the rhythm of urban activity, parallel with the venerable liturgical schedule observed by the Church. Bells now chimed from secular belfries, and by the end of the thirteenth century, mechanical clocks began striking the hour.

From the twelfth century onwards, cities moreover became cultural centres in their own right. The new teaching afforded in the rising urban schools now taught lay folk, too, how to read, write and calculate. In the wake of economic renewal came that of jurisprudence, with a host of new callings in the field of law: southern Europe saw a spectacular rise in the number of notaries public.

ECONOMIC DEVELOPMENT

From the tenth century on, indeed perhaps ever since the seventh, the medieval West enjoyed a steady economic rise which hardly suffered a break, not even in the fourteenth century, whose crisis was rather one of growth than of decline.

But development at first was mainly rural. A Europe which fed on white bread and quantities of meat began to emerge, while the drinking map split the continent between a beer quaffing North and a wine-bibbing South. A sense of taste in the distinct gastronomic meaning of the term – returned with the thirteenth-century appearance of actual cooking manuals, encouraged not only by patrons from the nobility, both religious and secular, but even among the burghers. Rural growth, best observed in the great plains of north-east Europe and also in Lombardy, Flanders and Normandy, fed a population which probably tripled between the seventh and fourteenth centuries, rocketing from 15 million to 50 million in Western Europe alone, and from 27 million to 73 million in Europe as a whole.

Not that most of Europe was yet safe from the vagaries of weather or natural disaster. Famines had almost entirely disappeared by the thirteenth century but returned with a vengeance in the fourteenth, while child mortality remained severe.

Improved craftsmanship and a budding industry made themselves felt most in metallurgy, building and textiles, which spawned in turn a demand for luxuries and the appearance of true fashions. The wearing of furs became widespread, from the costly pelisses of the wealthy and powerful to the more modest pelts of simple burghers. A burgeoning taste for bright colours created a tremendous demand for dyes. Colours, indeed, were fraught with symbolic connotations and served as an elaborate expression of the knightly code itself (heraldry was adopted by all professional and social categories).

The spectacular growth in trade spurred resumption of an economy based on coinage. The available quantity of gold and silver coins of Byzantine and Arab origin no longer satisfying demand, Western Europe – to crown as it were its own economic rise – again began minting its own gold and high-value silver pieces ('groats') (see Plates 193 d and 194, a, b and c).

The greatest fairs of thirteenth-century Europe were those held in the French province of Champagne, where products from the North were exchanged for those from the Mediterranean South.

Major international trade – involving a 'world economy' (*Weltwirtschaft*) which implicated all of Europe – dealt mainly with such costly goods as silks, gold and silver plate, and spices. The lion's share of this trade fell to the Italians and especially to the Lombards. Fourteenth- and fifteenth-century Italians created true banks and subsidiary firms which united banking with trade. The most famous of such firms became the one founded by the Medici of Florence.

Reliance on a monetary economy and the growth of large-scale trade did, however, raise serious religious problems for Christian Europe. For merchants to deal thus in money, to wax rich, to extract interest, and as it were to speculate on the very flow of time (time being a dimension considered by the Church to pertain to God alone), caused such merchants to come to be looked upon in the same light as usurers. It took some years for the Church to sort out those mercantile activities regarded as permissible from those to be ruled out as illicit, and so to allow Christian merchants to hone just those pre-capitalist skills which now permitted them to take their full place in a Christian society – while partly rehabilitating the use of money itself (along with the dignity of labour). Indeed, the very way in which Latin Christendom thus found a place for such a budding capitalism within its own system of values provided, in turn, one of the main historical conditions for the future development of Western Europe.

TECHNOLOGICAL BREAKTHROUGHS

Breakthroughs in technology were what rendered such economic growth possible, not only through outright inventions but also by means of improvement and better distribution of previously known techniques.

The basic raw material of the Middle Ages was wood, but the age increasingly resorted to stone and iron. The thirteenth century expanded the exploitation of iron, lead, copper and coal mines.

The most important source of energy was furnished by mills. Watermills in town and country alike powered forges and such activities as fulling, tanning, brewing, sawing, paper making and so on. The windmill appeared in the late twelfth century. The mill thus became a true industrial machine (see Plate 17).

Transport improved only slowly. Merchants found greater safety by organizing into convoys. The most important breakthroughs occurred in naval techniques: ships increased in tonnage (from the Mediterranean *nave* to the Hanseatic *kogge*) and sturdier and far more practical and mobile stern rudders replaced the older lateral rudders (see Plates 23–25). Improved rigging now included the lateen sail. The astrolabe and other instruments for measuring the declination of the stars were further perfected, while the spread of compasses allowed far better maps to be drawn (see Plate 141). Late medieval European ships were prepared to venture forth into high seas and were not necessarily forced to drop anchor with the onset of the cold season. Late fifteenth-century Venice's arsenal, a true naval factory where warships and trading vessels alike were built and repaired, became Europe's first 'modern' industrial enterprise. By the turn of the sixteenth century, Europe enjoyed the technical means to discover, and conquer, the world.

Progress in farming involved greater use of iron for tools, along with a host of new implements and methods, including adoption of the wheeled plough with mould-board, the harrow, the shoulder-harness for horses, which avoided pressing on the windpipe, and crop rotation over a three-year period, allowing for a considerable extension of land under cultivation. The trend towards more rational and informed farming was reflected, in the thirteenth and fourteenth centuries, in the appearance of agricultural treatises, – and in the increasing use of natural fertilizers (see Plates 5, 6).

The major innovation in crafts and industrial techniques, besides the windmill and its derived uses, was the vertical pedal loom or spinning wheel, known by the end of the thirteenth century. In building yards, various apparatuses for leverage were perfected, and the wheelbarrow made its appearance. As in many other societies, military demand spurred technical progress. The age of heavy wooden siege machines yielded to artillery, which by the fifteenth century stimulated metallurgy, especially in Lombardy and several German regions (see Plate 44).

An outstanding breakthrough was the camshaft, which allowed a continuous movement to be converted into an alternating one, and thereby harnessed water pressure to power hammers, mallets and pounders. In the fourteenth and fifteenth centuries, two technological innovations linked to the world of aesthetics and knowledge found promising practical application: window glass, a derivative of the art of stained glass; and paper, whose production soared in response to the rising demand for books.

At issue here was the hesitant and highly sensitive borderline, in European civilization, between the perceived role of the craftsman or manual labourer, whose status was despised or at any rate regarded as inferior; and the perceived role of the artist, as an eminent individual in a position to break out of the mould of anonymity and social mediocrity. The twelfth century came up with the concept of 'mechanical arts', alongside the so-called 'liberal arts', to account for such techniques and crafts as those involved in farming, building, metalwork, the forging of arms and armour, and so on. Gothic carving gave material form to Western Europe's ongoing debate between the active and the contemplative life.

Technical progress in commerce bore an obvious cultural component. Book-keeping, including double-entry book keeping, along with the writing of handbooks for traders and the spreading use of letters of credit, were a consequence of the new level of learning available to the merchant – and goaded his demand for more. The common skills involved in reading, writing and arithmetic brought the two worlds of commerce and culture increasingly closer. The late medieval merchant was generally a cultured individual who appreciated, and often sponsored, works of art. Indeed he might be an actual author himself. Florence in particular, in the fourteenth and fifteenth centuries, spawned a flowering of such merchant-writers (see Plate 103).

EDUCATION AND LEARNING (SEE MAP 7)

Christianity overtly rejected the philosophy of the ancient pagan world but nevertheless took over the encyclopaedic ordering of knowledge and other intellectual tools derived from Greek Aristotelianism, as well as, and above all, the educational curriculum which the Romans themselves had inherited from Greece. The Church Fathers preserved Latin as their cultural language and made room for the systematic grading known as the Seven Liberal Arts (made up of the *trivium*, which comprised grammar, rhetoric and dialectic, and the *quadrivium*, comprising arithmetic, geometry, astronomy and music).

The Carolingian renaissance purified current Latin usage and reintroduced a culture based on book learning along with the study of a good number of classical authors.

The structure of medieval Christianity's system of thought, based on classical foundations, was erected by such sixth century Italian thinkers as Cassiodorus, from the monastery he directed, and especially Boethius (480–525), who was both an official to the heretical Arian king Theodoric and a major philosopher and logician in his own right. Boethius' *Consolation of Philosophy*, tinged as it was with a strong neo-Platonic strain, became in turn one of the classics of later medieval thought which itself always remained steeped in neo-Platonic tradition. Hardly less significant was the

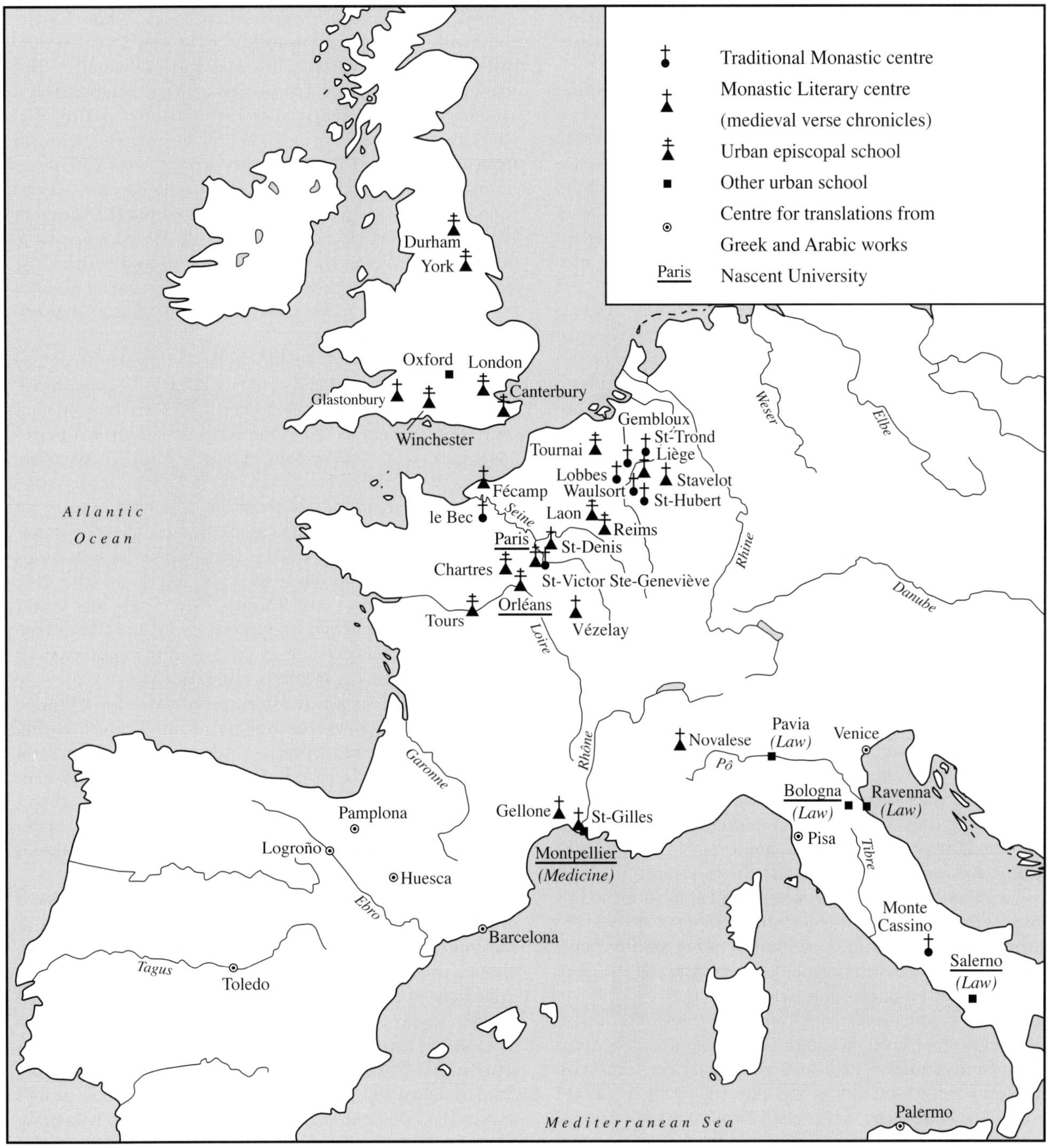

Map 7 Intellectual centres in Western Europe during the twelfth century (Le Goff, J., 1964, *Civilisation de l'occident medieval*, Flammarion-Arthaud).

succeeding contribution of Christian thinkers from the British Isles in the years immediately before and during the Carolingian age. Such men included the Venerable Bede (673–735), both a naturalist and a great historian of the early English Church; Alcuin (*c.* 735–804), a trained rhetorician who inspired Charlemagne's educational reforms on the continent; and the ninth century's own John Scotus *Erigena* (that is, 'The Irishman'), one of the profoundest philosophers of the entire Middle Ages. In Italy again, the Lombard chronicler, Paul the Deacon (720–*c.* 800), a monk at Monte Cassino, added his own, Germanic component to the growing fabric of medieval Christian learning.

Late classical antiquity's encyclopedic tradition in summarizing learning was especially pursued in a Christianizing strain by the Spanish bishop Isidore of Seville (*c.* 570–636), in his *Book of Origins or Etymologies*, and later by the German Benedictine monk Rhabanus Maurus (*c.* 780–856), abbot of Fulda and then archbishop of Mainz (see Plate 163).

Western Christendom received Greek and Arab influences through Spain and southern Italy (see Plates 72, 73). Palermo under its twelfth-century Norman kings and thirteenth-century Emperor Frederick II became a melting-pot for Greek, Arabic and Latin cultures, which in turn stimulated the teaching of medicine in Salerno and Montpellier. A Spanish journey inspired the encyclopedic learning of Gerbert d'Aurillac, who presided as Pope Sylvester II over the turn of the eleventh century, the fateful year 1000. Scientific and intellectual exchange owed a great deal to the essential role of translators. At least until the thirteenth century, intellectual life further benefited from frequent contacts between Christians and Jews, who enjoyed their own flourishing centres of learning in such cities as Toledo, Narbonne and Troyes (see Plates 76–79).

The Italian-born abbot of Le Bec in Normandy, and later archbishop of Canterbury (1093–1109), Anselmo of Aosta, was the true founder of scholasticism: that is, the venture to demonstrate the truth of faith in the light of reason according to Anselmo's own famous definition: *Fides quaerens Intellectum*, 'Faith in quest of Intellect'. This approach furnished a crucial guideline for European thought. The mental ferment of the tremendous twelfth century shifted intellectual life from monastic to urban schools. For this was the century of theology (a term coined by Abélard, who turned this intellectual discipline into something like a science), where it shone in such centres as Laon and then Chartres: whose teaching held Nature to lie at the very heart of Christian philosophy. The Cathedral Chapter of Notre Dame in Paris sheltered its own famous school, known as 'Saint Victor'. The same century saw a major resumption in the study of law. The University of Bologna sponsored both a revival of ancient Roman jurisprudence and the true birth of canon law (with the *Decretals* of the monk Gratian in about 1140). Finally, the twelfth century brought about a specifically Christian form of humanism, whereby the Socratic tradition was Christianized in accordance with the Biblical assertion that 'God created man in his own image'.

Twelfth-century urban intellectuals became professionals. The guilds which brought together masters and students gave birth to universities. These sought papal support to secure autonomy from local or national powers, whether priestly or lay. They also delivered bachelor's and doctor's degrees after examination. This was Europe's first case of social advancement based not on birth but tested merit. The nascent universities organized into faculties of arts, medicine, Roman law and canon law, and theology; drafted programmes; and taught according to the method of scholasticism, whereby authority and reason were combined through resort to both spoken lectures and book learning. The scope of the universities was international. Masters and students wandered from one university to another, wrote and communicated in Latin, and in the major institutions earned doctoral degrees recognized as valid in all Western Christendom. Students at each institution grouped into nations, so called on account of their common geographical origin rather than in terms of 'nationality' in the modern sense. Poorer students enjoyed access to the universities through grants which ensured both their lodging and course of study in colleges. (One such college, founded in the mid-thirteenth century, by the churchman Robert de Sorbon in Paris, became famous and later gave rise to the Sorbonne.) Twelfth-century masters earned their stipends from students' fees. Those of the thirteenth century were usually clerics who received only minor orders but still lived on ecclesiastical benefices. But the thirteenth-century University of Paris also witnessed violent clashes between 'secular' clerical masters and 'regular' clerical masters: that is, in the latter case, masters who stemmed from one of the two mendicant monastic orders, Dominicans or Franciscans. The new ideas taught by the 'regular' masters found great favour with students but incurred the hatred of their fellow 'secular' scholars, not only on acount of the competition offered by the 'regulars' but also because the 'regulars' owed first loyalty to their orders rather than to corporate solidarity (for instance, in the case of masters' strikes).

The most famous university scholars in thirteenth-century Paris were, on the one hand, two Franciscans, the Englishman Alexander of Hales and the Italian Saint Bonaventure; and on the other hand, two Dominicans, the German Albertus Magnus and the Italian Saint Thomas Aquinas (see Plate 127).

The only extant universities of the thirteenth century are found in Italy (with Bologna as the first and greatest centre for the study of law), France (Paris was Christendom's theological centre, but there were also important schools in Orléans, Toulouse and Montpellier, with the latter specializing in medicine), England (Oxford and Cambridge offered the best instruction in the arts of the *quadrivium* or scientific disciplines), and Spain (at Salamanca).

But the founding of universities spread to the rest of Europe in the fourteenth and fifteenth centuries, including Germany (Heidelberg, 1386), Bohemia (Prague, 1348), Poland (Cracow, 1364), Scotland (St Andrews, 1413), Brabant (Louvain, 1425), Portugal (Lisbon and Coimbra, 1290), Austria (Vienna, 1365), Basel (1459), Sweden (Uppsala, 1477), Denmark (Copenhagen, 1478), and other spots in Christendom.

Previous university teaching of the arts was rendered obsolete by the new theological humanism of the thirteenth century, which found expression in the great synthetic works, known as *summae*, which have been aptly compared to cathedrals of thought. But such teaching in turn suffered decline under competition from philosophy, while the faculties of theology became increasingly involved in repression (by 1270 and 1277, the bishop of Paris was already condemning a whole list of opinions taught by his own city's university). Medicine and law developed only by becoming increasingly secular disciplines, although they thereby played a highly important social role in training new elites (see Plates 133 a, b, c, d, e).

Still, the balance struck, by the twelfth century, between faith and reason was medieval thought's finest legacy to what became Europe's traditional attempt to find a means of harmonizing the dictates of reason with those of the heart.

ART AND LITERATURE

Medieval Europe had no specific words to designate art and literature as such. These were hardly recognized by medieval men and women as precisely defined fields of activity in themselves. 'Art' (Latin *ars, artis*) continued to be perceived as something pertaining and close to craftsmanship. Still, 'art' very much involved carved or painted images, and these pointed to a hidden realm of which these images purported to be mere reflections. 'Art' was hence the mirror wherein medieval humanity looked upon itself, and through which it sought to look upon the world. In contrast to Judaism and Islam, Christianity allowed the figurative depiction of human beings – and even of God in human form. Such an attitude rendered the arts an essential element of Christian humanism (see Plates 59–62).

Stone castles rose towards the end of the tenth century, and their architectural development through the eleventh to fifteenth centuries betrayed the steady replacement of their military function by a purely residential one, whereby the feudal lord gradually turned into the Renaissance noble or prince.

Two successive forms of art spread throughout all Latin Christendom: the Romanesque in the eleventh and first half of the twelfth century, and the Gothic from the second half of the twelfth century onwards (see Plates 74–75).

Romanesque creativity was as sharply marked in sculpture as in architecture and should hardly be judged by the austere condition in which so many Romanesque churches find themselves today, stripped of their erstwhile ornamentation down to bare structural essentials. Romanesque churches were once highly coloured and adorned, with painted sculptures and walls draped with embroidered hangings and tapestries.

But, towards the middle of the twelfth century, there began to spread, from its cradle in Île-de-France, a new form of art which later detractors (beginning with Lorenzo Valla in the fifteenth century and followed by the classically minded critics of the seventeenth and eighteenth centuries) came to brand as 'Gothic', that is to say, 'barbaric': a derogatory term which the nineteenth-century Romantics, however, converted into one of praise. This style bore the stamp of a new architectural feature: the pointed arch, which afforded greater height for buildings and more variety in vaulting. Another mark of this art was its relentless search for ever more light: whence soaring stained-glass windows, as at Chartres. Finally, the structures of this style aimed to obey a rational order, similar to that of scholastic thought itself.

Only the very greatest cathedrals of Gothic Europe may be listed here: in France, the Abbey Church of Saint-Denis begun by Abbot Suger as early as 1144, followed by the structures at Sens, 1164, Laon, mid-twelfth century, Notre-Dame of Paris between 1163 and 1200, Chartres between 1194 and 1220, Reims, Amiens and Bourges in the course of the thirteenth century, and Albi from 1282; in England, Canterbury from 1174, Lincoln between 1192 and 1235, Salisbury between 1220 and 1258, and Wells from 1185-1190; in the German lands, Cologne's unfinished cathedral was begun in 1248 and that of Strasbourg in the second half of the thirteenth century; in Flemish Hainaut, Tournai (1243–1255); Spain's mid-thirteenth-century cathedrals in Toledo, Burgos and Léon show strong French influence; in Italy, construction of Florence's Santa Maria dei Fiori began in 1296.

Gothic also flourished in secular buildings intended for collective or private use, such as the communal palaces or town halls in German and especially Italian cities (Siena, Florence, Venice and the like), the covered markets (at Ypres and Cracow), the isolated castles or urban mansions of nobles and princes, and the stone dwellings of richer burghers.

How ever much it shone in larger architectural feats, Gothic displayed no less brilliance in sculpture and painting (as in frescoes and miniatures). Italy's contribution here was outstanding. In the second half of the thirteenth century, Nicola Pisano and his son Giovanni carved the great cathedral pulpits of Siena, Pistoia and Pisa, where they stated a truly classical monumental style in sculpture. In painting, the sixteenth-century Renaissance came to regard an all-round master like Giotto (*c.* 1266-1337) as a forerunner, that is, as the first true artist in the modern sense.

Moreover, gothic form triumphed in the so-called minor arts of metalwork and carved ivories and alabaster, while domestic arts bore witness to heightened refinement in dwellings: as in furniture, tapestries, glass vessels, ceramics and embroidered stuffs – thus creating Europe's nascent visual setting.

Gothic finally asserted the worth of the individual and of private life. Realistic portraiture appeared in the early fourteenth century, and decisive technical improvement was yielded by the development of oils (attributed to the Van Eyck brothers in the early fifteenth century) and easel painting. Art here entered domestic space, and made it its own (see Plates 173, 174).

Another major development made itself felt in both the visual arts and literature. This was a return to a taste for narrative, or 'stories'. Major new pictorial cycles depicted the lives of Jesus or the saints, and sought to express the very sequence of time.

Even by the mid-twelfth century, Gothic art betrayed a tendency to exaggerate its own forms: whence its evolution into the Perpendicular, and, finally, Flamboyant styles, Gothic's own form of the Baroque. A bold but still harmonious masterpiece heralds this turning point in Gothic: the *Sainte Chapelle* or Holy Chapel in Paris, built for the sainted King Louis IX within his own palace to shelter therein the relics of Christ's Passion.

As mainly known to us through the various visual or literary arts, the five senses of men and women were addressed with increasing subtlety and refinement as the medieval period unfolded. Sight, for example, was enticed by the new art of perspective in painting, whose development began in the thirteenth century. The sense of smell was tickled not only by holy incense but increasingly by 'all the perfumes of Arabia'. Taste was flattered by new concoctions in the kitchen. Touch revelled in sweeter contacts as poets began evoking caresses upon a woman's body *qui tant est souef*, 'which is so soft', as François Villon's verse would put it in the fifteenth century (see Plate 118). And finally, fresh nuances in hearing increasingly solicited the attention of medieval men and women. Music was regarded as one of the sciences of the *quadrivium* and loomed, with architecture, as one of the great European arts. Instrumentation broke new auditory ground with the successive appearance of the organ, the lute, of the viol, the harp, the trumpet and the virginal, all accompanied, above all, by fresh demands on the human voice. For a long time, singing had been strongly influenced by ancient Greek traditions, but a new form of chant arose in a purely Roman environment: this was the Gregorian plainsong, whose European spread and popularity were much encouraged by Charlemagne. Polyphony appeared in the twelfth and thirteenth centuries, notably with the great school of Notre Dame in Paris. No more than any of the other arts could music fail to echo the general upsurge in sensitivity in the fourteenth century, but the resulting *ars nova* was a truly modern art. Currents of folk music continued to run beneath manifestations of learned music, but these are difficult for us to detect (see Plate 179).

In the field of *belles lettres*, Latin yielded ground in the twelfth century to the various vernaculars. The first dominant genre here was war poetry, the epic, which generally centred on the figure of a hero with his lineage, and became elaborated into cycles. The oldest preserved vernacular epic actually known to us (in a very early eleventh-century written form) is the probably eighth-century Anglo-Saxon poem *Beowulf*, although the German *Niebelungenlied*, while only consigned to script in about 1200, draws on legendary lore – dwelling on themes of vengeance – going back to the sixth century AD. The late eleventh-century *Song of Roland* heralded in writing the great French-language epic cycle embroidered around the idealized figure of Charlemagne, bestowing fine literary form on the heroic image cherished by a warlike feudal nobility. Such imagery found corresponding expression in Spain's *Song of El Cid* (1140) and also in the singular flourishing of Old Norse epics which occurred in Iceland: the poems of the *Edda* cycle composed between the seventh and thirteenth centuries, and then the sagas of the twelfth and thirteenth centuries, stand out as being among the most original productions of Western medieval literature. Such heroes as Roland, Charlemagne, Siegfried (or Sigurd) and El Cid thereby became permanently etched upon Europe's imagination.

The twelfth century also brought to light the romance, still one of the West's major literary genres. This emphasized narrative with a strong storyline: generally, here, the tale of an individual or couple under the spell of love – that is, courtly or modern love, associated with death. Underlying Celtic myth nourished such romances, which, while composed in verse in the twelfth century (as in the works of Chrétien de Troyes), were turned into prose in the thirteenth. Steeped in knightly atmosphere, courtly romance featured love and adventure which most often ended in death.

New, prodigious figures hereby enriched Europe's imaginary landscape: King Arthur and his knights of the Round Table, Merlin the magician, and that haunting and mysterious goal of knightly quest, the Holy Grail. The thirteenth-century Church managed to impart spiritual and Christian meaning to this mythological world which welled up from an ancient barbarian past. But courtly romance imposed on Europe its own vision of that tragic couple of myth, Tristan and Isolde, incarnations of an irresistible and magical force of love, one impossible to satisfy, and which just as irrevocably lured them to their deaths (see Plate 178).

The rise of lyric poetry underscored and provided counterpoint to such epics and courtly romances, as sung by the *troubadours* of southern France (in the Provençal language), the *trouvères* of northern France (in Old French), and Germany's own *Minnesänger* (as in the love lyrics of the early thirteenth-century Walther von der Vogelweide) (see Plate 177). Late thirteenth-century Italy's *dolce stil nuovo* ushered in a more spiritualized and precious vein.

The monastic ideal of the early Middle Ages had frowned on the expression of mirth, which now forced its way to the surface in such short, merry tales as the *fabliaux*. The theatre, whose first ties were to liturgy, emerged from within the Church into the public square to satisfy the tastes of a new audience of rich burghers. By the close of the Middle Ages, plays had developed two distinct genres, farce (the jester or buffoon became an important character both at court and in literary works), and 'moralities' or 'passions', still performed before church portals, and which notably dramatized the Passion of Christ.

In the thirteenth century, use of the French language spread throughout Europe almost like a second Latin. Two French works here enjoyed amazing success: the realistic and satirical animal fables of *Reynard the Fox* (written between 1180 and 1250), and the two-part poetic, allegorical and naturalistic *Romance of the Rose*.

Italy, however, produced the literary genius in which the poetry of the Middle Ages found its crowning expression, Florence's Dante (1265–1321), author of *The Divine Comedy* (see Plate 180).

While the humanistic literary current began to break with medieval tradition after Petrarch (1302–1374), who was the first to stigmatize the 'Middle Ages' as such, the short story or *novella* was best featured in those two fourteenth-century masterpieces, Boccaccio's Italian *Decameron* (*c.* 1350) (see Plate 103), followed several decades later by Chaucer's English *Canterbury Tales*.

IDEAS, SENSITIVITY AND OUTLOOK

Medieval civilization felt the need to think, and to act, in accordance with a system of Christian values based on obedience to the teachings of God and his Church, and thereby to compensate for its own quite correctly perceived material and intellectual weakness in the face of threatening and still very poorly harnessed forces of nature. Society was regarded as lying under the arbitrary will of a god of wrath – however good in his essence – whose anger might be at any time unleashed through the agency of an ever-present deceiver and tempter: the Devil (see Plate 131). Hence medieval resort to the help of authorities, both Christian and also ancient pagan, in the field of learning. The greater part of medieval cultural activity therefore consisted of quotations, borrowings, glosses, commentaries and, basically, compilations. What cultural innovation was allowed lay mainly in one's choice of authorities – one might, for instance, introduce and quote new authorities – and in one's fresh ways of ordering and interpreting the same set of texts and ideas. Europeans grew used to regarding themselves as inheritors or pupils, although by the twelfth century they had begun to show increasing awareness of themselves as *moderni*, 'modern' folk, as opposed to the 'ancients' – not that the Middle Ages had any conception whatsoever of what we would regard as 'progress'. Medieval Christendom saw the perfecting of humanity as a process that followed a literally ascending path (for Christianity is a heaven-oriented creed), but also one that widened humanity's horizons (through conquests on Earth and mastery over the sea), and one that stressed increased internalization of one's personal, social, professional and spiritual life.

The individual and collective vulnerability of medieval men and women lent particular force to the passions that rent their emotional life. Although medieval society was strongly masculine in tone and professed to regard Eve's daughters as dangerous beings ever since the fall of their mythic mother, still women held sway over household, family and emotional matters, and definitely influenced public life and even government – the tremendous development of the cult of the Virgin Mary from at least the twelfth century onwards was an eloquent sign of women's rising status. Children were of course the targets of all their parents' care, love and teaching, but childhood in itself was hardly regarded as charged with any special value, and rather considered an inherently unstable and dangerously vulnerable age to be outgrown as soon as possible. A pall, however, lay over minds. Thoughts took the steering or dominating form of outright obsessions, not to mention sheer fear. There was fear of natural disaster, fear of the Devil and damnation, and fear of an apocalyptic end to the world.

A chief obsession concerned sin. The Church taught that sin lay at the root of the whole human condition. Carnal sin was accorded prime importance, in the light of the Church Fathers' gloss of original sin as having been mainly a sexual one. Sin took root in vice, and to overpower sin constituted the main issue at stake in the spiritual struggle waged to secure eternal heavenly bliss. The Church drew up a scale of the 'Seven deadly sins', pride, covetousness, wrath, envy, lust, gluttony, sloth – down which an unrepentant sinner slid to damnation. The only corrective to this obsession with Hell was provided by a doctrine which finally emerged in the later twelfth century whereby a third otherworldly location was conveniently invented: Purgatory, where the departed might be purged of their non-deadly sins in order to gain admittance to Paradise.

A further obsession of the age was a haunting fear of the unseen and the supernatural. Medieval men and women were convinced that all visible things remained permeated by other, invisible realities, with no definite borderline and certainly no yawning gap between them. For the supernatural might make itself apparent on Earth at any moment. Hence belief in the importance of dreams (a belief long disapproved of by the Church as a pagan attitude), widespread concern with visions and general credulity regarding miracles, for these were precisely perceived as so many supernatural manifestations of divine power. After the start of the twelfth century, however, closer attention to nature caused a broadening interest in nature's own marvels – which might be wonderful, rare or surprising, but still remained conceived as part of the natural order. Europeans resumed efforts to distinguish the holy from the secular and the supernatural from the natural, while attempting to define the benevolent field of the properly miraculous and wonder-filled as strictly opposed – in so far as possible – to the magic and malevolent realm of Satan and his demons, witches and warlocks: to be excluded (see Plate 131).

Still another obsession concerned memory. As a civilization still dominated by the spoken word, medieval society could hardly afford to do without cultivating highly efficient powers of memorization. Social life and legal precedent long remained predicated upon custom, that is, upon tradition as transmitted by memory – especially the memory of the aged. Clerics elaborated complex mnemonic techniques, known, indeed, as 'the arts of memory'. But such primacy granted to memorization tended to hinder the rise of history proper, that is, a rational and critical organization of memory in order to account for events perceived as occurring along a linear flow of time – from Creation, through the Incarnation, down to the 'Last Days' and Day of Judgement – perhaps after a millennium or longed-for 'Thousand-Year Rule' of the elect on Earth. The primacy of memory rather privileged a more circular view of time, one that dwelt on the ceaseless return of a yearly liturgy that commemorated the earthly life of Christ.

Belief in a supernatural order, regarded as an actual world of truth hovering closely over this lower Earth – itself considered a mere imperfect and flawed reflection of this higher reality of things – created an obsession with symbolism. Symbolic systems included numerals, thought to express the hidden mathematical order of the world, as well as hosts of images and the full range of colours, all in turn held to be fraught with meaning.

The social and political obsessions of the age rested on the notions of hierarchy and order, but ambiguously enough, an attendant obsession with liberty never lay far off. For liberty bore two faces. Freedom, to be sure, belonged only to the privileged: to churchmen as opposed to laymen, and to noblemen as distinct from serfs and bondsmen. But such a concept of freedom in itself already implied notions of independence and nurtured the thought that obedience might be denied to illegitimate or tyrannical authority. This was the early seed of a far distant democratic age.

The major turning-point in the history of Western Christendom's ideas, values and outlooks occurred in the twelfth and thirteenth centuries. A new conception of sin now laid stress on a sinner's intentions rather than on his actual deeds, whence the practice of confession had to be reviewed. The fourth Lateran Council (1215) bound all the faithful to confess at least once a year, individually and to the ear of a priest. Confessors and penitents together thus plumbed the depths of conscience, and this, many centuries later, ultimately led to introspection and psychoanalysis. Judicial practice, hitherto centred on accusation, now shifted to a new stress on confession, which might have been an improvement had not such procedure become twisted by a thirteenth-century Church bent above all on suppressing heresy – whence creation of the Holy Office of the Inquisition intent on extorting confession through torture.

All the while, scorn for this lower world slowly yielded to a more positive appreciation of the earthly surface: an attitude which finally brought the values of Heaven back down to Earth. Not that religious zeal abated in any way. The new attitude lay in this: values once regarded as attainable only in Heaven, beyond the threshold of death, were now perceived as extant and apparent on this very Earth. A human being might now gain salvation, not in opposition to this world, but through it. Labour thus became a form of participation in God's creation and a positive means towards redemption. Time, once thought to belong only to God, now too could serve the purposes of salvation; and those who dealt in time, like the merchants, found new legitimacy. For their part, scholars who dispensed science – another of God's hitherto virtually inviolable treasures – now made available an entirely permissible knowledge, the better to master both conditions on Earth and ways of access to Heaven. Holy symbolism no longer cloaked numerals as taboo but allowed them to play their useful role in the here and the now for operations of arithmetic. The earthly city in turn ceased to be spurned as merely a perverse reflection of the City of God but came to be considered as a polity, whose power was justified if ordered in the interest of the commonweal. Even the human body found rehabilitation. Entertainment, games and leisure were allowed if they contributed to the recovery of bodily strength after labour – and pleasure itself might be justified within certain forms and limits. Scholasticism applied itself to defining licit conditions for various human activities, and a sense of nuance and measure prevailed where previously matters had stood – in the Manichaean manner – only in stark terms of absolute good or evil. Possible exceptions to various prohibitions now became legion. Europe began treading here the increasingly tolerant path of casuistry. Meanwhile, the individual began to emerge from the community: through the practice of confession, the painting of his or her portrait, and a spell for his or her soul in Purgatory.

The crisis of the fourteenth century ushered in the 'Waning of the Middle Ages', to borrow J. Huizinga's expression: 'The sharp savour of life offered contrasts so violent as to dispense a mingled scent of blood and roses.' Flamboyant piety now exhausted itself in overwrought emotions and sheer fancies, contemplation of death sank into a taste for the macabre which dwelt on corpses, skulls and skeletons, while the great theme in painting and poetry became the dance of death.

The ideal of chivalry itself took on flamboyant forms in dress, adornment and even the unrealistic policies pursued by knightly princes. An age of sumptuous entertainments became suffused with the recurrent fashionable motif of melancholy. Spirited tales of knighthood reached romantic heights in this autumnal phase of the dying Middle Ages. Such were the English *Morte d'Arthur* by Sir Thomas Malory (published in 1485), Spain's *libros de caballería* like the *Amadís of Gaul* by García Rodriguez de Montalvo (published in 1508), and the great Italian *romanzi*, including Luigi Pulci's *Morgante the Giant* (1460–1480) and Ariosto's masterpiece *Orlando Furioso* (which first appeared in 1520, with a definitive edition in 1532).

But several brilliant trends of medieval civilization survived and still pursued their course through the sixteenth century; indeed our conventional term 'Renaissance' conceals the fact that there was a continuous succession of 'rebirths' throughout the Middle Ages. The Carolingian renaissance of the eighth and ninth centuries was such a 'rebirth', followed by another in the tenth which has only recently been recognized, and then by a third major 'rebirth' in the twelfth. The so-called 'great' Renaissance had its origins in thirteenth-century Italy and already becomes very apparent by the thirteenth century in the writings of Petrarch, who explicitly turned his back on a 'middle age'. Italy, which lay culturally somewhat apart from the European medieval mainstream, spearheaded the fifteenth century's 'rebirth' in the environment provided by Florence's civic-minded humanism, with the many-sided genius of the Hellenizing philosophers Pico della Mirandola (1463–1494) and Marsilio Ficino (1433–1499) and such combined architects, painters and sculptors as Brunelleschi (1377–1446), who crowned the city's cathedral with a dome (see Plate 180), Leon Battista Alberti (1404–1472), Leonardo da Vinci (1452–1519) and Michelangelo (1475–1564). The new humanism spread north to France, where Jacques Lefèvre d'Etaples (*c.* 1450–1537) translated the Bible and Aristotle. But things medieval persisted well into the heart of the sixteenth century. The Reformation, in a sense, was the first heresy to succeed. 'Courtesy' became the code of the 'courtier', as in Baldassare Castiglione's *Il Cortegiano* (1528), while 'prowess' changed into 'honour' and 'virtue'. Even the new printing presses, before turning to spread the message of humanism, served to publish traditional religious writings.

The modern age's lengthy period of incubation came about in the midst of plague and battle, poised as it were between melancholy and folly. Sebastian Brandt published his *Ship of Fools* in Basel in 1494, while Erasmus of Rotterdam dedicated his *In Praise of Folly*, in the opening years of the sixteenth century, to England's Sir Thomas More, future author of *Utopia*.

BIBLIOGRAPHY

BLOCH, M. 1939–40. *La Société féodale*, 2 vols. Paris.

BORST, A. 1973. *Lebensformen ins Mittelalter.* Frankfurt am Main, Propyläen.

CAPITANI, O. 1979. *Medioevo passato prossimo.* Bologna, Il Mulino.

CURTIUS, E. R. 1948. *Europaischer Literatur und lateinisches Mittelalter.* Berne, Francke.

DE LORT, R. 1982. *La vie au Moyen Âge.* Paris.

DEMIANS D'AMBAUD, G. 1968. *Histoire artistique de l'occident médiéval.* Paris.

DUBY, G. 1976. *Les trois ordres ou l'imaginaire du féodalisme.* Paris.

——. 1978. *Le temps des cathédrales. L'art et la société.* Paris.

FLASCH, K. 1986. *Das philosophische Denken im Mittelalter. Von Augustin zu Machiavelli.* Stuttgart.

FOCILLON, M. 1965. *Art d'occident.* Paris.

FUHRMANN, H. 1987, 1989. *Einladung ins Mittelalter*, Munich. Beck.

GENICOT, L. 1961. *Les lignes de faîte du Moyen Âge.* Tournai.

GUREVICH, A. 1985. *Categories of Medieval Culture* (translated from Russian 1972).

——. 1988. *Medieval Popular Culture: Problems of Belief and Perception.* Cambridge.

——. 1992. *Historical Anthropology of the Middle Ages.* Polity Press, Cambridge.

HEER, F. 1961. *Mittelalter*, George Weidenfeld & Nicolson.

HUIZINGA, J. 1919. *Herfsttijd der Middeleeuwen.*

KANTOROWICZ, E. H. 1957. *The King's Two Bodies. A Study in Medieval Political Theology.* Princeton.

KÖHLER, E. 1956. *Ideal und Wirklichkeit in der höfischen Epik.* Tübingen.

LADNER, G. B. 1965. *Ad imaginem Dei. The Image of Man in Medieval Art.*

——. 1983. Images and Ideas in the Middle Ages.

LE GOFF, J. 1964, 1984. *La civilisation de l'occident mediéval*, Paris.

——. 1968. *Hérésies et sociétés dans l'Europe préindustrielle.* Paris, The Hague.

——. 1985. *L'imaginaire mediéval.* Paris.

——. (ed.) 1990. *L'uomo medievale.* Rome and Bari, Laterza.

LOPEZ, R. 1962. *Naissance de l'Europe* (IV–XIVe siècles). Paris

MITRE, E. 1976. *Introducción a la Historia de la Edad Media Europea.*

MOORE, R. I. 1967. *The Formation of a Persecuting Society. Power and Deviance in Western Europe*, 950–1250. Oxford.

MORRALL, J. B. 1967. *The Medieval Imprint.* London.

MURRAY, A. 1978. *Reason and Society in the Middle Ages*, Oxford.

SOUTHERN, R. W. 1953. *The Making of the Middle Ages.* London.

STANESCO, M.; ZINK, M. 1992. *Histoire européenne du roman médiéval.* Paris.

TABACCO, G.; MERLO, G. G. 1981. *La civiltà europea nella storia mondiale. Medioevo V–XV sec.*

VOLPE, G. 1965. *Il Medio Evo.* Florence.

VON DEN STEINEN, W. 1965. *Homo caelestis. Das Wort der Kunst im Mittelalter*, 2 vols.

WHITE, L. JR. 1962. *Medieval Technology and Social Change.* Oxford.

ZUMTHOR, P. 1972. *Essai de poétique médiévale.* Paris.

——. 1980. *Parler au Moyen Âge.* Paris.

12

EAST AND SOUTH-EAST EUROPE

12.1

ETHNIC AND POLITICAL CHANGES IN THE BALKAN PENINSULA

Vasilka Tăpkova-Zaimova

ETHNIC MOVEMENTS AFTER THE SIXTH CENTURY (SEE MAP 8)

Its geographical position made the Balkan peninsula one of the nerve centres in the formation of post-Roman Europe. From the fourth century onwards, the Eastern Empire had to deal with groups of 'barbarians' who were sporadically crossing the Danube frontier. But the problem of migrating tribes became much more complicated from the sixth century (especially the second half), when the Slav and Avar–Slav peoples stepped up their invasions, thus precipitating an ethnic and demographic crisis.

Taking over from the Germanic tribes that had preceded them, the Slavs, following the routes leading from

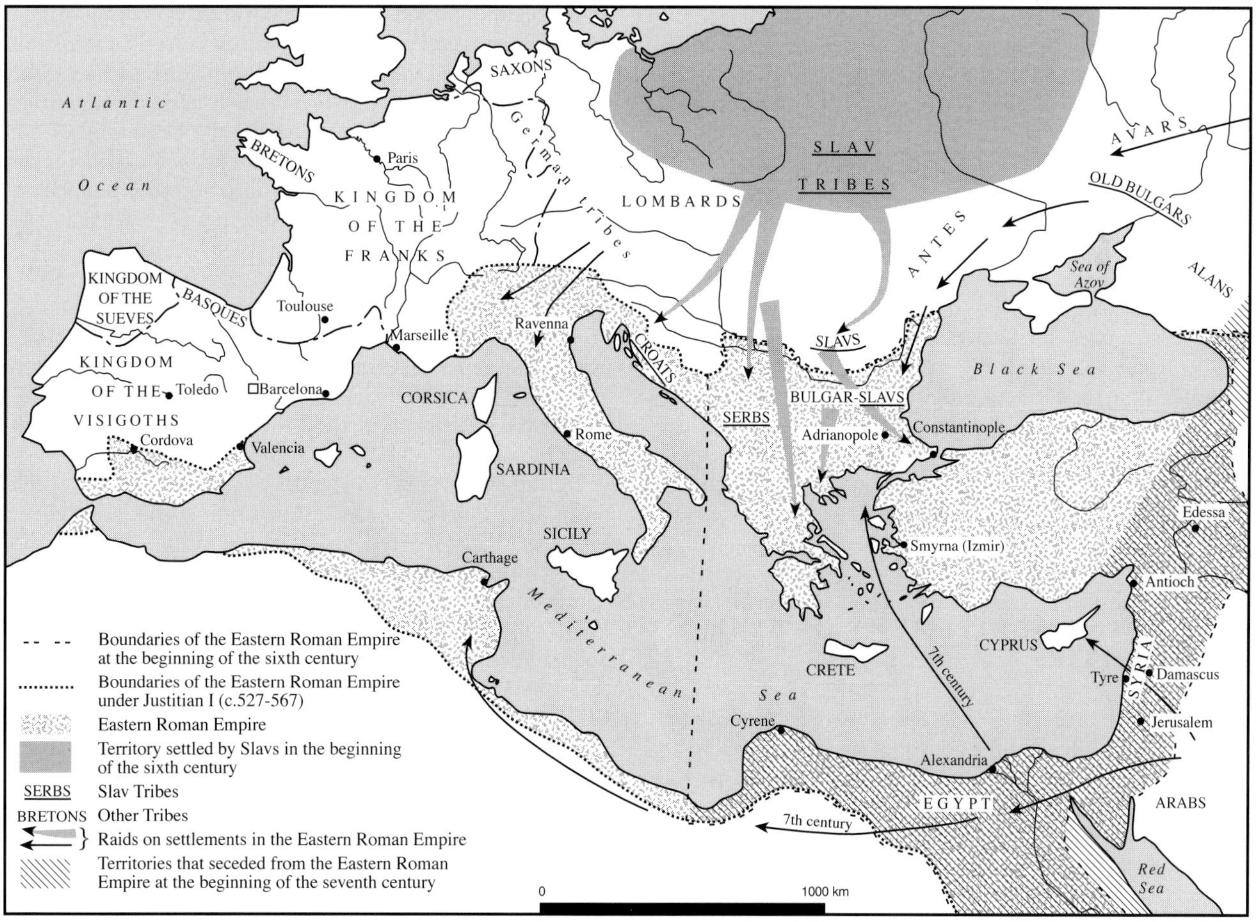

Map 8 Ethnic movements in Central and South-Eastern Europe in the sixth and seventh centuries.

sub-Carpathian Ukraine and Volhynia to the eastern slopes of the southern Carpathians, began their wanderings through Slovakia and Pannonia, on the one hand, and the Wallachian plain, on the other, and so entered the Danubian provinces (Ditten, 1978; Teodor, 1984). Until the beginning of the sixth century, there was a sort of Slav infiltration of the Danube frontier. This small-scale migration was not reflected in the works of contemporary authors but can be glimpsed from the evidence of archaeology and linguistics (Tăpkova-Zaimova, 1966).

The tribes and tribal confederations began to penetrate in large numbers from the reign of Justinian I (527–565), following the old land routes or waterways that were tributaries of the Danube. Some of them who had invaded Pannonia were included as 'Beivolk' in expeditions organized by the Avar khaganate, that is, as infantrymen who followed the shock cavalry of those former nomads already settled between the Danube and the Tisza (Avenarius, 1974; Pohl, 1988).

By the end of the sixth or the beginning of the seventh century, the Slavs of Dacia, who had been organizing their own campaigns, and the Avar–Slavs of Pannonia, had penetrated into the two Moesias (Danubian provinces), into Illyricum and neighbouring lands along the Adriatic (Kovačević, 1981). Furthermore, there is evidence of their presence already south of the Haemus range, in Macedonia, Thessaly and as far as the Peloponnese, if we are to believe the lessons of numismatics and toponymy (Zaimov, 1975; Nystazopoulou-Pelekidou, 1986). With their small hollow sailing vessels *(monoxylae)*, carved from a single tree trunk, they were then engaging in piracy in the islands of the Aegean Sea.

The first campaigns south of the Danube were largely the work of the Slavs of Dacia but partly of the Slavs of Pannonia (the so-called 'Bulgar' group). They were joined during the first half of the seventh century by other South Slavs, the Serbo-Croats, who were fewer in number. These headed towards the western parts of the peninsula. It seems, in addition, that there were two waves of Serbo-Croatian migrants: the second apparently occurred after 626, that is, after the failure of the great Avar–Slav campaign southwards and eastwards when Constantinople was besieged. But despite the absence of the Emperor Heraclius (610–641), the capital of the Byzantine Empire was saved and the withdrawal of the Avars to the eastern Alps opened the way to the Serbo-Croats.

The Serbs occupied the area between the Dinaric Mountains and the Neretva, which empties into the Adriatic, and further south, the Zahumlje, the Travunia and the Dioclea. Further north and west, the Croats settled partly in Dalmatia and partly on the Sava, a tributary of the Danube (Dalmatian Croatia and Pannonian Croatia) (Kovačević, 1981).

PERMANENT SETTLEMENT OF SLAV COMMUNITIES

In their wanderings, the Avar–Slavs usually followed the great military routes and the course of rivers,. but the Avars would usually return to their lands once the expedition was over; in their nomadic traditions, they were chiefly interested in looting and booty. But the Slavs gradually settled in the devastated and deserted areas and on lands left waste. A marked fall in the general level of provincial culture became apparent. This phenomenon of a break with the achievements of late antiquity was above all visible in the towns along the Danube, and this was so despite the efforts of the government in Constantinople to fortify the Danubian *limes*. But even inside the empire, urban life became somewhat fossilized in numerous, once flourishing urban centres, where trade suffered big damage. From the seventh century, too, a certain ruralization of towns became evident. In general, traces of cash circulation in the Danube provinces and even in Dalmatia end in the first half of the seventh century (Ferjančić, 1984; Jurukova, 1969).

But the notion that the Balkan provinces completely disintegrated is exaggerated. It is true that events and the fact that the central government was quite unable to enforce tax collection in some areas encouraged particularisms. The preferred location of the territorial units that contemporaries called 'Slavinias' or 'Sclavinias' was in interior regions which for varying periods remained largely autonomous of the provincial government (Litavrin, 1984). But some of them ended up being reduced to the rank of tributary people and subject to the provincial regime of the Byzantine Empire. This process really became marked from the reign of the emperors of the Isaurian dynasty and continued into the ninth century. Many of these tribal groups or confederations gradually blended into the Bulgar state and gave its Slavic ethnic character to the area of Danubian Bulgaria (Angelov, 1971).

THE BULGARS SOUTH OF THE DANUBE: DANUBIAN BULGARIA

Among the 'barbarians' who invaded the lands south of the Danube in the sixth and seventh centuries, contemporaries invariably mentioned the Bulgars, mostly of Turkic origin, who from the end of the fifth century were in the pay of the empire in its campaigns against the Goths of Italy. The Utrigurs and Kutrigurs, who were already permanently settled on the shores of the Sea of Azov by the beginning of the sixth century, made their presence felt in the Balkans on several occasions (Karayannopoulos, 1978), either as invaders or (as was the case with the Kutrigurs) as *foederati* in the service of Justinian I. Moreover, this system, which was inherited from the previous period, was also pursued in relations with the Slavs and others: the *foederati* (called 'friends' or 'allies' from the sixth century) were granted permission to settle with their own chiefs in depopulated frontier regions. There, with varying degrees of loyalty to the central government, they took on the obligations of border guards.

During the 630s in the steppes east and north-east of the Sea of Azov, there existed a state formation of Onogur–Bulgars led by the Khān Kovrat, an ally of Byzantium. His writ ran over vast lands to the north of the Dniepr, to the east of Azov over Kuban and to the west as far as the Tauric Chersonese (the Crimea). This 'Great Bulgaria' or 'Volga Bulgaria' did not last very long; after Kovrat's death it fell under the blows of a nomadic grouping of Turks from Western Asia, the Khazars. The Bulgars began to withdraw westwards and southwards: some infiltrated into the khaganate of the Avars by taking part in their campaigns. Another group of Bulgars followed Asparuch, presumably Kovrat's son, towards the Danube delta, where they settled while keeping control of the lands up to the Dniestr (Dimitrov, 1987).

It was from there that Asparuch's attacks on the lands to the south of the Danube and towards the Black Sea began. Having overcome the Byzantine army, the Bulgars secured recognition of their state on the Danube by a treaty with Constantinople (681), when their raids began to be directed at the fortifications on the Haemus range (Vojnov, 1956).

Danubian Bulgaria covered lands inhabited by a Slav population, the 'seven tribes' and the Severi, probably *foederati* of Byzantium. Although it cannot be regarded as a faithful copy of Volga Bulgaria, for the absence of steppes limited the great wanderings typical of the nomadic model, it nevertheless retained its traditional military structure. Moreover, the presence of a population of Slav cultivators ensured the material base of the military nucleus and the development of an economy that was partly agrarian.

Such was the demographic framework in which the continual wars with Byzantium in the eighth and the first part of the ninth century unfolded. The Bulgar khāns preserved their pagan traditions and their power, which they claimed was of divine origin, and invariably defended their claims to a state against Byzantium's imperial ideology. In a succession of armed confrontations, the Byzantine *basileus* (emperor) Nicephorus I lost his life after an expedition to the north of the Balkan range as far as the Bulgar capital (811). A victorious campaign by Bulgar forces in eastern Thrace as far as the Black Sea ensued; the Khān Krum only halted before the gates of Constantinople.

After a period of respite which followed the conversion of Bulgaria by Prince Boris (864 or 865), the confrontation resumed with renewed ferocity in the reign of Simeon (893–927). After several victorious campaigns in which he almost took the Byzantine capital, Simeon laid claim to the title of *basileus* (*tsar*) of the Bulgars and 'Romans', by which he even sought to remove the Byzantine emperor from the Balkan provinces. This title of *basileus* relating solely to the Bulgarian territories, was recognized by Constantinople for his son Peter after a dynastic marriage with a Byzantine princess (Tăpkova-Zaimova, 1979; Fine, 1983).

It was also during these centuries that the national consolidation of Bulgaria was achieved, along with the cultural synthesis between the more numerous Slavs, who imposed their language, and the Bulgars, who were to bequeath their name to this national identity that was born of two ethnic elements. These complex processes had a significant impact on the formation of other states among the Balkan Slavs, notably the Serbs and the Croats (see Plates 150–153).

SLAV STATES IN THE WESTERN PARTS OF THE PENINSULA

As a result of the wars between Byzantium and the Avars and the ethnic movements that followed in the western provinces of the peninsula, within Rascia a core of Slav communities fused together, and it was from this core that the Serb nation was to arise at the beginning of the ninth century (Čirković, 1964). A sort of system of internal vassalage came into being among a few princes, among whom Vladimir bore the title of 'archon' (*knez*) in the 820s. This indicates that the archaic structures characteristic of the western regions of the peninsula had already evolved and that this Serb entity really was a state. The state unity of Croatia was more difficult to achieve, chiefly because of the involvement of the political interests of Byzantium, which partly retained its rule over the Dalmatian coast, and those of the empire of Charlemagne and his successors in eastern Franconia. A sort of balance came into being between so-called Dalmatian Croatia and its Prince Borna, on the one hand, and Pannonian Croatia with its Prince Ljudevit. The conflict between them in the 820s already indicates serious attempts at political integration. Finally, as early as 852, Prince Trpimir had signed a charter as 'prince (*knez*) of the Croats' and at the beginning of the tenth century Tomislav was called *'rex Croatorum'* ('king of the Croats'). At this time, there was also a well-established ecclesiastical organization and an administrative apparatus serving the central power. But it was a situation that did not last: the presence of the Hungarians in Pannonia at the end of the ninth century and beginning of the tenth once again complicated the political situation to the detriment of the Slavs in the western part of the peninsula (Klaić 1971; Fine, 1983).

The name of Bosnia appears for the first time in the middle of the tenth century. This region, which cannot be considered as enjoying true political autonomy for a long time, was bordered by Croatia to the west and Serbia to the east. But by the end of this same century it was asserting its own political life, and its ruler took the title of *ban* (Čirković, 1964).

The formation of national states in the Balkans had the effect of sharpening the latent conflict between Byzantium and Bulgaria, which, in the time of Simeon, succeeded in integrating the Serbian territories within its borders, claiming to remove the empire from the system of political vassalage of the peninsula (Tăpkova-Zaimova, 1979). This was a continuing competition which was ended only at the beginning of the eleventh century by the wars of Basil II (976–1025). He defeated the Bulgarian *tsar* Samuel and his heirs and re-established over the peninsula the political authority of Byzantium, which now once again, bordered the Danube and the Adriatic Sea.

All these events brought the Romanians and the Albanians on to the historical scene. There were no written records in their respective languages at the time, and Byzantine sources are silent on the processes that lay behind the formation of these two Balkan nations. The Albanians, descendants of the Illyrians, went through a long period of Romanization followed by Slavification before asserting their national identity in the Middle Ages, when relations in the Balkans were complex. The earliest reference concerning them in Byzantine sources therefore dates back to the second half of the eleventh century.

The same holds for the Romanians, who do not appear under their ethnic name in any Byzantine or Bulgar source until the time of Tsar Samuel's wars in Macedonia. The earliest records concerning them relate to the Romanized population south of the Danube, who were called Walacks at the time (Berza and Buda, 1980; Murnu, 1984).

It was only after the eleventh century that political relations between the Byzantine Empire and the Balkan peoples still fighting for state autonomy took a somewhat different turn.

BIBLIOGRAPHY

ANGELOV, D. 1971. *Obrazuvane na bŭlgarskata narodnost* [The Formation of the Bulgarian Nation] (in Bulgarian with English and German summaries). Sofia.

AVENARIUS, A. 1974. *Die Awaren in Europa*. Bratislava, pp. 130–131.

BAKALOV, G. 1985. *Srednovekovnijat bŭlgarski vladetel: titulatura i insignii* [The Bulgarian Ruler in the Middles Ages: Titles and Insignia] (in Bulgarian). Sofia, pp. 96–144.

BUDA, A. 1980. Quelques questions de l'histoire de la formation du peuple albanais, de sa langue et de sa culture. In: *Studia albanica*, I, pp. 41–61.

ĆIRKOVIĆ, S. 1964. *Istorija srednjovekovne Bosanske države* [History of the Bosnian State in the Middle Ages] (in Serbian). Belgrade, pp. 40 *et seq.*

——. 1981. *Istorija srpskog naroda* [History of the Serb People] (in Serbian). Belgrade, pp. 141–155.

DIMITROV, D. I. 1987. Asparuchovite bŭlgari prez poslednite dve desetiletija na VII v. [The Bulgars of Asparuch in the Last Two Decades of the 7th Century]. In: DIMITROV, D. I. (ed.) *Prabŭlgarite po severnoto i zapadnato Černomorie* [The Proto-Bulgars on the Northern and Western Pontus] (in Bulgarian). Varna, pp. 195–206.

DITTEN, H. 1978. Zur Bedeutung der Einwanderung der Slawen. *Byzanz im 7. Jahrhundert. Untersuchungen zur Herausbildung des Feudalismus.* Berlin, pp. 73–160.

FERJANČIĆ, B. 1984. Invasions et installation des Slaves dans les Balkans. *Villes et peuplement*, pp. 101–109.

FINE, J. V. A. 1983. *The Early Medieval Balkans* , I. Michigan, pp. 141 *et seq.*

——. 1983. *op. cit.*, pp. 248 *et seq.*

Istorija srpskog naroda [History of the Serb People], *op. cit.*, pp. 143–145.

JURUKOVA, J. 1969. Les invasions slaves au Sud du Danube d'après les trésors monétaires en Bulgarie. *Byzantinobulgarica*, Sofia, Vol. 3, pp. 255-264.

KARAYANNOPOULOS, J. 1978. *Istoria tou Vizantinou Kratous* [History of the Byzantine Empire] (in Greek), Vol. I. Thessaloniki, pp. 597–600.

KLAIĆ, N. 1971. *Provjest Hrvata u ranom srednjem vjeku* [History of the Croats in the High Middle Ages] (in Croatian), Zagreb, pp. 55 *et seq.*

KOVAČEVIĆ, I. 1981. *Istorija srpskog naroda* [History of the Serb People] (in Serbian), Vol. I. Belgrade, pp. 108-124.

Les peuples de l'Europe du sud-est et leur rôle dans l'histoire. 1969 (Berza, M. Roumanie; Buda, A. La place des Albanais dans l'histoire européenne du VIIIè au XVIIIè s.) Actes du premier colloque international des Etudes balkaniques et Sud-Est européennes. Sofia, III, pp. 51 *et seq.*, pp. 57 *et seq.*

LITAVRIN, G. G. 1984. Slavinii VII–IX vv. Social nopolitičeskie organizacii Slavjan [The Slavinias, 7th to 9th Centuries. Socio-Political Organizations of the Slavs]. *Etnogenesis narodov Balkan i Srednego Pričernomorija. Linguistika, istoria, arheologia* [Ethnogenesis of the Peoples of the Balkans and the Middle Pontus. Linguistics, History, Archaeology] (in Russian), Moscow, pp. 193–203.

MURNU, G. 1984. *Studii istorice privitoare la tretucul Românilor de peste Dunăre* [Historical Studies on the Past of the Romanians from the Far Side of the Danube] (in Romanian), pp. 67–77.

NYTSTAZOPOULOU-PELEKIDOU, M. 1986. Les Slaves dans l'Empire byzantin. *The 17th International Byzantine Congress. Major Papers.* New York, pp. 348–352.

POHL, W. 1988. *Die Awaren. Ein Steppenvolk im Mitteleuropa* (567–822). Munich.

PRIMOV, B. 1981. *Istoria na Bŭlgaria* [History of Bulgaria] (in Bulgarian), Vol. 2. Sofia, pp. 133–142.

TĂPKOVA-ZAIMOVA, V. 1966. *Našestvia i etničeski promeni na Balkanite, VI–VIIv.* [Invasions and Ethnic Changes in the Balkans in the 6th–7th Centuries: in Bulgarian, French summary] (in Bulgarian) Sofia, Academy of Sciences, pp. 567 *et seq.*

——. 1979. L'idée byzantine de l'unité du monde et l'Etat bulgare. In: TĂPKOVA-ZAIMOVA, V. (ed.) *Byzance et les Balkans à partir du VIè s.* London: Variorum Reprints, No. XVIII, pp. 293 *et seq.*

——. 1979. Genèse des peuples balkaniques et formation de leurs Etats. L'expérience bulgare. Byzance et les Balkans à partir du VIè s., *op. cit.* No. XX, pp. 71 *et seq.*

TEODOR, D. G. 1984. Origines et voies de pénétration des Slaves au sud du Danube (VIe–VIIe ss), *Villes et peuplement dans l'Illyricum protobyzantin. Actes du Colloque organisé par l'Ecole française de Rome* (Rome, 12–14 May 1982) (Paris), pp. 63–84.

VOJNOV, M. 1956. Za Părvija dopir ne Asparuhovite bălgari săs slavjanite i za datata na osnovavaneto na bŭlgarskata dŭržava [The First Contact Between the Bulgars of Asparuch and the Slavs and the Date of the Foundation of the Bulgarian State: in Bulgarian with French Summary]. *Bulletin de l'Institut d'histoire bulgare*, Sofia, Vol. 6, pp. 453–478.

ZAIMOV, J. 1975. Beitrag zur Erforschung der Bulgarischen Namen in Griechenland. *Zeitschrift für Balkanologie*, Jahrgang XI, Heft 1, Munich, pp. 105–116.

12.2

THE CHRISTIANIZATION OF THE SLAVS AND OTHER ETHNIC GROUPS, PARTICULARLY THOSE NEAR THE BLACK SEA

Vasilka Tăpkova-Zaimova

Christianity as the official religion began to be established in south-eastern Europe from the ninth century. It was a process that in places lasted over a century and was everywhere influenced by the long rivalry between the Church of Rome and that of Constantinople.

DIOCESAN CENTRES IN THE BALKAN PROVINCES

During the centuries of invasions and great political upheavals, especially in the seventh–eighth centuries, the activity of the old diocesan centres in Illyricum, the two provinces of Moesia on the Danube, Macedonia, and so on, had gradually diminished or even in some places stopped altogether. The great acquisitions of the time of Justinian I, whose work of construction and fortification involved not just public buildings in the great urban centres but also churches, gradually lost their lustre (see Map 9 and Plate 145). Such was the case, for example, with Sirmium in Pannonia, Justiniana Prima (Caričingrad, near Niš), Marcianopolis on the Black Sea, and so on (Mirković, 1981). But the sees continued their work of ecclesiastical organization much more on the coast of the Pontus and the Aegean, not to mention the territories of Greece proper, where there were few or no periods of interruption.

From as early as the end of the fourth century, there had been attempts to evangelize settled populations and migrant tribes. Such was the case with the 'Besses' (that is, the Thracians south of the Haemus), who had converted in the fifth century, and the Goths settled around Nicopolis and Istrum south of the Danube. These Goths had adopted the arianism of the Emperor Valens (364–378), and their bishop Ulfila had even translated part of the Scriptures into their own language (Tăpkova-Zaimova, 1979). The Crimean Goths were also Christianized in the late fourth century. This region of the northern Pontus remained continuously under Byzantine administration. Thus the Church of Constantinople retained its sees there despite the complex relations in the seventh–eighth centuries between Byzantium and the Khazars and the Bulgar groups who penetrated as far as the town of Phanagoria – one of the better-known fortresses of Justinian I's time (Zubar, 1991).

After the 840s, the iconoclasm crisis was settled in Byzantium, and imperial authority emerged triumphant over the separatist tendencies of the Anatolian aristocracy. Religious activity therefore became particularly intense in the Slav world, not only in the south-east but also towards Pannonia and Moravia, as competition between Rome and Constantinople in organizing missions was stepped up in the middle of the ninth century. Politically, the existence of the empire of Charlemagne had greatly complicated relations with Constantinople. The Frankish Empire quickly fell apart, it is true, but the princes who succeeded him challenged Byzantium's rights over Illyricum and the western parts of the Balkan peninsula. The fact was that some of the Bulgar lands, especially Serbia and Croatia, had been part of the old diocese of Illyricum, which had been removed from the jurisdiction of Rome for almost two centuries (Peri, 1983).

CYRIL AND METHODIUS – APOSTLES TO THE SLAVS

Such was the East–West situation when the organization of the mission of Cyril and Methodius was dreamed up in Constantinople. It was largely the work of the flexible and far-sighted policy of the patriarch Photius.

The Slavs of Moravia, Bohemia, Pannonia and Carantania (Slovenia), converterd between the seventh century and the middle of the ninth, had prelates under Western control when Cyril and Methodius' apostolate began in Moravia in 863. Accompanied by a group of missionaries that they had trained, the two brothers, who were natives of Thessaloniki, went there under an agreement between Emperor Michael III and Moravian Prince Rostislav. Their mission had been preceded by a period of preparation during which they had translated part of the Scriptures into the Slav dialect, which was to develop into the language known as Old Bulgarian. The alphabet invented by Cyril for this purpose, known as Glagolitic, was later simplified and became known as Cyrillic (Dujčev *et al.*, 1983) (see Plate 106).

The mission of Cyril and Methodius initially encountered favourable conditions in Moravia and then in Pannonia. The training of an indigenous clergy and the flexible adaptation to the needs of a Slav population that could receive a Christian education in a language they understood quickly produced good results. But after some time the opposition of the Bavarian clergy made itself felt. The two brothers were obliged to go to Rome to clear themselves of having introduced Slavic into the liturgy and received approval of their work from Pope Hadrian II. But Cyril was not to leave Rome again; he died there in 869. Methodius continued his

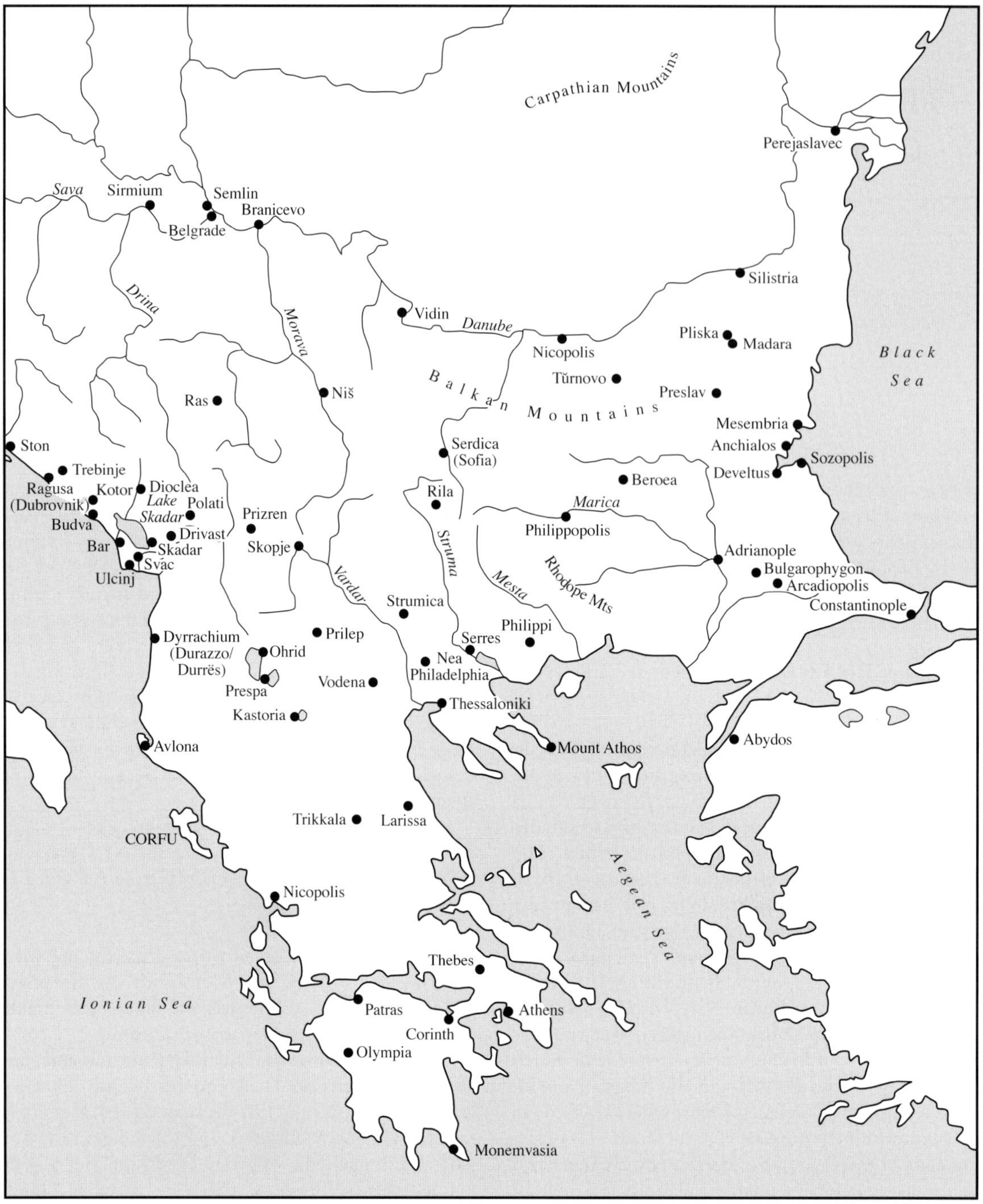

Map 9 Major early medieval towns in the Balkans (after Fine, J. V. A., 1983, *The Early Medieval Balkans*, Michigan).

apostolate in Pannonia and Moravia, where, after further tribulations and having suffered a period of imprisonment by the Bavarian clergy, he ended his days in 885.

The mission of Cyril and Methodius left its mark on the religious and cultural life of the Slavs of Central Europe (Vavřínek, 1963). Nevertheless, it ended in failure: the two brothers' disciples were expelled from Moravia but were welcomed south of the Danube, where Prince Boris of Bulgaria was in the process of laying the foundations of the religious life of his country. Christianity had been introduced into Bulgaria as its official religion two decades earlier (864 or 865).

OFFICIAL CHRISTIANITY IN BULGARIA: GROWTH OF THE SLAVONIC–BULGAR CULTURE

The conversion of Bulgaria did not go smoothly. The pre-Christian Bulgar khāns jealously preserved the 'law of the ancestors'. The Bulgars who, like other Turkic peoples, chiefly adored a celestial divinity (the god Tangra or Tengri), practised a true cult of the personality of the head of the community (in the case of the head of state, 'crowned by God').

But it seems that Christianization by Byzantine missionaries had won ground among some of the Slavs included in the

Bulgar state, who at the time were still practising a form of pre-Christianism closely linked to the forces of nature (Perun was the god of thunder) and corresponding to the way of life of an agrarian population.

The general political situation, and some military setbacks, notably against the Serbs and the Croats, led Boris to convert in dramatic circumstances: part of the Bulgar aristocracy revolted, however. In the eyes of this aristocracy, loyalty to the old customs represented independence from the Byzantine Empire.

By his act of conversion, Boris accepted the position of political vassalage that was necessarily that of a prince newly accepted into the Christian community (Giuzelev, 1981; Vojnov, 1962). But he adopted a line of conduct which was to end in the organization of an autocephalous Church. Initially playing Rome against Constantinople (he had attempted to establish relations with Pope Nicholas I), Boris ended by accepting from Byzantium an archbishop who took charge of the Bulgarian Church (see Plate 153). Later, in the reign of his son Simeon, the Bulgarian Church was raised to the rank of a patriarchate (Bakalov, 1985).

Meanwhile, and thanks to the welcome given to the representatives of the mission of Cyril and Methodius, Boris succeeded in organizing a cultural life on a grand scale: the two main centres where Naum and Clement, two disciples of Cyril and Methodius, worked, and who had their own disciples, were Great Preslav, the capital of Christian Bulgaria, and Ohrid in Macedonia. In the space of a few decades, a Bulgarian–Slav literature developed there which not only performed a mediating function but also created cultural models in European orthodoxy (Obolensky, 1963; Tăpkova-Zaimova and Simeonova, 1987).

BETWEEN CONSTANTINOPLE AND ROME: RELIGIOUS LIFE IN THE WESTERN PARTS OF THE PENINSULA

The Christianization of the western parts of the Balkan peninsula and the South Slavs who had settled there had begun, as was the case with the other Slavs in the Balkans, in the seventh century, if we are to believe the more or less legendary account of the Emperor Constantine Porphyrogenitus. It is believed that the official conversion to Christianity in the Serb and Croat principalities must be dated to the 820s, when renewed Byzantine expansion began in Dalmatia, followed by anti-Byzantine movements among the local population. After Croatian Dalmatia, with the exception of the Neretljani, who long remained pre-Christian, Christianization gradually penetrated into the areas away from the Adriatic – Bosnia, Serbia and Slavonia on the Sava, a tributary of the Danube. This process was especially significant during the rule of Emperor Basil I (867–886) and the patriarch Photius. The episcopal centre of Nin in northern Dalmatia played an important role in the mid- and late ninth century, but it was eliminated at the beginning of the tenth century during the struggles between Rome and Constantinople for primacy in the organization and ecclesiastical jurisdiction of Croatian Dalmatia. In any event, it seems that it was the metropolitan centres of Dalmatia and Pannonia that sent missions to 'Christian Serbia', as Constantine Porphyrogenitus called it at the beginning of the tenth century. The first Christian names to be found in Serbia are those of the grandchildren of Prince Vlastimir, who were born in the 870s (Ćirković, 1992; Maksimović, 1992).

The political particularism that marked relations among the western parts of the Balkan peninsula had a definite influence on ecclesiastical organization in the Adriatic territories until the beginning of the eleventh century, when Byzantium erected a see at Dyrrachium (Durrës in modern Albania) whose activity was to thwart that of Split (Spalato) in Croatian Dalmatia, in obedience to Rome. At the same time, the Serbian Church was concentrated around the see of Rascia (Naumov, 1988).

CONVERSION OF THE EASTERN SLAVS

The conversion of the Eastern Slavs was part of Byzantium's great initiative aimed at christianizing the Slavic world. But despite the success of the missions of Constantinople on the southern shore of the Crimea among the Goths who had settled there and despite the contacts between this population and the Eastern Slavs, inhabitants of the so-called steppes of southern Russia (the Černjakov culture in which Iranian features are also found), there is no record of the existence of Christian communities in the seventh and eighth centuries. Nor did any such communities exist at an earlier date among this so-called 'Scythian' population, which lived along the northern shore of the Pontus and the lower Dniestr. Thus it was in a later phase, in the second half of the ninth century, that the missions from Constantinople turned towards the principality of Kiev, which had already organized the Eastern Slavs politically (Vodoff, 1989).

This route, which led 'Varangians to Greece', as the Russian Chronicles put it, was in the first place a trade route, but it was also the route that the army of the Kievan princes followed in their campaigns against the Byzantine capital. In the 860s, the Russian fleet almost reached the walls of Constantinople. Almost a century later, in 957, Princess Olga was baptized, also in Constantinople, but was unable to impose the new religion on the court of Kiev and among the aristocracy; an approach on her part to the German Emperor Otto I was also fruitless. It was only in 989 that Prince Vladimir officially received baptism after his marriage to the sister of Emperor Basil II. The Russian Church was organized under the leadership of missionaries sent from Byzantium. Representatives of the Bulgarian clergy took part in introducing the Scriptures (Rogov, 1988) (see Plates 157–160).

RELIGIOUS MOVEMENTS OUTSIDE ORTHODOXY

In the Middle Ages, continuity in orthodoxy was the strength of South-Eastern and Eastern Europe. But that does not mean that the strength was not contested by nonconformist religious movements. The religious disputes, which were basically theological differences, sometimes took on the appearance of social revolts, mainly among people living a rather isolated life away from the towns and diocesan centres.

Such were the Bogomils in Bulgaria in the tenth century. They rejected ecclesiastical hierarchy and the worship of icons, simplified the service of the sacraments and espoused an extreme dualism in their understanding of Christianity (Angelov, 1979). Campaigns of repression, sometimes carried out by the Byzantine and Bulgarian governments together, had the aim of thwarting the growth that this movement was enjoying in the second half of the tenth century. But in the eleventh–twelfth centuries, during the period of renewed Byzantine expansion in the Balkans, the Bogomils sometimes made common cause with other rebels against the Byzantine regime. It was at the end of this period that Bogomil doctrines also spread outside the borders of Bulgaria. Traces can be found, with some local variations, in Bosnia, where the 'national' Bosnian Church (Ecclesia Sclavoniae) existed until the Ottoman period (Dragojlović, 1987; Čirković, 1987). The influence of Bogomilism was also felt in Western Europe in the late twelfth and thirteenth centuries in the dualist communities of the Patarenes, the Cathars and the Albigensians. The name Bulgars (Old French 'Bougres', 'Bougarans', 'Bougrès') even spread there as a name to describe heretics in general (Primov, 1960).

The name of the Paulicians, the other heretics in the Byzantine provinces of Asia Minor, was known in the seventh–eighth centuries and especially the ninth century (Loos, 1974). Massive deportations of Paulicians to Thrace and elsewhere publicized their doctrine, which was close to that of the Bogomils, in other parts of the Balkans too. In their writings, authors of the time who assumed the task of refuting these doctrines often lumped together all these heretics, who posed a lasting administrative and ecclesiastical problem for the Byzantine Empire.

Furthermore, in relations between the Church of Rome and that of Constantinople, there were, now and again, confrontations which inevitably left their mark on the intellectual and political life of Europe as it was being formed.

BIBLIOGRAPHY

ANGELOV, D. 1979. *Il Bogomilismo – un eresia bulgara*. Bulzoni, Rome.

BAKALOV, G. 1985. *Srednovekovnijat bŭlgarski vladetal: titulatura i insignii* [The Medieval Bulgarian Ruler: Titles and Insignia] (in Bulgarian). Sofia, pp. 96–113.

ČIRKOVIĆ, S. 1981. *Istorija srpskog naroda* [History of the Serb People] (in Serbian), I. Belgrade, pp. 150–153.

——. 1987. Bosanska crkva u bosanskoj državi [The Bosnian Church in the Bosnian State]. In: *Prilozi za istoriju Bosni i Herzegovini* [Materials for the History of Bosnia and Herzegovina] (in Serbian), Vol. I, Sarajevo, pp. 191–254.

DRAGOJLOVIĆ, D. 1987. *Krstjani i jeretička crkva bosanska* [The Christians and the Bosnian Heretic Church] (in Serbian). Belgrade.

DUJČEV, I.; KIRMAGOVA, A.; PAUNOVA, A. 1983. *Kirilometodievska bibliografia 1940–1980* [Cyril and Methodius'Bibliography]. Sofia.

GIUZELEV, V. 1981. *Istoria na Bŭlgaria*, [History of Bulgaria] (in Bulgarian), 2. Sofia, pp. 213–234.

LOOS, M. 1974. *Dualist Heresy in the Middle Ages*. Prague.

MAKSIMOVIĆ, L. 1992. The Christianization of the Serbs and the Croats. In: *The Legacy of Saints Cyril and Methodius to Kiev and Moscow*, Thessaloniki, pp. 167–184.

MIRKOVIĆ, M. 1981. *Istorija srpskog naroda* [History of the Serb People] (in Serbian), I. Belgrade, pp. 99–105.

NAUMOV, E. P. 1988. Čerkovnaja organizacija y političeskoj strukture serbskih i horvatskih zemel (konec IX.–načalo XII. v.) [Ecclesiastical Organization in the Political Structure of the Serb and Croat Lands – Late 9th to Early 10th Centuries]. In: *Prinjatije hristianstva narodami Central'noj i Jugo-vostočnoj Evropi i Kreščenije Rusi* [Reception of Christianity by the Peoples of Central and South-Eastern Europe and Christianization of Russia] (in Russian). Moscow, pp. 85–103.

OBOLENSKY, D. 1963. St. Cyril and Methodius, Apostles of the Slavs. *St Vladimiros Seminary Quarterly*, New York, pp. 9 *et seq*.

PERI, V. 1983. Gli 'jura antiqua' sulla patria dei Bulgari – un 'topos' canonico per un risveglio missionario, In: *Atti dell'8° Congresso internazionale di studi sull'alto medioevo*. Split, pp. 226–268.

PRIMOV, B. 1960. Medieval Bulgaria and the dualistic heresies in Western Europe. *Etudes Historiques*. Vol. I, Sofia, pp. 89–103.

ROGOV, A. I. 1988. Kul'turnyje svjazi Kievskoj Rusi s drugimi slavjanskimi stranami v period jejo hristianizacii [The Cultural Relations of Kievan Russia with the Other Slav Countries During the Period of Christianization]. In: *Prinjatije hristianstva, op. cit.*, pp. 207–234.

TĂPKOVA-ZAIMOVA, V. 1979. Istoria na Bŭlgaria [History of Bulgaria] (in Bulgarian), I. Sofia, 1, pp. 405–413.

TĂPKOVA-ZAIMOVA, V.; SIMEONOVA, L. 1987. Aspects of the Byzantine cultural policy towards bulgaria in the epoch of Photius. In: *Byzantine and Europe: First International Byzantine Conference*, Athens, pp. 153–163.

VAVŘÍNEK, V. 1963. Die Christianisation und Kirchenorganisation Grossmährens, *Historia*, Prague, pp. 5–56.

VODOFF, V. 1989. *Naissance de la chrétienté russe: la conversion du prince russe Vladimir de Kiev en 988 et ses conséquences*. Paris, pp. 48–61.

VOJNOV, M. 1962. Njakoi vŭprosi vŭv vrŭzka s obrzsuvaneto na bŭlgarskata dŭržava i pokrŭstvaneto na bŭlgarite [Some Problems Relating to the Formation of the Bulgarian State and the Evangelization of the Bulgars]. *Bulletin de l'Institut d'histoire*, 10 (in Bulgarian), Sofia, pp. 287–307.

ZUBAR, V. M. 1991. *Proniknovenije i utverždenije hristianstva v Hersonese Tavričeskom* [Penetration and Confirmation of Christianity in the Tauric Chersonese] (in Russian). Kiev.

12.3
LITERARY AND ARTISTIC FORMS OF EXPRESSION

12.3.1
LITERARY FORMS OF EXPRESSION

Vasilka Tăpkova-Zaimova

The literatures of the Southern and Eastern Slavs developed within the cultural sphere referred to as 'Orthodox Slavdom'. At the outset, the inspiration for these literatures was religious: their purpose was to serve the missionaries in their work among the newly converted Slav populations. Hence translations and adaptations of Byzantine texts were numerous.

BULGARIAN LITERATURE: THE FIRST NATIONAL LITERATURE

Slavic–Bulgarian literature stemmed directly from the tradition inaugurated by Saints Cyril and Methodius (Georgiev *et al.*, 1962; Kuev, 1981). The earliest works written in the language which came to be known as Old Bulgarian, and which stood in distinctly close relationship to the spoken tongue, appeared in the second half of the ninth century, and in the early tenth.

The Gospels of Assemanius, of Zographus and a few other texts were transcribed into Glagolitic characters, while the Codex Suprasliensis and the Book of Sava, among other works, were written in the Cyrillic alphabet (see Figures 25a and b). Most of these written monuments go back to the late ninth (or the tenth) century. The main centres where the literati plied their trade under the rules of Boris and Simeon were at Preslav and Ohrid. Clement, often called Clement of Ohrid, made important stylistic contributions to Church oratory through his 'Praises' and 'Hymns', composed on the occasion of the major religious festivals, and which later had a considerable impact in other Orthodox Slavic lands (Kliment Ochridski, 1970–1977). Labouring as both an apostle and an educator, Clement fully deserved to be referred to as a 'Second Paul, speaking unto the Second Corinthians – the Bulgarians'.

In Preslav, Chabr the Monk wrote his 'Letters', a polemical tract which defended the achievement of Saints Cyril and Methodius and laid stress on the importance of the Slavic alphabet (Kuev, 1967). The same ideas occur in the 'Acrostic Prayer' by Constantine of Preslav, the first poetic essay in Bulgarian literature (Graševa, 1994). In the introduction to his 'Učitelno evangelie' (Gospel of Instruction, a collection of Sunday sermons), Constantine of Preslav further wrote that 'those peoples without letters are naked peoples'. Another of the Preslav literati of the time, John the Exarch, composed a 'Hexameron' or account of the creation of the world in six days, drawing for inspiration on works on the same theme in Byzantine literature going back to the age of Saint Basil. John's 'Hexameron' opens with an impressive description of the Bulgarian capital, and this preface included a portrait of Tsar Simeon, seated on his throne (Aitzetmuller, 1958).

The flowering of Bulgarian literature came about under the patronage of the court at Preslav. Boris saw literature as a further means for weaning Christian Bulgaria from a dependency on Constantinople, which was not only religious in nature, but also political. For his part, Tsar Simeon also took up the pen: he even came to be referred to as the 'new Ptolemy' in light of the interest he took in letters. The first translations of Greek chronicles go back to Simeon's rule. Collections of didactic narratives also continued to be composed. The best-known such collection, the 'Zbornik of Simeon', was carried over into Kievan Russia after the conversion of the Russians in 989, and was copied in 1073 under the title of 'Zbornik of Svetoslav', after the name of the Kievan prince, which replaced that of Tsar Simeon in the preface (Simeonov zbornik, 1991).

SLAVIC LITERATURE IN SERBIA AND CROATIA

Literary production in Preslav and Ohrid could not long fail to provoke considerable repercussion in such areas as Rascia or the territories along the Neretva river. Liturgical works like the Gospel of Miroslav and the Gospel of Vukan were written in Serbian towards the end of the twelfth century (Kašanin, 1975 ; Bogdanović, 1980). As early as the tenth and eleventh centuries, however, local chroniclers had already composed annals which, although now lost, furnished useful materials to that highly informed imperial writer, the tenth-century Byzantine ruler Constantine Porphyrogenitus (Kašanin, 1975). The Presbyter of Duklja wrote his major chronicle of the maritime regions in, probably, the middle of the twelfth century. Based on local annals or chronicles of the Adriatic coast, this work was originally written in Latin, but side by side with an extant Latin manuscript of the text dating from the fifteenth century, we have a Croat translation from the sixteenth (Mošin, 1950).

Glagolitic script was introduced into Croatia and Slovenia at a time when the mission of Saints Cyril and Methodius was still being carried out in Lower Pannonia. After Methodius' disciples were expelled from Great Moravia, some of their number were welcomed in Croatia, where they continued however to face hostility from the Bavarian clergy. The Glagolitic alphabet nevertheless remained in partial use until the sixteenth century (Hamm, 1963). But in Dalmatian Croatia, Latin was preserved for official use, as in all other countries oriented towards the Church of Rome.

Literary developments in medieval Serbia were encouraged by the ruling princes and their families. Saint Sava, who belonged to the ruling family of the Nemanids and who was appointed archbishop of Serbia, stands out among this area's literati. He also worked with zeal to preserve close relations between the Orthodox Churches, and died in Tùrnovo, the capital of the Bulgarian Assenids, while returning from a mission to Nicaea (Istorija srpskog naroda, 1981).

This was only the beginning of close ties which were pursued on the initiative of the representatives of the Tùrnovo school of literature. In subsequent years, literary production in Bulgaria's capital came to have a decisive impact in the regions to the north of the Danube, that is, in the Valachia, in Moldavia, and in Russia – especially toward the close of the fourteenth century, when Ottoman Turkish penetration of Bulgarian territory provoked a large-scale northbound emigration of literati from Tùrnovo.

OFFICIAL LITERATURE AND POPULAR 'LOW' LITERATURE

Parallel to official literary production, a literature known as 'apocryphal' and 'historic-apocalyptic' spread widely throughout Bulgaria and, later, Serbia, etc. This consisted of popular tales (whence the name 'low literature'), which, while also of religious inspiration, presented a more naïve and altogether rather simplistic cosmogony (Tăpkova-Zaimova; Miltenova, 1996). Such writings contained 'prophecies' on the 'end of days' and the succession of 'earthly kingdoms' before the Second Coming, lore which became very much to the taste of the peoples in western Bulgaria and Serbia. Such lore was later linked to the tragic fate of Prince Lazar Hrebeljanović, who fell at the Battle of Kosovo (Dragojlović, 1976 ; Mihalčić 1989).

But lore of this kind also sometimes came close to the religious and philosophical representations of the Bogomils. The direct works of these 'heretics' have been little preserved, since they were marked for persecution and destruction. Only a twelfth-century Latin version makes known to us 'The Secret Book of the Bogomils'. Better-known is the 'Treatise Against the Heretics' penned by the Bulgarian priest Cosmas, who lived under the rule of Tsar Peter (927–969 or 970) (Begunov, 1973). This work mercilessly castigates those who swerve from the true faith, but rings with a very personal tone – one of the most individual to survive from this age – and was much used through the following centuries as a weapon against heretics in Serbia and Russia.

Standing as it were midway between the official and 'low' literatures were those narratives woven around 'historical' matter, that is, which reproduced the legends of classical Greek antiquity. Such were the 'Alexander Romance' and the 'Tale of Troy', which penetrated the Balkans from the West and which reached not only Byzantium but also Serbia and Bulgaria. Poetic romances of this sort became very popular during the period after the Crusades (Marinković, 1962, 1969).

LITERATURE IN KIEVAN RUSSIA

As in the other Slavic lands, such literature grew up to serve the purposes of the Church after the conversion of Prince Vladimir. In addition to renditions of Scripture, this period also saw translations from the Byzantine chronicles. Medieval Bulgaria played an important role in the work of literary transmission and religious education.

Legends and oral tradition, and the recollection of memorable feats of arms, found a durable reflection in epic songs, known as *blyiny*, such as those where the well-known hero, Ilja Murometz, fights for his country's freedom. Travelling bards and their accompanying musicians, using instruments of a national type, wandered the vast plains and were listened to by different classes of the population. The great Russian epic, the 'Lay of Prince Igor', going back most probably to the second half of the twelfth century, thus came into circulation shortly after Igor's campaigns against the Cumans (Lihačev, 1978: pp. 132–204).

'The Tale of Bygone Times' is a Russian chronicle assigned by tradition to the chronicler Nestor (twelfth century). Nestor laboured in the 'Great Laura' of Kiev, where he also wrote lives of saints. In fact, 'The Tale of Bygone Times' is not a personal work as it includes several textual layers, which accumulated through the course of at least half a century (Lihačev, 1978: pp. 22–110).

The cities of medieval Russia preserve a rather strange form of documentation: charters written on elm bark. Pieces found in Novogorod date to the eleventh century (Janin, 1975).

SLAV ORTHODOXY AND LITERARY PRODUCTION IN THE MONASTERIES

Translation of the texts of the Old and New Testaments by Saints Cyril and Methodius and their disciples marked the initial stage of literary communication within Slavic Christendom. Adaptations of the major monuments of canon law constituted a second stage. But the writing of the lives of saints played a considerable role in what amounted to a spiritual fusion. Monasteries on Mount Athos multiplied after the close of the tenth century, and these included not only Greek establishments but also Serbian (founded by Saint Sava), Bulgarian, Russian, and later Vlach. The production of literature and especially of saints' lives became increasingly abundant. Hence arose a vast cultural area where literary ties were pursued without interruption down to a time far later than the chronological framework assigned to the Middle Ages (Picchio, 1981, 1984).

BIBLIOGRAPHY

AITZETMULLER, R. 1958–1975. *Das Hexameron des Exarchen Johanne*, 1–7, Graz.

BEGUNOV, J. 1973. *Kosma presviter v slavjanskih literaturah* [Cosmas the Priest in Slavic Literature] (in Russian). Sofia.

BOGDANOVIĆ, D. 1980. *Istorija stare srpske knlizevnosti* [History of Old Serbian Literature] (in Serbian). Belgrade, pp. 29–140.

DRAGOJLOVIĆ, D. 1976. Mit o 'zlatnom veku' i 'nebesnom kraljevsvu' u staroj srpskoj književnosti [The Myth of the "Golden Age" and the "Heavenly Kingdom" in Old Serbian Literature]. In: *Prilozi za književnost, jezik, istoriju i folklor* [Contributions to Literature, Language, History and Folklore] (in Serbian), 42, pp. 1–4.

GEORGIEV, E.; DUJČEV, I.; VELČEV, V.; DINEKOV, P.; ANGELOV, B. 1962. In: *Istorija na bùlgarskata literatura* [History of Bulgarian Literature] (in Bulgarian), Vol. I. Sofia, pp. 23–242.

GRAŠEVA, L. 1994. Konstantin Preslavski. In: *Kirilo-Metodievska Enciklopedija* [Encyclopaedia of Cyril and Methodius] (in Bulgarian), Vol. II, Sofia, pp. 426–440.

HAMM, J. 1963. Vom kroatischen Typus der Kirchenslavschen. In: *Wiener slawishen Jahrbuch*, Vol. X, pp. 11–39.

Istorija srpskog naroda [History of the Serb People] 1981 (in Serbian). Vol. I. Belgrade, pp. 238–240.

JANIN, V. L. 1975. Komplex berestjannyh gramot N. 519–521 [The complex of Charters written on elm-bark N. 519–521]. In: *Obsčestvo i gosudarstvo feodaljnoj Rossii* [Society and State of Feudal Russia]. pp. 30–39

KAŠANIN, M. 1975. *Srpska knjizevnost srednjem veku* [Serbian Literature in the Middle Ages] (in Serbian). Belgrade, pp. 15–108.

KLIMENT OCHRIDSKI 1970–1977. *Šabrani săčinenija* [Complete works] (in Bulgarian). Vol. I–III. Sofia.

KUEV, K. 1967. *Černorizec Harbr* [Harbr the Monk] (in Bulgarian). Sofia.

——. 1981. In: *Istorija na Bùlgaria* [History of Bulgaria] (in Bulgarian).Vol. II. Sofia, pp. 310–323.

LIHAČEV, D. S. 1978. Velikoe nasledije [The Great Heritage] (in Russian). Moscow.

MARINKOVIČ, R. 1962. Južnoslovenski roman o Troiu [The South Slav Romance of Troy]. *Anali filozofskog fakulteta* [Annals of the Faculty of Philosophy] (in Serbian), Vol. I, Belgrade, pp. 9–66.

——. 1969. *Srpska Alexandria* [The Serbian Alexander Romance] (in Serbian), Belgrade.

MIHALČIĆ, R. 1989. Verski koreni [The Roots of Faith]. In: *Junaci Kosovke legende* [The Heroes of the Legend of Kosovo] (in Serbian). Belgrade, pp. 212–229.

MOŠIN, V. 1950. *Ljetopis popa Dukljanina* [The Chronicle of the Cleric of Duklja] (in Croatian). Zagreb.

PICCHIO, R. 1981. Mjastoto na starata balgarska literatura v kulturata na srednovkovna Evropa [The place of Old Bulgarian Literature in the Culture of Medieval Europe]. In: *Literaturna mišal* (in Bulgarian), Vol. XXV, 8, pp. 19-36.

——. 1984. The impact of ecclesiastic culture on old literary technics. In: *Medieval Russian Culture*, BIRNBAUM, H. and PLIER, M. S. (eds). University of California Press, Berkeley, Los Angeles London, pp. 247–279.

Simeonov sbornik [Collection of Simeon] 1991 (in Bulgarian). Vol. I. Sofia.

TĂPKOVA-ZAIMOVA; MILTENOVA, V.-A. 1996. *Istoriko-apokaliptičnata Knižnina văv Vizantija i v srednovenkovna Bălgarja* [The Historical-Apocalyptic Literature in Byzance and in medieval Bulgaria] (in Bulgarian with French abstract). Sofia.

12.3.2
ARTISTIC FORMS OF EXPRESSION

Vasilka Tăpkova-Zaimova

The Byzantine East's artistic superiority exerted a decisive influcncc on thc shaping of national cultures in the Balkans. Such a cultural impact mostly found expression through literature and the arts, which stamped this region with its own distinctive traits in the life of medieval European civilization.

In Byzantium, as in other Christian countries, architecture, and especially ecclesiastical architecture, tended to dominate other forms of artistic expression. The basilica became widespread as a model for church design as early as the fourth century, with its oblong form best illustrated by the early sixth-century Sant'Apollinare Nuovo in Ravenna. Church architecture was further elaborated upon, however, during the reign of Justinian I (527–565), with a dome now crowning a polygonal base as at San Vitale in Ravenna. Justinian's most famous edifice is Saint Sophia in Constantinople, the model for the new, Byzantine central type of church covered by a dome (see Plate 145). But longitudinal basilicas continue to be found in Thessaloniki, the towns of the Pontus and the Adriatic, and in the provinces of the interior – wherever Christianity had, with the help of a well-orginazed diocesan centre network, taken more or less firm root. Furthermore, the building of churches went hand in hand with urban administration, as well as with that of religious observance. This was the case in a number of places, such as Marcianopolis between the Danube and the Black Sea, Ratiaria and Durostorum on the Danube, Augusta Traiana to the south of Mount Haemus, Serdica (now Sofia), Justiniana Prima near Niš, Spalato (Split) on the Adriatic, and so on (see Plate 63).

It was a desire to bring Christianity to the Crimean Goths that prompted the building of a number of basilicas in the Tauric Chersonese (Crimea), which was always a Byzantine province. These basilicas, too, date from the reign of Justinian I.

The building of religious centres was resumed after a gap of nearly two centuries. Indeed, following the settlement of the Slavs in the Balkan provinces, some of the initial gains of evangelization were lost, and the practice of Christianity was slow to penetrate these isolated and pre-Christian Slavic realms. In Danubian Bulgaria, where cultural life was sponsored by the proto-Bulgarian aristocracy, the old Caucasian and Iranian traditions were preserved and, in a manner of speaking, superimposed on the remains of provincial Byzantine culture.

The first pre-Christian capital, Pliska, located between the Danube and the Haemus (Balkan) mountain range, bears the clear stamp of this distant civilization: it boasted a double enclosure built of massive stone (the outer wall surrounds a 'camp' 23 square kilometres in area), monumental palaces, public buildings of impressive dimensions – all built during the eighth century and the first half of the ninth century.

A number of graffiti drawings on the blocks of stone, and numerous so-called 'proto-Bulgarian' inscriptions in Greek, together recount the exploits of the Bulgarian khāns. The Horseman of Madara is a stone relief located 20 km from Pliska; symbolizing the idea of power, the dual power of a ruling sovereign and grand priest, this is an impressive and unique monument in the artistic history of the Balkans. Sculpted lions stood before the gates of the fortified towns.

However, after the mid-ninth century, once Christianity has been adopted as the official religion in Bulgaria, monuments of Christian culture replaced those of the preceding period. John the Exarch, writing in the reign of Simeon, describes the magnificence of the palace in Preslav, which aroused the admiration of local inhabitants and foreigners alike.

Yet the building of churches was always the favourite subject of writers of that period. A more or less legendary text asserts that a figure as early as Simeon's father, Boris I (the Converter) (see Plate 153), had seven churches built. These were most certainly episcopal centres, where new churches were built in the old basilican tradition, even though that design had already been abandoned in the Byzantine capital. Archaeological excavations in the region of Pliska have brought to light nineteen such churches, the most important of which is the Great Basilica standing outside the town walls. Others have been discovered at Preslav (see Plate 155) and in the surrounding area; with regard to monasteries, special mention should be made of Ravna (about 60 km west of Varna).

The style characteristic of this period is also to be found in the church of Saint Sophia at Ohrid (eleventh century), which was in the diocese of Saint Clement, the first disciple of Cyril and Methodius, and in the church at Bregalnica, also in Macedonia. The church of Saint Achilleus, on the island of Lake Prespa in Macedonia, is also a basilica. It formed part of the residence of Tsar Samuel in the late tenth century.

In the ninth and tenth centuries in the recently converted Balkan countries, as in Byzantium in the same period, cross-shaped churches became the rule. One such church is the church of Preslav, called the Round Church (the church is a rotunda) or the gold-gilded Church, because of its decoration. Deep niches alternating with straight columns, a richly decorated floor and detailed carving all contribute to its artistic wealth.

Churches built on a central plan, with minor differences of detail, make their appearance in Macedonia (churches built on the cross-in-square plan), and in western parts of the peninsula.

At Kotor (Cataro) on the Adriatic, the first single-naved church goes back to AD 809. To this period also belong the churches of the Holy Trinity at Zadar, of the Holy Archangel at Prizren, and Saint Peter near Novi Pazar.

Some of the churches in Dalmatia are built according to a plan in which six or eight apses are formed around a central nave. These churches show similarities both to the churches of Great Moravia and to those built in the tradition of Cyril and Methodius. This plan, comprising several apses on either side of a central nave, is not peculiar to this part of Europe; it is also found in the same period in Armenia and Georgia.

Several specific traits are found in the towns of the central and eastern parts of the Balkan peninsula as they developed in the thirteenth and fourteenth centuries. The then Bulgarian capital, Veliko Tŭrnovo, and the town of Červen near present-day Ruse on the Danube, are surrounded by ramparts crowning steep rock faces; in this they differ from the former capitals of Pliska and Preslav. Groin vaults predominate in the construction of churches (the churches of Saint Peter and Saint Paul at Tŭrnovo; Saint Nicholas and Saint Panteleimon at Bojana near Sofia). Their outer walls contain shallow arched niches, in which the play of light and shadow is enhanced by ceramic decorations. The Pantokrator and Saint John Alitourgetos churches of Mesembria (now Nesebŭr) overlook the Black Sea.

Sculpture was used mainly for decorative purposes. We have already noted in the palace of Preslav the palmettes and rosettes, and other details reminiscent of western Asia. As has already been suggested, other sculpted forms recall the pre-Romanesque western style, which is particularly characteristic of the northern borderlands of Croatia and the Adriatic seaboard.

The period following the defeat of the Byzantine iconoclasts had a noticeable influence on iconography in the Balkan region. Among the most remarkable frescoes of the tenth to thirteenth centuries are those of the church of St George, a rotunda at Sofia (late tenth century) (see Plate 154), those of the church of Saint Sophia at Ohrid, which are somewhat later, the church of Saint Peter at Raška (eleventh century), Saint Michael at Ston in Dioclea (eleventh century), and finally the frescoes of the church of Saint Panteleimon at Nerezi near Skopje (1164) and the church of Saint George at Kurbinovo in Macedonia (1191). The frescoes of these churches are all masterpieces; their mosaics are less well preserved. However, what remains is sufficient to conclude that the same style and techniques were used, for example, in the churches of Saint Demetrius, Saint Sophia and so on at Thessaloniki (see Plate 146). A characteristic form of iconography in the period following the ninth century is the painted ceramic icons manufactured in the monasteries around Preslav, the Bulgarian capital at that time; the workshops of those monasteries produced a considerable quantity of decorative ceramic work (see Plate 155). In the production of manuscript books (in Bulgarian, etc.) illumination occupied pride of place.

In the thirteenth and fourteenth centuries, mural painting in Bulgaria and Serbia achieved remarkable results in a realistic style which arose in the Byzantine post-iconoclast period. There were also major achievements in eleventh- and twelfth-century local monuments, such as the monasteries of Bačkovo (in the Rhodope Mountains), Nerezi and Kurbinovo, which have already been mentioned. Particularly remarkable in this respect are the frescoes of the church of Bojana (1259), as well as those of the churches of Berende and Zemen in western Bulgaria, Hreljo's tower at the monastery of Rila, the rupestrian churches of Ivanovo in northern Bulgaria, and the frescoes of the Serbian monastic churches of Studenica, Sopoćani, Mileševa (thirteenth century) and Dečani (fourteenth century) (see Plate 152).

As elsewhere, the applied arts were in great vogue in South-Eastern and Eastern Europe. Illumination had pride of place in the production of manuscript books (Bulgaria, Russia) (see Plates 151 and 153). Made of gold, silver or bronze, flat-tipped and wire-bound bracelets, necklaces set with precious stones or decorated with cloisonné enamel, and encolpion crosses are among the artifacts found by archaeologists along the route taken by the Slavs towards the south. The development of silver mines in Bosnia subsequently boosted this type of artistic production, and the manufacture of luxury cloth became more widespread when Byzantium lost its monopoly of the production of silk in Europe after the twelfth century.

The nomadic tradition of tying decorations to the battle dress of warriors and to their cavalry horses was still alive in the ninth century in the Balkans. In this respect, the golden treasure of Nagy Szent Miklós (Kunsthistorisches Museum, Vienna) is of considerable artistic interest.

The popular culture of the Southern and Eastern Slavs is relatively poorly documented. Their rich folklore (songs, dances, musical instruments) forms an elaborate system of ideas concerning nature, society and humanity. In the Balkans, pre-Christian traditions (of Slavic origin) sometimes combined with throwbacks to Graeco-Roman or Thraco-Illyrian antiquity. Examples of such syncretism are the cult of Saint George, who in some areas resembles the Thracian Horseman, or various popular icons, in which Saint Elijah wielding his thunderbolt is strikingly reminiscent of the Slavic god of thunder, Perun.

BIBLIOGRAPHY

ALEKSOVA, B.; MANGO, C. 1971. Bargala: A Preliminary Report, *Dumbaron Oaks Papers*, 25, pp. 265–281.

BEŠEVLIEV, B. 1963. *Die protobulgarischen Inschriften*. Berlin.

CAIKANOVIĆ, N. 1973. *Mit i religia u Srba* [Myth and Religion among the Serbs] (in Serbian). Belgrade.

ČANEVA-DEČEVSKA, N. 1988. *Cŭrkovnata arcitektura v Bŭlgaria prez XI–XIV v.* [The Ecclesiastical Architecture in Bulgaria, XI–XIV s.] (in Bulgarian, with Russian and English abstracts). Sofia.

DŽUROVA, A. 1980. *1000 godini bŭlgarska rŭkopisna kniga* [A Thousand Years of Bulgarian Manuscript Books] (in Bulgarian, with German, English and Russian abstracts). Sofia.

GEORGIEVA, I. 1985. *Bulgarian Mythology*. Sofia.

GRABAR, A. 1967. *Die Kunst des frühen Christentums: Von den ersten Zeugnissen christlicher Kunst bis zur Zeit Theodosius I.* Munich.

HODINOTT, R. F. 1963. *Early Byzantine Churches in Macedonia and Southern Serbia*. London.

Istorija srpskog naroda [History of the Serbian People] (in Serbian), Vol. 1, pp. 230, 273–296, 408–433.

Istorija na bŭlgarskoto izobrazitelno izkustvo. 1976 [The History of Bulgarian Decorative Art] (in Bulgarian). Sofia, pp. 67, 101–103, 125, 209–265.

IVANOVA-MAVRODINOVA, V. 1967. *L'art et la culture du premier Etat bulgare*. Sofia.

KRAUTHEIMER, R.; ĆURČIĆ, S. 1986. *Early Christian and Byzantine Architecture*. Harmondsworth.

MARASOVIĆ, T. 1988. *The Byzantine Component in Dalmatian Architecture from the 11th to 13th Century*. Belgrade.

MAVRODINOV, N. 1959a. *Le Trésor de Nagy-Szent-Miklós*. Budapest.

——. 1959b. *Starobŭlgarskoto izkustvo* [Old Bulgarian Art] (in Bulgarian), Vol. I. Sofia, pp. 281–290.

MILLET, G. 1919. *L'ancien art serbe: Les Eglises.* Paris, pp. 41–46.

MOUTZOPOULOS, N. 1989. Byzantinische und nachbyzantinische Baudenkmäler aus Kleinprespa und aus Hl (German). In: *I basiliki tou hagiou Achilliou stin Prespa* [The Basilica of Saint Achilleus at Prespa] (in Greek and other languages) Thessaloniki, No. 4, pp. 259–307.

PURKOVIĆ, M. 1985. *Srpska kultura srednjega veka* [Serbian Culture in the Middle Ages]. Himmelstühr, pp. 80 *et seq.*

RADOJČIĆ, S. 1964. Prilozi najstarijeg Ohridskog slikarstva [Contributions of the Oldest Ohrid Painting] (German abstract available). *Recueil des travaux de l'Institut d'études byzantines.* Vol. VIII, No. 2, Belgrade, pp. 354–382.

RYBAKOV, A. 1982. *Kievskaja Rus' i russkie knjažestva, XII–XIIIdd* [Kievan Rus' and the Russian Principalities, Twelfth–Thirteenth Centuries]. Moscow, pp. 75 *et seq.*

STRIČEVIĆ, D. 1961. La rénovation du type basilical. *Actes du XIIe Congrès des études byzantines: Rapports.* Vol. VII, Ochrid, pp. 187 *et seq.*

TOKAREV, S. A. 1957. *Religioznije verovanija vostočnoslavjanskih narodov* [The Religious Beliefs of the Eastern Slavic Peoples] (in Russian). Moscow–Leningrad.

TOTEV, T. 1979. Icônes peintes en céramique de Tuzlălăka à Preslav. In: *Culture et art en Bulgarie.* Sofia, pp. 65–73.

VAKARELSKI, H. 1974. *Ethografia na Bŭlgaria* [Ethnographie of Bulgaria] (in Bulgarian). Sofia.

VAKLINOV, S. 1977. *Formirane na starobŭlgarskata kultura* [The Formation of Old Bulgarian Culture] (in Bulgarian with English, German, Russian and French abstracts). Sofia, pp. 79–166, 208–220.

ZUBAR, V. M.; PAVLENKO, J. V. 1978. *Chersones Tavričeskij* [The Tauric Chersonese] (in Russian). Kiev, pp. 69–76.

13

CENTRAL AND NORTHERN EUROPE

Lucien Musset

This vast area, in the earlier part of the Middle Ages, experienced widely different fortunes, and it was only from the eleventh and twelfth centuries that a common fate – that of progressive assimilation to the civilization of the West – began to bring the various parts closer to one another, although diversity nevertheless remained very much in evidence.

In the seventh century, nearly every one of these different parts was still at an extremely archaic stage of evolution. Writing was certainly known to a large number of the Germanic peoples (runes) but was very little used; a monetary economy was unknown (precious metals were appreciated for their weight, and especially as raw material for the art of the goldsmith); urban development was only faintly beginning to take shape, and forest zones (except on the Pannonian plain) still stretched over considerable expanses; political fragmentation remained the rule, with unstable formations hardly beyond the tribal stage. Only those few territories which had once been dependencies of the Roman Empire showed a little more progress, especially Bavaria and its neighbouring regions.

The various peoples who occupied Central and Northern Europe can hardly be fitted into any system of classification except according to linguistic criteria. To the north, Scandinavia, the Danish islands and Jutland were home to peoples who spoke a Nordic variety of Germanic (the extreme north, however, was partly populated by Lapps, whose language is akin to Finno-Ugric). The southern shores of the Baltic, from the Vistula to the neighbourhood of Kiel, and their hinterlands stretching even further south to the Carpathians and the middle reaches of the Danube, had just been occupied by various Slavic groups, who also spilled over as far as Bohemia and the eastern foothills of the Alps. The Pannonian plain had long been the region where semi-nomadic peoples, originating from Asia, had finally come to a halt, as was the case, in the seventh century, with the Avars. Finally, the northern slopes of the Alps were nearly everywhere occupied by Germanic peoples, speaking Westic dialects (although a few pockets of Romance speech did survive) (see Map 10).

Relatively stable monarchical structures probably already existed in a few parts of the Scandinavian world (as in central Sweden and the Danish islands) and among the Bavarians and the Avars. They emerged only somewhat later among the Slavs. Only the western fringes of Central Europe had truly organized states, that is, the Merovingian kingdoms, whose centre lay in Gaul, and Lombard Italy – but the influence of these had barely yet begun to make itself much felt further to the north and east. Thus Lower Saxony remained stubbornly recalcitrant to any such organization until the time of Charlemagne, although Thuringia and Bavaria did already clearly betray some of its effects.

Modifications to this equilibrium first came about as early as the seventh century as a result of the creation of less rudimentary formations among the Slavs of Central Europe. The most ancient known occurrence of this concerns Bohemia, around AD 625, when a Frankish subject, Samo, who had come as a merchant (perhaps dealing in slaves), began to organize those territories corresponding to modern Czechoslovakia while waging struggles against both the Avars and the Merovingians. But nothing else took shape before the second third of the ninth century, when other, less short-lived, constructions made their appearance, such as 'Greater Moravia' – based on a nobility with fortified castles. It was able to welcome, in 862, the first great Christian mission yet to reach the Slavs – that of the brothers Constantine and Methodius, who came from Thessaloniki after passing through Byzantium and then through Rome. Henceforth the Slavs of Central Europe were able to organize on foundations recognized as valid by such Westerners as the Carolingians and then the Ottonians, who came to accept them, as their conversion to Christianity spread, into a sort of 'brotherhood' of Christian monarchies.

Those Slavs who dwelt closest to the Baltic were not able to follow this same path until a considerable time later, although their social evolution had already made some headway, as shown by the existence of numerous urban settlements, especially in the basin of the Vistula. Here, at the end of the tenth century, there appeared a second area where a monarchy took shape around the family of the Piasts, amongst the Polans (Poland). Official conversion occurred around 990, and Prince Mieszko was recognized by both the Byzantine empire and the papacy. The regions further west, between the Oder and the Elbe, remained both much less organized and also stubbornly rebellious to Christian influences until the eleventh and even twelfth centuries.

Henceforth, the existence of crowns consecrated by the Church, religious sees (as at Gniezno in Poland), and political and matrimonial alliances between Western rulers and Slavic princes, ensured that these princes enjoyed a status of near equality with the rulers of the older Christian monarchies, even though most of them continued to be more or less obviously overshadowed by the Holy Roman Empire. A Christian art, with architecture in stone, symbolized this new

Map 10 Northern and Central Europe (draft Musset, L.).

situation, as did the adoption of Latin as the sole means of written expression (for the attempt to use Slavic dialects as Church languages failed in Central Europe). The fate of these populations thus sharply diverged from that of both the Slavs to the East and the majority of the Slavs in the Balkans.

The political collapse of the Avars (796) under a Frankish offensive, followed by the complete disappearance of this people, left a free zone on both banks of the middle Danube. Up-river as well as along the southern banks and as far as the eastern spurs of the Alps, the regions thus freed were occupied by Germans from Bavaria, who laid the foundations for what would become Austria. Down-river, the Pannonian plain, from 895 onwards, became home to a new steppe people of mostly Finno-Ugric (but also partially Turkic) stock, the Hungarians (Magyars), who finally came to a standstill in these parts at the end of the tenth century after terrorizing half of Europe with their cavalry raids. Their dynasty, the Arpadians, accepted baptism and received a royal crown from the pope in AD 1000, while an archbishop's see was established, shortly afterwards, at Esztergom on the

Danube. This people then settled down slowly to sedentary life. The Slavs of Central Europe in this way lost almost all contact with those in the Balkans.

The Balts, living between the delta of the Vistula and the Gulf of Finland, did not follow in the footsteps of the Slavs. Until the thirteenth century, they remained unfamiliar with even incipient political organization, and averse to any Christian penetration.

The Scandinavian world, from the close of the eighth century to the middle of the eleventh, experienced a remarkable phase of expansion and restructuring commonly known as the 'Viking age', since the raids of the Vikings (or 'seaborne pirates') were its most obvious manifestation in the eyes of Westerners. After a period of relative isolation from the sixth century onwards, the Scandinavians suddenly discovered, shortly before AD 800, that, lying beyond the seas, and without any overwhelming obstacles in their way, awaited all manner of wealth they might secure, thus allowing their chiefs, once home again, to assert their social superiority by surrounding themselves with dependants, buying land and enjoying conspicuous luxury. This new attitude was linked to considerable technical progress in both shipbuilding and navigational skills on the high seas, progress whose first stages are seen splendidly illustrated on the carved stelae found on the island of Gotland, in the central Baltic. The Scandinavinans now knew how to build large, undecked ships, propelled by both oar and sail, satisfactorily stable, very manoeuvrable both at sea and on rivers, and easy to beach without the need for a proper port. This was a type of craft which varied little before the twelfth century (see Plates 20, 165–167).

Simultaneously, in order to draw profit from the riches thus plundered from far and wide, trading posts grew up where booty, and slaves, could be exchanged for luxury products. Emporia of this kind already existed in several easily accessible sites, such as Helgö in Sweden, a little to the west of Stockholm. From the eighth century, these trading posts developed in a spectacular way, particularly Hedeby, lying on the Danish and German borderlands at the base of the Jutland peninsula; Ribe situated a little further north-west; and Birka on Lake Mälar, in central Sweden. Here, Christian and Muslim merchants willingly flocked, for fat profits could be made where a pre-monetary economy (that of Northern Europe) thus came into contact with monetary ones (those of the West and the Islamic world (see Plate 193c).

Launched at first as a result of individual initiatives, spurred on by local chiefs and recruiting their men from all over the North, the first Viking ventures appear to have been uncoordinated and launched without any pre-established plan. They were simply launched with an eye to taking advantage of whatever occasion happened to offer itself. Nevertheless, a few broad traits do emerge fairly clearly.

The Swedes sailed mainly to the eastern shores of the Baltic, then moving inland up the rivers, they discovered, beyond the tracts inhabited by Finns and Balts, those countries populated by Eastern Slavs. Beyond the confines of present-day Russia, they touched upon the fringes of both the Greek Empire and the Islamic world. The Swedes went as far as northern Iran, the Caucasus and Constantinople. Along the way, they managed to live, in more or less peaceful symbiosis, with the most varied peoples, and to find profitable employment as mercenaries or traders where they were not mere pirates.

The Danes showed relatively little interest in the lands lying to the east and south. Their momentum led them west, in the direction of the Frankish States (whose division considerably favoured their ventures) and of the Anglo-Saxon kingdoms (which were, however, able to put up a more effective resistance). Danish raids quickly took on the aspect of organized military expeditions, first on a seasonal basis, then several times a year, and their goal, over and above sheer booty, was first to extort tribute ('Danegeld'), and then finally to secure lands to be exploited for their own benefit, often after formal cessions.

The Norwegians operated in a far more scattered way, mostly sailing to the Celtic countries to the west and to the empty, or sparsely populated, lands of the North Atlantic – the Islands of Scotland, the Faeroe Isles, Iceland and, later, Greenland and the extreme north-eastern shores of North America, not forgetting such coasts as those of the White Sea beyond the North Cape. The Norwegians were not so much interested in commercial ventures as in colonizing territories overseas which would allow them to do a little farming and a great deal of cattle breeding, transhumant to a greater or lesser extent as in their own homelands. On occasions, but in no really systematic way, they pushed as far as both the Christian and Islamic shores of Spain, and on into the western Mediterranean.

How are we to account for what must have lain at the roots of this extraordinary dynamism, this almost unlimited expansion – even though it involved only very small numbers? Was there demographic pressure? This is hardly likely because except in a few odd districts, Scandinavia was then still very thinly populated. Was it because of some sort of religious fanaticism, as Western monks chose to believe? This is to be ruled out, since Norse cults were closely linked to their native soil and were difficult to export. More probably involved was a social structure where upward mobility always remained possible for those who struck it rich and could surround themselves with dependants by means of lavish gifts, buy slaves and lands, and so parade their wealth and experience. Sometimes there might, however, be added an ulterior political motive, as in Denmark, where the preoccupation was to avoid the fate which had befallen neighbouring Saxony, annexed by Charlemagne.

The 'first Viking age', which began soon after 780, ended in about the first third of the tenth century – after wreaking appalling havoc in both Gaul and England. A half-century lull followed, during which the North paused, as it were, to get its breath, enjoy its acquired wealth, consolidate its hold over conquered lands (in Russia, Normandy and northern England), learn the ways of money and so adapt to a new economic organization, and finally to make its first intellectual contacts with Christendom – very intermittently in the cases of Sweden and Norway, more intimately in Denmark, which alone in this age showed the beginnings of monarchy.

Between 980 and roughly 1066, there occurred a 'second Viking age', which affected a more restricted area and was mainly the work of the Danes. The Danes managed to conquer England temporarily with Canute, and so founded a sort of empire straddling the North Sea, although they failed to spread their power to Norway. They came up against the rivalry of still another Scandinavian power, that of Normandy. In the meantime, Anglo-Danish circles maintained their grip over English society, and thus transmitted to the Nordic world a host of fertile ideas (institutional ones in the main) while playing a decisive role in the conversion of the North to Christianity.

From these events, Northern Europe emerged transformed, with monarchies of varying solidity and a network of towns, acknowledging allegiance to the Latin Church, using money, and ready gradually to adopt the main features of Western civilization. The pace of this process differed widely depending on the country. It began in Denmark, followed with some delay by Norway, and much later still by Sweden – but nowhere did it result in total assimilation. Throughout the Middle Ages, Norwegian circles (both in Norway itself and especially in Iceland) preserved an autonomous culture, based on widespread use of their national language alongside Latin, and all three countries kept an original system of law, close in spirit to the Germanic legal codes which had prevailed in the Merovingian age. This legal system left the bulk of judicial and legislative powers to hierarchically organized assemblies (*ting*) at the level of district, province, or kingdom, and this regime everywhere lasted until at least the thirteenth century. However, while the language in the tenth century had still been more or less uniform, it broke up into widely diverging strains from the thirteenth so that it rapidly became impossible for Scandinavians to understand one another.

Denmark, which turned its back on any further expansion beyond the North Sea in the closing decades of the eleventh century, underwent profound reorganization. Several of its towns, all of them bishops' sees, began to play a decisive economic and administrative role – thus Ribe and Aarhus on Jutland; Roskilde on the isle of Sjaelland; and Lund in Scania. Aristocratic houses with extensive lands established themselves in positions of authority. The monarchy, stabilized as a dynasty, found support in the Church and imposed its authority, taking advantage of its monopoly of minting coins and of its very ancient right to muster the country's naval forces, a right which no doubt took on systematic form as a result of the influence of Anglo-Saxon institutions. To be sure, conflicts between members of the royal family were many, and bloody. The grandees sometimes reacted with very great violence and soon began to build castles on the Western model – yet royal predominance always ultimately prevailed after each bout of civil war. Rural shrines and dressed-stone cathedrals multiplied, bearing witness to very real prosperity. At the close of the twelfth century, Denmark was a regularly organized monarchy, in every way comparable to those of the West, even though still lacking a fixed capital.

The reign of Valdemar the Great (1157–1189) marks a kind of high-point in this regard. Valdemar consolidated the defences of his kingdom, sealed an alliance with the Church, which proceeded to canonize his father, undertook a kind of crusade against the Slavs on the island of Rügen and in Pomerania, and began to encourage a brilliant culture expressed in Latin, a culture symbolized soon after by the writing of a national history, drawing on both classical tradition and the Nordic legacy, by the cleric Saxo Grammaticus (shortly after 1200). An archbishop's see had been set up in Lund in 1103, with initial supremacy over all of Scandinavia. It enjoyed outstanding lustre, particularly under Absalom, its archbishop from 1178 to 1201. Absalom, a person as gifted in intellectual as in political matters, understood the importance of the site which commanded the Straits and so founded there the future capital, Copenhagen. He began to send large numbers of students to the schools in Paris and took up arms against the pagan Slavs. Enormous profit was derived from the fisheries in Scania and the trade fair resulting from them.

Norway had been hard put to it to effect its unification in the last years of the ninth century along a coastal roadway (the country's name means 'North Way') and around a dynasty originating from the area around Oslo Fjord. These results were challenged both by local chiefs (especially by those in the North) and by the Danish kings (who were attempting to establish their protectorate over the south). Finally, after much fighting, the saint-king, Olaf (1016–1030), a former Viking, imposed a return to unity as well as Latin Christianity, although civil wars between royal pretenders were a feature of the eleventh and twelfth centuries. Nevertheless, a number of towns came into being: Oslo, Bergen and Trondheim. These became bishops' sees, and the latter had its own archbishop in 1152 after the visit of an English legate, who profoundly reformed the local Church. Norwegian influence slowly waned in the Scottish islands, the Viking spirit giving way to that of the Crusades. King Sigurd thus went to Palestine as early as 1109. Latin civilization here reached its peak at the end of the twelfth and the beginning of the thirteenth centuries, along with that of Iceland. A highly original form of wooden architecture prevailed in rural areas, while the towns saw an influx of merchant colonies, mostly German, interested in the trade in fish, wood and butter. Nevertheless, the country remained basically rural and seafaring (see Plate 168).

Sweden experienced a slower and more complex evolution. Its various populations – the *Svear* around Lake Mälar, the *Götar* further to the south, and finally the inhabitants of Gotland – belonged to different traditions. Conversion was far from over at the close of the eleventh century, and dynasties remained unstable until the middle of the thirteenth. The towns took a long time to emerge from the models of the Viking age. Uppsala did not have an archbishopric until 1164, while Stockholm did not exist until the last third of the thirteenth century. Expansionist traditions long continued to draw Swedes eastwards. At the end of the thirteenth century, they began colonizing the coastal islands and shores of Finland and several districts of Estonia. The conversion of the Finns came about only in the thirteenth century, but competition from the Russians made itself felt here (Carelia had to be yielded to them), and also from the Danes (in the northern third of Estonia). Finally, there was the German thrust, in the form of the two military orders, the Teutonic Knights and the Knights of the Sword, who conquered the approaches to the Gulf of Riga. In the meantime, Swedish supremacy became established throughout the northern part of the Baltic zone, while the discovery of mining potential – with iron and copper – brought the kingdom an obvious prosperity that attracted merchants to its towns.

Shortly afterwards, the Scandinavian world was rent asunder by disputes of a new kind between opposing views of the relation between crown and Church, between immigrants and native populations and between the increasingly feudally minded leaders of the aristocracy and the traditionalists prevailing in rural areas. New military techniques came into use after 1134, and it was now knights and mercenaries, often German, who made up the nucleus of the armed forces. The nobility began fortifying its residences. Each country reacted in its own way. The monarchy emerged ultimately consolidated in Denmark and Sweden but very nearly ruined in Norway, whose ancient dependencies lost their autonomy (as did Iceland in 1264). Old rights gradually vanished. Architecture was renewed, with the now widespread use, especially in the towns, of a building material learned from frequenting the routes of the South: brick. In summary, the second half of the Middle Ages differed profoundly from the first.

We are most familiar with the struggles between the aristocratic bishops and the crown. In Denmark, these clashes led to tragic consequences in the closing years of the thirteenth century. Hundreds of people were banished, the kings had to yield a large proportion of their resources to German lords, mostly from Holstein, and outright anarchy prevailed at the beginning of the fourteenth century. In Norway, King Sverre (1177–1202), whose right to the throne was dubious, managed to assert himself against the supporters of the bishops. His descendants in the thirteenth century managed to build up a solid and distinguished monarchy, steeped in English and French culture, which attracted merchants to its capital cities, Bergen and then Oslo. These kings framed a body of legislation which left considerable scope to the Church. At the end of the thirteenth century, however, a crisis, both political and economic, ruined the country. Norway was reduced to obtaining its supplies of grain from northern Germany and became dependent on the cities of the Hanseatic League, particularly Lübeck, while its aristocracy drew ever closer to that of Denmark.

In Sweden, the new dynasty of the Folkungar strengthened its position and completed the conquest of Finland. The towns developed, and mining activities played an increasingly important role. However, unrest grew at the end of the twelfth century, while the landed aristocracy seized the reins of power. German colonies proved more welcome here, especially on the island of Gotland, which was incorporated to a greater or lesser extent into the Germanic Hanseatic League and enjoyed extreme prosperity, as evidenced by the fortifications in Gotland's capital, Visby, and by the construction of a hundred or so stone churches adorned with frescoes and stained glass. Gotland in fact lay at the end of the trade route with Russia (Novgorod). Although it came late to acknowledging Christian ideals (slavery was not outlawed there until 1335), Sweden did provide the Catholic Church with one outstanding personality – Saint Bridget (1303–1337), the founder of the only religious Order to have originated in Scandinavia (see Plate 175).

The condition of the rural population worsened everywhere. The kings' permanent financial straits, the strengthening of the military feudal order, civil wars and epidemics took their toll by reducing the former peasantry to a state of dependency bordering in some cases (as in Denmark) on servitude. On the other hand, the ruling classes, increasingly infiltrated as they were by German immigrants, organized and became powerful. They adopted Western ideas and provided the driving force behind the state councils, which, by the end of the thirteenth century, had become the main organs of government. Crown officers and landed grandees in the fourteenth century formed a 'council of the realm' and seized the reins of political power. Finally, Scandinavia took the first steps towards achieving a measure of intellectual autonomy, since universities came into being at much the same time (1477–1478) in Uppsala and Copenhagen, although their influence long remained very restricted and their links with the German universities were strong.

As did other European regions, Scandinavia at the end of the Middle Ages experienced a powerful drive towards unification, favoured by dynastic circumstances and by the converging interests of the ruling classes. This was the 'time of unions', begun in 1319 between Sweden and Norway, then taken up with its own interests in view by the Danish crown after its own house had been vigorously put in order under King Valdemar Atterdag (1340–1385). After a complicated series of events, union was officially sealed between all three kingdoms at Kalmar in 1397, to the benefit of the Queen-Regent Margrete I. This union, which never really took effect since nationalities, state 'councils' and armed forces remained distinct, functioned mostly to the greater profit of Denmark, the richest of the three, which took great advantage of Norway's obvious decline.

Sweden, whose economy was developing rapidly, very soon showed considerable hesitation about the union. Blunders committed by the union's second ruler, Eric of Pomerania, provoked a first general uprising in 1434. This insurgency failed, but others broke out in every succeeding generation until Sweden finally recovered its independence in all essentials in 1471, although at first without providing itself with a stable dynasty. Denmark's king then tried to wrest the country back in 1520 by violent means ('the Stockholm bloodbath'), but had to give up the attempt. Sweden fully recovered its freedom under the kings of the Vasa family.

The consequences of these unions varied widely. To begin with, virulent political hostility between Denmark and Sweden lasted until the nineteenth century, but an enduring link forged between Denmark and Norway survived until 1814, as did the link with Norway's former dependencies (into the twentieth century). Norway indeed almost lost its national language in favour of Danish, and it did not revive (and even then rather artificially) until the nineteenth century. Nevertheless, because of the unions, Scandinavia as a whole reacted similarly when, in the sixteenth century, the problem of the Reformation arose. Despite their profound differences, the Scandinavian lands unanimously welcomed the Reformation in its Lutheran form and rejected the Catholic tradition.

Developments in Central Europe also proceeded apace after AD 1000, although along very different paths. A large portion of this region fell within the orbit of the Holy Roman Empire and so was subject to a process of colonization which resulted in the Germanization of wide areas. The organization of the rest revolved around three poles – Poland, Bohemia and Hungary – which themselves drew less solid bodies such as Lithuania into their orbit. The end of the Middle Ages witnessed here a yearning for political unification similar to that in Scandinavia (and in the Iberian peninsula). There were really lasting consequences only in Poland and Lithuania, which, until the end of the eighteenth century, formed a single state, although only in dynastic terms. Union failed between Poland and Hungary and touched only glancingly on Bohemia. Economic and social processes did not bring about enduring ties. The Germanic world sometimes played the role of a screen, and sometimes that of a transmission belt, between Western and Southern Europe on the one hand, and Central Europe on the other, very nearly to the exclusion of all other forms of influence. Here too, the towns, and the aristocracy, provided the main channels for German imports.

Among the Poles, who were united by Mieszko I at the end of the tenth century, there rapidly grew up a state which grouped the various tribes around a 'little Poland'. This Polish state did not include the lands between the Oder and the Elbe, which were also exposed along the coast to Scandinavian influences, but it contended with Bohemia for control over its southern reaches. Poland's Slavic neighbours to the west, who had remained staunch pagans, formed a barrier and for a long time prevented some of the German pressures from making themselves fully felt, so allowing the Piast state to preserve considerable autonomy in the face of the Holy Roman Empire. A new art developed in Poland with stone churches in the towns, influenced partly by the legacy of

Greater Moravia and partly by the examples of Ottonian Germany. As in Bohemia, many Polish churches were at first circular in plan, but the basilical form finally became more common. The Church's autonomy was organized around the archbishop's see at Gniezno, founded in AD 1000 by Boleslas I with Emperor Otto III's permission. Latin culture was gradually adopted, although one that followed original paths.

Further south, Bohemia, since the close of the ninth century, had replaced Greater Moravia as the centre of political gravity for the Central European Slavs. Moravia and Silesia were Bohemian dependencies. Bohemia's chiefs, the Prémyslids, had occasionally adopted the royal title since 1085 (and were to do so permanently after 1212), but from 1004, the country was formally incorporated into the Holy Roman Empire. The Bohemian Church, after being briefly attached to the Bavarian see at Ratisbon, secured its own bishop's see at Prague in 973 (and a second one for Moravia at Olomouc in 975). Ecclesiastical foundations multiplied after the middle of the eleventh century, and the culture which developed here expressed itself in writing in Latin alone. The Slavic dioceses remained attached to the German archbishop's see at Mainz.

The regions between the Oder and the Elbe, however, failed to organize politically. Divided as they were among many tribes, from the tenth century onwards they were the target of attempts at political and religious conquest on the part of Germany and also, along the coast, from Denmark. The tribes' rejection of Christian missions ultimately resulted, in the twelfth century, in outright crusades waged against them, the first being launched in 1107 and the main one in 1147. Finally, although a number of chiefs did manage to preserve part of their authority after their conversion, most of the country was subjected to, and administered by, Germans, especially Saxons and Westphalians. A network of new towns grew up along the Baltic coasts and the main routes leading east. The economic way of life inaugurated by their burghers, who were in the main German, was based on exports of grain and imports of manufactured goods. This was one of the reasons for the existence of the Hanseatic League, a federation of merchant towns. Nevertheless, a Slavic peasantry managed to survive here and there, in small pockets of varying compactness, until the eighteenth century along the middle reaches of the Elbe, and down to our own day around Lausitz.

Hungary evolved along parallel lines. It still offered shelter to, and assimilated, the scattered remnants of various steppe peoples who had wandered westwards (such as the Petchenegs at the end of the eleventh century and the Kumans in the twelfth). The outstanding issue here was first the settling down of the Magyars to a sedentary form of life, then their acceptance of a Christian and Latin form of civilization. Decisive stages were a defeat at the hands of the Germans in 955 at Lechfeld near Augsburg, then the securing of a royal crown by Stephen in 1000 and the organization of a Church. The full triumph of these new ways had to wait, however, until the last third of the eleventh century. Only the western fringes of the Pannonian basin were lost to German colonization. Elsewhere, German immigration affected only the towns and, somewhat later, the mining areas in the mountain ranges around Hungary (Slovakia and Transylvania). The ethnic make-up of the kingdom remained very much mixed. Besides Hungarians and Germans, there were Slavs, numerous both in the north (Slovaks) and in the south (Croats), as well as Latins (Romanians) in Transylvania. The dominant element, however, was still Magyar.

The gradual build-up of Poland around two unified nuclei, that of the Polans along the middle Vistula, and that of the Vislans in the area of Cracow, came about through the sovereigns of the Piast dynasty. These were energetically supported by their own armed forces and ruled from Cracow. They set members of their family over the country's regional dukedoms but in the twelfth century were forced to sustain struggles against the heads of aristocratic clans with bases in strongly fortified towns. Assemblies regulated the lives of the local communities. The country's princes assumed royal titles on a regular basis only after the middle of the twelfth century. Their dependence upon the Holy Roman Empire was rarely made clear, but Poland's membership of the Latin Church did take root and the kingdom even sent out its own missions – albeit with little success – to its Baltic neighbours.

In the meantime, German pressure increased in the western territories and along the coasts, while in the north, the Order of Teutonic Knights established itself in Prussia. In 1241, the appearance of Mongol armies who had crossed the expanses of Russia began to raise formidable problems. The still pagan Lithuanians imposed themselves as a dangerous power. Crisis threatened everywhere. The monarchy nevertheless recovered its strength, although with the extinction of the national dynasty, Bohemia's kings secured the Polish throne at the outset of the fourteenth century. Like Bohemia, Poland briefly acknowledged the rule of an Angevin family – actually an Italian branch of the Capetians – between 1370 and 1386. After this particular interlude, the Polish aristocracy thought it wiser to make an alliance with the Lithuanian state against the Teutonic Knights, provided that the Lithuanians accepted Christianity. This they did, officially, in 1385. Union under the new dynasty of the Jagiellons proved effective. The Teutonic Knights were defeated and permanently restricted to East Prussia (battle of Grünwald or Tannenberg, 1410).

Poland and Lithuania thus formed a union based on personal ties but solid enough to spread across a considerable sweep of territory, the eastern limits of which nevertheless remained somewhat ill-defined. At one point, this union even managed to include Bohemia and Hungary, although these latter additions were rather artificial affairs with few lasting consequences. They remained quite distinct national entities. Hence only the alliance between Poland and Lithuania proved durable, and it underwent further consolidation in the sixteenth century (the Union of Lublin in 1505) under a king who was no longer hereditary but elected. The rural nobility (*szlachta*) arrogated to itself many powers, wielded by means of 'diets', whence the curious 'noblemen's democracy' which would so stamp the sixteenth and seventeenth centuries. The towns, many of which adopted German legislation (from Lübeck and especially Magdeburg), evolved a way of life that more and more came to resemble that of the Germanic world, even though a culture in the national language did flourish in the course of the fifteenth century. Cracow received its university in 1364. Many Jews, driven out at this time from Western Europe, found shelter on Polish soil. On the whole, a power of the first order seemed to be on the rise, but one which would have to deal with a Turkish threat to the south and then with Russian competition to the east (see Plate 176).

Bohemia also saw its German population make considerable progress along its western and southern fringes, in the mining regions and in the main towns. The Slavic element reacted strongly, although the national dynasty of the Prémyslids died out in 1306 and the crown was then disputed for many years between the Houses of Habsburg and Luxembourg. Under the latter, the country enjoyed great prosperity, even though the policy of these rulers was more concerned with acquiring prestige and imposing their sovereignty over external lands lying between Poland and the Holy Roman Empire. The founding of the University of Prague (1348), which rapidly exerted considerable influence, marked an essential stage in the country's intellectual development. There was an intense ferment of ideas in the theological field, especially among the Czechs (see Plate 61).

This was the context in which there appeared, in the early years of the fifteenth century, a highly original thinker (although he was influenced by ideas much akin to those of the Englishman John Wycliffe) – Jan Hus. Hus demanded a reform of the Church and resort to the Gospels as the main source of faith – a true precursor of Protestantism. Repeatedly condemned by the religious hierarchy, but supported by the Czech population, Jan Hus was finally excommunicated (1411), hauled before the Church Council at Constance, and executed (1415). The majority of Bohemian Slavs held him to be a martyr and rose up in a mass in support of his ideas – notably that of communion for all – often pushing theological speculation to very bold limits. An outright war of religion broke out in which the Czechs showed considerable mettle, zeal and indeed fanaticism. Their armed bands long held the princes and crusaders at bay, and launched raids deep into eastern Germany (as far as the Baltic), Moravia and Hungary. Divisions nevertheless appeared among the extremists, and then a measure of understanding was reached with Rome. After the extreme violence of these struggles, the country was left practically ruined. Violent unrest had lasted here for more than two generations. After this, Bohemia temporarily passed under the sovereignty of the Polish–Lithuanian dynasty of the Jagiellons (1471).

In Hungary, once the Mongol threat in the thirteenth century had ebbed, the main political problems resulted from the dying out of the national dynasty of the Arpadians at the end of the fourteenth century. The Angevin kings reorganized the state, which henceforth had a stable capital in Buda, an aristocracy of 'magnates' and nobles who found expression in an assembly ('diet'), where the language they used was Latin, and a well-enough structured local administration made up of 'comitats'. Civilization in the towns and particularly in Buda – which boasted its own university by 1389 – was distinguished and easily on a par with Western standards, although the traces that it might have left behind were later largely wiped out by the Ottoman conquest. Hungarian missionaries played their part in the policy of Catholic expansion towards Asia. The crown attempted to establish itself firmly over the Slavic lands along the Adriatic coast (Croatia and Dalmatia), widened its contacts with Italy, and at a very early date received the first rays of the dawning Renaissance. The Hungarian monarchy shone under its national princes of the fifteenth century (John Hunyadi, Mathias Corvinus), but already the Ottoman Turks were closing in on the country's southern borders around 1440. Nothing overcame this threat, despite numerous attempted counter-attacks in the Balkans, and repeated calls for solidarity to be shown by Western Christians.

BIBLIOGRAPHY

CAMPBELL, J. G. 1980. *The Viking World*. London.

DVORNIK, F. 1949 *The Making of Central and Eastern Europe*. London.

FASOLI, G. 1945. *Le incorsioni ungare in Europa nel secolo X*. Florence.

GIEYSZTOR, A. 1961. Recherches sur les fondements de la Pologne médiévale. Etat actuel des problèmes, In: *Acta Poloniae Historica*, IV, pp. 7–33.

GRAUS, F. 1986. *Die Nationenbildung der Westslawen im Mittelalter*. Sigmaringen.

GRAUS, F; LUDAT, H. 1967. *Siedlung und Verfassung Böhmens in der Frühzeit*. Wiesbaden.

HENSEL, W. 1960. *Les origines de l'état polonais*. Warsaw.

HOMAN, B. 1940. *Geschichte des ungarischen Mittelalters*. Berlin.

MUSSET, L. 1961. *Les peuples scandinaves au Moyen Âge*. Paris.

——. 1971. *Les invasions. Le second assaut contre l'Europe chrétienne*. Paris.

ROESDAHL, E. 1989. *Vikingernes verden. Vikingerne hjemme og ude*, 3rd edn. Copenhagen.

Settimane di studio del centro italiano di studi sull'alto medioevo XVI, i normanni e la loro espansione in Europa nell'alto medioevo. 1969. Split.

Settimane di studio del centro italiano di studi sull'alto medioevo XXX. Gli slavi occidentali e meridionali nell'alto medioevo. 1983. Split.

14

THE EXPANSION OF EUROPEAN INFLUENCE

José-Luis Martín Rodríguez

EUROPEAN CULTURAL DEVELOPMENT: SCHOOLS OF TRANSLATORS, AND CO-OPERATION BETWEEN MUSLIMS, CHRISTIANS AND JEWS

Coexistence in the Iberian peninsula and in southern Italy between Christians and Muslims made these areas into cultural intermediaries between East and West from the tenth century. A number of Christian monasteries in the north of the peninsula were then already familiar with the Indian numerical system as this had been spread by an Arabic-writing mathematician of Persian origin, Al-Khwārizmī (d. *c.* 846), in a book of which a Latin version has been preserved, in Toledo, under the title *Algorithmi de Numero Indorum*. During these same years, several technical innovations also reached Europe such as the windmill, the means for the conservation of snow, the drawing off of water from beneath river beds, the lateen sail and paper, which was manufactured in Turkestan as early as the eighth century AD and known by the early tenth century in Tunis, whence its use spread to Sicily and southern Italy at the same time as it became known in Spain – where paper was already being used for various works written in the middle of the tenth century in several northern Spanish monasteries.

Along with these technical innovations, the Arabs introduced texts on mathematical and astronomical subjects to Europe, which were being translated into Latin at a very early date. One such instance was the writings conveyed to the Catalan monastery of Ripoll by monks who had fled Cordova, and of whose content and circulation we are informed through the biography of Gerbert d'Aurillac, a monk whose life history was literally transformed when Count Borrell of Barcelona paid a visit to his monastic community in 967. The monastery's abbot asked the count if the 'liberal arts' were known in his domains, and on being answered in the affirmative, begged the nobleman to take his monk Gerbert back with him to Catalonia. Thus Gerbert was able to study mathematics there with diligence and in great depth, according to his disciple and biographer, Richer, who also describes how Gerbert accompanied the count three years later to Rome in a visit which happened to coincide with that of the Holy Roman Emperor Otto I, who marvelled in turn at the monk's knowledge of music and astronomy, and attached him to his own person. In time, Gerbert rose to become pope under the name of Sylvester II, but above all, he became famous for his learning in arithmetic, geometry, music, medicine and astronomy, studied by means of the translations from Arabic into Latin done in Spain and Italy, and either copied by – or transcribed on the orders of – Gerbert himself, whose passion for books appears clearly enough in his letters like those sent to the Abbot of St Julien in Tours, or to the monk Rainardo of Bobbio, from whom he requested works on astrology, rhetoric and optics.

Translations and translators

While the most important stages in the spread of Arabic learning throughout Europe certainly occured in the twelfth and thirteenth centuries, one may still speak of the existence of a specialized school of translators in Cordova as early as the tenth century. This may be inferred from an account, by the Cordovan Muslim historian Ibn Juljul, concerning the 'fate' of the book known as the *De Materia Medica* of Dioscorides (see Plates 126, 130). This work was first translated in the ninth century from the Greek into Arabic, in Baghdād, by Stephen the Greek, then further revised by the Nestorian Christian Arab Ḥunayn ibn Isḥāq – although in both cases in rather incomplete form, since neither the Greek nor the Arab translator was sufficiently familiar with the pertinent technical vocabulary and left many words in their original Greek, failing to discover exact equivalents in Arabic. This, however, was the translation used throughout the Islamic world until 948, when the Byzantine emperor sent the caliph of Cordova numerous gifts, among which was a copy of the treatise of Dioscorides in its original Greek and the *Historia Adversus Paganos of Orosius* in its original Latin. To these gifts, the Byzantine emperor added a note reminding the recipient of the need for a translator who should also be versed in medical lore if full profit were to be derived from the work of Dioscorides. Three years later, at the caliph's request, the Eastern Roman emperor this time sent the monk Nicholas, proficient in both Latin and Greek, to Cordova, where he immediately made contact with a group of local physicians, including the Jewish doctor Ḥasday ibn Shaprūt. These men were extremely interested in learning what the text of Dioscorides had to offer. With the co-operation of such specialists, it proved possible to render the Greek work fully into Arabic without making mistakes or leaving any words untranslated, except for a few minor cases.

The system of translation used did not differ much from that followed in the Islamic East since the early Muslim centuries. This system required collecting the largest possible number of versions in order to settle upon a critical text, and so offer the most suitable translation. The caliphs took pains to collect written works through either purchases or exchanges of gifts, or as demands for tribute – or spoils of war – in the form of books surrendered to enrich the libraries of Islam. Not all these translations were correct, since although the most suitable translator was sought, he would occasionally delegate his work to persons less skilled than himself, or who were unfamiliar with the material to be rendered. In some cases, two individuals revised a single work, one of them reading the translation and the other the original version. Frequently, the same work might be retranslated several times over, as we learn from the above-mentioned Ḥunayn ibn Isḥāq, who tells us what happened with the text known as the *Book of Sects* by the Greek physician Galen. This had first been rendered into Syriac by an inferior translator, then revised by Ḥunayn ibn Isḥāq himself at the age of twenty, who based his revision on a Greek manuscript of poor quality then in his possession. Many years later, however, once Ḥunayn had access to several better Greek manuscripts, he was able to establish a sounder text, and so compare this with the older Syriac version and thereby correct it, and then further render this improved Syriac reading into Arabic in turn. Often enough, as in this case, resort would have to be made to an intermediate language, as with Syriac in the East, but it could be Spanish Romance in the West, whence the references to teams of translators, that is, groups of men involved in translating first from Arabic into Spanish Romance, and thence into Latin.

The Jews as spreaders of Islamic culture

Spanish Jewish culture was strongly influenced by that of the Muslims and reached its maturity under the so-called 'taifas kings', that is, under the Spanish Muslim princelings who rose to power in the wake of the disintegration of the caliphate of Cordova in the early eleventh century. The taifas kings welcomed the Jews to their courts as administrators and officials while tolerating – if not indeed encouraging – manifestations of Hebrew culture in their small kingdoms of Grenada, Zaragoza, Valencia, Denia and Badajoz. The grammatical and philological studies undertaken at this time revealed the basic grammatical and philological laws of the Hebrew language and contributed to the purification of literary Hebrew. Translated into Latin, these studies were the source from which the Renaissance scholars, in turn, learned their Hebrew.

The second generation began their lives in Islamic lands and moved to Christian territories when Al-Andalus (the southern part of Spain, then under Islamic rule) came under the occupation of the North African Almoravid dynasty. Moses ben Ezra (1055–1135), who acknowledged ties of friendship and co-operation with Muslim scholars in Granada, was thus forced to seek refuge in Castile, from where he moved on to Navarre and Aragon before finally settling in Barcelona. To this scholar is attributed one of the golden rules of translation: to concentrate on the meaning and not render literally, since languages do not have identical syntax. The third generation carried on its work entirely within the Christian kingdoms, whence both Hebrew and Islamic culture spread throughout Europe thanks to the labours of such men as Moshe Sefardi, Abraham ben Ezra, and Yehuda ben Tibbon and his son Samuel.

Moshe Sefardi, who upon his conversion to Christianity took the name of Petrus Alphonsus or Pedro Alfonso (Chaucer's 'Piers Alfonce'), became personal physician to King Henry I of England and was the first person to make Arabic astronomy and mathematics known in Northern Europe. His efforts to spread culture induced numerous Europeans to travel to Spain in order to make contact with those sciences, which other Jews were already spreading among the Hebrew communities in southern France. Thus Abraham ben Ezra of Tudela (1092–1167) travelled between 1140 and 1167 through the main cities of Italy, France and England, teaching Spanish–Arabic learning and writing numerous works on matters philosophical, grammatical, mathematical and astronomical, in both Hebrew and Latin. Yehuda ben Tibbon (1120–1190) was born in Grenada and died in Marseilles. He became known as the 'Father of Translators' on account of his work and also that of his sons, who translated works on philosophical subjects (including those written by Spanish Jews in Arabic) and on grammar and religion. One of his nephews eventually came to teach in the Faculty of Medicine in Montpellier, while another member of his family translated into Hebrew and into Latin the works of Averröes and Aristotle, in addition to many other scientific treatises for the German Emperor Frederick II (see Plates 76, 133).

The schools of translators

The presence in Spain of Mozarabs (Christians who had experienced Islamic rule) and Jews, who could both speak and read Arabic and who were thus able to transmit the knowledge which had come to Al-Andalus from the East, was brought into sharp focus at the beginning of the twelfth century by various Muslim writers, who recommended that books on scientific matters should not be sold to Jews or Christians, since these would then translate them and attribute their authorship not to Muslims but to members of their own creeds – or else leave out the names of the authors altogether, as can actually be seen in the case of a number of manuscripts preserved in monasteries in northern Spain.

During these same years, the Jewish convert Petrus Alphonsus was writing, in Latin, his *Disciplina Clericalis*, a collection of moral fables of Eastern origin which came to be very widely circulated throughout Europe. Meanwhile, in Tarazona, under the authority of Bishop Michael (1119–1152), a true school of translators was at work whose most important representative was Hugo Sanctallensis. Here works on astronomy, mathematics, astrology, alchemy and philosophy were translated. Nor were translations lacking of the Qur'ān itself, as the efforts of Peter the Venerable, Abbot of Cluny, bear witness. Determined to carry on the struggle against Islam on ideological grounds but unable to do so because he did not know what it taught, he sought out and paid for specialists in the Arabic language, who, advised by a Muslim translated the Qur'ān into Latin. We have the names of these translators: Robert of Ketton, Hermann of Dalmatia, Peter of Toledo and Muḥammad 'the Saracen'.

The coexistence in Toledo, after the Christian capture of the city in 1085, of Muslims, Jews, and Mozarabs and other Christians (both Spanish and non-Spanish), quickened the pace of translation, although not to the point of resulting in an actual school or body of translators, as is sometimes claimed. Translations were carried out in Toledo because in this city were preserved a large number of works, because cultured Mozarabs and Jews continued to flock there, having been expelled from southern Spain by the Almoravid rulers or their successors, the Almohad caliphs, and because Toledo's own archbishops favoured and encouraged the translators. These included the above-mentioned collaborators of Peter the Venerable, to whom we owe numerous translations of works on astronomy, alchemy, algebra and astrology. There was also John of Seville, the author of more than thirty-seven translations and original works. On some occasions, the translators worked as teams, as was the case with the cleric Dominicus Gundissalvus (Domingo Gundisalvo) and his partner Avendauth (Ibn Dāwud), a convert from Judaism, with their renditions of the Arabic philosophers.

In the second half of the twelfth century, Gerard of Cremona was working in Toledo, and translations continued into the thirteenth century there with Marcus of Toledo, the Italian Plato of Tivoli, Rudolph of Bruges and the Englishman Michael Scot. During his reign, King Alfonso X of Castile encouraged translation work there into both Latin and Castilian, while in Burgos, Bishop García Gudiel (1273–1280), with the Christian Juan González and Solomon the Jew, continued to translate Avicenna; then all three men pursued their labours in Toledo when García was appointed Archbishop there (1280–1299). The fame then enjoyed by Islamic science has been thrown into sharp relief by one translator, Daniel of Morley, who relates how he left his native England in search of wider knowledge and so moved to Paris, where, however, he says he found only 'fatuous windbags' for teachers. Therefore, being aware that in Toledo the scientific learning of the Arabs was then being taught, he at once hurried there to learn from the best scholars in the world. To conclude this account, we shall just call to mind how one particular Arabic work was translated into Castilian, Latin and French, and so could have come to the knowledge of Dante and provide a thematic basis for *The Divine Comedy*. This Arabic text, in its Latin version known as the *Liber Scalae* or 'Book of the Ladder', was a collection of legends pertaining to the other-worldly journey made to Hell and Heaven by the Prophet Muḥammad. This was translated into Castilian for King Alfonso X before 1264, and Bonaventure of Siena later translated it into Latin and French, in either of which versions it could have been known to Dante (see Plate 180).

According to Vernet, 47 per cent of the works translated into Latin, and so known to Europe, dealt with what we might call the exact sciences (mathematics, astronomy and astrology), philosophical texts accounted for 21 per cent; medical subjects for 20 per cent; and the occult sciences (geomancy and alchemy) for 4 per cent. The rest were works on religion and physics. The Latin translators ignored strictly philological and literary works, which, however, were carefully studied and translated by the Jews, perhaps because of the close linguistic affinity between Hebrew and Arabic.

EXPANSION TOWARDS THE EAST: MILITARY ORDERS AND THE CRUSADES; MEDITERRANEAN COMMERCE AND THE MARITIME REPUBLICS; TRAVELLERS AND DIPLOMATS

European history from the close of the eleventh century to the second half of the thirteenth gravitates around the Crusades, the campaigns launched from the West in order to recapture the Holy Law for Christendom and ensure its links with Europe. But any survey of these expeditions calls first for look, however brief, at the situation in both Europe and the Eastern world.

The European world, Byzantium and the Islamic East

From AD 1000, improved climatic conditions, internal peace and the modernization of agricultural techniques brought about a considerable increase in production and productivity and an increase in population. The excess population moved into the cities or sought new areas in which to settle outside Europe, as can be seen in the German drives to the East, the Spanish *Reconquista* or some of the first Crusades. The participants here were peasants down on their luck or the younger sons of the nobility who could not accept the role allotted to them by a society where a monetary and commercial economy was becoming increasingly important. Control over long-distance trade was basically in the hands of Venice and Genoa, and this led these two Italian cities to co-operate actively in the undertaking of the Crusades, with the aim of securing privileges or territorial enclaves in order to maintain their commercial activities – and, where necessary, neither city hesitated to use the Crusaders as shock troops to push their own competitors aside.

The search for new lands and the commercial interests of the Italian cities do not alone suffice to explain the Crusades, which were first and foremost manifestations of both medieval piety and of power attained by the Roman pontiffs, who considered themselves, and acted as, the spiritual and political leaders of all Christendom, and who saw in the Crusades an ideal opportunity to reaffirm this power at the same time as they freed the Holy Land from the presence of the Muslims. But manifestations of piety underwent a change at this time. The above-mentioned economic circumstances have much to do with this, for the widening of human horizons led Europeans to look for the remission of their sins not only in prayer and alms giving but also in visits to places hallowed by the presence of miraculous virgins, apostles, relics and so on, that is to say, in pilgrimages – of which those made to Rome, Santiago de Compostela and Jerusalem attained lasting world fame. These pilgrimages linked devotion with a taste for adventure, which in some cases could be very dangerous, as in the case of travel to the Holy Land, which could be reached only after a lengthy voyage requiring an armed escort. This was therefore not a peaceful but a military pilgrimage; this was the Crusade, whose leadership came to be assumed by Rome.

By the middle of the eleventh century, the Church was well on its way to freeing itself of the tutelage of the secular powers and was ruled by pontiffs won over to reformist ideas, which resulted, after 1059, in restricting the election of popes to the College of Cardinals. This cancelled the rule enforced by Otto I of Germany, who, after dominating Rome militarily in 963, had determined that no pope should be elected without imperial consent. By the end of the eleventh century, however, the popes were no longer content to demand their independence and that of their clergy. They sought to assert their authority over all the faithful, lay and ecclesiastical alike, not excepting kings and emperors. The Crusade, as a military expedition with a religious goal, offered Rome the best opportunity to test the extent to which its authority was accepted and the extent to which kings and emperors were willing to unite under the pontifical banner. A successful outcome to the Crusades would have signalled Rome's triumph not only throughout the West but also over the entire Christian world, that is to say both Byzantium and those Eastern areas dominated by Islam, where there survived Christian communities which did not accept Roman supremacy and preserved a liturgy and dogma distinct from Roman usage.

The political situation in the East could only encourage these expeditions, which were already facilitated by the economic, social, political, and religious and ecclesiastical situation of the European world. The growing differences between East and West since Roman imperial times found ecclesiastical expression in the formation of two Christendoms – the Orthodox or Eastern, ruled from Constantinople, and the Western, ruled from Rome. The definitive break occurred in 1054, when the bishop of Rome and the Byzantine patriarch mutually excommunicated one another; and political differences were added to religious ones, for in the second half of the eleventh century, the Normans under Robert Guiscard occupied Byzantine territories in southern Italy and began to threaten the Greek coasts – although these problems did not prevent Byzantium from turning to the West for military assistance after the Turks occupied Anatolia in 1071. Rome made tremendous moral capital out of this request, which provided a pretext for the First Crusade, in which Norman contingents predominated, both from Normandy itself and from southern Italy.

The unfolding of the Crusades

Pilgrimage to Jerusalem, even though restricted to very small groups, had existed since at least the fourth century, when the grotto of the Holy Sepulchre, the hill of Calvary and the remains of the Holy Cross were discovered. In these hallowed places, basilicas were erected to which ecclesiastics and religious communities were appointed in order to attend to the services of worship and to meet the needs of the pilgrims who thronged, for example, for the feast day of the Exaltation of the Cross, shown to the faithful on 14 September. To these early pilgrims, Europe owed a great number of the relics venerated in its churches and shrines.

The number of pilgrimages fell when the Muslims occupied Palestine in the seventh century, a period which coincided with the impoverishing of the West and internal wars among the Germanic kingdoms, rendering difficult and dangerous any travel whatsoever. But with the Carolingian recovery, new impulse was given to travel to the Holy Land, and not only was a personal pilgrimage there attributed to Charlemagne but also the signing of an agreement with the Caliph Hārūn al-Rashīd to guarantee the safety of pilgrims. At least until 1009, pilgrims were not molested by the tolerant Muslims, who also respected the Christian communities already settled in the Holy Land.

The number of pilgrimages depended not so much on the Muslims in Palestine as on the difficulties and perils of the journey there and many people began to make the journey only when two means of access became truly practicable – an approach by sea, when the Mediterranean had become converted into an Italian lake; and an approach by land, once the Hungarians had finally settled down in Europe in the second half of the tenth century and the invasions begun in the fifth century AD had come to an end. It was Saint Stephen, the king and national Hungarian hero, who opened the Way to Jerusalem, with inns and hospitals at regular intervals, just as the Way to Santiago was opened up at the other end of Europe at about the same time. But whether by land or sea, pilgrimages depended on the goodwill of Byzantium, and this was obviously forthcoming when the Byzantines appealed for help after suffering their crushing defeat at the hands of the Turks at Manzikert in 1071.

The West's response to Pope Urban II's appeal at Clermont in 1095 obeyed both religious and economic impulses. The liberation of Jerusalem, demanded and directed by the Church, was a motive sufficient in itself to attract Christians. Miracles and prodigies held to have occurred everywhere testified to the justice of the cause, and the hope of securing remission for one's sins through pilgrimage added to the conviction of saving one's soul if one died in the course of the venture, swayed Western Christians to take part in the undertaking. In addition, Jerusalem was described in Biblical language as the land of milk and honey, as the new promised land, and those hard on their luck, those whom Europe was incapable of feeding, flocked to the standard of the Crusade in the hope of finding new lands in which to live or over which to exercise an authority denied them in the West because they were the younger sons of noble families. Some were pilgrims who thought to return home again. Others took their wives and children with them in search of the promised land. For many, the symbolic Jerusalem was replaced by a more earthly Jerusalem of mortar and stone, and alongside such Crusades as that of the 'Paupers' or that of the 'Children', led by the likes of Peter the Hermit and Stephen the Shepherd, we find Crusades commanded by feudal lords such as Godfrey of Bouillon and his brother Baldwin, Robert of Normandy, and Bohemond of Taranto. These were the men who carved out principalities for themselves in Antioch, Edessa and Jerusalem and so provoked the reaction of the Muslims in Egypt, who in turn threatened the Latin presence in the East.

It was thus against Egypt that one of the Crusades came to be directed. This depended, for the transport of its fighting men, on the ships of Venice, whose neutrality, along with that of the other Italian port cities, was therefore purchased by the Egyptian sultan with the offer of important trade privileges in his domains. The tardy arrival of the Northern Crusaders on the Italian coast freed Venice from its obligations and transformed the Crusaders into debtors for a voyage which had failed to materialize. Venice suggested that the Crusaders discharge their debt by helping the Venetians to occupy Zara, a Dalmatian port then in Hungarian hands. When this city had been captured in 1202, it was proposed that the Crusading army might restore the deposed emperor to his throne in Byzantium. This offer was of interest to all: to the Venetians for the trade privileges it might entail, and to the Crusaders because the emperor was offering men and money for the Egyptian campaign, that is, for the Crusade. Alexius IV was restored to his throne, and to meet his pledges imposed new taxes, against which his population then rose in revolt. The Crusaders thereupon took Constantinople by storm in 1204 and elected as the new emperor one of their own, Baldwin of Flanders. Venice enjoyed the greatest triumph. It ingratiated itself with Rome by replacing the Greek Orthodox patriarch by a Venetian who observed Roman rites, while reserving for itself three-eighths of the conquered city – the sectors most suitable for its commercial activities. Baldwin and his successors used the imperial title, but they were not true emperors, only lords of a mere quarter of the empire. Of the rest, half went to the Venetians and the other half was shared out among the Crusader leaders, who held their lands as fiefs under the theoretical sovereignty of the Latin Emperor. The Byzantine aristocracy partly regrouped around Theodore Lascaris, a member of the Greek imperial family, who from Nicaea attempted to restore the Greek Empire in wars against the Latins, Bulgarians, Turks, and other Byzantine lords who ruled the despotate of Epirus and the kingdom of Trebizond. In 1261, with the help of the Genoese, the Nicaean Greeks recovered Constantinople and restored the Byzantine Empire, which had been destroyed by the Crusaders (see Plates 63, 64).

The military orders

The Latin domains in the Holy Land were not fated to survive, but another creation of the Crusades would endure. This was the institution of the military orders, created to protect and assist pilgrims. In Jerusalem there had existed, since the middle of the eleventh century, a brotherhood whose members devoted themselves to the care of pilgrims in the inn and hospital which they possessed next to the Church of Saint John. From 1119, this charitable brotherhood was transformed into a religious order, dedicated not only to caring for the pilgrims but also to defending them militarily. From their old hospital and their proximity to the Church of Saint John, they took both the names under which they became known – the Order of the Hospital, or Order of Saint John. This transformation was due no doubt to the example set in 1118 by Hugh of Payns, a Crusader from Champagne, who with eight companions founded a religious and military brotherhood with the aim of protecting pilgrims on their way to the Holy Land. Their work was acknowledged by the king of Jerusalem, who ceded to these brethren part of the dependencies of his royal palace, the ancient Temple of Solomon, whence the name of this order – that of the Temple.

The members of these two orders were at once monks and warriors, subject to the vows of poverty, chastity and obedience. While the Hospitallers combined their former charitable work with the task of defending pilgrims, the Templars were an exclusively military organization. Their soldier-monks rode down to the Palestinian port cities to greet the pilgrims, served them as armed escorts on their way to Jerusalem and accompanied them on their pilgrimage. The West's favourable response to the creation of these orders caused a rapid increase in the number of their knights, and with them their military potential, which was used by the king of Jerusalem for fighting the Muslims, either in the open field or from the fortresses and castles entrusted to the knights throughout the kingdom. In imitation of these orders, there arose others in Jerusalem, and also in other areas of Christendom threatened by the Muslims. Such were the Order of the Holy Sepulchre, whose foundation was attributed to Bishop Arnulph of Jerusalem; the Order of the Teutonic Knights, set up by German Crusaders, which transferred its field of activity to the German lands and merged with the Order of the Knights of the Sword in order to conquer Estonia and Livonia in the thirteenth century; and in the Iberian peninsula, the Orders of Santiago, Calatrava and Alcántara in twelfth-century Castile, along with the Order of Aviz in Portugal and, for the purpose of ransoming captives, the Order of Our Lady of Mercy in Barcelona, which was founded in the thirteenth century.

Until 1291, the Crusaders – and with them the orders – kept their hold on the Palestinian port of Saint John of Acre, but the initial reason for their existence disappeared with the loss of this ultimate Latin possession in the Holy Land. The Knights of Saint John defended Cyprus after the fall of Acre, and in 1310 conquered Rhodes, as a result of which they also came to be known as the Knights of Rhodes, and then later of Malta, after the island granted to them by Emperor Charles V when they were driven out of Rhodes by the Turks. The Templars, for their part, having lost all military reason for their existence, aroused jealousy in ecclesiastical and political circles alike, for the knights were accused of practices and beliefs contrary to the Faith. Above all, the French crown took an interest in liquidating this order, which had begun by lending money to pilgrims to help them to make their journey and ended up by becoming bankers to the monarchy of France. Their trial, begun in 1307, closed in 1312 with a decree of dissolution of the order signed by Pope Clement V.

Travellers and diplomats

When Europe came into direct contact with the Eastern world through the Crusades, this turned out to be only the initial stage in a lengthy process which culminated in the discovery of America in 1492. The Crusaders had made their way to the East either overland or across the Mediterranean, from which there set out the missionaries, diplomats and merchants to whom Europe was ultimately to owe its knowledge of Central Asia, China and the Indies – the areas which Christopher Columbus thought it possible to reach by travelling in the entirely opposite direction, by sailing the Atlantic westwards.

Central and Eastern Asia first became known to Europe through the travels and accounts of the monks John of Piano Carpini and William of Rübruck, ambassadors of the pope and of Saint Louis of France to the Great Khān of the Mongols. These monks were the authors of a *Historia Mongolorum* and of an *Itinerarium*, respectively. The journey of the first occurred in the years 1246–1247, and that of the second in 1253–1256, and their narratives excited the imagination of Europeans, awed by the report of these vast new spaces, the many peoples dwelling there, their customs and their ways of life. Carpini and Rübruck rubbed shoulders in the court of the Great Khān with Chinese, Koreans, Tibetans, Muslims from Turkestan and Persia, Russians, and ambassadors hailing from India – all territories which hitherto had been little more to Europeans than legends.

These and other missionary-ambassadors blazed the trail for the European merchants in Central Asia. In 1250, the Venetians Niccoló and Matteo Polo entered the Mongol dominions and reached Sarāy, capital of the Golden Horde, to whose leader, Berké, they offered their wares. This khān graciously acknowledged their gesture, and as a great Mongol lord, bestowed upon the two brothers goods twice the value of what he himself had received from them, encouraging them to sell this merchandise in his lands, a task which took Niccoló and Matteo a full year before they decided to make their way back to Venice. But the return journey by the same way no longer proved possible because of the outbreak of wars between Mongol chiefs, hence the two Venetians had to find another path home, which took them through the cities of Bukhārā and Samarkand, commercial centres where the trade routes of China, southern Russia, India and the Near East through Persia converged.

For the first time, the West had come into direct contact with the Silk Road, and the Venetians (see Plate 40) followed this ancient track in the company of Mongol ambassadors making their way to China in order to pay their respects to the Great Khān, Qubilay (see Plate 245). This overlord, who resided in 'Cambaluc' or Khān-Balygh to the north of present-day Beijing, showed considerable interest in the European world and asked the Venetians to act as his ambassadors to the pope, requesting him to send to China learned men capable of teaching the Christian religion and doctrine. After delivering Qubilay Khān's message, the two Polo brothers left again for China in 1271 with a letter from the pope to the Great Khān and taking with them this time Niccolò's own son, Marco. This journey came to an end twenty-five years later, and Marco then described his wanderings in 1298 in the text variously known as *The Book of Marvels, The Million*, or *The Description of the World*. Marco Polo's accounts were further confirmed and supplemented by Eastern travellers reaching Europe, and by missionaries established in Asia (see Plate 121).

IBERIAN EXPANSION IN THE ATLANTIC OCEAN: FROM THE RECONQUISTA TO THE DISCOVERY OF AMERICA AND THE PORTUGUESE EXPEDITIONS ALONG THE AFRICAN COASTS

Trade and travel towards the East beyond the Mediterranean became more difficult from the second half of the fourteenth century owing to clashes between Mongol chiefs and the anarchy prevailing in India after 1351. The economic consequences were not long in making themselves felt. Silk and spices became rarer, their prices doubled on European markets, and the trading cities of the Mediterranean lost importance, especially after the shores of the eastern Mediterranean came under the control of the Ottoman Empire.

Henceforward, the route to India and China would have to go via the Atlantic, following the sea route first opened at the end of the thirteenth century by the Genoese brothers Ugolino and Vadino Vivaldi, who fitted out two ships in 1291 to try to reach India through the Straits of Gibraltar in what has been considered a precursor to the voyage of Christopher Columbus. The ships were lost, and ten years later a son of Vadino tried to follow their course along the African coast but got no further than the Moroccan shores, where he was informed that the Genoese ships had been wrecked. While the first expeditions ended in disaster, it took more than this to dishearten the Italians. In the early fourteenth century, the Genoese Lancialotto (Portuguese 'Lançarote') Malocello reached the Canaries, and in 1341 a combined Genoese and Florentine expedition reached Madeira and, possibly, the Azores. Around the same time, in 1339, a cartographer in Majorca, Angelino Dulcert, included in his *portolano* a representation of the River Niger on whose banks there reigned an immensely rich king. In 1346, the navigator Jaume Ferrer left Majorca bound for the 'river of gold', but he too failed to return, perhaps because Mediterranean ships were not the most suitable for sailing in Atlantic waters. It would ultimately fall to the Atlantic countries, Portugal and Castile, to make the new discoveries – the Portuguese along the African shores as far as India and the Castilian vessels, commanded by Christopher Columbus, across the Atlantic to America.

The Portuguese discoveries

The existence of an African gold-producing centre had been known since antiquity, as were also the caravan trails linking this centre and the cities on the Mediterranean and Atlantic coasts of North Africa. At the end of these routes in the late Middle Ages, there were colonies of Genoese, Catalan and Majorcan merchants, who purchased large quantities of gold and slaves there. A further step was taken in 1415 when the Portuguese conquered and occupied the Moroccan port of Ceuta in a campaign which has been described as a prolongation of the *Reconquista*, the struggle against the Muslims, although today multiple motives have been recognized as underlying this expedition, which was, at once both military and religious. There was the search for gold, slaves, ivory, silk and spices but also the thirst for glory and wealth on the part of the nobility, and then the interests of the merchant class of Lisbon and Porto in the control of Ceuta, not only for its commercial importance but also in order to put an end to piracy and, moreover, to obstruct Castilian expansion into Morocco, from which Portugal acquired a large proportion of the wheat that it consumed.

The expedition against Ceuta enjoyed the support of Rome. Two years before the actual conquest, the Holy See even appointed an archbishop for 'Carthage' and in 1420 conceded to Prince Henry the Navigator, who was the driving force behind the Portuguese campaigns, the management of the assets of the Order of the Knights of Christ in order to finance attacks against the Muslims in Africa or elsewhere. From Ceuta and the Portuguese coast, numerous expeditions, both privately financed and officially backed, made their way down the Atlantic shoreline before rounding Cape Bojador in 1434. In addition to these expeditions, the Portuguese undertook others to the islands lying off the North African Atlantic coast – the Canaries, Madeira and the Azores – lands certainly known since the fourteenth century but as yet hardly explored and in no way settled. Many Castilian, Portuguese and Catalan expeditions sailed for the Canaries in the fifteenth century with specific economic ends in view (slaves and natural dyes in particular), although the Catalans abandoned this route at the end of the century, leaving the Castilians and Portuguese as the main contenders in the struggle for control over the archipelago. The first occupation of the Canary Islands took place in 1402 by Norman and French sailors and men-at-arms in Castilian service. Then Henry the Navigator tried, without success, to occupy Gran Canaria between 1424 and 1434. Two years later, Castile secured from Pope Eugene IV official recognition of its sovereignty over these islands, despite which the contest with Portugal lasted until 1480.

Between 1434 and 1444, meanwhile, Portuguese vessels reached Cape Verde and discovered the mouth of the River Senegal (see Plates 24, 25), and from then on made rapid progress. Guinea, Sierra Leone and the Cape Verde Islands were reconnoitred in 1460. Exploration was closely followed by the establishment of trading posts like the one at Arguim, set up in 1443 and immediately converted into a major commercial centre from which Portugal obtained slaves, gold, spices and ivory, the abundance of which is revealed by the names given by the discoverers to these areas (see Plate 124): the Coast of the Grains of Paradise (*malagueta* or 'fools' pepper'), the Ivory Coast (see Plate 265), the Gold Coast, the Slave Coast. In 1482, Diogo Cão reached Gabon, the Congo and Angola; and in 1488, Bartolomeu Dias discovered the passage to India when his ships rounded the Cape of Good Hope.

Christopher Columbus

The Portuguese expeditions had made it possible to understand and overcome the difficulties of navigation out of sight of land, and it is possible that voyages were already made much further west but were not pursued for lack of interest, since no new lands had been discovered, although the existence of such lands was nevertheless believed in. In the years prior to 1490, legends and rumours were in circulation among the sailors of the Azores and Madeira about lands in the west, and there has been speculation about the possibility of a 'pre-discovery', a voyage about which Columbus might have had precise news. But whether he was so informed or not, it is obvious that at a given point in his life, Columbus became firmly convinced of the feasibility of reaching the eastern coast of India by sailing across the ocean, as his own writings clearly show. He always attributed this conviction to divine inspiration, buttressed however by his own experience at sea in Portuguese service, and by the accumulated knowledge then available in such books as the *Geography* of Ptolemy, the accounts of Marco Polo, the *Historia Rerum Ubique Gestarum* ('History of Deeds in All Parts') by the Italian Renaissance humanist Aeneas Sylvius Piccolomini (who eventually became pope under the name Pius II), and the *Imago Mundi* or 'Image of the World' by the French cardinal Pierre d'Ailly, writings from which Columbus concluded that by sailing towards the west, he might reach Asia within a matter of days.

Columbus's project was turned down by the Portuguese court. Not that Lisbon's experts did not believe in the theoretical possibility of so reaching India, but they shared here the opinion of the Italian cartographer Toscanelli that the distance was much greater than that indicated by Columbus, which is why they thought that it would be easier to reach the East by going around the coast of Africa. Spurned in Portugal (1485), Columbus moved to Castile, where he wandered for years searching for backing for his venture, only to be turned down again because he spoke of only 800 leagues separating the Canary Islands and the Indies, whereas the experts held that the figure had to be more like 2,500 leagues – that is, for practical purposes, an insurmountable distance given the means available at the time. Despite this adverse judgement, however, the Catholic sovereigns of Spain did not dismiss the visionary navigator outright but rather took pains to point out that while it was not possible for them to help him at the present time, they could still offer him grounds for hope for the future. The opportunity presented itself in 1489 when the war with Grenada appeared nearly won, and when it was learned that Bartholomeu Dias had rounded the Cape of Good Hope, by which Portugal had found the route to the Indies.

The rekindling of Castilian hostilities against Grenada delayed agreement for the project, however, and it was not until 2 January 1492, when Grenada surrendered, that Queen Isabel and King Ferdinand, judging the enterprise not excessively costly given the benefits that might ensue, granted Columbus permission to realize his long-standing dream. On 17 April, the Capitulations of Santa Fe were signed, bestowing upon the Genoese sailor the office and dignity of 'Admiral of the Ocean Sea', and title to all the islands and stretches of mainland he might discover or win. Four months later, weighing anchor in the port of Palos, the discoverers bound for the 'Indies' set sail and reached a New World on 12 October 1492 (see Map 11).

BIBLIOGRAPHY

ALPHANDÉRY, P.; DUPRONT, A. 1959–1962. *La Cristiandad y el concepto de Cruzada*, 2 vols. UTEHA, Mexico.

ARRANZ, L. 1987. *Cristobal Colón*. Historia 16. Madrid.

ATIYA, A. S. 1962. *Crusade, Commerce, and Culture*. Bloomington, Indiana.

CAHEN, C. 1983. *Orient et Occident au temps des croisades*. Paris.

CHAUNU, P. 1969. *L'Expansion européenne du XIIIè au XVè siècle*. Paris.

CORTESÃO, J. 1960. *Os descobrimentos portugueses*, 2 vols. Lisbon.

DIAS, M. N. 1963–1964. *O capitalismo monarquico português, 1415–1549*, 2 vols. Coimbra.

GARCÍA, E. L. 1990. *Primera travesía colombina. Aspectos meteorológicos*. Salamanca Universidad.

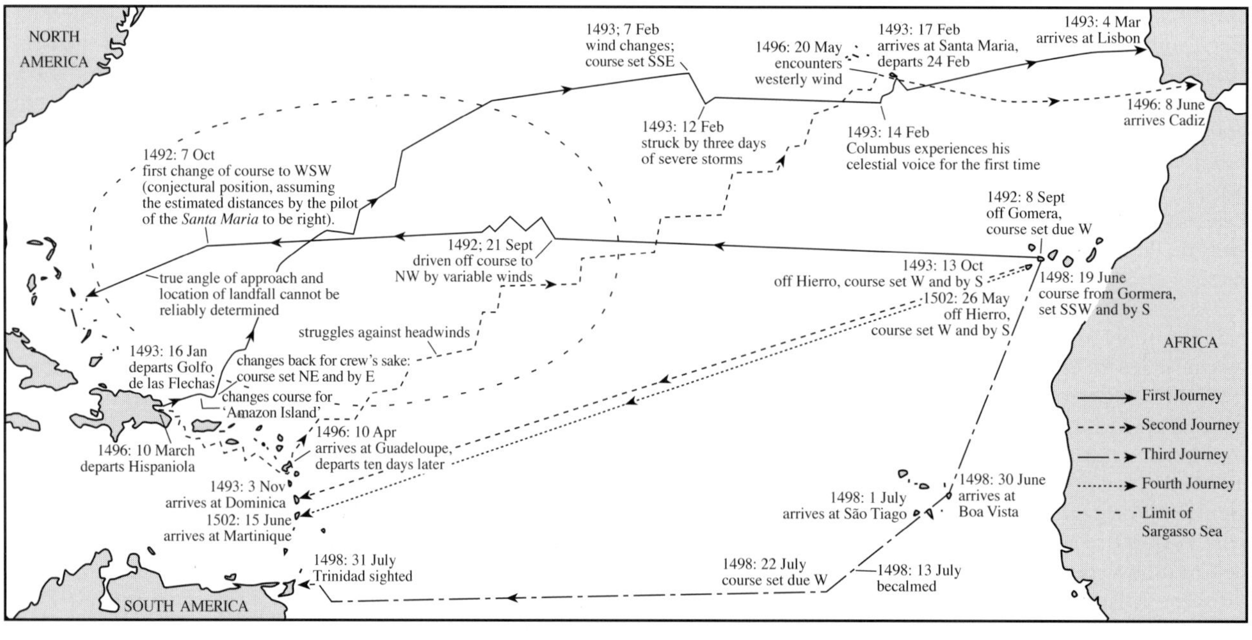

Map 11 Christopher Columbus' voyages to America (after Fernandez-Armesto, 1991, *Columbus*, Oxford University Press).

GODINHO, V. M. 1963–1971. *Os descobrimentos e a economia mundial,* 4 vols. Lisbon.
——. 1990. *Mito e mercadoria, utopia e prática de navegar. Séculos XIII–XVIII.* Difel, Lisbon.
GUILLEMAIN, B. 1969. *L'Eveil de l'Europe (1000–1250),* Paris.
LEMAY, R. 1963. Dans l'Espagne du XIIè siècle. Les traductions de l'arabe au latin. In: *Annales, Economies, Sociétés, XVIII,* Paris, pp. 639–665.
LOMAX, D. 1976. *Las Órdenes Militares en la Península Ibérica durante la Edad Media.* Universidad Pontifica, Salamanca.
LUCENA, M. 1982. *Descubrimiento y fundación de los reinos ultramarinos.* Rialp, Madrid.
MENÉNDEZ PIDAL, R. 1951. Como trabajaron las escuelas alfonsíes, In: *Nueva Revista de Filologia Hispánica,* pp. 363–380.
——.1956. *España, eslabón entre la Cristiandad y el Islam.* Madrid.
'Militia Christi' e Crociata nei secoli XI–XIII. 1992. In: *Atti della undecima settimana internazionale di studio,* Méndola, Università Cattolica, Milan.
MILLAS VALLICROSA, J. M. 1987. *Estudios sobre la Historia de la Ciencia Española,* 2 vols. Consejo Superior de Investigaciones Científicas, Madrid.
MORALES, F. 1971. *Historia del descubrimiento y de la conquista de América,* Madrid.
OLLIVIER, A. 1967. *Les Templiers.* Bourges.
PROCTER, E. S. 1945. The Scientific Work of the Court of Alfonso X of Castile: the King and his Collaborators. *Modern Language Review* 40, pp. 12–29.
ROMANO, D. 1971. Le opere scientifiche di Alfonso X e l'intervento degli ebrei. In: *Acts of the International Congress on East and West in the Middle Ages: Philosophy and the Sciences.* Accademia dei Lincei, pp. 677–711, Rome.
ROUX, J. P. 1967. *Les explorateurs au Moyen Âge.* Paris.
SAENZ-BADILLOS, A. 1991. Literatura hebrea en la España Medieval. Universidad Nacional de Educación a Distancia, Madrid.
SÁNCHEZ-ALBORNOZ, C. 1956. *El Islam de España y el Occidente.* Settimane di Studio, Split, XII, pp. 149–389.
SETTON, M. K. 1976–1978. *The Papacy and the Levant* (1204–1571). 2 vols. Madison, Wisconsin.
SEWARD, D. 1971. *The Monks of War: The Military Religious Orders.* London.
TAVIANI, P. E. 1974. *Cristoforo Colombo: la genesi della grande scoperta,* 2 vols. Novara. (Spanish trans., Barcelona 1983).
VARELA, C. 1984. *Cristobal Colón, textos y documentos completos,* Madrid.
VERNET, J. 1978. *La cultura hispanoárabe en Oriente y Occidente.* Barcelona.
——. 1982. *El Islam y Europa.* Barcelona.
WOLFF, P. 1971. *L'Eveil intellectuel de l'Europe.* Paris.

15

THE CORRIDOR BETWEEN EUROPE AND ASIA

15.1
THE KIEV RUS'

Anatoly P. Novoseltsev

After the expansion of the Protoslavs to the south-west and east from the region of their initial settlement (the fifth–eighth centuries), three groups betweeen Slavs gradually became distinct (Western, Southern and Eastern), with each representing a synthesis between Slavs proper, as bearers of the language, with various other ethnoses who adopted the Old Slavonic language.

The Eastern Slavs who inhabited the vast territory covering parts of present-day Ukraine, Belarus and the Russian Federation, later continued their expansion to the east and north-east. In the eighth–ninth centuries, there emerged the early Eastern Slavic political entities (principalities), the most important of which were the southern (Kievan) principality; the northern principality – with its centre later to become the city of Novgorod; and possibly the Polotsk principality. From the late eighth century and especially in the ninth century, some of the Eastern Slavic principalities came under the sway of Scandinavian (Varangian) *konungs* (kings), while the rest fell under that of the Khazarian khaganate. The name Rus' (Russia) also came to the Eastern Slavs from the north; as early as the tenth century it was accepted by all Eastern Slavs as a common self-name. In Rus', the Varangians were quickly Slavonized.

Sometime in the last quarter of the ninth century, the Eastern Slavs and some of the other tribes (Finnic, Baltic and Iranian) formed a union initiated from the north (from the land of the Ilmen Slavs) and situated mainly along the then vital trade route from the Baltic to the Black Sea ('The route from the Varangians to the Greeks'). This union was centred around Kiev in the south, its rulers bearing the title of great prince or *Khakan* of the Rus' (borrowed from the Khazars). Throughout the major part of the tenth century, this Old Russian state represented a specific federation of semi-independent principalities and lands directly ruled from Kiev.

During the tenth century, the great princes struggled to liquidate the vassal principalities and fought against the Khazarian khaganate, which fell to their onslaught in the 960s during the reign of Prince Sviatoslav Igorevich. The reforms of Princess Olga (mother of Sviatoslav) practically put an end to the ancient 'poliudie' (the seasonal collection of tribute by the prince and his *druzhina* (armed retinue) in the dependent lands) and established more stable systems of taxation. The foreign policy of the Old Russian State was increasingly focused on various contacts with Byzantium, as fixed in the partly preserved treaties between Rus' and the empire. These contacts were determined at that time by the leading role of Kiev, which was interested in exporting its locally produced goods to Constantinople.

The early attempts at embracing Christianity undertaken in the 860s and under Princess Olga are also linked with Kiev. Nevertheless, the ultimate Christianization of the country took place only in the late 980s under Vladimir Sviatoslavich, who made this religion official. Rus' received its Christianity from Byzantium, from where the first bishops and priests arrived. In general, the highest hierarchy of the Church in Old Rus' prior to the Mongol invasion was Greek, and we know only two metropolitans who were Russians by birth (Hilarion in the eleventh and Klim in the twelfth century). The Church's hierarchs did not interfere, however, in the worldly affairs controlled by Kiev's great princes. By the late tenth century, the latter had liquidated all local princes, but in their stead Vladimir Sviatoslavich (980–1015) appointed his numerous sons to rule over the provinces. The sons had to take into consideration local separatist tendencies, which took form in uprisings headed at first by Sviatopolk and then, just before Vladimir's death, by Iaroslav, ruler of Novgorod, the second most important city of Rus'. After Vladimir's death, the Polotsk principality seceded, and Rus' was divided between Iaroslav and his brother Mstislav along the Dnieper (after the latter died in 1036, Iaroslav unified the state and ruled alone).

The strife between the sons of Iaroslav the Wise and the descendants of Iziaslav Vladimirovich of Polotsk was aggravated by the dominance of the Cumans (Kypchaks) over the southern steppe, where they had defeated the formerly victorious Petchenegs. From that time onwards, Old Russian princes alternated between wars against the Cumans and alliances with them against common enemies, often their own closest relatives.

In the second half of the eleventh and the first third of the twelfth century, Rus' remained unified, although the Liubech Congress of 1097 had established the right of individual princes to rule hereditarily in their lands. The basis of the emerging fragmentation was formed by the rise and strengthening of private landed property (belonging to individual princes, monasteries, *boyars* or nobles and so on) which took place at that very time, in the second half of the eleventh and in the early twelfth century. This process was not synchronous, however, in different parts of Rus'.

The temporal growth of Russian power under Vladimir Monomakh (Great Prince between 1113 and 1125) was soon replaced by the triumph of feudal fragmentation. In the twelfth century, Rus' had two major centres of gravity – the north-east (Vladimiro-Suzdalian Rus') and the south-west (Volynia–Galicia). Novgorod stood apart, transformed into a specific feudal republic with the rich *boyars* and merchants engaged in domestic and international trade. Nevertheless, Novgorod strongly depended on its neigbhours, first of which was Vladimiro-Suzdalian Rus'. Initially, there was a fierce struggle for Kiev and the title of Great Prince, but in the second half of the twelfth century, Kiev began to lose its importance, especially for north-eastern Rus'. The encroachments of the Cumans were on the rise, although peaceful relations with the nomads also continued to some extent. Rus' became more and more fragmented by the multiplying descendants of the semi-legendary Riurik, and at the moment of the Mongol invasion (1220s–1230s) there was not a single principality capable of leading the struggle against the foreign enemy. The international prestige of Rus', which had been previously closely linked with various parts of Europe, sharply declined.

Little is known about the culture of pagan Rus'. Most of the data pertain to the religious beliefs of the Eastern Slavs before their conversion to Christianity, although the scope of even this information is extremely limited. 'Initial Chronicle', when describing the first religious reform of Vladimir Sviatoslavich, mentions the establishment by him of an official pantheon of several, predominantly South and Eastern Slavic deities. The Pantheon was headed by Perun, the patron of the prince and his *druzhina*. Also mentioned are several deities of heavenly bodies, first of all the sun, then the winds and so on. Some of them (for example Khors) originated from the Iranian Scythian–Sarmatian environment, for some of those Iranians had been assimilated by the Eastern Slavs and had become part of the Old Russian ethnos. It is remarkable that these ancient pagan deities were worshipped even by some representatives of the upper class of Russian society long after the adoption of Christianity (for example Khors, Troyan and so on). Apart from them there were numerous other deities, some kind, others evil, who would also be worshipped hundreds of years after the tenth century (various house spirits, wood goblins, the Rod (clan-spirit) and so on).

It is likely that before the Conversion, Rus' had not been familiar with masonry, and all its cult buildings, even its early Christian ones (as that of Saint Elias' in Kiev), had been of wood. The first recorded stone structure, the Church of the Tithes in Kiev, was erected in 996 by Vladimir.

The zenith of architecture came under Iaroslav the Wise when several churches dedicated to 'Holy Wisdom' or Saint Sophia were constructed (in Kiev, Novgorod and Polotsk).

Then, during the eleventh–twelfth centuries, Rus' was decorated with a large number of stone buildings (both religious and secular), some of which have survived (mainly in the Novgorod region and in Vladimiro-Suzdalian Rus').

The problem of the emergence of the written language in Rus' is equally difficult. There are some reasons to suggest that as early as the tenth century, that is, even before the adoption of Christianity, the generally used form of the Slavonic written language (in Cyrillic characters) was applied in the country on an official level and even between individuals. Nevertheless, the written language became widespread in Rus' only after the adoption of Christianity, when the princes began opening schools in the churches, and the scribes took to copying Slavic books, while translators into a Slavonic language understood by all Slavs began their intense activity. An original Old Russian literature also came into being, marked by such early milestones as the 'Sermon on Law and Grace' by Metropolitan Hilarion. The age of Iaroslav the Wise saw the first known composition of annals (although maybe some were written at an earlier date).

Unfortunately, only a small part of Old Russian literature, mainly of an ecclesiastic nature, has survived. The most famous among the secular monuments of literature is 'The Lay of Igor's Regiment', an anonymous account of the unsuccessful campaign of the Seversk princes against the Cumans in 1185. The poem is full of pathetic calls to unify Rus' against the nomads (calls so uttered in verse, though unnoticed by the rulers, on the very eve of the Mongol invasion).

The preserved frescoes of the Kiev cathedral of Saint Sophia, and the church decorations of north-eastern Rus', give some examples of Old Russian art. They include vignettes of daily life, depictions of princes and their families, scenes of hunting, and so on.

The decisive factor in Old Russian culture was its close co-operation with Byzantium, with Western Europe and partly with the Near East, all of which influenced the country's cultural types and forms. For example, Old Russian icon painting emerged and developed under an explicit Byzantine influence. On the other hand, Old Russian architecture, including that of churches, was based on ancient local traditions: thus developing a specific architectural colour which became increasingly manifest in the following centuries.

The achievements of Old Russian culture were later shared by the three Eastern Slavic peoples (Russian, Ukrainian and Belarusian), based on the Old Russian ethnos, and characterized by local specific features which became even more intensely prominent between the fourteenth and sixteenth centuries after the Mongol invasion in a very complex historic environment (see Plates 157–160).

BIBLIOGRAPHY

GREKOV, B . D. 1949. *Kievskaja Rus'* [Kievan Rus]. Moscow.

GRUSHEVSKI, M. 1991–1993, *Istorija Ukraini – Rusi.* [A History of Rus – Ukraine], 3 vols. Kiev.

IPAT'EVSKAJA LETOPIS' [The Ipatiev Chronicle]. 1909. In: *Polnoe Sobranie russkih letopisej* [Collected Russian Chronicles], Vol. II. St Petersburg.

LITAVRIN, G. G.; BAGRYANORODNY, K. 1991. *Ob upravlenii imperiej* [On the Governance of Empire], 2nd edn. Moscow.

NOVOSELTSEV, A. P. 1992. Drevnerusskoe gosudarstvo [The Old Russian State] In: *Istorija Evropy.* [A History of Europe], Vol. 2. Moscow.

PRESNYAKOV, A. E. 1993. *Knjažoe pravo v Drevnej Rusi* [The Law of the Prince in Ancient Rus']. Moscow.

SEDOV, V. V. 1982. *Vostočnye slavjane v VI–XIII vv* [The Eastern Slavs in the Sixth to Thirteenth Centuries]. Moscow.

SHCHAPOV, Y. N. 1989. *Gosudarstvo i cerkov' Drevnej Rusi X–XIII vv.* [State and Church in Ancient Russia of the Tenth to Thirteenth Centuries]. Moscow.

15.2
THE ARMENIANS

Viada Arutjonova-Fidanjan

Throughout the Middle Ages, Armenia, along with the entire Caucasus region, stood at the crossroads of the major routes linking East and West: routes used both for trade and war, at the very nexus of differing confessional and cultural streams. Between the seventh and the fifteenth centuries, Armenia thus found itself successively locked in a vice between the Byzantine Empire and the Crusading states of Frankish Christian Europe, on the one hand, and on the other, a sequence of Islamic powers: the 'Abbāsid caliphate, then the Seljuk sultanate, and finally the Ottoman Empire. With the gradual decay of the caliphate, Byzantium waged a vigorous counter-offensive against the Arabs in alliance with the rulers of Armenia in an inexorable drive to the East. With the restoration of full Armenian statehood at the end of the ninth century, the frontier between Byzantium and the Islamic polities shifted from a mere military barrier into a virtual land bridge, over which passed the great caravan trade routes leading from India, China and Central Asia to Constantinople and the Black Sea ports. The hitherto rapid decline of Armenia's cities into so many Arab frontier garrison towns was halted, then reversed, as these same cities revived and indeed flourished as commercial way-stations along the Transcaucasian route between the caliphate and Byzantine Asia Minor, whence merchants could push on to south Russia and the Volga regions. Such towns as Dvin, Van and Nakhchavan bloomed anew, while new urban centres like Ani, Kars, Artsn, Mush, Lori and Kapan were founded and soon became large cities in turn. All this urban prosperity was based on international trade. Between the eighth and the eleventh centuries, the bulk of Armenia's urban population was made up of merchants and artisans plying their crafts in *gortsatuns* (workshops). Weaving enjoyed a boom, with a rising production in woollen and silken textiles of all sorts: drapes, brocades, carpets. Work in metal was widespread and highly finished: items wrought included tableware in copper, tools, and weapons. Ani was renowned for the skill of its jewellers, while its potters fashioned not only ordinary earthenware but also refined artifacts of translucent white faience in imitation of Chinese porcelain.

While Byzantium secured political control over most of Armenia in the tenth and eleventh centuries, this was conducive to further economic prosperity for the country's various feudal kingdoms and principalities. Short-lived decline in the wake of Seljuk invasion was followed hard upon, as early as the turn of the twelfth and thirteenth centuries, by fresh economic growth, in reward for the successful struggle put up against the Seljuks by both the Armenians and a now united Georgia. Brisk trade across the Black Sea through the port of Trebizond actually multiplied. Armenian merchants enjoyed contact with the Crimea, the Cuman steppe, Rus' and Poland, while trading with both Venice and Genoa. The feudal monarchy founded by the Rubenid dynasty on the Mediterranean itself, the Armenian kingdom of Cilicia, also engaged in large-scale trade. The kingdom's main port, Ayas, emerged in the thirteenth century as a major commercial centre between East and West. But then, in the latter half of the thirteenth century, both the Transcaucasian lands and the Armenian kingdom of the Rubenids were subjugated by the Mongol state of Hūlāgū (Hülegü) Khān and his heirs, and Armenia's economy and civilization alike suffered the steepest decline.

Armenia's culture had been one which absorbed the most varied influences, through its peculiar geographical and historical position between East and West.

By the opening of the seventh century, Armenia had developed a civilization which was a synthesis of different Hellenistic traditions, not only as directly inherited by the Armenians themselves, but also as filtered through neighbouring Syria and Sasanian Iran. The cities of the surrounding Byzantine world, including Constantinople itself as well as Athens, Alexandria and Edessa, still preserved the treasures of the science, literature and arts of classical antiquity. Here Armenian youth, the mainstay of their country's 'Philhellenic' school, went for their higher education. One of the greatest Armenian disciples of Hellenistic learning in the seventh century was Anania Shirakatsi, whose encyclopaedic range embraced mathematics, astronomy, cosmography and geography; he founded the 'art of computation' in his country and wrote the 'Armenian Geography'. The legacy of the Greek, Syrian and Roman theatre, blended with local traditions of theatralized pagan rites, gave birth to Armenia's own drama, which was to endure for many centuries. The seventh century also saw the zenith of Armenian architecture, which found its most shining expression in the Temple of Zvartnots ('Vigilant Forces'), a three-tier composition, with a central cupola.

The advent of the Arabs, between the late seventh and the ninth centuries, ushered in a period of economic and cultural decay. Levond, whose 'History' continues to 788, writes of exorbitant taxes, the eradication of whole noble houses, commoners slaughtered, and desperate resistance. The struggle for liberation, however, produced not only its expected crop of martyrs but also a heroic epic, *David Sasunskiiy*. But then the collapse – at any rate in Armenia –

of the caliphate's rule, the restoration of the Armenian statehood by the Bagratids, and the rise of Byzantine cultural influence, especially in the epoch of renewed imperial expansion (tenth to eleventh centuries), were all beneficial to the cultural development of Armenia.

Scholars tend to see the Armenian ethos as a monolithic entity. But the interrelations and mutual influence between the Armenian and Byzantine worlds, to a large extent, took place at the level of the Armenian–Chalcedonian community, which differed profoundly from the majority of the Armenian *ethnos* in both confessional and cultural aspects. The civilization of the Armenians–Chalcedonians belonged to a type of open-minded culture rare in the Middle Ages, one which absorbed and transformed different influences. Over the centuries, and most actively from the sixth to thirteenth, the Armenian Chalcedonians played a leading role as intermediaries who not only ensured constant contact between Byzantium, Armenia and Georgia, but also created a special cultural environment. The frescoes of those churches built for Armenian–Chalcedonian patrons (the Church of Tigran Honents in Ani, Plindzahank (Akhtala) Kirants, Kobayr) are a synthesis of the artistic traditions of Armenia, Byzantium and Georgia.

The powerful historiographical tradition encouraged in the 'Age of the Bagratid Rulers' gave rise to works by both regional (Vaspurakan, Aluank, Syunik) and national historians such as the *Catholicos* Hovhannes Drashanakertsi, Stepannos Taronetsi (tenth century) and Aristakes Lastivertsi (eleventh century), all of them nobles or *Vardapets* of high rank, who spoke against feudal fragmentation and saw their aim in promoting the idea of a common fatherland, as a correlate to their National Church. Their works contain a treasury of data on Armenian, Georgian, Syrian and Byzantine affairs, as also are those of their followers: Matteos Urhaetsi (twelfth century), who described the events between 952 and 1136, Smbat Sparapet the Cilician historian, whose 'Chronicle' embraces the years 951–1276, Kirakos Gandzaketsi (thirteenth century), an eye-witness and chronicler of the Mongolian encroachments, and Stepannos Orbelyan (thirteenth century), the highly educated author of the'History of the Country of Sisakan', who depicted the history of Syunik against the general background of the history of both Armenia and her neighbours. From the late thirteenth to the seventeenth centuries, Armenian historiography is represented mainly by minor chronicles only. But in the early fourteenth century, by order of the Pope Clement V, the Cilician historian Hetum ('Frère Hayton') wrote a'History of the Tartars'. Written in French, this work was immediately translated into Latin and became one of the most popular narratives about the East in medieval Europe, and was later further transcribed into nearly all the European languages (Babayan, 1981).

The development of Armenian philosophy was highly influenced by Grigor Pahlavuni (990–1058), a prominent scholar, philosopher, rhetorician and poet. A new stage in the development of philosophic thought came in the thirteenth to fourteenth centuries with the advent of prominent followers of Nominalism: Vahram Rabuni, Hovhannes Vorotnetsi, Grigor Tatevatsi. The most famous work in the sphere of jurisprudence was the 'Code of Laws' by Mkhitar Gosh (1130–1213), which reflects the legal norms of Medieval Armenia. It was used not only in Armenia but also in the Armenian colonies in Europe. The 'Code of Laws' by Smbat Sparapet (based on the one by Gosh) was visibly influenced by both Byzantine and Latin Law.

Of similar high quality was the level reached in the tenth to fourteenth centuries by Armenian *belles-lettres,* especially lyrics. The first great lyrical poet of Armenia was Grigor Narekatsi (950–1003). His masterpiece, the 'Book of Lamentations', offers the most perfect expression, in words, of that same artistic vigour which then inspired Armenian architects, stone carvers and miniaturists.

However, the central place in the fine arts of medieval Armenia (twelfth to thirteenth centuries and later) belongs to book illustrations. Their major features were clarity of composition, expressiveness and maturity in the selection of colours, and decorative sense reflected in the abundance and beauty of their ornaments. Toros Roslin and the artists of his school in Cilicia (in the second half of the thirteenth century) developed the art of the Armenian miniature to perfection. Along with brilliant decoration, lavish use of gold and wealth of colours, Toros introduced true human beings with all their worldly passions into the realm of the miniature. Toros Roslin the Elder, a contemporary of Giotto and Dante, can be rightfully ranked among the great masters of the Early Renaissance (Drampyan, 1969).

In the thirteenth to fifteenth centuries, Armenian lay poetry continued its development with Frik (thirteenth century), Constantine Erzrkatsi (*c.* 1250–1340), Arakel Bagischetsi and Mkrtich Nagasch (seventh to fifteenth centuries).

In the thirteenth century, several magnificent palaces and temples were erected (palace of Sargis in Ani, palace of Sahmadin in Mren, monuments in Sjunik), but after the second half of the fourteenth century, both architecture and the fine arts in general began to decline.

Nevertheless, education in Armenia remained strong. Apart from primary schools, which had existed in Armenian monasteries since time immemorial, high schools or *vardapetarans* also came into being in the eleventh to fourteenth century (Ani, eleventh to thirteenth century; Sis, twelfth to thirteenth century; Gladzor, thirteenth to fourteenth century; Tatev, fourteenth to fifteenth century) to give instruction in theology, mathematics, astronomy, geometry, history, geography, grammar, music, philosophy and rhetoric. Many of their graduates became prominent figures in arts and culture (see Plate 156). The Armenian science between the tenth and fourteenth centuries was especially strong in the fields of historiography, philosophy and jurisprudence.

BIBLIOGRAPHY

AGAYAN, T. P. *et al.*; MNATSAKANYAN, A. S.; HARUTYUNYAN V. M. 1976. The Armenian Culture IX–XI Centuries; KHACHERIAN L. G. *et al.* The Armenian Culture, XII–XIV Centuries. In: AGAYAN, T. P. *et al.* (eds) *History of the Armenian People*, Vol. III. Erevan, pp. 345–395, 789–879 (in Armenian).

BABAYAN, L. O. 1981. *Historiographic Essays in the History of Armenia (Ninth to Thirteenth Centuries).* Erevan (in Armenian).

DRAMPYAN, R. G. (ed.) 1969. *Armenian Miniatures.* Erevan (in Russian).

15.3
THE GEORGIANS AND OTHER CAUCASIANS

Viada Arutjonova-Fidanjan

Between the seventh and fifteenth centuries, Georgia, like its neighbour Armenia, suffered the impact of one warlike expansionist force after another: the Arabs, the Byzantines, the Seljuks, the Mongols. The loosening of the 'Abbāsid caliphate's grip in the later ninth century allowed Georgia to recover its statehood and revive its trade at home and abroad under its own branch of the Armenian royal house, the Bagratids. David IV the Builder especially, the most famous of the Georgian Bagratids, but also his successors, vigorously supported commerce and so permitted Georgia to resume its full place in the world's economy, while they struggled against feudal particularism and redeemed their cities from the power of feudal lords. In the eleventh and twelfth centuries, such Georgian towns as Tbilisi, Rustavi, Chunani and Samshvilde became important centres for trade and the crafts. Such Georgian urban crafts, which had increasingly flourished since the country's ninth-century revival – and would continue to thrive well into the thirteenth – included, among others, joinery, stone carving, heavy and light metalwork, ranging from jewellery to fine metal tableware in copper, silver and gold, the firing of ceramics, the blowing of glass, the tanning of leather goods and manufacture of footwear, the weaving of textiles and cutting of fine clothing in cotton, silk or wool, and finally the production of such writing materials as parchment. Georgia's towns traded not only with Armenia but as far afield as Byzantium, Persia, Arabia and Egypt, exporting pottery, furs, wool, cotton, silk, and such textile products as clothes and carpets, while importing sugar and also much jewellry from Baghdād, and 'Greek' textiles and brocades stitched in gold from Constantinople. More precious stuffs came from neighbouring Armenia. Hence many merchants and artisans peopled Georgia's cities between the ninth and thirteenth centuries. Georgia's autocephalous Church, too, played a leading role in the country's economic life: monastic fiefs flourished, crafts also thrived in the monasteries, and the Church in turn dealt in trade both foreign and domestic. But while the Church in Armenia actively supported the centralizing policies of the Armenian Bagratid princes against feudal dissidence, the Georgian high clergy enjoyed far too many close links with their own country's nobility. Such links the Georgian Bagratids had to take harsh measures to cut, notably by replacing outright appointments to church offices with ecclesiastical elections. Georgia's full unification enabled it to take an active part in Near Eastern international politics. By the second half of the thirteenth century, the Georgian kingdom had extended its sway not only over all the Georgian lands proper but also over the whole of eastern Armenia and indeed over a major portion of northern Asia Minor. The Georgian Bagratids bore the title of kings of the Abkhazians (western Georgia), of the Kartvelians (Kartli and Mescheti), of the Rans, of the Kachs (Ereti, Kacheti), and of the Somechs (Armenians), and also claimed suzerainty over the neighbouring Muslim *Shāhanshāhs* and *Shīrvānshāhs*, so 'ruling from Nikopsia to Derbent'.

Although the Caucasus boasted a tremendous variety of ethnic groups, these had lived cheek by jowl for so long that their common culture ended by showing unmistakable signs of unity. The Russian orientalist N. Ia. Marr was the first to introduce the concept of a 'Caucasian cultural world', and the work of many succeeding Caucasologists has gone far to prove the soundness of such a notion. Common Christianization, for one thing, at the outset helped to strengthen such Caucasian cultural unity. The cult of Saint Gregory of Armenia, as the holy patron who first brought the Gospel to the entire Caucasus, long overshadowed veneration for the figures of more local patron saints. But then dogmatic differences steadily subverted the unity of the three Churches of Armenia, Georgia and Caucasian Albania (that is, modern Shīrvān), and finally split and destroyed it in 726 at the Council of Manazkert, which pitted an Armenian Monophysite see against a Georgian–Chalcedonian one. Albania's Church came under the jurisdiction of Armenia's *Catholicos*. But even many years after this split, an eleventh-century Georgian author like Leontius Moveli could still write of the initial spiritual unity of all the Caucasian peoples (Toumanoff, 1963).

The cultural flowering of Georgia proceeded apace with the blossoming of its written language. Between the seventh and ninth centuries, a heavily bookish, churchly idiom tended to prevail, as in the 'Martyrdom of Abo of Tbilisi'. But then, in the ninth and tenth centuries, a literary idiom emerged that was used to translate texts from Arabic, Greek, Armenian Persian and Syriac, with renderings so lively and popular that they seem to be the original writings of Georgian authors themselves. Indeed, original saints' lives in Georgian (such as 'The Life of Saint Gregory Xandsteli' by Giorgi Merchule) also appeared. Medieval Georgian cultural history always shows the powerful influence of the Georgian monasteries, then active both within and without the country's borders. Vigorous literary work was carried out in the Monastery of Shatberd, whose scriptorium turned out the tenth-century 'Shatberd collection of texts'. This collection not only included a number of original Georgian texts, such as 'The

Life of Saint Nino' and the account of 'The Conversion of Georgia', but also crucial medieval Georgian renderings of important classical Greek texts, ranging from an abstract of the founding Greek grammar composed by Dionysius of Thrace in the first century BC (this 'Art of Grammar' is preserved within the 'Textbook'), to an Armeno-Georgian recension of the famous late Greek 'Physiologus' or Bestiary. Scientific Georgian literature of the eleventh century was represented by the works of Giorgi of Athos and Euphrem Mtsire, and history by a 'Chronicle of Georgia'. Euthymius of Athos, a learned translator, also worked in the field of jurisprudence, which he enriched by writing his 'Minor Nomocanon' (canon of laws).

Georgian monasteries in Sinai, Palestine (including Jerusalem), Cyprus and Mount Athos housed renowned translators, philologists and other scholars both Georgian and Armenian (of the Chalcedonian rite). These monkish scholars played the role of a cultural link between medieval Caucasian society and the Byzantine and Near Eastern worlds lying beyond. For indeed, their intimate knowledge not only of classical Greek but also of Arabic and Persian writings allowed them to transmit much Eastern lore to the medieval West, as in the case of the 'Tale of Barlaam and Ioasaph', a rendering into Greek – through Georgian – from an Arabic version of what was ultimately the story of the Buddha (Grekov, 1953). In the eleventh and twelfth centuries, in addition to translations from the Greek, the works of such outstanding Persian-language narrative poets as Firdawsī (the *Shāh-Nāmeh* or 'Book of Kings'), Niẓāmī ('The Romance of Khusraw and Shīrīn') and Gurgānī ('the Romance of Vīs and Rāmīn') also now appeared in Georgian versions. Philosophical thought in Georgia was best represented in the neo-Platonic works of John Petritci, who wrote in the monastery of Bachkovo in the Balkans. Historiography was illustrated by the 'History of the King of Kings, David' (David IV the Builder, 1089–1125); by the works of three chroniclers of Queen Tamar (1184–1213); and by an anonymous author of the fourteenth century, who described political events in thirteenth- and fourteenth-century Georgia. The tenth to the thirteenth centuries were an age of splendour for Georgian architecture, both sacred and secular, as well as a brilliant period for painting in fresco and miniature and also for the applied arts (especially the chasing of gold and the inlaying of cloisonné enamels).

Medieval Georgian civilization found its consummate expression in secular poetry. The most famous literary work of this classical age was the poem 'The Knight in a Tiger's Pelt' by Shota Rustaveli, dedicated to Queen Tamar. The poet directed all his attention here to portraying living human beings, depicted with all the complexity of their feelings, passions and thoughts. The poet further manifested his deep-lying humanism in the expression of his love, admiration and advocacy of spiritual freedom for women, in his stated idea of the brotherhood of individuals from different peoples, and in his profession of selfless devotion to his fatherland. Rustaveli may be considered the founder of a new Georgian literary language (Baramidze, 1984). His poem ranks among the masterpieces of world literature, combining as it does the blended legacy of classical Greek philosophical ideas with Georgian folklore, along with a keen knowledge of the poetry then being written in Persian.

Ever since the tenth century, Persian had been the chief literary language of those vast regions of the Islamic world stretching to the east of the Arab lands, from Transcaucasia as far as India. In the eleventh- and twelfth-century Caucasian region, Persian was now the chosen vehicle of expression for such Muslim poets of Āzerbaijān as Qaṭrān, Khāqānī, Falakī and especially Niẓāmī of Ganjeh.

Niẓāmī (1141–1209) was an outstanding lyrical poet, philosopher and humanist. His five great narrative poems – 'The Treasury of Mysteries', 'Khusraw and Shīrīn', 'Laylā and Majnūn', 'The Seven Icons', and the *Iskandar-Nāmeh* or 'Romance of Alexander' – constitute so many social and philosophical meditations with digressions into history, combined with the theme of love (see Plates 112, 113, 218). References to Armenian and Georgian themes are scattered throughout his works, and in turn he exerted profound influence not only on the literature of the Islamic East but also on the poetry of his Christian neighbours in Transcaucasia: especially on Georgian secular verse (Gulazade, 1984). For not only princes from Christian Georgia and Islamic Shīrvān together thronged the court of Queen Tamar – their poets flocked thither as well.

Thus the tale of 'The Son of the Blind One', long popular among Armenians and Ossetes, passed into the language of Turkic Āzerbaijān in multiple folkloric adaptations, of which the most widespread finally became known under the name of *Kör-oghli*, the heroic epic of the Oghuz people. Students of the other great Turkic epic, 'The Book of Dede Korkut', find therein many traces of Caucasian reality and folklore resulting from contacts between so many different peoples living within basically the same geographical, historical and cultural environment (Muradjan, 1984).

It has now been verified that the secular architecture of the Armenian city of Ani in turn deeply influenced neighbouring Islamic architecture, while Seljuk ornamentation drew to a great extent on deep-rooted Caucasian motifs: 'the (Seljuk) mausoleums of Akhlat, Erzerum and Vostan are the architectural fruit of a grafting, as it were, from age-old Christian Armenian and Georgian church-building' (Orbeli, 1963).

However complex, the Caucasian cultural world of the tenth, eleventh and twelfth centuries thus represented a true unity. Such unity was partly that imparted by the age itself, for this was a time when Islam penetrated the Caucasus as a cultural ingredient that would henceforth be permanent – so that mosque and church 'stood close to each other', as the tenth-century Arabic-writing geographer Iṣṭakhrī chose to put it. Since eleventh- and twelfth-century Armenia, Georgia and their Islamic neighbours so much enjoyed a similar social setting, marked by vigorous urban growth, powerful dynasties and a splendid court life, it is no surprise that their shared cultural climate gave rise to such close resemblances in artistic taste as well: best mirrored in Rustaveli's 'Knight in the Tiger's Pelt', Niẓāmī's 'Khusraw and Shīrīn' and the architectural monuments of Ani.

In the twelfth and thirteenth centuries, the world of the Caucasus underwent far-reaching ethnic, political and cultural changes. These dissolved the traditional framework of national and political particularisms, resulting in new contacts and mutual penetration between the 'Christian world of the Caucasus' and the 'World of Islam'.

Then, with the later thirteenth and fourteenth centuries, this cultural and political flowering of Georgia and its Caucasian neighbours was cut short by the Mongol invasion.

The period from the thirteenth to the fifteenth centuries has therefore left us with only a handful of major works in literature, art and architecture. Monuments of note include the late thirteenth-century church in Metechi; the Church of Saint Sabbas in the monastery of Safari; and the fifteenth-century monastery of Chule in Samzche. Artists, however, increasingly resorted to decorating their architecture, not with expensive carved stone, but with frescoes. In the second half of the fourteenth century, a 'Ritual of Georgian Court Life' was drawn up. Finally, the close of the fifteenth century spawned a new version of the Georgian collection of chronicles, the 'Kartlis Tschovreba', dedicated to political events in the country in the eleventh and twelfth centuries: the so-called 'version of Queen Anne'.

BIBLIOGRAPHY

BARAMIDZE A. G. 1984. Georgian Literature. In: BERDNIKOV, G. P. *et al.* (eds) *History of World Literature,* Vol. II. Moscow, pp. 314–319 (in Russian).

GREKOV, B. D. 1953. Culture of Georgia. In: GREKOV, B. D. (ed.) *Essays in History of Peoples of the USSR, Ninth-Thirteenth Centuries,* Part I, pp. 578–596 (in Russian).

GULIZADE M. YU. 1984. *The Literature of Azerbaijan.* In: BERDNIKOV, G. P. *et al.* (eds) *History of World Literature,* Vol. II. Moscow, pp. 328–336.

MARR, N. IA. 1934. *Ani.* Academy of Sciences Press, Moscow–Leningrad, pp. 37–38 (in Russian).

MURADJAN, P. M. 1982. *Caucasian Cultural World and the Cult of Grigor the Enlightener. Caucasus and Byzantium,* Vol. 3. Erevan, pp. 5–20 (in Russian).

——. 1984. *The New Developments in the Caucasian World. Caucasus and Byzantium,*Vol. 4. Erevan, pp. 153–154 (in Russian).

ORBELI, I. A. 1963. *Selected Works.* Academy of Sciences Press, Erevan, pp. 364–365 (in Russian).

TOUMANOFF, C. 1963. *Studies in Christian Caucasian History.* Washington, pp. 88 *et seq.*

15.4
THE CRIMEANS

Sergei P. Karpov

Throughout all the periods of its history, the Crimea, or 'Taurica' as it was known to the ancients, was a zone where different civilizations acted upon one another. Many ethnic groups made up its population. In both ancient and medieval times, the urban centres dotting the peninsula's southern coast maintained close contact not only with Asia Minor but also with the nomadic and semi-nomadic populations of the steppe hinterlands to the north.

By the sixth century, both southern Crimea and its eastern reaches – around the city of Bosporus – had been incorporated into the Byzantine Empire. The other parts of Taurica were inhabited by Sarmato-Alans and Goths – with the latter already partly assimilated by the former. A large ancient Greek *polis*, Chersonesus, remained the major urban centre of Byzantium's possessions in the peninsula. Chersonesus minted its own coinage and exchanged goods of local or Byzantine manufacture for corn and animal products – especially furs – from the hinterland. Under the Byzantine Emperor Justinian I, a chain of strongholds was built both along the shore and in the central mountainous part of the peninsula to protect the empire's holdings against the nomads. Such forts included Alouston (modern Alushta), Gorzouvitai (Gurzuf), Mangup and Eski Kermen. The spread of Christianity was accompanied by intensive construction of churches and baptistries in the towns and larger settlements. Several shrines decorated with marble and mosaics have been discovered by archaeologists at the sites of Chersonesus, Mangup and Parthenitai along the southern shore.

In the seventh century, Crimea's towns suffered decay as the peninsula lapsed into increasing ruralization, with raids by the Khazars becoming ever more intense by the end of the century. In the eighth century, the major part of Crimea thus came under the sway of the greater Khazar state, while proto-Bulgarian tribes also settled in the peninsula at the same time. But the eighth and ninth centuries also saw a relative return to economic prosperity. Old towns were rebuilt and new settlements founded in eastern and south-western Taurica. High-quality pottery, both glazed and unglazed, increasingly replaced rougher, rustic homemade ware.

The crisis of iconoclasm in Byzantium provoked the flight to the Crimea of Greek orthodox monks and others still faithful to the worship of icons, who rejected what was then the religious policy of Constantinople's emperors. The refugees founded cave monasteries hewn from cliff faces along the Crimean littoral and in the mountainous interior. Various architectural and decorative features connect these rock-cut churches and chapels with those found in Anatolia, especially in Cappadocia. The first cross-shaped church with central cupola known in the Crimea, Saint John Prodromus in Bosporus (modern Kerch), goes back to this period of the turn of the eighth and ninth centuries. Four bishoprics then existed in the Crimea: those of Chersonesus, Gothia, Sougdaia and Bosporus. In *c.* 861, Saint Constantine, or Cyril, conducted a mission to the Crimea in an attempt to convert the Khazars.

Khazar rule was shaken by Petcheneg incursions in the late ninth century and was finally annihilated by the prince of Kiev, Sviatoslav, in 965. Taking advantage of their own victory over Sviatoslav in 971, the Byzantines re-annexed Gothia. Yet by the end of the tenth century, eastern Taurica with its city of Bosporus, or Kerch, had come under the sway of the Russian Tmutarakan' principality. Thereafter the Crimea, and especially Chersonesus, after a short occupation by Vladimir, prince of Kiev (who had been baptized in 988), again became an important way-station for trade, this time between Byzantium, Kievan Rus' and the nomads of the northern Black Sea steppe area. The craftsmen of Chersonesus proved to be skilled carvers in bone and wood and produced fine ware in metal and glass. Their articles, especially glazed red pottery and glass bracelets, were imported in large numbers by Kiev, Novgorod, Smolensk and the Volga region. The artistic style and type of the Crimean cities' production show considerable syncretism, blending patterns borrowed from Constantinopolitan and Syrian models with original local features. In general, Crimean craftsmanship was able to absorb influences from the Near East and from the Byzantine, Slavonic and nomadic worlds. To these were added, from the thirteenth century onwards, increasing influences from the Latin West.

Between the late eleventh and early thirteenth centuries, the Crimea was dominated by the Cumans. The port of Sougdaia (Sudak) now became the main political and trading centre of Taurica. After the fall of Constantinople to the Crusaders in 1204, Chersonesus and the other Byzantine possessions acknowledged the authority of the Greek Empire of Trebizond. Several independent principalities arose in the Crimea, such as Theodoro (Mangup), ruled by the Greek dynasty of the Gabrades, Kirk-Yer, and others. For its part, the sultanate of Rum, in Anatolia, made its own attempt to seize Sougdaia. This period of political instability ended with the conquest of the entire peninsula by the Mongols, or 'Tatars', in 1239–1242. The Crimea soon became an *ulus* (or appanage belonging to a Mongol family branch) of the Golden Horde, which itself corresponded to the great western subdivision of the Mongol Empire. The first independent khān of the Golden Horde, Berke (1257–1266), ordered a list drawn up of the entire tax-paying population of his empire. This included the Crimea. Berke further initiated the regular minting of Juchid coins in the Crimean towns. The steady conversion to Islam of the Tatar population in the Crimea began under Berke's rule. Full Islamization was achieved under Öz Beg (r. 1312–1342), whose reign saw the spread of Arabic and Persian literary culture. From the fourteenth century onwards, dervish fraternities, mostly from Asia Minor, spread the teachings of Ṣūfism, or Islamic mysticism, among the Muslims of the Crimea.

But the wars which devastated eastern Asia Minor in the thirteenth and fourteenth centuries also caused significant Armenian Christian migration to the Crimea's towns. Armenians were active in trade and crafts, and their monasteries (Surb Hach and others) were renowned for their finely illuminated manuscript production.

Meanwhile, since the 1260s, Crimean ports had become so many sea terminals for the caravan routes bound for Europe from the Volga region, Central Asia, India and China. This is what spurred the Italian maritime republics to found trading stations in these same ports. In 1265, Genoese merchants thus settled in Caffa (the former Theodosia). Caffa became the most important of a string of Genoese Black Sea colonies, which also included – among many other ports – Cembalo (Balaklava), Vosporo (Kerch) and Soldaia (Sudak). The Venetians, in fact, had first settled in Soldaia in *c.* 1287, but their Genoese rivals seized this colony from them in *c.* 1365. In order to stimulate the spread of Roman Catholic missions in the area and also to put the Italian settlements on a proper ecclesiastical footing, the papacy elevated Vosporo to the status of an archdiocese in the early fourteenth century. The Franciscans and Dominicans in turn founded chapter houses in Caffa, Soldaia and Vosporo, whence to propagate Catholicism throughout 'northern Tartary'.

This 'Latin' presence in the Crimea introduced many new factors into the region's social and cultural development. Caffa became a major clearing house for trade in slaves to the Levant, as well as a central meeting point for the exchange of goods, and attendant technologies and cultural outlooks, from the most varied countries. Caffa's own unique *lingua franca* arose between the thirteenth and fifteenth centuries. The famous *Codex Cumanicus*, a Latin–Persian–Cumanic dictionary, was most probably compiled in Caffa in *c.* 1303. A century or so later, a teacher of grammar who practised and wrote in Caffa itself, Alberto Alfieri, following the European fashion of his day, composed a Latin allegorical poem, the *Octoad* (that is, 'eight chapters'), in which he not only described political struggles in Milan and Genoa but also took care to describe Caffa graphically as well. Fortified structures at Caffa, Soldaia and Cembalo, whose towers and walls still partly survive, yield clear evidence of the Crimea's integration into the system of economic and political relations then prevailing in the Mediterranean world, as do the notarial acts and books of accounts preserved in the archives of Venice and Genoa. Despite periods of sharp confrontation with both the khāns of the Golden Horde and local Tatar rulers, the Italian settlements managed to survive – they had no other choice – by nurturing multilateral relations with the different peoples of the Black Sea region, the Caucasus, Anatolia, and the Russian, Danubian, Polish and Lithuanian lands. Caffa itself was inhabited by Greeks, Armenians, Tatars, Slavs, Caucasians, Wallachians, Jews and others, with the 'Latins' there very much a minority although they constituted the uppermost social level.

Different cultural traditions may also be traced in the principality of Theodoro. Both its architecture (the complex of palace buildings at Mangup) and wall painting (the frescoes in the sepulchral church of Eski Kermen and in the cave chapel of Cherkes Kermen) reflect a pure late Byzantine style. But the system of fortifications at Mangup and Kalamita followed not only local and Byzantine practices but also and especially Genoese models. Marble slabs with inscriptions and coats of arms of the princes of Mangup bear a combination of Byzantine, Tatar and Italian decorative elements.

Solghat (Eski Krim) was the most important Tatar town in the Crimea between the thirteenth and fifteenth centuries. A sumptuous mosque with incorporated *madrasa* (Qur'ānic school) was built here in 1314 by Khān Öz Beg. Its carved portal is a masterpiece of Islamic stone cutting. The *türbes* or mausoleums at Chufut Kal'e and Eski Yurt also show the close relation between Crimean Tatar building styles and Seljuk architectural traditions in Asia Minor. In Kīrk Yer, in the central Crimea, a fortified settlement of Karaims, or Crimean Jews, also came into being in the fourteenth century. The settlement boasted an excellent library of Hebrew books and served as a religious and cultural focus for the Karaims until the nineteenth century.

A separate Crimean khānate arose between 1430 and 1440 in the wake of the disintegration of the Golden Horde. Then, in 1475, all the Crimea's Genoese colonies, as well as the principality of Theodoro, were conquered by the Ottomans. The Crimean khāns of the Girāy dynasty acknowledged the Ottoman sultans as their overlords. The Crimean khāns organized their state along military lines, with stress on cavalry and horses provided by the stock-breeding Tatar tribesmen. The khānate's finances relied heavily on external tribute, whether enforced or seized through external raids against the khānate's northern neighbours. The Crimean khāns moreover profited from the slave trade in addition to the weighty taxes they levied on their indigenous Christian peasantry (in contrast to the much lighter taxes they required from their Muslim Tatar subjects). The capital of the khānate – Bāghche Sarāy – became an important centre for Islamic civilization. Outstanding architects built here the Palace of the Khāns, the mausoleum (*türbe*) of Hājī Girāy (1501) and a *madrasa* (1500), which became well-known in eastern Islamic lands for the quality of its Qur'ānic learning. A mosque in Gözlev (Evpatoriya) was even erected by the famous Ottoman architect Sinān (1552). But Greek monasteries also continued to exist, and to be built, in the Crimea.

Notwithstanding much cruel devastation, high cultural traditions thus continued to exist in the Crimea throughout the medieval period, mirroring the close contact, and fruitful interaction, of Christian, Islamic and other civilizations (see Plate 37).

BIBLIOGRAPHY

BALARD, M. 1978. *La Romanie Génoise (XIIè–début du XVè siècle).* Rome–Genoa.

BARANOV, I. A. 1990. *Tavrika v epokhu rannego srednevekovya* [Taurica in the Early Medieval Epoch]. Kiev.

BENNIGSEN A. *et al.* 1978. *Le Khanat de Crimée dans les Archives du Musée du Palais de Topkapi.* Paris.

BRĂTIANU, G. 1969. *La Mer Noire.* Munich.

KARPOVV, S. P. (ed.). 1991. *Prichernomor'e v srednie veka* [The Black Sea in the Middle Ages]. Moscow.

MĪZ, V. L. 1991. *Ukrepleniya Tavriki X–XV vv.* [The Fortifications of Taurica, Xth–XVth centuries]. Kiev.

VASILIEV, A. 1936. *The Goths in the Crimea.* Cambridge. X.

YAKOBSON, A. L. 1974. *Krīm v srednie veka* [The Crimea in the Middle Ages]. Moscow.

III: The Muslim World and its Arabian Zone

INTRODUCTION

Abdul Aziz Duri

When in 622 Muḥammad left Mecca, his native town, for Yathrib (Medina), where a small community of his followers awaited him, no one could possibly have imagined the momentous consequences that would ensue from what even the hostile Quraysh of Mecca must have deemed not an unduly alarming episode. But within the next ten years, the Prophet achieved the triumph of his faith within the Arabian peninsula; and his death (632) did not, despite a rising of the Bedouin tribes, stop the expansion of Islam. Under the non-dynastic ('pious') caliphs (632–661), the great Sasanian Empire of Iran was destroyed, and the rich eastern lands of the Byzantine Empire (Syria, Palestine and Egypt) overrun. In spite of internal divisions, leading to repeated serious revolts, one of which ultimately consumed it, the Umayyad caliphate (661–750) kept up the momentum of expansion, which placed the Arab pennants on the banks of the Indus and the Syr Daryā in the east and the Pyrenees and the Atlantic coast on the west. Islam as a religion has flourished largely within these geographical limits, the most notable changes since then having been its spread in Asia Minor (Turkey), sub-Saharan Africa, South Asia, Malaya and Indonesia, and the loss of its presence in Spain (see Map 12).

One of the most remarkable features of the Arab conquests, rapid and extensive as they were in their initial phase, was

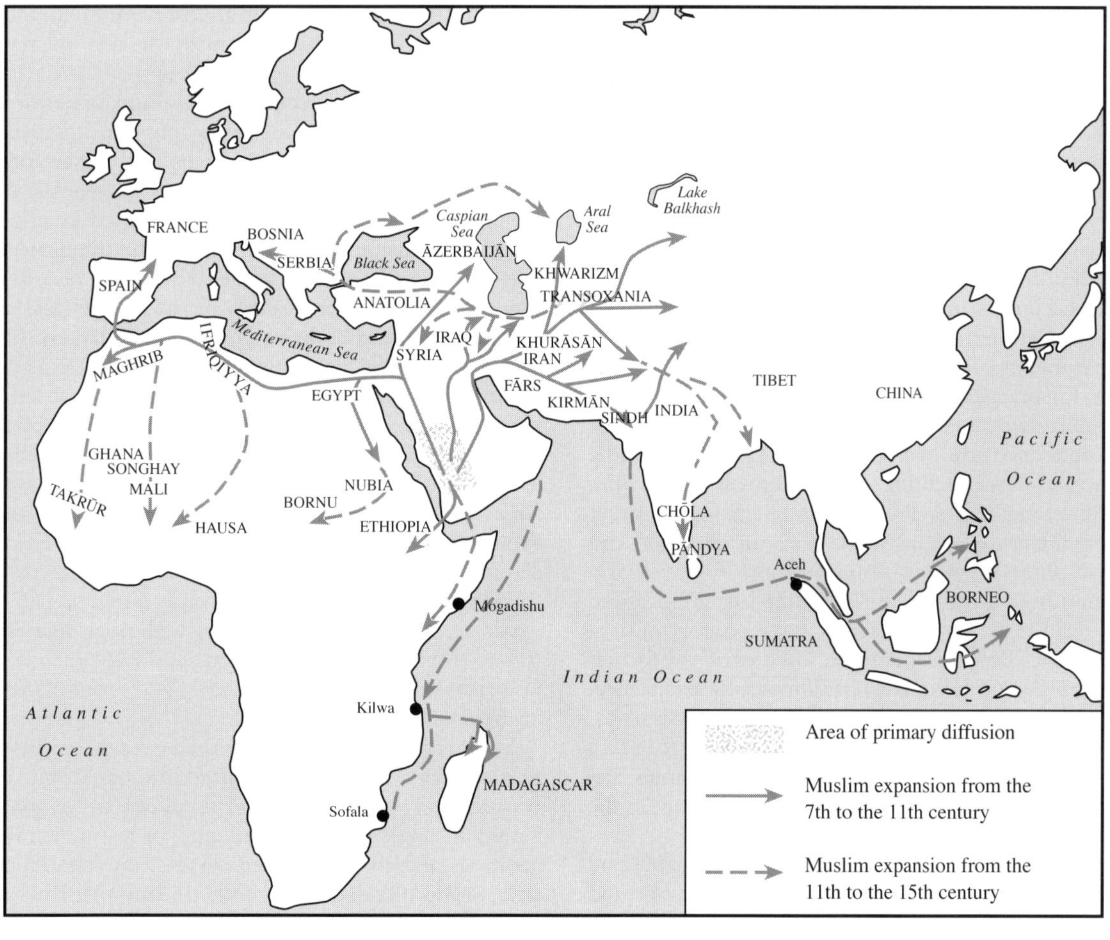

Map 12 The spread of Islam throughout the Old World, from the seventh to the fifteenth century (draft Mantran, R.).

the transformation of the desert conquerors into an elite presiding over an international civilization that not only identified itself with the faith of the invaders but also adopted their language. Even when, with the decline of the 'Abbāsid caliphate (750–1258), the political unity of Islam passed away for good, the Arabic language and the common faith, as well as the links of commerce, reinforced by the annual *ḥajj* pilgrimage to Mecca, bound together Islam's different regions through the sharing of a single 'high' culture and many common features of social and material life.

One of the most prominent shared features of life was the city. It is true that most of the tribes which formed the original ranks of the Arab conquerors were Bedouin or desert nomads; but power essentially had rested with the Quraysh, who were much more at home in the mercantile and urban world. Camp cities like Kūfa (Iraq) and Qayrawān (North Africa), where the Arab soldiery, preserving their tribal quarters, first tended to settle, were in time succeeded by true cities, developed and made prosperous by the caliphs: both old ones, like Damascus, capital of the Umayyads, and new ones like Baghdād, the 'Abbāsid capital, and Cairo, capital of the Fāṭimids. The flourishing urban life in the Islamic world stood in sharp contrast to the decline of towns that marked the 'Dark' and Middle Ages in Western Europe. In the Islamic world, well-frequented caravan routes connected the major cities, and, characteristically, it was these routes that formed the basic grids for the Arab geographers' descriptions of the world known to them. Not only craft products, but also crafts and techniques travelled along these routes. Paper manufacture spread rapidly along them, once it had been learned from the Chinese in Transoxania, in the eighth century, just as the geared waterwheel, the *sāqiya*, spread steadily from the Mediterranean in the reverse direction.

The Islamic world, by reactivating the Silk Road overland to China, and by supporting the Arab–Iranian navigation of the Indian Ocean and the Arab navigation of the Mediterranean, helped to join the various countries of East and West in a web of commerce. There was never as strong a breach in Mediterranean trade in and after the seventh century as Pirenne had tended to assume, although, undoubtedly there were in certain regions, and during certain periods, breakdowns in commerce owing to Arab military and naval operations.

The cultural life of this large zone was stamped by the use of Arabic for practically all purposes of learning from the eighth century onwards. It replaced Middle Persian, Greek, Syriac, Coptic and Latin, even for Jews and Christians writing on philosophical and scientific subjects in the Islamic world. One of the strengths of Arabic came to be the large amount of learned literature in Greek (of both the Hellenic and Hellenistic phases) that was translated into it as well as a certain amount of Indian scientific (mainly astronomical and mathematical) texts. Once it became the repository of such a rich heritage, the language began to be enriched further by fundamental contributions in both philosophy and science. Al-Rāzī (Rhazes) (860–932), Ibn Sīnā (Avicenna) 980–1037, al-Bīrūnī (973–1048), Ibn Rushd (Averroës) (1126–1196) and Ibn Khaldūn (1332–1406) are some of the names that lent lustre to medicine, science and philosophy (and, in the case of Ibn Khaldūn, to sociology).

There was another source of development of history and biography in Arabic, that is, the dedication to collection and recording of oral traditions (*ḥadīth*) of the events of the Prophet's life (*sīra*), which formed the basis of the theologians' recapitulation of the Prophet's conduct (*sunna*), setting the model for all believers. While these narrations led to the early compositions of the history of the Prophet (for example, Ibn Isḥāq, 704–767), testing of the *ḥadīth* narrators' credibility led to the undertaking of biographical researches. The *Tārīkh* of Ṭabarī (839–923) is, perhaps, the greatest work of history of the early phase.

The development of Islamic theology led to the formation of a comprehensive legal system (*fiqh*) under the four major Sunni schools (Ḥanafite, Mālikite, Shāfi'ite and Ḥanbalite) and the Shī'ite (Ja'farī) school during the eighth and ninth centuries. Within the realm of theological doctrines, al-Ash'arī (874–936) carried out a crusade against Mu'tazilite beliefs, reputedly based on a partial appeal to reason. By the tenth century, the detailed contours of the legal system and theology of Islam had been drawn, giving the social life of Muslims a large degree of uniformity despite the many differences in the opinions of the schools and the surviving influences of local custom.

The execution of Manṣūr Ḥallāj (858–922), for his assertion 'I am God', marked the public emergence of the hitherto esoteric beliefs of Ṣūfism; henceforward, Ṣūfism charted a course parallel to that of orthodox theology by stressing love, not expectation of reward or fear of punishment, as the basic factor behind man's submission to God. Ṣūfism became an open cult, with its own rites, organization and texts. Sharing a common antipathy to rationalism, it won recognition from al-Ghazālī (1058–1111), one of the great theologians and scholars of Islam. But Ṣūfism evolved further, and with Ibn al-'Arabī (1165–1240) came the theory that all existence is an emanation of the Being, and thence the belief in absolute monism *(waḥdat al-wujūd)*. Islam thus developed a rich variety of religious thought, although almost correspondingly there was a perceptible decline in the realm of scientific achievement.

Under Islam, the older geographical and historical regions largely preserved their identities, but the linguistic map changed phenomenally. From being the spoken tongue of the warriors emerging from the sparsely peopled Arabian peninsula, Arabic became not only the language of officials, scholars, merchants and townsmen of the subjugated lands, but, from the Euphrates to the Atlantic, it also began to supplant the common dialects of the villages and deserts. Even the nomadic Berbers of North Africa largely shifted to Arabic within the first millennium of Islam. In the absence of any large-scale migrations such as those that led to the imposition of Germanic and Turkish languages over large areas in roughly the same period, the spread of Arabic must be deemed a remarkable achievement. Only in the Iranian zone did it stop at being just an officials' and scholars' language. From the tenth century began the revival of Persian, in its classical incarnation, drawing richly upon Arabic vocabulary and forms of verse, although rigorously reiterating its 'Aryan' structure. Its splendid renaissance, with poets like Firdawsī (*c.* 940–1020), Rūmī (1207–1273) and Ḥāfiẓ (d. 1389), and historians like Rashīdu'ddīn (1248–1318), is one of the glories of the civilization of Islam.

Some art traditions also flourished over the entire Islamic world, like 'Saracenic' architecture based on arcuate construction, with domes and minarets, and emphasis on light and space; and the 'arabesque', or low-relief, floral or geometrical decoration. There was also a universal fascination with beautiful calligraphy, both on stone and on skin or paper, the Kūfic style succeeded by the stately *naskh* and the beautiful *nasta'līq* (see Plates 70, 71, 107–114).

There was a similar openness to diffusion of institutional forms. If the mosque was, from the beginning, the basic unit of congregational worship everywhere, the *khānqāh* (hospice) came to be a common sight once Ṣūfism had spread; and with the eleventh century began the age of the endowed *madrasa* (college), a major institution of higher education in Islam.

There was, without doubt, a considerable degree of hierarchy in Muslim society as well as despotic authority; and social inequities, such as slavery and disabilities of women, were present practically everywhere. Islam in its eastern part also suffered considerably during the Mongol conquests, precisely when its romance with science and philosophy was nearing its eventide. And yet its achievements were already so brilliant that Islamic civilization can legitimately claim a significant place in the history of humanity during the period with which this volume deals.

16

THE RISE OF ISLAM

16.1
THE RISE OF ISLAM IN ARABIA

Abdul Aziz Duri

Islam arose in the first half of the seventh century in the Arabian peninsula, a land of sparsely peopled deserts and oases. Unified by a new faith, proclaimed by Muḥammad as the Prophet of God, the Arabs rapidly created an empire and a dazzling civilization. It is now recognized that theirs was more than a mere nomadic movement caused by some little understood cycle of climatic or demographic change. Attention is now more particularly riveted to the accumulation over time of complex conditions developing within Arabia, such as the spread of oasis agriculture, emergence of urban settlements, growth of caravan trade, and a certain cultural unification based on the spread of a standard Arabic language replacing the various dialects of both nomadic and sedentary communities. These various factors were already by the sixth century tending to give to the Arab tribes on the Byzantine and Iranian frontiers a new political strength and an urge to expand at the expense of their neighbours.

By the seventh century, lands on the middle and lower Euphrates and parts of Mesopotamia had been largely Arabized. In Syria, Arab tribes spread towards the east and south-east of that country. As a threat arose from these nomadic incursions, the Byzantines encouraged the rise of Arab federate allies, the Tanūkh, Ṣaliḥ and Ghassān, in the fourth–sixth centuries. They were made Byzantine vassals to protect the frontier, ward off tribal raids and provide auxiliaries to the Byzantine army. The Lakhmids were similarly situated in subordination to Iran. The tendency towards creating larger political entities within Arabia can be discerned in the traditions about the expedition of Imrū' l-Qays of Kinda to Najrān in south-west Arabia, the Sabā'ite expeditions to Qaryāt al-Faw, and later, Abraha's campaign againt Huluban and some tribes (552?).

The Ghassānids and Lakhmids participated in the wars between Byzantium and Iran, but at times they showed independence of their respective paramount powers. The line of the Lakhmids ended in 602, and the Ghassānids also in the early seventh century. The Kinda, from Ḥaḍramaut, held Qaryāt al-Faw, a caravan centre on the road from south-west Arabia to the Gulf, and moved north; this tribal federation played an important role in the fifth and sixth centuries in Najd and Yamāma. However, the federation disintegrated, and the Kinda returned to Ḥaḍramaut in about 570. The Ghassānids protected trade routes: namely the northern part of the incense route, including Wādī l- Sirḥān, as well as trade markets (*aswāq*) in Dūma and Buṣrā. They patronized poetry, and used Arabic in their documents and in their churches. The Lakhmids protected the trade route from Yemen running through Ḥīra. Ḥīra became an important town, and a centre for Christianity. Its script developed from the (Nabatean) Aramaic, and it was from this that the Arabic script of the sixth century was derived: Arabic poetry too flourished here. The Kinda also contributed much to Arabic poetry, especially its poet and ruler Imrū' l-Qays, and its political aggrandisement possibly led to the spread of literary Arabic in southern Arabia.

In later Islamic tradition this period was designated as one of *jāhiliyya* ('ignorance') and remembered as one of heroism and of tribal conflicts, the *ayyām al-'Arab* ('Arab battles') and of the crystallization of the tribal code of honour (*murūwa*). However, it must be remembered that the penetration of Judaism and Christianity in many parts of Arabia, meant that there would be some familiarity everywhere with monotheistic notions and with ethical systems different from those of mere tribalism. Literary Arabic, superseding tribal dialects, developed and spread over the whole peninsula by the fifth century. Pre-Islamic Arabic poetry reached its climax in the sixth century, when the present Arabic script was adopted by Mecca.

The sixth century saw the gradual rise of Mecca as a caravan city and a sacred place. Tradition attributes to Qusay (early fifth century) the entry of the Quraysh into historical prominence. The spread of reports about the sanctuary (*ḥaram*) of the Ka'ba at Mecca, and of the Quraysh as descendants of Ismā'il (Ishmael son of Abraham) and as guardians of the Ka'ba, helped in securing the friendship and attachment of the nomads to the Quraysh townsmen and merchants; and pilgrimages were often combined with trade fairs. Though it had a pantheon of deities, Mecca had traces of monotheistic ideas: the trio of al-Lāt, 'Uzzā and Manāt were held to be daughters of Allāh; and the Ḥanīfs saw themselves as followers of the religion of Abraham, and, therefore, monotheists.

A station on the incense route, Mecca depended on trade even for its provisions. From local commerce it extended its activities to international trade. The fall of Palmyra and the continued wars between Byzantium and Iran favoured the growth of the 'incense' route, away from the war zone, while the fall of the Ḥimyār tribe paved the way for the power of the Quraysh. Public affairs at Qurayshite Mecca were dealt with by the *mala* or council of men of wealth and of recognized 'noble' families; tribal ties were perceptibly weakened by the growth of commerce so that Quraysh polity could be termed a rough oligarchy.

It was in this modestly prosperous town that Muḥammad was born. On his life and the contents of his prophetic preaching the most primary source is the Qur'ān, the collection of the revelations (*waḥī*) that he proclaimed to have received from God, and in which God is the speaker and Muḥammad the immediate addressee. The texts of the revelations, collected together after the Prophet's death (632), are not arranged in a chronological order, and the occasion and context of the individual revelations are often known only from later reports and commentaries. Broadly, they are classified into those which were received at Mecca, in or before 622, and those received at Medina (622–632); the former are largely concerned with belief, while in the latter there is much that is of a legislative character, crucial for the organization of a distinct social community.

Reports about the Prophet as heard from eye-witnesses were spread about and began in time to be recorded, becoming known as *ḥadīth*. From such oral reports systematic accounts of the Prophet's life and actions (*sīra/maghāzī*) came to be written. The first works on *sīra* belonged to the second half of the seventh century, written by Abban ibn 'Uthmān (*c.* 713) and 'Urwa ibn al-Zubayr (94/712), to be elaborated by Zuhrī (741) and others of his generation. The first full-scale *sīra* was produced by Zuhrī's student, Ibn Isḥāq (761). With Wāqidī (823) and Ibn Sa'd (844), the genre reached its maturity in plan and content. A tendency towards exaggeration developed with time; and popular stories, often quite unhistorical, grew apace. The historian needs to discount much of the pious literature of the latter type.

The Prophet was probably forty years old when he received the first call of his mission (*c.* 609), and his mission at Mecca lasted about thirteen years, whereafter in 622 he migrated to Medina. Most reports put his birth at about 570, but much uncertainty about the actual year prevails.

Little is known of Muḥammad's life before the call to Prophethood. He was of a respected family, but of modest resources. His early life had been difficult. Born an orphan (Qu'rān, xciii. 6), he lost his mother early, and soon thereafter his grandfather, 'Abdu'l-Muṭṭalib. He was really brought up by his uncle Abū Ṭālib, and spent the first four or five years of his life in the desert with the Banī Sa'd, looking after the pasturing sheep of some Meccans. He also went to Syria as a boy with his uncle, in a caravan. Pious traditions assert that he did not take part in idol-worship, and Muḥammad might, indeed, have been inclined to the beliefs of the Ḥanīfs, the Meccan monotheists.

Muḥammad is called *ummī* (vii, 157), generally explained as 'illiterate', but some indicate that this is because he could not read the (Jewish and Christian) scriptures (xxv. 4, 5); and *ummī* might also have meant one who was not of Jewish descent (cf. lxii.2)

At twenty-five, he married Khadīja, a rich widow, who engaged in credit and commerce. She had employed him in her trade to Syria and other places (twice to Jurash), and was impressed with his character and honesty. She always stood by him, and bore him four daughters and two sons, both of whom died young.

At Mecca, Muḥammad became known as *al-amīn* ('the honest one'), and before his Prophetic call arbitrated on how the Black Stone in Ka'ba was to be set in place when the building was being rebuilt. This good repute might have been due in part to his increasing spiritual concerns, with periods of seclusion and devotions (not unfamiliar, though, in Mecca) in a cave at mount Ḥīra, and then visions in dreams. Yet the first revelation shook him deeply.

Sūra xcvi.1 ff. is believed to have been the first revelation; other revelations (starting with lxxiv.1 1–5) followed, and continued till his last days. *Waḥī* (revelation) to him was auditory: it is said to have come at times like the ringing of bells, or through an angel who recited the words to him (lxxv.16–18, lxxxvii.6). The *Waḥī* came to him as to previous prophets (iv.163).

The mission in Mecca, once Muḥammad had come to terms with his call, was initially secret, but three years later, it was proclaimed openly (xv.94). Conversions began with his family and friends and, then, the clan, Mecca being naturally especially addressed (vi. 93). The Revelations came in Arabic, the tongue of his own people (xiii.37; xxvi.194–5, 198–9), but were meant for all peoples, as indicated in some Meccan verses (e.g. vi.90, xiii.38; xxv.1).

The basic elements of the faith were developed in the Meccan period to be elaborated and supplemented by legislative and practical measures at Medina later. Belief in one God and in the Day of Judgement (lvi.2, 6–46; lxxxiii.1–6) were its essential elements and the most insistently emphasized, as also a rejection of polytheism and idol worship. 'Submission' to God (*al-Islām*) was held to be the essence of piety, and the worship of Him its outward expression (iii. 18–19). Ethical values like honesty, kindness, modesty, and chastity are stressed. Respect and obedience to parents, respect for others' rights and charity, especially to the poor and orphans, are prescribed (ii.177; iv.36; xvii.26). Liberation of slaves was highly commended (xc.13; also iv.92; lviii.3).

Of the five 'pillars' of Islam, the prayers were set early in Mecca (xcvi.9–10; lxxxvii.14–15) and their times defined (iv.101–3). Fasting was first prescribed for one day (*'ashūrā*) as practised by the Jews (10 *Tishri*), and by the Quraysh as well. The fast of Ramadhān was decreed in Medina in 624(ii.183–188). Pilgrimage to Mecca was next made obligatory (ii.158,189,196). Paying alms was recommended in Mecca (li.19; xxvii.3), but became obligatory (xxxiii.33) with their quantum defined, in Medina.

The *qibla* (direction of prayers) was initially towards Jerusalem, but it was changed to Mecca in 624 (ii.144, 149). This change is significant, since it underlined the relation of Islam with Abraham, the traditional founder of the Ka'ba (ii.127). Islam was proclaimed as a return to the religion of Abraham (Ibrāhīm) (ii.130-135), who was a Ḥanīf and a Muslim (iii.67). In practical terms, Islam undoubtedly gained in Arabia with its holiest of holies identified with a recognized pilgrim centre of the Arabs.

The Prophet's mission first went on largely unopposed until he began to denounce the heathen gods and so seemingly denied the Meccans' ancestral beliefs (xi.62) and undermined faith in the gods of their sanctuary, very crucial to their position as the Ka'ba's guardians. Especially the wealthy became increasingly opposed to the new call, for it could threaten their trade, since the *ḥajj* and the sacred months were of great importance to Mecca (xxviii.57). Muḥammad's small but growing sect of followers first included his wife Khadīja, and young cousin ʿAlī (later the fourth caliph, 656–661), his close friend Abū Bakr (the first caliph, 632–634), ʿUmar (caliph, 634–644) and ʿUthmān (caliph, 644–656). They were to show, with others, an extreme fortitude in loyalty to the Prophet in all the harsh circumstances that now ensued.

Muḥammad was exposed to accusations (xxiii.70) and ridicule (xv.11, 95; vi.10). Though owing to the support of Abū Ṭālib and his clan there was no danger to his life, plots against him were made in secret (viii.30; xxi.3; xliii.80). Converts with no tribes to protect them, especially the poor and the slaves, suffered heavily.

As Muḥammad could not protect his followers he advised them to emigrate to Abyssinia, and some (reputedly eleven men and four women) did so in the fifth year of his preaching. A year later over eighty emigrated, though some returned. The Quraysh took severe measures and drove the Prophet's clan of the Banī Hāshim and Abū Ṭālib to the latter's *shiʿb* (valley) and boycotted them. It may, however, not have been as hard as was supposed later on; and the ban collapsed three years later (619).

Muḥammad, however, lost his wife Khadīja, and Abū Ṭālib, in the meantime, and could not by himself get the required support in Mecca. He tried to establish himself at Ṭāʾif, south-east of Mecca, and failed; and then during the pilgrimage season he contacted the people of Medina: at first (620), six were converted, in the second season (621), twelve. Muṣʿab ibn ʿUmayr was now sent with them to propagate the faith. By the third season (622), Islam spread in Medina and many of that town met the Prophet secretly at ʿAqaba, and paid homage to him.

In 621 the Prophet told his followers of the *Isrāʾ* (night journey to Jerusalem) and *miʿrāj* (ascension to Heaven) (xvii.1, 60). ʿĀisha stated that both journeys were made spiritually, while another wife of the Prophet claimed that both were physical acts. Ibn Isḥāq thought both to be possible, while later Muslim tradition strongly asserted a physical journey in both cases, being cited as miracles that were held to be a necessary mark of prophethood.

Muḥammad now directed his community in Mecca to emigrate to Medina and about seventy did so fairly openly; he himself followed secretly, with Abū Bakr. The Quraysh did not wish Muḥammad to be out of their sight, but he evaded them and arrived in Medina on 24 September 622.

The migration to Medina could with hindsight be judged a momentous event. In one step, an unarmed religion became a state; and Muḥammad now combined the mantle of the Prophet with that of a statesman. Its importance became so clear even to contemporaries that the Muslim lunar calendar was assigned the *hijra* ('migration') for its epoch, when it was instituted under the second caliph, ʿUmar (634–644).

Once at Medina, Muḥammad set himself energetically to work. First a mosque was built, with quarters for the Prophet. The 'emigrants' (*muhājirūn*), received by the Muslims of Medina, designated 'Helpers' (*Anṣār*), had to be settled in houses of their own on land granted by the *Anṣār*. A *muʾākhāt* (brotherhood) was instituted; usually a *muhājir* allied himself with an *anṣārī*, obtaining support even to the extent of inheritance, which practice was later abrogated after the Muslim success at Badr (624).

At Medina, some arrangement became necessary to define the relations between Muslims and the others and to organize the affairs of the emerging polity. This was mainly done in the *ṣaḥīfa* (charter) or *kitāb* (writ). This document announced the formation of an *umma* (community) bound by faith, contained a compact with the Jewish tribes, and provided a kind of constitution for the functioning of the young state under the Prophet's control.

Tribes survived as units for some social functions, but loyalty to the *umma* began to take precedence over tribal affiliations. Matters of war or peace were decided by the Prophet, and he was the arbiter in any differences among the people covered by the compact. Medina was considered *ḥaram* (sanctuary), while the Quraysh were seen as the main enemy.

The struggle with the Quraysh had started with limited raids on some of their small caravans in 623, and these soon threatened the trade of the Meccans. The Prophet concluded agreements with tribes in the vicinity to ensure their co-operation or neutrality. A raid carried out in a sacred month (led by Ibn Jahsh) was considered justified (ii.217). One such raid to capture a major caravan led to the battle of Badr. The Quraysh were alerted and though the caravan passed safely, they felt that their trade was threatened and decided to strike. In an uneven battle at Badr (see viii.5–7), the Muslims were yet victorious (624), their success seeming to them to come from the support of the Lord (viii.9, 12, 17). The rules for division of the spoils of war were now defined (viii.41), and the treatment of prisoners prescribed. The duty of *jihād* too was now formally imposed on all Muslims.

The Quraysh prepared for revenge, and, aided by their allies (of Thaqīf, ʿAbd Manāt and Aḥābish), moved in a large body towards Mecca. The Muslims' position weakened, when ʿAbdullāh ibn Ubay withdrew with his people; and the Prophet himself declined to let a regiment of Ibn Ubay's Jewish allies fight with him. The encounter at Uḥud (23 March 625) resulted in a major reverse for the Muslims (iii.152). But the Quraysh could not win a decisive victory and withdrew.

After Uḥud Muḥammad continued his policy of raids on caravans, and on tribal groups suspected of enmity. It was clear that the Quraysh, despite their success at Uḥud, were not still able to ensure safety for the trade route to Syria. They now tried to raise a fresh alliance of tribes to attack Medina. Muḥammad planned to stay in Medina and to dig a ditch, to protect the open part (north) of the city. The siege lasted fifteen days (May 627). It was a critical time for Muslims (xxxiii.10–11): the 'hypocrites' (*munāfiqūn*) wavered, while the Jewish tribe of Qurayza tended to side with the enemy (xxxiii.26). However, the failure of the besiegers' cavalry to break through the defences, stormy weather and mutual suspicions between the allies led to the failure of the siege (xxx.9, 25). The Quraysh not only failed in their confrontation with Muḥammad, but their trade also declined as well as their prestige.

The Prophet had made separate compacts (*muwādaʿa*) with the Jews who were divided among tribes and clans. Their help, or at least their neutrality, in case of any attack on Medina, was imperative. Since they were the 'people of the Book', he had at first treated them gently and hoped to win them over. However, the Jews rejected the claim that Muḥammad stood in succession to their prophets, and this embittered relations. The Jewish Qaynuqāʿ turned hostile after Badr (viii.58). They were besieged but allowed to leave Medina with their families (624). The Qur'ān then warned against alliances with Jews and Christians (v.51, 57).

About a year later came the clash with the Jewish tribe of the Banū' l-Naḍīr. They were accused of conspiring against the Prophet, warned, and besieged; some of their palm trees were cut (lix.5), then they were allowed to leave for Khaybar and Syria with their goods, except arms, while their land was made *fay* (public property) for the Prophet (lix.6) (625).

The Jewish Qurayza were dealt with in 627, immediately after the raising of the siege by the Quraysh, during which they were suspected of aiding the besiegers. They were punished with a massacre of their menfolk and enslavement of women and children. The number of those killed may, however, have been exaggerated by pious tradition.

The Prophet did not, in this phase of success, want to destroy the Quraysh, his own tribe, and of great prestige among Arabs; he wished only to neutralize their opposition. The new attitude is shown in the Ḥudaibiyya expedition. Muḥammad decided to visit Mecca in 628 as a religious act (*'umra*) and to make a show of Muslim strength. The Prophet avoided the army sent by the Quraysh and came to Ḥudaibiyya (about nine miles from Mecca). After negotiations, an agreement was reached, viz., a truce for ten years; all other people made free to make alliance with either Muḥammad or with the Quraysh; and Muslims to be allowed to visit Mecca the next year. In spite of some unpleasant details, Ḥudaibiyya proved to be a victory for Muḥammad (xlviii, 18–21): Islam spread still more rapidly; and its followers multiplied.

The turn of Khaybar, a fertile oasis north of Medina with rich palm groves inhabited mainly by Jews, came next, since the Banū' l-Naḍīr had moved to settle there. The Prophet marched quickly against them (628): Khaybar was conquered, the land of its inhabitants was considered booty, but the Jews were left to cultivate it for half the produce. A campaign against Mu'ta (southern Syria) (629), now undertaken, proved unsuccessful: its three leaders and a few others were killed, and Khālid ibn Walīd, later to be so famous, led the withdrawal.

The truce with the Quraysh was held to have been broken by the attack of its allies, the Banū Bakr, on the Khuzā'a, allies of the Muslims, who appealed to the Prophet. The response was quick: a large force left Medina (630), the Quraysh leader, Abū Sufyān, who came to mediate, saw no way out, adopted Islam, and advised the Quraysh to surrender. Significantly, there was now little opposition (except from some leaders of the Makhzūm clan). The Prophet clearly wanted to win over the Quraysh, instructed his troops not to use force, and declared a general amnesty (s.xvi/126). He entered Mecca in January 630, and the Ka'ba was cleared of idols. It was the victory that opened the gates for all Arabs to join Islam (*sūra*, cx, 'victory', was now revealed).

The new strength of Islam was shown when the Hawāzin and Thaqīf rose to challenge the Prophet's power. The Muslims moved, aided by a levy from the Quraysh, and a bitter struggle with the Bedouin tribes followed. The Hawāzin were defeated, 630 (ix.29), while the Thaqīf entrenched themselves, with provisions, in their fort. The Hawāzin accepted Islam, their captured women and children being freed, but the Thaqīf stood the siege (630) and the Muslims withdrew. About a year later their delegation came to announce their acceptance of Islam and a peaceful rendering of allegiance.

Now that much of Arabia was firmly under his authority, the Prophet turned north, gathered a large force from Medina and the allied tribes, including the Quraysh, and announced his destination as Tabūk, on the way to Syria (630). The objective is not clear; but from Tabūk Muḥammad decided to return to Medina.

The Prophet turned to peaceful ways to propagate his mission, the *da'wā*. Year 9 AH (630) is called the year of the *wufūd* ('delegations'), in reference to the advent of deputations from different tribes and clans, especially from central and south Arabia, to announce their conversion and allegiance. During the *ḥajj* pilgrimage of this year, it was announced that no polytheists would be allowed to enter the Ka'ba hereafter (ix.28); and war was now declared upon them (ix.5).

In 632, the Prophet led his last pilgrimage to Mecca. In a farewell address attributed to him he stressed equality among Muslims, the sanctity of property and blood, and the discarding of Jāhiliyya (pre-Islamic) pacts and obligations. Preparations were now made for another campaign against southern Syria, but the Prophet fell ill and passed away on 7 June 632.

Muḥammad's achievement in his lifetime had been great, but the historical consequences of his mission were only just beginning to unfold at the time of his death. Abū Bakr is said to have declared upon the Prophet's death: 'Those who worshipped Muḥammad, should know he is dead; but those who worship Allāh know Allāh is alive and immortal'. The words, possibly apocryphal, bear a much larger significance than was perhaps intended when they were uttered (or recorded). The entire historical context in which Islam was to be practised as a faith was to change fundamentally by its own triumphs. The strong will of the first caliph Abū Bakr (d. 634) and the statesmanship of his successor, 'Umar (634–644), played their part in first saving Islam within the Arabian peninsula and, then, in initiating and maintaining its dramatic expansion in other lands as a military power. This expansion and the conversion of other peoples ultimately gave new strength and content to the universality that was always implicit in the strong monotheism of Islam, where worship is due to God from all mankind.

BIBLIOGRAPHY

AL-'ALĪ SĀLEH. 1988. *Al-Dawla fī-'Ahd al-Rāsul* (The State in the time of the Prophet). al-Majma 'al-'Ilmī al-'Irāqī. Baghdād.

ANDRAE, T. 1960. *Muhammed, the Man and his Faith* (trans. by Menzel, T.). Harper Torchbooks. New York.

AL-BALĀDHURĪ. 1959. *Anṣāb al-Ashrāf* (The Noble Companions), ed. by M. Hamidullah. Dār al-Ma'ārīf. Cairo.

BLACHERE, R. 1952. *Le problème de Mahomet.* PUF. Paris.

BUHL, F. 1961. *Das Leben Muhammeds* (The Life of Muhammad), 3rd edn. Heidelberg.

DARWĀZA, M. L. 1384 AH/AD 1965. *Sīrat al-Rasūl* (The Life of the Prophet), 2 vols, 2nd edn. Cairo.

GIBB, H. A. R. 1969. *Mohammedanism.* Oxford University Press, Oxford.

HAMIDULLĀH, M. 1959. *Le Prophète de l'Islam, sa vie, son oeuvre.* Vrin, Paris.

IBN-HISHĀM. *al-Sīra al-Nabawiyya* (The Life of the Prophet), 4 vols, M. al-Saqqa *et al.* (eds). Dār Ihva'-Turāth al-'Arabī. Beirut.

Majmū 'āt al-Wathāiq al-Siyāsiyya li'l-'Ahd al-Nabawī wā'l-Khilāfa al-Rāshida (Collection of Documents Pertaining to Policy at the Time of the Prophet and the First Four [Orthodox] Caliphs), 2nd edn. Cairo.

MAQRĪZĪ 1941. *Imtā 'al-Asmā* (Delight in Names). Maḥmūd Shākir (ed). Cairo.

RODINSON, M. 1961. *Mahomet.* Paris. English transl. *Mohammed.* Penguin Books, Harmondsworth, 1971.

ṬABARĪ. 1976–1977. *Tārīkh al-Rusūl wa'l-Mulūk* (History of the Prophets and Kings), 10 vols, 2nd edn. A. F. Ibrāhīm (ed.). Dār al-Ma'ārif. Cairo.

'UMARĪ, A. D. 1991. *al-Sīra al-Nabawiyya al-Ṣaḥīḥa* (The Sound History of the Life of the Prophet), 2 vols. Qatar.

WĀQIDĪ. 1966. *Kitāb al-Māghāzī* (The Book of Military Campaigns). 3 vols. Marsden Jones (ed.). London.

WATT, W. M. 1960. *Muḥammad at Mecca*, Oxford.

——. 1962. *Muḥammad at Medina.* Oxford.

16.2
THE SOURCES OF ISLAM

Azmi Taha Al-Sayyed

When Muḥammad announced that he was the messenger of Allāh (God), it was made clear that he was otherwise a man just like any other (Qur'ān, iii.144) and that the religion he propagated, termed *Islām*, or submission (to God) (vi. 125, etc.) was offered to all, without compulsion (ii.256; cix.6). Allāh's own words constituted the Qur'ān; and the words of the Prophet and his deeds, which were later called *sunna*, supplemented the commandments of the Qur'ān. These two (later considered to be the two sources of Islam) were deemed to constitute the totality of the belief and practice of the faith during the lifetime of the Prophet. But after his death (632), questions soon arose on which direct guidance was not available in the Qur'ān or in the reports circulating about the Prophet's words and actions. This necessitated the definition of rules deduced from principles found in the Qur'ān and the *sunna*. This came to be known later as *ijtihād* (endeavour) and to be treated as the third source of Islam.

Of the three sources, the Qur'ān is naturally held by Muslims to be the primary one, being God's Word. But words need to be understood, and traditional Muslim interpretation has recognized that some Qur'ānic verses denote single specific meanings (*muḥkamāt*), while others have more than one possible meaning (*mutashābihāt*). Several verses have their meanings defined and limited by reference to contexts, often provided only by *sunna* reports. The work of interpreting the Qur'ān by such means constitutes *tafsīr*, in which realm al-Ṭabarī (d. 923) is widely held to have made the most monumental contribution.

In matters of creed, the Qur'ān lays emphasis on the belief in the One God, who is the Creator of all, is beneficent and benevolent and is the Lord of all creation and beings within it, and who rewards as well as chastises, in this world and on the Day of Judgement, when the dead shall be resurrected. God is served by angels, among whom is Gabriel (*Jibrā'īl*, who conveyed the revelations to Muḥammad. The believers are warned against the fallen angel Shayṭān (Satan) or Iblīs, who seeks to seduce mankind to evil. The exegeses of these issues take a considerable space in the Qur'ān, in particular as to what pertains to Allāh, and to His qualities. The Qur' ān underscores obedience to Allāh, since this is the purpose for which He has created man. This act of obedience is called 'worship' (*'ibādah*), which refers to those acts which conform to Allāh's orders, including religious rites. The essential rites are the 'five pillars' of Islam, namely, the verbal testimony (*shahādah*) that 'there is no god but Allāh, and Muḥammad is the prophet of Allāh'; the offering of the five prescribed prayers during the day and night (*ṣalāt*); fasting in the month of Ramaḍān (*ṣawm*); prescribed almsgiving (*zakāt*); and the pilgrimage to Mecca (*ḥajj*) at least once in the lifetime of the person who is capable of doing so.

The Qur'ān explicitly claims that the creed of Islam is identical to the creeds propagated by earlier divine revelations received by Abraham, Moses and Jesus (ii.136). Though the Jews and Christians are accused of having altered the divine books delivered to both Moses and Jesus (ii.140), they are still called 'People of the Book' (ii.113, iv.153, 171, v.18–19, etc.) and are summoned to what the Qur'ān calls 'the common word' (*Kalimah Sawā'*) between them and the Muslims (iii.64).

The second major element which the Qur'ān comprehends is that of the *sharī'a*, which is the practical and legal side of religion.

The *sharī'a* found in the Qur'ān includes law on such matters as the rules for dividing inheritance between heirs; provision for punishments for stealing and adultery; a specified maximum number of wives (four); and prohibition of gambling, usury and some items of food and drink, especially pork and wine.

Much space is devoted in the Qur'ān to man's conduct, notably behaviour towards others. The Qur'ān emphasizes the principle of equality of man, in that every person is descended from one father, that is, Adam; and Adam was created from dust (ii.213; iii.59; vii.26, 27); and it sets piety (*taqwā*) as the criterion for distinction (*cf.* lix.18).

The concept of good morals is associated in the Qur'ān with 'righteousness', or what Allāh commands, whereas 'evil' is linked with what He prohibits. There is considerable emphasis in the Qur'ān on praiseworthy conduct, such as clemency, self-control, respect for the elderly, dutifulness towards parents, good treatment of women, especially wives, and of relatives, treating one's neighbours amicably, refraining from lies and slander, and helping the sickly and the needy (e.g. xi.86; xxvi.1, 165; xxix. 7; xxxi.13; xivi. 14; lv.8; lxx.19–34).

Sunna (traditions of the Prophet), the second 'source' of Islam, is held to comprise everything that was said, done or agreed to by Muḥammad. Verbal *sunna* comprises the utterances of the Prophet with regard to Islamic legislation and forms the major part of the Prophetic tradition. But the *sunna* also includes all those reported deeds of the Prophet that were intended to serve as models, for example for the ways to perform ablutions (*wuḍū'*), prayers (*ṣalāt*) and pilgrimage (*ḥajj*), or carry out judicial actions. Still another category of *sunna* comprises 'what was agreed upon' (*taqrīr*), represented by the Prophet's silence on some utterances and actions that Muslims made in his presence.

There are several verses of the Qur'ān where Muslims are urged to obey the Prophet (e.g., xlviii.33; xlviii.17), to see him as an example, to quote from him, and imitate him. The Prophet's 'companions' used to relate to people what they had heard from the Prophet, or saw him do. This is why the traditions have also been called *ḥadīth*, or oral statements. The Ummayad caliph 'Umar ibn 'Abd al-'Azīz (719) ordered that all such reports be collected and written down. There was thus a considerable lapse of time between the original report and its first record. Muslim scholars thus had to devise some method of checking the authenticity of the traditions. Their major concern was with the credibility of each of the named original narrators and successive transmitters. In the ninth century, two large collections of *ḥadīth* were compiled, by al-Bukhārī (d. 870) and by Muslim (d. 875), both obtaining the title *al-Ṣaḥīḥ* ('sound' or 'correct'), owing to the belief that these were selected according to the best standards of authenticity. Shī'ite scholars, it is true, tend to question the validity of much of such *ḥadīth* collection, generally urging the reliability of only such *ḥadīth* narrations as are traced to the Prophet's cousin and son-in-law, 'Alī. Modern critical research too has raised many problems regarding the evolution of the traditions and the authenticity of individual narrations (Schacht, 1950).

The *sunna* complements the Qur'ān. This means that many legal principles which are not directly to be found in the Qur'ān are derived from the *sunna*. As examples one can cite the injunction to provide adequate support for a wife, how to deal with the inheritance of a grandmother, and the prohibition of marriages with persons related in specified ways and of the eating the meat of certain animals.

Ijtihād, the third 'source' of Islam, literally means 'an effort' made by a competent jurist to derive legal rules from the Qur'ān and *sunna* for matters on which there is no clear statement in either of these two sources. It is, therefore, subordinate to, and delimited by, the Qur'ān and the *ḥadīth*.

There exists a kind of collective *ijtihād*, called 'consensus' (*ijmā'*), that is, customs or rules on which all Muslim scholars have openly or tacitly agreed (*ittifāq*). Many (excluding Shī'ite theologians, however) regard consensus (*ijmā'*) as a reliable source of the *sharī'a*. Foremost among other principles governing *ijtihād* – and the only valid one, according to al-Shāfi'ī (d. 820) – is deduction by *qiyās* or analogy: the jurist looks for a precedent in the Qur'ān or *sunna* which may resemble the case he is examining. If he finds one, he applies the same legal principle to the case before him.

There is also another method of *ijtihād*, much resorted to in the Ḥanafite school, though rejected by al-Shāfi'ī: this is called 'common interests' (*istiṣlāḥ*): whenever anology is not available, the jurist examines whether a particular course, if adopted, would result in a judgement of public interest or utility (*maṣlaḥah*).

The story of the arrangement and elaboration of Muslim law (*sharī'a*) after the Prophet's death (632) can only be briefly set out here. His non-prophetic functions were deemed to devolve to his successors (*khalīfas*), the caliphs, beginning with Abū Bakr (632–634), followed by 'Umar I (634–644), 'Uthmān (644–656) and 'Alī (656–661). Under these non-dynastic 'pious' caliphs, all of whom were companions of the Prophet, the Islamic Arab Empire was created, and the caliphs, especially 'Umar I, took a number of financial, fiscal and administrative measures for the empire's governance. Later jurists, such as Abū Yūsuf (d. 798), took these into account as legitimate pieces of legislation.Since there was no fixed law of caliphal succession, the challenge to the claims of 'Alī, the Prophet's cousin, by Mu'āwiya, the founder of the Umayyad dynasty (661–750), and the death of 'Alī's son (the Prophet's grandson) Ḥusayn at Karbalā (680) while challenging the claims of the Umayyads, led to the formation of the *Shī'a*, the 'party', in favour of the Prophet's house. The Shī'ites developed in time the theory of the *imām*, a religious leader from the Prophet's house, capable of perfect legislation by means of *ijtihād*. The Fāṭimid caliphate of Egypt (969–1171) belonged to a section of this sect (Ismā'īlīs). Subsequently, most Shī'ites, particularly in the eastern Islamic lands, tended to accept the line of the Twelve *Imāms* (with Ismā'īl and his branch excluded), which ended with the disappearance of the twelfth imām in 873. Thereafter, the function of *ijtihād* has had to be exercised by such theologians as obtain by their learning the status of *mujtahids*.

Among the majority of Muslims, who in contradistinction to the Shī'ites called themselves *Ahl Sunna*, 'followers of the *Sunnah*', or Sunnis, there developed four major 'rites' (*madhhabs*) or schools of jurisprudence, founded by Abū Ḥanīfa (d. 767), Mālik ibn 'Anas (d. 795), al-Shāfi'ī (d. 820) and Aḥmad ibn Ḥanbal (d. 855), respectively. They have differences (*ikhtilāf*) among themselves on matters of principle, such as the scope of *rāy* (personal opinion) and *istiḥsān* (choice of the 'better' course), as well as on numerous matters of detail. But in sum the differences as to substance of law are not fundamental; such being also the case between these Sunni schools and the *madhhab* of the 'Twelve' Shī'ites traced to the sixth *imām* Ja'far al-Ṣādiq (d. 765). All four Sunni 'rites' came to be regarded as legitimate by Sunnis: one had to choose a particular school alone for oneself, although the choice often came to be made by the territory or community to which one belonged. Most Sunnis in medieval times held that with the establishment of these schools 'the gate of *ijtihād* was closed'; yet some theologians, like the Ḥanbali scholar Ibn Taymiyya (d. 1328) continued to acknowledge the need for *ijtihād* though prescribing rigorous constraints under which it could be exercised.

If man's relations with man were a major concern underlying the elaborate construction of the *sharī'a*, Islam as a faith (*dīn*) was deeply concerned with man's relations with God. The very Qur'ānic expression, *islām* (vi.125; lxi.7; xxxix.22), means man's 'submission' to God; and the nature of God and the nature of man's relationship with him were necessarily the objects of ever-growing reflection and speculation within Islam in its first millennium.

With the Mu'tazila, traced to Wāṣil ibn 'Aṭā (d.761), began an urge to systematize and partly, perhaps, to rationalize theological principles. God was so absolute that words used in the Qur'ān to suggest anthropomorphic representations of him were to be treated as figurative only; God's justice is infinite and, therefore, predetermined; the Qur'ān is created, not eternal, for God is unique in His eternity. These ideas exercised considerable influence until the tenth century, when al-Ash'arī (d. 935) contested its major premises and laid the basis of much of the later Sunni theology of dependence upon *manqūl* (the received text) as against the products of reason (*ma'qūl*). The Qur'ānic words about God were to be taken as they are: man is incapable of grasping God's absoluteness in His attributes; God's grace, like His justice, is also infinite; and the Qur'ān is not created, but eternal. All these matters came to be the concern of *'ilm al-Kalām* or scholastic theology.

Philosophical ideas, generated notably by the increasing familiarity with Greek thought, showed their influence in the writings of Ibn Sīnā (Avicenna) (d. 1037) with his interest in the 'first cause', gnosis, and the eternity of the soul. Ibn Rushd (Averroes) (d. 1198) attempted to define truth which could be reached both by received knowledge and by reason. Already, however, al-Ghazālī (d. 1111) had taken up the cudgels against philosophical speculations and so heavily reinforced the dogmatic system of theology which al-Ash'arī had formulated.

In the meantime, a spiritual wave developed which was to exercise considerable influence on Muslim higher thought as well as popular beliefs. This was the mystical movement known as Ṣūfism (*ṣūf*, woollen garment), which seems to have essentially originated in a spurning of the idea of reward or punishment as a factor impelling one to obey God. The only admissible impulse could be love. The saying was attributed to the woman *ṣūfī*, Rābi'a al-Adawīya (d. 801): 'Love of God hath so absorbed me that neither love nor hate of any other thing remains in my heart' (quoted in Gibb, 1953, p. 133). The object of spiritual endeavour was then the elimination (*fanā*) of self, which would at once be communion (*wiṣāl*) with God. It was for such a claimed communion that the celebrated ṣūfī Manṣūr al-Ḥallāj was executed (922). But Ṣūfism spread despite such persecution (on the whole, occasional), and from al-Ghazālī, it obtained a *de jure* recognition. With Ibn al-'Arabī (d.1240), a new trend began within Ṣūfism that of monism and pantheism (or, at least, qualified pantheism), which transformed the basis of much of ṣūfism throughout the Islamic world, notably in its eastern and central parts. It is to be remembered that despite their differences with orthodox theologians ('*ulamā*'), the *ṣūfīs* by no means rejected the *sharī'a*, and they also insisted that the Ṣūfic truths had descended to them from Muḥammad through a chain (*silsilah*) of successors traced to him usually through 'Alī. By its own perception, therefore, Ṣūfīsm was imbedded firmly in the very prophethood of Muḥammad and represented the most total submission of the believer (*mu'min*) to God. This perception was naturally not shared by the mainstream theologians, many of whom continued to express their suspicions of the mystic path (*ṭarīqah*) as a challenge to the formal law (*sharī'a*). Despite such suspicion, Ṣūfism retained its appeal for those who were drawn to the prospect of spiritual experiences; and the Ṣūfī's objective of self-annihilation (*fanā*) in his love of God inspired great devotion. This spirit is especially reflected in the Persian poetry of Rūmī(1207–1273), Ḥāfiẓ (d. 1389) and Jāmī (1414–1492); and in Arabic there is an early representative too – the Egyptian Ibn al-Fāriḍ (d. 1235).

BIBLIOGRAPHY

Articles on Islam, Al-Ḳur'ān, Ḥadīth and Idjtihād. In *Encyclopedia of Islam* (new edition). 1986–1993. E. J. Brill. Leiden.

COULSON, K. 1964. *History of Islamic Law.* Edinburgh University Press, Edinburgh.

GIBB, H. A. R. 1953. *Mohammedanism, an Historical Survey*, 2nd edn. London. Now reprinted as *Islam.*

GRUNEBAUM, I. G. E. VON. 1961. *Islam: Essays in the Nature and Growth of Cultural Tradition,* 2nd edn. London.

LEVY, R. 1957. *The Social Structure of Islam,* 2nd edn. Cambridge.

MORGAN, K. W.(ed.) 1958. *Islam Interpreted by Muslims.* Ronald Press, London.

NICHOLSON, R. A. 1914. *The Mystics of Islam.* London.

——. 1921. *Studies in Islamic Mysticism.* London.

SCHACHT, J. 1950. *The Origins of Muhammadan Jurisprudence.* Oxford.

The Holy Qur'ān. 1968. English Translation and Commentary by Yusuf Ali. Dar-el-Arabiah, Beirut.

TRITTON, A. S. 1962. *Islam: Belief and Practice.* Hutchinson, London.

WATT, W. M. 1961. *Muhammad: Prophet and Statesman.* Oxford University Press, Oxford.

16.3

THE FORMATION OF THE EARLY ISLAMIC POLITY AND SOCIETY: GENERAL CHARACTERISTICS

Clifford Edmund Bosworth

When in 632 Abū Bakr became caliph (*khalīfa* literally, 'successor' (of the Prophet Muḥammad) and temporal head of the nascent Islamic community in Mecca and Medina, there were no precedents in either the urban or tribal societies of north and central Arabia for the future development of the Muslim polity. Now, such questions posed themselves as, what was to be the relationship of the head of the community with the body of the faithful? How was he to be chosen? What was the theological justification for his rule? How were the demands of the factions which early grew up with differing interpretations of the Qur'ān and *sunna* of the Prophet to be reconciled? These were questions to be resolved, if possible, within the Muslim community. But beyond this was a wider question, as the momentum of Arab conquest grew, and more and more lands of the Middle East and North Africa fell under Arab Muslim rule, that of the changing relationship between the Muslim Arab military aristocracy and their subject populations – Aramaeans, or Nabataeans (the indigenous people of Syria and Iraq), Jews, Copts, Greeks, Berbers, Hispano-Romans and Persians – since considerable parts of these peoples gradually adopted the Islamic faith and became theologically, at least, fellow Muslims and so spiritual equals of the ruling Arab elite. This was to be primarily a question of the political, financial and legal status of the new Muslims. But behind it was a wider social and cultural question, involving opposing currents of symbiosis and tension between the Arabs, military conquerors from the most closed and least developed part of the Arabian peninsula, its centre, and their newly-acquired subjects, of whom the Persians, in particular, had a glorious past and a sense of enduring national identity beyond anything which the Arabs could claim. The Persian people were to adopt whole-heartedly the Islamic faith of the Arabs but, unlike most other peoples, retain their own Iranian language. The process of symbiosis between the Arabs and the so-called 'Ajam (meaning, above all, the Persians) was to result in the evolution of a common Arabo-Persian Islamic culture, but this was to take three or four centuries to achieve.

The topic of the nature of the Muslim community and its leadership dominated almost totally the course of events during the period of the Rāshidūn or 'Rightly Guided' caliphs, (632–661). Abū Bakr (632–4), 'Uman (634–44), 'Uthmān (644–56) and 'Alī. At this earliest period of military expansion, first within Arabia and then outwards into the Near Eastern lands of the Byzantines and the Iraqi and Persian lands of the Sasanian emperors, the infant Muslim community comprised the *levée en masse* of the Arab tribesmen, the *muqātila* or warriors; only within the army could one become a full citizen of the nascent Islamic community and enjoy the rights of a conquering people, above all, entitlement to a stipend from the state. The caliph had to be a successful war leader, if not commanding armies personally, at least organizing war and sending out competent field commanders; Mu'āwiya, the first Umayyad caliph (661–680), owed his triumph over the last Rightly Guided caliph, the pacific and unwarlike 'Alī, in large degree to his experience as commander in warfare against Byzantium in Syria and the eastern Mediterranean and his famed quality of *ḥilm*, definable as a combination of statesmanship, shrewd judgement and magnanimity. Under the Rightly Guided caliphs, the choice of leader was not yet fixed. The first four caliphs all came from clans of the Meccan tribe of Quraysh, although all of them also had some bond of personal relationship, by blood or marriage, with the Prophet; the precedent was thus laid down for both Sunnī and Shī'ite Muslims that, in the words of a tradition attributed to Muḥammad, 'this authority shall not depart from my tribe'. In all cases, this was sealed by some form of acclamation or approval, even if only by a small group of leaders of the community rather than the mass of believers.

After a period of internal dissent, and civil war (656–661), which claimed the lives of Caliphs 'Uthmān and 'Alī, one of the Meccan clans, Umayya, succeeded in establishing a hereditary line within its members for ninety years (661–750), even though the principle of father–son succession was not really to become general till under the succeeding 'Abbāsid dynasty. Nevertheless, Umayyad claims were challenged in Arabia and Iraq by a rival Meccan family, the Zubayrids, for eight years (683–691), during which time there was both an Umayyad caliph and an anti-caliph. Also, the members of the family of Muḥammad's cousin and son-in-law 'Alī, who had acted as the fourth Rightly Guided caliph, considered that they had a divinely granted right to the caliphate or imamate (*imām*:'exemplar, model leader'), and their schemings and resentments particularly after 'Alī's son Husayn's death in battle with Umayyad forces at Karbalā in Iraq (681), were to be skilfully utilized (but their claims ultimately set aside) by the 'Abbāsids in their underground propaganda of the years 720–747 and open rebellion of 747–750, which overthrew the Umayyads and substituted the rule of another Meccan family, that of the 'Abbāsids from the clan of Hāshim. Thus we have in this period the genesis of the Shī'ite movement in favour of the 'Alids, descendants of 'Alī, but in Umayyad times it was more an unchannelled trend of thought and emotional feeling for the house of 'Alī than the coherent movement which it was later to become, with its own legal and theological system. More immediately dangerous for the Umayyads were the Khārijites or 'secessionists', a radical, egalitarian sect which held to a rigorous interpretation of the Qur'ān as supreme arbiter in all questions of politics and society, holding that there was no special divine mandate for Quraysh to be the sole providers of leaders of the Muslim community, the Caliph–Imāms, but that the most pious Muslim, 'even a black slave', was the one best qualified for the office. The Umayyads, and the early 'Abbāsids likewise, had to contend with violent, largely unsuccessful rebellions by the Khārijites in Syria, Iraq and Persia, although by the ninth century Khārijism had been mastered in the caliphal heartlands and pushed out to the peripheries, to Khurāsān and Sīstān in the east, Oman in the south-east of the Arabian peninsula and Berber North Africa in the west. Hence, while Shī'ism was to consolidate itself, to attract adherents and to grow powerful and influential in the Islamic world (as seen in the establishment of the Fāṭimid caliphate in North Africa, Egypt and Syria in the tenth century), Khārijism was to survive only vestigially.

Apart from the Khārijite threat, the main internal threat to peace and stability during the Umayyad period came not from internal sectarian or outside military threats but from factional and tribal disputes amongst the Arabs themselves. That the rivalry and antagonism of the two groups which emerged in early Umayyad times, the Qays or North Arabs and the Yemen or South Arabs, had any pre-Islamic antecedents is unlikely, and any differences of geographical location in early Arabia went back to the distant past. They seem to have become embodied in struggles over pasture lands in northern and central Syria and Mesopotamia, and in contending for offices and influence within the central and provincial Arab government, but the divisions were carried, with the migrations of the Arab tribes, to places like Egypt and Khurāsān in eastern Persia. They certainly contributed to a weakening of the military basis of the Umayyad caliphate, so that the later caliphs tried to move beyond dependence on tribal contingents to more professional bodies of troops. However, this was not achieved in time successfully to confront and defeat the 'Abbāsid revolutionary movement, which had recruited discontented Arab tribesmen in Khurāsān to its banner, appealing to a feeling that the distant Umayyad government in Damascus was neglectful of their interests.

Before they were thus finally overwhelmed, the Umayyad dynasty had produced some leaders of outstanding military ability, such as Mu'āwiya, Marwān I, (684–685) 'Abd al-Malik (685–705), Walīd I (705–715), and Hishām, (724–743), who had successfully surmounted various political and military crises and extended the boundaries of the 'Abode of Islam' from Transoxania in the east to the Pyrenees and Atlantic shores in the west. Nevertheless, their own dominance as an Arab ruling dynasty and the military dominance of an Arab tribal aristocracy were being slowly eroded by the transformation of Islamic society and the numerical increase in converts during their period of rule. Increasingly in the later seventh and early eighth centuries, it became difficult to ignore claims to social recognition and a role in the structures of power from the non-Arab converts to Islam, especially as these converts were especially equipped with the expertise and knowledge to man the administrative infrastructure of the empire; only at the end of the seventh century did Arabic begin to replace such languages as Coptic, Greek and Persian in the *dīwāns* or government departments. The converts had first to secure a footing in the socially dominant Arab class by enrolling as *mawālī* ('clients') of the Arab tribes, and for long they remained the subjects of much social and cultural discrimination, despised, for instance, as marriage partners by the Arabs. In the ninth and tenth centuries, under the 'Abbāsids, representatives of the *mawālī*, long by that time as skilled as native Arabs in the Arab legal, theological, philological and literary sciences, were to challenge Arab dominance (in the literary and cultural movement of the so-called Shu'ūbiyya, that of the *shu'ūb* 'nations', of the Qur'ān) and substantially to secure social equality; by that time, anyway, the Arabs had long lost their monopoly of political and military power.

But all this was in the future for the Umayyads, and it was the financial aspect of the mass movement of conversion to Islam which was immediate and pressing for them. The so-called *dhimmīs* or 'protected peoples', that is, the non-Muslim possessors of written scriptures, were liable, according to Qur'ānic prescription, to the *jizya* or poll tax. The exact nature and development of the taxation system under the Umayyads continues to be the subject of debate, but it is clear that when non-Muslims converted to Islam, they thought that they would henceforth be much freer from tax liabilities. Hence, by the end of the seventh century, many non-Arab rural cultivators in the richest province of the caliphate, Iraq, were leaving their lands and flocking to such Arab garrison cities as Baṣrā and Kūfa, becoming Muslims and claiming the status of *mawālī*. We know that tax revenue from Iraq dropped considerably at this time, just at a point when the state's demands for money for public buildings, palaces, irrigation works and so on was increasing. Hence the policy of a governor of Iraq and Persia like al-Ḥajjāj Yūsuf (d. 714) (see Plate 191(a)) was to round up runaway peasants and send them back to their villages, where taxation could be reimposed on them. This policy was followed by subsequent governors, equally concerned at the diminution of state revenues arising from the processes of conversion and flight to the anonymity of towns and garrison cities. But opponents of the Umayyad dynasty were now able to portray the governors' attempts to deny or restrict rights claimed by the *mawālī* as attempts to deny access to Islam in the religious sense, so that the 'pious opposition' in Medina and other places could stigmatize the Umayyads as enemies of Islam. The efforts of 'Umar II (1717–1720) to give a colour of piety to the Caliphate and grant tax concessions to past (but not future) converts proved to be of little avail.

Substantial numbers of *mawālī* had taken part in the rebellion in Persia and Iraq at the opening of the eighth century led by Ibn al-Ash'ath, which nearly toppled the Umayyad caliphate, and their grievances became a further strand in the discontent which culminated in the overthrow of the dynasty and the dilution of Arab ethnicity as the ordinary embodiment of Islamic religion. In other words, the end of the Umayyad period marks a transition from the mode of early conversion in which the non-Arab had to become the client of an Arab tribe, that is, to some extent enter into Arab ethnicity (something like the equation of religion and ethnic identity involved in Judaism), to a later mode of conversion which distinguished adherence to Islam from ethnic identification with the Arabs and *'urūba*, Arabness. Hence, in the ensuing 'Abbāsid period, it became much easier to be, say, both a Persian and a Muslim, that is, one did not have to give up one's Persian ethnicity in becoming a Muslim.

The French historian Gaston Wiet (1953) spoke of 'l'empire néo-byzantin des Omeyyades et l'empire néo-sassanide des

Abbassides', portraying the Umayyad caliphate, based in Damascus and much concerned with the war with the Greeks, as in some degree the heir of Byzantium in the empire's former Near Eastern territories, just as the 'Abbāsid one, based on Baghdād, was to look eastwards and to adopt much of the political ethos and cultural inheritance of the ancient Persian emperors. Following on from this analysis, the Umayyad period may be viewed as part of late antiquity, the transition from the classical world of Greece and Rome to the mediaeval and early modern worlds of the Christian European and the Islamic Middle Eastern empires.

Although land warfare along the Taurus Mountains frontier and naval warfare in the eastern and central Mediterranean, including two sieges of Constantinople (672–673, 716–717), characterized the Umayyad period, there was no rigid prohibition of cultural contacts. The two empires of the Byzantines and the Arabs shared a common world view, a teleological vision of human history which started with the Creation and closed with the end of the world and the Last Judgment, and they treated each other as equals. The achievements of the Greeks, above all in such practical sciences as mathematics, mechanics, astronomy and medicine, were valued by the Arabs, and a secretary of the Caliph Hishām commissioned the translation into Arabic of a series of letters purportedly from Aristotle to his most celebrated pupil, Alexander. The Greek imprint in the administrative practice of the secretarial and financial departments in Muslim Syria and Egypt remained strong, and it was only 'Abd al-Malik (685–705) who made the *naql al-dīwān*, the transition to the use of Arabic language in the bureaucracy, and the Greek system of accounting procedure continued in practice to be used beyond the Umayyad period. In minting practice, the gold *solidus* of Emperor Heraclius was used essentially by the Muslims of the western half of the caliphate until 'Abd al-Malik's coinage reform of the early 690s and the introduction of purely Islamic aniconic gold dīnārs (see Plates 191(a–c), 192(a)). We know little about Umayyad court ceremonial and organisation, compared with the extensive information available on those of the 'Abbāsids and Fāṭimids; hence it is difficult to discern whether any influences from the Byzantine court in Constantinople reached the caliphs in Damascus, modifying the Umayyads' original conception of themselves as elevated tribal chiefs. But it does seem certain that the Arabs in Syria were not indifferent to, or insensible of, the aesthetic qualities of the fine, stone-built Byzantine palaces and churches to which they became heirs. Not infrequently, the Arabs took over churches or parts of churches for their own purposes of worship. Hamilton Gibb (1967) suggested that 'Abd al-Malik's building of the Dome of the Rock (see Plate 45) and his son Walīd I's building of the Aqsā Mosque in Jerusalem show a conscious desire to emulate and surpass the fine cathedrals of the Christians at Edessa and elsewhere, a suggestion confirmed by some Arabic historical traditions. There is also a persistent story in later Islamic historians that Walīd requested, and received, aid from the Byzantine emperor for the decoration of the Umayyad Mosque in Damascus and the Mosque of the Prophet in Medina, for which Greek craftsmen and supplies of mosaic cubes were sent.

Oriental influences during the Umayyad period did not assume the significance which they were to have in ensuing times, when the new, eastwards orientation of the 'Abbāsid caliphate and the inflow of Persians into the military guard of the first caliphs and into the higher administrative ranks (including what was to evolve into the vizierate) began a gradual symbiosis of the Arabic and Persian cultures. But Arabic poets of the Umayyad period begin to use an increasing number of Persian loan words (especially those relating to material culture, words absent from the original vocabulary of the desert nomad Arabs) – such words having already appeared in the work of the pre-Islamic poets and in the text of the Qur'ān – and in the later Umayyad period we have the beginning of a translation movement which made Middle Persian works available to an Arab audience. This movement is particularly associated with Ibn al-Muqaffa' (d. 756), who worked as a secretary for various Umayyad governors and who brought to the Arab ruling classes information on the ancient Persian traditions of statecraft and kingly power. That there was by then an interest in such things – at least by those outside the rigidly Arabocentric religious and legal classes – is shown by Hishām's reportedly showing an interest in Sasanian Persian history and ruling practices.

BIBLIOGRAPHY

ARNOLD, T. W. 1924. *The Caliphate.* Oxford.

BOSWORTH, C. E. 1983. The Persian Impact on Arabic Literature. In: A. F. L. BEESTON *et al.* (eds) *The Cambridge History of Arabic Literature. Arabic Literature to the End of the Umayyad Period.* Cambridge, pp. 483–496.

——. 1996. Byzantium and the Arabs. War and Peace between Two World Civilisations. In: *idem, The Arabs, Byzantium and Islam. Studies in Early Islamic History and Culture. No. XIII.* Aldershot, Hants.

CRONE, P. 1980. *Slaves on Horses. The Evolution of the Islamic Polity.* Cambridge.

——. 1994. Were the Qays and Yemen of the Umayyad Period Political Parties? In: *Der Islam,* Vol. 71, pp. 1–57.

CRONE P.; HINDS, M. 1986. *God's Caliph. Religious Authority in the First Centuries of Islam.* Cambridge.

DENNETT, D. C. 1950. *Conversion and the Poll Tax in Early Islam.* Cambridge, Mass.

Encyclopaedia of Islam, new edition. 1960. Leiden, Arts. Khalīfa; Mawlā; Umayyads.

GARDET, L. 1967. *L'Islam, religion et communauté.* Paris.

GIBB, H .A. R. 1962. Arab–Byzantine Relations under the Umayyad Caliphate. In: S. J. SHAW and W. R. POLK (eds) *Studies on the Civilization of Islam.* Boston, pp. 47–61.

GOLDZIHER, I. 1967–71. Arab and 'Ajam. In: *idem, Muslim Studies,* trans. C. R. BARBER and S. M. STERN, 2 vols. London. Vol. 1, pp. 89–136.

GOODMAN, L. E. 1983. The Greek Impact on Arabic Literature. In: A. F. L. BEESTON *et al.* (eds) *The Cambridge History of Arabic Literature. Arabic Literature to the End of the Umayyad Period.* Cambridge, pp. 460–482.

GRABAR, O. 1964. Islamic Art and Byzantium. In: *Dumbarton Oaks Papers,* Vol. 18, pp. 69–88.

——. 1973. *The Formation of Islamic Art.* New Haven, Conn.

GRUNEBAUM, G. E., VON, 1946. *Medieval Islam, A Study in Cultural Orientation.* Chicago.

——. 1970. Ch. The Umayyads. In: *Classical Islam, A History. 600–1258.* London, pp. 64–79.

HAMIDULLAH, M. 1970. Le Chef de l'état à l'époque du Prophète et des califes. In: *Recueils de la Société Jean Bodin,* 20, pp. 481–514.

HAWTING, G. R. 1986. *The First Dynasty of Islam. The Umayyad Caliphate AD 661–750.* London and Sydney.

KENNEDY, H. 1986. *The Prophet and the Age of the Caliphates. The Islamic Near East from the Sixth to the Eleventh Century.* London and New York.

WATT, W. M. 1971. God's Caliph. Qur'ānic Interpretations and Umayyad Claims. In: C. E. BOSWORTH (ed.) *Iran and Islam. In Memory of the Late Vladimir Minorsky.* Edinburgh, pp. 565–574.

——. 1973. *The Formative Period of Islam.* Edinburgh.

WIET, G. 1953. L'empire néo-byzantin des Omeyyades et l'empire néo-sassanide des Abbassides. In: *Journal of World History,* Vol. 1, pp. 63–70.

17

EXPANSION OF ISLAM AND ASPECTS OF DIVERSITY IN ASIA, AFRICA AND EUROPE

17.1

POLES OF EXPANSION FROM ARABIA

Saleh Ahmed Al-Ali

Among the most important results of the Prophet's work was a growing stability of the central authority and an emerging sense of 'Arabism', an Arab identity transcending tribalism. Yet these did not uproot the tribal allegiance of most of the nomads and their chiefs, who did not assimilate the new Islamic ideas and rebelled against the first caliph, Abū Bakr (632–634), who succeeded, however, in quelling them and imposing effective authority over the whole peninsula, with Medina as the centre, and in expanding the state beyond the confines of the Arabian peninsula. The outward spread of the Arabs into surrounding regions was a process which had begun long before the advent of Islam. There had been a gradual, natural and peaceful process of nomad migrations.

The study of the Islamic conquests must distinguish, on the one hand, between the motives which impelled the Arabs on the path of conquest and, on the other, the factors which contributed to their success. With regard to their victories, two factors were crucial. First, there was the new situation of the Arabs after they had adopted Islam and unified into a single state. Second, there was the political situation prevailing in the Orient at the time of the emergence of Islam. For centuries past, the region had been divided between the Byzantine and Sasanian Empires. Both of these were suffering from economic exhaustion due to the constant warfare between them, which exhausted their treasuries and undermined their military machinery, as well as to the religious schisms, which spilled over into political life. Each of the two empires governed numerous ethnic groups with different cultures and outlooks.

Other factors which helped the Muslim Arabs to victory within a relatively short space of time were, on the one hand, the personal qualities of a people inured to hardship and climatic extremes and, on the other, military advantages of swift movement in small formations. This combination of elements made it easier for them to confront the slow-moving and cumbrous regular armies. Moreover, Arab advance came as something of a surprise for both Byzantium and Persia. Not only were they unprepared for this style of fighting, but they did not expect a serious threat from the Arabian peninsula. The Persian defences were concentrated on the northern front facing the Byzantines, and the surprise attack from the south proved a lethal blow. Their capital, Ctesiphon, was neither far nor well protected from a danger coming from the south. Its fall caused the whole political structure to collapse. With Byzantium, on the other hand, although the Arabs launched their attacks from unexpected directions, the outcome was not as decisive. The Byzantine Empire's strong points compelled the Arabs to launch a series of attacks, which exhausted their forces and compelled them to call a halt at the Taurus Mountains. Thus, rather than collapsing swiftly like the Sasanians, the Byzantines were able to hold on to some of their territories and provincial capitals.

AIMS AND MOTIVES

Several broad fundamental aims and motives impelled Muslims to conquest, as is the case with almost all other great conquests in history. Here the initial impulse came from the supreme command of the early Caliphs who had been the earliest Muslims and the companions of the Prophet. This had enabled them to assimilate his views, and to feel the necessity to put them into practice. The ideals were well clarified in the sayings of the Prophet, and in the main orientation of his deeds. At issue was the creation of a far-reaching political system in which the word of God would reign supreme, and dominated by Islam in its broadest cultural sense. This allowed other ideas and systems, provided they did not undermine the new order's main principles. Such aims were clearly assimilated by the top directors of the policy, and extended in various degrees to the whole body of Muslims who believed that God supported them and rewarded those who die in his cause.

This supreme ideal towered above, though it did not exclude the purely material ambition a gaining booty. In the early stage of conquests, in any case, booty was scanty and the effect of the great victories did not yet make itself felt.

THE CONQUEST OF IRAQ

Iraq was the richest province in the Sasanian Empire: its southern borders were a continuation of Arabia without any geographical barrier separating them. Therefore, since remote times, the Arabs had infiltrated into Iraq and altered its ethnic structure. The Sasanians supported the Mundhirī Arab dynasty in Ḥīra to protect its western boundaries from any threat from the desert. When in AD 602 that dynasty fell, the barrier fell with it, and the nomadic Arabs intensified their skirmishes which met with some success, while the Sasanians suffered internal troubles and economic decline.

One of the chief Arabs thus attacking the Iraqi frontier was Al-Muthana, with a group of his tribe, the Bakr. When Caliph Abū Bakr quelled rebellious movements in Arabia, Al-Muthana approached him, and linked his activities with Islam. Abū Bakr then ordered Khālid Ibn Al-Walīd to move to the borders of Iraq and control the sporadic Arab activities there. Khalīd advanced towards the borders, defeated some of the Sasanians, occupied Ḥīra and the adjacent areas west of the Euphrates, and reached north, toward the borders of the Byzantine domains. Abū Bakr then ordered Khālid to move and join the Muslim forces on the frontier of Syria; Al-Muthana was left to carry on the activities of the Arabs against the Sasanians.

'Umar succeeded Abū Bakr as caliph (634). He modified the policy of Islamic military operations, permitted former dissidents, who had not been allowed by Abū Bakr to join the Muslim armies, to do so, and thus large numbers of Arabs flocked to participate in the conquests. 'Umar did not hesitate to send them immediately to the frontiers. He also accorded high priority to military operations on the frontier of Iraq, and lost no time dispatching from Medina an army commanded by Abū 'Ubayda al-Thaqafi, who was defeated however, in the Battle of Jisr, near Babylonia; but 'Umar immediately sent another force, chiefly Yemenites commanded by Jarīr, who defeated the Persians at a battle near Ḥīra. 'Umar followed this victory by sending a large force of around 20,000 men, drawn mainly from the Arabs of Yemen and North Nejd commanded by Sa'd Ibn Abī Waqqās, a veteran from Mecca. After elaborate preparations he met a well-trained Persian army, commanded by the Sasanian general Rustam. After three days of fierce fighting in Qādisiya on the border of the desert west of Ḥīra, the Arabs defeated the Sasanians. The battle was significant, since it left the rich lands in the middle of Iraq undefended, and raised the morale of the Arabs who, after a few months' pause, continued their advance and entered Ctesiphon, the capital of the Sasanians, who withdrew without serious resistance. The defeated Sasanian forces regrouped at Jalawla, 260 km east of Ctesiphon, but the Arabs soon defeated them, and so secured control over Iraq.

The remnants of the Sasanian army withdrew to the foothills of the Zagros mountains, and regrouped their available forces to fight the Arabs in a fierce battle at Nihāwand (641). The Arabs won a decisive victory and the Sasanian army was completely shattered. The Persian king Yazdagird fled, and the burden of the defence now fell on local Persian princes; there was no longer any major organized resistance. The path was open for the Arabs to sweep over the entire Persian plateau.

THE SYRIAN FRONTIERS

Syria had been the first main target of Arab expansion. It is adjacent to Ḥijāz and had ancient, ethnical and commercial ties to it. The Prophet organized a number of campaigns in the region, concluded treaties with the headmen of many towns and tribes, and also received delegations from many of them.

When Abū Bakr had quelled the rebellions and secured hegemony over Arabia, he sent four armies to Syria, each of which numbered 7,000 men, and fought the Byzantines in a number of indecisive battles.

When 'Umar became Caliph, he appointed Abū 'Ubayda as general commander of the Arab forces, and the Byzantines suffered a crushing defeat at the battle of Yarmūk. The Arabs immediately followed up their victory by taking the remaining cities of Syria, capturing the towns of Palestine and the coast with ease. Following a series of treaties, Damascus capitulated in 636, Jerusalem in 638, and Caesarea in 640. Even so, the first years of the conquest were not all that easy, and the Muslims faced many difficulties in controlling Syria. Moreover, their military strength was greatly weakened in 638 by the plague of Amwās. Meanwhile, the Byzantines gathered their forces in the nearby Taurus Mountains, and their fleet still controlled the Mediterranean. As a result, it was necessary for the Arabs to redistribute their forces over many centres, and to fortify several coastal towns. This secured them against any serious attack from the Byzantines armies.

THE CONQUEST OF EGYPT

After the conquest of Syria, it was only natural that the Arabs should turn their attention to Egypt. 'Umar dispatched 'Amr ibn al-'Ās with a force of 4,000 men who followed the coastal road and entered Egypt through Rafah, Suez and Al-Farma. 'Amr was further reinforced with some 10,000 troops, defeated the Byzantines at 'Ayn Shams and Babylon-on-the-Nile, and led a force which conquered Alexandria after three months' resistance. As a result, the whole of Egypt was occupied by 642. The Islamic forces then proceeded rapidly westwards, and occupied Bạrqa and Tripoli (642).

CONQUEST OF THE JAZĪRA (NORTHERN MESOPOTAMIA) AND ARMENIA

Following the conquest of Palestine and Syria, the Arabs turned their attention to Al-Jazīra (northern Mesopotamia) because of its strategic and commercial importance. The majority of the population here were both Aramaeans and Arabs. The Muslim armies advanced to Mosul from lower Iraq, followed by another advance from Syria two years later. The towns of the Jazīra, including Ḥarrān, Rāha (Edessa), and Nisibis, fell to them in 641–642.

The Arabs then turned towards Armenia. They suffered many setbacks in their campaigns, and it was not until 652 that they finally succeeded in gaining control of the country.

CONQUEST OF THE IRANIAN PLATEAU

After a short pause following the conquest of Iraq, Caliph 'Umar granted permission to the Arab forces to advance onto the Persian plateau. The military operations there were far from easy: whereas in Iraq they had been fighting in a country they knew fairly well and where they were helped by the local Arab tribes, they faced on the Iranian plateau a land different in climate and culture. Actually, several towns in this plateau resisted strongly, rebelled against the new rulers, and had to be reconquered.

By 649, the Arabs had completed their conquest of the Persian plateau, but needed another five years to achieve full control over the main towns of Khurāsān (present north-eastern Iran and northern Afghanistan), which they attacked during the caliphate of 'Uthmān.

EXPANSION DURING THE UMAYYAD CALIPHATE

The first wave of conquests in the fifteen years following the Bedouin rebellions or, 'wars of apostasy', then, was a great success, even exceeding the objectives of the caliphate in Medina. This was followed by a second great wave of conquests during the Umayyad period, extending north, west and east. Caliph Mu'āwiya waged war in Anatolia in 663, and besieged Constantinople in 668 by land and sea. However, this campaign failed to gain its objectives. In 672, however, the Arabs captured the island of Rhodes, followed by Crete. An attempt was also made to conquer Sicily. But, the failure of the siege of Constantinople led to the loss of control of the Islands by the Arabs. In 676 Mu'āwiya sent 'Uqba ibn Nāfi' from Barqa to conquer North Africa. 'Uqba established the first Muslim outpost in North Africa at Kairouan, which paved the way for the conquest of the whole of the Maghrib. However, control over the coast of North Africa changed hands repeatedly between the Arabs and Byzantium. This was particularly due to the Berber inhabitants of the Maghrib, whose loyalties shifted from one side to the other until they submitted finally to the Arabs.

In the reign of 'Abd al Malik and his son Walīd, conquests were achieved in both the east and the west. The new governor Mūsā ibn Nuṣayr consolidated the Arab hold over the Maghrib, and Ṭāriq ibn Ziyād, his deputy, seized Tangiers and Ceuta on the straits between Morocco and Spain. He was followed by Mūsā ibn Nuṣayr who pursued the Arab victories and conquered Iberia (Spain) which the Arabs knew as 'Al-Andalus' (Andalusia). This occurred in the years 710–713, although some areas remained unconquered until 759. By 721, the area under Muslim control extended deep into Europe proper with the Arabs carrying out numerous raids into France. In 732, the Arabs, under 'Abd al-Raḥmān al-Ghāfiqī, were defeated by Charles, 'mayor of the palace' of the Frankish Kingdom, at the battle of Poitiers. The pope conferred on Charles the title of 'Martel', or Hammer of God.

In the east, the conquest of Transoxania and parts of Turkestan was now completed through the efforts of several governors, the most prominent of them being Qutayba ibn Muslim. Bukhārā fell in 712 and Samarkand in 713. Sind was conquered in the years 708–713 by the commander Muḥammad ibn al-Qāsim al-Thaqafī. Military operations, supplies and reinforcements to the eastern front were controlled by the governor of Iraq, Ḥajjāj ibn Yūsuf al-Thaqafī.

Constantinople was besieged for the second time in 716 by a sea and land campaign launched by the Caliph Sulayman ibn 'Abd al-Malik. Once again, however, the siege was a failure, and the new caliph' 'Umar ibn 'Abd al 'Azīz, had to order the army to withdraw.

Yazíd ibn al-Muḥallab, governor of Iraq and the east, was able to recover the Caspian Sea provinces – Quhistān, Jurjān and Ṭabaristān. However, the subjugation of some of these lands, such as Ṭabaristān, remained only nominal, and Yazíd was content to levy an annual tribute.

By the beginning of the eighth century, the hegemony of the central authority became weakened in various places. In the Maghrib, the Berbers rose in rebellion, defeating the Muslims in the battle of Al-Ashraf in 741, but caliph Hishām ibn 'Abd al-Malik succeeded in recovering the Maghrib. But the Berbers made clear their opposition to the Umayyad regime by embracing the Khārijite sect of Islam, and more particularly the Ibāḍī observance thereof.

Andalusia could well have been lost through quarrels between the Arabs themselves, but Caliph Hishām realized the situation in 742, sent a new governor, and Umayyad authority was re-established.

In Transoxania, the local rulers of Farghāna and Kush broke their peace with the Muslims, and there were rebellions in Sind. Thus ended the second wave of conquests. It was now necessary for the Islamic state to consolidate its gains rather than expand further.

For the first time in history, the Arabs were able to conquer all the regions of Western Asia and to annex to their state the lands of North Africa, Andalusia, Transoxania, Turkestan and Sind. In so doing, they prepared a suitable geographical environment for the growth of a shared culture under the aegis of Islam, but by no means confined to Muslims alone, (see Map 12).

BIBLIOGRAPHY

ABU ZAKARIYYĀ AL-AZDĪ. 1967. *Tārīkh al-Mawṣ il* (History of Mosul). Cairo.

AL-'ALI, S. 1955. *Muḥāḍarāt fī Tārīkh al-'Arab* (Lectures on the History of the Arabs). Baghdād.

'ALI, J. 1961. *Tārīkh al-'Arab fi l-Islām* (History of the Arabs in Islam). Baghdād.

ARNOLD, T. 1924. *The Caliphate.* Oxford.

AL-BALĀDHURĪ. *Ansāb al-Ashrāf* (Lineages of the Noble Ones). Cairo, Vol. 1, n.d.; Vol. 1, pt. 4, Vol. 2, Beirut, 1974; Beirut, 1979; Vol. 5, Jerusalem, 1983.

AL-BULDĀN FUTŪḤ (*Conquests of the Lands*). 1866. Leiden. Also Cairo, 1956.

AL-DĪNĀWARĪ. 1888. *Kitāb al-Akhbār al-Ṭiwāl* (Book of the Lengthy Reports). Leiden.

DONNER, F. 1981. *The Early Islamic Conquests.* Princeton.

DURI, A. 1960. *Muqaddima fī Tārīkh Sadr al-Islām* (Introduction to the History of the Heartland of Islam). Beirut.

GIBB, H. 1923. *The Arab Conquest of Central Asia.* London.

IBN 'ABD AL-HAKAM. 1914; 1922. *Kitāb Futūḥ Miṣrwa l-Maghrib wa l-Andalus* (Book of the Conquest of Egypt, the Maghrib and Spain). Arabic text ed. by H. Massé (Le livre de la conquête de l'Egypte, du Maghreb et de l'Espagne), Cairo 1914. Arabic text also ed. by C. C. Torrey, The History of the Conquest of Egypt, North Africa and Spain, Yale University Press, New Haven, Conn. 1922. Partial French trans. with corresponding extracts of Ibn 'Abd al-Hakam's Arabic text, Conquête de l'Afrique du Nord et de l'Espagne, ed. and trans. by A. Gateau, Algiers 1948.

IBN AL-ATHIR. 1851–1876. *Al-Kāmil fi l-Tārīkh* (The Perfection in Chronicles). Leiden. New edn. 1987, Beirut.

IBN A'THAM AL-KŪFĪ. 1300 AH/AD 1883. *Al-Futūḥ* (The Conquests). Persian trans., Bombay; Arabic text, 1986, Beirut.

IBN HISHĀM. 1955. *Al-Sīra al-Nabawiyya* (The Life of the Prophet). Cairo.

IBN IDHĀRĪ. 1948–1951. *Al-Bayān al-Mughrib* (The Wondrous Elucidation). Leiden.

IBN ISḤĀQ. 1976. *Al-Maghāzī wa l-Siyar* (Feats of Arms and Biographies). Rabat.

IBN KHAYYĀṬ, Khalifa. 1967. *Kitāb al-Tārīkh* (Book of Chronicles). Najaf.

IBN SA'D. 1960. *Tabaqāt* (Categories). Beirut.

IBN SALLĀM. 1353 AH/AD 1934 . *Kitāb al-Amwāl* (Book of Wealth). Cairo.

LEVI-PROVENÇAL, E. 1950. *Histoire de l'Espagne musulmane.* Paris.

LEWIS, B. 1950. *The Arabs in History*. London.
MANTRAN, R. 1967. *L'expansion musulmane, viiè–ixè siècles*. Paris.
SHABAN, M. A. 1971. *Islamic History*, Vol. I. Cambridge.
SHOUFANY, E. 1972. *Al-Riddah and the Muslim Conquest of Arabia*. Toronto
AL-ṬABARĪ. 1881. *Tārīkh al-Rusul wa l-Mulūk* (The Chronicle of Prophets and Kings). Leiden. Also Cairo, 1986. French trans. by H. Zotenberg, Chronique, Paris 1867–1874 and 1980.
'URWA IBN AL-ZUBAYR. 1982. *Maghāzī* (Feats of Arms). Riyadh.
YAḤYĀ IBN ĀDAM AL-QURASHĪ. 1958. *Kitāb al-Kharāj* (Book of Taxes). Leiden.
YĀQŪT AL-RŪMĪ. 1866–1873. *Mu'jam al-Buldān* (Compendium of Lands). Leipzig.
——. 1907–1931. *Irshād al-Arīb ilā Ma'rifat al-Adīb* (Skilful Guidance unto the Learning of a Cultured One). Leiden.
AL-WĀQIDĪ. 1989. *Kitāb al-Ridda* (The Book of the Apostasy). Paris.

17.2

ARAB EXPANSION IN THE MUSLIM WORLD

Saleh Ahmed Al-Ali

ESTABLISHMENT OF NEW CITIES

Their great early victories enabled the Arabs to add to their new state large rich regions; consequently, there emerged the necessity to establish fixed centres to station permanent armies in the conquered regions. Since this might mean soldiers losing contact with their old homes and becoming rooted in the newly conquered regions, the centres were established to this end in border areas where the climate was suitable for the Arabs and the camels which served them. These centres were: Baṣrā in the south of Iraq and Kūfa in the centre; Al-Fusṭāṭ at the head of the delta in Egypt; Jawatha in Bahrein; and Al-Jābiyah in Syria. The last two did not keep their importance for long, while the other three cities grew in stature with the passing of time. In addition, 'Umar also considered Medina, the home of the caliphate, to be one of these centres. These new centres were called *amṣār* (plural of *miṣr*): 'cities'.

Organization of the new cities

The new cities were established at much the same time in the various regions as soon as the Arabs had established their authority. Though separated by great distances, they were similar in design and organization. Each was established in proximity to an old existing city, that is, Baṣrā next to Ubulla, Kūfa next to Ḥīra and Fusṭāṭ next to Heliopolis. They served as administrative headquarters of the regions conquered by the army and were responsible for maintaining law and order and extending the boundaries. In the main their Arab population came from various regions of the Arabian peninsula who had taken part in the conquests.

These new cities were permanent camps for the army, administrative centres, and community settlements in which social, economic and intellectual activities could be carried out under the aegis of the Islamic state. Arabic became the language of all their inhabitants, many of whom were already of Arab origin.

In each city, the main focus was the mosque, which was allocated space sufficient to accommodate all worshippers and a large adjoining square, together with an area set aside for the residence of the governor and the few departments associated with his work. These were the only public buildings. At first they were simple structures of clay, sun-dried bricks and reeds. But by the beginning of the Umayyad period, however, high walls came to surround these buildings, and elaborate colonnades rose. Besides offering space for prayers – and particularly Friday prayers – the mosque served other purposes also; it was used by the Qāḍī to examine legal matters, and by the governor to issue public instructions and orders. The mosque could also serve as a military headquarters offering shelter to the governor. In addition, it was a centre for poetry recitations and political meetings.

A number of main streets led off from the mosque square to the edges of the city, and between them lay a warren of narrow intersecting lanes and alleys. The land between the main streets and side roads was allocated to the different clans, each such allotment being designated by the clan name. Individual allotments were then distributed among its members who would build their own houses, first from mud and reeds and later from sun-dried brick. The clan continued to own the allotment, even if some of its people migrated to other towns, and there was some intermixing. The allotments retained their clan names for centuries despite influxes of unrelated newcomers or the decay that followed the emigration of large numbers of clan members.

The non-Arab population of the new cities

From their earliest days, these cities were also settled by non-Arabs, some of whom were often foreign soldiers who had joined the Arabs, such as the Asāwira and the Sayābija in Baṣrā, the Ḥamrā' al-Daylām in Kūfa and the Ḥamrā' in Fusṭāṭ.

Other non-Arabs flocked to these centres in search of work or fortune. They settled mainly around the markets and so came to be known as the 'people of the *sūq*' as opposed to the Arabs, who were the 'people of the mosque'. Thus they fulfilled many services needed in the city. Many of them became Muslims and established ties with the Arabs in economic, social and intellectual life. Some of them acquired wealth and attained high rank in religious studies, but in general the Arabs regarded them with distrust and even contempt. Besides, they were not included in the register of stipends and donations. Therefore they were deprived of security which the Arabs enjoyed, which caused acute tension threatening to stability and order.

The arrival of non-Arabs did not alter the basic character of the city as a centre of the Arab Muslim armies. This combination of an Arab, military and Islamic character distinguished these cities from earlier Arab towns.

Financial organization

The Arab warriors received an annual stipend and monthly provisions from the state. The stipend ranged from a minimum of 200 *dirhams* in Iraq and 20 *dīnārs* in Syria and Egypt, to a maximum of 2,500 *dirhams* or 200 *dīnārs* per annum. At the lower end of the range it kept the fighters out of poverty, while at the upper end, it was a mark of esteem for service which, though considerable, was by no means a fortune.

The expenses were met from the revenues of the provinces conquered by the particular city. This system led to an impoverishment of the rural areas, and to the accumulation of money in the cities, encouraging industry and commerce and making them important economic centres. This in turn gave rise to a class of wealthy people, and a developed market. The ordinary rural population, however, remained largely unaffected by this development of the market.

The status of Arabic and Arab culture in the new cities

The overwhelming majority of the Arab population of the new cities helped to reinforce the privileged position of the Arabic language and of Arab social, political and cultural activities. Arabic also enjoyed a high status because it was the language of the Qur'ān, of Islamic rituals, of the courts and of the political elite. Its large vocabulary and flexibility, in the course of time, made it the spoken language of the masses in large parts of the empire for both literary expression and everyday use. Other factors also contributed to the spread of Arabic as an international language throughout the wide domains of the Islamic state, where it was spoken by many and used as the only written tongue by intellectuals.

The Arabs who settled in such cities brought with them their varied lore fraught with the world of their emotions, feelings, proverbs, maxims, tales and poetry. Thanks to the freedom afforded by the state, they had the opportunity to extend their horizons and to rub shoulders with people of other cultures. Thus, the use of Arabic became extremely widespread as it emerged as a language of culture and scholarship. Distinguished scholars appeared who owed their success to a traditional interest in the humanities, and also to the attitude of the Islamic state which supported intellectual pursuits, in addition to a financial system which guaranteed a minimum acceptable level of existence to the Arab settlers. Another important element was the fact that the period of military service was relatively short, each man being called to arms for no more than one season every three years.

ISLAMIC STUDIES

The Qur'ān was so important that it was studied from every aspect, and these studies soon developed into such Qur'ānic sciences as recitation, etymology and interpretation. Other studies were connected with various facets of Islam, including the sayings of the Prophet and events of his life, jurisprudence and the like. Though these subjects were studied by Arab and non-Arab scholars alike, the main requirement became a thorough understanding of Arabic. For all these reasons, the use of Arabic spread and reinforced the link between Arabism and the universal principles of Islam. Consequently, in the course of time, less emphasis was placed on pure Arab lineage, and a more humane, universalist outlook gradually came to take its place (see Plates 107–109).

ESTABLISHMENT OF FURTHER NEW MILITARY BASES FOR THE ARABS

The expansion of the Islamic state necessitated the establishment of additional new military bases for the Arab warriors. They were located in secure areas but not far from places where the frontiers of the state were most vulnerable. As its northern shores and frontiers were threatened by Byzantium, Syria was the first region to see the establishment of such bases. They were located first in Damascus and Ḥumṣ and in Palestine, then in Qinnaṣrin and subsequently in Al-Jazira province and the northern regions such as Rāha (Edessa), Raqqa, Mosul and Ardabīl.

In the east, the warriors were stationed in various centres such as Qazwīn, Marāgha and Tabrīz in Āzerbaijān, as well as in Rayy, Iṣfahān, Māsbadhān and Karaj. Additional bases followed in Qom, Jurjān and Shīrāz, but more important were the Arab settlements in Khurāsān founded in the middle of the reign of Mu'āwiya, (673) when Arab forces were dispatched to consolidate Arab rule and to push forward into Transoxania. The force, numbering 50,000 men with their families, was stationed chiefly at Marw, Nīshāpūr, Ṭūs, Marw-al-Rūdh, Herāt, and later in Balkh. After a further wave of expansion, Bukhārā and Samarkand were used as military camps for the Arab forces brought from the cities to guard and extend the frontiers of the Islamic state.

In North Africa, the Arabs established their military camp in the early years of the Umayyad caliphate at Kairouan; and when Spain was added to their domains, they settled in many centres, the main ones being Cordova and Seville.

The settlements in these new centres relieved the population pressures in the earlier cities. The new settlers retained cultural links with the places they had come from and some continued to own property there. Moreover, they maintained the same general organization as in the earlier cities and continued to receive their monthly and annual stipends. They also kept their tribal structures and organization, as well as their Arabic language, ideas, and Islamic religion, although they also adopted some of the non-Arab features of the surrounding civilizations where they settled.

The new bases where the Arabs settled in their second wave migrations, though still referred to as 'cities' (*Amṣār*), were old established centres of population, with a majority of non-Arab inhabitants keeping their homes and ways of life. In this regard, the new bases differed from the earlier cities which had been new settlements where a majority of Arab inhabitants had not forged close ties with the original inhabitants.

The Arab forces in Khurāsān took part in the political events which marked the end of the Umayyad caliphate. They were responsive to the calls of the parties in Iraq opposed to the Umayyads, and played a decisive role in the rebellion and subsequent rise to power of the 'Abbāsids.

Although the new settlements did not initially enjoy the same active intellectual life as the earlier cities, they would come to rival them during the early years of the 'Abbāsid dynasty. In any event, despite their geographical disparity, all these centres had certain features in common, namely strong attachment to Arabic and a concern to maintain and propagate Islam.

BIBLIOGRAPHY

ABU L-FARAJ AL-IṢFAHĀNĪ. *Kitāb al-Aghānī* (The Book of Songs). Būlāq, 1284–5 AH (= AD 1871–72); 20 vols; Vol. 21, Leiden, 1306 AH (= AD 1888); index, Leiden, 1900.

AL-'ALĪ, S. 1969. *Al-Tanẓīmat al-Ijtimā'iyya wa l-Iqtisādiyya fi l-Basṛa fi l-Qarn al-Awwal al-Ḥijrī* (The Social and Economic Constitution in Baṣrā in the First Century of the Islamic Era). Beirut.

——. 1988. *Al-Dawla fī 'Ahd al-Rasūl* (The State in the Time of the Prophet). Baghdād.

——. 1989. *Dirāsāt fi l-Idāra al-Islāmiyya* (Studies in Islamic Administration). Baghdād.

AL-BALĀDHURĪ. *Ansāb al-Ashrāf* (Lineages of the Noble Ones). Vol. 11, Greif Swold, 1883; Vol. 5, Jerusalem, 1936, repr. 1983; Vol. 4, B, Jerusalem, 1938; Vol. 4, part III, Beirut, 1978.

DENNET, D. B. 1950. *Conversion and the Poll Tax in Early Islam. Cambridge.*

DURI, A. 1960. *Muqaddima fī Tārīkh Ṣadr al-Islām* (Introduction to the History of the Heartland of Islam). Beirut.

FAIṢAL, SH. 1978. *Al-Mujtama'āt al-Islāmiyya* (Islamic Societies). Beirut.

GIBB, H. 1969. *Mohammedanism*. London.

IBN 'ABD RABBIH. 1940. *Al-'Iqd al-Farīd* (The Peerless Necklace). Cairo.

IBN 'ASĀKIR. 1333 AH (= AD 1915). *Tārīkh Dimashq* (History of Damascus). Damascus.

IBN AL-ATHĪR. 1851–76. *Al-Kāmil fi l-Tārīkh* (The Perfection in Chronicles). Leiden. Also Beirut, 1987.

IBN DURAYD. *Al-Ishtiqāq* (Etymology). Göttingen, 1854; also Cairo, 1958.

IBN KHALDŪN. *Al-Muqaddima* (An Introduction to History). Beirut, 1886. Also Cairo, 1958. English trans., *The Muqaddimah*, by F. Rosenthal, 3 vols, Princeton, 1958, repr. 1967.

IBN AL-NADĪM. 1347 AH (= AD 1929). *Kitāb al-Fihrist* (The Book of the Catalogue). Cairo. English. trans. by Bayard Dodge, *The Fihrist of al-Nadīm,* 2 vols, New York, 1970.

IBN QUTAYBA. 1904. *Kitāb al-Shi'r wa l-Shu'arā* (The Book of Poetry and Poets). Leiden. Arabic text of the introduction only also edited with French trans. by M. Gaudefroy-Demombynes, *Ibn Qotaïba: Introduction au Livre de la poésie et des poètes*, Paris, 1947.

——. 1925. *'Uyūn al-Akhbār* (Sources of Reports). Cairo.

——. 1931. *Sharḥ Adab al-Kātib* (Gloss concerning the Culture of the Scribe). Cairo.

AL-JĀḤIẒ. 1933. *Rasā'il* (Epistles). Cairo.

——. 1938–1947. *Al-Ḥayawān* (The Animals). Cairo.

——. 1948. *Al-Bayān wa l-Tabyīn* (Proof and Demonstration). Cairo.

——. 1958. *Al-Bukhalā'* (The Misers). Cairo.

AL-JAHSHIYĀRĪ. 1938. *Kitāb al-Wuzarā' wa l-Kuttāb* (The Book of Viziers and Scribes). Cairo.

JUYNBOLL, O. H. A. (ed.) 1982. *Studies on the First Century of Islamic Society*. Carbondale, Ill.

AL-KINDĪ. 1959. *Kitāb al-Umarā' wa Kitāb al-Quḍāt* (The Book of Emirs and the Book of Judges). Beirut.

AL-MAS'ŪDĪ. 1861–77. *Murūj al-Dhahab* (The Meadows of Gold); Arabic text with French trans., *Les Prairies d'Or*, by C. Barbier de Meynard and Pavet de Courteille; Arabic text revised by Ch. Pellat, Beirut 1965; repr. Arabic text, Beirut, 1987.

MORONY, M. 1983. *Iraq after the Muslim Conquest*. Princeton.

AL-MUBARRAD. 1874. *Al-Kāmil* (The Perfect One). Leipzig.

SAUNDERS, J. J. 1965. *A History of Medieval Islam*. London.

AL-SHĀFI'Ī. 1983. *Kitāb al-Umm* (The Motherbook). Beirut.

AL-SHĪRĀZĪ. 1981. *Ṭabaqāt al-Fuqahā'* (Grades of the Jurists). Beirut.

AL-ṬABARĪ. 1881. *Tārīkh al-Rusul wa l-Mulūk* (The Chronicle of Prophets and Kings). Leiden. Also Cairo, 1986. France trans. by H. Zotenberg, *Chronique*, Paris, 1867–74 and 1980.

UDOVITCH, A. L. (ed.) 1981. *Studies in Economic and Social History*. Princeton.

WĀKI. 1947. *Akhbār al-Quḍāt* (Reports Concerning Judges). Cairo.

WELLHAUSEN, J. 1902. *Das Arabische Reich und sein Sturz*. Berlin. English trans. *The Arab kingdom and its Fall*, Calcutta, 1927.

AL-YA'QŪBĪ. 1969. *Tārīkh* (Chronicle). Leiden.

AL-ZUBAYR IBN BAKKĀR. 1972. *Al-Akhbār al-Muwaffaqiyyāt* (Reports Concerning Favoured Matters). Baghdād.

17.3
THE IRANIAN RENAISSANCE AND THE RISE OF THE NATIONAL LANGUAGE AND LITERATURE

Ehsan Yarshater

THE DEMISE OF AN EMPIRE AND THE WANING OF A RELIGIOUS CULTURE

To appreciate the Persian cultural renaissance after the Islamic conquest, it is necessary to recall what had waned or vanished as a result of this conquest, what Persians were doing between the demise and rebirth, and in what circumstances and forms the revival took place. Persia suffered a decisive defeat at the hand of the Muslim Arab armies in 642 at the battle of Nihāwand, which the Arabs named the 'victory of victories', (*fatḥ al-futūḥ*). It sounded the death knell of a powerful empire that the Arabs had regarded for centuries with awe and admiration. Within a decade, Persian provinces succumbed one after another to the advancing Arab forces. The inglorious murder of the fugitive Yazdgird III, the last Sasanian king of kings, by a miller in 652, sealed the fate of the long-enduring dynasty (224–652) and one of the superpowers of the time (the other being the Byzantine Empire). The conquest also ended the hegemony of the powerful Zoroastrian church, which had held sway over the country in close tandem with the Sasanians.

At about the time of the advent of Islam, Persia had become debilitated by protracted wars with Byzantium, excessive taxation (from which the aristocracy and the priesthood were exempt), and the abuses of royal and sacerdotal powers. The later Sasanians, wrapped as they were in their pomp and vainglorious luxury, presented to the outside world the empty splendour of a shining shell; the Arab invasion broke the shell, exposing the exhaustion within. Internal strife and rivalry between the great feudal houses had almost paralysed the state machinery, and the country was ripe for a social upheaval.

THE ADVENT OF ISLAM IN PERSIA AND THE TRANSFORMATION OF PERSIAN SOCIETY

Islam arrived at an opportune moment, with a fervent spiritual message and a brave and dedicated army to back it. The combination proved irresistible, and the process of conversion to Islam began. Some were converted by persuasion, and sometimes under conditions of war. In Transoxania and Khurāsān, for instance, where the inhabitants of some of the major cities offered military resistance and rebelled after defeat, Islam was often imposed. Even though the Zoroastrians were eventually treated like Jews and Christians as a 'people of the (divine) book' and were therefore allowed to keep their religion and be protected in exchange for the payment of a poll tax, conversion to Islam, particularly in the urban centres, continued and in time gathered momentum. The increasingly negative and humiliating attitude towards those who chose to keep their faith (such as denying them public jobs, reduced punishment for crimes against them, and favouring in matters of inheritance the converts in a household at the expense of the steadfast), accelerated the process. Within about a hundred years the country assumed an Islamic visage, at least in the cities.

None the less, some chose to migrate to India in order to escape the indignities inflicted on them; their descendants are the Parsis of India and Pakistan, who have preserved the religious texts and rituals of Zoroastrianism, in living contact with their brethren in Persia. In the countryside and in the less accessible regions, people tolerated the hardships of keeping to their convictions much longer. Fārs, the birthplace of the Sasanians, still had a significant Zoroastrian population in the tenth century, and pockets of the faithful have continued to this day in Yazd and Kirmān provinces, keeping alive a knowledge of Zoroastrian lore. Even those who had converted often found it necessary to attach themselves, following a pre-Islamic Arabian custom, to an Arab tribe or clan and become its *mawlā* (pl. *mawālī*) or 'client' in order to have the protection of the tribe and find a social foothold. The number of these clients grew rapidly, and they soon became a very significant force in the cultural and political arena of Islam.

In the meantime, Arabic, the language of the conquerors, the Qur'ān and daily prayers, took root in Persia among the elite. Under Hajjāj ibn Yūsuf, the governor of Iran and Iraq (661–714), Arabic script replaced the Pahlavi alphabet in the *dīwān* or government offices, paving the way for the adoption of the Arabic system of writing for Persian in general.

Conversion to Islam meant major transformations in the religious outlook, tenets and practices of erstwhile Zoroastrians. Ahura Mazda was replaced by the all-powerful Allāh, whose absolute unity would admit no partners; Ahriman, the prince of darkness, lost independent status, being replaced in the popular mind by Satan, a creature of God; fire temples gave way to mosques; fasting, rejected earlier as a devilish practice (as hunger was a creation of Ahriman), and pilgrimage to Mecca became incumbent upon the faithful, who now faced Mecca for their daily prayers and buried their dead instead of exposing them to birds of prey; the elements (fire, water, earth and air) lost their sanctity;

and dogs, which were favoured animals and whose presence was necessary in some religious rituals to validate them, came to be regarded as ritually unclean. The Zoroastrian clergy, who were the main repositories of Persian lore and learning, fell from authority; anything that smacked of Manichaean Mazdakite or Magian beliefs became suspect. Persians began to preach Islam and to fight its holy wars.

Cultural life, too, went through major transformations. Pahlavi books, their script no longer understood, fell into disuse and, as a result, a major connection with the Persian past was severed and Persia was drawn more closely into the Islamic orbit. Arabic loan words – first religious and administrative terms, and later others – made increasing appearances in Persian. Persians wrote Arabic poetry, and Persian metrical patterns were adapted to Arabic quantitative meters. Scholars discussed the literary arts in terms of Arabic prosody and rhetoric (see Plate 109).

PERSIAN PARTICIPATION IN THE FURTHERANCE OF ISLAMIC CIVILIZATION

Having accepted Islam, Persians now devoted themselves to consolidating Islam and making it respond to the intellectual, theological and juridical needs of the more sophisticated people of the Middle East, as did the cultured Muslims of Iraq, Syria, North Africa and Spain. They translated their major literary works and histories into Arabic, including the *Khwadāy-nāmag*, or *Book of Lords*, an account of Persian national history and legends; *Kalīla wa Dimna*, a collection of fables of Indian origin, current in Persia (see Plates 210–211); many historical novels and works of wisdom literature; books on manners and court etiquette; and scientific treatises. They also applied themselves to the furthering of Islamic learning. The roster of Islamic scholars in early and classical periods is studded with the names of scholars of Persian stock (Yarshater, 1998, pp. 4ff., 54ff.). Their preponderance is such that Ibn Khaldūn, the celebrated fourteenth-century Arab historian, concluded that with few exceptions most Muslim scholars in both the religious and intellectual sciences were Persian (*'ajam*) and that when a scholar was of Arab origin, he was Persian in language and upbringing and had Persian teachers, and this in spite of the fact that Islam arose in an Arabic milieu and its founder was an Arab (Ibn Khaldūn, 1958, III, p. 311). And a modern scholar of Islam writes:

> In the final analysis I think it is impossible to deny that Islam owes more to its vanquished, non-Arab, converts than to the few victorious Arab tribesmen and that is a truism for 'centre' as well as 'edge'. . . . Islam as a religion and a political theory must in the first place thank its *mawālī* for what it grew into.
>
> (Juynboll, p. 483)

The contribution of Persians in promoting the cause of Islam and enriching its culture (Browne, 1902-1924: I, pp. 251ff), apart from the sheer number of Persian scholars (Brinner, in *EI2*, I, pp. 112; Hodgson, p. 446; Yarshater, 1998, pp. 90–94), may be gauged by the fact that such luminaries as 'Abd al-Hamīd Kātib, the founder of Arabic epistolary style and the 'father of Arabic prose' (al-Qādī, 1992: p. 223); Ibn Muqaffa' (d. 756), writer, translator, political theorist and the initiator of Arabic literary prose (Latham, 1990: pp. 154–164; Latham, *EIr.*, VIII; Shaked, 1984: pp. 31–40); Ibn Ishāq (d. 767), early biographer of the prophet of Islam (Gillepsie, 1970); Abū Hanīfa (d. 767), eminent jurist and founder of the Hanafite School of Islamic law; Sībawayhi (d. 793?), the foremost early grammarian of Arabic; Muḥammud Khwārazmī (d. 847), the famous mathematician and geographer and father of algebra; Ibrāhīm Mawsilī (d. 804) and his son Ishāq (d. 850), prominent musicians; Ibn Qutayba (d. 887), distinguished scholar and literateur; Bāyazīd (d. 875), Junayd (d. 910) and Hallāj (d. 922), notable mystics; Muḥammad ibn Jarīr Tabarī (d. 923), the author of the most important history written in Arabic; Rhazes (Abū Bakr Rāzī, d. 925), the eminent physician and philosopher Avicenna (d. 1037), the foremost physician (author of the *Canon of Medicine*) and the greatest philosopher of the Islamic world; Abū Rayhān Bīrūnī (d. after 1050), the premier Islamic savant and polymath; Ghazālī (d. 1111), the most influential Islamic theologian; and the authors of the six Sunni canonical collections of *ḥadīth* were all of Persian extraction (Safā, 1953–1992: I, p. 74). However, it is only fair to say that the common faith of the Muslims and the use of Arabic as the *lingua franca* for scholarship tended to blur national and regional differences between scholars.

With the Islamization of Persia and the wholehearted and effective participation of Persians in the building and promotion of the fledgling Islamic culture, one would have thought that Persia would be absorbed, as were Syria, Iraq and Egypt, into the Arab world, abandoning its own traditions and abdicating its cultural distinction. But this was not to be. Persia rose again, if not politically, at least culturally and linguistically, and in doing so laid the foundation for a second phase of Islamic civilization.

THE REVIVAL OF THE PERSIAN LANGUAGE AND THE RESUMPTION OF LITERARY ACTIVITY

The Persian renaissance took place in the ninth century, almost two hundred years after the demise of the Sasanian Empire. A simmering attachment to the national heritage and pride in a remembered past had continued. These sentiments did sometimes flare into the open and challenge the Arabizing and levelling tendencies of Islam. One such manifestation of national pride was the attitude and cultural orientation of Persian secretaries (*kātibs*) and administrators of the *dīwān*, in particular during the period that has been labelled the 'Golden Age of Islam' (749–847) (Mas'udī, 1965–1979: paras 585, 630; Mas'udī, 1894: pp. 87, 100; Barthold, 1968: p. 197; Gibb, 1953: pp. 63–64). Jāḥiẓ, the famous literateur of the tenth century, accused these secretaries, in a long passage of his treatise devoted to their reproof, of studying and valuing only the wisdom of Sasanian sages, disdaining Islamic sciences, and disparaging Arabic traditions (Jāḥiẓ, 1988: pp. 122–125; Bosworth, in *EIr, I*, p. 91; Qādī, 1992: p. 238). Another such manifestation was seen in the Shu'ūbiyya movement, which flourished in the eighth–tenth centuries and sought to prove the superiority of non-Arabs, particularly Persians, over Arabs by extolling the virtues of the former and expounding the shortcomings of the latter (Goldziher, 1967–1971: I, pp. 137–198; Gibb, 1953: pp. 62–73).

Several events had a decisive effect on the prompting and emboldening of such sentiments. One was the leadership of Abū Muslim and his remarkable success in demolishing the Umayyad caliphate in 749 and bringing the 'Abbāsid revolution to fruition. The Umayyads stood for Arab hegemony and were accused of lording it over non-Arab Muslims and treating them, against the dictates of the Qur'ān, as inferior citizens. The 'Abbāsid propagandists presented a broader view of Islam and promised greater scope for the *mawālī*. The army that crushed the Umayyads, although ethnically mixed, was of a decidedly Khurāsānian character (Jāḥiẓ, 1948: III, p. 366; Sharon, 1983: pp. 19ff) and used Persian as its language of communication (Tabarī, 1879–1901: III/l, pp. 50ff; Daniel, 1979: pp. 74; Sharon, 1983, p. 67; Levy, 1953: p. 74). Abū Muslim's resounding victory and the accession of the 'Abbāsids, who distrusted tribal loyalties (Tabarī, 1879–1901: III/l, pp. 25, 414, 444; Daniel, 1979, p. 46, n. 112), opened the way for full participation by the Persians in the affairs of the Islamic state (Tabarī, 1879–1901: III/2, pp. 1142; Qādī, 1992: p. 238). This inspired the Persians with a new sense of confidence. When al-Mansūr, the second 'Abbāsid caliph, ordered the murder of AbūMuslim, it offended the Khurāsānians as a treacherous act of ingratitude and incited a number of religio-political uprisings in the region.

In 821, Tāhir, the able general of 'Abbāsid Caliph al-Ma'mūn, who was of Persian extraction, was appointed governor of Khurāsān. He and his descendants ruled eastern Persia as a semi-independent dynasty for fifty-two years. Their rule partly coincided with the beginning of the weakening of the political power of the caliphate and heralded the rise of local dynasties and the loosening of caliphal grip on the more distant areas.

One such dynasty was the Saffārid (first phase: 867–901), which may be said to have formally inaugurated the Persian renaissance. The founder of the dynasty was Ya'qūb ibn Layth (r. 867–879), a soldier of unusual courage and ability who had risen from plebeian circumstances (his father was a coppersmith) to become ruler of all of eastern and southern Persia and to march on Baghdād and challenge the 'Abbāsid caliph al-Mu'tamid. When a poet in his entourage wrote a poem eulogising him in Arabic, as was the fashion in the 'Abbāsid and Tāhirid courts, he remonstrated by asking why poems should be written in a language that he could not understand; whereupon Muḥammad ibn Wasīf, who was in charge of his official correspondence, wrote a panegyric ode (*qasīda*) addressed to Ya'qūb in New Persian, and this (according to the anonymous author of *The History of Sīstān*, who cites the poem) was the beginning of poetry in that language.

However, this claim of primacy cannot be quite accurate; there are traces, even specimens, of poems written under the Tāhirids (Rypka, 1968: pp. 135–136), including two pieces by Hanzala of Bādghīs in quantitative meters (Lazard, 1962–1964: I, p. 53; II, p. 12; Safā, I, pp. 163–182), and it is only reasonable to assume that attempts to compose in native meters as well as Arabic moulds must have been made sporadically even earlier, but the results have not reached us (de Blois, 1992, pp. 42–58). However, the impetus given by Ya'qūb to writing poems in Persian began a tradition which was taken up and developed by the Sāmānids, the true champions of the Persian literary renaissance.

The Sāmānids (819–1005) were from Balkh, in northern Afghanistan, and traced their origin to Bahrām Chōbīn, the famous general of the Sasanian Hurmazd IV. The founder of their fortunes, Sāmān, embraced Islam, and al-Ma'mūn (see Plate 215) appointed his four grandsons to various governorships in Transoxania. In 875, one of these, Nasr ibn Ahmad, received the governorship of the entire region. His brother and successor, Ismā'īl, consolidated his power and secured the borders of his domain against the attacks of the pagan Turks on the north-eastern fringes. In 900, he earned the gratitude of Caliph al-Mu'tamid for defeating and capturing 'Amr ibn Layth, the successor of the Saffārid Ya'qūb, and was rewarded with the addition to his domain of Khurāsān, where the Tāhirids and Saffārids had ruled. His writ was now obeyed from the Jaxartes River *(Syr daryā)* in the north to the borders of India in Afghanistan; he also exercised suzerainty over a number of local satellites in the outlying regions, such as Khwārazm in the north and Sīstān in the south.

By securing the borders, keeping the trade routes open and the caravans safe, and by maintaining the confidence of the 'Abbāsid caliphs, the Sāmānids succeeded in making their realm prosper. They were credited with the fair treatment of their subjects. Their court in Bukhārā and Samarkand became a centre of learning and a haven for scholars, authors and poets. They instituted a system of government based on the 'Abbāsid model, itself largely adopted from the Sasanian prototype (Barthold, 1968: p. 197; Goldziher, 1967–1971: I, pp. 108ff; Lewis, in *EI2*, I, p. 17b). Accordingly, they entrusted the management of their administration to a vizier, a well-trained man of culture and experience who headed a number of governmental departments or *dīwāns*. The administrative, fiscal and juridical scheme that the Sāmānids instituted became a model for subsequent dynasties; it was followed by the Ghaznavids, adopted by the Seljuks and continued in its essentials until the Mongol invasion and beyond, well into the nineteenth century (see Plates 195, 216).

The significance of the Sāmānids lies not only in providing an administrative example of long duration but even more, in their sponsorship of a vigorous cultural rebirth and their encouragement of Persian poetry and prose, and this without withholding their support from Arabic writing. Their court, which was emulated by their successors, was adorned by a number of poets, including Rūdakī, the father of Persian poetry and panegyrist of the Sāmānid Nasr ibn-Ahmad (914–943), Mas'ūdī of Marw, Shahīd of Balkh, Muḥammad Farālāwī, Abū Shakūr of Balkh, Abū Shu'ayb of Herāt, Hakīm Maysarī, the author of a medical manual in verse, Abu'l-'Abbās of Rabanjan, Abū Tāhir Khusravānī, Abu'l-Mu'ayyad of Balkh, Daqīqī of Tūs, Kasā'ī of Marv, Ma'rūfī of Balkh, Valvālijī, Badī' of Balkh, Munjīk of Tirmadh, Tāhir Chaghānī, Āghājī, 'Amāra of Marv, Kashī Īlāqī, and Abu'l-Haitham of Jurjān ('Awfī, 1903: I, pp. 2–28; Hidāyat, 1957–1961, pp. 130ff; Browne, 1902–1924: I, pp. 445–480; Safā, 1953–1992: I, pp. 369–456; de Blois, 1992: I, s.v.; Lazard, 1962–1964: II, pp. 23–194). To this impressive list we must add the name of the great epic genius of Persia, Firdawsī, who completed the first version of his monumental epic, the *Shāh-Nāmeh*, before 1000, during the Sāmānid period, but in the end had to dedicate it to the unappreciative Ghaznavid Mahmūd (998–1030).

The poetry of the Sāmānid period, the tenth century, is distinguished first by its great variety: extant specimens include lyric, epic, didactic, narrative, panegyric, philosophical, satirical and invective genres; and second, by its maturity, considering its youth, not only in terms of ideas and sentiments but also with respect to language and expression. The best of these poems have nothing archaic about them, even if, compared with later Persian poetry, they are unadorned, concise and straightforward. They reveal a rich culture of deep roots. The poetry of this period is also noted for its youthful and buoyant spirit, the sunny temper and generally positive attitude towards life that shine through it. Although contemplative thought is not alien to Sāmānid poets, they are not given to renouncing the world, harbouring ascetic or mystical sentiments and disparaging the pleasures of mundane life. Love of nature and joyful appreciation of things beautiful or pleasurable radiates from their poetry. A virile tone governs the cadences and syncopated rhythms of the poems. Similes and short metaphors or tropes in which two images are likened together (such as lip and ruby, eyebrow and bow, teeth and pearls), the observance of congruity or *tanāsub*[1], and tropes based on the personification of ideas (for example, the hand of destiny, eyes of greed) are the chief rhetorical figures; extended similes, however, are not favoured. Lyrics, often addressed to young male companions, are of a light and playful nature; the pathos born of unrequited love or the inaccessibility of the beloved, typical of the lamentations of the *ghazal*-writers of the later periods, do not colour Sāmānid poems, even though a brooding awareness of the passage of time and the fickleness of fortune is not lacking.

Pride in Persia's past prompted an intense interest in the pre-Islamic history of the country and its legends. Several heroic epics recounting the legendary history of Persia were written: for instance one by Mas'ūdī of Marw, another in prose by Abu'l-Mu'ayyad of Balkh, neither of which has survived; and yet another in prose by Abū Mansūr Ma'marī (or Mu'ammarī), the vizier of Abū Mansūr Muḥammad, the Sāmānid governor of Khurāsān, of which only the introduction has been preserved; and one in verse by Daqīqī, who started on the history of Gushtāsb and the coming of Zoroaster but did not live long enough to complete it. The culmination of these attempts was Firdawsī's monumental epic, the *Shāh-Nāmeh*, or 'Book of Kings'. A copious work of nearly 50,000 couplets, which incorporates the 1,000 lines by Daqīqī, it recounts traditional Iranian history from the mythological first world king, Gayōmarth, to the last Sasanian monarch, Yazdgird III. It is an epic of great vigour and beauty, with engrossing episodes, dramatic events, ethical precepts, romantic stories and philosophical musings, raised by the genius of Firdawsī to poetic heights worthy of its lofty content. A passionate attachment to the ideas and ideals of ancient Persia and its chivalric traditions informs the pages of the *Shāh-Nāmeh*. The careers of its noble warriors, which form the greater and most eloquent part of the epic, are shaped by their faith in their duty as defenders of the integrity of Iranian lands and its symbol, the institution of monarchy. Better than any other work, the *Shāh-Nāmeh* represents the prevailing patriotic spirit among eastern Iranians, once they had regained their confidence and set out to revive their cultural and literary distinction, a concern that continued in subsequent centuries. In this context, the *Shāh-Nāmeh* became a pillar of national pride and identity and has helped to maintain this identity throughout turbulent periods of Persian history, when the country was invaded and conquered by the Turks, the Mongols and the Tatars.

It was also in the tenth century, under the Sāmānids or their vassals, that New Persian prose made its début as a language of science and learning, thus ending the monopoly of Arabic in these fields. Persian epistolary style, which had under the Umayyads and through the innovative epistles of Abu'l 'Alā Sālim (Latham, 1990: pp. 154–164) and 'Abd al-Hamīd Kātib inspired the Arabic writing style, was now revived by the cultivated secretaries of the Sāmānid era. Economic prosperity and a stable polity encouraged attention to cultural activities, increased readership, and boosted the production of books and the formation of libraries. Avicenna's description of the rich library of the Sāmānid Nūh ibn Mansūr (976–997) in Bukhārā attests to the cultural affluence of the era. We owe several important pioneering prose works to this renaissance of Persian letters. These include Abu 'Alī Bal'amī's rendition of Tabarī's monumental Arabic history by order of Sāmānid ruler Mansūr ibn Nūh (961–976); *Tafsīr-i Tabarī*, a translation of Tabarī's copious commentary of the Qur'ān by order of the same ruler, who summoned the leading doctors of Islamic law in his realm and obtained a decree that it was permissible for Persians to read and recite the Qur'ān in Persian; *Hudūd al-'ālam* or the 'Regions of the World', an anonymous geographical treatise; Abu'l-Hasan Kharaqānī's mystical work *Nūr al-'ulūm*; Abū Bakr Juvaynī's *Hidāyat al-muti'allimīn* or 'Guidance for Learners', a textbook of medicine; Abū Rayhān Bīrūnī's *at-Tafhīm*, an introduction to the science of astronomy[2]; and Avicenna's *Dāneshnāme-yi 'Alā'ī*, a course of philosophy[3] (logic, metaphysics, mathematics and natural sciences) and others.

THE SPREAD OF ISLAMIC PERSIAN CULTURE AS A SECOND PHASE OF ISLAMIC CIVILIZATION

The Persian culture that was revived in eastern and northeastern Iran after some 200 years of gestation, at a time when the classical Islamic civilization was beginning to show signs of decline, continued to develop and grow under the subsequent dynasties that ruled in Persia. These rulers, notably the Ghaznavids (first phase 977–1038), the Seljuks (in Persia and Iraq, 1038–1194), and the Khwārazmshāhs (1077–1231), who were Turkic and originated in the steppes of Central Asia, embraced Persian culture and its literary tradition wholeheartedly, and became earnest exponents and propagators of that culture and tradition (von Grunebaum, 1970: p. 150). The Ghaznavid Mahmūd's court is renowned for the number of distinguished Persian poets it generously supported, and the courts of the Seljuks Malekshāh (1072–1092) and Sanjar (1118–1157) boasted of major poets. A branch of the Seljuks took Persian language, art and letters to Anatolia, as did various Muslim dynasties hailing from Afghanistan and Transoxania in the case of India, a process which was accelerated when the Ottomans absorbed smaller Turkish houses in Anatolia in the fourteenth and fifteenth centuries (Gibb, 1900–1909: I, p. 29), and as the Delhi Sultanate of the thirteenth and fourteenth centuries consolidated its administrative control in northern India and the Deccan; when Bābur, a Tīmūrid prince, moved to India and occupied Delhi in 1526 and founded the Mughal Empire, Persian language and culture were already widespread in his domain. Thus, Persian language, literature, art, fashion and manners were diffused far and wide, and were enriched by the support and participation of people from other lands, so that when Baghdād fell in 1258 to the Mongols, and the unifying institution of the caliphate virtually disappeared, Persia emerged as the seat of a vigorous, productive and expanding culture, while the western lands of Islam, once the seat of a brilliant culture, exhausted and debilitated, sank into a period of impotent sterility, soon to become a possession of the Ottoman Empire (Yarshater, 1998, pp. 74ff.). The Mongol Īl-khāns and their successors, among them the Tīmūrids, further spread and established Persian culture in their possessions, with the Persian language serving as the vehicle of administration and polite discourse (Hodgson, 1961–1974: II, p. 486; Spuler, p. 472; Fahir Iz, pp. 683–688, 692). Persian literature was written from the Bosphorus to the Bay of Bengal (Toynbee, 1939: V, pp. 514ff). Persian poetry, its ideas, images and conventions, set the model for the poets in the eastern lands of Islam, irrespective of the language in which they wrote. Thus, when in the sixteenth century the eastern, non-Arab societies of the Islamic world were articulated in three great empires, the Ottoman, the Safavid and the Mughal, their literary culture was founded on the Persian model (Yarshater, 1998, pp. 85ff., 96ff). In the meantime, Arabic literature, which had shined so brightly during the Golden Age of Islam, had, like Arab political power, ebbed to a low point.

Thus, the Persian renaissance, which had its beginning in the Saffārid period and its blossoming under the Sāmānids, provided the Islamic world with a second phase of cultural vitality, development and productivity, which lasted well into the eighteenth century, when it was challenged and eclipsed by the ever-increasing impact of the West.

NOTES

1 This consists of introducing or bringing together in a verse, in a seemingly effortless manner, words which are related by association or contrast, such as sun and moon, day and night, the four elements, parts of the body, etc.

2 This is apparently a Persian version of an Arabic work by Bīrūnī, made either by him or one of his contemporaries; see Lazard, 1963: pp. 58–62; Bosworth in *EIr, IV*, pp. 274–276.

3 Although this work was written in Iṣfahān and dedicated to the Kākūyid ruler 'Alā al-Dawla Muḥammad, Avicenna like Bīrūnī, who later joined the Ghaznavid court, was born and bred in Transoxania and was originally attached to the Sāmānid court; Bīrūnī originally belonged to the Afrīghid circle in Khwārazm.

BIBLIOGRAPHY

ANON. 1935. *Tārīkh-i Sīstān.* ed. M. T. Bahār. Zavvār, Tehran. Trans. M. Gold. 1976. *The Tārīkh-e Sistān.* ISMEO, Rome.

ARBERRY, A. J. 1958. *Classical Persian Literature.* George Allen & Unwin, London.

'AWFĪ, MUḤAMMAD. 1903. *Lubāb al-albāb,* 2 vols, ed. Browne, E. G. Luzac & Co. and E. J. Brill, London and Leiden.

BARTHOLD, V. V. 1968. *Turkistan down to the Mongol Invasion.* 3rd edn, trans. V. Minorsky (Gibb Memorial Series, No. 5), ed. C. E. Bosworth. Luzac & Co, London.

BAUSANI, A. 1968. La Letterature Neo-persiana. In: A. PAGLIARO,; A. BAUSANI, (eds) *La Letteratura Persiana.* Sasoni-Accademia, Roma, pp. 138–318.

DE BLOIS, F. 1992. *Persian Literature. A Bio-bibliographical Survey,* Vol. V, part 1. Poetry to AD 1100. Royal Asiatic Society, London.

BROWNE, E. G. 1902–1924. (Reissued as a set, 1928) *A Literary History of Persia.* 4 vol. Cambridge University Press, Cambridge.

Cambridge History of Islam. 1970. Eds Holt, P. M.; Lambton, A. K. S.; Lewis, B.; 2 volumes. Cambridge University Press, Cambridge.

DANIEL, E. L. 1979. *The Political and Social History of Khurasan under Abbasid Rule 747–820.* Bibliotheca Islamica, Minneapolis and Chicago.

Encyclopedia of Islam (EI2). 1960–1999. Vols. I–IX. Leiden.

Encyclopedia Iranica (EIr). 1985—. Vols. I–IX. London, Costa Mesa, and New York.

ETHE, H. 1904. Neupersische Litterature. In: W. GEIGER and E. KUHN (eds) *Grundriss der iranischen Philologie.* Karl J. Trubner, Strasbourg. II, pp. 212–368.

GIBB, E. J. W. 1900–1909. repr. 1958–1967. *A Literary History of Ottoman Poetry,* 6 vols. (Gibb Memorial Series). Luzac & Co., London.

GIBB, H. A. R. 1953. The Social Significance of the Shu'ūbiyya. In: *Studia Orientalia Ioanni Pedersen Dicata.* Munksgaard, Copenhagen, pp. 105–114.

GILLEPSIE, C. C. 1970. Dictionary of Scientific Biography, 15 vols. Charles Scribner's Sons, New York.

GOLDZIHER, I. 1967–1971. *Muhammedanische Studien.* Trans. S. M. Stern and C. R. Barber, ed. by S. M. Stern as *Muslim Studies,* 2 vols. George Allen & Unwin, London.

GRUNEBAUM, G. E. von. 1970. *Classical Islam. A History, 600 A.D.–1258 A.D.* Trans. Katherine Watson. Aldine, Chicago.

HIDĀYAT, R. 1957–1961. *Majma'al-fuṣaḥā',* 6 vols. Amīr Kabīr, Tehran.

HODGSON, M. G. S. 1961–1974. *The Venture of Islam. Conscience and History in a World Civilization,* 3 vols. University of Chicago Press, Chicago.

IBN KHALDŪN. 1958. 2nd edn. 1967. *The Muqaddima, an Introduction to History,* Trans.Franz Rosenthal, 3 vols. (Bollingen Series, XLIII). Princeton University Press, Princeton.

IZ, FAHIR. Turkish Literature. In: *Cambridge History of Islam (q.v.).* II, pp. 652–694.

JĀḤIẒ, 'Amr ibn Baḥr. 1948–1950. *al-Bayān wa'l-tabyīn.* ed. Muḥammad Hārūn, 4 vols. Beirut, 2nd edn, repr. Dār al-Jīl and Dār al-Fikr, n.d.

——. 1988. *Kitāb dhamm akhlāq al-kuttāb.* In: *Rasā'il al-Jāhiẓ,* ed. 'A.Muhannā. Dār al-Ḥadātha, Beirut, pp. 119–134.

JUYNBOLL. 1955. In: *Journal of the American Oriental Society* 115/3, (*JAOS*), p. 483.

LATHAM, J. D. 1990. Ibn al-Muqaffa' and Early 'Abbāsid prose. In: *The Cambridge History of Arabic Literature. 'Abbāsid Belles-Lettres,* eds. Ashtiany, J. *et al.* Cambridge University Press, Cambridge, pp. 48–77.

LAZARD, G. 1962–1964. *Les premiers poètes persans,* 2 vols. Librairie d'Amérique et d'Orient, Paris and Tehran.

——. 1963. *La langue des plus anciens monuments de la prose persane.* C. Klincksieck, Paris.

LEVY, R. 1953. Persia and the Arabs. In: A. J. ARBERRY, (ed.) *The Legacy of Persia.* Clarendon Press, Oxford.

MAS'ŪDĪ, Abu'l-Ḥasan. 1894. *Al-Tanbīh wa'l-ishrāf,* ed. M. J. de Goeje (Bibl. Geog. Arab. V III). E. J. Brill, Leiden.

——. 1965–1979. *Murūj al-dhahab,* 7 vols, ed. Pellat, C. Jāmi'a al-Lubnāniyya, Beirut.

MUḤAMMADĪ, M. 1995. *Farhang-i Īrānī.* 3rd, revised edition of 1944 issue. Tūs, Tehran.

NAFĪSĪ, Sa'īd. 1965. *Tārīkh-i naẓm u nathr dar Īrān wa dar zabān-i fārsī.* Furūghī, Tehran.

QĀḌĪ, Wadād. 1992. Early Islamic State Letters: The Question of Authenticity. In: *The Byzantine and Early Islamic Near East, I, Problems in Literary Source Material.* Cameron, A.; and Conrad, L. I. (eds). Darwin Press, Princeton.

QAZVĪNĪ, M. 1933. Muqaddima-yi qadīm-i Shāhnāma, in Bīst Maqāleh, Part 2. Ed. 'Abbās Iqbāl. Matba'a-yi Majles, Tehran, pp. 1–64.

RYPKA, J. 1968. *History of Iranian Literature.* D. Reidel Publishing Co., Dordrecht.

ṢAFĀ, Dh. 1953–1992. *Tārīkh-i adabiyyāt dar Irān.* 5 volumes in 8 parts. Ibn Sīnā *et al.*, Tehran.

SHAKED, Sh. 1984. From Iran to Islam: note on some themes in transmission. In: *Jerusalem Studies in Arabic and Islam* 4, pp. 31–67.

SHARON, M. 1983. *Black Banners from the East.* E. J. Brill, Leiden.

SPULER, B. Central Asia from the Sixteenth Century to the Russian Conquests. In: *Cambridge History of Islam (q.v.),* I, pp. 468–494.

ṬABARĪ, Abū Ja'far Muḥammad ibn Jarīr. 1879–1901. *Ta'rīkh al-rusul wa'l-mulūk,* ed. de Goeje, M. J. *et al.,* 3 parts in 15 vols. E. J. Brill, Leiden.

TOYNBEE, A. *A Study of History,* 13 vols. Vol. I, 1935. *Introduction: The Genesis of Civilization.* 2nd edn, 1951. Vol. V, 1939. *The Disintegration of Civilizations.* Oxford University Press, London.

YARSHATER, E. 1998. *The Persian Presence in the Islamic World,* eds Hovannisian, Richard and Sabagh, G. Cambridge University Press, Cambridge.

17.4
THE TURCO–MONGOL PERIOD

Françoise Aubin

For a period beginning in the eleventh century and lasting for 300 years, historians must direct their attention towards Central Asia, the epicentre of a number of upheavals whereby the destinies of lands at opposite ends of the Eurasian landmass became intertwined. The nature of this Central Asian world, a vast expanse between the borderlands of the great empires, was fashioned by a common factor, the difficulty of procuring and making the best use of water (see Map 13).

The answer found by the Turkic and Mongol nomads, both originating from the centre of what is now Mongolia, was to keep their groups permanently on the move, driving their flocks – their equivalent of both capital and interest – over their habitual grazing grounds of varying widths, in the mountainous or semi-desert steppe lands, which represented their means of production. In the Middle Ages, these nomads, whose harsh environment made them combative, were ever ready, with their families and livestock, to answer the call to arms of a charismatic leader. The sedentary populations of the oases practised agriculture with the help of irrigation. The relationship between the two types of economy and social organization and the two ways of life could be, according to the time and the place, either complementary or conflictual (Adshead, 1993: Chapter I, pp. 4–26).

From the point of view of the spread of Islam, the heart of Central Asia lies in western Transoxania, between two rivers which flow into the Aral Sea, the Syr Daryā to the north and the Āmū Daryā to the south (the classical Jaxartes and Oxus): Transoxania or, as the Arab geographers called it, the *Mā warā' an-Nahr* ('what is beyond the river' that is, the Āmū Daryā), the farthest outpost of the Islamic expansion into Central Asia in the eighth century. Under the Iranian Sāmānid dynasty (864–999/1005), its brilliant cultural centres, Bukhārā and Samarkand (Uzbekistan), became independent centres of Sunni Ḥanafī Islamization through the medium of the Persian language, a process that was still active towards the east until the dawn of the twentieth century (see Plate 195).

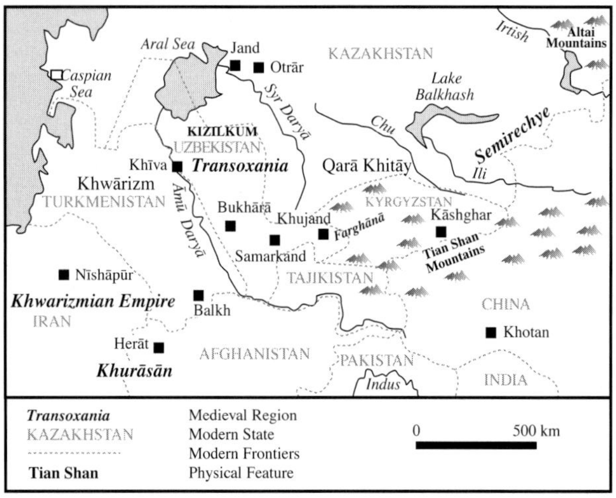

Map 13 Central Asia: important medieval geographical areas (draft Aubin, F.).

TURKIC AND ISLAMIC EXPANSION IN CENTRAL ASIA (ELEVENTH–TWELFTH CENTURIES)

By the very end of the tenth century, the push towards the west and south-west by the confederations of Turkic nomads, which had gone on intermittently since the sixth century, resulted in the establishment in Transoxania of dynasties of Turkic origin that had converted to Islam.

The confederation referred to by modern historians as the Qarākhānids developed a decentralized authority, which in the eleventh century split into two branches. The Eastern Khānate, which extended from the shores of Lake Balkhash to cover the south-east of Kazakhstan (Semirechye, the 'seven rivers region', subsequently a stronghold of some of the most powerful political entities), present-day Uzbekistan (medieval Farghāna) and the south-west of eastern Turkestan (the Xinjiang region of China), with its flourishing cultural centres of Kāshghar and Khotan, encouraged the expression of a Turkic identity and the emergence of an Islamic literature in Turkic, the first of its kind. The Western Khānate in Transoxania assimilated the local Iranian Islamic tradition into its own culture.

The Ghaznawid Sultanate (977–1186) was a Persian-speaking political entity set up in what is now northern Afghanistan and eastern Iran. This dynasty was drawn not from the tribal aristocracy of the steppes but from the ranks of the Sāmānids' Turkic slave soldiers; its external policy was one of aggression and conquest, but in domestic affairs it fell under the spell of the Persian language and culture and developed a refined urban civilization (see Plate 216).

Towards the middle of the eleventh century, a great Turkic military power emerged as a champion of Sunnism, which was upheld by the Baghdād caliphate in a world in which Shī'ism was steadily gaining ground. These were the Seljuks

(Saljūqs) (1038–1194), Turkmen still close to their nomadic and military origins, whom the Ghaznawids had enlisted to defend Khurāsān (eastern Iran) and who were to dominate Transoxania, Iran, Iraq and Anatolia. It is to this period that not only the restored supremacy of Sunnism, but also the institutional and architectural model of the *madrasa* (colleges for the study of religion and jurisprudence) and the innovative organization of Ṣūfī mystics into *ṭarīqāt* ('ways') belongs (A. Bausani, 'Religion in the Saljuq Periods', in Boyle, 1968: Chapter 3, pp. 283–302).

Another geopolitical entity occupying a prominent place in the process of Islamization in Central Asia was Khwārazm (Khorezm), the region of Khīwa along the lower reaches and delta of the Āmū Daryā, between present-day Uzbekistan and Turkmenistan. The fourth and final dynasty of the Khwārazm-shāhs, which held sway there from 1097 to 1220 and made it the principal regional power of the period, is celebrated for having opposed the caliphate but also for its remarkable cultural influence. Thus, for instance, the country was involved in the establishment of the system of Ṣūfī *ṭarīqat*, and the founder of the Kubrawīya remained active there until the Mongol massacres in 1220.

The diversification of Sunni Islam by the growth of Ṣūfism is beyond doubt the most notable feature of this period, which was dominated by the first Turkic Muslim dynasties.

THE RESURGENCE OF PRE-ISLAMIC RELIGIONS AND THE MONGOL DOMINATION (TWELFTH–THIRTEENTH CENTURIES)

During the twelfth and thirteenth centuries, however, Islam in Central Asia was rocked by new onslaughts from the east. First came the Qarā-Khitāy (1123–1218), a breakaway branch of a non-Chinese dynasty of northern China (the Liao, most probably pre-Mongols) who, after being driven out by other invaders coming down from the Manchurian forests, in 1116–1123, fled the Chinese sphere of influence, bringing with them to the now Muslim region between Lakes Balkhash and Issyk-Kul a nomadic confederation type of organization overlaid with Chinese cultural traits. After fierce fighting, the Qarā-Khitāy managed to impose direct or indirect rule over the neighbouring regions from 1141 onwards , keeping on the Qarākhānids and Khwārazm-shāhs as their vassals.

For nearly two centuries thereafter, Transoxania was thus under non-Muslim suzerainty. The tolerance, or indifference, of the Qarā-Khitāy in religious matters allowed Nestorianism (a heterodox form of Christianity that arose in the fifth century) to thrive to the east of Transoxania, Manichaeism (a doctrine that arose in Iran in the third century) and Buddhism to be revived in Kāshgharia (see Plate 54).

The invasion by the Mongols under Chinggis Khān (Chinggis Khān, c.1162–1227), a century after that of the Qarā Khitāy, showed the nomads' light cavalry at its most effective: on one side of Asia, Beijing and northern China fell to the Mongols in 1215 (southern China followed in 1279); on the other, in a welter of blood and horror, Kāshgharia and the Qarā-Khitāy region succumbed in 1218, Transoxania in 1219–1220 and proud Khwārazm (Khwārizm) and eastern Khurāsān in 1221. Under Chinggis Khān's immediate successors, the Mongols continued their inexorable advance. The Seljuk sultanate of the West was defeated in 1243, and the 'Abbāsid caliphate of Baghdād in 1258 (see Plates 12, 243, 248).

Even today, it is difficult to make a balanced and unemotional assessment of Chinggis Khān's empire (see Map 29) since the Mongol techniques for conquest, foreshadowing in this respect the total war of modern times, included the use of systematic propaganda to build up their own image. The destruction of cities, the massacre of urban populations and the reversion of irrigated land to desert were all tragedies, which, however, varied considerably in their impact, much greater in Central Asia than in China; but the decline which in many areas followed the Mongol occupation had already set in before the invasion. Although the fall of Baghdād marked the end of the 'Abbāsid caliphate, that emblem of universal Islam, the role of the caliphate had in fact long been under attack from jurists, mystics and any number of sultans.

On the other hand, the *pax mongolica*, encompassing all of Chinggis Khān's dominions, was neither as calm nor as durable as has often been suggested (Allsen, 1987; Fletcher, 1986; Franke, 1994). It really remained in effect only until the death in 1259 of the fourth Great Khān, Möngke, Chinggis Khān's grandson; it had only a token existence during the reign of his successor, Qubilay, the ruler of China from 1260 to 1294, and was practically non-existent thereafter. Nevertheless, the Mongol explosion of the first half of the thirteenth century was the first global event in world history (Adshead, 1993: Chapter 3, pp. 53–77). As a result of a policy of general mobilization of available human resources and a lively intercontinental trade, people and cultures met and mingled as never before in the pre-industrial age. China, which was least affected by the phenomenon, took from the Muslim world only a few new techniques, relating to calendar, astronomy, architecture, hydraulics and military science. The salient fact for China was the introduction, in the thirteenth and fourteenth century, from Transoxania and the Middle East, of Islam, which prospered there, being assimilated rapidly and totally into the Chinese environment.

Through such exchanges, Europe gained both a vision of the world which would later spur it on to undertake voyages of discovery and a number of Chinese technical innovations, such as gunpowder, movable-type printing, segmental-arch bridges, lock gates and postal relays, to name but a few. Transoxania, the Middle East and Russia were to remain influenced by Chinese administrative and fiscal methods. The benefits of cultural syncretism in Īlkhānid Iran (1256–1335) included innovations in miniature painting, in the writing of historical and geographical works, and in medicine; at the same time, Iranian mathematics and astronomy spread to Byzantium, China and India.

THE RESUMPTION OF ISLAMIZATION AND THE REASSERTION OF REGIONAL IDENTITIES (FOURTEENTH–FIFTEENTH CENTURIES)

By the time the Mongols were expelled from China by the Ming in 1368 and fell back on their ancestral steppe land (present-day Mongolia), now empty of its original Turkic inhabitants, the political entities they had founded had already vanished, though the memory of Chinggis Khān has remained alive in Central Asia right up to the 1990s as a symbol of the legitimacy of political power and as the ultimate model of good government.

In a matter of decades, in the second half of the thirteenth and the first half of the fourteenth century, the Mongol aristocracy, in their western possessions, were Turkicized and drew closer to the substratum of sedentary local populations. They were also islamized under the impetus of an increasingly dominant Ṣūfism – the Ṣūfī order most popular in modern times in Central Asia and China, the Naqshbandīya, arose during the fourteenth century.

With Tamerlane – in Turkic, Temür; in Persian, Tīmūr (-i Lang, 'the Lame'), 1336–1405 – the round of murderous conquests began again, but during the century following his death Central Asia experienced, arising from the ruins of the Chinggis Khān's Chaghatāy khānate, a spectacular cultural and spiritual renaissance under Tīmūr's descendants, the Tīmūrids (1405–1507), in the centres of high Turco-Persian culture in Transoxania and Khurāsān and in particular in the cities of Samarkand and Herāt, the dazzling capitals of a new Chaghatāy (Uzbek) and Persian (Tājīk) ethnocultural identity (see Plates 26, 27, 186, 218).

At the beginning of the sixteenth century, Central and Western Asia suddenly took on the shape they have to this day. The great Islamic power was now the Ottoman Empire. Originating in the thirteenth century as a small outlying Turkmen emirate of the Seljuk sultanate, dedicated to waging holy war against Byzantium, by the beginning of the sixteenth century the Ottoman Empire stretched from the Balkans to the Arab lands. The fall of Cairo, where the caliph then resided, in 1517, is a date as laden with symbolism as the taking of Baghdād by the Mongols two and a half centuries earlier.

From the Īlkhānid Iran of the Mongols, split into rival principalities during the fourteenth century and ravaged first by Tīmūr and then, during the fifteenth century, by various Turkic tribes, Ṣafawid Iran, which proclaimed Shī'ism its national religion, emerged in 1502.

In 1480, the Grand Duchy of Moscow shook off the yoke of the Chinggis Khān Golden Horde, which it had borne since 1240, and began to claim Russian suzerainty over the Muslim Turkic khānates descended from the Horde. While the Kazakh hordes occupied the region between the Caspian and Semirech'ie, where their descendants continue to live as nomads to this day, Uzbek (Özbeg) migrations reintroduced a nomadic regime into Transoxania based upon the survivors of the Golden Horde, and drove out the Tīmūrids, one branch of whom went on to found the Mughal Empire of the sixteenth–eighteenth centuries in northern India in 1526.

Mogholistan, the last heir of Chinggis Khān's turkicized khānates, which for its part remained a nomad state, was founded by a branch of the Chaghatāy in the 1360s to the east of Lake Issyk-Kul but was limited after 1508 to the western part of eastern Turkestan (that is, Xinjiang, to the east of the Tian Shan Mountains). During the first half of the sixteenth century, Islam finally became established in this region, as well as further east in Uighuristan (eastern Chinese Turkestan, the region of Turfān and Hami), while nomadism declined, giving way to a civilization centred on the oases. Apart from a further Mongol occupation of eastern Turkestan from the sixteenth to the eighteenth century, Central Asia had become for its greater part Turkic and Islamic by the beginning of the sixteenth century.

BIBLIOGRAPHY

ADSHEAD, S. A. M. 1993. *Central Asia in World History*. Macmillan, Basingstoke.

ALLSEN, T. T. 1987. *Mongol Imperialism: The Policies of the Great Qan Möngke in China, Russia, and the Islamic Lands, 1251–1259*. Berkeley and Los Angeles.

BARTHOLD, W. 1968 (1st edn. 1928). *Turkestan Down to the Mongol Invasion*, 3rd edn. Luzac (E. J. W. Gibb Memorial Series, V), London.

BASILOV, V. N. 1989. *Nomads of Eurasia*. Trans. M. F. Zirin. Natural History Museum of Los Angeles County; Los Angeles, Seattle.

BOYLE, J. A. (ed.) 1968. *Cambridge History of Iran*, Vol. V. *The Saljuq and Mongol Periods*. Cambridge.

Encyclopaedia Iranica. Vols IV and V. 1990 and 1992. Bukhārā, Central Asia, Chaghatayid Dynasty, Chinese Turkestan.

Encyclopaedia of Islam. Vols I–VII. 1960–1991 Leiden. s.v. Baghdād, 'Caghatay', 'Cingiz Khān', 'Cingizids', 'Farghānā', 'Ghaznawids', 'Ilek-khāns or Karakhānids', 'Īlkhāns', 'Karā Khitāy', 'Khwārazm', 'Mā warā' al-Nahr', 'Mongols'.

FLETCHER, J. 1986. The Mongols: Ecological and Social Perspectives, *Harvard Journal of Asiatic Studies*, Vol. 46, No. 1, pp. 11–50.

FOURNIAU, V. 1994. *Histoire de l'Asie centrale*. Paris. (Que sais–je? No. 2821).

FRANKE, H. 1994. Sino-Western Contacts Under the Mongol Empire'. In: FRANKE, H. (ed.) *China Under Mongol Rule*. Aldershot, Variorum (Variorum Collected Studies Series, CS 429). Text No. VII, first published in: *Journal of the Royal Asiatic Society*, Vol. VI, Hong Kong, 1966, pp. 49–72.

INALCIK, H. 1973. *The Ottoman Empire: The Classical Age, 1300–1600*. London.

LAMBTON, A. K. S. 1988. *Continuity and Change in Medieval Persia: Aspects of Administrative, Economic and Social History, 11th–14th Century*. London.

MORGAN, D. 1986. *The Mongols*. Oxford.

PLETNEVA, S. A. 1982. *Kochevniki Srednevekov'ja: Poiski istoricheskih zakonomernostej* [Nomads of the Middle Ages: Search of Historical Regularities]. Moscow.

SEAMAN, G. (ed.). *The Nomads: Masters of the Eurasian Steppe*. Vol. I, 1989, *Ecology and Empire: Nomads in the Cultural Evolution of the Old World*. Vol. II, 1991, *Rulers from the Steppe: State Formation on the Eurasian Periphery*. Vol. III, 1992, *Foundations of Empire: Archaeology and Art of the Eurasian Steppes*. Ethnographics; University of Southern California, Los Angeles.

SOURDEL, D.; SOURDEL, J. 1968. *La civilisation de l'Islam classique*. Paris.

17.5
THE WEST OF ISLAM

17.5.1
AL-MAGHRIB, SPAIN AND SICILY

Younes Shanwan

It is an elementary fact of geography that much of the North African coast, comprising the Mediterranean shores of Morocco, Algeria and Tunisia, and the hump around Ben-Ghazi in Libya, share with Spain, southern France and Italy a common climate marked by mild winters with moderate rain and dry summers; and this gives rise to a common class of vegetation which, like the climate itself, bears the name 'mediterranean'. With the Straits of Gibraltar at the western end, and the Sicilian Channel at the eastern, the western Mediterranean appears like a fairly well enclosed lake providing easy access to all the lands that ring it. There are other affinities too: if the central Spanish plateau is semi-arid, marked by cool winters with slight rain and summers warm and dry, similar conditions are found across the Gibraltar Straits in the southern slopes of the Atlas range. Both zones thus constitute natural grounds for pastoralism, existing side by side with agriculture carried on in the more rain-favoured areas, where vines and palm trees flourish. It is therefore not surprising that for nearly a millennium before the Islamic intrusion, the western Mediterranean had been a distinct historical unity. Within it Rome and Carthage had fought for mastery; and the Roman Empire and then Christianity had embraced the entire region. It might therefore have been expected that once the Arabs broke into North Africa from their base in Egypt, they would inevitably seek to convert the western Mediterranean as a whole into an Islamic lake.

The conquest of the Maghrib began with the Arab occupation of Barca in Libya in 643, soon after the fall of Alexandria (642). It was followed by an expedition passing through Tripolitania into Ifrīqiyya (Tunisia) in 647. But the two countries were truly subjugated only during 663–670 by the Umayyad commander 'Uqba ibn Nāfi', who reputedly founded the great camp city of Qayrawān in Ifrīqiyya (670). During his second term of appointment (680–683), he marched through Algeria and Morocco to reach the Atlantic. The Arabs in the Maghrib encountered the Berbers, similar in many ways, with their camel-based nomadism and tribal system, to the Arabs of the desert. Two successive rebellions under Kusayla and a prophetess (*kāhina*) were suppressed, and a long and tortuous process of conversion and Arabicization of the Berber tribes began. The last Byzantine outpost of Carthage was captured in 697, and the Berber prophetess defeated and put to death in 701 by one of the most successful Umayyad governors, Ḥassan ibn al-Nu'mān. In 705, Mūsā ibn Nuṣayr took charge of the Arab dominions in the Maghrib, and it was under him that the turn of Spain came.

Spain was at that time under the rule of the Visigoths. Witiza, the last legitimate ruler of the dynasty, had been succeeded in the capital, Toledo, by Roderic, his commander. Julian, the ruler of Ceuta, having some dispute with him, offered to assist Mūsā ibn Nuṣayr in invading al-Andalus (the Arabs' name for the whole Iberian peninsula, not simply Andalusia or southern Spain). In 710, Ṭarīf ibn Abī Zar'a led a reconnaissance raid to the island which still bears his name (Tarifa). In 711, Ṭāriq ibn Ziyād, a Berber commander, crossed the straits, the site of his arrival later being named after him (Gibraltar), and defeated Roderic at Wādī Lago. The way into al-Andalus now lay open. By 716, the Muslims had taken Cordova, Toledo, Seville, Zaragoza, Pamplona and Barcelona. The speed of the conquest was facilitated by the internal conflict among the Visigoths and a lack of resistance on the part of sections of the population, who now received, as Juan Vernet points out, a wide measure of self-government and a burden of taxes lower than those prevailing earlier. Nor was anyone compelled by force to become Muslim.

The arrival of the Umayyad fugitive 'Abd al-Raḥmān (731–788) in al-Andalus in 755, and his founding in 756 of a dynasty independent of the 'Abbāsids, did not result in al-Andalus becoming separated culturally from the Maghrib or the east; indeed, it increasingly relied on the east in matters of learning and culture. 'Abd al-Raḥmān himself sought to have in al-Andalus reminders of his homeland (Syria), so he built a castle named Ruṣāfa, after the castle of his grandfather Hishām in Syria; he had a seedling palm tree planted in Ruṣāfa and built a residence especially for women singers from Medina in Cordova.

A number of Muslim groups made their home in al-Andalus: Arabs and Berbers, Spanish Muslims (*muwalladūn*), clients of Arab tribes (*mawālī*), and Slavs; so did non-Muslims, Jews and Christians. The newly arrived Syrian armies settled there (741) under Bilj ibn Bishr al-Qushayrī. Men from

Damascus settled in Elvira; from Jordan in Rayyo; from Palestine in Sidonia; from Homs in Seville; from Qinnasrīn in Jaén; from Egypt in Beja; and a division in Tudmīr. The soldiers from Syria gave the names of their own cities to their new places of settlement, and contacts between the Syrian settlers in al-Andalus and their homeland were maintained for quite some time.

It is clear from the distribution of the Arab tribes that the Arabs, in their two branches of ʿAdnān (northern Arabs) and Qaḥṭān (southern Arabs), settled in the cities in the south-eastern part of Spain. The Berbers, on the other hand, settled in the more arid mountainous regions of al-Andalus. Owing to the proximity of their homeland, they were far more numerous than the Arabs and jealous of Arab supremacy.

The Berbers in al-Andalus were from two groups, the Butr and the Baranis; Nafza, Miknāsa, Hawwāra and Madyūna were of the Butr, while Kutāma, Zanana, Maṣmūda, Malīla and Ṣanhāja were of the Barānis. The Zanāna came from the region of Cétif; the other Barānis came from further east along the Mediterranean. The Nafza and Miknāsa in al-Andalus were settled between the region of Galicia and the city of Cordova; the Hawwāra and Madyuna settled in Santáver.

The *musālima* were Christians who, in large numbers, changed their religion to Islam during the period of the conquest and the emirate. The *muwalladūn* were second-generation Muslims, and these came to make up the majority of the Muslim inhabitants of al-Andalus. Being the original inhabitants, they considered that the Arabs had robbed them of most of the good things in their land. From among them came the well-known revolutionary ʿUmar ibn Ḥafsūn, who, in the late ninth century, raised the most serious revolt that the Umayyads had to face. As the great historian of Arab Spain ibn Ḥayyān (d. 1076) describes it: 'The *musālima* took the side of the *muwalladūn,* and the Christian *dhimmīs* [protected peoples] joined in with them; together they rallied against the Arabs in response to the call of Ibn Ḥafsūn' (Ibn Hayyan, 3:1).

The Mozarabs (*mustaʿrabūn*) were Christians who, while living among the Muslims, held to their Christian faith but were Arabized in language and culture. Subordinate to, and alongside Arabic, there was the common language of al-Andalus, a Romance tongue (*ʿajamiyya*); and then there were the Berber dialects. The long coexistence within one region of diverse peoples, religions and cultures led to mutual influence, although the Arabic and Islamic elements were obviously stronger. The Christian north, according to Menéndez Pidal, was subject to the general decline of the Roman world in the west since it had been cut off from the Greek world; in contrast, the Islamic south flourished, sharing in the general revival brought to it by Arab civilization. Arabic itself was becoming richer as a language of science and culture, a process to which al-Andalus in time so significantly contributed.

With its numerous cities, al-Andalus was a fertile and prosperous country, of which Ibn Ḥawqal said:

> 'I entered Andalus at the beginning of the year 337 [AD 948], at which time the ruler was Abū-l-Mutarrif ʿAbd al-Raḥmān ibn Muḥammad [ʿAbd al-Raḥmān III, r. 912–961] . . . there was great prosperity, and the major part was cultivated and inhabited. Everywhere we find flowing water, trees and rivers of freshwater; it is an accessible land with good conditions, where both the upper classes and the ordinary people can lead prosperous and comfortable lives.'

The security and settled conditions in the period of the caliphate led to an increase in population and attracted many people from the Maghrib to al-Andalus. This gave the impetus to ʿAbd al-Raḥmān III to build, near Cordova, the city-palace of Madīnat al-Zahrāʾ, whose construction can be seen as an exemplar of Islamic cities in Andalus; he began with its great mosque, the centre of social life in Islamic cities.

From Spain, the Arabs crossed early into southern France and already by 720 had occupied Narbonne. The check received by them at Poitiers (732) from Charles Martel may have been given more significance by hindsight than it actually possessed, for the Arab foothold in southern France remained small and short-lived thereafter. The 'Saracen raiders', outposts established on the coast of Provence from 890 onwards were of even lesser long-term consequence.

Unlike southern France, Muslim presence in Sicily was of a much longer duration and had a greater cultural impact. The Arab–Berber conquest of Sicily, originally began under the auspices of the Aghlabids of Qayrawān in 827, and the emirate in Sicily lasted till the Norman conquest (1060–1091). Two outposts were established briefly on the Italian mainland, in Bari (*c.* 847–871) and Taranto (850–880). Islamic influences did not by any means disappear with the fall of Muslim political dominance. The Andalusian traveller Ibn Jubayr visited Sicily and said of its ruler William I (acc. 1154), son of Roger II, who had been the patron of the geographer al-Idrīsī:

> 'He places great confidence in the Muslims, trusting them in all his most important affairs; even the superintendent of his kitchen is a Muslim. . . . One of the strange facts about him is that he reads and writes Arabic. . . . The officers who are the eyes of his government and carry out orders by his authority are Muslims too; every one of them observes the fast at its appointed times, voluntarily and seeking recompense [from Allāh], and gives alms seeking the approval and favour of Allāh.'

Next to Moorish Spain, Norman Sicily therefore served as the channel by which much of Arabic learning was transmitted to the medieval West (see Plates 65–69, 72, 73).

BIBLIOGRAPHY

ARIE, R. 1990 (2nd edn). *Etudes sur la civilisation de l'Espagne musulmane,* Leiden/New York; Spanish trans., 1982. *España Musulmana (siglos VIII–XV).* Barcelona.

GARCĪA GÓMEZ, E. 1967. *Andalucía Contra Berbería.* Madrid.

GONZÁLEZ PALENCIA, Á. 1945. *Historia de la Literatura Arábigo-Andaluza.* Madrid.

IBN AL-ʾABBĀR. 1963 (1st edn), 1987 (2nd edn). *Al-Ḥulla Al-Sayrāʾ* (The Fruitful Adornment), 2 vols, ed. by Ḥusayn Muʾnis. Cairo.

IBN ḤAWQAL. 1870–1873. *Kitāb al-Masālik wa l-Mamālik* (Book of Roads and Countries, also referred to as the *Opus Geographicum*), 1st edn of Arabic text by J. M. De Goeje, 2 vols (with text of al-Iṣṭakrī), Leiden; 2nd edn of Arabic text by Kramers, 1 vol. Leiden, 1938.

IBN ḤAYYĀN. 1937. *Kitāb al-Muqtabis fī Tārīkh Rijāl al-Andalus* (i.e. collected surviving 'citations' from Ibn Ḥayyān on the history of the leading personalities of Muslim Spain); 1st edn by M. Antuña, *Chronique du règne du calife umaiyade ʿAbd Allâh à Cordoue.* Paris; other editions: Cairo 1971; Beirut 1973; P. Chalmeta ed., Madrid 1979.

IBN ḤAZM. 1962. *Jamharat Ansāb l-ʾArab* (Collected Genealogies of the Arabs). ed. by Hārūn. Cairo.

——. 1980. *Rasāʾil Ibn Ḥazm* (Epistles of Ibn Ḥazm). 4 vols, ed. by Iḥsān ʿAbbās. Beirut.

IBN 'IDĀRĪ. 1848–1851. *Kitāb al-Bayān al-Mughrib fī Akhbār Mulūk al-Andalus wa l-Maghrib* (The Book of Wondrous Discourse upon the Chronicles of the Kings of Muslim Spain and Morocco); 1st edn of Arabic text by R. Dozy, 2 vols, Leiden; 3rd vol. of Arabic text ed. by E. Lévi-Provençal, Paris 1930; re-ed. of Arabic text in 4 vols, Beirut 1980. French trans. by E. Fagnan, Algiers 1901–1904.

IBN JUBAYR. 1858. *Riḥla* (Journey); 1st edn. of Arabic text by W. Wright. Leiden; 2nd corrected edn. by J. M. De Goeje. Leiden 1907; new Arabic edn, Beirut.

IBN AL-QUṬIYYA. 1868. (The Son of the Gothic Lady), *Tārikḥ iftitāh al-Andalus* (History of the Conquest of Spain), 1st edn of Arabic text by P. de Gayangos, E. Saavedra and F. Codera, Madrid; re-ed. Beirut 1956; Spanish trans. by J. Ribera, *Historia de la Conquista de España*. Madrid 1926.

IBN SA'ID. 1964. *Al-Mughrib Fī Hula al-Maghrib* (Marvels upon the Adorned Robe of the West). Cairo.

LÉVI PROVENÇAL, E. 1950–1953. *Histoire de l'Espagne musulmane, 711–1030*, 3 vols. Paris/Leiden.

MAKKĪ, M. 1961–1964. Ensayo sobre las aportaciones orientales en la España musulmana (Essay on the Eastern Contributions to Muslim Spain). In: *Revista del Instituto Egipcio de Estudios Islámicos*. Vol. IX YX (65–231), Vols. XI and XII (7–140). Madrid.

AL-MAQQARĪ. 1855–1861. *Nafḥ al-Ṭīb* (Fragrant Scents), 1st edn of Arabic text, *Analectes sur l'histoire et la littérature des Arabes d'Espagnes,* ed. by Dozy, Dugat, Krehl and Wright. Leiden; re-ed. of Arabic text by Iḥsān 'Abbās, 8 vols, Beirut 1988; partial Engl. trans. by Pascual de Gayangos, *The History of the Mohammedan Dynasties in Spain*. London 1840.

MENÉNDEZ PIDAL, R. 1977. *España, eslabón entre la Cristiandad y el Islam* (Spain, a Threshold between Christendom and Islam). Madrid.

TORRES BALBAS, L. 1985. *Ciudades hispanomusulmanas* (Spanish–Muslim Cities), 2nd edn. Madrid.

VERNET, J. 1978. *La Cultura hispanoárabe en Oriente y Occidente*. Barcelona; French trans. by G. Martínez Gros, *Ce que la culture doit aux Arabes d'Espagne*. Paris 1988.

17.5.2
THE SUDAN AND COUNTRIES SOUTH OF THE SAHARA

Djibril Tamsir Niane

In Africa south of the Sahara – unlike Egypt and the Maghrib, where conversion to Islam followed external conquests – the religion spread mainly through traders and scholars. People at some levels of society adopted Muslim lifestyles and customs long before they were actually converted. In West Africa (Mauritania, Senegal), during the warfare of the eleventh century, the Almoravids found that many Berber and Black tribes had already been converted to Islam. The Sudan, the upper Nile and East Africa were Arabized at the same time as they were converted, but throughout the region generally the indigenous population assimilated Islam while retaining a strong cultural identity.

THE ISLAMIZATION OF THE WESTERN AND CENTRAL PARTS OF SUB-SAHARAN AFRICA

As early as AD 666 – only forty-six years after the birth of Islam – Muslim troops led by 'Uqba ibn Nāfi', the Arab conqueror of Egypt, reached the Fezzān and Khawār oases. In 682, an expedition left the Sousse region of southern Morocco for black Africa. In 734 Ḥabīb ibn Abī 'Ubayd al-Fihrī, 'Uqba's grandson, led a victorious foray to the south of the Sahara and reached the kingdom of Ghana, bringing back gold and slaves.

Although these expeditions were more in the nature of raids than of conquests or missionary campaigns in the name of Islam, they did bring Muslims into contact with the Black peoples and made them aware of the wealth of the region.

It fell to merchants to establish lasting relations with Black Africa by organizing trading caravans. While the conquerors' orthodox Islamic faith took root in the Maghrib, it was the 'dissidents' or Khārijites who were to introduce the new religion south of the Sahara. Their base was the North African town of Tāhert, where they established a strong community led by *imāms*. For two centuries, Tāhert, a meeting point for traders from Baṣrā, Kūfa and Kairouan, provided a bridgehead into Black Africa. In 903, a Tāhert trader, Ibn al-Ṣaghīr, praised the sense of justice and hospitality of the Khārijite *imām*, who succeeded in attracting traders so that 'the roads leading to the Ṣūdān [that is, sub-Saharan Africa] and countries to the east and west were opened up to contacts and trade.' Gifts and missions were exchanged between Tāhert and the rulers of the Sudan as early as the eighth century. (Ibn Al-Saghīr, 1980.) Ibāḍī traders belonging to a Khārijite sect were to be found in all the Sahel towns, in Takrūr, Ghast, Kumbi and Gao. A distant Ibāḍī influence lingered on in the shape of the minarets of West African mosques.

Although the Ibāḍī were concerned only with trade and did not seek to impose their beliefs on others, they did have a great influence on their Black trading partners, who adopted the Muslim way of life even before converting to Islam.

By the time the conversion of the kings began in the eleventh century, most of the urban population had already been Islamized. In the tenth century, the Songhai king of Gao (Mali) converted to Islam; archaeological excavations have uncovered the funeral stelae of the royal family dating from that time.

More information is available about the conversion of the kings of Takrūr (Senegal) and Malel (Mali). The former converted in 1030, even before the Almoravids had imposed Islam on the Berber tribes of Mauritania. According to the Arab geographer al-Bakrī, Ouardjabi, the king of Takrūr, then set about spreading the religion to other cities (Al-Bakrī, 1857), he even provided an army for his son, who joined the Almoravids in their campaign of conquest in the Maghrib.

The king of Malel (Mali) converted in about 1050, in highly significant circumstances. Drought had been ravaging the country for many years and despite many sacrifices of oxen to the spirits, the king could not make it rain. An Arab living at the court suggested that he call on Allāh. The king agreed, performed his ablutions with the Arab and prayed throughout the night. At dawn, the long-awaited rain began to fall and the delighted king converted, the royal family and the entire court following his example.

In the central Sudan, the Kānem peoples, like those of Takrūr and Ghana, were won over to Islam well before their rulers converted. The *Mai* (king) of Kānem, Hummay Djilimi (1080–1097), converted and founded a Muslim dynasty, and his son and heir made the pilgrimage to Mecca.

The animists' unfamiliarity with proselytization was generally propitious for the spread of Islam. They were not at all wary of the Muslims and were even eager to obtain their amulets and charms. This is why Muslims were welcomed in the courts and why the kings often sought the prayers of the scholars and marabouts who lived at court.

The Almoravids

The Berber peoples of Mauritania were Islamized to only a small degree in the eleventh century. The Berber chief Yaḥyā ibn Ibrāhīm then decided to enforce the strictest orthodoxy: he used the services of a scholar called Ibn Yāsīn, who founded a *ribāṭ* (fortified 'convent'), where he shut himself up with his disciples to study. They emerged around 1054 and launched a *jihād*. These Almoravids (a distorted form of Al-

Murābiṭūn – 'people of the *ribāṭ*') imposed orthodoxy on all the tribes of the Maghrib and established a huge empire taking in parts of North Africa and Spain.

In 1076, the Kaya Maghan, king of Ghana, the most powerful kingdom in West Africa, converted to Islam. Kumbi, his capital, had for a long time had an Arab quarter with mosques, and some of the Kaya Maghan's own advisers were Muslims (Al-Bakrī, 1857). As happened elsewhere in West Africa, the ruler's conversion sounded the death knell of Khārijism. The Soninke or Sarakole, who made up most of Ghana's population, were to become fervent propagators of Islam.

The Almoravid conquests resulted in population movements. According to Senegalese tradition, after the conversion of Ouardjabi the Serer, who lived by the river in the Fouta Toro region, migrated westwards to escape Islam and took refuge in Siro, on the Atlantic coast.

The medieval empires of the western and central parts of sub-Saharan Africa were at their height in the thirteenth to fourteenth century. Under the Mali empire, many of the Soundjata's heirs made the pilgrimage to Mecca, and *Mansa* (prince) Mūsā I returned from the holy places with an architect who built the mosques at Gao and Timbuktu (1325). It was during the reign of *Mansa* Sulaymān (1332–1358) that Ibn Baṭṭūṭa visited Mali and stayed in the capital, Niani (see Plate 259) (Ibn Baṭṭūṭa, tr. 1956–1971).

Trade flourished and the Malinke and Sarakole merchants travelled all over the vast empire, even taking Islam beyond its borders. Timbuktu, Niani, Jenné and Gao also became renowned centres of learning. Their influence was felt as far as the area round Lake Chad. The *Chronicle of Kano* records the arrival of Malian traders, who introduced Islam to Kano in the fourteenth century.

In the central sub-Saharan area, the Hausa, Islamized at an early stage, propagated the new religion. Merchants like the Soninke and Malinke, they established many trading cities such as Kano, Zaria and Katsina, which also had famous schools.

Thus, between the seventh and fifteenth centuries, Islam made constant progress in Black Africa from Senegal to Lake Chad; practically all the Sahel region was Islamized. There were only two pockets of resistance, the Mosi within the Niger Bend and the Bambara along the river, but Islam continued to win converts because of the traders, who knew no borders.

ISLAM IN SUDAN AND EAST AFRICA

The name *Sūdān* ('land of the black people') in this context applies only to Upper Egypt or Nubia. This region had been converted to Christianity, and the Christian kingdoms of Nubia survived until the fourteenth century. Islam started to encroach upon this bastion of Christianity in an entirely different way.

From the seventh century onwards, in the wake of their conquest of Egypt, the Arabs tried to gain the ascendancy in the upper Nile, but the fierce resistance of the Christian kings obliged them to make peace. This led to the signing of the famous Bakt, the convention that for six centuries was to govern relations between the Muslim rulers of Egypt and the Christian kings of Nubia. The Bakt established a close interdependence between the two political systems (*EI*[2], 1960–).

Two separate kingdoms emerged in Nubia: Maqurrah and Alwah.In Nubia, Islamization took place slowly and was accompanied by a movement of the Arab population towards the south, which resulted in the whole country becoming arabized. As the Bakt had established the rules governing trade between the two regions, Muslim traders were free to enter and leave Nubia as they wished. The first Arab immigrants settled mainly between the valley of the upper Nile and the Red Sea, establishing several communities that lived on good terms with the local population.

From the eleventh century onwards, there was a large-scale movement of Kabila Arabs from Egypt to Nubia. These tribes, which had fallen foul of the Ayyūbids and the Mamlūks, sought refuge in Nubia, provoking Arab–Nubian clashes when they began to arrive in large groups in the twelfth century. The Mamlūk sultan Baybars (1260–1277) adopted an offensive policy towards Nubia in order to safeguard his southern borders.

In the fourteenth century, this pressure led to the conversion of the kings of Maqurrah. An Arabic source relates how the cathedral of Dunqula was turned into a mosque in 1317 (see Plate 273). Sayf al- Dīn 'Abdallāh al-Nāṣir, a Nubian king who had converted to Islam, was installed by the Mamlūks. The decline of Maqurrah was marked by the Arabization of the royal family and the aristocracy. The kings chosen by the Mamlūks no longer stood for anything, and Maqurrah lost its vitality as an organized state. In fact, Nubia was taken over by the Arab immigrants.

Alwah did not escape the Arabization process either. Also in the fourteenth century, the Arabs settled in the heart of the country, near Soba. Arbadji, a city founded in 1475, marked the southern limit of Arab expansion.

It can thus be seen that the conversion of Nubia to Islam was not a clear-cut process. Traders played a decisive role, here as in the rest of sub-Saharan Africa, at least to begin with, but Arab infiltration was the distinctive feature of the Islamization of Nubia. Christianity lived on there for several generations, however, and churches survived until the sixteenth century. Nubia, later to become Sudan proper, was from the fifteenth century onwards a complex Arab-African entity, a 'microcosm of Africa'. It was the meeting point of two worlds: the lands of the nomads and tropical Africa.

In East Africa, Islam made its appearance during the very first century of Islam. This region, on the shores of one of the busiest seas in the world, had been in contact with the outside world since the earliest times. The coastal strip, which the Arabs called the 'land of the *Zanj*' ('negroes'), provided an outlet to the sea for a fertile hinterland whence came gold, ivory and slaves.

Muslim traders first made their appearance in the coastal towns in the seventh century. Arabs and Persians settled there, building up strong relations with the indigenous peoples of Bantu extraction. As in Senegal, Mali and Kānem, Islamization affected the urban populations before the conversion of the king and his court.

However, Islamization was mainly the work of traders who arrived from the Persian Gulf and in particular those from the town of Shīrāz. These contacts between Arabs, Persians and indigenous peoples gave birth to the Swahili civilization and a language, Kiswahili, which is Bantu-based but has borrowed most of its vocabulary from Arabic. It was used as a *lingua franca* throughout the coastal region before becoming the common language of the entire region.

The Swahili civilization was at its height between the twelfth and fifteenth centuries. Arab, Persian and Indian immigrants became intermingled to such an extent with the Bantu population that the term 'Swahili' cannot be considered to apply either to an ethnic or to a social community.

In the fourteenth century (1332), the Arab traveller Ibn Baṭṭūṭa described Mogadishu as a great Muslim city where scholars were welcomed with honour by the sultan, a city bustling with activity where commerce was king (Ibn Baṭṭūṭa, tr. 1956–1971).

By the thirteenth century, Kiswahili had become a written language, using Arabic script, and was employed for the purposes of religion, trade and law. Official documents such as the codes of rights and privileges governing society were put into writing.

One of the natural consequences of the spread of Islam was the building of mosques. Whereas towns and villages in West Africa continued to be mud-built, in East Africa stone came into use. The Kilwa excavations have brought to light various artifacts from this civilization, such as oil lamps and vases, which confirm the Arab–Persian influence.

Masterpieces of Swahili Islamic architecture were built in Kilwa under the reign of Sultan al-Ḥasan ibn Sulaymān II (1310–1333) (see Plates 35, 271, 272).

As elsewhere south of the Sahara, it was thanks to commerce that this civilization came into being, prospered and grew. As in Takrūr, Timbuktu and Jenne, once the pattern of trade was disturbed the civilization went into decline. This overly great reliance on almost commerce alone was one of the weaknesses of Swahili civilization.

BIBLIOGRAPHY

ABŪ 'ABD ALLĀH MUḤAMMAD IBN IBRĀHĪM IBN HABĪB AL-FAZĀRĪ. Eighth-cent. (AD) geographer quoted by AL-MAS'ŪDĪ in the *Murūj al-Dhahab* (*'Meadows of Gold'*), ed. of Arabic text with Fr. trans., *Les Prairies d'Or,* by C. Barbier de Meynard and Pavet de Courteille, Paris 1861–1877, Vol. I, p. 39. Arabic text revised by Ch. Pellat, Beirut 1965. Arabic reprint., Beirut 1987.

AL-BAKRĪ, ABŪ 'UBAYD ABD ALLĀH. 1857. *Kitāb al-Masālik wa al-Mamālik* (Book of the Pathways and Kingdoms). Portion of Arabic text ed. with French trans. (*Description de l'Afrique septentrionale*) by Baron William MacGuckin de Slane, Algiers 1857; reprint of French text, Adrien Maisonneuve publ., Paris 1965.

CHITTICK, H. N. 1963. Kilwa and the Arab Settlements of the East African Coast. In: *Journal of African History*, 4, 2, pp. 179–90. Oxford University Press, London/New York.

——. 1966. Kilwa, a Preliminary Report. In: *Azania* I, pp. 1–36. Nairobi.

——. 1974. *Kilwa: an Islamic Trading City on the East African Coast.* Nairobi/London.

Encyclopaedia of Islam. 2nd edn. (*EI*²), 1960– (in progress). Brill, Leiden.

IBN 'ABD AL-ḤAKAṂ 1914; 1922. Kitāb Futūh Misr wa al-Maghrib wa al-Andalus (*Book of the Conquest of Egypt, the Maghrib and Spain*). Arabic text ed. by H. Massé (*Le livre de la conquête de l'Egypte, du Maghreb et de l'Espagne*), Cairo 1914. Arabic text also ed. by C. C. Torrey, *The History of the Conquest of Egypt, North Africa and Spain*, Yale University Press, New Haven, Conn. 1922. Partial French trans. with corresponding extracts of Ibn 'Abd al-Ḥakaṃ's Arabic text, *Conquête de l'Afrique du Nord et de l'Espagne*, ed. and trans. by A. Gateau, Algiers 1948. [Chronicle deals with conquest of Kawas (AD 666) and Sousse (AD 734).]

IBN BAṬṬŪṬA. 1853-1859. *Rihla* (*Journey*) full medieval Arabic title: *Tuḥfat al-Nuzzār fī 'Ajā'ib al-Amsār* (Gift unto the Observers Concerning the Marvels of the Lands). First edn of Arabic text with French trans. by C. Defrémery and B. R. Sanguinetti, 4 vols. Paris 1853–1859. English trans. by H. A. R. Gibb, *The Travels of Ibn Battūta*, Hakluyt Society, Cambridge, 1956–1971. Arabic text only: *Rihla Ibn Battūta*, ed. by Talāl Harb, *Dār al-Kutub al-'Ilmiyya.* Beirut 1992.

IBN HAWQAL. 1873; 1938. *Kitāb Ṣūrat al-Arḍ* (Book of the Figure of the Earth). Arabic text ed. by M. J. De Goeje (1873), Leiden; and J. H. Kramers (1938), Leiden. French. trans. by J. H. Kramers and G. Wiet, *Configuration de la Terre.* Paris 1965.

IBN KHALDŪN. 1868 edn *Kitāb al-'Ibar* (Book of Admonition = Universal History), Arabic text, 7 vols. Būlāq, 1868; Beirut 1958. Partial French trans., 4 vols. by Baron W. MacGuckin de Slane, *Histoire des Berbères et des dynasties musulmanes de l'Afrique septentrionale*, Algiers, 1852–1856; reprint Paris 1925–1926. New complete French trans., 7 vols. Beirut 1956–1959.

IBN AL-SAGHĪR. 1980. *Chronique sur les Imams rustamides de Tāhert* (Chronicle of the Rustamid Imāms of Tāhert). Arabic text with English trans. In: *Actes du XIVè Congrès International des Orientalistes*, pp. 3–132; see English text p. 5, n. 5. Paris 1980.

AL-IDRĪSĪ. 1864–1866. *Kitāb Nuzhat al-Mushtāq fī 'khtirāq al- Afāq or Kitāb Rujjār* (Book of Delight unto him who would Wander through Distant Horizons, or Book of Roger – after the work's twelfth-century patron, King Roger II of Sicily). Partial edn of Arabic text with French. trans. by A. Dozy and M. J. De Goeje, *Description de l'Afrique et de l'Espagne.* Leiden.

AL-'UMARĪ, IBN FAḌL ALLĀH. 1924. *Masālik al-Absār fī Mamālik al-Amsār* (Glances of the Eyes throughout the Districts of the Lands); Arabic text, Cairo 1924. French trans. by M. Gaudefroy-Demombynes, *L'Afrique moins l'Egypte,* Paris 1927. [See ch. 10 on Mali.

18

THE ISLAMIC WORLD: SOCIAL AND MATERIAL LIFE, CLASSES AND COMMUNITIES

18.1

SOCIETY AND MATERIAL CULTURE OF THE ISLAMIC WORLD

Mounira Chapoutot-Remadi and Radhi Daghfous

THE GEOGRAPHICAL ENVIRONMENT

'Islam was born of the desert' (De Phanhol, 1993), or rather in its oases: the greater part of the Arabian peninsula is made up of 'harsh, isolated land, almost entirely given up to the desert'(Miquel, 1977 a: p. 22). Three parts of it may be distinguished: a mountain barrier running along the Red Sea inland towards the west, the Ḥijāz; the highlands rising to the south, the Yemen; and, stretching between these twin regions, the tablelands of Najd. These last merge into the even more arid, reddish lands of the Rub' al-Khālī or 'Empty quarter' to the south-east, and of the Nafūd to the north, halfway between 'Aqaba on the Red Sea and Kuwait on the Gulf. From here, the Arabs went forth to carve out an immense empire from the Indus to the Atlantic. The enormous space occupied by the Arabs, which in time became the Islamic world, formed a band of territories stretching almost entirely through the arid and sub-arid zones. Here precipitation is insufficient, and agriculture relies almost completely on irrigation, while the deserts were home to nomadism. The great deserts to the east are the Arabian Desert and the Persian Desert; and in the west stretches the Sahara. Among these wastelands, making up one compact mass, are to be found vast stretches like the Sahara with its sandy *ergs*, and stony *hammadas*, or rocky wastes as in Iran or small deserts like the Sinai. But while Islam was poorly favoured by climate, it did enjoy an exceptional position by controlling the crossroads of the great trade routes: it was 'the region of all the isthmuses' (Lombard, 1977 a), and it had agriculturally rich habitable zones in river valleys such as those of the Nile, the Euphrates, the Oxus and the Syr Daryā, besides innumerable smaller valleys and oases.

SOCIETY

The social and economic life of the Bedouin, and his marginalisation

Living as they did in the flatlands and deserts of northern and central Arabia, the Bedouin tribes moved in search of grazing for their camels, raided oases and caravans to improve their meagre resources, and fought one another over control of the water holes and herding paths scattered across the peninsula (Eickelman, 1981: pp. 63–81). But the Bedouin also flocked on market days to the oases, which produced dates and grain, to barter what they raised against what the settled folk farmed or crafted. Some took part in the trade which passed through the Ḥijāz, as protectors to the caravans which carried incense and spices from the south and south-east to the Mediterranean lands, after the decline of south Arabia and the interruption suffered by the Euphrates and Gulf commercial route as a consequence of the wars between the Byzantines and Persians. By the sixth century, the Bedouin had become familiar with new social and economic conditions, with the conversion of a certain number to Judaism or Christianity. On the social plane, the Bedouin began tracing their origins back to a common, eponymous ancestor hero; this acknowledgement ensured a certain amount of social cohesion, while family links between respective tribal clans were thereby recognized (see Plate 182).

The nomads and semi-nomads were the agents for the rapid expansion of the Arabs and of Islam. But while they did not at once abandon their ancient customs, many became acclimatized to city life as they populated the new Islamic centres which grew from tribal 'camps' into urban settlements. Nevertheless, their expansion did not transform the economy of the conquered regions, nor did it signify an extension of nomadism. There were two types of nomads in the Islamic world: the great camel nomads, and the seasonal sheep-herding nomads (De Planhol, 1993). The Arabian nomads had always been in contact with the settled populations of oases and towns. When they did settle down, they often 'brought back to life' lands which had been deserted and so left fallow by former owners. The great Arab Muslim landed gentry in fact took keen interest in the yield of their farms. Not Islam nor the Arab conquerors, then, but the fiscal policy of the later caliphs, and the overreaching of their tax collectors and then military mercenaries, caused some lands to be abandoned and revert to desert.

The Umayyad caliphs relied on an Arabian aristocracy founded on birth and kinship ties to one of the two great tribal confederations of the peninsula, the 'Adnān and the Qaḥṭān (Rodinson, 1979). The dynasty's main weakness resulted from the tribal infighting which often impelled the caliphs to indulge in a balancing act whereby imperial policy favoured now one tribal group, now the other. Arabs made up the majority of the warriors listed in the registers of the *dīwān*. They drew annual pensions and gifts in money and kind. This wealth had originated in the allotment of booty from the conquests, and in the revenue derived from the provinces.

The 'Abbāsid caliphs stripped the tribes of their military functions by cancelling their pensions. The nucleus of the army was now made up of Khurāsānīs (Iranians including Arabs settled in Iran), an elite corps devoted to the regime (Shaban, 1971; 1976; Kennedy, 1986). For a while a troop of loyalist Arabs, the *'Arab al-Dawla* or 'State Arabs', was maintained, but soon lost importance. For soon the majority of the armed forces came to consist of specially trained bond men, mainly Turks from Central Asia. So the Arab tribesmen gradually left the *amṣār* or 'city camps', some to resume a nomad life which they had never really altogether abandoned, while others settled down on their acquired lands. This period, then, is when the name 'Arab' came to be restricted to nomads alone. The gradual autonomy of the provinces to the east and west of the 'Abbāsid Empire turned into a series of independent states. However, some Arab nomads did extend their sway over upper Mesopotamia and northern Syria to found short-lived but brilliant Bedouin dynasties, like that of the Ḥamdānids in Mosul and Aleppo in the tenth century, then that of the Mirdassids in Aleppo again.

The value system of the Bedouin was based on a recognition of specific traits which might be cited as toughness of character, a taste for poetry and eloquence, a touchy sense of honour reinforced by notions of kinship solidarity and respect for hospitality, and a self-glorification in those human qualities (boldness, courage, generosity, self-control, but also craftiness) believed to make up manliness, *muruwwa*. In addition, the Bedouin claimed to speak the purest form of Arabic.

Islam at its birth could not ignore either the conditions which Arab tribal life imposed, or the Bedouin ideal. But the new faith did modify pre-Islamic values in a major way. Thus as soon as Muḥammad was established in Yathrib (Medina), he proposed Islamic brotherhood, *mu'ākhāt,* in place of clan solidarity, *'aṣabiyya*, and so created the concept of a community, or *umma*, including all Muslims regardless of tribal origin.

The Muslim conquerors, for the most part, were gradually assimilated into the older urban civilizations of the East (Mesopotamia, Syria). Those Bedouin most firmly set in their old ways were ultimately pushed back into the desert: so were the tribes of the Banū Hilāl and the Banū Sulaym, whom the caliph 'Abd al-Malik at the outset of the eighth century deported to the isthmus of Suez, there to serve as caravan transporters, or carry on with their life of wandering and raiding. Generally the value system of the Bedouin underwent profound alteration under the impact of Islam and its expansion.

Taken in all, the Bedouin Arabs were gradually pushed back to the sidelines of society; yet as a way of life, nomadism did not disappear, either in Arabia, or in the other lands conquered by the Muslims (such as Iraq, Syria, Egypt). One question whether it is possible entirely to accept the argument defended by a number of Orientalists and geographers, including Renan, Marçais, Xavier de Planhol, that Islam is 'essentially an urban creed'.

Life in the city and in the desert (*bādiya*)

Life certainly differed enormously between the desert, or *bādiya*, and the farmed countryside, or *rīf*. In the towns – which ranged in Iraq from the military tribal camps that were turning into cities (*amṣār*) like Kūfa and Baṣrā, to later foundations like Baghdād – the basic activities remained trade and crafts. The same was the case in Syria, Egypt, Iran, the North African cities of Kairouan and Mahdiyya and Tunis and Fez, or in the Spanish metropolis of Cordova. In Arabia, however, Mecca and Medina had become the twin religious poles of Islam, the first because it sheltered the shrine of the Ka'ba, and the second, the tomb of the Prophet. Nevertheless, the basic cell of society remained the family. The aristocratic urban family clung to survivals of Bedouin family practice by grouping together all survivors of its different generations as well as its clients or *mawālī*. But at poorer levels, the once extended family was reduced to a more elemental nucleus as it broke up under the pressure of having to secure a livelihood.

The important everyday features of the Islamic city were the market or *sūq* (pl. *aswāq)* and the *qayṣariyya,* which grouped more or less specialized shops clustered around the main mosque. Moreover, such religious buildings as the main mosques or *jawāmi'*, where Friday sermons were preached, and the smaller 'parish' mosques or *masājid*, where ordinary worship was offered, marked each city with their particular stamp, along with the theological colleges or *madrasas*, which appeared in the Seljuk period (eleventh century), the public baths or *ḥammāms* regarded as mandatory adjuncts to houses of worship, and the public fountains or *sabīls* (see Plate 184).

Such towns needed to be administered. When towns rose in popular revolt, as happened on occasions in Central Asia, one can discern aspirations to local autonomy and dissatisfaction with the normal system of urban officialdom became obvious. The city was mostly populated by legally free members of the Islamic community, but also by hosts of slaves, and by the tributary folk or *dhimmīs*. All city-dwellers lived in demarcated quarters along the lines of ethnic group, common regional origin or shared creed. Each quarter boasted its own house of worship, public bath and small market or *suwayqa*, along with its public oven.

Outside the city limits, too sharp a contrast should not be drawn between nomadic Bedouin herders and settled peasant farmers, for between these extremes existed graded differences. Certain regions were completely given over to agriculture, and here all stock-breeding was in the hands of the farmers. But in other regions, peasant farmers and nomadic shepherds shared use of the soil. In some places, seasonal migrations of the herds between lowlands and highlands were the rule, and farming would also be practised, but on a seasonal basis, by the nomad herders themselves. Finally, there were areas where the great nomads held complete sway, and peasant serfs farmed the oases on behalf of their nomad lords. Too often, the opposition between 'desert and sown' has been overstated: the activities of stock-breeders and farmers were mostly complementary. However, the balance in power between the two sides was somewhat delicate. In some caravan oasis-cities, merchants controlled all markets and palm groves. In other cases, nomads ruled over oasis peasants, worked them as a labour force, along with outright slaves, or exacted tribute from them, the *khuwa*. Here such a situation coloured the nomads' value system. Imbued with a sense of their own free ways, they would tend to consider themselves superior not only to the *fallāḥīn* or peasants, but even to town folk.

Several natural factors might upset the balance between herding and farming. The gradual desiccation of the Sahara is attested, and this certainly affected the ratio between grain and olive production, on the one hand, and pastoralism, on the other. Or demography might come into play, as where a spurt in nomad population overtaxed resources. When kings managed to extend their sway a great distance over the plains, farming spread there to meet the needs of heightened urban consumption. The breaking points were reached, especially in the tenth and eleventh centuries: Turkish nomads penetrated Iran and Anatolia, the Hilālī Bedouin burst into Ifrīqiyya, and Berbers from the edges of the Sahara swept north as far as Andalusia.

The role of the city in promoting cultural life

Ibn Khaldūn states that in his day, the arts were 'numerous only in cities. The quality and the number of the crafts (lit. 'arts', *ṣanā'i'*) depend on the greater or lesser extent of civilization in the cities and on the sedentary culture and luxury they enjoy, because (the arts) are something additional to just making a living' (Ibn Khaldūn, 1958). In addition to its political, economic and religious roles, the Islamic city also served as a crucible for intense intellectual activity and as the centre where Islamic and Arabic literary culture was fully elaborated. This literary culture crystallized in the ninth century, but certain of its genres, like poetry, went back to the pre-Islamic age (Miquel, 1969; Wiet, 1966).

The Islamic city, with its political function as seat of power and its intellectual role as centre of creativity, did much to further cultural life. The example set by Baghdād was followed by all the provincial capitals: Damascus, Cordova, Kairouan and later Mahdiyya, then Tunis, Fez and Cairo. Patronage extended by the rulers and rich city-dwellers encouraged urban literary production. In the ninth century, the Barmecide viziers were protectors of letters and the arts. In the tenth, Sayf al-Dawla al-Ḥamdānī who held his court at Aleppo was a great literary patron. The famous poets al-Mutanabbī and Abū Firās and the no-less celebrated anthologist Abu-l-Faraj al-Iṣfahāni, author of the 'Book of Songs' or *Kitāb al-Aghānī*, dedicated their works to him. The tenth century possibly saw the apex of Islamic culture.

The three leading strata of urban society

The ranking officials

At the head of the cities there stood, first of all, the governors, who represented central authority in the person of a caliph, vizier, provincial governor, sultan or emir. Several viziers and bevies of officials formed the entourage of each ruler. Scribes or *kuttāb* carried out the administrative and financial duties of the *dīwāns* or bureaux. Gradually such *dīwāns* became diversified under the 'Abbāsids to deal with 'domestic affairs, foreign affairs, finance, the army, diplomatic correspondence (with copies for the archives), the postal system (with censorship of mail), general communication, and propaganda' (Gardet, 1977). To dwell on military and police matters: Baghdād's prefect of police kept public order and had his own troops distinct from those of the regular army and his own swarm of financial officers. These officers, the *'ummāl*, collected taxes. The *muḥtasib*, at once a censor of morals and a warden of Islamic morality, kept watch over public behaviour and repressed economic fraud. Justice was pronounced by the *qāḍī* according to Islamic law. The army was still made up of Arab tribesmen under the Umayyads; but, as mentioned above, under the 'Abbāsids it was increasingly formed of Khurāsānī levies and then of Turkish bondsmen. Several army chiefs received the governments of whole provinces, and so became quasi-autonomous rulers. Other officers stemming originally from the Persian province of Daylam became in the tenth century lords protector to the caliphs, and so took the title of 'Emir of the Emirs', *amīr al-umarā'*: this was the Būyid House, itself of Shī'ite persuasion. Rulers of provinces, sultans and emirs, then surrounded themselves with the same kind of bureaucratic staffs as the caliphs of Baghdād, and maintained troops organized along the same lines.

The merchants

The conquests resulted in the creation of a vast and unified economic empire whose outstanding feature was the linking of the Mediterranean and the Indian Ocean. The merchants (Rodinson, 1966; 1970; Ibrahim, 1990) played a leading role in the cities. Great merchants constituted what M. Rodinson has called a 'capitalist sector'. Greater and lesser merchants alike were known as *tujjār*; the richer sort either imported foodstuffs and raw materials from the countryside into the city, or on a wide scale specialized in import-and-export trade over long distances, and were then known as *rakkādūn*. These were the men who organized caravans and chartered ships. Some, the *khuzzān*, specialized in storing goods in vast warehouses, others traded wholesale. Jewish merchants participated as actively in all this trade as did Christians. Cloth, spices, raw and wrought goods and jewellery, fetched great profits. The very richest stayed home, while their caravan leaders and ship captains plied the trails and sea lanes on their behalf.

Among the merchant class, the money changers, whose task was to assess the exact value of coins, served as true auxiliaries of the authorities: indeed, these were the men often rewarded with the farming of taxes. The merchants were often learned men, because they dealt in books of accounts and letters of credit, were aware of the art of codes and secret messages, and were familiar with Indian numerals; in sum, they resorted to the new techniques in payment, credit and banking, and took advantage of the intensity of monetary circulation to concentrate great wealth in their own hands. They became polished men who sported their learning and taste in poetry, no longer hesitated to play the part of patrons of the arts, while also embellishing religious buildings and endowing pious foundations, *madrasas*, fountains and other works of public interest. They added to their role as social benefactors by offering bed and board to budding scholars and their masters, and sheltering passing pilgrims. Finally they exercised their sway over the intellectual life of the city by offering encouragement to the literati, notably the poets, and subsidizing their works. A number of wealthy merchants even became viziers (Sourdel, 1960). Goitein speaks of the rise of 'the merchant bourgeoisie' in this classical age (Goitein, 1968).

Scholars

The *'ulama'*, or 'learned ones', could be both men of religion and men of science: they remained in touch with rulers and the ruled alike, linked as all classes were to the culture of the mosque. Scholars were respected by their contemporaries, and Islamic cities took pride in their presence and number. Such men might travel widely in quest of learning and gather many disciples themselves. Among the scholars listed and classified in the biographical works and dictionaries known as *ṭabaqāt* and *tarājim,* are to be found specialists in the traditional sayings of the Prophet, exponents of Qur'ānic exegesis, legal experts, theologians, judges, physicians, mathematicians, astronomers, physicists and philosophers.

From among the ranks of the scholars were recruited many religious officials and even civil servants: the *muftīs*, *qāḍīs*, notaries assessors (*'udūl*), court witnesses (*shuhūd*), and the *muḥtasibs* (censors of morals). Some taught in the universities that were sheltered under the roofs of mosques or, in a later age, in the *madrasas*.

Next to the divines, there was also a place for the literati and secular scholars who gravitated around the ruler and his court. Such men included many converts of Persian as well as Byzantine origin, in addition to ethnic Arabs. Louis Gardet has distinguished three main groups of literati: 'the scribes; the polymaths and moralists; and the philosophers and scholars' (Gardet, 1977). The first category, that of the scribal secretaries *(kuttāb)*, ended by forming a powerful caste of its own whence many higher officials were drawn. Specialized works were written to deal with their training. Scribes were expected to command a large store of knowledge in the most varied fields of learning, and to possess a kind of humanism, then known as *adab*. The second category, that of the polymaths, tended to popularize philosophy and learning: those amongst them who became most widely known included writers and scholars al-Jāḥiẓ, al-Tawḥīdī, and Miskawayh. The third category, that of philosophers and the learned, constituted the real glory of this classical age: with the astrologer al-Kindī under Caliph al-Ma'mūn, the philosopher al-Fārābī at the court of Sayf al-Dawla, Ibn Sīnā at the courts of the Shī'ite emirs of Hamadhān and Iṣfahān, as well as men like Jābir ibn Ḥayyān, al-Khwārizmī, al-Bīrūnī and Ibn al-Ḥaytham.

Relations between community and state

The community or *umma* was above all a religious entity, whose binding link was Islam. And yet in the very beginning, the *umma* as established by the Prophet Muḥammad in Medina – under the 'Medinan Constitution' known as the *ṣaḥīfa* (Serjeant, 1964; 1978; Watt, 1956) – had been open to all dwellers of the oasis, even non-Muslims. Regarded as partners in the *umma* were the local *anṣār* or 'companions' from the Aws and Khazraj tribes, their Jewish members included, and the 'emigrants' or *muhājirūn* from Mecca. Later, the notion of belonging to the community was reserved for Muslims alone, regardless, however, of ethnic origin: Arabs, Persians, Berbers, Turks and others. The *umma* as a whole was considered to be organized into a state headed by a caliph, who wielded significant powers at least down to the tenth century. The caliph was surrounded by a number of auxiliaries and officers of government responsible for discharging precisely defined functions: justice, the army, police, fiscal policy, imperial and provincial administration and the bureau for correspondence. Members of the *umma* were taught to feel a sense of solidarity as Muslims. Even where Muslims deferred in obedience to this or that temporal ruler, they never recognized the ruler as a source of legislation (which was a Qur'ānic matter) (Lapidus,1975). Such an attitude became all the more marked when the central authority of the caliphate disintegrated and power passed to rulers of doubtful legitimacy and often ethnically foreign to their subjects.

Centralization and resistance

We should bear in mind that authority had been centralized from the very first, indeed since the birth of the Islamic state under the guidance of the Prophet Muḥammad. The Umayyads and then the 'Abbāsids had reinforced such centralization by equipping the state with systematic organs of government and specialized personnel: scribes, ranking officials placed at the head of the various bureaux or *dīwāns*, viziers, *qāḍīs*, and *muḥtasibs*. What mitigated such centralization was the more or less lively provincial resistance to it in various regions of the empire.

Although Islam as a religion did not make any ethnic distinctions, regional sentiments could not but exist within the *Dār al-Islām* or 'Abode of Islam' (Haarmann, 1980; Al-Dūrī, 1987). It is therefore legitimate to speak of a Persian provincial feeling, and of Egyptian, Berber, Kurdish or Daylamite forms of particularism. Such trends, from the tenth century onwards, spawned provincial dynasties which enjoyed independence of the caliphate to a greater or lesser degree. Such regional powers became very apparent as the ninth century progressed; in the far western provinces of the empire, these included the Aghlabids in Ifrīqiya and Idrīsids in Morocco; in the eastern provinces, the Ṭāhirids and Ṣaffārids in Khurāsān, the Sāmānids in Transoxania, then the Ghaznavids in Afghanistan and India; finally, such powers sprang up in the Near East itself, with the Ṭūlūnids and then Ikhshīdids in Egypt, the Ḥamdānids in northern Syria, and the Ziyādids and then Yu'furids in the Yemen.

All these regional particularisms were shot through with sectarian movements inflamed by the religious disputes over the legitimacy of political power after the death of the Prophet: hence the rise of the Qarmaṭ state in Baḥrayn, of the imāmate of Tāhert, and of the Zaydite state in the Yemen. An even more serious break in the *umma's* unity was marked by the birth of two rivals to the 'Abbāsid caliphate: the Umayyad in Spain, and the Fāṭimid in the Maghrib and then in Egypt.

There were also social revolts, the gravest of which was that of the Zanj, slaves in lower Iraq.

Ethnic diversity: the *Shu'ūbiyya*

After the efforts at imperial unification by the Umayyads and early 'Abbāsids, the Islamic world was splintered by infiltration of new peoples. This sharpened a general picture of an ethnic, heterogeneous mosaic: Iranians to the east, Turks in Central Asia, Arabized Semites in Mesopotamia (Aramaeans) and Syria (speakers of Syriac), Copts in Egypt, Berbers in North Africa, Blacks in the *Bilād al-Sūdān* ('Land of the Blacks') ranging from Ethiopians or *Ḥabash* to the peoples of Mali, as well as the indigenous inhabitants and Slav mercenaries of Spain – not to mention imported slaves of various origins everywhere. All these peoples mingled with the Arabs and for the most part converted to Islam. However, Arabization did not spread to Iran to the degree it did elsewhere. Here, Persian continued to be spoken, although since Arabic remained the language of the faith, the Iranians read the Qur'ān in Arabic and adopted much Arabic vocabulary. The

Iranians clung to many of their traditions, and took pride in their accomplishments, reflected in disputes which touched upon the respective merits of Arabs and non-Arabs (*'Ajam*) in the formation of Islam (Gibb, 1953; Goldziher, 1967; Mottahedeh, 1980).

Written sources have immortalized these debates under the name of *shu'ūbiyya* ('pertaining to peoples'). The word *shu'ūbiyya* comes from a seminal passage in the Qur'ān (49: 13). The *shu'ūbiyya* controversy arose from the pretensions of the *shu'ūb*, 'peoples', that is to say the conquered peoples, to impose their moral and intellectual ideals on the community. The origins of the movement went back to the end of the Umayyad period; its advocates then confined themselves to calls for equality amongst all Muslims, Arabs or *mawālī*: hence such *shu'ūbi* apologists had often been called *Ahl al-Taswīya*, 'the people of equality'. With the coming to power of the 'Abbāsids, conditions changed and the Persian *mawālī* gained such social parity with the Arabs that by the end of the eighth century the very word *mawālī* fell into disuse.

While the notion of *shu'ūbiyya* was used on certain rare occasions by political movements displaying a notable 'ethnic' or 'regional' character, like that of the Ṣaffārids, still most *shu'ūbī* advocates were not really politically oriented and remained for the most part loyal servants to the caliphate. In the tenth century, a great literature made its appearance in a new form of the Persian language: Persian epic poetry, of pre-Islamic origin and dealing with the traditional history of Iran and its kings, returned to the fore with the 'Book of Kings', or *Shāh-Nāmeh,* by the poet Firdawsī in AD 1010 (Von Grunebaum, 1955). This rebirth of Persian literature did not mark any trend towards separatism, however, but only reaffirmed specifically Iranian glories. Rivalries between the various Islamic peoples came to be expressed here and there, but the *shu'ūbiyya* movement as such found its advocates mainly in Andalusia and in Persia, with this difference that the Persian revival was more far-reaching.

Under the 'Abbāsids, the trend moved towards a motivating 'national consciousness' among Iranians. The growing Iranian influence was reflected as the 'Abbāsids drew their viziers from the Barmakī family of Khurāsān (eastern Iran), and from the Banū Sahl, also of Persian origin. The *shu'ūbiyya* movement also reflected the shift in the imperial centre of gravity from the Mediterranean towards Asia. From the ninth century, Islam shows much territorial exploration towards the north and the east: witness the journey of Ibn Faḍlān towards the Volga and the Russian world; of 'Alī ibn Dulāf to China; and finally that of Sulaymān the Merchant, who reached Eastern Asia through the Gulf and the Indian Ocean, and whose adventures later served as models for those ascribed to the famous Sindbād the Sailor.

The elite and the masses

Muslim authors when describing society used two main concepts, that of *khāṣṣa* to designate the elite or aristocracy, and that of *'āmma* to refer to the common people or masses, thereby opposing them (Brunschvig, 1962; Ziyāda, 1982). But these were not so much two social classes as varied groups, with their own traits and hierarchies.

The elite included those persons who gravitated around the ruler – caliph, sultan or prince – and such palace dignitaries came from very different social circles. First, mention must be made of the 'military aristocracy'. This was made up of ranking officers or emirs. Its important responsibilities were leading armed expeditions and maintaining internal order. This aristocracy provided one part of the circle of dignitaries serving on the caliph's council. Ultimately, the military emirs came to play a predominant role in government and the empire. But the other aristocracy, that of the secretaries, was formed mainly of the great scribal administrators, the *kuttāb*, who directed the major bureaux or *dīwāns* found in all Islamic capitals: Baghdād, Cairo or Cordova. This select group also included such magistrates as the *qāḍīs*, the judges and jurists. All these men constituted an intellectual elite, an aristocracy of learning and faith. But the great traders also belonged to the elite, since merchants and bankers might furnish the ruler with funds in case of need.

The *'āmma* was far from constituting a social class: rather a series of diversified masses living both in the cities and in the countryside in difficult and indeed harsh circumstances – not to mention the lot of the slaves.

The urban mass was made up of petty craftsmen grouped into guilds. These craftsmen also functioned as petty shopkeepers, since they sold their own handiwork: bakers, butchers, grocers, water carriers, caterers, cooks, pastry chefs, weavers, barbers, tanners. Individuals without work, or those who plied the inferior and despised trades, took part in many urban uprisings.

The truly destitute as well as marauders in Islamic cities were known as the *'ayyārūn* (literally 'vagrants'), who organized into distinct groups in eleventh century Iraq and Iran: groups bound by ties of solidarity known as *futuwwa*. Such *'ayyārūn* played their part in the political and religious disturbances which frayed the social fabric of the Iraqi and Persian cities. In Syria, the corresponding groups were known as the *aḥdāth*, or 'young ones', who actually took over from the authorities wherever these fell into abeyance.

To these various urban groups should be added the dispossessed in the countryside, ruined farmers and landless sharecroppers, whose fate was particularly harsh. They were crushed by taxes which rose at the same time as the cost of living, forcing them off the land to swell the ranks of the urban poor and share in its uprisings, whether in Iran, Egypt or Syria. Caliph al-Ma'mūn put down a revolt by the *Zuṭṭs* or gypsies of lower Mesopotamia and deported them to the Byzantine frontier.

The *'āmma* of the cities made up a poverty-stricken and restless populace whose way of life differed little from that of the rural poor; they formed an explosive social force whose outbursts shook Baghdād from the ninth to the eleventh centuries (Sabari, 1981). Nor should the disturbing element created by nomads in the towns be left out of account.

Taken in all, Islamic society remained hierarchically patterned and fairly rigidly segregated. It was based upon an aristocratic organization of power of dual origin, one religious, the other secular. What the distinction made between an aristocratic elite and the people at large implied, was that all the elements of this society were far from being integrated.

Islamic 'feudalism'

Was there such a thing as Islamic feudalism? The term seems inappropriate but stubbornly lives on. Poliak first used it in 1936, and despite the studies and strong stands taken on the issue by Claude Cahen, the institution is still found referred to erroneously in this way (Lewis, 1950). In fact, the actual system of fiscal and military organization, based on the *iqṭā'*, had little in common with Western European feudalism.

The professionalization of the army under the 'Abbāsids led to a system of wage payments based on taxation. Even though the exact number of standing troops is not known, the army's social weight multiplied in proportion to the amount of money expended on it. In addition to wages, soldiers received allocations in kind, and further clothes and gifts on the occasion of a ruler's accession, or a festival. The army bureau, the *dīwān al-jaysh*, turned into a major cogwheel in the imperial administrative machine. On its registers were inscribed the names of the men, their places of birth, genealogy and physical traits. The entire fiscal system of the state was mobilized on the soldiers' behalf: the administration of taxes and land holdings, the drawing up of land surveys, periodic reassessments of the tax base, accounts of revenues and their redistribution. Out of a budget which soared to 16 million dīnārs at its height under the 'Abbāsids, more than half was earmarked for the upkeep of the armed forces.

At the outset, the caliphs assigned to their officers various lands selected from among the holdings of the state. Recipients were expected to manage their estates properly, and thereby be in a position to pay their *zakāt*, or charity tax, here specifically known as a *qaṭā'ī* or one 'pertaining to estates'. Such lands were ceded on long-term mortgageable leases. But soon enough lands to assign in this fashion no longer remained. Thus appeared another form of concession: officers were granted the right to levy the tax on the 'tax-lands' (*kharāj*) of a given district, and from these levied sums they were expected to pay their own *zakāt*. Such a concession was known as an *iqṭā'* (Cahen, 1953), and it is the assignment of such a concession, in return for an officer's services, that has been regarded by a number of scholars as a system comparable to European feudalism. True, the *iqṭā'* did reinforce the authority of those who derived profit from the land. But it did not result in the privatization of power, or in hereditary landed property. Nor did it modify the nature of social ties. In the ninth century, the beneficiary of such an arrangement, known as a *muqṭa'* (or *iqṭā'* – holder), was made responsible for the upkeep of irrigation works and proper exploitation of the soil. To be sure, he would at the same time try to swell his revenues and reduce his expenses. He might do so by granting his peasants, at a price, 'protection' rights or *talji'a* against both bandits and extortion on the part of his own tax collectors. But such traits betrayed the limits to an emir's local influence. He did not exercise judicial functions in the manner of a European feudal baron. And whatever lands he acquired as his private property were legally broken up among his heirs after his death.

The manner in which taxes were collected is what formed the very basis of the *iqṭā'*. It was left to the emirs and tax-farmers to levy the imposts from which, keeping the difference, they paid their own lump sum. This system became generalized under the Būyids (Bosworth, 1967) in Iraq, then in Iran under the Seljuks, coming to be known as an *iqṭā' istighlāl*, a 'harvesting'. A beneficiary might be granted the right to levy in taxes the amount corresponding to his own military fee, while the states preserved close control over the services he owed the state as a consequence. But no stable or institutional link became established between an emir and his tenants. The first consequence was a harsher lot for those peasants so subjected to military exactions, with a heavier burden in land taxes and a rising price in granted 'protection' or *ḥimāya*.

The Seljuks (Lambton, 1965; 1988) and their vizier Niẓām al-Mulk tried to reform the system set up by the Būyids by shifting beneficiaries from one *iqṭā'* to another every few years, and limiting grants of an *iqṭā'* to emirs only. While Khurāsān under the Sāmānids and the Ghaznavids did not adopt this system, the Seljuks spread their own model of the *iqṭā'* to Iran. Tribal chiefs and Seljuk princes thereby came to command vast holdings. In the closing period of the dynasty, the *iqṭā'* ceded by the Seljuks tended to grow ever larger and become more numerous, and especially more long-lasting, even tending to become hereditary.

In Syria, Nūr al-Dīn and Salāh al-Dīn (Saladin) made the *iqṭā'* hereditary (Irwin, 1977). A *muqṭa'*, thus assured that he might bequeath his *iqṭā'* to his heirs, was expected to take a keener interest in improving his land's produce and protecting his peasants.

In Egypt (Rabie, 1970; 1972; Al-'Arīnī al-Bāz, 1956; Tarhān, 1968), the Ṭūlūnid and then Fāṭimid dynasties also adopted the *iqṭā'* as a way of funding their armies. Localities were farmed out to officers for collecting *kharāj* or 'tax'; the farms were revocable. With Saladin's rule, the *iqṭā'* also became hereditary in Egypt. In the period of Mamlūk rule, the *iqṭā'* lost its hereditary status again, and the sultans changed beneficiaries very often to avoid concentrations of local power. The Mamlūks' institution of a three-tiered hierarchy of emirs explains the corresponding hierarchy of their land grants. Moreover, there existed a difference between the *iqṭā's* of the highest emirs, and inferior *iqṭā's* granted to soldiers from the *ḥalqas* or 'circles' (units of free men).

Slavery and its sources

Like all ancient and Near Eastern cultures, Islamic civilization, was familiar with slavery (Gordon, 1987; Lewis, 1971). Above all, a slave represented muscle power to be used in the house, on plantations, in mines, in the cities and in the army (Ayalon, 1951; Crone, 1981; Pipes, 1980). Originally, there were three sources for procuring slaves: captives taken in battle; slaves purchased from the *Dār al-Ḥarb* ('Abode of War') or territories lying beyond the pale of Islamdom; and children born to slave mothers already in Islamic lands. Three main territories for acquiring slaves were available to Muslim dealers from beyond the frontiers: the 'Land of the Slavs' or *Bilād al-Saqāliba*, Central and Eastern Europe; the 'Land of the Turks' or *Bilād al-Atrāk*, Turkestan and Central Asia; and the 'Land of the Blacks' or *Bilād al-Sūdān*, the scrublands which fringed the African forest. During the age of conquests, the slave trade yielded great profits. Many prisoners were captured by the Muslims in war. But by the eleventh century, the pagan Slavs were converting to Christianity, and the pagan Turks to Islam. The only source still exploitable lay in Africa, but here, too, the zone was shrinking as Islamization proceeded. Still, raids conducted along the non-Islamized coasts continued to feed the slave trade.

Slaves imported from the three zones mentioned above were not all set to the same tasks. Black bondsmen were mainly allotted domestic service and also, in some cases as in Lower Iraq and Aghlabid Ifrīqiyya, plantation work. Black bondswomen were used as concubines and wet nurses. Slav bondsmen were highly sought by the aristocracy and often gelded to serve as eunuchs and personal bodyguards to the rulers. The Umayyad caliphs of Cordova in particular collected a guard of 10,000 Slavs, while the Aghlabid emir Ibrāhīm I, surrounded himself with a guard of 5,000 Blacks (Talbi, 1966). Finally, Turkish bondsmen made excellent soldier material; the trend to buy Turkish slaves for the army began under Caliph al-Ma'mūn and neared a peak under al-Mu'taṣim with his troop of 70,000 Turks.

Slaves were a prized commodity, hence one that offered occasion for fraud: as we learn from two small treatises for slavers written by Ibn Buṭlān and Muḥammad al-Ghazālī, where both discuss how to 'touch up a slave' (the better to sell despite defects) (Rosenberger, 1987).

A slave was the master's property, to be bought, sold or bequeathed: not, however, as in Roman law, as 'a thing', but as a person with rights and duties. While Islam confirmed the slave's status, it did try to mitigate his condition. A bondsman had to be treated correctly 'with justice and mildness'; he could spend his own money as he chose; he could marry. Slave children could not be sold without their mother before the age of seven. The *muḥtasib* or censor was expected to see to it that slaves were not subjected to harsh treatment. A bondswoman taken as a concubine by her master saw her issue born into slavery; but if she became the 'mother of a son', *umm walad*, then she was assured of manumission upon her master's death. However, if her master wished to take her unto himself as a lawful wedded wife, then he had first to emancipate her. Nevertheless, a slave might not inherit or bequeath: *'lā yarith wa lā yūrith'*. In case of death, a slave's belongings reverted to his master. Still, the Qur'ān sanctified the manumission of slaves as a pious deed. Moreover a bondsman had the right to buy back his freedom – but then as a freedman he still remained very closely tied to his former master, sometimes indeed marrying one of his master's daughters. Many freedmen played a political or military role of primary importance in the Islamic world : two such were Ibn Ṭūlūn and Kāfūr, who both rose to become governors of Egypt and then founders of dynasties, the Ṭūlūnids and the Ikhshīdids.

A domestic bondsman was not always treated unkindly. His master might entrust him with a commercial venture, or have him instructed in a craft: many thus came to manage their masters' wealth. Others were instructed to become tutors to their masters' children. Bondswomen often received careful education, with training in music and singing: as *qiyān* (Pellat, 1963; Chapoutot-Remadi) or 'songstresses' they fetched high prices, and several became famous for the poetry they wrote, learning they displayed or music they composed. Less refined *jawārī* or 'handmaids' were employed as domestics. The harshest living conditions fell to the plantation slaves on the vast estates of lower Iraq or North Africa. Troops of Black bondsmen were put to draining and improving the Baṭā'iḥ or marshlands of lower Iraq to raise sugar cane (Popovic, 1976; Al-Sāmir, 1971; Talbi, 1982).

Urban autonomy

The Islamic city is usually depicted as standing in contrast to both the city of classical antiquity and to the medieval European commune. It was indeed rather amorphous and lacking in distinct character given its full integration into the imperial administrative system. In the very early days of Islam, to be sure, local communities in both the Sasanian territories and the former Byzantine provinces had preserved a significant margin of self-administration. But as the regime became more firmly grounded, and Islam more widespread, the new administrative order in formation made its presence felt gradually in the cities, which were, after all, the effective centres of all material and spiritual life, as well as the seats of government throughout all lowlands. A number of officials and magistrates held all powers. A governor's subordinates included the qāḍī, the prefect of police or *ṣāḥib al-shurta*, and such bodies of militia as the *Aḥdāth*, notably in Syria (Ashtor, 1956; 1958) and upper Mesopotamia. These institutional officers were supposed to represent the community's unifying government. In fact, they might pivot around and come into play against the regime as factors or elements of a 'local-minded urban resistance'. But the truly autonomous elements of resistance in Islamic cities in their classical age were far more spontaneous eruptions and had nothing to do with the official institutions. Textual sources speak here of various ties of solidarity or *'aṣabiyya* that might be forged between small groups or factions. Older surviving ties might link tribal kinsmen, or a sense of brotherhood bind fellow believers, or alliances be struck between subjects of the same principality. The ties of *'futuwwa* ('groups of young braves') and *'iyāra* ('groups of vagrants') also came into play. Mainly in the former Sasanian lands, the *fityān* – members of a *'futuwwa'* brotherhood – were hostile to the established authorities in such cities as Kūfa, Baṣrā, Baghdād, Rayy and the cities of Khurāsān. The *fityān* were suppressed, but in those towns insufficiently policed, they still made their influence felt sometimes by enrolling in the armed patrols of the watch – or *shurṭa* – themselves. In those provinces which had once belonged to the old Byzantine domains, such as Syria and Egypt, the *Aḥdāth* banded behind a *ra'īs* or 'captain', and so formed true urban militias themselves.

The *'ayyārūn* ('vagrants') were true outlaws, outcasts who had lost all means of livelihood, including ruined craftsmen from the outskirts of such cities as Baghdād. Like the *fityān*, the *'ayyārūn* forged their own ties of solidarity. They reappeared whenever the urban authorities betrayed signs of weakness to rob, loot and impose other exactions, including the levying of outright 'protection' money, or *ḥimāya*.

The existence of a town's sense of autonomy, in the face of princes and military regimes perceived as foreign by local populations, basically found expression in the importance assumed by such groups as the *fityān* and the *aḥdāth*. In the Islamic West, Ibn Baṭṭūṭa mentions the *suqūr* ('hell children'), which he compared to the *shuṭṭār* ('scoundrels') of Iraq and the *zu'ār* ('highwaymen') of Syria, but the social trait at issue here seems mostly to have been one found in the Eastern lands.

Corporations

The Islamic world was, without any doubt, familiar in its urban centres with organized professions (Cahen, 1970) and forms of collective solidarity. In the Islamic town, crafts were allotted, topographically, to different quarters. Thus manufacturers of fine textiles, or dealers in books, as well as the practitioners of other crafts associated with wealth such as goldsmiths, bankers and others, tended to ply their trades near the city centre, close to the main mosque. Messy crafts requiring water, such as those of dyers and tanners, were restricted to the periphery. Trades dealing with food were to be found throughout a city's different quarters, while those trades linked to commercial exchanges with the outside world set up shop in the suburbs or near the city gates.

Besides the privately owned trades – some of which might furnish the State with free deliveries in lieu of taxes – were those professional activities directly linked to the state: public works, arsenals, shipyards for the war fleet, mining extraction, mints or *dār al-ḍarb* ('abode of striking'), manufactures of papyrus, and especially the workshops where *ṭirāz* was woven: that is, the royal cloth works (Cahen, 1964). Royal manufactures of precious stuffs were to be found in all political capitals. In the *ṭirāz* workshops, luxury textiles, stitched in gold and silver, were woven for the wardrobe of the ruler and his retinue. Famous stuffs included 'muslin' from Mosul (Mawṣil) and 'damask' silks from the Syrian capital.

The manufacture of sweets, as well as glass works, potteries and tanneries, required only modest dimensions and simple tools. Workshops here were organized in rudimentary fashion: with each headed by a master surrounded by journeymen and apprentices. Trades involving food were very numerous, such as those plied by bakers, spice vendors, butchers, greengrocers, water carriers, sherbet sellers, *kebab* vendors, pastry chefs and keepers of roadside food stalls. Some crafts were considered 'vile' (Brunschvig, 1962): those of weavers of inferior stuffs, apothecaries who applied cupping glasses and barber-surgeons generally, tanners, wine merchants, and pigeon trainers.

Surveillance of the markets was ensured by the *muḥtasib* or censor (Essid, 1993). This official's authority was bestowed by the *qāḍī*, and not by the members of the market's various professions. Handbooks describing his office, or *ḥisba,* defined his prerogatives. He was responsible for seeing that transactions were carried out in a regular manner, weights and measures were kept accurate and only sound coins were tendered. In larger urban centres the *muḥtasib* was assisted in his task by several minor officials. Each of these was known as an *amīn* ('trustworthy one') in the West, or as an *'arīf* ('knowledgeable one') in the East, and was supposed to be a specialist in a given craft.

The administrative organization of the trades did not, strictly speaking, amount to that of corporations, in the sense in which a guild-type corporation is mainly defined: 'a private association which groups together the masters of the same craft, regulates how a such craft is to be carried on, and provides a framework for the activities of its members even outside their regular working hours: especially those activities pertaining to the members' worship and mutual assistance'. Such a type of organization did not come into existence in the Islamic world before the sixteenth century, notwithstanding arguments to the contrary by Louis Massignon and Maurice Lombard. These scholars have thought it possible to recognize the existence of actual guild-type corporations in the *futuwwa* groups (Cahen, 1953b; 1955), and Ismā'īlī cells of mystical initiation (Marquet, 1961), which became widespread among urban workers by the tenth century. One must, however, acknowledge that many trades have indeed only become known to us from the lists of the names of various medieval Islamic religious scholars (names which often do point to their connection to a particular craft), and that there is evidence of at least some form of corporate solidarity, at any rate in Central Asia, by the thirteenth century. Still, not until the sixteenth century did it become fully permissible to speak of specific rules drawn up for each corporation, and of actual mystical initiation required for admission into a particular craft group.

The place of women

Women (Keddie (ed.), 1992) played only a limited role in medieval Islamic society. Nevertheless, some measures enjoined in favour of women by the Qur'ān and *sunna* ('tradition') do show that their lot, in pre-Islamic Arabia at least, had been even harsher. Killing off baby girls was forbidden (Qur'ān 16: 57–59) and their right to life affirmed in several verses of the Qur'ān. Legally, a woman remained always a minor, but she did enjoy certain precisely defined material guarantees. The Qur'ānic *sūra* on women permitted a man to take four legally wedded wives, as well as any number of concubines: but equality amongst all four spouses was enjoined, as well as kind treatment for concubines (Qur'ān 4: 2–3). Islam also laid down rules for marriage, along with prohibitions of incest (Qur'ān 4: 22–24). The same Qur'ānic *sūra* listed a woman's rights concerning her dowry, trousseau and inheritance: and such rules on marriage and inheritance were certainly an improvement on the past.

But these rights most certainly did not amount to equality with men. The first verse of the same *sūra* on women stresses female inferiority to males according to the very order and circumstances of Creation.[1] According to the *sharī'a* (Islamic law), a woman had to be protected by a male tutor, whether this was her father, her brother or other close kinsman; such a tutor enjoyed the right to marry her with her consent. She owed her husband obedience, and he, in return, owed her kind treatment and upkeep. Men took advantage of their right to pronounce divorce. To be sure, a woman too had the right to demand divorce in certain instances: as in cases of impotence, insanity, leprosy or denial of her rights – but then she, for her part, had to resort to the *qāḍī*. Inequality also showed itself in laws on inheritance. On the death of her spouse, a widow received one-eighth of his wealth; the rest was divided between his issue, if he had any, in the proportion of two parts to each son for one part to each daughter; the widow received a quarter of the deceased's wealth if he had no issue; if all his issue were daughters alone, then two-thirds of the deceased's inheritance remained theirs (Qur'ān 4: 11–12): Again according to the *sharī'a*, a woman's testimony was equal to only half of a man's, and no testimony was valid if it was that of women only.

Shutting up women within doors was the most obvious example of their unequal status. The pattern of the Islamic city, and of Islamic dwellings, was dictated by this insistence on purdah. The notion of *ḥaram*, meaning that which is both sacred and forbidden, was basic to the allotment of public and private spaces within the city. A house's structure was fundamentally an enclosed space, shielded from view, the domain of women: its very architecture and design observed the logic of purdah (Brunschvig, 1947). If a woman did step out into the street, despite the repeated prohibitions of theologians, then she did so veiled and draped in a shapeless garment so as to prevent the contours of her body from being discerned (Chapoutot-Remadi, 1995). Still, she so appeared in the *sūqs*, merchants' shops, cemeteries, mosques, and on feast days. In the large cities, even *dhimmī* women wore the veil (Talbi, 1994) (see Plate 188).

Some of the poorer free women were forced to take up work as domestic servants or spinners in the textile industry ('Abd-al-Rāziq, 1973; Schatzmiller, 1994). Other women, who were slaves, could become singing girls, and some were sought for both their beauty and their talent. Within the ranks of the political or religious aristocracy, some women, albeit very few, even became reigning queens (Mernissi, 1990; Chapoutot-Remadi, 1977), while others left their mark on the urban pattern of the larger cities by sponsoring the construction of mosques, *madrasas*, mausoleums and other monuments, some of which have survived down to our own day[2]. Still other women became distinguished for their learning, notably as transmitters of *ḥadīth*, and thereby found a place in the great biographical dictionaries (Berkey, 1979).

The model woman who primarily came to a Muslim male's mind would be one of the 'chosen ones', that is, either the Prophet's wives Khadīja, Ḥafṣa, 'Ā'isha and Mary the Copt and the Prophet's own daughter Fāṭima, or the hosts of ṣūfī women regarded as protective saints who might even intercede with God. The mausoleums of these ṣūfī women were to be found in every city, and the literature on saints dwelt upon their 'virtues'. However, cloistered and shut out of view, many women did manage to leave their stamp upon the imagination of Islam, from the heroines of Arabic love poetry to the protagonists of tales like those in *The Thousand and One Nights* (see Plate 187).

Migrations

Thoughout the medieval period, the Islamic world experienced whole series of migrations of peoples from one land to another. Especially noteworthy are the movements of the nomadic and semi-nomadic Hilālī tribes in the eleventh century and of the contemporary Turkish Seljuk tribes, followed by the great Mongol invasions of the thirteenth century (Roux, 1984). The important two-pronged migrations of the Berber tribes towards Spain and Egypt have also been studied, particularly the two great Berber dynasties which swept out of southern Morocco to conquer nearly the entire Islamic West: the Almoravids and Almohads. But there have been fewer studies devoted to smaller-scale migrations like those of the Armenians or Kurds (Ashtor, 1972; Cahen, 1971), or even to such important movements as those which involved whole social categories like merchants, scholars or pilgrims.

In the east, the first phase of the Arab invasions had coincided with the irruption into Transoxania of Turkish war bands of the Oghuz tribe from the seventh century (Cahen, 1988). In the eleventh century, the Seljuks, as leaders of the Oghuz, overcame the Ghaznavids and took over the cities of Iran. The Seljuk ruler Ṭughril Beg entered Baghdād, ended the government of the Būyid house and founded his own military regime, which was then carried on by his successors Alp Arslān and Malik Shāh. The Seljuks also annexed parts of Syria and invaded Asia Minor (Cahen, 1934). The invasion of the Seljuk Turks had important repercussions on the Islamic world as a whole. They gradually annexed Anatolia and reinforced Sunnism. The social balance was modified (Cahen, 1973; 1982) by the intrusion of Turkish military elements and by the sway of a host of Turkish principalities from Transoxania to Mesopotamia. This first Turkish migration led to others still, such as the advance of the Khwārizmians who obtained a fleeting presence in Western Iran in the thirteenth century, while the Shahrāzūriya Kurds moved into Syria over the same period.

A second period of migration bears the stamp of the Mongols (Roux, 1993) who swept as far as Syria by the middle of the thirteenth century. The Mongols penetrated Iran (Ayalon, 1963; Morgan, 1988) in 1220s, took Baghdād in 1258 and moved on to invade the rest of Iraq and Syria before their advance was stopped at 'Ayn Jalūt in 1260 by the Mamlūks. The Mongol invasion wrought havoc in the eastern Islamic world. In the earlier stage of their rule, the shamanistic Mongols showed tolerance for other beliefs, even allowing Nestorian Christianity and Buddhism to flourish – but in the latter half of the thirteenth century within Islamic lands they converted massively to Islam (see Plate 12).

In the Islamic West, the first major migration was that of the nomad Arabs of the Banū Hilāl and Banū Sulaym tribes who moved in the mid-eleventh century into Ifrīqiyya (Tunisia and part of Algeria), whence they spread to the rest of the Maghrib. These nomads originally came from Najd and the Ḥijāz. A number of their families were removed on orders of the Umayyad caliph Hishām in 727 to Egypt, to serve as camel drivers. The Fāṭimids deported the Hilāl and Sulaym tribes to the region of Ḥawf in Upper Egypt in 978. These same tribal elements were sent into Ifrīqiyya by the Fāṭimid caliph al-Mustanṣir in the middle of the eleventh century, for two reasons, partly to punish his rebellious vassal, al-Mu'izz the Zīrid, and partly to throw these tribes out of Egypt, whose whole economic and political balance they had badly upset.

The Hilālī migration involved some 200,000 individuals and had important consequences for Ifrīqiyya (Tunisia and part of Algeria) and the Maghrib. It contributed to the linguistic Arabization and religious Islamization of Ifrīqiya's countryside, while weakening the Zīrid régime and so contributing to the rise of a series of city-states both in the interior and along the coast. As a result of Hilālī inroads, sedentary farming shrank, and pastoralism increased, in the Ifrīqiya region. In economic terms, the arrival of the Hilālī tribes thus led to a decline in agriculture and to a shift of trade routes to the sea[3].

Other invasions and migrations in the West involved Berber ethnic groups, albeit in smaller numbers. First came the Almoravids (Bosch-Vila, 1956) who surged up from the western Sahara and carved out an empire covering much of the Maghrib and all of Islamic Spain, hitherto rent between contending city-states ruled by those known (in Spanish) as the *Reyes de Taifas*, or 'party kings'. In the twelfth century, the Almoravids were replaced by still other Berbers, the Almohads (Garcin, 1987), who overran nearly the entire Maghrib and founded their own distinctive regime.

TECHNIQUES; MATERIAL CULTURE

Techniques of irrigation and preservation of water

Much of the Islamic world lacked regular rainfall. Some oases enjoyed only intermittent flood water, while others benefited from a constant supply. In the first case, access to water and soil had to be collective. In the second case of constant supply, water and soil could be private family property. An individual user, then, enjoyed free access to water if the watering system belonged to him privately, but he had to take his turn if the system was a collective one.

The case was different with those oases which nestled beneath foothills and so received a permanent water flow fed by rain and snow on the highlands, as with the *wādīs* (dry river beds) of southern Morocco, or the Barāda in Syria, and the Oxus. But further irrigation still required elaborate work.

For many oases lying on the plains, underground water tables might be tapped. In most such cases, the water had to be hoisted above the level of the fields to be worked. This would require winch and pulley, or bucket and balancing pole: hence the Egyptian *shādūf*, or the Andalusian and Syrian *noria* or water wheel (see Plates 16, 18).

Another system allowed conveyance of an underground water flow to the surface without the need for hoisting, by taking advantage of a slope wherever the soil to be irrigated was set lower than the water tapped. In this case, an underground gallery was tunnelled out which followed the slope, leading the water tapped uphill, which this gallery served to drain, downhill to the fields, which the same gallery now irrigated as a canal. This was the system, originally Iranian, known as *qanāt*, which then spread both eastwards and westwards throughout the Islamic world; local variant names include *kārēz*, *foggara* and *khettara* (Goblot, 1979).

The spread of plant species

Arabic-language sources (Miquel, 1980; Cahen, 1977(a); Chapoutot-Remadi, 1974; Bolens, 1974; Marin and Waines, 1994) provide us with a spectrum of the plant and animal species then known to the Arab and Islamic world. Differences might be pointed out between the concerns of the settled folk and those of the nomads, and also between the 'old crops' of the Mediterranean raised according to dry farming methods – grain, olives, vines – and the imported 'new crops' that relied on irrigation: rice, sugar cane, oranges, dates. The spread of such crops was connected to the way the Islamic world itself had been formed by linking two zones: the Mediterranean and the Indian Ocean. These twin types of farming, dry and irrigated, complemented one another and created in turn a high demand for variety in foods in Islam's urban centres. The texts themselves stress the difference between seeds, which must be sown, and the yield derived from shrubs.

Rice (Canard, 1959) spread to the Mediterranean basin from India and lower Mesopotamia, where it had been a familiar product even before the Christian era. Thence it came to be grown in the Ghawr, watered by the Jordan, as well as in the Fayyūm and other oases of Egypt, in Yemen, in the Iranian region of Khūzistān, around the Caspian Sea, in Khurāsān and other parts of Central Asia, in Morocco's Sous valley, and finally in Spain's lowlands along the banks of the Guadalquivir and around Valencia.

Sugar cane spread from east to west, in both the hot and warmer temperate zones. Introduced from India into Mesopotamia in the sixth century, it was carried farther in the wake of Islam, reaching Egypt by the end of the eighth century, where the richest lands were allotted to it (Ashtor, 1972). It was also grown around the shores of the Caspian Sea, the Aral Sea and the Persian Gulf, as well as in Khurāsān, Khūzistān, Fārs, Kirmān, along the Syro-Palestinian coast, in Yemen, Sicily, Spain along the valley of the Ebro, and in Morocco's Sous.

Plants for the kitchen garden, shrub and floral, were outstanding features of Islamic farming and spread throughout the Mediterranean. First should be mentioned melons, watermelons, cucumbers and pumpkins, ultimately adopted in Western Europe around 1400. Leguminous plants were mainly farmed in Egypt and Syria–Palestine. Condiments like pepper, caraway, cumin, cloves, saffron, mustard, sesame and ginger came mostly from India. Medicinal plants were also grown in gardens. Fragrance was yielded by sandalwood, spikenard, musk, amber and incense, the products of Arabia. Perfumes were moreover derived from flowers. Fārs was home to attar of roses, exported to China, the Maghrib and India.

Olives were harvested in Ifrīqiyya, Syria and Spain. Olive groves also spread to Morocco. Egypt consumed other kinds of cooking oil as well: sesame, coleseed, horseradish, linseed and castor.

The date palm is Mesopotamia's own tree: here the largest groves were to be found. But even before Islamic times the date palm had made its way to southern Syria, Egypt and southern Tunisia. In the Islamic period, it continued to gain ground in northern Syria, Cilicia, Spain and the western Sahara.

Vines were to be found everywhere in the Mediterranean world, but the main producing countries were Palestine, northern Syria, the Nile delta, Ifrīqiyya's 'Sahel' or *Sāḥil* (the Tunisian steppelands north of the Sahara), and southern Spain.

Fruit trees grew in orchards wherever soil and irrigation allowed and were much to be seen in the green belts around the cities. Orange and lemon trees came from India to Oman, spread to Mesopotamia, were thence introduced into Syria in the tenth century, and from there were brought to Sicily, southern Morocco, Malaga in Spain, Egypt and Cyrenaica. The rarest and most exotic species were fetched from remote regions to be planted in royal gardens. Spain imported fruit trees from Persia and Syria, and Cairo from the Ghūṭa oasis in Damascus. Mulberry plants were also grown thickly in gardens: not only for their fruit but also for their leaves, on which silkworms fed to yield true silk.

As for other industrial plants (Lombard, 1978), linen was widely cultivated in Mesopotamia, the Caspian lands, Egypt (notably in the Fayyūm oasis), the Maghrib, Sicily and Spain. Cotton was grown from Morocco to Seistān (south-west Afghanistan) with important yields in such areas as Syria. Dyes were obtained from henna, saffron, carthamum and madderwort: thus yellow, orange and red hues were obtained more or less everywhere. Indigo grew along the banks of the Nile, and lent its own name to the colour blue (*nīla*) in Islamic languages.

The spread of animal species

The dromedary (De Planhol, 1993; Bulliet, 1975; Hill, 1975) or one-humped camel became familiar to humans about a thousand years after the two-humped Central Asian variety: it is attested in Arabia between about the sixteenth and fourteenth centuries BC. However, the domestic dromedary became widespread in North Africa only in the very first centuries AD. Between the eighth and eleventh centuries, camel zones stretched between Central Asia, Iran and Mesopotamia on the one hand, and Arabia, Ethiopia, Nubia and the western Sahara, on the other. Thereafter, the camel was introduced into northern Syria, Asia Minor, the steppes of southern Russia, Spain and the West African Sudan. Lighter or heavier animals, capable of bearing different amounts of burden, were selected, bred and raised in various areas according to required purpose (see Plates 182–184).

The Persian horse (Lombard, 1978) spread to the Gulf and India. The Barbary horse was to be found in every country of the Mediterranean basin. The Turco-Mongol horse made its way to China and to Eastern and Central Europe alike, while the Syrian horse was taken to Najd and thence, again, to the Persian Gulf, India and the Mediterranean lands (see Plate 12). The donkey seems to have become as widespread as the horse. Egypt reared the finest asses and exported them to the Maghrib (see Plate 11).

Sheep were herded wherever the textile craft so required, and indeed their numbers multiplied throughout the rangelands of the Fertile Crescent, in Transoxania, and on the Iranian plateau. Spain's merino sheep, which derives its name from the Merinid (Banū Marīn) dynasty of Morocco, is a cross between Moroccan and Spanish breeds and yielded a wool much in demand in Europe. The Spaniards borrowed from the Berbers a system which turned into Christian Spain's own corporation of sheep-herders with a communal approach to sheep breeding itself: the *mesta*. Not that raising sheep went without harming crops and woodlands, especially the latter; Spain's *mesta*, too, was responsible for much damage to local vegetation.

Climate restricted the raising of cattle, although these animals might yet be found in Morocco's Atlantic lowlands, in the Algerian *tell*, in Spain, and in Egypt, whence cattle were exported to Iran, Āzerbaijān, Armenia and Khūzistān. The Indian buffalo found a new home in the marshlands of lower Iraq, where it was brought by the *Zuṭṭs* or gypsies and thence was taken as far as the Orontes valley in northern Syria (see Plates 18, 185).

Eastern and Mediterranean gardens: their spread to Europe

'The gardens of Islam' (Marçais, 1957) are an outstanding trait in the civilization of Muslims. Everywhere throughout the Qur'ān, the garden looms powerfully as promised land. According to Georges Marçais, the art of gardens spread with Islam, moving east to west and specifically from Persia to Iraq, and thence as far as Spain. Islam appears to have received its horticultural techniques for shrubs and irrigated plantations from Persia, along with its knowledge of the *qanāt*. Thence derived the 'Abbāsid pleasure grounds at Sāmarrā' and those of the Fāṭimids in Cairo, the Aghlabids and Fāṭimids in Kairouan, and the Ḥafṣids in Tunis: gardens all comparable to so many royal parks, with a *birka* or pond in their midst serving both to irrigate and to adorn, and bedecked with pleasure boats.

The *munya*, or 'dream', appears to have been introduced into Andalusia by the Umayyads: as a caliph's demesne, or gentleman's residence with plantation, on a city's outskirts. A *raḥal* designated a gentleman's landed property, which yielded him 'both pleasure and crops'. Either of such Andalusian estates might be compared to royal parks elsewhere (Barrucand, 1988; Lagardère, 1993). Modern Spanish designates the Andalusian garden under all its aspects as a *huerta*, which is at once horticultural and agricultural.

The Egyptian *ghayṭ* or *bustān* (Behrens-Abouseif, 1992) resembled the Moroccan Berber *agdāl* in so far as it also combined a garden with a plantation. The *riyāḍ* (pl.) or *rawḍa* (sing.), a type found in both North Africa and Andalusia although not in Egypt, corresponded rather to a 'town garden' serving to beautify an inner space in residential architecture (see Plate 187).

Topography of the trade route infrastructure: caravans, ports and ships

What must be distinguished here are the maritime routes in the Mediterranean and the Indian Ocean, and the land routes; there was also Eastern and South Eastern trade, as well as Western and African trade.

The main ports of embarkation in the Gulf were Baṣra, Sīrāf and Hormuz at least down to the eleventh century, then Ṣūḥār and Masqaṭ. Navigators were mainly Omani and Iraqi Arabs, and Persians. They sailed to ports on the coasts of Malabar and Sri Lanka, then on to Malacca, to the port of Qalā north-west of modern Singapore, and then as far as Indochina and even China with its port of Guangzhou, in Arabic 'Zaytūn'. Colonies of Muslims dotted the shores of this sea lane. Merchants brought back aloeswood, teak, porcelain, brazilwood and Malaysian tin. Ships on the home voyage sailed from India to Arabia or detoured along the east coast of Africa before returning to the Persian Gulf. In East Africa, Gulf merchants flocked to the trading ports along its coast or to neighbouring islands as far south as Zanzibar, the Comoros and Madagascar (see Plate 200).

In the Red Sea, ties had long existed between Yemen, Ethiopia and Somalia; ships sailed north as far as Jidda, the port for Mecca and Medina, much thronged in the pilgrim season. Egyptian merchants reached Jidda by way of the Red Sea port of 'Aydhāb after crossing the eastern desert from Qūs. Ships from the two gulfs of Qulzum and Wayla (on either side of Sinai) also made their way down to Jidda and rounded Arabia by hugging the coast as far as Baṣrā. Two ports which played a major role in this trade were Aden in Yemen and Ṣūḥār in Oman, both regarded as 'anterooms to China' (Miquel, 1980).

Next to this great sea lane should be considered the land routes crossing Asia. These consisted mainly of two large networks. The so-called Silk Road linked China to the Mediterranean by traversing all Asia from east to west, through a chain of oases leading through Iran to Iraq via Baghdād and Mosul, and on to Aleppo, where the route forked towards the cities of the Syrian lowlands on the one hand and Constantinople on the other. The second great route was a more northern one, the 'Fur Road' winding up to the Polish, Russian and Siberian evergreen forests. Hoards of 'Abbāsid and especially Sāmānid coins, found near the shores of the Baltic and throughout Scandinavia, testify to the importance of a trade which yielded slaves and furs to the Islamic world (see Plate 193c).

To the far west of the empire, sea lanes led from Morocco's Atlantic coast to the Mediterranean through Gibraltar. Andalusia was connected to the Moroccan ports through a network of criss-crossed sea lanes, and also to Carolingian Gaul by land routes. Both Jewish and Mozarab (Spanish Christian) merchants passed through the cities of Spain's northern marches to reach Gaul. Muslim pirates thrived in the tenth century, especially raiding the coasts of Provence and Italy. In the central Mediterranean area, ships sailing from Ifrīqiyya gained Sicily and Egypt. The Aghlabids studded their eastern Tunisian coastline with *ribāṭs* (forts) and *maḥāriss* (watchtowers), both to protect their kingdom and to serve as military bases for expeditions. This trend was pursued by the Fāṭimids in Tunisia, where they founded Mahdiyya and so managed to secure their grip to a certain extent over the Mediterranean. Naples, Gaeta and Amalfi enjoyed commercial ties with both the North African coast – based here on the slave trade – and Byzantium. Moreover, Constantinople was linked to northern Italy through Greece and the Adriatic.

Land routes connected Egypt with Ifrīqiyya and the rest of the Maghrib, and many paths traversed North Africa from east to west. Kairouan was at a major crossroads. Caravan cities like Tāhert and Sijilmāsa were the starting points for caravan trade with Black Africa through the desert, where salt and manufactured goods were exchanged for slaves and gold. Several southern Maghribi towns flourished as a result of this trade: Aghmāt, Tamdoult, Tozeur and Tubna. Tāhert's considerable prosperity was eclipsed by that of Sijilmāsa from the tenth century, when the Fāṭimids extended their sway over the central Maghrib (see Plate 192d).

Muslim merchants controlled most of the trade during this early phase, but Ibn Khurdādhbeh (early ninth century) informs us that Russian traders brought such northern produce as slaves and furs into the Islamic world, while Jewish traders, known as the 'Radhanites', were very active in his day. The existence and origin of this group has provoked much debate. Radhan is the name of a district of the Sawād, east of the Tigris: Christianized Assyria and the land of Babylon have both been called 'land of Radhan'. Originally, the 'Radhanites' may have been Iraqi Jews who then went to settle in the Carolingian Empire in Narbonne, where they would have enjoyed a special status: their knowledge of many languages allowed them to move about and penetrate deeply into the Islamic world – and even to reach the East Asia, and so link both East and West.

In the eleventh century, a Fusṭāṭ–Mazāra–Mahdiyya–Almería axis appeared and brought profit to al-Andalus (Islamic Spain). Along this line, Mediterranean trade revived after a long period of flourishing piracy. While in this period the main point of contact between Islam and Byzantium had been reduced to Trebizond on the Armenian route, merchants from Amalfi, moving along the Fusṭāṭ-Almería axis, forged ties with Ifrīqiyya and what was then Islamic Sicily, and set up a trading base in Cairo, whence they carried on a lively business with Egypt.

This revival of Mediterranean trade was possibly connected with changes in the Asian routes. Trade shifted after 870 to the coastline of Fārs and yielded most profit to Sīrāf, which supplied Shīrāz, and to Hormuz. But when the Qarmaṭians, based in Bahrein, interrupted and quickly ruined this traffic, the merchants quit the Persian Gulf and resorted to the Red Sea route by way of Aden. Eastern Asian goods were unloaded in Aden, then trans-shipped to 'Aydhāb, whence they were borne overland to Fusṭāṭ and the Mediterranean; in the fourteenth century, the opening of a port at Quṣayr encouraged the use of the Suez route. Fur routes suffered a decline as a result of Turkish pressure on Transoxania and Khwārizm and the rise of a new political power centre on the marches of India, Ghaznī – whither merchants now repaired. Asian trade routes tended increasingly to converge on Egypt, the new centre of the Levant and the necessary commercial crossroads between the Far East and Europe until the Age of Discovery.

Travellers moved in caravans or formed maritime convoys. Our sources dwell on the carrying of goods by camel or mule, for which simple tracks sufficed. Land traffic in the Islamic world basically moved over paths with pack trains, and not on wheels. Richard Bulliet (1975) demonstrates how the use of the camel had supplanted that of the wheel before the rise of Islam, and holds that such use was not a sign of regression in itself, given the economic advantages of resorting to this beast of burden for transport. Nor had wheeled vehicles disappeared everywhere: they remained in use wherever conditions of climate allowed. On the most frequented thoroughfares, especially those near major towns, caravanserais were built – known variously as *khān* in Syria, *wikāla* in Egypt and *funduq* in the Maghrib – to shelter merchants and their goods (see Figure 26). In the cities of the Maghrib, the *qayṣariyya* served to store especially costly goods. Many such buildings were put up by rulers and nobles, and the revenue they generated was set aside as a *waqf* or pious endowment for the upkeep of religious establishments (mosques, *madrasas* or *zāwiyas*). Bridges also were laid over certain rivers (Al-Hassan and Hill, 1986).

Maritime commerce relied on seasonal winds, such as the monsoons of the Indian Ocean, for travel to India and China. India-bound ships from the Gulf sailed in January, and returned in July.

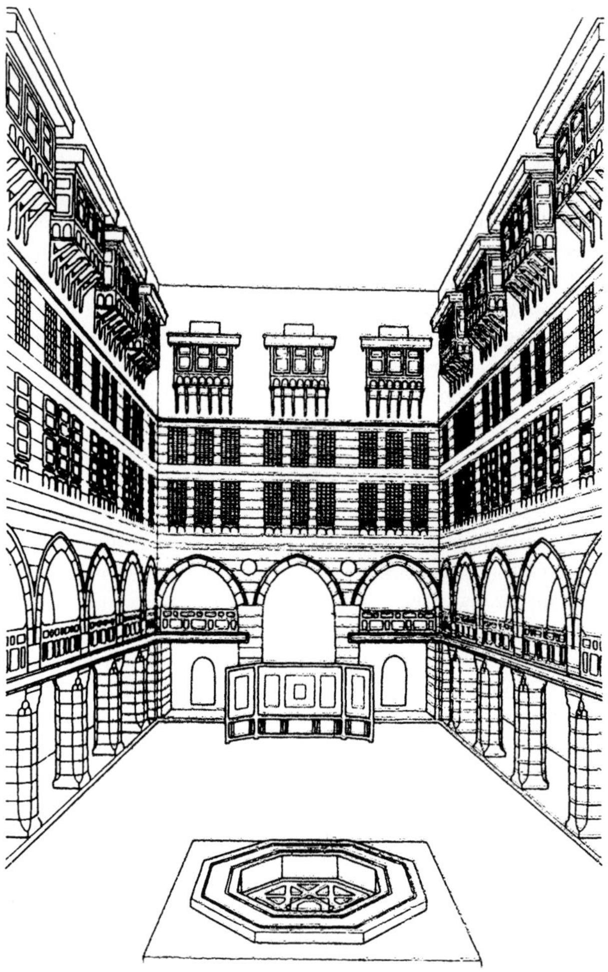

Figure 26 Courtyard of a *funduq* or *khān*, a hostelry and storehouse for caravans, merchants and their goods, Cairo, fifteenth century. The English 'caravanserai' derives from the Persian word for this institution, Kārawān-Sarāy, 'enclosure for caravans'. Animals were stabled and goods stored on the ground floor; merchants lodged in the upper galleries (after Gabrieli, F. *et al.*, *Maometto in Europa*, Verona 1983, p. 78).

Red Sea shipping (Cahen, 1969, Serjeant, 1978(b)) developed mostly after the tenth century. The great harbour here was Aden on the southern coast of Arabia. To this port sailed Indian vessels and Chinese junks alike, whose cargoes were then transferred to Arab *dhows* plying the Red Sea. Winds and reefs made most navigation dangerous in the northern Red Sea, and *dhows* usually preferred to dock at 'Aydhāb, on the African shore, whence camels conveyed the merchandise in a land journey of fifteen days to Aswān and Qūṣ: where the goods were again embarked, on river craft, to follow the Nile to Cairo and the Mediterranean.

When Christian ships docked at Alexandria, Damietta, Tinnīs, Rosetta (Rashīd) or Nastarū, lists of the passengers and goods were drawn up. Cargoes were unloaded and conveyed to a *funduq*. Foreigners were generally quartered in these ports and paid an excise tax usually equivalent to a tithe.

The Arabs played a key role in the progress of navigation, transmitting to the West such inventions as the lateen sail, first used for Red Sea craft; the magnetic needle of Chinese origin; the stern-post rudder; and the use of sea charts, which Southern Europeans came to know as *'portolanos'* (Fahmī, 1973; Al- Nakhīnī, 1974; Chapoutot-Remadi, 1995) (see Plates 21 and 22).

The monetary system

The Islamic world's monetary system (Ehrenkreutz, 1959; 1963) was based on coinage minted from either one of two metals: the silver standard inherited from the Sasanian silver *drachma* and the gold standard, which was a legacy of the Byzantine gold *solidus* or *nomisma*. This system was taken over from the past and continued to function until the Umayyad caliph ʿAbd al-Malik ibn Marwān (Grierson, 1960; 1979; Cahen, 1982(b))undertook a true monetary reform by unifying all coinage in circulation into either a silver *dirham* (2.97 g) or a gold *dīnār* (4.25 g), whose stamped inscriptions were Arabized and symbols made to conform to Islam. The first gold coinage was minted in Syria and Egypt, and the first silver issue in Iraq. The new coinage gradually spread throughout the Islamic world, and *dīnārs* found their way as far as southern Russia and Western Europe. This dual minting helped to link hitherto insulated monetary systems and gradually imposed the dual or bimetallic (gold and silver) standard throughout the Mediterranean basin. By the end of the ninth century, a *dirham* was held to be 7/100 of a *dīnār*, and the normal exchange rate between gold and silver was set at 1:10.

However, by the tenth century, devaluations of gold and silver had reduced the legal coinage to an ideal standard only: currencies now differed from one region to the next. While silver coinage became the rule in those areas that had once been part of the Sasanian Empire – Iraq, Iran, Afghanistan and Central Asia – as well as in Spain, gold coinage held sway in the former Byzantine domains of Syria, Egypt (Cahen, 1984) and North Africa, as well as in Arabia. True small change consisted of coins minted of copper or bronze, the *fils*, from a Byzantine model. While this copper coin served for small everyday transactions, the *dirham* was used for more significant trade, and the *dīnār*, the standard monetary unit of the medieval Islamic world or 'dollar of the Middle Ages' (Cipolla, 1956), was resorted to mainly for the payment of major sums such as a province's tribute or fiscal contribution.

Mints existed in both the imperial capitals and the major provincial centres. In each workshop, minters, smelters and engravers plied their trade. By reason of the influx of gold in the Islamic world – through the booty derived from the conquests, which put much hoarded yellow metal back into circulation, and then especially because of trade in Sudanese gold (Cahen, 1981) – the influence of gold reached its widest extent in the tenth century. Silver's domain shrank in the face of gold's, despite the exploitation of the Hindu Kush silver mines, until the trend was reversed in the course of the thirteenth century.

Moreover, monetary deposits encouraged the development of banks and the role of bankers. The latter saw to the smooth functioning of their money shops in the cities and perfected a system of credit by improving techniques of exchange: with letters of exchange, commissions and promissory bills – whence such Italian techniques as the *commenda* (Udovitch, 1970). Their term for promissory note or bill, *sakk*, now survives in 'cheque' (see Plates 190–194).

Currencies and problems of trade between Europe and the East

The Islamic world at first had only a few goldfields of its own, in Arabia and on the marches of Armenia. But in Asia, gold came in from the Caucasus, the Urals, the Altai, Tibet and Turkestan. And far more gold reached the Muslims from the *Bilād al-Sūdān*, or Land of the Blacks: that is, the entire stretch between the Nile and the Red Sea, Nubia–Ethiopia, and West Africa. Moreover, Islam procured its own silver from mines in Spain, northern Iran, Afghanistan and Central Asia. Its copper was mined in Central Asia and the Caucasus, in upper Mesopotamia, in Cyprus, in the Kabyle highlands of Algeria, in Morocco's Dra and Sous valleys, and in Spain. But tin – Arabic *qaṣdīr* from Greek *kassiteros* – had to come from two main outside sources: the British Isles and Malaysia, whose produce was known as *qʿalaʾī*.

Concerning trade between Europe and the East in this period, historians and numismatists have engaged in much lively debate (Lombard, 1971b).[4] It is difficult to take sides, given the inadequacy of the data. At any rate, several regional nexuses of trade ought to be distinguished here: that between Central Asia and Eastern Europe; another between Yemen and the Indian Ocean; a third between the Near East and Byzantium; a fourth between the Maghrib and Black Africa; and finally a North African and Spanish nexus with Sicily and the rest of Mediterranean Europe. We should therefore do away with an over-simplified vision of a merely three-way trade between only three units, the Islamic, the Byzantine and the Western European, with a flow of various precious metals and currencies between them. Instead, we should look to the very variegated economic spaces that were opening up in their midst.

By the close of the sixth century, the minting of gold coinage began to be modified in the West and ceased to imitate Byzantine models. Then, in the eighth century, a reverse trend occurred in the West, and silver coinage now imposed itself in place of a gold.

The presence of Arab gold coins in Italy and in England dating from between 750 and 870, and of Arab silver coins in Sweden dating from 890, bears witness to the fact that Islamic expansion had in no way been responsible for a general break in currency relations in Western Europe. An end to the inflow of African gold as a result of Arab raids in the Mediterranean may have served as a catalyst, forcing the West to take stock of its own possibilities and economic needs, thus resulting in the creation of its own silver-based *denarius*. In any case, the existence of a form of trade playing upon the differing exchange rate between gold and silver is hardly likely, for this is a period when we actually find traces of an increased presence of Islamic gold in the West. The circulation of gold *dīnārs* is attested not only by scatterings of such coins found throughout Western Europe but also by mention in texts dated between 770 and 970, especially in Italy and in England.

In the Scandinavian world, eastern Arab coins struck between 870 and 930 arrived in enormous quantities: 200,000 such coins have been found along the Baltic shores, in Russia and especially in Sweden, with 60,000 on the island of Gotland alone; 25,000 have been recovered in Poland, and 4,000 as far as Denmark. The coins came from Baghdād or from the Central Asian Sāmānid dynasty and have been linked to the silver mines at Shāsh (modern Tashkent in Uzbekistan) and in the Panjshēr Valley (Afghanistan), allowing us to infer that a new trade route had opened in this direction. The multiplication of such coins in circulation in the West around the end of the tenth century shows the coexistence in Europe of different monetary traditions. Spain and southern Italy remained embedded in the Mediterranean world, and so were familiar with coinage based on various metals and minted according to both Byzantine and Islamic models. Meanwhile, the rest of Europe abided by a silver standard alone. This trend was only reversed with the permanent resumption of the minting of gold in the West, in 1252 by Genoa and Florence, in 1285 by Venice (see Plates 190–194).

NOTES

1 Male/female inequality due to Creation was also the prevailing view in medieval Christendom (J. Delumeau, 1978).
2 Like the mausoleum of Queen Chagarat al-durr in Cairo built by her and many other religious monuments of Ayyubid and Mamlūk times in Damascus and Cairo. And we can see the mosque and the *madrasa al-tawfiqiyya* built by Princess 'Atf in Tunis in the Hafsid period.
3 The file on the Hilālī continually gets thicker, and the issue arouses lively debate (Cahen, 1971; Berque, 1978: pp.53–67; Daghfous, 1977; 1995).
4 See also the ideas of the Belgian historian Henri Pirenne, who argued that the Arab conquests provoked a major rupture in the Mediterranean economy.

BIBLIOGRAPHY

'ABD AL-RĀZIQ, A. 1973. *La femme au temps des Mamlūks*. Institut français d'archéologie orientale. Cairo.
ABDELKEFI, J. 1989. *La Médina de Tunis*. Paris.
'ABDUL LATIF 'ABDULLAH IBN DUHAISH. 1989. Growth and Development of Islamic Libraries. *Der Islam*, LXVI/2, pp. 289–302.
AL-'ARĪNĪ AL-BĀZ. 1956, *Al-Iqṭā' al-ḥarbī zamān salāṭīn al-Mamālīk*. (The War Fief of the Mamlūk Sultans). Cairo.
ARNALDEZ, R. 1991. Les théories classiques de la guerre sainte, *Les religions et la guerre (Judaïsme, Christianisme, Islam)*. Paris, pp. 375–385.
ASHTIANY, J. *et al.* (eds). 1990. *Abbassid Belles Lettres*. Cambridge University Press, Cambridge, New York.
ASHTOR, E. 1956. L'administration urbaine en Syrie médiévale. *Revista degli Studi orientali*, 31, pp. 71–128.
——. 1958. L'urbanisme syrien à la basse époque, *Revista degli Studi orientali*, 33, pp. 181–209.
——. 1972. Migrations de l'Irak vers les pays méditerranéens. *Annales ESC*, XXVII, No.1, pp. 185–214.
——. 1976. *A Social and Economic History of the Near East in the Middle Ages*. London.
ATIYA, A. S. 1968. *History of Eastern Christianity*. London.
AYALON, D. 1951. *L'esclavage du Mamelouk*. Jerusalem.
——. 1961. Furūsiyya Exercises and Games in the Mamlūk Sultanate. *Studies in Islamic History and Civilization, Scripta Hierosolymitana*, Jerusalem, Vol. IX, pp. 31–62.
——. 1963. The European Asiatic Steppe: A Major Reservoir of Power for the Islamic World. *Proceedings of the 25th Congress of Orientalists*, Moscow, II, pp. 47–52.
BARRUCAND, M. 1988. Gärten und gestaltete Landschaft als irdisches Paradies: Gärten im westlichen Islam. *Der Islam* 65/2, pp. 244–267.
BEESTON, A. F. L. *et al.* (eds) 1983. *Cambridge History of Arabic Literature: Arabic Literature to the End of the Umayyad Period*. Cambridge University Press, Cambridge, New York.
BEHRENS-ABOUSEIF, D. 1992. Gardens in Islamic Egypt. *Der Islam*, 69/2, pp. 302–312.
BELKHODJA, M. H. 1992. Guerre et paix dans l'optique de la tradition musulmane: Les religions et la guerre. *Der Islam*, pp. 357–371.
BERARDI, R. 1979. Espace et ville en pays d'Islam.In: D. CHEVALLIER (ed.) *L'espace social de la ville arabe*, Paris, p. 107.
BERKEY, J. 1979. Women and Islamic Education in Mamlūk Egypt. In: D. CHEVALLIER (ed.) *Women in Middle Eastern History, L'espace social de la ville arabe*, Paris, pp. 143–163.
BERQUE, J. 1958. Cité éminente, les villes. Ecole Pratique des Hautes Etudes, Paris, pp. 50–63.
——. 1978. Les Hilaliens au Maghreb. *De l'Euphrate à l'Atlas*, I. *Espaces et moments*, Paris, pp. 53–67.
BOLENS, L. 1974. *Les méthodes culturales au Moyen Âge d'après les traités d'agronomie andalous: traditions et techniques*. Geneva.
BOSCH-VILA, J. 1956. *Les Almoravides*. Tétouan.
BOSWORTH, C. E. 1967. Military Organization Under the Buyids. *Oriens*, XVIII–XIX.
BRUNSCHVIG, R. 1947. Urbanisme médiéval et droit mulsulman, *Revue des études islamiques (REI)* (reprinted in *Mélanges d'Islamologie*, Vol. II, 1976, pp. 7–36).
——. 1962. Les métiers vils en Islam. *Studia Islamica (SI)*, Vol. XVI, pp. 41–60 (reprinted in *Etudes d'Islamologie*, Paris 1976, Vol. I, pp. 145–166).
BULLIET, R. W. 1975. *The Camel and the Wheel*. Harvard University Press, Cambridge, Mass.
CAHEN, C. 1934. La campagne de Manzikert d'après les sources musulmanes. *Byzantion*, IX, pp. 613–642.
——. 1953a. L'évolution de l'iqtā' du IXè au XIIIè siècle, *Annales ESC*, pp. 25–52.
——. 1953b. Notes sur les débuts de la futuwwa d'al-Nāsir. *Oriens*, VI, pp. 18–22.
——. 1955. Mouvements et organisations populaires dans les villes de l'Asie musulmane au Moyen Âge: milices et associations de futuwwa. *Recueils de la Société Jean Bodin*, VII, *La ville*, pp. 273–288.
——. 1960. Réflexion sur l'usage du mot féodalité. *Journal of Economic and Social History of the Orient (JESHO)*, III, pp.2–20. Leiden.
——. 1964. Un texte inédit relatif au Tirāz égyptien. *Arts Asiatiques*, XI, pp. 165–168 (reprinted in *Makhzūmiyyāt*, pp. 190–193).
——, 1965. Y a-t-il eu des corporations professionnelles dans le monde musulman classique? Quelques notes et réflexions. In: HOURANI, A. H.; STERN, S. M. (eds) *The Islamic City*, Proceedings of the Oxford Symposium, Oxford, 1970, pp. 51–63.
——. 1966. Le commerce musulman dans l'Océan Indien au Moyen Âge, *Sociétés et compagnies de commerce en Orient et dans L'Océan Indien*. 8th Maritime History Symposium, Beirut, Service d'Edition et de Vente des Publications de l'Education Nationale, Paris, 1969, pp. 179–193.
——. 1970a. *L'Islam des origines au début de l'empire ottoman*. Paris. (reprinted 1995).
——. 1970b. L'imigration persane des origines de l'Islam aux Mongols, *Convegno internazionale sul tema: la Persia nel Medioevo*, Roma. *Atti del Academia Nazionale dei Lincei*, CCCLXVIII, No. 160, Rome, 1971, pp. 181–193.
——. 1971. Notes sur les Hilaliens et le nomadisme (Miscellanea). *JESHO*, XIV, pp. 63–68.
——. 1973. Nomades et sédentaires dans le monde musulman du milieu de moyen âge. In: RICHARDS, D. S. (ed.) *Islamic civilization, 950–1150*. Oxford, pp. 93–104 (reprinted in *Les Peuples Musulmans*, pp. 423–437).
——. 1977a. *Les peuples musulmans dans l'histoire médiévale*. Damascus.
——. 1977b. *Makhzūmiyyāt, Etudes sur l'histoire économique et financière de l'Egypte médiévale*. Brill, Leiden.
——. 1981. L'or du Soudan avant les Almoravides: mythe ou réalité. *Le sol, la parole et l'écrit, Mélanges en hommage à Raymond Mauny*, Société française d'Outre-Mer, Paris. Vol. II, pp. 539–545 (first published in *Revue française d'histoire d'Outre-Mer*, 66, 1979, pp. 169–175).
——. 1982a. Le rôle des Turcs dans l'Orient musulman médiéval. *Le cuisinier et le philosophe, Mélanges Maxime Rodinson*, Paris, pp. 97–102.
——. 1982b. Deux questions restées sans réponse sur la réforme monétaire de 'Abd al-Malik. *Mélanges offerts à Raoul Curiel, Studia Iranica*, XI, pp. 61–64.
——. 1983. Orient et occident au temps des croisades. Paris.
——. 1984. La circulation monétaire en Egypte des Fātimides aux Ayyubides. *Revue numismatique*, 6th series, XXVI, pp. 208–217.
——. 1988. *La Turquie pré-ottomane*. Institut français d'études anatoliennes, Istanbul and Paris.
CANARD, M. 1959. Le riz dans le Proche-Orient. *Arabica*.

CHALMETA, P. 1973. *El Señor del Zoco en España*. Instituto Hispano-árabe de cultura, Madrid.
CHAPOUTOT-REMADI, M. 1974. L'agriculture dans l'empire mamlūk d'après al-Nuwayrī. *Cahiers de Tunisie*, pp. 23–45.
——. 1977. Chagarat al-durr, esclave mamlūke et sultane d'Egypte. *Les Africains*, Paris, pp. 101–128.
——. 1995a. Femmes dans la ville mamlūke. *JESHO*, pp. 145–164.
——. 1995b. La médecine, un maillon entre Orient et Occident. In: ANNABI, H.; CHAPOUTOT-REMADI, M.; KAMMARTI, S. (eds) *Itinéraire du savoir, les temps forts de l'histoire tunisienne*, CNRS-ALIF-IMA, Paris.
——. 1996. *Liens et relations au sein de l'élite mamlūke sous les premiers sultans bahrides, (648/1250–741/1340)*. Damascus.
——. forthcoming. Les esclaves musiciennes: l'époque mamlūke. *Mélanges 'Abd al-'Aziz al-Dūrī*.
CIPOLLA, C. 1956. *Money, Price and Civilization in the Mediterranean World*. Princeton.
COOPER, R. 1977. Agriculture in Egypt, 640–1800, *Geschichte der islamischen Länder, Handbuch der Orientalistik*, Leyde-Cologne, pp. 188–204.
CRONE, P. 1981. *Slaves on Horses*. London.
DAGHFOUS, R. 1977. Contribution à l'étude des conditions de l'immigration des tribus arabes (Hilāl and Sulaym) en Ifrīqiya. *Cahiers de Tunisie*, Nos. 94–98, pp. 23–60.
——. 1995a. La migration des Hilâliens au Maghreb et ses répercussions (in Arabic) *Histoire de la nation arabe*. Alecso Publication, Tunis.
——. 1995b. *Le Yaman islamique des origines jusqu'à l'avènement des dynasties autonomes* (I/III A.H–VII/IXè s.), Tunis.
DELUMEAU, J. 1978. *La peur en Occident, XIVè–XVIIè siècles: une cité assiégée*. Paris.
DENNET, D. C. 1951. *Conversion and the Poll Tax in Early Islam*. Cambridge.
DJAIṬ, H. 1986. Al-Kūfa – *Naissance de la ville islamique*. Paris.
AL-DŪRĪ 'ABD AL-'AZĪZ, 1945. *al-'Asr al-'Abbāssī al-Awwal* (The First 'Abbāsid Age), Baghdād.
——. 1987. *Al-Takwīn al-Tārīkhī lil-Umma al-'Arabiyya* (The Historical Formation of Arab Community). Beirut.
EBIED, R. Y.; YOUNG, M. J. L. 1976. Les Arabes ont-ils inventé l'Université? *Le Monde de l'Education*, pp. 41–42.
EHRENKREUTZ, A. S. 1959. Studies on the Monetary History of the Near East in the Middle Ages, the Standard of Fineness of some Types of Dīnārs. *JESHO*, Vol. II/part 2, pp. 128–143.
——. 1963. Sequel, II, The Standard of Fineness of Western and Eastern Dīnārs Before the Crusades. *JESHO*, Vol. VI/part 3, pp. 243–278.
EICKELMANN, D. F. 1981. *The Middle East, An Anthropological Approach*. London.
ESPERONNIER, M. 1985. Al–Nuwayrī: les fêtes islamiques, persanes, chrétiennes et juives. *Arabica*, XXII (1), pp. 80-101.
ESSID, Y. 1993. *At–Tadbīr Oikonomia, Pour une critique des origines de la pensée économique arabo-musulmane*. Tunis.
FAHMI, 'ALĪ M. 1973. *Muslim Naval Organization in the Eastern Mediterranean, from the Seventh to the Tenth Century*. New Delhi.
GARCIN, J. C. 1984. Toponymie et topographie urbaine médiévale. *JESHO*, XXVII, p. 140.
——. 1987. Les Almohades, *Encyclopédie berbère*, IV. Edisud, Aix-en-Provence.
——. *et al.* 1995. *Etats, sociétés et cultures du monde musulman médiéval*, Xè-XVè siècle, Vol. 1, Paris.
GARDET, L. 1954. *La cité musulmane: vie sociale et politique*. Paris (2nd edn. 1961).
——. 1977 *Les Hommes de l'Islam*. Paris.
GIBB, H. A. R. 1953. The Social Significance of the Shu'ūbiyya. *Studia Orientalia Ianni Perdersen*, Haunia, pp. 105–114.
GOBLOT, H. 1979. *Les Qānāts, une technique d'acquisition de l'eau*. Paris; The Hague; New York.
GOITEIN, S. D. 1968. The Rise of the Middle Eastern Bourgeoisie in Early Islamic Times. *Studies in Islamic History and Institution*, Leiden, pp. 217–242.
——. 1967, 1971, 1975, 1981, 1985. *A Mediterranean Society*.
GOLDZIHER, I. 1967. *Muslim Studies*, Vol. I. pp. 137–163, London.
GORDON, M. 1987. *L'esclavage dans le monde arabe*, VIIè–XXe siècle. Paris.
GRIERSON, P. 1960. The Monetary Reform of 'Abd al-Malik. *JESHO*, III, pp. 241–264 (reprinted in *Dark Ages Numismatic*, Variorum Reprints, London, 1979, No. XV).
HAARMANN, U. 1980. Regional Sentiment in Medieval Islamic Egypt. *BSOAS*, Vol. XIII.
——. 1984. The Sons of the Mamlūks as Fief-holders in Late Medieval Egypt. In: TARIF KHALIDI (ed.) *Land Tenure and Social Transformation in the Middle East*, Beirut, pp. 141–168.
AL-HASSAN, Y.; HILL, D. R. 1986. *Islamic Technology. An Illustrated History*. UNESCO, Paris.
HILL, D. R. 1975. The Rôle of the Camel and the Horse in the Early Arab Conquests, In: PARRY, V. J. AND YAPP, M. E. (eds) *War, Technology and Society in the Middle East*. Oxford University Press, New York, Toronto.
HODGSON MARSHALL, G. S. 1974. *The Venture of Islam*, 3 vols. University of Chicago Press, Chicago.
HOURANI, A. 1991. *A History of the Arab Peoples*. Harvard University Press, Cambridge, Mass.
HUMPHREYS, R. S. 1992. *Islamic History, a Framework for Inquiry*. American University in Cairo Press, Cairo.
IBN KHALDŪN, 1858. *Al-Muqaddima*, Quatremère, E. (ed.), 3 vols (Paris: Duprat). English. trans. F. Rosenthal, 3 vols, Princeton, Bollinger, 1958.
IBRAHIM, M. 1990. *Merchant Capital and Islam*. University of Texas Press, Austin.
IRWIN, R. 1977. Iqṭā' and the End of the Crusader States. *Eastern Mediterranean Lands in the Age of the Crusades*. Warminster, pp. 62–73.
JACQUART, D.; MICHEAU, F. 1990. *La médecine arabe et l'Occident médiéval*, Paris.
KEDDIE, N. R. (ed.) 1992. *Women in Middle Eastern History. Shifting Boundaries in Sex and Gender*. Yale University Press, New Haven and London.
KENNEDY, H. 1986. *The Prophet and the Age of the Caliphates*. London and New York.
KING, D. 1987. *Islamic Astronomical Instruments*. Variorum Reprints, London.
KISTER, M. J. 1971. Rajab is the Month of God: A Study in the Persistence of an Early Tradition. *Israel Oriental Studies*, I, pp. 191–223.
——. 1979. Sha'bān is my Month: A Study of an Early Tradition. *Studia Orientalia memoriae D.H. Baneth Dedicata*, Jerusalem, pp. 15–27.
——. 1989. Do Not Assimilate Yourself . . . . *Jerusalem Studies in Arabic and Islam*, 12, pp. 321–371.
LAGARDÈRE, V. 1993. *Campagnes et paysans d'al-Andalus VIIIè–XVè siècles*. Paris.
LAMBTON, A. K. S. 1965. Reflections on the Iqṭā'. In: MAKDISI, G. (ed.) *Arabic Studies in Honor of H.A.R. Gibb*, Leiden, pp. 358–376.
——. 1988. The Iqṭā', state land and crown land, *Continuity and Change in Medieval Persia*, London, especially pp. 97–129.
LAOUST, H. 1965. *Les schismes dans l'Islam*. Paris.
LAPIDUS, I. M. 1967. *Muslim Cities in the Later Middle Ages*. Cambridge, Mass.
——. 1975. The Separation of State and Religion, *IJMES*, VI, pp. 363–385.
——. 1988. *A History of Islamic Societies*. Cambridge University Press.
LEWIS, B. 1950. *The Arabs in History*. London.
——. 1971. *Race and Color in Islam*. New York.
LOKKEGAARD, F. 1951. *Islamic Taxation in the Classical Period*. Copenhagen.
LOMBARD, M. 1971a. *l'Islam dans sa première grandeur (VIIIè–XIè siècle)*. Paris.
——. 1971b. *Monnaie et Histoire de Mahomet à Charlemagne*, Paris.
——. 1974. *Les métaux dans l'ancien monde du Vè au XIè siècle*. Paris, The Hague.
—— 1978. *Les textiles dans le monde musulman. VIIè–XIIè*. Paris, The Hague, New York.

MARÇAIS, G. 1957. Les jardins de l'Islam. *Mélanges d'histoire et d'archéologie de l'Occident musulman*, Vol. I, pp. 236–256.
MARIN, M.; WAINES, D. 1994. *La alimentación en las culturas islámicas*. Madrid, pp. 11–21.
MARQUET, Y. 1961. La place du travail dans la hiérarchie ismaïlienne des Ikhwān al-Safā, *Arabica,* VIII, pp. 225–237.
MERNISSI, F. 1990. *Sultanes oubliées*. Paris.
MEYERHOF, M. 1984. *Studies in Medieval Arabic Medicine, Theory and Practice*. Variorum Reprints, London.
MIQUEL, A. 1969. *La littérature arabe*. Paris.
——. 1967, 1975, 1980, 1988. *La géographie humaine du monde musulman jusqu'au milieu du XIè*, Paris, The Hague.
——. 1977. *L'Islam et sa civilisation (VIIè-XXè s.)*. Paris.
MONROE, J. T. 1970. *The Shu'ūbiyah in al-Andalus*. Berkeley, p. 69.
MORABIA, A. 1994. *La notion de jihād dans l'Islam médiéval, des origines à al-Ghazālī*, Paris.
MORGAN, D. A. 1988. *Medieval Persia, 1040–1797*. London and New York.
MOTTAHEDEH, R. P. 1980. The Shu'ūbiya controversy and the social history of early Islamic Iran. *IJMES VII/2*, pp. 161–182.
AL-NAKHĪLĪ, D. 1974. *Al-Sufūn al-Islāmiyya 'alā Ḥurūf al-Mu'jam*. Alexandria.
NASR, S. H. 1993. *Sciences et savoir en Islam*. Paris.
PELLAT, C. 1963. *Les esclaves-chanteuses de Gāhiz, Arabica,* X, pp. 121–147.
——. Kayna, *EI²*, IV, pp. 853–857.
——. 1986. Cinq calendriers égyptiens. Cairo.
PIPES, D. 1980. *Slave Soldiers in Islam: The Genesis of a Military System.*
DE PLANHOL, X. 1993. *Les Nations du Prophète, Manuel géographique de politique musulmane*. Paris.
POLIAK, A. N. 1936. La féodalité islamique, *REI*, pp. 247–265.
——. 1937. Some notes on the feudal system of the Mamluks. *JRAS*, pp. 97–107.
——. 1939a. The Ayyubid Feudalism. *JRAS*, pp. 428–432.
——. 1939b. *Feudalism in Egypt, Syria and Lebanon 1250–1900*. London.
POPOVIC, A. 1976. *La révolte des esclaves en Iraq*. Paris.
POUZET, L. 1988. *Vie et structures religieuses dans une métropole islamique*. Beirut.
RABIE, H. 1970. The Size and the Value of the Iqṭā' in Egypt 564–741/1169–1341 AD. In: COOK, M. (ed.) *Studies in Economic History of the Middle East*, London, pp. 129–138.
——. 1972. *The Financial System of Egypt A.H. 564–741/ AD. 1169–1341*. London; *cf.* Cahen, C., *JESHO*, XVI/Part I, pp. 107–111; Chapoutot-Remadi, M., *Arabica*, XX/1973, pp. 323–325.
RODINSON, M. 1966. *Islam et capitalisme*. Paris.
——. 1970. Le marchand musulman. In: RICHARDS, D. S. (ed.). *Islam and the Trade of Asia.*
——. 1979. *Les Arabes*. Paris.
ROSENBERGER, B. 1985. Maquiller l'esclave, el-Andalus (XIIè–XIIIè siècle). Proceedings of the Third International Symposium of Grasse, *Les soins de beauté*, CNRS, Faculty of Literature and Human Science, Nice, 1987, pp. 319–347.
ROUX, J. P. 1960. *Les Explorateurs au moyen âge*. Paris.
——. 1984. *Histoire des Turcs, deux mille ans du Pacifique à la Méditerranée*. Paris.
——. 1993. *Histoire de l'empire mongol*. Paris.
SABARI, S. 1981. *Mouvements populaires à Bagdad à l'époque abbasside, IXè–XIè siècle*. Paris.
AL-SĀMIR, F. 1971. *Thawrat az-Zanj* (The Revolt of the Zanj). Baghdād.
SAMSO, J. 1978. Un calendrier tunisien d'origine andalouse? – du XIXè siècle. *Cahiers de Tunisie*, XXVI, pp. 67–84.
SARTON, G. 1960. *Introduction to the History of Science*, 2 vols. Baltimore.
SCHATZMILLER, M. 1994. *Labour in the Medieval Islamic World*. Leiden.
SERJEANT, R. B. 1964. The Constitution of Medina. *Islamic Quarterly*, VIII, pp. 3–16.
——. 1978a. The Sunnah Jāmi'ah Pact with Yathrib Jews, and the Taḥrīm of Yathrib. Analysis and Translation of the Documents Comprised in the So-called Constitution of Medina. *BSOAS*, XII, pp. 1–42.
——. 1978b. Maritime Customary Law off the Arabian Coasts, *Sociétés et Compagnies de Commerce*, pp. 195–207.
SHABAN, M. A. 1971. *Islamic History I*. Cambridge.
——. 1976. *Islamic History II*. Cambridge.
SIRAT, C. 1988. Le parchemin, Le papier. *Le livre au moyen âge*, Glénisson, J. (ed.), preface by L. Holtz, Paris, CNRS, pp. 22–23, 32–33.
SOUISSI, M. 1995. Les mathématiques et l'astronomie entre Ifrīqiyya et Maghreb and Les Sharfī et la cartographie. In: ANNABI, H.; CHAPOUTOT-RAMADI, M. AND KAMMARTI, S. (eds) *Itinéraire du savoir, les temps forts de l'histoire tunisienne*, CNRS-ALIF-IMA, Paris.
SOURDEL, D. 1960. *Le vizirat abbasside*, 2 Vols. Damascus.
SOURDEL, D.; SOURDEL-THOMINE, J. 1968. *La civilisation de l'Islam classique*. Paris.
TALBI, M. 1966. *L'Emirat aghlabide*, p. 136.
——. 1982. *Etudes d'histoire ifriqiyenne et de civilisation musulmane médiévale*. Tunis.
——. Les courtiers en vêtements en Ifrīqiyya au IXè–Xè siècle d'après les Masā'il al-Samāsira d'al-Ibyānī, *Etudes d'histoire ifrīqiyenne*, pp. 231–262.
——. Droit et économie en Ifrīqiyya au IIIe/IXe siècle. Le paysage agricole et le rôle des esclaves dans l'économie du pays. *Etudes d'histoire ifrīqiyenne*, pp. 185–230.
——. 1994. Vivre dans la cité, *Les différents aspects de la culture islamique, l'individu et la société en Islam, sous la direction de Bouhdiba* (Abd al-W.), UNESCO Publishing, Paris, pp. 444–448.
TARHĀN, I. 1968. *Al-Nuẓūm al-Iqṭā'iyya fī al-Sharq al-Awsaṭ fī al-'Uṣūr al-Wusṭā*, (The Iqṭā' System in the Medieval Middle East). Cairo.
TROUPEAU, G. 1954. Le livre des règles de conduite des maîtres d'école. *REI*, pp. 81–182.
UDOVITCH, A. L. 1970. *Partnership and Profit in Medieval Islam*. Princeton University Press.
VERNET, J. 1978. *La cultura Hispanoárabe en Oriente y Occidente*, 2nd edn. Barcelona.
VON GRUNEBAUM, G. E. 1955. Firdausi's concept of history. *Islam: Essays in the Nature and Growth of a Cultural Tradition. Comparative Studies of Cultures and Civilizations*, No. 4, REDFIELD, R. and SINGER, M. (eds) *The American Anthropologist*, Vol. 57, No. 2/2, pp. 168–184.
WATT, M. 1956. *Muḥammad at Medina*. Oxford.
WATSON, A. M. 1983. *Agricultural Innovation in the Early Islamic World: The Diffusion of Crops and Farming Techniques*, 700–1100. Cambridge University Press, Cambridge.
WIET, G. 1966. *Introduction à la littérature arabe*. Paris.
——. 1969. Fêtes et jeux au Caire. *Annales Islamologiques* VIII, pp. 99–128.
YOUSKEVITCH, A. P. 1976. *Les mathématiques arabes (VIIIè–XVè siècle)*, trans. by Cazenave, M. and Jaouiche, K., Paris.
ZIYADA, K. 1982. Al-Khissīs wa'l-nafīs fī al-madīna al-islāmiyya, al-fi'āt fī al-madīna al-islāmiyya (Base-born and Noble-born in the Islamic City, gangs in the Islamic City'). *al-Fikr al-'Arabi*, No. 29, 4th year, pp. 153–161.

18.2
NON-MUSLIMS IN ISLAMIC SOCIETY

Benjamin Braude, Irfan Habib, Kamal Salibi and Ahmad Tafazzoli, co-ordinated by Mounira Chapoutot-Remadi and Radhi Daghfous

While Islam as a religion does not recognize, indeed militates against, racial pride and all ethnic segregation, it does legalize religious distinctions. Thus the non-Muslims – Christians, Jews, Zoroastrians, Hindus, and even Sabeans and Samaritans – were recognized as 'protected ones' and so received the status of *dhimmīs* (Fattal, 1958), which allowed them freedom of worship, movement, residence and self-administration along their own religious lines on payment of a special poll tax, the *jizya* (Dennet, 1951; Løkkegaard, 1951). These tolerated communities were defined either as 'People of the Book' (Stillman, 1967; Lewis, 1984), that is, possessors of a revealed Scripture, or as 'People of the Pact', with whom an agreement of protection had been concluded (this was also known as the Pact of 'Umar).

From the ninth century onwards, polemics between the spokesmen for the various creeds did break out, ultimately on account of underlying fear that their respective faithful might abjure and of concern to keep their respective flocks in the fold. Even so, such polemics could not prevent considerable interpenetration between the faiths in Near Eastern society at least down to the eleventh century. To be sure, many non-Muslims had by then already converted to Islam, and so had ceased to pay the *jizya*. But such new converts in the Umayyad age formed only an inferior category known as the *mawālī*, or 'clients'. They had not been admitted to enjoy equal status with the Muslim Arabs in this very beginning of the Islamic era. At the same time, they were also forbidden to revert to their original creeds on pain of charges of apostasy, *ridda* and a death sentence. Meanwhile, between Muslims and non-Muslims lay a heavy financial discrimination which weighed most on the poorer 'protected ones', as well as a legal discrimination which proved harsh to any *dhimmī* opposed in a lawsuit to a Muslim.

THE JEWS

Benjamin Braude

Jewish life in medieval Islam constituted one of the great periods of cultural achievement in Jewish history (Braude and Lewis (eds), 1982). In the centuries after the rise of Islam, Arabic, usually written in Hebrew characters (Judaeo-Arabic), became one of the dominant vehicles for Jewish religious, literary, scientific, and philosophical expression. In Andalusia, Egypt and Iraq, Jewish intellectuals thereby contributed not only to the culture of their own communities but also to that of Islamic and world civilization. The result was the creation of what has been called the Judeao-Islamic tradition, a term with considerably more historical reality than the Judaeo-Christian tradition to which it may be compared. The effects of this tradition were not limited to high culture, for they also transformed the everyday experience of Jews. Its most remarkable element was the conversion of Middle Eastern Jewry as a whole from speakers of Aramaic to native speakers of the *lingua franca*, Arabic. A key indicator of the degree and speed of Arabization was the Arabic translation of the Bible by Saadia Gaon (892–942). The acceptance of the *lingua franca*, a relatively unusual phenomenon in pre-modern Jewish experience, is clear testimony to the success of integration into Arab society at large and to the openness of Jewish and Muslim societies to each other.

Moses Maimonides (1135–1204), philosopher, jurist, physician and communal leader, was the most illustrious figure of this age. The vicissitudes of Maimonides' career illustrate both the opportunities afforded and the threatening obstacles confronting the Jews. At the age of thirteen, his tranquil and secure life in Cordova, the leading city of Andalusia, was violently disrupted by the invading Muwaḥḥidūn (Almohads), an extreme millenarian Muslim movement from the South of Morocco, which attempted to unify all the entire Muslim West under their rule.

The Muwaḥḥidūn conquered all the North African lands, then occupied Andalusia ('Inān; 1965). They could not tolerate any other interpretation of Islam (so Muslims who would not submit were 'purged'), and they also refused to observe the tolerance precribed by the *sharī'a* for the 'People of the Book'. They tried to impose conversions on Jews and Christians. It is probably at this time that Christianity disappeared from North Africa. Jews suffered, but resisted (Hirshberg, 1974), and the later Almohads permitted the *dhimmīs* to practise their religion in accordance with the law.

Maimonides and his family fled and after nearly two decades of further threats and dangers eventually settled in Cairo. It was his skill as a physician that brought him honour and respect as he rose to the height of his profession in the royal court of Ayyūbid Egypt, where he peacefully ended his days. In Egypt, Jews played an important role not only in medicine but also in government, especially in Fāṭimid times, when Ya'qūb ibn Killis became a vizier in 977, and many others Jews played important roles in the Egyptian and Syrian administration.

In addition to the intellectual role that the Jews of Islam played in the cultural life of the age, they also made another contribution, which has been chronicled in an invaluable source. Jews helped to build the flourishing international economy which united and supported the Muslim world from India to Spain. Their records are preserved in the Geniza, a storehouse attached to a synagogue in the medieval quarter of Cairo, where the pious buried paper on which Hebrew script appeared, for its sanctity made it too precious to destroy. In the twentieth century, scholars, most notably S. D. Goitein,[1] have unearthed these random records – shopping lists, deeds to property, poetry, sacred manuscripts and business correspondence – to reconstruct an entire world which otherwise would have been be lost to posterity. Documents from the Geniza are one of the most useful sources for the study of the reality of medieval Islamic society as a whole.

CHRISTIANS

Kamal Salibi

In the Muslim world, historical communities of indigenous Christians have existed mainly in the lands of the Fertile Crescent (Iraq, historical Syria – comprising today's Syria, Lebanon, Jordan and Palestine/Israel), Egypt and North Africa.

When the Arabs conquered these countries, they neither forced nor encouraged the urban and rural Christians to convert to Islam. Instead, they guaranteed them the right to continue in the practice of their religion, provided that they paid the *jizya*. Their gradual conversion to Islam, between the eighth and ninth centuries, brought about the first appreciable reduction in numbers of the Christian faithful in Syria, and more so in Iraq (Bulliet, 1979; Levitzion, 1979).

During the early Muslim centuries, Christian Arabs in Syria and Iraq contributed to its enrichment of Islamic civilization in science, medicine and philosophy, by transmitting the Greek heritage in these fields through a monumental series of translations.

In Egypt, the Christian Copts (Little and Northrupp, 1990) probably continued to form the majority of the population until the time of the Crusades. The same may have been true of the Christians (Melchites, Jacobites and Maronites) in Syria. They played a very important role in the administration of these countries, specially as *kuttāb* or secretaries, and they monopolized the financial *dīwān* offices, until Mamlūk times. In both lands, however, the numbers of the Muslims were to grow in due course, reducing the Christians to minorities which became proportionally smaller with time.

Normally protected by the Muslim state authority, the Christians of the Arab lands rarely experienced persecution; and what persecution they did experience was never systematic or prolonged. Like the Jews, their condition worsened under Almohad rule, and they disappeared from North Africa in the middle of the twelfth century (Talbi, 1990). The Crusades were a partial factor because Muslim rulers began to suspect that their Christian subjects might, in time of war, collude with the enemy: the Byzantines, for example, then with the Franks. But in fact, with the signal exception of the Spanish Christians linked to the Church of Rome, the other Christians in the East, mainly belonged to dissident churches which had broken off from the main body of Christendom on account of Christological disputes.

ZOROASTRIANS

The late Ahmad Tafazzoli

Zoroastrianism, the religion of Zoroaster, the ancient Prophet of Iran, was the official faith of Iran during the Sasanian period (AD 226–635). There was some uncertainty among the Muslim authorities as to whether the Zoroastrians should enjoy the same minority rights as the Jews and the Christians. But because of their great population and their long experience in administering the affairs of the country, they had to be considered as a 'People of the Book'. Thus, they had the choice of converting to Islam, or paying the poll tax (*jizya*). The great majority, especially in the cities, preferred to convert to Islam; however, a substantial number still remained within the Zoroastrian fold for quite some time.

Under the four orthodox caliphs (AD 632–661) the rights of the Zoroastrians to have their fire temples, freedom to perform their religious practices, and to celebrate their feasts, were generally respected. Umayyad rule (AD 661–750) brought forth a harsher policy. The rise of the 'Abbāsids, with the help of Iranian Muslims, did not augur a change for the better. During the rule of Caliph al Ma'mūn (AD 813–833), however, the spirit of tolerance became somewhat dominant. Most of the extant Zoroastrian books in Middle Persian (Pahlavi) were written down in the ninth century, and in Islamic sources, Zoroastrian scholars are quoted as authorities on the history, culture and religion of ancient Iran.

In Khurāsān and eastern Iran, Zoroastrians had to suffer a more difficult life, because Muslim rulers tried to convert them by force, as in the late tenth century. Those who were steadfast in their faith immigrated by sea to Gujarāt in Western India where in time they formed a prosperous community. Little is known about Zoroastrians in Iran during the thirteenth–fifteenth centuries. Yazd and Kirmān remained the two main centres of the Zoroastrians in Iran. But under the Safavid rule their conditions seem to have worsened and in the eighteen century, Sultan Ḥusain (1694– 1722) ordered their conversion to Islam and the demolition of their temples.

HINDUS

Irfan Habib

The Arabs encountered Hindu populations for the first time when the Umayyad commander Muḥammad ibn Qāsim conquered Sind and southern Punjab in 710–714. It was natural for the conquerors to extend to the Hindus the status of *dhimmīs*, in line with what had been done in respect of the Zoroastrian ('Magian') peoples of Iran. They were to pay the land tax, *kharāj*, and the poll tax, *jizya*, the former alone apparently collected from the countryside, the latter from the towns, at three standard rates. The collection was left to the Brahmans, who were the priests as well as tax collectors in the previous regime. The Brahman priests were permitted to conduct worship of their idols, and to receive gifts as heretofore. Moreover, the restrictions and repressive rules imposed on the 'outcasts' under the Brahmanical caste system were expressly confirmed and continued.[2] Since this area remained under Arab control until it came under the Ghaznavids in the eleventh century, these arrangements seem to have served as the model for the succeeding regimes.

Under the Delhi sultans (1206–1526), the poll tax was not levied in the countryside. The land-tax, indifferently called *kharāj* or *jizya*, or *kharāj-jizya*, was levied on both Hindu and Muslim peasants. The *jizya* as poll tax, however, seems still to have been levied on Hindus in towns, the Brahmans as priests being exempt. Under Fīrūz Tughluq (1351–1386), it was imposed, at least on paper, on (Hindu) peasants, but perhaps only fleetingly; as fleeting, perhaps, was its extension in the towns to cover Brahmans (Rayachaudhuri and Habib,

1982. In the fifteenth century, references to the poll tax practically disappear; and it is very difficult to know what kind of tax or taxes the Mughal emperor Akbar actually did away with when he formally abolished the *jizya* on Hindus in 1564.

Tolerance and persecution (Ali, 1991) might be found to alternate in history. Hindu temples were destroyed in war and expeditions. But in 857, an Arab governor in the North-West Frontier Province of Pakistan, in a bilingual inscription, could use the Hindu invocation *Om* (God); the Ghōrid conqueror Mu'izzu'ddīn ibn Sām (d. 1206), in some of his gold coins, could picture the Hindu goddess Lakshmī, a feature pronounced, by a numismatic authority as without parallel in Muslim history.

The tolerance was extended to religious preaching as well, though persecution of heretics and individual Hindu divines sometimes occurred. The opening up of the highest ranks to Hindu nobles and officers by the Sultans was an important feature of the Delhi sultanate. Similarly, Sultan Zainu'l 'Ābidīn of Kashmir (1420–1470) had a large number of Brahman ministers and officers. In Bengal, one of the Hindu nobles, Ganesh, became sovereign (1415–1418) without converting to Islam, though his son and successor did undergo conversion (Habib and Nizami (eds), 1970/1982).

These facts remind us that, despite the rulers in large parts of India being Muslims from the thirteenth century onwards, Muslim communities accommodated themselves to coexistence with a large and fairly stable Hindu majority, so that it is difficult to speak of a simple 'Muslim society' in India. The Hindus provided the bulk of the rural aristocracy and dominated the spheres of commerce and credit. To a considerable extent, they were governed by their own customs and laws. The subcontinent could hardly ever fit into the Muslim theologians' concept of *Dār al-Islām*, and law and theology had inevitably to concede a great deal of ground to statesmanship, and, above all, to simple convenience.

NOTES

1 The monumental study by S. D. Goitein on the Jews of this age is based on the documents of the Geniza in Cairo and without a doubt remains the most important work not only on this issue, but even on the society and economy of the medieval Islamic and Arab world as a whole. See Goitein, 1967–1988.

2 This information is given from the remarkable Arabic collection of contemporary narratives and documents surviving in a literal thirteenth-century Persian translation, the *Chachnāma*. See Daudpota, 1939, pp. 207–216.

BIBLIOGRAPHY

('ABD ALLĀH) 'INĀN MUḤAMMAD. 1965. *'Asr al-Murābitīn wa al-Muwahhidīn fī alMaghrib wa al-Andalus* (The Age of the Almoravids and Almohads in North Africa and Spain), 2 vols. Cairo.

ATHAR ALI, M. 1991. Encounter and Efflorescence: The Genesis of Medieval (Indian) Civilization. *Proceedings of the Indian History Congress*, 50th Session (Gorakhpur), Delhi, pp. 2–9.

BOYCE, M. A. 1977. *Persian Stronghold of Zoroastrianism*. Oxford.

——. 1979. Zoroastrians. London, Boston, Henley.

——. 1992. Zoroastrianism. Costa Mesa, California and New York.

BRAUDE, B.; LEWIS, B. (eds) 1982. *Christians and Jews in the Ottoman Empire. The Functioning of a Plural Society*, Vol. I: *The Central Lands*, ix, 449, Vol. II: *The Arabic speaking Lands*, ix, 248, Holmes & Meier Publishers, New York.

BULLIET, R. W. 1979. *Conversion to Islam in the Medieval Period: An Essay in Quantitative History*. Cambridge, Mass.

CERETTI, C. G. 1991. *An 18th-Century Account of Parsi History, the Qesse-ye Zardoshtān-e-Hendustān* (The Story of the Zoroastrians in India). Napoli.

COHEN, M. 1994. *Under Crescent and Cross. The Jews in the Middle Ages*. Princeton University Press, Princeton.

CUOQ, J. 1984. *L'Église d'Afrique du Nord du IIè au XIIè siècle*. Paris.

DAUDPOTA, M. (ed.) 1939. *Chachnāma*. Delhi.

DENNET, D. C. 1951. *Conversion and the Poll-Tax in Early Islam*. Cambridge, Mass.

EDULJI, H. E. 1991. *Kisseh-i Sanjān*. Bombay.

FATTAL, A. 1958. *Le Statut légal des non-musulmans en pays d'Islam*. Beirut.

GERVERS, M.; BIKHAZI, R. J. (eds) 1990. *Indigenous Christian Communities in Islamic Lands, Eighth to Eighteenth Centuries*. Pontifical Institute of Mediaeval Studies, Toronto.

GOITEIN, S. D. 1967–1988. In: *A Mediterranean Society: The Jewish Communities of the Arab World as Portrayed in the Documents of the Cairo Geniza*. Berkeley.

HABIB, M.; AND NIZAMI, K. A. (eds) 1970/1982. *Comprehensive History of India*, V. New Delhi, pp. 754, 1151–1152.

HALKIN, A. 1956. *The Judaeo-Islamic Age*. In: SCHAWARTZ, L. W. (ed.) *Great Ages and Ideas of the Jewish People*. Random House, New York. XXVII, pp. 215–263.

HIRSCHBERG, H. Z. 1974. *A History of the Jews in North Africa*. Leiden, I.

KARAKA, D. F. 1884. *History of the Parsis*, 2 vols. London.

LEVITZION, N. (ed.) 1979. *Conversion to Islam*. New York.

LEWIS, B. 1984. *The Jews of Islam*. Princeton University Press, Princeton, XII.

LITTLE, D. P.; NORTHRUPP, L. 1990. In: *Indigenous Christian Communities*. Toronto, pp. 253–262; 263–288.

LOKKEGAARD, F. 1951. *Islamic Taxation in the Classic Period*. Copenhagen.

MODI, J. J. 1934. *Qisseh-i Zardushtiān-i Hindūstān* (The Story of the Zoroastrians in India). Bombay.

QURESHI, I. H. 1942. *The Administration of the Sultanate of Delhi*. Lahore.

RAYCHAUDHURI, T.; HABIB, I. (eds) 1982. *Cambridge Economic History of India*, I. Cambridge, pp. 60–67.

SADIQI, G. 1993. *Jonbeshhā-ye Dīnī-ye Īrānī dar Qarnhā-ye dovvom-ō sevvom-e Hejrī* (The Iranian Religious Movements in the Second and Third Centuries AH). Tehrān.

SPULER, B. 1952. *Iran in Früh-islamischer Zeit*. pp. 183–204.

STILLMANN, N. 1967. *The Jews of Arab Lands: A History and Source Book*. Philadelphia, the Jewish Publication Society of America.

TALBI, M. 1990. In: *Indigenous Christian Communities*. Toronto, pp. 313–351.

TRITTON, A. S. 1970. *The Caliphs and their Non-Muslim Subjects: A Critical Study of the Covenant of 'Umar*. London, A. S. Cass.

19

ARABIA AND THE EASTERN ARAB LANDS (AL-MASHRIQ)

Farouk Omar Fawzi

POLITICAL AND ADMINISTRATIVE CONDITIONS (FROM THE MID-EIGHTH TO THE MID-ELEVENTH CENTURY AD)

The success of the 'Abbāsid *da'wa* ('call, appeal': missionary movement or religious propaganda), and the 'Abbāsids' attainment of the caliphate, marked an important turning point in the history of state and society in Islam. The importance of the 'Abbāsid victory lies in the radical changes which followed it in both the political and cultural spheres. The 'Abbāsids themselves were the first to emphasize that their movement was a revolution, and for that reason they gave their new system the title *dawla* (lit. 'change of time, turn of fortune', and by extension 'state, polity') (al-Mubarrad, I, p. 144).

Careful examination of the emergence of the 'Abbāsid *da'wa* and its consequences throughout the early days of the 'Abbāsid era clearly demonstrates the importance of the role of the Arabs and their active participation in the 'Abbāsid movement. Most of its political propaganda was directed against the Umayyad dynasty and those Syrians who were its beneficiaries. The leaders of the *da'wa*, and subsequently the caliphs of the new state, were Hāshimī, Arabs. Similarly, the backbone of the historical bloc (*cf.* al-Jābirī, 1992: pp. 329 ff), comprising various groups which supported the movement and then the state, consisted of Arab tribes, in particular the Yamānī and Rabī'a tribes, and the Iranian *mawālī* (sing. *maulā* 'client converts': non-Arab converts during the first century of Islam, who acquired status by attachment to an Arab tribal group; the term more commonly meant 'freedmen' later in the 'Abbāsid period). The Arabs (including the Banū Hāshim) continued to occupy the main political, administrative and military posts, and the caliphs relied upon them for all difficult tasks and delicate situations (Omar, 1970: *passim*). To be more precise, while the Arabs in the early 'Abbāsid period did not lose their central position, there was greater scope for non-Arabs to gain a share of power.

The new regime led to important social changes. The warriors were gradually superseded by new social groups, including merchants, small traders and craftsmen, land owners, secretaries (employees in government offices), scholars, jurists and others. At the same time, the main cities underwent a transformation from military bases to urban centres endowed with cultural facilities, markets and schools. This should come as no surprise, for this was the age of the rich Islamic civilization that sprang from the mingling of numerous peoples, all with a variety of experiences. Its cities became the focus of social, economic and intellectual activities. This new Islamic Arab civilization was not just an updated version of Sasanian or Byzantine civilization, as some scholars have seen fit to suggest (Wiet, 1953) but had an identity of its own deriving from both Islam and Arab traditions, while liberally incorporating elements from neighbouring or earlier civilizations.

The expansion of cities, the complexity of urban life in all its different aspects, the development of the countryside and expansion of agricultural holdings, and the growth of professions, crafts and trade, led to the appearance of new types of organization. The forerunners of craft organizations appeared, such as the guilds, which began to develop in clearer fashion in the ninth and tenth centuries.

Political conditions

The first 'Abbāsid caliph, Abū l-'Abbās 'Abdullāh ibn Muḥammad (*al-Saffāḥ*, the 'shedder of blood', the generous), was formally acclaimed caliph in the mosque of Kūfa in October 749. Abū l-'Abbās bequeathed the caliphate to his brother Abū Ja'far 'Abdullāh (al-Manṣūr), who acceded to the office in July 754.

Historians are agreed that it is al-Manṣūr who was the real founder of the new dynasty, and that it was he who built up its power and renown. 'It was he who established the state, organized the kingdom, drew up regulations, instituted law and devised whatever was needed' (Ibn al-Ṭiqṭaqā, 1899; English trans., 1947: p. 160). In fact, al-Manṣūr dealt successfully with all dangers confronting the caliphate.

His era witnessed a fundamental change in the central administration: the powers of the government offices became established and new offices were instituted. He worked to introduce centralization and began by establishing a regular army, bound by ties of loyalty to the state; he built a new capital, *Madīnat al-Salām* ('the city of peace': Baghdād), as a centre for the government administrative offices and a headquarters for the military; the building process lasted from 758 to 766. Then al-Manṣūr began to build al-Ruṣāfa to the east of the Tigris and ordered his heir, al-Mahdī, to settle it and develop it. Al-Manṣūr's plan was to keep the caliphal succession in his own line, so he prepared his son Muḥammad to inherit the caliphate after his death. To that end, he spread propaganda widely, naming him al-Mahdī; this eventually compelled the legal heir, 'Īsā ibn Mūsā, to step down in his favour, and al-Mahdī was proclaimed caliph in October 775.

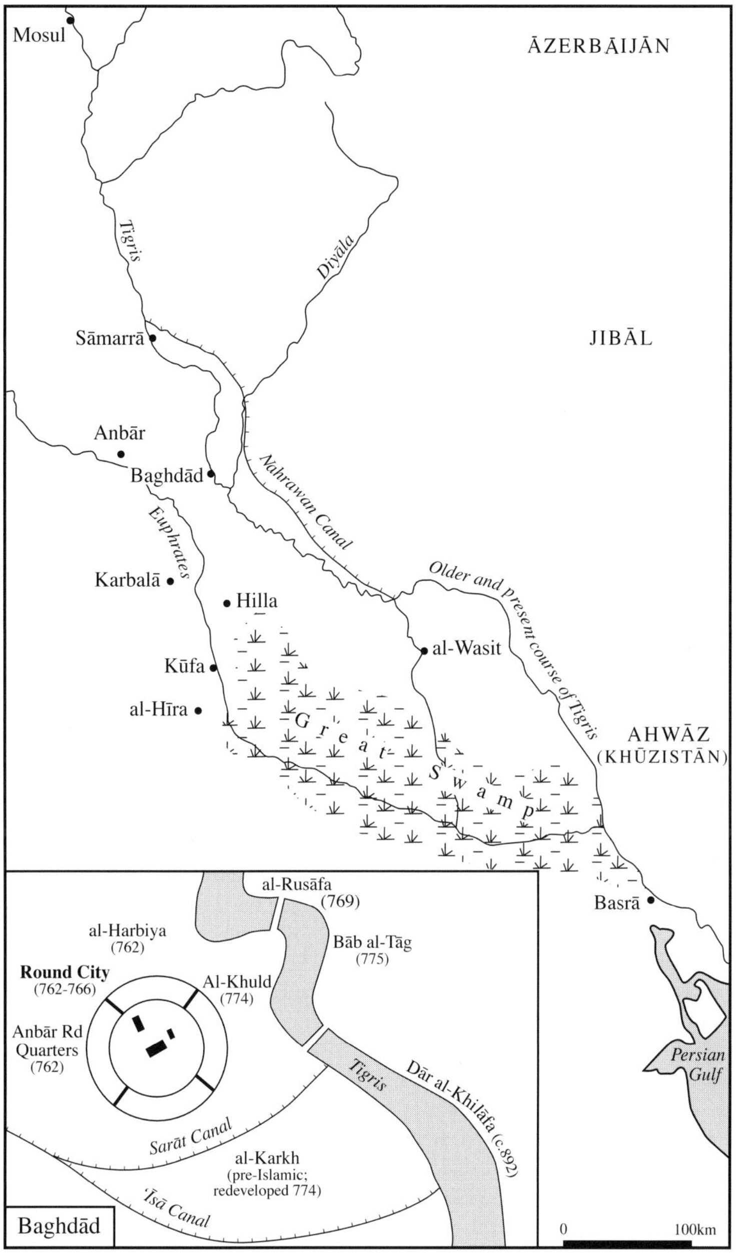

Map 14 Iraq in the early ʿAbbāsid era (after Lapidus, I. 1984).

In comparison with the severity of al-Manṣūr, the caliphate of the ʿAbbāsid al-Mahdī was characterized by political stability and economic prosperity, and moves towards reconciliation. He also devoted considerable attention to fighting the *zindīqs* (free-thinkers, heretics or agitators), who were a new religious group. He established a government office with the specific aim of pursuing and punishing the *zindīqs*.

Baghdād (see Map 14) expanded, its markets and properties flourished, the building of al-Ruṣāfa was completed, and new government offices were established. Al-Mahdī involved himself in the *jihād* (religious war of conquest) and there was much military activity in both summer and winter. The ʿAbbāsid campaigns extended as far afield as India, Transoxania and Anatolia. Under the influence of Khayzurān, al-Mahdī conceived the idea of appointing his sons Mūsā al-Hādī and Hārūn al-Rashīd as his heirs.

Mūsā al-Hādī assumed the caliphate in August 785, but his rule did not last long – he died suddenly in mysterious circumstances about a year later. Hārūn al-Rashīd succeeded as caliph in September 786; the personality of al-Rashīd is undoubtedly the best-known and most famous of all the ʿAbbāsid caliphs, not only in popular legend but also in historical accounts (Omar, 1977). The accounts concerning him and his policies are varied and contradictory, however. Some of these accounts portray al-Rashīd as a caliph who was not concerned with the affairs of his subjects but 'entrusted the affairs of his subjects to the Barmakids'; other stories minimize their role and highlight that of other personalities who played a role parallel to that of the Barmakids in administration and politics.

The era of al-Rashīd saw significant achievements in the fields of building, urban development, and civilian government and institutions. The caliph was concerned to ensure security and stability in the far-flung regions of the caliphate. He aroused fresh enthusiasm for the *jihād* and himself led the army into the heart of Byzantine territory, even reaching the outskirts of Constantinople – the first time in ʿAbbāsid history. He concerned himself with the frontier regions and reorganized them administratively and militarily. He also paid great attention to the fleet in the Mediterranean, reconstructing harbours and furnishing them with garrisons. These achievements, in addition to progress in both culture and the sciences, brought him widespread fame in the then known world; embassies from the kingdoms of the Carolingian Franks, for example, hastened to Baghdād to strengthen their diplomatic ties. Trade and agriculture revived, and new ways were devised of assigning a portion of produce in payment of the *kharāj* (land tax). Homes were built for the sick and for lepers. The ʿAbbāsid institution of the wazīrate began to assume a new shape: its functions and powers were clarified. In this way, the age of al-Rashīd, with all its cultural and intellectual advances, seemed a golden age. And yet, certain incidents foreshadow the coming political fragmentation and the beginning of administrative break-up. The appearance of separatist tendencies in the east and the west and some governors' abuse of power caused difficulties to the central government in Baghdād.

Hārūn al-Rashīd granted the succession first to his sons Muḥammad al-Amīn, ʿAbdullāh al-Maʾmūn and al-Qāsim (al-Muʾtamin). He divided the administrative districts of the state between them and was the first caliph whose three sons were all acknowledged as caliph after his death. Al-Ṭabarī reports the words of the common people: 'He cast dissension among them, and the outcome of what he did had dire consequences.' Hārūn al-Rashīd died in the city of Ṭūs in Fārs while on his way to suppress the movement of Rāfiʿ ibn al-Layth; he was succeeded by Muḥammad al-Amīn in April 809. His reign, which lasted until 813, was one of civil war, a result of the strife with his brother al-Maʾmūn. Baghdād was besieged for fourteen months, during which al-Amīn and his supporters put up a fierce resistance, fighting street to street; finally, al-Amīn was killed by the army of Ṭāhir ibn al-Ḥusayn in September 812 (Ibn Ṭayfur, 1904, pp. 52 ff.).

Although al-Maʾmūn had already proclaimed himself caliph in Khurāsān and the east in general in March 811, official acknowledgement came only in September 812, when the insignia of the caliphate were sent from Baghdād. He decided to establish himself in Marw (Merv), the centre of Khurāsān, on the advice of his *wazīr* al-Faḍl ibn Sahl, whose personality overshadowed that of the caliph. He tried to introduce Persian customs in court procedure and the state (see Plate 215), and sent his brother al-Ḥasan ibn Sahl to be governor of ʿIrāq. But ʿIrāq, as the traditional centre of the ʿAbbāsid caliphate, swiftly made clear its opposition to the new policies of al-Faḍl ibn Sahl, and the people of Baghdād remained in opposition, and in July 817 proclaimed a rival ʿAbbāsid caliphate to that of al-Maʾmūn. All this compelled al-Maʾmūn to return to ʿIrāq in 819 and to rid himself of ʿAlī al-Riḍā and the *wazīr* al-Faḍl ibn Sahl.

In the final year of his reign, al-Maʾmūn decided to make Muʿtazilism the official religious rite of the state, which it remained until the reign of al-Mutawakkil. The first ʿAbbāsid caliphs were not known to have any official preference for one rite over another, despite their leaning towards *ahl al-ḥadīth* (the followers of Prophetic tradition: the Traditionists) and their friendly relations with certain prominent scholars of *ḥadīth*. Al-Maʾmūn favoured men of learning, thinkers, philosophers and speculative theologians, and he was clearly impressed by the rational arguments of the Muʿtazilīs, who defended Islamic doctrine by the new methods of logic and debate taken over from the Greek tradition. However, the controversy aroused by the Muʿtazilīs at that time, in which they were supported by al-Maʾmūn, was the question of the created nature of the Qur'ān, which led to what is termed the *miḥna* ('ordeal, trial'), or inquisition. The Muʿtazilīs declared that the Qur'ān was created – in other words that it was neither eternal nor pre-existent – since the contrary would imply that the Qur'ān shared one of the attributes of God, namely pre-existence, which would be an infringement of *tawḥīd* (the doctrine of the oneness of God). For this reason, the Muʿtazilīs came to be known as *aṣḥāb at-tawḥīd* (the adherents of the oneness of God). The Muʿtazilīs also emphasized free will, claiming that human beings have a choice in what they do, that they are responsible for their own actions and are thus deserving of reward or punishment in the hereafter. From this they came to be called *ahl al-ʿadl* ('the people of justice'). But in reality, when the Muʿtazilīs came to power they persecuted those who opposed their views, and there followed the *miḥna* inquisition, in which suffering was inflicted on such scholars as Aḥmad ibn Ḥanbal and his followers, and Aḥmad ibn Naṣr al-Khuzāʿī. The *miḥna* produced violent reactions, which could well have led to much bloodshed, had it not been for the judiciousness and prudence of Caliph al-Mutawakkil.

Al-Maʾmūn died while on campaign against the Byzantines and was buried in Ṭarṭūs, in August 833. His heir, ʿAlī al-Riḍā, had died in 819. Shortly before his final illness, al-Maʾmūn nominated his brother al-Muʿtaṣim as heir.

The personality of Caliph al-Muʿtaṣim was totally different from that of his predecessor; he was not so much concerned with ideas, culture and the sciences as with military affairs and war. Thus the Muʿtazilī school was maintained not because the new caliph had any particular faith in it but simply because he followed his predecessor's policy and was guided by his injunction. He reorganized the army and recruited a greater number of Turks, giving them preference over other troops. He put an end to many of the disturbances which had previously troubled the state, in particular the movement of the Khurramīya under the leadership of Bābak in Āzerbaijān, the Jibāl and the Euphrates Jazīra, and the conspiracy of al-Afshīn, the powerful Turkish commander.

Another result of employing Turks in the ʿAbbāsid army and administration was the building of Sāmarrāʾ in 835 and the transfer there of the centre of the state; Sāmarrāʾ became the headquarters of the army and the government offices (see Plate 206). Perhaps the most important factor behind the transfer of the capital was the cultural divide between the urbane inhabitants of Baghdād and the rough nomadic Turkish soldiery, which led to conflict between the two groups. However, Sāmarrāʾ did not become a substitute for Baghdād, which remained the centre of culture, learning and trade, although it momentarily lost its position as capital of the ʿAbbāsid caliphate until 892.

Al-Wāthiq was acknowledged as caliph on the day of al-Muʿtaṣim's death in January 843. During his reign, a greater share of power went to some Turkish military commanders, such as Ashnās, Waṣīf, Ītākh and Bughā the Elder. The influence of the Muʿtazilīs remained strong, especially that of Aḥmad ibn Abī Du'ād, one of the two persons on whose opinion the caliph relied, the other being the *wazīr* Muḥammad ibn ʿAbdulmalik az-Zayyāt.

Al-Wāthiq did not nominate a successor to the caliphate, which left the field wide open for the military and civil bureaucracy to intervene in the choice of the new caliph. This set a dangerous precedent, which was to have dire consequences for the future of the caliphate. Al-Mutawakkil came to power with the support of certain Turkish military commanders and leading Mu'tazilīs. From the start, he tried to pursue a new policy by forming a bloc of loyal supporters who were to regulate the administration, put an end to corruption and gradually endeavour to reduce the influence of the military in politics and the administration. His hostility to the Mu'tazilīs and his severity towards the supporters of the 'Alids and protected non-Muslims (*dhimmīs*) won him the support of some religious jurists, and hence some sections of the populace. He tried to exploit this support in his confrontation with the Turkish military faction as he began to realize the danger it posed to the caliphate.

These and other measures, such as the transfer of the old Sāmarrā' units from Sāmarrā' to Damascus and then to Ja'farīya, and finally their incorporation within the newly formed army, led to resentment among the Turkish commanders. So they had him assassinated and chose his son al-Muntaṣir, who had plotted with them against his father. The reign of al-Mutawakkil was notable for the abandonment of Mu'tazilism as the official rite of the state. However, al-Mutawakkil pursued a moderate and tolerant policy in his dealings with the Mu'tazilī leaders; indeed, had he not been in power and taken steps to prevent a clash, there would have been a harsh reaction against the Mu'tazilīs responsible for the *miḥna*. The Mu'tazilīs were a cultivated group of people, who were somewhat extreme in their use of rational and logical argumentation. The caliph's action to end their influence was in response to a desire emanating from within the community, especially under Ash'arite aspirations.

Al-Mutawakkil's policies gradually contributed to the emergence of what came to be known as the rite of *ahl al-sunna wa-l-jamā'a* (the people of the *sunna* (the sayings and actions of the Prophet as a legal precedent, as transmitted in the *ḥadīth*) and of the community), which was still in the process of formation. In addition to his edict, in which he exhorted the faithful to 'command good and forbid evil', and attacked the Mu'tazilīs, he also urged *ḥadīth* scholars to disseminate the *ḥadīth* among the people and encouraged authors to write about the doctrine and the foundations of religion. So 'Alī ibn Rabbān al-Ṭabarī wrote his work *al-Dīn wa-l-dawla* ('Religion and State'), and al-Jāḥiẓ wrote his treatise *Fī l-radd 'alā l-naṣārā* ('In Reply to the Christians'). The aim of these and other writings was to publicize the virtues of Islam and to refute its opponents' arguments. However, the legal experts and leaders of *ahl al-ḥadīth*, including Aḥmad ibn Ḥanbal, were still wary of the ruler; and the 'Abbāsid caliphs did not now take sides with respect to competing rites or schools of religious law and did not compel anyone to adhere to a particular rite.

Following the assassination of al-Mutawakkil in the first military coup of the early 'Abbāsid period, the military commanders felt secure, for no one was left to threaten their interests, and their influence became predominant in the nomination and removal of caliphs and in controlling the affairs of state.

This period is characterized by the emergence in the east and west of regional political entities – an indication of the political weakness of the central government. At the same time, some of these entities played a part in the war against the Byzantines (the Ḥamdānids) or against non-Muslim Turks and Hindus (Sāmānids and Ghaznawids), and spread Islam to new regions. The political disintegration may not have been wholly pernicious but rather a reflection of the cultural diversity within the unitary civilization of the Muslim community, especially when we recall that the vitality of the 'Abbāsid caliphate had very nearly been exhausted, rendering it incapable of playing a leading role. So these new entities played a part in the spread of Islam and gave encouragement in their own courts to religious scholars, jurists, men of letters and philosophers. They produced thought, culture and science of great importance for the development of Arab Islamic civilization, which, with all its values and traditions, retained its supreme hold over society. In other words, the emergence of these political entities constituted a series of relative changes which resulted in a transformation of the political geography of the Islamic world. And yet, Islamic civilization retained a permanence and continuity which transcended the fluctuating national boundaries and the various separatist movements. Al-Andalus (Spain) broke away in the days of al-Manṣūr, followed by al-Maghrib (north-west Africa) and Ifrīqiyya (present-day Tunisia) and the Ṭāhirids in Khurāsān in the days of al-Rashīd and al-Ma'mūn; then the Ḥamdānids appeared in the Euphrates Jazīra, the Ṭūlūnids (868) and Ikhshīdids in Egypt, and the Fāṭimids in al-Maghrib and Egypt; the Zaydīs appeared in Ṭabaristān (864), the Ṣaffārids in Fārs (867), and the Sāmānids in Transoxania and Khurāsān (873); the Ibāḍī Khārijīs successfully founded an Ibāḍī imāmate of their own in 'Umān (Oman) in 750, as did the Ibāḍī and Ṣufrī Khārijīs in the Maghrib and North Africa (Bosworth, 1967; De Zambaur, 1927).

The 'Abbāsid caliphate not only faced internal struggles between political factions in the state and the army but was also opposed by other movements whose aim was to overthrow the dynasty completely; such were the risings of the Zanj, the Qarmaṭīs (Carmathians) and the Ṣaffārids.

The Zanj were African slaves who were forced to work in land reclamation in the southern parts of 'Irāq; they were joined by slaves from the neighbouring towns and villages. They worked in large bands, without regular pay, and their daily food ration was no more than a little flour, dates and gruel. Their leader, 'Alī ibn Muḥammad, was not himself a black slave, but becoming aware of their wretched circumstances he began to promise them land and wealth. He adopted a religious mantle, presenting himself as a long-awaited *mahdī*, which drew them to him, and he led them in a violent uprising in 869. At first he succeeded in gaining control of Baṣrā and the surrounding area, as well as Ahwāz and Wāsiṭ, pursuing a strategy of violence and terrorism against his opponents. He was helped also by the disaffected Arab tribes in the region. However, al-Muwaffaq, the caliphal heir, managed to mobilize the army and undertook a series of military and administrative actions which enabled him to gain victory over the Zanj rebels in 883.

The movement of the Qarmaṭīs, in the region of the Persian Gulf and western 'Irāq, had organizational and doctrinal links with the Ismā'īlīs and helped to spread discontent in the Gulf, western 'Irāq and southern parts of Syria. They were joined by Bedouin tribes in southern 'Irāq and Bahrein. From about 900, the Qarmaṭīs, led by Abū Sa'īd al-Jannābī, launched a series of attacks against the caliphal army in the regions of Hajar, Baṣrā and Kūfa, and several regions of Syria; there was great slaughter and devastation in the areas they attacked. The Qarmaṭīs reached the peak of their power after 913, when Abū Ṭāhir ibn Abī Sa'īd al-Jannābī took over the leadership of the movement after his father had been killed. He inflicted many defeats on the caliphal army, plundered numerous cities and caravans of pilgrims and traders, and committed horrible massacres. This brought about a violent reaction in Baghdād against the *wazīr* Ibn al-Furāt, who was suspected of collusion with the

Qarmaṭīs. In 929, Abū Ṭāhir attacked Mecca during the annual pilgrimage; he killed pilgrims at the Holy Mosque in Mecca and removed the sacred Black Stone and took it to Hajar. Abū Ṭāhir thus continued his attacks undeterred until his death in 943, which, however, marked the beginning of the decline of Qarmaṭī power as conflicts emerged within the movement itself. They showed a readiness to negotiate with the Baghdād government, and with the Būyids after the latter took control of Baghdād, for the purpose of dividing up profits from both land and sea trade, and this is what happened. Furthermore, the involvement of the Qarmaṭīs in the internal struggles between the various political factions within the ʿAbbāsid caliphate, especially in the Būyid period, led to the fragmentation of their power, and they suffered a number of debilitating setbacks which gradually undermined their influence.

At the end of the period of military chaos, on the eve of Būyid rule, the ʿAbbāsid caliphate had clearly entered a phase of decline; there were continual disturbances, troubles and separatist uprisings, while no one could be found to thwart Byzantine ambitions; furthermore, the economy was in decline and corruption was on the increase.

Tuzun, the leader of the Turks, who coveted the post of *amīr al-umarā'* (commander-in-chief), managed to enter Baghdād in 942 and was appointed by the caliph al-Muttaqī as commander-in-chief, in which post he remained until his death in 945. He was succeeded by his secretary Ibn Shīrzād, whose tenure lasted only three months, ending with the unopposed entry into Baghdād of Aḥmad ibn Būya (Muʿizz al-Dawla) in the same year (Ibn Khaldūn: p. 162).

The next period, in which the Būyids presided over the fate of the ʿAbbāsid caliphate, lasted from 945 to 1055. The Būyids originated from the region of Daylam, to the south of the Caspian Sea. They were a warlike people, among whom Islam of the Zaidī rite had spread towards the end of the eighth century. The Būyids ʿAlī, al-Ḥasan and Aḥmad, sons of Abū Shujāʿ Buwayh, first came to prominence as soldiers fighting in the armies of local warlords, but they took advantage of the political and economic chaos to divide up the regions of Fārs among themselves. Thus ʿAlī (ʿImād al-Dawla) became commander of Fārs, and al-Ḥasan (Rukn al-Dawla) of the Jibāl, while Aḥmad ibn Būya (Muʿizz al-Dawla), after taking control of Ahwāz, headed for ʿIrāq, and Baghdād. He entered the city in January 946 and met Caliph al-Mustakfī, who gave him and his two brothers the titles by which they became known. Muʿizz al-Dawla subdued the Ḥamdānids in the north, suppressed the activities of the Turkish army in Baghdād and dealt with the Barīdīs in Baṣrā. Muʿizz al-Dawla could not abide Caliph al-Mustakfī and deposed him less than two weeks after he entered Baghdād, replacing him with his cousin, to whom he granted the title of al-Muṭīʿ li-Llāh. Thus began what Minorsky calls the Iranian intermezzo between the period of Arab rule from the beginning of Islam and the Turkish invasion in the eleventh century.

The Būyids founded a hereditary principality at the heart of the ʿAbbāsid caliphate, and in this they were supported by an army composed mostly of Daylamīs and Turks. The caliphate thus became a purely formal institution, which the Būyids left in place simply for administrative and opportunistic reasons. All authority was wielded by the Būyid *amīr al-umarā'* (commander-in-chief). In terms of civilization and culture, the tenth century represents – as Mez says (Mez, Arabic transl., 1957) – the era of the renaissance of Islam. During this period, five caliphs reigned in succession; from al-Mustakfī bi-Llāh to al-Qā'im bi-Amr Allāh. They retained only the obligatory mention in the *khuṭba* (Friday sermon) and the title of caliph; and even some of these symbols, and a number of other signs of the caliphate, the Būyid commanders shared with the caliph.

The institution of the wazīrate had been created in the early ʿAbbāsid period as an official post with a relatively well-defined mandate and important responsibilities, although the *wazīr's* influence remained to a large extent subject to the will of the caliph during the early ʿAbbāsid period. Even so, the *wazīr*, who was chosen from the civil bureaucracy (or in Claude Cahen's phrase, 'the aristocracy of secretaries'; Cahen, 1970: p. 150), was considered to be the supreme head of the central administration. In the Būyid period, the authority of the ʿAbbāsid wazīrate vanished completely, and each caliph had a secretary (*kātib*, pl. *kuttāb* 'scribe, secretary') to look after his affairs. In contrast, the Būyid king, or commander-in-chief, had a *wazīr* who enjoyed great influence, even though the *wazīr* at this time was liable to have his property confiscated when he was dismissed.

As a result of social development and the complexity of all aspects of urban life, there arose a number of schools of law, whose purpose was to regulate the affairs of daily life. Thus there came into being the science of *fiqh* (Islamic jurisprudence), which was divided into two schools: that of *ahl al-ḥadīth* in the Ḥijāz and that of *ahl al-ra'y* (the proponents of individual judgement) in ʿIrāq. ʿAbdullāh ibn al-Muqaffaʿ may have been the first to mention the codification of legislation, which enabled information to be derived from a single source. Caliph al-Manṣūr attempted, with Mālik ibn Anas, to produce a comprehensive work on jurisprudence for the reference of jurists and judges within the system.

Connected with the development of legal institutions is the appearance of the *ḥisba* (al-Māwardī, 1966: p. 260). This was a religious–civil post; in addition to overseeing the market and the guilds, its powers included the preservation of public morality, the prevention of monopolies and counterfeit coinage, and the supervision of prices. The penetration of opposition movements into the market guilds added a further duty to the tasks of the *muḥtasib* (holder of the *ḥisba*), namely that of keeping an eye on political activities which were opposed to the state. The early ʿAbbāsids' keenness to investigate grievances, and to oversee this institution directly, was rooted in a notion which they promoted actively, namely that they had come in order to purvey justice and to act in accordance with the Qur'ān and *sunna*. The judge Abū Yūsuf (Abū Yūsuf, 1932: pp. 111–112) insisted on the need for the caliph himself to preside in person over the investigation of grievances and thus ensure that awareness of his concern reached the provinces, in order that evil-doers should take fright and no longer dare to commit their evil deeds.

While the post of chief justice (*qāḍī l-quḍāh*) had been established in the days of the early ʿAbbāsids, the Būyid period in the tenth century saw the emergence of a new post called *aqḍā l-quḍāh* (supreme justice) in view of the proliferation of judges with the title *qāḍī l-quḍāh* in the same town. Abū l-Ḥasan al-Māwardī, author of *al-Aḥkām al-sulṭānīya* ('The Imperial Statutes'), was the first to receive this title, in 1037, since he was on excellent terms with the Būyid commanders. The post of judge was among those which were monopolized by certain well-known families and so became a quasi-hereditary office in the ninth and tenth centuries. One of these families was that of Abū l-Shawārib, from which eight judges were appointed in Baghdād and sixteen in other regions; another was the family of Banū Abī Burda. Despite what has been said about the partisan policies of the Būyids, the judges at this time were extremely varied in their personal interpretations and rulings; they included Mu'tazilīs, Ẓāhirīs and Shāfi'īs. The four judges of Baghdād in the reign of 'Aḍud al-Dawla were Mu'tazilīs, while the chief justice was a Ẓāhirī. Judges of whatever rank or school of law continued to view their office as a religious one, closely linked to the institution of the caliphate in Baghdād, and to consider that one of their tasks was to uphold the faith in the face of radical or extremist currents such as the Ismā'īlīs, the Bāṭinīs, the atheists and the *zindīqs* (Ibn al-Jawzī, 1938: Vol. 7, pp. 226, 264; Kabir, 1959).

At the beginning of the 'Abbāsid era, the military institution underwent a significant change when for the first time in the history of the Islamic state there came into being what might be called a professional standing army in which people from Khurāsān, both Arabs and *mawālī*, were enrolled on an individual rather than a tribal basis. They were registered in the military office according to the names of their towns and villages, not of their tribes, and they were bound by ties of loyalty to the state, which provided their training, supplies and equipment. As time passed, the 'Abbāsids came to recognize the urgent need for new blood in the army and launched a concerted drive to recruit mercenaries, in particular Turks and other inhabitants of the Islamic east.

When the Būyids gained control of Baghdād, it was the army commanders who wielded effective power. At the beginning of their rule, the Būyids were unable to reorganize the army or ensure the support of an army composed of Daylamīs, to whom the Būyids belonged. This was because the Daylamīs themselves, as mercenaries, were accustomed to giving their allegiance to a commander who gave them what they wanted. So they would go from one commander to another, depending on what advantages they could gain. This situation gradually led the Būyids to rely more on the Turks as an effective force with which to keep down the Daylamīs when they rebelled.

Social and economic conditions

The 'Abbāsid revolution has been described as a 'bourgeois revolution' because it reflected the aspirations of the middle class, which had begun to appear in the urban centres, gradually acquiring wealth and influence. Viewed in a social context, the 'Abbāsid revolution was the expression of a crisis in society which had its roots in the social, economic and political circumstances at the end of the Umayyad era. The revolution was a response to those circumstances and gave added impetus to factors promoting the spread of urban phenomena in society.

Baghdād, the capital of the new dynasty, built by al-Manṣūr soon after the start of the 'Abbāsid era, was a perfect illustration of these new tendencies in society. In his choice of site, the founding caliph had given due consideration to those factors which might contribute to Baghdād's development as an urban centre, such as easy communications, good soil and climate, abundant water, and the site's potential for development as a centre of trade. Stability and coexistence within a well-defined space such as Baghdād led, for reasons of mutual interest, to greater mingling of the various populations, and this in turn gradually weakened tribal loyalties and strengthened the geographically based urban spirit.

From the outset, Islam had been favourable to the sedentary way of life: urban settlement was encouraged, and major new cities were built. The Arabs who settled in these cities and urban areas found new sources of livelihood in agriculture, trade and crafts. Meanwhile, the various schools of law and Islamic groups encouraged the study of *sharī'a* (Islamic law) and science. The struggle between tribal traditions and new Islamic concepts intensified, but the process of social change continued apace.

First the 'Abbāsid revolution and later the established state urged a more global view of Islam. The first 'Abbāsids endeavoured to enlarge the basis of their support to include a greater proportion of *mawālī* and other groups, in addition to Arabs. However, at the beginning of the 'Abbāsid era, the Arabs were still the most dominant group in society. The importance of the Arabs as a fighting force was clear, and they were the major factor behind the success of the 'Abbāsids, whose caliphs were Arabs and proud of their heritage; in their court, they encouraged Arab traditions and customs and gave precedence to the Banū Hāshim and consulted them in important matters. Arabs formed the majority of the companions of the caliph, who numbered as many as 700 in the reign of al-Manṣūr, and in al-Mahdī's reign 500.

The second group in society were the *mawālī*, who were not a uniform social group some were not badly off. They had begun to prosper towards the end of the Umayyad era and in the early 'Abbāsid era, since they were engaged in trade and crafts, owned land and enjoyed the protection of the dynasty or the clans loyal to it. The *mawālī* flocked to the large cities and their numbers increased, as they sought a new position in the social structure. Some of them became scholars, specializing in *ḥadīth*, jurisprudence and similar studies, naturally learning from Arab scholars, who were foremost in the field. In addition, the development of the administrative machinery gave rise to a need for employees to work in the government offices. The *mawālī* formed the majority of the secretaries in the central and regional government offices both before and after these shifted to using Arabic.

The emergence of the *mawālī* in the 'Abbāsid era, and the fact that they played a more prominent role than previously, was due solely to the time factor and historical evolution. The 'Abbāsids stressed the values of urban life and gave impetus to the process of collaboration and intermixture between the numerous social groups, including the *mawālī*. This contributed to the growth of these groups and the appearance of new skills in many different areas of life. All this gave rise to a new standard for social classification which rejected the idea of race (blood descent) and replaced it with the criteria of culture, and allegiance to Islam and its principles (Ibn Khaldūn: Vol. 3, p. 507).

The third group in society was the *dhimmīs*: non-Muslims belonging to one of the religious communities, who had a recognized and tolerated but subordinate status in the Islamic polity, and who, in return for paying the *jizya* (poll tax on non-Muslims), enjoyed protection, comprising the Jews, Christians, Sabians and Magians. Like the *mawālī*, the *dhimmīs* engaged in crafts, trades and manufacture; during the 'Abbāsid period they also included *wazīrs*, physicians, financial inspectors, translators and religious scholars. Suspicions that *dhimmīs* spread scepticism about Islamic beliefs or that some of them were in league with the Byzantines were taken by some of the early 'Abbāsid caliphs to justify hard measures against the *dhimmīs*. However, the measures they adopted were largely formal, as shown by the fact that *dhimmīs* continued to be employed in the administration and at court, and to play an active part in public life. The remarks of al-Jāḥiẓ (d. 869), the famous author of the 'Abbāsid era, attest the intermixing between *dhimmīs* and Muslims and the remarkable social and economic level that the *dhimmīs* had attained. Each community had a leader who was responsible for them before the state and appointed by the caliph's decree; special ceremonies were held for each of these dignitaries on his assumption of office. The head of the Christians was called the *Jāthalīq* (Catholicos) and the head of the Jews *Ra's al-Jālūt*, the 'Head of the *Gālūth* (diaspora)'. They were subject to the *jizya*, which they paid in return for protection and a guarantee of safety and security. Exemptions were granted to children, women, the old and infirm, monks, and sick persons unable to work.

The Magians were included with the *dhimmīs* from a very early date in the Islamic state and were treated as *ahl al-kitāb*, 'People of the Book', and thus paid the *jizya*. As to Magians (followers of Zoroaster), Christensen reckons that the influence of Zoroastrianism continued in many parts of Fārs, though their ranks continued to thin through conversion to Islam. As for the Sabaeans, it seems, from a conversation between al-Ma'mūn and a group of Sabaean notables, that they had their own independent religious identity and beliefs, which differed from those of the other *dhimmīs*. By origin they were star worshippers and called themselves Ḥarrānīs. However, their small numbers, the secret nature of their beliefs and their deliberate isolation meant that their social impact was slight. They were prominent as translators in the *Bayt al-Ḥikma* (the House of Wisdom) in Baghdād, and as astronomers, goldsmiths and metal engravers; and some of them achieved important administrative positions at that time.

The fourth social group was that of the slaves (al-Jāḥiẓ, *Risāla fīl-qiyān*). Slavery had been known to various societies long before Islam and was a manifestation of acute social disparities. Islam introduced a number of mitigations to the system of slavery and prescribed certain restrictions which alleviated the suffering of slaves and encouraged their manumission, which led to the contraction of this class as time passed. One source of slaves in Arab Islamic society was prisoners of war, who were counted as booty; the second source was through purchase. Furthermore, some feudal lords used to offer slaves in partial payment of the annual tax imposed on them, or as a gift to the caliph or governor. The slaves brought into eastern Islamic territories were mainly of two kinds: those drawn from the coasts of East Africa and those of Byzantine, Slav or Turkish origin. The slave trade prospered as a result of conquests and growth of trade. In Islamic society, slaves were freed on various grounds: religious, humanitarian, personal and economic; but the relationship between the former slave and master remained, and was regulated by certain obligations connected with inheritance and the payment of blood money. At the official level, the state concerned itself with the condition of slaves, and the supervision of slave markets was one of the responsibilities of the *muḥtasib*. The slaves themselves varied in status, education and occupation. Some won the confidence of their masters and became their trade agents, helped to administer their various businesses, or worked as house servants, especially those who had been made eunuchs. Some attained high rank in the army, politics or the administration. On the other hand, the Zanj, who were forced to work in the reclamation of marshlands in the south of 'Irāq (the *baṭīḥa*), suffered extreme hardships, which led them to revolt, around the mid-ninth century; as we have seen, their revolt lasted fifteen years before being crushed.

The individual in Islamic society was free to choose the profession or craft he wished to exercise; our sources (al-Dūrī: 1959, p. 154) mention many professions in which craftsmen moved gradually up the scale from apprentice to journeyman to master. The *Ikhwān al-Ṣafā'* (Brethren of Purity) compiled a classification of occupations, preferring some to others. The prestige of some crafts, such as goldsmithing and perfumery, derived from the materials used in them; the importance of others, such as weaving, ploughing and building, stemmed from people's need for them; yet others, such as porters and menial workers, offered general services; some, such as musicians, painters, artists and the like, were highly respected in themselves for their skill or art. The practitioners of such occupations were often organized in guilds. Religious–political movements tried to attract and make use of the more active groups of master craftsmen. The state thus had to increase its vigilance over the guilds in the market through the offices of the *muḥtasib* and the police.

Just as the traditional view of merchants changed, so it changed towards crafts, which had previously been looked down upon; people came to respect them and consider them honourable (al-Jāḥiẓ, *Kitāb al-bukhalā'*, p. 51). Many traditionists and jurists of that time were engaged in various professions and crafts, which were no longer the preserve of the *mawālī* and *dhimmīs*; Arabs worked in them as well.

'Abbāsid society was an urban one, whose cities were centres of trade and manufacturing. Hence the markets in Islamic cities were the natural location for the activities of merchants and craftspeople. It seems that the tendency for the practitioners of each craft to congregate in a single market, which began in the middle of the seventh century, reached its peak in the markets of Baghdād. Caliph al-Manṣūr realized the importance of the physical site and its potential for commercial prosperity when Baghdād became capital of the new state. From its founding in 762, large numbers of labourers, manufacturers, craftspeople and merchants moved there, which gave it its international character as a 'metropolis' and influenced the development of the city's urban characteristics. This is clear from the words of al-Khaṭīb al-Baghdādī (al-Khaṭīb al-Baghdādī: Vol. 1, p. 119):

> Baghdād was unrivalled all the world over for its magnificence and splendour, the number of its scholars and great men, the distinction of its elite and common people . . . the number of its palaces, houses, roads, streets, shops, markets, lanes, alleys, mosques, baths, architectural styles [*ṭuruz*] and *khāns* [caravanserais]; for its excellent air, its sweet water, its cool shade . . . for the great number of its citizens, and the numerous buildings and people in the days of al-Rashīd.

Al-Manṣūr moved the markets out of the city to al-Arbāḍ in 774 for reasons of security, and allotted separate rows and buildings to each guild. The people of each trade had recognized streets for their houses and shops, and no corporation or trade mingled with another.

Islam was concerned with the position of the family within society and was anxious to ensure its cohesiveness. Islam also respected women and made provision for women as individuals with certain rights in law. Their status was thus protected throughout the seventh century and a large part of the eighth century. However, since concubinage continued to be permitted, the large numbers of slave girls and the increase in wealth and luxury all had an adverse effect on the position of women; free women were isolated and kept secluded from society. Jealousy was one reason for the employment of eunuchs in households, and this led to increased trade in eunuchs, who were described by contemporary authors such as al-Jāḥiẓ and Abū Hayyān al-Tawḥīdī. Even so, a number of women achieved prominence in religion, literature and political life, in works of charity and piety, in building and in public service, both at the beginning of the 'Abbāsid era and in later periods. In Baghdād and other cities, we find women who were learned *ḥadīth* scholars, under whom great men *ḥadīth* scholars studied. Such women included Shahda al-Ibarī, Tajannī al-Wahbaniyya and Zaynab al-Sha'riyya, and many others in the fields of poetry, literature, politics, music and singing (al-Khaṭīb al-Baghdādī: Vol. 14, pp. 430–447).

Al-Ya'qūbī, in his book *Mushākalat al-nās li-zamānihim* ('The Resemblance of People to their Time'), says that people are more in tune with their generation than they are with their own parents, and that people follow the religion of their rulers; this claim is borne out by the various manifestations of public life in this period. New traditions and social etiquette were introduced, some adopted first by the court and the upper echelons of society, then by the rest of the people. This change, however, did not take place all at once, but gradually. By the time of al-Rashīd, the acquisition of singing girls and slave girls, sessions of singing and music, wine drinking and openly improper poetry, all became widespread, so that al-Rashīd's time was known as the 'age of wedding festivities'. Al-Ya'qūbī relates how Caliph al-Amīn's addiction to promoting young court slave boys (*ghilmān)* led to Umm Ja'far taking pretty, shapely slave girls and dressing them like male youths. The rich then began taking such girls with close-cropped hair and called them *al-ghulamiyyāt* (female youths).

The high standard of living among the elite and the wealthy social groups attached to them prompted an interest in food and the introduction of new types of food, which were described in the numerous cookery books written in this period and later, some of which are mentioned in *al-Fihrist* ('The Index') of Ibn al-Nadīm (Ibn al-Nadīm: p. 424). Dishes were of numerous sorts, some popular and ordinary, others rare and costly. There was a great variety of fruit, sweetmeats and appetizers.

The urban trend in Islam grew and developed during the 'Abbāsid period. The state endeavoured to provide public services to society, and the jurist Abū Ḥanīfa, who lived at the beginning of this period, considered that the poor were all equally deserving of the maximum alms entitlement, which was less than 200 *dirhams* or 20 *dīnārs* in his time. Al-Māwardī, writing at the end of the period under consideration (eleventh century), mentioned three classes of the poor: (1) the man working in the market and earning a living, but whose income was insufficient, whom one *dīnār* might raise from wretched poverty to a better level; (2) the poor man who needed alms because of incapacity or illness or the large size of his family, who should receive more alms than the first; and (3) the poor workman who could earn enough for himself and his family, and should therefore receive no alms. The state was thus expected to intervene to provide public services and vital necessities for the common people, and especially the poor, by various means, including *mabarrāt* (charitable contributions to the needy and the weak) and *jirāyāt* (daily rations). In al-Manṣūr's reign, a special official was appointed to distribute daily rations to the blind, orphans and old women; in the reign of al-Mahdī this was extended to lepers and those in prison. 'When [al-Mahdī] rode out, large sacks of money were carried with him, and with his own hand he bestowed gifts on whoever asked for something; and other people imitated him.' Al-Rashīd provided manifold services and gifts to the people and was famed for building halting places/rainwater cisterns on the road to Mecca, Medina, Minā and 'Arafāt; he built accommodation for his frontier troops. Zubayda is famous for supplying many public services, and providing halting places/rainwater cisterns, irrigation works and places for ritual ablution around the Great Mosque; she had fountains and irrigation works built at 'Arafāt and Minā and wells dug on the road to Mecca, setting aside estates as endowments. She gave money for hospitals and set aside, for the frontier lands and the poor, estates with a revenue of 100,000 *dīnārs*. Al-Manṣūr enlarged the Great Mosque, a project continued by his son al-Mahdī, in 776 and 780. The state built prisons, roads and bridges and protected them from the depredations of thieves and highway robbers. It is related that the *wazīr* 'Alī ibn 'Isa Ālī al-Jarrāḥ wrote to the physician Sinān ibn Thābit, in a year which saw much sickness:

> May God prolong your life, I have been thinking about those in prison, for as they are so numerous and live in such harsh conditions they are liable to suffer from sicknesses . . . so, may God enable you, you should appoint physicians to visit them every day, with drugs and potions . . . and treat any sick men and alleviate their illnesses.

Certain wealthy men and great men of the state also contributed to the provision of these services.

While luxury and entertainment were typical of the 'Abbāsid age, opposite phenomena also emerged in society: asceticism and seclusion. These ascetics and pious recluses displayed extreme devotion and aloofness from the normal activities of life. This movement was a form of spiritual or social reaction against class disparities and social evils as well as the frivolity, shamelessness, luxury and political anarchy which followed the era of strength and prosperity at the beginning of the 'Abbāsid age. Massignon (1922) says that the inclination to asceticism and mysticism usually arises from an internal agitation which seizes the soul and leads people to rebel against social injustices. This is not only in opposition to others but starts as a struggle with the self. Sufyān al-Thawrī (d. 777) wrote advising one of his friends: 'Seek obscurity . . . For at one time, when people met they used to benefit from one another; but today that has gone, and salvation lies in avoiding them' (Mez, Arabic trans.: Vol. 2, p. 28).

Our information on social phenomena increases as we move on, so that we know much more about the tenth century than about the beginning of the 'Abbāsid age. It is to be expected that tangible social changes should have occurred when the Būyids came to preside over the fate of the 'Abbāsid caliphate during the tenth century and the first half of the eleventh century. However, the values of the new Arab Islamic civilization appear to have had a considerable impact on society: they became the predominant elements thereof and worked as a factor for unity and homogeneity among the inhabitants, with all their variety of customs, traditions, cultures, languages and religions. The regions subject to Būyid rule comprised numerous peoples, including Arabs, Persians, Turks, Daylamīs, Kurds and Zuṭṭs (gypsies). This diversity of peoples was more apparent in the cities than in the countryside. Despite what has been said of the Būyid commanders' partiality to the Zaydī rite, or sometimes the Imāmī rite, some of them, such as 'Aḍud al-Dawla, were favourable to the Mu'tazilīs. There is no indication that they understood these rites, or even that their Islam was of a very rigorous sort. This is strongly suggested by the fact that the religious allegiances of the people remained virtually unchanged from what they had been at the beginning of the 'Abbāsid era. The Ḥanafī, Shāfi'ī and Ẓāhirī rites were still predominant within the Būyid sphere of influence, although there were here and there centres of Zaydīsm, Mu'tazilism, Imāmism and Ismā'īlism. No fierce rivalry occurred between these rites until the end of the tenth century and again in the eleventh century (Munaimina, 1987).

Adam Mez (Arabic trans.: Vol. 2, p. 268) notes that it was the custom of the caliphs, commanders and kings to found small resort towns, which beginning in the mid-ninth century sprang up in both the east and the west of the Islamic Empire. Al-Hāshimīya was built beside Kūfa and al-Ruṣāfa beside Baghdād, both in the early 'Abbāsid era; later, al-Ja'farīya was built near Sāmarrā', al-Qaṭā'i' beside Fusṭāṭ, Raqqāda near Qayrawān, and Kurd Fanā-Khusrau beside Shīrāz in 'Aḍud al-Dawla's reign, for Fārs was then the most prosperous region. In 'Irāq, 'Aḍud al-Dawla' restored Baghdād after it had been badly damaged in insurrections and sectarian disturbances. Al-Rūdhrāwarī says: 'he sought the good of Baghdād . . . he worked to revive its prosperity, he built the hospital, and gave it great endowments, and sent there various types of equipment and medicine from all over; traces of these achievements can still be seen today' (Al-Rudhrawārī, 1961: Vol. 3, pp. 68–69).

The Arabs' transition from a simple nomadic existence to complex urban life, and progress in all areas of civilization, led to greater attention being devoted to economic matters such as agriculture, trade and manufacture. At the beginning of the 'Abbāsid era, the state endeavoured to foster the budding urbanization and economic prosperity. The strength of the trend may be gathered from a statement attributed to Caliph al-Mu'taṣim: 'In development there are praiseworthy concerns, the first of which is to cultivate land, for on it all people depend, it yields the land tax, money is plentiful, and cattle live on it; prices are low, there is much profit, and income expands.'

The varied climate, abundance of water, geographical location and the provision of security were essential factors in the growth of agriculture and the variety of crops in the eastern Islamic regions at this time. The clearest indication of this comes from the land tax registers, which, despite their small number, amply demonstrate the agricultural prosperity of the provinces. Indeed, agriculture was the cornerstone of the economy: agricultural lands expanded around the cities and in the countryside, and in many parts of the empire there was double cropping.

The systems of land tenure and exploitation were always important matters for the middle layers of society, for land remained the chief means of production despite the flourishing of crafts, manufacturing and trade in the 'Abbāsid era. To begin with, one should note the diversity of systems of land tenure and cultivation at this time. The early 'Abbāsid caliphs were aware of the excesses that had occurred in the system of land tenure and the rate of taxation during the Umayyad period, so they endeavoured to develop agriculture and encourage the wealthy to acquire land and invest their own money in it. The position of jurists regarding these developments, in general, was to try to reconcile *sharī'a* with the existing circumstances; so their position evolved according to the changes in the agricultural system, though some rejected the 'excesses', which in their view were not in accordance with *sharī'a*.

When the state began to decline, from the late ninth century, the caliphs were compelled by political circumstances to appoint leaders in the regions and grant them financial powers in the supervision and taxing of agricultural land. The method of *ḍamān* (tax farming) spread as a method of exploiting land and subsequently developed into what is known as 'administrative *iqṭā'*', whereby victorious commanders gained absolute control of the lands under them. In this transitional stage, there emerged within the framework of a decentralized state a type of grant which was administered by military or civil governors, and which Shaban therefore calls an 'administrative military grant'. Lambton considers that this was a development which was intermediate between the *ḍamān* (tax farm) and the Būyid military grant. Cahen believes that it was a system of land tenure which developed from the *ḍamān* grant; whereas al-Dūrī considers that various types of land grant were current in this period, before the Būyid military grant assumed its definitive form. Other types of land tenure remained as they had been in the time of the early 'Abbāsids, allowing for variation in some of the titles. The caliphal estates were called 'imperial estates' (*ḍiyā' sulṭānīya*), and a clear distinction was made between *iqṭā' al-tamlīk* (grants of appropriation), in which the *iqṭā'* holder owned the land outright and could bequeath it, and *iqṭā' al-waẓīfa* (grants of office), which were not hereditary and, whether military or civil, could be annulled by the caliph. When a *wazīr*, leader or commander assumed office, he received grants of *iqṭā'* land, which were recovered from him after his removal and handed over to his successor. *Waqf* lands continued to be administered by the *qāḍī*, although the *wazīr* 'Alī ibn 'Īsā Āl al-Jarrāḥ created a special government office called *dīwān al-birr* (the office of pious works), the function of which was to administer *waqf* lands.

In the Būyid period, there was a definite shift in the system of land tenure. The Būyids considered the land seized by them as their property, as booty won by might. When they found themselves unable to pay the army's stipends they had recourse to the military grant system, which led to the decline of agriculture and consequently to a deficit in treasury revenues. From the early tenth century, there was a monetary crisis which the state did its best to cope with, but the crisis grew worse with the coming of the Būyids because of their extravagance and poor administration, and the great number of disturbances and conflicts at that time. Last but not least was their constant readiness to yield to all the financial demands of the army. The Būyids proceeded to introduce a military land grants system: they granted lands to military leaders as substitute for pay, and gave whole regions to the troops, who could then extract their pay from the revenue of the land, so in the course of time they gained ownership of the land, through protection or other methods. Military grants thus increased in the time of 'Aḍud al-Dawla, who gave the army grants from *waqf* lands and seized imperial estates to give to Būyid commanders. AD 945 was a decisive turning point, when land grants became mainly military and such military land grants began to predominate over other types of land tenure.

Mineral resources were plentiful in many regions of the east. Mez tells us that the east produced silver and the west gold; the gold mines were situated in Upper Egypt and the Sūdān, while the largest silver mines were in the Hindū Kush and especially in the Panjshū Valley, north-east of Kabul.

Pitch, petroleum and salt were extracted from the Earth and were considered almost as important as water. Pitch was used for coating bath-houses, the walls of houses and boats, and for waterproofing generally; in Khāniqīn and Bākū, there were large oil wells, which were very profitable. Our sources indicate that crude oil existed in numerous regions of Fārs, 'Irāq, Central Asia, the Arabian peninsula, Egypt and Āzerbaijān. The first reference to its use in war is from 752, when al-Maqdisī said of Fārs: 'Its earth is full of minerals.' These included iron, lead, silver, mercury, sulphur, petroleum and salt. Petroleum bubbled up out of the earth in Dārābjird in Fārs. In Kirmān and Khurāsān, there were also iron mines, and al-Tha'ālibī tells us that among the best-known precious stones in the tenth century were turquoise from Nīshāpūr, pearls from 'Umān (Oman), chrysolite from Egypt and carnelian from Yemen.

In view of the abundance of raw materials of agricultural, animal and mineral origin, and the great demand engendered by the high standard of living, the Islamic regions in the east were actively engaged in numerous types of manufacturing, especially textiles, which reached a high level of refinement and development in this period, especially in Fārs, Khurāsān and Egypt. Types of woven fabric varied to meet the demand for clothing, curtains, carpets, rugs, coverings, cushions and so on. The manufacture of dyes was closely connected with textiles; the colours used were extracted from plants, and sometimes minerals.

The manufacture of scents such as rose water and of soap was the speciality of large cities like Baghdād and the cities of Fārs, which were noted for the extraction of essences from plants and seeds. In Baghdād, there was a special market for scents, and Kūfa was known for its gillyflower oil. The city of Jūr (Gūr, Fairūzābād) was famous for the manufacture of rose water of such abundance and quality that it came to be known as *jūrī* rose water.

Paper (*kāghad*) was the new material used in writing, instead of *qirṭās* made from parchment and papyrus. It had begun to be used at the beginning of the 'Abbāsid era, and its use spread in the first half of the ninth century; manufacturing techniques progressed and the number of paper factories in Baghdād increased. This well-known 'Baghdādī' paper was used by the drafters of official documents in government offices, and by booksellers and calligraphers in copying the Qur'ān and other books. In Baghdād, there were also shops for the sale of paper. This period thus constituted an important turning point in the manufacture of paper, which spread to many lands. The various types of Samarkand paper made obsolete the old-style Egyptian *qirṭās*, as al-Tha'ālibī tells us (Shaban, 1971–1976, Arabic trans.: Vol. 2, pp. 89 ff.). In Fārs, black ink was made for writing, although it was of a lower quality than Chinese ink (Ibn Ḥawqal, p. 262) (see Plate 108).

In addition, there were other crafts, such as the manufacture of arms sustaining the 'weapons market' in Baghdād; smithery for the manufacture of tools, scales and engravings; leather working; preservation of dried fruit; and wine production from grapes. The wine shops were mostly within or near monasteries, which were surrounded by vineyards. The flourishing long-distance trade of the tenth century is described by Mez as 'one of the splendours of Islam . . . Muslim traders occupied the first rank in international trade' (Mez, Arabic trans.: Vol. 2, p. 271). From a commercial angle, the ninth and tenth centuries constituted an important turning point in the trend towards luxury and opulence in Arab society. Baghdād and Alexandria set the prices of luxury goods throughout the world. A number of factors contributed to the development and prosperity of trade during the 'Abbāsid era, especially in the tenth century and later. Foremost was perhaps the favourable attitude of Islam towards trade, and the increased demand of the new urban society for both basic necessities and luxury goods. Second, there was the geographical location of the Islamic east, which enabled it to command the routes of international trade between the East and the Mediterranean. And finally, there was the relative security and prosperity enjoyed by the Arab Islamic world, in which some part was undoubtedly played by the concern of the state to patrol and maintain roads, ensure security for caravans, deal with highway robbers, and prevent market fraud through the *muḥtasib*.

Intellectual life

An intellectual movement began, broadly speaking, with the dawn of Islam. By the time the 'Abbāsids came to power, the formative stage of this movement had given way to a period of consolidation, and by the tenth century it was fully mature and flourishing. Many factors contributed to this intellectual awakening, including encouragement by the state, personified by the 'Abbāsid caliphs and various high officials, of scholars and men of letters. The emergence of different schools of jurisprudence, scholastic theology and philosophy, the rivalry between various Islamic groups, the variety of social and religious structures, which included both Muslims and *dhimmīs*, all contributed to the richness of intellectual endeavour from the very outset of the 'Abbāsid era. The intellectual awakening, which reached its peak in the tenth century and later, can legitimately be attributed to the high cultural level reached by Islamic society in various fields, the atmosphere of relative security and freedom, and, last but not least, the openness to other cultures and ideas. The universal nature of Islam encouraged cultural and intellectual cross-fertilization and interaction in order to ingest what was deemed useful in other civilizations.

Much was written in the early 'Abbāsid era in both the traditional and rational sciences, or sciences of the ancients. The *Bayt al-Ḥikma* played a prominent part in translating Greek work into Arabic; al-Manṣūr was 'the first caliph to have ancient books translated. In his day, Muḥammad ibn Isḥāq (al-Manṣūr) wrote *Kitāb al-Maghāzī* ('The Book of the Prophet's Military Campaigns'). Abū Ja'far studied science and narrated *ḥadīth*, and in his days knowledge was of a high level' (al-Ya'qūbī: p. 54).

There was no deliberate division of work or activities in society, and there may be some exaggeration in the hypothesis put forward by some historians (Wellhausen, 1902; Van Vloten, 1894) that there was social, economic and political discrimination against the *mawālī* in the Umayyad period. Certainly, under the 'Abbāsids, the situation was different: there is little reason to be astonished by Ibn Khaldūn's remark that 'most of the people of learning in Islam were non-Arabs' (Ibn Khaldūn: p. 173). The Arabs were naturally mainly occupied with politics, government and war in the very early days of Islam, while the role of the *mawālī* was bound to emerge gradually in numerous spheres, including learning and culture. It was the pioneering Arabs who taught the *mawālī* and encouraged them to play a part in the new Islamic society. According to one account, 'when the first [Arab] experts died, jurisprudence in all countries became the preserve of the *mawālī*' (Yāqūt al-Ḥamawī, article on Khurāsān).

Sa'īd ibn al-Musayyab al-Qurashī was the jurist of Medina before Zayd ibn Aslam and others appeared there; Sa'īd ibn

Jubayr, the jurist of Kūfa, learned from ʿAbdullāh ibn ʿAbbās, and al-Ḥasan al-Baṣrī from ʿImrān ibn Ḥaṣīn and al-Nuʿmān ibn Bashīr; Muḥammad ibn Sīrīn learned from Abū Hurayra, ʿAbdullāh ibn ʿUmar and Anas ibn Mālik; these *mawālī* scholars duly learned from Arab teachers. All of Baṣrā came out to accompany the *maulā* al-Ḥasan al-Baṣrī to his final resting place, and Aḥmad ibn Ḥanbal said of the *maulā* Saʿīd ibn Jubayr, 'There is thus no one in the whole world who could not benefit from his knowledge.' There is little justification for Ibn Khaldūn's suggestion that society in the first Islamic centuries was a Bedouin society, and that learning was therefore the province of the *mawālī*, because the Arabs despised them and barred them from becoming involved in matters of state.

At the beginning of the ʿAbbāsid age, partly as a result of vigorous translation activity, there arose the science of *kalām* (scholastic theology), which relied upon logic, argumentation and debate. Public meetings under the Barmakids were full of scholars and literary men of many different schools, so that Caliph al-Rashīd was compelled to prevent debate and discussion in the mosques and streets. But Caliph al-Maʾmūn, who was sympathetic to the Muʿtazilī rite, encouraged discussion and organized debating sessions among the scholars. Among the most famous scholars of Islamic theology (*kalām*) at this time were Wāṣil ibn ʿAṭāʾ, ʿAmr ibn ʿUbayd, al-ʿAllāf and al-Naẓẓām.

This period saw the emergence of a sizable elite of scholars in various branches of knowledge. Al-Khalīl ibn Aḥmad al-Farāhīdī was the first to codify the rules of grammar, the first to compile a dictionary, called *Kitāb al-ʿayn* ('The Book of the Source'), and the first to write on prosody. Sībawaih was an outstanding grammarian, and ʿAbdullāh ibn al-Muqaffaʿ was well known for his prose and his translation from Pahlavi (Old Persian) into Arabic. He was followed by Ibn Qutayba al-Dīnawarī and al-Jāḥiẓ, who were among the most productive authors of the period. Some scholars, such as Yaḥyā ibn al-Ḥārith al-Dhimārī (d. 762) and Hamza ibn Ḥabīb al-Zayyāt (d. 772), specialized in the details concerning alternative readings of the Qurʾān. Hārūn ibn Mūsā al-Baṣrī (d. *c.* 786) was the first to subject the readings to critical scrutiny, and specialists in *tafsīr* began to collect and record all that had been passed down to them, without checking its accuracy: one such specialist was Muqātil ibn Sulaymān al-Azdī (d. 767).

The Muʿtazilīs attempted to interpret the Qurʾān on a rational basis. One of the first of these was Abū Bakr al-Aṣamm (d. 854). Arabic scholars such as al-Farrāʾ (d. 822) wrote works elucidating the more obscure verses of the Qurʾān, usually entitled 'the Meanings of the Qurʾān'. Similarly, jurists of this period wrote books which they called 'Qurʾānic Precepts'. Al-Kisāʾī, al-Aṣmaʿī, Abū ʿUbayda and Khalaf the grammarian, were interested in the language and its rules and literature. Al-Mufaḍḍal al-Ḍabbī presented his *Mufaḍḍalīyāt* ('Al-Mufaḍḍal's Anthology') to Caliph al-Mahdī (Rosenthal, pp. 108 ff.).

Muslims were interested in *ḥadīth*, since this was one of the sources of legislation. In the ninth century, the two prominent writers on this subject were Muḥammad ibn Ismāʿīl al-Bukhārī (d. 869) and Muslim ibn al-Ḥajjāj al-Qushayirī (d. 874), both authors of works entitled *al-Ṣaḥīḥ* ('The Authentic'), the most famous books on *sunna*. The science of jurisprudence emerged at this time and crystallized into two schools: *ahl al-ḥadīth* in the Ḥijāz and *ahl al-raʾy* in ʿIrāq. Prominent jurists included Mālik ibn Anas in Medina, Abū Ḥanīfa al-Nuʿmān in Kūfa, and later Muḥammad ibn Idrīs al-Shāfiʿī, Aḥmad ibn Ḥanbal and Jaʿfar al-Ṣādiq. These men wrote a number of works recording their rulings.

An innovative trend in poetry appeared in the early ʿAbbāsid period, Abū Nuwās being the most famous of such poets. Poetry had many aims and themes: al-Buḥturī was notable for his admirable descriptions, Abū Tammām al-Ṭāʾī for his philosophical musings, Ibn al-Rumī for the profundity of his imagery, and Bashshār ibn Burd for the variety of his themes and the accuracy of his descriptions. Each legal school or sect had its own poets, who wrote poetry in order to propagate the views of the school or sect. In this way, a variety of poets emerged whose verses could be political, sectarian or ascetic, or which dealt with themes of love or opulence.

History in Islam had its roots in the *ḥadīth* of the Prophet. Just as there were two schools of jurisprudence, so there were two schools of history, representing two distinct tendencies: the Islamic tendency (traditionalists), centred on Medina in the Ḥijāz, and the tribal tendency (genealogical), based in Kūfa and Baṣrā in ʿIrāq. The early historians, who were also *ḥadīth* scholars, were influenced by the *ḥadīth* scholars' method of criticism of both the text and the chain of transmission of the narrative. They were interested in the Prophet's military campaigns and his biography, a discipline which was derived from the science of *ḥadīth* and which focused on the entire lifetime of the Prophet. The first historical studies at the beginning of the ʿAbbāsid age were undertaken by a group of writers, including Mūsā ibn ʿUqba (d. 758), Muʿammar ibn Rāshid (d. 767), Muḥammad ibn Isḥāq (d. 767) and ʿAbdulmalik ibn Hishām (d. 813). Ibn Isḥāq, author of *al-Sīra* ('Biography of the Prophet'), and after him Muḥammad ibn ʿUmar al-Wāqidī, author of *al-Maghāzī* ('The Prophet's Military Campaigns') (d. 822) and Muḥammad ibn Saʿd (d. 844), author of *al-Ṭabaqāt al-kubrā* ('The Great Biographical Dictionary') are considered the pioneer historians; they were also *ḥadīth* scholars, but to a lesser degree.

The second school, which was interested in genealogies, legendary deeds, battles and tribal glory, comprised a group of chroniclers and genealogists who lived in the main cities of ʿIrāq. They included ʿAwāna ibn al-Ḥakam (d. 764), Abū Mikhnaf (d. 774), Sayf ibn ʿUmar (d. 796), Naṣr ibn Muzāḥim (d. 827), and al-Madāʾinī (d. 839). The most famous genealogists were Muḥammad ibn al-Sāʾib al-Kalbī and his son Hishām; then Abū l-Yaqzān, followed by Muṣʿab az-Zubayrī (d. 850).

Thanks to the spread of trade, the undertaking of all manner of land and sea voyages, and the translation of numerous texts from foreign cultures, the first books of geography and travel began to appear in rapid succession during the ʿAbbāsid age. *Kitāb al-masālik wa-l-mamālik* ('The Book of Itineraries and Kingdoms') by Ibn Khurdādhbih was the first geography book of its kind, written at the beginning of the 'Abbāsid era. When the ʿAbbāsid state was founded in ʿIrāq, there were at least two centres of foreign culture (especially Greek culture) near Baghdād. The first was Ḥarrān, whose people were Sabaeans, who knew Arabic and Greek and thus helped to translate Greek works into Arabic. The second was Jundīshāpūr in Ahwāz (Khūzistān), which provided a haven for Greek philosophers and physicians suffering persecution; it subsequently became a centre for the teaching of Greek learning in that region. Thanks to the establishment of the *Bayt al-Ḥikma*, the early ʿAbbāsids had a variety of books translated on philosophy, medicine, astronomy, mathematics, alchemy and other subjects. Among the most celebrated translators of this period were Thābit al-Ḥarrānī, Ḥunayn ibn Isḥāq, Qusṭā ibn Lūqā and the Nawbakht family. Vast sums were spent, especially by al-Rashīd and the Barmakids, by al-Ma'mūn and the family of Mūsā ibn Shākir, to acquire books on the sciences of the ancients and have them translated into Arabic. This movement had the desired results, and a number of Muslim scholars became prominent in various fields: they assimilated the ancient learning, and added new disciplines which contributed to the progress of human science and culture. These scholars included Muḥammad ibn Mūsā al-Khwārizmī in algebra, Jābir ibn Ḥayyān in alchemy, al-Ḥajjāj ibn Arṭā'a in architecture, 'Imrān ibn al-Waḍḍāḥ in arithmetic, Abū Ma'shar the astronomer, al-Ḥārith the astrologer, Abū Sahl ibn Nawbakht in the science of the stars, and Jabrā'īl ibn Bukhtyashū', Ibn Māsawayh and Ḥunayn ibn Isḥāq in medicine (al-Nashshār: Vol. 1, pp. 76 ff.). In addition, the arts of building and ornamentation began to claim the attention of the Muslims in this early part of the 'Abbāsid era, especially after the construction of Baghdād, Sāmarrā' and al-Ja'farīya, and the various buildings and public service utilities in those cities (Cresswell, 1938–1940; Grabar, 1972).

Perhaps the most noteworthy feature of the following period (ninth to tenth centuries) is that scholarly endeavour did not necessarily follow the vicissitudes of the political situation. For the Islamic east was in administrative turmoil and politically fragmented, and Turkish commanders and Būyid kings did not know Arabic well and so could not appreciate its literature or understand the significance of the rational sciences. Nevertheless, their courts were full of scholars, whom they vied with one another to attract and encourage. In view of the competition between rulers to attract scholars, it seems that the attitude of society towards the sciences had changed: from being considered mere crafts – apart from the sciences of religious law – and viewed with contempt, they came to be accorded prominent status in society.

During this time, 'Irāq continued to occupy pride of place in the Islamic world on the scholarly front, and most intellectual activity, in the form of schools, libraries, book sellers, copyists and authors, was concentrated in Baghdād, as is clearly shown by al-Khāṭīb al-Baghdādī's *Tārīkh Baghdād* ('History of Baghdād'), with its accounts of scholars in various fields.

Despite Caliph al-Mutawakkil's disestablishment of Mu'tazilism as the official rite of the 'Abbāsid state, the movement continued to play an active role in intellectual affairs. Among the best-known Mu'tazilī scholars at this time were Abū 'Alī al-Jubbā'ī and his pupil Muḥammad ibn 'Umar al-Ṣaymarī, as well as the chief *qāḍī* 'Abduljabbār (d. 1024). Abū l-Ḥasan al-Ash'arī (d. 941) was a pupil of al-Jubbā'ī, but he opposed the Mu'tazilīs and formed an independent school which attracted numerous scholars, including Abū Ḥāmid al-Isfarā'inī, who taught in Baghdād until his death in 1015. *Fiqh* (jurisprudence) flourished in 'Irāq, and there were many *mujtahidīn* (Islamic jurisconsults formulating independent decisions in legal or theological matters), such as Dā'ūd al-Ẓāhirī (d. 883) and Muḥammad ibn Jarīr al-Ṭabarī (d. 922) author of the *Tafsīr* ('Exegesis') and the *Tārīkh* ('History') and one of the most learned people in the jurisprudence of the various rites, and finally the Mu'tazilī al-Zamakhsharī, author of *al-Kashshāf* ('The Unveiler'). The Ḥanbalīs (Makdisi, 1985: pp. 216 ff.) had great influence in this period; their leaders were 'Abdullāh ibn Aḥmad ibn Ḥanbal (d. 902) and Abū Bakr 'Abdullāh ibn Dā'ūd al-Azdī al-Sijistānī (d. 928).

Ṣūfī doctrine became more elaborate during this period; it possibly borrowed ideas from Greek and Indian philosophy through *al-Ḥārith al-Muḥāsibī* (d. 857) and subsequently flourished with al-Junayd (d. 909), who said: 'Ṣūfism is the purity of one's personal relationship to God.' Al-Ḥallāj, killed in 921 for claiming communication with God, was one of his pupils.

As a result of the conflicting opinions regarding the legal sciences and the humanities in general, there arose what was known as the literature of doctrinal divergence and the principles of debating, which entailed comprehending a viewpoint and then refuting it. Books of jurisprudence and the various accounts and biographical dictionaries are full of historical examples of the treatment of controversial cases, from which we may cite Abū Ḥanīfa, who said: 'This is our position, and we do not compel anyone to hold this opinion, nor do we say that anyone must accept it unwillingly; if anyone has something better, then let him come forward' (al-Alwānī: 1981: p. 91).

In the field of language and literature, Muḥammad ibn Durayd al-Azdī al-'Umānī (d. 933) wrote several books, the most famous of which are *al-Jamhara* ('The Gathering Together') and *al-Ishtiqāq* ('Derivation'). He was followed by Abū 'Alī al-Qālī, author of *al-Amālī* ('The Dictations'), Abū Sa'īd al-Sīrāfī, and last but not least Abū Bakr ibn al-Anbārī (d. 939), who wrote on various literary and legal subjects. There were also numerous poets who composed verses on various themes.

In historical writing (Muṣṭafā, 1979: Vol. 2, pp. 68 ff.), there was a noticeable increase in historical material from the beginning of the ninth century onwards, for a variety of reasons, including the stability of state institutions, the availability of records to historians, and the vigorous translation activity, which provided new information to historians, who were in the habit of travelling in order to see and hear for themselves at first hand. One of the most prominent historians of this period was Aḥmad ibn Yaḥyā al-Balādhurī (d. 892), who wrote on the conquests and on genealogies; another was Aḥmad ibn Ya'qūb al-Ya'qūbī (d. 897), who wrote on history and geography. He and his contemporaries Abū Ḥanīfa al-Dīnawarī (d. 895) and Muḥammad ibn Muslim ibn Qutayba (d. 889) gave expression to a comprehensive view of history and a concept of world history. However, it is Muḥammad ibn Jarīr al-Ṭabarī (d. 922) who represents the highest level of historical writing achieved by the Muslims thus far. His view of history and historical writing was influenced by his education as a jurist and *ḥadīth* scholar, as is evident in his book *Tārīkh al-rusul wa-l-mulūk* ('History of the Prophets and Kings').

A new trend in historical writing emerged in the shape of local histories of specific regions, which were arranged either chronologically or biographically. Such were *Kitāb Futūḥ Miṣr wa-Akhbārihā* ('The Book of the Conquests of Egypt and the Accounts Thereof') by Ibn 'Abdulḥakam (d. 870), *Tārīkh Baghdād* ('History of Baghdād') by Ibn Abī Ṭāhir Ṭayfūr (d. 893), *Tārīkh al-Mawṣil* ('History of Mosul') by Abū Zakarīyā al-Azdī (d. 945) and *Akhbār Makka* ('Chronicles of Mecca') by Muḥammad 'Abdullāh al-Azraqī (d. *c.* 858).

By the beginning of the tenth century, the cultural movement had reached full maturity. *Al-Fihrist* ('The Index') by Ibn al-Nadīm (d. *c.* 988) gives an idea of the great number of authors in the various branches of learning. The second generation of Būyids, in both 'Irāq and Fārs, were more favourably inclined to the Arabic language and to culture and learning; among them, we may draw particular attention to Prince 'Aḍud al-Dawla and the *wazīrs* Ibn al-'Amid al-Ṣāḥib ibn 'Abbād and al-Muhallabī, whose scholarly gatherings were veritable intellectual forums, and whose libraries were treasure houses of Islamic and foreign thought.

The Būyid 'Aḍud al-Dawla (al-Tha'ālibī: Vol. 2, p. 216) favoured the company of men of letters, poets and scholars who came to his court in Shīrāz or Baghdād. Miskawayh gives us a clear picture of 'Aḍud al-Dawla's position with regard to the intellectual issues of his day, his interest in the traditional and the rational sciences, and his patronage of a number of astronomers, physicians, philosophers and men of letters. Al-Maqdisī described 'Aḍud al-Dawla's library in Shīrāz, which rivalled those of al-Ṣāḥib ibn 'Abbād and Ibn al-'Amīd and that of the Sāmānids in Bukhārā. Ibn al-'Amīd was the *wazīr* of the Būyid Rukn al-Dawla; he was well versed in logic, architecture, philosophy and the natural and religious sciences, as well as literature. Miskawayh worked for him as curator of his library, which contained books in all branches of science and literature. He was the host of a celebrated gathering attended by scholars and writers. Al-Ṣāḥib ibn 'Abbād was a pupil and friend of Ibn al-'Amīd; he became *wazīr* to Mu'ayyid al-Dawla and Fakhr al-Dawla. Al-Ṣāḥib was a Mu'tazilī who pursued legal, literary and linguistic studies. He was learned in *ḥadīth*, Islamic theology and the principles of religion. He held scholarly gatherings, which were well attended.

Interest in learning and patronage of books and libraries were not confined to these *wazīrs*; their example was followed by others, such as Abū 'Abdullāh Sa'dān, *wazīr* to Ṣamṣām al-Dawla, and Abū Naṣr Sābūr, *wazīr* to Bahā' al-Dawla, who founded for the benefit of scholars a house at Karkh in Baghdād called *Dār al-'Ilm* (the House of Learning) in which he collected over 10,000 volumes. Abū l-'Alā' al-Ma'arrī referred to it in an ode, as did al-Sharīf al-Raḍī in Baghdād.

In 988, Sharaf al-Dawla built an observatory such as there had been in the time of the 'Abbāsid al-Ma'mūn; he appointed Ibn Rustam al-Kūhī as its administrator, and Abū Ḥāmid al-Asṭurlābī as his assistant.

This period also witnessed the first attempts to revive Iranian culture. We have already referred to the social consequences of the *shu'ūbīya* movement, which emerged in the early part of the 'Abbāsid era. From a cultural point of view (Gibb, 1953) this was a trend which was hostile to the Arabic language and heritage, taking pride in the non-Arab heritage and reviving those cultures.

The second trend contemporary with *shu'ūbīya* at the beginning of the 'Abbāsid era was that of the *zindīqs* (Vajda, 1938). While scholars differ as to the precise technical and linguistic meaning of this term, the official and historical understanding at that time was of a new Manichaeism: an organized intellectual movement whose adherents sought the spread of Manichaeism; hence the perceived danger to Islam, especially as Manichaean literature in Arabic, Persian and Syriac was widespread. Manichaean writers objected to the Qur'ān with regard to both style and content and rejected the 'celestial' (revealed) religions. Al-Jāḥiẓ attacked the *zindīqs* and lumped them together with the *shu'ūbīs*.

While at the beginning of the 'Abbāsid era, the *shu'ūbīs* and *zindīqs* failed, the religious, linguistic and, in general, cultural heritage of the Persians was preserved in some regions of Īrān, such as Fārs and Khurāsān. But the Daylamī Būyids, who had gained control of the western regions of Īrān, especially Fārs, were not conscious of any real connection with Persian culture, and when they took control of 'Irāq they were drawn into the vigorous Arab Islamic culture; indeed, they became enamoured of it and worked to promote it. Under the Persian Sāmānids, Khurāsān began to play a part in reviving the new Persian culture. In fact, the movement to revive Persian culture had begun with the translation activity in the early 'Abbāsid period, and had gained strength during the period of the separatist movements in the east at the time of the Ṭāhirids and Ṣaffārids; this movement reached its zenith in the time of the Sāmānids in the tenth century, in the works of Rūdakī, Bal'amī and Firdawsī (d. *c.* 1020). Thus the contribution of the Būyids to the Persian cultural movement was limited in comparison with their role in enhancing Arabic learning.

This period, in which all branches of Islamic thought were flourishing, also witnessed an intellectual struggle between the various schools of jurisprudence and scholastic theology. This struggle emerged in the early 'Abbāsid period, and developed and reached maturity with the advent of the Seljuks (mid-eleventh century). Despite the continued political fragility inherent in the existence of a weak 'Abbāsid caliphate in Baghdād, controlled by the Būyids and under threat from the Fāṭimids in Egypt and Syria, who sent missionaries throughout the Islamic world spreading their Ismā'īlī doctrine, and from the conflict in the eastern parts of the Islamic world between the Ghaznavids and the new Turkish power (the Seljuks), the intellectual renaissance continued to develop, and there was interaction and conflict between the *ahl al-ḥadīth* (later known as *ahl al-sunna wa-l-jamā'a*), and the Mu'tazilīs, Shī'īs, Ṣūfīs, philosophers and others (Goldziher, 1910; Watt, 1973: pp. 33 ff.).

Just as the Būyids protected prominent Shī'īs and Mu'tazilīs, they also encouraged philosophers. 'Aḍud al-Dawla set aside a special place in his palace for wise men and philosophers to gather, so that their learning thrived and prospered. They included the *Ikhwān al-Ṣafā'* and Ibn Sīnā (d. 1036), who is considered to have been the leading philosopher at the end of the tenth century. He attempted to reconcile Islam with philosophy, an attempt which prompted criticism from the scholastic theologians and the jurists (Afnan, 1958: pp. 71 ff.).

A controversy arose between Sunnī scholars and a group of Ṣūfīs, who began to emerge in the last part of the ninth century and in the tenth century, and who distanced themselves from *sharī'a*, the law of Islam, considering that they possessed illumination and revelation; they interpreted religious observances in an esoteric manner and abrogated obligatory religious duties. Disputation between *Ṣufīs* and orthodox theologians became inevitable. The debate generated works such as Abū Naṣr al-Sarrāj al-Ṭūsī's (d. 988) *Kitāb al-luma' fī l-taṣawwuf* ('The Glittering Book of Ṣūfī Mysticism'), and Abū 'Abdurraḥmān al-Sulamī's (d. 1021), *Ṭabaqāt al-ṣūfīya* ('Biographical Dictionary of the Ṣūfīs'); they were followed by Abū l-Qāsim al-Qushayrī (d. 1072) and his famous treatise in which he sought to bring Ṣūfism back into line with Islamic law and cleanse it of the subversive doctrines that had become attached to it.

Last but not least, in the latter part of the tenth century and the early eleventh century, there was a noticeable intellectual rapprochement between the Imāmī Shī'īs and the Mu'tazilīs, despite the fact that their schools of thought were so clearly contradictory, a point underscored by various controversies, some of which have already been mentioned. While aspects of Mu'tazilī thought are present in the work of some Imāmī Shī'ī scholars of the tenth century, such as Sheikh al-Mufīd, al-Ṭūsī and al-Sharīf al-Raḍī [al-Sharīf al-Murtaḍā?], the influence was not long-lasting.

Mu'tazilī thought underwent a period of revival in various places in the Islamic east, such as Rayy, with the Mu'tazilī *wazīr* al-Ṣāḥib ibn 'Abbād, Ahwāz (Khūzistān), Shīrāz and Hurmuz in Fārs. Faced with this groundswell, Caliph al-Qādir bi-Llāh issued a decree in 1018 that whoever taught that the Qur'ān was created was an infidel and could legally be executed.

However, al-Qādir bi-Llāh was unable to carry through his final plan (al-Bayhaqī: p. 80), which was to put an end to Būyid power in Baghdād. For his supporter Maḥmūd of Ghazna died in 1030, and in the following year the caliph himself died. So the Būyids continued to control Baghdād until supplanted by a new eastern power, the Turkic Seljuks.

AL-MASHRIQ BETWEEN 1050 AND 1500

In 1050, 'Abbāsid Caliph al-Qā'im bi-Amr Allāh conferred upon the Seljuk ruler Ṭoghrïl titles commensurate with his status, such as *rukn al-dīn* ('the pillar of religion'); these titles served as confirmation by the caliphate of the legitimacy of the Seljuk sultanate. It should be noted that all was not well at the centre of the 'Abbāsid caliphate: the caliph had been stripped of his temporal power by the Būyid kings, who had taken over the reins of government. In the last days of the Būyids, a prominent Turk, Abū l-Ḥārith Arslān al-Basāsīrī, enjoyed increasing power; at the same time, conditions were deteriorating in Baghdād as a result of sectarian fighting, and relations had soured between the Turks, the effective power in Būyid Baghdād, and their Būyid masters. For all these reasons, the caliph appealed to Ṭoghrïl Beg as the one person who could save the caliphate. In 1055, Ṭoghrïl Beg decided to go to Baghdād, where he received a warm welcome, and put an end to Būyid rule. It appears that he hoped to unite the Islamic world under his banner. Consequently, he was not content merely to subject the various kingdoms of the caliphate to his overlordship but rather proclaimed himself *sulṭān* of all the kingdoms within his sphere of influence. In so doing he introduced a new order into the Islamic world, and the caliph was forced to confirm and submit to this *fait accompli* (al-Rāwandī, 1960: p. 157; al-Husainī, 1933: p. 14). Ṭoghrïl Beg was able to save the 'Abbāsid caliphate from collapse when later, in his absence, al-Basāsīrī gained control of Baghdād and broadcast propaganda for the Fāṭimid caliphate from the pulpits of Baghdād for approximately a year.

After Ṭoghrïl Beg's death, he was succeeded on the throne by Alp Arslān, who had become famous for his battles against the Byzantines, in particular the celebrated battle of Malazgird (Mantzikert) between himself and the Byzantine emperor, Romanus Diogenes (26 August 1070). This victory opened the gates of Anatolia and allowed the Muslim Turks to flood into it, particularly once most of the Byzantine forces standing as a bulwark in their way had been routed (Ibn Al-Athīr: p. 109; al-Rāwandī: p. 189).

His successor Malik Shāh succeeded in expanding his empire by taking possession of the greater part of Anatolia, except for the coastal areas. He also took Syria from the Fāṭimids and gained control of the Jazīra, or upper Mesopotamia. Malik Shāh took as his *wazīr* Niẓām ul-Mulk, who had served in the same capacity to Malik Shāh's father Alp Arslān. Niẓām ul-Mulk is the author of the famous Persian tract on polity and administration, the *Siyasat-Nāmeh*.

Following the death of Malik Shāh and the assassination a month previously of his *wazīr* Niẓām ul-Mulk, there was considerable unrest in the Seljuk empire. There was a struggle between the various Seljuk princes for the throne, and this led to the break-up of the Seljuk empire into four parts: the Seljuks of Iran and Iraq (1092–1194), the Seljuks of Kirmān (1092–1187), the Seljuks of Syria (1082–1117) and the Seljuks of Rūm (Rome), or Anatolia (1092–1308). Of these the Seljuk sultanate in Anatolia (Ibn al-Athīr: p. 28; F. Omar, 1983: p. 82) proved to be one of the most important and long-lived of the various Seljuk states.

In general, the Seljuks adopted Islamic practices with regard to their administrative, military and financial systems (see Plate 193 (c)); they were also influenced by the practices and culture they found in Iran (see Plates 197, 206). At the same time, they continued to be guided in their social life by their long-standing Turkic traditions; more generally, cultural and scientific progress continued quickly during the Seljuk period. The conflict between theology and science was brought to a high point by the refutations of rational policy by al-Ghazālī (d. 1111), who, however, sought to reconcile theology and Ṣufism, Muḥyī l-Dīn ibn al-'Arabī (d. 1240), Ibn Taimīya (d. 1328) and others. The attitude of the Seljuks, especially during the rule of the *wazīr* Niẓām ul-Mulk, was favourable to learning (see Plates 114, 126, 182–185). They contributed to the revival of Islamic science and culture, and established schools known as *Niẓāmīyas* in the various sciences and arts (see Plates 11, 18, 108, 210). They also built in numerous major Islamic cities teaching hospitals (*shifā-khāneh*) in which, in addition to their basic function, medical training was provided.

This period was characterized by the spread of Ṣūfī mystic orders, particularly in Anatolia. Ṣūfī convents, which dispensed teaching and training, were known by various names, such as *tekke* and *zāwiya*. Subsequent to the Seljuk period the Akbarīya, established by Muḥyī d-Dīn ibn al-'Arabī (d. 1240), and the Mawlawīya (Turkish Mevlevī), established by Sulṭān Walad ibn Jalāl ud-Dīn Rūmī, became two of the most important Ṣūfī orders; these were followed by the Qādirīya, established by 'Abdulqādir Gīlānī (al-Jīlānī) (Ibn al-Athīr: 1962, pp. 170 ff.; Ibn Shaddād, 1953: p. 122). The increasing strength of Ṣufism provoked a rigorous attack on it by Ibn Taymiya (d. 1328) (Ibn al-Athīr, 1963: pp. 170 ff.; Ibn Shaddād, 1953: Vol. 1, p. 122).

From the eleventh to the thirteenth century, campaigns were waged by the 'Franks' (Crusaders) against Syria and Egypt. The enfeebled 'Abbāsid caliphate in Baghdād was unable to contribute actively to the military and political response to the Frankish invaders, but it gave its support and blessing to the efforts of 'Imād ud-Dīn Zangī, his son Nūr ud-Dīn Maḥmūd, and later Ṣalāḥ ud-Dīn al-Ayyūbī (Saladin) to block the path of the invaders (Abū Shama, 1956: pp. 410 ff.).

The avowed aim of the Frankish campaigns was to gain control of the Holy Land in Palestine, and in particular of Jerusalem (see Plates 45, 46). However, they were driven not only by religious but also by secular goals, including political, economic and commercial aims. The first Crusaders' kingdom encompassed numerous cities in greater Syria, and in particular Jerusalem in 1099. The Franks founded four Crusader principalities in greater Syria: the kingdom of Jerusalem, the principality of Antioch (Anṭākiya), the county of Tripoli (Ṭarābulus) and the county of Edessa (Turkish: Urfa; Arabic: al-Ruhā'). When the Franks attacked Egypt in 1161, the Fāṭimid Caliph al-'Āḍid appealed to Nūr ud-Dīn Maḥmūd for help. Nūr ud-Dīn sent Shīrkūh and Ṣalāḥ ud-Dīn al-Ayyūbī, who expelled the Franks. Ṣalāḥ ud-Dīn overthrew the Fāṭimid dynasty in 1171 and had the *khuṭba* (Friday sermon) recited in the name of the 'Abbāsid caliph. In 1173, relying on his own efforts and resources, Ṣalāḥ ud-Dīn united Egypt and greater Syria. In 1192, he engaged the Crusaders in the Battle of Ḥaṭṭīn, from which he emerged victorious and managed to recover Jerusalem. The *sulṭāns* who succeeded him were not as powerful, but the power of the Crusaders was also waning, and the Mamlūk *sulṭāns* in Egypt and greater Syria managed to deal with them definitively after they had defeated the Mongols at 'Ayn Jālūt in 1260 (see Plates 30, 31).

The efforts of the *atabegs* and the Ayyūbids were complementary to the scientific and intellectual endeavours of the Great Seljuks and were aimed at reviving the spirit of *jihād* (holy war) and resistance to the Isma'īlī ('assassin') and extremist currents that had spread extensively within the Islamic world at that time. The building of schools continued, and Nūr ud-Dīn established two schools in Aleppo (Ḥalab). Nūr ud-Dīn also established Ṣūfī *khānaqās* (convents) for both men and women for the purpose of devotion, study and writing. Ṣūfī scholars enjoyed official esteem, particularly on the part of Nūr ud-Dīn, who placed his trust in them. Nūr ud-Dīn was also keen to promote the teaching of *ḥadīth* (the sayings and practices of the Prophet), and he granted such teaching establishments sizeable religious endowments (*waqf*), which enabled the teachers and students to devote themselves to the pursuit of knowledge. Among the prominent scholars and thinkers of this period were 'Imād ud-Dīn al-Iṣfahānī, Quṭb ud-Dīn of Nīshāpūr 'al-Ḥāfiẓ' ('the depository of the tradition') Ibn 'Asākir. Like Nūr ud-Dīn Maḥmūd, Ṣalāḥ ud-Dīn al-Ayyūbī built many schools and Ṣūfī convents, endowing them handsomely with religious endowments.

The circumstances of the Islamic east (*al-Mashriq*) in this period, including the Frankish invasion and the spread of *Isma'īlī* ideas, may have influenced the contemporary curriculum, which focused on teaching *ḥadīth* and *fiqh* (jurisprudence), urging people to *jihād*, and reviving the spirit of martyrdom by teaching about *jihād* and other subjects conducive to stiffening people's resistance. Al-Qāḍì l-Fāḍil ('the excellent judge') had a school for the teaching of the Qur'ān. Bahā' ud-Dīn ibn Shaddād was among those who were prominent in intellectual circles, along with other thinkers who had graduated from the Seljuk *Niẓāmīya* schools a generation or more previously.

A great disaster befell the eastern Islamic world with the arrival of the Mongols. The Mongols were originally a nomadic people living in the area of north-eastern Asia known as the Mongolian plateau. These tribes fell into internal struggles, the outcome of which was that Chinggis Khān became their sole leader. He founded an empire which stretched from the borders of China to Turkestān. Chinggis Khān began his conquest of the Islamic world in 1219 when he invaded the state of Khwārizm, which had arisen on the ruins of the state of the Seljuks of Iran and Iraq. While the Khwārizm-Shāh 'Alā' ud-Dīn Muḥammad ibn Tekish (1219–1199) had managed to subdue the rulers of Transoxania and Khurāsān, he was unable to withstand the Mongol onslaught; his forces collapsed on their first encounter with the Mongols, and he fled to an island in the Caspian Sea, where he died. Chinggis Khān's armies invaded Iran and gained control of most of its territory. Chinggis Khān died in 1227, having divided his empire between his sons. He was succeeded by his son Ögödäy, under whose rule the Mongols captured all the territory of the Khwārizm-Shāh Jalāl ud-Dīn Mengüberti, thus paving the way for them to penetrate further west. During the reign of Tolui's eldest son Möngke, the Mongols, led by Hülegü, attacked the 'Abbāsid caliphate. Weak and fragmented, and on its last legs, the caliphate was unable to withstand the Mongol invasion; the capital Baghdād fell to the Mongols in 1258 and was largely destroyed, and Iraq became part of the Mongol Empire. Although Mongol forces entered Syria and gained control of large parts of it, they were repelled, especially at the battle of 'Ayn Jālūt between the Mongols and the Mamlūks in 1260. Having seized the 'Abbāsid domains, Hülegü began to rule practically independently and founded the Īl-Khānid dynasty, which lasted until 1335 and had its capital at Marāgha in Āzerbaijān. During the reign of Ghazan Khān (1295–1304), the Mongols converted to Islam. Indeed, Ghazan Khān adopted Islam as the official religion of the Īl-Khānid state, although his formal links with the Mongol Empire continued. The Mongols, having been drawn into the cities and cultural centres of Islam, assimilated Islamic civilization and adopted its heritage and thought. In this way, the processes of sedentarization and urban development were resumed after only a short pause (B. Spuler, 1968: pp. 58 ff.) (see Plate 12).

The last Īl-Khānid *sulṭān* died in 1335. With no son to succeed him on the throne, this led to the break-up of the Īl-Khānid state, and the rulers of the various regions declared their independence. One of the foremost of these rulers was Ḥasan-i Buzurg (the Great), who in 1339 founded the Jalāyirid state comprising Iraq, Khūzistān and Diyār Bakr. After his death in 1356, his successors undertook to expand the state, but it fell prey to Tīmūrid invasions. The desolation caused by Tīmūr in Iraq and Syria was devastating. After occupying Asia Minor, Tīmūr entered Syria in 1400, destroying towns and massacring their inhabitants. In 1401, he took Baghdād by surprise and wrought a great massacre there. Tīmūr used to build towers of the skulls of the people massacred on his orders. His invasion of Syria obliged him to come face to face with the Ottomans. This aspect, however, does not concern us here.While the Jalāyirids managed to recover some of their territory, their struggle with the Tīmūrids ended only with the death of Tīmūr-i Lang (Tamerlane) in 1404, and the dynasty finally fell when the last of its *sulṭāns*, Aḥmad, lost his life at the hands of the Turkmen prince Qarā Yūsuf of the Qarā Qoyunlu (see Plates 185, 186).

The Qarā-Qoyunlu (black sheep) were a branch of the Oghuz Turks. To begin with, they submitted to the Jalāyirids, but by the late fourteenth century, Qarā Muḥammad had managed to found a Qarā-Qoyunlu principality, and his son Qarā Yūsuf transformed this principality into a state. Initially, however, Qarā Yūsuf was not able to expand the area of the Qarā-Qoyunlu state, since a Tīmūrid line (*khaṭṭ*) had been established. After Tīmūr's death, Qarā Yūsuf embarked upon two battles against the Tīmūrids. He seized Tabrīz and Āzerbaijān and transferred his administrative centre to Tabrīz. Following his victory in the battle between him and Aḥmad Jalāyir, the gates of Arab Iraq stood open, and he proceeded to occupy it.

After Qarā Yūsuf's death, his successor was unable to continue in power, for a dispute arose between him and his brothers, who appealed to Tīmūr's son Shāh Rukh to intervene. During the reign of Jahān Shāh, the state expanded in size, extending from Khurāsān to the borders of the Ottoman state. Jahān Shāh lost his life following his campaign against the Āq-Qoyunlu state, and this led in 1467 to the fragmentation of the Qarā-Qoyunlu, which was unable to withstand the raids of the Āq-Qoyunlu, who gradually gained control of his possessions.

The Āq-Qoyunlu (white sheep) were also Oghuz Turks. Individual Āq-Qoyunlus participated in Tīmūr's campaigns against Iraq and Syria, and Tīmūr granted them the region of Diyār Bakr as a fiefdom; they established a principality there in 1402. Ūzūn (tall) Ḥasan was one of the most celebrated rulers of this state; he established an orderly and extensive state and transferred its capital from Diyār Bakr to Tabrīz. After the death of Ūzūn Ḥasan in 1478, the struggle for power between the princes intensified; a number of weak rulers succeeded one another, and the state was divided into several parts. While circumstances were thus deteriorating, the Ṣafawids were gathering strength under Shāh Ismā'īl I, who managed to gain control of the regions under Āq-Qoyunlu influence in Iran. He then marched on Iraq, which he occupied (J. E. Woods, 1976: pp. 23 ff.).

The Ṣafawids (R. M. Savory, 1980: pp. 76 ff.) belonged to a Turkmen dynasty which included Shaykh Ṣafī ud-Dīn, the ancestor of Shāh Ismā'īl I. Ṣafī ud-Dīn was the founder of the Ṣafawīya Ṣūfī order, which became widespread among the Turkmen tribesmen. After his death in 1334, the leadership of the order passed to Ṣafī ud-Dīn's son and then to his grandsons, the foremost of whom was Ismā'īl Ṣafawī, who succeeded in raising at an army of disciples of his father and grandfather in Ardabīl. He undertook a series of military operations which enabled him eventually to gain control of Tabrīz, the Āq-Qoyunlu capital, to found a Ṣafawid state there, and then to extend that state's influence to the rest of Iran and Diyār Bakr. In 1508, he took Baghdād. But he suffered a crushing defeat in the Battle of Chāldirān in 1514 at the hands of the Ottoman *sulṭān* Selīm I, who seized large parts of the Ṣafawid dominions in the west, including, temporarily, the capital, Tabrīz, which was recovered a year later. Shāh Ismā'īl remained in power until his death in 1524. Shāh Ismā'īl's proclamation in 1501 established Twelver Shī'ism as the official and compulsory religion of his empire and began the process of the conversion of the whole country, until then largely Sunnī, to Shī'ism. Syria, on the other hand, passed into the hands of the Ottomans.

BIBLIOGRAPHY

'ABDULJABBĀR (Mu'tazilī *qāḍī* (judge)). 1966. *al-Mughnī fī abwāb at-tauḥīd wa-l-'adl* (The Dispenser in Matters of Unity and Justice). Cairo.

ABŪ SHĀMA. 1956. Al-*Rawḍatayn fī Akhbār al-Dawlatayn* (The Book of the Two Gardens concerning the Two Dynasties), Vol. 1, Cairo, pp. 410 ff.

ABŪ YŪSUF. 1932. *Kitāb al-kharāj* (The Book of Land Tax). Cairo.

AFNAN, A. 1958. *Avicenna*. London.

Akhbār al-daula al-'abbāsīya (An Account of the 'Abbāsid State). 1971. Beirut.

ALLARD, M. 1965. *Le problème des attributs divins dans la doctrine d'Al-Ash'arī et de ses premiers grands disciples*. Beirut.

AL-ALWĀNĪ, T. J. 1981. *Adab al-ikhtilāf fī l-Islām* (The Literature of Doctrinal Divergence in Islam). Herndon, USA.

AMĪN, A. n.d. *Duḥā l-Islām* (The Forenoon of Islam). Beirut.

——. *'Zuhr al-Islām* (The Midday of Islam), Vol. 1, 1945, Beirut; Vol. 2, 1952, Cairo; Vol. 4, 1964, Cairo.

AL-ASH'ARĪ. *al-Ibāna 'an usūl al-diyāna* (Exposition of the Foundations of Religion). Cairo, n.d. English translation by W. C. Klein, 1940, New Haven, Conn.

ASHTOR, E. 1976. *A Social and Economic History of the Near East in the Middle Ages*. London.

AZIZI, M. 1938. *La domination arabe et l'épanouissement du sentiment national en Iran*. Paris.

BADAWĪ, A. A. 1988. *Al-Tārīkh as-siyāsī wa-l-fikrī li-l-madhhab al-sunnī* (Political and Intellectual History of the Sunnī Rite). Cairo.

AL-BAGHDĀDĪ. 1973. *al-Farq bayn al-firaq* (The Distinction between the Sects). Beirut.

AL-BALĀDHURĪ. 1978. *Ansāb al-ashrāf* (The Genealogies of the Nobles). Beirut.

AL-BAYHAQĪ. 1956. *Tārīkh al-Bayhaqī* (al-Bayhaqī's History). Arabic trans. from Persian. Cairo.

AL-BĪLĪ, O. I. 1989. *A Study of Some Aspects of the Reign of al-Mu'tasim*. Qatar.

BOSWORTH, C. E. 1967. *The Islamic Dynasties: A Chronological and Genealogical Handbook*. Edinburgh.

BOWEN, H. 1928. *The Life and Times of Ali Ibn Isa*. Cambridge.

BUSSE, H. 1975. Iran under the Buyids. In: *Cambridge History of Iran*, Vol. 4, pp. 250–304. Cambridge.

CAHEN, C. 1963. Points de vue sur la révolution 'abbāside. *Revue Historique*, pp. 295–338.

——. 1965. L'évolution de l'*iqṭā'* du IXè au XIIIè siècle. In: Cahen (ed.) 1977, pp. 238 ff.

——. 1970. *L'Islam des origines au début de l'Empire Ottoman*. Paris.

CHRISTENSEN, A. 1944. *L'Iran sous les Sassanides*. Copenhagen.

COULSON, N. J. 1964. *A History of Islamic Law*. Edinburgh.

——. 1969. *Conflicts and Tensions in Islamic Jurisprudence*. Chicago.

CRESSWELL, A. 1938–1940. *Early Muslim Architecture*, 2 vols. Oxford. 2nd revised edition of Vol. 1, 1969. Reprinted: New York, 1980.

DE GOEJE, M. J. 1886. *Mémoire sur les Carmathes du Bahrain*, 2nd edition. Leiden.

DE ZAMBAUR, E. 1927. M*anuel de généalogie et de chronologie pour l'histoire de l'Islam*. Hanover.

DENNET, D. 1939. Marwān ibn Muhammad. Unpublished thesis, Harvard University.

DJAIT, H.; AL-KUFA. 1986. *Naissance de la ville islamique*. Paris.

AL-DŪRĪ, A. A. 1945a. *Dirāsāt fī l-'usūr al-'abbāsīya al-muta'akhkhira* (Studies in the Late 'Abbāsid Period). Baghdād.

——. 1945b. *Muqaddima fī tārīkh sadr al-islām* (Introduction to the History of Early Islam). Baghdād.

——. 1959. Nushū' al-asnāf wa-l-hiraf (The Development of Guilds and Trades). *Majallat Kullīyat al-Adab wa-l-'Ulūm* (Journal of the Faculty of Literature and Science). Baghdād.

——. 1960. *Baḥth fī nash'at 'ilm al-tārīkh 'ind al-'arab* (Study on the Emergence of the Science of History among the Arabs). Beirut. English trans.: L. Conrad, *The Rise of Historical Writing among the Arabs*, Princeton, 1983.

——. 1970. Nash'at al-iqtā' fī l-mujtama'āt al-islāmīya (The Emergence of Feudal Tenure (*iqtā'*) in Islamic Societies). In: *Majallat al-Majma' al-'Ilmī al-'Irāqī* (Journal of the Iraqi Academy of Sciences), Vol. 20, pp. 14–25.

——. 1977. *Tārīkh al-'Irāq al-iqtiṣādī fī l-qarn al-rābi' al-hijrī* (Economic History of Iraq in the Fourth Century AH), 2nd edition. Beirut (1st edition, Baghdād, 1948).

ESS, J. van. 1971. *Frühe mu'tazilitische Haeresiographie* (Heresiography of the Early Mu'tazilīs). Beirut.

FATTĀḤ, I. A. 1974. *Nash'at al-falsafa al-ṣūfīya wa-taṭawwuruh* (The Genesis and Development of Ṣūfī Philosophy). Beirut.

GABRIELI, F. 1929. *Al-Ma'mūn e gli 'Alidi* (Al-Ma'mūn and the 'Alids). In: *Morgenländische Texte und Forschungen*, Vol. 3. Leipzig.

GIBB, H. A. R. 1953. The Social Significance of the Shu'ūbiyya. In: *Studia Orientalia Ioanni Pedersen Dicata*. Copenhagen, pp. 105–114. Reprinted in H. A. R. Gibb, *Studies on the Civilization of Islam*, edited by S. J. Shaw and W. R. Polk, Boston, 1962, pp. 62–73.

——. 1961. Government and Islam under the Early Abbasids: The Political Collapse of Islam. In: *Colloque de Strasbourg, 1959: L'élaboration de l'Islam*. Paris, pp. 114–127.

——. 1962. Article on 'Tārīkh' (History). In: *Studies on the Civilization of Islam*. Boston.

GOITEIN, S. D. The rise of the Near Eastern bourgeoisie. *Islamic Culture*. Vol. 23.

GOLDZIHER, I. 1910. *Vorlesungen über den Islam* (Lectures on Islam). Heidelberg. French translation by F. Arin, *Le dogme et la loi de l'islam*. Paris, 1920. English translation by R. and A. Hamori, *Introduction to Islamic Theology and Law*. Princeton, 1981.

GRABAR, O. 1972. *Studies in Medieval Islamic Art.* London.
GRUNEBAUM, G. E. von. 1953. *Medieval Islam: A Study in Cultural Orientation,* 2nd edition. Chicago.
AL-HAMADHĀNĪ. 1961. *Takmilat Tārīkh al-Ṭabarī* (Supplement to the History of at-Ṭabarī). Beirut.
HILĀL AL-ṢĀBĪ. 1919. *Kitāb al-tārīkh* (The Book of History). Cairo.
——. 1958. *Kitāb al-wuzarā'* (The Book of Ministers). Cairo.
——. 1964. *Rusūm dār al-khilāfa* (Customs of the Caliph's Palace). Baghdād. Trans. by E. A. Salem 1977: *The Rules and Regulations of the Abbasid Court.* Beirut.
AL-HUSAYNĪ. 1933. *Akhbār al-daula al-saljūqīya* (Account of the Seljuk Empire). Lahore, p. 14.
IBN AL-ATHĪR. 1963. Al-*Tārīkh al-bāhir fī l-daula al-atābakīya* (The Brilliant History of the Regime of the *Atābegs).* Cairo, pp. 170 ff.
——. 1965–1967. *al-Kāmil fī l-tārīkh* (The Complete Chronicle), 13 vols. Beirut.
IBN AL-FAQĪH. 1885. *Mukhtaṣar Kitāb al-buldān* (Summary of the Book of Countries). Leiden.
IBN ḤAWQAL. 1938. *Kitāb Sūrat al-ard* (The Book of the Configuration of the Earth). Kramers ed. Leiden.
IBN AL-JAWZĪ. 1938. *al-Muntaẓam fī tārīkh al-mulūk wa-l-umam* (The Well-Ordered History of Kings and Nations). Hyderabad.
IBN AL-JIQJAQĀ. AH 1317/AD 1899 *Kitāb al-Fakhrī* (Fakhr's Book). Cairo. (English trans. by C. E. P. Whitting, London, 1947).
IBN KHALDŪN. 1975. *al-Muqaddima* (The Prolegomena). Beirut.
IBN KHURDĀDHBEH. 1889. *Kitāb al-masālik wa-l-mamālik* (The Book of Itineraries and Kingdoms). Leiden.
IBN AL-MUQAFFA'. 1960. *Risāla fī l-ṣaḥāba* (Epistle on the Companions of the Prophet). Beirut.
IBN AL-MURTAḌĀ. 1952. *Ṭabaqāt al-mu'tazila* (Biographical Dictionary of the Mu'tazilīs). Beirut.
IBN AL-NADĪM. 1347 AH/AD 1929–1930. *Al-Fihrist* (The Catalogue), Arabic text, 2nd edn. Cairo. English trans. by B. Dodge.
IBN QAYYIM AL-JAWZĪYA. 1965. *Ahkām ahl al-dhimma* (Statutes Relating to the *Dhimmīs).* Cairo.
IBN SHADDĀD. 1953. *Al-A'lāq al-khatīra fī dhikr umarā' al-Shām wa-l-Jazīra* (Weighty Nuggets concerning the Princes of Shām (Syria) and the Jazīra (Upper Mesopotamia)), Vol. 1, ed. D. Sourdel, Damascus, p. 122.
IBN TAYFŪR. 1904. *Kitāb Baghdād* (The Book of Baghdād). Leipzig.
IBN TAYMĪYA. 1964. *Minhāj al-sunna al-nabawīya* (The Path of the Prophetic Tradition). publ. Maktabat Dar al-'Uruba.
AL-IṢFAHĀNĪ, ABŪ L-FARAJ. AH 1284–1285/AD 1867–1868. *Kitāb al-aghānī* (The Book of Songs). Būlāq.
AL-IṢṬAKHRĪ. 1961. *Kitāb al-masālik wa-l-mamālik* (The Book of Itineraries and Kingdoms). Cairo.
AL-JĀBIRĪ, M. A. 1992. *al-'Aql al-siyāsī al-'arabī* (The Arab Political Mind). Beirut.
AL-JĀḤIẒ. *Kitāb al-Bukhalā'* (The Book of Misers). Damascus.
——. 1938. *Kitāb al-ḥayawān* (The Book of Animals). Cairo.
——. *Rasā'il* (Letters), edited by A. Harun. Cairo.
——. al-Radd 'alā l-naṣārā (Reply to the Christians). In: *Rasā'il* (Letters), pp. 16–18.
——. Risāla fī l-qiyān (Letter concerning Maidservants). In: *Rasā'il* (Letters), p. 70.
AL-JAHSHIYĀRĪ. 1938. *Kitāb al-wuzarā' wa l-kuttāb* (The Book of Ministers and Secretaries). Cairo.
AL-KHAṬĪB AL-BAGHDĀDĪ. AH 1349/AD 1930. *Tārīkh Baghdād* (History of Baghdad). Cairo.
KABIR, M. 1956. Cultural Development under the Buwayhids of Baghdād. *Journal of the Asiatic Society of Pakistan,* Vol. 1.
——. 1959. Administration of Justice during the Buwayhid Period. *Islamic Culture,* Vol. 33.
——. 1961. The Religious Background to the Rise and Fall of the Buwayhid. *Indo-Iranica,* Vol. 1.
LAMBTON, A. K. S. 1965. Reflexions on the *Iqṭā'*. In: G. MAQDISI (ed.) *Arabic and Islamic Studies in Honour of A. R. Gibb.* Leiden, pp. 358–376.
——. 1980. *Theory and Practice in Medieval Persian Government.* London.
LAOUST, H. 1961. *Les schismes dans l'Islam.* Paris.
LAPIDUS, I. 1988. *A History of Islamic Societies; Part I: The Origins of Islamic Civilization: The Middle East from Goa to 1200.* Cambridge.
LASSNER, J. 1970. *The Topography of Baghdād in the Early Middle Ages.* Detroit.
——. 1980. *The Shaping of Abbasid Rule.* Princeton.
——. 1984. *Khitat Baghdād fī l-'usūr al-'abbāsīya al-ūlā* (Plans of Baghdād in the Early 'Abbāsid Period). Arabic translation of 'Notes on the Topography of Baghdād'. Baghdād.
LE STRANGE, G. 1924. *Baghdād during the Abbasid Caliphate.* Oxford.
LEVY, R. 1957. *The Social Structure of Islam.* Cambridge.
LEWIS, B. 1937. The Islamic Guilds. *English Historical Review.*
——. 1940. *The Origins of Ismailism.* Cambridge.
——. 1966. Government, Society and Economic Life under the 'Abbāsids and Fātimids. *Cambridge Medieval History,* new edition. Cambridge.
LOMBARD, M. 1971. *L'islam dans sa première grandeur.* Paris.
——. 1978. *Les textiles dans le monde musulman.* Paris.
MAKDISI, G. 1962–1963. Ash'arī and the Ash'arites in Islamic Religious Thought. *Studia Islamica,* Vol. 17, pp. 37–80; Vol. 18, pp. 19–39.
——. 1985. Hanbalite Islam. In: M. Schwartz (ed.) *Studies on Islam.* New York.
AL-MAQDISĪ (*also* al-Muqaddasī) 1906. *Ahsan al-taqāsīm ilā ma'rifat al-aqālīm* (The Best Divisions for Knowledge of the Regions), 2nd edition. Leiden.
MASSIGNON, L. 1922. *Essai sur les origines du lexique technique de la mystique musulmane,* 2nd edition. Paris, 1945.
AL-MAS'ŪDĪ. 1873. *Murūj al-dhahab wa-ma'ādin al-jawhar* (The Meadows of Gold and the Mines of Precious Stones). Edited and translated by Barbier de Meynard, Paris.
AL-MĀWARDĪ. 1966. *al-Aḥkām al-sulṭānīya* (The Principles of Government). Cairo. French trans.: E. Fagnan. *Les statuts gouvernementaux.* Reprinted. Paris, 1982.
MEZ, A. 1922. *Die Renaissance des Islams.* Heidelberg. English trans.: S. Khuda-Bukhsh; D. S. Margoliouth, *The Renaissance of Islam,* London, 1937. Reprinted: Beirut, 1973; New York, 1975.
MINORSKY, V. 1932. *La domination des Daylamites.* Paris.
MIQUEL, A. 1967–1980. *La géographie humaine du monde musulman jusqu'au milieu du XIe· siècle.* Paris.
MISKAWAYH. 1914. *Tajārib al-umam* (The Experiences of the Nations). Cairo.
MOSCATI, S. 1946. Le Califat d'al-Hādī. *Studia Orientalia,* Vol. 13, No. 4.
——. 1946–1949. Studi storici sul califfato di al-Mahdī (Historical Studies on the Caliphate of al-Mahdī). In: *Orientalia,* Vols 13, 14.
AL-MUBARRAD. 1956. *Kitāb al-kāmil (fī l-adab)* (The Compendium (of Literature)). Cairo.
AL-MURTAḌĀ. 1967. *al-Amālī* (The Dictations). Beirut.
MUSṬAFĀ, S. 1979. *al-Tārīkh al-'arabī wa-l-mu'arrikhūn* (Arab History and the Historians). Beirut.
NETTON, I. R. 1982. *Muslim Neoplatonists: An Introduction to the Thought of the Brethren of Purity.* London.
NÖLDEKE, T. 1892. A Servile War in the East. *Sketches from Eastern History* (English trans. by J. S. Black). Edinburgh.
OMAR ('UMAR), F. 1968. 'The Composition of the Early 'Abbāsid Support'. *Journal of the Faculty of Literature and Science.* Baghdād.
——. 1969. *The 'Abbāsid Caliphate.* Baghdād.
——. 1970. *Ṭabī'at al-da'wa al-'abbāsīya* (The Nature of the 'Abbāsid *Da'wa).* Dār al-Irshād, Beirut.
——. 1971. Hārun al-Rashīd. *Encyclopaedia of* Islam, 2nd edition. Leiden.
——. 1973. *al-'Abbāsīyūn al-awā'il* (The Early 'Abbāsids). Beirut. Vol. 2 (author: Vol. I, Beirut, 1971; Vol. II, Damascus, 1973; Vol. III, Amman, 1982).
——. 1974. Barmakids. *Encyclopaedia Britannica,* 15th edition.
POPOVÍC, A. 1986. *La révolte des esclaves en Iraq: IIIè–IXè siècle.* Paris.
QUDĀMA IBN JA'FAR. 1889. *Kitāb al-kharāj wa-sinā'at al-kitāba* (The Book of Land Tax and the Craft of Secretaryship). Leiden.
AL-QUSHAYRĪ. 1915. *al-Risāla al-qushairīya* (The Epistle of Qushayrū). Cairo.
AL-RĀWANDĪ. 1960. *Rāhat al-sudūr* (Repose of Hearts) (Arabic trans.

from the original Persian). Cairo, p. 157.

ROSENTHAL, F. 1952. *A History of Muslim Historiography*. Leiden. 2nd revised edition, 1968.

——. 1970. *Knowledge Triumphant: The Concept of Knowledge in Medieval Islam*. Leiden.

AL-RŪDHRĀWARĪ. 1961. *Dhail Tajārib al-umam* (Supplement to the Experiences of the Nations). Cairo.

SADIGHI, G. H. 1938. *Les mouvements religieux iraniens au IIè et au IIIè siècle de l'Hégire*. Paris.

SATO, T. 1982. The Iqtā' System of 'Irāq under the Buwayhids. *Orient*, Vol. 18, pp. 82 ff.

SAVORY, R. M. 1980. *Iran under the Safavids*. Cambridge, pp. 76ff.

SHABAN, M. A. 1970. *The 'Abbāsid Revolution*. Cambridge.

——. 1971–1976. *Islamic History: A New Interpretation*, 2 vols. Cambridge. (Arabic trans. al-Tārikh al-Islami. Tafsir jadid, Beirut, 1986).

AL-SHAYKHALĪ, S. D. 1976. *al-Aṣnāf wa-l-ḥiraf fī l-'aṣr al-'abbāsī* (Guilds and Trades in the 'Abbāsid Age). Baghdād.

AL-SHĪRĀZĪ. 1949. *Sīrat al-Mu'ayyad fī l-Dīn dā'ī l-du'āh* (Biography of the Chief Missionary, al-Mu'ayyad fī l-Dīn). Cairo.

SOURDEL, D. 1959–1960. *Le vizirat abbaside de 749 à 936 (132 à 324 de l'Hégire)*, 2 vols. Damascus.

SPULER, B. 1968. *Die Mongolen in Iran, 1220–1350*. Berlin, pp. 58 ff.

SUBARI, S. 1981. *Mouvements populaires à Bagdad à l'époque abbaside: IXè-XIè siècles*. Paris.

SUBḤI A. M. 1969. *Nazarīyat al-imāma ladā al-shī'a al-ithnā 'asharīya* (The Theory of the Imāmate among the 'Twelver' Shī'īs). Cairo.

AL-SUBKĪ. AH 1324/AD 1906. *Tabaqāt al-shāfi'īya* (Biographical Dictionary of the Shāfi'īs). Cairo.

AL-ṢŪLĪ. 1938. *Akhbār al-Rādì wa-l-Muttaqī* (Accounts of al-Rādì and al-Muttaqī). London.

AL-ṬABARĪ. 1881. *Tārīkh al-rusul wa-l-mulūk* (History of the Prophets and Kings). Leiden. (Persian translation by Bal'amī, Cawnpore, 1906; French translation of the Persian text by H. Zotenberg, Paris, 1867–1874).

AL-TANŪKHĪ. 1921. *Nishwār al-muḥāḍara*. English trans.: D. S. Margoliouth. *The Table-Talk of a Mesopotamian Judge*, 2 vols. London.

ṬARKHĀN, I. A. 1968. *al-Nuẓūm al-iqṭā'īya fī al-sharq al-auṣat fī l-'usur al-wusṭā* (Systems of Feudal Tenure in the Middle East in the Middle Ages). Cairo.

AL-THA'ĀLIBĪ. 1974. *Yatīmat al-dahr* (The Orphaned Daughter of Fate). Cairo.

TRIMINGHAM, J. S. 1971. *The Ṣūfī Orders in Islam*. Oxford.

TRITTON A. S. 1930. *The Caliphs and their Non-Muslim Subjects: A Critical Study of the Covenant of Umar*. Oxford. Reprinted: London, 1970.

TYAN E. 1960. *Histoire de l'organisation judiciaire en pays d'Islam*, 2 vols. Leiden.

UDOVITCH, A. L. (ed.) 1981. *The Islamic Middle East, 700–1900: Studies in Economic and Social History*. Princeton.

'UTHMĀN, A. 1967. *Qāḍī l-quḍāh 'Abduljabbār* (The Chief Judge 'Abduljabbār). Beirut.

VAJDA, G. 1938. Les zindiqs en pays d'islam au début de la période abbaside. *Revista degli studi orientali*, Vol. 17, pp. 173 ff.

VLOTEN, G. van. 1894. Recherches sur la domination arabe, le chiitisme, et les croyances messianiques sous le Khalifat des Omayades. In: *Verhandelingen der Koninklijke Akademie van wetenschappen te Amsterdam, Afdeeling Letterkunde*. Deel I, No. 3. Amsterdam.

WATT, W. M. 1973. *The Formative Period of Arabic Thought*. Edinburgh.

WELLHAUSEN, J. 1902. *Das arabische Reich und sein Sturz*. English trans. by M. G. Weir, *The Arab Kingdom and its Fall*. Calcutta, 1927. Reprinted: Beirut, 1963.

WIET, G. 1953. L'empire néo-byzantin des Omayyades et l'empire néo-sassanide des 'Abbāsides. *Cahiers d'histoire mondiale*, UNESCO, Paris, Vol. 1, 1953, pp. 63–71.

WOODS, J. E. 1976. *The Aqquyunlu: Clan, Confederation, Empire*. Minneapolis and Chicago, pp. 23 ff.

AL-YA'QŪBĪ. 1892. *Kitāb al-buldān* (The Book of Countries). Leiden.

——. AH 1323/AD 1905. *Mushākalat al-nās li-zamānihim* (The Resemblance of People to their Time). Tehrān.

——. AH 1377/AD 1957. *al-Tārīkh* (The History). Najaf.

YĀQŪT AL-ḤAMAWĪ. 1955–1957. *Mu'jam al-buldān* (Geographical Dictionary). Beirut.

20

NORTH AND NORTH-EAST AFRICA

20.1

MIṢR (EGYPT)

Ayman Fu'ad Sayyid

TILL THE END OF FĀṬIMID RULE (1171) (SEE MAP 15)

Political history

From the time of the Arab conquest in 640, Egypt remained a governorship of the caliphate, ruled successively from Medina, Damascus and Baghdād. During this period, while governors were sent or appointed by the caliphs, the Byzantine elements of administration, with Greek as the official language, were gradually supplanted by new institutions and offices, with increasing use of Arabic. Immigrant Arabs, constituting the *wujūh* (elite), had by the end of the eighth century replaced the Copts in the more important positions in tax administration; and under the 'Abbāsid caliphs, a number of Khurāsānid officials too were sent to Egypt. Conversions to Islam grew steadily among the Egyptian population, and with it spread Arabic speech. There was some nomadic Arab immigration as well. But it must be remembered that by the ninth century, a large number of Egyptians were still Christians, and Coptic was perhaps still the language of the majority.

It was in 868 that the 'Abbāsid caliphs' governor, Aḥmad ibn Ṭūlūn (d. 884), succeeded in founding the first independent state in Egypt. But his ambitions did not go further than setting up in Egypt a hereditary dynasty that recognized the sovereignty of the 'Abbāsid caliphate. In 905, the Ṭūlūnid dynasty was overthrown by an 'Abbāsid army. This renewal of direct rule from Baghdād came to an end when the Ikhshīdids took power in 935, marking a return to autonomous rule.

During the Ikhshīdid period (935–969), following the rule of its founder Muḥammad ibn Tughj (935–946), real power was wielded by Kāfūr, an able Nubian eunuch who controlled the administration of the realm. The Fāṭimid caliphs were in power now in much of the Maghrib; they sent their missionaries and succeeded in winning over a number of the inhabitants. Kāfūr's death in 968 removed the last obstacle to the Fāṭimid takeover of Egypt.

The conquest of Egypt in 969 under the famous Jawhar, general of the Fāṭimid caliph al-Mu'izz (935–975), did not mean simply the replacement of one regime by another; practically, it amounted to a religious, political and social *coup d'état*. Egypt was now governed by a dynasty that did not recognize, even nominally, the caliph of Baghdād but sought by all means to overthrow him. The new regime was at once imperial and revolutionary. The Fāṭimid rulers were the leaders of a great religious movement whose ambition was no less than to bring the whole world of Islam under their control. They saw themselves as the true *imāms* on the principle of divine right from inheritance, on the basis of their claim to be the descendants of the Prophet's daughter Fāṭima and his cousin 'Alī, through Ismā'īl, the son of *imām* Ja'far al-Ṣādiq (d. 765). The Fāṭimid state in Egypt drew its strength from its capacity to profit to an unprecedented extent from the many social and ethnic communities that made up the Egyptian people. They took advantage of foreign elements, especially Maghribīs, Turks, Daylamites and Armenians; and they also relied on the Copts and other non-Muslims by putting them in charge of administrative and financial affairs and appointing them to leading government offices, from which the Sunnis were kept away.

The religious followers of the Fāṭimids, however, remained a minority. This deprived the Fāṭimid rulers of the positive support of the bulk of the country's population. But if for quite a long period they commanded the population's passive acceptance, this was due to the flourishing economy and the general prosperity that Egypt enjoyed under them as a result of their political successes. Moreover, the Fāṭimids gained support from non-Muslims by adopting a policy of religious tolerance towards them, except for the persecution they endured under the caliphate of al-Ḥākim (996–1021). Otherwise, non-Muslims experienced under the Fāṭimids an era of prosperity and tolerance. The Sunnis, however, were not treated in the same liberal way.

The Fāṭimids developed considerable naval and military power, especially in the late tenth and eleventh centuries under the caliphs al-'Azīz (975–996), al-Ḥākim, al-Ẓāhir (1021–1036) and al-Mustanṣir (1036–1094), operating in the Mediterranean and strongly maintaining their hold on Syria. Only the original North African possessions were lost to

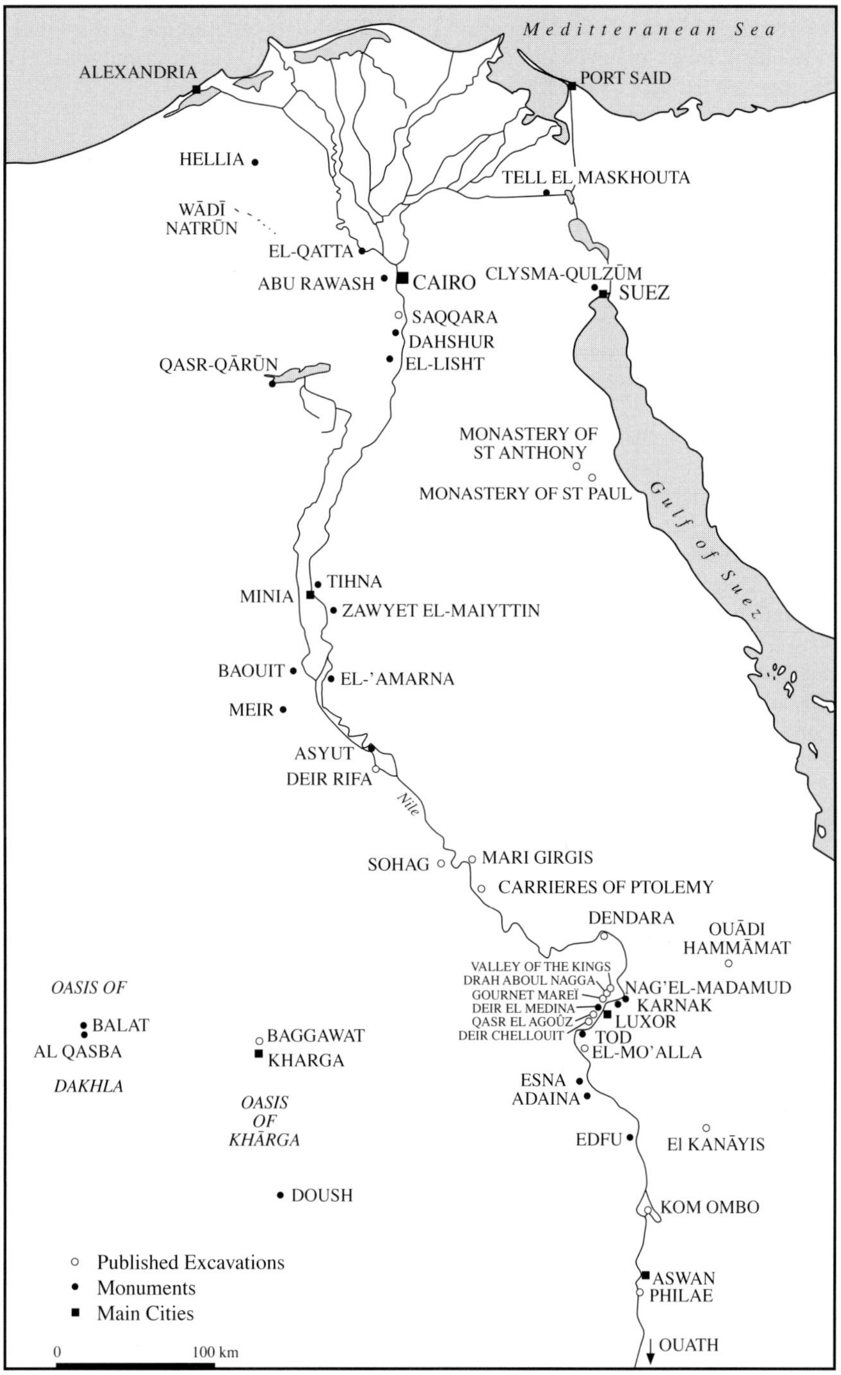

Map 15 Egypt.

the Zīrids in 1051. The Fāṭimid dominance over Yemen, gained in 1047, was important for their revenues owing to the lucrative spice trade with India which it commanded; and the Fāṭimids also controlled the export of Sudanese gold. There were considerable exports of woollen fabrics, linen and glassware to Europe from Egypt itself, in which trade Venice and Genoa participated. Economically, therefore, the Fāṭimid regime, in its hey-day, was an undoubted success.

In the latter half of the eleventh century, the Fāṭimids' political decline began. The Seljuk invasion of Syria (1069–1070) and the Crusader principalities sapped their power. The strong administration of the two Armenian viziers and commanders, Badr al-Jamālī (d. 1094) and his son al-Afḍal (d. 1121), could not stem the decline. In 1171, the dynasty was overthrown by the last vizier, Salāḥ al-Dīn, the famous Saladin, who established the Ayyūbid dynasty.

Intellectual developments

Early Sunni schools

The beginnings of Islamic intellectual life in Egypt are shrouded in obscurity. A *ṣahīfa* by 'Abd Allah ibn Lahī'a (eighth century) has been preserved on papyrus with its account of traditions relating to the Last Judgement.

At a very early period, the Mālikite doctrine took on great importance in Egypt; it is said to have been introduced by a *mawlā* (non-Arab Muslim), 'Abd al-Raḥīm ibn Khālid

(d. 779). The Mālikite doctrine held sway unchallenged until 813, when Imām Ibn al-Shāfi'ī came to Egypt and quickly acquired numerous disciples. He preached until his death in 820. The Ḥanafite doctrine was occasionally represented by a Ḥanafite judge sent from Baghdād but came up against local resistance. The Mālikite and Shāfi'īte doctrines held the field until the arrival of the Fāṭimids:

Ismā'īlism

A phase of vigorous attempts to promote Ismā'īlism (the religious sect headed by Fāṭimid rulers as *imāms*) was made under the Fāṭimids. Jurists and theologians, were awarded pensions to teach the Ismā'īli doctrine in the 'Amr mosque at Fusṭāṭ (Cairo). The mosque of al-Azhar also benefited. In 988, Caliph al-'Azīz is said to have bequeathed to thirty-seven *fuqahā'* (theologians) a residence near al-Azhar, with a trust to provide for their maintenance.

Dissension was caused by al-Ḥākim's encouragement of belief in his being a divine incarnation, a belief still held by the Druze of Syria and Lebanon. His disappearance or assassination (1021) led to a complete disavowal of al-Ḥākim's claim by the Fāṭimid *da'wā* (missionary establishment), and to the persecution of its adherants.

Learning and libraries

The most remarkable effort by the Fāṭimids to promote learning was to be seen in the *dār al-ḥikma* ('House of Wisdom') founded by Caliph al-Ḥākim in 1005. This was the true cultural centre of Cairo and Egypt at the time and foreshadowed the *madrasas* (schools) founded half a century later by the Seljuk sultans. The founder of this institution wanted it to resemble the *bayt al-ḥikma* ('Dwelling of Wisdom') created by the 'Abbāsid al-Ma'mūn in Baghdād; al-Ḥākim took great care over its organization and furnished a special building for it. A superb library was installed with collections transferred from the caliph's own library. The library was open to the public, and work there was facilitated by the provision of materials needed for transcription such as paper, ink and pens.

Al-Musabbiḥī has left a fine description of the Fāṭimids' royal library. We are told by another source that it had 18,000 books devoted to the ancient sciences. Ibn al-Ṭuwayr and Ibn Abī Ṭayy reports that 'it contained more than 200,000 bound volumes and a few unbound ones.'

Sunnism under the Fāṭimids

Once the Fāṭimids had completed their conquest of Egypt, Sunnism was practically forbidden. But al-Fusṭāṭ, the country's capital city, still remained strongly attached to Sunnism.

Alexandria too remained a centre of Sunnism. A large number of theologians from North Africa and Andalusia visited the city throughout the period; one of them was Abū Bakr Muḥammad ibn al-Walīd al-Ṭurṭūshī, a Mālikite scholar who settled in Alexandria in 1097 after spending some time in Baghdād. The sources speak of a school in Alexandria in which al-Ṭurṭūshī taught.

Shortly after the death of Caliph al-Āmir in 1130, Sunni doctrines began to take hold again. In 1136, Caliph al-Ḥāfiẓ appointed a Sunni, Riḍwān ibn Walakhshī as vizier, who a year later built a school in Alexandria to teach the Mālikite doctrine. Fourteen years later, another Sunni vizier, al-'Ādil ibn al-Sālār, ordered the construction in the same city of a second school, but this time for the Shāfi'ite doctrine.

Scientific development

Under the Fāṭimids, great strides were made in science, especially medicine and astronomy. We have space only to introduce some of the most important scholars.

Ibn al-Haytham (965–1039) was one of the foremost Arab mathematicians and probably the greatest Arab natural philosopher. Born in Baṣrā in about 965, he went to Egypt during the reign of al-Ḥākim (996–1021), where he unsuccessfully attempted to regulate the course of the Nile. Most of his numerous writings – a few of them very short – were devoted to mathematics and physics, but he also covered philosophical and medical subjects. His best-known work is the *Kitāb al-Manāẓir* ('Book of Optics'), which was translated into Latin under the title 'Alhazen' in the twelfth century.

Abū'l-Ḥasan 'Alī ibn Riḍwān al-Miṣrī (d. 1061), the chief physician of Egypt at the time of Caliph al-Mustanṣir, was the author of medical texts and also a polemicist. About twenty of his works have survived. Ibn Riḍwān showed a profound knowledge of ancient medicine but was not an original thinker: he simply expounded the thinking of Hippocrates and Galen. Among his most important works is a treatise on health and diseases in Egypt and Cairo, 'On the prevention of bodily ills in the land of Egypt', which deals with the plague and its cause, and with preventive measures and rules of hygiene, and includes a medical topography of Cairo and its suburbs in his time.

Ibn Yūnus al-Ṣadafī (d. 1009), was one of the most renowned Muslim astronomers. His important treatise on astronomy, *al-Zīj al-kabīr al-Ḥākimī*, or 'great almanac dedicated to al-Ḥākim' (which has not, it seems, been preserved in its entirety) was begun around 990 and completed shortly before the death of its author. Ibn Yūnus mentioned a great many astronomical observations (eclipses and other phenomena), some of which dated back to his predecessors in the ninth and tenth centuries, while others had been made by himself in Cairo. Taken as a whole, this work contains the most extensive list of astronomical observations in medieval times till then known: Ibn Yūnus describes the research of his predecessors with the greatest care; and, when he criticizes the errors and inaccuracies contained in their works, his tone is remarkably modern. The observations reported by him have been studied by Newcomb, who was struck by their potential usefulness for estimating the secular acceleration of the Moon. Ibn Yūnus also made some original contributions to plane and spherical trigonometry.

Architecture

Almost nothing worthy of note in art or architecture from the pre-Ṭūlūnid period has survived, apart from the 'Amr mosque in al-Fusṭāṭ, whose importance is not so much archaeological as historical, and the Nilometer on the isle of Rawḍa, which was re-erected in 861. The real history of Islamic architecture in al-Fusṭāṭ began with the Ṭūlūnids. Though the mosque of Ibn Ṭūlūn is all that remains, the certainty of its date makes it one of the most important landmarks of Cairo's architecture.

The first Fāṭimid mosque in Egypt, the al-Azhar mosque, was probably built (970) to resemble the Ibn Ṭūlūn mosque. Though much of the original building no longer remains, the shape of the vast central court (*al-ṣaḥn*) surrounded by porches with Persian arches, and the form of the prayer hall with its five bays running parallel to the wall of the *qibla*, conform to the original design (see Plate 204).

The mosque of al-Ḥākim (990–1013), was also designed after the mosque of Ibn Ṭūlūn, but here the brick pillars are more slender and there are other new features, such as the monumental entrance, clearly inspired by the one in the Fāṭimid mosque of al-Mahdiyya in North Africa.

This type of porch can also be seen on a much smaller scale in the Fāṭimid mosque of al-Aqmar (1125) (see Plate 70) and in the Mamlūk mosque of al-Ẓāhir Baybars (1266), where it reaches an impressive size with lateral façades decorated with three blind arcades, as against two in the al-Ḥākim mosque and only one at al-Mahdiyya.

At the al-Aqmar mosque, the façade is decorated with a rich covering of foliated ornaments and inscriptions, the first instance of this in Cairo. It also displays a more complex and elaborate use of *muqarnas* ('stalactite' corbellations).

The Fāṭimids also built a new kind of sanctuary in Egypt (see Plate 32), a memorial above the tombs of the principal 'Alīds buried in that country. The most ancient of these, whose ground plan is still intact, is the 'Martyr Ground of al-Juyūshī', at the top of the Muqaṭṭam hills.

EGYPT FROM 1171 TO 1517 (SEE MAP 15)

Political history

The Ayyūbids (1171–1250)

Salāḥ al-Dīn ibn Ayyūb (Saladin), himself a Kurd officer of Nūr al-Dīn (d. 1174), the rising potentate of Syria, became vizier to the Fāṭimid ruler in 1169 under a shadow of the army sent by his master. In September 1171 he proclaimed the abolition of the Fāṭimid caliphate and, with it, Egypt's return to formal allegiance to the 'Abbāsid caliphate in Baghdād. The Ismā'īlī call to prayer was prohibited, Sunnism became the official sect, and the Shāfi'ī school was particularly favoured.

Saladin (d. 1193) founded the Ayyūbid dynasty, as he struggled both to restore the country's prosperity and to control all its avenues of approach to Egypt by land by assigning the territories to his various kinsmen. He introduced into Egypt the system of *iqṭā*'s (territorial tax assignments) to support his army, and also reorganized a fleet. His concerted effort in pursuit of his counter-crusade bore fruit, and the Franks were defeated at Ḥaṭṭīn in 1187, whereafter Saladin took Jerusalem. His reconstituted fleet simultaneously thwarted Byzantine and Western raids from the sea.

The true organizer of the Ayyūbid confederation was Saladin's brother and successor, al-Malik al-'Ādil, (*sulṭān*, 1200–1218). Like Saladin, he reserved no specific demesne for himself, the lands being shared out between three of his sons, while Aleppo fell to one of Saladin's sons, al-Ẓāhir Ghāzī.

Not much time elapsed, however, before dissensions broke out amongst al-Malik al-'Ādil's sons, and unity between their possessions was never realized except for short spells. All these princes were wary, however, of expensive military activities and developed trade ties with the West, so Egypt gradually replaced the Crusader states as the focus of the Levant trade.

The Mamlūks (1250–1517)

The strains attendant on the two military crises provoked by French King Louis IX's Crusade (1249–1250) and then the invasion of Syria by the Mongols (1259–1260), helped to bring about the fall of the Ayyūbids in Egypt and Syria – and their replacement by the Mamlūks of the so-called Baḥriyya regiment (*Baḥr*, Egyptian name for the Nile). The Baḥriyya were a military grouping of originally *Qipchāq mamlūks* or Turkish armed bondsmen, formed by the Ayyūbid sultan al-Malik al-Ṣāliḥ Ayyūb (1240–1249).

Aybak al-Turkumānī, one of the *baḥriyya* officers, took the throne as al-Malik al-Mu'izz in 1250. But when the Mongols began invading Syria in 1259, a powerful mamlūk officer, Quṭuẓ, usurped the sultanate. With another mamlūk, the famous Baybars, he led an expeditionary force into Palestine and defeated the Mongols at *'Ayn Jālūt* on 3 September 1260. But soon afterwards Baybars led a group of conspirators, who murdered Quṭuẓ, and took the sultanate for himself.

The true founder of the Mamlūk sultanate, Baybars, had a relatively long reign (1260–1277), during which he succeeded in ensuring internal stability.

Baybars sought to legitimize his power by setting up an 'Abbāsid prince in Cairo with the title of caliph, and in June 1261 securing from this puppet caliph an official delegation of full powers to himself as the universal sultan of Islam. The descendants of this 'Abbāsid prince were in turn duly recognized as caliphs in Egypt and Syria until the Ottoman conquest.

Baybars's dynasty did not long survive him. One of his former colleagues in arms, Qalāwun al-Alfī, usurped the throne in August 1279. The logic of the new political system now became clear: the new regime was so structured as to make transmission along family lines very difficult. Power rather depended upon the loyalty of a group of mamlūks to the person of the particular prince to whom their fate was linked. Qalāwun (d. 1290) himself was the second major figure of the new sultanate, and he repeated Baybars's triumph over the Mongols, at Ḥims, in 1281. But while lineal descendants of his son, al-Nāṣir Muḥammad (1310–1341), did succeed one another on the throne, the fact that twelve sultans held sway over a period of less than half a century betrays how weak they really were.

Then, in November 1382, a mamlūk of Circassian origin, Barqūq ibn Anas, deposed the House of Qalāwun and usurped the sultanate. The new sultan's power rested upon the *Burjiyya mamlūks*, 'they of the Tower', from their quarters in the towers of Cairo citadel. The regiment itself was founded by Qalāwun. These Circassian mamlūks were to retain power in Egypt and Syria until the Ottoman conquest of 1517.

Throughout the fourteenth and fifteenth centuries, the Mamlūk sultanate of Cairo appeared as the leading power in the Arab world. The Mamlūk sultans strove to control the Mediterranean shoreline from Cyrenaica to as far as Anatolia. An essential complement of this northward policy was extension of their influence to the south over the Red Sea and far into the interior of the African continent.

The decline of the Īlkhānid state in the first quarter of the fourteenth century contributed to the shift the major currents of world trade to Egypt by the second half of the same century. While the Italians and the Catalans held a monopoly over Mediterranean trade, Egypt's own *Kārimī* merchants dominated trade within the Islamic lands. This age marked the zenith of the Kārimī merchants' activities, which not only involved them in dealing with local produce but also took them as far afield as Yemen, the Indian Ocean and Sudanese Africa. Mamlūk Egypt probably reached the apogee of its prosperity during the reign of al-Nāṣir Muḥammad (1310–1341), when canals were dug in the Nile delta, considerably extending cultivation. Great building activity took place under him at Cairo. A treaty made by him with the Mongols (Īl-khānids) in 1323 confirmed the Euphrates as the boundary between the two powers.

Mamlūk Egypt entered a long period of economic difficulties after al-Nāṣir Muḥammad's death in 1341, as bubonic plague known as the 'Black Death' struck both Syria and Egypt with virulent force. Plague broke out again and again for the next 150 years, with grievous long-term impact upon Egypt's population. This in turn led to a fall in crop production and so of the tax resources and wealth of the Mamlūk regime. This reason for the long-term weakening of the Mamlūk power tends now to be more stressed, rather than the alleged fall in Mamlūk revenues owing to the Portuguese diversion (after 1498) of part of the Eastern trade from the Mediterranean to the Cape of Good Hope.

Military factors too perhaps contributed to the Mamlūk decline, although the Mamlūks were among the first in the Islamic world to take to gunpowder, weapons based on which are described by al-Qalqashandī (d. 1418); and matchlocks were possibly in use by the reign of Sultan Qā'it Bay (1468–1496). However, these weapons proved to be of little avail in 1516–1517 against the Ottoman armies, which had taken still more extensively to the new arms.

Religious life

Under the Ayyūbids, the structure of Fāṭimid Ismā'īlism was rapidly demolished; the succeeding Mamlūks too continued to affirm their loyalty to Sunni orthodoxy. The Mamlūk rulers used both the Ḥanafite and Mālikite schools to counterbalance the local Shāfi'īte dominance. This is illustrated by the appointment of the famous Tunisian scholar Ibn Khaldūn (d. 1406), a Mālikite, as grand judge after his arrival in Egypt in 1382. The Mamlūks also patronized Ṣūfic establishments, an attitude which brought them into conflict with the Ḥanbalite scholar Ibn Taymiyya (d. 1328) in Damascus.

One of the greatest religious institutions to develop under the Mamlūks was the mosque of al-Aẓhar. This mosque had suffered complete neglect under the Ayyūbids. With the Mamlūks, this situation changed, and al-Aẓhar's flourishing as both mosque and academy dates from this period. Sultan Baybars added new buildings, encouraged the teaching of the sciences and restored to the shrine its privilege of housing the pronouncing of the *khutba*. Nor did al-Aẓhar merely benefit from the favour of local rulers: its fortunes rose in ever greater measure as a result of the havoc wrought by the Mongols in the East and by the retreat of Islam in the West, events which together provoked the disappearance, or at any rate the decline, of many once-flourishing ancient *madrasas* (see Plate 204).

Literature and learning

By the fourteenth century, Arabic had become the common spoken language of Egypt, completely supplanting Coptic. As Arabic itself was being simultaneously supplanted by Persian as the principal literary language in the eastern Islamic world, and as, with the thirteenth-century Mongol conquests, Iraq went into a political eclipse, Egypt (with Syria as its appendage) became the chief centre of Arabic literature and learning (see Plates 90, 110, 140, 217).

Arabic poetry of the *ghazal* (lyric) type found a notable figure in al-Bahā' Zuhayr (d. 1187); and soon afterwards 'Umar ibn al-Fāriḍ (d.1235) wove Ṣūfic themes in the traditional idiom of wine and love. Religious poetry of the reverential kind received its classical expression in the panegyric on the Prophet, the *al-Burda*, by al-Buṣīrī (d. 1296). In the late Mamlūk period, Ibn Sudūn (d. 1464) wrote humorous and satirical poems drawing upon colloquial speech.

Stately secretarial prose (*inshā*) was provided a model by al-Qāḍi al-Fāḍil (d. 1199), and later by al-Qalqashandī (d. 1418). From Ibn Abī Uṣaybī'a (d. 1270), we get early examples of the colloquial Arabic idiom in use in 'good society'.

Egyptian Arabic literature of this period was especially rich in historical works, notably those of Al-Maqrīzī (d. 1442) and Ibn Taghrībirdī (d. 1469), the latter criticizing the former's anti-Turkish bias. Ibn Ḥajar al-'Askalānī (d.1449) showed immense industry in compiling analytical manuals on *ḥadīth* narrations; he also authored biographies of scholars. Al-Maqrīzī compiled biographies of Egyptian scholars; and the polymath al-Suyūtī (d. 1503) produced biographies of philologists.

Al-Qalqashandī's *Ṣubh al-'Ashā* is an important repository of historical and geographical information about the Islamic world, besides having a value as an *inshā'* manual.

While the famous collection 'The One Thousand and One Nights' (*Alf Layla wa Layla*) seems to have obtained its final form after the Ottoman conquest (1517), there is little doubt that most of its stories, derived from various civilizations, had already been compiled within the Mamlūk period, with some stories inserted that were purely of Egyptian origin.

The Mamlūks, being of Turkish extraction, encouraged translations of Arabic and Persian works into old Anatolian Turkish, and Sultan Qā'it Bay (d.1496) left behind a collection of verses in that language. Mamlūk Egypt has thus had a role to play in the evolution of literary Turkish.

Architecture

The coming to power of the Ayyūbids in Egypt in no way modified building techniques and added few elements to the system of decoration. Since the institution of the *madrasa* had been a Sunni creation for the purposes of teaching *fiqh*, it was widely known in Egypt in this age. Most of the buildings raised by the Ayyūbids have disappeared. The most important to have survived down to our own day are the walls and citadel of Saladin (1176–1184); the mausoleum of Imām al-Shāfi'ī (1211); and the tomb of Sultan al-Malik al-Ṣāliḥ Ayyūb (1250).

The Mamlūk sultans added new types of monument to those known to Egypt in the Fāṭimid and Ayyūbid periods. The *madrasa* was developed; the *khānqāh* or Ṣūfī convent was introduced into Cairo and drew its inspiration from the *madrasa*, even though the most ancient of its kind founded in Egypt, that of Sā'id al-Su'adā (1173–1174), was an Ayyūbid creation. Henceforth, the tombs of sultans and other exalted individuals would adjoin either a *khānqāh* or a *madrasa*, to which would be added, by the end of the period under consideration, a *sabīl* or drinking fountain, completed by a *kuttāb* or elementary school.

The Mamlūk age was moreover quite familiar with mosques adorned with porticoes, such as the mosque of Baybars (1269) and the mosque of al-Nāṣir Muḥammad in the citadel (1318–1335), while the mosque of al-Mu'ayyad Shaykh (1415–1420) near the Bāb Zuwayla was the last such porticoed shrine to be built in Mamlūk Cairo.

The *madrasa* tended to gradually replace the mosque, and indeed several mosques actually adopted the ground plan of the *madrasa*, while *madrasas* based on a cruciform ground plan progressively eliminated all other types. The *madrasa* of Sultan Ḥasan (1356), one of the greatest monuments in Cairo, is the most accomplished of such cruciform-patterned *madrasas* of the fourteenth century. In the Circassian period, *madrasas* outnumbered mosques, and the cruciform ground plan remained the preferred pattern for *madrasas* of all four Sunni rites.

Throughout the Mamlūk period, the citadel remained the seat of government of the sultan. The most important building activity carried out under the Mamlūks in the citadel occurred under al-Nāṣir Muḥammad; construction here included a large mosque with porticoes (1318), and the palace known as the 'Piebald Castle', *al-Qaṣr al-Ablaq* (1314), on account of the two-coloured arch-stones making up the arches of the main Hall or *qā'a*. The palaces of the emirs, which in Maqrīzī's day covered the southern slopes of the Citadel's embankment, have now completely disappeared.

BIBLIOGRAPHY

Note: *EI*² = *Encyclopaedia of Islam*, 2nd edn. Leiden.

ALLOUCHE, A. 1994. *Mamluk Economies. A Study and Translation of al-Maqrīzī's Ighāthah.* University of Utah Press.

AYALON, D. 1977. *Studies on the* Mamlūks *of Egypt.* Variorum Reprints, London.

——. 1997. The End of the Mamlūk Sultanate, *SI* LXV, pp. 125–148.

BLACHERE, R. 1973. La Fondation du Caire et la renaissance de l'humanisme arabo-islamique au IVè siecle. In: *Colloque International sur l'Histoire du Caire.*

CAHEN, C. 1960. article: 'Ayyūbids', *EI*², I, pp. 796–807.

——. 1970. *L'Islam des origines au debut de l'Empire ottoman.* Paris.

——. 1983. *Orient et Occident à l'époque des Croisades.* Paris.

CANARD, M. 1965. Article: 'Fatimides' *EI*² II, pp. 870–884.

CRESWELL, K. A. C. 1952, 1958. *The Muslin Architecture of Egypt, I. Iksids and* Fāṭimids, *II. Ayyūbids and early Mamlūks.* Oxford.

DAHMANNS, F. J. 1975. *Al-Malik al-'Ādil. Ägypten und der Vordere Orient in den Jahren 589/1193 bis 615/1218,* Giessen.

DARRAG, A. 1961. *L'Egypte sous le règne de Barsbay, 825–841/ 1422–1438.* Damascus.

ECHE, Y. 1967. *Les Bibliothèques arabes publiques et semi-publiques en Mésopotamie, en Syrie et en Egypte au Moyen Âge.* Damascus.

EHRENKREUTZ, A. S. 1972. *Saladin.* Albany, NY.

ELISSEEFF, N. 1977. *L'Orient musulman au Moyen Âge (622–1210).* Paris.

FU'AD SAYYID, A. 1992. *al-Dawla al-fāṭimiyya fī Miṣrtafsirun dgadīd,* Cairo.

——. 1997. *La Capitale de l'Egypte jusqu'à l'époque Fatimide.* Beirut.

GARCIN, J.-C. 1976. *Un centre musulman de la Haute Egypte médiévale: Qus.* Cairo-IFAO.

——. 1995. *Etats, sociétés et cultures du monde musulman médiéval, Xè–XVè siècles: I, L'Evolution politique et sociale.* Paris.

GOITEIN, S. D. 1967. *A Mediterranean Society,* Vol. I: *Economic Foundations.* Princeton.

GOLDSTEIN, B. R. 1971. article: 'Ibn Yūnus', *EI*², III, pp. 969–970.

GOTTSCHALK, H. L. 1958. *Al-Malik al-Kāmil von Ägypten und seine Zeit.* Wiesbaden.

HOLT, P. M. 1991. article: 'Mamlūks', *EI*², VI, pp. 314–331.

——. 1995. *Early Mamluk Diplomacy (1260–1290). Treaties of Baybars and Qalāwān with Christian Rulers.* Brill, Leiden.

HUMPHREYS, R. 1977. *From Saladin to the Mongols.* Albany, NY.

'INĀN, MUḤAMMAD 'ALĪ. 1958. *Tārikh al-Jāmī' al-Azhar* (History of the Mosque of al-Aẓhar). Cairo,

IRWIN, R. 1986. *The Middle East in the Middle Ages. The Early Mamlūk Sultanate, 1250–1382.* London.

JOMIER, J. 1960. article: 'al-Aẓhar', *EI*², I, pp. 813–821.

KHOURY, R. C. 1981. Une description fantastique des fonds de la bibliothèque royale, hizanat al-kutub au Caire. In: *Actes du IXè Congres de l'Union européenne des arabisants et islamisants,* Leiden, Brill, pp. 123–140.

LABIB, S. 1965. *Handelsgeschichte Ägyptens im Spätmittelalter 1171–1517.* Wiesbaden.

LEV, I. 1999. *Saladin in Egypt.* Brill, Leiden.

LEWIS, B. 1949–1950. The Fāṭimids and the route to India. *Revue de la Faculté des Sciences économiques,* Université d'Istanbul, XI, pp. 50–54.

LYONS, M. C.; JACKSON, D. E. P. 1982. *Saladin.* Cambridge.

MAQDĪSĪ. 1906. *Aḥsan al-Taqāsīm fī ma'rifad al-aqālīm,* ed. Goeje, Leiden, Brill.

MAQRĪSĪ. 1853. *Khiṭaṭ: al-mawā'iz wal-i'tibār fī dhkr al-khiṭaṭ wal-athār,* 1–2. Būlāq.

——. 1934–72. *al-Sulūk li ma'rifat duwal al-mulūk,* ed. Muh. M. Ziāda and S. 'Āshūnr. Cairo.

MEINECKE, M. 1992. *Die Mamlukishe Architektur in Ägypten und Syrien (648/1250 Bis 923/1517).* Gluckstadt.

MIQUEL, A. 1971. L'Egypte vue par un géographe arabe du IV/Xè siècle: al-Muqaddasī. *Annales Islamiques,* X, pp. 109–139.

MUSABBIHI. 1978–1984. *Akhbār Miṣr* (fragment), ed. A. F. Sayyid, T. Bianquis and H. Nissar. Cairo.

PETRY, C. 1994. *Protectors or Praetorians? The Last Mamlūk Sultans and Egypt's Waning as a Great Power.* State University of New York Press.

RABBAT, N. O. 1995. *The Cairo Citadel.* Brill, Leiden.

ROGERS, M. 1978. article: 'al-Kāhira', *EI*², IV, pp. 424–440.

SCHACHT, J. 1971. article: 'Ibn Riḍwān', *EI*², III, pp. 969–970.

AL-SHINNĀWĪ. 1983. *'Abd al-'Azīz, Al-Azhar, Jāmi' wa Jāmi'a* (Al-Aẓhar, Friday Mosque and University). Cairo.

SOURDEL, D.; SOURDEL, J. 1983. *La civilisation de l'Islam classique.* Paris.

THORAU, P. 1987. *Sultan Baibars I. von Ägypten,* Wiesbaden; *The Lion of Egypt, Sultan Baybars I and the Near East in the Thirteenth Century,* English version with additions by P. M. Holt, London, 1992.

VERMULAN, U. and DE SMET, D. 1995. *Egypt and Syria in the Fatimid, Ayyubid and Mamluk Eras.* Leuven.

VERNET, J. 1971. article: 'al-Haytham', *EI*², III, pp. 811–812.

WIET, G. 1932. *L'Egypte arabe.* Paris.

20.2
AL-MAGHRIB

M'hammad Benaboud

The cultural and scientific history of the Maghrib has been rather neglected by historians despite its many points of interest. Within the region, one may say that Ifrīqiyya, which comprised present-day Tunisia and eastern Algeria, calls for special attention during the period *c.* 650–1000 and Morocco *c.* 1000–1500 (See Map 16).

The cultural development of the Maghrib was characterized by its ability to continuously incorporate new external elements. With the rise of the Almoravid state and its incorporation of Al-Andalus, that is, Islamic Spain (eleventh century), the Andalusian cultural element was introduced in the Maghrib with much vigour. As an independent political state during the period of the Umayyad caliphate, Al-Andalus had tangled with the Fāṭimid caliphate in Ifrīqiyya over Morocco. Now subdued by the Almoravids, the Andalusians imposed their cultural hegemony over the Maghrib. Maghribī art, architecture, science and knowledge in general were strongly marked by Andalusian culture throughout the period of the 'Almoravids', (*al-Murābiṭūn, c.* 1064–1145), the 'Almohads' (al-Muwaḥḥidūn, *c.* 1120–1269), and the 'Merinids' (*Banū Marīn,* 1259–1420). The most important cities in the Maghrib like Kairouan (*Qayrawān*), Tlemcen (*Tilimsān*), Ceuta (*Sibṭa*) or Fez (*Fās*), bore strong traces of Andalusian culture. Scholars in the Maghrib who attained universal acclaim between the eleventh and fourteenth centuries such as the jurist *al-Qāḍī* 'Iyad (1083–1149), the philosopher Abu-l-Walīd ibn Rushd (Averroës, 1126–1198), the encyclopedic fourteenth-century scholar and politician Ibn Marzūq of Tlemcen, or the historian and philosopher of history Ibn Khaldūn, were all closely associated with Al-Andalus.

The development of culture in the Maghrib during the periods of the Almoravids, Almohads and Merinids was stimulated by two elements: the rulers and the *'ulamā'* (scholars). For rulers, we may cite the examples of Al-Mahdī Ibn Tūmart (d. *c.* 1130), himself an established scholar, Ya'qūb al-Manṣūr al-Muwaḥḥidī (r. 1162–1184) and Abu 'Inān Al-Marīnī (r. 1348–1358), who established schools in different Moroccan cities. The abundant availability of financial support for cultural projects during the period of the Almohads and Merinids (1257–1559) explains much of the progress in science and culture attained during this period. From the side of the *'ulamā'* came the judicial tradition, which constituted the general framework for the development of Mālikism.

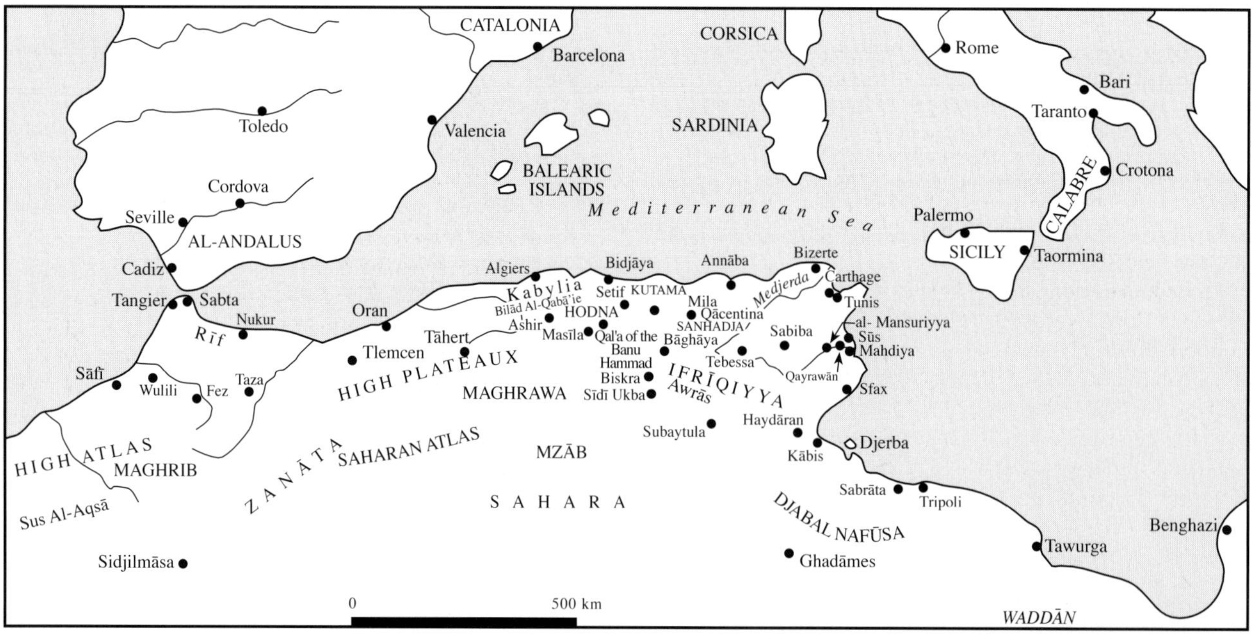

Map 16 The Maghrib in the Middle Ages (after Hrbek, I. 1984, in *General History of Africa,* Vol. IV).

MĀLIKISM

Mālikism refers to a school of law established by its founder Mālik ibn Anas in Medina during the eighth century, but it also designates a cultural movement in the Maghrib. It became the official rite in many parts of the Maghrib and Al-Andalus. The causes behind the success of Mālikism in the Maghrib are a subject of controversy, as is the question of defining the term. Mālikism came to cover so many aspects of cultural life in the Maghrib that it could be considered an expression of the cultural development in this region.

Mālikism first appeared in Ifrīqiyya in the eighth century before spreading to other parts of the Maghrib, including Morocco. During the course of its development, it underwent a number of transformations that enriched it immensely. The origins of Mālikism are still vague, although Myklos Moranyi has recently studied the earliest sources by Māliki scholars. Moranyi's study indicates that the contribution of many Maghribī scholars in Ifrīqiyya to the development of Mālikism was important even in the embryonic stage. The mutations of Mālikism in both the Maghrib and Al-Andalus over the centuries could be considered a result of its ability to adapt to new developments and socio-cultural conditions.

Although Mālikism has traditionally been considered by some as an obstacle to the development of free thought in the Maghrib and Al-Andalus, recent studies have adopted more positive approaches towards it. Mālikism was adopted as the official rite in the Maghrib by several dynasties. During the eleventh century, the Almoravids adopted it as the official school of law and of theology, their state being the first to unite an extensive territory that ranged from Marrakesh and Cordova in the north and Ifrīqiyya in the east. The success of Mālikism as an official school does not imply that it was imposed by force but rather that it enjoyed such popular support that the state decided to adopt it as its official rite. The Mālikī jurists and scholars who became politically powerful under the Almoravids gained wide popularity through their opposition to non-Islamic taxation and other unpopular measures. Mālikism was also popular because some of its principles, such as *al-maṣāliḥ al-mursala,* which gave priority to the 'higher interests' in some cases, enabled it to adapt to social changes over many centuries and under many states.

Mālikism was also successful culturally because it succeeded in orientating culture in the Maghrib and Al-Andalus even during the periods of states which opposed each other ideologically. The exclusive association of Mālikism with particular states like that of the Almoravids appears to be overstressed. The literary productivity of the *'ulamā'* during this period contradicts the commonly propagated idea that this was a period of cultural and intellectual stagnation.

The contribution of Mālikism is clear in several aspects of cultural life in the Maghrib during the period of the Almoravids. The first was the publication of numerous works in various branches of knowledge. Bio-bibliographical dictionaries have recorded an impressive number of publications from the periods of the Almoravids and the Almohads in *fiqh* or jurisprudence, as well as in history and literature. Examples of such dictionaries include Ibn Bashkuwal's *Kitāb Al-Sīla* or Ibn Al-'Abbār's *Al-Takmila li Kitāb Al-Sīla,* which deal with eleventh- and twelfth-century scholars. Second, the high calibre of some of the intellectual figures of the period such as al-Qāḍī 'Iyād in the field of jurisprudence reflects the high quality of culture during this period. Al-Qāḍī 'Iyād supported the Almoravids and opposed the Almohads politically, while defending Mālikism in his biographical dictionary of Mālikī jurists entitled *Tartīb Al-Madārik wa Taqrīb al-Masālik ilā Ma'rifat Madhhabi-l-Imām Mālik.* Third, popular contributions to the cultural developments of this period are important because they formed the basis for the success of Mālikism as a cultural tradition. The popular dimension of Mālikism is reflected, for example, in the fact that it continued to flourish even during the period of the Almohads, the great opponents of the Almoravids, the patrons of Mālikism.

The idea that the Almohads formed a state that constituted the antithesis of that of the Almoravids needs careful examination. It is necessary to distinguish between the position of al-Mahdī ibn Tūmart, the founder of the Almohad dynasty, towards Mālikism and his position towards Mālikī jurists (*fuqahā'*). His attitude towards Mālikī jurists was clearly antagonistic, because he accused them of relying on Mālikī texts rather than on scriptural sources, thus introducing a human element into the field of *fiqh* or jurisprudence. Second, he accused them of attributing corporal elements to Allāh; that is, of conceiving God through man. These fundamental differences led to Al-Mahdī's opposition to the *fuqahā'* of the Almoravids, a policy which was continued by his successor 'Abd al-Mu'min (r. 1129–1162).

However, from his own point of view, al-Mahdī's attitude towards Mālikism was positive. He is the author of an abridged version of Mālik ibn Anās' *Al-Muwaṭṭa'* entitled *Muhādhi-l-Muwaṭṭā,* in which he reproduced the texts of the Prophet's sayings in Mālik's *Al-Muwaṭṭa.* Through this book, al-Mahdī' intended to organize the spiritual life of his followers.

It is important to note that al-Mahdī ibn Tūmart's differences with Mālikī scholars were limited in extent. He agreed with them on the two main sources of Islamic jurisprudence, namely the Qur'ān and the *Ḥadīth* (sayings of the Prophet). To a certain extent, he even agreed with them on such principles as the need to rely on *ijmā'* or consensus and *qiyās* or analogy. However, he disagreed with them on the definition of consensus when he limited this consensus to the companions of the Prophet from among the inhabitants of Medina (Mālikism accepts the consensus of all the inhabitants of Medina who were contemporary with the Prophet). He also disagreed with the *fuqahā'* of the Almoravids on the question of analogy, rejecting *qiyās al-shahīd* (analogy based on a witness) and supporting *al-qiyās al-shar'ī* (legal analogy) or reasoning by analogy by deducing the unknown from the known.

Although the Almohads did introduce certain innovations at the dogmatic and cultural levels, Mālikism continued to flourish during their period. Rather, the Almohads enriched Mālikism by supporting new cultural trends in the Maghrib and Al-Andalus, which they also ruled. Free thought flourished during their period as it had not done previously. Some of the most eminent intellectual figures who lived during their period include different blends of Andalusian philosophers and theologians whom the Almohads patronized, such as Ibn Ṭufayl, author of *Ḥayy ibn Yaqdhān,* precursor of Daniel Defoe's *Robinson Crusoe,* Ibn Rushd (Averroës), one of the most famous Andalusian philosophers as well as a jurist and medical doctor, and Ibn Bajja (Avempace). Abu-l-Ḥajjāj Yūsuf Al-Miklatī is the author of a refutation of philosophers in theology (*'ilm al-kalām),* entitled *Lubab al-Nuqūl.* Such works had been forbidden by the Almoravids. New sciences flourished during this period, such as mathematics and Qur'ānic sciences. The mathematician Ibn al-Yasmīn Al-Fāsī wrote a work on algebra in rhymed verse (*urjūza*). It is also important that Mālikism continued to flourish after the Almohad period, and most particularly under the Merinids whose regime followed immediately afterwards and lasted until the fifteenth century.

It is necessary here to note the contribution of Andalusian Mālikī scholars to Mālikism in Morocco. Since political frontiers were abolished during part of this period, while geographical proximity was permanent, religious and cultural ties between Mālikī jurists and scholars of both countries were maintained throughout the medieval period. Their continued cultural contact with Islamic West Asia and Egypt (the *Mashriq*) constituted another unifying factor. The impact of Andalusian Mālikī jurists like Abu-l-Walīd Al-Bājī or Ibn ʿAbd al-Barr was very strong in the Maghrib. However, the importance of Mālikism in the Maghrib is perhaps most strongly symbolized by al-Qāḍī ʿIyād, with his high intellectual calibre, fervent defense of Mālikism and lifelong dedication to the study of jurisprudence. His monumental work *Tartīb al-Mādarik* illustrates various aspects of the development of Mālikism as a cultural force in the Maghrib and Al-Andalus. The introduction to this work constitutes a fervent defence of Mālikism as a rite, a mode of thinking and an approach to life. The highly developed techniques applied by al-Qāḍī ʿIyād include the presentation of the criticism of Mālikism by other Islamic schools before refuting them and justifying the various positions of Mālikism.

Another interesting feature of his book lies in his methodology at the level of classification, which revolved around the objective of defending Mālikism. He included only Mālikī jurists and began his work with a defence of Mālik ibn Anās and his thought. He then divided his book into groups or categories of Mālikī jurists according to generations and subdivided into regions. The Maghrib and Al-Andalus were each treated as an important region, so that it was possible to find the biographies of Maghribī scholars of each generation in different volumes of the work. Al-Qāḍī ʿIyād engaged in sharp polemical discussions with such prestigious authorities in the *Mashriq* as the Iraqi Muʿtazilite jurist al-Zamakhsharī. His great reputation has been summarized in the saying: 'Without ʿIyād, the Maghrib would not have been known'. The role of the Mālikī '*ulamā*' in the promotion of culture and learning was thus fundamental in the Maghrib.

LIBRARIES, COPYISTS AND CALLIGRAPHERS

Libraries played an extremely important cultural role in the Maghrib throughout the medieval period, as a number of recent studies by such authors as Muḥammad al-Manūnī and Binbin have demonstrated. These libraries were numerous and often highly specialized. The production and distribution of manuscripts was partly a reflection of the widespread educational activity in the Maghrib during the medieval period, reaching its peak during the Almohad and Merinid periods. Books in Maghribī libraries were carefully preserved even during the thirteenth century, when the great libraries in some of eastern Islam's great cultural centres, such as Baghdād, were destroyed during the Mongol invasions. Although libraries were less important in the Maghrib than in Western and Central Asia, they were saved because of the relative stability of the region during the Merinid period.

The history of books in the Maghrib during the medieval period is closely associated with the paper industry, and the work of scholars as authors, as well as the role of scribes in writing these books, including specialized calligraphers. We have some information concerning some of the techniques and materials used by Maghribī copyists and calligraphers.

Arabic calligraphy is believed to have been introduced to the Maghrib during the Islamic conquest of the seventh century. There is a reference to the beautiful handwriting of Sāliḥ al-Barghwatī, who ruled from 744. The eleventh-century Andalusian geographer Al-Bakrī refers to calligraphers in Fez during the early tenth century. Arabic calligraphy was used in Kairouan at an early stage, adopting both the *kūfī* and *naskhī* scripts. Several tenth-century manuscripts written in the *kūfī* script have been discovered in Kairouan. Al-Qāḍī ʿIyād refers to the oldest Maghribī calligrapher, the *faqīh* Abū ʿUthman Saʿid ibn Khalf Al-Riyyāḥī, who copied most of the works on Mālikism existing at the time (see Plate 107).

Maghribī calligraphy underwent radical transformation when the Andalusian script gradually replaced that of Kairouan under the Almoravids. Another change introduced during the Almoravid period was the increasing use of paper instead of *al-riqq* or leather hide, particularly deerskin. Paper manufacture flourished in Fez, where 104 paper factories have been recorded. Several copyists lived in Fez during the Almoravid period, including Yaḥyā ibn Muḥammad ibn ʿAbbād al-Lakhmī (twelfth century) who worked for the Almoravid rulers.

The Almohad period is considered as the golden age of Maghribī calligraphy because it was during this period that this tradition was transformed into a specialized art. It was taught by professionals, and some calligraphers specialized in making copies of specific books such as the Qur'ān. The calligraphers experimented with all the known Arabic scripts of the period. Some of the famous calligraphers taught this art to the Almohad princes. ʿAbd Allāh ibn Sulaymān al-Hārithī, who died in 1215, was the teacher of the children of Almohad Caliph Yaʿqūb al-Manṣūr in Marrakesh. The thirteen children of Caliph ʿAbd al-Mu'min were all calligraphers. Al-Murtaḍā, one of the Almohad rulers, wrote beautifully in three different scripts. Perfection in the art of calligraphy was considered a status symbol, so that the Andalusian poet Ibn Mujbir praised the *Amīr* ʿUmar ibn ʿAbd al-Mu'min as a distinguished calligrapher. The Almohad ruler al-Murtaḍā had a special department for copyists and calligraphers.

Manuscript binding also flourished during this period, adopting sophisticated artistic forms. Caliph ʿAbd al-Mu'min held a special celebration for the beautiful cover which was brought to Marrakesh from Cordova, made for a copy of the Qur'ān reputedly belonging to the third caliph, ʿUthmān. ʿUmar ibn Murjiʿ al-Ishbīlī was charged with decorating the cover of this Qur'ān with jewels. Book binding was so common that Abū ʿAmr Bakr al-Ishbīlī wrote a book on binding, describing the use of sophisticated techniques. It is possible to study some of these bindings which have survived.

The paper industry flourished during this period: there were 400 paper factories in Fez during the reigns of Yaʿqūb al-Manṣūr and his son al-Nāṣir. A quarter of the city was called al-Kaghghāṭin after the paper-makers. One of the city gates of Fez was named *Bāb al-Warrāqīn*, or 'Gate of the Calligraphers', and one of the streets in Ceuta, where the paper industry prospered greatly, was named *Ziqāq al-Warrāq* or 'Street of the Calligraphers'. We may remember that paper had not yet been introduced in Christian Europe, despite geographical proximity.

The art of calligraphy was highly appreciated in the Maghrib during the Almohad period, and numerous calligraphers received notice along with the great scholars and jurists in the bio-bibliographical dictionaries such as al-Marrākushī's *Al-Dhaylu wa-l-Takmīla.* These include Muḥammad ibn Aḥmad al-Marrākushī (d. *c.* 1193), and Muḥammad ibn Aḥmad Al-Sabṭī (fl. 1119). Some of these calligraphers specialized in the art of decorating books as well. Some of their works have reached us, such as that of the Almohad Caliph Abū Ḥafṣ 'Umar al-Murtaḍā, including a copy of the Qur'ān in ten volumes, which he transcribed in 1267, using several scripts, including the Maghribī *mabsūṭ* and the Mashriqī *thuluthī* and *naskhī* scripts. The same Almohad caliph also copied Mālik ibn Anās' famous *Al-Muwaṭṭa'* in two volumes, which have reached us.

Calligraphy was so popular that women, some of whom had emigrated from Al-Andalus, took to it during the Almohad period. These include Sa'īda bint Muḥammad al-Ṭutīlī, who worked as a copyist with her sister in Marrakesh, and Warqā' bint al-Ḥājja al-Ṭulayṭuliyya (d. *c.* 1145), who became famous in Fez for her beautiful calligraphy. The large number of Andalusian copyists and calligraphers who emigrated to Morocco, and who are referred to in the biographical dictionaries, explains the introduction of Andalusian calligraphy to the Maghrib and its direct influence on Maghribī calligraphy, which also continued to borrow from Mashriqī calligraphy. The same calligrapher often wrote in both Maghribī and Mashriqī scripts.

During the Merinid period, copyists and calligraphers continued to prosper in such cities as Marrakesh, Meknès, Taza, Ceuta and Salé. This art even became widespread in rural areas in a degraded form, which the famous historian Ibn Khaldūn (fourteenth century) criticized. It was during the Merinid period that the Maghribī script, which had been strongly marked by the Andalusian script, took its definite form. The Maghribī script of the Merinid period differed from the Andalusian script in some respects. This stemmed from different forms of letters, the omission of the dots on some letters and the avoidance of the division of a word between the end of one line and the beginning of the next.

The newly developed Maghribī script of the Merinid phase was divided into five types, each of which served a specific purpose. The first, *al-mabsūṭ* was used to write copies of the Qur'ān. It is still used for decorative purposes. The second, *al-mjahwar,* was commonly used not only at the popular level but also by the Merinid sultans in their official correspondence, and by the sultans of the Alaouite dynasty (established 1669) such as Muḥammad IV. The third, *al-musnad or al-zamānī* was used in legal documents and personal records. The fourth, *al-msharqī*, altered by the influence of Maghribī calligraphers, was used for decorative purposes. The fifth, *al-kūfī,* an altered version of the Mashriqī *kūfī* script, was used for writing on deerskin. This script was also used for decorating stones or plaster walls in mosques, schools, tombs and so on (see Plate 111).

Calligraphy prospered during the Merinid period, and the public libraries of this period became centres of work by copyists and calligraphers. The latter specialized in the Qur'ān or in specific types of books. One of the main reasons for the improvement in the quality of calligraphy was the introduction of improved techniques and writing tools. These tools often took extravagant forms in the Merinid courts, where such precious metals as silver and gold were used. The paper industry continued to flourish in cities like Fez, but it had declined by the end of the Merinid period in comparison with other regions like Baghdād, Syria or Egypt, which produced paper of much higher quality. European paper from Venice and other European regions was now imported and used in many parts of the Maghrib, although scholars in Fez and Al-Andalus continued to use locally produced paper. Al-Wansharīshī reports in his compilation of juridical decrees, entitled *Al-Mi'yār,* that Ibn Marzūq's grandson was asked to issue a decree in 1409 on the legality of using imported paper from Europe, and he wrote a treatise on the subject. Notable calligraphers of this period include Sārah bint Aḥmad al-Ḥalbiyya (twelfth century), and Abū Yaḥyā ibn Fākhir al-'Abdārī Al-Ṣalawī (d. 1301), who is believed to have produced twenty copies of the Qur'ān. Sultan Abu-l-Ḥasan 'Ali al-Marīnī (d. 1351) is described as an excellent calligrapher in Ibn Marzūq's *Al-Musnad.* He personally made copies of the Qur'ān, which he sent to several mosques, including those in Medina, Mecca and Jerusalem. Another royal calligrapher was Abū 'Inān (d. 1358). He made a copy of a book on the Prophet Muḥammad's sayings now preserved in the General Library in Rabat. This copy is written in a beautiful Maghribī style called *mjahwar* with a strong Andalusian influence. Muḥammad al-Manūnī has examined the works of more than seventy copyists and calligraphers of the Merinid period in his history of the libraries in Morocco. The copyists and calligraphers of this period were also very productive. For example, Muḥammad ibn Sa'id al-Ru'ayni al-Fāsī (d. 1376) copied more than 150 books besides his own books. Calligraphers were generally held in high esteem, as is illustrated by the pursuit of that skill by the sultans mentioned above, or by judges like the Qāḍī of Marrakesh, Abu-l-Ḥasan 'Alī Al-Maṣmūdī al-Saktī.

DEVELOPMENT OF THOUGHT

The development of thought in the Maghrib between 600 and 1492 was characterized by diversity, dynamism and originality in a number of branches. The diversity of this thought is explained by numerous factors, such as the development of different branches of knowledge in the Maghrib and the existence of two religious traditions, Muslim and Jewish. Several sources such as bio-bibliographical dictionaries reflect the different branches of knowledge which flourished in the Maghrib: some Maghribī thinkers were extremely original and creative. It is also significant that within the range of Maghribī thought, Jewish thinkers also succeeded in developing another aspect of this thought, thus complementing the contribution of Muslim thinkers.

Muslim thinkers

Some of the fields of knowledge to which Maghribī scholars contributed most decisively included the religious sciences comprised within Mālikism, the *'ilm uṣūl al-dīn,* dealing with the foundations of religion, the *uṣūl al-fiqh* the foundations of jurisprudence, mysticism, and the philosophy of history. Ibn Abī Zayd al-Qayrawānī and Saḥnūn are considered to have laid the foundations for the early development of Mālikī thought in the Maghrib. Abū Bakr Muḥammad al-Murādī al-Ḥaḍramī (d. 1095) from the Almoravid period and al-Mahdī' Ibn Tūmart from the Almohad period contributed decisively to the development of political thought and theology, respectively. Abu-l-Ḥasan al-Shādhilī (d. 1253) of the Almohad period contributed to the final orientation of

Maghribī Ṣūfism, which developed within the range of Mālikism before spreading to such remote areas as Egypt and many parts of Africa. Ibn Khaldūn (fourteenth century) was an original thinker not only as a philosopher of history but also in other fields such as the sociology of history and the history of sociological thought.

Given its situation in the Mediterranean world, the Maghrib imported ideas from either the Mashriq or Al-Andalus, just as it had previously done from Rome. However, the Maghrib also contributed to the field of thought, although this factor has been largely overlooked. For example, the early Mālikī scholars of Ifrīqiyya such as Ibn Abī Zayd al-Qayrawānī, Saḥnūn and many others developed the foundations of Mālikism in the Maghrib before it spread to Al-Andalus. Al-Mahdī Ibn Tūmart contributed to the development of theology through his book *A'azzu mā Yuṭlab*. Al-Shādhilī developed a blend of mysticism that was to mark the beginning of a new tradition of Ṣūfism in the Maghrib which continues today. Yet the best example of the originality of a Maghribī thinker is perhaps Ibn Khaldūn, whose *Muqaddima* or 'introduction' to his history of the world represents a landmark in the development of historiography not only in the Maghrib but also in the entire Islamic world.

Al-Murādī al-Ḥaḍrami contributed to political thought with his *Kitāb al-Siyyāsa* or 'Book of Politics'. This book reflects political theory and practice during the Almoravid period. It is clear from the introduction to the work that the author addressed a ruler and through him the people. It is equally clear from the complete title of the book that its main subject was the administration of a state. Al-Ḥaḍrami's work should be placed in the more general context of interest in politics during the Almoravid period. A work on the same subject appeared in Al-Andalus during the same period, that is, Ibn Ḥazm Al-Andalusī's *Naqṭ Al-'Arūs* on the categories of rulers. Unlike this work, which consists of an introduction to the political history of many states and peoples, al-Ḥaḍramī's work stands out for its theoretical dimension. Since it was meant to advise a ruler on how to administer his state, al-Ḥaḍramī combined a pragmatic way of reasoning, an appeal to experience, and an ethical and epistemological dimension which stresses the need to rely on knowledge when wielding power. The themes which al-Ḥaḍramī discusses reflect a sophisticated political theorist in which the religious dimension is almost totally absent. The sources for this work could be divided into philosophical and political. The author was probably familiar with philosophical sources as a result of his interest in theology *(kalām)*. It is interesting that he had digested the sources of his period to produce an original work. The predominantly political dimension of the work reflects the author's profound reflection on the political developments of the Almoravid period, and perhaps most interestingly, his capacity to express reality in the form of theory.

Ibn Khaldūn (1332–1406) represents the highest example of Maghribī thought (see Plate 123). His *Muqaddima* stands out as a major contribution to the philosophy of history and constitutes a profound reflection on the sociological and historical development of historical thought and theory. The main contribution of this work lies in the fact that it encompasses so many disciplines, including those which attract the interest of modern scholars, notably sociology; other disciplines pursued include urbanism, economics, philosophy, politics, linguistics, anthropology, ethnology, psychology, geography and religious sciences such as Qur'ānic studies. Whether Ibn Khaldūn was the founder of a new science is perhaps not very important. What is so extraordinary about his work is that he contributed as no other thinker had done until then to producing a work that stands out so strongly for its combination of the theoretical and practical dimensions, and its ability to relate historical thought to so many disciplines.

Jewish thought

The importance of Jewish thought in the Maghrib derives from three factors: its continuity over many centuries; its existence in different parts of the Maghrib, ranging from Ifrīqiyya to Morocco; and its close contact with the Islamic currents of thought in the Maghrib, which it complemented. It is important to observe that Jewish thought continued to flourish in the Maghrib under Islamic dynasties of different ideological orientations, including the Aghlabids, the Zīrids and the Ḥafṣids in Ifrīqiyya and the Almoravids, Almohads and Merinids in Morocco. Some of the earliest Arabic sources refer to Maghribī Jewish tribes such as the Fendelawa, Neffoussa and Fazzāz. This early presence of the Jews illustrates the continuity of the contribution of this important element in Maghribī history. The cultural and intellectual affiliation of Maghribī Jews is reflected linguistically: the Jews usually wrote in Judaeo-Arabic or Judaeo-Berber, that is, Arabic or Berber but in the Hebrew script.

The development of Jewish thought ran parallel to Islamic thought in the Maghrib. It could be divided into religious and secular thought. The first category developed exclusively within the Jewish community, while the second was closely linked to the main intellectual currents in the Maghrib.

The Biblical text constituted a model for Maghribī Jews, just as the Qur'ān was a model for Muslims. In both cases, communities adopted religious criteria as a model for shaping their beliefs. The comparison between Jewish and Muslim Maghribī thought is equally interesting at the level of education, since Maghribī Jews adopted an educational system similar to that of the Muslims, relying heavily on the memorization of Biblical and Talmudic texts just as the Muslims memorized the Qur'ān.

Similarities between Maghribī Jews and Muslims are also interesting at other levels. They shared common popular beliefs, such as the worship of saints, common religious stories derived from Biblical and Qur'ānic sources, and a common popular literature (with the same stories using either Islamic or Jewish names). Maghribī Jews also shared the same music with Maghribī Muslims. Like the Muslims, the Jews played both Andalusian music and different forms of popular music such as the *malḥūn*, and their music was strongly marked by both Andalusian and Mashriqī influences.

Jewish culture and thought differed from one region to another, given the existence of a variety of different languages, dialects and literary traditions in the Maghrib. The language of the Jews in the Maghrib was strikingly different from that of the Andalusian Jews, because while that of the latter was a highly developed language as a result of their numerous works, the Maghribī Jews jealously conserved a classical language that respected traditional models. This fact is clearly illustrated in the development of two different language theories among the Jews of the Maghrib and those of Al-Andalus, which formed the basis of the debate between Dunāsh ibn Labraṭ Al-Fāsī of the tenth century and his students, who defended the need to continue the application of the Biblical language, and the Andalusian Menāḥem ibn Sarūj (910–970) and his followers.

Jewish thought flourished in most of the important Maghribī cities. Over the many centuries of our period, the Jews of Kairouan developed different branches of knowledge down to the tenth century, after which they emigrated to other cities in Ifrīqiyya. In the studies of Jewish theology, Joseph Ben Nissim Ben Josias, founder of a Hebrew university, stood out. Medicine also developed among the Jews of this city, as is illustrated by such doctors as the famous Isaac Ben 'Amrān Hamoussalem and his student Isaac Israeli (tenth century), who wrote several works on fevers, diets and medical ethics. One of Maimonides' disciples, Yossef ibn Aknīn, was born and lived in Ceuta and was the author of several works in Arabic, such as his *Introduction to the Talmud*. The most important Maghribī Jewish linguist, Yehuda ibn Quraysh, who is considered the father of Hebrew grammar, was born in Tāhert and lived in Fez during the ninth century. He was familiar with the Qur'ān and with Arabic as well as with other Semitic languages, and adopted a comparative approach to teaching Hebrew. It was in Fez, particularly during the tenth century, that Jewish thought flourished most, and here Arabic grammar and literature in particular enriched Hebrew learning in various ways. Important Jewish philological and religious figures who lived in Fez include Dunāsh ibn Labraṭ and David Ben Abraham al-Fāsī during the tenth century, and Yehuda Hayūdj during the eleventh. David Ben Abraham al-Fāsī represented one of the most conservative blends of Judaism, the Karaites, who accepted only those scriptures revealed in Hebrew. One of the most famous Jewish philosophers, Yehuda Ben Nissim ibn Malka, was also from Fez. Some of the most famous Andalusian Jewish thinkers, such as Simon Ben Semaḥ Duran, emigrated to Algiers during the fourteenth and fifteenth centuries. The development of Jewish thought in the Maghrib thus left an important mark on the intellectual history of this region during the medieval period and even afterwards.

LITERATURE AND SCIENCE

The Maghrib experienced a rich development of literature during this period. While the contribution of Berber and Arab elements predominates in Maghribī literature, other ethnic and religious groups also enriched it. These include sub-Saharan African, Andalusian and Jewish elements. The degree of importance of each of these groups in Maghribī literature varies from one part of the region to another and from one period to another. Both tribalism and urbanism are strongly reflected in it, given that, unlike Al-Andalus, the Maghrib was essentially inhabited by nomadic Berber and Arab tribes alongside settled communities.

In Ifrīqiyya, the Aghlabid period produced refined poetry during the eighth and ninth centuries, which led to the golden age of the literary experience during the Zīrid period (*c.* 984–1148). It then declined, to be revived by the Ḥafṣids from the thirteenth to the beginning of the sixteenth century. In Morocco, the sources reflect a very limited literary activity during and immediately after the Idrīsid period, but literary production flourished during the periods of the Almoravids, Almohads and Merinids.

Literary expression took different forms during the Almoravid period. Poetry was the most prestigious literary genre. Noted Maghribī poets included Ibn Rāshiq al-Qayrawānī, who emigrated from Ifrīqiyya to settle in Al-Andalus during the eleventh century, where he died in extreme poverty.

One of the main factors which stimulated the development of literature in the Maghrib was official patronage. This phenomenon reached its peak during the Merinid period, but it flourished as early as the Almoravid period as a result of contacts with Al-Andalus. Even the local rulers in both Al-Andalus and cities like Salé attracted poets and scholars to their courts to compete with those who gathered around the Almoravid ruler. During this period, poets were patronized by such rulers as the Amīr (*emir*) Ibrāhīm ibn Yūsuf ibn Tāshufīn, Tāshufīn ibn 'Alī and Muḥammad ibn al-Ḥāj. The literary figures at the Almoravid palace of Marrakesh included poets such as 'Abd al-Jalīl ibn Wahbūn and Abu-l-A'mā aṭ-Ṭuṭili as well as the historian of the Almoravids, Yūsuf ibn As-Sayrafī. Poetry was appreciated by people of both sexes and of different classes. One woman poet known to us from this period is al-Ḥurra Hawwā'. Most of the Almoravid jurists were men of letters, and some were poets as well.

Almoravid poetry was dominated by religious themes such as *jihād*, or mysticism. E. García Gómez stresses other features of Almoravid poetry such as its popular trend as represented by Ibn Quzmān, who composed new forms of poetry such as *az-zajal* and *al-muwashshaḥ*, alongside the conservative trend of Ibn Khafāja and Ibn az-Zaqqāq in what was at this time the Almoravid province of Al-Andalus.

Prose also developed in original ways in the Maghrib during the Almoravid period and most particularly in correspondence (*rasā'il*). Al-Qāḍī 'Iyād of Ceuta represents this literary genre in its multiple facets. He exchanged letters on juridical, theological and literary matters with numerous scholars in Ifrīqiyya and the Mashriq. Some of the letters which he wrote were not meant to be answered. Other types of letters which stand out for their high literary quality are *al-rasā'il al-ikhwāniyya*, which could be translated as 'fraternal letters'. The strong cultural contact between the Maghrib and the Mashriq during the Almoravid period resulted from the recognition of the Islamic caliphate at Baghdād by the Almoravids, who even sent official diplomatic missions such as one headed by Abū Bakr ibn al-'Arabī. Maghribī scholars who travelled to Mecca in order to perform their pilgrimage often visited other scholars in Egypt, Syria, Palestine and Iraq. It is interesting to observe that correspondence emanating from Morocco through Ceuta crossed the entire Mediterranean Sea to Mahdīya in Ifrīqiyya, to Alexandria in Egypt, where the famous scholar Abū Bakr Aṭ-Ṭurṭushī lived, and to parts of West Asia.

The *rasā'il* of the Almoravid period can be classified into several categories. The case of the *rasā'il* of al-Qāḍī 'Iyād is representative of this genre: he wrote his 'letter' to the Prophet Muḥammad, in which the spiritual dimension is dominant; then he wrote letters to living literary figures, in which a literary dimension stands out; and finally, he wrote letters to other scholars on legal or religious matters in which the juridical or technical dimension predominates. Each type of these letters reflects different techniques, forms of expression and idiom. He wrote on a wide range of subjects, from nature to women. Another form of literary expression which prospered in the Maghrib under the Almoravids was literary criticism. Here, too, 'Iyād contributed significantly.

The period of the Almohads saw still greater literary development. Several factors contributed to this, such as the existence of stability, the propagation of literature in both official circles and at the popular level, financial assistance by rulers to the literati, and the expansion of education. The literature of the period was marked by its high literary quality and was stimulated by a privileged intellectual class, the *ṭalabāt al-ḥaḍar*. Some of the literary figures of this period such as Ibn Ḥabbus al-Fāsī, Abu-l-'Abbās al-Jirawī, Ibn Khabbāza, Abu-r-Rabī' Sulaymān al-Muwaḥḥidī, Abū Zayd al-Fazzāzī and Abū Ḥafṣ al-Aghmatī as-Sulamī, can be considered as representative of Maghribī literature at the summit of its development. Some of the poetic forms which characterize this period included eulogies of the Prophet Muḥammad, court poetry and mystical poetry. New literary forms appeared such as epic poetry, the *muwashshaḥ* and *zajal*. Other forms of literary expression which flourished during this period included *rasā'il* or 'letters' of various types such as official correspondence. Abū Ja'far ibn 'Aṭiyya produced a manual for writing official letters which continued to be adopted in both Al-Andalus and the Maghrib during the following centuries. Another class of writing which appeared during the Almohad period was hagiography, which is represented by Ibn az-Zayyāt at-Tadīlī's *Kitāb At-Tashawwuf Ilā Rijāl At-Taṣawwuf*, Abu-l-'Abbās al-'Azafī as-Sabṭī's *Kitāb Da'amat Al-Yaqīn fī Za'āmat al-Muttaqīn* and Muḥammad ibn Qāsim At-Tamīmī al-Fāsī's *Al-Mustafād fī Manāqib Al-'Ubbādi wa-z-Zuhhād*. These works drew on both historical information and the imagination of their authors. The literary models of the Almohad period were imitated during the Merinid period without much innovation, with very few exceptions such as new metrics (*'arūḍ al-balad*).

Travel accounts could be considered as among the greatest Maghribī literary achievements, reflecting the contact of the Maghrib with other cultures. The motivation behind these travels could be religious as well as educational and political. Merinid travel accounts stand out in Maghribī literature and include detailed descriptions of both the Maghrib and the Mashriq. Examples of this literary genre from the fourteenth century include Ibn Rashīd's writings in which he describes Tunisia, Syria, Palestine and the Arabian peninsula. Al-'Abdārī describes the Maghrib beginning from Tlemcen in Algeria and going on to Tunisia, Libya and Egypt as well as Arabia. Al-'Abdārī sharply criticized the societies in the cities and the rural areas which he visited. Other travellers of the Merinid period include Al-Tujībī and Abū Ya'qūb al-Bādīsī. The most remarkable travel account is certainly that of Ibn Baṭṭūṭa (*c.* 1304–1378), which included a detailed account of the cities, traditions, religious and even fauna of Asian countries like India and China, and practically the entire Islamic world. Ibn Baṭṭūṭa also serves as an important source for the history of the Maghrib, the Mashriq and farther Asia.

Although much less developed than literature and culture in general, science also flourished in the Maghrib, including geography, medicine, mathematics, engineering and astronomy.

The development of many branches of science in the Maghrib between the eleventh and fifteenth century was naturally influenced by the close cultural ties which developed between Morocco and Al-Andalus during the Almohad and Merinid periods. The Merinid Caliph Ya'qūb al-Manṣūr created an impressive psychiatric hospital at Marrakesh which has been described by the historian 'Abd al-Wahīd al-Marrākushī as one of the greatest in the world and one of the physicians of this hospital came from Denia in eastern Spain. In this hospital, there was a special section for men and another one for women, as well as a special department for operations. Al-Marrākushī describes the beautiful building and gardens of this hospital in detail. The Andalusian influence is also clear from the names of the native places of the doctors of the Almohad caliphs. Caliph 'Abd al-Mu'min's physician came from Seville, Caliph Yūsuf's from Cordova, Caliph al-Manṣūr's from Zaragoza and Caliph al-Mustanṣir's from Beja in Portugal.

Medicine flourished during the Almoravid and Almohad periods but underwent a period of stagnation and decline during the Merinid period. Still, Abu-l-Ḥasan 'Alī at-Tadīlī al-Fāsī was the author of a work on epidemic diseases entitled *Al-Maqāla Al-Ḥikamiyya fi-l-Amrāḍ Al-Wabā'iyya*, and Abu-l-Faḍl al-Ṣalawī, who lived during the thirteenth and fourteenth centuries and worked in the psychiatric hospital of Salé, wrote a number of medical works, including one on epidemiology and nutrition entitled *Kitāb Al-Aghḍiyya*.

Other sciences which flourished in the Maghrib include mechanical and hydraulic engineering. We also find works relating to business such as Abu-l-Ḥasan 'Alī ibn al-Qaṭṭān's (d. 1230) work on weights and Abu-l-'Abbās Aḥmad al-Azadī al-Sabṭī (1161–1264), who wrote a work on weights and the value of money.

Mathematics is another science that flourished in the region. Abu-l-'Abbās al-Sabṭī wrote *Al-Lubab fī Masā'il al-Ḥisāb*. The mathematician Abu-l-Ḥasan ibn Farḥūn studied mathematics in Fez. Abū 'Abd Allāh Muḥammad ibn Al-Yasmīn (d. 1208) wrote several poems on different branches of mathematics such as algebra.

Some of the most famous Maghribī mathematicians who lived between the thirteenth and fifteenth century include Abū 'Alī al-Ḥasan al-Marrākushī (fl. 1272), Abu-l-'Abbās Aḥmad al-Khaṭīb ibn al-Qunfudī of Constantine (Algeria) (d. 1407), Ya'qūb al-Muwaḥḥidī, who lived in southern Morocco during the fourteenth century, Abu-l-Ḥasan 'Alī ibn Ḥaydar of Tadla, Morocco (d. 1413), and Abu-l-'Abbās Aḥmad al-Azadī, known as Ibn al-Bannā', who lived and died in Marrakesh (1256–1321). Ibn al-Bannā' wrote fourteen books on mathematics, including *Kitāb al-Talkhīs fi-l-Ḥisāb, Risāla fi-l-Misāḥa* and *Al-Uṣūl wa-l-Muqaddimāt fī Sinā'at al-Jabr*.

The Maghrib also made contributions to agronomy, much under the influence of Andalusian agronomists of the eleventh and twelfth centuries. Agronomists of the Merinid period include the famous Ibn al-Bannā', just mentioned, who was the author of two agronomical works, entitled *Mukhtaṣar fī Kitāb al-Filāḥa* and *Risāla fi-l-Anwā'*. His other publications include works on Qur'ānic exegesis, theology, jurisprudence, mysticism and the occult sciences.

During the Almohad period, the development of geography as an independent field of study is particularly represented by Abū 'Abd-Allāh Muḥammad al-Idrīsī, who was of Maghribī origin, being born in Ceuta in 1100; Idrīsī died in Sicily in 1166, and his many contributions to geography are described in Chapter 21 of this volume.

Other Maghribī geographers of the Almohad period whose works have been lost, but who have been cited by later sources, include Ibn Fāṭima and 'Abd Allāh Ibn Hārūn, who was known as 'the Chinese' because of his extensive travels in China.

The fact that geography flourished in the Maghrib is clear from the geographical dimension of many historical works. Examples of twelfth-century Almohad works include 'Abd al-Wahīd Al-Marrākushī's *Al-Mu'jib* and the anonymous author of *Al-Istibṣār*. The former describes the provinces of the Maghrib and Al-Andalus, their cities, rivers, frontiers and mineral resources, while the latter describes Maghribī cultural traditions in different cities of the region, as well as cities and rivers. We have already mentioned travel accounts under literature: these naturally served as major sources of geographical information.

ARCHITECTURE

Architectural expression in the Maghrib differed from period to period to such an extent that Aghlabid architecture has little resemblance to Almoravid, Almohad or Merinid architecture. While the first was strongly marked by the Mashriq, the latter was essentially Andalusian. The Aghlabid *amīr* Ziyādat Allāh of Ifrīqiyya (present-day Tunisia) demolished the mosque of Kairouan, first built in 670 and rebuilt in 836. This mosque is characteristic of Aghlabid art with its courtyard, which covers two-thirds of its surface area, and its 'Abbāsid-style *mihrāb* with its large square ceramic tiles. This mosque also includes a beautiful, finely sculptured *minbar*, considered the oldest in the world to be preserved intact, with small panels of carved teak. The columns of the mosque were erected in the shape of a T (see Plate 202). This mosque served as a model for many others, including the Zaytūna mosque in Tunis, built in 864. The Aghlabid palaces in Raqqāqa, not far from Kairouan, were influenced by Umayyad and 'Abbāsid art and included large hydraulic systems such as aqueducts, and large water reservoirs like the famous 'Aghlabid pool', which has been perfectly preserved. These palaces also had beautiful gardens. Aghlabid art constituted a symbiosis of cultural currents, particularly of 'Abbāsid and Syrian arts. Despite a limited Andalusian influence during the ninth century, which is visible, for example, in the domes (*qubba*) on the mausoleums of saints in the cities and countryside, the Aghlabid and Fāṭimid periods were largely inspired by the Mashriq, until its abrupt end with the invasions of the Banū Hilal.

The Almoravid and Almohad empires (1069–1259) dominated the entire Maghrib and large parts of the Iberian peninsula or Al-Andalus. Almoravid and Almohad architecture began to be strongly marked by Andalusian trends. For example, Almohad monuments which were built in Al-Andalus, such as the Torre de Oro and the Giralda of Seville, or the Hassan tower in Rabat and the Koutoubia (*Kutubiyya*) mosque in Marrakesh, represent the same architectural blends (see Plate 203 and Figure 27). Because the Almoravid and Almohad empires dominated the entire Maghrib, Andalusian influences spread from the Atlantic coast to Kairouan. Following the Banū Hilal invasions (1057), Ifrīqiyya was ripe for receiving Andalusian influences during the Almoravid and Almohad periods, which continued during the Ḥafṣid period that followed.

Following the collapse of the Almohad empire, three dynasties sprang up in the Maghrib: the Merinids in Fez (1229–1465), the Banū 'Abd al-Wadd in Tlemcen (1235–1255); and the Ḥafṣids in Tunis (1235–1554). It is interesting to contrast certain architectural features of the Ḥafṣid and Merinid periods, because they represent two different traditions in the two geographical extremities of the Maghrib.

Like other artistic forms in the Maghrib, the diversified architecture of the thirteenth to the fifteenth century was essentially religious, and certain buildings of this period are renowned as symbols of specific dynasties. A comparison of the mosques of Kairouan in Ifrīqiyya, Al-Qarawiyyīn in Fez and the Koutoubia in Marrakesh illustrate the contrast in the Maghribī mosques as expressions of a variety of distinct cultural traditions. One is struck by the contrast between the relatively small round minaret of Kairouan in Tunisia, which appears to be lost in the mosque's enormous courtyard reflecting Mashriqī artistic influences, and the enormous square Hassan tower in Rabat, which majestically overlooks the Abū Raqraq River and the city of Salé, or the Koutoubia minaret in Marrakesh, which, like the Hassan tower, stands out for its enormous size (see Plates 201, 202, 203). Unlike all the above-mentioned minarets, the rather plain Al-Qarawiyyīn minaret in Fez, built earlier during the Idrīssid period, does not stand out in the context of the covered building of the mosque and appears to be lost among the numerous houses surrounding it. Together these minarets represent Aghlabid, Idrīssid, Almohad and Merinid traditions, respectively.

Both the Ḥafṣids and the Merinids built many mosques, which were designed to serve religious, educational and political needs, *madāris* (sing. *madrasa*) or schools, which sometimes included dormitories in the same building, and *zawāyā* (sing. *zāwiya*) or religious brotherhoods. Some Tunisian mosques of the Ḥafṣid period resemble Moroccan architecture. This is clear in the Almohad influence on the mosque of the Qasḅa, built in Tunis in 1235, with its square minaret, fourty-three columns and the *muqarnas* or stalactite-like decorations on its dome. Other mosques of the Ḥafṣid period, such as the Al-Hāwa mosque founded by Princess 'Aṭif, lack a courtyard. Moroccan influence is also present in the *zawāyā* which were built in Ifrīqiyya during the Ḥafṣid period, such as the *zāwiya* of Sīdī Ben 'Aroūs (after the Benī 'Aroūs in northern Morocco) built in Tunis, or that of Sīdī Qāsim Al-Jalīzī, built in a suburb of Tunis, where the saint's grave was erected on the Moroccan model with a green-tiled pyramidal roof. This *zāwiya* also includes a mosque built on the Andalusian model. When the Ḥafṣids rebuilt the Zaytūna mosque, which had been badly damaged during the twelfth century, they introduced such elements as a *mīda* or ablutions room, and a court with galleries and new doors, some of which strongly evoke the Andalusian style. The Ḥafṣid rulers built the first *madrasa* in Tunis in 1249, called al-Madrasa al-Shama'iyya, but the Merinids developed more sophisticated schools such as those in Fez. Other schools built by the Merinids include a well-preserved architectural jewel, the *madrasa* of Salé, with its simple *mihrāb* and classroom, and a fountain for ablutions in a small courtyard surrounded by little rooms where students lived on the first and second floors. The perfect handling of this tiny space, accompanied by Moroccan–Andalusian decorations in mosaic tiles, wood and stone, represents Merinid art at its best.

Other architectural expressions are reflected in the public and private baths (*ḥammām)* or in the markets such as the *Sūq al-'Aṭṭārīn* in Tunis. The influence on Ḥafṣid architecture represents a combination of Mashriqī art inherited from the Aghlabid period and Andalusian art as transmitted under the Almoravids and the Almohads.

Architecture of the Merinid period represents a revitalization of Andalusian art (see Plates 111, 201). Like the conservative scholars and saints of the Merinid period, their buildings included Ṣūfī fraternities, and schools to educate the state's bureaucracy. Decorative elements of the Merinid period combined elements from the Almoravids and the Almohads as well as from the Naṣrids of Spain (1232–1492). Architecture of the Merinid dynasty stands out for the striking imprint it left on the architecture of the major cities of the Maghrib, including their capital Fez and Tlemcen, the capital of the Banū Zayyān from the mid-thirteenth to the mid-fourteenth century. The contrast is sharp between the continuous internal troubles and setbacks in the Maghrib (for example Ifrīqiyya) and in Al-Andalus, where the disastrous battle of Las Navas de Tolosa (1212) was a symbolic harbinger of the end of Islamic Spain, and the continued cultural dynamism so clearly expressed in architecture. About twenty major constructions and architectural expansions were executed during the reigns of Abū Sa'īd 'Uthmān, Abu-l-Ḥasan 'Alī and Abū 'Inān Fāris al-Marīnī (1310–1348) alone.

The architecture of the Merinid period is characterized by the fact that decorative elements of different blends reflecting previous Andalusian trends assume great prominence. Unlike the simplicity of Almoravid buildings and the monumental scale of Almohad buildings, the luxurious and highly elaborate surface decoration of Merinid buildings is very marked, even when the buildings are large, such as the Bū'nāniyya *madrasa* of Fez with its dormitory housing more than a hundred students.

Most of the mosques from the Merinid period have not survived intact, but the period is perhaps best known for its great theological schools, which usually included a mosque and a dormitory. Monuments from this period include the restoration of the Al-Qarawiyyīn mosque and the tomb of Mūlay Idrīs in Fez, the enlargement of the *Jāma' Al-Kabīr* (great mosque) in Tāza, with its ribbed dome over the *mihrāb,* which enabled the penetration of light, and the redecoration of the *Jāma' Al-Kabīr* in New Fez, built in 1276. Decorative innovations in this mosque include the dome over the first bay of the mosque and the colourful minaret in the north-west corner of the courtyard. Some of the decorative elements which were introduced include the combination of bricks and *zullayj* (glazed Andalusian ceramic mosaic) on the minaret and an upper register of stellar tile patterns.

The survival of various theological schools from the Merinids period in Fez, Meknès and Salé is possibly explained by their continued use. These schools had some factors in common, such as courtyards covered entirely with geometric, floral and epigraphic designs in carved stucco, cedarwood, marble and *zullayj,* and they all had a fountain or pool below the students' small cells. The arcades in these courts, and other decorative motifs, constitute a reminder of the Alhambra palace of the Naṣrid period. Although the architecture of the Merinids resembles that of the Naṣrids in Al-Andalus, some of the schools built by the Merinid rulers, such as the *madrasa* of Salé, reflect Almohad influences as well. These schools are characterized by a variety of sizes and artistic forms. The large size and luxury of the Madrasat Aṣ-Ṣaffārīn (1271) and the Madrasat Abū 'Inān (1355) in Fez contrast with the simplicity and small size of the Madrasat As-Sbā'iyyīn, which housed no more than eleven students.

Archaeological excavations may unearth more monuments from the Merinid period, such as Abū 'Inān Al-Marīnī's *zāwiya,* which has been discovered in the ruins of Chellah in Rabat, with a courtyard around a large pool. Other non-religious monuments of this period include city walls, gates, baths, aqueducts, fountains and storehouses; even the remains of a palace have been discovered near Tlemcen. A residential tower stands in Belyunesh near Ceuta, and several small houses of the period have been discovered at Al-Qaṣr As-Saghīr between Ceuta and Tangiers (1997).

BIBLIOGRAPHY

'ABD AL-HAMID, S. Z. 1979. Tārīkh al-Maghrib al-'Arabī min al-Fath ilā Bidāyat 'Usūr al-Istiqlāl (History of the Arab West (Maghrib) from the (Islamic) Conquest to the Beginning of the Era of Independence), 2 vols., Al-Ma'ārif Publishers, Alexandria. pp. 436, 641.

'ABD AL-JALIL, A. 1987. Madkhal ilā Tārīkh al-Mūsīqā l-Maghribiyya (An Initiation into the History of Maghribī Music). 'Alam al-Ma'rifa (World of Knowledge Publishers). Kuwait.

——. 1988. Al-Mūsiqā l-Andalusiyya l-Maghribiyya (Andalusian and Maghribī Music). 'Alam al-Ma'rifa. Kuwait.

'ABD AL-WAHHAB, H. H. 1972. *Waraqāt 'an al-Hadāra al-Maghribiyya bi l-Ifrīqiyya al-Tūnisiyya* (Documents on Maghribī Civilization in Tunisian Ifrīqiyya). Vol. 1. Tunis.

ABU DAYF AHMAD, M. 1986. Athār al-Qabā'il al-'Arabiyya fi l-Hayāt al-Maghribiyya, mundhu l-Fath al-'Arabī ilā Suqūt al-Dawla al-Mustaqilla (Traces of the Arabian Tribes in Moroccan Life, from the Time of the Arab Conquest until the Fall of the Independent State) (AH 23–296 / AD 643–909). Vol. 1. Dār al-Nashr al-Maghribiyya (The Moroccan Publishing House). Casablanca.

ABU LUGHOD, J. 1980. Rabat: Urban Apartheid in Morocco. Princeton.

ABUN-NASR, J. M. 1975. A History of the Maghrib. Cambridge.

BENALHAJ SOULAMI, J. 1986. La vie littéraire au Maghreb sous les Almohades (515–668/1121–1269), 2 vols. Thèse de Doctorat de 3e cycle, Université de Paris IV–Sorbonne.

BENCHEKROUN, M. B. A. La vie intellectuelle marocaine sous les Mérinides et les Wattassides (XIIIe, XIVe, XVe, XVIe siècles). Rabat.

BOUYAHYA, C. 1972. La vie littéraire en Ifrīqiyya sous les Zirides. Tunis.

DJEBBAR, A. 1980. Enseignement et recherches mathématiques dans le Maghreb des XIIIe–XIVe siècles). Typescript, Université de Paris–Sud.

ETTINGHAUSEN, R.; GRABAR, O. 1989. The Art and Architecture of Islam 650–1250. Reprinted: London.

HOAG, J. D. 1975. Islamic Architecture. Milan.

ISMA'IL, M. 1980–1992. Susyulujiyyat al-Fikr al-Islāmī (The Sociology of Islamic Thought), Vols 1–3. Dār al-Thaqāfa (Cultural Heritage House Publishers). Casablanca.

JULIEN, C. A. 1969. Histoire de l'Afrique du Nord, Tunisie–Algérie–Maroc, de la conquête arabe à 1830, 2nd edn. Paris.

KABLY, M. 1986. Société, pouvoir et religion au Maroc à la fin du Moyen Âge. Paris.

KRACHKOVSKII, I. I. 1949. Istoria arabskoi geograficheskoi literatury (A History of Arabic Geographical Literature). Moscow/Leningrad. Arabic trans.: Tārīkh al-Adab al-Jughrāfī al-'Arabī. Beirut, 1957.

LAROUI, A. 1970. L'histoire du Maghreb, un essai de synthèse. Paris.

LOMBARD, M. 1971. L'Islam dans sa première grandeur (VIIIe–XIe siècles). Paris.

MANUNI, M. 1983. Al-Masādir al-'Arabiyya li Tārīkh al-Maghrib, min al-Fath al-Islāmī ilā Nihāyat al-'Asr al-Ḥadīth (Arabic Sources for the History of Morocco, from the Islamic Conquest to the End of the Present Period), Vol. 1. Kulliyyat al-Adab bi l-Ribāt (Rabat Literary College). Casablanca.

——. 1988. Al-'Ulūm wa l-Adab wa l-Funūn 'alā 'Ahd al-Muwahhidīn (The Sciences, Literature and the Fine Arts in the Age of the Almohads). Dār al-Maghrib li l-Tarjama wa l-Nashr (Moroccan House for Translation and Publication). Rabat.

——. 1991. Tārīkh al-Wirāqa l-Maghribiyya, Sinā'āt al-Makhtūt al-Maghribī min al-'Asr al-Wasīt ilā Fatrat al-Mu'āsira (The History of Paper Manufacture in Morocco, and the Arts of the Moroccan Manuscript Book from the Medieval Age to the Present Period). Kulliyyat al-Adab bi l-Ribāt. Casablanca.

MURADI (AL-) AL-HADRAMI, A. M. 1981. Kitāb al-Siyāsa aw al-Ishāra fī Tadbīr al-Imāra (The Book of Policy, or Guide to the Management of Rulership). ed. Sami al-Nashshār Dār al-Thaqāfa. Casablanca.

MUSA, I. 1983. Al-Nashāt al-Iqtisādī fi l-Maghrib al-Islāmī khilal al-Qarn al-Sādis al-Hijrī (Economic Activity in the Muslim West during the Sixth Islamic Century (= thirteenth century AD)). Dār al-Mashriq (House of the East Publishers). Beirut–Cairo.

Al-Nazariyya al-Khaldūniyya wa Tafsīr al-Adab al-Maghribī (Ibn Khaldūn's Viewpoint and the Interpretation of Maghribī Literature). In: Al-Manāhil (Springs), No. 40, September 1992, pp. 124–165. Rabat.

RAZZUQ, M. 1991. Dirāsāt fī Tārīkh al-Maghrib (Studies on the History of the Maghrib). Casablanca, Ifrīqiyya/Al-Mashriq.

SHAHIDI (AL-), H. 1983. *Adab al-Rihla bi l-Maghrib fi l-'Asr al-Marīnī* (Travel Literature in Morocco in the Merinid Age), Vol. 1. Rabat.

SHAQQUR, A. 1983. *Al-Qādī 'Iyād al-Adīb (Al-Adab al-Maghribī fī Dhill al-Murābitīn)* (Judge 'Iyād the Lettered One: Maghribī Literature under the Aegis of the Almoravids). Dār al-Fikr al-Maghribī (House of Moroccan Thought). Tangier.

TALBI, M. Al-Dawla al-Aghlabiyya 184–296/800–909 (The Aghlabid State, AH 184–296/AD 800–909). Dār al-Gharb al-Islāmī (House of the Islamic West). Beirut.

ZAFRANI, H. 1983. Mille ans de vie juive au Maroc. Maisonneuve et Larousse. Paris.

21

MUSLIMS IN THE IBERIAN PENINSULA, THE MEDITERRANEAN COAST AND ITS ISLANDS

Manuel Sánchez Martínez

There is an Arab proverb, quoted by U. Rizzitano, which says that 'science is a grain seed which sprouted in Medina, was winnowed in Baghdād, ground in Kairouan, sifted in Cordova and eaten in Fez.' Although some important steps in this imaginary journey of science are missing, it would be difficult to find another metaphor which evokes more succinctly the process of transmission of oriental culture to the Western world. It is our aim to observe the vicissitudes of this transfer of knowledge within the area of the western Mediterranean a little more closely, but not before providing the background of political history which is essential to an understanding of this momentous event.

With the occupation of Visigothic Hispania in 711, the Islamic Empire reached the westernmost confines of the known world. The subsequent conquest of Sicily (827–878) converted the western Mediterranean into a true melting pot where oriental influences mingled with those from the Maghrib to produce a cultural amalgam of extraordinary vitality. Thanks to the profound impact of Islamic culture, the Iberian peninsula and Sicily, which belonged to Christendom, were effective channels for the transmission to Western Europe of the cultural heritage of antiquity, as translated and commented upon by Muslims. In this sense, the 'seed' of science, to carry on the metaphor quoted above, was finally digested in the Western world, thereby making the intellectual life of the first European universities more fertile.

THE WESTERN MEDITERRANEAN – A MUSLIM LAKE (SEVENTH TO EARLY NINTH CENTURY)

After the conquest of Egypt, the Arab Muslims began to push onwards towards Ifrīqiyya and, in 670, 'Uqba ibn Nāfi' founded Kairouan (Qayrawān) as a base for expeditions to the West. After the occupation of these territories the maritime campaigns in the central and western Mediterranean began, the first incursion into Sicily taking place in 652. It is worth noting that these expeditions (like all those which occurred in the eighth century) were of an official nature and carefully planned from the Orient or from Ifrīqiyya. The *wāli* ('governor') of this province, Mūsā ibn Nūṣayr, was charged with leading the offensive against the West (705–708). Once the Maghrib had been subdued, the scene was set for the conquest of Hispania.

The first century of al-Andalus and the Muslim conquest of Sicily

In July 711, by the River Guadalete, the (mostly Berber) troops mobilized by Ṭāriq ibn Ziyād, a client of Mūsā ibn Nuṣayr, defeated the Visigothic army and thus began the conquest of their territory. Ṭāriq advanced on Toledo, the Visigothic capital, where he met up with Mūsā himself, who had disembarked in the peninsula with an army composed mostly of Arabs. Brilliant campaigns led to the occupation of the cities of Zaragoza, León, Pamplona and Barcelona, so that five years after Ṭāriq disembarked a large part of Hispania was under the control, albeit patchy, of the Arabs and Berbers. It would be impossible to explain the speed and relative ease with which the conquest proceeded without taking into account two factors: the degree of internal disorder within the Visigothic state and society, and the skill of the Muslims, who, by using the same tactics as in the Orient in the seventh century, offered their conquered subjects highly favourable terms.

The following years saw the conquest of territories on the other side of the Pyrenees: Narbonne, Nîmes and Carcassonne were occupied in 725 and, proceeding up the Rhône valley, the Muslims reached Bourgogne, where they torched Autun. However, their advance was checked at Poitiers by the Franks under Charles Martel (732), and the Muslims were forced to retreat to Narbonne. In any case, Muslim control of the Languedoc (the area between the Pyrenees and the Rhône) was very tenuous, and the Franks were skilful enough to exploit the internal crisis in al-Andalus in the middle of the eighth century to recover Narbonne in 759.

Just as had occurred in the East in former times, there also arose in al-Andalus the inevitable conflict between the far-off state of Damascus and the conquerors. This conflict was exacerbated by the confrontation between those Muslim Arabs who had arrived first and successive waves of immigrants. So, two fundamental factors were involved in the great crisis of 740–755: conflicts over land ownership; and ethnic strife between Arabs and Berbers as well as between different Arab groups.

In support of the great *khārijī* uprising in the Maghrib, the Berbers of al-Andalus in turn rebelled against the Arab oligarchy. Riding down from the mountainous areas in the centre of the peninsula, they defeated the *wālī* Ibn Qaṭṭan. At that juncture, the caliph of Damascus sent 10,000 soldiers from the military circumscription *(jundīs)* of Syria to crush the rebellion. The *jundīs* did manage to defeat the Berbers, but they also deposed Ibn Qaṭṭān and set up their own leader, Balj, in Cordova. Imminent civil war was averted only by the arrival of a new governor, Abū-l-Khaṭṭār, who settled the Syrians in different provinces: the *jund* from Damascus in the Grenada/Almería area, those from Ḥims in Seville, and so forth. It must be stressed that the settlement of the *jundīs* in the middle of the eighth century ushered in the process of 'Syrianization' of Andalusian culture and manners, and with it the transmission of techniques and knowledge from the Orient to the West.

The Marwānī prince 'Abd al-Raḥmān escaped the extermination of the Umayyads of Damascus which followed the triumph of the 'Abbāsid revolution (750). Taking refuge among the Berbers of the Nakūr region, he established contacts with the Umayyad clients in al-Andalus to prepare his entry into the peninsula. Finally, in 755, 'Abd al-Raḥmān disembarked in al-Andalus. Having defeated the *wālī* al-Fihri and set himself up in Cordova, he inaugurated the period of the Umayyad emirate independent of Baghdād, which would last for almost two and a half centuries. During the period of 'Abd al-Raḥmān I (755–788), Syrian cultural traditions were strengthened by the mass influx of Marwāni Umayyad clients, who were the mainstay of the dynasty. A number of anecdotes yielded by the sources allow us to glimpse the nostalgia for Syrian cultural *mores* which pervaded the court at Cordova. During the reign of his successor, Hishām I (788–796), important campaigns were mounted against the Christian kingdoms of the north, which brought considerable booty to al-Andalus. But, from the cultural point of view, the most outstanding feature was the adoption of the *Mālikī* rite. As we shall see later, the extreme rigour of this school was to have decisive consequences in the field of speculative thought. The Islamic jurists (Arabic *faqīhs*, whence Spanish *alfaquíes*) of al-Andalus were characterized by their extreme intransigence (harshly condemned by Ibn Ḥazm at the beginning of the eleventh century) when confronted with any attempt to break the dominance of Mālikite orthodoxy.

The Islamic presence in the western Mediterranean and the occupation of the Iberian Peninsula did not immediately halt the process of urban decline or the decadence of maritime trade, characteristic phenomena since the crisis of the late Roman Empire. In fact, all the old cities on the verge of being revitalized by the Muslims, and the centres of political decision making of the new territories conquered by Islam, were situated in the interior of their respective countries, whether the Maghrib or al-Andalus. The coastal strips, on the other hand, languished on the fringes of political control and appeared almost devoid of important urban settlements. It is precisely from these coastal areas that numerous pirate expeditions set sail for the islands and coasts of the western Mediterranean throughout the ninth century. Very little is known about these incursions: given their peripheral nature on the fringes of political control, they are scarcely mentioned by Arab sources, and we must be content with Latin texts, which give scattered mention of the misdeeds – sometimes exaggerated – of the *Sarraceni* and *Mauri*, who swarmed throughout the Latin Sea. The expedition against Mallorca (798 and 799), which possibly set sail from the eastern coasts of al-Andalus, barely controlled by the emir of Cordova, fits into this category. So do the incursions against Corsica and Sardinia (from 806 to 810), Pantelleria (806), Ponza, Ischia and Lampedusa (812), Civitavecchia (813) and so on. The raids mounted from al-Andalus stopped for a time around 813. This hiatus might be related to the appearance of Andalusians in the eastern basin of the Mediterranean (P. Guichard). In 816, a group of Andalusians seized Alexandria, making that port the base for their forays. Having been expelled from Egypt, they disembarked in Crete where, in 827, they founded an independent emirate which lasted until the Byzantine reconquest of the island in 961. But if for the time being al-Andalus no longer gave cause for disquiet, new attacks against the islands and the Italian coasts were being launched from Ifrīqiyya, a land practically independent under its Aghlabid dynasty since 800.

In 827, an expedition made up of Arabs, Berbers and Andalusians, and led by the prestigious jurist Asad ibn al-Furāt, set sail from Sousse bound for Sicily and disembarked in Mazara. The conquest of the island was slow and laborious: the attempt to open a road to Syracuse proved fruitless, and the old Greek colony resisted the Muslims' assaults for a further fifty years. Only after the Arab occupation of Palermo (831) did the consolidation of the territory begin with the fortification of urban settlements and the construction of defensive enclaves: Cefalú fell in 859 and finally, after a long siege, Syracuse. With the occupation of Syracuse in 878, Byzantine dominion over the island disappeared. Around the same time (870), the conquest of Malta, which had been overrun by the Muslims in the early ninth century, was finalized. Here the occupation was swift and absolute and the process of Islamization equally profound. The Arabic language, from which Maltese is derived, reigned supreme.

However, while the conquest of Sicily proceeded slowly, the Muslims intensified their incursions into the south of Italy. It is worth pointing out that the astounding success of many of these expeditions would be inexplicable but for the fact that the Muslims encountered internal complicity, offered by the rivalries and complex play of local interests, which set principalities and cities against one another. Thus, in 835 the Muslims meddled in the confrontation between Naples and the principality of Benevento, which led them to sack Brindisi (838). On the Adriatic, the emirate of Bari was founded (847), and thence expeditions against the Italian and Greek coasts were launched. At approximately the same time the Muslims occupied Taranto and threatened Venetian maritime trade in the area. In the Tyrrhenian Sea, the Muslims anchored in the Gulf of Naples whence to prepare two spectacular incursions against Rome. Roman basilicas situated outside the city walls were sacked in 846. In 849 the expedition was finally checked at Ostia through military operations co-ordinated by Pope Leo IV. From the mid-ninth century onwards, the Carolingians strove to halt the Muslim advances in the south of Italy, and taking over their colonies of Bari and Taranto in 876 and 880, respectively. But Arab forays, mounted from a semi-permanent base at Garigliano, continued along the coasts of Campania and the Latium (882–915). On an almost annual basis, monasteries in the region (Monte Cassino, Farfa) suffered dramatic assaults. Only after 885, with the Byzantine reconquest, were the Muslims expelled to the east of the line between Gargano and Salerno.

Nevertheless, there was a resurgence of piracy by Muslims towards the end of the ninth century in other areas of the western Mediterranean. This was the case of the base at Fraxinetum (La Garde-Freinet, near the Gulf of Fréjus) established around 890. From this operations centre, the Muslims reached the Alpine passes, where they fell upon pilgrims and merchants to such telling effect that, in the mid-tenth century, trade between the rest of Europe and Italy was seriously affected. After a number of frustrated attempts, the colony of *Fraxinetum* was finally destroyed in 972–973.

The cultural splendour of Al-Andalus under the Umayyads. Fāṭimid and Kalbid Sicily

By the turn of the eighth and ninth centuries, new features emerged in the society of al-Andalus, precursors of the great change to occur by the mid-ninth century. Unlike the preceding period, the main uprisings which broke out against the reign of al-Ḥakam I (796–822) were not tribal in nature but prompted by a new kind of society striving to make itself heard, a society in which the *muladīs* (native peoples converted to Islam) and Mozarabs (Christians living in Islamic territory who clung to their faith) gained increasing prominence. It should be borne in mind that, as the structures of the Umayyad state were consolidated, the dynasty tended to recruit its servants from among those foreign to the Arab tribal environment such as *muladīs*, Mozarabs, Berbers and slaves of European origin, who held eminent positions in the civil and military administration of the emiral stronghold. On the other hand, the settlement of Arab Muslims had stimulated the development of crafts and commerce to satisfy the needs of the Arab aristocracy, so that a century after the conquest, artisans and merchants formed an essential part of the urban social structure. The serious revolt of the Arrabal (or suburb of Cordova) against Emir al-Ḥakam I in 818 was led by merchants, artisans and students of Islamic law and theology and may be regarded as the violent expression of all these concerns, the fruit of a new society in ferment. The rebellion was harshly repressed, and some of those who took part fled to Alexandria and later settled in Crete.

The reign of ʿAbd al-Raḥmān II (822–852) brought an important change of direction with regard to the previous period, both from the point of view of the organization of the Umayyad state and in the cultural sphere. In the course of this period, the political and cultural models which had triumphed in the ʿAbbāsid East were assimilated: from the institutional standpoint, a strict hierarchy of palace officials was set up and chancery services and fiscal administration were reorganized; in the cultural sphere, fashions prevalent in Baghdād spread throughout the peninsula. The prestige of the Umayyad state extended throughout the Mediterranean basin and found expression in the diplomatic relations established with Byzantium and the client relationship set up with the Rustamid dynasty of Tāhert, a commercial emporium linked to the Sahara trade routes.

Despite the magnificence of this façade, the ferment of dissidence, silenced by the brutally repressive policy of al-Ḥakām I, came to the surface during the period of the emirs Muḥammad (852–886), al-Mundhir (886–888) and ʿAbd Allāh (888–912). By the end of the century, al-Andalus had splintered into a mosaic of independent seigniories (Arab, Berber, *muladī*), which almost caused the downfall of the emirate of Cordova. AD 890 was particularly critical: the emir controlled only the city of Cordova and its environs, while the rest of the territory was fragmented into a multitude of autonomous territories.

Between 912 and 929 the new emir, ʿAbd al-Raḥmān III, undertook the task of subduing the rebellious enclaves in al-Andalus while, at the same time, launching the first campaigns against the Christian kingdoms. In 929, one year after suppressing the Andalusian revolt, the emir of Cordova assumed the title of caliph. Although the proclamation of the caliphate was a sign of the military superiority of the Umayyad state in al-Andalus and beyond, the decision was also precipitated by events in the Maghrib. In 910, the Fāṭimid *mahdī* had taken the title 'Emir of the Believers', thus shattering for the first time the religious unity of the Islamic Empire ruled from Baghdād. As the relative unification of the Maghrib by the Fāṭimids posed a very serious threat to Andalusian trade routes in North Africa, the proclamation of the Cordovan caliphate might serve as an effective ideological cover just when the struggle against the 'heretical' caliphate of the Maghrib was being planned.

The reigns of ʿAbd al-Raḥmān III (929–961) and al-Ḥakam II (961–976) mark the zenith of the caliphate of Cordova. Their military undertakings consolidated the prestige of the Umayyad dynasty beyond the frontiers of al-Andalus, thus helping to guarantee the security of their trade routes as well as providing considerable booty for the caliph and those who took part in the campaigns. With regard to the kingdoms to the north, at one stage Cordova even played the role of arbiter in the internal politics of the Christian kings, as a consequence of which there was a constant flow of emissaries between Barcelona, León and Castile and the caliphate. But the prestige of the Umayyad state reached even farther afield, to the point of exchanging of ambassadors with Byzantium, the Ottonian Empire and Pope John XII himself. It hardly seems necessary to stress the importance of these exchanges from the cultural point of view.

The earliest symptoms of the crisis within this monumental political edifice may be glimpsed beneath the apparently splendid raiment of the foreign policy enacted by Muḥammad ibn Abī ʿĀmir. This personage of obscure origin used every means at his disposal to attain the summit of maximum power and overthrow the legitimate caliph, Hishām II. In 981, he assumed the title al-Manṣūr bi-l-llāh and other appellations strictly reserved for the position of caliph. In order to win the support of Mālikite circles, he made a great display of strict piety, exemplified by the brutal expurgation of the great library gathered by al-Ḥakam II and an excessive extension of the great mosque at Cordova. But the most effective instrument for securing power was war: suffice it to say that he mounted numerous campaigns against the Christian kingdoms, including the deadly campaigns waged against Santiago de Compostela and Barcelona.

To return to Sicily for a moment: the establishment of the Fāṭimid caliphate in Tunisia and its sway over a large part of the Maghrib also had immediate consequences for the island. Considering himself the heir to the deposed Aghlabid emirs, the Fāṭimid caliph appointed governors to the island, but, due to the tenacity of Sicilian resistance, the island did not fully enter the sphere of the Fāṭimid Caliphate until 917. New conflicts rent Fāṭimid Sicily, which was not pacified until the arrival of the *wālī* al-Ḥasan ibn ʿAlī in 948, under whom Kalbid government began. Although theoretically dependent upon the Fāṭimid caliphate, the island in fact became a hereditary emirate, particularly when, during the last third of the tenth century, the Fāṭimid political centre of gravity shifted from the Maghrib to Egypt. Under the Kalbids (948–1053), Islamic Sicily lived through its moment of greatest splendour. From the military point of view, it is worth remembering the defeat of Emperor Otto II at Cortone (982), which may be regarded as the last great Muslim victory over Christians on Italian soil (U. Rizzitano). Some years before, in 972–973, Sicily was visited by the Eastern traveller Ibn Ḥawqal, who has left us an extraordinary description of the island at the time of its zenith. He tells of the density and fierceness of the population of Sicily, of the abundance and variety of its crops and its progress in irrigated agriculture, but, above all, Ibn Ḥawqal provides a detailed description of the city of Palermo with its five districts and 300 mosques, its well-stocked markets, its great congregational mosque and its intense intellectual life.

As M. Lombard points out, Islamic conquests in both the East and West helped to break down the relative isolation of important economic centres, favouring the formation of a vast area within which people, ideas, products and techniques could circulate unhindered. Al-Andalus very soon felt the benefits of the Islamic conquest, so that the peninsula received a rich technological arsenal which relatively rapidly also spread to the Western Christian world. The channels through which knowledge and techniques flowed from East to West, facilitated in large measure by the conquest of the strategic platform of Sicily, were many and varied. Sometimes it was the result of specific political circumstances: as already said, scarcely thirty years after the conquest, the settlement of the *jundīs* of Syria sparked off an intense process of imitation of the culture of the East, giving rise to the so-called 'Syrianization' of the environment. Suffice it to say that the planting of mulberry trees and the raising of silkworms around the middle of the eighth century in the provinces of Ilbira and Jaén probably developed as a result of the settlement in these areas of *jundīs* from Damascus and Qinnaṣrīn. A century later, it was the turn of cultural models from ʿAbbāsid Baghdād at the court of ʿAbd al-Raḥmān II: in this process of transmission, a notable role was played by the Iraqi musician and cantor Ziryāb (d. 857), who introduced the fashions of the court of Hārūn al-Rashīd to Cordova. Less spectacular, but at least equally – if not more – effective, were other channels for transmission such as the frequent journeys to the East of intellectuals, whose purpose might be pilgrimage or commerce but who took advantage of their stay to learn from Eastern masters. The embassies were also a good vehicle for transmission: to quote but one example, *Materia Medica* by the Greek physician Dioscorides (first century AD) reached Cordova as a gift from the Byzantine Emperor Constantine VII to ʿAbd al-Raḥmān III. But it was trade links which did most for the transfer of products, techniques and cultural patterns from the East to the West: the Jewish physician Ḥasdāy ibn Shaprūt echoed the importance of Andalusian foreign trade in the tenth century when he said:

> 'Here we see hordes of merchants who flock in great numbers from the most far-flung foreign lands, particularly Egypt, bringing perfumes, precious stones and other valuable objects for the use of princes and magnates, as well as other Egyptian products which we ourselves require.'

The most direct consequences of the Islamic occupation were felt in the field of agriculture. The expression 'Arab agricultural revolution' has been used to refer to the way new species were introduced and, above all, to the spectacular way in which they spread throughout the Islamic world. Most of these species (rice, durum wheat, sugar cane, cotton, citrus fruits such as oranges, lemons, limes and grapefruits, bananas, watermelons, spinach, artichokes and aubergines) were cultivated in Asia (India, Iran and so on) and, when Islam occupied the lands of the ancient Sasanian Empire, the eastern provinces of the Muslim world became the gateway through which such products could circulate freely towards Mesopotamia, Egypt, the Maghrib, Sicily and al-Andalus. The introduction to Sicily and the Iberian Peninsula of these and many other crops was closely related to the increased use of irrigation: networks of irrigation channels, elevation machines (from the simple wellsweep to the giant Persian waterwheel) and the Iranian technique of the *qānāt* – amply documented on the island of Mallorca – were widely used in al-Andalus (see Plate 16). In fact, the greater part of Spanish vocabulary relating to irrigation is Arabic in origin. The same can be said of Sicily, where words of Arabic origin related to agriculture and horticulture survive in Sicilian dialect. Thanks to the *Kitāb al-anwāʾ*, a work more commonly known as the 'Cordova Calendar', written in the tenth century by ʿArib ibn Saʿd and the Mozarab Rezemund, we have access to important information regarding the crops grown and the cultivation techniques used in al-Andalus during the caliphate. Apart from such traditional crops as cereals, vines and olives, the Islamic impact is to be seen, above all, in horticulture and tree cultivation and, particularly, in plants used for textiles and dyes. The cultivation of linen and cotton (probably introduced into the peninsula at the end of the ninth century), as well as that of silk, were the basis of an important Andalusian textile craft industry, production, according to the sources, being exported to the Christian kingdoms to the north, the Maghrib, Egypt, and as far away as the confines of Arabia.

As would seem logical, we must wait until the mid-ninth century and, more specifically, until the caliphal period to find the first identifiable fruits in the fields of Andalusian thought, science and literature. Naturally, this was only possible after profound Islamization of the country and consolidation in the peninsula of a rich and diversified urban society comparable to the Islamic societies of the East. Neither must we forget the importance of the patronage of caliphs such as ʿAbd al-Raḥmān III and al-Ḥakam II, who, as leaders of a state enjoying great prestige, turned their courts into magnets for scholars and men of letters and provided a stimulus for intellectual life. Thus, for example, the arrival of Dioscorides' *Materia Medica* during the reign of 'Abd al-Raḥmān III led to the setting up of a team sponsored by the Jewish physician referred to above, Ḥasdāy ibn Shaprūt, and made up of a Byzantine monk, a Sicilian Arab with a knowledge of Greek and five Andalusians, all of whom worked not so much to translate Dioscorides' text as to adapt it for use in al-Andalus (see Plate 130). Later, during the reign of al-Ḥakam II, this group was joined by Ibn Juljul (d. after 994), who was to become the physician of Hishām II. His work, *The Generations of Physicians and Sages,* is one of the most ancient collections of biographies of physicians: indeed, among the sources used for the book were works by Latin authors such as Orosius, Saint Jerome and Isidore of Seville, translated here into Arabic for the first time. A later period saw the rise of another physician, Abū-l-Qāsim al-Zahrāwī (d. 1013) (in Latin: 'Abulcasis'), the author of a medical encyclopedia, part of which was translated into Latin by Gerard of Cremona in Toledo in the twelfth century. This work, which was widely circulated throughout the West, soon became the standard work on surgery.

But the patron *par excellence* of the caliphal period was al-Ḥakam II, at whose court intellectuals gathered from both the East and Ifrīqiyya. It is said that his library housed 400,000 volumes, and it became the most important library in the Western world. As we have already shown, it was drastically expunged by al-Manṣūr and, apparently, did not survive the crisis of the caliphate. The mathematician and astronomer Abū-l-Qāsim Maslama al-Majrīṭī (that is, 'he from Madrid') (d. 1007), 'the principal mathematician of his period in al-Andalus whose knowledge of astronomy is more extensive than that of any man before him' according to the eleventh-century historian Ibn Ṣāʿid, flourished during the reign of al-Ḥakam II. He wrote a treatise on commercial arithmetic, a short treatise on the astrolabe and a translation into Arabic

(a)

(b)

(c)

(d)

Figure 27 Islamic architecture in Cordova (Spain), tenth century AD: (a) the Mosque: double-horseshoe arches of the main prayer hall; (b) the Mosque: multi-lobed arches of the caliph's private prayer space; (c) the Mosque: the *mihrāb* or prayer-niche indicating the direction of Mecca; (d) the caliph's palace in the Cordovan suburb of Madīnat al-Zahrā': detail of carved blind window, in stone (after Otto-Dorn, K., *Kunst des Islam*, Baden-Baden 1964, pp. 119, 121).

of Ptolemy's *Planispherium*. He also wrote commentaries on and adapted the astronomical Tables of al-Khwārizmī to the meridian of Cordova. Maslama founded an important school which, as we shall see later, yielded its principal fruits during the '*ṭā'ifa* kingdoms'. It is interesting to observe that the phenomenon of transmission of cultural knowledge from al-Andalus to the Christian world to the north was extremely swift: many Mozarab monks settled in Christian monasteries in the mid-tenth century passed on Andalusian knowledge. One of the most outstanding examples was the monastery of Santa María de Ripoll in Catalonia, whose texts are 'the oldest known testimony of Islamic influence on the culture of the western world' (J. Vernet). Not for nothing did Gerbert of Aurillac, the future Pope Sylvester II, travel to Ripoll around 960 and correspond with the translators of the Ripoll circle.

Prior to the eleventh century, philosophical speculation in al-Andalus developed with difficulty due to the intransigence of the *Mālikī* clergy. Ibn Masarra (883–931) was the first undisputed figure of Andalusian thought. Possibly of *muladī* or convert stock, Ibn Masarra followed the *Mu'tazilī* doctrines professed by his father until, having been denounced by the *faqīhs* (*alfaquíes*) for defending the theory of free will, he was forced to leave for the East, where he had the opportunity to hear the teaching of a number of masters. On his return to al-Andalus, he was able to enjoy the climate of relatively greater tolerance which prevailed during the period of 'Abd al-Raḥmān III. Withdrawing to the mountains of Cordova, he formed an ascetic community where he imparted his doctrine. When al-Manṣūr came to power, the winds of intransigence blew once more and the followers of Ibn Masarra had to disperse and live in hiding.

As with all things related to the cultural life of al-Andalus, we must wait for the second half of the ninth century to see the fashions imported from the East by the poet and musician Ziryāb give way to the galaxy of poets and prose writers who flourished during the period of the Spanish caliphate. It must be realized that Andalusian poetry was born and developed in close relation to Eastern poetry: the metres, genres and metaphors were the same as those used in 'Abbāsid Baghdād. Among the caliphal poets we might single out Ibn 'Abd Rabbihi (d. 939), who cultivated the *urjūza* or historical poem and was the author of *'Iqd al-Farīd*, an encyclopedic text adapted to the literary genre of the *adab*, and Abū 'Abd al-Malik Marwān (d. 1009), a great-grandson of 'Abd al-Raḥmān III. Two outstanding poets lived through the crisis of the caliphate: Ibn Darrāj al-Qasṭalli (d. 1030), known as the 'Mutanabbī of al-Andalus' who, having sung the exploits of al-Manṣūr and his son, left Cordova to travel around some of the *ṭā'ifa* courts, ending his days in Denia; and Ibn Shuhayd (d. 1035), an excellent representative of the neo-classical poetry of al-Andalus.

The essence of the art of al-Andalus under the emirate and caliphate is embodied in two buildings: the mosque at Cordova and the palace city of Madīnat al-Zahrā'. The great prayer hall was begun by 'Abd al-Raḥmān I in 785, and early construction made use of Roman and Visigothic materials. The mosque was enlarged during the reign of 'Abd al-Raḥmān II, but the most important extension was carried out under al-Ḥakam II, which is to say at the height of the caliphate. The *qibla* wall and the *mihrāb* were covered with mosaics made by specialists brought from Byzantium, whilst the marble and capitals were worked using a drilling technique and finished using finest polychromy. Before this prodigious wall stretch the naves with alternating red and black columns, and the multi-lobed arch makes its appearance in caliphal art. In the mosque at Cordova the 'Abbāsid tradition finally triumphed over earlier Roman, Visigothic and Syrian influences (see Figure 27a–d and Plates 65–69). Madīnat al-Zahrā', a typical palace city in the purest Islamic tradition, was built by 'Abd al-Raḥmān III in 936 in the foothills of the mountains of Cordova. The chroniclers furnish detailed and picturesque descriptions of this short-lived city (it survived for only seventy-five years): they tell of the number of squared stones and columns used in its construction, of the city walls, its orchards, fountains, halls, gardens, pools, details of the decoration, and so on. Today, Madinat al-Zahrā' is an immense expanse of ruins where successive excavations have been carried out regularly since 1910. In view of the splendid remains which have been uncovered, one might be excused for wondering whether the chroniclers' descriptions really were exaggerated.

With reference to Sicily, in view of the scant information available concerning cultural life there in the ninth and tenth centuries, it would seem that the only sciences cultivated were those relating to religion. As U. Rizzitano reminds us, it is possible that the succession on the island of two dynasties – the Aghlabid and the Fāṭimid – with their different doctrinal principles and antagonistic political programmes, may have frustrated intellectual life and the emergence of thinkers and scholars of renown. From the outset Sicily, like al-Andalus until the beginning of the eleventh century, was a staunch bastion of Mālikism. It should not be forgotten that the leader of the expedition which conquered the island – Asad ibn al-Furāt – introduced that school of thought to North Africa and that Aghlabid Ifrīqiyya was the hub of the most rigorous Maghribī brand of Mālikism. Thus in Sicily we find only scholars who cultivated those sciences directly related to the Qur'ān: men like Ibn Ḥamdūn al-Kalbī (d. 883) and, above all, Al-Qaṭṭān, also known as Ibn al-Kahhāla (d. 895 or 901), who was the author of a number of works which helped Mālikism to take a stronger hold on the island. Perhaps the unbroken monopoly of this school was the cause of such scant interest in philosophical speculation. The sources reveal no trace of the study of astronomy, medicine or mathematics in Sicily, although information about some of the medical studies carried out in neighbouring Kairouan probably did reach the island.

THE ELEVENTH CENTURY: POLITICAL CRISIS AND CULTURAL SPLENDOUR IN AL-ANDALUS AND KALBID SICILY

In the course of the eleventh century, a page was turned in the history of the Muslim presence in the western Mediterranean. The balance of power, which had remained to the advantage of Islam till the end of the tenth century, was overturned, yielding the initiative to the Christian kingdoms of northern Spain and to the cities of Pisa and Genoa in Italy. The histories of the Iberian Peninsula and Sicily coincide in more than one respect during this period. The political unity of the caliphate of Cordova shattered into a mosaic, extraordinarily shifting and ever-changing in the course of the century, of almost thirty small states (*'mulūk al-ṭawā'if'*, *ṭā'ifa'* or 'party kings'), frequently involved in confrontations with one another and incapable of offering effective resistance to the Christian kingdoms of the north. Similarly, the latter days of Kalbid Sicily also saw the fragmentation of the island into myriad rival local powers, a situation which favoured the Norman conquest. These internal circumstances were used to advantage by the Christian knightly class which arose as a result of the so-called 'feudal revolution' and by the powerful maritime 'republics' of Italy. In fact, once the threshold of AD 1000 had been crossed, the demographic and economic recovery of Christendom became evident in its spectacular expansion to the detriment of Islam. Although some bold Spanish-Arab raids in the Mediterranean are recorded at the beginning of the eleventh century (such as the expedition against Sardinia by King Mujāhid of Denia), the maritime routes passed into the control of Pisa and Genoa: Sardinia was recovered for Christendom in 1016 and once again in 1050; the Pisans assaulted Bona (1034); the Pisans and Genoese attacked Mahdiyya (1087); the Catalans and Pisans raided the Balearics (1114–1115), whilst the Normans set in train the conquest of Sicily in 1061. In al-Andalus, the advances of the Christian kingdoms pushed the frontier as far as the River Tagus, and very soon the emblematic and strategic city of Toledo fell to them (1085). However, in contrast to these grave events, the material prosperity and cultural vitality attained in cities such as Seville, Zaragoza, Toledo and Palermo remained extraordinary. Andalusian culture carried the heritage of the caliphate to its zenith in the eleventh and twelfth centuries: figures such as Ibn Ḥazm, Maimonides and Averroës sufficed to raise the rank of literature, medicine and philosophy of al-Andalus to one of the highest places of honour in the annals of universal letters and science. If the Islamic cultural tradition was checked in Sicily by the Christian conquest, still it yielded excellent fruits during the Norman period.

Al-Andalus under the *Ṭā'ifa* rulers

Although ʿAbd al-Malik continued the expansionist policy of his father al-Manṣūr, the caliphate had been dealt a mortal blow. In the years 1009 and 1010, a series of events occurred which symbolized the new situation perfectly: for the first time, the Spanish-Arab forces which disputed control of the caliphate of Cordova appealed to the sovereigns of the Christian north for help, inverting the trend which had been traditional for a century; the sack of Cordova by the Christians marked the onset of feudal aggression against al-Andalus. Furthermore, during the reign of Sulaymān al-Mustaʿīn (1013–1016), the Berbers who rendered services to this caliph received various provinces as their reward, thus opening the gates to the political fragmentation of al-Andalus and foreshadowing the future *ṭā'ifas*. This is not the place to describe in detail the events which dogged the final painful days of the caliphate: suffice it to say that between 1023 and 1031 there was a succession of three *marwāni* (Umayyad) caliphs in the midst of the general crisis of a state devoid of fiscal resources whose control extended little further than the environs of Cordova. In 1031, a Cordovan noble, occupied the Alcázar (royal palace) and expelled the last Umayyad caliph, Hishām III. The era of the republic of Banū Jawhar had dawned in Cordova while al-Andalus re-formed around new political structures, the 'party kings' (*mulūk al-ṭawā'if*).

But before Cordova lost its position of cultural supremacy to Zaragoza, Toledo and Seville, there arose in the former capital of the caliphate one of the great figures of Andalusian philosophy and literature, the great polymath Ibn Ḥazm (994–1063). Given the crucial years through which he lived, Ibn Ḥazm knew first the glory of a vizierate, then the bitterness of imprisonment and the pain of exile. In fact, his loyalty to the Umayyad cause cost him the confiscation of his goods, and he was forced to flee Cordova and seek asylum in a number of cities. In Mallorca, he enjoyed the protection of the governor Ibn Rāshiq, around whom a brilliant cultural group had formed. Later, the short-lived return of the Umayyads secured for him the vizierate under the caliphs al-Mustaẓhir and al-Muʿtadd, but, having fallen from favour once more, in 1027, he abandoned political life and devoted himself to writing the greater part of his work. His untiring dispute against the narrow-minded Malikid circles, his non-conformism at any cost, and his later position against the ʿAbbādids of Seville, made manoeuvring in the tortuous political life of the eleventh century difficult. The public burning in Seville of some of his works brought a haughty response from Ibn Ḥazm: 'You may burn the paper, but you will not be able to burn what it contains, for I carry it in my breast. . .' His work is extensive – it is said that at his death he left 400 manuscripts – and covers all the human sciences of his day. The principal work in the field of science is his *Critical History of Religions, Sects and Schools*, which is an impressive comparative study of different religions in which Ibn Ḥazm reveals a capacity for erudition and a subtlety which are truly prodigious. However, the work which best sums up his philosophical attitude, psychological intuition and talent both as a poet and writer of prose is the *Ṭawq al-Ḥamāma* ('The Ring of the Dove'), a splendid treatise on love, sprinkled with abundant anecdotes drawn from the life of the author, a book which is one of the richest sources of information and suggestive anecdotes available to anyone eager to learn about Cordovan civilization during the twilight of the caliphate. Running parallel in a way to the life of Ibn Ḥazm was that of the Cordovan Ibn Zaydūn (1003–1070), the greatest neo-classical poet in the history of al-Andalus. Like Ibn Ḥazm, he lived through the convulsive days of the crisis of the caliphate, held the post of vizier (in Cordova under the Banū Jawhar and in Seville under al-Muʿtadid) and was the victim of intrigues which brought about his downfall. The most personal poems of Ibn Zaydūn – such as his incomparable *qaṣīda an-nūn* deal with his relationship with the Umayyad Princess Wallāda, whose lost love he evokes in the gardens and surroundings of Cordova in poems which display something almost approaching Western Romantic sensitivity.

The little *ṭā'ifa* courts tried to emulate in almost every detail the ways of the lost caliphate: this had immediate repercussions in the field of culture. On the one hand, each sovereign had to attract a sufficient number of cultured people capable of carrying out the necessary bureaucratic tasks but, at the same time, beholding himself in the caliphal mirror, each *emīr* set himself up as a patron trying to surround himself with a brilliant court, each vying with its neighbour to attract scholars and poets to sing the praises of the dynasty. So, for example, according to the historian Ibn Ḥayyān, the court at Zaragoza was comparable to the resplendent Cordova of the caliphate: the king 'gathered there many personages who had formed part of the brilliant entourage of al-Manṣūr, such as his secretary-poets Ibn Darrādj and Sāʿid, thereby ensuring their dithyrambic verses, the propaganda of the age' (M. J. Viguera). In the period of Al-Muqtadir (1046–1081), the Aljafería Palace was built at Zaragoza: this is one of the few examples of Andalusian art under the *ṭā'ifas* which has survived to this day. The same might be said of the court of the *ṭā'ifa* at Denia under the patronage of Mujāhid (1017–1040) and his son Iqbāl al-Dawla: the city became one of the most active cultural centres in the Mediterranean, its influence reaching as far as the Balearic Islands, which fell within its jurisdiction at that time. To the court of Mujāhid came intellectuals from the East and other parts of al-Andalus, such as the great philologist Ibn Sīda of Murcía. Similarly, having decided to emulate his namesake, who founded the 'House of Knowledge', in Baghdād, King al-Maʾmūn (1037–1074) turned Toledo into the foremost scientific centre in the peninsula by extending his patronage to a group of astronomers. If Toledo was the capital of science, Seville was the most brilliant centre for Andalusian poetry and music. Under the Banū Abbād, and particularly during the reign of al-Muʿtamid (1069–1091), under whom the dynasty attained the summit of its political and cultural pre-eminence, the Sevillian state could, at some stage, dream of restoring the territorial unity of the caliphate, especially after it annexed the former capital, Cordova.

As pointed out above, the undisputed capital of Andalusian science was Toledo under King al-Maʾmūn ibn Dhi-l-Nūn.

The *qāḍī* of the city, Ibn Ṣā'id (d. 1070), was charged with enacting the scientific programme of the sovereign: he composed a treatise on astronomy (now lost), but above all he was the author of a work, *Ṭabaqāt al-Umam* ('The Book of the Category of Nations'), which has been considered the first systematic and coherent text written on the social history of science. It was in this environment that the great al-Zarqallī (Latin: Azarquiel) worked. Al-Zarqallī, the first European astronomer before Kepler, according to Millás Vallicrosa drew up the so-called 'Toledo Astronomical Tables' which were later to serve as the basis for those of Alfonso X. He also invented an apparatus called the *azafea*, which made the astrolabe much easier to use. The eleventh century was indeed the great era of Andalusian astronomy, when the disciples of Maslama of Madrid flourished, among them Ibn as-Samh (d. 1035), the author of commentaries on Euclid's *Elements*, and Ibn al-Ṣaffār (d. 1035), who compiled astronomical tables based on the Indian method of the Sindhind and wrote a treatise on the astrolabe.

Toledo was also one of the centres for Andalusian agronomy: the physician and pharmacologist Ibn Wāfid (d. 1074), a disciple of Abu-l-Qāsim, planted the so-called 'Garden of the King' in the capital of the *ṭa'ifa'* where he carried out interesting experiments in the acclimatization of species. He also wrote a treatise on agriculture which was to have a decisive influence in the Spanish renaissance. His successor as overseer of the 'Garden of the King' was Ibn Baṣṣāl, whose voluminous *summa* on agronomy was translated into Castilian in abbreviated form in the later Middle Ages. After the fall of Toledo to the Christians, Ibn Baṣṣāl went to Seville, where he created a new royal garden and came into contact with another group of agronomists that included Ibn Ḥajjāj, Abū-l-Khayr and al-Tighnarī, a native of Grenada. This rich seam of texts on agronomy was drawn together in the *Kitāb al-Filāḥa,* written by the Sevillian Ibn al-'Awwām (*c.* 1175). This work was translated into Castilian in the eighteenth century and must have influenced many of the agricultural experiments carried out during the Enlightenment. The agricultural science of al-Andalus drew on the traditions of classical antiquity (such as the Romans Varro and Columella), but also on the works of authors of the late empire and Byzantium, as well as on the famous 'Nabataean Agriculture' by Ibn Waḥshiyya, without forgetting the continual experiments carried out in that immense laboratory which was the whole *Dār al-Islām*. The application of these techniques meant that the land became much more productive than in the past due to a better knowledge of the different types of soil, more frequent tilling and fertilization of the land.

As already mentioned, the home of Andalusian poetry during the eleventh century must be sought in the Seville of the 'Abbādids and, more specifically, around the sovereign al-Mu'tamid. The most renowned poets of al-Andalus, Sicily and Ifrīqiyya flocked to Seville. Ibn 'Ammār, raised to the dignity of vizier thanks to his great friendship with the sovereign and his talent as a poet, also went to Seville. This courtly atmosphere, where – according to García Gómez – an impromptu poem might be rewarded with the title of vizier and poetry was a merchandise to be bought and sold, favoured the development of a lyric poetry which, to a certain extent, was, however, false and affected, as may be seen in many of the poems of Ibn 'Ammār himself.

The eleventh century was also prodigious in talented geographers. The genre of geographical itineraries grew up in the East during the tenth century, but it was two Andalusian geographers who developed it in the Islamic West. We refer here to the Almerian al-'Udhri (d. 1085), whose work of a historical–geographical nature is the best of its kind written in al-Andalus, and his disciple al-Bakrī (d. 1091), who, besides geography (only a fragment of his capital work the *Kitāb al-Mamālik wa-l-Masālik* has come down to us), cultivated theology, botany and philology. The field of history is dominated by the colossal figure of the Cordovan Ibn Ḥayyān (987–1076), who was capable of reflecting the society of his day: although largely lost, the fragments which do survive, written with overwhelming verve and passion, are the most lively and direct testimony of the turbulent history of eleventh-century al-Andalus.

In 1085, Toledo fell into the hands of Alfonso VI, king of Castile. As 'Abd Allāh, the last Zīrid king of Grenada said, this news 'resounded throughout all al-Andalus, filling its inhabitants with fright and extinguishing all hope of being able to continue living in that land.' The sovereigns of Seville, Badajoz and Grenada, laying aside their differences for a moment, appealed to the Almoravids for help, and thus it was that Yūsuf ibn Tāshufīn set foot in al-Andalus and inflicted a great defeat upon Alfonso VI at the Battle of Zallāqa or Sagrajas (1086). The second time that the Almoravid sovereign crossed over to al-Andalus was less auspicious for the *ṭā'ifas:* in 1090, Yūsuf occupied Grenada and Málaga,

Figure 28 Islamic architecture in Seville (Spain), twelfth century AD: original appearance of the minaret of the Great Mosque, Almohad Dynasty, *c.* AD 1190; drawing from a relief in the Cathedral of Burgos dated 1499; the minaret, subsequently much modified and changed into a church tower, is now known in Spanish as the 'Giralda' ('the weather-vane') (after Otto-Dorn, K. *Kunst des Islam*, Baden-Baden 1964, p. 125).

having obtained from the jurists opinions *(fatwas)* to provide canonical justification for the overthrow of their king and the legitimacy of the Almoravid occupation. Later came the turn of Seville, Almería and Murcia, whereas the Valencian *ṭā'ifa* held out under El Cid. Finally, when Yūsuf died in 1106, with the exception of Zaragoza, al-Andalus in its entirety had fallen into the hands of the Almoravids and a new chapter in Spanish history began.

The crisis of Kalbid Sicily

As had occurred in al-Andalus, the transition from the tenth to the eleventh century marked the beginning of a political crisis in Sicily, but the situation was hastened during the reign of the *emīr* al-Akhal (1019–1036) when external forces began to intervene in the internal affairs of the island: first the Zīrids of Mahdiyya and later the Byzantines. When the last Kalbid *emīr*, al-Samsam (1053) had been ousted, the territory was split into a number of local fiefdoms and power was disputed between different *qā'idis* such as Ibn al-Ḥawwās, 'lord' of Agrigento, Ibn al-Maklatī, 'lord' of Catania, and Ibn al-Thimna, 'lord' of Syracuse. Finally, after his defeat, Ibn al-Thimna appealed for help to the Normans, who, in 1061, were embarking upon the conquest of Sicily. The Normans persisted until the capitulation of Palermo in 1072. Despite such political upheavals, Sicilian Arab cultural life was at the height of its splendour when it was surprised by the Norman invasion. During the Kalbid period, traditional sciences, practised since the ninth century, flourished anew and, at the same time, new literary genres, such as poetry, developed finding an excellent breeding ground in the courtly atmosphere which surrounded the last Kalbid *emīrs*, similar to that which prevailed in the Andalusian *ṭā'ifas*.

In Palermo, the study of philology in particular flourished through the work of authors such as Ibn al-Birr and, above all, his disciple Ibn al-Qaṭṭān, a grammarian, historian and lexicographer who, having spent some time at Zaragoza, ended his days in Egypt. He composed an anthology of Arab–Sicilian poetry, part of which has survived to this day. An interesting juridical school, also dispersed by the conquest, formed around the members of the Mazāra group: Ibn 'Umar, called 'al-imām al-Mazārī', Ibn Muslim and Ibn Abi-l-Farāj. But foreign authors as well as native ones must also be remembered. The strategic situation of the island and the splendour of the Kalbid court attracted many intellectuals, who contributed to the transmission or advancement of studies in various disciplines: for example, in the course of the eleventh century, many Andalusians left the Iberian peninsula for political reasons and settled in Sicily, where they founded schools; this was the case of the lexicographer al-Rabā'ī and the philologist Ibn Mukram. This cultural relationship with al-Andalus was particularly fertile in the field of poetry. The greatest Sicilian poet, Ibn Ḥamdīs, whose 'Song Book' has been preserved in its entirety, probably ended his days in Mallorca (1132/3), after emigrating from 'Abbādid Seville and travelling through the Maghrib – in Aghmat, he shared his exile with al-Mu'tamid who had been banished by the Almoravids – and Ifrīqiyya. Although he was influenced by the neo-classical 'Abbāsid lyric poetry as represented by Mutannabī, the most personal feature of Ibn Ḥamdīs's poetry is reflected in the nostalgia with which he evokes the Sicily which was lost to him and in his lively descriptive fragments, which probably owe much to Andalusian influence.

AL-ANDALUS UNDER THE ALMORAVID AND ALMOHAD EMPIRES (TWELFTH AND THIRTEENTH CENTURIES) THE ISLAMIC HERITAGE IN CHRISTIAN SPAIN AND NORMAN SICILY

Around the year 1110, al-Andalus, unified once more, became a province dependent on the empire of Marrakech. Consequently, the early years of the twelfth century marked the culmination of Almoravid power in the peninsula, but it did not last long. In 1118, a great crusade led by Alfonso I of Aragon wrenched the city of Zaragoza from the Muslims and shortly afterwards, Tudela, Tarazona, Calatayud and Daroca. At about the same time, the first signs of the breakdown of political consensus in Andalusian territory also became apparent. Meanwhile, in the Maghrib 'Abd al-Mu'min proclaimed himself caliph and thus began the Almohad rebellion, which was finally to bring down the empire founded by Ibn Tāshufīn. After 1144, al-Andalus was subjected once again to political fragmentation and was divided into tiny states (the so-called 'second *ṭā'ifas*'). A large part of western Andalusia fell under the control of the Ṣūfi Ibn Qasī, while Sayf al-Dawla ('Zafadola') took over Jaén and Grenada, and a character called Ibn Mardānish set up an independent fiefdom in the eastern peninsula.

Summoned by the rebel Ibn Qasī, the Almohads disembarked in al-Andalus in 1146 and, as the Almoravids had done almost a century before, undertook the task of subduing the different *ṭā'ifas*. Finally, with the incorporation of the levantine regions, the Almohad Caliph Abū Ya'qūb Yūsuf set himself up in Seville and achieved the unification of al-Andalus once more, this time under an Almohad aegis. His successor, Caliph Abū Yūsuf Ya'qūb al-Manṣūr (1184–1199), under whom the Almohad dynasty reached its zenith (see Figure 28), dealt the kings of Navarre, Castile and León a harsh defeat at Alarcos (1195) which, for the historian al-Marrākushi, was a worthy retort to the Battle of Zallāqa a century earlier. However, with the fourth Almohad caliph, al-Nāṣir (1196–1213), the decline of the dynasty began: tribal insubordination in the Maghrib and the great Christian offensive in al-Andalus after 1208 marked the beginning of the end. With the defeat at Las Navas de Tolosa (1212), the frontier reached the Guadalquivir and the Christians began to penetrate the river valley, so that in a few years they had taken over the richest and most urbanized regions in the peninsula. Jaime I of Aragon conquered the Balearic Islands (1229) and the kingdom of Valencia (1238), while Fernando III of Castile occupied the 500-year-old capitals of Andalusian Islam: Cordova (1236), Jaén (1246) and Seville (1248). In 1232, Muhammad ibn Naṣr, 'lord' of Arjona, had begun to carve out a kingdom for himself in the south-east of the peninsula with Grenada, Málaga and Almería as its principal cities. When, in 1246, the king of Grenada became a vassal of the king of Castile, the Naṣrid kingdom of Grenada, the last Islamic political construction in the peninsula, was recognized.

Although it would be unwise to exaggerate its effects, there would seem to be no doubt that the change of atmosphere brought about by the establishment of Almoravid dominion in al-Andalus wrought important changes in the cultural sphere. Naturally, the disappearance of the patronage exercised by the many *ṭā'ifa* courts meant, for instance, a decline in poetic activity. Similarly, the pre-eminence of the *faqīhs* (*alfaquīes*) or Islamic clergy in the immediate surroundings of the Almoravid court also had an effect in the field of thought: the public burning in 1109 of the *Iḥyā'* by the theologian and mystic al-Ghazālī, whose ideas were contrary to Mālikid jurisprudence, will suffice as an example.

Belles Lettres in Seville under the Almoravids were rarer than loyalty and those who practised them, it was said, were 'heeded less than the moon in winter.' These words of the author Ibn Bassām will serve to illustrate what García Gómez has called the 'eclipse' of poetry in Seville during the Almoravid era. However, there were exceptions: in the Andalusian Levant two poets from Alcira raised neo-classical Hispano-Muslim lyric poetry to its peak, cultivating in particular floral poetry in their descriptions of the gardens of Valencia; these were Ibn Khafāja (d. 1138) – not for nothing was he nicknamed 'The Gardener' – and above all his nephew Ibn al-Zaqqāq, who revitalized the play of metaphors in old Arabic poetry. During the Almohad period, popular poetry was enriched by the invention, probably by Avempace, of the *zajal*. Written in vulgar Arabic, the *zajal* had a varied rhyme scheme and was studded with Romance words and colloquial expressions. The greatest exponent of the *zajal* was the Cordovan poet Ibn Quzmān (d. 1160). In contrast to the correct and, on occasion, affected classical poetry, the lyric poetry of Ibn Quzman represents 'a voice from the streets' (García Gómez) and enshrines the triumph of spontaneity: his *zajals*, gay and free in style, are also excellent cameos of daily life in al-Andalus in the mid-twelfth century (see Plates 187, 188).

If the eleventh century was the great period of Andalusian astronomy, the next two centuries witnessed the flowering of medicine and philosophy. In the field of medicine, the outstanding figure was the Sevillian 'Abd al-Malik ibn Zuhr (d. 1162) (Latin: 'Avenzoar'), who belonged to a dynasty of physicians which had flourished for a century. His most important work, the *Taysīr*, is a treatise on therapy and diet, written at the request of Averroës. Translated into Hebrew and Latin, the writings of Avenzoar were widely circulated during the Middle Ages. Better known as a philosopher, Averroës was also the physician of the Almohad caliph, Abū Ya'qūb, and the author of a great encyclopedia – the *Kitāb al-kulliyāt fi-ṭ-ṭibb*, translated into Latin under the title the *Colliget*: the seven books of this encyclopedia deal with anatomy, physiology, pathology, hygiene and therapy, interspersed with a wealth of digressions of a philosophical nature. Another outstanding figure in the field of medicine was the Andalusian Jew Moses ben Maymon, 'Maimonides' (d. 1204), who was physician to the sultan Saladin. His *Kitāb al-fuṣūl fi-ṭ-ṭibb* is a collection of 1,500 aphorisms taken from Galen. He also wrote seven other strictly original books on a variety of medical topics.

The neo-Platonist current which, in the tenth century, had inspired the thought of Ibn Masarra and his disciples, had an impact on the great development of the mystic school at Almería, under the direction of Ibn al-'Ārif. When the Mālikid *alfaquíes* had the work of al-Ghazāli burned, the Ṣūfīs of Almería openly condemned this action. Later, the Almoravid *emīr* ordered Ibn al-'Ārif and his disciple Ibn Barrajān to be deported to Marrakech, where they had to submit to an examination of their doctrines. Another disciple of Ibn al-'Ārif, called Ibn Qasī, organized a fragile 'kingdom' in the Algarve: at the *rābiṭa* of Silves, he raised the banner of rebellion against the Almoravids and persuaded the Almohads to intervene in al-Andalus. None the less, the greatest figure of Andalusian mysticism was Ibn 'Arabī of Murcia, called *Muḥyi al-Dīn*, the 'reviver of religion' (1165–1240), who travelled throughout al-Andalus, the Maghrib and the East, visiting Ṣūfī communities before his death in Damascus. Apart from his great works on Ṣūfī doctrine and spirituality, he wrote a 'Letter of Sanctity' (*Risālat al-quds*), which is an exceptional document dealing with his own life and the world of the Ṣūfīs in al-Andalus.

During this great century, philosophical life was dominated by the outstanding figures of 'Avempace', Ibn Ṭufayl, Averroës and Ibn Ṭumlūs. Ibn Bajja or 'Avempace' (d. 1138), from Zaragoza, was a physician, astronomer, musician and poet but, above all, he was the second greatest Andalusian philosopher after Averroës. In his work *Tadbīr al-mutawaḥḥid* ('The Rule of the Solitary'), in which he reveals his knowledge of Greek and Islamic philosophy – he quotes Plato, Aristotle, al-Fārābī and Avicenna among others – he took issue with mystic thought, maintaining that the path of humanity towards perfection runs parallel to the perfecting of reason, and that the final goal would be to attain pure intellect. The brilliant capital of Seville, where the Almohad Abū Ya'qūb Yūsuf surrounded himself with physicians and intellectuals, also attracted Ibn Ṭufayl (d. 1184), whose philosophical ideas are compiled in *Ḥayy ibn-Yaqẓān* ('Living Son of the Wakeful One'), a work which was widely circulated during the Middle Ages. Known, on account of its translation into Latin in 1672, as 'The Self-taught Philosopher', it tells the story of a child abandoned on a desert island who, by reason alone, acquired the most sublime knowledge. Attention has been drawn to the coincidences between this work of Ibn Ṭufayl and Daniel Defoe's *Robinson Crusoe* which was written at the beginning of the eighteenth century.

Averroës (d. 1198), the greatest of Arab philosophers, was born in Cordova into an illustrious dynasty of jurists. He studied there and later went to the Maghrib, where he was presented by Ibn Ṭufayl to Caliph Abū Ya'qūb al-Mansūr. He enjoyed the favour of the caliph, occupying the position of *qāḍī* of Seville and Cordova until, in 1195, the reconciliation of al-Manṣūr with the Mālikid circles led to his downfall: his works were burned, and he was banished from court. Although he was later reinstated, death came upon him suddenly in Marrakech a short time later. Most of his forty-six works deal with philosophy and medicine, although he also wrote books on theology, astronomy and jurisprudence. Averroës's transcendental work was his commentary on Aristotle, which, partially translated into Latin at the beginning of the thirteenth century by Michael Scotus, penetrated the Faculty of Arts in Paris, giving rise to so-called 'Latin Averroism' and provoking fierce disputes in Europe's emerging universities. It is hardly necessary to point out the contribution of the commentaries of Averroës to the introduction of Aristotelianism in the West. For this reason alone, they constitute a monument to the history of thought (see Plate 127).

Maimonides, whose activities as a physician have already been mentioned, was an exact contemporary of Averroës. In 1148, the persecution of the Jews unleashed by the Almohads forced him to flee Cordova and settle in Egypt. The most outstanding of his philosophical and theological works is the famous *Dalālat al-ḥā'irin* ('A Guide to the Perplexed'), in which he attempts to reconcile Hebrew theology with Islamic Aristotelianism (see Plate 76). As T. Burckhardt says, this and other writings by Maimonides 'fulfil the same role for Judaism as those of Saint Thomas Aquinas did for Catholic Christianity, that is, by incorporating Greek philosophy as transmitted and developed by the Arabs into the framework of the Jewish faith.' Ibn Ṭumlūs of Alcira, a disciple of Averroës who succeeded him as physician to the Almohad sultan, was the author of an 'Introduction to the Art of Logic'.

If Ibn Ṭumlūs did not live to see his native land invaded by the Catalan–Aragonese army, the same cannot be said for other men of letters. The defeat at Las Navas de Tolosa and the occupation of the cities of the Guadalquivir prompted many intellectuals to leave for North Africa and the Orient. As Ibn Khaldūn was to say a century later, when decadence overtook the Islamic capitals, 'the carpet of science was rolled up, with all that lay upon it . . . to be transported to other great Islamic cities.' But before that finally happened, Andalusian culture was to know a final moment of spendour in a corner of the extreme south-east of the Iberian Peninsula in the Naṣrid kingdom of Grenada.

Despite the Christian occupation, total in the case of Sicily and as yet incomplete in al-Andalus, the Muslim imprint in both territories was too profound not to leave its mark on the culture of the age. This was one of the most decisive moments in the history of science and thought: through the translations of Arabic works into Latin or Hebrew, a large part of the knowledge of antiquity and science cultivated in the Islamic world became known in Western Europe, enriching the intellectual life of its emerging universities such as Paris, Bologna and Montpellier.

In fact, many European scholars journeyed to the Christian kingdoms of the Iberian Peninsula, where a considerable number of Arabic manuscripts were to be found as well as people capable of translating them: Mozarabs or Jews with a knowledge of Arabic. Toledo, the so-called 'city of the three religions', held a prominent place in this process of transmission. Although there was no 'school' as such, in the sense of a centralized and carefully planned programme of activity, it is none the less true that almost all the intellectuals who worked in the peninsula (whether in Barcelona, León, Tarazona or Toledo) corresponded with one another and exchanged opinions and methods; some even taught in Toledo and reflected upon the organization of knowledge. Thus Toledo was not just a shelter for mere translators but one of the liveliest and most fertile centres of intellectual activity in twelfth-century Europe (see Plates 78, 79).

The names of some of those responsible for the transmission of scientific knowledge are known to us: Plato of Tivoli, who, in Barcelona and in collaboration with a Jew, translated the book of Ibn al-Ṣaffār on the astrolabe; Hugo of Santalla, who worked at Tarazona; or Hermann of Carinthia, who is reported to have worked in León and in the Ebro valley. However, the most important intellectual figure during the first half of the twelfth century was the enigmatic 'John of Seville' (his identity is still disputed), who translated a considerable number of Arabic scientific treatises into Latin. During the latter half of the century, the outstanding figure was Gerard of Cremona (1114–1187), who travelled to Toledo because only here could he have access to the *Almagest* of Ptolemy. Having learned Arabic, he set about his mammoth task, translating seventy works of philosophy (Aristotle's *Analytica Posteriora*, al-Fārābī, al-Kindī), mathematics (Euclid, Khwārizmī), astronomy (al-Farghānī, Ibn Qurra) and medicine (Galen, Rāzī, Avicenna and Abu-l-Qāsim), so that, according to J. Vernet, by the time of his death, the greater part of Oriental science, or of the science of antiquity as seen through Oriental texts, had been translated into Latin.

The activity of the Toledo translators continued throughout the thirteenth century. Before settling in the Sicily of Frederick II, Scotsman Michael Scotus (d. *c.* 1235) visited Toledo, where he translated, among other things, the zoological work of Aristotle. He is also credited particularly with the translation of some commentaries by Averroës on the work of that same Greek philosopher. Also worthy of note is the work of Hermann the German, who translated part of the philosophical works of Avicenna, al-Fārābī and Averroës. The decisive boost to the Toledo 'school' of translators was to come during the reign of Alfonso X 'the Wise' (1226–1288). This Castilian monarch was an important patron, who ordered a large corpus of Arabic works of a scientific and literary nature to be translated from Arabic to Castilian. In most cases, these translations were done by Jews with a knowledge of Arabic and the Romance tongues, such as members of the important Tibbonid family, foremost among whose members was Profeit Tibbon (d. 1305). The king of Castile showed a great interest in works dealing with astronomy and astrology: for indeed Toledo had been, as we have seen, the capital of Andalusian astronomy in the eleventh century. It was in Toledo that the so-called 'Alphonsine Tables' were drawn up by two Jews in 1272: these became the most frequently used astronomical tables in the Western world.

If the thirteenth century marked the zenith of the process of transmission of knowledge from the Muslim world to Christendom, it was because the immense achievements attained at the court of Alfonso X had been preceded by the activity organized in Sicily by Frederick II during the first half of the thirteenth century. It is now time to consider the situation on that Mediterranean island after the Norman occupation.

As has already been pointed out, the Norman conquest undoubtedly interrupted the rich cultural life of Kalbid Sicily to a large extent: with the flight of many jurists and poets to Egypt, the Maghrib and al-Andalus, some sciences and literary genres which had been traditional on the island for some time were no longer cultivated. But this mainly affected the intellectual elite. The majority of the Muslim population remained in Sicily, and traditional Islamic teaching continued in the many mosques which survived. Naturally, a decisive factor which nourished the fertile relationship between Christians and Muslims was the political tolerance shown by the Hauteville dynasty. It was during the reign of Roger II (1130–1154) that this policy yielded its first fruits: the monarch himself and some of his courtiers had a knowledge of Arabic, and Palermo became a centre of attraction for Muslim scholars, whose presence alleviated somewhat the flight of many masters as a result of the conquest. The most spectacular example was the work carried out at Roger's court by Idrīsī (d. 1166), one of the greatest geographers of Islam, with whom the genre of 'itineraries', developed in al-Andalus during the eleventh century, reached its peak. Born in Ceuta, Idrīsī studied in Cordova and, having travelled through various Eastern and Western countries, settled in Palermo. There, under the supervision of the Norman monarch himself, he drew up a map of the world in 1154, which represented a spectacular advance in the field of Islamic cartography. To illustrate it, Idrīsī gathered information from travellers, merchants, men of religion and ambassadors, which he used to write his great geographical work – the most extensive of its kind written in Arabic – soon to be known as the 'Book of Roger' since it was dedicated to the king of Sicily (see Plate 123). But Idrīsī was not the only learned Muslim attracted to Palermo: the astronomer Ibn 'Abd al-Mun'im also worked there, and poets such as al-Buḥturī or Ibn Bashrūn sang Roger's praises.

Ibn Jubayr, an Andalusian traveller who stayed for some time in Sicily around the end of the twelfth century (1184–1185), has left us a vivid picture of island society and the atmosphere at the Norman court. Ibn Jubayr had the opportunity to observe how Christians and Muslims lived together and saw the existence of many mosques where the faithful could practise their rites unhindered. But what surprised the Andalusian traveller most was the Muslim atmosphere which prevailed at the court of William II (1166–1189). The king, who could speak and write Arabic, surrounded himself with Arabic advisers (viziers and chamberlains directed by a *qā'id*), who were public officials and enjoyed the status of courtiers: he had Muslim physicians and astrologers, as well as a royal workshop for the manufacture of Islamic-type royal brocades (probably an offshoot of the Islamic usage of *ṭirāz*), where Muslim craftsmen worked.

A worthy emulator of Roger II in his interest in Arab-Islamic civilization was Frederick II of the House of Swabia (1197–1250). Like Roger II, Frederick proved capable of attracting Christian, Muslim and Jewish scholars, and he converted his Italian domains into a resplendent cultural centre. From this point of view, Frederick II was a worthy precursor of Alfonso X of Castile, and, under his patronage, the Sicilian court played the same role as Toledo was to play during the reign of King Alfonso, that is to say, it served as a channel for cultural transmission between East and West. Not in vain did Michael Scotus settle in Sicily after his fruitful stay in Toledo, and from there he contributed to the circulation of Aristotelian thought, as passed through the Arab-Islamic filter of Avicenna and Averroës. Scotus also wrote works on astrology and alchemy dedicated to the emperor. On his death, his place was taken by Theodore of Antioch, a true intermediary between Sicily and Arabic culture both Mid-Eastern and Maghribī.

Despite the already evident and resplendent heritage of Arab-Muslim culture at the Sicilian court of Manfred (1258–1266), translations continued to be made of Arabic texts on astrology, astronomy and mathematics, both on the island itself and in the Muslim colony of Lucera. This area of Apulia was to continue to receive ambassadors sent by the Mamlūks of Egypt and remained active as the last centre of Islamic culture in Italy until its destruction in 1300 (see Plates 72, 73, 213).

The end of Andalusian Islam: the Naṣrid kingdom of Grenada (1246–1492)

We have seen earlier how Muḥammad ibn Naṣr settled in Grenada and formed a small kingdom, soon to be enlarged by the addition of the Mediterranean cities of Málaga and Almería. By virtue of the so-called Jaén Pact (1246), Muḥammad accepted the status of vassal to Fernando III of Castile, and this dependence upon his powerful neighbour to the north was to be a defining feature of the political life of the sultanate for two and a half centuries. However, very soon this admittedly decisive influence mingled with that of the Banū Marin from the Maghrib: for the third time in Spanish history, a North African empire sought to intervene in the life of al-Andalus.

Having subdued some pockets of rebellion, the Naṣrid dynasty managed to consolidate its power during the second half of the thirteenth century, but the first half of the next century was characterized by the struggle for Gibraltar, the so-called 'War for the Straits'. In fact, once this sea route to the Atlantic had been opened up, various commercial interests vied with one another for control of Gibraltar: Genoa was affected most directly, but so were its commercial rivals, Catalonia and Mallorca. So the struggle for supremacy in the straits very soon became a struggle of international dimensions, bringing Castilians, Catalans, Mallorcans, Genoese and the new Merinid dynasty which had seized power in the western Maghrib into conflict. The small sultanate of Grenada had to show a very great measure of diplomatic tact and political prudence not to lose this game with so many players. After the bitter struggle for Gibraltar, which ended with the defeat of the Merinid Abū-l-Ḥasan at El Salado (1340) and the capture of Algeciras by the Castilians (1344), during the second half of the fourteenth century Grenada nevertheless reached the height of its political and cultural splendour. Under the *emīrs* Yūsuf I (1333–1354) and Muḥammad V (1354–1391), the most beautiful palaces and buildings of the Alhambra of Grenada were constructed, Yūsuf's *madrasa* was built and all the Naṣrid cities were embellished (see Plate 198). But the situation changed dramatically during the sombre fifteenth century in Grenada, which was the prelude to the final catastrophe: continual civil wars within the sultanate favoured Castilian pressure, which took the form of unceasing harassment along the frontier and the gradual occupation of fortresses. During the reign of Abū-l-Ḥasan (1464–1485) the process of political decomposition of Naṣrid Grenada entered its final phase. Nevertheless, in 1465 'Grenada, with its Alhambra, was one of the most grandiose and beautiful cities of the Islamic world': thus it has been described by one of the last Eastern travellers to visit it shortly before it fell. The systematic occupation of the sultanate began in 1482: the Catholic monarchs gradually conquered the peripheral areas (Málaga, Almería) until only the capital itself remained. On 2 January 1492, the capitulation of the sultan Abū 'Abd Allāh ('Boabdil' in Castilian texts) brought to an end the final stronghold of Islam on the soil of the Iberian Peninsula.

From the cultural point of view, and for obvious historical reasons, the tiny sultanate of Grenada was open to the most diverse influences, particularly those from neighbouring Castile but also from more distant places. It should not be forgotten that, with the end of the War of the Straits, the harbours between Valencia and Lisbon (and consequently also the Naṣrid ports) became important stopping places along the Atlantic sea route. Thus, Catalan, Mallorcan, Venetian and Tuscan merchants did business in the main commercial centres of the sultanate and, in some cases, they kept permanent consulates in Málaga, Almería and the capital itself. Above all, Genoese merchants settled in the greatest numbers and with the greatest persistence on Naṣrid soil, to such a degree that in the fifteenth century, Genoese penetration reached levels akin to colonial domination. Families such as the Spinola, Doria, Centurioni and Vivaldi grew rich by controlling the export of renowned Granadine silk (fine enough to compete with oriental silk), sugar and dried fruits.

Naturally, the intellectual prestige inherited by the kingdom of Grenada was felt most intensely in the Maghrib. Profound changes wrought in the physical and social landscape of Ḥafṣid Ifrīqiyya have indeed been attributed to contact with the Naṣrid world (M. Talbi), and the influence of Grenada also made a decisive contribution to the political configuration of the Zayyānid sultanate of Tlemcen, one of whose most important sovereigns was of Naṣrid culture and surrounded himself with Andalusian assistants. But the greatest influence is to be seen in the contacts of every kind (political, military, social, economic, artistic and intellectual) forged with Merinid Morocco: men of letters from Morocco taught at the *madrasa* at Grenada, and Naṣrid intellectuals (such as Ibn al-Khaṭīb himself among many others) travelled to and studied in Merinid Fez.

The sciences flowered in the sultanate, especially medicine, which was sorely tested during the Black Death of 1348, when interesting tracts were written by three renowned physicians, Ibn al-Khaṭīb, al-Saqūrī and Ibn Khāṭima. In the field of poetry, the outstanding figure was Ibn Zamrak (1333–1393), the author of numerous *qaṣīdas*, epigrams, impromptu verses and *muwashshaḥis*. The main characteristic of his poetic output (like that of Ibn al-Jayyāb, the other 'poet of the Alhambra') lies in that he composed almost all the poems which decorate the walls, fountains and niches of the Alhambra. Well might García Gómez say that 'Ibn Zamrak is perhaps in all the world the poet whose work has been published with the greatest luxury.'

But the field of intellectual production is undeniably dominated by the great figure of the polymath Ibn al-Khaṭīb (1313–1375). Historian, poet, author of works on medicine and treatises on mystical–philosophical themes, this author lived through the moments of greatest splendour of the Naṣrid sultanate during the second half of the fourteenth century and was, undoubtedly, the most powerful intellectual figure of the twilight years of Andalusian Islam. His main works are the *Iḥāṭa fi Tārīkh Gharnāṭa*, a beautiful description of the city and, above all, a complete biographical repertory of the personalities related to the city, and the *Lamḥa al-badriyya,* a collection of biographical sketches of the Naṣrid sovereigns. These works constitute two immense frescoes – intellectual and political, respectively – of the life of the sultanate until the mid-fourteenth century. Made known to Western readers under such hyperbolic titles as 'the Sallust of the Kingdom of Grenada' and 'the Prince of Arabian-Granadan Literature', Ibn al-Khaṭīb was the most perfect exponent of the twilight tone of Naṣrid literature, described by García Gómez as 'glosses on glosses, commentaries and erudition; reiteration, in poetry and prose, of art, topics and clichés from a former age'. In short, we have come far from the originality and intellectual vitality of the al-Andalus of two centuries earlier.

BIBLIOGRAPHY

GARCÍA GÓMEZ, G. E. 1971. *Poemas arábigoandaluces*. Espasa Calpe. Madrid.

GUICHARD, P. 1977. *Structures sociales 'orientales' et 'occidentales' dans l'Espagne musulmane*. Paris.

LÉVI-PROVENÇAL, E. 1950. *Histoire de l'Espagne Musulmane*, 3 vols. Paris.

RIZZITANO, U. 1975. *Storia e cultura nella Sicilia saracena*. Palermo.

VERNET, J. 1978. *La cultura hispano-árabe en oriente y occidente*. Barcelona.

IV: The Asian World

INTRODUCTION

Irfan Habib

If one is called upon to identify the major civilizations in the bulk of the Asian continent assigned to Part IV of this volume, one can perhaps readily mark three of them, at the beginning of our period (*c.* AD 600): the Chinese, the Indian and the Iranian. Of these, the last came under severe pressure from the seventh century onwards: the Arab conquests led to Arabic becoming practically the sole literary language for the following two centuries. It was through Arabic that the Iranian people made an impressive contribution to the study of Islam as well as to sciences received from Hellenistic sources. The spoken tongue of Iran underwent an enormous change, mainly by a generous absorption of Arabic vocabulary. At the same time, the migrations of Turkic people from the sixth century onwards initiated a long but steady process by which Iranian dialects such as Sogdianian and Khwārizmian began to be replaced by the offshoots of the young Turkic language. Persian ceased to be the spoken language over a larger part of Central Asia by the end of our period.

But, if the Iranian civilization seemed all but overwhelmed during the initial two centuries or more, a revival of Persian culture and language began in the tenth century and gained in strength as one century followed another. Soon, Persian, in its new incarnation, became the literary language of the whole eastern Islamic world, including its Turkic component; and from the eleventh century onwards, India also came increasingly under the sway of Persian language and culture.

With the establishment of the Delhi sultanate (1206–1526) began the substantive intrusion into India of both Islam and the Persian language and culture, exerting in time a profound effect on Indian civilization. The change is manifest enough in the technological sphere, marked, for example, by the arrival of paper, the spinning wheel and arcuate construction. India came to possess the great centres of Islamic learning and Persian literature; and interaction with classical Indian traditions led to a cultural efflorescence appearing to rise well above the smoke and destruction of invasion and dominance.

Chinese civilization was, perhaps, the least affected by external factors, despite the long-drawn out Mongol conquest (1211–1276), culminating in the Yuan Dynasty (1271–1368). From India, China had received Buddhism; and the seventh and eighth centuries saw perhaps the greatest number of Chinese pilgrims coming to India to learn and transmit the doctrine and its texts to their peers. But, essentially, the main developments in Chinese civilization stemmed from internal inspiration and processes. In many ways, our period contained moments of its greatest glory. China now gave some of its major inventions to the outside world – paper, the spinning wheel, the magnetic compass, printing and gunpowder, among others. The voyages of the Ming fleet under Zheng He (undertaken during 1405–1433) to South-East Asia and the Indian Ocean ports to East Africa, were remarkably bold enterprises by any reckoning. They were backed by the growth of crafts and commerce in China, of which Marco Polo (1254–1324) had given a glimpse to the world a century or more earlier.

Our period also saw nomadism play its most decisive role in history. Ibn Khaldūn (1332–1406), the North African historian and sociologist who thought that the relationships between nomadic tribalism and sedentary society were one of the main concerns of history, fittingly belongs to our period.

The Huns of earlier centuries still remain in the shadows, despite the terror they conjured up in countries as far apart as those of the Latin West and India. The Turks, on the other hand, have their history far better illumined. They proved to be the most successful nomads in historical times, beginning their expansion in the sixth century from their original homeland in the Gobi Desert of China and Mongolia. As they expanded under the cover of their first vast but ephemeral empire (sixth and seventh centuries), they became masters of steppes as well as agrarian zones. Very early, therefore, side by side with nomads, sedentary Turkic (or, at any rate, Turkish-speaking) populations also began to appear. The Turkish expansion accelerated under the Seljūqs or Seljuks (eleventh and twelfth centuries), and on the tailcoats of the Mongols (thirteenth and fourteenth centuries), until by the end of our period, the present limits of Turkic speech were largely established, extending from Asia Minor and the Volga to Xinjiang and Kirghizistan.

The greatest of the nomad empires proved to be that of the Mongols, founded by Genghis (Chinggis) Khān (r. 1206–1227). As the only empire coming close to a world empire, the balance sheet for it is not easy to draw. On the one hand, one sees the vast destruction and massacres that the Mongol armies perpetrated in conquered countries; on the other, the encouragement given by the Mongol rulers to trade and crafts, which V. Barthold underlined. As people of different civilizations came to their courts and served them in different parts of their vast empire, cultural cross-fertilization was bound to quicken. Islamic observatories were installed in Beijing; and Chinese-style 'paper' currency issued in Iran. Indeed, the Mongols are held to have made possible the transmission westwards of a number of inventions, not the least among them printing and gunpowder.

In these introductory remarks, one can only touch upon movements affecting large areas. But cultural contributions are seldom proportionate to the size of individual countries. Korea made notable contributions of its own to printing; and the Sanskrit-using kingdoms in South-East Asia preceded mainland India in the recorded use of both numeral place values and zero. Such facts should serve as a reminder that in the development of human civilization, every segment of humankind has made its own distinct contribution.

22

IRAN

Seyyed Hossein Nasr

The period 600–1600 coincides almost exactly with the first millennium of Islamic history as well as of the history of Islamic Iran.[1] The Persian Empire, ruled at the beginning of the seventh century by the Sasanians, was defeated in the battles of Qādisiyya (637) and Nahāwand (642), preparing the ground for the spread of Islam into the Sasanian realm, which reached from Iraq to the boundaries of China. The process of the Islamization of Iran, far from being rapid or by simple force of arms, was a gradual one[2] and took several centuries, during which the culture of pre-Islamic Persia became transformed and in turn coloured the Persian culture of the Islamic period. (See Plates 190a, 191b.) While the message of the Qur'ān transformed the intellectual and cultural landscape of Persia on the cultural level – although not the ritual and the judicial – there also occurred a process which some have called the Persianization of Islamic thought and culture (Frye, 1976). In any case, an Iranian or Persianate zone was created within the vast domain of Islamic civilization as distinct from the Arabic, a zone which had its centre in Iran itself but which stretched to all of Central Asia and later the Indian subcontinent and even western China (see Map 17).

THE CREATION OF PERSIAN ISLAMIC CULTURE

The cultural and intellectual life of the late Sasanian period preceding the rise of Islam has been already treated by other authors in Volume III and will therefore not be dealt with here (for example, Philippe Gignoux's chapter). The rise of Islam itself led to the creation of a major global civilization in which Iran was and has remained over the centuries one of its major centres. The Persians not only accepted the revelation of the Qur'ān, but were also instrumental to a large extent in the elaboration of the Islamic world view based upon the Qur'ān and *Ḥadīth*. They were among the first collectors of *Ḥadīth*, the most famous collection of *Ḥadīth* in the Sunni world being that of Bukhārī from the city of Bukhārā, which was a major centre of Persian culture in early Islamic history. They were also among the first commentators of the Qur'ān, as the names of Bayḍāwī, Zamakhsharī and Ṭabarī, all from Iran, demonstrate. Persian thinkers also helped to formulate Islamic cosmology, theology, jurisprudence, philosophy, mysticism and many other disciplines, which created a total world view, intellectual framework and social and ethical norm for themselves and for other Muslims.

This early period of the history of Islamic Iran was also marked by the major contribution of Persians to the elaboration of Arabic grammar and the development of Arabic prose, to which the names of Sībuwayh (Sībūyeh) and Ibn Muqaffa' amply testify (see Plate 210).

But the most important linguistic achievement of Persian culture in the period from the eighth to the tenth century is the creation of the Persian language on the basis of Pahlavi, Darī and the influences of Qur'ānic vocabulary. A language was born from this synthesis which became, after Arabic, the most important language of Islamic civilization, spoken by Iranians, Afghans and Tajiks to this day and understood by numerous generations of Turks, Indians and even Chinese Muslims (see sub-chapter 17.3) (see Plates 109, 112).

THE TRANSFORMATIONS OF IRANIAN STATE AND SOCIETY

Sasanian Persian society was a hierarchical one in which the two classes of Zoroastrian priests (*mūbads*) and the military and political aristocracy dominated, with the Persian king having at once a royal and a sacerdotal function. Society was held together by the teachings of a religion of Iranian origin and was ethnically fairly homogeneous. The stratification of society, however, became rather excessive and heavy during the Sasanian period and was one of the causes of the religious rebellions associated with Mānī and Mazdak. During the late Sasanian period, Persians were in fact awaiting a religious deliverer and many of them heartily embraced Islam, which promised the equality of all Muslims before God, in the hope of release from excessively oppressive social stratification.

The conversion of the people of the Iranian plateau to Islam was, however, a gradual one, and even 300 years after the downfall of the Sasanians there were sizeable Zoroastrian communities in Iran; even Manichaeism survived into early Islamic history. With the process of Islamization, the old class structures begin to change as Islam spread gradually from urban centres into the countryside. There was also a notable migration of Arabs into Iran, and many Persians became the *mawālī* (non-Arabs attached to Arabs) of this or that Arab tribe while they were being directly ruled by the Arab Umayyads. But the domination of Arabs during the Umayyad period (661–750) also caused a deep resentment among Persians, who considered themselves culturally superior to their Arab conquerors. Therefore, while the majority of Persians embraced Islam, an anti-Arabic political

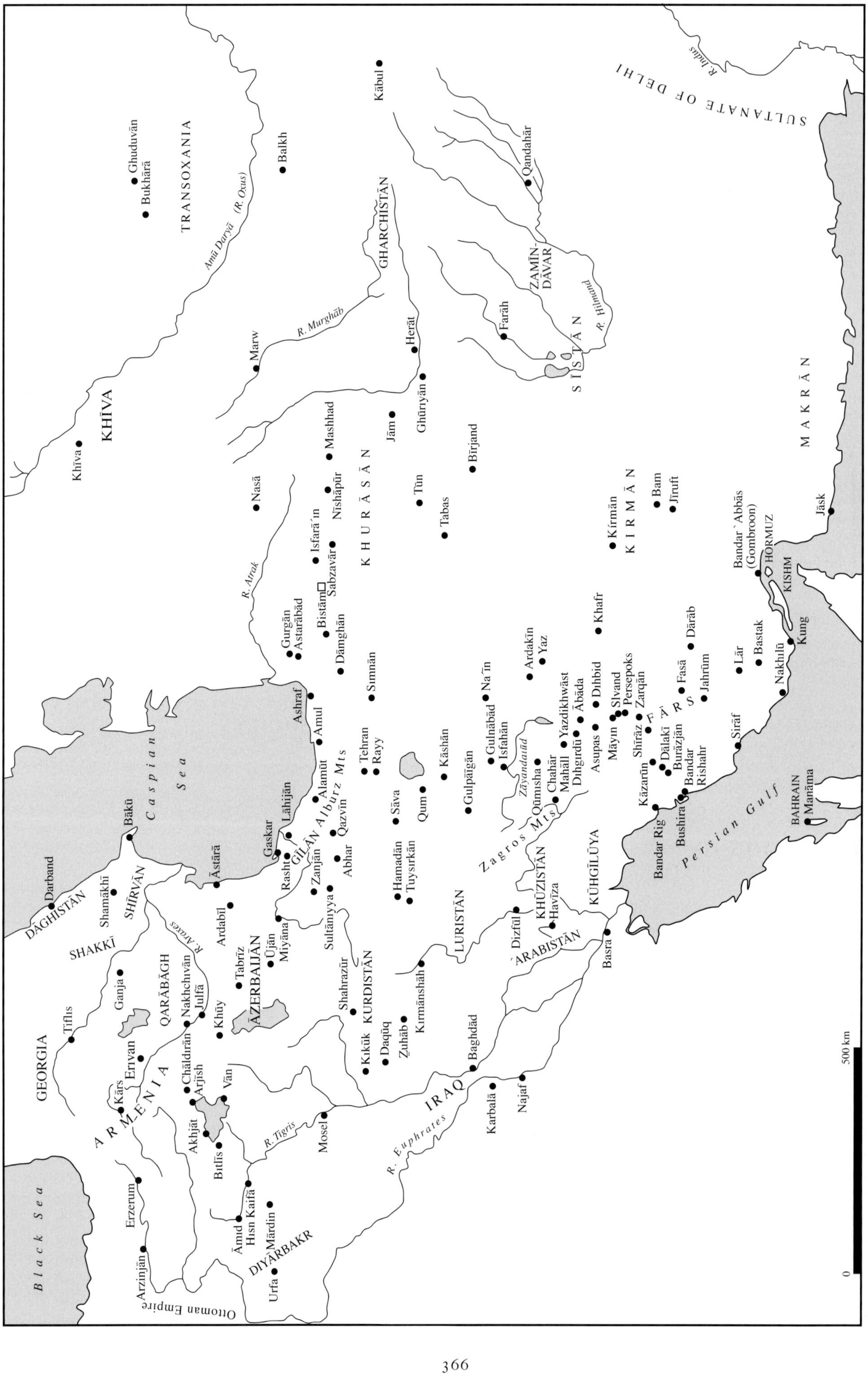

Map 17 Iran and its neighbours (draft S. H. Nasr).

and cultural sentiment set in. Some religious movements, such as that of Bābak-e Khurram Dīn in the ninth century, were crystallizations of Iranian sentiments of freedom against Arab domination expressing themselves in religious terms. But they did not sink their roots and disappeared fairly rapidly.

Of more enduring significance was the actual revolt of the Persian garrison of Khurāsān, led by a charismatic religious leader, Abū Muslim, who arose in the name of Islam and the family of the Prophet against the Umayyads, who had emphasized the Arabic element in favour of the universal perspective of Islam. The result of this uprising was the defeat of the Umayyads and the establishment of the 'Abbāsids, who built Baghdād as their capital near the old Sasanian capital of Ctesiphon. This event in turn marked not only a greater influence of Persian elements in the 'Abbāsid government, to the extent that much of the administration and bureaucratic structures were copied from Sasanian models (this emulation is to be seen even in the Umayyad period), but also greater local autonomy within Iran itself, leading in the ninth and tenth centuries to the establishment of local Iranian dynasties such as the Ṣaffārids, Sāmānids and Būyids.

There also developed at this time, in the context of the rivalry between Arab and Persian elements in the caliphate, the *shu' ūbiyya* movement, which openly espoused the cause of Persian culture and expressed a resentment against the Arab domination over Persian society. All this was taking place not only while the viziers of the 'Abbāsid caliphate and much of the central administration consisted of Persian elements, but also when Persians were making the most fundamental contributions to the institutions, religious thought, art, science and other major aspects of the new Islamic civilization.

In the tenth and eleventh centuries, Turkic tribes, descending south from the Aral mountains, conquered much of the northern areas of Iran and transformed them ethnically in a permanent fashion. Gradually, they gained political power with such dynasties as the Ghaznavids in the tenth century and the Seljuks in the eleventh and twelfth centuries. The latter, staunchly Sunni, in contrast to some of the earlier dynasties, which had general Shī'ite tendencies or were formally Shī'ite, supported the 'Abbāsid caliphate fully but were culturally completely Persianized. Many of their rulers were in fact among the greatest patrons of Persian literature. The migration of Turkic tribes led them gradually into present- day western Iran. From there, they pushed their way into Anatolia, Turkified the region and established Osmanli rule, which led finally in the fourteenth century to the foundation of the Ottoman Empire.

In Iran itself, this major event transformed the area of Āzerbaijān, whose people to this day speak Āzarī, a Turkic language, while also using Persian almost exclusively for literary discourse. This migration also brought a number of Turkic tribes to Iran such as the Qashqā'ī, tribes which were to play an important role in the later history of Iran and which have survived to this day. The Turkic migration into Iran marks the penetration of a second foreign force into Iran within a few centuries, the first being the Arabs. But in the second case, as in the first, Persian culture absorbed the new element, which brought new energy into society.

The most devastating and shocking invasion of Iran, however, was still to come. In the thirteenth century, the Mongols descended upon Transoxania, then Khurāsān, then the rest of Iran, laying waste some of its greatest cities, such as Nayshāpūr (Nīshāpūr), and destroying much of its irrigation and agriculture. Millions of people were killed as a result of this devastation, and many of the basic institutions of society were destroyed. Although the economic and social impact of this invasion was catastrophic, the Mongols did, however, respect learning to some extent: intellectual activity, far from dying out, saw a renaissance in the thirteenth and fourteenth centuries due to a large extent to the foresight of the Persian astronomer and philosopher Naṣīr al-Dīn Ṭūsī, who had gained the confidence of the Mongol ruler Hülāgū and was therefore able to salvage some schools and libraries, and preserve the lives of a number of men of learning (see Plates 12, 139).

It is interesting to note, however, that while Hülāgū had marched upon Baghdād and killed the last 'Abbāsid caliph, the symbol of the political unity of Islam, his grandson Uljaitü embraced Islam and took on the name Ṣultān Muḥammad Khudābandeh. The shamanistic and Buddhist Mongols were soon absorbed into the Islamic world. Furthermore, because of their rule over China and the facility they provided for exchange between China and Iran, they were instrumental in the remarkable revival of the arts, especially painting which reached such a peak of perfection with the Tīmūrids, the descendants of Tīmūr (Tamerlane), many of whom were great patrons of the arts and sciences (see Plates 186, 218).

On the social and political plane, however, the havoc wrought by the Mongol invasion, followed by the conquest of Iran by Tamerlane at the end of the fourteenth century, led to a period of turmoil, with local rule often accompanied by disorder and rapid change. Meanwhile, partly as a result of the destruction of the Sunni caliphate and partly because of the spread of certain Ṣūfī orders, which acted as a bridge between Sunnism and Shī'ism, the latter continued to spread in Iran until, at the end of the fifteenth century, the Ṣafavids reunited Iran under the banner of Shī'ism and established a national Iranian state.

RELIGION, THEOLOGY AND ṢŪFISM (MYSTICISM)

Religion

At the beginning of the seventh century, Iran was still predominantly Zoroastrian but with a number of Manichaeans and at least remnants of those who had embraced the religious revolt of Mazdak. There were also notable Christian communities, not only in lands such as Armenia which were more or less under the protection of the Sasanians, but also within Iran proper. Some of the oldest Jewish communities also lived in Iran in such areas as Hamadān and Iṣfahān. As already mentioned, the advent of Islam gradually transformed Iran into a predominantly Islamic country, but the pre-Islamic minorities continued, except for Manichaeism. Zoroastrianism itself became a minority religion, most of its adherents having converted to Islam during a period of over three centuries; a number among them migrated to India, forming the Parsi community, which is prominent in that country to this day. The Jewish community survived and was active in many domains, including medicine, pharmacology and music, while the Christian community, at the beginning, guardians of much of the Graeco-Alexandrian heritage particularly in medicine, increased in number during the Ṣafavid period with the migration under Shāh 'Abbās of many Armenians to Iran and the establishment of a community which was influential in the domain of crafts and trade.

As for Islam, at the beginning, that is, from the seventh to thirteenth centuries, Iran was predominantly Sunnī – in contrast to the prevalent view. But Shī'ism also found a home for itself from the beginning in Iran. The love of Persians for 'Alī and the 'Household of the Prophet' *(ahl al-bayt)* caused many descendants of the Prophet to take refuge in Iran from Umayyad and later 'Abbāsid persecution, and the country is dotted to this day with the mausoleums of the family of the Prophet, called *imām- zādehs,* which are places of pilgrimage and religious devotion, the most famous being those of Mashhad and Qum.

Theology

Until the Mongol invasion in the thirteenth century, however, Iran remained predominantly of the Shāfi'ī, Ḥanafī and to some extent Ḥanbalī schools. It produced numerous Sunni Qur'ānic commentators, collectors and scholars of *ḥadīth*, doctors of law and theologians *(mutakallimūn)*. It is sufficient to review the main texts used in Sunni religious universities *(madrasas)* such as al-Azhar University in Cairo to this day to realize the share of Persians in the development of classical Sunni learning. Especially in the tenth and eleventh centuries, when much of the 'Abbāsid caliphate was overrun by various Shī'ite forces, from the Būyids in Iran and Ḥamdānids in Syria to the Fāṭimids in Egypt and much of the rest of North Africa, Khurāsān became a bastion for the defence of Sunnism, and such figures as Imām al-Ḥaramayn Juwaynī (d. 1085) and Abū Ḥāmid Muḥammad al-Ghazālī (d. 1111) played a leading role in the intellectual defence of Sunni Islam. The Persian theologian, jurist and Ṣufī Ghazālī was perhaps the most influential scholar of Sunnism after the period of the establishment of Islam. Even during later centuries, the Persian contribution to Sunni theology continued, as is seen in the works of such thirteenth- to fifteenth-century figures as Fakhr al-Dīn Rāzī (d. 1209), Mīr Sayyid Sharīf Jurjānī (d. 1413), 'Aḍud al-Dīn Ījī (d. 1355) and Sa'd al-Dīn Taftāzānī (d. 1389), figures whose works are still taught in Sunni schools.

It is interesting to note that Shī'ite theology also had its centre in Iran. While most of the earlier Ismā'īlī thinkers, such as Abū Ya'qūb Sijistānī (d. 971), Abū Hātim Rāzī (d. 933), Ḥamīd al-Dīn Kirmānī (d. 1017) and Nāṣir-i Khusraw (d. *c.* 1075), who were both theologians and philosophers in the technical sense, were Persians, Twelve-Imām Shī'ite thought also developed primarily there. The authors of the four definitive collections of Shī'ite *ḥadīth* – Muḥammad ibn Ya'qūb Kulaynī (d. 940), Ibn Bābūyeh (d. 991) and Muḥammad Ṭūsī (d. 1068) – were from the central area of Iran and Khurāsān, as was the seminal early Shī'ite theologian Shaykh-i Mufīd (d. 1022). As for systematic Shī'ite theology, it came into being with another Persian figure, Khwājah Naṣīr al-Dīn Ṭūsī (d. 1273), whose *Tajrīd al-i'tiqād* ('Catharsis of Doctrine') is the most important work on Twelve-Imām Shī'ite theology.

THE SPREAD OF SHĪ'ISM

As mentioned already, it was during the two centuries following the Mongol invasion that Shī'ism of the *Ithnā-'asharī* or 'Twelve-Imām' School spread in Iran as a result of many religious, social and political factors, including the destruction of the 'Abbāsid Sunni caliphate, the conversion to Shī'ism of some of the most influential descendants of Hülāgū, who wielded political power and even ruled in Iran, and the spread of certain Ṣūfī orders with a messianic or mahdiist message, which played some role in the spread of Shī'ism. But it was the conquest and unification of Iran by the Ṣafavids, aided by the Turkic Qizilbāsh, that caused Iran to become predominantly Shī'ite, as it is today, and to inaugurate a period of flowering of Shī'ite theology and thought in general (see Nasr, 1991: pp. 395 ff.).

ṢŪFISM

Ṣūfism contains the esoteric teachings of Islam and has its origin in the esoteric meaning of the Qur'ān and the inner teachings and practices of the Prophet. It can be called Islamic mysticism, if this term is understood in its original sense of dealing with the divine mysteries. Ṣūfism was later to adopt many different languages for the expression of its teachings, and employ symbolism drawn from a multitude of sources ranging from Neoplatonist and Christian to Zoroastrian, Hindu and Buddhist. The inner teachings and practices of Ṣūfism do not originate from these sources, however, but from the Islamic Revelation itself. It was the universality of the teachings of Ṣūfism, as the esotericism of the last planar revelation whose finality has given it such a great power of synthesis, that permitted it to make use of so many symbols and forms for the exposition of its teachings based upon the doctrine of the Oneness of Ultimate Reality (*al-tawḥīd*), and the practice of means of attaining Oneness and reaching the One.

Ṣūfism derived from the companions of the Prophet, especially 'Alī ibn Abī Ṭālib, whence it came to be known to such early patriarchs of Ṣūfism as Ḥasan al-Baṣrī (d. 728) from whom it spread in turn in the eighth century to the rest of Iraq and later Khurāsān. In the ninth century the schools of Baghdād and Khurāsān became well known, each emphasizing a type of Ṣūfī spirituality. It is interesting to note that many of the most illustrious members of the school of Baghdād, such as Abu'l-Qāsim Junayd (902), were of Persian origin, while the school of Khurāsān with such major figures as Ibrāhīm Adham (d. 776 or 790), Bāyazīd Baṣṭāmī (d. 874), Ḥakīm Tirmidhī (d. *c.* 932), and Abu'l Ḥasan Kharraqānī (d. 1034), were of course all Persians. It is interesting to note that the great works of Ṣūfism in Arabic, written by Arabs themselves, were to appear in much later Islamic history, while in the early centuries, from the eighth to the twelfth, most of the Ṣūfī authors, including those writing in Arabic, were Persian. One need only recall the earliest classics of Ṣūfī ethics such as *Qūt al-qulūb* ('The Nourishment of Hearts') by Abū Ṭālib al-Makkī (d. 996), *Kitāb al-lumā'* ('The Treatise of Illumination') by Abū Naṣr al-Sarrāj (d. 988), the *Risālat al-qushayriyya* ('The Qushayrī Treatise') of Imam Abu'l-Qāsim al-Qushayrī (d. 1074) and *Kitāb al-ta'arruf* ('The Book of Introduction') of Kalābādhī (d. 990 or 994), all written in Arabic, and the Persian-language *Kashf al-maḥjūb* ('The Unveiling of the Masked') of Hujwīrī (d. *c.* 1071), the patron saint of Lahore. All these were written by Persians. Nor can one forget, in this context, Abū Ḥāmid Muḥammad al-Ghazālī's (d. 1111) *Iḥyā' 'ulūm al-dīn* ('The Revivification of the Sciences of Religions'), in Arabic, which is the most extensive and influential work of ethics in Islamic history.

Khurāsān remained the great centre of Ṣūfī activity during the early centuries of Islam, and produced in addition to those men named already, the brother of Abū Ḥāmid, Aḥmad al-Ghazālī, as well as many great Ṣūfī poets to whom we shall turn soon. But other Iranian cities were also centres of Ṣūfī activity. The most famous of the early Ṣūfīs, Ḥusayn ibn Manṣūr al-Ḥallāj (d. 922), hailed from near Shīrāz as did the great master of the exposition of Ṣūfī lore, Rūzbehān Baqlī (d. 1209). The most extensive early work on Ṣūfī hagiography was written by Abū Nu'aym al-Iṣfahānī (d. 1037), while Iṣfahān was also known in the tenth and eleventh centuries for Ḥanbalite Ṣūfīs such as Abū Manṣūr Iṣfahānī (d. eleventh century). Hamadān produced one of the earliest Ṣūfī poets, Bābā Ṭāhir (d. early eleventh century) and, two centuries later, one of the greatest intellectual figures of Ṣūfīsm, 'Ayn al-Quḍāt Hamadānī (d. 1132). One can point to almost all other areas of Iran and discover that major Ṣūfī figures hailed from there: Khwājeh 'Abdallāh Anṣārī (d. 1089) from Herāt, Abū Sahl Tustarī (d. 896) from Shūshtar in Khūzistān, Awḥad al-Dīn Kirmānī (d. 1237) from Kirmān, Afḍal al-Dīn Kāshānī (d. 1213–14) and 'Abd al-Razzāq Kāshānī (d. 1330) from Kāshān, Shaykh Maḥmūd Shabistarī (d. 1320) from Āzerbaijān, and so on (Schimmel, 1975).

It is also important to mention that many of the major Ṣūfī orders, such as the Qādiriyya, Suhrawardiyya, Mawlawiyya, Chishtiyya and Naqshbandiyya, which exercised the deepest influence upon lands ranging from the Philippines and China to Albania and Morocco, originated either in Iran proper or in the sphere of Persian culture. One cannot understand the religious and cultural history of much of Asia and Africa without taking into consideration these Ṣūfī orders (Nasr, 1971: Part I, pp. 3 ff.; Trimingham, 1971).

With the rise of the Ṣafavids, themselves based upon a Ṣūfī order originating from Ṣāfī al-Dīn Ardibīlī (d. 1331), confrontation began between the state and some of the Ṣūfī orders, especially the Ni'matullāhī: the most powerful Ṣūfī order in Iran at the time of the rise of the Ṣafavids. As a result, by 1600, the Ni'matullāhīs had already been almost decimated and took refuge in the Deccan in India, from which they returned to Iran only in the eighteenth century. The Qādiriyya and Naqshbandiyya orders survived among Iran's Sunni populations in Kurdistān and Balūchistān, while some of the other orders, such as the Dhahabī and Khāksār, continued to function in Shī'ite areas.

LITERATURE

As already mentioned, during the early centries of Islam, Persians wrote in Arabic, but gradually, by the ninth century, Persian literature began to see the light of day, as seen in surviving lines of poetry belonging to this period. Most poets, however, remained satisfied at this time with emulating both the great Arab poets and the meters and prosody of Arabic poetry.[3] In the tenth century, fully fledged Persian poetry was born with Abū 'Abdallāh Ja'far Rūdakī (d. 940), who hailed from the vicinity of Samarkand. He is said to have composed some one hundred thousand verses, thus transforming the classical forms of Arabic poetry into Persian ones. Only a few thousand verses of his poetry have survived, but he nevertheless remains the father and one of the most eloquent pillars of Persian poetry. He was followed in the eleventh century by such celebrated poets as Aḥmad Manūchihrī (d. *c.* 1040), who was attached to the Ghaznavid court. A man well versed in the religious sciences of his day, medicine and Arabic poetry (many of whose models he followed), Manūchihrī devoted much of his poetry to the description of nature. Another Khurāsanī poet of note of the same period, Abu'l-Qāsim 'Unṣurī (d. 1039), likewise belonged to the Ghaznavid court, and became famous for such works as the romance *Wāmiq wa Adhrā.*

Khurāsān remained the centre for the birth and growth of early Persian poetry, and it was here that the classical forms, such as the *qaṣīdah,* the *ghazal,* the *mathnawī* and the *rubā'ī* (quatrain), some adopted from Arabic, and others created by Persian poets themselves, were already developed by the eleventh century. In Khurāsān, the greatest epic poet of the Persian language, Ḥakīm Abu'l-Qāsim Firdawsī, was born, flourished and died in 1020. His *Shāh-Nāmeh* ('Book of Kings'), written in the rhyming couplet or *mathnawī* form, is the most important document of Iran's ancient past and the history of the Iranians as a distinct nation. This 'Homer of the Persian language' resuscitated the sense of identity of Iran's pre-Islamic past in a work written during the Islamic period by a pious person who, while opposed to the dominion by the Arabs over Iran, was profoundly Muslim and was called a Ḥakīm (sage) by his compatriots. In the *Shāh-Nāmeh,* the ancient Persian heroes, both historical and mythical, from Jamshīd and Farīdūn to Zāl and Rustam, and from Isfandiyār to the Sasanian kings, are brought to life in such a way that they remain alive to this day in the consciousness of Persians and other Persian speakers, such as the Tājīks and the inhabitants of the Persianized zone of Islamic culture in general. The literary masterpiece of Firdawsī is a key to the understanding of the national consciousness of Persians and a mirror in which Persian Muslims have, over the ages, reflected upon the myths of their ancient past.

After Firdawsī, the mainstream of Persian poetry became influenced to an ever greater degree by the ethos of Ṣūfism resulting in the treasury of Ṣūfī poetry to which we shall turn shortly. But there were also major poets who were not specifically Ṣūfīs, although Ṣūfism influenced them to some extent. Among the most eloquent of these poets was Ibrāhīm Khāqānī Shīrwānī (d. 1199), who served in the court of the rulers of Shīrwān but also travelled extensively in the rest of the Islamic world, including Iraq, where at the site of the ruins of the ancient capital of Ctesiphon, he composed one of the most eloquent *qaṣīdas* of the Persian language on the lessons that history teaches us about the transience of the world. Khāqānī, one of the most difficult poets of the Persian language, is the author of a famous *Dīwān* ('Collection'), as well as another well-known collection of poems called the *Tuḥfat al-'irāqayan* ('The Gift of the Twin Iraqs' (Arabic-speaking and Persian-speaking Iraq)).

A major poet whom Khāqānī befriended was Niẓāmī Ganjawī (d. 1209). Niẓāmī, who was to compose an elegy for his poet friend, was the author of a number of celebrated romances which possess great dramatic power and have become subjects for numerous minature paintings, romances contained in his *Quintet or Khamseh* such as *Laylī wa Majnūn, Haft Paykar* ('The Seven Bodies') and *Shīrīn wa Khusraw.* These works rank among the supreme masterpieces of the Persian language, and besides their dramatic quality, are replete with wisdom and philosophical insight. Niẓāmī was a highly educated and philosophical poet, and his works are of great interest for their cosmological symbolism as well as for their colour, imagery and power of story-telling. Like his great poet philosopher predecessor Nāṣir-i Khusraw, who was essentially a moralist poet, Niẓāmī was also profoundly concerned with ethical questions while dealing with the deepest aspects of human love. Many consider Niẓāmī to have kneaded the poetic 'body' into which Rūmī was later to breathe the 'spirit' of Ṣūfism. Niẓāmī was also the source for many a later poet, such as Amīr Khusraw, who lived and died in early fourteenth-century Delhi, and Jāmī, to whom we shall turn shortly (see Plates 112, 113, 218).

While the later age of Persian poetry became dominated by Ṣūfi poets, other genres of poetry did also continue to be written. With the advent of Shī'ism, a number of poets appeared known especially for their composition of elegies for the imāms, and depictions of the tragedies of Shī'ite history, the foremost among them being perhaps Muḥtasham Kāshānī (d. 1587). Gradually, a more complicated and ornate style of poetry developed known as the 'Indian style' (*sabki hindī*), among whose greatest masters was Sayyid Muḥammad 'Alī Tabrīzī also known as Ṣā'ib (d. 1675), who belongs to a period beyond the bounds of this essay.

Before turning to Ṣūfī poetry, a word must also be said about Persian prose of literary quality. Persian prose itself began to develop in the tenth and eleventh centuries, and several treaties or philosophy and the sciences were written in Persian by Ismā'īlī philosophers and such notable figures as Ibn Sīnā and Bīrūnī at this time. In the eleventh century, the philosophical writings of Nāṣir-i Khusraw, all in Persian, are especially significant from a literary point of view. But as works of literary art, it is especially the prose works of the Ṣūfīs and Illuminationist and mystical philosophers that are significant. One needs to mention in this context the *Munājāt* of Khwājeh 'Abdallāh Anṣārī of Herāt and especially the *Sawāniḥ* of Aḥmad al-Ghazālī (d. 1126), which is among the greatest literary masterpieces of the Persian language, engendering a whole literary genre to be seen later in the *Lama'āt* ('Divine Flashes') of Fakhr al-Dīn 'Irāqī (d. 1289) and the *Ashi' 'at al-lama'āt* ('Rays of Divine Flashes') and *Lamaḥāt* ('Sparkles') of Jāmī (d. 1492). As for philosophical prose, the works of 'Ayn al-Quḍāt Hamadānī (1131), Shaykh al-ishrāq Shihāb al-Dīn Suhrawardī (d. 1191) and Afḍal al-Dīn Kashānī are of exceptional importance from the point of view of literary beauty.

ṢŪFĪ POETRY

In many ways, Persian Ṣūfī poetry is the crown jewel of Persian literature and culture, containing the deepest ethos of Islam in general and the spiritual aspect of Persian culture in particular, in some of the most beautiful poetry to be found in any language. There is no language richer than Persian in mystical poetry. The universal message of this poetry changed the literary and even religious landscape of many lands outside Persia and helped to give birth to literatures ranging from Malay to Turkish. It even influenced numerous figures outside the Islamic world, ranging from the Bengali poet Tagore to Goethe and Emerson. Today, the translations of Rūmī into English vie in popularity in America with the works of the most famous poets of the English language.

The earliest Ṣūfī poems of which we have some knowledge are the moving and intimate quatrains of Bābā Ṭāhir 'Uryān from Hamadān and those attributed to the celebrated Khurāsānī, Shaykh Abū Sa'īd ibn Abi-l-Khayr (d. 1049). However, it is in the twelfth and thirteenth centuries that Persian Ṣūfī poetry reached the fullness of its development with Abu'l-Majd Sanā'ī (d. 1131), Farīd al-Dīn 'Aṭṭār (d. 1220) and Jalāl al-Dīn Rūmī (d. 1273), who followed each other in a progression that culminated with that supreme 'troubadour of the spirit', Rūmī (Schimmel, 1982). Sanā'ī, the first of this celebrated trio hailed from Khurāsān, as did 'Aṭṭār and Rūmī. Sanā'ī was at first a scholar of religious sciences who then turned to Ṣūfism and developed the *mathnawī* (rhymed couplet) form for the expression of Ṣūfī teachings, dealing with both divine knowledge and divine love. His *Ḥadīqat al-ḥaqā'iq* ('The Enclosed Garden of the Truth') reveals many of the inner mysteries of the Qur'ān and demonstrates his mastery of Islamic esotericism and the conditions of the spiritual path.

His successor, 'Aṭṭār from Nayshāpūr, was also a man of great learning and at the same time a lover of God who burned his ego in the fire of divine love in a state of ecstasy which caused him to pour forth his spiritual vision in a large number of poetic works such as the *Asrār-Nāmeh* ('Treatise of Divine Mysteries'), *Ilāhī-Nāmeh* ('The Book of God') and *Muṣībat-Nāmeh* ('Book of Afflictions'). His greatest poetic work is, however, the *Manṭiq al-ṭayr,* ('The Parliament of Birds') known in the West since Sylvestre de Sacy's nineteenth-century French translation. Numerous translations of this work into other Western languages have followed. 'Aṭṭār's 'Parliament of Birds' stands out among the foremost poetical masterpieces of the Persian language. But 'Aṭṭār was also a master of Persian prose, and his *Tadhkirat al-awliyā'* ('Memorial of the Saints'), dealing with the lives of Ṣūfī saints, is a unique literary masterpiece in this genre (see Plate 3).

The heritage of 'Aṭṭār was to pass to Jalāl al-Dīn Rūmī, whose father took him to Nayshāpūr to visit the venerable 'Aṭṭār when Jalāl al-Dīn was a young boy. Born in Balkh and driven away by the Mongol invasion, Rūmī was brought by his father to Anatolia where they settled. After studying the religious sciences and becoming a well-known teacher in this field, Rūmī's life was transformed by his meeting with the almost mythical wandering dervish, Shams al-Dīn Tabrīzī (a name meaning literally 'The sun of religion of Tabrīz'). This spiritual encounter caused the ocean of spiritual reality within Rūmī's being to erupt into gigantic waves, which produced the incomparable *Mathnawī* ('The Mystic Rhyming Couplets') and *Dīwān-i Shams-i Tabrīzī* ('The Poety-Collection of the Sun of Tabrīz). The *Mathnawī*, called by Jāmī the 'Qur'ān of the Persian language', is in reality a commentary upon the inner meanings of the Qur'ān and without a doubt the greatest mystical poetry of a didactic nature in Persian. As for the *Dīwān,* it is composed of 30,000 verses in *ghazal* form, with many different metres which are so rich in their variety as to make the work not only a treasury of ecstatic poetic utterance but also a treasury of Persian prosody. There is hardly any aspect of the mystery of human existence and man's quest for his origin as well as the nature of that origin in relation to the manifested cosmic order that is not treated in the greatest depth by Rūmī. An outstanding spiritual master who founded the *Mawlawiyya* Ṣūfī order, which wielded such influence in the Ottoman empire, Rūmī is deeply revered by both Persians and Turks, as well as by other Persian-speaking peoples. His main translator into English, R. A. Nicholson, considered him the greatest mystical poet who has ever lived. In any case, Rūmī marks the zenith of Persian Ṣūfī poetry and has remained an immense spiritual and cultural influence in Iran to this day.

Before proceeding any further with later Ṣūfī poets, a word should be said about the most famous Oriental poet in the West, who preceded 'Aṭṭār and who also hailed from Nayshāpūr, namely 'Omar Khayyām (d. *c.* 1132). Known to the West through the masterly but inaccurate rendition of his *Quatrains* into English by Edward Fitzgerald, Khayyām became almost a cult figure in Victorian England and has been associated by some with a hedonist and Epicurean philosophy. The real Khayyām, however, is much closer to the Ṣūfī tradition, especially if his well-known *Rubā'iyyāt* or *Quatrains* are studied in conjunction with his few surviving philosophical works, in which he extols Ṣūfism and expounds the gnosis or *ma'rifa* of the Ṣūfīs. Even his verses, if read carefully, are a basic reassertion of the absoluteness of the Absolute and the transience of all else, especially the many relative things which human beings take to be eternal and absolute but which, being relative, soon wither away.

One would think that Persian Ṣūfī poetry would have exhausted its creative possibilities with 'Aṭṭār and Rūmī, but such was not the case. The century after Rūmī witnessed the two great poets of Shīrāz, Sa'dī and Ḥāfiẓ, who brought the Persian language to the peak of its litereary perfection. Muṣliḥ al-Dīn Sa'dī (d. 1292) was a Ṣūfī of the *Suhrawardiyya* order, but his work is not concerned with Ṣūfism alone, although both of his celebrated masterpieces, the *Būstān* ('The Garden') and the *Gulistān* ('The Rose Garden'), contain some of the most beautiful verses of Persian Ṣūfī poetry. Rather, Sa'dī was a moralist poet and an astute observer of the human condition. His long life and far-ranging journeys allowed him to study the immense complexities of the human state. His works became a mirror of the realities he observed and studied, and for that reason he remains our best source for understanding the norms, values and ethos of Persian society to this day. His eloquence also became the ideal by which all later literature was judged, every generation of educated Persians has studied his *Gulistān,* and many have sought to emulate its language.

If Sa'dī was the poet of terrestrial human existence, Shams al-Dīn Ḥāfiẓ (d. 1389) was the poet of the celestial realities. The greatest lyric poet of the Persian language, this 'troubadour of the world of the Spirit' was a Ṣūfī who transformed the most sensuous of human experiences into spiritual realities and described the most exhalted divine mysteries in the language of human love and the vivid experiences of the world of the senses. In Ḥāfiẓ the process of the spiritualization of the corporal, and the corporealization of the spiritual, a major trait of Persian culture, reaches its peak, and his words possess an alchemical power upon the soul which only grows with familiarity. Like a ladder stretched from Earth to Heaven, Ḥāfiẓ attracts people of all inclinations from the most worldly to the most spiritual, and the universality of his poetry is unique. There is hardly any household in Iran in which his 'Poetry-Collection' or *Dīwān*, the only work he left behind, does not lie in a place of honour next to the Qur'ān. At the deepest level, Ḥāfiẓ was considered the 'messenger of the invisible world', in the Qur'ānic sense of the term, and his honorific title, *lisān al-ghayb* ('tongue of the invisible') is a most apt description of his basic function and cultural role.

Masterpieces of Persian Ṣūfī poetry continued to be written after Ḥāfiẓ, perhaps the most remarkable being the *Gulshani rāz* ('The Garden of Divine Mysteries') of Shaykh Maḥmūd Shabistarī (d. *c.* 1321). Already, in the thirteenth century, the teachings of the Andalusian sage Ibn 'Arabī were influencing Persian Ṣūfī literature, as can be seen in the works of Awḥad al-Dīn Kirmānī (d. 1238) and Fakhr al-Dīn 'Irāqī (d. 1289). This type of 'wisdom poetry' reached its peak with the short and inspired masterpiece of Shabistarī. Written in the space of a few days by a Ṣūfī who did not compose poetry otherwise, the *Gulshani rāz* ranks as one of the finest summaries of Ṣūfī teaching, presented in exquisite verse. No wonder it became one of the most famous and authoritative works of Ṣūfism in later centuries, and many commentaries were written upon it. Among other notable Ṣūfī poets of the period following Shabistarī, one might mention Shāh Ni'matallāh Walī (d. 1431), the author of a major *Dīwān* and the founder of the *Ni'matullāhī* order, the most widespread Ṣūfī order in Iran today. There were also a number of figures in India who wrote Persian Ṣūfī poetry following the fourteenth-century example of Amīr Khusraw. But the most important figure in later Ṣūfī poetry was the fifteenth-century 'Abd al-Raḥmān Jāmī, a Nanqshbandī Ṣūfī from Herāt who has been given the title of 'Seal of the poets' meaning 'he who closes the list' of the classical poets of the Persian language. Influenced at once by Rūmī and Ibn 'Arabī as well as 'Aṭṭār and Niẓāmī, Jāmī composed some of the most beautiful romances which have ever addressed human and divine love, such as *Yūsuf wa Zulaykhā*, which emulates the form of Niẓāmī's romances in the *Khamseh* but shows more direct concern with Ṣūfī teachings. Jāmī was also a major expositor of Ibn 'Arabī's thought, composing commentaries upon the Andalusian master's *Fuṣūṣ al-Ḥikam* ('Bezels of Wisdom') as well as independent works of highly literary quality such as the *Lawā'iḥ* ('Outward Signs'), which were even translated into Chinese. Altogether Jāmī was very popular in Islamic Asia, and not only in India and China, but also in the Malay world, where he played an important role in the formation of Malay literature.

During the Ṣafavid period, Ṣūfī poetry continued, although not at the same level of quality as during the Īl-Khānid and Tīmūrid periods. Among the most notable of the Ṣūfī poets of this period was Shaykh Bahā' al-Dīn 'Āmilī (d. 1621), at once a religious scholar and theological authority, and a mathematician and astronomer. His simply worded *mathnawīs,* such as *Nān wa ḥalwā* ('Bread and Sweetmeat'), have remained popular to this day. While new poets appeared on the horizon, the great masters of the classical period mentioned above continued, and still continue, to exercise the greatest spiritual and cultural influence in Iran. And it was the translation of their works from the late eighteenth century onwards, by such figures as Sir William Jones, that not only made Persian Ṣūfī poetry famous in the West but also caused it to exercise influence upon many major figures of European and American literature, such as Goethe, Rückert, Emerson and Tennyson (Yohannan, 1977).

PHILOSOPHY

Iran has always been a land known for its philosophy, as may be seen in the testimony of the Pythagoreans, the influence of certain Mazdaean themes upon Plato, the desire of Plotinus to join the Roman army so as to be able to reach Persia to study philosophy, and the fame of Zoroaster in the Hellenistic world as well as in the medieval and Renaissance West as a philosopher as well as a prophet. In the pre-Islamic period, however, philosophical thought remained enclosed within the context of religion, as one finds in other major oriental civilizations, and one must turn to such works as the *Dēnkart*, the *Chagand gumānik vichār* and the *Bundahishn* to discover the philosophical dimension of the Mazdaean world view. It is only in the Islamic period that philosophy becomes a distinct discipline, and on the basis of translations of Greek philosophical sources as well as of Indian and pre-Islamic Persian thought, and within the framework established by the Qur'ānic revelation, Islamic philosophy emerges as a major new intellectual perspective or even set of perspectives. During the Islamic period, Islamic philosophy was still closely related to religion, but it was now a discipline distinct from such religious subjects as theology and law.

Islamic philosophy is an integral intellectual tradition and cannot be divided along ethnic lines to satisfy various forms of modern nationalism. It certainly is not an Arabic philosophy, as the term 'Arabic' is understood in the contemporary context, any more than it is an Iranian philosophy. Although most works of Islamic philosophy were written in Arabic, many were in Persian, and although some of the greatest Islamic philosophers, such as al-Kindī and Ibn Rushd were Arabs, most were Persians, and it was in Iran and the Iranian zone of Islamic civilization that Islamic philosophy was to survive as an active intellectual tradition after the demise of Islamic philosophical activity in the Arab world, including the Maghrib and especially al-Andalusia in the thirteenth century.

EARLY 'PERIPATETIC' (*MASHSHĀ'Ī*) PHILOSOPHY

Although the first Islamic philosopher of that synthesis between Islam, Aristotelianism and Neoplatonism which came to be known in Arabic as *mashshā'ī* or 'Peripatetic' philosophy was the Arab Abū Ya'qūb al-Kindī, who flourished in Baghdād. Some of his most famous students, such as Abū Zayd Balkhī (d. 933) and Aḥmad ibn Ṭayyib Sarakhsī (d. 899), were from Khurāsān, and after the ninth century, Khurāsān became a major centre of Islamic philosophy (Corbin, 1993; Sharif, 1963–66; Nasr, 1996; Nasr and Leaman, 1996). Abū Naṣr Fārābī (d. 950), the father of Islamic political philosophy, whose *Ārā' ahl al-Madīnat al-Fāḍila* ('The Opinion of the People of the Virtuous City') is the fundamental text on this subject, was also a great commentator on Aristotle and the father of formal logic in Islamic thought. He hailed from Fārāb in greater Khurāsān and spent the first half of his life there before visiting Baghdād and finally settling in Damascus.[4] Fārābī completed the formation of Arabic philosophical vocabulary and established the main theses of the *mashshā'ī* school. His imprint is to be found on all later Islamic philosophy.

After Fārābī, the philosophical school of Baghdād was eclipsed by that of Khurāsān, where Abu'l-Ḥasan 'Āmirī (d. 992) wrote a number of works such as *al-Amad 'alā-l-Abad* ('Time Within Eternity') and *al-I'lām bi-Manāqib al-Islām* ('Declaration of the Virtues of Islam'), in which elements of Persian political thought of the pre-Islamic period were integrated into the tenets of the *mashshā'ī* school. He also dealt with the basic issue of the relation between reason and revelation which had also concerned Fārābī before him and nearly all the philosophers in Iran who were to follow.

'Āmirī was eclipsed to a large extent by the greatest of all *mashshā'ī* philosophers and the most outstanding and influential philosopher-scientist of Islam, Abū 'Alī ibn Sīnā (Avicenna) (d. 1037), who remains a cultural and almost mythical hero not only for Persians but also for several other nations. An exceptional genius who was already a celebrated philosopher and physician by the age of eighteen, Ibn Sīnā travelled from his city of birth (Bukhārā) to Jurjāniyya, and from there wandered from one city to another in Iran, such as Rayy, Iṣfahān and Hamadān for the rest of his life. And yet he wrote over 200 works, including the *Canon of Medicine (al-Qānūn fi'l-ṭibb)*, the most famous single work in the history of medicine, and the monumental encyclopedia of *mashshā'ī* philosophy and science, *Kitāb a-shifā'* ('Book of Healing'). Ibn Sīnā was also the author of the first work of *mashshā'ī* philosophy in the Persian language, the *Dānish-Nāmeh-yi 'alā'ī* ('The Book of Science dedicated to 'Alā' al-Dawleh'), which is of great liguistic significance and marks the beginning of the tradition of writing systematically thought out Islamic philosophy in the Persian language, a practice that became much more prevalent later, as we see in the works of Nāṣir-i Khusraw, Suhrawardī, Afḍal al-Dīn Kāshānī, Ṭūsī and others. With Ibn Sīnā, *mashshā'ī* philosophy reached its zenith, and he was able to create a vast synthesis which influenced all later Islamic thought. In Iran itself, his influence can be seen throughout all later centuries of Iranian history, despite the criticism brought against him and his school by Ash'arite theologians, especially al-Ghazālī and Fakhr al-Dīn Rāzī in the eleventh and twelfth centuries.

Ibn Sīnā's students, such as Bahmanyār ibn Marzbān (d. 1067) and Ḥusayn ibn Zayleh (d. 1048), continued his teachings through the eleventh century, but under the barrage of criticism unleashed by the theologians, *mashshā'ī* philosophy became eclipsed in Iran for a century and a half, while it flourished in al-Andalus. In Iran itself, the only notable philosophical figure in the twelfth century is Khayyām, who translated one of Ibn Sīnā's orations from Arabic into Persian: even though Khayyām remains much better known as a mathematician and poet, despite his very real philosophical importance. This eclipse of Ibn Sīnā's teachings was, however, only temporary. In the thirteenth century, his thought was revived by one of Iran's greatest philosophers and scientists, Khwājeh Naṣīr al-Dīn Ṭūsī, whose commentary upon Ibn Sīnā's last masterpiece, *al-Ishārāt wa'l-tanbīhāt* ('The Book of Directives and Remarks'), resuscitated the work of the master and re-established the *mashshā'ī* school as a living current of thought which has survived in Iran to this day.

THE INDEPENDENT PHILOSOPHERS

Although in Islamic philosophy schools dominate over individual interpretations of philosophy, there are a number of philosophers of note during this period who are of significance yet cannot be fully identified with any single school such as the *mashshā'ī* or the Ismā'īlī. Chief among them are Muḥammad ibn Zakariyyā' Rāzī (d. *c.* 932) and Abū Rayḥān Bīrūnī (d. *c.* 1051). Rāzī, celebrated as a physician and known in the West as Rhazes, was also a philosopher who considered himself the equal of Plato and Aristotle. He went so far as to deny the necessity of prophecy for those who could reach the truth through philosophy alone, a thesis totally rejected by Islam. As a result, most of his philosophical works have been lost, and he has therefore been praised and remembered mostly as a physician. But some of his philosophical works, such as *al-Sīrat al-falsafiyyah* ('The Philosophical Life') are extant and bear witness to his highly idiosyncratic philosophical stand.

In contrast to Rāzī, Bīrūnī stood firm in confirming prophetic revelation and its necessity, and yet, like Rāzī, he was also an outstanding scientist who was in fact attracted to Rāzī's works, of which he wrote a catalogue. One of the greatest of all medieval Islamic scientists, Bīrūnī did not write independent philosophical works but did criticize many theses of *mashshā'ī* natural philosophy in a series of questions and answers exchanged with Ibn Sīnā. In his *India*, considered the world's earliest work on comparative religion, he not only described the beliefs of the Hindus but also discussed many issues of general philosophical interest.

One must also mention the *Rasā'il* ('Treatises') of the Ikhwān al-Ṣafā' ('Brethren of Purity'), composed in the tenth century in Baṣrā in a milieu with both Arabic and Persian elements. Although later incorporated into Ismā'īlism, the *Rasā'il* were the product of a more general Shī'ite climate. In any case, whether considered as part of the Ismā'īlī school or as an independent philosophical composition, they contain an elaborate philosophical discourse with a strong Hermetico-Pythagorean colour which was widely read in different circles. If not of outright Ismā'īlī origin, the *Rasā'il* do reflect the philosophical aspects of thought in Shī'ite circles in Iraq and Iran during the tenth century.

THE SCHOOL OF ILLUMINATION (ISHRĀQ)

In the twelfth century, a major new school of Islamic philosophy, known as the 'School of Illumination' or *ishrāq*, was founded by the 'Master of Illumination' *Shaykh al-ishrāq*, Shihāb al-Dīn Suhrawardī, born in western Iran, educated in Iṣfahān and martyred in Aleppo. This astounding metaphysician integrated the angelology and cosmology of Mazdaean Iran with earlier Islamic philosophy, within the framework of Islamic gnosis (*ma'rifa, 'irfān*) and so created a new philosophical school which should properly be termed 'theosophical' (if this term were understood in its original and not current deviated sense). Suhrawardī's philosophy, besides representing one of the most important currents of thought in Iran itself ever since his death eight centuries ago, has exercised the profoundest influence upon Islamic thought in India as well, and also has had many followers in Ottoman Turkey. Suhrawardī wrote not only Arabic works of remarkable literary quality, especially his masterpiece, *Ḥikmat al-Ishrāq*, which his foremost student in the West, Henry Corbin, has translated as 'The Theosophy of the Orient of Light'; he also composed some of the most beautiful works of philosophical prose in the Persian language.

After a short hiatus, due to his execution for 'heresy', Suhrawardī's thought was revived in the thirteenth century by Muḥammad Shahrazūrī (d. *c.* 1288) and Quṭb al-Dīn Shīrāzī (d. 1311), both leading commentators of the *Ḥikmat al-Ishrāq*. Henceforth, numerous philosophers appeared, who identified themselves with the teachings of the 'Master of Illumination', such as Jalāl al-Dīn Dawānī (d. 1501 or 1502), and early seventeenth-century Mīr Dāmād. The 'School of Illumination' was also a major element in the new synthesis of various currents of Islamic thought wrought by Mullā Ṣadrā (d. 1640) after the end of the period under discussion in this essay.

ISLAMIC PHILOSOPHY IN IRAN FROM THE THIRTEENTH TO THE SIXTEENTH CENTURY AND THE SCHOOL OF IṢFAHĀN

Iran became the arena in which different currents of Islamic thought that had remained distinct in earlier Islamic history began to converge with each other between the thirteenth and sixteenth centuries. The philosophy of Ibn Sīnā, as resuscitated by Ṭūsī, the 'School of Illumination', the doctrines of Islamic gnosis associated with Ibn 'Arabī (d. 1240) and Ṣadr al-Dīn Qūnawī (d. 1274), and other various schools of Sunni and Shī'ite *Kalām*, gradually mingled. Some philosophers, such as Quṭb al-Dīn Shīrāzī, sought to combine *mashshā'ī* and *ishrāqī* doctrines; others, such as Afḍal al-Dīn Kāshānī, Ṣūfism and *mashshā'ī* teachings; and yet others, such as Dawānī, who belonged to the school of Shiraz, *Kalām* and *falsafah*. There were also those such as Ibn Turkeh (d. *c.* 1432) who attempted to unify *'irfān, mashshā'ī* and *ishrāqī* teachings into a whole, thereby preparing the ground for the major synthesis associated with the School of Iṣfahān.

In the sixteenth century, the grandmaster of later Islamic philosophy, Mīr Dāmād who was himself an *ishrāqī* interpreter of Ibn Sīnā, as well as a celebrated Shī'ite religious scholar, re-established the study of philosophy in Iṣfahān, beginning a new school which has come to be known as the School of Iṣfahān. It was, however, his student Mullā Ṣadrā who wrought the great synthesis of the schools mentioned above in what he called 'the transcendent theosophy' (*al-ḥikmat al-muta'āliya)*, concerning which he wrote a number of well-known works, chief among them *al-Asfār al-Arba'a* ('The Four Journeys'), which ranks with Avicenna's *Shifā'*, Avicenna's *Ishārāt* with its commentary by Ṭūsī, and Suhrawardī's *Ḥikmat al-Ishrāq*, as the most significant work of Islamic philosophy in Iran. Mullā Ṣadrā was also to have a major influence in India and has dominated the philosophical scene in Iran itself during the past three centuries. Like Suhrawardī but unlike Ibn Sīnā, who was so influential in the medieval West, Mullā Ṣadrā did not become known in the West until the present century, and it is only now that the significance of his philosophy *per se*, and its role within the philosophical tradition in Iran are becoming widely recognized.

THE SCIENCES AND TECHNOLOGY – BACKGROUND

During its several thousand years of history, Iran has been a centre of some of the most important scientific discoveries and technological inventions, going back to the smelting of iron on the Iranian plateau 8,000 years ago. From the Achaemenian period onward, the Persian Empire also exercised lordship over much of the land of the Greeks and was in contact with both India and, through the Silk Road, with China. Achaemenian kings had Greek physicians, while Sanskrit texts of medicine and astronomy were taught in Sasanian Persia. As for the Islamic period, it marks the zenith of scientific activity in Iran, and much of what is known as Islamic science was cultivated by Persians.

SCIENCE AND TECHNOLOGY IN ISLAMIC IRAN

As in the case of philosophy, so in the case of science, it is difficult to impose modern 'nationalistic' divisions upon Islamic science whose practitioners often crossed what are considered as 'national' borders today. We must limit our remarks, therefore, to those elements of Islamic science, understood to be seen as an undeniable unity, which were notably cultivated by Persians, and within the context of Persian and Persianate culture. Islamic science integrated the sciences of pre-Islamic civilizations, ranging from the Graeco-Alexandrian to the Indian and the specifically Iranian within the context of the Islamic world view, and, at the beginning, exclusively through the medium of the Arabic language, although later the Persian idiom also became a significant scientific language. Persian scientists, therefore, wrote in both Arabic and Persian and made the greatest contribution to the formation of Arabic as a language of science (Nasr, 1975–1991; 1987; 1995; King, 1986; Hartner, 1968; Hamarneh, 1983; Sezgin, 1970–1974; Ullmann, 1972). Islam seems to have inspired a greater degree of activity in the realm of 'abstract' and scientific and philosophical thought among Persians, as reflected in the sudden rise of scientific activity in Iran from the ninth century onward.

ASTRONOMY AND THE MATHEMATICAL SCIENCES

According to the traditional Islamic classification of the sciences, just as in the Pythagorean *quadrivium*, astronomy was regarded as a branch of the mathematical sciences, which for Muslims included, in addition to arithmetic, geometry and music, several other disciplines such as algebra and optics.

Islamic astronomy in Iran began on the basis of Sasanian astronomy and the *Zīj-i shahriyār* ('Royal Almanac') as well as *Kitāb al-ulūf* ('Book of Thousands'), which were both translated into Arabic. Later the Indian *Siddhāntas* became of central importance, followed by the *Almagest* of Ptolemy (Kennedy, 1983). Many Persian astronomers participated in the astronomical activities at al-Ma'mūn's court in Baghdād in the ninth century. During this century also, Abū Ma'shar al-Balkhī (d. 886) spread knowledge of Persian astronomy as well as astrology, while Muḥammad ibn Mūsā Khwārizmī (d. *c.* 863) was composing *Zījes* ('almanacs'). To this period also belongs 'Abbās al-Farghānī (d. *c.* 861), whose *Kitāb fi'l ḥarakat al-Samāwiyya wa Jawāmi' 'Ilm al-Nujūm* ('the Book on the movement of the heavens and the collected science of the stars'), also known as the *Principles of Astronomy,* marked a new chapter in the history of astronomy and was also very influential in the West. His contemporary Abu'l-'Abbās Nayrīzī (d. *c.* 922) composed one of the first commentaries upon the *Almagest.*

The tenth century was a particularly active one for the Islamic sciences in Iran. This century was witness to much new observation, with the composition of the major work on star configurations in Islam being the *Ṣuwar al-Kawākib* ('Figures of the Stars') of 'Abd al-Raḥmān Ṣūfī (d. 986), while Abu'l-Wafā' Buzjānī (d. 998) and Abū Maḥmūd al-Khujandī (d. 1000), both leading mathematicians, also did important astronomical work concerning the movement of the Moon and the Sun, respectively. The greatest astronomical work of the period, however, was *al-Qānūn al-Mas'ūdī* ('The Mas'ūdī Canon') of Bīrūnī, which summarized both the mathematical, and observational, astronomy of the day, and its history. Bīrūnī, who must be considered as one of the greatest of all Islamic scientists, also composed the first work on astronomy and astrology in the Persian language, entitled the *Kitāb al-Tafhīm* ('The Book of Astrology'), a work whose significance for the development of Persian as a scientific language can hardly be overemphasized (Nasr, 1993, pp. 105 ff.). Somewhat eclipsed during the Seljuk period, astronomy was revived during the Īl- Khānid period by Naṣīr al-Dīn Ṭūsī whose *al-Tadhkira* ('Memorial of Astronomy') and *Zīj-i Īl-Khānī* ('The Īl-Khānid Astronomical Tables') along with the works of his contemporary Quṭb al-Dīn Shīrāzī such as the *Nihāyat al-idrāk* ('The Limits of Comprehension'), mark, in many ways, the peak of Islamic astronomy. These works included a criticism of Ptolemaic planetary theory and new models for planetary motion. Later Persian works in astronomy up to 1600, such as those of 'Alī ibn Muḥammad Qūshchī (d. 1474) and the *Zīj* of Ulugh Beg (d. 1449), follow the school of Naṣīr al-Dīn founded in Marāgheh.

Astronomy in Iran during the Islamic period was also marked by great interest in new observations, which, indeed, characterized Islamic astronomy in general (see Plates 135, 139). This led, on the one hand, to the development of new instruments such as the astrolabe, quadrants, sextants, and so on, and, on the other, to the foundation of the observatory as a scientific institution. Astronomical instruments developed over the centuries from both a practical and artistic point of view, especially the astrolabe, some of whose best examples made in Tīmūrid and Ṣafavid Iran rank among the finest artistic masterpieces. The observatory established in Marāghehh by Ṭūsī during the rule of Hülāgū was the first fully fledged institution of its type in history, one in which a group of scientists collaborated together in both observation of the heavens and mathematical analysis of planetary motion (Sayili, 1960). It served as the model for the observatories of Samarkand and Istanbul and ultimately for the observatories of Renaissance Europe such as that of Tycho Brahe.

As for mathematics proper, almost all branches thereof witnessed remarkable development throughout the period under consideration (Matvievskaya and Rozenfel'd, 1983). As in astronomy, so in mathematics, the Greek, Indian and Iranian traditions blended and synthesized to form a unit from which Islamic mathematics, as such, took root and grew. The so-called 'Arabic' numerals themselves were adopted from Indian sources in Iran and appeared for the first time in Khwārīzmī's *al-Jām' wa'l-tafrīq bi Ḥisāb al-Hind* ('Addition and Subtraction in Indian Arithmetic'). This book brought Arabic numerals to the West, which is why the name of the Persian author of the work has survived in European languages to this day as words having to do with arithmetic or number theory, as with '*algorismo*' in Spanish and 'algorithm' in English. During later centuries, Persian mathematicians continued to show much interest in numerical theory and numerical series, as we see in the Ikhwān al-Ṣafā', Abū Bakr Karajī (d. *c.* 1020), Bīrūnī and, especially Ghiyāth-Dīn Jamshīd Kāshānī (d. *c.* 1436), with whom computation techniques reached their peak in Islam. He invented decimal fractions and is also credited with the invention of a computing machine. Later works in mathematics, such as Shaykh Bahā' al-Dīn 'Āmilī's *Miftāḥ al-ḥisāb* ('Key to Arithmetic'), are more or less summaries of Kāshānī's works.

In geometry, Muslims followed Greek mathematics, which they further developed extensively, however. In the ninth century, the Banū Mūsā brothers in Baghdād wrote on geometric figures and composed a recension of the *Conics* of Apollonius. In the tenth century, Nayrīzī and Abū 'Abdallāh Māhānī (d. *c.* 880) wrote notable commentaries upon Ptolemy. while Abū Sahl Kūhī (d. *c.* 988) turned to problems which had already been raised by Archimedes and Apollonius. In the twelfth century, the famous Persian poet Khayyām added a new chapter to the history of geometry when he re-examined the fifth postulate of Euclid concerning the parallel line theorem, a line of investigation later followed by Ṭūsī. But neither scientist pursued his research to its ultimate conclusion, which would have led him to non-Euclidian geometry.

Persian mathematics also had a major role to play in the development of plane and spherical trigonometry. The science of trigonometry as known today was established by Islamic mathematicians. One of the most important of these was the Persian Abu' l-Wafā' Buzjānī (d. 997 or 998), who wrote a work called the *Almagest* dealing mostly with trigonometry. He was also the first person to give a demonstration of the *sine* theorem for a spherical triangle. In his *Maqālīd 'Ilm al-Hay'a* ('Keys to the Science of Astronomy'), Bīrūnī treated all the trigonometric functions for the first time as a separate field of mathematics. In the thirteenth century, Ṭūsī's *Kitāb Shikl al-Qiṭā'* ('Book of the Figure of the Sector') established trigonometry once and for all as a distinct major branch of mathematics.

As for algebra, its origin in Islamic mathematics and even its name are derived from the title of the famous book by Khwārīzmī usually known as *Kitāb al-Jabr wa' l-Muqābalah* ('The Book of Compulsion and Equation'). On the basis of this seminal work, later mathematicians such as Khujandī and Karajī developed algebra extensively and prepared the ground for the works of Khayyām and Sharaf al-Dīn Ṭūsī (d. second half of the twelfth century) in algebraic geometry and algebra itself. The *Algebra* of Khayyām is the most complete work of its kind in Arabic, a work whose translation brought this important branch of mathematics to the West.

As far as physics and optics are concerned, one can only mention in the short space alotted here the study of weights and measures following the works of Archimedes by Bīrūnī and 'Abd al-Raḥmān Khāzinī (d. *c.* 1100), and the commentaries upon Ibn al-Haytham's masterpiece in optics, the *Kitāb al-Manāẓir* ('Optics'), by Kamāl al-Dīn Fārsī (d. *c.* 1320) in the thirteenth century, as well as the intense interest shown by his teacher Quṭb al-Dīn Shīrāzī in optics and the study of light in general. Moreover, from Ibn Sīnā onwards, Persian natural philosophers provided an important criticism of the Aristotelian theory of motion and proposed concepts which played a major role in the later development of mechanics and dynamics in the West (Nasr, 1995, pp. 139 ff.).

MEDICINE

As already mentioned, around AD 600, Jundishāpūr was the most important centre for medical studies in Western Asia and the Mediterranean world, one in which the Greek, Indian and Persian traditions came into contact. This centre was the immediate source for the great medical centre of Baghdād in the early 'Abbāsid period and provided the background for the tradition of Islamic medicine. By the ninth century, this earlier tradition had become completely transformed into Islamic medicine, and the first major works in the field began to appear in Arabic, starting with 'Alī ibn Rabbān Ṭabarī's (d. 1058) *Firdaws al-Ḥikma* ('Paradise of Wisdom'), the first systematic work of Islamic medicine characterized by its synthesis of Greek and Indian medicine (Elgood, 1951).

It is interesting to note that not only Ṭabarī but also the other three major figures who wrote systematic works of medicine in the tenth and eleventh centuries, namely Rāzī, Majūsī and Ibn Sīnā, were Persians. Muḥammad ibn Zakariyyā' Rāzī (Rhazes) was the greatest clinical physician of Islam and the author of the well-known medical encyclopedia *al-Ḥāwī* ('Continens'), along with another major opus, *Kitāb al-Malikī* ('Royal Book'), and was director of the famous 'Aḍud al-Dawla hospital in Baghdād. These works in turn found their culmination in Ibn Sīnā's *al-Qānūn* ('The Canon'), which is without doubt the most famous single work in the history of medicine in both East and West. Known as Avicenna in the Latin world, where he was entitled the 'Prince of Physicians', Ibn Sīnā created a synthesis which dominated Western medicine well into the Renaissance and continues to be followed in the Indian subcontinent, where it is referred to as *yūnānī* (Greek: literally 'Ionian') medicine (see Plate 133a–e).

The early masters synthesized not only Greek, Indian and pre-Islamic Persian medicine but also the Hippocratic and Galenic traditions within Greek medicine itself. They made many clinical observations, diagnosed for the first time several important diseases such as smallpox and expanded the pharmacopaeia to include not only what was known to Dioscorides but also the vast pharmacological knowledge of the ancient Persians and Indians. They studied the link between diet and health and the relation between psychological and physical health. They also paid much attention to public hygiene and the building of hospitals and dispensaries and extended the art of surgery, which reached its peak in Islamic medicine in Spain.

After Ibn Sīnā, the great tree of Islamic medicine branched out in several directions, including al-Andalus and the Maghrib, the Arab East, and later Turkey and the Indian subcontinent. While the influence of Persian physicians is to be seen in all these branches, it is especially later Islamic medicine in India that remained narrowly linked to the development of medicine in Iran itself, and in fact many of its most famous practitioners, until two centuries ago, were of Persian origin.

In Iran, nearly all later medical works were influenced profoundly by Ibn Sīnā. In the twelfth century, the theologian Fakhr al-Dīn Rāzī devoted a section in his scientific encyclopedia, the *Kitāb al-Sittīnī* ('Book of Sixty Sciences'), to medicine, following Ibn Sīnā closely. Also during this century, the first major medical work in Persian, entitled *Dhakhīreh-ye Khwārazmshāhī* ('Treasury dedicated to the King of Khwārīzm') by Zayn al-Dīn Ismā'īl Jurjānī (d. 1135–1136), was modelled upon the *Canon*. This work was also, perhaps, after the *Canon* the most influencial book in the later history of medicine in Iran and India. It also marked the beginning of a long series of works written on medicine in Persian, in both Iran and India, down to modern times. In fact, most of the works on Islamic medicine and pharmacology in the Indian subcontinent were written in the Persian language.

Medicine continued to flourish in Iran even after the Mongol invasion. During the Īl-Khānid period, Quṭb al-Dīn Shīrāzī wrote his *al-Tuḥfat al-sa'diyya* ('The Gift Presented to Sa'd'), considered as perhaps the most profound commentary upon the *Canon* ever written. The Īl-Khānid vizier, Rashīd al-Dīn Faḍlallāh (d. 1318), created a whole university city in Tabrīz, the Rab'-i Rashīdī ('The Rashīdian Quadrangle'), in which the teaching and study of medicine were especially emphasized. Not only did Rashīd al-Dīn write a medical encyclopedia himself, but he commissioned a work on Chinese medicine in Persian, a treatise which still survives. Likewise, in the Tīmūrid period, that is, in the fourteenth and fifteenth centuries, medical activity continued in many Persian cities, while some Persian physicians such as Ghiyāth al-Dīn Iṣfahānī wrote treatises for Ottoman sultans and even taught medicine in the Ottoman world.

During the Ṣafavid period, much of the activity of the Tīmūrid period continued. In fact the life of the most famous of all Ṣafavid physicians, Bahā' al-Dawleh, who was the first person to describe clearly hay fever and whooping cough, spanned the later Tīmūrid and early Ṣafavid periods. His *Khulāṣat-Tajārib* ('Quintessence of Experience'), based upon the model of Rāzī's *al-Ḥāwī*, is perhaps the most important medical work of the Ṣafavid era. During this time, there was also much interest in surgery, as seen in the *Dhakhīra-ye Kāmileh* ('The Perfect Treasury') of Ḥakīm Muḥammad (d. in the seventeenth century), devoted solely to surgery. The classical medical tradition continued to flourish to the end of the Ṣafavid period and even into the eighteenth- and nineteenth-century. Afshār, Zand and Qājār eras, when in Iran, as in most of the other Islamic lands, Western medicine began to replace the long Islamic medical tradition, if not completely, at least to a large extent, the only notable exception being the Indian subcontinent.

THE APPLIED SCIENCES AND TECHNOLOGY

Many other sciences were developed in Iran during the period under discussion, such as various branches of natural history and geography, which because of lack of space cannot be treated here. But a word must be said about some of the applied sciences and technology. Islamic science paid much attention to alchemy, which is both an art and a science of the soul and the cosmos, and not simply a prelude to chemistry. But those who sought to master the alchemical art also both developed instruments which are the forerunners of those used in present-day chemistry laboratories and dealt with the science of matter. Among the Islamic alchemists, the most famous was Jābir ibn Ḥayyān (eighth century), who is said to have hailed from Khurāsān. He was followed by Muḥammad ibn Zakariyyā' Rāzī, who was the first person to transform alchemy into a true chemistry and who is credited with the discovery of many substances, including alcohol as a substance to be used for medical purposes. The acid–base theory of chemistry has its origin in the sulphur–mercury theory of these and other alchemists.

Persians also developed the technology of building at this time. Although practically no written sources have survived concerning this field, the results, over the centuries, in the form of various architectural edifices, give one pause (see Plates 26, 27, 71, 89, 199). This is also true of many other technologies, such as the making of dyes which produced the brilliant colours of carpets, textiles and tiles that have survived over the centuries down to our own day. Likewise, Persians continued and expanded upon Sasanian techniques of metallurgy and irrigation, including the *qanāt* system, canals, dams and so on, many of which survive to this day. From metallurgy to glass making, from bricklaying to the dyeing of wool, numerous technologies were developed during the millennium considered in this essay, technologies which not only facilitated life for the people of the Iranian plateau but also made possible numerous works of Persian art, some of which rank among the greatest masterpieces of world art. Moreover, it was from Iran that many technologies of Chinese origin reached the Arab world and the West, chief among them the production of paper.

CONCLUDING COMMENTS

Persian culture, while open to many influences from both East and West, itself bloomed in nearly every aspect during the Islamic period. The Islamic culture of Iran made possible the flowering of philosophy, the sciences, literature and the arts in such a manner as to mark permanently those regions of Islamic civilization called 'Persianate' or 'Iranic' by many historians, as well as Islamic civilization as a whole. Its influence was also borne even beyond the confines of Islamic civilization, a civilization which Persia contributed so much to fashion, to India, China and South-East Asia in the East, and to both Byzantium and Latin Europe in the West. Classical Persian culture also remains the heart and soul of contemporary Iranian culture and is still very much alive. Far from being a matter of mere historical interest, this culture remains to this day what binds the people of Iran together, links them to their ancient past as well as to the rest of the Islamic world and even beyond the Islamic world, to humanity at large, thanks to the universal values espoused by its most perceptive and profound representatives.

NOTES

1 Throughout this essay, we have used both 'Iran' and 'Persia' and the adjectives which deriving from them, usually using 'Iran' for the name of the country (except when speaking of the Persian Empire) and 'Persian' for not only the language but also the culture and the people.

2 There is some debate concerning the rate of the spread of Islam in Persia, but in any case it is known that as late as the tenth century, there were sizeable Zoroastrian populations in Iran. On this issue, see Shaban, 1971: pp. 479–490; Shaban, 1970; Madelung, 1988; Zarrīnkūb, 1975; Spuler, 1952.

3 There are a number of histories of Persian literature from the classical work of E. G. Browne, to those of A. J. Arberry, J. Rypka and A. Bausani. But the most extensive and authoritative work in the field is that of Safā, Dh. *Tārīkh-ē adabiyyāt dar Īrān,* seven volumes of which have appeared thus far concerning the period from the earliest beginnings to the eighteenth and nineteenth centuries.

4 The first Islamic philosopher in Iran was not Fārābī but Īrānshahrī whose works have been lost, but references to his writings survive in the works of Bīrūnī, Nāṣir-i Khusraw and others. The Ismā'īlī philosophers, already cited, as well as the writer or writers of the mysterious *Umm al-kitāb*, which appeared in the eighth century, must also be mentioned among the earliest philosophical thinkers of Iran during the Islamic period.

BIBLIOGRAPHY

CORBIN, H. 1993. *The History of Islamic Philosophy*. London. (French original: *Histoire de la philosophie islamique*. Paris 1964).

ELGOOD, C. E. 1951. *A Medical History of Persia and the Eastern Caliphate from the Earliest Times until the Year AD 1932*. Cambridge.

FRYE, R. N. 1976. *The Heritage of Persia*. London.

HAMARNEH, S. K. 1983. *Health Science in Early Islam*, (ANEES, M. A. (ed.)). Blanco, Texas.

HARTNER, W. 1968. *Oriens–Occidens*. Hildesheim.

KENNEDY, E. S. 1983. *Studies in the Islamic Exact Sciences*. Beirut.

KING, D. 1986. *Islamic Mathematical Astronomy*. London.

MADELUNG, W. 1988. *Religious Trends in Early Islamic Iran*. Albany, New York.
NASR, S. H. 1971. *Islamic Spirituality – Manifestations*, Part I, pp. 3 ff.
——. 1975–1991. *An Annotated Bibliography of Islamic Science*. Tehran.
——. 1987. *Science and Civilization in Islam*. Cambridge.
——. 1991. Theology, Philosophy, and Spirituality. In: NASR, S. H. (ed.), *Islamic Spirituality – Manifestations*. New York, pp. 395 ff.
——. 1993. *An Introduction to Islamic Cosmological Doctrines*. Albany, New York. pp. 105 ff.
——. 1995. *Islamic Science – An Illustrated Study*. Chicago.
——. 1996. *The Islamic Intellectual Tradition in Persia*. London.
NASR, S. H.; LEAMAN, O. (eds) *History of Islamic Philosophy*. Routledge. London.
ROZENFEL'D, B. A. 1983. *Matemmatiki astronomy musul'manskogo svednevekov'ya i ikh trudy*. Moscow.
SAYILI, A. 1960. *The Observatory in Islam*. Ankara.
SCHIMMEL, A. M. 1975. *Mystical Dimension of Islam*. Chapel Hill, North Carolina.
——. 1982. *As Through a Veil*. New York. pp. 49 ff.
SEZGIN, F. 1970–1974. *Geschichte des arabischen Schrifttums*, Vols 3–5. Leiden.
SHABAN, M. A. 1970. *The 'Abbāssid Revolution*. Cambridge.
——. 1971. Khurāsān at the time of the Arab conquest. In: BOSWORTH, C. E. (ed.) *Iran and Islam*. Edinburgh. pp. 479–490.
SHARIF, M. M. (ed.) 1963–1966. *A History of Muslim Philosophy*. Wiesbaden.
SPULER, B. 1952. *Iran in frühislamischer Zeit*. Wiesbaden.
TRIMINGHAM, J. S. 1971. *The Sufi Orders in Islam*. Oxford.
ULLMANN, M. 1972. *Die Natur-und Geheimwissenschaften im Islam*. Leiden.
YOHANNAN, J. 1977. *Persian Poetry in England and America*. New York.
ZARRĪNKŪB, 'A. 1975. The Arab Conquest of Iran and its Aftermath. In: FRYE, R. N. (ed.) *The Cambridge History of Iran*, Vol. 4. Cambridge.

23

CENTRAL ASIA

Muhammad S. Asimov and Numan Negmatov

At the end of the seventh century and the beginning of the eighth, the territory of historical Bactria, Marghiana, Parthia, Sogdiana, Chorasmia (Khwārizm or Khwārizm), and the adjacent oases, steppes and mountains, were conquered by the Arab caliphate in a series of military incursions and campaigns, and the governorate of Khurāsān was established with its capital in the city of Marw (or Merw). In addition to Iran and Khurāsān, all the regions to the north and east of the Āmū Daryā were placed under the control of the governorate and were thereafter called by their new name: *Mā warā' al-nahr* (literally, 'that which lies beyond the river') or Transoxania, that is, the land beyond the River Oxus (Āmū Daryā) (Gafurov, 1972). The region later became known as Central Asia. In the seventh and eighth centuries, Transoxania thus fell within the economic, commercial and ideological orbit of a world power, the Arab caliphate.

The early medieval period saw the beginning of an extremely significant historical process, the emergence of the Tājīk people on the basis of the Soghdian, Bactro-Tokharian, Marghiano-Parthian (Khurāsānian), Khwārīzmian and Farghānan ethnic groups as well as the steppe and mountain Saka, Massagetai and Kangju tribal confederacies – the entire indigenous east Iranian ethnic, linguistic and cultural substratum of Transoxania. The ethnogenesis of the modern Tājīks, which began within the Sasanian state in Khurāsān, subsequently embraced Transoxania and was a largely completed within the borders of the Sāmānid state (see Map 18) in the vast expanses between the Hindu Kush and the Tian Shan Mountains, the Caspian Sea and the Pamirs (Negmatov, 1990).

In the sixth to eighth centuries, another historical process was initiated in the steppes of northern Transoxania and some regions in the basin of the Syr Daryā with the arrival and settlement of groups of Turkic tribes and clans, and the establishment in those areas of the first Turkic tribal confederacies, which formed the basis of the old Turkic substratum of the population, the first ethnic components of the region's future Turkic peoples (Baskakov, 1990).

The administration, military forces and missionaries of the Umayyad caliphate propagated Islam by every possible means and occupied Bukhārā, Samarkand, Marw, Balkh, Herāt as well as other towns both large and small (*The History of Bukhārā*, 1954). The Arab invasion resulted in the gradual erosion of many aspects of pre-Islamic culture.

The deprivation of political and religious freedom were responsible for a series of formidable mass rebellions against the Umayyads and gave rise to the cultural and intellectual movements of the seventh to tenth centuries. Of these, the movement and rebellions of the 'wearers of white garments', the followers of al-Muqanna', were particularly noteworthy, as was the protracted movement of cultural resistance offered by intellectuals known as the *shu'ūbiyya* (from the word for 'people').

The 'Abbāsids who seized power were therefore forced to alter their policy of government with regard to the eastern lands of the caliphate and began to draw the Persian, Tājīk and Turkic military and aristocratic elites into partnership in the government of the caliphate in general and the governorate of Khurāsān in particular. The future 'Abbāsid caliph al-Ma'mūn (813–833) was educated there (at Marw) for a number of years in the spirit of a highly cultured Iranian environment (see Plates 214, 215). The Barmakids of Balkh, the *afshīns* of Ustrushāna, the Ṭāhirids, the Ṣaffārids and lastly the Sāmānids were brought on to the historical stage. Opportunities were thus gradually created for the emergence of the semi-independent states of the Ṭāhirids and the Ṣaffārids, and then for the fully independent Tājīk state of the Sāmānids (819–999), with its capital in the city of Bukhārā. This strongly centralized state united all the territories populated by Eastern Iranians (Tājīks), from Ghaznī and Herāt in the south and Balkh, Nīshāpūr, Marw, Bukhārā, Samarkand, Khujand, Bunjikat, Khulbuk and Termez in the centre, to Gurganj and Taraz in the north.

The economic, political, technical and cultural resources of the country were brought together. For 150 years, farmers, craftsmen, traders, scholars, poets, architects and builders, protected from the destructive incursions of the nomads of the steppes and other outsiders, were able to go about their work and creative tasks in peace.

The statesmen Aḥmad ibn Asad and Ismā'īl ibn Aḥmad, the founders of the Sāmānid dynasty, entered the stage of history together with their cultured viziers Bal'amī and Jaiḥōnī (see Plate 195).

The intellectual achievements of the ninth and tenth centuries greatly influenced the development of society, its economy and the organization of the state. The Sāmānid period was, on the whole, a time in which local statehood and local traditions were regenerated and the economy bloomed. It was during the ninth and tenth centuries that the statehood of the Tājīk people was established. At the same time, Tājīk science and literature began to emerge on to a broader stage and thus to make their contribution to the welfare of mankind. It was during this period that classical Persian (Fārsī Darī) took shape in Khurāsān and Mā warā' al-nahr: it was to become the *lingua*

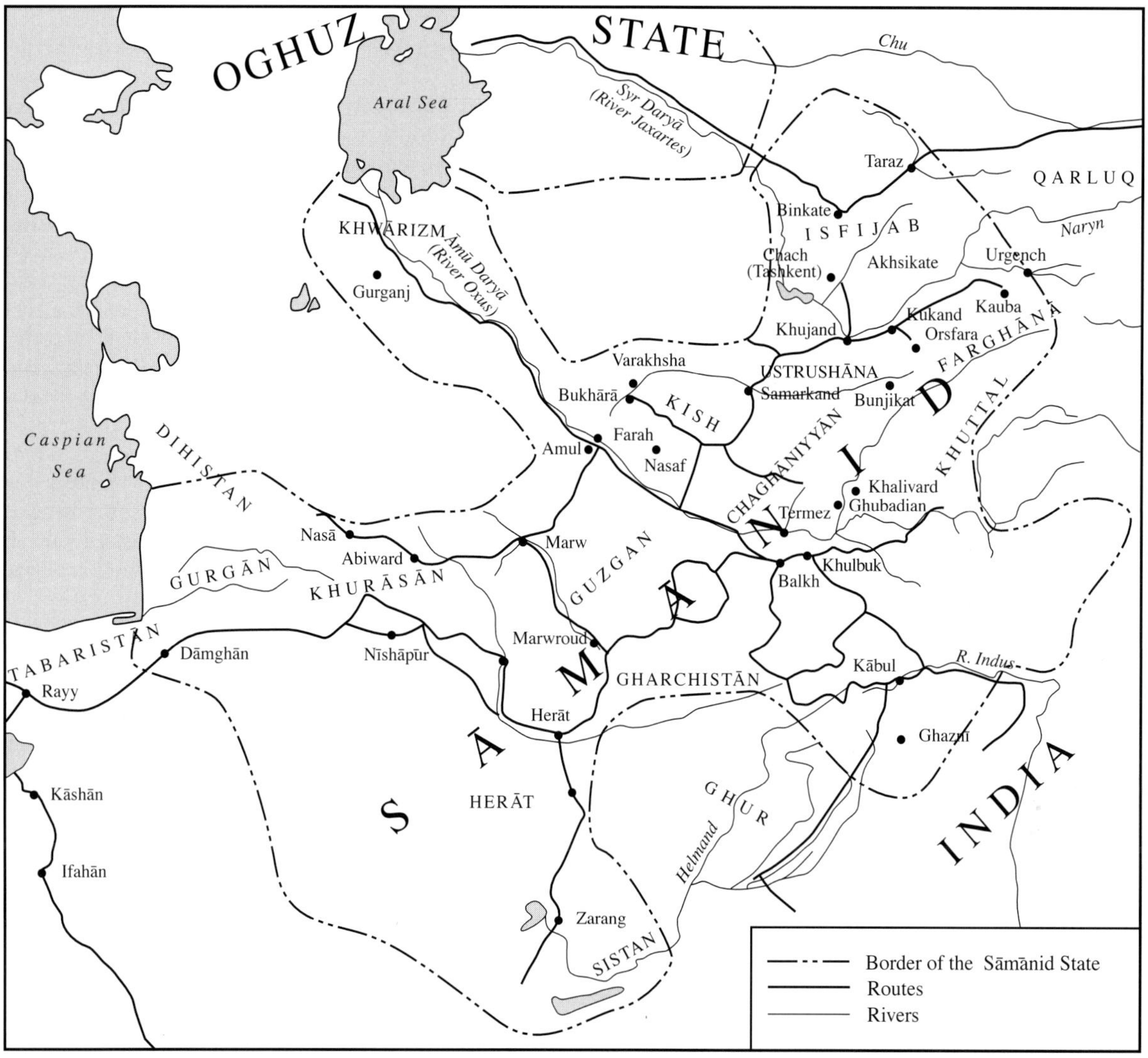

Map 18 The Sāmānid state between 874 and 999 (draft Negmatov, N.).

franca of a vast region of Asia and the medium for a poetry of universal renown. The well-known specialist in Iranian studies A. M. Oranskiiy (1960) has written that:

> When genuinely independent states with local dynasties were established in the ninth and tenth centuries in the eastern part of the Arab Caliphate, in Khurāsān, Sīstān and Mā warā' al-nahr, favourable conditions were created for the development of written literature in the Persian language, which had already become by that time the native tongue of the bulk of the population in those vast provinces.

In Bukhārā during the Sāmānid period, a galaxy of poets and writers created all the main genres of Tājīk–Persian poetry. Chief amongst them was Abū 'Abdallāh Ja'far Rūdakī, who was born in the Tājīk village of Piandjrūd, 100 km east of Samarkand. As a famous poet and musician, he was invited to the Sāmānid court in Bukhārā. Only a few thousand of Rūdakī's enormous legacy of some 1.3 million *bayts* (lines of verse) have been preserved. He established and brought to perfection the genres known as the *qaṣīda* (panegyric) and the *ghazal,* poems of deep reflection and wisdom. He was the author of several didactic poems, some verses of which have survived. Daqīqī laid the basis for the heroic epic, setting down 1,000 verses of the *Shāh-Nāmeh* (Book of Kings) before his tragic death. His efforts were continued by Firdawsī, 'whose creative work must, by its very nature, be ascribed to the Sāmānid circle' (*Istoriya persidskoy i tadzhikskoy literaturī*, 1970).

By virtue of its humanism, Firdawsī's *Shāh-Nāmeh* ranks among the masterpieces of world literature. Chief among the sources on which the poet drew in composing his work were the prose *Shāh-Nāmeh* of Abū Manṣūr and a book by Āzād Sarw Marvī. Firdawsī made extensive use of folk tales, ancient oral traditions and historical narratives. The philosophical and scientific ideas of the age were reflected in the *Shāh-Nāmeh,* together with ethical standards and folk wisdom. The *leitmotiv* of the work is the struggle of good against evil, the condemnation of fratricidal wars and the eulogizing of peace. The *Shāh-Nāmeh* contains the epic history of the Iranian emperors.

Epic poems were composed on themes drawn from the story of Alexander. 'Unṣurī wrote three epics which have not been preserved. These traditions were continued by Fakhr al-Dīn Gorgānī in the poem *Vīs ō-Rāmīn*, the plot of which is reminiscent of 'Tristan and Isolde'.

It was Avicenna who established the philosophical quatrain (*Rubā'ī*), brought to perfection by 'Omar Khayyām, who was also a native of Khurāsān.

The natural environment of the lower reaches of the Āmū Daryā and the Aral Sea region obliged the population to wage a constant, fierce struggle for existence, primarily involving the construction and maintenance of the infrastructure for irrigated agriculture and the supply of water to the towns. According to Herodotus, the Oxus (Āmū Daryā) was divided into 360 channels and flowed in forty branches into the Aral Sea. Irrigation systems were constantly being built and rebuilt in the region. The main canals were 60–70 km or more in length and 20–40 m wide. The canals were dug with different gradients on the upper and lower reaches in order to ensure that the water flowed at the speed required for the purposes of gravity-fed irrigation. There was also a technically complex and labour-intensive form of *kārēz* (underground) irrigation, consisting of infiltration galleries with vertical access shafts for construction and maintenance purposes. An extensive network of irrigation systems existed in the Zarafshān valley such as that in the Bukhārā oasis. Dams with sluices were built on the main channel of the Zarafshān in order to divert the water into channels. Water conservancy works were also undertaken in other areas of Transoxania (Gulyamov, 1957). The farmers who carried them out observed and drew inferences from their knowledge of seasonal and calendar cycles, reckoning by the Sun and stars; they made land surveys and agricultural observations, and studied the regular behaviour of the Āmū Daryā and Syr Daryā and the channels of their delta. In short, they amassed a body of knowledge about the land, water and environment which was vital for agriculture.

Mining and metallurgy underwent development. From written sources and archaeological material, a long list has been compiled of the mineral resources which were mined in Central Asia. In Badakhshān, Karrān, Rūshan and Shugnān there were garnets, rubies, silver, gold, lazurite, spinels, lapis lazuli, rock crystal and asbestos. Silver and gold were mined in Khuttāl and rock salt in the mountains of Makhastān. Gold, silver, hydrous sulphates, iron, copper, sal ammoniac and salt were to be found in Ustrushāna, while in Farghāna there were gold and silver mines and resources of mineral pitch, asbestos, iron, copper, lead, mercury, sal ammoniac, coal, tin, petroleum and other minerals. Īlak had silver and lead mines second in size only to the Panjshīr mines of the Hindu Kush in the tenth century; kaolin fire clay, crucible clay, millstone, alum, amethyst, serpentine and turquoise were also extracted.

Archaeologists and geologists have discovered the remains of entire ore-processing areas associated with mining in the valleys of the Bāzārdār and western Pshart in the Pāmīrs (tenth to twelfth centuries) and the remains of the largest medieval silver and lead mine at Koni Manṣūr in the Karāmazār hills near Khujand, where the remains of a miners' village dating from the ninth and tenth centuries have been found. More than ten large mines were worked in the region of Koni Manṣūr during the Middle Ages. The most important mines in the Īlak mountains after Koni Manṣūr were the deposits at Altyntepkan.

Archaeological and geological research has demonstrated that significant progress was made in the methods used to locate and mine deposits. The ore was extracted by sinking vertical and inclined shafts and excavating galleries and chambers, and also by open-cast mining. The pits reached depths in excess of 150 m. Fire setting was a method widely used in mining operations (the rock being heated by fire and cracked by means of cold water), but mining tools were then brought into play: iron and wooden wedges, stone or iron hammers, sledge hammers, picks and pickaxes, mattocks, spades, and so on. Shafts and galleries were reinforced with wooden props, posts and joists, stulls and pillars made of the actual rock. A 'high-tech' method was developed for flexible timbering. The mines were lit by lamps, ventilation was provided and water was drained off through underground channels. Ore was brought to the surface using wooden windlasses or along stepped passageways.

Great strides were made in the area of metallurgy in the tenth century. According to al-Bīrūnī, the smiths and metal-workers of Transoxania and Khwārizm produced four types of ferrous metal: wrought iron, mild steel, cast iron and crucible steel. One of the steel-making centres (for damask steel) was Herāt, where 'Indian' swords were also made from steel billets. Another important centre of the metallurgical industry was the town of Marsmand in the iron-ore district of Mink in Ustrushāna. It appears from the available evidence that the metallurgical and metal-processing techniques of the day were quite highly developed and scientific. The methods and technology of the metallurgical process had been comprehensively worked out. More specifically, progress was made in the production of lead and silver, and the process comprised fairly distinct stages (recovery, refinement and cupellation). There is evidence to show that the findings of alchemical research were put to use in metallurgy.

The development of irrigation and agriculture, especially in the ninth–tenth centuries, mining and metallurgy provided craft industries with a much greater variety of raw materials, and the growth of handicrafts was also assisted by the intensive development of the towns, where most craft goods were produced and consumed. Samarkand played an important role in the production of high-quality paper and transferred the technology of paper production from China to the Islamic World.

The most highly developed and socially important of the crafts was the weaving of many sorts of fabric, clothing and other articles from wool and cotton. Other branches included the manufacture of various metal utensils, tools and weapons, glazed and unglazed pottery – kitchenware, crockery, hollow-ware and everyday objects – glassware for cosmetic and pharmaceutical purposes, vases and other receptacles, window glass, and leather goods and clothing, not forgetting the sumptuous decorative and applied art of the jewellers working in metal, stone and manufactured materials (paste, glass, and so on). Woodwork and carving in metal, wood and *ganch* (stucco) were also of the highest order, as was the art of painters and sculptors. There were professional associations and guilds, schools and workshops established by architects, jewellers and artists who had attained the height of perfection in their craft. The historic towns of Samarkand, Marw, Bunjikat, Khulbuk, Termez, Penjikent, Varakhsha and many other medieval sites excavated by archaeologists and greeted with admiration by twentieth-century civilization were their creations (see Plate 214).

Many branches of knowledge experienced rapid development, including mathematics, astronomy, medicine, chemistry, botany, geography, geology, mineralogy, history, philosophy and literary studies (Dzhalilov, 1973).

Central Asia was, above all, one of the principal centres for the development of the exact sciences. A succession of brilliant scholars rose to prominence there whose works did much to assist the subsequent progress of medieval mathematics and astronomy both in the East and in Europe. One of their number was the outstanding Khwārizmian encyclopedist, mathematician, astronomer and geographer Abū Ja'far Muḥammad ibn Mūsā al-Khwārizmī (*c.* 780–*c.*

850), also known as al-Mājūsī, the founder of the mathematical school in the countries of the Arab caliphate. Al-Khwārizmī carried out most of his scholarly work in the Baghdād academy known as the *bayt al-ḥikma* or 'House of Wisdom'. In his treatise *Kitāb al-jam' wa' l-tafrīq bi ḥisāb al-Hind* ('The book of addition and subtraction according to the computation of India'), he introduced the Arabs, and Europe, to the Indian system of numerals for the first time (Sarton, 1949). In another treatise, *Kitāb al-mukhtaṣar fi ḥisāb al-jabr wa' l-muqābala* ('The Book summarizing computation through compulsion and substitution') al-Khwārizmī brought the term 'algebra' (*al-jabr*) into circulation. These two works on arithmetic and algebra brought al-Khwārizmī world renown. Another work of great importance was his *zīj* or astronomical almanac, consisting of astronomical tables accompanied by an account of theoretical astronomy: it was long used as the basis for later works in that field in the recension of the Andalusian astronomer Maslama al-Majrīṭī (*c.* 1007). In his mathematical geography *Kitāb ṣūrat al-arḍ* (or *Rasm al-rubū' al-ma'mūr*) ('Book of the Depiction of the Earth', or 'Picture of the Inhabited Quarters'), compiled in the form of *zīj* tables, he indicated the geographical position of 537 towns in seven climates and 209 mountains; he described seas, islands and rivers and boldly redefined the climates, compiling original maps. This work represented the beginning of a new age in geography and was put to further use in the eleventh-century Toledo Tables. In the twelfth century, it was translated into Latin, and the latinized form of his name, 'Algorismus', came to be applied to any system of counting (algorism) and any regular computational procedure (algorithm).

Other famous scholars included Aḥmad Abū' l-'Abbās al-Sarakhsī (d. 860–861), the author of works on algebra, arithmetic, music and logic; Aḥmad ibn 'Abd Allāh al-Marwazī (al-Ḥabash al-Ḥāsib), an authority on tangents, cotangents and tables thereof (d. *c.* 870); Abu Ma'shar Ja'far ibn Muḥammad al-Balkhī (d. 886), the author of forty works on astronomy; Abū l-'Abbās Aḥmad al-Farghānī (ninth century), who was known in Europe until the eighteenth century for his treatise *Kitāb fī-ḥarakat al-samāwiyya wa jawāmi' 'ilm al-nujūm* ('Book on the Movement of the Heavens and a Compendium of the Science of the Stars'), which was translated in the twelfth and thirteenth centuries into Latin and other European languages; the astronomer Abū Ḥāmid al-Asṭurlabī Saghanī (d. 989–990); the mathematician and astronomer Aḥmad Sājizī; Abū Naṣr ibn 'Irak from Khwārizm, the teacher of al-Bīrūnī; Abū Maḥmud al-Khujandī, the astronomer and builder of astronomical instruments; and Abū l-Wafā' al-Buzjānī (940–998), the trigonometrician.

Many Tājīk scholars made their mark on the history of geography: Ḥāfiẓ ibn Manṣur al-Marwazī (author of 'The Book on the Khurāsān Tax'); the man of letters and geographer Aḥmad al-Sarakhsī (d. 899); Abū' l-'Abbās Ja'far al-Marwazī; the famous geographer Ibn Khurradādhbih, the author of *Kitāb al-masālik wa' l-mamālik* ('Book of the Thoroughfares and the Kingdoms'); the founder of the classical school of Arabic-speaking geographers, Abū Zayd Aḥmad al-Balkhī (*c.* 850–934), the author of sixty works including *Ṣuwar al-Aqkālīm*; the geographer, traveller and poet Abu' l-Muayyad al-Balkhī (tenth century), the author of the *'Ajā'ib al-buldān*; Abū 'Abd Allāh Muḥammad al-Jayhanī, the cultured vizier of the emir Naṣr II Sāmānī; and the anonymous Tājīk geographer who was the author of the classical work *Ḥudūd al-'Ālam min al-Mashriq ila l-Maghrib*.

Medicine and medical practice made considerable progress during the Sāmānid period. The founder of the Sāmānid school of physicians was Abū Bakr Muḥammad ibn Zakariyyā al-Rāzī (865–925), who was known in Europe as Rhazes. Al-Rāzī wrote the first treatise in medical history on the subject of smallpox and measles, *Kitāb al-Jadari wa l-hasba.* He also wrote the large medical digest, *Kitāb al-Manṣūrī* ('The Book dedicated to Prince Manṣūr'), and the 'Comprehensive Book', *Kitāb al-Ḥāwī*. He systematized and enriched medical knowledge with his clinical experience, drawing on the works of the medical scholars of antiquity, in particular Hippocrates and Galen, and he 'made investigations on specific gravity by means of the hydrostatic balance. He also made an attempt to classify chemical substances' (Sarton, 1949).

Tenth-century medical scholars and practitioners also included Abū Bakr Ahawaynī al-Bukhārī or 'he of Bukhārā', author of *Kitāb-i Nabz* or 'Book on the Pulse' and *Kitāb-i Tashrīḥ* or 'Book on Anatomy'; Ḥakīm Maysarī, auhtor of *Dānish-Nāmeh* or 'Book of Wisdom'; the physician and pharmacologist Abū Manṣūr Munāfik al-Harawī or 'he of Herāt', author of a description of 585 medicines and remedies in Persian; Abū Manṣūr al-Bukhārī (d. 991), the author of a whole series of books on medicine, again in Persian; Abū Sahl Masīḥī (d. 1000), author of a book on medicinal herbs, the *Ṣad Bāb* or 'Hundred Chapters', and who was both one of the teachers of Abū 'Alī ibn Sīnā and a friend of al-Bīrūnī; the medical commentator Abū Sahl ibn 'Abd Allāh Nātilī; and the chemist Abu' l-Ḥākim Muḥammad ibn 'Abd al-Malik al-Khwārīzmī.

Successes in the area of medical science and practice prepared the way for the appearance of the most outstanding medical thinker of the Middle Ages, Abū 'Alī ibn Sīnā (Avicenna).

The development of medicine proceeded in close conjunction with that of chemistry. Chemists conducted many experiments, discovered new preparations, refined their methods for processing substances, and improved chemical apparatus. They left systematic descriptions of their research methods: dissolving, filtration, melting, distillation, calcination, amalgamation and so on.

Works of history and philology were also produced in the period from the seventh to the tenth centuries. They included the ten-volume compendium, 'The Sources of Knowledge', the sourcebooks *Kitāb al-ma'ārif* ('Book of Lore') and *Kitāb al-shi'r wa'l-shu'arā'* ('Book of Poetry and the Poets') and also the manual of secretarial skills, *Adab al-kātib* ('Good Manners for the Scribe'), by Ibn Qutayba (ninth century). Scholars in Central Asia also wrote a 'History of Baghdād' (Aḥmad ibn Abī Ṭāriḥ Tayfūr), a 'History of the Ṣaffārids' (Abū 'Abd Allāh Muḥammad al-Akhbārī), a 'History of Bukhārā' (Abū 'Abd Allāh Muḥammad al-Bukhārī) and *al-Tārīkh fī akhbār wulāt Khurāsān* ('History concerning the chronicles of the governorates of Khurāsām'), Abū 'Alī Ḥusayn ibn Aḥmad al-Salamī al-Bayhaqī). Lastly, the *Tārikh-i Bukhārā* or 'History of Bukhārā' was written by the illustrious Tājīk historian Abū Bakr Muḥammad ibn Ja'far Narshakhī (d. 959).

Especially noteworthy is the work of the outstanding Tājīk historian Abū 'Alī Muḥammad al-Bal'amī (d. 974), the Sāmānid vizier, who made an abridged translation from Arabic into Persian (*Fārsī-i Darī or Tājīk*) of the universal history of prophets and kings, *Tārīkh al-rusul wa' l-mulūk*, by Abū Ja'far Muḥammad ibn Jarīr al-Ṭabarī, with a number of additions drawn from the life of the Iranian peoples. Bal'amī's work enjoyed great popularity and was translated into Turkish and French and even back into Arabic.

Central Asian scholars collected an enormous amount of factual material about nature and society and carried out a great deal of research in a number of branches of science, thus preparing the ground for attempts to draw general conclusions therefrom. While such inferences had already been made by the two above-mentioned scholars and encyclopedists Muḥammad al-Khwārizmī and Zakariyyā al-Rāzī, the former in the fields of mathematics and astronomy and the latter in medicine and chemistry, it fell to the three remarkable encyclopedists Abū Naṣr al-Fārābī (873–950), Abū ʿAlī ibn Sīnā (980–1037) and Abū Rayḥān al-Bīrūnī (973–1048) to draw conclusions of a universal nature. All three were born in Central Asia, on the banks of one or other of its three great rivers, the Syr Daryā, the Zarafshān and the Āmū Daryā, in regions occupied by the east Iranians/Tājīks.

Abū Naṣr al-Fārābī: *Al-Muʿallim al-Thānī* ('The Second Teacher'); *Risāla fī Mabādiʾ Ārāʾ Ahl al-Madīnat al-Fāḍila,* the 'Model City', a treatise on good governance, 'The Origins of the Sciences'; 'What should be known before commencing the study of philosophy'; *Fuṣūṣ al-ḥikam* ('The Bezels of Wisdom'); commentaries on the problems of the introductions to the first and fifth books of Euclid; commentaries on the *Almagest* by Ptolemy; and a 'Treatise on what is right and wrong in the verdict of the stars'. His other works included the compendious *Kitāb al-mūsīqā al-kabīr* ('Great Book of Music').

Al-Fārābī, who possessed a universal mind combined with exceptional abilities, became one of the greatest thinkers of the early Middle Ages and a founder of rationalism in the East. His authority was particularly great in the fields of philosophy, logic, ethics and music. He was referred to as the 'second teacher', that is, after Aristotle.

Abū ʿAlī ibn Sīnā's works include: *Al-Qānūn fi' l-ṭibb* ('Canon of Medicine'); *Kitāb al-Shifa'* ('Book of Healing'); the *Dānish-Nāmeh* ('Book of Knowledge'); the *Kitāb al-ishārāt wa' l-tanbīhāt* ('Book of Signs and Admonitions'); the *Kitāb al-hidāyat* ('Book of Guidance'); *Rasāʾil fī asrār al-ḥikma al-mashriqiyya* ('Treatises on the secrets of Eastern wisdom'); *Risālat fi' l-nafs* ('Treatise on the soul') and many other works. At present, over forty of his works on medicine are known, about 185 on philosophy, logic and theology, thirty on astronomy and the natural sciences, three on music and also his literary work *Risālat al-Ṭayr* ('The Epistle of the Bird') and some excellent, socially acute verse in his native Tājīk language.

Ibn Sīnā was the outstanding scientist of the Middle Ages and an independent and original thinker. His works dealt with medicine, philosophy, logic, psychology, ethics, mathematics, cosmography, chemistry, botany, linguistics, music and other fields. He endeavoured to stimulate interest in the study of nature and attached great importance to experience and practice, the method of objective observation. His achievements were particularly remarkable in the areas of medicine, philosophy, logic and psychology. His greatest work was the *Qānūn fi'l-ṭibb,* a medical encyclopedia in five parts, a master work studied for many centuries by doctors in both the Islamic East and the Christian West and applied by them in their practice. It was translated into various languages, starting in the twelfth century, and was published in some thirty editions in Latin alone. It contains the general theory of medicine, anatomy, physiology, surgery, diagnostics, therapeutics, medicines, prophylactic measures and chronic diseases (see Plate 133a–e).

> Ibn Sīnā established the infectious nature of tuberculosis and the transmission of diseases by water and soil. His *Canon* contains many examples of good observation – distinction of mediastinitis from pleurisy; contagious nature of phthisis; distribution of diseases by water and soil; careful description of skin troubles; of sexual diseases and perversions; of nervous ailments. The Materia Medica [*Qānūn*] considers about 760 drugs.
>
> (Sarton, 1950)

Abū' l-Rayḥān al-Bīrūnī's works include 'Cartography', 'Astrology', 'Chronology' (Record of Past Generations), 'Spherics', 'Specific Weights', 'Geodesy', Chords', 'Shadows', 'Transits', '*Rāshikī*', 'The Science of the Stars', 'India', 'The Canon of Masʿūd on Astronomy and the Stars', 'Mineralogy' and 'Pharmacology'. These are the abridged titles of his most important works. Out of a total of 150 works, only twenty-six have survived to the present day, including some consisting of several volumes. His entire life was an epic during which he demonstrated genuine courage and produced an enormous corpus of scholarship.

'His critical spirit, toleration, love of truth [and] intellectual courage were almost without parallel in medieval times.' His achievements included an 'accurate determination of latitudes . . . Determination of longitudes . . . Al-Bīrūnī discussed the question whether the earth rotates around its axis or not, without reaching a definite conclusion . . . Investigations of specific gravity . . . Remarkably accurate determination of the specific density of 18 precious stones and metals . . . [He concluded that] the Indus Valley must be considered as an ancient sea basin filled up with alluvions' (Sarton, 1949).

The spread of Aristotelianism in the Islamic East is linked to the names of al-Fārābī and Ibn Sīnā. Following Aristotle, Ibn Sīnā advocated the idea of the co-eternal nature of the material world and its divine creator, and of the role of the senses in perception. In his works on medicine and natural science, he adhered to the principle of causality. The position of al-Fārābī and Ibn Sīnā conflicted with *kalām*, the official philosophy of Islam. The advocates of *kalām* (al-Ghazālī and Fakhr al-Dīn al-Rāzī) defended the idea of the creation of the world and asserted its dependence upon the will of God.

In the eleventh century considerable influence was acquired by Ismāʿīlism, to which was linked the philosophy of the Tājīk poet and thinker, Nāṣir-i Khusraw. The Ismāʿīlīs believed in the harmonic structure of the universe (or 'Macrocosm'), which they likened to that of the human body (or 'Microcosm'). Ṣūfism, a heterogeneous current of philosophy whose extreme doctrines combined a mystic pantheism with elements of humanism, became widespread between the tenth and thirteenth centuries. The principal exponent of Ṣūfī philosophy was the poet and thinker Jalāl al-Dīn Rūmī (a Balkhī), who was born in Balkh (Khurāsān) but lived and died in Konya, Turkey (or *Rūm*). According to Rūmī, the world is permeated by the struggle of opposites, striving to achieve harmony, and the material world is apprehended through opposites. In his *Masnavī* (or *Mathnawī*, 'rhymed couplets') and his collected odes or *Dīwān*, he propagated the idea of humanism.

In Central Asia, especially in Bukhārā, Islamic theology in the period under consideration witnessed a remarkable development of Qur'ānic exegesis and collections of the Traditions (*ḥadīth)* of the Prophet Muḥammad. The best-known of these collections was that of the Imām Muḥammad ibn Ismāʿīl al-Bukhārī (810–870), whose authority has been widely acknowledged, particularly among Iranian and Turkish Muslims.

Local pre-Islamic traditions were preserved in the fine arts. Thus, architecture developed on the basis of earlier traditions, continuing to employ customary techniques in relation to planning, construction and decoration. The traditional forms provided the basis even in the new forms of Islamic architecture. For example, the first types of Islamic mausoleum were influenced by the architecture of the early medieval house and pre-Islamic funerary buildings or temples. The basic stylistic canons and themes of traditional architectural decoration were maintained during the Islamic period (see Plate 195).

Testimony to the unified nature of the art of the Sāmānid period is provided by the many architectural monuments, paintings, carvings on wood, *ganch* (stucco) and clay, embossed and chased metal, jewellery, terracotta, fine pottery and glassware from Samarkand, Penjikent, Khulbuk, Sayod, Ajinatepe, Balaliktepe and Varakhsh and the wealth of wood carvings from the Zarafshān and Isfarīn valley.

These works reflect in astonishingly detailed and graphic fashion the enormous richness of the region's spiritual culture, ranging from epic and mythological heroes, including the heroes Jamshīd, Siyāwush and Rustam, to the divine and demonic pantheons of Ahura–Mazda, Mithra, Nanaya, Veshparkar, Afrāsiyāb, Zahhāk and others.

Secular themes played a very important part in the arts and were incorporated into a grand epic describing the struggle of the forces of Good and Light against the forces of Evil and Darkness. This was reflected in the panoramic mural paintings of episodes from Rustam's struggles against various demons and forces of darkness on the monuments of Penjikent in northern Tajikistan and in the compositions, many metres in length, in the Smaller Room of the Afshīn's Palace, on the carved wooden panel with episodes from the struggle between the forces of Farīdūn and the blacksmith Kāvah, and those of the murderous King Zahhāk and his troops, which is a masterpiece of world art. Another such masterpiece is the 'Capitoline she-wolf feeding the two infants Romulus and Remus', which is in the same palace in Bunjikat, the capital of Ustrushāna. Other monuments in Penjikent, Bunjikat and the other towns mentioned above exhibit an endless variety of themes which are also depicted with varying degrees of realism or stylization on absolutely all works of the applied arts – domestic utensils, ornaments, fabrics, clothing, liturgical objects and so on (see Plate 214).

At the end of the tenth century, a Turkic state was formed in the Semirech'e under a *khān* of the nomadic Yagma tribe, known to history as the Qarākhānids. In 999, the horde of the Qarākhānid Naṣr took Bukhārā, and the Sāmānid state fell under their assault. The Qarākhānid state stretched from Kashgar to the Āmū Daryā, and Mā warā' al-nahr remained under the control of the Qarākhānids for almost two centuries. Qarākhānid power collapsed in 1212 when the whole region of Mā warā' al-nahr was incorporated into the state of the Khwārizm-shāhs.

At the same time as the Qarākhanīd state was formed, an independent Ghaznavid state took shape in central and northern Afghanistan. Exploiting the fall of the Sāmānids, the Ghaznāvids brought Khurāsān, Khwārizm, Chaghāniyyān, Khuttal, Rayy and the Punjab under their control and thus made their state one of the most powerful in the Middle East.

Towards the middle of the eleventh century, a new Turkic state, that of the Seljuks (from the name of one branch of the Yabgu tribe), came into being in Khurāsān with its capital at the town of Marw. The Seljuks rapidly conquered Iran, Iraq, Azerbaijan, Kurdistan, Kuhistan, Armenia and Asia Minor.

The Seljuks being themselves nomads were obliged to employ Tājīks, Persians and settled Turks from the local aristocracy to run their state. In the second half of the eleventh century, a major political figure and statesman came to the fore: a Tājīk from Khurāsān, Abū 'Alī Ḥasan ibn Isḥāq, known by the title of Niẓām al-Mulk ('Order of the Kingdom'). This intelligent and educated man was vizier from 1063 to 1092. Drawing on the practices of the Sāmānids, Niẓām al-Mulk introduced order into the administration, endeavoured to restore Sāmānid cultural traditions and implemented a series of reforms curbing the arbitrary rule of military governors and feudal lords. Concerned to consolidate Seljuk power and to increase the revenues of the state, Niẓām al-Mulk also contributed to the development of culture and education and wrote a political treatise, the *Siyāsat-Nāmeh* or 'Book on Government', which set out the problems involved in the administration of the state.

In the course of the twelfth and thirteenth centuries, all or parts of Transoxania came under a number of other political formations: the Qarā-Khitāy from 1137 to 1216, the Khwārizm-shāhs, who held Khwārizm itself from the tenth to the beginning of the thirteenth century, and from the end of the twelfth century to 1220 also held the entire area from the north Caspian to the Persian Gulf and the Hindu Kush.

The general calamity to befall the people of the region struck in 1219–1220 with the arrival of the invading forces of Chinggis Khān. Their first blows were struck against Otrār, Khujand, Urgench, Bukhārā and Samarkand, which were subjected to merciless terror and the destruction of their means of livelihood and their culture. Under the Mongols, during the thirteenth and the first half of the fourteenth century, the Chaghatāy *ulus* (apanage) of the Mongol Empire became established in Transoxania. The collapse of urban life, culture, trade and agriculture of the first stage was only overcome towards the end of the thirteenth century. This was caused and assisted by the revival of the Great Silk Road and trade with China, and the monetary reforms undertaken at the beginning of the fourteenth century, which improved the situation in internal trade and handicrafts.

The penetration and settlement of nomadic Turks in Central Asia was continued by nomadic Mongols (Barlas, Ilairs and others) and caused a significant change in the ethnic, linguistic and cultural composition of the region.

The written tradition of Turkish literature in Central Asia began to crystallize during the eleventh, twelfth and subsequent centuries: among its sources were Maḥmūd Kāshgharī, Yūsuf Bālāsāghūnī, Ḥāfiẓ Khwārizmi, Turdī, 'Alī Shīr Nawā'ī, Zahīr al-Dīn Bābur, and Mashrab. This tradition provided the basis for the literatures of the Uzbeks, Kazakhs, Kirghiz, Uighurs, Turkmen and the Karakalpaks.

During the fourteenth and fifteenth centuries, Central Asia came under the rule of Tīmūr and the Tīmūrids. Tīmūr (1336–1405) entered the political arena in Mā warā' l-nahr and Khurāsān amid the fragmentation and feudal strife which prevailed in the 1350s and 1360s.

Under Tīmūr and the Tīmūrids, social relations reached their most developed state in Transoxania and Khurāsān. Considerable effort was invested in the expansion of agriculture and the extension of both the area of arable land and the irrigation network. Trades and crafts developed considerably, and trading relations with foreign countries were expanded. Urban development, architecture and building techniques made great progress and the applied arts thrived, including pottery, ceramics for facing buildings, embossed and chased metal-working, jewellery, weaving and embroidery. Drawing on the creativity of the local artistic culture as well as the creativity of the scholars, architects and artists, skilled artisans, calligraphers, poets, musicians and others brought in under duress from conquered countries, especially Iran, a syncretic style of architecture, architectural decoration and applied arts came into being in Transoxania, particularly in Samarkand and Shahr-i Sabz.

The art of the manuscript book, calligraphy and the miniature particularly flourished. Schools of remarkable calligraphers were formed in a number of cultural centres but especially in Herāt. These schools developed the style of writing known as *nasṭa'līq*, one of the major achievements of the art of calligraphy in the East. One outstanding work of this period was the recension of the text of Firdawsī's poem, the *Shāh-Nāmeh*, which remains a standard for excellence even today. Among the calligraphers of renown, mention may be made of 'Askar Herātī, Sulṭān 'Alī and Sulṭān Muḥammad Khandal. Among the miniaturists who achieved great fame, Khwājeh Muḥammad Naqqāsh and Mīrak Ustād were particularly prominent. The latter was the teacher of the very well-known Eastern artist Kamāl al-Dīn Bihzād, whose miniatures adorn many manuscript books in the world's major libraries and who left miniature portraits of his contemporaries, including an outstanding portrait of 'Alī Shīr Nawā'ī (see Plates 3, 26, 27, 112, 113, 186, 211, 218).

The fourteenth and fifteenth centuries witnessed a remarkable flowering of Tājīk–Persian and Turkish literature. We need only recall the names of Kamāl Khujandī, 'Ubayd-i Zakānī, Nāṣir-i Bukhārī, Salmān-ī Sāvaji, Badr Chāchī, Wāṣif, and Hilālī. In the sixteenth century, Samarkand and Herāt became the centres of Tājīk–Persian and Turkish literature. The most important poets of the age, 'Abd al-Raḥmān Jāmī (in Persian) and 'Alī Shīr Nawā'ī (in Turkish), lived and worked in those two cities (see Plate 113). Jāmī's literary heritage consists of three *dīwāns*, the Scroll stories of the 'Spring Garden' or *Bahāristān,* and seven major poems, grouped together as the *Haft Awrang* 'The Seven Thrones'). Among these latter poems, *Yūsuf and Zulaykhā, Laylā and Majnūn and 'The Wisdom of Alexander (or Iskandar),* are particularly worthy of note.

'Alī Shīr Nawā'ī produced four *dīwāns* and five major poems, collectively known as *The Khamsa* ('The Quintet'). His poems *Farhād and Shīrīn* and *Laylā and Majnūn* are especially popular. Under the pseudonym of Fānī, Nawā'ī also left a *dīwān* of verse in Persian.

During the emirate of Ulugh Beg, the social and educational functions of the *madrasa* were expanded and training was provided for officials, scholars and persons engaged in cultural activities as well as for members of the clergy. In the Ulugh Beg *madrasa* in Samarkand, lectures were delivered on astronomy and other natural sciences as well as on theological subjects (see Plate 136).

Mathematics and astronomy made particularly great strides in the course of the fifteenth century. Their progress was assisted by the construction of the Samarkand observatory, ordered by Ulugh Beg, and the establishment within the observatory of a whole school of science. Among the great scholars who worked there were Qāḍī-Zādeh Rūmī (1360–1428), Jamshid Kāshāni (Kāshī) (d. *c.* 1430) and 'Ala' al-Dīn 'Alī Kuishchī (d. 1474). The Fakhrī sextant, which was set up at the observatory and had a radius of roughly 40 m, was the invention of an earlier astronomer and instrument-builder, Abū Maḥmud al-Khujandī (tenth century). The accuracy of the observations made by the Samarkand observatory may be gauged, for example, from the fact that its latitude and the angle between the planes of the celestial equator and the ecliptic were determined to within a degree of error not exceeding several dozen seconds of arc. Such accuracy was exceptional for the time, considering that all observations were made with the naked eye. The most important work carried out in the observatory – the new astronomical tables – contain the theoretical bases of astronomy and a new catalogue of the positions of 1,018 stars, established for the first time since Hipparchus and with a level of accuracy unsurpassed until the observations of Tycho Brahe.

Many histories were compiled in the course of the fourteenth and fifteenth centuries. Of particular significance among these works were *Majma' al-Tawārīkh* by 'Abd Allāh ibn Luṭf Allāh, otherwise known as Ḥāfiẓ-i Ābrū, the *Ẓafar-Nāmeh* by Niẓām al-Dīn Shāmī, *Ẓafar-Nāmeh* by Sharaf al-Dīn Yazdī, and the multi-volume universal chronicle by Mīrkhwānd, *Rawẓat al-Ṣafā*. These works constitute primary sources for the history of Tīmūr and his age (see Plate 186).

In the fourteenth century in Central Asia, the famous Ṣūfī order of the Naqshbandī was established. The founder of this order was one Bahā' al-Dīn Muḥammad, usually known as Bahā' al-Dīn *Naqshband* ('The painter'). The Naqshbandī saints did not call on their followers to withdraw from the world like hermits but rather to 'dwell in the world' and ply 'honest labour' therein. Among the followers of the Naqshbandiyya Way, the 'masters' of the order, or *Khwājagān*, including such luminaries as *Khwājeh* ('master') Aḥrār, played an important role as spiritual leaders during the reign of Tīmūr and his successors.

The most spectacular urban development works under Tīmūr and his successors were carried out in the twin capitals, Samarkand and Herāt, and also in Tīmūr's birthplace, Shahr-i Sabz, and in the other major towns such as Bukhārā, Khujand and Termez. A major exercise in replanning was undertaken in Samarkand with the alignment of streets and quarters of the city: a new town centre, the *Rēgistān*, was created, with adjoining architectural complexes and the booths of craftsmen and traders. The magnificent buildings erected included Tīmūr's mosque, the Khānum *madrasa*, the Bībī Khānum mosque, the Shīr Dor *madrasa* and the *madrasa* of Ulugh Beg on the Rēgistān, along with the memorial complexes of the Shāh-i Zindeh and the Gūr-i Mīr. In Shahr-i Sabz stood the Āq-Sarāy ('White Palace'), the *Dār al-Ṭilāwat* ('House of the Goldsmiths') and the *Dār al-Siyādat* ('House of Lordship'). In Bukhārā rose the Ulugh Beg *madrasa* and a number of other buildings. In Khujand, a start was made on the creation of another city centre, the *Panjshambeh* 'Thursday market', with the *Saykh Muṣliḥ al-Dīn*, a complex of monumental religious buildings; in Herāt, a whole series of mosques and *madrasas* were built (see Plates 26, 27).

Gardens and parklands were laid out around Samarkand with palaces, pavilions, formal flowerbeds, irrigation systems and elaborate enclosures, including the *Bāgh-i Naqsh-i Jahân* ('The World-Depicting Garden'), *Bāgh-i Bihisht* ('Paradise Garden'), *Bāgh-i Dilgushā* ('Heart-Expanding Garden'), *Bāgh-i Shamāl* ('North Wind Garden'), *Bāgh-i Maydān* ('Polo-Field Garden'), *Bāgh-i Zāghān* ('Crows' Garden'), *Bāgh-i Chinār* ('Plane-Tree Garden'), and *Bāgh-i Naw* ('New Garden'), with a total of twelve according to written sources. New defensive walls with round towers, fortified gates and moats, were erected around the towns.

The art of the Tīmūrid age was characterized by the flowering of a radiant humanism. The search for innovation and breakthroughs is evident in the creative aspirations of this age's architects, painters, calligraphers and ceramicists, and it found expression in the immense and, at the same time, exquisite architectural complexes of Samarkand, Bukhārā, Herāt and Shahr-i Sabz, as well as in individual masterpieces like the mausoleums of Muḥammad Bashārā in Penjikent, of the *Gök-Gumbaz* ('Blue Dome') at Ura-Tyube, and of Khwājeh Aḥmad Yasavī in the town of Turkestan (Pugachenkova and Rempel, 1965).

Thus, Central Asia between the seventh and fifteenth centuries became one of the most culturally developed regions in the Islamic world. But Central Asian civilization also developed in close connecting with the cultures of virtually the entire old World, including those of Iran, China, the Indian subcontinent and the Arab lands. Central Asia was most intimately linked, however, with Iran.

Moreover the peoples of this general Central Asian / Iranian region often found themselves nearly all included within the boundaries of the same states, or identical polities. For their part, Tājīks and Persians were further united by a common language and literature. Full partners in this heritage, Central Asia's great poets in Persian, known the world over, include such names as Rūdakī, Nāṣir-i Khusraw, Firdawsī, 'Umar Khayyām, Sa'dī, Ḥāfiẓ, Kamāl Khujandī, Jalāl al-Dīn Balkhī (or Rūmī) and 'Abd al-Raḥmān Jāmī. To this list might even be added quite a few Persian-language poets from the Indian subcontinent, many of whom, like the outstanding master Amīr Khusraw of Delhi, boasted ancestors from Central Asia.

BIBLIOGRAPHY

Abuali ibn Sino (Abū 'Alī ibn Sīnā) i ego epokha (K 1000-lety so dnya rozhdeniya) (Abū 'Alī ibn Sīnā and his Age in Commemoration of the Millennium of His Birth). 1980. Dushanbe.

ASIMOV, M. S. 1985. *Al-Khwārizmī i opyt kul'turno-istoricheskogo sinteza.kn: Velikiy uchenyy srednevekoyya, Al-Khwārizmī. Materialy yubileynoy nauchnoy konferitsii, posvyashchonnoy 1200-letuiy so dnya rozhdeniya* (Al-Khwārizmī, and the Experience of a Cultural and Historical Synthesis: The Great Medieval Scholar al-Khwārizmī. Contents of the scientific conference marking his jubilee, in observance of the 1,200th anniversary of his birth'). Tashkent, pp. 13–15.

——. 1988. *Velichie Avitsenni: Torzhestvo Razuma. Materialy Mezhduradnogo seminara, posvyashchennogo 1000-letuiy so dnya rozhdeniya Abuali ibn Sino (Avitsenni)* (The Greatness of Avicenna: The Triumph of Reason. Contents of the international seminar, in observance of the millennium of the birth of Abū Alī ibn Sīnā (Avicenna)). *Donish*, Dushanbe (= *Dānish*, 'Knowledge'), pp. 3–18.

——. 1990. *Istoriko-kul'turnie aspekty etnogeneza narodov Sredney-Azii. Problemy etnogeneza i etnicheskoy istorii narodov Sredney Azii i Kazakhstana. Vyp. I. Obshshie voprosi* (Historical and Cultural Aspects of the Ethnogenesis of the Peoples of Central Asia). In: *Problems Concerning the Ethnogenesis and Ethnic History of the Peoples of Central Asia and Kazakhstan*; Part I: General Questions. Moscow, pp. 66–73.

BARTHOLD, W. 1928. *Turkestan down to the Mongol Invasion*. London.

BASKAKOV, N. A. 1990. *Osnovnye istoricheskie ētapy formirovaniya tyurksikh yazikov narodov Sredney Azii. Problemy etnogeneza i etnicheskoy istorii narodov Sredney Azii i Kazakhstana. Vyp. I, Obshchie problemy* (Basic Historical Stages in the Formation of the Turkic Speeches of the Peoples of Central Asia) In: *Problems Concerning the Ethnogenesis and Ethnic History of the Peoples of Central Asia and Kazakhstan*; Part I: General Questions. Moscow. p. 76.

BELENITSKY, A. 1968. *Central Asia*. Cleveland and New York.

BILALOV, A. I. 1980. *Iz istorii irrigatsii Ustrushany* (Concerning the History of Irrigation in Ustrushāna). Dushanbe.

AL-BĪRŪNĪ. 1879. *Al-Āthār al-Bāqiya* (Vestiges of the Past = *Chronology of Ancient Nations*). Ed. and trans. by Sachau; Vol.1: Arabic text; Vol 2: English trans. London.

BULATOV, M. S. 1978. *Geometricheskaya garmonizatsiya v arkhitekture, Sredney Azii IX–XV vv* (Geometrical Harmonization in the Architecture of Central Asia from the Ninth to the Fifteenth Centuries). Moscow.

DZHALILOV, A. D. 1973. *Iz istorii kul'turnoy zhizni predkov tadzhiskogo naroda i tadzhikov v rannem srednevekovye* (Concerning the History of the Cultural Life of the Ancestors of the Tājīk People and the Tājīks in the Early Middle Ages). Irfon (= *'Irfān*: 'Knowledge'). Dushanbe.

GAFUROV, B. G. 1972. *Tadzhiki. Drevneiyshaya, drevnyaya i srednevekovaya istoriya* (The Tājīks. Their Earliest, Ancient, and Medieval History'). Moscow, pp. 303–316.

GIBB, H. A. R. 1923. *The Arab Conquest in Central Asia*. London.

GULYAMOV, Y. A. G. 1957. *Istoriya orosheniya drevnego Khorezma s drevneyshikh vremen do nashikh dney* (History of the Irrigation of Ancient Khwārizm, from Earliest Times to the Present Day'). Tashkent.

AL-HASSAN, A., HILL, D. R. 1986. *Islamic Technology: an Illustrated History*. UNESCO, Paris.

KILCHEVSKAYA, E. V.; NEGMATOV, N. N. 1979. *Shedevry torevtiki Ustrushany* (Masterworks in chased metal from Ustrushāna). *Pamyatniki kul'turi. Novie otkrytiya*. In *Cultural Monuments: New Finds. Ezhegodnik* ('Yearbook'). Moscow.

LITVINSKIY, B. A. 1990. *Etnogenez i etnicheskaya istoriya narodov Sredney Azii i Kazakhstana v drevnosti i srednevekovye (teoricheskiy aspekt). Problemy etnogeneza i etnicheskoy istorii narodov Sredney Azii i Kazakhstana. Vyp. I. Oshchie voprosy* (The Ethnogenesis and Ethnic History of the Peoples of Central Asia and Kazakhstan in Antiquity and the Middle Ages: The Theoretical Aspect. In: *Problems Concerning the Ethnogenesis and Ethnic History of the Peoples of Central Asia and Kazakhstan*; Part I: General Questions, Moscow, pp. 21–41.

MANDELSHTAM, A. M. 1956. *Otrivok iz 'Poslaniya' Fatkhu b. Khakanu al Dzhakhiza* (An Extract from the *Risāla* or 'Epistle' of Fath ibn Khāqān al-Jāhiz). (*K istorii kul'tury Sredney Azii IXv.*). (Regarding the Culture of Central Asia in the ninth century). *Kratkie soobshcheniya Instituta istorii material'noy kul'turi, Vyp. 61* (Short Communications of the Institute for the History of Material Culture, Part I) pp. 28 ff.

MASSON, V. M. 1990. *Kul'turogenez i etnogenez v Sredney Azii i Kazakhstana, Vyp. I. Obshchie voprosy* (Cultural Genesis and Ethnogenesis in Central Asia and Kazakhstan; Part I; General questions). Moscow, pp. 42–53.

MEZ, A. 1922. *Die Renaissance des Islams*. Heidelberg. English trans. by S. K. Bukhshand and D. S. Margoliouth, *The Renaissance of Islam*. London.

MUKHAMEDZHANOV, A. P. 1978. *Istoriya orosheniya Bukharskogo oazisa* (History of the Irrigation of the Bukharan Oasis). Tashkent.

AL-NARSHAKHĪ, ABŪBAKR MUḤAMMAD. *Tārīkh-i Bukhārā* (Chronicle of Bukhārā: a twelfth-century Persian-language abridgement of the lost tenth-century Arabic-language original). Persian text publ. by Ch. Schefer, *Description topographique et historique de Boukhara par Mohammed Nerchakhy, suivie de textes relatifs à la Transoxiane*. Paris, 1892. Russian trans. by N. Lykoshin. Tashkent, 1897. Engl. trans. by R. N. Frye, *The History of Bukhārā*. Cambridge, Mass. 1954.

NEGMATOV, N. N. 1977. *Gosudarstvo samanidov* (The State of the Sāmānids'). Dushanbe.

——. 1985. *Nauchno-tekhnicheskie osnovy khorezmiyskoy tsivilizatsii i Muhammad al-Khwārizmī* (The Scientific and Technical Bases of Khwārizmian Civilization, and Muhammad al-Khwārizmī'). From the Al-Khwārizmī (1,200th birthday) commemoration volume. Tashkent, pp. 44–49.

——. 1990. *O kontseptsii i khronologii etnogeneza tadzhikskogo naroda* (Concerning the Concept and Chronology of the Ethnogenesis of the Tājīk People). In: *Problems Concerning the Ethnogenesis and*

Ethnic History of the Peoples of Central Asia and Kazakhstan; Part I : General Questions. Moscow, pp 85–97.

——. 1997. *Tajik phenomen: istoriya i theoriya*. Dushanbe.

——. 1998. The Samanid State. In: *History of Civilizations of Central Asia*, vol. IV. UNESCO Publishing, Paris.

NEGMATOV, N. N.; AVZALOV, R. Z.; MAMADZANOVA, S. M. 1987. *Khram i mechet' Bundzhikata na Kalai Kakhkakha I* (The Temple and Mosque of Bunjikat in Qal'a-yi Kakhkakha I). *Material'naya kul'tura Tadzhikistana*. In *The Material Cultural of Tajikistan. Donish* (= *Dānish* = 'Knowledge'). Dushanbe. Part I, pp. 177–210.

ORANSKIIY, A. M. 1960. *Vvedenie v Iranskuyu filologiyu* (An Introduction to Iranian Philology). Moscow, p. 27.

PUGACHENKOVA, G. A.; REMPEL, L. I. *et al.* 1982. *Ocherki iskusstva Sredney Azii* (Essays on the Art of Central Asia). Iskusstvo ('Art Publishers'). Moscow.

RYPKA, Y. (ed.) 1968. *History of Iranian Literature*. Dordreht.

SARTON, G. (ed.) 1950. *Introduction to the History of Science*, Vol. VI. Baltimore, pp. 563, 609, 710.

SINOR, D. (ed.) 1990. *The Cambridge History of Early Inner Asia*. Cambridge University Press.

24

TURKISH EXPANSION TOWARDS THE WEST

24.1

ISLAMIZATION OF THE TURKS, OGHUZ AND TURKMEN

Clifford Edmund Bosworth

THE FIRST CONTACTS OF THE TURKS WITH THE ISLAMIC WORLD

The Arabs first crossed the Oxus River (Āmū Daryā) into Central Asia or Transoxania (called by the Arabs 'the land beyond the river') in the second half of the seventh century and for several decades to come were mainly concerned with establishing their political authority over the indigenous Iranian peoples of Transoxania and Khwārazm (or Khwārizm). But we also have mention at this time of contacts with the Turks of the Central Asian steppes beyond the Syr Daryā, since Turkish contingents of the western Türk Empire or Türgesh seem at times to have aided the Soghdian princes against the incoming Arabs. The penetration of these Turks as far as the Soghdian 'Iron Gate', the Buzgala defile between Kish and Tirmidh on the Oxus (in the south-east of the modern Uzbek Republic) is mentioned in the Orkhon inscriptions in Mongolia, the royal annals of the Kök Türk Empire (first half of the eighth century).

Any contacts here between Arabs and Turks would, of course, be purely military clashes, those of opposing sides. It is true that Turks are occasionally mentioned in the earliest Arabic poetry, assuming that this is authentic, but these mentions seem merely to enshrine a vague knowledge, mediated via Iran, of the land of the Turks as an *ultima thule*. In early 'Abbāsid times, contacts between the Arab ruling classes in Transoxania and the Turks of the steppes continued at first to be inimical. We have various mentions in the Arabic chronicles of aid given to Arab rebels and to the local Iranian princes of Transoxania by the Turks, and it is *c.* 800 that we learn of the constituting of Turkish tribal confederations, arising out of the old Western Kök Türk Empire, such as those of the Qarluq in the Semirechye (the modern Kirghiz Republic and south-eastern Kazakh Republic) and north of the middle Syr Daryā, and of the Toghuz Oghuz on the lower Syr Daryā and the steppes to the north of the Aral Sea. But there now also begin to be some peaceful relations involving the Turks (see Chapter 24.2) as well as hostile ones, and these probably brought about the first conversions of Turks to Islam along the frontiers, although for long Islam remained only one of several of the higher religions, such as Nestorian Christianity, Buddhism and Manichaeism, which the tolerant and receptive steppe peoples espoused in addition to their indigenous shamanistic animism.

THE APPEARANCE OF THE TURKS AS MILITARY SLAVES

The first substantial entry of Turks from Central Eurasia into the Islamic lands took place in the ninth century, when the 'Abbāsid caliphs, from Hārūn al-Rashīd (786–809) onwards, started recruiting Turkish military slave soldiers (*ghulām*, pl. *ghilmān*, or *mamlūk*, pl. *mamālīk*), predominantly cavalrymen, in their new professional armies. It was believed – not always correctly, as events turned out – that these hardy warriors from the steppes would give single-minded loyalty to their masters, the caliphs, and, subsequently, to provincial governors and autonomous rulers in the outlying provinces of the caliphate – the Ṭāhirids, Ṣaffārids, Sājids and Būyids in Iran, the Ṭūlūnids, Ikhshīdids and Fāṭimids in Syria and Egypt, and so on. Such Turkish slaves were either captured in raids into the steppes of south Russia and Central Asia or were brought to slave markets in Transoxania and Transcaucasia as captives but also as mercenaries from internecine Turkish tribal warfare. It was in these towns, such as Bukhārā, Samarkand and Darband, that a process of Islamization began. At a later period, when the Islamic heartland was beset by external, non-Islamic pressures, such as the Christian Frankish Crusaders and the pagan Mongols, the idea was to become current that the Turks were a race divinely blessed, expressly sent by God to defend the frontiers of the Abode of Islam and to revivify the Muslim faith through an infusion of fresh piety; traditions (*ḥadīth*) gained currency in which the Prophet Muḥammad was said to have foretold this role for the Turks.

The influx of Turkish soldiers, purchased within or brought from the steppes and then converted to Islam, was to continue for several centuries. Out of such troops were to arise provincial dynasties of prime importance in medieval Islamic history, such as the Ṭūlūnids of Egypt and Syria (868–905), the Ghaznavids of eastern Persia, Afghanistan and northern

India (977–1186) and, above all, the line of rulers to be known as the Mamlūks, 'military slaves' *par excellence*, who ruled in Egypt and Syria 1250–1517. Jealous of their independence, the sovereigns of such lines were often at pains to rule as model Islamic rulers, conforming to the *sharī'a* or divine law. They followed earlier Iranian dynasties in their policies in revising ancient Iranian notions of sovereignty and statecraft. They also became great builders. Aḥmad ibn Ṭūlūn (868–883) built one of the great mosques of Cairo; Maḥmūd of Ghaznī (998–1030) (see Plate 216) achieved a great contemporary reputation as the upholder of orthodox Sunni Islam against dissident Muslims like the Mu'tazilīs and Ismā'īlīs and as 'hammer' of the infidel Hindus; whilst the Mamlūks (see Plate 217) secured renown throughout the Islamic world by reducing the last strongholds of the Crusaders on the Levant coast and stemming the apparently inexorable advance of the Mongols at the Battle of 'Ayn Jālūt in Palestine (1260). And such was the reputation of Turks as a military race that by the sixteenth century, rulers of Turkish origin controlled virtually all the Islamic lands from Algiers to Bengal, with the exception of the Arabian peninsula and sub-Saharan Africa.

THE FIRST NOMADIC POPULATION MOVEMENTS; THE APPEARANCE OF THE OGHUZ

So far, we have considered movements of Turkish peoples into Islam which involved professional soldiers and comparatively limited numbers; when their commanders themselves became rulers, they formed a military elite over masses of subjects who were mainly Persians or Kurds or Arabs or Armenians. But in the early eleventh century, the influx of Turks became a broader demographic movement, involving successive waves of peoples from Central Asia, the lands beyond the Oxus River and Syr Daryā, who were able to move into the Islamic lands once the power which had formed the north-eastern bastion of the Iranian world against pressure from the steppes, the Sāmānid dynasty (819–1005), had collapsed under the combined attacks of the Turkish Qarākhānids (see below) from the north and those of the Ghaznavids from the south and east. These new waves were not composed of military slaves, as the earlier influx had been, but of free bands of steppe nomads, mounted on horses and bringing with them their extensive herds and flocks. Although the first bands to cross the Oxus in the second quarter of the eleventh century numbered only a few thousands, the steady arrival of fresh contingents of Turkish nomads was, over a period of two or three centuries, to have long-term effects on the demography and environment of Transoxania and the 'northern tier' of the Middle East, the lands stretching from Afghanistan westwards through Iran to Anatolia. There, lands had their ethnic complexions gradually changed as Turkish peoples moved in and settled there. Thus Transoxania, from being an outpost of the ancient Iranian world, *l'Iran extérieur*, became almost wholly Turkicized, so that today, only Tajikistan remains of this ancient heritage. Parts of northern Khurāsān and almost all of Āzerbaijān had their Iranian populations overlaid by Turks. Armenia and Anatolia received great influxes of Turkish frontier warriors, *ghāzīs* and nomads, who assumed military and political dominance and in the end overwhelmed the local Armenian princes and the Greek empires of Constantinople and Trebizond; extensive areas of these provinces were Islamized.

The consequences of these Turkish migrations in the spheres of local economies and land utilization were equally marked. Some of the fertile oases of Transoxania, the upland plains of Khurāsān and Āzerbaijān, and the Anatolian plateau were highly attractive to the nomads and their beasts. The result was a gradual pastoralization of much of the land held by them there. This was combined with the spread of a system of landholding which had begun in the 'Abbāsid caliphate of the ninth century as a means of supporting civil and military servants, especially the professional Turkish ones, of the state, that of the *iqṭā'* or land grant, which conferred local fiscal rights on the holders and in large measure detached such estates and their cultivators from the control of central governments. Such processes tended to make for local particularism and a decentralization of power. Hence, while the Great Seljuk sultanate (see below), at its height under sultans Alp Arslān (1063–1073) and his son Malik Shāh (1073–1092), controlled an immense tract of territory from Turkestan to Syria, the hand of government was lighter than it had been under the powers whom the Seljuks had displaced; similarly, local historians of Transoxania note that taxes were lightened and political power there more diffused after the Turkish Qarākhānids had taken over from the Iranian Sāmānids.

Turks had for long lived on the northern fringes of the Sāmānid emirate of Transoxania. The Sāmānids had devoted considerable military efforts to maintaining their northern frontiers against the infiltration of Turks from the outer steppes, at times leading punitive raids there and establishing a series of *ribāṭs* or fortified posts along the frontiers, where enthusiastic fighters for the faith, *ghāzīs*, could congregate and could engage in *jihād*, the extension of the Islamic faith, against the pagans. On the other hand, there existed at the same time an economic and commercial symbiosis between the nomads, with the products of their herds and flocks, and the settled agriculturists, with their produce and their manufactured goods, such as textiles. That warfare along the frontiers in Central Asia was by no means the norm is shown by the evangelistic activity within the steppes of Ṣūfī *shaykhs* and other devotees, although little specific is known about these efforts. However, it is clear that Islam spread peacefully amongst the Qarluq tribes, a process traditionally marked by the conversion of their ruler, Satuq Bughra Khān, a Qarākhānid ruler in the mid-tenth century. It was most probably the Qarluq who were the driving force behind the Qarākhānid confederation which was to take over Transoxania from the Sāmānids at the end of the tenth century and rule there for over two centuries till the advent of the Mongols.

Under the Qarākhānids, those Turks who settled in cities adopted the high culture of the native populations and remained in close contact with the Uighur civilization of the Tarim basin. The first literary monuments of Turkic antiquity, Maḥmūd of Kashgar's *Dīwān Lughāt al-Turk* and Yūsuf's *Kutadgu Bilig,* were composed in this ambience.

The other great group of Turkish tribes in the steppes adjacent to the Sāmānid emirate, that of the Oghuz (for whom the term 'Turkmen', of uncertain derivation and significance, was also to appear in the eleventh century), was clearly in the tenth century at a lower cultural level than that of the Qarluq (on the evidence of the Arab traveller Ibn Faḍlān, who journeyed from Khwārizm to the kingdom of Bulghar on the middle Volga in 922 and, passing through the lands of the Oghuz on the Ust Yürt plateau to the mouths of the Ural and Emba rivers, found them nomadizing there). It was nevertheless from the Qiniq tribe of this tribal group that the

Seljuk (Seljūq, Saljūq) family sprang, with an eponymous ancestor Duqāq, father of Seljūq. We know of the family's presence around AD 1000 in Jand at the mouth of the Syr Daryā, and at some time towards the end of the tenth century the Seljuk family, and the parallel branch of that of the Yabghu or tribal chief of the Oghuz, became Muslim, although the mass of Oghuz tribesmen almost certainly remained pagan for a good while after this. Entry as mercenaries into the service of the declining Sāmānids gave the Seljuks a foothold within the Islamic lands, and they moved with their beasts to pastures in the neighbourhood of Bukhārā. Over the next decades, the Seljuks and their Oghuz followers were a factor in the civil warfare of the Qarākhānids and in the military policies of the Ghaznavids. Their depredations in northern Khurāsān, the north-eastern rim of the Iranian plateau, exasperated the Ghaznavid sultans, who expelled some of the Oghuz back to the Ust Yürt region but also put into train movements through northern Persia, so that by 1030 Turkmen bands had penetrated as far west as Āzerbaijān. The main body, under the Seljuk family's leadership, strengthened its position in Khurāsān, and by its superior mobility was able to defeat the more heavily armed but cumbersome Ghaznavid army at Dandānqān in the steppes between Merv and Sarakhs in 1040, and the whole of Khurāsān fell into their hands. It became a springboard for further Seljuk expansion across Persia, so that the leader Ṭughrul Beg was able to move his capital successively from Nīshāpūr to Iṣfahān to Rayy, and then in 1055 to enter Baghdād as protector of the 'Abbāsid caliph and as his liberator from tutelage by the Shī'ī Būyids.

THE CONSOLIDATION OF SELJUK POWER IN THE MIDDLE EAST AND THE FIRST RAIDS INTO ANATOLIA

Already in 1035 Ṭughrul and his kinsmen had styled themselves 'clients of the Commander of the Faithful' and at Nīshāpūr in 1038 Ṭughrul had assumed typically Islamic regnal titles and honorifics. There thus began the close attachment of the Seljuks to the cause of Sunnī orthodoxy and what was, in effect, a recognition of the moral and spiritual status of the 'Abbāsid caliph in Baghdād, while the temporal power within the Seljuk Empire remained firmly within the hands of the Great Seljuk sultans; it was only after Malik Shāh's death in 1092 and increasing successional strife between his sons and grandson that the caliphate could reassume much of its former executive power and become a significant force in the military and political affairs of Iraq and western Persia. Meanwhile, although Caliph al-Qā'im himself married a niece of Ṭughrul's, it required considerable diplomatic and financial pressure on an unwilling caliph before the latter finally agreed in 1062 to give one of his daughters in marriage to the unlettered Ṭughrul.

The Great Seljuk sultans, by Ṭughrul's death in 1064 masters of an extensive empire, do not seem to have had a conscious policy of militarily confronting the Byzantine Empire, which still enjoyed an ancient cultural and political prestige in Muslim eyes and which had, in the previous century or so, seemed impervious to Arab attacks. The sultans were content to consolidate their frontier in north-western Persia and Transcaucasia, subjecting the local Armenian princes and establishing a bulwark against the aggressive Christian kings of Georgia. But the Byzantine Empire was now no longer a closely knit unit with strong central direction from Constantinople. It was increasingly racked by succession disputes within the imperial family, the rebellions of ambitious generals, and rivalries between the various peoples of Anatolia (Greeks, Armenians, Syrians), while there occurred at the same time a general disappearance of the locally levied troops who had defended Anatolia against external attackers. Hence bands of Turkmen, largely independent or semi-independent of the Great Seljuk sultans, were now able to raid through Anatolia and sack such cities as Caesarea/Kayseri, Iconium/Konya and Amorion/'Ammūriyya. The opportunities for such raiding intensified after the Battle of Mantzikert/Malazgird in 1071, when Alp Arslān defeated Emperor

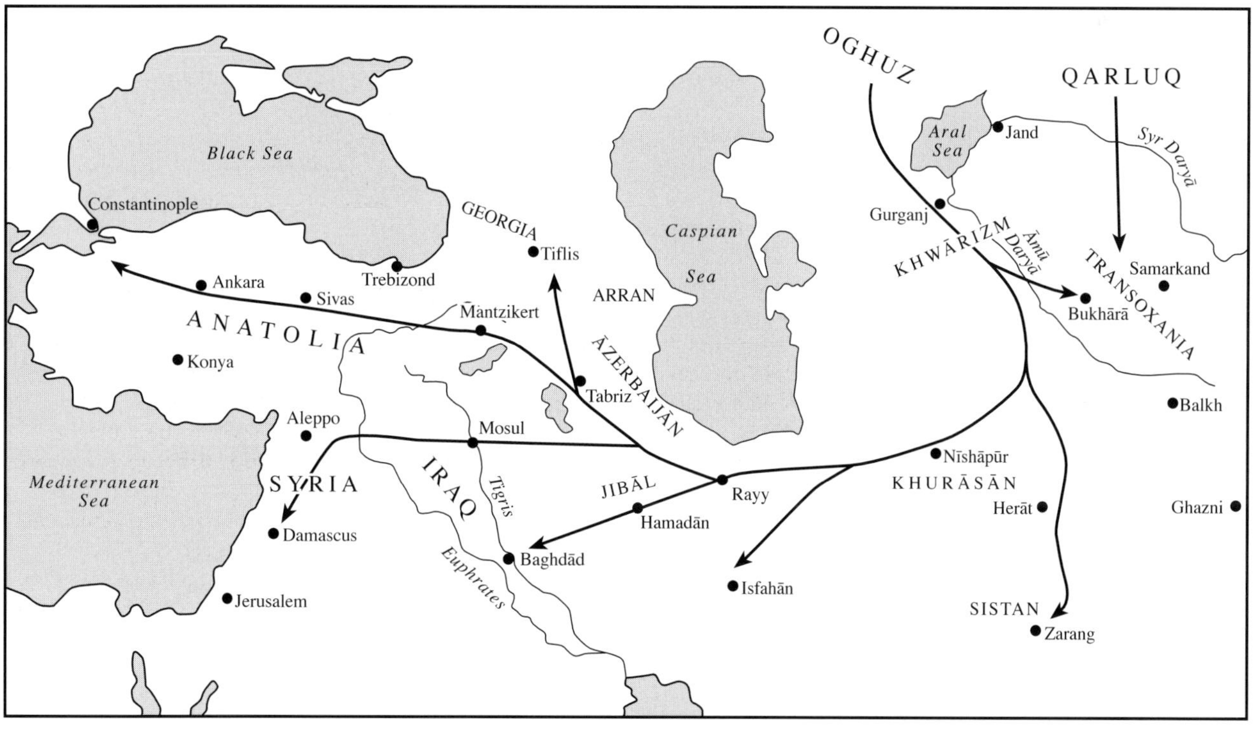

Map 19 Turkish migrations in the tenth and the eleventh centuries (draft Bosworth, C. E.).

Romanus Diogenes. The sultan himself was still not disposed to pit the military might of the Great Seljuk Empire against Byzantium, having pressing commitments in eastern Transcaucasia and Khurāsān, but the Turkmen bands could now raid as far as the shores of the Aegean Sea with impunity. Byzantine administrative authority effectively collapsed within Anatolia, and the region began to fragment, with competing groups striving for local power, such as Turkish emirates and the Frankish mercenary commander Roussel of Bailleul, in northern Anatolia, and the Armenian princes in the Taurus region; these last successfully established the nucleus of what became the kingdom of Little Armenia, which was to survive the Mongol invasions until the mid-fourteenth century.

THE ESTABLISHMENT OF THE TURKMEN GHĀZĪ PRINCIPALITIES AND THE SELJUK SULTANATE OF RŪM

It is soon after Mantzikert that we hear of the activities in Anatolia of the four sons of a member of the Seljuk family, Qutalmish or Qutlumush, and it was the descendants of one of these sons, Süleymān Shāh, who were to establish a local Seljuk sultanate, based first in Nicaea and then in Konya. For after Malik Shāh's death in 1092, Süleymān Shāh's son Qilij Arslān I managed to escape from captivity and was raised to the leadership of Turkmen bands at Nicaea/Iznik in north-western Anatolia, moving his capital to Konya after the Franks of the First Crusade recaptured Nicaea in 1097. It was really Qilij Arslan's son Mas'ūd I (1116–1155) who in the second half of his reign gained dominance over the Dānishmandids (see below) and consolidated the Seljuk sultanate of Rūm (in the mid-twelfth century, the titles *malik* ('king') and *sulṭān* seem to have both been applied to the Seljuk rulers) within what was nevertheless still a comparatively circumscribed area of central Anatolia, for Crusader backing enabled Byzantium to re-occupy northwestern Anatolia, while Greeks, Armenians and Franks held northern Syria and south-eastern Anatolia; but above all, other Turkmen principalities had arisen in northern and eastern Anatolia, making the Seljuks of Konya only one power among several. The leading emirate in northern Anatolia was that of the Dānishmandids, based on Caesarea and north-central Anatolia, and established by a Turkmen chief bearing the Persian name *dānishmand* ('scholar, learned man'); later, in the mid-thirteenth century, Dānishmand was to be the hero of an epic romance, the *Dānishmand-Nāmeh*, which connected him with earlier heroes of Islam, including the famed Arab warrior of Byzantine–Arab frontier warfare, Sīdī Baṭṭāl. During the first half of the twelfth century, the Dānishmandid emirate overshadowed that of the Seljuks in military power and its zeal in *ghazw* or raiding against the Christians, and in 1135 the 'Abbasid caliph and the Great Seljuk sultan in Iraq and western Iran bestowed on the Dānishmandid leader Ghāzī the title of *malik* as a reward for his services in the *jihād*. Further east, the Turkmen line of the Saltuqids was based on Erzerum and became involved in *ghazw* against the Greek Black Sea lands and the Georgians. From the coins of Saltuq and his son, it seems that they acknowledged as suzerains the Great Seljuks, that is, their connections were more with the Iraqi-Persian world than with the Anatolian principalities further west, although after the opening of the thirteenth century, the Saltuqid emirate became integrated with the expanding power of the Seljuks of Rūm. Also, in Enzinjan (Erzincan), Divriği and other towns of east-central Anatolia, one Mengüjek established a local line, concerning whose history little is known; again, this fell under the suzerainty of Konya, although it survived until the coming of the Mongols. Finally, the easternmost and south-eastern regions of Anatolia were dominated by further local lines which had been founded by Turkmen commanders of the Great Seljuk army, most notably those of the Artuqids in Diyārbakr and the Shāh Armanids of Akhlāṭ, but their connections, political and cultural, tended to be with the Arabo-Persian regions of upper Mesopotamia and western Persia rather than with the Anatolian lands further west.

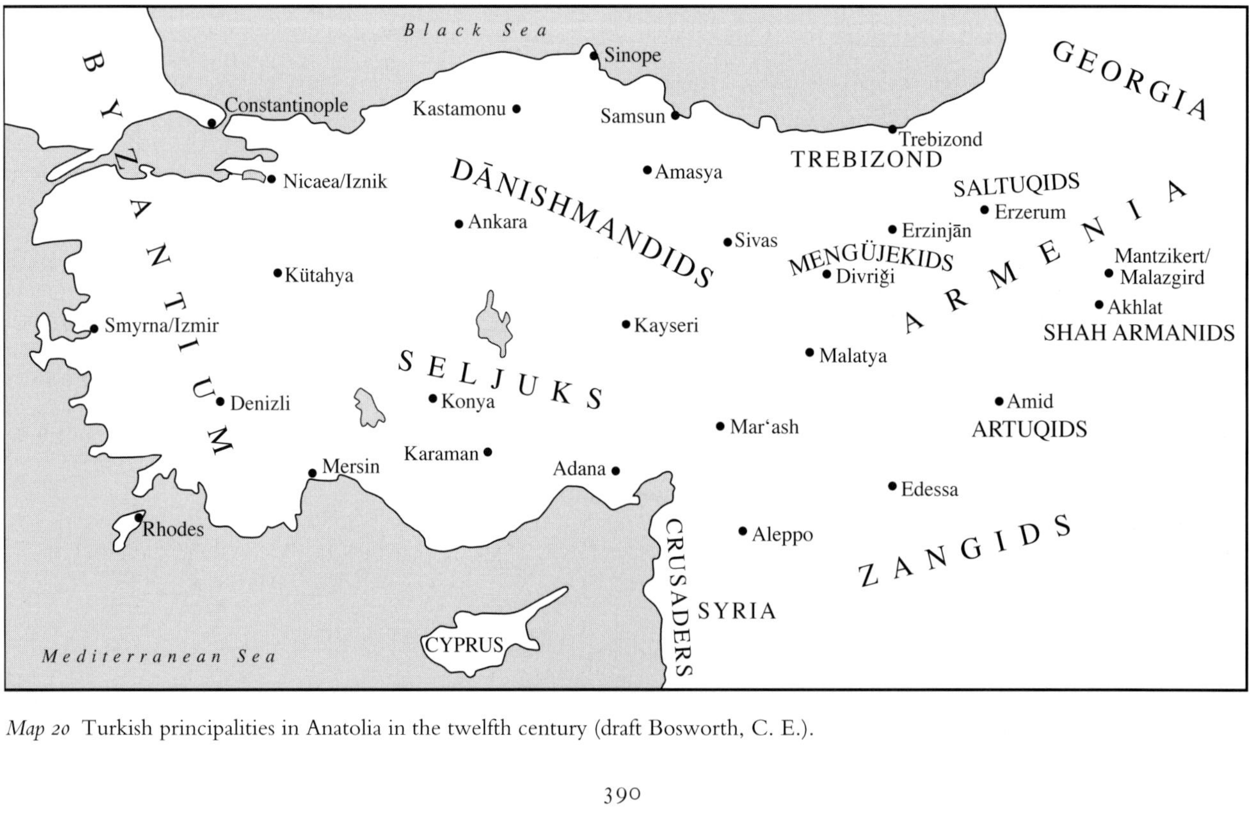

Map 20 Turkish principalities in Anatolia in the twelfth century (draft Bosworth, C. E.).

THE ZENITH OF THE SELJUK SULTANATE OF RŪM

The Seljuk sultanate of Rūm increased its power and influence as the Dānishmandids declined and after it had with difficulty in 1147 fought off from Konya a Byzantine army led by Emperor Manuel I Comnenus. Qilij Arslan II secured revenge for this last attack by inflicting a severe defeat on the emperor's army at Myriocephalon near Lake Egridir in 1176; after this, Byzantine hopes of reconquering Anatolia from the Turks faded, a recognition sealed by the capture of Constantinople in 1204 by the Fourth Crusade and the reduction of the Byzantine Empire in Anatolia to the region around Nicaea. For the Seljuks, the victory opened up the way to the Mediterranean shores and the ports of Antalya and Alanya, while towards the end of the twelfth century the Turkmen emir of Tokat captured Samsun, thus bringing Turkish arms to the Black Sea coast also, this being followed by the further conquest of Sinope. Whereas before this, the Turkish principalities of Anatolia had been essentially landlocked and confined to the interior plateau, they now had access to the sea. For the Seljuks, this was to mean exploitation of their position on the north–south trade route across Anatolia and trade relations with the Venetians – enemies of the Greeks – in Antalya, so that the sultanate benefited from Venetian trade with Alexandria. Commerce between the Black Sea ports and the great Crimean *entrepôt* of Sughdāq tended to be controlled by the Greek principality of Trebizond, but from 1225 to 1239, the date of the definitive conquest of southern Russia and the Crimea by the Mongols of the Golden Horde, the Seljuks were able, through Kastamonu and the Black Sea coastlands, briefly to establish their suzerainty in Sughdāq (1225–1227).

The vigorousness of the internal trade of Anatolia during the last years of the twelfth century and, despite the Mongol invasions of the 1240s (see below), during the whole of the thirteenth century, is shown by a marked rise in the construction of bridges across the rivers of Anatolia and of *khāns* (caravanserais) along the roads of Anatolia by the Seljuks and other local potentates, most of them directly financed by these rulers. Parallel with this was a great wave of religious building: elegant, medium-sized mosques, *madrasas* (colleges) and tombs, many of these buildings being still visible, in varying states of repair, today (see Plate 207). Military architecture and fortification necessarily flourished in this age of warfare, seen now in the walls of Alanya (the walls of Konya disappeared only within recent times). The palaces of the Seljuks at Qubādābād on the shores of the Beyshehir Lake have not, however, survived above ground, and one on the citadel at Konya is only fragmentarily preserved; knowledge about this form of domestic architecture is only now beginning to be obtained through archaeological excavation.

Material prosperity in the Seljuk sultanate went hand in hand with a rich religious and cultural life[1]. The process of Islamization on the Anatolian plateau was clearly a gradual one. The indigenous Christian populations suffered from the frequent warfare across the region and from the raids of indisciplined Turkmen, still largely unassimilated to Islamic religion and culture (it had been largely to keep these Turkmen from their own territories in Persia and Iraq that the Great Seljuks had been eager to deflect them westwards into Anatolia), and were open to the enslavement of their male children by the conquerors. In general, there was some movement of the Christian population from the central plateau to the maritime fringes and to mountain areas, where Turkmen power was only gradually and later extended, but substantial Christian elements remained in the towns and countryside of central Anatolia until the twentieth century. Some degree of intermarriage certainly took place between these peoples and the incoming Turkish groups, and contemporary Greek sources speak of a new generation of Anatolians of mixed ancestry, the *mixovarvarai*, who could be found in the forces of some Turkish chiefs. Such intermarriage, added to the social and legal disadvantages of non-Muslims living under Islamic rule, must have favoured a certain degree of conversion and contributed to some decline in the numbers of the Christians in Anatolia. Nevertheless, the situation of the Christians under Turkish rule in central Anatolia appears to have been more favourable than in the Arabo-Persian heartlands of the Abode of Islam. The Seljuk sultans of Rūm retained something of the tolerance towards, or indifference to, other faiths which characterized the Turks and Mongols in Central Asia: they married Greek and Georgian princesses; in their dominions, churches and monasteries remained; and the Greek clergy found no difficulty in maintaining their links with their patriarchate in Constantinople. It must also be remembered that the Turks were very probably, at this time, still a minority within the lands they ruled, and that the Graeco-Armenian Christian presence within Anatolia was, as noted above, to persist right up to the early part of the twentieth century.

The possibility of some degree of religious syncretism on the Anatolian plateau between Christianity and Islam has been discussed by scholars since the time of the British classicist F. W. Hasluck, but it is difficult to secure firm information about what was obviously an ill-defined trend. But there is no doubt about the liveliness of Islamic religious and cultural activity within the Seljuk sultanate, a vigour which was not only displayed in the spurt of religious building mentioned above. While the Arabic language retained its primacy in such spheres as law, theology and science, the culture of the Seljuk court and secular literature within the sultanate became largely Persianized; this is seen in the early adoption of Persian epic names by the Seljuk rulers (Qubād, Kay Khusraw, and so on) and in the use of Persian as a literary language (Turkish must have been essentially a vehicle for everyday speech at this time). The process of Persianization accelerated in the thirteenth century with the presence in Konya of two of the most distinguished refugees fleeing before the Mongols, Bahā' al-Dīn Walad and his son Mawlānā Jalāl al-Dīn Rūmī (1207–1273), whose *Mathnawī*, composed in Konya, constitutes one of the crowning glories of classical Persian literature. The settlement of Rūmī and his father in Konya also illustrates one of the salient features of religious life in the sultanate, the emphasis on Ṣūfism (Islamic mysticism). It was from its centre in Konya that the dervish order of the Mawlawiyya or Mevlevīs took shape after Mawlānā Jalāl al-Dīn's death under his son Sulṭān Walad, an order whose *dhikr* or form of corporate worship was to include listening to music (*samā'*) and dancing (*raqs*), features common to other Ṣūfī orders but raised to a high pitch of development by the Mevlevīs; these ceremonies can still be seen, albeit in a tourist-oriented form, at Konya today.

THE DECLINE AND DISAPPEARANCE OF THE SULTANATE

After the death of the great sultan Kay Qubād I in 1237, the sultanate fell into political decline, although intellectual life and material and commercial prosperity continued as before. Kay Qubād's successors were of inferior calibre but had to face a series of calamities for the state. A serious Turkmen rebellion under a charismatic religious *shaykh*, Bābā Isḥāq, was crushed in 1240, but shortly after this the Mongols appeared in Anatolia and defeated the Seljuk army at Köse Dagh to the east of Sivas (1243). Thereafter, the sultanate became a client, tribute-paying state of the Mongol Īl-Khāns. It enjoyed a period of calm under the skilful administration and *de facto* rule of the Seljuk official Mu'īn al-Dīn Parvāneh; but after the latter's death in 1277, Mongol governors took direct control, although the Seljuk dynasty, a shadow of its former self, lingered on as nominal rulers till 1308. After this, a new period in the history of Turkish Anatolia begins, that of its fragmentation into a series of petty principalities or *beyliks*, out of which were to arise the Ottomans.

NOTE

1 According to H. Inalcik, a member of the International Commission of the New Edition of the History, the unprecedented prosperity of Anatolia under the Seljukids was principally the outcome of the shift of the transcontinental and sea trade routes to Anatolia under the Mongol Empire in the thirteenth century.

BIBLIOGRAPHY

BARTHOLD, W. 1945. *Histoire des Turcs d'Asie Centrale*, French trans. Paris.

——. 1968. *Turkestan Down to the Mongol Invasions*, English trans., 3rd edn. Gibb Memorial Series, N. S. V. London.

BOSWORTH, C. E. 1970. The Turks in the Islamic Lands up to the Mid-11th Century. *Philologiae Turcicae Fundamenta*, Vol. 3. Separately published, Wiesbaden.

——. 1973. *The Ghaznavids, Their Empire in Afghanistan and Eastern Iran 994–1040*, 2nd edn. Beirut.

CAHEN, C. 1949. Le Malik-Nameh et l'histoire des origines Seldjukides. *Oriens*, Vol. 2, pp. 31–65.

——. 1968. *Pre-Ottoman Turkey. A General Survey of the Material and Spiritual Culture and History c. 1071–1330*. London.

GOLDEN, P. 1992. *An Introduction to the History of the Turkic Peoples*. O. Harrassowitz, Wiesbaden.

HASLUCK, F. W. 1929. *Christianity and Islam Under the Sultans*, 2 vols. Oxford.

KAFESOĞLU, I. 1988. *A History of the Seljuks. Ibrahim Kafesoğlu's Interpretation and the Resulting Controversy*. Trans., ed. and with an introduction by G. Leiser. Southern Illinois University Press, Carbondale and Edwardsville.

KÖPRÜLÜ, M. F. 1992. *The Seljuks of Anatolia. Their History and Culture According to Local Muslim Sources*. Trans. and ed. by G. Leiser, Salt Lake City.

TURAN, O. 1953. Les souverains seljoukides et leur sujets non-musulmanes. In: *Studia Islamica*, Vol. 1, pp. 65–100.

——. 1970. Anatolia in the Period of the Seljuks and the Beyliks. In: HOLT, P. M.; LAMBTON, A. K. S.; LEWIS, B. (eds) *The Cambridge History of Islam*, Vol. 1. *The Central Islamic Lands*. Cambridge, pp. 231–262.

VRYONIS, S. 1971. *The Decline of Medieval Hellenism in Asia Minor and the Process of Islamization from the Eleventh through the Fifteenth Century*. Berkeley, Los Angeles and London.

24.2
THE TURKMEN FORAYS INTO WESTERN ANATOLIA AND THE BALKANS

Robert Mantran

THE SELJUK SULTANATE AND TURKMEN PEOPLES

Firmly established on the Anatolian plateau since the beginning of the twelfth century, the Seljuk sultanate of Konya had, from the middle of the thirteenth century, to contend with two interconnected threats: the irruption into eastern Anatolia of Mongol troops, exerting pressure on central Anatolia which was destabilizing the Seljuks, and the arrival of additional Turkmen peoples from High and Central Asia driven westwards by the Mongols. These Turkmen were not welcomed by the sedentarized Turkish population, who regarded the Anatolian plateau as their own inalienable possession. Even though Turks were not in a majority on the plateau, they were sufficiently numerous and present for the name *Turchia* to be used at the end of the twelfth century by some Western chroniclers. Evidence for the presence of Turks is also to be found in some characteristic religious buildings (mosques, *madrasas* (in Turkish, *medreses*), tombs, and so on at Konya, Kayseri and Sivas), in cultural and religious contacts between Muslims and Christians (for example, the contacts with Jalāl al-Dīn-Rūmī at Konya), and in trade which attracted Genoese and Venetians and prompted the construction of numerous caravanserais. The Turkmen tribes were pushed back towards the sultanate's borders in the north, west and south adjacent to the lands held by the Byzantine emperors then operating from Nicaea and militarily too weak to stem the tide of new arrivals for long.

In 1261, the Byzantines recaptured Constantinople and then had to defend themselves against Latin-led attempts to win it back; this explains their peaceful policy towards the Turks of Anatolia, especially as the Turkmen tribes were not trying at this time to expand the territory attributed to them but rather to consolidate their settlements, organize their daily lives and establish relations with neighbouring populations, especially with the Greek cities that were the focal points of economic contact and exchange. Neither Byzantine nor Turkish sources make any mention of serious conflicts between Greeks and Turks in the last third of the thirteenth century, whereas they do mention the presence in Byzantine territory of Christianized Turks, admittedly few in number, who probably acted to some extent as intermediaries for contacts in the Aegean and Pontus hinterland. Nor do we know of any significant monument or building – especially religious building – erected at this time by the Turkmen, which suggests that they were not fully sedentarized, even if they were no longer entirely nomadic. They were certainly Muslims, but it is possible that their sense of being Turkish was stronger than their loyalty to Islam: their chiefs were called '*bey*' rather than '*emīr*' and bore Turkish rather than Muslim names, while their territory (*uj* or borderland) would be termed a *beylik* (emirate or principality), their system of government was rooted in Turkish traditions and they were spiritually under the influence of the heterodox dervishes, who were to some extent the successors to the shamans of Central Asia.

The disintegration and ultimate collapse of the Seljuk sultanate between 1280 and 1308 released the Turkmen *beys* from control and enabled them to take independent action; the Mongol sultans of Iran were too far away to be a threat, especially for the *beys* of western Anatolia, who would then turn out to be highly dynamic and aggressive, especially towards the Byzantines but occasionally towards their fellow *beys* in neighbouring *beyliks*. The concentration of relatively numerous Turkmen populations may have been a factor in expansion towards Byzantine territories.

TURKMEN EXPANSION TOWARDS WESTERN ANATOLIA

The expansion of the Turkmen established on the edge of the Anatolian plateau was directed towards occupation of the rich plains along the shores of the Aegean Sea and the Sea of Marmara. Emperor Andronicus II, who to save money had weakened his military grip in this area, tried unsuccessfully to arrange a military alliance with the Mongol ruler of Persia, Ghāzān Khān, and then launched against the *beys* the Catalan company of mercenaries of Roger de Flor and Ramón Muntaner (1304): their force, setting out from the peninsula of Cyzicus and advancing through western and southern Anatolia, marched as far as the area of the Cilician Gates, whence they returned by the same route to Constantinople. After their return, the Turkmen *beys* retook possession of the lands from which they had been momentarily driven. The expedition therefore achieved nothing for the Byzantines; indeed, it strengthened the offensives of the *beys*, who, in the next two decades, reached the shores of the Aegean and the Sea of Marmara. There is no doubt at all that these new offensives were largely the work of special Muslim combatants driven by powerful religious feelings. The attacks of these *Ghāzīs*, warriors for Islam, were helped by the disorganization of Byzantine frontier defences during this period. Poorly defended, the Greeks living in the rural areas of western Asia Minor, where the Byzantines by now held no more than a few fortified cities, did not hesitate long before rallying to the new masters.

The brunt of the Turkish pressure was brought to bear on two regions. One was the Aegean plain where, in the valleys of the Meander and Kaystras the *beylik* of the Aydinoğlu occupied Pyrgos, Ephesus, Nisa and first the acropolis and then the port of Smyrna, whence their leader Umur Bey raided the Greek islands in the Aegean. Further north, the Sarukhan *beylik* chose Magnesia of Sipylum (Manisa) as its capital and dominated all the area as far as the coast, with the sole exception of New Phocaea, which was in the hands of the Genoese; meanwhile, the *beylik* of Karesi controlled Pergamum, Adramyttium and the Troy peninsula. The other region under attack was Bithynia, where 'Osmān Bey, the eponymous founder of the Ottoman dynasty, established himself in the Sangarios valley (today called Sakarya) and then, after defeating the Byzantine forces (July 1301), extended his sway over western Bithynia and directly threatened Bursa, Nicaea and Nicomedia. These three cities fell to his son and successor Orkhān between 1326 and 1337. This Turkish advance was greatly facilitated by the Byzantine civil war between Andronicus II and Andronicus III, but also by a tolerant and conciliatory policy that won the support of the inhabitants: when places were conquered, no violence was used against the local population, who were perhaps also content to escape from the internecine quarrels of the Byzantines. It would seem that the conquered and their conquerors worked out a kind of *modus vivendi* regarding the ownership of property, work and land taxes.

The western *beys*, especially Umur of Aydin, took to the sea and raided Byzantine and Latin territories bordering on the Aegean, which prompted the organization of a relatively unsuccessful coalition against the Turkish corsairs. Here it is worth noting that the Turks, despite their 'landsman' reputation, built up active fleets which were probably manned to some extent by Greeks. In this part of western Anatolia, Umur of Aydin was so enterprising that John Cantacuzenus asked him for help in his struggle against John Palaeologus to win the throne of Byzantium.

THE RISE OF THE OTTOMAN BEYLIK

Based on the Asian side of the Dardanelles, the *beys* of Karesi took to piracy, while further east the Ottomans gradually put an end to the Byzantine presence in this region and occupied the *beylik* of Karesi. All that was left in Greek hands was the city of Chrysopolis (present-day Üsküdar – Scutari of Asia) and its suburbs and the Asian shore of the Bosphorus. A little later, the civil war that broke out between John Palaeologus and John Cantacuzenus in 1341 fired Ottoman ambitions: Umur Bey of Aydin was succeeded by the Ottoman Orkhān as the ally of Cantacuzenus, whose son-in-law he became. Orkhān took the opportunity to send troops into Thrace, where they remained (1352), and his example was followed by other Turkish chiefs. Twenty years later, the whole of Thrace was occupied and the city of Adrianople (Edirne) was taken (1361 and 1366). We have already mentioned the *ghāzī* spirit, or zealous propagation of Islam by military means if necessary, of the first Ottoman *beys*. But this argument smacks of hindsight, for it should not be forgotten that the Ottomans crossed over into Europe at the request of the Byzantines and that the Ottoman troops fighting in Asia Minor are known to have included Christians (see Map 21).

Although the Turkmen populations dependent on the Ottomans were originally not so much sedentary as seasonal

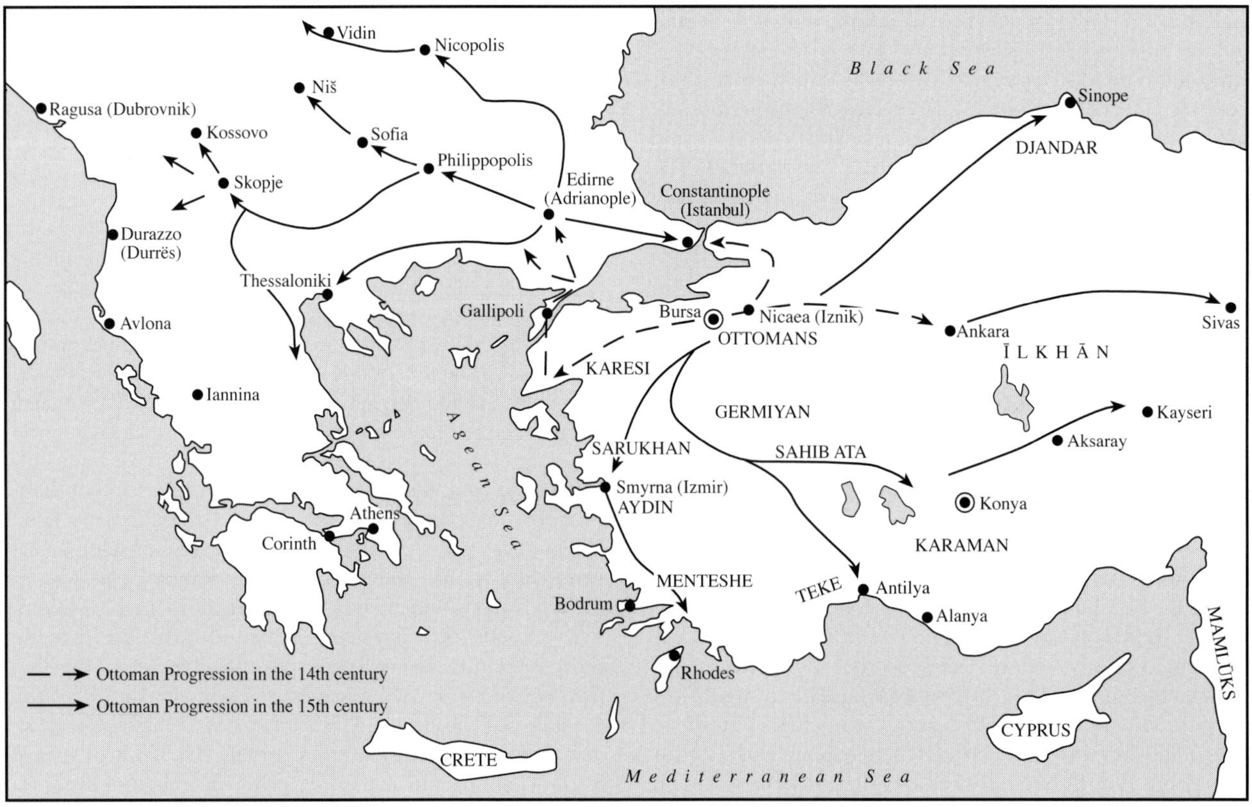

Map 21 Ottoman advances in the fourteenth and fifteenth centuries (draft Mantran, R.).

migrants, some of them had already chosen a sedentary or even urban existence before 1300; ʿOsmān, followed by Orkhān, made Yenishehir, then Bursa and later Adrianople, the centre of their state and, as in other cities likewise, erected religious buildings (mosques, *medreses*) and other public works such as baths, caravanserais and bridges. Under Orkhān, the organization and administration of the young Ottoman state took shape: the state belonged to the family; in accordance with Turkish tradition, a chief was chosen from the family, whose other members were given posts in the government council (*dīvān*) or in the administration of the province of Rumelia (Europe) after the conquests in Thrace; financial requirements were met by the income from Islamic taxes (as *jizya* and *ush)* but also from levies on land attributed to Ottomans or left in the hands of their former Christian owners for their lifetime (*timar*), taxes on trade, and booty. Fairly soon, city life became organized under the authority of a military chief and *kadi* (Arabic *qāḍī,* judge); corporations initially run by the *akhi* lodges (fraternities of craft workers) came into being along with an increasing number of Muslim religious communities around the mosques, *zāwiyas* (a fraternity's place of gathering and ritual) or *tekkes* (convents). The former shamanism of the Turkmen could be discerned in the more popular type of Islam practised by the dervishes (*bābā, abdāl*). The Turks lived as a minority alongside the numerous Greeks in western Asia Minor and Thrace: the Ottoman advance, although at the expense of the power of Byzantium, did not jeopardize the peaceful cohabitation of many groups in popular as well as elitist intellectual circles, and more especially of both Muslim and Christian clerics attracted by mysticism. Without going so far as to speak of conciliation between Byzantine Christianity and Turkish Islam, it can be claimed that contacts had already taken place in the second half of the thirteenth century around Ṣadr al-Dīn Qonevī and Mawlānā (Jalāl al-Dīn Rūmī). There was more dialogue in the fourteenth century, partly from political necessity but also because the Orthodox Christians were looking for ways of safeguarding their religious identity. Faced with the same adversary – the Latins – as the Muslims, the answer lay in an alliance profitable to both parties; this led to meetings, philosophical discussions, mystical comparisons and hence mutual influence. This accounts for the Turko-Islamic advance in a Byzantine Christian environment, which cannot be explained in sufficient depth by political and military events alone.

THE OTTOMAN FOOTHOLD IN EUROPE AND THE ADVANCE TOWARDS AN EMPIRE

During the reign of Murād I (1362–1389), first recognized as *bey* but later taking the title of *sulṭān*, the Ottomans advanced into Bulgaria and Serbia, whose sovereigns accepted their vassal status with varying degrees of willingness, and into Macedonia; threatened, the king of Hungary appealed to the West, but his forces were crushed at Nicopolis in 1396 by Bāyāzid I, who also laid siege to Constantinople (1394–1396). Through marriage, annexation and conquest, the *beyliks* of western and central Anatolia were absorbed into Ottoman territory, which had already become a large state on both sides of the Aegean under Beyazīd I (1389–1402).

In 1402, however, Tamerlane's attack on Asia Minor destabilized the Ottoman state for a decade; however, Mehmed I (1412–1421) and later Murād II (1421–1451) returned to an active policy of conquest which culminated in the fifteenth century with the capture of Constantinople by Mehmed II in 1453. During this period, a new political and religious phenomenon emerged in the Turko-Greek community: a Muslim mystic, Bedreddīn, and later his disciples, in contact with Greek religious circles, established a political movement directed against the Ottoman dynasty. The danger of a coalition between politicians and mystics enjoying support among the people led the Turkish sultans and the Greek religious authorities to join forces to eliminate the danger of secessions. This agreement and a very limited Islamization produced a religious and cultural melting pot characteristic of the Ottoman civilization, which would last until the nineteenth century.

In the sphere of administration and the economy, the Ottoman government introduced sultanic law codes side by side with the Islamic law which regulated the position of individuals in each province in relation to representatives of the central government. These collections of laws, updated, amended and from time to time adapted to circumstances, provided a safeguard for subjects against state officials who might be tempted to abuse their authority. They were the basis for the *kānūnnāmes* (organic laws) which were enacted by the sultans from the second half of the fifteenth century onwards. Conquered agricultural land was either left in the hands of the former holder or more often granted for life, under the *timar* or *ziyāmet* systems, to individual soldiers (*sipāhīs*) or civil officials, who were made responsible for administration, production, collecting taxes and, if necessary, mustering troops. It was under Bāyazīd I that the *devşirme* system of recruiting adolescents in the Christian families of the Balkans began. These boys, after conversion to Islam and a Turkish education, either entered the service of the government or palace or joined the army (as janissaries), where they would constitute the backbone of the Ottoman state's civil and military structure, especially from the reign of Mehmed II (1451–1481) onwards.

In spite of the temporary halt in 1402, the Ottomans, thanks to their liberal approach to government, were able to take advantage of the relatively favourable situation in their territories in Europe to undertake the rapid reconquest of the lands lost in Asia Minor. The advance resumed under Murād II towards Bosnia, Albania, Hungary, Transylvania and the Peloponnese, and towards Karaman in Asia Minor. When Mehmed II came to power, the only task left to complete the unification of the Ottoman state was the capture of Constantinople, which he accomplished on 29 May 1453. This date marks the true beginning of an 'Ottoman Empire' (see Plate 194 (d)).

BIBLIOGRAPHY

ANGELOV, D. 1956. Certains aspects de la conquête des peuples balkaniques par les Turcs. *Byzantinoslavica* 17, pp. 220–227.

BELDICEANU, I. 1989. Les débuts: Osmân et Orkhân. In: MANTRAN, R. (dir.) *Histoire de l'Empire ottoman*. Paris, Ch. I, pp. 15–35.

BELDICEANU, N. L'organisation de l'Empire ottoman (XIVe–XVe siècles). *Ibid*., pp. 117–138.

CAHEN, C. 1988. La Turquie pré-ottomane. Institut français d'Etudes anatoliennes. Istanbul-Paris.

INALCIK, H. 1954. The Ottoman Methods of Conquest. In: *Studia Islamica* ii, pp. 103–129.

——. 1973. *The Ottoman Empire. The Classical Age 1300–1600*. London.

KÖPRÜLÜ, M. F. 1928. Anadolu Beylikleri tarihine ait notlar (Notes on the History of the Beyliks of Anatolia), *Türkiyat Mecmuasi* II, Istanbul, pp. 1–32.
——. 1935. *Les origines de l'Empire ottoman*. Paris.
LEMERLE, P. 1957. *L'émirat d'Aydin, Byzance et l'Occident*. Paris.
TAESCHNER, F. 1929. Beiträge zur Geschichte der Achis in Anatolien (14.–15. Jhdt.). *Islamica*, IV, pp. 1–47.
VATIN, N. 1989. L'ascension des Ottomans (1362–1451). In: MANTRAN, R. (dir.) *Histoire de l'Empire ottoman*. Paris. Ch. II, pp. 37–80.
VRYONIS, S. 1971. *The Decline of Medieval Hellenism in Asia Minor and the Process of Islamization from the Eleventh through the Fifteenth Century*. Berkeley, Los Angeles and London.
WITTEK, P. 1934. *Das Fürstentum Mentesche*. Istanbul.
——. 1938. *The Rise of the Ottoman Empire*. Royal Asiatic Society Monographs, XXIII. London.
——. 1938. De la défaite d'Ankara à la prise de Constantinople, *Revue des Etudes Islamiques*. Paris, XII/1, pp. 1–3.

24.3
THE TURKMEN IN WESTERN ANATOLIA AND THEIR EMIRATES

Halil Inalcik

The displaced nomadic Turkmen groups pushed by the Mongols came and conquered western Anatolia and were later joined by sedentary folk, dervishes, members of the religious establishment, military leaders and administrative officials fleeing from the Mongol-dominated hinterland and seeking a new life on the western frontier. These sophisticated representatives of high Islamic culture helped the rustic Turkmen of the frontier to found viable sultanates and reorganized the newly settled territories after the traditions of the Islamic world from south-west Anatolia to the Sea of Marmara in the north. Over time, these emirates adapted themselves to the mercantile pursuits of the Italian city-states with which they had come into contact along the Aegean littoral and consequently actively participated in international trade. The port cities of western Anatolia served as export outlets for grain, cotton, wool and carpets, which were exchanged for the woollen manufactures and metals of Europe. Iranian silk was also an important item in the transit trade at these ports. Starting from the 1330s, the frontier Turks began to regard the Balkans as a kind of promised land. This powerful westward movement oscillated between phases of dramatic mass migrations and slow penetration,but its continuity and general direction remained constant. The main conduits for Turkish settlement and tribal movement in the Balkans in the fourteenth century were the Maritza River valley, the mountain passes of the western Balkan range (Stara Planina) and, in the southern districts, the *Via Egnatia* through Thessaloniki to Albania. The indigenous Greek and Slav inhabitants of conquered regions began to flee in large numbers under the shock of the initial frontier raids. None the less, once this violent raiding period was over and new emirates had been carved out of the conquered lands, the authorities sought ways of restoring the social equilibrium and encouraged conditions of peaceful coexistence between the new Turkish settlers and the indigenous populations. The two principal factors in the emergence of the Ottomans as empire builders among the emirates were, first, their success in achieving a reconciliation between the Muslim conquerors and indigenous Christian populations. In the period of the Turkmen emirates, the dominant social groups that represented Islamic frontier culture were the military rank and file, the *ghāzīs*, mostly of Turkmen origin, the popular dervishes, the (*faqīhs*), or Muslim clerics, and the *akhīs*, the leaders of the artisan fraternities. The heterodox dervishes were accepted by the newly arrived Turkmen of the frontier as their most revered religious leaders. These dervishes occupied a dominant position in the cultural and social life of Turkmen society. It was also the leaders of these popular orders who gave expression to a new literary synthesis in pure Turkish style which reconciled the disparate elements of inherited Turkic shamanism and forms of pantheistic mysticism that they encountered in Iran and Seljuk Anatolia. The popular, conciliatory system of beliefs which revolved around the figure of the dervish spread among the Christian masses, who lived together with the Turks in the newly conquered territories. The third major social group, the *faqīhs,* consisted of men of religion who had studied in a formal religious seminary. Despite the overwhelming influence of the dervishes in Turkmen society, the legal supremacy of the *sharī'a* was a principle that was formulated and generally accepted in the Ottoman state from the time of the first Ottoman rulers onwards. The fourth important organized social group in Ottoman society was the *akhīs*. In the opinion of the Moroccan traveller Ibn Baṭṭūṭa, who visited Anatolia in the 1330s, the *akhīs* constituted one of the most prominent and influential groups in both rural and urban settings. Ibn Baṭṭūṭa describes the *akhī* lodges in the Anatolian cities he visited as follows:

> They existed in all the lands of the Türkmens of al-Rūm, in every district, city and village. Nowhere in the world are there to be found any to compare with them in solicitude for strangers and in ardour to serve food and satisfy wants, to restrain the hands of the tyrannous, and to kill the agents of the police and those ruffians who join with them. An *akhī*, in their idiom, is a man whom the assembled members of his trade, together with others of the young unmarried men and those who have adopted the celibate life, choose to be their leader. . . .
>
> The *akhī* builds a hospice. . . . His associates work during the day to gain their livelihood, and after the afternoon prayer they bring him their collective earnings; with this they buy fruit, food, and the other things needed for consumption in the hospice. If, during that day, a traveller alights at the town, they give him lodging with them. What they have purchased serves for their hospitality to him . . . and after eating they sing and dance.
>
> (Gibb, H. A. R. 1956–1971, *The Travels of Ibn Baṭṭūṭa*, Vol. II, pp. 419–420. Hakluyt Society, Cambridge, Engl. tr.)

All these constituted the background to the Ottoman Empire, which channelled the westward movement of the Turks into the Balkans and united the Turkmen emirates in Anatolia and small states in the Balkans into an empire towards the end of the fourteenth century.

25

SOUTH ASIA

25.1
INDIA

Irfan Habib

SOCIAL AND ECONOMIC FORMATIONS

Indian feudalism, 600–1200

In Indian historiography, the period between the collapse of the last great north Indian empire of the first millennium, that of Harshavardhana (d. 648), and the beginning of the regime of the sultans of Delhi, 1206, is often designated 'late ancient' or 'early medieval'. In employing such nomenclature, most historians appear to have in mind mainly the continuous failure of Indian states of this period to achieve an imperial position or a high degree of centralization. Kosambi (1956) and Sharma (1980) have, however, invoked a more profound basis for demarcating these six centuries, namely, the dominance of 'Indian feudalism' (see Map 22).

Kosambi (1956: p. 243 ff.) ascribed to the process of craft diffusion the emergence of village isolation, which was the bedrock of the 'feudal' order. The conversion of the 'untouchables' or outcasts into a landless proletariat also appears to have been completed within the first millennium AD (Habib, 1993: p. 131). Village self-sufficiency undermined commerce, and the entire period up to 1000 is widely seen as one of urban decline (Sharma, 1987; Yadava, 1993: pp. 20–25). Gold and silver money tended to contract and even disappear, and this strongly suggests a decline in the number of large transactions (*cf.* Deyell, 1990; also Gopal, 1989).

As incidental statements by Yijing (*c.* 690) show, large land-holders seem to have enjoyed the option of cultivating their lands through hired servants and labourers, or getting them cultivated by peasants on a sharecropping basis (Takakusu, 1896: pp. 61–62). But, by and large, it was the peasants who cultivated the land and surrendered a part of their produce to the king or the intermediaries or other rural potentates. There is substantial evidence that they could be kept tied to their villages, though the existence of serfdom is disputable. The alienation of fiscal rights goes back to the Śaka and Śātavāhana rulers' grants to Brahmans in Mahārāshtra early in the second century. Grants on similar terms to the ruler's kinsmen, vassals and officials appear much later, at the earliest in the eighth century; they become numerous only in the eleventh. The appearance of these 'secular' grants synchronized with the emergence of what U. N. Ghoshal (1929) calls 'clan monarchies', in which the kingdoms tended to be divided up among members of the royal clan. Among such monarchies we may class the Gurjara-Pratīhāras, the Gāhaḍavālas and the Chāhamānas in northern India.

This development of an Indian variety of feudalism was possibly greatly accelerated by changes in military techniques and organization. By the seventh century, chariots had become obsolete, and cavalry was becoming important. The Sanskrit *rājaputra* (Prākrit *rāuta*, Hindi *rājpūt*), became the designation of the elite cavalry soldier. The *rājaputras* or *rāutas*, being mainly mounted lancers, could, collecting together, control a large territory, and, dispersing, hold individually its disparate parts. So with the *rājaputra* carving out villages in hereditary domains, there arose above him a class of potentates, variously styled *sāmanta, ṭhakkura, rāṇaka* or *nāyaka*. The king (*rāja, rāya*) tended to become the mere head of a confederacy of such chiefs. His power was eroded in almost exact correspondence to the growth in the flamboyance of his titles.

Southern India witnessed similar decentralized political structures, which provided the basis for B. Stein's (1980) thesis of the 'segmentary state'. Stein attributes the emergence of this state to a primitive peasant society (with no 'gentry' or 'lords'), marked by a two-*varṇa* (caste) system of Brahman (priests) and *Śūdras* (peasants): unlike northern India there were no recognized 'twice-born' castes of *Kshatriyas* (warriors) and *Vaiśyas* (merchants). However, there seems to be too much stress here on mere caste classification, and the thesis has not obtained wide acceptance, especially when it is applied to the Chōla Empire of the tenth and eleventh centuries (D. N. Jha, 1993: pp. 118–144).

The military and naval prowess displayed by the Chōlas (conquest of Sri Lanka, 993, and expeditions to Malaya and Sumatra) is certainly striking. The economic strength of Chōla power probably rested partly on the role that South India played in the Indian Ocean trade, serving as a convenient zone of trans-shipment between the Red Sea/Persian Gulf and South-East Asia. The royal monopoly of horses imported from Iran (Yule and Cordier, 1921: II, p. 340) gave added

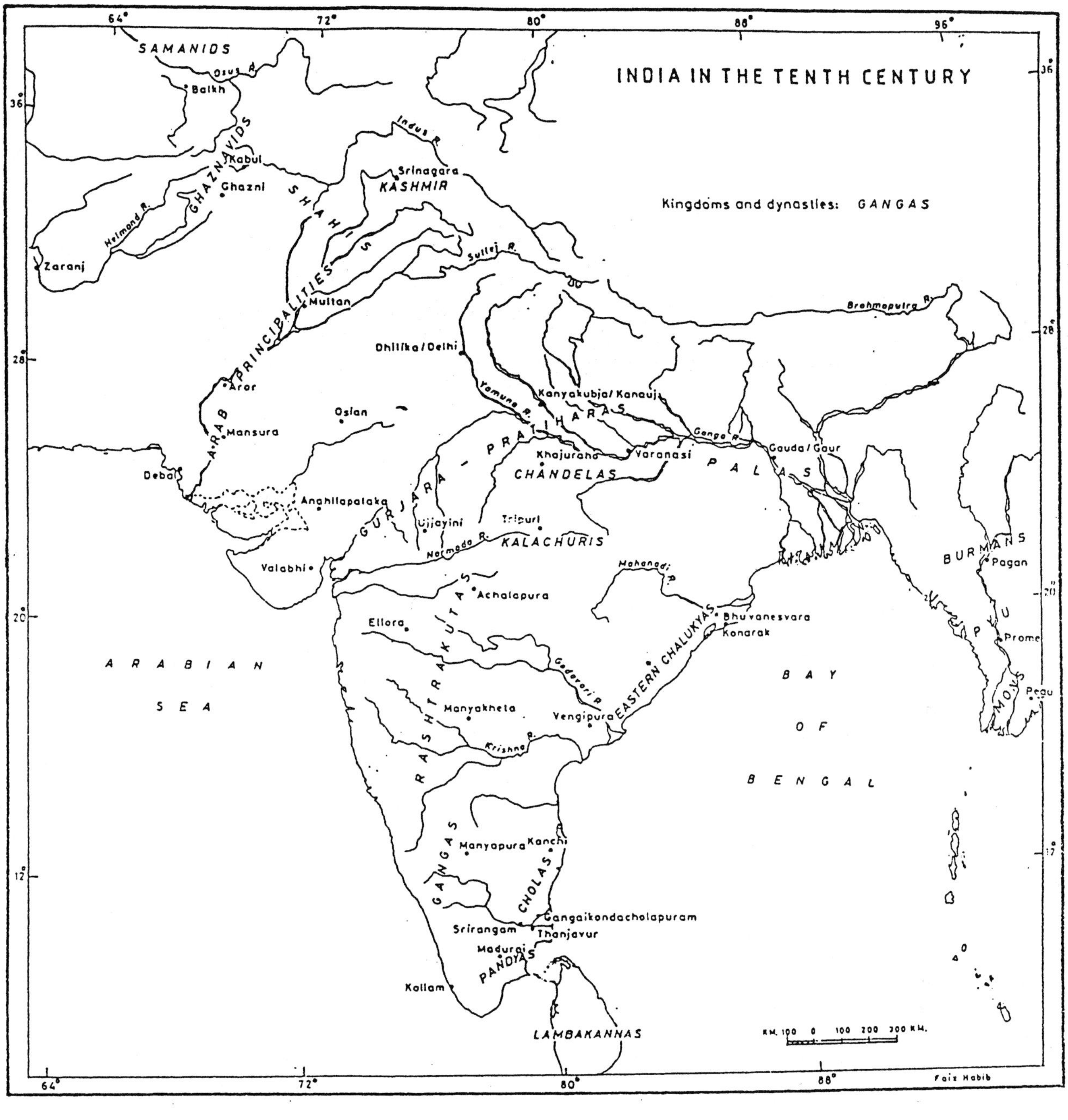

Map 22 India in the tenth century (map drawn by Habib, F.).

strength on land to the Chōlas, who claimed that their armies had subjugated even the powerful Pāla rulers of Bengal. For the rest, the same 'feudalizing' factors appear to have operated in the south as in the north.

'Indian Feudalism' on the social plane seems to have been related to changes in the caste system. It is possible that the caste system during this period became more rigid and took its classical shape. In 712–714, the Arabs, on conquering Sind, found (and continued) humiliating rules imposed on the pastoral community of the Jatts. Al-Bīrūnī (*c.* 1035) puts weavers very low even among the eight *antyaja* or outcasts, who, he says, could live only outside the towns and villages of the four castes (Sachau, 1910: p. 101). But by paying excessive attention to the letter of the *smṛitis* and the reports of his Brahman informants, al-Bīrūnī might be giving us a sterner picture than was warranted by reality. In the well-known late *Pañchatantra* story of the weaver masquerading as Vishṇu, the weaver claims to belong to the higher *Vaiśya* caste.

The increasing rigour in the caste system found its reflection in harsher customs imposed on women, of which *satī* (widow burning) among the higher castes was one illustration. In the seventh century, it was criticized by Bāṇa, but by the eleventh century it had become fairly widespread all over India (except in the extreme south) among rulers, nobles and warriors (Altekar, 1956: pp. 124–130). Documents dated 1230–1231 in the *Lekhapaddhati* show that women, when sold into slavery, legally lost their caste and family ties and could be obliged to do all kinds of work, in the house and the fields, including the dirtiest, under constant threat of torture (Gopal, 1989: pp. 71–80).

However, the caste system was not unchanging, and both resistance and vertical and horizontal shifts occurred. The

Kaivartas, listed among the outcast communities (*jātis*) in *Manusmṛiti,* rose in revolt in Bengal in the eleventh century, ultimately winning recognition as a 'clean' one by King Ballālasena (1159–1185). There was a similar transformation of the Jatts. Pastoral outcasts in seventh century Sind, they could challenge Maḥmūd of Ghazni (r. 1000–1030), fighting on boats, and were held to be *Śūdras* (the fourth caste) by al-Bīrūnī.

The medieval formation, 1200–1500 (see Map 23)

The Delhi sultanate was carved out of the conquests of Mu'zzu'ddīn of Ghōr (d. 1206), whose empire was the successor to that of Maḥmūd of Ghaznī (1000–1030). These two successive states passed on to the Delhi sultanate two major institutions: the *iqṭā'*, or transferable territorial tax assignment and military charge; and the *kharāj*, the tax rent. The sultans expected the maintenance of military contingents, mainly of mounted archers, from the holders of the *iqṭā'*s (*muqṭi's, wālīs*) and demanded payment of surplus revenues (*fawāẓil*). Certain areas were retained by the sultans under their direct control (*khāliṣa*), out of whose revenue they paid, either in cash or through sub-assignments, the soldiers belonging to the central army (*ḥashm-i qalb*).

In its tax resources, despotic centralization and military power, the sultanate was so different from the preceding polities of northern India that the term 'feudal' has been denied to it (Moreland, 1929: pp. 216–223). It is true that through most of the thirteenth century, despite the sultans' extensive domain in northern India, much of the land around their garrison towns remained *mawās*, or rebellious, and the chiefs (*rāṇakas* and *rāutas*) over much of the rest of sultanate merely paid tribute. But conditions began to change towards the close of the century. Under 'Alā'u'ddīn Khaljī (r. 1296–1316), Gujarat and central India were conquered and the larger part of the Deccan and south India subjugated. The first real all-India empire after the Mauryas (third century BC) was thus created. The territorial expansion was matched by an expansion of fiscal resources. The tax-rent (set at half the value of the produce) was rigorously imposed over a very large area, the fiscal claims of hereditary intermediaries (*chaudhurīs*) and village headmen (*khoṭs*) being heavily curtailed. The tax-grain (including grain sold by peasants to pay tax) was so large in its total quantity that by controlling its price, 'Alā'u'ddīn Khaljī was able to reduce and control prices of all commodities in the capital, Delhi.

Measures of expansion and centralization continued under 'Alā'u'ddīn Khaljī's successors. Bengal was re-annexed (1324) and the area of direct control extended almost to the extreme southern point of the Indian peninsula under Ghiyāṣ u'ddīn Tughluq (1320–1324) and Muḥammad Tughluq (1324–1351). The drive for greater control over the nobility led to the separation of the revenue charge from the military command within the *iqṭā'*s. The continuous pressure for larger tax realization led to agrarian uprisings, notably in the Dōāb near Delhi (1332–1334), and forced Muḥammad Tughluq to resort to a most interesting scheme of agricultural development based on the supply of credit to peasants.

In the closing years of Muḥammad Tughluq's reign, the political crisis intensified, with military officers (*amīrān-i ṣada*) rebelling in many regions, and the sultanate beginning to break up. The Vijayanagara Kingdom (1346) and the Bahmanī sultanate (1347) in the peninsula were now established. Some stability was attained for the Delhi sultanate under Fīrūz Tughluq (1351–1388), who gave substantial concessions to the nobility, making their territorial charges and offices practically hereditary. This naturally paved the way for the splitting away of the provinces as independent kingdoms (Bengal, Jaunpur, Gujarat, Malwa, Khandesh, Multan) after Fīrūz Tughluq's death. The process of disintegration was completed by Tīmūr's devastating raid (1398). After leading a precarious existence, the Sayyid dynasty in Delhi (1414–1451), gave way to the Lodīs (1451–1526), who extended their dominions to include a respectable portion of northern India. But Bābur's victory at Pānīpat (1526) put an end to the dynasty and led to the creation of the great Mughal Empire.

The successor states of the Delhi sultanate tended to retain its fundamental institutions. One was the heavy land tax (*māl*); the other, the territorial assignment against military obligation (*iqṭā'*), now known under different names: *wajh* and *sarkār* in the later Delhi sultanate; *muqāsa* in the Deccan sultanates; *paṭṭa* in Rajasthan; and *nāyaka* – 'captaincies' and *amara* tenures in Vijayanagara. In Vijayanagara, there was an undoubtedly conscious attempt to adopt certain administrative and military techniques of the sultanates, which partly explained its success against the Bahmanīs as well as the local powers.

The sultanates did not alter many of the fundamental institutions inherited from 'Indian feudalism'. The village community and caste system were not subverted, doubtless because they facilitated agrarian exploitation. The peasant, though theoretically deemed free (*ḥurr*), was not really free of extra-economic constraints. None the less, the political transformation was accompanied by important economic changes. One was the imposition of the cash nexus, along with the raising of the land tax to the level of rent. This led to a considerable expansion of 'induced' trade, especially in drawing food grains and other products to the towns. There was simultaneously a new phase of urban growth. Delhi and Daulatābād (Devgiri) rose in the fourteenth century to be two of the great cities of the world; and there were other large towns, like Multan, Kara, Jaunpur, Gaur, Cambay, Gulbarga and Vijayanagara. Numismatic evidence alters dramatically, as the Delhi sultans began their gold and silver mintage alongside copper from early in the thirteenth century, thereby evidencing brisk commerce with an abundance of large transactions. Despite the Mongol conquests of the western borderlands, India's external trade, both overland and oceanic, grew considerably during this period, it being now widely noted as an established fact that India was a large net importer of gold and silver (Digby, 1982: pp. 93–101).

External contacts led to important technological diffusions (see below), which in turn affected craft production. The spinning wheel, introduced by the fourteenth century, enlarged cotton textile production; and sericulture was established in Bengal by the fifteenth century. Paper manufacture was already well established in Delhi in the thirteenth century. Liquor distillation was reported to be an extensive industry in Delhi and its neighbourhood by the close of the thirteenth century. Building activity attained a new scale with the widespread use of lime and gypsum, and by the coming of vaulting techniques.

These developments had their reverse side as well. Slavery already existed in India, but the scale of enslavement probably grew substantially in the thirteenth and fourteenth centuries, as slaves were both captured in war and supplied in lieu of unpaid taxes. They were put to work at both domestic service and crafts (I. Habib, 1982: pp. 89–93). To some extent, slave

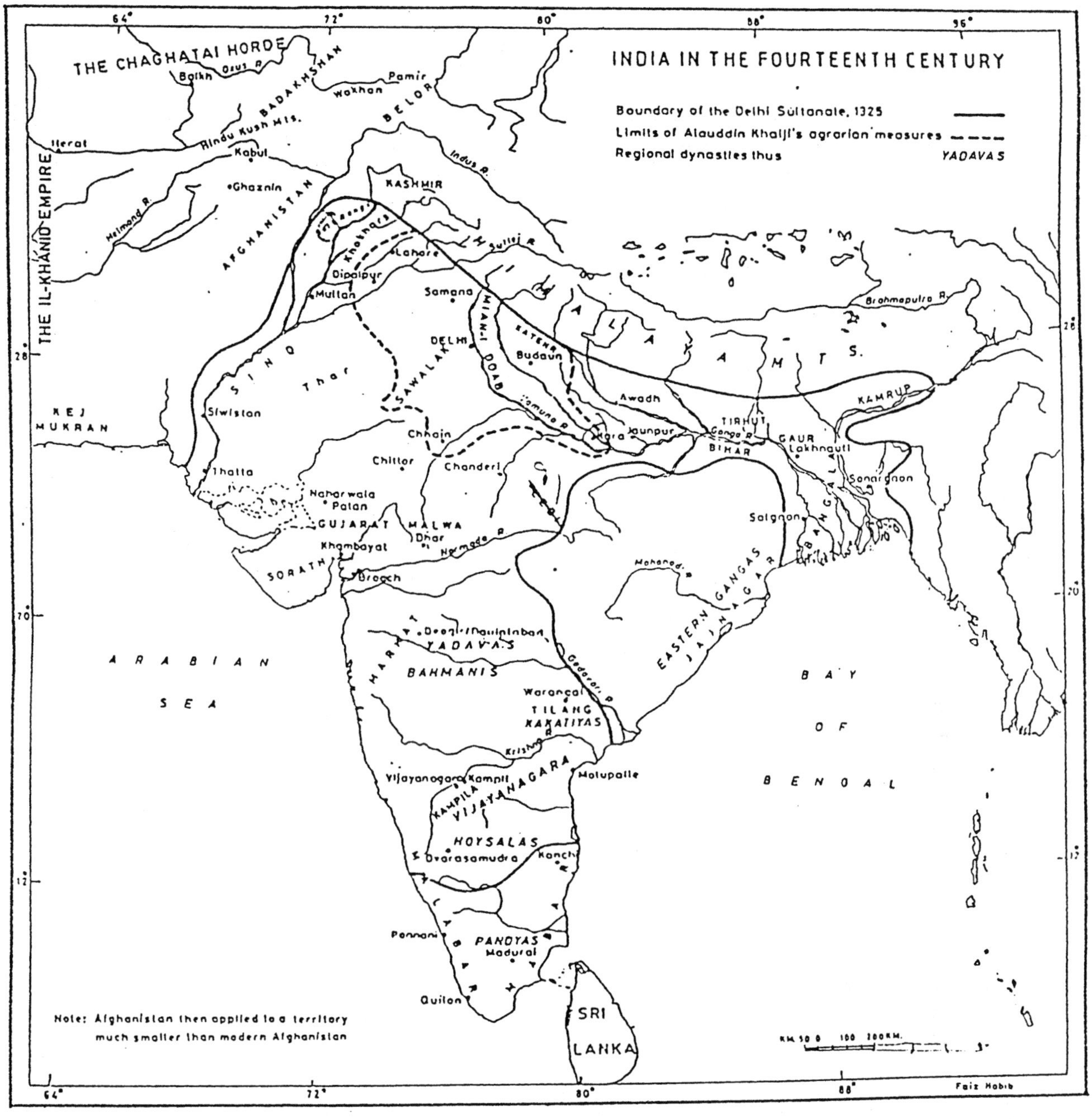

Map 23 India in the fourteenth century (map drawn by Habib, F.).

labour might have helped to circumvent the lack of availability of caste labour for new or expanding crafts, but the way that Hindū masons have left their marks, inscriptions and graffiti on important 'Saracenic' monuments that they helped to build shows that it was not long before many caste labourers too adapted themselves to the use of new techniques.

It is not easy to characterize the social formation that existed during the thirteenth–fifteenth centuries in terms of designations and definitions available in historical theory. The urban expansion, larger use of money and increase in trade distinguish it fundamentally from 'Indian feudalism'. The tax-rent equivalence suggests kinship with Marx's 'Asiatic Mode', provided that one is ready to ignore some other aspects postulated for the latter, such as tax payment mainly in kind and unstable towns. The two centuries, in fact, were marked by a shift to the cash nexus and saw much urban growth. It may therefore be safer at present to avoid a definite name for the Indian medieval formation.

TECHNOLOGY

Agriculture

As the number of crops cultivated by the Indian peasant grew in ancient times, with two major harvests within the year over most of India, irrigation became an increasingly important element of agricultural technology. Central India and the peninsula are eminently suitable for reservoirs created by embankments thrown across gorges or narrow outlets in hilly and undulating terrain. In the millennium *c.* 600–1500, India became one of the great zones of tank irrigation. Ruins of the great reservoir of Bhoja in central India (eleventh century) or the one at Madag in Karnataka (fifteenth century) show what immense works could be attempted. In the latter, one of the three earthen embankments was 260 m thick at the base and 30 m high, designed to fill a lake 18–26 km long, with single stones of 20 tonnes each to support platforms over gigantic sluices. The Grand Anicut, a masonry dam over 300 m long, up to 20 m thick and 6 m high, to take off irrigation canals from the Kaveri, was built under the Great Chōlas (eleventh century) or a little later.

In the north Indian plains, the expertise to excavate long canals from rivers which it was not yet possible to dam seems to have developed late. However, Fīrūz Tughluq (r. 1351–1388) was able to construct a network of canals from the Sutlej, Ghaggar and Kali rivers. He dug two canals from the Yamuna to form the predecessor of the modern West Yamuna Canal.

Much of India's irrigation was and still is derived from tapping underground water through wells. Oxen were used to draw up leather buckets by a rope over a pulley-wheel. In order to give a continuous flow, Indians made use of the *noria*, the *araghaṭṭa* of ancient texts. By the sixth century, the potgarland began to be hung over the well-wheel. When pin-drum gearing arrived from West Asia during *c.* 1200–1500, the well-wheel could at last be turned by cattle, and the *sāqiya* (the 'Persian wheel') was now employed all over north-western India.

References to the draw-bar, by which cattle could be made to move in circles to carry out threshing, or work the oil-mills and sugar-cane mills (and later on the *sāqiya*) have not been traced in early texts, and it is possible that its arrival in India from either the Mediterranean world or China is to be dated not much earlier than AD 700, whereafter references to threshing through circular treading have been found (Gopal, 1963–1964: p. 56).

Archaeologists have unearthed stills in Gandhāra (north-west Pakistan) in the early centuries of the Christian era, but more sophisticated devices of liquor distillation seem to have arrived from West Asia by the late thirteenth century. Stills (*bhaṭṭīs*) were now set up in towns and villages around Delhi to make liquor out of sugar syrup. By the fifteenth century, rice and coconut juice (toddy) were being distilled to yield strong liquor in Bengal.

Although India has an ancient history of wild and semi-domesticated silks (*eri*, *muga*, *tasar*), proper sericulture was not practised until the time of the Bengal sultanate (fifteenth century). Whether the art was learned directly from China or from Iran is not clear, but within two further centuries, Bengal had become one of the great silk-exporting regions of the world.

Crafts

In its major craft industry, cotton textiles, India has precedence over others in two devices: the worm-geared cotton gin for separating the seed from the fibre, illustrated in Ajanta frescoes (sixth century); and the bow scutch for separating the fibres themselves, mentioned in the *Jātakas* (early centuries AD). The latter device was adopted in the Islamic world (eleventh century) and reached Western Europe by the early fifteenth century.

In spinning however, India did not add anything to the almost universal whorl-and-spindle manipulated by the spinner's fingers. The crucial invention of the spinning wheel belonged to China (first century AD). This had arrived in India through Central Asia and Iran by the mid-fourteenth century and was then rapidly diffused. The corresponding improvement in weaving was secured by the addition of treadles to the loom, another early Chinese invention which is first described in India in 1468–1469.

Although ancient clay blocks have been found in India, it is not certain that these were used for printing cloth; and literary evidence for the practice is still lacking until we come to the fourteenth century, when the occurrence of words like *chhīpa* (cloth printer) and *chhāpa* (to stamp) in the context of textiles firmly attest to its presence. The art spread rapidly, and by the sixteenth century printed 'chintz' (*chhīnṭ*) had become a major variety of Indian textiles.

A totally new craft, which came inexplicably late, was paper manufacture. Why Indians continued with palm leaf, bark and cloth as writing materials when they could see Chinese like Yijing (in India, 671–695) using paper is hard to imagine. Paper manufacture is, however, attested in Delhi in the thirteenth century; in the fourteenth, it had become so cheap as to be used as a sweetmeat seller's packing material.

In metallurgy, the technique of tin-coating (*qala'ī*) came in the fourteenth–fifteenth centuries. This technique enabled the cheaper copper vessels to be used as cooking utensils and food containers instead of the more expensive bronze and brass vessels. India has a place in the early history of zinc separation: the metal had begun to be isolated by distillation at Zawar (Rajasthan) by the fourteenth century (Ambers and Bowman, 1994: pp. 107–109).

With the thirteenth century, a major transformation of techniques took place in the building industry. Ancient Indian stone and brick architecture had been almost wholly trabeate down to the thirteenth century. The structures were roofed by beams set on pillars or by sloping walls making towers. Such architecture demanded the use of larger stone blocks for larger buildings and discouraged the use of bricks, especially since mortar/cement was not used. But with the sultanate came the arch, vault and dome and the use of gypsum-and-lime mortar and of brick and rubble. This represented a wholesale change not only for monumental or public structures but also for middle-class urban housing and marketplaces.

Transport and navigation

The only camel depicted in ancient India was the two-humped Bactrian species, which could not serve in warmer climates. The one-humped dromedary is first referred to by Xuanzang in his account of Sind in the 640s (Watters, 1905: II, p. 252). The Arab invaders (early eighth century) also brought other breeds of the dromedary with them, and henceforth the animal became the mainstay of transport and draught work in north-western India. A herd of these camels is depicted in the Mandor frieze (twelfth century).

In navigation, the astrolabe (and sundial) must have made a considerable difference, since these instruments were not in use in India in pre-Islamic times. By the thirteenth century, the Chinese magnetic compass (needle floating on water) was also in use in the 'Indian seas'.

Military technology

The disappearance of the horse-drawn chariot as the principal element in the army appears to have become an established fact by the seventh century. This was accompanied by a growing emphasis on cavalry, as can be seen from the increasing frequency of the horseman's appearance in Indian sculpture. Yet the saddle which made possible the horseman's triumph in Europe in the early centuries of the Christian era, took a long time to come to India. Tenth-century sculptures at Khajuraho, despite numerous depictions of horsemen, fail to show the 'raised and concave saddle', though a stray piece of sculpture of about the same date does show it (Prakash, 1967: p. 88).

The diffusion of the iron stirrup was equally slow. It is not detected in a number of sculptured figures of horsemen, such as at Kanauj (ninth century), Bhubaneshwar (early eleventh), and Mandor (twelfth). A broad (wooden?) stirrup appears in Khajuraho sculptures (tenth century?), and a (leather?) ring-stirrup on the celebrated Konarak horseman (*c.* 1250). In Hoysala sculpture (twelfth–thirteenth centuries), the stirrup is universal but of leather and wood, only rarely of iron (Deloche: 1989, p. 31). The iron stirrup on the other hand, seems, to have been universal in the cavalry of the sultans' armies (thirteenth century onwards).

The third principal invention for cavalry, the horseshoe, also seems to have come with the Ghaznavid armies. It spread slowly; in the 1290s, Marco Polo reported that there were no farriers in south India to shoe imported horses (Yule and Cordier, 1921: II, p. 340).

The three cavalry inventions led to the mounted archer becoming the mainstay of the armies of the sultans. But the horseman's transformation from lancer to bowman proved even slower for the traditional Indian armies, as can be seen from the Hoysala sculptures, and it was only in the fifteenth century that the Vijayanagara emperors began to enroll mounted archers.

The Arabs invading Sind (712–714) made use of the recently discovered Greek fire (naphtha) and of ballistic missiles (*manjanīq*), which continued to be employed in the sultanate armies. Saltpetre-based pyrotechnic devices arrived from China *c.* 1400, and, in the fifteenth century, gun-powder-driven rockets were being used in the Deccan and possibly northern India (Khan, 1977: pp. 20–29). Bābur was to use guns and muskets with deadly effect at Pānīpat in 1526: the major agent of transmission here was the Ottoman Empire.

SCIENCE

The Indian tradition, 600–1200

It rarely happened in pre-modern times that a scientific theory was first developed in philosophical speculations and then used in practical applications affecting ordinary life. Yet in the development of zero and the decimal place-value system of numerals in India, the theoreticians' concepts seem to have been framed long before the beginning of our period (Sarma: 1992, pp. 400–405), while the actual use of such numerals in common writing and counting came only in the sixth century or later.

The earliest use of the place-value system in Indian inscriptions is found in the Mankani plates from Gujarat dated 346 in decimal notation (AD 595–596). The next certain reading occurs in an inscription in central India, similarly dated 849 (AD 791–792). In the ninth century, these numerals became general in inscriptions all over India. Zero appears as a dot in an eighth-century plate and as a fully drawn circle in plates of AD 870 and 876. Both place-values and zero have been found in Sanskrit or Sanskritic inscriptions in South-East Asia as early as the seventh century.

The Indian notational system was known in China by 718; and in the Islamic world, al-Khwārizmī (*c.* 825) gave an early exposition of it. In Western Europe, it came into use in the thirteenth century. What it has contributed to ease of counting the world over, with all the momentous consequences for commerce and science, hardly needs to be underlined.

The Indian decimal notation was itself the creation of a mathematical tradition of great vigour. It reached its high-water mark with Brahmagupta (b. 598) and his *Brāhmasphuṭa-siddhānta* (628). The level of mathematical advance is indicated by the subjects that this work covers: 'square and cube roots, rule of three, interest, progressions, geometry, including treatment of the right-angled triangle and the elements of the circle, elementary mensuration of solids, shadow problems, negative and positive quantities, cipher, surds, simple algebraic identities, indeterminate [and simple] equation of the first and second degrees' (Keith, 1920: p. 524). In many of these fields, Indian mathematicians (and in some of them, Brahmagupta alone) are not known to have had any predecessors.

Subsequent Indian writers enlarged on the earlier work. Algebraic signs (for example, for zero, *x*, and negative) appear in the Bakhshali Manuscript (seventh century) (Hayashi, 1985). Mahāvīra (*c.* 850) takes up a number of complex problems relating to interest. Bhāskara II (b. 1114) was the author of the *Līlāvatī*, a very systematic work on arithmetic, and the *Bījagaṇita*, on algebra. In the latter, he anticipates 'the modern theory of the sign convention' and works out the cyclic method (*chakravala*) of solving the Pellian equations $Nx^2 + 1 = y^2$, $Nx^2 + c = y^2$, recognized as a notable advance in the history of the theory of numbers (Sen in Bose, *et al.*, 1979: p. 169). Like Mahāvīra, he was also aware of the problem of square roots of negative numbers. Much of Indian mathematics, notably in the realm of extraction of square and cube roots, trigonometry and algebra, reached the Arabic world between the eighth and eleventh centuries and thence travelled to medieval Europe.

While the impetus behind mathematical research came mainly from problems of ordinary life, Āryabhaṭa I in his *Āryabhaṭīya* (499) had extended the mathematical method to solve problems of astronomy, which he put in an epicyclic mould. Varāhamihira (sixth century), author of the *Pañchasiddhāntika* and the *Bṛihatsaṁhitā*, followed Āryabhaṭa in supporting the true explanation of lunar and solar eclipses.

Brahmagupta was more systematic and comprehensive than his predecessors in the treatment of astronomical and mathematical themes in his *Brāhmasphuṭa-siddhānta* (628). He has, however, undermined his reputation by criticizing Āryabhaṭa for both his famous assertion of the Earth's daily rotation around its axis and his scientific explanation of the eclipses. In a later work, the *Khaṇḍakhādyaka* (665), Brahmagupta concentrates on simplifying and improving astronomical calculations while largely adopting Āryabhaṭa's system. Both his works passed into Arabic as *Sindhind* and *Arkand* in the eighth century and played their part in transmitting Indian astronomical theories to the Islamic world. The classical Arabic work in which the Indian astronomical tradition was critically described and analysed is al-Bīrūnī's *Kitāb al-Hind* (*c.* 1035); here too Brahmagupta is the last major authority used (Sachau, 1910).

A considerable amount of astronomical work was still done after Brahmagupta. Particularly noteworthy is the contribution of Bhāskara II, whose *Siddhāntaśiromaṇi* (1150) deals extensively with epicyclic–eccentric theories of planetary motions.

It is not clear how much of the literature of Indian medicine (*Ayurveda*) survives from the centuries before 600 without having undergone revision. That most of the traditional schools, with their texts, had already formed is, however, indicated by the Bower Manuscript (fourth century).

Our own period saw medical works appearing in considerable profusion. In the seventh century came the compendium of eight topics of medicine, the *Ashṭāṅgasaṁgraha* of Vāgbhaṭa, followed by the *Ashṭāṅgahṛidayasaṁhitā* of another Vāgbhaṭa. A very influential work on diagnosis and pathology, the *Rugviniśchaya*, was written in the ninth century by Mādhavakara. About the same time, Dṛiḍhabala revised and enlarged the *Charaka-saṁhitā*. Other compilations followed, notably the *Chikitsāsāra-saṁgraha*, a treatise on therapeutics by Chakrapāṇidatta (*c*. 1060).

An important feature of *Ayurveda* is its insistence on medication and abstinence, and recognition of elementary surgical practice. It also developed a fairly elaborate code of ethics for the physician. Superstition appears to have played little part in its substantive content.

Translations of both Suśruta and Charaka *Saṁhitās* appeared in Arabic by the ninth century, and *Ayurveda* was partly absorbed into Arabic medicine, the core of which nevertheless remained Greek. In South-East Asia, too, the *Saṁhitā* of Suśruta is referred to in a Campuchean inscription of the ninth century.

If astronomy was fuelled, in part, by astrological superstitions, alchemical beliefs (*rasavidya*) similarly led to chemical investigations. The urge to obtain the elixir of life was central to Indian alchemy, and mercury was the principal metal studied. Most of the *rasa* texts appear to have been written from the ninth century onwards, the *Rasaratnākara* of Nāgarjuna being assigned to that century.

From an early date, Sanskrit literature contains references to *yantras* or mechanical devices, real as well as mythical, but theoretical interest in technology was never strong in ancient India. Bhoja's *Samarāṅgaṇasūtradhāra* (eleventh century) is, therefore, a rare exception. Unfortunately, the mechanical devices described are largely fanciful, and the mechanical and chemical principles by which they were to work are often left obscure.

Interaction with Arabic–Persian sciences, 1200–1500

When *c*. 1035 Abū Rayḥān al-Bīrūnī (b. 973) in Lahore (Pakistan) wrote his celebrated study of Indian sciences, religion and customs, he brought to bear an unmatched rationality of approach and critical apparatus, creating truly 'a moment in history'. But within the next two centuries, a transformation had taken place within Islam, in which rationalism and science began to be looked at with increasing hostility, as in the writings of al-Ghazālī (d. 1111).

This ideological change must be borne in mind when we consider the consequences of the diffusion of Arabic and Persian learning in northern India after the Ghōrid conquests (*c*. 1200). Access to the massive richness of Arabic science was now achieved, but under increasing intellectual and religious constraints. The famous mystic Niẓāmu'ddīn of Delhi (d. 1324) denounced as heretical the scientists' assertion of planetary movements being self-propelled, and the historian Ẓiyā Baranī (1357) attacked the views of Muḥammad Tughluq (r. 1324–1351), who held the products of reason (*ma'qūl*) to be superior to the dictates of the sacred texts (*manqūlāt*), and kept company with scientists and philosophers.

It is, therefore, not surprising that little fundamental work in science was produced in India during the thirteenth–fifteenth centuries. The two areas in which most interest was shown were astronomy and medicine.

In astronomy, Amīr Khusraw is remarkable in declaring that the Earth rotates from west to east and revolves around the Sun (Siddiqui, 1994). Astrolabes and other observational instruments developed by Arab and Persian scientists began to be used; and Fīrūz Tughluq (r. 1351–1388) established an observatory at Delhi. Here the use of the Indian water clock (*ghaṛīāla*) was a significant addition to the mainly exotic instrumentation based on principles of the astrolabe.

In medicine, there was a recognizable attempt to use both the Graeco-Arabic and Indian systems. In the sultans' capital, Delhi, Milhaṇa (thirteenth century) wrote a notable work in Sanskrit on Ayurvedic therapeutics, the *Chikitsāmṛita*. Baranī mentions prominent Ayurvedic practitioners in Delhi in the early fourteenth century. When Maḥmūd Khajī built a hospital in Mandu (Madhya Pradesh, India) in 1442–1443, he ordered that medicines should be procured as were prescribed by both 'Islamic' and 'Brahmanical' physicians (Shihāb-Ḥakīm, 1968: p. 64). Finally, in 1512–1513, Bhuwah wrote in Persian the *Ma'dan-i Shifā'-i Sikandarshāhī*, a compilation based on all the major Ayurvedic texts in Sanskrit, the most important of which (Suśruta, Charaka) Bhuwah names in his preface.

RELIGION

The triumph of Brahmanism, 600–1200

When the Chinese monks Xuanzang (Yuan Chwang) (602–664) and Yijing (I-tsing) (635–713) visited India, Buddhism, in both its early Theravāda and later Mahāyāna forms, maintained a still strong presence. However, by the eleventh century, al-Bīrūnī could write about it only from hearsay. The evidence of the epigraphic record of donations to religious establishments and individuals and the evidence of the remains of religious structures is even more emphatic. At every level, it points to an increasing prosperity of the Brahmans and their cults, and to the decline of Buddhism.

One of the strengths of Brahmanism was undoubtedly its claim to lay down the social laws and ritual for the laity as part of the *dharmaśāstra*, in which Buddhism offered little or no competition. The basic texts of this law (*smṛitis*) continued to be composed until the beginning of our period, the last being that of Bṛihaspati, datable to the sixth or seventh century. Our period was mainly that of commentaries and compendia. The *smṛiti* of Nārada was commented upon by Asahāya (eighth century) and Yājñavalkya by Vijñāneśvara (eleventh). One of the earliest compendia is the *Smṛitikalpataru* of Lakshmīdhara (early twelfth century). These works prescribed for the caste system its religious basis as well as specific rites and rules. Although theory or prescription could differ considerably from actual practice, the connection of Brahmanism with the caste system always remained close and unshakable.

The other important aspect of Brahmanism, giving it an increasing space in the popular mind, was *bhakti* or devotionalism. Vaishṇavism had, by 600, developed a system in which Vishṇu could be conceived of as God, while his incarnations, especially as Kṛishṇa–Vāsudeva, could call forth a fervour of emotional attachment through devotional lore and the worship of his image. The growth of the cult can be seen in inscriptions from the fourth century onwards. Already in the eleventh century, al-Bīrūnī recognized a firm monotheism here, and, remarkably enough, could already see in the Bhagavad Gītā the central philosophical and moral text of Hinduism (Sachau, 1910: I, pp. 27–44). In the south, Vaishṇavism developed a distinct devotional cult, led by the Alvārs (sixth–ninth centuries), who sang in Tamil. These had successors in the Āchāryas, the first being Nāthmuni (tenth century). The personal divinity of Kṛishṇa, and the love that he ignited in the devotee, inspired one of the greatest creations of the Sanskrit language, Jayadeva's *Gīta-Govinda* (late twelfth century).

The cult of Śiva, as Supreme Creator and Destroyer, with his spouse, Pārvatī, representing energy, continued to be a rival to Vaishṇavism within the Brahmanical fold. It tended to assume diverse forms: there was, first, the orthodox or Purānic Śaivism. Outside of it the older worship of Śiva as *Paśupati* (Lord of Animals) became increasingly popular. In the south, the Nāyanārs (seventh–ninth centuries) gave a theistic thrust to Śiva worship and in their devotional songs made the spiritual path open to all, irrespective of caste. Śaivism too thus tended to develop its own *bhakti* tradition.

From a very early period, Śaivism provided in Pārvatī/Durgā, the female principle of creation, the fountain-head of Tantrism. A large body of Śiva worshippers followed the *Āgamas*, texts which, composed from the fifth century onwards, showed distinct Tantric influences. These were followed by the *Yamalas* (sixth–tenth centuries), evidencing a new pantheon in which various goddesses (for example, Kālika, Kāli) represented aspects of *śakti*, power or energy. The esoteric nature of many Tantric rites tended to conceal or overwhelm some of the higher ethical and moral elements, which the Tantric texts also extol (Avalon, 1952).

This was also a rich period for Brahmanical philosophical thought. The *Mīmāṅsā*, concerned essentially with a defence of Vedic ritual and practical prescriptions, had its spokesman in Kumārila (*c*. 700), who criticized Buddhist claims to knowledge while deriding the concept of illusion. The *Sāṁkhya* philosophy, which rested on a recognition of duality between matter and soul, and of the autonomous working of the transmigration of souls, received an exposition from Vāchaspati Miśra (*c*. 850) in his *Sāṁkhyatattvakaumudī*.

The most celebrated philosopher of this period was Śaṅkarāchārya (*c*. 750), who totally recast the tradition of the *Vedānta* (going back to the *Upanishads*), with its numerous contradictory speculations, into a single consistent system based on premises of the reality of non-duality (*advaita*) and the illusion of duality (*māyā*). To Śaṅkara, knowledge was everything, since the reality of God (*Brahman*) could only be grasped through it. *Karman* (works) was useful only for the empirical world. By setting forth a higher pantheism for knowledge and a lower level of illusion for practical conduct, Śaṅkarāchārya was able to reconcile his highest truth with all the multiplicity of beliefs and ritual of orthodox Brahmanism. He thus provided an ideological framework for 'a unity in diversity' with whose aid medieval and modern Hinduism could evolve into a single, increasingly monotheistic religion. Śaṅkara wrote a *bhāshya* or commentary on the *Brahma Sūtra* and various commentaries on the *Upanishads*. In spite of the efforts attributed to Śaṅkara and his disciples to promote his teaching, it naturally took time before his thought could gain a universal presence in India. His doctrine spread in northern India probably only in the fifteenth and sixteenth centuries.

The most influential onslaught on Śaṅkara's reading of *Vedānta* came from Rāmānuja (d. 1137), like him a southerner. He argued in *Vedāntasāra* and other works in favour of the separate existence of souls and for the achievement of perpetual bliss through *bhakti*, or devotion to the deity. He established a Vaishṇavite tradition, in which he was followed by Madhva (twelfth century), who asserted five fundamental 'dualisms' (*dvaita*), and by Vallabha (1376–1430), who combined monism with *bhakti*, and so heavily stressed the position of the preceptor of the devotee as to make him divine.

As for Buddhism, both its major components, the Theravāda and the Mahāyāna, were affected by its decline. Within the Mahāyāna School, which incorporated the concept of grace within an essentially non-theistic religion, Tantric tendencies began to develop, marked by an emphasis on the efficacy of *mantras* (incantations), *mudras* (finger positions) and rites. The principles are already present in the *Guhyasamāja* and *Mañjuśrīmūlakalpa* (sixth century). The cult of the Bodhisattva Avalokiteśvara, made into a divine personage, and his consort *Tārā*, the goddess of compassion, became increasingly popular. This Tantra-influenced Mahāyāna was to be the source of the later, Tibetan Buddhism.

Numerically small as the Jains were, their literary and cultural contributions in our period were considerable. Jain philosophy, in which the unity of change and permanence was strongly stressed, had its prolific spokesmen in Haribhadra (eighth century) and Hemachandra (d. 1172).

While the Brahmanical schools, the Buddhist sects and the Jains pursued different beliefs, they generally coexisted peaceably. Since, in this period, Sanskrit was the language they used most, they belonged to the same tradition of higher learning and thought. In spite of this common tradition, higher education was largely transmitted through sectarian religious institutions. Of these institutions, the Buddhist monastery of Nalanda, especially described by Xuanzang (*c*. 640), was the most highly reputed. It contained 'some thousands' of scholars, 'several hundreds being highly esteemed and famous' (Watters, 1905: II, pp. 164–170). This great monastic university lasted until well into the thirteenth century, surviving various political upheavals, including apparently a massacre by Muḥammad Bakhtyār Khaljī around 1200.

After Islam

Sind and southern Panjab passed into the control of the Umayyad caliphate in 712–714; and this marked the beginning of a substantive Muslim presence in India. Muslim merchants also settled in various ports on the western coast, especially in Gujarat and Kerala. Lahore under the Ghaznavids (eleventh and twelfth centuries) became an important Muslim settlement. With the Ghōrid conquests and the Delhi sultanate, Muslim communities appeared all over northern India during the thirteenth century. A similar process took place in the Deccan north of the Tungabhadra River in the fourteenth century, the faith, so to speak, following the flag.

By 1200, orthodox Islamic theology, with the *'ulamā'* or *dānishmands* (scholars) as spokesmen, had largely made peace with mysticism, whose votaries were the *ṣūfīs* or dervishes. The *ṣūfīs* ordinarily respected the domain of theology, just as the *'ulamā'* tolerated the *ṣūfīs'* practice of total subservience to the *pīr* or teacher, although *samā'*, the public recitation of love poetry addressed to God, still caused disputation.

Already a major work in Persian on mysticism, the *Kashfu'l-Maḥjūb*, had been written at Lahore in the late eleventh century by 'Alī Hujwīrī. In the thirteenth and fourteenth centuries, the Suhrawardī 'chain' (*silsila*) of mystics in Multan and the Chishtī in Delhi became very influential. The Chishtī *shaykh* Niẓāmu'ddīn offered a classical exposition of Ṣūfīsm of the pre-pantheistic phase in his conversations (1307–1322) recorded in the *Fawā'idu l-Fuwād*.

Ṣūfīsm began to turn pantheistic only when the ideas of Ibn al-'Arabī (d. 1240) began to arrive, first through the Persian poetry of Rūmī (1207–1273) and Jāmī (1414–1492), and then through the endeavours of Ashraf Jahāngīr Simnānī (early fifteenth century). It is remarkable that this wave of qualified pantheism should have begun to dominate Indian Islamic thought at about the same time that the pantheism of Śaṅkarāchārya's *Vedānta* was attaining increasing influence within Brahmanical thought. The identity of the two trends was at last explicitly recognized by Jahāngīr (1864: p. 176) early in the seventeenth century.

An important aspect of Islam in India was its very early appreciation of a long-term coexistence with Hinduism. The conqueror Mu'izzu'ddīn of Ghōr (d. 1206) had the image of the goddess Lakshmī stamped on some of his gold coins. Under the Delhi sultans, although Muslims dominated the upper levels of the nobility, the rural potentates remained mostly Hindu, and in the fourteenth century, Hindus were appointed governors and commanders. This attitude was reciprocated. Muslims served as officers and soldiers in the Vijayanagara Empire, and when Rānā Kumbha built his famous Victory Tower at Chittor in the fifteenth century, he took care to have the sculptured Hindu pantheon of deities surmounted by the name 'Allāh' carved many times in excellent Arabic calligraphy.

The question has often been raised as to how far Islam influenced developments of certain beliefs in Hinduism. The presence of Islam did not help to create a monotheistic trend in Hinduism; such a trend had long existed. But it probably did help to move it to a more central position, and to dilute to that extent the influence of Sāṁkhya belief in duality. Less certain is the extent to which the theoretical religious equality within the Muslim community generated criticism of the caste system raised within Indian society. The doubt arises because social hierarchy was in practice and in law a strongly established institution among Muslims, and one searches in vain for any explicit Muslim condemnation of the caste system in this period.

There was still another plane on which the influence of Islam could be felt: the concept of religion. To Arabs and Iranians, India was originally 'Hind' and the Indians were 'Hindus'. But as Muslim communities arose in India, the name 'Hindū' came, quite naturally, to apply to Indians who were not Muslims; and all the numerous religious beliefs current in India were put in one docket by the Muslims as the beliefs of Hindus. Correspondingly, a consciousness began to take shape among the Hindus (as from the fifteenth century they also began to call themselves) of a common framework of belief: starting from the existing body of internally conflicting beliefs, there was an increasing tendency to subject them to selection, synthesis and shifts of emphasis. The transformation of the massive Brahmanical tradition into Hinduism was thus largely on its own terms, however exotic the original impetus and the name.

The compilation of certain legal and philosophical texts helped to provide the basis of such a comprehensive view of Hinduism. In jurisprudence, Mithila (northern Bihar) took the lead, with Chaṇḍeśvara's *Smṛitiratnākara* (late thirteenth century) and Vāchaspati Miśra's *Vivādachintāmaṇi* (fifteenth century). In Mādhava's *Sarvadarśanasaṁgraha* (*c.* 1375), written in south India, sixteen *daranas* or systems (including the allegedly erroneous sects of Chārvākas, Buddhists and Jains) were presented as comprising the entire range of thought and theology of what would now be called Hinduism. The sixteenth school, *Vedānta*, is significantly held to be the most perfect of all the systems.

It is not surprising that a kind of popular monotheism began to emerge. In the thirteenth century, the Vīraśaiva or Lingayat sect of Karnataka entered history with Basava (b. 1125). In his system, there is only one God (*Para Śiva*), caste distinctions are denied, women given a better status, and Brahmans no longer monopolize the priesthood. The use of the Kannada language by the Lingayat preceptors undoubtedly indicated their popular character. A parallel but less organized trend was visible in Tamil Nadu, in the compositions of the Siddhars, who sang in Tamil of one God and criticized caste, Brahmans and metempsychosis.

Two shadowy figures seem to have played a part in transmitting the southern *bhakti* and monotheism to northern India. One was the calico printer Nāmdev (d. 1350) of Maharashtra, a rigorous monotheist who opposed image worship and caste distinctions. For this reason, he was seen in later tradition as a direct forerunner of Kabīr, the famous monotheistic teacher in northern India (*c.* 1500). Even more shadowy is Rāmānand (*c.* 1450), a Brahman follower of Rāmānuja, preaching at Varanasi, who in Brahmanical tradition is turned into the preceptor of most of the leading monotheistic preachers of the early sixteenth century (including Kabīr, for whom see Vol. V of this *History*).

Another tradition which grew in influence in our period was the Siddha-nātha tradition, going back to Gorakhnāth (tenth–eleventh century?) and earlier. It combined various Śaivite, Śaktic and Yogic beliefs in a kind of Tantric mysticism propagated by hosts of mendicants.

LITERATURE

Languages

As in most pre-modern civilizations, the literary languages tended to be different from those that ordinary people spoke. A large number of regional languages were spoken in India, and Amīr Khusraw (d. 1325) listed twelve of them. Sanskrit, India's great classical language, evolved as the language of priests, bureaucrats and the literati and had by the seventh century largely displaced Prākrit (more closely related to ordinary people's speech) throughout the country. Sanskrit retained its dominant position as the language of literature, administration and law until the end of the twelfth century, whereafter it had to share this position with Persian. Like Sanskrit, Persian too was entirely a language of the elite in India, confined to the rulers and the educated.

Outside the southern, Dravidian zone, Prākrit (current in some identified literary languages or dialects, such as Mahārāshṭrī, Saurasenī and Māgadhī) continued a fitful existence, being used mainly by the Jains. At the same time, a new species of literary language, termed Apabhraṁśa, appeared in recognizable forms by the sixth century out of mixtures of regional vernaculars with Prākrits and Sanskrit.

Modern regional languages have been traced to some literary fragments, originally datable to the twelfth century, in the case of Bengali, Oriya and Gujarati, and possibly Hindi (or rather one of the dialects which modern Hindi has supplanted and incorporated), and the thirteenth, in that of Marathi. The full-blown literatures of these languages, however, belong to a much later period.

Developments in the south were notably different. Tamil first appears in inscriptions around the time of Christ and afterwards in the *Sangam* texts as a literary language. In our period, it largely maintained its position, although Sanskrit tended to be the language of the priesthood and formal documents. The first inscription in Kannada belongs to the sixth or seventh century. Literature in Telugu has been traced to the eleventh century. Malayalam, the fourth major Dravidian language, achieved a firm literary status, distinct from Tamil, in the fifteenth century.

Sanskrit literature

But for the towering figure of Kālidāsa (*c.* 400), the 600 years, 600–1200, could be deemed to form the richest period of Sanskrit literature (see Plates 100, 101, 102).

At about AD 600 are placed a number of important Sanskrit writers, although the precise chronology of individual texts is often hard to determine. Bhartṛihari gave the last great exposition of Sanskrit grammar in his *Vākyapadīya* and was the author of three collections of lyrics and gnomic verse (*śatakas*). Daṇḍin wrote a grand romance, the *Daśakumāracharita,* the tales of ten princes as told by them, and a work on the science of poetics, the *Kāvyādarśa.* Subandhu's *Vāsavadattā* is another long romance, the style more complex and difficult than that of Daṇḍin.

But there is perhaps no more difficult an author than Bāṇa (*c.* 640). His *Harshacharita* is at once a romance and the biography of his royal patron, Harsha. His use of alliteration, words with double meanings and sonorous sounds made him a model for future writers, to the doubtful advantage of the language. The *Kādambarī*, Bāṇa's other famous work, is a narrative containing tales within tales. In spite of the complexity of his style and diction, Bāṇa has a sure sense of characterization and a capacity for portraying emotion and describing nature.

The first great extant dictionary in Sanskrit, the *Amarakośa* of Amarasiṁha, probably belongs to the eighth century. Vāmana (late eighth century) in his *Kāvyālaṁkāra* refined earlier ideas on poetry with his doctrine of *rīti* or style; he was followed by Bhāmaha, author of a work of the same title, but with a different categorization and allowances of weight to figures and qualities. The controversy as to whether sentiment or suggestion is the soul of poetry became important with the doctrine of *dhvani* found in Ānandavardhana of Kashmir (*c.* 850).

Bilhaṇa of Kashmir (late eleventh century), author of the *Vikramāṅkadevacharita,* a historical epic, is important in being the forerunner of India's first true historian, Kalhaṇa, the author of *Rājataraṅgiṇī* (1149), the annals of the rulers of Kashmir. Kalhaṇa's history becomes fairly accurate from about 850. Kalhaṇa has henceforward no heroes; he is able to analyse characters and circumstances and bring out denouements in a manner unsurpassed in Indian literature, except perhaps for Ẓiyā' Baranī (fl.1350).

The *Pañchatantra* 'animal tales', originating from India, became part of world literature. An early version of these was rendered into Pahlavi in the sixth century, and they were translated thence into Arabic by 750 under the title *Kalīla wa Dimna* (see Plates 210–211), from which other language versions came to be derived. But the further construction of these amoral didactic fables continued in India with the *textus simplicior* made in *c.* 1100. From this came Pūrṇabhadra's version (1199), while Nārāyaṇa's *Hitopadeśa* (eleventh–twelfth centuries), compiled in Bengal, is another version of the *Pañchatantra.*

It may be fitting to close this account of the late ancient phase of Sanskrit literature with Jayadeva (*c.* 1175), whose *Gītā Govinda* sings of Lord Kṛishṇa, Rādhā and the herdswomen (*gopīs*). Given the form of a dance-drama, its language, music, originality and spirit of devotion make it an inimitable achievement.

The establishment of the sultanates 'did not materially affect Sanskrit literature' (Mehendale and Pusalker, 1960: p. 464) – an important point to remember in considering the nature of the intrusion of Islam into India. It is true, however, that the general trend in Sanskrit was now scholastic rather than creative, and the major accomplishments were in the field of religion and law, as in the works of Mādhava and Vāchaspati Miśra. The influence of Arabic and Persian was yet little felt, although in the late fifteenth century, Śrīvara put the story of Yusuf and Zulaikhā in the form of a traditional Sanskrit love lyric, the last canto being dedicated to Śiva.

Persian

Persian literature came to India with its classic forms of poetry and traditions of prose already well formed. India for its part, also made important contributions to Persian literature.

The major figure in Persian poetry in our period was Amīr Khusraw (1253–1325), a poet who could rise to great lyrical heights in his *ghazals*. He could also affect all kinds of artificial prose, as in his *I'jāz-i Khusrawī*. He wrote five *maṣnawīs* (or *mathnawī-s*) or romances in rhymed couplets (*Panj Ganj,* 'The Five Treasures'), and a contemporaneous historical romance, the *Dewal Rānī Khiẓr Khānī*. His numerous metrical and prose historical works included the *Khazā'inu'l-Futūḥ* ('Treasures of Victories') and the *Nuh Sipihr* ('Nine Spheres'), containing the annals of sultans 'Alāu'ddīn Khaljī (1296–1316) and Quṭbu'ddīn Mubārak Khaljī (1316–1320). It could be argued that Amīr Khusraw wrote too much and that his views often shifted with those of his patrons; but his merits are still many. Of Turkish origin, he was India's first patriotic poet in Persian: in the *Nuh Sipihr,* he extols its climate, its languages, notably Sanskrit, its learning, its arts, its music, its people, even its animals.

Another branch in which Persian literature flowered in India was history. Two works stand out: Minhāj Sirāj's *Ṭabaqāt-i Nāṣirī* (1259–1260) and Ẓiyā' Baranī's *Tārīkh-i Fīrūz Shāhī* (1357). Minhāj's work is formally a world history but is remarkable for its detailed biographical notices of contemporary nobles and its information on the Mongols. Baranī is not only an annalist but also possesses a theory of history of his own, involving a triangle of conflict and adjustment between despotic monarchy, the established nobility and low-class upstarts. His powerful prose, simple and fluent, his capacity for critically portraying characters and analysing circumstances, and his conscious application of his own theory to his narrative make Baranī one of the great figures of medieval historiography. He also wrote the *Fatāwā-i Jahāndārī* on the science of statecraft.

There was much literature in the realms of theology, mysticism, law and sciences, in Persian as well as Arabic, but these mostly followed the traditional lines set in the Islamic world (see Plate 219).

Other Indian languages

This period saw the emergence as well as the disappearance of literature in Apabhraṁśa. Two works may require passing notice: the first, 'Abdu'r-Raḥmān's *Sandeśarasaka* (twelfth century), a metrical work on the separation of a woman from her beloved; and a collection of tracts written by Ṭhakkura Pherū in Delhi (1290–1320) on coinage, jewels, products and so on which form a unique literary source for economic history. Jain writing in both Apabhraṁśa and the Mahārāshṭri form of Prākrit remained considerable, one of the great names being Hemachandra (1088–1172), who also wrote profusely in Sanskrit.

Among the Indic regional literatures that emerged during this period, the earliest literary works are usually religious songs or secular ballads, first circulated by recitation and only later put into writing. In Gujarati, for example, the ballads (*rasa*) took a developed form from Vajrasena (*c.* 1170) onwards; Narasiṁha Mehta (d. 1481) composed devotional lyrics addressed to Kṛishṇa (see Plate 220).

The Dravidian languages generally exhibit a wider range in literature and greater maturity than their north Indian counterparts. This is shown by the earlier appearance of the epics in these languages. Of the *Rāmāyaṇa*, Kamban composed the Tamil version in the eleventh century; Pampā II, a Jain, the Kannada version in the twelfth or thirteenth; Ranganātha, the Telugu version in the thirteenth. In Telugu, Nanniah had begun a version of the *Mahābhārata* in the eleventh century; Villiputtūrar produced a Tamil version in the fourteenth; and Naranappa, a Kannada version in the fifteenth. Malayalam had its first possible literary text in the *Rāmacharitam*, based on the *Rāmāyaṇa*, in the fourteenth century. Besides religious and devotional poetry, there was also a certain amount of secular literature, as, for example, the humorous worldly verses (and episodes) attributed to the Tamil poet Kālamekam (fifteenth century?).

ART

Architecture

From the seventh century onwards, India witnessed the development of its classical architecture in stone. Until then, the extant architectural remains had overwhelmingly been in the form of monoliths, caves and buildings cut out of living rock. This mode of architecture continued to create its great monuments, such as Ellora and Elephanta. But the emphasis was now on stone construction.

In the fifth century, Bhitargaon in northern India had represented a possibility: a brick temple with a trabeate tower, but with a true arch over the doorway. However, it proved to represent a mere passing phase. The arch, vault and dome, as well as mortar/cement, remained strangers to Indian masons until the thirteenth century. As a result, if they built on a large scale, they had to have towering roofs, the walls tapering to meet at the top, or to have thick pillars, in order to bear the weight of heavy beams; resort had then to be made to larger and larger solid stone blocks. The inevitable effect of massiveness was relieved by a profusion of sculpture, with which these structures were increasingly endowed. The Brahmanical temple constitutes the principal product of this tradition of monumental architecture. Its sanctuary (*vimāna*) comprised the cella (*garbha gṛiha*), containing the idol or symbol of the deity and the spire (*śikhara*) over it. A pillared hall (*mandapa*) was attached to the sanctuary, sometimes with an intermediate chamber (*antarāla*), transepts and porch. Jain temples followed a similar plan.

Two styles, the so-called 'Indo-Aryan' (northern) and 'Dravidian' (southern) have been discerned within this broad tradition of temple architecture. The 'Aryan' *śikharas* are simple ribbed spires, the 'Dravidian' terraced towers; the 'Aryan' roofs tend to be flat or pyramidal, the 'Dravidian' more commonly globular (Fergusson, 1876).

Both these styles are present in early Chalukya architecture of the Deccan. At Ellora in Maharashtra was created the greatest building in India ever cut out of living rock, the Śaivite temple of Kailāśa (eighth century). Cut down vertically over a rectangular space of 100 by 60 m, the *śikharais* about 30 m high, the rock cutters followed the design of a stone-structured building with 'Dravidian' features.

At about the same time, Pallava architecture in south India also shifted from its rock-cut phase (seventh century) to the structural (eighth–ninth), both exhibiting classic 'Dravidian' elements. Of the monolithic kind are the seventeen temples (*rathas*) at Mamallapuram, south of Madras, crowned by the Shore Temple. Of the structural monuments, the most noteworthy seems to be the Kailāśanātha temple in Kanchi (*c.* 700).

The two great temples of the Chōlas, in Thanjavur (*c.* 1000) and Gangaikoṇḍacholapuram (*c.* 1025), excel all previous temples in size, the *śikhara* rising to 70 m from the base. The latter temple has also a very large, many-pillared hall (*maṇḍapa, chavadi*), a feature that was subsequently to become common.

In the final phase under the Pāṇḍyas (twelfth–fourteenth centuries) and their successors, the tendency began to enlarge the temple complex into a rectangular fort with strong walls, often concentric, enclosing open courtyards (*prakarmas*), and with massive gateways (*gopurams*) dwarfing the main shrine, as at Tiruvannamalai (*c.* 1300). These tendencies assumed their most emphatic form in the great temples of Madurai (completed seventeenth century) and Srirangam (built thirteenth–eighteenth centuries).

A different tradition within the Dravidian style is represented by the Hoysala temple architecture of the eleventh–thirteenth centuries, represented notably at Belur and Halabid. A high platform, an emphasis on horizontal divisions and the rich 'sculptured texture' of the *śikhara* are its distinctive features.

The 'Aryan' temple also had its early representatives in the Chalukya architecture at Aihole and Badami. But by the mere scale of constructional activity, Orissa took the premier position. Of the seventeen temples at Bhuwaneswar, spread over the period 750–1250, the greatest is the Liṅgarāja temple (*c.* 1000), its main large shrine surrounded by replicas, and enclosed by a solid wall (see Plate 225). The temple of Jagannāth at Puri (*c.* 1100) is of even more impressive proportions, the pyramid of its *diul* (sanctum) rising to about 70 m.

But the most striking achievement of Orissa architecture is undoubtedly the Sun temple at Konarak (the 'Black Pagoda') (*c.* 1250). Its designers saw the structure as the Sun god's chariot and added twelve giant wheels to support this illusion. The tower, whose upper portion has fallen, was extraordinarily high (75 m); and the richest sculpture was lavished on the building (see Plate 221).

A different version of the 'north Indian' style is presented by the group of Brahmanical and Jain temples at Khajuraho in central India (ninth–eleventh centuries). They attempt at grace and proportion rather than size; and rich surface treatment and sculpture of a high order contribute to their fame.

Towards the close of the twelfth century, India received a totally distinct tradition, the so-called 'Saracenic'. Its major characteristics were the use of arch, vault and dome, and the application of cement; it could achieve in consequence a lightness and grace that the earlier trabeate construction could not easily match. Its love of light and space and 'simple severity' seems to stand in sharp contrast to the 'plastic exuberance' of the Indian tradition (Chand, 1963: pp. 243–243).

The initial (thirteenth-century) phase of 'Saracenic' architecture showed the constraints that local skills placed on the exotic designs. The buildings of the Quwwatu'l-Islām Mosque (Delhi) (1190s) and Aṛhāī Din Kā Jhonpṛa (Ajmer) (early thirteenth century) thus had to erect 'false' arches and eschew true domes. Yet height could still be achieved. At an outer corner of the Quwwatu'l-Islām Mosque was built (early thirteenth century) the muezzin's tower, the famous Quṭb Mīnār (see Plate 209). Originally four-storeyed and rising to 78 m, fourteenth-century repairs made it five-storeyed, 80 m high: its height, the angular flutings, raised belts marking its storeys and the easy sloping of the tower upwards all combine to produce an impression of remarkable majesty.

The second stage arrived with the artisans' obtaining enough skill to construct the arch and the dome. The first extant true arch is found in Delhi in the tomb of Sultan Balban (d. 1287), and the first dome in the elegant 'Alā'ī Darwāza (1310).

In the first half of the fourteenth century, the city of Tughluqābād was laid out at Delhi. Here stands the tomb of Ghiyāṣu'ddīn Tughluq (d. 1324), a striking combination of red sandstone and marble, with battering walls set within a small fortress (see Plate 196). With some similarity of appearance is the mausoleum of Shāh Rukn-i 'Ālam at Multan (*c.* 1324). Under Fīrūz Tughluq (r. 1351–1388), construction on an exceptionally large scale took place at Delhi, sometimes impressive but generally utilitarian and plain. There were flashes of freshness, however, as in the arcaded terraces forming a stepped pyramid to provide a platform for the Aśokan pillar which Fīrūz had brought from near the Himalaya.

In the fifteenth century there developed a number of provincial styles, such as the Sharqī (centred at Jaunpur), Bengal (Gaur), Malwa (Mandu) and Gujarat (Ahmadabad). The Gujarat style, with its visible incorporation of elements from indigenous trabeate architecture and motifs, was to exercise considerable influence on Mughal architecture. In the peninsula, the Bahmanī architecture with its principal monuments at Gulbarga and Bidar (Karnataka) led to the later provincial styles of Golkunda and Bijapur. At Gulbarga, the Jāmi' Masjid (*c.* 1400) is remarkable for roofing an area of 10,200 m^2 aided by sixty-three small domes. Kashmir maintained an independent style of its own, based essentially on wooden construction and marked by pyramidal roofing.

It is surprising that the arcuate techniques exercised very little influence on the architecture of Vijayanagara (Karnataka) (fourteenth–sixteenth centuries). The great capital city, in its splendid religious and secular buildings, mainly follows the trabeate techniques and Dravidian style.

Sculpture

It may not perhaps be easy to name any other civilization which produced as much sculptured space in building stone as India did between 600 and 1500. Great temples were built of slabs of stone, every square inch of whose outer surfaces their builders generally sought to cover with carved figures and images. Much of the sculpture was religious in inspiration and illustrative of mythology. By *c.* 700, iconographic conventions had been strictly laid down to the utmost detail, and themes from the complex Śaivite and Vaishṇavite mythologies had fully supplanted the simpler *Jātaka* motifs of the earlier Buddhist sculpture.

That despite these constraints great art could be produced is shown pre-eminently by the sculptures at Ellora in the Brahmanical and Jain phases, such as those contained in the Kailāśa temple (eighth century). Here we have a series of justly famous sculptures: 'Śiva the ascetic', 'Śiva dancing'; 'Śiva warned by his consort Pārvatī of the demon Rāvaṇa'; and 'the river goddesses'. At Elephanta, near Bombay, among the many fine sculptures is the famous colossal image of the deity Maheśamūrti, his three heads suggesting compassion and wisdom. The effect was attained in these sculptures, as elsewhere in Indian art, by a fine delineation of posture and light touches given to eyes and lips.

In northern India, Buddhist sculpture had its last phase under the Pālas in Bengal and Bihar (eighth–twelfth centuries). This was notable for its art; but the two major traditions that have attracted the art historians' attention far more have been those of Orissa (eighth–thirteenth centuries) and Khajuraho (ninth–eleventh centuries). The panels of images and processions of figures are endless, but among them there could still be touching scenes like those of the simple Yashodhā making butter (at Bhuwaneshwar) or of a herd of deer in all their innocence (at Khajuraho). At Konarak (*c.* 1250) are examples of the sheer exhibition of power in the colossal statue of an elephant and a horse. In both Orissa and Khajuraho, free rein is given to eroticism, but neither the pornography nor the endless repetition can wholly obscure the art and skill employed (see Plates 52, 53, 100).

Such frank appeal to the sexual impulse is greatly restrained in south Indian sculpture, especially of the Śaivite tradition, but the art is marked by an increasing stiffness. However, a new dimension was given to sculpture in the south by the images made in copper and bronze, the most striking being that of the Naṭarāja, the 'Dancing Śiva' (see Plate 222).

In 'Saracenic' buildings, sculpture lost its crucial position. Only Arabic calligraphy, and geometrical and floral motifs carved on stone served to decorate the buildings. Such stone work, however, often showed great skill, and, as part of architectural design appears to reach the level of true art (see Plate 209).

Painting

The seventh century saw the last paintings put on the cave walls at Ajanta and Bagh; with them the classical period of ancient Indian painting seems to pass (see Plate 80). The 'medieval' tradition, whose early representation mingles with Ajanta survivals at Ellora (eighth–ninth centuries), is characterized by sharp lines, pointed angles, absence of colour modelling and an inclination towards variegated decoration. This 'medieval' element is stronger still in the wall paintings of south Indian temples (twelfth–fourteenth centuries) at Thanjavur and Tirumalai, among others. Finally, we have the Gujarat miniatures (beginning, *c.* 1100), usually in Jain manuscripts, where stylization reaches extremes (for example, both eyes shown in profile, one projecting) (see Plate 220).

A survival of the classical tradition, however, can be seen in the Pāla-period paintings of eastern India and Nepal, traceable in manuscripts until the thirteenth century (see Plate 101).

A tradition of wall painting, especially in private buildings, came with the Muslims. Book illustration might have received an impetus under Sino-Mongol influence from the thirteenth century onwards. A recognizable school developed in Malwa, where the manuscript of a dictionary, *Miftāḥu'l-Fuz̤alā'*, (1468–1469), was profusely illustrated: both the precision and the accuracy in these illustrations are admirable.

Music and dance

Our period saw Indian classical music and dance attain their mature forms. Indian music never developed a system of notation, so much of it had to be transmitted by vocalization, and much of its early history is therefore irretrievably lost. Important information on music is found in the *Nāṭyaśāstra* (third century?), but comprehensive texts on music came much later, such as Śarṅgadeva's *Saṁgītaratnākara* (early thirteenth century), followed by Dāmodara's *Saṁgītadarpaṇa*, and the anonymous *Ghunyatu'l-Munya* in Persian (1374–1375). The last-named work is good evidence of the patronage extended to Indian music at the sultans' courts.

The *Natyaśāstra* also laid down rules for dance (*nṛitya*). But for the physical poses and movements of Indian classical dances, our evidence comes mainly from the sculpture of our period (see Plates 222–224).

BIBLIOGRAPHY

ALI, M. A. 1990. The Medieval Civilization: Genesis and Efflorescence. Presidential Address in *Proceedings of the Indian History Congress, Gorakhpur Session, 1989–90*. Delhi.

ALTEKAR, A. S. 1956. *The Position of Women in Hindu Civilization*. Benares.

AMBERS, J.; BOWMAN, S. 1944. British Museum ^{14}C Measurements XXIII: Zawar Series, *Radiocarbon*, London, Vol. 38(1), pp. 107–109.

AVALON, A. (ed.) 1952. *Principles of Tantra*, 2nd edn. Calcutta.

BOSE, D. M.; SEN, S. N.; SUBBARAYAPPA, B. V. (eds) 1971. *A Concise History of Science in India*. New Delhi.

BROWN, P. 1951. *Indian Architecture* (Islamic Period). Bombay.

——. 1956. *Indian Architecture (Buddhist and Hindu Periods)*. Bombay.

CHAND, T. 1963. *Influence of Islam on Indian Culture*, 2nd edn. Allahabad.

CHATTOPADHYAYA, D. (ed.) 1982. *Studies in the History of Science in India*, 2 vols. New Delhi.

COOMARASWAMY, A. K. 1964. *The Arts and Crafts of India and Ceylon*, 2nd edn. New York.

DATTA, B.; SINGH, A. N. 1962. *History of Hindu Mathematics – A Source Book*. Bombay (single-volume edn).

DELOCHE, J. 1989. *Military Technology in Hoysala Sculpture*. New Delhi.

DEYELL, J. S. 1990. *Living without Silver: The Monetary History of Early Medieval India*. Delhi.

DIGBY, S. 1971. *War-Horse and Elephant in the Delhi Sultanate*. London, Oxford.

——. 1982. Contributions. In: RAYCHAUDHURI, T.; HABIB, I. (eds) *Cambridge Economic History of India*, I. London.

FERGUSSON, J. 1910. *History of Indian and Eastern Architecture*, 2nd edn. 2 vols. London.

GHOSHAL, U. N. 1929. *Contributions to the History of the Hindu Revenue System*. Calcutta.

GOPAL, L. 1963–1964. Article. In: *University of Allahabad Studies*, Ancient History Section. Allahabad.

——. 1989. *The Economic Life of Northern India, c. AD 700–1200*, 2nd (revised) edn. Delhi.

HABIB, I. 1980. Changes in Technology in Medieval India, *Studies in History*. Delhi, II(1).

——. 1982. Contributions. In: RAYCHAUDHURI, T.; HABIB, I. (eds) *Cambridge Economic History of India*, I. London.

——. 1995. *Essays in Indian History: Towards a Marxist Perception*. New Delhi.

HABIB, M.; NIZAMI, K. A. (eds) 1990. *A Comprehensive History of India*, V. New Delhi.

HAYASHI, T. 1985. *The Bakhsali Manuscript*. Rhode Island. (Ph.D. thesis, Brown University).

JAHĀNGĪR. 1864. *Tuzuk-i Jahāngīrī*. ed. Saiyid Ahmad, Ghazipur and Aligarh.

JHA, D. N. 1993. *Economy and Society in Early India*. New Delhi.

KEITH, A .B. 1920. *A History of Sanskrit Literature*. Oxford.

KHAN, I. A. 1977. Article. In: *Indian Historical Review*. Delhi, IV(1).

KOSAMBI, D. D. 1956. *An Introduction to the Study of Indian History*. Bombay.

MEHENDALE, H. A.; PUSALKER, A. D. 1960. In: MAJUMDAR, R. C. (ed.) *The History and Culture of the Indian People*, Vol. VI (*The Delhi Sultanate*). Bombay.

MORELAND, W. H. 1929. *Agrarian System of Moslem India*. Cambridge.

PRAKASH, V. 1967. *Khajuraho: a Study in the Cultural Conditions of Chandella Society*. Bombay.

QURESHI, I. H. 1942. *The Administration of the Sultanate of Delhi*. Lahore.

RAY, H. C. 1931. *The Dynastic History of Northern India*, 2 vols. Calcutta.

RAY, P. C. (ed.) 1956. *History of Chemistry in Ancient and Medieval India*. Calcutta.

SACHAU, E. C. 1910. *Alberuni's India*, 2 vols (translation). London.

SARMA, S. R. 1992. Article. In: KAPILA VATSYAYAN (ed.) *Kalātattvakośa: A Lexicon of Fundamental Concepts of the Indian Arts*. Delhi, New Delhi.

SHARMA, R. S. 1980. *Indian Feudalism, AD 300–1200*, 2nd edn. Delhi.

——. 1987. *Urban Decay in India* (*c.* 300–1000). New Delhi.

SHIHAB-HAKĪM. 1968. *Ma'āṣir-i Maḥmūd-Shāhī*. ed. Nurul Hasan Ansari, Delhi.

SIDDIQUI, I. H. 1994. Science and Scientific Instruments in the Sultanate of Delhi. Address in *Proceedings of the Indian History Congress*, 54th session (Mysore). Delhi.

STEIN, B. 1980. *Peasant State and Society in Medieval South India*. Delhi.

TAKAKUSU, J. 1896 (Translation of Yijing's I-tsing's) *A Record of the Buddhist Religion*. Oxford.

TRIPATHI, R. P. 1956. *Some Aspects of Muslim Administration*, 2nd edn. Allahabad.

WATTERS, T. 1905. *On Yuan Chwang's Travels in India, 629–645* AD, 2 vols. London.

YADAVA, B. N. S. 1973. *Society and Culture in Northern India in the Twelfth Century*. Allahabad.

YULE, H.; CORDIER, H. 1921. (Translation of) *The Book of Ser Marco Polo, the Venetian, Concerning the Kingdoms and Marvels of the East*. 2 vols. London. (Supplement, London, 1920).

25.2
SRI LANKA

Kingsley M. de Silva

Sri Lanka's close proximity to the Indian land mass made it easy for Indian influences, religious, cultural and political, to leave their stamp on the island's development over much of its long history. Equally importantly, separation from India by a narrow sea has enabled it to evolve a culture and civilization of its own, bearing the impress of its Indian origin but distinctive in its own way. The island's strategic location athwart the trade routes of the Indian Ocean brought other influences to bear upon it, primarily from South-East Asia but also from the Arab world and China (Bandaranayake *et al*, 1990: pp. 61–84, 179–190).

The history of Sri Lanka, from the seventh century to the end of the fifteenth, falls into two unequal parts. The dividing line is the thirteenth century, which marked the beginning of the collapse of Sri Lanka's irrigation civilization. The development and expansion of an intricate irrigation system was the key to the establishment, consolidation and maturation of the Sri Lankan civilization in the dry zone of the country, an extensive plain covering the northern half of the island and stretching southwards along the eastern coast to a smaller southern plain. Rice was the staple crop, but its cultivation was dependent on the vagaries of the north-east monsoon. Considerable technical expertise was required to provide and retain water in fields over long periods of time for successful rice cultivation. As settlements spread, it became necessary to insure against frequent drought. The solution devised was a highly sophisticated irrigation system remarkably attuned to the geological and geographical peculiarities of the island'. As early as the third century BC, Sri Lankan engineers had discovered the principle of the valve tower or valve pit to regulate the escape of water from man-made lakes or tanks. Some of these were of prodigious dimensions and demonstrated striking technological sophistication, as did the intricate network of canals that brought water to the fields they were designed to serve. Indeed, Sri Lanka's celebrated mastery of irrigation technology elevated it to the position of one of the great hydraulic civilizations of the ancient world.

The political system that evolved did not have the rigorous authoritarian and heavily bureaucratic structure which Karl Wittfogel, the theorist of the hydraulic civilizations, regarded as the key features of their polities. The Sri Lankan version was somewhat closer to European feudalism than to the social system of ancient China, Wittfogel's classic model of a hydraulic society. There were powerful countervailing forces in operation in Sri Lanka, including a zealously guarded particularist tradition; the influence of the *sangha* (the Buddhist order); the position of the *paramukhas* (Sanskrit 'pramukha' or chief) and the *kulina* gentry closely associated with the clan structure of Sinhalese society; and the wide diffusion of land ownership in a social structure in which the right to hold private property and to buy and sell land was securely established. Caste became, in time, the basis of social stratification. Castes had a service or occupational role as the primary distinguishing function, but in contrast to the Hindū Indian prototype, there was no religious sanction for caste in Sri Lanka's Buddhist society.

Two important nucleii of Sinhalese civilization developed in the north-central regions of the island, and control over them gave Sinhalese rulers the resources to extend their sway over the whole island during most of this period. There was a third core in Rohana, the dry zone of the south and south-east, which was settled almost simultaneously with the north-central plain. Literary sources as well as epigraphical and archaeological evidence would indicate that there were also settlements on the south-west coast, especially around some of the ports there. Despite the increase in the power of the ruler in Anuradhapura, the first of the great capital cities of ancient Sri Lanka, over the island, the problem of control over the outer provinces from the centre was just as intractable in Sri Lanka as it was in major kingdoms of the Indian subcontinent. Periodically, Rohana asserted its independence or served as a refuge for defeated Sinhalese kings or aspirants to the throne, but it was just as frequently controlled by the island's principal ruler and seems never to have rivalled the north-central region in economic power or population resources.

Buddhism, introduced to the island around the third century BC, became in time the state religion and the core of the culture and civilization of the Sinhalese. The intermingling of religion and 'national' identity has had a profound influence on the Sinhalese in generating a belief in a mission to protect and preserve Buddhism in their island home. The *sangha* became a powerful force in society, despite their sectarian disputes, and, in time, a notable restraining influence on royal authority.

Sri Lanka enjoyed enormous regional prestige as the home of Theravada Buddhism. After Buddhism virtually disappeared from its original Indian home, Sri Lanka came to be regarded by the Buddhists of Myanmar, Thailand and Cambodia as a second – almost a surrogate – holy land of Buddhism because of the relics of the Buddha preserved in the island's major centres of Buddhist worship. Sri Lanka's standing in the Buddhist world also attracted Chinese

Buddhist scholars to the island, and Chinese interest in general.

Stūpas or *chetiyas,* generally solid hemispherical domes enshrining relics of the Buddha and the more celebrated *illuminati* of early Buddhism, were among the most striking features of Sri Lanka's architecture in much of the period covered by this sub-chapter. The earliest of these were modelled on Indian prototypes, but in time they evolved a distinctive Sri Lankan style. They dominated the skyline of Anurādhapura and were awe-inspiring testimony to the state's commitment to Buddhism and evidence of the wealth at its command. Anurādhapura developed into a sprawling city and at the height of its glory was one of the great cities of ancient South Asia. The Abhayagiri, and the Jethavana in Anurādhapura, taller than the third pyramid at Gizeh in Egypt, were among the wonders of their time. The Jetavana was probably, the tallest single monument in the whole Buddhist world. The stone sculpture of the Anurādhapura kingdom included Buddha statues of various sizes, some of them exquisitely carved evocations of the concept of *samadi,* and some awe-inspiring standing Buddha images of colossal proportions, such as those at Avukana and Buduruvagala. While the Buddha image came to be regarded as a regular feature of Buddhist shrines in Sri Lanka, the moonstones, semicircular slabs richly decorated in low relief and placed at the foot of a stairway leading to major shrines, were central to the theme of worship. This motif, derived from Andhra, reached its fullest development in Sri Lanka. The earliest bronze sculptures discovered in Sri Lanka are representations of the Buddha seated in meditation. Stone played only a limited role in Sinhalese architecture and was usually restricted to ornamental details and ancillary features. But these latter have survived, while the woodwork which was the basis of Sinhalese architecture has not.

Polonnaruva, the capital in the eleventh century, was more compact but contained within its boundaries all the characteristic features of a capital city of ancient Sri Lanka, tanks, *stūpas,* palaces and parks and their architectural and sculptural embellishments. The link with South-East Asia left its mark on the architecture of some of the Buddhist monuments of that city and elsewhere.

While it is obvious that the Sri Lankan state of the period from the sixth to the thirteenth centuries would generally have had a very large agricultural surplus to invest in the establishment and growth of the large urban centres of Anurādhapura and Polonnāruva, the scale and complexity of the monuments there and the demands of the irrigation system for maintenance and expansion would appear to indicate that these agricultural surpluses on their own could not have sustained these enterprises. Quite clearly, profits from trade were large enough to supplement the agricultural surplus for these purposes. Archaeological excavations of recent times have turned up impressive evidence of the substantial regional and international trade of Sri Lanka, with its main ports and its capital city of Anurādhapura, serving as *entrepôts* in the maritime trade between China and the Arab world. These trading enterprises would have yielded large revenues to the state as well as considerable profits to the merchants involved in it.

Brahmanical practices appear to have been well established at the time Buddhism reached the island. Their salience, if not influence, diminished thereafter, but Hinduism emerged as the religion of the Tamil minority in the island after the sixth century AD. Trade links with the Indian Ocean states brought Islam to the island through small groups of Arab traders, who settled in the island from around the eighth century.

Apart from its expertise in irrigation technology and its Buddhist ethos, there were two others features which helped Sri Lanka to evolve a distinctive culture and civilization of its own. One was the linguistic homogeneity that emerged from the development and spread of the Sinhala language throughout the island. In its origins an Indo-Aryan language, Sinhala is unique to Sri Lanka. A rich literature in Sinhala, both prose and poetry developed from the sixth century. While the influence of Pali and Sanskrit styles and techniques were clearly seen in Sinhala literature, the latter evolved its own distinct identity as time went on. As an Indo-Aryan language it was cut off from its roots, that is, the Indo-Aryan languages in the north of India, by a large belt of Dravidian languages, and these latter, especially Tamil, also had an influence on Sinhala. And then there was the Sri Lankan historical imagination. Two chronicles, the *Mahāvamsa* (begun in the sixth century but most probably compiled somewhat later) and its continuation the *Chūlavamsa* (compiled in the twelfth century and continued in the fourteenth and eighteenth centuries) both written in Pali, provided a remarkably full and accurate account of the island's ancient and medieval history. Despite the shortcomings inevitable in such works compiled by *bhikkhus* (members of the Buddhist order) and the religious (including sectarian) biases inherent in them, the *Mahāvamsa* had no rival in any part of India as a historical source, and the *Chūlavamsa* was matched by very few Indian sources in comprehensiveness and accuracy. In this concern for the maintenance of the historical record, the point of comparison for Sri Lanka is not the Indian subcontinent but China and the Arab world.

The flourishing irrigation civilization of Sri Lanka's northern plain proved to be very vulnerable to invasion from south India. The earliest attacks came in the first century BC, but these increased in frequency and destructiveness after the sixth century AD. In the fifth and sixth centuries AD, a new factor of instability was introduced into the politics of peninsular India with the rise of the south Indian kingdoms of the Pandyas, Pallavas and Chōlas.

The Sinhalese contributed to their own discomfiture by calling in Dravidian assistance to settle disputed successions and dynastic squabbles. South Indian auxiliaries became, in time, a vitally important if not the most powerful element in the armies of Sinhalese rulers, and an unpredictable, turbulent group who were often a threat to political stability. They were also the nucleus of a powerful Tamil influence in the court. Sri Lanka was drawn into conflicts between these south Indian states and became an integral element in the power politics of that region. More important still, Tamil settlements on the island became sources of support for south Indian invaders.

In the middle of the ninth century, the Sinhalese intervened directly in the rivalries of the south Indian kingdoms, with disastrous consequences for themselves in provoking the hostility of the rising power and expansionist ambitions of the Chōlas. Under Rājarāja (984–1014) the Chōlas, with all of south India under their control, conquered the north-central plains of Sri Lanka and ruled this region as a province of the Chōla empire for nearly seventy-five years. The Chōlas established their capital at Polonnāruva in the north-east of the dry zone, and nearer the Mahaveli River, a shift determined as much for reasons of security as for economic considerations. They were eventually driven out of Sri Lanka in 1070 by Vijayabāhu I, with Rohana serving as his base of operations.

Once Vijayabāhu had regained control of Anurādhapura, he followed the Chōlas in retaining Polonnāruva as the capital.

During his reign of forty years, the country recovered from the ravages of the Chōla occupation, but Vijayabāhu left a disputed succession, and another period of extensive civil war followed, until stability was restored by Parākramabāhu I, who ruled at Polonnāruva from 1153 to 1186. He unified Sri Lanka under his control and built a remarkable series of irrigation works and public and religious monuments. The Parākarama Sāmudra (the sea of Parākrama), with an embankment nearly 16 km long at an average height of 13 m, was the greatest of the irrigation works of ancient Sri Lanka. But this vigorous revival of ancient grandeur under Parakramabahu I eventually exhausted the energies of the Polonnāruva kingdom. After him, came a brief decade of order and stability under Nissanka Malla (1187–1196) during which Polonnāruva reached the peak of its development as a capital city. Its architectural features rivalled those of Anuradhāpura. The four great statues of the Buddha which comprise the Gālvihāra complex are the summit of the artistic achievement of Polonnāruva. The Buddhist and Hindū bronzes of the Polonnāruva kingdom range from masterpieces to quite undistinguished works.

Renewed dissension among the Sinhalese and dynastic disputes attracted south Indian invasions, which culminated in a devastating campaign of pillage under Magha of Kalinga. The destruction wrought on this occasion was unparalleled. Sri Lanka's hydraulic civilization never recovered from the devastation. The waning and collapse of the irrigation civilizations of Sri Lanka's dry zone is one of the critical turning points in the island's history (Indrapala, 1971). The first and most important of the consequences that flowed from it was the relocation of the Sinhalese kingdoms in the south-west of the island, a development that was as much the cause as it was the result of a fundamental change in the economic resources of the state and in the nature of its revenue system. The change was from an overwhelming dependence on irrigation-based rice cultivation to rain-fed agriculture, with trade rising higher in the scale of the ruler's priorities than ever before. Cinnamon became one of the main export commodities. This was especially so in the principal Sinhalese kingdom. Muslim settlers in the island largely controlled its export trade. As this trade grew in importance, they settled in larger numbers in the coastal areas and in the ports, and then gradually penetrated into the interior.

Second, the invasion of Magha led directly to the formation of a Tamil kingdom in the island for the first time. The core of this kingdom was the Jaffna peninsula in the north of the island. The kingdom of Jaffna had a short but tempestuous history. Its power and influence in the country reached its peak in the fourteenth and early fifteenth centuries, after which it entered into a long decline until it succumbed to Portuguese power in the early seventeenth century. Its political status and influence changed dramatically from time to time: for a short period it was a very powerful kingdom, at others a satellite of expanding Dravidian states in southern India; and at times subjugated by the principal Sinhalese state of the day, it generally acknowledged its suzerainty. Parākramabāhu VI (1412–1467), the last Sinhalese ruler to bring the whole island under his rule, overran Jaffna in 1450. But Sinhalese control over the north, which he thus established was not maintained for long after his death, and Jaffna reasserted its independence.

The third of these trends was that the central region of the island began to stake a claim to an independent political role of its own. This was the origin of the Kandyan kingdom, which became in time the last of the Sinhalese kingdoms of the island.

Political instability was the bane of Sri Lanka's history throughout this period. The result was that when the Portuguese arrived in Sri Lanka in the early sixteenth century, they found the island divided into three independent and squabbling kingdoms (see Plates 55, 84, 223, 234).

BIBLIOGRAPHY

ARIYAPALA, M. B. 1968. *Society in Medieval Ceylon.* Colombo.

BANDARANAYAKE, S. 1974. *Sinhalese Monastic Architecture.* Leiden.

BANDARANAYAKE, S. *et al.* (eds). 1990. *Sri Lanka and the Silk Road of the Sea.* Colombo.

DEWARAJA, L. S. 1988. *The Kandyan Kingdom of Sri Lanka 1707–1782.* Colombo.

GEIGER, W. 1960. (BECHERT, H., ed.) *Culture of Ceylon in Medieval Times.* Weisbaden.

GUNASINGHE, P. A. T. 1987. *The Political History of Yapuhuwa, Kurungela and Gampala.* Colombo.

GUNAWARDANA, R. A. L. H. 1971. Irrigation and Hydraulic Society in Ceylon. *Past and Present*, 53, pp. 3–27.

——. 1982. Society Function and Political Power: A Case Study of State Formation in Irrigation Society. In: CLASSEN, H. J. M. and SKALNIK, P. (eds) *The Study of the State.* The Hague, pp. 133–154.

——. 1985. Prelude to the State. *Sri Lanka Journal of the Humanities*, VIII (1 and 2).

HETTIARACHCHY, T. 1972. *History of Kingship in Ceylon up to the 4th Century AD.* Colombo.

INDRAPALA, K. (ed.) 1971. *The Collapse of the Rajarata Civilization in Ceylon and the Drift to the South West: A Symposium.* Peradeniya, University of Ceylon.

KARUNATILAKA, P. V. B. 1988. Caste and Social Change in Ancient Sri Lanka. In: LIYANAGAMAGE, A. (ed.) *Studies in the Social History of Sri Lanka* (Social Science Review 4). Colombo, pp. 1–30.

LEACH, E. R. 1961. *Pul Eliya: A Village in Ceylon: A Study of Land Tenure and Kinship.* Cambridge.

LIYANAGAMAGE, A. 1968. *The Decline of Polonnaruwa and the Rise of Dambadeniya.* Colombo.

MENDIS, V. L. B. 1983. *Foreign Relations of Sri Lanka from Earliest Times till 1965.* Dehiwala, Tisara.

PARANAVITANA, S. (ed.) 1959–1960. *University of Ceylon History of Ceylon: From the Earliest Times to 1505, I, (1) and (2).* Colombo.

PATHMANATHAN, S. 1978. *The Kingdom of Jaffna*, Part I (c. AD 1250–1450). Colombo.

PIERIS, R. 1956. *Sinhalese Social Organization: The Kandyan Period.* Colombo.

RAGUPATHY, P. 1987. *Early Settlements in Jaffna: An Archaeological Survey.* Madras.

SOMARATNA, G. P. V. 1975. *The Political History of the Kingdom of Kotte.* Colombo.

25.3
NEPAL

Alexander W. Macdonald

During the period of our concern, Nepal, as a political and geographical entity, did not exist. Today, Nepal is a well-established nation-state. Its population is approximately 19 million and it occupies a territory shaped like an elongated rectangle stretching for 800 km along the southern slopes of the central Himalaya. To the north lies the Peoples' Republic of China. On the east, south and west, Nepal is bordered by India. Its capital is Kathmandu, today a polluted, international bazaar, situated in a small valley only 640 km^2 in extent which is practically in the centre of the country. It lies at the same altitude as the summit of Britain's Ben Nevis. Halfway between the hot, malarial plains to the south and the cold, Tibetan plateau to the north, the site of Kathmandu has been an important staging post on one of the principal routes of Indo-Tibetan and Sino-Tibetan trade.

Broadly speaking, there are four geographical zones in Nepal. Moving from south to north, one first crosses the plains of the Terai, which are a little above sea level and where the climate is subtropical; next one climbs through the middle hills, where the climate is temperate; higher up, difficult passes wind through the Himalaya themselves and behind them one discovers a few high valleys, where the climate is sub-alpine. These northernmost valleys are culturally and ethnically Tibetan. Five centuries or so ago, Mustang, for instance, was an important centre for the diffusion and reception of Buddhism. However, it was in the middle hills that the social, political and religious developments occurred which were to result in the unification of the peoples of Nepal.

Since long past, these hills have been inhabited by large Tibeto-Burman-speaking tribes – Magars, Gurungs, Rais, Limbus. Some time before the eleventh century, a people from the north-west known as Khas started moving eastwards into western 'Nepal', mingling with and sometimes intermarrying with the local populations as well as with immigrants from the south, some of whom were Rajputs. These Khas were the ancestors of today's Chetris (Sanskrit: *Kshatriya*), numerically the largest caste in the country. One of their rulers, Nagaraja/Nagadeva, founded a kingdom which, until the latter part of the fourteenth century, held sway over the west of 'Nepal' up to Gorkha, over present-day Kumaon and Garhwal and over Guge and Purang in south-west Tibet. The capital was at Sinja, and the political system was feudal and highly decentralized. The kings were Buddhists and patronized the construction of *stūpas* and temples: they left inscriptions on stone pillars found north of Surkhet in Sanskrit, Tibetan and Old Nepali. After the break-up of their authority, two confederations – the Baisi (22) in the Karnali and the Chaubisi (24) in the Gandaki zones – came to occupy the political scene: from them eventually emerged the small kingdom of Gorkha, situated 60 km north-west of Kathmandu.

The original inhabitants of the valley where Kathmandu is now situated seem to have been the Newars, who also spoke a Tibeto-Burman language, although their ethnic origins are varied. Much more historical material is available for tracing events in the valley than for any other part of the country. Over 190 inscriptions survive from the period 464–879 but less than a dozen for 879–1200. Architectural and sculptural remains, coins, accounts by foreign travellers such as the Chinese, and *vaṃshāvalīs* – written genealogical lists, the earliest of which were compiled in the fourteenth century – help the historian to reconstruct the past. Events are usually divided into periods according to the dynasty then reigning – the Lichchhavi, fifth to ninth centuries; the Thakuri, ninth to twelfth centuries; the Early Malla (1200–1382) and the Later Malla (1382–1768). Buddhism as well as Hinduism prospered under the Lichchhavi,who adopted Sanskrit as their state language. Many of Nepal's most famous monumental sculptures – Varaha, the boar incarnation of Dhum Varahi, the recumbent Vishnu at Balaju and Buddhanilakantha – date from the middle of the seventh century. In the seventh century, the king of Tibet is said to have married a princess from the valley called Bhrkuti.

During the Thakuri period, Gunakamadeva (980–998) founded Kathmandu. Lalitpur had become a centre of Buddhist Tantric learning by the tenth century, and students and scholars from India and Tibet came to study there. Traditionally, the large *stūpa* at Bodnath had been founded around 600. The earliest dated bronzes are from the eleventh century; by the fourteenth and fifteenth centuries Newar metalwork had reached its apogee. A Newar, whom the Chinese called A-ni-ko (1244–1306), led eighty artisans to China to work for the Yuan emperor. The first example of an illuminated manuscript dates from 1028, and by the thirteenth century a distinctive style of Newar painting had emerged.

An overview of events between the seventh and sixteenth centuries would emphasize the continuous movement of the Khas eastwards and the spread and development of their speech (Khaskura) into Nepali, the *lingua franca* of the entire country. However, it was only towards the end of the eighteenth century – after the period of our concern and subsequent to the capture of Kathmandu in 1769 by the

Hinduized Khas sovereign from Gorkha – that the country would start to assume its present-day geographical frontiers and manifest some degree of political and national cohesion. However, the *Kshatriya*-ization of the middle hills was already far advanced before the end of the sixteenth century. In the high valleys, the major source of architectural and artistic inspiration had been Buddhist and came from Tibet. In the Kathmandu valley, on the other hand, the Newars, whose artistic inspiration owed nothing to the Khas, produced in this time-span some of the finest examples of Hindu and Buddhist architecture, sculpture and painting extant in Asia. Raids by Khas of the Karnali between 1287 and 1334 did not succeed in putting an end to their artistic inventiveness. By the time of Jayasthiti Malla (r. 1382–1395), society in the valley had assumed many of its enduring aspects. Celibate monks were on their way out as a social force. Married Vajrayāna priests now lived peacefully alongside Hindu priests and *pūjāris*. The Newars had found their approximate ranks in the Hindu system of castes. They even seem to have invented the worship of the goddess Svasthani, today widespread among Hindūs throughout Nepal. And the *Svayambhu Purāṇa* which is invoked in justification of much present-day Buddhist practice may also date from this period.

BIBLIOGRAPHY

HUTT, M. *et al.* 1994. *Nepal: A Guide to the Art and Architecture of Kathmandu Valley*. Stirling.

MACDONALD, A. W.; VERGATI STAHL, A. 1979. *Newar Art: Nepalese Art from the Malla Period*. Warminster, Aris and Phillips; *Les Royaumes de l'Himalaya* MACDONALD, A. W. (ed.) 1982, Collection orientale de l'imprimerie nationale, Paris, pp. 5–25, 165–208.

SLUSSER, M. S. 1982. *Nepal Mandala: A Cultural Study of the Kathmandu Valley*. Princeton, New Jersey.

26

SOUTH-EAST ASIA AND THE ASIAN ISLANDS IN THE PACIFIC

Denys Lombard

As the countries bordering what has come to be called the 'South-East Asian Mediterranean' currently seek to discover, within the Association of South-East Asian Nations (ASEAN), the roots of a shared identity, they could well find it by looking to the history of these nine centuries, together with the prehistoric times that preceded them.

South-East Asia, which today seems so diverse in terms of both religion and politics, seems at that time to have opted for a single model, the model of the 'Indianized kingdom' (Coedès), closely associated, ideologically, with the spread of Hinduism and Buddhism and with that of the great myths of Indian origin (the *Ramāyāṇa*, the *Mahābhārata*, the Buddhist *Jātaka*, and so on). Linguistically, it must also be said that at that time Sanskrit acted as a sort of *koiné*, comparable to Latin in the West and, to some extent, English in South-East Asia today. However, here there was never a unified political structure, as there was in the Roman Empire established on both shores of the Mediterranean, but for many centuries a degree of cultural community persisted, which explains the many similarities that attempts are now being made to rediscover.

This simplified picture at once needs two major qualifications. The first is that this process of state formation was much more marked in the west (the Indochinese peninsula, Sumatra, Java, Bali, and so on) than in the east, where the islands (the Indonesian 'Far East', Mindanao, Luzon, and so on) remained aloof from the larger political and urban units for far longer. The second is that, even in the west, large areas, most of them mountainous, also remained outside the ambit of the great centralized systems and continued to function as reserves of natural products of greater or lesser value (timber, resins, scents, spices, medicinal plants, and so on) in relation to those states. Foreign traders were already coming to seek out these commodities from far away (mainly from China and India, but also from the Middle East). These areas also had inexhaustible reserves of men, so it was relatively easy to come and muster the manpower that the large kingdoms required.

All through the period under review, and for a long time thereafter (in some respects even well into the twentieth century), the lands of South-East Asia were covered by thick forest, broken in only a few spots by clearings of varying dimensions wherever conditions appeared propitious for a shift from a primitive slash-and-burn agriculture to permanent irrigation. Far removed from the areas where metal-working enjoyed its first successes (the valleys of the Huanghe and the Ganga), here the population lacked iron and only slowly improved their means to wage their struggle against the forest.

NEW SOURCES

For the most part, our knowledge of the history of these nine centuries for long depended on reconstructions made from epigraphic texts (several hundred inscriptions carved on stone or copper), the reports of foreign, mainly Chinese and Arab, travellers, and the examination of a few larger archaeological sites such as those in Java, at Pagan or at Angkor, which have been studied since the late nineteenth century. But in the last thirty years, numerous other sites have been located and excavated that have not yet been taken into account in syntheses. To mention only the most important ones, there are Kota China, Barus, Jambi and Palembang (Sumatra), Banten, Leles, Tuban and China (Java), the various sites at Lembah Bujang (Kedah, in the Malay Peninsula), the latest sites of the so-called 'Och-eo' culture (recently discovered by Vietnamese archaeologists in the Mekong delta), the recently identified site of the port of Van-don (in the Bay of Along), and the slightly better known site at Satingpra (in the Kra isthmus).

Moreover, throughout the region, there have been rapid advances in underwater archaeology (over fifteen ancient wrecks have been located, including the one at Pahang in Malaysia and those at Butuan in the Philippines), which are providing priceless information about ancient trading vessels and their cargoes.

THE EMERGENCE OF RICE-GROWING STATES

There can be no disputing that the key feature of the early part of the period under review here is the appearance of settled, organized agricultural societies. We know of their rise from stone inscriptions proclaiming the ambitions of lords or kings, who were anxious to advance rice growing and so founded villages or monasteries, while allocating to them a number of 'dependents': in short, organizing the space around them at the expense of the forest.

In fact, the process had begun much earlier in the delta of the Red River, where the Chinese model had been introduced in the time of the Han (111 BC). The urban site of Tong-binh (which would later become Thăng-long and then Hanoi) became a provincial headquarters in 607, but there is ample evidence of other older urban sites in the region (Co-loa, Long-biên, and so on). What was to become the land of the 'Viet' (Tonkin) was then inseparable from the land of the 'Yue' (modern Guangdong) – 'Yue' and 'Viet' indeed being simply two pronunciations of a single ethonym (denoted by the same ideograph). Until the tenth century, the region of north Viet Nam was an integral part of the Chinese Empire.

A comparable situation, although this time marked by the impact of India, arose later in other places in western South-East Asia: in the valley of the Irrawaddy, where the kingdom of Pyu flourished from the seventh century, using a Tibeto-Burman language (around Prome, a city with a surrounding brick-built wall); in the valley of the Menam, where archaeologists have rediscovered the remains of the Mon kingdom of Dvaravati; in the Mekong delta and southern Laos, where a kingdom took shape that Chinese sources describe after the sixth century by the name of 'Chen-la'; in western Java, where as early as the fifth century a king boasted of having caused a major canal to be dug; and in central Java, where the names of several kings (some of whom belong to the Buddhist 'Sailendra' dynasty) are well known to us from inscriptions from the seventh and eighth centuries onwards.

Alongside these kingdoms, which may be assumed to have been predominantly agrarian, there were also maritime *entrepôts* whose success rested on the trade that they conducted between a forest hinterland and traders from far-off countries. The best-known example is that of the kingdom of Srivijaya, made famous by both Arab travellers and Chinese pilgrims, a 'kingdom' whose centre was for a while Palembang and one of whose rulers declared himself 'great king' (*mahārāja*) in various inscriptions dating from the seventh century (and found all over southern Sumatra), but which must surely be interpreted above all as a system of *entrepôts*, situated at the mouths of the main rivers on both sides of the Straits of Malacca (*Melaka*). Chinese sources also mention several small trading ports on the coasts of the Malay Peninsula, as well as on those of Indochina, where inscriptions also reveal the existence of a busy maritime kingdom, the kingdom of Champa (in the area of Nha-trang and Phan-rang).

THE TRANSFORMATIONS OF THE NINTH AND TENTH CENTURIES

The ninth and tenth centuries saw a number of important changes, but we cannot yet be sure that they were all part and parcel of the same process. The agrarian kingdoms, only hazily known before then, arose and made their mark on the countryside with their enormous religious buildings, which compel admiration even today.

The most striking example is that of Angkor (whose name is a deformation of the Sanskrit *nāgara*, which means 'City', or better, the 'urbanized' space as against the still wild space of the forest). Its site was selected in 802 between the natural water tower formed by the sandstone range of the Kulen mountains and the great fish-filled lake of Tonle Sap, which also enabled direct access to the Mekong (and the sea). During the centuries that followed, the Khmer kings dug vast reservoirs (*baray*) to control irrigation, and, in a related move, built awe-inspiring mountain-temples which are all symbolic models of Mount Meru (the mountain which, in Hindu cosmology, is the axis of the world). Around the capital, or rather, the successive capitals, since each great king founded his own new one, a vast empire was organized which stretched eastwards beyond the Mekong and to the north and west controlled areas which are currently Laotian or Thai. In the time of King Jayavarman VII (thirteenth century), whose reign probably marked the zenith of the system, a whole network of royal highways, dotted with rest houses (*sala*), was maintained so as to make possible an ideal control of space (see Plates 82, 226, 229–231).

The ninth century also saw the formation of new kingdoms in the west, in the valley of the Irrawaddy: with those of Pegu in the south and Pagan in the north. The former was founded by the Mons (in 825) and grew as its maritime trade developed, the latter by the Burmese (in 849), who took advantage of the natural wealth of the Kyaukse basin (just below the confluence of the Irrawaddy and the Chindwin) to build a vast city, which was soon surrounded by magnificent Buddhist temples.

In Java, we get a glimpse of a similar rise of kingdoms, not so much from the study of urban sites (as yet poorly identified) but from the study of epigraphy and above all from the scale of the great monuments, built first in the centre of the island (the area known as Mataram, near Yogyakarta, where the temples at Borobudur were built in the ninth century, and then those at Sewu and Prambanan, in the tenth century) and then in the east, in the area of Kediri (twelfth century) and Singhasari (thirteenth century) (see Plates 224, 228).

In 1990, a charter engraved on copper was discovered in Luzon (near Laguna de Bay), a document that is so far unique but authentic and dating precisely from the year 822 of the Saka era (that is AD 900). This charter, written in a Nusantarian language which seems to contain some Tagalog terms, deals with the repayment of a debt and raises the fascinating problem of how far some places in the Philippine archipelago also experienced the existence of 'Indianized kingdoms'. Archaeologists have already drawn attention to some other 'old' agricultural regions, whose history is still little known but which might date from this first awakening: the land around Ifugao (in the far north of Luzon); and the region of Buayan (in southern Mindanao).

At the same time, the maritime kingdoms continued to pursue their commercial activities. In the eleventh century, the king of Srivijaya maintained relations with both the Chōla rulers of south India and the emperor of China. Dating from the same period, in Champa, some Arabic inscriptions have been found which are evidence of the intense traffic which from the ninth century at least linked the ports of the Persian Gulf with Guangzhou (by way of the *entrepôts* of the Straits of Malacca, the island of Tioman, the Cham coast and the island of Hainan). In 1177, the Chams attacked Angkor and for a time threatened the greatest South-East Asian kingdom of the time.

Mention must finally be made of one major event: in 939, the Viets freed themselves of Chinese suzerainty and proceeded to develop a strong nationalism in the face of pressure from their neighbours to the north. Their vitality was reflected not only by the strengthening of a well-organized state under a mandarinate (with the adoption of the examination system), but also by sustained aggressiveness towards their Cham neighbours. Thus a gradual southward advance of the Viets (*Nam-tiên*) began and, with it, an advance of the 'Sinic culture of the ideograph' at the expense of the 'Indianized' areas (see Plate 227).

THE BREAK OF THE THIRTEENTH CENTURY

While until the end of the thirteenth century the 'synchronisms' must be stressed only with considerable care, it is quite obvious that the 'Mongol moment' marked an important break in South-East Asia, just as it did in the rest of Eurasia. While the suddenness of the expeditions launched in the space of two decades by Qubilay Khān, not only against Japan (1274 and 1281) but also against Champa (1283–1285), Viet Nam (1285), Pagan (1287) and Java (1293), in a sense prefigured what much later would be the wave of Japanese conquest in 1942. It heralded, at the level of events, a long-term occurrence that is much more significant – the ever more active intervention of the 'sinicized world' or Chinese-type civilizations in the region. Except in Upper Burma, where they struck a heavy blow against Pagan, the Chinese–Mongol armies were generally defeated, in battles that later 'national' histories, notably in Viet Nam and Indonesia, would subsequently seek to present as emblematic. But that does not mean that their passage had no effects.

One of the most important of these effects was certainly the emergence of the Thai peoples into history. They were established with other 'minorities' (Yi, Hmong, Yao and so on) in the vast karstic mountain range situated north of the great valleys of the Indochinese peninsula, but, although converted to Buddhism and using scripts of Indian origin, they nevertheless spoke tonal languages (related to Chinese) and had long been exposed to a slow process of sinicization. Like the Vietnamese in the tenth century, they freed themselves from Chinese and Mongol suzerainty just as the Mongols were seeking to assert themselves more forcefully, and began to initiate their own 'historic' descent southwards, at the expense this time of the Mons and the Khmers. In the thirteenth century, they settled in the basin of the upper Menam, drove the Khmers out of Sukhotai and founded Chiang Mai (1296). In 1350, they founded Ayutthaya (Sanskrit, 'Ayudhya'), only 100 km from the sea, and made repeated attacks on Angkor (1353, 1393, 1431). Another group founded the Laotian kingdom of Lan Sang (1353). They brought with them a number of customs from the 'far north' such as the twelve-animal calendar cycle, which is well attested among Turco-Mongol peoples.

Another no less important consequence was the intensification of the Chinese diaspora. There were already a few Chinese communities in the *nanyang* or 'southern seas' – a generic term used in Mandarin long before the Europeans had coined the term 'South-East Asia' – notably at Angkor, where they are portrayed several times on the bas-reliefs at Bayon (thirteenth century). Indeed, one Chinese (Zhou Daguan) wrote a remarkable description of Angkor in 1296. But starting in the fourteenth century, these trading communities, which came mostly from Fujian but also from Guangdong, increased in numbers. By the beginning of the fifteenth century, the fleets of Admiral Zheng found Chinese settlers in virtually every port in the region.

The island of Java, situated in the far south of the area under review, remained somewhat apart from these new trends for rather longer. However, eastern Java in particular had its period of glory under the kings of Mojopahit (late thirteenth–early sixteenth century). This kingdom is quite well known from inscriptions and archaeology as well as from a number of literary texts (notably the *Nagarakertagama* dating from 1365), appears – rather, like that of Ayutthaya, with which it was contemporaneous – as both an old-style agrarian power and a maritime power. The fleets of Java were said to control a whole series of *entrepôts* at that time whose names, recorded on a map, correspond more or less to the area currently occupied by Indonesia (and Malaysia).

THE GROWTH OF MARITIME NETWORKS AND THE ADVENT OF ISLAM

In the fourteenth century, events in Central Asia, which had the effect of partly disrupting the ancient 'Silk Road' (that followed by Marco Polo in the thirteenth century), had the indirect consequence of intensifying traffic along the sea route and thus precipitating a great increase in trading activities all over the South-East Asian 'Mediterranean'.

The presence of Islam is attested by various tombs and mosques in Guangzhou as early as the ninth century, Quanzhou in the tenth century, Champa and eastern Java in the eleventh century, northern Sumatra in the thirteenth century and Malaya at the beginning of the fourteenth century. It was the main religion of these new traders and, wherever international trade developed, it was to become the religion of the elite, and then, in some regions, that of the majority. The model previously mentioned, that of the agrarian state, was gradually replaced by that of the port city, open to traders from elsewhere and devoted to trade. The first 'sultanate' of which there is evidence is that of Pasai (in northern Sumatra), which Marco Polo mentions and which Ibn Baṭṭūṭa from Tangiers describes very well in the mid-fourteenth century as a cosmopolitan crossroads.

The fourteenth and fifteenth centuries were marked by the spread of this sultanate model, first to Malacca (fifteenth century), then to Acheh (Aceh, Atjeh), at the northernmost tip of Sumatra, and to Demak, Chirebon (Cirebon) and Banten, on the north coast of Java (sixteenth century). Everywhere, these were cities of a new type, oriented towards the outside world, which sought not so much to manage a 'hinterland' (except to produce the pepper intended for export) as to control a commercial network. Foreign communities from the rest of Asia (among whom the first Europeans, Italians and Portuguese, would soon be seeking to carve a place), settled in distinct 'quarters' or 'compounds' (*kampung*) which bore the name of the ethnic group that they housed: *Kampung Keling* or 'Indian Quarter', *Kampung China* or 'Chinese Quarter', *Kampung Pegu* or 'Peguan Quarter', *Kampung Jawa* or 'Javanese Quarter', and so on.

Along with this expansion of trade went a new network of maritime routes further east, designed particularly to reach the Moluccas, whose spices were becoming much in demand on the world market. Several new *entrepôts* grew up all over the eastern part of the South-East Asian Mediterranean, maintaining relations with both the ports of eastern Java and those of Fujian, so as to cut out the ancient route along the Indochinese coast, which repeated attacks by Viet Nam against Champa (particularly the one that led to the fall of Vijaya in 1471) were also helping to weaken. These included the appearance of the sultanate of Brunei (fifteenth century) – which gave its name to the great island of Borneo, in the north of which it is situated – and Ternate (sixteenth century) in the north of the Moluccas. In the same way, there came into being in the archipelago that would later become known as the 'Filipino': the maritime entrepôts of Mindoro (the *Mayi* of thirteenth-century Chinese sources); old Manila (revealed by excavation of the archaeological site at Santa

Ana); and Butuan on Mindanao (well attested by numerous pieces of pottery and ancient wrecks).

By the end of the period under review, South-East Asia thus found itself enlarged more or less to the area it covers today; as for the cultural homogenization of its southern part (what is today Indonesia), it can be said that, through the gradual spread of Islam, this was already well under way.

SCRIPTS AND LANGUAGES

The multiplicity of languages and scripts used in the region is among the more serious difficulties facing the historian. But it is also a 'source' to the extent that it enables us to follow the efforts of different societies to master and then improve a particular technique.

We must first put on one side the case of Viet Nam, which had an ideographic script along with all the 'Yue' lands from their very first contacts with northern China. By the fourteenth–fifteenth century, the Vietnamese had developed an original script, known as *nôm*, with the aim of writing their own language with the help of Chinese characters adapted to the needs of phonetic notation.

Elsewhere in South-East Asia, use of the Indian syllabary (in the versions of it to be found in eastern and southern India), of which there are actually a few inscriptions dating from earlier periods (third century in the peninsula, fifth century in Java, sixth century in Sumatra), began to spread in earnest in about the seventh century and was gradually adapted to transcribe the vernacular languages. This syllabary, originally used to write Sanskrit, was gradually adapted to write the various languages of the region, which enables us to draw up a rough linguistic map of South-East Asia at the beginning of the period under review. The script was first used to write the Austroasiatic (Mon and Khmer) and Austronesian (Malay, Javanese, Balinese and Cham) languages, then to write Tibeto-Burman languages (Pyu and Burman) and, finally, after the 'Mongol moment' (thirteenth century) to write the Thai languages. Burman and Thai being tonal languages, the original syllabary had to undergo significant modifications during the shift.

From the fourteenth century, with the advances of trade and Islam, further changes occurred. The first Malay inscription in Arabic characters (found in the state of Trengganu, on the eastern coast of western Malaysia) dates from 1303 and heralds the drastic changes that were to occur in the archipelago from the fifteenth and sixteenth century onwards. Sanskrit finally ceased to be the *koiné*, to be replaced by Malay, which became for a long period the language of all trade, from the ports of Sumatra and the Malay Peninsula as far as the Moluccas. When, in 1521, Pigafetta reached the Moluccas with Magellan's fleet, he noted down a preliminary vocabulary of the 'strangers' in the place whose language was in fact already Malay.

As was the case throughout the Indianized world, the earliest writing was on stones, bronze plates and above all leaves (or *lontar*), that is leaves of the palmyra (*Borassus flabelliformi*), a very cheap material but not very durable. The few documents on leaves that have come down to us (such as the *Nagarakertagama* mentioned above) are ones that were piously copied from age to age; and virtually all the great archives that the agrarian kingdoms maintained have irretrievably disappeared. There is evidence of the use of paper (made by the Chinese technique) in Viet Nam from very early times, but it hardly spread in the archipelago, and after the seventeenth century most Malay manuscripts were written on European-made paper.

The solutions provided by scribes to the problems raised by adaptation of the Indian syllabary to the needs of the various vernacular languages are an interesting linguistic subject in their own right. Another indication is provided by the evolution of the rules of poetry (sometimes evidenced by the presence of a few treatises). Generally speaking, the whole 'Indianized' area moved gradually from the use of scanned versification (on the Indian model) to rhymed versification (on the Chinese model). This was an enormous change that raised many problems.

But the main importance of this spread of writing is surely that it signals the advent of a remarkable technique, on a par with the building of the great rice-growing cities, necessary to both the engineers and the administrators who would become experts in it and thus form, in every court, a significant 'mandarin' group. However, it should be observed that the Vietnamese were the only ones to borrow from China (as early as the eleventh century) the system of recruitment by examination.

TECHNOLOGICAL DEVELOPMENTS

For periods earlier than the sixteenth century, we lack theoretical texts that would enable us to trace the outlines of strictly 'scientific' thought, but the history of technology is rich, even though it often poses more problems than can currently be resolved. There are very few studies in this area, and while ethnologists have given clear descriptions of a whole range of 'traditional' techniques, few historians have yet sought their origin or reconstructed their evolution.

But it seems that a preliminary approximation would indicate that there were three 'technological revolutions' in South-East Asia. The first occurred well before the seventh century, although it is difficult to say precisely when it happened (and even exactly where). This is the so-called 'Neolithic' revolution, marked essentially by the domestication of rice (originally an aquatic plant) and the zebu (*Bos indicus*), the latter possibly occurring first in India and then being taken further east.

The second occurred at about the beginning of the period under review here, with the establishment of the great hydraulic systems and the building of monumental cities. It sought optimal exploitation of plant resources (which would change hardly at all until the arrival of American plants such as tobacco, sweet potatoes, maize and groundnuts, which occurred only from the sixteenth century onwards, essentially by way of the Philippines and Fujian), but it also sought to organize space on the grand scale, making the city of men a replica of the world of the gods. We are thinking here particularly of all the innovations consciously introduced (from Indian treatises, but also from China) by the architects of Cambodia and Java. For example, there were the architectural *trompe l'oeil* perspective effects, which have been particularly closely studied at Angkor. The technique of making tiles, of Chinese origin, and of ceramics also spread gradually through the countries of the peninsula: Viet Nam, Cambodia and Siam.

The third occurred after the thirteenth century and was associated with the emergence of port cities. Here the important development was the spread of coinage, which had long been known in Viet Nam but was still almost unknown in the other great agrarian cities (Prome, in the eighth century, being one of the few exceptions). In some places, such as Java, *sapeques* of Chinese provenance were used, but at Angkor there was only barter. The sultanate of Pasai was the first 'modern' state to mint its own gold coinage (late thirteenth century), and its example was followed by most of the sultanates (Malacca in the fifteenth century, Acheh in the sixteenth). Firearms too gradually spread, their use being reported in Java from as early as the thirteenth century (at the time of the Sino-Mongol invasion), and were well known in the Malay sultanates before the arrival of the Portuguese (Albuquerque seized a whole arsenal of them after his victory over Malacca in 1511). The flowering of the sultanates encouraged the development of a number of maritime techniques (use of the galley, for example) and of metal-working (gold working, *kris* technology, and so on).

But, as mentioned earlier in the context of the shift from scanned poetry to rhyming poetry, three basic developments need to be stressed here which (once again coming from the sinicized world) affected the whole of South-East Asia: (1) the shift from draped (Indian-type) clothing to sewn clothing (made with needles, and having buttons, and so on); (2) the shift from dwellings on stilts to dwellings on dry land (a process still under way in the twentieth century); and finally (3) with the introduction of furniture (beds, tables, and so on), the shift from a society using mats to one using chairs. More relevant still than the emergence of coinage (or of firearms), these three 'shifts' truly mark the advent of a new society.

LEGAL AND IDEOLOGICAL SYSTEMS

Study of the few legal texts that have been preserved by inscriptions (gifts of land or verdicts of tribunals) and above all study of the codes emanating from the agrarian kingdoms (the *Laws of Mojopahit* drawn up in Java in the fourteenth century, the *Lê Code* drawn up in Viet Nam in the fifteenth century), together with study of those emanating from the sultanates (such as the *Laws of Malacca* drawn up in the fifteenth century) give us a marvellous insight into the socio-political effects of the shift from the agrarian city to the trading city and enable us to trace the outlines of a radical development.

The agrarian city was built as a microcosm as a matter of principle, reflecting the divine macrocosm. The highly hierarchical societies in them were conceived as unchangeable (whether or not the Indian caste system was adopted in them). Around the divine king were his family, the great dignitaries of the court and then the senior mandarins, who represented his authority in the provinces. At the base were the village people, rather like serfs, some of whom came from the surrounding forests or neighbouring clearings, from where they had been abducted. The vision of space in them was simple and geometrical: it was that of the *mandala* of sedentary people, centred on an axis marked by the mountain-temple (or by the royal palace), with, round about, a concentric, directed layout that was reassuring in its apparent obviousness but in fact ruled out any initiative. Conversely, the conception of time in them was very complex, since it was not yet a matter of a measurement time, homogeneous and mathematical, but of a qualitative time whose various moments, the solemn and the informal alike, inevitably did not have the same value (and there was a very complicated body of calendrical knowledge claiming to be able to account for those different values).

The trading city, on the other hand, strongly inspired by Islam, came to the forefront in the thirteenth century, proclaiming its relationship with the rest of the world (and first and foremost, of course, with the peoples of the '*umma*' (in Malay, *ummat*), whose 'axis' was now in the direction of Mecca). In them, society was in principle more egalitarian, although there were always a few uprooted resident aliens who had become 'slaves', rather as happened with the *mamlūk* system in Egypt (although, in compensation, ideas about poverty and charity emerged). New clienteles came into being around notables (the *orang kaya*), who were usually major traders. Instead of gravitating around the figure of the king, as used to happen at the great ritual occasions in earlier days, the crowd (made up of men) now faced west at the collective Friday prayer, and the sultan had to be satisfied with kneeling in the front row. In this trade-oriented society, space became more 'geographical' and escaped centripetal forces. As for time, it very slowly ceased to be qualitative and became linear and directed, and in the shadow of this development, the taste for 'chronicles' if not for the 'meaning of history' began to make its appearance.

To conclude, there is thus reason to insist on this 'crisis of consciousness' experienced by South-East Asia during the period under review here. Having long been tempted by an ideology that has often been described as 'Indianized', but which it is doubtless much better to describe simply as 'agrarian', it saw the rise of some of the greatest kingdoms that Asia had yet seen (Angkor, Mojopahit) and then, under the effects of the impact of the Chinese and Mongols and of long-distance trade, it promoted a number of trading emporia (Pasai, Malacca, Acheh, Brunei, and so on), in no way second to Bruges or Genoa or Venice. That gives a hint of how much study of this region of the world might, by comparison, contribute to a better understanding of the concept of 'modernity'.

BIBLIOGRAPHY

AUNG THWIN, M. 1985. *Pagan. The Origins of Modern Burma.* Honolulu.

COEDÈS, G. 1964. *Les états hindouisés d'Indochine et d'Indonésie.* 3rd edn. Paris.

DUMARÇAY, J. 1986. *Le savoir des maîtres d'oeuvre javanais aux XIIIe et XIVe siècles.* Ecole Française d'Extrême-Orient: Paris.

GROSLIER, B. P. 1979. La cité hydraulique angkorienne: Exploitation ou surexploitation du sol. *Bulletin de l'Ecole Française d'Extrême-Orient.* Paris, 66, pp. 161–202.

KASETSIRI, C. 1976. *The Rise of Ayudhya: A History of Siam in the Fourteenth and Fifteenth Centuries.* Oxford University Press: Kuala Lumpur.

LÊ THÀNH KHÔI. 1982. *Histoire du Vietnam des origines à 1858.* Sudestasie: Paris.

LIAW YOCK FANG. 1976. *Undang-undang Melaka. The Laws of Melaka.* Nijhoff: The Hague.

LOMBARD, D. 1990. *Le carrefour javanais. Essai d'histoire globale,* 3 vols. Editions de l'Ecole des Hautes Etudes en Sciences Sociales: Paris.

MANGUIN, P. Y. 1980. The Southeast Asian Ship: An Historical Approach. *Journal of Southeast Asian Studies,* Singapore, 11, 2, pp. 266–276.

MILLIES, J. V. G. 1970. *Ma Huan, Ying-yai Sheng-lan, The Overall Survey of the Ocean's Shores (1433).* Hakluyt Society: Cambridge.

PIGEAUD, T. 1960–1963. *Java in the Fourteenth Century. A Study in Cultural History. The Nagara Kertagama by Rakawi Prapanca of Majapahit, 1365 AD,* third edition revised and enlarged by some contemporaneous texts with notes, translations, commentaries and glossaries, 5 vols. Nijhoff: The Hague.

WHEATLEY, P. 1961. *The Golden Khersonese: Studies in the Historical Geography of the Malay Peninsula before AD 1500.* University of Malaya Press: Kuala Lumpur.

WICKS, R. S. 1992. *Money, Markets and Trade in Early Southeast Asia. The Development of Indigenous Monetary Systems to AD 1400.* Cornell University Press, Southeast Asia Program: Ithaca, NY.

ZOETMULDER, P. J. 1974. *Kalangwan: A Study of Old Javanese Literature.* Nijhoff: The Hague.

27

CHINA

Guangda Zhang

Chinese historians have long been accustomed to viewing the whole span of their long history as a succession of dynasties with intermittent disunities, and to present Chinese history in terms of the dynastic cycle. In accordance with this customarily accepted traditional treatment of Chinese history, six dynastic periods are covered in this chapter, beginning at the end of the sixth century, when a reunified China emerged under the Sui (581–618) and extending to 1500, when the Ming (1368–1644) found themselves on the eve of being caught in a series of internal crises and external challenges. Four other intermediate dynastic periods are the Tang (618–907); the Five Dynasties and Ten Kingdoms (907–960); the Song (960–1279), Liao (Khitan, 916–1125), Jin (Jurchen, 1115–1234) and Yuan (Mongol, 1260–1368).

Expedient though it may be to arrange the enormous wealth of historical materials, dynastic cycles do not necessarily account for all the main guidelines of China's historical development. From the point of view of continuity, the cumulative changes in the socio-economic movement and the facets of a number of long-term cultural trends may be traced back to a remote date and certainly go beyond the dynastic frames. In the course of Chinese historical evolution, the span of more than nine centuries from 581 to 1500 stands midway between the ancient and the pre-modern periods, paving the way for the later phase of pre-modern China. Most Chinese, Japanese and Western scholars tend to view the late Tang and Song as a transitional period in the sense that many long-term trends of change that made subsequent Chinese society characteristically different from that of the preceding period – including the eventual decline of the old aristocracy and its kinship groups, final establishment of the autocratic regime, change in the appointment procedures of officials, the rise of scholar-officials and the dominance of a new bureaucratic elite, change in the commoners' social position, advances in agriculture, handicrafts, inter-regional trade and monetary economy, the proliferation of markets, and the growth of walled cities with their commercial suburbs – came to the fore in the late Tang and reached their culmination through the Song.

But these 900 years also encompass a most brilliant period, which witnessed China emerge as an Asian power from its former formative phase, with the further elaboration of its most enduring political order, the dazzling splendour of its literature and thought, and the ingenuity of its scientific and technological achievements. The Tang were not only prosperous on the economical level. On the political and cultural plane, Tang China was also the leading country of the East Asian world and exercised a far-reaching influence over its neighbours. The basic Tang institutions with their codified law and administrative statutes-regulations-ordinances (*ritsuryō-kyakushiki* in Japanese) system, inherited from the Sui, proved to be typical in medieval East Asia and served as an administrative model for neighbour societies as diverse as those of Korea, Japan, Viet Nam, the north-eastern kingdom of Bohai and the south-western kingdom of Nanzhao. It was during the Tang and Song that China gave a political pattern, a new form of Confucianism (Neo-Confucianism), a sinicized Buddhism and a Chinese script and literary culture to East Asia, and contributed its most important inventions – paper and printing, gunpowder, and the compass – to the whole world.

HISTORICAL SURVEY

Sui (581–617): reunification

China was reunited in 589 under the rule of Yang Jian, known as Sui Wendi (r. 581–604). That China achieved its unity by the Sui marks the end of a most important long-term development after its having been split into North and South for nearly four centuries: assimilation of the former alien nomadic peoples of the North, a process of the ethnic reconstruction of the Chinese race.

A man of great ability, Wendi made vigorous efforts to set up a strong centralized bureaucracy and emphatically asserted his emperor's power on the stern authoritarian principle. He reorganized the central government by coordinating a good number of governmental offices that had successively existed during the Han (206 BC–AD 220), Wei (220–265) and Jin (265–419). Affairs of state were conducted by a complex appararus of three central *sheng* (Secretariat, Chancellery and Department of State Affairs) and six *bu* (ministries) under the Department of State Affairs, assisted by nine *si* (boards or courts) and five *jian* (directorates). Inheriting a highly stratified society in which the aristocrats of the great 'notable' families monopolized the best positions in the localities as well as at court during the disunion period, he also attempted to break down their real socio-political prerogative, the monopoly of the official appointment held at all levels by hereditary great families since the Wei and Jin. It was Wendi who introduced such administrative practices as the appointment of all regular officials down to the prefecture and county levels by the central government or even by himself and implemented the 'rule of avoidance' which meant that main prefectural and county officials could not serve in their native place. He initiated an imperial examination system as a complementary instrument for gaining official recruits from the *literati*-official milieu.

Wendi began the construction of a nationwide communication system. He ordered the design of a great canal building project in 587. The first Grand Canal was accomplished by his son Yangdi (r. 605–618) between 605 and 610. This major transport artery was destined to play a vital role in economic exchange between the north and south and performed this function from this time to the end of the nineteenth century. Several great state granaries were constructed near the two capitals – Daxing (actual Xian) and Laoyang. By 609, the Sui had registered 8,907,536 households with a total population of 46,019,956.

Like the Qin in the third century BC, the Sui also had only two rulers. The Sui fell from power in 618 mainly because of Yangdi's oppressively tyrannical rule, his personal extravagance, his grandiose and ruinous undertakings, and a series of campaigns in Korea that exhausted the empire's material and manpower resources. But in spite of its short reign, the Sui was a prosperous and wealthy dynasty with plenty of innovations. Its new achievements in the establishment of a centralized system of government were to serve as a solid institutional foundation for the subsequent monarchical regime and benefited greatly its successor – the Tang – who enjoyed a stable and durable existence of almost three centuries, just as the Han (206 BC–AD 220) had followed the footsteps of the short-lived Qin (221–206 BC).

Tang (618–907)

Taking advantage of peasant rebellions, Li Yuan, a high-ranking official related by marriage to the Sui imperial house, proclaimed himself the new Tang Dynasty emperor in 618 (Map 24).

Building on earlier Sui political systems, the executive–administrative core of the Tang central government, the three Departments (*Zhongshu sheng, Menxia sheng*, and *Shangshu sheng*) and the six *bu* (ministries) under the *Shangshu sheng*, was totally modelled on that in use under the Sui. The *Zhongshu sheng* was an imperial secretariat, the chief responsibility of which was to draft the imperial edicts. The *Menxia sheng* (Chancellery) reflected the opinion of the high-ranked counsellors and had the right to review, revise and challenge a draft edict or order drawn up by the imperial secretariat. The *Shangshu sheng* (Department of State Affairs) and its six *bu* (ministries – personnel, finance, rites, war, punishments and public works) – was the working agency which implemented the definite decisions the other two *sheng* had reached.

The early Tang undertook a new codification of Sui law, comprising the general body of universally applicable administrative rules. This body of codified law (*lü*) and administrative statutes (*ling*) was revised about every twenty years. On these occasions, the code and statutes were regularly supplemented with regulations (*ge*) and ordinances (*shi*), issued by the Department of State Affairs and its subordinate central ministries, boards, courts and directorates. A centralized and uniform system of administration was thus assured by this systematic *lü-ling-ge-shi* revision effort.

Two of the best-known emperors in Tang history are Taizong (Li Shimin, r. 626–649) and Xuanzong (r. 713–755) (see Plate 237). Each presided over a brilliant court.

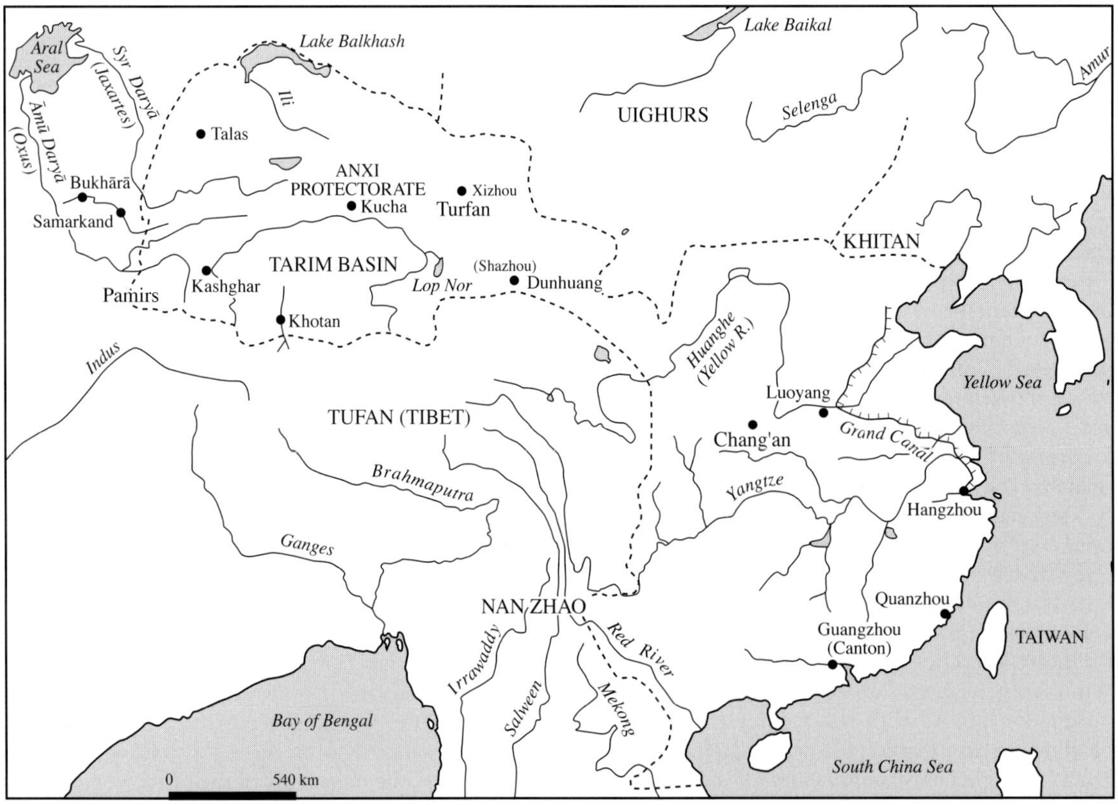

Map 24 The Tang Empire in 755 (draft Guangda Zhang).

Forceful and intelligent, Taizong was noted for his ability to select competent assistants and his eagerness to listen to the moral advice of his counsellors. Chiefly due to his socio-economic policies, rural economy was revitalized. Society was stable. People lived in peace and contentment. The number of people sentenced to death in 630 was alleged to be only twenty-nine in the whole country. His reign has been traditionally referred to and highly praised in Chinese history as the 'good government of the Zhenguan (reign title of Taizong)'.

After the splendid reign of Taizong, China saw the only woman sovereign in its history to reign in her own right. Wu Zetian (r. 684–705), the consort of ailing Gaozong, Taizong's successor, proclaimed herself Empress Wu in 690. She recruited support from the lesser families with scholar-official backgrounds by providing their members with greater advancement opportunities. Now new posts were filled by candidates from the examination system on a larger scale. The examination system as a test of the personal ability in gaining entry to the bureaucratic service proved to be a decisive blow at the old aristocracy since the Wei and Jin, a method in the long run to break the monopoly of socio-political power held by the upper aristocracy during the disunion period.

Xuanzong, Empress Wu's grandson, reigned over China for forty-five years. The first phase of his reign, labelled in Chinese history as the 'good government of the Kaiyuan (the reign title of Xuanzong, 713–741)', marks the zenith of prosperity and power of the Tang Dynasty. By 754, the Tang had 9,069,154 registered households and a total population of 52,880,488, twice as many as in the early Tang period.

Wide economic and cultural contacts with the outside world had effectively contributed to the Tang's prosperity. The horses, leather goods, furs, exotic costume of the north; the ivory, sandalwood, drugs, and aromatics of the south; the cotton and woollen textiles, glass, and gemstones of the West, together with Indian religion and astronomy; Persian and Sogdian gold and silver vessels, Manichaean Seven Luminaries, and Khotanese painting technique, made Chang'an, the Tang capital, the greatest cosmopolitan centre of the epoch. Visitors from all countries thronged the great Chinese cities. Together with them came the music and dancing girls of Central Asian and other origins.

But earlier in the 740s the Tang also suffered a steep decline. Whereas a wealthy but corrupt society posed more social and political problems, Xuanzong withdrew from active affairs into the pleasures of life, allowing things to take their own course. Special commissions (*shi*) holding extraordinary powers were set up one after another and entrusted by the emperor to cope with the most urgent fiscal affairs. In the face of the ever-threating menace of the Tibetans, resurrected Turks, Khitans and other frontier intruders, the militia of the early Tang had been gradually supplanted by recruited professional troops, and the emperor let his prime ministers confide to military commissioners (*jiedushi*) the command over all the forces along the frontiers. In the 730s, the vast frontier areas were organized into ten strategic military regions. The frontier commissioners of garrison army soon began also to assume charge of civilian administration.

The turning point was 745, when Xuanzong fell deeply under the influence of a new favourite, the imperial concubine Yang Guifei, who had been his daughter-in-law. Her relatives rapidly dominated the court. In 750, an aboriginal chieftain of Nanzhao, a kingdom in the south-west province of Yunnan, rebelled. An army sent to punish him was destroyed, involving a loss of 60,000 troops. In 751, Tang forces in Central Asia were beaten in a battle near the Talas River by the Arabs in league with the Qarlug Turks, a famous battle nineteen years after Charles Martel's victory over the Arabs at Poitiers in Europe.

At the end of 755, An Lushan, the military commissioner on the north-eastern frontier, revolted. The event taken in isolation was not of key importance, but it marks the beginning of a transition period in Chinese history. An Lushan threw the empire immediately into disarray. The government was unprepared as a result of an unbroken peace of more than 100 years.

The rebellion continued for eight years. The prefectures and counties around Luoyang were reduced to ruins. More significantly, perhaps, this disaster brought military adventurers to the forefront during the rebellion and afterwards military commissioners (*jiedushi*) remained a major force in the political life up to the end of the Five Dynasties (907–960). Arrogant and unruly, a number of new imperial military commissioners kept their private troops and bodyguards, exercised wide powers over their subordinate prefectures and counties, appointed their own officials, and recruited their subordinates from the *literati* who had failed to have themselves nominated in the central government after their civil service examination. They made their titles hereditary, thus bringing a considerable part of the Tang domain into the hands of independent or semi-independent warlords, called regional potentates (*fanzhen*). This led to a kind of regional separatism which meant a general decentralization of government power and to a fluctuating social situation which entailed the final decline of old aristocracy.

Two Tang emperors, Dezong (r. 779–805) and Xianzong (r. 805–820), made attempts to restore the fortune of the dynasty. A task of top priority was the reorganisation of taxation and finance, because civil and military administration as well as the court for their very existence relied upon the collection of rents and taxes. As an inevitable step that was the ultimate outcome of a long-term economic evolution and fiscal crises, Dezong, with the assistance of his chief minister Yang Yan, promulgated a new taxation system – the so-called two-tax system (*liangshuifa*). Under this system, taxes were levied primarily on property rather than on male adults as it had been in the past. This was a radical measure, for it recognized free private ownership and began the assessment of taxes in terms of money and property, a practice which remained the basis of the tax system down to 1581.

Under Xianzong, the Tang court regained a great deal of its power by implementing a tough policy towards the provinces. His success was based upon the palace armies, but the progressively effective control of the palace armies by eunuchs proved to be a disaster with grave consequences for his weak successors.

In the second half of the ninth century, the central authority, paralysed by the eunuchs' control and ministerial factions, was disintegrating with startling speed. Widespread discontent with the overall corruption of the administration and natural disasters led to a wave of peasant uprisings. The Tang nominally survived until 907, when Zhu Wen, once a leader of the peasants' revolt and now the most powerful warlord with a title of imperial military commissioner, deposed the puppet emperor and seized the throne, ushering in the period of the Five Dynasties and the Ten Kingdoms of Chinese dynastic history.

The Five Dynasties and the Ten Kingdoms (907–960); the Khitan (Liao)

The fifty-three years from 907 to 960 was a completely chaotic period in Chinese history, known as the Five Dynasties and Ten Kingdoms. Those in the north, Later Liang (907–923), Later Tang (923–937), Later Jin (937–947), Later Han (947–950) and Later Zhou (951–960) are called the Five Dynasties, while the nine states in the south and one in today's Shanxi province are given a general designation of the Ten Kingdoms. Three of the five dynasties – those of the Later Tang, Later Jin and Later Han – were founded by the Shatuo, a Turkic people by origin. Foreign tribes also invaded the north. This period of turmoil had its dark side. People were enduring hardship and deprivation caused by incessant wars and excessive taxes and levies. In the midst of political chaos, the heritage of the Tang survived only in relatively stable south-eastern and south-western China. With the help of immigrants from the central plain of China, the natural resources of the south were explored. From the ninth century on, south-eastern China, especially the lower Yangtze valley, witnessed a picture of continuous growth on the economic level and began to lead the country in agrarian developments. It was a decisive period of the gradual shift of the economic centre of gravity of China.

The far-reaching influence of the Tang culture had also stimulated the rise of the nomadic and pastoral peoples. Along the north-western frontier, the Tanguts (*Dangxiang*), a branch of a nomadic people of Tibetan stock, had established their kingdom (*Xixia*) to dominate the north-western passage to Central Asia. In Manchuria and eastern Mongolia, a new empire had emerged under the leadership of a largely pastoral people called the Khitan (*Qidan*). They probably spoke a language related to Mongol. Cathay, the name for north China in medieval Europe, and Kitai, the Russian name for China, derived from the name 'Khitan' or 'Khitai'. The Khitan founded the Liao Empire (916–1125) in 916. The Liao employed a dual system of administration, one for their own people that enforced tribal laws, another for the people of farming regions governed by the old Tang system.

Northern Song (960–1127) (see Map 25)

The Song (960–1279) had its beginning in usurping the throne of the preceding dynasty by Zhao Kuangyin (Taizu, r. 960–976), the military chief of the palace corps (see Plate 238). This was a commonplace happening during the period of the Five Dynasties, stemming from the institution of the imperial military commissioner since the mid-Tang and prevalent throughout the whole country for more than two centuries. It was therefore not without reason that much energy of the Song founder Zhao Juanyin, himself a typical representative of that military environment, was devoted to abolish the power of his military colleagues, who constituted a standing menace to the throne. The basic line laid down by Zhao Kuangyin was to bring about a political settlement whereby a single ruler wields the absolute power and keeps the military officers inferior and obedient to civil officials. A wide prevalence of war weariness among the population helped Zhao Kuangyin achieve his aim. Militarism was put to an end with relative ease.

But the system of imperial control over the army proved to have catastrophic consequences for the dynasty's destiny. The Song remained an empire feeble in terms of military

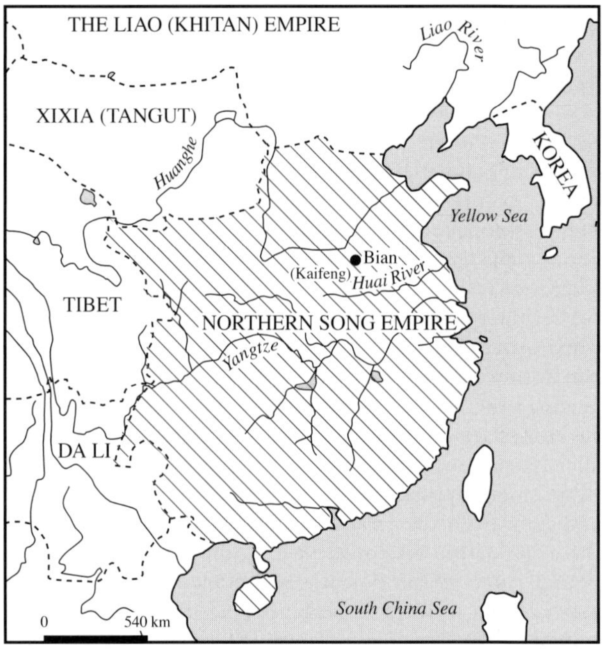

Map 25 The Northern Song Empire in 1111 (draft Guangda Zhang).

might and was always forced to buy peace by paying ever-increasing amounts of annual tribute as a result of the successive defeats against the Khitan, Tangut, Jurchen, and Mongols. Maintenance of a huge amount of troops imposed a steady and heavy strain on the government's fiscal and material resources.

The dynasty falls into two periods. The empire founded by Taizu with its capital at Bianliang (present-day Kaifeng) was called the Northern Song (960–1127). After one and a half centuries, the imperial court was driven by the Jurchen to the south of the Yangtze and eventually made its capital at Hangzhou, then Linan ('temporary safety', which means the provisional imperial headquarters, later known to Marco Polo as Quinsai, 'temporary imperial residence'). The empire, resigning itself to the 'temporary safety' situation until its final collapse, was known as the Southern Song (1127–1279).

To govern the reunited country, the Song elaborated a sophisticated system of checks and balances by distributing the scarcely clear-cut power or by dividing overlapping responsibilities over several bureaucrats. The authority of the grand councillors was partly shared by the other two separate agencies of the central government – the Bureau of Military Affairs and the State Finance Commission. Similar checks and balances were also set up in the network of functionally differentiated regional officials. Regular posts were overlaid with irregular agencies. Officials' formal titles had little relevance to their real functions.

With the concentration of power in the throne having been accomplished, the Song further stressed the Confucian ideal that a loyal subject did not serve two rulers. 'There are no two suns in heaven, nor two rulers in a state.' From the eleventh century onwards the ever expanding examination-recruitment system of the civil service formed the main channel for official nomination (illustration). The school of Hu Yuan (993–1059) was acclaimed as a model for the education of future idealistic officials through a combination of Confucian classical study and practical learning. Sun Fu (992–1057) and Li Gou (1009–1059), his contemporaries, were also famous teachers in the early Song. The noted scholar-official Fan Zhongyan (989–1052) set forth the principle of Confucian bureaucracy by putting concern for the good of the community at large ahead of the pursuit of their own interests. The true scholar-official 'should be first in worrying about the world's worries and last in enjoying its pleasures', he proclaimed. But, as time passed on, the civil service examination system became a stepping stone in selfish scholars' official careers.

After approximately eighty years of seeming stability, the Song court had to face a rapidly deteriorating socio-economic situation. By the middle of the eleventh century, the regular army numbered 1.25 million men. In 1065, defence expenditure consumed 83 per cent of the state's revenues (Smith, 1993, p. 81). But the Song lost every important battle on the frontier. The economic situation also worsened owing to increasing expenses for maintaining the motley host of redundant officials and to the payments of the annual tribute in silver and silk to the Khitan and Tangut. Concentration of farmland into the hands of the imperial family, nobles, officials, and landlords, the heavy burden of compulsory labour and services, and other abuses led to small-scale revolts in many places, even near the capital.

With the crises aggravated, Emperor Shenzong (r. 1067–1085) and many high officials were convinced that reforms were their first imperative. In 1069, Shenzong appointed Wang Anshi (1021–1086) his grand councillor and gave him the go-ahead to carry out reforms. One of the most noted poets and prose writers, and a particularly innovative stateman, Wang laid out his extensive programme of reform, known in Chinese history as the 'new policies' (*xin fa*). He elaborated the 'green shoots policy' (*qing miao fa*), by which local government provided seed loans to farmers during the sowing season to be repaid after harvest at a low interest rate. This was a first-aid measure to undercut the dependency of farmers upon landlords and moneylenders. He commuted public services and compulsory labour into graduated money payments. With these service-exemption payments, the government hired labourers instead. He carried out a more equitable land-tax scale based upon a land remeasurement and a reassessment of its productivity. He set up state warehouses to stablize the prices of basic commodities and to make a profit for government. He attempted to remedy the military weakness and enforce social security by enacting the neighbourhood and joint liability system (*baojia fa*).

The new policies produced some results. Government income increased to some extent. But all elements that Wang called 'engrossers', that is, large landlords, landowning officials, big merchants, and moneylenders, strongly opposed these reforms. After the death of Shenzong, the upright but conservative-minded historian Sima Guang (1019–1085) became grand councillor and most of the new policies were repealed. With the long-standing abuses returned, the government was dislocated in the bitter wrangling of the subsequent reform and anti-reform factions, and its miscalculation at the handling of the alignment policy with the Khitan or Jurchen led to the final fall of its capital into enemy hands.

Jin (Jurchen, 1115–1234); Southern Song (1127–1279)

In the last years of its existence, the Northern Song confronted a more menacing new power, the Jurchen, Tungusic-speaking tribes in Manchuria, ancestors of the Manchus. The Jurchen proclaimed the Jin Dynasty (1115–1234) in 1115 and crushed the Liao in 1125 with aid from the Song. More

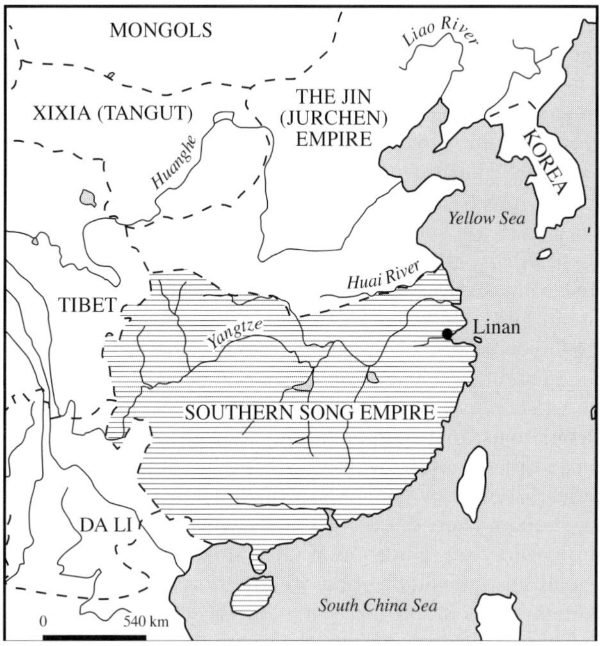

Map 26 The Southern Song Empire in 1208 (draft Guangda Zhang).

belligerent, the Jin took the Song capital, Kaifeng, after a long siege in 1127 and carried off the last emperor Qinzong and his father Huizong, putting a tragic end to the dynasty.

The Song forces withdrew southwards. Confucian-minded scholar-officials and patriotic generals established Gaozong (1127–1162), the only son of the former emperor Huizong, who had evaded capture, as successor. Thus began the Southern Song (1127–1279) (see Map 26).

The struggle between the Song and Jin for the possession of the Yangtze valley dragged on until 1142, when a peace treaty was concluded. The border was drawn along the Huai River. During the prolonged fighting, Gaozong showed an expressed preference for appeasement towards the Jin at any price. He had Yue Fei, a general who gained a wide reputation fighting the Jin, imprisoned for obstinately obstructing the peace negotiations and murdered in prison by the hand of his grand councillor Qin Gui. With the peace of 1142 concluded, the Song formally accepted inferior status as a vassal of the Jin and agreed to pay an annual tribute – 250,000 taels of silver and 250,000 bolts of silk. Although it was a great blow to Chinese pride, the peace purchased in 1142 basically was maintained for the remaining years of the Southern Song. Thus China was divided between north and south down to the Mongol conquest.

As regards the internal policy, the Southern Song court showed no such innovative initiative as the Northern Song once had displayed. In spite of its lack of political activism and the much smaller size of its territory, the Southern Song attained a level of general affluence that no earlier period ever had been able to attain. The Song was also a time of booming internal and maritime trade.

China within the Mongol orbit: Yuan (1271–1368) (see Map 29)

The Mongols, who rose to supremacy under the leadership of their talented military chief Temujin, originated from the Erguna River in what is today China's northernmost province, Heilongjiang. In 1206, at a diet (*kuriltai*) of the tribal chiefs at the source of the Onon River, Temüjin was recognized as universal ruler with the title Chinggis (Genghis) Khān. Within two decades Chinggis Khān had conquered surrounding states, bringing most of Eurasian territory under his rule. He died in 1227, but the Mongol campaigns were continued by his successors. The Jin dynasty finally fell in 1234 under the Mongol attacks. In 1264, Qubilay Khān (r. 1260–1294), a grandson of Chinggis Khān and the fifth grand Khān, was recognized as Great Khān. He transferred his capital to Beijing, called Khānbāliq ('Khān's town') in Mongolian and 'Cambaluc' in Turkic and in Marco Polo's book. In 1271, Qubilay adopted the Chinese name of Yuan and other imperial symbols, such as a reign title and an era name, for his dynasty. When Qubilay launched offensives against the Southern Song, the Song fortifications along the Yangtze River proved to be a formidable barrier for the Mongols. Both sides used gunpowder and a variety of explosive firearms in the fierce fighting. In 1276, the Mongol troops captured the Southern Song capital, Lin'an. A famous Song minister, Wen Tianxiang (1236–1282), organized desperate resistance. The whole of China was brought under the Yuan rule in 1279, the first foreign dynasty in Chinese history to govern the entire country.

The Mongols administered China in a manner as dualistic as that of the previous conquering dynasties, Liao and Jin. Most of the Mongol nobles attempted to impose on China a backward, pastoral mode of production, but Qubilay established a Chinese-style bureaucracy and relied largely on the Chinese sub-officials to rule the conquered subjects. One of his successors even restored the civil service examination system in 1315. Ethnically, the Yuan rulers classified the population into four categories. At the top were the ruling Mongols; beneath them were the *semu* ('coloured-eyed' peoples of Eurasia); then came the 'Hans' (the Khitan, Jurchen and north Chinese); at the bottom of the social ladder were the 'southerners'. As the subjects of the Southern Song surrendered last, they were most discriminated against.

The reunification of China promoted the assimilatation of the different peoples and reintegration of China's economy. Transportation markedly improved. A new Grand Canal system was constructed. Coastal shipping became an important means of grain transport. Modelled on the Song, a national paper currency was introduced. As the Mongol rule was a huge worldwide empire, the Yuan was also a time of unprecedented flourishing of external commerce and cultural exchange.

Eventually, the Yuan rulers and Mongol nobles proved incapable of exploiting their possessions in a sedentary agricultural country. They had at their disposal large numbers of peasants and artisans, but customarily treated them in accordance with nomad practice. They exacted *corvée* after having imposed excessively heavy taxes on peasants. Economic distress, combined with a series of natural disasters, aroused the peasantry to open revolt against the alien rule. The Mongol forces were defeated by the uncoordinated uprisings that spread all over China proper towards the middle of the fourteenth century. They finally retreated to their northern homeland without having been annihilated. The Yuan Dynasty ended in 1368, but the Mongols remained a menace from the northern border to the succeeding Ming Dynasty.

Ming (1368–1644): its early phase (see Volume 5 p.320, Map 27)

The founder of the new native dynasty was Zhu Yuanzhang. As an orphan of a tenant farmer, Zhu became a mendicant novice at an early age in a Buddhist monastery. He was drawn into a popular rebellion with a religious tinge called the 'Red Turbans' and emerged from the insurgent forces as a leader adept at seizing power. By early 1368, he had proclaimed himself emperor of the Ming Dynasty in Nanking, known as Taizu (1368–1398), with the reign title Hongwu (see Plate 239).

Taizu was a capable monarch but of a suspicious character. He succeeded in reconstructing a mechanism of highly centralized government to protect his hold on autocratic power. In 1380, when he purged the central government of its imperial secretariat in connection with the alleged conspiration of his grand councillor and divided its functions among six ministries (*liubu*). This crucial decision, tightening up all official performance under the emperor's close surveillance, and generally referred to in Chinese history as 'the abolition of the *zhongshu*', was meant to totally deprive the Imperial Secretariat of its traditional function in participating in the execution of state affairs. This step also marks the further reassertion of the autocratic imperial prerogative at the expense of the prime ministership, a long-term trend of the encroachment of the power of the emperor on that of the prime minister in Chinese history. A new organ called the grand secretariat (*neige*) was created to replace the abolished imperial secretariat. This group of high-ranking obedient officials, chiefly drawn from the Hanlin Academy, served thereafter as advisors for emperors; they assisted the emperors in dealing with memorials to the throne and in drafting imperial edicts. It constituted a part of the 'Inner Court', together with eunuchs. As a result, government operation under subsequent feeble or aberrant emperors suffered from inefficiency and the dominance of the palace eunuchs.

As the Mongols in retreat posed a constant threat to China from the north, the third Ming emperor, Chengzu (r. 1402–1424, with the reign title of Yongle), decided to transfer the capital in 1421 from Nanking to the site of the former Yuan capital, Khānbāliq. The reconstruction of the new capital, now given the name Shuntianfu ('Capital that follows the Mandate of Heaven'), took 15 years. With its orderly layout, it consisted of three rectangles, one within the other, the innermost of which was the imperial palace, known as the Forbidden City in present-day Beijing.

As a bulwark against the Mongol cavalry, the Ming rebuilt the old defensive Great Wall. The new Great Wall had a stretch of 6,350 km, divided into four garrison zones. Flanking the capital Beijing, the eastern wall, stretching from Shanxi province eastwards to Liaoning province with a length of 1,487 km, was built over successive mountain ranges, undulating with the peaks and ravines. Covered with bricks, the wall was 6 m thick at the base, sloping to 5.4 m at the top. The wall itself rose to a height of 8.7 m with battlements 2 m high on the northern side, from which the Mongol threat came. There were guard houses in the wall about every 70 m apart.

On the high seas, the early Ming was a period of expansion. Between 1405 and 1433, Chengzu dispatched seven huge naval expeditions, logistically prepared by his able fiscal minister Xia Yuanzhi and led by his Muslim eunuch admiral Zheng He (1371–1433). Each fleet consisted of 100 to 200 ships, up to sixty-two of which were 'treasure ships' (*bao chuan*). The biggest 'treasure ships' were 150 m long and 60 m wide, with twelve sails, and each was manned by 300 sailors. Well equipped with 27,800 experienced people, the fleets visited Java, Sumatra, the Malay archipelago, Sri Lanka, India, Arabia, the coast of the Red Sea and East Africa, and called at ports in more than thirty countries. Zheng He's ships set out with gold, silver, silks, porcelain, cloisonné and metal wares, and brought back lions, giraffes, ostriches, zebras and other exotic products. Zheng He's voyages pre-dated by half a century those of Vasco da Gama and Columbus (see Map 27).

The early Ming was also a great age for compilation projects. The greatest of all was a government-sponsored encyclopaedia which bore Chengzu's reign title – *Yongle Dadian* (Yongle Encyclopedia). It consisted of 22,000 volumes, running to 370 million characters.

For a century after Chengzu, the Ming enjoyed prosperity. Farm and handicraft production reached a new high level by the mid-Ming period. With the stimulus of the development of agriculture and handicrafts, the mid-Ming witnessed a fairly well-developed commodity economy in large commercial cities and market towns. The census of 1393 registered 60,545,812 people (Ho Ping-ti, 1959, p. 10). By the end of the fifteenth century, the Chinese population had increased to more than 100 million.

But while Europe had reached the great age of exploration, Ming society seemed to be trapped in nonactivity, and it began to lose its vigour and vitality. Thus, already during the mid-Ming the stage was set for the future political and cultural clash between China and the West.

ECONOMIC DEVELOPMENT AND SOCIAL CHANGES

China remained primarily an agrarian country with an agricultural civilization. The most noteworthy changes during the period under review were the southward migration of the Chinese people, the further development of intensive agriculture, and the diversification of the Chinese economy with the growth of industry and commerce.

Southward migration of the population

Wheat, several subspecies of millet, soy beans and rice were traditionally the key crops in China. As more and more dry farmland was progressively lost to erosion, and seasonal rainfall was becoming uncertain in the Huanghe valley, a constant grain shortage made the northern plains dependent on the agricultural resources of south China. The gradual shifting of China's agricultural base from the Huanghe valley to its southern provinces had begun as early as the mid-Tang. A migration wave gathered momentum when civil strife ravaged north China during the later phase of this dynasty; then the invasions of equestrian Liao and Jin nomads from the north since the Five Dynasties dislodged more people from their normal life. Those who migrated southwards to escape the war formed a fairly large proportion of the Song population. This demographic growth was all the more conspicuous in the south-eastern coastal regions during the Southern Song, because this was a far smaller empire, reduced by half in extent as a result of direct confrontation with its northern and northwestern neighbours. The growth of the population in South China was from about four million households around 750 to about 12 million in 1290 (Kracke, 1955, p. 480, note. 2).

Administrative control over economic activities during the early Tang: changes sprung from late Tang roots

During the Sui and early Tang, the main economic activities were regulated by a uniform system of codified administrative law, statutes, regulations and supplementary ordinances (*lü-ling-ge-shi*). According to the *tian ling* (land statutes) of the Tang, every male adult over 18 was meant to be assigned patches of arable land amounting to 100 *mu* (6.6 ha) by the

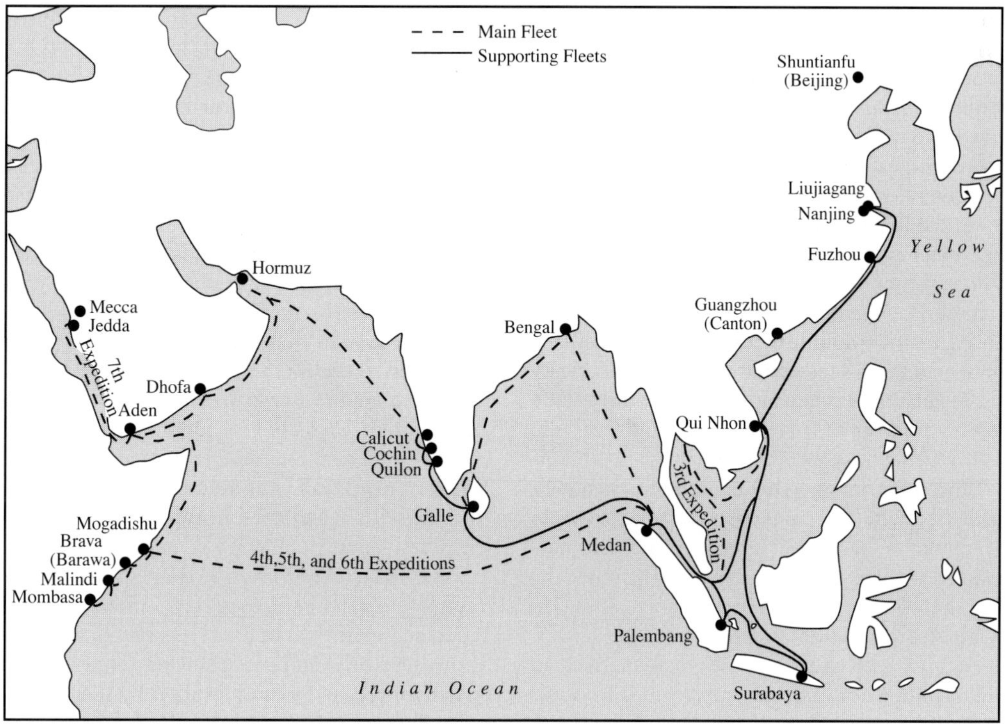

Map 27 Zheng He's voyages between 1405 and 1433 (draft Guangda Zhang).

government, 20 *mu* of which could be held in perpetuity while the remaining 80 were to be returned at his death or when he ceased to be a taxpayer at 60. This equal land allotment served as the prerequisite of the equally fixed head tax. Based on the *hu ling* (household statutes), the new census was to be carried out once every three years. It recorded the name and age of all members of each household and the status and landed possessions of each male adult. All taxable households had to pay annually, for each adult male family member, a head tax in grain (2 *piculs*) and in silk fabric (20 *chi*, about 7 m) or hemp cloth (25 *chi*). Each male adult was liable to twenty days of work for the central government and to a much longer period of work for the local authorities. But this kind of *corvée* and labour service could be commuted into a stipulated amount of silk fabric or hemp cloth or money instead. In the light of recent researches on the Tang texts concerning land allocation, rediscovered in Dunhuang and Turfan, most scholars are inclined to believe that as a legal system governing registration of landed property and its disposal, it remained in force until An Lushan's rebellion in the mid-eighth century, but that it was not implemented to the letter in any region, and probably not at all in the South. It seems to have been enforced in Turfan, but with many modifications to suit local conditions.

Large landed and residential estates were allotted to members of the imperial clan and hierarchically ranked officials. A prince could have 10,000 *mu* (666 ha) and a top rank official 6,000 (400 ha). Land was also granted in various amounts to various state institutions and to the Buddhist and Daoist establishments to serve as a fund for the expenses of government management, office-running expenditure, and the living cost of monks and nuns. As to officials' salaries, they were largely met by the rent from the land allotted to them and by the interest on funds of money allocated for similar purposes.

Giving first priority to agriculture, the government instructed officials on both the central and local levels to encourage farming. It was the duty of the district magistrates to supervise the peasants to do the necessary farm work in the right season and enforce various agricultural encouragement measures, such as the construction of irrigation facilities, water-control works, and public granaries. Huge labour-intensive undertakings were sponsored by special administrative organs and commissioners.

After the An Lushan rebellion (755–763), the Tang government had to give up the attempt to re-enact the system of equitable land allocations. As described above, the uniformly fixed headtaxes in grain and cloth based on this equal land allotment was replaced in 780 by the 'two-tax' system, a system of progressive taxation based on assessment of property of each household, especially on land acreage under cultivation, and collected twice in cash, respectively in summer and in autumn. Private land transactions became a common and widespread feature throughout the countryside.

The early Tang government also exercised a stringent control over the urban life and enforced strict regulations in matters related to trade. The urban populace was compartmentalized into rectangular wards, surrounded by walls. Much of the commercial activity in large cities was conducted within the designated walled-in market quarters. There had been only two great metropolitan markets in Chang'an and Loyang, and one in each prefecture. The hours of trading, quality of goods and categorization of the prices into three scales (as evidenced by the relevant documents discovered in Dunhuang and Turfan manuscripts), were all fixed according to the *shiyi ling* (statute of commerce) and subject to governmental supervision and regulations. From the mid-Tang on, traders began to roam free of government control and seek out their favourite markets. The old government market system (Twitchett, 1966, pp. 202–248) with its various restraints imposed on merchants gradually ceased to be effective.

In contrast to the early Tang years, when official supervision or regulation was imposed on agriculture, handicraft industry and trade in conformity with the codified administrative statutes, the mid-Tang government had to set up, after the An Lushan rebellion, a series of new fiscal institutions, such as state salt monopoly, to tap new financial resources. As a result of monetisation of taxation (the 'two tax' system) and the growth of commercial activity, the Tang government modified in many aspects its centralized economic control policy.

Agriculture

Advances in farming techniques and new methods of irrigation were instrumental in the increase of production in south China. The rise of agricultural production was also due, besides the introduction of early-ripening rice, to the reorganization of rural landholdings into large estates (*zhuang yuan*), the emergence of tenant rent systems, and the proliferation of cities as markets for cash crops.

During the Tang, Song and Yuan periods, the use of iron implements became increasingly widespread. The Tang plough with curved mouldboard, consisting of eleven parts in all, was described in detail by Lu Guimeng (? – *c.* 881) in his *Leisi Jing* (Canon of Spades). It was powered by water buffalo, the sole draft animal, in rice paddy farming.

Chinese agricultural growth also stemmed from the expansion of cultivated acreage. The farming area in China had been concentrated along the Huanghe River in ancient times but had expanded into the Yangtze valley by the Han period. After Tang and Song times, lands in the south were extensively cultivated. Intensive cultivation by introducing multiple crops and rotation systems had transformed once worthless acres to the most high-yielding fields. When in the plain no more wasteland was left to be opened up, an enormous amount of land in less accessible places was brought under cultivation in Song times, such as terraced fields on hill slopes and marshy fields around lakes reclaimed by building dykes. Terraced fields, which appeared for the first time during the Song, could be made fully productive by providing them with irrigation water. In Tang times, hydraulic power was largely used to activate waterwheels and mills. Early in the Southern Song, in addition to the man-powered square-pallet chain-pump, turned mainly by a man's foot (*longgu shuiche*, 'dragon-backbone waterwheel'), a new water-raising system, the animal-powered square-pallet chain-pump, was used to scoop water up to the shore and into ditches that led it into the rice fields. Water could be raised by as much as 30 m by such a device.

The *Nong Shu* (Treatise on Agriculture) by Chen Fu, completed in 1149 during the Southern Song Dynasty, gave a detailed treatment of the technique of raising rice seedlings in nursery beds and transplanting them in paddy fields, the 'constant renewal of soil fertility' by the use of manure, and other fertility preservation methods and, finally, the practice of sericulture, beginning with the planting of mulberry trees and ending with the rearing of cocoons. Another guidebook, also entitled *Nong Shu*, compiled during 1295–1314 by Wang Zhen, the noted agronomist of the Yuan Dynasty, is a large agricultural work. As magistrate of several counties in Anhui and Jiangxi provinces, Wang Zhen gave first priority to agriculture and often went to the rural areas for inspections. The basic concept of his work was that agriculture constitutes the foundation of the Chinese economy. It summed up the farming experience on a country-wide scale – the production practices of dry farmland in the Huanghe valley and rice-paddy cultivation in the region south of the Yangtze. It discusses various technologies and practices not only in farming but also in forestry, animal husbandry, sideline production, fishing, and many other related things such as improved tools and new mechanical devices (a kind of geared water-powered device with one waterwheel to drive nine millstones simultaneously, for example).

The introduction of early-ripening Champa rice around 1012 during the Song seems to have been an event of great significance. With a shortened ripening time of less than 120 days, this high-yielding variety of rice made two crops a year possible. Within a century, double-harvest rice steadily spread from the south into all paddy-field areas. Rice became the main staple crop.

Supplementary crops, such as sugar and tea, were also grown widely, and tea eventually became an essential commodity. Peasant households also engaged in the production of silk and hemp, and also later in tea production. In early Tang times, the chief silk-producing areas had been in the north-east, but after the An Lushan rebellion, silk-production began to increase rapidly in the Yangtze valley and Sichuan.

Cotton was first grown in the western regions (Serindia). Words for cotton appeared in Chinese poems from about the beginning of the ninth century. The cotton grown in the Turfan area was spun and woven into *diebu* (cotton cloth) and imported into China proper. But cotton was introduced to China as material for clothing and an article of commerce mainly from South Asia, especially from Champa and *Da-ba-tang*, an unidentified country in the 'Southern Ocean'. It seems that the technique of cotton planting was introduced in coastal Lingnan (present-day Guangdong province) by the beginning of the ninth century and became a crop in common use in China from the twelfth and thirteenth centuries (Goodrich, 1944, pp. 408–410). Huang Daopo, a woman from Songjiang (now one of the Shanghai townships), was an innovator in Chinese textile history. After the thirteenth century, cotton spinning and weaving emerged as extensive rural industries in China.

Chinese wine making has a long history. After the Tang conquest of Serindia, a new wine-making grape, 'horse-nipple grapes' (*maru putao*) and, with it, the technique of making grape wine, were introduced to China. According to Song records, people had known how to make spirits through double distillation since the middle or towards the end of the tenth century.

Emergence of the great estates: tenancy and hired labour

The free tenure of land became fairly common since the mid-Tang. The accumulation of landed wealth led to the formation of large private estates (*zhuangyuan*) from the mid-ninth century onwards. In 843–846, the temple wealth, especially the monastic farmland of large 'temple estates' (*sizhuang*) that had been set up in the course of hundreds of years as Buddhist foundations, were seized by the government and sold off on the occasion of the suppression of Buddhism. Provincial officials and new families of local landholding gentry of many regions were able to consolidate their fortunes by piecing together purchased or annexed plots into large estates. Having been dispossessed of their lands, many peasants became tenants of the 'encloser' or dependants of a powerful patron. Tenancy developed into a common practice.

By the Song, the status of most people in rural society was determined, above all, by the possession of land. The extensive development of the great estates led to the development of a master–subordinate relation between landlords and tillers. New categories of cultivator spread in rural society – *dianhu* (tenants) and *guyongren* (hired workers), – many of whom were probably classified as *kehu* (propertyless and migrant but free households) in the official registry. A proportion of small farmers found shelter from taxes and *corvée* under a rich and powerful landlord working land of their own, side by side with the lands rented from their patron.

An employer–employee contractual relation emerged. Hired labour was widespread during the Song period. Hired workers were employed by government-operated industries, military garrisons and handicraft workshops. There were thirty-six smelting plants in Xuzhou (in present-day Jiangsu province) in the late eleventh century, each of which employed more than 100 men. A record dated 1181 shows that an iron-ore foundry in Shuzhou (in present-day Anhui province) employed 500 labourers.

Handicraft industry

In early Tang times, artisans and craftsmen who had acquired a high degree of skill handed down in their families from generation to generation, or who possessed an outstanding manual dexterity, were kept in bondage to the government-operated factories. Government offices not only supervised these handicraft factories and industrial production but also exercised administrative control over the artisans, who were assigned slave status. Luxury objects, especially those of the highest artistic quality, produced by these highly skilled silk weavers, goldsmiths and porcelain makers, were destined for the court or noble households. By far the largest number of craftsmen worked in district capitals and cities. Take the silk textile industry for example. Various districts and towns sent their representative or unique silk fabrics to the imperial court as an annual tribute (*tugong*) – *jin* (brocade), *sha* (gauze), *luo* (leno), *ling* (damask), *duan* (satin), *chou* (silk), *rong* (velvet), *kesi* (silk fabric with large, stand-out jacquard patterns), and so on.

Besides the imperial and local factories, Tang handicraft production can be divided broadly into two groups: farm crafts and the products of individual craftsmen. Strictly speaking, farm crafts were merely subsidiary activities within agriculture, performed in the farmer's home with the help of his family during the slack season. Their products, such as those of hand weaving and basket plaiting, were generally indispensable items of daily life, not intended for the market. Individual craftsmen were engaged primarily in smithery, carpentry, weaving, dyeing, pottery, tanning, paper making, the manufacture of ink-sticks, or printing.

Song handicraft factories represented a higher stage of development in traditional Chinese skill-intensive industry.

Big salt-producing factories, some porcelain kilns and textile products were operated or supervised by the government. Some handicrafts, such as ink-stick manufacturing, paper making and book printing, reached a higher level of labour division and greater specialization with the aid of new devices or better processing. Besides, the tendency towards specialization became more pronounced in a number of industrial centres such as Jingdezhen, the 'porcelain town' of more than 300 kilns, in Jiangxi, the silk industry in Jiangnan, the cotton textile centres in Jiangsu and Zhejiang, the ironware-manufacturing centre of Foshan in Guangdong, and shipyards in southern harbours, chiefly Guangzhou (Canton), Quanzhou and Ningbo.

The characteristic form of organization in the urban handicraft industry was the master craftsman guild (*hang* or *zuo*). It seems that the master craftsmen associations remained as the main form of organization since the Tang, as evidenced by many guild inscriptions carved in the Buddhist caves in Fangshan district to the south-west of Beijing, and Longmen in the vicinity of Luoyang as well as by some Dunhuang documents concerning the painters and pigment guilds. In Song times, there were at least 160 guilds in Kaifeng and 414 guilds in the southern Song capital Linan.

Ferrous mining and metallurgy: the use of coal

An unprecedented demand for iron products – agricultural implements, weapons, iron currency, anchors, nails and prows for shipbuilding, heavy pans for salt processing, and so on – boosted the production of wrought iron. The Northern Song mines and smelters had an average annual iron output of 71,241,000 *jin* (approximately 35,600 tonnes) in 1049–1053, with an additional yearly yield of more than 200 tonnes in 1064–1067. By 1078, it is estimated that 75,000 – 150,000 tonnes of iron were being produced annually (Hartwell, 1962), but this is probably an overestimated figure.

Notable technical progress was also achieved in the extraction of other metals, such as gold, silver, copper, lead and tin.

The increasing demand for iron production in turn exerted increased pressure on the Song's timber resources and led to the use of coal, the 'black stone' known to Marco Polo.After having been used in cooking, coal was now also used as a fuel to smelt iron ores. From the relics of a Song coalmine in Hebi district in present-day Henan province, a vertical shaft was dug to a depth of 46 m. People had also learned to use coal as a fuel in daily life. More than a million households lived in the Hedong circuit (present-day Shanxi province), and the capital Kaifeng and its environs made wide use of coal for cooking.

Iron casting

From the Five Dynasties period onwards, the technique of casting large and massive iron objects made marked progress due to the application of clay moulds. Under the conditions of manual production, such massive castings demanded skilled labour and complex co-ordination. The gigantic iron lion of the Northern Zhou (954–960) in Cangzhou, Hebei province and the Northern Song iron pagoda in Danyang, Hubei province, are among the largest iron castings known in the world. The huge iron bell in the Great Bell Tower of Beijing was cast in 1420 during the reign of Emperor Yongle (Chengzu of the Ming). The bell stands 6.75 m high, with an outer diameter of 3.3 m and a lip thickness of 18.5 cm. It weighs 46.5 tonnes. More than 227,000 characters of seventeen Buddhist sutras and tantras were engraved on both the inside and outside.

Porcelain

Porcelain-making techniques progressed rapidly. Tang potters developed the famous glazed 'three-colour' (*sancai*, usually green, yellow and white). The beauty of the porcelain of the later period is due to its usually fragile body being coated with a glaze of one or more delicate colours. The so called *chianfeng cui se* ('the green of a thousand peaks') of the Yue kilns and the white porcelain of the Xing kilns by the Tang; *yu guo tian ching* ('serene sky after rain') of the Northern Zhou (951–960); *mise* ('secret' or 'forbidden' colour, said to have been so called because it was reserved for imperial use) of the Wuyue (907–978, one of the Ten Kingdoms, located in China's most rapidly advancing areas – in and near the lower Yangtze delta); *baijisui* ('hundredfold crackled veins') of the Ge kiln, *yingbai* ('jade white') and *tianbai* ('sweet white') of the Ding kiln, the 'brown moth and iron-coloured foot' of the Guan kiln, the 'black hare's fur' and the 'partridge spots' of the Jian kiln, and especially the *yaobian* (glaze variations resulted from firing, a process that makes the copper-red underglaze come out mottled, streaked or splashed) of the Jun kiln of the Song; *qing hua* (blue-and-white) and *qing hua you li hung* (blue-and-white in red glaze) of the Yuan, and jade-like white glaze and blue-and-white of the Ming are among the most famous porcelain types displaying distinctive glaze charm.

Structural innovations in kilns during the Song are important. The Longquan kiln, for instance, is dragon-shaped and built along the curve of a foothill. Its enormous cavity held more than 170 rows, each with a capacity of up to 1,300 pieces, which meant a total of 20,000–25,000 pieces at one firing. Well–distributed kiln heat is fully utilized by means of the curve in the middle, which serves as a damper, reducing the speed of the flames through the kiln (Institute of the History of Natural Sciences, *Ancient China's Technology and Science*, 1983, p. 198).

Shipbuilding and ocean navigation

The achievement in shipbuilding was another outstanding feature of Song technology. Ships of many types, the 'sand ship' and 'Fujian ship' among others, were built along the coast and rivers, including vessels that could accommodate 200 to 600 people. The government shipyards were engaged in building warships and grain carriers, while the civil dockyards constructed merchant ships and pleasure boats. A total of 3,337 vessels were built in 997. In 1974, a sturdy Southern Song ocean cargo ship was excavated near Quanzhou, Fujian province, then one of the world's biggest ports. Judging from the 34.5 m long, 9.9 m broad and 3.27 m high remains of the hull, it must have had a displacement of 374.4 tonnes. It seems that Song shipwrights developed a great variety of gigantic types of vessel. The great dragon boat was ballasted with 400 tonnes of iron in its hull to keep the ship steady. The paddle-wheel ship of the Song was 70–100 m long (the largest of which measured 110.5 m long by 12.6 m wide) and carried 700–800 men. A fleet of such ships was built by Gao Xuan, a general under Yang Yao who commanded a rebel peasant force on Dongting lake in Hunan province. The paddle-wheel warship of Yang Yao had a two- to three-storey deck-castle and was powered by over 1,000 men. The number of paddle-wheels increased from four with two axles for early types to eight, then to twenty-four and thirty-two, with the corresponding number of axles (Institute of the History of Natural Sciences, *Ancient China's Technology and Science*, 1983, p. 492).

As a result of socio-economic development and technical advances, China witnessed a naval power established on a permanent basis during the late Song, Yuan and early Ming. The Song navy was administered by a special government agency called *yanhai zhizhishi si* (the imperial commissioner's office for the control and organization of the coastal areas), instituted in 1132. The Jurchen invasion attempt in 1161 failed when its fleet was destroyed by the Song fleet under the command of Li Bao near the Chenjia Island off the coast of Shandong. This was the first naval battle fought with firearms in world history. In 1237, the Southern Song navy had grown to be an effective fighting force of twenty squadrons manned by nearly 52,000 men. After the Song, the Yuan court immediately embarked on a gigantic programme of shipbuilding. Shipping magnates, such as Pu Shougeng, a man of Western Asian origin, contributed their services and their ships to help in building the Yuan navy.

As mentioned above, early in the fifteenth century, Chengzu's eunuch admiral Zheng He led seven great naval expeditions between 1405 and 1433. On each voyage, he took a fleet of 100 to 200 ships.

Growth of commerce and paper money

On the socio-economic level, the Song witnessed the emergence of a commercial and monetary economy and the proliferation of cities and towns with an ever growing urban population, a phenomena that gained prominence for the first time in Chinese history. Especially significant to commerce was the proliferation of minor markets and fairs in the countryside, which in time developed into a network of impressive size. The development of the handicraft industry and substantial improvements in the transportation system helped extend the reach of the Song commercial economy. Taxes were assessed and levied in money. A large number of landlords and peasants who originally were isolated and self-sufficient, now came in touch with the market, and in varying degrees became involved in commercial operations. Sometimes lands were cultivated to produce cash crops.

Brisk trading led to the circulation of silver and a huge number of copper and iron coins. By the end of the Northern Song, the government's silver holdings reached the sum of approximately forty million taels. Annual output of copper cash rose to 1,830,000 strings early in the eleventh century, reaching a maximum of 5,060,000 strings in 1080 (Shiba, 1983, p. 92). Largely as a result of the chronic copper and iron coin shortage, great merchants issued drafts or money orders as a substitute. The first experiments of its kind, called 'flying cash' (*feiqian*), appeared as early as 811. The Song saw a wide application of this innovation geared to the needs of the booming commerce. Around the beginning of the Zhenzong's reign (998–1022), sixteen great merchants of Yizhou (present-day Chengdu, Sichuan province) issued a kind of note payable in cash, called *jiaozi*, as an expedient means of transaction on credit. In 1023, the Song government took over the issuing rights from the private business firms and converted *jiaozi* into a legal currency, and so the world's first printed paper money came into circulation. Paper money became the main currency during the Southern Song. In 1246, the seventeenth and eighteenth issues of *huizi* in the south-eastern region amounted to 650 million strings, aggravating long-standing inflation.

Urban life

Prosperity constitutes the central feature of Song urban life. There were probably five or more cities whose population exceeded half a million, including Kaifeng, Nanking, Ezhou and Chengdu. Linan (present-day Hangzhou), the Southern Song capital, had a resident population of 2 million within its walls and another 2 million in its suburbs. The famous Venetian traveller Marco Polo gave a vivid description of its huge size and its lively social life. Residential districts or regions with a more dense population arose outside the city, such as the *caoshi* ('hay market') in the southern suburb of Ezhou (present-day Wuchang, Hubei province).

City services such as the neighbourhood fire-fighting squads and the sewage disposal system grew. Many entertainment places in pleasure districts provided daily amusements with acrobats, jugglers, wrestlers, sword swallowers, snake charmers, kickball, puppet shows, dramas, amusing plays and storytellers. Teahouses, wine shops, restaurants and theatres had singing girls skilled in playing musical instruments. A twelfth-century long-scroll painting, 'Qinming Festival at the Riverside' by Zhang Zeduan, represents a series of colourful street scenes along the Bian River in Kaifeng, showing the activities of all walks of life in detail and recapturing the bustling atmosphere of the Northern Song capital's prosperity (see Plates 9, 241).

Social change in a transition period

As in the economic order, the Tang and Song were also major stages in the evolution of the social composition of the Chinese governing class. In Tang times, ninety-eight great aristocratic families provided the court with 369 prime ministers, but during the late Tang and the Five Dynasties period, when central power was weak and the reins of local government were held by the military, old aristocratic families could no longer maintain their social standing as the primary elite and hold their former position of dominance in government. The Song witnessed the emergence of a new professional bureaucratic elite recruited primarily from scholar-officials and the local gentry. This new class was based no more on birth or a good pedigree, but on education, one's career as an official in central and local government, and the possession of landed property. Related families of a region were usually organised into a clan for their common welfare, but they were totally different from the old great aristocratic families.

In a society gone commercial, ever-expanding economic activities entered into each of the once sharply distinguished four-part divisions – *shi* (scholar-officials), *nong* (farmers), *gong* (artisans) and *shang* (merchants) – of traditional Chinese society. The *shi* could not remain untransformed. The gap that had hitherto existed between the *shi,* who served the government and dominated society, and the *shang,* who engaged in trade and carried on commerce, was getting narrower. A major issue of argument among Song scholar-officials was how to regard commerce (Hymes and Schirokauer, 1993, p. 47). Officials were often engaged in mercantile pursuits. The Song government itself was usually involved in domestic trade and maritime commerce. A large share of the government's revenue came in the form of returns from state monopoly agencies for salt and tea. Even members of the imperial court held shares in private enterprises.

Although spectacular, these reversals came to the fore within tradition, or in other words, they were merely changes by traditional standards. It was just this steady process of expansion of commerce and social changes that had equipped the late Tang and Song to take its place in what is now usually termed the 'Tang–Song transition period'. It is true that most essential features of the last phase of pre-modern China owe their origins to this formative period.

NEO-CONFUCIANISM

Historically, Chinese traditional thought may be divided into three periods. The first is the classical period, conventionally termed the period of rival schools of thought, beginning with Confucius (551–479 BC) and lasting until the late third century BC, when the Qin (221–206 BC) created the first unified empire and laid a firm foundation of centralized and bureaucratic regime for the next two millennia. Confucianism, amalgamated with Legalist practice, was eventually installed as the orthodoxy in official life and ethics around 140 BC. However, Confucianism was on the wane from the third century AD, when neo-Daoism and Buddhism prevailed and were particularly influential in the sphere of religion. In the ninth century, intellectual interest began to move away from Daoism and Buddhism and back to ancient Confucian ideals after several centuries of eclipse. Then came the third period, that of neo-Confucianism, from the eleventh to the late nineteenth century.

The mid-Tang period witnessed a Buddhist impact on the metaphysical and ethical concepts of Confucianism. The Chan monk Zongmi (780–841), for example, inaugurated the subject of human nature, which was to arouse animated discussions. Mindful of his responsibilities as a Confucian and looking for traditional sources of thought, Han Yu (768–824), the most famous essayist in Chinese history, showed his deep concern in his writings about the topics dealing with mind (*xin*), nature (*xing*), and feelings or emotions (*qing*). Modelled on the Chan Buddhist school concept that truth is transmitted from mind to mind through a succession of patriarchs, Han Yu also advocated an orthodox transmission of Confucian *Dao* (way) through a line of early sage-rulers extending to Confucius and Mencius. His colleague Li Ao (d. *c.* 844) displayed an even more unmistakably Buddhist influence in his writings. His metaphysical concepts such as principle (*li*), nature (*xing*), and so on, can be traced to the Huayan and Tiantai schools, two pillars of sinicized Buddhism. The intellectual movement that was initiated by Han Yu and Li Ao in defence of Confucian ideals against Buddhist influences in the mid-Tang, effectively led to the overwhelming revival of Confucianism during the Song.

This reassertion of Confucian tradition, that had started from the implicit combination of Confucianism with Buddhism intermingled with Daoist terminology around AD 1000, was to be fully developed during the Southern Song; it culminated in a 'new' Confucian orthodoxy known to the Chinese as *lixue* (the 'learning of principle') or *daoxue* (the 'learning of the Way') and *xinxue* (the 'Learning of the Mind'), and as 'Neo-Confucianism' in Western literature. The neo-Confucianists, speculating on the governing forces of the universe, introduced the concept of 'principle' (*li*), as a substitute for the Buddhist emptiness (*sūnyatā*) and the Neo-Daoist non-being (*wu*). If there had ever been anything really 'new' in this phase of Confucianism, it was its metaphysical reasoning regarding such characteristic concepts – *li* (principle), *xing* (nature, the substance of the universe), *qi* (material force), and so on, the role of which had been negligible in ancient Confucianism. No less important than the metaphysical reasoning was the end in view and the result keenly sought after, which was neither Buddhist salvation nor Daoist immortality, but attaining 'cultivation of self and ordering of the state' (*xiu shen zhi guo*), or 'sageliness within and kingliness without' (*nei sheng wai wang*). It was to be realized through the working of the mind and the cultivation of moral values, complemented by scholarly disciplines, aimed at becoming an ideal man in the Confucian sense.

That *xinxue* or *daoxue* gained wider acceptance during the Song was also due to some peculiar circumstances. The significant shifting in the Song domestic policy towards developing a civil service to prevent the rise of any potential militaristic regional power, the expansion of the examination system for the recruitment of civil officials, and the related demand for a new type of education from the eleventh century onwards also contributed to the progress in the new exposition of Confucian doctrine. As the Song Dynasty finally resigned itself to its militarily inferior position *vis-à-vis* its northern neighbours, after all its vain efforts to achieve territorial unity, and there the Song court proved to be unwilling to effect any more reform or to fight a war for the recovery of the lost central plains, the only thing left for the Song scholars to do was insisting upon the superiority of the Chinese cultural tradition. Thoroughly disenchanted with the dismal political situation, many idealistic Confucianists withdrew from official service and committed themselves to learning and educational activities. Neo-Confucianism finally developed into an articulate and well-integrated philosophical system that synthesized metaphysics, ethics, social ideals, political aspirations and moral/intellectual self-cultivation.

Zhou Dunyi (1017–1073) has been regarded as the most important pioneer of Song Neo-Confucianism. Borrowing from Daoist doctrines and elaborating on the *I jing*, he composed the *Taiji tu* (Diagram of the Supreme Ultimate), in which he elucidated the origin of the 'heavenly principle' (*tianli*) and inquired into the beginning and end of all things, including those of the human being and his position in the universe. He held that the universe was an infinite, absolute entity evolved from the ultimate of non-being (*wuji*). The ultimateless (*wuji*) gave rise to the supreme ultimate or great ultimate (*taiji*). The supreme or great ultimate through movement or activity (*dong*) produces the *yang* (male). This movement or activity, having reached its limit, is followed by quiescence or tranquillity (*jing*), and by quiescence or tranquillity it produces the *yin* (female). By the transformation and the union of the *yang* and *yin*, water, fire, wood, metal, and earth are produced. All beings are formed through the interaction of the *yang* and *yin* and constituted of the five elements (*wuxing*: metal, wood, water, fire, earth). According to Zhou Dunyi, the five elements pertain to what he calls *qi*, which constitutes the basis of differentiation of things. Zhou Dungyi's cosmological speculations were further developed by Shao Yong (1011–1077) in his study of symbols and numbers.

The men who developed the concepts of *li* and *qi* and made them the central thesis of the new doctrine were Zhang Zai (1020–1077) and the Cheng brothers. Of the two concepts, Zhang Zai treated that of *qi* more fully and the Cheng brothers gave greater prominence to that of *li*. Zhang Zai regarded *li* not as above or different from *qi* but as the law according to which *qi* operates. The Cheng brothers, Cheng Hao (cognomen Mingdao, 1032–1085) and Cheng Yi (cognomen Yichuan, 1033–1108), bore a close relationship to their neo-Confucian contemporaries. They had Zhou Dunyi as their teacher, Shao Yong as their friend and Zhang Zai as their uncle. Carrying on Han Yu's thought, they advanced anti-Buddhist and anti-Daoist arguments. They rejected the concept of *li* (principle) as it was understood by the Tiantai and Huayan Buddhist sects, and they reinterpreted *li* as the direct cause of all phenomena and *qi* as the substance of the universe.

It is generally acknowledged that the 'school of *li*' of the Song and Ming was established by the Cheng brothers. They both argued that for a thing to exist, there must be its *li* (principle or reason), and *li* is inherent in the nature (*xing*) of man and other beings. But there is a shade of difference between these brothers in their ideas regarding *li*. But although they were slight, these seeds of difference were to pave the way for the emergence within neo-Confucianism of its two main schools: that of the Learning of Principle and that of the Learning of Mind. Convinced that Principle (*li*) is at the basis of all phenomena, the younger Cheng, Cheng Yi, was inclined towards the study of the physical world, which he believed to be real. 'All things in the world may be understood through this underlying principle' by speculative thinking and investigating. This school of the study of principle was to be further elaborated in the works of Zhu Xi (1130–1200) as the Learning of Principle. The standard saying of this Cheng-Zhu school is that 'nature is principle' (*xing* = *li*). For the elder Cheng, Cheng Hao, principle or heavenly principle is nothing more than the force inherent in any concrete object, and as such does not exist apart from such an object. From this point of view, innate knowledge exists without being acquired from outside, and therefore mind and its inner experience gradually assumed more importance than things. In later times, this theory came to be developed by Lu Jiuyuan (1139–1193) and Wang Shouren (cognomen Yangming, 1472–1529, the most eminent exponent of this intuitive school) and passed from the study of *li* into the study of mind. Man's mind is not the function of his nature but is rather the function of principle itself. 'mind is principle' (*xin* = *li*). 'All things are therefore complete within us.'

The Cheng brothers never discussed the supreme or great ultimate. It was left to Zhu Xi, a century later, to incorporate metaphysics, ethics, social and political ideals, individual discipline, and self-cultivation into a more fully integrated philosophical system. Zhu Xi inherited Cheng Yi's thought and also took into account the views of other neo-Confucianists of the Northern Song. According to Zhu Xi, the universe consists of abstract principles (*li*) in dynamic combination with the 'stuff' (*qi*) – the material cause that makes a thing concrete, and that constitutes the actualizing force in all phenomena. *Li* is never separable from the *qi*. Nevertheless, *li* pertains to what is 'above shapes' or prior to physical form (*xing er shang*), whereas the *qi* pertains to what is 'within shapes' or posterior to physical form (*xing er xia*). The summation of all principles is the supreme ultimate. Everything, in addition to its own particular principle which make it what it is, also holds within itself the supreme or great ultimate. In other words, things share the same supreme principle. The supreme or great ultimate is one, but as its functions, it is manifested in the innumerable concrete things, just as 'the moon reflecting itself in ten thousand streams' – 'principle is one but its manifestations are many'.

What was more important - for Zhu Xi was the *li* in the ethical and social domains of human concern. Man derives his nature from *li*, and his physical frame from the *qi*. Nature alone remains constant. The basic principles of morality such as benevolence, righteousness, propriety, wisdom, and good faith are endowment of *li*. In a word, human nature is identical with the supreme ultimate in all its completeness. Men differ because their material endowments are different as the tangible result of the particular combinations of *li* with *qi*, the latter being unequal in its purity in different individuals.

Then the question arose how to investigate principle. For Cheng Yi and Zhu Xi, principles are in things and one can penetrate into the principles of all external things and phenomena by *gewu* ('to investigate things') and *zhizhi* ('to extend knowledge'). Interpreted to mean 'investigating the principle (*li*) of things' and 'extending the knowledge of *li*', this *gewu* and *zhizhi* endeavor became the basic training requisite for the intellectual and moral cultivation of the literati class. The goal of every man is to fulfil the potentiality of his *li*. Man can achieve this by devoting himself to 'the cultivation of the self', for example through true self-understanding. As man's feelings arise from his physical frame, they become 'human desire' or, if they become excessive, 'selfish desire'. As any action motivated by excessive desire is immoral, man should preserve the heavenly principle (*cun tian li*) and extinguish human desire (*qu ren yu*). The renewal of society can be achieved through a sequence of well-defined steps and stages of individual and collective self-cultivation. Most of Zhu's voluminous writings, such as his *Commentaries on the Four Books* (*Si Shu – Great Learning, The Doctrine of The Mean; The Analects of Confucius and Mencius;* and *Reflections on things at Hand* (*Jin si lu*) – are destined for this purpose in the broadest terms.

Lu and Wang vigorously contended with this external approach. In contrast to the Cheng-Zhu school, Lu not only emphasized the central agency of the mind but also held that the mind is nothing other than principle. In Lu's view, to investigate principle is to investigate the mind. Since all men have the innate ability to do good, they naturally extend their knowledge into action. Wang further elucidated Lu's theory by emphasizing intuitive, rather than intellective, character of the mind. Calling principle (*li*) 'intuitive knowledge (*liangzhi*)', Wang regarded the 'extension of intuitive knowledge (*zhi liangzhi*)' as the main purpose of learning. To Wang, principle and things are a single entity, knowledge and action are identical (*zhi xing he yi*).

It is obvious that principles the neo-Confucianists investigated are not laws of nature in an epistemological sense. As indicated above, *gewu* or 'the investigation of things' and *zhizhi* or 'the extension of knowledge' as integral parts of the neo-Confucianist educational curriculum of self-education was merely aimed at gaining spiritual training and moral knowledge. Confucianism, the dominant ideology in China for more than two millenia, is largely a code of morality, and neo-Confucianism is a further metaphysical elaboration of the doctrine of human relationships. Its primary concern is how to achieve harmony in the family, an orderly management of the state and, finally, peace and well-being in society.

To the neo-Confucianists, loyalty, filial piety, benevolence, and righteousness (*zhong, xiao, ren*, and *yi*) were conceived as the embodiment of abstract principles in human nature. As a natural result, human relationships in Zhu Xi's interpretation proved to be most appealing to the autocratic rulers. The emphasis is on a person's moral obligations to others: subservience and obedience of children to parents, the young to elders, wife to husband, commoners to their superiors and officials, and officials to the sovereign. From the early fourteenth century, the neo-Confucianism was established as the sole state orthodoxy. By the end of the fourteenth century, when the Mongol conquerors took over China, Zhu Xi's *Commentaries on the Four Books* was adopted as the basic text of official instruction and the civil service examination system. The Ming and Qing (Manchu) rulers reconfirmed time and again Zhu's Confucianist orthodoxy and integrated its principal precepts into their 'sacred edicts', transforming it into a kind of imperial Confucianism.

But Confucian and neo-Confucian ideals also persisted as the lofty aspirations of some literati. For quite a long time in Chinese history, individual self-cultivation in a neo-Confucian spirit inspired the independent attitude of a number of scholar-officials and helped many intellectuals to learn to survive in adversity, nurturing their mind with moral values.

In recent years, some scholars argue that the Confucian legacy seems to have added a valuable contribution to the booming economies of East and South-East Asia. Moreover, some neo-Confucian values, as a source of inspiration for our own time, are believed to be instructive in shaping 'new selves' better adapted to the requirements of both the present and the future (de Bary, 1988, p. 138).

RITUAL AND RELIGION

Ancestor worship

Ancient Chinese religious belief may be characterized briefly as showing a conspicuous lack of a unifying religion and a plurality of the cults of local deities. Perhaps one of the cardinal practices running throughout the entire span of Chinese history and practiced by everyone from the highest imperial level down to the lowest social classes is ancestor worship. Confucianists emphasized that filial piety was the foundation of an ethical life which would contribute to regulate the family harmony and attain the ideal of social peace and political stability. Memorial services were strictly held and sacrificial offerings were regularly brought before the ancestor's memorial tablets. As Buddhism expanded its influence over all social strata during the Tang and Song, Buddhist clerics were involved in such memorial services, sometimes held in the monasteries, on behalf of the deceased ancestors, in the hope of getting their soul to be reborn in paradise. A great number of scrolls and manuscripts concerning the fast days, discovered in the cave-shrine of Dunhuang, reveal details of this kind of clerical participation.

Prescribed rituals

For more than two millennia of imperial history, performance of the rituals of birth, marriage and death in the prescribed manner was another characteristic of traditional Chinese daily life that unified Chinese of various social strata across time. At the highest, imperial level, formulized schedules and stereotyped procedures for routine rituals were classified into five categories: Sacrifices to Heaven, Earth, the land, the harvest, the ancestors, and other seasonal sacrificial or festive occasions (*ji*); death, mourning, funerals and offerings at regular intervals (*xiong*); military rites (*jun*); rules of hospitality on the occasion of receiving vassals and giving them audience (*bin*); weddings, clan banquets, country feasts and various auspicious omens (*jia*). As for officials and ordinary people, their life-cycle rituals – birth, marriage, death, and so on – were also duly arranged in conformity with prescribed rituals.

Buddhism

Buddhism came to China in the fourth century AD. By the time of the Northern and Southern Dynasties (420–589), it had become widespread, with a marked difference that practitioners in the north gave more attention to *dhyāna* (concentrated meditation) and those in the south to *prajnā* (wisdom). This was also the beginning of the age of the large-scale and systematic translation of Buddhist scriptures and commentaries. Through the combined efforts of non-Chinese Buddhist missionaries and their Chinese colleagues over ten centuries, the resulting Chinese version of the Buddhist canon is greater than that in any other language and preserves many texts of which the Pali/Sanskrit originals have been lost.

During the Sui and Tang, Buddhism reached its apogee as an inspiring force in social, religious and intellectual life. Different Mahāyāna schools emerged one after the other, adapting Buddhism to the Chinese way of thinking.

The teaching of the three stages (*san chieh chiao*) preached a doctrine of the universality of the Buddha nature and carried their teaching to the furthest extreme, that there was no distinction between Buddhist and non-Buddhist. This movement was suppressed by the Tang court. The syncretistic Tiantai school, with its tenets based on the *Lotus Sūtra*, elaborated a harmoniously co-ordinated presentation of Buddhist teachings propagated by different schools and formulated a system of theoretical study on the identity of *Bhūtatathatā* ('true suchness', known here as the 'single absolute mind') and the world of phenomena in the form of 'impure things'. The *Avataṃsaka* school ('Flowery Splendour' or *Huayan School*), whose basic canonical text is the *Avataṃsaka sūtra*, held the doctrine of the *Dharmadhātu* (the realm of Truth). They expounded the theory in the universal causation of the realm of phenomena and established a universal harmony between the realm of things (*shi fa jie*) and the realm of principle (*li fa jie*), a Buddhist synthesis of phenomenon and noumenon.

The famous pilgrim Xuanzang (602–664) was one of the greatest figures in the history of Chinese Buddhism. He travelled via Central Asia to India for seventeen years (629–645) and covered a distance of 25,000 km, leaving a detailed account of enduring value of his pilgrimage, entitled *Buddhist Record of the Western World (Xiyuji)*. Being the most learned scholarly monk of his time, he spent the remainder of his life in translation work in Chang'an, together with his disciples – 1,335 volumes of original Buddhist scriptures and commentaries were translated into Chinese by them. These translations have been recognized as standards in both style and accuracy. He also introduced the *Yogācāra* system of Buddhism into China and established the *Dharmalakṣana*

(*Faxiang*) School or the 'Ideation-Only' (*Weishi)* School, aiming at a subtle analysis of the nature of all phenomena in terms of the causal and conditional functions of the 'Storehouse-consciousness (*ālaya-vijñāna*).

During the eighth century the Tantric teachings of the Vajrayāra system of India were introduced into China by Jingangzhi (Vajrabodhi), Bukong (Amoghavajra) and others, giving rise to the Tantric sect in China. Other schools founded in China during the Tang dynasty upon the exposition of different scriptures and treatises were that of the 'Three-Treatise' or (*Sanlun School*), the Vinaya (Discipline or *Lü)* School, the Abhidharma-kośa ('Compendium of Philosophy') School, and *Satya-siddhi* (*chengshi*) School.

Most of these schools were short-lived. Of all the ten principal Chinese schools that arose during the Sui and Tang, only two, the Pure Land (*Jingtu*) School and that of Dhyāna (Meditation or *Chan)* School, remained active under the following dynasties because of their easier practice, aimed at the identification of mind with the innate Buddha. The Pure Land school promoted the recitation of the holy name of Amitābha Buddha, so that one might be reborn in his pure land. But the most uniquely Chinese and most influential school is that of Chan (*dhyāna*).

The southern branch in the traditional history of the Chan lineage propagated an intuitive way of instantaneous enlightenment. The Chan masters hardly ever expressed their approval of textual formulation (*bu li wen-zi*), nor did they rely on the sacred scriptures and metaphysical discourse. They usually addressed the adherents saying: 'Point directly to the human mind (*zhi zhi renxin*), see into the nature [of the mind] and attain Buddhahood (*jian xing cheng fo*)'. According to the highly revered sixth patriarch, Huineng (638–713), the human mind is originally pure. The only way to retrieve the original nature of the mind, that is, the innate Buddha mind, is to practise 'cultivation through non-cultivation', to rid the mind of any abiding, and prevent oneself from being carried away by thought in the process of thought. With an expressed preference for 'a transmission of Truth from mind to mind', they favoured a plain, direct, and practical approach to enlightenment and used various devices such as shouts, blows, enigmatic expressions, bizarre gestures and witty metaphors in a vernacular style to stimulate practitioners to awaken to the Buddha nature. By the effect of synthesizing the sublime with the common, some of the Chan masters came to a fuller realization that 'there is nothing very much in Buddhism', 'Spiritual understanding and divine functioning lie in carrying water and chopping firewood'.

As they were propagated and studied widely, the theories of the different schools of Buddhism in China had a great influence upon the educated class. This especially was the case with the Chan school, whose monastic community enjoyed a period of unprecedented material prosperity and spiritual influence during the Song under imperial and elite patronage.

Devotees' worship activities as reflected in the cave-temples of Longmen and Dunhuang

Empress Wu Zetian came from a very pious Buddhist family. As a concrete way of seeking divine favour she eagerly took on the role of Buddhist Empress and commissioned the carving of a great number of images at the great cave temple sites of Longmen near Luoyang, including the colossal statue of Vairocana, during her reign.

To the south-east of Dunhuang, the oasis town at the eastern end of the Silk Road in present-day Gansu province, lie the Mogao Caves, also known as *Qianfodong*, the Thousand Buddha Caves. Here more than a thousand cave-shrines were carved into the cliffs from the fourth to fourteenth century by devotees. Of the 480 extant grottoes, 60 to 70 per cent were done during Sui and Tang times. These cave-shrines, whose walls and ceilings are covered with murals illustrating the *Jātaka* tales and Buddhist *sūtras*, demonstrate all phases of iconographic and artistic development over 1,000 years and make up the richest repository of Buddhist art in the world. It is estimated that the Mogao cave paintings could cover a wall 5 m high stretching over 25 km if linked together. The caves are also famous for painted stucco statues, ranging from 33 m to 10 cm high, realistic in appearance and graceful in posture.

Many thousands of manuscript scrolls in bundles, a significant number of paintings, textiles and banners embroidered with Buddha images and portraits of donors had been sealed up in cave-shrine no. 17 since the early eleventh century. They were preserved intact in the dry atmosphere until this deposit was rediscovered in 1899 or 1900. Today, manuscript scrolls and paintings from this great treasure are separately kept in museums in London, Paris, St Petersburg, New Delhi and Beijing (see Plates 85, 87, 235).

Daoism

Daoism enjoyed a privileged status during the Tang because of the reigning house's claim to be descended from the deified Laozi. This pretence of being related to the legendary founder of Daoism served as a means of enhancing dynastic prestige. For most of the Tang Dynasty Daoism was prosperous, but Daoists had to compete with Buddhists. Of the three great traditions – Confucianism, Buddhism and Daoism – Daoism took precedence over the other two from 625.

Daoism received its greatest imperial preferential sponsorship during the reign of Xuanzong, sixth the emperor of the Tang. In 741, Xuanzong made Daoism a state doctrine. He inaugurated a separate Daoist examination (*daoju*) for recruiting students and scholars versed in Daoist classics into the civil service. He edited an imperial commentary to the *Daodejing* and distributed it throughout the empire. He also tried to compile all extant Daoist texts into a canon, as the Buddhists had done.

Daoism once again became the official religion in the early eleventh century. It witnessed an efflorescence in the twelfth century, especially during the reign of Huizong (1101–1125) of the Song. Huizong also edited an imperial commentary to the *Daodejing* and had the Daoist canon printed towards the end of his reign. Several new Daoist movements also developed under the Jin Dynasty (1115–1234) in the north. Among them, the ascetic Quanzhen (complete perfection) movement evolved into a fully fledged Daoist monastic tradition.

Manichaeism

Manichaeism was introduced into China by the Iranians, most probably by Sogdian missionaries and merchants in the sixth to seventh centuries, with 694 as the earliest registered date. It was in that year that a *fu-do-dan* (episcopus) from *Bosi*

(Persia) came to the Tang court presenting a '*Sūtra* of the Two Principles' (*Er zong jing*). The interest of the imperial court in the Manichaean religion appears mainly to have been associated with the reign of the empress Wu Zetian (684–705). In 731, a Manichaean priest was ordered, at the instruction of the emperor, to compile a treatise on the Manichaean teaching – '*The Compendium of the Teaching of Mani, the Buddha of Light*' (*Mani guangfo jiaofa yilue*) – only to have this religion absolutely prohibited the following year.

But Manichaeism again prospered after 763 in and around two Tang capitals, Chang'an and Luoyang, and in some other cities in inland China, when Bögü Qaghan, ruler of the powerful Uighur Khaganate in Central Asia, on whom the Tang court depended militarily to suppress the An Lushan rebellion, made Manichaeism his state religion in 762. As the Uighur Kaganate acquired wealth, mainly through trade with the help of the Manichaean Sogdians, the Uighur rulers fell under the Sogdians' influence in matters of religious faith as well as state policy. In 840, when the Uighur Khaganate lost its political dominance on the Mongol plateau and migrated westwards, Manichaeism lost its influence in China proper. In 843, with the broad-scale persecution of religions in China, Manichaeism too was strictly forbidden.

Nevertheless, it survived in disguise under a new name, *mingjiao* (religion of light), during Song and Yuan times, or even later, as it became more and more integrated with the peasant movements. It became a heretical secret religion, especially in the coastal provinces of Fujian and Zhejiang. Some Manichaean communities were absorbed by messianistic Buddhist sects, mixing the concept of the coming saviour, Maitreya. Telling evidence of its presence in this area is the identification of a site with a Manichaean temple now called *Cao'an*, situated 20 km south of Quanzhou (in present day Fujian province), mentioned in Song literature. This monument may be considered as the only Manichaean monastery now preserved in the world.

Another place of special interest for the present-day study of Manichaeism is Turfan and its surrounding countryside in Xinjiang (eastern Turkestan). Among the great variety of archaeological findings are Manichaean murals and manuscripts written in Iranian (Parthian, Middle Persian and Sogdian) and Turkic languages decorated with superb miniatures. It seems that the Manichaean community existed in the Turfan area (Sundermann, 1992, p. 64) until the rise of Mongol rule, but elsewhere, Manichaean temple were replaced by Buddhist sanctuaries from the eleventh century or even earlier (see Plate 54).

Mazdeism

Mazdeism, with its variant of the dualistic Persian Zoroastrianism, entered China with Persian missionaries and Sogdian merchants earlier than the other religions of Western Asia. Traces of Mazdean influences over syncretic Daoist writings have been detected by some scholars. It seems that such vaguely traceable evidence may suggest an even earlier date of entry.

Apparently, few Chinese adopted this religion, called *xian* in Chinese literature. During the Sui or earlier, a regular system of official sacrifices was instituted for foreign followers of this religion in China. *Sabao* (priests) were appointed in Chang'an and in the provinces by the Tang authorities. In 621, a *hu xien ci* ('Barbarian *Xian* Temple')was established in Chang'an. This was probably the first recorded Mazdean temple in Tang times. In 631, a *Muhu* (Magus) priest was received in audience at the imperial court. It is interesting to note that in Tang times the sinicized Sogdians of Dunhuang and Turfan, apparently Mazdean believers, displayed considerable community activities as evidenced by the literary documents found there.

Nestorianism

The earliest mention of Christianity with a certain date is 635, when a Nestorian mission from the country of Taqin (referring loosely to the Roman Orient or, more specifically, Syria) reached China. Nestorius died in *c.* 439, but already by 635 Aloben (*rabbouni*, the teacher) arrived in China, and a church was established in Chang'an in 638 with the original name *Posi hu si,* which was later changed to *Daqin si* in 745. In Tang times, the religion called itself *Jingjiao* (the 'brilliant religion'). Its best-known monument is a bilingual (Chinese–Syriac) stone inscription, entitled 'A Monument of the Diffusion through the Middle Kingdom of the Brilliant Teaching of Daqin', erected in 781 and rediscovered in 1625 not far from the site of the first church.

Some Christian manuscripts (Psalms, New Testament passages, and so on) in Syriac, Sogdian and Uighur Turkic languages were discovered in the ruins of many sites, including Bulayïq, Qoco and Qurutqa, in the Turfan region (Sims-Williams, 1992, pp. 43–44). A Chinese version of the hymn 'Gloria in Excelsis Deo' (*Jingjiao sanweimongdu zan,* 'A Hymn of the Brilliant Teaching to the Three Majesties, for obtaining Salvation') was found in the cave-shrine at Dunhuang (Collection Pelliot No. 3847 in the Bibliothèque Nationale in Paris).

Between 1000 and 1200, Christianity spread among the non-Chinese tribes along the northern frontiers of China, while it had disappeared from China proper. In Mongol times, the Turkic Öngüt tribesmen were largely Nestorian Christians. They left a large number of tombstones with inscriptions and crosses. Many members of Chinggis Khān's house, such as Güyük (r. 1246–1248), grandson of Chinggis Khān, were brought up in the Christian faith. From everywhere – Syria, Greece, France and the Caucasus – Christian priests and artisans flocked to his court. Sorqaqtani, mother of Mongka Khān (r. 1251–1259) and Qubilay Khān (r. 1260–1294), was a Nestorian Christian. With the Mongols, Nestorianism re-entered China and saw its final flourishing. The most famous Nestorian patriarchs in the Yuan capital, Khānbāliq (present-day Beijing), were Mar Jabalaha III (1245–1317) and his older companion Rabban Sauma (1230?–1294). Mar Jabalaha at least was an Öngüt. A chain of archbishoprics and bishoprics stretched from Samarkand to Khānbāliq. A Nestorian church in Khānbāliq and another in Ganzhou (Zhangye, in present-day Gansu province) were dedicated to Sorqaqtani. Another certain Nestorian relic of Yuan times is two carved stones in a temple called Shizi Si, the 'Holy Cross Temple' in the hills near Fangshan, 25 km south-west of Beijing.

Franciscan missions

In 1245, Pope Innocent IV dispatched the Italian Franciscan John of Plano Carpini to call on the Mongol Great Khān. Several years later, King Louis IX of France supported the Flemish Franciscan William of Rubruck to visit the Great

Khān's court. In about 1265, Nicolo and Maffeo Polo, merchants of Venice, reached Qubilay Khān's capital. They were quickly sent back with letters to the pope. In 1289, the Franciscan friar John of Monte Corvino (1246 or 1247–1328) was sent from Rome to be Archhbishop of Khānbāliq. He reached there in 1294, translated the Testament into Mongolian, made thousands of converts, and built two Catholic churches in 1298 (or 1299) and 1305–1306. When the Venetian merchants Nicolo and Maffeo Polo (father and uncle of the famous Marco) returned from their first visit to Qubilay Khān's capital in 1266, they again carried with them a request from the Great Khān for more than 100 Catholic priests, and in 1307 seven more Franciscans were sent to join John of Monte Corvino. Of the members of this mission, Peregrine was made Bishop of Zaitun (Quanzhou) in 1318. Later, Odoric of Pordenone reached China in 1323(?), and his countryman, the Franciscan John of Marignolli, in 1342. John of Marignolli presented a large Western horse to the Great Khān, and the horse created a deep impression at the court. Many *lettré-fonctionnaires* were ordered to compose poems in its honour. A census taken in about 1300 in Zhenjiang (in present-day Jiangsu province) listed the Christians together with other foreign residents. With the fall of the Yuan Dynasty, the Roman Catholic Church was expelled from China, but its return from Europe was only to be expected two centuries later.

Jews

Very little is known of the history of the Jews in China. A mutilated Judaeo-Persian fragment was found at Dandan-uiliq in the Khotan area of the Tarim basin (Stein, *Ancient Khotan*, Vol. I., pp. 306–309; 570–574; Vol. II., plate cxix). Another small manuscript of the ninth or tenth century in square Hebrew script was discovered in the cave-shrine at Tunhuang (*Journal Asiatique*, 1913, pp. 139–175). Jews were mentioned by Abū-Zaid among the foreign residents of Khanfu (Guangzhou) in the ninth century, then by Marco Polo in Khānbāliq in the thirteenth century and by other Franciscans in Khānbāliq and Zaitun (Quanzhou). The synagogue in Kaifeng seems to have been built in 1163.

Islam

Closer relations between the Chinese and the Arabs (known as 'Dashi' in Chinese literature, a name derived from the Persian *Tājīk*) seems to have existed since the second half of the seventh century. In 651, the first Arab embassy from the fourth caliph ʿUthmān, came to the court in Chang'an by land. Then, in about one hundred years from the mid-seventh to early ninth centuries more than thirty embassies came to China from the Arab lands. There is no precise date for the founding of the first mosque in China. It is reported that a mosque had been erected in Chang'an when an embassy in 725 or 726 led by Sulaymān and twelve companions reached there.

It is well known that the ʿAbbāsid caliphate was to a large extent dependent on revenues from commerce with India and China. Throughout most of the Tang and Five Dynasties period merchants from Arabia and Persia could be found in almost every big city of China. They came via overland and maritime routes. In the ninth century a maritime voyage from Persia to Guangzhou took 130 to 140 days. Thousands of Muslim merchants resided in the special foreign quarters. Some carried on trading in pearls, precious stones, jewels and silk. Others operated small shops selling grape wine and exotic foods. According to the Arabic sources of Abū Zayd and Masʿūdī, 120,000 Arabs and Persians perished in Guangzhou when the bandit army of Huang Chao sacked the city in 879.

At the same time, Chinese ships from Guangzhou, which during The Tang was China's main international port, called at ports as far as Sīrāf and Baṣra on the Persion Gulf. Chinese silk, handicraft products, and inventions like paper, the magnetic compass and gunpowder found their way to many countries in Africa and Europe through the Muslim world.

The real diffusion of Islam took place during the Yuan Dynasty. The Mongol rulers were well disposed toward this alien religion. From Yuan times on, Islam spread widely throughout China. The merchant Pu Shougeng was appointed as an official in the foreign trade administration in Fujian and Canton provinces by the Yuan court. When the noted traveller Ibn Baṭṭūṭa (1304–1377) came to China from Tangier in Morocco in 1347, he remarked that his Muslim way of life was deeply respected everywhere.

LITERATURE

Poetry

When China was reunited under the Sui and Tang, a group of poetic geniuses succeeded each other in capturing the vigour of the epoch and extirpating of the decadent and artificial trend of the preceding epoque. Poetry (*shi*) showed a renewed vitality and reached full maturity. It is generally recognized that the Tang Dynasty was the golden age of Chinese poetry. The Tang poets, while retaining older forms of poetry, developed new forms, *jintishi* or 'modern style verse'. The older forms were hereafter referred to as *gushi* or 'old-style verse'. Of the new developed forms the most important were the *jueju* (broken-off lined verse) and *lüshi* ('regulated verse'). *Jueju* consists of four five-syllable or seven-syllable lines (a quatrain), and *lüshi* of eight (two four-line stanzas), with strict requirements for verbal parallelism in the two middle couplets. Strictly speaking, these two forms were not new either, but now they were regulated by strict rules for the arrangement of level and oblique tones (*pingze*) according to patterns of tonal euphony (see Plates 95, 96).

By the middle of the eighth century, Tang poetry flourished under imperial patronage and attained its full splendour.Skill at poetry was essential for any one who was seeking acceptance in elite society and success in the civil service examination. Even the outstanding poets are too numerous to recapitulate here; the greatest by common consent are Li Bai (701–762) and Du Fu (712–770). They were contemporaries and friends, though different in temperament.

Li Bai, infatuated in his youth by the idea of *xia* (chivalry) and renowned for his love of wine and his fondness for the practice of Daoist immortality lore, proclaimed himself 'an immortal banished from Heaven'. Not abiding by all the strict rules for composing poetry, he impressed his contemporaries with the exceptional versatility of his literary talent and strong element of romantic fantasy. Li Bai's works are also widely known in Japan and Korea.

Du Fu was a more serious and thoughtful poet. With his deep understanding of life and society, he used his poetry to expose glaring social injustice. His most admired poems are those which give a lively description of the hardships, misery and sufferings inflicted upon the helpless people by the harsh government. Since most of his poems were written in eventful times when the Tang began to decline and accurately reflected the conditions of a complex, turbulent period, his work has been labelled as 'history in verse (*shishi*)' and he himself has been popularly acknowledged as the 'sage of poetry (*shisheng*)'.

From the ninth century onwards there appeared a corpus of satirical poems (*xinyuefu* – 'New Music Bureau Ballads') criticizing the abuses of government, of which Bai Juyi (772–846) was a prolific composer. One of the most influential poets after Du Fu, Bai Juyi wrote about sixty poems of social criticism, including 'Old Man with the Broken Arm', 'Old Charcoal Seller' and 'Salt Merchant's Wife'. Bai Juyi is also noted for his long narrative ballads, particularly the famous 'Song of Everlasting Remorse' and 'Song of the Lute Player'. Unlike Du Fu, who wrote in dense language, Bai Juyi composes his poems in a popular style with verbal plainness. He is said to have read his poems aloud to an illiterate old woman before he had finalized them, changing the wording until it was fully intelligible to her.

A second important poet of the ninth century, Han Yu (768–824), more famous as an essayist and the leader of the so-called *guwen* or 'classical prose' movement, advocated the use of clearer language and worked to introduce a greater freshness into verse.

Late Tang poetry saw a return to dense, allusive language. It was not until the eleventh century, in the mid-Song, that poetry regained its earlier creative vitality. Following the lead of major Tang poets, Song writers adopted a simple, elegant and refined style. Of the many noteworthy poets of Song times, the most renowned was Su Shi (cognomen Dungpo, 1037–1101). As a statesman, a versatile writer in almost all genres of *belles-lettres*, a painter and a calligrapher, this many-sided genius attained an unrivalled expressiveness in his verse and prose. His essays and poems are swift-moving and spontaneous like 'floating clouds in the sky and flowing water on the Earth', bearing no traces of having been 'carved and polished'. A second high point of Song poetry was reached in the closing years of the dynasty in the works of Lu You (1125–1210).

Nearly 50,000 Tang poems have been preserved. The 'Anthology of the Tang Dynasty', compiled as late as the eighteenth century, contains more than 48,900 poems by no less than 2,300 poets.

Emergence and development of the *'ci'*

Towards the end of the Tang Dynasty, a new poetic form, known as *ci*, had a distinct and increasing vogue. This kind of 'suitable-for-singing' lyric is characterized by lines of varying lengths, prescribed tonal patterns and being set to music. The first verse in *ci* form must have dated from the mid-Tang, as evidenced, among others, by a large number of anonymous works found in the famous deposit of sacred waste and manuscripts, sealed in a cave-shrine at Dunhuang in northwestern China, that was discovered at the beginning of the twentieth century. These texts seem to confirm that the *ci* was developed out of a popular folk song form that originated among singing girls and musicians. Later, the *ci* began to flourish as a major genre in its own right in the hands of the *literati*. From the late Tang and Five Dynasties to the early years of the Northern Song these lyrics were all written in *Xiaoling* form, or 'short snatches of lyric'. By the reign of Song emperor Renzong (r. 1023–1064), the longer *manci* or 'slow lyrics' had come into fashion. In time, the subject matter of *ci* was widened to include many themes hitherto treated only in classical *shi* form. Then musical specialists like Zhou Bangyan (r. 1056–1121) and Jiang Kuei (*c.* 1155 – *c.* 1221) created new rigorous metres. *Ci* acquired greater complexities of metre and rhyme, and in that form they have coexisted with *shi* down to the present day.

Of all *ci* writers of the Five Dynasties, the most remarkable seems to have been Li Yu (937–978) or Li Houzhu, the last ruler of the small kingdom of Southern Tang (937–975). Born in the seclusion of the palace and brought up by court women, Li Yu was a poet of pure feeling who never lost his unworldly innocence. Taken captive to the Song capital, oppressed by mingled feelings of sorrow and humiliation, he depicts happy memories of days gone by, giving vent to his grief and despair. Here are some excerpts of his *ci*:

> The water flows, the blossoms fall,
> the glory of spring is gone;
> In nature's domain and in the world of men.
> (Translated by J. Bonner, *Wang Kuowei*, p. 120)

> The high tower – who's to climb it with me?
> Autumn's clear vista as I've known it for so long,
> But past events have turned to emptiness,
> Become like things in a dream.
> (Translated by B. Watson, *The Columbia Book of Chinese Poetry*, p. 362)

He wrote *ci* as if to express universal human emotions, not just the poet's own personal anguish. 'Like Shakyamuni and Jesus Christ, Li Yu seems to have borne the guilt of all mankind', observed the outstanding scholar Wang Kuo-wei (1877–1927).

The Song Dynasty is regarded as the high point of this poetic genre. Many writers of the time became known for their *ci*. A monumental work, *Quan Song ci* (Complete Song *ci*), first published in 1940 and revised in 1964, contains more than 1,330 *ci* writers and 19,900 *ci* lyrics. In fact, at least 3,812 *ci* writers are mentioned in the literature of Song times. The above-mentioned scholar-official Su Shi played a prominent role in the development of *ci* by introducing more serious subject matter.

Memories of the Past at Red Cliff

> East flows the mighty river,
> Sweeping away the heroes of time past;
> This ancient rampart on its western shore
> Is Zhou Yu's Red Cliff of Three Kingdom's fame;
> Here jagged boulders pound the clouds,
> Huge waves tear banks apart,
> And foam piles up a thousand drifts of snow;
> A scene fair as a painting,
> Countless the brave men here in time gone by!
> I dream of Marshal Zhou Yu in his day
> With his new bride, the Lord Qiao's younger daughter,
> Dashing and debonair,
> Silk-capped, with feather fan,
> He laughed and jested
> While the dread enemy fleet was burned to ashes!
> In fancy through those scenes of old I range,
> My heart overflowing, surely a figure of fun,
> A man grey before his time.
> Ah, this life is a dream,

Let me drink to the moon on the river!
(From *Poetry and Prose of the Tang and Song*, translated by Yang Xianyi and Gladys Yang, Beijing, 1984, p. 255)

Like Su Shi, Xin Qiji (1140–1207) also wrote *ci* in a bolder, freer style and in vivid language. He was born in north China and, as a young man, joined the fighting to resist the Jurchen invaders. Later in the south he presented time and again memorials for recovery of the lost territory in the central plains. His *ci* express his lofty ideals and his deep concern for national unity.

Lu You was already well known at the age of 17 as a poet. A prolific poet, he wrote more than 9,000 *shi* and *ci* describing current events, the episodes of everyday life as well as his own feelings. What especially distinguishes him is that all his life he longed for the recovery of the lost territory. His work is noted for its ardent patriotism. The most famous example is his last poem he left to his son:

To My Son

Death ends all, that is sure,
But what grieves me is not to have seen our land united;
The day that our imperial arms win back the central plain,
Mind you sacrifice[1] and let your old man know!
(From *Poetry and Prose of the Tang and Song*, p. 286)

Li Qingzhao (1081–1145), an extremely erudite woman, is highly eulogized for her superb *ci*. She enjoyed several years of happiness after her marriage and produced fresh, beautiful work. Then her birthplace fell to the Jurchen and her husband died as they fled south. She wrote poignant lines expressing her loneliness and concern for her country.

Related to the *ci* but much longer in form is the *qu* or *sanqu,* which was to be set to the northern tunes. *Qu* constitutes an important element in Yuan drama.

The classical prose (*guwen*) movement during the Tang and Song

The great *literati* of the Han Dynasty wrote in a simple, natural prose style. After the Han prose was undergoing a transition from unadorned simplicity to artificial elegance. Many writers cherished a passion for flowery parallelism with an extensive use of historical allusions. This tendency towards ornateness became increasingly pronounced until it reached its highest development in the so-called *pianwen* or 'parallel prose' in the Six Dynasties period. Most *pianwen* writers took a delight in refining the wording and tailoring phrases in four or six characters, and they indulged in the skilful use of strict verbal parallelism (*pianti*).

During the early years of the Tang, essayists continued to model their style on the 'parallel prose' of the preceding period, especially in memorials to the imperial court and letters on formal occasions. But dissatisfaction with its artificialities was growing and in time a strong reaction against it took shape in the so-called classical prose (*guwen*) movement, headed by Han Yu and Liu Zongyuan (773–819). This literary movement, as suggested by its name, aimed at reform of the literary style by breaking through the stilted *pianwen* and reviving the lucid, unornamented prose of the Han Dynasty and earlier periods. It implies also an effort to propound Confucian moral teachings and elevate the status of Confucianism in opposition to Buddhism and Daoism. One of most famous essays of Han Yu is *Yuan Dao* or 'on the origin of the *Dao* (Way, Truth)', in which Han Yu, influenced by and following Chan Buddhist ideas, advanced a theory of orthodox transmission of the *Dao* through a line of early sage-rulers extending to Confucius and down to Mencius. Han Yu was surely not a philosophical thinker, he was better known as a master essayist. But his role, together with that of his contemporary Li Ao, as the formulator of the theory of *Dao*, was to have great intellectual significance. The school of Song and Ming neo-Confucianism derived its name from this theory. Another idea that Han Yu advocated with passionate eloquence concerns the role of prose as the vehicle for the propagation of *Dao*. In each case, he worked not only to make prose return to the classical style, but also to apply it to the realm of ideas.

With the passing of Han Yu and Liu Zongyuan, some of their followers took to write a genre of 'abstruse prose', which had the disadvantage of not being widely accepted. The result was a revival of parallel style (*pianti*) in prose as well as in verse during the closing years of the Tang. In the early Song the *pianti* prose which was called *shiwen* or 'contemporary style' and the verse which was labelled as *xikun* style became especially prevalent under the leadership of Yang Yi (974–1020), Liu Yun and others, because only essays and verse written in these styles were effective in securing fame and position. It was not until the eleventh century, when Ouyang Xiu (1007–1072) launched out into an extended defence of the *guwen,* that the classical prose movement yielded the eventual result. The statesman, historian, poet, and essayist Ouyang Xiu wrote in classical prose style memorials, letters, prefaces, epitaphs or funeral orations, and all genres of *belles-lettres*. His works were of such unexcelled lucidity and naturalness that many scholars-officials around Ouyang Xiu, notably the reformers Fan Zhongyan, Wang Anshi and some leaders who opposed Wang, such as Su Shi, modelled themselves on his style. By the time of Ouyang Xiu's death, *guwen* was firmly established as the accepted style for almost all types of prose writing. Since then, *guwen* have become the model of Chinese style until the literary revolution of 1919, after which *guwen* as a style of writing has gradually been replaced by vernacular Chinese.

In the Ming Dynasty, Mao Kun (1512–1601) collected the prose of Han Yu and Liu Zongyuan of the Tang and that of Ouyang Xiu, Su Shi, Su Shi's father Su Xun, Su Shi's brother Su Zhe, Wang Anshi, and Zen Kong of the Song – the last five people were all Ouyang Xiu's disciples – in a chrestomathy entitled *The Masterpieces of Eight Prose Masters of the Tang and Song Dynasties*. That honorific designation has remained attached to their names ever since.

Short stories (*Chuanqi*) of the Tang

In the Tang Dynasty, the short story or *chuanqi* developed from its brief, anecdotal forms of earlier periods into full novellas. In the early years of the Tang, Zhang Zhuo (660?–740?) wrote *You xian ku* (A Visit to a Fairy Cave), a famous work that 'envoys from the kingdoms of Silla and Japan were willing to pay gold for' (*Jiu Tang shu*, Ch. 149, p. 4024). It narrates how the author passes a night in stirring excitement with two young ladies when he is travelling on an official mission. From the middle of the eighth to the early ninth centuries this genre was popular. These Tang short stories give us a vivid, sometimes realistic characterization of daily life or of some special feature of contemporary society. A representative work is the story entitled *Everlasting Remorse*, written by Chen Hong, a *literati* contemporary of Bai Juyi who composed a long narrative ballad with the same theme and title. Both Chen's *chuanqi* and Bai's ballad give us a colourful description of the decadent and intoxicated life of the ruling group, indulging in pleasures and excitement, extravagant in expenditure and rivalling in luxuries, but in the meanwhile they express a true appreciation for the faithful love which triumphs over death. Similarly in the *Tale of a Pillow*, the hero Lu dreams that after having made rapid advances in his career he is thrown into prison on acount of slander, incurred by him in the pursuit of power and profit. Lu winds up his career in a state of a bitter remorse. *Prince Huo's Daughter* and *the Story of Yingying* describe the tragic love stories of women. The heroines bear their hard lot simply because they are unfortunate in their choice of lover. *The Old Man of the East City* reflects the horrors of war.

Most *chuanqi* writers possessed an attractive style. They created many social pictures with deft touches.

The rise of vernacular literature

Buddhist *sūtra* explanation played a very prominent part in broadening the subject material and promoting the vernacular style of Chinese literature. Some vernacular literary types, especially those related to oral performance, seem to have grown out of a popular tradition of expounding Buddhist texts in easily understandable colloquial language during the Tang Dynasty. Most temples had a meeting place where monks gave colloquial Buddhist lectures intended for poorly educated laymen and the illiterate masses. We find in the manuscript collection of the cave-shrine at Dunhuang a corpus of *changdao* (introductory *sūtra* chanting) and *sujiang* (lectures at a popular level) texts. Apparently, these colloquial Buddhist lectures and *chantefable* compositions in an alternating mixture of prose and verse were originally oral before being written down. They set the precedents to oral narratives like *bianwen* (popular narrative stories), a special genre of popular literature under Buddhist influence that prevailed during the late Tang and Five Dynasties. The storytellers' scripts (*huaben*) of the Song had a lot of features in common with *bianwen*. Many other types of vernacular literature, such as dramatic ballads in *zhugongdiao* form, lyrics set to the northern tunes known as *qu* or *sanqu*, are believed also to have originated in a similar way. In addition, the courtyards of many great temples of the Tang Dynasty were used for public purposes and provided various entertainment activities on the occasion of festivals and ceremonies which attracted large audiences of diverse social groups, including princesses.

The commercial expansion during the Song Dynasty gave a strong incentive to urban popular culture, including oral and theatrical performance. Consequently, the Song proved to be an important formative period for all kinds of vernacular literary and artistic forms in Chinese history.

Yuan drama

From the end of the Southern Song to the end of the Yuan Dynasty, the most striking advances in literature were made in the composite dramatic form, the *zaju*. The Yuan period was one of the great ages of drama. More than 200 dramatists are named in histrorical records and some 700 dramas were written, out of which about 150 are extant.

A Yuan drama was written primarily to be sung and acted. The above-mentioned *sanqu,* the lyrics or arias set to tunes that had already appeared in the entertainment quarters of the big cities in the Southern Song, were now incorporated into the sung passages of Yuan drama. Used in an operatic form of performance, *Sanqu* developed into *zaju*, the celebrated Yuan drama. Most of the Yuan *zaju* are well plotted. They are usually of four acts, sometimes with a prelude (*xiezi*), combining dialogue, acting, mime, dancing and various displays borrowed from acrobatic shows.

There were four great Yuan dramatists, Guan Hanqing, Wang Shifu, Bai Pu and Ma Zhiyuan, the most prolific and brilliant being Guan Hanqing and Wang Shifu.

Guan Hanqing (*c.* 1210–1300), a native of the Yuan capital, Khānbāliq, was once an official in the imperial medical academy. He wrote sixty plays on a wide range of topics during his lifetime. He had a wide experience of life and personal familarity with the ordinary daily life of the man in the street. His best-known work is *Snow in Midsummer*, a play about injustice. The innocent heroine has great courage and strength of character. Before her execution, she appeals to Heaven and Earth:

> Alas, Earth! you cannot distinguish good
> from evil, how can you yet be Earth!
> Alas, Heaven! you fail to uphold justice,
> you are Heaven in vain!

She firmly believes that Heaven and Earth will vindicate her innocence with snow in midsummer, the hottest period of the season.

Wang Shifu was active at the end of the thirteenth and beginning of the fourteenth centuries. He is best known for his masterpiece, *The Western Chamber*. The main theme of this play is the love between a young scholar and a girl of good family.

Early Ming novels

Novels written at the beginning of the Ming dynasty developed from popular storytellers' tales of Song and Yuan times. The most important are the *Water Margin*, the *Outlaws of the Marshes (Shuihu zhuan*, also known in translation as *All Men Are Brothers*) and the *Romance of Three Kingdoms (San guo zhi yanyi*). The *Water Margin* describes the heroic exploits and chivalrous adventures of a group of revolting peasants, fishermen, army officers, small functionaries and some landowners. Based on the Song storytellers' script *Tales of the Xuanhe Period*, this novel seems to have been recast by the great writer Shi Nai'an (*c.* 1296 – *c.* 1370) and then further modified by later authors. The *Romance of the Three Kingdoms* is ascribed to Luo Guanzhong, who is believed to have lived in the last seventy years of the fourteenth century. This novel gives a fictionalized history of the late Han and the subsequent stirring and troubled times – the period of the three kingdoms (220–280). It depicts the political and military struggle between different factions. These novels have had an immense literary and social influence on subsequent generations and are today known in nearly every Chinese household.

PAINTING

China's painting tradition reached a new height of accomplishment during the Tang Dynasty. Many celebrated masters of figure painting, such as Yan Liben, Wu Daozi, Zhang Xuan and Zhou Fang, were invited to the court and secured imperial patronage during the seventh and eighth centuries. Their style and manner in portraying the rulers of the past, worthy officials, foreign envoys, and court ladies found favour with emperors and enjoyed popularity in high circles. Yan Liben was said to have executed his figures in forthright lines which seemed as rigid as iron wire. The use of shading in different thicknesses made the figures stand out. Wu Daozi, the most famous Tang court painter, known as the 'painting saint', drew his figures, both religious and secular, with a more flexible line. Under his brush, a shawl or ribbon could be rendered so expressive of elegance that it appeared to be fluttering in the wind. Zhang Xuan's 'Ladies Preparing Silk' and Zhou Fang's 'Tuning the Lute and Drinking Tea' depicted court life in an exquisite and minute manner.

As Buddhism reached its culmination in China during the seventh and eighth centuries, leading artists also devoted themselves to the iconographical glorification of the numerous heavenly beings. Wu Daozi displayed a great talent in no less than 300 murals on the walls of the principal temples of the two capitals, Chang'an and Loyang. These murals of his and many others were executed on a large scale, just as stucco sculptures and embroided or polychrome woven figured silk banners and drawings that embellished and adorned the temples, enabled the believers to visualize the compassionate expression of Buddha and *bodhisattvas* and the colourful pageant of the Buddhist paradise.

The Tang Dynasty was also a period of progress in landscape painting. Li Sixun and his son Li Zhoudao developed *jinbi shanshui*, 'golden blue-green landscape', a formal style of painting depicting sumptuous details to meet courtly tastes. In the mid-eighth century, Wang Wei, a famous eighth-century poet and scholar, introduced a new type of ink landscape composition with freehand brushwork that made an aesthetic and artistic appeal to the *literati*. To literary scholars, a creative concept and spontaneous expression were far more essential than technical perfection, which, in their opinion, was the court painters' professional concern. The further *literati* trend away from the court-sponsored style of landscape painting was shown by employing the technique of 'breaking the ink' (Zhang Zao), spattering and splashing the ink onto the silk (Wang Mo also called Wang Qia) or by executing the painting with exaggerated features or in a distorted manner (Buddhist monk Guan Xiu).

During the period of the five Dynasties (907–960) and Ten Kingdoms (907–980), the great northern landscape painters were Jing Hao, Li Cheng, Guan Tong and Fan Kuan. The representatives of the less austere southern style were Dung Yuan and his follower Ju Ran. The firm style of the northern painters and the more spontaneous manner of the southern artists followed two distinct lines of development in Chinese landscape painting that have continued to modern times (see Plate 251).

The figure painting of the period was represented by Ku Hongzhong and Zhou Wenju. A remarkable work by Ku Hongzhong is 'The Night Entertainment of Han Xizai', which depicts the voluptuous, debauched life of the minister Han Xizai. Zhou Wenju was famous for his pictures of court ladies, female games players and musical entertainment. His 'Ladies Bathing Children' illustrates daily life in the inner palace.

Flower and bird painting came into its own as a separate branch of painting during the Five Dynasties. Huang Quan developed a skill called *mogu hua*, which means 'boneless painting, or wash without outline drawing', a technique mainly adopted by professional painters. Scholars admired the free sketches of Xu Xi. Their successor during the early Song was Cui Bo.

Song scholarly landscape painting was represented by a group of *literati* that included Su Shi, Mi Fu and his son Mi Youren, Wen Tong, and Li Gonglin (Li Longmian). Li Gonglin was a master of *baimiao*, plain-line painting, without colour, shading or wash. He was also reputed to be a great painter of horses. Scholarly painters valued close resemblance in spirit. They sought intellectual expression. Sometimes, they tried to gain a clearer expression of spontaneity, *'xie i'*, literally 'to write ideas', by 'lodging' their thoughts and feelings in 'borrowed forms of things', such as bamboo, mountains, even dried trees and weird rocks. Moreover, it became common practice from the Song for scholars to integrate poetry, painting and calligraphy into one drawing.

The Northern Song emperors were enthusiastic patrons of the arts, the most famous being Huizong (r.1101–1125). Huizong was the greatest imperial art collector, acquiring nearly 6,400 paintings by 231 masters, compiling a pre-eminent catalogue of paintings and dominating artistic and literary circles. He was himself an accomplished calligrapher and a painter chiefly of birds and flowers. He invited painters of exceptional merit to the imperial painting academy.

During the Southern Song, the academy of painting was re-established in the temporary capital, Linan. Elegant court-sponsored monochrome paintings of the Southern Song were characterised by precision and high technical standards. The four great masters were Li Tang, Liu Songnian, Ma Yuan, and Xia Gui.

Painting during the Yuan Dynasty, chiefly landscapes, broke with the imitations and conventions of the Song official academy. Scholarly painters cultivated characterizations of their own. Their paintings were thought to reveal the character of the author. For the freehand brushwork of this period, Huang Gongwang, Wang Meng, Wu Zhen and Ni Zan were most famous. They were called the four great painters of the Yuan.

SCIENCE AND TECHNOLOGY

During the Tang, Song and Yuan periods, scientific and technical knowledge reached a fairly high level. Official dynastic histories and some encyclopaedias were compiled during the Song Dynasty, together with treatises on calendars, astronomy, music and harmonics. Specialized treatises on agriculture and horiculture (*Nongshu*), medicine, acupuncture, architecture (*Yingzao fashi*), military technology (*Wu jing zongyao*), geography, cartography and 'the hundred techniques' were written by scholar-officials and specialists. Applied sciences and new techniques progressed when they provided clear benefit to the imperial court in particular and to the bureaucracy in general. Scholar-officials actually needed some knowledge in these branches of applied science and technology to perform their duties.

Mathematics

The Song and Yuan registered distinct advances in traditional Chinese mathematics. Song-Yuan mathematics is marked by its creativeness and a large number of works of a high level. It is chiefly represented by four great mathematicians: Qin Jiushao, Li Ye, Yang Hui and Zhu Shijie. Qin solved problems of higher numeric equations. Li introduced *tianyuanshu*, a type of matrix formed by rows of counting rods for solving equations. Yang simplified the counting-rod arithmetical operations by developing a number of mnemonic rhymes. Zhu's works embodied another two epoch-making achievements: the solution of multivariate simultaneous equations, and a method of solving problems of power finite differences (*Ancient China's Technology and Science*, comp. by the Institute of the History of Natural Sciences, 1983, pp. 54–55).

Improvements in counting-rod operation in traditional rod arithmetic led to bead arithmetic. The appearance of the abacus seems to have met a real demand for rapid calculations among commercial circles since the mid-Tang. Throughout the Song and especially the Ming mnemonic computational rhymes (*koujue*) thrived, bringing about significant and remarkable improvement in operations on the abacus.

The calendar and almanac

In the monographs on literature (*yiwenzhi*) of the official dynastic histories of the Tang and Song, works on the calendar and almanac were listed together with that of mathematics. Revision of the calendar was frequent under the Tang, because traditional Chinese calendars were not limited to the arrangement of years, months and days, but also included predictions of the movements of the Sun, the Moon and the five planets, forecasts of solar and lunar eclipses and the definition of solar terms. Of the numerous calendars mentioned in Tang historical records, Buddhist monk Yixing's Dayan Calendar occupied an important place. Promulgated in 728, it gave a far more accurate and precise calculation of the Sun's ecliptic motion and the apparent fluctuation in its apparent velocity. Yixing also made important contributions to mathematics, with the benefit of Indian influence. In fact, many books on calendar, almanac and astrology of the Tang were based on Indian and Western

Figure 29 The astronomical clock-tower built at Kaifeng in the eleventh century under imperial orders, relied on a highly sophisticated combination of water-driven gears (seen at right centre in the cutaway diagram above) to rotate an armillary sphere (under the thatched roof) and a celestial globe (located within the tower on the second floor). Additional gears turned the five horizontal discs at left centre, bringing a series of figures into view in the apertures along one wall of the tower. These jacks announced the time with placard, drum or gong (from Kotker, N.; Fitzgerald, C. P, *The Horizon History of China*, NY 1969, p. 155, after Needham, J., *Science and Civilization in China*, Cambridge 1952).

Asian systems. An *Almanac of the Seven Luminaries*, of Indian origin, had been in use since the seventh century. Amoghavajra, a monk-official, and his Chinese disciple translated and annotated Indian works on calendar computations. The Sogdian list of the Manichaean 'Seven Luminaries', transcribed in Chinese characters during the mid-Tang, has been found in the manuscript collection of the Dunhuang cave-shrine.

In 725, Yixing and his colleague Liang Lingzan built a water-driven mobile celestial globe with a clock. But the best representative of such astronomical instruments was a water-powered astronomical clock-tower (see Figure 29) designed and installed in 1088 by Han Gonglian under the sponsorship of Su Song, the then minister of personnel. This instrument was a great wooden structure more than 12 m high. According to *Xin yi xiang fa yao* (New Design for an Armillary Clock), written by Su Song himself in 1090, on the top platform of the clock-tower was an armillary, which was connected by gears to a water-powered drive mechanism: a waterwheel that rotated regularly as each water scoop on its rim was filled in turn. This device enabled the armillary to follow the motion of the natural celestial sphere and keep the Sun in the visual field of the observer. Under the top platform, in a chamber within, was the celestial globe, rotated mechanically to follow the spinning of the natural celestial sphere; it located the constellations. Below this chamber were the driving wheel and an ingenious and sophisticated system for time announcement. The wheel was provided with an escapement device.

Shen Gua (1031–1095) was another brilliant scientist in Northern Song times. He devised a twelve-period solar calendar and discovered the slight deviation towards the east of the magnetic compass, a deviation much greater in Song times than it is today. In his later years, he retired to Mengxi (Dream Stream) Garden and left his most famous work *Mengxi bitan* (Dream Stream Notes), in which we find the first account of the construction of relief maps, descriptions of fossils and many other scientific reports (magnetic compass, printing with movable type, and so on).

In Yuan times, Guo Shoujing (1231–1316), a great astronomer, geographer and expert on water conservation, developed a dozen instruments for astronomical observation and precise calculation. He computed the length of the year as 365.2425 days – only 26 seconds of error. His almanac/calendar has the same cycle as that of the Gregorian calendar (see Plate 134).

Paper making

Paper, although the method of making it was invented in China some time before the first century AD, came into extensive use as a writing material during the Tang and Song Dynasties. The massive needs of administration procedures and business transactions, the development of the civil service examination system and official fostering of scholarship all encouraged the increasing demand for, and further improvement of, paper.

Many innovations were made in paper-making techniques during this period. The paper for documents was made from the bark of a species of mulberry called *chu* (*Broussonetia papyrifera*), hence the general name of the paper was *chuzhi*. Hemp paper was paper of good quality called *mazhi*. Ratten, daphne-bark, rice- and wheat-stalk and bamboo were also introduced as raw materials in addition to the more commonly used hemp and mulberry bark. The manufacture of bamboo paper developed rapidly in south China, where bamboo was abundant. The wood or bamboo pulp was well beaten and pounded to give a uniform texture. Starch paste was used in the Tang as sizing and filler. In the Song Dynasty, a sticky vegetable juice called *zhi-yao* ('paper drug') replaced starch paste to soften the fibres and give an even distribution of fibres in the water suspension. An improved screen mould, densely woven from finely polished bamboo strips, was made for lifting a sheet of paper from the pulp.

Workshops for paper making could be found all over the country during the Tang. More than ninety paper factories were operating along the Yangtze in the major manufacturing centres of modern Jiangsu, Zhejiang, Anhui, Jiangxi, Hunan, and Sichuan provinces (Tsien Tsuen-Hsuin, 1985, p. 45). Paper of special quality, known as 'tribute paper' (*gongzhi*), was regularly levied on eleven districts of the empire. It seems that paper workshops also existed in the north-western region. Among the documents found in Turfan in 1972, one dated to 620 bears the name of paper craftman (*zhi shi*) Wei Xiannu. Another fragment furnishes some information about sending prisoners to work in local paper workshops.

Books on paper making appeared during this period, among them *Zhipu* (Manual on Paper) edited in 986, *Shu qian pu* (Manual on Sichuan Writing Paper) of the Yuan Dynasty, and Chapter 13 of the most noteworthy *Tiangong Kaiwu* (Explanation of the Works of Nature) written in 1637 by Song Yingxing of the Ming Dynasty.

Paper greatly aided the dissemination and preservation of literary and religious works. Apart from the extensive use of paper for copying and printing the Confucian classics, the publication of Daoist and Buddhist texts also required enormous amounts of paper. An enormous quantity of documents, manuscript scrolls, letters, various other texts, and paper artifacts dating from the fourth to the eleventh century have been rediscovered in a cave-shrine at Dunhuang and in the region of Turfan. Several hundred manuscripts of Buddhist, Daoist and Confucian scriptures from the Dunhuang grotto bear dated colophons, the earliest of which is a Buddhist *vinaya* text dated AD 406 (code number Stein 797 in the British Library).

Paper became widely used at every level of bureaucratic administration. In Tang times, for example, once every three years the government undertook a complete census of the population by commune (*li*), county (*xian*) and prefecture (*zhou*). The census registers discovered in Dunhuang and Turfan bear witness to the extreme care with which these documents were drawn up in accordance with the statute of the land. The necessary writing material – paper, brushes, ink and paper – were to be provided by charging one cash per individual member included in a given register.

Paper was also used for printing paper drafts and exchange certificates for salt and tea (*jiaoyin*). Paper money was originally called *chubi* (paper-mulberry money) and gradually became a true currency in use throughout the country. The issue of paper notes during the Song Dynasty (*jiaozi, huizi*) led the government to establish its own factories for manufacturing special paper for the notes, and this practice was continued in the following dynasties, Yuan and Ming.

Many kinds of paper were made for artistic uses, especially painting and calligraphy. From the Tang onwards, artists and the *literati* began to paint on paper. By the Song, paper had become the ideal medium for artistic expression. The most famous kind of paper for artistic purposes has been and still is *xuanzhi*.

The invention of printing

Then came the practice of wood-block printing. The text of an entire page was first written on a sheet of thin, translucent paper, which was glued face downwards on to a block, usually from the wood of the date or pear tree. The characters were then carved out in negative with a knife. The engraved wood-block was inked, a sheet of paper spread on it and brushed over gently and evenly, somewhat similar to the production of rubbings (in which case, the inscription is not cut in negative) (see Plate 115).

It seems that wood-block printing was invented in the seventh century, although no specimen dated earlier than the eighth century survives. The impetus for printing may have been the need for the massive copying of Buddhist texts, especially the need to reproduce an enormous number of Buddhist images. One of the main meritorious acts of Buddhist piety was copying texts and images. The world's oldest extant example of printing is a *dhāraṇī-sūtra* discovered in 1966 in a stupa in the Buddhist temple of Pulguk-sa, Kyŏngju, in south-east Korea. It is believed that this must have been printed between 704 and 751. Another piece of old printing dated approximately from the same period, Chapter 17 of the *Lotus Sūtra*, was found in Turfan. An almanac in widespread use was printed by wood-blocks and available on the market in the 830s in Sichuan, one of the centres of the block-printing trade. The world's earliest clearly dated printed work is an exquisitely engraved *Diamond Sūtra* found in the cave-shrine at Dunhuang, bearing the date 'Fifteenth Day of the Fourth Moon in the Ninth Year of Xiantong (reign title of Emperor Yizong of the Tang, AD 868).

During the period of the Five Dynasties and Ten Kingdoms, an increasing number of Confucian classics, Daoist scriptures, literary anthologies and encyclopedic works were printed, along with Buddhist *sūtras* and calendars. Private printing of books was also popular and thriving. The Song Dynasty saw further development in the workmanship of block-printing; Song editions are the most highly prized by collectors.

During the Song Dynasty, a worker by the name of Bi Sheng (?–1051) introduced a method of printing with movable type. As described in Shen Gua's *Mengxi bitan*, Bi Sheng started making baked clay types, one for each character, with duplicates depending on the frequency of use. For typesetting, a square iron plate with an iron frame was prepared and a layer of mixed resin, wax and paper ashes spread on it. When the plate was full of the arranged type, it was heated over a fire and pressed down with a wooden board so that the type was evened out over the melted mixture.

It is interesting to note that bronze blocks for printing paper money in the Song and Yuan periods are still extant today. As for movable type, many non-Chinese scripts have survived to the present. Several hundred wooden types in Uighur, dating from the beginning of the fourteenth century, found in Dunhuang, are now preserved in the Musée Guimet in Paris.

Gunpowder and firearms

Before the Tang, Chinese alchemists had already accumulated practical experience in dealing with 'fire drug' (*huoyao*), a mixture of saltpetre, sulphur and charcoal with instantaneously combustible and explosive properties. In early Tang times, Sun Simiao (581–682), a famous pharmacist-alchemist, picked up knowledge on the 'subduing of sulphur' for safe use in alchemy and devoted a technical discussion to this subject in his works. But more accounts of the use of gunpowder in weaponry appeared after the Five Dynasties. The earliest representation we have of a firearm is a scene on a Buddhist silk banner of *c.* 950, discovered in the cave-shrine at Dunhuang and now held in the collection of the Musée Guimet in Paris. It depicts, among other things, a demon watching the flames shoot out horizontally from a fire-lance, which he holds with two hands (Needham, 1985, pp. 8-11). From 1100 onwards, the Song Dynasty started to exploit the explosive potential of gunpowder in the wars with the Jurchen of the Jin. In AD 1000, Tang Fu presented models of *huojian* (fire arrows), *huoqiu* (fire balls), and *huojili* (barbed fire packages) to the Song emperor. In 1002, Shi Pu designed a number of fire grenades and arrows. In *Wujing Zong Yao* (Collection of the Most Important Military Techniques), a military compendium compiled by order of the Song emperor in 1040 and completed under the editorship of Zeng Gongliang in 1044, Zeng described many kinds of incendiary and explosive weapon and gave various prescriptions for making different gunpowder packages. The Northern Song government set up workshops to make gunpowder. About 1130, Chen Gui related in his *Shou cheng lu* ('A City on the Defensive') the use of the fire-lance against the attackers in a city north of Hankou. Towards the end of the Northern Song, new types of bursting fire weapon, *pilipao* ('thunderclap bombs') and *zhentianlei* ('heaven-shaking thunder'), came into use against the Jurchen. Another important advance in fire weaponry was achieved by peasant insurgents. Barrel firearms called *huoqiang* ('fire-lance') first appeared in 1132, then *tuhuoqiang* ('fire-spitting lance') in 1259. The barrel of such weapons was made from a thick bamboo tube.

Bronze and iron barrels of true explosive weapons appeared in the Yuan dynasty. They were called *huochong* (fire gun) and earned a sobriquet of *tongjiangjun* ('bronze generals'). The oldest *tongjiangjun*, now exhibited in the Beijing Historical Museum, was cast in 1332. It is the world's earliest surviving gun (see Plates 42, 43).

The magnetic compass

Artificial magnetism was discovered very early in China. At the time of the Song, the south-pointing fish – a thin leaf of magnetized iron cut into the shape of a fish and made to float on a bowl of water – and the south-pointing needle were mentioned in Zeng Gongliang's *Wujing Zong Yao* in 1044 and in Shen Gua's *Mengxi bitan* in 1086 (see Figure 30). Not much later than Shen Gua, a magnetized needle with an earth disc indicating the twenty-four direction points beneath it, a prototype of the modern mariner's compass, was used by necromancers and geomancers. Mention of such discs, called *diluo* or *luojingpan*, can be found in Zeng Sanyi's *Tong hua lu* (Discourse on the Cause of Things) of the Southern Song (J. Needham, *Science and Civilization in China*, Vol. 4, 1962, p.306).

The earliest Chinese report on the use of the compass at sea is found in *Pingzhou ketan* (Pingzhou Table Talk) written in 1119 by Zhu Yu of the Northern Song. In Zhu Yu's words, 'the sailors rely on the south-pointing needle in navigation when it is cloudy'. During the Southern Song, the compass came into wide use on Chinese merchant ships travelling to South-East Asia and India. In the Yuan Dynasty, all important sea routes were charted, with detailed marks of various locations on maritime routes on the compass.

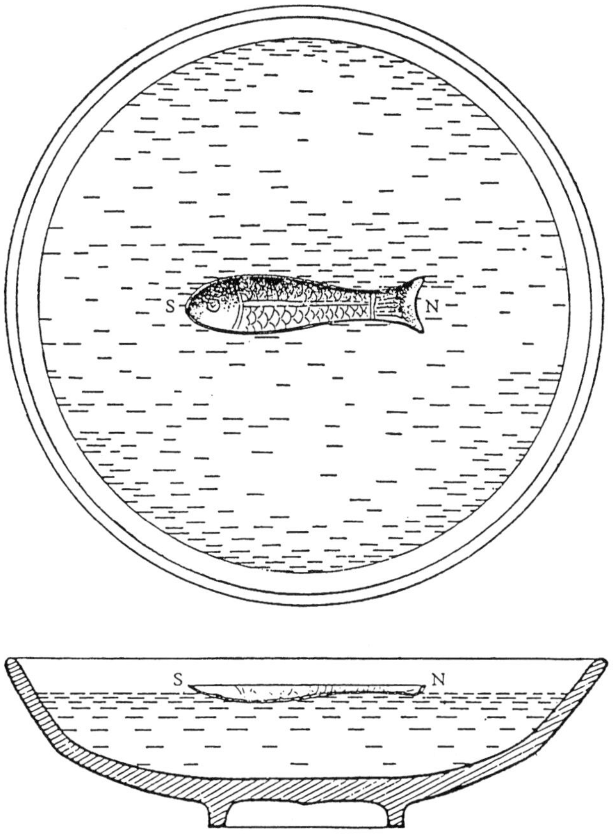

Figure 30 Early Chinese compass: floating metal fish in a bowl of water.

These charts were called *luopanzhen lu* (records of locations on the compass). They were mentioned in *Haidao jing* (Manual of Sailing Directions) and *Da Yuan haiyun ji* (Records of Maritime Transportation in the Great Yuan Dynasty). All models of the Chinese compass could have been transmitted westwards by Persian and Arabian merchants travelling on Chinese vessels in the twelfth and thirteeth centuries, and then to Europe via the Arab world.

Cartography

The Tang saw a great development of geographical works and map making. Following the six rules of indicating distances by a network of tiny squares in map making laid down by Pei Xiu (223–271), the greatTang cartographer Jia Dan (730–805) compiled a map of the whole empire from 785 to 801. This map, entitled *Hainei Hua Yi tu* (Map of both Chinese and Barbarian Peoples within the Four Seas), was about 9 m long and 10 m high, constructed on a grid scale of 1 *cun* (2.94 cm) to 100 *li* (1 Tang *li* = 18.000 *cun*). It depicted an area of 30,000 *li* from east to west and 33,000 *li* from north to south.

The Song and Yuan periods were the golden age of Chinese cartography. The two most magnificent monuments of Chinese mediaeval cartography still in existence were inscribed on stone in 1136. They are now preserved in the 'Forest of Steles' at Xian, the capital of Shanxi province. The first is entitled *Hua Yi Tu* (Map of China and the Barbarian Countries), the second *Yu ji tu* (Map of the Tracks of Yu). Both are about 1 m^2.

During the Yuan, Zhu Siben (1273–1337), a younger contemporary of the astronomer Guo Shoujing, completed his celebrated *Yu tu* (terrestrial map). His map was a large one and took ten years to prepare. It was then revised and enlarged by the Ming cartographer Lo Hunxian (1504–1564) under the title *Guang yu tu* (Enlarged Terrestrial Atlas).

NOTE

1 It was the custom, during sacrifice to the ancestors, to announce important family news to their spirits.

BIBLIOGRAPHY

BODDE, D. 1991. *Chinese Thought, Society, and Science. The Intellectual and Social Background of Science and Technology in Pre-Modern China.* Honolulu.

BOL, P. K. 1993. Government, Society, and State: On the Political Visions of Ssu-ma Kuang and Wang An-shih. In: HYMES, R. P.; SCHIROKAUER, C. (eds) *Ordering the World*, Berkeley, pp. 128-192.

DE BARY, W. T. 1981. *Neo-Confucian Orthodoxy and the Learning of the Mind-and-Heart.* New York.

——. 1983. *The Liberal Tradition in China.* Hong Kong.

——. 1988. *East Asian Civilizations: A Dialogue in Five Stages.* Cambridge, Mass.

——. 1989. *The Message of the Mind in Neo-Confucianism.* In: DE BARY, W. T.; CHAFFEE, J. W. (eds) *Neo-Confucian Education: The Formative Stage.* Berkeley.

EBREY, P. B.; GREGORY, P. N. (eds) 1993. *Religion and Society in T'ang and Sung China.* Honolulu.

ELVIN, M. 1972. The High-level Equilibrium Trap: The Causes of the Decline of Invention in the Traditional Chinese Textile Industries. In: WILLMOTT, W. E. (ed.) *Economic Organization in Chinese Society.* Stanford.

——. 1973. *The Pattern of the Chinese Past.* Stanford.

FENG YUANJUN 1983. *An Outline History of Classical Chinese Literature*, trans. by Yang Xianyi and Gladys Yang. Hong Kong.

GERNET, J. 1956. *Les aspects économiques du Bouddhisme dans la société chinoise du Ve au Xe siècle.* Saigon.

——. 1962. *Daily Life in China on the Eve of the Mongol Invasion 1250–1276* trans. by WRIGHT, H. M. London.

——. 1972. *Le monde chinois.* Paris.

GOLAS, P. J. 1980. Rural China in the Song. *Journal of Asian Studies*, Vol. 39, No. 2, pp. 291–325.

HARTWELL, R. A. 1962. A Revolution in the Iron and Coal Industries During the Northern Sung. *Journal of Asian Studies*, Vol. 21, No. 1, pp. 153–162.

——. 1967. A Cycle of Economic Change in Imperial China: Coal and Iron in Northeast China 75–1350. *Journal of the Economic and Social History of the Orient*, Vol. 10, pp. 102–159.

——. 1982. Demographic, Political, and Social Transformations of China, 750–1550. *Harvard Journal of Asiatic Studies*, Vol. 42, No. 2, pp. 354–442.

HO, PING-TI. 1959. *Studies on the Population of China, 1368–1953.* Cambridge, Mass.

HUANG, R. 1974. *Taxation and Finance in Sixteenth-Century Ming China.* Cambridge.

——. 1981. *1587: A Year of No Significance.* New Haven, Conn.

HUCKER, C. O. 1975. *China's Imperial Past. An Introduction to Chinese History and Culture.* Stanford.

HYMES, R. P.; SCHIROKAUER, C. (eds) 1993. *Ordering the World. Approaches to State and Society in Sung Dynasty China.* Berkeley.

INSTITUTE OF THE HISTORY OF NATURAL SCIENCES, Chinese Academy of Science. 1983. *Ancient China's Technology and Science.* Beijing.

KRACKE, E. A., JR. 1955. Sung Society: Changes within Tradition. *Far Eastern Quarterly*, Vol. XIV, No. 4, pp. 479–488.

LIU, J. T. C. 1988. *China Turning Inward: Intellectual Political Changes in the Early Twelfth Century.* Cambridge, Mass.

LIU, J. T. C.; GOLAS, P. J. (eds) 1969. *Change in Sung China. Innovation or Renovation?* Mass.

LIU XU *et al.* 1975, new imp. 1987. *[Jiu] Tang Shu*. Zhonghua Shuju, Beijing.

LO JUNG-PANG. 1955. The Emergence of China as a Sea Power during the Late Sung and Early Yüan Periods. *Far Eastern Quarterly*, Vol. 14, No. 4, pp. 489–503.

MCMULLEN, D. 1988. *State and Scholars in Tang China*. Cambridge.

MIYAKAWA HISAYUKI. 1955. An Outline of the Naitō Hypothesis and its Effects on Japanese Studies of China. *Far Eastern Quarterly*, Vol. 14, No. 4, pp. 533–552.

NEEDHAM, J. *et al. Science and Civilization in China*. Cambridge.

——. 1960 (2nd edn 1986). *Heavenly Clockwork. The Great Astronomical Clocks of Medieval China*. Cambridge.

——. 1985. *Gunpowder as the Fourth Power, East and West*. Hong Kong.

OU YANGXIU *et al.* 1974. *Xin Wu Dai Shi* [*Wu Dai Shi Ji*]. Zhonghua Shuju. Beijing.

——. 1975 (new imp. 1987). *Xin Tang Shu*. Zhonghua Shuju, Beijing.

OWEN, S. 1981. *The Great Age of Chinese Poetry: The High T'ang*. New Haven, Conn.; rev. JAS Vol. 42, No. 3, 1983.

ROSSABI, M. (ed.) 1983. *China Among Equals*. Berkeley.

SHIBA YOSHINOBU. 1970. *Commerce and Society in Sung China*, trans. by Mark Elvin. Ann Arbor, University of Michigan Center for Chinese Studies.

——. 1983. Sung Foreign Trade: Its Scope and Organization. In: ROSSABI, M. (ed.) *China among Equals*, pp. 89–134.

SIMA GUANG. 1956. *Zi Zhi Tong Jian* (*Comprehensive Mirror for Aid in Governance*). Guji Chubanshe. Beijing.

SIMS-WILLIAMS, N. 1992. Sogdian and Turkish Christians in the Turfan and Tun-huang manuscripts. In: *Turfan and Tun-huang: The Texts*. Florence, pp. 43–61.

SMITH, P. J. 1991. State Power and Economic Activism during the New Policies, 1068–1085. In: HYMES, R. P.; SHIROKAUER, C. (eds) *Ordering the World*, Berkeley, pp. 76–126.

SONG LIAN *et al.* 1976. *Yuan Shi*. Zhonghua Shuju. Beijing.

SUNDERMANN, W. 1992. Iranian Manichaean Turfan Texts Concerning the Turfan Region. In: *Turfan and Tun-huang. The Texts*. Florence, pp. 63–84.

TANG ZHANGRU. 1992. *Wei-Jin-Nanbeichao-Sui-Tang Shi Sanlun* (*Three Treatises on Wei-jin Northern and Southern Dynasties – Sui–Tang History*). Wuhan.

TOQTO *et al.* 1977. *Song Shi*. Zhonghua Shuju. Beijing.

TSIEN TSUEN-HSUIN. 1985. Paper and printing. In: J. NEEDHAM'S *Science and Civilization in China*, Vol. 5, Part 1.

TWITCHETT, D. 1963 (2nd edn 1971). *Financial Administration under the T'ang Dynasty*. Cambridge.

——. 1966. The Tang Market System. *Asia Major*, n.s. 12, part 2, pp. 202–248.

——. 1968. Merchant, Trade, and Government in Late Tang. *Asia Major*, n.s. 14, part 1, pp. 63–95.

——. (ed.) 1979. *The Cambridge History of China*, Vol. 3, Part 1: *Sui and T'ang China, 589–906*. Cambridge.

——. 1992. *The Writing of Official History under the T'ang*. Cambridge.

WATSON, B. 1984. *The Columbia Book of Chinese Poetry*. New York.

XU SONG (comp.). 1957 (reprint of 1809 MS). *Song Hui Yao Ji Gao*. Zhonghua Shuju. Beijing.

XUE JUZHENG *et al.* 1976. *[Jiu] Wu Dai Shi*. Zhonghua Shuju. Beijing.

YANG LIEN-SHENG. 1957. Buddhist Monasteries and Four Money-Raising Institutions in Chinese History. *Harvard Journal of Asiatic Studies*, Vol. 20, pp. 36–52.

YANG XIANYI; YANG, G. (trans.) 1984. *Poetry and Prose of the Tang and Song*. Beijing.

28

JAPAN AND KOREA

28.1
JAPAN

Francine Hérail

The period from the seventh to the sixteenth century in Japan falls into two main parts: until the twelfth century, the country had only one centre, the imperial court, and during that period Japanese civilization was for the most part in the hands of a civil aristocracy. From the late twelfth century onwards, a *shōgun*, or warrior chief, was mandated by the court to maintain order, thus creating a new centre of authority. Until the sixteenth century, several periods of internal unrest, culminating in the creation of small principalities, brought the warriors to the fore, many of whom were of humble social origin. Although they did not renounce the legacy of the court aristocracy, they were instrumental in popularizing and diversifying Japanese civilization and giving it its own distinctive character, different from that of China, its main model, and from that of Korea – both of which gave precedence to a bureaucratic elite recruited by examination.

FROM THE SEVENTH TO THE TWELFTH CENTURY

Adoption of the Chinese model: the 'state governed by codes'

The northern coast of Kyūshū is less than 200 km from Korea. The Japanese archipelago is close enough to the mainland not to be cut off from influences emanating from it, but far enough away for those influences to reach it later than they did Korea, and for it to be better protected against Chinese hegemony.

From the first century of the Christian era, the influence of China, whether direct or indirect, via Korea, became apparent in Japan. The chiefs of Yamato (present-day region of Nara and Ōsaka) used the services of Korean immigrants at a fairly early date, learning from them the rudiments of the classics and philosophy of China, and hence Chinese writing.

The language they spoke was different from Chinese, however: it was polysyllabic, whereas Chinese is monosyllabic; it used verbal suffixes and case enclitics, where Chinese has neither declensions nor conjugations; the verb was placed at the end of the sentence, whereas in Chinese it follows the subject. The inhabitants of Yamato had no writing system when they came into contact with the Chinese script made up of ideograms, each of which had its own meaning inseparable from the sound. By the first century AD, China already had a long written tradition and a rich collection of philosophical, historical, moral and poetic works. Yamato was still at the stage of a purely oral literature of stories and poems. It would take several centuries for it to become familiar with Chinese writing and sufficiently knowledgeable about Chinese works to be able to understand and interpret them.

It took the Japanese three centuries, from the seventh and eighth centuries onwards, to progress from a difficult notation for poems and genealogies using Chinese characters taken phonetically and reading Chinese texts in pure Chinese, to assimilate Chinese through their way of reading, and to invent a syllabary. In this way, they increased their range of means of expression: they could write in good Chinese, in the simplified Chinese used for administrative purposes, or in Japanese with a varying admixture of Sino-Japanese words (see Plates 98, 99).

Reading and writing Chinese was the key to Yamato's development. It looked to China for its institutions, a substantial amount of political morality and Buddhism. What is remarkable, however, is that the imitation of China was deliberate and organized and that the necessary adaptations were highly ingenious. The Chinese model was not imposed by a conquest or by the overwhelming proximity of a neighbour. It was decided upon by the Yamato court, probably because the latter did not wish to be outshone, in civilization at least, by the brilliant mainland empire.

By the end of the sixth century, there was a core of people at the Yamato court who could read and understand Chinese thought and were already well versed in Buddhism, which was officially adopted at that time. Tradition accords a prince of the ruling family, Prince Shōtoku (574–622) (see Plate 128), the honour of having inaugurated the policy of introducing Chinese institutions. He is supposed to have been the author of a basic legal text entitled 'Seventeen Articles Constitution', which echoes several Chinese texts. It is more than a constitution, being a collection of moral advice intended for the servants of the sovereign. He also took steps to become better acquainted with China by sending official missions accompanied by students, some of whom stayed on the mainland for several decades. From that time onwards, the Yamato court had a clear sense of its own identity and the ambition of placing itself on a level with the Sui Dynasty court, as is borne out by the letter which Yamato sent to it: 'The Sovereign of the Land of the Rising Sun to the Sovereign of the Land of the Setting Sun'. To China, this attempt to avoid appearing as some inferior tributary was unacceptable, but it consented to a degree of special treatment for the embassies of the eighth and ninth centuries by waiving the need for an official letter.

The seventh century was a period of reform, warring clans, testing of new institutions, the development of Buddhism, the founding of temples and the establishment of a Chinese-style capital under the management of the ruling family. It culminated in 702 with the coming into force of administrative and criminal codes which copied and amended the Tang codes.

The 'code-governed state' was ostensibly a centralized monarchy. The sovereign was assisted by a bureaucracy, which was admittedly not very numerous – a little under 1,000 functionaries for a population of 5–6 million – made up of individuals recruited on criteria of both birth and merit, who were given rank and position, graded annually and paid in kind from the official stores or, for the highest-ranking officials, out of revenue from paddy fields and households which were assigned to them. All business was brought before a council of prominent dignitaries, which submitted its proposals for decisions to the emperor. A central civil service, made up of bodies of unequal importance, was primarily concerned with running the court and the capital, which was Fujiwara-kyō from 694 to 710, then Heijō-kyō (Nara) until 784, and finally Heian-kyō (Kyōto), where it stayed. The court appointed a few provincial administrators to the sixty-eight provinces and islands, who were responsible for supervising all the activities of the people and ensuring that taxes were paid. To enable the population to pay the taxes, the Chinese system of dividing up paddy fields was adopted. Each individual received a plot of land for life (in order to pay taxes, the peasants lived for the most part from dry farming and slash-and-burn agriculture). These measures presupposed the keeping of population and land registers. Despite the assistance of local dignitaries chosen to be district and village administrators, these forms of supervision were cumbersome and could not be sustained. However, the bureaucratic pattern was not abandoned.

In material terms, too, Japan learned much from China, both directly and indirectly. It adopted Chinese measurements for cadastral surveys and building. Construction techniques were improved and diversified and the manufacture of tiles developed. At the beginning of the eighth century, the court endeavoured to dress exactly like the Chinese. The capital, set out like a chess board, and the layout and orientation of the palace, were small-scale reproductions of the Chinese capitals (see Figure 31).

Assimilation of Chinese influences

The first written texts in Japan, history and legislation, were in Chinese. Consequently, at first glance everything seems Chinese, from institutions and moral and political thought to the appearance of the capital, costumes and many customs. Conversely, however, imitating China seems to have enabled the Japanese to become aware of their own distinctive, original features, which they endeavoured to protect.

The very name of the country, Nihon, 'origin of the Sun' was chosen with reference to China and imposed by the Yamato court first in its dealings with Tang China and the Korean kingdom of Silla. It made it possible to avoid the expression Wakoku, land of the Wa, a word which the Chinese wrote with a character signifying dwarf (the Japanese themselves wrote it with the character *wa*, harmony, and read it as Yamato).

This name appears in the title of Japan's first real historiographical work, *Nihon shoki*, 'Chronicles of Japan', which was completed in 720 (it succeeded an initial work of 712, the *Kojiki*, 'Records of Ancient Matters', which was in a language incorporating considerably more Japanese, written in characters and thus difficult to interpret). When the court decided to extend its sway over the country to the past as well, and thus consolidate its power, it copied Chinese historiography. That is why mythology, the story of origins, was treated as history in Japan, and the generations of human rulers succeeded seamlessly the divine generations. The annals format was adopted at that time, as was the habit of compiling official history by committees of bureaucrats. This method of writing made it possible to establish precedents useful to those in power. But unlike the official histories of China, which contained sections devoted to the lives of ministers and other influential individuals, as well as the annals of the emperors and monographs on various aspects of the empire, the *Nihon shoki* and the histories which followed it focused on the emperor and the court and contained only the annals of each reign.

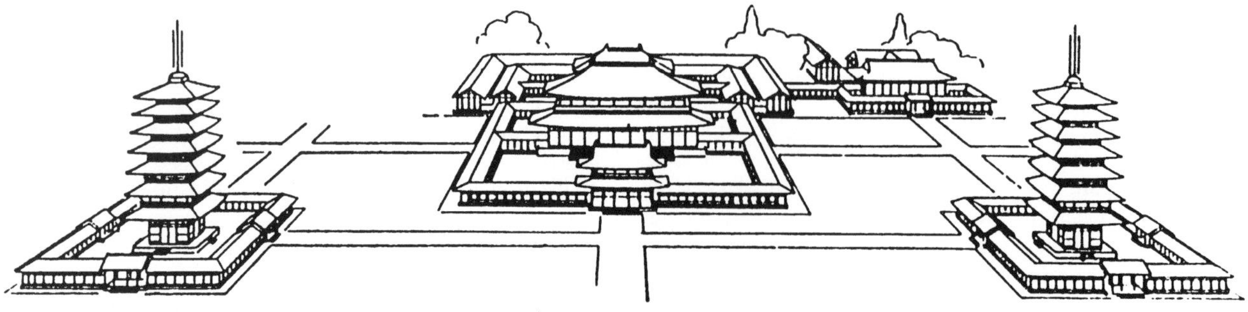

Figure 31 Schematic view of the Tōdaiji (Japan), eighth century (after Sickman, L.; Soper, A., *The Art and Architecture of China*, London 1956, p. 267).

It was by imitating China that Japan was able to establish its chronology. It borrowed the lunar–solar calendar that was used on the mainland and the practice of dividing time into eras, which rarely coincided with a reign. It was one of the emperor's prerogatives to choose the name of the era, thus demonstrating control over time. The emperor changed the name at irregular intervals in order to renew time, especially after a series of calamities. Japan was never willing to use the Chinese eras, as Korea had done, because to do so would have been a sign of subservience.

The term which came to designate the sovereign was also Chinese, *tennō*, which we translate as emperor. In fact, this word of Daoist origin designates the Pole Star, which is stationary, the axis on which the universe turns. The emperor is the centre, giving all things their meaning and place. Or, to follow another form of Chinese wording, the emperor is the child of the heavens and thus likened to the Sun, which radiates warmth and blessings and has a unique position: 'there are not two suns in the sky; there are not two sovereigns on earth'. Nevertheless, imperial ideology was not purely Chinese. The divine origin of the dynasty, asserted in the founding legends which were written down under the court's direction, bolstered the legitimacy and authority of the emperor, who reigned by virtue of the promise of long duration, eternal rule, given to her descendants by the divine ancestor, the great sun goddess worshipped at Ise, Amaterasu. The gift of the three regalia, mirror, sword and jewels, objects which should always be close to the emperor, lent weight to the promise. The emperor was the sole intermediary between Amaterasu and the country. On the grounds of this divine origin, Japan rejected the Chinese theory of the mandate of heaven that passed to a new dynasty when the previous one no longer deserved it.

Japan adopted China's political ideology. In theory, the emperor governed; all decrees came from him, and all reports had to be submitted to the emperor. The emperor was not an autocrat, however: taking advice was a duty. In Japan, the role of counsellor fell to prominent dignitaries. Subsequently, from the end of the tenth century, the advice came chiefly from the regent, *sesshō*, or, if the emperor had come of age, from the chief counsellor, *kampaku*. Under the fiction of the sole and unique responsibility of the emperor, all measures were in fact dictated to him by these persons. What made this divergence possible was a feature characteristic of Japanese society distinguishing it from the Chinese, which was patrilinear. In many instances, marriage in Japan was uxorilocal, and the maternal grandfather was responsible for the education of his grandchildren. The Fujiwara family was able to gain possession of the posts of regent and chief counsellor because its daughters married members of the imperial family, and from the middle of the ninth century it was thus able to assume the position of guardian of an emperor who was still a minor.

Doctrine made the emperor the benefactor of the people, with a duty to ensure that everyone had enough to live on and could work in safety. In order to achieve this, there was a need for a body of honest bureaucrats, capable of edifying and educating the people, to direct the work. Hence, in the space of 200 years, until the beginning of the tenth century, the court issued a great many highly detailed decrees and regulations.

From the outset, though, Japanese administration differed from Chinese. A first point, which is of secondary importance but revealing, is the care taken to make frequent use of terms different from those used by the Tang to designate the various bodies. Furthermore, not only did the size of the country and its small population warrant a smaller number of offices, but the structure of the civil service diverged from the Chinese in that no real distinction was made between the bodies which administered the court and those which administered the country as a whole.

After two centuries, the cohesion of the country and its administration rested not so much on a bureaucratic and impersonal kind of system as on personal and family connections forged in the bureaucratic circles of the capital, and between them and local dignitaries.

The political ideology of ancient China was not egalitarian. Inequality between beneficent superiors and obedient and eager inferiors, between young and old, guaranteed harmony. Each individual was obliged to work for the common good by carrying out the duties corresponding to his or her status. Japan apparently already had a sound tradition on this score: one of the first Chinese texts on the customs of the archipelago's inhabitants recounts that inferiors would prostrate themselves before superiors, which presupposes an already developed sense of hierarchy. Chinese thinking here reinforced a characteristic that was already present, and justified it.

Another feature of the 'regime of codes' imported from China was to take merit into consideration. There were competitive entrance examinations to the civil service, and officials were then assessed annually on merit in order to obtain promotion. Whereas in China the examinations tended to acquire increasing importance under the Song dynasty, in Japan the reverse held true and they diminished in importance. In the early ninth century, an upsurge of interest in China led to the creation of an official career in the arts, for which candidates were recruited by competitive examination. Some fine scholars distinguished themselves in it, and a number of them joined the group of high-ranking bureaucrats. One of the most brilliant of these, the great poet Sugawara no Michizane (845–903), even became a minister before falling from favour. But the scholars had neither the power nor, perhaps, the will to influence the way the country evolved and to impose merit-based recruitment and promotion. Japan remained committed to a system which emphasized birth yet did not altogether neglect merit.

There was one lesson from China which the Japanese court welcomed enthusiastically – the importance of ritual. It gave a different emphasis to rites than did the Confucian texts, in which their role was primarily to illustrate hierarchy, teach everyone to act according to status, and instil serenity and discipline. Belief in the power of rites over supernatural entities was not prominent. The Japan of ancient times emphasized religious ritual and believed firmly in its effectiveness, and throughout that period there was a marked increase in ceremonies. Administrative procedures themselves gradually became ritualized: form prevailed.

Buddhism reached Japan from China, at first mostly through Korea. The court made much of the promises contained in some *sūtras* of the Buddha's protection for the country of those kings who recited the *sūtras*, and it instituted a series of ceremonies for the prosperity and peace of the country and the health of the sovereign. The number of monks began to grow, particularly after the tenth century. Large monasteries were established, first at Nara, with the Hōryū-ji (founded by Prince Shōtoku), the Yakushi-ji and the Tōdai-ji, where a giant statue of the Buddha was built in the middle of the eighth century, the hypostasis of all Buddhas. At the same time the court set up two official temples in each province in further imitation of China. These monasteries were centres not only for ceremonies for the prosperity of the land but also for study of the doctrines of the various schools of Buddhism. Later, from the ninth century onwards, the two schools of Tendai and Shingon dominated the religious Buddhist scene; the former had both an exoteric and an esoteric branch, but the latter was purely esoteric.

The court protected Buddhism and at the same time made sure that it controlled it, partly to prevent tax evasion as the monks and their institutions were exempt from tax, and partly to prevent the power of Buddhist rites from being used ill-advisedly (see Plates 81, 236).

The protection granted by the court to Buddhism did not make it inclined to neglect ethnic divinities: on the contrary, as if to underscore its distinctiveness, Japan gave the blanket name of Shintō, 'the way of the gods', to all the legends and cults relating to the country's multitude of gods. It gave pride of place to the Office of Deities, which was directly answerable to the Council of State, the body at the head of the administration. The court was always very attentive to the worship of national deities. It kept a list of most of them in order to honour them with offerings at various dates in the year, either directly or through provincial governors. The celebrations at shrines always took precedence over Buddhist celebrations.

Lastly, Japan imported, together with the Chinese calendar, a whole set of so-called *yin* and *yang* doctrines whereby it was possible to identify propitious and unpropitious dates and good and bad directions on the basis of the position of real or imaginary planets or the gods associated with the five elements. A group of specialists in the lore of the calendar and divination was organized with the task of setting the dates for the court's activities and teaching which days should be 'taboo', either to avoid misfortune or for purification. In this field, too, a Japanese note was struck in the form of the obligations relating to cleanliness and the means to be used to purify oneself of contamination resulting in particular from contact with corpses, blood or persons in mourning.

So every Chinese import was assimilated and recast. From the middle of the ninth century, political decadence in China and then the disturbances which accompanied the fall of the Tang brought a temporary halt to the official missions to this country. Although the official missions did not resume for a long time, relations were maintained through Japanese monks travelling to China and the arrival of Chinese merchants in the north of Kyūshū. Japan continued to follow closely what was being written in China in the fields of philosophy, literature and Buddhism, and also developments in art (see Map 28).

The heyday of aristocratic civilization

By the beginning of the tenth century, Japan had naturalized the Chinese script: many of the characters now had a 'Japanese reading' as well as a 'Sino-Japanese reading', whose pronunciation tended to differ from that used in China. It had thus appropriated the wealth of Chinese thinking and literature and adapted them to its own needs.

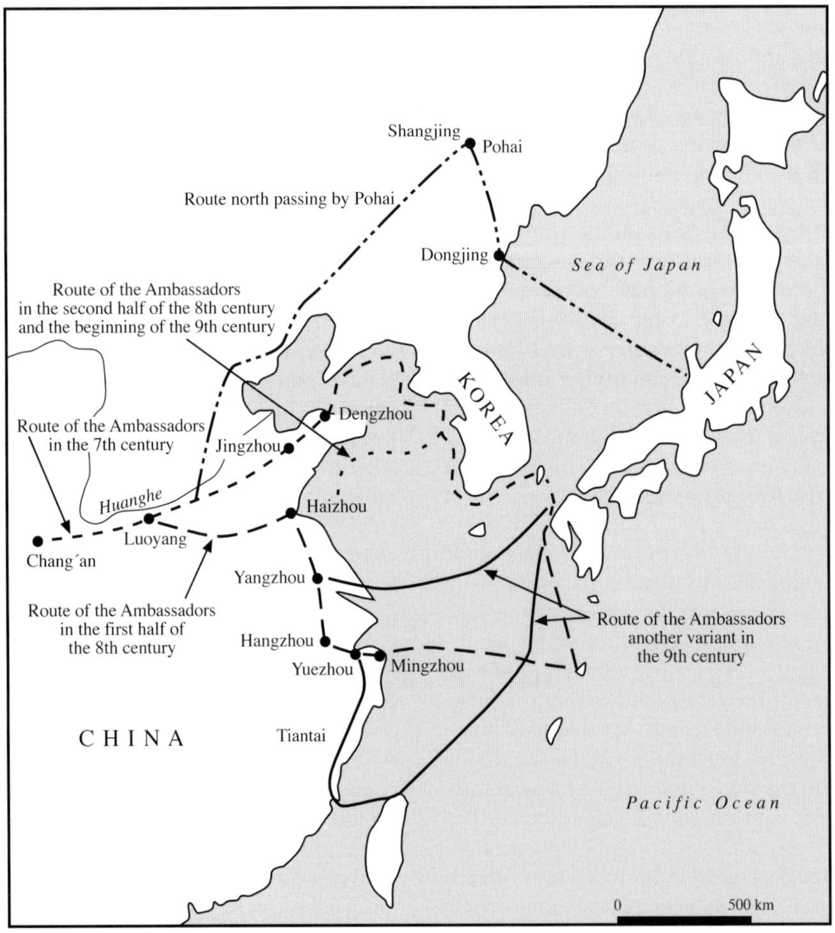

Map 28 Relations between China and Japan between the seventh and the ninth centuries (draft Herail, F.).

It distorted the institutions laid down by the codes. The court had retained the idea that it was responsible for the prosperity and security of the country and the moral character of the people, but it did not seek to achieve that ideal through constant interference in the life of the provinces, or strict supervision of the actions of its agents, or the rigorous application of the regulations on the division of paddy fields or the levying of taxes. It seemed more convenient to appoint a governor to each province who would be responsible for maintaining order and collecting and sending to the capital the produce that it needed. The court required a report only at the end of the term of office and would dismiss the governor only if there was disorder in the province or if the inhabitants sent a complaint to the capital.

So the court aristocracy lived on the basis of client relationships between it and the middle-ranking officials, the governors, and the latter sought to secure the services of subordinates. Personal connections thus began to undermine purely administrative practices.

The court did not, then, lose its sources of income, because it alone controlled the official selection of provincial governors, whom it always had the option of dismissing. During the eleventh century, it introduced a new method of managing its revenues, no longer relying only on the governors for its basic income. Estates of varying sizes were gradually removed from the authority of the governors, first by exempting them from taxes and then by ordering that no one should enter them to maintain order. These estates belonged to members of the imperial family, the great aristocratic families and religious orders, and were administered by their owners, who appointed stewards. These were sometimes the descendants of the original owners, who, in return for the right to continue running the estates, had chosen to hand them over to a powerful figure capable of protecting them from the demands of the governor.

In order to maintain its hold over the country, the court tended to rely on the authority that it derived from the divine origin of the dynasty. It focused a considerable part of its activities on organizing Buddhist and Shintō ceremonies, which were intended to win the protection of the Buddha and deities for the country, and court ceremonies designed to display its glory and the high degree of civilization that it had attained.

The life of the aristocracy was accordingly punctuated by festivals at shrines, principally those at Kamo, north of the capital, and Iwashimizu to the south, and others for which it merely sent messengers and offerings.

The Buddhist ceremonies in temples and aristocratic residences often lasted for a whole day, and sometimes for several days. They included a meal, the arrival in procession of religious dignitaries in sumptuous robes, chanting in Sanskrit, Chinese and Japanese, secular chants, and occasionally dancing.

The civil ceremonies were banquets accompanied by music and dancing, and sessions of composing Chinese poetry. Sometimes the court amused itself with debates on the classics or on Buddhist doctrine.

All the arts contributed to the beauty of these ceremonies. They took place in the palace or in the residences of the aristocracy, large groups of pavilions positioned symmetrically around a garden. The pavilions were spacious halls sheltered by broad, majestic roofs and surrounded by galleries supported on columns. The plain, brown wood, the cypress bark covering, wooden partitions and blinds gave the whole a dark, sober colouring relieved by the curtains decorated with red tassels, and by the trains of the high-ranking dignitaries and of the women who showed beneath the blinds. Painted screens were positioned so as to create partitions. The court had an artists' studio with painters attached to it (only their names remain). They painted Chinese-inspired landscapes and mythological scenes in the Chinese style, and Japanese landscapes and genre scenes depicting the seasons and the annual cycle of ceremonies in the Japanese style. Chinese and Japanese poems were written in calligraphy on the paintings. Later, in the twelfth century, painted scrolls were produced, illustrating secular and religious stories. One of the oldest, that of the *Genji monogatari* (The Tale of Genji), is also one of the most famous (see Plate 258). For Buddhist ceremonies, there were paintings which clearly corresponded to the standard iconography. The development of Amidism introduced a new motif, that of the descent of Amitābha appearing behind the mountains. Works produced in Japan, however, can always be distinguished from those coming from China by a different sense of space, as depth is not represented. Aristocrats also commissioned many religious statues from the workshops of image carvers, whose chief craft workers were honoured with religious titles. Japanese taste inclined less towards metal, clay and lacquer, favouring rather wood carving and more particularly the technique of assembling shaped wooden pieces vertically and horizontally (see Plates 81, 236).

Temples and aristocratic residences were positioned to face a garden, a sort of miniature world with a pool, river, standing stones and slopes. Very little remains of these palaces and gardens. A few objects, mostly boxes and writing desks, attest to the high degree of perfection reached in Japan in the art of lacquer. Japan perfected techniques brought over from China, in particular that of inlaying gold and mother-of-pearl. It also imported printing, which was invented in China. One of the oldest printed texts is apparently to be found in Japan and contains protective formulas which were placed in small pagodas in 770. Throughout the Middle Ages, texts were printed from boards of engraved wood in the major temples of the central region. Printed books were not really widespread until the end of the sixteenth century.

The court nobility had its heyday at the beginning of the eleventh century, when Fujiwara no Michinaga (966–1027) was chief counsellor and dominated the Japanese scene. For several decades, masterpieces proliferated, starting with those created by women. As they were unable to use the aristocratic language, Chinese, or to compose Chinese poems as did men, they wrote novels, such as the famous *Genji monogatari* by Murasaki Shikibu, private diaries, essays, like the *Makura no sōshi* by Sei Shōnagon (The Pillow Book of Sei Shōnagon), historical tales like the *Eiga monogatari* about the splendour of the Michinaga period, as well as poems in Japanese. Poetry was a common means of communication in this society, and poetry competitions were held occasionally. The works are imbued with emotions of love, jealousy, nostalgia, sadness, the sense of impermanence and a feeling for nature, and have no counterparts in China. This literature, which was largely the work of women and is the only one of its time to be still known, imitated and appreciated, distorted the image of aristocratic society, often describing it as more sophisticated and more committed to aesthetic values than it really was (see Plates 257, 258).

Men were, in reality, involved in power struggles. Aristocrats maintained companies of often violent retainers, and the major Buddhist monasteries had groups of pseudo-monks more concerned with fighting than with doctrine.

Life in the capital and the provinces was disrupted by murder, arson and robbery, at a rate which was probably considered acceptable until the middle of the twelfth century. After the middle of the eleventh century, however, a school of thought rooted in Buddhism, and bolstered by the belief that the gods might abandon the country if it was badly governed, spread pessimism and a feeling of living in decadent times throughout court circles. The theory that in 1052 the world had entered the final period of Buddhist law, the *mappō*, 'latter law', contributed to the success of Amidism, which was characterized by faith in Amitābha's power of salvation. The abandonment of the principles of the codes led some aristocrats to claim that the gods were angry and were allowing epidemics and other misfortunes to occur.

In order to subdue the unrest, the court delegated middle-ranking officials who gradually became specialized in fighting and recruiting troops. In 1156, after disputes over the succession in the imperial family, warriors, principally of the Taira and Minamoto families, sided with the opposing factions and then fought each other (see Plate 256). From 1159 to 1180, a Taira chief, Kiyomori (1118–1181), dominated the capital, thus undermining the traditional hierarchies and tarnishing the prestige of the court. The Minamoto took their revenge after 1180 and eliminated the Taira in five years of fighting, during which the capital was laid waste. A young emperor was drowned in the final defeat of the Taira at the battle of Dannoura. These wars, which left no region of the country untouched, are the subject of the famous *Heike monogatari* (The Tale of the Heike), a long saga recited by generations of storytellers throughout the land.

FROM THE TWELFTH TO THE SIXTEENTH CENTURY

The first *bakufu*, or warrior government

From the earliest times, local dignitaries had been horsemen and archers. In the Heian period, they had been ordered to police their provinces. In addition, many younger sons of officials who could not find work in the capital went to live in the provinces. Both categories could be given positions in local administration. In the twelfth century, the court-appointed governor more often than not merely sent a representative, while the rest of the staff was recruited locally. Local dignitaries, whatever their background, could also be appointed estate stewards. Many of them defended their rights, or attempted to win new ones, sword in hand. When central authority was weakened by the unrest and wars of the late twelfth century, which were combined with famine and epidemics in the central regions, Minamoto no Yoritomo (1147–1199), in exile in the east, taking advantage of an order by an imperial prince to drive out the Taira, sought to avenge his family's defeat in 1159 and put himself forward as a leader who could pacify the land.

Yoritomo was first and foremost an organizer rather than a warlord. He had not taken part in the main battles against the Taira but, very early on, he had tried to control the great warrior clans, first those in the east and then, as his army advanced westwards, those in the other regions. He confirmed the rights of those who declared themselves to be 'men of his house', *gokenin*, his vassals. From 1183, he was ordered by the court to maintain order in the east in the expectation that he would levy the taxes needed to meet the court's expenses. When he was officially entrusted with the mission of pursuing the Taira, considered to be rebels, he was also given the right to oversee the affairs of warriors in the rest of the country. He settled in Kamakura in the east, setting up there the offices of his house which dealt with the warriors, finance and justice, and recruited the staff in part from the low- and middle-ranking officials of the capital. In this way, the latter brought to the *bakufu* some of the traditions of the old administration and its judicial institutions. Finally, in 1192, the emperor conferred upon Yoritomo the title of *seii taishōgun*, abbreviated to *shōgun*, which would remain the title of the heads of the three successive *bakufu* until 1868.

As he had the right to appoint the provincial administrators in the east, and the military stewards and governors everywhere else, Yoritomo was in a position to reward faithful vassals, since these responsibilities entitled the incumbents to revenue, notably the right to keep a percentage of the estate tax raised on behalf of the lord of the estate, resident either in the capital or in the region.

The Kamakura *bakufu* took its final form only after 1221. Yoritomo died in 1199, leaving two young sons. The Hōjō, his wife's family, eliminated the two boys. After 1219, the shōgun was chosen from the Fujiwara family or the imperial family, but real power was exercised by the Hōjō, particularly by the one placed in authority, or regent, the *shikken*.

The court found it hard to endure the concessions it had been forced to make to Yoritomo. When it attempted to react, the *bakufu*'s warrior vassals did not obey the order of the court in 1221 to pursue Hōjō Yoshitoki as a rebel. The troops from the capital were defeated and *bakufu* authority emerged strengthened by the episode. A council, *Hyōjō-shū*, was set up composed of the chiefs, in many cases hereditary, of offices and representatives of the main vassal families. It was intended primarily to oversee property cases in which vassals, military stewards and military governors were involved. In 1232, the *bakufu* promulgated a code, *Jōei Shikimoku*, the Jōei Formulary, which remained the basis of legislation for the subsequent *bakufu*.

However, the court's institutions and laws were not abolished. It retained jurisdiction over the provinces and continued to receive complaints and give rulings. The court nobles and the imperial family owned estates throughout the country. The rights over these estates were complex and tangled and varied according to the circumstances: there were the rights of eminent landowners, which ranged from receiving a share of the taxes to appointing and replacing estate officials, rights of resident estate officials, rights of the military stewards appointed by the *bakufu*, rights of the owners of taxable land and rights of those who actually worked the land, who were in some cases distinct from the owners. There were inherent long-term risks in the estate system for the eminent landowners, the court nobles, but it was still providing them with an adequate income into the thirteenth century. The police bureau of the Heian court remained active in the capital during the thirteenth century, and indeed the court extended its protection to groups of artisans and merchants, seafarers who supplied fish and salt, and carriers living in the central regions and those of the Inland Sea, which were the most active areas. What authority remained to it, though, was mostly based on tradition and the prestige it retained, rather than on its strength.

In the latter half of the thirteenth century, when the country had to confront the Mongol threat, the *bakufu* alone took the decisions. The court merely ordered religious ceremonies and expressed its hopes. In both 1274 and 1281, this defence was substantially aided by the elements – typhoons and storms.

But after this final success, which gave them time to establish more firmly their influence over the west and the shipping routes of the Inland Sea, the Hōjō regime entered a period of decline. Although in the early days it had been adept at controlling its vassals, which enabled it to maintain order, it had to face up to the growing dissatisfaction of the *gokenin*, whose numbers had risen, who had become poorer as a result of divided inheritances, and who were increasingly in debt. Instances multiplied of misappropriation of revenue, disorder, and robbery by pirate gangs and rebels, while the Hōjō tended more and more to favour their own people over the *bakufu* vassals, and their entourage was torn by bloody disputes.

When Go-Daigo (1288–1339) became emperor in 1318, he started to plot to destroy the *bakufu* and restore the power of the court. After various incidents, which included the exiling of Emperor Go-Daigo in 1331 by the *bakufu*, the latter, deserted by a large proportion of its vassals, notably Ashikaga Takauji (1305–1358), fell in 1333 to warriors who were not *bakufu* vassals, such as the well-known Kusunoki Masashige, with whom some *gokenin* joined forces. Emperor Go-Daigo was able to return to Kyōto and attempt a restoration in the Kemmu era. In fact, that restoration was based on a misunderstanding, because the vassals of the Kamakura *bakufu* had not destroyed it in order to return to the old regime and did not wish to take orders from the institutions of Kyōto or to accept a review of the estate titles they held or had appropriated. The outcome was therefore the opposite of what Emperor Go-Daigo had hoped for, and the failed restoration led to a more rapid weakening of the court and its gradual despoilment. From 1335 onwards, Ashikaga Takauji's relations with the court deteriorated. In 1336, he banished Emperor Go-Daigo from the capital. Over the previous decades, the Kamakura *bakufu* had organized the succession to the throne by alternating between two branches descended from the emperor who had reigned from 1242 to 1246. When Emperor Go-Daigo, who was from the Daikakuji branch, set up his court in Yoshino, south of the Nara basin, it became possible to enthrone an emperor from the Jimyō-in line in Kyōto. There were thus two courts, and the country was plunged into a long period of conflict.

The chaotic destiny of the Ashikaga *bakufu*

Until 1392, there was a schism in the imperial family and two courts, the northern court in Kyōto and the southern court at Yoshino. The country was thus divided, but there was no clear frontier between the regions belonging to one or the other court. The supporters of each lived side by side, and many chose whichever would be in their best interests, with no compunction about changing sides or indeed withdrawing their allegiance from both. The emperor of the northern court conferred the title of *seii taishōgun* on Ashikaga Takauji, who claimed to be descended from the Minamoto (see Plate 14).

The Ashikaga *bakufu*, also known as the Muromachi *bakufu* after the district of the capital where the third *shōgun* settled, was a slightly modified version of the previous one. There was no regent, *shikken*, but a deputy *shōgun*, *kanrei*, whose office was not hereditary but was reserved for members of the three main families of military governors. The head of the warriors' bureau was also military governor of Yamashiro province and therefore in charge of policing the capital and supervising its large population of merchants and artisans. The members of four families were eligible for this position. The civil service bureau, which was in charge of finances, gained importance at the end of the fourteenth century when the *bakufu* began to derive funds from taxes paid by moneylenders and saké brewers.

The military governors appointed in each province belonged for the most part to families who shared a common origin with the Ashikaga, but that was not enough to guarantee their loyalty. In the previous period, they had been entitled only to punish murderers and armed robbers and to convene the *gokenin*. They had, however, taken advantage of the disturbances of the fourteenth century and of the need to fight the southern court's supporters to expand their prerogatives. They interfered in the administration of the estates and lands which remained under provincial control and obtained, often on a temporary basis, the right to raise taxes there or to take half of those due to the lords. They tended to keep back appeals which they were supposed to pass on to the *shōgun* court. The military governors often lived in the capital, and, as some of them were in charge of several provinces, they appointed representatives who sometimes seized the chance to fulfil their own ambitions. Those in the east reported to an Ashikaga of a cadet line who was established in Kamakura; those of Kyūshū were answerable to a governor-general of the island, Kyūshū *tandai*. They tried with varying degrees of success to subjugate and make vassals of the minor local warriors, estate officials and even paddy field owners whose work they supervised: in other words, both warriors and farmers.

Since the previous century, peasant communities had become organized and acquired some sort of legal status, since their undertakings (the earliest known one dates back to 1240) to pay a fixed amount of taxes were considered to be legally binding. By the end of the thirteenth century, some of them had drawn up their own regulations.

The contest was played out between four camps: (1) the landowners, court nobles and major religious establishments; (2) the minor provincial warriors; (3) the peasant communities; and (4) the *bakufu* representatives. The minor local warriors might team up with the peasants against the domain lords or submit to the military governor so that they could gain the right to control an estate or a peasant community. They might establish a league among themselves, *ikki*, to oppose the military governor. Military governors often had no scruples about exploiting court nobles and appropriating their rights. Peasants could take advantage of the disputes among their superiors, who depended on them for a living. On the whole, the major monasteries and shrines defended their property better than did the court nobility. Rural communities could also enter into alliances with local warriors and obtain their protection, but some of them simply took up arms and defended themselves.

After the reunification of the two courts in 1392, to the advantage of the northern court, the Ashikaga *bakufu* reached its apogee. The third *shōgun*, Yoshimitsu (1358–1408), after bringing to heel some of the big military governors, gave the country a few years of peace and prosperity. In addition to his position as *shōgun*, he persuaded the court to appoint him minister of the left in 1382, and grand minister of state in 1394 when he passed on the title of *shōgun* to one of his sons. The following year he became a monk, although he continued to run the *bakufu* through his son. He had the magnificent residence of Kitayama built in the hills to the north of Kyōto. In order to improve the state of his finances, which enabled him to buy loyalty and play the part of the grand aristocrat and patron of the arts, he renewed official – that is, unequal – relations with China. For the occasion he took the title of *ō*, prince or king, which was used by kings who were tributaries of China and excluded the emperor, who in this way was not compromised. He was able to obtain licences to trade with China and to sell them at a profit. His successor, dissatisfied with the unequal aspect of the relations, ended them and chose to give up the benefits of trade, but his own successor (his brother) reversed the decision and trade by licence continued, although it enriched the great *daimyō* (domain lords) and religious institutions, particularly the Zen temples, more than the *bakufu*. Since the fourteenth century and the end of the Mongol threat, activities which were half piracy and half trade had flourished in Kyūshū, Tsushima and throughout the west of the country. The *bakufu*'s endeavours to eliminate the supporters of the southern court from Kyūshū were broadly designed to gain a share of the profits from the trade with Korea and China. Among other things, it meant that currency could be imported, which Japan needed urgently for internal exchange, since the minting of coins had been suspended in the tenth century and would not resume until the end of the sixteenth century.

After the assassination of Yoshimitsu's second successor in 1441, the *bakufu* went into decline, although at the end of the century the *shōgun* Yoshimasa (1436–1490) was in a position to build the elegant residence of Higashiyama in east Kyōto, collect works of art there, organize poetry composition sessions and practise the tea ceremony. All central authority collapsed and the country entered a phase of rapid change, social transformation and the overturning of hierarchy, which contemporaries called 'inferiors overcoming superiors', 'subversion', *gekokujō*. The disturbances became more widespread after the Ōnin War (1467–1477), which, using the pretext of a dispute over succession in the shōgunal family, set two leagues of *daimyō* at each other's throats in the central regions. Historians refer to the period from 1467 to the fall of the Ashikaga *bakufu* in 1573 by the name of *Sengoku jidai*, 'warring country period'.

The end of the fifteenth century and the sixteenth century were times of rebellion and struggle, mainly in the central regions, but the rest of the country was not spared. Peasant communities enjoyed a certain autonomy, with their own assemblies, and they managed their common land and irrigation systems. When the inhabitants were dissatisfied with the local lord, they sometimes formed 'communes', also called *ikki*, to present their demands, often so violently that the word *ikki* has acquired the meaning of peasant revolt. After 1428, peasants and horse lenders frequently rose up to demand 'acts of grace', *tokuseirei*, edicts cancelling debts. In the capital, such riots targeted moneylenders, who were often defended by the *bakufu* because they paid taxes. In other cases, the revolt sought a reduction in land tax or the abolition of the customs posts set up on roads, of which there were many in the central regions. Sometimes they affected an entire province. Some rebels targeted the military governors. In 1487, the main inhabitants of Yamashiro province drove out the armies of the two rivals who were fighting for the title of military governor. For seven years, they tried to run the province by themselves, but failed. On the other hand, the Amidist sect known as Ikkōshū (sect of those who turn in one direction, who put their trust only in the Amida Buddha (Amitābha), another name for the True sect of Pure Land Buddhism) succeeded in administering Kaga province for 100 years.

Eventually, other disturbances like those of the Ōnin era shook the families of the military governors, the *daimyō* or 'great names'. The trend in warrior families was to designate only one heir, which led to frequent quarrels over succession in which the main vassals joined. In this way, several great *daimyō* houses were weakened and ambitious vassals were able to replace them, all the more easily because the military art allowed for neither total defeat nor total victory. Many people bore arms, and it was always possible to organize them into groups. Some of the sixteenth-century *daimyō* were descended from military governors, but others had newly emerged, sometimes from quite humble backgrounds. No *daimyō* managed to establish stable authority in the central regions. On the whole, each local lord tried to organize his territory, set up structures, levy taxes, legislate and above all secure the loyalty of warriors.

Nevertheless, in the midst of this turmoil, fighting and rivalry, there was progress on the economic front. In the sixteenth century, it was in the interest of each *daimyō* to enrich his territory by developing towns and markets, and growing crops like cotton. The impression that Japan was rocked by constant wars and revolts in the Middle Ages is not strictly true, since the disturbances were often short-lived and did not affect all the regions at the same time. This period was a time of renewal of the elites, economic progress, the emergence of new religious movements and the development of new literary genres.

Medieval civilization

The medieval era, especially the thirteenth century, was again a time of intense religious activity. Several new sects were established during the Kamakura period. Their doctrines were not really new or unknown in Japan, because they were for the most part contained in the doctrine of the Tendai school. The new sects fell into two groups: Amidism and Zen.

Amidism took off at the end of the tenth century as the fear grew that the age of the 'latter law', *mappō*, was beginning and when faith in the Buddha Amida's promise to save all who would turn to him appeared to be the only road to salvation. Three sects were born in the thirteenth century. The first was the Pure Land sect, Jōdoshū, founded by Hōnen (1133–1212), which advocated recital of the invocation of Amida but did not abolish monastic life. One of its more radical disciples, Shinran (1173–1262), considered that the observances of monks and nuns had no relevance to anyone who had faith in a higher power and trusted in Amida's promise. He established the True sect of Pure Land Buddhism, Jōdo shinshū. Shinran married and went to preach in the east. He organized groups of believers. After obscure beginnings, his descendants, in the person of Rennyo (1415–1499), had themselves acknowledged as hereditary leaders of the sect. It spread widely among villagers and by the end of the fifteenth century, as we have already seen, it dominated Kaga province. Its main centre in the sixteenth century, the Hongan-ji of Ishiyama (on the site of present-day Ōsaka) held out for a long time against Oda Nobunaga. Another monk in the thirteenth century, Ippen (1239–1289), spread devotion to religious observance in the form of dance, which was very popular among the people. He created the Amidist sect Jishū, which did not develop on the same pattern as the sect founded by Shinran (see Plate 81).

Zen (from Chinese *Chan*, itself derived from Sanskrit *Dhyāna*, 'awakening'), a method of meditation, is a way of achieving Enlightenment, that is of rediscovering, or revealing, the 'Buddha nature' which is within each of us. The Tendai sect was already familiar with these practices but did not focus its teaching on them. Unlike Amidism, which relied on the strength of Amida, Zen believed that awakening could be gained through the strength of the adept who emptied his or her mind by practising quiet sitting, *zazen*. Two monks, both trained in Tendai doctrine, went to China. The first, Eisai (1141–1215), returned with the Zen of the Rinzai school and the second, Dōgen (1200–1253), one of the greatest thinkers of the Middle Ages, brought back that of the Sōtō school. In Zen, written transmission is in theory considered inferior, although this has not prevented Zen monks from writing a great deal. Likewise, Zen is in theory opposed to esoteric Buddhism and its efficacious rites, which had been so popular in the Heian period. In practice, however, medieval Zen remained thoroughly imbued with Tendai esotericism. Monks, particularly those of the Rinzai school, were in great favour with the Kamakura and Muromachi *bakufu*. As many of them had made the journey to China, they played an important part in the transmission of neo-Confucian thinking. The Rinzai sect was organized on the Chinese 'Five Mountains' model, *Gozan*, with a hierarchy of monasteries and the appointment of superiors by the authorities. Zen produced many monks distinguished by their talent for Chinese poetry; their skill as diplomats, either in domestic disturbances or in relations with China; their financial competence – Zen monasteries made interest-bearing loans and took an active part in trade with China; their technical skills – the printing of religious texts and Chinese poems flourished in them; and their artistic talents – it was in Zen temples that the model of the dry garden was created, and the art of monochrome landscape painting was perfected by Shūbun and his pupil Sesshū (1420–1506) (see Plate 254).

A sort of reform of Tendai, shorn of its esoteric side, was carried out by the monk Nichiren, who founded the only home-grown Buddhist sect, that which bears his name or is sometimes called Hokkeshū because it is essentially based on the *Lotus Sūtra*. The sect found many disciples among the merchants and artisans of Kyōto. Nichiren had conceived a revulsion for Amidism, and the followers of his sect quite naturally found themselves opposed to the Ikkō sect, another name for Jōdo shinshū, which was widespread among the peasants on the outskirts of the capital, who were often in debt to city moneylenders. This hostility, like that which Tendai harboured against Amidism and the Nichiren sect, contributed substantially to the unrest of the fifteenth and sixteenth centuries.

Shintō was also flourishing. The era of pilgrimages to Kumano (in the south of the Kii peninsula) had begun in the twelfth century, and in the thirteenth century nobles, warriors and before long the common people went to Ise. The relationship between Buddhism and Shintō was reviewed: whereas at the beginning of the Middle Ages there had been a tendency to deify the reincarnations of the buddhas, thinkers such as Yoshida Kanetomo (1435–1511) reversed the relationship and made the deities the primary entities, of which the Buddhas were the incarnations.

The increasingly impoverished court nobility retained its reputation for refinement and courtesy. It cultivated what it considered to be its speciality, *waka* poetry, short poems of five lines: the court continued to order the compilation of official anthologies until the twenty-first and last of these in 1439. The ancient *gagaku* music endured, albeit in decline, until the fifteenth century. The Ōnin War, however, led to the dispersal of musicians and the loss of the court orchestras. Erudition was also one of the nobles' strong points and interests, particularly regarding everything to do with the old court, the cycle of celebrations, ceremonial, institutions and commentaries on the great works of the past. These themes were, for them, shot through with nostalgia. Through such studies they endeavoured to keep alive the memories of a past that seemed more and more glorious the more distant it became. They accordingly produced handbooks on protocol and encyclopedias on subjects such as *yin* and *yang* doctrines, customs, costumes and rites. A few names among many deserve mention. At the beginning of the thirteenth century, Fujiwara no Teika (1162–1241), compiler of the poetic anthology *Shin kokin wakashū* and publisher of earlier texts, was the first in a line devoted to the conservation of ancient poetry. In the fourteenth century, Kitabatake Chikafusa (1293–1354) wrote a handbook of ancient institutions, the *Shokugenshō,* and a history of the country, the *Jinnō shōtō ki*, 'Chronicle of the Direct Descent of Divine Sovereigns', which enjoyed an excellent reputation in the succeeding centuries. Tōnoin Kinkata (1293–1360) composed a small and comprehensive encyclopedia on the court, the *Shūgaishō.* Lastly, the great scholar of the fifteenth century was Ichijō Kaneyoshi (1464–1514), who was chief counsellor and author of commentaries on the *Genji monogatari*, *Kokin wakashū*, *Nihon shoki* and many other works. The Ōnin War dealt him a rude blow, too, when his library was burned down.

The warriors of the thirteenth century were mostly illiterate and more given to mounted archery at a moving target and other pleasures than to literature and the arts. The warrior elite, however, beginning with Minamoto no Yoritomo and later Ashikaga Yoshimitsu and Ashikaga Yoshimasa, far from despising the culture of the court nobles, endeavoured to learn from them and from the Zen monks who brought them the philosophy and arts of China. Medieval civilization did not only inherit aristocratic civilization, however. It was strengthened, too, by popular contributions such as the earlier entertainments known as *sarugaku* (sometimes translated as 'monkey dances') or tales sung by wandering storytellers, who ensured that the *Heike monogatari*, '*The Tale of the Heike*', became the best-known work in Japanese literature and the source of a great many Noh plays. It was in Kyōto where especially after the fourteenth century many warriors settled, and where there was a significant population of merchants, that the intermingling occurred. Even the outcast peoples, known as the *kawaramono* because they lived on the banks of the Kamo River, played a role in the artistic life of the time, particularly as garden designers. The group of people who looked after interior design, the positioning of art objects, the organizing of poetry composition sessions and the tea ceremony in the houses of the *shōgun* or the major *daimyō* was often made up of recruits with very humble backgrounds. These people were known as *dōbō*, and they concealed their origins under a form of religious name ending in *ami* (which denoted membership of the Ji sect), such as Zeami, the great Noh artist; Zenami, the garden designer; and Geiami, Nōami and Sōami, who managed the tea ceremony for Yoshimasa. In the fifteenth century, the rich merchant city of Sakai (the eastern part of present-day Ōsaka) also contributed to the flourishing of some forms of art, in particular all aspects of the tea ceremony.

The Middle Ages experienced two high points, in the early fifteenth century around Yoshimitsu (the period called

Kitayama, after the name of his villa) and at the end of the century under Yoshimasa (a period called Higashiyama, after the name of his residence). The symmetry and scale of the layout of the earlier great aristocratic dwellings had been abandoned in favour of a freer spatial arrangement of the pavilions. Zen monasteries had provided the model of small detached retreats, each with its own garden. The interior layout of the pavilions was altered. Walls multiplied, thus creating small rooms, the floor was entirely covered with matting, and translucent paper partitions between the outer gallery and the interior replaced wooden shutters and blinds. The decor of certain rooms – dais, alcove adorned with a painting or vase, flanked by asymmetrical shelves and cupboards – was created. This style was to dominate noble and bourgeois living spaces in the centuries to come.

The beginning of the fifteenth century saw the creation and development of Noh theatre, the theoretician, author and actor of which, Zeami (1363–1443), was a favourite of Yoshimitsu. This theatre had popular origins and initially also a popular audience. Likewise, the habit of several individuals composing linked verse, each responsible for half a *waka*, was highly popular among the community of minor warriors and merchants, even though the principle was already known but not much practised among the aristocracy, which preferred poetry competitions.

The tea ceremony, which began to be codified in the fifteenth century, influenced architecture, landscape gardening, ceramics, painting and flower arranging. The shōguns, and Yokimasa in particular, built up collections of objects and works of art connected with the tea ceremony. The first expert and theoretician, Murata Shukō (1423–1502), had been influenced by Zen. He had many disciples throughout the country, but the group from the rich merchant city Sakai merits particular attention – it was honoured by Takeno Jōō (1502–1555), then by Sen Rikyū (1521–1591), who served Toyotomi Hideyoshi and was associated with the warrior elite, but who died tragically.

No great novels have come down to us from the literature of this time, which instead was noteworthy above all for its poetry. Zen monks produced numerous collections of Chinese poetry (Gozan *bunkagu*, 'Five Mountains Literature') that contain great works – the earliest being strongly inspired by religious themes but becoming more worldly as time went by. One of the best-known poets, although marginal in relation to the others, is Ikkyū Sōjun (1394–1481), who lived as a wandering monk before returning to secular society. He felt most painfully the troubles of his time and criticized the decadence of the monastic establishment. One of his collections, *Kyōunshū*, 'The Crazy-Cloud Anthology', is still famous. He influenced both masters of the tea ceremony, such as Murata Shukō, and *renga* specialists. *Renga*, linked poetry, was the typical Japanese poetry form of the Middle Ages, produced in groups with each participant composing half a *waka*. The two main collections are *Tsukubashū* from the mid-fourteenth century, and from 1495, *Shinsen Tsukubashū*. The most frequently cited of many names are Sōgi (1421–1502) and Sōchō (1448–1532). Theoreticians of the art of tea and poets, like authors of Noh drama, came for the most part from the common people. This is characteristic of medieval civilization, together with a certain leaning towards original, non-conformist behaviour, as common among warriors as among the ordinary people.

When the Ashikaga *bakufu* was destroyed in 1573 by Oda Nobunaga (1534–1582), who had begun to reunify the country after the 'warring country' period, Japan had been in contact for 30 years with the Portuguese, who had brought firearms, soon to be manufactured in Japan itself. Such guns had played a role in the turn-of-the-century fighting which led to reunification under the authority of Toyotomi Hideyoshi (1536–1598), a *parvenu*. Further measures, such as the disarming of the population, the sharp distinction made between warriors and the rest of the people and the new land register, which abolished the last traces of the earlier domain system, consolidated unification. After a final battle at Sekigahara, Tokugawa Ieyasu (1542–1616) was able to found the third and last *bakufu* in 1603. Japan had entered a new age.

NOTE

1 The word 'civilization', which the author uses, must be understood in its French sense: the entire social phenomena of a religious, moral, aesthetic and technical nature common in a society.

BIBLIOGRAPHY

AKIYAMA, T. 1961. *La peinture japonaise*. Geneva, Skira.

BROWN, D. M. (ed.) 1993. *Ancient Japan*, Vol. 1. Cambridge. XXII <2> (*The Cambridge History of Japan*).

COLLCUTT, M. 1981. *Five Mountains: The Rinzai Zen Monastic Institution in Medieval Japan*. Council on East Asian Studies, Harvard University (Harvard East Asian Monographs, 85). Cambridge, Mass.

COOPER, M. (ed.) 1976. Introduction by DOI, T. *The Southern Barbarians: The First Europeans in Japan*. Palo Alto, Kodansha International in co-operation with Sophia University. Tokyo.

ELISSEEFF, V. AND D. 1980. *L'art de l'ancien Japon*. Paris,

FRANK, B. 1958. *Kata-imi et Kata-tagae, étude sur les interdits de direction de l'époque Heian*. Maison Franco-japonaise (Bulletin de la Maison Franco-japonaise, tome V, Nos. 2–4). Tokyo.

——. 1993. *Le panthéon bouddhique au Japon, collection d'Emile Guimet*. Réunion des musées nationaux. Paris.

GOMI, F. 1988. *Kamakura to Kyoto* (Kamakura and Kyoto). Vol. 5, Shōgakkan (Taikei Nihon no rekishi). Tokyo.

GROSSBERG, K. A. 1981. *Japan's Renaissance: The Politics of the Muromachi Bakufu*. Council on East Asian Studies, Harvard University (Harvard East Asian Monographs, 99). Cambridge, Mass.

HALL, J. W., MASS, J. P. (eds) 1988. *Medieval Japan: Essays in Institutional History*. New Haven, Conn. (reprinted, Stanford, California, Stanford University Press).

HALL, J. W., TOYODA, T. (eds) 1977. *Japan in the Muromachi Age*. Berkeley, Calif.

HALL, J. W., NAGAHARA, K., YAMAMURA, K. (eds) 1981. *Japan before Tokugawa: Political Consolidation and Economic Growth, 1500 to 1650*. Princeton, NJ.

HÉRAIL, F. (ed.) 1990. *Histoire du Japon*. Le Coteau, Horvath.

JOÜON DES LONGRAIS, F. 1958. *L'Est et l'Ouest*. Maison Franco-japonaise. Tokyo.

MASS, J. P. (ed.) 1982. *Court and Bakufu in Japan: Essays in Kamakura History*. New Haven, Conn.

——. 1979. *The Development of Kamakura Rule, 1180–1250: A History with Documents*. Stanford, Calif.

MASS, J. P., HAUSER, W. B. (eds) 1985. Foreword by JANSEN, M. B. *The Bakufu in Japanese History*. Stanford, Calif.

MORRIS, I. 1964. *The World of the Shining Prince: Court Life in Ancient Japan*. Knopf, New York, Oxford University Press, Oxford, England, (reprinted, Penguin Books, Harmondsworth, Middx, 1964; Tuttle, Tokyo, 1978).

NAGAHARA, K. 1988. *Nairan to Minshu* (Civil War and the Common People). Vol. 6. Tokyo, Shōgakkan (Taikei Nihon no rekishi).

NOMA, S. 1966 and 1967. *The Arts of Japan, I: Ancient and Medieval. II: Late Medieval to Modern* (trans. by ROSENFIELD, J. and WEBB, G.T.) Kodansha International. 2 vols. Tokyo, New York.

REISCHAUER, E.; CRAIG, A. M. 1989. *Japan: Tradition and Transformation.* Houghton Mifflin. rev. edn. Boston, Mass.

SUGIMOTO, M.; SWAIN, D. L. 1978. Foreword by SIVIN, N. *Science and Culture in Traditional Japan, A.D. 600–1854.* MIT Press (MIT East Asian Science Series, 6) Cambridge, Mass. (reprinted, Tuttle, 1989. Tokyo).

TANAHASHI, M. 1988. *Ōchō no shakai* (Heian Aristocratic Society), Vol. 4. Tokyo, Shōgakkan (Taikei Nihon no rekishi).

VARLEY, H. P. 1967. *The Ōnin War: History of its Origins and Background with a Selective Translation of the Chronicle of Ōnin.* Columbia University Press (Studies in Oriental Culture, 1). New York.

VERSCHUER, C. VON. 1987. *Le commerce extérieur du Japon, des origines au XVIe siècle.* Collège de France, Institut des hautes études japonaises. Maisonneuve et Larose. (Bibliothèque de l'Institut des hautes études japonaises). Paris.

WAKITA, H. 1988. *Sengoku daimyō* [Feudal Lords (*daimyō*) of the Sengoku Era], Vol. 7. Tokyo, Shōgakkan (Taikei Nihon no rekishi).

YAMAMURA, K. (ed.) 1990. *Medieval Japan*, Vol. 3. Cambridge, XVIII <3> (*The Cambridge History of Japan*).

YOSHIDA, T. 1988. *Kodai kokka no ayumi* (The Ancient State). Vol. 3. Shōgakkan (Taikei Nihon no rekishi). Tokyo.

YOSHIE, A. 1986. *Rekishi no akebono kara dento shakai no seijuku he* (From the Dawning of History to the Maturation of Traditional Society), Vol. 1. Yamakawa shuppansha (Nihon tsūshi). Tokyo.

28.2
KOREA

Li Ogg

THE PENINSULA UNDER THE DOMINATION OF SILLA

After several years of warfare, final victory in the struggle for mastery of the Korean peninsula went to the kingdom of Silla (57 BC to AD 918) at the expense of its neighbours, Koguryŏ (37 BC to AD 668) to the north and Paekche (18 BC to AD 660) to the west. To achieve its aim, Silla had to call on the assistance of the Chinese army of the Tang, whose sole motive in intervening in the war between the peninsular's states was to expand its territory to the east. The Chinese dynasty having shown that it wanted to gain control of the former territories of these defeated states, a new war broke out. Silla succeeded in repelling the Chinese northwards, but the Chinese did not 'grant' Silla control of the territories south of the Taedong River basin until 735.

Strongly influenced by its relationship with China, Sillan civilization underwent a radical change, particularly during the sixth and seventh centuries. The ruling class sought to adopt Chinese ways, as can be seen from the fact that courtiers at the royal court were already beginning to dress in the Chinese style by 649, and King T'aejong (654–661) wore clothes presented to him by the Tang emperor, a sure sign of 'submission' to Chinese civilization. In response to the need to train additional administrators to govern its enlarged territory properly, Silla established a national school (*kukhak*) in 682, where young aristocrats spent 9 years learning not only the Chinese art of government but also Chinese history and philosophy. None the less, it was not until 728 that trainees were allowed, with the permission of the Chinese emperor, to study at the Chinese State Institute (*guoxue*). In fact, of the fifty-eight such students who passed the final examinations of this college, a dozen did so well that they were awarded Chinese civil service titles.

Buddhist monks also made their way to China to complete their education, among them Wonch'ŭk (613–696) and Uisang (625–702). A disciple of the celebrated Xuanzang (Hsüan Tsang), Wonch'uk assisted, during his stay, in the translation of Buddhist scriptures into Chinese. Uisang is known as the founder in Silla of the Hwaŏm sect (in Chinese *Huayan*, in Sanskrit *Avatamsaka*). A few fortunate monks went as far as India, among them Hyech'o (Huichao in Chinese) (704 to ?), whose services, on his return in 728, were also enlisted, in China, for the translation of Buddhist scriptures into Chinese and who wrote, in Chinese, the well-known 'Diary of a Journey to the Five Countries of India'. From the end of the eighth century, faith in Amitābha and belief in 'rebirth in the western paradise' became widespread throughout the peninsula. The practice of salvationist religion was strongly encouraged by the monk Wŏnhyo (617–686).

In Silla, the Korean language was already being transcribed using a procedure known as *idu,* in which the Korean semantemes were represented by means of Chinese ideophones of an equivalent meaning, whereas the particles and suffixes peculiar to Korean were transcribed using the phonetic value of the Chinese characters.

As with temple architecture, for example the Pulguksa, Buddhist sculpture was also greatly influenced by that of the Tang, which itself borrowed from Central Asia and Graeco-Buddhist art. Most of the statues and bas-reliefs of this era, in particular the eighth-century examples from Sokkuram, near Kyŏngju, the capital of Silla, can be ranked among the masterpieces of this art form executed in Eastern Asia.

The people of Silla also learned the technique of making wood-block prints from the Chinese. This was borne out by the paper scroll, discovered in 1966, on which at the end of the seventh century was printed the Chinese translation of the *dharani* entitled 'Sūtra of Pure Light'. According to experts on Korea, this is believed to be the oldest example of xylographic printing in the world.

Prominent among the merchants engaging at that time in private trade between China and the peninsula was Chang Pogo (otherwise known as Kungbok or Kungp'a), who died in 846. Having served as an officer in the Chinese army doing garrison duty at Gansu, the starting-point of the routes to Central Asia, Chang was given the task by King Hŭngdok (826–836) of dealing with the pirates, both Chinese and others, who were then infesting the west coast of Korea. Being an enterprising character, Chang Pogo promptly set up his headquarters on the island of Wan, from where, with the aid of the junks at his disposal, he finally succeeded in controlling for himself part of the trade between China and Silla. This is a demonstration of what we know from other sources concerning the trading, both official and unofficial, and the privateering which was common at the time on the high seas off the coasts of the peninsula and as far down as the waters off the south of Japan.

The bitter struggles between rival factions of an aristocracy vying for political power meant that towards the end of its existence, and especially in the ninth century, the monarchy was in turmoil. The disorder that resulted eventually brought the country to a state of indescribable chaos and, from the beginning of the tenth century, the situation was made worse by revolts of peasants, organized in armed bands. One of the peasant leaders, Wang Kŏn (877–943), established a kingdom called Koryŏ (918–1392), and in 936 received the peaceful 'submission' of Silla.

THE ERA OF KORYO (918–1392)

Early in its history, in 993 and 1010, Koryŏ had to deal with the invading armies of the Khitans under the Liao Dynasty (907–1125). Later, in 1115, the Jurchen, founders of the Jin Dynasty (1115–1234), threatened the existence of Koryŏ, which had to submit to them in 1125. This series of disturbances instigated by the Jurchen gave renewed influence to the military, who, though traditionally regarded with disdain by the educated civil servants, were nevertheless one of the two ruling classes in the establishment or *yangban* (literally, 'two classes'). In 1170, General Chŏng Chungbu (?–1178) carried out a successful *coup d'état.* Other generals followed each other in the most important positions in government, thus establishing a period of military dictatorship which was to last about 250 years. Early in the thirteenth century, the threat from the Mongols crystallized and their cavalry invaded the territory of Koryŏ in 1231. 'Resident commissars' arrived to impose the will of the Mongol Empire on the whole peninsula. In the meantime, the Koryŏ court took refuge on the island of Kanghwa and remained there until 1270, putting up such resistance as it could to the intransigent demands of the Mongol authorities. After the submission of the Koryŏ court, the Mongols enlisted its considerable support in attempting two invasions of Japan, in 1274 and again in 1281. Both attempts failed on account of violent storms, the *kamikaze*, which burst on the invading armies and prevented them landing on the Japanese coast. The Mongol dynasty of Yuan was overthrown in 1368 by the dynasty known as the Ming. The question of obedience to this new Chinese dynasty brought about the downfall, in 1392, of the kingdom of Koryŏ, which then fell victim to inevitable political and economic decline.

With its 2 million inhabitants, the Korea of the Koryŏ era, despite many invasions and their disastrous consequences, enjoyed extraordinary prosperity, the beneficiaries of which were the nobles. Evidence for this is to be found in a complaint by one Ch'oe Sŭngno to the reigning monarch, which reads: 'The wealthy are constantly trying to outdo each other and are building large houses. (In doing so) . . . they succeed merely in depleting their family fortunes. They are also oppressing the peasantry.' On another occasion, during the reign of King Yejong (1105–1122), a civil servant named Han Anin criticized the extravagant lifestyle of the nobility. In 1168, King Uijong (1124–1170) personally attacked such ways of living: 'Luxury has become the norm. Silk brocade is used for everyday wear, and gold and jade for household crockery.' In the *Koryŏ sa* (History of Koryŏ) (chapter CXXIX, we note that criticism was levelled at a certain Ch'oe Ch'unghŏn for having had more than 100 houses demolished so that he could build a house of his own and for having accumulated there and in two other properties in the capital a vast amount of wealth in the shape of gold, precious jades, coins and grain. From the same source, we learn that this important person had a guard which watched over him at home and escorted him whenever he went out, and with such pomp that one might have thought that he was setting off for war. It cannot be emphasized enough just how vast were the sums that these aristocrats felt obliged to spend in order to maintain their rank and not 'lose face'. In addition to these expenses, there was the largesse distributed to the usually quite large numbers of clients which every person of note felt constrained to support if not to feed.

Protected by the court, Buddhism flourished in Koryo, but at the same time the monks were tolerant of shamanist practices and beliefs. On his return from two years spent in China, Uichŏn (1050–1101), also known as Master Taegak, worked from 1086 to achieve a synthesis of doctrine. It combined the doctrines of Kyo (in Chinese, *jiao*) teaching, that is, those of the five principles of *vinaya*, *dharma*, *dharmata*, *nirvāṇa* and *avamtamsaka*, according to which awakening and deliverance can be attained only by thorough knowledge of the canonical scriptures. At the same time, it unified the sects of the *dhyāna* (Korean: *Son*, Chinese: *Chan*, Japanese: *Zen*), who believed that awakening and deliverance are attained only through meditative asceticism. Apart from its theological significance, it also represented an attempt to secure a dominant position for two doctrinal sects, the Ch'ondae (in Chinese Tiantai) and the Hwaum (Chinese: *Huayan*), both of which were under the tutelage of Uichŏn, and thus to enlist, for the pious ruling dynasty (Uichŏn being the fourth son of King Mujong (1047–1083), the protection against natural disasters and fate which the Buddha, the *bodhisattvas* and the exorcistic incantations of the *darani* (*dhārani*) represented in the eyes of the aristocratic elite of Koryŏ, who were as pragmatic as they were superstitious. Although this striving for unity, taken up by the monk Chinul (also known as Pojo; 1158–1210), explains the syncretic nature of Korean Buddhism from this time, the motive behind it may also have been to permit closer supervision of the activities of the heads of these sects, who are known to have been members of the aristocracy.

The Chinese-style poetry of the Koryŏ period is strongly influenced by ideas derived from the schools of *Mahāyāna*, *nirvāṇa*, Amitābha and *dhyāna.* All this makes it possible to understand why the dynasty of Koryŏ undertook the publication of the Tripitaka in order to expel from its territory the Khitan invaders, who had come from Manchuria. Even more prodigious were other actions undertaken at the time of the Mongol invasions. As a means of securing the protection of the Buddha, the court decreed in 1236 that the Buddhist scriptures should be engraved on plates and several copies printed. This impressive project was begun in Kanghwa and completed in 1251. Today these plates, totalling 81,137 in number, are kept in Haein-sa, a temple in the province of Northern Kyŏngsang. Contrary to what was hoped, disasters occurred in the intervening period, which caused a serious loss of confidence in the protective power of Buddhist scriptures and images.

Another technique introduced from China in the first half of the twelfth century was the art of celadon, which, in the hands of the Koreans, reached near perfection. It achieved recognition in China itself, the most exquisite examples being the black and white encrusted vases which are said to have been made by Korean potters in the second half of the twelfth century. Besides vases, the ceramics of the Koryŏ period included braziers, perfume burners, dishes, flasks and cups, some of which were used for tea, others for alcoholic drinks; and decorative pieces such as tortoises, dragons, the *kilin* or unicorn, monkeys, hares, ducks, geese, fish, the calabash, the lotus blossom and bamboo shoots.

Advances in printing techniques were especially noteworthy. In Chapter XI of the *Tongguk Yi Sangguk chip* by the scholar Yi Kyubo (1168–1241), we read that twenty-eight copies of a book entitled *Sangjong yemun*, or Summary of Rituals, written during the reign of King Injong

(1123–1146), had been printed using movable metallic type. The exact date of printing is unknown, and the book itself has not survived. However, this is largely made up for by a copy of the second of the two volumes of the *Pulcho chikchi shimch'e yojŏl*, or 'Spiritual Identification with the Buddha through Zen', the colophon of which tells us: 'This book was printed using metallic type in the Hŭngdŏk temple near Ch'ŏngju in the seventh month of the seventh year of Xuanguang (1372)'. This priceless cultural relic is now in the French National Library in Paris.

The scholars of Koryo, having introduced the neo-Confucianism of Zhu Xi (1130–1200) to Korea in the twelfth century, took delight in exposing the vices of Buddhist monks and corrupt civil servants, whose unjust and shameful machinations inevitably dragged the country into total ruin. Under the Yi dynasty (1392–1910), these same scholars, profiting from the change of dynasty, established orthodox neo-Confucianism on a firm footing (see Plates 86, 97, 125).

BIBLIOGRAPHY

BALAIZE, C. *et al.* 1991. *La Corée.* Collection Que sais-je? Paris.
COURANT, M. 1985. *La Corée ancienne à travers ses livres.* Centre d'Etudes coréennes du Collège de France. Paris.
GARDINER, K. H. J. 1969. *The Early History of Korea.* Honolulu.
GOMPERTZ, G. ST. G. M. 1963. *Korean Celadon and other Wares of the Koryo Period.* London.
HENTHORN, W. E. 1963 *Korea: The Mongol Invasions.* Leiden.
JEON, SANG-WOON. 1974. *Science and Technology of Korea.* Cambridge, Mass.
KIM, CHE-WON; KIM, WON-YONG. 1966. *Corée, 2000 ans de création artistique*, Bibliothèque des Arts. Paris
KIM, WON-YONG. 1986. *Art and Archaeology of Ancient Korea.* Seoul.
LEE, KIBAIK. 1984. *New History of Korea.* Seoul.
LEE, P. H. 1969. *Lives of Eminent Korean Monks: The Haedong Kosung chon.* Cambridge, Mass.
LI, OGG. 1989. *La Corée des origines à nos jours.* Paris and Seoul.
——. 1980. *Recherche sur l'antiquité coréenne – ethnie et société de Koguryŏ.* Centre d'Etudes coréennes du Collège de France. Paris.

29

SIBERIAN–MANCHURIAN HUNTING PEOPLES

29.1

SIBERIAN AND MANCHURIAN PEOPLES: NOMADISM

Michail V. Vorobyev

There are hardly any historical sources for the vast territory of Siberia, and this is particularly true of the period from the seventh to the fifteenth century, at which point writing was established almost everywhere. In this section, we can make only the most generalized statements about the history and culture of Siberia. What follows must therefore be taken with reservations. Siberia did have tribal and early state structures, but mainly in the southern regions, which were to form the periphery of the Turkic and Uighur khaganates and the *ulus* states of the Mongol Empire. It is not always possible to extend what is said about those structures to the whole of Siberia.

In the sixth to the eighth century, the Turkic Tie-lie and Tiu-kiu tribes entered history in the Sayan and Altai mountain ranges and the Minusinsk basin. After a conflict with the Ru-ran, the Tie-lie tribes established the Old Turkic khaganate (552–745) with its base in the Altai. Many local tribes, for instance the Enisei Kyrgyz, fell under its sway, and more than once its influence was seriously challenged by China. The basis of the Turkic economy was nomadic herding, supplemented with hunting, and iron was used to make weapons. A form of writing was devised using rune-type characters. Internal instability led to the division of the khaganate into an eastern part (in Central Asia from 583) and a western part (in Central Asia from 562).

The Uighurs rose to prominence as successors to the Old Turkic khaganate after its final collapse. In the fifth to the eighth century, they had been part of the Ru-ran khaganate and subsequently of the Turkic khaganate. The foundations of the Uighur khaganate (750–840) were established in the basin of the Selengi, Orkhon and Tola rivers. Nomadic herding was the mainstay of the economy, although they knew how to plough, irrigate and produce iron goods. They used their own version of the Old Turkic writing system.

The Old Kyrgyz lived on the Yenisei. They had established a military union as early as the seventh century, and in the middle of the ninth century they destroyed the Uighur khaganate and formed one of their own. The Kyrgyz khaganate (840–1209) was the first genuine union to be formed by an Old Turkic tribe located for the most part in Siberia. Its economy was based on agriculture and herding. Crafts (iron working and pottery) and trade came to be vitally important. The Old Kyrgyz had their own writing system and literature.

As the Mongols conquered more territory from the thirteenth century onwards, the natural development of a local state system in Siberia and Manchuria was brought to a halt. From the middle of the thirteenth century, with the emergency of the *ulus* system, the entire region apart from the extreme north was divided up into new formations headed by the immediate descendants of Chinggis Khān: there was the Wugede (chief) *ulus* in the Far East; the Chagatai (Chaghatāy) *ulus* in eastern Siberia, and the Juchi (Jöchi) *ulus* (Golden Horde) in western Siberia. Siberia and Manchuria became the northern divisions of these *ulus*. After the break-up of the Golden Horde in the 1420s, the Sibir khanate was formed in western Siberia (it fell at the end of the sixteenth century). Russia established relations with it at the end of the fifteenth century.

Events in Manchuria in the same period appear to be clearer, for two main reasons. What happened in Manchuria depended largely on local conditions, and the information has come down to us thanks to the continuity of the Chinese historical tradition. Some peoples had already left the scene when our period begins; others had acquired new ethnonyms, and still others were making their first appearance.

After the fall of the Sianbi Empire, its lands were taken by the Ku-mo-xi (or Ku-mo-hi). They were grouped in the Chahar region and divided into five territorial units. Each group grazed its own herds, using carts with felt tents to follow them. The Ku-mo-xi were renowned for hunting, shooting from the saddle and for their raids, especially against the Khitan. When the Ahuei clan rose to prominence among them, it became the leader of their union of territories. In the seventh century, the Ku-mo-xi were subjugated by the Turkic khaganate, but as early as 629 the excursions into China began again. In 660, the Ku-mo-xi rebelled but in 710 their leader went to China, without, however, renouncing formal vassal status with the Turks. In 847, there was a serious uprising of the northern Ku-mo-xi, which was crushed. In 868, they sent one last embassy to China and in 911 or thereabouts the Khitan took control of their territories, the economy of which was very dependent on Chinese fabrics and grain.

The territory of the Shi-wei was on the River Zeya. They were hunters and herders, and they used only primitive cultivation methods (with hoes and ploughs). The men worked off the bride price in their bride's parents' home over a period of three years. Moves were organized with vehicles pulled by oxen, on which were transported cabins made of hides. Metals (iron and gold) were bartered in Korea. There were up to five ethnic Shi-wei territorial groups. From the seventh to the ninth century, they controlled the northern part of Inner Mongolia, part of Liaonin province and the left bank of the Amur. In 629, they took sable to China, thus acknowledging the overlordship of the Tang Dynasty, and in the eighth to the ninth century such trips became regular occurrences. The population lived in separate nomadic encampments without an overall leader. In the seventh century, there were seventeen main encampments, the smaller containing a thousand and the larger several thousand households. Ranging over a large territory, their economic activities varied according to the type of area occupied.

In the first half of the seventh century, the eastern and south-eastern regions of Manchuria became part of the Korean kingdom of Koguryo (Chinese: Gaogyüli). This kingdom had been a force to be reckoned with in the region and on the Korean peninsula for over 500 years. It was a strong, independent state with a high level of culture, but in the period under consideration it was engaged in constant and bitter warfare with China, which would lead to its downfall in 668.

The Mo-he and their ancestors had long been living in the now liberated northern lands of Koguryo. They comprised seven autonomous tribes distinguished by the size of their standing army. Each tribe lived in its own territory, the whole group of territories occupying the area around the Sungari, Ussuri and Amur rivers. The Mo-he lived in separate settlements, each with its own chieftain. They bred horses and pigs, used horses to cultivate the land, grew millet, wheat and rice and obtained salt through evaporation. Marriages were concluded with the consent of the bride and groom, but adultery was severely punished. The various Mo-he tribes operated autonomously – at least four sent their own embassies to China. At the turn of the sixth and seventh centuries, the Changboshan Mo-he became vassals of Koguryo, and after the latter's fall became subjects of the Tang Dynasty. From 622, the Mo-he sent fairly regular embassies to China with gifts, all of which indicates some sort of consolidation. The leader of one of the tribes, Tudiji, became the leader of the union, made the position hereditary and strengthened links with China. His own tribe consisted of a thousand families (5,000–6,000 people), with 1,000 domestic slaves, and the rich had several hundred pigs. In 688, the Mo-he suffered a heavy defeat at the hands of the Chinese.

The Su-mo Mo-he joined forces with the Koguryo to establish the state of Bohai (698/713–926) on the east Manchuria coast and in north-east Korea. It was the first true state with a developed structure to be set up by a people of Manchuria. The leader proclaimed himself king, a title which was immediately recognized by China, but he then went further – he introduced his own currency for the years of his reign, a sign of 'self-will' in the eyes of the Chinese emperor. The Chinese concluded an alliance with the Hei-shui Mo-he behind Bohai's back in 723, and the Bohai people responded with a raid on Dengzhou in Shandong in 732, but in the following year neighbouring Silla attacked Bohai. In this complex situation, the people of Bohai tried to strengthen their position by moving their supreme capital north to the Huhan River in 755. Without breaking their close links with China (from 100 to 130 embassies in 200 years), they established relations with Japan in 727, which they kept up until the collapse of their own state. Until 818, Bohai controlled a number of tribes in northern Manchuria. Based on the model of China, Bohai set up a ramified system for the administration of its territory with both central and local government apparatus and bureaucracy, an interesting feature being the existence of five capitals. A complicated social structure was developed, headed by the royal family, beneath whom came several dozen families of dignitaries, followed by the service class, then free commoners, and finally subjects and slaves. The economy was fairly diverse but essentially agricultural. Farmers leased their land from the state and paid the exchequer taxes. A variety of specialized crafts were practised. Both the distinctive Bohai and Chinese writing systems were used, and there was significant literary output. The level of spiritual culture was high, and Buddhism, with its temples, monks and *sūtras*, flourished. The archaeological remains of Bohai confirm the existence of a culture more advanced than any known before in Manchuria.

The Hei-shui Mo-he were the northernmost and strongest of the seven tribes of the Mo-he union. They had settled along the middle and lower Amur and the lower reaches of the Sungari, and in 628 they made their presence known by sending an embassy to China. By that time, a tribal union of sixteen clans was taking shape around them. Following their visit to China in 722, clearly with a grievance against Bohai, a Chinese district, Bolizhou, was set up on their territory and the leader was given a Chinese first name and surname – Li Xian-cheng. The economy was of the same type as that of the other Mo-he tribes. Constant pressure from Bohai led some of the Hei-shui Mo-he to recognize its authority, while the rest migrated to Korea. Judging by archaeological finds around the Amur (including the Troitskoe village dig) the Hei-shui Mo-he had also settled the left bank of the Amur. Weapons testifying to links with the right bank and with the Jurchen have been found in graves with horses (see Plates 246–250).

The Khitans had for many years lived south of the Shara-Muren River and north of Huanglong. Towards the beginning of our period they were divided into eight tribes. Although they did their own hunting and cattle raising, they waged battle only when all the tribes agreed to do so, with the supreme ruler playing a significant role in the decision-making process. According to information from sometimes contradictory sources, the supreme ruler was elected to the position and could be replaced. Members of the council of elders were elected for periods of up to three years. The beginning of the seventh century found the Khitan subjects of the Turks, although individual tribes did maintain relations with China (607), and some even went over to the Chinese (621, 648). There was an uprising against the Chinese in 696, which was suppressed with difficulty in 699. From 715, Chinese government structures were established in the lands of the pacified Khitans. In 744, the Khitans became vassals of the Uighurs but in 842 they transferred their allegiance to the Chinese. In 906, the leader Apoki made a deal with the chieftains of the other seven tribes and became the Khitan's sole leader. In 907 – the year of the fall of the Tang Dynasty – he announced that he had created his own state. Chinese advisers helped him in this undertaking. In 916, he built a supreme capital (Shangjing) and proclaimed himself emperor. The Ku-mo-xi and Shi-wei had been subdued even before the establishment of the state. In 926, the Khitans overwhelmingly defeated Bohai and set up in its place a tiny vassal principality, Dongtan, with Apoki's son at its head (926–936). In addition to their military exploits, the Khitans were active culturally: they established their own scripts, a large one (920) and a small one (924), and laid the foundations of a dual system of administration, one for the Khitans themselves and another for the conquered peoples (921). The destruction of Bohai did not make the situation in that part of Manchuria much easier for the Khitans. The Wu-re tribe on the Yalu River set up the principality of Dingan (938–1112), which maintained relations with China. Five countries (Wuguo, 1019–1073) formed a sort of federation on the lower reaches of the Sungari River. The whole of eastern and north-eastern Manchuria was populated by 'restless' Jurchen, who paid tribute to the Khitans. Their 'peaceful' kinsfolk to the south were completely under the control of the Khitans. By 947 – the year when they adopted the name Great Liao – the Khitans had founded the first empire to cover the whole of Manchuria and some neighbouring territories too. However, their most comprehensive and outstanding conquests were made beyond the frontiers of Manchuria, in Korea, northern China and Mongolia. Their influence on the situation in Manchuria was indirect. They introduced the five-capitals system (1044), four of which were situated in their own lands, which were where they built imperial tombs, memorial and funerary stelae, Buddhist temples and pagodas, schools and colleges and pottery kilns, and printed Buddhist *sūtras*.

The might of the Khitans was smashed by the Jurchen (nüchen, nüzhen), their recent neighbours, indeed vassals. A new supreme tribal chief chosen in 1113, Aguda, had within a year seized the important border town of Ningjianzhou. In 1115, Aguda proclaimed himself emperor of the new state of Jin (*Chin*) and in the following year he liberated his kinsfolk in Liaodong. In 1122, an agreement was concluded with the Chinese Song Dynasty to wage war together on the Liao; although the fighting was almost exclusively done by the Jurchen, it ended with the complete destruction of the Liao in 1125. The Jurchen extended their political power further afield than the Khitans. All of Manchuria and a series of outlying regions, the left bank of the Amur and eastern Mongolia, fell into their hands. As early as 1125, the war against the Liao developed into a war against the Song. But even more glorious victories and extensive conquests awaited the Jurchen in north (1126–1130) and central (1130–1136) China. Most of the neighbouring countries on the mainland recognized the suzerainty of the Jin. Manchuria remained Jurchen territory, although an organized mass migration of Jurchen to China began in 1114 and lasted until 1188. In 1133, both the captive Song emperors were sent to Wuguocheng (one died there in 1135). Until 1153, the entire empire was run from Shangjing – it was only in 1153 that its supreme capital was transferred to Yangjing (Beijing). Rebellious Khitans were resettled in Manchuria in 1177, but even when the Jurchen were at their apogee, Manchuria retained its ethnic diversity. In 1143, the Meng-gu tribes rose up and escaped Jin control. In 1161, the Khitans rebelled and the uprising was crushed with difficulty. In 1181, the Jurchen were obliged to set up a major defensive system to ward off the Mongols on the northern border of the empire and in 1192 to the north-west, yet even so it was through Manchuria that the enemy came and destroyed the Jin empire.

As they gained control, the Jurchen reinforced the militarized territorial Meng-an and Mou-ke units, which had become the government's economic and military strongholds. Manchuria was given its own administrative and territorial structure, which included the five-capitals system, three being to the north of the Great Wall. At first, a dual system of administration operated, their own for the Jurchen and one they were accustomed to for the Chinese, but they were gradually unified. Jurchen families were provided with land, animals and equipment, for which they paid a special tax with a team of draught oxen. Two systems of writing were developed very early on, one with large characters in 1119 and one using small characters in 1138, and from 1172 it was compulsory for the Jurchen to learn them. Around the 1160s, a determined effort was made to translate selected philosophical and scientific works from Chinese into the Jurchen language. The intensive military defence construction in the region was highly original, with extensive earthworks and open-plan fortresses. The bulk of the population remained shamanist with only the administrative elite appreciably affected by Chinese culture (Buddhism, neo-Confucianism). The Jurchen were the first people of Tungus origin to set up their own empire, as early as the Middle Ages. Their culture strongly influenced both contemporaries and descendants, in Manchuria and on the left bank of the Amur.

New times came for Manchuria in 1212, when the armies of Chinggis Khān swept in while the main Jurchen forces were held up in China. The Mongol armies soon turned to the south, but taking advantage of the situation in Manchuria the Khitans defected and set up their own structure, Great Liao (1213–1217), and the local Jurchen commanders also set up Great Jin or eastern Xia (1215–1233). By the early 1230s, the power of the Jurchen in Manchuria had been smashed, and the Mongol commanders given large *ulus* estates which were independent of the centre. It was not until 1267 that Qubilay Khān divided Manchuria into districts and 1272 that he organized a household census. By 1288, Manchuria had become, in administrative and territorial terms, part of the Yuan (Mongol) Empire. However, the real interests and power of the Mongols were confined to southern Manchuria, bordering north China and Korea, and 150 years of Mongol rule left scarcely a trace of their presence in Manchuria, nothing of even a military or administrative nature. After suffering defeat in China in 1368, the Mongols withdrew to Manchuria, where they held out for around twenty more years, having established the northern Yuan (1370–1387). Under the Mongols, the local population dropped sharply and went into decline: agriculture gave way to hunting and a sedentary way of life to nomadism, while Jurchen and Shui Da-da authorities in military settlements were obliged to plough the land. Other indigenous peoples had to hand over part of what they obtained from hunting and gathering, such as sable, hunting falcons and ginseng.

The fall of the Yuan Dynasty and its governing institutions left Manchuria in a completely disorganized state. Debilitated Jurchen, Shui Da-da ('river Tatars'), Ye-ren and Wu-zhe led a primitive existence on its territory until liberation from the Mongol yoke opened the way for the economic and social rehabilitation of these peoples. The market in horse rearing revived and individual tribes managed to consolidate (Jurchen Jianzhou). The newly established Chinese Ming Dynasty (1368–1644) unintentionally played the role of catalyst in the regeneration process. Having firmly grasped the message of history – that all invasions of China come from the north – the Chinese turned their attention to Manchuria, immediately after liberation. Chinese administration was very promptly re-established in southern Manchuria, where the Chinese population was still fairly substantial. The territory (Liaodun and Liaosi provinces) was divided by defensive earthworks. The lands to the north of the earthworks were watched over by guards (around 400 of them) headed by loyal local chieftains, and Jianzhou became the strongest structure in that region (from 1403). There was another defensive strip further to the north which was backed up by fortifications. The Nuerkan region was set up in 1404 as further reinforcement but without a clearly defined northern frontier. The degree of Chinese control diminished the further north the area. Posts were reserved more for local leaders than for Chinese, and at the beginning of the sixteenth century a whole system of local government was developed on the basis of these posts.

In 1410 and 1432, the Chinese launched two major exploratory and colonizing operations. These expeditions (the first of 1,000 people on twenty-five ships, the second 2,000 on fifty ships) crossed Manchuria and sailed to the mouth of the Amur. Here, on Tyr Island, they built a Buddhist temple and memorial stelae with inscriptions in Chinese, Jurchen and Mongolian. As far as we know, these stone inscriptions reflect the cultural, linguistic and ethnic composition of the region's population at that time.

BIBLIOGRAPHY

BUTIN, Y. M. 1984. *Koreya. Ot Chosona k trem gosudarstvam (II v. do n.e. – IV v. N.e.)*.('Korea – From Chason to the Three Dynasties, 2nd cent. B.C.–4th cent. A.D.). Novosibirsk.

CHANG POCHÜEN. 1985. *Tungbei difang shigao. Changchun.* 1893.*Chinding Manzhou Yüanliu Gao*. Hangzhou.

EBERHARD, W. 1942. *Kultur und Siedlung der Randvölker Chinas.* Leiden.

GIBERT, L. DE. 1934. *Dictionnaire historique et géographique de la Mandchourie*. Hong Kong.

——. 1968. *Istoriya Sibirii. T.1: Drevnaya Sibir'*.('History of Siberia. Vol. 1: Ancient Siberia.') Leningrad.

——. 1986. *Istoriya narodov vostochnoi i tsentral'noi Azii s drevneishikh vremen do nashikh dnei*.('History of the People of Eastern and Central Asia from earliest times to our own day.') Moscow.

HAMBIS, L. 1956. The Ancient Civilization in Manchuria. *East and West* (Rome), Vol. 7, No. 3, pp. 218–227.

LEE CHI RING, KANG IN SUK. 1976. *Koguryo shi yŏngu*. Pyongyang.

——. 1958. *Litai kētsu chuanchi hueipien*. Vols. I and II, Parts 1 and 2. Beijing.

LI CHI. 1932. Manchuria in History. *The Chinese Social and Political Science Review* (Shanghai), Vol. 16, No. 2, pp. 1–43.

MACGOVERN, W. M. 1939. *The Early Empires of Central Asia*. Leiden.

RINOUE MASAFUMI. 1989. *Chugoku kodai-no sho minzoku*. Tokyo.

SHIRATORY, K. (ed.). 1914. *Beiträge zur historischen Geographie des Manschurei*. Tokyo.

VOROBYEV, M. V. 1961. *Drevnyaya Koreya. (Istoriko-arkheologicheskie ocherki)* ['Ancient Korea (historical and archeological essays.')]. Moscow.

29.2
THE TURKISH AND MONGOL PEOPLES OF THE STEPPES: PASTORAL NOMADISM

Louis Bazin

From the beginning of the seventh century to the end of the fifteenth, the scale of the westward movement of nomadic herdsmen from the Asian steppes grew. The Turks were the first to migrate, followed in the thirteenth century by the Mongols under Chinggis Khān. Both peoples established empires where they took up a partially sedentary way of life and intermingled with the local population, a process that included cultural and linguistic exchanges (see Plates 185, 186, 243–245).

The steppes of Asia cover a huge area, from the shores of the Pacific to those of the Caspian Sea, south of the great forests of Siberia and north of China, Tibet, India and Iran, from which they are separated first by the Great Wall of China and then by high mountain ranges. They are particularly suited to extensive livestock rearing. The Tian Shan and Altai mountains which divide them down the middle, can be crossed in some places. The slopes of the mountain massifs that occur in parts of the steppes, especially to the east, provide summer pastures. The generally rich grasslands become sparse in arid areas without actually disappearing, and true deserts (saline or waterless) occupy only a small area. On the gently undulating plains that predominate, travel on horseback can be very fast (around 50 km a day during military campaigns).

Horsemanship and the rearing of horses were a speciality of the Turkish and Mongol nomads.[1] During the period under consideration, their herds often ran into hundreds or even thousands. Horses provided their usual means of travel and were the principal source of their military might and, through barter, an important factor in their economy. Their horsemen played a vital role in war, usually giving them superiority over sedentary opponents. They were past masters in training warhorses, and their mounted archers were formidable; their tactics were based on mobility, encirclement or simulated retreat, during which they would shoot arrows backwards and then do a sudden about-turn. The outcome of battles was largely dependent on the horsemen, since the foot soldiers' main task was to win territory. The main weapons used were the composite bow, the sword (later replaced by the sabre) and the lance. They were made from wood, horn and iron, which both Turks and Mongols were good at producing and working. Leather, reinforced by iron plates where possible, protected the men and some of the horses. Speed of movement, which is essential for nomads, ruled out heavy weapons. Only the sedentary populations built fortresses, usually with ditches and earth banks, and defence works were built only around camps intended for long-term occupation (see Plates 12, 248).

At every level of tribal organization, all males who were fit and sufficiently strong underwent constant military training from puberty onwards and could be mobilized at any time by the local chiefs and formed into groups according to the tribal hierarchy. The nomadic herdsmen were also warriors throughout their adult lives; their goals in war were to conquer grazing land and to capture livestock, slaves and other booty. Another of their practices was immediately to enrol and train surviving enemy soldiers in their own ranks, which could boost their numbers considerably within a short space of time. This amply accounts for the fact, surprising at first sight, that Turkish or Mongol warlords who set out with a relatively small number of men soon found themselves at the head of huge armies and quickly gained control of vast areas of land, thus acquiring unheard-of wealth and power.

The way of life of both the Turkish and Mongol nomads was broadly similar. The meat and milk of their flocks and herds – mostly sheep – provided their staple diet. Sheep, whose fatty tails can store water, thus allowing them to survive in arid regions, were raised in very large numbers in the steppes. In well-watered areas, such as the north of what is now Mongolia, cattle were also raised. Goat rearing was less important. Bactrian camels, used only as beasts of burden or for trading caravans, and whose double hump also stores water, could get by well on the resources of the steppes, and they provided a limited but much appreciated contribution to the nomad economy.

Hunting was a favourite activity that brought some variety to the daily fare. Important chiefs often organized great hunts, for which whole tribes would be mobilized. Vegetables and plants, sometimes gathered, formed only a very small part of the diet, since only the sedentary populations practised agriculture, but as the nomads often imposed their suzerainty on those populations they usually demanded tribute in the form of grain, as well as other contributions in kind (and also in cash).

Tribute, which was also imposed on other, subjugated nomads, the spoils of war and booty from raids were also prized resources, sometimes providing the great chiefs with luxury items such as alcohol and silk.

When the fruits of conquest were in short supply, the nomads could be self-sufficient: wool from their sheep was turned into felt for the traditional round, domed tents known as *yūrts* (see Plate 85) and lighter tents, and was also used in clothing and in weaving carpets and bags; skins and leather were utilized in many different ways; nomad craft workers fashioned articles from metals, including precious metals, wood and horn, and they were also skilled in basket making.

In peacetime, the Turks and Mongols engaged in trade, willingly exchanging livestock (horses, sheep, camels) and craft products (woollen goods, felt, carpets, leather, tanned skins, and so on) for other goods. These exchanges took the form of barter or used lengths of (Chinese) silk or (local) woollen fabric of a strictly defined size, a more common form of currency than metal coins in the Asian steppes. Moreover, as the Turks and Mongols largely controlled the overland trade routes between China and Western Asia, they levied tolls on the caravans using them.

The nomads' military might fed their economy, which in turn provided keep for their armies, and the armies swelled in number by enlisting prisoners and by conscription among the subject peoples. The outcome of wars, in which rival tribes of both Turks and Mongols frequently clashed, continually altered the political landscape of the steppes: a string of defeats would reduce – sometimes to nothing – the territory occupied by the defeated tribal confederacies, but a series of successes could soon enable victorious confederacies to extend their territory, even to the point of creating empires.

Without going into detail about those empires' political and military history, we shall merely give a brief account of their expansion, duration and dissolution before evaluating the role they played in the cultural development of humanity.

Around 600, the first great Turkish empire, that of the Turkic peoples proper, a tribal confederacy originally from the Altai mountain region, stretched from the bend of the Yellow River to the Aral Sea, taking in Mongolia and the steppes of Central Asia up to and beyond the Āmū Daryā, but it was in fact already divided, on side of the Altai mountains, between the eastern Turkic peoples of Mongolia and the western Turkic peoples. Between 630 and 680, Tang Dynasty China, which had adapted its military technology to that of the Turks and exploited dissension between chiefs and tribes, managed to impose its hegemony over almost all the former empire. In 682, after a revolt against the Chinese protectorate, a second, independent, Turkic Empire was established in Mongolia, but military expeditions by its rulers against the western Turkic chiefs aimed at restoring unity failed to put the great empire of the sixth century back together, and the tribes in the western part split up into rival factions. The history of the Turkic Empire of Mongolia is fairly well known from Chinese sources and from the inscriptions on the funerary stelae of its main leaders (including the famous Orkhon inscriptions) dating from about 700 to 735, the oldest known texts in any Turkic language. This empire collapsed in 742, following a tribal uprising that ended in the hegemony in Mongolia of another Turkish-speaking people, the Uighurs. In 763, the Uighur ruler converted to Manichaeism and made it the state religion. The invasion of Mongolia by another race of Turkish-speaking people, the Kirghiz of the Yenisei, in 840 drove out the Uighur tribes, who withdrew south-westwards into the eastern part of the Tian Shan Mountains and the oases of the Tarim basin, regions where the indigenous peoples were Indo-Europeans (Tokharians), most of them Buddhists. The new Uighur state developed in what would later be known as Chinese Turkestan, and it had good relations with Tang-dynasty China. A large part of the Uighurs settled in the oases, and Buddhism became the principal religion in the towns. The subjects of this new state, whose capital was Khocho, near Turfan, are often (and wrongly) called 'Uighurs of Turfan'; 'western Uighurs' would be a better term. A few groups of the Uighurs driven out of Mongolia emigrated to Kansu and established their capital in the town of Kan-Chou (Ganzhou).

Initially, the western Uighurs came together to form a new empire stretching as far as the Tun-huang (Dunhuang) region and Transoxania, maintaining contacts with both the Chinese and with the Soghdians, eastern Iranians from Bukhārā and Samarkand, and they gradually absorbed the Tokharians of the oases. In the early eleventh century their empire shrank, but they held on to the oases of the Tarim basin and the Turfan region until, in the second quarter of the twelfth century, they were forced to submit to the Qarā-Khitāy and, in 1209, became vassals of Chinggis Khān and faithful subjects of the Mongol Empire.

The Qarā-Khitāy were a Mongol-speaking people whose ruling class was strongly Chinese-influenced. They came from the tribal confederacy of the Khitan (the Mongol plural of Khitāy), which had invaded northern China as far as the area south of Beijing and whose rulers had reigned there between 936 and 1122, adopting Buddhism and Chinese culture. When northern China was invaded by the (pre-Manchu) Jurchen, the Qarā-Khitāy fled and overran the principalities of the Qarākhānides, Islamized, sedentary Turks who at the time ruled the area from Kashgar to Bukhārā – and carved out an empire that included the Ili valley, Uighuria and Transoxania. The Qarā-Khitāy then came into conflict with the Khwārizm-Shāhs (Khiva region), who had once been their subjects before rebelling, and then in 1210–1211 against the Naiman of the Altai mountains, and were defeated. Fighting between Khwārizmians and Naiman during the years that followed opened the way for the great Mongol invasion.

Mongolia did not remain long in the hands of the Kirghiz of the Upper Yenisei after their conquest of 840. They were driven out by the Khitan in 920. The situation in the region thereafter was permanently unstable, with waves of Mongols migrating from the north-east pushing the Turkish-speaking nomads westwards. East–west movements were also taking place on the Siberian fringes of the Turco-Mongol world, resulting in the arrival of new waves of Turks in Central Asia and even as far west as Europe, whose eastern steppes were invaded by, among others, the Kuman (Kipchak) from the upper Ob and Irtysh regions. The greatest upheavals, starting in the early thirteenth century, were, however, to result from the extraordinary scale of the conquests of Chinggis Khān and his successors, and the creation of a huge Mongol Empire in Eurasia (see Chapter 30).

When this empire fell apart, losing its territories in Anatolia, Mesopotamia and Iran in 1335, its dominion in China in 1368 and in Transoxania and the neighbouring regions, annexed by Tīmūr (Tamerlane), between 1370 and 1405 (see Chapters 22 and 23), the main power centre of Chinggis Khān's Mongols shifted to eastern Europe, with the Golden Horde and its dependencies. After 1370, Mongolia itself went through a period of anarchy. It should be pointed out that the Mongols, in their far-ranging expansion outside their land of origin, had gradually intermingled with the Turkish populations, many of whom had converted to Islam, so much so that many Mongols had become Turkish-speaking Muslims. By the end of the fourteenth century, east of the Tian Shan Mountains the Mongols retained their nomadic way of life and culture, and there were still nomad tribes living in the steppes and semi-desert regions to the west, the great majority of them Turkish-speaking and often Islamized, albeit superficially; but urbanization and the trend towards a sedentary life had made great progress. There were no more great nomad states left in the steppes in either Asia or Europe.

Since the history of the socio-cultural, intellectual and religious development of the Muslim world (Part III) and, more specifically, of the Islamized Turkish and Mongol peoples (Part IV, particularly Chapters 23, 24 and 30) is dealt with elsewhere in this work, we shall discuss here only the history of those Turks and Mongols who did not convert to Islam. There are in this respect broad similarities between the traditions and development of the two ethno-linguistic groups, which often make it possible to refer, conventionally, to those socio-cultural phenomena common to them as 'Turco-Mongol'.

The Turco-Mongol societies of nomadic herdsmen and warriors during the period under consideration (seventh to fifteenth century) have practically the same, strongly hierarchical structures, similarities which extended into their systems of kinship and alliances. The basis of social organization was the extended family of the patriarchal type, whose head was the eldest in patrilinear descent. It was also patrilocal: on marriage, the wife ceased to belong to her father's family and she and her children became members of her husband's family. Unless there were exceptional circumstances, she lived in the conjugal tent, which was often the same one her parents-in-law lived in. Several families descended from the same male ancestor constituted a clan. In accordance with specific conventions of alliance, the sons of one clan married the daughters of another, but the sons of the latter were not allowed to marry the daughters of the former. The preferred type of marriage was one in which the young man married the daughter of a maternal uncle (contrary to Arab tribal custom, in which he married the daughter of a paternal uncle). The chains of alliance that thus existed between clans could spread very wide. Polygamy was allowed but was only common among important chiefs. The first wife theoretically had authority over the others, and her sons took priority, by order of age, in the paternal inheritance, the eldest taking over the functions of authority. For the highest of these functions, at the head of large tribes, of tribal confederacies and especially of established states, however, this transfer of power was subject to ratification by an assembly of chiefs and notables, which could choose another brother, nephew or paternal uncle of the deceased. This often led to armed confrontations: when for instance Qapghan Qaghan, the ruler of the Turkic people of Mongolia, died in 716, he was succeeded not by his eldest son but by the son of his elder brother, the former emperor Elterish Qaghan, who was proclaimed ruler by one of these assemblies, setting off a brief civil war in which the descendants of the dead leader were wiped out. On the Mongol side, great assemblies of tribal chiefs proclaimed Temüjin as khān of his tribal group, then as Great Khān of all the Mongols in about 1197, and finally Chinggis Khān (universal ruler) in 1206, although he did not inherit any of those offices, having been left an orphan at the age of 12.

Within a strongly hierarchical ethno-political structure, from the family to the clan and on to the tribal faction, the tribe, the tribal federation, the great confederacy of tribes, and finally the kingdom or empire, civilian and military authority filtered up and down, thus ensuring that the ruler's decisions were enforced and that troops were mobilized. These tribal structures were not permanent and were not necessarily the result of descent from a common ancestor. While basically ethnic, they were also political, forming and dissolving as politico-military circumstances changed. The old saying 'woe betide the vanquished' was the practical rule.

The structures of family and of matrimonial alliances were equally flexible, despite the principles laid down by tradition. Adoption could replace filiation; males could become blood brothers by drinking from the same cup in which they had mixed their blood, as in the Scythian custom described by Herodotus; the children of slave concubines taken as 'spoils of war' could be made legitimate and integrated into the clan. In short, society was not set in its ways. In fact, the ethnic composition of many tribes changed in the course of migrations. Among princes and rulers with diplomatic contacts, marriages with foreign women, Chinese for instance, or between Turks and Mongols, were frequent. Furthermore, anyone who entered the tribal structure by adoption, alliance or choice was no longer a 'foreigner'. The strength of Turco-Mongol society lay in the fact that, despite being highly structured and hierarchical, it was nevertheless open.

This openness, this freedom from exclusion and racism, tended towards universalism, in line with the politico-religious ideology common to Turks and Mongols, which was based on the Utopian idea of a universal sovereign appointed by Heaven. In the epitaph (732) to his brother Kül Tegin, the Turkic ruler of Mongolia Bilgä Qaghan proclaimed himself 'celestial' and, immediately after referring to the creation of the world and the appearance of humans, added: 'Over the humans reigned my ancestors Bumin Qaghan and Istämi Qaghan.' The Mongol Emperor Möngkä, in a letter to Louis IX of France in 1254, wrote: 'Such is the commandment of Eternal Heaven: there is only one God in Heaven and only one sovereign on Earth, Chinggis Khān, the son of God'; Chinggis Khān had died in 1225 but continued to reign in the person of his grandson, the Great Khān Möngkä.

The Turco-Mongol imperial religion was dominated by the God of Heaven Tengri, absolute master of the universe, who delegated and inspired a universal sovereign on Earth. According to eighth-century Turkish inscriptions in Mongolia, Umay, a subsidiary divinity to Tengri, was a mother goddess who protected the empress, mothers and young children. Sacred earth and water are also mentioned, but it was Tengri who made all decisions, on Earth and in Heaven. The Mongols' laws were promulgated 'by the force of Eternal Heaven'.

This supreme celestial God could also become, under the same name, the one God of monotheism for those Turks and Mongols who converted to Christianity (usually the Nestorian form) or to Islam, but the same name could also be used to refer to any divinity in other religions such as Manichaeism, which in 763 became the state religion of the Uighurs of Mongolia, or Buddhism, which had followers among the aristocracy of the Turkic peoples of Mongolia from the middle of the sixth century onwards and which later became the main religion of the Uighurs and, during the second half of the thirteenth century, of the eastern Mongols. The religious policy of the Turco-Mongol rulers who did not convert to Islam was one of the greatest tolerance, with a strong tendency to syncretism; this syncretism can be clearly seen in the way the later Uighurs welded Manichaeism – adopted in its Chinese form, in which Mānī was the Buddha of Light – with Buddhism. The non-Islamized Mongol rulers, whether they remained faithful to the old religion of Tengri or converted to Buddhism, left the Nestorian Christians entirely free to practise their religion and even received Catholic missionaries in the mid-thirteenth to mid-fourteenth century: their subjects' religion was of little importance to them as long as the subjects prayed for the rulers. This religious eclecticism was one consequence of the Turco-Mongol leaders' basic universalism, and it fostered peace within their states, whose mission was one of universality.[2]

The religion of the common people among the Turkish and Mongol nomads was a form of shamanism similar to that which can still be found today among certain Turkish-speaking peoples in Siberia and among some of the Buryat Mongols. It existed alongside the worship of Tengri but did not merge with it. It was based on a generalized animism, attributing supernatural powers to plants and animals as well as to mountains, rivers and lakes in a world peopled with countless spirits over which the shaman had extensive powers: sometimes he would even journey through space to influence Tengri and the divinity of the underground world, Erlik 'the Powerful' (corresponding to the Buddhists' Yama). These beliefs, whose original form is little known for lack of documentary evidence, gradually absorbed elements of other religions, especially Buddhism. The shaman was both a soothsayer and a healer. He could also be a formidable sorcerer, a practitioner of black magic. Some shamans specialized in magical control of the weather, particularly rain making.[3]

The Turco-Mongol peoples in general, and their leaders in particular, showed great curiosity about different religions, viewing them with an indulgence that could lead to conversion, and even successive conversions, or to syncretic mixtures of beliefs. During the period under consideration, these peoples always included small groups of scholars (nearly always priests: Buddhist, Manichaean or even Christian), who translated religious or similar texts from various sources. It was the Uighurs who left the largest number of important texts from this time, either translated or adapted from Tokharian, Soghdian, Sanskrit or especially Chinese. Many of the original texts have been lost, and only the Turkish translations survive; they are major sources of religious and cultural history in regard to the religions mentioned above as well as to certain aspects of Chinese Daoism, Sino-Buddhist divination, and Chinese and Indian astrology and astronomy, with their extremely complex technical applications in the composition of calendars and almanacs.

Also of prime importance are the original Turkish and Mongol texts recording indigenous history and traditions. The texts in question are mainly, on the Turkish side, the eighth-century funerary inscriptions which have been preserved in Mongolia. The most famous of these, and rightly so, are the Orkhon inscriptions (732 and 735), which trace the history of the Turkic peoples in epic style and eloquently set forth the political doctrine of Emperor Bilgä Qaghan. Historically linked to them are the later Uighur inscriptions in Mongolia. From the same period, and continuing into the tenth century, are the epitaphs left by the Turkish-speaking peoples, including the Kirghiz, of the upper Yenisei. There are ten times as many of these and, although mostly short and rather simple, they are very original documents, providing a wealth of socio-cultural information; in a direct and spontaneous style, they refer to the personal and family life of the deceased, the goods and chattels he left behind, the social functions he fulfilled and the grief of his loved ones. On the Mongol side, the most substantial historical source is undoubtedly the *Secret History of the Mongols* (completed shortly after 1240), which has come down to us in the form of a Chinese phonetic transcription of the Mongol text. A sizeable work narrated in a lively style, it is filled with evocative details and includes genealogical myths, clan traditions, the biography of Chinggis Khān and his brothers, the ins and outs of his rise and conquests, and the circumstances of his succession. It is a text of a force and originality rarely equalled in the historiography of the period and an exceptional ethnological document.

In trying to evaluate the contribution of the non-Islamized Turco-Mongol peoples of eastern Turkestan and Central Asia to the cultural development of humanity between 600 and 1500, we should remember that these nomadic, pastoral peoples, who for a long time had little contact with the great sedentary civilizations, only adopted the use of writing at a late stage, the Turks in the sixth century and the Mongols in the thirteenth century. Before then, their traditions were handed down orally, and all that remains of them are a few accounts recorded more or less accurately by foreign historiographers, leaving us poorly placed to judge their culture at an earlier period. For the period after the establishment of the first Turkic Empire in Mongolia and Central Asia in the middle of the sixth century, however, and even more so after the huge Mongol Empire was set up in the thirteenth, there is a fairly well-documented record of their ways of life, socio-economic conditions, civilian and military organization, ideology and beliefs. The scale of their involvement in material and cultural exchanges by land throughout Asia, from China to Europe and the Islamic world, also becomes apparent: these peoples indeed were largely in control of the 'Silk Roads' followed by the caravans that carried this intercontinental trade.

This central position, which brought the Turco-Mongols into contact with the greatest sedentary civilizations in Eurasia, gave them a major role in the transmission of material goods and techniques, as well as cultural wealth and scientific discoveries, from east to west and *vice versa*. Overland trade, which they controlled and in which they took part, supplemented the seaborne trade, which is currently better known, and directly affected the inland regions. A well-known example is the export of silk to the West, followed by that of Chinese silkworm-rearing techniques, but equally important was the export of the related techniques of paper making and printing, which also came from China. As early as the tenth century, paper was in common use among the Uighur Turks and, following the Chinese example, they were beginning to carve groups of characters for printing out of wood.[4]

However, it was from west to east that an alphabetic form of writing spread among the Turco-Mongol peoples, based on the alphabet of the Soghdians (an Iranian people of Transoxania who led caravans and engaged in trade, playing a major cultural role in Central Asia), a cursive Turkish script developed around AD 600 and was used in the thirteenth century as a model for the Mongol alphabet, which in turn was the source of the alphabet used by the Manchus, who ruled China from the mid-seventeenth century until 1911. Under the Tang Dynasty, the Soghdians and Turks passed on elements of Irano-Turkish culture to the Chinese, especially as regards music and musical instruments. There was even a fashion for 'turqueries' in dress, poetry, song and theatre among the Chinese aristocracy. It was largely through the Turco-Mongols that the Western world learned about China and its culture. The high point of cultural communication between the east and west of Eurasia in the Middle Ages was under the Mongol Empire, especially during the reign of the Great Khān Qubilay (1214–1294), the protector of Marco Polo. Thus, for instance, contact between Chinese and Arab astronomical traditions enabled significant progress to be made in that field.

The Turco-Mongol peoples were not merely transmitters of others' cultures. While maintaining their own traditions in the social sphere, they were also very receptive to scientific and technical influences from the great sedentary cultures as well as to religious influences, and they melded different cultures together, which worked to their advantage and ensured the power and development of the 'empires of the steppes' that they established. It is true that their military conquests were often accompanied by great cruelty and wrought havoc among the vanquished, but their acute sense of organization, a legacy of their strongly hierarchical tribal structure, subsequently enabled them to establish states in which new, mixed cultures grew up in symbiosis with the subject populations (with whom they merged to a greater or lesser extent), and these constitute their contribution to world culture.

EDITOR'S NOTES

Professor Irfan Habib, whom we thank, made the following pertinent remarks. The passages in quotes are taken from him.

1 It is important to mention 'the role of the Turks in technological transmission, any reference related to the horse collar, horseshoe and iron stirrup.' 'All these transmissions from China/Siberia to West Asia and Europe occurred in the very period (sixth to eleventh centuries) when the Turkic nomadic diffusion could have played a very important role in them.'

'There is also the possibility that the spinning-wheel, first recorded in Iran, India and Western Europe almost simultaneously in the thirteenth–fourteenth centuries, reached these areas from China, the country of its original invention either through the Mongols or through an earlier Turkic channel (for example, the Seljuks?).'

2 'Some reservations should be made about the identification of the Turco-Mongol *Tengri* with God (in a monotheistic sense) alone. In the eleventh century, Kāshghari, the author of the famous Turkish–Arabic dictionary, noted that the pagan Turks called not only the sky *Tengri* but also any large mountain or tree that they worshipped.'

3 'The assumption that shamanism was prevalent among pagan Turkic tribes generally seems to need reconsideration, since there seems to be practically no reference to 'shaman' and 'shamanism' pre-thirteenth century.'

Care should be taken, in any event, not to project into the distant Turco-Mongol past the modern (and in any case varied) forms of Siberian shamanism, about which little was known before the nineteenth century. The presence of *seers* among the Turks is mentioned in ancient Chinese and Byzantine sources, such as Kāshghari in the eleventh century ('*al-kāhin*'); this author also records that they practised magic incantation (*ruqyāt*). These 'sorcerers' (ancient Turkish: *qam*) present analogies with the shamans, and the same word (*qam, xam*) is used today to designate the Siberian Turkish shamans, although their practices have certainly changed over the centuries.

4 'The transmission of paper making to Europe went through a different route than printing. The Turks were involved only in helping to bring Chinese paper makers to Samarkand. The transmission further onwards was through the Arabs. In transmitting printing, the Mongol Empire seems to have played the crucial role.'

The importance of the spread of paper in the West is often emphasized but 'the participation of the Turks in transmitting paper to India (via Xinjiang as well as Samarkand) was of equal importance. And, of course, paper use in the Islamic world was of great significance in the spread of learning within it.'

Some chronological details: invention of paper in China around AD 100; use of paper in the Turfan region before AD 400; Chinese paper makers, who were made prisoners of war after the battle of Talas, were installed in Samarkand by the Arabs in AD 751; paper making in Baghdād from AD 793 onwards and from AD 950 in Muslim Spain; from there, a gradual expansion into Europe, where the use of parchment long remained dominant.

BIBLIOGRAPHY

ABE, T. 1955. *Nishi Uiguru kokushi no kenkyū* [Étude de l'histoire nationale des Ouigours occidentaux]. Kyoto.

BAZIN, L. 1991. *Les systèmes chronologiques dans le monde turc ancien.* Akadémiai Kiado/Editions du CNRS. Paris and Budapest.

CHAVANNES, E. 1903. *Documents sur les Tou-kiue* (Turcs) *Occidentaux.* Académie Impériale, St. Petersburg.

——. 1904. *Notes additionnelles sur les Tou-kiue (Turcs) Occidentaux.* Académie Impériale, St. Petersburg.

CLEAVES, F. W. 1949. The Mongolian Names and Terms in the 'History of the Archers' by Grigor of Akanc. *Harvard Journal of Asiatic Studies.* Vol. XIII, pp. 400–443.

GROUSSET, R. 1941. *L'empire des steppes.* reprint 1960, Paris.

——. 1941. *L'empire mongol (première phase).* Paris.

HAENISCH, E. 1948. *Die Geheime Geschichte der Mongolen.* Harrassowitz, Leipzig.

HAMBIS, L. 1969. *Documents sur l'histoire des Mongols à l'époque des Ming.* Paris.

——. (ed.) 1955. Marco Polo. In: *La description du Monde.* Paris.

HAMILTON, J. R. 1955. *Les Ouïgours à l'époque des cinq dynasties.* Paris, reprint 1988.

——. 1986. *Manuscrits Ouïgours du IXe–Xe siècle de Touen-houang,* 2 vols., Vol. XXIII, Paris.

HOWORTH, SIR HENRY. 1876. *The History of the Mongols,* 4 vols. London, reprint 1927.

KWANTEN, L. 1979. *Imperial Nomads: A History of Central Asia 500–1500.* Leicester.

LEMERCIER-QUELQUEJAY, C. 1970. *La paix mongole.* Paris.

LIU MAU-TSAI, 1958. *Die chinesischen Nachrichten zur Geschichte der Ost-Türken (T'u-küe),* 2 vols (annotated translation of Chinese origins). Harrassowitz, Wiesbaden.

MACKERRAS, C. 1972. *The Uighur Empire, According to the T'ang Dynastic Histories,* Vol. IX. Asian Publications Series, No. 2, Canberra.

MORGAN, D. 1949. *The Mongols.* New York, reprint 1986, Oxford.

PELLIOT, P. 1949. *Histoire Secrète des Mongols.* Complete Mongolian text and French translation of Chaps. I–VI. Librairie d'Amérique et d'Orient, Paris.

PINKS, E. 1968. *Die Uiguren von Kan-chou in der frühen Sung-Zeit (960–1028).* Asiatische Forschungen, Band 24, Vol. XI, Wiesbaden.

ROUX, J. P. 1984a. *La religion des Turcs et des Mongols.* Paris.

——. 1984b. *Historie des Turcs.* Paris.

——. 1993. *Historie de l'empire Mongol.* Paris.

RUBROUCK, G. DE. 1993. *Voyage dans l'empire mongol* (1253–1255), CLAUDE-CLAIRE; KAPPLER, R. (eds), Paris.

30

THE MONGOL EMPIRE

Shagdaryn Bira

THE FOUNDATION OF THE MONGOL STATE BY CHINGGIS KHĀN: THE CAMPAIGNS OF CONQUESTS

The geographical position of Mongolia in the heartland of Central Asia was the main environmental factor that determined the specific character of the historical and cultural development of its inhabitants. 'The Great Steppe of Mongolia', which represents a huge grazing land, was most favourable for animal husbandry.

Animal husbandry required no less knowledge, skill and technique than agriculture. A nomad could not survive unless he could adapt to the challenges of the steppe environment. Hence, a huge amount of knowledge and experience of animal husbandry, a folk science of the Mongol nomads, was accumulated. The traditional technology of the making of animal products and the processing of raw materials, although it was limited and of a home-made character, was well developed and provided the nomads with the necessities of life. By the beginning of the thirteenth century, the nomadic society of the Mongols had reached a high level in its social and cultural progress. Its traditional social system underwent drastic transformations. The primitive clan structure bound together through blood relationships actually came to an end. The social consciousness of the members of Mongol society was determined more by their common socio-economic interests, and territorial factors and common ethno-cultural bonds acquired more and more meaning in the relations between tribes and tribal confederacies.

It was in 1206, after having successfully carried out several decisive battles against his most powerful rivals, that Chinggis Khān (*c.* 1162–1227) convened a Quraltai, the assembly of Mongol nobility, at the head of the Onon River. At this Quraltai, he was proclaimed ruler of all the Mongols, with the rank of Khān and the title of Chinggis (*Secret History of the Mongols*, Vol. 1, p. 141; *History of the Mongolian People's Republic*, Vol. 1, pp. 170–191). The event meant, in fact, the birth of a new state in Mongolia; a unified Mongol state.

In 1206–1211, Chinggis Khān was busy with the establishment and reorganization of civil and military administration. Administratively, Mongolia was divided into three great tümens or 'myriads' – the left, the right and the central – each of them in its turn consisting of tens, hundreds and thousands. One of the important measures undertaken by Chinggis Khān in the field of civil administration was the codification of laws, under the title of 'Yeke Jasa' (the Turkic derivative – Yāsā) ('The Great Law'). Although this law has not yet been found, data from various sources prove beyond doubt the existence of the written version of 'The Great Jasa'.

In general, the Great Jasa represented a code of laws which is said to have been prescribed by Chinggis Khān for the various spheres of social life. Thus it had laid down the juridical basis for the newly born Mongol state. Moreover, with the creation of the Mongol Empire, it eventually became the most authoritative handbook of the Mongol jurisprudence, to be strictly followed through the expansion of the empire for decades.

In the fifteenth year of the reign of Chinggis Khān, that is, 1220, the capital city of Mongolia – Qarāqorum - was founded in the valley of the Orqon River (Cleaves, 1952). Shortly after the creation of strong political and military machinery, Chinggis Khān embarked on the path of expanding his power.

In 1219–1224, he had successfully carried out his campaigns of conquest against Khwārizm-Shāh 'Alā' al-Dīn Muḥammad's empire, which at that time was on the decline due to internal discords and feuds. As a result, all the lands of this empire with their great cities, Samarkand, Bukhārā, Urgench, Utrar (Otrar), Nīshāpūr, Marw, and so on, were occupied by the Mongols. Most of the great centres of culture were turned into ruins and their population massacred. Cities like Balkhi and Shahr-i Ghulghula (Bāmyān) were completely destroyed by the invaders.

It is likely that the traditional form of submission typical of all steppe empires must have corresponded with Chinggis Khān's general conception. According to this, it was more important to master the peoples as an 'appanage' (*ulus*) rather than to govern the territories of the conquered countries. With regard to sedentary societies, Chinggis Khān preferred to ensure economic exploitation of these countries by tax collection and tribute.

It is true that he was hugely successful in all his enterprises, mainly due to his superiority in military strength. No less a role was played by him as a military genius and great politician of his time. The light cavalry mounted on tough, swift-footed Mongol horses and equipped with bows was the main strength of Chinggis Khān and his successors. Besides this, the Mongols were highly innovative in the art of warfare, taking over new techniques and improving them with the help of Chinese and Muslim experts.

THE WORLD EMPIRE OF THE MONGOLS (SEE MAP 29)

Unlike Alexander, whose empire did not even survive his death, Chinggis Khān left a great nomadic empire which during the reigns of his successors became the largest empire that had existed to that date.

Chinggis Khān's successors, although declaring their adherence to the commandments of their great predecessor, in fact departed from his fundamental principle of staying outside 'civilization' and not sacrificing the ideals of the nomads for the sake of others. Ögödäy (1229–41), Güyük (1246–1248) and Möngke (1251–1259) continued to expand their empire by conquering great sedentary societies.

The empire of the Mongols can usually be divided into five major parts, mostly according to geographical principles: Mongolia itself as the centre of the empire, beginning with the rise of Chinggis Khān and ending with the death of Möngke Khān in 1259; the Yuan Empire in China, beginning with the enthronement of Qubilay; the Īl–Khāns in Persia; the Golden Horde in Russia; and the Chaghatai khānate in Central Asia. Despite the fact that the Mongol Empire represented a conglomeration of various peoples and countries, cultures and socio-economic structures, it had many common features and important similarities that made it a coherent entity almost for the whole period of its existence. On the other hand, one cannot deny that there were specific differences and incompatibilities between the subdivisions of the empire, which ultimately resulted in its disintegration.

Yehü Chucai, the great Khitan adviser of the Mongol Khāns, is said to have repeated the old Chinese admonition to Ögödäy: 'Although the empire can be conquered on horseback, it cannot be ruled from a horse' (Kwanten, 1979, p. 142). There is no doubt that the Mongol khāns realized

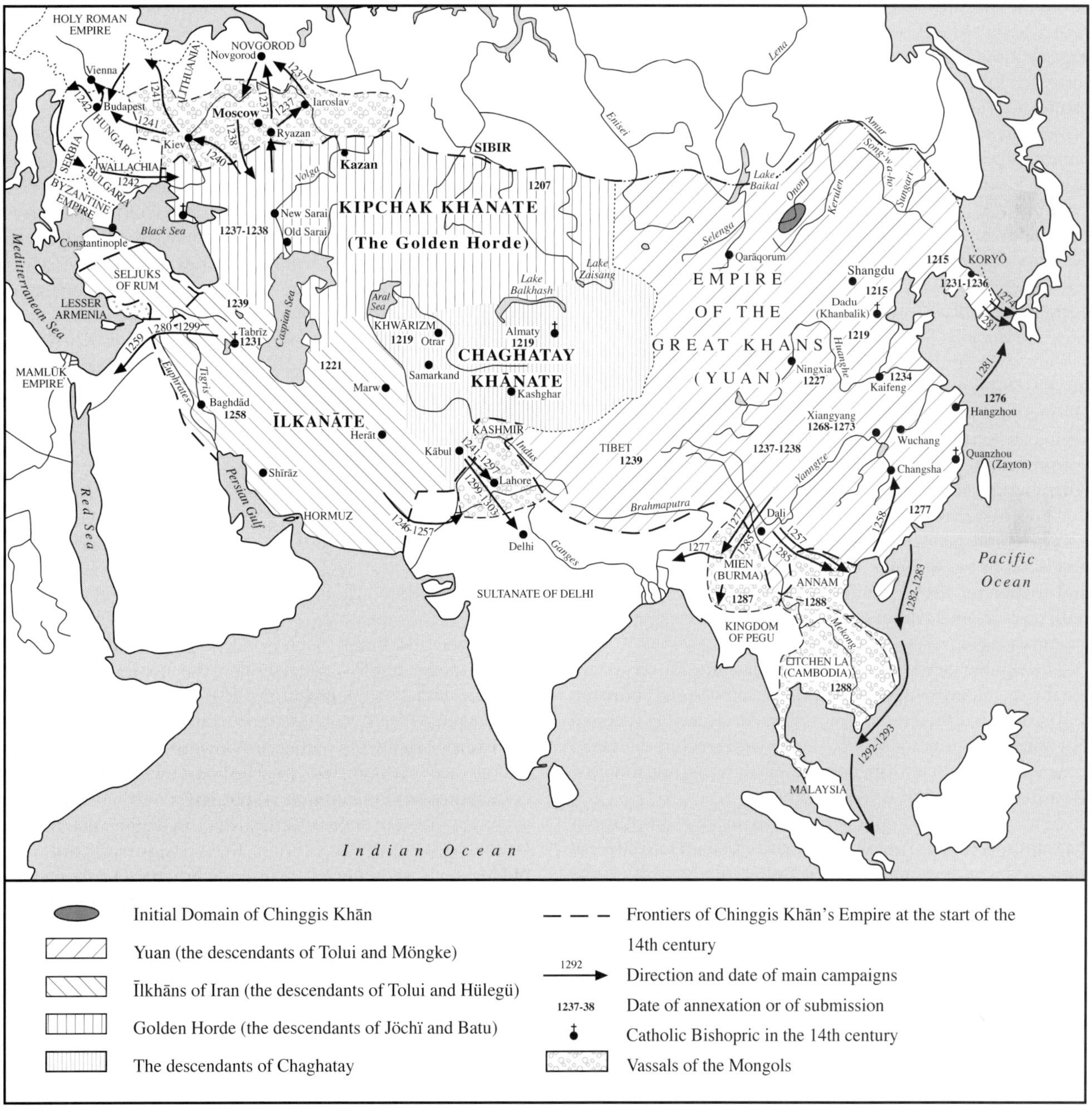

Map 29 The Mongol Empire: conquests and campaigns (thirteenth century), (after Aubin, F. in *Encyclopaedia Universalis*, volume 11, 9th edition, p. 250, 1977).

this when they were faced with the problem of governing their empire. Whatever it might be, the successors of Chinggis Khān made a historical attempt to govern the empire by creating an administrative system that combined traditional nomadic, political and military institutions with the centralized, bureaucratic administrative structure of the Chinese and Persian–Central Asian models.

In the process, the traditional institutions of nomadic society had acquired especial significance, having been, in many instances, modified to conform with new historical circumstances. By that period the Quraltai, the oldest form of political institution among the nomads, had assumed much more importance than it had ever had before. It had become a real assembly of elite Mongol leaders – princes and nobles – acting on the basis of old traditions and customs to handle most important matters of state, like the acclamation of a khān, questions of war, and the establishment of law and policy.

The Mongol Empire was created through military conquest, and the Mongol khāns regarded the army as the most basic of all the imperial institutions. Military organization, based on the decimal system, had not only been sustained for generations of khāns but had also served as the model of the army constructed by later followers and pretenders to the right of the members of Chinggis Khān's family throughout Central Asia. A new, important element of the Mongol army structure during the post-Chinggis Khān period was the institution of the *tamma*. *Tamma* forces were originally established by order of the central imperial government with the purpose of maintaining conquered territories. Some *tamma* ultimately became the nuclei of the permanent military forces of the empire's subsidiary khanates, such as Hülegü's Īl-Khānate in Persia.

One of the very first institutions introduced by the Mongols in the conquered territories was the horse mail service (Mongolian *jam*, Turkic *yam*). Its beginnings go back to Chinggis Khān himself, but as a worldwide network of communication it acquired its shape in 1234, when Ögödäy Khān began setting up post stations in his own domain.

The structure of the system was based on the erection of a post station (*jam*) at stages equivalent to a day's journey, that is about 25–30 miles. The stations held stocks of horses and fodder for those who travelled. Normally, messenger traffic was about 25 miles a day, but express messengers could go much faster.

The significance of the expanded communication system for the development of relations between various countries and peoples is difficult to overestimate. Along its roads moved not only the couriers of Mongol khāns with speedily delivered orders and items of information, but also envoys, missionaries, merchants and all kinds of adventurers.

The Mongols invented some other original institutions and offices which did not only function efficiently in different parts of the empire, but left their noticeable imprint on the later civil administration and the government of conquered countries. One of the key institutions in the Mongols' administration on the local level of the empire was the office of *daruγachi*. The institutional system of 'daruγachi' had been set up in all the Mongolian ruled regions of Eurasia – Persia, China and Russia. The term '*daruγachi*' (in Chinese: *ta-lu hua-ch'ih* (*dala huachi*), in Russian: '*daruga*' or its Turkic equivalent '*bašqaq*', in Persian: dārūghā) was widely known all over the empire: the Imperial Mongol officers (judges).

Mongol khāns also introduced various forms of taxation in the regions of their empire. They had to procure the best way of economic exploitation of the conquered peoples all over the empire.

The first three successors of Chinggis were staunch adherents of maintaining Mongolia as the centre of their empire. In this respect the reign of Möngke was the most important period in the history of the empire. It was during his reign that the Mongol Empire not only expanded greatly, but eventually acquired a firm organizational form. Möngke Khān managed to create an efficient administrative system for ruling the empire from the centre in Mongolia. He established the supremacy of the Great Khān in Qarāqorum over any prince, regardless of his lineage, and over any clan or family alliance. The Great Khān had to preside over a strong bureaucratic structure staffed by supranational personnel which included, besides the Mongols themselves, Uighurs, Khitans, Chinese, Central Asians and Persians.

There is no doubt that the unprecedental upheaval of the Mongol nomads could not but be accompanied by great changes in their social and cultural life. Society in Mongolia had been gaining a more feudal-like character. The primitive clanship structure was no longer characteristic of the Mongol society. The statehood of the Mongols had acquired its fully fledged form and functioned efficiently. With the creation of the world empire, the traditional concept of the Mongols concerning the khān's power and its function had undergone considerable modification under the influence of the political systems and chancellery practices of sedentary peoples. The empire had been attaining more and more symbiotic features on the basis of the traditional institutional structures both of the nomadic and the sedentary societies.

The Mongols awarded great significance to the ideological foundation of their political supremacy from the view-points of different religions that had become well known to them.

The Secret History of the Mongols propagated a concept of the heavenly origin of the 'golden clan' of Chinggis Khān. It is said in the very beginning of the book that Chinggis Khān takes his origin from Börte Chinya, who was 'born with the destiny from Heaven above' (SHM, p. 2). Another legend referred to in the same book says that Alan-goa, the legendary foremother of the Mongols, was miraculously conceived with Light and gave birth to her son Bodonchar, the direct ancestor of Chinggis Khān's clan (SHM, p. 4). These legendary accounts were assigned to develop two important concepts of the origin of Mongol khānship – those of Heaven and Light. Such concepts could have appeared among the Mongols as a final result of the meeting of different religious and cultural traditions. It is true that the worship of Heaven (*Tengri*) was inherent in shamanism, and it was the bedrock of the old Mongolian khānship conception. But it does not exclude that the Heaven-sanctioned khānship conception of the Mongols might have, in the final phase of its evolution, been inspired by the highly developed political doctrine of the Chinese, the doctrine of the mandate of Heaven (*t'ien-ming* or *tianming*) (de Rachewiltz, de, 1973). Moreover, we can go still further in order to discover another stratum of influence, this time, the influence of a more distant civilization, that is, the Iranian, or to be more exact, the Zoroastrian–Manichaean concept of Light which might have inspired the Mongols to elaborate their own version of an immaculate conception of Alan-goa by means of Light (Bira, 1989).

The sources bear witness to the idea that the celestial mandate and the extraordinary origin of Chinggis Khān's clan were eventually developed into the original imperial concept which inspired the Mongols in their empire-building activities.

The historical conditions that prevailed in Mongolia naturally favoured its cultural development. Although it is not certain when the Mongols first became familiar with the Soghdian–Uighur script, which in turn goes back to the Pheonician–Aramaic system of writing, it is most probable that the fully fledged usage of the script had actually begun with the chancellery practice of the Mongol state in the reign of Chinggis Khān. And since that period the tradition of writing and learning had been uninterruptedly kept among the Mongols. The earliest known form of Mongol writing was carved in rock, the so-called 'Chinggis inscription' dated from *c.* 1225. This was a monument erected in honour of Esünge, Chinggis Khān's nephew (*c.* 1190–1270).

As the great literary monument, one has to refer to the *Secret History of the Mongols* (*Mongol — un Niucha Tobchiyan*) supposedly written between 1228 and 1240 on the bank of the river Kerulen. The author of the book is not known. But this earliest surviving literary monument of the Mongols was a heroic epic as well as history. It represents the richest treasure-house of Mongolian folklore. The book may be divided into three parts – the genealogy of the ancestors of Chinggis Khān, stories about his life and heroic deeds, and a short section on Ögödäy Khān. The main theme was developed in the second part in which legendary accounts give way to more reliable historical data.

As known from historical sources, there were some other historical books, such as the *Altan debter* ('Golden Book') which was widely used by Persian historian Rashīd al-Dīn (see below).

During the period of the Mongol empire, with the subsequent settling down of Mongol khāns in China and Iran, the literary activities of the Mongols shifted from Mongolia to the respective conquered countries, and it was there that the Mongols entered into direct contact with developed traditions of literature and learning. Mongol khāns particularly patronized history writing, resorting to the service of historians from the different countries. Due to the domination of the Mongols, Mongolian historical traditions gained the leading position throughout the empire, and the family history of Chinggis Khān and his clan was regarded as an official history. The legend of Alan-goa, the foremother of the 'Golden clan', was kept in high respect and enjoyed extraordinary popularity throughout the empire from Iran to Tibet.

During the period of the Mongol Empire the geographical outlook of widely separate peoples was broadened as it had never been before. Travellers and merchants were the main disseminators of first-hand information about diverse countries and peoples. The Mongols and their Empire had not only become the focus of world interest, but they themselves had accumulated rich knowledge about the countries and the peoples which they had incorporated into their empire. *The Secret History of the Mongols* displays not only a remarkably accurate knowledge of the geography of Mongolia itself, but also contains fairly realistic information on foreign countries, their towns and peoples.

The Europeans who visited Mongolia and China, like the Franciscan John of Piano Carpini, Friar William of Rubruck, Marco Polo and others, transmitted a wealth of information on Mongolia and other Asian countries to their countrymen, while Arab and Persian travellers introduced the countries of Central Asia and the Middle East to the Mongols and the Chinese.

Despite the cruelty that accompanied the conquests, religious fanaticism was, however, alien to the Mongols. They pursued the policy of religious tolerance in their multinational empire. And it is difficult to think that this policy was determined simply by the indifference or ignorance of the Mongols, as some scholars suppose. Rather, it was a premeditated policy necessitated by 'holding the soul' of their subjugated peoples belonging to different ethnic groups and beliefs. Almost all the great world religions had become well known to the Mongols during this period. Under Möngke, the Nestorians held a privileged position. As witnessed by William of Rubruck, the Franciscan Friar who met Möngke Khān, the Mongol khān's official attitude towards different religions was as follows:

> We Mongols believe that there is but one God, by Whom we live and by Whom we die, and towards Him we have an upright heart. But just as God gave different fingers to the hand, so has He given different ways to men.
>
> (The mission of Friar William of Rubruck, 1990)

Mongolia had for a while become a meeting place of different peoples, cultures and religions. Qarāqorum, the capital of the empire, was a cosmopolitan city, where one could meet Christians, Muslims, Buddhists and Chinese, Hungarians, Russians, Western Europeans, Armenians and others. The city was linked to all parts of the Empire by the wide network of roads along the horse relay post stations. Embassies from all over the world, including the European kingdoms and the papacy, undertook the long voyage to the Mongol court. The Franciscan Friars John of Piano Carpini and William of Rubruck, who visited Mongolia during the reigns of the khāns Güyük and Möngke, left remarkable accounts of their travels, which are first-hand source materials on the history of the Mongols.

The travel accounts, for instance, give lively descriptions of the artistic activities within Qarāqorum and the open display of works of art (see Figure 32). Friar William of Rubruck was greatly impressed by the khān's palace and a large tree at its entrance made of silver by Master William of Paris. He writes that the Khān's palace resembled a church, with a middle nave and two sides beyond two rows of pillars and three doors on the south side. There were two quarters in the city; one was for the 'Saracens' (Persians), where there were bazaars and where many traders gathered; the other was the quarter of the 'Cataians', Chinese who were craftsmen. There were also large palaces belonging to the court secretaries and twelve Buddhist temples, two mosques and one Christian church (Mission of Friar William of Rubruck, 1990, p. 221). According to another source, under the reign of Ögödäy, a foundation to a Buddhist edifice was laid, which was completed by Möngke. A great *stūpa* covered with a tall pavilion constituted rooms around which there

Figure 32 Granite tortoise near the ruins of the palace at Qarāqorum (Mongolia), thirteenth century. This sculpture once served as a base for a stone stela bearing an official inscription (drawing after Kiselev, in Phillips, E. D., *The Mongols*, London 1969).

were arranged the statues of various Buddhas, completely in accordance with the indication of the *sūtras* (Cleaves, 1952) (see Plates 233, 247).

The city was enclosed by a mud wall and had four gates. At the east gate, millet and other kinds of grain were sold; at the west gate, sheep and goats were on sale; at the south gate, cattle and wagons; and at the north gate, horses.

THE MONGOL KHĀNATES AND THEIR CULTURAL EXCHANGES

The Yuan Empire

The empire was founded by Qubilay Khān, who ruled China from 1260 to 1294. He concentrated his attention on securing Mongol rulership in the greatest sedentary society. Qubilay Khān unified the northern and southern parts of China which had for centuries been separated from one another. Although Mongol rule in China was one of foreign domination, in the reign of Qubilay Khān the situation in the country much improved, and by the end of his rule China became a unified, flourishing and powerful nation, developing active contacts with many countries of the world.

Qubilay was a great innovator who introduced quite a new type of policy into the building-up of the steppe empire. Having inherited a world empire, Qubilay did not confine himself to relying only on the Chinese administrative and political practice, but was able to take advantage of mobilizing all that he could find useful in his multi-national empire.

In principle the Mongols did not change the traditional Chinese system of bureaucracy and administration much, but they had their own concepts and practice of rule, and they innovated some characteristic military and administrative institutions in China. Qubilay was well familiar with Confucianism, and he was surrounded by Chinese Confucian advisers. Nevertheless, in his policy he preferred Buddhism, which he ultimately declared the state or imperial religion. He, together with the members of his family, converted to Buddhism. Tibetan sources testify that Qubilay Khān established close relations with the Sa-Skya sect. He invited its abbot, hPhags-pa bla-ma bLo gRos rGyal-mTshan (1235–1280), to his court, and placed him at the head of the Buddhist church in his empire, having granted him the title of *Guoshi* or 'Imperial Preceptor'. His spiritual authority was skilfully exploited by Qubilay Khān in his religious policy. In his numerous works hPhags-pa bla-ma proclaimed the Mongol khāns as *Chakravartins* – 'universal emperors', thus making them equal with the great ancient Indian Buddhist emperors. Qubilay Khān is said to have founded the policy of 'two principles', which meant a close alliance between the Throne and the Altar, that is, the khān's power and doctrine (*dharma*) (Bira, 1978).

Qubilay Khān's religious and other policies were more or less continued by his successors. Buddhism continued to be prestigious at the Mongol court.

As a daring attempt of innovation on the part of Qubilay Khān in the field of culture, one has to mention his initiative to introduce a new writing system. In 1269, he issued the decree by which a new script was introduced. The creator of the script was the above mentioned hPhags-pa blama, and the script was meant to be adopted for transcribing all the diverse languages of the Empire's peoples instead of the then existing scripts – Mongol, Chinese and others. The script was called 'hPhags-pa script' after the creator's name, or 'square script' because of the square form of its letters, and 'state script' (*Guozi*) according to its designation. The adoption of the new script by Qubilay Khān was quite in accord with the cosmopolitan spirit of the age. It was the blend of the different writing systems that were known then in the Empire. It was mainly constructed on the basis of the Tibetan letters which, in turn, derived from the Indic script, but it had to be written in the vertical as the Mongol Uighur script, and its letters had a square shape as the Chinese characters; lastly, it used a vertical bar that linked the writing units, something similiar to the linking line of the Nāgari script, although with characteristic differences.

While ruling China, the Mongol khāns could not neglect the great validity of Confucian statecraft. Qubilay and his successors in particular had, after all, to be guided by the pragmatic ideas of Confucianism. They used the Chinese people's own institutions and traditional bureaucracy system to consolidate their administrative power in China. Qubilay Khān wanted to have all the prerequisites to be regarded as a 'Son of Heaven'. In this way the absolute power of the khān might be guaranteed. He was not only the legitimate successor of Chinggis Khān, but also the 'Son of Heaven' in China, and a 'Chakravartin' in Tibet.

On the other hand, Qubilay was the Great Khān of the Mongol Empire as a whole. He enjoyed the support and recognition of the rulers of the other parts of the empire. His policy had, in a wider sense, acquired a much more cosmopolitan character. The Mongol khān was surrounded by a great variety of advisers and defectors, ready to serve at the Mongol court. Qubilay Khān tried to create a multiracial, supranational administration; this permitted Mongols, Muslims, Tibetans, Chinese and others to collaborate in the service of the empire.

It is characteristic that during the reign of the Yuan emperors, relations by land between East and West reached their highest point of development hitherto. Overseas trade between China and India, Southeast Asia and Persia also further developed.

Collaboration between Chinese and Arab–Iranian astronomers in turn was very close, and most fruitful. In 1267, Qubilay Khān invited the Iranian astronomer Jamāl al-Dīn to China to transmit his discoveries. In the *Yuan shih* (*shi*), a couple of pages are devoted to plans or models of astronomical instruments from 'Western countries' – these were sent by Hülegü Khān or his successor to Qubilay Khān through the hands of the above-mentioned Jamāl al-Dīn in person (Needham, 1979a). Among these instruments (altogether seven) were diagrams of an armillary sphere, sundials, an astrolable, a terrestrial globe, and a celestial globe (Franke, 1966).

It was under the Yuan Dynasty that the great Chinese astronomer Guo Shoujing (1231–1316) who took high post at the Mongol court had created one of the most important astronomical observatories of the age at Daidu (Beijing) (Plate 134). There, he and his famous Iranian colleague Jamāl al-Dīn carried on their research works. The Iranian astronomer offered a new calendar, known in Chinese as *Wannian Li* ('Calendar for Ten Thousand Years'), to Qubilay. His Chinese counterpart, Guo Shoujing, used the Iranian diagrams and calculations to build his own instruments and to devise his own calendar, the *Shoushi Li* ('Calendar Delivering the Season'), which with minor revisions was employed through the Ming Dynasty. The calendar was based on the most accurate astronomical calculations. It was reckoned that one year was equal to 365 days 2 hours 42 minutes 5 seconds (Chiu Shu-Sin, 1984) (the real time occupied by the earth in one revolution round the sun being 365 days 5 hours 48 minutes 46 seconds).

Arab–Iranian medicine also enjoyed great popularity in China under Mongol rule. In 1285, 1288 and 1290 he dispatched envoys to South India to seek not only precious goods but also skilled craftsmen and doctors. Two branches of the Guanhui si (Imperial hospitals), composed primarily of Iranian and Central Asian doctors, were established in Kaiping and in north China to treat the Emperor and the Court. Qubilay also sought to obtain medicines from Korea. Thirty-six volumes of Arab–Iranian medicinal recipes were placed in the court library. Qubilay established an imperial academy of medicine (Chinese *Taiyi guan*).

The Mongols are known to have used Chinese and Central Asian experts in the fields of engineering and technology from the beginning of their conquests. Some Iranian and Central Asian experts were involved also in hydraulic engineering works in China. Sayyid Ajall Sham al-Dīn, the Arab engineer, who was the Governor of Yunnan, did much for the irrigation of the Kunming Basin (Needham, 1979b). There was another great Arab engineer, called Shams (1278–1351). He was the author of a treatise on river conservation, the *Hefang tougyi* ('Comprehensive Explanation of River Conservation'), published in 1321. Apart from hydraulic engineering, Shams is described in his biography as having been an expert in astronomy, geography, mathematics, and musical or rather acoustical theory.

It was during the Yuan period that the Mongols came into direct contact with a variety of cultures – Chinese, Tibet-Buddhist, Arab–Iranian and Central Asian. Buddhism's culture and literature spread widely among the Mongols. Buddhist literature was translated into Mongolian from different languages, mostly Tibetan. In the first decade of the fourteenth century, the great Mongolian scholar Choyijiodser was actively engaged in translating Buddhist texts into Mongolian and writing his own works. He translated the famous Buddhist treatise, the Boddhicharyavatara by Shantideva, and wrote his own commentary on it, and this commentary was published in 1312 in Uighur–Mongol script in hundreds of copies. The Mongolian tradition ascribes to him the composition of the first Mongolian grammar, the '*Jirüken-ü tolta*' after the model of Sanskrit and Tibetan grammars. The Buddhist *sūtra* known as '*Beidou jijing*' in Chinese, and as '*Doloγan ebügen neretü odun-u sudar*' in Mongolian ('The *Sūtra* of the Great Bear'), was translated from Chinese into Uighur in 1313, and into Mongolian in 1328. The Mongolian translation was block-printed in 2,000 copies. In the Yuan period, the famous work of Sa-skya Paṇḍita Kun-dGa' rGyal-mTshan, the '*Subhāṣitaratnanidhi*' (Mong. *Sayin ügetü erdeni-yin sang*), was also translated into Mongolian and was published in the hPhags-pa script, the four-page fragment of which were discovered in Turfan (Chinese Turkestan) at the beginning of the twentieth century. Scholars are of the opinion that Sonomgara's translation of the same book as it survived in the Uighur Mongol script, also belongs to the Yuan period.

Not a few Mongols mastered the Chinese language and Chinese writing. They took an active part in literary and translation activities, and some of them even wrote their works in Chinese. In collaboration with the Mongols, worked the Uighurs, the Tanguts, the Chinese and the Central Asians. The Mongol scholar Temürdashi, together with his Chinese, Uighur and Tangut colleagues, worked on a compilation of the histories of the Liao, Jiu and Yuan dynasties. Chagan, a native of Khotan known as a polyglot, translated into Chinese several Mongolian books, like the '*Tobchiyan*', a Mongol history mentioned in the *Yuan Shi*, the history of the campaigns of Chinggis Khān, and better known by its Chinese name '*Zhenguri qinzheng Lu*' because preserved only in its Chinese version and in other languages. In 1307 Bolodtemür, then Assistant of the Left in the Secretarial Council presented to the Khān Qaisan (r. 1307–1311), a Mongolian version of the famous Confucian book '*Xiaojing*' in 'state script', that is, in hPhags-pa script. The khān decreed that this work contained the most profound utterances of Confucius, and that all, from the nobility to ordinary people, should act according to it. He ordered to cut blocks and print it, and copies of the work were widely distributed. Some scholars consider that Bolodtemür was the author of the Mongolian version of the *Xiaojing* in the hPhags-pa script. Scholars also are of the opinion that there must have existed an earlier version of the Mongolian translation of this book, because, since 1229, the *Xiaojing* had been elucidated for members of the Mongol imperial family. One or more of these early versions may have served as a basis for the translation, in 1307, in hPhags-pa script, and also for the Mongolian translation of the same book which has reached us in Uighur Mongol script (de Rachewiltz, 1982).

It is characteristic that some Central Asian works were also translated into Mongolian. The poems of Muḥammad al-Samarqandī were translated into Arabic, Persian, Uighur, and Mongolian. But only a few strophes of the Mongolian version have survived, representing a unique specimen of early Mongolian translation.

It is certain that the stories of the famous 'Romance of Alexander' were already known to the Mongols in the thirteenth century. Möngke Khān's Minister Maḥmūd Yalavach once related to his sovereign a story from the Muslim version of the Alexander Romance, and the Mongol khān 'was extremely pleased with it' (Rashīd al-Dīn, 1971). It was a true sensation when, in the 1950s, scholars discovered and identified the anonymous and fragmentary text of a Mongolian version of the Alexander Romance (Poppe, 1957; Cleaves, 1959). It is supposed to have been translated in the early fourteenth century from its Uighur Turkish version. The Romance of Alexander (in Mong. *Sulqarnai*, from Persian – Zu-l-Qarnayn, itself from the Arabic Dhu-l-Qarnayn) was widely spread in Ethiopic, Syriac, Arabic, Persian, and Turkish versions throughout the Near East and Central Asia since an early date. The Mongolian fragmentary version, in which the quest of immortality seems to be the predominant theme, consists of four distinct episodes: (1) the ascent upon Mount Sumer; (2) the descent to the bottom of the sea; (3) the descent to the land of darkness; and (4) The return to the city of Misir.

As a result of the literary and translation activities of the Mongols, their written language acquired its classical form which continued to develop, indeed, well into modern times. The rules of spelling were set, and the lexicon of the language was enriched by new words and expressions, including loan words from different languages, mostly from Sanskrit (in Soghdian–Uighur forms), Chinese and Tibetan. It was culturally important that the Mongols had mastered the Chinese technique of block printing. The Mongolian books published by way of block printing were not only available to more readers and bibliophiles, but had more chances to be inherited by later generations. Since that period, block printing practice was continuously preserved among the Mongols until the very recent past, and produced a great amount of books.

The reign of the Mongol khāns in China lasted altogether for a century. Although not a few Mongols among the ruling elite in China were acculturated, and assimilated Chinese civilization, still, the Mongol ruling class, in its majority, was not assimilated. Scholars have pointed out that the Mongols were remarkably successful in maintaining many features of their way of life, from culinary and dress customs and language to military organization, throughout the whole period of their domination in China.

The Īl-Khānate

With the foundation of the Īl-Khānate by Hülegü (1256–1265), Persia and Iraq, together with much of Anatolia, were brought definitively under Mongol control. The Īl-Khānate existed for 70 years. The dynasty of the Īl-Khans was subject to the Great Khānate. The prestige of the Great Khāns, particularly that of Qubilay, was immense, and the connection between China and Persia remained strong and friendly under Mongol rule. This factor greatly favoured the development of relations between the two great centres of civilization.

Under Mongol rule, the Mongol–Chinese impact on Persia and the Middle East became stronger than ever before. In Persia, as in China, the Mongols were confronted with a flourishing culture. The Mongol conquest, particularly at its initial stage, caused great damage to this culture, simply because a great number of intellectuals and artisans were annihilated or forcefully deported to Mongolia and China.

The Mongols could not offer anything culturally superior in exchange for what they had destroyed. However, what could be regarded as a positive point in favour of the Mongols was the fact that they played an active intermediary role in introducing some East Asian elements into the Persian culture and religion. To take the case of religion , for example, Islam, hitherto a relatively homogenous culture, now underwent several drastic changes.

The policy of religious tolerance pursued by the Mongols directly resulted in the revival of non-Islamic traditions in Persia. While the Mongol attitude towards religion was undoubtedly driven by political motives, the role of the Kerait princesses, who were Nestorian Christians and married into the family of the Chinggisids, cannot be underestimated. One has to refer to the achievements of Sorqoqtani, Tolui's wife, whose three sons Möngke, Qubilay and Hülegü, became famous sovereigns. She is well known to have been the Kerait princess, and a practising Christian. She may have influenced her sons. Hülegü, the founder of the Īl-Khānate, was also married to a Christian princess from Kerait, whose name was Doquz Khātūn. Hülegü's son Abāqā, who succeeded his father, also had a Christian spouse, named Maria.

Nestorian Christians were influential in the Īl-Khānate. Some served the Īl-Khān's court as Mongol ambassadors to the countries of Europe. For instance, Rabban Sauma and Mark were two Uighur Nestorians whom Qubilay and Arghun used as their own envoys to foreign countries (see Figure 8).

The most intriguing aspect of religious life under the Īl-Khān's was the fact that Buddhism enjoyed a brief period of official favour. That was a distant reflection of the general religious policy of the Mongol Empire. Hülegü displayed sympathy towards Buddhism. He had his appanage in Tibet: the Phag mo Grupa, one of the great Buddhist centres of Tibet, was under his jurisdiction. With his successors, especially in the reign of Arghūn, Buddhism was increasingly favoured. Through Buddhism, some Tibetan religious and cultural influence reached Persia through the Mongols. Nevertheless, material evidence of Mongol-Tibetan Buddhism in Persia is very scant, for Buddhist monuments were destroyed or converted to Islamic use after the conversion of the Mongol rulers to Islam. Only a few Buddhist ruins exist near Marāgheh.

Perceptible East Asian, Mongol, Buddhist and Chinese influence may be noticed on examples of Persian painting of the Mongol and post Mongol periods. For instance, a pair of miniatures in the Miscellany Collection H. 2152 of the Topkapi Library made for the Tīmūrid prince Bāysunghur, and mainly composed of Īl-Khānid and Tīmūrid pictorial and calligraphic works, apparently show that the Mongol Buddhist painting style and motifs were so influential that they were pursued by later generations of artists in the Tīmūrid period (Esin, 1977; Needham, 1979c).

The Īl-Khāns are known to have patronized and promoted sciences and scholarship. The famous philosopher and astronomer, Naṣīr al-Dīn al-Ṭūsī (1201–1274), was one of Hülegü Khān's advisers. Hülegü Khān entrusted him with the creation of an astronomical observatory at Marāgheh in Āzerbaijān, south of Tabrīz. The observatory was equipped with the best instruments constructed up to that time, and the library is said to have contained over 400,000 volumes. The observatory was a meeting place for scientists from different countries. The illustrious Muslim astronomer from Spain, Yaḥyā ibn Muḥammad ibn Abi l-Shukr al-Maghribī al-Andalusī is known to have worked there.

One has to refer to the remarkable work of Rashīd al-Dīn (1247–1318) on medicine. He served the Mongol rulers in Persia as court physician, and occupied the high post of prime minister. About 1313, he prepared an encyclopedia of Chinese medicine called *Tansūq-Nāmeh-yi Īl Khān dar Funūn-i 'Ulūm-i Khiṭā'ī* ('Treasures of the Īl Khān on the Sciences of Cathay'). The work dealt with the various subjects of Chinese medicine: sphygmology (pulse lore), anatomy, embryology, pharmaceutics and so on.

Historiography enjoyed particular attention and patronage from the Īl Khāns, who were naturally interested in immortalizing 'great deeds', their own and those of their predecessors. For this purpose, they recruited the connoisseurs of old times and historians from different nations, and made available their archives and official chronicles for those who wrote history. As illustrations, one might refer to the two famous Persian works *'Tārīkh-i Jahān-Gushā'* ('The History of the World-Conqueror'), by Atā Malik Juwaynī (1226–1283) and the *'Jāmi' al-Tawārīkh'* ('The Compendium of Histories') by Rashīd al-Dīn. Both authors held high political positions in the Īl-Khānate, and were eye-witnesses and participants in many important events that took place in these days. Juwaynī began working on his book during his residence in Qarāqorum in 1252–1253 at the suggestion of his Mongol friends from the court of Möngke Khān. He must have completed his work after his return to Iran, sometime after 1260.

Rashīd al-Dīn wrote his book in 1300–1311 by order of the Īl-Khāns Ghazan and Öljeitü. His 'Compendium of Histories' was the world's first real universal history, that is, a general history of all the Eurasian peoples with whom the Mongols had come into contact. Beginning with Adam and the Patriarchs, the book recounts, besides the history of the Mongols,the history of the pre-Islamic kings of Persia, of

Muḥammad and the caliphate down to its extinction at the hands of the Mongols in 1258; of the post-Islamic dynasties of Persia; of Oghuz and his descendants, the Turks, the Chinese, and the Jews; of the Franks and their emperors and popes; and of the Indians, with a detailed account of Buddha and Buddhism (Boyle, 1971).

The last, third volume of the history was a geographical compendium containing 'not only a geographical and topographical description of the globe as it was then known . . . but also an account of the system of highways in the Mongol Empire, with mention of the milestones erected at imperial command, and a list of postal stays' (Jahn, 1964).

Rashīd al-Dīn had the unique opportunity of obtaining the assistance of scholars from different nations resident at the Īl-Khān Court. The history of India was composed with the help of the Kashmīrī hermit Kamalashri, and the history of China with the assistance of Mongol and Chinese connoisseurs of history like Bolud Chingsiyang, who is likely to have been the chief authority on contemporary China.

The main place in the book was given to the history of the Mongols which was based almost exclusively on native sources many of which are now lost. Rashīd al-Dīn had the privilege to avail himself of the assistance and favour of influential Mongols, like Bolud Chingsiyang (Pulad chinksak), and Ghazan Khān himself. We have every reason to think that all the materials pertaining to the Mongols, and which Rashīd included in detail in his book, must have been retold or especially prepared for him by his Mongol colleagues from Mongol sources, as good as the famous *Altan debter* ('Golden Book') which was always preserved in the treasury of the khāns' court and which was referred to in many places by the author. Scholars rightly assume that the first draft of the earliest parts of the Jāmi' al-Tawārīkh was not originally written in Persian, and goes back to a Mongolian version, most probably compiled by Bolud Chingsiyang and other Mongol genealogists. Consequently, the monumental history became a multilingual affair which was edited in Persian, Arabic, and perhaps also in Mongolian and East Turkic (Togan, 1962). While reading the parts of the Persian historian's book devoted to the Mongols, including the history of the successors of Chinggis Khān, no matter in whatever language – in the original Persian or in the modern English or Russian translation, any Mongol can easily discover for himself the surprisingly traditional Mongol manner and style of history narration which so greatly contrasts with that of Persian Islamic history writing.

The Golden Horde and the Chaghatai khānate

The role of these two khānates in the cultural life of the empire was not so great. Unlike the khānates in China and Iran, they actually kept aloof from the main streams of cultural exchanges, representing only peripheral offshoots of the Empire. The two khānates were nearer to each other, and the territories were mostly populated by different groups of Turkish people who were closer to the Mongols both ethnoculturally and linguistically, and the level of their sociocultural development was not higher than that of the Mongols. In the steppe lands of conquered territories the Mongols found favourable conditions for their nomadic way of life, and they easily came into direct contact with their Turkish counterparts.

Although the khāns of the Golden Horde ruled over Russia, they did not settle in the depths of its territory. When Bātū Khān (1236–1255), the founder of the Golden Horde, wished to have his residence, he preferred to build his capital Saray in the delta of the lower Volga, not far from Astrakhān. The Dasht-i Qipchāq with its grazing lands attracted the Mongols more than the great cities of Russia. The Qipchāq steppe was the core of the Golden Horde, which is why the latter was also known as the Qipchāq Khānate.

As far as Russia is concerned, once it was severely devastated by invasion, it came under Mongol vassalage. And the indigenous Russian lands, as a matter of fact, were not administratively included in the territory proper of the Mongol horde. The old Russian princely administration system was on the whole maintained. Russia was subject to heavy tribute and taxes.

Chaghatai received from his father Chinggis Khān the lands from the country of Uighurs in the east to Bukhārā and Samarkand in the west. In fact, the khānate was created long after the death of Chaghatai Khān (d. 1242), by whose name it has gone down in history. It was Alughu (d. 1265/66) who actually founded an independent Mongol Khānate; he even expanded the former Chaghatai domains by bringing the whole of Central Asia under his sway.

The unification of so many different peoples under the strong power of the Mongols obviously promoted the meeting, and integration, of their different cultures and traditions. It is noteworthy that the 'specific gravity' of non-Islamic, Mongol–Turkish elements increased, greater than ever before, in the socio-political and cultural life of the Central Asian peoples. The Mongols brought their own cultural elements – their language and writing, their faith, their nomadic mode of life, as well as their khānship tradition and knowledge of polity and experience. In the Golden Horde, the Mongol language and script were used in official documents. Some *yarlyks* (Turkic, in Mongolian, *jarlig*), the charters of the Khāns, written in the Mongol script, have survived down to our day, dating from the end of the fourteenth century. To this period also belong the last coins of the Khān Taktamish, on which the Khān's name was recorded in the Mongol script.

On the other hand, Mongol domination in the khānates enhanced all that was Turkish, and Turkish elements eventually came uppermost. It should be pointed out that the Mongols in both khānates were considerably outnumbered by the Turks, and these Mongols, after all, had to be assimilated in the local ethno-cultural milieu where Islam and Islamic culture had prevailed since the pre-Mongol period. The Mongols were converted to Islam, and such Mongol clans as the Barlas, Dughlat, Jalāyir and others, were Turkicized; but they continued to play an active role in the history of Central Asia even after the fall of Mongol rule. They are known to have given rise to some prominent emirs, like Tughluk Tīmūr from the Barlas, who later founded the great empire of the Tīmūrids, on the model of the khānates of the Chiggisids in Central Asia.

Scholars may argue whether there was a *Pax Mongolica* or not, and whatever the political and military consequences of the conquests may have been, the fact is that the Mongol empire had brought the great majority of the lands of Eurasia, with their different peoples and cultures, under one authority. It was likely the first and the last experience of humankind to have united, within one set of boundaries, the largest land empire that the world had ever known; and its cost was steep and could hardly be justified. Nevertheless, one ought to take into account that under the specific historical conditions of the age, a worldwide contact of peoples and cultures had been developing, and a fruitful exchange of material and intellectual wealth took place between the peoples of the world, with considerable after-effects for the further progress of humankind (see Plates 12, 243–248).

EDITORS' NOTE

1 As the contributors' typescripts were communicated to the members of the International Commission of this New Edition of the History, Halil Inalcik sent the following note, which we reproduce here: 'The Mongol Empire's impact on World History in transferring Chinese technology to the west is very important: silk exports from China to the Mediterranean and the Black Sea made it possible to develop silk industries in Italy; also the Asiatic trade route shifted from the Indian Ocean and the Red Sea to Anatolia and the Black Sea (Heyd, 1879)'.

BIBLIOGRAPHY

BIRA, S. 1978. *Mongolskya Istoriographya XIII–XVII vekov.* [Mongolian Historiography of the 13th–17th centuries], Moscow, pp. 78–91.

——. 1989. The Traditional Historiographical Mutual Relationship between India and Mongolia. In: BIRA, S. (ed.) *Mongolia and India*, Ulan-Bator, pp. 30–33.

BOYLE, J. A. 1971. Introduction to his English translation of Rashid al-Dīn's book '*The Successors of Chinggis Khan*', New York and London, p. 7.

CHIU SHU-SIN. 1984. *Survey on the History of the Yuan Dynasty* (Mongolian translation). Hayilar, Inner Mongolia.

CLEAVES, F. W. 1952. The Sino-Mongolian Inscription of 1346, *HJAS*, Vol. 15, Nos 1–2.

——. 1959. An Early Mongolian Version of the Alexander Romance (translated and annoted). *Harvad Journal of Asiatic Studies*, Vol. 22, pp. 2–99.

ESIN, E. 1977. A Pair of Miniatures from the Miscellany Collections of Topkapi. *Central Asiatic Journal*, 21 (1), p. 15.

FRANKE, H. 1966. Sino-Western Contact under the Mongol Empire. *Journal of the Royal Asiatic Society* (Hong Kong Branch), 6, p. 60.

HEYD, W. 1879. *Geschichte des Levantechandels im Mittelalter* (trans. in 1885–1886. Histoire du commerce du levant au Moyen Age, 2 vols, ed. F. RAYNAUD, Leipzig.

——. 1966. *History of the Mongolian People's Republic* (in Mongolian). Ulan-Bator, Vol. 1, pp. 170–191.

JAHN, K. 1964. The Still Missing Works of Rashīd al-Dīn. *CAJ*, IX/2, p. 7.

KWANTEN, L. 1979. *Imperial Nomads.* Leicester. p. 142.

Mission of Friar William of Rubruck, The. 1990. (Trans. by JACKSON, P. and MORGAN, D.) p. 221. London.

NEEDHAM, J. 1979a. *Science and Civilisation of China*, Vol. 3 (reprinted in 1979, Cambridge University Press, London. p. 49).

——. 1979b. *Science and Civilisation of China*, Vol. 1, p. 141.

——. 1979c. *Science and Civilisation of China.* Vol. 1., p. 218.

POPPE, N. 1957. Eine Mongolische Fassung der Alexandersage. *Zeitschrift*, 107, pp. 105–109.

RACHEWILTZ, I. DE. 1971. *Papal Envoys to the Great Khāns.* London, p. 136. cf. *The Mission of Friar William of Rubruck* (trans. by JACKSON, P. and MORGAN, D.) London, 1990, p. 236.

——. 1973. Some Remarks on the Ideological Foundation of Chinggis Khān's Empire. *Paper on Eastern History*, No. 7, pp. 21–26.

——. 1982. The Preclassical Mongolian Version of the Hsiao-ching. *Zentralasiatische Studien*, Vol. 16, p. 18.

RASHĪD AL-DĪN. 1971. *The Successors of Chinggis Khān.* (Trans. by BOYLE, J. A.). New York and London, p. 212.

Secret History of the Mongols, The (*SHM*). 1982. (Trans. and edited by CLEAVES, F. W.) Cambridge, Mass., and London, Vol. 1, pp. 2, 4, 141.

TOGAN, A. Z. V. 1962. The Composition of the History of the Mongols by Rashīd al-Dīn. *CAJ*, Vol. VII, No. 1, p. 64.

31

THE TIBETAN CULTURAL AREA

Yonten Gyatso and Fernand Meyer

CONQUERING KINGS AND CULTURAL COSMOPOLITANISM (SEVENTH–NINTH CENTURY)

At the beginning of the seventh century, Chinese chroniclers noted the appearance, in the distant heart of the high plateau that stretches to the north of the Himalaya, of a population that they referred to as *Tufan*. Their territory, the local name for which was *Bod*, was to be known in Europe in the Middle Ages as Tibet. The hereditary chief of the valley of the Yarlung, a southern tributary of the Brahmaputra in what would become central Tibet, had just added considerably to his domains by absorbing those of the neighbouring chiefs. This expansion was taken much further under his son Songtsen Gampo (d. 649), whom indigenous tradition was to see as the real founder of the Tibetan state and its institutions. His dynastic successors gave this hegemony imperial dimensions, and until the disintegration of central power in the middle of the ninth century, Tibet was a territorial and military power to be reckoned with in Central Asia.

Our knowledge of the political and cultural history of Tibet during this period, still far from complete, derives from contemporary evidence (archaeological remains, Chinese annals, important Tibetan documents discovered in the grottoes of Dunhuang in the Chinese province of Gansu) and from later Tibetan historiography.

The Tibetan plateau has been inhabited since Palaeolithic times. The oldest of Tibet's prehistoric sites appears to go back 50,000 years, and such sites are spread over the territory. The population was probably of diverse origins. The Tibetan language, spoken by the population groups that formed the nucleus of the new state, is related to Myanmar within the Tibeto-Burman family of languages, which is itself usually connected, in a remote association, with the huge Sino-Tibetan group. From the seventh century, military expansion brought in groups which were considered as alien at the time but which were rapidly assimilated: the kingdom of Zhangzhung in the west of the high plateau, whose language seems to have been similar to that of some modern languages or dialects of the western Himalaya, and Turco-Mongol and Tibeto-Burman groups to the north-east and the east. Moreover, Tibetan troops were often demobilized on the frontiers of the empire, thus establishing new populated areas which have largely been maintained to the present day. By the second half of the seventh century, the Tibetans controlled huge stretches of territory beyond the already vast high plateau itself, and these conquests brought them into contact with brilliant civilizations. To the south of the Himalayan watershed, the kingdom of the valley of Kathmandu – the Nepal of the ancient sources – became a vassal, and the Tibetan army even ventured onto the Gangetic plain. These regions still bore witness to the achievements of classical Indian culture at its apogee during the Gupta Empire (320–*c.* 500). To the east, the Tibetans came into contact, sometimes as allies, sometimes as foes, with the mighty Tang Dynasty of China (619–907), with which they vied in the north for hegemony over the Tarim basin, where the cosmopolitan oasis cities along the Silk Road had long blended Chinese, Indian and Iranian influences. During the eighth and at the beginning of the ninth century, Tibetan expansion continued westwards to the upper basin of the Indus and the Karakorum, where the culture was essentially Indian, and even further afield, to the regions from which the Persian Sasanian Empire had recently been ousted by Arab armies. At the other end of 'High Asia', the kingdom of Nanzhao in the north of the present-day Chinese province of Yunnan was held in vassal status throughout the eighth century, and Tibetan troops occupied the region of Dunhuang at the eastern end of the Silk Road from the end of the eighth to the middle of the ninth century. Throughout these areas, Buddhism constituted a powerful cultural force. The unification, under Tibetan authority, of this vast geographical area in the heart of Asia enabled men, objects and ideas to move unimpeded over great distances.

The administrative requirements of the new state and its foreign contacts resulted in the adoption of a system of writing. According to Tibetan tradition, it was King Songtsen Gampo who ordered its creation during the first half of the seventh century on the basis of an Indian alphabet. At the same time, the Tibetans acquired grammar, which would provide them with a powerful tool of linguistic analysis. Tibetan culture, which was still essentially oral at that period, was by no means rudimentary. It was already based on the mixed economy which would remain one of its characteristic features, and which linked it to Western Asia: cereal growing alongside stock breeding, which called, to differing degrees, for a sedentary or a nomadic way of life. Alongside the tents, which could be enormous and were sumptuously decorated when providing shelter for the king, the ancient sources also mention defensive stone architecture: citadels marking the centres of power, towers, and houses with several floors and flat roofs. The essential features of later Tibetan architecture were already in evidence here: load-bearing walls, flat roofs, monumental architecture. The methods of construction and the materials employed also link Tibetan architecture to Western Asia, setting it apart from Chinese architecture. The annals of the Tang note with admiration the great dexterity of Tibetan metalwork: zoomorphic objects, figures (sometimes articulated), miniature cities and so on, in gold or silver, along with lamellated armour which entirely covered the body of a rider and his mount, and finally, iron suspension bridges. Contemporary Tibetan texts attest to the existence of a rich oral tradition, which found expression in antiphonal choral singing and in a variety of religious representations and practices in which sacrifice and mountain worship played a major role, although we do not know whether they also formed part of a systematized religion linked to royalty. Funerals involved particularly elaborate rituals, and among the very numerous necropolises, most of which have only recently been discovered, those of the kings are distinguished by the impressive size of the burial mounds, none of which has been excavated. The sovereign was indeed invested with sacred attributes, which were manifested in supernatural powers associated with the celestial origin of the dynasty. His power was none the less circumscribed by that of mighty vassals, holders of huge fiefs, who participated in government. The highly developed civil and military organization of the state exhibited features also found in China and among Turco-Mongol population groups.

At the end of the eighth century, the Tibetan dynasty attributed to their ancestor Songsten Gampo – who thus became a founder hero – the introduction of Buddhism as well as the foundation, at the beginning of the previous century, of the Great Temple at Lhasa. Even if he was not the devout Buddhist glorified by subsequent tradition, the oldest parts of the sanctuary could well date from the seventh century.

In fact, royal patronage of Buddhism only became decisive under the reign of Thisong Detsen (755–797), who made it the state religion and founded the first Tibetan monastic community at Samye (*c.* 775). From that period, the court provided the needs of both monks and secular Tantrists. They were also exempt from taxes and military duties. At a later period, the sovereign assigned land to the monks together with tenant families to work it. The influence of Buddhism grew stronger still from the beginning of the ninth century, when monks were called upon to play a political role of the first importance and thus began to encroach on the prerogatives of the nobility, a section of which was hostile to the new religion.

The arrival of Buddhist missionaries in Tibet combined with cultural contacts and interest in the religious teachings of neighbouring countries gave rise to considerable activity in the field of translation, mainly from Sanskrit and Chinese, under the aegis of the royal dynasty. Foreign artisans were brought in to build and decorate the interiors of temples and monasteries, some of which, according to Tibetan historians, were based on Indian models. It would appear that these buildings blended Indo-Nepalese, Chinese and Central Asian influences with indigenous technical traditions to form an eclectic style of which very few traces now remain. Thus paintings on canvas produced at Dunhuang for Tibetan customers, perhaps by Tibetan artists, were executed in a style which was directly influenced by India and was undoubtedly among those current in central Tibet at the time. As it turned to Buddhism, the Tibetan kingdom also opened up to traditional Indian and Chinese sciences such as medicine, astrology and divinatory computation.

TWILIGHT OF THE DYNASTY AND RENAISSANCE OF BUDDHISM (NINTH–TWELFTH CENTURY)

Nobles opposed to the growing political and economic influence of Buddhist monasticism began to lay plots. In 838, they assassinated the devout King Repachen and replaced him with his brother Langdarma, who, according to tradition, decided to eradicate Buddhism. In fact, the persecution was probably directed not so much at Buddhism as such but at its monastic structures and their association with the state. When Langdarma was assassinated in turn, conflicts for the succession dislocated central political authority and led to the loss of control of the periphery of the Tibetan linguistic and cultural area, which then stretched, as by and large it does now, from the populated 'Tibetan' regions of the Chinese provinces of Gansu Qinghai and Yunnan to the east, to Ladakh (India) in the west. Local chiefs carved out independent fiefdoms and the vast expanse of often awe-inspiring mountainous territory at an average altitude of 4,500 metres broke up into feudal domains. While Buddhism, at least in the monastic form linked to the court, underwent an eclipse that was to last for roughly one and a half centuries in central Tibet during this troubled and little known period, this did not happen in the outlying areas, where it maintained its hold to a greater or lesser degree and where, in any case, it was strengthened by the influence of other neighbouring Buddhist centres. Thus it was that the cultural renaissance referred to in Tibetan tradition as 'the later diffusion' of Buddhism began on the eastern and western marches of the Tibetan area at the end of the tenth century. At the western extremity of the old empire, for example, descendants of the Yarlung dynasty in the second half of the ninth century founded a group of kingdoms, including Ladakh, which were in contact with Kashmīr, where Buddhism, especially in its most recent Tantric forms, was flourishing. Monastic ordination had to be reintroduced. Tantric rituals and mystic practices had been maintained to some extent by the secular clergy in the villages and hermitages, but they seemed to have been corrupted. A return to the sources of Buddhism was therefore required. Whereas a wide variety of cultural contacts had been maintained under the monarchy, at this stage the Tibetans turned essentially to India. This interest had the support of the sovereigns of western Tibet, who sent a group of young men, including the renowned Rinchen Zangpo (958–1055), to gather Buddhist teachings in Kashmir and in northern India. But the reintroduction of Buddhism also owed much to individuals who crossed the Himalaya to Nepal and India on their own initiative. In return, Indian, Kashmiri and Nepalese masters came to teach in Tibet. One of the first was Atīśa (982–1054), a great scholar from the famous monastic university of Vikramáśīla in Bengal. At the same time, there were Tibetans who went to sit at the feet of the *mahāsiddhas* or 'great accomplished', those *yogis* who, outside the more conventional tradition represented by Atīśa, claimed to rise above scholasticism and the contingencies of monastic rule through direct mystical experience of the highest tantras, considered at the time to offer the swiftest path to Awakening. Thus Tibet became the ultimate inheritor of Indian Buddhism and its associated sciences: epistemology, erudite poetry, lexicography, medicine, astrology, divination and calendar calculations, arts and technical skills, and so on, before they fell into jeopardy as a result of the Muslim conquests at the end of the twelfth century in northern India, and two centuries later in Kashmir. The valley of Kathmandu, which was spared these upheavals, continued to exert considerable influence on Tibetan Buddhism and, especially, art.

During the second propagation of Buddhism, there was much translation from the Sanskrit, both of new teachings and of texts which had come down from the period of the monarchy and needed revision. Tibetan masters gathered disciples around them, monks or secular Tantrists according to the orientation of their practices, to whom they passed on the teachings of Indian origin that they had acquired, thus establishing communities, some of which would develop into specific religious schools. While this diligent compilation of the Indian Buddhist tradition was going on, Tibetan authors not only began to compose volumes of exegesis but also produced a great range of original writings: works of spiritual edification and moral maxims drawing on the heritage of folk tales, biographies, histories, collections of rituals, mystical songs, medical treatises, and so on. The 'rediscovered' texts also began to spread at this time: these works were said to have been hidden under the monarchy and brought to light by those predestined to discover them. The renaissance of Buddhism was accompanied by the rise of another organized religion known as *Bon*, which was linked by tradition to the dynastic period. With many similarities to Buddhism, it never attracted more than a small minority, although it managed to build up a strong following in particular areas.

Indian models continued to define the structure of religious architecture, subject to the use of indigenous building techniques adapted to local conditions. Again following the Indian tradition, religious statuary was displayed amidst a rich iconography painted on walls or on cloth hangings (*thangka*) using a technique similar to gouache. The Buddhist pantheon evoked in the texts and represented in paintings in accordance with strict iconometric rules was by that period both profuse and diverse, including a number of indigenous deities added in Tibet as protectors of the doctrine.

The art of the period was profoundly influenced, directly or by way of Nepal, by the style which had developed in north-east India under the Pāla-Sena dynasty (eighth to twelfth century). The Buddhist art sponsored by the sovereigns of western Tibet, examples of which are provided to this day by the sites of Tholing, Tabo and Alchi (tenth and eleventh centuries), was more strongly influenced by the art of neighbouring Kashmir.

RELIGIOUS HIERARCHS AND FOREIGN PROTECTORS (THIRTEENTH–SIXTEENTH CENTURY)

During the second propagation of Buddhism, religious, cultural and artistic activities proliferated and flourished, gradually transforming the country and shaping its future. However, Tibet remained divided into feudal territories, and some ruling families placed themselves at the head of religious schools. Reunification was, however, imposed on the country in the thirteenth century by a recently established and rapidly expanding foreign power, the Chinggis khānid Mongols. In 1244, Godan Khān recognized in Sakya-pandita, the influential hierarch of the Sakyapa school, the authority through which he might exercise Mongol sovereignty over Tibet. This association of lay patron and Buddhist master acquired its full political and religious dimensions when it was taken over and institutionalized by Phagpa (1235–1280), the nephew and successor of Sakya-pandita, and Qubilay Khān, who founded the Yuan Dynasty on ascending the Chinese imperial throne in 1271. Until its fall in 1368, the Mongol dynasty continued to bestow its patronage on the Sakyapa hierarchs, who had become imperial chaplains, even when its own declining authority no longer enabled it to defend their temporal prerogatives in Tibet effectively. The Sakyapa were, in fact, ousted in about 1354 by another noble family, which headed another religious order, the Phagmodupa. The new political authority, which the Mongol court could only confirm as it was unable to intervene, reorganized the territorial administration of central Tibet in a bid to restore a more specifically Tibetan model.

It was at this stage that the scholars of the 'Land of Snows', after mastering and assimilating the vast heritage of India, produced the first of their own great works of synthesis and classification in the areas of doctrine, mysticism, iconography and science. At the same time, the canonical literature of India was assembled in two enormous corpuses, the *Kanjur* and the *Tanjur*, in the fourteenth century. Xylographic printing, although known in ancient times, was not practised on any significant scale until the fifteenth century, at a time when the saint Thangtong Gyelpo is also thought to have established the Tibetan theatrical tradition. A wealth of oral literature still circulated through all layers of society, even among the literate elite, and was already a vehicle for certain themes which would much later become part of the epic cycle of the hero Gesar.

The close political and religious relations established between Tibet, reunified under the aegis of the Sakyapa then the Phagmodupa, and the China of the Yuan had major cultural and economic implications. On the one hand, the Tibetan monasteries received generous donations from the Mongol court. The Tibetan lords in charge of the districts, some of whom were allied by marriage to the House of Sakya, sponsored large religious foundations. Craftsmen from the Yuan court invited to work in central Tibet brought with them new architectural and decorative styles and came into contact not only with Tibetan but also with Nepalese artists, large numbers of whom had been sent for by the Sakyapa. Some features of Mongol civilian and military administration were also introduced into Tibet at that time. On the other hand, the Mongol patronage enjoyed by Tibetan Buddhism even within China created a substantial demand for specific figurative representations and liturgical objects. This demand was initially satisfied by Tibetan and Nepalese artists brought in by the Sakyapa hierarchs, who created a Sino-Tibetan art style of enduring popularity.

In central Tibet, as may still be seen at the monastery of Shalu, which was restored and enlarged at the beginning of the fourteenth century, the old Tibetan post-Pala style, the new Chinese influences and the contemporary Nepalese style were juxtaposed rather than integrated during this period. These major stylistic trends, dominated by Indo-Nepalese traditions, can still be distinguished in the magnificent religious complex built at Gyantse at the beginning of the fifteenth century, just before they merged, with varying proportions depending on the style of the region or the school concerned, into fully mature Tibetan painting.

The advent of the Ming Dynasty (1368–1644) in China had no direct repercussions on the political situation in Tibet, although the emperors of the new dynasty took over the patronage of the prelates of the various schools of Tibetan Buddhism and the granting of appointments, merely ratifying *de facto* situations. At the beginning of the fifteenth century, Tsongkhapa (1357–1419) founded the Gelugpa school, the last great Tibetan religious order. Its rapid expansion would embroil it in the territorial conflicts which followed the loss of the temporal hegemony of the Phagmodupa in 1435. These political vicissitudes did not, however, affect religious and artistic activity in Tibet itself or exchanges with Ming China. The first xylographic edition of the canonical corpus of teachings attributed to the Buddha, the *Kanjur*, was produced in Beijing in 1410 under imperial patronage during the Yongle period. It was illustrated by a complete pantheon in the Sino-Tibetan style inherited from the Yuan, which it helped to popularize. From that period until the fall of the dynasty, the imperial workshops also cast a large number of magnificent statues in the same style. These were widely distributed and influenced the art of central Tibet from the end of the sixteenth century onwards. At the same time, contemporary Chinese decorative painting gave rise to the emergence of a new Tibetan pictorial style associated with the Karmapa order.

The recently established Gelugpa school, enmeshed in the recurrent political conflicts which continued to trouble Tibet throughout the sixteenth century, found powerful allies among the Mongols starting in 1577, when the Mongols began to convert to the form of Tibetan Buddhism preached by the Gelugpas. It was with Mongol military support that Tibet was once again reunified in the following century under the Gelugpa in the person of the fifth Dalai Lama, whose reign would mark a golden age for Tibetan culture, which had reached what may be considered its classical maturity (see Plate 83).

BIBLIOGRAPHY

BECKWITH, C. I. 1987. *The Tibetan Empire in Central Asia.* Princeton.

BOGOSLOVSKIJ, V. A. 1972. *Essai sur l'histoire du peuple tibétain.* Paris.

CHAYET, A. 1994. *Art et archéologie du Tibet.* Paris.

KARMAY, H. 1975. *Early Sino-Tibetan Art.* Warminster, United Kingdom.

MACDONAL, A. 1971. Essai sur la formation et l'emploi des mythes politiques dans la religion royale de Srong-btsan sgam-po'. In: *Etudes tibétaines dédiées à la mémoire de Marcelle Lalou.* Paris.

PAOLA MORTARI VERGARA; BÉGUIN, G. 1987. *Demeures des hommes, sanctuaires des dieux. Sources, développement et rayonnement de l'architecture tibétaine* (bilingue italien-français). Rome.

PARFIONOVITCH, Y.; MEYER, F; DORJE, G. 1992. *Tibetan Medical Paintings.* London.

PRATAPADITYA PAL. 1983. *Art of Tibet.* Los Angeles.

RHIE, M. M.; THURMAN, R. A. F. 1991. *Wisdom and Compassion. The Sacred Art of Tibet.* New York.

RICCA, F.; LO BUE, E. 1993. *The Great Stupa of Gyantse*, London.

SCHROEDER, U. VON 1981. *Indo-Tibetan Bronzes.* Hong Kong.

SNELLGROVE, D. 1987. *Indo-Tibetan Buddhism.* London.

SNELLGROVE, D.; RICHARDSON, H. 1968. *A Cultural History of Tibet.* London: Weidenfeld & Nicolson, Reprint: Boulder, Ed. Prajna Press, 1980.

SNELLGROVE, D.; SKORUPSKI, T. 1979–1980. *The Cultural Heritage of Ladakh*, 2 vols. Warminster, United Kingdom.

STEIN, R. A. 1972. *Tibetan Civilization.* Stanford.

TUCCI, G. 1973. *Transhimalaya.* London.

——. 1980. *Tibetan Painted Scrolls*, 2 vols. Kyoto.

——. 1988–1989. *Indo-Tibetica*, 7 vols. New Delhi.

URAY, G. The Narrative of Legislation and Organisation of the mKhas-pa'i dga'-ston'. In: *Acta Orient. Hung.*, XXVI, 1, pp. 11–68.

VITALI, R. 1990. *Early Temples of Central Tibet*, London.

V: The African Continent

INTRODUCTION

Sékéné Mody Cissoko

In the present state of historical research on Sub-Saharan Africa, the period from the seventh to the sixteenth century is marked by a flowering of civilizations throughout most of the continent. That is why the term 'Middle Ages', which has a special connotation in European history, can have no real meaning for Africa. Even the two temporal limits (600 and 1492) are problematic. The first does not correspond to any historical fact. Islam only really penetrated into sub-Saharan Africa during the period from the eighth to the tenth century. Nor does the date 1492 have any significance for Africa, which saw the arrival of the first Portuguese expeditions in the middle of the fifteenth century and opened up to them as the century went on. In fact, except for the east coast, the history of Africa mainly unfolds in the interior rather than on the ocean shores. Indeed, the period in question has to include a good part of the sixteenth century in many areas, since there was continuity and no sudden break in the flow of historical events (see Map 30).

Study of this period is beset with difficulties which limit our knowledge of Africa's past. Since the use of alphabets and writing to preserve the cultural heritage was unknown throughout practically the whole of Sub-Saharan Africa, our knowledge of its history comes from external sources of Arab and European provenance. The penetration of Islam into Sub-Saharan Africa after the conquest of Egypt in the seventh century gave rise to contacts and exchanges of all kinds between Muslims (Arabs and Berbers) and Africans. Travellers, clerics, merchants and warriors came into contact with the African world and produced a large amount of information, which now provides some of the main sources for the history of Africa. They include such major writers as Ibn Ḥawkal (tenth century), al-Bakrī (eleventh century), al-Idrīsī (twelfth century), Ibn Ṣa'id (thirteenth century), Ibn Faḍl Allāh al-'Umarī (fourteenth century), the great traveller Ibn Baṭṭūṭa (fourteenth century) and Ibn Khaldūn (fourteenth century), all of whose works have become classics among the sources in Arabic.

Gradually falling under Islamic influence from the eighth to the tenth century onwards, some regions of sub-Saharan Africa witnessed an upsurge in intellectual activities, producing major cultural figures in Timbuktu, Walata, Kānem Bornu, and so on. Historians from Timbuktu, such as Maḥmūd Ka'ṭī (fourteenth century), Aḥmad Bābā (sixteenth century) and 'Abd al-Raḥman al-Sa'dī (seventeenth century), and from Bornu, such as Ibn Fartuwa (sixteenth century) and others more or less well known, have left behind remarkable historical works in the form of chronicles which, supplemented by oral traditions, have provided the basis for writing the history of Africa. The oral sources in some regions are extremely rich and are indispensable to a knowledge of even the very distant past. Other disciplines such as ethnology, linguistics and, above all, archaeology have greatly contributed to the discovery of African civilizations. The first Portuguese navigators, such as the Venetian Ca' da Mosto (1450), Bartolomeu Dias (1488) and Vasco da Gama (1498), who sailed along the African coast from the Atlantic to the Indian Ocean, also provide extremely trustworthy sources. Thus, the history of Africa in the period in question, based as it is on reliable sources of different origin and date, is relatively well known and covers a time when African civilizations flourished and the continent opened up to some extent to the external world. Clearly, though, the sources have their limits for an understanding of the scientific, technical and cultural development traced by the authors of this volume. Archaeology, though still in its early stages, has been of great assistance in establishing the dates of African history and describing the environment and activities of the peoples of Africa. More recent research has enabled us to fill in the gaps and omissions of ancient historiography on the civilizations of Sub-Saharan Africa, which occupy an important place in the history of humankind during the so-called medieval period. Part V of this volume deals exclusively with sub-Saharan Africa, which is a vast area extending from the Sahara to the Cape of Good Hope and from the Atlantic Ocean to the Indian Ocean. It is divided into several climatic zones (Saharan-tropical-savannah, rainforest and so on) and contains two large deserts (the Sahara and the Kalahari). It is bordered by two great oceans (the Atlantic and the Indian Oceans), which either cut it off from the outside world or enable it to communicate with the rest of humankind. Its foremost characteristic is the diversity to be found in its geography, populations and cultures, which conceals another feature: the predominance of major human and cultural groups. Accordingly, this volume deals with four major historical areas: West Africa; the central and southern areas settled by the Bantu; the Nilotic–Ethiopian region; and the east coast and islands of the Indian Ocean.

West Africa, generally known as the Sudan, rose to prominence as a result of the emergence of large empires (Ghana, Mali, Songhay, Kānem Bornu), powerful states and brilliant civilizations in the Hausa and Yoruba worlds. Contacts with Islam and major trans-Saharan and inter-regional trading links encouraged the development of an urban civilization (Sahelian and Yoruba) and a great expansion of the creative arts, especially in the Bight of Benin.

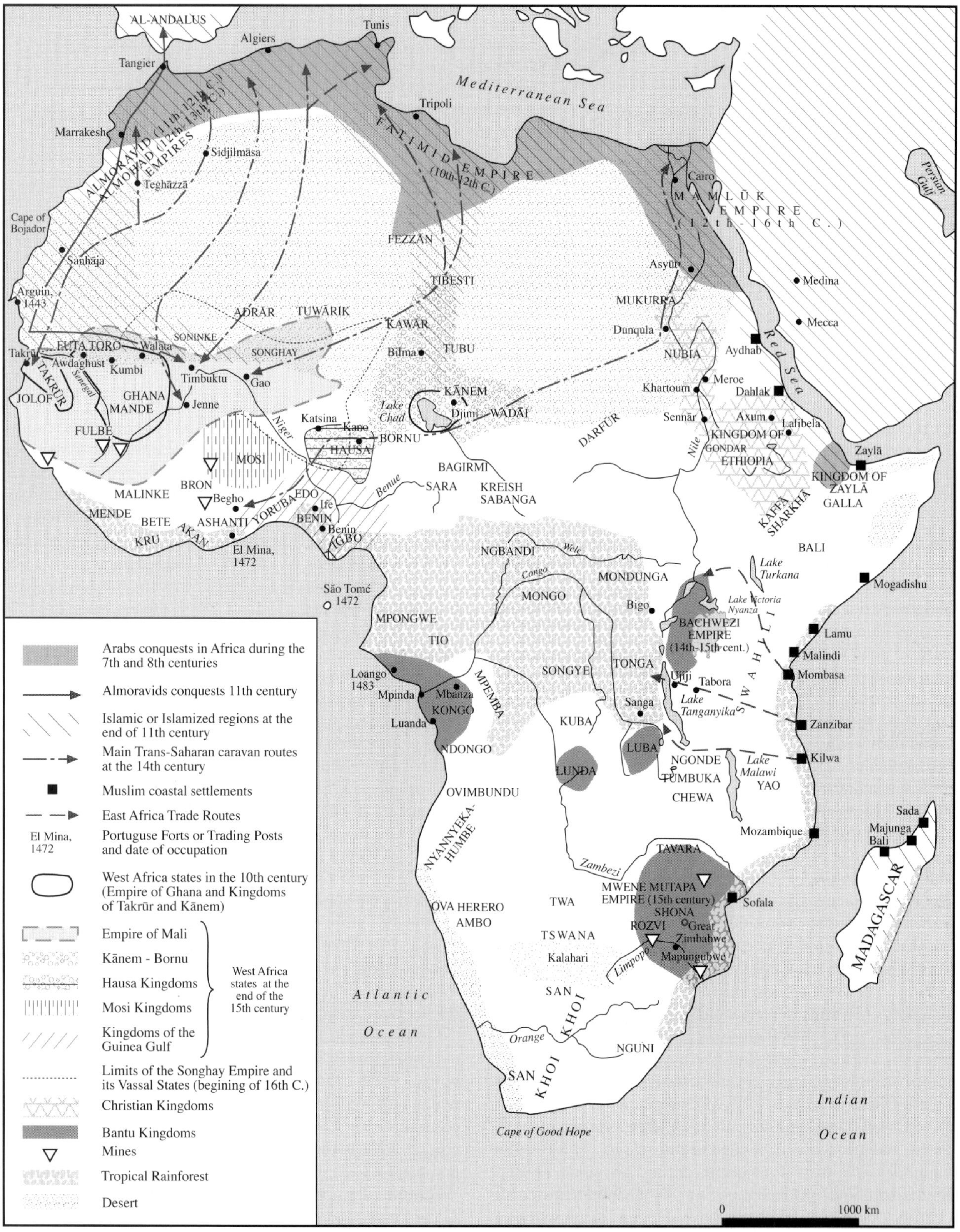

Map 30 Africa between the seventh and the fifteenth centuries.

The history of Central and southern Africa, which was mainly populated by the Bantu, who spread over most of the region, is now well known as a result of archaeological studies, oral traditions and written sources, especially Portuguese. The distinctive feature of this period is the migrations and settlement of peoples and the birth and development of states such as Zimbabwe and Mwene Mutapa (tenth to fifteenth century) and the Teke, Kongo, Lunda and Luba kingdoms between the twelfth and the sixteenth century.

Nilotic and Ethiopian Africa, which played a leading role in the ancient history of the continent, established contacts at a very early date with the Red Sea and the Mediterranean world, from which Christianity arrived. Meroë and Axum were important metal-working centres prior to the period with which we are concerned. Christian Nubia (of the Coptic rite) developed a civilization of its own and resisted Islamic influence until the fifteenth century. The same is true of Ethiopia, which struggled for centuries to preserve its Christian religion and finally united around dynasties such as the Solomonids.

As for the east coast of Africa, peopled by the Bantu (the Zanj), and the adjacent islands (Madagascar and the Mascarene Islands), their history is clearly marked by their external relations with the Arab–Islamic world and even with the Asian world, which brought about changes in population (Madagascar), in economic and social development and in Bantu culture. From the tenth to the thirteenth century, Islam encouraged the development of an urban civilization (the cities of Kilwa, Mogadishu, Mombasa, Zanzibar, Pemba and so on) along the whole of the east coast. Arabic, mixed with the Bantu languages, gave rise to Swahili, a new language and culture, which expanded throughout the region.

These large regions, which form the basis for this part of the volume, made progress – to a greater or lesser extent – in all fields of development. Among the most important factors affecting African civilization in this period were the major population movements throughout the continent, particularly in Central Africa, where Bantu migrations lasted the whole of the first millennium. Arab or Arab–Berber peoples settled in Sahelian Sudan, Nilotic Sudan, Ethiopia and along the east coast and thereby helped to shape the human physiognomy of Africa with effects lasting to the present day.

Africa, like other parts of the world, was deeply influenced by the expansion and establishment of Islam in many regions, particularly in the Sudano-Sahelian area, along the Red Sea and in the lands of the Zanj. Islam helped to bring about a profound transformation of African societies and cultures which, while preserving their own identities, came to form part of the Arab–Islamic world and experienced true economic and social development. Western Sudan, where trans-Saharan trade with the Maghrib and the East was of major importance, saw the appearance of genuine metropolises with local and foreign merchant communities and university cities such as Walata, Timbuktu, Jenne, Kano, Katsina and Bilma.

Throughout this period, however, Islam affected only a very small part of Sub-Sahara, that is, the fringes, and consequently did not sweep away the underlying cultural traditions but adapted itself to them so as to put down its own roots. Thus most parts of the continent, despite some degree of receptivity to external influences, developed their own civilizations differing from region to region and from people to people. At this period, African society was organized on the basis of clans, tribes and ethnic groups, and peoples were defined by their ethnic affiliation, for example Mandingo, Songhay, Yoruba, Fang, Kongo and Shona. All over the continent, peoples organized themselves into states, some of which, like Mali and Kongo, covered immense areas.

Generally speaking, African societies were based on farming, hunting and fishing. Agriculture (cereals, tubers, cassava, cotton and spices) and stock rearing were mostly directed towards serving local needs rather than external trade with the Arab world or, from the fifteenth century onwards, with European countries. Technologies already known prior to the period under discussion were developed and improved by craftsmen working in metal (iron, copper and zinc), wood (various tools) and clay, while advances were also made in fishing and sailing. On the other hand, such major external inventions as the wheel, the ship, the plough and gunpowder were not used even though they were known to travellers and pilgrims. Animism still remained the basis of religious beliefs in most parts of the continent. Even in Islamized areas of Sub-Sahara, ancestral beliefs and the worship of divinities linked to the natural world determined the way that people behaved and formed their view of the world.

Animism gave decisive impetus to artistic creation in some regions, such as the Yoruba and Bantu worlds (see Plate 269), which produced artefacts (statuettes in wood, metal and clay) that bear witness to this day to the artistic genius of Africans of that period.

All these aspects will be considered in these four chapters, taking due account of the distinctive features of each region. The treatment varies depending on how plentiful the sources are. Thus, Islamized Africa has been dealt with in greater detail than Bantu Africa, and socio-political aspects have received greater attention than science and technology. It being impossible to cover everything in so few pages, many gaps will be found. However, an attempt is made to touch upon all the essentials of the subject and to provide insights into the social and cultural history of Africa as it developed during the centuries covered by this period.

BIBLIOGRAPHY

AL-BAKRĪ, ABU 'UBAYD ALLĀH. 1857. *Kitāb al-Masālik wa l-Mamālik* ('Book of the Pathways and Kingdoms'). Portion of Arabic text ed. with French. trans., *Description de l'Afrique septentrionale*, by DE SLANE, W. M, Algiers 1857; repr. of French text, Adrien Maisonneuve publ., Paris 1965.

CA' DA MOSTO, A. D. 1550. *Le navigazioni* ('The Navigations'). Italian text in collection of RAMUSIO, G. B., *Navigazioni e viaggi* (Venice); Vol. 1 of complete edition of RAMUSIO by MILANESI, M., EINAUDI publ., Turin 1978. English trans. in CRONE, G. R., *The Voyages of Cadamosto, and Other Documents on Western Africa in the Second Half of the Fifteenth Century*, Hakluyt Society, London, 1937.

FERNANDES, V. 1940; 1951. *O manuscrito Valentim Fernandes*, ed. by the Academia portuguesa de história, Lisbon 1940. Portuguese text edn with French trans. by MONOD, T., TEIXEIRA DA MOTA, A., MAUNY, R., *Description de la côte occidentale d'Afrique, 1506–1510*. Centro de estudios da Guiné Portuguesa, Bissau, No. II, 1951.

IBN BAṬṬŪṬA. 1853–1859. *Riḥla* ('Journey'; full medieval Arabic title: *Tuḥfat al-Nuẓẓar fi 'Ajā'ib al-Amṣār*, 'Gift unto the Observers concerning the Marvels of the Lands'). English trans. by H. A. R. GIBB, *The Travels of Ibn Battūta*, Hakluyt Society, Cambridge, 1956-1971. Arabic text only: *Rihla Ibn Battûta*, ed. by Talāl Harb, Dār al-Kutub al-'Ilmiyya, Beirut 1992.

IBN HAWQAL. 1842; 1873; 1938; 1965. *Kitāb Sūrat al-Ard* ('Book of the Figure of the Earth'). Arabic text edn by DE GOEJE, M. J. (1873), Leiden; and KRAMERS, J. H. (1938), Leiden. Partial French trans. by DE SLANE, W. M., *Description de l'Afrique*, Paris 1842; full French trans. by KRAMERS, J. H. and WIET, G., *Configuration de la Terre*, Paris 1965.

IBN KHALDŪN. 1868 ed. *Kitāb al-'Ibar* ('Book of Admonition' = 'Universal History'). Arabic text, 7 vols, Būlāq, 1868; Beirut, 1958. Partial French trans, 4 vols, by DE SLANE, W. M., *Histoire des Berbères et des dynasties musulmanes de l'Afrique septentrionale*, Algiers, 1852–1856; repr. Paris 1925–1926. New complete French trans., 7 vols, Beirut 1956–1959.

KA'TI, MAHMŪD. 1913–1914; 1964; 1981. *Tārīkh al-Fattāsh* ('Chronicle of the Investigator'). First edn of Arabic text with French trans. by HOUDAS, O., and DELAFOSSE, M., Paris 1913–1914; repr. with rev., Paris 1964; UNESCO repr. of first edn, Maisonneuve, Paris 1981.

LEO AFRICANUS. 1550. *Descrizione dell'Africa*. Original Italian text in collection of RAMUSIO, G. B. (Venice); Vol. 1 of complete edition of RAMUSIO by MILANESI, M., EINAUDI publ., Turin 1978. English trans. by PORY, J., *The History and Description of Africa, by Leo Africanus*, London 1600; repr. by BROWN, R., London 1896.

PACHECO PEREIRA, D. 1898. *Esmeraldo de Situ Orbis* ('The Emerald, concerning the Situation of the World'). Sixteenth-century English trans. by G. H. T. Kimble, Hakluyt Society, London 1937.

AL-SA'DĪ, 'ABD AL-RAHMĀN. 1898; 1900; 1964. *Tārīkh al-Sūdān* ('Chronicle of the Sudan'). First edn of Arabic text by HOUDAS, O. and BENOIST, E., Paris 1898. French trans. by HOUDAS, O., Paris 1900, repr. with revised trans., Maisonneuve, Paris 1964.

AL-'UMARĪ, IBN FAḌL ALLĀH. 1924. *Masālik al-Abṣār fī Mamālik al-Amṣār* ('Glances of the Eyes throughout the Districts of the Lands'); Arabic text, Cairo 1924. French trans. by GAUDEFROY-DEMOMBYNES, M., *L'Afrique moins l'Egypte*, Paris 1927.

32

WEST AFRICA

32.1
THE PEOPLES

Sékéné Mody Cissoko

West Africa covers several million km², stretching almost unbrokenly from the Atlantic Ocean to Lake Chad and from the Sahara Desert to the Gulf of Guinea. Its basic feature is the climate, which played a decisive role in the history of settlement.[1] A succession of three tropical climatic zones can be distinguished: in the north the Sahara, then its southern fringe, the Sahel, and finally the vast area of the Sudan, which covers the whole of the interior. While the first is generally desert, the Sahel has a rainy season three or four months long with isohyets between 100 and 400 mm. The Sudan has a higher rainfall, which rises as one moves southwards. Savannah and cereals are predominant up to 800 mm of rainfall; beyond that, ever-thicker forest extends southwards towards the ocean. This is the region of root crops and fruits, including the famous kola nut, which marks the difference between north and south.

Much of the region is also watered by two great rivers: the Senegal flowing from east to west and the Niger from the south up into the northern Sahel, where it makes an enormous bend and then turns south again to flow into the Gulf of Guinea. Within each subregion, especially in the south, there are many water courses of varying dimensions that favour the settlement and movement of peoples.

Overall, West Africa is thus an area favourable to human settlement. It was peopled from very early times with a population that varied in time and space. Prehistorians accept that there was settlement in Neolithic times in the Sahara, which at that time was still wet, watered by streams with fish and crocodiles and inhabited by giraffes, elephants and other animals. The sole human skeleton found in West Africa is that of Asselar man (in northern Mali), which is dated to the Neolithic period. With the drying out of the Sahara between the fourth millennium and *c.* 1500 BC, the peoples settled there scattered in every direction and especially from the north southwards and from the east westwards. The medieval period experienced two great settlements, the Whites and the Blacks, who have shaped the human face of West Africa to the present day.

THE WHITES

A distinction must be made between two types of White peoples: the Libyco-Berbers and the Berber–Arabs. The former are known from earlier times than the latter. We have evidence from antiquity of the Garamantes, a Libyco-Berber people whose chariots crossed the Sahara between the Niger and Chad. In medieval times, various Libyco-Berber peoples, all of them nomadic, occupied the Sahara and the Sahel.

In the west the Ṣanhāja ruled, occupying the whole region from the Atlantic Ocean to the longitude of Timbuktu. They were subdivided into several subgroups: the *Goddala*, near the Atlantic Ocean, the *Lemṭūna*, wielding political power, and the *Messufa* in the east, controlling the trans-Saharan trade to the Niger bend. The first two formed a powerful confederacy in the eleventh century which fuelled the Almoravid movement and conquered the whole of the western area as far as Spain. In the eleventh century, Awdaghust, grown rich on the salt and gold trade, was a great cosmopolitan Sanhaja metropolis with Blacks and *Nefuza*, *Luata*, *Zenāta* and *Nefzawa* Berbers from the north.

The second Libyco-Berber subgroup was made up of *Tamāshaq*-speaking people (the Banū Tamāshaq) known as the *Tuareg*. From medieval times down to the present day they occupied the centre and east of the western part of the Sahara from Tassili N'Ajjer and the Hoggar in the north to the Niger bend and the Aïr in the east. Azaoud, Adrar des Ifoghas and the Aïr were the chief centres of these veiled nomadic Berbers who controlled the trans-Saharan routes through Tadmekka and Takedda, their chief markets. Contact with the Blacks in the Niger valley went back to very early times. Some tribes even founded Timbuktu in the twelfth century and others were demographically submerged by their own Black slaves, the *bellah*, for sometimes these were far more numerous than their masters.

The second group of Whites, the Berber–Arabs, occupied the western part, almost the whole of Mauritania. The arrival of the Arabs goes back to the Islamic expansion of the seventh century. While Chad (the area of Kāwār) was reached in 666 by the forces of the Arab conqueror ʿUqba ibn Nāfiʿ, sub-Saharan West Africa only came into contact with the Arabs in the eighth century. Umayyad Arab warriors defeated and captured by the Ghana empire, the al-Ḥunayn, were very quickly assimilated. Thus, until the invasion by the *Banū Hilāl* Bedouin tribes sent against the Tunisian Zīrids by the Egyptian-based Fāṭimids in the eleventh century, there were only a few isolated Arabs in West Africa, traders, holy men or travellers. In the fourteenth and fifteenth centuries, *Hilālian* and *Maqil* Arabs coming from the north occupied the whole of Mauritania, subjugating the Ṣanhāja and thereby controlling the great trans-Saharan trade routes. Thus, by the fifteenth and sixteenth centuries, through Islam, the Arabic language and civilization had imposed themselves on all the Berbers, except for the Tuareg, and resulted in bringing to birth a new people, the Berber–Arabs.

The presence must also be noted of a few Jewish enclaves in some parts of the Sahara, such as Tuat. At Tendirma, in the Niger Bend, the *Ta'rīkh al-Fattāsh* mentions a large Jewish colony living by market gardening and agriculture.

Thus, it can be seen that Berber (Libyco-Berber or Berber–Arab) settlement was limited to the desert or semi-desert areas of West Africa. But it was not always homogeneous or isolated from the Blacks who made up the bulk of the population of West Africa.

THE BLACKS

Historians now acknowledge that in Neolithic times the Sahara was inhabited by Black or Negroid peoples who were sedentary and practised agriculture, hunting, fishing and cattle herding. With the drying out of the Sahara, the Black peoples moved southwards, eastwards and westwards, with some, like the Ḥarrātīn, remaining isolated around a number of oases.

This migration continued into our period, which saw the virtually final settlement of Black peoples in that part of the southern Sahara known to the Arabs as the 'Bilād al-Sūdān', 'the land of the Blacks'. Depending on the prevailing climate, there were three areas of Black settlement: the Sudan–Sahel zone (northern Sudan climate) covered with grassland and savannah, the southern Sudan zone covered with savannah, and the Guinean zone, well watered and forested.

These three zones were occupied during migrations that went on for centuries and the peoples forming family and cultural-type communities ended up forming ethnic groups of varying sizes living mainly by agriculture, hunting or fishing. The largest and best known in the Sahel–Sudan area were the Wakore (Soninke) and Wangara (Mandingo) peoples. The Soninke or Sarakolle were settled in the southern Sahel, where they founded the empire of Ghana in the first millennium AD. They were farmers and traders and over the centuries they spread all over the area, from the Senegal Valley to the Niger Bend, in the southern Sudan, where their migrations continue down to the present day. The Mandingo (Malinke, Bambara, and so on) occupied the two southern banks of the Niger and the Senegal at a very early date, where agriculture (mainly cereals), hunting and mineral deposits (gold, iron) enabled them to form political organizations that were unified in the fourteenth century by the empire of Mali. The Mandingo, having become traders (*Diola*) and 'marabouts' (*murābiṭūn*, Islamic holy men) as well as conquerors, spread out all over West Africa as far as Hausaland (fourteenth century) and the forest regions along the Atlantic coast. There thus came into being a multifaceted Mandingo settlement covering much of West Africa.

This movement is comparable with that of the Fulani. It is not possible to be certain about the origin of this people, but it is highly likely that they lived in the Sahara in Neolithic times before moving southward, their language and culture remaining Negro-African. The Fulani were herdsmen and nomads and through their continuous migrations came to inhabit a good part of the Sahel area from west to east: Takrūr or Futa before the fourteenth century, then Bakhunu and Masina in the fifteenth and sixteenth centuries.

In addition to these three large ethnic groups spread all over the region, other no less important peoples settled all over the Sudan–Sahel region. In Senegambia there were the Wolof, the Serer and the Diola, and in the Niger bend, the Voltaic groups including the Kurumba, the Gurma, the Dagomba and above all the Mosi, founders of famous kingdoms in the Middle Ages. The Songhay, living around the eastern stretch of the Niger, were fishermen, farmers and warriors, and in the fifteenth and sixteenth centuries dominated the whole valley of the river from Hausaland in the east to Jenne in the west.

Between the Niger and Lake Chad, the Hausa, who had been moving in gradually from the east and north since the seventh century, settled in city states which grew rapidly thanks to their situation where routes in the zone crossed. The seven cities (the *Hausa bakwai*) regarded as 'ancestors' (Daura, Kano, Katsina, Zaria, Gobir, Biram, Rano) were major markets enjoying relations with all the countries in the subregion: Bornu to the east, the Yoruba, Jukun and Nupe lands to the south, and the cities of the Sahel to the north.

In general, little is known about the history of the countries of 'Guinea' south of the Sudan before the arrival of the Portuguese in the fifteenth century. The area was not, however, in the least isolated from the Sudan–Sahel zone, which it supplied with kola nuts, salt and slaves, and Mandingo peoples moved through it right down to the coast. Overall, it was forested but also showed many areas of savannah. It had been settled from a very early date and also showed many autonomous ethnic groups living by agriculture, gathering, fishing and hunting.

From Senegambia to the Ivorian coast, writers portray a host of independent peoples living in village or lineage communities and clinging to their animist beliefs. The Diola, Balante and Felupe were farmers; the Bainuk, Beafada, Landuma, Baga, Bulom, Kissi, Kru and many others yield evidence of dense settlement which probably goes back to Neolithic times.

From the Kru coast to the Gulf of Benin a large group of peoples (Akan, Ewe, Fon, and so on) made their living from a variety of activities in the forest, savannah and along the lagoons. The Akan probably came from the north, from the Chad–Benue region, in several stages. In a series of movements they came to occupy the whole subregion, mixing with other peoples and splitting into ethnic subgroups over the centuries. Some fractions, in contact with the Sudanese savannah, devoted themselves to the famous trade in kola nuts and gold; the market at Begho or Bitu (in the north of modern Ghana) was already a centre well known to Mandingo traders. Akan societies were made up of independent lineage-based communities in which matrilineal succession predominated. Some of them freed themselves in the sixteenth and seventeenth centuries to become ethnic subgroups moving off in all directions.

Between these peoples and the world of the Sudan, in the

transition zone between forest and savannah, the Yoruba people established themselves, coming from the north-east in successive waves between the sixth and eleventh centuries. Farmers and skilled craftsmen, the Yoruba founded cities that were remarkable for their political organization, religion and artistic output. Ifẽ, Oyo and above all Benin (Edo), which aroused the admiration of European navigators in the sixteenth century, had a major influence on all the neighbouring peoples.

These few examples show that the settlement of West Africa was not so different from what it is today. The main peoples were already almost in place. Of course, there was a difference between the peoples of the Sudan and Sahel, who were generally organized into hierarchical state societies, and those in the south who were more integrated into the framework of lineages and village organizations, with economic and cultural exchanges over a limited geographical area.

As for the size of the population, it is safe to say that the area was on the whole quite populated. Of course, settlement was not evenly spread over the whole area. Some regions were totally empty, others densely populated. Thus, compared to what they are today, the cities of the Sudan and Sahel were even overpopulated.

The Niger bend, Hausaland, Yorubaland and Benin contained a host of villages, the networks of which indicate the density of the medieval population. European writers who visited the West African coast had the same impression of a large and scattered rural population. The extravagant figures of the numbers in royal armies or imperial suites given in the Arabic sources are also indicative of a very numerous population in the Sudan-Sahel region. The trans-Saharan slave trade, climatic problems and various disasters do not seem to have excessively hindered the growth of population and the economy in general.

NOTE

1 Throughout this article we shall refer to works which are based on Arab and Portuguese sources. The most important being Ibn Ḥawkal (tenth century), al-Bakrī (eleventh century), al-Idrīsī (twelfth century), al-'Umarī (fourteenth century) and Ibn Baṭṭūṭa (fourteenth century), the two Sudanese *ta'rīkhs* of Timbuktu (fifteenth to seventeenth century), the fifteenth-century Portuguese authors including Valentim Fernandes, Diogo Gomes and Ca' da Mosto, and the Italian–Arab Leo Africanus (sixteenth century).

BIBLIOGRAPHY

(See Chapter 32.3.)

32.2
THE ECONOMY

Sékéné Mody Cissoko

The period between the seventh and fifteenth centuries saw significant economic development, especially in the area of trade.

THE RURAL ECONOMY

Agriculture remained the chief occupation of the peoples of West Africa. Knowledge of how to work iron and copper was acquired before the fifth century BC[1] and revolutionized rural life (see Plates 261, 262). The hoe in various forms enhanced the productivity of labour. Blacksmiths and other craftsmen, whether organized into castes or not, worked to produce vital implements such as hoes, axes, knives, scythes, fish-hooks, weapons (spears and arrows) and various items needed for domestic and rural life. The result was that production and population grew, and peasants' living conditions improved. Farms were family units since land belonged not to an individual, and rarely to a political authority, but almost always to the family of the first occupants. Naturally, there were exceptions in the rich river valleys (Niger, Senegal) where land was taken by power holders and worked by their captives and tributaries in return for tithes on the harvests.

Current farming practices included fallow, clearing and burning to prepare fields before the rains, the use of animal manure, and so on. In the valleys of watercourses (especially the Niger) and around oases and wells, irrigation and watering were used to keep market gardening going.

Agricultural production varied from one climatic zone to another. While date trees and various varieties of wheat predominated in the Sahel, and cereals (millet, sorghum, fonio, rice), various pulses, gourds, onions and so on in the Sudan, tubers, palms, plantains[2] and spices (malagetta pepper) were peculiar to the forest zones. Cotton was a major crop and revolutionized clothing in the Sudan, especially in Islamized areas. Overall, in its techniques and the variety of species grown, West African agriculture was reasonably productive and managed to meet the needs of the population.

Herding coexisted alongside agriculture, each village usually having its animals. Some nomadic tribes in the Sahel zone, such as the Ṣanhāja Berbers, the Tuareg and the Fulani, even specialized in the large-scale herding of cattle, sheep and camels, living always on the move and in symbiosis with peasant communities. In our period, hunting and fishing were important. The abundance of game in the Sudan early on gave rise to brotherhoods of hunters who were magicians to a greater or lesser degree, or at any event warriors, who in some countries achieved royal powers. Probably before the seventh century, groups of fishermen (Sorko, Bozo, Somono) had already monopolized fishing on the Niger and its tributaries. Along the Atlantic coast, in the fifteenth century, Portuguese navigators encountered boats without sails fishing not far from the shore. Fishing and hunting thus introduced a significant quantity of proteins, both for food and for trade. Smoked or dried fish was carried all over West Africa and into the heart of the Sahara.

TRADE AND CITIES

Economic activity in West Africa was dominated by the development of trade between local and regional communities but above all with the world across the Sahara and the Mediterranean. West Africa became involved in the world economy and underwent major social, cultural and political changes.

The development of trade was shaped by various factors including the general security that prevailed both north and south of the Sahara. Powerful political organizations (the Sudanese empires, the city-states) ensured security and order, protecting the people and markets. The Moroccan traveller Ibn Baṭṭūṭa, who crossed the empire of Mali in 1352–1353 from north to south and west to east, is full of praise for the general peace and sense of justice among the Blacks.

Trade could thus develop unhampered, carrying local products and goods from the north to the great markets that came into being in the Sudan–Sahel area in Yorubaland and Benin. The second key factor was the great productivity of West Africa, a consequence of the technological revolution involving iron and copper along with the existence of a number of raw materials that were much sought after, such as gold and salt. West Africa had famed gold mines in various places, and these in fact supplied the Mediterranean and Europe with most of its gold before the discovery of the mines in the Americas. It was thus a vital pole in trade, the various elements of which we must now examine.

Routes and means of communication

Despite its apparent vastness, isolation and lack of interest in the Atlantic Ocean, West Africa was not cut off from the world. Major routes linked its various parts to one another and crossed the Sahara to reach the Mediterranean and the Atlantic.

Donkeys, very hardy animals, pack oxen and, above all, slaves provided the bulk of transport south of the Sahel. There were corporations of donkey drivers in most trading centres. In the mid-fifteenth century, the navigator Ca' da Mosto reported caravans of slave porters in the forest region, and this was current practice throughout West Africa.

The major rivers (Senegal, Niger, Gambia) and streams played a vital role in the transport of merchandise. The Niger, almost at the limit of where trans-Saharan caravans broke bulk, was the home of the great Sudanese markets including Timbuktu, Jenne, Dia and Gao, and those in Hausaland, Yorubaland and at the river mouth. It was the natural route for north–south and east–west trade. Every writer stresses the intense activity on the river, used by thousands of big canoes for almost ten months of the year. Some canoes could carry up to five tonnes of merchandise in addition to many travellers. The crew used oars and not sails. Portuguese writers in the fifteenth century, who described the activity on these rivers, were struck by the absence of sails, all along the Atlantic coast.

The main routes taken by trans-Saharan trade varied over the period between the seventh and fifteenth centuries. The westerly routes predominated until the twelfth century. They ran from southern Morocco (Tamedelt) and Tafilelt (Sijilmāsa) towards the then flourishing empire of Ghana. With the insecurity that reduced activity at the Mauritanian salt mines, starting in the eleventh and twelfth centuries, the caravans would get their supplies at Teghazza, deeper in the desert but more oriented towards the Nigerian Sudan. The latter's routes were longer, with less security and fewer watering points; they linked the oases and major markets of the northern Sahara, principally Tuāt, with the cities of Walāta and, finally, Timbuktu and Gao. The Saharan staging point, Teghazza, supplied the caravans with rock salt, a product that was the mainstay of the Sudan–Sahel trade. Through Tuāt linked to Tafilelt (southern Morocco), Tlemcen (Algeria), Tuggurt (Tunisia) and the Fezzan (Libya), the cities of the Sudan came into contact with the trade of the Mediterranean and Europe. Gao, the eastern pole, was in touch with the great Saharan markets (Tadmekka or Es-Sūq), the copper mines at Takedda and, beyond, the Kāwār region, which produced rock salt. The old, even ancient routes, the ones used by the Garamantes starting from the Libyan coast, and going by way of the Fezzan and Takedda to reach the Niger bend or Lake Chad, or the ones used by the Romans through Kāwār towards Lake Chad, still continued to be plied, indeed even more so during the medieval period.

Thus, it can be seen that the two sides of the Sahara were linked to one another by routes that made possible the exchange of goods, people and ideas. Caravans stopped at the great outlets of the southern Sahel (Ghana, Walāta, Timbuktu, Gao, Katsina, Kano); from there, new routes led southwards into the forest area and even to the coast. Jenne, on the Bani–Niger, the Hausa cities and other intermediary points acted as stores and centralized and distributed goods from the north as well as those coming from the south.

Traders, trading techniques, weights and measures

Petty trade involved sellers and buyers of goods of all sorts, but trade proper was in the hands of a specific category of traders, big or small.

At the local or regional level, travelling hawkers, alone or in groups, frequented local markets and sold a bit of everything. Very early on, trans-Saharan trade awakened a trading vocation in certain ethnic groups which provided large-scale traders. The Wakore (Soninke), Wangara (Malinke) and Hausa were active participants in trade all over the western Sudan. The Hausa chronicles acknowledge the key role of the Wangara in the commercial and Islamic expansion of the Hausa cities in the fourteenth century. Throughout the Middle Ages, their activities gradually spread from the Sahel to the savannah and the forest, as far as the Atlantic coast, to which they carried goods, Islam and their own culture.

The Hausa and Yoruba traders dominated the Gulf of Guinea, where a new group – the women traders – came into being. In the Gulf of Benin and the Akan world, the chiefs, possessors of gold and slaves, were active participants in trade, which they turned to their own advantage. Berber–Arab traders conducted trans-Saharan trade. North Africans established in all the major cities of the Sudan came chiefly from Morocco and Algeria (Tlemcen) but also from Tunisia, Libya and Egypt. People from the great oases of the Sahara and the Sahel dominated the markets. Those from Tuāt, Tafilelt, the Fezzan, Dra, the Mauritanians (Tishit, Chingueti, Wadane), the Messufa and the Berabiche carriers formed a trading bourgeoisie with their quarters and cultural traditions in many cities of the Sudan and the Sahel.

Alongside them mention must be made of the city dwellers themselves, most of whom lived by trade through brokerage. They were middlemen between the traders from the north and those from the south, they had shops and houses, they could store and resell as prices fluctuated, and as such they were almost always winners. It has been rightly said that all the inhabitants of Timbuktu were in business; in any case, they certainly derived sure profits from the city's long-distance trade.

Traders and the world of business were organized under the auspices of freedom of trade. The most common type of organization, both among the Berber–Arabs and among the Sudanese, was family-based. The big traders worked with the members of their families, their retainers and their friends in the various markets. We know the example of the al-Maqqarī brothers in the thirteenth century, based in Tlemcen, who divided up their business across the Sahara and the Sudan under the leadership of a chief. There were individual traders and hawkers, of course, but there were also traders' guilds linked by agreements and sharing the profits made.

West African traders had gone beyond barter and used all the techniques employed in the north of the continent: advertising, credit, bills of exchange, travelling salesmen, action on prices by controlling supply and demand, use of couriers and express communications, and so on. Trade was not conducted with coins as the Africans had not minted any, but by the use of intermediate products that were just like currencies: cowries (*Cyprea moneta*) (see Plate 274), cotton fabric, salt, and so on. It is true that in some southern areas the Arab sources mentioned silent trade in the seventh to eleventh centuries, in which sellers and buyers practised barter of goods without seeing one another. Barter had not disappeared but was kept for particular exchanges. The account money of Arab origin, the *dīnār*, equivalent to the *mithqāl* (4.72 g), was the most widely used in trans-Saharan trade and in large-scale dealings where traders dealt in thousands of dīnārs. The Arab traveller Ibn Ḥawkal, passing through Awdaghust at the end of the tenth century, claims to have seen a bill of exchange for 42,000 dīnārs there, a sum that he regarded as exceptionally large in the Muslim world. Cowries were used in small and medium-scale trade. Until the fifteenth century, they were imported from the Maldive Islands and Indonesia by Muslim traders, but at the beginning of the sixteenth century their value collapsed with massive European imports.

Traders used scales of all sizes, measures of weight, capacity and length being adapted to local conditions and the products being traded. In the Islamized countries along the Sahel–Sudan border area, 'the Prophet's *moud*' (a local measure), the *mithqāl* and the quintal were used; elsewhere, and especially in the forest areas inhabited by the Edo, the Akan and others, a range of metal and wooden objects were used as units and means of measurement.

Markets

In West Africa, the marketplace was in the centre or just outside the city, in the open air or often built up. It housed people displaying goods, sellers, buyers, men, women, foodstuffs, local products; trade was usually by barter.

Major business was conducted in houses, shops and stores situated inside the market or inside the city. Such was the case in the big cities of the Sudan and the Sahel.

Markets and fairs were held on a regular basis, every three, five or eight days and attracted a vast crowd of traders, customers and all sorts of onlookers. The market was in effect a show, a festival, a place of popular culture where ideas were exchanged. Order prevailed there under the watchful eye of an agent of the powers that be who saw to the policing of the market and monitored transactions and weights and measures and raised the taxes due.

The big markets were to found above all in the Sudan-Sahel area, in the staging posts or termini of the principal routes (Awdaghust, Ghana, Walāta, Timbuktu, Gao, Tadmekka, Takedda) and in their counterparts in the Sudan (Silla, Niani, Dia, Gundiuru, Bure, Katsina, Kano). Further south, on the border between the savannah and the forest, there were the markets at Oyo, Ife, Benin and Bida (Nupe) and, in the forest, Bitu or Begho, and the mining centres in Akan lands. The Portuguese navigators in the second half of the fifteenth century found markets of all sizes along the Atlantic coast from the mouth of the Senegal to that of the Niger. They recorded intense business activity in the valley of the Gambia, in Sierra Leone, on the Gold Coast, along the lagoons and in the kingdom of Benin. These markets, often held regularly, were great centres where people from the surrounding areas came to exchange their products, especially gold and spices, which would later encourage the establishment of European trading posts along the coast.

What was generally being sold in these African markets? In addition to local products, long-distance international trade brought products from the Mediterranean, Europe, the Maghrib, the Orient, the Sahara and the whole of the West African hinterland. It was based above all on two main products: salt and gold. Rock salt, the most sought-after, came from mines in the Sahara. Awlil, on the coast of Mauritania, was being worked before the eleventh century. Idjil and Teghazza provided most of the output in the twelfth to fifteenth centuries. The mines in Kāwār served the countries north-east of Gao and above all the Hausa cities and Kānem-Bornu. Rock salt, carried in bars by special 'salt'caravans (known as the *azalai*) by the Berabiche and Messufa tribes, supplied all of West Africa along the trans-Saharan routes. Sea salt, exploited on the Atlantic coast, was not so easy to transport and preserve. Trade in sea salt was not as widely developed as that of Saharan salt and seems not to have gone far beyond the coastal areas.

The gold of the Sudan was the chief object of trade with foreigners in Africa during the medieval period. From a very early date it attracted Berber–Arab traders; some writers even believed that it grew like plants in Ghana! West Africa was indeed rich in gold. The best known mines were deep inside the Sudan. The mines at Bambuk and Falémé (Galam) provided powder (*tibar*), those at Bure, Lobi and Wassulu excellent quality nuggets. From the Akan lands, which the *Tā'rīkhs* call 'Bitu', and from Timbuktu, came quantities of gold, which in the fifteenth century would finally cause the European navigators to establish themselves on the coast known as the 'Gold Coast'. African mines thus supplied significant quantities of gold to world trade.

European historians such as Gautier, Braudel and Heers have stressed the role of gold from the Sudan in the world economy in the fourteenth to sixteenth centuries, before the discovery of the mines in America. Gold was the chief wealth of the Sudan; cities such as Ghana, Timbuktu, Jenne and Gao owed their reputation to it. The cities of the Maghrib, Italian cities (Genoa, Pisa, Milan, Venice), the coastal areas of Spain and Portugal, in particular the island of Majorca, and the Muslim East (Egypt) took the bulk of the trade in Sudanese gold. The Sudan thus contributed to the Renaissance of Europe. West Africa also exported slaves, cereals, dried fish, shea nuts, cotton goods (especially from the Hausa cities), spices, ivory and kola nuts from the forest zone.

From the north came the bulk of the goods exchanged: fabrics of all sorts (Venetian and Genoese cloths, haberdashery, women's mantles, and other textiles from the Maghrib), metals (copper, Saharan silver, tin, iron), weapons (spears, daggers, swords), jewellery, glass goods, beads, cowries, paper, books, items of ironmongery and everyday life. In addition, there were the highly sought-after Arabian horses and camels from the oases and the Sahel. By the mid-fifteenth century, European trade on the Atlantic coast was carrying more or less the same range of goods, but above all fabrics, metal items, pieces of jewellery, beads, ironmongery, in short the whole range of cheap trade goods.

Overall, the balance was in deficit for West Africa, which consumed more than it exported. Trade was based on raw materials and not on local production, which at the time was essentially rural. Outside a few cities such as Timbuktu, Kano or Bida (Nupé), where local craftware had reached a high level of productivity, it seems that trade in the period from the seventh to the fifteenth century had not led to economic and technological development comparable to that of Europe over the same period. While it had not produced major transformations in the productive apparatus, it had on the other hand led to major changes in the natural and cultural environment of West Africa. It was through trade that Islam became established all over the Sudan and the Sahel and that Africa opened up to the world of the Mediterranean and Europe as a key economic partner.

The cities

One of the consequences of the development of trade was the emergence of cities and urban living throughout the area. From the fringes of the Sahara to the countries of the Gulf of Benin, cities with several thousand inhabitants arose everywhere along the main trade routes. In 1324, *Mansa* Mūsā, the emperor of Mali, even told his hosts in Cairo that his empire contained 400 cities (see Plate 259)!

Timbuktu, Jenne, Benin and Kano, great markets or political capitals, may be taken as typical cities. Each had a population of several thousand: almost 100,000 for Timbuktu in the sixteenth century,[3] 30,000–40,000 for Jenne and as many for Benin in the fifteenth century (see Plate 34).

Timbuktu, like other cities in the Sudan and the Sahel, had a cosmopolitan and multiracial population, living solely on trade and related activities. Situated on the River Niger, and so serving as the port for the Sahara, it was a real commercial metropolis with its markets and its many mosques, including the two most famous ones, the Jingereber and the Sankore. Its fine houses with terraces and often with upper storeys reveal a beautiful style of Sudanese architecture. Timbuktu was a religious and intellectual capital and, as such, at the end of the fifteenth century, brought together famous teachers and a host of students from every ethnic group and every race. Jenne on the Bani–Niger, its twin to the south, in contact with the markets of the savannah and the forest and with the gold mines in Mande and the interior, was densely populated and inherited the cultural tradition of Jenne–Jeno, the oldest known city in the region before the Christian era.[4] Converted to Islam in the fourteenth century, Jenne was embellished with the finest architectural jewel of the Sudanese style, the famous mosque of Prince Koï Komboro. Like Timbuktu, it was not built on a geometric plan. The houses, close together, separated by twisting lanes and lacking much in the way of hygienic conveniences, were built in terraces with a hall and inner court.

Benin, visited by Portuguese navigators in the fifteenth century, had an altogether different appearance. Built on a rectangular plan, surrounded by walls open at the ends of the four great boulevards that crossed at right angles, the city of Benin, the political capital of the kingdom, looked almost modern. European visitors were greatly struck by the layout of the houses along streets bordered by trees, the decorations and architectural structure of the royal palace and the homes of the aristocracy, and the exceptional cleanliness of the city. As for Kano, founded in the late eleventh century, it grew through its domination of neighbouring villages. With a long, high wall pierced by seven gates, the palace (*gida*), enlarged at the end of the fifteenth century by King Rimfa, and its numerous mosques, Kano became the most important political and Islamic capital of Hausaland. As the great commercial meeting point between the northern Sahel, Bornu-Kanem and above all Nupe and Yorubaland, its market centralized and distributed the products of every region. It exported most of its large output of cotton goods, which were usually indigo-dyed, to the north. It was home to true city dwellers, who lived by trade, crafts and market gardening in the neighbouring suburbs.

These few examples of urban development are the signs of change and movement in West African societies from perhaps before the seventh century.

NOTES

1 Ironworking was mastered in West Africa before the fifth century (see Plates 261, 262). Historians cite iron as being imported (from Meröe in the fourth century BC or from Phoenician North Africa before or after AD) or mined locally from a continent rich in iron.

2 According to some writers, the plantain banana was introduced from Asia to the east coast of Africa at the beginning of the medieval period. It reached the forest and then West Africa, where it was called the banana well before the introduction of another species by the Portuguese at the beginning of the sixteenth century (Mauny, 1961; Marees, 1605).

3 Sékéné Mody Cissoko gives this estimate, which is much higher than the 25,000 inhabitants given by R. Mauny in *Tableau géographique*, p. 497.

4 According to two American archaeologists, Roderick J. and Susan K. McIntosh in *Afrique Histoire*, 7, 1983, Jenne–(Jeno) goes back to the third century BC and flourished in the seventh century AD.

BIBLIOGRAPHY

(See Chapter 32.3.)

32.3
SOCIETIES AND POLITICAL STRUCTURES

Sékéné Mody Cissoko

THE SOCIETIES

Like the peoples, the societies varied greatly in time and space. The peoples of the Sahel and the Sudan, all affected by economic exchanges which often altered social relations and encouraged mixing and social integration, did not have the same appearance as the southern and forest peoples, who were more independent and integrated into family and tribal-type structures.

From this time, it is possible to speak of people of millet (savannah) and people of yams (in the south) in terms of their life-styles and their cultures. Within each zone, the societies had different levels of development. In Timbuktu and Jenne, a commercial or intellectual bourgeoisie open to the world was superimposed on peasant communities with age-old traditions and ways of life unchanged for centuries. Overall, however, apart from a few small isolated groups living since Palaeolithic times by hunting, fishing and cultivation, the West African population was made up of peasant farmers living in a subsistence economy in villages, with little division of labour.

The family in the broad sense, the clan or the tribe, embraced people with a common ancestor, real or legendary. The clan, with its name, its piece of land and its own organization, was the key feature of most societies. It was supposed to ensure its members' safety and what they needed to survive. Mandingo oral traditions place the birth of the Keita, Konate (Mansaring), Soussoukho-Doumbia (Boula), Traore and Camara clans before Sundiata (thirteenth century). Society in the time of the empire of Ghana, the oldest one known, was already deeply clan-based with princely clans (Wague) and servile ones (Kussa). This type of organization covered the whole of the western Sudan even after the establishment of Islam. The clan, headed by its elder in a village which broke up into daughter villages, often covered a large area, big enough to be a potential centre of political power. The clans or sub-clans also freed a large number of their members with the continuous emigration of peoples. Thus by the fifteenth and sixteenth centuries, some clan names no longer corresponded to a real community but a remote or fictional one. The same was true of the tribes, very much alive in the Sahel and forest zones where the communities retained their cohesion, better to protect themselves against the environment and their neighbours. Whatever the community under consideration, clan or tribe, the striking feature is how strongly structured it was and how powerful the kinship ties binding the members together were. Thus the privilege of age gave power to the elders and priority to the oldest (fathers, elder brothers) while dividing the group into age groups. These, from the oldest to the youngest, had their own organization, with their leaders and rules, and took on some specific tasks related to the work and safety of the free community.

Communal society evolved during the period into a hierarchical society and lost some of its coherence and cohesion in many parts of the western Sudan. The technological revolution, following the appearance of iron and other metals, accelerated the division of labour and the appearance of specific social strata in all the activities of the community. Thus the increase in the size of the rural population, and therefore of needs, the opening up of villages to commercial exchanges, the migration of peoples over the centuries and inter-ethnic mixing led to profound social changes. The rural communal society weakened, and the dominant relations between men ceased to be those of blood and a common ancestor.

In the Sudan–Sahel zone, by the end of the fifteenth century, the differentiated society predominated, ordered almost in a hierarchy according to the status of the individuals, their property and their social activities. The new hierarchical society headed the underlying community, became stronger and took on power like that of a state.

Men were thus ranked in three categories by status: the free, the unfree and the craftsmen, whether into organized castes or not. Free men seem to have formed the majority of the population, especially in the southern or forest areas. Domestic slavery appears to have been dominant and slaves by birth or house slaves enjoyed almost the same rights as free men. In Mali and Songhay, slaves generally lived in village communities and enjoyed a degree of freedom in return for the payment of levies on their output. In Benin, where human sacrifice was an everyday practice, the victims came from the then very numerous royal slaves. In this area, as far as the lands of the Yoruba and Akan where many craft workers lived (weavers, smiths, jewellers, potters, artists of various sorts), the notion of caste was unknown, unlike the Sudan and the Sahel, where it appeared at a date previous to our period. Everyone carrying on a specialized activity or a craft belonged to an endogamous but not untouchable caste. Smiths and musicians (griots and genealogists) enjoyed great influence and performed economic, political and social functions out of all proportion to their numbers, especially in the monarchical societies. The opening of long-distance inter-regional and trans-Saharan trade made possible the formation of a commercial and intellectual aristocracy and led to the emergence of a whole range of craftsmen in all urban activities – weavers, dyers, jewellers, cobblers, potters, carpenters, smiths, fishermen, carriers, weighers, butchers and so on – a whole detribalized world tied into the market and trade economy.

Some social strata, who had early specialized in business, even ended up forming quasi-ethnic trading groups, such as the Wakore (Soninke) and the Wangara (Malinke), terms used to describe any trader in the Sudan. The political aristocracy appeared with the birth of states. The new political formations were the work of the dominant clans, both noble and slave or caste ones. The new aristocracy lacked a monopoly over the land, which remained communal property but it drew its power, wealth and influence from the exercise of government. In the Hausa and Yoruba cities, as in the Sudanese empires, this aristocracy remained open to the elite of other social strata since government, despite appearances, had not wholly lost its community character.

THE POLITICAL STRUCTURES

The communal society with its gerontocratic organization was headed by the council of elders, led by the patriarch of the clan or tribe. The council was made up of the chiefs (elders) of the various clan or village lineages and deliberated on all the problems of the group. It took its decisions by consensus and those decisions were carried out by the age-groups.

With the appearance of the new differentiated and hierarchical society, relations between men were governed by objective rules and subordinate to a strict authority. Everywhere in West Africa, state-type powers appeared overlying societies and countries. All across West Africa, from the Sudanese empires (Ghana, Mali, Songhay, Mosi) to the Senegambian kingdoms (Takrūr, Jolof, Serer) and the Hausa and Yoruba city states, states were formed that organized people and territories. Writers in this period give a host of details about the Sudanese empires which were federations or confederations of kingdoms under the leadership of a warrior ethnic group united around a dominant clan. The king of Mali or the *naba* of the Mosi was an almost sacred figure, surrounded by a court with strict protocol. Hereditary power in a princely lineage drew its legitimacy from ancestral traditions and rarely from force of arms. The ruler was assisted by a royal council made up of princes but also including leaders of the captives, free men, castes (griots), and some tributary communities.

The council guided the king, acted as judge at every level, and supervised the government responsible for managing affairs. In Ghana and Mali, the king entrusted government responsibility to a prime minister (*vizier*) aided by numerous dignitaries heading departments including finance, the army, foreigners, the palace, and so on. The empire was divided into conquered provinces and tributary kingdoms. The former were governed by governors (the Mandingo and Songhay *farin* or *farba*) appointed by the ruler. The latter retained their autonomy under the leadership of their legitimate dynasty but had to pay tribute in kind and provide quotas of soldiers. In the large Islamic trading cities such as Timbuktu, Jenne and Walata, the *qāḍī* dispensed justice and enjoyed great and unchallenged prestige.

The state extracted significant resources from customs, with import and export duties being paid at the border. To a large extent, the development of the Sudanese states depended on each country's resources. Taxes on certain products and in particular gold and salt, war booty, a variety of tributes, the products of the royal domains, gifts, slaves, and so on, gave a solid base to royal power, which usually maintained an administration, a numerous clientele and a sizeable army. Alongside the royal guard, some states, such as Mali and Songhay, maintained standing armies of several thousand men in some provinces (see Plate 15). But the army was only brought together in large numbers in the event of war; then it would be made up not simply of the royal troops but above all of quotas supplied by the tributary princes. The Sudanese state covered very considerable areas. In the fourteenth century the empire of Mali stretched from the Atlantic Ocean (Senegal) to Gao (see Map 30). Thus geography determined that it should be highly decentralized into a sort of federation of various ethnic groups, each enjoying real autonomy. Among the Hausa, the state was smaller in size, political unity having never been achieved over the whole country. The city, surrounded by a fortress, formed the heart of power by the fourteenth century. Thus the kingdom, including the city and the surrounding villages, was under the leadership of a king (*sarki*) elected by the notables of the various communities. The *sarki* entrusted the running of the country to a prime minister (*galadima*) assisted by the leading individuals responsible for the administration, the army, finance, religion, and so on. Power was by nature moderated and checked by the local aristocracy.

This pattern resembled that of the Yoruba cities, where power retained a degree of democracy. It was actually a group of almost autonomous towns that formed the kingdom of Oyo, the country's leading political unit. Each town and its surrounding area was governed by a senate (*bale*) whose members, co-opted from the urban bourgeoisie, monitored the administrators, who worked in pairs. The *bale* was responsible to the people to whom it rendered account. At the head of the kingdom, the king of Oyo (*alafin* of Oyo) was elected by the council of state of seven members (the *Oyo-mesi*), who were not nobles but were the real power holders, even capable of ordering a ruler to commit suicide.

Unlike the Yoruba manner of ruling, Benin in the twelfth to the fifteenth century had an absolute monarchy. The king (*oba*) was deified and lived according to a mystical ritual, with human sacrifice. He was surrounded by an aristocracy of hereditary grand counsellors (the *orizama*) and numerous dignitaries representing the various territorial communities, but chosen by him and dependent on his will (see Plates 267–269).

Apart from this unique case, everywhere all over West Africa, power was shared to a greater or lesser extent between the ruler and the heads of the various communities. Geographical conditions, the low level of economic and technological development and the sense of community tempered social differentiation, explaining why power was relatively decentralized and moderate. In sum, West Africa experienced, with varying degrees of success, every form of state, from patriarchal chieftaincy to municipal democracy.

BIBLIOGRAPHY (Chapters 32.1–32.3)

ADAMU, M. 1984. The Hausa and the Neighbours in Central Sudan. In: *General History of Africa*, UNESCO, California, Vol. IV, pp. 266–300.

ADDE. 1972. *La croissance urbaine en Afrique noire* (CNRS), Paris.
Atlas Jeune Afrique. 1973. Le continent africain. Paris.
AL-BAKRĪ, ABŪ 'UBAYD ALLĀH. 1857. *Kitāb al-Masālik wa l-Mamālik* (Book of the Pathways and Kingdoms). Portion of Arabic text ed. with French trans., *Description de l'Afrique septentrionale*, by W. M. de Slane, Algiers 1857; repr. of French text, Adrien Maisonneuve publ., Paris 1965.
BOAHEN, A. A. 1974. Who are the Akan? In: *Bonduku Seminar Papers*.
BOHANNAN, P.; DALTON, C. 1962. *Markets in Africa*. Illinois.
BOVILL, E. W. 1933. *Caravans of the Old Sahara: An Introduction to the History of Western Sudan*. London.
——. 1958. *The Golden Trade of the Moors*. OUP, Oxford.
BRAUDEL, F. 1946. 'Monnaies et civilisation: de l'or du Soudan à l'argent d'Amérique', *Annales ESC*, I. Paris.
CAHIER AFRIQUE NOIRE' 5, 1982. Histoire des villes et des sociétés urbaines en Afrique noire: les villes précoloniales. Paris.
CISSÉ, Y. T.; KAMISSOKO, W. 1988. *La grande geste du Mali, des origines à la fondation de l'empire*. Paris.
CISSOKO, S. M. 1975. *Tombouctou et l'empire songhay: épanouissement du Soudan nigérien aux XVe–XVIe siècles* (NEA) pp. 20–22. Paris.
CROWDER, M. 1962. *The History of Nigeria*. London.
CROWDER, M.; AJAYI, J. F. A. (eds) 1971. *The History of West Africa*. London.
CUOQ, J. 1975. *Recueil des sources arabes concernant le Bilād al-Sūdān* (CNRS). Paris.
DESCHAMPS, H. *Les institutions politiques en Afrique*. Collection 'Que sais-je?', No. 549, Paris.
DIAGNE, P. 1967. *Pouvoir politique traditionnel en Afrique occidentale*. Présence africaine. Paris.
——. 1981. *Le concept du pouvoir en Afrique*, UNESCO.
DIOP, C. A. 1960. *Afrique noire précoloniale*. Présence africaine. Paris.
FERNANDES, V. 1940; 1951. *O manuscrito Valentim Fernandes*, ed. by the Academia portuguesa de história, Lisbon 1940. Portuguese text ed. with French trans. by T. MONOD, A. TEIXEIRA DA MOTA, R. MAUNY, *Description de la côte occidentale d'Afrique, 1506–1510*, Centro de estudios da Guiné Portuguesa, Bissau, No. II, 1951.
FORTES, M.; EVANS-PRITCHARD, E. 1947. *African Political Systems*. Oxford University Press. Repr. London/New York 1987.
GAUTIER, E. F. 1935. 'Le problème de l'or au Moyen Âge', *Annales d'histoire économique et sociale*. Paris.
GENERAL HISTORY OF AFRICA, UNESCO, California, Vol. IV: 1984. Vol. III: 1988.
GOMES EANES DE AZURARA. *Crónica do descobrimento e conquista de Guiné* (1453). (Chronicle of the Discovery and Conquest of Guinea). Portuguese text: Santarém ed., Paris 1841; J. de Bragança ed., Oporto (Pōrto) 1937; A. J. Dinis Días ed., Lisbon 1949; Reis Brasil ed., Lisbon 1989. English trans. in G. R. Crone, *The voyages of Cadamosto, and other documents on Western Africa in the Second Half of the Fifteenth Century*. Hakluyt Society, London, 1937.
GRAY, R.; BIRMINGHAM, D. 1970. *Precolonial African Trade*. Oxford University Press.
HEERS, J. 1958. 'Le Sahara et le commerce méditerranéen à la fin du Moyen Age', *Annales de l'Institut d'Etudes Orientales*, No. XVI. Paris.
HERODOTUS. *Histories*. Book IV, § 183. (Loeb edn of the Greek text with English trans.: A. D. Godley, 4 vols. London/Harvard 1921–1924.)
IBN BAṬṬŪṬA. 1853–1859. *Riḥla* ('Journey'; full medieval Arabic title: *Tuḥfat al-Nuẓẓār fī 'Ajā'ib al-Amṣār*, 'Gift unto the Observers concerning the Marvels of the Lands'). First edn of Arabic text with French trans. by C. Défrémėry and B. R. Sanguinetti, 4 vols. Paris 1853–1859. English trans. by H. A. R. Gibb, *The Travels of Ibn Baṭṭūṭa*, Hakluyt Society, Cambridge, 1956–1971. Arabic text only: *Riḥla Ibn Baṭṭūṭa*, ed. by Ṭalāl Ḥarb, Dār al-Kutub al-'Ilmiyya, Beirut 1992.
IBN ḤAWQAL. 1842; 1873; 1938; 1965. *Kitāb Ṣūrat al-Arḍ* (Book of the Figure of the Earth). Arabic text edn. by M. J. De Goeje (1873), Leiden; and J. H. Kramers (1938), Leiden. Partial French trans. by Baron William MacGuckin de Slane, *Description de l'Afrique*, Paris 1842; full French trans. by J. H. Kramers and G. Wiet, *Configuration de la Terre*, Paris 1965.
IBN KHALDŪN. 1868 edn. *Kitāb al-'Ibar* ('Book of Admonition' = 'Universal History'). Arabic text, 7 vols, Būlāq, 1868; Beirut, 1958. Partial French trans., 4 vols, by W. M. de Slane, *Histoire des Berbères et des dynasties musulmanes de l'Afrique septentrionale*, Algiers, 1852–1856; repr. Paris 1925–1926. New complete French trans., 7 vols. Beirut 1956–1959.
KA'TI, MAHMUD. 1913–1914; 1964; 1981. *Tārīkh al-Fattāsh* (Chronicle of the Investigator). First edn of Arabic text with French trans. by O. Houdas and M. Delafosse, Paris 1913– 1914; repr. with rev., Paris 1964; UNESCO repr. of first edn, Maisonneuve, Paris 1981.
KI ZERBO, J. 1972. *Histoire de l'Afrique noire*, pp. 161–164, Hatier, Paris.
LA CHAPELLE, F. DE. 1969. Esquisse d'une histoire du Sahara occidental, *Hespéris*, X. Paris.
LOMBARD, J. 1965. *Structures de type féodal en Afrique noire*. Paris.
MARÉES, P. DE. 1605. *Description et récit historique du riche Royaume d'Or de Guinée*. Amsterdam.
MAUNY, R. 1961. *Tableau géographique de l'Ouest africain au Moyen Âge* (Mémoire, IFAN). Paris.
MONOT, T. 1939. *Contribution à l'étude du Sahara occidental*. Paris.
MONTEIL, C. 1929. Les Empires du Mali, *BCHS AOF*, XII. Dakar.
——. 1951. Problèmes du Soudan occidental: juifs et judaisés. *Hespéris*, XXXVIII. Paris.
PACHECO PEREIRA, D. 1898. *Esmeraldo de Situ Orbis* (The Emerald, concerning the Situation of the World). Sixteenth-century. Portuguese text ed. by R. E. de Azevedo, Lisbon, other Portuguese editions: A. da Epiphanio da Silva Dias, Lisbon 1905; D. Peres, Lisbon 1954. Portuguese text ed. with English. tr. by G. H. T. Kimble, Hakluyt Society, London 1937. French trans. by R. Mauny, Bissau, Publicações do Centro de estudos da Guiné Portuguesa, No. XIX, 1956.
PALAU MARTÍ, M. 1964. *Le roi dieu du Bénin*. Paris.
PERÈS, H. 1937. Relations entre le Tafilelt et le Soudan . . . du XIIIe au XIVe siècle. In: *Mélanges géographique et oriental*. Tours, pp. 409–414.
ROBERT, D. S.; DEVISSE, J. 1970. *Tegdaoust. I. Recherches sur aoudaghost*. Paris, Vol. 1.
RODERICK, J.; MCINTOSH, S. K. 1983. In: *Afrique, Histoire*, 7. Paris.
RYDER, A. F. C. 1984. From the Volta to Cameroon. In: *General History of Africa*, UNESCO, California, Vol. IV, pp. 339–370.
AL-'UMARĪ, IBN FAḌL ALLĀH. 1924. *Masālik al-Abṣār fī Mamālik al-Amṣār* (Glances of the Eyes throughout the Districts of the Lands); Arabic text, Cairo 1924. French trans. by M. Gaudefroy-Demombynes, *L'Afrique moins l'Egypte*, Paris 1927.

32.4
RELIGIONS

32.4.1
TRADITIONAL AFRICAN RELIGIONS

Isaac Adeagbo Akinjogbin

In most West African communities, religion permeated all aspects of societal activities, be it politics, economics, interpersonal relationships and even food. Births and burials were eminently religious affairs. In order, therefore, to understand the West African community, one had to understand its religious beliefs and practices.

Between AD 600 and 1500, three religious practices existed in West Africa. The first was traditional African religion (TAR), which was indigenous and based on the total historical and philosophical experiences of West Africans. The second was Islam, which was introduced in the eleventh century AD. From then, through the pious activities of rulers of Sudanese states, particularly those of Mali, Songhay and Kānem, Islam was to blossom into a major socio-political force in West Africa by the sixteenth century AD. The third religious practice was Christianity, introduced five centuries after Islam. Since the introduction of the latter two religions the religious experiences of West African communities were then characterized by intense interactions between TAR and foreign religions (Greenberg, 1946; Nadel, 1970). The former had often tended to influence the latter, thus leading to revivalist movements in the latter from time to time (Hiskett, 1984). This section will deal with the TAR first because it continued to influence the lives of most West Africans; and second, in order to understand the nature of its beliefs.

TAR has often been regarded as the lowest form of religion (P'Bitek, 1970) and has been described in such derogatory terms as 'animism', 'paganism', 'fetishism' or 'voodooism'. Some say these could be described only as 'mysteries' rather than religions. Indeed, both Muslim and Christian missionaries would contend that until the introduction of their religions, West Africans had no so-called 'proper' religion of their own.

The denigration of TAR has been based on the observation that it featured man-made religious objects such as amulets, mascots, talismans, charms and such-like objects and that it practised rituals that were repulsive to human dignity (Adediran 'Biodun, 1985). What is often overlooked, however, is that most world religions at one stage or another have incorporated such man-made objects and practised such repulsive rituals. TAR indeed makes a distinction between such ritual objects and the deities worshipped. Among the Akan, for example, *Suman* (Charm) is not the same as *Obosom* (Deity) nor is *Ebo* (Sacrifice) among the Yoruba the same as *òrìsà* (Deity). The man-made objects and rituals were designed either to help the worshippers' concentration or to aid in the propitiation of the deity, which was the main object of worship.

In spite of the multiplicity of intercessionary deities, West Africans were not polytheistic. Throughout West Africa, the concept of a supreme being, who was above all and controlled all, was common and universal (Oduyoye, 1983). He was worshipped as the almighty creator of all things (including the intercessory deities), the giver of all lives, the controller of all destinies and the ultimate judge of human actions, since he saw and knew all things. Generally, no physical representation of him was included in the local pantheons where the deities were collected, because He was regarded as lying beyond the understanding of human beings.

However, the assumption should not be that the concepts of monotheism across West Africa were uniform. They could not be, since they were not introduced from any single source; rather, what appears clear was that the concepts were *similar* within each language group, with each developing its own particular concept from its own historical experience and world view. The fact that these concepts were recorded by modern scholars does not necessarily mean that modern scholars invented the words. For instance, Bolaji Idowu wrote on *Olodumare*, the Yoruba High God, in the 1950s. This does not mean that Bolaji Idowu invented either the word or the concept. The Spanish missionaries who visited the Aja Coast (modern Republic of Benin) in the late fifteenth and early sixteenth centuries recorded the people's concept of monotheism and published their findings in a book called *Doctrina Christiana*. A study of John Mbiti's works would suggest that such similarity went across sub-Saharan Africa. In spite of such similarities, however, the supreme being was given different names in different parts of West Africa (Imasogie, 1985; Mbiti, 1977). Thus in Mende he was called Ngewe or Leve (supreme creator).

Tenda	*Hounnounga*	(The unknown)
Akan	*Onyame*	(The supreme being)
Ewe	*Mawu-se*	(God – The supreme God)
Gun	*Mawu/Lisa*	(The supreme creator)
Yoruba	*Olodumare*	(Almighty)
Edo	*Osanobua*	(Creator of the world)
Urhobo	*Oghene*	(Lord of all)
Nupe	*Tsoci*	(The owner of us, our lord)
Tiv	*Aondo Gba Tar*	(God, the carpenter)
Yako	*Ubasi*	(Creator)
Bamum	*Nyinyi*	(The omnipresent)
Igbo	*Chineke Chukwu*	(Creator – great spirit)
Dogon	*Amma*	(Supreme being)
Songhai	*Irkoy*	(The almighty)
Hausa	*Ubangiji*	
Kpelle	*Gerze*	
Gbauda	*Ngala*	
Maman	*Wala*	
Kisi	*Hala*	

It is noteworthy that the local name by which the supreme being was known was always in the singular and was not a generic term. He had no images or visible representations, because he was too mighty for any human mind to contemplate. His power was such that ordinary mortals could not approach him directly, only through intermediaries.

These intermediaries were the deities. They were believed to be especially created by God Almighty as messengers and special assistants. This is probably one feature that makes TAR distinct from other major world religions. The deities included ancestral spirits and supernatural beings. There were also those associated with environmental features such as hills, rivers and trees, which were regarded as dwelling places of deities. Similarly, some plants and animals which played prominent roles in the historical development of the community were regarded as totems or emblems with which a sacred relationship was forged.

This is why the list of West African deities is not fixed; nor are there necessarily the same deities to be found in different localities. The historical experiences of people in various localities dictated the deities that existed in such localities. The general conception was that all things, animate and inanimate, were endowed with spirits that could communicate with God. If certain objects were exceptional for their size (such as trees, rivers, rocks or mountains, or if particular human beings were exceptionally endowed with uncommon charismatic attributes, then these were usually credited with an unusual portion of God's spiritual gift. Examples abound all over West Africa where large rivers – Gambia, Senegal, Niger, Volta, Mano, Oueme, Ogun, Osun, Benue and so on – were venerated by peoples through whose territories they passed primarily because they supported life: through agriculture, food (fish), transportation and so on. Similarly, rocks and hills, such as Futa Jallon, Atakora, Dala and Adamawa, were deified for the protective roles they played in times of war. The peoples of the West African middle zone, finding the rugged terrain of the region adequate for refuge from their bellicose northern and southern neighbours, created a large number of hill-related deities which still exist today among such people as the Dagomba, Mosi, Tallensi, Borgu, Jukun and Tiv. In the same way, a large number of local heroes and heroines were to be found among the pantheons of various peoples ranging from eponymous founders like Bayajida (Hausa), Oduduwa (Yoruba) to political initiators like Osei Tutu (Asante) and Sango (Yoruba). This proliferation of gods and goddesses will tend to suggest that West African peoples solved similar problems with the use of similar environmental features without one necessarily learning from the other (Akinjogbin, 1978).

There were other spirits or mystical powers which were recognized and reckoned with in the scheme of things. These included agents of witchcraft, magic and sorcery. Because of these, people took advice from diviners to help them deal with urgent problems. In addition, there were charms, amulets and so on which were used for protective and offensive purposes. Finally, TAR features elaborate rituals, sacrifices and ceremonies which were closely connected with various aspects of life – agriculture, child bearing, treatment of diseases, prevention of calamities and so on. In this wise, there was a link between religion and science. Often, the local priest was a compendium of knowledge about the physical, economic and human geography of his community. This knowledge, believed to have been conferred on him by the gods, he would put at the disposal of the community after adequate consultation with the gods. In this wise the deities were benevolent. For they existed for the peaceful ordering of the society.

Although TAR dealt primarily with the here and the now, it none the less reflected the quest of West Africans to comprehend the forces of nature that control them as all the other world religions did. This led to an attempt to understand the unknown and the hereafter. This quest in turn gave rise to the art of geomancy practised across West Africa (Trantman, 1939; Bascom, 1966; Abimbola, 1976). Even though the details differed from one locality to another, the practices which involved divination through kola nuts, cowrie shells, palm nuts or sand, were similar, giving the impression that they originated from a common source. Known as *Ifa* among the Yoruba, *Afa* among the Nupe, *Fa* among the *Fon*, *Ipe* among the Obudu of south- east Nigeria, and *Agbigba* among the Cross River peoples of Nigeria, geomancy developed into a highly organized system of education covering a host of disciplines such as history, mathematics, theology, agriculture, psychology, physical sciences, physiology, medicine and philosophy, designed to solve emerging problems that might confront individuals or the community at large (Abimbola, 1968; Opeola, 1988).

Although the indigenous religious practices in West Africa have been described as 'traditional', they were not static. On the other hand, they incorporated considerable changes in accordance with the historical experiences of the various peoples. The introduction of Islam and Christianity, for instance, had far-reaching influences on the indigenous religions, just as these in turn influenced local practice of these foreign religions. The story during the period under consideration was one of accommodation and conflict. For instance, while by the end of the eleventh century AD Islam had made an appreciable success in West Africa, having been adopted by the ruling dynasty of Gao, one of the major trading centres, it was clear to the immigrant merchants who brought Islam to West Africa that they had to adapt the religion to local practices (Hiskett, 1984). This led to religious syncretism, which occasioned frequent *jihāds* to purify Islamic practice in West Africa but which overall enhanced the prestige of the religion and contributed to its widespread diffusion, particularly in the savannah region by AD 1600. With the expansion of commercial activities and the establishment of large imperial frameworks, Muslim clerics enjoyed widespread patronage, and Islamic practices were commonly adopted, even though, in most cases, they were also adapted to suit local situations. On the other hand, Christianity, introduced in the last quarter of the fifteenth century, was less tolerant of the indigenous religious practices of the peoples of West Africa. It totally rejected attempts by the local peoples to adapt the new religion to their own traditional practices. This resulted in the failure of the early attempts to implant Christianity in West Africa (Ryder, 1969), at a time when foreign and indigenous Muslim clerics were making rapid progress at Islamization.

BIBLIOGRAPHY

(See Chapter 32.5.)

32.4.2
ISLAM AND CHRISTIANITY

Sékéné Mody Cissoko

Medieval West Africa was no stranger to the great movements taking place at that time in Asia and Europe. Its relative isolation was broken in the eleventh century by the arrival of Islam, which had already conquered the entire north of the continent, from Egypt to the Atlantic Ocean.[1] In the fifteenth and sixteenth centuries, the Portuguese caravels brought Christianity although this did not take hold. Thus, in some regions, traditional cultures absorbed the new monotheistic and universalist beliefs and formed a symbiosis with them in a highly original syncretism.

Islam reached the Sahara as early as 666 with the expedition of 'Uqba ibn Nāfi' in the Fezzān and Kāwār, but would have to wait until the ninth and tenth centuries for its real introduction to the western Sudan that is, Sudan–Sahel. Trade across the Sahara and travellers of all sorts and every ethnic extraction brought Islam further into West Africa every year, and by the end of the period under consideration (sixteenth century) it had even reached some forest and coastal regions. It thus became a reality in Africa, and West Africa became part of the world of Islam.

From the Senegambian coast to Lake Chad, from the Sahel to Yorubaland, Islam took hold by adapting to traditional society and beliefs. The great imperial monarchies (Mali and Songhay), the Takrūr and north Hausa aristocracies, to mention but a few, were converted and maintained close relations (economic, religious and cultural exchanges, migrations) with the Islamic and Afro-Asian world. For instance, every year thousands of African pilgrims visited Mecca, Egypt and the Nilotic Sudan. Arab Muslim intellectuals, *sharīfs* and entrepreneurs also came to West Africa, and some settled there permanently. It was above all with the Berber and Arab Maghrib that links in all fields were most intense, and the two regions even constituted an African Islamic unit.

Thus West African Islam took on the features of urban, elitist Islam. It was established in the cities of the Sahel (Chinguetti, Waddan, Timbuktu, Gao, Agadir and Tadmekka) and Sudan (Jenne, Dia, Niani, Silla, Gonjour, Kano, and Katsina), which were the area's major trade centres. It also contributed to the development of Sudanese town planning, characterized by densely populated towns with storeyed houses, monuments such as mosques (like the Sankore *djinguereber* in Timbuktu, see Plate 34) and the tombs of *askiyas* (kings) in Gao, built in the approximate shape of pyramids (Sudanese style), which survive in contemporary architecture.

Islam brought writing and Islamic science and helped to construct a new African society. Berber, Arab and especially Black African intellectuals spread the new religion, not through *jihād*, or holy war but by converting the political and merchant elite. Schools played an important role and made genuine intellectual development possible in the Sudan–Sahel region. Each 'marabout' (divine) had a Qur'ānic school where the basics of Arabic and the Qur'ān were taught. Some cities, such as Walata, Jenne and above all Timbuktu, opened what amounted to universities, the one in Timbuktu being the most famous (Cissoko, 1996). Besides the 150 to 180 Qur'ānic schools in the city, the Sankore mosque, in the north-east, attracted thousands of students in the sixteenth century around well-known teachers such as Muḥammad Bagayokho, the *qāḍī-s* 'Umar and Muḥammad Akit, Anda Ag Muḥammad, the great scholar Aḥmad Bābā (Hunwick, 1980, 1981), and so on.

The subjects taught included the classic sciences of Islam (theology land law) and Arabic language and literature, dialectics, astronomy, medicine, history and so forth. Illustrious teachers produced remarkable works well up to the standard of the great doctors of eastern Islam. A number of the works of Aḥmad Bābā (late sixteenth century) have now been recovered, and he appears to have been the greatest scholar of his time, as much for his vast erudition (grammar, theology, history, law, and so on) as for the depth of his thinking and his impact on the intelligentsia of the Maghrib and the Sudan. He himself, however, admired the works of his mentor Muḥammad Bagayokho, which, unfortunately, have not yet all been discovered.

The two *Tārīkhs* of Timbuktu, the *Tārīkh al-Fattāsh* of the Soninke Muḥmūd al-Qāti' and his descendants (fifteenth to sixteenth century), and the *Tārīkh al-Sūdān* of 'Abd al-Raḥmān al-Sa'di (seventeenth century), inspired by the works of Aḥmad Bābā, testify to the advanced level of historical research using a rigorous method close to that of modern science.

The influence of Islam neverthless remained confined to a tiny area of West Africa. Even in the Sudan–Sahel region, Islam penetrated only superficially into the countryside and the Sudanese savannah. It must be recognized that even in its zone of expansion, Islam did not do away with traditional beliefs. The most typical case is that of the Songhay, Soninke and Malinke, who came into contact with Islam very early on, but who assimilated it by adapting it to their own environment and their age-old beliefs. Thus it was that, from that time onwards, Islam took root, by virtue of tolerance and adaptability to African circumstances (Monteil, 1964).

Christianity, which arrived with the Portuguese navigators of the fifteenth and sixteenth centuries, did not take hold in West Africa. The caravels were filled more with navigators and goods to sell than with missionaries. The first voyages in the fifteenth century were genuine adventures along the Gulf of Guinea, and it was only in the sixteenth century that they were accompanied by the establishment of trading posts, especially in the Gulf of Benin.

The Cape Verde Islands alone inhabited by the Portuguese and their slaves, boasted the first church, but this had no impact on the continent.

NOTE

1 There are many works on this subject, which has become almost a classic of African medieval history. Without seeking to be too exhaustive, we would refer to Volumes III and IV of UNESCO *General History of Africa*, and the *Encyclopaedia of Islam*. Also: Guethner, 1984; Triaud, 1973. See also the bibliography in Part III, Chapter 17.5.2 of this volume.

BIBLIOGRAPHY

CISSOKO, S. M. 1996. *Tombouctou et l'Empire Songhay*. L'Harmattan, Paris.

Encyclopaedia of Islam, 1960. 2nd edn. (EI²) E. J. Brill. Leiden.

General History of Africa. UNESCO, California. Vol. IV: 1984. Vol. III: 1988.

GUETHNER, P. 1984. *Histoire de l'islamisation de l'Afrique de l'Ouest, des origines à la fin du XVIème siècle*. Librairie orientaliste P. Guethner, Paris.

HUNWICK, J. O. 1980. Gao and the Almoravids: A Hypothesis. In: SWARTZ B. K. and DUMETT R. F. (eds) pp. 413–430.

HUNWICK, J. O., MEILLASSOUX, C.; TRIAUD, J. L. 1981. La géographie du Soudan d'après Al-Bakrī'. Trois lectures. In: *Le Sol, la Parole et l'Ecrit*. Vol. I, pp 401–428.

MONTEIL, V. 1964. *L'Islam noir*. Seuil, Paris.

Tārīkh al-Fattāsh. 1913. French trans. O. Houdas, Paris. Al-Sadi: HOUDAS, O.; DELAFOSSE, M. (ed. and French trans.). Paris.

TRIAUD, J. L. 1973. Islam et société soudanaises au Moyen Âge: étude historique. In: *Recherches voltaïques, N16*. Collège de France, Paris.

32.5
ARTS AND SCIENCES

Isaac Adeagbo Akinjogbin

Religion gave rise to various forms of artistic expression from Sierra Leone to the Cross River and from the coast to the savannah. The systematic development of an urban culture following the Neolithic Revolution in West Africa was conducive to artistic development. Thus, from the turn of the first millennium AD, West African artists worked with available local materials, be they stone, wood or metals, to produce both religious and secular objects. The Yoruba, Edo, Akan, Baule and Bambara are among the most famous groups in West African art history (Fraser and Cole, 1972; Goldwater, 1964). Others who are well known include the Igbo, Nupe, Efik and Mende.

The large assemblage of artistic objects collected from different parts of West Africa indicates that the same ideas informed their production and suggest that the whole region belonged to the same artistic tradition, with a historical progression from basketry to lithic sculpture, to pottery, and finally to metallurgy (Willet, 1967). Basketry and stone sculpture definitely pre-dated the seventh century AD. Thereafter, plastic arts became prominent, particularly as stable urban settlements began to emerge in various parts. The contacts with Islam no doubt had a great impact on traditional art (Bravmann, 1974), as evidenced by the proliferation of oriental architectural styles in western and central Sudan by the sixteenth century AD. From the tenth century AD, metalwork appears to have taken over as the predominant material for the production of various artistic forms. The metals used included copper, brass, bronze, lead and iron. This last stage of development did not, however, obliterate the former mediums, as West African artists continued to use stone, wood and clay alongside the metals (see Plates 15, 260–270). Indeed, in areas where they were available, gold and ivory were equally employed. For instance, among the Soninke of Old Ghana, the Akan of Modern Ghana and the Baule of Côte d'Ivoire, gold was popularly used while ivory was a major item from the forest region of modern Côte d'Ivoire to Nigeria.

The forms and objects produced with these materials are many and varied, and they constitute part of the outstanding artistic heritage of humanity. In the rocky caves, there are engravings and paintings depicting human activities. In the forest zone there are wood carvings used as masks for various religious ceremonies, such as initiation or judiciary. A large number of wooden and terra cotta images represent gods, goddesses and ancestors. The bronze and brass heads of Ife and Benin (see Plate 267), some of them life-size, represent famous kings and warriors both male and female (Kaplan, 1981; Rottray, 1959). Nor were these all. The Baule and the Akan worked gold into fine ornaments. The Edo used ivory to produce such household utensils as spoons and combs. All over West Africa, potsherds, a by-product of clay industry, were used to pave the courtyards of shrines and houses of famous men as well as popular streets. Then there was the production of beads, which developed between the twelfth and fifteenth centuries. These were used by royalty and noblemen and women (Thompson, 1970). Ife and Benin became famous centres of bead production, but the industry was widespread throughout West Africa, because stones containing crypto-crystalline forms of silica were generally distributed all over the area.

The craftsmen's skills, the materials and forms they produced, were well developed by the time the Portuguese arrived on the coast of West Africa in the 1470s. The quantity, variety and sophistication of the works of art were directly related to urbanization and to favourable socio-economic conditions. The emergence of stable political systems gave people the opportunity to express their thoughts. The division of labour and the consequent wealth generated in such societies left enough for rich people to patronize art, and thus support the section of the population engaged in the production of artwork. Ife, Benin and Manso, which had strong monarchies and which were the nuclei of major polities with extensive spheres of influence, were also centres of great artistic civilization (see Plates 265–270).

By far the vast majority of the art works were produced under royal patronage. For example in Benin, the artists were organised into guilds called *igun,* and each *igun* was affiliated to a palace chieftaincy group. The guild of brass casters (*igun enomwon*) and the guild of ironworkers (*igun ematon*) were affiliated to the *Iwebo* palace chiefs. The guild of carvers (*igun igbesamwon*) and the guild of weavers (*igun owina*), on the other hand, were affiliated to the *Iweguae* palace chiefs. Through these palace chiefs, the king (*oba*) patronized and controlled the workers. Royal demands channelled through different palace chiefs produced healthy competition and experimentation (Igbafe, 1980).

The indigenous religions of West Africa also gave rise to scientific developments. The continuous quest to unravel the mystery of the unknown led to major innovations, particularly in the fields of medicine, agriculture and technology (Dalziel, 1955; Field, 1961; Verger, 1967). The development of medical science was probably the best example of this link. The local priests possessed immense knowledge of herbs and roots and knew how to use them to cure diseases and sickness. Treatment often involved rites and there were some cultic groups that specialized in the treatment of various ailments. These included the *Dibia* (Igbo), *Babalawo* (Yoruba), *Simo* (Baule) and the women's secret societies of the Mende. Through experience built up in handling various ailments over the years, and through a series of experiments with new herbs, roots and curative methods, the local medicine men developed new methods and improved their therapeutic skills (Bascom, 1969).

Similar experimentations led to major developments in agricultural and food sciences. Rock paintings, engravings and various artefacts reveal attempts to domesticate different varieties of plants and animals suited to particular geographical environments. For instance, there are paintings dating to about the eighteenth century AD depicting certain species of animals which are now extinct but which presumably were domesticated at the time. These are, in addition, animals such as cattle, goats and guinea fowl, which appear to have been domesticated by the sixteenth century (Blake, 1937). The widespread manufacture of Neolithic implements testify to early attempts at plant domestication. Crops like yam, oil palm, pumpkin, sorghum, millet, melon, cowpea, African breadfruit, okro and malaguetta pepper were indigenous to West Africa and domesticated at an early date (Isichei, 1983; Shaw, 1972; Davies, 1965). When crops like banana, plantain, water yam, cocoyam, onion, cassava and maize were introduced, continuous experimentation led to the production of varieties suited to the West Africa environment. From these crops, both indigenous and adopted, the peoples of West Africa developed various recipes which are a contribution to the development of food science.

The development of agriculture was enhanced by technological advancement as there were also developments in industrial science. The first major breakthrough would appear to be the invention of mining and working of iron. By the second century AD, iron extractive industries were already established in the south-eastern fringe of the Sudan, from where ironworking technology appeared to have become diffused in a south-westerly direction to other parts of West Africa (Diop, 1968). For instance, by AD 500 at Daima in the western basin of Lake Chad, archeological investigations indicate remarkable technological advancements that involved the working of iron and improvement in animal husbandry with the domestication of a number of animal species, including cattle, sheep and goats (Shaw, 1969). By AD 700, an extensive ironworking culture existed on the Jos plateau. Here, evidence of early Iron Age working, including wrought iron objects, iron slags, tuyeres, figurine fragments and domestic pottery, have been uncovered. Known as the Nok culture, the area was to become a major dispersal centre for iron technology in West Africa.

Because of its hard nature, iron was used to manufacture a variety of implements, tools and weapons. In most West African communities, there were rituals associated with the mining and working of iron, and deities associated with iron occupied important positions in the local pantheon. Extensive iron ore deposits existed and were mined by local blacksmiths. Blacksmithing became an important economic activity. The major centres of ironworking industries were located in areas where the local soil was of a ferrous type, containing iron deposits. Available traditions all over West Africa show that many of the state founders and prominent personalities from the eighteenth century AD were either blacksmiths or were closely associated with blacksmithing. By AD 1500, the industries of West Africa were already turning out high-quality iron weapons, shields and implements.

There was also the development of other metallurgical industries. As early as the eighteenth century, gold was already a popular article of trade in the Sudan, and the first centralized state in the region, Wagadugu, derived its fame from the gold-mining activities of its citizens. Before the sixteenth century, other Western African peoples developed techniques of mining and working various minerals such as gold, copper, brass, bronze, beads and salt. Thus, by the close of the fifteenth century, a prominent feature of the economy of West Africa was the extensive commerce sustained by agriculture and the extractive industries developed over the centuries through scientific experimentations.

It is undeniable that there were major technological developments in different parts of West Africa before the sixteenth century. Yet, the scientific initiatives of the period failed to take West Africa to great technological heights. The question might legitimately be asked: why was West Africa unable to advance beyond the levels reached by 1502? The fundamental reason for this is that the scientific innovations were not fully developed. The nature of West African society itself was responsible for this. In the indigenous societies, knowledge was transmitted orally; therefore much depended on memory and what the individual transmitter could remember or was willing to relate. Also, most of the artistic and industrial pursuits were lineage-based. Each lineage often attempted to monopolize and therefore jealously guard the knowledge of its particular skill. Furthermore, the association of many of the scientific practices with rituals made them not easily practicable to the non-initiated. Many of the industrial works were carried out in secrecy, and the larger community, who were uninitiated, could not have the opportunity of acquiring the necessary knowledge or skill through observation and practice. Even for the initiated, apprenticeship might involve a long and perilous period of sacrifice, which discouraged and stultified the interest of many. The sum total of these is that as a generation died out, part of the scientific knowledge it had put into practice died with it.

Lastly, there was the slave trade, which created general panic and disrupted the peaceful pursuit of life, creating an atmosphere inconducive to scientific pursuits and often resulting in the export of the most enterprising members of the society, who could otherwise have been engaged in the development of the sciences.

BIBLIOGRAPHY (Chapters 32.4.1 and 32.5)

ABIMBOLA, W. 1968. Ifa as a Body of Knowledge and as an Academic Discipline. *Lagos Notes and Records*. Lagos.

——. 1975. *Sixteen Great Poems of Ifa*. UNESCO. Lagos.

——. 1976. *Ifa: An Exposition of Ifa Literary Corpus*. Ibadan.

ADEDIRAN. B. 1985. The External Factor in the Development of an African Historiography. *Islam and the Modern Age*. New Delhi. Vol. XVI/3, pp. 127–145.

ADEGBOLA, B. A. (ed.). 1983. *Traditional Religion in West Africa*. Ibadan.

AKINJOGBIN, I. A. 1978. *History and Nation Building*. Ile-Ife.

AKINJOGBIN, I. A.; OSOBA, S. O. (eds.) 1980. *Topics on Nigerian Economic and Social History*. Ile-Ife, pp. 19–34.

BASCOM, W. R. 1966. Odu Ifa, the Names of the Signs. *Africa*. Cambridge, pp. 408–421.

——. 1969. *Ifa Divination: Communication Between Gods and Man in West Africa*. Bloomington, Indiana.

BLAKE, J. W. 1937. *European Beginnings in West Africa, 1485–1578*. London, pp. 79–80.

BRAVMANN, R. A. 1974. *Islam and Tribal Art in West Africa.* Cambridge.
DALZIEL, J. M. 1955. *The Useful Plants of West Tropical Africa.* London.
DANQUAH, J. B. 1968. *The Akan Doctrine of God.* London.
DAVIES, O. 1968. The Origins of Agriculture in West Africa. *Current Anthropology.* London.
DIOP, L. M. 1968. Métallurgie et l'âge du fer en Afrique. *Bulletin de l'IFAN.* Dakar.
DOUGLAS, M.; KABERRY, P. M. (eds) 1969. *Man in Africa.* London.
FIELD, M. J. 1961. *Religion and Medicine of the Ga People.* London.
FORDE, D. I. (ed.) 1970. *African Worlds: Studies in the Cosmological Ideas and Social Values of African Peoples.* London.
FRASER, D; COLE, H. M. 1972. *African Art and Leadership.* Madison, Wisconsin.
GOLDWATER, R. 1964. *Bambara Sculpture.* New York.
GREENBERG, J. 1946. *The Influence of Islam on a Sudanese Religion.* New York.
HISKETT, M. 1984. *The Development of Islam in West Africa.* London.
IDOWU, E. B. 1973. *African Traditional Religion.* London.
——. 1977. *Olodumare: God In Yoruba Belief.* London.
IGBAFE, P. A. 1980. The Pre-Colonial Economic Foundations of the Benin Kingdom. In: AKINJOGBIN, I. A.; OSOBA, S. O. (eds) *Topics on Nigerian Economic and Social History.* Ile-Ife, pp. 19–34.
IMASOGIE, O. 1985. *African Traditional Religion.* Ibadan.
ISICHEI, E. 1983. *A History of Nigeria.* London, pp. 21–83.
KAPLAN, F. S. (ed.) 1981. *Images of Power, Arts of the Royal Court of Benin.* New York.
LOUIS-VINCENT, T.; RENÉ, L. 1975. *La terre africaine et ses religions.* Paris.
LUCAS, E. O. 1948. *The Religion of the Yoruba.* Lagos.
MAUPOLL, B. 1943. La géomancie à l'ancienne côte des esclaves. Paris.
MBITI, J. S. 1977. *Concepts of God in Africa.* London.
——. 1977. *African Religions and Philosophy.* London.
——. 1986. *Introduction to African Religion.* London.
MERCIER, P. 1962. *Civilisation du Bénin.* Paris.
MURDOCK, G. P. 1959. *Africa: Its Peoples and Their Culture History.* New York.
NADEL, S. F. 1970. *Nupe Religion.* London.
ODUYOYE, M. 1983. Polytheism and Monothesism: Conceptual Difference. In: ADEGBOLA, B. A. (ed.) *Traditional Religion in West Africa.* Ibadan.
OPEOLA, S. M. 1988. A Way of Applying Science Education to Interpret Ifa Literary Corpus. *ODU: Journal of West African Studies.* Ile-Ife, No. 33, pp. 149–162.
P'BITEK, O. 1970. *African Religions in Western Scholarship.* Kampala.
PALAU-MARTI, M. 1964. *Le roi-dieu au Bénin, sud Togo, Dahomey, Nigeria occidentale.* Paris.
PARRINDER, E. G. 1962. *African Traditional Religion.* London.
——. 1962. West African Religion. London.
——. 1969. *Religion in Africa.* London.
ROTTRAY, R. S. 1959. *Religion and Art in Ashanti.* London.
RYDER, A. 1969. *Benin and the Europeans, 1485–1897.* London, pp. 24–84.
SHAW, T. (ed.) 1969. *Lectures on Nigerian Prehistory and Archaeology.* Ibadan.
——. 1972. Early Agriculture in Africa. *Journal of the Historical Society of Nigeria.* Ibadan.
SMITH, E. W. (ed.) 1961. *African Ideas of God.* London.
THOMPSON, R. F. 1970. The Sign of a Divine King: An Essay on Yoruba Bead Embroidered Crown with Veil and Bird Decoration. *African Arts.* Los Angeles, 3, pp. 8–17; 74–78.
TRANTMAN, R. 1939. La divination à la Côte des esclaves et à Madagascar. *Memoires de l'IFAN.* Dakar.
VERGER, P. 1957. *Notes sur le culte des Orisa et Vodun à Bahia, la baie de tous les saints au Brésil et l'ancienne côte des esclaves en Afrique.* Institut Français d'Afrique Noire, Dakar, Mémoires, No. 51.
——. 1967. *Awon Ewe Osanyin* [Yoruba Medicinal Plants] Institute of African Studies, Osogbo. No. 8.
WILLET, F. 1967. *Ife, in the History of West African Sculpture.* London.

33

NUBIA AND THE NILOTIC SUDAN[1]

Yūsuf Faḍl Ḥasan

The civilization of medieval Nubia is undoubtedly better known than that of its predecessors, thanks partly to the richness of archaeological finds from Lower Nubia and Dunqula, partly to the considerable body of information contained in medieval Arabic writings, and for the last stage, from Sudanese oral traditions (Monnert de Villard, 1938; Adams, 1977; Ḥasan, 1967, pp. 172–213). Nubian civilization like that of Pharaonic Egypt and the kingdom of Napata – Meroë or Kush (750 BC–AD 350) – was based on the narrow strip of the Nile between the First Cataract and the confluence of the Blue and White Niles. It was hence largely a civilization of a settled people (Shinnie, 1967, p. 62). There the main centres of authority blossomed.

In the wake of the period of disintegration that followed the downfall of the kingdom of Meroë, three independent kingdoms arose. They are loosely called *Bilād al-Nūba* in contemporary Arabic sources, and their inhabitants are *al-Nūba* or Nubians. This region also constituted the eastern part of what medieval Muslim geographers called *Bilād al-Sūdān*, the 'Land of the Blacks'. It referred to the belt of sub-Saharan Africa that extended from the Red Sea to the Atlantic Ocean. By the end of the nineteenth century, however, the term 'Sudan' came to be increasingly restricted to the territories south of Egypt, that is to Nubia and the Beja lands. The 'Nilotic Sudan' refers to those riverain territories as far as Sinnar.

The first of the three Nubian kingdoms from the north was Nobatia (al-Marīs in Arabic), with its capital at Bājrash (modern Faras), extending between the First and the Second Cataracts. The second, Makuria (al-Muqurra in Arabic), embraced the middle Nile region, which extended up to the Fifth Cataract (and possibly further to the South at al-Abwāb) (Monnert de Villard, 1938, p. 153; Hasan, 1967, p. 6). When the Arabs attacked Dunqula in AD 651–652, it was the capital of the two northern kingdoms. However, the two regions were administered differently, and the two names, Nobatia and al-Muqurra, continued to be used for centuries (Kirwan, 1935, pp. 60–61).

The third kingdom was Alodia ('Alwa in Arabic); its capital was Soba, a few miles south of modern Khartoum. 'Alwa's southern border is difficult to determine; however, its influence seems to have extended as far as Sinnar, where Christian remains were found (Crowfoot, 1927, XIII; p. 142; Arkell, 1959, XL, 45).

The eastern and western frontiers of Nubia were marked largely by the extent of cultivable land on both banks of the Nile, which at times might extend up to a mile or two. The rest was desert sparsely populated by nomads. The most important among these desert dwellers were the Beja of the eastern desert. The deserts were traversed by caravan routes that connected Nubia with tropical and West Africa, Egypt, and the Red Sea ports.

In the limited cultivable lands of Nobatia and al-Muqurra, Nubians practised *selūka* cultivation in the low flood plains and also in the natural depressions or basins to which flood water was guided when the Nile was high. Higher flood plains were irrigated by water-lifting devices, which had been introduced in Meroitic times: these were the hand-operated *shadūf* or crane, and the ox-driven *sāqiya* or water-wheel.

'Alwa had more fertile lands, first along the banks of the Nile and its two main tributaries, and second the rain-cultivated grasslands of the Butana and the Gezira – the land between the Blue and the White Niles (Adams, 1977, 20, pp. 52–54).

Although the economy of the three kingdoms depended mainly on farming, it was supplemented, besides trade, by pastoral activities to which people turned as an alternative in times of hardship. In 'Alwa, in areas where there is adequate rainfall to sustain the rearing of sheep and camels, a mode of nomadic or semi-nomadic existence was followed.

The intermediary position that Nubia occupied between the advanced civilizations of the Mediterranean world, and the cultures of tropical Africa, made it responsive to many cultural and ideological developments. From Pharaonic Egypt and its successor states, Nubia received increasing Egyptian influence which left indelible marks on nearly all facets of Kushite civilization. The scope of this impact included religious beliefs, temples, burial practices, building techniques, and irrigation implements.

CONVERSION OF NUBIA TO CHRISTIANITY

Between the seventh and the sixteenth centuries, Nobatia, al-Muqurra and 'Alwa were affected by two major cultural tides which were to become dominant factors in the history and the culture of these kingdoms. The first was the evangelization of Nobatia, al-Muqarra and 'Alwa in about AD 580 and Christianity's continued domination for more than 800 years.

However, no sooner had Christianity become the prevailing faith in those states than the second cultural tide,

Islam, emerged in Egypt, Nobatia and al-Muqurra. Gradually it attained prominence, filling the cultural vacuum engendered by the disintegration of Nubian Christianity. The process of Christianization began with the arrival of persecuted Christians from Egypt. It was later reinforced by the arrival of two formal missionary groups representing two rival Christian doctrines: the Melkites, or Dyophysites, and the Jacobites, or Monophysites: the Melkite sect stood for the official creed of the Church of Byzantium, which upheld the decree of the Council of Chalcedon of AD 451. The council attributed two separate natures to Jesus Christ. The Monophysites (generally identified with the Egyptian Coptic Church) were declared heretics by the Council of Chalcedon because they championed the doctrine of the single nature of Christ.

The details of conversion need not detain us here. It suffices to state that by 580 the formal process of conversion, notably among members of the ruling elite, had been realized in all three kingdoms. Although the Monophysites gradually dominated the Nubian scene, there is also evidence to confirm that the Melkite rites continued to exist for a long time. After the seventh century, the Nubian Church developed strong ties with the Monophysite Coptic Church and virtually became an integral part of it. From the eighth century, the Nubian Church acknowledged the patriarch of Alexandria, the head of the Coptic Church, as its spiritual superior. It was he who appointed bishops, many of whom were probably of Egyptian origin, a practice that continued almost to the time when the Muslims took over political power.

The acceptance of Christianity by the Nubians introduced a fundamental change in the ideological domain of their civilization. The new faith became an essential factor in the cultural life of the Nubians and brought about significant changes which set it apart from earlier and later eras of Sudanese history.

The impact of Christianity was manifested in burial practices, buildings, decorations and symbols. Probably the best example to demonstrate the rapidity of transformation from pagan beliefs to Christianity was the changeover from pagan to Christian funerary customs, where Christianity introduced a completely different form of burial. The ancient practice of burying material goods with the deceased disappeared, as did the belief in the divinity of kings. Stripped of his former attributes, the king was no longer the central figure in Christian Nubia. People began to glorify a 'heavenly king' who exercised greater sway over people's minds and souls than did the state. The former beliefs were superseded by new canons of faith, of art, of architecture and of literature. In short, throughout the Middle Ages, the Christian faith continued to be the most important stimulus of Nubian civilization (Ḥasan, 1967, pp. 8–9; Adams, 1977, pp. 439–440, 481–501; Shinnie, 1978, p. 557; Gadallah, 1959, XL, pp. 38–42; Torok, 1988, pp. 70–71).

THE *BAQT* TREATY

The Islamic conquest of the Byzantine province of Egypt in AD 641–642 decisively altered Egypt's status both politically and ideologically. First, having become a province of the Islamic caliphate, Egypt gradually developed into an influential Arabized and Islamized country. Second, Egyptian hostility to Byzantine domination and the Melkite Church, while facilitating the Arab conquest, earned the Monophysites a favourable position in the eyes of the Arab rulers. The Monophysite Coptic Church emerged as the national church with a great measure of autonomy. As a result of these two developments, it is not surprising that the Coptic Church was to exercise a great influence in the development of the Nubian Church and on its arts, architecture and literature. The close association between the two churches was further affirmed by the conclusion of the *Baqt* treaty (Adams, 1977, pp. 446, 506-7).

Muslim intervention in Nubia was probably instigated by the frontier raids that Nubians launched in support of their fellow Christians in Egypt. The Arabs launched two major campaigns: one in 641–642, and another in 651–652. They met gallant resistance from the famous Nubian archers. In the second campaign, to be sure, the Nubians were particularly frightened by the catapults which bombarded the cathedral of Dunqula. Still, having failed to defeat their enemy decisively, the Arabs accepted the Nubians' bid for peace. The settlement reached was no more than a 'truce of security', or non-aggression pact, by which neither side would attack the other. It also recognized the mutual commercial interests of the two countries. Both sides agreed that Nubians would deliver annually 400 slaves to the Muslim governor in Egypt in exchange for food stuff and clothing. Muslims were allowed to enter Nubia as traders but not as settlers, and the same advantage was conferred on the Nubians when entering Egypt (al-Maqrīzī, 1922, III, pp. 290–293; Ibn 'Abd al-Ḥakam, 1920, p. 189; Ḥasan, 1967, pp. 20–24; Hinds and Sakkout, 1981, pp. 210–216). This agreement, commonly known as the *Baqt*, continued to be honoured in principle and endured as the bedrock of Muslim–Nubian relations for six centuries. In short, it contributed towards the establishment of a good basis for peace and economic prosperity, both of which were important characteristics of medieval Nubian civilization.

It was probably at this time that Nobatia was incorporated into al-Muqurra. Dunqula became the chief centre of political authority for the two regions. However, Nobatia maintained its lead in economic and cultural growth. The organization of commercial transactions between al-Muqurra and the Islamic world in accordance with the provisions of the *Baqt* treaty seem to have led to the expansion of that traffic beyond the traditional markets, and to the advantage of both sides (Adams, 1977, pp. 453–454, 464, 501–506). Nubians exported slaves, dates, copper, ivory, pottery (and gold from the Eastern Desert) in exchange for manufactured goods, like textiles, glass and ceramics and also food provisions (Michalowski, 1981, p. 335; Jakobielski, 1986, p. 232). To comply with the *Baqt* treaty and to satisfy the increasing demand for slaves, Nubians as middlemen had to procure them from an ever-widening area to the south-west of Nubia (Al-Iṣṭakhrī, 1870, pp. 41–42; Nāṣirī Khusraw, 1945, p. 46; Ḥasan, 1967, p. 46).

After the seventh century, Muslim traders were allowed to settle freely in Lower Nubia. The establishment of a free zone trading area and the active participation of Muslim merchants led to the introduction of a monetary economy based on Islamic coinage. Relations with Egypt were handled by the governor of Nobatia, the eparch or *Ṣāḥib al-Jabal*, in the name of the king. The central region, south of the Second Cataract, remained closed to foreign merchants. There the king had a monopoly over commerce (as well as sole ownership of land) which was conducted by barter (Adams, 1977, pp. 461, 504–505; Torok, 1975, p. 296; Jakobielski, 1986, p. 232).

ARCHITECTURAL DEVELOPMENT: HOUSES

At the beginning of the eighth century both al-Muqurra and Nobatia enjoyed an environment of prosperity which was mirrored in the expansion of their settlements, with building activity both religious and secular (Adams, 1977, pp. 488–494, 501).

The housing sector went through some architectural development: in the early Christian period houses were small, cramped, unsystematically planned and imperfectly constructed of stone and mud brick. Houses had flat roofs made of wooden beams, thatch (or straw mats) and clay. After AD 900, houses became larger, better shaped and were built of baked brick. A standard house would include one or two front rooms, one or two small store rooms connected with a narrow passage ending at an indoor latrine at the back of the house (Adams, 1977, p. 491). Such concern for an internal 'sewerage system' demonstrated a significant development in medieval Nubian house architecture.

By the thirteenth century, houses tended to be smaller but were stoutly built with thick walls. The change in design, and later architectural evolution, were due to two factors. First, villages in northern Nubia had to contend with the encroaching sand dunes that moved across from the desert. Second, the same period witnessed the commencement of internal political unrest and the intrusion of Mamlūk armies in Nubian affairs, a point that will be taken up later. The stoutly built houses, though better equipped for coping with sand encroachment, were probably not suitable for defence purposes.

The answer came in the form of a two-storey house unit that looked like a 'miniature castle'. The defensive characteristics and architectural features demonstrated in the two-storey house units were the accomplishment of professional architects. These master builders, whether Nubians or immigrants, were probably stimulated by the spirit of military feudalism which by the twelfth century had engulfed Europe and Western Asia. From there the new spirit seemed to have radiated into Nubia. Military feudalism together with the defensive approach led to the development of the two-storey house unit, just discussed, and then the 'blockhouse'. The first structure was regarded as a 'de luxe' house. The second, though similar in design, was immensely larger, and normally built on a commanding location in the village. It probably served as a 'haven' into which the village community could retire, together with its basic requirements in supplies, in times of danger. Castle-building as such did not, however, make much headway in Lower Nubia beyond the 'blockhouse' phase. Elsewhere, the chief 'feudal lords' used older Meroitic fortifications, while others were satisfied with the big two-storey houses. Castle construction probably attained its fullest development in al-Muqurra, in the region between the Third and the Fifth Cataracts (Adams, 1977, pp. 515–518).

SACRED ARCHITECTURE: NUBIAN CHURCHES

Almost from the outset, Nubian Christians evolved artistic and literary traditions of their own. It was in the domain of ecclesiastical architecture, mural decoration, domestic industries – notably pottery – and religious literature that they made significant achievements. Church building was an important branch of sacred architecture. Hence, it is not surprising that in nearly all Nubian settlements the church occupied a focal point (Jakobielski, 1988, p. 216).

Nubian architects, once affected by the tenets of the new faith, modelled their church architecture on that of the Byzantine Empire. Though virtually severed from direct contacts with the main Christian architectural centres abroad, Nubian architects attempted to emulate advanced architectural patterns and to improve their technical methods (Gartkiewciz, 1982, p. 9).

The basilican pattern, which prevailed in northern Nubia, is an elongated building, oriented east–west and divided into a nave and two aisles. The earliest Nubian churches were identical with those of Egypt. However, with the discovery of the church of Dunqula by the Polish archaeological mission in 1964, it became clear that sacred architecture was also stimulated by other patterns. The layout of the Dunqula old church manifests the concept of the central cruciform design in a rectangle (or a combination of that of the cruciform church and that of the church with granite columns) (Jakobielski, 1982a, p. 52; Jakobielski, 1988, pp. 216–217) (see Plate 273).

By the eighth century, the Nubian Church had achieved a number of distinguishing architectural features, which were observed for many centuries. These included a narrow passage moving behind the apse and connecting the two corner rooms, and the expansion of the sanctuary area at the expense of the nave. Another architectural development was the gradual decrease in the size of the church. By the middle of the eleventh century it had shrunk further and become less elaborate; indeed it was drastically simplified. This was the time when churches too were affected by the sweeping sand dunes. It was probably in response to such a threat that the 'cupola church' concept was introduced. The 'new' church had a square layout covered by a tall central cupola (Adams, 1977, pp. 476–477; Jakobielski, 1988, pp. 217–219).

A two-storey royal building, long recognized as a church, is still intact in Dunqula. It was constructed at the turn of the eighth century. It contained the King's throne hall and was once decorated with murals (Jakobielski, 1988, p. 200). In 1317, the royal building was converted into a mosque by King Sharaf al-Dīn 'Abdallāh al-Nāṣir Barshambū (Ḥasan, 1967, p. 124 and note 180 (p. 244)). It continued to be used for religious purposes until recently.

Nubian architectural ingenuity and cultural development is best demonstrated by the great cathedral at Faras, which was marvellously excavated by the Polish archaeological mission. The cathedral, though roofless, was in a good state of preservation, thanks to the windblown sands that covered it completely for centuries. This majestic edifice was originally built in the seventh century. It had a nave and two aisles. In 707, the cathedral was magnificently rebuilt and markedly enlarged. It incorporated a nave and four aisles. Between the middle of the eighth and the end of the twelfth centuries a series of fine paintings were executed on the walls of the cathedral, some of which were superimposed on the top of earlier ones (Shinnie, 1978, p. 575).

MURAL ART

Earlier architectural decorations of Nubian churches seem to have been restricted to the use of sculptured capitals, lintels, door jambs and cornices either of stone or wood. By the seventh century this pattern was substituted by brightly coloured figurative mural paintings. Inspired by Byzantine frescoes and mosaics, these paintings became the loftiest embodiment of Christian Nubian civilization. This development was evidenced, at first, by the discovery of fragments of coloured plaster in abandoned churches all over Nubia. The largest finds of mural decorations were those from the Faras Cathedral, and from the two small churches of ʿAbdāllah Nirqī and Tino. The complete collection of paintings from the three named churches is without parallel in the annals of medieval Christian Africa: 120 separate, brightly coloured paintings were skilfully removed from the walls of Faras Cathedral. In addition to the religious scenes, such as that of the Nativity, Christ and the Virgin Mary, there were portraits of saints, archangels, bishops, and scenes from the Old and New Testaments.

The paintings show the dominance of Coptic influence as well as those radiating from Byzantium, Syria and Palestine. Nubian touches, particularly in style, execution and details, are easily detected.

An example of local traits is the representation of ethnic Nubians (bishops or rulers) in a shade darker than that given to Christ, the Holy Family, the saints and the angels, who were normally shown with a white complexion (see Plates 56, 276–278).

Religious representation was by no means restricted to the church; it embraced a wide range of facets of daily life. Walls of houses were periodically decorated with protective inscriptions from the Bible. Surfaces of pottery vessels were also decorated with similar devices. Some people carried leather amulets in which a protective passage of Holy Scripture was written (Adams, 1977, pp. 464–496; Adams, (a), 9–10).

DOMESTIC ARTS

Pottery making is an ancient tradition in which Nubians have excelled since Meroitic times. In the early Christian period Nubian pottery was simple in decoration, emulating patterns of Roman red ware. By the end of the eighth century wares were produced in abundance, with a wide variety of bowls, vases and jars decorated in bright colours depicting geometric, floral and animal motifs. Such were the luxury wares, skilfully manufactured, elegantly decorated and hence highly prized, as distinct from standard eating bowls and cooking pots (Shinnie, 1978, p. 570; Adams, 1977, pp. 496–498).

The new artistic tradition of pottery making, known as classic Christian pottery, was abundantly produced in various centres. In the tenth or eleventh century, production was abruptly discontinued. In the late Christian period, however, pottery making flourished again and recovered its pre-eminence and elegance. At this juncture, the Nubians succeeded in effecting 'a closer control of firing temperatures and atmospheres which allowed the production of vessels in various shades of orange and yellow' (Shinnie, 1978, p. 498).

From the middle of the thirteenth century, the art of wheel-made pottery degenerated rapidly, both in quantity and in quality, and by the end of the Christian period it had reached its lowest ebb. Consequently, production was discontinued and local demand was satisfied by the hand-made wares shaped by women as was the case in pre-historic times (Shinnie, 1978, pp. 520–521).

Weaving of wool and camel hair was one of the important domestic crafts. Nubian woollen robes were mostly smartened up with alternating bright colours or, infrequently, chequered patterns. Nubian artisans forged iron tools (such as hoes and knives), ornaments (like pectoral crosses) and also gold and silver medallions of holy figures. Domestic crafts included leather work (like sandals, thongs and whips), matting, basketry, artistically made plates or *ṭabaqs*, wooden tools, and grinding stones. Palm-fibre products seem to have developed into a specialized industry like wheel-made pottery. The latter was part of a wide trading network while the former (including cooking pots or *kantushes* and buckets or *qadūses* used in drawing up water by *sāqiyas* or *shadūfs*) were not (Adams, 1977, p. 500; Jakobielski, 1988, p. 206; Adams, (a), p. 14).

LITERATURE AND LANGUAGES

At the time Christianity penetrated Nubia, there was no established written language. Meroitic was close to being extinct. Greek was very little used, mostly in issuing proclamations. However, as it was the language of the Egyptian Church, it also became the liturgical language of Nubia after the triumph of Christianity. When the Egyptian Church severed its relations with Byzantium, it adopted the Coptic tongue. The Nubian Church did not switch to Coptic but continued to use Greek all through the Middle Ages: texts and Nubian inscriptions were written in Greek.

From the seventh century, both Coptic and Old Nubian gradually attained some prominence as the language of documents and inscriptions (specially in Nobatia). Coptic enjoyed the moral support of the Egyptian clergy and monks who performed a significant role in the evolution of Nubian culture. Old Nubian was the contemporary indigenous language of Christianized Nubians written in the Coptic alphabet.

Several hundred fragments of parchment (and later on paper), and painted mural inscriptions were discovered in churches and monasteries. They are mainly of a religious nature and for the most part canonical. This religious literature does not seem to have displayed 'any novelty' except for introducing Old Nubian as a vehicle of writing. Medieval Nubian literature, like sacred architecture and mural paintings and other cultural and artistic manifestations, seems to have been under the guidance of the clerical establishment. The surviving literature includes five complete books of prayer or breviaries, numerous fragments of the Gospels, lives and sayings of saints, sermons and rituals, all typical of early Christian writings. These texts exhibit wide linguistic diversity – namely Greek, Coptic and Old Nubian.

Arabic was used in diplomatic and commercial contacts, particularly in Lower Nubia. There, in places like Qaṣr Ibrīm, a multilingual (Nubian and Arabic) society flourished.

Although the general public was illiterate throughout this period, knowledge of writing was probably more extensive in medieval Nubia than in earlier times (Shinnie, 1974, pp. 41–47; Shinnie, 1978, pp. 573–575, 580–581; Adams, 1977, pp. 447–448, 484–485; Jakobielski, 'Polish Excavations at Old Dongola', 1969. In: Dunkler, E. (ed.) *Kunst und Geschichte Nubiens in Christlicher Zeit*, Recklinghausen, 1970, quoted in Adams, 1977, p. 485).

THE DECLINE OF NUBIAN CIVILIZATION

The rise of the Mamlūk sultanate in Egypt (1250–1517) marked the beginning of a new chapter in Muslim–Nubian relations. The Mamlūks ordered immediate resumption of the *Baqt* treaty and delivery of its arrears. Failing to achieve this objective, they launched a series of campaigns with the help of Arab tribesmen against al-Muqurra, which lasted for a century. Before the Mamlūks started their armed offensive, Dāwūd, the Nubian monarch, feeling isolated after the Mamlūk acquisition of Sawākīn, initiated an offensive policy when, in 1272, he sacked 'Aydhāb, Egypt's rich commercial port on the Red Sea.

The Mamlūk armies overran Nobatia and al-Muqurra several times, thus underminimg its political structure and paving the way for its ultimate fall. Other factors were conducive to the same conclusion. Members of the royal family, torn by dynastic discord, sought Mamlūk support against their rivals.

The Christian kingdom of Nubia had virtually ceased to exist when one of the claimants, Sayf al-Dīn 'Abdallāh Barshambu, who adopted Islam while in detention in Cairo, was raised to the Nubian throne by Mamlūk forces on 29 May 1317. Although the Islamization of the kingly office was a grave blow to the Christian Nubian monarchy, it did not mean the end of the Christian faith or the Christian civilization. These were to last for about another century and a half. Furthermore, Christian political authority was not completely wiped out as was generally thought (Ḥasan, 1967, pp. 106–120, 125).

A Christian kingdom, Dotawo, persisted to the end of the fifteenth century. It comprised the southern part of Lower Nubia. A leather scroll from Qaṣr Ibrīm, dated 1464, discloses that King Joel and Bishop Merki, both of Nubian origin, were then residing at Qaṣr Ibrīm; twenty years later they were still alive at Gebel Adda (Ḥasan, 1967, pp. 109–110, Adams, 1977, pp. 531–536, 541–542).

However, despite the gradual disintegration of the Church as an establishment, Christianity continued to linger on, and in a few isolated places possibly to the end of the sixteenth century. Nubian pilgrims were seen in Palestine in the fourteenth and fifteenth centuries (von Suchen, 1895, p. 103; Fabri, 1987, p. 209). The final blow to the Christian fabric in Nubia was inflicted by nomad Arabs, who, harassed by the ruling elite in Egypt, especially the Mamlūks, began to infiltrate in small numbers from the tenth century. Some of those Arabs settled in Nobatia and intermarried with the Nubians. Benefiting from the matrilineal system of succession, some of these immigrants, like the Banū al-Kanz, inherited local chieftainships. They gradually became virtual masters of al-Mātis, married into the royal family in Dunqula and seized the Nubian throne in 1323. Thus the Christian Nubian dynasty became both Arabized and Islamized (Ḥasan, 1967, pp. 98–99, 111, 119, 120). The slow migratory movement escalated towards the end of the thirteenth century and continued for about two centuries. Migrant Arabs poured in large numbers, either as part of the Mamlūk troops along the Nile, or independently. The latter followed the eastern route, where many Arabs from Egypt and directly from Arabia across the Red Sea had already settled in the Beja lands. The new arrivals trekked on into the Butāna and the Gezīra; the rest crossed the Nile to the plains of Kurdufān and Dār Fūr. There they met other migrants who followed the western bank of the Nile and broke off via Wādī al-Milik, Wādī al-Muqaddam to Kurdufān, Dār Fūr and Chad. Before this irruption slowed to a trickle, the lands of the kingdom of 'Alwa were nibbled away by the marauding Arabs who dealt a *coup de grâce* to the impoverished capital, Soba, in about 1450 (Ḥasan, 1967, pp. 42, 90, 124–125, 128, 132, 135).

Little has been said about the cultural and artistic development of al-Muqurra and even less about that of 'Alwa. The reason for this silence is that we have no data comparable to what has been yielded by Nobatia. Indeed most of the general remarks made on this subject are based on detailed examples more typical of Nobatia, where the region between the First and Second Cataracts was extensively investigated archaeologically just before it was inundated by the High Dam at Aswān. Although scant archaeological data have been obtained from the southern regions, al-Muqurra and 'Alwa, many important sites await to be studied.

The history of 'Alwa is generally obscure. Soba was hardly mentioned in contemporary sources. According to archaeological evidence, the kingdom of 'Alwa was apparently in decline as an independent state by the twelfth century. The king of al-Abwāb, whose kingdom was created within 'Alwa's northern borders, received more attention in Arabic sources. Prior to the early days of the Mamlūk sultanate, the impact of the Muslims was felt only in the commercial transactions that flourished between 'Alwa and the Islamic world. With increasing Mamlūk intervention in al-Muqurra, Muslim influence was clearly enhanced (Mufaḍḍal, 1919; II, p. 237; Ibn 'Abd al-Ẓāhir, 1961, pp. 143–144; Ḥasan, 1967, pp. 128–130).

As in al-Muqurra, the Church played a significant role in the culture of the southern Nubian kingdom. Byzantine influence was clearly demonstrated in the basilican plans of recently excavated (1981–1983) churches. Each of the two churches, designated A and B, was larger in area than the Faras Cathedral. The same site also reveals 'the continued use of Greek as late as the eleventh century' (Welsby; Daniels, 1991, XVIII, p. 9). However, with mounting Muslim pressure, the Church became more isolated and received no effective guidance. In the middle of the thirteenth century, the patriarch of Alexandria suspended the dispatch of priests to 'Alwa. John of Syria, who visited 'Alwa some time before 1520, stated that there were still 150 churches; whereas at the time of Abū Ṣāliḥ al-Arminī (*c.* 1203) there were no less than 400. According to Álvares, the people were so lacking in Christian instruction that they were 'neither Christians, Moors, nor Jews and that they live in the desire of being Christians' (Álvares, 1961, II, p. 461; Abū Ṣāliḥ, 1894, p. 120). The weakening of the Church was one aspect of the general decline of the kingdom of 'Alwa. By the second half of the fourteenth century, it had proved quite powerless to withstand the pressure of the Bedouins.

With the disappearance of the central government in Dunqula and later in Soba, chaos prevailed. The nomadic Arab tribes overran most of the territories of al-Muqurra and 'Alwa. The role of these nomads and their depredations in Nubia is succinctly explained by the celebrated Arab historian Ibn Khaldūn. He states: 'at their [the Nubians'] conversion to Islam, payment of *jizya* (poll tax) ceased. Then several clans of the Arab tribes of Juhayna dispersed throughout their country and settled there. They assumed power and filled the land with disorder and chaos '(Ibn Khaldūn, 1958, V, pp. 922–923). The prevalence of a climate of insecurity is also substantiated by archaeological evidence. The development of defensive structures, alluded to before, was probably consequential to the large-scale Arab movements of population that hit the area towards the end of the thirteenth century. Although the general pattern of infiltration was probably a peaceful one, the occurrence of clashes with farmers, local rulers and caravan leaders was inevitable. Nomads by their predatory disposition were the hereditary foes of settled peoples and organized states.

The unruly demeanour of these nomads was by and large responsible for ruining the valuable trade that thrived along the Nile. That trade had been the prime ingredient of Nubian prosperity. With the loss of peace and the devastation of the basis for its economic prosperity, Christian Nubian civilization could not survive.

It is true that these unlettered Bedouins had little regard for settled life and the refinements associated with it, but they were not the entire cause of the decline of Nubian civilization. In addition to the factors cited above, the Nubian monarchies had betrayed signs of decay well before the Mamlūk onslaught. Both al-Muqurra and ʿAlwa were then more than 700 years old. The Mamlūk incursion had weakened al-Muqurra beyond recovery. The Nubian archers could no longer match the professional Mamlūk fighters. The Nubian Church had become more detached from daily affairs. Spiritual support from the see of Alexandria was waning, and the dispatch of priests to either Dunqula or Soba was discontinued in the thirteenth century. The decline of trade was partly due to external factors. Since the conclusion of the *Baqt* treaty, Nubian trade had been integrated into the trade of the Muslims and as such became susceptible to world economic fluctuations in supply and demand, as well as to shifts in the major trade routes. The closure of the gold and emerald mines in the eastern desert, and the drop in demand for slaves, might have had a negative result (Ḥasan, 1967, pp. 49, 58, 80–81, 129). The advancing spirit of military feudalism, expressed in the appearance of feudal lords, defensive structures and escalating rivalry between claimants to the Dunqula throne, were further marks of the general decline. All these factors contributed collectively to the collapse of the Nubian monarchy and the disintegration of Christian Nubian civilization. The Bedouins delivered the final blow. The peaceful, prosperous, artistic civilization of Christian Nubia came to an end. All trace of a state or an organized Church disappeared. Long-distance trade faded, and so did the art of writing, and artistic and architectural traditions. Wheel-made decorated wares were abandoned, and only the practice of hand-made pottery was retained (Adams, 1977, p. 521).

In the anarchy that prevailed, social regression seemed to have encompassed Nubian society. In the vacuum that emerged the seeds of a new culture, a new faith and a new written language were implanted. The transformation from a Christian Nubian to an Islamic Arab culture was as great as that from a Kushite to a Christian.

THE ARABIZATION AND ISLAMIZATION OF THE SUDANESE PEOPLE

The Arabization and Islamization of the Nubians and other Sudanese communities were the direct result of the penetration of large numbers of nomadic Arab tribes, over many centuries, a process which dwindled towards the end of the fifteenth century. At first, the Arabs set up their tents along the desert fringes and gradually forced their way to the banks of the Nile, where they settled. Those who took up permanent residence intermingled and intermarried with the local inhabitants, repeating a process which had already been at work in al-Māris. By dint of the area's matrilineal practice, they fell heirs to positions of leadership and/or property. Others carved their own domains by means of political manipulation or military strength. Hence, slowly, successive sections or provinces of the Nubian states fell to the Muslim Arabs. The newcomers, mostly nomads, outnumbered the farmers and other permanent dwellers along the Nile and prevailed over them.

The infiltration of Arab nomads in large numbers, and their permanent abode in Nubia, adjusted the 'ecological balance between the desert and the cultivated land'. The nomads and semi-nomadic Arabs who were not attracted by a settled life were able, by virtue of their mobility and martial disposition, to exercise considerable influence over the farmers. Indeed, the military balance was tilted, possibly for the first time in Sudanese history, away from the riverain peoples, in favour of the steppe and desert tribes (Adams, 1977, pp. 548, 590).

The twin processes of Arabization and Islamization largely accomplished during the 'Dark Period' (1317–1504), went hand in hand. Large sections of the Sudanese people became Arabized and assimilated into the tribal structure. They adopted Arab genealogies and customs, and those who were thoroughly Arabized exchanged their native language for Arabic. However, the great majority of the Nubians north of the Fourth Cataract and the Beja, who were the first to have felt the impact of Arabic culture and Islamic ascendancy, continued to speak their own languages to the present day. The ethnic and cultural assimilation was a two-way process involving both the Arabization of the original inhabitants and the indigenization of the Arab immigrants. The dominance of Arab culture suggests, among other factors, that the Arab invaders arrived in large numbers and hence were able to exert substantial influence on the Sudanese peoples. The preponderance of nomadism among the newcomers meant that their cultural impact on the nationals was largely uniform. But the nomads were faced with substantial environmental differences that compelled them, in certain instances, to shift from use of camels to that of cattle while trekking in the southern parts of Kurdufān and Dār Fūr while clinging to a nomadic existence. The degree of Arabization seems to have been closely correlated with the number of arrivals. It was greatest in the areas between the Fourth Cataract and Sinnār along the Nile, in the Butāna, the Gezīra and the northern plains of Kurdufān and Dār Fūr. There the same process of acculturation took place. Within this broad framework, the degree of Arabization varied from tribe to tribe. Furthermore, compared with those Arabs who opted for a sedentary life together with the Arabized Nubians, the nomadic Arabs – sheep and camel breeders – probably mingled less with the indigenous population. Yet regardless of a few exceptions – consisting basically of nomadic Arab tribes – the term *ʿArab* was increasingly stripped of its ethnic significance (Ḥasan, 1967, pp. 135–136, 167, 174–176).

In sum, after at least two centuries of close association between the Arabs and the peoples of the Sudan, an ethnically and culturally Arabized hybrid emerged. A focal point in this evolution was the widespread adoption of 'Arab' ancestry, at times even among those who hardly spoke Arabic but who truly embraced the Islamic faith. Indeed, the close association of Islam with 'Arab' identity implied in the minds of new converts that being a Muslim meant becoming an Arab.

The process of Islamization in Nubia was inseparably bound up with Arabization. The dissemination of Islam was initially the work of two distinct groups of Muslims. The first were the traders, who, though limited in the scope of missionary activity, propagated Islam while conducting their own commercial contacts, which lasted for about eight centuries.

The second were the nomads who invaded the country. The great majority of these nomads, though themselves not well versed in Islamic doctrine and not inspired by missionary zeal, were in fact mainly responsible for the Islamization of the people of the Sudan. This was accomplished primarily by their intermingling and intermarrying with the local population (Ḥasan, 1971, pp. 75-76).

The scope of Islamization was not restricted to the riverain Nubians, who were adherents of Christianity, but also included the followers of African beliefs living in the stretches of grasslands. The latter areas offered wide opportunities for Islamic ascendancy. Although the spread of Islam at this stage, the 'Dark Period', was probably little more than nominal, the efforts of the two pioneering groups were strengthened by the works of some Muslim teachers. Sudanese oral traditions specify two religious teachers. The first was Ghūlām Allāh Ibn 'Āyd, a scholar from Yemen who visited Dunqula towards the end of the fourteenth century. He decided to settle there because 'the place was in extreme perplexity and error for lack of learned men. He built the mosques and taught the Qur'ān and religious sciences' (MacMichael, 1922, II, p. 35 (B.A. Arabic Ms. No. 573) (see Plate 273). The second was Ḥamad Abū Dunnāna, a Moroccan *Ṣūfī* missionary who introduced the Shādhiliyya order in the Sudan in about the second half of the fifteenth century. Although the impact of these two men could not have been great, they stand out as the pioneers of religious education in the country. However, real Islamization began with the coming of the 'Abdallābī kings and the Funj sultans to power.

According to a vigorous Sudanese tradition, the fall of Soba was achieved primarily by the Arab tribes under the leadership of 'Abdallāh nicknamed *Jammā'* or the 'gatherer' (Holt, 1960, XXII, pp. 1–12; Ḥasan, 1972, pp. 23–37). In about 1450, he established the first Arab state in the Sudan, probably along tribal lines, and ruled the country from Qarrī about 50 miles north of Soba. By the beginning of the sixteenth century, this newly established Arab kingdom had to contend with a formidable enemy – the Funj. There is much controversy surrounding their remote origin. They were a dark-skinned people who established their hegemony over the southern region of the Gezīra. Sudanese traditions credited them with an Arab ancestry; however, they were probably only recent converts to Islam. At Arbajī, in about 1504, the two powers clashed, and the Funj reduced the 'Abdallabī king to the position of a viceroy. From Sinnār, the dynastic capital, the Funj ruled over both the Arabs and their non-Arab subjects as far as the Third Cataract. In the south, the frontier of the Funj Islamic sultanate (and that of Islam) was stabilized more or less along latitude 10–11° N. East of the Nile, their authority covered the Beja country, while to the west, Kurdufān remained a bone of contention between them and the Islamic kingdoms of Tagalī, the Musabba'āt and the Fūr (Holt, 1963, IV, pp. 39–55; Ḥasan, 1965, XLVI, pp. 27–32).

The establishment of a strong government under the Funj sultans provided the country with a measure of unity and stability that prepared the ground for proper Islamization. Under the guidance of the Funj kings and Arab chiefs, individual scholars, mainly jurists and *Ṣūfīs* from Egypt and the Ḥijāz, were welcomed and encouraged to settle (Ḥasan, 1971, p. 75).

According to Ibn Ḍayf Allāh, the native author of the *Ṭabaqāt*, a biographical dictionary of holy men and jurists, Maḥmūd al-'Arakī was the first Sudanese to study in Cairo. On his return, in the first half of the sixteenth century, he established a school of learning. He taught Islamic law; and no less than seventeen schools were founded by his students on the lower waters of the White Nile. Another jurist who studied Māliki law in Cairo, was Ibrāhīm al-Būlād ibn Jābir, (fl. 1570), who introduced the teaching of two Mālikī textbooks: namely the *Risāla* of Ibn Abī Zayd al-Qayrawānī (d. 996) and the *Mukhtaṣar* of Khalīl ibn Isḥāq (d. 1563). He, his brothers and their descendants were instrumental in propagating the tradition of learning in many parts of the country (Ibn Ḍayf Allāh, 1992, pp. 40–41, 45–46, 250, 344). Once Islamization had progressed far into Nubia, educated Nubians migrated to areas where it had not yet progressed much. Among the first pioneers in this respect were the Maḥas Nubians, who migrated during the first half of the sixteenth century from the area between the Second and Third Cataracts to the banks of the Nile and the Blue Nile near Soba. Their residence there led to the development of important religious centres. Soon many religious schools or *khalwas* littered the whole area between the Fourth Cataract and the Gezīra (Trimingham, 1949, note 2, p. 99).[2] However, the attempt of trained Muslim scholars to raise the level of religious sophistication was not an easy task in such a vast, isolated and backward country.

The arrival of Shaykh Tāj al-Dīn al-Bihāri of Baghdād, a follower of the Qādirī *Ṣūfī* order, in 1577 led to the growth of the distinctive features of Islamic culture in the Sudan. During his 7-year stay, he initiated a number of prominent Sudanese into the Qādirī order. The *Ṣūfī* missionaries introduced a more popular and less exacting type of Islam. When *Ṣūfism* was disseminated in the Sudan it was already affected by some unorthodox practices and here, in the absence of a strong intellectual stimulant, many superstitions were assimilated. The *Ṣūfī* path continued to flourish until it won over the hearts of the majority of Muslims. Indeed, mystics became more revered than jurists. However, the two functions of a jurist and a *Ṣūfī* were eventually amalgamated in one person, the *faqīh*, who were the instruments of the new ideological and cultural change (Ibn Ḍayf Allāh, 1922, pp. 41, 127–128; Ḥasan, 1971, pp. 80–82).

The supremacy of Islam and Arabic culture dates from the rise of the Islamic Funj Sultanate. The *sharī'a*, the law of Islam, was gradually implemented (Kropacek, 1984, p. 415). A case in point was the change from a matrilineal system of succession to patrilineal practice. In the new cultural climate, the *Khalwa* symbolized the basic expression of the new faith and its cultural manifestations. There both the written elements of the new faith and *Ṣūfī* practices were taught. In short, the stage was set for the further growth of both the Islamic faith and Arab culture, which would ultimately pave the way for more cohesion among the diverse ethnic groups and the different cultural entities of the Nilotic Sudan and its gradual absorption into the Arab world. The pioneering Nubians became an integral part of the new Afro-Arab-Islamic cultural transformation that embraced large tracts of the Nilotic Sudan. Thus a new chapter in the cultural history of the Nilotic Sudan was begun: one to which the conclusion has not yet been written.

NOTES

1 In writing this chapter, I have drawn a lot from the works of many scholars, especially those of Nubian archaeologists and historians. Foremost among them are the works of Professors W. Y. Adams, S. Jakobielski and P. L. Shinnie. To all I would like to express my gratitude. I am also thankful

to Professor Ahmad M. A. al-Hakem, chairman, Sudan National Board for Antiquities and Museums, for supplying me with photographs of material kept in the museum.

2 It seems to me that the Mahass had emigrated earlier than suggested, I think towards the end of the fifteenth century.

BIBLIOGRAPHY

IBN 'ABD AL-ḤAKAM. 1914; 1922. *Kitāb Futūḥ Misr wa l-Maghrib wa l-Andalus* (Book of the Conquest of Egypt, the Maghrib and Spain). Arabic text ed. by MASSÉ, H. (*Le livre de la conquête de l'Egypte, du Maghreb et de l'Espagne*), Cairo 1914. Arabic text also ed. by TORREY, C. C., *The History of the Conquest of Egypt, North Africa and Spain*, Yale University Press, New Haven, Conn. 1922.

IBN 'ABD AL-ZĀHĪR; MU'ĪN AL-DĪN. 1960. *Tashrīf al-Ayyām wa l-'Usūr fī Sīrat al-Malik al-Mansūr* (The Nobility of the Days and the Ages in the Course of Life of the Victorious King). Cairo.

ABŪ SĀLIḤ AL-ARMANĪ. 1894. *Tārīkh al-Shaykh Abī Sālih al-Armanī*.(Chronicle of the Shaykh abū Sālih al-Armanī Abī) EVETTS, T. A. (ed.). Oxford.

ADAMS, W. Y. 1977. *Nubia: Corridor To Africa.* Allen Lane, London.

——. (a). *Medieval Nubia: Another Golden Age.* (in press).

——. (b). *The Ballana Kingdom and Culture: Twilight of Classical Nubia.* (in press).

ÁLVARES, F. 1989. *Verdadeira informação das terras do Preste João das Indias (1540).* New edn., Lisbon. English trans. by BECKINGHAM, C. F., HUNTINGFORD, G. W. B. Hakluyt Society, Cambridge, II. 1961.

ARKELL, A. J. 1959. Medieval History of Darfur and Nilotic Sudan. *Sudan Notes and Records*, Vol. XL, pp. 44–47.

CROWFOOT, J. W. 1927. Christian Nubia. *Journal of Egyptian Archaeology*. Vol. XIII, pp. 141–150.

IBN DAYF ALLĀH, MUḤAMMAD AL-NŪR. 1990. *Kitāb al-Tabaqāt fī Khusūs al-Awliyā' wa l-Sālihīn wa l-'Ulamā' wa l-Shu'arā' fī Sūdān* (Book of Categories regarding the Saints, Worthies, Learned Divines, and Poets of Sudan). Ed. by ḤASAN, Y. F. Khartoum.

FABRI, F. 1897. The Book of Wanderings of Brother Felix Fabri. *The Library of the Palestine Pilgrims Text Society*, Vol. VII, pp. 373, 435. London.

GADALLAH, F. F. 1959. The Egyptian Contribution to Nubian Christianity. *Sudan Notes and Records.* Vol. XL, pp. 38–42.

GARTKIEWIEZ, P. M. 1982. *New Outline of the History of Nubian Church Architecture.* In: MOORSEL P. VAN (ed.) *New Discoveries in Nubia.* Proceedings of the Colloquium on Nubian Studies. The Hague, 1979, Leiden, pp. 9–10.

——. 1987. Nubian Church Architecture: Unity or Distinctness. In: HAGG, T. (ed.). *Nubian Culture Past and Present.* Stockholm.

ḤASAN, Y. F. 1965. The Umayyad Genealogy of the Funj. *Sudan Notes and Records.* Vol. XLVI, pp. 27–32.

——. 1967. *The Arabs and the Sudan. From the Seventh to the Early Sixteenth Century.* Edinburgh.

——. 1971. External Islamic Influences and the Progress of Islamization in the Eastern Sudan Between the Fifteenth and Nineteenth Centuries. In: ḤASAN, Y. F., *Sudan in Africa*, Khartoum, pp. 73–86.

——. 1972. *Muqaddima fi Tārīkh al-Mamālik al-Islāmiyya fi al-Sūdān al-Sharqī*, (Introduction to the History of the Islamic Kingdoms in Eastern Sudan). Beirut.

HINDS, M.; SAKKOUT, H. 1981. A Letter from the Governor of Egypt to the King of Nubia and Muqurra Concerning Egyptian–Nubian Relations in 141/785. In: AL-QĀDĪ W. (ed.) *Studia Arabica and Islamica*, Beirut, pp. 209–29.

HOLT, P. M. 1960. A Sudanese Historical Legend: The Funj Conquest of Soba. *Bulletin of the School of Oriental and African Studies.* Vol. XXII, pp. 1–17.

——. 1963. Funj Origins: A Critique and New Evidence. *Journal of African History,* Vol. IV, pp. 39–55.

AL-ISTAKHRĪ, IBRĀHĪM IBN MUḤAMMAD. 1870. *Kitāb Masālik al-Mamālik* (Book of the Routes of the Kingdoms). de Goeje, M. J., ed. of Arabic text. Leiden.

JAKOBIELSKI, S. 1982a. A Brief Account on the Churches of Dongola. In: MOORSEL, P. VAN (ed.) *New Discoveries in Nubia.* Proceedings of the Colloquium on Nubian Studies. The Hague, 1979, Leiden, pp. 51–56.

——. 1982b. Remarques sur la chronologie des peintures murales de Faras aux VIIIe et IX siècles. In: JAKOBIELSKI, S. (ed.) *Nubia Christiana.* Warsaw, pp. 141–172.

——. 1986. North and South in Christian Nubian Culture: Archaeology and History. In: MOORSEL, P. VAN (ed.) *Nubian Culture Past and Present.* Stockholm.

——. 1988. Christian Nubia at the Height of its Civilization. In EL FASI, M. (ed.) *General History of Africa.* Vol. III, *Africa from the Seventh to the Eleventh Century.* UNESCO, Paris, pp. 194–223.

IBN KHALDŪN. 1868. ed. *Kitāb al-'Ibar* ('Book of Admonition' = 'Universal History'). Arabic text, 7 vols, Būlāq, 1868; Beirut 1958. Partial French trans., 4 vols, by Baron W. MacGuckin de Slane, *Histoire des Berbères et des dynasties musulmanes de l'Afrique septentrionale*, Algiers, 1852–1856; repr. Paris 1925–1926. New complete French trans., 7 vols, Beirut, 1956–1959. [See Vol. V of the 1958 Beirut Arabic edn.]

KIRWAN, L. P. 1935. Notes on the Topography of the Christian Nubian Kingdoms. *Journal of Egyptian Archaeology.* Vol. XXI, pp. 60–61.

KROPACEK, L. 1984. Nubia from the Late 12th Century to the Funj Conquest in the Early 15th Century. In: NIANE, D. T. (ed.) *General History of Africa.* Vol. IV. *Africa from the Twelfth to the Sixteenth Century.* UNESCO, Paris, pp. 398–422.

MACMICHAEL, H. A., 1922. *A History of the Arabs in the Sudan.* Cambridge, 2 vols.

AL-MAQRĪZĪ. 1922. *Kitāb al-Mawā'iz wa l-I'tibār bi-Dhikr al-Khitat wa l-Āthār.* (Book of Admonitions and Exhortation in the Mention of Land-Tracts and Traces). WIET, G. (ed.). Cairo, Vol. III.

MICHALOWSKI, K. 1981. The Spreading of Christianity in Nubia. In: MOKHTAR, G. (ed.) *General History of Africa.* Vol. IV, *Ancient Civilizations of Africa.* UNESCO, Paris, pp. 326–340.

MONNERT DE VILLARD, U. 1938. *Storia della Nubia Cristiana.* Pontificio Institutum Orientalum Studiorum, Roma.

MUFADDAL IBN ABĪ L-FADĀ'IL. 1919. *Al-Nahj al-Sadīd wa l'Durr al-Farīd fī mā ba'd Tārīkh Ibn al-'Āmid* (The Proper Path and Peerless Pearl in What Follows upon the Chronicle of Ibn al-'Āmid'). BLOCHET, E. (ed.) Vol. II. Paris.

NĀSIR-I KHUSRAW. 1881; 1945; 1992. *Safar-Nāmeh* (The Book of Travels). Persian text ed. with French trans. by SCHEFER, C. Paris, 1881. Standard Persian text ed. by M. D. Siyāqī, Tehran AH 1370 (solar) = AD 1992. Arabic trans. by M. al-Khashshāb, Cairo 1945.

PLUMLEY, J. M. 1982. The Christian Period in Nubia as Represented on the Site of Qasr Ibrim. In: MOORSEL, P. VAN (ed.) *New Discoveries in Nubia.* Proceedings of the Colloquium on Nubian Studies. The Hague, 1979, Leiden, pp. 100–110.

SHINNIE, P. L. 1967. *Meroë: A Civilization of the Sudan.* New York.

——. 1974. Multilingualism in Medieval Nubia. In: ABDALGADIR MAHMOUD ABDALLA, (ed.) *Studies in Ancient Languages of the Sudan.* Khartoum, pp. 41–47.

——. 1978. Christian Nubia. In: FAGE, J. D. (ed.) *The Cambridge History of Africa.* Cambridge, Vol. II, pp. 556–588.

SUCHEN, L. VON. 1895. Description of the Holy Land. *The Library of the Palestine Pilgrims Text Society*, Vol. VII. London.

TOROK, L. 1975. Money, Economy and Administration in Christian Nubia. In: *Etudes Nubiennes.* Colloque de Chantilly, pp. 2–6, 7, 1975, 287–311.

——. 1988. Late Antique Nubia. In: *History and Archaeology of the Southern Neighbour of Egypt, c. 4th–6th Century AD.* Budapest.

TRIMMINGHAM, J. S. 1949. *Islam in the Sudan.* Oxford.

WELSBY, D. A.; DANIELS, C. M. 1991. *Soba, Archaeological Research at a Medieval Capital on the Blue Nile.* Memoir 12, British Institute in East Africa, London.

34

ETHIOPIA

E. J. Van Donzel

At the beginning of the seventh century AD, the kingdom of Aksum came into close contact with Islam. Muslim sources report on friendly relations between the Prophet Muḥammad and the *Najashi*, the king of Ethiopia. During the so-called *first ḥijra*, the Prophet sent a number of his followers to the *Najashi*, who received them in a friendly manner (EI[2], 1960). In the first half of the eighth century, the *najashi* figures among the 'family of kings' from whom the Umayyad caliphs sought to derive legitimacy (Erlich 1994, p.11). The positive attitude of Islam towards Ethiopia is still reflected in a well-known tradition of the ninth century, according to which the Prophet said: 'leave the Ethiopians alone as long as they leave you alone' (Erlich in: EI[2], 1994, pp.14 ff.). Traditions such as these may have contributed to the often quoted statement, attributed (Trimmingham, 1952, p. 52) to Ibn Ḥawqal, according to which Abyssinia was not subject to the *jihād*. However, Ibn Ḥawqal says only that there was no war (*ḥarb*) then going on in the land of the Beja (Erlich in: EI[2], 1994, pp. 14 ff.). After AD 750, when the 'Abbāsids transferred the centre of Muslim power from Damascus to Baghdād, Ethiopia disappeared from view for the Muslims, except as a provider of slaves (Van Donzel, 1988, pp.113–121).

It is generally stated that Islam cut off Ethiopia's contacts with the outside world. The new religion indeed blocked connection between Ethiopia and its ally Byzantium, but this isolation had already begun when the Persians, opposed to Byzantium, around AD 575 forced the Ethiopians to leave South Arabia which they had conquered in about AD 525.

Thrown back upon its own resources, politically and culturally, the kingdom of Aksum began to expand southward. The period between the eighth and the thirteenth centuries is often referred to as 'the dark centuries'. This term, however, is only acceptable if it is understood to mean: 'lacking historical documents'. A notable exception are the spectacular rock-hewn churches at Lalibala (or Lalibela), which date from the twelfth–thirteenth centuries (see Plate 280). It was during this long period that the Semitico-Cushitic culture, the characteristic feature of Ethiopia, came into being.

ENVIRONMENT AND TECHNIQUES (Pankhurst, 1961)

Agriculture

Marco Polo (d. 1324) writes that Ethiopia abounded in all the necessities of life, and he speaks of wheat, meat, milk and sesame as agricultural products. Ibn Faḍl Allāh al-'Umarī (d. 1349) also mentions the well-known *tef* (*Erogrostis abyssinica*), and underlines that two harvests could be obtained per year. Three centuries later, Portuguese authors still praised the country's fertility. Ploughs were digging sticks, equipped with handles for breaking the topsoil; they were drawn by oxen, which were also used for treading the corn. Selection of crops was brought about by differences in altitude. *Qat* (*Catha edulis*) (Schoppen, 1978), believed to be native to Ethiopia, was introduced into the Yemen during the reign of the Rasūlid al-Malik al-Mu'ayyad Dā'ūd (r. 1296–1322), while coffee, according to Arab tradition, was brought from Ethiopia to Arabia in the fifteenth century (Kahwa; Becca in *EI*[2], 1994, p. 34). One of the most important textiles was cotton. Sugar cane is mentioned in the fourteenth and fifteenth centuries, but honey must have been used since early times for the manufacturing of mead. Fruits included banana, citron, lemon, pomegranate, apricot and grapes; vines, however, were introduced only in the seventeenth century.

Land

According to tradition, Menelik I, son of King Solomon and the Queen of Sheba and the first king of Ethiopia, divided the land into three equal parts: one for the Crown, one for the Church, and one for the people. It would seem that, until 1974, the wealth and power of Crown and Church were indeed based on this tradition. In theory, all land was owned by the emperor, so that every cultivator was his tenant. The collectivity of cultivators of land, therefore, had to provide for the maintenance of the government, including the provincial one, for the army, and for the Church. Part of the land of the Church was worked by priests and monks, the rest being hired out to the peasants (Ullendorff, 1960, p. 188).

Tax payments to the lord or to the emperor consisted of a portion of the crop, a certain amount of cloth, or a pot of honey and an occasional fowl.

Trade and currency

Trade was carried out mainly by Muslim and non-Ethiopian merchants, the local Christians considering it as an inferior pursuit. According to Ibn Faḍl Allāh al-'Umarī, barter was used both by the Muslims in their sultanates and by the

Christians in their kingdom. It is generally believed that coins were used in the Aksumite kingdom from the third through the ninth–tenth centuries. After that, gold coins, and in general coins with Greek inscriptions became infrequent, which indicates that international trade was in decline. Currency was then replaced by gold bars, salt and iron bars, while in the north, coarse cotton cloth and pepper were also used. Iron mines were found in most parts of the country, especially near Aksum and in Lasta. For the Muslim merchants, iron was the normal medium of trade, and the Agaw exchanged it against gold, which was brought from the regions south of the Blue Nile.

Blacksmiths, silversmiths, potters and other manual workers were looked down upon. These crafts were exercised by the Falasha, the 'Jews of Ethiopia'.

Slavery

Slavery in Ethiopia is already mentioned in the *Periplus Maris Erythraei* (first century AD), and Ethiopian slaves were found in Mecca before Islam. In Ethiopia, the institution was based on Mosaic law, and later sanctioned in the *Fetha Nagast*. The establishment of Muslim trading centres along the roads leading from the Red Sea ports inland increased the slave trade, which in its turn favoured Islamization, because becoming a Muslim was the only way for a captured Christian to avoid slavery: according to Muslim law, a Muslim could not be enslaved by a Muslim. The Arab geographers al-Idrīsī (d. *c.* 1165) and Ibn Ṣa'id al-Maghribī (d. 1286), as well as the Italian traveller Ludovico di Varthema (d. 1510), relate that Ethiopians, captured in great numbers by Muslims, were exported as slaves to Mecca, Cairo, south Arabia, Persia and India. According to Ibn Faḍl Allāh al-'Umarī, castration was explicitly forbidden by the emperor, but it was carried out by brigands in a region known as Waslu, where Muslim merchants used to take their slaves. R. Pankhurst (1961, p. 388) calculated that in the early nineteenth century, the annual export of slaves from Ethiopia may have amounted to 25,000. This would suggest that, out of a population of perhaps 10 million, something like 2.5 million were carried away in one century. On the basis of these calculations, it may safely be said that, in the period under consideration, the slave trade from Ethiopia across the Red Sea and the Sudanese border was a thriving business.

THE ETHIOPIAN CHRISTIAN KINGDOM AND ISLAM

600–1270

During the expansion southwards, military colonies were established in the land of the Agaw. By the beginning of the tenth century, the Arab historians Ibn Ḥawqal, al-Mas'ūdi and al-Ya'qūbī, the only sources available for this period, speak of a great kingdom ruled by the *Najashi*, to whom the Cushitic Sidama of the Shoa plateau had become tributary. According to the *History of the Patriarchs of Alexandria* (Evetts, 1904, p. 171), a pagan queen, probably of Sidama (Damot) origin, persecuted and killed the Christian king of Ethiopia (Tamrat, 1972, pp. 38–39). The Christian kingdom was further weakened by strife within the Church. 'The stability of the kingdom was clearly dependent on the integration of the Agaw peoples, who were now brought within the effective orbit of Monophysite Christianity' (Ullendorff, 1960, pp. 61–62). Such an integration took place in religious matters, for at a certain moment the Zagwe kings, who were of Agaw stock, were converted to Christianity. The centuries-old opposition between Semites and the Cushitic peoples, however, remained, as is clear from the apparent enmity between the Aksumite-oriented clergy and the Zagwe monarchs (Van Donzel, 1997a).

It was in this period of internal weakness of the Christian kingdom that Islam began to move in. From the Dankali and Somali coasts, from eastern Shoa, from Harar in the east and from Lake Zway in the south-west, it spread among the Beja in the north and the Sidama in the south. Muslim merchants who brought their religion to the markets of the villages along the trade routes, began to demand freedom of worship, turning to Egypt for support, but the Christian king and his clergy rejected their requests. 'Thus there began the historic role of Egypt as the champion of Islam in Ethiopia' (Tamrat, 1972, p. 46) and, one may add, of the Ethiopian king as the champion of the Copts in Egypt. A prominent role on the Egyptian side was played by Badr al-Jamālī (d. 1094), the Armenian *vizier* of al-Mustanṣir bi-llāh, the Fāṭimid caliph in Cairo (Van Donzel, 1999). Although on both sides the claim to protect the other's minority was just a powerless threat, the two countries were linked to one another, even if for opposite reasons. The Ethiopian Church, and consequently the Ethiopian State, were linked to the patriarch of Alexandria, the head of the Church who appointed the metropolitan bishop of Ethiopia. Through the patriarch, the Ethiopian Church and State had to deal with the caliph and his *viziers* as well. In Egypt, it was believed that the Ethiopians were able to block the Nile, or to divert its course to the Red Sea. This legend was to play a role in relations between the two countries (Van Donzel, 1997b).

While Islam grew in the south-east, important changes were taking place in the north. The Semitic kingdom of Aksum was losing its political and military power to the Cushitic Agaw, in particular to those of Lasta. Under the Zagwe dynasty (*c.* early twelfth century–1270). Aksum was replaced by the new capital Roha, in Lasta, later to be renamed Lalibala, after the best-known king of the dynasty, to whom the eleven world-famous rock-hewn churches are ascribed (see Plate 280) (Gerster, 1968; Van Donzel, 1997a).

In 1270, the Zagwe dynasty was overthrown by Yekuno Amlak, who was said to be a descendant of Delnaod, allegedly the last king of Aksum, and the reputed 'restorer' of the dynasty of the Solomonides.

1270–1500

By now, the Christian kingdom reached from Shimazana and the River Marab in the north to the northern part of the Shoa plateau in the south, and from the river Takaza, the southern Begemdir and the eastern tributaries of the Blue Nile in the west to the edge of the Shoa plateau in the east (Tamrat, 1972, p. 212). An intermittent state of war existed between this more or less united Christian kingdom, and the seven petty Muslim states of Ifat, Dawaro, Bali, Hadiya, Arababni, Sharkha and Dara. In 1285 Ifat overthrew the sultanate of the Makhzumi in eastern Shoa which, according to tradition, had been founded in AD 896–897 (Trimingham, 1952, pp. 58, 64).

Yekuno Amlak's son Yagbea Syon (1285–1294) was the first Ethiopian ruler to dispatch a letter to the Ethiopian community in Jerusalem. In 1290, one of the Ethiopian delegates, perhaps the leader, was a Muslim (Cerulli, 1943, p. 89). Future kings were to follow this procedure in their relations with Egypt.

Yekuno Amlak's grandson Amda Syon (1314–1344) is considered as the champion of the struggle against the Muslim states. The fusion of Church and State, which for centuries to come was to be the chief characteristic of Ethiopia, began to take shape.

For their communication with the Red Sea ports, the Christians were dependent on the Muslims. In order to redress this situation, Amda Syon attacked Ifat, which was destroyed. At first the Christian forces met strong resistance, but in the end Damot and Hadiya surrendered. In order to keep the Ethiopian trading routes open, the king attacked Dawaro, Mora and Adal.

During the troubled years in Egypt around the middle of the fourteenth century, when five caliphs succeeded one other in fifteen years (1348–1363), the Copts were persecuted by the Cairene populace. King Sayfa Arad (1344–1371) took up the position of protector of his co-religionists. On the Egyptian side, Patriarch Marcos (1348–1363) was ordered to send a delegation to the Ethiopian king, so that he should put an end to the hostile actions against the Muslims. Meanwhile, the centre of Muslim power had been transferred from Ifat to Adal, from where the trading routes could better be controlled. King Dawit (1380–1412) led several campaigns against Adal and even reached Zaylā, where the Muslim leader Sa'd al-Dīn was captured and killed.

Since 1270, the Ethiopian kingdom had expanded considerably. In the south, Damot and Hadiya had been conquered, and the influence of the Christians was strongly felt in the Sidama region. Gojjam was attacked under King Yishaq (1413–1430), and, in the north-west, the Falasha country was gradually brought under Christian control. All these conquests had opened up vast regions, into which the Ethiopian Church was about to penetrate. The Falasha, who usually refer to themselves as *Beta Isra'el* or 'House of Israel', used to live to the north of Lake Tana in Begemdir, Semien, and Dambiya. They are Ethiopians of Agau stock practising a peculiar kind of Judaism. This has given rise to the claim that they are 'the Jews of Ethiopia'. They are first mentioned in the royal chronicles of King Amda Syon. According to Ullendorff, the Falasha are descendants of those elements in the Aksumite kingdom who resisted conversion to Christianity. Their so-called 'Judaism', then, is merely a reflection of those Hebraic and Judaic practices and beliefs which were implanted in parts of south-west Arabia in the first post-Christian centuries and subsequently brought into Abyssinia (Ullendorff, 1960, pp. 111–112). Kay Kaufman Shelemay, on the other hand, attempts to demonstrate that the *Beta Israel* not only are part of their Ethiopian environment, but also were shaped by it (Kaufman Shelemay, 1986, p. 17).

Already in the early years of the Solomonids, a religious revival had started at Dabra Damo in Tigré, where Iyasus Mo'a, born *c.* 1211, arrived in about 1241. In 1248 he traveled south and settled on the island of Lake Hayq. One of his disciples there was Takla Haymanot, the great saint of the Ethiopian church, born in Shoa in about 1215. Their encounter led to a lasting controversy between Dabra Hayq and Dabra Libanos, then called Dabra Asbo, the monastery in Shoa founded by Takla Haymanot. Ba-salota Mika'el, Iyasus Mo'a's successor, continued the opposition against lax morals (such as monks and nuns living together), and openly attacked King Amda Syon for having two wives and keeping numerous other women. In 1237, the new metropolitan Ya'qub arrived in Ethiopia. In contrast to his predecessors, who used to side with the king, he distanced himself from the court, supported the reform movement of the monasteries, and tried to convince King Sayfa Arad that he should keep only one wife. But the king sent him back to Egypt, and banished the reform-minded monks to the southern part of the country. As a result, the regions around Lake Zway were opened up to evangelization. The other great saint of the Ethiopian Church in the Middle Ages is Ewostatewos (*c.* 1273–1352), who founded a community in Sara'e, the region north of Aksum. Around 1337 he left Ethiopia and went to Cairo, Palestine, Cyprus and finally to Armenia, where he died. The reason for his leaving his homeland was the dispute about the Sabbath. He strongly supported the view that the Sabbath should be celebrated in the same way as Sunday. The opposition of his order, called the 'House of Ewostatewos', against the metropolitan and the patriarch in Alexandria was such that they were excluded from receiving the holy orders. Consequently, the communities of the order were almost completely separated from the Church. For the celebration of holy mass, they obtained ordained priets from elsewhere, but the latter were only admitted after they had done penance for having been members of other communities (Tamrat, 1972, p. 212). The anti-Sabbath group, which followed the doctrine of the Coptic Church of Alexandria, was supported by King Dawit, by the greater part of the monasteries and by the new metropolitan Bartolomewos, who had arrived in Ethiopia in 1398–1399. At a synod held in 1400, the followers of Ewostatewos were condemned, but they refused to give in. By 1403, they had been permitted to observe the Sabbath but had to accept the supremacy of the Church of Alexandria and the leadership of the metropolitan. The king evidently wanted to bring the parties together, but the influence of the 'House of Ewostatewos' kept growing while the prestige of the metropolitan diminished (Rodinson, 1964, pp. 11–19). The defenders of the Sabbath found confirmation in the Apostolic Canons (Perier, 1912; Muyser, 1937, pp. 89–111), in the monastic *Rules of Saint Pachomius* which had been translated from Greek at an earlier date, together with the *Life of Paul the Hermite* and the *Life of Saint Anthony*, works which had been fundamental to Christian monasticism (Cerulli, 1956, pp. 25–26).

During the reign of King Zar'a Ya'qob (1434–1468), considered as one of the great kings of Ethiopia for his military campaigns and his church reforms, the observance of the Sabbath was revived. The king found a staunch supporter in the prominent scholar and writer Ghiorghis of Sagla. The monks of Dabra Libanos, however, remained strongly attached to the practice of the Church of Alexandria. Zar'a Ya'qob then sought the cooperation of Mika'el and Gabri'el, the two Egyptian bishops who had succeeded Bishop Bartolomewos. At a council at Dabra Mitmaq in Shoa, which was presided over by the king and attended by the two bishops, the followers of Ewostatewos and the abbots of the leading monasteries, the followers of Ewostatewos agreed that the holy orders should be administered by the Egyptian bishops, who in their turn authorized the observance of the Sabbath in the Ethiopian Church. Other subjects of discussion at the council were the Persons of the Trinity, the unity of God, the Stephanites, who rejected the cult of the Cross and the veneration of the Virgin Mary, and the Mikaelites, who denied that God can be known (Taurat, 1966 p. 226; Hammerschmidt, 1967, pp. 56–57, 62).

After the successful outcome of the council, Zar'a Ya'qob began to reform the church whose impact, in his view, was far from satisfactory. The lands of the conquered peoples were distributed as fiefs among the newly arrived Christian officials (Tamrat, 1972, pp. 98–103; 231), but the clergy were unable to transmit any form of education, Christian or other. The most urgent problem was the lack of priests and deacons, and so the king sent Bishop Mika'el to Amhara and Bishop Gabri'el to Shoa. Each of the major monasteries was given its own religious sphere of influence. Zar'a Ya'qob directed harsh measures against pagan worship and encouraged baptism by rewarding new converts. Every Christian should go to church on Saturdays and Sundays, and a priest was to go for the weekend to any group of Christians who lived too far from a church to attend services. Every Christian should also have his father confessor – until recently a distinctive feature of the Ethiopian Church – whose recommendation was necessary before being admitted to holy communion. Zar'a Ya'qob also ordered that each church should have a library with religious books for instruction. Consultation with witch doctors, offering sacrifices to pagan gods and the use of magical prayers were forbidden on pain of death. Every Christian should have the names of the Father, Son, and Holy Ghost branded upon his forehead, and the sign of the Cross had to be fixed on dresses, weapons and even ploughs. Strict observation of the numerous fasting and holy days was controlled by the abbots, assisted by royal troops, members of the royal house and confidents. Notwithstanding the threat of the patriarch of Alexandria that anyone who opposed the king's measures would be excommunicated, political unrest was due to follow. Zar'a Ya'qob himself, though a strict reformist, remained polygamous, superstitious and inclined to harshness. Yet, the revival of Ethiopian literature and the reorganization of the Church are his lasting achievements.

INTER-STATE RELATIONS

Relations with Egypt

Until the sixteenth century, Ethiopia remained alone in its struggle against Islam. So far there are no Ethiopian documents to prove, even indirectly, that the Crusaders had any contact with Ethiopia (Cerulli, 1943, pp. 20–26; Newbold, 1945, pp. 220–224). But by the time the crusades period came to an end with the capture of Acre by Mamlūk sultan al-Ashraf Khalīl (1291), European powers had begun to think of Ethiopia as a possible ally in the fight against Islam. The famous legend of the Blue Nile was taken up in Western military plans. On the Ethiopian side, at least among the Ethiopians in Jerusalem, there was the wish to learn more about the Christians in the West. But direct contact with Europe was not yet established. King Amda Syon (1314–1344) led a successful campaign to the north and even reached the Red Sea, but this was far from constituting a threat to Egypt. Relations between Ethiopia and Egypt became tense under King Sayfa Arad (1344–1371). Under Sultan al-Sāliḥ Salāh al-Dīn Sāliḥ (1351–1354), unrest in Egypt led to persecution of the Copts. Churches were destroyed, church land was confiscated and Coptic scribes dismissed (*EI*[2], 1994, s.v. Mamlūks; ibid. s.v. al-Salah, al-Malik). According to an Ethiopian source, Patriarch Marcos (1348–1363) informed Sayfa Arad that he had been imprisoned by the sultan. When the Ethiopian king marched northwards, the sultan gave in. According to another version, it was the Ethiopian Muslims who were persecuted and who appealed to the sultan for help (Tamrat, 1972, p. 253).

The Egyptian historian al-Maqrīzī relates (Quatremère 1811, pp. 276–277) that King Dawit (1380–1412) in 1381 had marched as far as Aswān, and that Patriarch Matewos (1378–1408), on the sultan's orders, had written to him that he should put an end to hostilities. Al-Maqrīzī's story is confirmed by Ethiopian sources (Tamrat, 1972, p. 255), some of which indicate that it was King Dawit's aim to go to Jerusalem.

Under Zar'a Ya'qob, military colonies were established on the Eritrean plateau. Several districts were grouped together and placed under the Bahr-Nagash or governor of the coastal provinces. Zar'a Ya'qob also sent a friendly letter to the Circassian Sultan Barsbāy (1422–1437) requesting his protection for his Christian subjects and respect for their churches. But in 1441, Patriarch Yohannes XI (1428–1453) wrote that Barsbāy had ordered the demolition of the church of Mitmaq (al-Makta). Zar'a Ya'qob then had a new church built at Eguba in Tagulat, which he named Mitmaq (Cercelli, 1943, p. 12; Perruchon, 1893, p. 56). In a strongly worded letter, he admonished Sultan Jaqmaq (1438–1452) that the persecution of the Copts was a breach of the complete freedom granted them by previous Muslim rulers, because Christian property had been confiscated and their churches desecrated. He himself, he wrote, behaved well towards the Muslims in Ethiopia, on whom not even the poll tax – he used the Arabic term *jizya* – was levied, and remarked that he could divert the course of the Nile but would not do this out of fear of God, and because he was concerned about the great sufferings that would follow. He requested the sultan to pursue traditional good relations. Jaqmaq sent an envoy with gifts, but rejected Zar'a Ya'qob's request that churches be rebuilt (al-Sakhawī, 1896, pp. 67–72; Wiet, 1938, pp. 124–125). The king then retained the Egyptian envoy and, after his great victory of 1445 over Badlay, the Muslim ruler of Adal, had him mistreated. In retaliation, Jaqmaq had Patriarch Yohannes severely beaten. He sent another message to Ethiopia, demanding the release of the envoy.

Relations with Europe

In the Middle Ages, Ethiopia was, for Europeans, the 'land of Prester John'. Legends about the powerful Christian monarch who ruled in Central Asia and attacked Islam from the rear were perhaps already circulating before 1141, when the Mongol Khitāy defeated the troops of the Seljuk sultan Sanjar in the Katwan Steppe in Ushrushana. The news of this victory reached the Crusaders, and thence Christian Europe. In the course of time, the Prester's kingdom was identified as 'High Ethiopia'. Well into the seventeenth century, many legends around 'Prester John' circulated in Europe.

The first European monarch to send a message to Ethiopia was King Henry IV of England (1399–1413), who had visited the Holy Land in 1392. The purpose of his letter seems to have been King Dawit's participation in a Crusade. The first Ethiopian mission to Europe is reported in 1402 (Cerulli, 1943, p. 208). King Yishaq (1413–1430) is said to have written to European rulers proposing a Christian alliance against Islam (al Maqrīzī, 1790, p. 8). In 1427, he sent a delegation to King Alfonso of Aragon in Valencia (De la Roncière, 1925, pp. 115–116). In 1432, Pietro of Naples returned from Ethiopia, where he had been on a mission sent out by the

Duke of Berry. He had stayed in Ethiopia for some years and had married an Ethiopian woman (Schefer, 1892, p. 148). In 1450, Zar'a Ya'qob sent another mission to King Alfonso, which was led by Pietro Rombulo, a Sicilian (Trasselli, 1941, p. 176; Creone, 1902, pp. 71–72, 75–76) who had stayed in Ethiopia for a long time. With his three Ethiopian companions, he was received by Pope Nicholas V (1447–1455), but there is no indication that this visit is to be considered a rapprochement with the Roman Catholic Church. Nor had there been an official delegation of the Ethiopian Church to the Council of Florence in 1441 (Tamrat, 1972, p. 265). King Alfonso answered that he would send artisans and masons, but it is not known whether they ever reached Ethiopia. European documents mention two other missions sent by King Alfonso, one in 1452, the other in 1453. Towards the end of the fifteenth century, several Europeans were living at the Ethiopian court. One was Pêro de Covilhã, a Portuguese sent to the East in 1487 by King João II of Portugal. Álvares gives his history in chapter civ of his work. Another European was the Venetian Nicolao Brancaleone, who had arrived in Ethiopia in 1480 (or 1487). He is said to have painted a picture of the Virgin and Child, which gave great offence to the Ethiopians because the child was held in his mother's left arm. Álvares met both of them when he arrived in Ethiopia in 1520 (Beckingham-Huntingford, 1961, p. 279).

In 1477 King Ba'eda Maryam (1468–1478) convened a council, where the question was raised whether the spiritual dependence on the Coptic Church in Alexandria should remain in force.

His successor, King Eskender (1478–1494), was crowned at the age of six. Power was in the hands of Ras Amda-Mika'el, who at the council of Matmaq in 1450 strongly defended the view that the Ethiopian Church should remain dependent on the Church of Alexandria. He found a formidable opponent in Ileni (Zan Ḥayla, d. 1522), a princess from Hadya who had been married to Zar'a Ya'qob in 1445. During the reign of Ba'eda Maryam, she had played the role of queen mother, the king having lost his own mother. Under Eskender's young son Amda Syon II (1494), civil war broke out. King Na'od (1494–1508) gained successes in his campaigns against Bali and Dawaro, but there were many defections in the Christian army, while the Muslim attacks increased in intensity. King Na'od lost his life in a battle against Ifat. The small states of Ifat, Bali and Dawaro, meanwhile, had become centres of Muslim power. It was in these regions that Ahmad Grañ was to win his earliest and most decisive victory in 1529. He was also welcomed by the Falasha, the Agaw south of Lake Tana, and in Hadya and Ganz. Only in Shoa, north of the river Awash, in eastern Gojjam, in Dambya and in Wagara had state and religion become welded strongly enough to resist the invading Muslims.

Literature

In the period under consideration, Ethiopian literature was for the greater part of a religious Christian nature. It reflected the way in which Church and State grew together and remained interdependent. Before AD 600, the Bible, including the so-called Deutero-canonical books, had been translated from Greek, together with works on monasticism, some writings of Cyril of Alexandria, parts of the homilies of various Fathers of the Church, and the *Fisalgos* or 'Physiologurs' (the moralized 'Bestiary'). Although no manuscripts older than the thirteenth century seem to have survived, the maturity shown in the works of that period reveals a long tradition of writing (Cerulli, 1956, p. 35). Literary activity seems to have started towards the end of the thirteenth century with translations from Arabic. The first was that of the *Legend of the Prophet Habacuc*, finished on 15 October 1293, apparently during the reign of Yagbe'a Syon (1285–1294). The *Senodos*, a juridical and religious work containing the canons of the Coptic Church, was translated around 1300. Many works, for the greater part hagiographies written in Arabic, were translated into Ethiopic under the patronage of the metropolitan Salama (1350–1390). They were intended to redress dissident ideas which were circulating in the monasteries. The most important work of this period, however, is the *Senkessar* (Synaxarium), a collection of short notices and lives of saints, to be read on the day of the saint's commemoration (see Plates 49, 279) (Cerulli, 1956, pp. 69–70; Guidi, 1932, pp. 34–35, 75, 81; Wallis Budge, 1928).

Great literary activity was developed during the reign of King Amda Syon I (1314–1344). His victorious campaigns are described in a chronicle, written between 1331 and 1344 (Perruchon, 1889, pp. 271–363, 381–494; Cerulli, 1956, pp. 37–43). A work which the Ethiopians consider as fundamental is the *Kebra Nagast* or 'Glory of the Kings', composed by Isaac, a cleric from Aksum, between 1314 and 1322. Intended to serve as the biblical basis for the Solomonid dynasty (see Plate 49), it relates above all the story of King Solomon and the Queen of Sheba, the birth of their son Menelik I, the latter's journey to Ethiopia, the clandestine transport of the Ark of the Covenant from Jerusalem to Aksum, and Menelik's coronation as the first king of Ethiopia. A smaller part is devoted to stories and explanations, which would prove that the most important sovereigns of the world descend from Israel, the kings of Ethiopia themselves being of a higher descent, namely from Jesse. At the end of the work, Isaac remarks that the *Kebra Nagast* was translated from Coptic into Arabic in 1225 – i.e. during the reign of the Zagwe, probably of King Lalibala – but that it could then not be translated into Ethiopic because 'those who are reigning are not Israelites' (Cerulli, 1956, pp. 43–52; Bezold, 1905; Wallis Budge, 1922; Ullendorf, 1960, pp. 143–144, Van Donzel, 1997a, Aethiopica).

An original Ethiopian work is the *Mashafa mestir za-samay wa-medr* 'Book of the Mysteries of Heaven and Earth' (Perruchon, 1907; Grebaut, 1911; Wallis Budge, 1935). Written by the monk Yishaq, a disciple of Abbot Ba-hayla Mika'el, the work is of an apocalyptic character and consists of four parts which deal with the mysteries of the Creation and the rebellion of the angels, with an esoteric interpretation of the Apocalypse, an interpretation of the mystery of the Divinity and a cabalistic explanation of calculations and numbers found in Holy Scripture.

To the fourteenth century probably also belongs the *Zena Eskender* or 'The [Christian] Story of Alexander [the Great]'. This romance seems to be an original Ethiopian work, vaguely inspired by Pseudo-Callisthenes' *History of Alexander.* The unknown author regards Alexander, a model of chastity and continence, as an early Christian king of Ethiopia, who obtained the power to perform his mighty deeds through fasting and prayer (Wallis Budge, 1933, pp. 236–256). From the fourteenth century also date war songs in honour of Amda Syon, celebrating his victories over the Muslims of Wag, Hadiya and Bali. Most of the poetry of this period, however, is religious songs, for example in honour of the martyr Mercurios, the martyrs of Najran and the crucifixion (Cerulli, 1956, pp. 62–67).

Gadls or 'Acts'

A *gadl* is a life of a saint, tending towards hagiography. Many were written in the times of Amda Sion and Sayfa Arad in order to support the views of leading monks in questions concerning the relation between Church and State. Much attention is given to the fact that these monks insisted on the strict observance of religious prescriptions, and to the opposition between the metropolitan and the secular clergy on the one hand, and the monasteries on the other. The *gadls* contain a great variety of themes, but they are unanimous in attacking King Amda Syon I for having married his deceased father's wife, a practice which was common among the Sidama and in the Kaffa. King Sayfa Arad was attacked for his polygamy. Other subjects common to these *gadls* are charges of simony against the metropolitan bishop and of calumny against the monks by the secular clergy, and the dispute about the date on which Christmas Day should be celebrated. The best-known *gadls* are those of Philippos, the third abbot of Dabra Libanos, of the above-mentioned Ba-salota Mika'el, of Samuel, abbot of Dabra Wagag in south-eastern Shoa and a contemporary of King Dawit I, of Anorewos, abbot of the monastery of Sigaga, a disciple of Takla Haymanot and a great admirer of Ba-salota Mika'el, and of Aaron the Thaumaturge, abbot of Dabra Daret in Begemdir (Tamrat, 1972, p. 275).

Another group of *gadls* are those of the Zague kings Lalibala, Na'akweto la-Ab and Yemerhanna Kristos and of Lalibala's queen Maskal Kebra. Most were probably written in the fifteenth century, but a manuscript of King Lalibala's *gadl*, in the possession of the British Museum, dates from the fourteenth century (Wright, 1877, no. 719).

Still another cycle of *gadls* is formed by those of Iyasus Mo'a, founder of Dabra Hayq (d. 1292), and of Takla Haymanot, founder of Dabra Libanos (d. 1313). In the *gadl* which carries his name, Iyasus Mo'a is credited with having 'restored' the Solomonid dynasty in 1270, an honour claimed for Takla Haymanot in the *gadl* which carries his name.

Meanwhile, literary activity in the north sought to glorify the monasteries of Tigré. The *gadl* of the so-called Nine Saints describes how nine Syrian monks, who in the sixth century were persecuted by the Byzantines for their Monophysite faith, fled to Ethiopia. These biographies, however, are not adaptations of historical events, as was the case with the *gadls* mentioned above. The best-known *gadls* of this cycle are those of Za-Mika'el Aragawi, founder of the monastery of Dabra Damo in Tigré, of Libanos or Mata, to whom the translation of the Gospel of Matthew is specifically attributed, of Garima, of Pantalewon, of Afse and of Yared, the putative author of the *Deggua* or Ethiopian church music.

In southern Ethiopia, *gadls* were composed of the lives of personalities who were active in those regions, such as Gabra Manfas Qeddus, founder of the monastery of the Zukwala in southern Shoa, and of John the Oriental (Yohannes Mesrakawi), also called John of Sagaro, the name of the monastery which he founded in Menz.

According to Cerulli (Cerulli, 1943, *Il libro*; 1956, pp. 105 ff.), one of the most important works of Ethiopian literature, and certainly the most typical, is the *Ta'amra Maryam* or 'Miracles of Mary'. It had its origin in France towards the middle of the twelfth century, and spread widely over Europe while taking up many local elements. It thus became a large collection of stories, legends and traditions. Between 1237 and 1289, one of its versions was translated into Arabic. This version, enriched in the same way as those in the West, was translated into Ethiopic towards the end of the fourteenth century. The Ethiopian text, itself also enriched by local stories and traditions, contains important testimonies of events which happened in the fourteenth century. King Zar'a Ya'qob ordered the 'Book of Miracles' to be read in church, and so a canonical series of thirty-three stories came to be established, much smaller than the very large collection of stories known elsewhere. In the Ethiopian version Cerulli has identified stories originating from Spain, Italy and France. From the Near East there are stories from Syria (Saint Mary of Saidna, near Damascus), from Palestine (Jerusalem, Bethlehem), from Egypt (the monastery of Samuel of Qalamon, Scete, al-Maktas (Mitmaq), Qusqam), and from Ethiopia itself during the reigns of Dawit I and his son Zar'a Ya'qob.

Zar'a Ya'qob

King Zar'a Ya'qob deserves special mention. Having spent a number of years in the royal prison of Mount Geshen in Amhara (Tamrat, 1972, p. 275), he set out to put an end to the internal dissensions in the state, and to fight the heresies of the Stephanites and the Mikaelites. Several works carry his name, either because he wrote them himself, or because they were written under his supervision. The *Mashafa Berhan* or 'Book of Light' and the *Mashafa Milad* or 'Book of the Nativity' contain exhortations to resist the enemies of the throne, directions against practices and usages judged incompatible with the Christian faith, regulations against magical practices and the cult of pagan deities, and long refutations of the Stephanites and the Mikaelites. The *Mashafa Berhan* describes the organization of the 'House of Ewostatewos'. Zar'a Ya'qob is also the author of two smaller works, the 'Book of Essence' and the 'Custody of the Sacrament'.

The time of Zar'a Ya'qob, described as the central period of Ethiopian literature, also produced 'one of the most beautiful jewels of Ethiopian poetry' (Cerulli, 1956, p. 147), namely the war song in honour of King Isaac (1414–1429). Religious poetry, such as *Egziabher nagsa* or 'God reigns', ordered by Zar'a Ya'qob and consisting of a collection of hymns, is of lesser artistic value. The *Arganona Maryam* or 'Harp of Mary', composed at the request of Zar'a Ya'qob by an otherwise unknown George the Armenian, is a collection of hymns praising the Virgin Mary. The themes, such as 'the Beatitudes', are taken from the Bible.

King Na'od (1494–1508) composed poems on the Eucharist, the Virgin Mary and Saint Michael which are still in use today.

Finally, the fifteenth century produced the beginning of a genre of poetry known as *qene* and practised today. According to a widely spread saying, the *qene* belongs to its author, the creature to its Creator, i.e. only the author of a *qene* fully appreciates his own poetry, just as the Creator alone has a complete knowledge of His creatures (Hammerschmidt, 1967, pp. 126–127; Ullendorff, 1960, p. 109).

Architecture

No building executed in bricks and mortar dating from the period under consideration seems to have survived. It may even be asked whether any such building ever existed, for no lime is found in Ethiopia. Public buildings, churches in the first place, were generally built in stone, with mostly a rectangular form in northern Ethiopia, as can still be seen in Dabra Damo, and a round form in southern regions. All churches had a threefold division. The innermost part, square in form, was called *meqdes* or 'holy of holies', where the *tabot* was kept, a simple table of wood or stone, which was put on the altar for the celebration of the Eucharist. In the circle around the *meqdes*, called *qeddest*, holy communion was administered. It was also the place for the non-officiating clergy. The outside ambulatory, where the *debteras* or cantors sang the hymns, was called *qene mahlet*. The three divisions were connected by three doors, while the separating walls were decorated with images, painted on cloth (Hammerschmidt, 1967, pp 126–127; Ullendorff, 1960, p. 109).

The world-famous churches at Lalibela in the province of Lasta (see Figure 33) consist of huge rectangular pieces of rock, laid free on the four sides by excavating big trenches in the surrounding solid rock. The isolated block in the centre was then shaped into a church, both internally and externally. The construction of the eleven churches is attributed to King Lalibala of the Zagwe dynasty. They were probably constructed to form the nucleus of the new capital of Roha, which should replace the former capital of Aksum. According to Ethiopian tradition, the churches were hewn out to replace Jerusalem after Saladin had conquered the Holy City in 1187 (Van Donzel, 1997a, Aethiopica). Recently, a great number of other remarkable rock churches have been described (Geister, 1968) (see Plate 280 and Figure 33).

The usual type of house was the so-called *tukul*, a round hut with a cone-shaped roof, able to stand up to winds and heavy rain. The roof became watertight by the smoke rising from the fireplace. The skeleton of the hut was made of tree trunks, the gaps being filled with branches tied together with straw and then padded with *ciqa*, a fermentation of mud and straw, cement having been unknown during the period under consideration. The plastering often could not stand up to heavy rainfall. Air and light entered by a low entrance, windows being unknown. In the north, where rainfall was in general lighter than in the south, the houses, usually built of stone, had flat roofs (Ullendorff, 1960, pp. 175–176).

Manuscripts and Painting

'No other country has written so much on parchment as Ethiopia has' (Leroy, 1961, p. 6). Although papyrus grows in Ethiopia, and notwithstanding the long-standing relations with Sudan and especially Egypt, there is as yet no evidence that papyrus was used in Ethiopia as a writing medium. Paper, introduced into Egypt as early as the eighth century, seems to have found its way only very slowly into Ethiopia, despite the fact that the Greek term *kertas* is frequently used in Ge'ez literature. Ethiopian manuscripts made of paper were very rare before the nineteenth century (Pankhurst, 1961, p. 353). They mostly came from places outside the country where scribes were active, such as Cairo, Alexandria, Jerusalem and Rome. On the coastal regions of the Red Sea, paper was used by Jewish Egyptian merchants for their reports to Egypt (Sergew

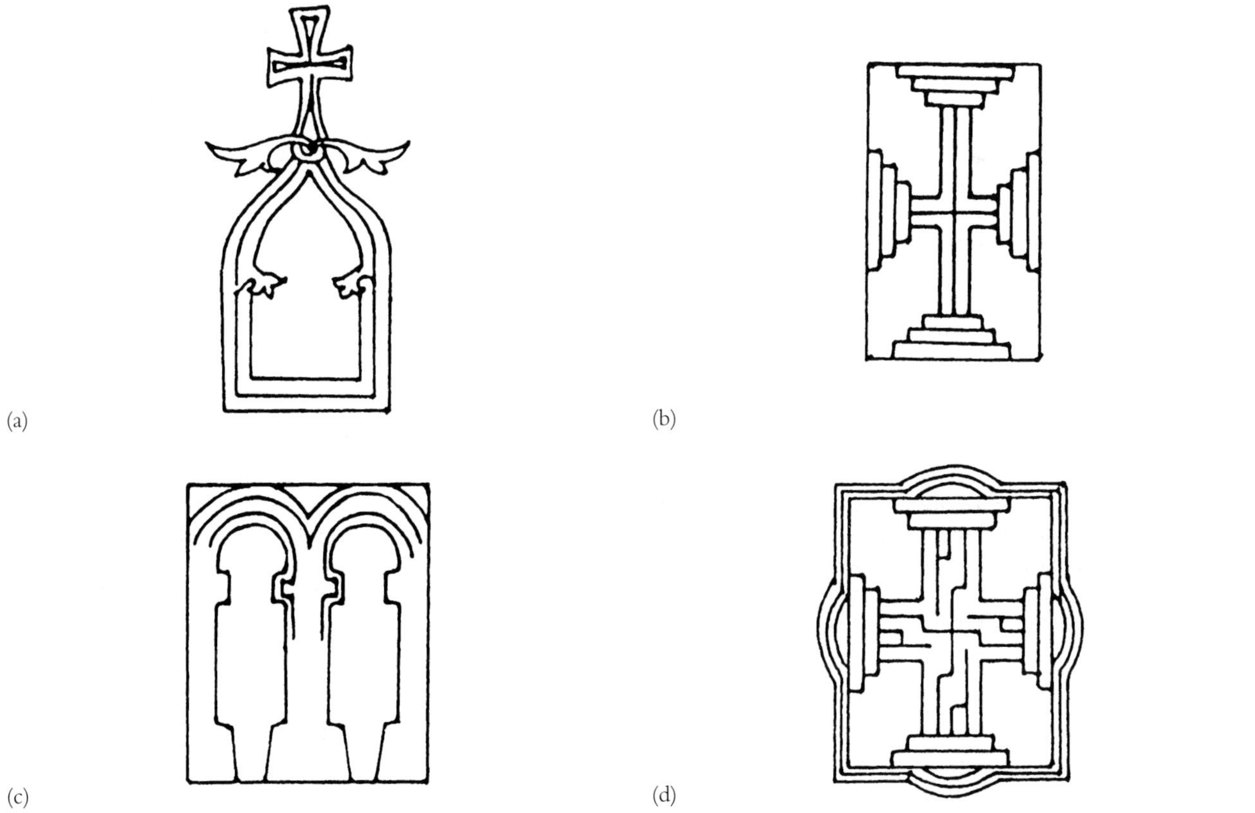

Figure 33 Sculpted windows from three rock churches in Lalibela (Ethiopia), turn of the twelfth and thirteenth centuries: (a) Church of Beta Ghiorghis; (b) Church of Beta Mariam; (c) and (d) Church of Beta Mikael (after Beckwith, C.; Fisher, A., *The Horn of Africa*, London 1990, p. 16).

Hable Sellasie, 1981), and probably also by the Muslims.

Most of the Ethiopian manuscripts are illustrated. The illuminations were done mainly on vellum because goatskin is of higher quality than sheepskin. For some of the largest manuscripts, as many as 100–150 goats must have been killed to provide the necessary parchment. Quires usually consist of five sheets, i.e. ten folios or twenty pages, each quire having a consecutive number. There are generally two columns to one page, the largest manuscripts having three columns, the smaller only one. The bindings consist of thick wooden boards, often covered with leather. The entire volume is placed in a case with straps to be carried over the shoulder (Ullendorff, 1960, p. 141). Very few Ethiopian manuscripts are older than the fourteenth century, but those dating from that period show calligraphy of a high degree of perfection, which points to an already existing calligraphic tradition. The painters and illuminators were priests and monks, who wished to transmit their messages of religious instruction in a direct way. The paintings therefore are vivid, colourful and comprehensible, with less emphasis on elegance or finesse (see Plates 49, 279).

Painting in general was done mainly on canvas and on walls in churches. It is considered to have been influenced by Byzantine, Syriac and Coptic styles. One of the most popular paintings, on all sorts of material and in a great variety of versions, depicts the story of King Solomon and the Queen of Sheba, as related in the *Kebra Nagast* (see Plate 49). Another widespread painting was the icon called *kwer'ata re'esu* or 'the blow on his head', representing Jesus being struck on the head with the reed (Matthew 27). It is brought in connection with the 'chapel of the abuse' in Jerusalem, which came into Ethiopian hands in the second half of the fifteenth century (Cerulli, 1943, pp. 265–275; 1947, pp. 109–129; Chojnacki, 1985). Finally, mention should be made of Saint George of Lydda, who is one of the most popular saints (Wallis Budge, 1930).

Music

Ethiopian music and especially hymnography still await further study, in particular the so-called *Deggua* or 'Hymnary', a collection of hymns popularly attributed to Yared. The earliest recension dates from the fifteenth century. Almost all manuscripts of the *Deggua* contain a form of musical notation, the signs of which consist of letters, dots and circles placed above the relevant syllable. They indicate the raising or lowering of the voice as well as other modes of voice production.

The musical instruments used in church were the lyre of six or ten strings (*kerar*), the harp of eight or ten strings (*begena*), the one-stringed *mesenko*, the tambourine (*kebero*), the long drum (*negerit*) and the sistrum (*senasel*). Singing in falsetto, hand-clapping and marking the beat with the prayer-stick (*mekwamya*) – also serving as a support for the debtera during the long services – were parts of religious ceremonies (Ullendorff, 1960, p. 172; Kaufman-Shelemay, 1986).

BIBLIOGRAPHY

BECCARI, C. 1903–1913. *Rerum Aethiopicarum Scriptores Occidentales irediti a saeculo XVI ADXIX.* 15 vols. Rome.

BECKINGHAM, C. F.; HUNTINGFORD, G. W. 1961. *The Prester John of the Indies*, 2 vols. Cambridge University Press. London, New York, Toronto.

BEZOLD, C. 1905. Kebra Nagast. Die Herrlichkeit der Könige. *Abhandlungen der Königlichen Bayerischen Akademie der Wissenschaften.* Munich.

CERULLI, E. 1943, 1947. *Etiopi in Palestina. Storia della Communità Etiopica di Gerusalemme*, 2 vols. La Libreria dello Stato, Rome.

——. 1943. *Il libro etiopico dei Miracoli di Maria e le sue fonti nelle letterature del Medio Evo-latino.* Rome.

——. 1947. Il 'Gesù percosso' nell'arte etiopico e le sue origine nell'Europa del XV secolo. *Rassegna di studi etiopici.* Vol. VI.

——. 1956. *Storia della letteratura etiopica.* Nuova Accademia Editrice, Milan.

CHOJNACKI, S. 1985. *The 'Kwerata Re'esu': its iconography and significance; an essay in the cultural history of Ethiopia.* Istituto Universitario Orientale. Naples.

CREONE, F. 1902, 1903. La politica orientale di Alfonso di Aragone. *Archivio storico per le Provincie Napolitane.* Vol. 27.

Encyclopaedia of Islam, 1960. 2nd edn. (EI²). E. J. Brill, Leiden.

ERLICH, H. 1994. *Ethiopia and the Middle East.* Lynne Rienner Publishers, Boulder, London.

EVETTS, P. T. A. (ed.) 1904. *Patrologia Orientalis I*, fasc. 2.

GERSTER, G. 1968. *Kirchen im Fels. Entdeckungen in Äthiopien.* Kohlhammer, Stuttgart.

GRÉBAUT, S. 1911. Le livre des mystères du ciel et de la terre. *Patrologia Orientalis.* Vol. VI, 3.

GUIDI, I. 1932. *Storia della letteratura etiopica.* Istituto per l'Oriente. Rome.

HABLE SELLASIE, S. 1981. *Bookmaking in Ethiopia.* Leiden.

HAMMERSCHMIDT, E. 1967. *Äthiopien. Chrisliches Reich zwischen Gestern und Morgen.* Otto Harrassowitz, Wiesbaden.

KAUFMAN SHELEMAY, K. 1986. *Music, Ritual, and Falasha History.* African Studies Center, Michigan State University, East Lansing.

LEMMA, T. 1975. *Ethiopian Musical Instruments.* Addis Abeba.

LEROY, J. 1961. *Aethiopien. Buchmalereien.* Einleitung Jules Leroy. Texte Stephen Wright und Otto A. Jäger. New York Graphic Society in Übereinkunft mit der UNESCO.

AL-MAQRĪZĪ. 1790. *Al-Ilmam bi-akhbār man bi-ard al-Habasha min mulūk al-Islam.* ed. and trans. RINCK, F. T. Leiden.

MUYSER, J. 1937. Le samedi et le dimanche dans l'église et la littérature coptes. Appendix to TOGO MINA, 1937. *Le martyre d'Apa Epima.* Cairo.

NEWBOLD, D. 1945. The Crusaders in the Red Sea and the Sudan. *Sudan Notes and Records.* Vol. XXVI, Part 2.

PANKHURST, R. 1961. *An Introduction to The Economic History of Ethiopia from Early Times to 1800.* Lalibela House. Addis Ababa.

PÉRIER, J. and A. 1912. Les canons des Apôtres. *Patrologia Orientalis*, vol. VII.

PERRUCHON, J. 1889. Histoire des guerres d'Amda Seyon, roi d'Ethiopie. *Journal Asiatique.* Série 8, tome XIV.

——. 1893. *Les chroniques de Zar'a Ya'qob et de Ba'eda Maryam.* Paris.

——. 1907. Le Livre des Mystères du Ciel et de la Terre. *Patrologia Orientalis.* Vol. I, 1.

QUATREMERE, E. 1811. *Mémoires géographiques et historiques sur l'Égypte et sur quelques contrées voisines*, 2 vols. Paris.

RODINSON, M. 1964. Sur la question des 'influences juives' en Ethiopie. *Journal of Semitic Studies*, Vol. IX.

RONCIERE, C. DE LA. 1925. La découverte de l'Afrique au Moyen Âge. *Mémoires de la Société Géographique d'Égypte.* Vol. IV.

AL-SAKHAWĪ. 1896. *Al-Tibr al-masbūk fi Dhayl al-Sulūk.* Cairo.

SCHEFER, C. 1892. *Le Voyage d'Outremer de Bertrandon de la Brocquière.* Paris.

SCHOPPEN, A. 1978. *Das Qat. Geschichte und Gebrauch des Genussmittels Catha Edulis Forsk.* Yemen.

TAMRAT, T. 1966. Some Notes on the Fifteenth-century Stephanite 'Heresy' in the Ethiopian Church. *Rassegna di Studi Etiopici*, Vol. XXII. Rome.

——. 1972. *Church and State in Ethiopia 1270–1527.* Clarendon Press. Oxford.

TRASSELLI, C. 1941. Un Italiano in Etiopia nel secolo XV: Pietro Rombulo di Messina. *Rassegna di studi etiopici.* Vol. 1.

TRIMINGHAM, J. S. 1952. *Islam in Ethiopia.* Oxford University Press. London, New York, Toronto.

ULLENDORFF, E. 1960 (3rd edn 1973). *The Ethiopians. An Introduction to Country and People.* Oxford University Press. London, New York, Toronto.

VAN DONZEL, E. J. 1988. *Ibn al-Jawzī on Ethiopians in Baghdad.* In: BOSWORTH, C. E. E.A. (ed.) 1988. *The Islamic World. From Classical to Modern Times. Essays in Honor of Bernard Lewis.* The Darwin Press, Princeton, NJ.

——. 1997a. Ethiopia's Lalibala and the fall of Jerusalem in 1187. *Aethiopica* I. Hamburg.

——. 1997b. The legend of the Blue Nile in Europe. *The Nile, Civilizations, History, Myths.* Proceedings of the Congress held in Tel Aviv 1997.

——. 1999. Badr al-Jamālī, the Copts in Egypt and the Muslims in Ethiopia. *Festschrift C. E. Bosworth* (EI²). E. J. Brill, Leiden (forthcoming).

WALLIS BUDGE, E. A. 1922. *The Queen of Sheba and her only Son Menyelek.* London.

——. 1928. *The Book of the Saints of the Ethiopian Church.* Cambridge University Press. Cambridge.

——. 1930. *George of Lydda, the patron saint of England. A study of the* Cultus *of St. George in Ethiopia.* Luzac and Co. London.

——. 1933 (repr. 1976). *The Alexander Book in Ethiopia.* Oxford University Press. London.

——. 1935. *The Book of the Mysteries of Heaven and Earth.* London.

WIET, G. 1938. Les relations égypto-abyssines sous les sultans mamelouks. *Bulletin de la Société d'Archéologie copte.* Vol. IV.

WRIGHT, W. 1877. *Catalogue of the Ethiopian Manuscripts in the British Museum Acquired since the Year 1847.* No. 719. London.

35

THE EAST COAST AND THE INDIAN OCEAN ISLANDS

35.1
ENVIRONMENT AND TECHNIQUES

Edward A. Alpers

Stretching 3,000 km from southern Somalia to southern Mozambique, the east coast of Africa has represented one of the longest and most important human frontiers of the continent for the past two millennia. Because of its great extent, even excluding its northern and southern extremities, we should expect that over time there would be many complex interactions along this coast, with multiple variations. And, indeed, there were. What is most surprising, however, is that during the era covered by this volume, there emerged along this vast frontier a distinct African civilization that encompassed not only the coast and its offshore islands but also stretches of coastal Madagascar and the Comoro Islands. The forces that contributed to and shaped the emergence of this civilization are the subject of this sub-chapter.

The environment of the coast as far south as Madagascar is dominated by the regime of seasonal monsoon winds that prevail in the western half of the Indian Ocean. The monsoons determined the annual economy of the coast throughout this period, dictating not only the agricultural cycle but also communication and exchange of goods both across the Indian Ocean and with the peoples of the interior of the continent. Beginning in November and ending by March, the north-east monsoon prevails. The months following the north-east monsoon are dominated by greater equatorial equilibrium in pressure systems, which brings with it the major season of heavy rains. As the long rains end by about June, the south-west monsoon becomes established and is most reliable from July until September until a second, less powerful period of equatorial equilibrium is established by October. Basically, the year can be divided into two somewhat unequal parts, blowing in from South and South-West Asia during the north-east monsoon and from East Africa towards those regions during the south-west monsoon, with two intervening, shorter transitional seasons. However, it should also be noted that the amount of rainfall diminishes somewhat both north and south from the modern Kenya–Tanzania border, while the period of heaviest rains is later in the north than it is to the south.

At the beginning of our period, there is good evidence that the coast was occupied by north-eastern Bantu-speaking agriculturalists who practised a broadly shared culture that is associated with the ceramic tradition known as Tana ware.[1] These people generally practised a mixed agriculture based on the hoe cultivation of grains and legumes, as well as certain fruits; they also kept livestock and supplemented their diets by fishing and hunting. In the north, among Sabaki speakers, there is evidence of intense interaction with southern Cushitic speakers that is reflected in the vocabulary of cattle-keeping (Nurse; Spear, 1985). Leaving aside the cultural transition that occurred at the end of the first millennium with the rise of the Swahili and Comoran languages within the Sabaki subgroup and the introduction of Islam (see sub-chapters 35.2 and 35.3), let us turn to the specific techniques employed by the peoples of the coast during this era in building their culture.

The deep roots of agriculture on the coast derive from the earliest antecedents of the Bantu-speaking populations of East Africa. The principal grains cultivated were eleusine, millet and sorghum, with rice becoming more significant in some areas, such as the Comoro Islands; local varieties of beans and peas were prominent among cultivated legumes. In addition, sugar cane, yams, pumpkins and cucumbers were grown, as were some limited tree crops. Later, certainly by the end of the first millennium, both bananas and coconuts had been introduced from Asia and spread along the coast and to the coastal islands. The linguistic evidence indicates a broad proto-Bantu vocabulary for farming that suggests the kind of seasonal agricultural pattern that we know is imposed by the monsoon regime. Some form of bush fallowing cultivation must certainly have obtained throughout this period. Grains not only provided food as porridge but were probably also brewed as beer, while archaeological evidence of earthenware ovens at some coastal sites indicates the baking of bread by the late twelfth century (Chittick, 1975, Vol. I, p. 35; Chittick, 1982, p. 60).

Although primarily cultivators, the people of the coast also supplemented their diets by keeping livestock, fishing and hunting. Honey was also consumed as a product of either bee-keeping or gathering wild honey. Archaeological remains of livestock bones, as well as literary sources, indicate clearly that cattle, sheep, goats and chickens were consumed to varying degrees, depending on the location of a settlement. Fishing, primarily carried out in shallow waters by spearing, casting nets or with traps, is also attested to in both the archaeological and literary records, as is the hunting of sea turtles and dugongs. Based on a systematic analysis of faunal remains, including both animal and fish bones, which was undertaken by British archaeologist Mark Horton and Kenyan osteologist Nina Mudida at Shanga in Kenya, it has been calculated that the percentage of protein in the local diet increased steadily from about AD 800 to about 1400, with domestic livestock other than chickens only becoming significant after about 1050 (Horton and Mudida, 1993). Parallel faunal evidence from the Comoro Islands suggests a similar pattern of consumption, while at the same time emphasizing the significance of both fishing and local variation, depending on the site of a particular settlement (Wright, 1992).

We have already noted that a broadly shared ceramic tradition linked these geographically dispersed communities of the coast and its offshore islands. Until the expansion of Islam and the significant urban development that accompanied greater integration of the coast into the wider world of the Indian Ocean around the turn of the millennium, local pottery overwhelmingly predominated in all the coastal sites that have been excavated. Allowing for considerable local variation, according to East African archaeologists F. T. Masao and H. W. Mutoro, 'The two diagnostic local wares of this period are bag-shaped cooking pots with incised decoration on rim and shoulder and red burnished ware' (Masao and Mutoro, 1988, p. 594; *cf.* Wright, 1993, p. 660), as well as various bowls and lamps.

We know that the people of the coast manufactured iron. Evidence of both smelting and forging occurs in the earliest deposits at Manda and Shanga in the Lamu archipelago of Kenya, at several sites on Zanzibar, at Kilwa in southern Tanzania, and at Chibuene in southern Mozambique, although the archaeological record provides little idea of the range of implements produced. Other manufactures attested to by archaeology include shell beads, which are abundant on Zanzibar, and terracotta spindle whorls from the first half of the second millennium, which indicate the spinning and weaving of cotton textiles. Some evidence also attests to the production of sea salt by evaporation along the Tanzanian coast, where salt continues to be thus produced in this way today (Chittick, 1975). In fact, despite the lack of a continuous archaeological or literary record, we can assume the steady development of a quite varied and sophisticated technology along the coast and islands of East Africa throughout this period.

Perhaps there is no better example of the absence of evidence as it relates to coastal technology than our gap in all that relates to every aspect of seafaring. Although there is external, literary evidence for the existence of sewn boats from the *Periplus of the Erythraean Sea* (*c.* AD 130–140) and from the Portuguese at the end of the fifteenth century, as well as from some wall engravings at several sites within the chronological confines of this volume, we possess no physical evidence for these apparently ubiquitous sailing vessels (Chittick, 1980). Despite this disappointment, however, there can be no doubting that coastal sailing, including the ability to navigate across the channels that separate the mainland from the major offshore islands, such as Zanzibar and the Comoros, must have constituted an important component of the technology and scientific knowledge of coastal dwellers during this period (see Plate 22). The very range of their distribution and their shared coastal culture provide vivid testimony to that effect.

The one area of environment and technique where we do enjoy abundant evidence is architecture. Before the ninth century, most coastal dwellings were rectangular (though some were round before being supplanted by rectangular houses) and built of mud and wattle with thatched palm fronds for roofing, a style that persists among ordinary folk right up the present. With the great expansion of international trade and urban development, including the introduction of Islam, which will be discussed in the following two sub-chapters, sufficient accumulation of wealth occurred to make possible the emergence and elaboration of a distinctive building style that drew for its inspiration upon local materials such as coral rag and mangrove poles, local notions of design and decoration, as well as broader ideas of Islamic architecture then obtaining in the western Indian Ocean. Coral was quarried, lime mortar was produced by burning coral, plaster and concrete were also derived from this lime, and over time techniques evolved from simple block construction on mud mortar to more permanent, complex, aesthetically nuanced design features that included lime mortar foundations and poured mixtures of concrete and coral rubble, which allowed greater plasticity, such as vaults and domes. Domestic architecture led the way at Manda from the end of the first millennium, with squared coral blocks and mud mortar being used for the foundations of mud-and-wattle structures and then for coral rag walls. A similar pattern seems to have obtained at Kilwa in the first centuries of the second millennium. By the thirteenth century, mosque building pioneered the new technique at Shanga, followed a century later by an explosion of domestic building in stone, while at Kilwa these developments were coterminous. Eventually, during the height of coastal prosperity in the thirteenth and fourteenth centuries, the extraordinary complex known as Husuni Kubwa at Kilwa Kisiwani was built, as well as a greatly expanded mosque. This same period also witnessed the construction in coral rag and lime mortar of a unique feature of coastal East African architecture, the so-called pillar tombs, striking examples of which were erected during the heyday of Shanga, *c.* 1320–1440. All of this building activity clearly bears witness to the development of highly skilled artisans on the East African coast, such as the influential workshop 'of exceptionally high quality porites carving that existed in early twelfth century Zanzibar' (Horton, 1992, p. 8). Nevertheless, while smaller sites along the coast also adopted this building style, it is important to remember that the majority of people probably still lived in mud-and-wattle houses in what was becoming an increasingly hierarchical society (see Plates 35, 200, 271, 272).

NOTE

1 Earlier designations for 'Tana ware' (Abungu; Mutoro 1993, p. 702) include both 'early kitchen ware' and 'Swahili ware'. Closely related contemporaneous ceramic traditions have been identified at Monapo in northern Mozambique and Chibuene in southern Mozambique (Sinclair *et al.*, 1993, pp. 419–420, 423–424) as well as in the Comoros (Wright, 1993, p. 660).

BIBLIOGRAPHY

(See Chapter 35.5.)

35.2
TRADE AND URBAN DEVELOPMENT

Edward A. Alpers

Although in earlier works like those of Justus Standes (1899) and Reginald Coupland (1938), all cultural and commercial growth in East Africa was attributed to exogenous influences emanating from the Indian Ocean, a strong case can be made for indigenous factors contributing to the rise of trade and urban development in the region.

Our starting point at the beginning of this period should be from a perspective that envisions the region as a series of adjacent sub regions connected loosely along the length of the coast by the western borders of the Indian Ocean. Put differently, we should not at this time view the coast as the centre of activity (even though it is the focus of our attention in this sub-chapter) but as a frontier for scattered communities who had occupied the coast as part of the general expansion of Bantu-speaking peoples in East Africa. Those people who had settled along the coast necessarily maintained significant relationships with the people of the hinterland, to whom, in most cases, they were related by speech and culture, although in the north these interactions also involved southern Cushitic speakers (see sub-chapter 35.1). With respect to trade and the larger sub-regional economies of the times, we can surmise the existence of a coast–interior regional symbiosis in which goods and, particularly, foodstuffs were exchanged as part of a socio-economic system that also involved kinship and marriage exchange. This sort of system of exchange was founded upon the uneven distribution of natural resources, such as iron and salt, as well as on the differential influence of ecological niches on both agricultural and pastoral production. The particular advantage of coastal dwellers in such a system was their access to high-quality sea salt, on the one hand, and to the products of the sea, including fish and shell beads. These networks also constituted the structural basis for regional strategies for dealing with famine, when the availability of foodstuffs across ecological zones became especially critical.

Granted that the evidence for this reconstruction during this era is fragmentary, but it does conform to what we know in considerable detail about later periods of coastal history. Moreover, evidence from the second half of the first millennium does exist. For example, Kenyan archaeologists George Abungu and Henry Mutoro (1993) present a powerful example of this sort of subregional network linking the coastal settlement of Ungwana, which was founded at the end of the first millennium at the mouth of the Tana River in Kenya, with the lower and middle reaches of the Tana valley. This valley, they suggest, comprises a complex, interdependent system of quite varied ecosystems that have historically supported agriculturalists, pastoralists and hunter–gatherers. The links between coast and interior are attested to by the linguistic evidence and shared ceramic tradition cited above. Archaeological evidence of trade, however, is thin. One reason for this weakness in the evidence may be that most of the goods traded between interior and coast were perishable, such as foodstuffs 'and other organic materials which would not be visible in the archaeological record' (*ibid.*, p. 703). Oral traditions, by contrast, speak to important connections among the peoples of the Tana valley and the coast, as they do between other peoples of the coast and the hinterland folk. In addition, social links often joined extended kinship groups in coastal communities with counterparts in the hinterland, such as the American historian Berg (1968) has described in detail for the period after 1500 at Mombasa. Indeed, there are hints of these sorts of connection in oral traditions collected along the length of the coast. Nor should they surprise us: coastal settlements provided a gateway to the resources of the Indian Ocean for peoples of the interior, while hinterland communities controlled access to the wealth of the continent. If we regard the pioneers of coastal settlement as operating on the farthest frontier of the continent, coast–interior symbiosis makes perfect sense.

Just as it is difficult to identify physical evidence of trading within these subregional zones, it is hard to distinguish exchange between coastal communities from the broader patterns of oceanic trade during the earlier centuries of this period. Clear evidence of the latter dates from the ninth and tenth centuries, however, with examples of imported ceramics from the Middle East and, occasionally, from China, being most prominent in coastal sites. Settlements were widely scattered, small and self-sufficient, probably best described as villages rather than towns until the eleventh century. Although there were surely Muslim individuals resident in many of these settlements during this period, the absence of mosques in all but a few (the earliest being noted at Shanga from the late eighth century) indicates that Islam was still a minority faith along the coast. What is most important to note here is that these settlements owe their genesis to the initiative of East African peoples, as the archaeological evidence irrefutably indicates.

Each of the major excavations of coastal settlements reveals that beneath the more enduring, sometimes spectacular stone architecture that dates to the heyday of coastal prosperity in the later centuries of this era, there was a pre-existing foundation of African habitation. The most striking example comes from Shanga, where Horton's work has revealed a core of both round and rectangular hut sites and a rectangular central cattle enclosure that bears a striking resemblance to the spatial organization of mainland communities in the adjacent hinterland. But the same assertion can be demonstrated by evidence from such widely separated communities as existed at Mombasa, on Zanzibar, at Kilwa, and in the Comoro Islands.

Overseas trade flourished just as certainly throughout this early period. The archaeological record everywhere indicates the steadily increasing presence of imported ceramics, while scattered evidence from the African side suggests that ivory and tortoiseshell were exported. These fragmentary hints are attested to more fully by the literary evidence. The Arab traveller and geographer al-Mas'ūdī, who last visited East Africa in 916–917, specifically mentions both of these items. Other exports that are referred to in the written record include ambergris, cotton cloth, leopard skins, iron, incense, wood and spices. Without knowing either their precise provenance or anything about the mechanisms of the trade, there is also testimony to traffic in slaves from East Africa, since we know that there was a large population of enslaved *Zanj* – the term universally used by Arab writers to describe the peoples of this part of Africa, though also including the Horn – in the great salt flats of lower Iraq in the ninth century. Finally, perishable goods like cloth were almost certainly an important component of Indian Ocean imports to the coastal communities at this time, as they were in later centuries.

From the beginning of the second millennium, and then with greater momentum towards the end of the twelfth century, both trade and urban development intensified along the coast and offshore islands. Site surveys indicate, for example, that the number of settlements, both large and small, increased significantly. Stone buildings began to appear at the more important sites and then to proliferate with increasing prosperity. The size of the major towns expanded – Kilwa, for example, expanded to cover an area of 30 ha in the eleventh century (Wright, 1993, p. 667) – and their character became increasingly hierarchical and Muslim (see Map 31). There is some evidence to suggest that the major towns also threw off, or at least inspired, the establishment of smaller towns, as more people were drawn to the bright flame of the robust Indian Ocean commerce of the thirteenth and early fourteenth centuries. For the heyday of coastal trade and urban development, the archaeology of coastal settlement has unearthed a rich architecture that features many large domestic (and perhaps commercial) buildings, as well as numerous mosques, some of impressive size and design. From a situation described by Horton for late eighth-century Shanga in which Muslims were clearly in a minority, to that at Mtambwe Mkuu on Pemba Island in Tanzania, where in the eleventh–twelfth centuries excavation of a cemetery suggests 'a mixed population of Muslims and

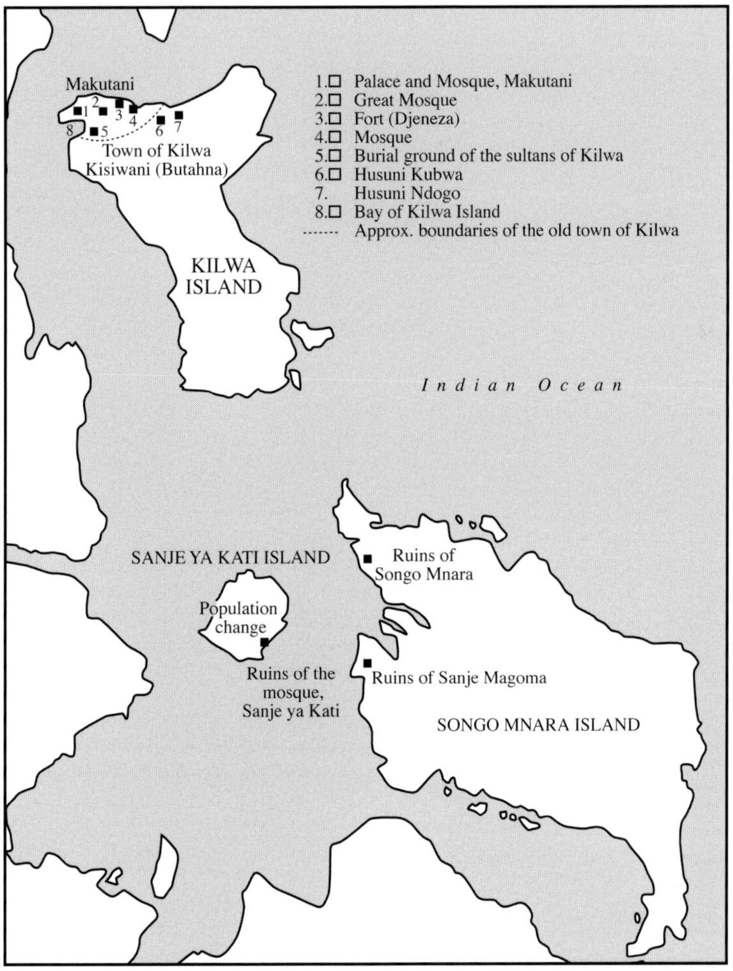

Map 31 Island and town of Kilwa: the map is based on English Admiralty Chart N-661, from archaeological excavations carried out by the British Institute in East Africa, directed by Neville Chittick, and from information provided by medieval Arab authors (draft Matveiev, V. V., 1984).

non-Muslims who were buried together' (Horton, 1992, pp. 2–3), we emerge into the mid-fourteenth century to encounter the great Arab traveller, Ibn Baṭṭūṭa, whose descriptions of both Mogadishu and Kilwa leave no doubt that the peoples in the towns of the coast were Muslim, even if the peoples of the mainland were not (see Chapter 35.5).

The cause of this sharp rise in prosperity was the increased exploitation of the gold trade, which was based upon mined ore in the Zimbabwe plateau that was then traded overland to the southern coast of Mozambique at Sofala, a site that was apparently dominated first by Mogadishu and then by Kilwa. A further vivid sign of the wealth that the gold trade produced, and of its ramifications for all the major coastal towns of the period, is the appearance of locally minted coinage, primarily in copper, although some were struck in silver and a few isolated examples in gold. Coins were minted at Kilwa, Mogadishu and Zanzibar, but it seems clear from a hoard of mainly Fāṭimid silver and gold coins from the mid-eleventh century at Mtambwe Mkuu that the wider world of Islam provided the model for doing so. What all of this demonstrates is that by the end of our period, coastal East Africa and its associated islands were inexorably bound up with the wider Muslim world and, through it, to both the Mediterranean and the Orient. This was not a new phenomenon, as the *Periplus* reminds us, but with the advent of Islam and its expansion around the entire Indian Ocean basin, together with the increased trading activity of the last three centuries of this epoch, this part of the African world found itself more deeply influenced by these currents than ever before (see Plates 22, 35, 200, 271, 272).

BIBLIOGRAPHY

(See Chapter 35.5.)

35·3
ARAB–MUSLIM CULTURES AND LOCAL CULTURES ON THE EAST COAST OF AFRICA AND THE INDIAN OCEAN ISLANDS

Victor Matveyev

A distinctive, original culture, forming a single entity in its own right, emerged on the east coast of Africa and on the Indian Ocean islands as a result of contacts between several peoples. Its emergence was the outcome of economic, social and cultural processes taking place within local society. The information we have comes from archaeological evidence, written sources in Arabic, Persian and Chinese, and oral and written sources in Swahili. However, this information is still, however, somewhat scant and does not give a full picture of the historical and cultural background of the region. The most important are the African sources in Swahili and in some cases Arabic, since, together with factual data, they afford insights into the internal organization and rationale of life in East African society. Such information is characteristically missing from all the non-African sources, foremost among which are those in Arabic. They and others furnish a fair amount of factual information, but their authors interpreted what they saw and learned from the conventional standpoint of their own, usually Muslim, societies. The archaeological evidence is irrefutable *per se*, but it leaves room for differences in interpretation and dating. Furthermore, archaeological excavations yield only artefacts made of durable materials. In a tropical climate, objects of vegetable origin soon perish.

The population of the region was not homogeneous. It was predominantly made up of Africans speaking languages of the Bantu group. A lesser proportion was made up of strangers to the region who became either temporary or permanent inhabitants. This group was composed of Arabs, Persians, Indians and others. They seem to have accounted for only a small segment of the total population but were still sufficiently numerous for the Africans to have classified them as minor groups – the Wa-arbu, Wa-shamu and Wa-shirazi. The local population groups, too, were heterogeneous. The majority were peoples and groups who had come to the coast and the islands relatively recently and maintained their traditional tribal relations. The remaining inhabitants had been living on the coast for a relatively long time, and although they too adhered to some of the traditions of their tribal society, they were more advanced in their social and cultural relations. The first group was called *Zanj* by Arab sources. The second group were the Swahili (from the Arabic word 'sāḥil', plural 'sawāḥil', meaning 'coast'). It should be noted that in the Arab sources the term '*Zanj*' is used to designate the more recent arrivals only where it appears alongside the term 'Swahili'. When there is no such conjunction it is used to designate the whole of the population of East Africa and the islands and also other peoples. It is first found in Arab sources in the seventh century and probably existed even earlier. The word *sawāḥil,* meaning 'Swahili', was first mentioned by al-Jāḥiẓ (767–869). It was in the seventh century that a single culture first began to emerge out of the cultural melting-pot of all these groups. The seventh to the tenth century was the period of its formation; the tenth to the twelfth century that of its rise; in the fourteenth century it was at its height; and the fifteenth century saw its decline and fall after the invasion of the Portuguese. The Swahili people played the predominant part in forging this culture, which is sometimes known as the Swahili civilization. Its development was stimulated by transoceanic trade with the Middle East, following the regular monsoon winds.

The contribution of the various peoples to the establishment of this culture was varied but equally valuable and crucial. The Zanjī of the mainland territories and the largest islands preserved and sustained the most vital aspects of culture, without which society could not have survived, namely agriculture and, in some places, cattle breeding and hunting for large animals. The latter provided goods for trading – elephant tusks, rhinoceros horns and leopard skins. The Zanjī also clearly engaged in other activities such as woodworking, wickerwork and, in the later period, cotton growing, spinning and weaving.

The Swahili population seems to have engaged in the same pursuits, but not everywhere and on a very much smaller scale. Their activities were focused more on fishing and catching other marine creatures, collecting shells, pearl diving and so on, and such related activities as seafaring, boat building and astronomy. In addition, they are also known to have engaged in gold and iron extraction, and to some extent ironworking and slave raiding, using the products of nearly all these activities largely for trade, in exchange for porcelain from the countries of the West and East Asia and beads and textiles of various kinds. They constructed small dwellings, and in the eleventh and twelfth centuries construction in stone and blocks of coral made its appearance.

The foreigners brought with them Islam and the whole body of knowledge and rules associated with it, including its legal system (in the thirteenth and fourteenth centuries) and also the knowledge and skills specific to their own countries.

The ideological conceptions of the African, Zanjī and Swahili peoples were basically those of a pre-class society. It would be a mistake, however, to classify East African society in the seventh century as a primitive communal one. Still, this age and subsequent periods saw the decline of this society and the isolation of the tribal rulers from the new elite of influential people that emerged from among those who had grown rich on trade. The new social system was underpinned by increasing inequality in the ownership of property. The earliest records of states date from the tenth century. In this context, the egalitarian principles of primitive communal ideology became redundant. A new ideology was needed, and it was Islam that met that need. Specific confirmation of this is found in al-Mas'ūdī's reports for AD 916. In them, he writes about the rulers of both the Zanjī and the Swahili and also about the island of Qanbalu (Pemba), which was inhabited by Muslims who spoke the Zanjī language. They ruled over the island, holding the Zanjī living there captive. It is thus obvious that the Swahili were Muslims and that the Zanjī represented a socially more simple and more backward people.

The acquisition, at some stage apparently between the tenth and thirteenth centuries, of a written language was a major event in the development of the Swahili culture. Drawing on the Arabic alphabet, this written language was not just a simple borrowing but rather a creative utilization of ready-made material. Research by the Russian scholar V. M. Misyugin has demonstrated that a thorough knowledge of the Swahili language was required to be able to decipher the texts, indicating that it was the Swahili people themselves who devised their written language, essentially for the purposes of commerce, accounting and other records.

Maritime trade led the Swahili people to establish numerous coastal and island settlements, many of which were transformed with the passage of time into cities that were initially composed of simple, traditional huts and subsequently of buildings in stone, beginning with mosques (in the eleventh and twelfth centuries) and followed in the fourteenth and fifteenth centuries by edifices with other functions. The methods of construction depended on local conditions and circumstances; the most outstanding examples of this architecture are the great mosque at Kilwa (which has been restored) and the palace complex of Husuni Kubwa (see Plates 35, 271, 272).

By the twelfth century, what was still a multi-ethnic Swahili society had come into existence, with a language that had developed over the past five centuries. East Africa never became an Arabic-speaking region; Islamization occurred peacefully, and interaction between the Swahili and Arabic languages resulted in the enrichment of the former by essential everyday words borrowed from the latter.

The break with their earlier beliefs and the adoption of Islam meant that the Swahili people had to find a place for themselves in the ideological, historical and political cosmography of the Islamic world. The result was a whole series of ethnogenetic legends linking the origins of the entire people or of its ruling family with a well-known Islamic personage or with some Near Eastern dynasty. Virtually all the cities of East Africa, and indeed almost all of the African countries reached by Islam, have such legends, which serve as the basis for the idea that the founders of East African culture were Arabian or Persian. This does not mean that this is what happened in reality, or that the roots of the Swahili culture were not essentially indigenous. This is at variance with our own thesis, which attributes endogenous roots to the culture of East Africa and can also be substantiated. Misyugin considered the Swahili written sources less as chronicles of events than as legal records of dynastic accessions to power. This in turn helped to clarify the nature and rules of succession. It appears that in the ruling dynasties of the East African city-states power was handed down through the male line, but from the generation of fathers and uncles to the generation of the sons rather than directly from father to son and – within one generation (*ndugu*) – from the older to the younger brothers. The women of the ruling clan were the repositories of this power, but its acquisition depended upon marriage, a ceremony that was also the occasion for its transmission to the next in line. In order to conserve power, intermarriage within the ruling clan was practised. However, it seems that marriage outside the clan sometimes occurred, thereby opening the gates of power to a male outsider. This would appear to have been the case of Sulaymān, the founder of the al-Nabhani dynasty of Paté, whose marriage to a woman of the ruling clan forms the basis of a number of ethnogenetic legends.

Such pretensions to a false lineage have been confirmed in more modern times, with various East African groups or clans claiming Arabian or Persian origins despite their incontestably African roots. And so the existence of the described system of inheritance among the rulers of East African settlements and cities demonstrates that these rulers were Africans (Swahilis), not Arabs or Persians, who had a different system of inheritance.

All the above goes to show that the culture of the people of the East African mainland and islands, formed under the influence of local society, absorbed features from a variety of sources but remained fundamentally local, African and Swahili.

BIBLIOGRAPHY

CHITTICK, H. N. 1974. *Kilwa: An Islamic Trading City on the East African Coast.* Nairobi.

——. 1980. *L'Afrique de l'Est et l'Orient: les ports et le commerce avant l'arrivée des Portugais.* Paris, pp. 15–26.

FREEMAN-GRENVILL, G. S. P. 1962. *The Medieval History of the Coast of Tanganyika.* London.

——. 1962. *The East African Coast: Selected Documents from the First to the Earlier Nineteenth Century.* Oxford.

INGRAMS, W. H. 1931. *Zanzibar, Its History and Its People.* London.

MASAO, F. T.; MUTORO, H. W. 1988. East African Coast and the Comoro Islands. In: *General History of Africa.* Vol. III. UNESCO, Paris, pp. 586–615.

MATHEW, G. 1966. The East African Coast Until the Coming of the Portuguese. In: OLIVER, R.; MATHEW, G. (eds) *History of East Africa.* Oxford, pp. 94–128.

MATVEIEV, V. V. 1984. The Development of Swahili Civilization. In: *General History of Africa.* Vol. IV. UNESCO, Paris, pp. 455–480.

——. 1960. *Northern Boundaries of the Eastern Bantu (Zinj) in the tenth century, according to Arab sources.* Oriental Institute, Moscow.

MISIUGIN, V. M. 1966. Suakhiliiskaia khronika srednevekovnogu gosudarstva Pate: La Chronique swahili de l'état médiéval du Paté. In: *Africana, Kultura i iazyki narodov Afriki.* Akademiia nauk SSR. Trudy Instituta etnograffii iu. N. N. Miklukho-Maklaia, n.s., 90, Afrikanskii etnograficheskii sbornik, 6, Moscow.

MIKLUKHO-MAKKAIA, M. S., 90, Afrikanskii etmograficheskii sborinik, 6, Moscow.

OLIVER, R. 1970. Afrique orientale. In: DESCHAMPS, H. (ed.) *Histoire générale de l'Afrique noire des origines à 1800.* Paris, pp. 424–432.

STIGAND, C. H. 1966. *The Land of Zinj.* London.

35.4
MIXED CULTURES OF MADAGASCAR AND THE OTHER ISLANDS

Rafolo Andrianaivoarivony

The Indian Ocean, with its many seas, has from the earliest times been the scene of long-distance navigation, which by the first centuries AD, had led sailors to become proficient in using the monsoons, the key to sailing between India, the Persian Gulf, the Red Sea and the East African coast (see Plate 22). The peopling of Madagascar in the middle of the first millennium AD and of the Comoros in the eighth–ninth centuries was a consequence of the voyages of sailors and traders from the Indonesian archipelago, South-East Asia, south India, the Persian Gulf and the Red Sea to the western Indian Ocean. However, the peopling of the Mascarenes, Mauritius (Île-de-France), Réunion (Île Bourbon), Rodriguez and the Seychelles did not begin until the seventeenth century, although these other islands were well known to Arab seafarers in the 'Middle Ages'.

The Indian Ocean, linking Oceania, Asia and Africa, brought the peoples and cultures that came to settle in Madagascar and the Comoro Islands and engendered a mixing of cultures in these islands: Austronesian, East African (Bantu) and superficially Arab–Islamic in Madagascar, and Arab–Islamic, East African and superficially Austronesian in the Comoros.

We have no intention here of trying to determine how much each influence contributed to the civilization of the islands but intend rather to describe these mixed cultures in their new environment, and also to look at the cultural and technological creativity of these societies during the period under consideration, from 600 to 1492.

SETTLEMENTS AND TRANSFORMATIONS OF THE ENVIRONMENT

From the seventh to the thirteenth century, by which date most of the peopling of Madagascar was finally complete both along the coast and in the interior, immigrants arrived in waves, each with their own cultural characteristics. There were Afro-Indonesians from south-east Borneo (seventh–ninth centuries) who had probably stayed some considerable time on the East African coast, thus initiating the perfect symbiosis of Austronesian and East African cultures visible on the soil of Madagascar; then 'Shīrāzīs' landing in both the Comoros and northern Madagascar in the eleventh century, followed in the twelfth century by Islamized groups: the *Zafiraminia* (descendants of Raminia), who, after a short stay in the north of the island, finally settled in the south-east, and the *Antalaotse* group ('People of the open sea'), an urbanized trading people who settled on the islands and at the ends of the bays on the north-west and north coasts, like the 'people of the coast' and the Swahili towns of East Africa. At the same time, more Indonesians, influenced in varying degrees by Bantu civilization, were landing in the Bay of Antongil, in the east north-east of the country, intent on occupying the interior of the island. Finally, in the thirteenth century, in the south-east of the country, other Islamized groups arrived, the *Zafikazimambo* (descendants of *Kazimambo*) and the *Antemoro-Anakara* (people of the coast), who knew the *sorabe* script ('big writing'), which transcribed the Malagasy language into Arabic letters long before the adoption of the Roman alphabet in 1820.

The transformation of the Malagasy environment began with the first arrivals, and each new settlement led to the cutting down of vast areas of forest and to the clearing of large tracts of land, first for grubbing and then to develop the low ground and valleys through rice growing. This led to the disappearance, by the eleventh or twelfth century, of most of the big fauna such as the giant lemur (*Archaeolemur*), the giant land tortoise (*Geochelone grandidieri*), the ratite ('elephant bird', *Aepyornis*) and the dwarf hippopotamus (*Hippopotamus lemerlei*).

Human beings' arrival in the Comoro Islands – Ngazidja or Grand Comoro, mountainous and lacking permanent rivers, Mwali or Mohéli, Ndzwani or Anjouan, and Maoré or Mayotte with their welcoming fertile soils and permanent rivers – took the same form as it did in Madagascar. First, small groups of Afro-Indonesians arrived perhaps as early as the fifth century AD (Masao and Mutoro, 1990, p. 633); then, between the eighth and tenth centuries, there were successive but small waves of Arabs who were not yet Islamized (graves that have been discovered confirm this). This high period was marked by the so-called Dembeni culture (Wright, 1984, 1992; Allibert, 1990), to which we shall return below. The Islamized groups arrived between the eleventh and fourteenth centuries, notably the Shīrāzīs associated with the expansion of Islam into the south-west Indian Ocean and converting the whole archipelago.

TYPES OF SETTLEMENT AND FRAMEWORKS OF EXISTENCE (see Map 32)

Types of settlement varied according to the period and place and might be simple or fortified. The former have left few remains and are sometimes difficult to locate in the absence of anything to mark their boundaries. Such, in Madagascar, are the fishermen's sites in the south (Sarodrano, fifth century; Talaky, eleventh century), the rock shelters and caves in the north, including Andavakoera, dated to AD 405, currently the oldest known site in the Great Island, or the sites of rudimentary dwellings along waterways (Beropitike, eleventh century, in southern Madagascar) or near sources of water (sites in Mahafale country, fifteenth century). In the Comoros, there are small hamlets dating from the twelfth century. Some of these sites have sizeable stone structures such as dry stone enclosures or *manda* in central and southern Madagascar (fourteenth–sixteenth centuries), believed to be pens for animals, and architectural remains (houses, graves, mosques) in the trading posts along the coasts of the Comoros and north Madagascar, flourishing by the ninth century in the Comoros and by the eleventh–twelfth centuries in Madagascar.

Fortified settlements were built on hills or defensive hilltops with wall fortifications in the Comoros from the fifteenth century, and with ditches, that is, defensive moats, in Madagascar from the eleventh century if not before. These sites with ditches are located in the central Malagasy Highlands and the far south-east, and the oldest ones currently known are Ambohimanana (eleventh century) and Ankadivory (twelfth century), both in the area of Antananarivo.

The old Malagasy dwellings of the time were built with perishable materials (wood, leaves, bark, branches and so on) and were rectangular in shape, as in Indonesia, standing on piles in wet areas, on stone supports in the highlands and directly on the ground in the warm areas of the south and west. They varied in area from 20 to 30 m², and in the sixteenth century might reach up to 50–70 m² in the case of royal huts. They were aligned on a north–south axis with openings to the west and a blind wall to the east to keep out the cold trade winds. The organization of living space was

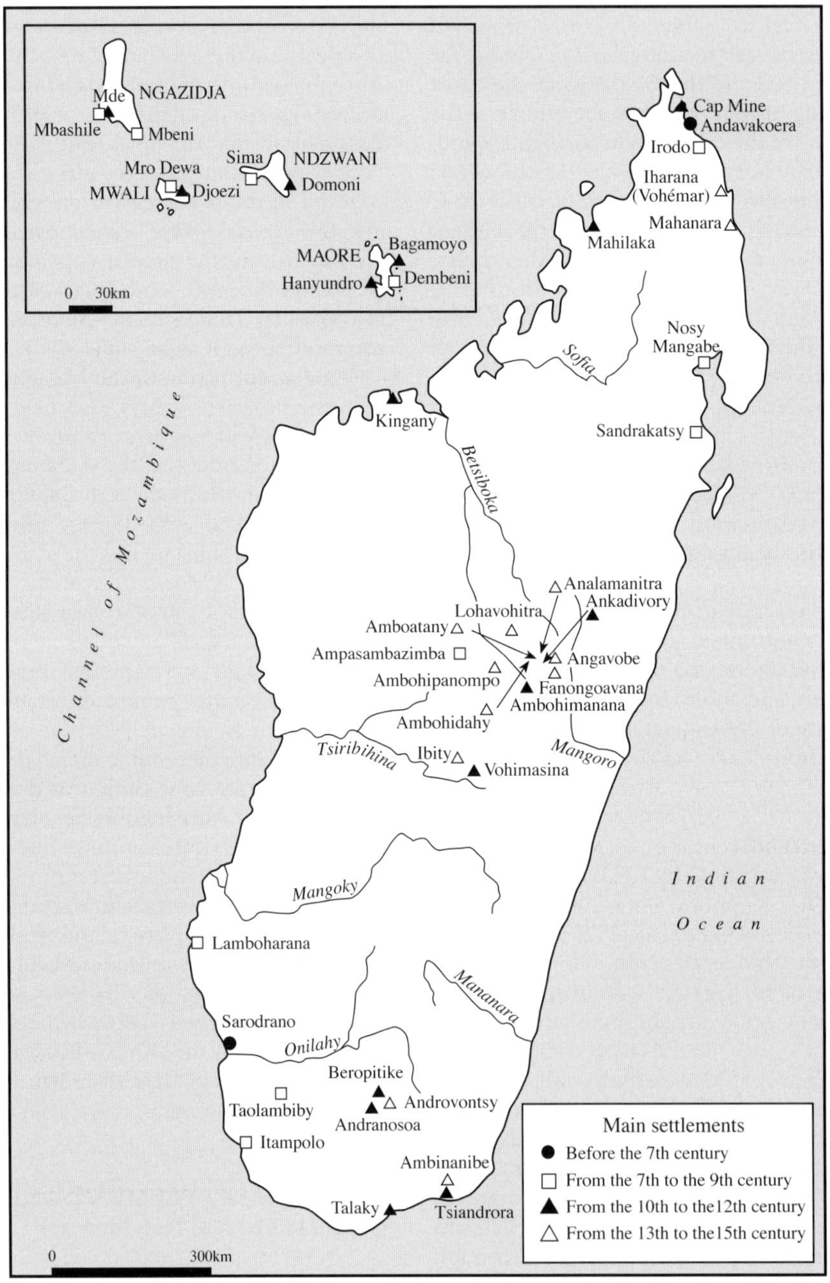

Map 32 Archaeological sites known and dated in Madagascar and the Comoros from the period 600 to 1500 (draft Rafolo, A.).

governed by the relief and particular configuration of each site, but it was generally the north side that was given priority, except in the southern parts of the island, where it was rather the south side.

In the Comoros, stone was used as the foundation for houses from the very earliest cultural periods of the eighth–tenth centuries, the most typical sites of which were Dembeni (Maoré) and Old Sima (Nzwani). The use of stone developed with Islam, but most houses were built of plant materials.

LIFE-STYLES AND TECHNOLOGY

Life-styles

Slash-and-burn agriculture, an old Indonesian and African technique, was a vital necessity for people who were used to other agricultural traditions such as the cultivation of paddy or hill rice. This had to wait until the valleys has been made ready and the forest had been cleared. Large numbers of burnt rice grains discovered at Dembeni (ninth century) and some sites in the interior of Madagascar (Fanongoavana, thirteenth century and Lohavohitra, fifteenth century) testify to the practice of rice growing. In addition to this, in the Comoros, millet, leguminous plants, coconuts, bamboo, bananas and taro were grown in cultivated plots (Wright, 1992), and the same plants were also found in Madagascar along with sugar cane and Asian yam. Roots and forest fruits were also gathered.

The life-style of the hunter–gatherer does not seem to have predominated except in some regions of Madagascar, and it always needed to be backed up by agriculture. There is evidence of animal husbandry at all sites of the period in Madagascar and the Comoros on account of the large quantities of bones of zebus (*Bos indicus*), oxen (*Bos taurus*), sheep, goats and pigs (*Sus scrofa domesticus*, particularly at Dembeni, well before the arrival of Islam). Malagasy sites in the interior include enclosures reminiscent of the Bantu kraals of East Africa, from where the use of cattle as capital also came. Insectivores were hunted such as the tenrec (*Centetes ecaudatus*) and the ericulus (*Ericulus telfairi*) in the Comoros from the eighth to eleventh century, and in southern Madagascar in the eleventh century. The meat of African river hogs (*Potamochoerus larvatus*) was eaten in many Malagasy sites, and large fauna were hunted as late as the thirteenth century in the far north of the island (Dewar and Rakotovololona, 1992). Fishermen in coastal sites in both Madagascar (Sarodrano, Talaky) and the Comoros (Bagamoyo, tenth–thirteenth centuries, on Maoré) relied on a diet dominated by seafood such as fish, crustaceans, turtles and shellfish caught with harpoons, hooks, lines and nets. The non-coastal populations also engaged in fishing.

Technology

The people that made landfall in Madagascar and the Comoros brought with them their own technology and skills, which they adapted in the light of the types and above all the quality of the materials available in their new environment.

Wood, an abundant and readily available material, was used to build dwellings and make domestic and some funerary furniture, musical instruments, crockery, weapons and traps, and some regions may legitimately be described as having a plant civilization.

The strong influence exerted by local resources also appears in pottery, which shows specific features resulting from the creative spirit of the people. Thus the Malagasy selected earths for clays, along with mica, quartz or feldspar for degreasing and graphite to mix with their clay or for use as a glaze. They made their pottery entirely by hand, and firing was done in the open air at low temperatures (500–800°). The shapes of vessels and decorative motifs, the same all over the country, are evidence of a true cultural unity with circulation of techniques. One finds bowls, jars, pitchers, cooking pots (the oldest reminiscent of those made of soapstone in the Islamic staging posts), earthenware water coolers, graphitized legged plates, typical of the central highlands, oil lamps and ladles made of fired clay. In addition to these, there were toys and a few instruments such as spindle-whorls. Forms and styles developed naturally over the centuries, but what emerges is a remarkable cultural continuity stretching right through the period and even beyond. Decorative motifs are solely geometric, for example impressions of small triangles or small circles, or herringbone, parallel or cruciform incisions, in relief or chased. In the Comoros, the original feature of local ceramics is the tradition of decoration with shells with indented edges, including the Arca type mentioned by the archaeologists H. Wright at Dembeni and C. Allibert at Bagamoyo. The second original local ceramic ware is that known as 'Dembeni graphitized red' with a polished, graphitized red slip. The rest of what was produced was of common manufacture and has similarities with some ceramics in Malagasy or Swahili staging posts. Thus the carinated ceramics of the Majikavo phase (eighth century) resemble those of Irodo (north-east Madagascar) and Manda, and the ceramics of the Hanyundru phase (eleventh–thirteenth centuries) those of Mahilaka in north-west Madagascar. The most common vessels are large-diameter hollow dishes, sometimes carinated, glazed with a red burnish with graphitized bands and sometimes displaying Arca decoration. Next come globular-shaped pots with narrow openings.

Where the working of stone was concerned, the ancient Malagasy quarried granite by thermal shock. Soapstone, abundant in the north-eastern and south-eastern regions, and used in the making of cooking pots, was cut out with knives and then turned and/or gouged.

Metal-working, brought by the first migrants, has left many remains (instruments, slag, workshops, grindstones, weapons, ornaments) in pre-ninth–tenth-century sites on the coasts of Madagascar and the Comoros and in pre-twelfth-century ones in central and southern Madagascar. The early Malagasy made iron from powdery ore or iron-bearing rocks in small clay furnaces using charcoal as fuel and limestone ($CaCO_3$) as a flux (Radimilahy, 1985, pp. 63–66). Evidence of the working of precious metals such as gold and silver is provided by the discovery of grindstones of various shapes in a number of interior sites in Madagascar.

Leather working, basket making and weaving have left few traces, and these date solely from the late period (twelfth–fourteenth century), for example metal hooks, bone polishers, traces of basketwork reproduced by chance on the bottom of vessels before firing, and spindle-whorls.

TRADE AND THE DEVELOPMENT OF TOWNS

The large number of imported objects found testifies to the existence of intense trade along maritime routes linking the islands in the south-west Indian Ocean to East Africa, the Red Sea (and from there certainly to the Mediterranean), the Persian Gulf (especially to the port of Ṣīraf) and the Far East by way of South India, South-East Asia and Indonesia. Between the seventh and the eleventh century, this trade was carried on chiefly by Austronesian traders, and Madagascar exported, among other products, aromatics, medicinal plants and spices (Domenichini-Ramiaramanana, 1990; Domenichini, 1988). Some non-Islamized Arab merchant-traders were also present in the Comoros (Wright, 1992). Between the twelfth century and the end of the fifteenth, trade in the region fell under Arab domination, and the islands became part of the Islamic world and economy. This connection, and Arab influences, brought into Malagasy culture such items as the lunar calendar, astrology, the names of the days, the *sorabe* script, the vocabulary of divination, the use of monetary units and of scales, and the prohibition on eating pork.

In the Comoros, the successive settlements of Muslim traders introduced cultural traditions very close to those of the Swahili world, whose trading posts had their Malagasy equivalents in the *antalaotse* settlements along the north-west and north-east coasts. The expansion of their activities, mainly oriented towards the open sea, transformed them into true towns, initially rather small, covering 8–15 ha like Dembeni, Sima and Domoni (Ndzwani) during the Hanyundru period in the Comoros, and later larger, like Mahilaka, covering up to 60 ha, according to research in progress by Radimilahy. The 'ports' consisted of sandbanks on which dhows would be driven ashore to unload and load at low tide. They would then wait for the high tide to take to sea again. Goods carried (and sometimes reaching areas far away from the coast like central and southern Madagascar) included agricultural produce such as spices, various liquids (water, oils, syrups), slaves, vast amounts of Sasanian–Islamic pottery (earthenware jars, bowls), sgraffiato vessels after the eleventh century (marbled enamel and slipware Islamic pottery), so-called Dembeni graphitized red ceramic pottery, soapstone cooking pots from Madagascar, red cornelians from India, pottery from western Indochina (martaban), 'blue and white' and 'yellow and black' Chinese porcelain, willow green Chinese celadonware (plates, bowls, pots, teapots and so on), glass as early as the tenth century, bronze mirrors, ambergris and many other goods of which no trace or memory survives.

The west Indian Ocean in general, and Madagascar in particular, were during the entire period a meeting point for neighbouring peoples throughout the Indian Ocean. The huge island was thus a centre for the dissemination of ideas and all kinds of merchandise and plants to the east coast of Africa. Yet the flow was equally rich in the opposite direction, because a large part of the population, a number of cultural components, the Islamic religion and many commercial products passed through East Africa before reaching Madagascar.

EVOLUTION OF FORMS OF GOVERNMENT

It is likely that the migrants in every period had known complex concepts and forms of political and social organization in the countries from which they came or in which they had lived temporarily. Nevertheless, it was not yet necessary to establish them in the lands to which they came, either in Madagascar or the Comoros, given the size of the communities and their isolation. An elementary organization to manage the economy and religious practices of small areas was sufficient until the twelfth century, when the numbers in the groups had become such that it was necessary to adopt a different, more suitable system of organization such as the state, that is a supra-ethnic authority (Vérin, 1992), the idea of which may have come from some outside influence. This change of political organization did not occur at the same time in all regions: in Madagascar, some did not experience it until the nineteenth century. It occurred in the Comoros with the establishment of the *fani* (the first Muslim chiefs) in the twelfth–thirteenth centuries and the regime of the sultanates starting in the fifteenth century, and in Madagascar starting in the twelfth century with the advent of kingdoms in various parts of the island and city states in the main trading posts (Vérin, 1975, 1992).

RELIGION AND BELIEFS

The religion of the ancient Malagasy rested on God who created everything (*Zanahary, Andriamanitra*), the ancestors who were supposed to watch over the living, the spirits of nature, charms deemed to protect the holder or cause harm to others, and divination based on lucky or unlucky spells (*vintana*) and geomancy (*sikidy*). The *ombiasa* (diviner-healer), *mpisikidy* (diviner) and *mpitan-kazomanga* (holder of a charm which was, and still is, widespread throughout western and southern Madagascar), constituted what might be called the 'holy men' of Malagasy traditional religion (Vig, 1973). The ancient Malagasy invoked God, the ancestors or the spirits, in various sacred places such as the north-east corner of a house, graves, certain stones, trees, mountains, springs, lakes and so on. This religion withstood the expansion of Islam, which was able to take root superficially only along the north-west and north-east coasts of the island. In the Comoros, on the other hand, particularly because of the limited extent of the archipelago and the small number of inhabitants, Islam, initially Shī'ite (eleventh–thirteenth centuries) and later Sunni (fourteenth century), was able to take over completely and make a deep mark on the civilization of the islands.

The arrival of Islam in this part of the Indian Ocean was due to several factors, including trade and religious persecution. Sects and brotherhoods which were regarded as heretical – particularly certain Ṣūfic sects, which were not welcome everywhere as they were considered obscurantist, mystical and too irrational – were forced into exile, sometimes very far away. Thus the western Indian Ocean, already well known to Arab merchants and navigators, offered refuge: those who were persecuted as they went into exile were welcomed in East Africa and the Comoros by the local populations who had settled there before them and were subsequently converted to the Qur'ānic faith.

BIBLIOGRAPHY

ALLIBERT, C., ARGANT, A.; ARGANT, J. 1983. Le site de Bagamoyo (Mayotte), *Etudes Océan Indien*, Paris, No. 2, pp. 5–10.

——. 1990. Le site de Dembéni (Mayotte, Archipel des Comores), *Etudes Océan Indien*, Paris, No. 11, pp. 63–172.

CHANUDET, C.; VÉRIN, P. 1983. Une reconnaissance archéologique de Mohéli, *Etudes Océan Indien*. Paris, No. 2, pp. 41–58.

DESCHAMPS, H. 1972. *Histoire de Madagascar*. Paris.

DEWAR, R.; RAKOTOVOLOLONA, S. 1992. La chasse aux subfossiles:

les preuves du onzième siècle au treizième siècle, *Taloha*. Antananarivo, No. 11, pp. 4–15.

DOMENICHINI-RAMIARAMANANA, B. 1990. Madagascar. In: *General History of Africa* Vol. III. UNESCO, Paris, pp. 681–703.

DOMENICHINI, J. P. 1988. *L'Histoire de Madagascar aujourd'hui*, Antananarivo.

ESOAVELOMANDROSO, F. V. 1984. Madagascar and the Neighbouring Islands from the 12th to the 16th Century. In: *General History of Africa*. Vol. IV. UNESCO, Paris, pp. 597–613.

MASAO, F. T.; MUTORO, H. W. 1990. The East African Coast and the Comoro Islands. In: *General History of Africa*. Vol. III (UNESCO, Paris.), pp. 586–615.

OTTINO, P. 1976. Le Moyen Âge de l'Océan Indien et les composantes du peuplement de Madagascar. *Asie du Sud-Est et Monde Insulindien* (ASEMI). Paris, Vol. VII, Nos. 2–3, pp. 3–8.

RADIMILAHY, C. 1985. *La métallurgie ancienne du fer à Madagascar* Musée de l'Université Antananarivo.

RAFOLO, A. 1987–1988. L'alimentation carnée chez les anciens Malgaches. In: *Nouvelles du centre d'art et d'archéologie*. Antananarivo, Nos. 5–6, pp. 22–26.

——. 1989. *Habitats fortifiés et organisation de l'espace dans le Vonizongo (Centre-ouest de Madagascar); le cas de Lohavohitra*. University of Paris-I, doctoral thesis. Paris.

RASAMUEL, D. 1984a. Alimentation et techniques anciennes dans le Sud malgache à travers un dépotoir du XIe siècle. In: *Etudes Océan Indien*. Paris, No. 4, pp. 81–109.

——. 1984b. *L'ancien Fanongoavana*. University of Paris-I, Third Cycle thesis. Paris.

——. 1989. Madagascar (Archéologie). In: *Universalia*. Encyclopaedia Universalis, Paris. pp. 229–233.

TOUSSAINT, A. 1961. *Histoire de l'Océan Indien*. Paris.

VÉRIN, P. 1975. *Les échelles anciennes du commerce sur les côtes nord de Madagascar*. Service de reproduction des thèses, 2 vols. Lille.

——. 1990. *Madagascar*. Paris.

——. 1992. Etats ou cité-états dans le nord de Madagascar. *Taloha*. Antananarivo, No. 11, pp. 65–70.

VÉRIN, P.; WRIGHT, H. T. 1981. Contribution à l'étude des anciennes fortifications de Ngazidja (Grande Comore). In: *Asie du Sud-Est et Monde Insulindien (ASEMI)*. Paris, No. XI, pp. 289–303.

VIG, L. 1973. *Les conceptions religieuses des anciens Malgaches*. Impr. Catholique. Tananarive.

WRIGHT, H. T. 1984. Early Seafarers of the Comoro Islands: the Dembeni Phase of the IXth–Xth Centuries AD. *Azania*. Nairobi, No. XIX, pp. 13–59.

——. 1990. Trade and Politics on the Eastern Littoral of Africa AD 800–1300. In: *Urban Origins in Eastern Africa/Working Papers 1989*. Central Board of Swedish Antiquities. Stockholm.

——. 1992. Early Islam, Oceanic Trade and Town Development on Nzwani: the Comorian Archipelago in the XIth-XVth Centuries AD, *Azania*. Nairobi, No. XXVII (in press).

35.5
INTERNATIONAL IMPORTANCE OF THE REGION

Edward A. Alpers

Like all cultures, we can safely assume that the people of the evolving Swahili culture of the eastern coast of Africa and the offshore islands regarded themselves as living at the centre of the universe. From a world history perspective, however, indeed even from the more immediate larger perspective of the Indian Ocean or the continent of Africa, this region was at the periphery of the known world. Yet it was by no means unknown, and with the birth, rise and expansion of Islam it was drawn increasingly into the dominant international currents of commerce and culture. Nevertheless, throughout these 900 years the primary attraction and international significance of this broad region of the Africa world was as a source of otherwise unobtainable luxury goods. Despite some considerable indigenous cultural achievements, it was not regarded by outsiders as a source of cultural inspiration or of world leadership.

At the beginning of this long era, the isolation of the region in *c.* 600 appears to have been greater than at the beginning of the first millennium AD, when the *Periplus* suggests that it was a well-known, if far-flung, part of the wider Mediterranean world. And we have seen from our previous discussion of trade and urban development (see sub-chapter 35.2) that it remained relatively marginal until after about AD 1100. One explanation that is sometimes given for this situation is the major interruption caused in the early march of Muslim commerce in the Indian Ocean world by the revolt of the Zanj slaves in lower Iraq and the Persian Gulf between 866 and 883, which shut down the major ports of the Gulf and severely hindered maritime trade. If one accepts that the Zanj slaves came from the coast, or at least through trade at the coast, notwithstanding the fact that we cannot with any certainty identify their origins except to note that they were not speakers of Arabic, then it is evident that coastal East Africa had a powerful impact on the 'Abbāsid caliphate in the later ninth century.

By the time of Mas'ūdī's last visit to East Africa, only three decades later, the groundwork for the flourishing commercial relations that would obtain in subsequent centuries was already laid and it is possible to begin to observe the impact of cultural influences emanating from the Muslim world on coastal society. For example, in describing the ivory trade at the coast, Mas'ūdī notes that most of the ivory was shipped from the coast to Oman, whence it was forwarded to India and China, lamenting that 'if it was not shipped to these destinations, ivory would be very abundant in Muslim lands'. In China, he explains, ivory was carved into walking sticks that were carried by all officials, as well as in temple fixtures, while in India it was used to manufacture dagger handles and sabre guards, but especially chessmen and backgammon pieces (Mas'ūdī, 1965, pp. 323–324). About half a century later, argues Horton, 'a radical change took place' in European culture, both Christian and Muslim, with the advent of remarkable carvings in elephant ivory, the bulk of which he suggests 'came from East Africa' (Horton, 1987, p. 86). What we can see in these tenth-century developments is the international recognition of the superiority of African elephant ivory, especially that from East Africa, because of its suitability, for intricate carving.

As the fame of raw materials from East Africa spread throughout the known world, curiosity about the region increased accordingly. Just as the coastal inhabitants were the gatekeepers to the interior, Muslim traders provided the physical connections between the coast and the outside world. Arab and Indian dominance of the Indian Ocean trading system ensured that access to and knowledge of East Africa and the islands was mediated almost exclusively through Arab channels. The various Arab literary sources that follow Mas'ūdī's account bear eloquent testimony to this reality. At the same time, because of its proximity to the heartlands of Islam, East Africa provided an extensive, and therefore safe, haven for various Muslim dissidents, whether theological or political, from southern Arabia and the Persian Gulf, as well as a frontier of opportunity for adventurous souls. The complex history of settlement and Islamic development along the coast provides ample evidence for this reconstruction, even if the details remain a source of much scholarly contention. What we do not know, regrettably, is to what extent people of the coast participated in the dissemination of popular, as opposed to literary, knowledge and images of East Africa during this period, as surely they must have done. There can be little doubt that coastal people participated as seamen in the trade of the Indian Ocean, even if the international shipping lanes were the nearly exclusive preserve of Arab, Persian and Indian vessels. And like seafarers everywhere, at least in the ports of the region, including the Red Sea, they must have exchanged tales of their homeland that excited the imagination of their listeners. We will never be able to document this lost history, but it must surely have had its effect.

There is no better way to capture the flavour of this world and its reputation internationally than to listen to the eyewitness testimony of Ibn Baṭṭūṭa, who spent several days during his travels in 1331 at each of the two most important towns on the coast, Mogadishu and Kilwa. Ibn Baṭṭūṭa describes Mogadishu as:

a town of enormous size. Its inhabitants are merchants possessed of vast resources; they own large numbers of camels, of which they slaughter hundreds every day [for food], and also have quantities of sheep. In this place are manufactured the woven fabrics called after it, which are unequalled and exported from it to Egypt and elsewhere.
(English tr. Gibb, 1956–71, Vol.II, pp. 419–420.)

Since he was not a merchant but a man of letters, Ibn Baṭṭūṭa was made a guest of the *qāḍī* instead of being hosted by a local broker. He was introduced to the ruler of the town, who was known by the title of *shaykh* and who spoke both the local language (it is not clear whether this means Somali or Swahili) and Arabic. When he was received by the *qāḍī*, who was 'an Egyptian by origin', he was served 'some leaves of betel and areca nuts', both products of South Asia and characteristic of Indian hospitality, and his hands were washed in 'rose water of Damascus'. The food served to Ibn Baṭṭūṭa reflected influences from India, the Persian Gulf and Africa, while his description of a set of clothing given him to wear for Friday prayers similarly mirrors these cosmopolitan influences. Other influences noted by the great traveller include the manner in which the *shaykh* was greeted by his followers, which 'is the same as the custom of the people of al-Yaman', and the four canopies each mounted by the figure of a gold bird, which British Arabist H.A.R. Gibb identifies as deriving from the ceremonial parasols of Fāṭimid Egypt. The following day, Ibn Baṭṭūṭa attended the weekly judicial hearings at the *shaykh's* residence, noting that some cases were decided according to Islamic law, others according to customary law (Gibb, 1962, Vol. II, pp. 375–378).

After resting at Mombasa for a single night, an indication that this town, which was to become the centre of international rivalry between the Portuguese and the Omani Arabs after 1500, had not yet achieved such prominence within the coastal political economy, the Moroccan jurist proceeded to Kilwa, 'a large city on the sea coast, most of whose inhabitants are Zinj [*sic*], jet-black in colour'. There he learned about the sea route to Sofala and the time it took to reach the country of the interior of southern Africa, from where gold came down to the coast at Sofala. Kilwa impressed him as 'one of the finest and most substantially built towns', and he observed that its inhabitants 'are for the most part religious and upright, and Shāfi'ites in rite'. One senses that Kilwa was at the edge of the Muslim world for Ibn Baṭṭūṭa by his comment that the sultan 'used to engage frequently in expeditions to the land of the Zinj [*sic*] people, raiding them and taking booty', a fifth of which he would set aside for pious works as prescribed in the Qur'ān. While commenting further upon the sultan's piety, humility and generosity, Ibn Baṭṭūṭa mentions by name several *sharīfs* from both Iraq and the Ḥijāz who were visiting Kilwa, yet further testimony to the place that it held in international consciousness (Gibb, 1962, Vol. II, pp. 379–381) (see Plate 35).

Recognition of the importance of coastal East Africa during this period was not restricted to either Arabs in particular or Muslims in general. The dissemination of luxury items from the continent to Asia and the Mediterranean must have sustained its reputation as a region of considerable wealth, or at least as a place from which one could gain such wealth. Yet there is disappointingly little information to be gleaned from Indian sources on either East Africa or Africans in India during this entire epoch (Talib, 1988, pp. 731; Devisse with Labib, 1984, p. 656). Chinese sources, however, provide some insight into the highly negative way in which Zanj slaves were portrayed while at the same time marking East Africa as a place of some noteworthiness because of its natural resources. Finally, in a bold series of seven recorded voyages between 1405 and 1433 involving unusually large fleets, the Chinese ventured out for themselves into the Indian Ocean, reaching East Africa twice, in 1417–1419 and 1421–1422. In the first voyage, the fleet touched at Malindi, on the Kenya coast north of Mombasa, and its leaders sent a giraffe to the imperial court, which was regarded as an omen of good fortune. In the second, both Mogadishu and Barāwa, further south on the Banadir coast of Somalia, were reached and intriguing descriptions of their inhabitants recorded (Talib, 1988, pp. 731–733; Devisse with Labib, 1984, p. 658; Wheatley, 1975; Shen, 1995: for a recent critical review of the way in which these sources have sometimes been misinterpreted and misused).

The fifteenth century witnessed some shifting fortunes along the coast, as Kilwa and Mogadishu declined somewhat in significance and Mombasa, Malindi and Zanzibar expanded their influence. Viewed regionally, however, while still considered to be at the periphery of world affairs, coastal East Africa and its islands enjoyed an established place in that world. Nevertheless, when the Portuguese entered the waters of the Indian Ocean at the end of the fifteenth century, although they clearly had considerable knowledge of the wealth of the Orient, particularly in spices, they possessed little knowledge of the rich regional culture that flourished along the coast of East Africa (see Plates 22, 200, 271, 272).

BIBLIOGRAPHY (Chapters 35.1, 35.2, 35.5)

ABUNGU, G. H. O.; MUTORO, H. W. 1993. Coast–Interior Settlements and Social Relations in the Kenya Coastal Hinterland. In: SHAW, T. *et al.* (eds) *The Archaeology of Africa: Food, Metals and Towns*. London, New York, pp. 694–704.

BERG, F. J. 1968. The Swahili Community of Mombasa, 1500–1900. *Journal of African History*. London, Vol. IX, No. 1, pp. 35–56.

CHITTICK, H. N. 1974. *Kilwa: An Islamic Trading City on the East African Coast*. British Institute in Eastern African, Nairobi. 2 vols (Memoir No. 5).

——. 1975. An Early Salt-Working Site on the Tanzanian Coast. *Azania*. British Institute in Eastern African. Nairobi. Vol X, pp. 151–153.

——. 1980. Sewn Boats in the Western Indian Ocean, and a Survival in Somalia. *The International Journal of Nautical Archaeology and Underwater Exploration*. London, Vol. 9, No. 4, pp. 297–309.

——. 1982. Medieval Mogadishu. *Paideuma*. Wiesbaden, No. 28, pp. 45–62.

COUPLAND, R. 1938. *East Africa and its Invaders*. Oxford.

DEVISSE, J. (in collaboration with LABIB, S.) 1984. Africa in Inter-Continental Relations. In: NIANE, D. T. (ed.) *General History of Africa, IV: Africa from the Twelfth to the Sixteenth Century*.UNESCO, Paris; London, Berkeley, pp. 635–672.

HARRIS, J. E. 1971. *The African Presence in Asia*. Evanston, Ill.

HORTON, M. September 1987. The Swahili Corridor. *Scientific American*. Washington, XXX, pp. 86–93.

——. 1992. Archaeology and the Early History of Zanzibar. Paper presented at the International Conference on the History and Culture of Zanzibar, Zanzibar.

HORTON, M.; MUDIDA, N. 1993. Exploitation of Marine Resources: Evidence for the Origin of the Swahili Communities of East Africa. In: SHAW, T. *et al.* (eds) *The Archaeology of Africa: Food, Metals and Towns*. London, New York, pp. 673–693.

IBN BATTŪTA. 1853–1859. *Riḥla* ('Journey'; full medieval Arabic title: *Tuḥfat al-Nuẓẓār fī 'Ajā'ib al-Amṣār*, 'Gift unto the Observers concerning the Marvels of the Lands'). First edn. of Arabic text with French trans. by C. Defrémery and B. R. Sanguinetti, 4 vols, Paris 1853–1859. English trans. by H. A. R. Gibb, *The Travels of Ibn Baṭṭūṭa*. Hakluyt Society, Cambridge, 1956–1971. Arabic text only: *Rihla Ibn Baṭṭūṭa*, ed. by Talāl Harb, Dār al-Kutub al-'Ilmiyya, Beirut 1992.

MASAO, F. T.; MUTORO, H. W. 1988. The East African Coast and the Comoro Islands. In: EL FASI, M.; HRBEK, I. (eds) *General History of Africa, III: Africa from the Seventh to the Eleventh Century*. UNESCO, Paris; London, Berkeley, XXV, pp. 586–615.

AL-MAS'ŪDĪ. 1861–1877. *Murūj al-Dhahab* (The Meadows of Gold); Arabic text with French trans., *Les prairies d'or*, by C. Barbier de Meynard and Pavet de Courteille; Arabic text revised by Ch. Pellat, Beirut 1965; repr. Arabic text, Beirut 1987.

MATVEYEV, V. V. 1984. The Development of Swahili Civilization. In: NIANE, D. T. (ed.) *General History of Africa, IV: Africa from the Twelfth to the Sixteenth Century*.UNESCO, Paris; London, Berkeley, pp. 455–480.

NURSE, D.; SPEAR, T. 1985. *The Swahili: Reconstructing the History and Language of an African Society, 800–1500*. Philadelphia.

SHEN, J. 1995. New Thoughts on the Use of Chinese Documents in the Reconstruction of Early Swahili History. *History in Africa*. Madison, Vol. 22, pp. 349–358.

SINCLAIR, P. J. J. 1982. Chibuene: An Early Trading Site in Southern Mozambique. *Paideuma*. Wiesbaden, 28, pp. 149–164.

SINCLAIR, P. J. J. *et al.* 1993. A Perspective on Archaeological Research in Mozambique. In: SHAW, T. *et al.* (eds) *The Archaeology of Africa: Food, Metals and Towns*. London, New York, pp. 409–431.

STRANDES, J. 1961. *The Portuguese Period in East Africa* (Berlin, 1899). Translated by Jean F. Wallwork; edited with topographical notes by KIRKMAN, J. S., East African Literature Bureau, Transactions of the Kenya Historical Society, Nairobi, Vol. II.

TALIB, Y. 1988. based on a contribution by Samir, F., The African Diaspora in Asia. In: EL FASI, M.; HRBEK, I. (eds) *General History of Africa, III: Africa from the Seventh to the Eleventh Century*,UNESCO, Paris; London, Berkeley, pp. 704–733.

UNESCO. 1980. *Historical Relations Across the Indian Ocean*. Report and papers of the meeting of experts organized by UNESCO at Port Louis, Mauritius, 15–19 July 1974. *The General History of Africa*: Studies and Documents 3. Paris.

WHEATLEY, P. 1975. Analecta Sino-Africana Recensa. In: CHITTICK, H. N.; ROTBERG, R. I. (eds) *East Africa and the Orient: Cultural Syntheses in Pre-Colonial Times*. New York, London, pp. 76–114; Appendix 2, pp. 284–290.

WRIGHT, H. T. (with contributions by KNUDSTAD, J. E.; JOHNSON, L. W.; REDDING, R. W.) 1992. Early Islam, Oceanic Trade and Town Development on Nzwani: The Comorian Archipelago in the XIth–XVth Centuries AD. *Azania*. British Institute in Eastern Africa, Nairobi, Vol. XXVII, pp. 81–128.

——. 1993. Trade and Politics on the Eastern Littoral of Africa, AD 800–1300. In: SHAW, T. *et al.* (eds) *The Archaeology of Africa: Food, Metals and Towns*. London, New York, pp. 658–672.

36

CENTRAL AND SOUTHERN AFRICA

Isidore Ndaywel è Nziem

Central and southern Africa, the vast area that stretches from about 4°N to the Cape of Good Hope in South Africa, less the space between a line drawn from Lake Victoria to Lake Malawi and the Indian Ocean, represents more than a third of the continent and over half of sub-Saharan Africa! This area exhibits the greatest variety of geographical features, with its mountains, the highest points on the continent; and its great rivers such as the Zambezi and the Limpopo, which flow into the Indian Ocean, or the Orange and the Congo, which flow into the Atlantic.

Its plant cover is a sort of reproduction, in reverse, of the situation in West and North Africa. After the savannah, which covers the northern part of Central Africa, there is a vast forested area dominating the lands bordering the Equator and the main waterways; then the great southern grasslands stretch out which, to the south-west, eventually give way to the Kalahari Desert and ultimately the temperate countryside of its southernmost tip. Overall, the climate is tropical, except for the region along the Equator – Gabon, southern Cameroon and Democratic Republic of the Congo (D.R. of the Congo) – where it is equatorial, and the south-western part of the area – Namibia, Botswana and western South Africa – where it is Sahelian or even desert. It is easy to understand why the population density is low, except for a few pockets such as Rwanda and Burundi, the areas around large urban centres and the southern coastal zone (van Chi-Bonnardel, 1973, pp. 25–41).

Until about AD 1000, this part of the continent remained practically isolated from the rest of the world, apart from a few influences coming from Indonesia, recorded along the eastern coast. Yet it too had been occupied from a very early date, as witness the many stone industries that have been identified there by prehistoric archaeology[1].

In southern Africa the autochthonous layer, the oldest layer in the present-day population, consists of hunter–gatherers and pastoralists, known as Bushmen and Hottentots, respectively. Manifestly related to each other, and very similar in physical type, the two population groups speak similar languages and share very similar subsistence techniques and material culture. They later came to be called Khoikhoi, in the case of the Hottentot pastoralists, and San, in the case of the Bushmen hunters, the juxtaposition of the two names giving the term Khoïsan (Parkington, 1981, pp. 639–670). At the beginning of the Christian era, they were joined in this habitat by iron-using people who had come from further north.

The San probably represent the oldest populations on the continent. Originally they were not indigenous to the Kalahari and may perhaps have occupied parts of the Sahara, where there are caves which contain rock paintings of a style similar to those produced in south-western Africa. As for the Khoikhois, they may well be the result of inter-mixing between San and white invaders from the north-east. Their dispersal area seems to have been the Great Lakes region, and they probably only reached southern Africa after the migration of the San.

In central Africa, the scattered Pygmies, who still survive today in remote areas, are described as the remains of the original population of the region. They live in scattered groups in the upper valley of the Ituri to the east of the Democratic Republic of the Congo, in the forest of Gabon and southern Cameroon and in the valleys of the Ubangi and the Sangha (Schebesta, 1957; Vansina, 1966a, pp. 53–69). This group of indigenes was probably scattered all over this region of the continent, living for the most part by gathering, hunting and fishing, and obtaining cereals and tubers in exchange for game meat. Their visibly small size is probably the source of the tales about 'small men with big heads' recorded by Bantu traditions about the earliest masters of the land, who ended up being driven out by the newcomers. In order to justify their behaviour in confiscating the best lands available, these migrants tell in their conquering traditions how the 'small men' had been driven out all the more easily because they were unable, once they had fallen down, to get up unaided because of the weight of their heads. That is how they were so easily decimated.

In reality, things were not quite so simple as the tales suggest, and the earliest masters of Central Africa were not all Pygmies. Already at this early date the existence of human groups similar to present-day Bantu has been noted. Apparently, the stories of the beginnings had borrowed the etiological form only to justify a *de facto* situation in which the coming of the newcomers had led to the absorption of the certainly less numerous pre-existing groups. They were defeated, absorbed and integrated because the dominant groups had the advantage over them of having mastered the techniques of metallurgy, the domestication of animals and farming.

However, some little groups of these archaic populations isolated themselves in the most inhospitable areas in order to safeguard their autonomy, which is what explains the existence today of Pygmies, San and Khoikhois in the demographic make-up of Central and southern Africa.

THE GREAT MIGRATIONS (see Map 33)

Migrations, as consequences of the demands of subsistence, were a permanent, even unchangeable feature in sub-equatorial Africa. According to the seasons, it proved to be indispensable to go in quest of land with more abundant game and better able to produce a supply, as soon as those being exploited began to yield less or became too far from where people were living.

While not instantaneous, mobility was thus an integral aspect of behaviour as a condition of survival. And this was not always conscious and automatic since, logically, removal ought, in principle, to have been envisaged only after possibilities of getting supplies on the spot had been exhausted. Similarly, the constant need to move dwellings nearer to areas of gathering that were forever moving farther away created an almost imperceptible expansionary movement that only became apparent to the whole population years later.

The great migrations that occurred here were of a quite different kind. They were made necessary as the remote consequences of drives from areas in the north following the gradual drying out of the Sahara. In addition, there were surely other push factors in different places such as famines, epidemics, wars or simply the spirit of adventure.

The first migratory movement was that of the dispersion of the Bantu (Obenga, 1985; 1989). There is a long history to the problem of precisely identifying this population group. Linguistics was the first to observe that the great majority of the peoples occupying the southern third of the continent use closely related languages.

In 1862, on the basis of similarities between the words for 'people' in these various languages (*bato* in Duala, *bot* in Fang, *baaru* in Tio, *bantu* in Kongo, *banto* in Mongo, *vear* in Ngwii, *baar* in Ding, *baat* in Bushong, *bantu* in Luba, *abantu* in Rwanda, *vanhu* in Shona and *abantu* in Herero), W. Bleek dubbed this group of languages 'Bantu'. The fact is that the similarities among them are too significant for them to be a matter of chance or mere borrowing; they are rather evidence of a common origin. Consequently, the original language was called 'proto-Bantu', the language that, it was assumed, gave rise to this family of languages when it disappeared in a dynamic process of linguistic fragmentation.

Starting with the work of H. Johnston (1886), the first serious hypotheses began to be made as to the location of

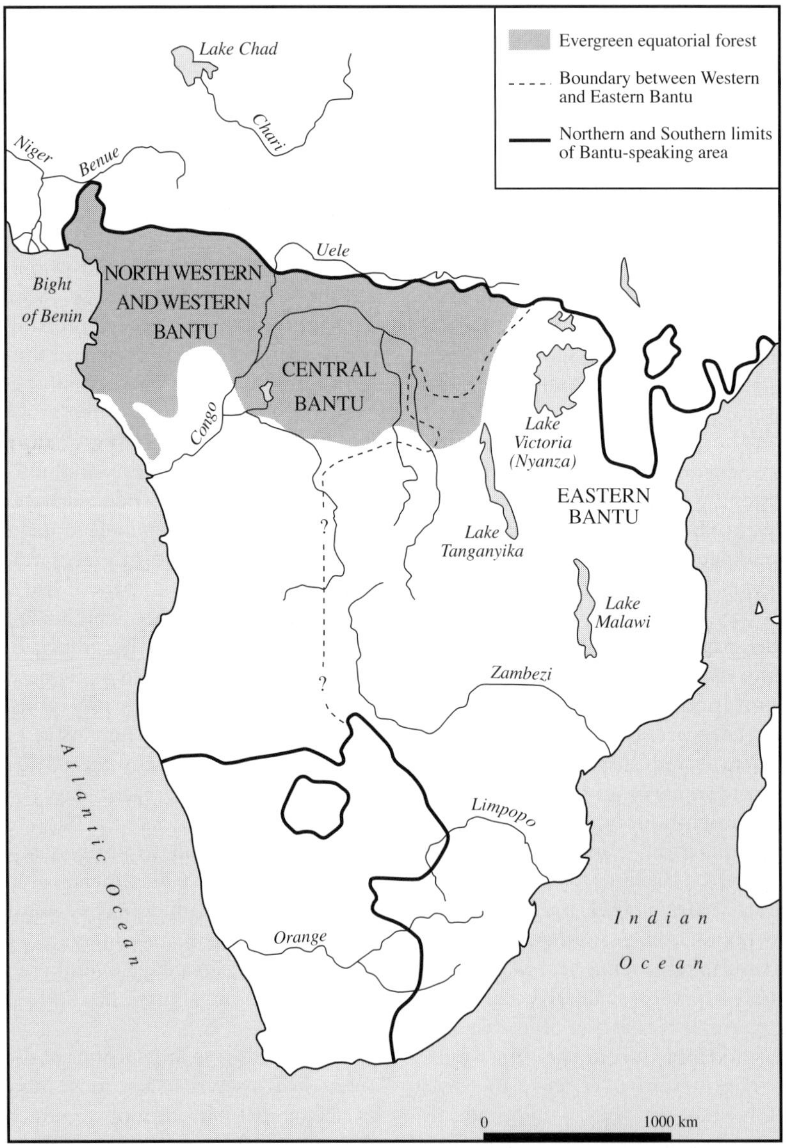

Map 33 Bantu expansion in central and southern Africa (after Vansina, J., 1988, *General History of Africa*, Heinemann-UNESCO).

the cradle of this common archaic language and so to determine its geographical location and thereby the origin of the Bantu. From that, attempts began to be made to reconstruct the process of their dispersal over the continent. Several specialists devoted their lives to solving this problem: some of them linguists, and others belonging to other disciplines including archaeology, anthropology and history[2].

This widespread interest, involving many different approaches, over several decades, has not necessarily led to greater enlightenment. On some aspects, it has even been a source of new confusion[3]. Evidence of this may be seen in the fact that in the current state of research, it is still very difficult to determine precisely the origins of the Bantu and the reasons for their expansion all over sub-equatorial Africa. For all that, the very principle of 'migration' is not as clear-cut as it might seem. The Bantu languages may have spread without thereby meaning that there was any corresponding movement of population, as in the case of the Romance languages, which spread all over Western Europe from the Latium without involving any significant migration by the people of the Latium; or of the Arabic language and culture which extended into most of Egypt and other parts of North Africa without involving a large-scale expansion of population from the Arabian peninsula.

The distinguished historian Roland Oliver put forward the first plausible theory to explain the history of the Bantu expansion from their original homeland all over the continent as far as South Africa: he suggested that the apparently conflicting hypotheses of Greenberg and Guthrie were in fact complementary. With the help of more recent data, this history could be summarized as follows, at least until some new evidence suggests otherwise.

The Bantu-speaking peoples were settled on the Nigerian–Cameroonian plateau, more precisely in the area of the middle Benue, just where these two countries meet. Their expansion southwards began in the Neolithic, between 1000 BC (or even earlier) and 400 BC (de Maret; Nsuka, 1977, pp. 43–66). It continued over a long period in four stages: first, the very rapid migration, along the Congo waterways, of small groups speaking 'pre-Bantu' languages, from the forests of central Cameroon and the Ubangi to similar regions south of the equatorial forest, where the environment is similar to that of their original homeland; then a gradual consolidation and settlement of the migrant peoples and their expansion through the woodland belt extending from coast to coast and embracing the Central African region between the mouth of the River Congo on the west coast and the River Rovuma in Tanzania on the east coast; later, a rapid Bantu penetration into the more humid region north and south of the area of their former lateral expansion; and finally, the occupation of the remainder of present Bantu Africa. The whole process was not completed until about AD 1500 (Lwanga-Lunyiigo and Vansina, 1988, pp. 140–162).

Starting from the northern savannah, this movement split into two with one great branch moving down the western side and one down the eastern side of the continent. There are thus two groups of Bantu languages: western Bantu languages (especially those of the Kongo group), and eastern Bantu languages (notably those of the Great Lakes region), which spread farther south.

Along the western 'route', the group's ancestral language is thought to have still been spoken during the first millennium AD, between the River Alima and the forest, on the right bank of the Congo, which is a transitional zone between the forest and the savannah, like the original homeland. From there, this original language spread out, fragmenting as it did so, carried by fishermen along the various rivers in the region and by individuals moving from village to village. The advance was so rapid that it left no traces of the pre-existing autochthonous languages, which were absorbed or invaded by the languages of these fisher people.

In the eastern area, the eastern proto-Bantu settled on the western shores of Lake Tanganyika in three successive waves between 600 and 400 BC or later. The first was made up of the ancestors of the Lega-Gura people of the eastern Democratic Republic of the Congo, to the west of the western Rift Valley system; then those of the Lacustrine Bantu of Rwanda, Burundi and eastern Uganda, and finally by those of the Tuli of East, Central and southern Africa. The diffusion of metallurgy observed from the Great Lakes to Transvaal and Natal may correspond to this linguistic expansion from the Great Lakes to the Cape. This great expansion was the major feature of the demographic identity of the region as a whole, complemented by internal movements carving up the area among smaller communities.

But this demographic identity of the whole region was only fully achieved with the later arrival of other peoples. In the northern savannah of Central Africa, Sudanese and Nilotic elements mixed with Bantu speakers so closely as sometimes to borrow their languages, as in the case of the Alur in the north-eastern Democratic Republic of the Congo. More generally, this mixing laid the basis for the emergence of ethnic groups with a hybrid culture such as the Zande, the Mangbetu and the Ngbandi[4].

In Malawi, as throughout eastern, central and southern Africa, this further influx of population was also provided by the Negroes of Zanzibar; while in southern Africa, it was by the immigration of the Boers and other peoples from Europe and Asia. But that did not prevent the development of a regional culture by the end of the first millennium AD and the creation of social and economic institutions to organize life in this space.

TECHNIQUES AND ENVIRONMENT

The stories of migrations make it possible to identify the type of environment that was best suited to the old subsistence way of life. They were the intermediate zones between the forest and the savannah. Such a situation gave access to the abundant and varied plant and animal products of the forest without having to suffer the disadvantages of such an environment because of its unhealthiness, scale and wildness. At the same time, the products of the savannah were available too to complement those of the forest and guarantee survival.

The earliest techniques developed were those that had to with subsistence, collecting food and producing it. The technique of capturing animals for meat, a supremely male activity, initially involved simple trapping. Hunting with nets was an innovation in this quest for appropriate technology to 'harvest' animal products. Then, gradually, it came to be accompanied by use of the spear, a prelude to the invention of the arrow, although some of these peoples seem to have moved directly to the arrow, a short spear which has the advantage of not requiring human energy, necessarily limited, to be projected over any considerable distance. This activity, like fishing, was unreliable, subject as it was to chance. Hunting was not necessarily successful, and access to meat was therefore unpredictable.

The most permanent harvesting of foodstuffs involved plant products, an activity acknowledged as supremely a woman's activity. Varieties of vegetables, fruits, insects and caterpillars were gathered. Such an activity involved identifying such edible products as existed in the environment. The amount of such knowledge varied from group to group, depending on the peculiar features of its habitat, which is the explanation for the extreme variation in food habits that can still be observed today.

Among the western Bantu, perception of edible vegetables and fruits was based on observation of animals. The wild mushroom was deemed not to be poisonous and therefore fit for consumption when it was found to be eaten by millipedes; similarly, wild fruits eaten by monkeys were in principle edible.

The need to introduce or transport plant species that produced food in the areas of supply and protect them from any danger of destruction – notably from fires – created conditions favourable to the development of pre-agricultural practices. This concern, gradually leading to the domestication of plants, led to the autonomous invention of agriculture at the beginning of our era. Shifting slash-and-burn agriculture is most likely the remnant of this ancient manner of producing part of the needed foodstuffs in order to escape, at least in part, the imperious necessity of gathering.

There is as yet no complete inventory of food plants of local origin. It is known that most of them are food crops such as varieties of yam, squash and bean; cereals such as sorghum, millet and finger millet; oleaginous plants and stimulants such as the Elaeis palm and the kola nut, respectively; not to mention a variety of vegetables, as yet not adequately identified by ethnobotany, which constituted the main domestically grown vegetables of the region.

Agricultural activity was enhanced between 400 and 200 BC by contributions from plants originating from Asia, such as rice, Asian yams, taro, probably sugar cane and bananas and their many varieties, which meant that they could be used both as a basic foodstuff and as a supplement[5].

As for herding, it remained a marginal activity, separate from agriculture and the work of specialized ethnic groups such as the Khoikhois of the Kalahari, nomad peoples of the Tanzanian grasslands or Tutsi pastoralists of Rwanda and Burundi in the Great Lakes region. Not that agriculturalists did not engage in any stock raising themselves (small livestock, poultry, pigs, goats and sheep), but this was limited to subsidiary activities which hardly impinged on the subsistence economy. Even recently, it was not uncommon for a peasant to recoil from eating 'domestic meat' and to eat only 'bush meat', whereas he did not observe the same discrimination when it was a matter of plant products, wild or domestic.

Domestication – notably of certain species of dog – preceded the acquisition through diffusion of many animal species such as hens, ducks, goats and sheep. The local provenance of the dog is made clear by its place in domestic life. Dogs were used as hunting aids, as libation offerings in rituals and to provide meat. The introduction of goats and sheep in arid regions displaced the dog from the two latter functions and left it to specialize in the role of hunting companion[6].

The predominance of agriculture was only possible because it was backed by knowledge of iron. It was the use of iron, much more than the mere resort to fire, that made possible a significant amount of forest clearing and possibly tilling. However, despite this know-how and the available space, agricultural activity was limited in scope. Use of the hoe and machete rather than the plough imposed restrictions which could have been overcome by double-cropping. But the crops grown, basically tubers and local cereals, did not really lend themselves to this, and it only became possible with the introduction of maize. Traditional agriculture has thus remained at a rudimentary level, despite its long standing and its association with knowledge of iron.

In Central Africa, archaeology customarily associates the early Iron Age with the dimple-based pottery known in the interlacustrine area, including Kivu in the Democratic Republic of the Congo. The dating that it yields confirms the chronology established from the remains of the necropolises at Sanga and Katoto on the upper Lualaba (Congo), which is evidence that knowledge of iron was something acquired in the earliest centuries of the Christian era[7]. It is practically the same in southern Africa, where mastery of metallurgical techniques is attested south of the River Limpopo as early as the fourth or fifth century AD at the latest (Phillipson, 1981, pp. 671–692; Posnansky, 1981, pp. 533–550). South of the Zambezi, the early Iron Age cultures of the first millennium were replaced during the eleventh and twelfth centuries by societies whose pottery was more smoothly finished, and which also made human figurines in clay and imported pearls, glass and other objects. These communities are thought to have been responsible for the construction of the impressive monument of Great Zimbabwe (see Plates 33a, b) (Fagan, 1984, pp. 525–550).

SOCIO-POLITICAL ORGANIZATION

The individual and the community

Apart from the use of features of the environment, the autochthonous and migrant peoples could not have occupied the available space without developing an internal social organization. The family provided the foundation for the earliest needs for close organization.

The first distinction that stood out was the particular relationship among blood relatives, a relationship from which other humans were excluded. And kinship itself could not withstand the need to introduce internal divisions. Kinship by marriage could not be treated in the same way as kinship by consanguinity, inevitably the most important relationship because it is undeniable. To make it a useful principle of organization, particularly in the matter of inheritance, custom came to accept only one of two modes of filiation, matrilinear or patrilinear. Thus 'blood brothers' were recruited in accordance with one or other of these principles, and rarely by both at once[8]. Of the two modes of descent, matrilinear organization is the older; it existed in areas where the patrilinear system now prevails (de Heusch, 1972, pp. 99–111; Cheikh Anta Diop, 1960).

Within the consanguineous community, the individual belonged to the same 'class' as those with whom he shared the same family ties. Consequently, all brothers stood in the relation of 'fathers' to any child that one of them might have. This explains the simplification of terms of address. Not only the biological father but all his real and classificatory brothers were equally addressed as 'father'. It was the same with other positions within the extended family.

This structure makes it possible to locate the existence of family 'classes', those comprising parents and grandparents, distinguished from those comprising children and grandchildren. Within the 'class', relations were based on reciprocity, while between them they were hierarchical: one would talk with one's brother and not with one's father or one's uncle. Yet this cleavage between 'juniors' and 'elders' was nuanced by the relations between alternate generations. It was not uncommon for them to share a joking relationship[9].

As for kinship by marriage, it had its foundation in the need to form relations, through the marriage bond, between family communities. An individual could offer his family community the chance of several alliances through resort to polygamous unions.

In Central Africa, alliances that were regarded as particularly desirable could be made the object of renewal by other marital unions, so that these be not forgotten and kin not be lost to sight. These *preferential* marriages were preferably contracted between cross cousins, or between a grand-daughter and her classificatory grandfather, most commonly the grandfather's great-nephew.

The family units

Here, as elsewhere, family units of several different sizes existed, ranging from the smallest to the most complex social organizations. It should be noted that since the conventional nuclear family is the meeting point of two consanguineous communities, it could not be seen as a subdivision of one of them. The minimal family, 'nuclear lineage', the smallest unit of the matrilineage or the patrilineage, was rather the one made up of the mother and her children in matrilineal descent or, in patrilineal descent, the father and his children (Ndaywel è Nziem, 1981, pp. 272–282). From this 'minimal family', other social constructs were built up, among which the clan represents the maximal stage and the lineage the intermediate structure.

The lineage, a grouping of blood relations who are still able to trace how they are related, was generally limited to three or four generations and rarely more. But that did not mean that consanguinity beyond that limit was therefore neglected, since it was embraced by the brotherhood of the clan, the 'clan' being the macro-structure embracing all those who claimed kinship with one another even if they were unable any longer to remember the precise nature of it. To track down that relationship and thereby avoid the possibility of incestuous unions, society forged formal criteria by which 'clan brothers' recognized one another. Thus every clan had a definite name, one or more food taboos and sometimes a motto (including in that case reference to the food taboo). Through the correspondence of these elements of identity, even people who had previously known nothing of each other could identify their common clan membership[10].

The clan thus possessed a capacity for extension that was ultimately unmeasurable, since no one could say a priori where it ended, except through a general survey of a given space. In reality, as men were always moving, its extension in principle went beyond ethnic boundaries, so that clan brotherhood came into competition with ethnic brotherhood. If the area of clan extension could go beyond the boundaries of ethnicity, conversely ethnic society could embrace a variety of clans, which were in reality so many segments of more extensive and larger clan units that had overflowed the limited frameworks of ethnic groups. The clan was thus inter-ethnic, just as the ethnic group was, in its morphology, a multi-clan affair (Vansina, 1980, pp. 135–155; Perrot, 1985, pp. 1289–1305).

From the family to the political

Acknowledgment of the principle of hierarchy underlay the political praxis already at work, as we have seen, in the family. In this way lineages, within a single clan unit, were ranked in some hierarchical order, just as clans might be in a given grouping. The terminology sanctioning these relations of subordination was borrowed from the family. Thus the most common distinction was between the political structure of the 'elder' and those of the 'juniors' or the 'husband' structure and the 'wives' structures. The move from family organization to political organization visibly occurred on the basis of this same cleavage, through the distinction between 'elder' villages and 'junior' villages.

Starting from that differentiation, the time eventually came when the 'royal' or 'aristocratic' clan was distinguished from other similar formations (Balandier, 1970). The ideology of kinship buttressed kingly power by giving kings a religious dimension. The king was eventually regarded as superhuman, endowed with supernatural powers and able to communicate with the unseen world. He was thus able to use the forces of nature and was considered to be the author of any innovation, including technological innovations. He was a universally imposing figure, whose power could be challenged only by another 'superhuman', which meant another member of his own clan.

The clan and the ethnic group are the two structures that seem to have made it possible to invent political structures on the basis of the organization of the family, although they diverged in their mode of operation. For while the clan was a collection of families, the ethnic group was a cultural community identified in principle by use of the same language and resort to the same social institutions[11]. The ethnic group thus operated as an association of clans, more precisely of sub-clans that shared the same cultural references and were conscious of this shared membership. And ethnic citizenship was determined by membership of one of the affiliated clans.

Of these two social formations, the clan is obviously the older. In the proto-Bantu stage, it constituted a community of residence. But with the migrations and the mixing with peoples met in the new places of residence, it was no longer possible for all the Bantu to use the same language. If this differentiation posed a problem, it was more so because of the demands of exogamy. For, at all costs, marriage partners had to be recruited in other kinship networks. The wives recruited ended up adopting the language of their husbands. It can be said that as a result of their presence, the same language came to be used by the majority of clans, that is, the clan of the husbands and the clans of the many wives from other villages. This new multi-clan linguistic community constituted a new social structure, the genesis of ethnicity. The clan, a homogeneous reality in terms of kinship, would now co-exist with the ethnic group, a multi-clan formation, which it had engendered.

Ethnic groups would grow in importance. With the demands of removals, the first ones segmented in turn and gave rise to other similar units. These developed in widely differing ways depending on circumstances and the dynamism of the existing aristocracies. Some would equip themselves with internal hierarchies to the point where they constituted political units; others would evolve in the direction of greater fragmentation, creating a multiplicity of other similar structures; others again, absorbing here and there an excessively large number of autochthonous or new immigrants, would be transformed into composite cultural units. Whatever the case, this institution ended up becoming a mode of organization valid for the whole of sub-Saharan Africa. In places where it led to a process of political construction, it was supported and consolidated by structures enabling the tip of the hierarchy to supervise and protect its lower levels. The regular payment of tribute was a sign of recognition of and allegiance to the supreme authority, and any interruption signalled a political challenge or a desire for independence.

Ethnic structures remained distinct from specifically political units: village, lordship or chiefdom, kingdom and empire: a single ethnic group could have within it several political societies, just as one political society could embrace several ethnic groups. The first case was that of Shi society in Kivu (Democratic Republic of the Congo), which embraced several kingdoms, the best known of which are Kabare and Ngweshe (Bishikwabo, 1982), or that of the only Lunda group which was able to produce several political aristocracies in the southern Democratic Republic of the Congo and northern Angola and Zambia such as that of *Mwant Yav, Kasanje, Kazembe, Lwena* and *Kiamfu* (Vansina, 1966b). Also relevant to this model is the situation of the political space between the Kalahari and the Sofala region on the Indian Ocean, at least after the death of the *mwene mutapa* (king) who had secured its conquest and political organization. Two rival states emerged and fought each other throughout the eighteenth century: that of the *Karanga* and that of the *Rozwi*. Yet both together made up the ethnic community of the *Shona* (Ki-Zerbo, 1978, pp. 188–189). The second case is the more common one of the great majority of African kingdoms and empires that ever existed and which, each time, brought together a number of ethnic groups. For example, the word *Kuba* originally denoted an ethnic grouping, but the kingdom bearing this name included Bushong, Luba, Mongo and Kete. In such situations, the dominated groups would adopt the customs of the conquerors, and even their traditions, as did the Mbundu, who were subjected to the court of the king of Kongo, or else a composite language such as the Kuba language would emerge (Vansina, 1964; 1974, pp. 171–184). In reality, 'ethnic groups' constituted peoples as distinct from 'families' and 'states'.

Trade and commerce

In this space, until after AD 1000, the most important economic institution was the market. This was the mechanism chiefly responsible for orienting regional and inter-regional trade. Generally speaking, Central and southern Africa were hardly affected by the international trading connections that developed in other areas, except for the trading zone centred on the Copper Belt, which was indirectly in contact with the Indian Ocean before 1100, while the integration of part of Zimbabwe and Transvaal into an international network was an even more recent development (Devisse; Vansina, 1988, pp. 750–793).

The distinction between local and inter-regional markets was valid both in terms of products and in terms of the origin of traders. Local markets brought together customers from a village and its surrounding area, while inter-regional markets, offering a wider range of goods, brought together traders sometimes from far away. The goods sold were not only everyday consumer items; there were also craft products.

Each region had its calendar for markets to ensure that they did not all occur on the same days. In some areas, such as the western southern savannah, the imperatives of the market led to the development of a system for computing time. On the basis of changes in the Moon, which during the month has four quarters of seven days, seven four-day weeks were introduced to fill the month. And the traditional week included a special market day, distinct from the days devoted to rest and farming.

The circulation of goods through markets could not have grown to any great degree had there not been some fiscal system, which initially must have been simple barter. Two goods of the same value were exchanged.

When the circulation of goods became more intense, it became no longer easy to continue with this type of valuation. Gradually, the idea developed of doing so using a single product. Some products, such as shells, cloth and metal objects, acquired a twofold importance: they became both objects and media of exchange.

There is evidence of use of shells (called *nzimbu*) on the coast of Angola (see Plate 274). Their exploitation was in the hands of the king, who was responsible for putting the available money into circulation. The product was doubtless chosen because of its durability and indivisibility; it could even be standardized. Using a calibrated sieve, small shells could be separated from big ones; measuring baskets were made which contained an exact number of shells (Dartevelle, 1953; Balandier, 1968 p. 122).

As for cloth, by its very nature it was one of the earliest products of human industry to have served as an object of trade. It was used as clothing, as everyday currency and as prestige currency in matrimonial transactions. But it was a less rigorous instrument and had the disadvantage that it could not be standardized, although it constituted the most widely used medium of exchange in Central Africa.

Some instruments of exchange were made from metals, notably copper and iron, locally made products. Iron was also at once a commodity and a currency; use of it pre-dates that of copper, since there is evidence of it as early as the fifth century AD, when it was used in the form of a collar or bar. Resort to copper, obviously less widely available, had a greater impact because of the expansion of 'crosses' – cruciform ingots. The area where these were produced was in principle restricted to the Copper Belt (Democratic Republic of the Congo–Zambia), where they were used to 'purchase' women and slaves as well as to acquire craft products; but these products can be found as far away as the coast of India, proving the development of long-distance trade towards the end of the first millennium AD.

All these social, political and economic structures are evidence of a greater mastery of space. During the second millennium AD, the peoples of Central and southern Africa would demonstrate even greater creativity and construct socio-economic systems whose growth and development were halted only by the intervention of outside forces.

Art and forms of expression

The invention of the plastic arts depends on a conjunction of three elements: human beings' need to express themselves; the use of a physical material as a means of expression; and the existence of plastic forms of expression which are intelligible to all who belong to the same culture.

The practice of the plastic arts throughout Central and southern Africa confirms the desire of the populations of this area to express themselves in this way. This means of expression seems to have been a corollary of the need to make utensils, and hence the need to prepare standardized instruments to serve the same purpose. This is demonstrated by the fact that the materials used to make the utensils are the same as those used for the plastic arts, which could be of mineral (soft stone, ceramics, iron, copper), plant (wood) or animal (ivory, shell) origin. Other things began to be imprinted on these materials, whether they were made into utensils or not. The artistic dimension was always directed towards the inhabitants of the invisible world, divinities and the spirits of the ancestors. Artistic activity was thus eminently religious, whether as an instrument of prayer, supplication, blessings or curses.

What underlying reasons can be found for this approach? The most simple are probably the most likely to be right. The quest for the absolute is innate the world over. And in this part of the world, the massive scale of the natural environment (rivers, lakes, mountains, forest, savannah), together with its sudden and sometimes pitiless onslaughts (drought, epidemics, attacks of wild animals) and its equally immense generosity, providing far in excess of expectations or hopes (abundance of animals to be hunted, fish to be caught and fruit and berries to be gathered, many types of medicinal herbs), could have accentuated the need to control events and feel more secure. If this were found to be the case, we should have an explanation not only for the direction of this artistic activity but also for its distinguishing features.

Art objects produced in Central and southern Africa practically always serve some kind of purpose. Their anonymous creators worked on the basis of pre-established canons (Mabiala Mantuba, 1994), which makes it possible to identify the geographical area covered by a particular model, and in principle also to identify the historical period with which it was associated, as W. Gillon (1984)[12] has attempted to do.

Archaic sculpture is understood to consist of objects, generally of clay, unearthed in the course of excavations (see Plate 275). Pre-classical sculpture is more refined and made out of less fragile materials – stone and bronze, for example. This category includes the eleventh-century stone figurines from Zimbabwe, from which base the Mwene Mutapa kingdom, a centre of the stone culture, spread its influence over surrounding areas (Bastin, 1984, pp. 50–52). Stone carvings were also produced in the kingdom of the Kongo (west Democratic Republic of the Congo, north-west Angola), representing political leaders or heads of families (*mintadi* and *bitumba*). When the person passed away, the carving was placed on his tomb, where it continued to provide protection for the community. The classical period, which came next, was an outstandingly productive one in terms of traditional African art. Practically all the objects produced by Africans for their own purposes which were found by Europeans in the hands of the autochthonous population belong to this period. In fact, many objects found by Europeans up to the turn of the last century which carry on this tradition should be placed in this category, as distinct from *modern* sculpture, whose themes and purposes both show signs of external influence.

There are several ways of classifying the African arts by geographical area. The most common is to distinguish forest cultures from those of the savannah. The distinguishing feature of forest sculpture is its religious symbolism, evident in the masks and statues of the equatorial zone. The Ngbaka, Mbole, Yela and Lega peoples of the Democratic Republic of the Congo, for example, are well known for the oval anthropomorphic or zoomorphic masks which enabled the living to benefit from the continuing presence and protection of the spirits of their ancestors. The Zande and the Mangbetu who live in this area stand out for their exceptional artistic sensitivity and the special status of both their artists and their craft workers (Neyt, 1981, pp. 21–71).

In the central and southern savannah, art was associated more with the aristocracy, being involved in political life, and the development of art was connected with the chiefs and kings. This is also a feature of the art of the peoples of the grasslands of Cameroon (Bangwa, Bamileke and Bamoun) in the northern savannah.

There were several important artistic centres in the central savannah, such as those of the *Pende*, *Cokwe*, *Luba* and *Songye* cultures. In all of them the basic symbols relate both to the sphere of magic/religion and to the political and military sphere (Cornet, 1972, pp. 17–286). The most remarkable example is the Kuba kingdom, whose capital consisted of huts each of which was almost a work of art in itself. The splendour of the court, the ingenuity and refinement lavished on the palaces, particularly in the royal enclosure, the variety of the masks that could be worn for ceremonies and the beautiful bead-embroidered raffia weaves worn by the king and high officials all bear witness to the high level of achievement of this political culture in the heart of Central Africa (Cornet, 1982).

In the architectural field, the most spectacular case is the Zimbabwe space, occupying the region between the Zambezi and the Limpopo and marked by the monumental ruins of major stone-built dwellings. These constructions remain somewhat enigmatic on account of their gigantic proportions and their mysterious origins. Nowadays, at least, there is absolutely no doubt about the African origin of the undertaking, since it was produced with local materials in accordance with architectural principles that had prevailed in the region for centuries[13].

The scale of the ruins near the town of Masvingo (previously Fort Victoria) is such that they represent the quintessential Zimbabwe, the Great Zimbabwe. Several parts of the complex can be distinguished. First, there is the Great Enclosure, representing the most spectacular part with its average height of 7.3 m and its thickness of 5.5 m at the base and from 1.3 to 3.6 m at the top, decorated with a herringbone motif over a length of 52 m. Then there is a series of parallel walls and internal enclosures and, in a corner, two conical towers. Finally, farther away on a hill is the Acropolis, the remains of a colossal fortification. Between this and the internal enclosures, vestiges of dwelling houses are scattered over the valley. Even though this array of scant data is difficult to interpret because of the huge amount of pillage the site has suffered, it may be supposed that they were clearly related to the hierarchical order and that this impressive construction was the abode of the Great Zimbabwe sovereign. This state certainly came before the monumental architecture that characterized it. The most intense occupation of the site must have started in about the eleventh century, but no stone wall can have gone up before the thirteenth century. For it was then or a little later, in the fourteenth century, that the first structures were built below the Acropolis. The Great Enclosure was built only gradually, during the fifteenth century (Fagan, 1985, pp. 579–588) (see Plates 40a, b).

Statues were admittedly rarer in southern Africa, but concern with sculpture found expression in other objects such as the elegant curved head-rests in wood, with a beautiful patina, of the Shona in Zimbabwe, the fertility dolls made of gourds and beads of the Nguni and, later, the snuff or gunpowder holders of the Sotho (Bastin, 1984, pp. 381–384). Statuettes, masks and other highly prized objects reflected major preoccupations and at the same time continued to play a functional role in everyday life.

NOTES

1 On this, see the special issue of *Etudes d'histoire africaine* (IX–X, 1977–1978), devoted to 'archaeology in Central Africa' and the synthesis of available information by Muya, 1987. On the excavations on the upper Lualaba, vital for knowledge of the archaeological history of the region, see the work of de Maret, 1985.

2 The best-known studies are those by Johnston, 1919–1922; Guthrie, 1962, pp. 273–282; Greenberg, 1972, pp. 189–216; Oliver, 1966, pp. 361–376.

3 In: *Le phénomène bantu et les savants*, 1981 (pp. 495–503), Vansina denounced the danger of adopting an interdisciplinary approach without following it through properly in studies of the Bantu, so that 'the hypotheses of one discipline are taken as certainties in others'. The warning still remains very apposite and stands as a new source of difficulties in the study of the history of the Bantu.

4 On the particular identities of these populations the reader is referred to the following writings: Thuriaux-Hennebert, 1964; Ngbakpwa te, 1992.

5 On the early history of food plants in sub-Saharan Africa see the works by Portères, 1962, pp. 195–210; Portères and Barrau, 1981, pp. 687–705.

6 Some communities in Central Africa still use dogmeat in certain situations or in exceptional circumstances.

7 See the special issue of *Etudes d'histoire africaine*, IX–X, 1977–78 devoted to 'archaeology in Central Africa'; Van Noten *et al.*, 1981, pp. 620–638.

8. So-called omnilinear descent is in reality a situation in which two unilinear descents co-exist (and not one in which there is a combination of the two), as among the Lunda, where 'popular' descent is matrilinear and 'aristocratic' descent is patrilinear (Crine-Mavar, 1974, pp. 87–90).

9 Because of this closeness between alternate generations, children could be greeted as 'father' or 'mother' by their own parents, by virtue of the closeness that existed between them and their grandparents who are the parents of their parents.

10 Without confirmation from physical anthropology, nothing can show whether this social kinship is really based on sharing of one and the same biological inheritance.

11 The case of the Tutsi and Hutu ethnic groups in Rwanda and Burundi who speak the same Kinyarwanda and Kirundi languages, shows that there are exceptions to the rule and that distinct ethnic groups, conscious of their difference, can share the same languages (Chrétien, 1985, pp. 129–166).

12 This author has distinguished four distinct periods in the history of the plastic arts in Africa. First, the archaic period (*c.* 500 BC–AD 800), followed by the pre-classical period (ninth to seventeenth century), the classical period (seventeenth to nineteenth century) which provides all the exhibits for museums, and finally the modern period (1900 to the present).

13 Fagan (1985, p. 588) notes that this architecture was the culmination of broad enclosures reserved for the chief, except that the banco had been replaced by stone since there was abundant granite in the vicinity.

BIBLIOGRAPHY

BALANDIER, G. 1968. *Daily Life in the Kingdom of the Kongo from the Sixteenth to the Eighteenth Century*. London.

——. 1970. *Political Anthropology*. London.

BASTIN, M. L. 1984. *Introduction aux arts plastiques d'Afrique noire*. Arnouville.

BISHIKWABO, C. 1982. *Histore d'un etat shi en Afrique des grands lacs: Kaziba au Zaïre (c. 1850–1940)*. Leuven [PhD thesis in History].

CHRETIEN, J. P. 1985. Hutu et Tutsi au Rwanda et Burundi. In: AMSELLE, J. L.; MBOKOLO, E. (eds) *Au coeur de l'ethnie*, Paris.

CORNET, J. 1972. *Art de l'afrique noire au pays du fleuve Zaïre*. Brussels.

——. 1982. *Art Royal Kuba*. Milan.

CRINE-MAVAR, B. 1974. L'avant-tradition zaïroise. *Revue zaïroïse des Sciences de l'Homme*. Kinshasa.

DARTEVELLE, E. 1953. *Les nzimbou, monnai du royaume du Congo*. Brussels.

DEVISSE, J.; VANSINA, J. 1988. Africa from the Seventh to the Eleventh Century: Five Formative Centuries. In: *General History of Africa*, Vol. III. UNESCO, Paris, California, pp. 750–793.

DIOP, C. A. 1960. *L'unité culturelle de l'Afrique noire*. Paris.

FAGAN, B. M. 1984. The Zambezi and Limpopo Basins: 1100–1500. In: *General History of Africa*, Vol. IV. UNESCO, Paris, California, pp. 525–550.

GILLON, W. A. 1984. *Short History of African Art*. London.

GREENBERG, J. 1972. Linguistic Evidence Regarding Bantu Origins. *Journal of African History*, 12, 2. London.

GUTHRIE, M. 1962. Some Developments in the Pre-History of the Bantu Languages. *Journal of African History*, 3, 2. London.

HEUSCH, L. DE. 1972. *Le roi ivre ou l'origine de l'Etat*. Paris.

JOHNSTON, H. 1919–1922. *A Comparative Study of the Bantu and Semi-Bantu Languages*, 2 vols. Oxford.

KEIM, C. 1979. Precolonial Mangbetu rule: Political and Economic Factors. In: *Nineteenth Century Mangbetu History*, PhD thesis, Indiana University.

KI-ZERBO, J. 1978. *Histoire de l'Afrique noire d'hier à demain*. Paris.

LWANGA-LUNYIIGO, S.; VANSINA, J. 1988. The Bantu-speaking Peoples and their Expansion. In: *General History of Africa*, Vol. III. UNESCO, Paris, California, pp. 140–162.

MABIALA MANTUBA-N. 1994. *Méthodologie des arts plastiques de l'Afrique noire*. Cologne.

MARET, P. DE. 1985. *Fouilles archéologiques dans la vallée du haut Lualaba*, 2 vols. Tervuren, MRAC.

MUYA, K. 1987. *La préhistoire du Zaïre oriental*, 2 vols. Brussels.

NDAYWEL È NZIEM, I. 1981. Histoire clanique et histoire ethnique: quelques perspectives méthodologiques. In: *Les Civilisations anciennes des Peuples des Grands Lacs*. Paris, pp. 272–282.

NEYT, F. 1981. *Arts traditionnels et histoire au Zaïre*. Brussels.

NGBAKPWA, TE M. 1992. *Histoire des Ngbandi du Haut-Ubangi (des origines à 1930)*. Doctoral thesis, Brussels.

OBENGA, T. 1985. *Les Bantu, langues, peuples et civilisations*. Paris.

——. (ed.) 1989. *Les peuples bantu, migrations, expansion et identité culturelle*, 2 vols. Paris.

OLIVER, R. 1966. The Problem of the Bantu Expansion. *Journal of African History*, 7, 3. London.

PARKINGTON, J. E. 1981. Southern Africa: Hunters and Food-Gatherers. In: *General History of Africa*, Vol. II. UNESCO, Paris, California, pp. 639–670.

PERROT, C. H. 1985. L'appropriation de l'espace: un enjeu politique pour une histoire du peuplement. *Annales*, 6, pp. 1289–1305.

PHILLIPSON, D. W. 1981. The Beginning of the Iron Age in Southern Africa. In: *General History of Africa*, Vol. II. UNESCO, Paris, California, pp. 671–692.

PORTERES, R. 1962. Berceaux agricoles primaires sur le continent africain. *Journal of African History*, 3, 2. London.

PORTERES, R. and BARRAU, J. 1981. Origins, development and expansion of agricultural techniques. In: *General History of Africa*, Vol. I. UNESCO, Paris/London.

POSNANSKY, M. 1981. Introduction to the Later Prehistory of Sub-Saharan Africa. In: *General History of Africa*, Vol. II. UNESCO, Paris, California, pp. 533–550.

SCHEBESTA, P. 1957. *Les pygmées du Congo-Belge*. Namur.

THURIAUX-HENNEBERT, A. 1964. *Les Zande dans l'histoire du Bahr el Ghazal et de l'Equatoria*. Brussels.

VAN CHI-BONNARDEL, R. (ed.) 1973. *Grand Atlas du continent Africain*. Paris.

VAN NOTEN, F. *et al.* 1981. Central Africa. In: *General History of Africa*, Vol. II. UNESCO, Paris/London.

VANSINA, J. 1964. *Le royaume kuba*. Tervuren, MRAC.

——. 1964. Le phénomène Bantu et les savants. In: *Le sol, la parole et l'écrit. Mélanges offerts à R. Mauny*. Paris.

——. 1966a. *Introduction à l'ethnographie du Congo*. Kinshasa.

——. 1966b. *Kingdoms of the Savanna: a History of the Central African States until European Occupation*. Madison, Wisconsin.

——. 1974. Les langues bantoues et l'histoire: le cas kuba. In: *Perspectives nouvelles sur le passé de l'Afrique noire et de Madagascar, Mélanges offerts à H. Deschamps*. Paris, pp. 171–184.

——. 1980. Lignage, idéologie et histoire en Afrique équatoriale. In: *Enquêtes et documents d'histoire Africaine*, 4, pp. 135–155.

VI: Civilizations of the Americas

INTRODUCTION

Christine Niederberger and Louis Bazin

The problems of periodization raised in this volume, as planned to cover the span of time between around AD 600 and 1492, when Christopher Columbus and his crew discovered the 'New World', are particularly complex so far as the history (or rather protohistory) of the American continent and its islands is concerned. In fact, the beginning of this period was mainly chosen in light of an event of considerable importance for the 'Old World', namely the rise and spread of Islam – which, however, in no way concerned the future 'New World' in the Americas in the centuries under consideration here.

'Americas' in the plural is the proper expression. While the American continental mass admittedly stands sharply marked out between the Atlantic and Pacific Oceans, as a geographical unit from north to south and east to west it has nevertheless shown considerable diversity ever since 'pre-Columbian' times: when languages, ethnic groups, ways of life, types of social organization and systems of beliefs were numerous and varied as much as prevailing climates and environments. Distances are enormous from one end of the American continent to another: for instance, the Bering Strait is as far from Tierra del Fuego as from Dakar or the Cape of Good Hope. Such a geographical span is wider than the most immense continental reaches within Eurasia. Moreover, natural barriers – mountains, forests, deserts and even the bottleneck formed by the narrow isthmus of Panama – slowed communications and exchange and, with few exceptions, contributed to the scattered character of human occupation and its fragmentation among so many ethnic groups, languages and socio-political formations.

Such fragmentation was duly noted by the first European conquerors of the 'New World' and by the Catholic missionaries in their wake, who faced so many idioms to learn in order to impart their religious message. This linguistic variety has lasted to an important degree even down to our day, although major regroupings have since occurred around those great traditional tongues which remain the legacy of the ancient federating peoples (Quechua, Maya, Aymara, Guaraní, Aztec-Náhuatl and others).

A major hurdle to overcome when writing the history of the different American groups lies in the fact that so few of these 'nations' – with the exception of, for example, the Maya, the Zapotecs, the Mixtecs or the Aztecs – have left any written documents. The Aztec graphic system, as used shortly before the Spanish Conquest, remains arduous to decipher, consisting as it does of sheer picture puzzles. But, the highly complex graphic code of the Maya of the 'classic' age – in their case, a true system of writing based on both glyphic and syllabic elements – has now been to a great extent deciphered, thanks to the tenacity of scholars and the help of computer technology. We are thus currently in a position to consider that this success will henceforth yield us considerable information on the history and culture of pre-Columbian times (see Map 34).

Although the first European conquerors could not decipher local written documents at hand, they did not fail to obtain and consign, from native informants, a large set of historical, economic and socio-cultural data concerning the pre-Hispanic world. Learned Spaniards (members of religious orders for the most part), and also descendants of the native aristocracies, noted down these oral traditions in written documents, today of inestimable value. Still, in all types of culture, oral transmission must be treated with caution; nor can historical research rely entirely upon it. Lastly, it must be noted that for remoter periods, our knowledge has to bear heavily on archaeological evidence – upon which so many of the authors of this volume have had to depend.

Now, while this volume does essentially address historical matters, for Part VI, which deals with the civilizations of America (or better, the Americas), we have preferred the term 'protohistory' specifically because the American continent, in the period under consideration, had not yet entered the field of historical research as such, for such a phase implies a full use of written material. Different explanations can be adduced for such lack. To begin with, at the time of the 'discovery' in 1492, understanding of some writing systems, such as that of the Maya civilisation of the first millennium AD, had already largely disappeared. Nor should one forget the systematic burnings or *autos-da-fe* of pre-Columbian manuscripts carried out by the early sixteenth-century Spaniards in areas like the Maya lowlands and the Valley of Mexico, where the princes of local reigning dynasties had built up true 'libraries' covering broad intellectual domains from politics and economic matters to geography and poetry.

The existence of such written materials rules out, therefore, the term 'prehistory'. Moreover, in the light of the kind of research carried out today, information of at least partly 'historical' value has indeed been recovered from both oral tradition and from the sixteenth-century ethno-historical sources. Not to be neglected either are the surviving ways of preparing and consuming food, and also surviving settlement patterns and farming systems, which are the great legacy of the pre-Columbian age.

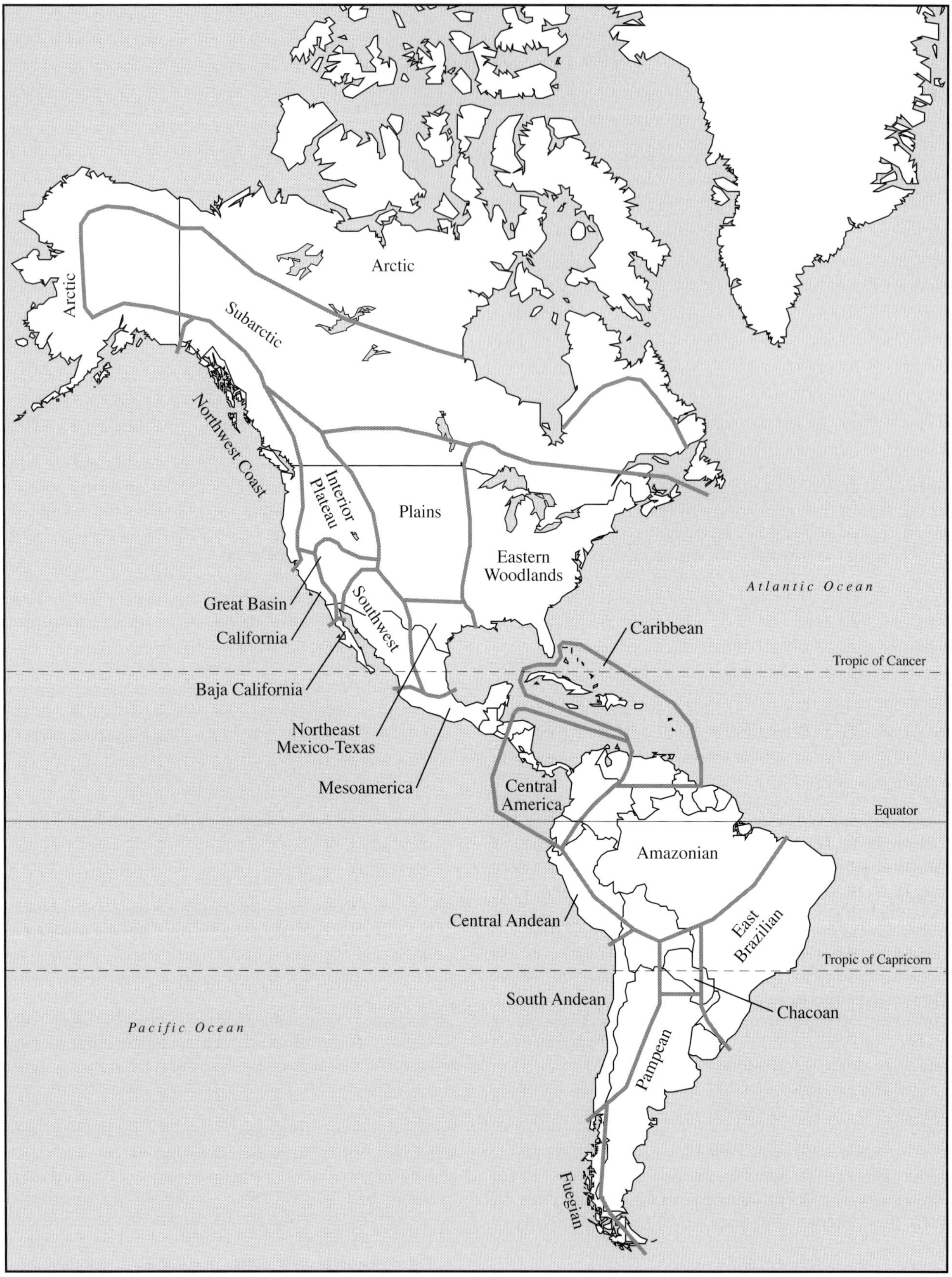

Map 34 American culture areas (Schmidt, P., 1971).

All in all, in our effort to write – or attempt to reconstitute – the history of humanity in the Americas between the early seventh century AD and the fatal date of 1492 (a turning point followed by grim warfare, mutual acculturation and widespread economic fallout), we possess a considerable mass of data: although such data betray a rather heterogeneous nature pertaining not only to history but also (if not more so) to archaeology, anthropology and even to the rapidly progressing field of comparative linguistics.

The relative importance of each of these four fields of study varies profoundly, depending on the region considered. But all four approaches do supply us with complementary information, in particular for the two great cultural areas separated by the isthmus of Panama and the highlands of Colombia. These areas are:

1 *Mesoamerica*: whose southern and eastern zones – including Yucatán and Guatemala – were dominated by the Maya, creators of a high civilization, while other regions were occupied by a myriad of different ethnic groups, including the Zapotecs and the Mixtecs, who held sway over a vast territory around Oaxaca. The Aztecs, later arrivals in the Valley of Mexico, adopted in part the culture of the local dynasties they encountered and founded a large and brilliant capital which lay at the heart of a theocratic and militaristic empire that was still expanding at the time of the Spanish Conquest;
2 *The central Andes*: here the Incas founded an equally highly civilized theocratic empire, socially organized around a legally elaborate communal basis (excluding all private ownership of the soil) with one dominant language, Quechua. The civilization of the Incas did use a system for consigning information by material means, but this system remains little understood.

Three prominent groups, the Maya, the Aztecs and the Incas, created major political organizations, with languages that have either survived down to our days (Maya, Náhuatl) or have even continued to spread (Quechua). The high cultural level of these groups in a way assisted the conquerors in securing considerable information concerning their traditional history and customs.

Currently, international scholarship (beginning with Latin America's own scholars) has pressed historical research much further, with a wide geographical perspective regarding not only the various cultural aspects of these two highly privileged regions of Mesoamerica and the central Andes now but looking beyond: to the neighbouring northern regions of Mexico and other cultural areas of North, Central and South America.

The authors of Chapters 38 and 39 of the present volume have thus been able to assess the cultures considered by making full use of the indispensable data supplied by both history and archaeology. But cases still occur where a given author must rely on the information supplied by archaeology alone (when dealing, for example, with that part of America stretching between Mesoamerica to the north, and the central Andes to the south).

Other authors, by combining the methods of archaeology with those of cultural anthropology, have been in a position to present data concerning food-procurement systems, settlement patterns, trade, socio-political organization, funerary practices and systems of belief.

However, regarding those chapters dealing in the present volume with North America (from the Arctic nearly down to the Tropic of Cancer) and including the lands of present-day Canada, the United States and northern Mexico, the nature of the data here differs radically from that available in areas farther south. Evidence here is scarcer and is supplied mostly by ethno-history and archaeology. Icelandic probes (984 – *c.* 1000) under Erik the Red along the south-east coast of Greenland and under his son Leif Eriksson along those of 'Vinland' (southern Labrador) remained only short-lived episodes, virtually devoid of consequences. True exploration of North America had to wait until 1497.

The authors of sub-chapters 37.1 to 37.5 in the present volume could not rely on historical sources, properly speaking, but had to resort instead to the approach of the prehistorian, using data yielded by archaeological finds, which, fortunately, have recently been turning up in increasing abundance.

The interpretation of such finds had to be, in some cases, deduced, or induced, through ethnographical, linguistic and historical information emanating from a later date; such a methodological framework (expressed in a specific terminology) often pertains to theories of cultural evolution taken up and refined by such American anthropologists as J. Steward and E. Service since the 1950s. Since such methodology often proves unfamiliar to readers more at home with classical historical research, the editors of Volume III thought it wise to add the following remarks (p. 533) to their introduction to Part VIII, 'The Americas', a section mostly written in light of this particular scholarly approach; we can do no better than to quote these remarks here anew:

> In this section, the reader will note that William T. Sanders and Philip Weigand use terminology that is derived from evolutionary cultural anthropology to identify and describe prehistoric social, political, economic institutions and systems. The terminology in question includes terms like band, tribe, chiefdom, state, ranking, stratification and urbanism. These scholars consider archaeology as part of the general field of anthropology and therefore many of their concepts derive from the broader field.

The findings of North American archaeological fieldwork – as analysed in sub-chapters, 37.1 to 37.5 – have led to a remarkable breakthrough and offer us a better understanding of ancient societies of the US south-west and the quasi-urban societies of the Mississippi valley: however, they do not yet permit any precise delimitation of periods. In any case, adherence to a theoretical principle of strict obedience to a chronological span set between *c.* AD 600 and 1492 made little sense in this context and had no scientific foundation. Our authors have therefore boldly chosen to ignore it, while taking care not to repeat the information already contained in Volume III. The editors responsible for this volume have accepted this waiver of a rule which, in present circumstances, would hardly have been literally applicable here anyway.

Data presented by the articles dealing with pre-Columbian North America, then, offer a vast survey of territorial organization, food resources (derived from hunting, gathering, fishing and the earlier stages of farming), technical skills, social structures, artistic expression, cosmo-visions, funeral rites, warfare and, so far as possible, linguistic segmentation and evolution down to the Spanish Conquest.

Particular attention has been paid to the study of North American botanical remains and cultivated plants. The inventory is here characterized by the introduction and development of an increasing number of cultivars from Mesoamerica in addition to local botanical species. Analysis of some types of complex socio-political structure and mythological belief also betrays, in given zones, clear influences from the south.

In fact, Part VI deals with American cultures before the Americas actually entered the mainstream of world history as such: hence a clear-cut contrast with other portions of this volume (save perhaps for the sections pertaining to Oceania), for which – as in Europe, Asia and much of Africa – a wealth of written documentation becomes available, in ever-greater quantities, from even the outset of this chronological span beginning around AD 600.

But the contrast lies not only between the abundance, or scarcity, of explicitly historical sources. Methods, too, notably differ between those appropriate for classical historical studies and those required for protohistory, with the latter essentially relying on archaeological data and theories of cultural evolution which are still the subject of much debate on the very continent, America, where they were first developed methodologically – and where they are already being supplemented to a great extent by other types of theoretical approach.

But even beyond the issue of theories or methods, there remains here a solid body of acquired data, with soundly argued interpretation and a no less stimulating set of questions raised: all of which offers the reader a remarkable synthesis of the long and extraordinarily complex cultural path followed by pre-Columbian America.

37

NORTH AMERICA

37.1
NORTH AMERICAN ARCTIC CULTURES

Jean Aigner

The North American Arctic littoral zone stretches 77,000 km from Alaska in the west to Labrador and Greenland in the east (see Map 35). It is bordered by the Bering Sea, and the North Pacific, Arctic and North Atlantic Oceans. It includes the treeless Arctic littoral zone, plus, for our discussion, the maritime grasslands of the Aleutian Islands and the adjacent forested coast of Pacific Alaska. The littoral coincides with the major, traditional adaptational foci of the Esk–Aleut-speaking peoples of North America and with the past or modern seasonal foci of several groups of Athabaskan–Eyak- and Algonkian-speaking peoples. In all, the population is estimated at around 90,000 individuals in pre-contact times. This discussion concentrates on the Esk–Aleut speakers of Aleut, Yu'pik and Inupiaq and their history, particularly between 700 and 1500, but it necessarily includes their earlier history as well. The ethnic names for these peoples are Aleut, Yuit and Inuit.

Throughout the Arctic littoral zone there are significant differences in the annual distribution, variety and density of littoral resources, relating to climate, longitude and latitude, degree of insularity and coastal complexity. Generally speaking, resource complexity and density are greatest in the west on the North Pacific and Bering Sea coasts. This is especially true in the Aleutian Islands–Kodiak region, where ice-free conditions and marine upwelling systems support vast intertidal, marine mammal, fish, and bird faunas. Resources are somewhat less diverse and rich in the region of the Bering Strait, with its migratory bowhead whales, bearded and ringed seals, and walruses. They are less again along the deep fjords of west Greenland. Resources are least

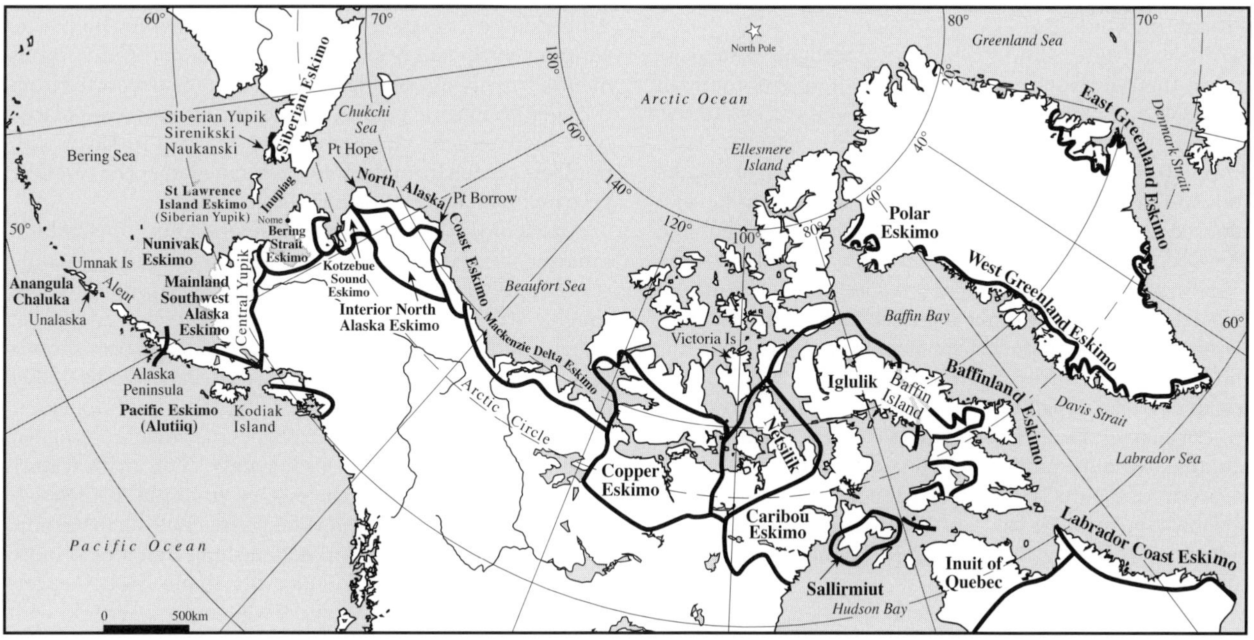

Map 35 Key to tribal territories in the Arctic (*Arctic*, 1984, Smithsonian Handbook of North America).

along the ice-choked Arctic Ocean coast, particularly in the central Canadian Arctic. Here and in a few other subareas ,the terrestrial animal resources assume more economic importance.

Subregional variations in resources influenced population structure and density, community size, mobility, and societal and technological complexities. Ranked societies with features of chiefdoms developed among the most sedentary, long-term Aleut and Koniag (Kodiak area) communities. The rich and elaborate burials of members of noble families attest to their wealth and importance. Young and old, male and female members of these families received differential treatment at death as well as in life. Villages formed themselves into loose political alliances in the eastern Aleutians, for example, recognizing lead villages and prominent chiefs. Warfare and chiefdom-type social organization probably developed and became increasingly common in the latter prehistoric period (after 700).

Ranked village society existed on the Bering Strait within the largest of the Arctic whaling communities, which numbered 300 souls or more. Some villages attained a large size and were organized into subvillage units around whaling captains and associated ritual houses. Other villages of historically related groups were small, with a single captain, a crew and their families. The captains had to maintain preeminence by virtue of continued success in whaling. The technical and social aspects of whaling adaptation developed and began to spread some time between 700 and 1000.

Egalitarian villages of the Bering Sea and west Greenland fishers and sea mammal hunters were relatively more mobile than ranked villages. Their shifting settlements were generally smaller and less permanent. At one extreme the villages of the Yukon and Kuskokwim attained some permanence, based on salmon runs, with seasonal forays to the coast for seals. More typically, however, communities fished and hunted on the coast and along the coastal tundra. They shifted residence up to half a dozen times during the year and frequently moved the main, winter, village location.

Most mobile of all were the peoples in the central Canadian Arctic, who lived in small, fluid bands of 25–50 people. Impermanence of personnel and settlements were typical, as groups fished, hunted game in the interior, and caught seals through the winter ice.

Although today and in the past we recognize language and cultural divisions within the Aleut, Yuit and Inuit, all groups share a common Asian origin. Some 18,000–16,000 years ago at the peak of the last ice advance, mean sea level dropped by 100 m. Eastern Siberia and most of Alaska constituted a single land mass called Beringia. The vast exposed land was dry tundra–steppe. Glaciers prohibited access to, and use of, the coasts of Southwest Alaska, eastern Canada, and Greenland until about 8000 BC. The northern Arctic Ocean coast was not then habitable. The southern Bering Sea coast supported sea mammals, fishes, avifauna and some invertebrates. With warming, the ice melted and sea level rose, separating the landmass into Asian and American parts. Holocene coastlines changed, with isostatic rebound, tectonism and erosion processes affecting both the location of coasts and their subsequent preservation. Specifically, through the late Pleistocene and Holocene periods, the Bering Sea coastline became longer, more convoluted and richer.

Most archaeologists believe that the ancestors of the Aleuts, Yuit and Inuit gradually expanded south-eastwards along the coast from Asia toward Alaska between 18,000 and 10,000 years ago. A journey along the coast undoubtedly took several millennia as groups adjusted to warmer climates, more open water, less winter ice and a wider variety of marine resources. This testing ground served them well, for we find our earliest example of a people with a subarctic Aleut-style adaptation more than 9,000–8,500 years ago on Anangula, just off Umnak Island, in the eastern Aleutian Islands.

This earliest recorded coastal village perches upon the coast, overlooks sea mammal and fishing grounds, and is near seasonal bird rookeries. The village consists of a number of 3 × 5 m semi-subterranean houses, some with small stone-lined hearths which contain greasy residue. The general features of village location, architecture, reconstructed maritime economy and even use of space may be traced to later villages in the eastern Aleutians until, 4,000 years ago at Chaluka on Umnak Island and at other sites, we have a continuous record of Aleut people and village life.

Some time prior to the first Russian contacts recorded in 1759, hierarchically ranked, chiefdom-level societies developed. In the east, the communities of 100 or more lived together in one or more semi-subterranean, communal longhouses, 25–50 m long and 5–10 m wide. Society recognized nobles, commoners and slaves, the latter usually captive Aleuts or Yuit. It is said that a noble had the power of life and death over a slave.

A noble and his family enjoyed wealth, although they were not relieved from economic pursuits. These included open-water fishing, fowling and sea mammal hunting from kayaks and from the shore, collecting birds and eggs from nests and rookeries, salmon fishing with spears, hooks, traps and perhaps nets, and collecting invertebrates on the strand flats and more plants on shore. A flexibility in economic assignments (except hunting from kayaks, the purview of men) and sophistication in technology and organization of the economy, coupled with the rich and diverse resources of the Aleutians, supported a large human population and complex social organization.

In life, members of an Aleut society or polity distinguished themselves by their dress and ornament in terms of both rank and polity affiliation. At death, the wealthy of all ages were accorded burial which involved considerable time and effort in preparing and clothing the deceased. Aleutian mummies, deliberately eviscerated, are well known, spanning the 1700s. Mummy caves had been in use for far longer. Other forms of burial involving considerable labour are also reported from the later prehistoric period. In one, the pit grave was placed on a high hillside. A large mound of earth surfaced with boulders carried from the shore was raised over the carefully prepared and dressed body of the deceased.

Archaeological study of the development of hierarchical ranking, longhouses and chiefdom organization is only recently under way. Surveys on Unalaska and Umnak Islands suggest a recent trend, probably between 700 and 1500, toward differentiation in architecture. Village sites show a mix of house sizes, with many small, oval single-family houses and several large, multiple-family or wealthy dwellings. Some of these houses assume complex shapes and are subrectangular with ancillary oval pits at each corner. The main feature might be 15 m long plus the pits, each 5 m in diameter. It is possible to envision these dwellings stretched out to become longhouses, with several pits added along the sides as more families are incorporated under the single roof. Reports contend that internal house space was assigned by rank, with the chief at the eastern end and lesser-ranked families arrayed in descending order to the west.

The south-western Arctic littoral zone stands out because maritime living is most ancient, continuities in way of life are most striking, and the social complexity ultimately achieved is greatest for the entire region. The period from 700 to 1500 saw the final development of ranked chiefdoms in favourable parts of the island chain.

In the adjacent North Pacific, the Kodiak area shows parallel, though less striking, developments. The maritime adaptation is recorded, with the currently earliest known sites there more than 6,000 years old. There is evidence to suggest that material culture became progressively more elaborate, reaching an apogee, along with aspects of burial ceremonialism, after 700. By the time of Russian contacts in the mid-1700s, chiefdom-type arrangements had developed. It would appear that the period between 700 and 1500 saw population increase, greater competition, and the emergence of new social adaptations.

For the Bering Sea, Bering Strait, and Arctic Ocean coasts, the period from 700 to 1500 can be seen as one of great change, with the ethnogenesis of many societies. The linguistic diversity of the Yu'pik-Inupiaq and the Yu'pik languages reflects time depth for occupation and divergence, which is clear in the archaeological record of the Bering Sea coast. The less differentiated and far flung Inupiaq attest to recent population movement, also indicated in the archaeological record all across the Arctic north.

Archaeologists usually discuss whether or not the pioneering Bering Sea culture received stimulus mainly from the south or north. It is perhaps as likely that the earliest coastal people have their history on the submerged Beringian coast which in Holocene times was retreating eastwards. People simply moved with the coast. As the sea level rose, the Bering Sea coast lengthened, providing new territory for residents. Those in the south were in contact with the North Pacific groups, and vice versa, based on some shared styles. Those in the north had closest communications with the Siberian side of the Bering Strait.

In the historic period, the Bering Sea hunters and fishers showed significant adaptational variations related to the particular mix of resources the local region offered. The south coast with its sea mammals and salmon rivers saw a focus on those economic pursuits. Communities with permanent dwellings occurred on the Alaska peninsula streams at least 3,000 years ago. Houses at one site are 4 m on a side and are dug slightly into the soil. Each house was entered through a covered entryway, contained a hearth and showed charred salmon bones on the floor. Seasonal forays to the coast for sea mammals and fish were undoubtedly associated with this. At various times, in the interior caribou may have been of some importance too. Sealing equipment, which must have required a strong maritime component, is also found early.

After 700, the archaeology of the region documents the maritime hunting–fishing foci of the adaptational system. The Yukon and the Kuskokwim rivers with their major salmon runs have been the focus for permanent fishing communities of 50–100 people for millennia. Continuity in adaptation and aspects of material culture may be traced to the historic period. As early as 2,000 years ago, we find remains preserved on the Yukon delta, beneath deep silts. A regional Eskimo (Yu'pik) culture is indicated thereby, with wooden masks attesting to its wealth of ceremonial activities. Over time, villages spread upriver. Continuity in the tradition leading to historic groups is present throughout the period from 700 to 1500. Expansion of northerners at the same time contributed to local population displacements and more widespread technological innovations were introduced from the same direction. Local group boundaries and identities were shifting during this period.

The Alaskan side of Bering Strait, including the Seward peninsula and north-west Alaska, is a mosaic of resource zones. Major points such as Point Hope may have had abundant sea mammal and caribou resources nearby. The northern Seward peninsula in recent times had a caribou herd which, combined with coastal seals, provided most resources. The southern Seward peninsula groups were marine hunters and fishers. Historically, groups traded surplus resources and met in summer at trade fairs. At times they formed alliances to repulse advancing Siberians. There is every reason to expect subcultural diversity in the prehistoric past.

Archaeological evidence of the northern Bering Sea coastal peoples is at least 4,000 years old. At Cape Krusenstern, camps of seal hunters record a material culture which also spread across the eastern Arctic at the same time. Both the Alaskan (Arctic Small Tool) and eastern peoples (Pre-Dorset/Independence I) have a coastal and tundra hunting culture, with the focus primarily upon seals and caribou. Much of the north lies beyond the zone of salmon runs. The stone tool technology of the northern Bering Sea and Arctic Ocean coasts has technological links, although not necessarily cultural links, to the Siberian 'Neolithic'.

The earliest northerners may have been pioneer Arctic hunters from coastal northeast Asia, perhaps augmented by Alaskans who adopted their ways. Or they may have been an older northern Bering coast culture whose stone tool technology was heavily influenced from Siberia. Apparently they were the first to exploit an open Arctic Ocean coastal zone and their spread was rapid. Perhaps local game was at first unwary of these new predators. The history of these people after coming to America is better known for the eastern Arctic than in Alaska. Nonetheless, archaeologists propose that the later Norton and Ipiutak groups along the northern Bering Sea–Bering Strait coast of Alaska were connected with these pioneers. Ipiutak culture is dated to 400/500–1200. Many examples are late and in marginal areas of the north. The groups may have avoided competition for prime coastal areas with newly arrived Bering Strait groups.

The Norton and Iputak economic focus was coastal whenever feasible. Seals, walrus and caribou were mainstays at the Bering Strait. During warm phases, salmon reached the Nome area and they were added to the game sought. Generally, communities were small and groups moved several times during the year. Their technological repertoire was perfectly adequate for life in the north, but not competitive against Bering Strait cultures who filtered into the northern Norton and Ipiutak territories after AD 500. The latter engaged in cooperative hunting from umiaks, used detachable harpoons and drag floats, and had dogsleds and sophisticated devices for hunting seals at their breathing holes.

Only in zones of unusual resource richness did the Alaskan northerners achieve the maximum of sedentariness, personal wealth and comfort which their technology and social arrangements permitted. Point Hope is one such place; seals, walrus, small whales and caribou are available all year. These were effectively captured with the repertoire of techniques ascribed to northern groups more than 4,000 years ago and maintained over the ensuing millennia.

Point Hope was a particularly prosperous Ipiutak community occupied for several centuries, beginning around 400–500. The locale is known for its several hundred plank-and-log houses and its remarkable cemetery. The latter produced burials accompanied in some cases by beautifully and intricately carved, nonutilitarian ivory and antler objects. The individuals buried may have been shamans. Several log-tomb burials included composite bone face masks and ivory inlays in the eye sockets. The village houses are square and substantial, with interior low benches and central fireplaces. Some, at least, had covered entries in which meat was stored. Houses varied somewhat in size and wealth, but differences may relate only to personal achievement. It is not enough to suggest ranking or social differentiation of the magnitude seen in the Aleutians and Kodiak. Some of the differences in household goods are related to the occupants – an apparent bachelor in some instances of small (2 × 2 m) houses; a family with several children and associated extra adults in others (5 × 5 m) with much gear, miniature equipment and toys. Overall, the community appears to have been stable, wealthy and secure, particularly by Arctic coast standards.

Ipiutak village at Point Hope did not, however, endure, although its people and their adaptational strategies clearly contributed to the historic peoples of the northern Bering Sea coast. And as was mentioned earlier, populations south of Seward Peninsula, in particular, have longstanding archaeological records suggesting continuity. Beginning about 1000 there was an infusion of cultural innovations into the Bering Sea coast with adaptational strategies from coastal Siberia and St. Lawrence Island. Furthermore, linguistic evidence suggests a recent (about 1500) expansion of Inupiaq-speaking groups into the northern Bering Sea coastal region.

The original inhabitants of the Arctic Ocean coasts and tundra spread from the west more than 4,000 years ago. These early peoples living above the Arctic Circle had many adaptational similarities to the modern Inuit; at the same time, aspects of technologies and practices for open water hunting and whaling from sophisticated kayaks and umiaks, efficient breathing hole sealing, and use of dogs for sleds were absent or poorly developed. Archaeological remains of their bone tool technology and food refuse attest to a coastal–tundra hunting and fishing adaptation. But while ringed seals, bearded seals and walruses are reported, migrating harp seals, which are agile, and larger whales are rarely found in these sites. Inland hunting of musk ox, caribous, polar bears, hares, foxes and birds is recorded, and fishing for char is likely. A number of aspects of the lithic technology of these groups fit into the Siberian 'neolithic' stone working traditions, as mentioned above. Whatever the nature of the connections, pre-Dorset people and their adaptation are closely similar to later Yuit and Inuit. Their adaptation permitted them to pioneer across the Arctic. They are especially well represented in a core area around the Foxe Basin–Hudson Strait and, during times of warmer climate, in the High Arctic, above 75°N.

The initial push across the Arctic coast more than 4,000 years ago coincides with the end of a period of ameliorated climate. Pre-Dorset/Independence I populations reached the large High Arctic islands of the Canadian archipelago and Greenland. Most of them left the northern coasts with the onset of cold around 3,500 years ago. People reached the core lands as early as this date and continued to occupy them. At times, the cold sent more groups south along the Labrador coasts, where they displaced Maritime Archaic Indians who were seasonal users of the coast. The colonizers of the Arctic coasts maintained themselves until about 1000, the time of the incursion of Thule (Inuit) peoples.

Late Dorset (500–1000) and Terminal Dorset (1000–1500) represent continuations of the original population and cultural adaptation. The first warming trend in a millennium sent Late Dorset people into the High Arctic. Late remains include artistic pieces, most serving magical purposes, which are small but outstanding examples of carving. Most shelters are ephemeral windbreaks and small family tents, but a late Dorset development seems to be the building of long, unroofed, stone-outlined enclosures. These measure 5–7 m wide and around 14 m long; one example is 32 m. The enclosures contain little refuse and are interpreted as gathering places for ceremonies during the snowfree parts of the year. None the less, late Dorset groups saw their populations, or at least traits of their culture, diminish as Thule newcomers from the west advanced after 1000. Thus, identifiable late Dorset settlements are increasingly uncommon, with their population either reduced or assimilated into Thule communities.

The failure of Dorset is attributed to aspects of their economy and social organization. Although successful for 3,000 years, they were disadvantaged when faced by Thule culture. Dorset people hunted near the settlement, within a day's walk. They sealed in narrow channels rather than at sea. They took animals where they were most abundant, especially the least wary among them. They focused on bird rookeries rather than on harder-to-capture migratory fowl. Their technology remained conservative. The timing of band movements was key to group success and several failures during the annual round could greatly weaken the band. It has been suggested that Dorset groups could not withstand sharing territory with Thule groups, who travelled long distances by umiak and dogsled, had more specialized equipment and who were better organized for co-operative hunting.

The Siberian Yuit (speakers of Sirenikski, central Siberian, and Naukanski languages of Yu'pik) may be traced back about 2,000 years. Their historic roots lie in the heavily maritime sea mammal hunting cultures of the Punuk, Diomede, and St. Lawrence islands and the coast of Chukotka. These are known as Old Bering Sea/Okvik, (0–700) and Punuk (700–1500). Punuk and the American mainland variant, Birnirk, contributed to the formation of the Thule adaptation, about 1000, which gave rise to the historic Inuit. The cultural traditions which lie behind the northern maritime adaptation of Old Bering Sea/Okvik have yet to be identified.

Punuk, beginning near 700, is distinguished by a quantity of decorated objects and implements, ground slate projectiles, knives and *ulus* (women's knives), crude pottery and a wide variety of distinctive bone and ivory harpoon heads and spears. During early Punuk times, people intensified their use of technological complexes for spring–summer open water kayak hunting, which used detachable harpoons and inflated skin floats, and for winter sealing through breathing holes in the ice. Shaman's gear was common. The dog drawn sled was present. The focus on hunting large sea mammals culminated in social changes. A whaling boat owner-captain (*umialik*) emerged to achieve high status in his community, which now organized around him, his whaling crew and their families, and the men's house (for work and ceremonies). Settlements increased in number as well as size and whalebone houses became larger. There was increased population and inter-village contact and conflict. Slat-armour of bone, new spears, reinforced bows and wrist guards appear in the record at this time.

Growing competition in the northern maritime areas may have sent some groups to the American mainland by 500.

Birnirk is known at the major sea mammal hunting stations in the Bering Strait area, including Point Hope. While some sites show whaling, others indicate the focus was on seal hunting from the ice and open water. Birnirk houses at Point Barrow are 2.5 × 3 m with a long entrance tunnel. Sleeping platforms were set at the back. Heat and light came from lamps. The village population was probably small. At Cape Krusenstern, the community consisted of two small houses. The focus was on seals and caribou here. Contacts with Ipiutak culture are indicated in some of the stone tool styles.

The newly arrived Birnirk groups were successful. For example, they had a competitive advantage over the indigenous Norton hunter–fisher groups in the Cape Nome area. Birnirk was able to carry on by sealing all year round when Norton adaptation was evidently stressed beyond its limits by a decrease in adadromous fish (during a cold phase) and a low in the caribou cycle.

Both Punuk and Birnirk play roles in the emergence of the Thule in America around 900. The Thule people spread eastward within a century or two. Their cultural-adaptational development and spread are attributable to two or three interacting factors. One is the coalescence of technology and social organization which occurred in Punuk and was suitable to cooperative hunting of large sea mammals and spring whales from umiaks. The second was a warm climatic oscillation (900–1350) which increased the Arctic open-water zone and sent bowhead whales and other large sea mammals into the Arctic Ocean, making its coasts more attractive to northern maritime hunters. A third was population pressure in northeast Siberia, due to displacements northward. Archaeologists suggest that the Punuk people were moving eastward under this pressure and in concert with an expansion of their preferred habitat areas as warming continued. Punuk groups brought the whaling organization and economy to Alaska. One reading of the evidence suggests that there was close social interaction between the Punuk and the Birnirk and the outcome was the Thule.

Where it emerged in Alaska along the Bering Strait, in locations like Point Hope, Point Barrow and Cape Prince of Wales, the Thule maintained and enlarged their whaling communities. The many miles between the great whaling villages could be covered by boat and sled. Summer trade fairs regularly heightened community contacts. Seward peninsula and North Slope groups participated too. Here and at Cape Krusenstern, the whaling villages gave way to sparsely populated settlements of single room houses. The economy was forced to do without the huge increase to subsistence brought by a whale, and as a result fishing was emphasized and community mobility increased.

Thule groups wielded large numbers of tools and gadgets related to their activities, and moved more and heavier household supplies between settlements. A variety of weapons permitted hunting both on sea ice and in open water for birds, seals and whales. Large, well-built houses with cold-trap entrances and raised sleeping platforms increased house warmth. Beyond the equipment, Thule social organization was adaptively superior. Whaling crews and their leaders formed more permanent villages with established leadership, specialization of duties, organization of labour, and mechanisms for taking concerted action.

Within a few hundred years the Thule had reached Greenland. The presumed route, given the distribution of early Thule sites, lay across the mainland coast south of Victoria Island, then north-east along Victoria and across southern Devon Island, continuing along eastern Ellesmere Island to north Greenland. Some of these High Arctic Thule groups subsequently moved south. It is unclear if earlier Thule peoples had also come into the low Arctic as part of the initial push eastward.

Between 1100 and 1300, there was a marked expansion of the Thule population to virtually all of the Arctic save Labrador, Quebec and the most north-westerly islands. Settlements included those with permanent winter houses (large, semi-subterranean stone, sod and whalebone structures). Interiors were elaborate and had meat lockers, raised platforms with storage beneath, and baleen mats for added insulation. Summers were spent in tents. High Arctic sites increased as people spread north across Greenland and down its east coast. But the most notable new growth was in the south. Population growth is attributed to favourable environmental circumstances, the absorbing of the Late Dorset folk, and the receiving of fresh immigrants from the west.

During the favourable period of climate, 900–1350, the Thule peoples appear as organizing for open-water whaling whenever the opportunity presented itself. Whaling gear included weaponry, the umiak, and cooperative hunting (boats included the harponeer, helmsman, and several paddlers). However, catching a bowhead whale could not be counted on by every whaling village each year. In the eastern Arctic, the mainstays for a community were seals, caribou, and walrus. The Thule peoples also drew on other resources such as hares, birds, musk ox (when present), eggs and clams, for which they used a variety of highly specialized tool kits and gadgets. The hunting kayak is represented, and there is evidence for ice hunting from floe edge and through breathing holes. Evidence of metal and European objects from Baffin Island and Greenland demonstrates early contact with the Norse, further north than Norse accounts suggest.

The Thule culture began changing after 1250. There were major expansions southward, increasing adaptational heterogeneity. Between 1350–1500 and later, Thule culture adjusted to changing resources by focusing more on walruses, caribous, narwhal or musk ox. This redistribution and differentiation of Thule culture is associated with a climatic change which saw colder summers and, on Baffin Island and Greenland, advancing glaciers. In parts of the north, drifting pack ice in summer may have been so extensive that summer boating was ruled out. Southwards, fast ice along the shore stayed longer and may have hampered launching umiaks while shortening the deep-water hunting season. Increased size of drifting ice fields would have greatly reduced whale habitat areas across the Arctic. Archaeological evidence indicates this reduction in whaling after 1400. By 1600, Thule societies were well adapted to local ecological situations and formed the groupings known to early explorers.

37.2
NORTH-WESTERN NORTH AMERICA

Roy L. Carlson

North-west North America includes that territory west of the Rocky Mountains, south of the Arctic and north of the Great Basin. It fronts onto the Pacific Ocean and has sometimes been called the 'salmon area' because this fish was so basic and vital to the aboriginal cultural system which evolved within its boundaries. In modern terms, the North-west includes the Alaska panhandle, most of the province of British Columbia, the entire state of Washington, western Oregon, north-west California, and the western fringes of Idaho and Montana. The North-west is often divided into two culture areas: the North-West Coast, which lies between the coastal mountain ranges and the Pacific Ocean; and the Columbia–Fraser Plateau, which is situated between the coastal mountains to the west and the Rockies to the east and is drained by the two major river systems which give the area its name. Much archaeological research has been undertaken in these two areas, demonstrating that the ethnographic cultures were the end-products of long-standing prehistoric cultural traditions (see Map 36).

Warming of the coast by the Japanese Current results in a rainy, temperate climate with relatively short periods of freezing winter temperatures in the north, and sometimes none at all in the south.

Coniferous forests of spruce, fir, hemlock and most importantly the western red cedar (*Thuja placata*) covered the coast from sea-shore to timber line. Vegetation in the interior plateaux was sparser and much more varied; large expanses of grassland and sagebrush were present, and pine and Douglas fir dominated the forests. Deciduous trees such as the trembling aspen also covered large areas in the far northern part of the plateau; winters were longer and colder and summers hotter than on the coast. These factors made it more difficult in the plateau to earn a living and kept population densities lower than on the coast.

The coastal mountains of British Columbia, which become the Cascade Range in Washington and Oregon, separate the coast from the plateau. Major rivers systems link the two areas, however, and not only provide a migration route for the anadromous salmon and oolichon to spawn but also served as the main routes of human communication between the two areas. The Fraser and Columbia Rivers with their vast drainage basins and numerous large tributaries were the most significant routes, but the medium-sized Klamath, Stikine and Skeena also served this purpose, as did the smaller Nass and Bella Coola, which flow into deep fjords. A continuous protected coastal waterway from Lynn Canal in Alaska south to Puget Sound in Washington state provided an unparalleled north–south transportation route for peoples with a maritime technology. East–west traffic was linked to this route at the mouths of most major rivers and by a short overland route in southern Puget Sound which linked the Columbia and its tributaries to the system.

Aboriginally, this area was the home of an estimated 150,000 to 200,000 people speaking dozens of different languages but who were in many other respects quite similar. Variations in culture were also based on divergent culture history and the unequal distribution of natural resources, which resulted in different population densities and differing potentials for the support of administrative and craft specialists not engaged in the food quest. Peoples in the better-endowed regions achieved a higher level of cultural elaboration than those in poorer regions. In much of the anthropological literature these language groups are referred to loosely as tribes, even though their members were not organized on a political basis but on the basis of ethnicity, and recognition of the common language and culture. The village, not the tribe, was the basic unit of political organization. Villages were linked by bonds of kinship and reciprocity with other villages. The system was based on a network of social relationships throughout the area and resulted in interaction spheres which crossed physiographic and linguistic boundaries. There is no reason to believe that there was any greater political complexity in the prehistoric period. The larger named 'tribes' of anthropological study are the products of the post-contact period of amalgamation, when the survivors of different local village groups united into one or several villages. Population densities were probably always highest on the coast, with its warmer climate and access to marine as well as terrestrial and riverine resources, and lowest in the northern interior with its harsher enviroment.

The languages spoken in the North-west have been grouped into ten families by the linguists M. D. Kinkade and W. Suttles. These scholars point out that much of the phonology, grammar and semantics cross-cut these language families and indicate interaction between them over a long period of time. A significant accomplishment was the ability to absorb words and concepts from neighbouring languages and incorporate them into their own language. Some interior Athabascan-speaking groups have taken over the Tlingit language in its entirety. Such borrowings probably accompanied intermarriage and the spread of material goods throughout the various regions by trade. Contact between groups prehistorically is shown by the widespread distribution of obsidian, seashells of many species, and specific tool types

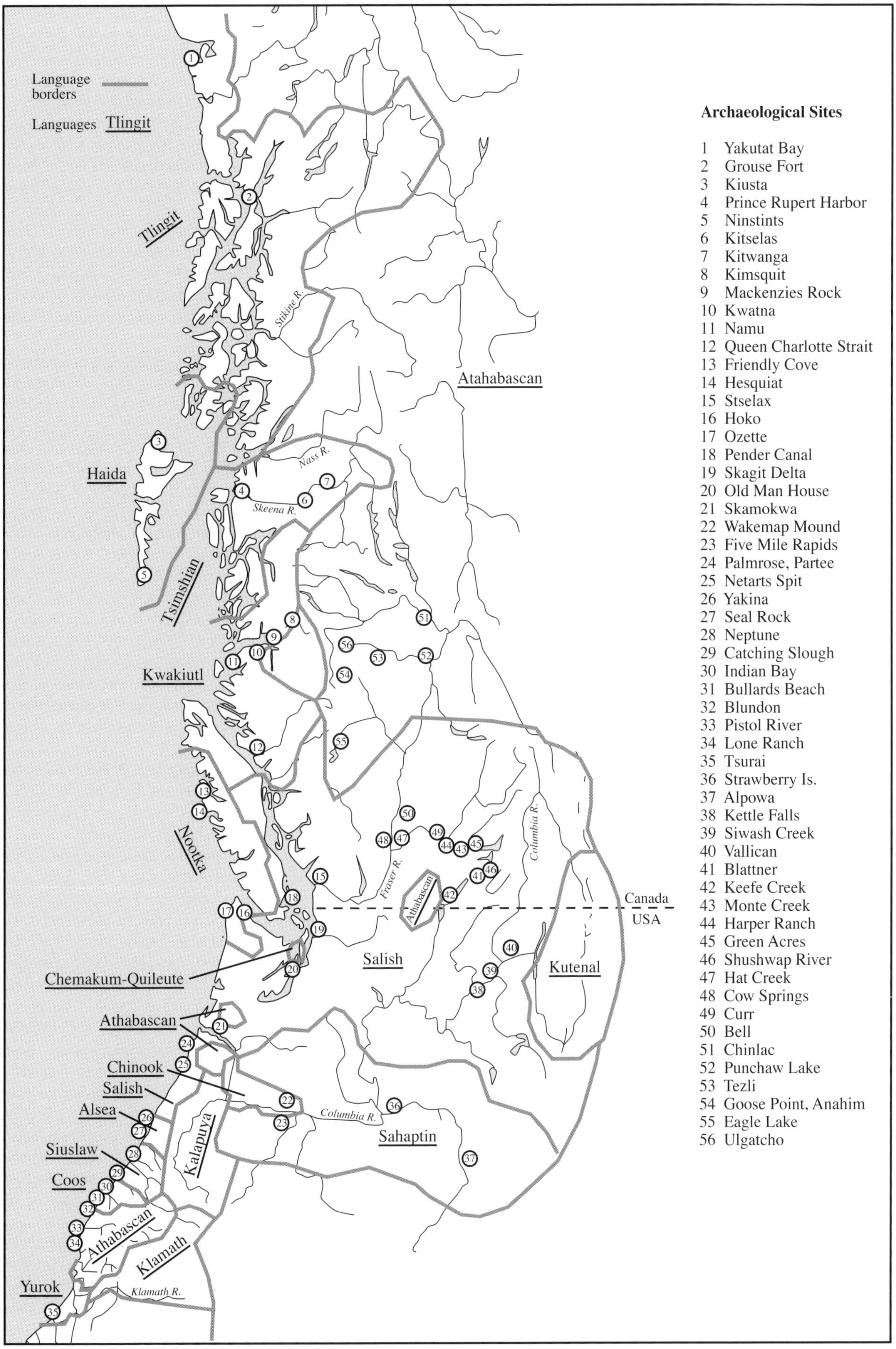

Map 36 Language groups, rivers and significant archaeological sites or localities on the North-West Coast of North America, 700 to 1500 (Carlson, R. L.; Schmidt, P.).

such as nephrite adze blades far from their points of origin.

There are a considerable number of excavated sites which have yielded cultural components of the late pre-contact period. In many such sites these components grade imperceptibly into either or both the earlier prehistoric period and the later period of European contact. The better-known sites are briefly described in this section region by region, beginning with the northern North-West Coast, and their locations are plotted on Map 36.

On the northern North-West Coast in Tlingit territory are a number of sites at Yakutat Bay and the site of Grouse Fort at the mouth of Lynn Canal. On Queen Charlotte Island in Haida country are Kiusta at Cloak Bay and Ninstints on Anthony Island. It is still uncertain how long the latter site, which has been designated a World Heritage Site by UNESCO, was actually occupied prior to the period of the fur trade. In Prince Rupert harbour in Tsimshian territory are many excavated late period sites, and up the Skeena River valley are sites in Kitselas Canyon and the mighty fortress of Kitwanga.

To the south on the central coast of British Columbia the most significant locality for excavated sites of the period is Kwatna Bay, which ethnographically was the home of peoples speaking both the Salish language of the Bella Coola and the Kwakiutl language of the Bella Bella. The remains of a large plank house dating to 1280 were excavated at the village of Nutlitliquotlank. Nearby, at the site of Axeti at the mouth of the Kwatna River, the remains of a fence-type fish weir and a waterlogged deposit containing basketry hats, bentwood box fragments, curved one-piece wooden fish hooks, composite fish hooks, storage baskets, cedar bark mats, rope, wooden splitting wedges, wooden chisel handles, and a complement of stone and bone tools, were discovered. Some excavation has also been undertaken at Kimsquit and at Mackenzie's Rock on Dean Channel. The latter is so named because it was the farthest point reached by the explorer Alexander Mackenzie when he crossed the continent in 1793. The site of Namu at the mouth of Burke Channel in Bella Bella territory has provided a 10,000-year record of continuous occupation.

The west coast of Vancouver Island and the north-west tip of the state of Washington is the territory of the Nootkan-speaking peoples. Major excavations have been undertaken in sites in four localities – Friendly Cove, Hesquiat, Hoko and Ozette. The latter site has yielded a greater quantity and variety of data from the late prehistoric and early historic periods than any other site on the coast. The reason for this is that Ozette was a village in full flower when it was covered by a mudslide which resulted in the preservation of nearly the entire complement of wood and fiber artefact types which under normal circumstances are lost to decay. The Makah Tribal Museum at Neah Bay houses this marvelous collection. The Nootkan speakers and possibly their immediate neighbours to the south were the only North-West Coast peoples actually to venture into the Pacific in pursuit of whales, and much whaling equipment and ritual paraphernalia were preserved at Ozette. Yuquot at Friendly Cove was the village of the famous whaler and chief Maquinna of the fur trade period of the early nineteenth century. Excavations there have demonstrated that whaling technology goes well back into pre-contact times to at least 800.

The Strait of Georgia and Puget Sound region was the home of coastal Salish-speaking peoples. Much less is known about the early ethnography than in regions to the north and west. The sea otter, prized by the fur traders, was not common, and there are fewer accounts by traders and explorers. In addition, the region came under the heavy impact of European colonists and missionaries, and local culture declined more rapidly than in areas to the north. Nevertheless, this region abounds in archaeological sites and is one of the heartlands for the early development of native arts. Late-period sites which have been excavated are Old Man House on Puget Sound, the birthplace of Chief Seattle (Sealth), Stselax Village at the mouth of the Fraser River, sites on the Skagit delta, and a number of seasonal sites in the San Juan and Gulf Islands. The village of Siwash Creek at the mouth of Fraser Canyon has yielded late prehistoric materials. Excavations at Stselax were within a standing plank house of the Musqueam Indians and indicated a level of cultural development in the late pre-contact period equal to that of other coastal peoples.

There are many known sites along the lower Columbia River, the Oregon coast and in north-west California. The lower Columbia region was devastated in 1830 by an epidemic of what is thought to have been malaria, so ethnographic data are not as complete as for many other regions. There are at least 152 known village sites of the Chinook, Clatsop, Kathlamet and Wishram peoples, at least eight of which are known to have late prehistoric components. Wakemap Mound on the Columbia River near the Dalles is probably the most famous of these sites. Lewis and Clark visited Wakemap in 1803 and noted that it was abandoned by that time. Excavation has proved it to be rich in art work and to belong to the late prehistoric period. Five Mile Rapids directly across the Columbia River from Wakemap has the longest local archaeological sequence, extending from nearly 10,000 years ago to historic times. Of 168 known sites on the northern and central Oregon coast and 135 on the southern coast, at least nineteen belong in part to the late prehistoric period. Many are shell middens, and many show evidence of plank houses and other typical coastal customs. Netart's Sand Spit in Tillamook territory is probably the best-known site. In north-west California, the village of Tsurai on Trinidad Bay transcends the period from prehistory to history.

Along the middle and upper Columbia and the middle Fraser river systems are a great many village sites. Unlike the coast, where the wooden plank house was the favoured dwelling, the peoples of the plateau preferred the semi-subterranean pit house. Other types of sites also occur – cache pits, platforms for temporary dwellings, scatterings of debris left from making stone tools, roasting pits, and rock art sites. The associated cultural complexes of the plateau pattern are winter pit house villages, underground cache/storage pits, seasonal food-gathering camps, heavy reliance on anadromous fish resources, earth ovens for cooking plant food, woodworking tools, chipped stone arrow points for hunting, geometric and biomorphic carvings, pictographs and petroglyphs, tubular pipes for smoking, and exchange systems involving obsidian, soapstone, nephrite and seashells. Many perishables such as basketry, cordage, netting and skin clothing were undoubtedly part of this culture, which in many of its aspects goes far back into prehistory; the earliest known pit house is at the site of Alpowa and dates to about 5,000 years ago. Many of these sites show evidence of occupation dating to both historic and prehistoric periods. Some of the better known and dated late pre-contact sites are Vallican, Blattner, Keefe Creek, Monte Creek, Harper Ranch, Curr, Green Acres, Shushwap River, Hat Creek, Cow Springs and Bell in British Columbia, and Kettle Falls, Alpowa and Strawberry Island in

Washington. About 1730, the introduction of the horse into the plateau, by other Indian peoples to the south, changed the aboriginal pattern to a degree, particularly in the open, unforested parts of the plateau.

In the upper Fraser drainage of the plateau, in the territory occupied by the Athabascan-speaking Carrier and Chilcotin, are at least nineteen sites of the late prehistoric period that have been tested or excavated. The most important of these are Chinlac, Punchaw Lake, Tezli, Goose Point, Eagle Lake and Ulgatcho. These sites exhibit much the same cultural remains as those in the Salish and Sahaptin parts of the plateau to the south, except for the absence of stone and bone sculpture. Ethnographically, art work was in birch bark and other perishable objects, so this absence is not surprising. Pit houses are present, but so are large plank houses of wood of a type clearly borrowed from the coast and sometimes referred to as 'potlatch houses', suggesting that this coastal custom was also borrowed, and may have been one of the reasons for adopting this house type. Whether this borrowing took place before AD 1500 or later is unknown. It is also uncertain how long the ancestors of the Carrier and Chilcotin were actually living on the upper Fraser and its tributaries. They may have been relatively recent arrivals from the Yukon and interior Alaska, where the largest group of northern Athabascan speakers still lives. The archaeological evidence is equivocal on this point, and different archaeologists present widely differing interpretations of the data.

CULTURAL COMPLEXES AD 700–1500

Data from the archaeological sites mentioned in the preceding section and from the relevant ethnographies indicate that the significant cultural complexes of this period in the North-west were based on the native inhabitants' scientific knowledge of the plants and animals with whom they shared the landscape, and on their technical skills in transforming the products of nature into tools, clothing, housing, transportation and food. First and foremost was their ability to wrest a living from the environment without the aid of either agriculture or metal tools. None of the peoples of this area grew plant food or kept domestic animals, except for dogs. Their livelihood was based on their fishing, hunting and collecting abilities, and on knowledge of food preservation. Salmon was more important than all other foodstuffs, except in the upriver reaches of the main river systems.

One anthropologist has counted sixty-three variations in devices used during the ethnographic period solely for procuring salmon. Archaeology corroborates this count to the extent that the most common artefact type found in sites of the late pre-contact period on the coast is the small bone barb, which was used as the hook portion of composite fish hooks, leisters, herring rakes and other fishing devices, which attest to the development of a significant fishing technology. These artefacts, and the large numbers of fish bones with which they are found, testify to the knowledge of not only how to take salmon but also halibut, cod, herring, oolichon, rockfish and other species using a multitude of hooks, traps, weirs and nets. The same types of fishing tool are found in the plateau but are not as common; much larger numbers of small, chipped stone points for arrows are found there than on the coast, which is evidence of the greater importance of hunting in the plateau. Carbon isotope studies of prehistoric bone samples from sites on the middle and upper Fraser River drainage indicate that protein of marine origin, which had to have been salmon, constituted from 40 to 60 per cent of the protein in the diet of these interior peoples, and that this reliance on salmon gradually declined with distance upriver. Comparable studies are not available for the other river systems, but the same results can be expected – the further from the sea, the less the reliance on salmon and the more on terrestrial products. The habits of sea mammals were also known and important on the coast, particularly for the Nootka, who were successful whale hunters. Hunting of land mammals was practised by all groups.

Botanical knowledge was also of great importance for subsistence, medicine, handicrafts, and house and canoe building. In western Washington alone at least 135 different plants were in common usage. These ranged from hemlock, whose inner bark was widely used for food, to the bark of flowering dogwood, which was used as a laxative, to the western red cedar used for canoes, houses and many other artefacts. Comparable knowledge of the properties of plants was known by the peoples of the other north-western regions. Archaeological evidence for extensive prehistoric processing of edible roots has recently been found in the upper Hat Creek valley of British Columbia – eleven large (2.77 to 5.0 m in diameter) subsurface pits lined with quantities of rocks have been excavated. Sixteen species of edible roots of plant species used for food during the ethnographic period are present in the immediate area. The eleven excavated root-roasting pits range in age from 800 BC to the time of European contact. Knowledge of the heat-retaining properties of stone, and the amounts of heat required to bake and steam, but not destroy, foodstuffs, was required for success in preparing plant foods for storage and consumption. The bulb of the wild camas lily was prized for food throughout the North-west and traded into those regions where it was not found. Considerable knowledge was required to distinguish it from the death camas, from which it can be differentiated only when in bloom. In the far north-western part of California, acorns were an important food. Here the technical knowledge of leaching was known and used to remove the poisonous tannic acid to make them edible. Among the Klamath, the seeds of wokas, the yellow water lily, were an important staple. A specialized two-handled muller was evolved to use in grinding these seeds. The preceding examples are only a very small part of the considerable botanical knowledge of the native north-westerners, who in addition to using plants for food relied heavily on bark, wood and roots to make the many necessary containers for cooking and storage such as have been found at Ozette. They understood the physical properties of these natural resources and used this knowledge to their advantage.

The entire way of life was based on the scheduling of seasonal movements of inhabitants of entire villages in order to take advantage of the salmon runs and other seasonally available foodstuffs found in ecological zones ranging from the seashore to alpine meadows. To be of maximum value, such resources had to be not only collected but also preserved and stored. Only then were they of use for winter consumption, for trade and for the support of specialists such as chiefs, shamans and craftspeople, who spent only part of their time in the food quest. Preservation was accomplished by air drying in places such as the Fraser Canyon, with its continuous upriver warm wind in late summer, by smoking where air drying was impractical, by immersion in oil, and by placing in underground pits, where temperatures remained cool. At the late period Carrier Indian village of Chinlac on the Stewart River in the upper Fraser drainage, over 2,000 cache pits were recorded on the ridges behind the village. Cache pits in fewer numbers are known from many other sites in the plateau and from coastal sites such as Kitselas Canyon. At the canal site on Pender Island are layer upon layer of clam shells associated with small circular hearths, where it is thought clams were dried for trade and winter use. Many other shell middens show these same features. Storage requirements were met through the institution known as the winter village, where preserved foods were kept for use during the winter months.

The winter village, which consisted of a group of semi-subterranean pit houses on the plateau and from one to many large wooden plank houses on the coast, was not only the place to store food surpluses for winter but also the most important socio-political unit throughout this area. On the coast, the large dwellings and concentrated population of the winter months facilitated ceremonial life and encouraged the production of arts and crafts. Surplus foodstuffs were controlled by a chief, who was responsible for their redistribution and who used them to support his relatives, to fulfill potlatch obligations and to support part-time specialists. Ozette again provides the best archaeological data on which to base such inferences, although most excavated coastal winter village sites have yielded some non-utilitarian art objects. Most North-West Coast art objects were made of wood, and unfortunately wooden objects are only rarely preserved. The smaller size of the plateau pit houses probably made them less useful for economic and ceremonial endeavours, although some of the larger ones could well have been community houses rather than dwellings and been used for these purposes.

Slavery and warfare were also aspects of ethnographic coastal society and were well integrated into the economic system. Slaves were obtained by raids on adjacent settlements and were used to produce handicrafts and collect foodstuffs for their owners. This system is difficult to document with archaeological data. Artefacts which are clearly war clubs go back at least 3,000 years on the northern North-West Coast, and there are the occasional burials of warriors from more recent periods. A few skeletons also show fractures of the lower left forearm, which probably resulted from warding off blows in hand-to-hand combat. It is known that the Tlingit were superior warriors who harassed the Russians unmercifully during the early historical period. Fortified settlements and retreats on steep prominences are common features over most of the coast and probably belong to the late prehistoric as well as to the historic periods. Petroglyphs in a late style from Jump-across Creek near Kimsquit show warriors carrying heads and were put there probably to commemorate a raid by a famous warrior. There is clear evidence of conflict in the late prehistoric period on the plateau in the form of people killed by arrows, but slavery and warfare were probably less institutionalized than on the coast.

An essential achievement of the peoples of the North-west was their ability to transform stone, bone and wood into tools, houses and canoes. This ability was dependent on their knowledge of both technical skills and the properties of animal products, plants and minerals. The coastal groups harboured craftsmen who were outstanding in working wood for both utilitarian items such as houses and canoes and ceremonial items such as masks, totem poles and feast dishes. In the ethnographic period, this skill was most highly developed among the Tlingit, Haida and Tsimshian of the northern coast of British Columbia and the Alaska panhandle. The splitting and planing adzes found in sites on the northern coast are unparalleled elsewhere in the North-west. The Haida were renowned for their large, skillfully crafted dugout canoes, which were traded widely, and for the intricately carved totem poles which dominated their villages of plank houses. In the forests of the Queen Charlotte Islands, particularly in the Yakoun drainage, are the archaeological evidences of the canoe-building industry in the forms of massive cedar logs adzed into canoe shapes, but for unknown reasons never completed, and of cedars with test holes cut into them to test the quality of the wood.

At one time, some scholars thought that the high development of wood sculpture was dependent on the introduction of metal tools by European traders. It is now known that this is not the case; the sculptural tradition as shown by numerous carvings in stone and bone, by waterlogged wood carvings, and by the presence of many woodworking tools, goes far back into prehistory and was truly a native accomplishment. Variations exist from region to region in the amounts and kinds of craftsmanship in wood, but the basic toolkit – wedges, chisels, adze blades and mauls – is evident prehistorically throughout the coast and plateau. Wood working was highly developed by at least 3,500 years ago and has roots which probably go back to much earlier local pebble chopper industries.

The evidences of pre-contact art provide the best information on pre-European belief systems. Ethnographically, the custom of intervening with destiny by invoking spirit power either with the aid of a shaman or through individual spirit helpers was universal throughout the area, although varied in practice from region to region. Cultural achievements in the arts were based on two fundamental goals – enhancement of prestige and bringing the supernatural to one's assistance. The former was typical of the coast and the latter of both the coast and the plateau. On the coast, surplus goods were concentrated in the hands of a chief, who used them to promote the fine arts and to pay specialists in painting and sculpture to create works of art which both enhanced his prestige and served as reminders to one and all of the perogatives and traditional history of his family. Masked dances and gift-giving feasts called 'potlatches' accompanied these public validations of wealth and perogatives. A written script was absent, but the art tradition took its place and served to transmit family history from generation to generation through public display of art objects and the recounting of traditional histories with which they were associated.

The wealth of art on the coast is best shown archaeologically by the outstanding finds at Ozette, which seem to date later than the period under discussion, mostly between 1500 and 1850, and by a series of small carvings in antler which show masks, spirit helpers and shamanistic symbols from the Pender Canal site, which dates much earlier, to between 2000 and 1500 BC. At both sites are carvings of the thunderbird, the owl and wolf, and other spirits important to the aboriginal way of life. On the plateau, the most widespread art forms are the rock art depictions of guardian spirit visions, but there are also portable stone and antler carvings important to shamanism. Also in remote localities on the plateau are rock cairns and walls probably erected by adolescents in their quests for spirit power.

At Ozette are looms for weaving dog and goat hair blankets and spindles and whorls for making the yarn. At both Ozette and Kwatna, fishing and sea mammal hunting equipment, wooden boxes made by bending and steaming, woven baskets, and other objects testify to the skill of craftspeople. Preservation by waterlogging at these late sites as well as at earlier ones such as Hoko and Musqueam, which date to 2,500 to 3,000 years ago, shows the long continuity of basket making, steaming and bending wooden fish hooks, and other industries.

The significant scientific and cultural achievements of the peoples of the Pacific North-west originated long before the period 700 to 1500. The archaeological record indicates both that this is the case and that there has been little cultural change over the last 4,000 years or more. Expertise in marine transportation, subsistence and technology has been present for the last 10,000 years on the northern and central North-West Coast. The earliest inhabitants, who were there at that time, could not have survived without this expert knowledge. Direct evidence for some use of salmon up the rivers goes back into prehistory for about 7,500 years, and data from the coast at the site of Namu indicate that salmon was the main staple by at least 4,000 years ago. Indirect evidence suggests that the seasonal subsistence system based on scheduling of group movements to take advantage of the best salmon runs was also present by this period. Preservation technology and the winter village must also have been in use, although unequivocal evidence has yet to be found. Data from the Pender Canal site indicate that both the memorial potlatch, the most widespread type of potlatch known ethnographically from the coast, and the North-West Coast tradition of sculptural art, originated about 3,500 years ago.

These accomplishments, and the scientific knowledge and technical skills on which they were based, formed the foundations of North-west culture. It was such a successful system that North-west culture persisted with little change until the time of European-derived influences. Certainly, there were some alterations in response to environmental shifts and other documented natural causes which brought about local populations dislocations. There was also the introduction of new technologies, such as the bow and arrow, which appeared about 500, and new customs such as pipe smoking, which came in somewhat later, but these introductions altered the overall way of life very little. Even today, much of the aboriginal scientific and cultural knowledge, which goes far back into prehistory, is still important in the native communities of North-western North America.

BIBLIOGRAPHY

CARLSON, R. L. (ed.) 1983. *Indian Art Tradition of the Northwest Coast.* Archaeology Press, Simon Fraser University, Burnaby.

FLADMARK, K. R. 1986. *British Columbia Prehistory.* National Museum of Man, Ottawa.

GREENGO, R. E. (ed.) 1983. *Prehistoric Places on the Southern Northwest Coast.* Thomas Burke Memorial Washington State Museum, Seattle.

GUNTHER, E. 1945. *Ethnobotany of Western Washington.* Seattle.

KINKADE, M. D.; SUTTLES, W. 1987. New Caledonia and Columbia (Linguistics). In: *Historical Atlas of Canada,* Vol. I. Toronto.

KIRK, R.; DAUGHERTY, R. D. 1978. *Exploring Washington Archaeology.* Seattle.

KROEBER, A. L. 1939. *Cultural and Natural Areas of Native North America.* Berkeley.

LAGUNA, F. DE. 1972. Under Mount Saint Elias: The History and Culture of Yakutat Tlingit. Smithsonian Contributions to Anthropology, Vol. 7, Washington, DC.

LOVELL, N. C.; CHISHOLM, B. S.; NELSON, D. E.; SCHWARZ, H. P. 1986. Prehistoric Salmon Consumption in Interior British Columbia. In: *Canadian Journal of Archaeology,* Vol. 10, pp. 99–106.

37·3
THE EASTERN WOODLANDS OF NORTH AMERICA

James B. Stoltman

The eastern woodlands of North America is a large, complex and highly diverse area, both enviromentally and in terms of the adaptive patterns of its native peoples (see Map 37). It was during the interval 700 to 1500 that agriculturally based economies first became widespread in the area and highly complex social systems rose to prominence in many regions, some attaining a scale and level of social sophistication approaching those of Mesoamerican societies. The two centuries following 1500 saw the arrival of increasing numbers of European immigrants, progressively intensified cultural interaction between the newcomers and the native peoples, and the eventual decimation or displacement of most native populations. The period between 700 and 1500, then, constitutes the last chapter in the story of human history in the Eastern Woodlands that can be characterized as purely native American.

CULTURAL BACKGROUND *c.* 700

An archaeological map of the eastern woodlands for about 700 would show a complex mosaic of regional cultural expressions. Because of the enormous regional diversity, it is difficult to generalize about the eastern woodlands without distorting the complex picture of differential cultural adaptation that archaeological research has pieced together for the area.

Most cultures of this time are referred to as 'Late Woodland'. Such societies were generally characterized by small, autonomous village communities with egalitarian social organization and were sustained primarily by hunting and gathering, sometimes supplemented by cultivated garden products. The construction of earthen mounds for human burial was a widespread practice, although the amount of energy expended on tomb construction and grave furniture acquisition had declined noticeably in contrast to mortuary practices of the Early and Middle Woodlands stages. An especially distinctive constituent of the technological inventory of these Late Woodland societies was the manufacture of ceramic containers. While Late Woodland ceramics were generally fashioned into simple jar forms from pastes tempered with crushed rock, sand, or grog, a wide range of regional ceramic traditions has been recognized. An especially noteworthy feature of the geographic distribution of these ceramic traditions is the basic regional integrity that persisted across the Middle Woodland/Late Woodland interface leading up to 700. In other words, regional continuity in both culture and population seems to have been the primary operative process across the landscape of the eastern woodlands at this time.

In some ways, use of the term 'Late Woodlands' as an archaeological taxon has serious drawbacks. It is often used to designate a period, especially 400 to 1000, but the persistence of typologically Middle Woodland cultures throughout this interval in parts of the north-east, mid-Atlantic and Appalachian regions renders the term unsuitable for such use on a pan-eastern scale. More important, however, is the problem that the inclusion of a wide range of cultures in a single taxon like 'Late Woodland' encourages the view that all somehow shared in a recent common ancestry. Nothing could be further from the truth. It is for this reason that Late Woodland is best viewed taxonomically as a stage, that is, a purely homotaxial grouping of cultures that are not necessarily related to one another in any temporal or cultural-historical sense. It is in this sense that the term is used here.

Some examples of Late Woodland cultures dating to *c.* 700, all of which can be seen to have had local antecedents in their respective regions, include Weeden Island in north Florida; Coles Creek in the lower Mississippi valley; Fourche Maline in the trans-Mississippi south; Miller III, McKelvey and Hamilton in the Midsouth; Patrick and Raymond in southern Illinois; Newtown in southern Ohio; and Effigy Mound and Princess Point in the Great Lakes region. It was Late Woodland societies such as these that provided the matrix into which the seeds of social complexity were sown and eventually germinated by 1000.

MAJOR CULTURAL TRENDS: 700–1000

Four widespread socio-cultural trends are especially characteristic of the interval between 700 and 1000: (1) agricultural intensification; (2) the construction of civic–ceremonial centres with platform mounds and associated religious institutions that integrated multi-community social units; (3) the emergence of ranked, hierarchical social systems; and (4) certain technological innovations. Although influences from Mesoamerica have frequently been cited to account for these developments, the current archaeological record provides no firm evidence of significant outside cultural contacts at this time. Instead, it is more reasonable to view this as a time of largely indigenous culture change, presumably as a result of increased communication and interaction among various Late Woodland peoples.

Categories of Sites

Late Woodland ■		Middle Mississippi ▲
1 Hoecake		22 Cahokia
2 Miller		23 Angel
3 Effigy Mounds		24 Nodena
4 McKelvey		25 Winterville
5 Princess Point		26 Moundville
6 Owasco		27 Zebree
7 Townsend		28 Hiwasee Island
8 Guida Farm		29 Dallas
9 Raymond		30 Martin Farm
10 Lewis		
11 Baytown		**Lower Valley ◆**
		31 Lake George
Oneota ○		32 Greenhouse
12 Midway		33 Toltec
13 Utz		34 Fatherland
14 Huber		
15 Humphrey		**South Appalachian ●**
		35 Town Creek
Fort Ancient □		36 Irene
16 Baum		37 Etowah
17 Madisonville		38 Lamar
		39 Woodstock
Caddoan ◇		
18 Crenshaw		**Gulf △**
19 Spiro		40 Kolomoki
20 Harlan		41 Weeden island
21 Davis		42 Fort Walton
		43 McKeithen

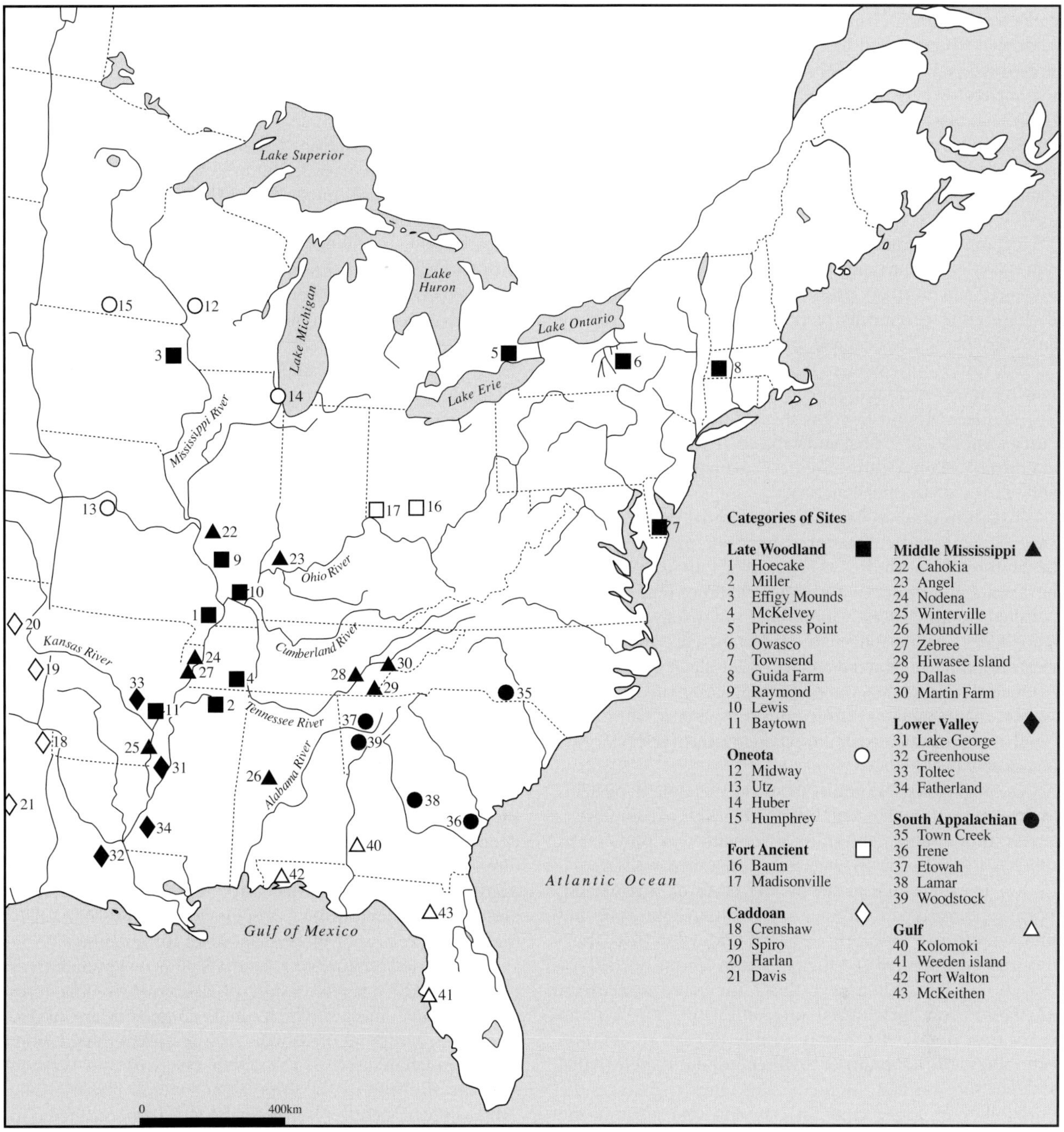

Map 37 Eastern woodlands of North America (Stoltman, J. B.; Schmidt P.).

Agricultural intensification played a critical role in the cultural transformations that highlight the 700–1000 period. This process cannot be attributed to the introduction of new cultivars, with the possible exception of beans, for maize and squash, along with native cultivars such as sunflower, sumpweed, maygrass, knotweed, and goosefoot, had been under cultivation in many eastern regions well before 700. A burgeoning body of evidence in the form of charred plant remains argues convincingly that maize, despite its appearance by 200, did not become a dietary staple in the eastern woodlands before 900. There is currently no satisfactory explanation to account for the timing of this trend. Certainly an adjustment period, both for the plant and its new users, was required after the initial arrival of maize, for it was a tropical crop in a temperate enviroment. One possibility,

still largely hypothetical, is that warmer climates (the neo-Atlantic climatic episode) facilitated the spread of maize cultivation at this time. Another popular view attributes maize intensification to population pressure; however, population pressure is an extremely elusive concept to confirm empirically. Care must be taken not simply to accept increased site size as such evidence, since population nucleation can occur unaccompanied by overall population growth.

The spread of civic–ceremonial centres with platform mound–plaza complexes as their nuclei is symptomatic of important social, political and religious changes that also transpired during this interval, principally in the south-east. While such civic–ceremonial centres became common from Florida to Oklahoma only after 900–1000, there is no need to look beyond the Eastern Woodlands for their origin. More likely, the platform mounds with religious, mortuary or elite residential structures on top that are the hallmark of these centres evolved from simpler flat-topped mounds that recur in a variety of Late and even Middle Woodland contexts from the lower Mississippi valley (at Marksville and in Coles Creek culture) across Tennessee to North Carolina (at Pinson and Garden Creek), through Georgia (at Annewakee Creek, Mandeville and Kolomoki) to the Weeden Island culture in north Florida.

The presence of monumental public works in the context of preplanned communities and the existence of high-status residential and mortuary precincts suggest that by 1000 some of these civic-ceremonial centres were administered by hereditary elites. For example, between 900 and 1000 at the Cahokia site in south-western Illinois, construction had begun on two important mounds aligned along the site's north–south axis: Monk's Mound (a colossal platform over 30 m high with a basal area of 7.3 ha) and Mound 72 (which contained 200 burials, many clearly of elite personages, while others were clearly of sacrificial victims.

What distinguishes the civic–ceremonial centres of the 900–1000 era and thereafter from their predecessors in the Eastern Woodlands is the unambiguous association of the former with intensive maize agriculture and with the so-called South-eastern Ceremonial Complex, as broadly defined; this is a term applied to a widely shared, cross-cultural set of religious beliefs and practices whose clearest expression is seen in the elaborate iconography appearing on distinctive copper, marine shell, ceramic, and stone items commonly found in high-status burial contexts in sites from north Florida to eastern Oklahoma.

Two technological innovations are useful, if perhaps sometimes overemphasized, horizon markers of this period. A new, more permanent house style, with wall posts set in trenches instead of individual holes (so-called wall–trench houses) became widespread by the close of this period, appearing in parts of Tennessee and Arkansas before 900 and then widely in the south-east and mid-west thereafter. Presumably, the increased investment in labour needed for such house construction reflects increased sedentism associated with agricultural intensification. The second innovation involved a highly visible change in ceramic technology, the adoption of shell tempering. Experimental evidence suggests that the use of shell temper enhances the workability of some kinds of clay and also permits the construction of thinner, yet stronger, vessel walls with improved heat-transmitting qualities. It is presumed that these advantages led to the widespread adoption of shell tempering in the south-east and mid-west following its inception, apparently in parts of Arkansas and Missouri, shortly after 700. While it is reasonable to accept the prevailing view that shell tempering of ceramics was an innovation of the native peoples of the Middle Mississippi valley province, care must be taken not to equate the spread of this technology with the 'radiation' of a people. A third important technological innovation, the bow and arrow, probably made its initial appearance a little earlier, but it first became widespread during this period.

In much of the literature on the Eastern Woodlands, the transformation of the Late Woodland stage, through these technological innovations, agricultural intensification, civic–ceremonial centre development and increased social complexity is equated with the emergence of the Mississippian stage or tradition, which then persisted to the time of European contact over most of the south-east.

THE MISSISSIPPIAN CONCEPT

The term 'Mississippian' is one of the most venerable and familiar terms in the literature of North American prehistory. So popular is the term that archaeologists are continually inventing new definitions in order to maximize its usage. Unfortunately, the new definitions often contradict the old, and since old definitions are like old soldiers (they never die), the literature is awash with conflicting usages of the term. The objective here is not to resolve this issue but to describe the major alternatives in order to make explicit the approach that we shall use in my attempt to analyse the cultural patterning observable in the archaeological record from 700 to 1500.

The term 'Mississippi' or 'Mississippian' as an archaeological taxon derives from a name, Middle Mississippi, that W.H. Holmes (1903) coined for one of the eleven ceramic provinces into which he subdivided eastern North America in his pioneering study of the area's prehistoric ceramics. This province, which centred upon the contiguous portions of the states of Illinois, Kentucky, Missouri, Arkansas, and Tennessee, was distinguished by its shell-tempered ceramics fashioned into varied and often complex forms.

In the 1930s, the archaeological meaning of Middle Mississippi was broadened by the addition of numerous traits, such as platform mounds, wall–trench houses, and polished stone discoids, that were associated with the province's distinctive ceramics. At the same time, an even more inclusive designation, 'Mississippi Pattern', was introduced that included both the new Middle Mississippi complex and a series of typologically similar complexes in the Ohio and upper Mississippi valleys. All subsequent efforts to redefine the Mississippian concept have had to contend with this deeply entrenched artefact-based ('formal' as opposed to temporal or spatial) definition. Whatever else Mississippian might be, it invariably includes or ressembles the late prehistoric cultural complexes of the central Mississippi valley that were the basis of Holmes' original formulation.

Today, the literature of Eastern Woodlands prehistory is characterized by a wide range of definitions of the term 'Mississippian', most of which can be assigned to one of two categories: temporal or formal. As a temporal designation, Mississippian is used in the south-east and mid-west to connote the interval of time within which typologically 'Mississippian' cultures had flourished, usually considered to have been from *c.* 900/1000 to the time of European contact. Because cultures considered to be 'Mississippian' under virtually all formal definitions of the term do not occur in many parts of the Eastern Woodlands, the term is unsuited for use as a truly pan-eastern period. Thus, in large areas of the Great Lakes, north-east, and mid-Atlantic regions, the term 'Late Woodland' is used instead to designate the same period.

Whether or not a Mississippian period is recognized, most archaeologists today utilize some kind of formal definition of Mississippian, usually referring to it as a culture, a tradition or a stage. While there is no doubt of the primacy of form over time in the derivation and continued use of the Mississippian concept, there is little agreement among archaeologists over what criteria to use in the formal definition. A popular approach is to limit the term Mississippian to those complexes possessing the basic traits used by the formulators of the Mid-west Taxonomic Method when they expanded the term 'Middle Mississippi' from a ceramic province to a fully fledged archaeological assemblage.

In this usage, which might be termed the 'restricted cultural' approach, Mississippian and Middle Mississippi are essentially equivalent terms.

In contrast to the 'restricted cultural' approach, the recent literature has seen a number of scholars advocate what might be referred to as the 'broad behavioural' approach to defining Mississippian. For example, in an influential synthesis published in 1967, Griffin suggested that the term 'Mississippian' be used to denote those societies that had 'developed a dependence upon agriculture for their basic, storable food supply', thereby encouraging the extension of the Mississippian designation to non-Middle Mississippi cultures in the trans-Mississippi south, lower Mississippi valley and south Appalachian regions. In a similar vein, emphasizing past socio-economic behaviour instead of material culture, Smith (1978) has defined Mississippian societies as those characterized by 'a ranked form of social organization and . . . a specific complex adaptation to linear, environmentally circumscribed floodplain habitat zones'. In yet another recent effort to define Mississippian more in terms of past behavior than artefact assemblages, Knight (1986) has proposed that Mississippian be regarded as 'a shared ritual pattern'. Besides emphasizing behaviour, whether economic, social or ritual, instead of material culture, these recent efforts to redefine Mississippian in formal (as opposed to temporal or spatial) terms share a common effect. They all entail a broader application of the term than is true of the 'restricted cultural' approach, in each case subsuming varying numbers of non-Middle Mississippi societies under the rubric of Mississippian.

By now, it should be clear that the term 'Mississippian' means many things to many people. Recognition of this situation is essential if one is to understand the literature of Eastern Woodlands prehistory; however, it would be futile at this time to seek consensus over a 'best' usage. After all, this is not purely a semantic issue. Each of the usages of the term Mississippian reflects a different problem orientation and a different perspective on the past. While the search for new perspectives on the past must be continually encouraged, eastern prehistorians will eventually have to confront the issue that continued redefinition of the same term is counterproductive to clear communication. Until that point is reached, however, we are destined to be bombarded with multiple and often conflicting definitions of the term. In such a context, one can only hope that authors are explicit in stating their objectives and in explaining their usage of the term and that they remain consistent in that usage, at least within a single work.

The objective of this chapter is to provide an overview of the primary cultural processes operative within the Eastern Woodlands during the interval 700 to 1500. Thd main thesis is that the primary cultural processes operating in the Eastern Woodlands throughout this period were the persistence of diverse regional technological and adaptive patterns, enriched by varying degrees of inter-regional interaction but not associated with major population movements. To avoid ambiguity in the discussion of this issue, the term 'Mississippian' will be avoided altogether; instead, only names for specific regional manifestations, like Middle Mississippi or south Appalachian or Caddoan, will be employed. This approach might be described as 'from below', in contrast to 'from above', in that greater emphasis is placed upon documenting and explaining the nature of inter-regional variability than upon recognizing pan-regional similarities.

CULTURAL PATTERNS IN THE EASTERN WOODLANDS, 700–1500

It is not just the available data but also how one approaches the archaeological record, whether 'from above' or 'from below', that influences how one perceives the past. This point can be illustrated through a metaphor, the distinction between a layer cake and a multi-strand rope. When the prehistory of a large and complex area like the Eastern Woodlands is approached 'from above' (that is, searching for pan-regional regularities), periods or stages are the most effective organizational devices. Viewed from this perspective, there is a tendency to perceive prehistory as a giant cake composed of a series of sequential layers. Most recent efforts to synthesize the prehistory of parts of the Eastern Woodlands have used this approach (for example, Funk 1983; Griffin 1983; Muller 1983; Smith 1986; Steponaitis 1986). As is amply evident from the results, numerous valuable insights have been gained through the recognition of the various 'layers'. Venerable terms like 'Late Woodland' and 'Mississippian', as well as newer terms such as 'Emergent Mississippian', are typically employed to refer to the 'layers' and serve to focus attention on widespread developmental trends that might otherwise go unnoticed. In contrast to this approach is that 'from below', the best example of which is seen in the work of Caldwell (1958). By stressing the importance of inter-regional variation, and seeking explanations for how these regional differences arose and were maintained, this approach tends to perceive prehistory more in the form of a complex rope composed of multiple, intertwined strands.

If we approach the post-700 prehistory of the Eastern Woodlands 'from below', the first and best-known 'strand' we are likely to encounter is that generally referred to as Middle Mississippi. Since its formal definition in the 1930s, archaeological research has progressively unravelled this strand, demonstrating not only that it was composed of a number of regional variants but also that each of the regional variants had a prolonged history and even an independent ancestry. The view of Middle Mississippi as a unitary culture that radiated from a single central Mississippi valley homeland is now untenable. Instead, Middle Mississippi is better conceptualized as a group of largely autonomous regional cultures that 'grew up' together through a mutually beneficial process of cultural exchange and interaction both with one another and with non-Middle Mississippi cultures. This basic viewpoint was presented over four decades ago by Griffin (1946), but it had enjoyed only mixed acceptance until recently.

The greater willingness of prehistorians now to accept a polyphyletic view of Middle Mississippi origins can no doubt be attributed to a steadily mounting body of evidence suggesting continuity between individual Middle Mississippi regional cultures and local expressions of the Late Woodland stage in the same region. For example, the Middle Mississippi variant found in the American Bottom (that is, Cahokia and its hinterlands) is clearly rooted in a southern Illinois Late Woodland culture (Late Bluff) that is distinctly different from the McKelvey/West Jefferson continuum of northern Alabama, which underlies the Moundville culture or the Mason/Banks and Hamilton/Martin Farm continua, which underlies the mature Middle Mississippi cultures of west and east Tennessee.

With the unitary-origins view of the Middle Mississippi culture group now in serious doubt, the time is perhaps ripe for a critical rethinking of the Mississippian concept in general in Eastern Woodlands prehistory. There is a decided tendency in the literature to discuss Mississippian as singular rather than as plural, as in 'the expansion of Mississippian culture' or 'expansion of the Mississippian cultural adaptation', which is, we submit, an unanticipated correlate of the prevailing approach 'from above'. If 'Middle Mississippi' must be conceptualized as a pluralistic rather than a unitary cultural entity, as current evidence suggests, how then can we expect to use the larger, more inclusive concept of Mississippian in a singular sense without creating an oversimplified picture of eastern woodlands prehistory?

The fundamental problem in the use of the Mississippian construct in the 'broad behavioural' sense is not that a primary dependence upon agriculture, or a complex agricultural adaptation to floodplain habitats, or a specific shared ritual pattern did not occur or do not merit recognition, but that these practices were more broadly distributed than the Middle Mississippi cultural province. Because of the intimate historical and etymological connection between the Middle Mississippi and Mississippian concepts, it is virtually impossible to use the latter in a way that is totally free from the connotation that the non-Middle Mississippi cultures included in it (for example, Lower Valley, Caddoan, South Appalachian or Gulf) were also cultural descendents of the former. At the very least, this is a highly debatable view. It is a view that is in need of much closer critical scrutiny, which is hardly encouraged within the conceptual framework of the 'broad behavioural' approach. It is for this reason that the term 'Mississippian' has been eschewed in this chapter.

There is no doubt that considerable cultural interaction occurred between the Middle Mississippi cultural province and surrounding regions after *c.* 900–1000. When viewed 'from below', however, it is equally clear that, across the south-east (the traditional 'Mississippian' province), at least four major non-Middle Mississippi cultural 'strands', or traditions, co-existed and maintained recognizable identities from well before 700 until the time of European contact: Gulf, South Appalachian, Lower Valley and Caddoan.

The Gulf Tradition, as exemplified by the Weeden Island and Fort Walton cultures, flourished on the coastal plain in north Florida, southern Georgia and southern Alabama. Sand-tempered, incised-punctated ceramics, sometimes with modelled adornos, along with communal mortuary offerings of 'killed' ceramic vessels in mounds but not in individual graves, reflect a basic continuity linking the two cultures. In addition, it should be pointed out that civic–ceremonial centres with platform mounds, plazas, and at least hints of important social differentiation in mortuary practices are evident in Weeden Island culture well before Fort Walton.

To the north of this region, in central and north Georgia, much of South Carolina and south-western North Carolina, sand-tempered ceramics with distinctive carved-paddle, complex stamped designs serve as the hallmark of the South Appalachian tradition, which persisted throughout this period. Here too it is important to note that platform mound construction occurred well before 'Mississippian' times.

To the south and west of the Middle Mississippi cultural province, centring on the Mississippi valley below the Arkansas River, is the setting for the Lower Valley tradition exemplified by the Coles Creek and Plaquemine cultures. A long history of grog-tempered ceramics occurs in this region, with platform mounds and hints of social differentiation appearing prior to 900 in Coles Creek culture.

The last of the four major non-Middle Mississippi traditions in the south-east is Caddoan, located in the trans-Mississippi south region immediately west of the lower Mississippi valley. Characterized by polished, engraved ceramics often tempered with bone, by high-status group burials, and by a distinctive dispersed farmstead–vacant ceremonial centre settlement pattern, the Caddoan tradition shows a 'seamless' continuity with the preceding Fourche Maline culture.

In each of the above four south-eastern regions, as in the central Mississippi valley, intensive maize agriculture, civic–ceremonial centres, ranked social systems and ceramic innovations like shell tempering became widespread only after 900–1000. It is thus a common practice in the literature to refer to the later stages of all of these regional traditions as Mississippian to connote their taxonomic equivalence. There is great merit to such an observation 'from above', but at the same time there is a hidden cost, namely, the danger that the cultures included under this rubric will be regarded as descendents of the Middle Mississippi cultural group. The available archaeological evidence overwhelmingly contradicts such a view, suggesting instead that Middle Mississippi cultures were as much the beneficiaries as the donors in a complex network of cultural interaction that characterized the Eastern Woodlands during this interval.

While complex social systems were evolving throughout much of the south-east, cultures generally to the north of the Ohio River followed a different developmental trajectory. As in the south-east, evidence for agricultural intensification becomes widespread after 1000. However, since the main cultivar, maize, is a tropical grass, there were important environmental limits (roughly the 120 days frost-free line) beyond which effective maize agriculture was impractical. In addition, the paucity of rich, naturally rejuvenated, easily tilled alluvial soil, so common in the major river valleys of the south-east and favoured by agriculturalists there, also was an important constraint upon the intensity with which maize could be cultivated across most of the northern half of the eastern woodlands. For most maize cultivators of the mid-west and north-east, soil infertility or inaccessibility (because of flood susceptibility or poor drainage) and short growing seasons were such effective deterrents to intensive agriculture that the practice of shifting cultivation in deciduous forest-covered upland settings had to be adopted. This upland cultivation strategy was generally associated with smaller-scale and less sedentary settlement systems than were possible for the intensive riverine cultivators of the south-east and was no doubt an important factor in the failure of ranked social systems to evolve over most of the mid-west and north-east.

In many portions of the mid-west, the shift from the Late Woodland practice of tempering pottery with grit to the 'Mississippian' practice of using shell temper is associated with the appearance of intensified maize agriculture *c.* 1000. The two best-known regional expressions of this trend are the Oneota culture in the upper Mississippi valley and the Fort Ancient culture in the central Ohio valley, both of which are characterized by the earliest sedentary agricultural villages in their respective areas. Neither of these cultures, however, shows evidence of the more complex forms of ranked social organization that characterize most Middle Mississippi societies. The apparently abrupt appearance of these cultures and their general typological affinities to Middle Mississippi cultures have contributed to the long-standing belief that they had been either derived from or inspired by Middle Mississippi cultures. Indeed, in the Mid-western Taxonomic Method, Oneota and Fort Ancient were placed in the Upper Mississippi phase of the Mississippi Pattern, and thus were commonly included (and often still are) under the rubric of 'Mississippian' (Deuel, 1937; Griffin, 1943, 268–302).

There seems little doubt that the emergence of both cultures involved the transformation of local Late Woodland societies through interaction with the Middle Mississippi cultural world. Exactly how this interaction occurred, however, is a complex and hotly debated topic. The introduction of Middle Mississippi practices through a migration of new peoples into both the upper Mississippi and central Ohio valleys has been postulated. In the central Ohio valley, incremental changes in ceramic technology between the Late Woodland Cole and Newtown phases and the earliest Fort Ancient phases, Baum and Anderson, coupled with the absence of 'pure' Middle Mississippi assemblages, argue persuasively against the migration theory of Fort Ancient origins. By contrast, in the upper Mississippi valley, the absence of an unambiguous intermediate complex between local Late Woodland manifestations (for example, effigy Mound culture) and early Oneota phases, along with the presence of assemblages in north-west Illinois, south-east Minnesota and southern Wisconsin that have the clear impress of the American Bottom variant of the Middle Mississippi culture group, permit the migration theory to maintain its viability. There is a large body of evidence to indicate that cultural influences (whether via population movements or not) emanating ultimately from Cahokia were widespread in the upper Mississippi valley region during the interval 1050–1200. Depending upon how one interprets the available radiocarbon dates, these Cahokia influences were either correlated with the emergence of Oneota culture from a presumed Late Woodland forerunner after *c.* 1050 or were greeted by an already extant Oneota complex that is postulated to have evolved at least a century earlier as an adaptative response to intensive maize agriculture, which preceded the primary wave of Cahokia interaction.

Beyond the geographic limits of Oneota and Fort Ancient cultures after 1000, the northern half of the Eastern Woodlands, as well as the eastern seaboard as far south as South Carolina, were characterized by a myriad of local cultural complexes generally assigned to the Late Woodland stage. The shifting cultivation of maize was widely practised among these peoples, although the extent to which it was a dietary staple varied considerably. Generally, the Late Woodland peoples of the adjacent portions of the states of Michigan, Ohio, West Virginia, Pennsylvania and New York, along with southern Ontario in Canada, were the most dependent upon maize cultivation. Indeed, recent carbon isotope analyses of human bones from Monongahela culture contexts in the West Virginia panhandle indicate that these Late Woodland people were virtually identical to Fort Ancient peoples in their dietary intake of maize, while both were more dependent upon maize than all currently known Middle Mississippi peoples! This creates an interesting dilemma for those who would like to define Mississippian in terms of a primary dependence upon agriculture.

More sedentary lifestyles are evident among the various Late Woodland peoples across the Great Lakes to the eastern seaboard after 1000 as substantial year-round communities appear in the archaeological record in abundance for the first time. The widespread appearance of stockaded villages indicates that inter-community social conflict was not limited to the more populous regions of the south-east. With the possible exception of the Powhatan of the Virginia coastal plain, all of the known Late Woodland and historic peoples of the northern half of the Eastern Woodlands had egalitarian social systems.

As with the Mississippian concept in the south-east, Late Woodland in the Great Lakes and north-east must be understood to connote a grouping of cultures that are taxonomically equivalent, not necessarily cultures that shared a common ancestry. Indeed, viewed 'from below', the Late Woodland stage in the northern half of the Eastern Woodlands can be seen to have the structure of a complex rope composed of a large number of independent but intertwined 'strands', or persisting regional traditions. The overall geographic patterning visible in the archaeological record of Late Woodland peoples after 1000, commonly attributed to population movements in the earlier literature, now increasingly appears to have resulted from cultural interaction among stable regional populations. Further diversity was added to the northern Late Woodland world through differential interaction with 'Mississippian' cultures to the south. Eastward of the upper Mississippi valley (where Cahokia interaction with its northern hinterlands was so prominent between 1000 and 1200), the primary source of 'Mississippian' influences seems to have been Fort Ancient culture. Southern Michigan and northern Ohio mark the north-eastern limits of ceramic assemblages that have incorporated such 'Mississippian' practices as shell temper and the use of handles on jars into otherwise Late Woodland contexts. There is certainly no need to invoke migrations to account for the appearance of such 'Mississippian' traits along the northern peripheries of Fort Ancient culture (see Plates 283–288).

BIBLIOGRAPHY

BADGER, R. CLAYTON, R. and L. A. (eds) 1985. *Alabama and the Borderlands from Prehistory to Statehood*. The University of Alabama Press.

BAREIS, C. J.; PORTER, J. W. (eds) 1984. *American Bottom Archaeology*. Urbana, Illinois.

BRAIN, J. P. 1976. The Question of Corn Agriculture in the Lower Mississippi Valley. In: *Southeastern Archaeological Conference Bulletin*. 19: 57–60.

CALDWELL, J. R. 1958. *Trend and Tradition in the Prehistory of the Eastern United States*. American Anthropological Association Memoir 88.

CUSTER, J. F. (ed.) 1986. *Late Woodland Cultures of the Middle Atlantic Region*. Newark, Delaware.

DEUEL, T. 1935. Basic Cultures of the Mississippi Valley. *American Anthropologist*, 37(3): 429–445.

——. 1937. The Application of a Classificatory Method to Mississippi Valley Archaeology. In: COLE, F. C.; DEUEL, T. (eds) *Rediscovering Illinois*, Chicago, pp. 207–219.

FAULKNER, C. H. 1972. The Mississippian–Woodland Transition in the Middle South. *Southeastern Archaeological Conference Bulletin*, 15: 38–45.

FORD, R. I. (ed.). 1985. *Prehistoric Food Production in North America*. University of Michigan, Museum of Anthropology, Anthropological Papers 75.

FOWLER, M. L. 1974. Cahokia: Ancient Capital of the Midwest. Addison-Wesley Module in Anthropology No. 48.

——. 1975. A Pre-Columbian Urban Center on the Mississippi. *Scientific American*, 233(2): 92–101.

FUNK, R. E. 1983. The Northeastern United States. In: JENNINGS, J. D. (ed.) *Ancient North Americans*. San Francisco, pp. 302–371.

GIBBON, G. E. (ed.) 1982. *Oneota Studies*. University of Minnesota Publications in Anthropology.

GRIFFIN, J. B. 1943. *The Fort Ancient Aspect: Its Cultural and Chronological Position in Mississippi Valley Archaeology*. Ann Arbor, Mich.

GRIFFIN, J. B. 1946. Cultural Change and Continuity in Eastern United States Archaeology. In: JOHNSON, F. (ed.) *Man in Northeastern North America*, Papers of the Robert S. Peabody Foundation for Archaeology, 3: 37–95.

——. (ed.) 1952. *Archaeology of Eastern United States*. Chicago.

——. 1967. Eastern North American Archaeology: A Summary. In: *Science,* 156 (3772): 175–91.

——. 1983. The Midlands. In: JENNINGS, J. D. (ed.) *Ancient North Americans*. San Francisco, pp. 242–301.

HOLMES, W. H. 1903. Aboriginal Pottery of the Eastern United States. *Twentieth Annual Report of the Bureau of American Ethnology*, pp. 1201.

JENNINGS, J. D. (ed.). 1983. *Ancient North Americans*. San Francisco.

JOHNSON, F. (ed.) 1946. *Man in Northeastern North America*. Papers of the Robert S. Peabody Foundation for Archaeology.

KNIGHT, V. J., JR. 1986. The Institutional Organization of the Mississippian Region. *American Antiquity,* 51(4): 675–687.

MCKERN, W. C. 1939. The Midwestern Taxonomic Method as an Aid to Archaeological Culture Study. *American Antiquity,* 4(4): 301–313.

MASON, R. J. 1981. *Great Lakes Archaeology*. New York.

MILANICH, J. T.; FAIRBANKS, C. H. 1980. *Florida Archaeology*. New York.

MORSE, D. F.; MORSE, P. A. 1983. *Archaeology of the Central Mississippi Valley*. New York.

MULLER, J. 1983. The Southeast. In: JENNINGS, J. D. (ed.) *Ancient North Americans*. San Francisco, pp. 372–419.

RITCHIE, W. A. 1965. *The Archaeology of New York State*. New York.

SMITH, B. D. 1984. Mississippian Expansion: Tracing the Historical Development of an Explanatory Model. *Southeastern Archaeology*. 3(1): 13–32.

——. 1986. The Archaeology of the Southeastern United States: From Dalton to de Soto, 10,500–500 B.P. *Advances in World Archaeology*. 5: 1–92.

STEPONAITIS, V. P. 1986. Prehistoric Archaeology in the Southeastern United States, 1970–1985. *Annual Review of Anthropology,* 15: 363–404.

STOLTMAN, J. B. (ed.) 1986. *Prehistoric Mound Builders of the Mississippi Valley*. The Putman Museum, Davenport, Iowa.

WILLEY, G. R. 1966. *An Introduction to American Archaeology*, Vol. 1. Englewood Cliffs, New Jersey.

37·4
THE GREATER SOUTH-WEST

Linda S. Cordell

NATURAL ENVIRONMENTS, SUBSISTENCE AND SETTLEMENTS

The Greater South-west is an environmentally diverse region centring on the states of Arizona and New Mexico in the United States and Chihuahua and Sonora in Mexico, and including portions of Utah, Colorado, Texas, Coahuila, Durango and Sonora (see Map 38). Landscapes include forested mountains, desert basins, grassland plains and wooded mesa country. Elevations range from near sea level to peaks of 4,265 m. The entire region is united by its arid to semi-arid climate and by variability that makes reliance on horticulture difficult. Nevertheless, aboriginally, the peoples of the Greater South-west cultivated corn, beans, squash, cotton and tobacco. It is the horticultural tradition and its concomitants (relatively permanent villages and dense population) that set the South-west apart from cultures to the west, east and north. In contrast to Mesoamerican cultures to the south, highly stratified, state-level society and urbanization were not features of the prehistoric greater south-west. Rather, there were shifts to and from apparently egalitarian to weakly stratified social systems over the course of millennia.

The Greater South-west has a large and diverse Indian population today which includes descendants of societies known archaeologically. Four major prehistoric cultural traditions are recognized in the archaeological literature: the Hohokam, the Patayan, the Mogollon and the Anasazi. Hohokam territory lay between the Gila and Salt River drainages of central Arizona, as well as the adjacent low deserts, where rainfall is scant and desert vegetation predominates. The Hohokam are considered generally ancestral to the modern Pima and Papago. The Patayan occupied the Colorado River valley and adjacent uplands, which are cooler, wetter and wooded. The modern Yuman-speaking tribes are considered generally descendants of the Patayan tradition. Mogollon culture occupied the southern and eastern portions of the basin-and-range province, with its associated volcanic mountain masses. Grassland valleys predominate at lower elevations, but woodland and forested mountains occur at higher elevations. Although most archaeologists suggest that the Mogollon were ancestral to some modern Pueblo peoples of New Mexico and Arizona, a link with the Tarahumara of Chihuahua has also been suggested. The term 'Anasazi' is applied to the prehistoric culture centred on the San Juan River drainage and the Colorado Plateau. At times in the late prehistoric period, Anasazi villages also extended eastwards onto the Great Plains. Anasazi territory includes vast areas of nearly horizontal rock formations, cut by steep canyons. Wooded and forested mountains and grassland valleys also cover much of the terrain. Not only is precipitation too scant to ensure agricultural success, but throughout much of the northern half of the Greater South-west, the growing season may be inadequate for reliable crops. Continuity between the Anasazi and the modern Pueblos is universally acknowledged. In the sixteenth century, Athapaskan speakers, whose ultimate homeland was in interior Canada and Alaska, moved into New Mexico and began spreading west and south into territory abandoned by or used only sporadically by the Pueblos. The descendants of these newcomers are the modern Navajo and Apache.

Prehistoric south-westerners adopted their major crops (maize, beans, squash and cotton), and agricultural technology from Mesoamerican peoples, among whom the plants were domesticated. Maize was present in the South-west by about 1500 BC. Although people came to depend more upon their crops over time, the crops had been accepted within a very ancient hunter–gatherer tradition that retained its importance. Wild plants, such as mesquite and cactus in the desert areas, and pinyon nuts, wild grass seeds, fruits and berries in higher-elevation areas, were always part of the south-westerner's diet. Dogs were ubiquitous domesticated animals, and turkeys were domesticated among the Anasazi. Yet, hunting retained major importance. Deer, antelopes, bighorn sheep, jack rabbits, cottontail rabbits, smaller game, birds and, where available, fish were components of the subsistence system.

Between 700 and 1500, most groups depended on domestic crops for a major portion of their livelihood, and this dependence required various technological devices and skills to enhance agricultural success. In the Hohokam area, irrigation was essential, and Hohokam irrigation systems are impressive by any standard. At least 580 km of prehistoric Hohokam irrigation canals have been mapped in the vicinity of Phoenix, Arizona, alone. Hohokam canals were generally U- or V-shaped in cross-section and lined with mixtures of clay and loam. Away from the major rivers, the Hohokam cultivated outwash fans, where possible. Brush diversion dams and ditches, low brush dikes, embankments and small ditches were used to divert runoff to fields where corn and cotton were grown in locations receiving less than 25 cm of rainfall per year. The Mogollon and Anasazi also used a variety of waters and soil-control devices, depending on the particular conditions and topographic features available. In

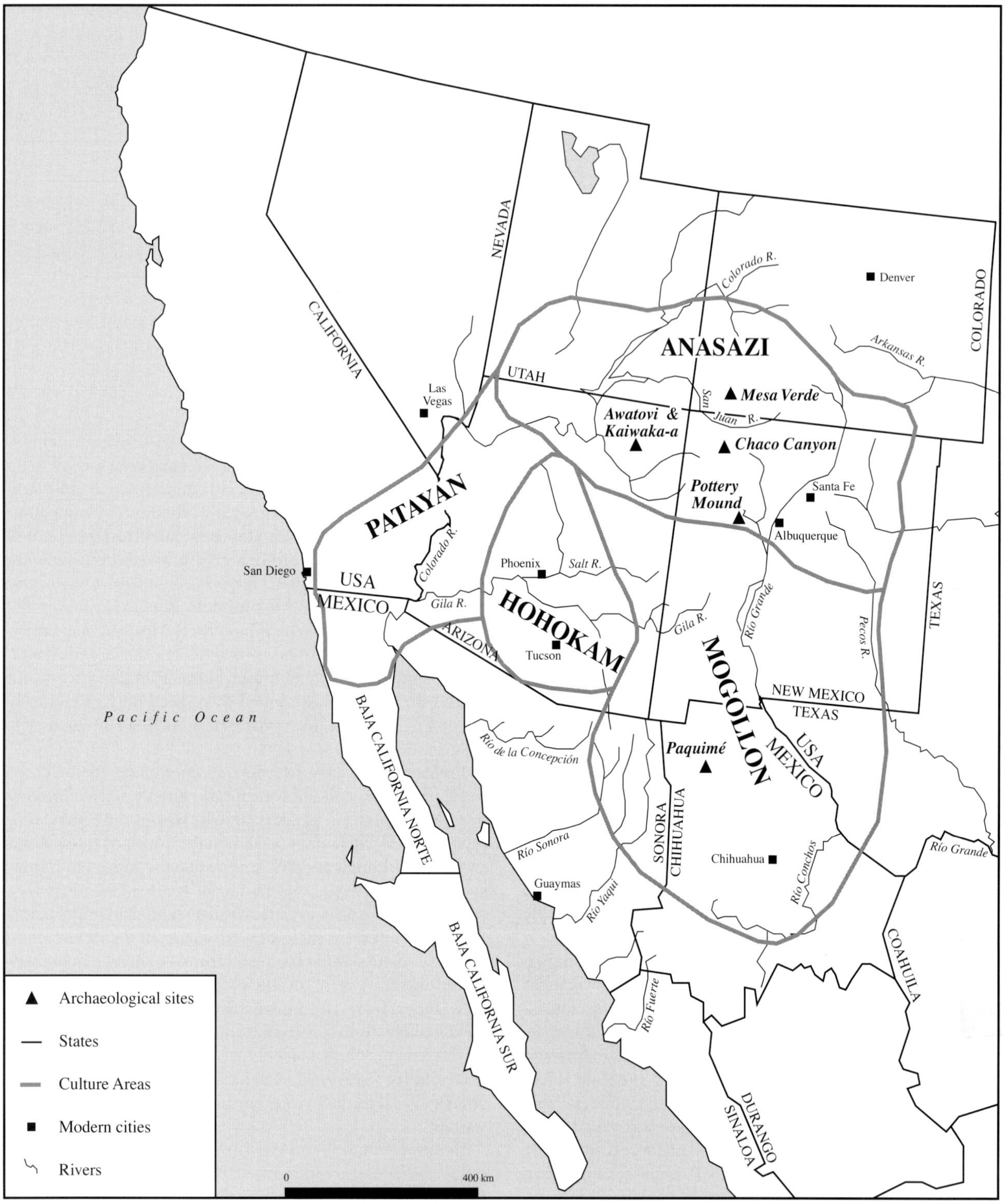

Map 38 North America's greater south-west with prehistoric culture areas and archaeological sites mentioned in the text (Cordell, L.; Schmidt, P.).

some areas, they used irrigation systems with series of canals, ditches and headgates. Elsewhere, they built series of terraces and bordered gardens on hillsides and stone check dams across *arroyos*. Some Anasazi fields consist of stone-bordered gardens with a mulch of fist-sized gravel. Gravel mulch, which serves to stabilize soil temperatures as well as retain moisture, seems to have mitigated the effects of short growing seasons in some areas. Although built to provide water for domestic use, rather than for agriculture, the Anasazi also constructed reservoirs, such as at Mesa Verde.

Although difficult to prove in the absence of writing systems and documents, prehistoric south-westerners probably relied on a combination of accurate astronomical knowledge and ritual in order to ensure the success of crops. Various specialists within modern south-western Indian communities are responsible for making celestial observations in order to predict the solstices. Archaeo-astronomers have suggested that some architectural features may have been used as solstice windows in prehistoric times. In addition, clay pipes and cane cigarettes for tobacco are recovered archaeologically and may have served in 'cloud-making' rituals, as they do among some modern South-western Indians.

By 700, most south-western peoples were living in villages or hamlets, although these varied in architectural style and degree of permanence (see Plate 281). From 700 to about 1250, the Hohokam occupied settlements composed of spatially separated dwellings of nuclear or extended family units. Their houses, referred to as pit houses, had floors excavated slightly below the surface of the ground and superstructures of pole and brush. After 1250, multi-storey, adobe-walled 'great houses', and single-storey, adobe-walled compounds were built in the Hohokam area. In the upland Patayan area, from about 700 to 1000, circular or oval pit houses were arranged in loosely aggregated settlements. After 1000 and until about 1200, settlements over much of the upland Patayan area are single-storey masonry structures of eight to ten contiguous rooms. Architectural remains from that portion of the Patayan area along the lower Colorado River are not known. In historic times, the Yuma tribes planted fields in the Colorado floodplain but moved to higher elevations during the winter. The structures associated with the agricultural season were ephemeral, their locations changing from year to year depending upon the course of the river. If the prehistoric Patayan followed a similar strategy, this would account for the lack of structural or stratified archaeological sites along the river.

The Mogollon and Anasazi also occupied loosely aggregated pit house villages. These were replaced by about 850 or 900 by single- and then often multi-storey, contiguous-roomed pueblos in the Anasazi area. The change from pit house to single-storey pueblo houses occurred in about 1000 in the Mogollon region. In the Anasazi area, during the eleventh and twelfth centuries, some pueblos were built of three and four storeys. Particularly at Chaco Canyon and other locations within the San Juan basin, the pueblos were large, highly formalized masonry structures with multi-storey, terraced room blocks, central plaza areas, and large circular, semi-subterranean ceremonial chambers referred to as *kivas*. Multi- and single-storey pueblos, constructed of stone or adobe, with several plaza areas, and either circular or rectangular *kivas*, continued to be constructed in the Anasazi area into historic times and are occupied by Pueblo Indians today. The temporal variation in architectural styles, along with stylistic changes in pottery, are the basis of divisions in the phase chronologies used by South-western archaeologists. In fact, the development of chronologies has received great emphasis in South-western archaeology, so that very local areas such as river valleys often have unique phase schemes.

ARTS, CRAFTS, TRADE, RELIGION AND REGIONAL INTEGRATION

Hand-shaped pottery decorated with coloured paint was produced throughout the south-west as a domestic craft and as an item of trade. Designs, both geometric and figurative, were skillfully executed with mineral or vegetable-based paints. A true iron-based glaze was used in some areas but only as a decorative pigment never completely covering vessel surfaces. The ceramic art of the Mimbres branch of the Mogollon and that of the inhabitants of Paquimé (Casas Grandes), Chihuahua, are particularly well known and admired today (see Plates 282a, b, c, e, f).

Jewellery and ornaments of shell and stone were also made in abundance and traded over great distances. The Hohokam are particularly well known for their shell work. Most of the shell (for example, *Glycymeris* and *Cardium*) was obtained from the Gulf of California. This was fashioned into carved and cut bracelets and pendants, rings and beads. Life forms such as frogs, birds and snakes were common motifs carved into shell. A sophisticated technique of using acid to etch designs onto shell was also practised. Hohokam shell-work was traded throughout their homeland as well as to the Mogollon and Anasazi. The Hohokam and the Anasazi fashioned inlayed items using jet, turquoise and shell. The Anasazi made extensive use of shell beads and mined, traded and crafted turquoise into a variety of beads and pendants. Jewellery of lignite and serpentine is also known from Anasazi sites.

Athough perishable, and therefore not often recovered from archaeological contexts, colourful, intricately woven textiles are known from throughout the prehistoric South-west. Yucca, agave, milkweed, mesquite, juniper bark, fur, hair, feathers and domestic cotton were dyed a variety of bright colours. Archaeologically recovered textiles include twills, tapestry weaves, gauze weaves and tie-dye. During the late prehistoric period in the Pueblo area, *kiva* walls were sometimes painted with elaborate and colourful murals. Those of Pottery Mound and Kuaua in the Rio Grande area and Awatovi and Kawaika-a in Hopi country preserved multiple layers of wall paintings that included a variety of naturalistic scenes, some elements of which are identifiable by modern Pueblo Indians.

The most abundant, diverse and elaborate evidence of craft production comes from excavations in the En Medio period ruins of Paquimé. Lost-wax casting was used to produce copper bells and axeheads. Other copper objects included sheet-copper armlets, disk beads, rings and pendants. Vast quantities of shell items were also produced, including *Strombus* shell trumpets.

As Woodbury (1979) indicates regarding social integration in the Greater South-west, there is 'weak stratification of society, but with successful communal efforts for building religious structures and for large-scale irrigation; emphasis on ceremonial elaboration and on religious rather than political controls.' The religious structures, preserved archaeologically, include platform mounds and ball courts among both the Hohokam and the residents of Paquimé, *kivas* and great *kivas* among the Anasazi, and great *kivas* among the Mogollon. Among northern branches of the Anasazi, towers may also have served as religious buildings. The importance of these features is indicated by the considerable labour invested in their construction. *Kivas* continue to be used for religious functions among the modern Pueblo Indians. Despite the religious conservatism of these peoples, in the absence of written records, it is not possible to know the extent of the similarities with past religious practices, or to know the precise religious functions of ball courts and platform mounds where these occur.

Throughout most of the prehistoric period, peoples of the Greater South-west lived in relatively small, dispersed villages. Today, the various native Indian communities are politically independent of one another. Yet it appears as though regionally integrated systems flourished for brief intervals during the prehistoric period. The earliest of these (*c.* 950–1150) arose in Chaco Canyon. The system involved more than seventy sites in the San Juan Basin that were constructed in a highly stylized and homogeneous fashion and linked to the canyon sites by an extensive system of prehistoric roadways. Within this system, there was trade in ceramics and turquoise and possibly other goods. As indicated above, Paquimé seems to have been the centre of a well-developed regional system that involved specialized craft production and trade. Elaborate water-control features, roads and signalling stations were aspects of both the Chaco and Paquimé systems. Dating the Paquimé development is disputed: nevertheless, dates in the twelfth to the fifteenth centuries seem reasonable.

Less well-documented regional systems have been suggested for the eleventh-century Hohokam and for the fourteenth-century western Pueblo. The Hohokam system may have involved extensive trade networks (especially for shell and minerals), religious interactions, and co-ordination functions for irrigation systems. The western Pueblo system may have entailed the exchange of subsistence goods (especially agricultural products) regulated by elite individuals who exchanged certain kinds of ceramics among themselves.

The arrival of Europeans in the South-west in 1540 effectively prohibited any further steps towards development of purely native complex societies. European diseases decimated South-western populations; livestock greatly altered native economies, and European settlements and political organization disrupted native systems of trade, exchange and inter-community dependence. It is a tribute to the resilience and spirit of the native populations that so much of their traditional beliefs and life-ways survive into the twentieth present.

BIBLIOGRAPHY

CORDELL, L. S. 1984. *Prehistory of the Southwest.* Orlando.

HAURY, E. W. 1976. *The Hohokam, Desert Farmers and Craftsmen: Excavations at Snaketown, 1964–1965.* Tucson, Arizona.

HIBBEN, F. C. 1975. *Kiva Art of the Anasazi at Pottery Mound.* Las Vegas.

KENT, K. P. 1983. *Prehistoric Textiles of the Southwest*, School of American Research. Albuquerque, New Mexico.

ORTIZ, A. (ed.) 1979. *Southwest. Handbook of North American Indians,* Vol. 9. Smithsonian Institution, Washington.

——. 1983. *Southwest. Handbook of North American Indians,* Vol. 10. Smithsonian Institution, Washington.

REYMAN, J. E. 1976. Astronomy, Architecture, and Adaptation at Pueblo Bonito. *Science,* 193: 957–962.

WOODBURY, R. B. 1979. Prehistory: Introduction. In: Southwest, ORTIZ, A. (ed.) *Handbook of North American Indians*, Vol. 9, pp. 22–30, Smithsonian Institution, Washington.

37·5
NORTH-EASTERN MEXICO

Jeremiah F. Epstein

AREA GEOGRAPHY AND CULTURAL ECOLOGY

The geographical area under consideration comprises the Mexican states of Tamaulipas (north of the Soto de la Marina River), Nuevo León, Coahuila, eastern Chihuahua and the adjacent parts of Texas (see Map 39). All Indian groups within this region were hunter–gatherers. In contrast, tribes living to the west and south were agricultural peoples with Mesoamerican affiliation; the northern border was inhabited by various tribes whose culture was derived from the Plains or Eastern Woodlands.

Three major physiographic features dominate the region. On the eastern border is the gulf coastal plain, which slowly rises in elevation until it reaches the tall and rugged mountains of the Sierra Madre Oriental. West of the Sierra is the basin-and-range country of the Mesa del Norte. The major drainage for the entire region is the Rio Grande, into which empty the San Juan River in Tamaulipas, the Sabinas River in Coahuila and the Conchos River in Chihuahua. The only significant body of standing water was located in south-western Coahuila, where the Nazas River fed into the Parras basin and formed the Laguna Mayran.

North-eastern Mexico is hot and dry; without irrigation, agriculture is impracticable. Vegetation consists of mesquite, thorny shrubs, cactus, agaves and desert grasses. Variations in elevation, soil type and availability of water combine to produce a variety of enviromental niches. Except for mesquite, trees are scarce; however, cottonwood and oak can be found along river courses, and pine and juniper grow in high elevations. Today, the mammals most frequently observed are deer, rabbits, jack rabbits, squirrels and javelina. In the sixteenth century, bison ranged in northern Coahuila.

THE ABORIGINAL CULTURE IN THE SIXTEENTH CENTURY

North-eastern Mexico is one of the least-known areas in North America. Early historical sources, beginning with Cabeza de Vaca, who lived among the Indians in 1534–1535,

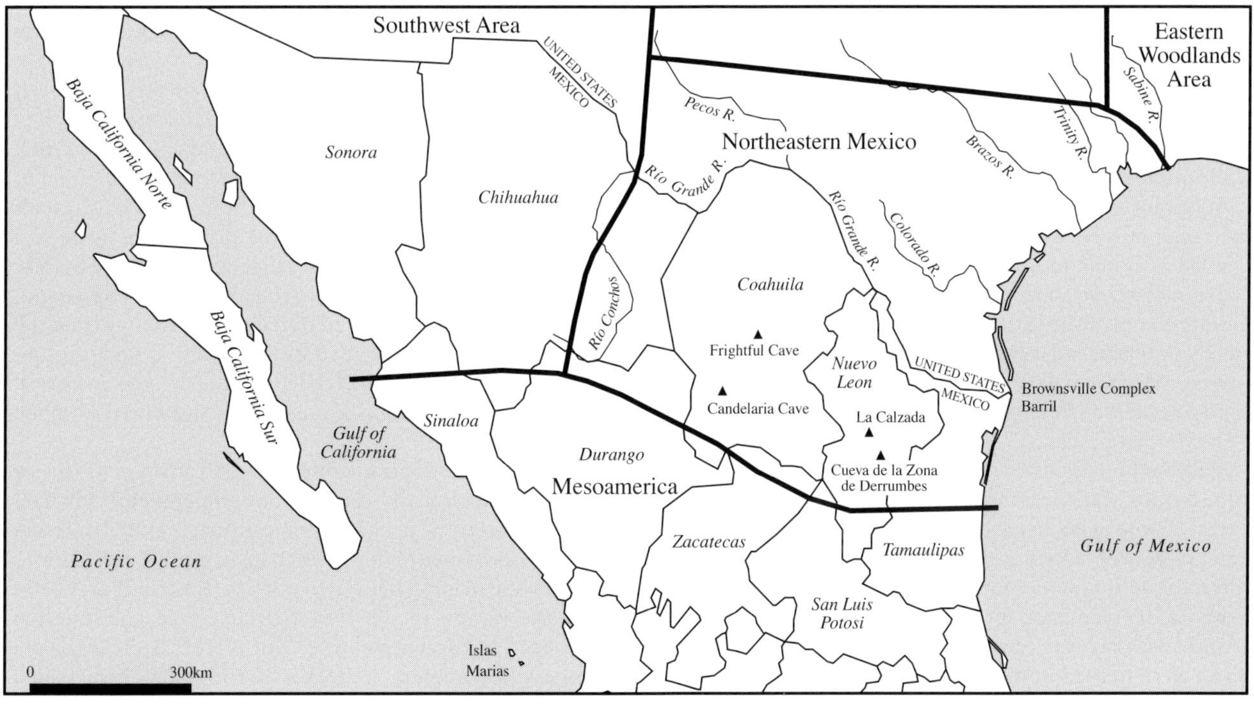

Map 39 North-eastern Mexico culture area (Epstein, J. F.; Schmidt, P.).

emphasize the linguistic and cultural diversity of the hundreds of native groups but supply little specific information about their languages. During the seventeenth century, as a result of invasions of Spanish settlers from the south and Apache from the north, the Indians were displaced from their original territories; by the nineteenth century, most were extinct. As a result, modern scholars are reluctant to make positive assertions about the distribution of sixteenth-century Indian tribes in North-eastern Mexico and the languages they spoke until more data are available.

The diversity of language and culture described by Cabeza de Vaca in the early sixteenth century and by Alonso de León in the seventeenth century makes it difficult to generalize about the culture for the whole area and to link archaeological materials with specific populations. The characteristic features of settled peoples have not been detected; there is no evidence of agriculture, villages, writing, medicine, science or sculpture. According to historical sources, the trappings of religion – deities, priests, temples, ritual – were absent. The magico-religious element was embodied in the shaman, who effected cures by removing offending objects (that is, little sticks, pieces of bone) from the body. The major ceremonial activity involving all members of the group was the dance, *mitote*, which was held frequently to ward off dangers or to celebrate glad tidings. The *mitote* often lasted two or three days.

Although Cabeza de Vaca and Alonso de León provide little data on culture patterns, they found the Indian diet and foraging way of life sufficiently interesting to describe it in some detail. The Indians of north-eastern Mexico lived by hunting and gathering. Each group had its own foraging territory in the winter and shared its summer territory, when food was most abundant. Settlements moved frequently, relocating whenever the local food supply was depleted. Aboriginal structures, which were made of flexible poles and covered with mats, grass, or cane, could be taken down or erected easily. A small hearth was usually located in the centre of the structure. The average-size house may have held eight to ten people; the average settlement had possibly fifteen houses.

Generally, men wore no clothing. Sources indicate that some women covered their pubic areas with grass or cordage; others wore deerskin skirts embellished with beads or strings of snail shell, animal teeth and hard seeds. Among some groups, people wore robes of rabbit skin. Sandals were worn in thorny regions.

Aboriginal diets were highly varied, although the amounts and range of food eaten depended on seasonal availability. The list of animal foods included large and small mammals – deer, rabbits, rats, mice – as well as birds, snakes and insects. Among the plants mentioned are maguey roots and stalks, prickly pear fruit and leaves, mesquite pods, fruits, and cactus flowers. Maguey stalks were cooked for two days to make them palatable, and mesquite pods were pounded into a flour with wooden pestles.

Skills for finding water and food were impressive. Among some groups, water was carried in hollowed-out prickly pear leaves. Those who lived close to the Río Grande stored water in gourds, which were gathered after they had floated down the Río Grande during the flood season. Along the coast, canoes were used for fishing; fish were caught in traps or shot with arrows. Shellfish were eaten when available. Bison were hunted in northern Coahuila.

While the hunting and fishing techniques imply a bountiful food supply, this was not the case. Early historians noted that the Indians were close to starvation during the winter, often going for days without food. This suggests that regardless of the season, groups relied on whatever foodstuffs were available.

ARCHAEOLOGY

Archaeological research indicates that the historical pattern described above for most of North-eastern Mexico existed essentially unchanged for thousands of years. The major innovation, the bow and arrow, was introduced approximately between 500 and 700. Initially, bows were used concurrently with the *atlatl* (spear thrower) and the rabbit stick, but the *atlatl* was no longer in use by 1000.

The archaeological data emphasize the difficult nature of aboriginal life. Evidence of foraging is found in rock shelters and from open camp sites, the latter being recognized by clusters of hearths. Animal bones and dried faeces from cave deposits (the Late Coahuila Complex at Frightful Cave, the Linares Phase materials at Cueva de La Zona de Derrumbes and at La Calzada in Nuevo León) confirm the eclectic nature of the foraging diet and provide evidence for a few items not mentioned in the historical accounts.

Most striking is the fact that almost all of the artifact remains are connected with the food quest. Hunting and gathering activities are indicated by bows, arrows, rabbit sticks, carrying baskets and nets. Food preparation is implied in grinding stones for breaking up wild seeds, nuts and small animal bones; mortar holes in solid rock attest to centuries of pounding mesquite bean pods with wooden pestles. Various methods of cooking are indicated: clusters of burnt rock hearths for roasting; wooden tongs for handling the hot rocks used in stone boiling; fragments of burnt baskets, probably used in parching seed. The abundance of sandals preserved in almost every dry rock shelter is archaeology's most dramatic document of the extensive walking required by the foraging life.

Burial data do not indicate continuity between the archaeological and ethnohistorical data. Historical sources note that shamans were cremated while other individuals were buried in fields, the remains often covered with prickly pears and rocks to deter scavenging animals. As of this writing, however, no cremations or burials in open sites have been discovered. The few burials found so far were unearthed from midden deposits in rock shelters and are of two types: flexed and secondary bundle (the bones only, as opposed to the whole body, were collected and buried). Grave goods are scarce, a suggestion that status distinctions were not important. With the exception of secondary bundle burials, the dead do not appear to have been given special treatment. These unrelated variations in burial practices imply that the same rock shelters were used by culturally distinct groups, confirming the cultural diversity noted by the historical sources. But the absence of cremations and burials in open sites is puzzling.

Although the adoption of the bow and arrow is the major innovation within the region, contemporaneous changes occurring along the periphery indicate local cultural diversity and trade and contact with other areas. In south Texas, various groups were making their own pottery (Epstein *et al.*, 1980). Near the mouth of the Rio Grande, some communities specialized in carving pendants out of conch shells (Barril, Brownsville complex), some of which may have been traded as far as south-western Coahuila (Campbell, 1960). These people also traded with the Huastecs in southern Tamaulipas.

A remarkable mortuary practice (Mayran complex) appeared in south-western Coahuila, where hunter–gatherers had contact with Mesoamerican peoples to the west and south. This complex is best documented at Candelaria Cave in the Bolsón de Delicias and dates to about 1250. The energy expenditure represented by both the grave goods and the method of interment is impressive. The dead, wrapped in blankets of fine woven yucca fibre along with their own tools, clothing and adornments, were carefully placed in deep, difficult-to-reach subterranean sinkholes far from the habitations. The burial adornments included strings of marine shells from both the Pacific coast (*Olivella dama*) and the Gulf of Mexico (*Marginella apicina, Oliva reticulares*). Additional burial goods indicate connections with seventeenth-century shamanistic practices: cut deer antler to be thrown in the fire during ceremonies, deer skulls, which may have been used as headdresses, and scarifiers, which were used to draw blood. Another cave, called La Paila, contained decorated gourds and other trade items from the Mesoamerican cultures of Western Mexico.

It is not clear who these people were or precisely where they lived. They may have been more sedentary hunter–gatherers or perhaps Mesoamericanized Zacatecans from the south. Although there is continuity between this mortuary cult and the historical period with regard to shamanism, the Spanish friars who settled in the Laguna region in the early seventeenth century wrote nothing about people weaving fine fabrics; nor is there mention of a mortuary cult or of long-distance trade in marine shells.

It appears that the mortuary complex was defunct a century or so before the Spanish conquest. Its demise may well have been linked to the general collapse of Mesoamerican cultures in Chihuahua, Zacatecas and Durango around 1350–1400. While the causes of that collapse are not known, the harsh environment of northern Mexico must have played a significant role.

BIBLIOGRAPHY

AVELEYRA ARROYO DE ANDA, L.; MALDONADO-KOERDELL, M. AND MARTÍNEZ DEL RÍO, P. 1956. *Cueva de la Candelaria.* Memorias del Instituto Nacional de Antropología e Historia. V. México.

CABEZA DE VACA, A. N. 1984. The Narrative of Álvar Núñez Cabeza de Vaca. In: HODGE, F. W. (ed.), *Spanish Explorers in the Southern United States 1528-1543*. Texas Historical Society, Austin, pp. 1–126.

CAMPBELL, T. N. 1983. Coahuiltecans and Their Neighbors. In: STURTEVANT, W. B. (gen. ed.) *Handbook of North American Indians*, Vol. 10. Southwest, pp. 343–358. Smithsonian Institution, Washington, DC.

EPSTEIN, J. F. 1969. *The San Isidro Site: An Early Man Campsite in Nuevo León, Mexico.* Anthropological Series, Department of Anthropology, University of Texas at Austin.

EPSTEIN, J. F.; HESTER, T. R.; GRAVES, C. (eds) 1980. *Papers on the Prehistory of Northeastern Mexico and Adjacent Texas.* Special Report No. 9, Center of Archaeological Research, The University of Texas at San Antonio, San Antonio.

LEÓN, A. DE. 1975. Relación y Discursos del Descubrimiento, Población, y Pacificación de Este Nuevo Reino de León, In: GARCÍA (ed.) *Documentos inéditos o muy raros para la Historia de Mexico.* Mexico, Vol. 60, pp. 97–101.

MACNEISH, R. S. 1958. *Preliminary Archaeological Investigations in the Sierra de Tamaulipas, Mexico.* Transactions of the American Philosophical Society 48, Part 6.

38

MESOAMERICA AND CENTRAL AMERICA

38.1

MESOAMERICA

Paul Gendrop, Jaime Litvak King and Paul Schmidt

CENTRAL AND NORTHERN AREAS

The fall of the great city of Teotihuacán should be seen as much more than merely an episode in the history of a culture. This metropolis had dominated Mesoamerica for close to 600 years and had imprinted its image on the culture of the elites throughout the area (see Map 40). Most of the main cities grew because they had become trading links in the Teotihuacán domain or had adapted to that role as a matter of survival. Merchandise, in the guise of products from all the climates in Mesoamerica, went to the centre and was exchanged for goods from other provenances. Foreign dynasties had married into the Teotihuacán nobility, and the figure of the long-nosed water god came to be enshrined in reliefs and paintings in far away regions.

Teotihuacán became the heir to an expanded Olmec territory. It took 400 years for the highland city to become the most important settlement in Mesoamerica – a great focal node. The end of Teotihuacán required the rearrangement of the whole area. Cities fell and rose because of their position relative to the former trading network.

The collapse of Teotihuacán did not affect every region in the same way. Oaxaca had disconnected itself from the network long before, at the time of the Monte Albán IIIb phase, and consequently there is no evidence in the region that echoes happenings in the Valley of Mexico. The north-east Huastec culture seems to have hardly noticed the event. El Tajín, in northern Veracruz, and the Sierra Gorda of Querétaro, the source of cinnabar, directly linked to the Huasteca, seem to have not only survived but actually flourished when their trade no longer had to compete with Teotihuacán-dominated central Mexico.

Sites peripheral to the Valley of Mexico, like Cholula and Cacaxtla to the east, and Xochicalco to the south, as well as many other sites and regions that had clearly been linked to the mighty domain, show a clear change in their materials that can be dated to the fall of Teotihuacán. In the case of the last two sites, their relations with the Gulf Coast area, and through it, with the Maya region, increased noticeably, and there are good examples, in monumental art, mural painting and pottery exemplifying these relations: Xochicalco's well-known relief showing seated men with characteristic Maya headdresses; the recently discovered Maya-style murals at Cacaxtla; and Maya vaults in Guerrero, Oxtotitlán and Xochipala.

The general layout of the whole region was affected. The strong monofocality that Teotihuacán had impressed upon it, at least until when its domain began to deteriorate around 600, was never replaced by another power as strong as the Classic city. A period of dispersion followed, with Xochicalco, from central Mexico, seeming to try to fill the power vacuum. The dispersion of Xochicalco-influenced artefacts, including figures with crossed hands, show that the possible route of contact followed the Balsas River to Oaxaca, and from there to Chiapas, to the south-east. Between 750 and 900, Xochicalco traits are found at many sites: Tenango, in the Valley of Toluca, to the west, being among the most important. There is a very probable, as yet unexplained, link between the Xochicalco and El Tajín styles. However, Xochicalco did not succeed in gaining hegemony, and for 150 years the different geographical components of Mesoamerica seem to have followed their own paths with very few attempts at more than local hegemony.

Possible evidence for the re-establishment of the trading network, at least in a reduced and localized version, is the distribution of the red-on-buff Coyotlatelco ware that seems to encompass the valleys of Toluca, Morelos, Puebla and Mexico. This ware is found in Teotihuacán, in households built over the ruins of the city, and it pre-dates the Toltec Mazapa Red-on-Buff ware in many sites.

After 900, a number of strong regional sites emerge. The Valley of Oaxaca region seems to have been dominated by the Mixtec, a folk previously known to have lived in the mountains to its north-west, and may even have been a major component of the population in the city of Cholula. They appear to have conquered the Valley of Oaxaca – inhabited mainly by Zapotec people – where they settled in the already existing cities. They re-used the abandoned centre of Monte Albán as a burial ground for their chieftains. Tula, in central Mexico, populated by the historically documented Toltec, grew to become the dominant centre for the region, its

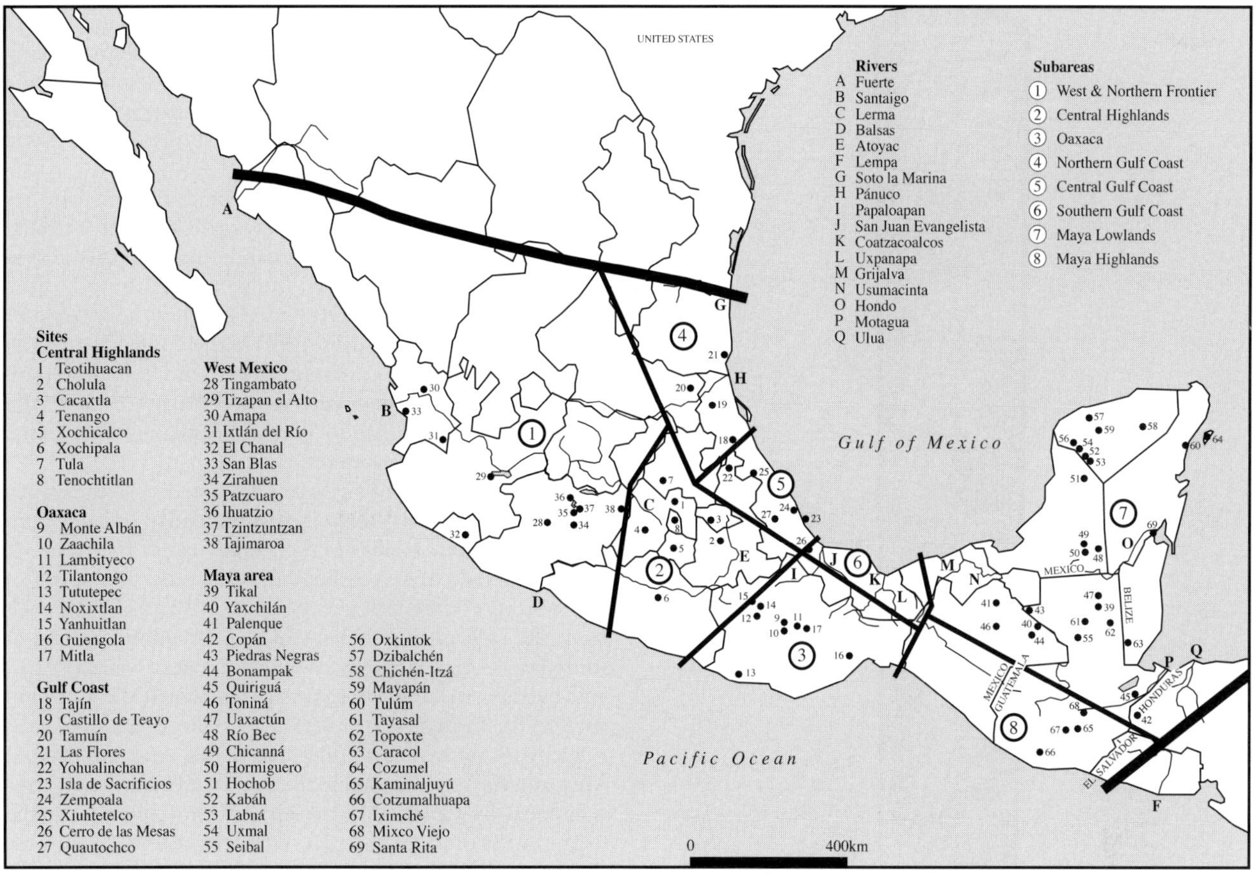

Map 40 The Mesoamerican culture area (Schmidt, P.).

influence extending far beyond its immediate area, probably reaching the Maya zone. Evidence for this is apparent in the architecture of buildings at Chichén-Itzá, Náhuatl names for Maya rulers in the northern Yucatán Peninsula, and local lore stating that chieftains were required to receive their emblems of power in a place called Tula (see Plate 299).

The Toltec domination shows not only the emergence of a new central power vying for control over the whole Mesoamerican area but also the re-emergence of commerce in several directions. Although the Toltec Mazapa ware, especially its flat figurines, is important evidence for the expansion of Tula's domain, the main trade wares of the time are not Toltec in origin. Fine Orange ware seems to come from the extreme south-eastern part of the Gulf region, and Plumbate – the only pre-Hispanic glazed ware – is held to have been made in the southern section of today's Mexico–Guatemala border. One of their most characteristic types of sculpture, the reclining *Chac Mool* statues, appears to have a West Mexican origin.

The Toltec are formally the first Mesoamerican metal users. The culture area is oddly late in the development of a number of technologies, contrasting harshly with previous achievements in science, astronomy and mathematics: it has yet to be compared with Central and South America, mainly the Andean region, where metalworking appeared much earlier.

Mesoamerican metal never seemed to have reached the state where its use as a tool could have spurred changes in society. Copper, gold and some silver were the principal materials, although copper mixed with tin, in a bronze-like alloy, is believed by some researchers to have been in use. However, the evidence for this alloy comes from artifacts in private collections and is, consequently, not trustworthy. The use of metal seems to have penetrated from Central America into West Mexico, spreading mainly to Oaxaca and reaching as far as Yucatán. Most metal objects have been found in ritual contexts, jewellery associated with burials and sacrificial situations. A number of needles and small implements have been found as part of normal household debris.

Focal sites, which would be thought of as rich sources of metal pieces, have not been extremely so. Although it is a fact that the Spanish conquerors were able to gather a considerable amount of gold, the quantity does not compare with Peru. Metal sources were mostly rivers, where gold nuggets were gathered. Pre-Hispanic copper mines have been found, but they are in marginal areas in west Mexico, there being no evidence that their economic input meaningfully affected the region. Most of the gold work seems to have been imported from Costa Rica. Metalworking techniques were limited to hammering and lost wax; the control of high temperatures was lacking in Mesoamerica.

The Toltec ascendancy did not last long. Tula, according to Aztec narrative, seems to have been destroyed by northern barbarians around 1000. Central Mexico again became the scene of a fluid situation where rival towns, mainly Texcoco, Culhuacán and Azcapotzalco, competed for a purely local overlordship, although their alliances linked them to other chiefdoms in other areas. Documents from after that time, like the Codex Xolotl, show people armed with the bow and arrow, which was supposed to have been a northern introduction that affected warfare and hunting by replacing the *atlatl*, the traditional dart thrower, which appears to have been a symbol of rank (see Figure 34).

Toltec domination did not cover as much territory as Teotihuacán. Although not well known, and local lore offers

contradictory versions, it is fairly certain that some settlements had achieved regional ascendancy and were developing ruling traditions. After the fall of Tula, central Mexico remained a conglomerate of market cities fighting between each other, without a clear winner until the establishment of the Aztec as the main force after 1428.

Aztec expansion is amply documented, reaching further than any previous force into the Maya area, collecting tribute from the coast of Chiapas and establishing a trading post at Zinacantán in the Chiapas highlands. Although they depended on cacao for currency, they were never able to gain control of its principal sources in the Gulf Coast region of Tabasco. When they attempted to extend their dominion into West Mexico, they were severely beaten back by the Tarascans of Tzintzuntzán, whose ascendancy was halted only by the Spanish conquest.

Aztec domination of Mesoamerica lasted until the arrival of the European conquerors, who were joined by Indian groups welcoming them as allies in their fight against the Aztec. It was hampered, from the beginning, by the difficulties of transport due to the lack of large mammals and of the wheel, from the lack of the concept of a multi-ethnic empire as something different from a town's conquest of other villages, and by their own social organization, which did not lend itself to the formation of a strong centralized, national unit.

Little is known regarding the social organization of Mesoamerican groups before the Aztecs. Even the numerous references by Colonial historians and chroniclers as to the organization of the Aztec government have to be taken with little more than a grain of salt because of the interests of the informants and of the lack of acceptable comparative models available to Europeans at the time.

Tenochtitlán, the Aztec capital, a huge city with a population said to have numbered over a quarter of a million, seems to have been in the process of changing from an agricultural capital to a truly metropolitan urban node. Its society shows at the same time a powerful, inaccessible ruler, resembling a mixture of both a European monarch and a Zulu chieftain. There was centralized regulation of trade and market, but at the same time an earlier mode of land distribution and ownership subsisted. Religion seemed to be ruled by a powerful priesthood, linked with the monarchy, with characteristics which made it hark to the traditional agricultural deities; at the same time, some of the main gods appear to have been local tribal protectors, very much related to the Náhuatl cosmogonical legends (see Plates 300–307).

There is no information on Teotihuacán social organization. Archaeological evidence paints a huge city, certainly much larger than a traditional chiefdom government could have ruled. Previous stereotypes had it as a peaceful and non-military site, but evidence to the contrary is emerging in many places. Tula, according to historical sources, was either ruled by a dual monarchy, too easily identified with religious and civil matters by historians, or the scene of rivalry between chiefs, the limits of whose domains were not very clear at the time.

By the time of the Aztec, the chiefdom was in transition to a more territorial, less tribal form of organization. Ahuizotl, one of the last Aztec rulers, tried to reform a growing

Figure 34 *Átlatl* or spear-thrower, Mixtec or Aztec (Mexico), wood and gold leaf, *c.* AD 1400. Museo di Antropologia e Etnologia, Florence (after Levinson, J. A. (ed.) *et al.*, *circa* 1492: *Art in the Age of Exploration*, Yale and London 1992, p. 561).

bureaucracy, including the granting of government posts to persons not in the nobility, but his measures were overturned by his successor.

At the time of the Spanish Conquest, Mesoamerican culture was in flux. Territorial domination by the Aztecs was clearly in danger and irrevocably on its way out. Its society was undergoing change from its previous local scope to the possible formation of new units that approximate our concept of a state. Its technology, although primitive, would have adopted the use of metal, which, in turn, would have caused further social changes. What the Spanish found was a world in the midst of critical change. Their arrival at that precise point only made conquest that much easier and prepared the ground for the rapid acceptance of European religion, technology and customs.

OAXACA

Like Teotihuacán, Monte Albán suffered a steep decline and, although not entirely abandoned, it ceased to be a metropolis (perhaps, as some authors have suggested, the pressure justifying the costly upkeep of a major population centre on the heights where Monte Albán is located disappeared with the collapse of Teotihuacán). Zapotec centres developed in the western arms of the Valley of Oaxaca (Cuilapán, Zaachila) as they did to the east (Lambityeco), and continued the Zapotec tradition even if they never reached the size of the old Classic capital. From the mid-seventh to mid-eighth century, Lambityeco represented one of the purest examples of Zapotec art of the Late Classic period. Its funerary architecture and the altars around the courtyards provide some of the best preserved examples of the characteristic Oaxaca *tableros* with their relief panels always underlined by a fine recessed band creating sharp lines of shade that help to define the principal architectural volumes. A rare example of conservation is the modelled and painted relief decoration at the centre of each recessed panel at Lambityeco, and likewise the remarkably fine faces of old people at the entrance to Tomb 6 and the large masks of Cocijo, the god of thunder and rain (the Zapotec equivalent of the Mexican Tláloc, the god Tajín at Veracruz, or the Maya Chac).

In this region, which contributed so much to the creation of a Mesoamerican system of 'glyphic' writing and counting (see Plate 94), stelae tended to be replaced by 'genealogical registers' carved on stone tablets and recording marriages and other events. Zaachila attempted to achieve political domination for a time but did not succeed, perhaps because of the incipient expansion of the highlanders of the nearby Mixteca, who developed an independent regional style (the *Ñuiñe* style) expressed in the use of large monolithic blocks (with glyphic inscriptions in relief at Huamelulpán) at the corners of their artificial platforms.

In fact, the Mixtec entered the stage of Mesoamerican history during the Post-classic period, during which time their expansion towards the Valley of Oaxaca began. From that time onwards, one of the main cultural features of the Mixtec elite was to be an exaggerated emphasis on the purity of its lineage and its concern to express that purity in complex genealogical codices whose unmistakable style would influence many facets of the Mesoamerican world in the last centuries before the Spanish conquest.

The prince of Tilantongo and lord of Tututepec, 8 Deer 'Jaguar Claw', who is the hero of many Mixtec codices, embodies perfectly the type of historical account contained in such 'genealogical codices'. Born on the day 8 Deer in the year 12 Reed (1011) in Tilantongo, this prince chose Tututepec on the coast as his operational base, and from there established a bureaucratic state. An attempt was made during his reign to consolidate the Mixteca politically: like the change in the calendar, this change may have been inspired by the Toltec model. An ingenious system of cultivation known locally as *lama-bordo*, which made more intensive farming possible, was also developed in the valleys of Nochiztlán and Yanhuitlán in Mixteca Alta. For his conquest of Acatepec in 1044, 8 Deer was honoured in the following year: his septum was pierced and a nose plug inserted with great ceremony; he may have travelled to Tula for that purpose.

Curiously, lineage came to be so important among the members of the Mixtec aristocracy that it occasionally outweighed attachment to their place of origin: hence the high mobility of some of those princes who, armed with the prestige conferred by their high rank and escorted by their faithful *tay situndayu* (a kind of personal serf), were able to settle where they pleased. This practice, consolidated by marriage and other types of alliance, largely explains the virtual control exercised by Mixtec minorities over the Zapotecs of the Valley of Oaxaca during the Late Post-classic period as well as the final transfer of the Zapotec capital from Zaachila to Guiengola in the Isthmus of Tehuantepec.

Jewels made of gold, silver, and rock crystal and, in general, objects worked in bone, shell, and wood (such as those found in the famous Tomb 7 of Monte Albán, an old Zapotec tomb reused for the burial of Mixtec princes) give us some idea of the amazing luxury with which the Mixtec aristocracy surrounded itself: collars and large pectorals, rings and nail guards finely cast in gold by the lost-wax process; fanholders, sceptres, spearthrowers (the typical Mesoamerican *átlatl*), and so on. Although metalworking developed late in comparison with Central and South America, far from negligible technical and aesthetic levels were soon achieved, as Mixtec jewellery amply demonstrates.

Such skills in the fine arts (also expressed in pottery with delicate, faultless polychrome decoration) constitute one of the many arguments deployed on the subject of the real intellectual authors of late buildings such as those at Mitla, the last sacred Oaxacan city. There has, indeed, been much discussion about the cultural identity of this site, whether Zapotec or Mixtec. Weighing the pros and cons, it would seem that we can identify in the architecture of Mitla the essential elements of the Zapotec *tablero*, in which the decorative friezes were sculptured, the stylistic feature which marked the Classic period in what would here be the last stage of its development. Although it retains its unmistakable appearance, it is now reduced to the role of a frame which throws into relief the superb variations on the step-and-fret motif. Fret was, incidentally, an ornament quite widely used in Mesoamerica (actually appearing on occasion in Classic Zapotec architecture), and while it is particularly abundant in the decoration of Mixtec ritual pottery of the Post-classic period, it emerges with special prominence in the Late Classic architecture of Puuc in Yucatán, along with another feature found at Mitla: the slight but deliberate outward inclination of the façades. Moreover, the fact that residential areas now predominated over ceremonial areas may reflect a general change towards a life lived more often in palaces. The murals adorning certain monolithic lintels of some of the palaces at Mitla are clearly in a style similar to that of the Mixtec genealogical codices. Some observations of a more general nature are, however, in order in this connection.

In this discussion on the Mixtec presence at that time, we should not lose sight of one very important point: although Toltec political and cultural influence dominated during the first phase of the Post-classic period throughout Mesoamerica (retaining until the Aztec period a legendary aura that made it seem synonymous with art and refinement), it was the Mixtec artistic traditions that were to predominate, especially in what are referred to as the minor arts, during the last three centuries of pre-Hispanic life, to the point of becoming the supreme manifestation of the 'good taste' of the age, at the Aztec court and also in other regions. Thus, for example, a clear 'Mixtec codex' style is visible in the murals at Tulum in Quintana Roo and in those of Santa Rita in Belize; the forms of Mixtec ceramics dominate the Mesoamerican scene at this time as Toltec forms had done shortly before (or, even further back, Teotihuacán forms). Given this dual trend in Post-classic culture, we may therefore speak of a combination – at various levels – of Toltec and Mixtec elements, and it is particularly significant that whenever one encounters an exceptionally refined object from the period close to the *Conquista*, it is nearly always referred to as 'Aztec' or 'Mixtec'. It is well known that, as Aztec power was consolidated towards the end of the fifteenth century, the new Aztec masters had the most renowned artists and artisans of the day brought to Mexico–Tenochtitlán: first among the latter were those from the 'Mixteca–Puebla' region, which at the time covered the area from the central valleys of Oaxaca to the Puebla–Tlaxcala Valley.

The conquest of Oaxaca was certainly no easy task for the Aztec, whose most warlike king, Ahuizotl, was routed at Guiengola on the Isthmus of Tehuantepec by the Zapotec king, Cocijoeza.

THE MAYA AREA

While the years from 650 to 700 show a marked cultural decline for Teotihuacán and Monte Albán, they coincide in the Maya lowlands with the beginning of the greatest splendour of the Classic Period.

The year 681 witnessed the restoration at Tikal of the old dynasty, the most brilliant representative of which during the second quarter of the fifth century had been Cielo Tormentos, whose origins clearly lay in Teotihuacán. That event provided the occasion for the inauguration of the first of the twin-pyramid complexes that would continue to be built in the city at the transition from one *katún* to the next. This architectural ensemble consists of a large artificial terrace, at the eastern and western ends of which rise two identical step-pyramids, simple raised ceremonial platforms with no temple at their apex, and stairways on either side. Opposite the eastern pyramid there are usually nine pairs of flat, unadorned stelae and altars, whereas, on the perpendicular axis to the south, there is a long, low building, usually with nine doors, and to the north an enclosure entered through a doorway in the form of a Maya arch: the enclosure contains a pair of sculpted monoliths, the stela of which depicts the ruling prince in the ritual pose of the sower.

In 682, the prince ascended the throne of Yaxchilán: possibly a usurper from the area of Puuc in the north-east of the Yucatán peninsula, he, and his successor, gave the art of Yaxchilán a particularly sensual quality.

At about the same time, the prince Pacal completed the construction of his secret mausoleum in the Temple of the Inscriptions at Palenque, where he would be buried amid great pomp in 684. The founder of a line of princes who were patrons of the arts, Pacal was perhaps the first to make the city of Palenque a truly revolutionary phenomenon on the Maya artistic scene, which, orchestrated mainly from Tikal, had until then dominated practically the whole of the Maya area. The architecture produced at Palenque in those years – the purest expression of which would be the three temples in the 'group of the Cross' – appears to be the logical outcome of a series of challenges to the architectural traditions that had prevailed up to that time in the Maya lowlands.

The battlements, light but solid in design, rise directly out of the middle wall, thereby giving greater scope for width and flexibility to the two lengthwise corridors. The downward thrust is reduced by all possible means (integral niches, transverse vaulting, thin walls, wide openings, upper moulding running parallel to the intrados of the vault, and so on); and the final result is a building that is both light and elegant, combining structural logic and solidity with a number of aesthetic achievements and great refinement. The battlements and mouldings and the main façade are covered with delicate modelled stucco reliefs; in the inner sanctuary, built into the rear wall, a number of large stones worked in fine relief – which here replace the above-mentioned monolithic stelae – tell of the reigning dynasty, its religious beliefs and its cult of ancestor worship.

The year 692, which was particularly significant for the arts, also marked, in the field of science, the introduction of the calculation of lunar months, with the glyphic dates at Copán. This event, together with the customary observations of the movements of the Sun and Venus, gave Maya astronomical calculations (which Copán had been improving since the sixth century) a degree of accuracy that placed Maya astronomy far above the level achieved at that time by the rest of the world. The Maya tropical year, as calculated by the astronomer-priests of Copán, was 365.2420 days long, a surprisingly accurate figure differing by only 3/10,000 of a day per year from our modern calculations.

The eighth century began at Tikal with the construction of Temple I (also called the Temple of the Giant Jaguar from a motif carved in wood on one of the interior lintels). This monument epitomizes the architecture of that city, which represents the culmination of the trend towards the vertical that had been visible centuries earlier and which was accentuated by such features as the recessed angles of the base and the majestic battlements towards the rear of the temple.

The delicacy of the bas-reliefs at Palenque, the exuberance of the free-standing and attached sculpture of Copán, not to mention the proper feeling for composition and the sensual relief of Piedras Negras and Yaxchilán, make the sculptural production of the central Maya area during the eighth century, by its sheer diversity and scale, one of the artistic high points of the pre-Columbian world.

Curiously, in spite of the fact that Teotihuacán was in steady decline by that time, its cultural influence shone again with renewed brilliance in the Maya area. And just as many Teotihuacán iconographic features appeared (such as the 'sign of the year' or the mask of Tláloc) among the attributes and regalia of numerous princes, so, too, architectural bases were constructed with more or less literal versions of the *talud-tablero* motif of Teotihuacán.

Wall painting achieved surprising heights at Bonampak. The sense of composition in certain scenes (only observable in outstanding pieces of sculpture such as Stela 12 or Lintel 3 at Piedras Negras) combined with the lifelike quality of many postures and a particularly warm and vibrant palette, place the master of Bonampak in a category apart (see Plate 296). To all of the above must be added finely executed pottery, often covered with what amounts to a mythical world in miniature, and delicate objects carved in wood, bone, jade and other semi-precious stones.

At the risk of oversimplification, it may be said that the finest Maya art in the central area was produced during the eighth century. Palenque, for instance, produced its stucco reliefs in the palace and its 'scribe's tablet'; Toniná its free-standing sculptures of captives; Yaxchilán its finest stone lintels; Piedras Negras the impressive sequence of stelae turned out during each *hotún* (or period of five ritual years of 360 days) for a period of more than two centuries without interruption; Copán its finest stelae, its altars and its attached sculptures; Quiriguá its colossal, elaborate monoliths, either stelae or the famous 'zoomorphs', a real 'tropical nightmare' (see Plates 92, 93, 294, 295, 297).

While participating to a much lesser degree in the 'cult of the stela' which had taken such a hold further south, the northern Maya area made a remarkable contribution to the enrichment of the Maya repertoire, especially in the areas of architecture and attached sculpture, in which it adopted plans tending more towards the geometric, with sharper outlines, calling on artists with a less suave technique. There were two main centres of development in the Yucatán peninsula from the seventh century on, if not earlier: the regions of Río Bec and Puuc.

The Río Bec style produced the strange 'tower complexes' (as in the well-known Temple B or Río Bec B) between the seventh and eighth centuries and created the most fantastic portals in the form of snake jaws (as in Building II at Chicanná and Hormiguero or – in the region of Los Chenes, further north – the main buildings at Hochob and Tabasqueño). The architecture of the Puuc region underwent a more complex series of metamorphoses, producing, towards the beginning of the eighth century, architectural styles dominated by colonnaded porticos (a feature which is virtually absent from classical Maya architecture further south) and finding diverse uses for the Maya vault, which, besides covering interior spaces, here generates passageways running under stairways or forms the admirable monumental arches such as those at Kabah, Labná and Uxmal. The architecture produced by these same cities in a 'peninsular' synthesis between the end of the ninth and the middle of the tenth centuries (that is, at an exceptionally late date) expresses one of the most outstanding styles ever produced in Mesoamerica and the last of the Classic Maya world. We need only mention, in this connection, such examples as the Codz-Poop at Kabah, the arch at Labná, the Nuns' Quadrangle and the Governor's Palace at Uxmal, where a sure touch in the handling of volumes is combined with rich and well-balanced sculptural ornament.

It should be noted that, at the time when Puuc was experiencing its most creative period, the rest of the Maya world practically without exception had already fallen into decline. Evidence of elements foreign to the traditions that had dominated the Maya lowlands until that period appeared at Palenque as early as 799, in 810 at Polol, and between 849 and 889 at Seibal. And, as signs of cultural hybridization made their appearance, so the Maya cities, one after the other, ceased to erect stelae and other date-bearing monuments at regular intervals, as they had done for centuries past, thus marking the beginning of the end: Copán (801), Yaxchilán (807), Piedras Negras and Quiriguá (810), Oxkintok (869), Jimbal and Uaxactún (889). It is particularly significant, in this context, that whereas nineteen Maya cities erected monuments bearing dates in order to commemorate the end of a *katún* (9.18.0.0.0) in 790, only twelve were continuing to observe the practice in 810 (9.19.0.0.0); and the decline proceeded rapidly, with only three monuments being inaugurated at the start of *baktún* 10 (10.0.0.0.0). The end came in 909 (10.4.0.0.0) with only two known dates in the outlying sites of Toniná (Chiapas) and Dzibalchén (Quintana Roo).

It is no easy matter to form a cultural assessment of this Classic Maya period. Beyond the dazzling effect of the arts there is our admiration for the special ability of the Maya to deduce a coherent system from astronomical observation, which not only includes one of the two known forms of zero but also achieves surprising precision in the calculation of the solar year and launches into incredible feats of speculation such as the calculation of the occultations of the planet Venus in periods of millions of years! Aside from its intrinsic beauty, the Dresden Codex is also eloquent in this respect.

The few Maya codices that survived the Spanish Conquest have enlightened us as to certain aspects of the beliefs of the ancient Maya between the end of the Classic period and the arrival of the *conquistadores*. Thus, a page from the Troano Codex clearly shows the cyclic conception of phenomena so deeply rooted in Mesoamerican thinking: first we see the rain god Chac tending a plant; next comes Ah Puch, the god of death, uprooting the same plant. Such was the inexorable – and essential – cycle of life and death, seen as two facets of the same reality. Similarly, on the fantastic, monster-laden portals (which, like the one at Chicanná, are apparently related to the cult of Itzamná the creator), signs of life and death alternate with celestial, terrestrial and underworld symbols in an unending and awesome struggle of opposites and complementary aspects.

With certain variations according to region, we see in Maya monumental art the procession of many of the gods of a colourful pantheon. Kinich Ahau, the Sun god, stands out among the large stucco masques of Kohunlich; the central finial of the Stairway of the Jaguars at Copán is the face of the god of the planet Venus, while fine busts of singing youths emerge from opening flowers on the frieze of Temple 22 in the same city: incarnations of the young maize god. In Yucatán, where water is in short supply, the obsessive cult of the rain god was translated in the Codz Poop at Kabah into the litany-like repetition over the entire façade of hundreds of large masks of Chac with his wide, hooked nose.

Whereas the cult of Chac was very popular, especially in the northern Maya area, some deities were more esoteric than others and must have remained the near exclusive preserve of a certain power-holding elite, since they are frequently associated with the attributes of Chac (as the 'god of the mannikin-sceptre'). Thus, in Palenque, the throne-room (or House E) has as an ornamental border a 'heavenly host' that turns into a two-headed monster; and guarding the tomb of king Pacal are the *Bolontikuu*, or 'nine lords of the night'. Some themes, such as the 'maize tree' (or 'tree of life') at Palenque, are almost exclusively local. There is also a legion of mythological beings (often identifiable with legends of more recent periods) which populate monuments, ritual ceramic ware, codices and other objects. In the absence of written sources which might help us to understand this fascinating Classic world, efforts have been made to interpret it by analogy with oral traditions collected, like the *Popol Vuh*, in the last century: the legendary narratives of those traditions appear to refer on occasion to scenes that are represented in the art of the Classic period. At the same time, there are various indications that many cultural traits disappeared with the collapse of the Classic world. Thus, of the complex system for calculating dates known as the Long Count, only a simplified and much less accurate version, the Short Count, remained on the eve of the Spanish Conquest.

Whatever the many and complex reasons for the Maya collapse, the clear point revealed by archaeology is that, by the beginning of the tenth century – the beginning of the Post-classic period – all the Maya cities in the southern lowlands had been abandoned, save a few Puuc cities (such as Uxmal and Chichén Itzá) (see Plate 298). From that time on, apart from several isolated late settlements such as Tayasal on Lake Flores or Topozté on Lake Yaxhá, this trend would be confined to two main areas: the southern Maya area (particularly the Guatemalan highlands, where the *Tohil Plomiza* pottery was produced, the most famous of the Toltec period, with its anthropomorphic and zoomorphic vases and its peculiar metallic lustre due to the graphite in the clay) and the northern part of the Yucatán peninsula together with the coastal strip from Campeche to Quintana Roo.

Chichén Itzá, which had developed from the end of the Classic period under Puuc influence, spanned the first half of the Post-classic period (from the end of the tenth century to the beginning of the thirteenth), representing the last great pre-Hispanic development: the so-called 'Maya–Toltec episode' which, according to the oral traditions of the Mexican high plateau, was brought about by a Toltec contingent from far-off Tula led by the legendary man-god Quetzalcóatl. Some modern authors see in the new Chichén Itzá much more than a simple Toltec 'colony' in Maya territory and assign it a more active role in the gestation of the Toltec phenomenon. Be that as it may, there is a strong element of cultural hybridization in which the warlike and bloodthirsty Toltec repertoire is combined to varying degrees with the great Maya architectural tradition inherited from Puuc. The monumental architecture with its attached sculpture reflects every level of hybridization. The characteristics of an astronomical observatory, which we sense in so many other buildings or architectural ensembles of the Classic period, are clearly visible in the case of the Caracol. And gold discs depicting struggles between the two ethnic groups stand out among the gold jewellery found in the Sacred Cenote (or well) alongside some zoomorphic pieces in the Coclé style brought from Panamá.

Mayapán, which became the dominant city after Chichén Itzá from 1224 to 1461, is in many respects no more than a very poor copy of the latter, although it endeavoured in vain to revive some of the old Maya traditions of the golden age, such as the erection of date-bearing stelae and the arrangement of buildings in quadrangles. However, the practice of the Long Count had long been abandoned in favour of a simplified but less precise system known as the Short Count. On the other hand, the beliefs and ancient prophecies survived in oral tradition, which was so deeply rooted in those regions: assembled under the title of the Books of *Chilam Balam*, they constitute one of the most important indigenous sources of documentation. In architecture and the other branches of the arts, however, nothing could curb the gradual degeneration, which reached such a stage that, scarcely one century after the fall of Mayapán, when the Spaniards embarked on the conquest of Yucatán, they found the entire peninsula in a state of complete cultural and political chaos; only some small towns on the Caribbean coast of Quintana Roo, such as Tulum, appear to have escaped this chaos, but their pleasant appearance masks a poverty of execution and a cramped use of space which clearly reflect the cultural level of the age. This did not prevent the island of Cozumel from being at the time one of the most renowned centres of pilgrimage of the Maya area, with its sanctuary dedicated to Ixchel, the companion of Itzamna, goddess of the Moon and patroness of medicine and childbirth.

At the time when Yucatán was rent by the rivalries of a string of decadent small states, the Guatemalan highlands at the other extremity of the Maya area constituted the other hub of a civilization which was still alive, if relatively decadent and hybrid in several respects. This region, which had played a decisive role during the formative period and which, after producing at Kaminaljuyú a real Teotihuacán enclave, had only participated to a limited extent in the splendour of the Maya Classic period, none the less succeeded in creating an interesting cultural centre in Santa Lucía Cotzumalhuapa, apparently inspired to some extent by Teotihuacán elements. The successive migrations would later highlight a gradual process of 'Mexicanization', until the fortified cities of the age (such as Iximché, Mixco Viejo and Cahyup), with their twin temples and their broad stairways divided into short flights through the succession of vertical (*tablero*) and inclined (*talud*) volumes presented more similarities with the Chichimec and Aztec traditions then ruling on the central Mexican plateau than with the old Classic Maya traditions of the lowlands. The Quiché and other warlike peoples of the Guatemala highlands, aware and also proud of their distant Mexican descent, did not therefore cease to boast of their ancient Maya cultural extraction, of which they preserved a very lively oral tradition; two of the finest jewels in that tradition, the *Popol Vuh* and the marvellous epic poem *Rabinal Achi*, were collected during the last century.

THE GULF COAST

The non-Maya Mesoamerican Gulf coast is usually divided into three fairly distinct areas: the northern or Huastec area, extending approximately from the Soto de la Marina River in the north to the Cazones River in the south; the central area, from the Cazones River to the Papaloapan River; and the southern area, reaching as far as the Tonalá River.

The northern area

At the time of the Conquest this area was inhabited by speakers of Huastec, a member of the Maya language family. At one time they may have occupied the central Gulf Coast, eventually being cut off from the Maya area by the intrusion of other linguistic groups – Totonacs and Nahuas. Very little archaeological excavation has been carried out in the area. As with other Mesoamerican regions, the Post-classic horizon can be divided into Early (900–1200) and Late (1200–1500) periods.

The Early Post-classic period (900–1200) shows evidence of central Mexican Toltec expansion into the area, as can be seen by the ceramics at sites such as Castillo de Teayo. This site has a stepped pyramid 11 m high with a staircase facing north-west and the remains of a temple on top. The construction material consisted of irregular stones using lime and sand mortar. Outstanding stones on the body were used to hold a thick layer of stucco in place. Little archaeology has been carried out at this site because it is mostly covered by a modern town. Another impressive city is Cacahuatenco. It has a great number of pyramids of which one, El Castillo, which is 45 m at the base, bears some resemblance to the pyramid of El Castillo at Chichén Itzá in Yucatán.

Round buildings are characteristic of this area, perhaps the best examples being from the sites of Tamuín and Las Flores. Also typical are a variety of carved shell objects: bracelets, miniature human skulls, earplugs, and gorgets, the last two with finely incised representations of the culture hero Quetzalcóatl.

Notable also is large stone statuary. Representations of humans with conical hats, pyramidal skirts and realistic facial features, were carved in low relief on limestone slabs, only the head being carved in the round. On the back of some of these statues is the representation of a cranium. The arms and legs of these statues are covered with low-relief carving, indicating the use of scarification. The most outstanding sculpture is 'the adolescent', which was carved in the round; it is 1.45 m high, naked, showing the genitals, and carries a baby on its back. Both arms and the right leg are covered with low-relief carving. Finely carved and intentionally slightly crooked stelae with symbols relating to Quetzalcóatl are typical.

It is possible that many of the Early Post-classic period traits continue into the Late Post-classic period (1200–1500); however, the most salient new feature occurs in ceramics. Effigy vessels in a white ware painted with reddish-brown or black motifs are characteristic, many of them having stirrup spouts. The painting is used to emphasize facial features; the motifs, combinations of rectangles, circles, and triangles have been compared to the motifs on Anasazi pottery of the south-west United States; however the vessel forms are different.

The central area

The Early Post-classic period (900–1200) is the florescent period of El Tajín, the largest known pre-Hispanic city on the Gulf Coast from any period, and one of the largest in Mesoamerica. Its architectural style, based on inverted slopes, cornices, niches, panels of 'greek' key-patterns, large open windows, and flat roofs of up to 85 cm thick without needing any kind of internal reinforcement, spreads over more than 10 km^2 of hills covered with dense rain forest. El Tajín and Cholula share the interesting distinction of being the two major Classic-horizon cities that were not abandoned by 900. However, while Cholula was still a major centre at the time of the Spanish conquest, El Tajín had been abandoned by 1200.

Major constructions were carried out at El Tajín during this period: a building with seven columns 1.10 m in diameter covered with bas-reliefs; the South Ball Court, containing six panels of very finely carved bas-reliefs depicting personages and ballplayers, and decorated with scrolls, a style which is shared with the decoration found on *palmas*, yokes, and axeheads, objects which may be related in some way to the ball game because they are shown on the panels, as were tunnels connecting various parts of the site.

Yohualinchán is another large site that has much in common with El Tajín. There are many sites which have ball courts, tunnels, pyramids and large platforms: Paxil, Aparicio, Cerro Montoso, Isla de Sacrificios, the earliest period of Zempoala, the last period of Xiuhtetelco, Cuetlaxtlán and Upper Cerro de las Mesas.

As in many other parts of Mesoamerica, this period is identified by Toltec traits, especially ceramics such as Mazapa-ware plates decorated with multiple parallel wavy red lines. A fine orange ware in the form of flower vases with pedestal bases, probably produced locally, is widely distributed throughout the area and other parts of Mesoamerica. A glazed variety of the fine orange ware has been found at Isla de Sacrificios.

Although the really large sites such at El Tajín, Yohualinchán, and Xiuhtetelco were abandoned by the Late Post-classic period, by this time the overall number of sites had increased notably. At the time of the Spanish conquest there was one large city: Zempoala, the last Totonac capital. The chronicler Bernal Díaz del Castillo calculated its population at 30,000 inhabitants and marvelled at its wide streets and shining houses. The city extends over 5 km^2 of the coastal plain. Only the central part of the city has been excavated, where ten groups of buildings have been uncovered. Among these are a pyramid with thirteen levels, various smaller pyramids and a round structure made out of merlons, which also decorate the top of various other buildings.

The name 'Zempoala' means 'abundance of water', and this is evident in the city's sophisticated water supply system. Aqueducts carried water to stone-lined underground canals, which branched throughout the city. The system employed for supplying houses with water consisted in a slightly inclined canal leading to a house reservoir, while another canal led out of it towards another house, and so on. Once the last house had been supplied, the channel leading out of it was directed to an irrigation canal.

Towards the end of this period, strong central Mexican influence is evident in both ceramics and architecture. Polychrome ceramics, alabaster vessels and cruciform tombs pertaining to the Puebla–Mixteca complex, centred at Cholula, are found at many sites, from Zempoala southwards to the area called the Mixtequilla. At Quautochco, there is an Aztec style pyramid of four levels.

WEST MEXICO

The term 'West Mexico' has traditionally been applied to the area covering the present states of Nayarit, Sinaloa, Jalisco, Colima, Michoacán, and parts of Guanajuato, Querétaro and Guerrero. The area cannot be characterized in terms of a cultural tradition due to the lack of adequate exploration; only a handful of archaeological sites have been excavated. Most of the characteristics of the Classic horizon (100/300 to 900) of central and southern Mesoamerica are either not present or their presence is at best patchy in West Mexico. Evidence is lacking for an Olmec base during the Pre-classic horizon, the dual calendar system of 260 and 365 days, writing, and urbanism. Except for Tingambato, a site in Michoacán that has a Teotihuacán-like layout, the use of stone masonry in building is quite scanty. While in central and southern Mesoamerica there is a clear break between the Pre-classic village organization and Classic urbanism between 100 and 300, in West Mexico no such change is evident. Whether this is due to lack of exploration or whether it just does not occur, it has given rise to much discussion concerning the relationship of this area to the rest of Mesoamerica, either as a marginal part of the greater culture area, which did not develop at the same rate, or as an entirely different culture area.

During the Post-classic horizon (900–1521), contacts with central Mexico are more notorious. This horizon is divided into two periods: the Early and Late Post-classic. The first of these is identified mainly by the appearance of Toltec traits from central Mexico, while the second is identified primarily with the Tarascan empire centred in Michoacán.

In the Early Post-classic (900–1220), metallurgy makes it appearance in Mesoamerica. Its earliest appearance occurs in the southern area of West Mexico, in the Balsas river drainage, around 700–800. Shortly thereafter, during the Early Post-classic period, it spreads throughout West Mexico and the rest of Mesoamerica. Hammered copper bells and rings have been found at various sites such as Tizapán el Alto and Amapa, while beads made of iron pyrite have been uncovered as far north as Amapa on the north-west Pacific coast.

At this time, Toltec expansion reached all corners of West Mexico. The evidence for this consists mostly of ceramic wares such as Plumbate, Fine Orange bowls and vases, red-on-brown painted plates called *Coyotlatelco,* globular jars with criss-crossing brushed white lines, and flat clay figurines which are characteristic of Tula, the Toltec capital, in the central highlands. Alabaster and polychrome ceramic vessels in the Mixteca–Puebla style, from the east and south-east of the Valley of Mexico, have been found as far north as Sinaloa, bordering on an area which is definitely no longer Mesoamerican. A large variety of ceramics indigenous to the area, including cloisonné, incised wares, polychromes, bichromes and plain wares complete the ceramic picture.

Prismatic obsidian blades, grinding stones, mortars, ground stone palettes, clay spindle whorls, and turquoise mosaics are widespread.

Burial customs are not as well known from West Mexico as from other areas of Mesoamerica. One outstanding feature of this period seems to be the disappearance of shaft tombs, characteristic of earlier periods. Primary flexed and sitting burials are known from Tizapán el Alto, and incineration of the dead on platforms from Amapa.

Both public buildings and houses appear to have been made out of wattle-and-daub, and often built on top of small earthern mounds. It is not until the Late Post-classic period that masonry is more common.

During the Late Post-classic period at the site of Ixtlán del Río, in Nayarit, a round stone platform with twin temples on top which are surrounded by a wall with cross-shaped openings, has been excavated. The site also has an extensive habitation zone and an obsidian workshop.

The largest known sites from this period outside the Tarascan sphere of influence are El Chanal in Colima and San Blas in Nayarit. The ceremonial centre of El Chanal, which is of urban dimensions, has five large pyramids with staircases and, possibly, a ball court. Clay figurines of dancers and warriors, as well as the burnt bones of over 100 individuals, have been found. Numerous petroglyphs, including one representation of the rain god Tlaloc, have been located, including some on the stones used to build the pyramids. Objects of copper, silver and gold occur in burial offerings. At San Blas, sites of up to 500,000 m^2 have been located, one with as many as 246 mounds. Located as they were by the sea, a large portion of the diet of the inhabitants seems to have consisted of oysters. Petroglyphs were also found here.

The Tarascan kingdom

The best-known culture of West Mexico is the Tarascan kingdom. With successive capitals at the cities of Zirahuen, Patzcuaro, Ihuatzio and Tzintzuntzan, the Tarascans dominated most of the present state of Michoacán and parts of Guanajuato, Querétaro and Guerrero. Their culture is described in several sixteenth-century Spanish sources. Their history, prior to the Late Post-classic period, is unknown. Perhaps this is due to insufficient archaeological reconnaissance, but at the moment they seem to appear on the Mesoamerican scene suddenly, without any antecedents. Their language is not related to any other Mesoamerican language; its closest relative, according to linguists, is Quechua, the language spoken by the Incas of the central Andes. The Aztecs attempted to conquer the Tarascans but failed miserably in a historic battle at Tajimaroa, an eastern Tarascan outpost.

Little is known of the Tarascans outside the Patzcuaro lake area. Here the economy depended to a large extent on the lake. Like their language, the architecture of their ceremonial buildings is unique to Mesoamerica. At Tzintzuntzan, they built what are called *yácatas*, which consist of several combined rectangular and circular stepped buildings placed on top of a very large rectangular platform. At Ihuatzio, the ceremonial centre consists of twin pyramids, side by side, with a large quadrangle in front of them; this is slightly reminiscent of the Aztec pyramids, which have two staircases leading to twin temples.

Tarascan sculpture and stonemasonry is crude compared with other arts and crafts where they excelled, such as paper-thin obsidian cylinders and highly polished obsidian noseplugs. They were gifted metallurgists, specializing in hammered copper. To this day a town across the lake from Patzcuaro, Santa Clara del Cobre, depends almost entirely on this craft. Gold was also worked.

Tarascan ceramics are among the finest of pre-Hispanic Mesoamerica. Beautiful black-on-red wares and black, red, white, and yellow polychromes of a great plastic variety: double bowls, kidney-shaped plates, stirrup handles, pitchers and pipes are outstanding.

BIBLIOGRAPHY

BERNAL, I. 1965. Archaeological Synthesis of Oaxaca. *Handbook of Middle American Indians*, Vol. III, Part 2, pp. 788–813. Austin, Texas.

CASO, A. 1969. *El tesoro de Monte Albán.* INAH, Mexico.

COE, M. D. 1966. *The Maya.* New York.

COVARRUBIAS, M. 1956. *Indian Art of Mexico and Central America.* New York.

CULBERT, T. P. (ed.) 1973. *The Classic Maya Collapse.* Albuquerque, New Mexico.

DAVIS, N. 1973. *The Aztecs: A History.* Norman, Oklahoma.

FLANNERY, K.; MARCUS, J. (eds) 1983. *The Cloud People: Divergent Evolution of the Zapotec and Mixtec Civilizations.* New York.

GENDROP, P. 1978. *Les Mayas. 'Que Sais-Je?'*, Paris.

——. 1983. *Los estilos Río Bec. Chenes y Puuc en la arquitectura maya.* UNAM, Mexico.

MOSER, C. L. 1977. *Nuiñe Writing and Iconography of the Mixteca Baja.* Nashville, Tennessee.

PADDOCK, J. (ed.) 1966. *Ancient Oaxaca: Discoveries in Mexican Archaeology and History.* Stanford, California.

THOMPSON, J. E. 1970. *Maya History and Religion.* Norman, Oklahoma.

——. 1977. *The Toltecs, Until the Fall of Tula.* Norman, Oklahoma.

38.2
CENTRAL AMERICA

Wolfgang Haberland

Central America was culturally part of a larger entity occupying the space between the central Andes in the south and Mesoamerica to the north (see Map 41). Central America borders on Mesoamerica. The boundaries here, rather impermanent and vague, are thought to be the Río Jiboa in central El Salvador and the Río Uloa in western Honduras. Its southern boundary is placed in the Atrato Depression of north-western Colombia. Central America, therefore, comprises the present states of Panama, Costa Rica and Nicaragua, as well as eastern El Salvador and most of Honduras.

Geographically, Central America is a narrow land bridge between the Caribbean Sea and the Pacific Ocean. Its interior is mountainous; except for Panama, it is dominated by numerous and often still active volcanoes. The Pacific coastal strip is frequently narrow, interrupted by mountain spurs jutting out from the interior.In contrast to this, the plains

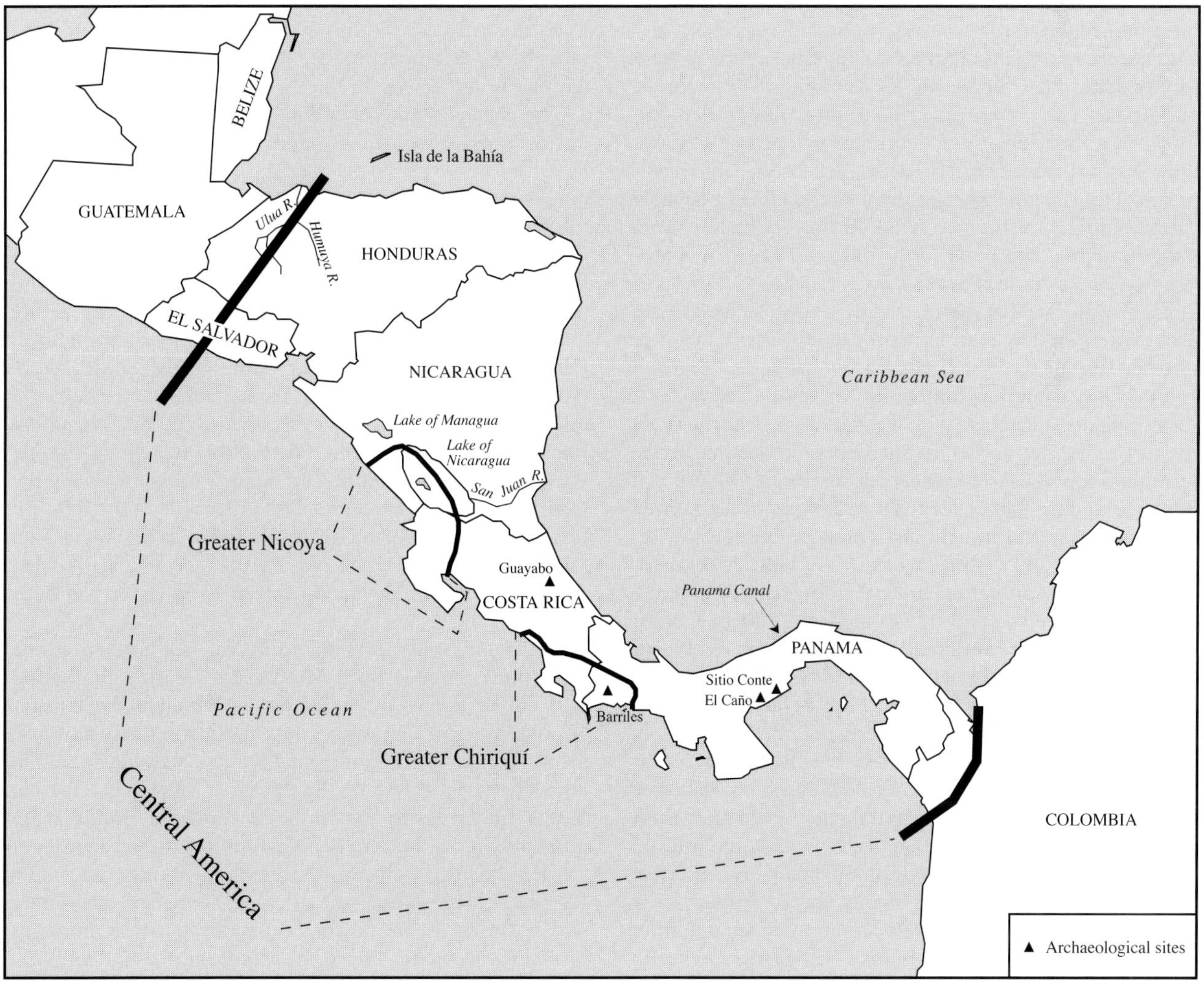

Map 41 Central America (Haberland, W.; Schmidt, P.).

along the Caribbean coast are, with the exception of central Panama, wide and continuous. This compartmented landscape gave rise to very different climatic and ecological conditions and made communication difficult.

Central American history, before 1500, can only be reconstructed by archaeological means, rarely supplemented by controversial accounts of early colonial times. The Caribbean coast is largely unexplored, there being large regions along the Pacific coast and in the interior which are unknown or have been only superficially investigated. Therefore, our understanding of the developments, influences and migrations are based on rather flimsy grounds. They will certainly be subject to serious revision in the future. Also hampering our understanding is the nature of the Central American cultural entities and political units: there are neither overall cultural links nor cultural spheres covering most or all of Central America. More often cultural units are rather small, due both to the broken nature of the landscape and to the various external influences.

The period around 700 was a time of upheaval. The old order disappeared, less through internal causes than through outside influence and pressure. This old order had developed through many centuries and was specifically Central American in its expression. Economically, its many and diverse cultures were based on maize agriculture, with beans, cucurbits and sweet manioc as other important cultigens. Diet was supplemented by root and tree crops, collecting wild foods, hunting and, where possible, by fishing and mollusk collecting. Slash-and-burn agriculture was present, but in the highly fertile volcanic soils of the northern and central sections of Central America, long fallow periods were not necessary.

That gave rise to permanent fields, and villages therefore remained settled for several centuries. A long and copious rainy season made irrigation unnecessary. No large states existed. The most we can infer are small chiefdoms, probably not exceeding a few villages. No detectable 'capitals' existed at that time. An exception to this rule was Panama, where ceremonial centres such as El Caño in Coclé and Barriles in Chiriquí were present. Here, a higher political order may have existed. In Coclé, the heads of these petty states were buried in lavishly furnished graves, accompanied by gold and slaves. The contemporary burials of chiefs in Nicoya (Costa Rica) contained a set of special stone objects: elaborately carved seats of power (often erroneously called *metates*), mace heads, and greenstone pendants, all signs of rank. We can therefore assume that at least the beginning of a stratified society was present throughout Central America.

Technologically, stone work was well developed, including statues in central and western Panama and the already mentioned seats of power in Greater Nicoya. Most of the ceramics were well made and elaborately decorated with incising, modelling, stamping, and so on. Painting was restricted to bi- and trichromes. True polychromes were only present in central Panama. Here, too, metal, especially gold, was used and manufactured (see Plate 308). This knowledge, as well as the polychromy and the more elaborate political structures, may reflect influence from the south (Colombia). Religious beliefs are not yet well understood. Burials, with their grave goods, point to belief in an afterlife. Female clay figurines, often sitting spread-legged, may represent fertility goddesses, while paintings and/or sculptures of animals or animal-headed human beings may represent other deities or 'masters of animals'. Among them, the alligator or its derivations ('dragons') are especially prominent (see Plates 309–310). Shamans rather than priests administered to the spiritual needs and corporal ailments.

The first change ocurred in the south. About 600, the Barú volcano in Chiriquí erupted, putting an end to the Aguas Buenas (or Bugaba) culture, which had flourished since about 700 BC. Somewhat later, cultures vaguely related to those in central Panama established themselves in Greater Chiriquí (Chiriquí province in Panama, Valle del General, Diquis, and Osa peninsula in Costa Rica), bringing with them, among other items, polychrome pottery and, perhaps, metallurgy. This 'Classic Chiriquí' culture, as well as its contemporaries in central Panama (the eastern part is scarcely known), existed till the advent of Europeans. The central Panamanian cultures continued in the same vein as before 700, but were gradually impoverished, perhaps by the loss of their gold manufacturing monopoly. At the time of the Conquest a rather large number of petty principalities existed along the Pacific coast. Their territories often extended into the interior, sometimes up to the continental divide, thus integrating different ecological regions and establishing economically self-sufficient entities.

Warfare was endemic and resulted in the ascendancy of a privileged warrior class. Another consequence was the fortification of the main settlements by log palisades and, sometimes, ditches. These settlements, of up to 1,500 inhabitants, consisted of round buildings with log or cane walls and conical thatched roofs. No permanent stone buildings were present, perhaps due to the fact that most of the larger settlements were situated on the coastal plains. Even the 'palaces' of the rulers seem to have been nothing more than enlarged houses. Whether there were special temples is unknown.

The change at the other end of Central America, that is, its north-western part, was spurred not, as far as we know, by natural causes but by invasions from Mesoamerica, perhaps the result of the changes taking place in Central Mexico at this time, that is, the fall of the Teotihuacán empire or trade network. The catastrophic third-century eruption of the Ilopango, which made about 10,000 km^2 in central and western El Salvador uninhabitable for centuries, had already disrupted the age old trading route from Mexico and highland Guatemala along the Pacific shore. New routes were established, one following the Uloa drainage, especially the Río Humuya to the Río Guascorán, which drains into the Fonseca Bay of the Pacific coast and hence along the old coastal route to the south. The other was by boat along the Caribbean coast of Honduras and Nicaragua to the Río San Juan and up that river to Greater Nicoya and the Costa Rican highlands. After 600, the old trails along the Pacific were reopened after the devasted areas of El Salvador had been resettled.

Archaeologically and historically, the first group to arrive in Central America from Mesoamerica during the period under discussion were the Chorotega, who settled in Greater Nicoya (Nicoya Peninsula and Guanacaste in Costa Rica, isthmus of Rivas and Ometepe Island in Nicaragua) around 800. They probably came by the Uloa route, since the Las Vegas polychrome ceramics of central Honduras are intimately related to the Papagayo polychrome ceramics of Greater Nicoya. Polychrome ceramic painting, often on a whitish or beige background, is, together with some pottery shapes and motifs, the most obvious innovation the Chorotega brought with them. Among the motifs, animals and mythical beings like the feathered serpent, the jaguar and the turkey point to the north. The latter might even have been introduced at that time to Central America. Other innovations are not as clear cut: Chorotega might have initiated secondary urn burials in Greater Nicoya, but it was obviously popular only in the northern (Nicaraguan) parts, as was the brushing of the exterior surface of domestic pottery, shoe-shaped vessels, and life-sized stone statues of human and mythical beings. The reasons for the differences between northern and southern Greater Nicoya are not yet understood.

In any case, it was probably only a rather small group of immigrants that arrived in Greater Nicoya and blended peacefully with the old inhabitants, gradually producing a culture or number of cultures containing elements of Mesoamerican as well as Central American origin, sometimes mixed with yet unexplained components. The fact that no 'higher level' in the economic and/or political sphere was attained is specially striking: agricultural activities did not change; in some places they even seem to have diminished, as along the Bahia de Culebra where mollusk collecting attained greater importance than ever before. Politically, small chiefdoms continued, without any indication of a 'supreme chief' directing all or most of the people living in Greater Nicoya. This 'stagnation' in significant sections of culture can only be explained through economic factors: the older 'Central American' inhabitants had already attained a stage of optimal exploitation of their surroundings, which even the influx of new people and new ideas could not improve.

This perseverance of a rather early stage of political development was also significant for all other known cultures in Central America. Slash-and-burn agriculture with maize, beans, cucurbits and, in some places, manioc as staples continued, supplemented by other root and tree crops. Gathering of nuts, fruits and so on, as well as molluscs, continued, as did hunting and fishing. No large towns, stone houses or tall pyramids were constructed. The only artificial hills – with one exception – are low burial mounds, occurring especially in central Costa Rica and Greater Chiriquí. They contain large numbers of individual burials, sometimes in stone-walled and/or stone-roofed graves. Retaining walls and stone markers, sometimes carved, are further elements of these mounds. Crafts such as pottery making, stone cutting, and weaving were obviously part-time occupations and not the work of specialists. There might, however, have been some exceptions: metalworking, particularly in gold, which gradually spread north from central Panama to at least the Costa Rican highlands and perhaps even to the southern part of Greater Nicoya, was pursued by itinerant professionals, travelling from one 'court' to another, manufacturing the ornaments to order. Some pottery, like the thin, well-fired and standardized San Miguel bisquit of Greater Chiriquí, may also have been produced by specialists, but this was certainly the exception.

Politically, Central America continued to be fragmented into numerous petty chiefdoms, often at war with one another. No larger states existed, nor were there any known attempts to create one. The dissected landscape is often cited as a reason for the failure of such states to arise, but this is a weak argument since it did not prevent the rise of larger political structures in Mesoamerica. Rather, an absence of tasks necessitating the co-operation of large numbers of people, like the creation of irrigation systems or raised fields, none of which have been found up to date in Central America, may have been the determinant for the lack of higher political organization. Whatever the reason, Central America remained a rather crazy quilt of chiefdoms and diverse, loosely linked cultures.

Trade inside Central America, as well as with the adjoining areas, played a significant role in the dissemination of ideas and techniques. Gold objects and techniques had already been introduced to Panama from Colombia before the time under discussion, from where it spread north. This first one-sided trade later became a two-sided affair, with Colombian gold objects reaching Costa Rica, while Panamanian gold work was found as far south as the Cauca valley. This trade, more or less restricted to the Pacific side of the isthmus, was brisk, with foreign styles often so 'fashionable' that local copies were made and even exported further along the line: Panamanian copies of so-called 'Darien pendants' ended up in the Cenote of Chichén Itzá. What else was traded between Panama and Colombia is still a matter of discussion, not the least because of our very limited knowledge about the archaeology of eastern Panama (the Darien gap). There is, furthermore, a feeling that other, stronger influences (even migrations) from South America reached far into Central America, travelling perhaps along the still widely unexplored Caribbean coast. They may be responsible for a number of yet unexplained phenomena. One of these concerns Guayabo de Turrialba and related sites on the Atlantic slope of central Costa Rica. This settlement contains groups of low, circular and truncated pyramids, certainly the substructures of dwellings. They are stone-faced, are ascended by stairs or ramps and face rectangular courts. Cobblestone roads, stone bridges and subterranean water conducts are other elements of these settlements. They are unique in Central America and remind one strongly of Tairona villages in the Sierra Nevada de Santa Marta of Colombia, but no direct connections have been established. Also the last intrusion on Ometepe Island, Nicaragua, dated around 1400, has, ceramically, a strong South American feeling, but again proof is lacking.

That knowledge of faraway regions was present is shown by the fact that the first news the Spaniards obtained about the Inca Empire of Peru came from inhabitants of Panama, including a description of llamas. Some stone and ceramic sculptures from Greater Chiriquí and Costa Rica may even depict this animal, which never lived in Central America.

Trade with Mesoamerica continued all the time along the routes outlined above. Tohil Plumbate pottery from Pacific Guatemala has been found in Greater Nicoya and Las Vegas, and polychrome ceramics from central Honduras in Tula, central Mexico. Shortly after 700, the first gold objects were introduced into southern Mesoamerica (Copán, Tazumal) from Costa Rica. Around 900, metalworking became known in Mexico, its origin being, at least in part, Panama. Certainly, many other items, which left no traces in the archaeological record, were traded between the two culture areas, like the Murex-dyed purple textiles from Greater Nicoya, alluded to in early colonial records.

Along with trade, pressure from Mesoamerica continued. The last invasion occurred in the fourteenth or fifteenth century, when the Nahua-speaking Nicarao entered Nicaragua and settled along the western shores of Lake Managua. Curiously, no pyramids or other buildings have been found which could be assigned to them. Only one pottery type, Managua polychrome, shows sufficient Mexican elements to be attributed to invaders. They were, most probably, again only a rather small group, splintered off from the Pipil, who in turn had occupied western and central El Salvador (the southern frontier of Mesoamerica) a short time before. The significance of the Nicarao in Central American cultural history has obviously been blown out of proportion by the Spaniards, with whom they collaborated willingly.

Our knowledge of non-archaeological achievements here and elsewhere in Central America is hopelessly inadequate. No written sources of native origin existed, and the early conquerors left only a few and often garbled accounts about the original culture. The oral traditions, certainly present, are now lost, with scarcely a trace, as are most of the musical compositions. Only the instruments (flutes, pan-pipes, trumpets, rattles, drums) survived. Lost, too, is the medical knowledge, any calendar which might have existed, and those other cultural elements which do not manifest themselves in non-perishable remains.

By 1500, Central America had almost turned into a meeting place of Meso- and South American cultures. Perhaps a century later these culture areas would have communicated directly, a new era would have dawned, with unforeseeable consequences in the cultural and political realm. European conquest prevented these developments.

BIBLIOGRAPHY

LANGE, F. W.; STONE, D. Z. (eds) 1984. *The Archaeology of Lower Central America.* A School of American Research Book. New Mexico.

ROUSE, I.; ALLAIRE, L. 1978. Caribbean. In: TAYLOR, R. E.; MEIGHAN, C. W. (eds) *Chronologies in New World Archaeology*, pp. 431–481. New York.

39

SOUTH AMERICA

39.1

THE CARIBBEAN AREA AND THE ORINOCO–AMAZON REGION

Mario Sanoja and Iraida Vargas Arenas

HIERARCHICAL CHIEFDOM SOCIETIES IN NORTHERN SOUTH AMERICA COLOMBIA: THE ATLANTIC COAST (see Map 42)

The Momposina depression

Around the seventh century AD, various tribal groups seem to have reached a lifestyle corresponding to chiefdoms. In the region of the lower Magdalena there were already groups living in dwellings built on platforms of trampled earth, the stability and territorial permanence of which are proved by the great depth of the archaeological deposits found there.

These communities lived mainly by growing maize and cassava, and by hunting and fishing. These activities must have been fruitful enough to allow demographic expansion, which is revealed by the increasingly complex nature of their society in general. This is evident in the existence of numerous hamlets, each of which is associated with extensive cemeteries where burials in funeral vessels are the predominant feature.

In some places, such as Betancí-Viloria and at the archaeological sites of Bajo San Jorge, the communities introduced very advanced cultivation techniques for growing maize and cassava in the areas periodically flooded by the Magdalena River. Proof of this is offered by the hundreds of hectares of raised cultivation fields, which allowed planting to take place annually in drained and irrigated soils.

The hierarchical nature of these indigenous communities in Bajo San Jorge and Bajo Sinú is revealed by such social features as the differential treatment given in burial to some corpses, which were interned in large clay vessels with richer and more varied funeral objects than common individuals. In certain tombs rich ceramic offerings were included, allowing us to surmise the existence of dignitaries or perhaps priests, who exercised power. Some kind of centralized authority and a structure of delegated power was required to co-ordinate, build and look after the extensive raised fields, and to plan the seasons for sowing and harvesting the crops. The excellence, both in design and manufacture, of the pottery and gold and silver work, suggests the existence of groups of specialists, whose output seems to have been intended for ceremonial use.

The Sierra Nevada de Santa Marta

Between the sixth and eighth centuries, Tairona society developed in the Atlantic region of Colombia. Its main settlements were in the Sierra Nevada de Santa Marta.

The Taironas were particularly remarkable for their skill in architecture, metallurgy, pottery and hydraulic works. This material basis of their society suggests the existence of social relations which heralded the breakdown of tribal society. This is an essential feature for the analysis of the historical dynamics of tribal hierarchical lifestyles (chiefdoms and fiefdoms) which existed in north-western South America, since in certain cases, although inequality did exist between the ruling houses and those they governed, goods and services continued to be distributed between autonomous hamlets. When hierarchical chiefdom lifestyles brought tribal society to the point of extinction, social relations of a statist nature, if not an outright state, appeared. Hierarchical organization is evident in every sector of society: in the territorial aspect, in the unequal relations between settlements of different sizes, and in the cycles of production, distribution and consumption of goods and services. The ceremonial centres characteristic of certain hierarchical chiefdoms also contain numerous hierarchical elements in regard to house design, public service buildings and work areas.

As far as their political organization was concerned, the Taironas were grouped around densely populated ceremonial centres of very complex structure. The buildings were placed on platforms surrounded by stone walls reached by means of staircases. These centres, like those in Costa Rica, were connected by roads paved with stones. They were also connected to the secondary centres and the hamlets surrounding each one.

In many cases, there were systems for harnessing the water from springs and rivers, and public buildings for civic and

Map 42 The circum-Caribbean and Orinoco–Amazon areas from 700 to 1600 (Schmidt, P.).

religious purposes. At the ceremonial centres not only is labour differentiation by sex and age apparent, but the existence of specialized producers is also evident as well as workshops for pottery making, gold- and silversmithing, stone-carving, and bone-working.

The goods and services generated at these production centres were distributed throughout the peripheral areas through markets and merchants who transported the goods over long distances and exchanged objects of silver and gold, beads, blankets and clay vessels, for raw materials such as emeralds, gold, fish and other products. Some of these items, such as clay vessels decorated using modelling or incising techniques and objects carved in stone, would appear to have reached the Sierra Perijá and the north-western shore of Lake Maracaibo.

Agriculture was based on maize production. There were complex canal systems, ponds for storing water for irrigation, and terracing to permit cultivation of the hillsides while preserving the plant layer.

The importance of ceremony is to be seen in the presence of large circular wooden temples situated on large artificial platforms. Decorated pottery provides information regarding the items used in these ceremonies and the hierarchical nature of society by showing human figures in high relief. These represent priests or warriors wearing complicated headdress and with faces covered by impressive masks.

When the Spaniards arrived in the sixteenth century, the urban centres were inhabited by thousands of people. The chronicles of the period stress the existence of specialized potters, silver- and goldsmiths, stonecarvers, and the presence of a civil and religious class which exercised political power in each of the districts or regions into which the society seems to have been divided.

Between the tenth and sixteenth centuries, each Tairona district or region was organized in accordance with a hierarchical scheme which included a principal regional centre, characterized by monumental architecture and a structure of ceremonial civil power which regulated the social life of the whole region. Around this main centre there were secondary centres which also had monumental buildings, ceremonial–civic and residential areas. Going down the hierarchical ladder we then find hamlets with very simple stone structures and small habitation mounds, and, finally, isolated houses and seasonal settlements.

The pyramidal organization of the regions and districts into which the Tairona territory was divided contrasts with the absence of global cohesion between the groups which governed each one. It would appear that rivalries existed and violent wars were waged between the civil, military and priestly authorities, although, under certain circumstances, they could form confederations or temporary alliances for their mutual defence. This rivalry between different sections of society seems characteristic of certain tribal lifestyles where the population developed state-like or quasi-state social relations. It would also appear to be a general characteristic of the nascent class society which developed without forming supra-state forms of socio-political control, as was the case of the city-states of ancient Greece. This phase has been called the imperial phase of Tairona society.

The Cundiboya region

The Muiscas were the latest settlers of this region. The first Europeans found a densely populated region divided into two large zones called the *Zipazgo* and the *Zacazgo*. The first of these was governed by an authority called the *Zipa* and the latter by the *Zaque*. It would appear that each of these great subdivisions was also made up of a number of other areas governed by chieftains forming a federation under the control of each of these overlords.

The populations of both regions were frequently involved in struggles for control of territory or hamlets in order to extract tribute from them. The governing class was organized on matrilineal lines. The members of this class lived in large dwellings which the Spanish chroniclers called 'palaces' on account of their size and magnificence, and they were normally carried in richly adorned litters.

The principal chieftains wielded absolute power over their subjects. No one was allowed to see their faces, and anyone who requested an audience was required to offer them a gift.

Palaeo-pathological studies of the Muisca population indicate that their society was stratified in terms of sex and social condition among both men and women. In the Soacha region, skeletal evidence shows that women had little opportunity to eat meat, but that they consumed large amounts of carbohydrates. This is revealed by the high incidence of illnesses caused by under-nourishment.

The Spanish chronicles tell of the existence of polygyny in Muisca society. In archaeological terms this is seen in the presence of an inordinately high number of women in cemeteries such as the cemetery at Soacha. Skeletal remains show that the women came from different groups from the men, which would seem to indicate the existence of matrimonial alliances of a patrilocal or virilocal nature. Some of the women seem to have enjoyed a better-balanced diet than others, indicating that certain women had a privileged social status which allowed them to receive certain food offerings from their menfolk. On the other hand, the incidence of artificial cranial deformities is greater among the women.

It is possible that weaving and pottery making were important tasks assigned to women, in which case polygyny might have been a method of gaining direct access to the labour of a large number of women. The existence of a variety of different types of spindles, generally made of stone, and of decorative designs reveals the complexity of spinning and possibly weaving techniques which existed among the Muiscas.

On the other hand, the skeletal remains of the male population are remarkably homogeneous, which would confirm that males remained in their parents' hamlet after marriage. As among the women, some skeletons belonged to men who were stronger and taller than the rest. These skeletons are usually associated with spear or arrow points made from fragments of human bone. This might indicate the existence of a warrior caste which enjoyed a superior socio-economic status.

Muisca gold- and silversmithing seems to have been a highly specialized activity which attained a high degree of expertise, and it may have been a purely male activity. As may be observed from the complex knowledge of metal chemistry and amalgams necessary to make *tumbaga,* as well as the techniques for the design of moulds for metal-casting, the silver- and goldsmiths must have formed a very specific group of specialists. Their production, eminently opulent in nature, must have been distributed along the trade routes which existed within Muisca territory and beyond. Their produce or ideas also reached areas as remote as Panamá, Costa Rica and north-western Venezuela (see Plates 313–315).

Archaeological data confirm the strongly hierarchical nature of Muisca society. This coincides with the elaborate ceremonial associated with the appointment of the *Zacazgo* or *Zipazgo* Overlord, which so greatly impressed the Europeans.

The presence of necropolises with different types of funeral structure, such as shaft-tombs with a number of lateral chambers and burial domes where the dead were buried with offerings, and burials directly in the earth in collective cemeteries also reveals the degree of social stratification attained in Muisca society.

Religion was centred around sun worship. Large temples were devoted to adoration of the Sun and the Moon. There were also ceremonial 500 m^2 fields, marked off on the south and east by columns of stone. In the centre of these ceremonial fields were stone monoliths or columns which appear to have been used to measure the passage of the solstices and the equinoxes. This leads us to surmise the existence of specialists (priests) devoted to the study of time who offered their knowledge in exchange for tributes or offerings.

Although wooden temples devoted to the cult of astronomical deities appear to have existed, such as the Sun temple at Sogamoso and the Goranchacha temple at Tunja (offering proof of formalized religious activity), the Muiscas also seem to have participated in more individualized ceremonial activities, which are revealed by the presence of shrines or ceremonial sites situated in caves or open spaces. Offerings of pottery, stone instruments and necklaces were deposited there as a kind of tribute to other deities or natural spirits which governed or controlled certain aspects of the surrounding environment.

The economy was based on the cultivation of such crops as maize, cotton and other varieties of tuber crops typical of the Andean highlands, such as potatoes and *ulluco*. The existence of observatories like those mentioned above is an indication of the importance of predictions for planning agricultural activities. In some areas of Muisca territory, irrigation channels were dug as well as artificial terraces for hillside cultivation.

Networks seem to have existed for the distribution of finished products and raw materials both within and beyond the boundaries of Muisca territory. There were also market centres where trade took place between the different communities. This also fostered regional integration of the various ethnic groups which made up Muisca society. Among the products which circulated through these networks were salt, obtained mainly from the Zipaquirá mines, pottery, gold and silverwork, cotton cloth, tobacco, *yopo* and coca leaf.

The structure and layout of archaeological sites related to Muisca society seem to indicate one type of settlement pattern based on scattered hamlets and a nuclear type, where a number of hamlets, whose inhabitants were linked by blood ties, were grouped together. There may also have been ceremonial and cult centres where a considerable number of people gathered on a seasonal basis.

Muisca society, like the other societies which occupied a large part of the intermontane valleys of Colombia between the sixth and fifteenth centuries, may be classified as hierarchical chiefdoms, that is, societies 'where inter-hamlet relationships became truly political. Specialization of social tasks in some or one of the hamlets, together with the breakdown in that hamlet of intra-hamlet kinship ties (except in family units) and the replacement of these with political and status links between the different lineages of the hamlet, led to the rise of a locality which was dominant in the political, religious and economic spheres. Inter- and intra-hamlet reciprocity, within the tribal territory, gave way to relationships of subordination, which were expressed by means of tributes which had to be paid to the main centre and to the *cacique* or main chief, who could, at one and the same time, be the sole military chief or priest, or political, military and religious chief, among a class of lesser subordinate lords who fulfilled the same functions in their own localities. The need also arose for a military body not only to defend the tribal territory but to guarantee the annexation of new territories and the payment of tributes' (Vargas Arenas, 1990: 112–116).

VENEZUELA (see Map 42)

The north-western shore of Lake Maracaibo

The northern region of the Lake Maracaibo basin seems to have lain on the periphery of the hierarchical societies which developed along the Caribbean coast of Colombia, giving rise to a situation similar to the hierarchical chiefdoms or fiefdoms which continued to exist within the nascent Mesoamerican class-based society, not as mere left-overs from a tribal structure but as organic socio-political units within the state relationship between the centre and the periphery. In this regard, we see that by the sixteenth century, extensive networks existed linking northern Colombia and the regions to the south and west of Lake Maracaibo. These networks were important not only for the distribution of raw materials and objects of value such as the so-called gold *aguilillas* or *caracuríes* but also for the distribution of perishable produce such as salt, fish, maize, animal pelts and woven cotton blankets, as well as to maintain a system of alliances with friendly and reliable intermediaries (and also for maintaining a route for spiritual exchanges: magico-religious concepts, rituals in the cult of the dead, fertility rites, cures, and so on) in order to guarantee a degree of compatibility in the relationships of subordination or complementarity which might be established between the state society and the hierarchical or egalitarian societies on the periphery.

The Andean region

The settlement of the upper reaches (between 1,000 and 3,000 m) of the Andean mountains in the south-west of Venezuela by tribal peoples seems to have begun around AD 600. The first communities, known as the Miquimú phase, lived in simple hamlets built on the river banks: they may have practised agriculture, hunting and river fishing.

At the Miquimú site, it is worth noting the presence of winged pendants in the form of bats carved in stone, similar to those already seen among the hierarchical chiefdoms of the Quíbor valley in the northern Andes from at least the beginning of the common era, which were made with semi-precious stones, seashells or animal bones.

Important changes seem to have occurred in the life of the Andean communities, particularly in the tenth century. In the Sierra de Mérida there appear communities known as the San Gerónimo phase, characterized by the presence of square houses associated with underground chambers called *mintoyes,* which would appear to have been used in some cases as tombs and, in others, possibly as silos to store food.

During this period there is evidence of the construction of terraces for hillside cultivation and of simple irrigation systems. These techniques, which had been used throughout the Andean region for many centuries, only reached the Quíbor valley and may be related to the period of greatest expansion of the tribal society in that region, its incipient breakdown, and the expansion of hierarchical chiefdoms in the north-west of South America.

The economy of the Venezuelan Andean communities was based on the cultivation of maize, potatoes, cassava, cuiba and the Peruvian carrot.

The agrarian system which developed in the region allowed fairly stable hamlets to grow up, not only because it was easy to obtain a more varied and lucrative production but also because the investment in public works, such as the construction and maintenance of cultivation terraces and irrigation channels, meant the formation of a system of collective land possession and farming capital which constantly stengthened the links between the community and the land.

Pottery in these communities was simply decorated. The techniques used were modelling and incision, and the most typical shapes were three- or four-legged vessels in the form of incense burners.

Sculpture in stone was another important vehicle of Andean aesthetic expression, the most noteworthy manifestations being female figurines and winged pendants in the shape of bats. At some sites, such as Mocao Alto in the state of Mérida, there were workshops for the manufacture of pectorals and serpentine plates which may then have been distributed to other communities in the Andean region and beyond by the barter system.

Ceremonialism seems to have attained a level of formalism and complexity greater than in other areas of Venezuela. It finds expression in shrines and offering sites situated in caves or in rocky fissures in the most inaccessible parts of the cold wastelands, and, according to the Spanish chroniclers, in little wooden temples attended by priests. The presence of winged pendants in the shape of bats may be a kind of cult to the dead, as well as a form of expression aimed at reinforcing the socio-political integration of the Andean communities.

Most ethnologists seem to agree that the archaeological manifestations which begin around the tenth century are associated with the ethnic groups which lived in the region in the sixteenth century. These are known as the Timotes or Timotís, and the Cuicas are a dialectal variation of this group. The Timoto-Cuicas, but above all the Timotes, would have occupied the highlands above 2,000 m, while the Cuicas would have settled below that altitude. This would not have been an inflexible scheme, however, as archaeology shows, since the Timotes also seem to also have settled on the lower eastern slopes of the Venezuelan Andes, particularly in the Canaguá, Pahuey and Santo Domingo river basins, leaving extensive cemeteries in the Turbio Valley and perhaps also in the Quíbor Valley, to the north of the Andes. From the linguistic point of view, they have been included in the Macrochibcha family, and their presence has been explained as an extension of the Chibcha hierarchical chiefdoms which developed simultaneously in the Cundiboya region of Colombia. By the tenth century, the north-west of Venezuela was a historical region where indigenous peoples linked to the hierarchical chiefdom lifestyle had been settled since the second or third century in the sub-Andean valleys. According to archaeological data and the chroniclers of the sixteenth century, the Andean peoples and the peoples of north-western Venezuela had reached a peaceful *modus vivendi* in the region. In the sixteenth century, good trade links existed between the Andean Cuicas and the Caquetís, who controlled north-western Venezuela. They even shared the same settlements, as was the case at Hacarygua (possible Acarigua in the present state of Portuguesa). From the archaeological material found at the pre-Columbian cemetery at Cerro Manzano, the possibility that groups of Timotís or Cuicas even settled in the valley of the River Turbio, where the city of Barquisimeto stands today, may be considered.

Despite the friendly relations between Timoto–Cuicas and Caquetís, significant differences in their political organization may be observed. Scattered settlements, based on independent hamlets fortified by palisades or surrounded by moats, seem to be characteristic of the former. In some cases, the dwellings seem to have been inhabited by nuclear families.

There is no evidence to suggest that chieftains with great political power or control over numerous hamlets existed, although religion seems to have played an integrating role within the Timoto–Cuica communities. The role of doctors, priests and diviners was exercised by *mohans*, who practised their rites, not only in caves and at shrines, but also in the little wooden temples which existed in different places in the Andean area, as was the case at Escuque, where Icaque, a female deity, was worshipped, possibly linked to fertility rites.

The temple dedicated to Icaque served as a meeting point for the indigenous people who came from many parts of the Andean region of Venezuela to bring her tributes in the form of balls of thread or cotton blankets, *quiteros* or *quiripas* (necklaces made of shell or bone beads), human skulls, venison, salt, and so on. Access to the temple was forbidden to all those who were not priests or *mohans*; the latter held divining rites and ceremonies of propitiation to ensure the success of the harvests inside the temple.

It is clear that ceremonial life, as expressed in the corporate activity of the *mohans* or priests, was a mechanism for social integration in the region which would seem to have lain beyond the authority of the local chieftains. The Timoto–Cuica priests seem to have formed a body of public servants whose main aim was to serve as mediators between the gods and ordinary people.

The north-west region

The historical region of north-western Venezuela is a vast territory which extends in a north–south direction from the Caribbean to the northern foothills of the Venezuelan Andes, and from west to east from the eastern coast of Lake Maracaibo to the hills which form the western edge of the Lake Valencia basin. From the beginning of the common era, archaeological evidence points to the presence of hierarchical chiefdoms which controlled both the Quíbor and River Turbio valleys and the surrounding mountainous regions, as well as the valleys covered by tropical forest which connect the Caribbean and the Lake Valencia basin.

The level of development attained by the communities of the historical region of north-western Venezuela was maintained until the seventh to tenth centuries of our era, when qualitative changes occurred. The whole region began to be occupied by people who made polychrome pottery, whose shape, modelling, and incised decoration differ from the pottery previously found in the region. The earlier pottery had been polychrome and geometrical, with highly stylized motifs enclosed in squares, trapeziums and triangles marked out by solid black, white or red lines and organized around a circular space which was the central focus for the development of the decoration.

By the tenth century, archaeological evidence suggests the existence in the valleys of the Carora region of indigenous peoples who had attained a high level of development. There we find medium-sized hamlets with earth platforms reinforced by stone walls, which served as the base for dwellings. They are associated with extensive cultivation terraces, pools for storing water, and irrigation systems. During the Sicarigua phase, the hamlets were associated with collective work areas for grinding maize, and many carved *metates* (curved grinding stones) for this purpose are found there.

Between the tenth and fifteenth centuries, the indigenous population spread out towards the other valleys in the region, as well as towards the foothills of the Andean region, setting up settlements like those of the Guadalupe phase, characterized by circular groups of ten to twelve habitation mounds built with trampled clay (in some cases they are pyramidal in shape) which enclosed a circular space or kind of plaza, where numerous *metates* were also found. In a radius of 4 to 5 km around these groups of mounds other related archaeological sites existed, without mounds, which appear to have been subsidiaries of the former. In some of these great centres the expansion and vertical growth of the artificial mounds led to a real ring or extensive circular ridge of trampled clay being formed enclosing the central plaza. In others, such as the El Mosquitero site, smaller habitation mounds were built around a large habitation mound. These were only 4–5 m in diameter and sometimes served as burial structures. In one of these, inside the top clay layer, bottle-shaped kilns had been built to fire pottery, whereas 2 m further down there appeared a row of large clay vessels covering what would appear to be a cremation burial ground. The vessels associated with such burials are similar to those made at sites such as Mirinday, in the Andean foothills. Other similar burial grounds have been located at sites without mounds, near Guadalupe.

The structures at habitation sites such as El Botiquín show that the use of domestic space may have been hierarchical: the characteristic here is a central communal hearth surrounded by smaller hearths. As far as domestic appurtenances are concerned, all the hearths shared the same sets of cooking vessels – large globular containers, porringers or bowls, gourd containers and tripod vessels with polychrome decoration. Although everyone ate a basic diet consisting of rabbit, agouti and iguana meat, as well as freshwater fish, land slugs, fowl and maize, still, meat from large mammals, such as deer, seems to have been reserved for those who used the central hearth. Use of arrowheads made of bone was also restricted to those who gathered around this central hearth.

Archaeological evidence from the Guadalupe phase indicates a process of population concentration in hierarchized domestic living spaces. The same trend is also evident both in the differentiation of social functions and in the social distribution of goods obtained or produced by the community. Parallel to this is the differentiation of territorial space in a hierarchy of sites ranging from complex central communities such as Los Arangues and Sicarigua, to subsidiary mound centres such as Guadalupe, El Mosquitero, El Botiquín and Oroche, which in turn had subsidiary habitation sites without mounds, such as Ojo de Agua. The above would seem to indicate the existence of a power centre, possibly the seat of the Overlord of the region, who would exercise control over other peripheral centres of population of lesser importance left under the authority of a minor chieftain who, in turn, would control a limited region populated by smaller, less complex hamlets.

Between the seventh and sixteenth centuries, the indigenous population inhabiting the Carora, Quíbor and Turbio valleys was ethnically homogeneous. Similar vessel shapes are found with peculiar stylistic interpretations in the polychrome decoration of the pottery in the low Andean valleys of the state of Trujillo; these, at that time, must have been populated by Cuica groups; and more of these vessels have been discovered on the shores of the Caribbean in Falcón State, shores which may have been inhabited by Caquetí groups.

The Spanish chronicles of the sixteenth century seem to indicate that the indigenous population in the modern states of Falcón, Lara and Yaracuy were of Arawak stock. If we were to assume that they were the manufacturers of the late polychrome pottery in the region, it is possible to maintain that they also spread towards the valleys in the northern Venezuelan Andes, intermarrying and forming alliances with the Cuicas. This might link them with the process of socio-political integration which was taking place among the Caquetí peoples of the region in the sixteenth century, where the institution of the *Diao*, or Lord of Lords, is worthy of note. The *Diao* was at one and the same time the religious and military leader – the repository of great magical and religious power – and all the communities of that vast region paid tribute to him. He was carried on a hammock so that his feet would not touch the ground. These communities would seem to have been hierarchical societies, where power was inherited. An entourage of relatives surrounded the *Diao*, and a distinguishing feature of the military orders was that they were symbolically 'related' to certain animals such as the jaguar.

What we are seeing here may be lifestyles characteristic of the final phase of the tribal production mode which signified the breakdown of the tribal structure. It may also be that social relations of a state type were beginning to emerge. These would be evident in a form of political domination which would be expressed by territorial hierarchization, but they would not yet have reached the point of differentiating between cities and peasant settlements, as is the case of the Taironas.

The Lake Valencia basin

After the seventh century, the Lake Valencia basin was occupied by indigenous populations known archaeologically as the Valencia Phase. This colonization seems to have been the result of migrations from the Middle Orinoco and the River Apure basin, both of which are identified with the so-called Arauquín tradition. Apart from the lake region, by the period 1150–1550, the Valencia people already controlled not only the extensive valleys of the present states of Carabobo and Aragua, but intermontane valleys such as the Caracas valley and others in Miranda state such as the Venezuelan Antilles.

There were central villages of greater importance with a number of lesser hamlets around them. One of the central villages seems to have been situated on the south-east shore of the Lake, and coincides with a series of extensive habitation mounds such as Tocorón, La Mata, Camburito and El Zamuro.

Three types of settlement may be identified within the chiefdom: those which were located in the interior in the intermontane valleys surrounding the lake; those situated on the fringe of the Caribbean shore; and those situated on islands and islets off the central Venezuelan coast.

For the reasons given above, the Lake Valencia chieftain exploited the resources from a great variety of environments, either directly or through a network of subject hamlets. This helped optimize and diversify production, thus guaranteeing sustained growth of the tribal territory with the subjection and/or complementary nature of the peripheral hamlets.

Products, goods and raw materials were regularly exchanged between the sites forming the central nucleus and the peripheral sites, particularly seashells of different types, which were used to make body ornaments, hooks, and so on.

All the sites had a large number of cultural features in common with the central village, particularly pottery. Nevertheless, it is evident that works of public interest, particularly terracing works, were concentrated, as might be expected, at the lakeside sites which constituted the seat of centralized power.

The variety of burial procedures practised is evidence that inequalities existed. Some individuals were buried in large clay urns accompanied by pottery offerings, luxury goods and sacrificed animals, particularly dogs and monkeys, whereas others were buried directly in the earth with simpler offerings or none at all.

As well as a hierarchization of space revealed by the construction of funeral, habitation and agricultural mounds, the existence of the specialized or semi-specialized production of some goods, particularly luxury ceramic items and other raw materials such as amber, shell, jadeite and gold, may be inferred.

From the sum of the archaeological evidence analysed we may consider that the Lake Valencia basin constitutes 'what might be called 'an archaeological zone of optimal conflux' since the soil was rich, fauna were abundant, there was plenty of fresh water, the climate was benign, there were flat areas protected from the strong winds, the rainfall pattern was excellent and stable, and access to other ecosystems was easy. All these features provide the natural conditions for implementing the highly productive and profitable work method which strengthened the self-dynamic qualities of the Araquinoid social base. This is to be seen in the process of reorganization of the workforce, demographic and territorial expansion, and the subjection of egalitarian communities within an extensive network of hamlets joined by their cultural relationship or (it would seem) domination' (Vargas Arenas, 1990: 238–239).

Although some authors have identified the hierarchical chiefdoms of the Lake Valencia basin with Carib peoples, also on the basis of ethno-historical data, they regard them as Caquetís. The archaeological evidence points to a link between the Valencian sites and the hierarchical chiefdoms of the Great Antilles.

The Orinoco basin

Around the seventh century, the region of the middle and lower Orinoco had fallen, either directly or indirectly, under the sway of the Arauquín tradition. This middle Orinoco tradition might be regarded as related to a mixed egalitarian lifestyle, despite the presence of sites with habitation mounds scattered along the rivers of the region. Barrancas, situated on the lower Orinoco, is the most developed phase of one of the vegeculture egalitarian lifestyles which existed in the area. Neither of the two which existed in this region reached the degree of social hierarchization attained by the peoples of Orinoco origin in the centre of Venezuela.

The economy of these communities was based on the cultivation of cassava, a staple food, and maize, which was used mainly to make *chicha*, a fermented drink consumed in ceremonies and at social events. After the seventh century, the expansion of the Arauquín tradition reached its zenith with the occupation of all the hamlets which had previously been under the control of the Barrancas tradition.

Between the seventh and sixteenth centuries, the population of the Lower Orinoco increased generally with a corresponding increase in the production and consumption of agricultural produce and an obvious decrease in game and fish. Pottery production also increased, and a corollary of this was a deterioration in the aesthetic excellence of the decoration which had been one of the distinctive characteristics of the previous Barrancoid society.

It would appear that the expansion of the Arauquín people in the lower Orinoco provoked the development of sub-traditions such as the Macapaima. Evidence of this is the establishment of simple centres such as those which exist where the Caroní River flows into the Orinoco. Some of these centres continued to exist until the seventeenth century. Like the Barrancoid villages, the Macapaima settlements were relatively stable, showing an increase in population, in the production, processing and consumption of cassava in the form of cassava flour bread (*cazabe*), and in the manufacture of and demand for pottery. However, domestic spaces were, at one and the same time, dwellings, burial grounds and workshops for a variety of productive activities. This feature clearly links them with one of the vegeculture egalitarian lifestyles which were prominent in the lower Orinoco.

On the basis of ethno-historical data from the region and according to the sixteenth-century testimony of Sir Walter Raleigh regarding the hamlets at the mouth of the Caroní River, some authors have suggested that the peoples who dominated the Orinoco basin between the seventh and sixteenth centuries may have been related to Carib peoples. The archaeological research carried out by Sanoja and Vargas Arenas in that region shows the existence of large villages inhabited by people related to the Macapaima sub-tradition which, at the beginning of the seventeenth century, was related to Carib peoples who inhabited the banks of the Orinoco in the south of the state of Anzoátegui. Since Macapaima seems to be an offshoot of the Arauquín tradition, regarded as an exponent of Carib culture, the Arauquinoid groups which migrated to the Lake Valencia basin around 700 must also have been Caribs.

The north-eastern region

According to Steward and Faron (1959), analysis of ethno-historical data would allow us to establish that by the sixteenth century, hierarchical chiefdoms associated with the Palenque, Cumanagoto and Chaima peoples existed on the north-eastern coast of Venezuela. However, according to Vargas Arenas (1990: 216), the archaeological evidence is not conclusive enough to define with certainty the existence of this kind of society in the region, and she is of the opinion that we can only speak with any authority of communities related to a vegeculture egalitarian lifestyle, possibly largely related to peoples of Carib origin, who, around the same time, had begun to occupy a large part of the Lesser Antilles.

THE EASTERN CARIBBEAN ISLANDS (see Map 42)

The Lesser Antilles

The indigenous island hamlets which existed on the Lesser Antilles between the seventh and fifteenth centuries would appear to have been relatively simple and sparsely populated. The existence of numerous petroglyphs, burials with offerings and anthropomorphic sculptures in stone denote influences from both the continent and the Greater Antilles. Ethno-historical inferences based on the sixteenth-century inventories of Peter Martyr of Anghiera and Labat (in Fewkes, 1914) reveal the existence of hamlets or dwellings in the vicinity of the shore or on the river banks with good fishing facilities, sea or land molluscs, and game. One type of building served as a general dwelling, and another type occupied the central position in the hamlet: the latter was used as a kind of shrine where the *zemis* or ritual stones were kept. Some hamlets had up to twenty or thirty houses laid out in a circular pattern around a central plaza. Each house was inhabited by a kinship group comprising the head of the household, his wives and unmarried children.

The Greater Antilles

In the Greater Antilles, comprising Boriquen (Puerto Rico), Quisqueya or Haiti (Santo Domingo and Haiti) and Cuba, the most noteworthy historical feature between the seventh and sixteenth centuries was the emergence of hierarchical chiefdoms known as the Taíno culture or Boca Chica tradition, which brought profound changes in settlement patterns, socio-political organization and ceremonial life. A feature of note is the construction of different types of artificial mound structures on trampled earth which served as sites for communal dwellings, fields for the cultivation of cassava and maize and burial grounds. In some cases, the mound complexes are situated around a *pelota* or *batey* field which is marked out by rows of stones, sometimes decorated with petroglyphs.

In some cases, real necropolises developed where the craftsmanship of the burial offerings, consisting of ceramics and objects sculpted in stone and shells, was excellent in the extreme. On the other hand, the design and manufacturing techniques of the stone and wooden statues also achieved a high degree of complexity. Foremost among these are the sculpted, pyramid-shaped stones called *zemis*, which represent *Yuca-hu Bagua Maorocotí*, the cassava god.

The people lived by growing bitter cassava, which was turned into cassava flour bread *(cazabe)* as in northern South America, as well as maize and a variety of tuber crops, and also by fishing, collecting marine produce and hunting. The dominant cultivation system was the slash-and-burn method, and vegeculture was the main component. This is evident from the protagonism of the deity Yuca-hu in Taíno mythology. On the other hand, cassava flour cakes made on dishes for baking maize bread (*budares*), decorated by using the incision technique, are reminiscent of the Barrancoid peoples of the lower Orinoco and the Saladoids of north-eastern Venezuela. By using finer cassava flour, they could make a kind of bread destined for consumption by the most important chieftains. Each side of this bread was decorated with geometric or biomorphic motifs which may have been linked to the lineage of the person in question.

By the end of the fifteenth century, Taíno society had become aristocratic in nature and highly stratified. The most prominent position was occupied by the main chieftains whose position may have been determined by matrilineal descent. These were followed by an entourage of *nitaínos* or 'nobles' and then by servants or slaves called *naboría*. A class society may have existed. We believe that Taíno society, or the Boca Chica tradition, may be set alongside the hierarchical chiefdoms of Venezuela, Colombia and southern Central America. The latter represent the upper phase or breakdown point of tribal society, which is marked by the development of hierarchical social relationships of a state nature, a fundamental feature which is gradually transformed so that states and the juridical apparatus of a class society may develop.

Among the most outstanding features of the Boca Chica tradition are the institution of the *pelota* game *or batey*, and all the paraphernalia associated with it, such as 'yokes' (*yugos)* and 'elbows' (*codos*) richly sculpted in stone. These highly remarkable items suggest the possibility of a link with Meso-america, via the Yucatán peninsula, between the seventh and ninth centuries (see Plates 289–293).

THE AMAZON DELTA (see Map 42)

Around the sixth century, the population known archaeologically as the Marajoara phase made its appearance in the delta of the Amazon River, displacing the simple horticultural communities which continued to live as the early settlers had done since the beginning of the last millennium BC, and where the cultural influence of the Tupi-Guaraní from southern Brazil was beginning to be felt.

The most outstanding material characteristics of the Marajoara society are the large artificial mounds of trampled earth and the manufacture of polychrome pottery of very complex design. The mounds differed according to their use: groups of small, low habitation mounds with dwellings set directly on top, each of which may have been a collective dwelling. Each group of habitation mounds was associated with at least one burial mound, the largest of which might be 225 m long, 30 m wide and 10 m high.

Analysis of burial grounds from the Marajoara phase shows both chronological differences in burial practices as well as differences in the way the dead were treated. In the oldest layers, burials in large undecorated urns or urns, decorated using polychrome painting or excision techniques and covered with a semi-globular vessel which served as a lid, are the commonest. Some skeletons, possibly female ones, were accompanied by a kind of *tanga* or ceramic covering for the pubic area decorated with polychrome motifs, as well as mini-vessels and offerings of sacrificed animals. In the more recent strata, cremation displaces secondary burials: the urns used are smaller and less ornamented, and the custom of associating pubic coverings with burials is abandoned. Some burials were associated with a number of other urns, whereas other skeletons were buried directly in the earth. The above would seem to indicate important changes which must have taken place in the social relations of the Marajoara people, particularly the disappearance of simple differentiation by sex, which existed in egalitarian societies, and its replacement by certain forms of inequality, which gave some individuals the privilege of being buried accompanied by the mortal remains of other people who may have formed their entourage.

Archaeological evidence reveals the existence of some degree of organization of labour for collective purposes, such as the construction of habitation or burial mounds, and considerable production of material goods for non-reproductive purposes, such as burial offerings. Roosevelt (1987) has put forward the idea of a chiefdom in the lower Amazon, based on the existence not only of dwellings and terracing works but also of sites, concentric in layout, where groups of communal dwellings are distributed around a central area and surrounded by large earth walls. The population of these sites was approximately 360 to 1,200 people.

The Marajoara phase stands out from the other pre-Columbian peoples in the Orinoco–Amazon basin on account of its socio-historical development. Its origins and subsequent insertion into a region so isolated and far from the main South American civilizations has given rise to a number of hypotheses regarding its formation. Of these we wish to consider the hypothesis of Clifford Evans and Betty Meggers (1968), who locate its origins in the Napo phase on the eastern slopes of the Ecuadorean Andes, despite the fact that carbon-14 dating for that region (1168 and 1320) is later than for the lower Amazon. According to these authors, the Marajoara people would have broken away from a developed sub-Andean context, becoming gradually decultured and devolving towards the tropical jungle culture level due to their inability to adapt to the environment of the lower Amazon. On the other hand, Roosevelt (1987) appears to favour an Amazonian cultural origin.

The proof or refutation of both hypotheses must take account of the fact that in history things do not happen by chance but in response to clearly established social needs. Bearing in mind the volume of information which we possess at the present time regarding the Amazon region, it is difficult to consider the Marajoara phase as a kind of sudden mutation which split away from very simple local societies. Its characteristics clearly associate it with other similar societies – and we believe that they are hierarchical – which would appear to have existed in the region of the Bolivian Amazon. However, in this regard, we cannot limit our consideration to a single quantitative criterion, such as the existence of habitation mounds at Marajó and in the Bolivian Amazon, which may be interpreted differently according to the socio-historical contexts in which they occur. Marajoara probably did not begin in the Lower Amazon, but neither do we believe that peoples evolve or regress historically. The complex societies which existed in the sixteenth century along the Santarem and Tapajos Rivers are conclusive evidence that the emergence of the indigenous societies of the lower Amazon is the result of the general dynamics prevalent in the Andean and Amazon areas. Their penetration into the mouths of the Amazon meant the beginning of complex local changes which coincided with other similar processes in northern South America, Central America and the Antilles. Nevertheless, these Amazon societies must be analysed by developing theories about them not only as a quantitative phenomenon but, fundamentally, also by taking account of their qualitative content.

BIBLIOGRAPHY

CASSÁ, R. 1974. *Los taínos de La Española.* Universidad Autónoma de Santo Domingo. Dominican Republic.

CRUXENT, J. M.; ROUSE, I. 1961. *Arqueología cronológica de Venezuela,* 2 vols. Washington, DC.

EVANS, C.; MEGGERS, B. 1968. *Archaeological Investigations on the Rio Napo, Eastern Ecuador.* Washington, DC.

FEWKES, W. 1914. *Relations of Aboriginal Culture and Environment in the Lesser Antilles.* Contributions of the Heye Museum, No. 8, New York.

OSGOOD, C.; HOWARDS, C. 1943. *An Archaeological Survey of Venezuela,* No. 27. New Haven, Conn.

RALEIGH, SIR WALTER. 1595. *The discovery of the large, rich, and beautiful Empire of Guiana, with a relation of the great and golden city of Manoa (which the Spaniards call El Dorado). Performed in the year 1595 by Sir Walter Raleigh, Knight.* In: R. HAKLUYT, *Voyages and Discoveries* (London, 1598-1600). J. Beecham ed., London 1972, pp. 386–410.

ROOSEVELT, A. C. 1987. Chiefdoms in the Amazon and Orinoco. In: DRENNAN, R.; URIBE, C. A. (eds) *Chiefdoms in the Americas.* Maryland.

SANOJA, M.; VARGAS, I. 1987. *Antiguas formaciones y modos de producción venezolanos.* Monte Avila Editores. Caracas [2nd edn].

STEWARD, J.; FARON, L. 1959. *Native Peoples of South America.* New York.

VARGAS ARENAS, I. 1990. *Arqueología, ciencia y sociedad.* Caracas.

39.2
THE CENTRAL ANDES

Luis Millones

A glance at the long cultural history of the Andes shows that supremacy alternated between the coastal and highland societies (see Map 43). If we take the Formative or Chavín culture as our point of reference, we see that, from 1000 BC, highland culture was the ideological and cultural powerhouse of northern Peru. This was followed by a period lasting from AD 200 to AD 700, which archaeologists call the Early Intermediate period or the period of the master craftsmen, when the dominant culture was that of the desert oases of the coast, which developed into centres known as Mochica culture in the north and Nazca in the south. It has been suggested that such swings in ideological and socio-political supremacy were linked to much more general phenomena of environmental change, but this is a subject for future research.

During the period which concerns us here, cultural development seems to have revolved around the southern mountains of Peru and northern Bolivia, the Collao plateau, where the first organizations that can with some degree of certainty be called states emerged, shortly afterwards reaching their zenith as a political entity in the central highlands of Peru in what is now the department of Ayacucho. Although this view is not held unanimously by specialists, there is evidence to suggest that qualitative and quantitative changes did occur in the organization of human settlements, the layout of architectural spaces and the crystallization of an ideology which 'humanized' the figures of the Andean pantheon, which is to say that the deities were endowed with a solid human shape. This may have coincided with the decadence of theocratic political moulds, the loss of importance of the priestly castes and the replacement of the ceremonial centres with true cities.

The Tiwanaku and Wari sites may serve to demonstrate this.

TIWANAKU OR THE CITY ON THE ROOF OF THE WORLD

If we think in terms of a constituted state, the regional history of Tiwanaku (or Tiahuanaco) is ancient. On the site of the same name, 3,850 m above sea level and covering an area of 3 km by 1.5 km, this is one of the highest cultural centres or capitals in the world. Situated on the Collao plateau, near Lake Titicaca, it reached its zenith during the period known as Classical Tiwanaku, which probably developed between AD 500 and 900. The capital was surrounded by other secondary centres, such as Lukurmata, Pajchiri, Oje, Khonko and Wankané, which are also situated in the vicinity of Lake Titicaca on each side of the modern border between Peru and Bolivia, including Esteves Island.

The emergence of these power centres around Lake Titicaca must be related to the changing water level of the lake, which stabilized at the level we know today some time between 2000 BC and the beginning of the common era. The Pukara centre preceded Tiwanaku. Pukara, which lies about 60 km from Lake Titicaca, heralded the social development which was to come. However, as its predominance was short-lived (400 BC to AD 100), it did not attain such a high profile as Tiwanaku, although, during its 500 years of existence, the ruling priests used well-defined trade caravans of llamas to control, or at least influence, the economy of the population of an area which stretched from Cuzco in the north (about 150 km away) to northern Chile to the south, about 900 km away.

In ideological terms, it may be argued that the walking-stick god who was proclaimed by the rulers of Tiwanaku and Wari has clear precedents in Pukara iconography.

Long before its expansion, it would appear that considerable power was concentrated at the site of Tiwanaku itself. This may be seen in the construction of the semi-subterranean temple in the north-eastern sector of the monumental area. Inside this temple, a stone stela with an image which would seem to represent a bearded person stands out. Other monuments, such as Kalasasaya and Pumapuncu, denote what must have been the physical structure which preceded political and ideological expansion. The system of buildings is completed by the Akapana pyramid located at the centre of the site, directly to the south-east of the Kalasasaya precinct. This is the tallest and most voluminous structure on the site.

Lake Titicaca is known to have been a great centre for farming experiments, on account of the different microclimates developed in the vicinity and the flora and fauna found there. One technique found during this period which takes these conditions into account is the technique known as *waru waru*. This technique of cultivation on raised terraces offers a number of advantages, such as improved drainage, retention of humidity, irrigation, easier weeding and a certain increase in the fertility of poor soils. Several different types of raised terrace were used, and knowledge of this technique may have reached the Llanos de Mojos on the eastern slopes of the Andes, in a possible attempt to colonize the jungle area. But the economy and subsistence of the altiplano depended upon the domestication of *camelidae*,

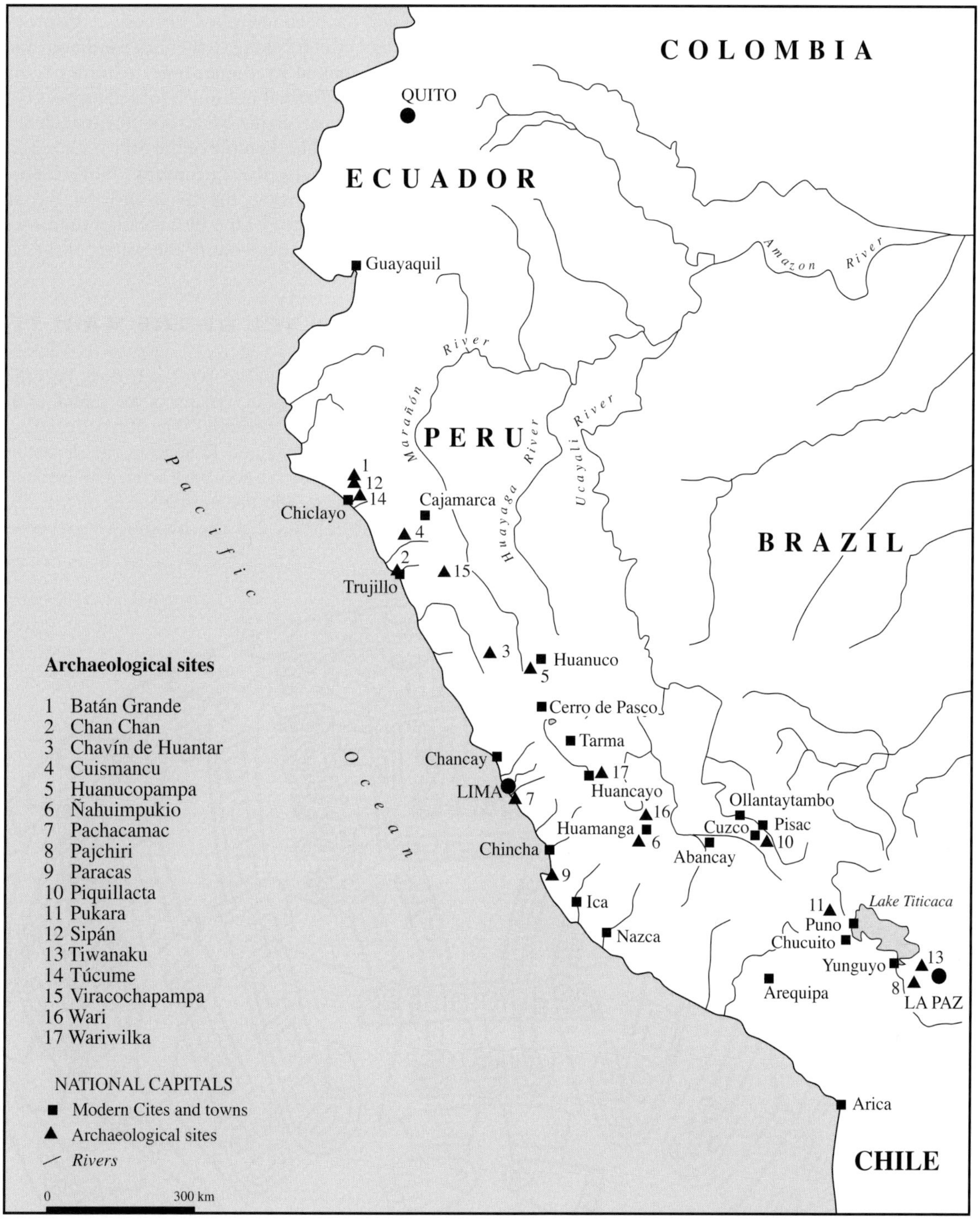

Map 43 The Central Andes from 700 to 1600 (drawn by Millones, M.).

which were used for many purposes and made it possible for caravans to transport both high-quality goods and ideology. It must be remembered that pastoral activity, particularly as part of a central political system, was a formidable weapon of expansion. With the aid of llamas and alpacas, the routes to the coast and the jungle were opened up (see Plate 323).

The stone architecture and sculpture of Tiwanaku suggest a complex religion, whose iconography may be traced back to the remote anthropomorphic figures of Chavín in the northern mountains of Peru around 1000 BC. In 1932, the North American archaeologist Wendell Bennett discovered the reddish-coloured stone monolith which now bears his name. The monolith, which must have stood in the sunken patio of the semi-subterranean temple mentioned earlier, was transferred to La Paz. It stands 7.3 m high, which makes it the largest sculpture in the Andean region. It depicts a noble or deified person, splendidly attired and wearing a very ornate headdress. In one hand he seems to be holding a ceremonial vessel or *kero* and in the other a staff of command.

To obtain the andesite stone and transport it to Tiwanaku must have involved a great deal of planning and a huge labour force. It is highly likely that the materials came from the Copacabana Peninsula and were transported across Lake Titicaca. But the job did not end there. Once the stone reached the ceremonial centre, the sculptors had to create and reproduce the central motifs of a very complex cult which continued to linger right up to the arrival of the Europeans.

Of all the structures at Tiwanaku, the most noteworthy is the Gate of the Sun (Puerta del Sol) which is now situated on one side of Kalasasaya in a spot which was not its original position. The Gate of the Sun was cut from a block of lava, and the central frieze depicts one of the most important images of the Tiwanaku religious pantheon. The dominant figure, which is about 70 cm high, is anthropomorphic and wears a mask from which rays end in circles or animal heads project like sunbeams. The body is highly ornate and the legs are very curtailed. In his hands he carries two staffs, the lower ends of which are shaped like a condor's head.

A variety of different interpretations have been put forward to explain the figures on the Gate of the Sun, on both sides of which, apart from the figure described above, there are other beings that appear to be paying homage to the central figure, bowing or kneeling before him or running out to meet him. These are all winged figures, and they are shown in profile looking towards the staff god (as he is usually known) (see Figure 35). Their heads are either like that of the central figure or condor heads, and in both cases they carry staffs similar to the one carried by the central figure. The staff god has been identified variously as Viracocha and Illapa, both of which belong to the Inca pantheon, and their images were sacked by the European hordes soon after Pizarro's arrival. There is not much formal support for these interpretations, as we do not have a documentary description of the *Coricancha* (The Temple of the Sun at Cuzco) images as they were seen by the Europeans. Nevertheless, the ideological link between the Incas and the lake area is undeniable. In fact, one of the Inca creation myths says that the founding couple arose out of the waters of the lake.

THE EMERGENCE OF THE WARI STATE

Some 30 hectares constitute what can now be called the heart of the archaeological remains of the capital of the first imperial experiment in the Andes. The site is situated between the cities of Huamanga and Huanta in the department of Ayacucho, about 3,000 m above sea level. The area occupied by the ruins is vast, and the impression is one of disorder, which would indicate that the buildings were erected in

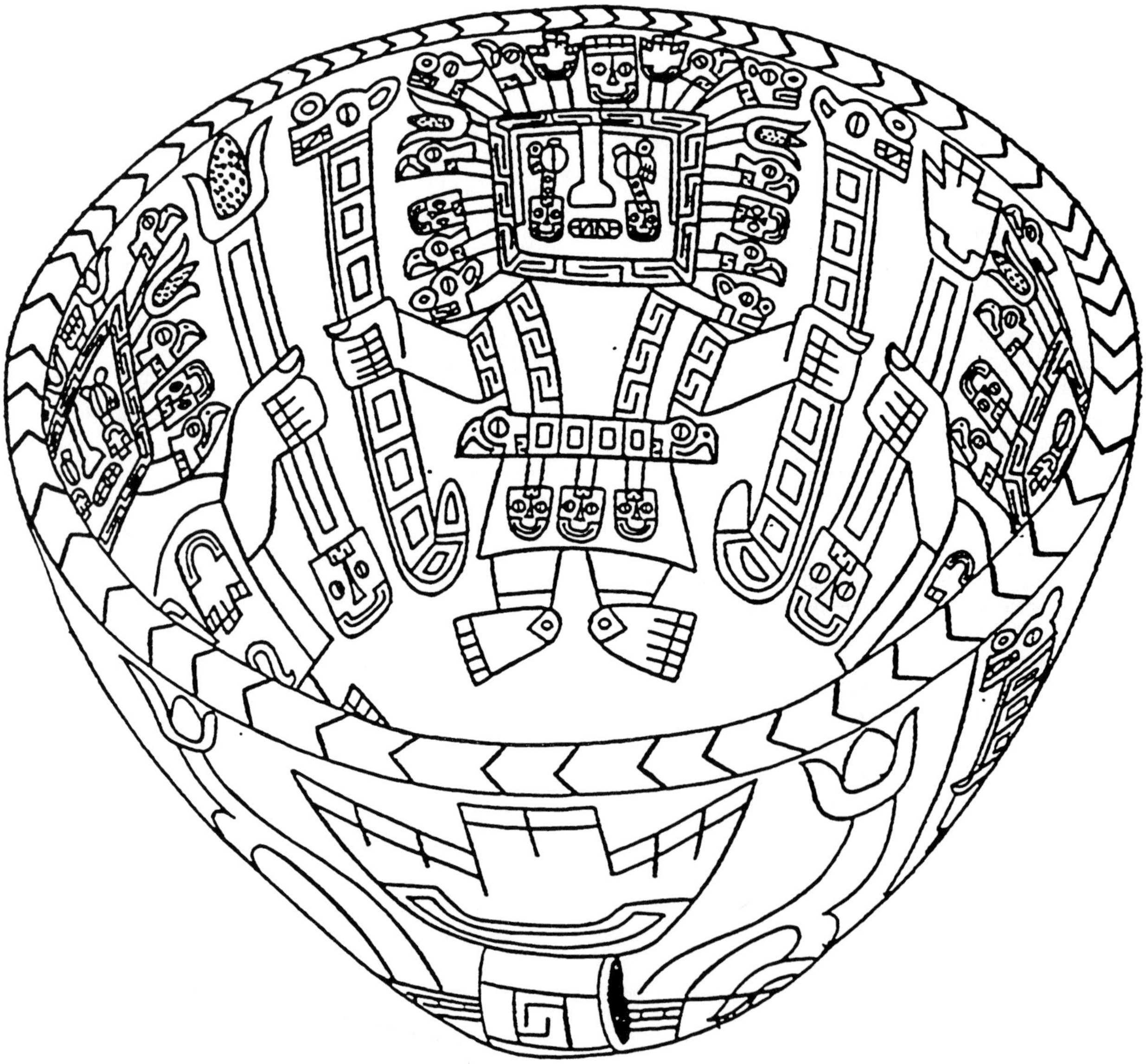

Figure 35 The 'Staff God' or 'Weeping God' of Tiwanaku or Tiahuanaco (Bolivia). A large urn, found in Nazca (Peru), dating from the Tiwanaku or Tiahuanaco coastal occupation (AD 1000–1300), (after Hagen, V. W. von, *Realm of the Incas*, NY 1957, p. 29).

different periods. This proves that the site was occupied continuously. Furthermore, what appears to us today to be a jumble of fragments would in their day, and owing to the complexity of the society which lived there, have belonged to precincts which had separate functions. The site has also been sacked on numerous occasions.

Around AD 500, Wari had a semi-subterranean temple built of rectangular and polygonal stones whose edges fitted together perfectly. However, the square structure and the absence of vertical carved stones make it different from its counterpart at Tiwanaku. The building is situated at the centre of the site, which, as we have already said, is covered with stone structures that it is difficult to arrange into distinct precincts. The number of precincts is estimated to be between three and thirteen, and this, in itself, is indicative of the absence of a detailed general plan of the site. However, the monumental architecture of rustic stone found at the nearby sites of Chaquipampa and Ñahuinpuquio is impressive. These sites may have preceded the concentration of power at Wari, whose inhabitants used the materials from these sites to build the new capital.

It is impossible to determine the number of inhabitants in the 'urban' area of Wari at its height with any degree of certainty. Estimates vary from 5,000 to 100,000. A realistic figure based on the possible density per hectare might be around 30,000, which would make it the largest sacred city in South America at that time. There are no reliable figures for Tiwanaku either, but it would appear not to have been larger than the Ayacucho capital. This takes us directly to the question of how this considerable mass of people survived.

Unlike Tiwanaku, Wari is situated on arid terrain with meagre watercourses. This contrasts with the high level of occupation and the quantity of goods produced by craft workshops. Even if we disregard this type of vestige and allow for the occupation of more productive areas, it is inconceivable that the people of Wari could have survived without bringing in supplies from distant places. This is one of the arguments put forward to explain Ayacucho expansionism. Demographic pressure and the ideological emergence of a god similar to the staff god would have promoted military conquest or the exchange of goods and ideas with other regions. It is important to note that, although Tiwanaku and Wari coincide in their central deity and the winged figures (angels) which accompany him, in Bolivia they are generally depicted in stone, whereas at Ayacucho they are depicted on ceramics, particularly large vessels which are painted all over including the interior, and in stone figurines like amulets. Another factor which differentiates between these two cultural complexes is the use of wooden tablets (for sniffing hallucinogens), which were very common at Tiwanaku but are not found at Wari.

We shall use Wari to explain the debate regarding the imperial nature of these cultural complexes. Naturally, the terminological debate regarding the validity of an interpretation based on the European experience could go on *ad infinitum*, but it is clear, on the basis of the urban layout and for stylistic reasons, that residential and ceremonial centres following the Ayacucho model were built at places far from Huamanga. This is the case of Viracochapampa in Huamachuco (northern mountains of Peru) and Pikillaqta near Cuzco. The same may be said of Pachacamac, where the Ayacucho influence lasted for a long time. On the northern coast, Wari appears to have reached a series of agreements with the Mochica people. This is evident in their later ceramics. In the east, their colonies probably settled in the Lower Apurimac region, beyond the jungle fringe marking the border with the Pano-speaking peoples, who were excellent travellers and very good traders, at least in later periods.

Little is known about this complex process. During the seventh and ninth centuries, the ancestors of today's Pano-speaking population (known as the Cumancaya period) had settled in Ucayali at the end of what we surmise was a migratory process. Successive waves of these people had pushed Arawak groups out of the alluvial plains of the Ucayali River and they, in turn, put pressure on the ancestors of the Amueshas, Asheninkas (Campas) and Machiguengas who must have established closer links (barter or subordination) with the Wari people or their descendants.

Current research is as yet unable to clarify the relationship between Tiwanaku and Wari. It is clear that an exchange of artistic motifs did take place. This may have occurred by way of the textiles transported by travelling peoples, such as the Callahuaya, with the aid of their camel-like animals, which would have provided the necessary means of transport. But the cultural context of both social entities would also support the theory of independent development.

By AD 1000, the political impact of Wari had disappeared, but not before it had laid the foundations of what would appear to be the first imperial experiment. Roads, tribute systems (particularly labour) and perhaps *mitimaes* (groups of people who were forced to settle lands far from their birthplace) may be the heritage bequeathed by Wari to the various 'kingdoms and confederations' which arose from its ashes. Later, close to Pikillaqta, its most diligent disciples would arise, the Incas.

THE NORTHERN COASTAL CULTURES

Around AD 600, a period known to archaeologists as the Early Intermediate Period or Period of the Master Craftsmen reached its peak on the coast of Peru. These names allude to the characteristics of the pottery and its highly elaborate artistic development in general and to the fact that the series of human settlements in the vicinity of the coastal rivers gave rise to highly differentiated local forms now freed from their common background, i.e. Chavín. Later the influence of the Wari–Tiwanaku cultural complexes would provide the independent coastal developments with a unifying characteristic.

Recent research would appear to indicate that the influence of the highland cultures was irregular, both in terms of span and the degree of control or trading links with the Mochica and Nazca peoples. Their influence was obviously felt most keenly on the south coast. To a degree, Wari arose as a result of the links between the local Ayacucho cultures, such as Huarpa, and the latter phases of Nazca culture.

In the north, the high profile of the city of Chan Chan and the spectacular monuments of the Moche, Chicama and Cao valleys detracted from the importance of the archaeological remains at Lambayeque. Furthermore, the discovery in 1988 of the tomb of the lord of Sipán made new research possible in the La Leche, Lambayeque and Saña valleys. As a result of this renewed interest, it can now be affirmed that two cultural developments with similar characteristics existed, one in the Moche and Chicama valleys and another in the Lambayeque valleys. Both these cultural environments may be broadly classified as belonging to Mochica culture, and cultural supremacy alternated between the two locations. At first, the dominant area was the one whose most important sites lie in the Moche valley. Later, power seems to have been divided between this valley and the Batán Grande sites which have become known as the Lambayeque or Sicán culture (see Plates 314, 315).

During the period which concerns us here, for a short time (AD 700–800) the Wari people made their influence felt in both the cultural centres of the north. As a result of this highland presence, the northern valleys grew stronger, and it is legitimate to refer to the Sicán kingdom of Batán Grande and the Chimú kingdom of Moche. Finally, around 1200, the lord of Chimú took the Lambayeque valleys by force and established his power, which lasted until the arrival of the Incas (1400).

Archaeologists have decided to use the term Chimú to refer to a series of cultural characteristics and to reserve the name Chimor for the pre-Columbian state which lasted up to the fifteenth or sixteenth century, when it competed with the Incas. Colonial documents tell us that the natives called themselves *Mochicas* at least up to the eighteenth century.

The archetypal northern monument of this period is Chan Chan (see Figure 36), which is very close to the Pacific and a few kilometres from the modern city of Trujillo. The central nucleus of the city covers an area of about 6 km^2, but the remains of walls and related constructions cover a radius of 20 km. The central area comprises nine or ten 'citadels', a word which is used to refer to closed precincts which surround the centre of Chan Chan. The largest of these 'citadels' is now known as Gran Chimú. It measures 550 by 350 m and is made of walls of adobe blocks 8 m high, although they may once have been higher (see Plate 316).

Prior to 1100, the site was a fair sized town with a population of between 7,000 and 8,000 inhabitants, all of whom made their living from agriculture and fishing. The members of the elite probably lived in the oldest citadels, such as those now known as Tello and Uhle, and it is speculated that these citadels were used as their tombs when they died. After this date, the Chimor kingdom spread along the coast maintaining trade links and alliances with Cajamarca. At its height, it would appear to have stretched from Tumbes in the north to Casma in the south, although some people maintain that it reached the Rimac valley, which would mean a minimum of 400 km.

Dwelling in a valley complex formed by meandering rivers, the Chimú people carefully worked a system of canals which enabled them to engage in constant agricultural production. The alluvial terraces situated on high ground drained naturally, but the land located on river banks tended to become saline owing to constant irrigation. The water supply for the Chan Chan site itself came from 140 wells situated within the 'citadels' and other internal buildings known as 'palaces' and those where the servants and lower-ranking population are thought to have lived. At the southern edge of the site a system of 'sunken gardens' was used. This involved digging down to the water table and sowing crops there. Cotton, maize and beans were the most important crops.

Given the physical structure of the Peruvian coastline, from ancient times a system of roads connecting the valleys was indispensable. The Chimor people made use of these road, traces of which still remain between Motupe and Chao and between Jequetepeque and Moche.

Around 1350, some changes become apparent which are indicative of expansive development. At this time, provincial administrative centres came into operation, such as Farfán in the Jequetepeque valley and Chiquito y Viejo in Chicama. The movement of skilled craftworkers, particularly weavers, goldsmiths, and wood- and stone-workers, towards Chan Chan is also apparent. The concentration of llamas in the valleys adjacent to the city is also worthy of note. This was because they could not be kept in the vicinity of the city

Figure 36 Chimú architectural decoration in moulded mud at Chan Chan (Peru), AD 1000–1466 (after Hagen, V. W. von, *Realm of the Incas*, NY 1957, p. 30).

owing to its desert characteristics.

There has been much speculation about the decadence of Mochica pottery at this time. Ideas in this regard must be revised in so far as a political entity like Chimú required considerable quantities of utilitarian vessels, and the use of moulds became commonplace in an attempt to satisfy the incessant demand. The commonest shape is the spherical pitcher with a slightly flattened spherical base and a stirrup neck. The tubular arc was usually inserted in the body of the vessel and a small figure (animal or human) was added to it. Human, animal, plant and fruit shapes are also found (see Plates 317–319).

As stated above, around 1400 the Chimor state conquered its neighbour at Lambayeque forming a significant political entity which made alliances in the northern mountains to act as a hedge against Inca expansion. In the Cajamarca and Huamachuco area, Inca and northern interests came into conflict, culminating in the outbreak of hostilities, the subsequent dispersion of the Chimor nobility and the carving up of their kingdom among rulers who were puppets of Cuzco.

THE LORDS OF THE CENTRAL COASTAL AREA

Three adjacent valleys formed by the Chillón, Rimac and Lurín Rivers cut through the desert of the central coast of Peru from north to south. Shortly beforehand, in the locality of Casma or Huarmey, the influence of the northern cultures declined, giving way to two possible local developments which are identifiable by their material remains, but which had little political impact. Everything would seem to indicate that neither one held sway over the other.

The small kingdom of Collique, or Collis as its original name appears to have been, flourished in the Chillón valley, clearly with a view to further expansion towards the mountains. Its mountain frontier was the Chaupiyunga region (at an altitude of about 1,500 m), where it came into contact with and fought against the Cantas, another ethnic group, for possession of the western slopes of the Andes, where a variety of coca leaf (*Erythroxylon novagranatense truxillense*) known to the Incas as *tupa* was grown and was regarded as superior to the variety produced on the eastern slopes.

To the north they bordered another small kingdom, the Chancay kingdom, which has left many pottery and textile remains but little historical information, and their monuments have scarcely been studied. To the south, the Rimac and Lurín valleys were dominated by the Pachacamac sanctuary.

The small Ichma fiefdom is probably buried beneath the streets of Lima. Pizarro's parade ground was located on what must have been their ceremonial centre, an oracle of local importance which gave its name to the Rimac River. This may be rendered as 'he who speaks'.

But none of its monuments could compete with the Pachacamac architectural complex. Situated in the Lurín valley, right by the seashore, this site has a long history of ideological control over the surrounding valleys. Its name is taken from one of the most important coastal gods, and more than one chronicler (Calancha, Santillán and others) tells how this deity received offerings comparable to the offerings made to the Sun, which was the official god of the Inca religion. The administration must have functioned rather like an indigenous version of the Vatican, with a priestly group which organized the cult and directed the pilgrimages coming from all over the Andes. The authority of this site was, clearly, severely undermined with the arrival of the Incas, who built a temple to the Sun and a precinct dedicated to the Sun priestesses *(acllas)* on sacred native ground. However, its prestige did not disappear altogether, and the last two Incas, Huascar and Atahualpa, consulted the oracle at Pachacamac to find out whether they would succeed their father Huaina Capac. If the Spanish chroniclers are to be believed, Huaina Capac was also a devotee of the coastal god.

The most notable pre-Inca buildings are the pyramids with ramps, I and II. These pyramids, which are made of clay, were probably used most intensively during the Late Intermediate Period, i.e. the period when the kingdoms and confederations prior to the Incas were being formed.

We do not know what links they maintained with the neighbouring Chincha kingdom, in the valley of the same name to the south of Lurín. The Chinchas were excellent sailors and travelled as far as the kingdoms of the north coast. At the same time, barter activity must have contributed to the expansion of the Pachacamac cult, whose priests demanded that replicas be built in the Chimú kingdom.

The prestige of Pachacamac must have owed a great deal to the fact that he was the 'god of tremors'. As the central coast is a seismic area, given to continual earth tremors, the faith of his believers did not diminish as the political sway of the site waned.

THE LAKESIDE KINGDOMS

At the break-up of Tiwanaku, when relatively fixed trade and caravan routes had been established, lakeside states and fiefdoms ruled by *curacas* vied for supremacy in the region. So far four such entities are known to have existed: the Collas and Lupacas in the north-east, and the Pacajes and Omasuyos in the south-east. The links between the former and the western valleys and the coast have been well documented by archaeological evidence. Allita Amaya pottery, which corresponds to the Lupacas, is closely related to such complexes as Churajón (Arequipa), whereas Kollau pottery, which would appear to have belonged to the Collas, is to be found at Alto Caplina (Tacna in Peru) and Azapa (Arica in Chile).

Of the groups mentioned above, the Lupacas (Lupaqa) have received considerable attention on account of the publication of *La visita hecha a la provincia de chuquito* (The Visit to Chuquito Province, by García Díez de San Miguel in 1567). This is a long administrative document in which the native population and the resources of the seven Chuquito villages, the ancient Lupaca centre, are quantified. The data was collected for tax purposes, but, independently of the aims of the visitor, the source provides us with historical information concerning the original population and how the people and the territory of the region were treated by Cuzco. Unfortunately, the nature of the document means that not much information is provided about aspects unrelated to taxes. Moreover, the information provided by the chronicles, centred on the Inca oral tradition, is particularly scanty and does not complement the material provided by this visit. The situation is not helped by the fact that these were Aymara-speaking people. Although a million people still speak this language today, the fact that they have lived side by side for almost two thousand years with Quechuas has diluted the cultural differences between the two. Aymara belongs to the linguistic family known as Jaqi, and only two other languages belonging to this group survive today, Jakuru and Jawki, both of which are spoken in Peru.

At the time of this visit, the Lupacas were concentrated along the shores of the lake (about 100,000 inhabitants), but they also inhabited the western slopes of the plateau. These were permanent settlements which maintained links with the home region. They herded flocks, grew maize, coca leaf or chillies, and collected salt and guano along the Pacific coast.

Both the Lupacas and the neighbouring kingdoms occupied lands beyond the limits of their own political centre, with the result that Lupaca settlements are to be found in Pacaqe territory and vice versa. This 'discontinuous landholding' system was not confined to complex political entities. In 1593, *curaca* fiefdoms and Camaná villages had small plots in neighbouring land. Was this a kind of strategy to protect their meagre crops against misfortunes such as frosts, or was it a way of ensuring their mutual dependence in order to prevent wars? As no convincing reply is available, it would be opportune to reflect on the matter using ecological criteria.

The land distribution pattern is like an archipelago, i.e. a series of 'islands' belonging to one system. The Lupacas showed how, in the Andean environment, it was necessary to have a presence in different ecological niches in order to ensure the resources essential for survival. In Chuquito, the 'islands' continued to depend on the lords who ruled from the shores of the lake, and these links were maintained far into the colonial period when the settlers claimed to belong to ethnic groups which had remained on the altiplano.

This hypothesis fits in with the idea of verticality as a mental picture of relationships in the Andean world and upholds the idea that the Collao plateau maintained close communications with the coasts of Peru, Chile and north-western Argentina. How ever valid this hypothesis may prove to be outside the region, this is something which is under review. In northern Peru it would appear that coastal pre-eminence ('inverted verticality' or the 'horizontal archipelago') climbed the slopes of the Andes, where the 'fiefdom' of Cuismancu or Guzmango (Contumazá, Cajamarca) would have paid tribute to Chimor with 'islands' which have even been detected on the eastern slopes of the mountain range.

Chuquito province was organized around the seven original villages (Chuquito, Acora, Llave, Juli, Pomata, Yunguyu, Zepita), divided, according to Andean custom, into two units *(alasaa* and *maasaa)* known in Quechua as *sayas*. According to the *quipus* (a system of knotted cords used to record statistics), the province comprised 28,080 households split between the two main ethnic groups, 15,778 Aymaras and 4,129 Urus. If we allow five members per household, this gives us a round figure of about 100,000 souls.

Who were the Urus? A dictionary compiled in 1612 defines them as: 'a nation of Indians of low intelligence despised by all, who are normally fishermen', but this is not how they are portrayed by the Chuquito document, which states that

> these people are no less intelligent and capable than the rest of the Aymaras, but they have been subjugated and oppressed to such a degree that they have not been allowed to be more noble . . . Melchor Alarcón (the royal scribe based in the region during the visit) has seen them work very well. Their fields or those of the overlords are the first to be sown in the province, and whether in the latter or in the fields of other Indians who give them coca leaf, beverages or some other payment in kind . . . and he knows and has seen . . . that the fields they work will be more fruitful and they are better than the Aymaras.

The existence of subject peoples is not unusual in the pre-European context, but the outstanding point here is that they are ascribed to a particular ethnic group and a special trade ('fishermen'). The contemptuous references may be explained by the fact that the source is Aymara.

The Incas ordered Urus and Aymaras to be transferred to Arica and Atacama. Whether or not they originated on the coasts of Chile or were familiar with that area at some time in the past is a matter open to debate. One story dated 1581 tells of 400 Urus from Atacama who 'were not baptised' and did not live in a concentrated settlement and paid allegiance to no one, although they did give fish to the lords of Atacama as a sign of vassalage. 'They are very primitive. They neither reap nor sow and live by eating fish alone'. Since the sixteenth century, the Urus, along with two other groups of fishing communities, the Camanchaca and Proanche, have been known generically as the Changos, and their presence has been detected in Antofagasta (Chile) at a late stage. Archaeological reports from Arica and Atacama suggest that the Changos' clothing was similar to that of the Aymaras. Remains of their household effects and food have been discovered alongside offerings and fishing tackle.

This was not the only ethnic group on the altiplano. The Chuquito, *Padrón de los indios más ricos de la Provincia* ('Census of the One Thousand Richest Indians in the Province') refers to the *ayllu* of Chuquilla hunters, who bear the brunt of derogatory remarks similar to those made against the Urus. It was said of them '. . . they are hunters. There are not many of them and they know nothing about anything except killing wild animals and practising idolatry. They are sorcerers and, as they never see Spaniards, they prefer to remain among their *huacas* (sacred place or object). From a later document, it may be inferred that the people of Hatun Colla had hunting grounds reserved for the Chuquillas (according to the provisions of the Tawantinsuyu). These areas were located on the very wet subalpine paramo and on the rainy, alpine tundra, where they set traps and fished. The Chuquillas must have occupied the high area surrounding the Colla heartland. There is not much more information available on them, but they must have prospered to a degree during colonial times. Their chief, Guarecallo, was recognized as a powerful person in the Chuquito *urinsaya*.

In political terms, the area around the lake must have been very unstable. The chronicles explain that this is why it was conquered, the conquest being attributed to the Inca Viracocha. According to a more extensive version, Cari, 'king' of Chuquito, and Zapana, lord of 'Hatun Colla', disputed the area. Their skirmishes alternated with frequent incursions to the Cuzco valley. Viracocha decided to put an end to this threat and, having overthrown the Canchis and made a pact with the Canas (both ethnic groups located near Cuzco valley), he sent messengers to the Collao. When the Incas managed to reach the plateau, they found that the situation was already defined: Cari had vanquished the Collas and made a pact with Cuzco symbolized by burying the vessel used to toast this new friendship. The native chronicler, Juan Santa Cruz Pachacuti, transcribed a hymn which reflects this alliance:

> You the lord of Cuzco
> And I the lord of Collao:
> Let us drink

Let us eat.
(And) let us agree
that neither (of us) is sad.
I who cling to silver
you who cling to gold
you who adore Viracocha
the sustainer of the world,
I who adore the Sun

Although in the text both rulers are attributed with equal status, this situation is not corroborated by the report by Garcia Díez de San Miguel referred to earlier. However, the Incas demanded a heavy tribute from their neighbours to the south: salt, potatoes, *quinua* and *camelidae* as basic resources; feathers and fine cloth as luxury items; labour to make ordinary cloth and shoes; skilled labour to make fine textiles and feather-work; *mitayos* (shift workers) to extract minerals and to labour in the construction of Cuzco buildings; *mitimaes* or settlers to tame far-off places; soldiers for military campaigns; wives for the Inca nobility and, finally, victims for human sacrifices. The Inca counterpart could not be more symbolic: blankets and *cumbi* (a fine cloth) shirts for the *curacas* and foodstuffs for the festivals decreed in the capital of the Tawantinsuyo. The Incas could not have been harsher with the land which saw the birth of their ancestors Manco Capac and Mama Ocllo.

THE LORDS OF THE CENTRAL MOUNTAINS

While a precarious alliance was being built up between the highland people and the kingdom of Chimú in the north of the country, the characteristics described for the domains and fiefdoms of the central coast made it difficult for them to maintain relations with their counterpart in the highlands.

If we examine the region between Huancayo, the Lake of Junín (also known as Bombón or Chinchaicocha) and the Chanchamayo valley in the high jungle, we find that during this period immediately prior to the Incas there were three ethnic groups with a large population. First of all there were the Huancas. The Huancas were perhaps the most numerous and they inhabited the lands irrigated by the Mantaro river, which stretch from Huancayo to Jauja, and all the interconnected valleys in this vicinity. Then there were the Tarmas or Taramas, whose lands extended from the Tarma valley to the eastern edge of the Junín puna. Finally, the slopes of the Andes which stretch as far as the Gran Pajonal were inhabited by the Asheninkas or Campas, whose population pattern was probably more akin to that of the Amazon peoples. It must be pointed out, however, that the Campas (and their neighbours the Amueshas) always maintained closer links with the highland peoples than the other peoples of the tropical jungle.

There is a considerable amount of colonial information on the Huancas, particularly because they, like the Cañaris of the Ecuadorean mountains, soon abandoned their status as vassals of the Incas to ally themselves with the Spanish army. This indicates that their relationship with the lords of Cuzco, who must have dominated the central mountains up to 1450, was a difficult one.

It is difficult to determine which political centre exercised authority over the Tarmas or the Huancas. The site with the highest density of buildings belongs to the largest group in the Yanamarca valley, but it would appear that this was not due to the need to establish intercommunal links but rather to a concentration of population which does not seem to have been repeated elsewhere. At this site, the plan clearly was to divide the built-up areas into equal constructions forming pairs which are repeated with some regularity. There is also the tendency to occupy the high ground, which would appear to indicate a certain defensive model. In any case, the most common buildings would appear to have been used for very local purposes, such as food-stores. This is also true of the Tarma, although on a smaller scale. The Palcamayo valley was the residential centre for this ethnic group, providing them with the best land.

The basic resource of both peoples was pasturing. As well as llamas and alpacas, they utilized the local fauna, the Chinchaicocha lake area being the place with the greatest variety of puna species. Like Lake Titicaca in the southern mountains, from ancient times this lake, though smaller, also provided the people of the central puna with a niche in which to experiment with and domesticate plants and animals. Its role in their ideology has not been studied. In any case, the Wariwilka temple, which was built by the Waris, would appear to have had a greater impact on the Huancas, who regarded it as their legendary place of origin.

One last word on the Campas. The heartland of their territory is the river system including the Apurimac river, which then joins the Mantaro, so becoming the Ene. Further downstream, this river joins the Perené to form the Tambo river, which flows into the Ucayali. These people, who lived in scattered autonomous groups along the rivers, maintained smooth links with the peoples of the highlands. It is noteworthy that in 1742, two centuries after Pizarro, an Andean mestizo took the name Inca Atahualpa (Juan Santos Atahualpa) and rallied the Indians to his call. The uprising halted the European advance for a century. Their leader was sanctified (Apo Capac Huaina or *Jesús Sacramentado* ('Jesus Transubstantiated')) and before the eyes of his followers was raised up into heaven, where he dwells among the Campa gods. As in the case of the Incas, for the Campas the most important deity was the Sun god.

THE CHANCAS, BETWEEN MYTH AND HISTORY

It is more difficult to find answers to questions regarding the formation of highland political entities after Wari, when we move to the territory of Ayacucho itself. With the fall of Wari, the great cities disappeared and were replaced by rather precarious human settlements that were generally located in the higher mountain reaches and were circular or square in design. Two kinds of poor quality pottery then evolved, one with cursive motifs and the other decorated in three characteristic colours: white and black on a red background, using geometrical designs.

If the chronicles are reliable, the original territory of the Chancas was situated in what is today the department of Huancavelica, as their creation myths have them arise out of the Choclococha lake in the Pipilchaca district. The lake lies at an altitude of 4,511 m and must be in the region of nine kilometres long by three kilometres wide. Originally its waters flowed into the Atlantic basin, forming the Pampas river, which divides the department of Ayacucho in two. Later its course was altered, and it now flows into the Ica river basin in order to irrigate the land in this region.

When the Europeans arrived, the lake was also known as Lake Acha, although the legendary memory of a battle between two Chanca leaders had given rise to its new name, which may be translated as 'the lake of the corn cobs'. According to local archaeologists, Chanca territory stretched from Castrovirreina (Huancavelica), including the whole of the department of Ayacucho and part of the department of Apurimac, as far as its natural boundary at the confluence of the Pampas and Apurimac rivers.

Following the pattern of the fiefdoms of the central mountains, there are no important monumental centres and their settlements are similar to those described above. The remains prove that they made their appearance in the Andes around AD 1100 and, like the rest of the peoples in the Cuzco area, they were absorbed around AD 1400.

When the chronicles refer to the Chancas, they always mention their warlike nature. As we shall see, this is due more to an Inca interpretation of their own history where the Chancas played a special role. They also allude to the local tradition according to which their ancestor was the puma, puma skins being used as ceremonial garments.

It is interesting that, although the Incas recognized Lake Titicaca as their place of origin in one of their myths, the birth of the Tawantinsuyu as a panregional state is attributed to the triumph of the Inca Pachacuti over the Chancas.

With slight variations, the Inca imperial saga tells how the Inca Viracocha was threatened by Uscovilca, the Chanca chief who was anxious to measure his strength against the lord of Cuzco. Inca Viracocha decided to put up no resistance and withdrew to the capital of his small kingdom with his son Urco, whom he had chosen as his successor. Another son, called the Inca Yupanqui, decided to take on the defence of Cuzco, and for this task he acquired divine assistance. According to some versions, the Sun, and according to others god Viracocha (not to be confused with his father, who was also called Viracocha), appeared to him in his dreams and promised him victory. For the final battle, the Inca Yupanqui must have been overwhelmed by the number of Chanca warriors, but the god fulfilled his promise and the stones surrounding the city turned into warriors and defeated the invaders.

The Inca Yupanqui took the name Pachacuti, overthrew his father and annulled the decision designating Urco as his successor. After a long reign, he then set up the institutions which laid the foundations of the empire of the four corners of the world.

The interesting point about this legendary tale is that it rejects the Ayacucho region as the origin of the political model later followed by the Incas. This conflicts with the archaeological evidence which shows that Wari was undoubtedly the first experiment in a transregional state whose structures, both physical (roads, *usnos* (state buildings), etc.) and administrative (*mitimaes, tambos* (store houses), *chaskis* (messenger)) must have been inherited by the Incas.

The story of Pachacuti sounds like an ideological fabrication aimed at claiming an identity which effaces any direct paternity. In this scenario, the Chancas, seen as the barbarian descendants of a lost grandeur, were the ideal rivals.

But this contemptuous vision could not be applied to the whole of their relationship with the Waris. In Vilcashuamán, the Incas built one of the most important ceremonial temples. The Villac Umu or High Priest travelled there before the ceremony which would consecrate him as the director of the religious life of the Incas.

THE CHILDREN OF THE SUN

None of the highland kingdoms which arose after the decline of Wari could compete with the supremacy of the coastal kingdom of Chimú, which controlled the northern coast and threatened the nearby mountains. Chimú had a compact system of government and an ideology which spread beyond its own frontiers, and its technology was unrivalled. However, once again the pendulum of power swung back towards the mountains, and the lords of Cuzco ranged over the Andean territory, paying particular attention to their northern neighbours.

Research has yet to provide us with a reasonable volume of knowledge regarding the Incas. This is partly explained by the fact that Cuzco has been inhabited continuously and the modern urban area stands above the old colonial and pre-Hispanic site. This poses logistical problems and arouses passions which make it difficult to carry out excavations on the site. Similar problems arise with the documentation, which, like all written documents preserved in Andean archives, is of poor quality, editions of which are limited. The documents are infinitely inferior to those of Mexico, for instance. Only in the past decade or so have critical editions begun to appear and ethnographic and folkloric works been produced, although these latter fields did receive considerable attention in the 1940s and 1950s.

Fitting together the fragments of information available, it would appear that around AD 1200 the Cuzco valley was divided into a series of *curaca* fiefdoms which were continually at war with one another, although no single one managed to dominate the region. The Incas, who arrived on the scene later, were not much different from the Sañu, Alcaviza or Ayamarca, who are regarded as the original inhabitants. They all share a common history of wars and rather precarious alliances where pacts against third parties are as common as marriages for dynastic reasons. This situation would seem to have changed when, at the initiative of the Inca group, work was begun to drain the marshy floor of the valley.

The above does not automatically belie the information attributed to the 'first dynasty', part of which undoubtedly constitutes a description of situations concurrent with the development of an embryonic state. Thus, in the early days, the Inca and the gods shared the Inticancha, a kind of palace cum ceremonial centre, and the Inca is attributed with performing works of magic, using talismans and spells, etc., which indicates that civil and religious powers, as we know them separately today, were closely linked.

As the Tawantinsuyu developed, however, this picture changed considerably, particularly because the growth of the ruling class required increased tributes and led to a divergence of interests. Furthermore, the roles of their technicians became specialized. For this to occur, a qualitative and quantitative leap was required to transform a more or less loose federation of *curaca* fiefdoms into an integrated state. The legendary language of the chronicles explains this through the 'war with the Chancas', which we have already mentioned.

In archaeological terms, the pottery which developed when the Inca Empire was at its height (1300 – 1500) would seem to be based on a local pottery called Killke, found mostly in the Huatanay River basin, which is one of the rivers closest to the monumental capital. Similarly, in the valley of the Lucre River, which is also close to Cuzco, the existence of artifacts reminiscent of Wari is well known. Another factor is its buildings, which recall the city of Pikillaqta, by then abandoned. The pottery found at Lucre, known as Qotakalli, reveals that it managed to survive the presence of the Ayacucho people and that the Killke and Qotakalli are two of the groups to have emerged during the power vacuum which occurred as a result of the decline of Wari.

In social terms, by counting and classifying each and every inhabitant of the city and reserving elite status for the members of the founding families, the lords of Cuzco were a double hierarchical group of ruling officials at the service of the Tawantinsuyu.

It is well known that their early campaigns followed the highland route and, having defeated the Chancas in the north, they had to turn southwards to bring the lakeside kingdoms under control. Then, once they had conquered the peoples of the north western mountains of Peru, they continued their fairly relaxed advance as far as Quito. The central coast was an area which they coveted and they reached it slowly and with planning. The same may be said of their entry into the Pachacamac sanctuary. As was pointed out above, it is easy to see how the Incas built over the sites reserved for the erstwhile powerful god of earthquakes of the Wari period. Sometimes the link is difficult to explain, as is the case of the 'Chincha fiefdom'. It appears that this fiefdom was a political entity with a centralized government and a barter economy which allowed these people to sail along practically the whole Peruvian coast on large rafts. When Atahualpa was captured in 1532 in Pizarro's ambush, many of the Spaniards thought the Inca was the lord of Chincha on account of his clothing and the number of servants accompanying him.

This contrasts with the destructive attitude imposed by the later Incas on the north coast, where Chan Chan was in a state of ruin when the first European saw it. There were differences of opinion, therefore, on whether to subject the vast territory finally ruled by the Incas or to make alliances. The Inca Empire, which extended from Pasto in Colombia to the Maule River in Chile, with the Amazon mountains as its eastern frontier, was the largest political organization ever to exist in the New World.

Curiously enough, the references to the eastern flank of the Andes are deprecatory. According to official propaganda, the 'Chunchos' or savages were not worth the effort of conquest. However, there is proof that attempts were made to conquer them on numerous occasions. Contrary to what one might expect, these attempts did not begin following the natural course of the Apurimac and Urubamba Rivers which surround the Cuzco region and then, further north, form the Ucayali. Albeit in vain, the Incas preferred to use the jungle area around Cuzco itself, beginning in the Yucay valley, setting up what was later to be their last stand, Vilcabamba; but they achieved little. Other later attempts were launched from the Madre de Dios to the north-east of Cuzco, but with equally meagre results.

Perhaps the machinery of social control worked best in population groups with well-known cycles, such as those based on a farming economy, where fairs and calendric meetings might receive the protection of a generous patron (the Inca or his officials) who would guarantee the administration of crops or newborn *camelidae*. The aim of building or redecorating monumental complexes (such as Huanucopampa) was to turn the act of subjecting the local groups into a celebration, as these groups would identify the buildings and Cuzco officials (or officials trained in Cuzco) as the organizers of their lives.

Like the rulers of Wari, the Incas made their architecture a symbol of their political presence. Some buildings, such as the *usno*, are to be seen in nearly every corner of the Tawantinsuyu. In some cases their vessels, austere and functional, e.g. the *keros*, carry on previous traditions and the decoration, which is mostly geometrical, must bow to the cultures which preceded them. But we should not be hasty to judge what we know mostly through written accounts rather than from the systematic excavation of Cuzco, which has not yet begun. The buildings that are visible in the capital have been occupied since 1532, and the fact that they have been used constantly, right up to the present day, makes the archaeological work, which ought to have been undertaken long ago, difficult to carry out. Even so, the ruins of the immediate past (Pisac, Ollantaitambo or Sacsaihuamán) give us some idea of what the city of cities of Pre-Columbian America must have been like (see Plates 320–322).

BIBLIOGRAPHY

BONAVIA, D. 1991. *Perú hombre e historia. De los orígenes al siglo XV.* Ediciones Edubanco, Lima.

CASAEVITZ, R.; SAIGNES, T; TAYLOR, A. C. 1988. *Al este de los Andes. Relaciones entre las sociedades amazónicas y andinas entre los siglos XV & XVII.* Ediciones Abya-Yala-IFEA, Lima and Quito.

COOK, A. G. 1994. *Wari y Tiwanaku: entre el estilo y la imagen.* Pontificia Universidad Católica, Lima.

GONZÁLEZ CARRÉ, E. 1992. *Los Señoríos Chankas.* Indea, Lima.

HUERTAS, L. 1990. Los chancas y el proceso distributivo en los Andes. In: *Historia y Cultura,* No 20. Lima.

ISBELL, W. H. 1985. El origen del estado en el valle de Ayacucho. In: *Revista Andina,* No. 1, pp. 57–106.

MANZANILLA, L. 1992. *Akapana: Una pirámide en el centro del mundo.* Instituto de Investigaciones, Mexico City.

MATOS, R. 1994. *Pumpu. Centro Administrativo Inka de la Puna de Junín.* Editorial Horizonte, Lima.

MILLONES, L. 1987. *Historia y poder en los Andes centrales (desde los orígenes al siglo XVII).* Alianza Universitaria, Madrid.

—. 1997. *El rostro de la fe. Doce ensayos sobre religiosidad andina.* Pablo de Olavide. El Monte, Seville.

MORRIS, C.; THOMPSON, D. E. 1985. *Huanuco Pampa. An Inca City and its Hinterland.* Thames & Hudson, London, Madrid.

MORRIS, C.; VON HAGEN, A. 1993. *The Inca Empire and its Andean Origins.* American Museum of Natural History, New York.

PARSONS, J.; HASTINGS, C. 1992. Late Intermediate Period. In: KEATING, R. W. (ed.) *Peruvian Prehistory.* Cambridge University Press, Cambridge.

RAYMOND, S. 1992. A View from the Tropical Forest. In: KEATING, R. W. (ed.) *Peruvian Prehistory.* Cambridge University Press, Cambridge.

RICHARDSON, J. 1994. *People of the Andes.* St. Rémy Press and Smithsonian Institution, Montreal.

ROSTOROWSKI, M. 1997. *Costa Peruana Prehispánica.* Instituto de Estudios Peruanos, Lima.

SHIMADA, I. 1995. *Cultura Sicán.* Edubanco, Lima.

TOPIC, J. R. 1985. Huari and Huanachuco. Paper prepared for Huari Round Table. Dumbarton Oaks (16–19 May 1985), Washington, DC.

TOPIC, T. L. 1990. Territorial expansion and the kingdom of Chimor. In: MOSELEY, M. E. and CORDY, A. C. (eds) *The Northern Dynasties, Kingship and Statecraft in Chimor.* Dumbarton Oaks, Washington, DC.

UCEDA, S.; MÚJICA, E. (eds) *Moche, propuestas y perspectivas.* Universidad Nacional de Trujillo and IFEA, Lima.

ZARZAR, A. 1989. *Apo Capac Huaina, Jesús Sacramentado. Mito, utopía y milenarismo en el pensamiento de Juan Santos Atahualpa.* Ediciones CAAAP. Lima.

39.3
SOUTHERN SOUTH AMERICA

Ana María Lorandi and Daniel Schávelzon

CULTURAL DEVELOPMENTS AFTER AD 700

The area of valleys and *punas* of Chile's *Norte Grande*, particularly Arica and San Pedro de Atacama, is linked to Pukará and Tiwanaku among other cultures of the altiplano (see Map 44). The influence of Pukará was particularly strong in the coastal valleys in the early period, giving way later to the Tiwanakus who had colonies in a number of valleys along the southern Peruvian coast and Arica, and whose links with San Pedro de Atacama would appear to have been commercial in nature. The development of this site did not depend on large centres: pottery designs, wooden tablets and spoons, and characteristic weaving, show autonomy and a certain degree of regionalism. The objects imported from the north or from the Puna and the valleys of Argentina prove that San Pedro was a redistribution centre. In the tombs there are red or black ceramic items from the central valleys such as Condorhuasi, or of the Isla de la Quebrada de Humahuaca type. All this forms a network associating local elements with Tiwanaku (around AD 800). In Arica, the influence of the altiplano in the hamlets of the middle period begins in the Pukará era during the Alto Ramírez phase. The later Maytas ceramics are from the Tiwanaku period.

Access to these valleys from the north was significant: maize, chillies, cotton and fish allowed them to obtain other resources in addition to potatoes and *llamas* from the highlands. During this period, the patterns of subsistence and obtaining surpluses were clearly undergoing expansion, due to colonization or trade. This explains the rise of Tiwanaku, which must have exploited these subsidiary areas to consolidate its political and religious power. At this time, surpluses, village development and the beginnings of urban development in the area converge to produce power centres with comparatively dependent marginal areas.

During the Middle Period (650–1000), north-west Argentina saw the expansion of the Aguada ideology. This culture (González, 1964) developed out of the Alamito complex of the Early Period on the eastern fringe of the north-west, and spread throughout the whole region. It probably overlaid and lived side by side with the bearers of the Ciénega culture, from the Catamarca centre, and it may have lasted and coexisted with other groups of non-Andean origin in the region, with their own patterns or offshoots from old cultural components.

The distribution of Aguada appears to be linked to cat-centred rituals and warrior characteristics, as can be seen in its iconography, complex decoration and the oniric forms, which may sometimes indicate shamanic cults. War and cult can be likely factors of social cohesion and coercion exercised by a wealthy elite. This decoration takes distinguishing forms in each region. In the Hualfín valley, incised black pottery is dominant, while at Ambato both painted and incised ceramics are found: large urns with decorated figures with body paint, or feline masks and large hook-shaped noses. In the north of La Rioja, pieces with polychrome painting predominate. The symbology, with elements represented in ceramics, metal and wood carvings, reveals the direct influence of Tiwanaku.

In the Aguada culture, pottery-making techniques advanced considerably, a number of different types being found at habitation sites and in refuse dumps. Different types of decoration are found using both painting and incision techniques. Among the former are the Aguada bicolour types, black designs on a reddish-yellow background, and black, red and tricolour Aguada, with black and crimson designs on a natural background. The decorative motifs are geometrical shapes or feline figures. The most common shapes are cylindrical and conical pitchers, globular and sub-globular pots and semi-spherical vessels or *pucos* with a mixed profile. There are also reddish-yellow anthropomorphic figures, generally nude images with large slant eyes and complicated hairstyles; the arms and legs are mere stumps.

Most of the figurines are in a standing position. The modelled male form predominates, although little stress is laid on sexual characteristics. There are also clay pipes with fantastic figures, human faces or feline, diabolical or monstrous images which were used as incense-burners. Human statuettes of soft stone, which are often replicas of the clay figurines, are found as well as cylindrical or keriform vases made of soapstone with feline figures or figures of warriors wearing complicated headdress and carrying head trophies and axes.

In the field of metallurgy, the casting technique was used more extensively: axes adorned with dragon figures or with feline images on the blade are found. The so-called 'discs' are noteworthy. The Lafone Quevedo disc, perhaps the most outstanding of this type, shows a central figure, whose head and chest are richly adorned, flanked by two feline figures on his shoulders which extend downwards in a dragon-like shape.

The settlement pattern is that of the hamlet, although at Ambato there are settlements with ceremonial mounds like those at Alamito in the previous period. In the north of La Rioja there are complex clusters of stone dwellings which

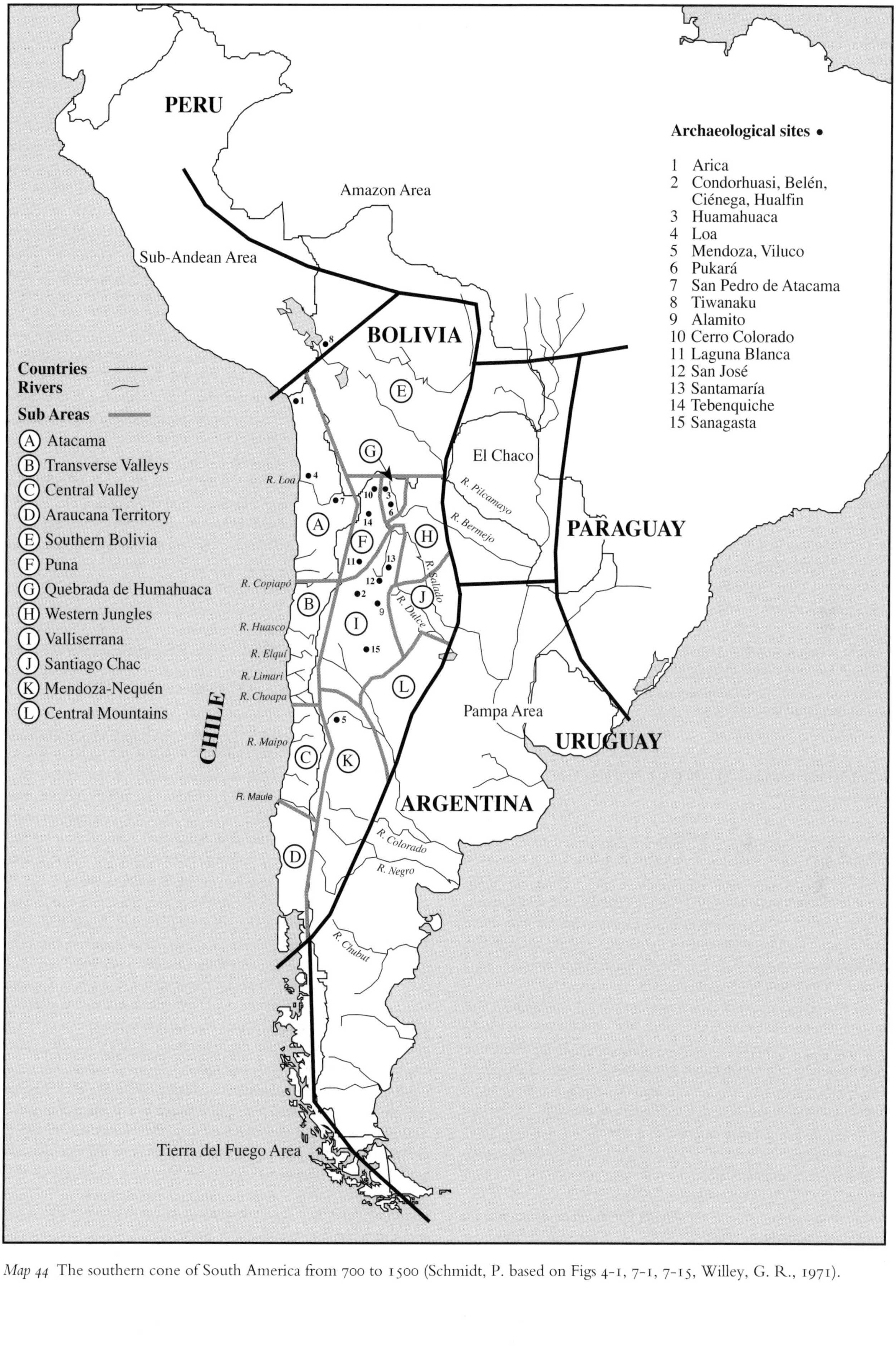

Map 44 The southern cone of South America from 700 to 1500 (Schmidt, P. based on Figs 4-1, 7-1, 7-15, Willey, G. R., 1971).

have been little studied to date. There is evidence of craftsmen with technical and artistic expertise in bronze metallurgy. In the rest of north-west Argentina the hamlet pattern of the Early Period continued. There are sites belonging to that period, such as Santa Ana de Abralaite on the northern Puna and the Cerro Colorado phase at Yave on the north-eastern Puna, which show no connection with the northern Puna, such as Laguna Blanca and Tebenquiche, except that the settlement pattern continues to be the hamlet linked to cultivation fields, cultivation terraces as in Santa Ana or mounds as in Cerro Colorado and Pozuelos.

There would appear to be no common stylistic pattern in pottery. On the whole the designs are geometrical. The sites were communities with good harvests and an emphasis on pasturing. They appear not to have formed large political units and show a settlement pattern based on segmented *puna* societies with no major changes.

In Quebrada de Humahuaca, on the other hand, a transition can be seen from small hamlets to large ones with larger structural elements, possibly associated with a more complex political model. This is the beginning of the formation of small power centres, with landed property located at different heights, which used the horizontal model of land rights. This situation may have had a bearing on social relationships, the exchange of women, or associations more symbolic and ritual in nature than political.

Aguada manifestations are also found in the extreme south of the Andean region in the north of the Cuyo area, particularly at San Juan. The dwellings in the settlements at the bottom of the valleys are built of long stretches of adobe wall erected at the same time. In the rest of Cuyo, the post-archaic or early model characteristic of the Agrelo culture continues, with stylistic links to the Molle complex in the centre and Norte Chico of Chile.

LATE REGIONAL DEVELOPMENT (1000–1480)

The transition from the Middle to the Late Period in the central area of north-west Argentina must have involved population changes. In the remaining areas similar situations are difficult to find, although in the north of Chile, occupation of the coastal valleys by people from the *altiplano* may have increased. The presence in the central area of people and features from the lowlands must have occurred in successive waves of migration to and settlement in the area.

Between 800 and 1000, once the sway of Aguada had passed, there are a number of regional complexes revealing great changes which become evident later. In general, the ceramics from these regional developments, like the ones at Sanagasta, Hualfín, Angualasto and San José, reveal stylistic elements which are a continuation of old models which had been weakened by the impact of Aguada.

In general, the period is characterized by technological advance, greater population density, and cultural units which extended throughout each of the main valleys, particularly in Hualfín, and the Calchaquí and Quebrada de Humahuaca valleys. Despite the cultural unity of these expansions, the political structure does not appear to have been equally united. There are chiefdoms with small territories and a tribute-producing base ranging from two or three to eleven villages each. The existence of forts in the interior of the valleys, one within sight of the other, and the colonial data which reflect constant conflict, reveal a relatively atomized organization which did not hinder the development of stable settlements, the construction of large villages with stone dwellings, which were frequently walled, and ceremonial centres of some size, with very extensive terracing as at Coctaca and increasing irrigation control.

Many valley communities set up colonies in the highlands of Aconquija, the Pampa Grande and the Sierra de Santa Victoria. From there they could control the wooded eastern slopes. Towards the Puna they had links with areas of pastureland and saltpans, which allowed them to increase their production base. The concentration of semi-urban population is notable in Quebrada de Humahuaca, the Calchaquí valleys and Hualfín, and the areas of the Humahuaca, Santa María and Belén cultures. Towards the south, in the Sanagasta culture, where conglomerate settlements are rarer, the hamlet pattern and dwellings surrounded by fields are more common.

In the north-east of the Puna, the Yavi Chico culture, dated between 930 and 1460, in the basin of the Yavi–La Quiaca, which flows into the Pilcomayo River, shows signs which link it with the Chicha populations of southern Bolivia. The settlement pattern varies between the semi-conglomerate and the conglomerate model. Their pottery also shows stylistic links with the little known complexes at Santa Victoria in the east and Pozuelos in the north of the Puna.

It is difficult to establish to what extent trading took place between the societies of the late period and how they obtained supplies. There is no clear evidence to show the existence of an organized market, even at Tastil, one of the largest settlements (12 ha) of the time. These conglomerations show a tendency towards specialization, such as large-scale manufacture of cloth which might have attracted local barter trade. According to Ottonello, 'however, even at Tastil, the general situation seems to have been the same as in the rest of the Andean heartland and, in particular, the southern highlands, that is, a search for self-sufficiency by controlling the maximum possible number of ecological niches, whose diversified produce complemented that of the core area, (Ottonello and Lorandi, 1987). This is apparent in both the Santa María and Quebrada populations, who extended their links to the Puna and the sub-Andean highlands, or in the population of the Belén culture, in the Hualfín valley, with settlements near Antofagasta on the northern Puna.

The late settlements on the Puna are concentrated in the Guatayoc–Salinas Grandes basin, at altitudes above 3,500 m. The Puna conglomerations are associated with extensive hillside cultivation areas and significant pasturing activity; the Puna is an area of passage linking valleys and canyons with the Atacama area. Connections with the southern *altiplano* would appear to have been less intense.

Relations between the cultures of southern Bolivia – where the so-called Southern Tricoloured Horizon predominates – and north-west Argentina, are revealed by the presence of sets of iconographical elements associated with the eastern highlands of the region which spread beyond the Andean area towards the lands of Chaco Santiago. For the time being, no links of geographical continuity can be established in the area, between these regions, linked by decoration motifs. However, the Aconquija highlands do show such links with the cultures of the altiplano, although they cannot be attributed to any specific contacts or relations.

While the influence of this link with the Bolivian highlands was very real, it was more, difficult for it to penetrate the valleys and canyons, where the political units managed to maintain comparative cultural independence, which gives them independent features such as the frequency of burials in urns or the construction of multiple sepulchres for burying adults, normally accompanied by an abundance of objects. There are often real cemeteries, although burial in village yards or in dwellings may be characteristic of Quebrada de Humahuaca and El Toro. The Puna, where graves are found in hollows or small caves in the hillsides, is the only area where this feature typical of the *altiplano* is apparent. Metalworking, particularly in bronze, developed enormously in the central valleys. Bronze was used in ritual objects, such as discs with anthropo-zoomorphic designs characteristic of this period.

Wood carvings were important at ritual sites. Painted and dressed, they represented guardian gods. The quality of pottery diminishes, but there are exceptions, such as at Santiago del Estero and Tucumán, the pottery of which was later held in high esteem by the Incas.

Funeral urns for children date from this period and region. In Santa María and Hualfín there are urns and *pucos*. Pitchers and a greater variety of shapes are characteristic of Quebrada de Humahuaca. Black pottery virtually disappears, giving way to bi- and tricoloured decorations which vary from one region to another.

In the sub-Andean mountains and in Santiago del Estero, the later patterns of settlement adapt to wooded conditions. In Santiago there are hamlets from 800 onwards which continued until colonial times. Debris from various activities is accumulated in mounds which formed a part of the settlements. Dams were built between these to retain rain and flood water. Burials are found there either in urns or at the bottom of the mounds, apparently with no burial objects.

At this time, the north of Chile became increasingly dependent upon kingdoms and fiefdoms of the altiplano. The coastal fiefdoms with important hamlet settlements, and ceramics in the style of San Miguel, Pocoma and Gentilar, contemporary with the Urco (*altiplano*) chiefdoms or confederations with special rights or links with the coastal valleys, form an extensive area. Complex networks of borrowings link the Uma populations of the eastern valleys with products from the coast.

Most of the information about this period in the Arica valleys is derived from burial objects; data about late settlements are scarcer and in some places links between the highlands and the coast are apparent. The middle valleys are important staging points for the traffic between the different regions. Huancarane, in the Camarones valley, and Cerro Sombrero, in the Azapa Valley, are evidence of this. Their materials reveal important settlements, with silos for food, or predominantly local cult centres; *altiplano* pottery is either limited to specific areas, such as at Huancarance, or is intrusive, as at Cerro Sombrero. In both cases, products of coastal origin, such as maize and chillies, are as widespread as those of highland origin.

Little is known about the late period at the Puna oases. Sites at the source of the Loa and the Toconce reveal altiplano patterns (Castro *et al.*, 1977). The burial ritual in *chullpas* is similar to that of the Aymaras. These are pastoral communities, but terracing and other indications, such as spades or wooden hoes, reveal that agriculture was practised. The *chullpa* type of construction at Toconce is not found on the Argentinian Puna, which would seem to indicate a greater degree of contact between the central *altiplano*, the Puna and the Chilean side.

In the extreme south of the Andean area, in Cuyo and the central mountains, changes in relation to the previous period are fewer. The pattern of small scattered settlements indicates the presence of segmented societies. In the north, the dominant ceramic style is that of Angualasto, and in the centre-south of Mendoza, the dominant culture is Viluco.

In Córdoba, scattered settlements, sometimes with semi-subterranean dwellings, characterize the cultural complex of the historical Comechingones. Incised pottery, figurines and bone tips are a part of a fairly uniform context typical of a mixed economy which stressed hunting and gathering without, however, ignoring agriculture.

CULTURAL MANIFESTATIONS IN NORTH-WEST ARGENTINA DURING THE LATE PERIOD

Contemporary cultural developments in the region are varied. The level attained can be seen in cases such as the three phases of settlement patterns at Belén. The first phase is that of the communal well-houses measuring 17 by 20 m and housing three or four families: these are found in groups of four or five. This is followed by isolated dwellings with stone walls which are subsequently grouped in semi-urban centres, mostly in strategic locations. The houses, which have a number of rooms, are rectangular with narrow doors. Metallurgy developed in parallel with Santa María. Metal discs are frequently used as smooth and decorated shields. There are axes, gauntlets and bells made of cast bronze, and a characteristic element is the small rectangular metal pendants with two zoomorphic figures facing one another. Pottery is generally made of red clay and the typical shape is that of the child's burial urn, 35 to 40 cm high, made of compact clay, well fired, deep red in colour and painted with black lines on red with geometrical decoration in horizontal bands. Drawings of vipers with two or more heads and fantastic animals may have a symbolic meaning.

The pattern of settlement in the Santa María culture went through different stages. At the beginning, the people lived in large communal houses, and the population, comprising extended families, must have been scattered throughout the countryside. Then there are hamlets with rectangular stone houses grouped together, forming true urban centres. During the last stage, the model of which might be Loma Rica (Catamarca), there are 210 dwellings with open spaces like plazas. The city walls are thick and they may have been used to walk upon. The dwellings have no doors, so access must have been through the roof.

The pottery is decorated using two or three colours of paint but no incision techniques are used, and modelling or engraving is rare. A typical decorative feature is a space completely covered with geometrical shapes. The characteristic type is called the Santa María design: large ovoid urns with three sections, a conical base, and an almost cylindrical neck with handles with humanoid faces. There are anthropomorphic elements, highly stylized batrachians and ñandús (American ostriches), as well as serpents.

Other styles are the polychrome Yocavil and the Yocavil red on white. The shapes are generally *pucos* or *keros*, some with zoomorphic reliefs on the brim. The *pucos* are decorated with stylized birds on the inside.

Metallurgy made great strides. There are discs, breastplates, axes, gauntlets and bells made of cast metals. The circular disc is the item of highest quality. The decoration on them contrasts with the severe, variegated decoration on the urns: here the surfaces are smooth and open and the lines are clean. The designs are figurative, such as human heads, serpents, anthropomorphic figures or any combination of these. On the reverse side there is no decoration, only two lugs which acted as handles for an armlet. Possession of one of these probably symbolized the power and status of the bearer.

Quebrada de Humahuaca was the main route by which the low-lying areas of the subtropical rainforests near San Salvador de Jujuy could reach the Puna and the Bolivian *altiplano*, and there had been lively trade and ethnic migration along this route since ancient times. The settlement pattern in this culture was that of dwellings grouped together at strategic points, with an estimated population of 200 inhabitants. The dwellings are rectangular in shape with stone walls and open onto cleared spaces like a plaza. There is pottery with decorative motifs in black on a red background. The decoration on the Tilcara type is fine and delicate. The common shapes are globular or ovoid vases with side handles, either with a narrow neck and horizontal handles or neckless. The designs are varied and complex, geometrical with vertical or horizontal bands. Metallurgy is rare and the decoration on it is poor. There are large bone cornets engraved with concentric circles, objects for use in textile manufacture and containers for stimulants.

Among the wooden objects are tablets for offerings, large knives for agricultural use, gauntlets and bells used to pasture the llama. It was common practice to bury adults inside the dwelling in circular sepulchres in the corners. Children were buried in urns. Headless individuals who have been found indicate a head trophy cult. Burial objects are varied, ranging from very rich to very poor, which shows that social differences were well defined.

Quebrada del Toro, like Humahuaca, was one of the routes to Bolivia, and the most representative site is Santa Rosa de Tastil, with a population of more than 2,500 inhabitants. The structures there are made of fairly low dry-stone walls opening onto an area of 12 ha. Dwellings are rectangular, square or irregular in shape. There are streets, squares and sepulchres for burials. There are no defensive structures.

This culture is remarkable for its textiles, for which it became a centre of manufacture and trade. The commonest items are caps, the use of which must have conferred a certain degree of social status. They were made of llama or vicuña wool using a simple in-weaving technique. Human hair was used, possibly in wigs. They used the tapestry technique: embroidery on the finished surface is noteworthy as well as the decoration using thick materials with locks of human hair. Their rupestrine art shows petroglyphs on stone walls or engravings on the surface of rock splinters of different sizes. These are figures with long legs and curly tails, anthropomorphic figures, camel-like animals and geometrical shapes formed using straight lines.

The dryness of the Puna has allowed wooden objects and articles of clothing made of perishable material, such as bags, combs, caps and hats, to be preserved. The most noteworthy of the wooden objects are the tubes for ingesting hallucinogenic substances, decorated with anthropomorphic and zoomorphic figures. The edges of some pieces are incrusted with semi-precious stones. These are accompanied by decorated bone or wooden tubes. Burials were in *chullpas*, little oven-like houses leaning against the walls, or in fissures in the rocks which can be seen in pictographs and petroglyphs.

The village of Yavi is a unique site. It has two settlement patterns one on agricultural land, with square and rectangular dwellings with foundations made of stone and mud mortar which rise a metre above ground level. On top of the foundations there is an adobe wall measuring 30 by 60 cm. The other type is rectangular dwellings with stone walls. The cultivation terraces are extensive.

The surface of the pottery is polished, and the decoration is black on red with fine line motifs. The commonest designs are fine cross-hatching, circles and rectangles which end in interwoven spirals. The typical shape is the globular vase with an anthropomorphic figure on the neck.

In the Sanagasta or Angualasto cultures, the settlement pattern is that of scattered communities. The dwellings on these sites, where there is no stone, are made of perishable material or *adobe*. Metalworking is inferior in quality to that of previous periods. Some wooden objects such as tablets and tubes are found, as well as arrow tips and bone pins, with a figure at the top, used to secure clothing.

Adults were buried directly in the ground with relatively poor burial objects. The characteristic feature is the pottery, particularly funeral urns for children made of thick clay in two or three colours. These are accompanied by *pucos* which served as lids. There are two types of urns, the first being the tricolour San José type, decorated in black on red or white. The decoration on the body of the urn consists of vertical bands with motifs such as ostriches, toads, serrated wheels or rosettes, and on the base entwined parallel lines, with transverse strokes between, forming large truncated S shapes. The other type, the geometric Shiquimil, is rougher.

THE INCA PERIOD

The chronicles permit us to surmise that these territories were conquered by Topa Inca, who received vassalage from the Tucumán Indians, then under pressure from groups of nomads from the Chaco anxious to take over the central valleys of the Argentine north-west. The Calchaquís, part of the Diaguitas from the south, and the Chillis put up resistance which was gradually overcome by the arrival of large contingents of Mitmakunas brought from the environs of Cuzco (de Sicuani), the northern *altiplano* or pre-Hispanic Tucumán itself. These contingent's were settled in the central valleys of Catamarca. The policy of bringing in settlers required the construction of administrative centres all along the trunk road which crosses the *puna* from north to south, in the Calchaquí valleys and their offshoots.

The imperial presence is relatively rare in the Norte Grande in Chile, where the Incas may have exercised power indirectly through the *altiplano* kingdoms. This is not so, however, in the transverse valleys of the Norte Chico and the centre where, as in north-western Argentina, resistance required an active and vigilant presence. Cuzco state control reached as far as the centre of Mendoza, as well as the Aconcagua valley by way of the Uspallata valley.

The Inca presence in these regions, with large administrative and craft centres, is considerable: *ushnus* for parliaments and rituals are evident. There are *tambos* of lesser status and high altitude centres and forts which protected the empire.

The number of Mitmakuna settlers is revealed by the incidence of foreign pottery styles and their influence on local ceramics, due to group contact in the same living spaces and while carrying out common chores. The importance of foreign pottery is so great that one is led to believe that part of the economy of the region was based on that activity. Intensive research has recently begun at Potrero-Chaquiaga, near Andalgalá, where crafts were the main activity. There is an aqueduct there which supplied one of the districts where pottery production and storage was concentrated.

Mining must have been important, particularly in Chile. In the chronicles there are registers of caravans carrying gold to Cuzco when Diego de Almagro arrived in 1534.

The Inca presence is clear in pottery, which shows Inca motifs, such as *aríbalos* or *aribaloids*, and flat dishes with handles in the shape of a duck's head and tail. There are metal axes destined for use in war, as shown by their improved edge and greater efficiency in comparison with those used previously in the region. The use of metal for practical purposes was widespread, as was gold and silversmithing to make objects for offerings, little llamas, hollow anthropomorphic figures and ornaments. Bronze *bolas* and puzzles are common. The widespread use of bronze weapons may have been one of the factors which facilitated the Inca conquest of this vast expanse of territory.

BIBLIOGRAPHY

BENNET, W. C.; BLEILER, E. F.; SOMMER, F. H. 1948. Northwest Argentine Archaeology. *Yale University Publications in Anthropology*, 38, New Haven, pp. 5–158.

GONZÁLEZ, A. R. 1963. Cultural Development in North Western Argentine. *Cultural Developments in Latin America*, pp. 102–117, Smithsonian Miscellaneous Collections, Washington.

GONZÁLEZ, A. R.; PÉREZ, J. A. 1975. *Argentina Indígena, Vísperas de la Conquista*. Paidós, Buenos Aires.

VII: Oceania and the Pacific

OCEANIA AND THE PACIFIC

Jacqueline de La Fontinelle and Michel Aufray

The term 'Oceania' is defined differently according to whether it is used in physical geography or the social sciences. Sometimes the word is used as a synonym for the term 'Pacific' and includes all the islands and coastlines bathed by the ocean of that name, but 'Oceania' may also apply only to the seas and islands of the central and western Pacific. Usage varies from author to author and age to age. Furthermore, despite their geographical location, Japan, the Philippines and Indonesia are regarded as belonging to Asia, while Australia, whose west coast is washed by the Indian Ocean, is placed sometimes in Oceania and sometimes on its own. Thus the extent of this 'marine continent' fluctuates according to the angle from which it is studied, and to the 'Oceania' of geographers, historians and economists must be added the uses ethnologists and linguists make of the term when they refer to Austronesian cultures and languages. The Austronesian group, characterized by affiliation to a family of languages, has representatives in continental Asia, the Philippines, Taiwan, Indonesia and Madagascar, as well as throughout the Pacific; the term 'Oceanian' is restricted either to the central and western zones of the Pacific or to the western zone alone. These difficulties go some way to explaining why writers continue to use the terminology suggested in 1831 by the French explorer Dumont d'Urville, one of those who discovered the 'Great Ocean'. He divided the Oceanian area into three zones, grouping the islands under three names: Micronesia ('small islands'), Melanesia ('black islands') and Polynesia ('many islands'). This division, based on geographical criteria but later applied to peoples and cultures, helped to spread racial prejudice against the Melanesians: the term 'Melanesia', describing high islands standing out black against the sky, was interpreted as referring to the skin colour of the inhabitants.

Micronesia includes the Marianas, the Marshall Islands and the Carolines, situated in the west of the Pacific and north of the Equator; Melanesia refers to the large, generally mountainous, islands of the south-west Pacific: Papua-New Guinea and the Solomon, Vanuatu, New Caledonia and Fiji archipelagoes; Polynesia includes all the archipelagoes of the central Pacific: Samoa, Tonga, Cook, Wallis and Futuna and French Polynesia, and extends northwards as far as Hawaii, eastwards to Easter Island and southwards to the three islands of New Zealand, the only archipelago outside the Tropics.

It was not until 1968, when the hypothesis of plate tectonics finally confirmed the Wegener theory of continental drift, that a history began to take shape of the peopling of Australia by living organisms, including the human race. Australia, as part of a single continent, Pangaea, by contrast with the vast ocean of Panthalassa, which was the precursor of the Pacific, was in contact with other continents such as Asia and South America from the Carboniferous period to the end of the Cretaceous period, as is proved both by fossils and by its present-day flora and fauna. Later, when Australia moved up towards the Tropic of Capricorn, it became the last remaining home of marsupials and egg-laying mammals or monotremes (echidna and duck-billed platypus). To the north of Australia, conditions which prevented other mammals from passing over from the Sunda continent to the Sahul zone (Wallace and Weber lines), gave rise to the idea that man was similarly unable to cross these expanses of sea. Since navigation was regarded as a Neolithic discovery, it was thought that the aborigines reached their habitat at only a late date. Dating of the Lake Mongo artifacts (now a desert zone) suggests that human occupation goes back to 50,000 years ago; and in the Northern Territory, near Kabadu, now a well-known tourist resort, the most recent carbon-14 dating shows that the imprints of hands on the walls of grottoes go back 60,000 years. These imprints thus become the most ancient deliberate testimony of the presence of man. It is moreover likely that as archaeology develops, we shall be led to push back still further the dates of the peopling of Australia by Aborigines.

The extent of time over which human beings dwelt on the continent accounts for the great linguistic variety and sophistication of the societies' artistic cultures – as they now appear to us today; previously, the fact that these peoples lived as hunter–gatherers and nomads meant that the invading explorers totally failed to understand them and refused, as 'civilized' persons, to accord them a place in human culture. So it came about not only that Australia did not officially enter into our history until several millennia after its peopling by human beings but also that nearly 200 years elapsed before the presence of the Aborigines was tolerated, and expressions of local cultures were grudgingly admitted to have any value. This being the case, obviously much has been irretrievably lost.

CONTACT WITH THE OUTSIDE WORLD

Some Asian and Indonesian peoples explored the ocean beyond their coasts. Of the contact with neighbouring areas we have only a little evidence in Chinese writings, although the Arabs, through the Malay world, probably had contact with the nearest Pacific islands. Before and during the first half of the sixteenth century, that is during the Ming Dynasty, Chinese ships sailed between the islands of the western Pacific and may have reached the coast of Australia (Needham, 1974, p. 171). Chinese junks have been found at Rossell Island, east of New Guinea, and at Futuna in western Polynesia (Guiart, 1983, p. 19). It is even possible that Chinese sailors reached the Hawaiian islands (Langdon, 1971, p. 23). But even where we have documentary evidence, it is difficult to identify the islands referred to, and the documents are obviously later than the exchanges themselves.

As far as European awareness of Australia is concerned, at the time of the Renaissance, there were vague indications that there existed a *Terra australis incognita*, which was assumed to 'balance' all the known land masses and to lie somewhere beyond the seas. Various European sailors discovered parts of Australia in the sixteenth and seventeenth centuries: Abel Tasman found the southern island 'Van Diemen's Land' (Tasmania) in 1642, while James Cook explored the east coast of the continent and claimed it for England in 1770.

The problem of a non-written 'history'

Australia has retained few and fragmentary traces of what its ancient societies were like. Present-day autochthonous cultures and languages show only very rare vestiges which have escaped two centuries of unbridled colonization. It will be remembered that until recent times, scientists disputed the right of Aborigines even to be called human beings, or to be recognized as of the same human race as their conquerors.

It must also be remembered that none of the Oceanian cultures had any form of writing, with the very limited exception of the *rongo-rongo* on Easter Island, which have yet to be fully deciphered. Moreover, few of these tablets engraved with signs escaped the destructive faith of Christian missionaries, and archaeological excavations have only recently been carried out systematically. Much remains to be discovered about humanity's long history in some parts of the Pacific and the way virgin lands may have been colonized.

The historical stability that used to be attributed to cultures 'without [written] history' is now being questioned, and it has to be accepted that societies whose existence we can only guess at were established and succeeded each other before the impact of European discovery. Polynesian oral tradition speaks of political change and the alternating worship of various 'gods' – Taaroa, Tane, Tu, Oro – expressing the taking of power by local groups. In Mare (Loyalty Islands, New Caledonia), the accounts of battles with the Eletok should be interpreted as the eradication of one group by another (Dubois, 1975). In Australia, the ancient cultures of the hunter–gatherers who first settled there were swept away by two centuries of frenzied European colonization, and the aboriginal languages and cultures that exist today are but the rare survivors of an utterly different world to which they still bear witness.

After rejecting the hypothesis that the traditional societies had a history and that they passed it on – without using writing – by means of 'myths', anthropologists now consider that myths not only lend themselves to analysis in Freudian or art terms but that they also contain hidden information about the past, part of which can be deciphered. Aboriginal literature is immensely rich, and a current theme is how humanization took place. 'The age of dreams', as it is interpreted, transports us into a world where the difference between nature, animals and human beings is constantly shifting. Everything is proteiform, and this explains the transformations which have taken place and which have made animals into ancestors with whom verbal communication is maintained only for the initiated, and regulates at one and the same time the nature and basic behaviour patterns of the family and society. It therefore seems that these documents attest the age-old establishment of human beings and not, for example, like the Polynesian documents, the arrival of human beings on uninhabited territory or its occupation by other humans. That which human memory was unable to retain of the past was transmuted into 'myths'. In this way, the confrontations between various groups, the ancestral paths followed and the sites of sacred places where tribes met periodically are stored in the memory of these Iliads and Odysseys going back to the dawn of time.

The historical hypotheses based on linguistic comparison

The nineteenth-century 'neo-grammarians' used linguistic comparison to establish the family relationship between Indo-European languages and so reconstructed a 'mother language', one which preceded the earliest surviving written documents.

Similarly, on the basis of the languages still spoken in the Pacific region, contemporary linguists have sought to establish typologies and suggest the model of a proto-language – but obviously without being able to use written documents. Otto Dempwolff studied all the material available to him and, between 1920 and 1938, suggested a model, proto-Austronesian, of the ancestor of the languages spoken today. His pioneering work has been developed and considerably enriched (especially with material from the languages of Taiwan). Later work by I. Dyen and A. Capell 'statistico-lexicography' has made it possible to suggest how ancient peoples settled in Oceania. The differences observed between present-day languages and between them and the reconstructed model presuppose a time factor: the degree of difference is a function of the number of centuries or millennia that have elapsed since the separation from the mother language. This technique makes it possible to advance approximate dates for the settlement of Austronesian peoples; archaeological discoveries may corroborate the estimated arrival of human beings on an island, but it will obviously never be certain that the form of the language spoken corresponded to that of the linguistic hypothesis.

Thus the historical and linguistic reconstruction hypotheses are both based on a number of unverifiable points. It is assumed that when the Austronesian travellers settled in Oceania they spoke, if not a single language, at least very closely related ones. It is still not known for sure where they came from, and the criteria on which theories are based have varied over the years: skin colour and blood counts (particularly before the Second World War), cultural or linguistic evidence. Many hypotheses have been advanced, including Indian or Dravidian origin, or that the Austronesians came from the coasts of China, South America or Borneo. It is interesting to note that today specialists will not advance a definitive answer: the 'Oceanian' peoples probably came from Asia, in any case from west of the Pacific, but the idea of isolated sea voyages from the coasts of America, particularly

South America, is not entirely discounted, as there is some evidence that supports the hypothesis. It was to demonstrate this possibility that Thor Heyerdahl sailed from Peru to the Tuamotu archipelago on a raft. The sweet potato seems to have come originally from South America and is now the staple food of areas far inland such as central New Guinea: this implies a very ancient relationship between America and Oceania. Certain physical and cultural characteristics such as the similarity between *marae*, Polynesian places of worship, and Maya temples, is remarkable, but in the present state of knowledge it is impossible to evaluate the importance of such voyages for the history of the Pacific.

Exactly how the Austronesians conquered the lands they discovered is also a matter of debate. While it is certain that the islands of the central and eastern Pacific were virgin lands and the Austronesians were the first to colonize them, in Melanesia, where linguistic and cultural differences are very great, an extremely ancient settlement may have preceded the waves of Austronesian immigration or, again, the islands may have been settled by successive waves of immigrants, all of whom were Austronesian. At present, attempts are being made to establish various colonization models which would fit in with archaeological discoveries: colonization may have been the result of the sudden or gradual eradication of earlier groups, or of merger with them, but all the possibilities must be considered: a small number of people arriving in a land already occupied, a massive incursion of foreigners, and so on; the material levels of the groups may have been different and to varying degrees in different cases, and so forth.

The traditional history of the Oceanians

The local oral tradition describing the arrival of the indigenous peoples and the establishment of agriculture is now beginning to be taken seriously. The island people have in fact told the story of their origins themselves. The 'myths', in particular, use a symbolic language to describe either the community's origin or the major problems the first settlers encountered. They tend to corroborate the hypothesis of very ancient settlement of some islands, and more recent settlement of others.

The ancestors are usually said to have come from another world. The choice of terrestrial or marine symbols is significant as it sometimes makes it possible to claim the land rights of the first occupant, at others to recall the external origin of a community. In this way, the peoples whose arrival goes back to ancient times, like those of Papua, Australia and Melanesia, have developed a chthonic symbolism to express the fact that they regard themselves as the first occupiers of the land and therefore have a right to it. This allegorical discourse uses tropes that refer to a stable universe, in particular that of the rocks, trees, tubers and reptiles to which the origin of human beings is attributed. This symbol is placed in a precisely situated context and becomes the protector of the line and the archetype of the community's political and territorial powers. In short, it is a mythical geography. The texts which recount the events of the 'dream time' are associated with the landscape and toponymy. Places and paths thus serve as the vectors of collective memory and constitute a sort of living history that the group uses to demonstrate its status as the oldest in the country.

Some Melanesian myths also contain characters at once ridiculous and dreadful: ogres, monsters and subterranean beings. The stories have historical meaning as they are the new arrivals' commentary on the original, defeated inhabitants. Conversely, some myths are the testimony of the earlier occupants seeing the foreigners arrive: sometimes they appear to be the harbingers of death – masks coming out of the sea to terrorize the people, huge, man-eating dogs, and so on – sometimes, they are seen as cultural innovators bringing fire, pottery and new plants.

The peoples who arrived more recently, like those in Polynesia, have told the story of their arrival in the form of an allegory whose tropes are borrowed from the marine world and associated with ancestors who came from the sea: the arrival of floating stones, islands fished out of the sea, migrations of birds, fish, sharks or turtles. Moreover, the persistence of the memory of their settlement is found again in the symbolism of social organization: the various parts of the pirogue and the position of the people on board during the initial voyage are reproduced on land in social hierarchy and roles; similarly, the architecture of their dwellings is reminiscent of the structure of boats.

It should also be pointed out that in traditional Polynesian societies, genealogies played an important role. Some of those which have come down to us extend over ten generations. Some European commentators have tried to use them to date the past of island groups. The information they provide is, however, extremely tenuous. Many of the genealogies were collected in the nineteenth century by European civil servants, travellers and missionaries. Connected as they were with political power and land ownership, many of them were falsified or distorted to enhance the authority and claims of one group to the detriment of another in the eyes of the colonial administration.

The archaeological data

Humanity already had a long history in this part of the world when Europe became aware of the existence of the islands. Our knowledge about human settlement in the region is recent and far from certain.

Archaeological research, which has been really significant only since the 1960s in the various parts of the Oceanian world, is constantly pushing back the dates of human occupation. It has been suggested that the first human settlement occurred during the Ice Age. Carbon dating gives the probable figure of 48,000 years BC for the carved stones of Lake Mungo in south-east Australia and 38,000 years BC for occupation of the Huon peninsula in north-east New Guinea. As far as western Melanesia, New Britain and New Ireland are concerned, it has recently been accepted that there has been a continuous human presence for 30,000 years, which suggests there may be other 'surprises' regarding the presence of human beings in places where it was thought only 'late' settlement had occurred.

THE HISTORY OF THE EARTH AND OCEANIAN HISTORY

If Oceanian prehistory is to be interpreted correctly, it must take the physical evolution of the planet into account. People from present-day Asia went and settled in the continents that occupied part of Oceania before the waters rose when the planet became warmer. To the west was the continent of Sunda in the Indonesian zone, and to the east, the continent of Sahul, including New Guinea, Australia and Tasmania, the two separated (Wallace's Line), which prevented placental animals spreading eastwards, thus enabling marsupials to survive but which, according to archaeologists, did not impede movements of people from New Guinea to the Solomon Islands. The distance between the islands, an average of 350 km, did not require very sophisticated navigation techniques.

Thus, after many different hypotheses and discussions, the result sometimes of ideological rather than scientific exchanges, the current view is that ancient peoples, becoming very diverse both biologically and culturally, settled in Australia, New Guinea and Melanesia at the end of the Pleistocene, and that there was rapid colonization in the second millennium BC, gradually spreading to the uninhabited islands. Speculation about the settlement of the Pacific is based not only on material remains but also on botanical surveys (introduction of cultivated plants, such as taro, yam and coconut palm) and zoological studies (presence of dogs and pigs, of Chinese or Indonesian origin, brought to some regions by human beings).

LAPITA CULTURE AND THE SPREAD OF THE AUSTRONESIANS

The early colonization of the islands of Oceania was attributed to a new culture, known as Austronesian, and heated controversy arose as to the origin of Lapita pottery – from the name of a site in New Caledonia. Lapita potsherds were found in Tonga as early as 1920 and were attributed to the Polynesians, a light-skinned people that Europeans considered superior to the other Oceanians. After the Second World War, when Oceanian archaeology really began to develop, some preconceived ideas had to be revised. Thus in the late 1950s the archaeologist J. Golson found pottery fragments in Melanesia comparable to those found in Tonga, thus showing that the Melanesians and Polynesians, despite their physical differences, shared the same cultural features. Linguistic and ethnological studies then confirmed the underlying unity of Austronesian cultures, seeing their very specificities as variations on the same ancient theme. The idea of two distinct races settling successively in the Pacific was called into question and then abandoned altogether. Today it is accepted that the Austronesians came from Asia and had time to develop different, successive cultures as they spread. The Lapita culture, so striking in its elaborate material remnants, is probably only one of the still tangible manifestations of the cultures of the Austronesian peoples.

These fragments of Lapita pottery reveal the successive stages in the rapid progression of the Austronesians towards the central Pacific. Their presence is attested about 3,000 years ago in the Solomon Islands, Vanuatu, New Caledonia and the Fiji archipelago, from where they carried their culture to Tonga and then Samoa around 1000 or 1200 BC. There remains no material evidence of Lapita culture beyond around AD 500.

The eastward population movement extended in Polynesia as far as the Marquesas Islands, where human presence is recorded around 120 BC. From there the Polynesians spread into central Polynesia (the Society and Cook Islands); then, in about the fourth century AD, they reached the Hawaiian Islands and, between AD 400 and 500, Easter Island. The expansion did not end until about AD 800 or 900 with the occupation of New Zealand.

These navigators knew astronomy and had navigation techniques, maps made of strips of wood bound together on which shells represented currents and islands, and boats capable of carrying them long distances (while the catamarans and outrigged pirogues were not suitable for the high seas, this was not true of the double pirogues, which were capable of carrying up to 200 people, livestock, lumber and provisions). The Marquesas are about 3,000 km from Hawaii and about the same distance from Easter Island.

RELATIONS BETWEEN THE ISLANDS

Vast networks of inter-insular alliances were formed whereby women and goods were able to be exchanged among Polynesian communities and also with the inhabitants of the more distant regions of Melanesia and Micronesia. It was during the sumptuous festivals, which brought together large numbers of people involved in the production of food and objects and served as occasions for ceremonial exchanges of the potlatch type and the sacrifice of pigs, that artefacts (chants and dances as well as manufactured items) were exchanged and alliances, rivalries and forms of power crystallized. Ethnologists have been able to see how some of these politico-economic and cultural exchanges still operate. Thus Malinowski described the *kula*: complex, codified systems of exchange, extending over several years, whereby mother-of-pearl breastplates, cowries and giant clams travelled from the coasts of the Trobriands, where they were gathered, to the high plateaux of New Guinea (whose inhabitants did not even have a name for the ocean, which remained outside their ken); between Vanuatu and New Caledonia and the Loyalty Islands, jadeite axes were exchanged for wives. The women of the Pacific were gardeners and potters and brought to the regions where they were sent both botanical discoveries and styles of pottery.

All these exchanges, which attest to the ancient links that existed between the different peoples, provided a means of cultural diffusion and, while not ensuring linguistic understanding, at least maintained the conditions for communication and, on the basis of a common heritage, over and above the great number of local differences, were certainly instrumental in establishing the cultural and linguistic constants that enable us today to identify 'Oceanian' traits.

BIBLIOGRAPHY

ALLEN, J.; WHITE, P. 1980. Melanesian Prehistory: Some Recent Advances. *Science*. Washington, No. 207, pp. 728–734.

——. 1989. The Lapita Homeland: Some New Data and an Interpretation. *Journal of Polynesian Society*. Auckland, Vol. 98, No. 2, pp. 129–146.

BEAGLEHOLE, J. C. 1966. *The Exploration of the Pacific*. London.

DAHL, O. 1976. *Proto-austronesian*. Scandinavian Institute of Asian Studies, series No 15. Curzon Press, London.

DEMPWOLFF, O. 1934; 1937; 1938. *Vergleichende Lautlehre des Austronesischen Wortschatzes*. Beihefte zur Zeitschrift für Eingeborenen Sprachen, Heft 15, 17, 18. D. Reimer, Berlin.

DUBOIS, M. J. 1975. *Mythes et traditions de maré – Nouvelle-Calédonie – Les Eletok*. Publications de la Société des Océanistes No. 35, Musée de l'Homme, Paris.

DYEN, I. 1963. *A Lexicostatistical Classification of the Austronesian Languages*. Memoir No 19. International Journal of American Linguistics. Baltimore.

GARANGER, J. 1987. L'archéologie océanienne: résultats et perspectives. *Journal de la Société des Océanistes*. Paris, Vol. 84, No. 1, pp. 101–102.

GOLSON, J. 1961. Report on New Zealand, Western Polynesia, New Caledonia and Fiji. Current Research in Pacific Islands Archaeology. *Asian Perspectives*. Hong Kong, Vol. 3, No. 2, pp. 166–180.

——. 1971. Both Sides of the Wallace Line: Australia, New Guinea and Asian Prehistory. *Oceania*. Sydney, No. 6, pp. 124–144.

GUIART, J. 1983. *La terre est le sang des morts*. Paris.

LANGDON, R. 1971. Les naufrages européens dans le Pacifique antérieurement à la période de Cook (trans. Jaunez, B.). *Bulletin de la Société des Etudes Océaniennes*, Papeete, tome XV, No. 1, No. 174, pp. 21-40.

MALINOWSKI, B. (re-ed.) 1989. *Les Argonautes du Pacifique*. Gallimard, Paris.

NEEDHAM, J. 1973. *Chinese Science; Explorations of an Ancient Tradition*. MIT Press, Cambridge, Mass.

ÖSTÖRAKOS. 1981. *Europeans and Islanders in the Western Pacific, 1520–1840*. Vienna, Institüt für Völkerkunder der Universität Wien.

SHARP, A. 1960. *The Discovery of the Pacific Islands*. Oxford.

SPATE, O. H. K. 1979. *The Pacific since Magellan, the Spanish Lake*, Vol. I. Canberra.

TERRELL, J. 1986. *Prehistory in the Pacific Islands*. Cambridge.

CHRONOLOGICAL TABLE

CHRONOLOGICAL

AD 500

WESTERN EUROPE		BYZANTIUM; CENTRAL, EASTERN AND NORTHERN EUROPE		MUSLIM WORLD	
		568	The Avars in Hungary.	570/571	Birth of Muḥammad.
		c. 580	The Slavs in the Balkans.		
590–604	Gregory I, Pope; foundation of the temporal power of the Papacy.				

600

WESTERN EUROPE		BYZANTIUM; CENTRAL, EASTERN AND NORTHERN EUROPE		MUSLIM WORLD	
		610–641	Reign of the Byzantine emperor Heraclius, victories over the Sasanians (622–628), creation of the 'themes' (Byzantine provincial governorates).	610	First relevations.
				612–613	Beginning of preaching.
613	Clotaire II, king of the Franks, unifies Austrasia, Neustria and Burgundy into a single state.				
615	Death of Saint Colomban, Irish Monk, founder of monasteries in Gaul and Italy.				
				622	The 'Hegira': Muḥammad's departure from Mecca to Yathrib (Medina). Beginning of the Muslim calendar.
				623	Founding of the Muslim community at Medina.
				630	Muḥammad enters Mecca. Destruction of the idols of the Ka'ba.

TABLE

ASIA AND OCEANIA (CENTRAL, SOUTHERN, EASTERN AND SOUTH EAST ASIA)		AFRICA		THE AMERICAS	
					AD 500
538	Introduction of Buddhism into Japan.				
552–630	First Turk Empire in Mongolia.				
553–630	Khanate of Western Turks in Central Asia.				
581–618	Sui Dynasty: unification of North and South China.				
593	Invention of printing in China by means of engraved wooden plates.				
595–596	First Indian inscription with decimal notation.				
					600
7th cent.	Bakhshali manuscript (India): first use of algebraic signs for zero, 'x' negative.	7th cent.	The Kingdom of Ghana, first political organization known in West Africa.		*Mesoamerica*
	Sri Lankan chronicle, *Mahāvamsa* in Pali.			600–900	Late Classic period in the southern Maya area. Sites like Palenque flourish.
	Rise of Buddhist kingdom of Sri Vijaya in Sumatra.				
600–1185	Absolutism in Japan.				
c. 600	The Indonesian Islands: Sumatra, Java and surrounding islands converted to Buddhism.				
602–664	Xuanzang (Yuan Chuang), Chinese Buddhist scholar and traveller, author of celebrated account of India.				
605	Foundation of Luoyang, city-palace in China.				
606–648	Reign of Harshavardhana in Northern India; his empire subsequently broke up into numerous states.				
	Last phase of classical Indian painting in Ajantā.				
618–907	Tang Dynasty in China.				
c. 628	India: Brahmagupta's treatise on mathematics and astronomy.				
630–635	The first Nestorians in China.				
630–680	Chinese protectorate over Mongolia and Turk Central Asia.				

WESTERN EUROPE *(cont.)*		**BYZANTIUM; CENTRAL, EASTERN AND NORTHERN EUROPE** *(cont.)*		**MUSLIM WORLD** *(cont.)*	
				632	Death of Muḥammad.
				632–634	Caliphate of Abū Bakr.
		634–662	Foundation of the Slav Empire of Bohemia–Moravia by Samo.	634–644	Caliphate of 'Umar ibn al-Khattāb.
		634	Monenergism (monothelitism), doctrine aiming at reconciling dualist orthodoxy and monophysism. Condemned in 649, then in 680–681, together with monophysism.	634	Arabs in Syria and Iraq: victory at Ajnadain.
636	Death of Isidore of Seville, Father of the Church, author of *Etymologies*, an encyclopedic treatise.			636	The Arabs in Iran: the victory at Qadisiyya; battle of Yarmuk in Syria.
				641	Major administrative measures under 'Umar.
				642	Foundation of Al-Fustāt (Egypt).
				644–656	Caliphate of 'Uthmān ibn 'Affān.
653	Conversion of the Longobards (Lombards) to Christianity.			653	Establishment of the text of the Qur'ān.
				656–661	Caliphate of 'Alī.
				660	Mo'āwiya proclaimed Caliph. Foundation of the Umayyad Dynasty (660–750). Damascus becomes the capital.
				670	First expansion in North Africa. Foundation of Qayrawān in Tunisia.
		673–677	Siege of Constantinople by the Arabs. Greek fire.		
		679	Foundation of the Bulgarian kingdom in Thrace by Isperich.		
				680	Death of Husayn, son of 'Alī, at Karbalā. Formation of shī'ism, religious and political opposition to Sunnism.
				c. 690	Arabic used as the administrative language; issue of the dīnār, Arab gold coin.
				691–695	The Dome of the Rock in Jerusalem completed by order of the Umayyad caliph 'Abd al-Malik.
				695–698	Conquest of the Maghrib.
700					
				705	Great Mosque of Damascus.
				705–714	Arabs in Transoxania.
				709	Al-Aqsā Mosque in Jerusalem.

ASIA AND OCEANIA (CENTRAL, SOUTHERN, EASTERN AND SOUTH EAST ASIA) *(cont.)*		**AFRICA** *(cont.)*		**THE AMERICAS** *(cont.)*	
		634–644	Conquest of Egypt by the Arabs.		
c. 640	India: Bāṇa, poet wrote *Harshacharita.*				
640–641	Tibet under Chinese domination.				
		641	Arabs in Nubia. They levy a tribute in slaves.		
c. 650	Sanskrit poem by Bhatti relating the story of Rāma.				
		652	Resistance of the Dunqula Kingdom to the Arabs.		
c. 663	Invention of porcelain in China.				
		666	'Uqba Ibn Nāfi's expedition in Kawār, in the Saraha.		
		670	First expansion of the Arabs in North Africa.		
682–742	New Turk Empire in Mongolia. Restoration of the Tengri religion against Sinicization and Buddhism in Mongolia.				
685	Buddhism becomes the state religion in Japan.				
692	Account of a voyage to Sumatra and India by the Chinese Buddhist monk Yijing (I-Tsing).				
		695–698	Conquest of the Maghrib by the Arabs.		
					700
699–759	Wang Wei, Chinese painter.				*Andes*
700–737	Period of great Turk inscriptions in Central Asia.			700–1100	The Wari Empire; main sites: Wari and Tihuanaco.
					Mesoamerica
				c. 700	End of the Classic period of Monte Albán Culture, the major city in the valley of Oaxaca.
701–762	Li Bo, Chinese poet.				
710	Construction of the royal palace at Nara (Japan).			*c.* 710	Foundation of Chichén-Itza in the Yucatán.

WESTERN EUROPE *(cont.)*		**BYZANTIUM; CENTRAL, EASTERN AND NORTHERN EUROPE** *(cont.)*		**MUSLIM WORLD** *(cont.)*	
711	Invasion of Spain by the Arabs. End of the Visigothic Kingdom.	717–741	Leo III the Isaurian, Byzantine emperor.	711–718	Conquest of Spain.
				712–714	Conquest of Sind (India).
719	St Boniface (680–754) begins his mission to evangelize Germany.				
		725	Edict of Leo III banning religious images; beginning of iconoclasm.		
732	Charles Martel triumphs over the Muslims at Poitiers.				
735	Death of the Venerable Bede, scholar of the Anglo-Saxon Church.				
				749–750	Abū l-'Abbās proclaimed caliph. Elimination of the Umayyads. Beginning of the 'Abbāsid Dynasty (750–1258).
				751	Victory of the Arabs over the Chinese at the Battle of Talas (Central Asia).
		753	Council of Constantinople condemning the use of images.		
				756	Creation of the Umayyad emirate of Cordova.
				762	Foundation of Baghdād, capital of the 'Abbāsids. First trading links with the Chinese, via Ceylon.
768	Charlemagne, king of the Franks. Crowned emperor in 800.				
		769	Beginning of Christianization in Corinthia.		
		780–802	Irene regent, later empress of Byzantium.		
783–804	Alcuin (737–804), Anglo-Saxon scholar, head of Charlemagne's Palatine ('Palace') School.				
				786	Mosque of Cordova (Spain).
				786–809	Caliphate of Hārūn al-Rashīd. Beginning of paper manufacture in Iraq, introduced from China.
		787 and 815	Council of Nicaea and Constantinople in favour of images.		

ASIA AND OCEANIA (CENTRAL, SOUTHERN, EASTERN AND SOUTH EAST ASIA) *(cont.)*		**AFRICA** *(cont.)*		**THE AMERICAS** *(cont.)*	
712–756	Xuanzong, emperor of China; encourages the arts and humanities.				
720–780	Han Gan, Chinese painter.	730–739	Arab trading posts in Pemba, Kilwa and Mogadishu.		
725	Foundation of an Imperial Academy of Sciences in China.				
		734	Failure of an Umayyad expedition against the Kingdom of Ghana (West Africa).		
735	Unification of Korea by the Kingdom of Silla.				
744–840	Uighur Empire in Mongolia.				
750	Sugar cane reaches Egypt from India.				*Mesoamerica*
Second half of 8th cent.	India: The Saivite Temple of Kailasa at Ellora.			*c.* 750	Destruction and abandonment of Teotihuacán.
				750–900	Period during which independent states, such as Xochicalco and Cacaxtla, develop in the Central Highlands of Mexico between the fall of Teotihuacán and the rise of the Toltec Empire.
					North America
				750–1500	Anasazi, Mogollon and Hohakan cultures in the south-west of North America. Development of the Mississippian tradition in the central Mississippi valley and of Effigy Mounds in the upper Mississippi valley.
					Central America
					Development of the Polychrome tradition.
763	Manicheism, state religion in Mongolia.				
768–824	Han Yu, Chinese essayist and philosopher.				
771	The Lamas first monastery in Tibet, near Lhasa.				
788–820	Śaṅkara, Indian thinker, propounder of Vedantic pantheism.				

WESTERN EUROPE *(cont.)*		**BYZANTIUM; CENTRAL, EASTERN AND NORTHERN EUROPE** *(cont.)*		**MUSLIM WORLD** *(cont.)*	
793	First Viking raids in Ireland and England.				
				Last 8th cent.	Kahlīl and Sībawayhī, lay the foundations of Arabic grammar and lexicography.
800					
		c. 800	Foundation of the Viking Danish Kingdom.	800	Idrīsids in Morocco (800–930). Foundation of Fez.
				800–847	Al-Khwārizmī, astronomer, inventor of algebra.
804	Construction of Charlemagne's Palatine ('Palace') chapel of Aix-la-Chapelle.				
807	Foundation of Hamburg. Expansion of Christianity in Northern Europe.				
		810–813	Sieges of Constantinople by the Bulgarians.		
		817	Death of Theophanes the Confessor, Byzantine chronicler.		
				826–902	Conquest of Sicily by Aghlabids of Ifrīqiyya (Tunisia).
827	Egbert unifies seven Anglo-Saxon kingdoms and becomes king of Anglia, which he defends against the Vikings.			*c.* 827	Introduction of the Mu'tazilah, a philosophical doctrine introducing reason alongside faith, into state dogma.
		829	Preaching of the Gospel in the Scandinavian lands by Angsar. Death of the patriarch Nicephorus, opponent of the iconoclasts, author of a 'Short History' (602–769).		
				830	Foundation of the 'House of Wisdom' *(Bayt al-Hikma)* in Baghdād, great intellectual centre.
				836	Construction of the Great Mosque of Qayrawān in Ifrīqiyya (Tunisia).
842	Oaths of Strasbourg, in which early forms of French and German first emerge as official languages. Europeans adopt stirrups from Spanish Arabs: rise of heavy cavalry (knights).	842–843	End of iconoclasm; restoration of orthodoxy in Byzantium.		
843	Treaty of Verdun: division of the Frankish Empire among the three sons of Louis the Pious: Charles the Bald (West Frankish kingdom), Louis the German (East Frankish kingdom), and Lothair (Lothairinga, territories from Frisia to Italy).				
Second half of 9th cent.	Viking incursions all along the Atlantic coast of Europe.			*c.* 850	The Turks in Transoxania.
852	Formation of the first guilds in the North of Europe.				
		860	The Magyars settle along the Danube. Foundation of Novgorod.	(801)–860	Al-Kindī, astronomer and philosopher.
		After 860	Merchants from Kiev in Constantinople.		
		862	Foundation by Rurik of the Russian Empire of Novgorod.		

ASIA AND OCEANIA (CENTRAL, SOUTHERN, EASTERN AND SOUTH EAST ASIA) *(cont.)*		**AFRICA** *(cont.)*		**THE AMERICAS** *(cont.)*	
		789	Kaya Maghan Cisse, emperor of Ghana.		
794	Kyoto (Heian) becomes the imperial capital of Japan.				
					800
800	Construction of the Buddhist temple of Borobudur in Java.	*c.* 800	Foundation of the Kānem Kingdom. (Central Africa)		*Mesoamerica*
				c. 800	Bonampak frescoes. Decline of the Maya culture in the southern lowlands. Practically all the cities abandoned.
802	Worship of the God-King in Cambodia.				
805	The use of tea, originally from China, spreads to Japan.				
		808	Creation in Western Sudan of a Sanhāja Empire. Foundation of the City of Awdaghust.		
		833	Al-Khwarīzmī mentions the cities of Ghana and Gao.		
840–1209	Uighur Kingdom of Eastern Turkistan.				
850	Melanesia: appearance of populations in New Caledonia.	*c.* 850	Formation of the Muslim Kingdom of Ifāt (East Africa). The Dya'Ogo founds the Takrūr Kingdom (West Africa).	850/900–1500	Development of the Northern Maya Culture (Rio Bec and Chenes), and later development of cities such as Mayapan and Chichén Itza in Northern Yucatán.

WESTERN EUROPE *(cont.)*		**BYZANTIUM; CENTRAL, EASTERN AND NORTHERN EUROPE** *(cont.)*		**MUSLIM WORLD** *(cont.)*	
		863	Slavic translation of the Gospel by Cyril and Methodius; conversion of Slavic Moravia.		
		864	Conversion to Christianity of Boris, the Bulgarian leader.		
		865	Foundation of the Russian Empire of Kiev.		
		867–1056	Macedonian Dynasty founded by Basil I (867–886) in Byzantium.		
				868–906	The Tūlūnids in Egypt.
				869–883	Revolt of black slaves (the *Zanj*), in Lower Iraq.
				(810)–870	Al-Bukharī, traditionalist, collector of hādīth.
		872	Foundation of the Kingdom of Norway.		
				877–907	Revolt of Qarmatians in Iraq.
				879	Ibn Tūlūn's Mosque in Al-Fustāt.
881	Appearance of 'fiefs' *Poème de Sainte Eulalie*, first poem in old French.				
		885–965	Khazar Empire in Southern Russia.	885	Death of Ibn Khurdādhbih, chief section of the Postal service in Baghdād, traveller and geographer
				891	Death of Ya'qūbī, geographer (*Book of the Countries*), Iraq.
				892	Death of al-Balādhurī, historian (*The Book on the Conquests of Countries*), Iraq.
		895	Arpäd founds the Hungarian Kingdom of the Danube.		
900					
				Early 10th cent.	Deposit banks, exchange offices, relations with India, China, Russia.
905	St James of Compostela (northern Spain), place of pilgrimage.				
		c. 907	Expedition of the Russian Prince Oleg against Constantinople (Treaty in 911).		
				909	Entry of 'Ubayd Allāh into Qayrawān. Establishment of the Shī'ite Caliphate of the Fātimids.
910	Foundation of the monastery of Cluny (France), which becomes the chief centre of the monastery reform movement.				
911	Normandy, fief of the 'Norman' (Viking) chief Rollo.				
		913–959	Constantine Porphyrogenitus, Byzantine emperor and writer (*The Book of Ceremonies*).		
				921	The Fātimids, in control of the Maghrib. Foundation of Mahdiya (Tunisia).

ASIA AND OCEANIA (CENTRAL, SOUTHERN, EASTERN AND SOUTH EAST ASIA) *(cont.)*		**AFRICA** *(cont.)*		**THE AMERICAS** *(cont.)*	
868	First clearly dated printed book: Chinese Buddhist sutra, Dunhuang.				
876–82	Peasant revolt in China				
889	Foundation of Angkor, capital of the Khmer Kingdom in Cambodia.				
		890	The kings of Kūkya extend their authority over Gao (West Africa).		
Late 9th cent.	End of the Pallava Dynasty in the south of India. Beginning of the expansion of the Chōla Dynasty.				
					900
		c. 900	Foundation of the State of Benin (West Africa.		*Mesoamerica*
				900–1200	Period of domination by the Toltec Empire (capital: Tula) over central and northern parts of Mesoamerica. Domination of El Tajín over the north–central Gulf Coast and Cempoala on the central Gulf Coast.
907	Fall of the Tang Dynasty in China. Division of the Empire into North China and South China.				
		c. 908	The Arabs in the Horn of Africa.		
916	Foundation of the Qidan (Khitan) Empire in Mongolia.				
		918	Dislocation of the Sanhāja Confederation.		
		921	The Fātimids in control of the Maghrib.		

WESTERN EUROPE *(cont.)*		**BYZANTIUM; CENTRAL, EASTERN AND NORTHERN EUROPE** *(cont.)*		**MUSLIM WORLD** *(cont.)*	
				921–922	Account of Ibn Fadlān's travels among the Bulgarians on the Volga.
				922	Execution in Baghdād of the Sūfī preacher Abū Manṣūr al-Hallāj (858–922).
				(839)–923	al-Tabarī, historian, wrote the *History of the Prophets and Kings* in Persian.
		927	Extension of the Bulgarian Empire under Tsar Symeon.		
				929	Institution of the Umayyad Caliphate of Cordova by 'Abd al-Rahmān III.
		c. 930	The Vikings found the free State of Iceland.		
		935	Death of St Venceslas, Duke of Bohemia.		
936	Otto I, king of Germany; crowned emperor in Rome in 962.			936	Foundation of the city-palace of Madīnat al-Zahrā near Cordova.
		940	The 'Bogomils' found a socio-religious movement in Bulgaria.		
			The king of Denmark, Harald Bluetooth, adopts Western Christianity.		
		941–944	Attacks by the Russian prince Igor against Constantinople. Treaty in 944.		
				956–957	*The Meadows of Gold* by the historian Mas'ūdī (Egypt).
		964	Foundation of the Laura (monastery complex) on Mount Athos.		
				965	Death of al-Mutanabbī, Arabic poet (Syria).
		966	Western Christianity becomes state religion in Poland.		
				969	Conquest of Egypt by the Fātimids. Foundation of Cairo and the al-Azhār Mosque (979).
		976–1025	Reign of the Byzantine emperor Basil II Bulgaroctonus, 'the Killer of the Bulgars'.		
				977–997	Sebüktigin, Turkish governor of Ghaznī, (Afghanistan), extends his authority over parts of Iran and India.
				977–988	*Picture of the World* by the geographer Ibn Ḥawqal.
987	Hughes Capet elected and crowned king of France (987–996).	987	Baptism of the Russian prince Vladimir.	987	Revolt of Zīrid Berbers who declare themselves autonomous in Ifrīqiyya.
988	Guild of London.				
991	Invasion of England by the Danes.				
				996–1021	Caliphate of the Fātimid al-Hākim in Cairo; his mysterious death gives rise to the Druze religion.
		997	Foundation by Stephen I (crowned in 1001) of the Hungarian Kingdom.		
				998–1030	Reign of Mahmūd of Ghazni, independant sovereign in Afghanistan and India.

ASIA AND OCEANIA (CENTRAL, SOUTHERN, EASTERN AND SOUTH EAST ASIA) *(cont.)*		**AFRICA** *(cont.)*		**THE AMERICAS** *(cont.)*	
		922	Foundation of the main Hausa cities: Kano, Katsina, Zaria, Gobir.		
935	Foundation of the Kingdom of Korea by Wang-Kŏn.				
937–975	Dong Yvan, Chinese painter, active.				
947	North China incorporated into the Khitan Empire (renamed Liao).	947	The Malays arrive in Madagascar.	947–999	*Mesoamerica* Reign of the legendary Toltec sovereign Acalt Topiltzin, who took the name of Quetzalcóatl ('Feathered Serpent').
954–960	Cast-iron lion of Northern Zhou (China).				
		956	The Nubians attack Aswan and occupy Upper Egypt.		
960	Reunification of China under the Song Dynasty (960–1279).				
		969	Conquest of Egypt by the Fātimids. Treaty between Nubia and Egypt, zenith of Nubia.		
973	The Chālukya Dynasty in the Deccan (India).				
978–*c.* 1014	Lady Muraski in Japan: *The Tale of Genji.*				
		c. 990	The king of Ghana seizes Awdaghust, visited by the Arab traveller Ibn Ḥawqal.		
993	Chōla conquest of Sri Lanka; expelled, 1070.				
998–1186	The Ghaznavid Dynasty in eastern Persia, Afghanistan and the Punjab: Islam spreads to north-west India.				

WESTERN EUROPE *(cont.)*		**BYZANTIUM; CENTRAL, EASTERN AND NORTHERN EUROPE** *(cont.)*		**MUSLIM WORLD** *(cont.)*	
999	Gerbert of Aurillac, first Frenchman elected Pope (Sylvester II, 999–1003), brings the Poles and Hungarians into the Church of Rome, introduces Spanish–Arabic mathematics.				
1000				(1003–) c. 1075	Nāsir-i Khusraw, poet and traveller.
				1004	*The Book of Kings* by the Persian poet Firdāwsi.
1006	St Philibert's Church in Tournus (France), first flowering of Romanesque architecture.				
		1008	Complete Christianization of Sweden.		
1010	Foundation of a school of medicine in Salerno.			1010–1030	Disintegration of the Umayyad Caliphate of Spain; creation of small independant emirates.
1015–1035	Canute (c. 994–1035), king of Denmark and England.				
		1021	First compendium of Russian laws published in Novgorod.		
1023	Treatise on music by Guido of Arezzo (polyphony and earliest notation of music).				
1037	Mainz Cathedral (Romanesque architecture).			(980)–1037	Ibn Sīnā (Avicenna), physician and politician of Khurāsān.
				1037–1063	Toghrïl Beg, architect of the rise of Seljuk Turks in Iran and Iraq.
		1040	Construction of Cathedral of Saint Sophia, in Kiev, in Byzantine style.		
1042	Edward the Confessor, king of England.			1042	Beginning of the Almoravid Dynasty in the south of Morocco.
		1045	Foundation of a school of law and a school of philosophy in Constantinople.		
		1047	Annexation of the Kingdom of Ani by the Byzantines. Foundation of Oslo.		
				(973–)1050	Death of al-Bīrūnī, scientist, Indologist, encyclopedist.
				1052	Invasion of Ifrīqiyya by the Banū Hilāl and Banū Sulaym Arab tribes sent by the Fātimids.
1054	Schism between the churches of Rome and Constantinople.	1054	Split between the Churches of Rome and Constantinople.	1054–1062	Expansion of the Almoravids in the Maghrib.
1059	The Norman Robert Guiscard, duke of Apulia and Sicily.				

ASIA AND OCEANIA (CENTRAL, SOUTHERN, EASTERN AND SOUTH EAST ASIA) *(cont.)*		**AFRICA** *(cont.)*		**THE AMERICAS** *(cont.)*	
					1000
c. 1000	Polynesia: in Tahiti, plates-formes of stones (*marae*), temples with interior courts. Easter Islands: first temples with monumental statues.	*c.* 1000	Zimbabwe. Trade with the East coast visited by Arab navigators.		
1004	Treaty imposed on Northern Song by the Liao.				
11th cent.	Bengal: Kaivarta's revolt.				
		1010	Dyā Kosoy, Songhay king of Kūkya converted to Islam at this time according to the *Tārikh al-Sūdān*, a 12th-cent. source. He settles its capital at Gao (West Africa). Beginning of Omar Diyābā's Reign (d. 1040) in the Takrūr (Middle Senegal).		
c. 1025	The great temple at Gangaikondacolapuram.				
c. 1035	*India* by al-Birūnī (Ghanzī), in Arabic.				
		1042	Beginning of the Almoravid Dynasty in the south of Morocco.		
1044–1287	First Burmese Empire. Capital: Pagan.				
				c. 1050–1200	*Andes* Decline of the Tihuanaco civilization. Development of regional states such as Chanchán in the North and Chancay in the Central Andes.
?–1051	Bi Sheng, Chinese inventor of printing with movable type.				
		1054–1062	Expansion of the Almoravids in the Maghrib.		
		1054–1076	Offensive of the Almoravids against the Ghana Empire which now becomes Muslim.		

WESTERN EUROPE *(cont.)*		**BYZANTIUM; CENTRAL, EASTERN AND NORTHERN EUROPE** *(cont.)*		**MUSLIM WORLD** *(cont.)*	
				1062	Foundation of Marrakech, Morocco.
1066	Battle of Hastings. Conquest of England by William 'the Conqueror', Duke of Normandy.				
		1067	Cuman Turks in Southern Russia.		
		1071	Defeat of the Byzantines by the Seljuk Turks at Manzikert.	1071	Victory of the Seljuks over the Byzantines at Manzikert. Seljuk inroads into Rūm (Anatolia).
1073–1085	Gregory VII elected Pope. Reformer of the Church, opponent of Emperor Henry IV, champion of theocracy and of the papacy's sole right to appoint bishops instead of their investiture by secular kings.				
1075	*'The Domesday Book'* of England.	1075	Death of John Xiphilinus, jurist and patriarch of Constantinople.	(1003–) *c.* 1075	Nāṣir-i Khusraw, poet and traveller.
		1078	Death of Michael Psellus, Byzantine philosopher, politician and historian.		
		1081	Victory of Alexius Comnenus (1081–1118), founder of the Comnenian Dynasty (1081–1185).		
		1083–1148	Anna Comnena, Byzantine princess, author of *The Alexiad.*		
		1083	Settlement of Venetian merchants in Constantinople.		
1085	Capture of Muslim Toledo by the Castilians. Beginnings of massive Spanish–Arab cultural influences on Western Europe.			1085	Muslims lose Toledo to the Castilians.
				1086	The Almoravids in Spain.
1088	High School of Law at Bologna.			1088	Great Mosque of Iṣfahān, Iran.
		1091	Elimination of the Petcheneg Turks in Thrace.		
1093	Ogival vaulting in the Cathedral of Durham.				
1095	Council of Clermont. Sermon of the Crusade.	1095	Council of Piacena (Italy), Byzantine emperor Alexius I asks for the Pope's help against the Turks.		
1098	Foundation of Cîteaux Abbey.				
1099	Jerusalem captured by the Crusaders.			1099	Capture of Jerusalem by the Crusaders (First Crusade).
1100					
		First half of 12th cent.	Mosaics of St Sophia of Constantinople.		
1102–1125	Beginning of the Communal Movement in the North of France and The Netherlands.				

ASIA AND OCEANIA (CENTRAL, SOUTHERN, EASTERN AND SOUTH EAST ASIA) *(cont.)*		**AFRICA** *(cont.)*		**THE AMERICAS** *(cont.)*	
1060	Work of Chakrapanidatta on therapeutics.			*c.* 1060	Foundation of the Inca Empire by the semi-mythical King Manco Capac (1022–1107).
		c. 1065	Al-Bakrī describes West Africa.		
1069–1076	Reforms in China by the Chancellor Wang Anshi (1021–86): new tax, administrative and military laws.				
1069	Sima Gwang (1019–86): *Chronological History of China.*				
		1070	The king of Mali, Mansa Baramandama, converted to Islam.		
		1085	King Hummay, sovereign of Kānem-Bornu, converted to Islam.		
1090	The Kashfu l-mahjūb, a Persian-language work by 'Alī Hujwirī on ṣūfism (Lahore).				
					1100
After 1100	Polynesia: demographic expansion in the Marquesas and migration to the Tamotu Islands and New Zealand.	12th cent.	Expansion of the Yorubas (West Africa) – Ife metalwork. Foundation of the Shona Dynasty of Mwene Mutapa (East Africa).		
		c. 1100	Foundation of Timbuktu, initially a simple Tuareg camp site. Foundation of the Empire of Mali.		*Andes*
				c. 1100	Beginning of the Chibcha culture on the high plateaux of Bogotá in Colombia.
				After 1100	Foundation of Cuzco; gradual rise in hegemony of the Incas.
1101–1126	Chinese emperor Huizong, painter and calligrapher.				
1102	Use of the compass at sea by the Chinese.				

WESTERN EUROPE *(cont.)*		**BYZANTIUM; CENTRAL, EASTERN AND NORTHERN EUROPE** *(cont.)*		**MUSLIM WORLD** *(cont.)*	
1104	'The Song of Roland', an epic poem perhaps by the Norman bard Turoldus, in Old French.				
		1111	Establishment of Pisan merchants in Constantinople.	1111	Death of al-Ghazāli, (b. 1058) theologian, jurist and critic of 'philosophers', in Iran.
1115–1153	St Bernard, abbot of Clairvaux. Preacher of the Second Crusade, he struggles against the Cathars and corruption within the Church.				
		1118–1143	John I Comnenus.		
1119	Order of the Templar Knights.				
1122–1157	Peter the Venerable, abbot of Cluny, instigator of the translation of the Qur'ān into Latin (1141).			1122	Beginning of the Almohad Dynasty, with Ibn Tūmart, in the south of Morocco. Death of Harīrī author of the *Māqāmāt*.
1132	Gothic abbey church of St Denis in France: beginnings of Gothic architecture.				
1137	Founding of a school of medicine at Montpellier in France.				
1138	The Staufens, new German Dynasty, supported by the Pope.				
		1143–1180	Manuel I Comnenus.		
				1144	The Christian city of Edessa captured by Zenkī (a Seljuk Turk), cause of the Second Crusade.
				1150–1159	Conquest of Morocco by the Almohads who obtained a foothold in Spain (Almeria, Seville, Grenada).
1152–1190	Frederick I Barbarossa, emperor of Germany.				
1154–1189	Henry Plantaganet, king of England.	1154	Victory of Sweden over the Finns – Christianization of Finland.		
		1156	Establishment of Genoese merchants in Constantinople.		
1157	The legend of 'Tristan and Iseult' (Old French poem). Arthurian romances of Chrétien de Troyes (d. 1183).				
				1158	Nūr al-dīn in Damascus. Kutūbiyya Mosque in Marrakesh.
1162	Beginning of the construction of Notre Dame in Paris Cathedral.				
				1165	Death of al-Idrisī (b. *c.* 1099), geographer.
		1169	Vladimir, capital of the Russian State of Vladimir – Suzdal.		

ASIA AND OCEANIA (CENTRAL, SOUTHERN, EASTERN AND SOUTH EAST ASIA) *(cont.)*	**AFRICA** *(cont.)*	**THE AMERICAS** *(cont.)*
	1107 Foundation of Zanzibar.	
1113–1150 Reign of Suryavarman II: zenith of the Khmer Empire.		
	c. 1120 Kilwa supplants Mogadishu and wins the Sofala gold trade monopoly; becomes capital of a Muslim merchant state in which the Swahili civilization develops (East Africa).	
	1122 Beginning of the Almohad Dynasty in the south of Morocco.	
1123–1146 Reign of Injong of Korea, during which metallic movable type used for printing.		
1125 Founder of monotheistic sect of Lingayats, Bāsava, born (South India).		
1126 Conquest of the North of China by the Jin (Jurchen) of Manchuria.		
c. 1130 Manufacture of gunpowder by the Chinese.		
1130–1209 Qarā Khitay Empire, sinicized pre-Mongols in Central and Eastern Asia.		
1130–1140 Temple of Angkor-Vat in Cambodia.		
1137 The Genji Roll representing life at the Japanese Court. Death of Rāmanuja, proponent of *bhakti* and critic of Śaṅkara.		
1140–1210 Laing Kai, Chinese painter.		
1150 The *Rājataranginī*: great history of Kashmir by Kalhana.		
1151 Spread of Christianity among Mongol tribes in Central Asia.		
c. 1162–1227 Chinggis Khān, Mongol conqueror.		
1162 Xhu Xi's book on the Chinese in daily life.		

WESTERN EUROPE *(cont.)*		**BYZANTIUM; CENTRAL, EASTERN AND NORTHERN EUROPE** *(cont.)*		**MUSLIM WORLD** *(cont.)*	
				1171	Saladin (Salāḥ al-Dīn) sultan of Egypt: the Ayyūbid Dynasty. Great Mosque of Seville.
1175	Beginning of the construction of Canterbury Cathedral in Kent.				
1179–1223	Advent of Philippe Auguste, king of France.				
				c. 1180	Karīmī merchants in the Indian Ocean.
				1180–1192	The Khwārizm-Shāhs in control of Iran and Baghdād.
		1181	Establishment of German merchants in Novgorod.		
		1185–1205	Political anarchy in Constantinople.		
				1187	Victory of Saladin over the Latins at Hattīn. Jerusalem recaptured.
1189-1199	Richard the Lion Heart, king of England.				
1189–1192	Third Crusade.				
1190	Appearance of the compass, a Chinese invention transmitted by the Arabs, in the Mediterranean.			1190	Death of ʻAttār, Sūfī poet of Nīshāpūr.
				1190–1192	The Third Crusade.
				1192	Saladin allows Christian pilgrims access to the Holy Sepulchre.
				1193	Death of Saladin (b. 1137). Division of his states (Syria, Palestine, Egypt). The 'Giralda' of Seville (minaret of the Mosque).
1195	The Teutonic Knights. The Hohenstaufen in control of Sicily.			1195	Victory of the Almohads over the Castilians at Alarcos.
1197	Pope Innocent II. Zenith of pontifical power.				
				(1126)–1198	Ibn Rushd (Averroës) of Cordova, jurist and philosopher.
				Late 12th cent.	Minaret of Jām in Afghanistan.
1200					
c. 1200	The 'Nibelungenlied', Old German epic poem.				
1202	Appearance of 'Arabic' numerals in Italy (Leonardo Fibonacci of Pisa).				
		1203	Autocephalous Bulgarian Church.		
1204	Constantinople captured by the Crusaders of the Fourth Crusade. *Parzival*, by the German poet Wolfram von Eschenbach, zenith of Arthurian romance.	1204	Constantinople captured by the 'Latins' (Fourth Crusade) – Foundation of the 'Latin Empire' of Constantinople and 'Latin' states of Peloponnese, Athens and Thessaloniki. Foundation of the Greek Empire of Trebizond (1204–1461).	(1135)–1204	Ibn Maymūn (Maïmonides) of Cordova, Jewish theologian and physician.

ASIA AND OCEANIA (CENTRAL, SOUTHERN, EASTERN AND SOUTH EAST ASIA) *(cont.)*		AFRICA *(cont.)*		THE AMERICAS *(cont.)*	
1172	Death of Hemachandra, Indian writer and philosopher (b. 1088). Flowering of bronze sculpture in South India and Sri Lanka.				
c. 1175	Jayadeva's poem on Krishna, the *Gita Govinda*.				
1177	Angkor (Cambodia), sacked by the Chams.				
1181–1218	Reign of Jayavarman VII, builder of Angkor Thom (Cambodia).				
1184	Reform of the Chinese language by Zhu Xi separation of colloquial language from written language.				
(1114)–1186	Bhāskara II, Indian mathematician and astronomer, established the laws of planetary movements.				
1186–1193	Conquest of northern India by the Ghūrid Mu'izzuddīn. Capture of Delhī (1193).				
1192–1867	Reign of the Shōguns in Japan.				
1199	The Qutb Minār of Delhī: beginnings of Indo-Muslim architecture.				
		Late 12th cent.	First coins issued by the sultan of Kilwa.		
					1200
1200	Song School of painting in China				*Mesoamerica*
				After 1200	Migration of the Aztecs from the north-west to the Upper Valley of Mexico.
c. 1200	Marquesas Islands: the *Tohua*, rectangular village squares lined with terraces and houses.	*c.* 1200	Lalibela, Zagwe king of Ethiopia, builder of rock convents and churches.	1200–1500	The Aztec Empire with its capital at Tenochtitlán founded in 1325 (now Mexico City). The Tarascan Empire with its capitals at Ihuatzio and Tzintzuntzán.
		1200–1235	Western Sudan dominated by the Soso.		

WESTERN EUROPE *(cont.)*		**BYZANTIUM; CENTRAL, EASTERN AND NORTHERN EUROPE** *(cont.)*		**MUSLIM WORLD** *(cont.)*	
		1204–1222	Theodore I Lascaris, founder of the Byzantine Empire of Nicaea (1204–1261).		
1209	St Francis of Assisi, apostle of poverty, originator of the Order of the Franciscans, one of earliest Italian poets			(1141–)1209	Nīzāmī, Persian poet of Gandja.
1211	Cathedral of Reims in France.				
1212	Battle of Las Navas de Tolosa: collapse of Muslim power in Spain.			1212	Battle of Las Navas de Tolosa: defeat of the Almohads by the Castilians, collapse of Muslim power in Spain.
1214	Battle of Bouvines, consolidation of French monarchy.				
1214–1294	Roger Bacon, English philosopher and theologian.				
1215	Magna Carta. University of Paris.				
1216	The Order of the Dominicans.				
1218–1250	Frederick II, emperor of Germany.				
				1220	'Alā al-dīn Mosque in Konya, Turkey.
				1220–1237	Kayqubād I, Zenith of the Seljuk Sultanate of Rūm.
1226–1230	Prussia taken by the Teutonic Knights.				
1226–1270	Reign of Louis IX (Saint Louis) in France.				
				1229–1574	The Hafsid Dynasty in Tunisia.
1235–1250	The Sainte-Chapelle, Paris (zenith of Gothic architecture and stained glass).			1235–1239	The Mongols complete the conquest of Iran.
				1236	Cordova taken by Ferdinand III of Castile.
				1236–1393	The Ziyānids in Algeria.
				1237	Independence of the Nasrids in Grenada.
				1240	Death of Ibn Arabī (born Spain), one of the greatest Muslim mystics, in Damascus.
		1242	Victory of Russia's Alexander Nevsky over the Teutonic Knights.		
1245	Westminster Cathedral in London.				
				1248	Capture of Seville by Ferdinand III.
				1248	Death of Ibn al-Baytar, of Málaga, author of works on botany.
1249	Oxford University.	1249	Foundation of Stockholm.		
				1250	The Mamlūks seize power in Egypt and in Syria in 1260.

ASIA AND OCEANIA (CENTRAL, SOUTHERN, EASTERN AND SOUTH EAST ASIA) *(cont.)*		AFRICA *(cont.)*		THE AMERICAS *(cont.)*
1206	Chinggis Khān enthroned as sovereign unifies Mongolia. Quṭbuddīn Aibak (d. 1210) founded the Delhi Sultanate.			
1211–1215	North China conquered by the Mongols.			
1219–1230	All the territories from Korea to Western Russia fall to the Mongols.			
1227	Ögödäy enthroned as Great Khān of the Mongols (d. 1241); Bātū, grandson of Chinggis Khān, made overlord of the western part of the Mongol Empire (the 'Golden Horde') (d. 1256).			
1228–1240	*Secret History of the Mongols* written by anonymous Mongol author.			
		1230–1255	Sundiata Keïta, the emperor of Mali, defeats the Soso and ensures his hegemony.	
		1230–1259	Zenith of the Kānem during the reign of Dūnama Dibalami.	
		c. 1230	Trade with the Chinese on the East Africa coast; slave trade.	
1245–1246	John of Piano Carpini, Italian Franciscan (*c.* 1182–1252), in Mongolia and Central Asia.			
1246–1248	Kūyūk, Great Khān of the Mongols.			
c. 1250	The Temple of the Sun at Konarak, in eastern India.	*c.* 1250	Foundation of the Mosi Kingdom of Ouagadougou (West Africa). Rise of the coastal Kingdoms of Kongo (Central Africa). Yoruba's integration in the Kingdom of Ife (West Africa). Great Bantu migrations (Central and Southern Africa).	
1251–1259	Mōngke, Great Khān of the Mongols.			

WESTERN EUROPE *(cont.)*		**BYZANTIUM; CENTRAL, EASTERN AND NORTHERN EUROPE** *(cont.)*		**MUSLIM WORLD** *(cont.)*	
1252	First minting of the golden coin of Florence: the *Florin*.				
1255	University of Salamanca, Spain.				
1257	Cambridge University, England.				
				1258	Capture and sack of Baghdād by the Mongols.
				1260	The Mamlūks under Baybars defeat the Mongols at Ayn Jalut in Syria.
		1261	Constantinople recaptured by the Greeks.	1261	The 'Abbāsid caliph took refuge in Cairo.
		1261–1282	Michael VIII founds the Palaeologan Dynasty (1261–1453).		
1265	England's First Parliament. The *Summae* of St Thomas Aquinas (1225–1274), Italian Dominican who tries to reconcile faith and reason. Birth of Dante (d. 1321), Italian poet.				
1266	Birth of Giotto, Italian painter.				
1267	Manufacture of paper in Italy.	1267	The Genoese settles in Galata, a quarter of Constantinople.		
				1269	Marīnid Dynasty in Morocco: capital Fez.
1273	Rudolph of Habsburg elected emperor. Foundation of the Habsburg Dynasty (1273–1918).			1273	Death of Jalāl al-dīn Rūmī, Persian-language poet and mystic, whose son, Sultan Veled, created the Mevleviyah brotherhood, in Konya, Turkey.
1274	Council of Lyon on the Union of the Churches of Rome and Constantinople.				
				1277	Death of the Mamlūk Sultan Baybars.
				c. 1280– *c.* 1324	*Osman I*, bey of the Ottomans, eponym of the Osmanli or Ottoman Dynasty.
		1282–1328	Andronicus II, Byzantine emperor.		
1284	Minting of the Venetian ducat.			1284–1285	Qalā'un hospital and mosque in Cairo.
				1291	Fall of Saint-John of Acre, last Frankish stronghold in the East. Death of Sa'dī of Shīrāz, Persian writer in prose and verse.
				1295	Mecca under the control of the Mamlūks. The Alhambra of Grenada: final flowering of Islamic art in Spain.
c. 1298	Marco Polo's *Book of Marvels*.				

ASIA AND OCEANIA (CENTRAL, SOUTHERN, EASTERN AND SOUTH EAST ASIA) *(cont.)*		**AFRICA** *(cont.)*		**THE AMERICAS** *(cont.)*
1253–1254	William of Rubrouck, Flemish Franciscan (*c.* 1200–1293), on mission in Mongolia for Louis IX, king of France.			
1254–1322	Zhao Mingfu, Chinese painter and calligrapher.			
1255	Hulegu (Hulagu), Brother of Mongke, made overlord of Central and Western Asia, founder of the Īl-Khānid Dynasty (d. 1265).			
1258	Destruction of Baghdād by the Mongols.			
1260	Qubilay Khān (d. 1294), grandson of Chinggis Khān, Great Khān of the Mongols and founder of the Yuan Dynasty (1271–1368) in China. Established his capital in Beijing.			
1271–1292	Marco Polo in Central Asia and China where he spends 20 years.			
c. 1275–1315	Reign of Thai king Rama Kamhing, who instituted the Thai script.			
		1276	The Christian Nubian Kingdom of Mukurra (capital: Dunqula) comes under a Mamlūk protectorate.	
		1285	Foundation of the Sultanate of Kilwa. Strengthening of the Mali Empire under Mansa Sakura's reign (1285–1300).	
1290–1320	The Khalji Dynasty (Delhi sultanate).			
1295	Construction of the first Christian church in Beijing. Conversion of the Mongol Īl-Khāns to Islam under Ghazan (the Īl-Khān, 1295–1304).			
1296–1316	'Alā' u'ddīn Khaljī, most powerful of the Delhi sultans, reigned.			

WESTERN EUROPE *(cont.)*		BYZANTIUM; CENTRAL, EASTERN AND NORTHERN EUROPE *(cont.)*		MUSLIM WORLD *(cont.)*	
1300					
		Early 14th cent.	Saint Saviour in Chora (Kahriye Dajami) Constantinople: mosaics, final flowering of Imperial Byzantine art.	Early 14th cent.	End of the Seljuk Dynasty of Rūm. Independance of local Turkmen emirates. Yunus Emre, Turkish mystic poet.
1304–1373	Petrarch, Italian poet.				
		1308	Kiev supplanted by Moscow as seat of Russia's Orthodox patriarchate.		
1309–1376	The Popes in Avignon, France.				
				1312–1313	*Chronicles of the Kings of Andalusia and the Maghrib* by Ibn Idhārī.
1313–1375	Giovanni Boccacio, Italian poet.				
		1321–1328	Rebellion of the Byzantine Prince Andronicus the Younger against Andronicus II. Victorious with John Cantacuzenus's support, he becomes Andronicus III (1328–1340).		
				c. 1324–*c.* 1362	Reign of Orhan, bey of the Ottomans.
		1326–1331	Bursa and Nicaea taken by the Ottomans.	1326–1331	Bursa and Nicaea taken by Orhan.
				1328	Death of Ibn Taymiyya, Hanbalite theologian.
		1331	Advent of Stephen Dushan in Serbia. He invades Albania and Macedonia, and is proclaimed emperor at Skopje (1346); dies in 1355.		
		1332	Death of Theodore Metochites, scholar, philosopher and historian, head of the Imperial University under Andronicus II in Constantinople.	1332–1406	Ibn Khaldūn, historian and observer of society. *Muqaddima, Kitāb al-I'bār.*
		1333	Casimir III (1309–1370), king of Poland.		
		1335–1405	Theophanes the Greek, painter of icons and frescoes in Russia.		
1337	Outbreak of war between France and England (the Hundred Years War).			1337	The Marīnids in Tlemcen, Algeria.
		1340–1351	Hesychast controversy in Constantinople (Gregory Palamas).		
		1341–1347	Revolt of Jean Cantacuzenus against John V Palaeologus. Proclaims himself emperor of Byzantium (John VI, 1341–1355).		
1346	Defeat of the French by the English at Crécy. Siege of Calais. First appearance of gunpowder on European battlefields, beginning of the decline of knights.			1346	End of the Īl-Khānid Dynasty of Persia.
1347–1352	Black Death in Europe.				

	ASIA AND OCEANIA (CENTRAL, SOUTHERN, EASTERN AND SOUTH EAST ASIA) *(cont.)*		AFRICA *(cont.)*		THE AMERICAS *(cont.)*
					1300
1301–1374	Ni Zan, Chinese painter.				
1308	John of Monte Corvino, Archbishop of Beijing.	1307–1331	Reign of Mansa Musa, sovereign of Mali. Zenith of the kingdom.		
1318	Rashīd al-Dīn: author of *History of the World* and Īl-Khānid, minister, executed. Famous Indo-Persian poet Amīr Khusraw's *NuhSipihr*, marked by patriotism (d. 1325).	1315	Gradual Islamization of Nubia.		
1324–1351	Muḥammad Tughluq reigned: ambitions and innovative sultan of Delhi.				
		1325	Conquest of Gao and the Songhay Kingdom by Mansa Mūsā.		
		1328	In Ethiopia, the Christian Amhara Kingdom of Shoa subjugates the Muslim Sultanate of Ifāt.		
		1331	Visit by Ibn Baṭṭūṭa to Kilwa.		
1335	End of the Mongol Dynasty in Iran.	*c.* 1335	Foundation of Mbanza Kongo, capital of the Kongo Kingdom (Central Africa).		
c. 1335–1347	Moorish traveller Ibn Baṭṭūṭa's travels in India and China.				
1336	Vijayanagara Empire in southern India founded.	1336	Ali Kolen frees Gao and founds the Sonni Dynasty (West Africa).		
1343	Vijayanagara city established as capital.				
1347	Foundation of the Bahmanī, Kingdom in the Deccan (India).				
1350	First mention of spinning wheel in India.				*Mesoamerica*
c. 1350	Death of Namdev, an Indian monotheist.			*c.* 1350	The Mixtecs come to power in the west of the State of Oaxaca; their domination extended subsequently to Mounte Albán and other Zapotec centres to the East.
1350–1389	Zenith of the Majapahit Empire in the Indonesian archipelago.				
1350–1767	Kingdom of Ayutthaya in Thailand.				

WESTERN EUROPE *(cont.)*		**BYZANTIUM; CENTRAL, EASTERN AND NORTHERN EUROPE** *(cont.)*		**MUSLIM WORLD** *(cont.)*	
				1351–1358	Bū 'Ināniyya *madrasa* (school) in Fez, Morocco.
				1354	*Madrasa* of the sultan Hasan in Cairo.
		1360	Nicephorus Gregoras, theologian, philosopher, wrote a *Greek History*, opponent of the Hesychasts.		
		1362	Adrianople (Edirne) taken by the Ottomans and made their capital.	1362–1389	Murād I, Ottoman sultan.
				c. 1365	Creation of the Janissary corps by Murād I.
		1369	Submission of the Byzantine emperor John V to Catholicism in the hope of a Western Crusade against the Turks.	(1304–)1369 or (1304–) 1377	Ibn Baṭṭūṭa, Moorish traveller who travelled through the Muslim world from Spain to China and into sub-Saharan Africa from 1325 to 1353.
		1370–1371	Occupation of practically all of Macedonia by the Ottomans, Bulgaria reduced by the Ottomans to vassal status.		
		1370–1424	Ziska, leads Czech supporters of Jan Hus.		
1376–1384	Wycliffe, English reformer, refutes most of the Church's dogmas and supports the Peasants' Revolt.				
1378–1418	The Great Schism of the Catholic Church.				
1386	University of Heidelberg, Germany.				
1387–1390	Geoffrey Chaucer's *Canterbury Tales.*				
1388	The Swiss Confederation.				
		1389	The Serbs defeated at Kosovo by the Ottomans.	1389	Victory over the Serbs and death of Murād I at Kosovo.
				1389–1402	Bāyezīd I, Ottoman sultan.
				1390	Death of Hāfiz, Ṣūfī poet, in Shīrāz.
				c. 1395	Institution of *devshirmè* ('child-levy' among tributary Christians) by the Ottomans.
		1396	Battle of Nicopolis: defeat of the Hungarians and of the Western Crusaders by the Ottoman Sultan Bāyezīd I. Blockade of Constantinople by the Ottomans.	1396	Ottoman victory over a Western Crusade at Nicopolis.
					Tīmūr Lang ('Tamerlane'), in control of Iran and Iraq.
					'Anatolia Fortress', on the Bosphorus (Anadolu Hisar).
		1397	Union of Kalmar: unification of all the Scandinavian kingdoms.		

ASIA AND OCEANIA (CENTRAL, SOUTHERN, EASTERN AND SOUTH EAST ASIA) *(cont.)*		AFRICA *(cont.)*		THE AMERICAS *(cont.)*
1351–1388	Reign of Firūz Tughluq, sultan of Delhi and builder of canals, in North India.			
1353	Creation of the Lan-Xang Kingdom in Laos.	1353	Ibn Baṭṭūṭa visits Timbuktu.	
1357	The Indo-Muslim historian Ziyā Bārānī wrote the *Tārikh-i Firuzshāhī* (in Persian).			
		c. 1360	Foundation of the Kingdom of Jolof (West Africa).	
1363	Emergence of the Nō, Japanese drama.			
1364	Foundation of the Shan Dynasty, of Avā (central Burma).			
1368–1644	The Ming Dynasty, which expelled and succeeded the Mongol Yuan Dynasty.			
1370–1405	Reign and conquests by Tīmūr Lang (1336–1405) in Central Asia, Syria, Anatolia, southern Russia and northern India.			
c. 1375	Commentaries on Brahamminical schools by Mādhava Achārya.			
		c. 1380	Development of Zimbabwe in connection with the Eastern coastal trade.	
		1382–1411	Dawit I, king of Ethiopia, strives to contain Muslim pressure.	
		c. 1385	Zenith of Kano and Katsina. Beginning of the Islamization of the Hausa areas (West Africa).	
1397	Construction of the Golden Pavilion at Kyōtō.			
1398	Destruction of Delhī by Tīmūr Lang.			
1399–1420	Tīmūr Lang's programme of monuments at Samarkand.			
1392–1910	Yi Dynasty in Korea.			
End of 14th cent.	Polynesia: building of huge coastal temples (*marae*).	Late 14th cent.	Beginning of the exodus towards Chad of nomadic Arabs from Egypt driven by the Mamlūks. Tundjurs settle at Darfur, Kordofan and Waddaï.	

WESTERN EUROPE *(cont.)*		BYZANTIUM; CENTRAL, EASTERN AND NORTHERN EUROPE *(cont.)*		MUSLIM WORLD *(cont.)*	
1400					
1396–1475	Paolo Uccello, Italian painter; development of linear perspective.			Early 15th cent.	The Ak Koyunlu dominate the Eastern Anatolia territories of the Kara Koyunlu (Western Iran and Iraq).
1401–1402	First banks in Barcelona and Frankfurt.				
				1402	Defeat and capture of Bāyĕzid I at Anakra by Tīmūr Lang. Dislocation of the Ottoman State.
				1406	Gūr-i-Mīr, Tīmūr Lang's mausoleum in Samarkand.
		1410	Victory of Poles and Lithuanians over the Teutonic Knights at Tannenberg.		
		1410	Jan Hus condemned and burned for heresy at Constance.		
				1412–1421	Reconstruction of the Ottoman State by Mehmed I.
				1415–1420	'Green Mosque' in Bursa, Turkey.
				1415–1481	Mehmed II, surnamed the Conqueror (Fātih) Ottoman sultan.
		1420–1434	Crusade against the Hussites, Czech national movement.		
				1421–1451	Murād II, Ottoman sultan.
				1422–1438	Barsbay, Mamlūk sultan.
				1424	Ulugh Beg's observatory at Samarkand.
		1426	Andrei Rublev's icons in the Cathedral of Moscow.		
1429–1431	Joan of Arc (1412–1431).				
1431–1474	François Villon, French poet.				
1432	*Adoration of the Lamb* by Jan Van Eyck (*c.* 1390–1441); Flemish beginnings of oil painting and atmospheric perspective.				
1434–1464	Cosimo of Medici in Florence.				
1436	Dome of the Cathedral of Florence.				
		1438–1439	Council of Ferrara/Florence. Proclamation of the Union of the Churches, but rejected by the Byzantine people and its clergy.		
1439	Council of Ferrara/Florence: Union of the Churches of Rome and Constantinople.				

ASIA AND OCEANIA (CENTRAL, SOUTHERN, EASTERN AND SOUTH EAST ASIA) *(cont.)*		**AFRICA** *(cont.)*		**THE AMERICAS** *(cont.)*	
					1400
15th cent.	Gradual Islamization of Java, the coastal regions of Sumatra and Eastern Turkistan.	Early 15th cent.	The Songhay gradually take over Malil. Expansion of Benin.		*Andes*
1400	Mosque of jāmi 'Masjid Gulbarga (63 domes) in India.			1400–1500	Zenith of the Inca Empire under the reign of Pachacutec Yupanqui (1438–1471). Expansion over the high plateaux of Bolivia, the North-west of Argentina and Central Chile; under the reign of Huayan Capac (1493–1527), expansion to the borders of Colombia.
1405–1433	Chinese admiral, Zheng He's voyages in South China Sea and Indian Ocean.				
1406	Beijing: construction of the Forbidden City.				
1407	Java and the Malay states under Chinese domination.				
1410	Ashraf Jahāngīr Simnānī introduces Ibn 'Arabī's ideas in India.				
		1419–1460	Systematic exploration of the West African coast by the Portuguese.		
1420–1506	Sesshu, Japanese painter.	1420	First Luba Kingdom in Central Africa.		
1421	Completion of the Temple of Heaven in Beijing, declared Imperial capital.				
1423	India: Friday Mosque at Ahmadābād. Flowering of Indo-Muslim architecture.				
1425–1470	The Oïrat Empire (*Mongol-Kalmuck*) from Ili to Mongolia.				
					Mesoamerica
				1427–1440	End of Tepanec hegemony: conquest of a large portion of the valley of Mexico by the Aztec king Itzcoatl.
				1430–1472	Peaceful reign of Nezahualcóyotl of Tlaxcala; great builder and poet (Nahuatl language); his capital, Texcoco, becomes a major cultural centre.
1434	Phnom Penh, capital of Cambodia.				
		1435	The Tuaregs seize Timbuktu.		
		1440	Beginning of the Reign of Eware in Benin: zenith of the kingdom. Flowering of metalwork art.		
		1441	Beginning of the import of African slaves into Portugal.	1441	The Aztec ruler Moctezuma I ('Montezuma' I) brings vast territories in Central America under his authority.

WESTERN EUROPE *(cont.)*		BYZANTIUM; CENTRAL, EASTERN AND NORTHERN EUROPE *(cont.)*		MUSLIM WORLD *(cont.)*	
				(1363)–1442	Al-Maqrīzī, administrator, professor, author of the *Khitāt* (topography of Fustāt, Cairo, Alexandria) and of a *History of Egypt.*
1448	Invention of movable printing characters by Gutenberg in Mainz, Germany.	1448	Autocephalous Russian church.		
		1449–1453	Constantine XI Dragases, last Byzantine emperor.		
				Mid-15th cent.	The 'Blue Mosque' of Tabrīz: zenith of Islamic tile decoration in Iran. Flowering of Islamic civilization in Central Asia.
				1450–1535	Bihzād, miniature painter in Herāt: zenith of Islamic figurative art.
				Second half of 15th cent.	Ahmad Ibn Mājid, Arab navigator, pilot in the Indian Ocean; according to legend, reportedly guided Vasco da Gama towards India.
1452	Birth of Leonardo da Vinci, Italian artist.	1452	Death of Gemistus Plethon, Byzantine philosopher, theoretician of Neo-Platonism. Construction of the 'Rumelia' Ottoman fortress on the Bosphorus.	1452	Rumelia Fortress on the Bosphorus.
		1453	Siege of Constantinople by the Ottoman sultan Mehmed II; city taken on 29 May.	1453	Constantinople taken by Mehmed II. Called Istanbul, became capital in 1458–59.
				1454	First regulations (Kānūnnāmè) of Mehmed II on the organization of the Ottoman Empire.
1455	The Gutenberg Bible.				
1455–1485	The 'Wars of the Roses' in England.				
		1458	Ivan III sovereign of Russia (1458–1505)		
1460	Death of Prince Henry 'The Navigator', patron of Portuguese exploration of the African coast. 'The polyptych of St Vincent', by the Portuguese painter Nuno Gonçalves.				
1461–1483	Louis XI, king of France.	1461	Capture of Trebizond by the Ottomans. End of the Trebizond Empire, last Greek state.		
				1463–1471	The Mosque of Fātih in Istanbul.
				1463	Arsenal of Istanbul.
		1468	Death of George Scholarios (Gennadios), opponent of the Union of the Churches, first patriarch of Constantinople under the Ottomans.	1468–1469	Reign of the Mamlūk sultan Qāytbāy.
1469–1494	Lorenzo de Medici in Florence: rise of 'Renaissance' culture.				
		1474–1478	The Duchies of Rostov and Novgorod subjugated by Ivan III. Unification of the Russian Empire.		
				1475–1478	Topkapi Palace in Istanbul.
1478	Boticelli's *Allegory of Spring*, Florence: 'neo-paganism' in art.				
				(*c.* 1400)–1480	'Āshiqpāshāzāde, Ottoman chronicler.
1481	The Inquisition in Spain.	1481	End of the domination of the Golden Horde over Southern Russia.	(1481)–1512	Reign of the Ottoman sultan Bāyezīd II.
1482	Construction of the Sistine Chapel in Rome.				

ASIA AND OCEANIA (CENTRAL, SOUTHERN, EASTERN AND SOUTH EAST ASIA) *(cont.)*		AFRICA *(cont.)*		THE AMERICAS *(cont.)*	
		c. 1450	Creation of principalities on the right bank of the Senegal by the Peuls (Fulani) and the Lemtunas.		
		c. 1450–1497	Reign of Muhammad Rumfa, sultan of Kano, a great builder.		
1451–1526	Lodi Dynasty of Sultanate of Delhi. Hindi poetry of Kabīr of Benares: Hindu–Muslim spiritual synthesis.				
		1461	Colonization of the Cape Verde Islands by the Portuguese.		
		1464–1492	Reign of Sonni 'Alī who takes possession of Timbuktu and Jenne.		
		1465–1497	Reign of the sultan 'Alī Gajī ibn Dūnama in Bornu.		
1467–1477	Civil war in Japan. Destruction of Kyōtō.				
		1471	The Portuguese reach Cameroon and Gabon.		
1480	The painter Kāno Masanōbu founds the Kanō school in Japan.				
					Mesoamerica
				1481–1520	Greatest expansion of the Aztec Empire under Ahuitzotl (1481–1502) and Moctezuma II (1502–1520).

WESTERN EUROPE *(cont.)*		**BYZANTIUM; CENTRAL, EASTERN AND NORTHERN EUROPE** *(cont.)*	**MUSLIM WORLD** *(cont.)*	
1483	Births of Rabelais, Raphael and Luther.			
1485	Beginning of the Tudor Dynasty in England (1485–1603). Printing by Caxton of Sir Thomas Maloy's *Morte d'Arthur*, last of the great Arthurian romances in Medieval tradition. The Függer's first operations as bankers in Augsburg.			
1488	The Portuguese explorer Bartolomeu Dias reaches the Cape of Good Hope.			
1492	Grenada captured by the 'Catholic Monarchs' of Castile and Aragon. Beginning of the expulsion of Jews and Muslims from Spain. Christopher Colombus sights the islands of the Caribbean.		1492	Grenada taken by the Spanish. End of the Nasrid Dynasty. The Ottomans receive Jews, driven from Spain, in Thessaloniki and Istanbul. Death in Herāt of Jāmī, last great classical Persian poet, major mystical philosopher.
1494	Treaty of Tordesillas: division of the world by the Pope into Castilian and Portuguese spheres of influence.			
1498	The Portuguese explorer Vasco da Gama rounds Africa and reaches Calicut in India.			
			1499	Islam outlawed in Spain.
1500				
1500	The Portuguese explorer Perálves Cabral, following Vasco da Gama, touches on Brazil.			
			1501	Death in Herāt of Mīr 'Alī Shēr Nawā'ī, leading Turkish poet.

ASIA AND OCEANIA (CENTRAL, SOUTHERN, EASTERN AND SOUTH EAST ASIA) *(cont.)*		AFRICA *(cont.)*		THE AMERICAS *(cont.)*	
				1487	Consecration of the 'Templo Mayor' at Tenochtitlán.
		1488	Discovery of the Cape of Good Hope by the Portuguese Bartholomeu Dias.		
		c. 1490	First Catholic missions to Africa. Conversion to Christianity of the Empire of the Kongo.		
					Caribbean
				1492	Christopher Colombus lands at Guanahani (San Salvador), believes himself to be on the eastern rim of Asia.
		1493	Songhay Empire led for a century by the Askiya, a new Dynasty founded by Muhammad Ture or Sylla (1493–1528). Zenith of the University of Sankore at Timbuktu.		
					North America
				1497	John Cabot sails along part of the North American coast.
1498	Discovery of the Sea Route to the Indies by Vasco da Gama: landing at Calicut on the Malabar coast.	1498	Vasco da Gama rounds Cape of Good Hope and reaches Calicut, India.		

1500

		1500	Cabral touches Brazil before rounding the Cape of Good Hope and reaching Calicut, India.		*South America*
				1500	Brazil sighted by the Portuguese (Cabral): became a Portuguese colony.
		1504	Destruction of the Christian Nubian State, Alwā.		
1505	Beginning of Portuguese colonization of Sri Lanka (then Goa (1510), Malacca (1511).	1505	Kilwa occupied by the Portuguese. Beginning of the Portuguese colonization of Mozambique and slave trade with the Americas.		
				1507	The new continent called 'America' in honour of the Italian navigator Amerigo Vespucci, by the German cartographer Martin Waldseemüller.
1510	Portuguese capture of Goa, which became headquarters of Portuguese power in the East.				

INDEX

Bold page numbers refer to figures and maps; plate numbers are in **bold** and are prefixed by **Pl.**

Abbās al-Majūsī, Alī ibn 108
Abū Bakr 51, 131, 266, 267, 271
quells rebellion 274, 275
Abungu, George 526
Adelard of Bath 104, 115
Afghanistan 286
art and architecture **Pl. 208**, **Pl. 211**, **Pl. 216**
calligraphy **Pl. 112**
Afonso, Dom, King of Kongo 64
Africa
agriculture 75, 487
ancestors 26
animism 121, 487
arts and architecture **264–70**, 525, 530, 544–6, **Pl. 33–5**, **Pl. 259**, **Pl. 261–3**, **Pl. 271–3**, **Pl. 275**
Central and Southern:
agriculture 541–2
individuals
family and community 542–4
land and people 539
migrations **540**, 540–1
political structures 543–4
trade and commerce 544
Christianity 486–7, **Pl. 276–80**
East:
coins 528
international importance 536–7
Kilwa map **527**
land and agriculture 524–5
local cultures mix with Islam 529–30
Madagascar and islands' culture 531–4
trade and commerce 526–8, 536–7
urban development 527–8
education and scholarship 98–9
geography 11, 13, 110
government and law 63–4
historiography 111–12, 485
Islam 292–3, 500–1, 502
kinship 28
languages and writing 99
map **496**
population **14**, 20–1, 72
Portuguese sail around 247
pottery and ceramics 533, **Pl. 15**
scholarship 114–15
seafaring 90
search for gold 84
technology 487
West:
arts 504–5
currency and barter 493
geography 489
kinship and family 496
Libyco-Berbers and Berber-Arabs 489–90
markets 494
peasant communities 496–7
political structure 497
rural economy 492
settlement of Black people 490–1
slavery and social strata 496–7
towns and cities 494–5
traditional religions 499–501
agriculture **Pl. 2–6**
Africa 21, 487, 492, 505, 524, 533, 541–2
Arab land tenure 322
Asia 20, 428–9
Central America 590
cotton 429
Ethiopia 515
fertility preservation 428
great estates and hired labour 429
harnesses 88
hunter-gatherers 73
improved methods 18
India 401–2
irrigation 57, 380, 401–2, 411, 573–4
Islamic spread of plants and animals 304–5
mediaeval European progress 214
mills 74
North America 567, 570, 571, 573
olives 304
organization of production 78–9
pastoralists 73–4
plough horses speed grain farming 74
relation to city-state 42
rice 304, 419
rotation and multiple crops 428
silk 428–9
South America **75**, 596, 600, 612, 615
South-East Asia 20–1
Spain and Sicily 351, 354
spatial distribution of functions 75–6
sugar 304
vineyards 304
see also land
Aguadas 612, 614
Akan people 490
Aksum *see* Ethiopia

'Ala'u'ddīn Khalji 58
Albertus Magnus, St 106, 140
Aleut people 555–7
Alexander of Hales 216
Algeria 289
Ali (Muḥammad's cousin) 266, 271
Allibert, C. 533
Almohads 303
Almoravids 292–3, 303
Alphonsus, Petrus (Moses Sefardi) 243
America *see* Mesomerica; North America; South America
'Amilī, Shaykh Bahā' al-Din 371
'Amirī, Abu'l-Ḥasan 372
Amlak, Yekuno 516
Anasazis 573–6
Anatolia
  Christians 391
  emirates 397
  maps **389**, **390**
  Mongolian Īl-Khānate 476–7
  Seljuk rule 327
  sultanate of Rūm 390–2
  Turkish migration 289–90
Andalusia 106
  architecture 345
  Christian conquest of *ṭā'ifa* rulers 353–4
  cultural achievements 350–4, 356–7
  first century of Islamic rule 348–9
  Islamic scholars 341–2
  literature 343
  and the Maghrib 338–9
  Nasrid kingdom of Granada 356, 358–9
  political fragmentation 355–6
animals
  alpacas **Pl. 323**
  arctic 556, 558
  in art **Pl. 210–13**, **Pl. 255**
  camels and dromedaries 73–4, 84, 304, 402, 465, **Pl. 182–4**
  cattle 305
  dogs 542, 573
  donkeys 493
  fish 563
  game 573
  goats 465
  horses 73–4, 84, 304, 402–3, 465, 563, **Pl. 7–9**
  husbandry in Africa 524–5, 542
  nomad knowledge 470
  North America 573
  sheep 304–5, 465
  South America 598, 609
  transport **Pl. 7–9**
  water-raising work 428
  West African herding 492, 505
Anna Comnena 112
Anselmo of Aosta 216
Antilles (Greater and Lesser) 599–600
Apaches 573
Apollonios of Kition **Pl. 129**
Aquinas, St Thomas 140, 216, **Pl. 127**
Arabic language **99**
  calligraphy 145, 154, 340, **Pl. 112–14**
  Egypt 332, 336
  grammar and lexicography 112–13, 324
  histories 324, 325
  Ibn Ṭufayl 339
  influence on Persian 281, 282, 369
  the language of the faith 298–9
  learning and scholarship 98
  literature 156, 158, 324, 325, 336, **Pl. 187–8**
  scientific use 373–4
  SE Asia 417, 418
  state administration 272, 273
  translations and cultural diffusion 115, 242–3, 255
  use by Jews 311
  writing on East African culture 529–30
Arabs 94
  'Abbāsid caliphates 314–18, 319, 321, 322
  artistic expression 145
  Būyid caliphates 318–19, 321, 322
  camel transport 85–6
  classical Greek learning 176–7
  coins **Pl. 191–2**
  conquests in Europe 175, 210
  creation of Baghdad 319
  declining culture 317
  education and scholarship 323–7
  expansion of 600s 84
  high status in cities 279
  influence on Nubia and Sudan 511–13
  intellectual influence on Europe 210
  invade Constantinople 178–9
  Mecca before Islam 264–5
  migration 17–18
  military organization 279–80
  mineral resources 322–3
  new cities 278
  non-Arab Muslims 278
  organization of trade and manufacturing 320
  pastoralism 73–4
  philosophers 133
  political history 314–19
  population movement 72
  rise of Islam 264–7
  Ṣafawid dynasty 329
  seafaring in Indian Ocean 90
  Seljuk rule 327–9
  social and economic conditions 319–23
  state institutions 318
  technology and manufacturing 322–3
  towns and cities 80
  Umayyad dynasty 276, 279, 298
  uprisings 317–18
  see also Islamic culture
Aragawi, Za-Mika'el 520
Aramaic language 98
archaeology
  SE Asia and Islands 416
Archimedes 103
architecture
  Arabian cities 278
  arctic peoples 557, 559
  Balkan churches 232–3
  Buddhist temples 435
  building programmes 79, 80–1
  Byzantine Empire 188
  Carolingian Empire 203
  Central Africa 545
  churches and cathedrals **Pl. 28–9**, **Pl. 68–9**, **Pl. 74–5**
  East Africa 525, 530
  Egypt 334–5
  Ethiopia 521, **521**
  four arches **Pl. 195**
  France **Pl. 67–9**
  Gothic 218, **Pl. 28–9**
  imperial palaces 156–7
  Incas 611
  India 408–9
  Iran **Pl. 27**
  Iraq **Pl. 197**
  Islamic Spain and Sicily 352, **355**, **Pl. 198**
  Japan **448**, 456
  the Maghrib 345–7, **346**
  Malagasy 532–3
  Mayan 584–5, 586
  mediaeval Europe's castles and cathedrals 218
  Mesoamerica 164–8, 587, 588
  minarets **Pl. 202–9**
  mosques **Pl. 26**, **Pl. 65–6**, **Pl. 88–9**, **Pl. 199–201**
  North America 562–3, 564, 575
  Nubia 509

places of worship and commemoration 148–52
pyramids 164
religious functional spaces 152–3
Romanesque 218
Sāmānid state 383
South America 611, 615, **Pl. 38**
South East Asia 419
Sri Lankan shrines and monuments 411–12
Syria **Pl. 30**
Tibet 479–80
Tiwanaku 603–4
towns and cities **Pl. 32**, **Pl. 39–41**
walls and fortresses **Pl. 30–9**
Yemen **Pl. 189**
Argentina **612**, 612–16
Armenia 94, 252–3
Byzantine culture 191–2
Chalcedonian community 253
education and scholarship 252–3
Islamic conquest 275
migration 303
Seljuk invasion 252–3
art
Armenia 253
Balkans 233
Byzantine Empire 188–90, 191–2, 194
calligraphy 340–1, 409
Carolingian Empire 203
Chinese painting 440–1
Christianity **Pl. 56–64**
effect of migration and movement 143–8
Ethiopia 521–2, 522
European painting 218
folk and popular 158–9
icons 160, 194, 233, **Pl. 145–60**
illuminated manuscripts 189, 202, 384, 521–2
India 409–10
industrial 161
Mayan 584–5
Mesoamerica 164–8, **167**, **168**
Mongols 473, **473**
music and dance 410
Northwest American carvings 564–5
Nubian murals 509–10
painting 189
patronage 156–9
perspective from optics 116
piety and pleasure 159–61
Sāmānid state 383
sculpture 189–90
self-expression 161–2
symbols and representations of the sacred 153–6
Timurid Central Asia 384, 385
Vikings **Pl. 165–8**
West Africa 504
artisans and craftsmanship 76–7
Africa 504, 533, 544–6
Central Asia 380, 384, 385
China 429–30
Indian textiles 402
Islamic corporations 301–2
jewellery 77, 190
Mesoamerica 583, 587, 588, 591
metalwork **77**
North America 564–5, 575
organization of production 79–80
South America 594–5, 596–7, 615–16
tools 77
see also art; mining and metallurgy; pottery and ceramics; textiles
Āryabhaṭa 403
Al-Ash'arī 133
Ashikaga Takauji 453
Asia
agriculture 75
animal transport 85–6
arts and architecture 144, 146–7
cavalry **Pl. 12**
Central:
arts and architecture 380, 384, 385, Pl. 195, Pl. 214–15
astronomy Pl. 136
Persian language 385
principles of nomads 55–6
Sufism 287, 327, 382
technology 380
family model 37
geographical conditions 11
Islam 276
map **286**
population 14, 15, 16, 19–20
shamanism 120–1
South East
art and architecture **Pl. 226–32**
emergence of nations 416–20
languages and writing 419
legal and ideological systems 420
technology 419–20
trade and commerce 417, 418
Atīsá 480
'Aṭṭār, Farīd al-Dīn 370, 371
St Augustine of Hippo 176
Aurauquíns 599
Australia
animism 121
geography and geology 13, 621, 623–4
historiography 621, 622–3
population **14**
Avars 222, 235, 236
Averroës *see* Ibn Rushd
Aymaras 607
Aztecs **582**, **Pl. 1**
animism 121, 122
archaeological information 553
art and architecture 168, **Pl. 300–7**
calendars **Pl. 144**
government and law at time of conquest 66–7
rise of and conquest 582–3
sciences and mathematics 101
symbols of faith 156

Ba-salota Mika'el 517
Babylonians 102
Bacon, Roger 105, 116, 142
Badr, battle of 266
Bai Juyi 438, 440
Al-Bal'amī, Abū 'Alī Muḥammad 381–2
Balkans
architecture 232–3
the Byzantine context 178–80, 192
migrations and movements 175–6, **221**, 221–3
popular culture 233
Slavs 222–3, 225, **226**, 227
and the Turks 182, 395
see also Bulgaria; Serbia
Balts 237
Bāṇa 407
Bantus 486, 487, 539
language 540–1, 543
migrations 540–1
Banū Mūsā brothers 102, 103, 374
Kitāb al-Hiyal 104
Baranī, Ẓiyā' al-Dīn 58, 111, 407
Basil I of Byzantium 179
Al-Battānī 103
Baybars 335–6, 336
Al-Bayṭār, Abū Bakr 106
Béatrice de Bourbon **Pl. 173**
Becket, Thomas à **Pl. 169**
St Bede 216
Bedouin nomads **Pl. 182**

city life versus desert life 296–7
Nubia 511–12
social and economic life 295–6
St Benedict 211
Benin 485, 495
Bennett, Wendell 603
Berbers 289–90
Berg, F. J. 526
St Bernard 154, 211
Bhāskara II 102, 103
Bi Sheng 444
Bilgä Kagan 55, 56
Birnik people 559
Al-Bīrūnī, Abū' l-Rayhān 104, 105, 106, 108, 109, 372
astronomy 374
influence in India 403, 404
works and achievements 382
Boccaccio, Giovanni 218, **Pl. 103**
Boethius 215
Bogomils 124, 227–8
Cosmas's treatise against 230
Bohai 462, 463
Bohemia 235, 239–40, 240–1
Hussites 241
Bolivia **613**, 614
Bolud Chingsiyang 477
St Bonaventure 216
books *see* libraries; printing and books
St Boris **Pl. 158**
Boris of Bulgaria 227, **Pl. 153**
Borneo 418, 622
Bosnia 223, 228
Brahmagupta 102, 103, 403
St Bridget of Vadstena 239, **Pl. 175**
Britain
agriculture **Pl. 6**
architecture **Pl. 74**
constitution and parliament 212
expansion 212
Lindisfarne Gospels **Pl. 104**
Brunei 418
Buddhism
Amidism 451, 452, 454
architecture 149, 151–2, **Pl. 228**
art 145, **Pl. 80–7**, **Pl. 224**, **Pl. 230**, **Pl. 234**, **Pl. 236**
cave-temples 435
China 432, 434–5, 441, **Pl. 102**
decline in India 404, 405
Greater and Lesser Vehicles and beliefs 128–30
Japan 449–50, 451–2, 454–5
Korea 458, 459
Mongols 476
Nepal 414–15
Nichren 455
representation of the sacred 153, 154
sculpture 409
spread from India 57–8, 97, 129–30
Sri Lanka 411–12
stimulates wood-block printing 444
Tibet 130, 480
Turkic-Mongol nomads 467
Zen 454–5
Bukhārī, Muḥammad ibn Ismā'īl 383
Bulgaria 179, 192, 222–3, 395
Bogomils 227–8
conversion to Christianity 226–7
Cyrillic script **Pl. 106**
icons **Pl. 153–4**
literature 229, 230
Bumïn Kagan 55
Burdidan, Jean 105
burial *see* death and funeral rites
Burma *see* Myanmar
Burman language 419
Bushmen *see* San people
Buzjānī, Abu'l-Wafā' 375
Byzantine Empire
advance of the Turks 393–5, **394**
Arab expansion 274
architecture 232
arts 186, 188–90, **Pl. 57–8**, **Pl. 63**, **Pl. 145–50**
and Balkans 222–3, 227
coins **Pl. 190**, **Pl. 193**
before the Crusades 178–80
the Crusades and decline 180, **181**, 182
diffusion of culture 190–4
education and scholarship 99–100
falls to Turks 3, 138, 182
first Arab invasions 178–9
law 184, 187–8
medicine 187
military 184
recapture of Constantinople 393
relations with Latin West 136–8, 190–1
science and technology 187, **Pl. 129**
social structure and economy 184–5
split with West 175–7
state and administration 183–4
Turks in Anatolia 389–90, 391
without feudalism 177
see also iconoclasm

Cahen, Claude 299, 322
Caldwell, J. R. 568
calendars and time-keeping **442**, 442–3, **Pl. 1**
Aztecs **Pl. 144**
China **442**, 442–3
Japan 450
Mayans 584, 585
Mongols 474
calligraphy
China **Pl. 95**, **Pl. 96**
Cyrillic script **Pl. 106**
Islamic **Pl. 107–14**
Japan **Pl. 98–9**
Korea **Pl. 97**
Latin **Pl. 103–4**
Cambodia
art and architecture 151, **Pl. 227**, **Pl. 229–31**
Buddhism **Pl. 82**
early history 417
literature 98
monuments 57–8
ships 92
Campas 609
Cão, Diogo 64
Capell, A. 622
capitalism 214
Caquetí 598
Caribbean islands
Lesser and Greater Antilles 599–600
Caribs 599
Carolingian Empire **199**
administrative and religious structures 199–200
arts 203
assessment 203–4
coins **Pl. 194**
the Frankish kingdom before Pepin 195–6
images **Pl. 161–4**
intellectual culture 202–3
Pepin the Short 196–7
resources 201
rise of Charlemagne to Emperor 197–8
Verdun and break-up of empire 198–9
see also Charlemagne
Carpini, John of Piano 246
Castillo, Bernal Díaz 587
Cathars 124–5, 210
St Catherine of Siena 140
Central America *see* Mesoamerica

Chaan Muan II **Pl. 296**
Chaghatai Khān 477
Chaka 63
Champa 417, 418
Chan Chan 605–7, **606**, **Pl. 316**
Chancas 609–10
Chang Pogo 458
Chao Yuanfang 107
Charlemagne 138, **Pl. 161**
 administration 199–200
 assessment 203–4
 East-West European divide 176, 179
 land and resources 201
 rise to Emperor 197–8
Charles Martel 196, 276
 checks Arab advance 348
Charles the Bald 199, 201, 202, **Pl. 169**
Chattopadhyaya, B. D. 57
Chen Jingyi 105
Cheng brothers 433
Chichén Itzá 68
children
 boys' and girls' roles 34
 infant mortality 302
 infanticide 31
Chile **613**, 614
 Inca presence 616–17
Chimús 606, **606**, **Pl. 316**, **Pl. 319**
China
 administration 61, 426
 agriculture 61, 428–9, **Pl. 2**
 ancestors 26, 434
 arts 77, 144, 145, 147, 440–1, **Pl. 235**, **Pl. 237–42**, **Pl. 251**, **Pl. 252–5**
 Buddhism **87**, 129, **Pl. 85**
 calligraphy **Pl. 95**, **Pl. 96**
 cave-temples 435
 cities and towns 80, 431
 coins **Pl. 190**
 the compass 94
 Confucianism 125–6, 424–5
 Daoism 125
 economics 79, 427–8, 431, 443
 expansionism 3, 84
 family and kinship 24, 28, 29, 34
 Five Dynasties and Ten Kingdoms 424
 geography 109
 the Great Wall 426
 gunpowder and firearms 444
 handicrafts 429–30
 harnesses 88
 Hinduism **Pl. 54**
 historiography 111, 421
 inland waterways 93
 internal inspiration and processes 363
 Korea 458–60
 law 60–1
 maps **422**, **424**, **425**, **450**
 marriage 33
 medicine 105, **105**, 107, **107**
 military technology **Pl. 42–3**
 Ming dynasty 426–7
 Mongol adminstration 425–6
 music 161
 neo-Confucianism 432–4
 Northern Song Empire **424**, 424–5
 paper and printing 94, 159
 patronage in Tibet 481–2
 population 19, 72
 porcelain 76
 printing **Pl. 115**
 private contracts 61
 rebellions and revolts 423, 428
 religion 25, 121
 science **Pl. 134**
 science and mathematics 101–2, 103, 104, 105, 106
 seafaring 89, 90, 92–3, **Pl. 21**
 Siberian-Manchurian nomads 462–4
 silk 79–80
 social framework 36
 social order 431–2
 Southern Song Empire 425
 Sui unity 421–2
 Tang dynasty 421, 422–3
 technology 72, 82, **442**, 442–5, **Pl. 19**
 trade and commerce 423
 transmission of knowledge 114
 transport 88–9, **Pl. 9**
Chincas 607
Chinese language 112
 literature 437–40, **Pl. 95**
 Mongol literary use of 475
 in SE Asia 419
Chinggis (Genghis) Khān 56, 287, 328
 builds empire 383, 425–6, 463, 470
 portrait **Pl. 243**
 successors to empire **471**, 471–4
 universal heavenly sovereign 467
Christendom
 children 34
 East–West split 207–8, 209–10
 Ethiopia resists Islam 516–18
 family and marriage 24, 25, 28, 38
 fellowship and associations 36
 map **207**
 marriage 32
 Monophysite Coptics in Nubia 507–8, 511
 power and property 47
 primogeniture 35
 reconquest of Mediterranean lands 353–5
 serfdom 36–7
 sexuality 26, 30–1
 women's role 29
 see also Byzantine Empire; European culture; Orthodox Church; Roman Catholic Church
Christianity 141–2
 Africa 486–7, **Pl. 276–80**
 Anatolia 391
 architecture 149, **149**, **150**, 150–1, 152–3
 arts 144–5, 156, 160, **Pl. 56–64**
 the Balkans 226–7
 Carolingian empire 138–9
 China 436–7
 Coptic Church 136
 cult of Mary 29
 East–West split 99, 136–8
 Ethiopian literature and *gadls* 519–20
 Gregorian reform 139
 Hussites 241
 intolerance of indigenous practices 501
 Iran 367
 within Islamic lands 312, 320
 law 44–5
 monasticism, mendicants and brotherhood 140–1
 Nestorian 135–6, 436, 467, 476
 northern and central Europe 235–41
 pilgrimages 245
 religion outside orthodoxy 227–8
 representations of the sacred 153–5
 rival religions 124–5
 ruins of Roman empire 135, 138
 Scandinavia 238
 schism and Avignon popes 140
 spread to northern and central Europe 235–6
 symbols of faith 155
 West Africa 501, 502–3
 see also Orthodox Church; Roman Catholic Church
El Cid 354
Clark, William 562
class and hierarchies

Africa 542–3
Arab society 319–20
arctic North American 556–7
aristocracy and property 47
Chinese ranks 61
feudal system 211–12
Indian castes 37, 57, 127, 398–400
Japan 449, 450–2
Sri Lankan castes 411
Cokwe people 545
Collique/Collis 607
Columbia
art **Pl. 311–13**, **Pl. 315**
hierarchical chiefdoms 593–5
Columbus, Christopher 3, 84, 110, 551
navigation 118
voyages 247
communications
block-printing 94
post horses 94
Comneni dynasty 180, 184
Comoran language 524
Comoro Islands 524, 527
map **532**
settlement and life-style 531–3
trade 534
Confucianism 15, 125–6
Korea 460
Mongols 474
neo-Confucianism 432–4
Confucius 424, 432
Congo 541
Constantine the Great 183, **Pl. 145**
forged 'Donation' 197
Constantinople
fall of 3, 99, 138, 395
recapture 393
siege of 395
Umayyad seiges 273
Cook, James 622
Copts 312, 332
icons **Pl. 56**
language 98, 113, 510
Cordova, sack of 353
Costa Rica **589**, 590, 591
Coupland, Reginald 526
crime
Aztecs 67
law 48–9
Crimea (Taurica) 257–8, **Pl. 37**
Croatia 223
Crusades 137, 139, 141, 333
the Byzantine Empire 180
campaigns against Islam 327–8
context and origins 244–6
Ethiopia 518
military orders 246
weakens Europe 210
Cuicas 597, 598
St Cyril 101, 192, **193**
apostle to Slavs 225–6
influence on Slavic literature 229, 230
Czechs 101, 212–13, 241, **Pl. 60**

Dante Alighieri 142, 218, 244, **Pl. 180**
Daoism 125, 432, 435
Dawit 517, 518
Al-Dawla, 'Aḍud 326
death and funeral rites
Caribbean Islands 600
funerary masks **Pl. 311**, **Pl. 319**
India 38
mausoleums and tombs **Pl. 195–6**, **Pl. 275**
northeastern Mexico 578–9
South America 598–9, 615, 616
Deer 'Jaguar Claw' 583
Dembeni culture 533, 534
St Demetrius **Pl. 146**
Dempwolff, Otto 622
Denmark 212, 237–9
Dezong 423
Dias, Bartolomeu 110, 247, 248, 485
Al-Dīnawarī 106
Diocletian 183
Dioscorides 106
Arabic translation **Pl. 126**, **Pl. 130**
Materia Medica 351
Dōgen 455
Dominican Republic
art **Pl. 289**, **Pl. 291**
Du Fu 437–8
Du Wan 105
Duby, G. 43
Dyen, I. 622

Easter Islands 624
economic systems
Arab military 279
Carolingian empire 201
mediaeval European development 213–14
merchant hierarchies 79
monetary systems 214
organization of production 78–80
technological diffusion 77–8
education and scholarship
Arab intellectual life 323–7
Armenian Hellenism 252
Asia **Pl. 128**
Byzantium 186–7
Carolingian empire 201–2
China 96
founding of universities 216
grammar and lexicography 112–13
India 97
Iran 283, 284
Islamic culture 262–3, 297–8
Japan 96
Korea 96
The Maghrib 341–3
mediaeval Europe 215–17, **215**
'mirrors' 203
St Thomas Aquinas **Pl. 127**
translation and diffusion of knowledge 114–15
Egypt
agriculture 75
Arab conquest and Fatimid rule 332–3
architecture **146**, 334–5, 336–7, **Pl. 32**, **Pl. 70**, **Pl. 203**
arts 336, **Pl. 90**
the Ayyūbid dynasty 335
calligraphy **Pl. 110**
Copts 312, 332, 516, 518, 519
the Crusades 245
Ethiopia 516, 518, 519
intellectual development 333–4
Islamization 275, 293, 300, 333–4
Ismaʿīlism 334
learning and libraries 333
the Mamlūks 335–6
map **333**
religion 336
science and mathematics 334, **Pl. 142**
trade and economics 333, 335–6
Eliade, M. 122
English language 113
Ericsson, Leif 91
Erigena, John Scotus 202–3, 216
Erik the Red 553
Eriksson, Leif 553
Eskimo people
see under North America: arctic peoples

Estonia 238
Ethiopia 485, 487
  agriculture 515
  architecture 521, **521**, **Pl. 280**
  art **Pl. 49**, **Pl. 279**
  Christianity 98, 516–18
  and Islamic world 515–18
  Jews 517
  land owned by government 515
  language and culture 115
  literature and *gadls* 519–20
  manuscripts and illuminations 521–2
  music 522
  relations with Egyptian Copts 516, 518, 519
  relations with Europe 518–19
  trade and currency 515–16
ethnic relations 298–9
Euclid 103
European culture
  aftermath of Roman empire 195
  agriculture 75
  arts 161, 217–18
  astronomy 103–4
  Byzantium and Latin west 190–1
  currencies and Islamic trade 307–8
  economic development 213–14
  education and scholarship 99–101, **100**, 215–17, **215**
  the feudal system 211–12
  geography and exploration 110
  Greek–Latin divide 175–7
  historiography 112
  ideas and outlook 218–20, **Pl. 119–22**, **Pl. 124**
  languages 113
  literature 218
  mathematics 102–3
  medicine 108–9, **109**, **Pl. 127**, **Pl. 129**
  new states 212–13
  northern and central **236**
  population **14**, 17–19
  power of the Catholic Church 209–10
  printing **Pl. 117–18**
  science 107
  shamanism 120–1
  towns and cities 80, 81
  translation and diffusion of knowledge 114, 115–16
  wheeled transport 86–8, **87**
  see also Christendom
Evans, Clifford 600
Ewostatewos 517
exploration and expansion
  geographical and travel literature 324
  the 'New World' 84, 247
  Portuguese navigation 92, 247
  representations and images **Pl. 119–25**
  scientific knowledge from travels 118
  Spanish navigation 92
  travel writing 344
  travellers and diplomats 246–7
  Vikings 91
  Zheng He 92–3, 426–7, **427**
Eyck, Jan van **Pl. 174**
Eystein **Pl. 168**

Al-Faḍl ibn Sahl 316
families
  evidence 23–4
  incest 32
  Islam 320–1
  kinship and groupings 27–9
  law 48
  preservation from defilement 25–6
  property and inheritance 34–5
  religious regulation 23, 24–5
  role of elders 26
  self-identity 26
  three general models 37–8
  see also marriage; women
families and kinship
  Africa 64, 542–3
  ancestors 26
  birth rates 14
  children's place 34
  China 61
famine 15, 18
Al-Fārābī, Abū Naṣr 133, 372, 382
Al-Farghāni 104
Al-Farisi 105
Faron, L. 599
festivals and holidays 36
feudalism 43
  India 398–400
  Islamic forms 299–300
  origins and area 177
  place in European culture 211–12
  vassalage 47
Fibonacci, Leonardo of Pisa 102
Finland 236, 237, 238
  Swedish colonization 239
Finno-Ugric languages 101, 235
Firdawsī, Hakīm Abu'-l-Qāsim 98, 369, 379, **Pl. 12**, **Pl. 219**
France
  agriculture **Pl. 5**
  Arabs occupy Narbonne 290
  architecture **150**, **Pl. 28–9**, **Pl. 31**, **Pl. 36**, **Pl. 39**, **Pl. 67–9**, **Pl. 75**
  the astrolabe **Pl. 141**
  education and scholarship 216
  heraldry **Pl. 10**
  language 100, 161, 218
  mills and water wheels **Pl. 17**
  rid of England 212
  saint with spectacles **Pl. 132**
St Francis of Assisi 140
Franciscan missions 436–7, 473
Franks *see* Carolingian Europe; Charlemagne
Fujiwara no Michinaga 451
Fukuyoshio Omura 107
Fulani people 490
Fur Road 305

Gaelic language 101
Galen 108
Gama, Vasco da 72, 84, 110, 485
games and recreation 36
  Arab culture 321
  arts for pleasure 160–1
  Byzantine sports 187
  mediaeval Christian attitudes 220
Ganesh **Pl. 52–5**
García Gómez, G. E. 354, 356, 359
Gardet, Louis 298
geography 11, **12**, 13, 109–10
  cartography 445
  Idrisi 358
  the Maghrib 344
  Tajiks 381
  world views **Pl. 119**, **Pl. 122**, **Pl. 123**, **Pl. 124**
St George **Pl. 154**
Georgia 191–2, 254
  cultural flowering 254–6
  language 101
Gerard of Brussels 105
Gerard of Cremona 115, **117**, 244, 357
Gerbert (Pope Sylvester II) 102, 115, 242
German language 113, 235
Germanic people 235, 240
  Hanseatic League 212, 239, 240
  Holy Roman Empire 210
  influence on Western Europe 177
Ghana 497

Ghassanid confederation 264
Al-Ghāzalī, Abū Ḥāmid Muḥammad 133, 155, 262, 270, 368
Ghiberti, Lorenzo 116
Ghiyāṣ u'ddin Tughluq **Pl. 196**
Ghoshal, U. N. 398
Gibb, Hamilton A. R. 273, 537
Gibert y Sanchez, Professor Rafael 41
Gibraltar 358
St Gleb **Pl. 158**
Go-Daigo 453
Goitein, S. D. 312
Golson, J. 624
government *see* monarchy; nation-state; power
Granada 356, 358–9
Greek language
  Byzantine scholarship 186–7
  development of vernacular 101
  European preservation of classical sciences 99
  in Nubia 510
  translation and cultural diffusion 115–16, 176–7, 242–3, 325
Greenberg, G. J. 541
Greenland 559
Gregory IV, Pope **Pl. 163**
St Gregory VII the Great, Pope 139
Griffin, J. B. 568
Grosseteste, Robert 105
Guan Hanqing 440
Guatemala **589**, 590, 591
guilds 80
Gunawardana, R. A. L. H. 57
Guo Shoujing 103, 443, 474
Guoxi **Pl. 252**
Guthrie, M. 541
Guy de Chauliac 108

Habib, Professor Irfan 38–9
Habsburg, House of 240
Al-Ḥadrami, al-Murādī 342
Ḥāfiẓ, Shams al-Dīn 371
Hammer, Heinrich (Henricus Martellus) **Pl. 124**
Han Yu 438, 439
Hanīfa, Abū 51–2, 52–3
Al-Ḥāṣib, Ḥabash 102
Hassig, Ross 67
Ḥaṭṭin, battle of 328
Hausa people 490, 497
Hawaiian Islands 624
health and disease
  Arab hospitals 321
  attitudes towards defecation 25
  bubonic plague/Black Death 18, 21
  mediaeval Europe 213
  population factor 15
  see also medicine
Hebrew language 98, 113, 342
Hei-shui Mo-he nomads 462
Heilbroner, Robert 78
Henry, Prince (The Navigator) 247
Henry II, German Holy Roman Emperor **Pl. 170**
Henry II of England **Pl. 171**
heraldry **Pl. 10–11**
Hilali 303
Hindi language 407
Hinduism 15, 126–7
  art and architecture 149, 151, **151**, 153, 154, 155, 156, **Pl. 229**, **Pl. 235**
  co-existence with Islam 312–13, 406
  dance 155
  family 38
  funeral rites 38
  Ganesh **Pl. 52–5**
  influence in South East Asia 97
  sculpture **Pl. 222–3**
  symbols of faith 155
  Upanishads 405
historiography 111–12
  al-Rashid's 'Compendium of Histories' 476–7
  Armenia 253
  Byzantium 186
  Japan 448
  objectivity 4
  Oceania 622–3
  Tajiks 381–2
  Western history paradigm 71
Hohokams 573–6
Holmes, W. H. 568
Holy Roman Empire 241
Honduras **589**, 590
Hongwu **Pl. 239**
Horton, Mark 525, 527, 536
Hottentots *see* Khoikhois
Huancas 609
Huastec language 166, 586
Huizinga, J. 220
Huizong 441, **Pl. 254**
human rights 45
Ḥunayn ibn Isḥāq 115, 242, 243
Hungary 194, 236, 239, 240, 241
  Catholicism 241
  rise of state 213
Huns 363
hunter-gatherers
  New World 72–3
  taxes and tribute 79
  see also Mesoamerica; North America; South America
Hus, Jan 212, 241

Ibn Akhī Khizām 106
Ibn al-Athīr 111
Ibn al-Bannā 344
Ibn al-Haytham (Alhazen) 103, 116, 334
  Kitāb al-Mānaẓir 104, **104**
  Optical Thesaurus 105
Ibn al-Khatīb, Lisān al-Dīn 111, 359
Ibn al-Shātir 103, **103**
Ibn Bājja (Avempace) 104, 116, 133, 356
Ibn Baṭṭuṭa 528, 536–7
Ibn Ḥamdīs 355
Ibn Ḥanbal 133
Ibn Ḥawqal 290, 350
Ibn Ḥazm 353
Ibn Jubayr 290
Ibn Juljul 351
Ibn Khaldūn 51, 111, 142, 323, 324
  Arab world-view **Pl. 124**
  on cities 297
  on decadence of Islamic capitals 357
  native to the Maghrib 338, 342
  nomadism versus sedentary societies 363
Ibn Mājid, Aḥmad 110
Ibn Masarra 353
Ibn Qushtimur 106
Ibn Rāshiq al-Qayrawānī 343
Ibn Riḍwān al-Miṣrī, Abū-Ḥasan 'Ali 334
Ibn Rushd, Abu-l Walīd (Averroës) 104, 133, 262, 270
  and Aquinas **Pl. 127**
  in Cordova 356–7
  native to the Maghrib 338, 339
Ibn Ṣā'īd 351
Ibn Sīnā, Abū 'Alī (Avicenna) 262, 270
  the Canon of medicine 282, 375, **Pl. 133**
  philosophy 133, 326, 372
  The School of Illumination 373
  sciences 104, 105, 106, 107, 108, 109
  Tajik origins 281, 282
  works and achievements 282
Ibn Taghrībardī 111
Ibn Ṭufayl 133
Ibn Wahshiyya 106
Ibn Yūnus al-Ṣadafi 334

Ibn Zamrak 359
Ibn Zaydūn 353
Ibn Zurh, 'Abd al-Malik (Avenzoar) 356
Iceland 212, 553
iconoclasm
authority of Byzantium 225
Charlemagne condemns 198
East–West split 136, 153, 179
effect on Balkan icons 233
provokes flight to Crimea 257
Al-Idrīsī 358, 516
Ifriqiyya (Tunisia) 289
architecture **Pl. 202**
see also the Maghrib
Ikhwān al-Ṣafā 105
Ikkyu Sōjun 456
Iltutmish 58
Incas 616–17
animism 122
archaeology 553, 610–11
art and architecture 611, **Pl. 38**, **Pl. 320–3**
decimal system **68**
government and law at conquest 68–9
origins and empire 610–11
and other Andean cultures 605, 607, 609, 610
pottery 610–11
sciences and mathematics 101
India
ancestors 26
Arabic and Persian culture 404
architecture 408–9, **Pl. 196**, **Pl. 209**, **Pl. 221**, **Pl. 225**
art 409–10, **Pl. 80**, **Pl. 91**, **Pl. 222**
astronomy 103
Brahmanism 404–5
caste system 37, 57, 127, 398–400
creation of Mughal Empire 400
dance 155
Delhi sultanate 363, 400
development of Islam 405–6
education and scholarship 97, 114, **Pl. 100–2**
family 24, 37, 38
feudalism 398–400
Ganesh **Pl. 52–3**
geography 109
Hinduism 126–7
historiography 111
influence in SE Asia 418, 419
Jains 405, **Pl. 220**
languages 97, 112, 406–8
maps **399**, **401**
marriage 33
medicine 108
mixture of Hindus and Muslims 58, 312–13
as one of Polo's marvels **Pl. 121**
population 20
religion 25, 154, 155
satī 32, 33
science and mathematics 102, **102**, 104, 105, 403–4
seafaring 90
sexuality 31
ships **Pl. 22**
slavery 400
state structures 57–8
technology 400
towns and cities 81
transport 89
individuals
artistic self-expression 161–2
identity within families 26
Western Christendom's outlook 218–19
Indonesia
architecture **151**, **Pl. 228**
sculpture **Pl. 224**
seafaring 89–90
Inuit people 555, 556
Ipiutak people 558–9
Iran
agriculture **Pl. 3**
architecture **Pl. 71**, **Pl. 89**
arts 145, 147, **Pl. 212**
calligraphy **Pl. 109**
coins **Pl. 190**
ethnicity 298–9
Islamic conquest 275–6, 281–2, 365, 367
literature 98
map **366**
Mongolian rule 367, 476–7
mosques **Pl. 199**
non-Islamic religions 367–8
participation in spread of Islam 282
philosophy 371–3
revival of culture 284–5, 326, 363
science, medicine and technology 373–6
seafaring in Indian Ocean 90
Solomon **Pl. 50–1**
Sufi poets 369–71
theology 368–9
Turkic invasion 367
waning of pre-Islamic culture 281
Zoroastrianism 123, 312
see also Persian language
Iraq **Pl. 184**
architecture **Pl. 197**, **Pl. 206**
art **Pl. 210**
calligraphy **Pl. 113**
Islamic conquest 274–5
map **315**
mills and water wheels **Pl. 18**
Mongolian Īl-Khānate 476–7
seafaring in Indian Ocean 90
see also Arabs 317
Ireland
Books of Kells **Pl. 105**
Isidore of Seville 216
Islāh al-Majistī **117**
Islamic culture
alliances and treaties 53, 508
in Andalusia and Sicily 348–59
architecture 148, 149–50, 151, 152, **Pl. 26–7**, **Pl. 30**, **Pl. 32**, **Pl. 34**, **Pl. 65–6**, **Pl. 70–3**, **Pl. 88–9**
arts 145–8, **148**, 156, 160, **Pl. 90–1**, **Pl. 213**
astronomy 103, **103**
Bedouin life 295–6
centralization of authority 298
children 34
Christians within 312
community relations to state 298
Crusade campaigns 327–8
dance 155
east Africa 293–4
education and scholarship 279
Egypt 275, 293
Ethiopia 515, 516–18
ethnic diversity 278, 298–9, 311
expansion 3, 274–6
family and kinship 25, 27, 28, 29, 38
flourishing **261**, 261–3
form of feudalism 299–300
geography 109–10, 295
global view 319
heraldry **Pl. 11**
and Hindus 312–13
historiography 111
influence of Byzantium 192
interaction in the world 141–2
Iran 275–6
Iraq 274–5
irrigation and water preservation 303–4
Jerusalem **Pl. 45–6**
and Jews 266–7, 311–12

languages 112–13
law 318–19, 324
literature 98
lose Andalusia and Sicily 352–5
The Maghrib 289, 341–2
map of world **Pl. 123**
mathematics 102
medicine 108
merchants 297
Mesopotamia 275
military organization 299
minarets **Pl. 202–9**
Mongolian invasion 328–9
mosques 334–5, 336, 345–7, **346**, **Pl. 199–201**, **Pl. 271–3**
nation-states 50–1, 52
Nubia and Sudan 508, 511–13
'People of the Book' 320
philosophy 270, 371–3, 382–3
printing **Pl. 116**
resistance 298
revival in Persian phase 284–5
romance **Pl. 187–8**
science and mathematics 98, 104, 105–7, **Pl. 135–8**, **Pl. 139**, **Pl. 141**, **Pl. 142**, **Pl. 143**
sexuality 30
Sicily 290
slavery 300–1, 516
social hierarchies 299
Spain and Sicily 289–90
spread of plants and animals 304–5
sub-Saharan Africa 292–3
Syria 275
taxation 339
technology **Pl. 16**
towns and cities 80–1, 296–7
trade and commerce 305–6, 437
tranformation of Iran 365, 367
translation and cultural diffusion 114, 242–3
Turkic-Mongol nomads 286–7, 466–7
Ummayyad dynasty 271–3
urban officials 297
women 26, 302–3
and Zoroastrians 312
Islamic religion
Africa 485, 487
the amān 53
ancestors 26
Asia 418, 437
basic elements 265–6
Christian converts 290
co-existence with Hinduism 406
doctrines 131–4
East Africa 526, 528, 530, 534
emulating the Prophet 269
ḥadīth 269
ijtihād 268, 269
India 405–6
influence of Greek thought 132–3
Iran 368
jihād 52–3, 315, 328, 388
Khārijīs 131
law 50, 51–2, 58
marriage 32, 33
Mecca 148, **Pl. 181**
Muḥammad and his message 130–1, 265–7
Mu'tazilism 316–17, 325, 326–7
Qur'ān 98, 268–9
rise in Arabia 264–7
scholastic theology 324
Shī'īsm 131, 269, 326, 368
sources 268–70
spread 131, 133–4
the *sunna* 268–9
Sunnīsm 131, 269, 326, 333–4, 368, 389
symbols of faith 153–5, 155
West Africa 500–1, 502
see also Sufism
Italy
architecture **Pl. 40–1**
art **Pl. 61**, **Pl. 64**
city-states 212
migrations and invasions 175, 176
Ivan Alexander of Bulgaria **Pl. 153**

Jābir ibn Hayyān 106–7
Al-Jāḥiẓ 106
Jainism 128, 151, 405, **Pl. 220**
Jamal al-Dīn 474
Jāmī, 'Abd al-Raḥmān 371, 406
Japan
architecture **448**, 456
art **Pl. 233**, **Pl. 236**, **Pl. 253**, **Pl. 256–8**
Buddhism 129–30, 449–50, 451–2, **Pl. 81**
calligraphy **Pl. 98–9**
Chinese models 447–9
Confucianism 126
education and scholarship 114
family and marriage 24, 28, 29, 33, 34
historiography 111
and Korea 447
language 112
law 61
literature and drama 96, 158, 451, 455, 456, **Pl. 98–9**
map **450**
medicine 107–8
Ōnin War 454, 455
portrait of Ashikaga Takauji **Pl. 14**
religion 25, 121, 454–5
ritual 449, 450, 451, 455, 456
sciences and mathematics 102
sexuality 31
Shinto 126, 450
social framework 36, 37, 449, 450–2
warrior governments 452–4
Java 417, 418, 419
Al-Jazarī 104
Jenne 495, 496
Jerusalem
the Crusades 245, 246, 327–8
the Dome of the Rock 148–9, **Pl. 45–6**
Jesus Christ **Pl. 56–62**
icons **Pl. 147–9**, **Pl. 156**, **Pl. 159–60**
Jews 134–5
art and architecture **Pl. 76–9**
in China 437
the Crusades 210
the Dome of the Rock 148–9
encounters with Muḥammad 266–7
Ethiopia 517
in Iran 367
within Islamic culture 297, 311–12, 320, 342
Judaism 134–5
the Kabbala 134–5
scholarship and translation 242–3, 342–3
sexuality 30
Solomon **Pl. 47–51**
West Africa 490
written communication 94
Yiddish language 101
see also Hebrew language
John Cantacuzenus 394
John II Comnenus **Pl. 148**
John of Damascus 155
John of Holywood 102, 104
John of Seville 244
John Palaeologus 394
Johnston, H. 540–1
Jordanus Nemorarius 104–5
Judaism *see* Jews
Jurchen nomads 463, 464, 466

Justinian 175, 178, **Pl. 145**
law code 44–5, 187–8

Kalhaṇa 57, 111
Kamāl al-Dīn al-Damīrī 106
Kannada language 407
Al-Karajī 102
Karangas 544
Al-Kāshī 102
Zij-i Ulugh Beg 103
Kenya **Pl. 200**
Khadija, wife of the Prophet 265, 266, 303
Khaljī, Jalālu'ddīn 58
Khāqānī Shīrwān, Ibrāhīm 369
Al-Khayyām, 'Omar 102, 370–1, 379
mathematics 374, 375
Khazars 257
Al-Khāzinī, 'Abd al-Rahman 375
The Balance of Wisdom 104
Khitan nomads 424, 425, 462–3, **Pl. 246**
Khmer language 419
Khoikhois (Hottentots) 539
Khusraw, Amir 406, 407
Al-Khwārizmī, Abū Ja'far Muḥammad ibn Mūsā 102, 109, 110, 242, 380–1
Kiev 150, 194
Kilwa 527–8
Ibn Battuta describes 537
map **527**
Al-Kindī 106, 133
Kinkade, M. D. 560
kinship *see* families and kinship
Knights of Saint John 246
knowledge *see* education and scholarship; languages; literacy; literature; science and mathematics; technology
Kodai-no-Kimi, Layd **Pl. 257**
Köl Tegin 55
Kongo 63, 64
Koniag people 555, 557
Korea 61, 458–9
attacks Bohai 462
Buddhism 129, 458, 459, **Pl. 86**
calligraphy **Pl. 97**
domination by Silla 458–9
education and scholarship 96–7, 114
kingdom of Koryŏ 459–60
language 458
Manchurian nomads 462
map **450**
pottery and ceramics 459
printing 459–60
religion 96
trade and commerce 458
world-view **Pl. 125**
Kosambi, D. D. 398
Köse Dagh, battle of 392
Ku-mo-xi nomads 461–2, 463
Kuba language 544
Kurds 303
Kuwait **Pl. 107**

labour
given dignity by Church 211, 212
hired farm labour in China 429
organization of professions 301–2
urban riots of poor workers 213
Lakhmid confederation 264
Lambton, A. K. S. 322
land
Chinese allocation
political power 43
Landes, David 78
languages
Africa 99, 489, 540–1
communications 94
Cyrillic alphabet 192, **193**
grammar and lexicography 112–13
India 97, 406–8
Islamic lands 98
Japan 96
north west America 560
Orthodox Church uses vernaculars 100
reconstruction Oceania's history 622–3
SE Asia and islands 419
translation and translators 242–4, 357
Uighur script for Mongolian 97, **97**
vernaculars 100, 113
Western Europe 100–1
Laos (Lan Sang) 417, 418
Latin language
grammar and lexicography 113
nearly only written language in Europe 94
scholarship 100
translations of scholarship 115–16
law
administration of justice 44–5
alliances and treaties 45
Armenia 253
Byzantine 184, 187–8
Chinese 60–1
civil and criminal 48–9
death penalty 49
family 61
human rights 45
India 57–8
influence of Romans 48
Islamic 50–3, 318, 324
Japan 61
judicial procedures 49
Malikism in the Maghrib 339–40
marriage 33
Mesoamerica 66–8
Mongol empire 470
Mongols 472
private contracts 61
religion 44–5
SE Asian systems 420
slavery 301
sub-Saharan Africa 63–4
Leo VI of Byzantium 179
León, Alonso de 578
Lewis, Meriwether 562
Li Bai 437
Li Gonglin 441
Li Qingzhao 439
Li Ye 101
Li Yu 438
Li Yuan 422
libraries
Al-Ḥakam II's at Cordova 351
Arabs 326
Egypt 334
Islamic centres at Cairo and Bukhara 98
The Maghrib 340–1
Topkapi 476
see also printing
Libya 289
literacy
Aztecs 67
East Asia 96–7
Germanic people 235
literature
Andalusia 352
artistic self-expression 161
Bulgarian 229, 230
Byzantine 186
China 96, 437–40
Georgia 254–5
India's many languages 406–8
Japan 455, 456

lyric poetry 218
The Maghrib 343–4
monastic 230
for pleasure 161
popular 230
representation of the sacred 155
romance and myth 218
royal patronage 157–8
Russian 251
Slavic 229–30
Ṣūfī poets in Iran 369–70
Tajik and Turkic Asia 384
tales of chivalry 220
vernacular European epics 218
Lithuania 239, 240
Lombard, Maurice 302
Lombards 196, 197–8
Lothair 198–9
Louis the German 198–9
Louis the Pious 198, 202
Lu Jiuyuan 433
Lu You 439
Luba people 545
Luo Guanzhong 440
Lupacas 607–8
Luxembourg, House of 240

Machu Picchu **Pl. 321**
Mackenzie, Alexander 562
McNeill, William 93
Madagascar and East African islands 524
map **532**
political organization 534
religion 534
settlement and life-styles 531–3
Magellan, Ferdinand 84
The Maghrib 289
agriculture **Pl. 4**
the Almohads and Almoravids 338, 339, 345–7
art and architecture 345–7, **346**, **Pl. 88**
cultural development 338
libraries and calligraphers 340–1
literature 343–4
Mālikism 339–40
map **338**
Merinids 338, 341, 345–7
Muslim and Jewish scholars and philosophers 341–2
see also Algeria; Morocco; Tunisia
Magyars 18, 120, 121
Al-Māhānī 102
Mahāvīra 102
Al-Mahrī, Sulaymān 110
Maimonides (Moses ben Maimon) 134, 311
flees Cordova for Egypt 356, 357
Guide to the Perplexed **Pl. 77**
Malagasy language 531
Malawi 541
Malay Peninsula 418
languages 97–8, 419
Malayalam 407
Mali **263**, **Pl. 261**
art and architecture **Pl. 205**, **Pl. 264**
Catalan Atlas **Pl. 259**
Islam 292, 293
political structures 497
Al-Malik, Abd 273, 276
Mālik ibn Anas 52
Malik Shāh 327
Mālikism 339–40, 349, 353
Malinowski, B. 624
Malta 246, 349
Mamlūks 293, 335–6, **Pl. 217**
Manchuria 425, 461–4, 463
Manichaeism 123–4, 287, 326, 367, 435–6
Mansel, Jean **Pl. 119**
Al-Mansur (Abū Jaʿfar ʿAbdullāh) 314–15
Manṣûr Hallâj 262, 270, 325
Mansūr Muwaffaq, Abū 108
Manuel II Palaeologus **Pl. 150**
Manzikert, Battle of 245
Al-Maqrīzī 111, 518
Marajoaras 600–1
Marianos of Faras, Bishop **Pl. 276**
marriage 31–3
age 34
arrangements 33
birth rates 14–15
dowries 33
endogamy and exogamy 32
Islamic culture 302
kinship and incest 32
monogamy and polygamy 32
religious customs 15
Martini, Simone **Pl. 172**
Mary, Mother of Jesus **Pl. 145**, **Pl. 147**, **Pl. 148**, **Pl. 176**, **Pl. 276–8**
Masao, F. T. 525
Massignon, Louis 302, 321
Al-Mas'udī 530, 536
Al-Māturīdī 133
Mauritania **Pl. 262**
Mayans 584–6
animism 121–2
archaeology 553
arts and architecture 166, **167**, 584–5, 586, **Pl. 93**, **Pl. 294–8**
Chichén Itzá 586
language 551, 553
literature 586
science and mathematics 101, **101**, 103, 584, 585
Mazdaism *see* Zoroastrianism
McNeill, William 85
medicine **105**, 107–9, **Pl. 126**, **Pl. 129–33**
Andalusia 356
Byzantine Empire 187
drugs 119
Egypt 334
Ibn Sīnā's *Canon* 282, 375, **Pl. 133**
India 404
Iran 375–6
the Maghrib 344
Mongols 475
Tājīks 381
Meggers, Betty 600
Mehemed II, Sultan 138
Melanesia 121, 621, 623, 624
men
primogeniture 35
role of boys 34
Mesoamerica
agriculture 590
arts and architecture 164–8, **167**, **168**, **Pl. 92–4**, **Pl. 289–310**
context of pre-Columbian history 551–3, **552**
family and kinship 28, 29, 32
Guatemala to Panama **589**, 589–92
map of culture areas **581**
population 6, **14**, 21
pottery and ceramics 590–1
religion 121–2, 590
rise and conquest of the Aztecs 580–3
sciences and mathematics 101, **101**
trade and commerce 591
see also Aztecs; Toltecs
Mesopotamia 275
St Mesrop 101
metallurgy *see* mining and metallurgy
St Methodius 192, **193**, 225–6, 229, 230
Mexico
arts and architecture 164–8, **167**, **168**, 588, **Pl. 92**, **Pl. 94**, **Pl. 294–307**
Aztecs 66–7, 580–3

Gulf coast cultures 586–7
Mayans 584–6
northeastern culture 577–9
pottery 587, 588
Western cultures 587–8
Mez, Adam 322
Michael Scotus 357, 358
Micronesia 121, 621, 624
Middle East
camel/animal transport 85–6
geographical conditions 11, 13
migration and movements
Arabs 17–18
Austronesians 624
Balkans **221**, 221–3
Black people to West Africa 489–1
Central Africa **540**, 540–1
effect on artistic expression 143–8
Islamic culture 281, 303
pilgrimages 159, 245, 281, **Pl. 183**
and technology 71–2
Turkish nomads 388–9
world population 15–16
military organisation
Arabs 279–80, 316–17, 319
arms production 79
Aztecs 67
ballistic missiles 403
Bedouin warriors 295–6
Byzantine Empire 184
Carolingian Empire **Pl. 162**
cavalry **Pl. 12**
China builds the Great Wall as defence 426
feudalism 211
gunpowder and cannon 118
Incas 69
Indian technology 402–3
India's tax 400
Islamic culture 299
Japan's warrior government 452–4
Mesoamerica 590
mounted archers 403
technology **Pl. 42–4**
Turkic-Mongol nomads 465, 466, 470, 472
Turkish military slaves in Islamic lands 387–8
see also war and peace
Milutin, Prince **Pl. 152**
Minamoto no Yorimoto 452
Ming Taizi
family law 61
mining and metallurgy 118
Byzantine Empire 185, 187
Central Asia 380
China 430
coal 430
iron casting 430
Mesoamerica 581, 590
South America 595, 612, 615, 617
West Africa 494, 504, 505
Mīr Dāmād 373
Mississippian culture 568–9
Misyugin, V. M. 530
Mitmakunas 616
Mixtecs 165–6, 168, 580, 583–4, **Pl. 94**
Mo-he nomads 462
Mo'a, Iyasus 517, 520
Mochica people 602, 605–7, **Pl. 317–18**
Mogadishu 528, 536–7
Mogollons 573–6
Molucca Islands 418
Mombassa 527, 537
monarchy
Byzantine *basileus* 183
Carolingian empire 199–200
court and administration 44
feudalism and central power 211
hierarchical chiefdoms of Columbia 593–6
lordships reduce power 47
patronage of art 156–8
property linked with power 47
as a public institution 48
and religion **Pl. 169–72**
Scandinavia 238
source of power 43
sultans and nobles 58
Turkic-Mongols' universal heavenly sovereign 467
universal heavenly sovereign 474
see also nation-states; power relations
Mondino dei Luzzi 108
money
Africa 493–4, 544, **Pl. 274**
Carolingian 200
Chinese use of paper money 431, 443
coins **Pl. 190–4**
East Africa 528
Ethiopia 516
Islamic trade and currencies 307–8
mints 307
SE Asia 419
trading systems 81
Mongols 17, 18
absorbed into Islamic world 367
administration of China 425–6
adopt Uighur script for writing 97, **97**
art and architecture 146–7, 473, **473**, **Pl. 243–50**
block printing 475
Chaghatai khānate 471, **471**, 477
Chinggis Khān's empire 287, 363, 470–4
Confucianism 474
in the Crimea 257–8
distract Ottomans from Balkans 395
European travellers 246
Golden Horde 288, 471, **471**, 477
inscriptions and texts 468, 473
Iran 367
language and script 474, 475, 477
law 470, 472
literature and translations 147, 475
Manchuria 462, 463, 464
in Middle East 328–9, 471, **471**, 476–7
Nestorian Christianity 136
nomad's religion 467–8
pastoral nomads 74, 465–9
population shifts 72, 303
principles of rule 56
religious tolerance 473, 476
resurgence of pre-Islamic religions 287
scholarship 114
sciences and medicine 474–5
Secret History of the Mongols 56, 468, 472, 473
in Tibet 481, 482
transport **Pl. 13**
Turks 287–8, 383–4
universal heavenly sovereign 467, 474
Yuan Empire 471, **471**, 474–6
Morocco 289
calligraphy **Pl. 111**
mosques and minarets **Pl. 201**, **Pl. 204**
Moses ben Ezra 243
Mosi people 490
Mu Biao 105
Mudida, Nina 525
Muḥammad the Prophet 3
eulogies to 343–4
life and message 130–1, 265–7
triumph 261
writings about 262, 269
Muiscas 595
Al-Mu'izz 332
Al-Murādī 104

Murasaki Shikibu
  Tales of the Genji 451, **Pl. 258**
music
  Central America 592
  China 438, **Pl. 240**
  Ethiopia 522
  folk and popular 158–9
  mediaeval Europe 217–18
  for pleasure 161, **161**
Muslim, Abū 367
Al-Muʿtasim 316
Al-Mutawakkil 317
Mutoro, Henry W. 525, 526
Myanmar (Burma) 20, 417

Nahāwand, battle of 365
Nahuas 586
Náhuatl language 553
Namdev 406
nation-states
  alliances and treaties 45, 53
  cities 42–3, 48
  control of production 78
  councils and assemblies 44, 47
  Islamic concept 50–1, 52
  king's court 44
  as legal entities 42–3
  loyalty 43
  powerful dukedoms 47–8
  ruler and the ruled 43–4
  sovereign power 43
  West Africa 497
  see also monarchy; power relations
Navajos 573
navigation
  the astrolabe **Pl. 139–43**
  the compass 72, 94–5, 104, 444–5, **445**
  geography 110
  Indian technology 402
  nautical charts 91, 445
  scientific discoveries 118
  technology 91
  see also ships and shipping
Nazcas 602, **Pl. 314**
Needham, Joseph 94
  Science and Civilization in China 77
Nepal 414–15, **Pl. 102**
Nestorianism 135–6, 467, 476
  China 436
  Mongols 136, 436
New Guinea 624
Nicaragua **589**, 590, 591
Nicholas of Cusa 142
Niger **Pl. 260**
Nigeria **Pl. 265–70**
Nithard 176
Nizāmī Ganjawī 369–70
nomads
  animals 465–6
  Bedouin 295–6
  camels 73
  geographical conditions 11, 13
  horses 73–4
  Mongols 74, 465–9
  Nubia 511–12
  pastoralism 73–4
  population 17, 21
  principles of power and law 55–6
  Siberian-Manchurian peoples 461–4
  taxes and tribute 79
  Turks 465–9
  yurts **Pl. 185–6**
Normans 355, **Pl. 72–3**
North America
  agriculture 573
  animism 121
  arctic cultures **555**, 555–9
  art and architecture 557–8, 575, **Pl. 281–8**
  context of pre-Columbian history 551–3, **552**
  early exploration 91
  Eastern Woodlands 566–71, **567**
  family and kinship 28, 29, 32
  geographical conditions 13
  North-west culture and technology 560–5, **561**
  Northeastern Mexico 577–9
  population 6, **14**, 21
  pottery and ceramics **Pl. 282**, **Pl. 288**
  South-west **573**, 573–6
Norway 212, 237–9
Nubia
  Arabization and Islamation 511–13
  architecture 509
  Baqt Treaty with Muslims 508, 511
  history and three kingdoms 507
  literature and language 510
  Monophysite Coptic Christianity 507–8, 511
  mural art 509–10
  pottery and weaving 510
  see also Sudan
Al-Nuwayrī 106

Oaxaca 580, 583–4
Oceania
  defining 621
  European awareness 621–2
  geological history 621, 623–4
  historiography 622–3
  kinship 28, 29
  languages 622–3
  Lapita culture and migration 624
  population **14**
  relations between islands 624
Oda Nobunaga 456
Ögödäy Khan **Pl. 244**, **Pl. 247**
oil 322
St Olaf of Norway 238
Olga, Princess of Kiev 250
Oliver, Roland 541
Olmecs 121, 164–5, 166
Oranskiiy, A. M. 379
Oresme, Nicholas 105
Orkhān Bey 394, 395
Orson **Pl. 269**
Orthodox Church
  Balkan states 226–7
  diffusion of Byzantine culture 192, 194
  education and scholarship 99–101
  effect of iconoclasm 136, 156, 179
  the *filoque* controversy 138, 202
  icons 194, **Pl. 145–60**
  Kiev Rus 250–1
  split from Rome 99, 137–8
Osman Bey 393
Otto II **Pl. 149**
Ottoman Empire *see* Turks
Ouyang Xiu 439
Oyo 497

Pacal, Prince 584
Pachacuti, Juan Santa Cruz 608–9
Pagan 417, 418
Pahlavī language 115
Palenque **Pl. 297**
Pali language 412
Panama **589**, 591, **Pl. 308–10**
paper 98, 323
  China 443
  India 402
  The Maghrib 340
  Mongol empire 469

see also printing and books
Pareto, Vilfredo 78
pastoralism 73–4
Patayans 573–4
Paulicians 228
peasants
Byzantine serfs 185
China 423, 429
feudalism 211
India 398–9, 400
Japan 453
West Africa 496
Pecham 105
Pende people 545
Pepin the Short 201, 202
Persian language 113, 299
Arabic conquest 281, 282, 369
beautiful script 154
Central Asia 385
diffusion 255
India 97, 407–8
literature 98, 161, 192, 282–4, **Pl. 218**, **Pl. 219**
revival after Arabic period 283–4
Shāh-Nāmeh 284
Ṣufī poetry 369–71
synthesis 365
used by Seljuk rulers 391
Peru
art and architecture **Pl. 314**
see also Incas
Petchnegs 180
Petrarch (Francesco Petrarca) 112, 218
Peuerbach, G. 104
Philippines 417, 418
Philoponus, John 105
philosophy
Islamic Iran 371–2
neo-Confucianism 432–4
Tajik 382–3
Pierre d'Ailly 110
pirates
Asian coast 458
Mediterranean 91
Planhol, Xavier De 73
Plethon (George Gemistos) 186, 191
Poland 239–40
political structures *see* monarchy; nation-states; power relations
Polo, Marco 4, 93, 110, 141, 246, **Pl. 121**
Polo, Nicolo and Maffeo 437
Polynesia 621, 623, 624
animism 121
seafaring 89–90
Ponthium, Treaty of 176
population
bubonic plague/Black Death 18
cities 18
effects of shifts 71–2
estimates *14*
Europe 17–19
general trends 21
as a legal entity 43
migration *17*
patterns 13–15
world at 600 AD 15–16
world after 600 AD 16–17
Portugal
Africa 64, **Pl. 265**
art **Pl. 62**
exploration 212, **Pl. 24–5**
potlatch 564, 565, 624
pottery and ceramics
Byzantine 190
Central America 590–1
Chinese porcelain 76, 430
East Africa 525
Iran 76
Islamic Spain 76–7
Korea 459
Mexico 165, 166, 167, 168, 581, 587, 588
North America 570, 571, **Pl. 282**, **Pl. 288**
Nubia 510
Oceania 624
South America 596, 597, 607, 610–11, 615, 616, 617, **Pl. 317–18**, **Pl. 322**
steppe nomads **Pl. 249**
West Africa **Pl. 15**
power relations
Islamic centralization 298
link with property 47
nation-states 43
see also monarchy; nation-states
Prakrit language 406
Prester John 518
printing and books
block 72, 78, 94, 96, 475, **Pl. 115–18**
Boccaccio **Pl. 103**
China 94, 96, 444, **Pl. 115**
Korea 459–60
manuscript binding 340
movable type **Pl. 117**
Sanskrit manuscripts **Pl. 101–2**
xylographic 481, 482
see also calligraphy; libraries; paper
property and wealth 28, 34–5, 38
primogeniture 35
Puerto Rico
art **Pl. 290**, **Pl. 292–3**
Pygmies 539

Al-Qāḍi ʿIyād 343
Qādisiyya, battle of 365
Qarā-Khitāy nomads 466
Qin Jiushao 101
Qubilāy Khān 246–7
cultural communication of east and west 468
Manchuria 463
Nestorianism 436
portrait **Pl. 245**
'son of heaven' 474
Yuan Empire 426, 474–6
Quechua language 553, 588
Quetzalcóatl **Pl. 301**, **Pl. 305**
Qurʾān
calligraphy **Pl. 108**
Islamic law 50–3
Muḥammad's message 130–1
scholastic interpretation 324
Quraysh 265–7, 272
Qutan Xida 101

Rabanus Mauraus **Pl. 163**
Al-Raḥmān, ʿAbd 289, 349
Raḥmān, Abdu'r 408
Rāmānand 406
Al-Rashīd al-Dīn, Hārūn 315–16, 321, 375
'Compendium of Histories' 476–7
Mongol Persian court 476–7
Al-Rāzī, Abū Bakr Muḥammad ibn Zakariyyā' 107, 108, 115, 372, 381, 382
Red Sea 90
Reformation 239
religion
Africa 499–501, 534, 545
ancestor worship 26, 434
animism, shamanism and polytheism 120–3, 499–501
Aztecs 582
Bogomilism 124
Buddhism 128–30
Catharis 124–5
Central America 590

China 434–7
Daoism 125
defining 120
ecclesiastical patronage of art 156
Hinduism 126–7
interaction of faiths 141–2
Jainism 128
Japan 454–5
Judaism 134–5
Manichaeism 123–4
Mayans 585
mediaeval European belief in supernatural 219
Mongolian imperial sovereign/god 467
outside orthodoxy of Christianity 227–8
places of worship and commemoration 148–52
purity and defilement 25–6
reaction to Islam 287
regulation of family 23, 24–5
representations of the sacred 153–5
scholarship and learning 336
shamanism 397, 468, 578
Shinto 126
South America 595–6, 597
and the state 44, **Pl. 169–72**
symbols of faith 155–6
Turk nomads 55–6
Zoroastrianism 123–4
see also Buddhism; Christianity; Islam
Rhabanus Maurus 216
Richen Zangpo 480
Ricoeur, Paul 122
Robert d'Anjou **Pl. 172**
Robert of Chester 103
Roman Catholic Church
Donation of Constantine 197
education and scholarship 99–100, 201–2
feudal system 211–12
ideas and outlook 218–20
monasteries and monastic culture 210–11
obsession with symbolism 219
the papacy 209
power and property 47
relation to European states 209–10
repression of certain groups 210
seek Pepin's help 196–7
solidarity of religious groups 213
split with East 175–6
Ronan, C. A. 94
Roosevelt, A. C. 601
Rozwi people 544
Rublev, Andrei **Pl. 159–60**
Rübruck, William of 246
Rūdakī, Abū ʿAbdallāh Jaʿfar 369
Rumania 194
Rūmī, Jalāl al-Dīn 370, 371, 406
Russia
the Golden Horde 477–8
icons **Pl. 157–60**
Kiev Rus 250–1
language and literature 192, **193**, 229, 230, 251
population 18–19
Tatar rule 100
Rustaveli, Shota 255
Rwanda 64

Sabiki language 524
Saʿdī, Muṣliḥ al-Dīn 371
Ṣadrā, Mullā 373
Ṣalāḥ al-Dīn/Saladin 333, 335
Salish language 562
El Salvador **589**, 590
Sāmānid state 378–83, **379**, 388
Samarkand **Pl. 26**
San people (Bushmen) 539
Sanāʾī, Abu'-l-Majd 370
Śankarāchārya 127
Sanskrit language 57, 97, 115, 419, 481, **Pl. 101–2**
Indian literature 406, 407
Scandinavia 235
Christianity 238
rise of states 212
Viking age 237–9
science and mathematics
alchemy 106–7, 118
algebra 403
Arab culture 324–5, 344, 351–2, 354, 356–7
astronomy 98, 103–4, 374, 384, 404, 574, 584, 585, **Pl. 134–43**
Byzantine 187, 192
chemistry 118–19
China 96, 441–2
consequences and applications 116–19
decimal notation 403
diffusion of knowledge 242
Egypt 334
geography 118
Hindu–Arabic numerals 116
Incan decimal system 68, **68**
India 97, 403–4
Iran 373–6
mathematics 101–3, 374–5
Mayans 584
Mongols 474–5
natural sciences 73, 105–6, 563, 574
optics 116, **117**, 375
physics 104–5
rapid calculations 442
Tājīks 380–1
West Africa 504–5
see also medicine; technology
Sei Shonagōn
The Pillow Book 451
Seljuks 286–7, 303, 327–9, 393
Armenia 252–3
feudalism 300
Middle East and Anatolia 389–90
origins 383, 388–9
sultanate of Rum 390–2
Syrian invasion 333
Sen Gua 109
Senegal 292
Serbia 192, **221**, 222
icons **Pl. 152**
Ottoman advance 395
Sesshu Toyo **Pl. 253**
sexuality
adultery 33
birth rates 14
eroticism 31
male attitudes towards women 26
prostitution 31
Shāfiʿī 52, 53
Shelemay, Kay Kaufmann 517
Shen Gua 104, 443
Shenzong 425
Shi Nai'an 440
Shi people 544
Shi-wei nomads 462, 463
Shield Jaguar II **Pl. 295**
Shintō 126, 450, 455
ships and shipping
Asia and Indian Ocean 89–90, 418
Byzantine Empire 187
China 92–3, 430–1, **Pl. 21**
East Africa 525
Europe 90–1, 214, **Pl. 23**, **Pl. 24–5**
inland waterways 93, 426
maritime law 187
naval warfare 91, 92
North Atlantic 91–2, **92**
production and design 79, **Pl. 22**

trade sea lanes 305, 306
Vikings 237, **Pl. 20**
see also navigation
Al-Shīrazī, Quṭb al-Dīn 103, 375
Shona people 544
Shōtoku Taishi, Prince 102, 447–8, 449
Siberia 461
Sicily
cultural achievements 350–1, 352, **Pl. 72–3**
Islamic conquest 290, 348, 349
Norman conquest and rule 353, 354–5, 357–8
Siddhartha Gautama (Buddha) 128
Sīdī Baṭṭāl 390
Silk Road 19, 86, 88–9, 144
Arab expansion 262
topography 305
Turkco–Mongolian nomads 468
Silla *see* Korea
Sima Guang 111
Simeon of Bulgaria 179, 192, 223, 227
Simon of Genoa 106
Sinhala language 412
slavery
Africa 496–7, 505, 516, 529
human rights law 45
India 400
Islamic lands 300–1, 317, 320, 516
Native Americans 564
serfdom 36–7
sources of slaves 36
Slavs
in the Balkans 222–3, 225, **226**
Byzantine context 178
central Europe 235–6
Christianity 225–6, 227
education and scholarship 100
Kiev Rus 250–1
language and literature 101, 192, **193**, 229–30
migration and movement **221**, 221–3
rise of mediaeval states 212–13
social organizations 35–7
Solinus Polyhistor **Pl. 120**
Solomon **Pl. 47–51**
Somalia
coffee 73
Songhay 497
Songsten Gampo 479
Songye people 545
South Africa 541
South America
agriculture 596, 600, 612, 615
Amazon delta 600–1
Andean cultures 602–11, **603**, **604**, **606**
arts and architecture 594–5, 596–7, 615–16, **Pl. 311–23**
Caribbean islands 599–600
context of pre-Columbian history 551–3, **552**
family and kinship 28, 29, 32
geographical conditions 13
hierarchical chiefdoms 593–6, 600
map **594**
mining and metallurgy 615, 617
political organization 597, 598
population 6, **14**, 21
pottery and ceramics 596, 597, 607, 610–11, 615, 616, 617, **Pl. 317–18**, **Pl. 322**
religion 595–6, 597
southern lands **612**, 612–17
Venezuela 596–9
see also Incas
Spain
art and architecture 157, **Pl. 59**, **Pl. 65–6**, **Pl. 198**
astronomy 104
coins **Pl. 192**, **Pl. 193**
cultural role of Toledo 357
disappearance of Islam 212
exploration and conquest 212
Islamic culture 76–7, 289–90
Jaén Pact 358
languages and scholarship 100, 115
synagogues **Pl. 78–9**
technology **Pl. 143**
unity 212
see also Andalusia
sports *see* games and recreation
Sri Lanka 411–13, 412
agriculture 411
art **Pl. 55**, **Pl. 234**
Buddhism 411–12, **Pl. 84**
Standes, Justus 526
Stein, B. 57, 398
Steward, J. 599
Su Shi (Dungpo) 438–9
Su Song 103, 104, 443
Sudan 485, 487, 490–1, 497, 507
Arabs and Islam 292, 293, 512–13
art and architecture **Pl. 276–8**
education and scholarship 99, 114
see also Nubia
Ṣūfism 262, **Pl. 218**
basic beliefs 262, 270
borrowings from Greece and India 325
Central Asia 287, 327, 382
historical development 368–9
India 406
Nubia and Sudan 513
order of the Naqshbandi 384
Persian poetry 370–1
Suhrawardī, Shihāb al-Dīn 373
Sumatra 418, 419
Sun Simo 106, 107
Suttles, W. 560
Sviatoslavich, Vladimir 250, 251
Swahilis 114–15
Arab and Islamic influence 293, 529–30
language 94, 293, 524, 529, 530
Sweden 212, 237–9
Switzerland 212
Syon, Amda 517, 518, 519
Syon, Yabgea 516–17
Syria 275, 351
culture 113, 115, **Pl. 28**

Al-Ṭabarī, Muḥammad ibn Jarīr 111, 325, 381
Taino people **Pl. 289–92**
Taira-no-Shigemori **Pl. 256**
Taironas 593–5
Taizhong (Li Shimin) 422–3, **Pl. 237**
Taizu (Zhu Yuanzhang) 426, **Pl. 238**
Tājīks 378–83
Talas River, battle of 3, 423
Tamar, Queen of Georgia 255
Tamerlane/Tīmūr 19, 288, 383–4, 466
Arab lands 328–9, 367
enthronment **Pl. 186**
Ottomans 395
Tamil language 407, 412
Tang Shenwei 105
Tanguts 424, 425
Tanzania 527–8
Tarascans 588
Tarmas 609
Tasman, Abel 622
Tatar Empire 100
taxes
agricultural land of Arabs 322
Andean cultures 607
Byzantine Empire 183–4
China 427–8
Ethiopia 515
India 400

Islamic towns 297
Japan 451
legal rights 47
Mālikism 339
Mongols 472
power of 48
Umayyad poll tax 272, 311
technology
Africa 487, 533
agriculture 18, 74, 88, 214, 428
arctic peoples 558, 559
Byzantium 187
camshaft 214
Central Asia 380
China 19, 430
diffusion of knowledge 242
distillation and alcohol 118–19, 402
effect of population movements 71–2
firearms 419–20
gunpowder and weapons 118, 444
India 400, 401–3
Iran 376
mediaeval Europe 214
military 402–3
optical lenses 104
scents and soap 323
South-East Asia 419–20
water conservation and irrigation 57, 303–4, 321, 380, 401–2, 411, 573–4, 576, 587, 593, 594
waterclocks 116, 118
West Africa 492, 505
Western history paradigm 71
wheelbarrow 214
wind and water mills 116, 118, 214, **Pl. 16–19**
world diffusion 77–8
see also mining; navigation; printing; science and mathematics; textiles; transport
Tegin, Köl 55
Temüjin *see* Chinggis Khān
Teutonic Knights, Order of 240, 246
textiles 76, **76**
Arabs 323
Byzantine Empire 187, 190
cloth as medium of exchange 544
Indian technology 402
nomads 465–6
North America 575
Nubia 510
organization of production 79–80, 301–2
patronage 158–9
Persian carpets 376
silk 75, 79–80, 430
women's labour 302
Thābit ibn Qurra 102, 104
Thailand 20, 417, 419, **Pl. 232**
Thangtong Gyelpo 481
Themon 106
St Theodore **Pl. 155**
Theodore of Freiberg 105
Theophano, Empress **Pl. 149**
Thisong Detsen 480
Thomas à Kempis 140
Thule people 559
Tiahuanaco culture 69
Tibet
architecture 479–80
Buddhism 480, 481–2, **Pl. 83**
Chinese patronage 481–2
language 112, 419, 479
literature 480
Mongol power 481, 482
pre-Buddhist shamanism 121
state and culture 479–81
Timbuktu 99, 495, **Pl. 34**
Timotes 597
Tiwanaku 602–4, 605
Ṭoghrïl Beg 327
Toledo, battle of 354
Tolima people **Pl. 311–12**
Toltecs 67–8, 167, 580–1, 584, 586, **Pl. 299**
Tonyukuk 55
torture 45
Totonacs 586
towns and cities
Andean cultures 602–11, **603**
architecture **Pl. 32**, **Pl. 39–41**
autonomy 301
Bedouin 296–7
China 431, **Pl. 241–2**
East Africa 527–8
gardens and parks of Samarkand 384–5
Islamic culture 278, 301, 320–1, 322
market areas 82
mediaeval Europe 213
merchants 297
officials 297
patronage of art 158
role in economics and culture 80–1
scholars 297–8
SE Asia 420
social hierarchies 299
spatial distribution of functions 75–6
Tenochtitlán 582
Toyotomi Hideyoshi 456
trade and commerce
Africa 492–4, 526–8, 533–4, 536, 544
Andalusia 351
Arabs 264, 320
Aztecs 67
Baqt Treaty between Nubia and Muslims 508
barter and money systems 81
bookkeeping 214
business partnerships 91
Byzantine Empire 185
China 423, 431–2, 437
the Crimea 258
desert caravans 85–6
effect of military conquest 82
Egypt 333, 335
Ethiopia 515–16
family-based businesses 493
gold 494
hybrid trade languages 94
Islamic merchants 297
itinerant pedlars 82
ivory 536
Korea 458
marketplaces 494
mediaeval Europe 213–14
Mesoamerica 591
North America 575–6
Oceania islanders 624
pastoral nomads 466
risks to merchants 81–2
salt 493, 494
scents and soap manufacture 323
South-east Asia and islands 416
topography of trade routes 305–6
traders' guilds 493
urban market areas 82
weights and measures 494
see also money; Silk Road
translation and cultural diffusion
see education and scholarship
Transoxania *see* under Asia: Central
transport 85, 94–5, 214
arctic dog sleds 558
camels 85–6, 402
caravans 88–9, 306, **306**, **Pl. 182–4**
chariots 87, 89

general conditions 84
harnessing and wagons 72, 86–8, **87**, **Pl. 7**, **Pl. 262**
horseshoes 403
India 89
inland waterways 93, 402, 426, 493
land 85–9
mediaeval Europe 214
roads 88
saddles and stirrups 86, 402–3
seafaring 89–93
topography of trade routes 305–6
West Africa 492–3
wheelbarrows 88
see also animals; ships and shipping
tribes
as legal entity 43, 48
Tughluq, Fīrūz 58, 312, 400, 402, 404
Tughluq, Muḥammad 58, 400, 404
Ṭughrul Beg 389
Tungus people 120
Tunisia *see* Ifriqiyya
Turks
Anatolia 397
in Arab army 316–17
architecture **Pl. 207**
artistic expression 145–7
attachment to Sunni orthodoxy 389
Byzantine Empire 182, 393–5, **394**
calligraphy **Pl. 113**
coins **Pl. 194**
dervishes 397
identity 393
inscriptions and texts 468
invasion of Iran 367
Islam 286–7, 387
language and literature 113, 147, 461
migrations 72, 303, 363, 388–9, **389**
and Mongols 288, 477
nomadism 55, 465–9, **Pl. 185**
the Oghuz 388–9
Ottoman Empire 3, 18, 288, 394–5, 395
Qarākhānids 383, 388
religion of nomads 467–8
Rūm sultanate 390–2
Samanid state 378
shamanism 397
slavery 300, 387–8
social organization of nomads 467
southern Siberia 461
tribal warfare 387
see also Seljuks
Al-Tūsī, Khwajeh Naṣīr al-Dīn 102, 103, 109, **Pl. 139**
astronomy 374
Persian philosophy 367

Uhud, battle of 266
Uighurs 466, 467, 468
Ulugh Beg
Zīj-i Ulūgh Beg 103
ʿUmar 266, 271, 275
Upanishads 405
Uqlīdisī 102
Al-Urdī 103
Urus 607–8
Urville, Dumont d' 621
ʿUthman 266, 271

Vaca, Cabeza de 577–8
Vāgbhata 108
Valdemar Atterdag of Denmark 239
Valdemar the Great of Denmark 238
Valla, Lorenzo 112
Vandals 16
Vargas Arenas, I. 599
Varthema, Ludovico di 516
Venezuela 596–9
Venice **Pl. 23**, **Pl. 194**
architecture **Pl. 40**, **Pl. 64**
Verdun, Treaty of (843) 198–9, **199**
Viet Nam 20, 97, 126, 416–17, **Pl. 226**
Vikings 237–9, **Pl. 193**
exploration 91, 110
population shifts 72
sculpture and carvings **Pl. 165–8**
ships **Pl. 20**
Villani, Giovanni 112
violence
blood ties 27
rape 31
urban riots 213–14
Vogelweide, Walther von **Pl. 177**

Wādī Lago, battle of 289
Wakore (Soninke) people 490
Wang Shifu 440
Wang Shouren 433
Wang Tao 107
Wang Wei 441
Wang Xiaotong 101
Wang Zhen 105
Wangara (Mandingo) people 490
war and peace
jihād 52–3, 315, 328, 388
laws of states 45
Wari state 604–5, 610
Al-Wāthiq 316
Weber, Max 81
Wendi (Yang Jian) 421–2
whaling 556, 559
White Jr, Lynn 87–8
Wiet, Gaston 272
William of Ockham 105, 140
William Rubruck 473
Witelo 105
women 30–1
African agriculture 542
in art **Pl. 173–6**
authority 30
calligraphers in the Maghrib 341
childbearing 29
courtly love **Pl. 178**
Empress Wu 423
inheritance of property 35
Islamic culture 302–3, 320–1
literature 343
matrilineal societies 28, 63
menstruation 26
roles 29–30
satī/immolation of widows 399
sexuality 29, 30–1
status and male distrust 26
Turkco–Mongol social organization 467
see also families; marriage
Woodbury, R. B. 575
Wright, H. 533
Wu Daozi 441
Wu Zetian, Empress 423, 435

Xianzong 423
Xin Qiji 439
Xuanzang (monk) 57, 434
Xuanzong (emperor) 422–3, 435

Yang Hui 101
Yangdi 422
Ya'qob, Zar'a 517–18, 518, 519, 520
Yehuda ben Tibbon 243
Yemen 73, **Pl. 189**
Yiddish language 101
Yixing 442–3

Yorubas 485, 491, 497
Yoshimitsu 453–4
Yuan *see* Qubilay Khan
Yuit people 555, 556, 558
Yu'pik language 558

Al-Zahrāwī, Abū al-Qāsim 108
Zanjis 529, 530, 536, 537
Zanzibar 525, 527
Zapotecs 165–6, 167–8, 580, 583
Zhamaluding 103
Zhang Daoling 125
Zhang Juhang 106
Zhang Zai 104, 433
Zhang Zhuo 439
Zhao Kuangyin 424
Zhao Mengfu **Pl. 255**
Zheng He 72, 92–3, 98
Zhiji 111
Zhou Dunyi 432
Zhu Shijie 102, 442
Zhu Sifen 109
Zhu Xi 433–4, 460
Zhu Xiao 105
Zhu Yu 104
Zimbabwe 545, **Pl. 33**
Zoroastrianism 123–4
    Chinese Mazdeism 436
    continuing influence 320
    end of sway in Iran 281–2
    within Islamic lands 312
    Mazdaism 436
    pre-Islamic Iran 365, 367
Zulu 63

PLATES

Plate 1 Codex Fejérváry-Mayer, Aztec civilization, second half of the fifteenth century (Mexico). Pre-Colombian manuscript from Central Mexico, painted on treated deerskin. Shown here are the nine 'Lords of Nights' who govern the ritual 260-day calendar whose signs are distributed among the four directions of the universe (Courtesy of Liverpool City Museum, Liverpool, UK).

Plate 2 Chinese farmer with plough and twin yoked bullocks. Wall painting from tomb, Tang dynasty, seventh century (Reproduction from *Peintures murales des Han et des Tang*, foreign language editions, 1974, Courtesy National Administration for Cultural Property, Beijing, China).

Plate 3 Muslim farmer with plough and twin yoked bullocks. Detail from illustration to Persian-language mystic poem 'The Parliament of Fowles' *(Mantiq at-Tayr)* by twelfth-century poet 'Attār of Nīshāpūr (Iran); painting by Bihzād of Herāt (modern Afghanistan); manuscript dated 1483 (63.210.49 r) (Metropolitan Museum of Art, Fletcher Fund, New York, USA).

Plate 4 Single camel and pair of oxen draw ploughs in Roman North Africa. Roman provincial relief, second century AD(?). 'Harnessing a single camel by a strap over its shoulders and traces along its sides was an innovation in North Africa' (after R. W. Bulliet) (Stadtbibliothek, Trier, Germany).

Plate 5 French farmer with wheeled plough and twin yoked oxen. From the 'Very Rich Book of Hours of John, Duke of Berry' *(Les Très Riches Heures du Duc de Berry)*, France, 1413–1416; illumination by the Limbourg brothers for the month of March. Castle of noble House of Lusignan, marked by winged dragon of fairy Mélusine in the family crest, stands in background (Musée Condé, Chantilly, France).

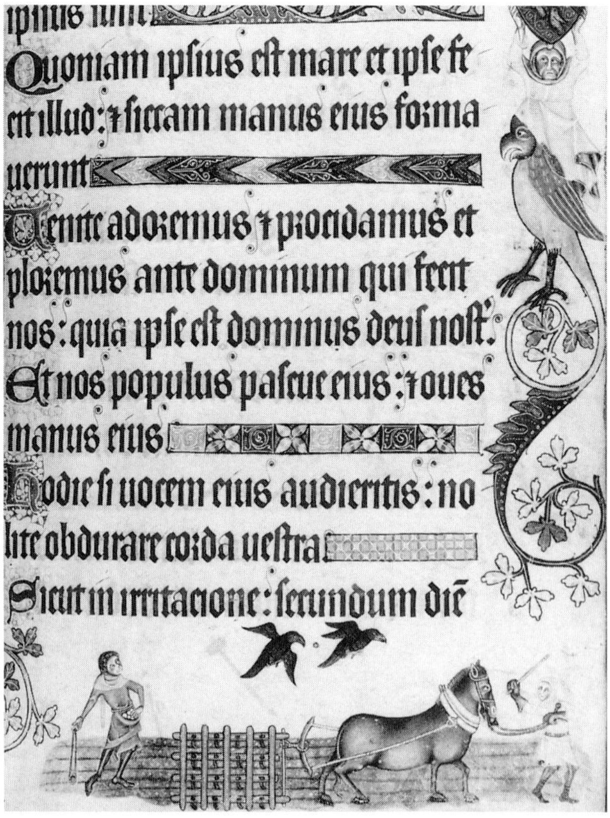

Plate 6 English farmer harrowing by means of 'a horse harnessed with an efficient horsecollar' (after R.W. Bulliet). From *Luttrell Psalter*, *c.* 1335–1340 (England) (By permission of The British Library, UK).

Plate 7 'Modern' horse collar harnessing in Europe. Horse-drawn cart, with horse collar around horse's shoulders: detail of Carolingian manuscript, German, *c.* 800 AD: 'The earliest illustration of 'modern' horsecollar harnessing in Europe. Though efficient harnessing may have been developed earlier in North Africa, the increase in use of horses for pulling waggons and ploughs dates from approximately this period. The ancient throat-and-girth-strap equine harness instead constricted the animal's neck and limited the force that it could apply' (after R.W. Bulliet) (Stadtbibliothek, Trier, Germany).

Plate 8 Horse-drawn cart going uphill, *Luttrell Psalter*. Horse-drawn cart with fully developed horse collar harness, and studded iron tyres, 1335–1340 (England) (By permission of The British Library, UK).

Plate 9 (a) and (b) Transport in former Chinese capital of Bienjing (modern Kaifeng): details from scroll 'Spring Festival on the River', by artist Zhang Zeduan, Song Dynasty, 1127 AD. Note carts both donkey-drawn (with collars) and bullock-drawn (with yokes); hand-pushed wheelbarrows; sedan chairs; pack-donkey trains; saddle horses; wheelwrights' shops; and taverns for travellers along street (Courtesy Beijing Summer Palace Museum, China).

Plate 10 Western European heraldry. From the 'Book of Tournaments of King René of Provence' *(Le Livre des Tournois du roi René)*. Illustration by Barthélémy d'Eyck, Franco-Flemish, *c.* 1460 (Bibliothèque Nationale, Paris, France).

Plate 11 Islamic heraldry. Illustration by artist al-Wāsitī to the Arabic-language 'Sessions' or *Maqāmāt* of the twelfth century prosodist al-Harīrī (Iraq) (By permission of The British Library, London, UK).

Plate 12 Central Asian cavalry. Farāmurz chasing the King of Kabul's army. Illustration to Persian-language 'Book of Kings' *(Shāh-Nāmeh)* by eleventh-century epic poet Firdawsī; Tabrīz (Iran) (Photo H. Lewandowski; Musée du Louvre, Paris, France).

Plate 13 Mongol princess in high-wheeled camel-cart crosses a river; eleventh or twelfth century. Poor road conditions throughout Eurasia and North Africa encouraged pack-trains and increasing preference for horseback riding over wheeled transport, especially since invention of stirrup; Song Dynasty (China) (In the care of the Museum of Far Eastern Antiquities, Stockholm, Sweden).

Plate 14 Japanese mounted Aristocrat. Portrait of the shōgun Ashikaga Takauji (1305–1358) (Moriya collection, National Museum, Kyoto, Japan).

Plate 15 West African equestrian figure. Ceramic, 70.5 cm; *c.* thirteenth to fifteenth century, Inland Delta Region (Mali) (Photo Franko Khoury; National Museum of African Art, Smithsonian Institution, Washington DC, USA).

Plate 16 Depiction of mill and water-wheel: Prince Bayād swoons by the river. Illustration to 'Romance of Bayād and Riyād' *(Hadīth Bayād wa Riyād)*, thirteenth century AD, Morocco or Islamic Spain (Courtesy of Biblioteca Apostolica Vaticana, Vatican)

Plate 17 French peasant woman bears grain to mill, with depiction of water-wheel. Illustration by artist Barthélémy d'Eyck for allegorical work *Le mortifiement de vaine plaisance* ('The Mortification of Vain Pleasure') by King René of Provence; Franco-Flemish, *c.* 1470. Influence of Spanish-Muslim agricultural techniques on Christian Europe was profound (Courtesy of Bibliothèque municipale de Metz, France).

Plate 18 Water-wheel moved by oxen. Illustration by artist al-Wāsitī to the 'Sessions' of al-Harīrī, 1237, Baghdād (Iraq). 'This device, often known by its Arabic name *sāqiya,* is still used from Morocco to India. Although not visible here, a chain of earthenware pots passing over the wheel descends to the bottom of the well; gears connect it to the wheel being turned by the oxen' (after R. W. Bulliet) (Bibliothèque Nationale, Paris, France).

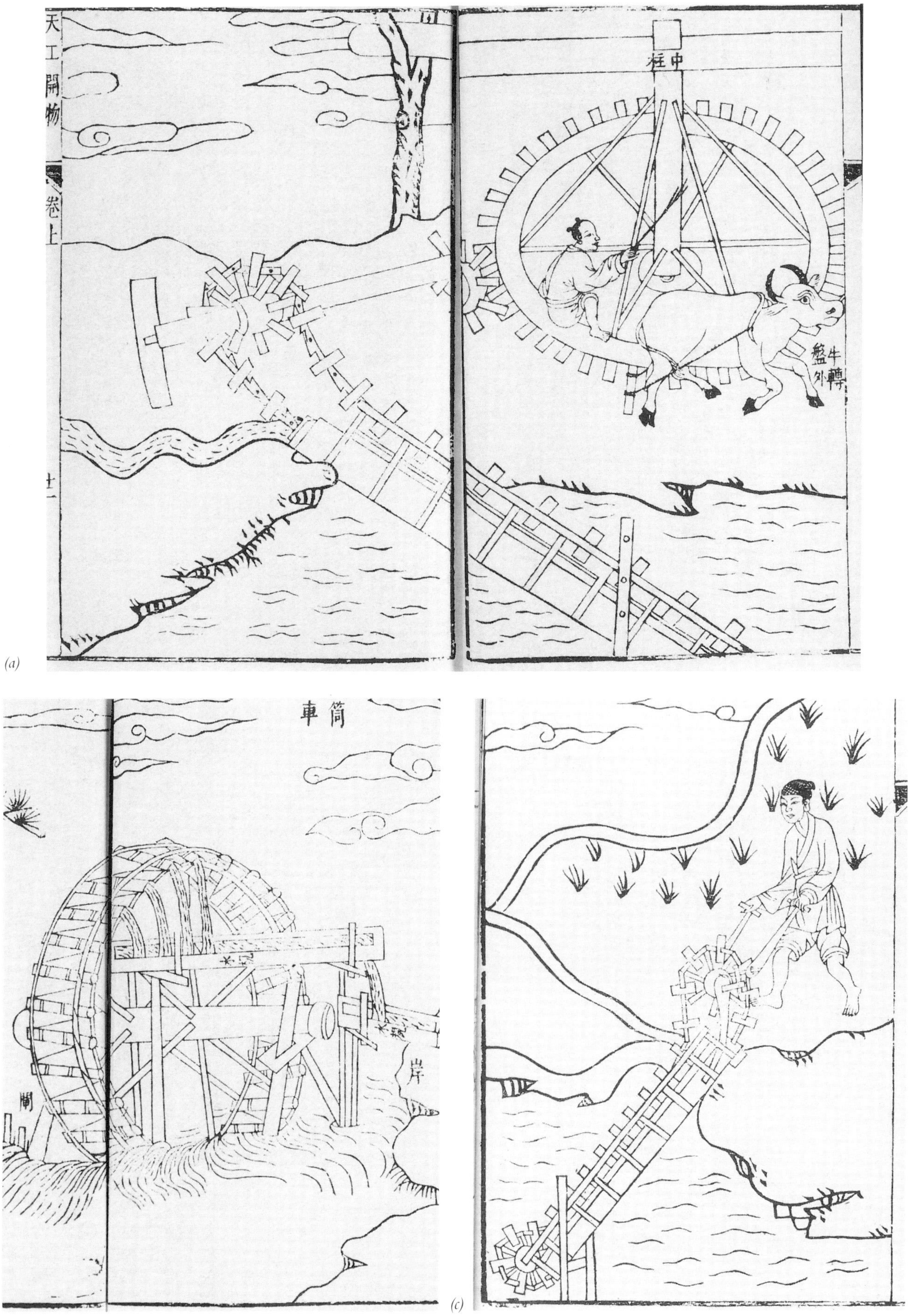

(a) *(b)* *(c)*

Plate 19 Harnessing water-power in China: *(a)* the *Niuche* or square-pallet chain-pump worked by ox; *(b)* the *Tongache* or square-pallet chain pump worked by water-wheel; *(c)* the *Bache*, the manually operated square-pallet chain-pump (mills and water-power) (Photos in Song Yingzing's *Tian Gong Kai Wu* (Exploitation of the Works of Nature), edition of 1637 re-edited by Zhonghua Shuju, 1959, Shanghai, China).

Plate 20 Viking ship (ninth century), found in Oseberg (Norway). This Norse ship, the best preserved in world, was still guided like the sea craft of antiquity, with detached steering oar lashed to its starboard side (Viking Ship Museum, Bygdøy, Oslo, Norway).

Plate 21 Chinese stern-post rudder. This detail from Zhang Zeduan's early twelfth-century scroll, 'Spring Festival on the River' depicts the earliest known example of a stern-post rudder in the world (Courtesy Beijing Summer Palace Museum, China).

Plate 22 Muslim dhow as used in the Gulf and Indian Ocean: illustration by al-Wāsitī for the 'Sessions' of al-Harīrī, 1237, Baghdād (Iraq). Crew members empty the bilge water. The planks of traditional Indian Ocean vessels like this one were sewn with palm fibres, rather than nailed, a usage attested in this region since at least the sixth century AD – but the distinctive new feature of this ship is its stern-post rudder with hinges, here shown to have been adopted from China and used by Muslim sailors in Indian Ocean waters by the thirteenth century. Note that Crew members and passengers were coming from Eastern Africa and Western and Southern Asia (Bibliothèque Nationale, Paris, France).

Plate 23 Venetian sailing craft, 'The Legend of Saint Ursula' by Vittore Carpaccio, Venice, end of the fifteenth century. These *carracks* for Mediterranean trade, one of which has been grounded for repairs, feature the rounded hull, stern-post rudder and square sail adopted from the Atlantic 'kogge' (Courtesy Museo dell'Accademia, Venice, Italy).

Plate 24 Early fifteenth-century Portuguese *caravela* as seen through a Spanish Muslim potter's eyes: glazed earthenware vessel with lustre decoration from Malaga, in the Islamic Nasrid kingdom of Granada, Spain, *c.* 1425–1450. The ship's square sail bears the arms of Portugal. The *caravela's* design – invented in fifteenth-century Portugal's shipyards – combines Atlantic and Mediterranean features with rounded hull, stern-post rudder and both square sail at mainmast and lateen sail at mizzenmast, the better to manoeuvre under all winds (Victoria and Albert Museum, London, UK).

Plate 25 Fully rigged Portuguese *caravela* under full wind aft (late fifteenth century); with rounded hull, stern-post rudder, square sails at bowsprite and mainmast, two furled lateen sails at the twinned mizzenmasts, and port-holes under the gunwales for artillery. Such floating fortresses, rigged for all seas, were launched by both Iberian powers for Atlantic and Indian Ocean conquest at the close of the fifteenth century (Engraving from the *Estoria do muy nobre Vespasiano Emperador de Roma*, Torre de Tumbo, Lisbon, 1496).

Plate 26 Building the Great Mosque of Tīmūr in Samarkand (Uzbekistan). Illustration by Bihzād of Herāt for the Persian-language *Zafar-Nāmeh* or 'Book of Victory', a chronicle of Tīmūr by Sharaf al-Dīn Yazdī, in a manuscript dated 1468 but illustrated *c.* 1488. Use of elephants by Central Asian Muslims for heavy construction work was adopted from India. Note sculpture yard, glazed-tile mosaic work on minaret and high-wheeled ox-cart of a design still used up until now in Mongolia (The John Work Garrett Library of the Johns Hopkins University, Baltimore, USA).

Plate 27 Building Castle Khawarnaq; illustrated by Bihzād of Herāt for the Persian-language tales of the twelfth-century poet Nizāmī of Āzerbaijān, in a manuscript dated 1494. Note burnt-brick architecture, pointed arch, scaffolding, hand-barrow and lime-pit (By permission of The British Library, London, UK).

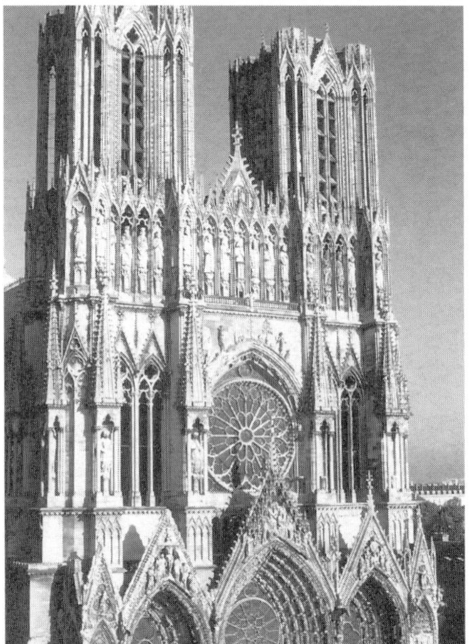

Plate 28 The Cathedral of Reims; built from 1211 to the end of thirteenth century (France) (Photo ICOMOS, Paris).

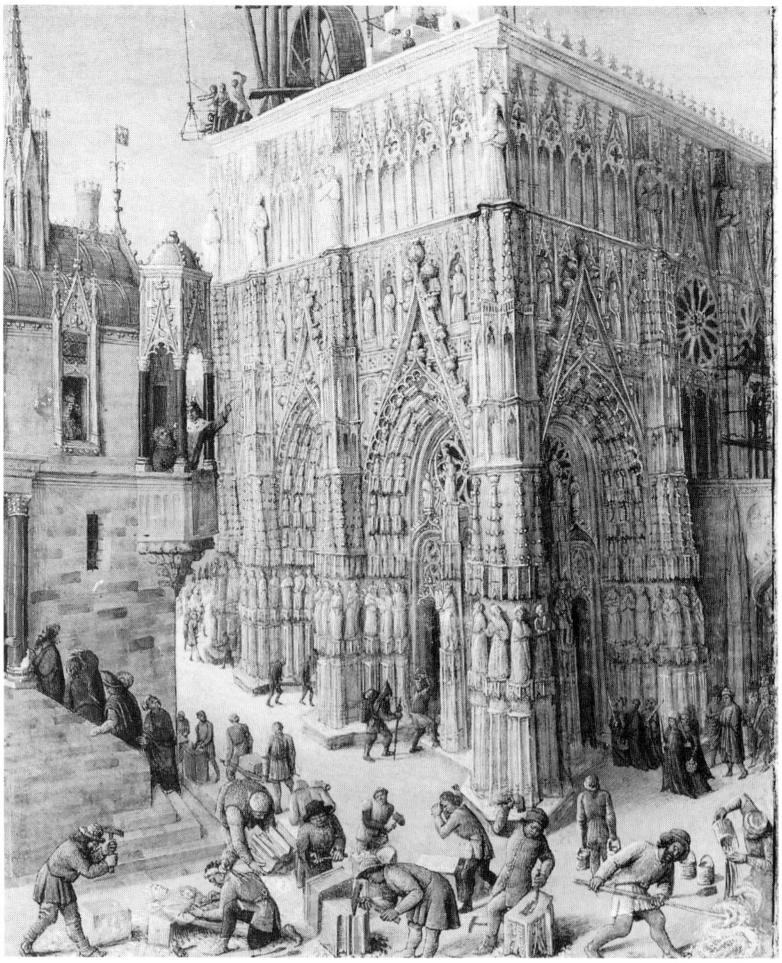

Plate 29 Depiction of a contemporary rising Gothic cathedral, Tours (France). Illustrated by Jean Fouquet, *c.* 1470, for a French rendition of the *Jewish Antiquities* (Antiquités judaïques) of Flavius Josephus (first century AD). Note sculpture yard, hoisting wheel and lime-pit (Bibliothèque Nationale, Paris, France).

Plate 30 Citadel of Aleppo (Syria); built by the Ayyūbid ruler Al-Malik al-Zāhir in 1209–1210, with gateway restored by the Mamlūk ruler Qānsūh al-Ghūrī in 1507 (Photo in Barbara Brend, *Islamic Art*, p. 101; British Museum Press, London, UK, 1991).

Plate 31 Krac des Chevaliers, Crusader castle; twelfth century (Syria). Note mutual influence between Christian and Muslim castle-builders (Photo Gérard Degeorge in Jean Favier, *La France médiévale*, Fayard, Paris, 1983, p. 453).

Plate 32 The Bāb Zuwayla, the *City ramparts*, Fātimid Dynasty; late eleventh century, Cairo (Egypt). The dome and minarets belong to the Mosque of Sultan Mu'ayyad, Mamlūk Dynasty, *c.* 1415 (Photo Ayman Fu'ad Sayyid).

Plate 33 The Great Zimbabwe, thirteenth to fourteenth centuries (Zimbabwe): (a) aerial view; (b) tower and ramparts. 'The construction of Zimbabwe's hilltop stronghold, and the Great Enclosure on the plain below must have required an effort comparable to that involved in the building of the Egyptian pyramids' (after V. V. Matveiev) (Photos in *The UNESCO Courier,* May 1984, pp. 68, 69).

Plate 34 Ramparts and minarets of the Mosque of Jingereber, Timbuktu (Mali); founded by Mansa Mūsā in 1325. No longer extant (Photo Roger-Viollet).

Plate 35 Gateway of fort of Kilwa Kisiwani, Kilwa Island (Kenya). Swahili civilization, fourteenth to fifteenth centuries (Photo Unwin, S. in *General History of Africa,* UNESCO, Paris, 1984, vol. IV, ch. 18).

Plate 36 Ramparts and moat, thirteenth century, Provins (France) (Courtesy of the Town Hall, Provins).

Plate 37 Genoese fortress at Soldaia, Crimea (Ukraine); fourteenth to fifteenth centuries, with small sixteenth-century mosque built by the Ottomans inside (Photo Sergei P. Karpov).

Plate 38 Fortress of Sacsahuamán, Cuzco ('Royal Eagle') (Peru); overlooking Inca capital of Cuzco, built between 1438 and 1500 (Photo L. Millones).

Plate 39 Fortified gateway of the 'Porte du Croux', Nevers (France); fourteenth century, with thirteenth-century cathedral tower in background (All rights reserved).

Plate 40 Northern European view of Venice: only major medieval European city not surrounded by walls because entirely protected by water (Italy). From manuscript of Marco Polo's 'Travels', *Il millione*, fourteenth century, Ms Bold. 264, fol. 218 r (Bodleian Library, Oxford, UK).

Plate 41. Italian fortified seaside town with citadel, drawbridge and keep, by Ambrogio Lorenzetti, *c.* 1318–1348 (Courtesy Pinacoteca, Siena, Italy).

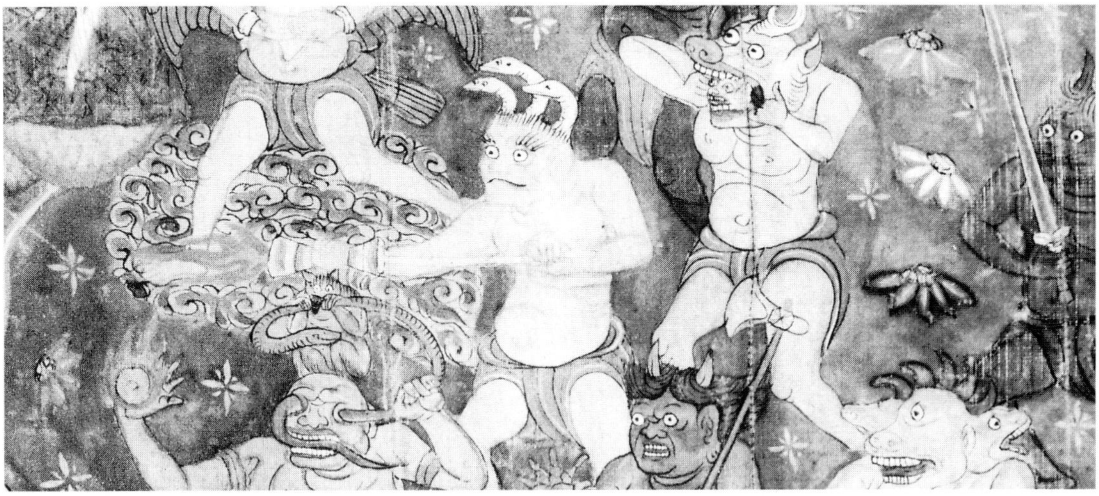

Plate 42. Demon with fire-lance on Buddhist banner (China); *c*. AD 950, earliest known representation of gunpowder (Musée Guimet, Paris, France).

Plate 43 Early bronze cannon cast in 1331 (China) (National Historical Museum, Beijing, China).

Plate 44 The English Earl of Warwick besieges the French fortified port of Caen with guns in 1417, during the 'Hundred Years' War' between England and France. From the *Chronicles of Richard de Beauchamp, Earl of Warwick*, or 'Beauchamp Chronicles', English, fifteenth century (By permission of The British Library, London, UK).

Plate 45 The Dome of the Rock, Jerusalem: Islamic, Umayyad Dynasty, built AD 687–691 by the caliph 'Abd al-Malik ibn Marwīn (Photo F. Alcoceba; UNESCO Photothèque, Paris).

Plate 46 Medieval French view of Jerusalem with the Dome of the Rock; fifteenth century. From *Passages d'Outremer* (Bibliothèque Nationale, Paris, France).

Plate 47 Judgment of Solomon, Hebrew prayer book, Tours (France); late thirteenth century, with Solomon as ideal ruler depicted as a contemporary French king (By permission of The British Library, London, UK).

Plate 48 Solomon with the Queen of Sheba symbolizing the wedding of divinely inspired Royal Wisdom with the human soul. From the portal of Notre Dame de Corbeil, France, late twelfth century (Musée du Louvre, Paris, France).

Plate 49 Solomon, regarded as the Founder of the Kingdom's Royal Line. From a Book of Psalms, Ethiopia, *c.* 1470 (Bibliothèque Nationale, Paris, France).

Plate 50 Solomon holds his magic seal as royal Master of all human beings, genies and animals, Tabrīz (Iran) (Topkapi Palace Library, Istanbul, Turkey).

Plate 51 Solomon, the Queen of Sheba and their minister Asaph borne by submissive genies. Style of Master Muhammad Siyāh-Qalam ('Black Pen'), probably Tabrīz, Iran, Turkmen period, fifteenth century. The image of the elephant-*jinn* ultimately derives from the Hindu god Ganesh (or Ganesha) (Topkapi Palace Library, Istanbul, Turkey).

Plate 52 Ganesh and his *Shaktī* or projected female counterpart, Khajuraho (India); eleventh to twelfth centuries. Reverence for Ganesh, one of the most important deities in the Hindu pantheon, spread far beyond India (Khajuraho Archaeological Museum, India).

Plate 53 Ganesh as Lord of Prosperity and patron of merchants; thirteenth century, Central India (British Museum, London, UK).

Plate 54 Ganesh and other Hindu deities (China). Fragment of a Manichean manuscript from Chinese Central Asia; eighth to ninth century (Courtesy Staatliche Museen, Preussischer Kulturbesitz, Indische Kunstabteilung, Berlin, Germany).

Plate 55 Ganesh in the royal pose enthroned upon the lotus, Polonnaruva (Sri Lanka); eleventh century (Anurādhapura, Archaeological Museum, India).

Plate 56 Christ as Pantocrator, in the pose of Imperial Protector, with Saint Menas. Eastern Christendom: Egypt, Coptic, icon on wood, *c.* AD 600. Early depiction of the bearded Christ which only prevailed by the sixth century (Photo H. Lewandowski; Musée du Louvre, Paris, France).

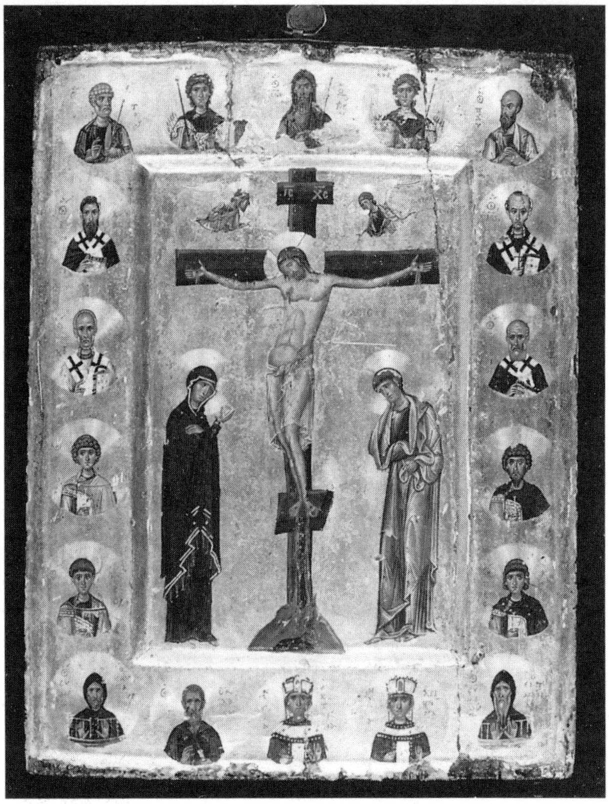

Plate 57 Christ as Man of Sorrows. The Crucified Saviour between the Virgin and Saint John. Eastern Christendom: Byzantine icon, twelfth century, from the Monastery of St Catherine, Sinai (Egypt).

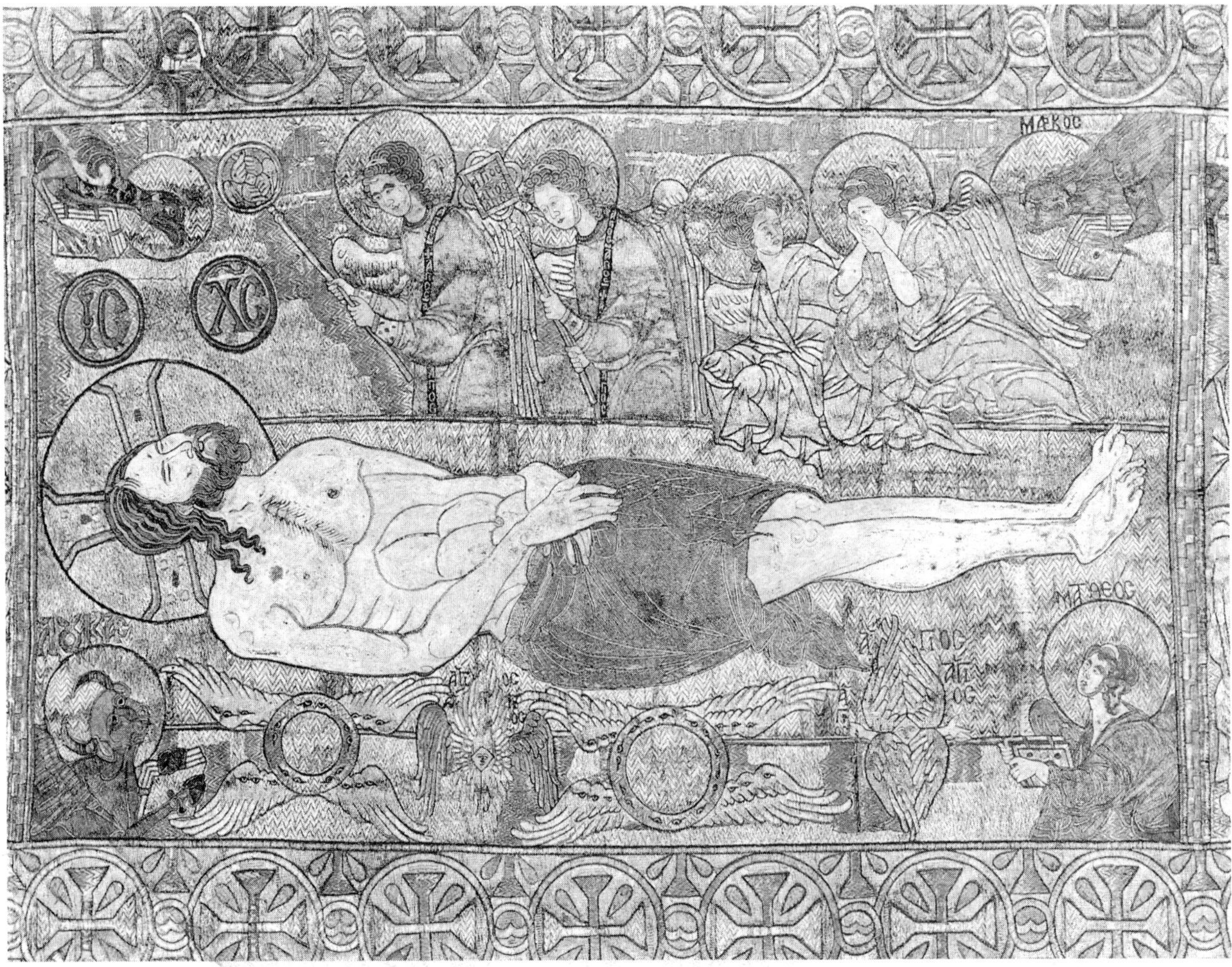

Plate 58 The Entombment (Epitaphios). Eastern Christendom: Byzantine embroidery, fourteenth century, Thessaloniki (Greece) (Courtesy Museum of Byzantine Culture, Thessaloniki, Greece).

Plate 59 Christ as Pantocrator, in the aspect of Wrath, Catalonia (Spain). Western Christendom: detail from the apse of the Church of Sant Climent de Taüll, *c.* 1123 (Courtesy Museu National d'Art de Catalunya, Barcelona, Spain).

Plate 60 Christ as Man of Sorrows, the Crucified Saviour, Arezzo (Italy). Western Christendom: detail of wooden crucifix, by Giovanni Cimabue, *c.* 1270. Church of San Domenico (Fototeca A.P.T., Arezzo, Italy).

Plate 61 Christ as Man of Sorrows bearing the wounds of the Cross, embracing his mother in Paradise, Prague (Czech Republic). Western Christendom: from the *Passion Book of the Abbess Cunegunda*, Prague, *c.* 1320 (Národní knihovna, Klementinum, Prague, Czech Republic).

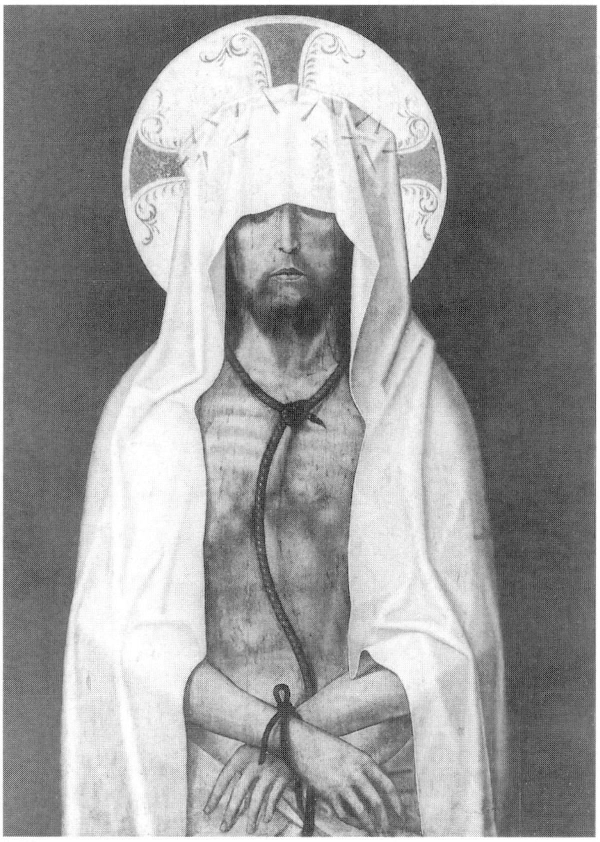

Plate 62 'Ecce Homo': Christ as both Man of Sorrows and Hidden Godhead. Western Christendom: fifteenth century (Portugal) (Museu de Arte Antiga, Lisbon, Portugal).

Plate 63 The Ascension of the Virgin as seen before the Imperial Basilica of the Holy Apostles in Constantinople. Illustration to the *Homilies on the Virgin* written by the monk James of Kokkinovaphos, first half of the twelfth century. The eleventh century building depicted here no longer exists (Bibliothèque Nationale, Paris, France).

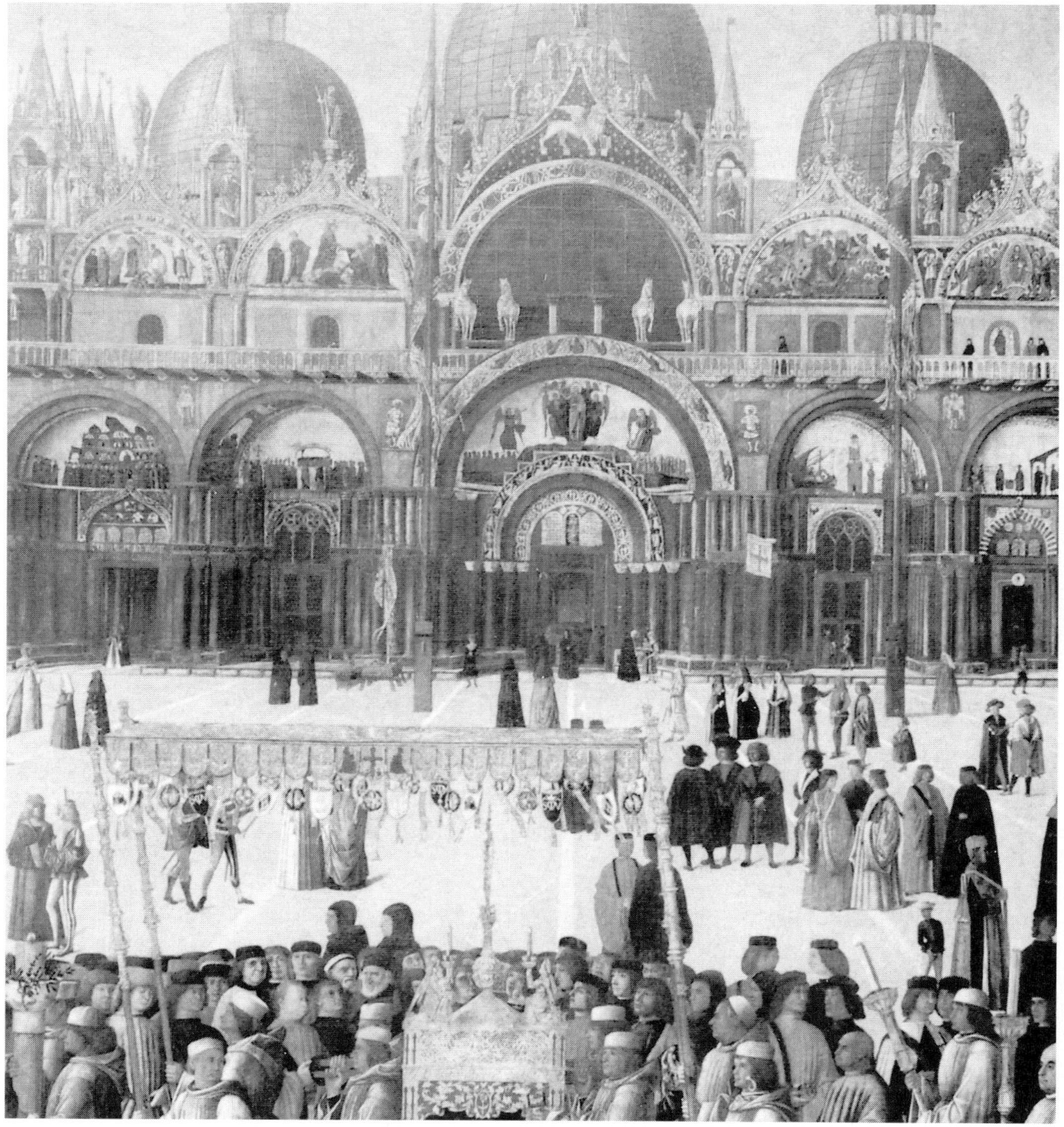

Plate 64 Procession of the Holy Cross before the Basilica of Saint Mark, Venice (Italy). Detail of oil painting by Giovanni Bellini, late fifteenth century. The Byzantine-type façade now shows fourteenth-century Gothic additions (Courtesy Museo dell'Accademia, Venice, Italy).

Plate 65 The Great Mosque of Cordova (Spain). Striped arches of the prayer hall. Islamic Spain, Spanish–Umayyad Dynasty, tenth century (Photo ICOMOS, Paris).

Plate 66 The private oratory of the caliphs in the Great Mosque of Cordova (Spain). Multi-lobed arches of the private oratory of the caliphs. Spanish–Umayyad Dynasty, tenth century (Photo ICOMOS, Paris).

Plate 67 Striped arches in the nave of the Abbey Church of Sainte Madeleine, Vézelay (France). Romanesque style with Cordovan influences, eleventh to twelfth centuries (Courtesy Office du Tourisme, Vézelay, France).

Plate 68 Striped arches in the cloisters of Notre Dame Cathedral, Le Puy en Vélay (France); twelfth century, Romanesque style with Cordovan influences (All rights reserved).

Plate 69 Multi-lobed arches of the portal of the Chapel of Saint Michel d'Aiguilhe, Le Puy en Vélay (France). Romanesque style with Cordovan influences, turn of the eleventh and twelfth centuries (Courtesy Office du Tourisme, Le Puy en Vélay, France).

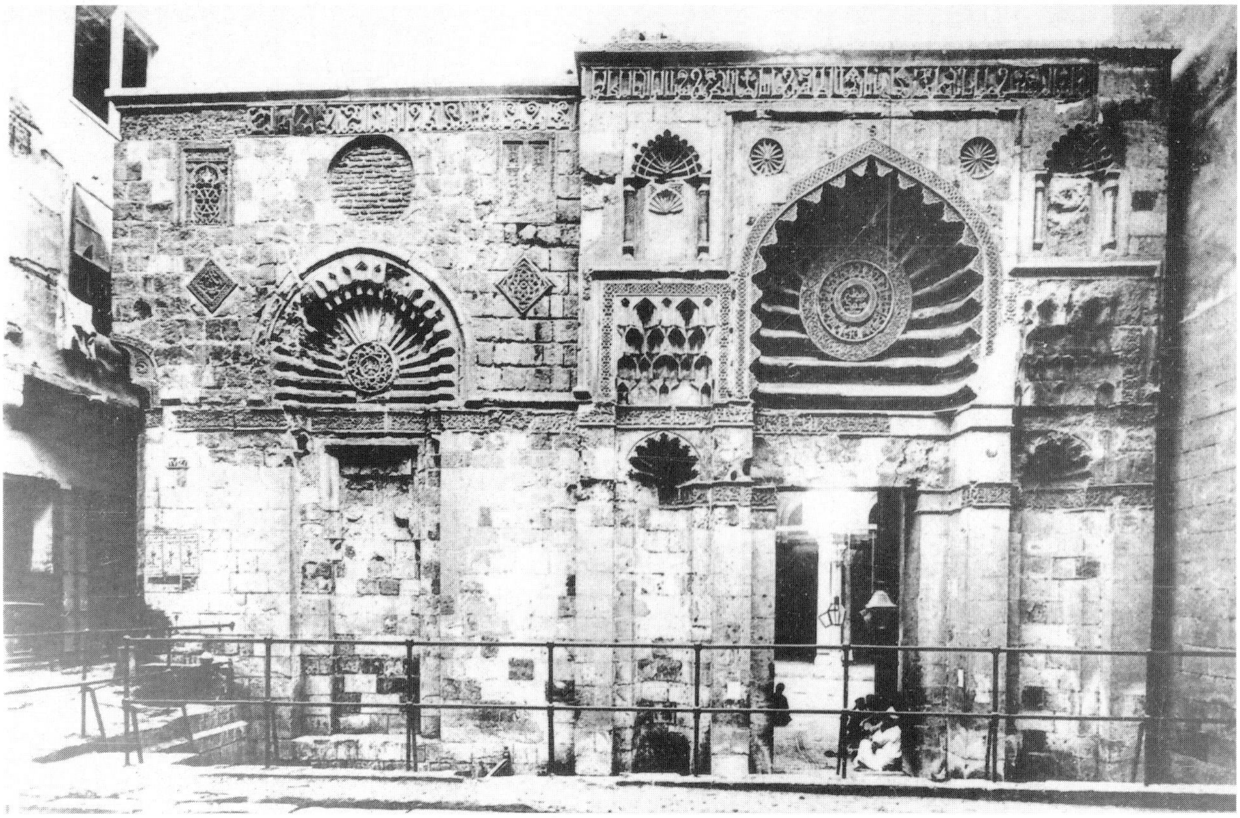

Plate 70 Blind pointed arches of the façade of the Mosque of al-Aqmar, Cairo (Egypt). Fāṭimid Dynasty, built AD 1125 (Photo Ayman Fu'ad Sayyid).

Plate 72 Fāṭimid-style blind pointed arches on the apse of the Cathedral, Monreale (Sicily). Norman Dynasty, begun 1174 (All rights reserved).

Plate 71 Pointed vaulting in the prayer hall of the Masjid-i Jāmi' ('Friday Mosque'), Isfahān (Iran). Seljuk Dynasty, construction begun in AD 1121 (All rights reserved).

Plate 73 Fāṭimid-style pointed arches in the cathedral cloister, Monreale (Sicily). Norman Dynasty, late twelfth century (All rights reserved).

Plate 74 Durham Cathedral (England); early twelfth century (Photo UNESCO World Heritage Center, Paris).

Plate 75 Cathedral of Saint Etienne, Bourges (France). Interior of the cathedral, *c.* 1200 (Photo UNESCO World Heritage Center).

Plate 76 Hebrew page from the *Guide to the Perplexed* by Maimonides (Spain); fifteenth century. Originally written by the Spanish-Jewish philosopher Maimonides (twelfth century) in Arabic although transcribed into Hebrew characters, then retranslated by French rabbis into Hebrew in the later thirteenth century (Courtesy *Judaism*, department of The Royal Library, Copenhagen, Denmark).

Plate 77 King David depicted as a contemporary French king, Tours (France). Hebrew prayer book, late thirteenth century (By permission of The British Library, London, UK).

Plate 78 Islamic-style windows in the Synagogue of El Tránsito, Toledo (Spain) (All rights reserved).

Plate 79 Mingled Hebrew and Arabic calligraphies in the Synagogue of El Tránsito, Toledo (Spain). This 'Moorish'-style synagogue was actually entirely built under Castilian Christian rule (fourteenth century) (All rights reserved).

Plate 80 Face of Prince Gautama as a *Bodhisattva*, Ajantā (India). Wall-painting; early seventh century (All rights reserved).

Plate 81 Face of the Bodhisattva Avalokiteshvara); symbol of Cosmic Mercy. Detail from a fresco of the 'Paradise of the Amitābha Buddha' (pronounced in Japanese: Amida). Sixth panel of the Temple of Hōryû-ji; Nara (Japan) late seventh century (All rights reserved).

Plate 82 The Buddha Shākyamuni meditates beneath the shelter of the Nāga or Cobra King, Ankor (Cambodia). Early Bayon style, end of the twelfth century; Hīnayāna Buddhism (Musée Guimet, Paris, France).

Plate 83 The Buddha Akshobhya meditates while touching the Earth; thirteenth century, Tibet, Mahāyāna Buddhism (All rights reserved).

Plate 84 The Bodhisattva Avalokiteshvara in royal pose, Veragala (Sri Lanka). Symbol of Cosmic Mercy; gilt bronze, crystal and precious stones, eighth to ninth centuries (Photo Jean-Louis Nou, National Museum, Colombo, Sri Lanka).

Plate 85 The Bodhisattva Avalokiteshvara in royal pose, Song Dynasty (China). Carved, lacquered and gilt wood. Song Dynasty, *c.* AD 1200 (Victoria and Albert Museum, London, UK).

Plate 86 The Bodhisattva Avalokiteshvara in royal pose (Korea). Ink, colour and gold on silk scroll, detail. Koryo Dynasty, fourteenth century (Courtesy of the Freer Gallery of Art, Smithsonian Institution, Washington DC, USA).

Plate 87 The Bodhisattva Avalokiteshvara seen as the guide of a human soul. Ink and colour on silk banner, Dunhuang, (China). Five Dynasties, tenth century (British Museum, London, UK).

Plate 88 The Great Mosque of Tlemcen (Algeria), AD 1136 (Photo Jean Mazenod in *L' Islam et l'art musulman*, Courtesy Editions Citadellas et Mazenot, Paris).

Plate 89 Oculus in the dome over the Tomb of the Ṣūfī master Shāh Ni'matullāh Walī, Māhān (Iran). The Divine as source of emanating light, Tīmūrid Dynasty, 1436 (All rights reserved).

Plate 90 Carpet page to a multi-volume Qur'ān, Cairo (Egypt). The Divine as source of an emanating maze of light: first page of Juz' IX, or ninth volume. Cairo; Mamlūk Dynasty, fourteenth century (By permission of The British Library, London, UK).

Plate 91 Tile decoration over the supposed tomb of the Ṣūfī master Shams-i Tabrīzī, Multān (Pakistan). Delhi Sultanate period, fourteenth century (Photo G. Degeorge, Paris, France).

Plate 92 'The Scribe', Palenque, Chiapas (Mexico). This relief panel represents King Ah kul Ah Nab (or Chaacal) III of Palenque; he reigned since AD 722 to 764. Limestone panel, Late Classic Period, AD 600–900; Maya Civilization (British Museum, London, UK).

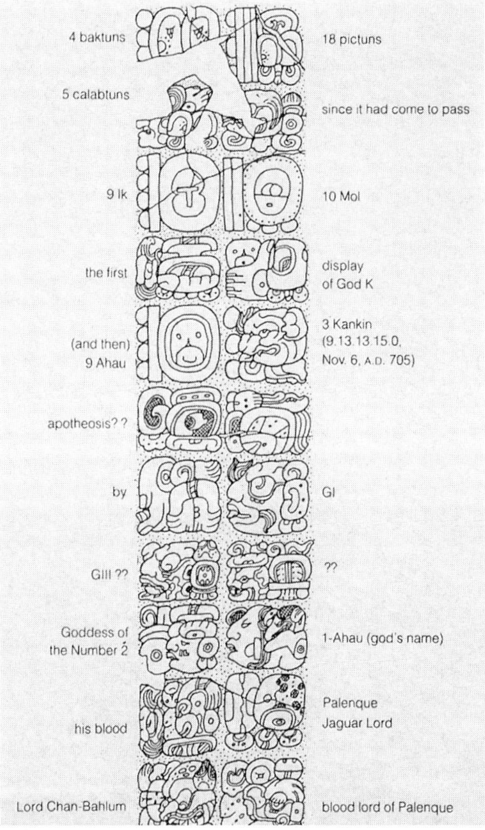

Plate 93 Maya characters or glyphs, Palenque, Chiapas (Mexico). Inscription in a limestone tablet in Temple 14, that celebrates king Chan-Bahlum II's defeat over the Lords of Underworld. Limestone Late Classic Period, AD 600–900 (dated 703 AD), Maya Civilization. After a drawing by Ian Graham, in Linda Schele and Mary Ellen Miller, *The Blood of Kings: Dynasty and Ritual in Maya Art,* New York, 1986, p. 273; interpretation of glyphs by L. Schele and M. E. Miller.

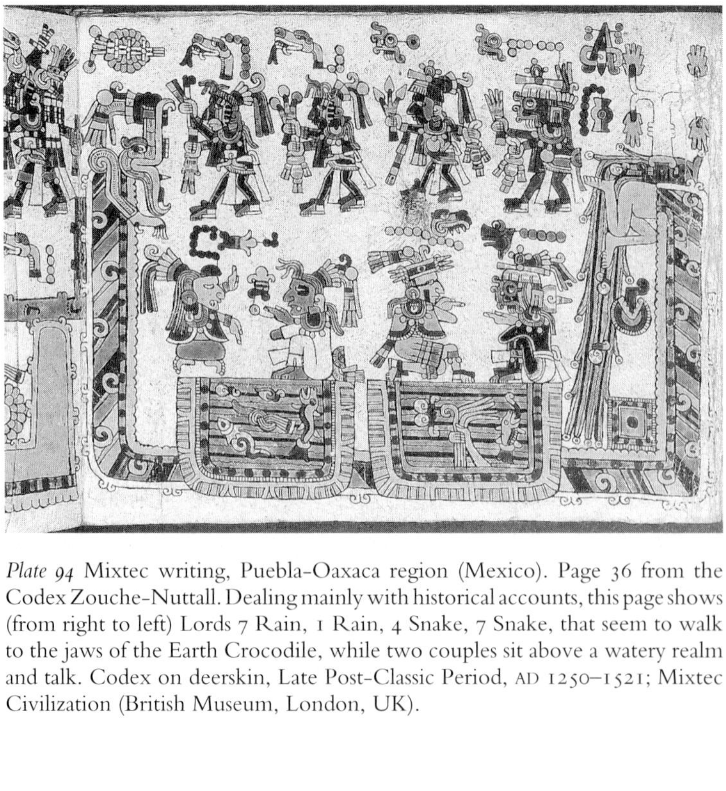

Plate 94 Mixtec writing, Puebla-Oaxaca region (Mexico). Page 36 from the Codex Zouche-Nuttall. Dealing mainly with historical accounts, this page shows (from right to left) Lords 7 Rain, 1 Rain, 4 Snake, 7 Snake, that seem to walk to the jaws of the Earth Crocodile, while two couples sit above a watery realm and talk. Codex on deerskin, Late Post-Classic Period, AD 1250–1521; Mixtec Civilization (British Museum, London, UK).

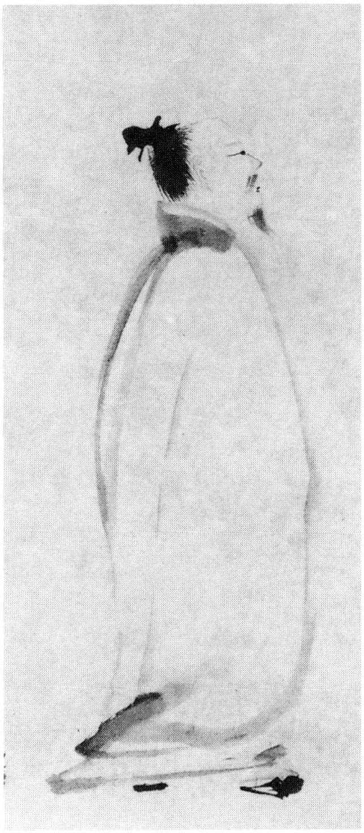

Plate 95 Portrait of the Tang poet Li Bo (701–762), Southern Song Dynasty (China); calligraphic brushwork by the painter-calligrapher Liang Kai; early thirteenth century (National Museum, Tokyo, Japan).

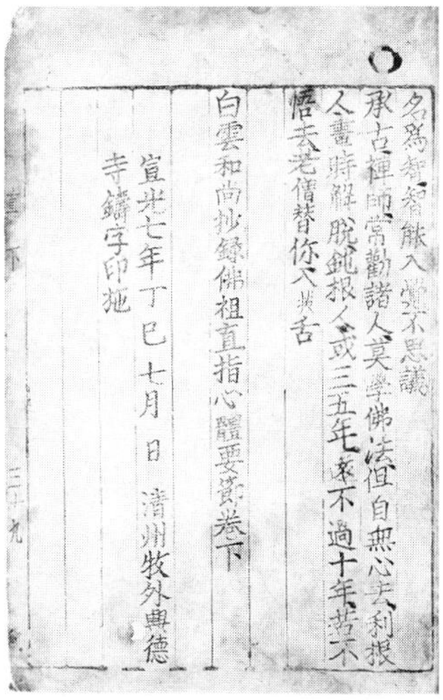

名爲智者能入不思議
承古禪師常勸諸人莫學佛法但自無心去利根
人當時解脫鈍根人或三五年遠不過十年若不
悟去老僧替你入拔舌
白雲和尚抄錄佛祖直指心體要節卷下
宣光七年丁巳七月 日 清州牧外興德
寺鑄字印施

Plate 97 Classically formed calligraphy. Final page of the *Pulch Chikchi Shimch'e Yojŏl* (the spirit's identification with the Buddha through the practice of Zen); Korea (date?) (Bibliothèque Nationale, Paris, France).

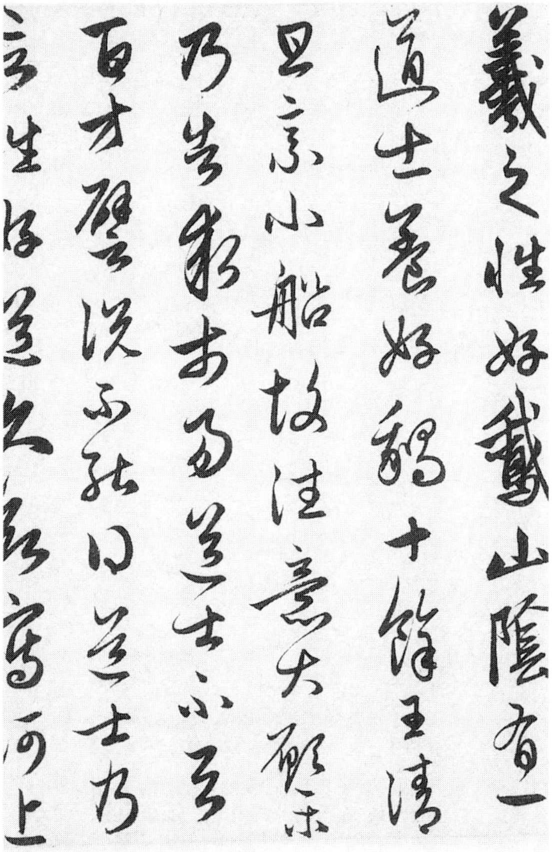

Plate 96 Cursive calligraphy, Yuan Dynasty (China). Detail of handscroll by the painter-calligrapher Zhao Mengfu (1254–1322) (Metropolitan Museum of Art, New York, USA).

Plate 98 Portrait of the poet Akahito with his Writing-Brush, Paper, and Scribe's Case, from the *Portraits of the Thirty-Six Master Poets* attributed to the artist Fujiwara Nobuzane (1176–*c.* 1265), Kamakura period (Japan) (All rights reserved).

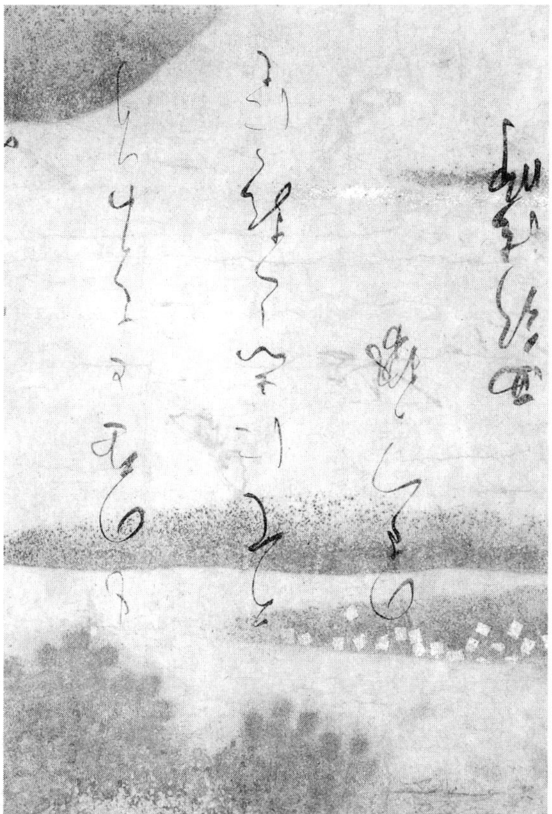

Plate 99 'Grass' calligraphy of verses by famous Poets, Kamakura period (Japan). Detail of a painting by the Emperor Fushimi (reigned 1278–1298) (Courtesy of Freer Gallery of Art, Smithsonian Institution, Washington DC, USA).

Plate 100 Educated Indian woman writing on a palm-leaf; eleventh century; Candella, Khajuraho (India) (Indian Museum, Calcutta).

Plate 102 Indian Buddhist missionary to China reading a Sanskrit manuscript. Painting from the period of the Yuan Dynasty (China) (National Palace Museum, Taipeh, Taiwan).

Plate 101 Astasāhasrikā-Prajnā-Pāramitā. Sanskrit manuscript on palm-leaf, tenth century (Nepal) (By permission of the British Library, London, UK).

Plate 103 Giovanni Boccaccio (1313–1375) at his writing-desk, with the figure of Fortune. Illustration to a French translation of his Latin-language *De Casibus Virorum et Feminarum Illustrium* 'Des cas des nobles hommes et femmes', *c.* 1415–1420, Paris (France) (cliché Bibliothèque Nationale de France, Paris, France).

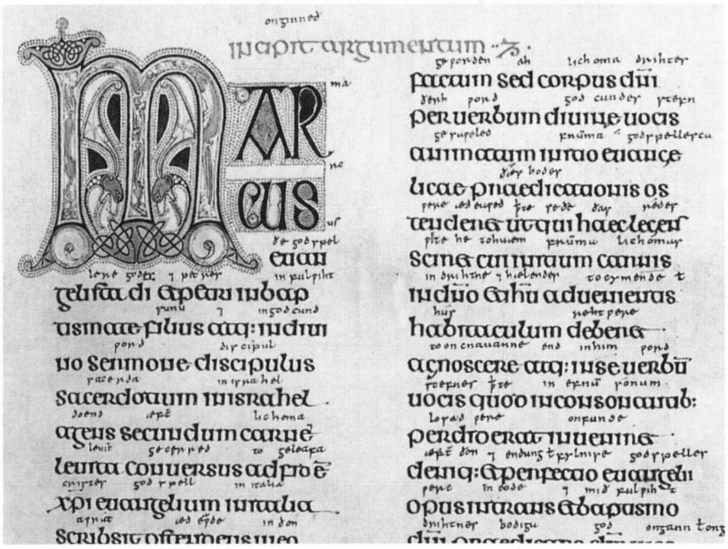

Plate 104 Marcus: initial to the Gospel of Saint Mark, from the Latin *Lindisfarne Gospels* by the scribe and illuminator Eadfrith of the island-monastery of Lindisfarne, AD 698 (England). An Anglo-Saxon translation appears between the Latin lines (By permission of The British Library, London, UK).

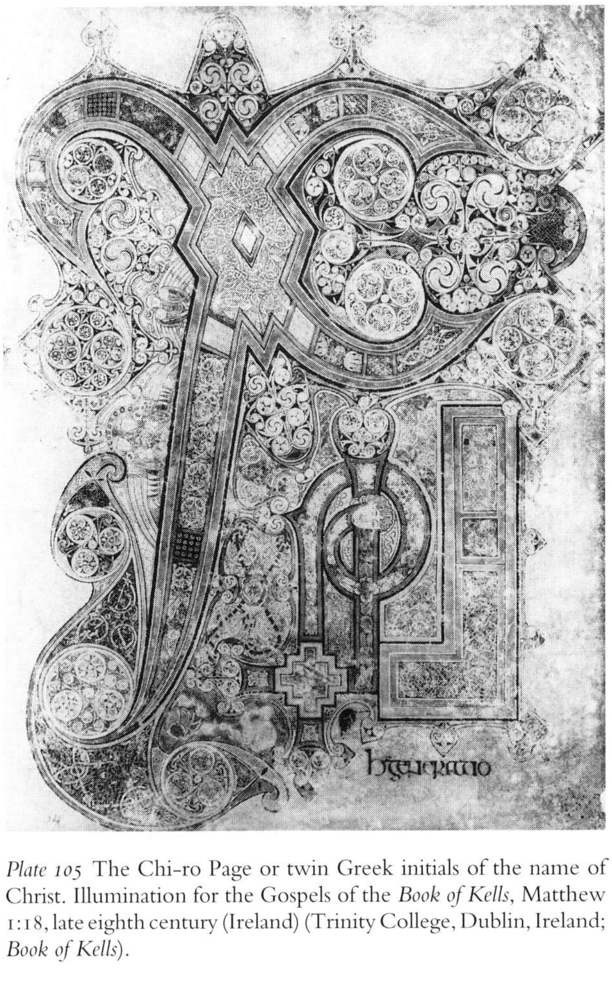

Plate 105 The Chi-ro Page or twin Greek initials of the name of Christ. Illumination for the Gospels of the *Book of Kells*, Matthew 1:18, late eighth century (Ireland) (Trinity College, Dublin, Ireland; *Book of Kells*).

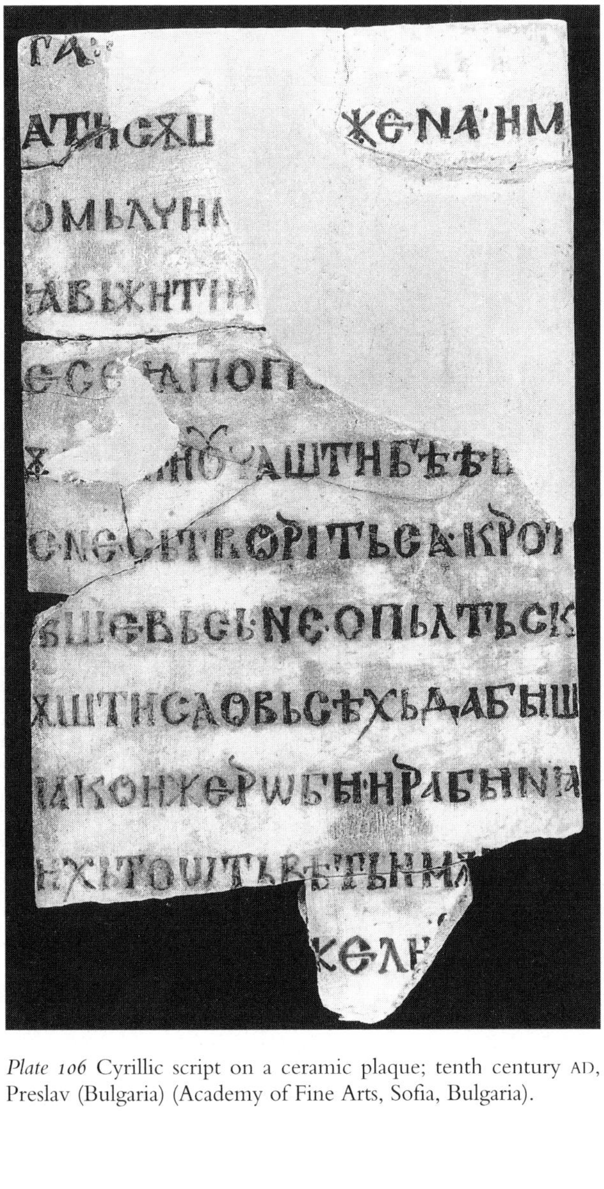

Plate 106 Cyrillic script on a ceramic plaque; tenth century AD, Preslav (Bulgaria) (Academy of Fine Arts, Sofia, Bulgaria).

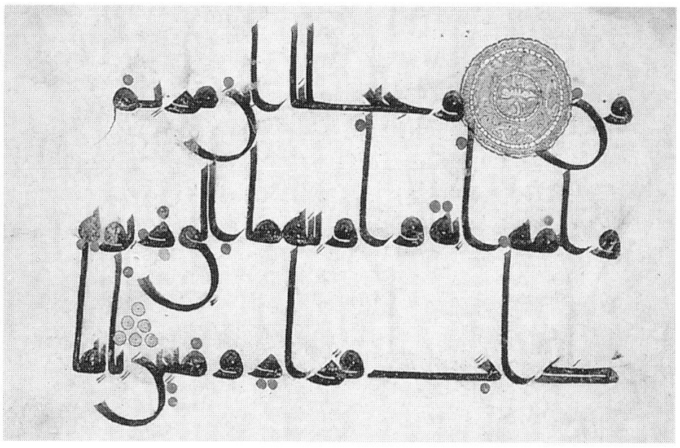

Plate 107 Page of Kūfī calligraphy from the Qur'ān on parchment. Fātimid Dynasty, tenth century AD (Al-Sabah Collection, Dār al-Athār al-Islāmiyyah, Courtesy of Museum of Islamic Art, Kuwait).

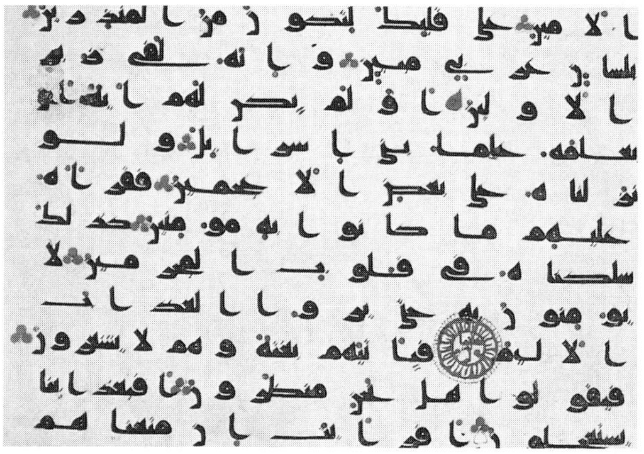

Plate 108 Page of Kūfī calligraphy from the Qur'ān on vellum; 'Abbāsid Dynasty, tenth century (Iraq) (By permission of The British Library, London, UK).

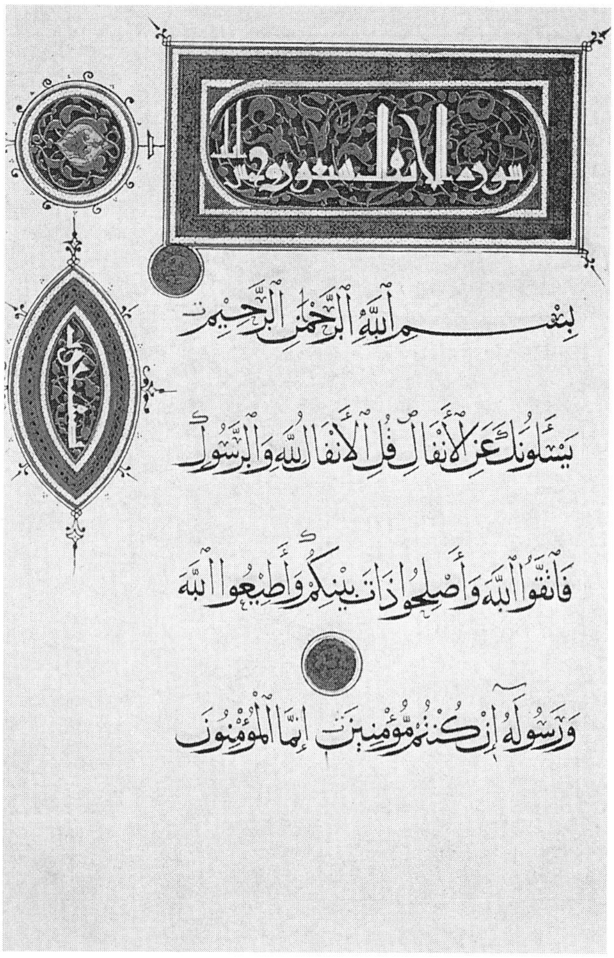

Plate 110 Page of Naskh (standard cursive) calligraphy from Qur'ān on paper, Mamlūk Dynasty, fourteenth century, Cairo, (Egypt) (By permission of The British Library, London, UK).

Plate 109 Blessing in Kūfī calligraphy on a slip-painted earthenware dish, Nīshāpūr (Iran); Sāmānid Dynasty, tenth century AD (Photo M. P. Chuzeville, Musée du Louvre, Paris, France).

Plate 111 Wall decorations in tiling and stucco with bands of thuluth: (cursive) calligraphy; *Madrasat al-'Attārīn* (Seminary of the Perfume-Sellers), Marīnīd Dynasty, fourteenth century AD, Fez (Morocco) .

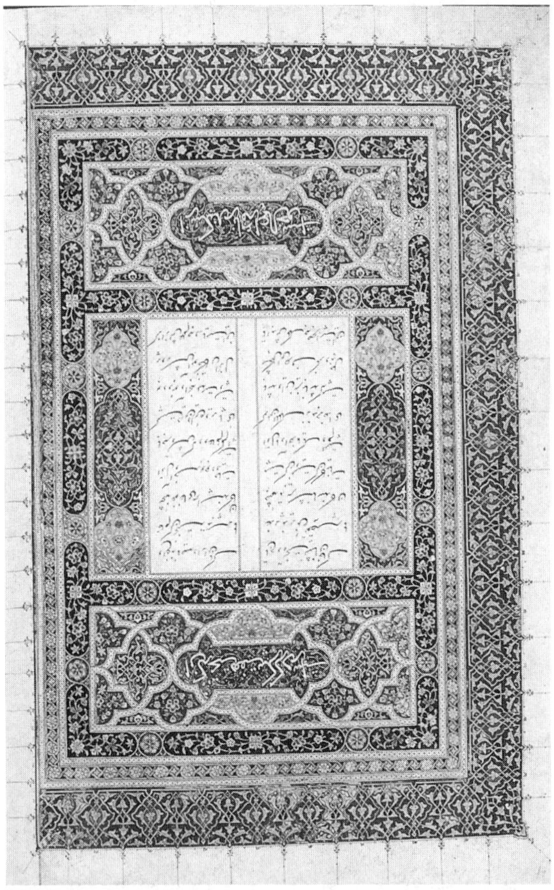

Plate 112 Arabic script as used for Persian in Nasta'līq ('hanging cursive') calligraphy. Opening illuminated page to the Khamseh or *Quintet* of Persian-language tales by the twelfth-century poet Nizāmī of Āzerbaijān, copied in Herāt in AD 1494–1495 (Afghanistan) (By permission of The British Library, London, UK).

Plate 113 Arabic script as used for Turkish in Nasta'līq ('hanging cursive') calligraphy; Illustration by the artist Qāsim Alī for the Turkish-language poems of Mīr 'Alī Shēr Nawāī (Mir Ali Sir Nevai), depicted (second from upper right) kneeling in a dream-vision in homage to the great Persian-language poets of the past from all parts of the Persianate cultural domain. From the *Sadd-i Iskandar* (Rampart of Alexander) of Mīr 'Alī Shēr Nawāī, copied in Herāt (Afghanistan) in AD 1483. Ms Elliot 339, fol. 95 v (Bodleian Library, Oxford, UK).

Plate 114 Arab scribe writing with a reed-pen upon his knee. Detail from an illustration by the artist al-Wāsiti for the Maqāmāt or 'Sessions' of the twelfth-century prosodist al-Harīrī; AD 1237, Baghdād (Iraq). (Bibliothèque Nationale, Paris, France).

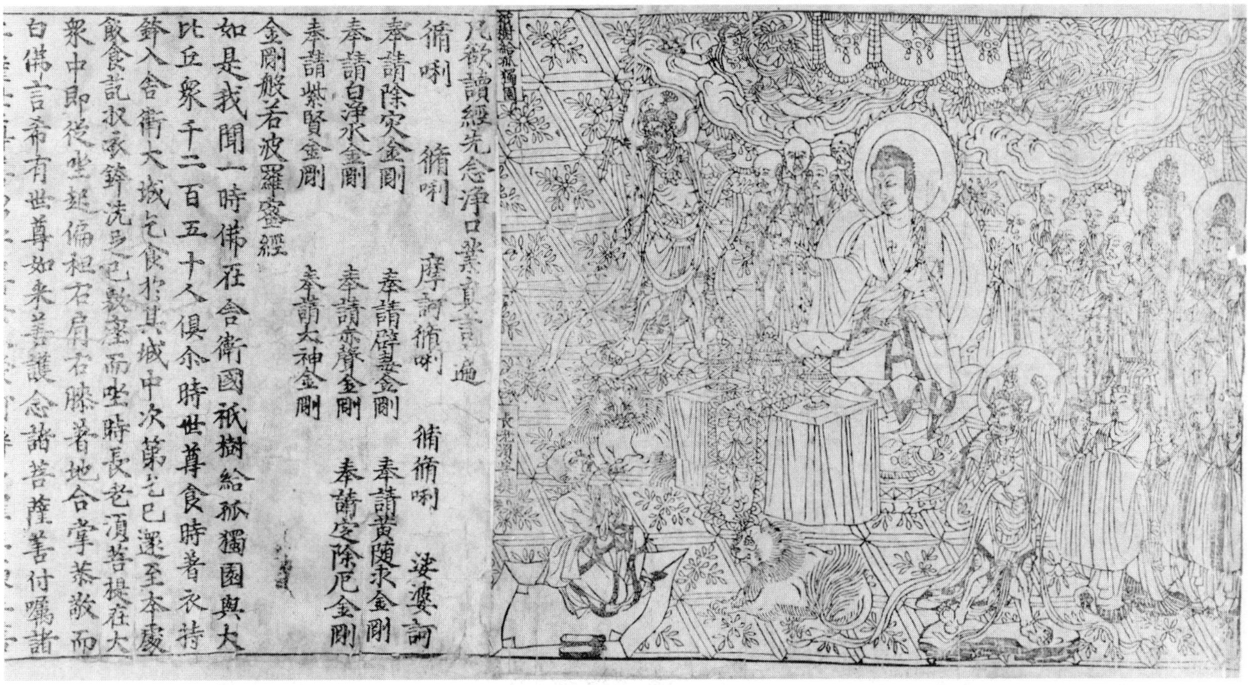

Plate 115 Chinese printing: the Chinese translation of the Sanskrit Diamond sutra. Frontispiece to the world's earliest known printed book; block-printed on paper, AD 868, Dunhuang (China) (By permission of The British Library, London, UK).

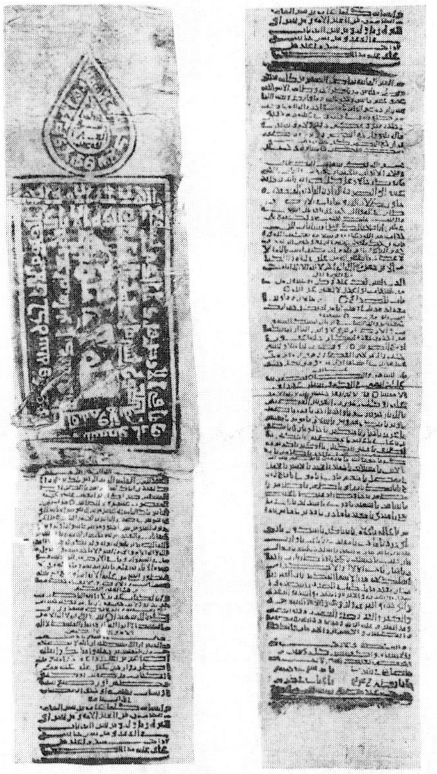

Plate 116 Arabic block-printing (West Asia); eleventh century(?). 'Printing in the Muslim world began perhaps in the 9th century, may have died out in the 14th, and could have inspired printing experiments in Europe' (after R. Bulliet) (Property of the Rare Books and Manuscript Collection of Columbia University Library, New York, USA).

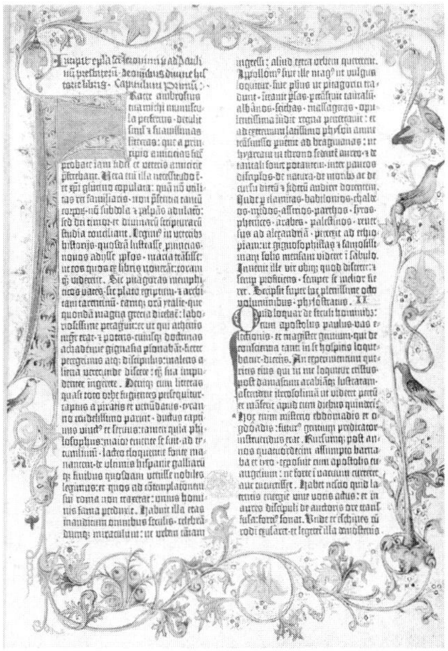

Plate 117 The 42-line bible in movable type, Mainz (Germany). Printed *c.* AD 1453–1455, probably by Gutenberg, Fust and Schöffer. (By permission of The British Library, London, UK).

Plate 118 The poet François Villon: frontispiece to the first edition of his work, with portrait in wood-block printing, and verse in movable type; Paris, printing press of Pierre Levet, 1489 (Bibliothèque Nationale, Paris, France).

Plate 119 The world as seen by the Franco-Flemish Jean Mansel: the three continents surrounded by the ocean stream as bequeathed by God to Shem (Asia), Cham (Africa) and Japheth (Europe). Cosmographical illustration to the *Fleur des Histoires* or 'Flower of Chronicles' by Jean Mansel, fifteenth century. (Bibliothèque royale Albert Ier, Brussels, Belgium).

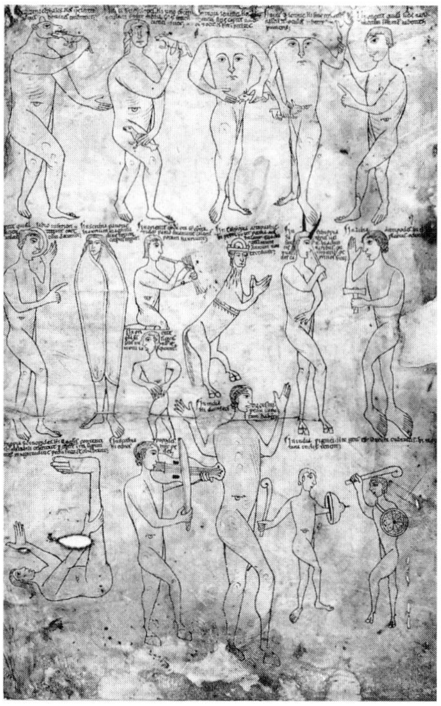

Plate 120 The monstrous creatures: a twelfth-century illustration to the works of Solinus Polyhistor (third century AD), twelfth century, Arnstein (Germany) (British Museum, London, UK).

Plate 121 Marco Polo samples the pepper crop on India's Malabar coast: illustration to a *Livre des merveilles* or 'Book of Marvels' copied for John the Fearless, Duke of Burgundy; Franco-Flemish, dated 1410 (Bibliothèque Nationale, Paris, France).

Plate 122 The Ptolemaic world map, second century AD, as published in Ulm (Germany), 1482. Africa here extends too far to the east and touches upon the fabled 'Golden Chersonese' (Malaysia), thereby erroneously transforming the Indian Ocean into a closed lake (Bibliothèque Nationale, Paris, France).

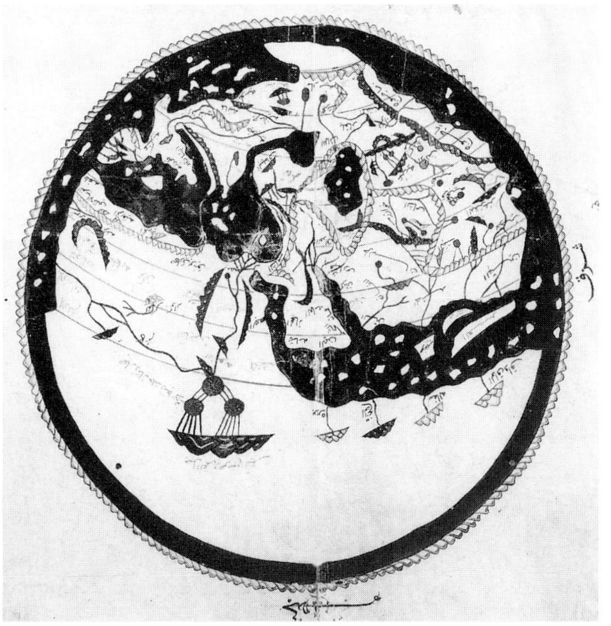

Plate 123 The medieval Arab world-view. Copy of map submitted by the Moroccan geographer al-Idrīsī of Ceuta (1100–1160) to the Norman Christian king of Sicily, Roger II, in the so-called *Kitāb Rujar* or 'Book of Roger', as reproduced in frontispiece to the manuscript of the *Muqaddima* or 'Introduction to Universal History' by the Tunisian philosopher-historian Ibn Khaldūn (1332–1406). Here an 'all-encompassing ocean' *(Bahr Muhīt)* surrounds the world-island and theoretically allows for an 'entry' *(madkhal)* between the Atlantic and Indian Oceans (Reproduced according to modern orientation, with North above) (Bodleian Library, Oxford, UK).

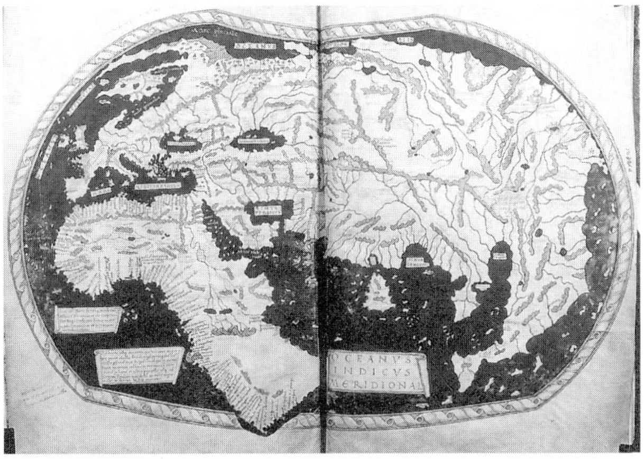

Plate 124 The world map of Henricus Martellus, Florence (Italy); dated 1489. The German cartographer Heinrich Hammer ('Henricus Martellus') was the first to record on this map the rounding of the Cape of Good Hope by the Portuguese in the preceding year, proving the Ptolemaic map wrong and that the Atlantic and Indian Oceans were indeed connected (By permission of The British Libary, London, UK).

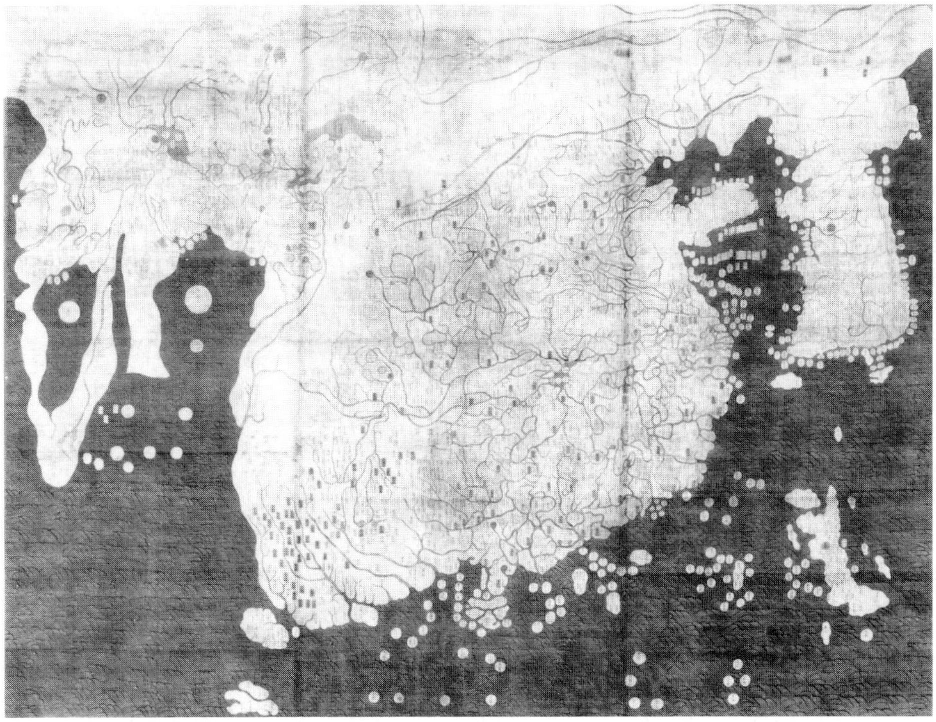

Plate 125 Detail of the Kangnido (Korea). A Korean world-map dated 1402. The detail of this copy, from 1470, follows, with the West shown above, the coasts of Malaysia, Indochina, China, Korea and the southernmost islands of Japan (Courtesy Ryûkoku University Library, Kyoto, Japan).

Plate 126 An Arabic translation of *De Materia Medica of Dioscorides*; AD 1229. The Transmission of Greek Learning to the Arabs. The Greek naturalist Dioscorides (1st century AD), copied in the Greek manner from a Byzantine manuscript but now wearing a Muslim turban, instructs two Muslim students (Bibliothèque Nationale, Paris, France).

Plate 128 Prince Shōtoku and his sons (Japan). The Transmission of Chinese Learning to the Japanese: 'Prince Shōtoku (AD 574–622) was a Buddhist and reformer who initiated direct cultural relations with the Sui Dynasty in 607. Japanese students were sent to China' (Japan) (Courbis images, London, UK).

Plate 127 The triumph of Saint Thomas Aquinas. Painting by Francesco Traini in the Church of Santa Caterina, Pisa, fourteenth century. The Transmission of Arab Learning to the Latins. Saint Thomas Aquinas (1225–1274), inspired by Christ, the Saints, and also by Plato and Aristotle, triumphs over the Spanish Muslim philosopher Ibn Rushd ('Averroës', 1126–1198) lying at his feet. 'But by quoting Latin translations of Averroës at length in apparent rebuttal, Saint Thomas thereby forced Western Christians to read this major Arab thinker thoughtfully and seriously – and this was perhaps the great Church Doctor's intention' (after Jacques Le Goff) (Photo Nicolò Orsi Battaglini Museo Nazionale, Firenze, Italy).

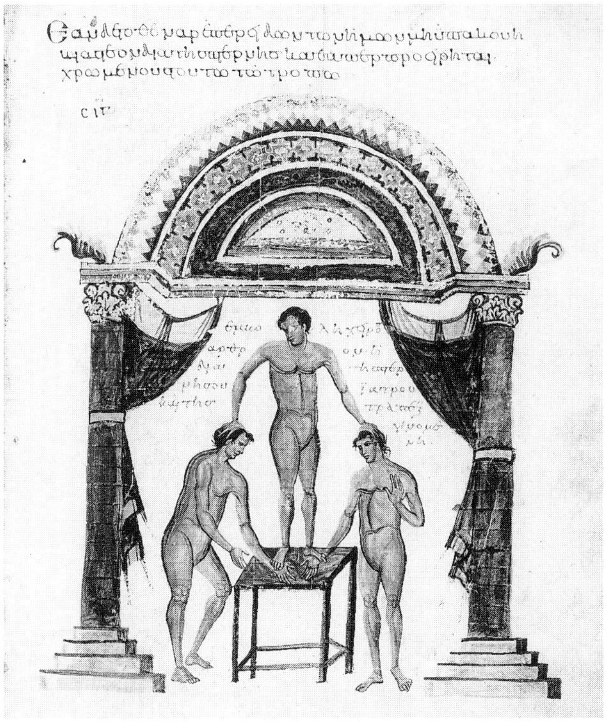

Plate 129 Miniature from a treatise on the dislocation of bones by Apollonios of Kition. Byzantine manuscript, Constantinople, tenth century (Biblioteca Medicea Laurenziana, Florence, Italy).

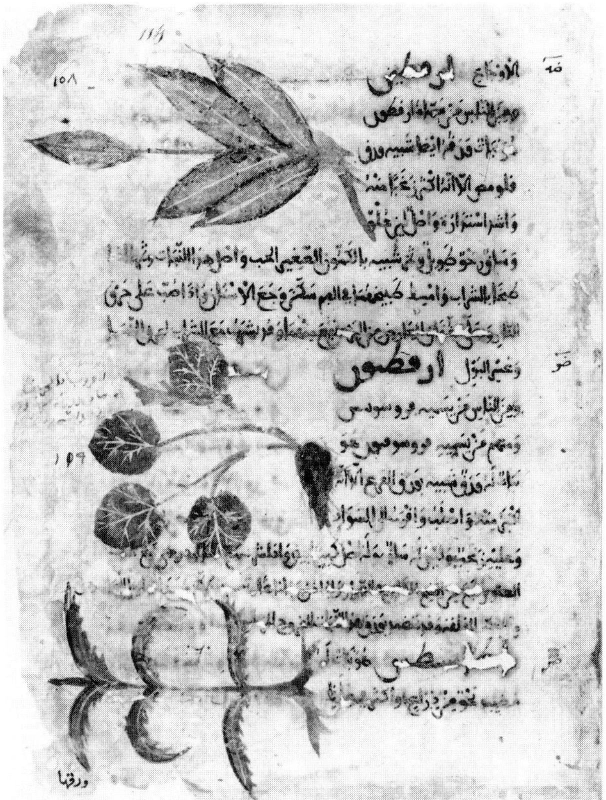

Plate 130 Page with a depiction of medicinal plants from an Arabic translation of *De Materia Medica of Dioscorides*; thirteenth century (Bibliothèque Nationale, Paris, France).

Plate 131 The Devil blows disease upon Job. Illustration to the *Moralia in Job* by Pope Gregory I (r. 590–604) (France). Early twelfth century (Bibliothèque municipale, Douai, France).

Plate 132 Church dignitary shown wearing spectacles. Cathedral of Meaux (France). Church dignitary (probably Saint Jerome): a rare fifteenth-century sculpture adorning the west portal of the thirteenth/fifteenth century. Spectacles are first attested in Western Europe in the fourteenth century (Courtesy Jean-Charles Périgaux, France).

(a)

(b)

(c)

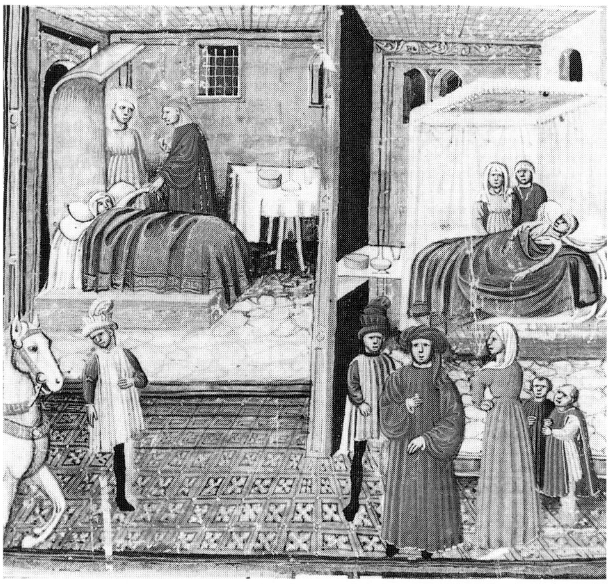

(d)

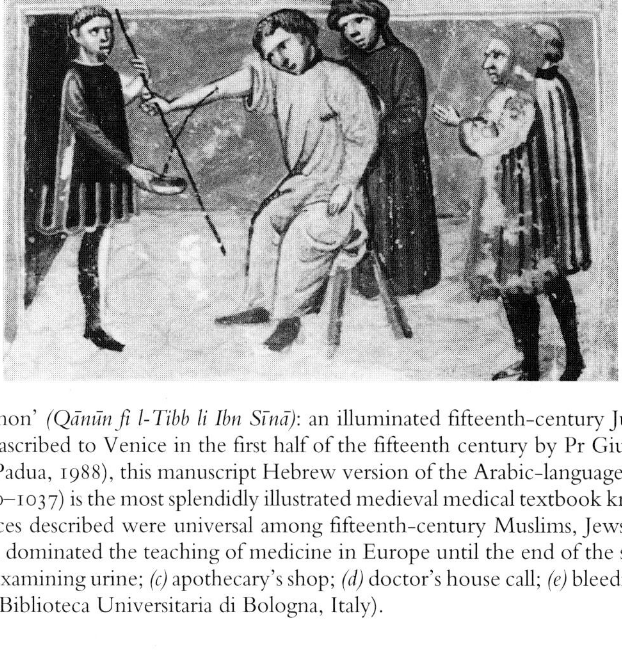

(e)

Plate 133 Avicenna's 'Medical Canon' *(Qānūn fi l-Tibb li Ibn Sīnā)*: an illuminated fifteenth-century Judaeo-Italian translation from the Arabic into Hebrew. Tentatively ascribed to Venice in the first half of the fifteenth century by Pr Giuliano Tamani *(Il Canon Medicinae di Avicenna nella tradizione ebraica,* Padua, 1988), this manuscript Hebrew version of the Arabic-language *Canon* by the great Central Asian scholar Ibn Sīnā or 'Avicenna' (980–1037) is the most splendidly illustrated medieval medical textbook known to exist. While the costumes and settings are Italian, the practices described were universal among fifteenth-century Muslims, Jews and Christians alike. In its Latin versions, the 'Canon' of Avicenna dominated the teaching of medicine in Europe until the end of the sixteenth century (after al-Hasan): *(a)* Avicenna lecturing; *(b)* doctor examining urine; *(c)* apothecary's shop; *(d)* doctor's house call; *(e)* bleeding (Photos Courtesy of Ministero per i Beni culturali e Ambientali, Biblioteca Universitaria di Bologna, Italy).

Plate 134 The astronomical observatory in Beijing (China). Built under the rule of the Mongol Emperor, Qubilay Khān (r. 1260–1294), Yuan Dynasty. (Photo from *Khubilai Khan. His Life and Times* by Morris Rossabi, University California Press Berkeley, Los Angeles, London, 1988).

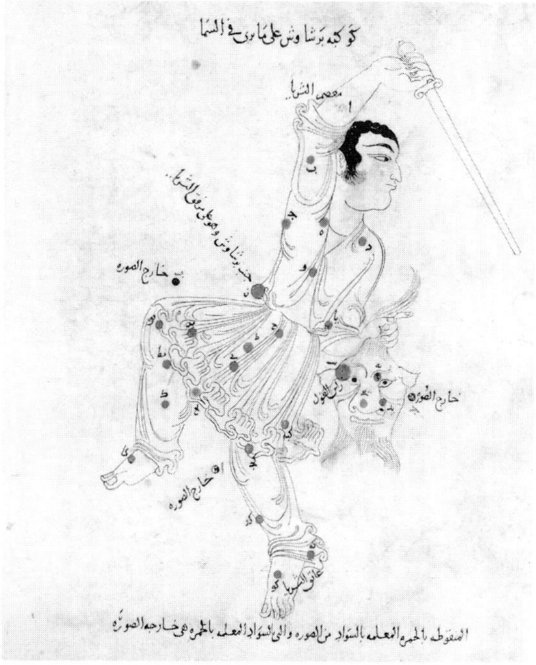

Plate 135 The constellation of Perseus (Iran). Illustration to the Arabic-language 'Book of the Fixed Stars' *(Kitāb al-Kawākib al-Thābita)* composed by 'Abd al-Rahmān al-Sūfī in *c.* AD 960, in Fārs; this text copied (probably in Fārs) in AD 1009, with drawing added several decades later. Ms Marsh 144, p. 111 (Bodleian Library, Oxford, UK).

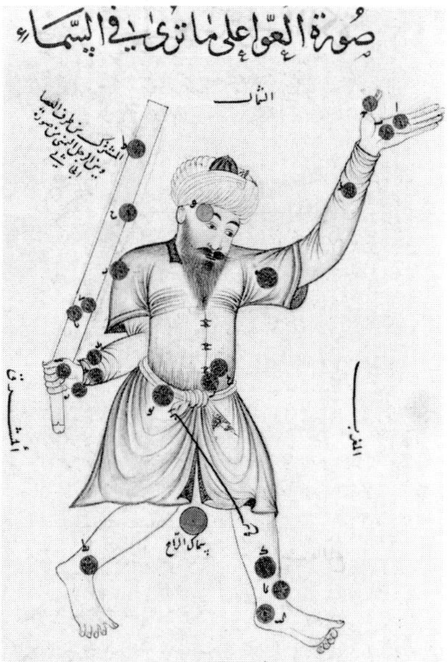

Plate 136 Central Asian representation of the constellation of Boötes. Illustration to the Arabic-language treatise of 'Abd al-Rahmān al-Sūfī, as copied for the astronomer-Prince Ulugh-Beg of Samarkand (modern Uzbekistan) in *c.* 1430–1440 (Bibliothèque Nationale, Paris, France).

Plate 137 The constellation of Aquarius. An illustration from the *Liber de stellis fixarum* (The Book of Fixed Stars), a thirteenth-century Latin translation of an Arabic treatise. (Bibliothèque Nationale, Paris, France).

Plate 138 Celestial globe (Iran). Dated AD 1430/1431 and signed by Muhammad ibn Ja'far ibn 'Umar al-Asturlābī ('The Astrolabe-Maker'), also known as Hilālī ('He of the Crescent Moon') (British Museum, London, UK).

Plate 139 The astrolabe (Iran). Miniature depicting the thirteenth-century Iranian scholar Nasīr al-Dīn al- Tūsī and his colleagues in their observatory at Marāgheh, in Iran; from a *Scientific Anthology* compiled and illustrated in Shīrāz in *c.* AD 1410 (Courtesy Istanbul Üniversitesi Rektorlügü, Turkey).

Plate 141 The astrolabe (France). Clerics measuring the heavens by the astrolabe. Illustration to the Psalter of Queen Blanche de Castille, mother to King Louis IX of France, thirteenth century (cliché Bibliothèque Nationale, Paris, France).

Plate 140 The astrolabe (Syria). Miniature depicting Aristotle, garbed as a Muslim scholar, instructing Arab pupils in the use of the astrolabe. Illustration to the Arabic-language 'Choice Wisdoms and Finest Sayings' *(Mukhtār al-Hikam wa Mahāsin al- Kalim)* by al-Mubashshir, first half of the thirteenth century (Istanbul, Topkapi Palace Library, Ahmet III, 3206).

Plate 142 The astrolabe (Egypt). Brass astrolabe made in Cairo in AD 1235–1236 by 'Abd al-Karīm al-Misrī (British Museum, London, UK).

Plate 143 The astrolabe (Spain). Brass astrolabe made in Islamic Spain by Ibrāhīm ibn Sā'id al-Sahlī, eleventh century (National Archaeological Museum, Madrid, Spain).

Plate 144 Stone of the Sun or Aztec calendar stone (Mexico). Basalt relief, diameter 360 cm, weight 25.5, metric tonnes, from the ancient Mexico-Tenochtitlán (Mexico City). The main image is the face of the Sun God, Tonatiuh, with protruding tongue in the form of a knife, and holding human hearts in his hands. He is surrounded by the symbolic depiction of the four previous ages, and successive rings displaying the glyphs of the twenty days, sun rays, jewels, and two Fire-Serpents facing each other. Late Post-Classic Period, AD 1325–1521, Aztec Civilization (Courtesy Institūto de Antropología e Historia, INAH, Mexico City, Mexico).

Plate 145 Emperor Constantine (right), as fourth-century founder of Constantinople, symbolically offers his walled city, and Emperor Justinian (left), as sixth-century founder of Hagia Sophia, symbolically offers his Church, to the Virgin and Child. Note halo around imperial as well as saintly figures. Lintel mosaic in Aya Sofya, Constantinople, tenth century (All rights reserved).

Plate 146 Saint Demetrius in the pose of Imperial Protector over the Archbishop (the religious authority) and the Governor (the secular authority) of Thessaloniki. Church of Saint Demetrius (Dimitriou), *c.* AD 635, Thessaloniki (Greece) (Courtesy Greek National Tourist Office).

Plate 147 The Christ-child as Imperial Pantocrator with the Virgin Enthroned, Byzantium. Icon on wood, Constantinople, *c.* AD 1200 (Andrew Mellon Collection, National Gallery of Art, Washington DC, USA).

Plate 148 Emperor John II Comnenus and Empress Irene, with the Virgin and Child. Mosaic panel from the south tribune, Aya Sofya, Constantinople, twelfth century (All rights reserved).

Plate 149 Christ crowns the German emperor Otto II and his Byzantine-born consort, the Empress Theophano, Byzantium. Ivory panel, Constantinople, tenth century (Photo R. M. N.; Musée du Louvre, Paris, France).

Plate 152 Prince Milutin of Serbia symbolically offers his church of the annunciation at Gracanica. Fresco, *c.* 1320 (Yugoslavia) (All rights reserved).

Plate 150 Emperor Manuel II Palaeologus. Manuscript illumination, Constantinople, first half of the fifteenth century, Byzantium (Bibliothèque Nationale, Paris, France).

Plate 151 Tsar Ivan Alexander of Bulgaria and his family. From the Gospels of Tsar Ivan Alexander, written and illuminated in 1355–6 in Tŭrnovo (Bulgaria) (By permission of The British Library, London, UK).

Plate 153 Baptism of the Bulgarians under Boris I in 865. Bulgarian manuscript (tenth century?) (Bulgaria) (Academy of Fine Arts, Sofia, Bulgaria).

Plate 154 Head of an archangel. Detail of a mural from the Church of Saint George in Sofia (Bulgaria), tenth century (Academy of Fine Arts, Sofia, Bulgaria).

Plate 155 Saint Theodore, ceramic icon from Preslav (Bulgaria). tenth century? (Academy of Fine Arts, Sofia, Bulgaria).

Plate 156 The Transfiguration. From a Gospel according to the Four Evangelists (Armenia) twelfth to thirteenth centuries (Freer Gallery of Art, Smithonian Institution, Washington DC, USA).

Plate 157 Baptism of the Rus' (Academy of Fine Arts, Sofia, Bulgaria).

Plate 158 Saint Boris and Saint Gleb, Moscow school. Icon on wood, late thirteenth or early fourteenth century (Russian Museum, St Petersburg, Russia).

Plate 159 The Trinity. Icon on wood by Andrei Rublev, Moscow, *c.* 1411. The Trinity, as symbolized by the Three Angels of Abraham (Tretyakov Gallery, Moscow, Russia).

Plate 160 The Saviour. Icon on wood by Andrei Rublev, Moscow, early fifteenth century (Tretyakov Gallery, Moscow, Russia).

Plate 161 Equestrian bronze statuette of Charlemagne; *c.* AD 800. Note that the Emperor still rides without stirrups (*L'Univers des Formes*. Gallimard, Paris, France).

Plate 162 Frankish mounted warriors, Carolingian Empire. Detail of an illustration to Psalm 59: The Campaigns of Joab; from the *St Gall Golden Psalter*, *c.* AD 841–883. The riders now use stirrups, of which this is the earliest known European depiction (*L'Univers des Formes*. Gallimard, Paris, France).

Plate 163 Rabanus Maurus (784–856), Abbot of Fulda, presents his book to Pope Gregory IV, Carolingian Empire. Manuscript illustration, early ninth century (Österreichische Nationalbibliothek, Vienna, Austria).

Plate 164 Saint John's mystic vision of the Adoration of the Lamb, Carolingian Empire. Illustration to the prologue by Saint Jerome for a volume of the Latin Gospels copied for Charlemagne's court, early ninth century. From the *Gospels of Saint-Médard de Soissons* (Bibliothèque Nationale, Paris, France).

Plate 165 Dragon-head, carved head-post from the Viking ship burial at Oseberg (Norway); *c.* AD 850. (Universitets Oldsaksamling; University Collection of Antiquities, Oslo, Norway).

Plate 166 Dragon-head, ornament to a horse's harness-bow from Mammen (Denmark). Gilt bronze (the wood is a modern reconstruction); ninth to tenth centuries (National Museum of Denmark).

Plate 167 Viking warrior's head from Sigtuna (Sweden). Carved post-ending fashioned out of an elk's antler; tenth to eleventh centuries (Photo Nils Lagergren; National Historical Museum, Sweden).

Plate 168 Head of King Eystein of Norway, Bergen (Norway); dated 1122, with crown bearing rune lettering and a cross, from the twelfth-century Mariae Kirke ('Mary's Church') (Photo Ann-Mari Olsen; Historisk Museum Universitet i Bergen, Norway).

Plate 169 The Frankish emperor Charles the Bald (843–877) receives a Bible in homage from the Abbot of the Monastery of Saint Martin de Tours. The emperor, surrounded by his lay nobility at the upper level, is blessed directly by the Hand of God, while the clergy stand respectfully below. From the *Bible of Charles the Bald*, *c*. AD 870 (Bibliothèque Nationale, Paris, France).

Plate 171 The ArchbishopThomas Becket slain in 1170 by the knights of King Henry II of England in his own Cathedral of Canterbury. Henry II was never able to live down the scandal of his Archbishop's martyrdom; the Church canonized Thomas as a saint. Miniature from a Latin Psalter, England, *c*. 1200 (By permission of The British Library, UK).

Plate 170 Rex a Deo Coronatus, German Emperor Henri II. 'The King Crowned by God': German Emperor Henry II (r. 1004–1024), represented crowned directly by Christ, receives from the saints Paul and Peter both his sword of secular power, and his staff – topped by a bishop's mitre – of religious power, making him in effect a priest-king (Bayerische Staatsbibliothek, München, Germany).

Plate 172 Robert d'Anjou, king of Naples, receives the crown on his knees from the sainted Bishop Louis of Toulouse; painting by Simone Martini of Siena, *c*. AD 1319–1320 (Courtesy Museo Nazionale di Capodimonte, Naples, Italy).

Plate 173 Queen Béatrice de Bourbon in the Basilica of Saint Denis (France); dated 1383, tomb effigy in the Basilica of Saint Denis (Photo R. Delon/Castelet, Paris, France).

Plate 174 The wedding of the Bruges-based Italian merchant Giovanni Arnolfini to Giovanna Cenami by Jan van Eyck, Bruges (Belgium). Oil painting; dated AD 1436 (National Gallery, London, UK).

Plate 175 Saint Bridget of Vadstena. Detail from a late fifteenth-century retable from Törnevall Church, Ostergötland (Sweden) (Photo J. Anderson, Historical Museum, Antikvarisk-Topografiska Arkivet, Stockholm, Sweden).

Plate 176 The Virgin of Kreuzlowa (Poland). Detail of wooden statue, fifteenth century (Courtesy National Museum, Cracow, Poland).

Plate 177 The Austrian lyric poet and knight Walther von der Vogelweide. Illumination from the *Manessischen Liederhandschrift* (poetry manuscript), Germany, early fourteenth century (Universitätsbibliothek, Heidelberg, Germany).

Plate 178 Courtly love: a kneeling knight and his lady, Westphalia (Germany). Painted coffer; *c.* AD 1330; 6.7 × 18.8 × 10.2 cm, 'Darstellung der Waffenreichung' (Westfälisches Landesmuseum für Kunst und Kulturgeschichte, Münster, Germany).

Plate 179 Musical notation: detail from the missal of Saint-Denis (France); *c.* 1350–1351. Modern musical notation is a medieval European invention ascribed to the Italian monk Guido d'Arezzo (*c.* 990–1050) (Victoria and Albert Museum, London, UK).

Plate 180 Dante admonishes the city of Florence by Domenico di Michelino, Florence (Italy); mid-fifteenth century. The painter evokes the entire three-part cosmology – Inferno, Purgatorio, Paradiso – of Dante's Divine Comedy, whose first verses appear in the poet's open book. Painting preserved in the Cathedral of Santa Maria dei Fiori, Firenze (Photo Nicolò Orsi Battaglini, Museo Nationale, Firenze, Italy).

Plate 181 Mecca, Mosque of the Ḥaram with the Ka'ba at the centre. The Ka'ba, a cube-like construction which houses the black stone towards which Muslims turn in prayer, is surrounded by a paved path along which pilgrims perform their ritual circumambulation. (Courtesy Serageldin, I).

Plate 182 Bedouin girl with camel herd. Illustration by the artist al-Wāsitī to the 'Sessions' or *Maqāmāt* of the twelfth-century prosodist al-Harīrī; AD 1237, Baghdād (Iraq) (Bibliothèque Nationale, Paris, France).

Plate 183 The setting out of a pilgrim caravan. Illustration by the artist al-Wāsitī to the 'Sessions' or *Maqāmāt* of the twelfth-century prosodist al-Harīrī; AD 1237, Baghdād (Iraq) (Bibliothèque Nationale, Paris, France).

Plate 184 Travellers in an Iraqi village. Illustration by the artist al-Wāsitī to the 'Sessions' or *Maqāmāt* of the twelfth-century prosodist al-Harīrī; AD 1237, Baghdād (Iraq) (Bibliothèque Nationale, Paris, France).

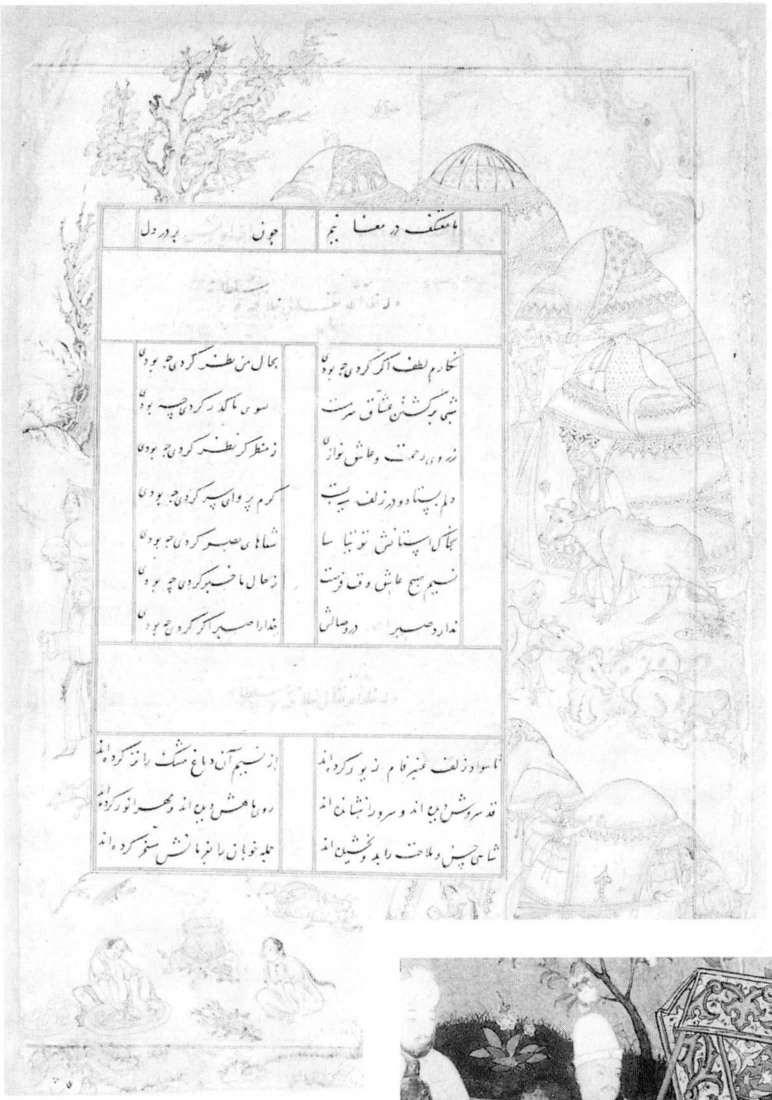

Plate 185 Nomad families with Turco-Mongol-style round felt tents (Yurts). Border illumination attributed to the artist Junayd for the Persian-language *Dīwān* (collected verse) of an acculturated Turco-Mongol ruler of Iraq and Western Iran, Sultan Ahmad Jalā'ir; *c.* AD 1405, Baghdād (Iraq) (Freer Gallery of Art, Smithsonian Institution, Washington DC, USA).

Plate 186 The feast of Tīmūr's enthronement beneath his royal *yurt*, Herāt (Afghanistan). Detail of an illustration of the accession of Tīmūr to power in the city of Balkh (modern Afghanistan) in AD 1370, by the artist Bihzād, for the Persian-language chronicle of Tīmūr by Sharaf al-Dīn Yazdī, the *Zafar-Nāmeh* or 'Book of Victory'; Herāt (modern Afghanistan), manuscript dated AD 1467–1468, illuminations added *c.* 1488 (The John Work Garrett Library of The Johns Hopkins University, Baltimore, USA).

Plate 187 Prince Bayād plays the lute before the Lady Riyād and her handmaidens. Illustration to the Arabic-language 'Romance of Bayād and Riyād' *(Hadīth Bayād wa Riyâd)*; Spain or Morocco, thirteenth century AD (Courtesy Biblioteca Apostolica Vaticana, Vatican).

Plate 188 The handmaiden Shamūl delivers a letter from the Lady Riyād to Prince Bayād. Illustration to the Arabic-language 'Romance of Bayād and Riyād' (*Hadīth Bayād wa Riyād)*. Muffled in a veil when out of doors, handmaidens like this served as a link between the divided worlds of upper-class women and men; Spain or Morocco, thirteenth century AD (Biblioteca Apostolica Vaticana, Vatican).

Plate 189 Traditional mansion (Yemen) (Photo Photothèque UNESCO, Paris).

(a) (b) (c) (d) (e)

Plate 190 Pre-Islamic coins: *(a)* Sasanian Iran: silver *drachma* of Emperor Khusraw II Parwēz r. AD 591–628, crowned with the wings of the god of war and victory, Verethragna (Bibliothèque Nationale, Paris, France). *(b)* Byzantium: reverse side of a gold *solidus* emitted by Emperor Constantine IV (r. AD 668–685), depicting the Cross on a staged platform flanked by the Emperors Tiberius II (r. 578–582) and Heraclius (r. AD 610–641) (Bibliothèque Nationale, Paris, France). *(c)* Byzantium: reverse side of another gold *solidus* emitted by Constantine IV, displaying the Cross on its staged platform (Bibliothèque Nationale, Paris, France). *(d)* Byzantium: reverse side of a gold *solidus* emitted by Justinian II (first reign: AD 685–695), depicting the Emperor holding the Cross on its staged platform (Bibliothèque Nationale, Paris, France). *(e)* Tang China: bronze coin of the 'Shun Tian Era' (*Shun Tian yuan bao* = AD 760), struck by Shi Siming in rebellion against the Tang (Bibliothèque Nationale, Paris, France).

(a) (b) (c) (d) (e)

Plate 191 Early figure-bearing coins of the Umayyad Dynasty: *(a)* Sasanian-type Umayyad silver *drachma* (dirham). Obverse. Struck for the first Umayyad caliph, Mu'āwiya ibn Abī Sufyān, with the Arabic inscription *Bismillāh* ('In the Name of God'), AD 661/2 at Dārābjird, Iran (Bibliothèque Nationale, Paris, France). *(b–c)* Byzantine-type Umayyad gold *solidus* (dīnār). Struck for the Umayyad caliph 'Abd al-Malik ibn Marwān between AD 691 and 694 in Damascus. Undated. Obverse shows the caliph in Byzantine-style cloak flanked by two officers. Reverse shows de-Christianized motif of a pillar, with cross-bar removed, on a staged platform, with the Arabic inscription *Bismillāh, lā Ilāha ilā-Llāh Waḥdahu, Muḥammad Rasūl Allāh* (In the Name of God, there is no god but God the One, Muḥammad is the Prophet of God) (Bibliothèque Nationale, Paris, France). *(d–e)* Byzantine-type Umayyad copper fals. Struck for the Umayyad caliph 'Abd al-Malik (r. AD 685–705) in Jerusalem. Undated. The obverse shows the caliph, with sword, in a so-called 'orant' or praying stance, with the Arabic inscription *Muḥammad Rasūl Allāh* (Muḥammad is the Prophet of God). The reverse still displays the Greek letter M, a value-sign (= '40 *nummi*) inherited from the Byzantines (Bibliothèque Nationale, Paris, France).

(a) (b) (c) (d) (e)

Plate 192 Islamic coins with inscriptions only: *(a)* Umayyad gold dīnār. Reverse. First issue, eschewing all figurative designs, struck for the Umayyad caliph 'Abd al-Malik ibn Marwān – in Damascus? – AD 696–697. The Arabic inscription reads Allāh Aḥad, *Allāh al-Ṣamad, lam yalid wa lam yūlad* (God is One, God is Eternal, He has neither begotten nor been begotten) (Bibliothèque Nationale, Paris, France). *(b–c)* Spanish Latin/Arabic Umayyad gold *solidus* or dīnār. Struck in AD 716–717 in both Latin and Arabic, but eschewing all figurative designs, in newly-conquered Spain, under the reign of the Umayyad caliph Sulaymān. Obverse (in Latin) shows a star. Reverse (in Arabic) displays the Islamic profession of faith (Bibliothèque Nationale, Paris, France). *(d)* Fāṭimid gold dīnār. Reverse. Struck – with gold dust from the bend of the river Niger – in Qayrawān (Tunisia) in AD 912–913 for the Fāṭimid emir 'Abdallāh, claimant to the caliphate against the 'Abbāsids, with his title on the reverse: *Al-Imām al-Mahdī Bi-Llāh.* The earlier Islamic dynasties enjoyed a virtual monopoly of access to the sources of African gold. (Bibliothèque Nationale, Paris, France). *(e)* Almoravid-type gold dīnar. Reverse. Struck in Seville (Spain) in AD 1144–1145 for the Almohad caliph Tāshfīn ibn 'Alī. (Bibiothèque Nationale, Paris, France).

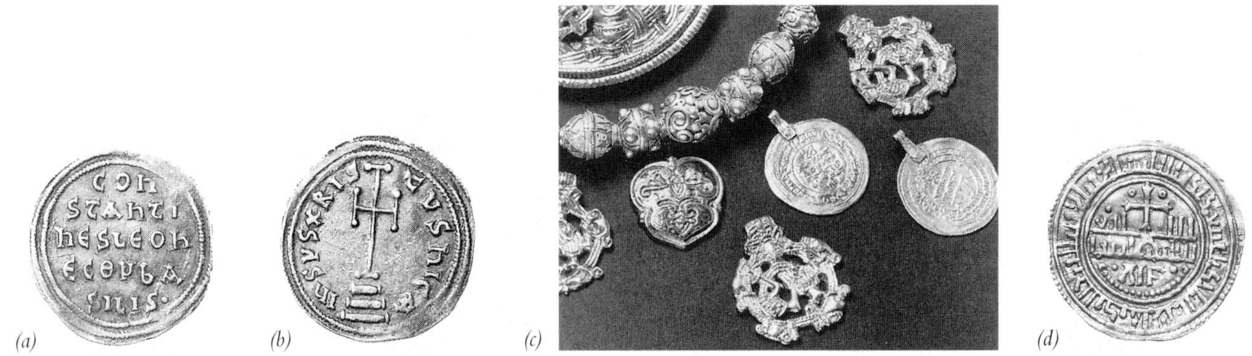

Plate 193 Impact of Islamic coins on Christian Europe: *(a–b)* Islamic-influenced Byzantine coinage: silver *miliarèsion* struck for Emperor Constantine V (r. 740–755, a partisan of the Iconoclasts, eschewing all imagery. Obverse (in Latin) bears the Emperor's name; reverse displays the Cross on its staged platform (Bibliothèque Nationale, Paris, France). *(c)* 'Abbāsid silver Dirhams from the Swedish Viking hoard of Vårby. Converted into pendants, these tenth-century AD 'Abbāsid coins from Iraq were found in a hoard of Viking jewellery concealed beneath a stone at Vårby, Södermanland, beside the water route from Stockholm to Helgö (National Historical Museum, Stockholm, Sweden). *(d)* Gold Almoravid-type *(maravedí)* Castilian dīnār. Obverse. Struck by King Alfonso VIII of Castile in Toledo in AD 1255. Early Christian Castilian coins closely imitated earlier Spanish-Arabic models, even to their inscriptions. Above the coin's Arabic calligraphy is stamped, however, a distinct Christian cross (Bibliothèque Nationale, Paris, France).

Plate 194 European-wide reversion to the gold standard: *(a)* Silver coin of Charlemagne. Struck at Mainz, Germany, between AD 806 and 814. Western Christian Europeans' resumption of gold coinage only occurred after their conquest of most of the cities of Islamic Spain, with their large reserves of West African gold, in the course of the thirteenth century (Bibliothèque Nationale, Paris, France). *(b)* Gold franc of King John the Good of France. Struck at Paris, France, in 1360 and known as the 'first franc' (Bibliothèque Nationale, Paris, France). *(c)* Venetian gold ducat. This issue was struck in Venice in 1485–1486 under Doge Marco Barbarigo, shown on the reverse kneeling in homage to Mark the Evangelist, the City's patron Saint. The Venetian ducat became the prevailing, standard currency of the fifteenth-century Mediterranean (Bibliothèque Nationale, Paris, France). *(d)* The first Ottoman gold coin: the Sultānī. Reverse. Struck in Constantinople (Qusṭanṭiniyya) AD 1478–1479 by Sultan Mehmed (Muḥammad) II. The Ottomans struck no gold coinage before their conquest of Constantinople in 1453; Sultan Mehmed II ordered this issue, based on the Venetian ducat's weight and standard, as befitting the new imperial dignity of his state (Bibliothèque Nationale, Paris, France; Cabinet des Médailles).

Plate 195 Mausoleum of Shāh Ismā'īl the Sāmānid, Bukhārā (Uzbekistan); *c.* AD 907. The design of this mausoleum in brickwork, dome and four pointed arches, which later inspired royal Muslim tombs in India, was ultimately derived from the pre-Islamic Sasanian design of the fire-temple (Persian *chār-tāq*, 'four arches') (Photo Photothèque UNESCO, Paris, France).

Plate 196 Tomb of Ghiyāṣ u'ddin Tughluq, Delhi (India); *c.* AD 1325 (Photo from reproductions in *Delhi: Architectural Remains of the Delhi Sultanate Period* by Tatsuno Yamamoto, Matsuo Ara and Takifusa Tsukinowa, published by the Institute of Oriental Culture, University of Tokyo).

Plate 197 Madrasa 'of the Citadel', Baghdād (Iraq); *c.* AD 1240–1250. Brickwork and pointed arches decorated in stucco worked into *muqarnas* or 'stalactites'. The earliest *madrasa* or centre of higher Islamic learning of this type was founded in Baghdād in the eleventh century AD (Photo G. Degeorge. In Flammarion/UNESCO, p. 46).

Plate 198 Court of Lions in the Alhambra (*al-Dār al-Hamrā'*: 'The Red Mansion', Grenada (Spain), built by the Nasrid ruler Muhammad V (r. 1354–1391). Brickwork and pointed arches decorated in stucco worked into *muqarnas* or 'stalactites', built around a patio and fountain (Photo ICOMOS, Paris).

Plate 199 Pointed blind niche or *mihrāb* indicating the direction *(qibla)* of Mecca for prayer, flanked on each side by a preacher's pulpit *(mimbar)*, fashioned in AD 1310 under the Mongol Il-Khān ruler Oljeytü in the eleventh century. Friday Mosque *(Masjid-i Jāmi')*, Iṣfahān (Iran) (Courtesy Kamzan Adl).

Plate 200 Multi-lobed pointed *mihrāb* (adorned with Chinese porcelains) of the Juma Mosque on Mafia Island (Kenya); late fourteenth or fifteenth century (Photo Unwin, S. in *General History of Africa*, UNESCO, Paris, 1984, vol. IV, ch. 18).

Plate 201 Multi-lobed horse shoe pointed gateway with *muqarnas* or 'stalactites', leading from the courtyard to the prayer hall, in the Qarawiyyīn Mosque, Fez (Morocco) – founded in AD 859, but much restored in the twelfth, fourteenth and seventeenth centuries (All rights reserved).

Plate 202 Minaret of the Great Mosque of Qayrawān (Tunisia).Umayyad Dynasty, AD 724; lantern and dome restored in the thirteenth century (All rights reserved).

Plate 204 Minarets of the Mosque of al-Azhar, Cairo (Egypt).The minarets are fifteenth and very early sixteenth-century Mamlūk Dynasty additions to the Mosque al-Azhar, founded in AD 976 by the Fātimids (Photo G. Degeorges; UNESCO Photothèque, Paris, France).

Plate 203 Minaret of the 'Booksellers' *(Kutubiyya)*, Marrakech (Morocco). Almohad Dynasty, twelfth century (Photo Roland Michaud, Rapho).

Plate 205 Minarets flanking the gateway to the Mosque of Jenne (Mali). Built of sun-dried mud, this style of mosque goes back to the fourteenth century, but requires constant restoration after the annual rains – hence the last reconstruction of the Mosque of Jenne occurred as late as 1935 (Photo ICOMOS, Paris, France).

Plate 206 Minaret of the Mosque of Sāmarrā (Iraq). 'Abbāsid Dynasty, in brickwork, AD 848–52 – often considered evocative of an ancient Mesopotamian ziggurat (Photo ICOMOS, Paris, France).

Plate 207 Twin stonework minarets flanking the gateway to the 'Blue *Madrasa*', *Gök Medrese*, Sivas (Turkey). Founded by the Seljuk sultans of Rūm in AD 1271/2. Later Ottoman pencil-shaped minarets derive from this style (All rights reserved).

Plate 208 Minaret of Jām (Afghanistan). Brickwork, stucco and blue tiling. Ghōrid Dynasty, *c.* AD 1162–1202. The minaret was discovered in the mountainous Afghan interior only in 1957 and was restored by UNESCO in 1975, but now lies under threat of collapse. The mosque and surrounding city have vanished (All rights reserved).

Plate 209 The Qutb Minār, Delhi (India). Red sandstone; begun by the Ghōrid conquerors of northern India in *c.* 1199–1200, in a synthesis of Ghōrid Afghan and local Hindu styles, top rebuilt in *c.* 1375 (Photo from reproductions in *Delhi: Architectural Remains of the Delhi Sultanate Period* by Tatsuno Yamamoto, Matsuo Ara and Takifusa Tsukinowa, published by the Institute of Oriental Culture, University of Tokyo).

Plate 210 Dimna the Jackal and the Lion-King, Baghdād (Iraq). Illustration to the animal fables of Kalīla and Dimna, in their eighth-century AD Arabic-language rendition by Ibn al-Muqaffa' from an ultimately Sanskrit original *(the Panchatantra)*; *c.* 1225 (Bibliothèque Nationale, Paris, France).

Plate 211 The Lion-King kills Shanzāba the Bull, while the jackals Kalīla and Dimna look on. Illustration to a later Persian rendition of the Kalīla and Dimna, copied in AD 1430 for Prince Bāysonqor of Herāt (Afghanistan) (Topkapi Palace Library, Istanbul, Turkey).

Plate 212 Figured tiles with animal and other motifs in cross and star patterns from the Kāshān workshops. Originally fired to adorn the walls of a shrine at Dāmghān (Iran), AD 1267 (Musée du Louvre, Paris, France; Département des Antiquités Orientales, Section islamique).

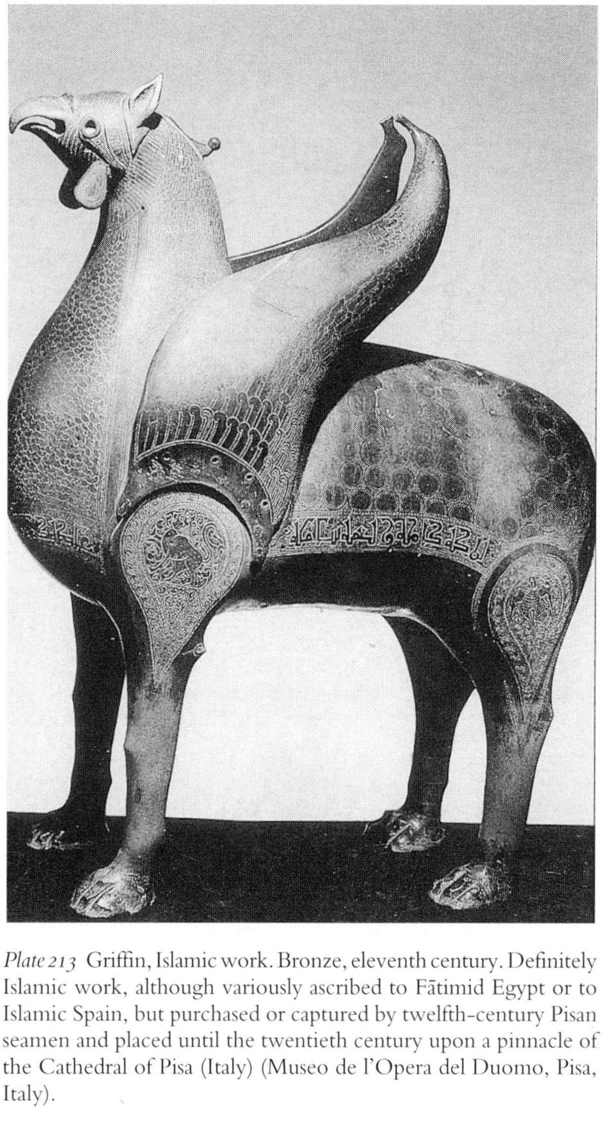

Plate 213 Griffin, Islamic work. Bronze, eleventh century. Definitely Islamic work, although variously ascribed to Fātimid Egypt or to Islamic Spain, but purchased or captured by twelfth-century Pisan seamen and placed until the twentieth century upon a pinnacle of the Cathedral of Pisa (Italy) (Museo de l'Opera del Duomo, Pisa, Italy).

Plate 214 Pre-Islamic Soghdian lords feasting cup in hand in the Sasanian royal pose. Fresco from Panjikent (Tajikistan), seventh century AD. Sasanian royal manners and étiquette profoundly influenced the style of Islamic court life from eighth-century 'Abbāsid times on (State Hermitage Museum/Terebenin, Saint Petersburg, Russia).

Plate 215 The 'Abbāsid caliph al-Ma'mūn feasting cup in hand in the Sasanian royal pose. Silver dish with gilding, probably from Marw (Turkmenistan), where al-Ma'mūn (r. AD 813–833) ruled as governor under the caliphate of his father Hārūn al-Rashīd (State Hermitage Museum/Terebenin, Saint Petersburg, Russia).

Plate 216 Muslim conqueror of north-west India (probably Sultan Mahmūd), enthroned in the Sasanian royal pose. Silver dish with gilding, attributed by V. Lukonin and I. Ivanov of the State Hermitage Museum, Saint Petersburg, to a workshop from Ghaznī (Afghanistan), early eleventh century AD. In addition to his twin-lion throne, associated in ancient Iranian lore with the fifth-century hero-king Bahrām Gōr, the Muslim ruler shown here is still depicted wearing a Sasanian-type crown with the wings of the god of war and victory, Verethragna (State Hermitage Museum/Terebenin, Saint Petersburg, Russia).

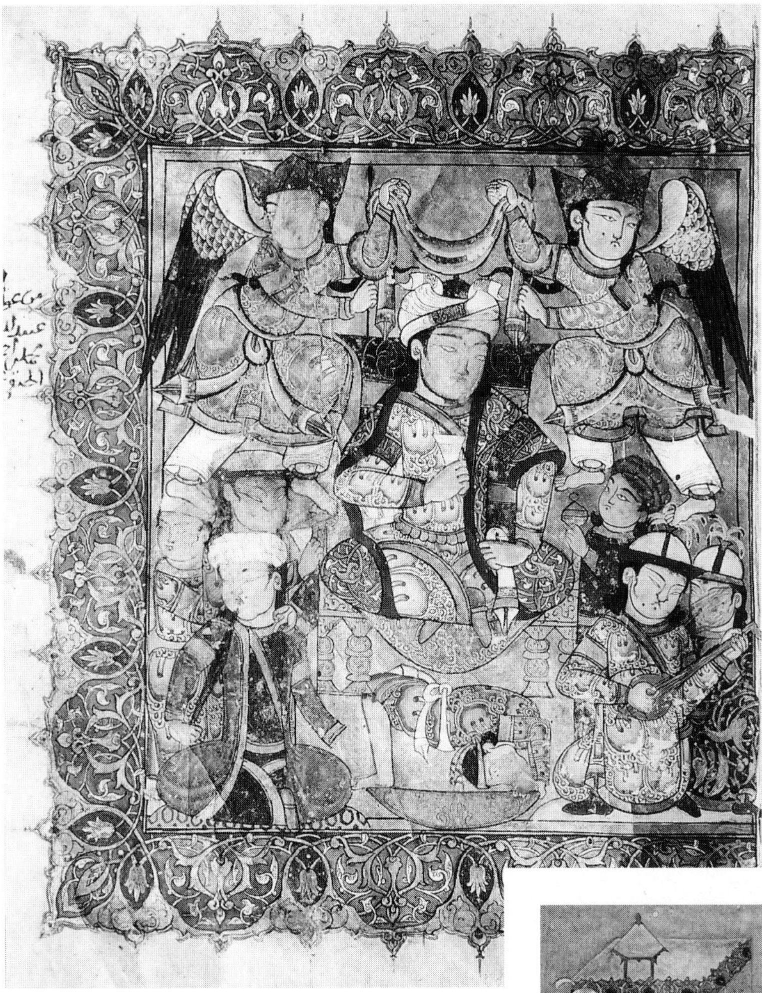

Plate 217 Mamlūk sultan feasting cup in hand in the conventional royal pose. Illustration to the *Maqāmāt* or 'Sessions' of the twelfth-century prosodist al-Harīrī, copied in Cairo (Egypt) in AD 1334 (Österreichische Nationalbibliothek, Vienna, Austria).

Plate 218 Sultan Husayn Mīrzā Bayqarā of Herāt humbles himself by night before a holy man. Illustration by the artist Bihzād to a two-part Persian-language 'Alexander Romance' *(Sharaf-Nāmeh and Eqbāl-Nāmeh)* by the twelfth-century poet Nizāmī of Āzerbaijān; the painter depicts the fabled conqueror with the features of his own reigning Sultan; the holy man appears as a contemporary Muslim Sūfī; while the castle in the background is an idealized rendition of the citadel of Herāt itself. From a *Khamseh* ('Quintet') of Nizāmī, Herāt (Afghanistan), AD 1494 (By permission of The British Library, London, UK).

Plate 219 The Iranian hero Siyāwush with his bride Farangish. Depicted as an Indo-Muslim royal couple. Illustration to a Persian-language 'Book of Kings' *(Shāh-Nāmeh)* of the eleventh-century epic poet Firdawsī, for the Muslim court of Gujerāt (India), *c.* AD 1450 (Photo Wettstein & Kauf; Museum Rietberg, Zürich, Switzerland).

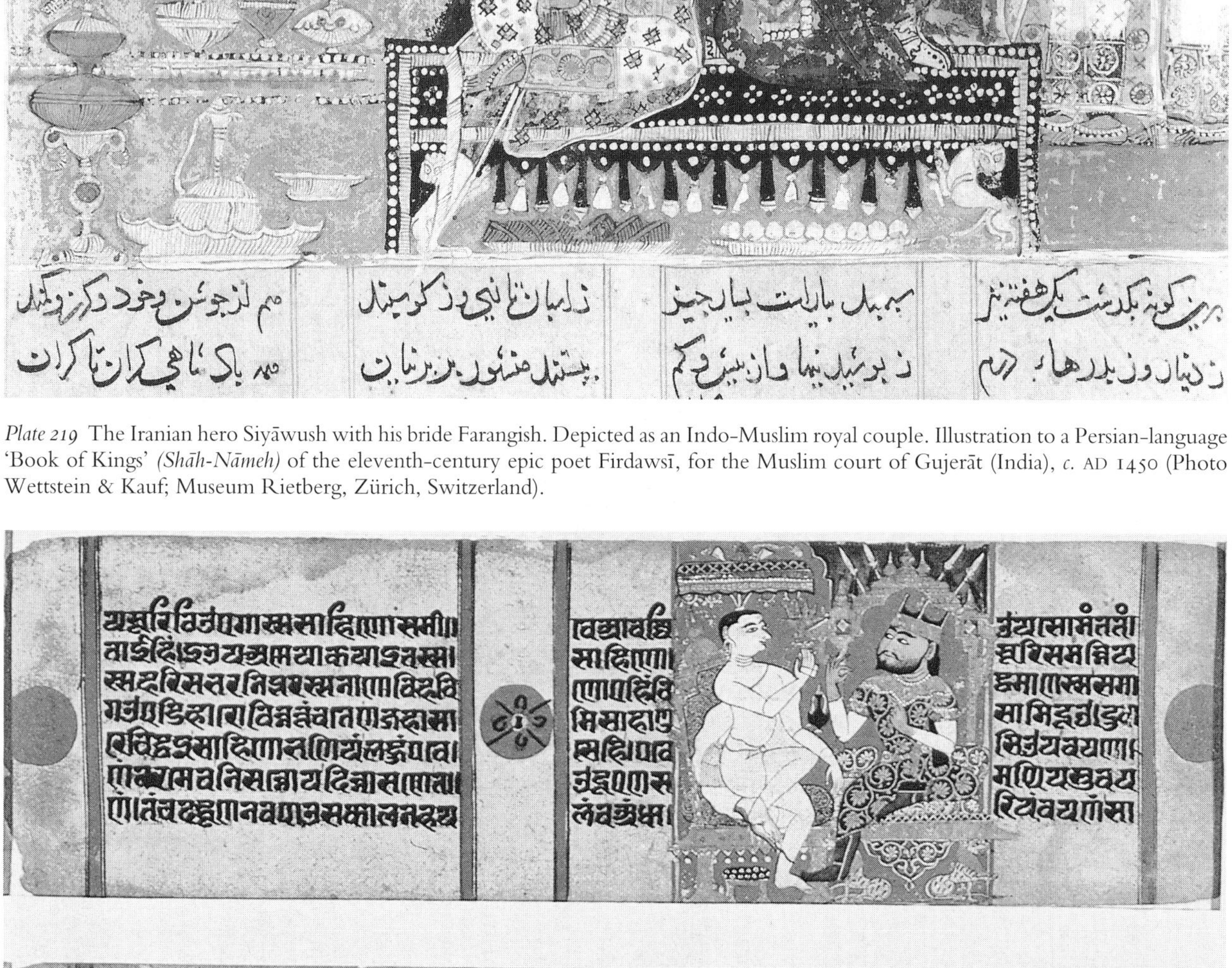

Plate 220 The Kalpasutra and the Kalakacharya Katha. Illustrations to the Jain scriptures, copied on paper in Gujerāt (India) in *c.* AD 1400 (All rights reserved).

Plate 221 The chariot-temple of the Jagamohan, Konarak, Orissa (India); thirteenth century AD (Photo ICOMOS, Paris).

Plate 223 Shiva Natarāja, Polonnaruva (Sri Lanka). Bronze; eleventh or twelfth century. A very close variant of the motif from India's neighbouring island (National Museum, Colombo, Sri Lanka).

Plate 222 Shiva Natarāja, Tāmilnādu (India), eleventh or twelfth century. The upper left hand holds a human cranium whence rises a flame (Musée Guimet, Paris, France).

Plate 224 Vajranrtya, goddess of the exuberant dance, Java (Indonesia). Bronze, one of eighteen statuettes from a Buddhist mandala. Central Javanese period, from Surocolo, early tenth century (Suaka Peninggalen Sejarah dan Purbakala, DIY, Bogem, Kalasan, Indonesia).

Plate 225 Lingarāja. Temple of Bhuvaneshwar, Orissa (India); tenth to eleventh century (Photo Archaeological Survey of India).

Plate 227 General silhouette of the Bayon, Angkor Wat (Cambodia). Khmer civilization, *c.* AD 1200, temple-mountain of King Jayavarman VII (1182–1220) (Photo ICOMOS, Paris).

Plate 226 Southern façade of the shrine of Po Klaung Garai, Binh-dinh (Vietnam). Cham civilization, late thirteenth century (Drawing after H. Parmentier, Inventaire descriptif des Monuments chams de l'Annam, Ecole Française d'Extrême-Orient (EFEO), Paris 1909; reproduced in B. Ph. Groslier, *Indochine, carrefour des arts*, coll. L'Art dans le Monde, édition Albin Michel, Paris, 1961, p. 201.)

Plate 228 Borobudur, Java (Indonesia). Gateway to the fifth balustrade yielding access to the three round terraces and to the central *stūpa*. Central Java, begun late eighth century AD. The Buddhist temple-mountain of Borobudur includes such Hindu motifs as this wrathful 'Face of Glory' *(Kirttimukha)*, the gateway through which all worshippers of Shiva must pass (Photo ICOMOS, Paris).

Plate 229 Ornamental front to a temple of Shiva at Banteay Srei (Cambodia). Khmer civilization, AD 967. The gods cause the two demons Sunda and Upasunda to turn from their rebellion and instead to strive against one another in rivalry by sending down to them the maiden Tilottāma. Nāga-s (cobras) adorn the sides (Musée Guimet, Paris, France).

Plate 230 The future Buddha Maitreya (Cambodia). Bronze, with silver. Khmer civilization, pre-Angkor period, *c.* eighth century AD (Musée Guimet, Paris, France).

Plate 231 Durga Mahisasuramardini (Cambodia). Grey sandstone. Khmer civilization, pre-Angkor period, style of Sambor Prei Kuk (Kompong Thom), first half of the seventh century AD (Photo John Gollings, Phnom-Penh, Cambodia, National Museum).

Plate 232 Crowned head of Buddha (Thailand). Bronze. Ayuthyā style, turn of the fifteenth and sixteenth centuries (Musée Guimet, Paris, France).

Plate 233 The drawing on the ceiling of the chamber in the tumulus of Koguryo (Photo Michail V. Vorobyev).

Plate 235 Many-armed Shiva seated upon the bull Nandī, Dandān-oilik (China). Painted wood, *c.* AD 600 (British Museum, London, UK).

Plate 236 A many-armed aspect of the Bodhisattva Avalokiteshvara, Kyōtō (Japan). Wood with lacquer and gold leaf, School of Jōkei, *c.* 1256 AD, Tōgenji Temple (From a reproduction of a postcard printed by P. J. Graphics Ltd, London W3 8DH, © the trustees of the British Museum, 1991. Courtesy of Tōgenji Temple).

Plate 234 Gal Vihāra, Polonnaruwa (Sri Lanka); eleventh to twelfth centuries (Courtesy H. W. Cowe, Colombo, Sri Lanka).

Plate 237 Emperor Taizhong of the Tang Dynasty (China). Reigned AD 627–649 (National Palace Museum, Taipeh, Taiwan).

Plate 238 Emperor Taizu of the Song Dynasty (China). Reigned AD 960–976 (National Palace Museum, Taipeh, Taiwan).

Plate 239 Emperor Hongwu, founder of the Ming Dynasty (China). Reigned AD 1368–1398 (National Palace Museum, Taipeh, Taiwan).

Plate 240 Three lady musicians, Tang Dynasty (China). Funerary figurines, terra cotta, eighth century AD (Courtesy Völkerkundesmuseum, Heidelberg, Germany).

Plate 242 A Ming Dynasty recreation of the painting 'Spring Festival on the River' (China). Detail of a Ming Dynasty recreation of the previous painting (Plate 241), *c.* AD 1600: an example of conscious archaizing revivalism of past Song cultural glory on the part of the Ming, who ruled from Beijing (The Metropolitan Museum of Art, New York, USA).

Plate 241 Dense urban crowds around the bridge in the twelfth-century Song capital of Kaifeng. Detail from the scroll by Zhang Zeduan, 'Spring Festival on the River', early twelfth century (Courtesy Beijing Summer Palace Museum, China).

Plate 243 Chinggis Khān (reigned *c.* 1160–1227) (Photo National Palace Museum, Taipeh, Taiwan).

Plate 246 (a)–(b) Khitan bronze funeral mask (Mongolia). Khitan period, AD 946–1125 (Photo Michail V. Vorobyev).

Plate 249 Ceramic tiles of Pohai (Photo Michail V. Vorobyev).

Plate 244 Ögödäy Khān (reigned *c.* 1229–1241) (Photo National Palace Museum, Taipeh, Taiwan).

Plate 247 Detail from a fresco in the Palace of Ögödäy Khān, Qarāqorum (Mongolia); thirteenth century AD. Frescos found under the Ögödäy Khān's palace in Quarāqorum (Photo in S. B. Kiselev, L. A. Evtuhova *et al.*, *Drevnemongolskiye goroda* (Ancient Mongolian Cities), Moscow, 1965, p.171, plate II).

Plate 250 Metallic amulet of the early inhabitants of the steppe (Photo Michail V. Vorobyev).

Plate 245 Qubilay Khān (reigned *c.* 1260–1294) (Photo National Palace Museum, Taipeh, Taiwan).

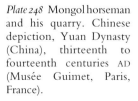

Plate 248 Mongol horseman and his quarry. Chinese depiction, Yuan Dynasty (China), thirteenth to fourteenth centuries AD (Musée Guimet, Paris, France).

Plate 251 'Hostelry in the Mountains'. Ink and light colour on silk by Yen Zuyu (Yen Tz'u-yu), late twelfth century, Chinese Daoist painting, Song Dynasty (China) (Freer Gallery of Art, Smithsonian Institution, Washington DC, USA).

Plate 253 'Autumn Landscape'. Vertical scroll, ink on paper, by Sesshu Toyo (1420–1506), Daoist painting (Japan) (National Museum, Tokyo, Japan).

Plate 252 'Autumn in the River Valley'. Detail of a handscroll, ink and light colour on silk, by Guoxi (Kuo Hsi), second half of the eleventh century, Chinese Daoist painting, Song Dynasty (China) (Freer Gallery of Art, Smithsonian Institution, Washington DC, USA).

Plate 254 'Five-Coloured Parakeet on Blossoming Apricot Tree', Song Dynasty (China). Academic study of a five-coloured parakeet. By the Emperor Huizong (Hui Tsung), Song Dynasty, r. 1101–1125, d. 1135. Handscroll; ink and color on silk; 53.3 × 125.1 cm (Maria Antoinette Evans Fund; Museum of Fine Arts, Boston, USA).

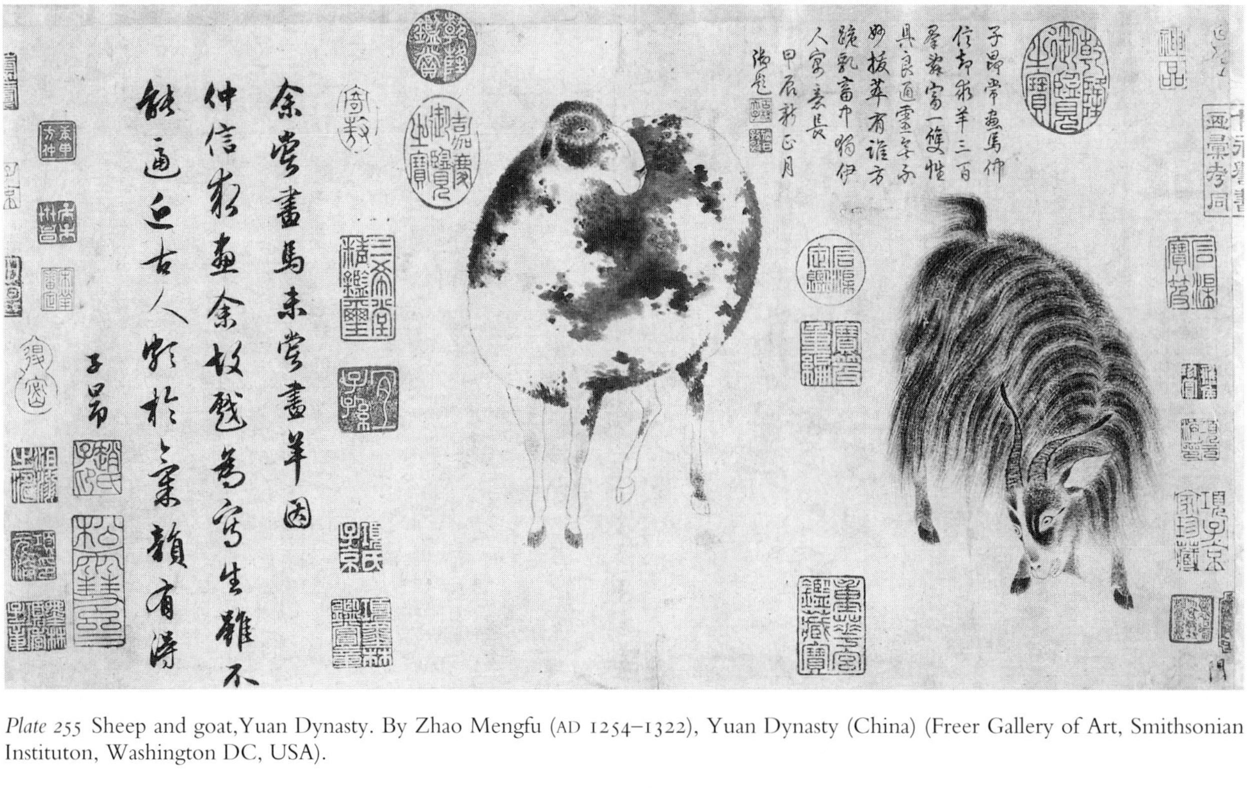

Plate 255 Sheep and goat,Yuan Dynasty. By Zhao Mengfu (AD 1254–1322), Yuan Dynasty (China) (Freer Gallery of Art, Smithsonian Instituton, Washington DC, USA).

Plate 256 The minister Taira-no-Shigemori (Japan). Vertical scroll, colours on silk, by Fujiwara Takanobu (AD 1142–1205) (Courtesy Kengaku Taniuchi, Kyoto, Japan).

Plate 257 Portrait of the Lady Kodai-no-Kimi, the poet (Japan). From the 'Thirty-Six Famous Poets' attributed to Fujiwara Nobuzane (1177–1265) (Courtesy Yamato Bunkakan Museum, Japan).

Plate 258 Prince Niu-no-Miya and his spouse Princess Uji (Japan). Illustration to the eleventh-century *Tales of Genji* by Lady Murasaki; horizontal scroll, colours on paper, first half of the twelfth century (Reimeikai Collection, Tokyo; on deposit with the Tokugawa Museum, Nagoya, Japan).

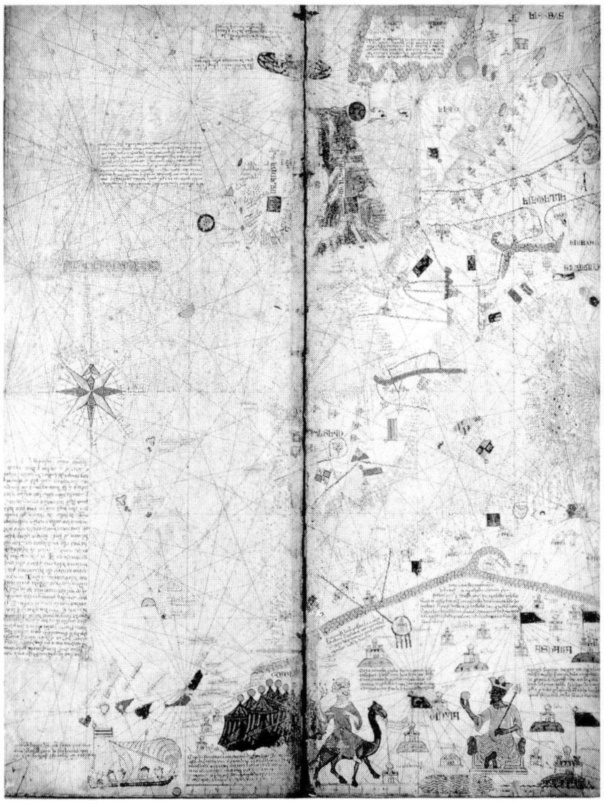

Plate 260 Couple: Terracotta statuettes (Niger); *c.* tenth century AD (Photo Gado, B. in *General History of Africa*, UNESCO, Paris, 1988, vol. III, ch. 28).

Plate 259 The international renown of the Mali Empire, which covered much of West Africa between the thirteenth and fifteenth centuries, is reflected in the famous *Catalan Atlas* (1375) produced by Abraham Cresques for King Charles V of France. Mali *(ciutat de Melli)* is prominently shown along with this portrait of its Mansa (emperor) wearing a European style crown. The ruler is holding a large nugget symbolizing Mali's fabulous wealth in gold. In front of him is a *Tuareg* chief on a camel (Bibliothèque Nationale, Paris, France).

Plate 261 Hairpin made of iron, twelfth century, Sanga (Mali) (Courtesy National Museum, Mali).

Plate 262 Horse's bit made of iron, fourteenth century, Kumbi Saleh (Mauritania) (Courtesy National Museum of Niamey, Niger).

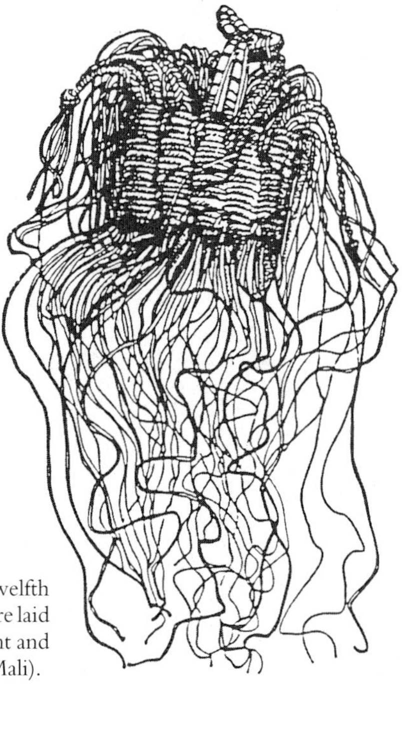

Plate 263 Cache-sexe, fibre and straw, eleventh to twelfth century, Sanga (Mali). Deceased Tellem women were laid in burial caves wearing a two-piece cache-sexe front and back tied by a belt (Courtesy National Museum, Mali).

Plate 264 Pre-Dogon statuette in wood, tenth century (Mali). (Photo Hughes Dubois Archives Musée Dapper, Paris, France).

Plate 265 Portuguese knight seen through West African eyes, kingdom of Benin (Nigeria). Ivory saltcellar, late fifteenth century. The Portuguese opened relations with the rulers of the Nigerian coast and brought horses mainly from the Futa region (in Modern Guinea) (Museu de Arte Antiga, Lisbon, Portugal).

Plate 266 Bronze roped pot, Igbo-Ukwu (Nigeria) (Photo Shaw, Th. in *General History of Africa*, UNESCO, Paris, 1984, vol. IV, chap. 14).

Plate 267 Bronze bust of a queen mother, Kingdom of Benin (Nigeria). Cast copper alloy and iron, Edo people; early sixteenth century (British Museum, London, UK).

Plate 268 Head of a young Oni (king), Ife (Nigeria). Bronze, *c.* thirteenth to fourteenth century AD (British Museum, London, UK).

Plate 269 Supposed portrait of Orson, spouse of the Olowo (king) Renrengeyen of Owo (Nigeria). Terracotta, Owo (Yoruba people), Nigeria, fifteenth century (Photo Shaw, Th.; in *General History of Africa*, UNESCO, Paris, 1984, vol. IV, ch. 14).

Plate 270 Decorative knob in bronze for a staff of office, Igbo-Ukwu, ninth century (Nigeria) (Courtesy National Museum Lagos, Nigeria).

Plate 271 The Great Mosque of Kilwa (Tanzania) (Photo in *The UNESCO Courier*, Paris, August–September 1979, p. 68).

Plate 272 Arches of the Great Mosque of Kilwa (Tanzania) (Photo in *The UNESCO Courier*, Paris, August–September 1979, p. 68).

Plate 273 A royal palace at Dunqula converted into a mosque in AD 1317 (Photo Y. F. Hasan).

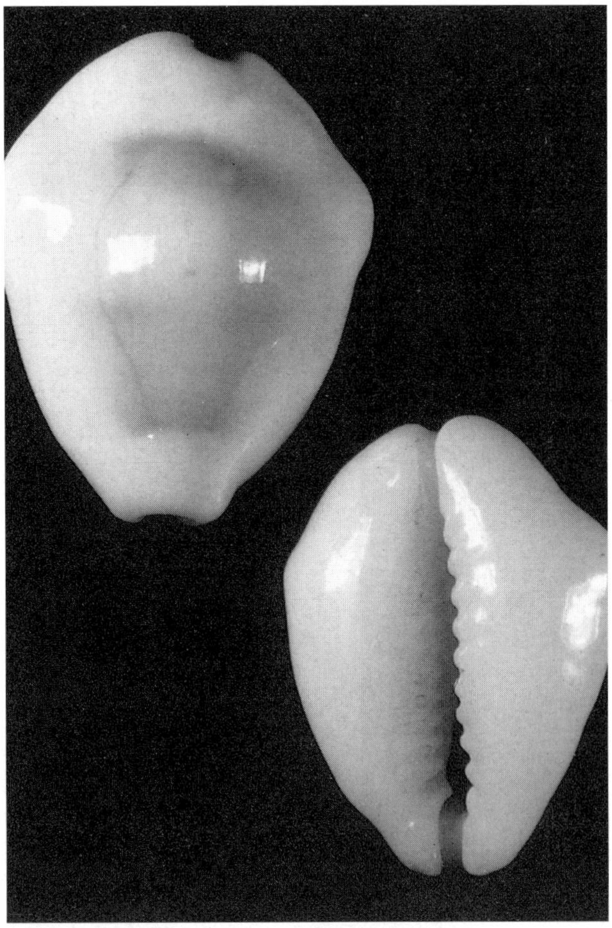

Plate 274 Money: cowries, *Cyprea moneta*. The cowrie served as currency in Africa (Photo in *The UNESCO Courier*, Paris, January 1990, p 23).

Plate 275 Tomb from the classical Kisalian period, tenth to fourteenth centuries, Sanga site (Photo Pierre de Maret in *General History of Africa*, UNESCO, Paris, 1988, vol. III, ch. 23).

Plate 276 Bishop Marianos of Faras (r. 1000–1036) protected by the Virgin and Child. Fresco from the church of Faras, Christian Nubia; early eleventh century AD (Sudan) (Photo Research Centre for Mediterranean Archaeology, Polish Academy of Sciences, Warsaw, in *General History of Africa*, UNESCO, Paris, 1988, vol. III, ch. 8).

Plate 277 Martha the Queen Mother with the Virgin and Child (Sudan). Fresco from the church of Faras, Christian Nubia; eleventh century AD (Photo Y. F. Hasan).

Plate 278 The Nativity. Fresco from the church of Faras, Chrisian Nubia (Sudan), eleventh century (Photo Y. F. Hasan).

Plate 279 Saint Mark (Ethiopia). Illumination to the Gospels in the Geez language; Ethiopia, early fourteenth century (Bibliothèque Nationale, Paris).

Plate 280 Rock-cut church of Beta Ghiorghis: *The Dwelling of Saint George*; late twelfth century AD, Lalibela (Ethiopia) (Photo Haberland E., Frobenius Institute in *General History of Africa*, UNESCO, Paris, 1984, vol. IV, ch. 17).

Plate 281 Cañon (Canyon) de Chelly: the *White House*, Cliffdweller Culture, Arizona (USA). Abandoned after the great drought of *c.* AD 1276–1299. *'Chelly'* is a Spanish rendering of Navaho *Tse-Yi*, 'Within the Rocks' (All rights reserved).

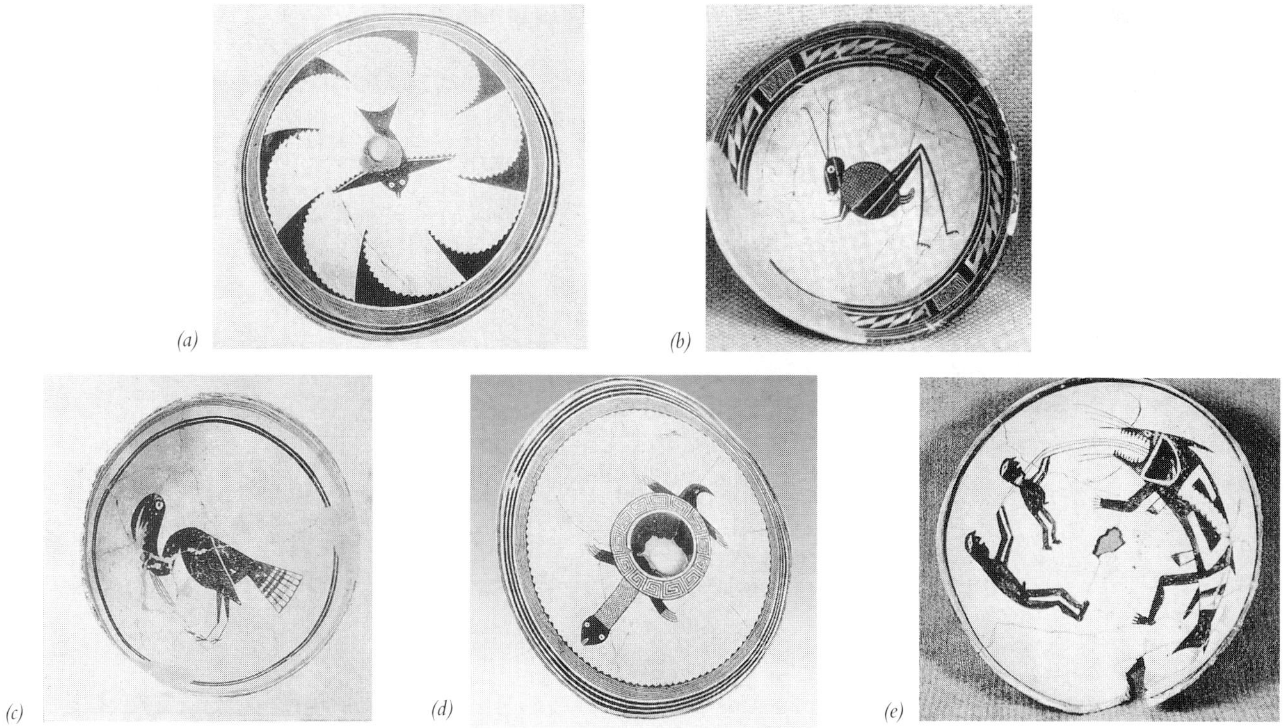

Plate 282 Painted pottery from Mimbres, New Mexico. *c.* twelfth century AD: *(a)* bird; *(b)* grasshopper; *(c)* turkey; *(d)* turtle; *(e)* mythological or ritual re-enactment scene (All rights reserved).

Plate 283 Deer figurehead. Wood, with detachable ears. Found in Key Marco, of the west coast of Florida (USA); Glades Culture, *c.* AD 1000 (All rights reserved).

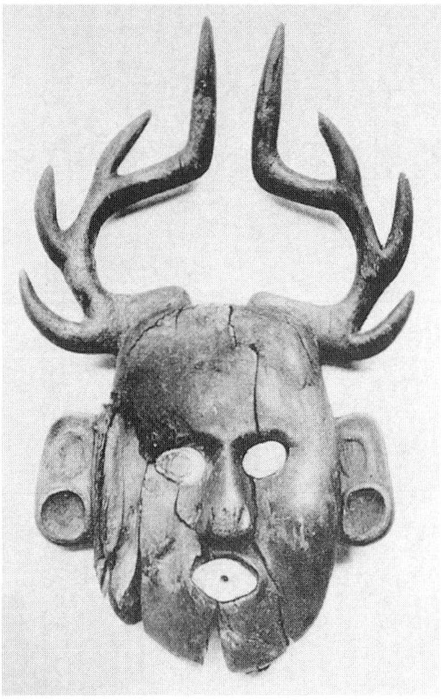

Plate 284 Antlered human head. Wooden mask, with shell inlay. From the Temple Mound, Spiro, Oklahoma (USA); Mound Builder Culture, AD 1080–1550 (All rights reserved).

Plate 285 Warrior's head. repoussé, copper plate. From the Temple Mound, Spiro, Oklahoma (USA); Cahokia Culture (?), *c.* AD 1000–1200 (All rights reserved).

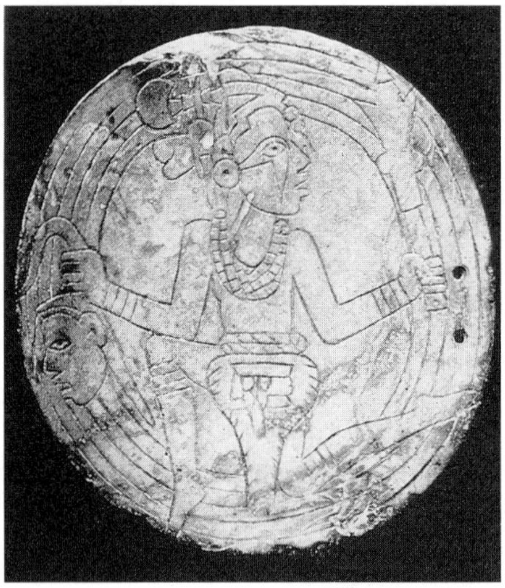

Plate 286 Warrior. Incised shell gorget. From Castilian Springs, Tennessee (USA); Caddo Mississippian Culture, *c.* AD 1300 (All rights reserved).

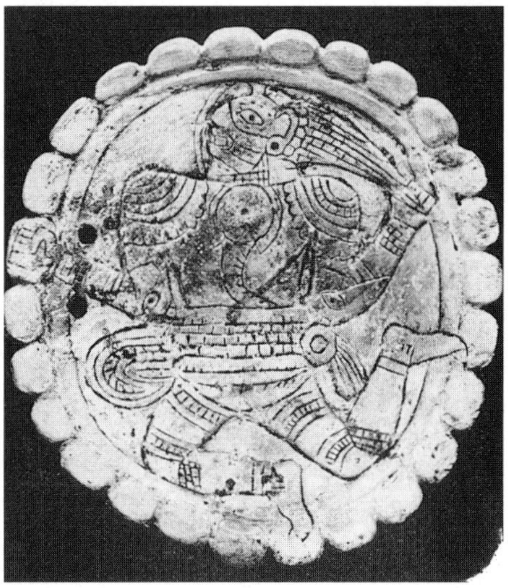

Plate 287 Dancing Shaman. Incise shell gorget. From the Temple Mound, Spiro, Oklahoma (USA). Caddc Mississippian Culture, *c.* AD 1300 (All rights reserved).

Plate 288 Human head effigy jar. Earthenware (Carson red on buff). Made in Arkansas, found near Panducah, Kentucky (USA). Middle Mississippian Culture (Nodena), AD 1400–1650 (All rights reserved).

Plate 289 Three-pointed stone, Santo Domingo (Dominican Republic). Stone carving from La Romana, Santo Domingo, representing a human head wearing a helmet; faces are carved as simple lines and hollows, and are intended to mean deities or 'zemís' related to fertility. AD 1000–1500, Taino Culture (Photo Dirk Bakker. Fundación García Arévalo, Santo Domingo).

Plate 290 Three-pointed stone, Río Piedras (Puerto Rico). This kind of sculptures represents male and female creator gods, as well as the god Yúcahu, the God of Cassava and therefore of food. Some scholars think that hollows were inlaid with beaten gold. AD 1000–1500, Taino Culture (Photo Dirk Bakker. Museo de la Universidad de Puerto Rico).

Plate 291 Spatula, Higüey, Santo Domingo (Dominican Republic). Carved from a seacow bone, in the shape of a bat with spread wings, it was used in the 'cohoba ritual': through the ingestion of powdered seeds of cohaba (acacia) Tainos induced vomiting to pursue ritual self-purification. 1000–1500 AD, Taino Culture (Photo Dirk Bakker. Fundación García Arévalo, Santo Domingo).

Plate 292 Dagger or Sceptre, anthropomorphic stone carving, Río Piedras (Puerto rico). Daggers or sceptres represent a seated human being, achieved through plain forms; the head is one-quarter of the total height of the body. 1000–1500 AD, Taino Culture (Photo Dirk Bakker. Museo de la Universidad de Puerto Rico).

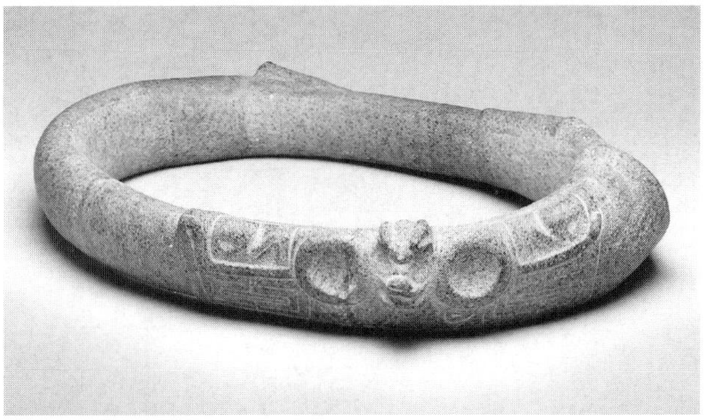

Plate 293 'Belt' or 'collar', Río Piedras (Puerto Rico). Stone carving associated with the ritual ballgame or 'batey', analogous to Mesoamerican practice. Belts probably protected the waist of the players, though they also could be trophies for the winners. 1000–1500 AD, Taino Culture (Photo Dirk Bakker. Museo de la Universidad de Puerto Rico).

Plate 294 Deified ancestor made manifest in the figure of a vision-serpent, Yaxchilan, Chiapas (Mexico). The serpent disgorges the founder of Yaxchilan's dynasty dressed as a warrior, wearing the 'Mask of Tlaloc', god of war and sacrifice. The founder reveals himself in a vision to the Lady Xoc after she has shed her own blood with a stingray-spine from her tongue. Limestone lintel from Yaxchilan, bearing the date corresponding to October 23, AD 681, Late Classic Period, AD 600–900, Maya Civilization (British Museum, London, UK).

Plate 295 Blood-letting ritual, Yaxchilan, Chiapas (Mexico). The Lady Xoc before her husband, King Shield Jaguar II, pulls a spiked thong through a hole in her tongue to induce a vision-trance and to invoke a vision-serpent. Limestone lintel dated 28 October, AD 709, Late Classic Period, AD 600–900, Maya Civilization (British Museum, London, UK).

Plate 296 Ruler and nobles with war captives, Bonampak, Chiapas (Mexico). King Chaan Muan II and nobles stand on top of a building, and several war prisoners are shown tied for sacrifice; this war took place on 2 August, AD 792. Distemper mural from Room 2 of Temple of the Paintings, Late Classic Period, AD 600–900, Maya Civilization (Courtesy Museo Nacional de Antropología, Mexico City, Mexico).

Plate 297 Head of a ruler, Palenque, Chiapas (Mexico). Modelled stucco head recovered from tomb beneath the Temple of Inscriptions, portraying King Pacal II (AD 603–683); his hair is combed and ornamented in a very fashionable style. Size of an actual human head; Late Classic Period, AD 600–900, Maya Civilization (Courtesy Instituto Nacional de Antropología e Historia, INAH, Mexico).

Plate 298 Pirámide del Adivino, Uxmal, Yucatán (Mexico). The Pyramid of the Sorcerer is one of the most impressive buildings of the ancient Maya city of Uxmal, because it shares two different architectonic styles called Chenes, dealing with zoomorphic monsters with opened jaws (doors), and Puuc, related to stone mosaic and geometrical designs. Late Classic to Early Post-Classic Period, AD 700–1250, Maya Civilization. (Courtesy Instituto Nacional de Antropología e Historia, INAH, Mexico).

Plate 299 Statue-columns, Tula, Hidalgo (Mexico). Four anthropomorphic columns carved in relief to represent the God of the Morning Star (Venus), a variation of god Quetzalcóatl as warrior; they wear panaches, a butterfly-like pectoral, a shield, and a spear-thrower. Basalt, height 400 cm; Early Post-Classic Period, AD 1000–1250; Toltec Civilization (Courtesy Museo Nacional de Antropología, Mexico City).

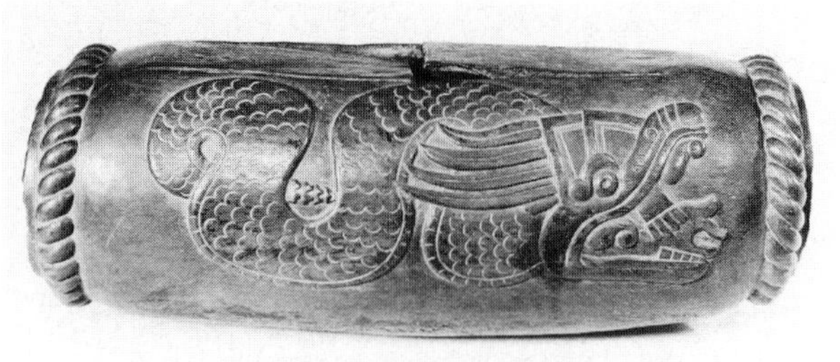

Plate 300 Drum with a serpent, Mexico City (Mexico). Carved on the surface of a drum made of wood, known as 'teponaxtle', the figure is that of a winding rattle-snake with open jaws, wearing a head-dress made of feathers. Wood, Late Post-Classic Period, AD 1325–1521, Aztec Civilization (Courtesy Instituto Nacional de Antropología e Historia, INAH, Mexico).

Plate 301 Quetzalcóatl in both human and serpent form, Mexico City (Mexico). The sculpture represents god Quetzalcóatl wearing a feathered-serpent dress. The god seats in a crouching position, and the serpent wraps itself around him; the head of the snake also functions as a helmet. Carved red porphyry, Late Post-Classic Period, AD 1325–1521, Aztec Civilization (Musée de l'Homme, Paris, France).

Plate 302 Crouching God, Mexico City. Almost naked, his head-dress has the folded paper shared by the deities of water, and from his mouth come out two teeth. These characteristics link the stone image to Tepeyollötli (Heart of the Mountains), rather than to Xiuhtecuhtli (Lord of Fire and of the Year). Carved basalt, Late Post-Classic Period, AD 1325–1521, Aztec Civilization. (British Museum, London, UK).

Plate 303 Turquoise mask, Mexico City. Possible mask of Tlaloc, God of Rain, his face is formed by two intertwined serpents. Perhaps part of the treasures yielded by the Aztec King Moctezuma II to Hernán Cortés in 1520. Turquoise and conch mosaic on wood, Late Post-Classic Period, AD 1325–1521, Aztec Civilization (Museum of Mankind, London, UK).

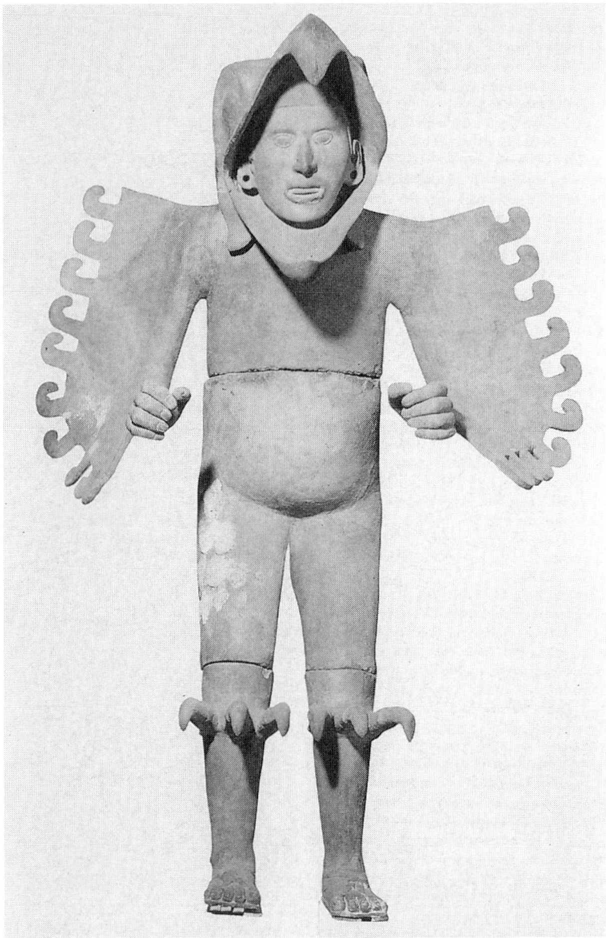

Plate 304 Eagle warrior, Mexico City. Recovered from the House of the Eagles at the Great Temple of Tenochtitlan. Warriors dressed in the attributes of eagles, with others dressed as jaguars, formed the élite of the Aztec armed forces. The eagle was associated with Huitzilopochtli, god of war and identified with the Sun. This hollow sculpture is slightly smaller than actual human size. Painted earth nware, Late Post-Classic Period, AD 1325–1521, Aztec Civilization (Courtesy Instituto Nacional de Antropología e Historia, INAH, Mexico).

Plate 305 Quetzalcóatl as lord of the winds offers a sacrifice, Mixteca-Puebla Region (Mexico). Polychrome manuscript illustration on animal skin, covered with stucco, from the Codex Fejérváry-Mayer. The content of this codex is mainly religious and ritual. Deerskin, Late Post-Classic Period, AD 1250–1500, Mixtec or Aztec Civilization (Liverpool City Museum, Liverpool, UK).

Plate 306 Double-headed serpent, Mexico City. Pectoral ornament, perhaps part of the treasures yielded by the Aztec King Moctezuma II to Hernán Cortés in 1520. Turquoise, coral and conch mosaic on wood, Late Post-Classic Period, AD 1325–1521, Aztec Civilization (Museum of Mankind, London, UK).

Plate 307 Aztec temple-pyramid, Mexico City. This is one of few Aztec shrines to have survived almost intact, visible at Santa Cecilia Acatitlan, north of Mexico City. Human victims were sacrificed on a stone situated at the edge of the upper platform. Late Post-Classic Period, AD 1325–1521, Aztec Civilization (All rights reserved).

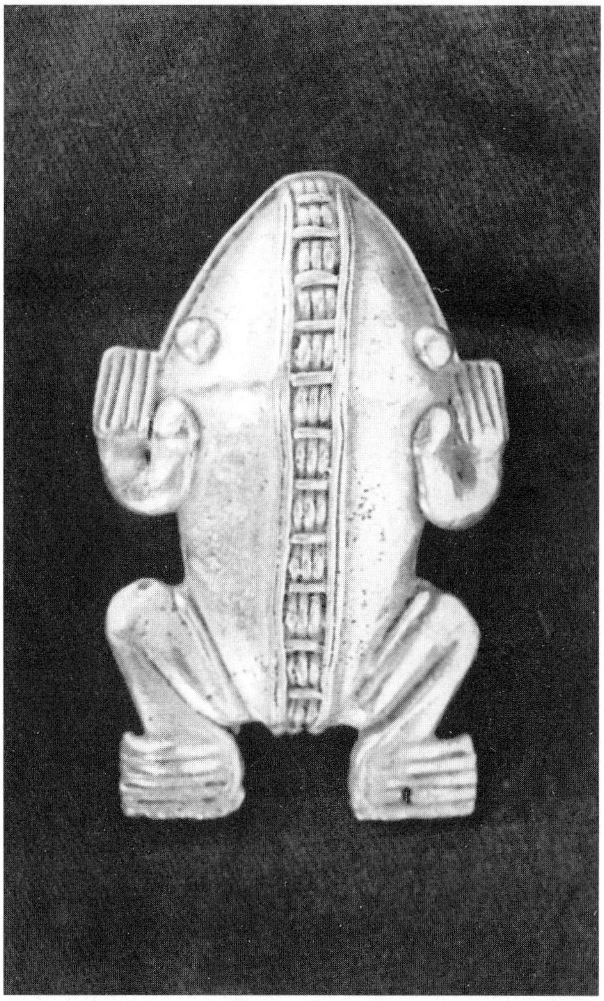

Plate 308 Golden frog, Panamá. One of most commonly represented animals, frogs are hollow pendants and/or part of necklaces. Such jewels were first done in wax, then covered with clay to form a mold, into which gold workers poured dow melted gold (or alloys of gold, silver and copper). Cast gold, AD 700–1500, Veraguas Style (Photo Wolfgang Haberland, Ahrensburg).

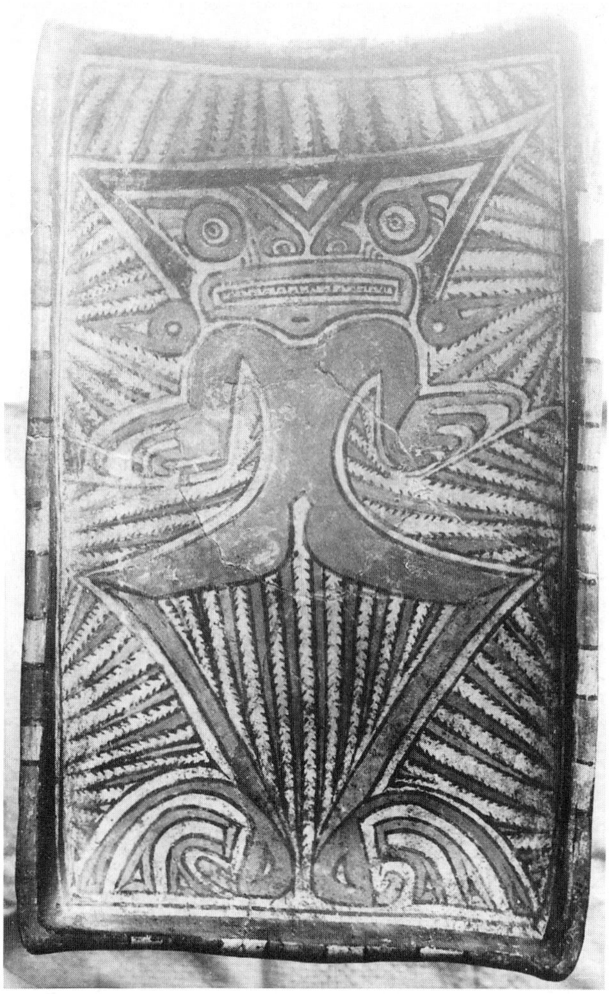

Plate 309 The 'Alligator' God, Río de Jesus, Province of Vereguas (Panamá). Identified as the 'Alligator' (sometimes as Frog) God, this frutera (recipient for fruits) shows a polychrome painting of an animal with geometrical traits: broad face, big mouth, short arms and long legs. AD 700–1500, Veraguas Style (Photo Wolfgang Haberland, Ahrensburg).

Plate 310 The 'alligator' God, Coclé (Panama). Another image of the squatting 'Alligator' God, who raises his arms to hold an object above his head. Depiction on a pectoral plaque made in hammered gold. AD 700–1300, Vereguas Style (Dumbarton Oaks Collection, Washington DC, USA).

Plate 311 Funerary mask, Tolima (Colombia). Images made of beaten gold, painted red and inlaid with emeralds, with masks, covered the faces of dead hierarchs to protect them in their journey to the Other-World. Gold, AD 600–1150, Quimbaya Culture (The Jan Mitchell Collection. Photo *The Art of Precolumbian Gold*, exhibition at the Metropolitan Museum of Art, New York, 1986, photo copyright of Metropolitan Museum of Art, New York, USA).

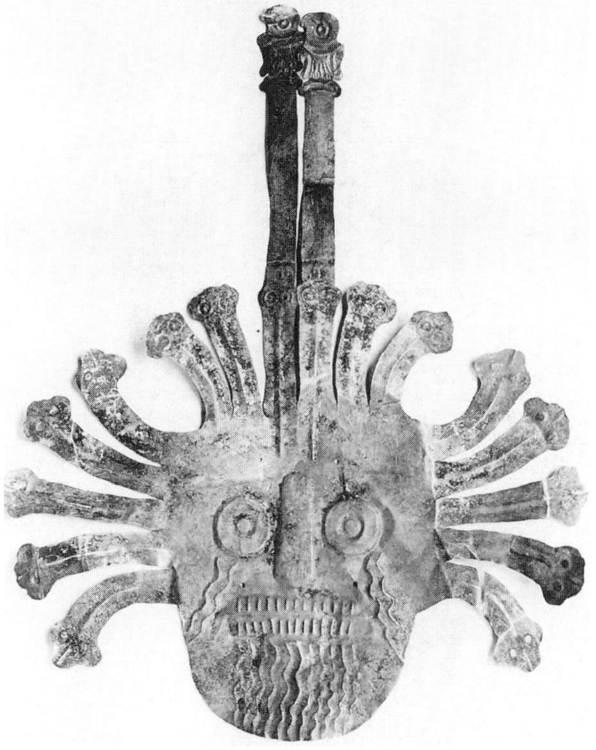

Plate 314 Gold mask, Nazca (Peru). Mask of a supernatural being, with a complex head- dress or hairdressing. Its iconography brings to memory similar images related to the cult of the creator god. Gold, AD 300–600, Nazca Culture (Musée de l'Homme, Paris, France).

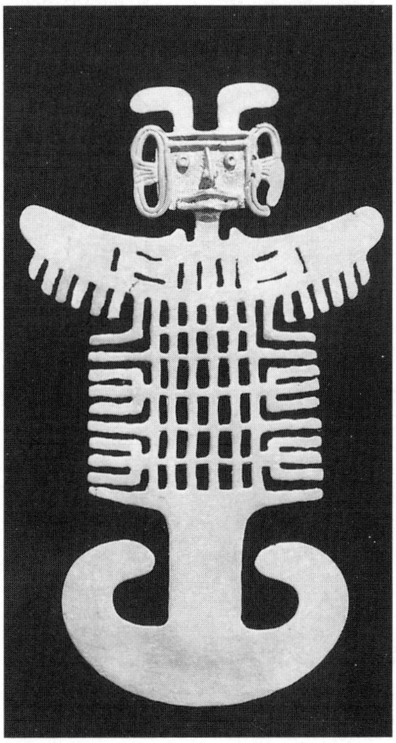

Plate 312 Stylized gold figure, Tolima (Colombia). A possible ritual knife, representing a bird with large ear-rings, perhaps associated to the cult of the Sun. Beaten gold, AD 600–1150, Quimbaya Culture (Michael C. Rockefeller Memorial Collection, The Metropolitan Museum of Art, Bequest of Nelson A. Rockfeller, New York, USA).

Plate 313 Cache figure, Tunja (Colombia). Geometrical and stylized human figure, his up- raised arms seem to hold two different objects. Gold, AD 1150–1540, Muisca or Chibcha Culture (The Jan Mitchell Collection. Photo: *The Art of Precolumbian Gold*, exhibition at the Metropolitan Museum of Art, New York, 1986, photo copyright of Metropolitan Museum of Art, New York, USA).

Plate 315 Ceremonial knife or 'Tumi'. Stylized gold figure, Tolima (Colombia). A ritual knife used in rituals or as scalpel to head-trepanning. It represents a human head with a semicircular roundhead-dress and big ear-rings. Cast gold with turquoise, AD 850–1150, Chimu Culture (The Jan Mitchell Collection. Photo: *The Art of Precolumbian Gold*, exibition at the Metropolitan Museum of Art, New York, 1986, photo copyright of Metropolitan Museum of Art, New York, USA).

Plate 316 Chan Chan, Tschudi (Peru). The great capital city of Chan Chan (20 km^2) is mainly built of adobe (sun-dried) bricks. Buildings or huacas display several motives of decoration: geometric form, animals, birds and fishes. One of them has been recognized as Ni, God of the Sea. Apogee *c.* AD 1200–1400, Chimu Culture (Photo L. Millones).

Plate 317 Anthropomorphic jar, Northern Peru. Made of two vertical halves, funerary jars were polished and painted in red, black and white,and usually had a 'stirrup-handle'. Among the most relevant are those with realistic human faces or 'portraits'. Pottery, AD 300–800, Mochica Culture (National Museum of Denmark, Copenhagen).

Plate 318 Pottery vessel with a Mythological scene (Peru). Polychrome motives often deal with religious, ritual or anecdotal scenes. In this example, a dancing shaman or priest disguises himself as an eagle and holds a plant in his right hand. Pottery, AD 300–800, Mochica Culture (Rautenstrauch-Joest-Museum, Köln, Germany).

Plate 319 Golden funerary mask, Lambayeque (Peru). A widespread artistic tradition in Andinamerica, gold masks had a protective purpose when put upon corpses, disposed of as funerary bundles. Beaten gold, red paint, emeralds, AD 1100–1300, Chimu Culture (Metropolitan Museum of Art, Bequest of Alice K. Bache, 1974 and 1977, New York, USA).

Plate 320 Pisaq terraces, Cuzco (Peru). Terraces served as bases for homes, temples and cultivated fields. AD 1400–1540, Inca Civilization (Photo L. Millones).

Plate 321 Machu Picchu, Cuzco (Peru). This city was built on the slopes of a mountain close to Urubamba River. One of the main buildings of Machu Picchu is the Temple of the Sun. Its ground plan looks like a horseshoe; its stone walls, perfectly chiselled, needed no mortar. The inner chamber kept the Sun God statue. AD 1400–1540, Inca Civilization (Photo L. Millones).

Plate 322 Pottery vessel (Peru), The Inca's Warriors. Vases or keros stand among the most skillful ceramic Inca items. Painted in brilliant colours (red, yellow, black, white) their motifs often mix geometric and anthropomorphic figures. This example displays a group of warriors or hunters. AD 1400–1540, Inca Civilization (Museo de América, Madrid, Spain).

Plate 323 Silver alpaca, Lake Titicaca (Peru-Bolivia). Found near the Sacred Rock on the island on Lake Titicaca, between modern Peru and Bolivia. Gold and silver work were highly developed during Pre-Columbian times in Andinamerica, as shown by this alpaca, identified by its slender neck and long wool. Alpacas were raised for wool and meat, unlike lamas which were used as beasts of burden. Silver, AD 1400–1540, Inca Civilization (American Museum of Natural History, New York, USA).